HOLT

Elements of
LITERATURE

Fifth Course

Kylene Beers

Carol Jago

Deborah Appleman

Leila Christenbury

Sara Kajder

Linda Rief

HOLT, RINEHART AND WINSTON

ISBN 978-0-03-036881-3
ISBN 0-03-036881-2
12 0868 16
4500600550   D E F G

Program Authors

Kylene Beers is the senior program author for *Elements of Literature*. A former middle school teacher, she is now Senior Reading Advisor to Secondary Schools for Teachers College Reading and Writing Project at Columbia University. She is the author of *When Kids Can't Read: What Teachers Can Do* and co-editor (with Linda Rief and Robert E. Probst) of *Adolescent Literacy: Turning Promise into Practice.* The former editor of the National Council of Teachers of English (NCTE) literacy journal *Voices from the Middle*, Dr. Beers assumed the NCTE presidency in 2008. With articles in *English Journal, Journal of Adolescent and Adult Literacy, School Library Journal, Middle Matters,* and *Voices from the Middle,* she speaks both nationally and internationally as a recognized authority on struggling readers. Dr. Beers has served on the review boards of *English Journal, The ALAN Review,* the Special Interest Group on Adolescent Literature of the International Reading Association, and the Assembly on Literature for Adolescents of the NCTE. She is the 2001 recipient of the Richard W. Halley Award given by NCTE for outstanding contributions to middle school literacy.

Carol Jago is a teacher with thirty-two years of experience at Santa Monica High School in California. The author of nine books on education, she continues to share her experiences as a writer and as a speaker at conferences and seminars across the country. Her wide and varied experience in standards assessment and secondary education in general has made her a sought-after speaker. As an author, Ms. Jago also works closely with Heinemann Publishers and with the National Council of Teachers of English. Her longtime association with NCTE led to her June 2007 election to a four-year term on the council's board. During that term she will serve for one year as president of the council. She is also active with the California Association of Teachers of English (CATE) and has edited CATE's scholarly journal *California English* since 1996. Ms. Jago served on the planning committees for the 2009 NAEP Reading Framework and the 2011 NAEP Writing Framework.

Deborah Appleman is professor and chair of educational studies and director of the Summer Writing Program at Carleton College in Northfield, Minnesota. Dr. Appleman's primary research interests include adolescent response to literature, multicultural literature, and the teaching of literary theory in high school. With a team of classroom teachers, she co-edited *Braided Lives,* a multicultural literature anthology. In addition to many articles and book chapters, she is the author of

Linda Rief, Alfred Tatum, Kylene Beers, Patrick Schwarz, and Carol Jago

PROGRAM AUTHORS continued

Critical Encounters in High School English: Teaching Literary Theory to Adolescents and co-author of *Teaching Literature to Adolescents.* Her most recent book, *Reading for Themselves,* explores the use of extracurricular book clubs to encourage adolescents to read for pleasure. Dr. Appleman was a high school English teacher, working in both urban and suburban schools. She is a frequent national speaker and consultant and continues to work weekly in high schools with students and teachers.

Leila Christenbury is a former high school English teacher and currently professor of English education at Virginia Commonwealth University, Richmond. The former editor of *English Journal,* she is the author of ten books, including *Writing on Demand, Making the Journey,* and *Retracing the Journey: Teaching and Learning in an American High School.* Past president of the National Council of Teachers of English, Dr. Christenbury is also a former member of the steering committee of the National Assessment of Educational Progress (NAEP). A recipient of the Rewey Belle Inglis Award for Outstanding Woman in English Teaching, Dr. Christenbury is a frequent speaker on issues of English teaching and learning and has been interviewed and quoted on CNN and in the *New York Times, USA Today, Washington Post, Chicago Tribune,* and *US News & World Report.*

Sara Kajder, author of *Bringing the Outside In: Visual Ways to Engage Reluctant Readers* and *The Tech-Savvy English Classroom,* is an assistant professor at Virginia Polytechnic Institute and State University (Virginia Tech). She has served as co-chair of NCTE's Conference on English Education (CEE) Technology Commission and of the Society for Information Technology and Teacher Education (SITE) English Education Committee. Dr. Kajder is the recipient of the first SITE National Technology Leadership Fellowship in English Education; she is a former English and language arts teacher for high school and middle school.

Linda Rief has been a classroom teacher for twenty-five years. She is author of *The Writer's-Reader's Notebook, Inside the Writer's-Reader's Notebook, Seeking Diversity, 100 Quickwrites,* and *Vision and Voice* as well as the co-author (with Kylene Beers and Robert E. Probst) of *Adolescent Literacy: Turning Promise into Practice.* Ms. Rief has written numerous chapters and journal articles, and she co-edited the first five years of *Voices from the Middle.* During the summer she teaches graduate courses at the University of New Hampshire and Northeastern University. She is a national and international consultant on adolescent literacy issues.

Leila Christenbury, Héctor Rivera, Sara Kajder, Eric Cooper, and Deborah Appleman

Program Consultants

Isabel L. Beck is professor of education and senior scientist at the University of Pittsburgh. Dr. Beck has conducted extensive research on vocabulary and comprehension and has published well over one hundred articles and several books, including *Improving Comprehension with Questioning the Author* (with Margaret McKeown) and *Bringing Words to Life: Robust Vocabulary Instruction* (with Margaret McKeown and Linda Kucan). Dr. Beck's numerous national awards include the Oscar S. Causey Award for outstanding research from the National Reading Conference and the William S. Gray Award from the International Reading Association for lifetime contributions to the field of reading research and practice.

Margaret G. McKeown is a senior scientist at the University of Pittsburgh's Learning Research and Development Center. Her research in reading comprehension and vocabulary has been published extensively in outlets for both research and practitioner audiences. Recognition of her work includes the International Reading Association's (IRA) Dissertation of the Year Award and a National Academy of Education Spencer Fellowship. Before her career in research, Dr. McKeown taught elementary school.

Amy Benjamin is a veteran teacher, literacy coach, consultant, and researcher in secondary-level literacy instruction. She has been recognized for excellence in teaching from the New York State English Council, Union College, and Tufts University. Ms. Benjamin is the author of several books about reading comprehension, writing instruction, grammar, and differentiation. Her most recent book (with Tom Oliva) is *Engaging Grammar: Practical Advice for Real Classrooms,* published by the National Council of Teachers of English. Ms. Benjamin has had a long association and leadership role with the NCTE's Assembly for the Teaching of English Grammar (ATEG).

Eric Cooper is the president of the National Urban Alliance for Effective Education (NUA) and co-founder of the Urban Partnership for Literacy with the IRA. He currently works with the NCTE to support improvements in urban education and collaborates with the Council of the Great City Schools. In line with his educational mission to support the improvement of education for urban and minority students, Dr. Cooper writes, lectures, and produces educational documentaries and talk shows to provide advocacy for children who live in disadvantaged circumstances.

Mabel Rivera, Harvey Daniels, Margaret McKeown, and Isabel Beck

Harvey Daniels is a former college professor and classroom teacher, working in urban and suburban Chicago schools. Known for his pioneering work on student book clubs, Dr. Daniels is author and co-author of many books, including *Literature Circles: Voice and Choice in Book Clubs and Reading Groups* and *Best Practice: Today's Standards for Teaching and Learning in America's Schools.*

Ben Garcia is associate director of education at the Skirball Cultural Center in Los Angeles, California, where he oversees school programs and teacher professional development. He is a board member of the Museum Educators of Southern California and presents regularly at conferences in the area of visual arts integration across curricula. Prior to the Skirball, he worked with classroom teachers for six years in the *Art and Language Arts* program at the J. Paul Getty Museum. Recent publications include *Art and Science: A Curriculum for K–12 Teachers* and *Neoclassicism and the Enlightenment: A Curriculum for Middle and High School Teachers.*

Judith L. Irvin taught middle school for several years before entering her career as a university professor. She now teaches courses in curriculum and instructional leadership and literacy at Florida State University. Dr. Irvin's many publications include *Reading and the High School Student: Strategies to Enhance Literacy* and *Integrating Literacy and Learning in the Content Area Classroom.* Her latest book, *Taking Action: A Leadership Model for Improving Adolescent Literacy,* is the result of a Carnegie-funded project and is published by the Association for Supervision and Curriculum Development.

Victoria Ramirez is the interim education director at the Museum of Fine Arts, Houston, Texas, where she plans and implements programs, resources, and publications for teachers and serves as liaison to local school districts and

Amy Benjamin, Ben Garcia, Robin Scarcella, and Judith Irvin

teacher organizations. She also chairs the Texas Art Education Association's museum division. Dr. Ramirez earned a doctoral degree in curriculum and instruction from the College of Education at the University of Houston and an M.A.T. in museum education from George Washington University. A former art history instructor at Houston Community College, Dr. Ramirez currently teaches education courses at the University of Houston.

Héctor H. Rivera is an assistant professor at Southern Methodist University, School of Education and Human Development. Dr. Rivera is also the director of the SMU Professional Development/ESL Supplemental Certification Program for Math and Science Teachers of At-Risk Middle and High School LEP Newcomer Adolescents. This federally funded program develops, delivers, and evaluates professional development for educators who work with at-risk newcomer adolescent students. Dr. Rivera is also collaborating on school reform projects in Guatemala and with the Institute of Arctic Education in Greenland.

Mabel Rivera is a research assistant professor at the Texas Institute for Measurement, Evaluation, and Statistics at the University of Houston. Her current research interests include the education of and prevention of reading difficulties in English-language learners. In addition, Dr. Rivera is involved in local and national service activities for preparing school personnel to teach students with special needs.

Robin Scarcella is a professor at the University of California at Irvine, where she also directs the Program in Academic English/English as a Second Language. She has a Ph.D. in linguistics from the University of Southern California and an M.A. degree in education-second language acquisition from Stanford University. She has taught all grade levels. She has been active in shaping policies affecting language assessment, instruction, and teacher professional development. In the last four years, she has spoken to over ten thousand teachers and administrators. She has written over thirty scholarly articles that appear in such journals as the *TESOL Quarterly* and *Brain and Language*. Her most recent publication is *Accelerating Academic English: A Focus on the English Learner*.

Patrick Schwarz is professor of special education and chair of the Diversity in Learning and Development department for National-Louis University, Chicago, Illinois. He is author of *From Disability to Possibility* and *You're Welcome* (co-written with Paula Kluth), texts that have inspired teachers worldwide to reconceptualize inclusion to help all children. Other books co-written with Paula Kluth include *Just Give Him the Whale* and *Inclusion Bootcamp*. Dr. Schwarz also presents and consults worldwide through Creative Culture Consulting.

Alfred W. Tatum is an associate professor in the Department of Curriculum and Instruction at the University of Illinois at Chicago (UIC), where he earned his Ph.D. He also serves as the director of the UIC Reading Clinic. He began his career as an eighth-grade teacher, later becoming a reading specialist. Dr. Tatum has written more than twenty-five articles, chapters, and monographs and is the author of *Teaching Reading to Black Adolescent Males: Closing the Achievement Gap*. His work focuses on the literacy development of African American adolescent males, particularly the impact of texts on their lives.

Critical Reviewers

Noreen L. Abdullah
Chicago Public Schools
Chicago, Illinois

Martha Armenti
Baltimore City College High School
Baltimore, Maryland

Jessica J. Asmis-Carvajal
Coronado High School
El Paso, Texas

Susan Beechum
Apopka High School
Apopka, Florida

Nilda Benavides
Del Rio High School
Del Rio, Texas

Melissa Bowell
Ft. Walton Beach High School
Ft. Walton Beach, Florida

Stacey Chisolm
Meridian High School
Meridian, Mississippi

Vincent Contorno
L.C. Anderson High School
Austin, Texas

Rita Curington
Athens High School
Athens, Texas

Melinda Fulton
Leon High School
Tallahassee, Florida

Holly Hillgardner
South Bronx Preparatory
New York, New York

Anna Yoccabel Horton
Highland Middle School
Gilbert, Arizona

Elizabeth Ignatius
Paul R. Wharton High School
Tampa, Florida

Tim King
Mason High School
Mason, Ohio

Barbara Kimbrough
Kane Area High School
Kane, Pennsylvania

Jennifer Moore Krievs
Midlothian High School
Midlothian, Virginia

Lynn V. Mason
Newark High School
Newark, Ohio

Vivian Nida
University of Oklahoma
Norman, Oklahoma

John Kevin M. Perez
Hampton Bays Secondary
   High School
Hampton Bays, New York

Judd Pfeiffer
Bowie High School
Austin, Texas

Aimee Riordan
Sun Valley High School
Monroe, North Carolina

Celia Rocca
Western High School
Baltimore, Maryland

Kelly L. Self
Alexandria Senior High School
Alexandria, Louisiana

Dr. Rosa Smith-Williams
Booker T. Washington High School
Houston, Texas

Kelly Southern
Ouachita Parish High School
Monroe, Louisiana

Jody Steinke
Quincy Senior High School
Quincy, Illinois

Kelly Swifney
Zeeland West High School
Zeeland, Michigan

Nichole Wilson
Mason High School
Mason, Ohio

Dr. Bernard Zaidman
Greenville Senior High School
   Academy of Academic
   Excellence
Greenville, South Carolina

FIELD-TEST PARTICIPANTS

Linda Brescia
HS for Health Professions
   and Human Services
New York, New York

Katherine Burke
Timber Creek High School
Orlando, Florida

Greg Cantwell
Sheldon High School
Eugene, Oregon

Cheryl Casbeer
Del Rio High School
Del Rio, Texas

Ms. Linda Chapman
Colonel White High School
Dayton, Ohio

Kim Christiernsson
Durango High School
Las Vegas, Nevada

Amanda Cobb
Timber Creek High School
Orlando, Florida

Marylea Erhart-Mack
University High School
Orlando, Florida

Yolanda Fernandez
Del Rio High School
Del Rio, Texas

Angela Ferreira
Hoover High School
San Diego, California

Dan Franke
Lemont High School
Lemont, Illinois

Ellen Geisler
Mentor High School
Mentor, Ohio

Luanne Greenberg
Coronado High School
El Paso, Texas

Colleen Hadley
Abilene High School
Abilene, Texas

Leslie Hardiman
Hoover High School
San Diego, California

Sandra Henderson
Lemont High School
Lemont, Illinois

Lee Ann Hoffman
Southeast High School
Bradenton, Florida

Jennifer Houston
Timber Creek High School
Orlando, Florida

Eva M. Lazear
Springfield North High School
Springfield, Ohio

Phil Lazzari
Lemont High School
Lemont, Illinois

Jacquelyn McLane
Cypress Creek High School
Orlando, Florida

Kathleen Mims
H. Grady Spruce High School
Dallas, Texas

Julie Moore
Monroe High School
Monroe, Wisconsin

Denise Morris
Rich Central High School
Olympia Fields, Illinois

Bunny Petty
Florence High School
Florence, Texas

Valerie Pfeffer
Durango High School
Las Vegas, Nevada

Bernadette Poulos
Reavis High School
Burbank, Illinois

Ann L. Rodgers
Currituck County High School
Barco, North Carolina

Narima Shahabudeen
East Orange Campus 9
High School
East Orange, New Jersey

Shari Simonds
Valley High School
Las Vegas, Nevada

Gail Tuelon
University High School
Orlando, Florida

Mandy Unruh
Brownsburg High School
Brownsburg, Indiana

Vanessa Vega
Irving High School
Irving, Texas

Elizabeth Weaver
Cypress Creek High School
Orlando, Florida

Tamera West
McQueen High School
Reno, Nevada

Erica White
Sherando High School
Stephens City, Virginia

Contents in Brief

Encounters and Foundations to 1800

"[In America] individuals of all nations are melted into a new race of men, whose labors . . . will one day cause great changes in the world."

—Michel-Guillaume Jean de Crèvecoeur

What Do You Think? How can people's beliefs affect their actions?

SKILLS FOCUS **Literary Skills** Evaluate and analyze the philosophical, political, religious, ethical, and social influences of a historical period.

Reading Skills Identify and understand chronological order; identify and understand graphic elements; use text organizers such as overviews, headings, and graphic features to locate and categorize information; read widely to increase knowledge of the student's culture, the culture of others, and the common elements across cultures; identify and understand elements of text structure (including headings and sections).

SKILLS FOCUS **Literary Skills** Understand and analyze the characteristics of Native American oral traditions; archetypes; setting; historical context.

Reading Skills Identify and understand cultural characteristics of a text; identify main ideas and supporting details.

COLLECTION **1** Native American Voices

COLLECTION 2 Voyages and Visions

SKILLS FOCUS **Literary Skills** Understand and analyze the philosophical, political, religious, ethical, and social influences of a historical period; the characteristics and use of the plain style; allusions; influence of the audience on a writer; the characteristics of satire; narrative accounts, including historical narratives; metaphor; historical and political contexts; conceits; imagery; philosophical context.

Reading Skills Analyze political context, especially political and social influences of the time. Summarize as a strategy for comprehension; identify main ideas and supporting details; summarize a text; analyze chronological order; identify/analyze tone; make inferences about an author's beliefs; analyze inverted syntax; analyze extended metaphor as a text structure; identify the writer's purpose or intent.

COLLECTION **3** Forging a New Nation

SKILLS FOCUS **Literary Skills** Evaluate and analyze the philosophical, political, religious, ethical, and social influences of a historical period. Understand and analyze characteristics of persuasion; style; the characteristics of a writer's style; the use of parallelism; symbolism; author's purpose; persuasive devices; the characteristics of autobiography; aphorisms.

Reading Skills Analyze persuasion/arguments in a text; recognize and analyze modes of persuasion, including appeals to reason and appeals to emotion; make inferences as a strategy for comprehension.

Informational Skills Analyze persuasion/arguments in a text.

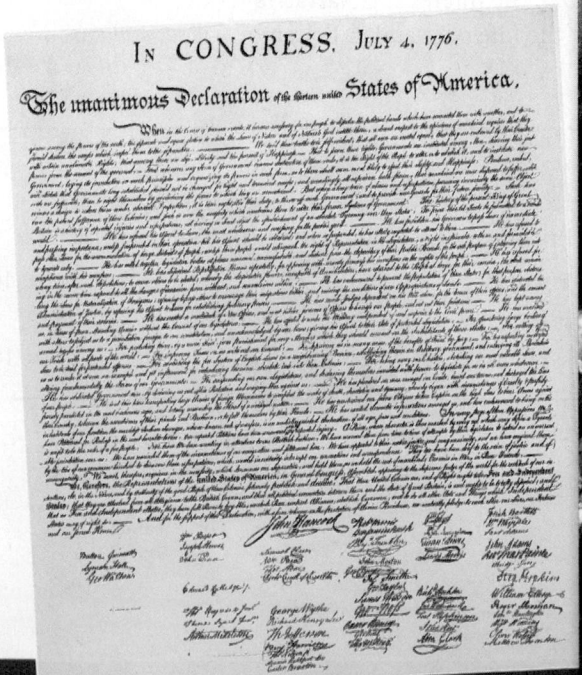

Imagination and the Individual: American Romanticism 1800–1860

"I unsettle all things. No facts are to me sacred; none are profane;
I simply experiment, an endless seeker, with no Past at my back."

—Ralph Waldo Emerson

SKILLS FOCUS Literary Skills Evaluate and analyze the philosophical, political, religious, ethical, and social influences of a historical period.

Reading Skills Identify and understand chronological order; identify and understand graphic elements; use text organizers such as overviews, headings, and graphic features to locate and categorize information; read widely to increase knowledge of the student's culture, the culture of others, and the common elements across cultures; identify and understand elements of text structure (including headings and sections).

What Do You Think? Where does an individual find inspiration?

COLLECTION **4** The Transforming
Imagination

SKILLS FOCUS Literary Skills Evaluate and analyze the philosophical, political, religious, ethical, and social influences of a historical period; analyze Romanticism; understand and analyze theme; metaphor; meter; sonnets; how imagery conveys meaning; figures of speech; historical context; philosophical context; paradox; parallelism; persuasive devices.

Reading Skills Read widely to increase knowledge of the student's culture, the culture of others, and the common elements across cultures; understand and analyze inverted sentences; annotate a poem; visualize imagery; identify the main idea of a text; monitor your reading for comprehension; read to understand style; make generalizations about a writer's beliefs; recognize persuasive techniques (logical, ethical, and emotional appeals).

COLLECTION 5 The Realms of Darkness

SKILLS FOCUS **Literary Skills** Evaluate genres and traditions in American literature; understand and analyze mood; symbolism; historical context; atmosphere; symbolic meaning; sound effects in poetry; characterization.

Reading Skills Make predictions as a strategy for comprehension; make inferences as a strategy for comprehension; use a variety of reading skills to understand literary and informational text; monitor your reading for comprehension; understand and analyze style, archaic words, word choice, language structures, and syntax; apply and monitor a variety of response and comprehension strategies; respond to graphics; retell key events; use oral interpretation to understand a poem; draw inferences about characters.

A House Divided: The Civil War Era and Its Aftermath 1850–1890

"'A house divided against itself cannot stand.' I believe this government cannot endure, permanently half slave and half free."

—Abraham Lincoln

SKILLS FOCUS **Literary Skills** Evaluate and analyze the philosophical, political, religious, ethical, and social influences of a historical period.

Reading Skills Identify and understand chronological order; identify and understand graphic elements; use text organizers such as overviews, headings, and graphic features to locate and categorize information; read widely to increase knowledge of the student's culture, the culture of others, and the common elements across cultures; identify and understand elements of text structure (including headings and sections).

SKILLS FOCUS **Literary Skills** Evaluate and analyze the philosophical, political, religious, ethical, and social influences of a historical period; understand and analyze diction; the characteristics of a writer's style; political context; refrain; oratory; repetition.

Reading Skills Determine the writer's purpose or intent; analyze a writer's perspective; identify and understand appeals to reason; identify and understand appeals to emotion, including loaded words; identify and understand the use of counterclaims/counterarguments in a text.

What Do You Think? How does conflict lead to change?

COLLECTION **6** Up from Slavery

COLLECTION 7 The Ravages of War

SKILLS FOCUS **Literary Skills** Understand and analyze elements of literature from American Romanticism and from the rise of realism; point of view; historical context; credibility in literature; situational irony; verbal irony; the characteristics of American Indian oratory, including repetition and tone.

Reading Skills Analyze the sequence of events in a text; make predictions; identify/analyze tone; identify and analyze emotional appeals in a text.

Informational Skills Understand and analyze author's purpose; analyze primary sources.

COLLECTION **8** Whitman and Dickinson— American Masters

SKILLS FOCUS **Literary Skills** Understand and analyze styles of poetry; the use of catalogs in poetry; the characteristics of free verse; biographical information; theme; symbolism; the use of parallelism; analogy; metaphor; exact rhyme and slant rhyme; style; epigrams; rhythm; irony; paradox; mood.

Reading Skills Understand and analyze the use of text structure in poetry; use paraphrasing or retelling as a strategy for comprehension; compare themes across texts; visualize the text; visualize imagery; compare and contrast poems; analyze poem structure; annotate a poem; summarize a text; monitor reading by paraphrasing.

Informational Skills Analyze rhetorical devices; analyze primary sources.

The Age of Realism 1880–1914

"What is character but the determination of incident? What is incident but the illustration of character?"

—Henry James

SKILLS FOCUS Literary Skills Evaluate and analyze the philosophical, political, religious, ethical, and social influences of a historical period.

Reading Skills Identify and understand chronological order; identify and understand graphic elements; use text organizers such as overviews, headings, and graphic features to locate and categorize information; read widely to increase knowledge of the student's culture, the culture of others, and the common elements across cultures; identify and understand elements of text structures (including headings and sections).

What Do You Think? What forces shape human character?

COLLECTION **9** Regionalism and Local Color

SKILLS FOCUS Literary Skills Understand and analyze regionalism; characterization; tall tales; the characteristics of satire; historical context; extended metaphor; style; setting.

Reading Skills Make predictions as a strategy for comprehension; understand vernacular; identify/recognize a writer's purpose; identify comic devices; make inferences such as conclusions, generalizations, and predictions, and support them using the text.

COLLECTION **10** Realism and Naturalism

SKILLS FOCUS **Literary Skills** Evaluate genres and traditions in American literature; understand and analyze realism and naturalism; irony; philosophical context; connotations; rhyme scheme; symbols.

Reading Skills Analyze historical context, especially political and social influences of the time; understand and analyze cause and effect; read closely for details; identify/recognize a writer's purpose.

Informational Skills Identify main ideas and supporting details.

UNIT 5

The Moderns 1914–1939

"Men travel faster now, but I do not know if they go to better things."
—Willa Cather

What Do You Think? How does progress challenge tradition and redefine society?

COLLECTION 11 Make It New!

COLLECTION 12 Modern American Fiction

SKILLS FOCUS **Literary Skills** Evaluate and analyze the philosophical, political, religious, ethical, and social influences of a historical period; understand and analyze Modernism; the protagonist and the antihero archetype; character motivation; setting; credibility in literature; tone; theme; stream of consciousness; political context; parody; foreshadowing.

Reading Skills Read for details; make inferences about characters; make inferences as a strategy for comprehension; analyze repetition; identify details; close reading; analyze cause and effect; make predictions as a strategy for comprehension.

Informational Skills Determine a speaker's message; analyze an author's beliefs; organize and record new information in systematic ways, such as notes, charts, and graphic organizers.

COLLECTION **13** The Harlem Renaissance

SKILLS FOCUS **Literary Skills** Evaluate and analyze the philosophical, political, religious, ethical, and social influences of a historical period; understand and analyze the Harlem Renaissance; the characteristics of autobiography; style; extended metaphor; metaphor; simile; rhythm; repetition; mood; political context.

Reading Skills Identify historical context; understand the use of text structure in poetry; compare and contrast poems; understand the writer's context; visualize the text; identify historical themes.

Informational Skills Analyze an author's arguments; identify and understand patterns of organization; identify comparison contrast organization.

The Contemporary Period
1939 to Present

"Everything is connected in the end."
—Don DeLillo

What Do You Think? What human needs and desires do we have in common?

COLLECTION 14 The Wages of War

COLLECTION 15 Contemporary Drama

COLLECTION 16 Contemporary Fiction

SKILLS FOCUS **Literary Skills** Understand and analyze characterization; static and dynamic characters; theme; conflict; credibility in literature; the characteristics of a writer's style; character motivation; biographical information; symbols; the use of catalog.

Reading Skills Draw inferences about characters; analyze the sequence of events in a text; analyze historical context, especially political and social influences of the time; learn through questioning; make predictions as a strategy for comprehension; make inferences about characters; analyze a writer's message; interpret/analyze details; identify and understand patterns of organization.

COLLECTION **17** Contemporary Nonfiction

COLLECTION **18** Contemporary Poetry

Comparing Texts

Selections by Alternative Themes

Selections are listed here in alternative theme groupings.

SELECTIONS BY ALTERNATIVE THEMES continued

SELECTIONS BY ALTERNATIVE THEMES continued

Selections by Genre

DRAMA

POETRY

SELECTIONS BY GENRE continued

NONFICTION AND INFORMATIONAL TEXT
APHORISMS

AUTOBIOGRAPHIES

BIOGRAPHY

CHRONICLE

DIARY

ESSAYS

SELECTIONS BY GENRE continued

UNIT INTRODUCTIONS

LITERARY FOCUS ESSAYS

READING FOCUS ESSAYS

HISTORY

SELECTIONS BY GENRE continued

POLITICAL ESSAY

POLICY STATEMENTS

SERMON

SPEECHES

Skills, Workshops, and Features

SKILLS

LITERARY FOCUS ESSAYS

READING FOCUS ESSAYS

LITERARY SKILLS

SKILLS, WORKSHOPS, AND FEATURES continued

READING SKILLS FOR LITERARY TEXTS

INFORMATIONAL TEXT SKILLS

VOCABULARY SKILLS
ACADEMIC VOCABULARY

LANGUAGE COACH

SKILLS, WORKSHOPS, AND FEATURES continued

VOCABULARY DEVELOPMENT: VOCABULARY SKILLS

WORKSHOPS
WRITING WORKSHOPS

PREPARING FOR TIMED WRITING

LISTENING AND SPEAKING WORKSHOPS

MEDIA WORKSHOP

FEATURES
LINK TO TODAY

ANALYZING VISUALS

SKILLS, WORKSHOPS, AND FEATURES continued

CROSS-CURRICULAR LINKS

LITERARY PERSPECTIVES

GRAMMAR LINKS

SKILLS REVIEW

LANGUAGE HANDBOOK

WRITER'S HANDBOOK

Why Be a Reader/Writer?

by Kylene Beers

File   Edit   View   Favorites   Tools   Help

Back   Forward   Stop   Refresh   Home   Search   Favorites   History   Mail   Print

Address   http://www.hrw.com/   Go

HOME   WHAT'S NEW   >>ARTICLES   PEOPLE   FAQ   CONTACT

The Story of the Sederand

In the following paragraph, you'll find several sentences that won't make much sense. There's a point to asking you to read these nonsense sentences, so play along, please!

Sederand is filled with blanderly grup. The grup is nanderlated in emublobbed corderices. These corderices flankle often and then, after flankling, rebolib into swabolines. The swabolines, unlike sederand, can be grizzled and then blubbed.

Internet

Now, answer the following questions:

1 What is sederand filled with?
2 Where is grup nanderlated?
3 What happens to corderice after flankling?
4 What can be done to swabolines that cannot be done to sederand?

Check your answers against the key printed upside down at the right of this page. How did you do? Maybe you did surprisingly well, even when you didn't understand—**really** understand—anything you read.

Now, read the paragraph again, and ask **your own** questions, what you **really** want to know about the paragraph—for example, "Just what is sederand?" Don't read on until you have at least one other question in mind.

Maybe you asked, "Why should I care about sederand?" You could have asked, "What's sederand got to do with me?" Maybe you even thought (don't be afraid to admit it), "Who cares?" Those are **GREAT** questions—**IMPORTANT** questions, actually—for two reasons:
1 They are the questions YOU thought of and asked.
2 They are the questions that make that paragraph meaningful to YOU.

CLICK HERE FOR SOME GREAT QUESTIONS!

Answers

1 Sederand is filled with blanderly grup.
2 Grup is nanderlated in emublobbed corderices.
3 After flankling, corderices rebolib into swabolines.
4 Swabolines can be grizzled and then blubbed.

ASKING QUESTIONS

It's easy in school to get caught up in answering other people's questions—teacher questions, test questions, textbook questions. After you graduate, your ability to respond to questions will be a much-needed skill throughout your life ahead.

Q: Your boss and co-workers will ask you questions. Your friends and your family will all ask questions. Wherever you go, questions, questions, questions:

○ Paper or ○ plastic?   When's the next bus? _____

○ Cash or ○ credit?   What's up after graduation? _____

○ Soup or ○ salad?   Who are you? _____

If you don't pause to ask your own questions, though, you're missing out on one of the most important ways to learn. **Why? Because the questions YOU ask mean the most.**

QUESTIONING WHILE READING

That's *why you should read.*

When you read with your own questions in mind, you are using the words on the page to learn more about YOURSELF and the world around you.

Throughout this book you'll find strategies and tips for improving your reading comprehension. You'll also find places where you are stopped and asked what the reading means *to you*. As you read, answer not only the questions that are posed to you but also the questions YOU wonder about.

QUESTIONING WHILE WRITING

That's *why you should write, too.*

While *reading* gives you information that helps you think about yourself and the world, *writing* **helps you crystallize your thoughts about yourself and the world.**

Being a writer is about something far bigger than making a certain grade: **Writing helps you think.**

Throughout this book you'll be given many opportunities to write. Instead of approaching these tasks as mere assignments to complete, try seeing them as opportunities to explore what YOU think and understand about the topic.

Kylene Beers
Senior Author
Elements of Literature

Kylene: At this stage in high school, you've already learned a great deal about reading and writing. You'll learn much more this year. And if you'll remember to ask your own questions as you read and to use writing as a way to think carefully, then perhaps you'll discover and articulate what is important to YOU and *why*.

Those insights will serve you well in the times ahead.   **SEND**

How to Use Your Textbook

Each time you get a new cell phone, you find it has more features than the last one.
Without looking at the instructions, you may miss out on the benefits of the phone.
It's the same with your textbook. This section introduces you to your book's features,
so that you can be successful from the beginning.

Unit Opener

As you look at the title and dates for each unit, think about what you might know already about that time period. Think about the **quotation**. What does it suggest about the literature of the historical period? Keep the **What Do You Think?** question in mind as you go through the unit. You may find that what you think about the period and its literature evolves as you work through the unit.

Time Line

In this book, you will study literature and events that occurred in both the recent and the distant past. The time line will help you to put it all in perspective. You'll see how history influenced literature and vice versa, including worldwide literary movements and historical events.

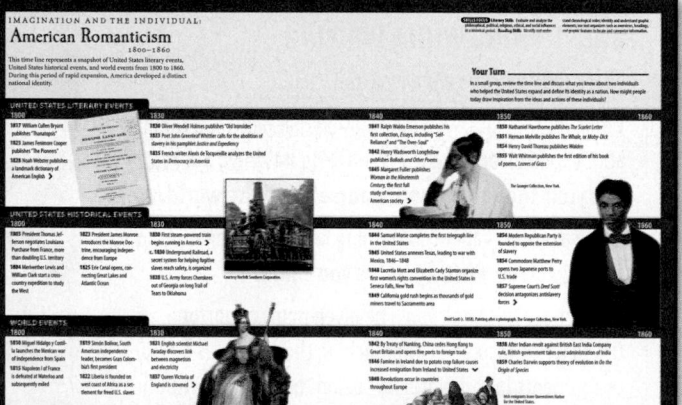

Introduction with Key Concepts

Often we say, "Cut to the chase," or, "Just give me the big picture." This is what **Key Concepts** does. For each unit, this feature provides the essentials about both the literature and the history of the time period. This understanding will be a foundation for your reading throughout the unit—how works of literature emerge in a time and place.

Link to Today

Though there has never been a century like this one in terms of instant communication, what makes us tick as humans hasn't really changed that much. Modern film makers draw on ancient epics, and modern history is driven by past history. **Link to Today** shows the connection and the relevance between events of the time period and our world today.

Collection Opener

A collection focuses on the major literary movements or literary works within the unit's time period. Each collection opener identifies the title of the collection—a clue to its contents—as well as a quotation that suggests a key theme or idea of the period. Try to notice the image on the opener page; consider what it suggests about the literary period.

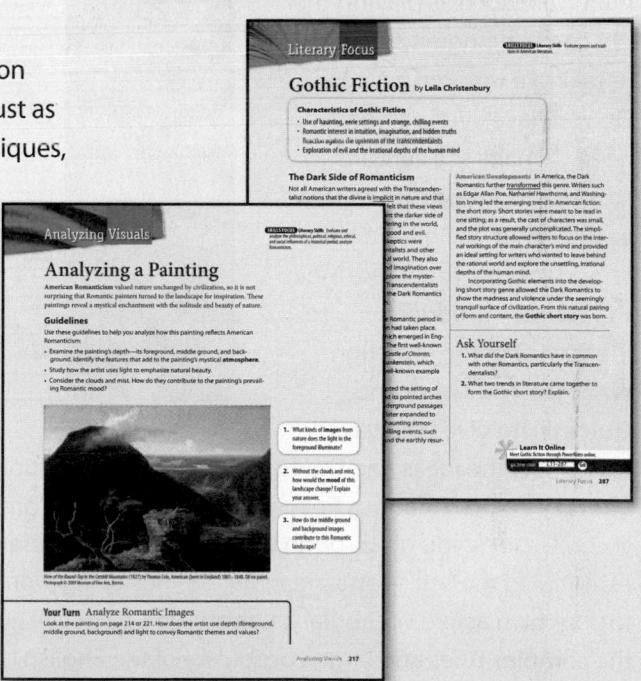

Literary Focus

The **Literary Focus** gives you necessary background on the literature and the time period you are studying. Just as Japanese anime has certain styles, themes, and techniques, the literary masters of the past had a framework within which they worked. **Literary Focus** helps you better understand that framework.

Analyzing Visuals

You are regularly immersed in images through television, magazines, street art, and billboards. Because visual media are so prevalent, you may find it challenging to think about them consciously and critically. **Analyzing Visuals** helps you apply your visual savvy to images and then connect those skills to the literary works you're reading.

How to Use Your Textbook

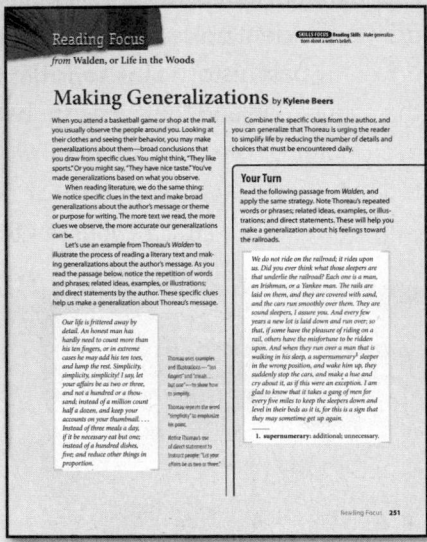

Reading Focus

Sometimes reading selections written in the past seems a little like trying to read something in another language that you barely know. **Reading Focus** gives you the keys to unlock the text. Is the word order changed in this poem? How did the writer use imagery to help the reader visualize the story in his mind? How is the sentence structure different from what we see in today's literature?

Literary Selection Pages
Preparing to Read

Before you do anything important such as playing the big game, going on a date, or taking a trip, you prepare. Do you have everything you need to make the venture successful? **Preparing to Read** ensures that you have all the important bits you need. **Meet the Writer** introduces you to the author of the selection. **What Do You Think** and **QuickWrite** give you ways

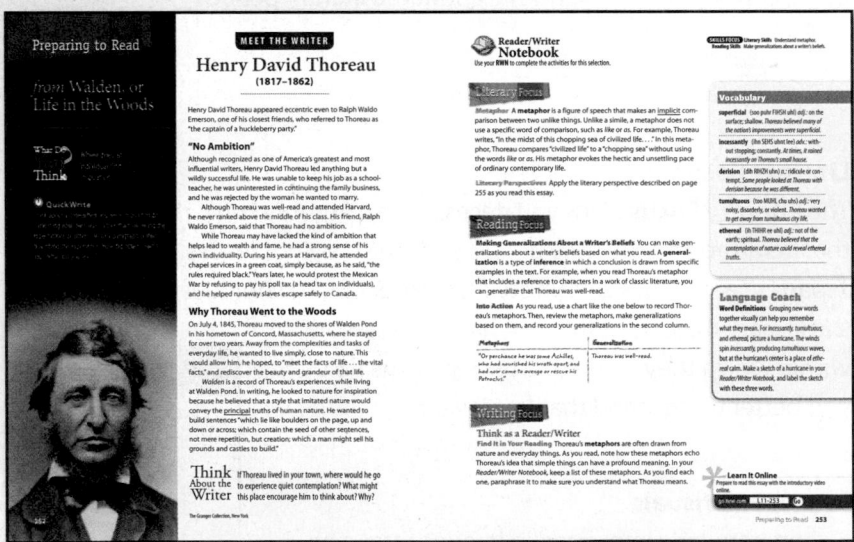

to connect the ideas and themes of the literary selection to your life. The **Literary Focus, Reading Focus,** and **Writing Focus** present the skills you will use as you go through the selection. **Vocabulary** lists the words essential to the selection's meaning, besides being words you should add to your own active vocabulary. **Language Coach** will guide you through the complex rules and large vocabulary of the English language.

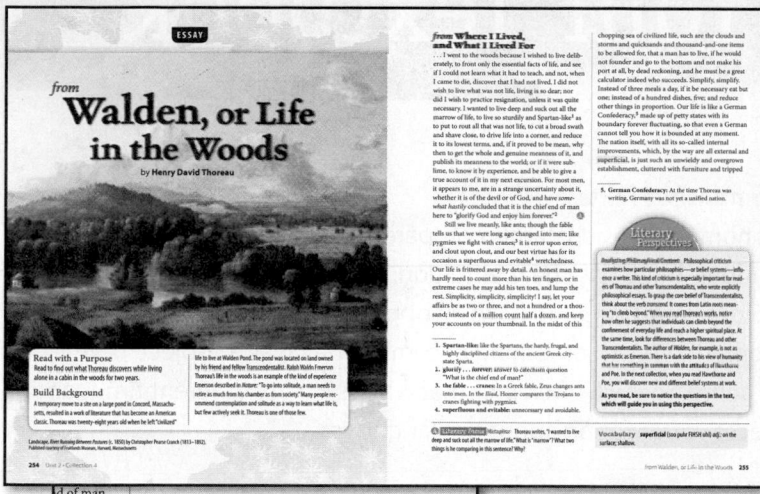

Selection

Which songs, movies, or stories from today do you think will captivate people fifty or even five hundred years from now? The few that survive will be the ones that help us grasp what it means to be human. The selections in this textbook are those universal ones that have survived. **Read with a Purpose** gives you a goal for your reading. **Build Background** provides any information you may need as context for the selection.

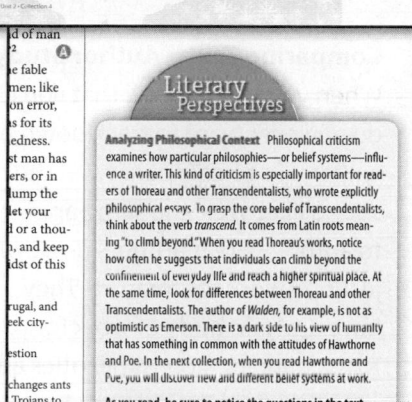

Literary Perspectives

Whether you are male or female, rich or poor, native or new to the U.S. influences how you see things. These same factors affect how authors write as well as how you read a piece of literature. **Literary Perspectives** helps you become aware of different perspectives, or lenses, for looking at literature to get a more complete view.

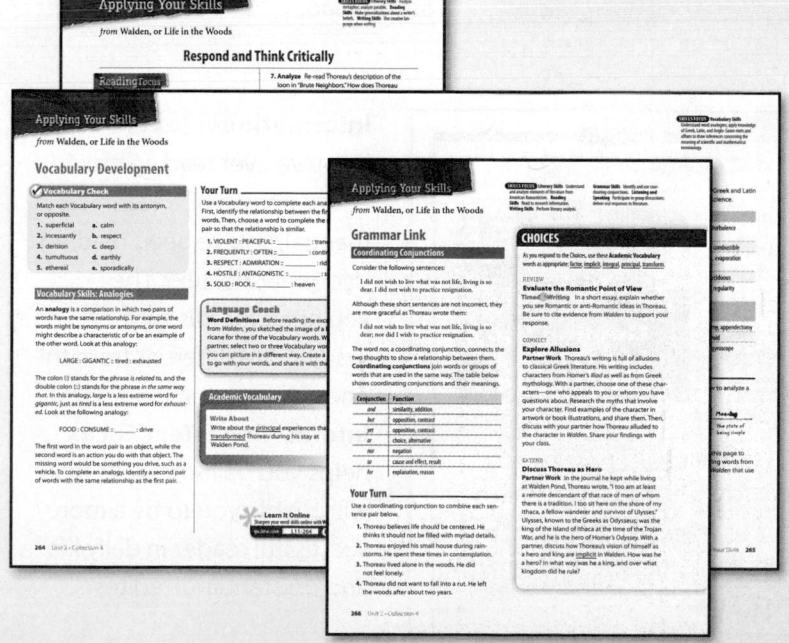

Applying Your Skills

Athletes, musicians, and artists all practice long and hard to perfect their skill. Games, performances, or exhibitions give them a venue for applying their skills. **Applying Your Skills** gives you the opportunity to apply the reading, literary and vocabulary skills you learned about before reading and then practiced throughout the selection. It shows how you are mastering the skills in each selection.

How to Use Your Textbook

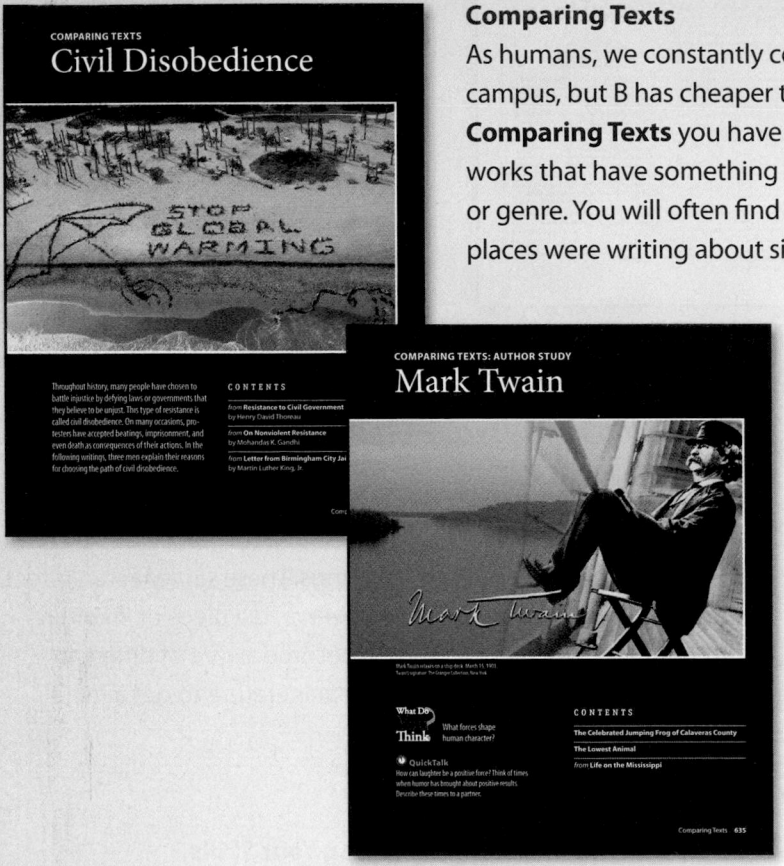

Comparing Texts

As humans, we constantly compare. College A has the prettiest campus, but B has cheaper tuition, and C is closer to home. In **Comparing Texts** you have an opportunity to compare several works that have something in common such as a subject, theme, or genre. You will often find that writers in very different times and places were writing about similar things.

Comparing Texts: Author Study

When you hear a band that you like, do you ever want to track down their earlier CDs to compare what they sound like? Well, the same applies to authors. Great authors don't write just one work of literature. They have a whole body of work for you to read and explore similarities and differences. In **Comparing Texts: Author Study** you'll dive into a number of works by an important author to make deeper connections as you read.

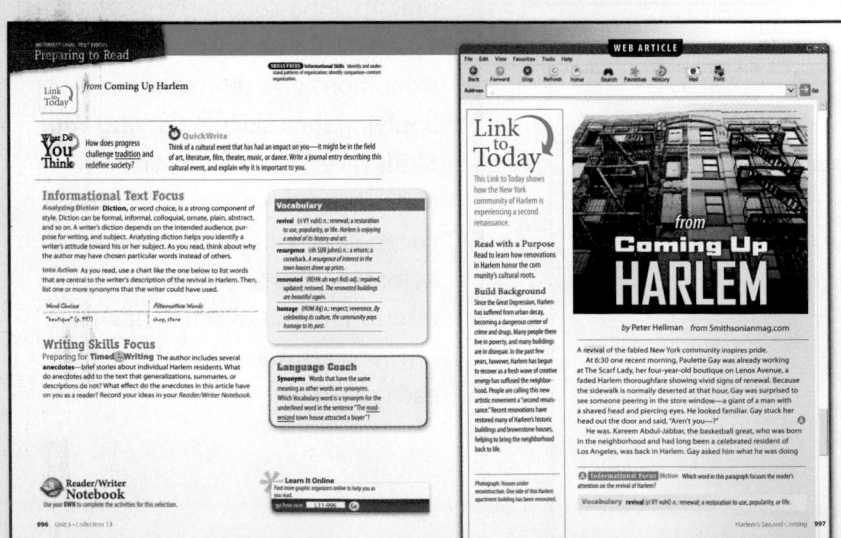

Informational Text Focus

If you've ever read an online encyclopedia or a technical manual, you've been reading informational text. The skills you need for this type of reading are different from the ones you use for literary text. **Informational Text Focus** helps you gain the skills that will enable you to be a more successful reader in daily life and on standardized tests.

Writing Workshop

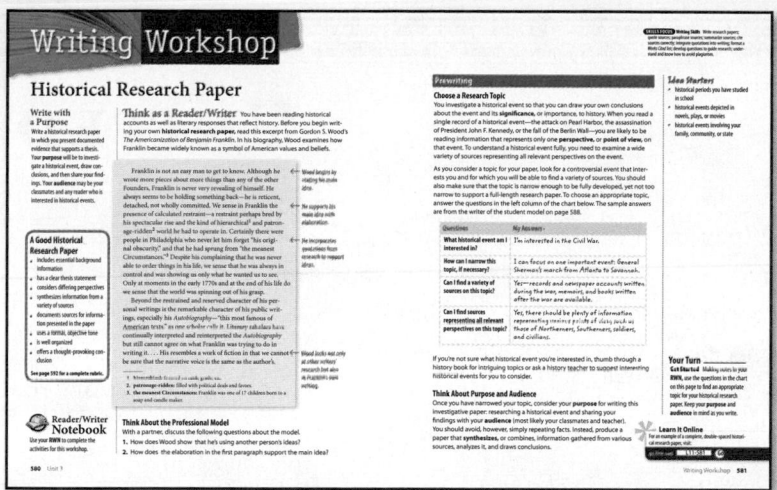

As you look forward to work, technical training, or college, you may wonder whether you'll leave writing behind in high school. The answer is most definitely "no." Any further education or career will require that you write, probably more than you have the past eleven or twelve years. **Writing Workshops** prepare you for that writing by helping you think through a piece of writing from the glimmer of an idea to the final version.

Preparing for Timed Writing

Have you ever nervously sat with a blank sheet of paper, trying to respond to a writing prompt, while the clock ticks ominously? **Preparing for Timed Writing** helps you practice for on-demand, or timed, writing so that you can realize your dreams of success.

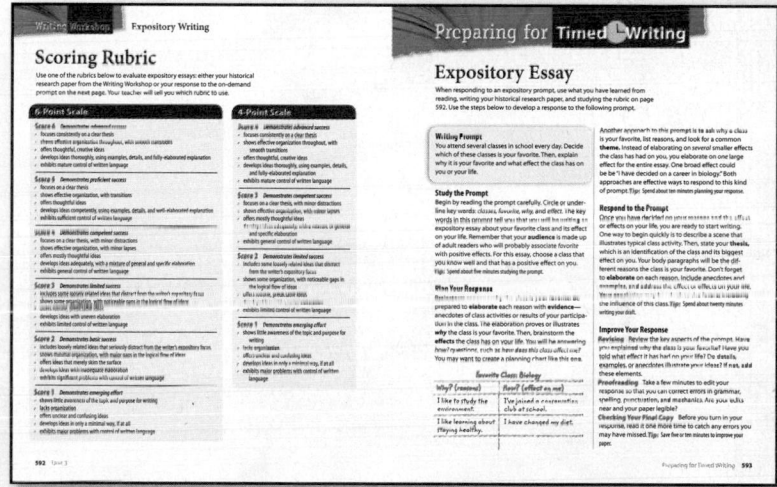

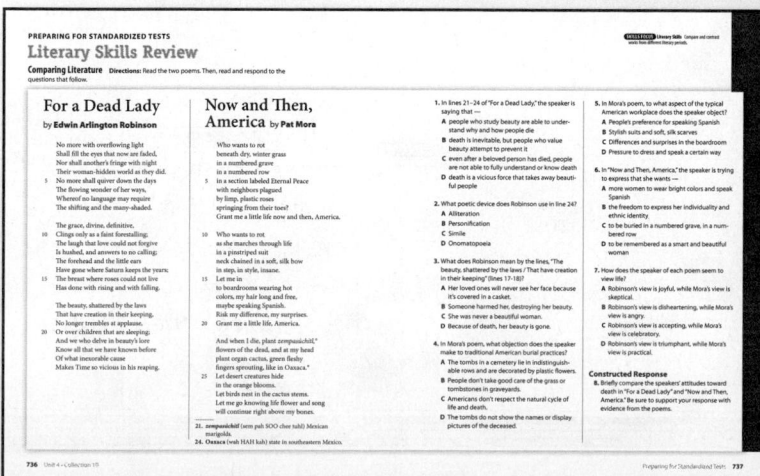

Preparing for Standardized Tests

Does the thought of taking a standardized test make you break out into a cold sweat? **Preparing for Standardized Tests** can reduce your anxiety by giving you the practice you need to feel more confident during testing.

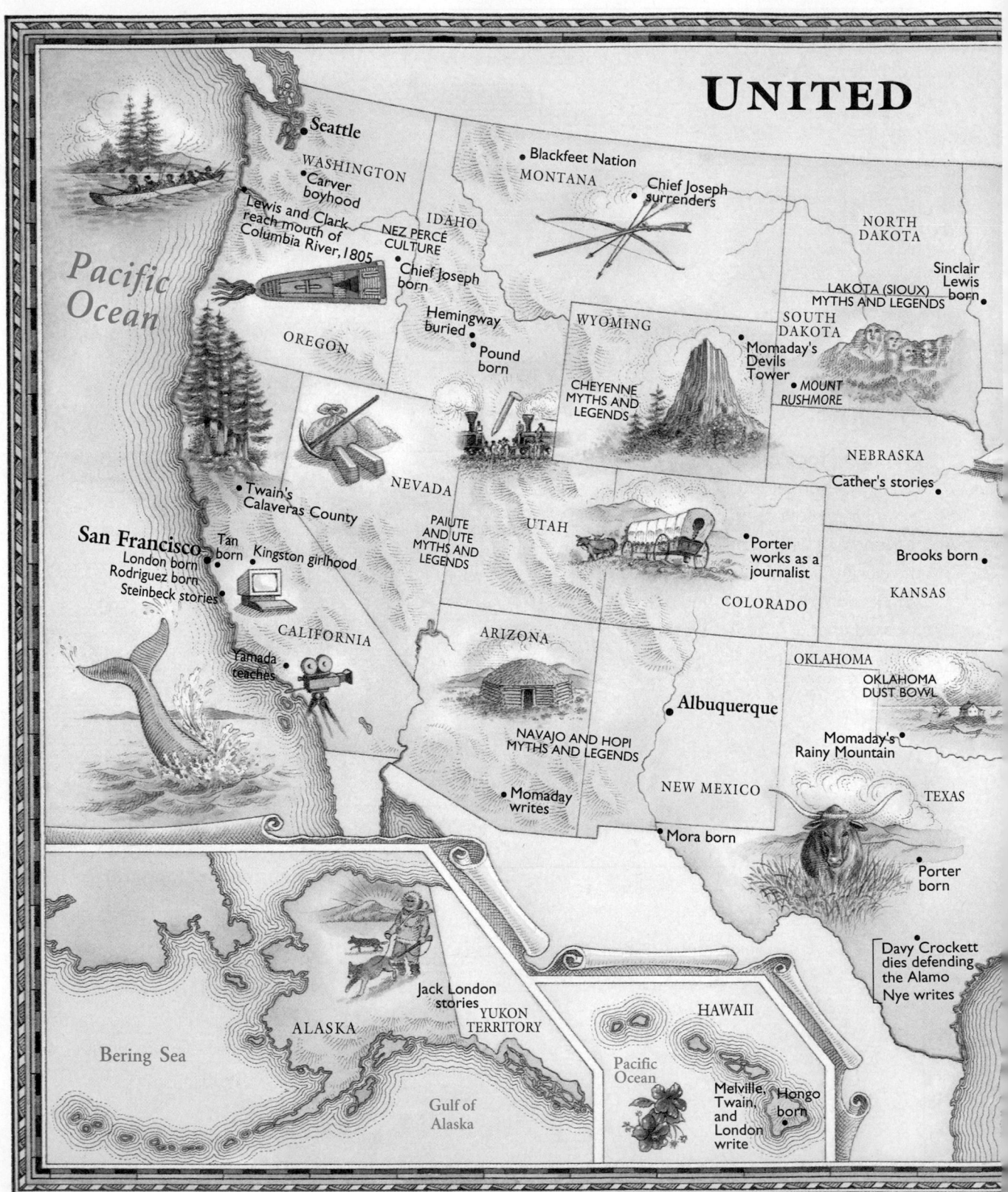

UNITED

Seattle

WASHINGTON

Carver boyhood

Lewis and Clark reach mouth of Columbia River, 1805

Pacific Ocean

IDAHO

NEZ PERCÉ CULTURE

Chief Joseph born

Hemingway buried

Pound born

OREGON

NEVADA

Twain's Calaveras County

San Francisco

Tan born

London born
Rodriguez born
Steinbeck stories

Kingston girlhood

CALIFORNIA

Yamada teaches

PAIUTE AND UTE MYTHS AND LEGENDS

ARIZONA

NAVAJO AND HOPI MYTHS AND LEGENDS

Momaday writes

Blackfeet Nation

MONTANA

Chief Joseph surrenders

WYOMING

CHEYENNE MYTHS AND LEGENDS

UTAH

NORTH DAKOTA

Sinclair Lewis born

LAKOTA (SIOUX) MYTHS AND LEGENDS

SOUTH DAKOTA

Momaday's Devils Tower

MOUNT RUSHMORE

NEBRASKA

Cather's stories

Porter works as a journalist

COLORADO

Brooks born

KANSAS

OKLAHOMA

OKLAHOMA DUST BOWL

Albuquerque

Momaday's Rainy Mountain

NEW MEXICO

TEXAS

Mora born

Porter born

Davy Crockett dies defending the Alamo

Nye writes

Jack London stories

YUKON TERRITORY

ALASKA

Bering Sea

Gulf of Alaska

HAWAII

Pacific Ocean

Melville, Twain, and London write

Hongo born

STATES

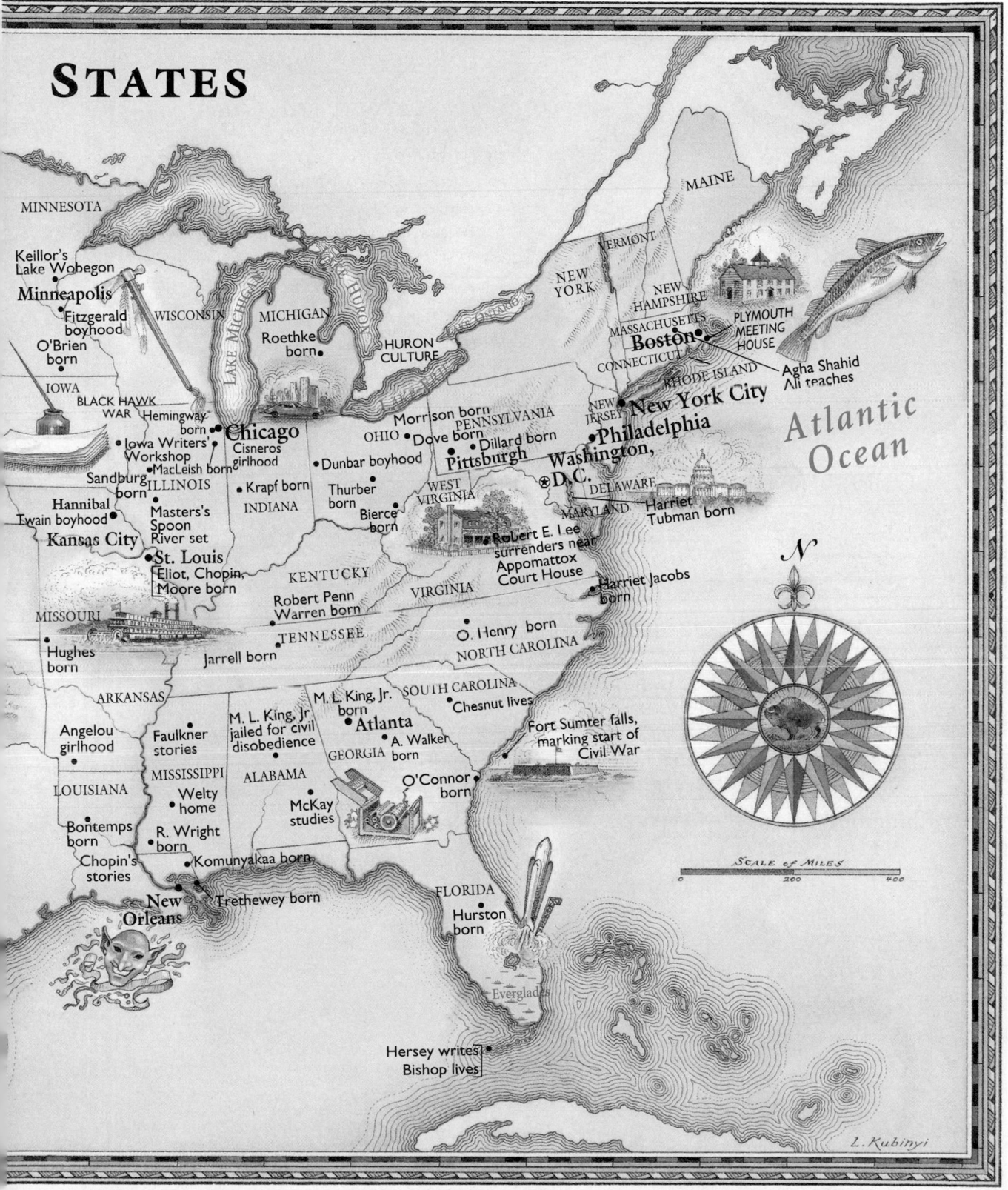

MINNESOTA

Keillor's
Lake Wobegon
Minneapolis
Fitzgerald
boyhood
O'Brien
born

WISCONSIN

IOWA

BLACK HAWK
WAR
Hemingway
born

Iowa Writers'
Workshop
MacLeish born
Sandburg
born ILLINOIS

Hannibal
Twain boyhood
Kansas City

Masters's
Spoon
River set
St. Louis
Eliot, Chopin,
Moore born

MISSOURI

Hughes
born

Chicago
Cisneros
girlhood

Krapf born

INDIANA

Dunbar boyhood

Thurber
born

Bierce
born

OHIO

Morrison born

Dove born

Dillard born
Pittsburgh

**Washington,
D.C.**

PENNSYLVANIA

WEST
VIRGINIA

Robert E. Lee
surrenders near
Appomattox
Court House

KENTUCKY

Robert Penn
Warren born

VIRGINIA

Jarrell born

TENNESSEE

O. Henry born

NORTH CAROLINA

ARKANSAS

Angelou
girlhood

LOUISIANA

Bontemps
born

Chopin's
stories

**New
Orleans**

Faulkner
stories

MISSISSIPPI

Welty
home

R. Wright
born

Komunyakaa born

Trethewey born

M. L. King, Jr
jailed for civil
disobedience

GEORGIA

ALABAMA

McKay
studies

M.L. King, Jr.
born
Atlanta

A. Walker
born

O'Connor
born

SOUTH CAROLINA

Chesnut lives

Fort Sumter falls,
marking start of
Civil War

FLORIDA

Hurston
born

Everglades

Hersey writes
Bishop lives

MAINE

VERMONT

NEW
YORK

NEW
HAMPSHIRE

MASSACHUSETTS

Boston

CONNECTICUT

RHODE ISLAND

NEW
JERSEY **New York City**

Philadelphia

DELAWARE

MARYLAND Harriet
Tubman born

PLYMOUTH
MEETING
HOUSE

Agha Shahid
Ali teaches

Harriet Jacobs
born

*Atlantic
Ocean*

LAKE MICHIGAN

MICHIGAN
Roethke
born

LAKE HURON

LAKE ONTARIO

HURON
CULTURE

N

SCALE of MILES

0   200   400

L. Kubinyi

A53

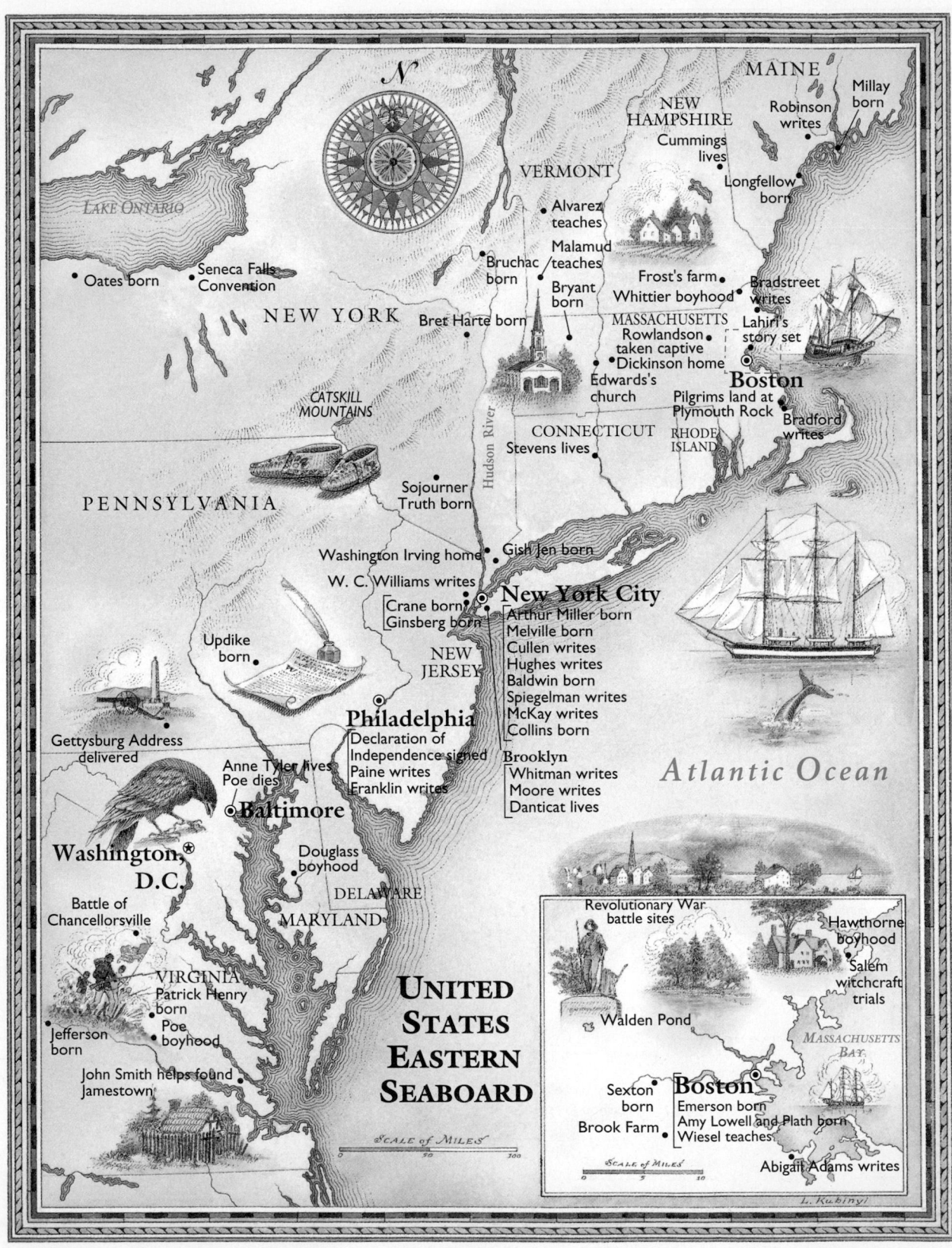

UNITED STATES EASTERN SEABOARD

MAINE
Millay born
Robinson writes
Longfellow born

NEW HAMPSHIRE
Cummings lives

VERMONT
Alvarez teaches
Malamud teaches
Bryant born

Frost's farm
Whittier boyhood
Bradstreet writes
Lahiri's story set

MASSACHUSETTS
Rowlandson taken captive
Dickinson home
Edwards's church

Boston

LAKE ONTARIO

Oates born
Seneca Falls Convention

NEW YORK

Bruchac born

Bret Harte born

CATSKILL MOUNTAINS

CONNECTICUT
Stevens lives

RHODE ISLAND

Pilgrims land at Plymouth Rock
Bradford writes

Hudson River

Sojourner Truth born

PENNSYLVANIA

Washington Irving home
W. C. Williams writes
Crane born
Ginsberg born

Gish Jen born

New York City
Arthur Miller born
Melville born
Cullen writes
Hughes writes
Baldwin born
Spiegelman writes
McKay writes
Collins born

NEW JERSEY

Updike born

Philadelphia
Declaration of Independence signed
Paine writes
Franklin writes

Brooklyn
Whitman writes
Moore writes
Danticat lives

Atlantic Ocean

Gettysburg Address delivered

Anne Tyler lives
Poe dies

Baltimore

Washington, D.C.

Battle of Chancellorsville

Douglass boyhood

DELAWARE

MARYLAND

VIRGINIA
Patrick Henry born
Poe boyhood

Jefferson born

John Smith helps found Jamestown

Scale of Miles
0   50   300

Revolutionary War battle sites

Hawthorne boyhood
Salem witchcraft trials

Walden Pond

MASSACHUSETTS BAY

Sexton born
Brook Farm

Boston
Emerson born
Amy Lowell and Plath born
Wiesel teaches

Abigail Adams writes

Scale of Miles
0   5   10

L. Kubinyi

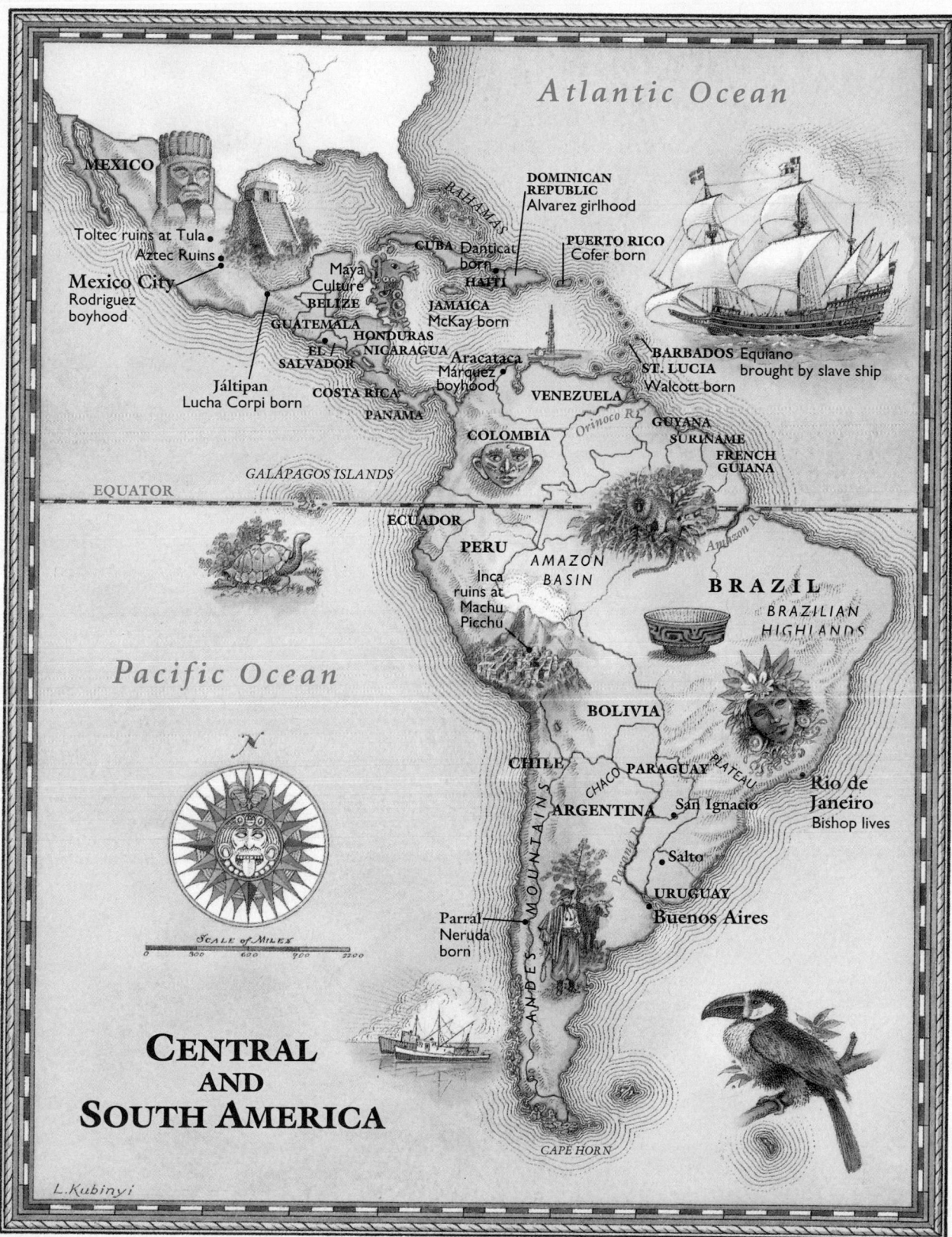

Atlantic Ocean

MEXICO

Toltec ruins at Tula
Aztec Ruins

Mexico City
Rodriguez
boyhood

BAHAMAS

DOMINICAN
REPUBLIC
Alvarez girlhood

CUBA Danticat
born

PUERTO RICO
Cofer born

HAITI

Maya
Culture

BELIZE

JAMAICA
McKay born

GUATEMALA

HONDURAS

EL
SALVADOR

NICARAGUA

Jáltipan
Lucha Corpi born

COSTA RICA

PANAMA

Aracataca
Márquez
boyhood

BARBADOS Equiano
brought by slave ship

ST. LUCIA
Walcott born

VENEZUELA

Orinoco R.

GUYANA

SURINAME

FRENCH
GUIANA

COLOMBIA

GALÁPAGOS ISLANDS

EQUATOR

ECUADOR

PERU

Inca
ruins at
Machu
Picchu

AMAZON
BASIN

Amazon R.

BRAZIL

BRAZILIAN
HIGHLANDS

Pacific Ocean

BOLIVIA

CHILE

PARAGUAY

PLATEAU

Rio de
Janeiro
Bishop lives

CHACO

ARGENTINA

San Ignacio

N

Paraná R.

Salto

SCALE of MILES

0   300   600   900   1200

Parral
Neruda
born

ANDES MOUNTAINS

URUGUAY

Buenos Aires

CENTRAL
AND
SOUTH AMERICA

CAPE HORN

L. Kubinyi

Encounters and Foundations to 1800

COLLECTION 1
Native American Voices

COLLECTION 2
Voyages and Visions

COLLECTION 3
Forging a New Nation

"[In America] individuals of all nations are melted into a new race of men, whose labors . . . will one day cause great changes in the world."

— **Michel-Guillaume Jean de Crèvecoeur**

What Do **You** **Think** How can people's beliefs affect their actions?

The Landing of the Pilgrims (1825) (detail), fireboard by Samuel Bartoll.

Learn It Online
Find out more about this historical period online.

go.hrw.com L11-1 **Go**

1

Encounters and Foundations to 1800

This time line presents a snapshot of United States literary events, United States historical events, and world events to 1800. During this period widespread political and cultural changes took place in the United States and around the world.

UNITED STATES LITERARY EVENTS

1500

1620–1647 William Bradford writes *Of Plymouth Plantation*

1650 Anne Bradstreet's *The Tenth Muse Lately Sprung Up in America* is published in England

1682 Mary Rowlandson chronicles her captivity during King Philip's War

1700

1700 Samuel Sewall publishes *The Selling of Joseph*, a tract against slavery

1728 William Byrd writes *The History of the Dividing Line*

1741 Jonathan Edwards ❯ delivers his vivid sermon "Sinners in the Hands of an Angry God"

> SINNERS
> In the Hands of an
> Angry GOD.
> A SERMON
> Preached at Enfield, July 8th 1741.
> At a Time of great Awakenings; and attended with remarkable Impressions on many of the Hearers.
> By Jonathan Edwards, A.M.
> Pastor of the Church of CHRIST in Northampton.
>
> Amos ix. 2, 3. Though they dig into Hell, thence shall mine Hand take them; though they climb up to Heaven, thence will I bring them down: And though they hide themselves in the Top of Carmel, I will search and take them out thence; and though they be hid from my Sight in the Bottom of the Sea, thence I will command the Serpent, and he shall bite them.
>
> BOSTON: Printed and Sold by S. KNEELAND and T. GREEN. in Queen-Street over against the Prison, 1741.

UNITED STATES HISTORICAL EVENTS

1500

c. 1500 Mohawk leader Dekanawida establishes the Iroquois Confederacy

1528 Spanish explorer Álvar Núñez Cabeza de Vaca lands in Florida

c. 1630 Great Migration of Puritans to New England begins

1690 Slavery exists in all English Colonies in North America ⌄

The Granger Collection, New York.

1700

1700 About 251,000 European settlers live in what is now the United States

1702 Yale college is founded

1712 First sperm whale captured by an American from Massachusetts

1716 San Antonio de Béxar is founded in present-day Texas

1718 The French found the city of New Orleans

1721 Smallpox epidemic hits Boston

1740–1745 The Great Awakening is touched off by a traveling English preacher

WORLD EVENTS

1500

1521 Aztec Empire falls to Spanish army

1605–1606 England's William Shakespeare writes *King Lear* and *Macbeth*

1632–1638 Mughal emperor Shan Jahan builds Taj Mahal in northern India ⌄

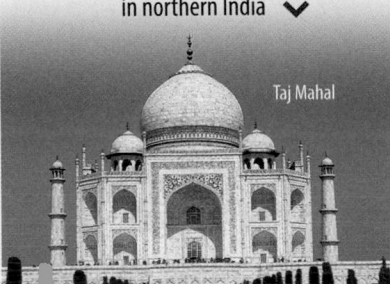

Taj Mahal

1700

1719 England's Daniel Defoe publishes *Robinson Crusoe*, considered one of the first English novels

1729 German composer Johann Sebastian Bach completes the oratorio *St. Matthew Passion*

1742 George Frideric Handel's *Messiah* is first performed, in Dublin, Ireland

1748 France's Montesquieu publishes *The Spirit of Laws*, a study of government later reflected in the U.S. Constitution

Your Turn

With a partner, review the time line and choose a few events that reflect the beliefs of a person or a group about a social or cultural issue. Discuss how you think these beliefs affected people's lives during this time period.

1750   **1780**   **1800**

1771 Benjamin Franklin begins to write his *Autobiography*

1773 Phillis Wheatley publishes *Poems on Various Subjects, Religious and Moral*

1775 At the Virginia Convention, Patrick Henry demands liberty from British rule

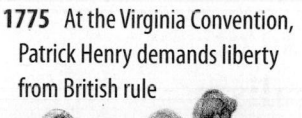

1787–1788 *The Federalist,* a series of essays by Alexander Hamilton, James Madison, and John Jay, urges voters to approve the U.S. Constitution

1789 Olaudah Equiano publishes *The Interesting Narrative of the Life of Olaudah Equiano*

1793 John Woolman writes *A Word of Remembrance and Caution to the Rich,* calling for the abolition of slavery

Patrick Henry addresses the Virginia Convention. The Granger Collection, New York.

1750   **1780**   **1800**

1752 Benjamin Franklin proves that lightning is a manifestation of electricity

‹ 1773 Boston Tea Party occurs in Boston Harbor

April 19, 1775 First shots of American Revolution are fired at Lexington and Concord, Massachusetts

July 4, 1776 Second Continental Congress adopts the Declaration of Independence

Boston Tea Party

October 1781 American Revolutionary War ends as British surrender at Yorktown, Virginia **›**

1789 George Washington is inaugurated as first president under U.S. Constitution

1790 First census in America sets population at about 3.9 million

1793 Invention of cotton gin leads to increase in slave labor

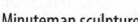

Minuteman sculpture

1750   **1780**   **1800**

1760 George III becomes king of England

1763 French and Indian War officially ends as Britain gains control of most French North American territory

1768 Ottoman Empire declares war on Russia

1778 France formally recognizes the United States of America and promises to send military help

1787 Austrian composer Wolfgang Amadeus Mozart finishes the opera *Don Giovanni* **›**

1789 French Revolution begins

1796 English physician Edward Jenner develops smallpox vaccine

1799 Napoleon Bonaparte becomes dictator of France

Mozart

3

Encounters and Foundations to 1800

About five hundred years ago, European explorers and Native Americans encountered each other for the first time. Later, in 1620, the first English Puritans landed at Plymouth, Massachusetts. Valuing self-reliance and industriousness, the Puritans carved out a new society. When the philosophy of rationalism spread from Europe to North America, the belief in the power of reason combined with an American sense of practicality. One byproduct of American rationalism was the mind-set that led to the Declaration of Independence and the American Revolution.

KEY CONCEPTS

Native Cultures Thrive in America

History of the Times Before the arrival of Europeans in the fifteenth century, the Americas were already home to thriving populations of American Indians. These societies, each of which was usually made up of a few thousand people, had extensive histories and diverse cultures.

Literature of the Times Native Americans created a rich oral tradition that includes myths, epics, songs, and chants. Their stories and poems, which were originally told in hundreds of different languages, often teach moral lessons and focus on the natural world.

Penn's Treaty with the Indians (1771–1772) by Benjamin West.

The Puritans Settle in New England

History of the Times English Puritans seeking religious freedom began to arrive in New England in 1620. Striving to lead exemplary lives, they valued self-reliance, hard work, and discipline. These qualities helped them build a new society in a vast and unfamiliar land.

Literature of the Times Puritan writers used the Bible as a model and preferred a simple, plain style. Diaries and histories were important forms of Puritan literature because they recorded the workings of God.

The Rise of Rationalism

History of the Times By the 1750s, many American thinkers had embraced rationalism, a philosophy that stressed the power of reason to discover truth. Rationalists principles influenced the great minds who conceived the Declaration of Independence and governed America after the Revolutionary War.

Literature of the Times In America, the Age of Reason was an age of pamphlets, since most literature served practical or political ends. This literature was rooted in the realities of organizing and governing the new nation.

SKILLS FOCUS **Literary Skills** Evaluate and analyze the philosophical, political, religious, ethical, and social influences of a historical period. **Reading Skills** Read widely to increase knowledge of the student's culture, the culture of others, and the common elements across cultures; identify and understand elements of text structure (including headings and sections).

UNIT 1 INTRODUCTION

KEY CONCEPT

Native Cultures Thrive in America

History of the Times

When European explorers arrived in our hemisphere about five hundred years ago, they were not alone. American Indians had been living here for thousands of years before the first Europeans encountered what they called the New World. As J. H. Parry states in his book *The Spanish Seaborne Empire,* "Columbus did not discover a new world; he established contact between two worlds, both already old."

The first interactions between Europeans and American Indians involved trading. Soon, a mutual curiosity led to increasing interdependence between the cultures. Europeans relied on American Indians to teach them survival skills, such as how to build canoes and shelters, how to make clothing from animal skins, and how to plant crops. In exchange, American Indians were eager to acquire European firearms, textiles, and steel tools.

In the early years of European settlement, American Indians vastly outnumbered the colonists. However, the settlers unwittingly exposed the native population to diseases to which they had no immunity, such as smallpox. Entire villages were wiped out by disease. Against great odds, many Native Americans survived the epidemics only to be forced off their lands by the colonists,[1] who no longer depended on their guidance.

Literature of the Times

Native American literature is rooted in oral tradition.[2] Storytellers were highly valued members of Native American communities. They passed down myths that answered questions about the origins of the world and the place of humans and animals

---

1. **colonists:** settlers or inhabitants of a colony, or a distant land.
2. **oral tradition:** literature that is spoken rather than written.

within it. Oral traditions captured the history of specific Native American groups, detailing their migrations and the challenges they faced after the arrival of Europeans.

Explorers' writings also contribute to our understanding of early Native American life. Alvar Núñez Cabeza de Vaca, an explorer from Spain, wrote a detailed account of the American Indians he encountered in his travels throughout what is now the southeastern United States.

Comprehension Check

What interactions took place between European settlers and Native Americans?

Fast Facts

Historical Highlights

- Dekanawida, a Mohawk visionary, unites American Indian peoples with the Iroquois Confederacy, c. 1500.
- Pilgrims land at Plymouth in 1620.
- Colonists battle the British in the Revolutionary War from 1775 to 1783.

Literary Highlights

- Columbus's journal, published in 1493, describes the North American continent and its people.
- Anne Bradstreet publishes the *Tenth Muse* in 1650.
- Benjamin Franklin publishes *Poor Richard's Almanack* in 1732.

Learn It Online
Find out more about this historical period online.

go.hrw.com | L11-5 | **Go**

The Puritans Settle in New England

History of the Times

In many respects, the American character has been shaped by the moral, ethical, and religious convictions of the English Puritans. Many historians feel that the Puritan ethic of thrift, hard work, and self-sufficiency contributed to the success of capitalism in the New World. The founding of a new society in North America was a business venture as well as a spiritual one. For the Puritans, the physical world and the spiritual world were closely intertwined. Because Puritans believed that wealth was a sign of God's favor, they strove to attain it. *[handwritten: monie is power]*

Spiritual matters also influenced Puritan government. In its eyes, a contract existed between God and humanity. This spiritual covenant was a useful model for social organization: Puritans believed that people should enter freely into agreements concerning their government. The Mayflower Compact, composed and signed while the Puritans were aboard the *Mayflower*, outlined how they would be governed in their new home. By using this contractual agreement, Puritans prepared the groundwork for American constitutional democracy. *[handwritten: no question power]*

Analyzing Visuals

Viewing and Interpreting In what ways has the artist captured the spirit and convictions of Puritanism as it is described on this page? What specific elements of the sculpture are particularly effective?

The Puritan (1883–86; this cast 1899 or after) by Augustus Saint-Gaudens (American, 1848–1907). Bronze; 30 1/2 × 18 1/2 × 13 in. The Metropolitan Museum of Art. Bequest of Jacob Ruppert, 1939 (39.65.53). Image ©The Metropolitan Museum of Art/Art Resource, NY.

used god to start a nation.

On the other hand, because the people holding the power in government based their <u>authority on religious tenets, their political views were sometimes uncompromising and harsh.</u> In 1692, about 150 people in Salem, Massachusetts, were accused of witchcraft. Twenty of those people were executed. Officials feared that the community's moral foundation was in danger and felt that they needed to take extreme action to save political unity.

Literature of the Times

The Bible provided a model for Puritan writing. Viewing each human life as a journey to salvation, the Puritans saw direct connections between biblical events and events in their own lives. Favoring a plain style of writing, they admired clarity of expression and avoided complicated figures of speech.

Diaries and histories—<u>the most common forms of Puritan writing—were believed to reflect the workings of God.</u> Likewise, captivity narratives, such as Mary Rowlandson's account of being captured by the Wampanoag, <u>were meant to reveal the path from sin toward God's grace.</u> Even Puritan poetry, such as the verse of Anne Bradstreet and Edward Taylor, reflected the Puritans' intense piety and strict self-discipline. The fiery sermons of Jonathan Edwards, a transitional figure <u>between Puritan America</u> and modern America, <u>urged people to awaken and seek spiritual salvation.</u>

Comprehension Check

Explain three ways in which Puritan beliefs influenced the colonists' lives.

Link to Today

Not-So-Personal Journals

The rise of the Internet has led many to call our age the "information age." Not since the invention of the printing press in the fifteenth century has a technology so radically transformed the availability of information.

One important development on the Internet has been the proliferation of Web logs, or "blogs." While early blogs were mostly personal diaries, millions of bloggers around the world—everyone from teenagers to political leaders—now use the Internet as a free public forum for their thoughts, ideas, and information.

While the journals and personal narratives of American colonists offered individuals the chance to share their stories with future generations, today's bloggers share theirs with a worldwide audience in real time. As more people turn to blogs for news and political viewpoints, traditional media like newspapers and television are gradually losing their once dominant hold on information. As bloggers become our new reporters and journalists, important questions are being raised about the reliability and quality of their information.

Ask Yourself

What do you think has contributed to the growing number of people who wish to share their personal views with the world?

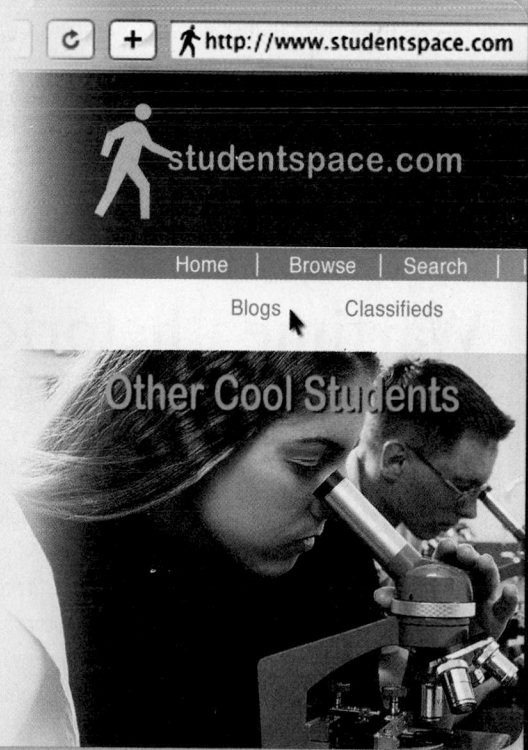

🔄 ➕ 🚶 http://www.studentspace.com

studentspace.com

Home | Browse | Search
Blogs | Classifieds

Other Cool Students

The Rise of Rationalism

History of the Times

In England, the political and social turmoil of the seventeenth century caused many people to question the divine right of monarchs. As a result, a new movement called the Enlightenment began to spread. Supporters of the Enlightenment believed in a philosophy called rationalism, or the belief that human beings can arrive at truth by using reason.

Like the Puritans, rationalists believed God had created the world. Yet, they disagreed with the Puritan notions of revelation,[3] divine providence,[4] and final judgment. Instead, rationalists felt God gave humanity reason to discover both scientific and spiritual truth, a viewpoint known as deism.

Rationalism and deism inspired the founders of the new country to call their peers to war, setting forth noble ideals of religious tolerance and individual liberty. Rationalist thought about relations among people, God, and natural law are the root of the Declaration of Independence.

3. **revelation:** the belief that God would choose to reveal himself at particular times to particular people.
4. **divine providence:** the belief that God plays a central but mysterious role in the workings of the universe.

The Artist in His Museum (1822) by Charles Willson Peale (1741–1827). Oil on canvas, 103 3/4 × 79 7/8 in.
Courtesy of the Pennsylvania Academy of the Fine Arts, Philadelphia. Gift of Mrs. Sarah Harrison (The Joseph Harrison Jr. Collection), 1878.1.2.

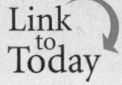
Link to Today

Wartime Rhetoric

Throughout history, calls to action have relied on the tools of literature. Compare Paine's call to arms in the Revolutionary War with Richard Nixon's attempt to renew the country's faith in the Vietnam War:

[A father], after speaking his mind as freely as he thought was prudent, finished with this unfatherly expression, *"Well! Give me peace in my day."* [But] a generous parent should have said, *"If there must be trouble let it be in my day, that my child may have peace";* and this single reflection, well applied, is sufficient to waken every man to duty.

—from *The Crisis, No. 1* by Thomas Paine, 1776

"I want to end the war to save the lives of those brave young men in Vietnam. But I want to end it in a way which will increase the chance that their younger brothers and their sons will not have to fight in some future Vietnam someplace in the world."

—from the Silent Majority speech by President Richard Nixon, November 3, 1969

Ask Yourself

Why might these leaders have invoked images of familial duty when discussing world conflicts?

Literature of the Times

Almost all American writing in the 1750s responded to unfolding political and social events, such as the struggle of Americans for independence from Britain, the struggle of women to gain equality with men, or the struggle of enslaved Africans to expose and end the horror of slavery.

Pamphlets were popular forms of writing during the years of the American Revolution. Thomas Paine, for instance, composed a series of sixteen pamphlets entitled *The American Crisis.* These writings commented on the Revolutionary War and gave encouragement to people involved in it.

Women and former slaves also produced significant pieces of American literature. Abigail Adams, wife of the second president John Adams, wrote famous letters to her husband calling for better treatment of women in the new nation. Phillis Wheatley, once enslaved, wrote poetry that expressed the hope that freedom and independence would one day be available to all. Olaudah Equiano recorded the horrifying details of slavery in his influential *The Interesting Narrative of the Life of Olaudah Equiano.*

Little strokes fell great oaks.

from *Poor Richard's Almanack* (1757) by Benjamin Franklin

Quite possibly the most famous piece of the time period was Benjamin Franklin's autobiography. Franklin made use of the autobiographical narrative, a form common in Puritan writing, but omitted its religious justification. Written in clear, witty prose, this account of the development of the self-made American provided a model for the story that would be told again and again in American literature.

Comprehension Check

How did rationalism differ from Puritanism, and what effect did rationalism have on the new American political system?

Wrap Up

Talk About . . .

With a partner, re-read the descriptions of Puritan beliefs and the Age of Reason. Using the Academic Vocabulary words **listed below,** discuss where you see evidence of these philosophies today.

Write About . . .

Many Native American myths answer fundamental questions about the world and human nature. How do stories answer such questions today?

Academic Vocabulary for Unit 1

Talking and Writing About Literature
Academic Vocabulary is the language you use to write and talk about literature. Use these words to discuss the literature you read in this unit. These words are underlined throughout the unit.

aspect (AS pehkt) *n.:* a side of something; part. *Do the positive aspects of the United States outweigh the challenges for recent immigrants?*

cite (syt) *v.:* quote as an authority; give as an example. *Read these stories, and cite some examples of the use of archetype.*

contemporary (kuhn TEHM puh rehr ee) *adj.:* living or happening at the same time. *How might the Puritans' experiences be similar to the experiences of contemporary refugees or pioneers?*

interpret (ihn TUR priht) *v.:* explain the meaning of. *Interpret the mythical elements in this creation story.*

perspective (puhr SPEHK tihv) *n.:* point of view. *How would the story be different if it were told from a different character's perspective?*

Your Turn

With a partner, summarize the main historical events and important types of literature that shaped this time period. Try to use the Academic Vocabulary words in your analysis.

Link to Today

This **Link to Today** provides a contemporary explanation of why Americans reinvent themselves to forge a common identity.

Build Background

U.S. immigrants often struggle to find a place in the United States while retaining the language, culture, and customs of the country from which they emigrated. As a result, second-generation Americans are often torn between assimilating into mainstream American culture and honoring their roots and family traditions. They struggle to answer the ever-present question, "What does it mean to be an American?"

Author Note

Gish Jen (1956–   ) is a second-generation Chinese American novelist and short-story writer. Her writings, which have appeared in *The New Yorker, The New York Times,* and other publications, revolve around the themes of immigration, ethnic identity, and cultural diversity. Jen was born in Scarsdale, New York, graduated from Harvard University, and now lives with her family in Cambridge, Massachusetts.

Read with a Purpose Read this essay to discover both the challenges and the positive aspects of life for recent immigrants in the United States.

Coming into the Country

by Gish Jen

In the Old World, there was one way of life, or 2, maybe 10. Here there are dozens, hundreds, all jammed in together, cheek by jowl,[1] especially in the dizzying cities. Everywhere has a somewhere else just around the corner. We newish Americans leapfrog from world to world, reinventing ourselves en route. We perform our college selves, our waitress selves, our dot-com selves, our parent selves, our downtown selves, our Muslim, Greek, Hindi, South African selves. Even into the second or third generation, we speak different languages—more languages, often, than we know we know. We sport different names. I am Gish, Geesh, Jen, Lillian, Lil, Bilien, Ms.

Jen, Miss Ren, Mrs. O'Connor. Or maybe we insist on one name. . . .

It's a kind of high, switching spiels, eating Ethiopian, French, Thai, getting around. And the inventing! The moments of grand inspiration: I think I will call myself Houdini. Who could give up even the quotidian[2] luxury of choosing, that small swell of power: to walk or to drive? The soup or the salad? The green or the blue? We bubble with pleasure. It's me. I'm taking the plane. I'll take the sofa, the chair, the whole shebang—why not?

Why not, indeed? A most American question, a question that comes to dominate our most private self-talk. In therapy-speak, we Americans like to give ourselves per-

---

1. **cheek by jowl:** close together.

2. **quotidian** (kwoh TIHD ee uhn): everyday; commonplace.

1915

2007

Analyzing Visuals

Viewing and Interpreting   One photograph shows early-twentieth-century immigrants at Ellis Island, New York. The other shows recent American immigrants at Miami International Airport. What do the two groups of immigrants have in common? And how might the process of entering the country contribute to the disorientation Gish Jen describes in "Coming into the Country"? Discuss your response with other students in your class.

mission. To do what? To take care of ourselves, to express ourselves, to listen to ourselves. We tune out the loudspeaker of duty, tune in to the whisper of desire. This is faint at first, but soon proves easily audible; indeed, irresistible. Why not go to town? Why not move away? Why not marry out? Why not? Why not? Why not?

To come to America is to be greatly disoriented for many a day. The smell of the air is wrong, the taste of the water, the strength of the sun, the rate the trees grow. The rituals are strange—the spring setting out of mulch, the summer setting out of barbecues. How willingly the men heat themselves with burgers! Nobody eats the wildlife, certainly not the bugs or leaves. And beware, beware the rules about smoking. Your skin feels tight, your body fat or thin, your children stranger than they were already. Your sensations are exhausting.

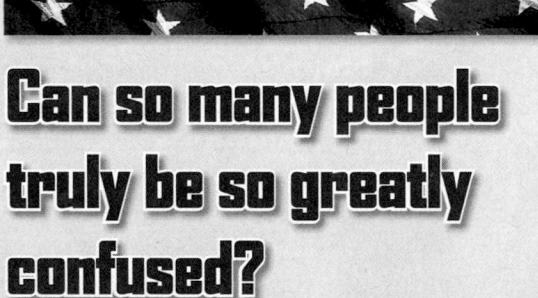

Can so many people truly be so greatly confused?

Yet one day a moment comes—often, strangely, abroad[3]—when we find ourselves missing things. Our choice of restaurants, perhaps, or our cheap gas and good roads; or, more tellingly, our rights. To be without freedom of movement, to be without freedom of speech— these things pain everyone. But to be without our freedom of movement, without our freedom of speech is an American affliction; and in this, as in many facets of American life, possession matters. The moment we feel certain rights to be inalienable, when we feel them to be ours

as our lungs are ours, so that their loss is an excision and a death, we have become American.

It's not always a happy feeling. For the more at home we become with our freedom, the more we become aware of its limits. There's much true opportunity in the land of opportunity, but between freedom in theory and freedom in practice gapes a grand canyon. As often as not, what we feel is the burn of injustice. A rise of anger, perhaps followed by a quick check on our impulse to act rashly; perhaps followed by a decision to act courageously. We gather here today to make known our grievance. For is this not America?

We wonder who we are—what does it mean to be Irish-American, Cuban-American, Armenian-American?—and are amazed to discover that others wonder, too. Indeed, nothing seems more typically American than to obsess about identity. Can so many people truly be so greatly confused? We feel very much a part of the contemporary gestalt.[4]

Yet two or three generations later, we still may not be insiders. Recently, I heard about a basketball game starring a boy from the Cochiti pueblo[5] in Santa Fe. The kids on his team, a friend reported, had one water bottle, which they passed around, whereas the kids on the other team each had his own. This was a heartening story, signaling the survival of a communal culture against the pressures of individualism. But did the Cochiti boy notice the other team? I couldn't help wondering. Did he feel the glass pane between himself and the mainstream, so familiar, so tangible, so bittersweet? Nobody has been here longer than we; how come our ways need protecting? Later a member of the pueblo told me that the Cochiti have started a

---

3. **abroad** (uh BRAWD): In a foreign country; overseas.

4. **gestalt** (guh SHTAHLT): A unified arrangement of individuals or parts. Here, the author uses *gestalt* to mean the complex arrangement of many cultures into a larger American culture.

5. **Cochiti pueblo:** A Native American community 55 miles north of Albuquerque, New Mexico. The pueblo language is Keres.

Analyzing Visuals

Viewing and Interpreting
These men and women are taking the U.S. Oath of Citizenship. In what ways do they illustrate Gish Jen's ideas about immigration today?

language-immersion program for the younger generation, and that it has been a success. They are saving their language from extinction.

Hooray! The rest of us cheer. How awed we feel in the presence of tradition, of authenticity. How avidly we will surf to such sites, some of us, and what we will pay to do so! We will pay for bits of the Southwest the way we will pay handsomely, in this generation or the next, for a home. Whatever that looks like, we find ourselves longing for some combination of Martha Stewart and what we can imagine, say, of our family seat in Brazil. At any rate, we can say this much: the home of our dreams is a safe place, a still place. A communal place, to which we contribute; to which we have real ties; a place that feels more stable, perhaps, than ourselves. How American this is—to long, at day's end, for a place where we belong more, invent less; for a heartland with more heart.

Ask Yourself

1. **Read with a Purpose** Does the author believe that the positive <u>aspects</u> of the United States outweigh the challenges for recent immigrants? <u>Cite</u> textual evidence to support your response.

2. What major difference does the author see between life in the "Old World" and life in the United States? Explain.

3. Jen states that "to come to America is to be greatly disoriented for many a day." Why does she believe this country is so confusing for new immigrants? Explain.

4. In what ways have you reinvented yourself throughout your lifetime? In what ways has the United States reinvented itself throughout its history?

Native American Oral Traditions

Ruins of Anasazi Cliff Dwellings

CONTENTS

"I am a feather
     on the bright sky
I am the blue horse
     that runs in the plain
I am the fish that rolls,
     shining, in the water."

— N. Scott Momaday

Native American Oral Traditions

by **Joseph Bruchac**

Characteristics of Native American Oral Traditions

- Provide explanations about the world and its origins
- Teach moral lessons and convey practical information
- Reflect the belief that the natural world includes both human beings and animals
- Respect speech as a powerful literary form

The Sun Still Rises in the Same Sky: Native American Literature

Few peoples have been as appreciated and, at the same time, as misrepresented as the many different cultures today called American Indian or Native American. Images of Indians are central to mainstream America, from Longfellow's misnamed epic poem *The Song of Hiawatha* (which actually tells the story of the Chippewa hero Manabozho, not the Iroquois Hiawatha) to the "cowboys and Indians" tradition of movies about the Old West. Yet it's only recently that the authentic literary voices of Native Americans have received serious attention. Native American literature has been a living oral tradition, but it was never treated with the same respect as European, or Western, literature. But Western literature itself has its roots firmly planted in the oral tradition—such ancient classics as the *Odyssey*[1] and *Beowulf*,[2] long before they were written down, were stories kept alive by word of mouth. The vast body of American Indian oral literature, encompassing dozens of epic narratives and countless thousands of stories, poems, songs, oratory, and chants, was not even recognized by Western scholars until the late 1800s. Until then, it was assumed that Native Americans had no literature.

Part of the problem scholars had in recognizing the rich traditions of American Indian literature was translating the texts from hundreds of different languages—a task often best done by Native Americans

Joseph Bruchac.

themselves. Over the decades, various American Indian writers—N. Scott Momaday, Louise Erdrich, Simon J. Ortiz, and Leslie Marmon Silko, among others—have revitalized Native American literature by combining their fluency in English with a deep understanding of their own languages and traditions.

We can make some important generalizations about American Indian oral traditions. First of all, Native American cultures use stories to teach moral lessons and convey practical information about the natural world. A story from the Abenaki people of Maine,

---

1. ***Odyssey:*** ancient Greek epic poem, attributed to Homer.
2. ***Beowulf:*** epic poem composed in Old English between A.D. 700 and 750.

oral Translation in a teaching was peace to others

for example, tells how Gluskabe catches all of the game animals. He is then told by his grandmother to return the animals to the woods. They will die if they are kept in his bag, she tells him, and if they do die, there will be no game left for the people to come. In this one brief tale, important, life-sustaining lessons about greed, the wisdom of elders, and game management are conveyed in an entertaining and engaging way.

American Indian literature also reflects a view of the natural world that is more inclusive than the one typically seen in Western literature. The Native American universe is not dominated by human beings. Animals and humans are often interchangeable in myths and folk tales. Origin myths may even feature animals as the instruments of creation.

All American Indian cultures also show a keen awareness of the power of metaphor. Words are as powerful and alive as the human breath that carries them. Songs and chants can make things happen—call game animals, bring rain, cure the sick, or destroy an enemy. For Native Americans, speech, or oratory— often relying on striking similes drawn from nature—is a highly developed and respected literary form.

Passed on from generation to generation, oral traditions preserve historical continuity. But these traditions are also, like the Native American peoples themselves, tenacious, dynamic, and responsive to change. The American Indian worldview is not that of a progressive straight line, but of an endless circle. This cyclical nature of existence is reflected both in the natural world itself, with its changing seasons and cycles of birth, death, and rebirth, and in Native American ceremonies repeated year after year. Each summer, for example, the Lakota people have their Sun Dance. In pre-Columbian times, they went to the Sun Dance on foot; after the coming of the Spanish, they rode horses to the annual event. Today, the Lakota arrive by automobile. While a European eye might see the technology of transport as the important point of this anecdote, to a Lakota the issue of changing transportation is unimportant. It is, after all, only a different way of getting to the same place. The sun still rises in the same sky.

Ask Yourself

1. What three generalizations does Bruchac make about American Indian oral traditions?

2. Identify three comparisons Bruchac makes between American Indian and Western views of the world.

 Learn It Online
Let *PowerNotes* introduce you to Native American oral traditions the multimedia way:

go.hrw.com | L11-16 | Go

SKILLS FOCUS Literary Skills Analyze the characteristics of Native American oral traditions.

Analyzing Native American Art

Most Native American art has everyday or religious uses; it was not created for display purposes. This <u>contemporary</u> example is the leather top of a traditional drum.

Guidelines

To analyze how this artwork reflects Native American oral traditions, use the following guidelines

- Consider the subject of the work. Is this image a part of a larger story? Is this just a small scene in a tale or myth? What do you think the story might be?

- <u>Interpret</u> the details of the artwork. Is the wolf image realistic?

- Think about why this object might be used in storytelling. How might a storyteller use a drum?

Wolf and Moon by Manuel Salazar.

1. How does the artist use the color and shape of the wolf's tongue to direct your attention?

2. Why has the artist chosen to make the trees so flat and simple? Why is the wolf colored black?

3. What story or message about the wolf does the artist convey through details of its face and other details in the artwork?

Your Turn Analyze Cultural Traditions

Look for more examples of Native American art from the Northwest coast of the United States. How traditional are the elements of this artwork, both in subject and in style?

Native American Myths

What Do You Think? How can people's beliefs affect their actions?

QuickTalk

When you were younger, did anyone tell you a story to address your curiosity about the world, perhaps to explain why the sky is blue or why it thunders during a storm? With a partner, share one of these stories or one that you made up yourself. Explain how it changed or reflected your view of the world.

INTRODUCTION

The Huron

"The Sky Tree" is a creation myth of the **Huron,** a Native American people of the eastern woodlands. Also known as the Wendat, the Huron consisted of four Native American tribes united by the Wyandot language. They lived along the St. Lawrence River, where they engaged in the fur trade. Over time, rivalry with other Native American peoples and European settlers forced the Huron west into the north-central United States and Canada and then into Kansas and Oklahoma.

The Sioux

"The Earth Only" comes from the **Teton Sioux,** a North American Plains Indian people who are sometimes called the Dakota. The Sioux were nomadic, following the buffalo and traveling across what is now Minnesota, North Dakota, and South Dakota. The Sioux forcefully resisted the westward expansion of the United States, but their power was eventually eroded by war and epidemic. Sitting Bull, named principal chief of the Teton Sioux in 1867, was the last Sioux leader to resist the rapid expansion of the U.S. government.

The Nez Perce

"Coyote Finishes His Work" has been handed down by the **Nez Perce,** a Native American people whose name comes from the French term for "pierced nose." The Nez Perce, a people of the Plateau culture, lived in what is now Idaho, Oregon, and Washington. Fierce conflicts, fueled by the opening of the Oregon Trail and the nineteenth-century gold rush, erupted over ownership of their land. In 1877, the Nez Perce leader, Chief Joseph, surrendered to federal troops with the now-famous words "I will fight no more forever."

The Blackfeet

"The Blackfeet Genesis" is a creation myth of the **Blackfeet,** a Native American people of the northwestern plains. Historically, the Blackfeet consisted of several related tribes that unified in times of war and to protect their land. The name Blackfeet comes from the tribal practice of dying moccasins black. Almost half of the Blackfeet living today reside in Blackfeet Nation, a reservation in northwestern Montana.

Think About the Myths In what ways do stories help preserve the cultures from which they come?

![Reader/Writer Notebook logo]

Reader/Writer Notebook

Use your **RWN** to complete the activities for these selections.

Literary Focus

Archetypes Most myths contain archetypes. An **archetype** is a very old imaginative pattern that appears in literature across cultures and is repeated through the ages. Archetypes include characters, plots, images, themes, and settings. For example, the tree in "The Sky Tree" is an archetype—that of the life-giving tree. Coyote in the Nez Perce myth is also an archetype—that of the trickster hero.

Reading Focus

Understanding Cultural Characteristics When you read works by members of different cultures, it is important to recognize differences in literary traditions. Since American Indian literature was handed down orally by storytellers, these pieces may lose some of their power in written form. As you read, try to imagine each piece being spoken by a skilled storyteller to an eager audience—or, better yet, read each piece aloud.

Into Action As you read, identify one archetype from each myth and list the archetype in a graphic organizer like the one below. Briefly note characteristics of that archetype. In the final row of the graphic organizer, note what the archetype indicates about the culture that produced it.

	The Sky Tree	The Earth Only	Coyote Finishes His Work
Archetype			
Characteristics			
Culture			

Vocabulary

endures (ehn DURZ) *v.:* keeps on; continues. *The earth endures longer than anything else.*

inhabited (ihn HAB uh tihd) *adj.:* lived in. *Old Man Above wanted the entire earth to be inhabited.*

revive (rih VYV) *v.:* return to life. *After the spirits reenter the bodies, they will revive.*

determined (dih TUR muhnd) *v.:* decided; concluded. *Old Man determined that humans should be created.*

Language Coach

Antonyms An antonym is a word that has the opposite meaning of another word. Some examples are *light/dark, simple/complicated,* or *growing/dying.* Look at the Vocabulary words above. Write down at least one antonym for each word.

Writing Focus

Think as a Reader/Writer

Find It in Your Reading Because these mythical stories were originally passed down orally from generation to generation, their syntax or sentence structure has a unique quality. As you read, note <u>aspects</u> of the syntax that seem to reflect an oral tradition and copy some examples in your *Reader/Writer Notebook.*

TechFocus As you read, think about how people today convey their own stories and myths.

Learn It Online
Get to know these Vocabulary words inside and out through Word Watch.

go.hrw.com   L11-19   Go

Read with a Purpose
Read to discover what each myth explains about traditions, beliefs, or the natural world.

Build Background
People have always asked questions about the origins of the world and about their place in the natural order of things. To answer their questions, people have told stories. These stories, called myths, are almost always connected to religious rituals. Myths help people explain the world they live in and their traditions.

The Sky Tree

In the beginning, Earth was covered with water. In Sky Land, there were people living as they do now on Earth. In the middle of that land was the great Sky Tree. All of the food which the people in that Sky Land ate came from the great tree. *Genesis* **A**

The old chief of that land lived with his wife, whose name was Aataentsic,[1] meaning "Ancient Woman," in their longhouse near the great tree. It came to be that the old chief became sick, and nothing could cure him. He grew weaker and weaker until it seemed he would die. Then a dream came to him, and he called Aataentsic to him.

"I have dreamed," he said, "and in my dream I saw how I can be healed. I must be given the fruit which grows at the very top of Sky Tree. You must cut it down and bring that fruit to me."

Aataentsic took her husband's stone ax and went to the great tree. As soon as she struck it, it split in half and toppled over. As it fell, a hole opened in Sky Land, and the tree fell through the hole. Aataentsic returned to the place where the old chief waited.

"My husband," she said, "when I cut the tree, it split in half and then fell through a great hole. Without the tree, there can be no life. I must follow it."

Then, leaving her husband, she went back to the hole in Sky Land and threw herself after the great tree.

As Aataentsic fell, Turtle looked up and saw her. Immediately Turtle called together all the water animals and told them what she had seen.

"What should be done?" Turtle said.

Beaver answered her. "You are the one who saw this happen. Tell us what to do."

"All of you must dive down," Turtle said. "Bring up soil from the bottom, and place it on my back."

Immediately all of the water animals began to dive down and bring up soil. Beaver, Mink, Muskrat, and Otter each brought up pawfuls of wet soil and placed the soil on Turtle's back until they had made an island of great size. When they were through, Aataentsic settled down gently on the new Earth, and the pieces of the great tree fell beside her and took root.

—from the Huron tradition,
retold by Joseph Bruchac

1. **Aataentsic** (ah tah EHNT sihk).

A Literary Focus Archetypes What other stories can you think of that include life-giving trees?

Sculpture du Nord by Sonny MacDonald, John Sabourin, Eli Nasogaluak, and Armand Vaillancourt.

The Earth Only

Wica'hcala kin	The old men
heya'pelo'	say
maka' kin	the earth
lece'la	only
tehan yunke'lo	endures
eha' pelo'	You spoke
ehan'kecon	truly
wica' yaka pelo'	You are right. **B**

The earth will never Die Jus+ Be ~~the~~ Jus+ life on it chanses.

—composed by Used-as-a-Shield
(Teton Sioux), translated in 1918

B **Reading Focus** **Cultural Characteristics** What parts of this myth might an experienced and skilled storyteller emphasize when telling it aloud? Why?

Vocabulary **endures** (ehn DURZ) *v.*: keeps on; continues.

Coyote Finishes His Work

From the very beginning, Coyote was traveling around all over the earth. He did many wonderful things when he went along. He killed the monsters and the evil spirits that preyed on the people. He made the Indians, and put them out in tribes all over the world because Old Man Above wanted the earth to be inhabited all over, not just in one or two places.

He gave all the people different names and taught them different languages. This is why Indians live all over the country now and speak in different ways.

He taught the people how to eat and how to hunt the buffalo and catch eagles. He taught them what roots to eat and how to make a good lodge and what to wear. He taught them how to dance. Sometimes he made mistakes, and even though he was wise and powerful, he did many foolish things. But that was his way. **C**

Coyote liked to play tricks. He thought about himself all the time, and told everyone he was a great warrior, but he was not. Sometimes he would go too far with some trick and get someone killed. Other times, he would have a trick played on himself by someone else.

[handwritten annotations: "1", "2", "4."]

[handwritten: 2.) This caused people to fear coyotes.]

Analyzing Visuals

Viewing and Interpreting How is Coyote described in this myth? How do the artists depict his trickster qualities in the paintings on this page and page 23?

Untitled (1922) by Fred Kabotie (Hopi).
School for Advanced Research, Catalog Number IAF.P201-14.

C **Reading Focus** **Cultural Characteristics** The first three paragraphs answer a number of questions about human beings. How might a storyteller have told this important part of the myth to an audience?

Vocabulary **inhabited** (ihn HAB uh tihd) *adj.*: lived in.

[handwritten: 2.) For the Black Feet they are in two places.]

He got killed this way so many times that Fox and the birds got tired of bringing him back to life. Another way he got in trouble was trying to do what someone else did. This is how he came to be called Imitator.

Coyote was ugly too. The girls did not like him. But he was smart. He could change himself around and trick the women. Coyote got the girls when he wanted. **D**

One time, Coyote had done everything he could think of and was traveling from one place to another place, looking for other things that needed to be done. Old Man saw him going along and said to himself, "Coyote has now done almost everything he is capable of doing. His work is almost done. It is time to bring him back to the place where he started."

So Great Spirit came down and traveled in the shape of an old man. He met Coyote. Coyote said, "I am Coyote. Who are you?"

Old Man said, "I am Chief of the earth. It was I who sent you to set the world right."

"No," Coyote said, "you never sent me. I don't know you. If you are the Chief, take that lake over there and move it to the side of that mountain."

"No. If you are Coyote, let me see you do it."

Coyote did it.

"Now, move it back."

Coyote tried, but he could not do it. He thought this was strange. He tried again, but he could not do it.

Chief moved the lake back.

Coyote said, "Now I know you are the Chief."

Old Man said, "Your work is finished, Coyote. You have traveled far and done much good. Now you will go to where I have prepared a home for you."

Then Coyote disappeared. Now no one knows where he is anymore.

Old Man got ready to leave, too. He said to the Indians, "I will send messages to the earth by the spirits of the people who reach me but whose time to die has not yet come. They will carry messages to you from time to time. When their spirits come back into their bodies, they will revive and tell you their experiences.

"Coyote and myself, we will not be seen again until Earthwoman is very old. Then we shall return to earth, for it will require a change by that time. Coyote will come along first, and when you see him, you will know I am coming. When I come along, all the spirits of the dead will be with me. There will be no more Other Side Camp. All the people will live together. Earthmother will go back to her first shape and live as a mother among her children. Then things will be made right."

Now they are waiting for Coyote. **E**

—from the Nez Perce tradition,
retold by Barry Lopez

Untitled (1922) by Fred Kabotie (Hopi).
School for Advanced Research, Catalog Number IAF.P201-18.

(handwritten notes)
3.) even Thouw you can Do it all Dose not my you are it all.

4.) whin one is two anoy all oth life BaD.

5) Cjoty Dos not want two lenve the fuhshgs

D **Literary Focus** Archetypes Have you read about, or watched, the adventures of other lovable, helpful trickster figures? Name one or more characters that share the trickster archetype with Coyote.

Vocabulary **revive** (rih VYV) *v.:* return to life.

E **Literary Focus** Archetypes The trickster often takes the form of an animal. What traits of Coyote cause him to function as a trickster?

The Blackfeet Genesis

A Chief of the Blackfeet Tribe (c. 1907) by Edward Curtis.

All animals of the Plains at one time heard and knew him, and all birds of the air heard and knew him. All things that he had made understood him when he spoke to them—the birds, the animals, and the people.

Old Man was traveling about, south of here, making the people. He came from the south, traveling north, making animals and birds as he passed along. He made the mountains, prairies, timber, and brush first. So he went along, traveling northward, making things as he went, putting rivers here and there, and falls on them, putting red paints here and there in the ground—fixing up the world as we see it today. He made the Milk River [the Teton] and crossed it, and, being tired, went up on a little hill and lay down to rest. As he lay on his back, stretched out on the ground, with arms extended, he marked himself out with stones—the shape of his body, head, legs, arms, and everything. There you can see those rocks today. After he had rested, he went on northward, and stumbled over a knoll[1] and fell down on his knees. Then he said,

---

1. **knoll** (nohl): a small, rounded hill.

"You are a bad thing to be stumbling against"; so he raised up two large buttes[2] there, and named them the Knees, and they are called so to this day. He went on farther north, and with some of the rocks he carried with him he built the Sweet Grass Hills.

Old Man covered the plains with grass for the animals to feed on. He marked off a piece of ground, and in it he made to grow all kinds of roots and berries—camas, wild carrots, wild turnips, sweetroot, bitterroot, sarvis berries, bull berries, cherries, plums, and rosebuds. He put trees in the ground. He put all kinds of animals on the ground. When he made the bighorn with its big head and horns, he made it out on the prairie. It did not seem to travel easily on the prairie; it was awkward and could not go fast. So he took it by one of

_____
2. **buttes** (byoots): steep, flat-topped hills.

its horns, and led it up into the mountains, and turned it loose; and it skipped about among the rocks and went up fearful places with ease. So he said, "This is the place that suits you; this is what you are fitted for, the rocks, and the mountains." While he was in the mountains, he made the antelope out of dirt, and turned it loose, to see how it would go. It ran so fast that it fell over some rocks and hurt itself. He saw that this would not do, and took the antelope down on the prairie, and turned it loose; and it ran away fast and gracefully, and he said, "This is what you are suited to."

One day Old Man determined that he would make a woman and a child; so he formed them both— the woman and the child, her son—of clay. After he had molded the clay in human shape, he said to the clay, "You must be people," and then he covered it up and left it, and went away. The next morning he went

F **Literary Focus** Archetypes What qualities of the creator archetype do you see in this passage? Cite details from the selection to support your answer.

Vocabulary **determined** (dih TUR muhnd) v.: decided; concluded. he chose To make a path in his life.

Native American Languages

Researchers estimate that when Columbus arrived in the Americas, approximately 2,000 independent peoples speaking at least 350 languages in about 60 language groups were spread across the North American continent. Because these languages were not written, many treasures in the oral tradition were lost or went undiscovered for years. In recent years, movements to revitalize Native American languages have been started to prevent additional loss of language and culture.

Ask Yourself
Why is it important to learn to speak or appreciate other languages?

to the place and took the covering off, and saw that the clay shapes had changed a little. The second morning there was still more change, and the third still more. The fourth morning, he went to the place, took the covering off, looked at the images, and told them to rise and walk; and they did so. They walked down to the river with their Maker, and then he told them that his name was Na'pi [Old Man]. = God. **G**

As they were standing by the river, the woman said to him, "How is it? will we always live, will there be no end to it?" He said: "I have never thought of that. We will have to decide it. I will take this buffalo chip and throw it in the river. If it floats, when people die, in four days they will become alive again; they will die for only four days. But if it sinks, there will be an end to them." He threw the chip into the river, and it floated. The woman turned and picked up a stone, and said: "No, I will throw this stone in the river; if it floats we will always live, if it sinks people must die, that they may always be sorry for each other." The woman threw the stone into the water, and it sank. "There," said Old Man, "you have chosen. There will be an end to them."

It was not many nights after that the woman's child died, and she cried a great deal for it. She said to Old Man: "Let us change this. The law that you first made, let that be a law." He said: "Not so. What is made law must be law. We will undo nothing that we have done. The child is dead, but it cannot be changed. People will have to die." **H**

—from the Blackfeet tradition,
retold by Joseph Bruchac

2.) if The woman was To have
not contested "old man"
her son would live Dont
chang what you cant
Bare.

G **Literary Focus** Archetypes Does the creator archetype described in this paragraph sound familiar to you? What other cultures that you know of have a similar archetype?

H **Reading Focus** Cultural Characteristics How might a storyteller dramatize the voices of the woman and Old Man? Why?

Applying Your Skills

Native American Myths

Respond and Think Critically

Reading Focus

Quick Check

1. Why does Aataentsic cut down the tree in "The Sky Tree"?

2. What does "Coyote Finishes His Work" promise for the future?

Read with a Purpose

3. From these myths, what can you conclude about how Native American peoples view traditions, beliefs, or the natural world?

Reading Skills: Understanding Cultural Characteristics

4. Review your chart on archetypes and their cultural characteristics. Add a final row in which you indicate what the archetype reminds you of in modern literature or media.

✔ Vocabulary Check

Match each Vocabulary word with its definition.

5. endures
6. inhabited
7. revive
8. determined

a. return to life
b. decided; concluded
c. lived in
d. continues

Literary Focus

Literary Analysis

9. Evaluate What do you think the poet of "The Earth Only" meant by "the earth only endures"? What does not endure?

10. Analyze Old Man in "Coyote Finishes His Work" says that when he returns, the earth "will require a change." What do you think he means?

11. Interpret Pick one of the myths to interpret, and explain what you think the mythical elements represent.

Literary Skills: Archetypes

12. Compare and Contrast Compare the use of archetypes in two of the myths. How is the usage different? How is it the same?

13. Extend What modern story or movie plot do you know that uses archetypes, and why do you think it uses those archetypes?

Literary Skills Review: Personification

14. Analyze Representing an object or animal as if it has the feelings or abilities of a person is called **personification**. How does the personification within each myth influence the myth's meaning? Why might a storyteller use an object instead of a person as a character?

Writing Focus

Think as a Reader/Writer

Use It in Your Writing Review your notes about the syntax, or sentence structure, of these oral traditions. Then, imitate their distinctive syntax as you write a brief mythical or fantastical story explaining a natural phenomenon, such as a hurricane, or something contemporary, such as space travel.

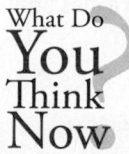 What Do You Think Now

How do these myths portray Native American beliefs about humankind's place in the world? How does your own view of your place in the world shape your beliefs?

Applying Your Skills

SKILLS FOCUS **Reading Skills** Identify and understand the cultural characteristics of a text. **Writing Skills** Write narratives.

Grammar Skills Identify and use verbs. **Listening and Speaking Skills** Adapt to the occasion when speaking: group presentations.

Native American Myths

Grammar Link

Regular and Irregular Verbs

To create the past tense of **regular verbs,** you may have to add *–ed* to the base form. The verb *return* is a good example; add *–ed* and you have the past tense form, *returned.*

Irregular verbs do not change forms as simply. In "The Sky Tree," both *go* and *throw* are verbs with irregular forms in the past tense:

> Then, leaving her husband, she <u>went</u> back to the hole in Sky Land and <u>threw</u> herself after the great tree.

Your Turn

Change the verbs in each sentence to past tense. Look out for irregular verbs. If you are unsure of how to change a verb to past tense, look up the verb in a dictionary.

1. As Aataentsic falls, Turtle looks up and sees her.
2. He kills the monsters and evil spirits that prey on the people.
3. He gives all the people different names and teaches them different languages.
4. Old Man covers the plains with grass for the animals.
5. They walk down to the river with their Maker, and then he tells them his name.

Writing Application Write a short, one-paragraph story using the past tense of all of the following verbs: *see, go, rise, cling, shake,* and *fall.* You can use the words in any order. Use your imagination to come up with an interesting tale. Then, share your story with a classmate.

CHOICES

As you respond to the Choices, use these **Academic Vocabulary** words as appropriate: <u>aspect</u>, <u>cite</u>, <u>contemporary</u>, <u>interpret</u>, <u>perspective</u>.

REVIEW

Discuss Cultural Differences

Partner Work With a partner, review the Introduction to each Native American group (or consult additional references to learn more). Compare the differences between Native American peoples' stories. What parts of their histories or cultures may account for the differences in stories that explain the same things? <u>Cite</u> historic events to support your ideas.

CONNECT

Be the Storyteller

TechFocus Remember that these myths were handed down as oral traditions. In groups, pick a myth and retell it through a multimedia presentation. Use audio and images to illustrate the myth. How does seeing and hearing these myths change or enhance your <u>perspective</u> and understanding of them?

EXTEND

Rewrite the Myth

Rewrite one of the myths to fit another genre, but be sure to retain its legendary, fantastic elements. (For example, make "The Earth Only" a memoir written by one of the old men.) Present your new version to the class, and discuss how genre changes a story.

For **CHOICES** see page 41. >

from **The Way to Rainy Mountain**

Identifying Main Ideas and Supporting Details by **Kylene Beers**

You head into a theater to see a movie and hear the people coming out repeatedly saying the name of the movie you want to see. What you can't hear, though, is what they are saying *about* the movie. The movie title is the topic of their conversation; what they are saying about the movie is the main idea. The comments that would answer who, what, when, where, why, and how questions are the details. Finding the main idea and details helps you understand what you're learning.

Writers sometimes state their main ideas directly in topic sentences. More often, main ideas are implied through the details. To identify a passage's main idea, look for the central thought that all of the sentences seem to support. For example, read the following excerpt from *The Way to Rainy Mountain:*

> In the late seventeenth century they began a long migration to the south and east. It was a journey toward the dawn, and it led to a golden age. Along the way the Kiowas were befriended by the Crows, who gave them the culture and religion of the Plains. They acquired horses, and their ancient nomadic spirit was suddenly free of the ground.

The first three sentences of the paragraph use some related words: *migration, journey,* and *along the way.* This repetition tells the reader that the idea of the Kiowas' movement across the plains is important and that their journey is related to the main idea. Each detail describes something the Kiowas acquire during the migration, such as cultural and religious knowledge and horses. The related words, combined with these details, imply that the journey was beneficial, which is the main idea of the paragraph. Use this process to help you find the main idea in any paragraph:

look for an idea that is repeated and emphasized, and the details that go with it.

Momaday expresses this main idea symbolically when he states, "It was a journey toward the dawn. . . ." Here, the dawn represents hope and a new beginning.

As you read the selection, think about the details that Momaday includes. Ask yourself why he might have included them, what they have in common, and what larger ideas they seem to support.

Your Turn

Read the following passage and work with a partner to identify the details. Then, determine the main idea by discussing what central thought the details seem to support.

> I do not speak Kiowa, and I never understood her prayers, but there was something inherently sad in the sound, some merest hesitation upon the syllables of sorrow. She began in a high and descending pitch, exhausting her breath to silence; then again and again—and always the same intensity of effort, of something that is, and is not, like urgency in the human voice. Transported so in the dancing light among the shadows of her room, she seemed beyond the reach of time.

Learn It Online

Find out more about main ideas and supporting details through *PowerNotes.*

go.hrw.com   L11-29   **Go**

from The Way to Rainy Mountain

What Do You Think?

How can people's beliefs affect their actions?

QuickWrite

Think about the core beliefs and values of your family or another family you know well. Where did these beliefs originate? How have they been shaped over the generations? Reflect on specific events or experiences in a family's history that influence its members' beliefs today.

MEET THE WRITER

N. Scott Momaday
(1934–   )

Link to Today

Native Americans have often been depicted in literature and other arts in the crudest of stereotypes, appearing as fearsome savages or noble but primitive warriors. You have only to look at movie westerns from the 1940s and 1950s to see how obvious the stereotypes were. Even American history textbooks reflected the popular view that white settlers "won" the West in a just war against Native Americans, whose resistance was unwarranted.

When the issue of civil rights for African Americans came to the forefront in the 1950s and 1960s, Native Americans brought their <u>perspective</u> to the struggle. Momaday and others spoke loudly and clearly of loss, injustice, and prejudice.

A Kiowa Journey

Pulitzer Prize WINNER

Navarre Scott Momaday, born in Lawton, Oklahoma, has Kiowa ancestors on his father's side and some Cherokee on his mother's. He studied creative writing and received his doctorate from Stanford University.

Momaday broke from the standard academic mold with three works grounded in his knowledge of Native American life. These included two memoirs, *The Way to Rainy Mountain* (1969) and *The Names* (1976). He also wrote a Pulitzer Prize-winning novel, *House Made of Dawn* (1968).

The Way to Rainy Mountain is part legend, part history, and part poetry. Momaday describes Kiowa history in an imagistic form that does not depend on straightforward narrative. On one page, he tells a Kiowa myth or legend; on the facing page, he includes a short excerpt from history and a personal memory of his own. In the mind of the reader, the inner truth blends with the outer, and emotion mixes with fact.

Momaday says that the journey to Rainy Mountain "is an evocation of three things in particular: a landscape that is incomparable, a time that is gone forever, and the human spirit, which endures."

Think About the Writer What advantage does personal history give Momaday for writing about the experience of the Kiowas?

Reader/Writer Notebook

Use your **RWN** to complete the activities for this selection.

Literary Focus

Setting The time and location in which a narrative takes place, or the **setting,** can create conflict, establish atmosphere, and help to develop characters. In this selection from *The Way to Rainy Mountain,* Momaday uses setting to establish **mood** and explore **theme**.

Literary Perspectives Apply the literary perspective on page 33 as you read this memoir.

Reading Focus

Identifying Main Ideas and Supporting Details The **main idea** of a paragraph or selection is the central thought the writer is trying to convey. **Supporting details** are the phrases containing information that supports the main idea. Momaday rarely states his main ideas in topic sentences; instead, he implies them through carefully chosen details. Often, these details take the form of vivid images of the natural world.

Into Action As you read, use a chart like the one below to identify the main ideas and supporting details of various paragraphs in the story.

Paragraph	Main Idea	Supporting Detail
1	The landscape has a powerful impact on the lone observer.	"brittle and brown" grass "cracks beneath your feet"

Writing Focus

Think as a Reader/Writer

Find It in Your Reading While some authors use it simply to establish place and time, **setting** is an integral part of Momaday's perspective in *The Way to Rainy Mountain.* As you read, use your *Reader/Writer Notebook* to take notes on the importance of setting to the story and characters. Record some of the rich **images** Momaday uses to make the setting come alive.

Vocabulary

infirm (ihn FURM) *adj.:* physically weak. *Grandmother became infirm in her old age.*

preeminently (pree EHM uh nuhnt lee) *adv.:* above all else. *To the Kiowas, warfare was preeminently a sacred business.*

luxuriant (luhg ZHUR ee uhnt) *adj.:* rich; abundant. *The mountain slope was luxuriant with all manner of wildlife and vegetation.*

tenuous (TEHN yoo uhs) *adj.:* slight; insubstantial; not firm. *As the U.S. continued its expansion, the Kiowas' hold on their land and heritage became more and more tenuous.*

opaque (oh PAYK) *adj.:* not transparent; not admitting light. *The windows were made opaque by thick layers of dust.*

enmities (EHN muh teez) *n.:* hatreds. *Deep-rooted enmities grew within the warriors as their land was taken from them.*

Language Coach

Etymology Choose a word from the Vocabulary list, and look up the meaning of its root (the part of the word that carries its basic meaning). How is the meaning of the root reflected in the word's definition?

Learn It Online
Learn more about Momaday and his world through these Internet links.

go.hrw.com   L11-31   **Go**

Link to Today

This Link to Today provides a unique look at the history of a Native American people and a reflection on the importance of memory.

Read with a Purpose

As you read, note each of the settings that Momaday describes and the meaning he associates with each place.

Build Background

This selection from N. Scott Momaday's memoir, *The Way to Rainy Mountain*, concerns the narrator's pilgrimage to his grandmother's grave. During his journey he relates his grandmother's background as a descendant of the Kiowa Native American group. As you read, keep in mind that most of the narrative takes place in the past, not the present.

from

THE WAY TO RAINY MOUNTAIN

by **N. Scott Momaday**

A single knoll rises out of the plain in Oklahoma north and west of the Wichita Range. For my people, the Kiowas, it is an old landmark, and they gave it the name Rainy Mountain. The hardest weather in the world is there. Winter brings blizzards, hot tornadic winds arise in the spring, and in summer the prairie is an anvil's edge. The grass turns brittle and brown, and it cracks beneath your feet. There are green belts along the rivers and creeks, linear groves of hickory and pecan, willow and witch hazel. At a distance in July or August the steaming foliage seems almost to writhe in fire. Great green and yellow grasshoppers are everywhere in the tall grass, popping up like corn to sting the flesh, and tortoises crawl about on the red earth, going nowhere in the plenty of time. Loneliness is an aspect of the land. All things in the plain are isolate; there is no confusion of objects in the eye, but *one* hill or *one* tree or *one* man. To look upon that landscape in the early morning, with the sun at your back, is to lose the sense of proportion. Your imagination comes to life, and this, you think, is where Creation was begun. **A**

I returned to Rainy Mountain in July. My grandmother had died in the spring, and I wanted to be at her grave. She had lived to be very old and at last infirm. Her only living daughter was with her when she died, and I was told that in death her face was that of a child.

I like to think of her as a child. When she was born, the Kiowas were living that last great moment of their history. For more than a hundred years they had controlled the open range from the Smoky Hill River to the Red, from the headwaters of the Canadian to the fork of the Arkansas and Cimarron. In alliance with the Comanches, they had ruled the whole of the southern Plains. War was their sacred business, and they were among the finest horsemen the world has ever known. But warfare for the Kiowas was preeminently a matter of disposition rather than of survival, and they never understood the grim, unrelenting advance of the U.S. Cavalry. When at last, divided and ill-provisioned, they were driven onto the Staked Plains in the cold rains of autumn, they fell into panic. In Palo Duro Canyon they abandoned their crucial stores to pillage[1] and had nothing then but their lives. In order to save themselves, they surrendered to the soldiers at Fort Sill and were imprisoned in the old stone corral that now stands as a military museum. My grandmother was spared the humiliation

of those high gray walls by eight or ten years, but she must have known from birth the affliction of defeat, the dark brooding of old warriors. **B C**

Her name was Aho, and she belonged to the last culture to evolve in North America. Her forebears came down from the high country in western Montana nearly three centuries ago. They were a mountain people, a mysterious tribe of hunters whose language has never been positively classified in any major group. In the late seventeenth century they began a long migration to the south and east. It was a journey toward the dawn, and it led to a golden age. Along the way the Kiowas were befriended by the Crows, who gave them the culture and religion of the Plains. They acquired horses, and their ancient nomadic spirit was suddenly free of the ground. They acquired Tai-me, the sacred Sun Dance doll, from that moment the object and symbol of their worship, and so shared in the divinity of the sun. Not least, they acquired the sense of destiny, therefore courage and pride. When they entered upon the southern Plains they had been transformed. No longer were they slaves to the simple necessity of survival; they were a lordly and dangerous society of fighters and thieves, hunters and priests of the sun. According to their origin myth, they entered the world through a hollow log. From one point of view, their migration was the fruit of an old prophecy, for indeed they emerged from a sunless world.

---

1. **pillage** (PIHL ihj): loot; steal.

A **Literary Focus** Setting What are some of the vibrant images and similes that bring the landscape to life in this paragraph?

B **Literary Perspectives** Historical Context How is the old stereotype of Native Americans as "ruthless savages" countered here?

C **Reading Focus** Identifying Main Ideas and Supporting Details The main idea of this paragraph is that the Kiowas went from rulers to prisoners on their own land. What details help support this idea?

Vocabulary **infirm** (ihn FURM) adj.: physically weak.
preeminently (pree EHM uh nuhnt lee) adv.: above all else.

Literary Perspectives

Analyzing Historical Context The "Cowboys and Indians" conflict in popular culture often stereotyped Native Americans as "savages" for defending their lands across North America from expansionist forces. Native American authors helped open the public's eyes to the Native American perspective on the United States' expansion. As you read, consider the historical and political circumstances that affected the characters in the selection.

As you read, be sure to notice the questions in the text, which will guide you in using this perspective.

Although my grandmother lived out her long life in the shadow of Rainy Mountain, the immense landscape of the continental interior lay like memory in her blood. She could tell of the Crows, whom she had never seen, and of the Black Hills, where she had never been. I wanted to see in reality what she had seen more perfectly in the mind's eye, and traveled fifteen hundred miles to begin my pilgrimage. **D**

Yellowstone, it seemed to me, was the top of the world, a region of deep lakes and dark timber, canyons and waterfalls. But, beautiful as it is, one might have the sense of confinement there. The skyline in all directions is close at hand, the high wall of the woods and deep cleavages of shade. There is a perfect freedom in the mountains, but it belongs to the eagle and the elk, the badger and the bear. The Kiowas reckoned their stature by the distance they could see, and they were bent and blind in the wilderness.

Descending eastward, the highland meadows are a stairway to the plain. In July the inland slope of the Rockies is luxuriant with flax and buckwheat, stonecrop and larkspur. The earth unfolds and the limit of the land recedes. Clusters of trees, and animals grazing far in the distance, cause the vision to reach away and wonder to build upon the mind. The sun follows a longer course in the day, and the sky is immense beyond all comparison. The great billowing clouds that sail upon it are shadows that move upon the grain like water, dividing light. Farther down, in the land of the Crows and Blackfeet, the plain is yellow. Sweet clover takes hold of the hills and bends upon itself to cover and seal the soil. There the Kiowas paused on their way; they had come to the place where they must change their lives. The sun is at home on the plains. Precisely there does it have the certain character of a god. When the Kiowas came to the land of the Crows, they could see the dark lees[2] of the hills at dawn across the Bighorn River, the profusion of light on the grain shelves, the oldest deity ranging after the solstices.[3] Not yet would they veer southward to the caldron of the land that lay below; they must wean their blood from the northern winter and hold the mountains a while longer in their view. They bore Tai-me in procession to the east.

A dark mist lay over the Black Hills, and the land was like iron. At the top of a ridge I caught sight of Devils Tower upthrust against the gray sky as if in the birth of time the core of the earth had broken through its crust and the motion of the world was begun. There are things in nature that engender[4] an awful quiet in the heart of man; Devils Tower is one of them. Two centuries ago, because they could not do otherwise, the Kiowas made a legend at the base of the rock. My grandmother said:

Eight children were there at play, seven sisters and their brother. Suddenly the boy was struck dumb; he trembled and began to run upon his hands and feet. His fingers became claws, and his body was covered with fur. Directly there was a bear where the boy had been. The sisters were terrified; they ran, and the bear after them. They came to the stump of a great tree, and the tree spoke to them. It bade them climb upon it, and as they did so it began to rise into the air. The bear came to kill them, but they were just beyond its reach. It reared against the tree and scored the bark all around with its claws. The seven sisters were borne into the sky, and they became the stars of the Big Dipper. **E**

From that moment, and so long as the legend lives, the Kiowas have kinsmen in the night sky. Whatever they were in the mountains, they could be

---

2. **lees** (leez): shelters.
3. **solstices** (SAHL stihs ihs): The solstices are the points where the sun is farthest north or south of the celestial equator, creating the longest (June 21) and shortest (Dec. 21) days of sunlight in the Northern Hemisphere.
4. **engender** (ehn JEHN duhr): cause; produce.

D **Literary Focus** Setting What does this paragraph say about the importance of land and place to the Kiowas?

E **Literary Focus** Setting How is this legend important to the setting of the story?

Vocabulary **luxuriant** (luhg ZHUR ee uhnt) *adj.:* rich; abundant.

At the top of the ridge I caught sight of

DEVILS TOWER

upthrust against the gray sky.

no more. However tenuous their well-being, however much they had suffered and would suffer again, they had found a way out of the wilderness.

My grandmother had a reverence for the sun, a holy regard that now is all but gone out of mankind. There was a wariness in her, and an ancient awe. She was a Christian in her later years, but she had come a long way about, and she never forgot her birthright. As a child she had been to the Sun Dances; she had taken part in those annual rites, and by them she had learned the restoration of her people in the presence of Tai-me. She was about seven when the last Kiowa Sun Dance was held in 1887 on the Washita River above Rainy Mountain Creek. The buffalo were gone. In order to consummate[5] the ancient sacrifice—to impale the head of a buffalo bull upon the medicine tree—a delegation of old men

journeyed into Texas, there to beg and barter for an animal from the Goodnight herd. She was ten when the Kiowas came together for the last time as a living Sun Dance culture. They could find no buffalo; they had to hang an old hide from the sacred tree. Before the dance could begin, a company of soldiers rode out from Fort Sill under orders to disperse the tribe. Forbidden without cause the essential act of their faith, having seen the wild herds slaughtered and left to rot upon the ground, the Kiowas backed away forever from the medicine tree. That was July 20, 1890, at the great bend of the Washita. My grandmother was there. Without bitterness, and for as long as she lived, she bore a vision of deicide.[6] **F** **G**

Now that I can have her only in memory, I see my grandmother in the several postures that were peculiar to her: standing at the wood stove on a winter

---

5. **consummate** (KAHN suh mayt): finish; make complete.

6. **deicide** (DEE uh syd): murder of a god.

Vocabulary **tenuous** (TEHN yoo uhs) *adj.:* slight; insubstantial; not firm.

F **Literary Perspectives** **Historical Context** In this paragraph, how are historical circumstances responsible for this defining moment in the grandmother's life?

G **Reading Focus** **Identifying Main Ideas and Supporting Details** Re-read the last sentence of this paragraph. Then, identify the paragraph's main idea and cite two details that support it.

morning and turning meat in a great iron skillet; sitting at the south window, bent above her beadwork, and afterwards, when her vision failed, looking down for a long time into the fold of her hands; going out upon a cane, very slowly as she did when the weight of age came upon her; praying. I remember her most often at prayer. She made long, rambling prayers out of suffering and hope, having seen many things. I was never sure that I had the right to hear, so exclusive were they of all mere custom and company. The last time I saw her she prayed standing by the side of her bed at night, naked to the waist, the light of a kerosene lamp moving upon her dark skin. Her long, black hair, always drawn and braided in the day, lay upon her shoulders and against her breasts like a shawl. I do not speak Kiowa, and I never understood her prayers, but there was something inherently sad in the sound, some merest hesitation upon the syllables of sorrow. She began in a high and descending pitch, exhausting her breath to silence; then again and again—and always the same intensity of effort, of something that is, and is not, like urgency in the human voice. Transported so in the dancing light among the shadows of her room, she seemed beyond the reach of time. But that was illusion; I think I knew then that I should not see her again. **Ⓗ**

Houses are like sentinels in the plain, old keepers of the weather watch. There, in a very little while, wood takes on the appearance of great age. All colors wear soon away in the wind and rain, and then the wood is burned gray and the grain appears and the nails turn red with rust. The windowpanes are black and opaque; you imagine there is nothing within, and indeed there are many ghosts, bones given up to the land. They stand here and there against the sky, and you approach them for a longer time than you expect. They belong in the distance; it is their domain. **Ⓘ**

Analyzing Visuals

Viewing and Interpreting Why do Native American artists so often take nature as their subject? What does this fact say about their culture?

Once there was a lot of sound in my grandmother's house, a lot of coming and going, feasting and talk. The summers there were full of excitement and reunion. The Kiowas are a summer people; they abide the cold and keep to themselves, but when the season turns and the land becomes warm and vital they cannot hold still; an old love of going returns upon them. The aged visitors who came to my grandmother's house when I was a child were made of lean and leather, and they bore themselves upright. They wore

---

Ⓗ **Reading Focus** Identifying Main Ideas and Supporting **Details** The main idea of this paragraph is that the narrator remembers his grandmother and that this memory is marked by a sense of great sadness. What details support this idea?

Ⓘ **Literary Focus** Setting Think about how land and nature are important to the Kiowas. Why might the narrator believe that houses belong in the distance?

Vocabulary **opaque** (oh PAYK) *adj.*: not transparent; not admitting light.

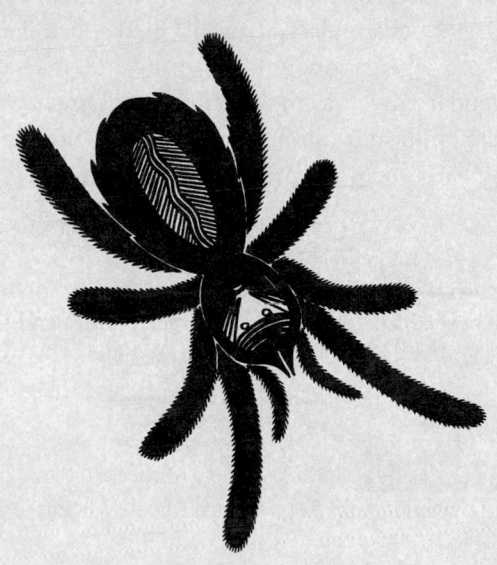

Illustrations by Alfred Momaday for *The Way to Rainy Mountain* © 1969 by the University of New Mexico Press.

great black hats and bright ample shirts that shook in the wind. They rubbed fat upon their hair and wound their braids with strips of colored cloth. Some of them painted their faces and carried the scars of old and cherished enmities. They were an old council of warlords, come to remind and be reminded of who they were. Their wives and daughters served them well. The women might indulge themselves; gossip was at once the mark and compensation of their servitude. They made loud and elaborate talk among themselves, full of jest and gesture, fright and false alarm. They went abroad in fringed and flowered shawls, bright beadwork and German silver. They were at home in the kitchen, and they prepared meals that were banquets.

There were frequent prayer meetings, and great nocturnal feasts. When I was a child I played with my cousins outside, where the lamplight fell upon the ground and the singing of the old people rose up around us and carried away into the darkness. There were a lot of good things to eat, a lot of laughter and surprise. And afterwards, when the quiet returned, I lay down with my grandmother and could hear the frogs away by the river and feel the motion of the air.

Now there is a funeral silence in the rooms, the endless wake of some final word. The walls have closed in upon my grandmother's house. When I returned to it in mourning, I saw for the first time in my life how small it was. It was late at night, and there was a white moon, nearly full. I sat for a long time on the stone steps by the kitchen door. From there I could see out across the land; I could see the long row of trees by the creek, the low light upon the rolling plains, and the stars of the Big Dipper. Once I looked at the moon and caught sight of a strange thing. A cricket had perched upon the handrail, only a few inches away from me. My line of vision was such that the creature filled the moon

---

Vocabulary   enmities (EHN muh teez) *n.:* hatreds.

like a fossil.[7] It had gone there, I thought, to live and die, for there, of all places, was its small definition made whole and eternal. A warm wind rose up and purled[8] like the longing within me. **J** **K**

The next morning I awoke at dawn and went out on the dirt road to Rainy Mountain. It was already hot, and the grasshoppers began to fill the air. Still, it was early in the morning, and the birds sang out of the shadows. The long yellow grass on the mountain shone in the bright light, and a scissortail[9] hied above the land. There, where it ought to be, at the end of a long and legendary way, was my grandmother's grave. Here and there on the dark stones were ancestral names. Looking back once, I saw the mountain and came away.

---

7. **fossil** (FAHS uhl): hardened remains of plant or animal life from a previous geological time period.
8. **purled** (purld): moved in ripples.

9. **scissortail** (SIHZ uhr tayl): species of flycatcher bird. The bird's distinctive tail is an average of thirteen inches long and is divided like scissors near its end.

J **Literary Focus** Setting Why might the narrator realize only now, years later, how small his grandmother's house is?

K **Literary Focus** Setting How is this image of the fossil in the moon similar to the legend of the seven sisters who ascended to the sky from Devils Tower?

Looking back once, I saw the mountain and came away.

Applying Your Skills

from **The Way to Rainy Mountain**

Respond and Think Critically

Reading Focus

Quick Check

1. Who are the Crows in this story?

2. How does Kiowa legend explain what looks like claw marks on Devils Tower?

3. What emotion does the narrator most associate with the memory of his grandmother?

Read with a Purpose

4. Why is setting so important in this memoir?

Reading Skills: Identifying Main Ideas and Supporting Details

5. As you read the selection, you identified the main ideas and supporting details of various paragraphs. Now, review some of the main ideas you identified. Then, identify the main idea of the selection. Explain your answer in two or three sentences, <u>citing</u> the text to support your response.

Paragraph	Main Idea	Supporting Detail
1	The landscape has a powerful impact on the lone observer.	"brittle and brown" grass "cracks beneath your feet"

Literary Focus

Literary Analysis

6. **Analyze** Most of this memoir was drawn from the narrator's memory and his knowledge of Kiowa history. How would the story change if it were told from the <u>perspectives</u> of different characters across history—for example, a Kiowa warrior, a nineteenth-century U.S. cavalry soldier, or the narrator's grandmother?

7. **Interpret** Why did the narrator want to visit his grandmother's grave?

8. **Evaluate** Some literature is criticized for having no plot. Could you apply this criticism to this selection? Is plot essential to a good narrative?

9. **Literary Perspectives** While reading the selection, you thought about the impact of history on the lives of the characters. How might the narrator's life have been different if the U.S. cavalry had not driven the Kiowas off their land?

Literary Skills: Setting

10. **Make Judgments** Look back at the description of the **setting** in the opening paragraph. Is it appropriate that the dead are buried at Rainy Mountain?

Literary Skills Review: Frame Story

11. **Analyze** A **frame story** is a literary device in which one story is enclosed in another. In this selection, which is the frame story and which is the enclosed tale?

Writing Focus

Think as a Reader/Writer

Use It in Your Writing Write a description of a setting that holds emotional significance for you. Like Momaday, use vivid images to capture your <u>perspective</u> and to make the setting appeal to readers' senses.

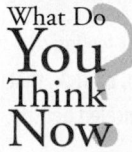 What Do You Think Now

How does the narrator's journey to Rainy Mountain change him? What significant event or experience in your life changed your outlook or influenced your behavior?

from **The Way to Rainy Mountain**

Vocabulary Development

✓ Vocabulary Check

Explain how each Vocabulary word in boldface below is used incorrectly.

1. The climber was feeling so **infirm** that she decided to climb another thousand feet.

2. The miser was **preeminently** interested in spending as much money as possible.

3. The fields were **luxuriant** due to the lack of rain.

4. Married fifty years, the couple celebrated their **tenuous** relationship.

5. I could see light through the **opaque** glass.

6. Because of their long-standing **enmities,** the two nations lived in peace.

Vocabulary Skills: Context Clues

Look at this example from *The Way to Rainy Mountain*:

"The windowpanes are black and **opaque;** you imagine there is nothing within, and indeed there are many ghosts, bones given up to the land."

The context clues state that the windowpanes are black and that they don't reveal what's on the other side. Therefore, you can infer that *opaque* means "not transparent" or "not admitting light." In this example, the word *black* serves as a **synonym,** or a word with a similar meaning, for *opaque*.

Look for these other types of context clues.

Type of Context Clue	Explanation	Example
Definition or restatement	Look for an actual definition or restatement of the word in more familiar terms.	She was feeling so **infirm, or sick,** that she canceled her trip.
Contrast	An unfamiliar word may be contrasted with a more familiar word or concept.	Her actions were based on **solid, not tenuous,** reasoning.
Example	Look for examples surrounding the unfamiliar word.	**Luxuriant** places **such as resorts** transformed the city.

Your Turn

For each boldface word below, list the context clues that could be used to determine the word's meaning. Then, label each context clue according to its type.

1. Unable to make up his mind, Robert **vacillated** between his options.

2. The event was a **debacle** and not the success Robert had hoped for.

Language Coach

Etymology Knowledge of roots can be a useful tool for unlocking word meanings. Review the footnoted words in this selection. Use a dictionary to determine each word's root. How might knowing the root help you decode the word?

Academic Vocabulary

Write About
Although Momaday's memoir is rich in tradition and memory, it is also modern. In a paragraph, explain the aspects of the memoir that reflect a contemporary perspective. Include text references.

Native American Myths /
from The Way to Rainy Mountain

CHOICES

As you respond to the Choices, use the **Academic Vocabulary** words as appropriate: aspect, cite, contemporary, interpret, and perspective.

REVIEW

Research Historical Information

Partner Activity Both N. Scott Momaday and the creators of the Native American myths address topics also found in reference works, such as the origins of various customs and the history of the Kiowa people. With a partner, choose one of these topics and research it using resources available online or in your library. Compare the presentation of the topic in the selecton with its treatment in the reference work. Why do you think Momaday and the Native American storytellers used the style they did? Which presentation was more informative or enjoyable? Why?

Compare History and Myth

Recall the following instances in the excerpt from *The Way to Rainy Mountain:* (1) the Kiowas getting horses; (2) the Kiowas entering the world through a hollow log; (3) how the Big Dipper came to be; (4) the Kiowas' nocturnal feasts. Which of these examples are factual, and which are legends? Arrange the events in a T-chart with one side labeled "Kiowa history" and the other side labeled "Kiowa myth." For each item, note why you think Momaday included it and why readers might find it appealing.

CONNECT

Describe a Natural Scene

Timed └Writing The selections in this collection discuss nature and its importance to all people. Think of an experience you have had with nature, whether it was watching a deer in a quiet forest or seeing the moon rise over a city skyline. What made this experience special for you? In a brief descriptive essay, describe your experience and say why it moved you so much. Include details that will allow your readers to visualize.

Create a Myth

Partner Activity With a partner, re-read the section about the creation of the Big Dipper in *The Way to Rainy Mountain* and about the creation of the bighorn sheep and the antelope in "The Blackfeet Genesis." Use an encyclopedia, Web site, or your own knowledge to help you choose another constellation or animal. See if there are any existing myths or legends about its creation. Together, create your own myth about how the constellation or animal came to be. Try to include dialogue in your myth.

EXTEND

Make a Visual

Review some of the vivid imagery used to describe settings in "The Sky Tree," "Coyote Finishes His Work," "The Blackfeet Genesis," and *The Way to Rainy Mountain.* Create a collage, painting, or drawing of what came to mind as you read. Your response to the piece may interpret the setting itself, illustrating the images and details in the selection, or it may address the importance of the setting to the characters involved.

Write a Memoir

Write your own memoir as Momaday did for the Kiowas. Choose an aspect of your culture that especially interests you. Consider family history, the culture of your community or region, or even a team or club to which you belong. Interview members of the culture you have chosen. Cite their stories and experiences alongside your own to create the memoir.

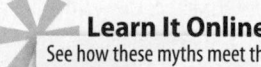

Learn It Online
See how these myths meet the modern world through these Internet links.

go.hrw.com   L11-41   **Go**

COLLECTION 2

Voyages and Visions

LITERARY FOCUS
American Narrative Tradition

CONTENTS

"For we must consider that we shall be as a city upon a hill, the eyes of all people are upon us. So that if we shall deal falsely with our God in this work we have undertaken, and so cause Him to withdraw His present help from us, we shall be made a story and a byword through the world. . . . "

— **John Winthrop, from a sermon delivered aboard the** *Arbella* **on the way to New England, spring 1630**

Amerigo Vespucci, Navigating by the Stars, French School.

SKILLS FOCUS Literary Skills Understand narrative accounts, including historical narratives; evaluate and analyze the philosophical, political, religious, ethical, and social influences of a historical period.

American Narrative Tradition

by **Leila Christenbury**

Influences on the American Narrative Tradition
- Writings of explorers who recorded early expeditions to the Americas
- Settlers' accounts of life in a new land
- Captivity narratives and other tales about colonial interactions with Native Americans
- Autobiographical writings by African slaves that helped the antislavery cause

A Tradition Is Born

A narrative is nothing more than a story—but good stories are central to most enduring literature. When you read narratives, look for who is telling the story and what he or she wants us to accept or believe.

The American narrative tradition, born of conflict, began with stories of European explorers' turbulent journeys across the sea. True events, often violent in nature and marked by controversy, became the basis of many narrative accounts of the nation's early years.

Travel Narratives The first European explorers undertook long, difficult journeys with a variety of goals. For example, Alvar Núñez Cabeza de Vaca set out from Spain to help conquer North America. He faced a series of misfortunes, and upon returning to Spain, wrote *La Relación*, a narrative of his expedition. *La Relación* documents the experiences of the first Europeans to cross the North American continent.

Tales of Life in North America After 1500, European settlers began to arrive in North America. Most of these settlers longed for land and for religious freedom, and narratives describing the vast possibilities of life in the Americas encouraged new settlers to realize their goals. Early American writings, such as Captain John Smith's *General History of Virginia, New England, and the Summer Isles* (1624), served as advertisements for what was called the New World. These narratives roused people's imaginations and promoted a widespread ambition to journey across the ocean to America.

The Bitter with the Sweet

Captivity Stories Not all narratives spoke glowingly of the New World. *A Narrative of the Captivity, Sufferings and Removes of Mrs. Mary Rowlandson* chronicled the author's kidnapping at the hands of the Wampanoag. "Captivity stories" such as Rowlandson's became one of the most widely produced forms of entertainment in North America. Unfortunately, these narratives also contributed to the decline of relations between American Indians and colonists.

Slave Narratives One of the most influential forms of early American literature was the slave narrative, an autobiographical account of the life of an enslaved person. Many such autobiographies, such as *The Interesting Narrative of the Life of Olaudah Equiano,* tell of the suffering that African slaves endured and of their intense desire for freedom. These narratives supported the abolitionist cause by revealing the horrors of slavery.

Ask Yourself

1. Name four types of early American narratives.
2. What are slave narratives, and how did they serve the abolitionist cause?

Learn It Online
Explore the American narrative tradition the multimedia way through *PowerNotes*.

go.hrw.com | L11-43 | **Go**

from
La Relación

Álvar Núñez Cabeza de Vaca
(c. 1490–c. 1560)

What Do
You
Think

How can people's beliefs affect their actions?

QuickTalk

Think about an experience you've had that did not go as planned. With a small group, discuss what happened and how you reacted to the unexpected events. Did they influence your outlook on life? How might this new perspective affect the way you react to unexpected events in the future?

Engraving of coat of arms belonging to King Charles V of Spain, from the cover page of *La Relación y Comentarios* by Álvar Núñez Cabeza de Vaca (1555 edition).

Álvar Núñez Cabeza de Vaca's narrative is a gripping adventure story. It is also a firsthand account of American Indians that urges readers to respect the humanity of native peoples.

A Grueling Journey

Álvar Núñez Cabeza de Vaca was born around 1490 to a noble family in Spain. His unusual name, which means "head of a cow," came from an ancestor who helped the Spanish win a battle by marking an unguarded mountain pass with a cow's skull.

As a teenager, Cabeza de Vaca joined the army. He participated in an expedition that set sail to Florida in June 1527. The Spanish conquistadors hoped to conquer North America and claim the land and its treasures for Spain. However, Cabeza de Vaca's journey was beset by disasters. Two ships were wrecked. Many sailors deserted, and many others died. By 1533, only Cabeza de Vaca and three other sailors survived. *La Relación* (The Narrative) reveals the suffering these men endured between 1528 and 1537 as they walked across Texas, New Mexico, and Arizona before reaching Mexico.

More Than a Travel Document

Spain sent several expeditions to conquer and colonize North America during the sixteenth century. *La Relación* is one of few surviving accounts of these journeys. First published in 1542, it is an informative document of American exploration. Written as a report to the king after Cabeza de Vaca's return to Spain in 1537, *La Relación* is an extraordinary travel journal as well as an important literary work. Cabeza de Vaca wrote about twenty-three Native American groups. He described their languages, rituals, diets, and migrations. After experiencing the hospitality of Native American peoples, Cabeza de Vaca began to argue against the brutal Spanish slave trade. He also encouraged his readers to respect Native Americans' dignity and land.

Think About the Writer

How do you think Cabeza de Vaca's travel report differed from what he originally expected to write for the king of Spain?

Reader/Writer
Notebook

Use your **RWN** to complete the activities for this selection.

Literary Focus

Audience The **audience** is the person or group of people for whom an author is writing. Authors often compose texts with particular readers in mind; this focus helps authors decide which details to include and what tone to use. Álvar Núñez Cabeza de Vaca wrote *La Relación* as a travel report for the king of Spain. To inform the king about his encounters in North America, Cabeza de Vaca uses a respectful tone and includes details that bring to life a land his audience has not experienced firsthand.

Reading Focus

Analyzing Historical Context To understand a work of literature fully, you may need to evaluate how it was shaped by the historical period in which it was written. The social and political beliefs of a time period often influence how authors portray people, places, and conflicts. Before you read *La Relación*, review the time line on pages 2–3 to get a feel for events that were happening during Cabeza de Vaca's time. As you read, consider how the historical context shapes Cabeza de Vaca's portrayal of Native Americans. How might the author's beliefs and those of his audience have influenced his descriptions?

Into Action As you read the excerpt from *La Relación*, use a chart like the one below to record details, such as descriptions or explanations, that reflect the **historical context** in which the text was written. Use the second column to analyze the social or political beliefs that might have influenced each detail.

Detail	Historical Context
"They thought themselves rich with the little bells and beads we gave them."	The Spaniards and the American Indians have different standards of wealth.

Vocabulary

calamity (kuh LAM uh tee) *n.:* great misfortune; disaster. *Cabeza de Vaca and his men suffered a calamity when their barge capsized.*

remnants (REHM nuhnts) *n.:* remains. *The remnants of their belongings had been on the barge.*

lamented (luh MEHN tihd) *v.:* cried out in sorrow. *The Indians lamented when they heard of the Spaniards' misfortunes.*

conferred (kuhn FURD) *v.:* talked things over; consulted. *Cabeza de Vaca conferred with his men before asking the Indians for help.*

beseeched (bih SEECHT) *v.:* begged. *The men beseeched the Indians for food and shelter.*

Language Coach

Suffixes Words that end with the suffix *–ity*, such as *calamity*, are usually nouns. Often, *–ity* turns an adjective into a noun, such as in the words *electricity* (from the adjective *electric*) or *similarity* (from the adjective *similar*). Write down three other words that end with the suffix *–ity*. What base word does each word come from?

Writing Focus

Think as a Reader/Writer

Find It in Your Reading *La Relación* is a travel document written for an **audience** that has never experienced the place or met the people the author describes. As you read, record in your *Reader/Writer Notebook* vivid details that bring the unfamiliar world to life.

Learn It Online
Improve your vocabulary with Word Watch online.

go.hrw.com | L11-45 | **Go**

from La Relación

by **Álvar Núñez Cabeza de Vaca**

translated by **Cyclone Covey**

Read with a Purpose

Read to discover how the writer's beliefs about American Indians change as a result of his surprising experiences.

Build Background

Cabeza de Vaca lived with the native peoples of what is now Texas for six years. He and the other survivors then decided to continue their journey to Mexico City, using American Indians as guides. They met and joined a party of Spanish soldiers on a slaving expedition, and in 1537 the men arrived in Mexico City. They had been traveling for more than eight years.

In 1527, Cabeza de Vaca was second in command of a disastrous five-ship expedition to establish a colony in Florida. After two ships went down in a hurricane and more than two hundred men drowned or deserted, the expedition landed in 1528 near present-day Tampa, Florida. The commander and his men wandered for six months in Florida, exhausted by hunger, disease, and Indian attacks. Finally, they built barges in an attempt to reach Mexico by sea. Most of the barges were lost, but Cabeza de Vaca's landed on an island off the coast of Texas. In this section of his narrative, Cabeza de Vaca describes an encounter with the Karankawa on what is thought to have been present-day Galveston Island, Texas.

Analyzing Visuals

Viewing and Interpreting
Review the introductory paragraph above. What difficulties will Cabeza de Vaca and the other survivors face? How are the difficulties conveyed in this image?

Chapter 19

The Indians' Hospitality before and after a New Calamity

As the sun rose next morning, the Indians appeared as they promised, bringing an abundance of fish and of certain roots which taste like nuts, some bigger than walnuts, some smaller, mostly grubbed[1] from the water with great labor.  **A**

That evening they came again with more fish and roots and brought their women and children to look at us. They thought themselves rich with the little bells and beads we gave them, and they repeated their visits on other days.

Being provided with what we needed, we thought to embark again. It was a struggle to dig our barge out of the sand it had sunk in, and another struggle to launch her. For the work in the water while launching, we stripped and stowed our clothes in the craft.

Quickly clambering in and grabbing our oars, we had rowed two crossbow shots from shore when a wave inundated us. Being naked and the cold intense, we let our oars go. The next big wave capsized the barge. The Inspector [Solís][2] and two others held fast, but that only carried them more certainly underneath, where they drowned.

A single roll of the sea tossed the rest of the men into the rushing surf and back onto shore half-drowned.

We lost only those the barge took down; but the survivors escaped as naked as they were born, with the loss of everything we had. That was not much, but valuable to us in that bitter November cold, our bodies so emaciated we could easily count every bone and looked the very picture of death. I can say for myself that from the month of May I had eaten nothing but corn, and that sometimes raw. I never could bring myself to eat any of the horse-meat at the time our beasts were slaughtered; and fish I did not taste ten times. On top of everything else, a cruel north wind commenced to complete our killing.

The Lord willed that we should find embers while searching the remnants of our former fire. We found more wood and soon had big fires raging. Before them, with flowing tears, we prayed for mercy and pardon, each filled with pity not only for himself but for all his wretched fellows. **B**

> ## ON TOP OF EVERYTHING ELSE, A CRUEL NORTH WIND COMMENCED TO COMPLETE OUR KILLING.

---

1. **grubbed:** dug.

2. **Solís:** Alonzo de Solís.

A **Literary Focus** **Audience** Why might Cabeza de Vaca's audience be interested in these specific details about the Indians' food-gathering methods and diet?

B **Reading Focus** **Analyzing Historical Context** How does the writer's mention of his faith reflect the historical context of the selection? What does it reveal about the audience to which Cabeza de Vaca writes?

Vocabulary **calamity** (kuh LAM uh tee) *n.:* great misfortune; disaster.
remnants (REHM nuhnts) *n.:* remains.

At sunset the Indians, not knowing we had gone, came again with food. When they saw us looking so strangely different, they turned back in alarm. I went after them calling, and they returned, though frightened. I explained to them by signs that our barge had sunk and three of our number drowned. They could see at their feet two of the dead men who had washed ashore. They could also see that the rest of us were not far from joining these two.

The Indians, understanding our full plight, sat down and lamented for half an hour so loudly they could have been heard a long way off. It was amazing to see these wild, untaught savages howling like brutes in compassion for us. It intensified my own grief at our calamity and had the same effect on the other victims. **C**

When the cries died down, I conferred with the Christians about asking the Indians to take us to their homes. Some of our number who had been to New Spain warned that the Indians would sacrifice us to their idols.[3] But death being surer and nearer if we stayed where we were, I went ahead and beseeched the Indians. They were delighted. They told us to tarry[4] a little while, then they would do as we wished.

Presently thirty of them gathered loads of wood and disappeared to their huts, which were a long walk away; while we waited with the remainder until near nightfall. Then, supporting us under our arms, they hurried us from one to another of the four big fires they had built along the path. At each fire, when we regained a little warmth and strength, they took us on so swiftly our feet hardly touched ground.

Thus we made their village, where we saw they had erected a hut for us with many fires inside. An hour later they began a dance celebration that lasted all night. For us there was no joy, feasting, or sleep, as we waited the hour they should make us victims.

In the morning, when they brought us fish and roots and acted in every way hospitably, we felt reassured and somewhat lost our anxiety of the sacrificial knife. **D**

---

3. **New Spain . . . idols:** New Spain was the Spanish colonial territory in the Americas that would eventually include Mexico, portions of Central and South America, the largest Caribbean islands, the Bahamas, Florida, and the southwestern United States. In Mexico, the Spanish conquistador Hernando Cortés had encountered Aztecs who practiced human sacrifice.

4. **tarry:** wait.

C **Reading Focus** Analyzing Historical Context What does this paragraph suggest about Europeans' views of American Indians at the time this account was written?

D **Literary Focus** Audience How might this paragraph and the previous one affect the audience's beliefs about Native Americans?

Vocabulary **lamented** (luh MEHN tihd) *v.:* cried out in sorrow.
conferred (kuhn FURD) *v.:* talked things over; consulted.
beseeched (bih SEECHT) *v.:* begged.

Applying Your Skills

from La Relación

Respond and Think Critically

Reading Focus

Quick Check

1. What happens to the Spaniards when they try to resume their journey?

2. Why are the Spaniards afraid of the Native Americans?

3. How do the Native Americans respond to the Spaniards' request for help?

Read with a Purpose

4. How do the writer's beliefs about Native Americans change? What causes the change?

Reading Skills: Analyzing Historical Context

5. As you read, you <u>cited</u> details about historical context and analyzed the beliefs of the time that might have influenced each detail. In a third column, comment on current social or political beliefs regarding each detail.

Detail	Historical Context	Current Context
"They thought themselves rich with the little bells and beads we gave them."	The Spaniards have a different standard of wealth than the American Indians do.	Today's global economy creates similar standards of wealth among many groups. There also exists a wide gap between rich and poor.

Literary Focus

Literary Analysis

6. **Interpret** Re-read Cabeza de Vaca's description of the Spaniards' state after their barge sinks. What words convey their desperation?

7. **Hypothesize** In the second paragraph, Cabeza de Vaca writes that the Indians "brought their women and children to look at us." What do you think the Indians thought when they saw the Spaniards? Why?

8. **Analyze** How does the title "The Indians' Hospitality before and after a New Calamity" communicate the main idea of the passage? What does the title reveal about the author?

Literary Skills: Audience

9. **Infer** How would this story have been different if Cabeza de Vaca had written it not for his king but for the native people that he met?

Literary Skills Review: Setting

10. **Evaluate** The **setting** is the time and location in which a narrative takes place. Explain how the setting of this selection affects its mood.

Writing Focus

Think as a Reader/Writer

Use It in Your Writing Write a paragraph about a place you or someone you know visited. Assume that your audience has never been to the place. Then, rewrite the paragraph for someone who has been there. How do your paragraphs reflect the differences in experience and knowledge of your audiences?

What Do **You Think Now** Do you think that reading *La Relación* would have caused readers during Cabeza de Vaca's time to change their views about Native Americans? Why or why not?

SKILLS FOCUS **Vocabulary Skills** Analyze word origins.

from La Relación

Vocabulary Development

Vocabulary Check

Match each Vocabulary word with its **synonym,** or word that has the same or almost the same meaning.

1. calamity	**a.** discussed
2. remnants	**b.** pleaded
3. lamented	**c.** disaster
4. conferred	**d.** mourned
5. beseeched	**e.** remainders

Vocabulary Skills: Cognates

Cognates are words from different languages that are related because they both come from the same original language. In fact, the term *cognate* comes from the Latin for "born together." English shares many cognate words with Spanish, even though English and Spanish aren't closely related languages. They're both distant cousins of a language called Indo-European, which was spoken thousands of years ago. English is much closer to languages such as German and Dutch. Throughout its history, though, English has had a great deal of contact with languages such as Latin, French, and Italian—all of which are closely related to Spanish—and has borrowed many words from these languages. Therefore, English shares numerous root words with Spanish. The chart below contains a few examples.

English word	Spanish cognate
athlete	atleta
creative	creativo
favorite	favorito
medicine	medicina

Your Turn

Many of the Vocabulary words in *La Relación* have Spanish cognates, or words in Spanish that are similar to them. The words in column A are from the selection. Use their appearance and pronunciation to match them to their Spanish cognates in column B.

A	B
calamity	conferir
remnant	calamidad
lament	lamentarse
confer	remanente

Language Coach

Suffixes Earlier you studied the noun-forming suffix *–ity.* Take a look at the Vocabulary word *remnant.* It contains the noun-forming suffix *–ant,* which can mean "person or thing that." (In the case of *remnant,* it means "something or someone that remains.") Look up the following *–ant* words in a dictionary, and list their base words and definitions: *aspirant, irritant, surveillant,* and *variant.*

Academic Vocabulary

Write About

What can you **infer,** or reasonably guess, about Cabeza de Vaca's perspective on the Karankawa from his commentary about their response to the Spaniards' misfortune? Cite passages from the selection that support your inferences.

Reading Focus

from Of Plymouth Plantation

Summarizing by **Kylene Beers**

Have you ever been unable to recall what happened in a chapter of a book you just read? You know you read it, but now you can't explain what it is you read.

Summarizing is a strategy that can help you understand while you read or check your comprehension when you've finished reading. A **summary** is a brief retelling in your own words. It focuses on big ideas and may include some, but not all, supporting details.

Summarizing requires you to break information into smaller parts and then put it back together in your own words. First, read a whole paragraph. Then, break it into parts and look at each sentence. Consider who or what each part is about and what is happening to or being said about the subject. For example, read this section from *Of Plymouth Plantation*.

> These troubles being blown over, and now all being compact together in one ship, they put out to sea again with a prosperous wind, which continued divers days together, which was some encouragement unto them; yet, according to the usual manner, many were afflicted with seasickness.

Now, you put it in your own words. What is the subject of this section? It is *travelers sailing together on one ship*. What happened to the travelers? *They became seasick*.

Continue this process on the next section.

> There was a proud and very profane young man, one of the seamen, of a lusty, able body, which made him the more haughty; he would always be condemning the poor people in their sickness and cursing them daily with grievous execrations; and did not let to tell them that he hoped to help to cast half of them overboard before they came to their journey's end, and to make merry with what they had; and if he were by any gently reproved, he would curse and swear. . . .

The subject of this section is a *young sailor* and what happens is that *he curses and threatens those who are ill*.

Repeat this process on the third and fourth sections.

> But it pleased God before they came half seas over, to smite this young man with a grievous disease, of which he died in a desperate manner, and so was himself the first that was thrown overboard.

The young sailor becomes ill, dies, and is thrown overboard.

> Thus his curses light on his own head, and it was an astonishment to all his fellows for they noted it to be the just hand of God upon him.

The other seamen are astonished and they believe his death to be the work of God.

Now you are ready to put the pieces together:

Crowded onto one ship, the passengers became seasick. A young sailor ridiculed and cursed them. He became ill, died, and was thrown overboard. The others believed his death was the work of God.

Your Turn

Using the strategy explained above, summarize the third paragraph of the excerpt from *Of Plymouth Plantation*. Then compare summaries with a partner. Discuss the similarities and differences between your summaries.

Learn It Online

Find the *PowerNotes* interactive introduction to summarizing online.

go.hrw.com | L11-51 | **Go**

from Of Plymouth Plantation

What Do You Think?

How can people's beliefs affect their actions?

⏱ QuickWrite

Think about a time when you faced a challenge, such as moving to a new place or learning how to overcome differences with another person. In a one-page journal entry, reflect on how your beliefs helped you overcome this challenge. What effect did this experience have on your beliefs?

William Bradford, original design by Cyrus E. Dallin, Plymouth, MA.

William Bradford
(1590–1657)

An independent thinker who worked for the common good, William Bradford led the Pilgrims after they landed at Plymouth.

Thinking Independently

William Bradford was the son of a prosperous farmer in Yorkshire, England. The Bible and the sermons of a Puritan minister inspired Bradford to begin attending the meetings of a small group of Separatists, people who disagreed with the Church of England's teachings. He joined them in 1606.

In 1608, under increasing pressure of persecution, Bradford's group of Separatists crossed the North Sea to Holland. The group sailed for America in 1620. They wanted to found a community in which they could live according to their beliefs.

Eventually, the group landed at Plymouth, Massachusetts. They created the Mayflower Compact, an agreement governing how they would live and work cooperatively in the new colony. In 1621, Bradford was elected second governor of the colony. He would be elected to the office thirty times. Many of Bradford's ideas, such as town meetings, continue to influence our politics and society.

Holding Together

As the Plymouth Colony prospered and grew, it gradually ceased to be primarily a religious community. The Pilgrims' dream of an ideal society gave way to the realities of life in a new land. Bradford even worked to help the society include people from all churches.

In 1630, Bradford began to write an annual account of the Plymouth settlement. Bradford wrote his chronicle every year, hoping it would inspire future generations to carry on the Pilgrims' ideals. The document was lost during the Revolutionary War. Almost a century later, Bradford's own volume was discovered in the library of the bishop of London. Bradford's work was first published as *History of Plymouth Plantation* in 1856. The manuscript finally returned to the United States in 1897 and can be seen today in Boston.

Think About the Writer

If Bradford were to help construct a document like the Mayflower Compact for your school, what issues do you think he would address?

Reader/Writer Notebook

Use your **RWN** to complete the activities for this selection.

Literary Focus

Plain Style At the beginning of his account, Bradford says he will try to unfold his story "in a plain style." Although his style may seem far from "plain" to modern readers because of its biblical quotations and allusions and its archaic syntax and vocabulary, Bradford's writing reflects the Puritan preference for plainness in all things. The Puritans thought that a plain style was more effective than a "high style" in revealing God's truth. The chief characteristics of **plain style** were simple sentences, everyday language, and direct statements. In contrast, "high style," which was in fashion in England at the time, used classical allusions, Latin quotations, and elaborate figures of speech.

Reading Focus

Summarizing To **summarize** a text means to retell it briefly in your own words. Summaries focus on the **main idea.** They may include key supporting details, but they do not include all of the details. Summarizing is especially helpful with selections such as Bradford's, which can challenge readers with its unfamiliar style.

Into Action As you read, use a chart like the one below to record and summarize challenging sentences or passages.

Passage (page #)	Summary
"These troubles being blown over, and now all being compact together in one ship, they put to sea again with a prosperous wind, which continued divers days together, which was some encouragement unto them; yet, according to the usual manner, many were afflicted with seasickness." (p. 55)	We were back at sea and the winds were calm, but then many of us became seasick.

Writing Focus

Think as a Reader/Writer

Find It in Your Reading Bradford uses simple diction and literal language to provide factual information. As you read, use your *Reader/Writer Notebook* to record passages in which Bradford uses simple words and literal language to tell about dramatic events. Think about how this straightforward language affects your understanding of each event.

Vocabulary

profane (pruh FAYN) *adj.:* not religious; contemptuous; disrespectful. *The profane sailor cursed the sick and suffering passengers.*

haughty (HAW tee) *adj.:* arrogant. *The haughty sailor mocked the passengers who became ill during the voyage.*

consultation (kahn suhl TAY shuhn) *n.:* a meeting to seek information or exchange ideas. *The Puritans and the Native Americans reached an agreement during a consultation.*

sundry (SUHN dree) *adj.* used as *pron.:* various; several. *The Puritans' ship barely survived through sundry of the storms.*

discourse (DIHS kawrs) *n.:* a written or spoken conversation. *After attending Samoset's discourse, the Puritans were able to communicate with the Native Americans.*

Language Coach

Spelling In English, the long /a/ sound can be represented by different letter combinations. Often it is represented with either the vowel combination *ai* or with *a* + consonant + *e*. Which word above contains the long /a/ sound? How is it spelled?

Learn It Online
Explore the Vocabulary words inside and out with Word Watch.

go.hrw.com L11-53

from Of Plymouth Plantation

by **William Bradford**

Drawing of the Plymouth Meeting House (1683).   Courtesy of the Pilgrim Hall Museum, Plymouth, Massachusetts.

Read with a Purpose
Read to learn about the hardships the Puritans faced as they tried to create new lives for themselves in America.

Build Background
For William Bradford, the hardships of the voyage to America did not end with the landing at Plymouth. In December 1620, while the *Mayflower* was anchored in Provincetown Harbor, Bradford and other men took a small boat ashore to scout for a place to land and build shelter. When they returned, Bradford learned that his young wife had fallen or jumped from the ship. Perhaps Dorothy Bradford was in despair when land was finally sighted and she did not see the hoped-for green hills of an earthly paradise. Beyond the ship lay only the bleak sand dunes of Cape Cod.

from Chapter 9

Of their Voyage, and how they Passed the Sea; and of their Safe Arrival at Cape Cod September 6 [1620].

These troubles[1] being blown over, and now all being compact together in one ship, they put to sea again with a prosperous wind, which continued divers[2] days together, which was some encouragement unto them; yet, according to the usual manner, many were afflicted with seasickness. And I may not omit here a special work of God's providence. There was a proud and very profane young man, one of the seamen, of a lusty,[3] able body, which made him the more haughty; he would always be condemning the poor people in their sickness and cursing them daily with grievous execrations;[4] and did not let to tell them that he hoped to cast half of them overboard before they came to their journey's end, and to make merry with what they had; and if he were by any gently reproved,[5] he would curse and swear most bitterly. But it pleased God before they came half seas over, to smite this young man with a grievous disease, of which he died in a desperate manner, and so was himself the first that was thrown overboard. Thus his curses light on his own head, and it was an astonishment to all his fellows for they noted it to be the just hand of God upon him. **(A)**

After they had enjoyed fair winds and weather for a season, they were encountered many times with crosswinds and met with many fierce storms with which the ship was shroudly[6] shaken, and her upper works made very leaky; and one of the main beams in the midships was bowed and cracked, which put them in some fear that the ship could not be able to perform the voyage. So some of the chief of the company, perceiving the mariners to fear the sufficiency of the ship as appeared by their mutterings, they entered into serious consultation with the master and other officers of the ship, to consider in time of the danger, and rather to return than to cast themselves into a desperate and inevitable peril. And truly there was great distraction and difference of opinion amongst the mariners themselves; fain[7] would they do what could be done for their wages' sake (being now near half the seas over) and on the other hand they were loath[8] to hazard their lives too desperately. But in examining of all opinions, the master and others affirmed they knew the ship to be strong and firm underwater; and for the buckling of the main beam, there was a great iron screw the passengers brought out of Holland, which would raise the beam into his place; the which being done, the carpenter and master affirmed that with a post put under it, set firm in the lower deck and otherways bound, he would make it sufficient. And as for the decks and upper works, they would caulk them as well as they could, and though with the working of the ship they would not long keep staunch,[9] yet there would otherwise be no great danger, if they did not overpress her with sails. So they committed themselves to the will of God and resolved to proceed. **(B)**

---

1. **troubles:** the transfer of passengers to the *Mayflower* after one of the other ships became unseaworthy.
2. **divers:** many.
3. **lusty:** energetic; robust.
4. **execrations:** angry words; curses.
5. **reproved:** reprimanded.
6. **shroudly:** shrewdly, used here in its archaic sense of "wickedly."
7. **fain:** archaic for "gladly."
8. **loath:** reluctant.
9. **staunch:** watertight.

(A) Literary Focus **Plain Style** Re-read the description of the sailor's death. Point out some examples of the everyday language and direct statements that Bradford uses in this passage. How does this straightforward account of the sailor's death help Bradford convey his belief that it was caused by God's will?

(B) Reading Focus **Summarizing** In this paragraph, what do the passengers and crew fear will happen, and how do they solve this problem? Cite evidence to support your response.

Vocabulary **profane** (pruh FAYN) *adj.:* not religious; contemptuous; disrespectful.
haughty (HAW tee) *adj.:* arrogant.
consultation (kahn suhl TAY shuhn) *n.:* a meeting to seek information or exchange ideas.

In sundry of these storms the winds were so fierce and the seas so high, as they could not bear a knot of sail, but were forced to hull[10] for divers days together. And in one of them, as they thus lay at hull in a mighty storm, a lusty young man called John Howland, coming upon some occasion above the gratings was, with a seele[11] of the ship, thrown into sea; but it pleased God that he caught hold of the topsail halyards[12] which hung overboard and ran out at length. Yet he held his hold (though he was sundry fathoms underwater) till he was hauled up by the same rope to the brim of the water, and then with a boathook and other means got into the ship again and his life saved. And though he was something ill with it, yet he lived many years after and became a profitable member both in church and commonwealth. In all this voyage there died but one of the passengers, which was William Butten, a youth, servant to Samuel Fuller, when they drew near the coast. **C**

But to omit other things (that I may be brief) after long beating at sea they fell with that land which is called Cape Cod;[13] the which being made and certainly known to be it, they were not a little joyful. After some deliberation had amongst themselves and with the master of the ship, they tacked about and resolved to stand for the southward (the wind and weather being fair) to find some place about Hudson's River[14] for their habitation. But after they had sailed that course about half the day, they fell amongst dangerous shoals and roaring breakers, and they were so far entangled therewith as they conceived themselves in great danger; and the wind shrinking upon them withal, they resolved to bear up again for the Cape and thought themselves happy to get out of those dangers before night overtook them, as by God's good providence they did. And the next

day they got into the Cape Harbor[15] where they rid in safety. . . .

Being thus arrived in a good harbor, and brought safe to land, they fell upon their knees and blessed the God of Heaven who had brought them over the vast and furious ocean, and delivered them from all the perils and miseries thereof, again to set their feet on the firm and stable earth, their proper element. . . .

But here I cannot but stay and make a pause, and stand half amazed at this poor people's present condition; and so I think will the reader, too, when he well considers the same. Being thus passed the vast ocean, and a sea of troubles before in their preparation (as may be remembered by that which went before), they had now no friends to welcome them nor inns to entertain or refresh their weather-beaten bodies; no houses or much less towns to repair to, to seek for succor.[16] It is recorded in Scripture[17] as a mercy to the Apostle and his shipwrecked company, that the barbarians showed them no small kindness in refreshing them, but these savage barbarians, when they met with them (as after will appear) were readier to fill their sides full of arrows than otherwise. And for the season it was winter, and they that know the winters of that country know them to be sharp and violent, and subject to cruel and fierce storms, dangerous to travel to known places, much more to search an unknown coast. Besides, what could they see but a hideous and desolate wilderness, full of wild beasts and wild men—and what multitudes there might be of them they knew not. Neither could they, as it were, go up to the top of Pisgah[18] to view from this wilderness a more goodly country to feed their hopes; for which way soever they turned their eyes (save upward to the heavens) they could have little solace or content in respect of any outward objects. For summer being done, all things stand upon them

10. **hull:** to float without using the sails.
11. **seele:** sudden lurch to one side.
12. **halyards:** ropes for raising a sail.
13. **Cape Cod:** They sighted Cape Cod in present-day Massachusetts at daybreak on November 9, 1620.
14. **Hudson's River:** They were trying to reach Manhattan Island. Henry Hudson had made his voyage in 1609 and had claimed the area for the Dutch, but the English did not recognize the Dutch claim.

15. **Cape Harbor:** now called Provincetown Harbor.
16. **succor:** aid.
17. **Scripture:** In the Acts of the Apostles (Chapter 28), Paul tells how the shipwrecked Christians were helped by the "barbarous people" of Malta.
18. **Pisgah:** mountain from which Moses first viewed the Promised Land.

C **Reading Focus** **Summarizing** Write a one-sentence summary of what happened to John Howland.

Vocabulary **sundry** (SUHN dree) *adj.* used as *pron.:* various; several.

Analyzing Visuals

Viewing and Interpreting Does this engraving represent hardships like those described on pages 56 and 57? Explain. (Observe the following: structures, objects, and people's postures.)

with a weather-beaten face, and the whole country, full of woods and thickets, represented a wild and savage hue. If they looked behind them, there was the mighty ocean which they had passed and was now as a main bar and gulf to separate them from all the civil parts of the world.... **D**

What could now sustain them but the Spirit of God and His grace? May not and ought not the children of these fathers rightly say: "Our fathers were Englishmen which came over this great ocean, and were ready to perish in this wilderness; but they cried unto the Lord, and He heard their voice and looked on their adversity,"[19] etc.? "Let them therefore praise the Lord, because He is good: And His mercies endure forever." "Yea, let them which have been redeemed of the Lord, show how He hath delivered them from the hand of the oppressor. When they wandered in the desert wilderness out of the way, and found no city to dwell in, both hungry and thirsty, their soul was overwhelmed in them. Let them confess before the Lord His lovingkindness and His wonderful works before the sons of men."[20]

from Chapter 11
The Starving Time [1620–1621].

But that which was most sad and lamentable was, that in two or three months' time half of their company died, especially in January and February, being the depth of winter, and wanting houses and other comforts; being infected with the scurvy and other diseases which this long voyage and their inaccom-

---

19. **they cried . . . their adversity:** paraphrase of Deuteronomy 26:7.

D Literary Focus **Plain Style** In this passage, Bradford dramatically describes the setting of the wintry Cape Cod sea coast. How does the style of this passage contrast with the plain style he uses to describe other aspects of the Pilgrims' experience in Cape Cod?

---

20. **Let them . . . the sons of men:** paraphrase of Psalm 107.

modate condition had brought upon them. So as there died sometimes two or three of a day in the foresaid time, that of 100 and odd persons, scarce fifty remained. And of these, in the time of most distress, there was but six or seven sound persons who to their great commendations, be it spoken, spared no pains night nor day, but with abundance of toil and hazard of their own health, fetched them wood, made them fires, dressed them meat, made their beds, washed their loathsome clothes, clothed and unclothed them. In a word, did all the homely and necessary offices for them which dainty and queasy stomachs cannot endure to hear named; and all this willingly and cheerfully, without any grudging in the least, showing herein their true love unto their friends and brethren; a rare example and worthy to be remembered. Two of these seven were Mr. William Brewster, their reverend Elder, and Myles Standish,[21] their Captain and military commander, unto whom myself and many others were much beholden in our low and sick condition. And yet the Lord so upheld these persons as in this general calamity they were not at all infected either with sickness or lameness. . . . **E F**

Indian Relations

All this while the Indians came skulking about them, and would sometimes show themselves aloof off, but when any approached near them, they would run away; and once they stole away their tools where they had been at work and were gone to dinner. But about the 16th of March, a certain Indian came boldly amongst them and spoke to them in broken English, which they could well understand but marveled at it. At length they

understood by discourse with him, that he was not of these parts, but belonged to the eastern parts where some English ships came to fish, with whom he was acquainted and could name sundry of them by their names, amongst whom he had got his language. He became profitable to them in acquainting them with many things concerning the state of the country in the east parts where he lived, which was afterward profitable unto them; as also of the people here, of their names, number and strength, of their situation and distance from this place, and who was chief amongst them. His name was Samoset.[22] He told them also of another Indian whose name was Squanto,[23] a native of this place, who had been in England and could speak better English than himself.

Being, after some time of entertainment and gifts dismissed, a while after he came again, and five more with him, and they brought again all the tools that were stolen away before, and made way for the coming of their great Sachem, called Massasoit.[24] Who, about four or five days after, came with the chief of his friends and other attendance, with the aforesaid Squanto. With whom, after friendly entertainment and some gifts given him, they made a peace with him (which hath now continued this 24 years)[25] in these terms:

---

21. **Myles Standish (c. 1584–1656):** a soldier who had been hired to handle the colonists' military affairs. Though not a member of the Puritan congregation, he nevertheless became a steadfast ally.

22. **Samoset** (SAM uh seht) **(1590?–1655):** a Pemaquid (PEHM uh kwid) from Maine.
23. **Squanto** (SKWAHN toh) **(1585?–1622):** one of the few survivors of the Pawtuxet (paw TUHKS iht), an Algonquian (al GAHNG kee an) people. He later joined Massasoit's Wampanoags (wahm pa NOH agz).
24. **Massasoit** (mas uh SOYT) **(c. 1580–1661):** sachem (chief) of the Wampanoags, who lived in the area that became Rhode Island and southern Massachusetts.
25. **With whom . . . this 24 years:** The treaty was kept faithfully until the reign of Massasoit's younger son, Metacomet (meht ah CAHM iht) (1639?–1676), also known to the colonists as King Philip.

E **Literary Focus** Plain Style This passage exemplifies plain style. How does Bradford describe the starving time? What effect might this matter-of-fact style have on how readers interpret the experience?

F **Reading Focus** Summarizing Summarize the long sentences that begin with "And of these" and "In a word." What is the main idea of each sentence?

Vocabulary discourse (DIHS kawrs) n.: a written or spoken conversation.

1. That neither he nor any of his should injure or do hurt to any of their people.
2. That if any of his did hurt to any of theirs, he should send the offender, that they might punish him.
3. That if anything were taken away from any of theirs, he should cause it to be restored; and they should do the like to his.
4. If any did unjustly war against him, they would aid him; if any did war against them, he should aid them.
5. He should send to his neighbors confederates[26] to certify them of this, that they might not wrong them, but might be likewise comprised in the conditions of peace.
6. That when their men came to them, they should leave their bows and arrows behind them. **G**

After these things he returned to his place called Sowams, some 40 miles from this place, but Squanto continued with them and was their interpreter and was a special instrument sent of God for their good beyond their expectation. He directed them how to set their corn, where to take fish, and to procure other commodities, and was also their pilot to bring them to unknown places for their profit, and never left them till he died. He was a native of this place, and scarce any left alive besides himself. He was carried away with divers others by one Hunt, a master of a ship, who thought to sell them for slaves in Spain. But he got away for England and was entertained by a merchant in London, and employed to Newfoundland and other parts, and lastly brought hither into these parts by one Mr. Dermer, a gentleman employed by Sir Ferdinando Gorges and others for discovery and other designs in these parts. . . . **H**

26. **confederates:** allies; persons who share a common purpose.

First Thanksgiving

They began now to gather in the small harvest they had, and to fit up their houses and dwellings against winter, being all well recovered in health and strength and had all things in good plenty. For as some were thus employed in affairs abroad, others were exercised in fishing, about cod and bass and other fish, of which they took good store, of which every family had their portion. All the summer there was no want; and now began to come in store of fowl, as winter approached, of which this place did abound when they came first (but afterward decreased by degrees). And besides waterfowl there was great store of wild turkeys, of which they took many, besides venison, etc. Besides they had about a peck of meal a week to a person, or now since harvest, Indian corn to that proportion. Which made many afterward write so largely of their plenty here to their friends in England, which were not feigned but true reports.[27] **I**

27. **Which made . . . true reports:** Although the specific day of the Plymouth colonists' first Thanksgiving is not known, it occurred in the fall of 1621. For three days, Massasoit and almost a hundred of his men joined the Pilgrims for feasts and games.

G **Reading Focus** **Summarizing** The Pilgrims and Massasoit agreed to a treaty with six terms. Read the terms carefully, making sure you understand to which person or group each personal pronoun (*he/his/him* and *they/their/them*) refers. With a partner, briefly summarize the treaty's main points.

H **Literary Focus** **Plain Style** Do you think Bradford's plain style determines what he tells and what he omits of Squanto's history? Explain your response.

I **Reading Focus** **Summarize** Summarize Bradford's account of the first Thanksgiving.

Applying Your Skills

from Of Plymouth Plantation

Respond and Think Critically

Quick Check

1. Why did the *Mayflower* return to Cape Cod?

2. During the first winter, about how many of the Pilgrims survived?

3. What were some of the foods at the first Thanksgiving?

Read with a Purpose

4. What actions did the Pilgrims take to survive the struggles they faced?

Reading Skills: Summarizing

5. As you read, you used a chart to record and summarize challenging sentences or passages. Add a third column to your chart in which you write down the main idea of each entry.

Passage (page #)	Summary	Main Idea
"These troubles being blown over, and now all being compact together in one ship, they put to sea again with a prosperous wind, ... yet, according to the usual manner, many were afflicted with seasickness." (p. 55)	We were back at sea and the winds were calm, but then many of us became seasick.	The journey was extremely difficult.

Literary Focus

Literary Analysis

6. **Compare and Contrast** Contrast the young sailor in the opening paragraph with the Native Americans the Pilgrims meet in the new land.

7. **Draw Conclusions** Why does Bradford use biblical allusions to describe the Pilgrims' conditions?

8. **Make Judgments** What does "The Starving Time" convey about the Puritans' attitudes toward suffering and self-sacrifice?

9. **Extend** How might the Puritans' experience be similar to the experiences of contemporary refugees or pioneers?

Literary Skills: Plain Style

10. **Analyze** Write down three of Bradford's sentences that contain elements of plain style, such as everyday language and direct statements. Recast these sentences into plain, modern prose. How did your changes affect the sound of the sentences?

Literary Skills Review: Allusion

11. **Evaluate** An **allusion** is a reference to someone or something that is known from history, literature, religion, politics, or some other aspect of culture. To what source does Bradford allude most frequently? Why?

Writing Focus

Think as a Reader/Writer

Use It in Your Writing Review your QuickWrite about a time you faced a challenge. Compare your style of writing to Bradford's. How is it similar or different? Might your style have differed if you had been writing in a formal situation? Explain.

 What Do You Think Now

How did the Puritans' beliefs influence the way they coped with obstacles they faced? Which particular traits helped them to survive?

Vocabulary Development

✓ Vocabulary Check

Complete the sentences below with the appropriate Vocabulary word.

profane
haughty
consultation
sundry
discourse

1. The _____ woman thought she was better than everyone else.

2. In _____ of the storms, fierce winds blew.

3. The workers and the managers will share their ideas about salary increases during their weekly _____.

4. We were shocked by the _____ words coming from the young child's mouth.

5. After her _____ with the doctor, the patient felt more informed about the topic.

Vocabulary Skills: Using a Dictionary

While you read, you may encounter words that are unfamiliar because they are **archaic,** or out of common use. Historical pieces such as Bradford's often contain archaic words or familiar words used in archaic ways. If the context clues do not help you understand the word's meaning, try looking up the word in a dictionary. A dictionary can provide a great deal of useful information about the word, including its meaning, part of speech, and **etymology,** or history.

In the selection, Bradford writes, ". . . fain would they do what could be done for their wages' sake. . . ." The following chart provides information you can learn from looking up the word *fain* in the dictionary.

Word: *fain*	
Meaning	"gladly"
Part of speech	adverb
Etymology	Middle English ("joyful"); Old English ("glad")

Your Turn

Using the previous chart as an example, fill out a similar chart for each of the words in the sentences below.

1. "These troubles being blown over, and now all being **compact** together in one ship . . ."

2. ". . . and on the other hand they were loath to **hazard** their lives too desperately. . . ."

3. ". . . they had now no friends to welcome them nor inns to entertain or refresh their weather-beaten bodies; no houses or much less towns to **repair** to, to seek for succor."

Language Coach

Spelling In the Language Coach feature on page 53, you studied spellings of the long /a/ sound. Now look at the short /o/ sound found in the Vocabulary word *haughty*. The letter combination *augh* represents the short /o/ sound in *haughty*. When you learn a new word, pay particular attention to which letters represent its vowel sounds. Other words represent the short /o/ sound with different combinations: *bought, haul, draw,* and *salt,* for instance. With a partner, list words that have a short /o/ sound and underline the letter combinations that represent the sound.

Academic Vocabulary

Talk About

With a partner, discuss your opinions on what sort of person you imagine William Bradford to be. Use examples from the text that help you <u>interpret</u> and understand his personality.

Preparing to Read

from
A Narrative of the Captivity . . .

What Do You Think

How can people's beliefs affect their actions?

QuickWrite

Think about a situation in today's world in which two groups of people (perhaps groups from different countries, political parties, or rival sports teams) are in conflict. Imagine that you are a member of one of the groups and that you come into contact with members of the other group. Jot down a first-person account of your experience.

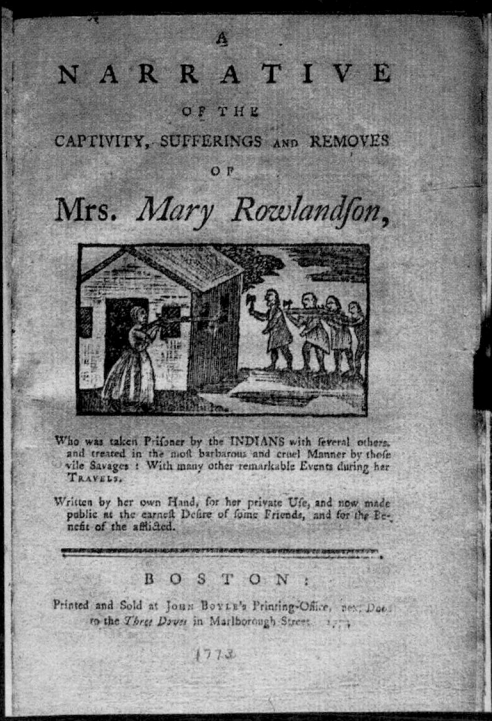

A
NARRATIVE
OF THE
CAPTIVITY, SUFFERINGS AND REMOVES
OF
Mrs. *Mary Rowlandson*,

Who was taken Prisoner by the INDIANS with several others, and treated in the most barbarous and cruel Manner by those vile Savages: With many other remarkable Events during her TRAVELS.

Written by her own Hand, for her private Use, and now made public at the earnest Desire of some Friends, and for the Benefit of the afflicted.

BOSTON:
Printed and Sold at John Boyle's Printing-Office, next Door to the Three Doves in Marlborough-Street. 1773.

1773

Mary Rowlandson
(c. 1636–c. 1711)

Captured in a violent raid, Mary Rowlandson displayed personal strength and a surprising sympathy for her captors.

Taken and Sold

From June 1675 to August 1676, the Wampanoag chief, Metacomet, led bloody raids on colonial settlements, including Lancaster, a frontier town thirty miles west of Boston. Mary Rowlandson, the wife of the Congregational minister, was a victim of one of the raids, caused by land disputes.

In February 1676, a Wampanoag raiding party carried away Rowlandson and her three children. The raiders wanted to trade their hostages for money. Conditions were harsh, and one of Rowlandson's children died within a week. After almost twelve weeks of captivity and near-starvation, Rowlandson's ransom was paid. She and her two surviving children were reunited with her husband.

In 1682, Rowlandson published her account of her ordeal. The book quickly became popular. Other colonial writers began to imitate her and write dramatic "captivity narratives."

Horror and Sympathy

Rowlandson's narrative presents a terrifying tale of frontier life. It also offers a perspective of the Puritans' belief that physical events had spiritual meaning. Rowlandson wished to show how her experience revealed God's purpose.

Rowlandson realized that her captors were barely better off than their prisoners. In a graphic passage, she describes her captors' efforts to find food: "They would pick up old bones and cut them to pieces at the joints, and if they were full of worms and maggots, they would scald them over the fire to make the vermin come out, and then boil them, and drink up the liquor . . . I can but stand in admiration to see the wonderful power of God in providing for such a vast number of our enemies in the wilderness, where there was nothing to be seen."

Think
About the
Writer

How would you survive the conditions that Mary Rowlandson endured? What qualities would help you to survive such conditions?

Title page of *A Narrative of the Captivity, Sufferings, and Removes of Mrs. Mary Rowlandson*. Published Boston 1773.

 **Reader/Writer
Notebook**

Use your **RWN** to complete the activities for this selection.

Literary Focus

Allusions An **allusion** is a reference to someone or something that is well known from history, literature, religion, politics, sports, science, or some other aspect of culture. The Puritans regarded biblical captivity narratives, such as that of the enslavement of the Israelites by the ancient Egyptians, as allegories representing the Christians' liberation from sin through the intervention of God's grace. Rowlandson views her experiences as a repetition of the biblical pattern and uses allusions to reflect her own situation. By using quotations from the Bible, Rowlandson places her experiences in the context of the ancient biblical captivity narratives.

Reading Focus

Analyzing Text Structures: Chronological Order Chronological order is the most common way for writers to tell a story or report events. Also called time order or sequential order, **chronological order** presents events in the order in which they occurred. Rowlandson tells of her experiences in chronological order and helps readers follow that order by referring to times of day and number of days since the previous event.

Into Action As you read, record in chronological order the important events of the selection in a time line like the one below.

Date	Saturday afternoon	nine days later, Feb. 18, 1675		
Important Event	Mary arrives in Wenimesset.	Sarah dies.		

Writing Focus

Think as a Reader/Writer

Find It in Your Reading As you read, notice how the author uses **allusions**. Think about her purposes in using them: How does the allusion strengthen the point she is making? In your *Reader/Writer Notebook*, interpret the allusions Rowlandson uses and how you think she wants them to affect the reader.

Vocabulary

tedious (TEE dee uhs) *adj.*: tiring; dreary. *The discomforts and difficulties of the long journey made it more tedious.*

lamentable (luh MEHN tuh buhl) *adj.*: regrettable; distressing. *The sick young girl was in a lamentable condition.*

entreated (ehn TREET ihd) *v.*: asked sincerely; begged. *She entreated the Lord for mercy.*

afflictions (uh FLIHK shuhnz) *n.*: pains; hardships. *Rowlandson was grateful to receive a Bible during her afflictions.*

plunder (PLUHN duhr) *n.*: goods seized, especially during wartime. *They found the Bible in the plunder after the fight.*

melancholy (MEHL uhn kahl ee) *adj.*: sad; sorrowful. *Reading comforted her during a melancholy time.*

repentance (rih PEHN tuhns) *n.*: sorrow for doing wrong; regret. *She believed she could find salvation through repentance.*

Language Coach

Parts of Speech The word *plunder* has both a noun and verb form; whereas *melancholy* has both an adjective and noun form. Look up the forms of each word in a dictionary. With a partner, write four sentences, each showing *plunder* and *melancholy* being used as a different part of speech.

 **Learn It Online**
Listen to this captivity narrative online.

go.hrw.com [L11-63] **Go**

A Narrative of the Captivity...

by **Mary Rowlandson**

<table>
<tr><td>

Read with a Purpose
Read to learn about the narrator's experience of being held captive in the wilderness.

</td><td>

Build Background
In the opening part of her narrative, Mary Rowlandson describes the attack on Lancaster, during which twelve people were killed and twenty-four taken captive, and the assault on her own house. During the raid, Mary and her six-year-old child Sarah, whom she calls her "babe," were wounded. The first part of this selection recounts the move of Mary and her captors from Princeton to Braintree, Massachusetts, two days after the raid.

</td></tr>
</table>

The Move to an Indian Village on the Ware River, Near Braintree (February 12–27)

The morning being come, they prepared to go on their way. One of the Indians got up upon a horse, and they set me up behind him, with my poor sick babe in my lap. A very wearisome and tedious day I had of it; what with my own wound, and my child's being so exceeding sick, and in a lamentable condition with her wound. It may be easily judged what a poor feeble condition we were in, there being not the least crumb of refreshing that came within either of our mouths from Wednesday night to Saturday night, except only a little cold water. This day in the afternoon, about an hour by sun, we came to the place where they intended, *viz.*[1] an Indian town, called Wenimesset, norward of Quabaug. . . . I sat much alone with a poor wounded child in my lap, which moaned night and day, having nothing to revive the body, or cheer the spirits of her, but instead of that, sometimes one Indian would come and tell me one hour, that your master will knock your child in the head, and then a second, and then a third, your master will quickly knock your child in the head. **Ⓐ**

---

1. *viz.:* abbreviation for the Latin word *videlicet*, for "namely.

Vocabulary **tedious** (TEE dee uhs).*adj.:* tiring; dreary.
lamentable (luh MEHN tuh buhl) *adj.:* regrettable; distressing.

Ⓐ **Reading Focus** **Chronological Order** How do the specific references to time in this paragraph make the introduction to the narrative more vivid?

Viewing and Interpreting
Examine the details in this depiction of an American Indian chief. Then, compare the visual image to the depiction of Native Americans in Rowlandson's narrative. If time allows, share your perceptions with a small group or with your class as a whole.

An engraving of King Philip, also known as Metacomet of Pokanoket. He was a *sachem*, or war chief, of the Wampanoag people.

This was the comfort I had from them, miserable comforters are ye all, as he said.[2] Thus nine days I sat upon my knees, with my babe in my lap, till my flesh was raw again; my child being even ready to depart this sorrowful world, they bade me carry it out to another wigwam (I suppose because they would not be troubled with such spectacles) whither I went with a very heavy heart, and down I sat with the picture of death in my lap. About two hours in the night, my sweet babe like a lamb departed this life, on February 18, 1675. It being about six years and five months old. It was nine days from the first wounding, in this miserable condition, without any refreshing of one nature or another, except a little cold water. I cannot but take notice, how at another time I could not bear to be in the room where any dead person was, but now the case is changed; I must and could lie down by my dead babe, side by side all the night after. I have thought since of the wonderful goodness of God to me, in preserving me in the use of my reason and senses, in that distressed time, that I did not use wicked and violent means to end my own miserable life. In the morning, when they understood that my child was dead they sent for me home to my master's wigwam: (by my master in this writing, must be understood Quanopin, who was a Sagamore, and married King Philip's wife's sister; not that he first took me, but I was sold to him by another Narragansett Indian, who took me when first I came out of the garrison). **B**
I went to take up my dead child in my arms to carry

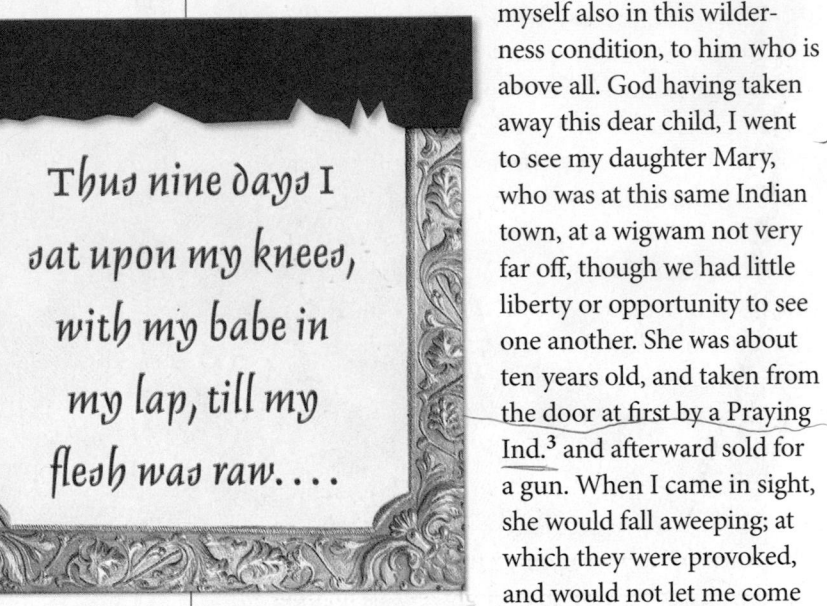

Thus nine days I sat upon my knees, with my babe in my lap, till my flesh was raw. . . .

it with me, but they bid me let it alone: There was no resisting, but go I must and leave it. When I had been at my master's wigwam, I took the first opportunity I could get, to go look after my dead child: When I came I asked them what they had done with it. Then they told me it was upon the hill: Then they went and showed me where it was, where I saw the ground was newly digged, and there they told me they had buried it: There I left that child in the wilderness, and must commit it, and myself also in this wilderness condition, to him who is above all. God having taken away this dear child, I went to see my daughter Mary, who was at this same Indian town, at a wigwam not very far off, though we had little liberty or opportunity to see one another. She was about ten years old, and taken from the door at first by a Praying Ind.[3] and afterward sold for a gun. When I came in sight, she would fall aweeping; at which they were provoked, and would not let me come near her, but bade me be gone; which was a heart-cutting word to me. I had one child dead, another in the wilderness, I knew not where, the third they would not let me come near to: "Me (as he said) have ye bereaved[4] of my Children, Joseph is not, and Simeon is not, and ye will take Benjamin also, all these things are against me."[5] I could not sit still in this condition, but kept walking from one place to another. And as I was going along, my heart was even overwhelmed with the thoughts of my

---

2. **. . . as he said:** The biblical allusion is to Job 16:2. In the passage cited, Job addresses those who try to console him. God had severely tested Job's faith by causing Job to lose his children and his money and to break out in boils all over his body.

3. **Praying Ind.:** American Indians who converted to Christianity were known as praying Indians. The Colonial assemblies allowed these converts to live in self-governing towns.

4. **bereaved:** suffering the death of a loved one.

5. **Me . . . against me:** Rowlandson quotes Jacob's lament in Genesis 42:36. Jacob had only his youngest son, Benjamin, at home.

B Literary Focus Allusions What do you think the narrator is alluding to when she says, "my sweet babe like a lamb departed this life?" How do you think she wants this comment to affect the reader?

condition, and that I should have children, and a nation which I knew not ruled over them. Whereupon I earnestly entreated the Lord, that He would consider my low estate, and show me a token for good, and if it were His blessed will, some sign and hope of some relief. And indeed quickly the Lord answered, in some measure, my poor prayers: For as I was going up and down mourning and lamenting my condition, my son came to me, and asked me how I did; I had not seen him before, since the destruction of the town, and I knew not where he was, till I was informed by himself, that he was amongst a smaller parcel of Indians, whose place was about six miles off; with tears in his eyes, he asked me whether his sister Sarah was dead; and told me he had seen his sister Mary; and prayed me, that I would not be troubled in reference to himself. . . . I cannot but take notice of the wonderful mercy of God to me in those afflictions, in sending me a Bible. One of the Indians that came from Medfield fight, had brought some plunder, came to me, and asked me, if I would have a Bible, he had got one in his basket. I was glad of it, and asked him, whether he thought the Indians would let me read. He answered, yes: So I took the Bible, and in that melancholy time, it came into my mind to read first the 28th chapter of Deuteronomy,⁶ which I did, and when I had read it, my dark heart wrought on this manner, that there was no mercy for me, that the blessings were gone, and the curses come in their room, and that I had lost my opportunity. But the Lord helped me still to go on reading till I came to Chapter 30 the seven first verses, where I found, there was mercy promised again, if we would return to Him by repentance; and though we were scattered from one end of the earth to the other, yet the Lord would gather us together, and turn all those curses upon our enemies. I do not desire to live to forget this Scripture, and what comfort it was to me. . . . **C**

6. **28th chapter of Deuteronomy:** In Deuteronomy 28, Moses warns that God will bless those who obey Him and curse those who do not.

The Sixth Remove

We traveled on till night; and in the morning, we must go over the river to Philip's crew. When I was in the canoe, I could not but be amazed at the numerous crew of pagans that were on the bank on the other side. When I came ashore, they gathered all about me, I sitting alone in the midst: I observed they asked one another questions, and laughed, and rejoiced over their gains and victories. Then my heart began to fail: And I fell aweeping which was the first time to my remembrance, that I wept before them. Although I had met with so much affliction, and my heart was many times ready to break, yet could I not shed one tear in their sight: but rather had been all this while in a maze, and like one astonished: But now I may say as, Psalm 137:1, "By the rivers of Babylon, there we sat down: yea, we wept when we remembered Zion." There one of them asked me, why I wept, I could hardly tell what to say: Yet I answered, they would kill me: "No," said he, "none will hurt you." Then came one of them and gave me two spoonfuls of meal to comfort me, and another gave me half a pint of peas; which was more worth than many bushels at another time. Then I went to see King Philip, he bade me come in and sit down, and asked me whether I would smoke it (a usual compliment nowadays amongst saints and sinners) but this no way suited me. For though I had formerly used tobacco, yet I had left it ever since I was first taken. It seems to be a bait, the devil lays to make men lose their precious time: I remember with shame, how formerly, when I had taken two or three pipes, I was presently ready for another, such a bewitching thing it is: But I thank God, He has now given me power over it; surely there are many who may be better employed than to lie sucking a stinking tobacco pipe. **D**

Now the Indians gather their forces to go against North Hampton: Overnight one went about yelling and hooting to give notice of the design. Where

C **Literary Focus** Allusions Compare the biblical allusions that Mary Rowlandson makes in this paragraph. How do the allusions reflect the narrator's state of mind in each instance? Why do you think she uses each allusion?

D **Literary Focus** Allusions How do the Bible verses that relate to Rowlandson's own experience enrich her narrative?

Vocabulary **entreated** (ehn TREET ihd) *v.:* asked sincerely; begged.
afflictions (uh FLIHK shuhnz) *n.:* pains; hardships.
plunder (PLUHN duhr) *n.:* goods seized, especially during wartime.
melancholy (MEHL uhn kahl ee) *adj.:* sad; sorrowful.
repentance (rih PEHN tuhns) *n.:* sorrow for doing wrong; regret.

Analyzing Visuals

Viewing and Interpreting
Do you find this representation of a kidnapping experience realistic or romanticized, or does it have elements of both? Cite evidence from Rowlandson's account to support your response.

Illustration from *Narrative of the capture and providential escape of Misses Frances and Almira Hall* (1833).

upon they fell to boiling of groundnuts, and parching of corn (as many as had it) for their provision:[7] And in the morning away they went. During my abode[8] in this place, Philip spoke to me to make a shirt for his boy, which I did, for which he gave me a shilling: I offered the money to my master, but he bade me keep it: And with it I bought a piece of horseflesh. Afterward he asked me to make a cap for his boy, for which he invited me to dinner. I went, and he gave me a pancake, about as big as two fingers; it was made of parched wheat, beaten, and fried in bear's grease, but I thought I never tasted pleasanter meat in my life. There was a squaw who spoke to me to make a shirt for her *sannup*,[9] for which she gave me a piece of bear. Another asked me to knit a pair of stockings, for

which she gave me a quart of peas: I boiled my peas and bear together, and invited my master and mistress to dinner, but the proud gossip, because I served them both in one dish, would eat nothing, except one bit that he gave her upon the point of his knife. . . .

The Move To The Ashuelot Valley, New Hampshire

But instead of going either to Albany or homeward, we must go five miles up the river, and then go over it. Here we abode awhile. Here lived a sorry Indian, who spoke to me to make him a shirt. When I had done it, he would pay me nothing. But he living by the riverside, where I often went to fetch water, I would often be putting of him in mind, and calling for my pay: At last he told me if I would make another shirt, for a papoose not yet born, he would give me a knife,

---

7. **provision:** a stock of necessary supplies.
8. **abode:** stay.
9. **sannup:** husband.

admire at the wonderful power and goodness of God to me, in that, though I was gone from home, and met with all sorts of Indians, and those I had no knowledge of, and there being no Christian soul near me; yet not one of them offered the least imaginable miscarriage to me. I turned homeward again, and met with my master, he showed me the way to my son. . . .

But I was fain[10] to go and look after something to satisfy my hunger, and going among the wigwams, I went into one, and there found a squaw who showed herself very kind to me, and gave me a piece of bear. I put it into my pocket, and came home, but could not find an opportunity to broil it, for fear they would get it from me, and there it lay all that day and night in my stinking pocket. In the morning I went to the same squaw, who had a kettle of groundnuts boiling; I asked her to let me boil my piece of bear in her kettle, which she did, and gave me some groundnuts to eat with it: And I cannot but think how pleasant it was to me. I have sometime seen bear baked very handsomely among the English, and some like it, but the thoughts that it was bear, made me tremble: But now that was savory to me that one would think was enough to turn the stomach of a brute creature.

One bitter cold day, I could find no room to sit down before the fire: I went out, and could not tell what to do, but I went in to another wigwam, where they were also sitting round the fire, but the squaw laid a skin for me, and bid me sit down, and gave me some groundnuts, and bade me come again: and told me they would buy me, if they were able, and yet these were strangers to me that I never saw before. . . . **E**

10. **fain:** archaic word meaning "glad; ready."

which he did when I had done it. I carried the knife in, and my master asked me to give it him, and I was not a little glad that I had anything that they would accept of, and be pleased with. When we were at this place, my master's maid came home, she had been gone three weeks into the Narragansett country, to fetch corn, where they had stored up some in the ground: She brought home about a peck and half of corn. This was about the time that their great captain, Naananto, was killed in the Narragansett country. My son being now about a mile from me, I asked liberty to go and see him, they bade me go, and away I went: but quickly lost myself, traveling over hills and through swamps, and could not find the way to him. And I cannot but

---

E **Reading Focus** **Chronological Order** How would you characterize the way in which, over time, Rowlandson's relationship with her captors changes?

Applying Your Skills

from **A Narrative of the Captivity**

Respond and Think Critically

Reading Focus

Quick Check

1. Briefly describe what happens to each of Rowlandson's children in the course of the selection.

2. Find details that reveal that Rowlandson's captors are themselves desperate to find food.

Read with a Purpose

3. How does the narrator's experience in the wilderness change her? Cite at least two examples.

Reading Skills: Analyzing Text Structures: Chronological Order

4. Consider how Rowlandson structures her narrative around the events you cited in your time line. Now, briefly explain the function of these events in the narrative.

✓ Vocabulary Check

Match each Vocabulary word with the word that is closest in meaning.

5. tedious   **a.** asked

6. lamentable   **b.** remorse

7. entreated   **c.** loot

8. afflictions   **d.** sad

9. plunder   **e.** tiresome

10. melancholy   **f.** unfortunate

11. repentance   **g.** hardships

Literary Focus

Literary Analysis

12. **Draw Conclusions** How does the narrator's religious faith influence her perspective? Explain.

13. **Interpret** Why do you think the narrator says, toward the end of the selection, "I was not a little glad that I had anything that they would accept of, and be pleased with"?

14. **Analyze** What conflicting attitudes, if any, does Rowlandson show toward her captors?

15. **Make Judgments** Would you describe Mary's captors as cruel or compassionate? Explain.

Literary Skills: Allusion

16. **Compare and Contrast** Describe at least two allusions to biblical stories that Rowlandson makes during her captivity. In what specific ways do Rowlandson's experiences resemble these biblical stories?

Literary Skills Review: Audience

17. **Analyze** A writer's **audience** is the group of people for whom he or she writes. Why might Rowlandson's narrative have been so popular in England? What parts of the narrative feel particularly suited to Rowlandson's audience?

Writing Focus

Think as a Reader/Writer

Use It in Your Writing Narrate an interesting journey or experience from your own life. Include allusions to a well-known story or song.

What Do You Think Now Which of Rowlandson's beliefs help her to endure captivity? Does a person's way of seeing the world affect his or her chances of survival in a challenging situation? How?

SKILLS FOCUS Literary Skills
Understand allusions; analyze the influence
of the audience on a writer. Reading Skills
Understand chronological order.

Vocabulary Skills Identify synonyms.
Writing Skills Employ literary devices for
effective writing; compare characters or historical figures; illustrate beliefs about life.

Grammar Skills Identify the subject of
a sentence; identify the predicate of a sentence; identify complements in sentences.

Grammar Link

Subjects, Verbs, and Complements

A word or word group that completes the meaning of
a verb is called a **complement**. Complements can be
nouns, pronouns, or adjectives. Notice how the boldface complements complete the meanings of the verbs
in the following examples.

      S   V   C

That movie is a **comedy.** [noun]

      S   V   C

The teacher asked **us** to quiet down. [pronoun]

    S   V   C

Sam is **anxious** about the test. [adjective]

Keep in mind that complements are never adverbs, and
complements are never in prepositional phrases.

> **Adverb**
> Angela works **late.** [*Late* tells how Angela works.]
>
> **Complement**
> The guests are **late.** [*Late,* an adjective, completes the
> meaning of the verb *are.*]
>
> **Prepositional Phrase**
> Mom and dad rode in the **bus.** [*Bus* is part of the
> prepositional phrase *in the bus.*]
>
> **Complement**
> Brian drove the **bus.** [*Bus* completes the meaning of
> the verb *drove.*]

Your Turn

Writing Application Construct four sentences from
these groups of sentence parts. Add no more than a
word or two to each group to form your sentences.

Subject	Verb	Complement
1. sky	looked	dark
2. you	send	invitation
3. Tom	tell	him
4. racers	are	weary

CHOICES

As you respond to the Choices, use these **Academic Vocabulary** words
as appropriate: aspect, cite, contemporary, interpret, perspective.

REVIEW

Vary the Sequence of a Story

Partner Work Choose a dramatic story from your
own experience or that of someone you know. Chart
the main events in the story. Then, create a second
chart with events rearranged to create flashbacks or
to tell the story in reverse, from end to beginning.
Tell your rearranged story to a partner. How does
telling the story in a different order change aspects
of the story, such as tone or meaning?

CONNECT

Analyze the Writer's Source of Strength

Timed └Writing In a brief essay, identify and
discuss Mary Rowlandson's ultimate source of
strength. How does her story compare with other
captivity stories you know about? Cite details from
Rowlandson's account in your response.

EXTEND

Create Art About Family

One of the thoughts that
sustains Rowlandson in her
captivity is the hope that
she will see her husband and
children again. The importance
of family is a thread that runs
throughout the narrative. Tell
your family about Rowlandson's
ordeal. Then, work with one or
more family members to create
a piece of artwork (such as a
collage or quilt) that expresses
your unity as a family.

American sampler, 1786. The
Granger Collection, New York.

from
The History of
the Dividing Line

What Do You Think? How can people's beliefs affect their actions?

⏱ QuickWrite

Think about a time you observed someone pursue pleasure at the expense of his or her responsibilities. Write a brief passage reflecting on how humor might be used to describe and address this situation or learn from it.

William Byrd II (c. 1724) attributed to Hans Hysing. Oil on canvas. Virginia Historical Society, Richmond, Virginia.

MEET THE WRITER

William Byrd
(1674–1744)

William Byrd is representative of the gentlemen planters of early Virginia. His *History of the Dividing Line* uses wit and humor to describe the early American frontier.

Renaissance Man

William Byrd was born in Virginia in 1674, the son of a wealthy landowner and merchant. He was educated in England, where he spent half his life. He preferred London to the American colonies because of its lavish homes, witty conversation, and gambling tables. During visits to Westover, his 2,000-acre home in Virginia, he tried to keep an active social and intellectual life.

Intellectual life in the colonies was split between the Puritans (or "Roundheads"), who disagreed with British intellectual and social trends, and the Cavaliers, who followed and enjoyed those trends. By and large, the Puritans settled in the northern colonies, while the Cavaliers settled in the southern colonies. Byrd shared the Cavalier perspective.

Byrd helped found the city of Richmond and established connections with powerful Virginia families, but his achievements outside the social sphere were even more impressive. Byrd was truly a Renaissance man. He translated Greek and Latin literature, composed poetry, wrote about mathematics, and experimented with farming. His library at Westover had almost 4,000 volumes. Writing a generation before Thomas Jefferson, Byrd displayed the same intellectual curiosity that his fellow Virginian would show later.

Surveyor and Philosopher

In 1728, Byrd joined a survey expedition to examine the disputed boundary between Virginia and North Carolina. On this trip, he began writing *The History of the Dividing Line*.

Byrd's work is far more than a simple record. Elegantly written and witty, it is filled with philosophical observations. It also includes many barbed comments about American colonial life. *The History of the Dividing Line* was found among Byrd's personal papers after his death and was published in 1841.

Think About the Writer How might Byrd comment on contemporary life in the United States? What would he find amusing?

Reader/Writer Notebook

Use your **RWN** to complete the activities for this selection.

Literary Focus

Satire Writers use **satire** to ridicule the shortcomings of people or institutions in an attempt to bring about change. Satire can cover a wide range of tones, from gentle mocking to harsh ridicule. For instance, Byrd uses satire not only to make fun of the missteps of the colonists but also to note how things could be done differently.

Reading Focus

Identifying Tone The **tone** of a work of literature is the writer's attitude toward the subject of the work, the characters in the work, or the audience reading the work. You can usually describe tone in a single word, such as *sad, ironic, happy, sarcastic,* or *critical*. Writers create tone through word choice and phrasing, or syntax. Byrd's choice of words and syntax helps create a satirical tone. His descriptions of incidents illustrate his main points in the piece.

Into Action As you read, use a chart to show how Byrd expresses a satirical tone throughout the selection. Note at least five words or phrases that help create this tone. Then, explain why each word or phrase is satirical.

Word or phrase, and how it is used	distemper (used in reference to adventurers' desire to go to America)			
Why it's satirical	makes the desire sound like a sickness, not a rational urge			

Writing Focus

Think as a Reader/Writer

Find It in Your Reading Byrd is writing a history, a record of actual events, yet his style is laced with humor. As you read, <u>cite</u> in your *Reader/ Writer Notebook* examples of how Byrd creates humor while describing historical events.

Vocabulary

frugality (froo GAL uh tee) *n.:* thrift. *The Company should have practiced less frugality when it sent colonists to North America.*

disdained (dihs DAYND) *v.:* refused; disapproved of; scorned. *Because many members of the colony disdained hard work, they later found that they did not have enough food.*

earnest (UR nihst) *adj.:* strong and firm in purpose; serious. *If the English had been earnest about living peacefully with the Indians, they might have considered Byrd's proposal about intermarriage.*

venerable (VEHN uh ruh buhl) *adj.:* deserving respect. *According to Bearskin, a venerable old man decides where American Indians go after death.*

haggard (HAG uhrd) *adj.:* looking worn from pain, hunger, worry, or fatigue. *To the newly arrived soldiers, the settlers looked haggard.*

Language Coach

Pronunciation Words are made up of syllabic, or units of sounds that contain a vowel and one or more consonants. In the syllabic pronunciations of the words above, each syllable is separated by a space. So, *earnest* has two syllables. Sometimes words are broken up into syllables without pronunciation information. For example, *earnest* can be broken up as /ear nest/ to show where the two syllables are.

 **Learn It Online**
Listen for Byrd's satire in the audio version of this selection online.

go.hrw.com L11-73 **Go**

FROM THE HISTORY OF THE DIVIDING LINE

by **William Byrd**

The Plantation (c. 1825) by an unknown American artist. Oil on wood (19 1/8" × 29 1/2").
The Metropolitan Museum of Art, NY. Gift of Edgar William and Bernice Chrysler Garbisch, 1963 (63.201.3).
Image ©The Metropolitan Museum of Art / Art Resource, NY.

Read with a Purpose
Read this selection to discover Byrd's strong, humorous opinions about how the English have colonized America.

Build Background
The History of the Dividing Line is one of two histories Byrd wrote about the survey of the disputed boundary. The first history was never intended for publication and is referred to as *The Secret History of the Line*. *The Secret History* is a behind-the-scenes account of the expedition, and its publication would have been scandalous. In his official history, Byrd begins his account with a lively description of England's colonization of America.

EARLY VIRGINIA COLONIES

As it happened some ages before to be the fashion to saunter to the Holy Land and go upon other Quixote adventures,[1] so it was now grown the humor to take a trip to America. The Spaniards had lately discovered rich mines in their part of the West Indies, which made their maritime neighbors eager to do so too. This modish[2] frenzy, being still more inflamed by the charming account given of Virginia by the first adventurers, made many fond of removing to such a Paradise.  Ⓐ

Happy was he, and still happier she, that could get themselves transported, fondly expecting their coarsest utensils in that happy place would be of massy silver.

This made it easy for the Company to procure[3] as many volunteers as they wanted for their new colony, but, like most other undertakers who have no assistance from the public, they starved the design by too much frugality; for, unwilling to launch out at first into too much expense, they shipped off but few people at a time, and those but scantily provided. The adventurers were, besides, idle and extravagant and expected they might live without work in so plentiful a country.

Westover (built c. 1730), William Byrd's plantation house, Charles City County, Virginia.

These wretches were set ashore not far from Roanoke Inlet, but by some fatal disagreement or laziness were either starved or cut to pieces by the Indians. Ⓑ

Several repeated misadventures of this kind did for some time allay[4] the itch of sailing to this new world, but the distemper broke out again about the year 1606. Then it happened that the Earl of Southampton and several other persons eminent[5] for their quality and estates were invited into the Company, who applied themselves once more to people the then almost abandoned colony. For this purpose they embarked about an hundred men, most of them reprobates[6] of good families and related to some of the Company who were men of quality and fortune. Ⓒ

The ships that carried them made a shift to find a more direct way to Virginia and ventured through the capes into the Bay of Chesapeake. The same night they came to an anchor at the mouth of Powhatan, the same as James River, where they built a small fort at a place called Point Comfort.

This settlement stood its ground from that time forward, in spite of all the blunders and disagreement

---

1. **Quixote adventures:** foolish adventures, like those taken by the mad hero of Miguel de Cervantes's novel *The Ingenious Gentleman Don Quixote de la Mancha.*
2. **modish:** fashionable; stylish.
3. **procure:** obtain; acquire.

4. **allay:** lessen; relieve.
5. **eminent:** well known for excellence.
6. **reprobates:** people without any sense of duty or decency.

Ⓐ **Literary Focus** **Satire** What historical event is Byrd referring to in the phrase, "saunter to the Holy Land"? What is satirical about the phrase? Cite and discuss a single ironic word in your response.

Vocabulary **frugality** (froo GAL uh tee) *n.*: thrift.

Ⓑ **Reading Focus** **Identifying Tone** The colonists of Roanoke Island mysteriously vanished, leaving behind the word *Croatoan* carved on a gatepost. To this day, no one has solved the mystery of the so-called "Lost Colony," but Byrd offers his own theory. How would you describe the tone of this theory? Why?

Ⓒ **Reading Focus** **Identifying Tone** Why is the phrase "reprobates of good families" ironic? What does this ironic phrase imply about the good families?

of the first adventurers and the many calamities that befell the colony afterward.

The six gentlemen who were first named of the Company by the Crown and who were empowered to choose an annual president from among themselves were always engaged in factions and quarrels, while the rest detested work more than famine. At this rate the colony must have come to nothing had it not been for the vigilance and bravery of Captain Smith, who struck a terror into all the Indians round about. This gentleman took some pains to persuade the men to plant Indian corn, but they looked upon all labor as a curse. They chose rather to depend upon the musty provisions that were sent from England; and when they failed they were forced to take more pains to seek for wild fruits in the woods than they would have taken in tilling the ground. Besides, this exposed them to be knocked in the head by the Indians and gave them fluxes[7] into the bargain, which thinned the plantation very much. To supply this mortality, they were reinforced the year following with a greater number of people, amongst which were fewer gentlemen and more laborers, who, however, took care not to kill themselves with work. These found the first adventurers in a very starving condition but relieved their wants with the fresh supply they brought with them. From Kecoughtan they extended themselves as far as Jamestown, where, like true Englishmen, they built a church that cost no more than fifty pounds and a tavern that cost five hundred. **D**

---

7. **fluxes:** dysentery; severe diarrhea.

D Literary Focus **Satire** What is satirical about the last sentence of this paragraph? What does this satirical comment tell you about Byrd's perspective?

Vocabulary disdained (dihs DAYND) *v.:* refused; disapproved of; scorned.
earnest (UR nihst) *adj.:* strong and firm in purpose; serious.

INTERMARRIAGE

They had now made peace with the Indians, but there was one thing wanting to make that peace lasting. The natives could by no means persuade themselves that the English were heartily their friends so long as they disdained to intermarry with them. And, in earnest, had the English consulted their own security and the good of the colony, had they intended either to civilize or convert these gentiles,[8] they would have brought their stomachs to embrace this prudent[9] alliance.

---

8. **gentiles:** here, nonbelievers. Historically, among Christians and Jews, *gentile* meant a pagan or nonbeliever. (*Gentile* comes from a Latin word meaning "foreigner.") The term is now more commonly used by Jews to refer to those who are not Jewish.
9. **prudent:** well thought out; careful.

Analyzing Visuals

Viewing and Interpreting
How does this image compare with the descriptions of Native Americans on the following page?

Indian Chief (c. 1585) by John White (1570–1593). Watercolor, 10 3/8" × 5 7/8".

THEY HAD NOW MADE PEACE WITH THE INDIANS, BUT THERE WAS ONE THING WANTING TO MAKE THAT PEACE LASTING.

The Indians are generally tall and well proportioned, which may make full amends for the darkness of their complexions. Add to this that they are healthy and strong, with constitutions untainted by lewdness and not enfeebled by luxury. Besides, morals and all considered, I cannot think the Indians were much greater heathens than the first adventurers, who, had they been good Christians, would have had the charity to take this only method of converting the natives to Christianity. For, after all that can be said, a sprightly lover is the most prevailing[10] missionary that can be sent amongst these or any other infidels.

Besides, the poor Indians would have had less reason to complain that the English took away their land if they had received it by way of a portion with their daughters. Had such affinities been contracted in the beginning, how much bloodshed had been prevented and how populous[11] would the country have been, and, consequently, how considerable! Nor would the shade of the skin have been any reproach at this day, for if a Moor may be washed white in three generations, surely an Indian might have been blanched in two. **E**

The French, for their parts, have not been so squeamish[12] in Canada, who upon trial find abundance of attraction in the Indians. Their late grand monarch thought it not below even the dignity of a Frenchman to become one flesh with this people and therefore ordered 100 livres[13] for any of his subjects, man or woman, that would intermarry with a native.

---

10. **prevailing:** convincing.
11. **populous:** crowded with people.
12. **squeamish:** easily offended or disgusted.
13. **livres:** former French monetary unit worth about a pound of silver.

By this piece of policy we find the French interest very much strengthened amongst the savages and their religion, such as it is, propagated[14] just as far as their love. And I heartily wish this well-concerted scheme don't hereafter give the French an advantage over His Majesty's good subjects on the northern continent of America. **F**

THE NATIVE RELIGION

In the evening we examined our friend Bearskin concerning the religion of his country, and he explained it to us without any of that reserve to which his nation is subject. He told us he believed there was one supreme god, who had several subaltern[15] deities under him. And that this master god made the world a long time ago. That he told the sun, the moon, and stars their business in the beginning, which they, with good looking-after, have faithfully performed ever since. That the same power that made all things at first has taken care to keep them in the same method and motion ever since. He believed that God had formed many worlds before he formed this, but that those worlds either grew old and ruinous or were destroyed for the dishonesty of the inhabitants. That God is very just and very good, ever well pleased with those men who possess those godlike qualities. That he takes good people into his safe protection, makes them very rich, fills their bellies plentifully, preserves them from sickness and from being surprised or overcome by their enemies. But all such as tell lies and cheat those they have dealings with

---

14. **propagated:** transmitted or spread.
15. **subaltern:** subordinate; of inferior rank or position.

E **Reading Focus** **Identifying Tone** Do you think Byrd's comment about the Moors and the American Indians is meant to be taken seriously? Why or why not?

F **Literary Focus** **Satire** How would you describe Byrd's diction, or choice of words, in describing the French people? Based on the words he uses, what would you say is Byrd's opinion of the French people?

Viewing and Interpreting What does village life, as depicted in this image of a Native American settlement, have in common with the afterlife Bearskin describes in this selection?

The towne of Pomeiock and true forme of their houses (1585–1587) by John White (1570–93)

he never fails to punish with sickness, poverty, and hunger and, after all that, suffers them to be knocked on the head and scalped by those that fight against them. **G**

He believed that after death both good and bad people are conducted by a strong guard into a great road, in which departed souls travel together for some time till at a certain distance this road forks into two paths, the one extremely level and the other stony and mountainous. Here the good are parted from the bad by a flash of lightning, the first being hurried away to the right, the other to the left. The right-hand road leads to a charming, warm country, where the spring is everlasting and every month is May; and as the year is always in its youth, so are the people, and particularly the women are bright as stars and never scold. That in this happy climate there are deer, turkeys, elks, and buffaloes innumerable, perpetually fat and gentle, while the trees are loaded with delicious fruit quite throughout the four seasons. That the soil brings forth corn spontaneously, without the curse of labor, and so very wholesome that none

G **Literary Focus** Satire Who was "knocked on the head" earlier in the selection? What might Byrd be implying about them by using the same phrase in his description of Bearskin's religion?

who have the happiness to eat of it are ever sick, grow old, or die. Near the entrance into this blessed land sits a venerable old man on a mat richly woven, who examines strictly all that are brought before him, and if they have behaved well, the guards are ordered to open the crystal gate and let them enter into the land of delight. **(H)**

The left-hand path is very rugged and uneven, leading to a dark and barren country where it is always winter. The ground is the whole year round covered with snow, and nothing is to be seen upon the trees but icicles. All the people are hungry yet have not a morsel of anything to eat except a bitter kind of potato, that gives them the dry gripes[16] and fills their whole body with loathsome ulcers that stink and are insupportably painful. Here all the women are old and ugly, having claws like a panther with which they fly upon the men that slight their passion. For it seems these haggard old furies[17] are intolerably fond and expect a vast deal of cherishing. They talk much and exceedingly shrill, giving exquisite pain to the drum of the ear, which in that place of the torment is so tender that every sharp note wounds it to the quick. At the end of this path sits a dreadful old woman on a monstrous toadstool, whose head is covered with rattlesnakes instead of tresses, with glaring white eyes that strike a terror unspeakable into all that behold her. This hag pronounces sentence of woe upon all the miserable wretches that hold up their hands at her tribunal. After this they are delivered over to huge turkey buzzards, like harpies,[18] that fly away with them to the place above mentioned. Here, after they have been tormented a certain number of years

---

16. **dry gripes:** stomach cramps.
17. **furies:** violent, vengeful women. In Greek and Roman mythology, the Furies are fierce avenging spirits.
18. **harpies:** evil mythological creatures with women's heads and birds' wings and legs.

AT THE END OF THIS PATH SITS A DREADFUL OLD WOMAN ON A MONSTROUS TOADSTOOL, WHOSE HEAD IS COVERED WITH RATTLESNAKES.

according to their several degrees of guilt, they are again driven back into this world to try if they will mend their manners and merit a place the next time in the regions of bliss. **(I)**

This was the substance of Bearskin's religion and was as much to the purpose as could be expected from a mere state of nature, without one glimpse of revelation or philosophy. It contained, however, the three great articles of natural religion: the belief of a god, the moral distinction between good and evil, and the expectation of rewards and punishments in another world. **(J)**

(H) Reading Focus **Identifying Tone** How does the tone of "The Native Religion" section differ from the tone of previous sections?

Vocabulary **venerable** (VEHN uhr uh buhl) *adj.:* deserving respect.

haggard (HAG uhrd) *adj.:* looking worn from pain, hunger, worry, or fatigue.

(I) Literary Focus **Satire** How is the winter country similar to what many of the colonists experienced? Do you think Byrd is implying that the colonists deserved the "winter country" of Bearskin's religion?

(J) Reading Focus **Identifying Tone** What does the phrase "as much to the purpose as could be expected from a mere state of nature" imply about Byrd's attitude toward Bearskin's religion? How do you know Byrd is satirizing the European attitude toward the nature-based religion of the American Indians?

Applying Your Skills

from The History of the Dividing Line

Respond and Think Critically

Reading Focus

Quick Check

1. What American colony does Byrd describe in his account?

2. According to Byrd, what is the error the colonists made in their dealings with the American Indians that the French did not make?

3. What elements of Bearskin's religion illustrate "the three great articles of natural religion"?

Read with a Purpose

4. What is Byrd's opinion of how the English have colonized North America?

Reading Skills: Identifying Tone

5. As you read, you <u>cited</u> words and phrases Byrd uses to create a satirical tone. Add a row to your chart in which you explain the effectiveness of each example. Does the example help Byrd make his point? Why or why not?

Word or phrase, and how it is used	distemper (used in reference to adventurers' desire to go to America)
Why it's satirical	makes the desire sound like a sickness, not a rational urge
Is it effective? Why?	Yes. Focus on disease conveys lack of control.

Literary Focus

6. **Analyze** What details lead you to believe that Byrd's description of Point Comfort is accurate?

7. **Interpret** <u>Cite</u> examples from the text that illustrate Byrd's attempts to understand and co-exist with the American Indians.

8. **Evaluate** Byrd describes many of the early colonists as clueless tourists who don't care to make friends with the American Indians. Byrd made efforts to get to know the American Indians and appreciate their culture. Why do you think Byrd's approach to living with the American Indians was not more widespread in the colonies?

Literary Skills: Satire

9. **Analyze** Writers use satire to ridicule the shortcomings of people or institutions, often to bring about change. How does Byrd's use of satire help you understand life in the early colonies? Why does Byrd use very little satire to describe his meetings with the American Indians? What change might Byrd have wanted to achieve?

Literary Skills Review: Figures of Speech

10. **Evaluate** A **figure of speech** is a word or phrase that describes one thing in terms of something else. It is not meant to be taken literally. What figures of speech does Byrd use to create a humorous effect?

Writing Focus

Think as a Reader/Writer

Use It in Your Writing Review your notes about how Byrd uses humor in his satire to describe historical events. Write a satirical paragraph about an event from your life or a historical event that interests you, and try to make it humorous.

 What Do You Think Now

What beliefs help people get through difficult circumstances? Are these beliefs universal?

SKILLS FOCUS **Literary Skills** Analyze the characteristics of satire; understand and analyze figures of speech. **Reading Skills** Analyze tone. **Vocabulary**

Skills Identify and correctly use synonyms; understand denotation and connotation. **Writing Skills** Incorporate satire and humor in writing.

Vocabulary Development

✓ Vocabulary Check

Match each Vocabulary word with its **synonym**.

1. frugality
2. venerable
3. disdained
4. earnest
5. haggard

a. sincere
b. scorned
c. exhausted
d. economy
e. honorable

Vocabulary Skills: Connotations

Denotations are the literal meanings of words. **Connotations** are the emotions or feelings that you associate with a word. For instance, if you were selling your grandfather's nineteenth-century table, you might describe it as either *old* or *antique*. Both mean that the table is not new and has been around a long time. The difference is that *old* **connotes,** or suggests, that the table might be in bad shape. *Antique* connotes that the table has only gotten better with age.

Here are some other examples of denotation and connotation:

Word	Denotation	Connotation
slick	slippery	suggests a lack of principle
polished	smooth, shiny	suggests that something is refined and elegant or that it might lack substance
hard	not soft; sturdy	suggests unfriendliness

Your Turn

Re-read the definition of each Vocabulary word below. Next, read each word's synonym. Explain the difference in connotation between the two words.

Word	Synonym	Difference in Connotation
frugality	stinginess	*"Frugality" can be a good thing, but "stinginess" implies mean and selfish behavior.*
disdained	disliked	
earnest	blunt	

Language Coach

Pronunciation The word *splints* has seven letters but only one syllable. The word has one vowel. All of the consonants in the word surround this vowel and blend to create one sound: /splihntz/. Knowing how many syllables a word has can help you pronounce it correctly. Using a dictionary, complete the chart below. Break each word into syllables by placing a space between them. Then, indicate the meaning of the word.

Word	Syllables	Definition
celebration	cel e bra tion	"a party or festival"
impetuous		
luminosity		

Academic Vocabulary

Write About
Describe William Byrd's <u>perspective</u> on early American life. <u>Cite</u> specific evidence from this selection to support your response.

from
The Interesting Narrative of the Life of Olaudah Equiano

 **What Do You Think**

How can people's beliefs affect their actions?

QuickWrite

Think about the last time you read or saw something—an article, a news report, or a documentary—that upset you and moved you to action. What made the message effective? If you wanted to bring about great change in the world, what would you write to spread the word and persuade others to act?

MEET THE WRITER

Olaudah Equiano
(c. 1745–1797)

In his narrative, Olaudah Equiano vividly describes cruel and horrifying <u>aspects</u> of the slave route known as the Middle Passage—the slaves' journey by sea.

Sold into Slavery

Olaudah Equiano's autobiography indicates that he was born in a part of West Africa that is now Nigeria. Slave traders kidnapped Equiano and his sister when he was only eleven years old. Equiano was separated from his sister and after some time put aboard a slave ship bound for the Caribbean.

Equiano saved enough money to buy his freedom in 1766, after having been enslaved for almost ten years. He eventually settled in England and worked as a free servant, a musician, and a barber. He also became active in the antislavery movement. When the abolition of the slave trade became a hotly debated issue in England, he visited abolitionist leaders and wrote letters to officials and newspapers. In 1789, his autobiography was published in England.

Equiano's account of the horrors he suffered struck a chord with northern abolitionists in the United States. His narrative is considered one of the first great black autobiographies.

New Debate

In recent years, newly found documents cast doubt on Equiano's early life. A baptismal record suggests he may have been born in North America. We are unsure if Equiano's account of the Middle Passage was written from memory, from hearing other people's stories, or from a blend of the two.

Even if the material in the autobiography is not Equiano's own story, it describes the real experiences of other slaves. Though we may never know the truth, Equiano's story remains an important work. It provides a window into how Western greed damaged eighteenth-century Africa, and it argues eloquently against the slave trade. Equiano and his narrative influenced many abolitionists to join the fight against slavery.

Think About the Writer Some people believe that it would not matter if Equiano never experienced the Middle Passage himself. Do you agree or disagree? Why?

Portrait of an African (c.1757–1760) (detail) attributed to Allan Ramsay (1713–1784). Oil on canvas.

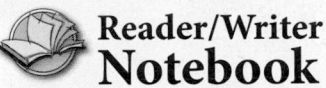

Reader/Writer Notebook

Use your **RWN** to complete the activities for this selection.

Literary Focus

Historical Narrative In narrative writing, an author recounts a series of events, often in chronological order. A **historical narrative** is an account of a significant event in history. In his account of the journey from Africa to Barbados aboard a slave ship, Equiano details the astonishment, horror, and helplessness of those who were captured.

Reading Focus

Making Inferences About an Author's Beliefs An **inference** is an educated guess based on what you already know and what you learn from reading a text. To make an inference while reading, look beyond what the author states directly and think about what is hinted, or implied. As you read Equiano's account, stay alert for passages that help you infer his beliefs about human nature and what he expects from life.

Into Action As you read, use a chart to record the author's beliefs. In the first column, list some of the major events of the narrative. In the second column, record Equiano's reactions to these events. Focus on the specific words he uses to describe them.

Major Events	Equiano's Reactions
arrival of a ship with its sails up	"astonishment"; "convinced it was done by magic"

Writing Focus

Think as a Reader/Writer

Find It in Your Reading In this selection, Equiano writes of events that happened to him in the past. To share his thoughts and reactions as he experienced them at the time, he writes in the past tense, as a person looking back on long-ago events. As you read, think about how using past tense affects the narrative. Record your thoughts in your *Reader/Writer Notebook*.

TechFocus As you read this selection, think about the different ways that a modern person might share a terrifying experience with the world.

Vocabulary

copious (KOH pee uhs) *adj.*: more than enough; plentiful. *Fish were copious in the ocean waters.*

avarice (AV uhr ihs) *n.*: greed; desire for wealth. *The avarice of the slave traders caused the cruel exploitation of many people.*

render (REHN duhr) *v.*: cause to become; make. *His fear will render him helpless.*

procured (pruh KYURD) *v.*: brought about; caused. *Some slaves procured their own freedom by saving enough money to purchase themselves.*

nominal (NAHM uh nuhl) *adj.*: existing in name only; not real. *Some slaves called the slave traders "nominal Christians" because the traders acted in a way that was inconsistent with the teachings of their religion.*

Language Coach

Word Associations When you learn a new word, think about other words you are familiar with whose meanings or ideas are related in some way. For instance, selfishness and envy are often associated with avarice. What other words might relate to *avarice*?

 Learn It Online
Find out more about Olaudah Equiano and his world through these Internet links.

go.hrw.com   L11-83   **Go**

FROM THE INTERESTING NARRATIVE OF THE LIFE OF OLAUDAH EQUIANO

by Olaudah Equiano

Read with a Purpose
Read to learn more about one man's experiences after being captured and transported as a slave.

Build Background
In the eighteenth century, the practice of capturing men, women, and children in Africa and selling them as slaves in North America was legal and lucrative. Equiano's account provides a firsthand description of the Middle Passage. The Middle Passage was the slaves' journey across the Atlantic Ocean. This journey, in which the captives were shackled together in crowded and unsanitary conditions, often took three months to complete. Many people died of dysentery, starvation, and suicide on the slave ships.

THE SLAVE SHIP

The first object which saluted[1] my eyes when I arrived on the coast was the sea, and a slave ship which was then riding at anchor and waiting for its cargo. These filled me with astonishment, which was soon converted into terror when I was carried on board. I was immediately handled and tossed up to see if I were sound by some of the crew, and I was now persuaded that I had gotten into a world of bad spirits and that they were going to kill me. Their complexions too differing so much from ours, their long hair and the language they spoke (which was very different from any I had ever heard) united to confirm me in this belief. Indeed such were the horrors of my views and fears at the moment that, if ten thousand worlds had been my own, I would have freely parted with them all to have exchanged my condition with that of the meanest[2] slave in my own country. When I looked round the ship too and saw a large furnace of copper boiling and a multitude of black people of every description chained together, every one of their countenances[3] expressing dejection and sorrow, I no longer doubted of my fate; and quite overpowered with horror and anguish, I fell motionless on the deck and fainted. When I recovered a little I found some black people about me, who I believed were some of those who had brought me on board and had been receiving their pay; they talked to me in order to cheer me, but all in vain. I asked them if we were not to be eaten by those white men with horrible looks, red faces, and loose hair. They told me I was not, and one of the crew brought me a small portion of spirituous liquor in a wineglass, but being afraid of him I would not take it out of his hand. One of the blacks therefore took it from him and gave it to me, and I took a little down my palate, which instead of reviving me, as they thought it would, threw me into

1. **saluted:** met.
2. **meanest:** lowest.

3. **countenances:** faces.

Slaves below decks on the Albaroz by Lt. Francis Meynell.
© National Maritime Museum, London.

Analyzing Visuals

Viewing and Interpreting Olaudah's narration emphasizes the smell of the ship. What aspects of the horrible conditions that Olaudah describes are represented in this painting? Cite details from the image to support your response.

the greatest consternation at the strange feeling it produced, having never tasted such any liquor before. Soon after this the blacks who brought me on board went off, and left me abandoned to despair. **Ⓐ Ⓑ**

I now saw myself deprived of all chance of returning to my native country or even the least glimpse of hope of gaining the shore, which I now considered as friendly; and I even wished for my former slavery in preference to my present situation, which was filled with horrors of every kind, still heightened by my ignorance of what I was to undergo. I was not long suffered to indulge my grief; I was soon put down under the decks, and there I received such a salutation in my nostrils as I had never experienced in my life: So that with the loathsomeness of the stench and crying together, I became so sick and low that I was not

able to eat, nor had I the least desire to taste anything. I now wished for the last friend, death, to relieve me; but soon, to my grief, two of the white men offered me eatables, and on my refusing to eat, one of them held me fast by the hands and laid me across, I think, the windlass,[4] and tied my feet while the other flogged[5] me severely. I had never experienced anything of this kind before, and although, not being used to the water, I naturally feared that element the first time I saw it, yet nevertheless could I have got over the nettings I would have jumped over the side, but I could not; and besides, the crew used to watch us very closely who were not chained down to the decks, lest we should leap into the water: And I have seen some of these poor African prisoners most severely cut for attempting to do so, and hourly whipped for not eating. This indeed was often the case with myself. In a little time

4. **windlass:** device used to raise and lower heavy objects, like a ship's anchor.
5. **flogged:** beat with a rod or whip.

Ⓐ Literary Focus Historical Narrative How does this narrative differ from an article written for a history textbook?

Ⓑ Reading Focus Making Inferences Why do you think Equiano fainted?

from The Interesting Narrative of the Life of Olaudah Equiano **85**

Viewing and Interpreting
What must it have been like to experience these inhuman conditions and, as Olaudah mentions, to be confused about what was going on?

Cross-section of a slave ship, from a manuscript on slavery by Jacques-Henri Bernardin de Saint-Pierre (late 18th century). Watercolor and ink on paper.

after, amongst the poor chained men I found some of my own nation, which in a small degree gave ease to my mind. I inquired of these what was to be done with us; they gave me to understand we were to be carried to these white people's country to work for them. I then was a little revived, and thought if it were no worse than working, my situation was not so desperate: But still I feared I should be put to death, the white people looked and acted, as I thought, in so savage a manner; for I had never seen among my people such instances of brutal cruelty, and this not only shown toward us blacks but also to some of the whites themselves. One white man in particular I saw, when we were permitted to be on deck, flogged so unmercifully with a large rope near the foremast[6] that he died in consequence of it; and they tossed him over the side as they would have done a brute. This made me fear these people the more, and I expected nothing less than to be treated in the same manner. I could not help expressing my fears and apprehensions to some of my countrymen: I asked them if these people had no country but lived in this hollow place (the ship): They told me they did not, but came from a distant one. "Then," said I, "how comes it in all our country we never heard of them?" They told me because they lived so very far off. I then asked where were their women? Had they any like themselves? I was told they had: "And why," said I, "do we not see them?" They answered, because they were left behind. I asked how the vessel could go? They told me they could not tell, but that there were cloths put upon the masts by the help of the ropes I saw, and then the vessel went on; and the white men had some spell or magic they put in the water when they liked in order to stop the vessel. I was exceedingly amazed at this account and really thought they were spirits. I therefore wished much to be from amongst them for I expected they would sacrifice me: But my wishes were vain, for we were so quartered that it was impossible for any of us to make our escape. **C D E F**

While we stayed on the coast I was mostly on deck, and one day, to my great astonishment, I saw one of these vessels coming in with the sails up. As soon as the whites saw it they gave a great shout, at which we were amazed; and the more so as the vessel appeared larger by approaching nearer. At last she came to an anchor in my sight, and when the anchor was let go I and my countrymen who saw it were lost in astonishment to observe the vessel stop, and were now convinced it was done by magic. Soon after this the other ship got her boats out, and they came on board of us, and the people of both ships seemed very glad

---

6. **foremast:** mast closest to the bow, or front, of a ship.

C **Reading Focus** **Making Inferences** Why were Equiano and the other prisoners whipped for refusing to eat?

D **Reading Focus** **Making Inferences** Why might Equiano imagine that the slave traders have no country of their own?

E **Literary Focus** **Historical Narrative** Why does Equiano call the ship "the hollow place"? What does this tell you about Equiano's understanding of what is happening to him?

F **Reading Focus** **Making Inferences** Why might Equiano believe that his captors are spirits rather than human beings?

to see each other. Several of the strangers also shook hands with us black people, and made motions with their hands, signifying I suppose we were to go to their country; but we did not understand them. At last, when the ship we were in had got in all her cargo, they made ready with many fearful noises, and we were all put under deck so that we could not see how they managed the vessel. **G H**

But this disappointment was the least of my sorrow. The stench of the hold[7] while we were on the coast was so intolerably loathsome that it was dangerous to remain there for any time, and some of us had been permitted to stay on the deck for the fresh air; but now that the whole ship's cargo were confined together it became absolutely pestilential.[8] The closeness of the place and the heat of the climate, added to the number in the ship, which was so crowded that each had scarcely room to turn himself, almost suffocated us. This produced copious perspirations, so that the air soon became unfit for respiration from a variety of loathsome smells, and brought on a sickness among the slaves, of which many died, thus falling victims to the improvident avarice, as I may call it, of their purchasers. This wretched situation was again aggravated by the galling of the chains, now become insupportable, and the filth of the necessary tubs,[9] into which the children often fell and were almost suffocated. The shrieks of the women and the groans of the dying rendered the whole a scene of horror almost inconceivable. Happily perhaps for myself I was soon reduced so low here that it was thought necessary to keep me almost always on deck, and from my extreme youth I was not put in fetters.[10] In this situation I expected

every hour to share the fate of my companions, some of whom were almost daily brought upon deck at the point of death, which I began to hope would soon put an end to my miseries. Often did I think many of the inhabitants of the deep much more happy than myself. I envied them the freedom they enjoyed, and as often wished I could change my condition for theirs. Every circumstance I met with served only to render my state more painful, and heighten my apprehensions and my opinion of the cruelty of the whites. One day they had taken a number of fishes, and when they had killed and satisfied themselves with as many as they thought fit, to our astonishment who were on the deck, rather than give any of them to us to eat as we expected, they tossed the remaining fish into the sea again, although we begged and prayed for some as well as we could, but in vain; and some of my countrymen, being pressed by hunger, took an opportunity when they thought no one saw them of trying to get a little privately; but they were discovered, and the attempt procured them some very severe floggings. **I**

One day, when we had a smooth sea and moderate wind, two of my wearied countrymen who were chained together (I was near them at the time), preferring death to such a life of misery, somehow made through the nettings and jumped into the sea: Immediately another quite dejected fellow, who on account of his illness was suffered to be out of irons, also followed their example; and I believe many more would very soon have done the same if they had not been prevented by the ship's crew, who were instantly alarmed. Those of us that were the most active were in a moment put down under the deck, and there was such a noise and confusion amongst the people of the ship as I never heard before, to stop her and get the boat out to go after the slaves. However two of the wretches were drowned, but they got the other and afterward flogged him unmercifully

---

7. **hold:** enclosed area below a ship's deck, where cargo is usually stored.
8. **pestilential:** deadly; harmful.
9. **necessary tubs:** toilets.
10. **fetters:** shackles or chains for the feet.

G **Literary Focus** Historical Narrative Why do you think Equiano included the detail that "the strangers also shook hands with us black people"?

H **Literary Focus** Historical Narrative Why didn't the crew want the slaves to see how they managed the ship? How does this detail add to your understanding of the way slave traders viewed slaves?

I **Reading Focus** Making Inferences What does Equiano mean when he says that he envies "the inhabitants of the deep"?

Vocabulary **copious** (KOH pee uhs) *adj.*: more than enough; plentiful.
avarice (AV uhr ihs) *n.*: greed; desire for wealth.
render (REHN duhr) *v.*: cause to become; make.
procured (pruh KYURD) *v.*: brought about; caused.

for thus attempting to prefer death to slavery. In this manner we continued to undergo more hardships than I can now relate, hardships which are inseparable from this accursed trade. Many a time we were near suffocation from the want of fresh air, which we were often without for whole days together. This and the stench of the necessary tubs carried off many. **J**

During our passage I first saw flying fishes, which surprised me very much: They used frequently to fly across the ship and many of them fell on the deck. I also now first saw the use of the quadrant; I had often with astonishment seen the mariners make observations with it, and I could not think what it meant. They at last took notice of my surprise, and one of them,

willing to increase it as well as to gratify my curiosity, made me one day look through it. The clouds appeared to me to be land, which disappeared as they passed along. This heightened my wonder, and I was now more persuaded than ever that I was in another world and that everything about me was magic. At last we came in sight of the island of Barbados, at which the whites on board gave a great shout and made many signs of joy to us. We did not know what to think of this, but as the vessel drew nearer we plainly saw the harbor and other ships of different kinds and sizes, and we soon anchored amongst them off Bridgetown. Many merchants and planters now came on board, though it was in the evening. They put us in separate

J **Literary Focus** **Historical Narrative** Based on this selection, describe the conditions aboard an eighteenth-century slave ship.

African American Heritage

Until recently, many obstacles have prevented African Americans from tracing their family trees back to Africa. Documents that genealogists use to trace a person's lineage often don't exist because records of slaves' births and deaths were poor and because laws prohibited slaves from owning land, marrying, and voting. Family lines are often unclear because so many slaves were separated from their relatives and were given their owners' names. Owners also sometimes forced women who were slaves to bear their children.

Recently, science has helped many African Americans, including the celebrity Oprah Winfrey, reclaim their history. Advances in genetic testing let interested people trace their ethnic heritage by having their DNA compared to samples gathered in large databases. DNA analyses can tell African Americans which African peoples share their genetic ancestry, and they can reveal the presence of European roots as well. Though this knowledge often raises new questions, it has the power to help create a sense of identity that comes from understanding one's past.

Ask Yourself

1. **If Equiano were alive today, do you think he would attempt to reconstruct his family tree? Cite details from the selection to support your answer.**

2. **Why do you think some people want to know about their genetic origins? What are they looking for?**

parcels and examined us attentively. They also made us jump, and pointed to the land, signifying we were to go there. We thought by this we should be eaten by these ugly men, as they appeared to us; and when soon after we were all put down under the deck again, there was much dread and trembling among us, and nothing but bitter cries to be heard all the night from these apprehensions, insomuch that at last the white people got some old slaves from the land to pacify us. They told us we were not to be eaten but to work, and were soon to go on land where we should see many of our countrypeople. This report eased us much; and sure enough soon after we were landed there came to us Africans of all languages.

We were conducted immediately to the merchant's yard, where we were all pent up together like so many sheep in a fold without regard to sex or age. As every object was new to me everything I saw filled me with surprise. What struck me first was that the houses were built with stories, and in every other respect different from those in Africa: But I was still more astonished on seeing people on horseback. I did not know what this could mean, and indeed I thought these people were full of nothing but magical arts. While I was in this astonishment one of my fellow prisoners spoke to a countryman of his about the horses, who said they were the same kind they had in their country. I understood them though they were from a distant part of Africa, and I thought it odd I had not seen any horses there; but afterward when I came to converse with different Africans I found they had many horses amongst them, and much larger than those I then saw. **K L**

We were not many days in the merchant's custody before we were sold after their usual manner, which is this: On a signal given (as the beat of a drum) the buyers rush at once into the yard where the slaves are confined, and make choice of that parcel they like best. The noise and clamor with which this is attended and the eagerness visible in the countenances of the buyers serve not a little to increase the apprehensions of the terrified Africans, who may well be supposed to consider them as the ministers of that destruction to which they think themselves devoted. In this manner, without scruple,[11] are relations and friends separated, most of them never to see each other again. I remember in the vessel in which I was brought over, in the men's apartment there were several brothers who, in the sale, were sold in different lots; and it was very moving on this occasion to see and hear their cries at parting. O, ye nominal Christians! might not an African ask you, Learned you this from your God who says unto you, Do unto all men as you would men should do unto you? Is it not enough that we are torn from our country and friends to toil for your luxury and lust of gain? Must every tender feeling be likewise sacrificed to your avarice? Are the dearest friends and relations, now rendered more dear by their separation from their kindred, still to be parted from each other and thus prevented from cheering the gloom of slavery with the small comfort of being together and mingling their sufferings and sorrows? Why are parents to lose their children, brothers their sisters, or husbands their wives? Surely this is a new refinement in cruelty which, while it has no advantage to atone for it, thus aggravates distress and adds fresh horrors even to the wretchedness of slavery. **M**

11. **scruple:** unease or doubt arising from difficulty in determining what is right.

K **Reading Focus** **Making Inferences** At first, Equiano is shocked to see men on horseback. How does his attitude change after he speaks to other Africans?

L **Literary Focus** **Historical Narrative** Equiano writes, "we were all pent up together like so many sheep in a fold without regard to sex or age." What does this comparison reveal about people's perspectives toward Africans at the time?

M **Reading Focus** **Making Inferences** In the final paragraph, what do you think Equiano is trying to convince his readers to believe or do? How can you tell?

Vocabulary **nominal** (NAHM uh nuhl) *adj.*: existing in name only; not real.

Applying Your Skills

from **The Interesting Narrative of the
Life of Olaudah Equiano**

Respond and Think Critically

Reading Focus

Quick Check

1. Who is Olaudah Equiano? From where does he come? To where is he taken?

2. What does Equiano see when he first looks around the ship? How does he react?

3. Why wasn't Equiano chained up during the journey, as many of the other prisoners were?

Read with a Purpose

4. Which of Equiano's reactions to his experiences as a slave did you find surprising or unexpected? Why?

Reading Skills: Making Inferences About an Author's Beliefs

5. While you read, you recorded major events in the narrative and Equiano's reactions to them. Add another column to your chart, and write inferences about Equiano's beliefs. Think about how inferring the author's beliefs, thoughts, and emotions enhances your comprehension.

Major Event	Equiano's Reactions	My Inferences about Equiano's Beliefs
arrival of a ship with its sails up	"astonishment"; "convinced it was done by magic"	He is unfamiliar with Western technology. He believes in the supernatural.

Literary Focus

Literary Analysis

6. **Analyze** Equiano uses the words *amazed* and *astonishment* several times. What effect do these words have on the mood of the narrative?

7. **Interpret** Paraphrase the last sentence of the selection, in which Equiano responds to the forced separation of enslaved families. What motive does he see in this cruel practice?

Literary Skills: Historical Narrative

8. **Extend** How did reading about historical events in the form of a personal narrative help you understand the events? What insights did you gain from Equiano's <u>perspective</u> that you might not have gained from an encyclopedia article on the treatment of slaves? Explain.

Literary Skills Review: Characterization

9. **Analyze** The process by which a writer reveals the personality of a character is **characterization.** Think about the character Equiano, not Equiano the writer, in the narrative. What do his actions and thoughts tell you about his <u>perspective</u> on life? What words would you use to describe him?

Writing Focus

Think as a Reader/Writer

Use It in Your Writing Think back to a time when you felt a sense of wonder or shock at something you did not fully understand. Using present tense, write a short piece describing this experience. Then, rewrite the piece using past tense. Which narrative gives a clearer sense of your experience?

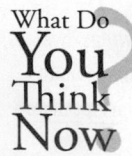

What Do You Think Now How do you think the slave trade shaped the beliefs of those who were enslaved? How did it shape the beliefs of those who captured, bought, and sold slaves?

Vocabulary Development

✓ Vocabulary Check

Match each Vocabulary word with its definition.

1. copious
2. avarice
3. render
4. procured
5. nominal

a. brought about
b. not real
c. plentiful
d. to cause to become
e. greed

Vocabulary Skills: Getting Information

Knowing a word's language of origin, its alternate definitions, and its synonyms and antonyms can help you understand and remember it. For example, if you look up the word *vessel*, you will find that the word is related to the Latin word *vas*, or vase. *Vessel* can mean "container," "watercraft," or "a tube or a canal," as in "blood vessel."

Look up the Vocabulary words in both a dictionary and a thesaurus. Complete a table like the one below by writing the definitions, origin, synonyms, and antonyms of each word.

Word	Definitions	Origin	Synonyms	Antonyms
copious	plentiful, abundant	Latin copia, "abundance"	numerous, bountiful, many	few, scarce, limited
avarice				
render				
procured				
nominal				

Your Turn

Each of the following words shares an origin with one of the Vocabulary words. Write down the Vocabulary word that has the same origin. Then, using your chart, write down what you think the word means.

1. nominate
2. cornucopia
3. secure
4. surrender

Language Coach

Word Associations Earlier you considered words similar in meaning to the Vocabulary word *avarice*. Now try *copious*, which means "abundant." Using a dictionary or thesaurus, develop a list of words similar in meaning to *copious*.

Academic Vocabulary

Talk About
With a partner, discuss the ironic aspects of the treatment of the slaves by the men who traveled thousands of miles to capture them. Does Equiano's perspective on these men support or negate the irony of the situation? Use specific references to the text to support your position.

Learn It Online
Learn more about the Vocabulary words with Word Watch online.

go.hrw.com   L11-91   **Go**

Applying Your Skills

from The Interesting Narrative of the Life of Olaudah Equiano

Grammar Link

Independent and Dependent Clauses

A **clause** is a group of words that contains a subject and a verb and that is used as part of a sentence. An **independent clause,** or main clause, expresses a complete thought and can stand by itself as a sentence.

S V

Example: She read three books last month.

A **dependent clause,** or subordinate clause, does not express a complete thought and cannot stand alone as a sentence.

S V

Example: that she read

The thought expressed by a dependent clause becomes complete when the clause is combined with an independent clause.

Example: The last book that she read was *The Great Gatsby.*

Your Turn

For each of the following sentences, identify the italicized clause as independent or dependent.

1. I did not win the race, *although I broke my personal record.*
2. *Because it was seen in the newspaper by hundreds of readers,* our advertisement succeeded in attracting more customers to our store.
3. *The family repaired the holes in their tents* before they left for their camping trip.
4. According to Beatrice, *Matt should have apologized years ago.*
5. The politician decided *that she would not run again.*

CHOICES

As you respond to the Choices, use these **Academic Vocabulary** words as appropriate: aspect, cite, contemporary, interpret, perspective.

REVIEW

Research the Slave Trade

Research Activity Research the economic reasons that the slave trade flourished in the seventeenth and eighteenth centuries. What did the slave owners gain? Why were African people targeted? Discuss other ways people in the Caribbean and North America could have handled their need for workers. Present your findings to the class.

CONNECT

Share Cultural Heritage

Partner Work Working with a partner, research which African peoples were enslaved most often. What aspects of their culture did they bring with them to North America? For each people, identify one cultural practice, food, or art form that they passed on to their descendants. How does this heritage live in people today? Share a food or other example of this cultural heritage with your class.

Gitaga drummers perform in Burundi.

EXTEND

Create a Modern Retelling

TechFocus People in contemporary times who have undergone terrifying experiences might share their stories through television interviews, documentaries, or movies. In a small group, create a modern retelling of Equiano's story in one of these forms to film or perform live for your class. Make sure that the chronological order of events is clear to your viewers.

The Puritan Worldview

A housewife and poet reflects on the loss of her house to fire. One minister composes a personal prayer; another delivers a fiery sermon. As you read, examine the religious beliefs at the core of these Puritan writings.

Self-Portrait (c. 1680) by Thomas Smith. Oil on canvas, 24 3/4" × 23 3/4".

CONTENTS

Here Follow Some Verses upon the Burning of Our House, July 10, 1666

What Do You Think?

How can people's beliefs affect their actions?

QuickWrite

What events inspire people to write poetry? Think of an event in your life that moved you strongly and affected your beliefs about the world. What happened? How did you feel? Write a few sentences describing your experience.

Anne Bradstreet (detail) (1948) by Harry Grylls. Stained glass.

Anne Bradstreet
(1612–1672)

Who would have guessed that the writer who would set in motion the history of American poetry would be an immigrant teenage bride? Anne Bradstreet was inspired by Shakespeare and the other great English poets, but the most important influence on her life and work was her strong Puritan faith.

Puritan Beginnings

Anne Bradstreet was born into a family of Puritans in England. At about the age of sixteen, she married a well-educated young Puritan named Simon Bradstreet. Two years later, in 1630, Anne, her husband, and her father voyaged to the region that would become the Massachusetts Bay Colony. There, her father and then her husband rose to prominence, each serving as governor of the colony. Meanwhile, Anne kept house and raised four girls and four boys. She also found time to write poetry, though she never sought publication.

Unexpected Recognition

Bradstreet's poems might never have come to light had it not been for her brother-in-law, John Woodbridge. In 1648, he went to England, and in 1650, without consulting the author, he published Bradstreet's poems under the title *The Tenth Muse Lately Sprung Up in America*. Some felt it was arrogant for a woman to aspire to earn a place among established male poets, but *The Tenth Muse* fared better with critics and the public than Anne expected (later even the learned Cotton Mather praised her work). She felt encouraged to write for the rest of her life.

Today, Bradstreet is mostly remembered for her later poems, which focus on personal aspects of life, such as the birth or death of children, her love for her husband, and her own illnesses and adversities. In a letter to her children just before she died, she writes, "Among all my experiences of God's gracious dealings with me I have constantly observed this, that He hath never suffered me long to sit loose from Him, but by one affliction or other hath made me look home, and search what was amiss."

Think About the Writer

Why do you think people resisted the idea of a female poet? Are those attitudes still with us today?

Reader/Writer Notebook

Use your **RWN** to complete the activities for this selection.

Literary Focus

Metaphor A **metaphor** is a figure of speech that compares two unlike things without using a word such as *like* or *as*. The Puritans rarely used elaborate figurative language; instead, they relied on a plain style that emphasized simple, clear language. Still, the **implied metaphor,** or metaphor not directly stated in the text, is a common and important device in Puritan literature, including Bradstreet's poem.

Literary Perspectives Apply the literary perspective described on page 96 as you read this poem.

Reading Focus

Analyzing Text Structures: Inversion To accommodate the demands of meter and rhyme, poets through the centuries have used **inversion.** In an inversion, the words of a sentence or clause are used out of normal word order, or syntax. For example, the first line of the poem reads, "In silent night when rest I took" instead of "In silent night when I took rest."

Into Action As you read Bradstreet's poem, pay close attention to her use of inversion. Then, to help you understand the poem, go through it line by line, and rewrite inverted lines in normal, "noninverted" order.

Line 1. Original Order	In silent night when rest I took
Normal Order	In silent night when I took rest
Line 2. Original Order	For sorrow near I did not look
Normal Order	

Vocabulary

piteous (PIHT ee uhs) *adj.:* deserving pity or compassion. *Observing the piteous sight of the ruined house and belongings, the speaker gains wisdom from the tragedy.*

consume (kuhn SOOM) *v.:* burn away; destroy. *Although the fire took her worldly goods from her, it did not consume her faith.*

vanity (VAN uh tee) *n.:* something valueless. *The speaker realizes that putting all her attention and security in her belongings is vanity.*

glory (GLOHR ee) *n.:* great beauty; splendor. *The speaker points out that her belongings here on earth do not compare to the glory of what awaits her in heaven.*

Language Coach

Antonyms Words that have opposite meanings from each other (or nearly opposite meanings) are called antonyms. For example, *worth* and *merit* are antonyms for *vanity*. Write down two antonyms for *consume*. Use a dictionary or thesaurus if you need help.

Writing Focus

Think as a Reader/Writer

Find It in Your Reading Implied metaphors—especially those written in the Puritan plain style—are more difficult to identify than directly stated metaphors. Although most of Bradstreet's images and words are literal, some are metaphorical. As you read, look for images and terms that could metaphorically represent other things or ideas.

Learn It Online
Check out the *PowerNotes* introduction to this poem online.

go.hrw.com   L11-95   **Go**

Read with a Purpose
Read to discover how the poet, to deal with loss, portrays an internal debate between herself and her soul.

Build Background
Rather than narrating a straightforward account of the burning of her house, Bradstreet records her spiritual journey from grief to solace and the realization that her love of material things has been in danger of eclipsing her love of things divine.

Here Follow Some Verses upon the Burning of Our House, July 10, 1666

by **Anne Bradstreet**

In silent night when rest I took
For sorrow near I did not look
I wakened was with thund'ring noise
And piteous shrieks of dreadful voice.
5   That fearful sound of "Fire!" and "Fire!"
Let no man know is my desire.
I, starting up, the light did spy,
And to my God my heart did cry
To strengthen me in my distress
10   And not to leave me succorless.°
Then, coming out, beheld a space
The flame consume my dwelling place.
And when I could no longer look,
I blest His name that gave and took,°
15   That laid my goods now in the dust.
Yea, so it was, and so 'twas just.
It was His own, it was not mine,
Far be it that I should repine;°
He might of all justly bereft°

20   But yet sufficient for us left.
When by the ruins oft I past
My sorrowing eyes aside did cast,
And here and there the places spy
Where oft I sat and long did lie:
25   Here stood that trunk, and there that chest,
There lay that store I counted best.

---

10. **succorless:** without aid or assistance; helpless.
14. **that gave and took:** allusion to Job 1:21, "The Lord gave, and the Lord hath taken away; blessed be the name of the Lord."
18. **repine:** to complain worriedly; to be displeased.
19. **bereft:** taken away; deprived.

Vocabulary piteous (PIHT ee uhs) *adj.*: deserving pity or compassion.
consume (kuhn SOOM) *v.*: burn away; destroy.

Literary Perspectives

Analyzing Historical and Political Contexts

Historical   Historicism is the study of how the social, economic, cultural, intellectual, religious, and political circumstances of a time period influence an author's work. This poem's context is the seventeenth-century Puritan colonies in North America. Considering Puritan perspectives on earthly and spiritual existence, how might a Puritan react to the sudden loss of all possessions?

Political   The study of gender in literature examines how concepts of masculinity and femininity influence an author's work. Puritan women's influence was often limited to the domestic sphere. How might Bradstreet's identity as a Puritan woman have influenced her reaction to the loss of her home?

As you read, be sure to notice the questions in the text, which will guide you in using these perspectives.

My pleasant things in ashes lie,
And them behold no more shall I. **Ⓐ**
Under thy roof no guest shall sit,
30 Nor at thy table eat a bit.
No pleasant tale shall e'er° be told,
Nor things recounted done of old.
No candle e'er shall shine in thee,
Nor bridegroom's voice e'er heard shall be.
35 In silence ever shall thou lie,
Adieu, Adieu, all's vanity.
Then straight I 'gin° my heart to chide,
And did thy wealth on earth abide?°
Didst fix thy hope on mold'ring dust?
40 The arm of flesh didst make thy trust?
Raise up thy thoughts above the sky
That dunghill mists away may fly.
Thou hast an house on high erect, **Ⓑ**

Framed by that mighty Architect,
45 With glory richly furnished,
Stands permanent though this be fled.
It's purchased and paid for too
By Him who hath enough to do.
A price so vast as is unknown
50 Yet by His gift is made thine own;
There's wealth enough, I need no more,
Farewell, my pelf,° farewell my store.
The world no longer let me love,
My hope and treasure lies above. **Ⓒ**

---

52. **pelf:** wealth or worldly goods (sometimes used as a term of contempt).

---

31. **e'er:** ever.
37. **'gin:** begin.
38. **abide:** to live, as in a place; to endure or tolerate.

Ⓐ **Reading Focus** **Analyzing Inversion** Rearrange the words in this line and the preceding line so that they are in normal order. How does this rearrangement affect the rhyme scheme?

Ⓑ **Literary Focus** **Metaphor** What is the "house on high"? Explain how this language is an example of implied metaphor.

Ⓒ **Literary Perspectives** **Historical Context** What aspects of Puritan society might have influenced Bradstreet's reaction to the fire that destroyed her house?

Vocabulary **vanity** (VAN uh tee) *n.:* something valueless.
glory (GLOHR ee) *n.:* great beauty; splendor.

Here Follow Some Verses upon the
Burning of Our House, July 10, 1666

Respond and Think Critically

Reading Focus

Quick Check

1. What awakens the poem's speaker?
2. Name two things the speaker loses when her house burns down.
3. Where is the speaker's "hope and treasure"?

Read with a Purpose

4. What points does the speaker make to herself in her internal dialogue?

Reading Skills: Analyzing Text Structures: Inversion

5. Add a third column to the chart in which you recorded inverted and normal word order in Bradstreet's poem. Using "noninverted" lines as a starting point, paraphrase each line of the poem.

✓ Vocabulary Check

Match each Vocabulary word below with its definition.

6. piteous   a. burn away; destroy

7. consume   b. something valueless

8. vanity   c. great beauty; splendor

9. glory   d. deserving pity or compassion

Literary Focus

Literary Analysis

10. **Interpret** Think about major Puritan beliefs as you re-read this poem. What philosophical beliefs about God and the purpose of human life are reflected in Bradstreet's poem?

11. **Draw Conclusions** *Pelf* usually refers to wealth acquired dishonestly. Why do you think the speaker calls her treasures "pelf" in line 52?

12. **Analyze** The speaker first narrates an incident and then draws conclusions from it. What line expresses the turning point of the poem?

13. **Literary Perspectives** History shows that the role of a Puritan woman in colonial America was in the household, as a manager of domestic chores. How does the focus of the poem reflect this Puritan role? How might the fire have disrupted Bradstreet's identity as a woman?

Literary Skills: Metaphor

14. **Infer** In Christian teachings, with what is fire usually associated? How might this metaphorical meaning of fire influence the speaker's decision to love the divine instead of the material?

Literary Skills Review: Meter

15. **Analyze** The pattern of stressed and unstressed syllables in a poem is called **meter**. Scan a few lines of Bradstreet's poem to determine the meter. Then, count the number of feet in each line. What kind of verse does Bradstreet use?

Writing Focus

Think as a Reader/Writer

Use It in Your Writing Think about a difficult event or situation. How did you or another person come to terms with it? Write a short poem about this event. Use an implied metaphor to express the resolution.

 What Do **You Think Now** How do Bradstreet's Puritan beliefs affect her response to the fire? How else might someone with a different set of beliefs respond to a similar event?

Grammar Link

Direct and Indirect Objects

A **direct object** is the noun, pronoun, or word group that tells who or what receives the action of the verb or that shows the result of the action: The direct object answers the question "Whom?" or "What?" after a transitive verb. For example, in the sentence "He sent flowers," the answer to "He sent *what*?" is *flowers*. *Flowers* is the direct object.

An **indirect object** is a noun, pronoun, or word group that precedes a direct object and tells *to* or *for whom* or *what* the action of the verb is done. For example, in the sentence "He sent her flowers," the indirect object is *her*. The flowers were sent to her.

Your Turn

Identify both the direct object and the indirect object in the underlined portion of each sentence.

1. As soon as Karen heard that John was sick, <u>she mailed him a care package.</u>
2. <u>The teacher gave the new student a kind smile</u> when he welcomed her to the classroom.
3. Every year <u>the restaurant serves the homeless a delicious holiday meal.</u>

Writing Application Review item 3 above. Now, write five sentences about a charitable organization with which you are familiar. What does the organization offer to people in need? Who are the people served? Include at least two direct objects and two indirect objects in your writing.

CHOICES

As you respond to the Choices, use these **Academic Vocabulary** words as appropriate: aspect, cite, contemporary, interpret, perspective.

REVIEW

Debate the Issue

Timed └Writing Bradstreet's poem portrays an internal debate between love for material goods and love for the divine. Choose one side of this debate to support in a persuasive essay. Review the poem and list all the points you find that support your perspective. In your essay, use these points to explain your position, and provide convincing reasons that might persuade others to support it.

CONNECT

Compare a Poem to Lyrics

Class Activity The regular meter and rhyming couplets of "Here Follow Some Verses . . ." give a musical aspect to the poem. Find a popular song that treats a similar theme or has a similar subject. Compare Bradstreet's poem to the song's lyrics, citing similarities and differences in a few short paragraphs. Play the song for the class, and present your findings.

EXTEND

Two Sides to Every Story

Think of an internal debate you've had with yourself. Write down the arguments on each side of the issue. Then, write down which side won or should have won. Write a poem, story, or essay that expresses both sides of the issue you've chosen as well as the resolution of the debate.

Learn It Online
Learn more about Anne Bradstreet through these Internet links.

go.hrw.com   L11-99   **Go**

Huswifery

 How can people's beliefs affect their actions?

QuickWrite

Have you ever felt unfairly judged because of your beliefs, or do you know of someone else who was? What happened? Write a paragraph or two about the episode.

Settler's house interior.
©The Shelburne Museum, Shelburne, Vermont.

Edward Taylor
(1642?–1729)

Edward Taylor's thoughtful, nonconforming vision found a voice in poetry.

Persecution and Faith

Born in Leicestershire, England, Taylor was raised in a family that held dissenting views about many of the practices of the Church of England. In 1662, the Act of Uniformity, which required ministers to subscribe to the prayer book, was contributing to the persecution of Puritans. Other acts also punished Puritans for disobedience. People ages sixteen and older faced severe consequences for attending religious services not conducted according to a certain set of rules. Pastors ejected from their posts could not live within five miles of where they had served, which essentially cut them out of their former communities. Taylor felt more and more uncomfortable in the religious climate of his country. He became determined to find the freedom that other Nonconformists had found in colonial America.

In 1668, Taylor sailed for Boston. After attending Harvard, he became pastor of a church in Westfield, Massachusetts, in 1671. Taylor stayed in Westfield for the rest of his life.

Hidden Brilliance

Taylor wrote an enormous amount of poetry. However, he allowed only a portion of one poem to be published during his lifetime. His grandson donated four hundred pages of manuscript to the Yale Library, where they sat quietly for many years. Although the author had requested that his work not be published, an editor collected and published Taylor's best poems under the title *The Poetical Works of Edward Taylor* in 1939. Taylor could not have known that his poems, which he had scrupulously hidden, would eventually earn him historical and literary prominence.

Think About the Writer If you had worked all your life on a creative project, would you want to keep it private—as Taylor did—or find a wide audience? Why?

Reader/Writer
Notebook

Use your **RWN** to complete the activities for this selection.

Literary Focus

Conceit A **conceit** is an elaborate metaphor or other figure of speech that compares two things that are extremely different from each other (in the case of the following poem, a lowly household task and salvation). A conceit often stretches the length of an entire poem, as in Edward Taylor's "Huswifery." In religious poetry a conceit can emphasize the underlying unity among all <u>aspects</u> of God's creation—high and low, familiar and strange. As a Puritan, Taylor believed that the miracle of grace consisted in mighty God consenting to join with lowly human beings. Thus, it was natural for him to compare the granting of grace to a housewife making homespun clothes.

Reading Focus

Analyzing Text Structures: Extended Metaphor An **extended metaphor** is a metaphor that is developed over several lines or with several examples. A **conceit** is a type of extended metaphor that compares two vastly different things. "Huswifery" develops an extended metaphor, or conceit, that begins with the poet comparing himself to a spinning wheel.

Into Action As you read Taylor's poem, pay close attention to how he develops his extended metaphor. Use a chart to keep track of the various <u>aspects</u> of the metaphor and to help you <u>interpret</u> the poem. (Look for materials mentioned, such as the spinning wheel, distaff, flyers, spool, reel, loom, cloth, dye, decorations, apparel.)

Materials	Connection to Spiritual Experience
Distaff	Holy Word—he wants his life to be "wound around" the Bible.
Swift Flyers	

Writing Focus

Think as a Reader/Writer

Find It in Your Reading A conceit is often a complex series of images that work together to support the overall comparison. As you read, pay close attention to the many different images that help complete the extended metaphor.

Learn It Online
Listen to this poem online.

go.hrw.com   L11-101   **Go**

Huswifery

by **Edward Taylor**

The Granger Collection, New York.

Read with a Purpose

Read Taylor's poem to learn about the Puritan belief that God shapes who we are and guides human purpose.

Build Background

Huswifery is an old spelling of *housewifery,* which means "the care and management of a household." In Puritan New England women were responsible for a wide range of tasks and duties in the household.

Make me, O Lord, thy Spinning Wheel complete.
　　Thy Holy Word my Distaff° make for me.
Make mine Affections thy Swift Flyers° neat
　　And make my Soul thy holy Spool to be.
5　　　My Conversation make to be thy Reel
　　And reel the yarn thereon spun of thy Wheel.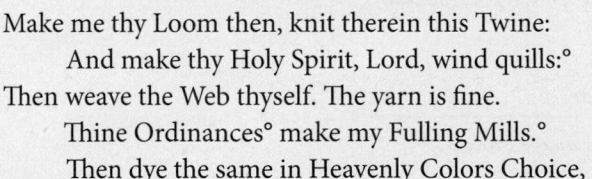

Make me thy Loom then, knit therein this Twine:
　　And make thy Holy Spirit, Lord, wind quills:°
Then weave the Web thyself. The yarn is fine.
10　　　Thine Ordinances° make my Fulling Mills.°
　　Then dye the same in Heavenly Colors Choice,
　　All pinked° with Varnished° Flowers of Paradise.

Then clothe therewith mine Understanding, Will,
　　Affections, Judgment, Conscience, Memory,
15　My Words, and Actions, that their shine may fill
　　My ways with glory and thee glorify.
　　　Then mine apparel shall display before ye
　　That I am Clothed in Holy robes for glory. **B**

2. distaff: On a spinning wheel, the distaff is a stick around which fibers are wound before they are spun into thread.
3. flyers: These help control the rate of rotation on a spinning wheel.
8. wind (wynd) **quills:** put twine around a spool.
10. ordinances: religious rules and laws. **fulling mills:** places for beating, pressing, and cleaning cloth.
12. pinked: decorated. **varnished:** embellished.

A **Literary Focus Conceit** What things are compared in the first stanza?
B **Reading Focus Analyzing Extended Metaphors** In Taylor's view, how is God like someone who spins thread, weaves cloth, and makes garments?

Respond and Think Critically

Reading Focus

Quick Check

1. With which part of the spinning wheel does the speaker associate her words?

2. How is the cloth decorated?

3. What does the speaker finally display for God?

Read with a Purpose

4. How does Taylor's poem illustrate the Puritan belief that all human purpose should be directed toward divine service?

Reading Skills: Analyzing Text Structures: Extended Metaphor

5. Think about how Taylor's extended metaphor fits together. Use the connections between making cloth and spirituality to determine the process described in the metaphor. Create a new table to show the major stages in this process and how they are organized into stanzas.

Overall Process	
Stage 1	In stanza 1, the speaker asks God to make him his spinning wheel—an instrument or tool in his hands. The stanza focuses on the making of thread.
Stage 2	
Stage 3	

Literary Focus

Literary Analysis

6. **Infer** *Housewifery* is "the care and management of a household." In the poem, what is the household that is being cared for and managed? Who is managing this household?

7. **Hypothesize** Taylor's poetry was not published until 1939. How do you think Puritans of his own day would have reacted to "Huswifery"? Explain.

8. **Draw Conclusions** What transformation does the speaker want to see in her life?

9. **Make Judgments** In this poem, how does the divine world interact with the physical world? How might this interaction contradict the Puritan belief that the importance of the divine far outweighs that of the physical?

Literary Skills: Conceit

10. **Interpret** To understand Taylor's complex conceit, it helps to identify its major components. Who represents the machines used to create the cloth and garment? What might the parts of the machines represent?

Literary Skills Review: Plain Style

11. **Analyze** The **plain style** of writing stresses simplicity and clarity of expression. Does the language of Taylor's poem adhere to the plain style? Explain.

Writing Focus

Think as a Reader/Writer

Use It in Your Writing Think of a device you use and list its components. For instance, a car's components can be tires, an engine, and so on. In a poem, compare the components to aspects of your personality.

 What Do You Think Now

"Huswifery" describes an exalted theme in humble, everyday ideas. How do Taylor's beliefs give his images dignity?

Preparing to Read

from Sinners in the Hands of an Angry God

What Do You Think?

How can people's beliefs affect their actions?

QuickWrite

Think about a time when you or someone you know felt so certain about a belief that it seemed necessary to persuade others to share that belief. How did you, he, or she try to convince others? Write a paragraph or two about the experience.

Reverend Jonathan Edwards (ca. 1750-55) by Joseph Badger (1708-1765). Oil on canvas. 77.5 x 64.8 cm. Bequest of Eugene Phelps Edwards. 1938.74. Yale University Art Gallery / Art Resource, NY. Yale University Art Gallery, New Haven, Connecticut, U.S.A.

MEET THE WRITER

Jonathan Edwards
(1703–1758)

Known for his fire-and-brimstone imagery, Jonathan Edwards was a brilliant, complicated man who straddled two worlds: the secular world of his time and the religious world of his Puritan ancestors.

Early Promise

Groomed to succeed his grandfather as pastor of the Congregational Church in Northampton, Massachusetts, Edwards entered Yale University when he was only thirteen. After his grandfather died in 1729, Edwards mounted the pulpit. He quickly established himself as a strong and charismatic pastor.

Science, reason, and observation of the physical world were important to Edwards. These disciplines confirmed his spiritual vision of a universe filled with the presence of God.

Great Awakening

Edwards's formidable presence and vivid sermons helped bring about the religious revival known as the Great Awakening, which began in the 1730s. It was marked by waves of conversions so intensely emotional that they amounted to mass hysteria at times.

The Great Awakening began when enthusiasm for the traditional Puritan religion was declining. Edwards became known for his extremism as a pastor. In his sermons, he didn't hesitate to accuse prominent church members—by name—of sinning. Edwards's strictness eventually proved to be too much for his congregation. In 1750, he was dismissed from his position.

After rejecting a number of other pastorships offered to him, Edwards relocated to the remote community of Stockbridge, Massachusetts. He spent eight years in virtual exile doing missionary work. He was then named president of the College of New Jersey but died three months later.

Edwards, known as "the last Puritan," had a hard time fitting in Puritan America or modern America. He never forgot his religious passion, which consumed his life. He wrote, "Grace is but glory begun, and glory is but grace perfected."

Think About the Writer

Edwards's convictions put him at odds with society. Would you risk being an outsider for your beliefs?

 **Reader/Writer Notebook**

Use your **RWN** to complete the activities for this selection.

Literary Focus

Imagery Writers often create vivid experiences for their readers by using **imagery,** language that appeals to the senses. Imagery describes sights, sounds, smells, textures, and tastes, the combination of which creates a dramatic and vibrant world. In this selection, Edwards uses terrifying imagery. He wants his listeners to experience the horrors he believes they will encounter if they do not repent of their sins and obey God's laws.

Literary Perspectives Apply the literary perspective described on page 107 as you read this sermon.

Reading Focus

Identifying Author's Purpose The **author's purpose** is the reason that he or she is writing. Authors may write to inform, to persuade, or to entertain. Sometimes they state their purpose directly. Other times, readers determine an author's purpose by paying close attention to the details and images in the selection. As you read, think about how and why the images are used, and monitor your reactions to them. Consider what reactions Edwards might want to elicit from his readers.

Into Action Use a chart like the one below to record Edwards's images and explore how they help him to achieve his purpose.

Image	How/Why It's Used	My Reaction
"the flames gather and flash about them . . ."	to show what will happen to "natural men"	I find the image frightening.

Vocabulary

incensed (ihn SEHNST) *adj.*: infuriated; angry. *He believes an incensed God will punish sinners.*

prudence (PROO duhns) *n.*: carefulness. *According to Edwards, sinners will not be protected from God's vengeance by their care, righteousness, or prudence.*

inconceivable (ihn kuhn SEE vuh buhl) *adj.*: unimaginable; beyond understanding. *Edwards preaches that although the idea may seem inconceivable, sinners in this life will face everlasting torment in the next.*

loathsome (LOHTH suhm) *adj.*: arousing hatred. *Edwards claims that God finds "natural men" loathsome.*

mitigation (miht uh GAY shuhn) *n.*: moderation; softening. *Their punishment will never get any easier; it will have no end and no mitigation.*

Language Coach

Pronunciation Words that have a /th/ sound followed by an /s/ sound can often seem like tongue twisters. With a partner, practice pronouncing the Vocabulary word *loathsome;* then try the words *paths* and— even trickier—*breadths.*

Writing Focus

Think as a Reader/Writer

Find It in Your Reading Edwards uses **repetition** to emphasize his points. As you read, record images and words that Edwards uses repeatedly, such as *wrath* and descriptions of the "pit of hell." Consider how repetition might affect a listener and how it contributes to Edwards's purpose.

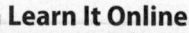 **Learn It Online**

Prepare to encounter this sermon through the *Power-Notes* video introduction online.

go.hrw.com L11-105   **Go**

from

SINNERS IN THE HANDS OF AN ANGRY GOD

by **Jonathan Edwards**

Read with a Purpose
Read this sermon to discover how Jonathan Edwards tried to persuade his congregation to reaffirm its faith.

Build Background
Jonathan Edwards delivered the sermon "Sinners in the Hands of an Angry God" at a time when colonists started to find answers to life's questions through science rather than religion. Some Puritans were abandoning their faith and not attending regular church services. In order to boost church membership, Puritan officials had softened the rules and, in Edwards's mind, allowed less-than-desirable candidates to join the church.

So that, thus it is that natural men[1] are held in the hand of God, over the pit of hell; they have deserved the fiery pit, and are already sentenced to it; and God is dreadfully provoked, His anger is as great toward them as to those that are actually suffering the executions of the fierceness of His wrath in hell, and they have done nothing in the least to appease or abate[2] that anger, neither is God in the least bound by any promise to hold them up one moment: The devil is waiting for them, hell is gaping for them, the flames gather and flash about them, and would fain[3] lay hold on them, and swallow them up; the fire pent up in their own hearts is struggling to break out: And they have no interest in any Mediator,[4] there are no means within reach that can be any security to them.

In short, they have no refuge, nothing to take hold of; all that preserves them every moment is the mere arbitrary will, and uncovenanted, unobliged forbearance[5] of an incensed God.

The use of this awful subject may be for awakening unconverted persons in this congregation. This that you have heard is the case of every one of you that are out of Christ. That world of misery, that lake

---

1. **natural men:** people who have not been "reborn."
2. **abate:** reduce in amount or intensity.
3. **fain:** archaic word meaning "happily" or "gladly."

4. **Mediator:** Jesus Christ. In general, one who intervenes between two parties in conflict.
5. **forbearance:** tolerance or restraint.

Vocabulary   incensed (ihn SEHNST) *adj:* infuriated; angry.

Sinners in Hell (1744). Woodcut from "The Progress of Sin" (detail).
The Granger Collection, New York.

of burning brimstone, is extended abroad under you.
There is the dreadful pit of the glowing flames of the
wrath of God; there is hell's wide gaping mouth open;
and you have nothing to stand upon, nor anything to
take hold of; there is nothing between you and hell but
the air; it is only the power and mere pleasure of God
that holds you up.   **Ⓐ**

You probably are not sensible of this; you find you
are kept out of hell, but do not see the hand of God in
it; but look at other things, as the good state of your
bodily constitution, your care of your own life, and
the means you use for your own preservation. But
indeed these things are nothing; if God should withdraw His hand, they would avail no more to keep you

---

Ⓐ **Reading Focus** **Author's Purpose** In your own words, define
the purpose of Edwards's sermon.

Literary Perspectives

Analyzing Philosophical Context This perspective asks us to
uncover and consider the philosophical arguments of the author
when we read literary works. Philosophical context refers to an
author's underlying assumptions regarding larger questions about
life and its meaning. An author's philosophy influences literary
texts in a variety of ways, including the form in which the text
is written and the overarching themes or messages the author
conveys. In this sermon, what aspects of Edwards's philosophy are
directly stated, and what are implied?

**As you read, be sure to notice the notes questions in the
text, which will guide you in using this perspective.**

from falling, than the thin air to hold up a person that is suspended in it.

Your wickedness makes you as it were heavy as lead, and to tend downward with great weight and pressure toward hell; and if God should let you go, you would immediately sink and swiftly descend and plunge into the bottomless gulf, and your healthy constitution, and your own care and prudence, and best contrivance, and all your righteousness, would have no more influence to uphold you and keep you out of hell, than a spider's web would have to stop a fallen rock. . . .

The wrath of God is like great waters that are dammed for the present; they increase more and more, and rise higher and higher, till an outlet is given; and the longer the stream is stopped, the more rapid and mighty is its course, when once it is let loose. It is true, that judgment against your evil works has not been executed hitherto; the floods of God's vengeance have been withheld; but your guilt in the meantime is constantly increasing, and you are every day treasuring up more wrath; the waters are constantly rising, and waxing more and more mighty; and there is nothing but the mere pleasure of God that holds the waters back, that are unwilling to be stopped, and press hard to go forward. If God should only withdraw His hand from the floodgate, it would immediately fly open, and the fiery floods of the fierceness and wrath of God, would rush forth with inconceivable fury, and would come upon you with omnipotent power; and if your strength were ten thousand times greater than it is, yea, ten thousand times greater than the strength of the stoutest, sturdiest devil in hell, it would be nothing to withstand or endure it. **B**

The bow of God's wrath is bent, and the arrow made ready on the string, and justice bends the arrow at your heart, and strains the bow, and it is nothing but the mere pleasure of God, and that of an angry God, without any promise or obligation at all, that keeps the arrow one moment from being made drunk with your blood. Thus all you that never passed under a great change of heart, by the mighty power of the Spirit of God upon your souls; all you that were never born again, and made new creatures, and raised from being dead in sin, to a state of new, and before altogether unexperienced light and life, are in the hands of an angry God. However you may have reformed your life in many things, and may have had religious affections,[6] and may keep up a form of religion in your families and closets,[7] and in the house of God, it is nothing but His mere pleasure that keeps you from being this moment swallowed up in everlasting destruction. However unconvinced you may now be of the truth of what you hear, by and by you will be fully convinced of it. Those that are gone from being in the like circumstances with you, see that it was so with them; for destruction came suddenly upon most of them; when they expected nothing of it, and while they were saying, peace and safety: Now they see, that those things on which they depended for peace and safety, were nothing but thin air and empty shadows. **C**

The God that holds you over the pit of hell, much as one holds a spider, or some loathsome insect over the fire, abhors you, and is dreadfully provoked: His wrath toward you burns like fire; He looks upon you as worthy of nothing else but to be cast into the fire; He is of purer eyes than to bear to have you in His sight; you are ten thousand times more abominable in His eyes than the most hateful venomous serpent is in ours. You have offended Him infinitely more than ever a stubborn rebel did his prince; and yet it is nothing but His hand that holds you from falling into the fire every moment. It is to be ascribed to nothing else, that you did not go to hell the last night; that you was suffered to awake again in this world, after you closed your eyes to sleep. And there is no other reason to be given, why you have not dropped into hell since you arose in the morning, but that God's hand has held you up. There is no other reason to be given why you have not gone to hell, since you have sat here in the house of God,

---

6. **affections:** feelings.
7. **closets:** rooms for prayer and meditation.

B **Literary Focus** **Imagery** What effect does the image of rising waters create? Why might Edwards want to create that effect?

C **Reading Focus** **Author's Purpose** How does citing (and thereby exposing) the attempts of parishioners to maintain the appearance of religious devotion strengthen Edwards's argument?

Vocabulary **prudence** (PROO duhns) *n.:* carefulness.
inconceivable (ihn kuhn SEE vuh buhl) *adj.:* unimaginable; beyond understanding.
loathsome (LOHTH suhm) *adj.:* arousing hatred.

O SINNER!
CONSIDER THE
FEARFUL DANGER
YOU ARE IN.

Sinners in Hell (1744). Woodcut from "The Progress of Sin" (detail).   The Granger Collection, New York.

provoking His pure eyes by your sinful wicked manner of attending His solemn worship. Yea, there is nothing else that is to be given as a reason why you do not this very moment drop down into hell.   **D**

O sinner! Consider the fearful danger you are in: It is a great furnace of wrath, a wide and bottomless pit, full of the fire of wrath, that you are held over in the hand of that God, whose wrath is provoked and incensed as much against you, as against many of the damned in hell. You hang by a slender thread, with the flames of divine wrath flashing about it, and ready every moment to singe it, and burn it asunder;[8] and you have no interest in any Mediator, and nothing to lay hold of to save yourself, nothing to keep off the flames of wrath, nothing of your own, nothing that you ever have done, nothing that you can do, to induce God to spare you one moment. . . .

---

8. asunder: into pieces.

It is *everlasting* wrath. It would be dreadful to suffer this fierceness and wrath of Almighty God one moment; but you must suffer it to all eternity. There will be no end to this exquisite horrible misery. When you look forward, you shall see a long forever, a boundless duration before you, which will swallow up your thoughts and amaze your soul; and you will absolutely despair of ever having any deliverance, any end, any mitigation, any rest at all. You will know certainly that you must wear out long ages, millions of millions of ages, in wresting and conflicting with this almighty merciless vengeance; and then when you have so done, when so many ages have actually been spent by you in this manner, you will know that all is but a point to what remains. So that your punishment will indeed be infinite. Oh, who can express what the state of a soul in such circumstances is! All that we can possibly say about it gives but a very feeble, faint representation

D Literary Perspectives **Philosophical Context** What two creatures does Edwards compare sinners to in this passage? From his comparisons, what can you interpret about Edwards's views on the nature of humankind?

Vocabulary **mitigation** (miht uh GAY shuhn) *n.:* moderation; softening.

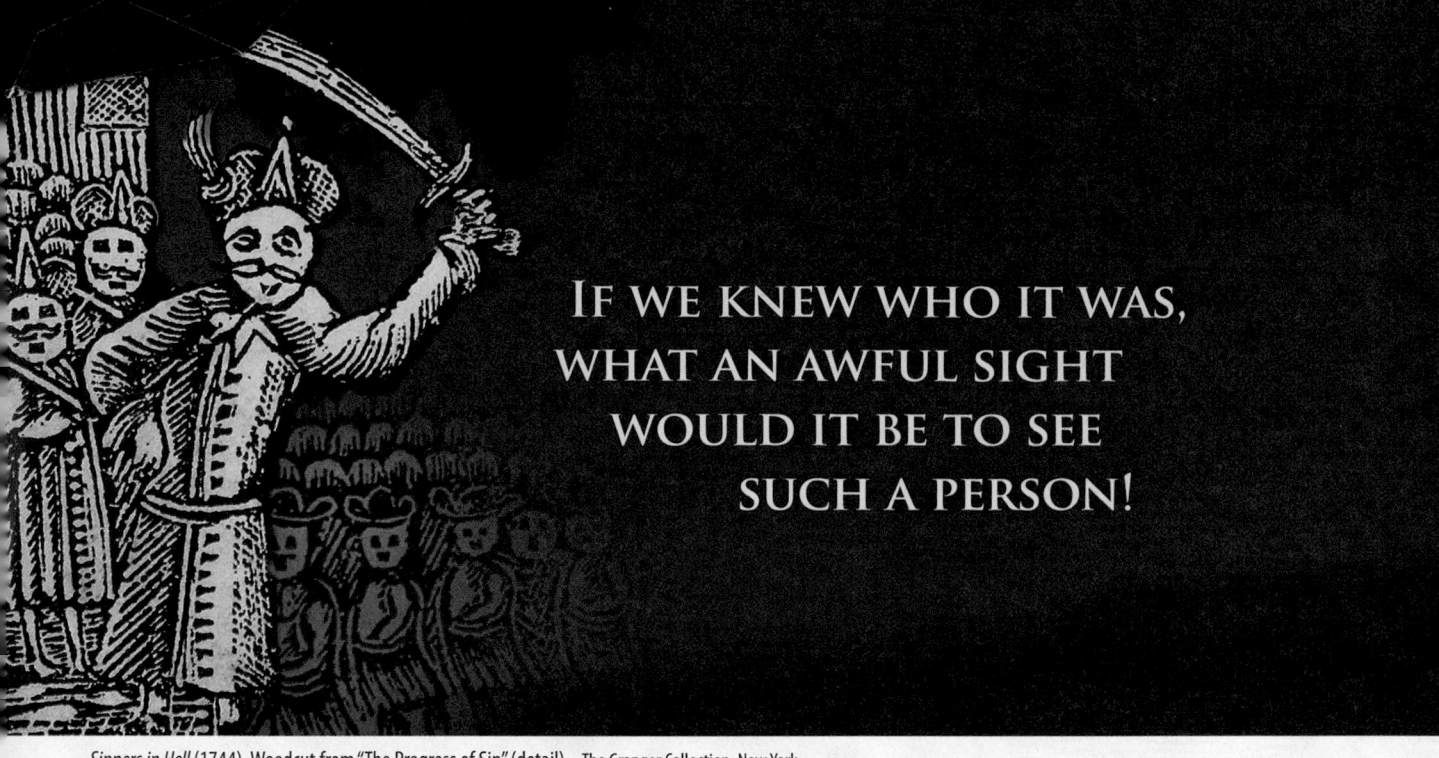

IF WE KNEW WHO IT WAS,
WHAT AN AWFUL SIGHT
WOULD IT BE TO SEE
SUCH A PERSON!

Sinners in Hell (1744). Woodcut from "The Progress of Sin" (detail). The Granger Collection, New York.

of it; it is inexpressible and inconceivable: For "who knows the power of God's anger?" **E**

How dreadful is the state of those that are daily and hourly in the danger of this great wrath and infinite misery! But this is the dismal case of every soul in this congregation that has not been born again, however moral and strict, sober and religious, they may otherwise be. Oh, that you would consider it, whether you be young or old! There is reason to think, that there are many in this congregation now hearing this discourse that will actually be the subjects of this very misery to all eternity. We know not who they are, or in what seats they sit, or what thoughts they now have. It may be they are now at ease, and hear all these things without much disturbance, and are now flattering themselves that they are not the persons, promising themselves that they shall escape. If we knew that there was one person, and but one, in the whole congregation that was to be the subject of this misery, what an awful thing would it be to think of! If we knew who it was, what an awful sight would it be to see such a person! How might all the rest of the congregation lift up a lamentable and bitter cry over him! But, alas! Instead of one, how many is it likely will remember this discourse in hell? And it would be a wonder if some that are now present should not be in hell in a very short time, even before this year is out. And it would be no wonder if some persons that now sit here, in some seats of this meetinghouse, in health, quiet, and secure, should be there before tomorrow morning. Those of you that finally continue in a natural condition, that shall keep out of hell longest, will be there in a little time! Your damnation does not slumber; it will come swiftly and, in all probability, very suddenly upon many of you. You have reason to wonder that you are not already in hell. It is doubtless the case of some whom you have seen and known that never deserved hell more than you, and that heretofore appeared as likely to have been now alive as you. Their case is past all hope; they are crying in extreme misery and perfect despair. But here you are in the land of the living and in the house of God, and have an opportunity to obtain salvation. What would not those poor damned hopeless souls give for one day's opportunity such as you now enjoy!

E **Reading Focus** **Author's Purpose** How does this paragraph develop Edwards's concept of an "*everlasting* wrath"?

And now you have an extraordinary opportunity, a day wherein Christ has thrown the door of mercy wide open, and stands in calling and crying with a loud voice to poor sinners; a day wherein many are flocking to him, and pressing into the kingdom of God. Many are daily coming from the east, west, north, and south; many that were very lately in the same miserable condition that you are in are now in a happy state, with their hearts filled with love to him who has loved them and washed them from their sins in his own blood, and rejoicing in hope of the glory of God. How awful is it to be left behind at such a day! To see so many others feasting, while you are pining and perishing! To see so many rejoicing and singing for joy of heart, while you have cause to mourn for sorrow of heart, and howl for vexation of spirit! How can you rest one moment in such a condition? . . . **F**

Therefore, let everyone that is out of Christ now awake and fly from the wrath to come. The wrath of Almighty God is now undoubtedly hanging over a great part of this congregation: let everyone fly out of Sodom.[9] "Haste and escape for your lives, look not behind you, escape to the mountain, lest you be consumed."[10]

---

9. **Sodom:** in the Bible, a city so wicked that God destroyed it, sparing only one man, Lot, and his family.
10. **"Haste and escape . . . lest you be consumed":** from Genesis 19:17, the words spoken by an angel of God to Lot, warning him to flee Sodom and never look back.

F **Literary Focus** Imagery How do the images of Jesus Christ opening the doors and the sinners flocking to him for mercy affect the mood of the sermon?

Analyzing Visuals

Viewing and Interpreting Edwards reminds his audience repeatedly of how fragile life is here on earth. Why does he emphasize this tombstone's point that one should "Remember death"?

Applying Your Skills

from Sinners in the Hands of
an Angry God

Respond and Think Critically

Reading Focus

Quick Check

1. According to the sermon, what keeps sinners out of hell?

2. According to Edwards, how can sinners obtain salvation?

Read with a Purpose

3. Why do you think Edwards points out that sinners "have no refuge, nothing to take hold of"?

Reading Skills: Identifying Author's Purpose

4. While reading, you recorded the author's images, analyzed their use, and reflected on your reactions. Do any of Edwards's images seem intended to evoke a similar response? Highlight any patterns you find, and then write a sentence that identifies the author's overall purpose.

Image	How/Why It's Used	My Reaction
"the flames gather and flash about them…"	To show what will happen to "natural men"	I find the image frightening.
"that lake of burning brimstone…"		

Author's Purpose: _____

Literary Focus

Literary Analysis

5. **Analyze** How does Edwards appeal to those in his audience who believe they are not sinners, and not in danger of the fate he describes?

6. **Evaluate** Would Edwards's mode of persuasion be effective today? Why or why not?

7. **Literary Perspectives** Judging from his sermon, what underlying philosophical beliefs does Edwards hold? What underlying assumptions does he have about the nature of both humans and God?

Literary Skills: Imagery

8. **Infer** Why do you think Edwards uses the image of God's hands to describe God's power? What makes this an effective image?

Literary Skills Review: Metaphor

9. **Interpret** A **metaphor** is a form of figurative language that directly compares two unlike things without using comparison words such as *like* or *as*. Edwards compares his listeners' powerlessness to a spider web stopping a plummeting rock. Explain what his listeners' lack of power and the spider web have in common, and why this metaphor is effective.

Writing Focus

Think as a Reader/Writer

Use It in Your Writing Edwards's use of repeated words and images helps convey his message by arousing fear in his listeners. Write a persuasive essay in which you try to convince someone to change his or her behavior. Include words and images that make your plea dramatic, and repeat them where appropriate to strengthen your appeal.

What Do You Think Now Edwards's beliefs motivate him to try to change the lives of others. Do you think this desire is common among people with strong beliefs? Why or why not?

Vocabulary Development

Choose the **synonym,** or word with almost the same meaning, of each Vocabulary word.

1. incensed
2. prudence
3. loathsome
4. mitigation
5. inconceivable

a. unimaginable
b. carefulness
c. moderation
d. angry
e. offensive

Vocabulary Skills: Prefixes and Suffixes

Prefixes are word parts attached to the beginning of a word, and **suffixes** are word parts attached to the end of a word. Most prefixes and suffixes change a word's meaning and part of speech. However, some suffixes, also called inflectional endings, simply change a word's number or tense. For example, –ed changes present tense to past tense, and –s turns a singular noun into a plural noun. The following table contains examples of some common prefixes and suffixes.

Prefix or Suffix	Meaning or Function	Example
–ed	puts a verb in the past tense	planted; deflated
–ence	state or condition	patience; independence
–some	like; characterized by	quarrelsome; troublesome
–tion	action or process; state or condition	attention; prevention
con–, com–	together; completely	concentrate; combine

Your Turn

Use the chart to help you answer the following questions:

1. Which word is an adjective, *loathe* or *loathsome*?
2. Explain the difference between *mitigation* and *mitigate*.
3. In the selection, *incensed* is a participle, or a verb used as an adjective. Write a sentence that uses *incensed* as a past-tense verb.
4. Describe a situation in which someone acts with *prudence*.

Language Coach

Pronunciation The suffix –*tion* is pronounced "shuhn." Work with a partner to pronounce the Vocabulary word *mitigation* correctly. Then practice saying the following words with the same suffix: *elevation, invitation, condition, completion, application.*

Academic Vocabulary

Write About
Edwards compares God's wrath to several things. In a short essay, cite at least three comparisons that he makes, and explain how the comparisons heighten one's awareness of humanity's perilous state.

from **Sinners in the Hands of an Angry God**

Grammar Link

Subject-Verb Agreement

Subject-verb agreement is essential to writing coherent, clear sentences. A verb should agree in number with its subject: Singular subjects take singular verbs, and plural subjects take plural verbs. Consider this incorrectly written sentence:

The sinners dangles over the pit of fire.

Dangles should be *dangle* to agree with the subject *sinners*. This sentence is correct:

The sinners dangle over the pit of fire.

Your Turn

Choose the verb in parentheses that agrees with each subject given.

1. Jon (*say, says*)
2. people (*go, goes*)
3. we (*think, thinks*)
4. Cara and Eliza (*run, runs*)
5. elephant (*appear, appears*)
6. dancing (*provide, provides*)
7. to lie (*are, is*)
8. the group (*want, wants*)
9. houses (*have, has*)
10. they (*see, sees*)

Writing Application Imagine you were part of Edwards's congregational audience. Write four sentences describing what each of the following people might think or feel while listening to Edwards's sermon: you and your spouse, two young children, a know-it-all, and a person living a secret life. For each sentence, underline the subject once and the verb twice, making sure your subject-verb agreement is correct.

CHOICES

As you respond to the Choices, use these **Academic Vocabulary** words as appropriate: aspect, cite, contemporary, interpret, perspective.

REVIEW

Illustrate the Images

"Sinners in the Hands of an Angry God" contains dramatic images, such as sinners dangling perilously over the pit of hell or an arrow aimed at a sinner's heart. Choose one image, and explain why it is effective. Comment on why the image is powerful not only to people of times past but also to contemporary people.

CONNECT

Compare and Contrast Author's Purpose

TechFocus Edwards's sermon was extremely powerful to his listeners. Find a recording of a modern song, speech, or poem with words that you find powerful. Compare and contrast the purposes of the two works, as well as the techniques Edwards used to bring his sermon alive, with the techniques used in the modern piece. Present your comparison to your class, citing specific examples from each work.

EXTEND

Write a Speech

Listening and Speaking Choose a cause about which you are passionate. Write a speech to persuade people to join your cause. You may wish to include techniques such as dramatic imagery and emotional appeals. Read it aloud to test the strength of your syntax and organization. Often, stumbling on a word or running out of breath signals awkward phrasing. Revise any awkward sentences. Present the speech to the class.

COMPARING TEXTS
Wrap Up

SKILLS FOCUS Writing Skills Write comparison-contrast essays; compare literary works.

The Puritan Worldview

Writing Focus

Writing a Comparison-Contrast Essay

Determine Your Essay's Focus What is the Puritan worldview? How do the three authors you have read express Puritan ideas? Use these questions to guide and focus your thoughts as you plan your essay.

Identify Similarities The three selections you have read—two poems on domestic subjects and a sermon about sin and punishment—provide insight into a way of life dominated by Puritan beliefs. Because Puritanism is central to these writers, consider focusing your comparison on the religious beliefs reflected in these writings or on the role religious belief played in the daily lives of the writers and their <u>contemporaries</u>.

Explore Differences Perhaps the more challenging part of this comparison-contrast essay is to identify the contrasts among the selections. Ask yourself the following questions to assist your analysis:

- Do the authors have different **purposes** for writing? What are they?
- Do the authors use **language** differently? Explain.
- Do the authors employ different **tones** as they write? What are the different tones?
- Do the writers reflect different **historical and political** <u>perspectives</u> of their time? If so, how?

Make notes about how each work reflects the elements in the questions above. Review your notes to decide which elements reflect significant similarities or differences. Then choose the elements you want to use.

Develop a Thesis Statement Use the most interesting ideas from your notes to develop your thesis statement. In a comparison-contrast essay, the thesis identifies how the selections are similar and/or different. Make your thesis statement clear and specific.

Save any details or examples for the body of your essay. For an example, look at the following thesis statement.

> Bradstreet, Taylor, and Edwards clearly illustrate the dominating force of religion in Puritan New England, but differences in purpose reveal a radical difference between the tone of the poems and the tone of the sermon.

Organize Your Essay Because you will compare and contrast three selections from Puritan literature, use the following method to organize your essay:

1. First element of similarity or difference
   - Discussion of Bradstreet, with evidence from her poem
   - Discussion of Taylor, with evidence from his poem
   - Discussion of Edwards, with evidence from his sermon
2. Second element of similarity or difference
   - Discussion of Bradstreet, Taylor, and Edwards, as above, with evidence to illustrate this element

Complete your plan by following the same structure for each element of similarity or difference.

Draft Your Comparison-Contrast Essay As you write, remember to include evidence from each of the three selections, including quoted and paraphrased text. If you cannot find the supporting evidence you need, examine your notes again and revise your thesis.

What Do **You** **Think** **Now** Bradstreet, Taylor, and Edwards each expressed strong Puritan beliefs. How did their beliefs shape their lives?

Forging a New Nation

Washington Crossing the Delaware River (1851) by Emanuel Gottlieb Leutze (1816–1868).

CONTENTS

Link to Today

"O ye that love mankind! Ye that dare oppose, not only the tyranny, but the tyrant, stand forth!"

— Thomas Paine

Literary Focus

SKILLS FOCUS Literary Skills Evaluate and analyze the philosophical, political, religious, ethical, and social influences of a historical period.

Political Writing by **Leila Christenbury**

Influences on Early American Political Writing

- Ideas and principles from Europe's Age of Reason, particularly the ideals of rationalism
- Emergence of deism and its influence on America's leaders and writers
- Conflict between British rule and American Colonists seeking independence
- Spread of self-published political writing

The Power of Reason

When America revolted against Great Britain in 1776, the Colonists' actions were fueled by influential political writings in favor of independence. The writers who helped inspire the American Revolution based their arguments on the ideals of **rationalism.** Rationalism, a movement that marked the beginning of the Age of Reason in Europe in the seventeenth century, is based on the belief that human beings can discover truth by using reason rather than by relying solely on religious faith or intuition.

Rationalists, like Puritans, believed that God created the natural world and its laws. However, unlike Puritans, rationalists thought that the universe operated without divine intervention. They believed that people could understand the world and guide their lives by their capacity to reason. This belief, which was shared by many of America's Founders, came to be known as **deism.**

The idea that all people are free to use reason to better their lives became part of the Colonies' justification for independence from Britain. This idea provided the foundation for the most important political documents in American history and literature: the Declaration of Independence and the U.S. Constitution.

The Argument for Revolt Throughout the diverse American Colonies, political writing helped unite people in the cause for independence. Early American leaders spread their ideals by sponsoring publication of their own words and making them widely available to the Colonists. *Common Sense,* a forty-seven-page pamphlet published by Thomas Paine in January 1776, is considered

by many to be the most important written work justifying American independence. The document used rationalism as the basis for its carefully reasoned argument in favor of revolt. In his discussion, Paine contests the reasons for remaining a colony, as in this passage:

> I challenge the warmest advocate for reconciliation to show a single advantage that this continent can reap by being connected with Great Britain.

COMMON SENSE;

ADDRESSED TO THE

INHABITANTS

OF

AMERICA,

On the following interesting

SUBJECTS.

I. Of the Origin and Design of Government in general, with concise Remarks on the English Constitution.

II. Of Monarchy and Hereditary Succession.

III. Thoughts on the present State of American Affairs.

IV. Of the present Ability of America, with some miscellaneous Reflections.

Man knows no Master save creating HEAVEN,
Or those whom choice and common good ordain.
THOMSON.

PHILADELPHIA;
Printed, and Sold, by R. BELL, in Third-Street.
MDCCLXXVI.

Paine also uses principles of deism to present reasons for American independence:

> Everything that is right or reasonable pleads for separation. The blood of the slain, the weeping voice of Nature cries, 'TIS TIME TO PART. . . . The republican form of government is the best because it is founded on the most natural principles.

The eloquent forcefulness of *Common Sense,* published at a time when the Colonies were on the verge of taking action against the British Crown, helped turn the tide of public opinion. Proof of its influence lay in the sheer number of pamphlets distributed. At a time when the population of the Colonies was approximately two and a quarter million, the pamphlet sold a half million copies. In December 1776, Paine continued to influence public opinion by publishing a series of pamphlets called *The American Crisis* that urged Americans not to give up the fight for independence.

Founding a New Nation

The words of early American political writers not only aroused passion for independence but also lay the foundation for an emerging nation. While Paine used a journalistic perspective to present his ideas to the masses, other revolutionary leaders, such as Patrick Henry and Thomas Jefferson, used political rhetoric within the halls of government. Both Henry and Jefferson used their rhetorical skills to guide American leaders toward building a new nation.

At the second Virginia Convention in March 1775, Patrick Henry delivered his famous "Give me liberty, or give me death!" speech after other delegates had argued for compromise with Britain. Like Paine, Henry sought to sway his audience by using rationalism. He reminded delegates that all peaceful options had failed, and he depicted the decision to compromise or to fight as a choice between slavery and freedom. Henry's speech successfully persuaded the delegation to arm the Colonies against Britain. This decision proved

to be a key step on the road to independence, and Henry's words became a battle cry that would echo throughout American history.

The following year, the Second Continental Congress appointed a committee to draft a declaration of independence. Jefferson was one of the document's main authors, and he helped infuse it with rationalist ideals that inspired him and his fellow leaders. In the Declaration, Thomas Jefferson and the other authors took the ideas and thoughts that had led to their revolt and used them as the basis for the new nation's independent government. The Declaration of Independence became the first American document to describe the ideal relationship between a government and its people. Underlying this relationship, which emphasized the rights of individuals, was a belief in all humankind's capacity—and freedom—to reason.

Ask Yourself

1. In what ways did the philosophies of rationalism and deism contribute to American independence?

2. What role did pamphlets and political speeches play in the decision to declare independence from Britain?

3. How did political writing allow individuals to affect the development of an entire nation? How does this power of the individual reflect the principles upon which the United States was founded?

 Learn It Online
Learn more about this historical time period with the introductory video, "Forging a New Nation" online.

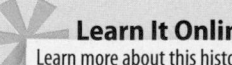 go.hrw.com L11-118 **Go**

Speech to the Virginia Convention

Analyzing Persuasive Techniques

by **Kylene Beers**

SKILLS FOCUS Reading Skills Analyze persuasion/arguments in a text.

Think about a time when you read an advertisement or watched a television commercial that made you want to buy something. Did the ad make you feel as though you just had to have that product? What aspects of the ad were particularly persuasive? Did it appeal to your sense of reason, to your emotions, or to a mixture of both reason and emotion?

Consider this: Wouldn't you say that many decisions you make are based on both your intellect *and* your feelings? Like advertisements, effective persuasive writing often appeals to logic and emotion. **Logical appeals** use facts, statistics, and examples to influence an audience. **Emotional appeals** use words, images, and anecdotes to arouse a reader's feelings, hopes, and beliefs.

In Patrick Henry's "Speech to the Virginia Convention," Henry uses both logical and emotional appeals to persuade his audience to arm themselves against the British. Read this excerpt from his speech, and imagine what thoughts and feelings a person hearing Henry's speech at the time might have experienced:

> I ask gentlemen, sir, what means this martial array, if its purpose be not to force us to submission? Can gentlemen assign any other possible motives for it? Has Great Britain any enemy, in this quarter of the world, to call for all this accumulation of navies and armies? No, sir, she has none. They are meant for us; they can be meant for no other. They are sent over to bind and rivet upon us those chains which the British ministry have so long been forging.

Notice Henry's appeal to logic when he refers to the factual situation of the British buildup of military forces in the Colonies. Note also that there is a shift in Henry's appeal from logic to emotion as he plays on

his audience's fears with the images of the British forging chains that fetter (or restrain) the Colonists. Henry knows that his listeners will shrink back in horror at the idea of being placed into chains, and he uses strong, vivid language to focus in on that fear.

When you draft a persuasive speech, it is important to predict how an audience might respond to your arguments. Henry is well aware of which details will sway his audience. By blending logical and emotional appeals and by tailoring his speech to his audience, Patrick Henry's words had the power to change a nation.

Your Turn

Read the following passage from Henry's speech, and analyze his use of persuasive techniques. What appeals does he employ? How can you tell?

> Sir, we have done everything that could be done, to avert the storm which is now coming on. We have petitioned; we have remonstrated; we have supplicated; we have prostrated ourselves before the throne, and have implored its interposition to arrest the tyrannical hands of the ministry and Parliament. Our petitions have been slighted; our remonstrances have produced additional violence and insult; our supplications have been disregarded; and we have been spurned, with contempt, from the foot of the throne.

Learn It Online

Practice analyzing persuasive techniques in modern media online at the MediaScope mini-site.

go.hrw.com   L11-119   Go

Speech to the Virginia Convention

What Do You Think? How can people's beliefs affect their actions?

QuickTalk

Think of a time when you were persuaded to do something. With a partner, talk about why you were persuaded. What made the argument persuasive?

Portrait of Patrick Henry by Asahel L. Powers.
© Shelburne Museum, Shelburne, Vermont.

MEET THE WRITER

Patrick Henry
(1736–1799)

Patrick Henry—a tall, somber-looking man who dressed like a preacher—is recognized as one of the most persuasive orators in American Colonial history.

An Uncertain Start

Born in a frontier region of Virginia, Henry was raised in a cultured but modest environment. During his youth the Colonies were in the midst of the religious revival known as the Great Awakening, and Henry often accompanied his mother to hear the sermons of traveling preachers. When he was a young man, Henry made several unsuccessful attempts at storekeeping and farming before discovering his true calling: the law.

A Stirring Speaker

In 1765, the twenty-nine-year-old lawyer was chosen to represent his region in the Virginia House of Burgesses. Henry's speech against the Stamp Act was the first of the two most famous speeches in American Colonial history. The second, his "liberty or death" speech, came ten years later, in 1775, as the Colonies neared the breaking point with England.

Following the Boston Tea Party in December 1773, the British closed the port of Boston. They also instituted other harsh measures that Colonists referred to as the Intolerable Acts. When people protested these acts, the British eased the Colonies' taxes on several conditions. One condition was that the Colonists must fully support British rule.

On March 23, 1775, after several delegates of the Virginia House of Burgesses gave speeches in favor of compromise with the British, Henry rose to defend his resolution to take up arms against Britain. As the speech reached its climax, Henry is said to have grabbed an ivory letter opener and plunged it toward his chest as he said, "Give me liberty, or give me death!"

Henry's emotional words persuaded the delegation, and the Virginia Convention voted to arm its people against England. A month later, on April 19, 1775, the Battle of Lexington in Massachusetts ignited the Revolutionary War.

Think About the Writer How might Henry's childhood exposure to various preachers have influenced his eventual success as an orator? Explain.

Reader/Writer
Notebook

Use your **RWN** to complete the activities for this selection.

Literary Focus

Persuasion A form of speaking or writing meant to convince an audience to take a specific action is called **persuasion.** Effective persuasion appeals to both **logic** and **emotion.** For example, in "Speech to the Virginia Convention," Patrick Henry persuades his audience to take up arms against England by appealing to their patriotism and to their mistrust of the British government.

Literary Perpectives Apply the literary <u>perspective</u> described on page 123 as you read this speech.

Reading Focus

Analyzing Persuasive Techniques One persuasive technique, known as **logical appeal,** provides reasons and examples to support a particular opinion or course of action. Another technique, known as **emotional appeal,** uses words and images to stir an audience's feelings.

Into Action As you read Henry's speech, use a chart like this one to keep track of the logical and emotional appeals he uses. In the first column, write down persuasive words, phrases, and sentences, noting where they appear in the text. Then, in the second column, indicate whether the quotations appeal to logic or to the audience's emotions.

Words, Phrases, and Sentences (page #)	Logical or Emotional Appeal?
"But different men often see the same subject in different lights" (p. 122)	logical appeal
"Shall we acquire the means of effectual resistance, by lying supinely on our backs?" (p. 126)	emotional appeal

Writing Focus

Think as a Reader/Writer

Find It in Your Reading Persuasive writers intentionally choose words that are emotionally charged. As you read, record in your *Reader/Writer Notebook* at least four examples of words and phrases that Henry uses to convey strong emotions. Be sure to note which emotions the words and phrases evoke.

Vocabulary

solace (SAHL ihs) *v.:* comfort. *Henry does not believe that the behaviors of the British ministry can solace the Colonists.*

insidious (ihn SIHD ee uhs) *adj.:* sly; sneaky. *Their insidious expressions gave away their true beliefs.*

supplication (suhp luh KAY shuhn) *n.:* plea; prayer. *Henry declares that their supplication toward Britain has gone unanswered.*

avert (uh VURT) *v.:* prevent; turn away. *Nothing could avert the coming war.*

spurned (spurnd) *v.:* rejected. *Every attempt at reconciliation has been spurned.*

inviolate (ihn VY uh liht) *adj.:* uncorrupted. *Henry believes that freedom should be inviolate.*

adversary (AD vuhr sair ee) *n.:* opponent. *Britain's ministry does not believe the Colonies are a dangerous adversary.*

vigilant (VIHJ uh luhnt) *adj.* used as *n.:* those who are watchful. *Henry believes that in times of crisis, the vigilant are just as important as the strong.*

Language Coach

Substantives Sometimes adjectives can function as nouns. For example, in the Vocabulary list above, *vigilant* is an example of an adjective that is used alone to represent a group of people. *Vigilant* normally modifies a noun: the vigilant people. This kind of adjective is known as a **substantive.**

Learn It Online
Meet this speech through the *PowerNotes* video introduction online.

go.hrw.com L11-121 Go

Speech to the Virginia Convention

by **Patrick Henry**

Read with a Purpose

Read to discover why Patrick Henry believes his country should go to war.

Build Background

Patrick Henry was known as a fiery public speaker and a staunch opponent of the British government. In March 1775, at a church in Richmond, Virginia, Henry addressed the second Virginia Convention to urge them to prepare for war. His words "Give me liberty, or give me death!" have since served as the foundation for attempts to preserve civil liberties around the world. Although Henry's 1775 speech is one of the most famous in American oratory, no manuscript of it exists. William Wirt, a biographer of Henry, used notes of people who were present to piece together the traditionally accepted text forty years after the speech was delivered .

Mr. President:[1] No man thinks more highly than I do of the patriotism, as well as abilities, of the very worthy gentlemen who have just addressed the House. But different men often see the same subject in different lights; and, therefore, I hope that it will not be thought disrespectful to those gentlemen, if, entertaining as I do, opinions of a character very opposite to theirs, I shall speak forth my sentiments freely and without reserve. This is no time for ceremony. The question before the House is one of awful moment[2] to this country. For my own part I consider it as nothing less than a question of freedom or slavery; and in proportion to the magnitude of the subject ought to be the freedom of the debate. It is only in this way that we can hope to arrive at truth, and fulfill the great responsibility which we hold to God and our country. Should I keep back my opinions at such a time, through fear of giving offense, I should consider myself as guilty of treason toward my country, and of an act of disloyalty toward the majesty of heaven, which I revere above all earthly kings. **Ⓐ**

---

1. **Mr. President:** Peyton Randolph (1721–1775), president of the second Virginia Convention.
2. **awful moment:** great importance.

Ⓐ **Reading Focus** **Analyzing Persuasive Techniques** What persuasive technique does Henry use in the first two sentences of his speech? What do you think he is trying to accomplish?

Mr. President, it is natural to man to indulge in the illusions of hope. We are apt to shut our eyes against a painful truth, and listen to the song of that siren, till she transforms us into beasts.[3] Is this the part of wise men, engaged in a great and arduous struggle for liberty? Are we disposed to be of the number of those who, having eyes, see not, and having ears, hear not, the things which so nearly concern their temporal salvation? For my part, whatever anguish of spirit it may cost, I am willing to know the whole truth; to know the worst and to provide for it.

I have but one lamp by which my feet are guided; and that is the lamp of experience. I know of no way of judging of the future but by the past. And judging by the past, I wish to know what there has been in the conduct of the British ministry for the last ten years, to justify those hopes with which gentlemen have been pleased to solace themselves and the House? Is it that insidious smile with which our petition[4] has been lately received? Trust it not, sir; it will prove a snare to your feet. Suffer not yourselves to be betrayed with a kiss. Ask yourselves how this gracious reception of our petition comports with these warlike preparations which cover our waters and darken our land. Are fleets and armies necessary to a work of love and reconciliation? Have we shown ourselves so unwilling to be reconciled, that force must be called in to win back our love? Let us not deceive

Literary Perspectives

Analyzing Style This perspective builds on what you have learned about authors' techniques, such as figurative language, imagery, characterization, and other literary tools that writers use to help convey the mood, tone, and theme of a literary text.

You probably have noticed that different authors use these techniques to create very recognizable styles. An author's style is like a literary fingerprint. When you analyze an author's style, consider sentence structure, vocabulary, use of images, and recurring themes or topics. As you read Henry's speech, consider what literary techniques he uses to form his famously persuasive style.

Be sure to notice the questions in the text, which will guide you in using this perspective.

---

3. **listen . . . beasts:** In Greek mythology, the sirens are sea maidens whose seductive singing lures sailors to wreck their boats on coastal rocks. In the *Odyssey*, Circe, a witch, transforms Odysseus's men into swine after they arrive at her island home. Henry's allusion combines these two stories.

4. **our petition:** The First Continental Congress had recently protested against new tax laws. King George III had withdrawn the laws on certain conditions, but the Colonists were unwilling to accept his conditions.

Vocabulary **solace** (SAHL ihs) *v.:* comfort.
insidious (ihn SIHD ee uhs) *adj.:* sly; sneaky.

Patrick Henry before the Virginia House of Burgesses (1851) by Peter F. Rothermel.

Red Hill, Patrick Henry National Memorial, Brookneal, Virginia.

ourselves, sir. These are the implements of war and subjugation;[5] the last arguments to which kings resort.

B

I ask gentlemen, sir, what means this martial array,[6] if its purpose be not to force us to submission? Can gentlemen assign any other possible motives for it? Has Great Britain any enemy, in this quarter of the world, to call for all this accumulation of navies and armies? No, sir, she has none. They are meant for us; they can be meant for no other. They are sent over to bind and rivet upon us those chains which the British ministry have been so long forging. And what have we to oppose to them? Shall we try argument? Sir, we have been trying that for the last ten years. Have we anything new to offer on the subject? Nothing. We have held the subject up in every light of which it is capable; but it has been all in vain. Shall we resort to entreaty and humble supplication? What terms shall we find which have not been already exhausted? Let us not, I beseech you, sir, deceive ourselves longer Sir, we have done everything that could be done, to avert the storm which is now coming on. We have petitioned; we have remonstrated; we have supplicated; we have prostrated ourselves before the throne, and have implored its interposition to arrest the tyrannical hands of the ministry and Parliament. Our petitions have been slighted; our remonstrances have produced additional violence and insult; our supplications have been disregarded; and we have been spurned, with contempt, from the foot of the throne. In vain, after these things, may we indulge the fond hope of peace and reconciliation. There is no longer any room for hope. If we wish to be free—if we mean to preserve inviolate those inestimable privileges for which we have been so long contending—if we mean not basely to abandon the noble struggle in which we have been so long engaged, and which we have pledged ourselves never to abandon until the glorious object of our contest shall be obtained, we must fight! I repeat it, sir, we must fight! An appeal to arms and to the God of Hosts is all that is left us!

C

---

5. **subjugation:** conquest; domination.
6. **martial array:** warlike display.

B **Literary Perspectives** **Analyzing Style** To what is Henry appealing by describing the actions of the British government? Which images are most effective? Why?

C **Literary Focus** **Persuasion** Which words in this paragraph do you find most persuasive? Why?

Vocabulary **supplication** (suhp luh KAY shuhn) *n.:* plea; prayer.
avert (uh VURT) *v.:* prevent; turn away.
spurned (spurnd) *v.:* rejected.
inviolate (ihn VY uh liht) *adj.:* uncorrupted.

Patrick Henry's eyeglasses.
Virginia Historical Society, Richmond, Virginia.

They tell us, sir, that we are weak; unable to cope with so formidable an adversary. But when shall we be stronger? Will it be the next week, or the next year? Will it be when we are totally disarmed, and when a British guard shall be stationed in every house? Shall we gather strength by irresolution and inaction? Shall we acquire the means of effectual resistance, by lying supinely on our backs, and hugging the delusive phantom of hope, until our enemies shall have bound us hand and foot? Sir, we are not weak, if we make a proper use of the means which the God of nature hath placed in our power. Three millions of people, armed in the holy cause of liberty, and in such a country as that which we possess, are invincible by any force which our enemy can send against us. Besides, sir, we shall not fight our battles alone. There is a just God who presides over the destinies of nations; and who will raise up friends to fight our battles for us. The battle, sir, is not to the strong alone; it is to the vigilant, the active, the brave. Besides, sir, we have no election.[7] If we were base enough to desire it, it is now too late to retire from the contest. There is no retreat, but in submission and slavery! Our chains are forged! Their clanking may be heard on the plains of Boston! The war is inevitable—and let it come! I repeat it, sir, let it come! **D**

It is in vain, sir, to extenuate[8] the matter. Gentlemen may cry peace, peace—but there is no peace. The war is actually begun! The next gale that sweeps from the north will bring to our ears the clash of resounding arms! Our brethren are already in the field! Why stand we here idle? What is it that gentlemen wish? What would they have? Is life so dear, or peace so sweet, as to be purchased at the price of chains and slavery? Forbid it, Almighty God! I know not what course others may take; but as for me, give me liberty, or give me death! **E**

---

7. **election:** choice.
8. **extenuate:** weaken.

D **Literary Focus** Persuasion   Describe the use of persuasive appeals in this paragraph. What effect might Henry's reference to God have on his audience?

E **Literary Focus** Persuasion   Would Henry's final words have persuaded you to act? Why or why not?

Vocabulary **adversary** (AD vuhr sehr ee) *n.*: opponent.
vigilant (VIHJ uh luhnt) *n.*: those who are watchful.

SKILLS FOCUS **Literary Skills** Analyze characteristics of persuasion; analyze rhetorical questions. **Reading Skills** Analyze modes of persuasion, including appeals to reason and appeals to emotion. **Writing Skills** Write persuasive essays or articles.

Speech to the Virginia Convention

Respond and Think Critically

Reading Focus

Quick Check

1. What does Henry believe is the issue at the heart of the debate?

2. How has Henry <u>interpreted</u> Britain's enlarging of its navies and armies?

3. Why does Henry believe it is useless to "cry peace"?

Read with a Purpose

4. What does Henry foresee happening if the country does not fight Britain?

Reading Skills: Analyzing Persuasive Techniques

5. While reading, you identified logical and emotional appeals in the speech. Now, review your notes. Add a third column, and explain why each appeal is effective.

Words, Phrases, and Sentences	Logical or Emotional Appeal?	Why It Works
"But different men often see the same subject in different lights"	logical appeal	It makes sense that reasonable people disagree.
"Shall we acquire the means of effectual resistance, by lying supinely on our backs?"	emotional appeal	

Literary Focus

Literary Analysis

6. **Interpret** In the third paragraph, how has "the lamp of experience" affected Henry's views about the British?

7. **Analyze** What metaphors does Henry use in the fourth paragraph? How do these metaphors contribute to his purpose?

8. **Extend** Because his audience was familiar with the Bible and classical mythology, Henry knew certain allusions would be effective. Find two allusions in Henry's speech. How would each allusion relate to the conflicts in Virginia in 1775?

9. **Literary Perspectives** How is the overall effectiveness of Henry's speech dependent upon his style? What elements of style—word choice, figurative language, rhetorical questions—are most effective in his speech? Explain.

Literary Skills: Persuasion

10. **Infer** Persuasion involves the use of logical and emotional appeals to sway an audience. Why would Henry use both types of appeals?

Literary Skills Review: Rhetorical Questions

11. **Analyze** Henry makes use of **rhetorical questions**—questions that are asked for effect. Find the series of rhetorical questions in the fifth paragraph. How do they make Henry's speech more presuasive?

Writing Focus

Think as a Reader/Writer

Use It in Your Writing Write a persuasive paragraph about a controversial topic that interests you. Fill your paragraph with words and phrases that are modeled on the examples that you found in Henry's speech.

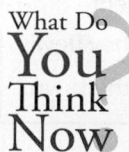 What Do You Think Now

Is it important that leaders such as Patrick Henry have passionate beliefs? How might this passion influence their own lives and the lives of the people they lead?

Applying Your Skills

Speech to the Virginia Convention

Vocabulary Development

✓ Vocabulary Check

Match each Vocabulary word with its definition.

1. supplication
2. avert
3. inviolate
4. adversary
5. vigilant
6. solace
7. insidious
8. spurned

a. those who are watchful
b. comfort
c. uncorrupted
d. plea or prayer
e. sly or sneaky
f. rejected
g. opponent
h. prevent or turn away

Vocabulary Skills: Synonyms

Because the words you choose say something about who you are, deciding how to express yourself in writing can be just as personal as deciding what to wear.

What should you do when your writing doesn't convey what you want? Focus on the word that isn't quite right, and look for a better word with a similar meaning. Use a dictionary or thesaurus to find **synonyms** that allow you to say exactly what you mean.

Synonyms for *noise*:

din, uproar, cacophony, clamor, racket, roar, disquiet, caterwauling

Notice that the synonyms above all mean "noise," but they have specific connotations and are used in different contexts as in the following examples.

Examples:

The rambunctious children made a horrible *din*.

The crowd was in an *uproar* after the incident.

The birds made a *cacophony* of sound as they flew.

The tornado *roared* as it spiraled through the town.

Your Turn

Replace the word *flew* in each sentence with one of the following synonyms: *swooped, floated, soared.*

1. The rocket burst from the launch pad and *flew* into the sky.
2. Across the field the hawk *flew* down and captured its prey.
3. Leaves *flew* to the ground and rustled underfoot.

Language Coach

Substantives The English language is filled with expressions like "the good" and "the brave." In both of these cases, the main word in each phrase is actually an adjective but functions as a noun. These kinds of adjectives, called **substantives,** can act as either the subject or the object of a verb.

The brave are willing to fight for what's right.

Working with a partner, write a short paragraph that includes at least three additional examples of substantives.

Academic Vocabulary

Talk About

In a small group, discuss how Patrick Henry's <u>perspective</u> on the aggressive actions of one country toward another can be applied to <u>contemporary</u> situations around the world. Provide specific examples to support your arguments.

Learn It Online

Learn more about synonyms with the *WordSharp* interactive tutorial online.

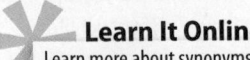 go.hrw.com L11-128

SKILLS FOCUS Vocabulary Skills Identify and correctly use synonyms. **Grammar Skills** Understand verb tenses; use consistent verb tenses. **Listening and Speaking Skills** Adapt to purpose when speaking to persuade.

Writing Skills Write comparison-contrast essays; address potential objections; support persuasive arguments and opinions with reasons and evidence.

Grammar Link

Sequence of Verb Tenses

A verb's **tense** indicates the time of the action or the state of being that is expressed by the verb.

> **Present tense**
> Henry <u>believes</u> that war <u>is</u> necessary.
> **Past tense**
> Henry <u>believed</u> that war <u>was</u> necessary.

The tense usually remains consistent within a written work. For example, something written in the **past tense** usually remains in the past tense. However, it is sometimes necessary to shift tense to show the correct sequence in time.

> **Necessary Shift**
> Henry <u>believed</u> that war <u>was</u> necessary because the Colonists <u>had exhausted</u> all other alternatives. *The Colonists had exhausted alternatives* before *Henry believed war was necessary.*

In this example the tense shifts from the past tense (*believed, was*) to the **past perfect tense** (*had exhausted*) to show that one past action took place before another. Watch out for unnecessary shifts in tense.

> **Unnecessary Shift**
> Henry <u>believes</u> that war <u>had been</u> necessary.

Your Turn

Writing Application Rewrite the following sentences by correcting any errors in verb tense. Consider the correct sequence of events, and watch for unnecessary shifts in tense.

1. Freedom is important to the Colonists because they wanted to follow their own paths.

2. We consider previous attempts and then decided upon a course of action.

3. Henry had hoped that it would not be thought disrespectful if he speaks his mind freely.

CHOICES

As you respond to the Choices, use the **Academic Vocabulary** words as appropriate: <u>aspect</u>, <u>cite</u>, <u>contemporary</u>, <u>interpret</u>, <u>perspective</u>.

REVIEW
Recite a Speech

Paired Activity With a partner, take turns reading Patrick Henry's speech aloud. As you read, use vocal inflection to communicate the emotion Henry may have felt as he delivered his speech. Do you think he would have spoken quickly or slowly? How long might he have paused after each question? How do you think his tone might have changed from the beginning to the end of the speech?

CONNECT
Research a Contemporary Leader

Timed ⏲ Writing In today's society, forms of persuasion bombard us constantly. Advertisements, newspapers, magazines, and other people want to influence our opinions. Think of a <u>contemporary</u> leader who, like Henry, wants to persuade people to take a specific action. Compare and contrast Henry and this leader in a short essay. Be sure to <u>cite</u> specific similarities or differences in your essay.

EXTEND
Counter the Argument

Everyone knows that there are at least two sides to every argument, but not everyone knows that you can win an argument by addressing your opponent's issues. Henry effectively addresses his opponents' issues in "Speech to the Virginia Convention." How do you think his opponents at the convention responded to his speech? Imagine that you are one of Henry's opponents in the debate about going to war. Prepare an argument that addresses his points and supports your own. You may need to do some research in order to better understand the issues.

Preparing to Read

from The Crisis, No. 1

What Do You Think?

How can people's beliefs affect their actions?

⏱ QuickWrite

Think of a time when you or someone you know wanted to make a new start—perhaps in school, in an extracurricular activity, or in a relationship. What kinds of changes did you or someone else make? What beliefs or attitudes led to these changes? Write a paragraph about the experience.

Thomas Paine
(1737–1809)

Thomas Paine was the most persuasive writer of the American Revolution. *Common Sense,* which he published in 1776, has been called the most important pamphlet in U.S. history.

A Slow Start

Thomas Paine, the poorly educated son of a corset maker, was born in England and spent the first thirty-seven years of his life drifting through various occupations. He was fired from his job as a tax collector in 1774 for attempting to organize the employees in a demand for higher wages. Like many others, Paine came to America to make a new start.

With a letter of introduction from Benjamin Franklin, whom he had met in London, Paine went to Philadelphia, where he worked as a journalist. As the conflict between England and the Colonies grew, he quickly identified with the Colonists. In January 1776, he published *Common Sense,* in support of American independence. The forty-seven-page pamphlet denounced King George III and asserted that a continent should not remain tied to an island.

Hero and Outcast

After the Revolution, Paine lived peacefully in New York and New Jersey until 1787, when he returned to Europe. He became involved in radical politics in France and supported the French Revolution. In 1791, he began to compose *The Rights of Man,* a call to the English to overthrow their king. When *Rights* was published, England tried Paine, who was living in France, for treason and banned him from the island. Paine was later imprisoned in France for being a citizen of England, an enemy nation. Paine was freed only after an American minister insisted that he was actually an American.

Paine's final notable work, *The Age of Reason,* laid out the principles of deism. The book was controversial in America. When Paine returned to the United States, he was considered a dangerous radical and an atheist. Though Paine died an outcast, his writings continue to inspire people today.

Think About the Writer

Paine played important roles in many political activities during his life. How do you think he would want to be remembered? Explain.

Reader/Writer Notebook

Use your **RWN** to complete the activities for this selection.

Literary Focus

Style A writer's **style** is the distinctive way that he or she uses language. Style is largely determined by sentence structure, word choice, and use of **figurative language** and **imagery.** In *The Crisis, No. 1,* Paine uses a combination of styles. He mixes direct, common speech with heightened expressions that are sharpened by dramatic rhetorical and literary techniques. In the opening line of his essay, Paine's use of **alliteration** makes his message memorable: "These are the times that try men's souls."

Reading Focus

Analyzing Persuasive Techniques Persuasive writers use a variety of appeals to develop their arguments. By citing evidence, facts, and statistics, a writer can appeal to the audience's **logic,** or reason. By using figurative language and personal experiences, the writer can arouse the **emotions** of the audience.

Into Action As you read *The Crisis,* watch especially for two literary techniques—an **analogy** that compares King George III to a thief and an **anecdote** about a tavern keeper and his child. In a chart like the one below, list clues that identify each example as an appeal to reason or an appeal to emotion.

	Analogy	Anecdote
Clues: appeal to reason		
Clues: appeal to emotion	Paine refers to the king as "a common murderer, a highwayman, or a housebreaker."	

Writing Focus

Think as a Reader/Writer

Find It in Your Reading Paine enhances the emotional effect of his writing by using vivid figurative language, such as his use of the term *summer soldier* to describe someone who fights only when fighting is easy. In your *Reader/Writer Notebook,* note some vivid figures of speech that Paine uses. How do they enhance his work?

Vocabulary

tyranny (TIHR uh nee) *n.:* cruel use of power. *Thomas Paine wants to end Britain's tyranny over the Colonies.*

impious (ihm PY uhs) *adj.:* irreverent. *Paine considers Parliament's Declaratory Act impious because it claims godlike power.*

ravage (RAV ihj) *n.:* violent destruction. *The ravage created by Sir William Howe and his British soldiers appalled Americans.*

relinquished (rih LIHNG kwihshd) *v.:* given up. *Paine does not believe that God has relinquished care of the Colonists.*

pretense (PREE tehns) *n.:* false claim. *Under what pretense could the tyrant King George III look to heaven for help?*

dominion (duh MIHN yuhn) *n.:* rule; the right to govern. *The Colonists would settle for nothing less than a release from foreign dominion.*

eloquence (EHL uh kwuhns) *n.:* expressive or graceful manner of speech. *Paine's eloquence helps make his writing persuasive.*

Language Coach

Prefixes You might know that the word *incapable* means "not capable" and that the prefix *in—* means "not." You might not know, however, that the *im—* in *impious* comes from the same prefix. When the negative prefix *in—* appears before the letters *b, m,* or *p, in—* changes to *im—,* making the word easier to pronounce.

Learn It Online
Sharpen your vocabulary skills with Word Watch online.

| go.hrw.com | L11-131 | **Go** |

from
The Crisis, No. 1

by **Thomas Paine**

Read with a Purpose
Read to discover how Thomas Paine uses his persuasive ability to lift the spirits of a nation at war.

Build Background
In 1776, the Continental army was exhausted, demoralized, and outnumbered by the enemy. Thomas Paine joined the army as it retreated from New Jersey to Philadelphia. On the way, he began to write a series of sixteen pamphlets called *The American Crisis* that urged Americans to tough it out and keep fighting. In December 1776, General George Washington's troops listened to a reading of the first pamphlet a few days before the army recrossed the Delaware River to attack the British-held city of Trenton, New Jersey.

These are the times that try men's souls. The summer soldier and the sunshine patriot will, in this crisis, shrink from the service of his country; but he that stands it NOW, deserves the love and thanks of man and woman. Tyranny, like hell, is not easily conquered; yet we have this consolation with us, that the harder the conflict, the more glorious the triumph. What we obtain too cheap, we esteem too lightly; 'tis dearness only that gives everything its value. Heaven knows how to put a proper price upon its goods; and it would be strange indeed, if so celestial[1] an article as FREEDOM should not be highly rated. Britain, with an army to enforce her tyranny, has declared that she has a right (*not only to* TAX) but "to BIND *us in* ALL CASES WHATSOEVER,"[2] and if being *bound in that manner,* is not slavery, then is

---

1. **celestial:** heavenly.
2. **to bind . . . whatsoever:** In response to protests, Parliament repealed the Stamp Act (which taxed all commercial and legal documents in the Colonies) on March 17, 1766. Also that day, it passed the Declaratory Act, giving Parliament the right "to make laws . . . to bind the Colonies and people of America . . . in all cases whatsoever."

Vocabulary **tyranny** (TIHR uh nee) *n.:* cruel use of power.

Statue of Thomas Paine in Norfolk, England, where he was born.

there not such a thing as slavery upon earth. Even the expression is impious, for so unlimited a power can belong only to God. **A B**

Whether the independence of the continent was declared too soon, or delayed too long, I will not now enter into as an argument; my own simple opinion is, that had it been eight months earlier, it would have been much better. We did not make a proper use of last winter, neither could we, while we were in a dependent state. However, the fault, if it were one, was all our own; we have none to blame but ourselves. But no great deal is lost yet; all that Howe[3] has been doing for this month past, is rather a ravage than a conquest, which the spirit of the Jerseys[4] a year ago would have quickly repulsed, and which time and a little resolution will soon recover.

I have as little superstition in me as any man living, but my secret opinion has ever been, and still is, that God Almighty will not give up a people to military destruction, or leave them unsupportedly to perish, who have so earnestly and so repeatedly sought to avoid the calamities of war, by every decent method which wisdom could invent. Neither have I so much of the infidel in me, as to suppose that he has relinquished the government of the world, and given us up to the care of devils; and as I do not, I cannot see on what grounds the king of Britain can look up to heaven for help against us: A common murderer, a highwayman,[5] or a housebreaker, has as good a pretense as he. . . . **C**

I once felt all that kind of anger, which a man ought to feel, against the mean[6] principles that are held by the Tories:[7] A noted one, who kept a tavern at Amboy,[8] was standing at his door, with as pretty a child in his hand, about eight or nine years old, as I ever saw, and after speaking his mind as freely as he thought was prudent, finished with this unfatherly expression, *"Well! Give me peace in my day."* Not a man lives on the continent but fully believes that a separation must sometime or other finally take place, and a generous parent should have said, *"If there must be trouble let it be in my day, that my child may have peace";* and this single reflection, well applied, is sufficient to awaken every man to duty. Not a place upon earth might be so happy as America. Her situation is remote from all the wrangling world, and she has nothing to do but to trade with them. A man can distinguish himself between temper and principle, and I am as confident, as I am that God governs the world, that America will never be happy till she gets clear of foreign dominion. Wars, without ceasing, will break out till that period arrives, and the continent must in the end be conqueror; for though the flame of liberty may sometimes cease to shine, the coal can never expire.

America did not, nor does not want force; but she wanted a proper application of that force. Wisdom is not the purchase of a day, and it is no wonder that we should err at the first setting off. From an excess of tenderness, we were unwilling to raise an army, and trusted our cause to the temporary defense of a well-meaning militia.[9] A summer's experience has now taught us better; yet with those troops, while they were collected, we were able to set bounds to the progress of the enemy, and—thank God!—they are again assem-

---

3. **Howe:** Sir William Howe, commander in chief of the British forces in America during the Revolution.
4. **Jerseys:** New Jersey was at this time divided into East Jersey and West Jersey.
5. **highwayman:** thief who patrolled the highways and robbed travelers.
6. **mean:** low.

7. **Tories:** those who supported British rule in the American Colonies.
8. **Amboy:** Perth Amboy, New Jersey.
9. **militia:** By "militia," Paine means an army of citizens quickly raised to meet an emergency. An army would be better equipped and well trained.

A Literary Focus **Style** What comparison does Paine employ in the third sentence? What is the effect of this comparison?

B Reading Focus **Analyzing Persuasive Techniques** What evidence is provided in this paragraph as an appeal to logic? What effect would it have on the Colonists?

C Literary Focus **Style** What appeals to emotion does Paine use here to rally the Colonists against the king? Consider his loaded words.

Vocabulary **impious** (ihm PY uhs) *adj.:* irreverent.
ravage (RAV ihj) *n.:* violent destruction.
relinquished (rih LIHNG kwihshd) *v.:* given up.
pretense (PREE tehns) *n.:* false claim.
dominion (duh MIHN yuhn) *n.:* rule; the right to govern.

bling. I always consider militia as the best troops in the world for a sudden exertion, but they will not do for a long campaign. Howe, it is probable, will make an attempt on this city;[10] should he fail on this side the Delaware, he is ruined: If he succeeds, our cause is not ruined. He stakes all on his side against a part on ours; admitting he succeeds, the consequence will be, that armies from both ends of the continent will march to assist their suffering friends in the middle

states; for he cannot go everywhere; it is impossible. I consider Howe the greatest enemy the Tories have; he is bringing a war into their country, which, had it not been for him and partly for themselves, they had been clear of. Should he now be expelled, I wish with all the devotion of a *Christian,* that the names of Whig[11] and Tory may never more be mentioned; but should the Tories give him encouragement to come, or assistance if he come, I as sincerely wish that our next year's arms

10. **this city:** Philadelphia.

11. **Whig:** Colonist who supported the Revolution.

From the original painting by Mort Künstler, *The World Turned Upside Down.* © 2006 Mort Künstler, Inc.

Analyzing Visuals

Viewing and Interpreting How does the artist's choice of perspective, or point of view, affect your sense of this scene? Why do you think the the artist chose to show these two armies from this particular vantage point?

may expel them from the continent, and that congress appropriate their possessions to the relief of those who have suffered in well doing. A single successful battle next year will settle the whole. America could carry on a two years' war by the confiscation of the property of disaffected[12] persons; and be made happy by their expulsion. Say not that this is revenge, call it rather the soft resentment of a suffering people, who, having no object in view but the *good* of *all,* have staked their *own all* upon a seemingly doubtful event. Yet it is folly to argue against determined hardness; eloquence may strike the ear, and the language of sorrow draw forth the tear of compassion, but nothing can reach the heart that is steeled with prejudice.

Quitting this class of men, I turn with the warm ardor of a friend to those who have nobly stood, and are yet determined to stand the matter out: I call not upon a few, but upon all; not on *this* state or *that* state, but on *every* state; up and help us; lay your shoulders to the wheel; better have too much force than too little, when so great an object is at stake. Let it be told to the future world, that in the depth of winter, when nothing but hope and virtue could survive, that the city and the country, alarmed at one common danger, came forth to meet and to repulse it. Say not that thousands are gone, turn out your tens of thousands;[13] throw not the burden of the day upon Providence, but *"show your faith by your works,"*[14] that God may bless you. It matters not where you live, or what rank of life you hold, the evil or the blessing will reach you all. The far and the near, the home counties and the back, the rich and the poor, will suffer or rejoice alike. The heart that feels not now, is dead: The blood of his children will curse his cowardice, who shrinks back at a time when a little might have saved the whole, and made *them* happy. (I love the man that can smile at trouble; that can gather strength from distress; and grow brave by reflection.) 'Tis the business of little minds to shrink; but he whose heart is firm, and whose conscience approves his conduct, will pursue his principles unto death. My own line of reasoning is to myself as straight and clear as a ray of light. Not all the treasures of the world, so far as I believe, could have induced me to support an offensive war, for I think it murder; but if a thief breaks into my house, burns and destroys my property, and kills or threatens to kill me, or those that are in it, and to *"bind me in all cases whatsoever,"* to his absolute will, am I to suffer it? What signifies it to me, whether he who does it is a king or a common man, my countryman, or not my countryman; whether it be done by an individual villain or an army of them? If we reason to the root of things we shall find no difference; neither can any just cause be assigned why we should punish in the one case and pardon in the other. **D**

> ## Quitting this class of men, I turn with the warm ardor of a friend to those who have nobly stood, and are yet determined to stand the matter out.

---

12. **disaffected:** here, disloyal to the American cause.
13. **thousands . . . tens of thousands:** "Saul hath slain his thousands, and David his ten thousands" (1 Samuel 18:7).

14. **show . . . works:** "Show me thy faith without thy works, and I will show thee my faith by my works" (James 2:18).

D **Reading Focus** Analyzing Persuasive Techniques Paine refers to his own reasoning as "straight and clear as a ray of light." Do you agree with him, or do you believe that his appeal is based more on emotion than on logic?

SKILLS FOCUS Literary Skills Analyze a writer's style. **Reading Skills** Analyze modes of persuasion, including appeals to reason and appeals to emotion. **Vocabulary**

Skills Demonstrate knowledge of literal meanings of words and their usage. **Writing Skills** Write persuasive essays or articles.

from The Crisis, No. 1

Respond and Think Critically

Reading Focus

Quick Check

1. How will the Americans be consoled for their hardships?

2. Why does Paine believe that God will favor the Americans over the British?

3. Why does Paine say that General Howe is "the greatest enemy the Tories have"?

Read with a Purpose

4. Many of Paine's statements are memorable and moving. Which statements might still encourage people to face conflicts? Why?

Reading Skills: Analyzing Persuasive Techniques

5. While reading, you listed clues that identify two examples from Paine's essay as appeals to reason or emotion. Review your chart. In three sentences, explain how each example works individually. Then, explain how they work together.

✓ Vocabulary Check

Match each Vocabulary word with its meaning.

6. tyranny   a. elegant speech

7. impious   b. false claim

8. ravage   c. irreverent

9. relinquished   d. savage destruction

10. pretense   e. gave up

11. dominion   f. cruel, oppressive power

12. eloquence   g. right to rule over

Literary Focus

Literary Analysis

13. **Analyze** What is Paine's main purpose for writing *The Crisis*? What do you think are the most powerful details supporting that purpose?

14. **Evaluate** Consider these lines from Paine's essay: "Not a place upon earth might be so happy as America. Her situation is remote from all the wrangling world, and she has nothing to do but to trade with them" (page 133). Do these lines reflect America's situation today? Explain.

Literary Skills: Style

15. **Analyze** Writers' styles can be defined in part by their use of imagery. What images appear at the beginning of the essay, and how do these images relate to the author's overall purpose?

Literary Skills Review: Metaphor

16. **Evaluate** A **metaphor** compares two unlike things without using comparison words such as *like* or *as*. Explain the following metaphor: "Though the flame of liberty may sometimes cease to shine, the coal can never expire" (page 133). Do you agree or disagree with this idea?

Writing Focus

Think as a Reader/Writer

Use It in Your Writing Create your own persuasive flier about an issue in your school or community. Use vivid figurative language like Paine's in your work.

What Do **You Think Now**

How do you think Paine influenced people's beliefs about the war? Cite specific examples from the text.

Political Points of View

Today in the United States every citizen is guaranteed equal treatment under the law, freedom to express ideas openly, and the right to vote. When the Declaration of Independence was written, however, only white males could vote. Many groups in our country have had to fight to gain equal rights. In the following selections you will see a variety of viewpoints on freedom, equality, and government.

CONTENTS

from

The Autobiography: The Declaration of Independence

What Do You Think?

How can people's beliefs affect their actions?

🕐 QuickWrite

In a few paragraphs, reflect on how your education has influenced your belief system. Examine how your learning experiences in and out of school have helped you become the person you are today.

Thomas Jefferson
(1743–1826)

Inspired by the Enlightenment, Thomas Jefferson used the power of words to help the United States win independence.

Prepared for Success

Jefferson was born in the red clay region of what is now Albemarle County, Virginia. Jefferson's father, a surveyor and magistrate, died when his son was fourteen. However, he had already provided Jefferson with a classical education and a large estate.

After attending the College of William and Mary, the brilliant and versatile Jefferson became a lawyer and a member of the Virginia House of Burgesses. He advocated for the rights of personal liberty and religious freedom. In 1774, he wrote a pamphlet that rejected the parliamentary authority of Britain. Two years later, the Second Continental Congress chose him to help draft the Declaration of Independence.

Political Power Figure

During the American Revolution, Jefferson served as the governor of Virginia. Afterward, he devoted himself to family and research. When his wife died in 1782, however, he returned to public life. He served as U.S. minister to France, secretary of state, and vice president. He served as the nation's president from 1801 to 1809.

Jefferson believed in the rights of individuals and states to govern themselves as much as possible. He doubled the size of the United States in 1803 with the Louisiana Purchase. Despite his achievements, Jefferson avoided public fanfare. A president, he thought, should neither act nor look like a king.

In 1826, both Jefferson, age eighty-three, and the former president John Adams, age ninety, became ill. Both men hoped to live to see the fiftieth anniversary of U.S. independence. Jefferson died the morning of July 4, several hours before Adams, whose last words were, "Thomas Jefferson still survives."

Think About the Writer

If Jefferson were alive today, would he think that personal liberty and religious freedom are widespread in the United States? Explain your answer.

Reader/Writer Notebook

Use your **RWN** to complete the activities for this selection.

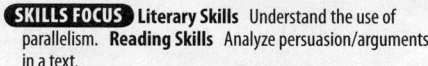

SKILLS FOCUS **Literary Skills** Understand the use of parallelism. **Reading Skills** Analyze persuasion/arguments in a text.

Literary Focus

Parallelism The repetition of sentences, clauses, or phrases with identical or similar structures is called **parallelism** or **parallel structure.** Parallelism is a device commonly used in public documents and speeches, often for dramatic effect. In this selection, when Jefferson cites the truths that are "self-evident," he begins each clause with *that*. He also begins a long series of paragraphs with the words *He has*. His use of parallelism creates a stately rhythm, or cadence, in the Declaration.

Literary Perpectives Apply the literary perspective described on page 141 as you read this selection.

Reading Focus

Analyzing Arguments The fight for equality is a universal conflict, one that has occurred—and is still occurring—in many cultures and in many nations. The Declaration of Independence is famous for its poetic and well-founded **arguments** against unfair treatment of the American Colonists at the hands of King George III.

Into Action Create a chart like the one below to examine how Jefferson uses parallelism to construct his arguments. In your own words, record arguments in the left-hand column, noting where they appear in the text. In the right-hand column, point out the parallel structure in each argument.

Summary of Argument	Use of Parallelism in Argument
All people are born with inalienable rights, and the government's responsibility is to secure these rights. (p. 141)	Each clause in the list of self-evident truths begins with "that."

Writing Focus

Think as a Reader/Writer

Find It in Your Reading Exposition is a form of discourse in which something is explained. Examine how Jefferson uses exposition in the opening paragraphs of the Declaration of Independence to provide background information about the Colonists' demand for equality. Record your findings in your *Reader/Writer Notebook*.

Vocabulary

despotism (DEHS puh tihz uhm) *n.*: rule by a tyrant or king with unlimited power. *The Colonists have the right to throw off the despotism of the English king.*

assent (uh SEHNT) *n.*: agreement. *The king would not give his assent to laws the Colonists created to address their needs.*

tenure (TEHN yuhr) *n.*: length of time that an office is held. *The judges' tenure depended on the whims of the king.*

perfidy (PUR fuh dee) *n.*: betrayal of trust. *The British rulers committed acts of perfidy against the American Colonists.*

opprobrium (uh PROH bree uhm) *n.*: shameful conduct. *The king's opprobrium pushed the Colonists to pursue their independence.*

redress (rih DREHS) *n.*: correction for a wrong done. *Because England committed many crimes against the American Colonists, the Americans sought redress.*

Language Coach

Double Consonants Three of the Vocabulary words above have examples of **double consonants,** or occurrences in which the same consonant appears twice in a row. Words with double consonants can be tricky to spell since, in many cases, neither letter is individually pronounced. When you are uncertain about whether a word should have a double consonant, the best thing is to compare the word to another that you already know how to spell. So, *redress* will suggest to you that *congress* has a double *s*.

Learn It Online

Prepare to read the Declaration of Independence through the video introduction online.

go.hrw.com   L11-139   **Go**

from

The Autobiography:
THE DECLARATION OF INDEPENDENCE

by **Thomas Jefferson**

Read with a Purpose

Jefferson says that people's beliefs are evident in what they accept and in what they reject. Read to learn how the beliefs and values of the delegates to the Second Continental Congress are reflected in what they accepted and rejected in the Declaration.

Build Background

Four other writers worked with Thomas Jefferson on the draft of the Declaration that was submitted to Congress: John Adams of Massachusetts, Roger Sherman of Connecticut, Robert Livingston of New York, and Benjamin Franklin of Pennsylvania. These other writers made few changes, but Congress insisted on major alterations. Jefferson was upset by what he called "mutilations" of his document.

In *The Autobiography,* Jefferson chronicled the alterations Congress made. The underlined passages in the Declaration of Independence show the parts Congress omitted from the original. The words added by Congress appear in the margins.

In June 1776, the Second Continental Congress appointed a five-person committee including Thomas Jefferson to write a document declaring the Colonies' independence from Britain. The signing of the Declaration of Independence launched a full-scale rebellion against Britain. Tension also mounted within the newly formed United States. John Dickinson, one of Pennsylvania's representatives to the Second Continental Congress, led the conservative opposition to the Declaration and refused to sign the document, alleging that the Colonists were not ready for such a fight. In the excerpt from his autobiography, Jefferson explains some of the problems with the original draft of the document, of which he was the main author.

Congress proceeded the same day to consider the Declaration of Independence, which had been reported and lain on the table the Friday preceding, and on Monday referred to a committee of the whole. The pusillanimous[1] idea that we had friends in England worth keeping terms with, still haunted the minds of many. For this reason, those passages which conveyed censures[2] on the people of England were struck out, lest they should give them offense. The clause too, reprobating[3] the enslaving the inhabitants of Africa, was struck out in complaisance[4] to South Carolina and Georgia, who had never attempted to restrain the importation of slaves, and who, on the contrary, still wished to continue it. Our northern brethren also, I believe, felt a little tender under those censures; for though their people had very few slaves themselves, yet they had been pretty considerable carriers of them to others. The debates, having taken up the greater parts of the 2d, 3d, and 4th days of July, were, on the

---

1. **pusillanimous:** cowardly; lacking in courage.
2. **censures:** strong, disapproving criticisms.
3. **reprobating:** disapproving of; condemning.
4. **complaisance:** desire to please.

evening of the last, closed; the Declaration was reported by the committee, agreed to by the House, and signed by every member present, except Mr. Dickinson. As the sentiments of men are known not only by what they receive, but what they reject also, I will state the form of the Declaration as originally reported. The parts struck out by Congress shall be distinguished by a black line drawn under them; and those inserted by them shall be placed in the margin, or in a concurrent column.

A Declaration by the Representatives of the United States of America, in General Congress Assembled

When, in the course of human events, it becomes necessary for one people to dissolve the political bands which have connected them with another, and to assume among the powers of the earth the separate and equal station to which the laws of nature and of nature's God entitle them, a decent respect to the opinions of mankind requires that they should declare the causes which impel them to the separation. **Ⓐ Ⓑ**

We hold these truths to be self-evident: that all men are created equal; that they are endowed by their creator with inherent and inalienable rights;[5] that among these are life, liberty, and the pursuit of happiness; that to secure these rights, governments are instituted among men, deriving their just powers from the consent of the governed; that whenever any form of government becomes destructive of these ends, it is the right of the people to alter or to abolish it, and to institute new government, laying its foundation on such principles, and organizing its powers in such form, as to them shall seem most likely to effect their safety and happiness. Prudence, indeed, will dictate that governments long established should not be changed for light and transient causes; and accordingly all experience hath shown that mankind are more disposed to suffer while evils are sufferable, than to right themselves by abolishing the forms to which they are accustomed. But when a long train of abuses and usurpations,[6] begun at a distinguished[7]

certain

---

5. **inalienable rights:** rights that cannot be taken away.
6. **usurpations:** acts of unlawful or forceful seizure of property, power, rights, and the like.
7. **distinguished:** clearly defined.

Ⓐ **Reading Focus** Analyzing Arguments What is the purpose of the first paragraph? How does it lend credibility to the document's arguments?

Ⓑ **Reading Focus** Analyzing Arguments What does Jefferson's reference to "the laws of nature and of nature's God" suggest about his religious and philosophical beliefs?

Literary Perspectives

Analyzing Style This perspective builds on what you have learned about authors' techniques, such as figurative language, imagery, characterization, and other literary tools that writers use to help convey the mood, tone, and theme of a literary text.

You have probably noticed that different authors use these techniques to create very recognizable styles. An author's style is like a literary fingerprint. When you analyze an author's style, consider sentence structure, vocabulary, use of images, and recurring themes or topics. What elements of style make Jefferson's writing stand out for you?

As you read, be sure to notice the questions in the text, which will guide you in using this perspective.

period and pursuing invariably the same object, evinces a design to reduce them under absolute despotism, it is their right, it is their duty to throw off such government, and to provide new guards for their future security. Such has been the patient sufferance of these colonies; and such is now the necessity which constrains them to expunge their former systems of government. The history of the present king of Great Britain is a history of unremitting injuries and usurpations, among which appears no solitary fact to contradict the uniform tenor of the rest, but all have in direct object the establishment of an absolute tyranny over these states. To prove this, let facts be submitted to a candid world for the truth of which we pledge a faith yet unsullied by falsehood.   **C** **D** **E**

alter

repeated
all having

C **Reading Focus** **Analyzing Arguments** Humans are born into many situations that are not equal. Some are born into poverty; and some, into wealth. Some are born into situations in which their talents are nurtured, and some are not. To what kind of equality is Jefferson referring?

D **Literary Focus** **Parallelism** Read aloud the list of self-evident truths at the start of the paragraph. How does the use of parallel structure enhance the sound of the passage?

E **Literary Focus** **Parallelism** Why might Jefferson have chosen to make the clauses "it is their right" and "it is their duty" parallel?

Vocabulary **despotism** (DEHS puh tihz uhm) *n.:* rule by a tyrant or king with unlimited power.

Photograph from the movie *Jefferson in Paris* (1995) starring Nick Nolte.

He has refused his assent to laws the most wholesome and necessary for the public good.

He has forbidden his governors to pass laws of immediate and pressing importance, unless suspended in their operation till his assent should be obtained; and, when so suspended, he has utterly neglected to attend to them.

He has refused to pass other laws for the accommodation of large districts of people, unless those people would relinquish the right of representation in the legislature, a right inestimable[8] to them, and formidable to tyrants only.[9]

He has called together legislative bodies at places unusual, uncomfortable, and distant from the depository of their public records, for the sole purpose of fatiguing them into compliance with his measures.

Writing materials used at the signing of the Declaration of Independence, Independence Hall, Philadelphia, Pennsylvania.

He has dissolved representative houses repeatedly <u>and continually</u> for opposing with manly firmness his invasions on the rights of the people.

He has refused for a long time after such dissolutions to cause others to be elected, whereby the legislative powers, incapable of annihilation, have returned to the people at large for their exercise, the state remaining, in the meantime, exposed to all the dangers of invasion from without and convulsions within.

He has endeavored[10] to prevent the population of these states; for that purpose obstructing the laws for naturalization[11] of foreigners, refusing to pass others to encourage their migrations hither, and raising the conditions of new appropriations of lands. **G**

He has <u>suffered</u> the administration of justice <u>totally to cease in some of these states</u> refusing his assent to laws for establishing judiciary powers.

obstructed / by

He has made <u>our</u> judges dependent on his will alone for the tenure of their offices, and the amount and payment of their salaries.

He has erected a multitude of new offices, <u>by a self-assumed power</u> and sent hither swarms of new officers to harass our people and eat out their substance. **H**

---

8. **inestimable:** invaluable; priceless.
9. **formidable to tyrants only:** causing fear only to tyrants.
10. **endeavored:** attempted; tried.
11. **naturalization:** process by which foreigners become citizens.

F **Literary Focus** **Parallelism** The paragraphs that begin with *He has* refer to King George's abuses against the Colonists. How does the use of parallelism affect this long series of paragraphs?

G **Reading Focus** **Analyzing Arguments** What is the main idea of the paragraphs that list King George's offenses? How does this idea relate to the Colonists' right to rebel against the Crown?

H **Literary Perspectives** **Analyzing Style** What loaded words—or words with strong emotional overtones—does Jefferson employ in this paragraph? How do these words strengthen his argument? How do they affect his style? Explain your response.

Vocabulary **assent** (uh SEHNT) *n.:* agreement.
tenure (TEHN yuhr) *n.:* length of time that an office is held.

Viewing and Interpreting How has the artist depicted the process of writing and revising the Declaration?

The Drafting of the Declaration of Independence in 1776 by Jean Leon Jerome Ferris (1863–1930). Oil on canvas.

He has kept among us in times of peace standing armies and ships of war without the consent of our legislatures.

He has affected to render the military independent of, and superior to, the civil power.

He has combined with others[12] to subject us to a jurisdiction foreign to our constitutions and unacknowledged by our laws, giving his assent to their acts of pretended legislation for quartering large bodies of armed troops among us; for protecting them by a mock trial from punishment for any murders which they should commit on the inhabitants of these states; for cutting off our trade with all parts of the world; for imposing taxes on us without our consent; for depriving us [ ] of the benefits of trial by jury; for transporting us _in many cases_ beyond seas to be tried for pretended offenses; for abolishing the free system of English laws in a neighboring province,[13] establishing therein an arbitrary government, and enlarging its boundaries, so as to render it at once an example and fit instrument for introducing the same absolute rule into these states; for taking away our charters, abolishing our most valuable laws, and _colonies_ altering fundamentally the forms of our governments; for suspending our own legislatures, and declaring themselves invested with power to legislate for us in all cases whatsoever. **Ⓘ**

He has abdicated government here withdrawing his governors, and _by declaring us out of his protec-_ declaring us out of his allegiance and protection. _tion, and waging war against us_

He has plundered our seas, ravaged our coasts, burnt our towns, and destroyed the lives of our people. **Ⓙ**

He is at this time transporting large armies of foreign mercenaries[14] to complete the works of death, desolation, and tyranny already begun with circumstances of cruelty and perfidy [ ] unworthy the head of a civilized nation. _scarcely paralleled in the most barbarous ages, and totally_

He has constrained our fellow citizens taken captive on the high seas, to bear arms against their country, to become the executioners of their friends and brethren, or to fall themselves by their hands.

He has [ ] endeavored to bring on the inhabitants of our frontiers, the _excited domestic insurrection_ merciless Indian savages, whose known rule of warfare is an undistinguished _among us, and has_ destruction of all ages, sexes, and conditions of existence.

He has incited treasonable insurrections of our fellow citizens, with the allurements of forfeiture and confiscation of our property.

---

12. **others:** members of British Parliament and their supporters and agents.
13. **neighboring province:** Quebec, in Canada.
14. **mercenaries:** professional soldiers hired to serve in foreign armies.

Ⓘ Reading Focus **Analyzing Arguments** To what general sphere of interest do all the actions in this paragraph refer? What is the main idea of the paragraph?

Ⓙ Literary Focus **Parallelism** What are the parallel structures within this sentence?

Vocabulary **perfidy** (PUR fuh dee) _n.:_ betrayal of trust.

He has waged cruel war against human nature itself, violating its most sacred rights of life and liberty in the persons of a distant people who never offended him, captivating and carrying them into slavery in another hemisphere, or to incur miserable death in their transportation thither. This piratical warfare, the opprobrium of infidel powers, is the warfare of the CHRISTIAN king of Great Britain. Determined to keep open a market where MEN should be bought and sold, he has prostituted his negative[15] for suppressing every legislative attempt to prohibit or to restrain this execrable commerce. And that this assemblage of horrors might want no fact of distinguished die,[16] he is now exciting those very people to rise in arms among us, and to purchase that liberty of which he has deprived them, by murdering the people on whom he also obtruded them: thus paying off former crimes committed against the LIBERTIES of one people, with crimes which he urges them to commit against the LIVES of another. **Ⓚ**

In every stage of these oppressions we have petitioned for redress in the most humble terms: Our repeated petitions have been answered only by repeated injuries.

A prince whose character is thus marked by every act which may define a tyrant is unfit to be the ruler of a [ ] people who mean to be free. Future ages will scarcely believe that the hardiness of one man adventured, within the short compass of twelve years only, to lay a foundation so broad and so undisguised for tyranny over a people fostered and fixed in principles of freedom.

  free

Nor have we been wanting in attentions to our British brethren. We have warned them from time to time of attempts by their legislature to extend a jurisdiction over these our states. We have reminded them of the circumstances of our emigration and settlement here, no one of which could warrant so strange a pretension: that these were effected at the expense of our own blood and treasure, unassisted by the wealth or the strength of Great Britain: that in constituting indeed our several forms of government, we had adopted one common king, thereby laying a foundation for perpetual league and amity with them: but that submission to their parliament was no part of our constitution, nor ever in idea, if history may be credited: and, we [ ] appealed to their native justice and magnanimity as well as to the ties of our

  an unwarrantable
  us

  have
  and we have conjured[17] them by

---

15. **negative:** veto.
16. **fact of distinguished die:** clear stamp or mark of distinction. Jefferson is being sarcastic here.
17. **conjured:** solemnly called upon.

Ⓚ Reading Focus Analyzing Arguments   It is well known that Thomas Jefferson owned slaves. Nevertheless, based on this material omitted from the Declaration by the Congress, what does his opinion of slavery seem to be?

Vocabulary   **opprobrium** (uh PROH bree uhm) *n.*: shameful conduct.
redress (rih DREHS) *n.*: correction for a wrong done.

common kindred to disavow these usurpations which were likely to interrupt our connection and correspondence. They too have been deaf to the voice of justice and of consanguinity,[18] and when occasions have been given them, by the regular course of their laws, of removing from their councils the disturbers of our harmony, they have, by their free election, reestablished them in power. At this very time too, they are permitting their chief magistrate to send over not only soldiers of our common blood, but Scotch and foreign mercenaries to invade and destroy us. These facts have given the last stab to agonizing affection, and manly spirit bids us to renounce forever these unfeeling brethren. We must endeavor to forget our former love for them, and hold them as we hold the rest of mankind, enemies in war, in peace friends. We might have been a free and a great people together; but a communication of grandeur and of freedom, it seems, is below their dignity. Be it so, since they will have it. The road to happiness and to glory is open to us too. We will tread it apart from them and acquiesce in the necessity which denounces[19] our eternal separation [ ]! **L**

would inevitably

We must therefore

and hold them as we hold the rest of mankind, enemies in war, in peace friends.

---

18. **consanguinity:** kinship; family relationship.
19. **denounces:** archaic for "announces" or "proclaims."

L **Reading Focus** **Analyzing Arguments** What is the main idea of this deleted passage? Do you think this paragraph added to Jefferson's arguments about equality? Explain.

HISTORY LINK

The History of the Document

The Declaration of Independence is one of the most important documents in American history. Today it is on display in Washington, D.C., behind a bullet-resistant glass case, surrounded by tight security. The United States has always been concerned about protecting this document. During the Revolutionary War the Continental Congress traveled with the document as they moved around, avoiding the British forces. During World War II it was briefly transferred to Fort Knox, Kentucky, and kept safely hidden away because of fears that America's enemies would attempt to destroy the document that marks the beginning of U.S. history.

Ask Yourself
Why do think protecting this document has always been so important to Americans?

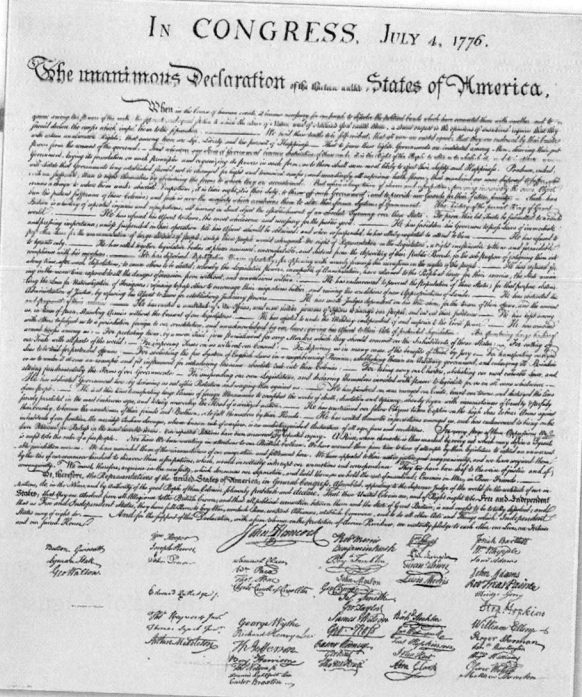

The Declaration of Independence.

Declaration of Independence, July 4, 1776 by John Trumbull (1756–1843). Oil on canvas.

We, therefore, the representatives of the United States of America in General Congress assembled, [ ] do in the name, and by the authority of the good people of these states reject and renounce all allegiance and subjection to the kings of Great Britain and all others who may hereafter claim by, through or under them; we utterly dissolve all political connection which may heretofore have subsisted between us and the people or parliament of Great Britain: And finally we do assert and declare these colonies to be free and independent states, and that as free and independent states, they have full power to levy war, conclude peace, contract alliances, establish commerce, and to do all other acts and things which independent states may of right do. **M**

And for the support of this declaration, [ ] we mutually pledge to each other our lives, our fortunes, and our sacred honor.

The Declaration thus signed on the 4th, on paper, was engrossed[20] on parchment, and signed again on the 2d of August.

appealing to the supreme judge of the world for the rectitude of our intentions,

colonies, solemnly publish and declare, that these united colonies are, and of right ought to be free and independent states; that they are absolved from all allegiance to the British crown, and that all political connection between them and the state of Great Britain is, and ought to be, totally dissolved;

with a firm reliance on the protection of divine providence,

---

20. engrossed: written in final draft.

M **Literary Perspectives** Analyzing Style Just as Jefferson uses vivid verbs—*refused, abdicated, plundered, constrained, incited*—in the list of charges against the king, he uses equally vivid verbs to describe the actions the Colonists are taking against the Crown. What is the effect of these verbs?

SKILLS FOCUS **Literary Skills** Analyze the use of parallelism; analyze characteristics of persuasion. **Reading Skills** Analyze persuasion/arguments in a text. **Writing Skills** Use parallelism correctly.

from The Autobiography:
The Declaration of Independence

Respond and Think Critically

Reading Focus

Quick Check

1. Why did Congress make cuts to the Declaration?

2. What is the main idea or main argument of the Declaration?

3. How does Jefferson feel about Congress's edits?

Read with a Purpose

4. How would you describe the beliefs and values of the delegates based on what they accepted and rejected?

Reading Skills: Analyzing Arguments

5. While reading, you examined parallelism in Jefferson's arguments about equality. Add a column to your chart, and explain how parallelism affects the meaning of each argument.

Summary of Argument	Use of Parallelism in Argument	Effects of Parallelism on Argument
All people are born with inalienable rights, and the government's responsibility is to secure these rights.	Each clause in the list of self-evident truths begins with "that."	The parallelism suggests that the ideas listed are equally important.

Literary Focus

Literary Analysis

6. **Interpret** Which changes seem to have been made to the Declaration of Independence for stylistic reasons, such as brevity or clarity, and which changes for political reasons? Explain.

7. **Extend** What insights about revision have you gained by reading this selection? Explain.

8. **Evaluate** Which version of the Declaration makes a more powerful argument for freedom, Jefferson's original text or Congress's revised text?

9. **Literary Perspectives** Judging from the writing in this selection, how would you describe Jefferson's style?

Literary Skills: Parallelism

10. **Compare and Contrast** Rewrite a few arguments from the text without using parallel structure. Are the arguments as effective without parallel structure? Why or why not?

Literary Skills Review: Loaded Words

11. **Interpret** The Declaration of Independence uses **loaded words,** or words with strong emotional overtones, to achieve its purpose. Using the word *despotism* to suggest that King George is a cruel tyrant is an example of loaded language. Re-read the second paragraph of the Declaration and gather other examples of loaded words. What effect does each have on the persuasiveness of the document?

Writing Focus

Think as a Reader/Writer

Use It in Your Writing The exposition at the beginning of the Declaration of Independence clarifies the document's purpose by summarizing the wrongs committed and listing the inalienable rights these wrongs violated. Write an argument against a wrong done to a person or group. Using parallel structure, write a brief list of the rights that have been violated.

What Do **You Think Now?** How did the unjust actions of the British government motivate the Colonists to change their lives?

from **The Autobiography:
The Declaration of Independence**

Vocabulary Development

✓ Vocabulary Check

Answer *true* or *false* to each of the following statements, and briefly explain your answer.

1. A leader ruling with **despotism** is fair and open.
2. If people show **assent,** they are in disagreement.
3. Someone's **tenure** refers to his or her time in office.
4. A person acting with **perfidy** is someone to be trusted.
5. **Opprobrium** deserves to be rewarded.
6. If someone hurts your feelings, you would want him or her to **redress** the situation.

Vocabulary Skills: Terms Used in Political Science and History

English has many words with origins in other languages. Many English words relating to law, politics, history, and education are borrowed from Latin or Greek. In reading political documents such as the Declaration of Independence, you will encounter many terms that come from one of these languages.

The best place to learn a word's origin—its **etymology**—is a dictionary. Most dictionaries include a bracketed etymology next to the definition. Here's part of a dictionary entry for the word *tyrant*:

> tyrant (TY ruhnt) *n.* [Middle English *tirant* < Old French *tiran, tirant* < Latin *tyrannus* < Greek *tyrannos*] 1. a brutal, oppressive ruler

The etymology of *tyrant* shows that the English word originates from (<) the Middle English word *tirant,* which in turn comes from the Old French *tiran* or *tirant.* The Old French words come from the Latin word *tyrannus,* which derives from the Greek word *tyrannos.*

Your Turn

Use a dictionary to research the etymology and meaning of each of the following political and historical terms. Record your information in a chart like the one below.

abdicate	judiciary	insurrection
colonies	democracy	constitution

Word	Etymology	Meaning
abolish	Latin *abolere,* "destroy"	to do away with

Language Coach

Double Consonants Working with a partner, look over the following list of words with double consonants. Then, using these words as models, come up with at least two other words that contain the same double consonant. For example, *different* should suggest *differentiate.* Use a dictionary to check to make sure that your words are correctly spelled.

different	**opposition**
irreversible	**bellicose**

Academic Vocabulary

Write About
In short written response, explain how the various <u>perspectives</u> of the delegates also represent concerns present in America today.

 **Learn It Online**
Use Word Watch online to get to know these Vocabulary words inside and out.

go.hrw.com L11-150   Go

Grammar Link

Choosing the Correct Pronoun Case

Case is the form that a pronoun takes to show its relationship to other words in a sentence. There are three pronoun cases: **nominative** (used as subjects), **objective** (used as objects), and **possessive** (used to show possession). Within each case, the forms of the personal pronouns indicate number, person, and gender.

	Nominative Case	Objective Case	Possessive Case
Singular			
First Person	I	me	mine
Second Person	you	you	your, yours
Third Person	he, she, it	him, her, it	his, her, hers, its
Plural			
First Person	we	us	our, ours
Second Person	you	you	your, yours
Third Person	they	them	their, theirs

Your Turn

Identify each personal pronoun in the sentences below. Then, identify its case; number (whether it is singular or plural); person; and, if applicable, its gender.

1. In the opening paragraphs, he sets forth the inalienable rights of humanity.
2. The king refused to approve laws that would help them.
3. You should learn how to be an effective and peaceful leader.

Writing Application Using pronouns, write a brief one-paragraph summary of the major charges against King George in the Declaration. Make sure that your pronouns are in the appropriate case and number.

CHOICES

As you respond to the Choices, use these **Academic Vocabulary** words as appropriate: aspect, cite, contemporary, interpret, perspective.

REVIEW
Examine History

Class Presentation Research the events surrounding and leading up to the writing of the Declaration of Independence. Find specific events that serve as examples of the king's unjust behavior and perfidy. Present the events to the class.

CONNECT
Research Dramatic Interpretations of Historical Events

Research popular entertainment based on the American Revolution, and find a movie or play that interests you. Obtain your teacher's approval to watch it. After viewing the film or play, write a summary of the work and a report on how it brought the events and era to life.

The Crossing (2000), a movie about the American Revolution.

EXTEND
Organize, and Declare Grievances

TechFocus Imagine that a tyrannical mayor has been elected in your community and is oppressing area teenagers with unjust curfews and restrictive laws. Form a group of representatives, and discuss how to formulate and present your grievances to the mayor's administration in a modern form. Use modern technology to illustrate the mayor's tyranny and to share your grievances. Then, present your modern Declaration to the class. Try to include at least one example of parallelism in your presentation.

Preparing to Read

DEKANAWIDA

from The Iroquois Constitution

ABIGAIL ADAMS

Letter to John Adams

ELIZABETH CADY STANTON

from Declaration of Sentiments . . .

What Do You Think? How can people's beliefs affect their actions?

 **QuickTalk**

Think of a time when you or someone you know envisioned a more fair and equitable way of doing something, such as dividing up chores or changing a school rule. How did you go about suggesting a change? How did others react to the suggestion? With a partner, discuss the situation and its outcome.

Dekanawida
(dates unknown)

According to legend, around 1500, a Mohawk visionary named Dekanawida convinced the five Iroquois nations to unite to establish peace and protect "life, property, and liberty." The resulting Iroquois Confederacy created the Iroquois Constitution, which gives members equal voice in the nations' affairs, spells out a system of checks and balances, guarantees religious freedom, and grants women extensive political power.

Abigail Adams
(1744–1818)

Although Abigail Smith had no formal education, she was a voracious reader. In 1764, she married John Adams, delegate to the First Continental Congress and future president. While John's duties kept him away, Abigail managed their farm, raised four children, and wrote more than three hundred letters. In 1776, Abigail wrote to her husband about the Declaration of Independence, urging him to consider the rights of women.

Elizabeth Cady Stanton
(1815–1902)

Elizabeth Cady was studying law in her father's office when she became aware of the inequalities women faced. In 1840, she married the abolitionist Harry Stanton. On their honeymoon at the World Anti-Slavery Convention, Cady Stanton met Lucretia Mott. Women were denied admission to the convention; as a result, Stanton and Mott began to plan a women's rights convention. It was held in 1848 in Seneca Falls, New York. There Stanton read the Declaration of Sentiments, calling for laws providing women voting rights and equal treatment.

Think About the Writers If these writers were alive today, would they be satisfied with gender and race equality in the United States? Explain.

from The Iroquois Constitution

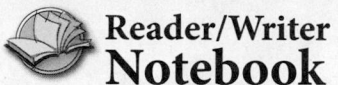

Reader/Writer
Notebook

Use your **RWN** to complete the activities for this selection.

Literary Focus

Symbolism A **symbol** is a person, place, thing, or event that has meaning in itself yet also stands for something more than itself. **Personal symbols** are created and developed by authors within their own works. **Public symbols** have a more universal meaning. The Iroquois Constitution uses several public symbols to represent political concepts.

Reading Focus

Analyzing Arguments The fight for equality is a universal conflict. The Iroquois Constitution created a political alliance of five major groups of Native Americans in an effort to bring about peace. In the constitution, Dekanawida argues that peace will arise from a society that guarantees a fair government, political and religious freedom, and respect for all people.

Into Action As you read, use a concept map like the one below to keep track of the symbols in Dekanawida's arguments about equality and freedom in the Iroquois Confederacy. How do the symbols convey a vision of a peaceful confederacy of nations?

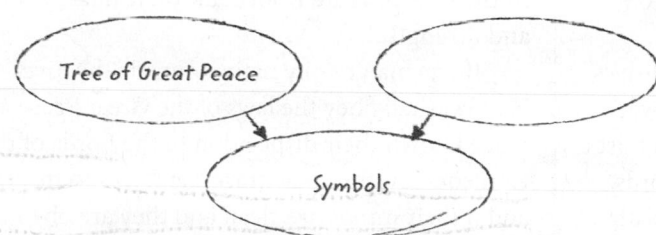

Tree of Great Peace

Symbols

Writing Focus

Think as a Reader/Writer

Find It in Your Reading The symbols in the Iroquois Constitution, such as the Tree of the Great Long Leaves, reflect a deep respect for the natural world. In your *Reader/Writer Notebook,* record the symbols of nature in the selection. How does nature imagery enhance the selection and represent the ideas of peace and equality?

Learn It Online
Let these letters and speeches come alive through the audio versions online.

go.hrw.com   L11-153   **Go**

from The Iroquois Constitution

by **Dekanawida**

Read with a Purpose
Read to learn how Iroquois beliefs about equality and freedom are reflected in the ideals that continue to shape American life.

Build Background
At the time that the Iroquois Constitution was framed, the Iroquois did not have a written language. After a written language was developed, the Iroquois Constitution was written from oral sources. The date of its original oral composition is not definitely known. Some new scholarship suggests that it may have originated three centuries earlier than 1451, the date on which most scholars have agreed until now. The Seneca's oral history mentions that the Iroquois Great Law of Peace was adopted shortly after a total eclipse of the sun. According to new research, such an eclipse was evident in upstate New York, where the Seneca convened to ratify their union, on August 13, 1142.

Tree of Great Peace

I am Dekanawida and with the Five Nations' Confederate Lords I plant the Tree of the Great Peace. I plant it in your territory, Adodarhoh, and the Onondaga Nation, in the territory of you who are Firekeepers.

I name the tree the Tree of the Great Long Leaves. Under the shade of this Tree of the Great Peace we spread the soft white feathery down of the globe thistle as seats for you, Adodarhoh, and your cousin Lords.

We place you upon those seats, spread soft with the feathery down of the globe thistle, there beneath the shade of the spreading branches of the Tree of Peace. There shall you sit and watch the Council Fire of the Confederacy of the Five Nations, and all the affairs of the Five Nations shall be transacted at this place before you, Adodarhoh, and your cousin Lords, by the Confederate Lords of the Five Nations.

Roots have spread out from the Tree of the Great Peace, one to the north, one to the east, one to the south, and one to the west. The name of these roots is The Great White Roots and their nature is Peace and Strength.

If any man or any nation outside the Five Nations shall obey the laws of the Great Peace and make known their disposition to the Lords of the Confederacy, they may trace the Roots to the Tree and if their minds are clean and they are obedient and promise to obey the wishes of the Confederate Council, they shall be welcomed to take shelter beneath the Tree of the Long Leaves. **(A)**

We place at the top of the Tree of the Long Leaves an Eagle who is able to see afar. If he sees in the distance any evil approaching or any danger threatening he will at once warn the people of the Confederacy. **(B)**

(A) **Literary Focus** Symbolism How do the roots literally and metaphorically represent strength?

(B) **Literary Focus** Symbolism The Iroquois chose the eagle as a symbol because they associated it with foresight. The eagle is also a symbol of the United States. What other symbolic associations does the eagle carry for Americans?

Leaders

The Lords of the Confederacy of the Five Nations shall be mentors of the people for all time. The thickness of their skin shall be seven spans—which is to say that they shall be proof against anger, offensive actions, and criticism. Their hearts shall be full of peace and goodwill and their minds filled with a yearning for the welfare of the people of the Confederacy. With endless patience they shall carry out their duty and their firmness shall be tempered with a tenderness for their people. Neither anger nor fury shall find lodgment in their minds and all their words and actions shall be marked by calm deliberation. **C**

Clans

The lineal descent of the people of the Five Nations shall run in the female line. Women shall be considered the progenitors of the Nation. They shall own the land and the soil. Men and women shall follow the status of the mother.

Symbols

Five arrows shall be bound together very strong and each arrow shall represent one nation. As the five arrows are strongly bound this shall symbolize the complete union of the nations. Thus are the Five Nations united completely and enfolded together, united into one head, one body, and one mind. Therefore they shall labor, legislate, and council together for the interest of future generations.

War and Peace

I, Dekanawida, and the Union Lords, now uproot the tallest pine tree and into the cavity thereby made we cast all weapons of war. Into the depths of the earth, down into the deep underearth currents of water flow-

Analyzing Visuals

Viewing and Interpreting Describe the characteristics of this man's clothes. Is there anything about his clothes that might be considered symbolic—that might have greater significance? Explain.

Not-to-way, or the Thinker, an Iroquois Chief (1835–1836) by George Catlin.

ing to unknown regions we cast all the weapons of strife. We bury them from sight and we plant again the tree. Thus shall the Great Peace be established and hostilities shall no longer be known between the Five Nations but peace to the United People. **D**

C **Reading Focus** **Analyzing Arguments** In this paragraph, what kinds of leaders does the constitution describe? How would this brand of leadership promote equality?

D **Literary Focus** **Symbolism** What is the symbolic meaning of burying the weapons of war deep in the earth? How do the pine tree and the currents of water add to this symbol?

Letter to John Adams

Reader/Writer Notebook

Use your **RWN** to complete the activities for this selection.

Literary Focus

Author's Purpose The **author's purpose** is the reason that he or she is writing. Authors write to inform, to persuade, or to entertain. Sometimes authors state their purposes directly. Other times, readers must determine the purpose by paying close attention to the details in the text. In her letter, Adams implies that men treat women as the British have treated the Colonists. How does this comparison help Adams achieve her political purpose?

Reading Focus

Analyzing Arguments In this heartfelt letter, Abigail Adams pleads with her husband to represent the voice of oppressed women as he and the other Founders draft the Declaration of Independence.

Into Action In the left-hand column of a chart, record Adams's arguments about gender equality as you read. In the right-hand column, explain how each argument helps Adams achieve her purpose.

Argument	How the Argument Helps Adams Achieve Her Purpose
"Do not put such unlimited power into the hands of the Husbands."	Her husband witnessed the consequences of unlimited power at the hands of King George III. Adams is trying to appeal to her husband's sense of justice.

Writing Focus

Think as a Reader/Writer

Find It in Your Reading **Loaded words** have strong emotional overtones and often elicit intense reactions. In your *Reader/Writer Notebook,* write down the loaded words, such as *tyrants,* that Adams uses in her letter. Make notes about why Adams might have used each word.

Vocabulary

foment (foh MEHNT) *v.:* stimulate; provoke. *Abigail Adams threatens to foment a revolt against the tyranny of men.*

impunity (ihm PYOO nuh tee) *n.:* immunity from harm or punishment. *With almost complete impunity, men could treat women cruelly and dishonorably.*

Language Coach

Common Phrases The word *impunity* is regularly introduced by the preposition *with,* to create the phrase "with impunity," indicating that someone did, or is able to do, something without fear of punishment. You will only rarely see *impunity* used alone.

 Learn It Online
Get to know the Vocabulary words through Word Watch online.

go.hrw.com   L11-156   **Go**

Letter to John Adams

by **Abigail Adams**

Read with a Purpose

Read to find out how Abigail Adams urges her husband to consider the rights of women when he helps draft the founding documents for a new nation.

Build Background

Abigail Adams wrote this letter when events were building toward the Revolutionary War. Parts of the letter describe a British military presence in Boston, where the Adams family owned a house. The house was briefly occupied by the British, a common occurrence in the Colonies. British occupation was a chief complaint in the Declaration of Independence.

March 31, 1776

I long to hear that you have declared an independency—and by the way in the new Code of Laws which I suppose it will be necessary for you to make I desire you would Remember the Ladies, and be more generous and favorable to them than your ancestors. Do not put such unlimited power into the hands of the Husbands. Remember all Men would be tyrants if they could. If particular care and attention is not paid to the Ladies we are determined to foment a Rebellion, and will not hold ourselves bound by any Laws in which we have no voice, or Representation. **Ⓐ**

That your Sex are Naturally Tyrannical[1] is a Truth so thoroughly established as to admit of no dispute, but such of you as wish to be happy willingly give up the harsh title of Master for the more tender and endearing one of Friend. Why then, not put it out of the power of the vicious and the Lawless to use us with cruelty and indignity with impunity. Men of Sense in all Ages abhor[2] those customs which treat us only as the vassals[3] of your Sex. Regard us then as Beings placed by providence under your protection and in imitation of the Supreme Being make use of that power only for our happiness. **Ⓑ**

A Adams

---

1. **tyrannical:** harsh; cruel; unjust.
2. **abhor:** turn away from in disgust; hate.
3. **vassals:** servants; subjects.

Ⓐ Literary Focus Author's Purpose What does Adams threaten that women will do if they are not given equal rights?

Ⓑ Reading Focus Analyzing Arguments How does Adams use religion to support her argument that men should consider women's rights?

Vocabulary **foment** (foh MEHNT) *v.:* stimulate; provoke.
impunity (ihm PYOO nuh tee) *n.:* immunity from harm or punishment.

from Declaration of Sentiments...

Reader/Writer Notebook

Use your **RWN** to complete the activities for this selection.

Literary Focus

Persuasive Devices Persuasion is a form of discourse that uses emotion or reason to convince a reader to think or act in a certain way. **Persuasive devices** include appeals to emotion and appeals to reason. An **emotional appeal** stirs up anger, sympathy, or other feelings. An appeal to reason shows **logical** connections between the argument and the real world. By using highly charged language in her list of men's abuses against women, Stanton appeals to both logic and emotion.

Reading Focus

Analyzing Arguments The fight for equality is a universal conflict. The Declaration of Sentiments, written in 1848, was a key document in the early days of American feminism and the fight for women's rights.

Into Action Use a chart first to summarize the arguments made in the Declaration. Then, explain why each argument is a logical appeal, an emotional appeal, or both.

Argument About Equality	Emotional or Logical Appeal, or Both?
Women have never been permitted to vote.	Logical, because it's a fact.

Writing Focus

Think as a Reader/Writer

Find It in Your Reading Parallel structure, or **parallelism,** is the repetition of words or phrases with similar grammatical structure, often used to emphasize or reinforce an author's argument. In your *Reader/Writer Notebook,* record examples of parallelism in Stanton's declaration. Make notes about how the use of parallelism affects the arguments' meanings.

TechFocus Stanton wrote her declaration in an effort to publicize the plight of women in her day. What other means might she have used to publicize her cause had she had access to today's technologies?

Vocabulary

covenant (KUHV uh nuhnt) *n.:* binding agreement; compact. *Stanton wants to form a covenant with men that ensures equal treatment for women.*

chastisement (chas TYZ muhnt) *n.:* punishment. *She protests the fact that men can subject women to chastisement without fear of punishment.*

remuneration (rih myoo nuh RAY shuhn) *n.:* payment. *Women are receiving little remuneration for employment.*

prerogative (prih RAHG uh tihv) *n.:* exclusive right or privilege. *Stanton says that men stole the prerogative to control women's destinies.*

abject (AB jehkt) *adj.:* hopeless. *Men have forced women to lead abject lives, with few options as to what they can do or be.*

Language Coach

Synonyms The five Vocabulary words above give a good sense of the richness of the English language. All five words have synonyms that are used in most everyday settings: *agreement, punishment, payment, right,* and *hopeless.* Each Vocabulary word, though, suggests something slightly different from these commonly used synonyms. Choose one of the Vocabulary words and its synonym. Then, write a brief explanation of how the two words are different in meaning.

Learn It Online

Explore modern methods of persuasion at the Media-Scope mini-site online.

go.hrw.com L11-158 **Go**

from
Declaration of Sentiments of the Seneca Falls Woman's Rights Convention

by **Elizabeth Cady Stanton**

Read with a Purpose
Read to learn how Stanton's arguments for women's rights echo the language and arguments in the Declaration of Independence.

Build Background
Elizabeth Cady Stanton is invariably linked with her lifelong friend and allied suffragist Susan B. Anthony. In the early years of their relationship, Stanton had young children and was unwilling to travel, so she wrote speeches for Anthony to deliver throughout the country. Although many ideological splits in the suffrage movement occurred over the years, Stanton and Anthony continued to stress a woman's right to vote.

Analyzing Visuals

Viewing and Interpreting What aspects of being a woman in the nineteenth century are depicted in this photograph? How might Stanton have responded to this depiction?

Elizabeth Cady Stanton and her daughter, Harriot. Daguerreotype.

When, in the course of human events, it becomes necessary for one portion of the family of man to assume among the people of the earth a position different from that which they have hitherto occupied, but one to which the laws of nature and of nature's God entitle them, a decent respect to the opinions of mankind requires that they should declare the causes that impel them to such a course.

We hold these truths to be self-evident: that all men and women are created equal; that they are endowed by their Creator with certain inalienable rights; that among these are life, liberty, and the pursuit of happiness; that to secure these rights governments are instituted, deriving their just powers from the consent of the governed. . . .

The history of mankind is a history of repeated injuries and usurpations on the part of man toward woman, having in direct object the establishment of an absolute tyranny over her. To prove this, let facts be submitted to a candid world. **Ⓐ**

He has never permitted her to exercise her inalienable right to the elective franchise.[1]

---

1. **inalienable . . . franchise:** right to vote, which cannot be taken away.

Ⓐ Reading Focus Analyzing Arguments How would you summarize the differences between Stanton's declaration and Thomas Jefferson's?

He has compelled her to submit to laws, in the formation of which she had no voice.

He has withheld from her rights which are given to the most ignorant and degraded[2] men—both natives and foreigners.

Having deprived her of this first right of a citizen, the elective franchise, thereby leaving her without representation in the halls of legislation, he has oppressed her on all sides. **B**

He has made her, if married, in the eye of the law, civilly dead.

He has taken from her all right in property, even to the wages she earns.

He has made her, morally, an irresponsible being, as she can commit many crimes with impunity, provided they be done in the presence of her husband. In the covenant of marriage, she is compelled to promise obedience to her husband, he becoming, to all intents and purposes, her master—the law giving him power to deprive her of her liberty, and to administer chastisement.

He has so framed the laws of divorce, as to what shall be the proper causes, and in case of separation, to whom the guardianship of the children shall be given, as to be wholly regardless of the happiness of women—the law, in all cases, going upon a false supposition of the supremacy of man, and giving all power into his hands.

After depriving her of all rights as a married woman, if single, and the owner of property, he has taxed her to support a government which recognizes her only when her property can be made profitable to it.

He has monopolized nearly all the profitable employments, and from those she is permitted to follow, she receives but a scanty remuneration. He closes against her all the avenues to wealth and distinction which he considers most honorable to himself. As a teacher of theology, medicine, or law, she is not known.

He has denied her the facilities for obtaining a thorough education, all colleges being closed against her. **C**

He allows her in Church, as well as State, but a subordinate position, claiming Apostolic[3] authority for her exclusion from the ministry, and, with some exceptions, from any public participation in the affairs of the Church.

He has created a false public sentiment by giving to the world a different code of morals for men and women, by which moral delinquencies which exclude women from society, are not only tolerated, but deemed of little account in man.

He has usurped the prerogative of Jehovah himself, claiming it as his right to assign for her a sphere of action, when that belongs to her conscience and to her God. **D**

He has endeavored, in every way that he could, to destroy her confidence in her own powers, to lessen her self-respect, and to make her willing to lead a dependent and abject life.

Now, in view of this entire disfranchisement[4] of one half the people of this country, their social and religious degradation—in view of the unjust laws above mentioned, and because women do feel themselves aggrieved, oppressed, and fraudulently deprived of their most sacred rights, we insist that they have immediate admission to all the rights and privileges which belong to them as citizens of the United States. . . .

---

2. **degraded:** disgraced; corrupted.

3. **Apostolic:** of the Apostles; directly from Jesus or the Gospels.
4. **disfranchisement:** act of taking away the rights of citizenship, especially the right to vote.

B **Literary Focus** Persuasive Devices Give two examples of Stanton's use of highly charged language in her list of abuses of women's rights. Explain how each example affects the argument's meaning.

C **Reading Focus** Analyzing Arguments How does the lack of education promote inequality?

D **Literary Focus** Persuasive Devices Summarize the argument in this paragraph. Does it appeal to logic or to emotion? Explain.

Vocabulary **covenant** (KUHV uh nuhnt) *n.:* binding agreement; compact.
chastisement (chas TYZ muhnt) *n.:* punishment.
remuneration (rih myoo nuh RAY shuhn) *n.:* payment.
prerogative (prih RAHG uh tihv) *n.:* exclusive right or privilege.
abject (AB jehkt) *adj.:* hopeless.

SKILLS FOCUS Literary Skills Analyze symbolism; analyze author's purpose; analyze persuasive devices.

Reading Skills Analyze persuasion/arguments in a text.

from **The Iroquois Constitution / Letter to John Adams /**
from **Declaration of Sentiments...**

Respond and Think Critically

Reading Focus

Quick Check

1. According to the Iroquois Constitution, who owns the land?

2. According to Abigail Adams, how should men treat women?

3. How does Stanton describe married women?

Read with a Purpose

4. What core beliefs about freedom and equality appear in all three documents? Explain.

Reading Skills: Analyzing Arguments

5. In these selections you encountered arguments from three different time periods. Use a chart first to summarize each selection's overall argument and position on social equality. Then, describe how these documents apply to life today.

Selection	Overall Argument	How It Applies Today
"Iroquois"	Peace requires equality, checks and balances, and religious and political freedom.	
"Letter"		
"Sentiments"		

Literary Focus

Literary Analysis

6. Extend How realistic is the Iroquois portrait of ideal leadership? Do you see these qualities in leaders today?

7. Evaluate Do you see any flaws in the reasoning in these three documents? Explain.

8. Make Judgments Has the passage of time made any of the writers' points of view irrelevant, or are their ideas timeless? Explain.

Literary Skills: Symbolism / Author's Purpose / Persuasive Devices

9. Interpret How do symbols affect the tone of the Iroquois Constitution? How might the document change if it didn't contain symbols?

10. Infer Do you think Adams believed she could help women's plight? Explain what you think Adams hoped to accomplish in her letter.

11. Analyze What is Stanton's primary mode of persuasion—emotion or reason? Support your answer with examples from the text.

Literary Skills Review: Argument

12. Make Judgments An **argument** appeals to both reason and emotion to convince someone to think or act a certain way. Based on your reactions to these texts, is an appeal to reason more effective than an appeal to emotion? Support your answer with textual evidence.

Writing Focus

Think as a Reader/Writer

Use It in Your Writing Write a persuasive letter convincing a state or community leader to support an issue of importance to you. Try to use symbols, loaded words, and parallel structure to add power and depth to your arguments.

What Do You Think Now

How does inequality motivate people? Why are negative situations often the driving force behind social progress?

from The Iroquois Constitution / Letter to John Adams / *from* Declaration of Sentiments…

Vocabulary Development

✓ Vocabulary Check

Choose the synonym, or word with almost the same meaning, of each Vocabulary word.

1.	covenant	a.	punishment
2.	chastisement	b.	dismal
3.	remuneration	c.	provoke
4.	prerogative	d.	compensation
5.	abject	e.	immunity
6.	foment	f.	privilege
7.	impunity	g.	compact

Vocabulary Skills: Terms Used in Political Science and History

A word's origin and development is called its **etymology.** Most dictionaries give the etymology of a word in brackets after its pronunciation and the abbreviation for its part of speech. Check the introduction of a dictionary for an explanation of how it organizes entries and what symbols and abbreviations it uses. Here is the beginning of a dictionary entry for *foment:*

> **foment** (foh MEHNT) *vt.* [L *fomentum,* a bandage < L *fovere,* to keep something warm to help it grow] to promote the growth of (something); incite

The etymology of *foment* shows that it comes from the Latin word *fomentum,* which means "a bandage." *Fomentum* comes from a Latin verb—*fovere*—that describes how heat promotes the growth of something. (For the Romans, a bandage kept the skin warm and in this way helped the skin regrow.) The English word *foment* retains this idea of helping something to grow or to develop.

Even if you already know a word, exploring its etymology can enrich your understanding of its meanings.

Your Turn

Use a dictionary to research the etymology and meaning of the following political and historical terms. Record your information in a chart like the one below.

covenant	declare	independence
consent	franchise	representation

Word	Etymology	Meaning
foment	L *fomentum,* "bandage" < *fovere,* "to keep warm"	to stir up or incite

Language Coach

Synonyms Working with a partner, complete the chart below by filling in all of the **synonyms** you can for each word. Then, discuss with your partner how each word suggests something slightly different from its synonyms.

Word	Synonyms
slowly	leisurely, unhurriedly, deliberately, lazily
control	
watch	

Academic Vocabulary

Write About
How does a person's perspective affect his or her opinion about inequality?

Wrap Up

SKILLS FOCUS Writing Skills Write comparison-contrast essays; write narratives. **Listening and Speaking Skills** Participate in formal/informal discussions and conversations; adapt to purpose when speaking: to persuade.

Political Points of View

Writing Focus

Writing a Comparison-Contrast Essay In what ways are the selections in Political Points of View alike and different? Re-read the selections to clarify your ideas. Then, write a short essay in which you compare and contrast two or three of the documents. You might choose to write about

- the way that the selections make their appeals or arguments
- the historical impact of the documents
- the documents' viewpoints on and promotion of social equality
- the viewpoints on women's rights in the various selections
- the expressed purposes of the selections

Review the elements of a successful comparison-contrast essay.

An effective comparison-contrast essay

- clearly states in the essay's opening paragraph what is being compared and contrasted
- conveys a main idea within a thesis statement
- is organized logically and effectively
- cites text passages to support ideas where appropriate
- contains few or no errors in spelling, punctuation, and grammar

What Do **You Think Now** Do you think we will ever live in a society completely free of inequality? How close do you think we are to reaching that goal?

CHOICES

As you respond to the Choices, use these **Academic Vocabulary** words as appropriate: aspect, cite, contemporary, interpret, perspective.

REVIEW

Review Chronology

Group Activity Review the time period of each selection by researching the historical events leading up to and surrounding the creation of each document. Create a time line that includes when each document was written (or composed). Then, fill in the time line with significant events related to the texts. After you finish, discuss with your group how reviewing the historical context of the selections deepens your understanding of them.

CONNECT

Connect the Past to Today

Timed Writing In an essay, identify and explain at least two issues presented in these selections that are represented in contemporary media today. Use specific examples from the texts and current media to support your argument.

EXTEND

Write a Story

Choose the document you read that you find most compelling or persuasive. Write a fictional narrative about a character who was alive when the document was created. How does this character react to the ideas and views expressed in the document? Your story should express your own point of view about the selection.

Preparing to Read

from The Autobiography
from Poor Richard's Almanack

What Do You Think

How can people's beliefs affect their actions?

QuickWrite

Write a short journal entry about a time when you or someone you know set out to achieve self-improvement. What was the goal, and what was the plan for accomplishing that goal? Were the efforts at self-improvement successful? Why or why not?

Benjamin Franklin
(1706–1790)

Boston-born Benjamin Franklin quickly rose from poverty to distinction, though he had to quit school to earn a living. By age twenty-four, Franklin was a prosperous merchant, owner of a successful print shop, and publisher of *The Pennsylvania Gazette*. He helped found the Academy of Philadelphia (which became the University of Pennsylvania), the American Philosophical Society, and the first public library in the United States. Franklin, a gifted scientist and inventor, invented an open heating stove (called a Franklin stove), bifocal eyeglasses, a type of harmonica, and a rocking chair that could swat flies.

Diplomat and Statesman

Franklin possessed uncommon talents as a diplomat, and he used these skills in the service of his country. In London, Franklin lobbied for the Colonies in their dispute with Britain and hoped to bring about a reconciliation that would prevent war. Franklin's wit and charm made him popular in London for many years; he once said that while in the city, he was invited out to dinner six nights a week. But by 1774, the stress between Britain and its Colonies had become too great. Franklin gave up his hopes for peace and sailed for the Colonies in 1775.

When Franklin arrived home, he learned that the first battles of the Revolutionary War had been fought. After helping Thomas Jefferson draft the Declaration of Independence in 1776, Franklin left for Paris to negotiate the treaty that brought the French into the war on the side of the Colonies. When the war ended, he helped mediate the peace. In 1787, Franklin served as a member of the Constitutional Convention. His death three years later was cause for international mourning.

Franklin's practicality, like the success story of his life, is typically American, but it has not been universally admired throughout the nation's history. The American novelist Herman Melville deplored Franklin's lack of imagination: "Jack-of-all-trades, master of each and mastered by none—the type and genius of his land. Franklin was everything but a poet."

Think About the Writer

How do you think Franklin was able to accomplish so much in so many fields?

Benjamin Franklin (detail) by Jean-Baptiste Greuze, after French, 1725–1805. Canvas (28 5/8 × 22 5/8 in.), detail. Gift of Adele Lewisohn Lehman. Photograph © Board of Trustees, National Gallery of Art, Washington.

from **The Autobiography /**
from **Poor Richard's Almanack**

Reader/Writer
Notebook
Use your **RWN** to complete the activities for these selections.

Literary Focus

Autobiography When a writer tells the story of his or her own life, the result is an **autobiography.** The word *autobiography* comes from the Greek words meaning "self," "life," and "writing." The following excerpt from Franklin's *Autobiography* illustrates his insights into the strengths and weaknesses of human nature.

Aphorisms An **aphorism** is a short, witty saying that offers a significant truth about life. Franklin collected his insights as aphorisms in *Poor Richard's Almanack*.

Reading Focus

Making Inferences When you read, you make educated guesses based on clues in the text and on your own knowledge and experience. These guesses are called **inferences.** You often need to look beneath the surface of a text to infer the writer's implicit, or suggested, thoughts.

Into Action As you read the excerpts from *The Autobiography* and *Poor Richard's Almanack*, use a chart for each selection to record words, phrases, or statements that you think provide clues to Franklin's attitudes and beliefs about human nature. Combine your knowledge with these details to infer Franklin's views.

Poor Richard's Almanack	Franklin's Views on Human Nature
"Three may keep a secret if two of them are dead."	People can't keep secrets.

Writing Focus

Think as a Reader/Writer

Find It in Your Reading In his *Autobiography*, Franklin looks back with gentle irony on himself as a young man. In your *Reader/Writer Notebook*, cite examples of Franklin's use of irony. What words or phrases seem to mock the idealism and expectations of his younger self?

TechFocus As you read these selections, consider what Franklin might think of the modern United States.

Vocabulary

arduous (AHR ju uhs) *adj.:* difficult. *Franklin finds the path to moral perfection an arduous one.*

rectitude (REHK tuh tood) *n.:* correctness. *It is easier to write about rectitude than to sustain it.*

facilitate (fuh SIHL uh tayt) *v.:* make easier. *According to Franklin, the acquisition of some virtues will facilitate the acquisition of others.*

subsequent (SUHB suh kwuhnt) *adj.:* following. *He thinks temperance will create a foundation for the subsequent virtues on his list.*

eradicate (ih RAD uh kayt) *v.:* eliminate. *Franklin hopes it will take only thirteen weeks to eradicate bad behavior.*

Language Coach

Collocations The way words combine or are arranged in a language is **collocation.** An important part of using a word is choosing the right collocation for it. Take *facilitate*, for instance. A common adverb used with *facilitate* is *further*. A common verb phrase used with *facilitate* is *[be] designed to*. Write two sentences, one with "further facilitate" and one with "is designed to facilitate" or "are designed to facilitate."

Learn It Online
Find out more about Franklin online.

go.hrw.com 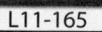 L11-165 **Go**

from
The Autobiography

by **Benjamin Franklin**

Read with a Purpose
Read to discover the philosophy of a man whose wisdom, humor, and diplomacy helped shape the United States of America.

Build Background
Franklin began *The Autobiography* when he was sixty-five. Although he worked on it intermittently for years, he never finished it and it was not published during his lifetime. When Franklin was a teenager, he worked as an apprentice—an employee who works without pay while learning a trade—for his older brother James, who printed a Boston newspaper. Disputes arose between the brothers, and the younger Franklin fled Boston for Philadelphia to escape from a second indenture, or contract of service, that his brother had forced him to sign. This selection begins with Franklin's arrival in Philadelphia.

Arrival in Philadelphia

I have been the more particular in this description of my journey, and shall be so of my first entry into that city, that you may in your mind compare such unlikely beginnings with the figure I have since made there. I was in my working dress, my best clothes being to come round by sea. I was dirty from my journey; my pockets were stuffed out with shirts and stockings, and I knew no soul nor where to look for lodging. I was fatigued with traveling, rowing, and want of rest, I was very hungry; and my whole stock of cash consisted of a Dutch dollar, and about a shilling in copper. The latter I gave the people of the boat for my passage, who at first refused it, on account of my rowing; but I insisted on their taking it. A man being sometimes more generous when he has but a little money than when he has plenty, perhaps through fear of being thought to have but little. **A B**

Then I walked up the street, gazing about till near the market house I met a boy with bread. I had made many a meal on bread, and, inquiring where he got it, I went immediately to the baker's he directed me to, in Second Street, and asked for biscuit, intending such as we had in Boston; but they, it seems, were

A **Reading Focus** **Making Inferences** What kind of "figure" does Franklin imply that he has since made of himself?

B **Reading Focus** **Making Inferences** Franklin has almost no money and is very hungry. Why then does he insist on paying for his passage on the boat? Based on this action, what can you infer about his character?

Analyzing Visuals

Viewing and Interpreting Look at this painting, and consider the message it sends about Franklin. What meanings might the quills, the lightning, and his fine clothes be intended to convey? How does this image contrast with Franklin's description of himself as a young man arriving in Philadelphia?

Portrait of Benjamin Franklin (1789) by Charles Willson Peale (1741–1827). Oil on canvas.

not made in Philadelphia. Then I asked for a three-penny loaf, and was told they had none such. So not considering or knowing the difference of money, and the greater cheapness nor the names of his bread, I bade him give me three-penny worth of any sort. He gave me, accordingly, three great puffy rolls. I was surprised at the quantity, but took it, and, having no room in my pockets, walked off with a roll under each arm, and eating the other. Thus I went up Market Street as far as Fourth Street, passing by the door of Mr. Read, my future wife's father; when she, standing at the door, saw me, and thought I made, as I certainly did, a most awkward, ridiculous appearance. Then I turned and went down Chestnut Street and part of Walnut Street, eating my roll all the way, and, coming round, found myself again at Market Street wharf, near the boat I came in, to which I went for a draft[1] of the river water; and, being filled with one of my rolls, gave the other two to a woman and her child that came down the river in the boat with us, and were waiting to go farther. **C**

Thus refreshed, I walked again up the street, which by this time had many clean-dressed people in it, who were all walking the same way. I joined them, and thereby was led into the great meetinghouse of the Quakers[2] near the market. I sat down among them, and, after looking round awhile and hearing nothing said, being very drowsy through labor and want of rest the preceding night, I fell fast asleep, and continued so till the meeting broke up, when one was kind enough to rouse me. This was, therefore, the first house I was in, or slept in, in Philadelphia. . . . **D**

---

1. **draft:** gulp or swallow.
2. **Quakers:** members of the Religious Society of Friends, a Christian group founded in the seventeenth century.

C Literary Focus **Autobiography** Why do you think Franklin mentions the first impression he made on his future wife? What does it reveal about his character?

D Reading Focus **Making Inferences** Based on Franklin's experience in the Quaker meeting house, what inferences can you draw about the Quakers Franklin met?

E Literary Focus **Autobiography** Where in this paragraph does Franklin seem to be mocking his younger self? Explain your answer.

Arriving at Moral Perfection

It was about this time I conceived the bold and arduous project of arriving at moral perfection. I wished to live without committing any fault at any time; I would conquer all that either natural inclination, custom, or company might lead me into. As I knew, or thought I knew, what was right and wrong, I did not see why I might not always do the one and avoid the other. But I soon found I had undertaken a task of more difficulty than I had imagined. While my care was employed in guarding against one fault, I was often surprised by another; habit took the advantage of inattention; inclination was sometimes too strong for reason. I concluded, at length, that the mere speculative conviction that it was our interest to be completely virtuous,[3] was not sufficient to prevent our slipping; and that the contrary habits must be broken, and good ones acquired and established, before we can have any dependence on a steady, uniform rectitude of conduct. For this purpose I therefore contrived the following method. **E**

In the various enumerations of the moral virtues I had met with in my reading, I found the catalog more or less numerous, as different writers included more or fewer ideas under the same name. Temperance, for example, was by some confined to eating and drinking, while by others it was extended to mean the moderating every other pleasure, appetite, inclination, or passion, bodily or mental, even to our avarice and ambition. I proposed to myself, for the sake of clearness, to use rather more names, with fewer ideas annexed to each, than a few names with more ideas; and I included under thirteen names of virtues all that at that time occurred to me as necessary or desirable, and annexed to each a short precept,[4] which fully expressed the extent I gave to its meaning. **F**

---

3. **virtuous:** morally excellent; pure.
4. **precept:** rule of moral conduct; principle.

F Literary Focus **Autobiography** Skim over the virtues listed in red type in the next column. If you were writing your own autobiography, which virtue would you describe as your strongest? Why?

Vocabulary **arduous** (AHR juh uhs) *adj.:* difficult.
rectitude (REHK tuh tood) *n.:* correctness.

These names of virtues, with their precepts, were:

1. **Temperance.** *Eat not to dullness; drink not to elevation.*

2. **Silence.** *Speak not but what may benefit others or yourself; avoid trifling[5] conversation.*

3. **Order.** *Let all your things have their places; let each part of your business have its time.*

4. **Resolution.** *Resolve to perform what you ought; perform without fail what you resolve.*

5. **Frugality.** *Make no expense but to do good to others or yourself; i.e., waste nothing.*

6. **Industry.** *Lose no time; be always employed in something useful; cut off all unnecessary actions.*

7. **Sincerity.** *Use no hurtful deceit; think innocently and justly, and, if you speak, speak accordingly.*

8. **Justice.** *Wrong none by doing injuries, or omitting the benefits that are your duty.*

9. **Moderation.** *Avoid extremes; forbear resenting injuries so much as you think they deserve.*

10. **Cleanliness.** *Tolerate no uncleanliness in body, clothes, or habitation.*

11. **Tranquility.** *Be not disturbed at trifles, or at accidents common or unavoidable.*

12. **Chastity.** *Rarely use venery[6] but for health or off-spring, never to dullness, weakness, or the injury of your own or another's peace or reputation.*

13. **Humility.** *Imitate Jesus and Socrates.[7]* **Ⓖ**

My intention being to acquire the habitude of all these virtues, I judged it would be well not to distract my attention by attempting the whole at once, but to fix it on one of them at a time; and, when I should be master of that, then to proceed to another, and so on, till I should have gone through the thirteen; and, as the previous acquisition of some might facilitate

---

5. **trifling:** unimportant; shallow.
6. **venery:** sex.
7. **Socrates** (SAHK ruh teez) (470?–399 B.C.): Greek philosopher who is said to have lived a simple, virtuous life.

Ⓖ **Reading Focus** Making Inferences If the adjective *trifling* means "unimportant" ("avoid trifling conversation"), what can you infer about the meaning of the noun *trifles* ("be not disturbed at trifles")?

Ben's Lightning Bells

Benjamin Franklin Drawing Electricity from the Sky (detail) by Benjamin West. Oil on canvas.

Benjamin Franklin was extremely curious about the natural world, and his need to know led to scientific experiments and inventions that improved many people's lives. Franklin created the first bifocals, the first odometer, and an early furnace called the Franklin stove. Above all, he was fascinated by electricity. After conducting his famous key-and-kite experiment, he attached a metal rod to the roof of his house to attract lightning. He used wires to connect the lightning rod to a set of bells inside his house. When there was lightning in the air, electricity would run through the rod and the wires, and the bells would ring. Franklin could then observe and experiment with his favorite natural phenomenon.

Ask Yourself
Which virtues from Franklin's list may have contributed to his many scientific pursuits and inventions?

---

the acquisition of certain others, I arranged them with that view, as they stand above. *Temperance* first, as it tends to procure that coolness and clearness of head, which is so necessary where constant vigilance was to be kept up, and guard maintained against the unremitting[8] attraction of ancient habits, and the

---

8. **unremitting:** not stopping; persistent.

Vocabulary **facilitate** (fuh SIHL uh tayt) *v.:* make easier. **subsequent** (SUHB suh kwuhnt) *adj.:* following.

Temperance							
Eat not to dullness. Drink not to elevation.							
	S	M	T	W	T	F	S
T							
S							
O							
R							
F							
I							
S							
J							
M							
Cl							
T							
Ch							
H							

Form of the pages for Franklin's book of virtues.

force of perpetual temptations. This being acquired and established, *silence* would be more easy; and my desire being to gain knowledge at the same time that I improved in virtue, and considering that in conversation it was obtained rather by the use of the ears than of the tongue, and therefore wishing to break a habit I was getting into of prattling, punning, and joking, which only made me acceptable to trifling company, I gave *silence* the second place. This and the next, *order,* I expected would allow me more time for attending to my project and my studies. *Resolution,* once become habitual, would keep me firm in my endeavors to obtain all the subsequent virtues; *frugality* and *industry* freeing me from my remaining debt, and producing affluence and independence, would make more easy the practice of *sincerity* and *justice,* etc., etc.

Conceiving then, that, agreeably to the advice of Pythagoras[9] in his Golden Verses, daily examination would be necessary, I contrived the following method for conducting that examination. **H**

I made a little book, in which I allotted a page for each of the virtues. I ruled each page with red ink, so as to have seven columns, one for each day of the week, marking each column with a letter for the day. I crossed these columns with thirteen red lines, marking the beginning of each line with the first letter of one of the virtues, on which line, and in its proper column, I might mark, by a little black spot, every fault I found upon examination to have been committed respecting that virtue upon that day.

I determined to give a week's strict attention to each of the virtues successively. Thus, in the first week, my great guard was to avoid every[10] the least offense against *temperance,* leaving the other virtues to their ordinary chance, only marking every evening the faults of the day. Thus, if in the first week I could keep my first line, marked T, clear of spots, I supposed the habit of that virtue so much strengthened, and its opposite weakened, that I might venture extending my attention to include the next, and for the following week keep both lines clear of spots. Proceeding thus to the last, I could go through a course complete in thirteen weeks, and four courses in a year. And like him who, having a garden to weed, does not attempt to eradicate all the bad herbs at once, which would exceed his reach and his strength, but works on one of the beds at a time, and, having accomplished the first, proceeds to a second, so I should have, I hoped, the encouraging pleasure of seeing on my pages the progress I made in virtue, by clearing successively my lines of their spots, till in the end, by a number of courses, I should be happy in viewing a clean book, after a thirteen weeks' daily examination. . . . **I** **J**

---

9. **Pythagoras** (pih THAG uh ruhs): Greek philosopher and mathematician of the sixth century B.C.
10. **every:** archaic for "even."

H **Reading Focus** **Making Inferences** What does Franklin's plan reveal about his character?

I **Reading Focus** **Making Inferences** Based on your knowledge of Franklin's life, how successful do you think his project was? Explain.

J **Literary Focus** **Autobiography** Franklin wrote his autobiography when he was an elderly man. How might the book be different if he had written it when he was young?

Vocabulary **eradicate** (ih RAD uh kayt) *v.:* eliminate.

from

Poor Richard's Almanack

by **Benjamin Franklin**

Read with a Purpose
Read to experience Franklin's legendary sense of humor and insight into human nature.

Build Background
With the publication of *Poor Richard's Almanack* in 1732, Franklin found his biggest publishing success, and he continued to publish his almanac for twenty-five years. Almost every household had an almanac. Almanacs calculated the tides and the phases of the moon, forecast the weather for the next year, and even provided astrological advice. Many almanacs also supplied recipes, jokes, and aphorisms. Poor Richard was an imaginary astrologer with a critical wife named Bridget. One year, Bridget wrote aphorisms to answer those her husband had written the year before on female idleness. Another time, Bridget included "better" weather forecasts so that people would know the good days for drying their clothes. Franklin's practicality shows itself not only in the content of his almanacs but also in the way he put them together. He borrowed wit and wisdom from a variety of sources. He printed old sayings translated from other languages, lifted some aphorisms from other writers, and adapted other aphorisms from popular and local sources. An American to the core, Franklin never hesitated to rework what he found to suit his own purposes. For example, Franklin skimmed all previous editions of the almanac and reused phrases to compose a single speech on economy in the 1758 almanac. This speech, titled "The Way to Wealth," has become one of Franklin's best-known works. It has been mistakenly believed to represent Poor Richard's wisdom. Poor Richard often called for prudence and thrift, but he just as often favored extravagance.

Title page of the first edition of Benjamin Franklin's almanac.
The Granger Collection, New York.

INDUSTRY NEEDS NOT WISH, AND HE THAT LIVES UPON HOPE WILL DIE FASTING

THERE ARE NO GAINS WITHOUT PAINS: THEN HELP HANDS, FOR I HAVE NO LANDS

Analyzing Visuals

Viewing and Interpreting
This engraving stresses the importance of work. Judging from Franklin's aphorisms, what other aspects of life does Franklin find important?

Poor Richard Illustrated: Panel from an engraving, c. 1800, for Benjamin Franklin's publication, with the mottoes, "Industry Needs Not Wish, And He That Lives Upon Hope Will Die Fasting" and "There Are No Gains Without Pains: Then Help Hands, For I Have No Lands." The Granger Collection, New York.

1. Love your neighbor; yet don't pull down your hedge.
2. If a man empties his purse into his head, no man can take it away from him. An investment in knowledge always pays the best interest.
3. Three may keep a secret if two of them are dead.
4. Tart words make no friends; a spoonful of honey will catch more flies than a gallon of vinegar.
5. Glass, china, and reputation are easily cracked and never well mended.
6. Fish and visitors smell in three days.
7. He that lieth down with dogs shall rise up with fleas.
8. One today is worth two tomorrows.
9. A truly great man will neither trample on a worm nor sneak to an emperor.
10. A little neglect may breed mischief; for want of a nail the shoe was lost; for want of a shoe the horse was lost; for want of a horse the rider was lost; for want of the rider the battle was lost.

11. If you would know the value of money, go and try to borrow some; he that goes a-borrowing goes a-sorrowing.
12. He that composes himself is wiser than he that composes books.
13. He that is of the opinion that money will do everything may well be suspected of doing everything for money.
14. If a man could have half his wishes, he would double his troubles.
15. 'Tis hard for an empty bag to stand upright.
16. A small leak will sink a great ship.
17. A plowman on his legs is higher than a gentleman on his knees.
18. Keep your eyes wide open before marriage, half shut afterward.
19. Nothing brings more pain than too much pleasure; nothing more bondage than too much liberty. Ⓐ Ⓑ

Ⓐ **Literary Focus** Aphorisms Which aphorisms on this page have similar messages? Explain.

Ⓑ **Reading Focus** Making Inferences Infer some possible purposes of aphorisms, based on the aphorisms you have read here. When and why do people use aphorisms?

Applying Your Skills

SKILLS FOCUS **Literary Skills** Analyze the characteristics of autobiography; analyze aphorisms; analyze author's purpose. **Reading Skills** Make inferences as a strategy for comprehension.

from The Autobiography / *from* Poor Richard's Almanack

Respond and Think Critically

Reading Focus

Quick Check

from **The Autobiography**

1. What is Franklin's condition in life when he arrives in Philadelphia?

2. Describe the project Franklin undertook when he was a young man.

Read with a Purpose

3. After reading the excerpts from Franklin's writings, how would you describe his personality and character?

Reading Skills: Making Inferences

4. Review the inference charts you made as you read each selection. Match up similar inferences about Franklin's views, and then write a few sentences summarizing his main beliefs about human nature.

Literary Focus

Literary Analysis

5. **Interpret** In *The Autobiography*, Franklin writes about "arriving at moral perfection" just as he had earlier written about his arrival in Philadelphia. What does this similarity in his language reveal about Franklin's philosophical assumptions?

6. **Infer** In *The Autobiography*, Franklin discusses his attempt to learn the habit of virtues. What can you infer about his character from this discussion? Explain.

7. **Hypothesize** How do Franklin's aphorisms convey so much meaning in so few words? Explain.

8. **Analyze** Why do you think Franklin had a fictional character narrate *Poor Richard's Almanack*? Explain your response.

9. **Evaluate** Do you think aphorisms like those in *Poor Richard's Almanack* are helpful to people? Why or why not?

Literary Skills: Autobiography / Aphorisms

10. **Infer** Reactions to *The Autobiography* have sometimes been negative. What <u>aspects</u> of the autobiography might have been criticized?

11. **Interpret** Many of Poor Richard's aphorisms convey moral lessons. Choose one of the aphorisms, and restate it in your own words.

Literary Skills Review: Author's Purpose

12. **Compare and Contrast** Authors have many reasons, or **purposes,** for writing. They may write to entertain, inform, or persuade. Both Benjamin Franklin and Jonathan Edwards (page 106) wrote about their values, which were deeply rooted in Puritanism. Compare and contrast these authors' purposes.

Writing Focus

Think as a Reader/Writer

Use It in Your Writing Re-read the list of words that Franklin uses to mock his younger self. Review your QuickWrite. Then, rewrite your journal entry as if you were much older and were looking back on the goal and plan. Include words and phrases that gently mock any unrealistic ideals presented.

 What Do You Think Now

How does Franklin's drive to change his life and better himself compare with that of most people you know? Is Franklin a good role model? Why or why not?

Vocabulary Development

✓ Vocabulary Check

Fill in each blank with the appropriate Vocabulary word.

arduous
rectitude
facilitate
subsequent
eradicate

In order to _____ his task, Franklin tried to _____ everything that stood in the way of moral _____. It was an _____ program, but his _____ career proved it was worth the effort.

Vocabulary Skills: Context Clues

A word's **context**—the words and sentences that surround it—often gives clues to the word's meaning. When you encounter an unfamiliar word, try using context clues to infer the word's meaning. Look at the following example—one of the Vocabulary words from *The Autobiography.*

Context: "And like him who, having a garden to weed, does not attempt to <u>eradicate</u> all the bad herbs at once, which would exceed his reach and his strength . . ." (page 170).

Inferences: Franklin mentions *eradicating* weeds in a garden. He calls weeds "bad herbs." You know that weeds are bad for a garden and that people pull them. You can then infer that *eradicate* probably means "remove" or "get rid of."

Context clues: The words *weed* and *bad* are clues that help you understand the meaning of *eradicate.*

Your Turn

With a partner, read the first paragraph of "Arriving at Moral Perfection" (page 168). Look for context clues to the meaning of the word *inclination*, which Franklin uses twice in this paragraph. Define *inclination,* and discuss the context clues that support your definition.

Language Coach

Collocations Earlier you learned about **collocations,** the natural way words are often arranged.

Now take a look at some collocations for the Vocabulary word *eradicate:*

"successfully eradicate"

"an effort to eradicate"

"help eradicate"

"impossible to eradicate"

"eradicate [something] from"

With a partner, write example sentences using each collocation for *eradicate* listed above.

Academic Vocabulary

Talk About

Those who see Franklin as a symbol of American character often <u>cite</u> his self-reliance and independence. With a partner, <u>cite</u> examples from Franklin's *Autobiography* and *Poor Richard's Almanack* that support the view of Franklin as independent and self-reliant.

Learn It Online

Learn how to use context clues the interactive way—online with *WordSharp.*

go.hrw.com   L11-174   **Go**

Grammar Link

Pronoun-Antecedent Agreement

Writers use **pronouns**—words such as *she* and *it* that stand in for nouns—to make their writing flow smoothly. The word or word group for which a pronoun stands is called the **antecedent.** An antecedent almost always comes before its pronoun in a sentence or paragraph. (The word *antecedent* comes from Latin roots meaning "go before.") A pronoun and its antecedent agree in both number and gender.

In the following example from Franklin's *Autobiography,* pronouns and their antecedents are surrounded by the same shapes. Note that the pronoun *I* is unusual—it doesn't always have an antecedent. In nonfiction, *I* often refers to the author.

I met a boy with bread. I had made many a meal on bread, and, inquiring where he got it, I went immediately to the baker's he directed me to.

Your Turn

Fill in the blanks in the following sentences with pronouns that agree with their antecedents. Then, circle the correct antecedent.

1. Though Franklin had little money, _____ gave away some of his food.

2. The grateful woman fed _____ child.

3. Franklin created a plan to rid himself of all _____ faults.

4. His goals are lofty, aren't _____?

5. Ambitious readers can try to improve _____ own lives by following Franklin's plan.

CHOICES

As you respond to the Choices, use these **Academic Vocabulary** words as appropriate: aspect, cite, contemporary, interpret, perspective.

REVIEW

Present a Monologue

Group Activity In a small group, create a **monologue**, a speech delivered by a single character, based on the excerpt from Benjamin Franklin's *Autobiography*. Before writing, discuss which details to include and how you will preserve unique aspects of Franklin's writing, such as his vocabulary and tone. Choose a group member to perform the monologue, or break it into sections so each person can perform.

CONNECT

Introduce the Present to the Past

TechFocus Benjamin Franklin was very important in the creation of the United States. What would he think of the country today? In a small group, prepare a multimedia presentation introducing Franklin to the contemporary world. Use images, music, and text to explain modern life to him. In your presentation, keep in mind the personality and opinions of Franklin as they appear in these excerpts. Tune your presentation to his particular character and interests. Share your presentation with your class.

EXTEND

Write Aphorisms

Partner Work Access *Poor Richard's Almanack* on the U.S. Department of State's Web site, and choose one edition from which to read the preface and maxims. Then, meet with a partner who has read a different edition of the almanac and exchange your favorite aphorisms. Together, create several aphorisms of your own to share with the class.

Preparing to Read

Link to Today

The Man of Many Masks *from* The Americanization of Benjamin Franklin

What Do You Think

How can people's beliefs affect their actions?

⏱ **QuickWrite**

Think of someone you know who tends to avoid revealing personal information. Why might this person choose to conceal many of his or her beliefs? Write about what can be gained and lost from hiding your beliefs.

Informational Text Focus

Analyzing Author's Argument An **argument** is a form of persuasion that appeals to both reason and emotion to convince an audience to think or act a certain way. To make their arguments strong, authors often cite facts, show statistics, and display concrete evidence. In this selection, Gordon S. Wood argues that Benjamin Franklin was a "man of many masks," or a person who was hard to get to know.

Into Action To analyze Wood's argument, pay close attention to the facts, statistics, and evidence he uses to support it. In a concept map such as this one, list the support you find for Wood's argument.

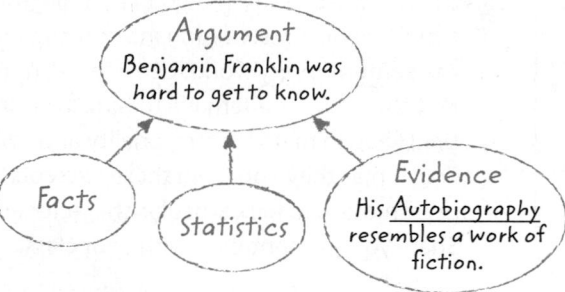

Argument
Benjamin Franklin was hard to get to know.

Facts

Statistics

Evidence
His *Autobiography* resembles a work of fiction.

Writing Focus Preparing for **Constructed Response**

As you read, make a list in your *Reader/Writer Notebook* of the quotations about Franklin that Wood borrows from other sources. Consider how each quotation supports Wood's argument. Why is it valuable to include quotations from others in a biography?

Reader/Writer Notebook

Use your **RWN** to complete the activities for this selection.

Vocabulary

reticent (REHT uh suhnt) *adj.*: hesitant to speak; quiet. *The author Gordon S. Wood claims that Franklin is reticent when it comes to speaking about himself.*

obscurity (uhb SKYUR uh tee) *n.*: the condition of being unknown. *Some people liked to remind Franklin that he lived his early life in obscurity.*

personas (puhr SOH nuhz) *n.*: public personalities. *Franklin hides his true identity behind many personas.*

pseudonymous (soo DAHN uh muhs) *adj.*: bearing a false name. *Franklin wrote many pseudonymous articles.*

rhetorical (rih TAWR uh kuhl) *adj.*: intended especially for display; artificial. *His rhetorical tricks often caused a great stir.*

berate (bih RAYT) *v.*: scold harshly. *In his writing, Franklin could mock and berate others skillfully.*

Language Coach

Word Roots In *pseudonym*, *pseudo–* means "false" and *–nym* means "name." Use the root *–nym* to help unlock the meaning of other English words such as *synonym*, *antonym*, and *anonymous*. Learn as much as you can about the roots of words.

Link to Today

This Link to Today provides a broad look at Benjamin Franklin's writing and what it does and does not reveal about his life.

Read with a Purpose
Read this article to discover how Benjamin Franklin maintained his privacy despite leading a very public life.

Build Background
This selection comes from Pulitzer Prize–winning author Gordon S. Wood's *The Americanization of Benjamin Franklin*, which was published in 2004. In the biography, Wood attempts to examine how Franklin, who for many years sympathized with the British, became widely known as a symbol of American values and beliefs. Americans often mistrusted Franklin during his lifetime. In fact, Franklin's death was mourned more widely in Europe than it was in the United States. Franklin's journey from rags to riches and his success in business received widespread attention only after his death. The inventor and writer became known as a model of self-improvement and industriousness. In this sense, the author argues, he was fully "Americanized."

The Man of Many Masks

from The Americanization of Benjamin Franklin

by **Gordon S. Wood**

Paris street sign Rue Benjamin Franklin, 16th arrondissement.

Franklin is not an easy man to get to know. Although he wrote more pieces about more things than any of the other Founders, Franklin is never very revealing of himself. He always seems to be holding something back—he is reticent, detached, not wholly committed. We sense in Franklin the presence of calculated restraint—a restraint perhaps bred by his spectacular rise and the kind of hierarchical[1] and patronage-ridden[2] world he had to operate in. Certainly there were people in Philadelphia who never let him forget "his original obscurity," and that he had sprung from "the meanest Circumstances."[3] Despite complaining that he was never able to order things in his life, we sense that he was always in control and was showing us only what he wanted us to see. Only at moments in the early 1770s and at the end of his life do we sense that the world was spinning out of his grasp.

Beyond the restrained and reserved character of his personal writings is the remarkable character of his public writings, especially his

---

1. **hierarchical:** focused on rank, grade, and so forth.
2. **patronage-ridden:** filled with political deals and favors.
3. **the meanest circumstances:** Franklin was one of seventeen children born to a soap and candle maker.

Vocabulary **reticent** (REHT uh suhnt) *adj.:* hesitant to speak; quiet.
obscurity (uhb SKYUR uh tee) *n.:* the condition of being unknown.

Viewing and Interpreting
Compare and contrast the image of Franklin depicted in this sculpture with the image Gordon Wood conveys in "The Man of Many Masks." Discuss your ideas with a small group or with the class as a whole.

View from below of the Benjamin Franklin National Memorial—James Earl Fraser, sculptor.

Autobiography[4]—"this most famous of American texts," as one scholar calls it. Literary scholars have continually interpreted and reinterpreted the *Autobiography* but still cannot agree on what Franklin was trying to do in writing it. Among the Founders, Jefferson and Adams also wrote autobiographies, but theirs are nothing like Franklin's. His resembles a work of fiction in that we cannot be sure that the narrative voice is the same as the author's. Indeed, much of

the reader's enjoyment of the *Autobiography* comes from the contrast between Franklin's descriptions of the "awkward ridiculous Appearance" the teenaged printer made upon his arrival in Philadelphia and "the Figure I have since made there." It is hard to interpret the *Autobiography,* since, as scholars have pointed out, Franklin moves between several personas, especially between the innocence of youth and the irony of a mature man.

In all of Franklin's writings, his wit and humor, his constant self-awareness, his assuming different personas and roles, make it difficult to know how to read

---

4. ***Autobiography:*** an incomplete self-portrait that was published after Franklin's death.

A Informational Focus Analyzing Author's Argument
The author notes that Franklin's *Autobiography* resembles fiction because "we cannot be sure that the narrative voice is the same as the author's." What does Wood mean? How does this statement support the author's argument that Franklin is hard to get to know?

Vocabulary **personas** (puhr SOH nuhz) *n.:* public personalities.

him. He was a man of many voices and masks who continually mocks himself. Sometimes in his newspaper essays he was a woman, like "Silence Dogood," "Alice Addertongue," "Cecilia Shortface," and "Polly Baker," saucy and racy and hilarious. At other times he was the "Busy Body," or "Obadiah Plainman," or "Anthony Afterwit," or "Richard Saunders," also known as "Poor Richard," the almanac maker. Sometimes he wrote in the London newspapers as "An American" or "A New England-Man." But other times he wrote as "A Briton" or "A London Manufacturer," and shaped what he wrote accordingly. During his London years he wrote some ninety pseudonymous items for the press using forty-two different signatures. For each of the many pieces he wrote both in Philadelphia and in London he had a remarkable ability to create the appropriate persona. Indeed, all of his many personas contribute nicely to the particular purpose of his various works, whether they are essays, skits, poems, or satires. "Just as no other eighteenth-century writer has so many moods and tones or so wide a range of correspondents," declares the dean of present-day Franklin scholars, "so no other eighteenth-century writer has so many different personae or so many different voices as Franklin." No wonder we have difficulty figuring out who this remarkable man was. **B**

Of all the Founders, Franklin had the fullest and deepest understanding of human nature. He had a remarkable capacity to see all sides of human behavior and to appreciate other points of view. He loved turn-

> # He was a man of many voices and masks who continually mocks himself.

ing conventional wisdom on its head, as, for example, when he argued for the virtue and usefulness of censure[5] and backbiting. But then again are we sure that he is not putting us on? He certainly enjoyed hoaxes and was the master of every rhetorical ploy. No American writer of the eighteenth century could burlesque,[6] deride, parody, or berate more skillfully than he. He could praise and mock at the same time and could write on both sides of an issue with ease.

It is easy to miss the complexity and subtlety of Franklin's writing. He praises reason so often that we forget his ironic story about man's being a reasonable creature. In his *Autobiography* he tells us about how he abandoned his youthful effort to maintain a vegetarian diet. Although formerly a great lover of fish, he had come to believe that eating fish was "a kind of unprovok'd Murder." But one day when he smelled some fish sizzling in a frying pan, he was caught hanging "between Principle and Inclination." When he saw that the cut-open fish had eaten smaller fish, however, he decided that "if you eat one another, I don't see why we mayn't eat you." And so he had heartily dined on cod ever since. "So convenient a thing it is to be a *reasonable Creature*," he concluded, "since it enables one to find or make a Reason for every thing one has a mind to do." **C**

---

5. **censure:** strong disapproval.
6. **burlesque:** to imitate in a way that makes fun of.

B **Informational Focus** Analyzing Author's Argument
What three qualities of Franklin's writing make him difficult to read? Choose one of these qualities, and explain why it adds to his mystery.

C **Informational Focus** Analyzing Author's Argument
Why do you think the author includes this anecdote about Franklin's vegetarianism? How does it support the author's argument?

Vocabulary **pseudonymous** (soo DAHN uh muhs) *adj.*: bearing a false name.
rhetorical (rih TAWR uh kuhl) *adj.*: intended especially for display; artificial.
berate (bih RAYT) *v.*: scold harshly.

Franklin's Arrival in Philadelphia by Newell Convers Wyeth (1882–1945/American). Oil on canvas.

None of the Founders was more conscious of the difference between appearance and reality than Franklin. Not only did he continually comment on that difference, but he was never averse to maintaining it. If one could not actually be industrious and humble, he said, at least one could appear to be so.

Although he wrote against disguise and dissimulation and asked, "Who was ever cunning enough to conceal his being so?" we nevertheless know that he was the master of camouflage and concealment. "We shall resolve to be what we would seem," he declared, yet at the same time he seems to have delighted in hiding his innermost thoughts and motives. "Let all Men know thee," Poor Richard said, "but no man know thee thoroughly: Men freely ford that see the shallows."

While sometimes bowing to the emerging romantic cult of sincerity, he remained firmly rooted in the traditional eighteenth-century world of restraining one's inner desires and feelings in order to be civil and get along. He never thought that his characteristic behavior—his artful posing, his role playing, his many masks, his refusal to reveal his inner self—was anything other than what the cultivated and sociable eighteenth century admired. He was a thoroughly social being, enmeshed in society and civic-minded by necessity. Not for him the disastrous assertions of antisocial autonomy and the outspoken sincerity of Molière's character Alceste in *Le Misanthrope*. Like many others of his day, Franklin preferred the sensible and prudent behavior of Alceste's friend Philinte, who knew that the pat of good sense was to adapt to the pressures and contradictions of society. Unlike, say, John Adams, Franklin never wore his heart on his sleeve; he kept most of his intentions and feelings to himself. He was a master at keeping his own counsel. As Poor Richard said, "Three may keep a Secret, if two of them are dead."

Franklin is so many-sided, he seems everything to everyone, but no image has been more powerful than that of the self-improving businessman. This modern image of Franklin began to predominate with the emergence of America's democratic capitalism in the early republic; and, like Alexis de Tocqueville's[7] description of that rambunctious democratic America, Franklin's personification of its values has had a remarkable staying power. Just as we continue to read Tocqueville's *Democracy in America* for its insights into the democratic character of our society in our own time nearly two centuries later, so too do we continue to honor Franklin as the Founder who best exemplifies our present-day democratic capitalist society. As the symbol of an American land of opportunity where one works hard to get ahead, Franklin continues to have great meaning, especially among recent immigrants. **(D)**

---

7. **Alexis de Tocqueville's:** Tocqueville was a scientist, politician, and historian best known for his analysis of nineteenth-century American society.

(D) Informational Focus **Analyzing Author's Argument** In this paragraph, the author mentions that Franklin has become a symbol. What does he symbolize? How might being seen as a symbol end up obscuring one's true identity?

Applying Your Skills

SKILLS FOCUS Reading Skills Understand and analyze persuasion/arguments in a text. **Vocabulary Skills** Demonstrate word knowledge.

The Man of Many Masks *from* The Americanization of Benjamin Franklin

Respond and Think Critically

Informational Text Focus

Quick Check

1. Which of Benjamin Franklin's writings is referred to as "this most famous of American texts"?

2. List some of the personas and "masks" that Franklin used in his writings.

3. Which of Franklin's images does the author claim is the most powerful?

Read with a Purpose

4. How did Franklin maintain his privacy despite leading a very public life?

Informational Skills: Analyzing Author's Argument

5. Look at the facts, statistics, and evidence you recorded in your concept map while you read. Underline the pieces of evidence you find most convincing. Explain your choices in a few sentences.

✓ Vocabulary Check

Match each Vocabulary word with its definition.

6. reticent	**a.** intended for show
7. obscurity	**b.** scold
8. personas	**c.** having a false name
9. pseudonymous	**d.** reserved
10. rhetorical	**e.** public identities
11. berate	**f.** state of being unknown

Text Analysis

12. **Infer** The author describes Franklin's "spectacular rise" and quotes Franklin about surviving "'the meanest Circumstances.'" What can you infer about Franklin's life from these statements?

13. **Compare and Contrast** How does Franklin's autobiography differ from the autobiographies of Jefferson and Adams, as Wood describes them? Explain.

14. **Interpret** Poor Richard, one of Franklin's personas, said, "Three may keep a secret if two of them are dead." How does it help you understand Franklin's choice to keep his identity private?

15. **Extend** The author asserts that Franklin symbolizes the "American land of opportunity." How does Franklin's life reflect this spirit? Why might Franklin still be a powerful symbol today, especially for recent immigrants? Explain.

Listening and Speaking

16. **Analyze** Benjamin Franklin used as many as forty-two different personas throughout his writing career. Choose three personas named in the text. In a small group, discuss what is unique about the personality, perspective, and attitude of each persona. Take notes as you discuss.

Writing Focus Constructed Response

Briefly explain how the author's use of quotations support's his argument in "The Man of Many Masks." Be sure to cite specific evidence to support your response.

What Do You Think Now How might people's beliefs about historical figures such as Benjamin Franklin motivate them to change their own lives?

Writing Workshop

Editorial

Write with a Purpose

Write an editorial that includes a clear position for your school newspaper on an issue that you feel strongly about. Your **purpose** is to persuade others to take a stand or to take action on this issue. Your **audience** is the students, staff, and community who read your school newspaper. Keep these readers in mind as you write.

A Good Editorial

- addresses an issue that is important to you
- conveys why the issue is important
- demonstrates evidence and reasoning to which the audience can respond
- uses rhetorical devices
- inspires readers to take a stand or take action on the issue

See page 190 for complete rubric.

Reader/Writer Notebook

Use your **RWN** to complete the activities for this workshop.

Think as a Reader/Writer You've seen how writers persuade readers to take action. In this workshop, you will persuade others by writing an **editorial.** Before you begin, read this excerpt from Stephen Jay Gould's article "A Time of Gifts," written shortly after the terrorist attacks of September 11, 2001.

> The patterns of human history mix decency and depravity in equal measure. We often assume, therefore, that such a fine balance of results must emerge from societies made of decent and depraved people in equal numbers. But we need to expose and celebrate the fallacy of this conclusion so that, in this moment of crisis, we may reaffirm an essential truth too easily forgotten and regain some crucial comfort too readily forgone. Good and kind people outnumber all others by thousands to one. The tragedy of human history lies in the enormous potential for destruction in rare acts of evil, not in the high frequency of evil people. . . . [E]very spectacular incident of evil will be balanced by ten thousand acts of kindness, too often unnoted and invisible as the "ordinary" efforts of a vast majority.
>
> We have a duty, almost a holy responsibility, to record and honor the victorious weight of these innumerable little kindnesses when an unprecedented act of evil so threatens to distort our perception of ordinary human behavior. I have stood at ground zero, stunned by the twisted ruins of the largest human structure ever destroyed in a catastrophic moment.....The scene is insufferably sad, but not at all depressing....In human terms, ground zero is the focal point for a vast web of bustling goodness, channeling unaccountable deeds of kindness from an entire planet—the acts that must be recorded to reaffirm the overwhelming weight of human decency.... My wife and stepdaughter established a depot on Spring Street to collect and ferry needed items in short supply... to workers at ground zero. Word spreads like a fire of goodness, and people stream in, bringing gifts, from a pocketful of batteries to a ten-thousand dollar purchase of hard hats....

← The introduction captures **readers' interest** with a bold statement.

← Gould clearly states his **opinion**.

← Gould gives **reasons** why he holds his opinion.

← Gould supports his reasons with **evidence**—examples of goodness.

Think about the Professional Model

With a partner, discuss the following questions about the model.

1. How does Gould persuade the reader to see his viewpoint?
2. How does he use language to stress the importance of his argument?

SKILLS FOCUS Writing Skills Write persuasive essays
or articles; support persuasive arguments and opinions with
reasons and evidence; address potential objections; include a
call to action; use the fundamentals of the writing process to
improve writing.

Prewriting

Choose an Issue

Inciting people to riot is a crime, but getting them to think about the **issues** is not. Which issues are important to you? What changes would you like to see in your school, in your community, or in the world?

- Talk to friends, classmates, and parents about issues of concern.
- Read your local newspaper to find out what issues people care about. Pay attention to editorials and letters to the editor.
- Attend student council meetings, school board meetings, or city or town meetings to see what issues are important to people.

Make a list of a few ideas that interest you and that might interest others. Do you have strong feelings about any of these issues? Choose one that you can make a convincing argument for or against in an editorial. The issue you choose should be something about which reasonable people can disagree—there's no point in arguing, for example, that cars should stop at school crosswalks.

Think About Purpose and Audience

Your **purpose** in writing an editorial is to persuade an **audience** of readers to share your opinion on an issue and to take action. To convince readers, you need to know something about them. Answer the following questions:

- How much do my readers know about the issue?
- What background information should I provide for readers who are unfamiliar with the issue?
- What are the concerns of readers who disagree with my position?
- What **counterarguments** can I use to address their concerns?
- What would motivate my readers to take action?

Identify Your Thesis

The **thesis statement** of an editorial (also sometimes called a **opinion statement, position statement,** or **proposition**) is a statement of the writer's opinion or position on the issue. Planning your thesis statement will help you focus your ideas and gather relevant evidence. You can use a graphic organizer like the one below to create your opinion statement. The example shown is based on the excerpt from "A Time of Gifts" shown on page 182.

The Issue	Position	Opinion Statement
The depravity or decency of people	More people are decent than are depraved.	"Good and kind people outnumber all others by thousands to one."

You may not have a definite opinion on your issue, yet. Your position may evolve as you gather more information about the issue.

Idea Starters

- What situation seems unjust or unfair?
- What makes you angry?
- What issue makes you want to take action?
- What issues are people in your school or community talking about?

Your Turn

Get Started In your **RWN,** freewrite ideas you have about the **issue** you have chosen. Decide on your **position,** and then write down your thesis, or **opinion statement.** Keep your audience and purpose in mind as you begin to write.

Learn It Online
To see how one writer completed this assignment, see the model editorial online:

 go.hrw.com L11-183

Support Your Opinion

Simply stating your opinion isn't enough to convince your audience to take your side of an issue. You must give your reader adequate **reasons** for your opinion. To persuade your readers, you should balance different kinds of appeals:

- **logical appeals**—give facts (statistics and examples) and expert opinions
- **emotional appeals**—use descriptive details, connotative language, and anecdotes that evoke emotions, plus rhetorical devices, such as repetition
- **ethical appeals**—show your experience, character, and trustworthiness, and call upon your reader's sense of right and wrong

Each reason should be supported by **evidence** that is relevant, or strongly tied to your issue. Kinds of evidence include

- **facts and statistics**
- **examples**
- **anecdotes** (short personal stories)
- **expert opinions**
- **cause-effect reasoning**

If the connection between a reason and its evidence isn't obvious, **elaborate** by explaining how the evidence supports your argument.

Examine the graphic organizer below to see how Stephen Jay Gould supports his opinion statement in "A Time of Gifts" with reasons and evidence. He provides additional reasons and evidence in the rest of his article, not excerpted in this workshop.

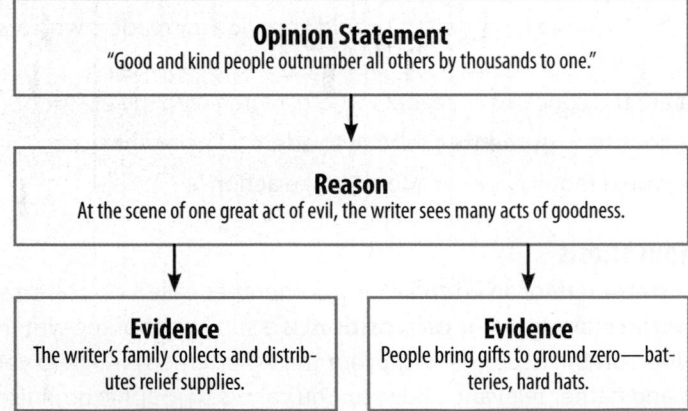

Opinion Statement
"Good and kind people outnumber all others by thousands to one."

Reason
At the scene of one great act of evil, the writer sees many acts of goodness.

Evidence
The writer's family collects and distributes relief supplies.

Evidence
People bring gifts to ground zero—batteries, hard hats.

The body paragraphs of your editorial should develop each of the reasons in your argument by presenting and elaborating on evidence.

Organize Your Support

A strong organizational structure can aid your editorial's persuasiveness. Consider using **order of importance**. Begin with your strongest reason to get your audience's attention, or save it for last to leave your audience with a strong impression. If you use your strongest reason last, consider opening with your second-strongest reason—to begin and end with your two best arguments.

Writing Tip

Some of your reasons may be **counterarguments,** or reasons that refute the reasons of the opposing viewpoint. For instance, Gould refutes the idea that the scene at ground zero is depressing.

Your Turn _____

Plan Your Support In your **RWN,** use a graphic organizer like the one on this page to plan support—**reasons and evidence**—for your opinion. If you like, add an additional row of boxes for **elaboration,** in which you explain how each piece of evidence supports the corresponding reason.

Drafting

Follow the Writer's Framework

As you write your first draft, remember to include reasons and evidence that support your opinion statement. Use your prewriting notes and organizers as a guide. You may want to structure your editorial according to the **Writer's Framework** to the right.

Use Rhetorical Devices

Rhetorical devices are methods writers use to enhance their arguments and make their writing effective. Try incorporating some of the following devices as you write your editorial:

- **Repetition** is the use of a word, phrase, or clause more than once for emphasis. Notice the repetition in this excerpt from a speech by Dr. Martin Luther King, Jr.:

  "**Let freedom ring** from Lookout Mountain of Tennessee! **Let freedom ring** from every hill and molehill of Mississippi. From every mountainside, **let freedom ring.**"

- **Rhetorical questions** are questions that are not meant to be answered but are asked for effect. For example, your editorial might ask, "Is our community brave enough to face this challenge?" (The obvious answer would be *yes*.)

- **Parallelism** is the repetition of the same grammatical form to express equal, or **parallel,** ideas. For example, you pair a noun with a noun, a phrase with a phrase, a clause with a clause, and an infinitive with an infinitive.

Framework for an Editorial

Introduction
- Attention-grabbing beginning
- Background information on the issue
- Clear opinion statement

Body
- Second-strongest reason and supporting evidence
- Other reasons and supporting evidence
- Strongest reason and supporting evidence

Conclusion
- Restatement of opinion
- Call to action

● Writing Tip

As you write your draft, think about your audience members and what evidence or argument will be most persuasive to them.

Grammar Link Using Parallelism

Parallelism is not only an effective rhetorical device; it is also an element of correct grammar and usage. Use parallel structure when you coordinate ideas, compare or contrast ideas, or link ideas with correlative conjunctions:

both . . . and   *either . . . or*   *neither . . . nor*   *not only . . . but also*

Notice how Stephen Jay Gould uses parallelism to contrast ideas:

> The tragedy of human history lies **in the enormous potential** for destruction in rare acts of evil, not **in the high frequency** of evil people. [prepositional phrase paired with prepositional phrase]

Reference Note For more on parallelism, see the Language Handbook.

Your Turn

Write Your Draft Use your plan for support, as well as the **Writer's Framework,** to write your first draft of your editorial. Use **repetition, rhetorical questions,** and **parallel structure** to enhance your argument.

Peer Review

Working with a peer, use the chart at the right to review each other's drafts. If you are confused by something in your partner's draft, ask questions. Give your peer-review partner specific, constructive suggestions about how to improve his or her editorial. When it is your turn to receive feedback, accept comments graciously and recognize them as a chance to improve your writing.

Evaluating and Revising

Read the questions in the left column of the chart below, and then follow the tips in the center column to see if you need to make revisions. The right column suggests techniques for revising your draft.

Editorial: Guidelines for Content and Organization

Evaluation Question	Tip	Revision Technique
1. Does the introduction catch the reader's interest?	**Highlight** sentences that serve to pull readers into the editorial.	**Add** a startling fact or opinion, an anecdote, or a rhetorical question that captures reader interest.
2. Does the introduction contain a clear opinion statement?	**Underline** the opinion statement. If it doesn't clearly identify the issue and your position, revise.	**Add** an opinion statement near the beginning of the editorial. **Replace** an unclear opinion statement.
3. Does the editorial include at least two convincing reasons? Is each reason supported by at least one piece of evidence?	**Circle** the reasons that support the opinion statement. **Bracket** facts, statistics, examples, anecdotes, expert opinions, and cause-effect reasoning.	**Add** reasons or **replace** weak reasons. **Add** evidence to support each reason.
4. Do rhetorical devices enhance the argument?	**Put a star** beside the sentences that contain repetition, rhetorical questions, and parallelism.	**Add** rhetorical devices, if necessary.
5. Are the reasons well organized?	**Number** the reasons and rank them according to their strength and persuasiveness.	**Rearrange** reasons so that they will have the greatest impact on the audience.
6. Does the conclusion include a restatement of the opinion and give a call to action?	**Underline** the restatement of your opinion. **Double underline** the call to action.	**Add** a restatement of your opinion. **Add** a call to action.

Read this student's draft and the comments about it as a model for evaluating and revising your own draft.

Safe Teen Driving

by Becca Aaronson, LBJ (Lyndon B. Johnson) High School

I've been driving to school since midway through my freshman year. I am a safe driver and love to drive.

Many people argue that teenagers should not be allowed to drive until 18 because of the threat new drivers pose to themselves and other people on the road. Taking away this privilege would be an injustice on many levels. Much of the maturity, responsibility, and independence teenagers develop in high school comes from driving. The same dangers would still exist if teenagers began driving at 18 rather than 16. At 18, they simply don't have their parents to put limitations on their freedom.

All drivers know that when they started driving, they were horrible: swerving into lanes, going the wrong way on one-way streets, slamming on the brakes at every stop sign. It's undeniable that the many accidents are caused by new drivers' inexperience—not age. If people began driving at 18, the age bracket with the most accidents would simply switch to 18-20.

*Becca's introduction includes a personal statement, but it does not grab the **reader's attention**.*

*She addresses the main **argument** of the **opposing viewpoint** and then clearly states her **position**.*

*Becca begins with her **strongest reason**—a **counterargument** to the opinion that accidents involving teens are a result of the driver's age.*

MINI-LESSON ▶ How to Catch Your Reader's Interest

Becca can revise her draft for a more effective beginning by catching the reader's interest with concrete, sensory details. Other good attention-getters are anecdotes, startling facts, or rhetorical questions. Notice that Becca's original draft lacks a "hook" to draw readers into her editorial.

Becca's Draft of Paragraph 1:

I've been driving to school since midway through my freshman year. I am a safe driver, and I love to drive

Becca's Revision of Paragraph 1:

Slip in the key, roll down the windows, push in the clutch, shift into gear, and carefully back down the driveway: my morning ritual. Then I check my rearview mirror and back slowly and carefully down the driveway.

I've been driving to school since midway through my freshman year. I am a safe driver, ~~and I love to drive.~~

Your Turn _____

Catch Reader Interest Read your draft, and then ask yourself which of the following would best help grab your readers' attention:

- concrete details
- an anecdote
- a startling fact
- a rhetorical question

Student Draft *continues*

This is Becca's **least strong reason**—parental oversight.

Her **evidence** includes cause-effect reasoning.

> In fact, there are advantages to learning to drive while you're still legally bound to your parents. When most teenagers begin driving, their parents put limitations on where they can go, who they can drive with, and what distractions should be eliminated. If people had to teach themselves to drive after the age of 18, they would be expected to be responsible, qualified drivers without any of the experience that comes from learning in slow steps. It is safer for teenagers to gain an awareness of how dangerous the road is under the supervision of experienced drivers—their parents. If I hadn't been taught this way, I know I wouldn't take the responsibility as seriously.

Becca's **second-strongest reason**—some families need teen drivers—is supported by a personal **anecdote**.

> Furthermore, special cases exist when families need someone to drive at an even younger age. For instance, my parents are divorced. I had to constantly travel between living arrangements. The fact that I could drive was a help to my entire family. My parents were tired of hauling baskets of clothing, sports equipment, and me, from house to house every week. It shouldn't be the government's decision as to whether a teenager is ready for a driver's license; it should be the family's decision.

Her conclusion **restates her opinion,** but it fails to include a call to action.

> The top priority should be creating safe drivers for the future. The first couple of years are hard for every new driver—of any age. However, if we spend time coaching our children to be safe, mature, and responsible, it is better that they have the opportunity to begin driving at 16, while still under parental supervision. Even if I do grind the gears once in a while, I am a more responsible person for having been given the opportunity to drive at 16.

MINI-LESSON ▶ How to Conclude with a Call to Action

Becca's draft ends by restating her opinion and including the vivid sensory image of grinding gears. However, she could strengthen her conclusion by adding a **call to action.** The purpose of persuasive writing is to create change. If there's a specific action your readers can take regarding your issue, direct them to do it. Becca adds a call to action to make her conclusion even more effective.

Becca's Draft of Paragraph 6:

> . . . Even if I do grind the gears once in a while, I am more responsible for having been given the opportunity to drive at 16.

Becca's Revision of Paragraph 6:

> Even if I do grind the gears once in a while, I am a more responsible person for having been given the opportunity to drive at 16. Talk to your parents, school administrators, and community leaders to make sure that 16-year-olds continue to have the opportunity to learn responsibility and independence as they learn to drive safely.

Your Turn

Add a Call to Action Ask a peer to read the final paragraph of your draft.

- Is there a specific action that you are asked to take on the issue?
- If so, is it reasonable, that is, something that you can do?
- Are the language and ideas persuasive enough to motivate you to take action?

Incorporate your partner's suggestions into your final draft.

Proofreading and Publishing

Proofreading

The last step in writing your editorial is to make sure your work is free of mistakes so that readers can focus on your ideas. Careless errors can make it hard for readers to follow your ideas, which can completely undermine your argument. Work with a peer to **proofread,** or **edit,** your work.

- Use reference materials, such as the Language Handbook in this book, to make sure you have avoided common errors.
- Use grammar- and-spell checkers, but don't depend on them solely. For example, a spell-checker will not catch an error in which you accidentally use *they're* when you intend to use *their*.
- Look for places where inserting commas would clarify **items in a series.**

> ### Grammar Link Using Commas with Items in a Series
>
> In your editorial, you might have listed **items in a series,** such as facts, examples, or parallel ideas. Be sure to use commas to separate items in a series. For instance, in Becca's conclusion, she uses commas to separate parallel ideas that are listed in a series.
>
> > However, if we spend time coaching our children to be safe, mature, and responsible, it
> >
> > is better that they have the opportunity to begin driving at 16, while still under parental
> >
> > supervision.
>
> **Reference Note** For more on using commas with items in a series, see the Language Handbook.

Publishing

Share your editorial with readers who are affected by the issue. Here are some ways to publish your editorial with a wider audience:

- Submit your editorial to a newspaper in your community.
- Post your editorial on a Web site that is focused on similar issues.
- Present your editorial at a school or community meeting.

Reflect on the Process In your **RWN,** write short responses to each of the following questions:

1. What constructive advice did you receive from your peer reviewer? How did it help you?
2. Did writing your editorial change your understanding of the issue you wrote about? If so, how?
3. How important is your evidence to the effectiveness of your editorial?

Proofreading Tip
Read your work aloud slowly to make sure that every sentence is complete. Remember to use parallelism to balance related ideas in your editorial.

Writing Tip
For clarity, some writers prefer always to use a comma before the conjunction (*and, or, nor*) in a series. Follow your teacher's instructions on this point.

Your Turn _____
Proofread and Publish Using the strategies and tips on this page, proofread your editorial to correct errors, including using commas with items in a series. When you are satisfied that your editorial is ready, use the publishing suggestions on this page to get it out to readers.

Scoring Rubric

Use one of the rubrics below to evaluate your editorial from the Writing Workshop or your response to the on-demand prompt on the next page. Your teacher will tell you to use either the six- or the four-point rubric.

6-Point Scale

Score 6 *Demonstrates advanced success*
- focuses consistently on a clear and reasonable position
- shows effective organization throughout, with smooth transitions
- offers thoughtful, creative ideas and reasons
- supports a position thoroughly, using convincing, fully elaborated reasons and evidence
- exhibits mature control of written language

Score 5 *Demonstrates proficient success*
- focuses on a clear and reasonable position
- shows effective organization, with transitions
- offers thoughtful ideas and reasons
- supports a position competently, using convincing, well-elaborated reasons and evidence
- exhibits sufficient control of written language

Score 4 *Demonstrates competent success*
- focuses on a reasonable position, with minor distractions
- shows effective organization, with minor lapses
- offers mostly thoughtful ideas and reasons
- elaborates reasons and evidence with a mixture of the general and the specific
- exhibits general control of written language

Score 3 *Demonstrates limited success*
- includes some loosely related ideas that distract from the writer's position
- shows some organization, with noticeable gaps in the logical flow of ideas
- offer routine, predictable ideas and reasons
- supports ideas with uneven reasoning and elaboration
- exhibits limited control of written language

Score 2 *Demonstrates basic success*
- includes loosely related ideas that seriously distract from the writer's persuasive purpose
- shows minimal organization, with major gaps in the logical flow of ideas
- offers ideas and reasons that merely skim the surface
- supports ideas with inadequate reasoning and elaboration
- exhibits significant problems with control of written language

Score 1 *Demonstrates emerging effort*
- shows little awareness of the topic and purpose for writing
- lacks organization
- offers unclear and confusing ideas
- demonstrates minimal persuasive reasoning or elaboration
- exhibits major problems with control of written language

4-Point Scale

Score 4 *Demonstrates advanced success*
- focuses consistently on a clear and reasonable position
- shows effective organization throughout, with smooth transitions
- offers thoughtful, creative ideas and reasons
- supports a position thoroughly, using convincing, fully elaborated reasons and evidence
- exhibits mature control of written language

Score 3 *Demonstrates competent success*
- focuses on a reasonable position, with minor distractions
- shows effective organization, with minor lapses
- offers mostly thoughtful ideas and reasons
- elaborates reasons and evidence with a mixture of the general and the specific
- exhibits general control of written language

Score 2 *Demonstrates limited success*
- includes some loosely related ideas that distract from the writer's position
- shows some organization, with noticeable gaps in the logical flow of ideas
- offers routine, predictable ideas and reasons
- supports ideas with uneven reasoning and elaboration
- exhibits limited control of written language

Score 1 *Demonstrates emerging effort*
- shows little awareness of the topic and purpose for writing
- lacks organization
- offers unclear and confusing ideas
- demonstrates minimal persuasive reasoning or elaboration
- exhibits major problems with control of written language

Persuasive Essay

When responding to a persuasive prompt, use what you have learned from reading, writing your persuasive essay, and studying the rubric on page 190. Use the steps below to develop a response to the following prompt.

Writing Prompt

Your school is debating whether to adopt a school uniform policy or to continue allowing students to choose what they will wear to school. Consider how each option affects the student population, the teachers, and the school environment. What is your position on the issue? In a persuasive essay, support your opinion with reasons and evidence.

Study the Prompt

Begin by reading the prompt carefully. Read it a second time, circling or underlining words that identify the type of writing, the issue, and any additional information that can help you focus your response.

Type of writing: persuasive essay
Issue: school uniform policy
Focus: how each option affects the student population, the teachers, and the school environment
Tip: Spend about five minutes studying the prompt.

Plan Your Response

Think about your own experiences with school uniforms. Use a chart like the one below to gather ideas.

School Uniforms	
Pros	
Cons	

The pros and cons are reasons for or against the policy. Decide which side of the debate you support. Keep in mind that you should choose your **position** based not only on the *number* of pros or cons but also on the *strength* of the ideas. Write down your **opinion statement:** your essay's topic and your opinion about it.

Reasons and Evidence The pros or cons you listed can become the **reasons** you use to support your position. Support each reason with **relevant evidence,** such as specific **facts, examples,** and **anecdotes.** Reasons and evidence should balance **appeals to logic, emotion,** and **ethics.** An effective response will often also address at least one **counterargument,** to show that you've considered both sides of the issue.

Organization Arrange your reasons and evidence by **order of importance,** presenting your second-strongest reason first, weakest reason next, and strongest reason last. **Tip:** Spend about ten minutes planning your response.

Respond to the Prompt

- Catch your reader's interest in your essay's **introduction;** then, present your opinion statement.
- Address each reason in a separate **body** paragraph, supporting each reason with specific evidence.
- In the **conclusion,** restate your position and issue a call to action, if you have anything specific you would like your readers to do in response to your essay.

Tip: Spend about twenty minutes writing your essay.

Improve Your Response

Revising Review the key aspects of the prompt. Is your position clear? Do you support it with reasons and evidence? Review your essay for organization of ideas, consistent tone, and strong overall arguments.

Proofreading Proofread, or edit, your essay to correct errors in grammar, spelling, punctuation, and capitalization. Make sure your edits are neat and the essay is legible.

Checking Your Final Copy Before you turn in your persuasive essay, read it one more time to catch any errors you may have missed. You'll be glad you took one more look to present your best writing. **Tip:** Save five or ten minutes to improve your draft.

Presenting and Evaluating Speeches

Speak with a Purpose

Adapt your written editorial into a persuasive speech, and deliver it to an audience. Then, listen to and evaluate the persuasive speeches of others.

Think as a Reader/Writer

As with reading and writing, speaking and listening are related processes. Like a writer, a speaker tries to convey ideas to others. Like a reader, a listener tries to understand someone else's ideas.

Effective persuasive speeches incorporate the same techniques that are used in good editorials. A speech, though, allows you to use your voice and body as well as words to make your point. Body language, voice inflection, and facial expressions help you communicate your arguments and convince your audience.

Adapt Your Editorial

Adapt the Content

To make your editorial sound natural and convincing when you present it aloud, you will have to make some changes to the introduction, body, and conclusion. Use ideas from the chart to adapt your editorial into a persuasive speech.

Introduction	Body	Conclusion
• Start with a thought-provoking quote that supports your ideas. • Paint a mental picture for your audience. Tell a vivid anecdote. • Quote an authority to support your opinion. • State your perspective in a simple, strong opinion statement. • Repeat your position for dramatic effect.	• Present your most convincing evidence and solid reasoning. • Choose points that will bring listeners to your side of the issue without making your speech too lengthy. • Determine if your listeners will respond more favorably to emotional appeals or logical appeals.	• End with a memorable finale. • Briefly summarize your strongest evidence. • Call your audience to take action, and be specific about what they can do. • Use a famous quote that your audience will remember after your speech ends.

Adapt the Organization

In your editorial, you chose between presenting your strongest evidence first and saving it for last. Now, choose which approach will have the greater impact on your listeners. Decide whether you will use a deductive or inductive approach when organizing your speech.

- In the **deductive approach,** you state your opinion in the introduction and give specific reasons and evidence for your opinion in the body.
- In the **inductive approach,** you present the reasons and evidence for your opinion first and offer your opinion in the conclusion.

Reader/Writer Notebook

Use your **RWN** to complete the activities for this workshop.

Deliver Your Persuasive Speech

Use Rhetorical Devices

The rhetorical devices you used in your editorial—repetition, parallelism, rhetorical questions, analogies—can be equally effective in your speech. Another effective device in persuasive speaking is to frame one or more of your arguments as a **syllogism**—a formula for presenting an argument, with two premises leading to an inescapable conclusion. Here are the parts of a syllogism, with examples.

Major Premise	The purpose of the 10:00 P.M. curfew for teens is to reduce the teen crime rate.
Minor Premise	Most teen crime occurs from 4:00 to 9:00 P.M.
Conclusion	The curfew will have little effect on teen crime.

Evaluate Persuasive Speeches

In many areas of life, you are asked to believe, support, or oppose certain ideas. Advertisers, politicians, and peers will try to persuade you to think or act in a certain way. You must be able to weigh evidence and analyze arguments. As you listen to your classmates' persuasive speeches and as you practice and write your own speech, look out for the following types of faulty logic and propaganda.

- An **overgeneralization** is based on too little evidence or evidence that ignores exceptions. *Adults just want to deny teenagers their rights. Otherwise, the curfew law would not have been approved.*

- A **red herring** takes a listener's attention away from the real issue or point. *The curfew law is the city council's attempt to usurp parents' authority.*

- **False causality** assumes one event caused another simply because one happened before the other. *Councilman Jones proposed the curfew after his store was robbed. The robbery is the reason he proposed it.*

- An attack **ad hominem** means attacking a person associated with the issue instead of the issue itself. *Mr. Lee, a longtime member of the city council, is well known for his dislike of children in general and teenagers in particular.*

- A **false analogy** draws an invalid conclusion from a comparison that is weak or unreasonable. *The city council understands modern teenagers about as well as most people understand the theory of relativity.*

- The **bandwagon** effect encourages listeners to act or think in a certain way simply because everyone else does. *The student council, the football team, and the entire cheerleading squad oppose the curfew. So should you.*

When you rehearse your speech, stick to solid methods of persuasion and avoid faulty logic and propaganda. When you listen to your peers, be alert for strengths as well as flaws in their methods of persuasion. Use these skills to analyze the messages of politicians and advertisers.

> ### A Good Persuasive Speech
> - focuses on an issue that has deep meaning for the speaker
> - includes specific and valid evidence
> - is dramatic and convincing
> - has practiced pitch, a serious tone, and appropriate volume at all points
> - uses appropriate gestures, pauses, and eye contact to maximize effectiveness

Speaking Tip

While preparing to deliver your speech, watch or listen to examples of persuasive speeches from current events or history. Think about how the speakers use their voices, their hands, and their facial expressions to create a sense of confidence.

 Learn It Online
Pictures, music, and animation can make your argument more compelling. See how on MediaScope.

go.hrw.com | L11-193 | Go

Literary Skills Review

Comparing Literature **Directions:** Read the following selections.
Then, read and respond to the questions that follow.

To My Dear and Loving Husband

by **Anne Bradstreet**

If ever two were one, then surely we.
If ever man were loved by wife, then thee;
If ever wife was happy in a man,
Compare with me, ye women, if you can.
5 I prize thy love more than whole mines of gold
Or all the riches that the East doth hold.
My love is such that rivers cannot quench,
Nor ought° but love from thee, give recompense.°
Thy love is such I can no way repay,
10 The heavens reward thee manifold,° I pray.
Then while we live, in love let's so persevere°
That when we live no more, we may live ever.

8. **ought:** archaic word meaning "anything." **recompense:**
repayment.
10. **manifold:** in many ways.
11. **persevere:** pronounced so
the last two syllables rhyme
with *ever*.

Love is not all

by **Edna St. Vincent Millay**

Love is not all: it is not meat nor drink
Nor slumber nor a roof against the rain;
Nor yet a floating spar to men that sink
And rise and sink and rise and sink again;
5 Love can not fill the thickened lung with breath,
Nor clean the blood, nor set the fractured bone;
Yet many a man is making friends with death
Even as I speak, for lack of love alone.
It well may be that in a difficult hour,
10 Pinned down by pain and moaning for release,
Or nagged by want past resolution's power,
I might be driven to sell your love for peace,
Or trade the memory of this night for food.
It well may be. I do not think I would.

1. The speaker in Bradstreet's poem states that her love for her husband is —

A less than her love of wealth and comfort

B greater than her love for God

C less than the love other women feel for their husbands

D as strong as, if not stronger than, any other woman's love

2. Bradstreet's poem ends with a **paradox**—an apparent contradiction that reveals a truth. Which of the following statements explains this paradox?

A People who are no longer alive on earth can be alive forever in heaven.

B People who don't love each other on earth will love each other in heaven.

C People should love each other while they're alive because life is short.

D People who don't love each other will die.

3. In "Love is not all," which of these points does the speaker make in lines 1–6?

A Love cannot let you down.

B Love cannot fill material needs.

C Love is less important than friendship.

D Love cannot last forever.

4. What **paradox** does the speaker in "Love is not all" point out in lines 1–8?

A Love is painful, yet it makes us happy.

B Loving oneself is more important than loving other people.

C Love cannot save lives, yet people can die without it.

D Loving people is more important than healing them.

5. Which of the following is a major stylistic difference between the two poems?

A Bradstreet's poem rhymes, and Millay's poem does not.

B Millay uses more religious imagery than Bradstreet.

C Millay's language is more contemporary than Bradstreet's.

D Bradstreet's poem is addressed to a person and Millay's is not.

6. Which of the following statements *best* expresses the shared **theme** of the two poems?

A It is easy to place a value on love.

B Love is always painful.

C It is hard to live without love.

D Love cures everything.

7. What is one way that each poem reflects the time period in which it was written?

A Bradstreet's poem reveals her Puritan devotion to God, and Millay's poem addresses more earthbound concerns.

B Bradstreet's poem questions a woman's place in society, and Millay's poem uses romantic imagery.

C Bradstreet's poem uses elaborate figures of speech, and Millay's poem does not.

D Bradstreet's poem praises love, and Millay sees love only as troublesome.

Constructed Response

8. Briefly discuss the contrast between the tone of Bradstreet's poem and the tone of Millay's poem. Be sure to cite specific evidence to support your response.

Vocabulary Skills Review

Context Clues **Directions:** Use the context clues in the following sentences to help you identify the meanings of the italicized Vocabulary words.

1. When Mary Rowlandson felt *melancholy*, or hopeless, she often turned to the Bible for comfort.

   In this sentence, *melancholy* means —

   A joyful

   B sorrowful

   C boring

   D angry

2. The slave traders' *avarice* drove them to cram the ships with as many people as possible so they could sell the people to make money.

   In this sentence, *avarice* means —

   A kindness

   B comfort

   C relief

   D greed

3. Devoted to the Colonists' cause, Patrick Henry *spurned* the idea that they could ever be happy under British rule.

   In this sentence, *spurned* means —

   A developed

   B rejected

   C revised

   D supported

4. Thomas Paine said that the Colonists would not be happy so long as they were subject to foreign control and *dominion*.

   In this sentence, *dominion* means —

   A interest

   B treasure

   C rule

   D thought

5. Benjamin Franklin's goal of moral *rectitude* was based on his ideas for proper moral conduct.

   In this sentence, *rectitude* means —

   A strength

   B wealth

   C correctness

   D harmony

6. According to Patrick Henry, the Colonists should see Britain as an *adversary*, not as a protector.

   In this sentence, *adversary* means —

   A friend

   B companion

   C neutral party

   D enemy

7. The Declaration of Independence states that King George hurt the Colonies by refusing to give his *assent* to laws that would support the common good.

   In this sentence, *assent* means —

   A denial

   B agreement

   C revenge

   D dictatorship

Academic Vocabulary

Directions: Choose the correct definition for the italicized Academic Vocabulary word from this unit.

8. An author's *perspective* is also his or her—

   A reputation

   B way of writing

   C point of view

   D personal history

SKILLS FOCUS **Writing Skills** Edit an editorial.

Writing Skills Review

Editorial **Directions:** Read the following paragraph from a draft of a student's editorial. Then, answer the questions that follow.

(1) Last week, the president of the local school board, Melinda C. Patterson, proposed a mandatory uniform policy for all public schools in the city. (2) Other districts have rejected such a policy. (3) Such a policy is ridiculous! (4) A mandatory uniform policy denies parents the right to choose their children's clothing. (5) Moreover, the school district will probably have to furnish uniforms for the students who can't afford them. (6) Such spending will be a misuse of funds, especially when school buildings are crumbling, teachers are grossly underpaid, and parents are losing faith in public schools.

1. Which sentence could replace sentence 3 to better convey the writer's opinion?

A Ms. Patterson's proposal has merit and should be adopted.

B Ms. Patterson's proposal will deny parents their rights.

C Ms. Patterson's proposal will cost taxpayers too much.

D Ms. Patterson's proposal should be rejected by the school board.

2. What evidence could the writer add to support the idea in sentence 5?

A School uniforms lower the social pressure students feel to fit in with their peers by dressing a certain way.

B School uniforms will impose a heavy financial burden on the students' families.

C School uniforms have been successful in decreasing disciplinary problems.

D School uniforms cost approximately fifty dollars per student, so the potential cost to taxpayers could be four million dollars.

3. Which rhetorical device does the writer use to enhance the effectiveness of sentence 6?

A A rhetorical question

B An analogy

C Repetition

D Parallelism

4. Which sentence should be deleted or moved to another paragraph to improve the coherence of the passage?

A 1

B 2

C 4

D 5

5. In which section of the editorial would this paragraph most likely be placed?

A The introduction

B The body

C The conclusion

D Any of the above

6. To adapt this passage to include in a persuasive speech, the speaker might —

A use only emotional appeals to convince an audience

B eliminate reasons that address listeners' concerns

C cut the conclusion to keep within the time limits of the presentation

D enliven the introduction to capture listeners' attention

FICTION

The Scarlet Letter

An adulterous woman is cast out from society. A self-righteous husband rages with vengeance. A minister tortures himself with secret guilt. In Nathaniel Hawthorne's powerful examination of the Puritan era, individuals come head to head with their society's strict moral code and examine their hearts, souls, and relationships in the process.

NONFICTION

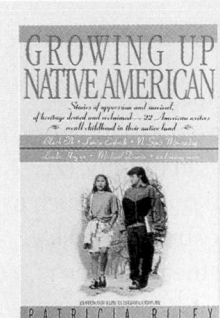

Growing Up Native American

This anthology, edited by Patricia Riley, combines more than one hundred years of fiction, essays, and autobiographies to portray coming-of-age from a Native American perspective. By exploring the loss of indigenous languages, the political devastation of the nineteenth century, the destruction of tribal identity, and the new hopes that took root during the twentieth century, *Growing Up Native American* provides both a historical and a personal look at the dignity and survival of fifteen nations in the United States and Canada.

FICTION

Hope Leslie

In this novel by Catharine Maria Sedgwick, two young women who seem worlds apart—Hope, a freethinking Puritan, and Magawisca, the daughter of a Pequot chief—forge a friendship based on their common experience of living in cultures they find repressive. As Hope works toward justice for women and Native Americans and Magawisca takes personal risks for the Puritan colonists, each woman finds an identity that transcends the restrictive boundaries of her society.

NONFICTION

Born in Slavery: Slave Narratives from the Federal Writers' Project, 1936–1938

http://memory.loc.gov/ ammem/snhtml/snhome.html

In the late 1930s, writers in the Works Progress Administration filled seventeen volumes with interviews and photographs of former slaves. This online compilation features more than twenty-three hundred first-person accounts and five hundred photographs digitized by the Library of Congress. Readers encounter the faces, emotions, and voices of those who experienced slavery firsthand.

POETRY
Complete Writings

As a young child, Phillis Wheatley was kidnapped and sold into slavery, but by age 14, she had published her first poem. Wheatley went from Africa to Boston, where the family who purchased her took the unusual step of educating her in reading, writing, and the classics. In 1773, she became the first African American to publish a book, a poetry collection; that same year she became a free woman. Wheatley's fans included Benjamin Franklin and George Washington, who requested an audience with her in 1776.

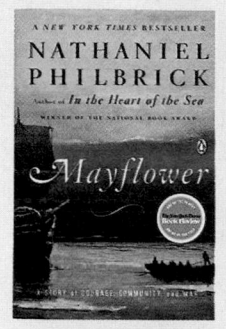

NONFICTION
Mayflower

What was the Pilgrims' voyage on the *Mayflower* really like? What actually happened at the first Thanksgiving? What was the true relationship between the Pilgrims and Native American peoples? In his myth-busting book *Mayflower,* Nathaniel Philbrick, winner of the National Book Award, goes beyond a simplistic saga of good versus evil to search for authentic answers to these and other questions about pre-Colonial life.

LETTERS
Letters from an American Farmer

Letters from an American Farmer tackled the question, "What is an American?" for Europeans who were curious to learn about this exotic new breed. It was written in 1782 near the end of the Revolutionary War. Its author, J. Hector St. John de Crèvecoeur, an aristocratic Frenchman who immigrated to New York, is credited with being the first person to discuss the concept of the melting pot and the American dream. Many of his observations about America remain true today.

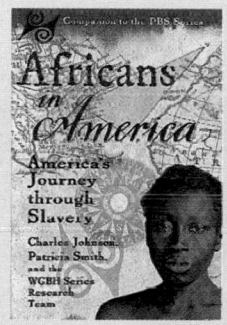

FICTION/NONFICTION
Africans in America

This volume chronicles the history of slavery in America. Patricia Smith's vivid narrative—which uses diaries, letter excerpts, and historical documents—is coupled with Charles Johnson's fictional histories to bring a new perspective to the slave experience, one told from the African point of view.

Learn It Online
For a study guide and PowerPoint presentation on *The Scarlet Letter*, visit *NovelWise.*

go.hrw.com L11-199 **Go**

IMAGINATION AND
THE INDIVIDUAL:

American
Romanticism

1800–1860

COLLECTION 4
The Transforming Imagination

COLLECTION 5
The Realms of Darkness

"I unsettle all things. No facts are
to me sacred; none are profane;
I simply experiment, an endless
seeker, with no Past at my back."

—**Ralph Waldo Emerson**

What Do
You
Think

Where does an
individual find
inspiration?

The Oxbow (the Connecticut River near Northampton) (1836) by Thomas Cole. Oil on canvas.

 Learn It Online
Learn more through the video "Imagination and the
Individual" online.

go.hrw.com   L11-201   Go

IMAGINATION AND THE INDIVIDUAL:

American Romanticism
1800–1860

This time line represents a snapshot of United States literary events, United States historical events, and world events from 1800 to 1860. During this period of rapid expansion, America developed a distinct national identity.

UNITED STATES LITERARY EVENTS

1800

1817 William Cullen Bryant publishes "Thanatopsis"

1823 James Fenimore Cooper publishes "The Pioneers"

1828 Noah Webster publishes a landmark dictionary of American English >

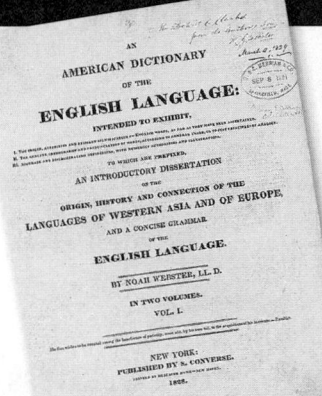

1830

1830 Oliver Wendell Holmes publishes "Old Ironsides"

1833 Poet John Greenleaf Whittier calls for the abolition of slavery in his pamphlet *Justice and Expediency*

1835 French writer Alexis de Tocqueville analyzes the United States in *Democracy in America*

UNITED STATES HISTORICAL EVENTS

1800

1803 President Thomas Jefferson negotiates Louisiana Purchase from France, more than doubling U.S. territory

1804 Meriwether Lewis and William Clark start a cross-country expedition to study the West

1823 President James Monroe introduces the Monroe Doctrine, encouraging independence from Europe

1825 Erie Canal opens, connecting Great Lakes and Atlantic Ocean

1830

1830 First steam-powered train begins running in America >

c. 1830 Underground Railroad, a secret system for helping fugitive slaves reach safety, is organized

1838 U.S. Army forces Cherokees out of Georgia on long Trail of Tears to Oklahoma

Courtesy of the Norfolk Southern Corporation.

WORLD EVENTS

1800

1810 Miguel Hidalgo y Costilla launches the Mexican war of independence from Spain

1815 Napoleon I of France is defeated at Waterloo and subsequently exiled

1819 Simón Bolívar, South American independence leader, becomes Gran Colombia's first president

1822 Liberia is founded on west coast of Africa as a settlement for freed U.S. slaves

1830

1831 English scientist Michael Faraday discovers link between magnetism and electricity

1837 Queen Victoria of England is crowned >

Your Turn

In a small group, review the time line and discuss what you know about two individuals who helped the United States expand and define its identity as a nation. How might people today draw inspiration from the ideas and actions of these individuals?

1840	**1850**	**1860**

1841 Ralph Waldo Emerson publishes his first collection, *Essays,* including "Self-Reliance" and "The Over-Soul"

1842 Henry Wadsworth Longfellow publishes *Ballads and Other Poems*

1845 Margaret Fuller publishes *Woman in the Nineteenth Century,* the first full study of women in American society ❯

1850 Nathaniel Hawthorne publishes *The Scarlet Letter*

1851 Herman Melville publishes *Moby-Dick; or, The Whale*

1854 Henry David Thoreau publishes *Walden*

1855 Walt Whitman publishes the first edition of his book of poems, *Leaves of Grass*

The Granger Collection, New York.

1840	**1850**	**1860**

1844 Samuel Morse completes the first telegraph line in the United States

1845 United States annexes Texas, leading to war with Mexico, 1846–1848

1848 Lucretia Mott and Elizabeth Cady Stanton organize first women's rights convention in the United States in Seneca Falls, New York

1849 California gold rush begins as thousands of gold miners travel to Sacramento area

1854 Modern Republican Party is founded to oppose the extension of slavery

1854 Commodore Matthew Perry opens two Japanese ports to U.S. trade

1857 Supreme Court's *Dred Scott* decision antagonizes antislavery forces ❯

Dred Scott (c. 1858). Painting after a photograph. The Granger Collection, New York.

1840	**1850**	**1860**

1842 By Treaty of Nanking, China cedes Hong Kong to Great Britain and opens five ports to foreign trade

1846 Famine in Ireland due to potato crop failure causes increased emigration from Ireland to United States ❯

1848 Revolutions occur in countries throughout Europe

1858 After Indian revolt against British East India Company rule, British government takes over administration of India

1859 Charles Darwin supports theory of evolution in *On the Origin of Species*

Irish emigrants leave Queenstown Harbor for the United States.

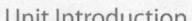

IMAGINATION AND THE INDIVIDUAL:
American Romanticism
1800–1860

By the beginning of the nineteenth century, Americans had forged an independent nation, but they had not yet created their own cultural identity. A new generation of writers, who called themselves Romantics and Transcendentalists, created a new kind of literature that emphasized imagination, feeling, individualism, and enthusiasm for nature. In many ways this literature reflected the optimism of American society at the time and defined the way we still view ourselves today.

KEY CONCEPTS

The Nation Expands

History of the Times The United States rapidly expanded westward after the Louisiana Purchase in 1803. A spirit of nationalism took hold as America grew and prospered. Industrialization and new waves of immigration caused cities to become overcrowded and polluted as conditions worsened.

Literature of the Times During the Romantic period, a new national literature developed. Romanticism, unlike rationalism, valued feelings over reason and logic, the power of imagination and the individual spirit, and the beauty of the natural world.

New Ideas Take Root

History of the Times Inspired by an awakening of intellectual and religious fervor, American reformers worked to improve society. They fought for better education, humane prisons, women's rights, the abolition of slavery, improved factory conditions, and other social reforms.

Literature of the Times An idealistic form of Romanticism, called Transcendentalism, sought to transcend, or go beyond, ordinary life through spiritual experiences in nature. Transcendentalists believed that to discover truth, one must transcend or see beyond the physical world and seek out the ideal world.

Differences Threaten National Unity

History of the Times Despite progress and prosperity, the United States felt the pull of conflicts over slavery, sectional differences, and economics. These struggles laid the groundwork for the Civil War. Friction with Native Americans also became a troubling issue as white settlers encroached on native lands.

Literature of the Times Another group of writers, known as Dark Romantics, explored the conflict between good and evil, the effects of guilt, and the dark underside of appearances. Unlike other Romantics, these writers did not believe that the spiritual truths found in nature are all harmless and good.

SKILLS FOCUS **Literary Skills** Evaluate and analyze the philosophical, political, religious, ethical, and social influences of a historical period. **Reading Skills** Read widely to increase knowledge of the student's culture, the culture of others, and the common elements across cultures; identify and understand elements of text structure (including headings and sections).

KEY CONCEPT

The Nation Expands

History of the Times

The size of the United States doubled at the beginning of the nineteenth century. When the Louisiana Purchase in 1803 added land between the Mississippi River and the Rocky Mountains, a new era of westward expansion began. Routes such as the Santa Fe Trail and the Oregon Trail brought a flood of settlers to the West—a mass migration that intensified with the Gold Rush of 1849. Thousands of Americans picked up and headed west, lured by dreams of wealth after gold was discovered at Sutter's Mill in California.

At the same time, a nationalist[1] spirit flourished in America, reflecting an optimistic belief in the nation's progress. The Industrial Revolution was changing the way people worked and lived. Americans saw what they could produce with the help of machines such as steam engines and mills. Transportation, communication, and commerce would never be the same. America was on the move.

With the rise of industry, cities became grimy, and the arrival of new immigrants caused overcrowding. By 1840, the U.S. population had grown to 17.1 million, up from 5.3 million in 1800. In New York alone, the population doubled between 1820 and 1840. In large eastern cities like New York, Boston, and Philadelphia, teeming tenements sprang up, while disease and crime made survival difficult.

Literature of the Times

The Romantic movement was in large part a reaction to rationalism. Romanticism provided expression for the discontent arising from the Industrial Revolution, which sought progress at all costs.

To rationalists, such as Benjamin Franklin, cities represented progress, economic success, and self-realization. To Romantic writers, the city was often a place of immorality, corruption, and death. The characteristic Romantic journey was to the countryside, which Romantics associated with independence, moral clarity, and healthful living. Romanticism was in many ways an appropriate vision for a nation expanding quickly toward new frontiers.

Comprehension Check

How did the United States expand both geographically and culturally during the early nineteenth century?

Fast Facts

Historical Highlights

- Rapid growth of industrialization, education, transportation, and cities transforms society.
- Numerous reform movements, centered in New England, seek to improve social conditions.
- Discontent over slavery intensifies as the abolitionist movement gains momentum.

Literary Highlights

- Romantic writings, such as Washington Irving's *The Sketch Book* (1820), look to feeling and imagination to reveal higher truths.
- Ralph Waldo Emerson's first collection of essays (1841) discusses Transcendentalist thought.
- Edgar Allan Poe, an influential Gothic writer, publishes *The Raven and Other Poems* in 1845.

---

1. **nationalist:** characterized by devotion to one's nation; patriotic.

Learn It Online

Learn more about this historical period online.

go.hrw.com | L11-205 | **Go**

New Ideas Take Root

History of the Times

An era of reform took hold in the first half of the nineteenth century. In 1826, the Lyceum movement began in Millbury, Massachusetts. Lyceum organizations pursued a number of goals, including educating adults, training teachers, establishing museums, and instituting social reforms.

The reform movement was also centered in New England. Horace Mann fought to improve public education. Dorothea Dix sought to relieve the horrible conditions in institutions for people with mental illnesses. William Lloyd Garrison and other abolitionists struggled to put an end to slavery. Feminists such as Elizabeth Peabody, Margaret Fuller, and Emma Willard campaigned for women's rights.

The abounding interest in social causes stirred up ideas both reasonable and crackpot. Numerous utopian projects—plans for creating a more perfect society—were developed. In 1840, Ralph Waldo Emerson wryly remarked that every man who could read had plans in his pocket for a new community. Emerson was speaking from personal experience, for he was a member of one of the most influential of these idealistic groups, the Transcendentalists.

Literature of the Times

At the heart of America's optimism and coming-of-age were a group of Romantics called the Transcendentalists, led by Ralph Waldo Emerson. Transcendentalism refers to the idea that in determining the ultimate reality of God, the universe, the self, and other important matters, one must transcend, or go beyond, everyday human experience in the physical world.

For Emerson, Transcendentalism was not a new philosophy but "the very oldest of thoughts cast into the mold of these new times." That "oldest of thoughts" was idealism, which had already been explained by the Greek philosopher Plato in the fourth century B.C. Idealists said that true reality was found in ideas rather than in the world as perceived by the senses. Idealists sought the permanent reality that underlies physical appearances. The Americans who called themselves Transcendentalists were idealists but in a broader, more practical sense. Like many Americans today, they also believed in human perfectibility, and they worked to achieve this goal.

Though Emerson was skeptical of many of the Transcendentalists' ideas and projects, he was the most influential and best-known member of the group, largely because of his lectures and books. Emerson's view of the world sprang not from logic but from intuition. Intuition is our capacity to know things spontaneously and immediately through our emotions rather than our reasoning abilities. Intuitive thought—the kind that Emerson believed in—contrasts with the rational thinking of someone like Benjamin Franklin. Franklin did not gaze on nature and feel the presence of a Divine Soul; Franklin looked at nature and saw something to be examined scientifically and used to help humanity.

Girls' Evening School (c. 1840) by unidentified artist, American. Graphite pencil and watercolor on paper, 34.3 × 45.9 cm (13 ½" × 18 ¹⁄₁₆").
Photograph © 2009 Museum of Fine Arts, Boston.

NOTICE.

AT the next regular meeting of the **UPPER ALTON LYCEUM,** To be held on *TUESDAY Evening, Feb. 11,* at the Seminary Hall, the following question, by order of the Society, will come up for debate :—

" *Has Congress power to abolish Slavery in the District of Columbia,* without the consent of the inhabitants thereof ?"

and Ladies are respectfully in-

An intense feeling of optimism was one product of Emerson's belief that we can find God directly in nature. God is good, and God works through nature, Emerson believed. Therefore, even the events that seem most tragic—disease, death, disaster—can be explained on a spiritual level. Death is simply part of the cycle of life. According to Emerson, we are capable of evil because we are separated from a direct, intuitive knowledge of God. But if we simply trust ourselves—that is, trust in the power each of us has to know God directly—then we will realize that each of us is also part of the Divine Soul, the source of all good.

Emerson's sense of optimism and hope appealed to audiences who lived in a period of economic downturns, regional strife, and conflict over slavery. Your condition today, Emerson seemed to tell his readers and listeners, may seem dull and hopeless, but it need not be. If you discover God within you, he suggested, your lives will partake of the grandeur of the universe.

Comprehension Check

How would reformers and writers in the Romantic Age describe an ideal society?

Link to Today

Factory Girl

She was only ten years old and couldn't even reach the top of the loom, but Harriet Robinson was already a factory worker in a textile mill. In 1824, the mills of Lowell, Massachusetts, badly needed workers, and Harriet was one of many young girls who flocked to the factory for jobs. She worked there for fourteen years.

Today, laws protect children under the age of fourteen from employment and entitle them to a free public education. In the early 1800s, however, children did not have these rights and protections.

In the early nineteenth century, child labor was common in New England mill towns because the mills could hire unskilled children with the oversight of a supervisor. Like Harriet, some of the girls working in textile mills were as young as ten, although most were sixteen to twenty-five. Many were earning money to send a brother to school. Along with other young girls, Harriet was a "doffer." She doffed, or took off, bobbins full of yarn from the spinning frames and replaced them with empty bobbins. The girls earned two dollars a week and worked fourteen-hour days, though the younger girls worked only a portion of every hour.

One of the first labor strikes in America occurred at Lowell in 1836. The strike, which protested a wage cut, was unsuccessful, but it marked the rise of a labor movement that led to better working conditions and wages for all. Over a century later, in 1938, a federal law was passed to limit child labor.

No record exists today of the name of this girl, who worked in a mill around 1850. Jack Naylor Collection.

Ask Yourself

For most people, how is today's workplace different than it was in Harriet's time?

Differences Threaten National Unity

History of the Times

Despite the progress and optimism that marked the first half of the nineteenth century, the United States faced a number of challenges. In the forefront was the issue of slavery. Though most Northern states had abolished slavery by the early 1800s, the number of slaves in the South increased as cotton plantations spread throughout the region. After working for abolition in their own states, many antislavery activists in the North wanted to put an end to slavery everywhere.

By 1840, abolitionists had recruited some 200,000 supporters to their cause. In addition, many free African Americans began organizing to free their "brothers in chains." As Southern slaveholders felt increasingly threatened, violence against abolitionists rose. Discord over this issue eventually erupted into an armed conflict: the Civil War.

Another challenge to peace and stability involved the treatment of Native Americans. In the early 1800s, many U.S. officials hoped that Native Ameri-cans would become farmers and blend into American society. Many Native Americans, particularly the Cherokee people, were forced to give up their way of life to take up farming and other livelihoods considered acceptable by the dominant white culture.

However, these efforts to adopt the lifestyle of their white neighbors did not ease the prejudice that Native Americans encountered. Those who switched to farming found themselves viewed as competition for valuable land. In 1830, Congress passed the Indian Removal Act, relocating Native Americans to territories now known as Oklahoma. The Cherokee were forcibly removed from their land. An estimated 4,000 Cherokee died on the 800-mile journey west that came to be known as the Trail of Tears.

Comprehension Check

What reaction did the Cherokee experience after making the transition to farming?

Link to Today

Environmental Pioneers

When you hear the words "going green," you might not think of the nineteenth-century writers Henry David Thoreau and Ralph Waldo Emerson. But their deep respect for nature is at the very core of today's environmental movement. For Thoreau and Emerson, it all began with concerns about the impact of industrialization on the nature and society.

Thoreau and Emerson continue to inspire today's conservation leaders and activists who seek to preserve a healthy environment, both for its own sake and for its part in the survival of humankind. As a result, you might see quotes like these from Thoreau or Emerson on a nature poster or brochure for a conservation group:

- "Behind nature, throughout nature, spirit is present." —Emerson
- "In wildness is the preservation of the world." —Thoreau

Emerson and Thoreau may not have been out there marching on behalf of endangered species, but their writings were among the earliest to call attention to the necessity of protecting America's natural treasures.

Ask Yourself

Explain in your own words what you think Emerson and Thoreau are saying in the quotations above. Do you think people today would find these slogans persuasive enough to change their attitudes? Why or why not?

The Trail of Tears (1838) by Robert Lindneux.
The Granger Collection, New York.

Literature of the Times

Emerson's idealism was exciting for his audiences, but not all the writers and thinkers of the time agreed with Transcendentalist thought. "To one who has weathered Cape Horn as a common sailor," Herman Melville wrote scornfully of Emerson's ideas, "what stuff all this is."

Some think of Nathaniel Hawthorne, Herman Melville, and Edgar Allan Poe as anti-Transcendentalists, because their views of the world seem so profoundly opposed to the optimistic views of Emerson and his followers. But these Dark Romantics, as they are known, had much in common with the Transcendentalists. Both groups valued intuition over logic and reason. Both groups, like the Puritans before them, saw signs and symbols in all events.

The Dark Romantics felt that Emerson had taken the ecstatic, mystical[2] elements of Puritan thought and ignored Puritanism's dark side—its emphasis on Original Sin, its sense of the innate wickedness of human beings, and its notions of predestination.[3] The Dark Romantics came along to correct the balance. In their works they explored the conflict between good and evil, the psychological effects of guilt and sin, and madness in the human psyche.

---

2. **mystical:** related to the belief that people can achieve direct knowledge of God.
3. **predestination:** religious belief that God has decided everything before people are born, including who is saved and who is not.

Wrap Up

Talk About . . .

With a partner, list conflicts that developed as the United States expanded in the nineteenth century. Are there similar conflicts in this country today? Explain. Try to use each Academic Vocabulary word listed below at least once in your discussion.

Write About . . .

The age of Romanticism in America has been called "the American Renaissance." A renaissance is a rebirth or reawakening. Write about a renaissance you see taking place in America or in your community today.

Academic Vocabulary for Unit 2

Talking and Writing About Literature
Academic Vocabulary is the language you use to write and talk about literature. Use these words to discuss the literature you read in this unit. The words will be underlined throughout the unit.

factor (FAK tuhr) *n.*: one element in a situation. *Conflict over land was a major factor leading to the forced removal of the Cherokee.*

implicit (ihm PLIHS iht) *adj.*: implied; suggested yet not plainly expressed. *What Romantic values are implicit in the poem?*

integral (IHN tuh gruhl) *adj.*: necessary for completeness; essential. *Gandhi's teachings are integral to the principle of civil disobedience.*

transform (trans FAWRM) *v.*: change in form or condition. *Transcendentalists believe in the power of individuals to transform their lives.*

principal (PRIHN suh puhl) *adj.*: most important; main. *One of the principal causes of the Civil War was conflicting views of slavery.*

Your Turn

Copy the Academic Vocabulary list into your *Reader/Writer Notebook.* Try to use these words as you outline the main ideas of the unit introduction and as you answer questions about the literature in the unit that follows.

ESSAY

Read with a Purpose Read to discover what Annie Dillard thinks a wild animal can teach her about how to live.

Living Like Weasels

by **Annie Dillard**

A weasel is wild. Who knows what he thinks? He sleeps in his underground den, his tail draped over his nose. Sometimes he lives in his den for two days without leaving. Outside, he stalks rabbits, mice, muskrats, and birds, killing more bodies than he can eat warm, and often dragging the carcasses home. Obedient to instinct, he bites his prey at the neck, either splitting the jugular vein at the throat or crunching the brain at the base of the skull, and he does not let go. One naturalist refused to kill a weasel who was socketed into his hand deeply as a rattlesnake. The man could in no way pry the tiny weasel off, and he had to walk half a mile to water, the weasel dangling from his palm, and soak him off like a stubborn label.

And once, says Ernest Thompson Seton[1]—once, a man shot an eagle out of the sky. He examined the eagle and found the dry skull of a weasel fixed by the jaws to his throat. The supposition is that the eagle had pounced on the weasel and the weasel swiveled and bit as instinct taught him, tooth to neck, and nearly won. I would like to have seen that eagle from the air a few weeks or months before he was shot: was the whole weasel still attached to his feathered throat, a fur pendant? Or did the

---

1. **Ernest Thompson Seton** (1860–1946): Naturalist and writer who fought to create parks for endangered animals. Later, he helped to establish the Boy Scouts of America.

Illustration of Thoreau's hut. From *Walden*.

Analyzing Visuals

Viewing and Interpreting
Judging by the photograph below, would you expect weasels to display the aggressive behaviors the author describes? Explain.

Short-tailed weasel, or ermine, western U.S.

eagle eat what he could reach, gutting the living weasel with his talons[2] before his breast, bending his beak, cleaning the beautiful airborne bones?

I have been thinking about weasels because I saw one last week. I startled a weasel who startled me, and we exchanged a long glance.

Near my house in Virginia is a pond—Hollins Pond. It covers two acres of bottomland near Tinker Creek with six inches of water and six thousand lily pads. There is a fifty-five mph highway at one end of the pond, and a nesting pair of wood ducks at the other. Under every bush is a muskrat hole or a beer can. The far end is an alternating series of fields and woods, fields and woods, threaded everywhere with motorcycle tracks—in whose bare clay wild turtles lay eggs.

One evening last week at sunset, I walked to the pond and sat on a downed log near the shore. I was watching the lily pads at my feet tremble and part over the thrusting path of a carp. A yellow warbler appeared to my right and

---

2. **talons:** the claws of an animal, especially a bird of prey.

flew behind me. It caught my eye; I swiveled around—and the next instant, inexplicably, I was looking down at a weasel, who was looking up at me.

Weasel! I had never seen one wild before. He was ten inches long, thin as a curve, a muscled ribbon, brown as fruitwood, soft-furred, alert. His face was fierce, small and pointed as a lizard's; he would have made a good arrowhead. There was just a dot of chin, maybe two brown hairs' worth, and then the pure white fur began that spread down his underside. He had two black eyes I did not see, any more than you see a window.

The weasel was stunned into stillness as he was emerging from beneath an enormous shaggy wild-rose bush four feet away. I was stunned into stillness, twisted backward on the tree trunk. Our eyes locked, and someone threw away the key.

Our look was as if two lovers, or deadly enemies, met unexpectedly on an overgrown path when each had been thinking of something else: a clearing blow to the gut. It was also a bright blow to the brain, or a sudden beating of brains, with all the charge and intimate grate of rubbed balloons. It emptied our lungs. It felled the forest, moved the fields, and drained the pond; the world dismantled and tumbled into that black hole of eyes. If you and I looked at each other that way, our skulls would split and drop to our shoulders. But we don't. We keep our skulls.

He disappeared. This was only last week, and already I don't remember what shattered the enchantment. I think I blinked, I think I retrieved my brain from the weasel's brain, and tried to memorize what I was seeing, and the weasel felt the yank of separation, the careening splashdown into real life and the urgent current of instinct. He vanished under the wild rose. I waited motionless, my mind suddenly full of data and my spirit with pleadings, but he didn't return.

Please do not tell me about "approach-avoidance conflicts."[3] I tell you I've been in that weasel's brain for sixty seconds, and he was in mine. Brains are private places, muttering through unique and secret tapes—but the weasel and I both plugged into another tape simultaneously, for a sweet and shocking time. Can I help it if it was a blank? . . .

I would like to learn, or remember, how to live. I come to Hollins Pond not so much to learn how to live as, frankly, to forget about it.[4] That is, I don't think I can learn from a wild animal how to live in particular—shall I suck warm blood, hold my tail high, walk with my footprints precisely over the prints of my hands?—but I might learn something of mindlessness, something of the purity of living in the physical senses and the dignity of living without bias or motive. The weasel lives in necessity and we live in choice, hating necessity and dying at the last ignobly in its talons. I would like to live as I should, as the weasel lives as he should. And I suspect that for me the way is like the weasel's: open to time and death painlessly, noticing everything, remembering nothing, choosing the given with a fierce and pointed will.

I missed my chance. I should have gone for the throat. I should have lunged for that streak of white under the weasel's chin and held on, held on through mud and into the wild rose, held on

---

3. **approach-avoidance conflicts:** This psychological term refers to situations in which a person is both attracted to and repelled by a situation.
4. **I come to Hollins Pond not so much to learn how to live as, frankly, to forget about it:** This statement parallels Thoreau's statement in *Walden:* "I went to the woods because I wished to live deliberately, to front only the essential facts of life, and see if I could not learn what it had to teach, and not, when I came to die, to discover that I had not lived."

fur, sniffing bird bones, blinking, licking, breathing musk, my hair tangled in the roots of grasses. . . . Could two live that way? Could two live under the wild rose, and explore by the pond, so that the smooth mind of each is as everywhere present to the other, and as received and as unchallenged, as falling snow?

We could, you know. We can live any way we want. People take vows of poverty, chastity, and obedience—even of silence—by choice. The thing is to stalk your calling in a certain skilled and supple way, to locate the most tender and live spot and plug into that pulse. This is yielding, not fighting. A weasel doesn't "attack" anything; a weasel lives as he's meant to, yielding at every moment to the perfect freedom of single necessity.

I think it would be well, and proper, and obedient, and pure, to grasp your one necessity and not let it go, to dangle from it limp wherever it takes you. Then even death, where you're going no matter how you live, cannot you part. Seize it and let it seize you up aloft even, till your eyes burn out and drop; let your musky flesh fall off in shreds, and let your very bones unhinge and scatter, loosened over fields, over fields and woods, lightly, thoughtless, from any height at all, from as high as eagles.

for a dearer life. We could live under the wild rose wild as weasels, mute and uncomprehending. I could very calmly go wild. I could live two days in the den, curled, leaning on mouse

Ask Yourself

1. **Read with a Purpose** What does Dillard think the weasel can teach her about how to live?

2. Dillard says that "the weasel lives in necessity and we live in choice." What does she mean by this distinction? Do you agree with her? Explain.

3. Meeting the weasel jolts Dillard into a new understanding of the animal and of herself. How does this essay affect the way you look at wild animals or at yourself? What lesson from Dillard's essay can you apply to your life?

4. How does this twentieth-century essay reflect the ideas of the nineteenth-century Transcendentalists described on pages 206–207?

The Transforming Imagination

LITERARY FOCUS
American Romanticism

CONTENTS

Yosemite Falls (c. 1865–1870) by Albert Bierstadt, (1830–1902). Oil on canvas.

"The gain of creation consists always in the growth of individual minds, which live and aspire, as flowers bloom and birds sing."

—Margaret Fuller Ossoli

SKILLS FOCUS **Literary Skills** Evaluate and analyze the philosophical, political, religious, ethical, and social influences of a historical period; analyze Romanticism. **Reading Skills** Read widely to increase knowledge of the student's culture, the culture of others, and the common elements across cultures.

American Romanticism by **Gary Q. Arpin**

Characteristics of American Romanticism

- Affirmation of feeling and intuition over reason
- Faith in imagination, inner experience, and youthful innocence, rather than educated sophistication
- Belief in the unspoiled natural world, as opposed to the artificiality of civilization
- Regard for individual freedom and the worth of the individual

A Reaction Against Rationalism

In the years after winning independence from the British and establishing a new nation, Americans began to form their own cultural identity. Writers calling themselves Romantics helped build this identity, and their work still influences the way Americans view themselves, their society, and the natural world.

Romanticism is the name given to schools of thought that value feeling and intuition over reason. The first rumblings of Romanticism were felt in Germany in the second half of the eighteenth century, and Romanticism strongly influenced literature, music, and painting in continental Europe and Britain well into the nineteenth century.

Romanticism developed, especially in Europe, in part as a reaction against rationalism. In the wake of the Industrial Revolution, with its squalid cities and miserable working conditions, people had come to realize the limits of reason. The Romantics believed that the imagination was able to discover truths that the rational mind could not reach. These truths were usually accompanied by powerful emotion and associated with natural beauty. To the Romantics, imagination, individual feelings, and wild nature were of greater value than reason, logic, and sophistication. The Romantics did not reject rational thought for all purposes; but for the purposes of art, they placed a higher value on intuitive, "felt" experience.

Romantic Escapism

The Romantics wanted to rise above what Edgar Allan Poe called "dull realities" and to find a realm of higher truth. They did so in two principal ways. First, the Romantics chose situations and settings from the more "natural" past or from worlds not at all like the grimy and noisy industrial age. They told tales of the supernatural and stories that harkened back to old legends and folklore. For example, the story by Washington Irving on page 290, "The Devil and Tom Walker," is based on an old European legend about a man who sells his soul to the devil for worldly riches.

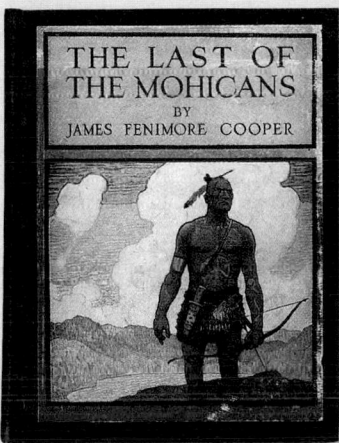

James Fenimore Cooper created romanticized American Indian characters.

Second, the Romantics tried to reflect on the natural world until dull reality fell away to reveal beauty and truth. This second Romantic approach is evident in many lyric poems. For example, in the poem "The Cross of Snow" by Henry Wadsworth Longfellow (page 229) a natural scene helps the speaker understand and express his deeply felt grief over the loss of his wife. This approach is similar to the way Puritans drew moral lessons from nature. The difference is one of emphasis and goal. The Puritans' lessons were defined by their religion. In nature the Puritans found the God they knew from the Bible. The Romantics, on the other hand, believed that contemplation of the natural world led to a more generalized emotional and intellectual awakening.

The American Novel and the Wilderness Experience

American Romantic novelists discovered that the subject matter available to them was very different from the subjects available to European writers. America provided a sense of limitless frontiers that Europe, so long settled, simply did not possess. The American novel developed hand-in-hand with westward expansion; the growth of a nationalist spirit; and, thus, the idealization of frontier life.

The novels of James Fenimore Cooper (1789–1851) clearly express these themes. Cooper explored uniquely American characters and settings: American Indians, backwoodsmen, frontier communities, and the wilderness of western New York and Pennsylvania. Most important, he created one of the first Romantic heroes in American literature: Natty Bumppo, a virtuous, skillful frontiersman whose simple morality, love of nature, distrust of town life, and almost superhuman resourcefulness mark him as a true Romantic hero.

American Romantic Poetry: Read at Every Fireside

The American Romantic novelists looked for new subject matter and new themes, but America's Romantic poets, who wanted to show that Americans were a sophisticated people, worked solidly within European literary traditions. Even when they constructed poems with American settings and subject matter, the American Romantic poets used typically English themes, meter, and imagery. They wrote in a style that a cultivated person from England who had recently immigrated to America might be expected to use.

The Fireside Poets—as the Boston group of Henry Wadsworth Longfellow, John Greenleaf Whittier, William Cullen Bryant, Oliver Wendell Holmes, and James Russell Lowell was called—were, in their own time and for many decades afterward, the most popular poets America had ever produced. They were called the Fireside Poets because their poems were read aloud at the fireside as family entertainment.

Daniel Day-Lewis as Natty Bumppo in *The Last of the Mohicans* (1992).

Limited by their literary conservatism, the Fireside Poets did not recognize the poetry of the future, which was being written right under their noses. Whittier's response in 1885 to the first volume of a certain poet's work was to throw the book into the fire. Ralph Waldo Emerson's response to that revolutionary poet was much more farsighted. "I greet you," Emerson wrote to Walt Whitman, "at the beginning of a great career."

Ask Yourself

1. How does Romanticism differ from rationalism?

2. In what two principal ways did Romantics try to rise above "dull realities"?

3. How were the goals of the American Romantic novelists different from the goals of the Fireside Poets?

 Learn It Online

Learn more about American Romanticism through *PowerNotes* online.

go.hrw.com | L11-216 | Go

SKILLS FOCUS Literary Skills Evaluate and analyze the philosophical, political, religious, ethical, and social influences of a historical period; analyze Romanticism.

Analyzing a Painting

American Romanticism valued nature unchanged by civilization, so it is not surprising that Romantic painters turned to the landscape for inspiration. These paintings reveal a mystical enchantment with the solitude and beauty of nature.

Guidelines

Use these guidelines to help you analyze how this painting reflects American Romanticism:

- Examine the painting's depth—its foreground, middle ground, and background. Identify the features that add to the painting's mystical **atmosphere**.
- Study how the artist uses light to emphasize natural beauty.
- Consider the clouds and mist. How do they contribute to the painting's prevailing Romantic mood?

1. What kinds of **images** from nature does the light in the foreground illuminate?

2. Without the clouds and mist, how would the **mood** of this landscape change? Explain your answer.

3. How do the middle ground and background images contribute to this Romantic landscape?

View of the Round-Top in the Catskill Mountains (1827) by Thomas Cole, American (born in England) 1801–1848. Oil on panel. Photograph © 2009 Museum of Fine Arts, Boston.

Your Turn Analyze Romantic Images

Look at the painting on page 214 or 221. How does the artist use depth (foreground, middle ground, background) and light to convey Romantic themes and values?

Thanatopsis

William Cullen Bryant
(1794–1878)

How does a country boy from western Massachusetts become the father of American poetry? In the farms, steepled towns, and mountain forests of the countryside, Bryant found connections between human life and the life of nature.

A Literary Prodigy

William Cullen Bryant's literary gifts were evident from an early age: By age nine, he was writing poetry and had earned a reputation as a prodigy. Though he was tutored for a career as a lawyer, his literary future was assured with the publication of "Thanatopsis." In his late twenties, he moved to New York City and for many years played the triple role of editor, critic, and poet.

Bryant became not only a famous literary figure but an influential voice in religion and politics, as well. An outspoken liberal, Bryant supported social reform, free speech, and the growing movement for the abolition of slavery.

The Father of American Poetry

When Bryant was still an adolescent, he read a book of poems that would transform his life: *Lyrical Ballads,* published in 1798 by his great English contemporaries, William Wordsworth and Samuel Taylor Coleridge. The book inspired Bryant, and he went on to become the first mature American Romantic.

Two other important factors supported the influence of English Romanticism on Bryant's poetry. One factor was Bryant's own growing attraction to the philosophy of deism, which held that divinity could be found in nature. The other factor was the geography of his surroundings, the wondrous beauty of which supported this philosophy. By the time he died, this country boy who translated the messages of English Romanticism into his native tongue was widely acknowledged as the father of American poetry.

What Do You Think?

Where does an individual find inspiration?

🕐 QuickTalk

Think of a time when you were inspired by something you read. With a small group of your classmates, discuss what you read and why it inspired you. In what specific way did this piece of literature influence your thoughts or actions?

Think About the Writer

If Bryant were alive today and could travel into space, what effect do you think that experience might have on his philosophical beliefs? Explain.

William Cullen Bryant (1833) by James Frothingham, American, 1786–1864. Photograph ©2009 Museum of Fine Arts, Boston.

Reader/Writer Notebook

Use your **RWN** to complete the activities for this selection.

Literary Focus

Theme In "Thanatopsis," Bryant reflects upon what happens to us after we die and how we should feel about death. Bryant's answers to these questions represent the **theme** of this poem—the central insight into human experience that a writer reveals in a literary work. As you read, pay special attention to lines 17–72, in which "the still voice" of Nature offers spiritual teachings.

Reading Focus

Identifying Inverted Sentences In order to maintain his meter and create certain **sound effects,** Bryant makes use of **inversion**—a reversal or rearranging of word order in sentences. The usual word order in English sentences is subject, then verb, then object or complement. If you're having trouble understanding a line or passage, look for the subject and the verb, and then restate the sentence in normal English word order.

Into Action As you read, use a chart like the one below to record lines with inversion, noting line numbers for each example. Underline the subject once and the verb twice. Then, rewrite the line in traditional word order. Finally, briefly restate the line in your own words.

Inverted Line	Line Written in Normal English Word Order	Line Restated in Your Own Words
"...from all around—/Earth and her waters, and the depths of air—/Comes a still voice." (lines 15–17)	From all around—/Earth and her waters, and the depths of air—/a still voice comes.	Nature has a soothing, calming quality.

Vocabulary

blight (blyt) *n.*: anything that takes away hope or causes ruin. *The thought of our own mortality is a blight on our happiness.*

clod (klahd) *n.*: lump of dirt or soil. *The farmer broke up the clods of dirt to plant his crops for the upcoming year.*

plod (plahd) *v.*: walk slowly or with difficulty. *All you can do is plod on when thoughts of death become overwhelming.*

mirth (murth) *n.*: happiness. *It is difficult to keep a sense of mirth when one thinks about dying some day.*

Language Coach

Multiple-Meaning Words Which of these words also means "a disease that affects plants"? Which word can also be used to describe "an ignorant person"? Use a dictionary to answer these questions.

Writing Focus

Think as a Reader/Writer

Find It in Your Reading Throughout his poem, Bryant uses **imagery** to evoke emotion. For example, in line 38, he describes the hills as "Rock-ribbed and ancient as the sun." As you read, use your *Reader/Writer Notebook* to record striking images that help convey the poet's theme.

Learn It Online
Listen to this powerful poem read aloud online.

go.hrw.com   L11-219   **Go**

Thanatopsis

by **William Cullen Bryant**

Read with a Purpose
Read to discover what nature can teach us about life and death.

Build Background
When Bryant was only sixteen years old, he coined the word *thanatopsis* by combining two Greek words, *thanatos,* "death," and *opsis,* "sight." The poem defines his new word and offers a different way of looking at and thinking about death.

To him who in the love of Nature holds
Communion with her visible forms, she speaks
A various language; for his gayer hours
She has a voice of gladness, and a smile
5 And eloquence of beauty, and she glides
Into his darker musings, with a mild
And healing sympathy, that steals away
Their sharpness, ere he is aware. When thoughts
Of the last bitter hour come like a blight
10 Over thy spirit, and sad images
Of the stern agony, and shroud, and pall,°
And breathless darkness, and the narrow house,°
Make thee to shudder, and grow sick at heart;—
Go forth, under the open sky, and list°
15 To Nature's teachings, while from all around—
Earth and her waters, and the depths of air—
Comes a still voice.— Ⓐ
              Yet a few days, and thee
The all-beholding sun shall see no more
In all his course; nor yet in the cold ground,
20 Where thy pale form was laid, with many tears,
Nor in the embrace of ocean, shall exist

11. **pall:** coffin cover.
12. **narrow house:** grave.

14. **list:** archaic for "listen."

Ⓐ **Literary Focus** **Theme** Notice how the speaker contrasts the "narrow house" in line 12 with the "open sky" in line 14. What feelings do these images evoke? How do these contrasting images work together to reflect the poem's theme?

Vocabulary **blight** (blyt) *n.:* anything that takes away hope or causes ruin.

Thy image. Earth, that nourished thee, shall claim **B**
Thy growth, to be resolved to earth again,
And, lost each human trace, surrendering up
25 Thine individual being, shalt thou go
To mix forever with the elements,
To be a brother to the insensible rock
And to the sluggish clod, which the rude swain°
Turns with his share,° and treads upon. The oak
30 Shall send his roots abroad, and pierce thy mold.

Yet not to thine eternal resting place
Shalt thou retire alone, nor couldst thou wish
Couch more magnificent. Thou shalt lie down
With patriarchs of the infant world—with kings,
35 The powerful of the earth—the wise, the good,
Fair forms, and hoary seers° of ages past,
All in one mighty sepulcher. The hills
Rock-ribbed and ancient as the sun,—the vales
Stretching in pensive quietness between;
40 The venerable woods—rivers that move
In majesty, and the complaining brooks
That make the meadows green; and, poured round all,
Old Ocean's gray and melancholy waste,—

28. rude swain: uneducated country youth.
29. share: short for "plow-share."

36. hoary seers: white-haired prophets.

B **Reading Focus** **Identifying Inverted Sentences** The main clause in this sentence, "shall exist / Thy image," is inverted. Identify the subject and verb, and then rewrite the clause in normal English word order. Why do you think Bryant inverted this clause?

Vocabulary **clod** (klahd) *n.:* lump of dirt or soil.

Are but the solemn decorations all
45 Of the great tomb of man. The golden sun,
The planets, all the infinite host of heaven,
Are shining on the sad abodes of death,
Through the still lapse of ages. All that tread
The globe are but a handful to the tribes
50 That slumber in its bosom.—Take the wings
Of morning,° pierce the Barcan wilderness,°
Or lose thyself in the continuous woods
Where rolls the Oregon,° and hears no sound,
Save his own dashings—yet the dead are there:
55 And millions in those solitudes, since first
The flight of years began, have laid them down
In their last sleep—the dead reign there alone.
So shalt thou rest, and what if thou withdraw
In silence from the living, and no friend
60 Take note of thy departure? All that breathe
Will share thy destiny. The gay will laugh
When thou art gone, the solemn brood of care
Plod on, and each one as before will chase
His favorite phantom; yet all these shall leave
65 Their mirth and their employments, and shall come
And make their bed with thee. As the long train
Of ages glides away, the sons of men,
The youth in life's fresh spring, and he who goes
In the full strength of years, matron and maid,
70 The speechless babe, and the gray-headed man—
Shall one by one be gathered to thy side,
By those, who in their turn shall follow them. **C**

      So live, that when thy summons comes to join
The innumerable caravan, which moves
75 To that mysterious realm, where each shall take
His chamber in the silent halls of death,
Thou go not, like the quarry slave at night,
Scourged to his dungeon, but, sustained and soothed
By an unfaltering trust, approach thy grave,
80 Like one who wraps the drapery of his couch
About him, and lies down to pleasant dreams. **D**

51. **Take . . . morning:** allusion to Psalm 139:9: "If I take the wings of the morning . . . ;" **Barcan wilderness:** desert near Barca (now al-Marj), in Libya, North Africa.
53. **Oregon:** early name for the Columbia River, which flows between Washington and Oregon.

Birch and Maples (1855) by Asher Brown Durand (1796–1886). Oil on canvas.

C **Literary Focus** **Theme** In lines 58–72, what comfort does the speaker offer? Do you find the images in these lines disturbing or comforting? Explain.

D **Literary Focus** **Theme** What claims does the speaker make about how we should live?

Vocabulary **plod** (plahd) *v.*: walk slowly or with difficulty.
mirth (murth) *n.*: happiness.

Applying Your Skills

Thanatopsis

Respond and Think Critically

Reading Focus

Quick Check

1. In lines 2–8, what does Nature do for those who communicate with her?

2. What decorates the "tomb of man" (ll. 40–45)?

3. In lines 50–57, what examples does the speaker use to explain that the dead are everywhere?

Read with a Purpose

4. According to the poem, what can nature teach us about life and death?

Reading Skills: Identifying Inverted Sentences

5. Review the examples of inversion you recorded in your chart. Then, in a new column, explain how each sentence connects to the theme.

Inverted Line	Line in Normal English Word Order	Line Restated in Your Own Words	How the Line Connects to the Theme
"...from all around—/ Earth and her waters, and the depths of air—/Comes a still <u>voice</u>."	From all around—/ Earth and her waters, and the depths of air—/a still voice comes.	Nature has a soothing, calming quality.	points out that nature can console us during our "darker musings"

✔ Vocabulary Check

Match each Vocabulary word with its definition.

6. blight
7. clod
8. plod
9. mirth

a. walk slowly; trudge
b. happiness
c. something causing ruin
d. lump of dirt or soil

Literary Focus

Literary Analysis

10. **Analyze** Lines 17–30 have a sad, tragic tone. How does the tone change in line 31? What images help create the change in tone?

11. **Summarize** Summarize the speaker's advice in lines 73–81. What images does the poet use?

12. **Evaluate** How effectively does the speaker convey his perspective on death? Explain.

Literary Skills: Theme

13. **Interpret** Some think this poem expresses a traditional view of the afterlife. Others find it an untraditional view—one in which those who die join Nature's great cycle instead of ascending into a heavenly kingdom. Which is a more valid reading of the poem's theme? Explain.

Literary Skills Review: Metaphor

14. **Interpret** A **metaphor** is a figure of speech in which two unlike things are compared. Identify two metaphors in the poem, and explain how they are used to support its theme.

Writing Focus

Think as a Reader/Writer

Use It in Your Writing Using the images in Bryant's poem as a model, write a short poem that expresses a vision of death. Include imagery that reveals your poem's theme.

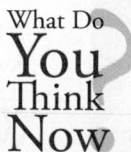

What Do You Think Now

Do you think the natural world of today would inspire Bryant? What kinds of places do you think he would choose to visit?

The Tide Rises, the Tide Falls

The Cross of Snow

QuickWrite

Think of a time when something that happened to you or someone you know inspired you to write. In a few paragraphs, consider what happened and why the event moved you to express yourself in this way.

MEET THE WRITER

Henry Wadsworth Longfellow
(1807–1882)

What image comes to mind when you think of a poet? For Americans, the image of Henry Wadsworth Longfellow—that of a wise and kind gray-bearded man living in a world of romance—has become the symbolic figure of the Poet.

A Popular Fellow

Longfellow was and still is the most popular poet America has ever produced. His poetry appealed greatly to an audience hungry for sermons and lessons. That audience wanted assurances that their cherished values would prevail over the new forces of history—such as industrialization—that were threatening to destroy them. The values Longfellow endorsed were positive forces in the making of the American character, but his tendency to leave these values unexamined led to poetry that often offered easy comfort at the expense of illumination.

Poet of Great Stature

Longfellow's early interest in foreign languages and literature led to an academic career and extensive travels in Europe. During one journey abroad, his wife died. Soon after, he became a professor of French and Spanish at Harvard and seven years later married his second wife, Franny Appleton. They settled into eighteen years of happy marriage, during which he produced some of his most celebrated poetry, including *Evangeline* (1847) and *The Song of Hiawatha* (1855).

By 1854, Longfellow had devoted himself to writing full time. Seven years later, though, tragedy struck when his wife died in a fiery accident. Longfellow tried to save her, smothering the flames with a rug, and was badly burned himself. Longfellow then devoted himself to his work with a religious and literary zeal. He lived a long and productive life, and two years after his death, his marble image was unveiled in the Poets' Corner in London's Westminster Abbey. He was the first American to be so honored.

Think About the Writer

Who do you consider the most popular poet in our era? What <u>factors</u> make him or her popular?

The Tide Rises, the Tide Falls

Reader/Writer
Notebook

Use your **RWN** to complete the activities for this selection.

Literary Focus

Meter: A Pattern of Sounds **Meter** is the pattern of stressed and unstressed syllables in a poem. A **foot** is a metrical unit of poetry made of at least one stressed syllable and one or more unstressed syllables. "The Tide Rises, the Tide Falls" is essentially **iambic**—that is, each metrical foot contains one unstressed syllable followed by one stressed syllable. However, in the first line, Longfellow pairs two stressed syllables in a metrical foot called a **spondee.**

Reading Focus

Annotating a Poem An **annotation** is simply a note about a text. Making notes about a poem while you read can <u>transform</u> your understanding of the poem's craft and meaning. To annotate a poem, jot down the meanings of unfamiliar words and paraphrase difficult lines. Write any questions or comments that you have.

Into Action As you read, use a chart like the one below to record your annotations. In the first column, record words or lines from the poem that require close attention, noting their line numbers. In the second column, write questions about, comments on, or paraphrases of these lines.

Word or Line	Annotations (questions, comments, or paraphrases)
"The twilight darkens, the curlew calls." (line 2)	Why does the poem begin at twilight? Twilight often symbolizes the last stage of life.

Writing Focus

Think as a Reader/Writer

Find It in Your Reading Poets sometimes repeat a word, phrase, or whole line to emphasize a central theme or image. The repetition of a whole line or a group of lines is a **refrain.** In your *Reader/Writer Notebook*, identify the refrain in this poem and note whether the **meter** is the same as or different from that of the rest of the poem.

TechFocus As you read this poem, consider the questions you have about it. What information would help you better understand the poem? Would the Internet or online databases help to provide this information?

Language Coach

Specialized Vocabulary Remember that in poetry, every word an author chooses is significant. Consider the words Longfellow uses to refer to animals in "The Tide Rises, the Tide Falls": *curlew* and *steeds.* You can find *curlew* defined in a sidenote to the poem. *Steeds* you will need to look up in a dictionary. You might even look up these words in an encyclopedia, where you can find additional information or images. What associations might these words have? Why might Longfellow have chosen these words instead of *bird* or *horses*? Keep in mind how the words sound, too.

Learn It Online
Plunge into this poem with a video introduction.

go.hrw.com   L11-225   **Go**

The Tide Rises, the Tide Falls

by **Henry Wadsworth Longfellow**

Read with a Purpose
Read to discover the fate of a lone traveler who walks along the ocean's shore.

Build Background
As a boy, Henry Wadsworth Longfellow lived in Portland, Maine, near the coast of the Atlantic Ocean. Imagery inspired by the coastal landscape plays a role in many of his poems. As he grew older, Longfellow reviewed his childhood memories through the lens of Romanticism. In poems written toward the end of his life, images from nature, such as the behavior of the water as the tide rises and falls, represent the vast cycles of nature—of which humans are only a very small part.

The tide rises, the tide falls,
The twilight darkens, the curlew° calls;
Along the sea-sands damp and brown
The traveler hastens toward the town,
5   And the tide rises, the tide falls. **Ⓐ**

> **2. curlew:** large, brownish shorebird with long legs.

Darkness settles on roofs and walls,
But the sea, the sea in the darkness calls;
The little waves, with their soft, white hands,
Efface° the footprints in the sands,
10   And the tide rises, the tide falls.

> **9. efface:** wipe out; erase.

The morning breaks; the steeds in their stalls
Stamp and neigh, as the hostler° calls;
The day returns, but nevermore
Returns the traveler to the shore,
15   And the tide rises, the tide falls. **Ⓑ**

> **12. hostler:** person who takes care of horses.

Ⓐ **Reading Focus** **Annotating a Poem** What happens in the first stanza of the poem? Make annotations that help you understand the setting, character, and action in this stanza.

Ⓑ **Literary Focus** **Meter** Read the poem aloud. How does the meter of the poem help create a sound like the rising and falling movement of the tides?

SKILLS FOCUS Literary Skills Analyze meter; analyze personification. **Reading Skills** Annotate a poem. **Writing Skills** Employ literary devices for effective writing.

The Tide Rises, the Tide Falls

Respond and Think Critically

Reading Focus

Quick Check

1. Summarize what happens to the traveler in the poem.

2. In the last stanza, what continues to occur despite the traveler's absence?

Read with a Purpose

3. What is the fate of the lone traveler? How might his journey represent the lives of all humans?

Reading Skills: Annotating a Poem

4. As you read, you recorded parts of the poem that require close attention. Now, add a third column in which you reflect on your annotations. Answer any questions you raised, and analyze any comments you made.

Word or Line	Annotations (questions, comments, or paraphrases)	Reflection on Annotation
"The twilight darkens, the curlew calls." (line 2)	Why does the poem begin at twilight? Twilight often symbolizes the last stage of life.	The twilight shows that the traveler is nearing the end of his life. In the second stanza, the twilight turns into complete darkness.

Literary Focus

Literary Analysis

5. Analyze How does the repetition of "the tide rises, the tide falls" express the poem's theme?

6. Interpret Though the rising and falling of the tide is the central image in the poem, other patterns and cycles are also present. What are they? How do they relate to the image of the tide?

7. Contrast What words in the third stanza hint at the traveler's fate? How does the image of the lively horses contrast with what probably has happened to the traveler?

8. Evaluate In an earlier poem titled "A Psalm of Life," Longfellow writes that at death, we may "leave behind us / Footprints on the sands of time." How does "The Tide Rises, the Tide Falls" echo and change this image?

Literary Skills: Meter: A Pattern of Sounds

9. Analyze Which words are repeated in lines 6–7? How does this repetition affect the rhythm and mood of these two lines?

Literary Skills Review: Personification

10. Interpret In a figure of speech called **personification,** an object or animal is given human feelings, thoughts, actions, or attitudes. What characteristics of a human does the poet give the sea and the waves in lines 7–9? What is the effect of the personification?

Writing Focus

Think as a Reader/Writer

Use It in Your Writing In your *Reader/Writer Notebook,* you identified the refrain of the poem and analyzed how it helped express the central theme. Think of an interesting image from nature, and write one line of poetry describing it. Then, write a short poem using this line as the refrain.

 What Do **You Think Now** Why do you think nature often inspires people to think about universal or fundamental questions?

For **CHOICES** see page 231.

Preparing to Read

The Cross of Snow

Reader/Writer
Notebook

Use your **RWN** to complete the activities for this selection.

Literary Focus

Sonnet A **sonnet** is a fourteen-line poem usually written in **iambic pentameter.** Lines of poetry written in iambic pentameter contain five iambs. An **iamb** is an unstressed syllable followed by a stressed syllable. The sonnet has two <u>principal</u> forms. The **Petrarchan,** or **Italian,** sonnet consists of an eight-line **octave** followed by a six-line **sestet.** The **Elizabethan,** or **Shakespearean,** sonnet consists of three **quatrains** (four-line stanzas) followed by a **couplet.** "The Cross of Snow" is a Petrarchan sonnet. The octave and sestet in a Petrarchan sonnet are usually related. The octave introduces the poem's subject, and the sestet responds to it.

Reading Focus

Visualizing Imagery Poets bring their ideas to life by using imagery, or language that evokes pictures or sensations. **Visualizing imagery** means making mental pictures of what you read.

Into Action As you read, use a chart like the one below to keep track of the images in the octave and the sestet. First, list the images in each part, noting the line number. Then, visualize each image and describe in your own words what you see.

	Image	Visualization
Octave	"sleepless watches of the night" (line 1)	The speaker can't sleep; he's pacing or tossing and turning.
Sestet		

Writing Focus

Think as a Reader/Writer
Find It in Your Reading The typical **rhyme scheme** in a **Petrarchan sonnet** is *abba, abba, cde, cde.* As you read this poem, take note of the rhyme scheme. Does it fit the traditional Petrarchan pattern? What word pairs does Longfellow rhyme?

Vocabulary

halo (HAY loh) *n.:* circular band of light. *The only thing illuminating the room was a halo of light around the candle.*

martyrdom (MAHR tuhr duhm) *n.:* painful death of a martyr. *Martyrdom almost always involves experiencing an enormous amount of pain and suffering.*

ravines (ruh VEENZ) *n.:* long, narrow valleys with steep sides. *The water from the melting snow formed the deep ravines.*

Language Coach

Related Words Build your vocabulary by learning clusters of related words. Since *halo* means "circular band of light," group it with *aura,* which describes light similar to a halo.

Learn It Online
Listen to this sonnet with the audio version online.

go.hrw.com   L11-228   **Go**

POEM

The Cross of Snow

by Henry Wadsworth Longfellow

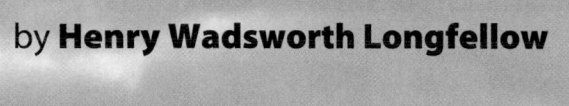

Read with a Purpose
Read to discover the multiple meanings of the image "cross of snow."

Build Background
Henry Wadsworth Longfellow wrote this poem eighteen years after his second wife, Fanny, died when a lighted match or hot sealing wax ignited her summer dress. Three years later Longfellow died without having shown the poem to anyone. Discovered among his papers, it was published four years later and immediately became one of his most famous poems.

Mount of the Holy Cross, Colorado.

> In the long, sleepless watches of the night,
>   A gentle face—the face of one long dead—
>   Looks at me from the wall, where round its head
>   The night lamp casts a halo of pale light.
> 5 Here in this room she died; and soul more white
>   Never through martyrdom of fire was led **Ⓐ**
>   To its repose; nor can in books be read
>   The legend of a life more benedight.°
> There is a mountain in the distant West **Ⓑ**
> 10   That, sun-defying, in its deep ravines
>   Displays a cross of snow upon its side.
> Such is the cross I wear upon my breast
>   These eighteen years, through all the changing scenes
>   And seasons, changeless since the day she died.

8. benedight: archaic for "blessed."

Ⓐ **Reading Focus** **Visualizing Imagery** Make a mental picture of the image "martyrdom of fire." What is Longfellow suggesting about his wife's character by using this powerful image? What other image reinforces this characterization of his wife?

Ⓑ **Literary Focus** **Sonnet** This line begins the sestet. How does this line signal a change in the poem's focus?

Vocabulary **halo** (HAY loh) *n.:* circular band of light.
martyrdom (MAHR tuhr duhm) *n.:* painful death of a martyr.
ravines (ruh VEENZ) *n.:* long, narrow valleys with steep sides.

Applying Your Skills

The Cross of Snow

Respond and Think Critically

Reading Focus

Quick Check

1. What happened to the woman in the picture?

2. What can you tell about the relationship between the speaker and the woman described in the picture?

3. What two crosses does the poem describe?

Read with a Purpose

4. What multiple meanings did you discover for the image "cross of snow"? Why might Longfellow have included the word "snow" to describe his personal cross?

Reading Skills: Visualizing Imagery

5. As you read the poem, you recorded the images and described your mental pictures. Review the information in your chart. Then, add a third column in which you explain how each image expresses the poem's meaning.

	Image	Visualization	Connection to the Poem's Meaning
Octave	"sleepless watches of the night"	The speaker can't sleep; he's pacing or tossing and turning.	helps suggest the speaker's loneliness and suffering
Sestet			

✔ Vocabulary Check

Match each Vocabulary word with its definition.

6. halo   a. long, narrow valleys

7. martyrdom   b. circular band of light

8. ravines   c. painful death of a martyr

Literary Focus

Literary Analysis

9. **Draw Conclusions** Why might Longfellow have chosen to use a cross as the symbol of his grief?

10. **Interpret** Explain how "sun-defying" (line 10) suggests conditions of weather and geology that might produce a permanent cross of snow on the side of a mountain. How does the poet relate this idea to his own feelings of grief?

11. **Extend** What universal human experience do you think Longfellow has expressed in this poem? How might this explain his popularity?

Literary Skills: Sonnet

12. **Interpret** What question or idea does the octave (lines 1–8) present? What answer or response does the sestet (lines 9–14) offer?

Literary Skills Review: Tone

13. **Interpret** The attitude a writer takes toward his or her subject, characters, or audience is **tone.** Describe the poem's tone. Which words create the tone, and how does it relate to the theme?

Writing Focus

Think as a Reader/Writer

Use It in Your Writing Try writing a sonnet of your own. In the octave, introduce your subject. Comment on your subject in the sestet. Follow the *abba, abba, cde, cde* rhyme scheme.

What Do You Think Now

Why do powerful emotions such as grief often inspire writing or other artwork? How might creative expression help people heal their grief?

Applying Your Skills

The Tide Rises, the Tide Falls /
The Cross of Snow

Grammar Link

Sentence Order: Inverted Sentences

In order to maintain the rhyme scheme of a poem, Longfellow often uses **inversion**—a reversal or rearranging of the usual word order in sentences. In English, the subject of a sentence usually comes before the verb, while the object or objects follow the verb. For example, in the sentence *The man climbed the mountain,* man is the subject, *climbed* is the verb, and *mountain* is the object. If you're having trouble understanding a line or passage, look for the subject and the verb, and then restate the sentence in normal English word order. For example, look at the following sentence:

> Several words said he.

In this line, *he* is the subject and *said* is the verb. *Words* is the object of *said.* In normal word order, the sentence looks like this:

> He said several words.

Your Turn

Rewrite each sentence in standard English word order. Identify the subject and verb in each sentence.

1. "Nor can in books be read / The legend of a life more benedight."

2. "Nevermore / Returns the traveler to the shore."

Portion of the original manuscript of "The Cross of Snow" by Longfellow.

CHOICES

As you respond to the Choices, use these **Academic Vocabulary** words as appropriate: factor, implicit, integral, principal, transform.

REVIEW

Annotate in Hypertext

TechFocus With a small group of classmates, create a hypertext version of "The Tide Rises, the Tide Falls." Create an HTML version of the poem, and hyperlink certain words to your group's questions, comments, and observations as well as information integral to understanding the poem. For example, you can offer comments on the poem's meter.

CONNECT

Compare Views

Partner Discussion The themes of "The Tide Rises, the Tide Falls" and "The Cross of Snow" involve death. With a partner, list and discuss the differences between the two poems' attitudes toward death. Are people's views on death different when they are talking about the concept of death than when they are grieving over a loved one?

EXTEND

Listen to Romantic Composers

The principal ideals of Romanticism can be found in the literature, art, music, and philosophy of the 1800s. Many of the great composers—Beethoven, Schubert, Chopin—were writing music during Longfellow's life. Find recordings of music written during the Romantic period to present to your class. Discuss similarities between the music and Longfellow's poetry. How is the Romantic view reflected in both?

 Learn It Online
Find out more about Longfellow and his poetry through these Internet links.

go.hrw.com   L11-231   **Go**

The Chambered Nautilus

What Do You Think?

Where does an individual find inspiration?

🕐 QuickTalk

Think about objects or scenes in the natural world that have meant something to you. Meet with a partner to discuss an aspect of nature that has led you to an insight about life or human nature.

Oliver Wendell Holmes
(1809–1894)

Oliver Wendell Holmes was a writer and teacher who is remembered for his wit, his wordplay, and his warm temperament.

A Doctor with a Sense of Humor

Holmes, a descendant of the Puritan writer Anne Bradstreet, was born into a respected Cambridge, Massachusetts, family. Bored with a brief stint studying law, he turned his attention to medicine. His wit was evident when, as a young physician opening his practice, he hung out a sign saying GRATEFUL FOR SMALL FEVERS.

Holmes later taught at Harvard, where he lectured on anatomy and physiology and later served as dean of the Harvard Medical School. An enthusiastic advocate for progress in medicine, Holmes spent a great deal of time giving lectures and writing. He published medical treatises, novels with medical themes, humorous essays, and many poems. His poem "Old Ironsides," about a famous battleship, was so popular it helped save the ship from being scrapped. (The ship was restored and remains a popular attraction today.) He is also credited with coining the term *anesthesia* ("without feeling").

A Fireside Poet

Holmes was part of a small group of American poets who were the first to rival British poets in popularity. Along with Henry Wadsworth Longfellow, John Greenleaf Whittier, James Russell Lowell, and William Cullen Bryant, he is known as one of the Fireside Poets, so called because they wrote about subjects geared for a family audience, and their work was often read aloud at the fireside.

Holmes and his friends founded the magazine the *Atlantic Monthly*, to which he contributed a series of lively essays eventually collected as *The Autocrat of the Breakfast-Table* (1858). The first volume of the magazine includes several poems; "The Chambered Nautilus" is one of the most famous. In addition to his medical, political, and humorous writing, Holmes also received recognition for writing biographies of his friends John Lothrop Motley (1879) and Ralph Waldo Emerson (1855).

Think About the Writer

Holmes was a multitalented man with varied interests. If he were alive today, what contemporary subjects do you think would intrigue him? What might he write about?

Reader/Writer Notebook

Use your **RWN** to complete the activities for this selection.

Literary Focus

Extended Metaphor A **metaphor** is a figure of speech that compares two unlike things without using the words *like* or *as*. Sometimes writers extend a metaphor—that is, they take it as far as it can logically be developed. An **extended metaphor** develops the comparison over a number of lines and with several examples. In "The Chambered Nautilus," Holmes compares the life span of the nautilus to the progress of the human soul. As you read the poem, pay attention to how he develops this metaphor.

Reading Focus

Finding the Main Idea The **main idea** of a poem is its <u>principal</u> message, theme, or insight—the point that the poet is trying to make. Holmes conveys his main idea about spiritual growth through an extended metaphor. As you read, focus on each part of the comparison. When you encounter difficult lines, you may need to re-read and then paraphrase them, or restate them in your own words.

Into Action To uncover the poem's main idea, use a chart like the one below to paraphrase various parts of the extended metaphor as you read.

Lines	Quotation	Paraphrase
1–2	"This is the ship of pearl, which, poets feign, / Sails the unshadowed main."	The chambered nautilus is like a ship made of pearl, and it is, as poets imagine, going on a voyage.

Vocabulary

venturous (VEHN chuhr uhs) *adj.:* bold; daring; adventurous. *The poet admires the venturous spirit of the chambered nautilus.*

unfurl (uhn FURL) *v.:* spread out or unfold. *To grow, the chambered nautilus will unfurl in a widening spiral.*

crypt (krihpt) *n.:* underground burial chamber. *The poet sees the broken chambered nautilus as a crypt that has been broken open.*

lustrous (LUHS truhs) *adj.:* shining, glossy. *Like many shells, the chambered nautilus has a lustrous surface.*

forlorn (fawr LAWRN) *adj.:* deserted; miserable; hopeless. *The chambered nautilus has been washed ashore, broken and forlorn.*

Language Coach

Word Definitions When you learn a new word, connect it to an image or word that will help you to remember the word and its meaning. With the word *unfurl,* for example, picture a flag spreading out in the wind or think of the rhyming word *uncurl.*

Writing Focus

Think as a Reader/Writer

Find It in Your Reading The Romantics believed that humans could find beauty and truth by reflecting on the natural world. As you read, notice the speaker's close observations of the nautilus's appearance and actions. In your *Reader/Writer Notebook,* make a list of words and images that reveal a careful attention to the natural world.

Learn It Online
Get to know the vocabulary words online with Word Watch.

go.hrw.com [L11-233] **Go**

The Chambered Nautilus

by **Oliver Wendell Holmes**

Read with a Purpose
Read to discover how the poet's observations of the natural world provide insight into the human soul.

Build Background
A relative of the octopus and the squid, the chambered nautilus is a snail-like sea creature native to the South Pacific and Indian Oceans. During its lifetime, the nautilus grows from the size of a tiny bead to the size of a pumpkin. As it <u>transforms</u>, the nautilus creates new chambers of its shell to house its body. The name *nautilus,* from a Greek word meaning "sailor," comes from an old belief that the creature could actually use its shell as a ship in which it sailed. Unique in many ways, the chambered nautilus inspired both the scientist and the poet in Oliver Wendell Holmes.

The first three stanzas of the poem are a meditation on the life and death of the nautilus. The final two stanzas use **apostrophe,** a direct address to someone or something that is not present.

This is the ship of pearl, which, poets feign,°
    Sails the unshadowed main°,—
    The venturous bark° that flings
On the sweet summer wind its purpled wings
5 In gulfs enchanted, where the siren° sings,
    And coral reefs lie bare,
Where the cold sea maids° rise to sun their streaming hair. **Ⓐ**

Its webs of living gauze no more unfurl;
    Wrecked is the ship of pearl!
10   And every chambered cell,
Where its dim dreaming life was wont to dwell,
As the frail tenant shaped his growing shell,
    Before thee lies revealed,—
Its irised° ceiling rent,° its sunless crypt unsealed!

1. feign (fayn): archaic for "imagine."
2. the unshadowed main: archaic for "the sunlit sea."
3. bark: archaic for "a sailing ship."
5. siren: in Greek mythology, one of a group of sea maidens whose seductive singing lures sailors to wreck their ships on coastal rocks.
7. sea maids: mermaids or sea nymphs.
14. irised (Y rihst): iridescent; rainbowlike. Iris is the Greek goddess of the rainbow. **rent:** torn.

Ⓐ Literary Focus Extended Metaphor In this stanza, Holmes compares the nautilus's shell to a ship. Choose three details he includes, and explain how they help extend the metaphor.

Vocabulary **venturous** (VEHN chuhr uhs) *adj.:* bold; daring; adventurous.
unfurl (uhn FURL) *v.:* spread out or unfold.
crypt (krihpt) *n.:* underground burial chamber.

Proportion

If you look at the photograph on page 234, you can see why artists admire the structure of the chambered nautilus shell. The shell spirals outward from the center in a beautiful, ever-widening curve. The nautilus has what artists call proportion—a pleasing balance between all the parts of an object or image. You can further appreciate the nautilus shell's natural perfection by looking at it in relation to what is called the golden section—an arrangement of ever-smaller rectangles, each a mirror image of the others. Look at the illustration; the eye can see it before the mind can grasp it.

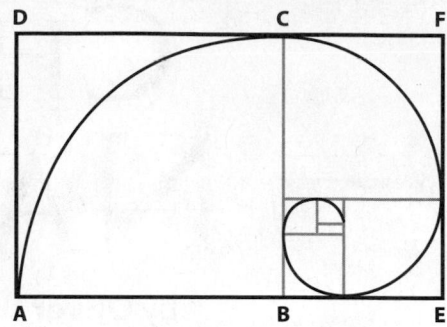

Golden section, with spiral showing proportion.

Ask Yourself

How can you tell that Holmes admired proportion in the chambered nautilus? Explain.

15 Year after year beheld the silent toil
     That spread his lustrous coil;
     Still, as the spiral grew,
He left the past year's dwelling for the new,
Stole with soft step its shining archway through,
20   Built up its idle door,
Stretched in his last-found home, and knew the old no more.

Thanks for the heavenly message brought by thee,
     Child of the wandering sea,
     Cast from her lap, forlorn!
25 From thy dead lips a clearer note is born
Than ever Triton blew from wreathèd horn!°
     While on mine ear it rings,
Through the deep caves of thought I hear a voice that sings:—

Build thee more stately mansions, O my soul,
30   As the swift seasons roll!
     Leave thy low-vaulted past! **Ⓑ**
Let each new temple, nobler than the last,
Shut thee from heaven with a dome more vast,
     Till thou at length art free,
35 Leaving thine outgrown shell by life's unresting sea!

26. than . . . wreathèd horn: echoes a line from "The World Is Too Much with Us," a sonnet by the English poet William Wordsworth (1770–1850): "Or hear old Triton blow his wreathèd horn." In Greek mythology, Triton is a sea god, often represented as blowing a trumpet made from a conch shell. *Wreathèd* means "coiled" or "spiral-shaped."

Ⓑ **Reading Focus** **Finding the Main Idea** How does the instruction to "Leave thy low-vaulted past!" relate to Holmes's main idea?

Vocabulary **lustrous** (LUHS truhs) *adj.:* shining; glossy.
forlorn (fawr LAWRN) *adj.:* deserted; miserable; hopeless.

SKILLS FOCUS **Literary Skills** Analyze extended metaphor; analyze allusion. **Reading Skills** Identify the main idea of a text. **Writing Skills** Develop descriptions with sensory details.

Respond and Think Critically

Reading Focus

Quick Check

1. Describe the chambered nautilus. What kind of creature is it? Where does it live?

2. What happens when the nautilus outgrows its chamber?

3. The third stanza makes an implicit comparison between the nautilus and a person who changes homes. What details contribute to this comparison?

Read with a Purpose

4. How does the poet's close observation of the nautilus lead to insights about the human soul?

Reading Skills: Finding the Main Idea

5. While reading the poem, you paraphrased difficult lines. Re-read the information in your chart. Then, add a column that shows how each line relates to the poem's main idea.

Lines	Quotation	Paraphrase	How It Relates to the Main Idea
1–2	"This is the ship of pearl, which, poets feign, / Sails the unshadowed main."	The nautilus is like a ship made of pearl, and it is, as poets imagine, going on a voyage.	The chambered nautilus is like the human soul on an earthly voyage.

Literary Focus

Literary Analysis

6. **Infer** Based on the images Holmes uses in the first stanza, what can you infer about his feelings toward the nautilus and its journey?

7. **Summarize** Summarize what has happened to the nautilus in the second stanza.

8. **Analyze** Who or what is the subject of the apostrophe in each of the last two stanzas? What is the main idea of each of these stanzas, and why do you think Holmes uses apostrophe here?

Literary Skills: Extended Metaphor

9. **Analyze** Step by step, explain the fifth stanza's extended metaphor comparing the life span of the nautilus and the progress of the human soul. Explain the "stately mansions" (line 29), the "low-vaulted past" (line 31), "each new temple" (line 32), the "outgrown shell" (line 35), and the "unresting sea" (line 35).

Literary Skills Review: Allusion

10. **Interpret** An **allusion** is a reference to someone or something from history, literature, religion, politics, science, or some other branch of culture. Summarize the lines that allude to Triton. Why might Holmes have wanted to allude to a Romantic poet?

Writing Focus

Think as a Reader/Writer

Use It in Your Writing Review your list of words and images that show Holmes's careful attention to the natural world. Choose something in nature that you find interesting. Write a short poem or paragraph describing it in detail.

What Do You Think Now

What do you think initially drew Holmes to the chambered nautilus as a poetic subject? Why do you think he found it inspiring?

from Nature
from Self-Reliance

What Do You Think?

Where does an individual find inspiration?

🕐 QuickWrite

Emerson found nature exhilarating. How does nature serve as a source of inspiration? Write a paragraph explaining the uplifting effects of nature.

Ralph Waldo Emerson (c. 1867) by William Henry Furness, Jr.

Ralph Waldo Emerson
(1803–1882)

Ralph Waldo Emerson was one of those rare writers who appealed both to intellectuals and to the general public. Emerson, an immensely popular lecturer, had a distinctly American perspective that denied the importance of the past. Instead, he urged people to focus on humanity and find inspiration in nature.

A Young Rebel

Emerson was born in Boston in 1803 to a family that was cultured but poor. After his father, a Unitarian minister, died when Emerson was seven years old, Emerson and his five siblings were raised by his mother and aunt.

Emerson entered Harvard at fourteen, and after graduation he prepared himself to become a minister, like the eight generations of Emersons before him. In 1829, at the age of twenty-five, he accepted a post at Boston's Second Church. He soon married Ellen Tucker, who died seventeen months later.

Emerson's grief coincided with a growing disbelief in some of the central doctrines of his religion. In 1832, he shocked his congregation by resigning from the ministry and setting off on an extended tour of Europe. There he met and conversed with the English Romantic poets William Wordsworth and Samuel Taylor Coleridge, as well as other influential writers.

A Trusted Guide

Returning to the United States in late 1833, Emerson settled in Concord, Massachusetts, and remarried. He began giving lectures, and his novel ideas eventually became popular.

With the author's growing fame, Concord became a destination for truth-seeking young people who looked to Emerson as their guide. The young responded to Emerson's predictions that they were on the verge of a new age; intellectuals responded to his philosophical ideas about the relations among humanity, nature, and God; and society as a whole responded to his optimism.

Although Emerson spoke publicly less often in his later years, his popularity did not diminish. He died in 1882.

Think About the Writer In what way did Emerson have to let go of the past in order to follow his own path in life?

from **Nature**

Reader/Writer Notebook

Use your **RWN** to complete the activities for this selection.

Literary Focus

Imagery In this essay, Emerson doesn't just *tell* us how he feels about nature. Instead, he uses vivid **imagery,** or words that appeal to the senses, to describe scenes in nature that move him. As you read, look for images that appeal to your senses. Notice how these images help you share the writer's experience.

Reading Focus

Monitoring Your Reading Nature provided Emerson with inspiring scenes and topics for serious reflection. To follow Emerson's thoughts, **monitor your reading** by pausing periodically to make sure that you understand what you have read. Use strategies such as summarizing the main idea and asking questions.

Into Action As you read, monitor your reading by filling in a chart like the one below. After reading each paragraph, write the main idea and a question you have about that paragraph.

Paragraph	Main Idea	Question
1	Looking at the stars gives one a sense of the sublime.	Why do the stars have an "admonishing smile"?
2		

Writing Focus

Think as a Reader/Writer

Find It in Your Reading Emerson's attitude toward nature is evident in his use of language. In describing scenes of nature, he uses vivid details and striking **images** to convey his impressions. As you read, use your *Reader/Writer Notebook* to record some of the descriptions of nature that you find especially interesting.

TechFocus As you read this essay, think about your own experiences with nature. To what extent has your exposure to the natural environment been affected by technological innovations such as television, video games, cell phones, and the Internet?

Vocabulary

transparent (trans PAIR uhnt) *adj.:* able to be seen through. *Earth's transparent atmosphere enables people to see the stars.*

admonishing (ad MAHN ihsh ihng) *v.* used as *adj.:* gently warning. *Emerson's admonishing remark tells us not to take the stars for granted.*

integrate (IHN tuh grayt) *v.:* form into a whole. *With his sensitive vision, the poet can integrate the objects of nature into a single impression.*

blithe (blyth) *adj.:* happy; carefree. *The poet feels blithe when he stands in the cool, refreshing air.*

egotism (EE guh tihz uhm) *n.:* thinking excessively of oneself. *His egotism and selfishness disappear when he experiences the beauties of nature.*

Language Coach

Roots The Vocabulary word *integrate* comes from *integer,* a word meaning "whole." In the excerpt from *Nature,* Emerson writes that a poet integrates separate aspects of nature into a complete picture. What other things or concepts can be integrated? With a partner, discuss what it might mean to integrate the following people or things: social groups, computer systems, ideas.

Learn It Online
Listen to this essay online.

go.hrw.com | L11-239 | Go

from NATURE

by **Ralph Waldo Emerson**

Upper Ausable Lake (1868) by Homer Dodge Martin.

Read with a Purpose

Read to discover how Emerson defines a "lover of nature."

Build Background

In his introduction to the book *Nature,* Emerson offers a clue to his purpose when he encourages his readers to look directly at nature. In this quest for original insight and a uniquely American literary expression, Emerson inspired the American renaissance. In *Nature* he made it clear that the magnificent American landscape itself could be an integral part of spiritual rebirth.

To go into solitude, a man needs to retire as much from his chamber[1] as from society. I am not solitary while I read and write, though nobody is with me. But if a man would be alone, let him look at the stars. The rays that come from those heavenly worlds, will separate between him and vulgar things. One might think the atmosphere was made transparent with this design, to give man, in the heavenly bodies, the perpetual presence of the sublime.[2] Seen in the streets of cities, how great they are! If the stars should appear one night in a thousand years, how would men believe and adore; and preserve for many generations the remembrance of the city of God which had been shown! But every night come out these envoys[3] of beauty, and light the universe with their admonishing smile.

The stars awaken a certain reverence, because though always present, they are always inaccessible; but all natural objects make a kindred impression, when the mind is open to their influence. Nature never wears a mean appearance. Neither does the wisest man extort all her secrets, and lose his curiosity by finding out all her perfection. Nature never became a toy to a wise spirit. The flowers, the animals, the mountains, reflected all the wisdom of his best hour, as much as they had delighted the simplicity of his childhood.

When we speak of nature in this manner, we have a distinct but most poetical sense in the mind. We mean the integrity of impression made by manifold natural objects. It is this which distinguishes the stick of timber of the woodcutter, from the tree of the poet.

The charming landscape which I saw this morning, is indubitably[4] made up of some twenty or thirty farms. Miller owns this field, Locke that, and Manning the woodland beyond. But none of them owns the landscape. There is a property in the horizon which no man has but he whose eye can integrate all the parts, that is, the poet. This is the best part of these men's farms, yet to this their warranty deeds[5] give no title. **Ⓐ**

To speak truly, few adult persons can see nature. Most persons do not see the sun. At least they have a very superficial seeing. The sun illuminates only the eye of the man, but shines into the eye and the heart of the child. The lover of nature is he whose inward and outward senses are still truly adjusted to each other; who has retained the spirit of infancy even into the era of manhood. His intercourse with heaven and earth, becomes part of his daily food. In the presence of nature, a wild delight runs through the man, in spite of real sorrows. Nature says—he is my creature, and maugre[6] all his impertinent griefs, he shall be glad with me. Not the sun or the summer alone, but every hour and season yields its tribute of delight; for every hour and change corresponds to and authorizes a different state of the mind, from breathless noon to grimmest midnight. Nature is a setting that fits equally well a comic or a mourning piece. In good health, the air is a cordial[7] of incredible virtue. Crossing a bare common, in snow puddles, at twilight, under a clouded sky, without having in my thoughts any occurrence of special good fortune, I have enjoyed a perfect exhilaration. Almost I fear to think how glad I am. In the woods too, a man

---

1. **chamber:** room in a house.
2. **sublime:** awe-inspiring. Here, Emerson refers to the divine.
3. **envoys:** messengers.

4. **indubitably:** without a doubt.
5. **warranty deeds:** legal documents showing property ownership.
6. **maugre** (MAW guhr): archaic for "in spite of; despite."
7. **cordial:** medicine, food, or drink that strengthens.

Vocabulary **transparent** (trans PAIR uhnt) *adj.:* able to be seen through.
admonishing (ad MAHN ihsh ihng) *v.* used as *adj.:* gently warning.
integrate (IHN tuh grayt) *v.:* form into a whole.

Ⓐ **Reading Focus** Monitoring Your Reading Paraphrase this paragraph. How does the poet use his unique vision to integrate the various parts of nature that he sees?

casts off his years, as the snake his slough,[8] and at what period soever of life, is always a child. In the woods, is perpetual youth. Within these plantations of God, a decorum[9] and sanctity reign, a perennial festival is dressed, and the guest sees not how he should tire of them in a thousand years. In the woods, we return to reason and faith. There I feel that nothing can befall me in life—no disgrace, no calamity (leaving me my eyes), which nature cannot repair. Standing on the bare ground—my head bathed by the blithe air, and uplifted into infinite space—all mean egotism vanishes. I become a transparent eyeball. I am nothing. I see all. The currents of the Universal Being circulate through me; I am part or particle of God. The name of the nearest friend sounds then foreign and accidental. To be brothers, to be acquaintances—master or servant, is then a trifle and a disturbance. I am the lover of uncontained and immortal beauty. In the wilderness, I find something more dear and connate[10] than in streets or villages. In the tranquil landscape, and especially in the distant line of the horizon, man beholds somewhat as beautiful as his own nature. **Ⓑ**

> IN THE WOODS, WE RETURN TO REASON AND FAITH. THERE I FEEL THAT NOTHING CAN BEFALL ME IN LIFE—NO DISGRACE, NO CALAMITY . . . WHICH NATURE CANNOT REPAIR.

The greatest delight which the fields and woods minister, is the suggestion of an occult[11] relation between man and the vegetable. I am not alone and unacknowledged. They nod to me and I to them. The waving of the boughs in the storm, is new to me and old. It takes me by surprise, and yet is not unknown. Its effect is like that of a higher thought or a better emotion coming over me, when I deemed I was thinking justly or doing right. **Ⓒ**

Yet it is certain that the power to produce this delight, does not reside in nature, but in man, or in a harmony of both. It is necessary to use these pleasures with great temperance. For, nature is not always tricked[12] in holiday attire, but the same scene which yesterday breathed perfume and glittered as for the frolic of the nymphs, is overspread with melancholy today. Nature always wears the colors of the spirit. To a man laboring under calamity, the heat of his own fire hath sadness in it. Then, there is a kind of contempt of the landscape felt by him who has just lost by death a dear friend. The sky is less grand as it shuts down over less worth in the population.

---

8. **slough** (sluhf): outer layer of a snake's skin, which is shed periodically.
9. **decorum:** orderliness.
10. **connate:** having the same nature.

11. **occult:** mysterious; hidden.
12. **tricked:** dressed up.

Ⓑ **Reading Focus** **Monitoring Your Reading** Re-read this long paragraph. What main ideas and supporting details are integral to Emerson's argument?

Ⓒ **Literary Focus** Imagery What image does Emerson use here? How does this image reveal Emerson's openness to nature's influence?

Vocabulary **blithe** (blyth) *adj.:* happy; carefree.
egotism (EE guh tihz uhm) *n.:* thinking excessively of oneself.

SKILLS FOCUS **Literary Skills** Analyze how imagery conveys meaning; analyze personification. **Reading Skills** Monitor your reading for comprehension. **Vocabulary** **Skills** Demonstrate knowledge of literal meanings of words and their usage. **Writing Skills** Describe a place; develop descriptions with sensory details.

Respond and Think Critically

Reading Focus

Quick Check

1. How does the poet's view of nature differ from that of a woodcutter or property owner?

2. How do people's views of nature change depending upon their circumstances?

Read with a Purpose

3. According to Emerson, what is a "lover of nature"? Would you consider yourself to be a lover of nature? Why?

Reading Skills: Monitoring Your Reading

4. Look over the questions you listed in your chart. Now add a fourth column to your chart in which you answer each question.

Paragraph	Main Idea	Question	Answer
1	Looking at the stars gives one a sense of the sublime.	Why do the stars have an "admonishing smile"?	They seem to know that people do not appreciate their beauty.

✔ Vocabulary Check

Answer the following questions, and justify your answers. Use the Vocabulary words in your answers.

5. How does looking into a star-filled, **transparent** sky affect one's outlook?

6. How can an **admonishing** remark to slow down make someone notice nature's beauty?

7. How can appreciating nature **integrate** one's fragmented thoughts?

8. Can one possess great **egotism** and still have a **blithe** spirit?

Literary Focus

Literary Analysis

9. **Analyze** What does Emerson mean by his statement that he is "not solitary when he reads and writes, though nobody is with me"?

10. **Compare and Contrast** Do you believe that "few adult persons can see nature"? Explain.

11. **Infer** What is the implicit message about city life in "In the wilderness, I find something more dear and connate than in streets or villages"?

Literary Skills: Imagery

12. **Interpret** Emerson writes that in the company of nature he becomes a "transparent eyeball." Describe this unusual image in your own words. How does it contribute to the essay's main idea?

Literary Skills Review: Personification

13. **Analyze** In the essay's first and last paragraphs, find two examples of **personification**—giving an object or animal human feelings, thoughts, or attitudes—and explain their effectiveness.

Writing Focus

Think as a Reader/Writer

Use It in Your Writing Choose a natural setting, and use colorful imagery to describe it. What thoughts and feelings do you experience in this setting?

What Do **You Think Now** What aspects of nature inspired Emerson?

For **CHOICES** see page 250. ❯

from **Self-Reliance**

Reader/Writer
Notebook

Use your **RWN** to complete the activities for this selection.

Literary Focus

Figures of Speech One sign of Emerson's poetic nature is the way he uses **figures of speech,** words or phrases that describe one thing in terms of another very different thing. Figures of speech—which include **simile, metaphor,** and **personification**—are not meant to be taken literally. In "Self-Reliance," Emerson uses a metaphor when he says, "Society is a joint-stock company." He is comparing society to a business where the shareholders or owners are held personally liable.

Literary Perspectives Apply the literary perspective described on page 245 as you read this essay.

Reading Focus

Understanding Figures of Speech In this essay, Emerson's figures of speech increase the reader's understanding of abstract ideas by framing the ideas in new ways. When you encounter a complex figure of speech, ask yourself, "Why did the writer choose this particular comparison?" and "What do the compared things have in common?"

Into Action When you come across a figure of speech, write it down and note the paragraph number in a chart like the one below. In the third column, tell what is being compared and what they have in common.

Paragraph	Figure of Speech	Comparison
1	"Imitation is suicide."	Imitating others can lead to the loss of one's self. In this sense, imitation is like suicide.

Writing Focus

Think as a Reader/Writer

Find It in Your Reading "Self-Reliance" is filled with memorable phrases and sentences. These short, clever statements that make interesting observations about life are called **aphorisms.** As you read, record in your *Reader/Writer Notebook* a few aphorisms from the essay.

Vocabulary

conviction (kuhn VIHK shuhn) *n.:* firm belief. *Emerson expresses his conviction that people should be self-reliant.*

manifest (MAN uh fehst) *adj.:* apparent; clear. *Emerson tries to make manifest the idea that people should trust themselves.*

predominating (prih DAHM uh nay tihng) *v.* used as *adj.:* having great influence or power. *A predominating principle in a person's life should be faith in oneself.*

transcendent (tran SEHN duhnt) *adj.:* excelling; surpassing. *Accept your transcendent destiny by living up to your full potential.*

aversion (uh VUR zhuhn) *n.:* strong or fixed dislike. *Those who are self-reliant may have an aversion to conformity.*

integrity (ihn TEHG ruh tee) *n.:* sound moral principles; honesty. *Act with integrity, and others will respect you.*

Language Coach

Roots *Integrity,* like the word *integrate,* comes from the word *integer,* which means "whole." Review the definition of the word *integrity.* In what way might the concepts of wholeness and honesty relate to each other?

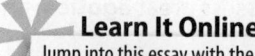

Learn It Online
Jump into this essay with the video online.

go.hrw.com | L11-244 | Go

from Self-Reliance

by **Ralph Waldo Emerson**

Read with a Purpose

Read to discover what <u>factors</u> Emerson includes in his definition of greatness.

Build Background

As a country founded on the beliefs of liberty and equality, America has cherished the importance of the individual. When Emerson's famous discussion of self-reliance first appeared in 1841, it appealed to the American spirit, and it continues to intrigue Americans today. In his speeches and writings, Emerson continually urged people to place their trust in themselves and their intuition, rather than in society and tradition.

There is a time in every man's education when he arrives at the conviction that envy is ignorance; that imitation is suicide; that he must take himself for better, for worse, as his portion; that though the wide universe is full of good, no kernel of nourishing corn can come to him but through his toil bestowed on that plot of ground which is given to him to till. The power which resides in him is new in nature, and none but he knows what that is which he can do, nor does he know until he has tried. Not for nothing one face, one character, one fact makes much impression on him, and another none. This sculpture in the memory is not without preestablished harmony. The eye was placed where one ray should fall, that it might testify of that particular ray. We but half express ourselves, and are ashamed of that divine idea which each of us

Vocabulary **conviction** (kuhn VIHK shuhn) *n.:* firm belief.

Literary Perspectives

Analyzing Historical Context Historical criticism reminds us that Emerson lived in this country at a particular historical moment, that his writing was shaped by his time, and that knowing something of his time can enhance our appreciation of his words. As you read this excerpt, keep in mind that it was published in 1841 and that the British Romantics influenced the American literature of the time. Remember that the optimism and individualism you will find in "Self-Reliance" are Romantic traits. Also remember that Emerson published this essay against the backdrop of the Industrial Revolution, which represented the opposite of what Romantics wanted for their world. Consider, too, that some of Emerson's fellow citizens owned slaves. What would slaveholders have made of this essay?

As you read, be sure to notice the questions in the text, which will guide you in using this perspective.

represents. It may be safely trusted as proportionate[1] and of good issues, so it be faithfully imparted,[2] but God will not have his work made manifest by cowards. A man is relieved and gay when he has put his heart into his work and done his best; but what he has said or done otherwise, shall give him no peace.

---

1. **proportionate:** balanced.
2. **imparted:** revealed.

Vocabulary **manifest** (MAN uh fehst) *adj.:* apparent; clear.

It is a deliverance which does not deliver. In the attempt his genius deserts him; no muse befriends; no invention, no hope.

Trust thyself: Every heart vibrates to that iron string. Accept the place the divine Providence has found for you; the society of your contemporaries, the connection of events. Great men have always done so and confided themselves childlike to the genius of their age, betraying their perception that the absolutely

A **Literary Perspectives** **Historical Context** What does Emerson say a person needs for fulfillment? What might have prevented readers of his time from obtaining this fulfillment?

The Veteran in a New Field by Winslow Homer (1836–1910).

trustworthy was seated at their heart, working through their hands, predominating in all their being. And we are now men, and must accept in the highest mind the same transcendent destiny; and not minors and invalids in a protected corner, not cowards fleeing before a revolution, but guides, redeemers, and benefactors, obeying the Almighty effort, and advancing on Chaos and the Dark. . . . **B**

These are the voices which we hear in solitude, but they grow faint and inaudible as we enter into the world. Society everywhere is in conspiracy against the manhood of every one of its members. Society is a joint-stock company in which the members agree for the better securing of his bread to each shareholder, to surrender the liberty and culture of the eater. The virtue in most request is conformity. Self-reliance is its aversion. It loves not realities and creators, but names and customs.

Whoso would be a man must be a non-conformist. He who would gather immortal palms[3] must not be hindered by the name of goodness, but must explore if it be goodness. Nothing is at last sacred but the integrity of your own mind. Absolve[4] you to yourself, and you shall have the suffrage[5] of the world. . . .

A foolish consistency is the hobgoblin of little minds, adored by little statesmen and philosophers and divines. With consistency a great soul has simply nothing to do. He may as well concern himself with his shadow on the wall. Speak what you think now in hard words, and tomorrow speak what tomorrow thinks in hard words again, though it contradict everything you said today—"Ah, so you shall be sure to be misunderstood"—Is it so bad then to be misunderstood? Pythagoras was misunderstood, and Socrates, and Jesus, and Luther, and Copernicus, and Galileo, and Newton,[6] and every pure and wise spirit that ever took flesh. To be great is to be misunderstood. . . . **C**

---

3. **he who . . . immortal palms:** he who would win fame. In ancient times, palm leaves were carried as a symbol of victory.
4. **absolve:** pronounce free from guilt or blame.
5. **suffrage:** vote; used here to mean "approval."
6. **Pythagoras . . . Newton:** great thinkers whose contributions to scientific, philosophical, and religious thought were ignored or suppressed during their lifetimes.

B **Reading Focus** **Understanding Figures of Speech** In the first sentence of this paragraph, what is the "iron string"? What is it being compared to? Why do you think the author chose this image?

C **Literary Focus** **Figures of Speech** Identify two figures of speech in this paragraph. What purpose does each one serve in the essay?

Vocabulary **predominating** (prih DAHM uh nay tihng) *adj.:* having great influence or power.
transcendent (tran SEHN duhnt) *adj.:* excelling; surpassing.
aversion (uh VUR zhuhn) *n.:* strong or fixed dislike.
integrity (ihn TEHG ruh tee) *n.:* sound moral principles; honesty.

Applying Your Skills

from **Self-Reliance**

Respond and Think Critically

Reading Focus

Quick Check

1. According to the selection, whom or what should every person trust?

2. What will make a person relieved and happy?

3. What attitude should individuals take toward conformity?

Read with a Purpose

4. According to Emerson, what <u>factors</u> define a great person? What does he suggest about the lives of great people?

Reading Skills: Understanding Figures of Speech

5. In your chart, add a column in which you state the purpose of each comparison and consider why Emerson compared the two things he did.

Paragraph	Figure of Speech	Comparison	Purpose
1	"Imitation is suicide."	Imitating others can lead to the loss of one's self. In this sense, imitation is like suicide.	It shows the serious consequences of failing to follow your own instincts.

Literary Focus

Literary Analysis

6. **Interpret** In the first paragraph, what do you think Emerson means by "that divine idea which each of us represents"? How is this philosophical assumption <u>integral</u> to the entire essay?

7. **Make Judgments** In the fourth paragraph, Emerson writes, "Whoso would be a man must be a non-conformist." Are his ideas too harsh toward those who conform to society's demands? Why or why not?

8. **Extend** Is there too much or too little emphasis on self-reliance and individualism today? What might Emerson think of today's focus?

9. **Literary Perspectives** What might a slaveholder think about this essay? What about a factory worker or an abolitionist? Explain your ideas.

Literary Skills: Figures of Speech

10. **Evaluate** Refer to the information you added to your chart in question 5. Which figure of speech do you find most effective? Why?

Literary Skills Review: Parallel Structure

11. **Analyze** The repetition of similar ideas in similar grammatical structures is called **parallelism.** When Emerson writes "envy is ignorance; imitation is suicide," he is using parallel structure. List other examples of parallel structure from "Self-Reliance," and explain the effect they create.

Writing Focus

Think as a Reader/Writer

Emerson's **aphorisms** concisely capture the essence of his beliefs about self-reliance. Choose a principle that you believe in, such as honesty or perseverance. Write a paragraph explaining the importance of this principle. Try to include an original aphorism about the principle.

What Do **You Think Now** According to Emerson, where do great people turn for inspiration? Why?

SKILLS FOCUS Literary Skills Analyze figures of speech; analyze the use of parallelism. Reading Skills Read to understand style. Vocabulary Skills Use

Greek, Latin, and Anglo-Saxon roots and affixes to understand vocabulary. Writing Skills Write to explain.

Vocabulary Development

✓ Vocabulary Check

Choose the synonym, or word with the same meaning, of each Vocabulary word.

1. aversion
2. conviction
3. integrity
4. manifest
5. predominating
6. transcendent

a. apparent
b. surpassing
c. powerful
d. dislike
e. honesty
f. belief

Vocabulary Skills: Latin Roots

Just as a mason uses bricks to build a structure, roots can be thought of as bricks that can be used to build new words. A **root** is a word part that carries the core meaning of a word. In many cases, roots combine with prefixes or suffixes to form complete words.

Many English words are built from Latin roots. Learning these roots can help you improve your vocabulary. The chart below contains some examples of Latin roots commonly found in English words, and some of the words in which they appear.

Root	Meaning	Examples
–cred–	believe	credible, credulous
–domin–	master	dominate, domain
–mon–	warn, remind	monument, monitor
–tag– –tact–	touch	contact, contagious
–vert–	turn	avert, reverse
–vict–	conquer	victor, convict

Your Turn

Use the chart in column 1 to help you answer the following questions.

1. Why might the word *conviction* come from a root meaning "conquer"? What idea do these two words have in common?
2. Describe the behavior of someone who acts with *integrity*.
3. Why might someone have an *aversion* to skunks?
4. What similarity of meaning exists between the words *predominating* and *domain*?

Language Coach

Roots Earlier you looked at *integer,* the root for both *integrate* and *integrity*. Remember that *integer*, which comes from Latin, means "whole." There are roots from other languages that also mean "whole". The following words all have roots that relate to wholeness: *heal, total, holistic, unite.* Look up each word in a dictionary, and list the language from which it is derived and the root that relates to the concept of wholeness.

Academic Vocabulary

Talk About
With a partner, discuss which <u>factors</u> distinguish self-reliance from selfishness or self-centeredness. Can self-reliance be taken too far?

Learn It Online
Learn more about roots with *WordSharp* online.

go.hrw.com L11-249 Go

SKILLS FOCUS **Writing Skills** Write to inform; deliver multimedia presentations. **Grammar Skills** Use clear pronoun references. **Listening and Speaking Skills** Deliver oral responses to literature.

Grammar Link

Clear Reference

A pronoun's **antecedent** is the noun to which it refers. Writers sometimes use pronouns without clear antecedents. Look at the example below:

> Emerson says that every person should trust his instincts.

In this example, whose instincts should every person trust—Emerson's or one's own? The sentence should be revised to make the reference clear.

> Emerson says that **people** should trust **their** instincts.

Look at the next example:

> According to Emerson, one way to avoid conformity is to listen closely when we hear them.

In this example, the plural pronoun *them* does not agree with the singular noun *conformity*. The pronoun probably refers to what Emerson calls "the voices which we hear in solitude," but the writer does not mention these voices. The sentence should be revised to clarify the reference.

> According to Emerson, one way to avoid conformity is to listen closely when we hear "the voices which we hear in solitude."

Your Turn

Correct the unclear pronoun references below.

1. Jon gave George the book of Emerson essays because it is his favorite.

2. Shining beautifully in the night sky, it is miraculous to behold.

3. When you read Emerson's essays, make sure to examine it thoroughly.

Writing Application Choose a piece of your own writing. Underline all the pronouns, and confirm that each pronoun has a clear antecedent. Revise any sentences with unclear pronoun references.

CHOICES

As you respond to the Choices, use these **Academic Vocabulary** words as appropriate: factor, implicit, integral, transform, principal.

REVIEW

Analyze the Essays

Group Discussion In "Nature" and "Self-Reliance," Emerson makes references to God and the divine but does not mention a specific set of religious beliefs. In a small group, discuss the principal role of spirituality in Emerson's philosophy. According to Emerson, what place should spirituality occupy in people's lives? Use passages from both essays to support your analysis.

CONNECT

Research the Misunderstood

In "Self-Reliance," Emerson lists several great thinkers who suffered during their lifetimes because people rejected their ideas. Conduct research into the life of someone you believe was great but misunderstood. Write about your findings in an essay, or present them to the class.

Self Portrait before Easel, 1888, by Vincent van Gogh (1853–1890)

EXTEND

Create a Digital Story

TechFocus Think about an encounter you had with nature that affected or transformed you, and create a digital story to share your experience. Write your script, and then choose images and sounds that will help you convey the experience and what it meant to you. Share your digital story with your class.

Learn It Online
Learn how to make a digital story online.

go.hrw.com | L11-250 | **Go**

Reading Focus

SKILLS FOCUS **Reading Skills** Make generalizations about a writer's beliefs.

from **Walden, or Life in the Woods**

Making Generalizations by **Kylene Beers**

When you attend a basketball game or shop at the mall, you usually observe the people around you. Looking at their clothes and seeing their behavior, you may make generalizations about them—broad conclusions that you draw from specific clues. You might think, "They like sports." Or you might say, "They have nice taste." You've made generalizations based on what you observe.

When reading literature, we do the same thing: We notice specific clues in the text and make broad generalizations about the author's message or theme or purpose for writing. The more text we read, the more clues we observe, the more accurate our generalizations can be.

Let's use an example from Thoreau's *Walden* to illustrate the process of reading a literary text and making generalizations about the author's message. As you read the passage below, notice the repetition of words and phrases; related ideas, examples, or illustrations; and direct statements by the author. These specific clues help us make a generalization about Thoreau's message.

Combine the specific clues from the author, and you can generalize that Thoreau is urging the reader to simplify life by reducing the number of details and choices that must be encountered daily.

Your Turn

Read the following passage from *Walden,* and apply the same strategy. Note Thoreau's repeated words or phrases; related ideas, examples, or illustrations; and direct statements. These will help you make a generalization about his feelings toward the railroads.

Our life is frittered away by detail. An honest man has hardly need to count more than his ten fingers, or in extreme cases he may add his ten toes, and lump the rest. Simplicity, simplicity, simplicity! I say, let your affairs be as two or three, and not a hundred or a thousand; instead of a million count half a dozen, and keep your accounts on your thumbnail. . . . Instead of three meals a day, if it be necessary eat but one; instead of a hundred dishes, five; and reduce other things in proportion.

Thoreau uses examples and illustrations—"ten fingers" and "meals . . . but one"—to show how to simplify.

Thoreau repeats the word "simplicity" to emphasize his point.

Notice Thoreau's use of direct statement to instruct people: "Let your affairs be as two or three."

We do not ride on the railroad; it rides upon us. Did you ever think what those sleepers are that underlie the railroad? Each one is a man, an Irishman, or a Yankee man. The rails are laid on them, and they are covered with sand, and the cars run smoothly over them. They are sound sleepers, I assure you. And every few years a new lot is laid down and run over; so that, if some have the pleasure of riding on a rail, others have the misfortune to be ridden upon. And when they run over a man that is walking in his sleep, a supernumerary[1] sleeper in the wrong position, and wake him up, they suddenly stop the cars, and make a hue and cry about it, as if this were an exception. I am glad to know that it takes a gang of men for every five miles to keep the sleepers down and level in their beds as it is, for this is a sign that they may sometime get up again.

_____

1. **supernumerary:** additional; unnecessary.

from Walden, or Life in the Woods

What Do You Think?

Where does an individual find inspiration?

QuickWrite

Think about a time when you were inspired to do something your own way, rather than following the expectations of others. Write a paragraph or two describing the experience. How did others react to you? What did you learn?

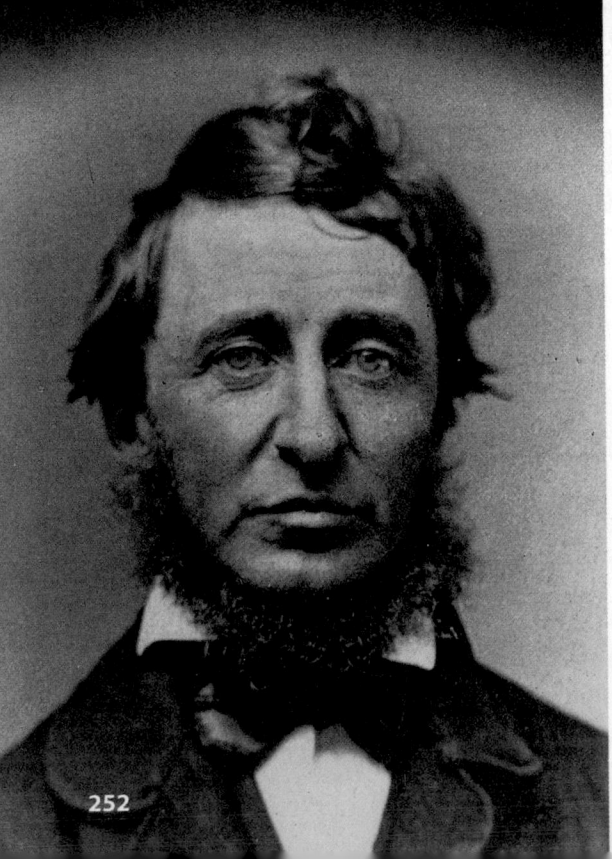

Henry David Thoreau
(1817–1862)

Henry David Thoreau appeared eccentric even to Ralph Waldo Emerson, one of his closest friends, who referred to Thoreau as "the captain of a huckleberry party."

"No Ambition"

Although recognized as one of America's greatest and most influential writers, Henry David Thoreau led anything but a wildly successful life. He was unable to keep his job as a school-teacher, he was uninterested in continuing the family business, and he was rejected by the woman he wanted to marry.

Although Thoreau was well-read and attended Harvard, he never ranked above the middle of his class. His friend, Ralph Waldo Emerson, said that Thoreau had no ambition.

While Thoreau may have lacked the kind of ambition that helps lead to wealth and fame, he had a strong sense of his own individuality. During his years at Harvard, he attended chapel services in a green coat, simply because, as he said, "the rules required black." Years later, he would protest the Mexican War by refusing to pay his poll tax (a head tax on individuals), and he helped runaway slaves escape safely to Canada.

Why Thoreau Went to the Woods

On July 4, 1845, Thoreau moved to the shores of Walden Pond in his hometown of Concord, Massachusetts, where he stayed for over two years. Away from the complexities and tasks of everyday life, he wanted to live simply, close to nature. This would allow him, he hoped, to "meet the facts of life . . . the vital facts," and rediscover the beauty and grandeur of that life.

Walden is a record of Thoreau's experiences while living at Walden Pond. In writing, he looked to nature for inspiration because he believed that a style that imitated nature would convey the principal truths of human nature. He wanted to build sentences "which lie like boulders on the page, up and down or across; which contain the seed of other sentences, not mere repetition, but creation; which a man might sell his grounds and castles to build."

Think About the Writer

If Thoreau lived in your town, where would he go to experience quiet contemplation? What might this place encourage him to think about? Why?

The Granger Collection, New York.

Reader/Writer Notebook

Use your **RWN** to complete the activities for this selection.

Literary Focus

Metaphor A **metaphor** is a figure of speech that makes an <u>implicit</u> comparison between two unlike things. Unlike a simile, a metaphor does not use a specific word of comparison, such as *like* or *as*. For example, Thoreau writes, "In the midst of this chopping sea of civilized life. . . ." In this metaphor, Thoreau compares "civilized life" to a "chopping sea" without using *like* or *as*. His metaphor evokes the hectic and unsettling pace of ordinary contemporary life.

Literary Perspectives Apply the literary perspective described on page 255 as you read this essay.

Reading Focus

Making Generalizations About a Writer's Beliefs You can make generalizations about a writer's beliefs based on what you read. A **generalization** is a type of **inference** in which a conclusion is drawn from specific examples in the text. For example, when you read Thoreau's metaphor that includes a reference to characters in a work of classic literature, you can generalize that Thoreau was well-read.

Into Action As you read, use a chart like the one below to record Thoreau's metaphors. Then, review the metaphors, make generalizations based on them, and record your generalizations in the second column.

Metaphors	Generalization
"Or perchance he was some Achilles, who had nourished his wrath apart, and had now come to avenge or rescue his Patroclus."	Thoreau was well-read.

Writing Focus

Think as a Reader/Writer

Find It in Your Reading Thoreau's **metaphors** are often drawn from nature and everyday things. As you read, note how these metaphors echo Thoreau's idea that simple things can have a profound meaning. In your *Reader/Writer Notebook*, keep a list of these metaphors. As you find each one, paraphrase it to make sure you understand what Thoreau means.

Vocabulary

superficial (soo puhr FIHSH uhl) *adj.*: on the surface; shallow. *Thoreau believed many of the nation's improvements were superficial.*

incessantly (ihn SEHS uhnt lee) *adv.*: without stopping; constantly. *At times, it rained incessantly on Thoreau's small house.*

derision (dih RIHZH uhn) *n.*: ridicule or contempt. *Some people looked at Thoreau with derision because he was different.*

tumultuous (too MUHL chu uhs) *adj.*: very noisy, disorderly, or violent. *Thoreau wanted to get away from tumultuous city life.*

ethereal (ih THIHR ee uhl) *adj.*: not of the earth; spiritual. *Thoreau believed that the contemplation of nature could reveal ethereal truths.*

Language Coach

Word Definitions Grouping new words together visually can help you remember what they mean. For *incessantly, tumultuous,* and *ethereal,* picture a hurricane. The winds spin *incessantly,* producing *tumultuous* waves, but at the hurricane's center is a place of *ethereal* calm. Make a sketch of a hurricane in your *Reader/Writer Notebook,* and label the sketch with these three words.

Learn It Online
Prepare to read this essay with the introductory video online.

go.hrw.com | L11-253 | **Go**

from Walden, or Life in the Woods

by Henry David Thoreau

Read with a Purpose

Read to find out what Thoreau discovers while living alone in a cabin in the woods for two years.

Build Background

A temporary move to a site on a large pond in Concord, Massachusetts, resulted in a work of literature that has become an American classic. Thoreau was twenty-eight years old when he left "civilized" life to live at Walden Pond. The pond was located on land owned by his friend and fellow Transcendentalist, Ralph Waldo Emerson. Thoreau's life in the woods is an example of the kind of experience Emerson described in *Nature:* "To go into solitude, a man needs to retire as much from his chamber as from society." Many people recommend contemplation and solitude as a way to learn what life is, but few actively seek it. Thoreau is one of those few.

Landscape. River Running Between Pastures (c. 1850) by Christopher Pearse Cranch (1813–1892).
Published courtesy of Fruitlands Museum, Harvard, Massachusetts.

from **Where I Lived, and What I Lived For**

. . . I went to the woods because I wished to live deliberately, to front only the essential facts of life, and see if I could not learn what it had to teach, and not, when I came to die, discover that I had not lived. I did not wish to live what was not life, living is so dear; nor did I wish to practice resignation, unless it was quite necessary. I wanted to live deep and suck out all the marrow of life, to live so sturdily and Spartan-like[1] as to put to rout all that was not life, to cut a broad swath and shave close, to drive life into a corner, and reduce it to its lowest terms, and, if it proved to be mean, why then to get the whole and genuine meanness of it, and publish its meanness to the world; or if it were sublime, to know it by experience, and be able to give a true account of it in my next excursion. For most men, it appears to me, are in a strange uncertainty about it, whether it is of the devil or of God, and have *somewhat hastily* concluded that it is the chief end of man here to "glorify God and enjoy him forever."[2] (A)

Still we live meanly, like ants; though the fable tells us that we were long ago changed into men; like pygmies we fight with cranes;[3] it is error upon error, and clout upon clout, and our best virtue has for its occasion a superfluous and evitable[4] wretchedness. Our life is frittered away by detail. An honest man has hardly need to count more than his ten fingers, or in extreme cases he may add his ten toes, and lump the rest. Simplicity, simplicity, simplicity! I say, let your affairs be as two or three, and not a hundred or a thousand; instead of a million count half a dozen, and keep your accounts on your thumbnail. In the midst of this

chopping sea of civilized life, such are the clouds and storms and quicksands and thousand-and-one items to be allowed for, that a man has to live, if he would not founder and go to the bottom and not make his port at all, by dead reckoning, and he must be a great calculator indeed who succeeds. Simplify, simplify. Instead of three meals a day, if it be necessary eat but one; instead of a hundred dishes, five; and reduce other things in proportion. Our life is like a German Confederacy,[5] made up of petty states with its boundary forever fluctuating, so that even a German cannot tell you how it is bounded at any moment. The nation itself, with all its so-called internal improvements, which, by the way are all external and superficial, is just such an unwieldy and overgrown establishment, cluttered with furniture and tripped

---

5. **German Confederacy:** At the time Thoreau was writing, Germany was not yet a unified nation.

---

1. **Spartan-like:** like the Spartans, the hardy, frugal, and highly disciplined citizens of the ancient Greek city-state Sparta.
2. **glorify . . . forever:** answer to catechism question "What is the chief end of man?"
3. **the fable . . . cranes:** In a Greek fable, Zeus changes ants into men. In the *Iliad,* Homer compares the Trojans to cranes fighting with pygmies.
4. **superfluous and evitable:** unnecessary and avoidable.

(A) **Literary Focus Metaphor** Thoreau writes, "I wanted to live deep and suck out all the marrow of life." What is "marrow"? What two things is he comparing in this sentence? Why?

Vocabulary superficial (soo puhr FIHSH uhl) *adj.:* on the surface; shallow.

up by its own traps, ruined by luxury and heedless expense, by want of calculation and a worthy aim, as the million households in the land; and the only cure for it, as for them, is in a rigid economy, a stern and more than Spartan simplicity of life and elevation of purpose. It lives too fast. Men think that it is essential that the *Nation* have commerce, and export ice, and talk through a telegraph, and ride thirty miles an hour, without a doubt, whether *they* do or not; but whether we should live like baboons or like men, is a little uncertain. If we do not get out sleepers,[6] and forge rails, and devote days and nights to the work, but go to tinkering upon our *lives* to improve *them,* who will build railroads? And if railroads are not built, how shall we get to heaven in season? But if we stay at home and mind our business, who will want railroads? We do not ride on the railroad; it rides upon us. Did you ever think what those sleepers are that underlie the railroad? Each one is a man,

an Irishman, or a Yankee man. The rails are laid on them, and they are covered with sand, and the cars run smoothly over them. They are sound sleepers, I assure you. And every few years a new lot is laid down and run over; so that, if some have the pleasure of riding on a rail, others have the misfortune to be ridden upon. And when they run over a man that is walking in his sleep, a supernumerary[7] sleeper in the wrong position, and wake him up, they suddenly stop the cars, and make a hue and cry about it, as if this were an exception. I am glad to know that it takes a gang of men for every five miles to keep the sleepers down and level in their beds as it is, for this is a sign that they may sometime get up again. . . .   **B C**

---

6. **sleepers:** British usage for "railroad ties," so called because they lie flat.

7. **supernumerary:** additional; unnecessary.

B **Literary Focus** **Metaphor** What point does Thoreau make by comparing human workers to railroad ties?

C **Reading Focus** **Making Generalizations About a Writer's Beliefs** What generalization would you make about Thoreau's view of "progress"?

Thoreau's journal entry, October 22, 1837.

from Solitude

. . . Some of my pleasantest hours were during the long rainstorms in the spring or fall, which confined me to the house for the afternoon as well as the forenoon, soothed by their ceaseless roar and pelting; when an early twilight ushered in a long evening in which many thoughts had time to take root and unfold themselves. In those driving northeast rains which tried the village houses so, when the maids stood ready with mop and pail in front entries to keep the deluge out, I sat behind my door in my little house, which was all entry, and thoroughly enjoyed its protection. In one heavy thundershower the lightning struck a large pitch pine across the pond, making a very conspicuous and perfectly regular spiral groove from top to bottom, an inch or more deep, and four or five inches wide, as you would groove a walking stick. I passed it again the other day, and was struck with awe on looking up and beholding that mark, now more distinct than ever, where a terrific and resistless bolt came down out of the harmless sky eight years ago. Men frequently say to me, "I should think you would feel lonesome down there, and want to be nearer to folks, rainy and snowy days and nights especially." I am tempted to reply to such—'This whole earth which we inhabit is but a point in space. How far apart, think you, dwell the two most distant inhabitants of yonder star, the breadth of whose disk cannot be appreciated by our instruments? Why should I feel lonely? Is not our planet in the Milky Way? This which you put seems to me not to be the most important question. What sort of space is that which separates a man from his fellows and makes him solitary? I have found that no exertion of the legs can bring two minds much nearer to one another. What do we want most to dwell near to? Not to many men surely, the depot, the post office, the barroom, the meetinghouse, the schoolhouse, the grocery, Beacon Hill, or the Five Points, where men most congregate, but to the perennial source of our life, whence in all our experience we have found that to issue, as the willow stands near the water and sends out its roots in that direction. This will vary with different natures, but this is the place where a wise man will dig his cellar. . . . **D**

D **Literary Perspectives** Philosophical Context How does this paragraph reveal the Romantic belief in the importance of the individual? Explain.

Analyzing Visuals

Viewing and Interpreting What does this landscape have in common with the kind of solitude Thoreau discusses in the excerpt above? Explain your response.

from **Brute Neighbors**

. . . One day when I went out to my woodpile, or rather my pile of stumps, I observed two large ants, the one red, the other much larger, nearly half an inch long, and black, fiercely contending with one another. Having once got hold they never let go, but struggled and wrestled and rolled on the chips incessantly. Looking farther, I was surprised to find that the chips were covered with such combatants, that it was not a *duellum*, but a *bellum*,[8] a war between two races of ants, the red always pitted against the black, and frequently two red ones to one black. The legions of these Myrmidons[9] covered all the hills and vales in my wood yard, and the ground was already strewn with the dead and dying, both red and black. It was the only battle which I have ever witnessed, the only battlefield I ever trod while the battle was raging; internecine[10] war; the red republicans on the one hand, and the black imperialists on the other. On every side they were engaged in deadly combat, yet without any noise that I could hear, and human soldiers never fought so resolutely. I watched a couple that were fast locked in each other's embraces, in a little sunny valley amid the chips, now at noonday prepared to fight till the sun went down, or life went out. The smaller red champion had fastened himself like a vise to his adversary's front, and through all the tumblings on that field never for an instant ceased to gnaw at one of his feelers near the root, having already caused the other to go by the board; while the stronger black one dashed him from side to side, and, as I saw on looking nearer, had already divested him of several of his members. They fought with more pertinacity than bulldogs. Neither manifested the least disposition to retreat. It was evident that their battle cry was "Conquer or die." In the meanwhile there came along a single red ant on the hillside of this valley, evidently full of excitement, who either had dispatched his foe, or had not yet taken part in the battle; probably the latter, for he had lost none of his limbs; whose mother had charged him to return with his shield or upon it.[11] Or perchance he was some Achilles, who had nourished his wrath apart, and had now come to avenge or rescue his Patroclus.[12] He saw this unequal combat from afar—for the blacks were nearly twice the size of the red—he drew near with rapid pace till he stood on his guard within half an inch of the combatants; then, watching his opportunity, he sprang upon the black warrior, and commenced his operations near the root of his right foreleg, leaving the foe to select among his own members; and so there were three united for life, as if a new kind of attraction had been invented which put all other locks and cements to shame. I should not have wondered by this time to find that they had their respective musical bands stationed on some eminent chip, and playing their national airs the while, to excite the slow and cheer the dying combatants. I was myself excited somewhat even as if they had been men. The more you think of it, the less the difference. And certainly there is not the fight recorded in Concord history, at least, if in the history of America, that will bear a moment's comparison with this, whether for the numbers engaged in it, or for the patriotism and heroism displayed. For numbers and for carnage it was an Austerlitz or Dresden.[13] Concord Fight! Two killed on the patriots' side, and Luther Blanchard wounded! Why here every ant was a Buttrick—"Fire! for God's sake fire!"—and thousands shared the fate of Davis and Hosmer.[14] There was not one hireling there. I have no doubt

---

8. **not a *duellum*, but a *bellum*:** not a duel, but a war.
9. **Myrmidons** (MUR muh dahnz): Achilles' soldiers in the *Iliad*. *Myrmex* is Greek for "ant."
10. **internecine:** harmful to both sides of the group.

11. **return . . . upon it:** echo of the traditional charge of Spartan mothers to their warrior sons: in other words, return victorious or dead.
12. **Achilles . . . Patroclus** (puh TRAH kluhs): In the *Iliad*, Achilles withdraws from the battle at Troy but rejoins the fight after his friend Patroclus is killed.
13. **Austerlitz or Dresden:** major battles of the Napoleonic Wars.
14. **Luther . . . Hosmer:** All these men fought at the Battle of Concord, the first battle of the Revolutionary War. Major John Buttrick led the minutemen who defeated the British. Isaac Davis and David Hosmer were the two colonists killed.

Vocabulary **incessantly** (ihn SEHS uhnt lee) *adv.:* without stopping; constantly.

I observed two large ants, **the one red**, the other much larger, nearly half an inch long, **and black**, fiercely contending with one another.

that it was a principle they fought for, as much as our ancestors, and not to avoid a three-penny tax on their tea; and the results of this battle will be as important and memorable to those whom it concerns as those of the Battle of Bunker Hill, at least.

I took up the chip on which the three I have particularly described were struggling, carried it into my house, and placed it under a tumbler on my windowsill, in order to see the issue. Holding a microscope to the first-mentioned red ant, I saw that, though he was assiduously gnawing at the near foreleg of his enemy, having severed his remaining feeler, his own breast was all torn away, exposing what vitals he had there to the jaws of the black warrior, whose breastplate was apparently too thick for him to pierce; and the dark carbuncles of the sufferer's eyes shone with ferocity such as war only could excite. They struggled half an hour longer under the tumbler, and when I looked again the black soldier had severed the heads of his foes from their bodies, and the still living heads were hanging on either side of him like ghastly trophies at his saddlebow, still apparently as firmly fastened as ever, and he was endeavoring with feeble struggles, being without feelers and with only the remnant of a leg, and I know not how many other wounds, to divest himself of them; which at length, after half an hour more, he accomplished. I raised the glass, and he went off over the windowsill in that crippled state. Whether he finally survived that combat, and spent the remainder of his days in some Hôtel des Invalides,[15]

15. **Hôtel des Invalides** (oh TEHL dehz an vah LEED): Home for Disabled Soldiers, a veterans' hospital in Paris, France. Napoleon I (1769–1821) is buried there.

I do not know; but I thought that his industry would not be worth much thereafter. I never learned which party was victorious, nor the cause of the war; but I felt for the rest of that day as if I had had my feelings excited and harrowed by witnessing the struggle, the ferocity and carnage, of a human battle before my door. . . . **E**

In the fall the loon (*Colymbus glacialis*) came, as usual, to molt and bathe in the pond, making the woods ring with his wild laughter before I had risen. At rumor of his arrival all the Milldam sportsmen are on the alert, in gigs and on foot, two by two and three by three, with patent rifles and conical balls and spyglasses. They come rustling through the woods like autumn leaves, at least ten men to one loon. Some station themselves on this side of the pond, some on that, for the poor bird cannot be omnipresent; if he dive here he must come up there. But now the kind October wind rises, rustling the leaves and rippling the surface of the water, so that no loon can be heard or seen, though his foes sweep the pond with spyglasses, and make the woods resound with their discharges. The waves generously rise and dash angrily, taking sides with all waterfowl, and our sportsmen must beat a retreat to town and shop and unfinished jobs. But they were too often successful. When I went to get a pail of water early in the morning I frequently saw this stately bird sailing out of my cove within a

E **Reading Focus** **Making Generalizations About a Writer's Beliefs** What images does Thoreau use to describe the ants in battle? Based on this passage, what generalization can you make about Thoreau's beliefs about war?

In the fall the loon . . . came, as usual, to molt and bathe in the pond, making the woods ring with his wild laughter before I had risen.

few rods.[16] If I endeavored to overtake him in a boat, in order to see how he would maneuver, he would dive and be completely lost, so that I did not discover him again, sometimes, till the latter part of the day. But I was more than a match for him on the surface. He commonly went off in a rain.

As I was paddling along the north shore one very calm October afternoon, for such days especially they settle onto the lakes, like the milkweed down, having looked in vain over the pond for a loon, suddenly one, sailing out from the shore toward the middle a few rods in front of me, set up his wild laugh and betrayed himself. I pursued with a paddle and he dived, but when he came up I was nearer than before. He dived again, but I miscalculated the direction he would take, and we were fifty rods apart when he came to the surface this time, for I had helped to widen the interval; and again he laughed long and loud, and with more reason than before. He maneuvered so cunningly that I could not get within half a dozen rods of him. Each time, when he came to the surface, turning his head this way and that, he coolly surveyed the water and the land, and apparently chose his course so that he might come up where there was the widest expanse of water and at the greatest distance from the boat. It was surprising how quickly he made up his mind and put his resolve into execution. He led me at once to the widest part of the pond, and could not be driven from it. While he was

16. **rods:** One rod measures 16½ feet.

thinking one thing in his brain, I was endeavoring to divine his thought in mine. It was a pretty game, played on the smooth surface of the pond, a man against a loon. Suddenly your adversary's checker disappears beneath the board, and the problem is to place yours nearest to where his will appear again. Sometimes he would come up unexpectedly on the opposite side of me, having apparently passed directly under the boat. So long-winded was he and so unweariable, that when he had swum farthest he would immediately plunge again, nevertheless; and then no wit could divine where in the deep pond, beneath the smooth surface, he might be speeding his way like a fish, for he had time and ability to visit the bottom of the pond in its deepest part. It is said that loons have been caught in the New York lakes eighty feet beneath the surface, with hooks set for trout—though Walden is deeper than that. How surprised must the fishes be to see this ungainly visitor from another sphere speeding his way amid their schools! Yet he appeared to know his course as surely underwater as on the surface, and swam much faster there. Once or twice I saw a ripple where he approached the surface, just put his head out to reconnoiter, and instantly dived again. I found that it was as well for me to rest on my oars and wait his reappearing as to endeavor to calculate where he would rise; for again and again, when I was straining my eyes over the surface one way, I would suddenly be startled by his unearthly laugh behind me. But why, after displaying so much cunning, did he invariably betray himself the moment he came up by that loud laugh? Did not his white breast enough betray him? He was indeed a silly loon, I thought. I could commonly hear the plash of the water when he came up, and so also detected him. But after an hour he seemed as fresh as ever, dived as willingly, and swam yet farther than at first. It was surprising to see how serenely he sailed off with unruffled breast when he came to the surface, doing all the work with his webbed feet beneath. His usual note was this demoniac laughter, yet somewhat like that of a waterfowl; but occasionally, when he had balked me most successfully and come up a long way off, he uttered a long-drawn unearthly howl, probably more like that of a wolf than any bird; as when a beast puts his muzzle to the ground and deliberately howls. This was his looning—perhaps the wildest sound that is ever heard here, making the woods ring far and wide. I concluded that he laughed in derision of my efforts confident of his own resources. Though the sky was by this time overcast, the pond was so smooth that I could see where he broke the surface when I did not hear him. His white breast, the stillness of the air, and the smoothness of the water were all against him. At length, having come up fifty rods off, he uttered one of those prolonged howls, as if calling on the god of loons to aid him, and immediately there came a wind from the east and rippled the surface, and filled the whole air with misty rain, and I was impressed as if it were the prayer of the loon answered, and his god was angry with me; and so I left him disappearing far away on the tumultuous surface. . . . **F**

from Conclusion

. . . I left the woods for as good a reason as I went there. Perhaps it seemed to me that I had several more lives to live, and could not spare any more time for that one. It is remarkable how easily and insensibly we fall into a particular route, and make a beaten track for ourselves. I had not lived there a week before my feet wore a path from my door to the pond side; and though it is five or six years

since I trod it, it is still quite distinct. It is true, I fear, that others may have fallen into it, and so helped to keep it open. The surface of the earth is soft and impressible by the feet of men; and so with the paths which the mind travels. How worn and dusty, then, must be the highways of the world, how deep the ruts of tradition and conformity! I did not wish to take a cabin passage, but rather to go before the mast and on the deck of the world, for there I could best see the moonlight amid the mountains. I do not wish to go below now. **G**

I learned this, at least, by my experiment: That if one advances confidently in the direction of his dreams, and endeavors to live the life which he has imagined, he will meet with a success unexpected in common hours. He will put some things behind, will pass an invisible boundary; new, universal, and more liberal laws will begin to establish themselves around and within him; or the old laws be expanded, and interpreted in his favor in a more liberal sense, and he will live with the license of a higher order of beings. In proportion as he simplifies his life, the laws of the universe will appear less complex, and solitude will not be solitude, nor poverty poverty, nor weakness weakness. If you have built castles in the air, your work need not be lost; that is where they should be. Now put the foundations under them. . . .

Some are dinning in our ears that we Americans, and moderns generally, are intellectual dwarfs compared with the ancients, or even the Elizabethan men. But what is that to the purpose? A living dog is better than a dead lion.[17] Shall a man go and hang himself because he belongs to the race of pygmies, and not be the biggest pygmy that he can? Let everyone mind his own business, and endeavor to be what he was made.

Why should we be in such desperate haste to succeed and in such desperate enterprises? If a man

---

17. **A living dog . . . lion:** Ecclesiastes 9:4.

F **Literary Perspectives** **Philosophical Context** How does Thoreau's description of the loon reflect the views of Transcendentalists?

Vocabulary **derision** (dih RIHZH uhn) *n.:* ridicule or contempt.
tumultuous (too MUHL chu uhs) *adj.:* very noisy, disorderly, or violent.

G **Literary Focus** **Metaphor** In this paragraph, Thoreau writes, "I did not wish to take a cabin passage, but rather to go before the mast and on the deck of the world, for there I could best see the moonlight amid the mountains. I do not wish to go below now." What is he comparing to a ship? How would the "cabin passage" differ from being "on the deck"?

> If a man does not keep pace with his companions, perhaps it is because he hears a different drummer.

does not keep pace with his companions, perhaps it is because he hears a different drummer. Let him step to the music which he hears, however measured or far away. It is not important that he should mature as soon as an apple tree or an oak. Shall he turn his spring into summer? If the condition of things which we were made for is not yet, what were any reality which we can substitute? We will not be shipwrecked on a vain reality. Shall we with pains erect a heaven of blue glass over ourselves, though when it is done we shall be sure to gaze still at the true ethereal heaven far above, as if the former were not? . . . **H**

The life in us is like the water in the river. It may rise this year higher than man has ever known it, and flood the parched uplands; even this may be the eventful year, which will drown out all our muskrats. It was not always dry land where we dwell. I see far inland the banks which the stream anciently washed, before science began to record its freshets. Everyone has heard the story which has gone the rounds of New England, of a strong and beautiful bug which came out of the dry leaf of an old table of apple-tree wood, which had stood in a farmer's kitchen for sixty years, first in Connecticut, and afterward in Massachusetts—from an egg deposited in the living tree many years earlier still, as appeared by counting the annual layers beyond it; which was heard gnawing out for several weeks, hatched perchance by the heat of an urn. Who does not feel his faith in a resurrection and immortality strengthened by hearing of this? Who knows what beautiful and winged life, whose

egg has been buried for ages under many concentric layers of woodenness in the dead dry life of society, deposited at first in the alburnum[18] of the green and living tree, which has been gradually converted into the semblance of its well-seasoned tomb—heard perchance gnawing out now for years by the astonished family of man, as they sat round the festive board—may unexpectedly come forth from amidst society's most trivial and handselled[19] furniture, to enjoy its perfect summer life at last!

I do not say that John or Jonathan[20] will realize all this; but such is the character of that morrow which mere lapse of time can never make to dawn. The light which puts out our eyes is darkness to us. Only that day dawns to which we are awake. There is more day to dawn. The sun is but a morning star. **I**

---

18. **alburnum:** sapwood; soft wood between the inner bark and the hard core of a tree.
19. **handselled:** given as a mere token of good wishes and therefore of no great value in itself.
20. **John or Jonathan:** John Bull and Brother Jonathan were traditional personifications of England and the United States, respectively.

I **Reading Focus** **Making Generalizations About a Writer's Beliefs** What do you think Thoreau means by these words: "Only that day dawns to which we are awake"? How does this statement reflect the beliefs that inspired him to move to Walden Pond?

H **Literary Perspectives** **Philosophical Context** What kind of philosophy does this paragraph reveal? Explain your answer.

Vocabulary **ethereal** (ih THIHR ee uhl) *adj.:* not of the earth; spiritual.

from **Walden, or Life in the Woods**

SKILLS FOCUS Literary Skills Analyze metaphor; analyze parable. **Reading Skills** Make generalizations about a writer's beliefs. **Writing Skills** Use creative language when writing.

Respond and Think Critically

Reading Focus

Quick Check

1. What are Thoreau's answers to the questions <u>implicit</u> in the title "Where I Lived, and What I Lived For"?

2. What arguments does Thoreau present in "Solitude" to demonstrate that he is not lonely in his isolated situation?

3. Why does Thoreau leave his life in the woods?

Read with a Purpose

4. What does Thoreau learn from living alone in a cabin in the woods? Cite details from the text that support your answer.

Reading Skills: Making Generalizations About an Author's Beliefs

5. As you read *Walden,* you kept track of Thoreau's statements and the generalizations you made from them. Write a sentence or two about what you have learned about Thoreau from his use of metaphors.

Metaphors	Generalization
"Or perchance he was some Achilles, who had nourished his wrath apart, and had now come to avenge or rescue his Patroclus."	Thoreau was well-read. Thoreau believes that allusions to classical literature help people understand everyday matters.

Literary Focus

Literary Analysis

6. **Interpret** What does Thoreau mean by "Simplify, simplify"? Do you think he has a valid point? Explain.

7. **Analyze** Re-read Thoreau's description of the loon in "Brute Neighbors." How does Thoreau **personify,** or give human attributes, to the loon?

8. **Evaluate** In "Conclusion," Thoreau writes, "If one advances confidently in the direction of his dreams . . . he will meet with a success unexpected in common hours." Do you agree that following one's dreams is <u>integral</u> to success? Explain.

9. **Literary Perspectives** What is the core belief of Transcendentalism, and how does Thoreau express this belief in these excerpts from *Walden*? Explain your response.

Literary Skills: Metaphor

10. **Analyze** Describe Thoreau's military imagery connected to ants. What is the purpose of this metaphor?

Literary Skills Review: Parable

11. **Draw Conclusions** A **parable** is a very brief story that teaches a moral or ethical lesson. What do you think is the lesson of the parable involving the bug in the wood table at the conclusion of *Walden*?

Writing Focus

Think as a Reader/Writer

Use It in Your Writing As you read, you noted Thoreau's metaphors based on nature and everyday things. Write a paragraph making an observation about your own surroundings. Use references to everyday things and at least one original metaphor.

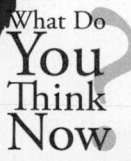

What Do **You Think Now** What did you learn from Thoreau's experience that might inspire you to make a change in your life? Explain.

from **Walden, or Life in the Woods**

Vocabulary Development

✓ Vocabulary Check

Match each Vocabulary word with its antonym, or opposite.

1. superficial   **a.** calm
2. incessantly   **b.** respect
3. derision   **c.** deep
4. tumultuous   **d.** earthly
5. ethereal   **e.** sporadically

Vocabulary Skills: Analogies

An **analogy** is a comparison in which two pairs of words have the same relationship. For example, the words might be synonyms or antonyms, or one word might describe a characteristic of or be an example of the other word. Look at this analogy:

LARGE : GIGANTIC :: tired : exhausted

The colon (:) stands for the phrase *is related to,* and the double colon (::) stands for the phrase *in the same way that.* In this analogy, *large* is a less extreme word for *gigantic,* just as *tired* is a less extreme word for *exhausted.* Look at the following analogy:

FOOD : CONSUME :: _____ : drive

The first word in the word pair is an object, while the second word is an action you do with that object. The missing word would be something you drive, such as a vehicle. To complete an analogy, identify a second pair of words with the same relationship as the first pair.

Your Turn

Use a Vocabulary word to complete each analogy. First, identify the relationship between the first pair of words. Then, choose a word to complete the second pair so that the relationship is similar.

1. VIOLENT : PEACEFUL :: _____ : tranquil
2. FREQUENTLY : OFTEN :: _____ : continuously
3. RESPECT : ADMIRATION :: _____ : ridicule
4. HOSTILE : ANTAGONISTIC :: _____ : shallow
5. SOLID : ROCK :: _____ : heaven

Language Coach

Word Definitions Before reading the excerpt from *Walden,* you sketched the image of a hurricane for three of the Vocabulary words. With a partner, select two or three Vocabulary words that you can picture in a different way. Create a sketch to go with your words, and share it with the class.

Academic Vocabulary

Write About
Write about the <u>principal</u> experiences that <u>transformed</u> Thoreau during his stay at Walden Pond.

Learn It Online
Sharpen your word skills online with Word Watch.

go.hrw.com   L11-264   **Go**

SKILLS FOCUS Vocabulary Skills

Understand word analogies; apply knowledge of Greek, Latin, and Anglo-Saxon roots and affixes to draw inferences concerning the meaning of scientific and mathematical terminology.

Vocabulary Skills: Greek and Latin Affixes

An **affix** is a word part that is attached to the beginning or end of a root word to make a new word. **Prefixes** are affixes that are added to the beginning of a word; for example, adding *un–* to the word *comfortable* makes a new word: *uncomfortable.*

The following chart shows some of the <u>principal</u> Greek and Latin prefixes used in math and science.

Latin Prefix	Meaning	Examples
co–, col–, com–, con–	with; together	coefficient, collide, compute, conduct
circum–	around	circumvent, circumnavigate
di–, dis–	away; lack	disinfect, dilute
re–	again; back	research, reproduce
Greek Prefix	**Meaning**	**Examples**
ant–, anti–	against; opposing	antibiotic, antidote
hypo–	under; below	hypothesis, hypodermic
poly–	many	polygon, polymer
micro–	very small	microcosm, microorganism

A **suffix** is an affix added to the end of a word. **Inflectional suffixes,** such as *–ing* or *–ed,* usually change the tense, person, or number of a word. **Derivational suffixes** carry their own meaning, and as a result, change the meaning of the root word. For example, the suffix *–less* added to the word *motion* makes the new word *motionless.*

The following chart shows some of the Greek and Latin derivational suffixes used in math and science.

Latin Suffix	Meaning	Examples
–ance, –ence	state or quality of being	buoyance, turbulence
–able, –ible	able to; likely to	malleable, combustible
–ion	action of; condition of	respiration, evaporation
–ous	full of	igneous, deciduous
–ity	state of; condition of	possibility, regularity
Greek Suffix	**Meaning**	**Examples**
–ectomy	cut	tonsillectomy, appendectomy
–oid	appearance; form	android, ovoid
–scope	see into	telescope, gyroscope

Your Turn

You can make a chart like the one below to analyze a word with a Greek or Latin affix.

Word	Affix	Root Word	Meaning
simplicity	–ity ("state of")	simple	the state of being simple

Use a dictionary or the affixes listed on this page to make affix analysis charts for the following words from *Walden*. Then, list three other words in *Walden* that use Greek or Latin affixes.

1. concluded
2. microscope
3. generously
4. disappear

Applying Your Skills

from **Walden, or Life in the Woods**

SKILLS FOCUS **Literary Skills** Understand and analyze elements of literature from American Romanticism. **Reading Skills** Read to research information. **Writing Skills** Perform literary analysis. **Grammar Skills** Identify and use coordinating conjunctions. **Listening and Speaking** Participate in group discussions; deliver oral responses to literature.

Grammar Link

Coordinating Conjunctions

Consider the following sentences:

> I did not wish to live what was not life, living is so dear. I did not wish to practice resignation.

Although these short sentences are not incorrect, they are more graceful as Thoreau wrote them:

> I did not wish to live what was not life, living is so dear; nor did I wish to practice resignation.

The word *nor,* a coordinating conjunction, connects the two thoughts to show a relationship between them. **Coordinating conjunctions** join words or groups of words that are used in the same way. The table below shows coordinating conjunctions and their meanings.

Conjunction	Function
and	similarity, addition
but	opposition, contrast
yet	opposition, contrast
or	choice, alternative
nor	negation
so	cause and effect, result
for	explanation, reason

Your Turn

Use a coordinating conjunction to combine each sentence pair below.

1. Thoreau believes life should be centered. He thinks it should not be filled with myriad details.

2. Thoreau enjoyed his small house during rainstorms. He spent these times in contemplation.

3. Thoreau lived alone in the woods. He did not feel lonely.

4. Thoreau did not want to fall into a rut. He left the woods after about two years.

CHOICES

As you respond to the Choices, use these **Academic Vocabulary** words as appropriate: factor, implicit, integral, principal, transform.

REVIEW
Evaluate the Romantic Point of View

Timed Writing In a short essay, explain whether you see Romantic or anti-Romantic ideas in Thoreau. Be sure to cite evidence from *Walden* to support your response.

CONNECT
Explore Allusions

Partner Work Thoreau's writing is full of allusions to classical Greek literature. His writing includes characters from Homer's *Iliad* as well as from Greek mythology. With a partner, choose one of these characters—one who appeals to you or whom you have questions about. Research the myths that involve your character. Find examples of the character in artwork or book illustrations, and share them. Then, discuss with your partner how Thoreau alluded to the character in *Walden*. Share your findings with your class.

EXTEND
Discuss Thoreau as Hero

Partner Work In the journal he kept while living at Walden Pond, Thoreau wrote, "I too am at least a remote descendant of that race of men of whom there is a tradition. I too sit here on the shore of my Ithaca, a fellow wanderer and survivor of Ulysses." Ulysses, known to the Greeks as Odysseus, was the king of the island of Ithaca at the time of the Trojan War, and he is the hero of Homer's *Odyssey*. With a partner, discuss how Thoreau's vision of himself as a hero and king are implicit in Walden. How was he a hero? In what way was he a king, and over what kingdom did he rule?

Civil Disobedience

Throughout history, many people have chosen to battle injustice by defying laws or governments that they believe to be unjust. This type of resistance is called civil disobedience. On many occasions, protesters have accepted beatings, imprisonment, and even death as consequences of their actions. In the following writings, three men explain their reasons for choosing the path of civil disobedience.

CONTENTS

Preparing to Read

 **What Do You Think?** Where does an individual find inspiration?

 **QuickWrite**

Write a paragraph explaining why you would or would not be moved to commit civil disobedience for a principle you believed in.

Literary Focus

Paradox A **paradox** is a statement that seems contradictory but actually reveals a truth. The premise of Thoreau's essay is a paradox: To be a good citizen, sometimes you must disobey the law. As you read, note how he uses paradox to express the complexities of civil disobedience.

Reading Focus

Recognizing Persuasive Techniques **Persuasive techniques** move an audience to think, feel, or act. They are commonly divided into three types of appeals. **Logical appeals** include evidence and reasons. **Ethical appeals** use widely accepted values or moral standards. **Emotional appeals** include language and anecdotes that arouse strong feelings.

Into Action As you read, use a chart like the one below to record Thoreau's persuasive appeals. Briefly summarize each appeal, and then indicate whether it is a logical, ethical, or emotional appeal.

Argument or Statement	Logical, Ethical, or Emotional Appeal?
asks reader to consider whether there can be, simultaneously, government and no government	logical

Writing Focus

Think as a Reader/Writer

Find It in Your Reading Thoreau uses **paradoxes** to challenge readers to view something in a different way. Use your *Reader/Writer Notebook* to record the paradoxes you find most intriguing or compelling, and briefly explain what truths they reveal.

 **Reader/Writer Notebook**

Use your **RWN** to complete the activities for this selection.

Vocabulary

expedient (ehk SPEE dee uhnt) *n.:* convenience; means to an end. *Government should be an expedient; it should not exist for the sake of existing.*

perverted (puhr VUR tihd) *v.:* misdirected; corrupted. *According to Thoreau, government is perverted when the few use it at the expense of the many.*

posterity (pahs TEHR uh tee) *n.:* generations to come. *Thoreau's ideas about civil disobedience have been recorded for posterity.*

alacrity (uh LAK ruh tee) *n.:* promptness in responding; eagerness. *Respond with alacrity to Thoreau's call to action.*

inherent (ihn HIHR uhnt) *adj.:* inborn; built-in. *The inherent purpose of government is to serve the people.*

insurrection (ihn suh REHK shuhn) *n.:* rebellion; revolt. *Would Thoreau lead an insurrection against unjust rulers?*

Language Coach

Prefixes Many of the words above contain prefixes: *expedient, perverted, inherent, insurrection*. The effect that a prefix has on a root word can vary, but most prefixes have a basic meaning or set of meanings. The *per–* in *perverted,* for example, generally means "thoroughly or completely."

from Resistance to Civil Government

by **Henry David Thoreau**

Read with a Purpose

Read to discover what Thoreau says about an individual's responsibility to his or her own conscience.

Build Background

In July 1846, Thoreau's stay at Walden Pond was interrupted by a night in jail. Thoreau was arrested because he refused to pay a poll tax that he believed would help finance the U.S. war with Mexico. He opposed the war because he believed it was an excuse to expand America's slaveholding territory. The police in Concord offered to pay the tax for Thoreau, but he refused the offer. He was forced, therefore, to spend the night in jail. Thoreau might have spent more time there, except that someone, probably his aunt, paid the tax for him. This night in jail was the inspiration for the essay known as "Resistance to Civil Government" or "Civil Disobedience." *For a biography of Thoreau, see page 252.*

I heartily accept the motto—"That government is best which governs least";[1] and I should like to see it acted up to more rapidly and systematically. Carried out, it finally amounts to this, which also I believe—"That government is best which governs not at all"; and when men are prepared for it, that will be the kind of government which they will have. Government is at best but an expedient; but most governments are usually, and all governments are sometimes, inexpedient. The objections which have been brought against a standing army, and they are many and weighty, and deserve to prevail, may also at last be brought against a standing government. The standing army is only an arm of the standing government. The government itself, which is only the mode which the people have chosen to execute their will, is equally liable to be abused and perverted before the people can act through it. Witness the present Mexican war, the work of comparatively a few individuals using the standing government as their tool; for, in the outset, the people would not have consented to this measure.[2] **Ⓐ**

---

1. **That . . . least:** This statement, attributed to Thomas Jefferson, was the motto of the New York *Democratic Review,* which had published two of Thoreau's essays.

2. **this measure:** On May 9, 1846, President James K. Polk received word that Mexico had attacked U.S. troops. He then asked Congress to declare war, which it did on May 13. Some Americans, including Thoreau, thought the war was unjustified. Because Thoreau would not pay taxes to support the war, he went to jail.

Vocabulary **expedient** (ehk SPEE dee uhnt) *n.:* convenience; means to an end.
perverted (puhr VUR tihd) *v.:* misdirected; corrupted.

Ⓐ **Reading Focus** **Persuasive Techniques** What logical argument does Thoreau use to persuade readers that the war with Mexico is unjust?

This American government—what is it but a tradition, though a recent one, endeavoring to transmit itself unimpaired to posterity, but each instant losing some of its integrity? It has not the vitality and force of a single living man; for a single man can bend it to his will. It is a sort of wooden gun to the people themselves; and, if ever they should use it in earnest as a real one against each other, it will surely split. But it is not the less necessary for this; for the people must have some complicated machinery or other, and hear its din, to satisfy that idea of government which they have. Governments show thus how successfully men can be imposed on, even impose on themselves, for their own advantage. It is excellent, we must all allow; yet this government never of itself furthered any enterprise, but by the alacrity with which it got out of its way. *It* does not keep the country free. *It* does not settle the West. *It* does not educate. The character inherent in the American people has done all that has been accomplished; and it would have done somewhat more, if the government had not sometimes got in its way. For government is an expedient by which men would fain[3] succeed in letting one another alone; and, as has been said, when it is most expedient, the governed are most let alone by it. Trade and commerce, if they were not made of India rubber, would never manage to bounce over the obstacles which legislators are continually putting in their way; and, if one were to judge these men wholly by the effects of their actions, and not partly by their intentions, they would deserve to be classed and punished with those mischievous persons who put obstructions on the railroads. **Ⓑ**

But, to speak practically and as a citizen, unlike those who call themselves no-government men, I ask for, not at once no government, but *at once* a better government. Let every man make known what kind of government would command his respect, and that will be one step toward obtaining it.

After all, the practical reason why, when the power is once in the hands of the people, a major-

ity are permitted, and for a long period continue, to rule, is not because they are most likely to be in the right, nor because this seems fairest to the minority, but because they are physically the strongest. But a government in which the majority rule in all cases cannot be based on justice, even as far as men understand it. Can there not be a government in which majorities do not virtually decide right and wrong, but conscience?—in which majorities decide only those questions to which the rule of expediency is

---

3. **fain:** archaic for "gladly; willingly."

Ⓑ **Reading Focus** **Persuasive Techniques** What is Thoreau's logical argument here? How does he enhance the emotional appeal of his argument?

Vocabulary **posterity** (pahs TEHR uh tee) *n.:* generations to come.
alacrity (uh LAK ruh tee) *n.:* promptness in responding; eagerness.
inherent (ihn HIHR uhnt) *adj.:* inborn; built-in.

I ask for, not at once no government, but *at once* a better government.

applicable? Must the citizen ever for a moment, or in the least degree, resign his conscience to the legislator? Why has every man a conscience, then? I think that we should be men first, and subjects afterward. It is not desirable to cultivate a respect for the law, so much as for the right. The only obligation which I have a right to assume, is to do at any time what I think right. . . .

It is not a man's duty, as a matter of course, to devote himself to the eradication of any, even the most enormous wrong; he may still properly have other concerns to engage him; but it is his duty, at least, to wash his hands of it, and, if he gives it no thought longer, not to give it practically his support. If I devote myself to other pursuits and contemplations, I must first see, at least, that I do not pursue them sitting upon another man's shoulders. I must get off him first, that he may pursue his contemplations too. See what gross inconsistency is tolerated. I have heard some of my townsmen say, "I should like to have them order me out to help put down an insurrection of the slaves, or to march to Mexico—see if I would go"; and yet these very men have each, directly by their allegiance, and so indirectly, at least, by their money, furnished a substitute. The soldier is applauded who refuses to serve in an unjust war by those who do not refuse to

Vocabulary **insurrection** (ihn suh REHK shuhn) *n.*: rebellion; revolt.

sustain the unjust government which makes the war; is applauded by those whose own act and authority he disregards and sets at nought; as if the State were penitent to that degree that it hired one to scourge it while it sinned, but not to that degree that it left off sinning for a moment. Thus, under the name of order and civil government, we are all made at last to pay homage to and support our own meanness. After the first blush of sin, comes its indifference and from immoral it becomes, as it were, *un*moral, and not quite unnecessary to that life which we have made. . . . **C**

I meet this American government, or its representative the State government, directly, and face to face, once a year, no more, in the person of its tax gatherer; this is the only mode in which a man situated as I am necessarily meets it; and it then says distinctly, Recognize me; and the simplest, the most effectual, and, in the present posture of affairs, the indispensablest mode of treating with it on this head, of expressing your little satisfaction with and love for it, is to deny it then. My civil neighbor, the tax gatherer, is the very man I have to deal with—for it is, after all, with men and not with parchment that I quarrel—and he has voluntarily chosen to be an agent of the government. How shall he ever know well what he is and does as an officer of the government, or as a man, until he is obliged to consider whether he shall treat me, his neighbor, for whom he has respect, as a neighbor and well-disposed man, or as a maniac and disturber of the peace, and see if he can get over this obstruction to his neighborliness without a ruder and more impetuous thought or speech corresponding with his action? I know this well, that if one thousand, if one hundred, if ten men whom I could name—if ten *honest* men only—aye, if *one* HONEST man, in this State of Massachusetts, *ceasing to hold slaves,* were actually to withdraw from this copartnership, and be locked up in the county jail therefor, it would be the abolition of slavery in America. For it matters not how small the beginning may seem to be: What is once well done is done forever. . . . **D**

I have paid no poll tax[4] for six years. I was put into a jail once on this account, for one night; and, as I stood considering the walls of solid stone, two or three feet thick, the door of wood and iron, a foot thick, and the iron grating which strained the light, I could not help being struck with the foolishness of that institution which treated me as if I were mere flesh and blood and bones, to be locked up. I wondered that it should have concluded at length that this was the best use it could put me to, and had never thought to avail itself of my services in some way. I saw that, if there was a wall of stone between me and my townsmen, there was a still more difficult one to climb or break through, before they could get to be as free as I was. I did not for a moment feel confined, and the walls seemed a great waste of stone and mortar. I felt as if I alone of all my townsmen had paid my tax. They plainly did not know how to treat me, but behaved like persons who are underbred. In every threat and in every compliment there was a blunder; for they thought that my chief desire was to stand the other side of that stone wall. I could not but smile to see how industriously they locked the door on my meditations, which followed them out again without let or hindrance, and *they* were really all that was dangerous. As they could not reach me, they had resolved to punish my body; just as boys, if they cannot come at some person against whom they have a spite, will abuse his dog. I saw that the State was half-witted, that it was timid as a lone woman with her silver spoons, and that it did not know its friends from its foes, and I lost all my remaining respect for it, and pitied it. . . . **E**

The night in prison was novel and interesting enough. The prisoners in their shirt sleeves were enjoying a chat and the evening air in the doorway, when I entered. But the jailer said, "Come, boys, it is time to lock up"; and so they dispersed, and I

---

4. **poll tax:** fee some states and localities required from each citizen as a qualification for voting. It is now considered unconstitutional in the United States to charge such a tax.

C Reading Focus **Persuasive Techniques** What ethical appeals does Thoreau make in this paragraph?

D Literary Focus **Paradox** According to Thoreau, how does his willingness to break the law improve government?

E Literary Focus **Paradox** Why does Thoreau not feel confined in prison?

heard the sound of their steps returning into the hollow apartments. My roommate was introduced to me by the jailer, as "a first-rate fellow and a clever man." When the door was locked, he showed me where to hang my hat, and how he managed matters there. The rooms were whitewashed once a month; and this one, at least, was the whitest, most simply furnished, and probably the neatest apartment in the town. He naturally wanted to know where I came from, and what brought me there; and, when I had told him, I asked him in my turn how he came there, presuming him to be an honest man, of course; and, as the world goes, I believe he was. "Why," said he, "they accuse me of burning a barn; but I never did it." As near as I could discover, he had probably gone to bed in a barn when drunk, and smoked his pipe there; and so a barn was burnt. He had the reputation of being a clever man, had been there some three months waiting for his trial to come on, and would have to wait as much longer; but he was quite domesticated and contented, since he got his board for nothing, and thought that he was well treated.

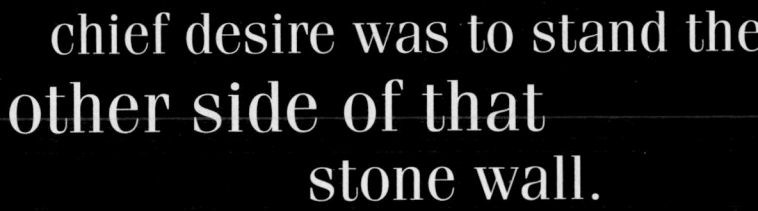

In every threat and in every compliment there was a blunder; for they thought that my chief desire was to stand the other side of that stone wall.

He occupied one window, and I the other; and I saw, that, if one stayed there long, his principal business would be to look out the window. I had soon read all the tracts that were left there, and examined where former prisoners had broken out, and where a grate had been sawed off, and heard the history of the various occupants of that room; for I found that even here there was a history and a gossip which never circulated beyond the walls of the jail. Probably this is the only house in the town where verses are composed, which are afterward printed in a circular form, but not published. I was shown quite a long list of verses which were composed by some young men who had been detected in an attempt to escape, who avenged themselves by singing them.

I pumped my fellow prisoner as dry as I could, for fear I should never see him again; but at length he showed me which was my bed, and left me to blow out the lamp.

It was like traveling into a far country, such as I had never expected to behold, to lie there for one night. It seemed to me that I never had heard the town clock strike before, nor the evening sounds of the village; for we slept with the windows open, which were inside the grating. It was to see my native village in the light of the middle ages, and our Concord was turned into a Rhine stream, and visions of knights and castles passed before me. They were the voices of old burghers that I heard in the streets. I was an involuntary spectator and auditor of whatever was done and said in the kitchen of the adjacent village inn—a wholly new and rare experience to me. It was a closer view of my native town. I was fairly inside of it. I never had seen its institutions before. This is one of its peculiar institutions;

for it is a shire town.[5] I began to comprehend what its inhabitants were about.

In the morning, our breakfasts were put through the hole in the door, in small oblong square tin pans, made to fit, and holding a pint of chocolate, with brown bread, and an iron spoon. When they called for the vessels again, I was green enough to return what bread I had left; but my comrade seized it, and said that I should lay that up for lunch or dinner. Soon after, he was let out to work at haying in a neighboring field, whither he went every day, and would not be back till noon; so he bade me good day, saying that he doubted if he should see me again.

When I came out of prison—for someone interfered, and paid the tax—I did not perceive that great changes had taken place on the common, such as he observed who went in a youth, and emerged a tottering and gray-headed man; and yet a change had to my eyes come over the scene—the town, and State, and country—greater than any that mere time could effect. I saw yet more distinctly the State in which I lived. I saw to what extent the people among whom I lived could be trusted as good neighbors and friends; that their friendship was for summer weather only; that they did not greatly purpose to do right; that they were a distinct race from me by their prejudices and superstitions, as the Chinamen and Malays are; that, in their sacrifices to humanity, they ran no risks, not even to their property; that, after all, they were not so noble but they treated the thief as he had treated them, and hoped, by a certain outward observance and a few prayers, and by walking in a particular straight though useless path from time to time, to save their souls. This may be to judge my neighbors harshly; for I believe that most of them are not aware that they have such an institution as the jail in their village.

It was formerly the custom in our village, when a poor debtor came out of jail, for his acquaintances to salute him, looking through their fingers, which were crossed to represent the grating of a jail window, "How do ye do?" My neighbors did not thus salute me, but first looked at me, and then at one another, as if I

had returned from a long journey. I was put into jail as I was going to the shoemaker's to get a shoe which was mended. When I was let out the next morning, I proceeded to finish my errand, and, having put on my mended shoe, joined a huckleberry party, who were impatient to put themselves under my conduct; and in half an hour—for the horse was soon tackled[6]—was in the midst of a huckleberry field, on one of our highest hills, two miles off; and then the State was nowhere to be seen.

This is the whole history of "My Prisons." . . .

The authority of government, even such as I am willing to submit to—for I will cheerfully obey those who know and can do better than I, and in many things even those who neither know nor can do so well—is still an impure one: To be strictly just, it must have the sanction and consent of the governed. It can have no pure right over my person and property but what I concede to it. The progress from an absolute to a limited monarchy, from a limited monarchy to a democracy, is a progress toward a true respect for the individual. Is a democracy, such as we know it, the last improvement possible in government? Is it not possible to take a step further toward recognizing and organizing the rights of man? There will never be a really free and enlightened State, until the State comes to recognize the individual as a higher and independent power, from which all its own power and authority are derived, and treats him accordingly. I please myself with imagining a State at last which can afford to be just to all men, and to treat the individual with respect as a neighbor; which even would not think it inconsistent with its own repose, if a few were to live aloof from it, not meddling with it, nor embraced by it, who fulfilled all the duties of neighbors and fellow men. A State which bore this kind of fruit, and suffered it to drop off as fast as it ripened, would prepare the way for a still more perfect and glorious State, which also I have imagined, but not yet anywhere seen. **(F)**

6. **tackled:** harnessed.

5. **shire town:** town where a court sits, like a county seat.

(F) Reading Focus Persuasive Techniques How does Thoreau use logic to support his argument for the rights of the individual?

Applying Your Skills

from **Resistance to Civil Government**

SKILLS FOCUS **Literary Skills** Analyze paradox; analyze theme. **Reading Skills** Analyze persuasive techniques (logical, ethical, and emotional appeals). **Vocabulary Skills** Apply knowledge of word origins. **Writing Skills** Write to express.

Respond and Think Critically

Reading Focus

Quick Check

1. According to Thoreau, what is the practical reason that the majority is permitted to rule? Why does he think majority rule can be a problem?

2. Why was Thoreau put in jail? How did his imprisonment affect his feelings about the government?

Read with a Purpose

3. How does Thoreau say a person should act if obeying a law conflicts with his or her conscience?

Reading Skills: Recognizing Persuasive Techniques

4. Review the arguments and statements in your chart. Then, add another column in which you analyze why each argument is persuasive.

Argument or Statement	Logical, Ethical, or Emotional Appeal?	Why Is the Argument Persuasive?
asks reader to consider whether there can be, simultaneously, government and no government	logical	Thoreau wants readers to consider how much control government should have over our lives.

✓ Vocabulary Check

Use a dictionary to look up the **etymologies,** or word origins, of the following Vocabulary words. Then, list the word origin for each word.

5. expedient
6. perverted
7. posterity

8. alacrity
9. inherent
10. insurrection

Literary Focus

Literary Analysis

11. **Interpret** How are Thoreau's perceptions of his fellow citizens changed by his night in jail?

12. **Analyze** How would civil order be <u>transformed</u> if each person always followed his or her conscience? Explain.

13. **Evaluate** Which of Thoreau's arguments did you find most convincing, and which did you disagree with? Briefly explain your opinions.

Literary Skills: Paradox

14. **Interpret** Identify the opposing ideas, and then explain the truth contained in this paradox from the essay: "I felt as if I alone of all my townsmen had paid my tax" (page 272).

Literary Skills Review: Theme

15. **Analyze** The **theme** of a literary work is the insight it offers into human experience. Unlike a work's subject, a theme is usually <u>implicit</u>—not stated directly—and must be inferred. What is the theme of Thoreau's essay?

Writing Focus

Think as a Reader/Writer

Use It in Your Writing Review the list of paradoxes Thoreau uses to convey his beliefs. Write a paragraph about something you believe in strongly, such as your opinion of a family responsibility. Include an original paradox to help express your idea.

What Do **You Think Now**

What aspects of Thoreau's "Resistance to Civil Government" might most inspire readers?

MOHANDAS K. GANDHI

from
On Nonviolent Resistance

DR. MARTIN LUTHER KING, JR.

from
Letter from Birmingham City Jail

What Do You Think?

Where does an individual find inspiration?

 **QuickWrite**

Think about a time when you or someone you know felt inspired to protest a rule you believed was unfair. Write a paragraph about how you protested. What were the strengths and weaknesses of this method? What other approach might you have used?

Mohandas K. Gandhi
(1869–1948)

Mohandas K. Gandhi, leader of India's fight for independence from British rule, is considered the father of his country. As a young lawyer, Gandhi worked for the rights of Indians living under the racist and repressive government of South Africa. From the 1920s to the mid-1940s, he led a prolonged *satyagraha* (noncooperation) campaign for Indian independence from the rule of Great Britain. Gandhi was often arrested and imprisoned and urged his followers to hold to the principles of nonviolent resistance even in the face of violent tactics by those in power.

After independence was granted by Britain, Gandhi, himself a Hindu, fought desperately—and in the end ineffectively—to ease the religious tension between India's Muslims and Hindus. In 1948, he was murdered by a Hindu fanatic. Today, Gandhi has mythic stature as the embodiment of civil disobedience.

Martin Luther King, Jr.
(1929–1968)

Dr. Martin Luther King, Jr., the brilliant leader of the U.S. civil-rights movement in the 1960s, was inspired by the ideas of both Thoreau and Gandhi. King's courageous commitment to nonviolent resistance captured the attention and respect of the nation.

In April 1963, King led a campaign in Birmingham, Alabama, to end racial segregation at lunch counters and discrimination in hiring. While he and his supporters were on a peaceful march toward city hall, the police turned fire hoses on them and then arrested them. While serving his sentence, King wrote his "Letter from Birmingham City Jail," which explains his philosophy of nonviolent resistance. Later that year, King gave his famous "I Have a Dream" speech, in which he expressed his faith that someday, all people would be treated equally. The Civil Rights Act of 1964 was passed soon after. During a 1968 trip to Memphis, Tennessee, King was assassinated.

Think About the Writers

If these individuals were alive today, what injustices do you think they would struggle against? Why?

from On Nonviolent Resistance

Reader/Writer Notebook

Use your **RWN** to complete the activities for this selection.

Literary Focus

Parallelism The repetition of similar grammatical structures for effect is **parallelism.** The key to parallel structure is balance, as in the following example from Gandhi's speech: "Send us to prison and we will live there as in a paradise. Ask us to mount the scaffold and we will do so laughing." Note the similar grammatical structure of the imperative verb followed by the same direct object (*us*) in each sentence. Both sentences are also compound, and both balance a command with the resisters' response.

Reading Focus

Recognizing Persuasive Techniques Speakers and writers who want to move an audience to think, feel, or act in a certain way use **persuasive techniques:** logical appeals, ethical appeals, and emotional appeals. (See page 268 for more about these three types.) In this speech, Gandhi uses all three appeals to convince his listeners that noncooperation is better than violence and war as a means of combating injustice.

Into Action As you read, use a chart like the one below to record the arguments Gandhi makes in his speech. Briefly summarize each one, and then determine whether it is a logical, ethical, or emotional appeal.

Argument	Type of Appeal
explains how the resisters will use peaceful methods to meet the government's challenges	logical, emotional

Writing Focus

Think as a Reader/Writer

Find It in Your Reading Gandhi uses **parallelism** as a persuasive tool in his speech. As you read, record examples of parallel structure in your *Reader/Writer Notebook*. After each example, briefly tell how the parallelism emphasizes an important point that Gandhi is trying to convey.

Vocabulary

conceded (kuhn SEE dihd) *v.*: admitted; acknowledged. *Gandhi conceded that war may lead to peace—but not a lasting peace.*

belligerents (buh LIHJ uhr uhnts) *n.*: nations, states, or their citizens at war. *When belligerents fight, everyone suffers.*

sovereign (SAHV ruhn) *n.*: person, group, or nation having supreme control. *A sovereign retains power only through consent of the governed.*

adorn (uh DAWRN) *v.*: enhance, as with ornaments. *We will not follow unjust rules; they will merely adorn the rule books.*

arbitrary (AHR buh trehr ee) *adj.*: based on personal preference or whim. *We will use noncooperation to fight arbitrary laws.*

Language Coach

Pronunciation Quite often in English, the same group of letters will be pronounced in very different ways. For example, the end of the word *sovereign* is pronounced /ruhn/. But the same letters in the word *reign* ("the period in which a monarch rules") are pronounced /rayn/. The reasons behind this are complex, but you should always be aware of this quirk of the English language.

* **Learn It Online**
Get to know the vocabulary words the interactive way—through Word Watch online.

 go.hrw.com | L11-277 | **Go**

from
On Nonviolent Resistance

by **Mohandas K. Gandhi**

Read with a Purpose
Read to see how Gandhi plans to fight injustice with *satyagraha,* or noncooperation.

Build Background
When Gandhi was working for Indian rights in South Africa, he edited and published a newspaper, *Indian Opinion.* He had read Thoreau's "Civil Disobedience," which made a "deep impression" on him. As he wrote years later, he "translated a portion for the readers of *Indian Opinion* [and] made copious extracts for the English part of the paper." Gandhi included a short biography of Thoreau and five columns of excerpts from "Civil Disobedience" that contained the essence of Thoreau's argument. Gandhi emphasized that Thoreau's "incisive logic is unanswerable" and that he "taught nothing he was not prepared to practice in himself."

There are two ways of countering injustice. One way is to smash the head of the man who perpetrates injustice and to get your own head smashed in the process. All strong people in the world adopt this course. Everywhere wars are fought and millions of people are killed. The consequence is not the progress of a nation but its decline. . . . Pride makes a victorious nation bad-tempered. It falls into luxurious ways of living. Then for a time, it may be conceded, peace prevails. But after a short while, it comes more and more to be realized that the seeds of war have not been destroyed but have become a thousand times more nourished and mighty. No country has ever become, or will ever become, happy through victory in war. A nation does not rise that way; it only falls further. In fact, what comes to it is defeat, not victory. And if, perchance, either our act or our purpose was ill-conceived, it brings disaster to both belligerents. **A**

A **Reading Focus** **Persuasive Techniques** What is Gandhi's principal argument against active, violent resistance to injustice? Is this argument a logical, ethical, or emotional appeal? Explain your answer.

Vocabulary **conceded** (kuhn SEE dihd) *v.:* admitted; acknowledged.
belligerents (buh LIHJ uhr uhnts) *n.:* nations, states, or their citizens at war.

But through the other method of combating injustice, we alone suffer the consequences of our mistakes, and the other side is wholly spared. This other method is *satyagraha*. One who resorts to it does not have to break another's head; he may merely have his own head broken. He has to be prepared to die himself suffering all the pain. In opposing the atrocious laws of the Government of South Africa, it was this method that

Gandhi marching in opposition to the British salt monopoly.

we adopted. We made it clear to the said Government that we would never bow to its outrageous laws. No clapping is possible without two hands to do it, and no quarrel without two persons to make it. Similarly, no State is possible without two entities, the rulers and the ruled. You are our sovereign, our Government, only so long as we consider ourselves your subjects. When we are not subjects, you are not the sovereign either. So long as it is your endeavor to control us with justice and love, we will let you to do so. But if you wish to strike at us from behind, we cannot permit it. Whatever you do in other matters, you will have to ask our opinion about the laws that concern us. If you make laws to keep us suppressed in a wrongful manner and without taking us into confidence, these laws will merely adorn the statute books. We will never obey them. Award us for it what punishment you like; we will put up with it. Send us to prison and we will live there as in a paradise. Ask us to mount the scaffold and we will do so laughing. Shower what sufferings you like upon us; we will calmly endure all and not hurt a hair of your body. We will gladly die and will not so much as touch you. But so long as there is yet life in these our bones, we will never comply with your arbitrary laws. **B**

B **Literary Focus** **Parallelism** Near the end of this paragraph, many sentences balance a government action with the resisters' response. How does the parallel structure of these sentences add to the persuasive effect of the speech?

Vocabulary **sovereign** (SAHV ruhn) *n.*: person, group, or nation having supreme control.
adorn (uh DAWRN) *v.*: enhance, as with ornaments.
arbitrary (AHR buh trehr ee) *adj.*: based on personal preference or whim.

Preparing to Read

Reader/Writer Notebook

Use your **RWN** to complete the activities for this selection.

Literary Focus

Questions Used in Argument Writers often pose questions as a way to advance or support their **argument.** Sometimes a question is used to set up an argument, and after posing it, the writer explores the answer in detail. Other times, the writer poses a **rhetorical question,** or a question that is intended for effect and that does not require an answer. Rhetorical questions often have seemingly obvious answers that support the speaker's or writer's argument. King weaves questions throughout his letter, posing both rhetorical questions and questions that he answers.

Reading Focus

Recognizing Persuasive Techniques Speakers and writers use **persuasive techniques**—logical appeals, ethical appeals, and emotional appeals—to move an audience to think, feel, or act in a certain way. (See page 268 for more about these three types.) King's letter includes all three persuasive techniques.

Into Action As you read, use a chart like the one below to record the arguments King makes in his letter. Briefly summarize each argument, and then indicate whether it is a logical, ethical, or emotional appeal.

Argument	Type of Appeal
points out that there are two types of laws—just and unjust	logical

Writing Focus

Think as a Reader/Writer

Find It in Your Reading As you read, pay close attention to the questions that King poses in his letter. Record them in your *Reader/Writer Notebook,* and explain how each question adds power to King's **argument** for civil disobedience.

Vocabulary

segregation (sehg ruh GAY shuhn) *n.:* separation of one racial group from another or from the rest of society. *In 1954, the Supreme Court outlawed segregation in public schools.*

application (ap luh KAY shuhn) *n.:* act of using; putting to use. *Some laws are just in principle but unjust in their application.*

evading (ih VAY dihng) *v.* used as *n.:* getting away from by trickery; avoiding. *King does not advocate evading just laws.*

anarchy (AN uhr kee) *n.:* disorder and confusion; lawlessness. *Defying laws arbitrarily and without consequence would lead to anarchy.*

arouse (uh ROWZ) *v.:* stir to action. *To arouse the conscience of the community, activists often break unjust laws and face penalties for doing so.*

Language Coach

Word Origins The word *anarchy* is made up of three parts: the prefix *an–,* meaning "no or not"; the root word *arch,* meaning "rule or authority"; and the suffix *–y,* meaning "condition or state." Put together, the parts mean "a state of no rule."

Learn It Online
Analyze persuasive techniques in modern forms of media online at the MediaScope mini-site.

go.hrw.com | L11-280 | **Go**

from

Letter from Birmingham City Jail

by **Dr. Martin Luther King, Jr.**

You express a great deal of anxiety over our willingness to break laws. This is certainly a legitimate concern. Since we so diligently urge people to obey the Supreme Court's decision of 1954 outlawing segregation in the public schools, it is rather strange and paradoxical to find us consciously breaking laws. One may well ask, "How can you advocate breaking some laws and obeying others?" The answer is found in the fact that there are two types of laws: there are just and there are unjust laws. I would agree with Saint Augustine that "An unjust law is no law at all."

Now what is the difference between the two? How does one determine when a law is just or unjust? A just law is a man-made code that squares with the moral law or the law of God. An unjust law is a code that is out of harmony with the moral law. . . .

An unjust law is a code inflicted upon a minority which that minority had no part in enacting or creating because they did not have the unhampered right to vote. Who can say that the legislature of Alabama which set up the segregation laws was democratically elected? Throughout the state of Alabama all types of conniving methods are used to prevent Negroes from becoming registered voters and there are some counties without a single Negro registered to vote despite the fact that the Negro constitutes a majority of the population. Can any law set up in such a state be considered democratically structured? **Ⓐ**

These are just a few examples of unjust and just laws. There are some instances when a law is just on its face and unjust in its application. For instance, I was arrested

---

Ⓐ **Literary Focus** Questions Used in Argument Are the questions in this paragraph rhetorical? For each, explain why or why not.

Vocabulary **segregation** (sehg ruh GAY shuhn) *n.*: separation of one racial group from another or from the rest of society.
application (ap luh KAY shuhn) *n.*: act of using; putting to use.

Friday on a charge of parading without a permit. Now there is nothing wrong with an ordinance which requires a permit for a parade, but when the ordinance is used to preserve segregation and to deny citizens the First Amendment privilege of peaceful assembly and peaceful protest, then it becomes unjust.

I hope you can see the distinction I am trying to point out. In no sense do I advocate evading or defying the law as the rabid segregationist would do. This would lead to anarchy. One who breaks an unjust law must do it *openly*, *lovingly* (not hatefully as the white mothers did in New Orleans when they were seen on television screaming, "nigger, nigger, nigger"), and with a willingness to accept the penalty. I submit that an individual who breaks a law that conscience tells him is unjust, and willingly accepts the penalty by staying in jail to arouse the conscience of the community over its injustice, is in reality expressing the very highest respect for law. **B**

B **Reading Focus** **Persuasive Techniques** Does King's final sentence appeal to readers' reason, emotions, or ethics? Why?

Vocabulary **evading** (ih VAY dihng) *v.* used as *n.*: getting away from by trickery; avoiding.
anarchy (AN uhr kee) *n.*: disorder and confusion; lawlessness.
arouse (uh ROWZ) *v.*: stir to action.

Applying Your Skills

from On Nonviolent Resistance /
from Letter from Birmingham City Jail

Respond and Think Critically

Reading Focus

Quick Check

1. According to Gandhi, how do strong people counter injustice? What happens to them in the process?

2. According to King, what must you accept if you engage in an act of civil disobedience?

Read with a Purpose

3. Why does Gandhi believe in *satyagraha*, or non-cooperation? Why does King believe that breaking the law is sometimes a moral act?

Reading Skills: Recognizing Persuasive Techniques

4. Review your chart on Gandhi's speech. Add a third column in which you note whether each argument uses parallelism. If it does, explain how the parallelism adds to the persuasive effect of the argument. Then, repeat the exercise with your chart on King's letter, but assess his use of questions rather than parallelism.

Argument	Type of Appeal	Parallelism?
explains how the resisters will use peaceful methods to meet the government's challenges	logical, emotional	Yes. The repetition of "we will" emphasizes that the resisters will meet every challenge.

Literary Focus

Literary Analysis

5. **Interpret** According to Gandhi, how can civil disobedience undermine the authority of an unjust government?

6. **Analyze** In the beginning of his letter, how does King try to gain the trust of those who might doubt him?

7. **Evaluate** In King's letter, he tries to make a careful distinction between his own disobedience and the actions of segregationists. What factors does he list to make that distinction? Do you think he successfully makes his case? Explain your opinion.

Literary Skills: Parallelism/Questions Used in Argument

8. **Evaluate** Both of these pieces employ a literary device as a persuasive technique. Gandhi uses parallelism, while King uses questions. Compare and contrast the use of these two devices. Which one do you find more effective, and why? How are their purposes similar or different?

Literary Skills Review: Author's Purpose

9. **Analyze** An **author's purpose** is his or her reason for writing, such as to inform, to persuade, or to entertain. Both Gandhi and King wrote in order to articulate their theories of civil disobedience. Which details in each selection are most effective in helping the writers convey their purposes? Why?

Writing Focus

Think as a Reader/Writer

Use It in Your Writing Review your notes on Gandhi's use of parallelism and King's use of questions. Choose a topic that you feel strongly about. Write a few paragraphs that present your point of view in a persuasive way. In your paragraphs, use parallelism and questions to help make your argument.

from **On Nonviolent Resistance** /
from **Letter from Birmingham City Jail**

Vocabulary Development

✓ Vocabulary Check

Match each Vocabulary word with its antonym, or opposite.

1. conceded		**a.** subject	
2. belligerents		**b.** integration	
3. sovereign		**c.** calm	
4. adorn		**d.** order	
5. arbitrary		**e.** allies	
6. segregation		**f.** denied	
7. application		**g.** rational	
8. evading		**h.** theory	
9. anarchy		**i.** confronting	
10. arouse		**j.** disfigure	

Vocabulary Skills: Etymology

English is a language full of borrowed words. Many English words originally come from Latin or from Old English, a language that traveled to England with the Anglo-Saxons in the fifteenth century. Other words derive from Greek, French, Spanish, and various Native American languages.

Most dictionaries give a word's etymology in brackets after its pronunciation and the abbreviation for its part of speech. For example, here's a dictionary entry for *adorn,* a word used in Gandhi's speech:

---

adorn (uh DAWRN) *v.:* [**L** *ad-,* to + *ornare,* fit out] **1** to be an ornament to **2** to put decorations on

---

The etymology of *adorn* shows that it comes from Latin terms for "to" and "fit out." To adorn something, then, is to add decorations to something, or to "fit it out." Learning the etymology of a word can help you better understand its meaning.

Your Turn

Working with a partner, use a dictionary to research the etymology and meaning of each Vocabulary word.

Word	Etymology	Meaning
adorn	Latin <u>ad-</u>, "to" and ornare, "fit out"	to be an ornament to; to put decorations on

Language Coach

Academic Language To talk about complex political and social issues, Gandhi and King use language that is equally complex and sophisticated. Yet the words they use do relate to familiar concepts and ideas: You might not call a group of people "belligerents," but you've certainly come across a group of "fighters."

For each Vocabulary word, think of a more plain-spoken synonym or phrase. Ask yourself how you would express this idea in your own words. Write up your list, and share it with the class.

Academic Vocabulary

Talk About

With a group of classmates, consider the following statements:

"Send us to prison and we will live there as in a paradise" (Gandhi)

"[Stay] in jail to arouse the conscience of the community." (King)

What ideas about moral action are <u>implicit</u> in these statements? What personal traits are <u>integral</u> to this kind of moral action?

SKILLS FOCUS **Reading Skills** Read in order to research self-selected and assigned topics. **Writing Skills** Write comparison-contrast essays; compare characters or historical figures. **Listening and Speaking Skills** Deliver informative presentations; adapt to occasion when speaking: discussions.

from Resistance to Civil Government / *from* On Nonviolent Resistance / *from* Letter from Birmingham City Jail

Writing Focus

Write a Comparison-Contrast Essay

Henry David Thoreau, Mohandas K. Gandhi, and Martin Luther King, Jr., were all driven by the events of their time. Thoreau wrote against war and slavery, Gandhi fought for his people's independence, and King fought for equal civil rights. Though they were inspired by different problems, the three writers chose the same solution: civil disobedience.

Each writer's view of civil disobedience was influenced by his cause and what he was trying to achieve. Write an essay comparing and contrasting the three causes and describing how each writer's cause affected his view. In your essay, consider the following questions:

- What was each writer's relationship to his cause?
- Could each writer hope to achieve his goals within his lifetime?
- Why did each writer choose civil disobedience? Why did each one believe that civil disobedience would help him achieve his goals?

Review the elements of a successful comparison-contrast essay.

An effective comparison-contrast essay

- clearly states in the essay's opening paragraph what is being compared and contrasted
- conveys a main idea within a thesis statement
- is organized logically and effectively
- cites text passages to support ideas where appropriate
- contains few or no errors in spelling, punctuation, and grammar

CHOICES

As you respond to the Choices, use these **Academic Vocabulary** words as appropriate: factor, implicit, integral, transform, principal.

REVIEW

Compare Situations

Timed └Writing Compare the reasons for Thoreau's and King's arrests. Was one more justified than the other? What do you think each action of civil disobedience achieved? In an essay, state your opinion, explaining your reasons in detail.

CONNECT

Find Peace on Earth

Listening and Speaking Nonviolent resistance is still practiced throughout the world. Research recent examples of people using civil disobedience to fight injustice. Share your findings in a class presentation describing the injustice and the methods being used in the struggle against it.

Julia "Butterfly" Hill occupies an ancient redwood tree to protest cutting redwoods down.

EXTEND

Define Your Philosophy

Group Activity In a small group, determine your own philosophy for battling injustice. What actions would you take? What would be the principal belief in your philosophy? Write a brief summary that describes your group's approach to fighting injustice.

What Do You Think Now

What's more important: inspiring others with words and ideas or taking concrete steps to change the world around you?

Learn It Online
Find out more about these writers and their causes through the Internet links online.

go.hrw.com | L11-285 | Go

CONTENTS

Link to Today

"They who dream by day are cognizant of many things which escape those who dream only by night."

— Edgar Allan Poe

Gothic Fiction by **Leila Christenbury**

Characteristics of Gothic Fiction

- Use of haunting, eerie settings and strange, chilling events
- Romantic interest in intuition, imagination, and hidden truths
- Reaction against the optimism of the Transcendentalists
- Exploration of evil and the irrational depths of the human mind

The Dark Side of Romanticism

Not all American writers agreed with the Transcendentalist notions that the divine is <u>implicit</u> in nature and that people are essentially good. Some felt that these views did not adequately take into account the darker side of human nature, the presence of suffering in the world, and the ongoing conflict between good and evil.

The Dark Romantics, as these skeptics were called, shared with the Transcendentalists and other Romantics an interest in the spiritual world. They also believed in the value of intuition and imagination over rationalism, and they wanted to explore the mysteries of human existence. Where the Transcendentalists saw goodness and hope, however, the Dark Romantics found madness, evil, and alienation.

European Beginnings During the Romantic period in European literature, a similar division had taken place. The result was the **Gothic novel,** which emerged in England in the late eighteenth century. The first well-known Gothic novel was Horace Walpole's *Castle of Otranto,* published in 1765. Mary Shelley's *Frankenstein,* which remains popular today, is another well-known example of the genre.

These tales of terror often adopted the setting of the medieval Gothic castle and used its pointed arches and vaults, dark dungeons, and underground passages to evoke fear. The term *Gothic* was later expanded to describe any fiction that created a haunting atmosphere and included strange and chilling events, such as live burials, horrifying tortures, and the earthly resurrection of corpses.

American Developments In America, the Dark Romantics further <u>transformed</u> this genre. Writers such as Edgar Allan Poe, Nathaniel Hawthorne, and Washington Irving led the emerging trend in American fiction: the short story. Short stories were meant to be read in one sitting; as a result, the cast of characters was small, and the plot was generally uncomplicated. The simplified story structure allowed writers to focus on the internal workings of the main character's mind and provided an ideal setting for writers who wanted to leave behind the rational world and explore the unsettling, irrational depths of the human mind.

Incorporating Gothic elements into the developing short story genre allowed the Dark Romantics to show the madness and violence under the seemingly tranquil surface of civilization. From this natural pairing of form and content, the **Gothic short story** was born.

Ask Yourself

1. What did the Dark Romantics have in common with other Romantics, particularly the Transcendentalists?

2. What two trends in literature came together to form the Gothic short story? Explain.

Learn It Online
Meet Gothic fiction through *PowerNotes* online.

go.hrw.com | L11-287 | **Go**

Preparing to Read

The Devil and Tom Walker

What Do You Think?

Where does an individual find inspiration?

QuickWrite

Washington Irving was inspired by folk tales and legends. Think of a story that you or someone you know finds inspiring. In a paragraph, explain what makes the story inspiring.

Washington Irving (1809) (detail) by John Wesley Jarvis. Oil on wood panel (33" × 26"), SS.62.2.
Historic Hudson Valley, Tarrytown, New York.

Washington Irving
(1783–1859)

Many people in England and the rest of Europe thought that America would never develop a literary voice of its own. Then Washington Irving arrived on the literary scene.

Satirist and Lawyer

Irving was the youngest son of a pious hardware importer and his wife. Despite his limited education, Irving had a genius for inventing fictional comic narrators. He became well known for these characters, including Jonathan Oldstyle, Gent., a caricature of British writers who could not accept the values of a new nation; and the mysterious Diedrich Knickerbocker, the imaginary author of a fake and comical history that ridicules the entire American past. The Knickerbocker book established Irving as the foremost New York satirical writer.

All this time Irving also practiced law, though his interest in it was lukewarm. In 1815, his father sent him to England to take charge of the failing overseas branch of the family business. Irving found the business beyond repair, but he fell in love with the British literary scene and stayed abroad for seventeen years.

An American Voice

While in England, Irving was greatly influenced by the novelist Sir Walter Scott, who advised him to read the German Romantics and find inspiration in folklore and legends. This advice helped shape Irving's future. He decided against putting further energy into business and gave himself entirely to writing. In 1817, he began to write stories based on German folk tales. His two most famous stories, "Rip Van Winkle" and "The Legend of Sleepy Hollow," adapt German folk tales to American settings. Irving collected his stories under the title *The Sketch Book,* which made Irving an international success.

Although Irving borrowed openly from European writers, he brought a fresh new voice to his material. It was an American voice—at times as inflated as a politician's, at times self-mocking. The young nation embraced this voice as its own.

Think About the Writer Until he was over fifty years old, Irving did not sign his own name to his work. Why did he wait so long?

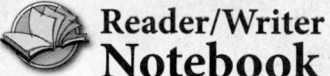

Reader/Writer Notebook

Use your **RWN** to complete the activities for this selection.

Literary Focus

Mood Mood—the overall feeling or atmosphere of a story, play, or poem—can be difficult to identify. After all, mood is intangible; you can't point to it in a text.

In order to identify a story's mood, start with the **setting.** Pay close attention to the details of time and place, and think about how the setting makes you feel. Look carefully at the writer's **diction,** or **word choice.** For example, in the first sentence of this story, the description of a "wooded swamp or morass" helps create a feeling of darkness and foreboding. Then, consider the **plot.** Does the story end happily, or does it present a bitter or tragic outlook on life? The mood of most stories can be described with one or two adjectives, such as *gloomy, sentimental,* and so on.

Reading Focus

Making Predictions When you make an **inference** about a text, you make an educated guess based on clues in the text and on your own knowledge and experience. A **prediction** is a special type of inference—an educated guess about what will happen later. As you read, you may discover that a prediction was incorrect, or you may learn something that transforms your understanding of the story. Adjusting your predictions as you read is an important part of active reading.

Into Action As you read, take notes in a chart like the one below. Identify clues in the plot, setting, or mood that suggest, or **foreshadow,** something that will happen later. Then, make a prediction based on each clue.

Clues in Plot, Setting, or Mood	Prediction
Captain Kidd is said to have buried hidden treasure under a huge oak tree.	Someone will find this buried treasure.

Writing Focus

Think as a Reader/Writer

Find It in Your Reading The **mood** of a story depends largely on how the author describes the setting. As you read, note words or phrases that describe the setting in a particularly evocative way, such as *morass* or *dark grove.* Write these words in your *Reader/Writer Notebook,* and point out how each one contributes to the story's mood.

Vocabulary

prevalent (PREHV uh lehnt) *adj.:* widely existing; frequent. *Earthquakes were prevalent in New England in the early eighteenth century.*

stagnant (STAG nuhnt) *adj.:* not flowing or moving. *The water in the swamp was stagnant.*

precarious (prih KAIR ee uhs) *adj.:* uncertain; insecure; risky. *Bargaining with the devil is a precarious business.*

obliterate (uh BLIHT uh rayt) *v.:* erase or destroy. *Tom could not obliterate the devil's signature.*

avarice (AV uhr ihs) *n.:* greed. *Tom's avarice drove him to make a deal with the devil.*

resolute (REHZ uh loot) *adj.:* determined; unwavering. *Despite the man's pleas, Tom was resolute in his decision to foreclose the mortgage.*

superfluous (su PUR flu uhs) *adj.:* more than is needed or wanted; useless. *Tom's piety was superfluous; it would not save him from the devil.*

Language Coach

Words Often Confused The word *avarice,* like its synonym *greed,* is sometimes confused with the word *envy.* Avarice and greed both refer to excessive desire. Envy involves desire, too; but a key feature of envy is a strong sense of resentment toward the owner of the desired object.

Learn It Online
Explore these Vocabulary words with Word Watch online.

go.hrw.com   L11-289   **Go**

THE DEVIL AND TOM WALKER

by **Washington Irving**

Read with a Purpose

Read to find out how a distinctly American writer adds his own spin to a well-known European tale.

Build Background

"The Devil and Tom Walker" is an American version of the archetypal story of Faust, the sixteenth-century German philosopher who sells his soul to the devil for knowledge and power. An **archetype** (AHR kuh typ) is an original or fundamental imaginative element or pattern that is repeated through the ages. An archetype can be a plot, an event, a character, a setting, or an object. The story of a person who sells his soul to the devil for worldly gain is an archetypal plot. The most famous and influential version of the tale is *Faust,* a play by Johann Wolfgang von Goethe (1749–1832). Each retelling of the Faust legend puts a different spin on the story, and its ending varies: The Faust character, for example, may face eternal flames, find forgiveness and love, or somehow cleverly beat the devil.

A few miles from Boston in Massachusetts, there is a deep inlet, winding several miles into the interior of the country from Charles Bay, and terminating in a thickly wooded swamp or morass. On one side of this inlet is a beautiful dark grove; on the opposite side the land rises abruptly from the water's edge into a high ridge, on which grow a few scattered oaks of great age and immense size. Under one of these gigantic trees, according to old stories, there was a great amount of treasure buried by Kidd the pirate.[1] The inlet allowed a facility to bring the money in a boat secretly and at night to the very foot of the hill; the elevation of the place permitted a good lookout to be kept that no one was at hand; while the remarkable trees formed good landmarks by which the place might easily be found again. The old stories add, moreover, that the devil presided at the hiding of the money, and took it under his guardianship; but this, it is well known, he always does with buried treasure, particularly when it has been ill-gotten. Be that as it may, Kidd never returned to recover his wealth; being shortly after seized at Boston, sent out to England, and there hanged for a pirate. **Ⓐ Ⓑ**

About the year 1727, just at the time that earthquakes were prevalent in New England, and shook many tall sinners down upon their knees, there lived near this place a meager,[2] miserly fellow, of the name of Tom Walker. He had a wife as miserly as himself: They were so miserly that they even conspired to cheat each other. Whatever the woman could lay hands on, she hid away; a hen could not cackle but she was on the alert to secure the new-laid egg. Her husband was continually prying about to detect her secret hoards, and many and fierce were the conflicts that took place about what ought to have been common property. They lived in a forlorn-looking house that stood alone,

and had an air of starvation. A few straggling savin trees,[3] emblems of sterility, grew near it; no smoke ever curled from its chimney; no traveler stopped at its door. A miserable horse, whose ribs were as articulate as the bars of a gridiron, stalked about a field, where a thin carpet of moss, scarcely covering the ragged beds of puddingstone,[4] tantalized and balked his hunger; and sometimes he would lean his head over the fence, look piteously at the passerby, and seem to petition deliverance from this land of famine.

The house and its inmates had altogether a bad name. Tom's wife was a tall termagant,[5] fierce of temper, loud of tongue, and strong of arm. Her voice was often heard in wordy warfare with her husband; and his face sometimes showed signs that their conflicts were not confined to words. No one ventured, however, to interfere between them. The lonely wayfarer shrunk within himself at the horrid clamor and clapperclawing;[6] eyed the den of discord askance;[7] and hurried on his way, rejoicing, if a bachelor, in his celibacy.

One day that Tom Walker had been to a distant part of the neighborhood, he took what he considered a shortcut homeward, through the swamp. Like most shortcuts, it was an ill-chosen route. The swamp was thickly grown with great gloomy pines and hemlocks, some of them ninety feet high, which made it dark at noonday, and a retreat for all the owls of the neighborhood. It was full of pits and quagmires,[8] partly covered with weeds and mosses, where the green surface often betrayed the traveler into a gulf of black, smothering mud: There were also dark and stagnant pools, the

---

1. **Kidd the pirate:** William Kidd (1645?–1701), known as Captain Kidd, a famous pirate in the late 1690s.
2. **meager:** thin.

3. **savin trees:** juniper trees.
4. **puddingstone:** rock consisting of pebbles embedded in cement.
5. **termagant** (TUR muh guhnt): quarrelsome, scolding woman.
6. **clapperclawing:** scratching or clawing with the fingernails.
7. **askance:** with a sideways glance.
8. **quagmires:** areas of land with soft, muddy surfaces; bogs.

Ⓐ Reading Focus **Making Predictions** What possible plot developments does the mention of buried pirate treasure invite?

Ⓑ Literary Focus **Mood** How would you describe the mood as the story opens? Which words from the first paragraph help create it?

Vocabulary **prevalent** (PREHV uh lehnt) *adj.*: widely existing; frequent.
stagnant (STAG nuhnt) *adj.*: not flowing or moving.

abodes of the tadpole, the bullfrog, and the water-snake, where the trunks of pines and hemlocks lay half drowned, half rotting, looking like alligators sleeping in the mire. **C**

Tom had long been picking his way cautiously through this treacherous forest; stepping from tuft to tuft of rushes and roots, which afforded precarious footholds among deep sloughs;[9] or pacing carefully, like a cat, along the prostrate trunks of trees; startled now and then by the sudden screaming of the bittern, or the quacking of wild duck rising on the wing from some solitary pool. At length he arrived at a firm piece of ground, which ran out like a peninsula into the deep bosom of the swamp. It had been one of the strongholds of the Indians during their wars with the first colonists. Here they had thrown up a kind of fort, which they had looked upon as almost impregnable and had used as a place of refuge for their squaws and children. Nothing remained of the old Indian fort but a few embankments, gradually sinking to the level of the surrounding earth, and already overgrown in part by oaks and other forest trees, the foliage of which formed a contrast to the dark pines and hemlocks of the swamp.

It was late in the dusk of evening when Tom Walker reached the old fort, and he paused there awhile to rest himself. Anyone but he would have felt unwilling to linger in this lonely, melancholy place, for the common people had a bad opinion of it, from the stories handed down from the time of the Indian wars, when it was asserted that the savages held incantations here, and made sacrifices to the evil spirit.

Tom Walker, however, was not a man to be troubled with any fears of the kind. He reposed himself for some time on the trunk of a fallen hemlock, listening to the boding cry of the treetoad, and delving with his walking staff into a mound of black mold at his feet.

As he turned up the soil unconsciously, his staff struck against something hard. He raked it out of the vegetable mold, and lo! a cloven[10] skull, with an Indian tomahawk buried deep in it, lay before him. The rust on the weapon showed the time that had elapsed since this deathblow had been given. It was a dreary memento of the fierce struggle that had taken place in this last foothold of the Indian warriors. **D**

"Humph!" said Tom Walker, as he gave it a kick to shake the dirt from it.

"Let that skull alone!" said a gruff voice. Tom lifted up his eyes, and beheld a great black man seated directly opposite him, on the stump of a tree. He was exceedingly surprised, having neither heard nor seen anyone approach; and he was still more perplexed on observing, as well as the gathering gloom would permit, that the stranger was neither Negro nor Indian. It is true he was dressed in a rude half-Indian garb, and had a red belt or sash swathed round his body; but his face was neither black nor copper color, but swarthy and dingy, and begrimed with soot, as if he had been accustomed to toil among fires and forges. He had a shock of coarse black hair, that stood out from his head in all directions, and bore an ax on his shoulder.

He scowled for a moment at Tom with a pair of great red eyes.

"What are you doing on my grounds?" said the black man, with a hoarse, growling voice.

"Your grounds!" said Tom, with a sneer, "no more your grounds than mine; they belong to Deacon Peabody."

"Deacon Peabody be d—d," said the stranger, "as I flatter myself he will be, if he does not look more to his own sins and less to those of his neighbors. Look yonder, and see how Deacon Peabody is faring."

Tom looked in the direction that the stranger pointed, and beheld one of the great trees, fair and

---

9. **sloughs** (slooz): swamps or marshes, usually parts of inlets.

---

10. **cloven:** split.

C **Literary Focus** Mood What mood does the description of the swamp create, and what words in particular heighten this mood? What might be Irving's purpose in creating this mood?

Vocabulary **precarious** (prih KAIR ee uhs) *adj.:* uncertain; insecure; risky.

D **Reading Focus** Making Predictions Tom is described here as a man who is not "troubled with any fears" that trouble other people. He does not worry about savages or evil spirits. What prediction does this description of Tom's character lead you to make? Explain.

flourishing without, but rotten at the core, and saw that it had been nearly hewn through, so that the first high wind was likely to blow it down. On the bark of the tree was scored the name of Deacon Peabody, an eminent man, who had waxed[11] wealthy by driving shrewd bargains with the Indians. He now looked around, and found most of the tall trees marked with the name of some great man of the colony, and all more or less scored by the ax. The one on which he had been seated, and which had evidently just been hewn down, bore the name of Crowninshield; and he recollected a mighty rich man of that name, who made a vulgar display of wealth, which it was whispered he had acquired by buccaneering.[12] **E**

"He's just ready for burning!" said the black man, with a growl of triumph. "You see I am likely to have a good stock of firewood for winter."

"But what right have you," said Tom, "to cut down Deacon Peabody's timber?"

"The right of a prior claim," said the other. "This woodland belonged to me long before one of your white-faced race put foot upon the soil."

"And pray, who are you, if I may be so bold?" said Tom.

"Oh, I go by various names. I am the wild huntsman in some countries; the black miner in others. In this neighborhood I am known by the name of the black woodsman. I am he to whom the red men consecrated this spot, and in honor of whom they now and then roasted a white man, by way of sweet-smelling sacrifice. Since the red men have been exterminated by you white savages, I amuse myself by presiding at the persecutions of Quakers and Anabaptists;[13] I am the great patron and prompter of slave dealers, and the grand master of the Salem witches."

---

11. **waxed:** become or grown.
12. **buccaneering:** robbery at sea; piracy.
13. **Quakers and Anabaptists:** In Puritan New England, where this story is set, Quakers were known primarily for their pacifism and refusal to take oaths, and Anabaptists were known for their opposition to infant baptism.

E **Reading Focus** **Making Predictions** What do you think the stranger is implying by showing Tom the trees marked with the names of wealthy and well-known men? What do you think will happen to these men?

HE NOW LOOKED AROUND, AND FOUND MOST OF THE TALL TREES MARKED WITH THE NAME OF SOME GREAT MAN OF THE COLONY, AND ALL MORE OR LESS SCORED BY THE AX.

"The upshot of all which is, that, if I mistake not," said Tom, sturdily, "you are he commonly called Old Scratch."

"The same, at your service!" replied the black man, with a half-civil nod.

Such was the opening of this interview, according to the old story; though it has almost too familiar an air to be credited. One would think that to meet with such a singular personage, in this wild, lonely place, would have shaken any man's nerves; but Tom was a hard-minded fellow, not easily daunted, and he had lived so long with a termagant wife, that he did not even fear the devil. **F**

It is said that after this commencement they had a long and earnest conversation together, as Tom returned homeward. The black man told him of great sums of money buried by Kidd the pirate, under the oak trees on the high ridge, not far from the morass. All these were under his command, and protected by his power, so that none could find them but such as propitiated[14] his favor. These he offered to place within Tom Walker's reach, having conceived an especial kindness for him; but they were to be had only on certain conditions. What these conditions were may be easily surmised, though Tom never disclosed them publicly. They must have been very hard, for he required time to think of them, and he was not a man to stick at trifles when money was in view. When they had reached the edge of the swamp, the stranger paused. "What proof have I that all you have been telling me is true?" said Tom. "There's my signature," said the black man, pressing his finger on Tom's forehead. So saying, he turned off among the thickest of the swamp, and seemed, as Tom said, to go down, down, down, into the earth, until nothing but his head and shoulders could be seen, and so on, until he totally disappeared. **G**

When Tom reached home, he found the black print of a finger burnt, as it were, into his forehead, which nothing could obliterate. **H**

The first news his wife had to tell him was the sudden death of Absalom Crowninshield, the rich buccaneer. It was announced in the papers with the usual flourish, that "A great man had fallen in Israel."[15]

Tom recollected the tree which his black friend had just hewn down, and which was ready for burning. "Let the freebooter[16] roast," said Tom. "Who cares!" He now felt convinced that all he had heard and seen was no illusion.

He was not prone to let his wife into his confidence; but as this was an uneasy secret, he willingly shared it with her. All her avarice was awakened at the mention of hidden gold, and she urged her husband to comply with the black man's terms, and secure what would make them wealthy for life. However Tom might have felt disposed to sell himself to the devil, he

---

14. **propitiated** (pruh PIHSH ee ayt id): gained the goodwill of.

15. **A great man had fallen in Israel:** popular expression, drawn from the Bible (2 Samuel 3:38), to refer to the death of a prominent member of the community.
16. **freebooter:** pirate.

F **Reading Focus** **Making Predictions** What do you predict Tom will do now that he is face to face with the devil? Explain.

G **Reading Focus** **Making Predictions** What do you think are the "conditions" the devil places on his bargain?

H **Literary Focus** **Mood** Describe the mood that the phrase "which nothing could obliterate" helps create.

Vocabulary **obliterate** (uh BLIHT uh rayt) *v.:* erase or destroy. **avarice** (AV uhr ihs) *n.:* greed.

ONE WOULD THINK THAT TO MEET WITH SUCH A SINGULAR PERSONAGE, IN THIS WILD, LONELY PLACE, WOULD HAVE SHAKEN ANY MAN'S NERVES.

was determined not to do so to oblige his wife; so he flatly refused, out of the mere spirit of contradiction. Many and bitter were the quarrels they had on the subject; but the more she talked, the more resolute was Tom not to be damned to please her.

At length she determined to drive the bargain on her own account, and if she succeeded, to keep all the gain to herself. Being of the same fearless temper as her husband, she set off for the old Indian fort toward the close of a summer's day. She was many hours absent. When she came back, she was reserved and sullen in her replies. She spoke something of a black man, whom she met about twilight hewing at the root of a tall tree. He was sulky, however, and would not come to terms: She was to go again with a propitiatory offering, but what it was she forbore to say.

The next evening she set off again for the swamp, with her apron heavily laden. Tom waited and waited for her, but in vain; midnight came, but she did not make her appearance: Morning, noon, night returned, but still she did not come. Tom now grew uneasy for her safety, especially as he found she had carried off in her apron the silver teapot and spoons, and every portable article of value. Another night elapsed, another morning came; but no wife. In a word, she was never heard of more. **I**

What was her real fate nobody knows, in consequence of so many pretending to know. It is one of those facts which have become confounded by a variety of historians. Some asserted that she lost her way among the tangled mazes of the swamp, and sank into some pit or slough; others, more uncharitable, hinted that she had eloped with the household booty, and made off to some other province; while others surmised that the tempter had decoyed her into a dismal quagmire, on the top of which her hat was found lying. In confirmation of this, it was said a great black man, with an ax on his shoulder, was seen late that very evening coming out of the swamp, carrying a bundle tied in a check apron, with an air of surly triumph. **J**

The most current and probable story, however, observes, that Tom Walker grew so anxious about the fate of his wife and his property, that he set out at length to seek them both at the Indian fort. During a long summer's afternoon he searched about the gloomy place, but no wife was to be seen. He called her name repeatedly, but she was nowhere to be heard. The bittern alone responded to his voice, as he flew screaming by; or the bullfrog croaked dolefully from a neighboring pool. At length, it is said, just in the brown hour of twilight, when the owls began to hoot, and the bats to flit about, his attention was attracted by the clamor of carrion crows[17] hovering about a cypress tree. He looked up, and beheld a bundle tied in a check apron, and hanging in the branches of the tree, with a great vulture perched hard by, as if keeping watch upon it. He leaped with joy; for he recognized his wife's apron, and supposed it to contain the household valuables.

---

17. **carrion crows:** crows that feed on decaying flesh.

Vocabulary **resolute** (REHZ uh loot) *adj.*: determined; unwavering.

I **Reading Focus** **Making Predictions** What do you think has happened to Tom's wife? Explain.

J **Literary Focus** **Mood** What words add to the mysterious mood of this passage? How does this passage add to the suspense about the fate of Tom's wife?

"Let us get hold of the property," said he, consolingly to himself, "and we will endeavor to do without the woman."

As he scrambled up the tree, the vulture spread its wide wings, and sailed off, screaming, into the deep shadows of the forest. Tom seized the checked apron, but, woeful sight! found nothing but a heart and liver tied up in it!

Such, according to this most authentic old story, was all that was to be found of Tom's wife. She had probably attempted to deal with the black man as she had been accustomed to deal with her husband; but though a female scold is generally considered a match for the devil, yet in this instance she appears to have had the worst of it. She must have died game, however; for it is said Tom noticed many prints of cloven feet stamped upon the tree, and found handfuls of hair, that looked as if they had been plucked from the coarse black shock of the woodman. Tom knew his wife's prowess by experience. He shrugged his shoulders, as he looked at the signs of a fierce clapperclawing. "Egad," said he to himself, "Old Scratch must have had a tough time of it!" **K**

Tom consoled himself for the loss of his property, with the loss of his wife, for he was a man of fortitude. He even felt something like gratitude toward the black woodman, who, he considered, had done him a kindness. He sought, therefore, to cultivate a further acquaintance with him, but for some time without success; the old black legs played shy, for whatever people may think, he is not always to be had for calling for: He knows how to play his cards when pretty sure of his game.

At length, it is said, when delay had whetted Tom's eagerness to the quick, and prepared him to agree to anything rather than not gain the promised treasure, he met the black man one evening in his usual woodman's dress, with his ax on his shoulder, sauntering along the swamp, and humming a tune. He affected to receive Tom's advances with great indifference, made brief replies, and went on humming his tune. **L**

By degrees, however, Tom brought him to business, and they began to haggle about the terms on which the former was to have the pirate's treasure. There was one condition which need not be mentioned, being generally understood in all cases where the devil grants favors; but there were others about which, though of less importance, he was inflexibly obstinate. He insisted that the money found through his means should be employed in his service. He proposed, therefore, that Tom should employ it in the black traffic; that is to say, that he should fit out a slave ship. This, however, Tom resolutely refused: He was bad enough in all conscience; but the devil himself could not tempt him to turn slave trader.

Finding Tom so squeamish on this point, he did not insist upon it, but proposed, instead, that he should turn usurer;[18] the devil being extremely anxious for the increase of usurers, looking upon them as his peculiar[19] people.

To this no objections were made, for it was just to Tom's taste.

"You shall open a broker's shop in Boston next month," said the black man.

"I'll do it tomorrow, if you wish," said Tom Walker.

"You shall lend money at two percent a month."

"Egad, I'll charge four!" replied Tom Walker.

"You shall extort bonds, foreclose mortgages, drive the merchants to bankruptcy—"

"I'll drive them to the d—l," cried Tom Walker.

"You are the usurer for my money!" said black legs with delight. "When will you want the rhino?"[20]

"This very night."

"Done!" said the devil.

"Done!" said Tom Walker. So they shook hands and struck a bargain.

A few days' time saw Tom Walker seated behind his desk in a countinghouse in Boston.

His reputation for a ready-moneyed man, who would lend money out for a good consideration, soon spread abroad. Everybody remembers the time of

---

18. **usurer** (YOO zhuhr uhr): one who lends money at excessive rates of interest.
19. **peculiar:** here, special or particular.
20. **rhino:** slang for "money."

K **Literary Focus** Mood In this passage, of what event does Tom see evidence? What is his mood upon seeing the evidence? How can you tell?

L **Reading Focus** Making Predictions Based on the devil's negotiating strategy, what do you expect the outcome of this story to be?

TOM NOTICED MANY PRINTS OF
CLOVEN FEET STAMPED UPON THE TREE,
AND FOUND HANDFULS OF HAIR,
THAT LOOKED AS IF THEY HAD BEEN
PLUCKED FROM THE COARSE BLACK
SHOCK OF THE WOODMAN.

© Mark J. Barrett 2005.

Governor Belcher,[21] when money was particularly scarce. It was a time of paper credit. The country had been deluged with government bills; the famous Land Bank[22] had been established; there had been a rage for speculating; the people had run mad with schemes for new settlements, for building cities in the wilderness; land jobbers[23] went about with maps of grants, and townships, and Eldorados,[24] lying nobody knew where, but which everybody was ready to purchase. In a word, the great speculating fever which breaks out every now and then in the country, had raged to an alarming degree, and everybody was dreaming of making sudden fortunes from nothing. As usual the fever had subsided; the dream had gone off, and the

imaginary fortunes with it; the patients were left in doleful plight, and the whole country resounded with the consequent cry of "hard times."

At this propitious time of public distress did Tom Walker set up as usurer in Boston. His door was soon thronged by customers. The needy and adventurous, the gambling speculator, the dreaming land jobber, the thriftless tradesman, the merchant with cracked credit; in short, everyone driven to raise money by desperate means and desperate sacrifices hurried to Tom Walker.

Thus Tom was the universal friend of the needy, and acted like a "friend in need"; that is to say, he always exacted good pay and good security. In proportion to the distress of the applicant was the hardness of his terms. He accumulated bonds and mortgages; gradually squeezed his customers closer and closer; and sent them at length, dry as a sponge, from his door.

In this way he made money hand over hand, became a rich and mighty man, and exalted his cocked

21. **Governor Belcher:** Jonathan Belcher (1681?–1757) was governor of the Massachusetts Bay Colony from 1730 to 1741.
22. **Land Bank:** loan system by which the province advanced money in exchange for mortgages on land. When the bank was outlawed, many people faced financial ruin.
23. **land jobbers:** people who buy and sell land for profit.
24. **Eldorados:** Spanish word meaning "the gilded"; places of fabulous wealth.

M **Literary Focus** **Mood** How does this plot development and the change of setting to Boston affect the story's mood?

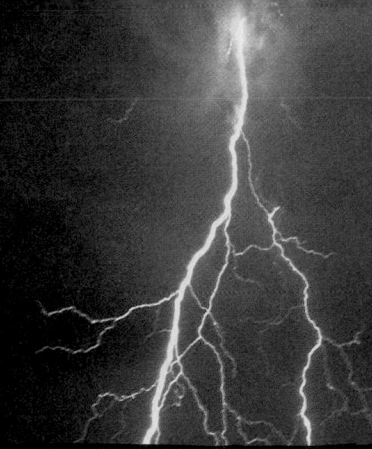

hat upon 'Change.[25] He built himself, as usual, a vast house, out of ostentation;[26] but left the greater part of it unfinished and unfurnished, out of parsimony. He even set up a carriage in the fullness of his vainglory, though he nearly starved the horses which drew it; and as the ungreased wheels groaned and screeched on the axletrees, you would have thought you heard the souls of the poor debtors he was squeezing.

As Tom waxed old, however, he grew thoughtful. Having secured the good things of this world, he began to feel anxious about those of the next. He thought with regret on the bargain he had made with his black friend, and set his wits to work to cheat him out of the conditions. He became, therefore, all of a sudden, a violent churchgoer. He prayed loudly and strenuously, as if heaven were to be taken by force of lungs. Indeed, one might always tell when he had sinned most during the week, by the clamor of his Sunday devotion. The quiet Christians who had been modestly and steadfastly traveling Zionward,[27] were struck with self-reproach at seeing themselves so suddenly outstripped in their career by this new-made convert. Tom was as rigid in religious as in money

matters; he was a stern supervisor and censurer of his neighbors, and seemed to think every sin entered up to their account became a credit on his own side of the page. He even talked of the expediency of reviving the persecution of Quakers and Anabaptists. In a word, Tom's zeal became as notorious as his riches. **O**

Still, in spite of all this strenuous attention to forms, Tom had a lurking dread that the devil, after all, would have his due. That he might not be taken unawares, therefore, it is said he always carried a small Bible in his coat pocket. He had also a great folio Bible on his countinghouse desk, and would frequently be found reading it when people called on business; on such occasions he would lay his green spectacles in the book, to mark the place, while he turned round to drive some usurious bargain.

Some say that Tom grew a little crackbrained in his old days, and that, fancying his end approaching, he had his horse new shod, saddled and bridled, and buried with his feet uppermost; because he supposed that at the last day the world would be turned upside down; in which case he should find his horse standing ready for mounting, and he was determined at the worst to give his old friend a run for it. This, however, is probably a mere old wives' fable. If he really did take such a precaution, it was totally superfluous; at least so says the authentic old legend, which closes his story in the following manner: **P**

One hot summer afternoon in the dog days, just as a terrible black thunder gust was coming up,

---

25. **cocked hat upon 'Change:** Tom's cocked hat was a three-cornered hat worn at the time. *'Change* is short for "the Exchange," a place where merchants and stockbrokers meet to do business.
26. **ostentation:** showy display.
27. **Zionward:** toward Zion, or Heaven.

N Reading Focus **Making Predictions** Tom's possessions are described in detail. What do you predict will happen to them?

O Reading Focus **Making Predictions** Do you think Tom's newfound religious zeal will help him cheat the devil? Why or why not?

P Literary Focus **Mood** How does the anecdote about Tom's horse <u>transform</u> the story's mood? Explain your response.

Vocabulary superfluous (su PUR flu uhs) *adj.:* more than is needed or wanted; useless.

Tom sat in his countinghouse, in his white linen cap and India silk morning gown. He was on the point of foreclosing a mortgage, by which he would complete the ruin of an unlucky land speculator for whom he had professed the greatest friendship. The poor land jobber begged him to grant a few months' indulgence. Tom had grown testy and irritated, and refused another day. **Q**

"My family will be ruined and brought upon the parish," said the land jobber. "Charity begins at home," replied Tom. "I must take care of myself in these hard times."

"You have made so much money out of me," said the speculator.

Tom lost his patience and his piety. "The devil take me," said he, "if I have made a farthing!"

Just then there were three loud knocks at the street door. He stepped out to see who was there. A black man was holding a black horse, which neighed and stamped with impatience.

"Tom, you're come for," said the black fellow, gruffly. Tom shrank back, but too late. He had left his little Bible at the bottom of his coat pocket, and his big Bible on the desk buried under the mortgage he was about to foreclose: Never was sinner taken more unawares. The black man whisked him like a child into the saddle, gave the horse the lash, and away he galloped, with Tom on his back, in the midst of the thunderstorm. The clerks stuck their pens behind their ears, and stared after him from the windows. Away went Tom Walker, dashing down the streets, his white cap bobbing up and down, his morning gown fluttering in the wind, and his steed striking fire out of the pavement at every bound. When the clerks turned to look for the black man, he had disappeared. **R**

Tom Walker never returned to foreclose the mortgage. A countryman, who lived on the border of the swamp, reported that in the height of the thunder gust he had heard a great clattering of hoofs and a howling along the road, and running to the window caught sight of a figure, such as I have described, on a horse that galloped like mad across the fields, over the hills, and down into the black hemlock swamp toward the old Indian fort; and that shortly after a thunderbolt falling in that direction seemed to set the whole forest in a blaze.

The good people of Boston shook their heads and shrugged their shoulders, but had been so much accustomed to witches and goblins, and tricks of the devil, in all kinds of shapes, from the first settlement of the colony, that they were not so much horror-struck as might have been expected. Trustees were appointed to take charge of Tom's effects. There was nothing, however, to administer upon. On searching his coffers,[28] all his bonds and mortgages were found reduced to cinders. In place of gold and silver, his iron chest was filled with chips and shavings; two skeletons lay in his stable instead of his half-starved horses, and the very next day his great house took fire and burnt to the ground.

Such was the end of Tom Walker and his ill-gotten wealth. Let all griping money brokers lay this story to heart. The truth of it is not to be doubted. The very hole under the oak trees whence he dug Kidd's money is to be seen to this day; and the neighboring swamp and old Indian fort are often haunted in stormy nights by a figure on horseback, in morning gown and white cap, which is doubtless the troubled spirit of the usurer. In fact the story has resolved itself into a proverb, and is the origin of that popular saying, so prevalent throughout New England, of "The Devil and Tom Walker." **S**

---

28. **coffers:** containers for money and valuables.

Q Reading Focus **Making Predictions** How does the phrase *terrible black thunder gust* influence your expectations about how this story will end?

R Literary Focus **Mood** How would you describe the story's mood when Tom is being carried off by the devil? What view of Tom does this scene convey?

S Literary Focus **Mood** How would you describe the mood as the story closes? What words or phrases create this mood?

Applying Your Skills

The Devil and Tom Walker

Respond and Think Critically

Reading Focus

Quick Check

1. Describe Tom Walker: Where does he live? What kind of personality does he have?

2. What bargain does Tom make with the devil?

Read with a Purpose

3. How would you describe Irving's spin on the Faust legend? How does Irving's version of the story reflect his beginnings as a satirical writer?

Reading Skills: Making Predictions

4. As you read, you made predictions based on clues you found in the text. Now, add another column to your chart. Use this column to evaluate whether your predictions were correct by recording what really happened in the story. Did any of the events in the story surprise you?

Clues in Plot, Setting, or Mood	Prediction	Actual Events
Captain Kidd is said to have buried hidden treasure under a huge oak tree.	Someone will find this buried treasure.	The devil uses the gold to tempt Tom.

Literary Focus

Literary Analysis

5. **Infer** How does the physical setting of the story reflect the moral decay of the characters and, indeed, of the whole society presented in this story?

6. **Analyze** Review the description of the devil when Tom first encounters him. What details suggest that he comes from a region of hellfire? What details refer to the devil's special dealings in America?

7. **Interpret** As the narrator tells the story, what tone prevails? Find details from the story that support your response.

8. **Extend** How would this story change if it were set in a time and place other than Puritan Boston? Would the theme remain the same? Who would the characters be? What bargain would they make with the devil?

Literary Skills: Mood

9. **Evaluate** Plot is a vital part of a story and has a great influence on its mood. How do the events of this story affect its mood? Which events seem to have the strongest influence?

Literary Skills Review: Stereotypes

10. **Make Judgments** Character types without individuality are **stereotypes** or **stock characters**. Tom Walker's wife is a stereotype of a nagging wife. When this story was published in 1824, people were not aware of how casually stereotypes were accepted. How do you feel about reading literature containing old stereotypes?

Writing Focus

Think as a Reader/Writer

Use It in Your Writing Review your QuickWrite in which you reflect on a tale you find inspiring. Write out the first two paragraphs retelling the story from memory. Identify the story's mood and include a description of the setting that evokes this mood.

 What Do You Think Now

What was Irving's purpose in writing "The Devil and Tom Walker"? What do you think inspired him to retell a tale rather than create a wholly original story?

Vocabulary Development

✔ Vocabulary Check

Match each Vocabulary word with its definition.

1. stagnant
2. obliterate
3. precarious
4. avarice
5. superfluous
6. prevalent
7. resolute

a. widely existing; frequent
b. not flowing or moving
c. determined; unwavering
d. greed
e. more than is needed or wanted; useless
f. uncertain; insecure; risky
g. erase or destroy

Vocabulary Skills: Context Clues

A word's **context**—the words and sentences that surround it—often gives clues to the word's meaning. Context can help you figure out the meaning of an unfamiliar word or a familiar word used in an unusual way. In "The Devil and Tom Walker," Irving tells us that Tom built a huge house "but left the greater part of it unfinished and unfurnished, out of *parsimony*" (page 298).

If you are unfamiliar with the word *parsimony*, context clues from the sentence can help you determine its meaning. Since Tom has plenty of money, he would leave his big house incomplete and unfurnished out of stinginess. *Parsimony* is another word for "stinginess" or "mean covetousness."

Different types of context clues are described below:

- A sentence may provide an example that illustrates the meaning of a difficult word.
- A sentence may use familiar language to define or rephrase an unfamiliar word.
- A sentence may provide a synonym or related word.
- An unfamiliar word might be contrasted with a more familiar word.

Your Turn

Explain how the context clues in each sentence help you understand the meaning of the italicized word.

1. You can find more mosquitoes in *stagnant* pools than in free-flowing bodies of water.

2. Tom was *resolute* in his efforts to avoid obliging his wife; he was determined not to sell himself to the devil to please her.

3. Tom had already lost his soul by dealing with the devil, so his last-minute efforts to save himself were *superfluous*.

4. The slippery swamp offered *precarious*, or uncertain, footholds.

Language Coach

Words Often Confused The word *precarious* has been confused with *dangerous*. To avoid this confusion, remember that *precarious* means unstable or unsure. Complete the following passage using *dangerous* and *precarious* once each.

Tom knew his day-to-day existence was _____, since the devil would eventually get his due. He should have known it was _____ to say, "The devil take me."

Academic Vocabulary

Talk About
In a small group, discuss how an attempt to fulfill his or her desires may transform someone's personality for the better, or, as in Tom Walker's case, for the worse. What factors might contribute to a positive or a negative transformation?

The Minister's Black Veil

What Do **You Think**

Where does an individual find inspiration?

QuickWrite

The narrator of this story remarks that the "saddest of all prisons" is a person's own heart. In a paragraph or two, reflect on what this means and how such "imprisonment" might inspire one to think or behave.

Portrait of Nathaniel Hawthorne (1840) by Charles Osgood. Oil on canvas. Peabody Essex Museum, Salem, MA.

Nathaniel Hawthorne
(1804–1864)

Nathaniel Hawthorne was born on one of the most significant dates and in one of the most recognizable places in American history: July 4, 1804, in Salem, Massachusetts, the site of the Salem witch trials. He was an unusually handsome man, with a loving and beloved wife. By midlife he had earned recognition as a writer and won the admiration of his contemporaries. Nevertheless, he became increasingly unhappy and withdrawn.

A Darkened Heart

Hawthorne's fiction is fueled by an awareness of the guilt that accompanies a Puritan conscience. This shadow of guilt appears to have darkened Hawthorne's life. The source of this darkness is thought to lie in Hawthorne's ancestors. William Hawthorne was a Puritan judge who persecuted Quakers; his son, John, was a judge during the Salem witch trials of 1692. He played a role in sentencing nineteen of the accused to death. Hawthorne often wondered if his family's later misfortunes were judgment for the acts of his two pitiless ancestors.

A Driven Writer

After attending Bowdoin College in Maine, Hawthorne set himself up in what he called the "dismal chamber," a room on the third floor of the family house in Salem. He isolated himself there for the next twelve years learning the craft of fiction. In 1837, Hawthorne emerged to publish *Twice-Told Tales*, a collection of stories that portray the human heart as a place where the secrets of past sins lurk. A brief sojourn at Brook Farm, an idealistic, experimental community founded by a group of Transcendentalists, did little to transform his dark spirits.

Hawthorne found success in 1850 with the publication of his masterwork, *The Scarlet Letter*. In 1851, he published another great novel, *The House of the Seven Gables*. With the onset of the Civil War, Hawthorne felt out of harmony with his times. Gloom continued to plague him until his death in 1864. Ralph Waldo Emerson thought that Hawthorne, no longer able to endure his solitude, "died from it."

Think About the Writer

What do Hawthorne's feelings about his ancestors tell you about his views on sin, guilt, and responsibility?

Reader/Writer Notebook

Use your **RWN** to complete the activities for this selection.

Literary Focus

Symbolism A **symbol** is a person, place, thing, or event that has meaning in itself but also stands for something more than itself. Hawthorne, like the other Dark Romantics, used symbolism in his writing. As the story's title suggests, Hawthorne's central symbol in this story is a "horrible black veil," a "dismal shade" that separates its wearer from the world.

Literary Perspectives Apply the literary perspective described on page 305 as you read this story.

Reading Focus

Making Inferences When you read, you make inferences all the time. When you make an **inference** about a character or event, you are making an educated guess based on details in the text and on your own knowledge and experience. For example, the opening paragraph of "The Minister's Black Veil" states that the children in Milford had "bright faces" and that the bachelors found the young girls pretty. From these details, you can infer that the mood on the Sabbath in Milford is cheerful and happy.

Into Action As you read, use a chart like the one below to record your inferences about the story's characters, events, and symbols. In column 1, list details from the text, noting the page number. In column 2, note what your own knowledge tells you about those details. In column 3, record your inferences based on the information in columns 1 and 2.

Details	My Knowledge	My Inferences
"Children, with bright faces, tripped merrily"; "bachelors looked sidelong at the pretty maidens." (p. 305)	Many of the words have a lighthearted, pleasant connotation.	The mood in Milford is cheerful and happy.

Writing Focus

Think as a Reader/Writer

Find It in Your Reading The black veil is the principal **symbol** in this story. As you read, notice how the author suggests the veil's meanings by describing the way it affects both the congregation's view of Mr. Hooper and Mr. Hooper's view of the world. In your *Reader/Writer Notebook*, write down details that help establish the meanings of the veil.

Vocabulary

inanimate (ihn AN uh miht) *adj.*: lifeless. *The black veil made everything in the world, whether living or inanimate, seem darker to Mr. Hooper.*

obscurity (uhb SKYUR uh tee) *n.*: darkness. *The black veil threw its obscurity between Hooper and the congregation.*

iniquity (ih NIHK wuh tee) *n.*: wickedness. *Were the congregants all hiding sinfulness and iniquity?*

ostentatious (ahs tehn TAY shuhs) *adj.*: deliberately attracting notice. *Their ostentatious laughter profaned the Sabbath.*

pensively (PEHN sihv lee) *adv.*: thoughtfully or seriously. *Elizabeth reacted pensively to Mr. Hooper's decision to wear the veil.*

antipathy (an TIHP uh thee) *n.*: strong dislike. *Is their antipathy toward the veil motivated by fear?*

plausibility (plaw zuh BIHL uh tee) *n.*: believability. *Is there plausibility to the rumor that Mr. Hooper had committed a great sin?*

Language Coach

Suffixes Adding a suffix may change many adjectives to nouns. Adding the suffix *–ity* to the adjective *obscure*, which means *dark*, transforms it into the noun *obscurity*, which means *darkness*. Changing a word from an adjective to a noun will also change the role it plays in a sentence since it has now become a different part of speech.

Learn It Online

For a preview of this story, see the video introduction online.

 go.hrw.com L11-303 Go

THE MINISTER'S BLACK VEIL
A PARABLE

by **Nathaniel Hawthorne**

Read with a Purpose

Read to learn how a minister's decision to cover his face with a black veil affects his congregation's views of guilt and sin.

Build Background

Like much of Hawthorne's best work, this story is set in the time of his Puritan ancestors, an era he said was "characterized by . . . gloom and piety." Hawthorne added the following note to the story: "Another clergyman in New England, Mr. Joseph Moody, of York, Maine, who died about eighty years since, made himself remarkable by the same eccentricity that is here related of the Reverend Mr. Hooper. In this case, however, the symbol had a different import. In early life he had accidentally killed a beloved friend; and from that day till the hour of his own death, he hid his face from men."

By adding the subtitle "A Parable" to this story, Hawthorne indicates the importance of the story's moral theme. A **parable** is a short, usually simple story, based on events from ordinary life, from which a moral lesson is drawn.

The sexton[1] stood in the porch of Milford meetinghouse, pulling lustily at the bell rope. The old people of the village came stooping along the street. Children, with bright faces, tripped merrily beside their parents, or mimicked a graver gait, in the conscious dignity of their Sunday clothes. Spruce[2] bachelors looked sidelong at the pretty maidens, and fancied that the Sabbath sunshine made them prettier than on weekdays. When the throng had mostly streamed into the porch, the sexton began to toll the bell, keeping his eye on the Reverend Mr. Hooper's door. The first glimpse of the clergyman's figure was the signal for the bell to cease its summons. **Ⓐ**

"But what has good Parson Hooper got upon his face?" cried the sexton in astonishment.

All within hearing immediately turned about, and beheld the semblance[3] of Mr. Hooper, pacing slowly his meditative[4] way toward the meetinghouse. With one accord they started, expressing more wonder than if some strange minister were coming to dust the cushions of Mr. Hooper's pulpit.

"Are you sure it is our parson?" inquired Goodman[5] Gray of the sexton.

"Of a certainty it is good Mr. Hooper," replied the sexton. "He was to have exchanged pulpits with Parson Shute of Westbury; but Parson Shute sent to excuse himself yesterday, being to preach a funeral sermon."

The cause of so much amazement may appear sufficiently slight. Mr. Hooper, a gentlemanly person of about thirty, though still a bachelor, was dressed with due clerical neatness, as if a careful wife had starched his band, and brushed the weekly dust from his Sunday's garb. There was but one thing remarkable in his appearance. Swathed about his forehead, and hanging down over his face, so low as to be shaken by his breath, Mr. Hooper had on a black veil. On a nearer view, it seemed to consist of two folds of crape,[6] which entirely concealed his features, except the mouth and chin, but probably did not intercept his sight, farther than to give a darkened aspect to all living and inanimate things. With this gloomy shade before him, good Mr. Hooper walked onward, at a slow and quiet pace, stooping somewhat and looking on the ground, as is customary with abstracted[7] men, yet nodding kindly to those of his parishioners who still waited on the meetinghouse steps. But so wonder-struck were they, that his greeting hardly met with a return. **Ⓑ**

---

1. **sexton:** church officer or employee whose duties may include maintenance, ringing the bells, and digging graves.
2. **spruce:** neat in appearance.
3. **semblance:** outward appearance.
4. **meditative:** deeply thoughtful.
5. **Goodman:** form of polite address similar to *Mister*.

6. **crape:** kind of black cloth worn as a sign of mourning; from the French *crêpe*.
7. **abstracted:** lost in thought.

Literary Perspectives

Analyzing Historical Context Thinking about historical context can help you understand the importance of the social and cultural characteristics of the time. The historical context of this story is the time of Hawthorne's Puritan ancestors. In Puritan New England, sin was a principal topic of sermons. Puritans believed that human beings were born in a state of sin resulting from the original sin of Adam and Eve. They also believed that people were predestined by God to be either saved from sin or damned. In addition to having original sin, human beings could sin by violating any of the Ten Commandments or by committing other offenses. How might the Puritans' beliefs about guilt and sin affect their emotions, their relationships, and their actions? How might the desire for salvation put a veil "on every visage"?

As you read, be sure to notice the questions in the text, which will guide you in using this perspective.

Ⓐ **Reading Focus** **Making Inferences** What is the mood in Milford? How do the villagers feel about going to the service? Cite details to support your inferences.

Ⓑ **Literary Focus** **Symbolism** Hawthorne says that the veil gave a "darkened aspect to all living and inanimate things." What does this mean, and how does it suggest that the veil has both a literal and a symbolic meaning?

Vocabulary **inanimate** (ihn AN uh miht) *adj.:* lifeless.

"I can't really feel as if good Mr. Hooper's face was behind that piece of crape," said the sexton.

"I don't like it," muttered an old woman, as she hobbled into the meetinghouse. "He has changed himself into something awful, only by hiding his face."

"Our parson has gone mad!" cried Goodman Gray, following him across the threshold.

A rumor of some unaccountable phenomenon had preceded Mr. Hooper into the meetinghouse, and set all the congregation astir. Few could refrain from twisting their heads toward the door; many stood upright, and turned directly about; while several little boys clambered upon the seats, and came down again with a terrible racket. There was a general bustle, a rustling of the women's gowns and shuffling of the men's feet, greatly at variance[8] with that hushed repose which should attend the entrance of the minister. But Mr. Hooper appeared not to notice the perturbation[9] of his people. He entered with an almost noiseless step, bent his head mildly to the pews on each side, and bowed as he passed his oldest parishioner, a white-haired great-grandsire, who occupied an armchair in the center of the aisle. It was strange to observe, how slowly this venerable man became conscious of something singular in the appearance of his pastor. He seemed not fully to partake of the prevailing wonder, till Mr. Hooper had ascended the stairs, and showed himself in the pulpit, face to face with his congregation, except for the black veil. That mysterious emblem was never once withdrawn. It shook with his measured breath as he gave out the psalm; it threw its obscurity between him and the holy page, as he read the Scriptures; and while he prayed, the veil lay heavily on his uplifted countenance. Did he seek to hide it from the dread Being whom he was addressing?

Such was the effect of this simple piece of crape, that more than one woman of delicate nerves was forced to leave the meetinghouse. Yet perhaps the pale-faced congregation was almost as fearful a sight to the minister, as his black veil to them.

Mr. Hooper had the reputation of a good preacher, but not an energetic one: He strove to win his people heavenward, by mild persuasive influences, rather than to drive them thither, by the thunders of the Word. The sermon which he now delivered, was marked by the same characteristics of style and manner, as the general series of his pulpit oratory. But there was something, either in the sentiment of the discourse itself, or in the imagination of the auditors, which made it greatly the most powerful effort that they had ever heard from their pastor's lips. It was tinged, rather more darkly than usual, with the gentle gloom of Mr. Hooper's temperament. The subject had reference to secret sin, and those sad mysteries which we hide from our nearest and dearest, and would fain conceal from our own consciousness, even forgetting that the Omniscient[10] can detect them. A subtle power was breathed into his words. Each member of the congregation, the most innocent girl, and the man of hardened breast, felt as if the preacher had crept upon them, behind his awful veil, and discovered their hoarded iniquity of deed or thought. Many spread their clasped hands on their bosoms. There was nothing terrible in what Mr. Hooper said; at least, no violence; and yet, with every tremor of his melancholy voice, the hearers quaked. An unsought pathos[11] came hand in hand with awe. So sensible were the audience of some unwonted attribute in their minister, that they longed for a breath of wind to blow aside the veil, almost believing that a stranger's visage[12] would be discovered, though the form, gesture, and voice were those of Mr. Hooper. **C**

At the close of the services, the people hurried out with indecorous[13] confusion, eager to communicate their pent-up amazement, and conscious of lighter spirits, the moment they lost sight of the black veil. Some gathered in little circles, huddled closely together,

---

8. **at variance:** not in agreement.
9. **perturbation:** state of alarm.

10. **the Omniscient** (ahm NIHSH uhnt): the all-knowing God.
11. **pathos** (PAY thos): feelings of pity, sympathy, and sorrow.
12. **visage:** face.
13. **indecorous:** improper; lacking good taste.

C **Reading Focus** **Making Inferences** How does the veil make Mr. Hooper's sermon more powerful to his congregation?

Vocabulary **obscurity** (uhb SKYUR uh tee) *n.:* darkness. **iniquity** (ih NIHK wuh tee) *n.:* wickedness.

with their mouths all whispering in the center; some went homeward alone, wrapped in silent meditation; some talked loudly, and profaned[14] the Sabbath day with ostentatious laughter. A few shook their sagacious heads, intimating[15] that they could penetrate the mystery; while one or two affirmed that there was no mystery at all, but only that Mr. Hooper's eyes were so weakened by the midnight lamp, as to require a shade. After a brief interval, forth came good Mr. Hooper also, in the rear of his flock. Turning his veiled face from one group to another, he paid due reverence to the hoary[16] heads, saluted the middle-aged with kind dignity, as their friend and spiritual guide, greeted the young with mingled authority and love, and laid his hands on the little children's heads to bless them. Such was always his custom on the Sabbath day. Strange and bewildered looks repaid him for his courtesy. None, as on former occasions, aspired to the honor of walking by their pastor's side. Old Squire Saunders, doubtless by an accidental lapse of memory, neglected to invite Mr. Hooper to his table, where the good clergyman had been wont[17] to bless the food, almost every Sunday since his settlement. He returned, therefore, to the parsonage, and, at the moment of closing the door, was observed to look back upon the people, all of whom had their eyes fixed upon the minister. A sad smile gleamed faintly from beneath the black veil, and flickered about his mouth, glimmering as he disappeared.

"How strange," said a lady, "that a simple black veil, such as any woman might wear on her bonnet, should become such a terrible thing on Mr. Hooper's face!"

"Something must surely be amiss with Mr. Hooper's intellects," observed her husband, the physician of the village. "But the strangest part of the affair is the effect of this vagary,[18] even on a sober-minded man like myself. The black veil, though it covers only our pastor's face, throws its influence over his whole person, and makes him ghostlike from head to foot. Do you not feel it so?"

"Truly do I," replied the lady; "and I would not be alone with him for the world. I wonder he is not afraid to be alone with himself!"

"Men sometimes are so," said her husband.

The afternoon service was attended with similar circumstances. At its conclusion, the bell tolled for the funeral of a young lady. The relatives and friends were assembled in the house, and the more distant acquaintances stood about the door, speaking of the good qualities of the deceased, when their talk was interrupted by the appearance of Mr. Hooper, still covered with his black veil. It was now an appropriate emblem. The clergyman stepped into the room where the corpse was laid, and bent over the coffin, to take a last farewell of his deceased parishioner. As he stooped, the veil hung straight down from his forehead, so that, if her eyelids had not been closed forever, the dead maiden might have seen his face. Could Mr. Hooper be fearful of her glance, that he so hastily caught back the black veil? A person, who watched the interview between the dead and living, scrupled[19] not to affirm, that, at the instant when the clergyman's features were disclosed, the corpse had slightly shuddered, rustling the shroud[20] and muslin cap, though the countenance retained the composure of death. A superstitious old woman was the only witness of this prodigy.[21] From the coffin, Mr. Hooper passed into the chamber of the mourners, and thence to the head of the staircase, to make the funeral prayer. It was a tender and heart-dissolving prayer, full of sorrow,

> THERE WAS NOTHING TERRIBLE IN WHAT MR. HOOPER SAID . . . AND YET, WITH EVERY TREMOR OF HIS MELANCHOLY VOICE, THE HEARERS QUAKED.

---

14. **profaned:** showed disrespect for.
15. **intimating:** indirectly suggesting.
16. **hoary:** white or gray, as with age.
17. **wont:** accustomed.
18. **vagary:** odd, unexpected action.

19. **scrupled:** hesitated.
20. **shroud:** cloth used to wrap a body for burial.
21. **prodigy:** something extraordinary or unexplainable.

Vocabulary ostentatious (ahs tehn TAY shuhs) *adj.:* deliberately attracting notice.

yet so imbued with celestial[22] hopes, that the music of a heavenly harp, swept by the fingers of the dead, seemed faintly to be heard among the saddest accents of the minister. The people trembled, though they but darkly understood him, when he prayed that they, and himself, and all of mortal race, might be ready, as he trusted this young maiden had been, for the dreadful hour that should snatch the veil from their faces. The bearers went heavily forth, and the mourners followed, saddening all the street, with the dead before them, and Mr. Hooper in his black veil behind.

"Why do you look back?" said one in the procession to his partner.

"I had a fancy," replied she, "that the minister and the maiden's spirit were walking hand in hand."

"And so had I, at the same moment," said the other. **(D)**

That night, the handsomest couple in Milford village were to be joined in wedlock. Though reckoned a melancholy man, Mr. Hooper had a placid cheerfulness for such occasions, which often excited a sympathetic smile, where livelier merriment would have been thrown away. There was no quality of his disposition which made him more beloved than this. The company at the wedding awaited his arrival with impatience, trusting that the strange awe, which had gathered over him throughout the day, would now be dispelled. But such was not the result. When Mr. Hooper came, the first thing that their eyes rested on was the same horrible black veil, which had added deeper gloom to the funeral, and could portend nothing but evil to the wedding. Such was its immediate effect on the guests, that a cloud seemed to have rolled duskily from beneath the black crape, and dimmed the light of the candles. The bridal pair stood up before the minister. But the bride's cold fingers quivered in the tremulous[23] hand of the bridegroom, and her death-like paleness caused a whisper, that the maiden who had been buried a few hours before, was come from her grave to be married. If ever another wedding were so dismal, it was that famous one, where they tolled the wedding knell.[24] After performing the ceremony, Mr. Hooper raised a glass of wine to his lips, wishing happiness to the new-married couple, in a strain of mild pleasantry that ought to have brightened the features of the guests, like a cheerful gleam from the hearth. At that instant, catching a glimpse of his figure in the looking glass, the black veil involved his own spirit in the horror with which it overwhelmed all others. His frame shuddered—his lips grew white—he spilt the untasted wine upon the carpet—and rushed forth into the darkness. For the Earth, too, had on her Black Veil. **(E)**

The next day, the whole village of Milford talked of little else than Parson Hooper's black veil. That, and the mystery concealed behind it, supplied a topic for discussion between acquaintances meeting in the street, and good women gossiping at their open windows. It was the first item of news that the tavern keeper told to his guests. The children babbled of it on their way to school. One imitative little imp covered his face with an old black handkerchief, thereby so affrighting his playmates, that the panic seized himself, and he well nigh lost his wits by his own waggery.[25]

It was remarkable, that, of all the busybodies and impertinent people in the parish, not one ventured to put the plain question to Mr. Hooper, wherefore he did this thing. Hitherto, whenever there appeared the slightest call for such interference, he had never lacked advisers, nor shown himself averse to be guided by their judgment. If he erred at all, it was by so painful a degree of self-distrust, that even the mildest censure[26] would lead him to consider an indifferent action as a crime. Yet, though so well acquainted with this amiable[27] weakness, no individual among his parishioners chose to make the black veil a subject of friendly remonstrance.[28] There was a feeling of dread, neither plainly confessed nor carefully concealed, which caused each to shift the responsibility upon another, till at length it was

---

22. **celestial:** heavenly.
23. **tremulous:** trembling.

24. **If . . . wedding knell:** reference to Hawthorne's story "The Wedding Knell." A knell is the ringing of a bell.
25. **waggery:** joke.
26. **censure:** expression of strong disapproval or criticism.
27. **amiable:** friendly; likable.
28. **remonstrance:** protest; complaint.

(D) Literary Focus Symbolism What might this vision of the minister and the maiden's spirit symbolize?

(E) Reading Focus Making Inferences What does the narrator mean when he says, "For the Earth, too, had on her Black Veil"?

Analyzing Visuals

Viewing and Interpreting Describe what is happening in this picture. Does knowing that this painting was created specifically to illustrate Hawthorne's short story influence how you interpret the mood of the image?

Illustration by Elenore Plaisted Abbot for "The Minister's Black Veil," from the 1900 edition of *Twice-Told Tales.*

found expedient to send a deputation[29] of the church, in order to deal with Mr. Hooper about the mystery, before it should grow into a scandal. Never did an embassy so ill discharge its duties. The minister received them with friendly courtesy, but became silent, after they were seated, leaving to his visitors the whole burden of introducing their important business. The topic, it might be supposed, was obvious enough. There was the black veil, swathed round Mr. Hooper's forehead, and concealing every feature above his placid mouth, on which, at times, they could perceive the glimmering of a melancholy smile. But that piece of crape, to their imagination, seemed to hang down before his heart, the symbol of a fearful secret between him and them. Were the veil but cast aside, they might speak freely of it, but not till

then. Thus they sat a considerable time, speechless, confused, and shrinking uneasily from Mr. Hooper's eye, which they felt to be fixed upon them with an invisible glance. Finally, the deputies returned abashed to their constituents, pronouncing the matter too weighty to be handled, except by a council of the churches, if, indeed, it might not require a general synod.[30] **F**

But there was one person in the village, unappalled by the awe with which the black veil had impressed all beside herself. When the deputies returned without an explanation, or even venturing to demand one, she, with the calm energy of her character, determined to

---

29. **deputation:** group of representatives.

---

30. **synod** (SIHN uhd): governing body of a group of churches.

F Literary Perspectives **Historical Context** In what way do the people's reactions to the veil reflect their Puritan beliefs? Explain.

chase away the strange cloud that appeared to be settling round Mr. Hooper, every moment more darkly
than before. As his plighted[31] wife, it should be her
privilege to know what the black veil concealed. At
the minister's first visit, therefore, she entered upon
the subject, with a direct simplicity, which made the
task easier both for him and her. After he had seated
himself, she fixed her eyes steadfastly upon the veil, but
could discern nothing of the dreadful gloom that had
so overawed the multitude: It was but a double fold of
crape, hanging down from his forehead to his mouth,
and slightly stirring with his breath.

"No," said she aloud, and smiling, "there is nothing terrible in this piece of crape, except that it hides a
face which I am always glad to look upon. Come, good
sir, let the sun shine from behind the cloud. First lay
aside your black veil: Then tell me why you put it on."

Mr. Hooper's smile glimmered faintly.

"There is an hour to come," said he, "when all of
us shall cast aside our veils. Take it not amiss, beloved
friend, if I wear this piece of crape till then." **G**

"Your words are a mystery too," returned the
young lady. "Take away the veil from them, at least."

"Elizabeth, I will," said he, "so far as my vow may
suffer me. Know, then, this veil is a type and a symbol,
and I am bound to wear it ever, both in light and darkness, in solitude and before the gaze of multitudes,
and as with strangers, so with my familiar friends. No
mortal eye will see it withdrawn. This dismal shade
must separate me from the world: Even you, Elizabeth,
can never come behind it!"

"What grievous affliction hath befallen you," she
earnestly inquired, "that you should thus darken your
eyes forever?"

"If it be a sign of mourning," replied Mr. Hooper,
"I, perhaps, like most other mortals, have sorrows dark
enough to be typified by a black veil."

"But what if the world will not believe that it is
the type of an innocent sorrow?" urged Elizabeth.
"Beloved and respected as you are, there may be whispers, that you hide your face under the consciousness

of secret sin. For the sake of your holy office, do away
this scandal!"

The color rose into her cheeks, as she intimated
the nature of the rumors that were already abroad in
the village. But Mr. Hooper's mildness did not forsake
him. He even smiled again—that same sad smile,
which always appeared like a faint glimmering of light,
proceeding from the obscurity beneath the veil.

"If I hide my face for sorrow, there is cause
enough," he merely replied; "and if I cover it for secret
sin, what mortal might not do the same?"

And with this gentle, but unconquerable
obstinacy,[32] did he resist all her entreaties. At length
Elizabeth sat silent. For a few moments she appeared
lost in thought, considering, probably, what new
methods might be tried, to withdraw her lover from
so dark a fantasy, which, if it had no other meaning,
was perhaps a symptom of mental disease. Though
of a firmer character than his own, the tears rolled
down her cheeks. But, in an instant, as it were, a new
feeling took the place of sorrow: Her eyes were fixed
insensibly on the black veil, when, like a sudden
twilight in the air, its terrors fell around her. She arose,
and stood trembling before him.

"And do you feel it then at last?" said he mournfully.

She made no reply, but covered her eyes with her
hand, and turned to leave the room. He rushed forward and caught her arm.

"Have patience with me, Elizabeth!" cried he passionately. "Do not desert me, though this veil must be
between us here on earth. Be mine, and hereafter there
shall be no veil over my face, no darkness between our
souls! It is but a mortal veil—it is not for eternity! Oh!
you know not how lonely I am, and how frightened to
be alone behind my black veil. Do not leave me in this
miserable obscurity forever!"

"Lift the veil but once, and look me in the face,"
said she.

"Never! It cannot be!" replied Mr. Hooper.

"Then, farewell!" said Elizabeth. **H**

She withdrew her arm from his grasp, and slowly

---

31. **plighted:** promised.

32. **obstinacy:** stubbornness; willfulness.

G **Literary Focus** Symbolism What does Mr. Hooper mean
when he says that "all of us shall cast aside our veils"? How does this statement transform your understanding of the veil as a symbol?

H **Reading Focus** Making Inferences How does Elizabeth feel
in this scene? How does Mr. Hooper feel? Support your answers with details
from the story.

"...I AM BOUND TO WEAR IT... THIS DISMAL SHADE MUST SEPARATE ME FROM THE WORLD."

departed, pausing at the door, to give one long, shuddering gaze, that seemed almost to penetrate the mystery of the black veil. But, even amid his grief, Mr. Hooper smiled to think that only a material emblem had separated him from happiness, though the horrors which it shadowed forth, must be drawn darkly between the fondest of lovers.

From that time no attempts were made to remove Mr. Hooper's black veil, or, by a direct appeal, to discover the secret which it was supposed to hide. By persons who claimed a superiority to popular prejudice, it was reckoned merely an eccentric whim, such as often mingles with the sober actions of men otherwise rational, and tinges them all with its own semblance of insanity. But with the multitude, good Mr. Hooper was irreparably a bugbear.[33] He could not walk the streets with any peace of mind, so conscious was he that the gentle and timid would turn aside to avoid him, and that others would make it a point of hardihood to throw themselves in his way. The impertinence of the latter class compelled him to give up his customary walk, at sunset, to the burial ground; for when he leaned pensively over the gate, there would always be faces behind the gravestones, peeping at his black veil. A fable went the rounds, that the stare of the dead people drove him thence. It grieved him, to the very depth of his kind heart, to observe how the children fled from his approach, breaking up their merriest sports, while his melancholy figure was yet afar off. Their instinctive dread caused him to feel, more strongly than aught else, that a preternatural[34] horror was interwoven with the threads of the black crape. In truth, his own antipathy to the veil was known to be so great, that he never willingly passed before a mirror, nor stooped to drink at a still fountain, lest, in its peaceful bosom, he should be affrighted by himself. This was what gave plausibility to the whispers, that Mr. Hooper's conscience tortured him for some great crime, too horrible to be entirely concealed, or otherwise than so obscurely intimated. Thus, from beneath the black veil, there rolled a cloud into the sunshine, an ambiguity of sin or sorrow, which enveloped the poor minister, so that love or sympathy could never reach him. It was said, that ghost and fiend consorted with him there. With self-shudderings and outward terrors, he walked continually in its shadow,

---

33. **bugbear:** source of irrational fears.

34. **preternatural:** abnormal; supernatural.

Vocabulary **pensively** (PEHN sihv lee) *adv.:* thoughtfully or seriously.
antipathy (an TIHP uh thee) *n.:* strong dislike.
plausibility (plaw zuh BIHL uh tee) *n.:* believability.

groping darkly within his own soul, or gazing through a medium that saddened the whole world. Even the lawless wind, it was believed, respected his dreadful secret, and never blew aside the veil. But still good Mr. Hooper sadly smiled, at the pale visages of the worldly throng as he passed by. **Ⅰ**

Among all its bad influences, the black veil had the one desirable effect, of making its wearer a very efficient clergyman. By the aid of his mysterious emblem—for there was no other apparent cause—he became a man of awful power, over souls that were in agony for sin. His converts always regarded him with a dread peculiar to themselves, affirming, though but figuratively, that, before he brought them to celestial light, they had been with him behind the black veil. Its gloom, indeed, enabled him to sympathize with all dark affections. Dying sinners cried aloud for Mr. Hooper, and would not yield their breath till he appeared; though ever, as he stooped to whisper consolation, they shuddered at the veiled face so near their own. Such were the terrors of the black veil, even when Death had bared his visage! Strangers came long distances to attend service at his church, with the mere idle purpose of gazing at his figure, because it was forbidden them to behold his face. But many were made to quake ere they departed! Once, during Governor Belcher's[35] administration, Mr. Hooper was appointed to preach the election sermon. Covered with his black veil, he stood before the chief magistrate, the council, and the representatives, and wrought so deep an impression, that the legislative measures of that year, were characterized by all the gloom and piety of our earliest ancestral sway. **J**

In this manner Mr. Hooper spent a long life, irreproachable[36] in outward act, yet shrouded in dismal suspicions; kind and loving, though unloved,

and dimly feared; a man apart from men, shunned in their health and joy, but ever summoned to their aid in mortal anguish. As years wore on, shedding their snows above his sable veil, he acquired a name throughout the New England churches, and they called him Father Hooper. Nearly all his parishioners, who were of mature age when he was settled, had been borne away by many a funeral: He had one congregation in the church, and a more crowded one in the churchyard; and having wrought so late into the evening, and done his work so well, it was now good Father Hooper's turn to rest. **K**

Several persons were visible by the shaded candlelight, in the death chamber of the old clergyman. Natural connections he had none. But there was the decorously grave, though unmoved physician, seeking only to mitigate[37] the last pangs of the patient whom he could not save. There were the deacons, and other eminently pious members of his church. There, also, was the Reverend Mr. Clark, of Westbury, a young and zealous divine, who had ridden in haste to pray by the bedside of the expiring minister. There was the nurse, no hired handmaiden of death, but one whose calm affection had endured thus long, in secrecy, in solitude, amid the chill of age, and would not perish, even at the dying hour. Who, but Elizabeth! And there lay the hoary head of good Father Hooper upon the death-pillow, with the black veil still swathed about his brow and reaching down over his face, so that each more difficult gasp of his faint breath caused it to stir. All through life that piece of crape had hung between him and the world: It had separated him from cheerful brotherhood and woman's love, and kept him in that saddest of all prisons, his own heart; and still it lay upon his face, as if to deepen the gloom of his darksome chamber, and shade him from the sunshine of eternity. **L**

For some time previous, his mind had been confused, wavering doubtfully between the past and the present, and hovering forward, as it were, at intervals,

---

35. **Governor Belcher's:** Jonathan Belcher (1681?–1757) was governor of Massachusetts Bay Colony from 1730 to 1741.
36. **irreproachable:** blameless.

37. **mitigate:** to make less painful.

Ⅰ Literary Focus **Symbolism** How does the black veil affect Mr. Hooper's relationship with the villagers?

J Literary Perspectives **Historical Context** What desirable effects does the veil have? What do these effects reveal about Puritans' attitudes toward sin and its consequences?

K Literary Focus **Symbolism** What does "rest" symbolize in this paragraph? What details in the text support your answer?

L Reading Focus **Making Inferences** What might Mr. Hooper have wanted, had he not felt obligated to wear the veil? What clues support your inference?

into the indistinctness of the world to come. There had been feverish turns, which tossed him from side to side, and wore away what little strength he had. But in his most convulsive struggles, and in the wildest vagaries of his intellect, when no other thought retained its sober influence, he still showed an awful solicitude lest the black veil should slip aside. Even if his bewildered soul could have forgotten, there was a faithful woman at his pillow, who, with averted eyes, would have covered that aged face, which she had last beheld in the comeliness of manhood. At length the death-stricken old man lay quietly in the torpor[38] of mental and bodily exhaustion, with an imperceptible pulse, and breath that grew fainter and fainter, except when a long, deep, and irregular inspiration[39] seemed to prelude the flight of his spirit.

The minister of Westbury approached the bedside.

"Venerable Father Hooper," said he, "the moment of your release is at hand. Are you ready for the lifting of the veil, that shuts in time from eternity?"

Father Hooper at first replied merely by a feeble motion of his head; then, apprehensive, perhaps, that his meaning might be doubtful, he exerted himself to speak.

"Yea," said he, in faint accents, "my soul hath a patient weariness until that veil be lifted."

"And is it fitting," resumed the Reverend Mr. Clark, "that a man so given to prayer, of such a blameless example, holy in deed and thought, so far as mortal judgment may pronounce; is it fitting that a father in the church should leave a shadow on his memory, that may seem to blacken a life so pure? I pray you, my venerable brother, let not this thing be! Suffer us to be gladdened by your triumphant aspect, as you go to your reward. Before the veil of eternity be lifted, let me cast aside this black veil from your face!" **M**

And thus speaking, the Reverend Mr. Clark bent forward to reveal the mystery of so many years. But, exerting a sudden energy, that made all the beholders stand aghast, Father Hooper snatched both his hands from beneath the bedclothes, and pressed them strongly on the black veil, resolute to struggle, if the minister of Westbury would contend with a dying man.

"Never!" cried the veiled clergyman. "On earth, never!"

"Dark old man!" exclaimed the affrighted minister, "with what horrible crime upon your soul are you now passing to the judgment?"

Father Hooper's breath heaved; it rattled in his throat; but, with a mighty effort, grasping forward with his hands, he caught hold of life, and held it back till he should speak. He even raised himself in bed; and there he sat, shivering with the arms of death around him, while the black veil hung down, awful, at that last moment, in the gathered terrors of a lifetime. And yet the faint, sad smile, so often there, now seemed to glimmer from its obscurity, and linger on Father Hooper's lips.

"Why do you tremble at me alone?" cried he, turning his veiled face round the circle of pale spectators. "Tremble also at each other! Have men avoided me, and women shown no pity, and children screamed and fled, only for my black veil? What, but the mystery which it obscurely typifies, has made this piece of crape so awful? When the friend shows his inmost heart to his friend; the lover to his best beloved; when man does not vainly shrink from the eye of his Creator, loathsomely treasuring up the secret of his sin; then deem me a monster, for the symbol beneath which I have lived, and die! I look around me, and, lo! on every visage a Black Veil!" **N**

While his auditors shrank from one another, in mutual affright, Father Hooper fell back upon his pillow, a veiled corpse, with a faint smile lingering on the lips. Still veiled, they laid him in his coffin, and a veiled corpse they bore him to the grave. The grass of many years has sprung up and withered on that grave, the burial stone is moss-grown, and good Mr. Hooper's face is dust; but awful is still the thought, that it moldered beneath the Black Veil!

---

38. **torpor:** dull or sluggish state.
39. **inspiration:** inhaling.

M **Reading Focus** **Making Inferences** What can you infer about the Reverend Mr. Clark's attitude toward the veil?

N **Literary Focus** **Symbolism** Why does Mr. Hooper claim to see a black veil on every human face? What is his final argument?

Respond and Think Critically

Reading Focus

Quick Check

1. How does the congregation respond at first to Mr. Hooper's black veil? Why?

2. What explanation does Hooper give to Elizabeth for wearing the veil? What arguments against wearing the veil does she make?

Read with a Purpose

3. How did the minister's veil affect his congregants' views of guilt and sin? Explain.

Reading Skills: Making Inferences

4. As you read, you recorded inferences. Review your chart. Then, add a column in which you write down how each inference affected your overall understanding of the story.

Details	My Knowledge/Experience	My Inferences	Effect on My Understanding of the Story
"Children, with bright faces, tripped merrily"; "bachelors looked sidelong at the pretty maidens."	Many of the words have a lighthearted, pleasant connotation.	The mood in Milford is cheerful and happy.	It helps show that sin lurks even in places that seem innocent.

Literary Focus

Literary Analysis

5. **Interpret** On page 312, the narrator states that the human heart is the "saddest of all prisons." Does this observation refer only to Hooper, or is it true of others in the story? Explain your response.

6. **Analyze** Would you describe this narrator's tone as neutral or emotional? Write down words and phrases that are <u>integral</u> to the story's tone.

7. **Evaluate** What would you say is the moral lesson this **parable** provides about our human existence?

8. **Literary Perspectives** How did your knowledge of Puritanism affect your comprehension of the story? How did reading the story add to your understanding of Puritanism?

Literary Skills: Symbolism

9. **Analyze** On his deathbed, Hooper says, "I look around me, and, lo! on every visage a Black Veil!" (page 313). What does Hooper mean? In what ways is Hooper's veil a symbol?

Literary Skills Review: Setting

10. **Evaluate** The **setting** is the time and location in which a story takes place. How does the setting of this story make it more believable?

Writing Focus

Think as a Reader/Writer

Use It in Your Writing Review the words and sentences that Hawthorne uses to help communicate the meanings of the veil. Choose an article of clothing that you or someone else has worn that you find symbolic of the wearer's personality. In a paragraph, describe the article of clothing.

 **What Do You Think Now** What inspired Hooper to wear the veil? Can you think of other ways he might have responded to the feeling or belief that motivated him to wear the veil? Explain.

SKILLS FOCUS **Literary Skills** Analyze symbolism; analyze setting. **Reading Skills** Make inferences as a strategy for comprehension. **Vocabulary Skills** Use

context clues in words, sentences, and para-graphs to decode new vocabulary; identify archaic words.

Vocabulary Development

✓ Vocabulary Check

Match each Vocabulary word with its definition.

1. antipathy
2. iniquity
3. obscurity
4. ostentatious
5. pensively
6. plausibility
7. inanimate

a. darkness
b. lifeless
c. strong dislike
d. wickedness
e. thoughtfully
f. showy
g. believability

Vocabulary Skills: Archaic Words

Language changes over time. New words appear, and some words become rare or drop out of use. **Archaic,** or old-fashioned, language sometimes makes read-ing works by writers like Hawthorne seem difficult to modern readers. **Context clues** can often help you figure out unfamiliar words as you read. Other words or phrases in the sentence and how the sentence is con-nected to the story around it may help you infer what the unfamiliar term means.

In the sentence, "As his *plighted* wife, it should be her privilege to know what the black veil concealed," *plighted* is an archaic term. First, begin by trying to understand as much as you can about what the rest of the sentence says. To whom does it refer? Elizabeth and Mr. Hooper. What is their relationship at this point in the story? They are engaged. What is their current situation according to the sentence? Elizabeth feels that because she is Hooper's *plighted* wife, she has a right to see beneath his veil. Are they married yet? No, they are not.

What kind of wife is Elizabeth if she is a *plighted* one? She is a wife-to-be, who is engaged, or has prom-ised, to marry Hooper. According to these contextual clues, *plighted* most likely means "promised," or engaged.

Your Turn

Which words in the following passages from the story are archaic? Locate the context in which each passage occurs in the story. Rephrase the passages in modern English. Are any of these words still in use today but with different meanings?

1. "So sensible were the audience of some unwont-ed attribute in their minister . . ." (page 306)
2. "A superstitious old woman was the only witness of this prodigy" (page 307).
3. "He well nigh lost his wits by his own waggery" (page 308).
4. "having wrought so late into the evening" (page 312)

Language Coach

Suffixes Some adjectives may be changed to nouns by adding the suffix *–ity* to the end of a word, such as changing *secure* to *security*. With a partner, underline transform the adjective in italics into a noun in the sentence below, and rewrite the sentence so that the new word works correctly. Change the wording as necessary, but keep the meaning of the sentence the same.

His intentions may have been *noble*, but people did not admire him.

Academic Vocabulary

Talk About
Appearance is a powerful factor in any soci-ety. With a partner, discuss whether you think someone's appearance reveals his or her identity, conceals it, or both. Support your opinion with specific examples.

SKILLS FOCUS **Grammar Skills** Identify and use independent clauses; identify and use subordinate clauses. **Literary Skills** Understand symbolism. **Reading** **Skills** Make inferences as a strategy for comprehension. **Writing Skills** Write reflective compositions.

Grammar Link

Independent and Subordinate Clauses

A **clause** is a group of words that contains a subject and a verb. **Independent clauses** express complete thoughts and can stand alone as sentences. **Subordinate clauses** are not complete sentences.

> Independent: Mr. Hooper's veil had a powerful effect.
> Subordinate: When he wore it over his face

A sentence can combine at least one independent clause with any number of subordinate clauses.

> Mr. Hooper's veil had a powerful effect when he wore it over his face.

Subordinate clauses act as adjectives, adverbs, or nouns. Adjective clauses tell *what kind, which one,* or *how many.* Adjective clauses begin with a **relative pronoun,** such as *who, whose, that,* or *which,* or with the **relative adverb** *where* or *when.*

> The veil, **which was made of simple black crape,** changed the minister's life.

Adverb clauses tell *how, when, where, why, to what extent,* or *under what condition.* Adverb clauses begin with a **subordinating conjunction,** such as *after, although, because,* or *until.*

> The veil changed the minister's life **because it kept anyone from getting close to him.**

Noun clauses act as subjects, predicate nominatives, or objects. Words used to introduce noun clauses include *how, that,* and *whether.*

> People understood **that Mr. Hooper refused to take off the veil.**

Your Turn

Re-read the first five sentences of *The Minister's Black Veil.* Then, indicate which sentences have subordinate clauses. Classify any subordinate clauses as adverb clauses or noun clauses.

CHOICES

As you respond to the Choices, use the **Academic Vocabulary** words as appropriate: factor, implicit, integral, principal, transform.

REVIEW

Understand Symbols

Group Activity In a small group, brainstorm a list of familiar symbols, such as the American eagle, a public symbol for the United States. Identify and discuss the meaning or meanings of each symbol. How can symbols help us communicate meanings in imaginative ways in life and in literature? If time allows, share your ideas with the class as a whole.

CONNECT

Write an Essay

Timed ⌐Writing In a brief essay, explain how the reactions of Hooper's parishioners to his veil reveal the nature of their own fears. Use evidence from the text to support your response.

EXTEND

Write a Reflective Letter

Mr. Hooper has been buried. Elizabeth is left alone, haunted by the memory of the man she loved but could not bring herself to marry. Write a letter from Elizabeth to a friend that recounts her thoughts and feelings about Mr. Hooper and the black veil. As you draft your letter, try to use language appropriate to Hawthorne's story. If possible, include some of the archaic words you encountered in Hawthorne's text.

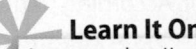

Learn It Online
Learn more about Hawthorne and his world through these Internet links.

go.hrw.com L11-316   **Go**

SKILLS FOCUS **Reading Skills** Use a variety of reading skills to understand literary and informational text; monitor your reading or comprehension; understand and analyze style, archaic words, word choice, language structures, and syntax.

Strategies for Understanding by **Kylene Beers**

Edgar Allan Poe's ornate writing is much like a Gothic mansion: a mix of dramatic features, complicated structures, and fantastic details. This style is ideally suited to Poe's explorations of the dark and winding paths of the human mind. The writing's depth and complexity, however, can also present challenges to readers. The following tips will help you understand difficult words and sentences in the text.

Breaking Down the Text Poe weaves rich language and specific allusions throughout "The Fall of the House of Usher." When you encounter an unfamiliar word or allusion, check the vocabulary definitions and footnotes or look it up in a reference source. You also might determine meaning through context clues.

Another challenging element is Poe's use of complex sentence structure. He frequently interrupts sentences with commas and dashes, often connecting several phrases in a complex order. It may be helpful to first locate the sentence's main subject and verb. Then, identify any objects, modifiers, and phrases. Breaking down complicated sentences piece by piece can help you unlock their meaning. In the following excerpt, Poe uses an unusual structure for a sentence setting up one of the story's main premises. The narrator states:

> Nevertheless, in this mansion of gloom I now proposed to myself a <u>sojourn</u> of some weeks.
>
> **sojourn** (SOH jurn) *n.*: short stay. *The narrator feels uncomfortable during his sojourn at Roderick's house.*

You may be unfamiliar with the word *sojourn*. Notice that the textbook defines *sojourn* and uses it in a sentence. (You will find both the definition and the sentence on the Preparing to Read page.) Next, you can break down the sentence parts. The main subject—the word *I*— is in the middle of the sentence. The verb is *proposed*. So, according to the sentence, the narrator has proposed (to himself) a short stay of some weeks in "this mansion of gloom."

Unraveling the Meaning When tackling Poe's longer sentences, like the one below, applying these tips can help unravel the meaning:

> Having deposited our mournful burden upon tressels within this region of horror, we partially turned aside the yet unscrewed lid of the coffin, and looked upon the face of the tenant.

Context clues—references to *coffin* and *horror*—can help you guess that the "mournful burden" is the coffin that they have "deposited" on "tressels," which must be some kind of coffin stand. To determine the sentence's main action, locate the subject (*we*) and verbs (*turned* and *looked*), which appear later in the sentence. Examining all of these pieces together can help you unravel the meaning of the sentence.

Your Turn

Using the suggestions in this essay, rewrite the following sentences to make them simpler to read and understand. If necessary, look up any unfamiliar words.

1. "Shaking off from my spirit what *must* have been a dream, I scanned more narrowly the real aspect of the building."
2. "To an anomalous species of terror I found him a bounden slave."

Learn It Online
Learn these strategies online through *PowerNotes*.

go.hrw.com | L11-317 | **Go**

The Fall of the House of Usher

What Do You Think? Where does an individual find inspiration?

QuickWrite

Think about how the circumstances of your life inspire and influence the choices you make. Write a few sentences explaining how life events or circumstances play out in your own life or in the life of someone you know.

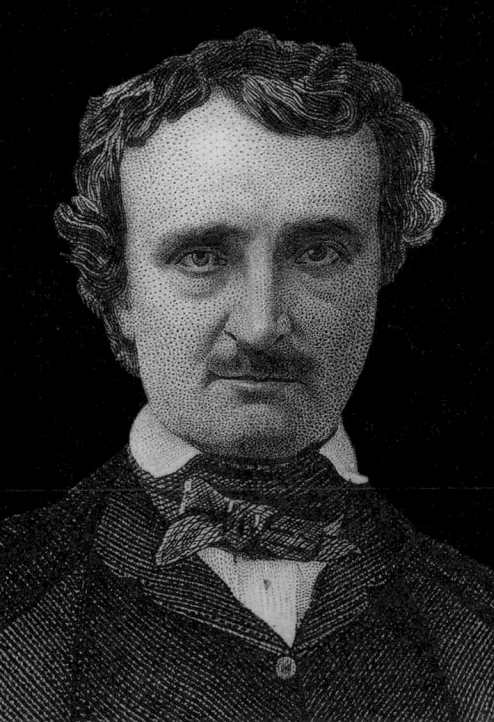

Edgar Allan Poe
(1809–1849)

Detective shows, ghost stories, horror movies—Edgar Allan Poe's influence <u>transformed</u> these genres for all subsequent readers. Poe pioneered modern tales of mystery and suspense that explored the darkest corners of the human mind.

Dark Beginnings

"The want of parental affection," wrote Poe, "has been the heaviest of my trials." His father, David Poe, was a mediocre traveling actor who drank heavily. He deserted Poe's mother, Elizabeth Arnold, when their second child, Edgar, was still a baby. A talented actress, she died on tour in Richmond, Virginia, and Poe became an orphan before his third birthday.

The boy was taken in by John and Frances Allan, a childless couple in Richmond. John Allan—an ambitious and self-righteous merchant—provided generously for Poe's early education, but he never formally adopted the boy.

Although Frances Allan was kind to the boy, Poe grew up feeling both the lack of a natural father and the disapproval of his foster father. John Allan made no secret of his disappointment in Poe—in his idleness, in his indifference to business life, and in his literary ambitions.

Breaking Away

At seventeen, Poe entered the University of Virginia. He did well in his studies but was resentful of the meager allowance Allan gave him. When Poe tried to earn extra money by gambling, he went deep into debt. On discovering these debts, Allan refused to help Poe and withdrew him from college.

After a bitter quarrel with Allan, Poe ran off to Boston. There, in 1827, he published a small volume of poems, *Tamerlane*. The book did not attract much attention, and Poe could find no other work. In despair he joined the army. He was promoted to the rank of sergeant major, but he disliked the enlisted man's life and asked Allan for help. At the request of his dying wife, Allan helped Poe enter the U.S. Military Academy at West Point.

While waiting to get into the academy, Poe published a second book of poems, *Al Aaraaf*, in 1829 and received his first real recognition as a writer. Soon after, Poe had himself dismissed from West Point and devoted his life fully to his writing.

Portrait of Edgar Allan Poe (1809–1849) by Ismael Gentz, (1862–1914). Engraving.

Exploring the Depths

Poe moved in with an aunt, Maria Poe Clemm, in Baltimore, Maryland. In 1835, he married her thirteen-year-old daughter, Virginia. The difference in their ages and Virginia's poor health resulted in a very odd marriage. Poe supported his family by working as an editor at various magazines and wrote when he could find the time.

In his tales built around the sleuth C. Auguste Dupin, "The Purloined Letter" and "The Murders in the Rue Morgue," Poe laid the foundations for the modern detective story. Poe inspired Sir Arthur Conan Doyle (1859–1930) to create Sherlock Holmes and inspired the Russian novelist Fyodor Dostoyevsky (1821–1881) to explore the criminal mind. Poe was a master of the psychological thriller, but his tales of the grotesque were not merely intended to shock and frighten: He wanted to explore the irrational depths of the human mind.

Triumphs and Tragedy

Poe produced a considerable body of work in spite of humiliating poverty and a serious drinking problem. Publication of his poem "The Raven" in 1845 brought Poe some fame at last, but not wealth.

When Virginia died of tuberculosis in 1847, Poe grew more unstable. In 1849, on his way home after a visit to see a woman he hoped to marry, Poe disappeared. A week later, he was found in a Baltimore tavern—delirious and in clothing that was not his and wet from a raging storm. Four days later, Poe died, and critics continue to wonder what happened in Baltimore.

Think About the Writer Do you think Poe's obsession with dark subject matter was the result of a difficult life? Explain.

Poe's stories have inspired numerous film adaptations.

Learn It Online
Find news, secrets, time lines, maps, and more about Poe at AuthorSpace online.

go.hrw.com   L11-319   Go

Preparing to Read

Literary Focus

Atmosphere Tales of horror such as Poe's often depend on **atmosphere,** or mood, to evoke terror. Poe uses elements of **Gothic fiction** to create a dark, foreboding atmosphere: a rotting mansion, mysterious illnesses, a person buried alive, and more.

Reading Focus

Strategies for Understanding In "The Fall of the House of Usher," Poe uses complex syntax, difficult vocabulary, and **allusions** (references to history, literature, or some other branch of culture). Use the following tips to increase your understanding as you read:

- Find the subject and verb in a long or complicated sentence.
- Read the footnotes that explain unfamiliar words and allusions. Use reference sources for other difficult or unfamiliar words or allusions.
- Use context clues to unlock the meaning of difficult words.

Into Action As you read, use a chart like the one below to help you make sense of this story and its atmosphere. In the left column, record a difficult word or phrase. In the right column, use the suggestions listed above to help you explain the word or phrase in conversational English.

Word or Phrase	Explanation
"the afterdream of the reveler upon opium—the bitter lapse into every day life—the hideous dropping off of the veil"	The narrator feels like someone who just woke up from a nightmare caused by drugs. He feels bitter and hungover. He sees life without a veil to disguise it, so life looks ugly to him.
Roderick Usher's "wildly importunate letter"	Usher has sent the narrator a frantic letter begging him to do something.

Writing Focus

Think as a Reader/Writer

Find It in Your Reading Poe establishes a gloomy **atmosphere** in the first sentence, and this atmosphere builds as the story develops. For example, the narrator describes Roderick as having "a cadaverousness of complexion; an eye, large, liquid, and luminous." In your *Reader/Writer Notebook,* note details <u>integral</u> to the story's dark atmosphere.

Reader/Writer Notebook

Use your **RWN** to complete the activities for this selection.

Vocabulary

pervaded (puhr VAY dihd) *v.:* spread throughout. *A deep, dark gloom pervaded every room of the house.*

sojourn (SOH jurn) *n.:* short stay. *The narrator feels uncomfortable during his sojourn at Roderick's house.*

inordinate (ihn AWR duh niht) *adj.:* excessive. *The house gives the narrator a feeling of inordinate gloom.*

palpable (PAL puh buhl) *adj.:* obvious; perceivable. *Roderick's madness is palpable to his boyhood friend.*

emaciated (ih MAY shee ay tihd) *adj.:* unusually thin. *Madeline's body is grotesque and emaciated when she falls upon her brother.*

morbid (MAWR bihd) *adj.:* diseased; unhealthy. *Roderick suffers from a morbid condition that affects how he hears music.*

obstinate (AHB stuh niht) *adj.:* stubborn. *Roderick was obstinate about placing Madeline's body in the vault.*

Language Coach

Etymology The word *pervade* comes from the Latin *per,* meaning "through," and *vadere,* meaning "go." To say that gloom pervades Poe's stories is to say that it "goes through" them. Look for these roots in words like *invade,* from the Latin for "to go in."

Learn It Online
Explore the Vocabulary words with Word Watch online.

go.hrw.com   L11-320   Go

THE FALL OF THE HOUSE OF USHER

by **Edgar Allan Poe**

Read with a Purpose
Read to discover what terrors await the narrator at the home of his childhood friend.

Build Background
It has been called "the definitive tale of horror," and indeed, Poe's

"The Fall of the House of Usher" has chilled the bones of many readers since it first appeared in *Burton's Gentleman's Magazine* in 1839. The story illustrates Poe's unique contribution to American literature—his exploration of the dark, often irrational world of the human mind. As the story unfolds, the narrator is drawn deeper into the madness infecting the family that inhabits the House of Usher.

Son cœur est un luth suspendu;
Sitôt qu'on le touche il résonne.[1]

—De Béranger

During the whole of a dull, dark, and soundless day in the autumn of the year, when the clouds hung oppressively low in the heavens, I had been passing alone, on horseback, through a singularly dreary tract of country; and at length found myself, as the shades of the evening drew on, within view of the melancholy House of Usher. I know not how it was—but, with the first glimpse of the building, a sense of insufferable gloom pervaded my spirit. I say insufferable; for the feeling was unrelieved by any of that half-pleasurable, because poetic, sentiment, with which the mind usually receives even the sternest natural images of the desolate or terrible. I looked upon the scene before me—upon the mere[2] house, and the simple landscape features of the domain—upon the bleak walls—upon the vacant eyelike windows—upon a few rank sedges[3]—and upon a few white trunks of decayed trees—with an utter depression of soul which I can compare to no earthly sensation more properly than to the afterdream of the reveler upon opium—the bitter lapse into everyday life—the hideous dropping off of the veil. There was an iciness, a sinking, a sickening of the heart—an unredeemed dreariness of thought which no goading of the imagination could torture into aught[4] of the sublime. What was it—I paused to think—what was it that so unnerved me in the contemplation of the House of Usher? It was a mystery all insoluble; nor could I grapple with the shadowy fancies that crowded upon me as I pondered. I was forced to fall back upon the unsatisfactory conclusion, that while, beyond doubt, there *are* combinations of very simple natural objects which have the power of thus affecting us, still the analysis of this power lies among considerations beyond our depth. It was possible, I reflected, that a mere different arrangement of the particulars of the scene, of the details of the picture, would be sufficient to modify, or perhaps to annihilate its capacity for sorrowful impression; and, acting upon this idea, I reined my horse to the precipitous brink of a black and lurid tarn[5] that lay in unruffled luster by the dwelling, and gazed down—but with a shudder even more thrilling than before—upon the remodeled and inverted images of the gray sedge, and the ghastly tree stems, and the vacant and eyelike windows. **Ⓐ**

Nevertheless, in this mansion of gloom I now proposed to myself a sojourn of some weeks. Its proprietor, Roderick Usher, had been one of my boon companions in boyhood; but many years had elapsed since our last meeting. A letter, however, had lately reached me in a distant part of the country—a letter from him—which, in its wildly importunate nature, had admitted of no other than a personal reply. The MS.[6] gave evidence of nervous agitation. The writer spoke of acute bodily illness—of a mental disorder which oppressed him—and of an earnest desire to see me, as his best, and indeed his only personal friend, with a view of attempting, by the cheerfulness of my society, some alleviation of his malady. It was the manner in which all this, and much more, was said—it was the apparent *heart* that went with his request—which allowed me no room for hesitation; and I accordingly obeyed forthwith what I still considered a very singular summons.

Although, as boys, we had been even intimate associates, yet I really knew little of my friend. His reserve had been always excessive and habitual. I was aware, however, that his very ancient family had been noted, time out of mind, for a peculiar sensibility of temperament, displaying itself, through long ages, in many works of exalted art, and manifested, of late, in repeated

---

1. *Son coeur . . . il résonne:* "His heart is a suspended lute; / Whenever one touches it, it resounds." From "Le Refus" ("The Refusal") by Pierre-Jean de Béranger (1780–1857).
2. **mere:** lake.
3. **sedges:** grasslike plants that grow in watery ground.
4. **aught** (awt): anything.

5. **tarn:** small but deep mountain lake. Its waters are dark from the decomposition of vegetation and lack of circulation.
6. **MS:** abbreviation for "manuscript."

Vocabulary **pervaded** (puhr VAY dihd) *v.:* spread throughout.
sojourn (SOH jurn) *n.:* short stay.

Ⓐ **Reading Focus** **Strategies for Understanding** Use the footnote to find the meaning of *tarn.* Why is this word effective in the passage?

deeds of munificent yet unobtrusive charity, as well as in a passionate devotion to the intricacies, perhaps even more than to the orthodox and easily recognizable beauties, of musical science. I had learned, too, the very remarkable fact, that the stem of the Usher race, all time-honored as it was, had put forth, at no period, any enduring branch; in other words, that the entire family lay in the direct line of descent, and had always, with very trifling and very temporary variation, so lain. It was this deficiency, I considered, while running over in thought the perfect keeping of the character of the premises with the accredited character of the people, and while speculating upon the possible influence which the one, in the long lapse of centuries, might have exercised upon the other it was this deficiency, perhaps, of collateral issue,[7] and the consequent undeviating transmission, from sire to son, of the patrimony with the name, which had, at length, so identified the two as to merge the original title of the estate in the quaint and equivocal[8] appellation of the "House of Usher"—an appellation which seemed to include, in the minds of the peasantry who used it, both the family and the family mansion.

I have said that the sole effect of my somewhat childish experiment—that of looking down within the tarn had been to deepen the first singular impression. There can be no doubt that the consciousness of the rapid increase of my superstition—for why should I not so term it?—served mainly to accelerate the increase itself. Such, I have long known, is the paradoxical law of all sentiments having terror as a basis. And it might have been for this reason only, that, when I again uplifted my eyes to the house itself, from its image in the pool, there grew in my mind a strange fancy—a fancy so ridiculous, indeed, that I but mention it to show the vivid force of the sensations which oppressed me. I had so worked upon my imagination as really to believe that about the whole mansion and domain there hung an atmosphere peculiar to themselves and their immediate vicinity—an atmosphere which had no affinity with the air of heaven, but which had reeked up from the decayed trees, and the gray wall and the silent tarn—a pestilent and mystic vapor, dull, sluggish, faintly discernible,[9] and leaden-hued. **Ⓑ**

WHAT WAS IT THAT SO **UNNERVED** ME IN THE **CONTEMPLATION** OF THE HOUSE OF USHER?

Shaking off from my spirit what *must* have been a dream, I scanned more narrowly the real aspect of the building. Its principal feature seemed to be that of an excessive antiquity. The discoloration of ages had been great. Minute fungi overspread the whole exterior, hanging in a fine tangled webwork from the eaves. Yet all this was apart from any extraordinary dilapidation. No portion of the masonry had fallen; and there appeared to be a wild inconsistency between its still perfect adaptation of parts, and the crumbling condition of the individual stones. In this there was much that reminded me of the specious[10] totality of old woodwork which has rotted for long years in some neglected vault, with no disturbance from the breath of the external air. Beyond this indication of extensive decay, however, the fabric gave little token of instability. Perhaps the eye of a scrutinizing[11] observer might have discovered a barely perceptible fissure, which, extending from the roof of the building in front, made its way down the wall in a zigzag direction, until it became lost in the sullen waters of the tarn.

9. **discernible:** noticeable.
10. **specious** (SPEE shuhs): seemingly sound, but not really so.
11. **scrutinizing:** carefully observant.

Ⓑ **Literary Focus** Atmosphere How does Poe use the tarn to reflect the atmosphere of the house?

7. **collateral issue:** relatives, such as cousins, who share the same ancestors but who are not in a direct line of descent.
8. **equivocal:** having more than one meaning.

Noticing these things, I rode over a short causeway to the house. A servant-in-waiting took my horse, and I entered the Gothic archway of the hall.[12] A valet, of stealthy step, thence conducted me, in silence, through many dark and intricate passages in my progress to the *studio* of his master. Much that I encountered on the way contributed, I know not how, to heighten the vague sentiments of which I have already spoken. While the objects around me—while the carvings of the ceilings, the somber tapestries of the walls, the ebon blackness of the floors, and the phantasmagoric[13] armorial trophies which rattled as I strode, were but matters to which, or to such as which, I had been accustomed from my infancy—while I hesitated not to acknowledge how familiar was all this—I still wondered to find how unfamiliar were the fancies which ordinary images were stirring up. On one of the staircases, I met the physician of the family. His countenance, I thought, wore a mingled expression of low cunning and perplexity. He accosted me with trepidation and passed on. The valet now threw open a door and ushered me into the presence of his master. **C**

The room in which I found myself was very large and lofty. The windows were long, narrow, and pointed, and at so vast a distance from the black oaken floor as to be altogether inaccessible from within. Feeble gleams of encrimsoned light made their way through the trellised panes, and served to render sufficiently distinct the more prominent objects around; the eye, however, struggled in vain to reach the remoter angles of the chamber, or the recesses of the vaulted and fretted[14] ceiling. Dark draperies hung upon the walls. The general furniture was profuse,[15] comfortless, antique, and tattered. Many books and musical instruments lay scattered about, but failed to give any vitality to the scene. I felt that I breathed an atmosphere of sorrow. An air of stern, deep, and irredeemable gloom hung over and pervaded all.

Upon my entrance, Usher arose from a sofa on which he had been lying at full length, and greeted me with a vivacious[16] warmth which had much in it, I at first thought, of an overdone cordiality—of the constrained effort of the *ennuyé*[17] man of the world. A glance, however, at his countenance, convinced me of his perfect sincerity. We sat down; and for some moments, while he spoke not, I gazed upon him with a feeling half of pity, half of awe. Surely, man had never before so terribly altered, in so brief a period, as had Roderick Usher! It was with difficulty that I could bring myself to admit the identity of the wan being before me with the companion of my early boyhood. Yet the character of his face had been at all times remarkable. A cadaverousness[18] of complexion; an eye large, liquid, and luminous beyond comparison; lips somewhat thin and very pallid,[19] but of a surpassingly beautiful curve; a nose of a delicate Hebrew model, but with a breadth of nostril unusual in similar formations; a finely molded chin, speaking, in its want of prominence, of a want of moral energy; hair of a more than weblike softness and tenuity;[20] these features, with an inordinate expansion above the regions of the temple, made up altogether a countenance not easily to be forgotten. And now in the mere exaggeration of the prevailing character of these features, and of the expression they were wont to convey, lay so much of change that I doubted to whom I spoke. The now ghastly pallor of the skin, and the now miraculous luster of the eye, above all things startled and even awed me. The silken hair, too, had been suffered to grow all unheeded, and as, in its wild gossamer texture, it floated rather than fell about the face, I could not, even with effort, connect its arabesque[21] expression with any idea of simple humanity. **D**

---

12. **Gothic . . . hall:** The hallway looked like a Gothic arch—high, pointed, and elaborately carved.
13. **phantasmagoric** (fan taz muh GAWR ihk): images appearing to change rapidly, like the events in a dream.
14. **fretted:** carved in an ornamental architectural design.
15. **profuse:** abundant.

16. **vivacious:** cheerful; lively.
17. *ennuyé* (ahn nwee YAY): French for "bored" or "jaded."
18. **cadaverousness:** paleness or gauntness, as a corpse.
19. **pallid:** pale.
20. **tenuity** (tuh NOO uh tee): fineness; lack of substance.
21. **arabesque** (ar uh BEHSK): strangely mixed; fantastic.

C **Reading Focus** Strategies for Understanding Read the sentence beginning with "While the objects around me . . ." Rewrite this sentence in a simpler form. Remove the dashes and elaborate clauses to get at the basic meaning of the sentence.

D **Literary Focus** Atmosphere Which words does Poe use to describe Roderick? How does the description of Roderick add to the eerie mood?

Vocabulary **inordinate** (ihn AWR duh niht) *adj.:* excessive.

In the manner of my friend I was at once struck with an incoherence—an inconsistency; and I soon found this to arise from a series of feeble and futile struggles to overcome an habitual trepidancy—an excessive nervous agitation. For something of this nature I had indeed been prepared, no less by his letter, than by reminiscences of certain boyish traits, and by conclusions deduced from his peculiar physical conformation and temperament. His action was alternately vivacious and sullen. His voice varied rapidly from a tremulous indecision (when the animal spirits seemed utterly in abeyance) to that species of energetic concision—that abrupt, weighty, unhurried, and hollow-sounding enunciation—that leaden, self-balanced and perfectly modulated guttural utterance, which may be observed in the lost drunkard, or the irreclaimable eater of opium, during the periods of his most intense excitement.

It was thus that he spoke of the object of my visit, of his earnest desire to see me, and of the solace he expected me to afford him. He entered, at some length, into what he conceived to be the nature of his malady. It was, he said, a constitutional and a family evil, and one for which he despaired to find a remedy—a mere nervous affection,[22] he immediately added, which would undoubtedly soon pass. It displayed itself in a host of unnatural sensations. Some of these, as he detailed them, interested and bewildered me; although, perhaps, the terms, and the general manner of the narration had their weight. He suffered much from a morbid acuteness of the senses; the most insipid[23] food was alone endurable; he could wear only garments of certain texture; the odors of all flowers were oppressive; his eyes were tortured by even a faint light; and there were but peculiar sounds, and these from stringed instruments, which did not inspire him with horror.

To an anomalous[24] species of terror I found him a bounden slave. "I shall perish," said he, "I *must* perish in this deplorable folly. Thus, thus, and not otherwise, shall I be lost. I dread the events of the future,

not in themselves, but in their results. I shudder at the thought of any, even the most trivial, incident, which may operate upon this intolerable agitation of soul. I have, indeed, no abhorrence of danger, except in its absolute effect—in terror. In this unnerved—in this pitiable condition—I feel that the period will sooner or later arrive when I must abandon life and reason together, in some struggle with the grim phantasm, FEAR."

> SURELY, MAN HAD NEVER BEFORE so **TERRIBLY ALTERED**, IN SO BRIEF A PERIOD, AS HAD **RODERICK USHER!**

I learned, moreover, at intervals, and through broken and equivocal hints, another singular feature of his mental condition. He was enchained by certain superstitious impressions in regard to the dwelling which he tenanted, and whence, for many years, he had never ventured forth—in regard to an influence whose supposititious[25] force was conveyed in terms too shadowy here to be restated—an influence which some peculiarities in the mere form and substance of his family mansion, had, by dint of long sufferance, he said, obtained over his spirit—an effect which the *physique* of the gray walls and turrets, and of the dim tarn into which they all looked down, had, at length, brought about upon the *morale* of his existence.

He admitted, however, although with hesitation, that much of the peculiar gloom which thus afflicted him could be traced to a more natural and far more palpable origin—to the severe and long-continued illness—indeed to the evidently approaching

---

25. **supposititious** (suhp uh zih TIHSH uhs): supposed; assumed; hypothetical.

Vocabulary **palpable** (PAL puh buhl) *adj.*: obvious; perceivable.

---

22. **affection:** ailment; disorder.
23. **insipid:** bland; without flavor.
24. **anomalous** (uh NAHM uh luhs): abnormal.

dissolution—of a tenderly beloved sister—his sole companion for long years—his last and only relative on earth. "Her decease," he said, with a bitterness which I can never forget, "would leave him (him the hopeless and the frail) the last of the ancient race of the Ushers." While he spoke, the lady Madeline (for so was she called) passed slowly through a remote portion of the apartment, and, without having noticed my presence, disappeared. I regarded her with an utter astonishment not unmingled with dread—and yet I found it impossible to account for such feelings. A sensation of stupor[26] oppressed me, as my eyes followed her retreating steps. When a door, at length, closed upon her, my glance sought instinctively and eagerly the countenance of the brother—but he had buried his face in his hands, and I could only perceive that a far more than ordinary wanness had overspread the emaciated fingers through which trickled many passionate tears. **E**

The disease of the lady Madeline had long baffled the skill of her physicians. A settled apathy, a gradual wasting away of the person, and frequent although transient affections of a partially cataleptical[27] character, were the unusual diagnosis. Hitherto she had steadily borne up against the pressure of her malady, and had not betaken herself finally to bed; but, on the closing in of the evening of my arrival at the house, she succumbed (as her brother told me at night with inexpressible agitation) to the prostrating power of the destroyer; and I learned that the glimpse I had obtained of her person would thus probably be the last I should obtain—that the lady, at least while living, would be seen by me no more.

For several days ensuing, her name was unmentioned by either Usher or myself: And during this period I was busied in earnest endeavors to alleviate the melancholy of my friend. We painted and read together; or I listened, as if in a dream, to the wild improvisations of his speaking guitar. And thus, as a closer and still closer intimacy admitted me more unreservedly into the recesses of his spirit, the more bitterly did I perceive the futility of all attempt at cheering a mind from which darkness, as if an inherent positive quality, poured forth upon all objects of the moral and physical universe, in one unceasing radiation of gloom.

I shall ever bear about me a memory of the many solemn hours I thus spent alone with the master of the House of Usher. Yet I should fail in any attempt to convey an idea of the exact character of the studies, or of the occupations, in which he involved me, or led me the way. An excited and highly distempered ideality[28] threw a sulfureous[29] luster over all. His long improvised dirges will ring forever in my ears. Among other things, I hold painfully in mind a certain singular perversion and amplification of the wild air of the last waltz of Von Weber.[30] From the paintings over which his elaborate fancy brooded, and which grew, touch by touch, into vaguenesses at which I shuddered the more thrillingly, because I shuddered knowing not why—from these paintings (vivid as their images now are before me) I would in vain endeavor to educe more than a small portion which should lie within the compass of merely written words. By the utter simplicity, by the nakedness of his designs, he arrested and overawed attention. If ever mortal painted an idea, that mortal was Roderick Usher. For me at least—in the circumstances then surrounding me—there arose

---

26. **stupor:** state of mental dullness; loss of the senses.
27. **cataleptical** (kat uh LEHP tih kuhl): Catalepsy is an emotional condition, associated with disorders such as epilepsy and schizophrenia, that may cause the victim to lose sensation and the ability to move the limbs or even the entire body. In a cataleptic attack, Madeline could be as stiff as a corpse.

---

28. **distempered ideality:** mental derangement.
29. **sulfureous** (suhl FYUR ee uhs): hellish; infernal. Poe's description probably comes from the yellowish color of sulfur, which is associated with the fires of hell.
30. **Von Weber:** Carl Maria von Weber (1786–1826), German Romantic composer.

E **Reading Focus** **Strategies for Understanding** The first sentence in this paragraph is interrupted by several dashes, but it can still be reduced to a basic statement that explains the main reason for Roderick's sadness. What is the source of his "peculiar gloom?" What effect do the dashes have on the pace of your reading?

Vocabulary **emaciated** (ee MAY shee ay tihd) *adj.:* unusually thin.

out of the pure abstractions which the hypochondriac contrived to throw upon his canvas, an intensity of intolerable awe, no shadow of which felt I ever yet in the contemplation of the certainly glowing yet too concrete reveries of Fuseli.[31]

One of the phantasmagoric conceptions of my friend, partaking not so rigidly of the spirit of abstraction, may be shadowed forth, although feebly, in words. A small picture presented the interior of an immensely long and rectangular vault or tunnel, with low walls, smooth, white, and without interruption or device. Certain accessory points of the design served well to convey the idea that this excavation lay at an exceeding depth below the surface of the earth. No outlet was observed in any portion of its vast extent, and no torch, or other artificial source of light was discernible; yet a flood of intense rays rolled throughout, and bathed the whole in a ghastly and inappropriate splendor.

I have just spoken of that morbid condition of the auditory nerve which rendered all music intolerable to the sufferer with the exception of certain effects of stringed instruments. It was, perhaps, the narrow limits to which he thus confined himself upon the guitar, which gave birth, in great measure, to the fantastic character of his performances. But the fervid *facility* of his *impromptus*[32] could not be so accounted for. They must have been, and were, in the notes, as well as in the words of his wild fantasias (for he not unfrequently accompanied himself with rhymed verbal improvisations), the result of that intense mental collectedness and concentration to which I have previously alluded as observable only in the moments of the highest artificial excitement. The words of one of these rhapsodies I have easily remembered. I was, perhaps, the more forcibly impressed with it, as he gave it, because, in the under or

---

31. **Fuseli:** Johann Heinrich Füssli (1741–1825), Swiss painter who lived in England and is known for scenes of horror and the supernatural.
32. ***impromptus*** (ihm PRAHMP tooz): spontaneous performances.

F **Literary Focus** **Atmosphere** Which details in the description of Roderick's music and art contribute to the story's atmosphere? How does the narrator respond to the music?

Vocabulary **morbid** (MAWR bihd) *adj.:* diseased; unhealthy.

Analyzing Visuals

Viewing and Interpreting This image foreshadows, or hints at, creepy happenings to come. How does the artist use color and lines to reflect Poe's eerie, disturbing atmosphere?

mystic current of its meaning, I fancied that I perceived, and for the first time, a full consciousness on the part of Usher, of the tottering of his lofty reason upon her throne. The verses, which were entitled "The Haunted Palace," ran very nearly, if not accurately, thus:

I

In the greenest of our valleys,
    By good angels tenanted,
Once a fair and stately palace—
    Radiant palace—reared its head.
In the monarch Thought's dominion—
    It stood there!
Never seraph[33] spread a pinion[34]
    Over fabric half so fair.

II

Banners yellow, glorious, golden,
    On its roof did float and flow;
(This—all this—was in the olden
    Time long ago)
And every gentle air that dallied,
    In that sweet day,
Along the ramparts plumed and pallid,
    A winged odor went away.

III

Wanderers in that happy valley
    Through two luminous windows saw
Spirits moving musically
    To a lute's well-tunéd law,
Round about a throne, where sitting
    (Porphyrogene!)[35]
In state his glory well befitting,
    The ruler of the realm was seen.

IV

And all with pearl and ruby glowing
    Was the fair palace door,
Through which came flowing, flowing, flowing,
    And sparkling evermore,
A troop of Echoes whose sweet duty
    Was but to sing,
In voices of surpassing beauty,
    The wit and wisdom of their king.

V

But evil things, in robes of sorrow,
    Assailed the monarch's high estate;
(Ah, let us mourn, for never morrow
    Shall dawn upon him, desolate!)
And, round about his home, the glory
    That blushed and bloomed
Is but a dim-remembered story
    Of the old time entombed.

VI

And travelers now within that valley,
    Through the red-litten[36] windows, see
Vast forms that move fantastically
    To a discordant melody;
While, like a rapid ghastly river,
    Through the pale door,
A hideous throng rush out forever,
    And laugh—but smile no more. **Ⓖ**

I well remember that suggestions arising from this ballad led us into a train of thought wherein there became manifest an opinion of Usher's which I mention not so much on account of its novelty (for other men have thought thus), as on account of the pertinacity with which he maintained it. This opinion, in its general form, was that of the sentience[37] of all vegetable things. But, in his disordered fancy, the idea had assumed a more daring character, and trespassed, under certain conditions, upon the kingdom of inorganization.[38] I lack words to express the

---

33. **seraph:** angel.
34. **pinion:** wing.
35. **Porphyrogene** (pawr FIHR uh jeen): Poe coined this word from *porphyrogenite,* the name once used to refer to royalty in Byzantine times. (The Greek word *porphyros* means "purple.") *Porphyrogene* means "one born to the purple" or "one of royal blood."

36. **red-litten:** red-lighted; Poe coined this archaic-sounding term.
37. **sentience** (SEHN shuhns): consciousness.
38. **kingdom of inorganization:** world of inorganic objects.

Ⓖ **Literary Focus** Atmosphere How do Verses V and VI of "The Haunted Palace" heighten the story's atmosphere?

full extent, or the earnest *abandon* of his persuasion. The belief, however, was connected (as I have previously hinted) with the gray stones of the home of his forefathers. The conditions of the sentience had been here, he imagined, fulfilled in the method of collocation of these stones—in the order of their arrangement, as well as in that of the many *fungi* which overspread them, and of the decayed trees which stood around—above all, in the long undisturbed endurance of this arrangement, and in its reduplication in the still waters of the tarn. Its evidence—the evidence of the sentience—was to be seen, he said (and I here started as he spoke), in the gradual yet certain condensation of an atmosphere of their own about the waters and the walls. The result was discoverable, he added, in that silent, yet importunate and terrible influence which for centuries had molded the destinies of his family, and which made *him* what I now saw him—what he was. Such opinions need no comment, and I will make none. **ⓗ**

Our books—the books which, for years, had formed no small portion of the mental existence of the invalid—were, as might be supposed, in strict keeping with this character of phantasm. We pored together over such works as the *Ververt et Chartreuse* of Gresset; the *Belphegor* of Machiavelli; the *Heaven and Hell* of Swedenborg; *The Subterranean Voyage of Nicholas Klimm* by Holberg; the Chiromancy of Robert Flud, of Jean D'Indaginé, and of De la Chambre; the *Journey into the Blue Distance* of Tieck; and *The City of the Sun* of Campanella. One favorite volume was a small octavo edition of the *Directorium Inquisitorum*, by the Dominican Eymeric de Gironne; and there were passages in Pomponius Mela, about the old African Satyrs and Ægipans,[39] over which Usher would sit dreaming for hours. His chief delight, however, was found in the perusal of an exceedingly rare and curious book in quarto Gothic—the manual of a forgotten church—the *Vigiliae Mortuorum*[40] *secundum Chorum Ecclesiae Maguntinae.* **ⓘ**

I could not help thinking of the wild ritual of this work, and of its probable influence upon the hypochondriac, when, one evening, having informed me abruptly that the lady Madeline was no more, he stated his intention of preserving her corpse for a fortnight (previously to its final interment), in one of the numerous vaults within the main walls of the building. The worldly reason, however, assigned for this singular proceeding, was one which I did not feel at liberty to dispute. The brother had been led to his resolution (so he told me) by consideration of the unusual character of the malady of the deceased, of certain obtrusive and eager inquiries on the part of her medical men, and of the remote and exposed situation of the burial ground of the family. I will not deny that when I called to mind the sinister countenance of the person whom I met upon the staircase,[41] on the day of my arrival at the house, I had no desire to oppose what I regarded as at best but a harmless, and by no means an unnatural, precaution.[42]

At the request of Usher, I personally aided him in the arrangements for the temporary entombment. The body having been encoffined, we two alone bore it to its rest. The vault in which we placed it (and which had been so long unopened that our torches, half smothered in its oppressive atmosphere, gave us little opportunity for investigation) was small, damp, and entirely without means of admission for light; lying, at great depth, immediately beneath that portion of the building in which was my own sleeping apartment. It had been used, apparently, in remote feudal times, for the worst purposes of a dungeon-keep,[43] and, in later days, as a place of deposit for powder, or some other highly combustible substance, as a portion of its floor, and the whole

---

39. **Ververt et Chartreuse ... Satyrs and Ægipans:** The books, authors, and subjects listed have to do with mysticism, magic, and horror.

40. *Vigiliae Mortuorum:* Latin for "vigil of the dead."
41. **person . . . staircase:** the physician.
42. **harmless . . . precaution:** Usher wishes to be sure the body will not be dissected. At the time, bodies were sometimes stolen and sold to medical students for study.
43. **dungeon-keep:** underground prison.

ⓗ Reading Focus Strategies for Understanding *Pertinacity* is the noun form of the adjective *pertinacious*. What does *pertinacious* mean? How does this word apply to Roderick in this passage?

ⓘ Reading Focus Strategies for Understanding Use the footnotes to learn what subject matter these books contain. Why do you think Poe tells us what books Usher and the narrator had been reading?

interior of a long archway through which we reached it, were carefully sheathed with copper. The door, of massive iron, had been, also, similarly protected. Its immense weight caused an unusually sharp grating sound, as it moved upon its hinges.

Having deposited our mournful burden upon tressels within this region of horror, we partially turned aside the yet unscrewed lid of the coffin, and looked upon the face of the tenant. A striking similitude[44] between the brother and sister now first arrested my attention; and Usher, divining, perhaps, my thoughts, murmured out some few words from which I learned that the deceased and himself had been twins, and that sympathies of a scarcely intelligible nature had always existed between them. Our glances, however, rested not long upon the dead—for we could not regard her unawed. The disease which had thus entombed the lady in the maturity of youth, had left, as usual in all maladies of a strictly cataleptical character, the mockery of a faint blush upon the bosom and the face, and that suspiciously lingering smile upon the lip which is so terrible in death. We replaced and screwed down the lid, and, having secured the door of iron, made our way, with toil, into the scarcely less gloomy apartments of the upper portion of the house.

And now, some days of bitter grief having elapsed, an observable change came over the features of the mental disorder of my friend. His ordinary manner had vanished. His ordinary occupations were neglected or forgotten. He roamed from chamber to chamber with hurried, unequal, and objectless step. The pallor of his countenance had assumed, if possible, a more ghastly hue—but the luminousness of his eye had utterly gone out. The once occasional huskiness of his tone was heard no more; and a tremulous quaver, as if of extreme terror, habitually characterized his utterance. There were times, indeed, when I thought his unceasingly agitated mind was laboring with some oppressive secret, to divulge which he struggled for the necessary courage. At times, again, I was obliged

---

44. **similitude** (suh MIHL uh tood): likeness.

to resolve all into the mere inexplicable vagaries[45] of madness, for I beheld him gazing upon vacancy for long hours, in an attitude of the profoundest attention, as if listening to some imaginary sound. It was no wonder that his condition terrified—that it infected me. I felt creeping upon me, by slow yet certain degrees, the wild influences of his own fantastic yet impressive superstitions. **J**

It was, especially, upon retiring to bed late in the night of the seventh or eighth day after the placing of the lady Madeline within the dungeon, that I experienced the full power of such feelings. Sleep came not near my couch—while the hours waned and waned away. I struggled to reason off the nervousness which had dominion over me. I endeavored to believe that much, if not all of what I felt, was due to the bewildering influence of the gloomy furniture of the room—of the dark and tattered draperies, which, tortured into motion by the breath of a rising tempest, swayed fitfully to and fro upon the walls, and rustled uneasily about the decorations of the bed. But my efforts were fruitless. An irrepressible tremor gradually pervaded my frame; and, at length, there sat upon my very heart an incubus[46] of utterly causeless alarm. Shaking this off with a gasp and a struggle, I uplifted myself upon the pillows, and, peering earnestly within the intense darkness of the chamber, harkened—I know not why, except that an instinctive spirit prompted me—to certain low and indefinite sounds which came, through the pauses of the storm, at long intervals, I knew not whence. Overpowered by an intense sentiment of horror, unaccountable yet unendurable, I threw on my clothes with haste (for I felt that I should sleep no more during the night), and endeavored to arouse myself from the pitiable condition into which I had fallen, by pacing rapidly to and fro through the apartment. **K**

I had taken but few turns in this manner, when a light step on an adjoining staircase arrested my atten-

---

45. **vagaries** (VAY guh reez): whims.
46. **incubus:** nightmare. In medieval times, some people believed that nightmares were caused by demons (incubi) who tormented the sleeping.

J Literary Focus **Atmosphere** What change in Roderick does the atmosphere in this paragraph reflect? What is the probable cause of this change?

K Literary Focus **Atmosphere** What details heighten the ominous character of the narrator's nighttime fears? What does this passage reveal about the narrator's state of mind?

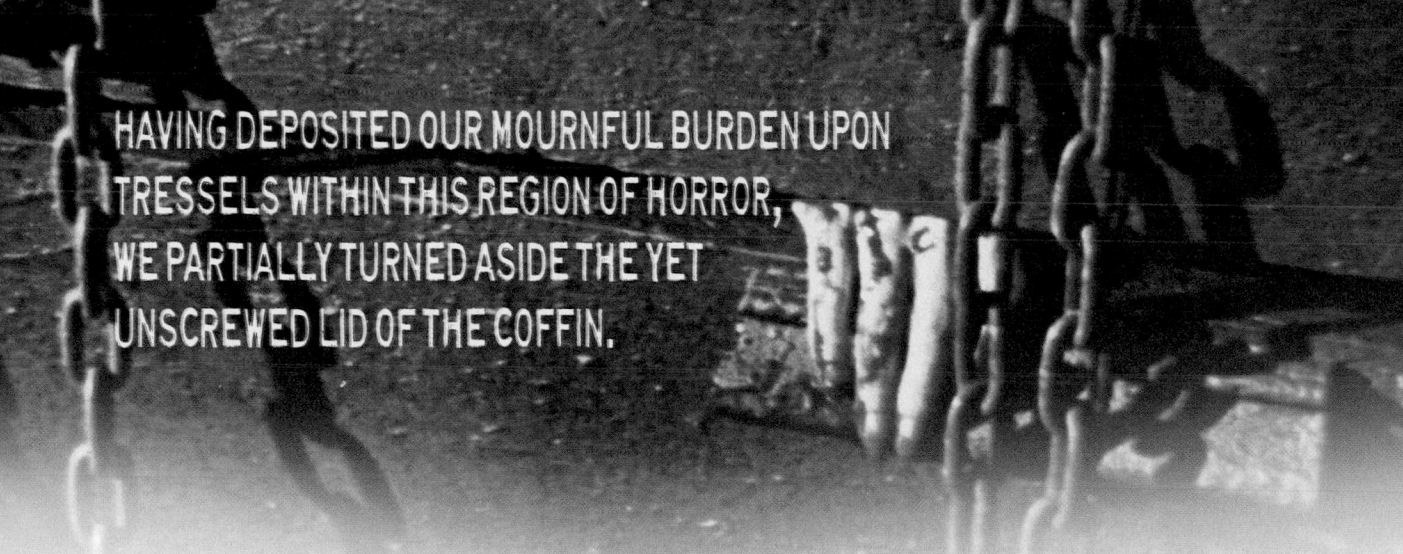

HAVING DEPOSITED OUR MOURNFUL BURDEN UPON TRESSELS WITHIN THIS REGION OF HORROR, WE PARTIALLY TURNED ASIDE THE YET UNSCREWED LID OF THE COFFIN.

tion. I presently recognized it as that of Usher. In an instant afterward he rapped, with a gentle touch, at my door, and entered, bearing a lamp. His countenance was, as usual, cadaverously wan—but, moreover, there was a species of mad hilarity in his eyes—an evidently restrained *hysteria* in his whole demeanor.[47] His air appalled me—but anything was preferable to the solitude which I had so long endured, and I even welcomed his presence as a relief.

"And you have not seen it?" he said abruptly, after having stared about him for some moments in silence—"you have not then seen it?—but, stay! you shall." Thus speaking, and having carefully shaded his lamp, he hurried to one of the casements, and threw it freely open to the storm.

The impetuous fury of the entering gust nearly lifted us from our feet. It was, indeed, a tempestuous yet sternly beautiful night, and one wildly singular in its terror and its beauty. A whirlwind had apparently collected its force in our vicinity; for there were frequent and violent alterations in the direction of the wind; and the exceeding density of the clouds (which hung so low as to press upon the turrets of the house) did not prevent our perceiving the lifelike velocity with which they flew careering from all points against each other, without passing away into the distance. I say that even their

exceeding density did not prevent our perceiving this— yet we had no glimpse of the moon or stars—nor was there any flashing forth of the lightning. But the under surfaces of the huge masses of agitated vapor, as well as all terrestrial objects immediately around us, were glowing in the unnatural light of a faintly luminous and distinctly visible gaseous exhalation which hung about and enshrouded the mansion. **L**

"You must not—you shall not behold this!" said I, shudderingly, to Usher, as I led him, with a gentle violence, from the window to a seat. "These appearances, which bewilder you, are merely electrical phenomena not uncommon—or it may be that they have their ghastly origin in the rank miasma of the tarn.[48] Let us close this casement—the air is chilling and dangerous to your frame. Here is one of your favorite romances. I will read, and you shall listen;—and so we will pass away this terrible night together."

The antique volume which I had taken up was the *Mad Trist* of Sir Launcelot Canning;[49] but I had called it a favorite of Usher's more in sad jest than in earnest; for, in truth, there is little in its uncouth and unimaginative prolixity[50] which could have had interest for the lofty and spiritual ideality of my friend. It was, however, the only book immediately at hand; and I indulged a

---

47. **demeanor:** behavior; conduct.

L **Reading Focus** Strategies for Understanding Look up any difficult words in this passage. What is Poe describing in this passage? How does the description contribute to the story's atmosphere?

48. **rank miasma** (my AZ muh) **. . . tarn:** The decomposing matter of the tarn could have given rise to swamp gas or electrical discharges that resulted in frightening optical illusions.
49. *Mad Trist* **of Sir Launcelot Canning:** a book invented by Poe for this story.
50. **prolixity:** wordiness.

vague hope that the excitement which now agitated the hypochondriac, might find relief (for the history of mental disorder is full of similar anomalies) even in the extremeness of the folly which I should read. Could I have judged, indeed, by the wild overstrained air of vivacity with which he harkened, or apparently harkened, to the words of the tale, I might well have congratulated myself upon the success of my design.

I had arrived at that well-known portion of the story where Ethelred, the hero of the *Trist,* having sought in vain for peaceable admission into the dwelling of the hermit, proceeds to make good an entrance by force. Here, it will be remembered, the words of the narrative run thus:

"And Ethelred, who was by nature of a doughty[51] heart, and who was now mighty withal, on account of the powerfulness of the wine which he had drunken, waited no longer to hold parley with the hermit, who, in sooth, was of an obstinate and maliceful turn, but, feeling the rain upon his shoulders, and fearing the rising of the tempest, uplifted his mace outright, and, with blows, made quickly room in the plankings of the door for his gauntleted hand; and now pulling therewith sturdily, he so cracked, and ripped, and tore all asunder, that the noise of the dry and hollow-sounding wood alarumed and reverberated throughout the forest."

At the termination of this sentence I started, and for a moment, paused; for it appeared to me (although I at once concluded that my excited fancy had deceived me)—it appeared to me that, from some very remote portion of the mansion, there came, indistinctly, to my ears, what might have been, in its exact similarity of character, the echo (but a stifled and dull one certainly) of the very cracking and ripping sound which Sir Launcelot had so particularly described. It was, beyond doubt, the coincidence alone which had arrested my attention; for, amid the rattling of the sashes of the casements, and the ordinary commingled noises of the still increasing storm, the sound, in itself, had nothing, surely, which should have interested or disturbed me. I continued the story:

"But the good champion Ethelred, now entering within the door, was sore enraged and amazed to perceive no signal of the maliceful hermit; but, in the stead thereof, a dragon of a scaly and prodigious[52] demeanor, and of a fiery tongue, which sate in guard before a palace of gold, with a floor of silver; and upon the wall there hung a shield of shining brass with this legend enwritten—

Who entereth herein, a conqueror hath bin;
Who slayeth the dragon, the shield he shall win;

And Ethelred uplifted his mace, and struck upon the head of the dragon, which fell before him, and gave up his pesty breath, with a shriek so horrid and harsh, and withal so piercing, that Ethelred had fain to close his ears with his hands against the dreadful noise of it, the like whereof was never before heard."

Here again I paused abruptly, and now with a feeling of wild amazement—for there could be no doubt whatever that, in this instance, I did actually hear (although from what direction it proceeded I found it impossible to say) a low and apparently distant, but harsh, protracted, and most unusual screaming or grating sound—the exact counterpart of what my fancy had already conjured up for the dragon's unnatural shriek as described by the romancer.

Oppressed, as I certainly was, upon the occurrence of this second and most extraordinary coincidence, by a thousand conflicting sensations, in which wonder and extreme terror were predominant, I still retained sufficient presence of mind to avoid exciting, by any observation, the sensitive nervousness of my companion. I was by no means certain that he had noticed the sounds in question; although, assuredly, a strange alteration had, during the last few minutes, taken place in his demeanor. From a position fronting my own, he had gradually brought round his chair, so as to sit with his face to the door of the chamber; and thus I could but partially perceive his features, although I saw that his lips trembled as if he were murmuring inaudibly. His head had dropped upon his breast—yet I knew that he was not asleep, from the wide and rigid opening of the eye as I caught a glance of it in profile. The motion of his body, too, was at variance with this idea—for he rocked from side

---

51. doughty (DOWT ee): courageous.

Vocabulary obstinate (AHB stuh niht) *adj.*: stubborn.

---

52. prodigious: of great size and power.

to side with a gentle yet constant and uniform sway. Having rapidly taken notice of all this, I resumed the narrative of Sir Launcelot, which thus proceeded: Ⓜ

"And now, the champion, having escaped from the terrible fury of the dragon, bethinking himself of the brazen shield, and of the breaking up of the enchantment which was upon it, removed the carcass from out of the way before him, and approached valorously over the silver pavement of the castle to where the shield was upon the wall; which in sooth tarried not for his full coming, but fell down at his feet upon the silver floor, with a mighty great and terrible ringing sound."

No sooner had these syllables passed my lips, than—as if a shield of brass had indeed, at the moment, fallen heavily upon a floor of silver—I became aware of a distinct, hollow, metallic, and clangorous, yet apparently muffled reverberation. Completely unnerved, I leaped to my feet; but the measured rocking movement of Usher was undisturbed. I rushed to the chair in which he sat. His eyes were bent fixedly before him, and throughout his whole countenance there reigned a stony rigidity. But, as I placed my hand upon his shoulder, there came a strong shudder over his whole person; a sickly smile quivered about his lips; and I saw that he spoke in a low, hurried, and gibbering murmur, as if unconscious of my presence. Bending closely over him, I at length drank in the hideous import of his words.

"Not hear it?—yes, I hear it, and *have* heard it. Long—long—long—many minutes, many hours, many days, have I heard it—yet I dared not—oh, pity me, miserable wretch that I am!—I dared not—I *dared* not speak! *We have put her living in the tomb!* Said I not that my senses were acute? I now tell you that I heard her first feeble movements in the hollow coffin. I heard them—many, many days ago—yet I dared not—*I dared not speak!* And now—tonight—Ethelred—ha! ha!—the breaking of the hermit's door, and the death cry of the dragon, and the clangor of the shield!—say, rather, the rending of her coffin, and the grating of the iron hinges of her prison, and her struggles within the coppered archway of the vault! Oh whither shall I fly? Will she not be here anon? Is she not hurrying to upbraid me for my haste? Have I not heard her footstep on the stair? Do I not distinguish that heavy and horrible beating of her heart? *Madman!*"—here he sprang furiously to his feet, and shrieked out his syllables, as if in the effort he were giving up his soul—"*Madman! I tell you that she now stands without the door!*"

As if in the superhuman energy of his utterance there had been found the potency[53] of a spell—the huge antique panels to which the speaker pointed, threw slowly back, upon the instant, their ponderous and ebony jaws. It was the work of the rushing gust—but then without those doors there *did* stand the lofty and enshrouded figure of the lady Madeline of Usher. There was blood upon her white robes, and the evidence of some bitter struggle upon every portion of her emaciated frame. For a moment she remained trembling and reeling to and fro upon the threshold—then, with a low moaning cry, fell heavily inward upon the person of her brother, and in her violent and now final death agonies, bore him to the floor a corpse, and a victim to the terrors he had anticipated.

From that chamber, and from that mansion, I fled aghast. The storm was still abroad in all its wrath as I found myself crossing the old causeway. Suddenly there shot along the path a wild light, and I turned to see whence a gleam so unusual could have issued; for the vast house and its shadows were alone behind me. The radiance was that of the full, setting, and blood-red moon, which now shone vividly through that once barely discernible fissure, of which I have before spoken as extending from the roof of the building, in a zigzag direction, to the base. While I gazed, this fissure rapidly widened—there came a fierce breath of the whirlwind—the entire orb of the satellite burst at once upon my sight—my brain reeled as I saw the mighty walls rushing asunder—there was a long tumultuous shouting sound like the voice of a thousand waters—and the deep and dank tarn at my feet closed sullenly and silently over the fragments of the "*House of Usher*."

---

53. **potency:** strength; power.

Ⓜ **Literary Focus** Atmosphere Although Poe already has us on the edge of our seats, how does he darken the atmosphere even more in this paragraph?

Applying Your Skills

The Fall of the House of Usher

Respond and Think Critically

Quick Check

1. How does the narrator feel when he first sees the House of Usher?

2. What does the narrator discover about the brother and sister after viewing Madeline in her coffin? What does this discovery help explain?

3. Why does Roderick go to the narrator's room near the end of the story?

Read with a Purpose

4. What happens to the House of Usher?

Reading Skills: Strategies for Understanding

5. Review the chart you used to record and explain difficult phrases. Then, write a few sentences discussing how the right column in your chart helps you to grasp the story's atmosphere.

Word or Phrase	Explanation
"the afterdream of the reveler upon opium—the bitter lapse into every day life—the hideous dropping off of the veil"	The narrator feels like someone who just woke up from a nightmare caused by drugs. He feels bitter and hungover. He sees life without a veil to disguise it, so life looks ugly to him.
Roderick Usher's "wildly importunate letter"	Usher has sent the narrator a frantic letter begging him to do something, perhaps to come here.

Literary Focus

Literary Analysis

6. **Interpret** What does the lyric "The Haunted Palace" reveal about Roderick's state of mind?

7. **Analyze** How does Poe bring the suspense to a climax?

8. **Evaluate** How convincing is Poe's treatment of the irrational mind? Consider descriptions of Roderick's state of mind and the workings of the narrator's imagination.

Literary Skills: Atmosphere

9. **Analyze** How does Poe use the setting in the final scenes to <u>transform</u> the story's atmosphere? How do the descriptive details of the house strengthen the story?

Literary Skills Review: Allegory

10. **Evaluate** An **allegory** is a story or poem that can be read on one level for its literal meaning and on a second level for its symbolic meaning. How might this story be read as an allegory of a journey into the human mind? What could the final *fall* of the house represent?

Writing Focus

Think as a Reader/Writer

Use It in Your Writing Poe relies heavily on atmosphere to envelop the reader in the dark world that he creates. Imagine that you are a character who has discovered a remote, abandoned house. Write a short scene in which you describe approaching and entering the house. Use details of setting to create an atmosphere like Poe's.

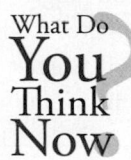 What Do **You Think Now** Where do you think Poe found inspiration for "The Fall of the House of Usher"? What details about Poe's life might help you understand this story?

For **CHOICES** *see page 358.* ›

Vocabulary Development

SKILLS FOCUS **Literary Skills** Analyze atmosphere; analyze allegory. **Reading Skills** Apply and monitor a variety of response and comprehension strategies.

Vocabulary Skills Understand denotation and connotation. **Writing Skills** Establish and develop setting; develop descriptions with sensory details.

✔ Vocabulary Check

Choose the Vocabulary word below that best completes each sentence.

1. She is being _____; nothing will persuade her.
2. I could feel his fear; it was _____.
3. After the hunger strike, he looked pale and _____.
4. _____ rudeness knows no boundaries.
5. He has a ___ obsession with violence.
6. Under the waterfall, the heavy mist ____ the cave.
7. Her _____ in Hawaii was restful.

   a. pervaded   **d.** inordinate   **f.** palpable

   b. obstinate   **e.** emaciated   **g.** sojourn

   c. morbid

Vocabulary Skills: Connotations

In addition to having dictionary definitions, or **denotations,** many words have associations or emotional overtones that affect their meaning. This additional, suggested meaning is a word's **connotation.** Synonyms often have similar dictionary definitions but different connotations. For example, both *firm* and *stubborn* can describe people who hold to their principles. The word *firm,* however, has a positive connotation, whereas *stubborn* has a negative one.

In "The Fall of the House of Usher," Poe uses words that create a gloomy atmosphere. At the outset, the narrator finds himself "within view of the melancholy House of Usher." The word *melancholy* means "sad," but by connotation, it suggests an atmosphere pervaded by gloom.

Consider the denotative and connotative meanings of the italicized words in these sentences from the story:

"I looked upon . . . the *bleak* walls."
"I reined my horse to the *precipitous* brink of a . . . tarn."

"An air of . . . *irredeemable* gloom hung over and pervaded all."

What impact does the connotation of the italicized word have in creating the atmosphere in each of these sentences?

Your Turn

Use four of the Vocabulary words in a short descriptive paragraph about a strange place you've visited or seen on television or in a movie. Then, using a dictionary or thesaurus, replace each Vocabulary word with a word that has a similar meaning but a different connotation. How do these changes affect both the meaning and the atmosphere of your paragraph?

Language Coach

Etymology You have already learned the Latin roots for *pervaded.* The other Vocabulary words for this story also have Latin roots. Choose two that you especially want to remember. Look them up, and see how the roots are related to the meaning.

Academic Vocabulary

Talk About
In a small group, talk about how elements <u>integral</u> to a Gothic atmosphere <u>transformed</u> Poe's short stories into masterpieces of horror.

Learn It Online
Learn more about connotations with *WordSharp.*

go.hrw.com   L11-335   **Go**

SKILLS FOCUS **Literary Skills** Understand atmosphere.
Reading Skills Respond to graphics.

Link to Today

This Link to Today gives a classic story new life with mood-drenched images.

from

The Fall of the House of Usher: A Graphic Version

by **Matt Howarth**

GRAPHIC CLASSICS: EDGAR ALLAN POE

THE FALL OF THE HOUSE OF USHER

POE/HOWARTH

Reader/Writer Notebook

Use your **RWN** to complete the activities for this selection.

What Do You Think? Where does an individual find inspiration?

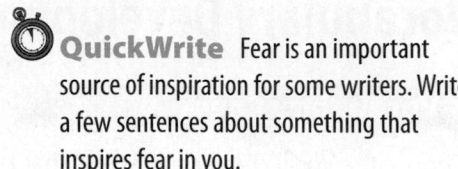

QuickWrite Fear is an important source of inspiration for some writers. Write a few sentences about something that inspires fear in you.

Literary Focus

Atmosphere Graphic novels create **atmosphere,** or mood, <u>principally</u> through visual elements. In this excerpt from a graphic version of "The Fall of the House of Usher," the artist Matt Howarth enhances Poe's atmosphere with a stark, black-and-white visual style that emphasizes shadows and darkness.

Reading Focus

Responding to Graphics When you read a graphic story, think about how the artist uses details and other visual elements to depict the action and to convey emotions.

Into Action As you read, use a chart like the one below to record what you notice about facial details, shadows, and other <u>factors</u> that affect the graphic story's atmosphere.

Faces	Shadows	Other Details
large black eyes with no pupil and no white	dark spiky shadow of scary character	black outside window, with streak of lightning

Writing Focus

Think as a Reader/Writer

Find It in Your Reading This graphic story uses shadows and images to create an eerie atmosphere. In your *Reader/Writer Notebook,* keep a record of story frames that most effectively convey the atmosphere.

Learn It Online
Explore modern versions of Poe with these links.

go.hrw.com   L11-336   **Go**

US $9.95
GRAPHIC CLASSICS
THE FALL OF THE HOUSE OF USHER, THE MASQUE OF THE RED DEATH & MORE!
EDGAR ALLAN POE
REVISED AND EXPANDED SECOND EDITION

No sooner had these syllables passed my lips, than I became aware of a distinct, hollow, metallic, reverberation. Completely unnerved, I leaped to my feet.

As I placed my hand upon his shoulder, there came a strong shudder over his whole person; and he spoke in a gibbering murmur, as if unconscious of my presence.

Bending closely over him, I drank in the hideous import of his words.

Yes, I hear it, and *have* heard it.

As if in the superhuman energy of his utterance there had been found the potency of a spell, the huge antique panels to which the speaker pointed threw back their ebony jaws.

It was the work of the rushing gust—but then without those doors there did stand the lofty and enshrouded figure of the lady Madeline of Usher. There was blood upon her white robes, and the evidence of some bitter struggle upon every portion of her emaciated frame.

For a moment
she remained trembling
and reeling to and fro
upon the threshold.

Then, with a low moaning cry, fell heavily inward upon the person of her brother, and in her violent and now final death-agonies, bore him to the floor a corpse!

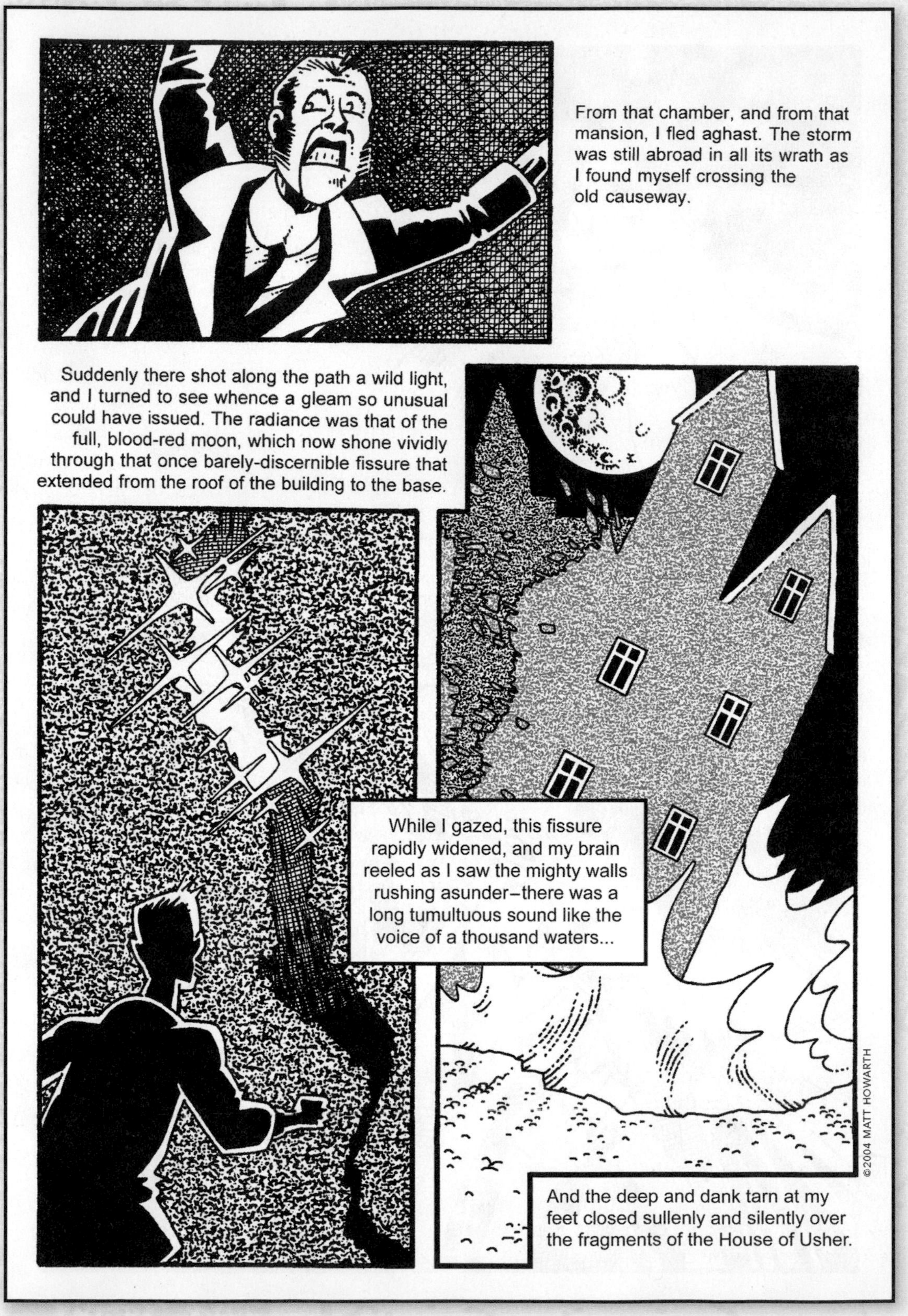

From that chamber, and from that mansion, I fled aghast. The storm was still abroad in all its wrath as I found myself crossing the old causeway.

Suddenly there shot along the path a wild light, and I turned to see whence a gleam so unusual could have issued. The radiance was that of the full, blood-red moon, which now shone vividly through that once barely-discernible fissure that extended from the roof of the building to the base.

While I gazed, this fissure rapidly widened, and my brain reeled as I saw the mighty walls rushing asunder—there was a long tumultuous sound like the voice of a thousand waters...

And the deep and dank tarn at my feet closed sullenly and silently over the fragments of the House of Usher.

©2004 MATT HOWARTH

Applying Your Skills

from **The Fall of the House of Usher: A Graphic Version**

Respond and Think Critically

Reading Focus

Quick Check

1. What important elements of the setting does the artist establish in the first frame?

2. How does the artist visually illustrate the force of the antique panels' opening?

3. In the first frame depicting Madeline Usher, how does the artist illustrate the fear felt by Madeline's brother and the narrator?

Reading Skills: Responding to Graphics

4. While reading, you used a chart to record facial details, shadows, and other <u>factors</u> that affect the story's atmosphere. Review your chart. Then, briefly explain how these visual elements contribute to the story's atmosphere.

Faces	Shadows	Other Details
large black eyes with no pupil and no white	dark spiky shadow of scary character	black outside window, with streak of lightning

Literary Focus

Literary Analysis

5. **Analyze** How does the artist's visual style reflect the horror in Poe's text?

6. **Interpret** In the first frame on the second page, why do you think the artist depicts the woman inside the closed coffin? Explain.

7. **Analyze** How does the artist make Madeline seem more like a ghost or demon than a real person? Explain.

8. **Evaluate** What is the most effective visual image in this excerpt? Explain your choice.

Literary Skills: Atmosphere

9. **Evaluate** Which elements of the artist's visual style do you think are the most effective in creating a dark, frightening atmosphere?

Literary Skills Review: Audience

10. **Hypothesize** The **audience** is the group of people that a writer wants to reach through his or her work. In some writing, such as speeches and essays, the audience is commonly a specific group of people. Other writing, such as most literary fiction, is intended for a general audience. Because the artist tells Poe's horror story in a graphic novel format, what audience do you think the artist has in mind? Explain your opinion, and support it with examples from the graphic novel.

Writing Focus

Think as a Reader/Writer

Use It in Your Writing Look back at the notes you took in your *Reader/Writer Notebook* about the frames that most vividly create the story's atmosphere. Now, choose one of these frames and imagine that you have been asked to produce a version in color. Explain what colors you would use, how you would use them, and how your color treatment would add to the story's atmosphere.

 What Do **You Think Now**

Stories inspired by fear are very popular with today's readers and moviegoers. What do you think accounts for their appeal? Explain your answer.

Preparing to Read

The Pit and the Pendulum

Literary Focus

Symbolic Meaning A **symbol** is a concrete object, a person, a place, or an action that works on at least two levels: It functions as itself, and it also implies a deeper meaning. For example, in "The Pit and the Pendulum," the total darkness in the narrator's cell might symbolize his own death, his captors' malice, or the "dark" dementia against which he struggles. A story's **symbolic meaning** emerges from an overall interpretation of its individual symbols.

Reading Focus

Retelling To understand what is happening in a story, review what has occurred already. As you read, stop periodically to **retell** the main events that have taken place so far. In your retelling, think about causes and their effects. Ask yourself, "What *caused* this event to happen?" and "What is the *effect* of this action?"

Into Action As you read, note significant changes in the narrator's circumstances or conditions. Stop at these points to retell what has happened. Each time you stop, use a chart like the one below to record the narrator's condition and to retell the events that caused it.

Causes	Narrator's Condition
1. He is tried by the Inquisition. 2. He hears his death sentence.	He hallucinates and faints.

Writing Focus

Think as a Reader/Writer

Find It in Your Reading Imagery is language that uses any of the five senses to evoke a picture or a concrete sensation. Imagery is integral to the terror Poe creates in "The Pit and the Pendulum." Such imagery includes the "smooth, slimy, cold" cell wall the narrator touches in the dark and the pendulum's hiss "as it sw[ings] through the air." In your *Reader/ Writer Notebook,* record some of the images based on the five senses that you think most effectively convey terror in the story.

TechFocus As you read, think about the experiences the narrator undergoes. How could you create the same sense of terror and horror in a visual form?

Reader/Writer Notebook

Use your **RWN** to complete the activities for this selection.

Vocabulary

lucid (LOO sihd) *adj.:* clearheaded; not confused. *The narrator is so exhausted that his thoughts are barely lucid.*

tumultuous (too MUHL chu uhs) *adj.:* violent; greatly agitated or disturbed. *The tumultuous motion of his heart awakens him from his dream.*

prostrate (PRAHS trayt) *adj.:* lying flat. *The narrator lies prostrate beneath the swinging pendulum.*

lethargy (LEHTH uhr jee) *n.:* abnormal drowsiness. *Lacking rest and nourishment, he is overcome by lethargy.*

averted (uh VUR tihd) *v.:* turned away. *When the burning light burst through the crevice, he averted his eyes.*

Language Coach

Word Choice Writers often choose a specific word or phrase to convey a particular sensation or mood precisely. Poe often includes more extreme versions of familiar words to illustrate the extreme situation of his narrator in "The Pit and the Pendulum." For example, the narrator is not merely thirsty, but is "consumed" by thirst. Explain the difference between each of these word pairs:

fall/plunge   eat/devour

Learn It Online

Get to know the Vocabulary words through Word Watch online.

go.hrw.com   L11-344   **Go**

The Pit and the Pendulum

by **Edgar Allan Poe**

Read with a Purpose
Read to experience the gripping atmosphere created by a master of suspense.

Build Background
"The Pit and the Pendulum" takes place during the final days of the brutal Spanish Inquisition (1478–1834). The Inquisition was a kind of religious court set up by the Catholic Church and the monarchy in Spain during the fifteenth century to accuse and punish those who failed to comply with the church or royal authority. Poe may have gotten the idea for this story from a book by Juan Antonio Llorente. Poe read a review of this book, which contains the following passage:

"The Inquisition was thrown open, in 1820, by the orders of the Cortes of Madrid. Twenty-one prisoners were found in it. . . . Some had been confined three years, some a longer period, and not one knew perfectly the nature of the crime of which he was accused. One of these prisoners had been condemned and was to have suffered on the following day. His punishment was to be death by the Pendulum. The method of thus destroying the victim is as follows: The condemned is fastened in a groove, upon a table, on his back; suspended above him is a Pendulum, the edge of which is sharp, and it is so constructed as to become longer with every movement. The wretch sees this implement of destruction swinging to and fro above him, and every moment the keen edge approaching nearer and nearer."

I was sick—sick unto death with that long agony; and when they at length unbound me, and I was permitted to sit, I felt that my senses were leaving me. The sentence—the dread sentence of death—was the last of distinct accentuation which reached my ears. After that, the sound of the Inquisitorial voices seemed merged in one dreamy, indeterminate hum. It conveyed to my soul the idea of *revolution*[1]—perhaps from its association in fancy[2] with the burr of a mill wheel. This only for a brief period, for presently I heard no more. Yet for a while, I saw—but with how terrible an exaggeration! I saw the lips of the black-robed judges. They appeared to me white—whiter than the sheet upon which I trace these words—and thin even to grotesqueness; thin with the intensity of their expression of firmness—of immovable resolution—of stern contempt of human torture. I saw that the decrees of what to me was Fate were still issuing from those lips. I saw them writhe with a deadly locution.[3] I saw them fashion the syllables of my name; and I shuddered because no sound succeeded.[4] I saw, too, for a few moments of delirious horror, the soft and nearly imperceptible waving of the sable draperies which enwrapped the walls of the apartment. And then my vision fell upon the seven tall candles upon the table. At first they wore the aspect of charity and seemed white, slender angels who would save me; but then, all at once, there came a most deadly nausea over my spirit, and I felt every fiber in my frame thrill as if I had touched the wire of a galvanic battery, while the angel forms became meaningless specters, with heads of flame, and I saw that from them there would be no help. And then there stole into my fancy, like a rich musical note, the thought of what sweet rest there must be in the grave. The thought came gently and stealthily, and it seemed long before it attained full appreciation; but just as my spirit came at length properly to feel and entertain it, the figures of the judges vanished, as if magically, from before me; the tall candles sank into nothingness! Their flames went out utterly; the blackness of darkness supervened; all sensations appeared swallowed up in a mad rushing descent, as of the soul into Hades. Then silence, and stillness, and night were the universe. **Ⓐ**

I had swooned;[5] but still will not say that all of consciousness was lost. What of it there remained I will not attempt to define, or even to describe; yet all was not lost. In the deepest slumber—no! In delirium—no! In a swoon—no! In death—no! Even in the grave all *is not* lost. Else there is no immortality for man. Arousing from the most profound of slumbers, we break the gossamer web of *some* dream. Yet in a second afterward (so frail may that web have been), we remember not that we have dreamed. In the return to life from the swoon, there are two stages: first, that of the sense of mental or spiritual; second, that of the sense of physical existence. It seems probable that if, upon reaching the second stage, we could recall the impressions of the first, we should find these impressions eloquent in memories of the gulf beyond. And that gulf is—what? How at least shall we distinguish its shadows from those of the tomb? But if the impressions of what I have termed the first stage are not, at will, recalled, yet, after long interval, do they not come unbidden, while we marvel whence they come? He who has never swooned is not he who finds strange palaces and wildly familiar faces in coals that glow; is not he who beholds floating in midair the sad visions that the many may not view; is not he who ponders over the perfume of some novel flower; is not he whose brain grows bewildered with the meaning of some musical cadence which has never before arrested his attention.

Amid frequent and thoughtful endeavors to remember, amid earnest struggles to regather some token of the state of seeming nothingness into which my soul had lapsed, there have been moments when I have dreamed of success; there have been brief, very brief, periods when I have conjured up remembrances

---

1. **revolution:** rotation; turning motion.
2. **fancy:** imagination.
3. **locution:** utterance; statement.
4. **succeeded:** followed.

---

5. **swooned:** fainted.

Ⓐ **Literary Focus** Symbolic Meaning The narrator sees the candles literally and then symbolically. What two different things does he say the candles symbolize for him?

which the lucid reason of a later epoch assures me could have had reference only to that condition of seeming unconsciousness. These shadows of memory tell, indistinctly, of tall figures that lifted and bore me in silence down—down—still down—till a hideous dizziness oppressed me at the mere idea of the interminableness of the descent. They tell also of a vague horror at my heart, on account of that heart's unnatural stillness. Then comes a sense of sudden motionlessness throughout all things; as if those who bore me (a ghastly train!) had outrun, in their descent, the limits of the limitless, and paused from the wearisomeness of their toil. After this I call to mind flatness and dampness; and then all is *madness*—the madness of a memory which busies itself among forbidden things.

Very suddenly there came back to my soul motion and sound—the tumultuous motion of the heart and, in my ears, the sound of its beating. Then a pause in which all is blank. Then again sound, and motion, and touch—a tingling sensation pervading my frame. Then the mere consciousness of existence, without thought—a condition which lasted long. Then, very suddenly, *thought*, and shuddering terror, and earnest endeavor to comprehend my true state. Then a strong desire to lapse into insensibility. Then a rushing revival of soul and a successful effort to move. And now a full memory of the trial, of the judges, of the sable draperies, of the sentence, of the sickness, of the swoon. Then entire forgetfulness of all that followed; of all that a later day and much earnestness of endeavor have enabled me vaguely to recall.

So far, I had not opened my eyes. I felt that I lay upon my back, unbound. I reached out my hand, and it fell heavily upon something damp and hard. There I suffered[6] it to remain for many minutes, while I strove to imagine where and *what* I could be. I longed, yet dared not, to employ my vision. I dreaded the first glance at objects around me. It was not that I feared to look upon things horrible, but that I grew aghast lest there should be *nothing* to see. At length, with a wild desperation at heart, I quickly unclosed my eyes. My worst thoughts, then, were confirmed. The blackness of eternal night encompassed me. I struggled for breath. The intensity of the darkness seemed to oppress and stifle me. The

---

6. **suffered:** allowed; tolerated.

Vocabulary **lucid** (LOO sihd) *adj.:* clearheaded; not confused. **tumultuous** (too MUHL chu uhs) *adj.:* violent; greatly agitated or disturbed.

HISTORY LINK

The Inquisition

Spain's Catholic monarchy established the Inquisition in 1478 to regain control of Spain's Muslim and Jewish populations. Moors (Muslims from North Africa) previously ruled the country for centuries, but along with Spain's large population of Jews, many converted to Christianity. In order to seize their property and destroy their influence, the monarchy used the Inquisition to find Spanish Jews and Muslims guilty of falsely converting to Christianity to protect their wealth. The Inquisition's methods included imprisonment, torture, and public execution. At its height, from 1483 to 1498, it ordered two thousand burnings at the stake, preceded by a religious ceremony called an auto-da-fé (Portuguese for "act of faith") in which the Inquisition publicly pronounced judgment and passed sentence on the accused. The Inquisition was temporarily halted in 1808 when Napoleon's army defeated Spain (General Lasalle's troops seized the city of Toledo), then briefly restored, but finally ended for good in 1834.

Ask Yourself
Why do you think Poe set his story during the Inquisition?

The Burning of the Books by Pedro Berruguete (1450–1504).

atmosphere was intolerably close. I still lay quietly, and made effort to exercise my reason. I brought to mind the Inquisitorial proceedings and attempted from that point to deduce my real condition. The sentence had passed; and it appeared to me that a very long interval of time had since elapsed. Yet not for a moment did I suppose myself actually dead. Such a supposition, notwithstanding what we read in fiction, is altogether inconsistent with real existence—but where and in what state was I? The condemned to death, I knew, perished usually at the autos-da-fé, and one of these had been held on the very night of the day of my trial. Had I been remanded to my dungeon, to await the next sacrifice, which would not take place for many months? This I at once saw could not be. Victims had been in immediate demand. Moreover, my dungeon, as well as all the condemned cells at Toledo, had stone floors, and light was not altogether excluded. **Ⓑ**

A fearful idea now suddenly drove the blood in torrents upon my heart, and for a brief period I once more relapsed into insensibility. Upon recovering, I at once started to my feet, trembling convulsively in every fiber. I thrust my arms wildly above and around me in all directions. I felt nothing; yet dreaded to move a step, lest I should be impeded by the walls of a *tomb*. Perspiration burst from every pore and stood in cold, big beads upon my forehead. The agony of suspense grew at length intolerable, and I cautiously moved forward, with my arms extended and my eyes straining from their sockets in the hope of catching some faint ray of light. I proceeded for many paces; but still all was blackness and vacancy. I breathed more freely. It seemed evident that mine was not, at least, the most hideous of fates.

And now, as I still continued to step cautiously onward, there came thronging upon my recollection

Ⓑ **Reading Focus** **Retelling** In your own words, retell what the narrator has been doing since he first regained consciousness.

a thousand vague rumors of the horrors of Toledo. Of the dungeons there had been strange things narrated—fables I had always deemed them—but yet strange, and too ghastly to repeat, save in a whisper. Was I left to perish of starvation in the subterranean world of darkness; or what fate, perhaps even more fearful, awaited me? That the result would be death, and a death of more than customary bitterness, I knew too well the character of my judges to doubt. The mode and the hour were all that occupied or distracted me.

My outstretched hands at length encountered some solid obstruction. It was a wall, seemingly of stone masonry—very smooth, slimy, and cold. I followed it up, stepping with all the careful distrust with which certain antique narratives had inspired me. This process, however, afforded me no means of ascertaining the dimensions of my dungeon, as I might make its circuit and return to the point whence I set out without being aware of the fact, so perfectly uniform seemed the wall. I therefore sought the knife which had been in my pocket when led into the Inquisitorial chamber, but it was gone; my clothes had been exchanged for a wrapper of coarse serge. I had thought of forcing the blade in some minute crevice of the masonry, so as to identify my point of departure. The difficulty, nevertheless, was but trivial; although, in the disorder of my fancy, it seemed at first insuperable. I tore a part of the hem from the robe and placed the fragment at full length and at right angles to the wall. In groping my way around the prison, I could not fail to encounter this rag upon completing the circuit. So, at least, I thought; but I had not counted upon the extent of the dungeon, or upon my own weakness. The ground was moist and slippery. I staggered onward for some time, when I stumbled and fell. My excessive fatigue induced me to remain prostrate; and sleep soon overtook me as I lay.

Upon awaking and stretching forth an arm, I found beside me a loaf and a pitcher with water. I was too much exhausted to reflect upon this circumstance, but ate and drank with avidity.[7] Shortly afterward, I

---

7. **avidity:** great eagerness.

resumed my tour around the prison and, with much toil, came at last upon the fragment of the serge. Up to the period when I fell, I had counted fifty-two paces, and upon resuming my walk, I had counted forty-eight more—when I arrived at the rag. There were in all, then, a hundred paces; and, admitting two paces to the yard, I presumed the dungeon to be fifty yards in circuit. I had met, however, with many angles in the wall, and thus I could form no guess at the shape of the vault, for vault I could not help supposing it to be.

I had little object—certainly no hope—in these researches; but a vague curiosity prompted me to continue them. Quitting the wall, I resolved to cross the area of the enclosure. At first, I proceeded with extreme caution, for the floor, although seemingly of solid material, was treacherous with slime. At length, however, I took courage and did not hesitate to step firmly—endeavoring to cross in as direct a line as possible. I had advanced some ten or twelve paces in this manner when the remnant of the torn hem of my robe became entangled between my legs. I stepped on it and fell violently on my face. **C**

In the confusion attending my fall, I did not immediately apprehend a somewhat startling circumstance, which yet, in a few seconds afterward and while I still lay prostrate, arrested my attention. It was this—my chin rested upon the floor of the prison, but my lips and the upper portion of my head, although seemingly at a less elevation than the chin, touched nothing. At the same time, my forehead seemed bathed in a clammy vapor, and the peculiar smell of decayed fungus arose to my nostrils. I put forward my arm, and shuddered to find that I had fallen at the very brink of a circular pit, whose extent, of course, I had no means of ascertaining at the moment. Groping about the masonry just below the margin, I succeeded in dislodging a small fragment and let it fall into the abyss. For many seconds I hearkened to its reverberations as it dashed against the sides of the chasm in its descent; at length, there was a sullen plunge into water, succeeded by loud echoes. At the same moment, there came a sound resembling the quick opening and as rapid closing of a door overhead, while a faint gleam of light flashed suddenly through the gloom and as suddenly faded away.

Vocabulary **prostrate** (PRAHS trayt) *adj.*: lying flat.

C **Reading Focus** **Retelling** Retell what has happened since the narrator found the wall.

I saw clearly the doom which had been prepared for me, and congratulated myself upon the timely accident by which I had escaped. Another step before my fall, and the world had seen me no more. And the death just avoided was of that very character which I had regarded as fabulous and frivolous in the tales respecting the Inquisition. To the victims of its tyranny, there was the choice of death with its direst physical agonies or death with its most hideous moral horrors. I had been reserved for the latter. By long suffering, my nerves had been unstrung, until I trembled at the sound of my own voice and had become in every respect a fitting subject for the species of torture which awaited me. **Ⓓ**

Shaking in every limb, I groped my way back to the wall; resolving there to perish rather than risk the terrors of the wells, of which my imagination now pictured many in various positions about the dungeon. In other conditions of mind, I might have had courage to end my misery at once, by a plunge into one of these abysses; but now I was the veriest[8] of cowards. Neither could I forget what I had read of these pits—that the *sudden* extinction of life formed no part of their most horrible plan.

Agitation of spirit kept me awake for many long hours, but at length I again slumbered. Upon arousing, I found by my side, as before, a loaf and a pitcher of water. A burning thirst consumed me, and I emptied the vessel at a draft. It must have been drugged; for scarcely had I drunk before I became irresistibly drowsy. A deep sleep fell upon me—a sleep like that of death. How long it lasted of course I know not; but when, once again, I unclosed my eyes, the objects around me were visible. By a wild, sulfurous luster,[9] the origin of which I could not at first determine, I was enabled to see the extent and aspect of the prison.

In its size I had been greatly mistaken. The whole circuit of its walls did not exceed twenty-five yards. For some minutes this fact occasioned me a world of vain trouble; vain indeed, for what could be of less importance, under the terrible circumstances which environed me, than the mere dimensions of my dungeon? But my soul took a wild interest in trifles, and I busied myself in endeavors to account for the error I had committed in my measurement. The truth at length flashed upon me. In my first attempt at exploration I had counted fifty-two paces, up to the period when I fell; I must then have been within a pace or two of the fragment of serge; in fact, I had nearly performed the circuit of the vault. I then slept, and upon awaking, I must have returned upon my steps—thus supposing the circuit nearly double what it actually was. My confusion of mind prevented me from observing that I began my tour with the wall to the left and ended it with the wall to the right. **Ⓔ**

I had been deceived, too, in respect to the shape of the enclosure. In feeling my way I had found many angles and thus deduced an idea of great irregularity; so potent is the effect of total darkness upon one arousing from lethargy or sleep! The angles were simply those of a few slight depressions, or niches, at odd intervals. The general shape of the prison was square. What I had taken for masonry seemed now to be iron, or some other metal, in huge plates, whose sutures or joints occasioned the depression. The entire surface of this metallic enclosure was rudely daubed[10] in all the hideous and repulsive devices to which the charnel[11] superstition of the monks has given rise. The figures of fiends in aspects of menace, with skeleton forms, and other, more really fearful images, overspread and disfigured the walls. I observed that the outlines of these monstrosities were sufficiently distinct, but that the colors seemed faded and blurred, as if from the effects

---

8. **veriest:** greatest.
9. **sulfurous luster:** glow like that of burning sulfur, which produces a blue flame. The word *sulfurous* also suggests the fires of hell.

---

10. **daubed:** painted crudely or unskillfully.
11. **charnel:** suggesting death. A charnel house is a tomb or place where bones of the dead are deposited.

Ⓓ **Literary Focus** Symbolic Meaning What symbolic connection does the narrator make between the falling bit of masonry and his own fate?

Ⓔ **Literary Focus** Symbolic Meaning What does the narrator's confused wandering symbolize?

Vocabulary **lethargy** (LEHTH uhr jee) *n.*: abnormal drowsiness.

of a damp atmosphere. I now noticed the floor, too, which was of stone. In the center yawned the circular pit from whose jaws I had escaped; but it was the only one in the dungeon.

All this I saw indistinctly and by much effort: for my personal condition had been greatly changed during slumber. I now lay upon my back, and at full length, on a species of low framework of wood. To this I was securely bound by a long strap resembling a surcingle.[12] It passed in many convolutions about my limbs and body, leaving at liberty only my head, and my left arm to such extent that I could, by dint of much exertion, supply myself with food from an earthen dish which lay by my side on the floor. I saw, to my horror, that the pitcher had been removed. I say to my horror, for I was consumed with intolerable thirst. This thirst it appeared to be the design of my persecutors to stimulate—for the food in the dish was meat pungently seasoned.

Looking upward, I surveyed the ceiling of my prison. It was some thirty or forty feet overhead and constructed much as the side walls. In one of its panels a very singular figure riveted my whole attention. It was the painted figure of Time as he is commonly represented, save[13] that, in lieu of[14] a scythe, he held what, at a casual glance, I supposed to be the pictured image of a huge pendulum, such as we see on antique clocks. There was something, however, in the appearance of this machine which caused me to regard it more attentively. While I gazed directly upward at it (for its position was immediately over my own), I fancied that I saw it in motion. In an instant afterward the fancy was confirmed. Its sweep was brief and of course slow. I watched it for some minutes somewhat in fear, but more in wonder. Wearied at length with observing its dull movement, I turned my eyes upon the other objects in the cell.

A slight noise attracted my notice, and looking to the floor, I saw several enormous rats traversing it. They had issued from the well which lay just within view to my right. Even then, while I gazed, they came up in troops, hurriedly, with ravenous eyes, allured by the scent of the meat. From this it required much effort and attention to scare them away.

It might have been half an hour, perhaps even an hour (for I could take but imperfect note of time), before I again cast my eyes upward. What I then saw confounded and amazed me. The sweep of the pendulum had increased in extent by nearly a yard. As a natural consequence its velocity was also much greater. But what mainly disturbed me was the idea that it had perceptibly *descended*. I now observed—with what horror it is needless to say—that its nether extremity[15] was formed of a crescent of glittering steel, about a foot in length from horn to horn; the horns upward, and the under edge evidently as keen as that of a razor. Like a razor also, it seemed massy and heavy, tapering from the edge into a solid and broad structure above. It was appended to a weighty rod of brass, and the whole *hissed* as it swung through the air. **F**

> I saw clearly the doom which had been prepared for me, and congratulated myself upon the timely accident by which I had escaped.

---

12. **surcingle** (SUR sihng guhl): strap that binds a saddle or a pack to a horse's body.
13. **save**: except.
14. **in lieu** (loo) **of**: instead of.

---

15. **nether extremity**: lower end.

F **Reading Focus** **Retelling** In your own words, retell what the narrator has discovered about the pendulum.

I could no longer doubt the doom prepared for me by monkish ingenuity in torture. My cognizance[16] of the pit had become known to the Inquisitorial agents—*the pit,* whose horrors had been destined for so bold a recusant[17] as myself—*the pit,* typical of hell and regarded by rumor as the ultima Thule[18] of all their punishments. The plunge into this pit I had avoided by the merest of accidents, and I knew that surprise, or entrapment into torment, formed an important portion of all the grotesquerie of these dungeon deaths. Having failed to fall, it was no part of the demon plan to hurl me into the abyss, and thus (there being no alternative) a different and a milder destruction awaited me. Milder! I half smiled in my agony as I thought of such application of such a term.

What boots it[19] to tell of the long, long hours of horror more than mortal, during which I counted the rushing vibrations of the steel! Inch by inch—line by line—with a descent only appreciable at intervals that seemed ages—down and still down it came! Days passed—it might have been that many days passed—ere it swept so closely over me as to fan me with its acrid breath. The odor of the sharp steel forced itself into my nostrils. I prayed—I wearied heaven with my prayer for its more speedy descent. I grew frantically mad and struggled to force myself upward against the sweep of the fearful scimitar.[20] And then I fell suddenly calm and lay smiling at the glittering death, as a child at some rare bauble.

There was another interval of utter insensibility; it was brief; for, upon again lapsing into life, there had been no perceptible descent in the pendulum. But it might have been long—for I knew there were demons who took note of my swoon and who could have arrested the vibration at pleasure. Upon my recovery, too, I felt very—oh! inexpressibly—sick and weak, as if through long inanition.[21] Even amid the agonies of that period, the human nature craved food. With painful effort I outstretched my left arm as far as my bonds permitted and took possession of the small remnant which had been spared me by the rats. As I put a portion of it within my lips, there rushed to my mind a half-formed thought of joy—of hope. Yet what business had *I* with hope? It was, as I say, a half-formed thought—man has many such, which are never completed. I felt that it was of joy—of hope; but I felt also that it had perished in its formation. In vain I struggled to perfect—to regain it. Long suffering had nearly annihilated all my ordinary powers of mind. I was an imbecile—an idiot.

The vibration of the pendulum was at right angles to my length. I saw that the crescent was designed to cross the region of the heart. It would fray the serge of my robe—it would return and repeat its operations—again—and again. Notwithstanding its terrifically wide sweep (some thirty feet or more) and the hissing vigor of its descent, sufficient to sunder these very walls of iron, still the fraying of my robe would be all that, for several minutes, it would accomplish. And at this thought I paused. I dared not go further than this reflection. I dwelt upon it with a pertinacity[22] of attention—as if, in so dwelling, I could arrest[23] *here* the descent of the steel. I forced myself to ponder upon the sound of the crescent as it should pass across the garment—upon the peculiar thrilling sensation which the friction of cloth produces on the nerves. I pondered upon all this frivolity until my teeth were on edge.

Down—steadily down it crept. I took a frenzied pleasure in contrasting its downward with its lateral velocity. To the right—to the left—far and wide—with the shriek of a damned spirit! to my heart, with the stealthy pace of the tiger! I alternately laughed and howled, as the one or the other idea grew predominant. **G**

Down—certainly, relentlessly down! It vibrated within three inches of my bosom! I struggled violently—furiously—to free my left arm. This was free only from the elbow to the hand. I could reach the

---

16. **cognizance:** awareness.
17. **recusant:** person who stands out stubbornly against an established authority.
18. **ultima Thule** (UHL tuh muh THOO lee): most extreme. The term is Latin for "northernmost region of the world."
19. **what boots it:** of what use it is.
20. **scimitar** (SIHM uh tuhr): sword with a curved blade, used mainly by Arabs and Turks.
21. **inanition:** weakness from lack of food.

---

22. **pertinacity:** stubborn persistence.
23. **arrest:** stop.

G **Literary Focus** Symbolic Meaning How does the phrase *damned spirit* reinforce the symbolic meaning of the dungeon?

latter, from the platter beside me, to my mouth, with great effort, but no farther. Could I have broken the fastenings above the elbow, I would have seized and attempted to arrest the pendulum. I might as well have attempted to arrest an avalanche!

Down—still unceasingly—still inevitably down! I gasped and struggled at each vibration. I shrunk convulsively at its every sweep. My eyes followed its outward or upward whorls with the eagerness of the most unmeaning despair; they closed themselves spasmodically at the descent, although death would have been a relief, oh, how unspeakable! Still I quivered in every nerve to think how slight a sinking of the machinery would precipitate that keen, glistening ax upon my bosom. It was *hope* that prompted the nerve to quiver—the frame to shrink. It was *hope*—the hope that triumphs on the rack—that whispers to the death-condemned even in the dungeons of the Inquisition.

I saw that some ten or twelve vibrations would bring the steel in actual contact with my robe, and with this observation there suddenly came over my spirit all the keen, collected calmness of despair. For the first time during many hours—or perhaps days—I *thought*. It now occurred to me that the bandage, or surcingle, which enveloped me, was *unique*. I was tied by no separate cord. The first stroke of the razorlike crescent athwart any portion of the band would so detach it that it might be unwound from my person by means of my left hand. But how fearful, in that case, the proximity of the steel! The result of the slightest struggle, how deadly! Was it likely, moreover, that the minions[24] of the torturer had not foreseen and provided for this possibility? Was it probable that the bandage crossed my bosom in the track of the pendulum? Dreading to find my faint and, as it seemed, my last hope frustrated, I so far elevated my head as to obtain a distinct view of my breast. The surcingle enveloped my limbs and body close in all directions—*save in the path of the destroying crescent.* **(H)**

Scarcely had I dropped my head back into its original position when there flashed upon my mind what I cannot better describe than as the unformed

half of that idea of deliverance to which I had previously alluded, and of which a moiety[25] only floated indeterminately through my brain when I raised food to my burning lips. The whole thought was now present—feeble, scarcely sane, scarcely definite—but still entire. I proceeded at once, with the nervous energy of despair, to attempt its execution.

For many hours the immediate vicinity of the low framework upon which I lay had been literally swarming with rats. They were wild, bold, ravenous—their red eyes glaring upon me as if they waited but for motionlessness on my part to make me their prey. "To what food," I thought, "have they been accustomed in the well?"

They had devoured, in spite of all my efforts to prevent them, all but a small remnant of the contents of the dish. I had fallen into a habitual seesaw or wave of the hand about the platter; and, at length, the unconscious uniformity of the movement deprived it of effect. In their voracity, the vermin frequently fastened their sharp fangs in my fingers. With the particles of the oily and spicy viand which now remained, I thoroughly rubbed the bandage wherever I could reach it; then, raising my hand from the floor, I lay breathlessly still. **(I)**

At first, the ravenous animals were startled and terrified at the change—at the cessation of movement. They shrank alarmedly back; many sought the well. But this was only for a moment. I had not counted in vain upon their voracity. Observing that I remained without motion, one or two of the boldest leaped upon the framework and smelled at the surcingle. This seemed the signal for a general rush. Forth from the well they hurried in fresh troops. They clung to the wood—they overran it and leaped in hundreds upon my person. The measured movement of the pendulum disturbed them not at all. Avoiding its strokes, they busied themselves with the anointed bandage. They pressed—they swarmed upon me in ever accumulating heaps. They writhed upon my throat; their cold lips sought my own; I was half stifled by their thronging pressure; disgust for which the world has no name swelled my bosom

---

24. **minions:** servants; followers.

25. **moiety** (MOY uh tee): part.

(H) **Reading Focus** **Retelling** Retell what has happened to the narrator since he first saw the rats coming out of the pit.

(I) **Reading Focus** **Retelling** How would you retell what the narrator has just done?

Medieval torture chamber, Regensburg, Germany.

and chilled, with a heavy clamminess, my heart. Yet one minute, and I felt that the struggle would be over. Plainly I perceived the loosening of the bandage. I knew that in more than one place it must be already severed. With a more than human resolution I lay *still*.

Nor had I erred in my calculations—nor had I endured in vain. I at length felt that I was *free*. The surcingle hung in ribbons from my body. But the stroke of the pendulum already pressed upon my bosom. It had divided the serge of the robe. It had cut through the linen beneath. Twice again it swung, and a sharp sense of pain shot through every nerve. But the moment of escape had arrived. At a wave of my hand my deliverers hurried tumultuously away. With a steady movement—cautious, sidelong, shrinking, and slow—I slid from the embrace of the bandage and beyond the reach of the scimitar. For the moment, at least, *I was free.*

Free!—and in the grasp of the Inquisition! I had scarcely stepped from my wooden bed of horror upon the stone floor of the prison when the motion of the hellish machine ceased, and I beheld it drawn up, by some invisible force, through the ceiling. This was a lesson which I took desperately to heart. My every motion was undoubtedly watched. Free!—I had but escaped death in one form of agony to be delivered unto worse than death in some other. With that thought I rolled my eyes nervously around on the barriers of iron that hemmed me in. Something unusual—some change which at first I could not appreciate distinctly—it was obvious, had taken place in the apartment. For many minutes of a dreamy and trembling abstraction, I busied myself in vain, unconnected conjecture. During this period, I became aware, for the first time, of the origin of the sulfurous light which illumined the cell. It proceeded from a fissure, about half an inch in width, extending entirely around the prison at the base of the walls, which thus appeared, and were, completely separated from the floor. I endeavored, but of course in vain, to look through the aperture.

As I arose from the attempt, the mystery of the alteration in the chamber broke at once upon my understanding. I had observed that, although the outlines of the figures upon the walls were sufficiently distinct, yet the colors seemed blurred and indefinite. These colors had now assumed and were momentarily assuming, a startling and most intense brilliance that gave to the spectral and fiendish portraitures an aspect that might have thrilled even firmer nerves than my own. Demon eyes, of a wild and ghastly vivacity, glared upon me in a thousand directions where none had been visible before, and gleamed with the lurid luster of a fire that I could not force my imagination to regard as unreal.

Unreal!—even while I breathed, there came to my nostrils the breath of the vapor of heated iron! A suffocating odor pervaded the prison! A deeper glow settled each moment in the eyes that glared at my agonies! A richer tint of crimson diffused itself over the pictured horrors of blood. I panted! I gasped for breath! There could be no doubt of the design of my tormenters—oh! most unrelenting! oh! most demoniac of men! I shrank from the glowing metal to the center of the cell. Amid the thought of the fiery destruction that impended, the idea of the coolness of the well came over my soul like balm. I rushed to its deadly brink. I threw my straining vision below. The glare from the enkindled roof illumined its inmost recesses. Yet for a wild moment did my spirit refuse to comprehend the meaning of what I saw. At length it forced—it wrestled its way into my soul—it burned itself in upon my shuddering reason.—Oh! for a voice to speak!—oh! horror!—oh! any horror but this! With a shriek, I rushed from the margin and buried my face in my hands—weeping bitterly.

The heat rapidly increased, and once again I looked up, shuddering as with a fit of the ague.[26] There had been a second change in the cell—and now the change was obviously in the *form*. As before, it was in vain that I at first endeavored to appreciate or understand what was taking place. But not long was I left in doubt. The Inquisitorial vengeance had been hurried by my twofold escape, and there was to be no more dallying with the King of Terrors. The room had been square. I saw that two of its iron angles were now acute[27]—two, consequently, obtuse.[28] The fearful difference quickly increased with a low rumbling or moaning sound. In an instant the apartment had shifted its form into that of a lozenge.[29] But the alteration stopped not here—I neither hoped nor desired it to stop. I could have clasped the red walls to my bosom as a garment of eternal peace. "Death," I said, "any death but that of the pit!" Fool! Might I not have known that *into the pit* it was the object of the burning iron to urge me? Could I resist its glow? Or if even that, could I withstand its pressure? And now, flatter and flatter grew the lozenge, with a rapidity that left me no time for contemplation. Its center, and of course its greatest width, came just over the yawning gulf. I shrank back—but the closing walls pressed me resistlessly onward. At length, for my seared and writhing body, there was no longer an inch of foothold on the firm floor of the prison. I struggled no more, but the agony of my soul found vent in one loud, long, and final scream of despair. I felt that I tottered upon the brink—I averted my eyes—

There was a discordant hum of human voices! There was a loud blast as of many trumpets! There was a harsh grating as of a thousand thunders! The fiery walls rushed back! An outstretched arm caught my own as I fell, fainting, into the abyss. It was that of General Lasalle. The French army had entered Toledo. The Inquisition was in the hands of its enemies. **J**

---

26. **ague** (AY gyoo): chills.
27. **acute:** of less than 90 degrees.
28. **obtuse:** of more than 90 degrees and less than 180 degrees.
29. **lozenge:** diamond shape.

Vocabulary **averted** (uh VUR tihd) *v.:* turned away.

J **Literary Focus** **Symbolic Meaning** What might Lasalle's arrival symbolize?

Applying Your Skills

The Pit and the Pendulum

Respond and Think Critically

Reading Focus

Quick Check

1. Why is the narrator in such a terrible situation?

2. How do the narrator's torturers initially try to kill him? How does he avoid this fate?

3. How does the narrator use rats to free himself?

Read with a Purpose

4. Why is the narrator able to survive his ordeals?

Reading Skills: Retelling

5. As you read the story, you retold events that cause key changes in the narrator's condition. Now, add a column to your chart in which you write down the effects of each change in the narrator's condition.

Causes	Narrator's Condition	Effects
1. He is tried by the Inquisition. 2. He hears his death sentence.	He hallucinates and faints.	He tries to determine if he is alive or dead. Eventually, he remembers what has happened to him.

Literary Focus

Literary Analysis

6. Evaluate List at least five of the horrifying details of the story's setting. Which detail did you find most effective in evoking horror? Why?

7. Analyze How do point of view and choice of narrator affect the story's tone and credibility?

8. Make Judgments Explain whether the last-minute rescue affects the story's credibility or appeal.

Literary Skills: Symbolic Meaning

9. Analyze Some critics read Poe's story symbolically, as the story of a man who dies and almost loses his soul in the pit of hell but is saved at the very end by God. Consider these questions:

- What might the pit symbolize?
- What do the pendulum and the painted figure holding a scythe represent?
- What sounds are usually associated with Judgment Day, as the world ends? Do you hear these sounds at the end of the story?

Using details from the text, explain whether this interpretation of the story's symbolism makes sense.

Literary Skills Review: Imagery

10. Make Judgments The use of language to evoke a picture or a concrete sensation of a person, a thing, a place, or an experience is called **imagery**. Which of the five senses do you think Poe's imagery appeals to most effectively? Include support from the text in your answer.

Writing Focus

Think as a Reader/Writer

Use It in Your Writing As you read, you recorded examples of imagery, based on the five senses, that make Poe's story terrifying. In a short paragraph, transform an everyday object (like a mirror or chair), that does not normally inspire fear, into something frightening by using imagery similar to Poe's. Include at least three of the five senses in your imagery.

 What Do **You Think Now** Poe's story was inspired by historical events. Why do writers and artists sometimes look to history for creative inspiration? Explain.

Vocabulary Development

✔ Vocabulary Check

Match each Vocabulary word with its antonym (or opposite).

1. lucid   **a.** confronted

2. tumultuous   **b.** upright

3. prostrate   **c.** energy

4. lethargy   **d.** confused

5. averted   **e.** peaceful

Vocabulary Skills: Etymology

Many English words have been borrowed from other languages. A large number of words come originally from Latin or from Old English, a Germanic language that traveled to England with the Anglo-Saxons in the fifth century. Because of the long history of English and English speakers' interactions with people from all over the world, English words have also been borrowed or derived from additional languages, including Greek (*academy*), French (*debris*), Spanish (*cargo*), Persian (*khaki*), Chinese (*tea*), Dutch (*trek*), and various Native American languages (*chocolate*).

The best source to use for the history of a word's origin and development—its **etymology**—is an unabridged or college dictionary. Many dictionaries include a bracketed etymology after a word's pronunciation and part-of-speech designation. The etymology includes the word's language of origin and its original meaning. For example, the etymology of the word *avert* looks like this:

[< L *a*–, from + *vertere,* to turn]

This etymology informs you that *avert,* which means "to turn away from," comes from the Latin words for "to turn" and "from."

Your Turn

Look up the etymology of the other Vocabulary words: *lucid, tumultuous, prostrate,* and *lethargy.* In a chart like the one below, list each word, its language of origin, and its original meaning. Think about how the meaning of each word relates to the meaning of the word or words from which it comes.

Word and Definition	Language of Origin	Original Meaning
avert: "to turn away from"	Latin	*a*–, from + *vertere,* to turn

Language Coach

Word Choice In the sentence, "She *opened* the door," you can replace *opened* with *flung* for a stronger effect. In the sentences below, replace the italicized word with a stronger word or phrase.

Hearing the train approach, he *hurried* into the station.

Academic Vocabulary

Talk About

People still love stories whose characters are miraculously saved from danger at the last minute. With a partner, discuss examples of these stories from movies or television. What <u>factors</u> continue to make these stories appealing to audiences?

 **Learn It Online**
Sharpen your vocabulary skills online with *WordSharp.*

go.hrw.com   L11-357   Go

The Fall of the House of Usher /
The Pit and the Pendulum

SKILLS FOCUS **Literary Skills** Understand and analyze elements of literature from American Romanticism. **Writing Skills** Analyze unique aspects of the text; write historical investigations; incorporate suspense. **Listening and Speaking Skills** Participate in formal/informal discussions and conversations; present persuasive arguments and share opinions.

CHOICES

As you respond to the Choices, use the **Academic Vocabulary** words as appropriate: <u>factor</u>, <u>implicit</u>, <u>integral</u>, <u>principal</u>, <u>transform</u>.

REVIEW
Discuss Opinions
Group Activity By the end of "The Fall of the House of Usher," the narrator's mind teeters between sanity and madness. Review the final scenes and the fantastic events that the narrator describes: the wild storm and glowing vapors, the sounds paralleling the story he reads, Madeline's return, and the house crumbling into the tarn. Do you think these events really occurred in the story, or were they projections of the narrator's madness? Discuss your opinions about these scenes in a small group. Be sure to support your thoughts with evidence from the story.

REVIEW
Analyze an Author's Technique
Timed **Writing** Poe is considered a Dark Romantic because he created stories that explore the inner self and irrational elements of the mind. How does Poe convey the states of mind of his characters? Write a brief essay in response to this question. Support your answers with details from the stories.

CONNECT
Create a Graphic Story
TechFocus The narrator of "The Pit and the Pendulum" describes his experience in vivid detail. Use a storyboard to plan a graphic story that includes images for each major scene. Try to convey the horror of the narrator's situation through the images you choose. Then, add text from the story to connect the scenes of your graphic narrative. Share your story with your class.

CONNECT
Research the Inquisition Worldwide
Class Presentation Although "The Pit and the Pendulum" is set during the Inquisition in Spain, the Inquisition also took place in France, Germany, Portugal, Italy, and Latin America. In your school library, research more about the Inquisition in countries besides Spain. Answer the following questions: What <u>factors</u> led to the Inquisition in these countries? Who were its victims? How were they punished? After completing your research, summarize your findings and share them with your class.

EXTEND
Create a Plot Outline
Partner Work "The Fall of the House of Usher" elaborates on a basic yet chilling premise: What if someone were buried alive? Many horror and suspense stories can be boiled down to similar "What if?" premises: What if someone were brought back from the dead? What if a madman were hiding in your home? Come up with three of your own "What if?" premises for a horror or suspense story. Share your ideas with a partner. Together, choose one "What if?" premise and create a plot outline for a story based on it.

EXTEND
Make an Escape
Much of the suspense in "The Pit and the Pendulum" is built around the narrator's narrow escape from the pendulum's blade. By making the narrator's escape seem impossible and then providing a clever and unforeseen solution, Poe creates a thrilling tale. Create your own impossible situation, and think of a clever solution. Write a one-page scene that describes your situation and solution in a suspenseful way.

Learn It Online
Plan your graphic story with the storyboarding template on the Digital Storytelling mini-site.

go.hrw.com | L11-358 | **Go**

Preparing to Read

The Raven

Reader/Writer Notebook

Use your **RWN** to complete the activities for this selection.

Literary Focus

Sound Effects "The Raven" is one of the most famous poems ever written. Like a song, the poem is catchy, with pleasing **sound effects.** It is a virtuoso performance in **internal rhyme**—rhyme that occurs within a line of poetry or within consecutive lines, such as the words *dreary* and *weary* in line 1. Poe also uses **alliteration,** or the repetition of a consonant sound. Sometimes this repetition creates **onomatopoeia**—the use of words with sounds that actually echo their sense. Line 13 echoes the sound of the "silken, sad, uncertain rustling" of curtains by repeating the /s/ sound. Poe also uses **refrain,** the repetition of a phrase or line, usually at the end of a stanza ("nothing more" in stanzas 1 and 3–7).

Language Coach

Onomatopoeia Words that sound like what they describe create **onomatopoeia**. When someone in a work by Poe screams, moans, or groans in response to a horrifying event, the sound of these words echoes that horror. Words with happier meanings, such as *chortle, chuckle,* and *giggle* can also produce onomatopoeia. With a partner, create your own list of five words that sound like what they describe and read your list aloud.

Reading Focus

Interpreting Meaning Through Oral Reading Reading the poem aloud or listening to an **oral reading** draws your attention to Poe's use of rhyme, onomatopoeia, and refrain. As you read or listen, bear in mind that literary sound effects—just like movie sound effects—have a purpose. Think about what Poe is trying to accomplish with the sound effects he creates in "The Raven."

Into Action In a chart like the one below, write down the sound effects in the poem. Determine whether each sound effect is internal rhyme, alliteration, onomatopoeia, or a refrain.

Line and Example	Type of Sound Effect
line 1: dreary and weary	internal rhyme

Writing Focus

Think as a Reader/Writer

Find It in Your Reading Poe uses a regular **rhyme scheme** throughout the poem. As you read, write down the end rhymes in your *Reader/Writer Notebook*—such as *lore, door,* and *more* in the first stanza. Try to determine the rhyme scheme of the poem.

TechFocus As you read, imagine how you might underline transform this spooky poem into a radio play. What sound effects could you use to bring the poem's mood to life on the air?

 Learn It Online
Encounter this poem the multimedia way through the introductory video online.

go.hrw.com   L11-359   **Go**

POEM

The Raven

by **Edgar Allan Poe**

Read with a Purpose
Read to discover how the meaning of a single word, *nevermore,* grows as it repeats throughout the poem.

Build Background
Before writing "The Raven," Poe asked himself the question, "Of all melancholy topics, what, according to the universal understanding of mankind, is most melancholy?" His answer: death. He then decided that the most poetic version of melancholy is the death of a beautiful woman. This topic is what the speaker ponders in "The Raven," and his sorrow is embodied by the poem's title character. Like much of Poe's writing, the poem explores one aspect of the dark side of human nature—in this case, what Poe called "that species of despair which delights in self-torture."

Once upon a midnight dreary, while I pondered, weak and weary,
Over many a quaint and curious volume of forgotten lore—
While I nodded, nearly napping, suddenly there came a tapping,
As of someone gently rapping, rapping at my chamber door—
5   " 'Tis some visitor," I muttered, "tapping at my chamber door—
      Only this and nothing more." **Ⓐ**

Ah, distinctly I remember it was in the bleak December;
And each separate dying ember wrought its ghost upon the floor.
Eagerly I wished the morrow;—vainly I had sought to borrow
10 From my books surcease° of sorrow—sorrow for the lost Lenore—
For the rare and radiant maiden whom the angels name Lenore—
      Nameless *here* for evermore.

10. surcease: end.

Ⓐ Literary Focus **Sound Effects** What is the poem's rhyme scheme? Which end rhyme is repeated throughout the poem?

And the silken, sad, uncertain rustling of each purple curtain
Thrilled me—filled me with fantastic terrors never felt before;
15 So that now, to still the beating of my heart, I stood repeating
" 'Tis some visitor entreating° entrance at my chamber door—
Some late visitor entreating entrance at my chamber door;—
        This it is and nothing more."

Presently my soul grew stronger; hesitating then no longer,
20 "Sir," said I, "or Madam, truly your forgiveness I implore;°
But the fact is I was napping, and so gently you came rapping,
And so faintly you came tapping, tapping at my chamber door,
That I scarce was sure I heard you"—here I opened wide the door;—
        Darkness there and nothing more. **B**

25 Deep into that darkness peering, long I stood there wondering,
        fearing,
Doubting, dreaming dreams no mortal ever dared to dream before;
But the silence was unbroken, and the stillness gave no token,
And the only word there spoken was the whispered word, "Lenore?"
This I whispered, and an echo murmured back the word, "Lenore!"
30   Merely this and nothing more.

Back into the chamber turning, all my soul within me burning,
Soon again I heard a tapping somewhat louder than before.
"Surely," said I, "surely that is something at my window lattice;°
Let me see, then, what thereat is, and this mystery explore—
35 Let my heart be still a moment and this mystery explore;—
        'Tis the wind and nothing more!"

Open here I flung the shutter, when, with many a flirt and flutter,
In there stepped a stately Raven of the saintly days of yore;°
Not the least obeisance° made he; not a minute stopped or stayed he;
40 But, with mien° of lord or lady, perched above my chamber door—
Perched upon a bust of Pallas° just above my chamber door—
        Perched, and sat, and nothing more.

Then this ebony bird beguiling° my sad fancy into smiling,
By the grave and stern decorum of the countenance it wore,
45 "Though thy crest be shorn and shaven, thou," I said, "art sure no
        craven,
Ghastly grim and ancient Raven wandering from the Nightly shore—
Tell me what thy lordly name is on the Night's Plutonian shore!"°
        Quoth the Raven "Nevermore."

B **Literary Focus** Sound Effects What refrains close the first four stanzas? Considering that these refrains rhyme with *Lenore,* what do you think is the purpose of this sound effect?

---

16. entreating: begging; asking.

20. implore: plead; ask.

33. lattice: shutter or screen
formed by strips or bars overlaid
in a crisscross pattern.

38. Raven . . . of yore: *Of yore*
is an obsolete way of saying "of
time long past." Poe's allusion is
to 1 Kings 17:1–6, which tells of
the prophet Elijah's being fed by
ravens in the wilderness.
39. obeisance (oh BAY suhns):
gesture of respect.
40. mien (meen): manner.
41. Pallas: Pallas Athena, the
Greek goddess of wisdom.
43. beguiling: charming.

47. Plutonian shore: Pluto is the
Greek god of the underworld—
the land of darkness—called
Hades (HAY deez). Hades is
separated from the world of the
living by several rivers, hence the
mention of a shore.

Much I marveled this ungainly° fowl to hear discourse so plainly,
50 Though its answer little meaning—little relevancy bore;
For we cannot help agreeing that no living human being
Ever yet was blessed with seeing bird above his chamber door—
Bird or beast upon the sculptured bust above his chamber door,
        With such name as "Nevermore."

55 But the Raven, sitting lonely on the <u>placid bust</u>, spoke only
That one word, as if his soul in that one word he did outpour.
Nothing farther then he uttered—not a feather then he fluttered—
Till I scarcely more than muttered "Other friends have flown before—
On the morrow *he* will leave me, as my Hopes have flown before."
60   Then the bird said "Nevermore."

Startled at the stillness broken by reply so aptly spoken,
"Doubtless," said I, "what it utters is its only stock and store
Caught from some unhappy master whom unmerciful Disaster
Followed fast and followed faster till his songs one burden bore—
65 Till the dirges of his Hope that melancholy burden bore
        Of 'Never—nevermore.' "

But the Raven still beguiling my sad fancy into smiling,
Straight I wheeled a cushioned seat in front of bird, and bust and
        door;
Then, upon the velvet sinking, I betook myself to linking
70 Fancy unto fancy, thinking what this ominous bird of yore—
What this grim, ungainly, ghastly, gaunt, and ominous bird of yore
        Meant in croaking "Nevermore." **C**

This I sat engaged in guessing, but no syllable expressing
To the fowl whose fiery eyes now burned into my bosom's core;
75 This and more I sat divining,° with my head at ease reclining
On the cushion's velvet lining that the lamplight gloated o'er,
But whose velvet-violet lining with the lamplight gloating o'er,
        She shall press, ah, nevermore! **D**

49. **ungainly:** unattractive.

75. **divining:** guessing; supposing.

C Literary Focus **Sound Effects** What sound effects does Poe employ in lines
69–72? What do they reveal about the speaker's state of mind?

D Reading Focus **Oral Reading** In the fourth and fifth lines of each stanza, Poe uses
repetition as well as internal rhymes and end rhymes. Read aloud the fourth and fifth lines in
this stanza and others. What mood do these sound effects create?

Gravestone marking Poe's burial site, Westminster
Cemetery, Baltimore, Maryland.

Then, methought, the air grew denser, perfumed from an unseen
    censer
80   Swung by seraphim° whose footfalls tinkled on the tufted floor.
"Wretch," I cried, "thy God hath lent thee—by these angels he hath
    sent thee
Respite—respite and nepenthe° from thy memories of Lenore;
Quaff,° oh quaff this kind nepenthe and forget this lost Lenore!"
        Quoth the Raven "Nevermore."

85   "Prophet!" said I, "thing of evil!—prophet still, if bird or devil!—
Whether Tempter sent, or whether tempest tossed thee here ashore,
Desolate yet all undaunted,° on this desert land enchanted—
On this home by Horror haunted—tell me truly, I implore—
Is there—*is* there balm in Gilead?°—tell me—tell me, I implore!"
90   Quoth the Raven "Nevermore."

"Prophet!" said I, "thing of evil!—prophet still, if bird or devil! **E**
By that Heaven that bends above us—by that God we both adore—
Tell this soul with sorrow laden if, within the distant Aidenn,°
It shall clasp a sainted maiden whom the angels name Lenore—
95   Clasp a rare and radiant maiden whom the angels name Lenore."
        Quoth the Raven "Nevermore." **F**

"Be that word our sign of parting, bird or fiend!" I shrieked,
    upstarting—
"Get thee back into the tempest and the Night's Plutonian shore!
Leave no black plume as a token of that lie thy soul hath spoken!
100   Leave my loneliness unbroken!—quit the bust above my door!
Take thy beak from out my heart, and take thy form from off my
    door!"
        Quoth the Raven "Nevermore."

And the Raven, never flitting, still is sitting, *still* is sitting
On the pallid° bust of Pallas just above my chamber door;
105   And his eyes have all the seeming of a demon's that is dreaming,
And the lamplight o'er him streaming throws his shadow on the floor;
And my soul from out that shadow that lies floating on the floor
        Shall be lifted—nevermore!

---

80. seraphim: highest of the nine ranks of angels.

82. nepenthe (nih PEHN thee): sleeping potion that people once believed would relieve pain and sorrow.
83. quaff: drink heartily.

87. undaunted: not afraid or discouraged.

89. Is . . . Gilead: literally, "Is there any relief from my sorrow?" Poe paraphrases a line from Jeremiah 8:22: "Is there no balm in Gilead?" Gilead was a region in ancient Palestine known for its healing herbs, such as balm, an ointment.

93. Aidenn: Arabic for "Eden; Heaven."

104. pallid: pale.

E **Reading Focus** **Oral Reading** Read line 91 aloud. What internal rhyme do you hear? What principal idea receives added emphasis from this sound effect?

F **Literary Focus** **Sound Effects** Why is the meaning of *Nevermore* in this stanza especially painful for the narrator?

Respond and Think Critically

Reading Focus

Quick Check

1. What is the poem's **setting,** or time and place?

2. Trace the main events of the story, from the rap on the door to the raven's sitting on the sculpture above the chamber door.

3. At the end of the poem, what does the speaker want from the raven? What does the raven do?

Read with a Purpose

4. How does repetition of the word *nevermore* <u>transform</u> the word's meaning and effect?

Reading Skills: Interpreting Meaning Through Oral Reading

5. In the chart you completed while reading aloud or listening to the poem, add a third column in which you examine how each sound effect relates to the poem's meaning.

Line and Example	Type of Sound Effect	How It Relates to Meaning
line 1: <u>dreary</u> and <u>weary</u>	internal rhyme	calls attention to the poem's bleak mood

Literary Focus

Literary Analysis

6. **Analyze** How would you describe the **mood,** or feeling, created by the poem's setting? Which images are <u>integral</u> to the mood?

7. **Interpret** The speaker's **tone,** or attitude toward his visitor, changes as the raven gradually <u>transforms</u> from a slightly comic figure into a demonic one. Trace these changes in tone. Is there evidence suggesting that the speaker is going mad? Explain.

8. **Interpret** What, in your opinion, does the raven symbolize? Why do you suppose Poe chose a raven rather than a different kind of bird to carry this meaning?

Literary Skills: Sound Effects

9. **Make Judgments** At times, Poe's use of alliteration seems excessive, such as in line 71, in which the hard *g* is repeated four times, almost resulting in a tongue twister: "this grim, ungainly, ghastly, gaunt, and ominous bird of yore." What is your opinion of Poe's use of alliteration? Is it successful in creating striking sound effects, or is it simply distracting? Explain your answer.

Literary Skills Review: Meter

10. **Analyze** The most obvious kind of **rhythm** in a poem is produced by **meter,** the regular pattern of stressed and unstressed syllables in a line of poetry. Each stanza in "The Raven" follows the same metrical pattern. What is the pattern? How does the pattern affect the poem's sound and meaning?

Writing Focus

Think as a Reader/Writer

Use It in Your Writing As you read, you recorded examples of Poe's use of end rhyme and determined the poem's rhyme scheme. Choose an animal, other than a raven, that you find haunting or sinister. Write a 6-line stanza that uses the same rhyme scheme as Poe's poem and briefly describes some of the characteristics that make that animal haunting or sinister.

 What Do **You Think Now** Why are death and other sorrowful topics such an inspiration for poets and other artists?

Grammar Link

Using Subordinating Conjunctions: Showing Relationships

An **adverb clause** is a subordinate clause that modifies a verb, an adjective, or another adverb. It specifies *how, when, where, why, to what extent,* or *under what condition.* Adverb clauses are introduced by **subordinating conjunctions,** which show the relationship between clauses and the words they modify.

- The subordinating conjunctions *as if* and *as though* introduce an adverb clause that tells *how.*

- *After, as soon as, before, once, since, until, when, whenever,* and *while* introduce a clause that tells *when.*

- *Where* and *wherever* introduce a clause that tells *where.*

- *Because* and *so that* introduce a clause that tells *why.*

- *As long as* and *than* introduce a clause that tells *to what extent.*

- *Although, if, in order that, provided that, though,* and *unless* introduce a clause that tells *under what condition.*

Your Turn

Complete these sentences by adding subordinating conjunctions, and identify the relationship between the adverb clause and the word it modifies.

1. The speaker is sad _____ Lenore has died.
2. The raven repeats the word *Nevermore* _____ it can express the sorrow in the speaker's heart.
3. The raven will stay _____ the speaker mourns.
4. Poe wrote "The Raven" _____ he decided death was the most melancholy subject.

Writing Application Write six sentences about Poe and the works you've read by him, one sentence for each category of adverb clause: *how, when, where, why, to what extent,* and *under what condition.*

CHOICES

As you respond to the Choices, use the **Academic Vocabulary** words as appropriate: factor, implicit, integral, principal, transform.

REVIEW

Analyze "The Raven"

Timed Writing In "The Raven," Poe waits until the seventh stanza, a third of the way into his poem, to introduce the principal character. Why do you think he waits so long to introduce the raven? What is the purpose of the first part of the poem? Write a brief essay addressing these questions.

CONNECT

Find Poe's Peers

Research Activity When "The Raven" was first published in 1845, it immediately became an integral part of the popular culture. In your school library, research culture and entertainment during the 1840s and 1850s. What else was popular during this period? Look for examples of music, poetry, fiction, plays, or visual art from the same period. Gather in a small group, and share one or two samples of your findings. Discuss how the different works compare to each other and to "The Raven."

"One more time."

One more time © Tee and Charles Addams Foundation.

EXTEND

Present Poe on the Radio

TechFocus With a small group, transform "The Raven" into a radio play. Decide who will be the narrator and in what voice he or she will speak. Then, create sound effects and/or music to accompany the poem. Rehearse your performance, and tape it for a presentation to your class.

Preparing to Read

from Moby-Dick

What Do You Think? Where does an individual find inspiration?

⏱ **QuickWrite**

Think of an experience from your past or someone else's past that still evokes strong emotions for you or that person. Write a paragraph about the experience and its effects.

MEET THE WRITER

Herman Melville
(1819–1891)

The central irony of Herman Melville's career is that his masterpiece, *Moby-Dick,* now considered one of the greatest American novels, was almost wholly ignored while its author was alive. Melville spent the last years of his life in obscurity and believed that he was a failure.

A Career at Sea

Melville was born into a distinguished Boston family, but his father went bankrupt in 1830 and died soon after. Faced with a grim life at home, Melville went to sea in 1839 on a merchant ship. A whaling expedition to the South Seas followed in 1841. A year and a half later, Melville jumped ship at the Marquesas Islands and then signed on to an Australian ship, which he deserted at Papeete. He roamed the islands of Tahiti and Moorea before joining a whaler to Honolulu and then enlisting on a U.S. Navy frigate. When his ship docked at Boston in October 1844, a career's worth of seagoing adventure had ended.

Spinning Tales of Adventure

In less than two years, Melville produced a book of slightly fictionalized travel memoirs, *Typee,* that became an immediate success. He published four other semiautobiographical sea tales between 1847 and 1850.

For his next project, Melville wanted to write an ambitious book that would exploit his whaling experience and seek the ultimate truth of human existence. The book, *Moby-Dick,* was finished in July 1851. Despite Melville's expectations, it failed to achieve success. Melville hoped to change his fortunes with the three novels he published in the next six years, but they were all poorly received. By 1866, he was earning so little as a writer that he had to take a job as a customs inspector.

Later, his wife's receipt of a small inheritance allowed Melville to work on *Billy Budd.* At his death in 1891, the novella lay unwanted in a desk drawer. Published thirty-three years later, it was acclaimed a masterpiece. Near the desk where Melville had worked, a note read, "Keep true to the dreams of thy youth."

Think About the Writer How might Melville's early misfortune have ultimately led to his success as a writer? Explain.

Reader/Writer Notebook

Use your **RWN** to complete the activities for this selection.

Literary Focus

Characterization The process by which a writer reveals a character's personality is called **characterization.** A writer can reveal a character by telling us directly what the character is like: benevolent, greedy, and so on. This method is called **direct characterization.** A writer can also present a character indirectly so that we can draw our own conclusions. Using **indirect characterization**, a writer describes the character's appearance, actions, thoughts, and feelings, and shows how other characters are affected by—and respond to—the character. This excerpt directly reveals Captain Ahab's personality <u>principally</u> through his words and actions. We also learn about Ahab's personality indirectly through the other characters' responses to him.

Reading Focus

Drawing Inferences About Characters You can determine what the text reveals about a character by **drawing inferences** based on the character's appearance, thoughts, words, and actions, and how others respond to the character. In this excerpt, you can draw inferences from the crew's reactions to Ahab.

Into Action As you read, use a chart like the one below to record how the harpooners (Queequeg, Tashtego, and Daggoo) and the mates (Starbuck, Stubb, and Flask) react to Ahab and his quest. Then, determine each character's feelings about Ahab by drawing inferences based on the characters' reactions.

Character	How the Character Reacts to Ahab and His Quest	How He Feels About Ahab
Stubb	He whispers his opinions to others and does not challenge Ahab directly.	He is afraid of Ahab.
Starbuck		

Writing Focus

Think as a Reader/Writer

Find It in Your Reading In this excerpt, Melville uses vibrant **dialogue** to bring his characters to life. In your *Reader/Writer Notebook,* record the key lines of dialogue that reveal the different characters' personalities.

Vocabulary

luster (LUHS tuhr) *n.:* brightness; shine. *Ahab's piece of Spanish gold sparkled with a rich luster.*

inarticulate (ihn ahr TIHK yuh liht) *adj.:* not uttered in distinct syllables or words; mumbled. *As Ahab paced the deck by himself, you could hear his inarticulate muttering.*

inscrutable (ihn SKROO tuh buhl) *adj.:* mysterious. *Starbuck did not support Ahab's inscrutable obsession with Moby-Dick.*

wreak (reek) *v.:* inflict. *Ahab was determined to wreak vengeance upon Moby-Dick.*

volition (voh LIHSH uhn) *n.:* will. *Ahab seemed to fill the men with his own intense volition.*

Language Coach

Multiple Meanings Some words are pronounced and spelled the same way, but they have more than one meaning. A phone may ring (verb), but when you wear a ring (noun) around your finger, the meaning of the word changes. With a partner, identify the word in each sentence below that has more than one meaning. Then, write a second sentence using an additional meaning of that word. You can check a dictionary to verify the different meanings.

1. He asked to ship this package later.
2. I am scheduled to work on the night shift.
3. She wants to coin a new word.

Learn It Online
Listen to this excerpt online.

go.hrw.com | L11-367 | Go

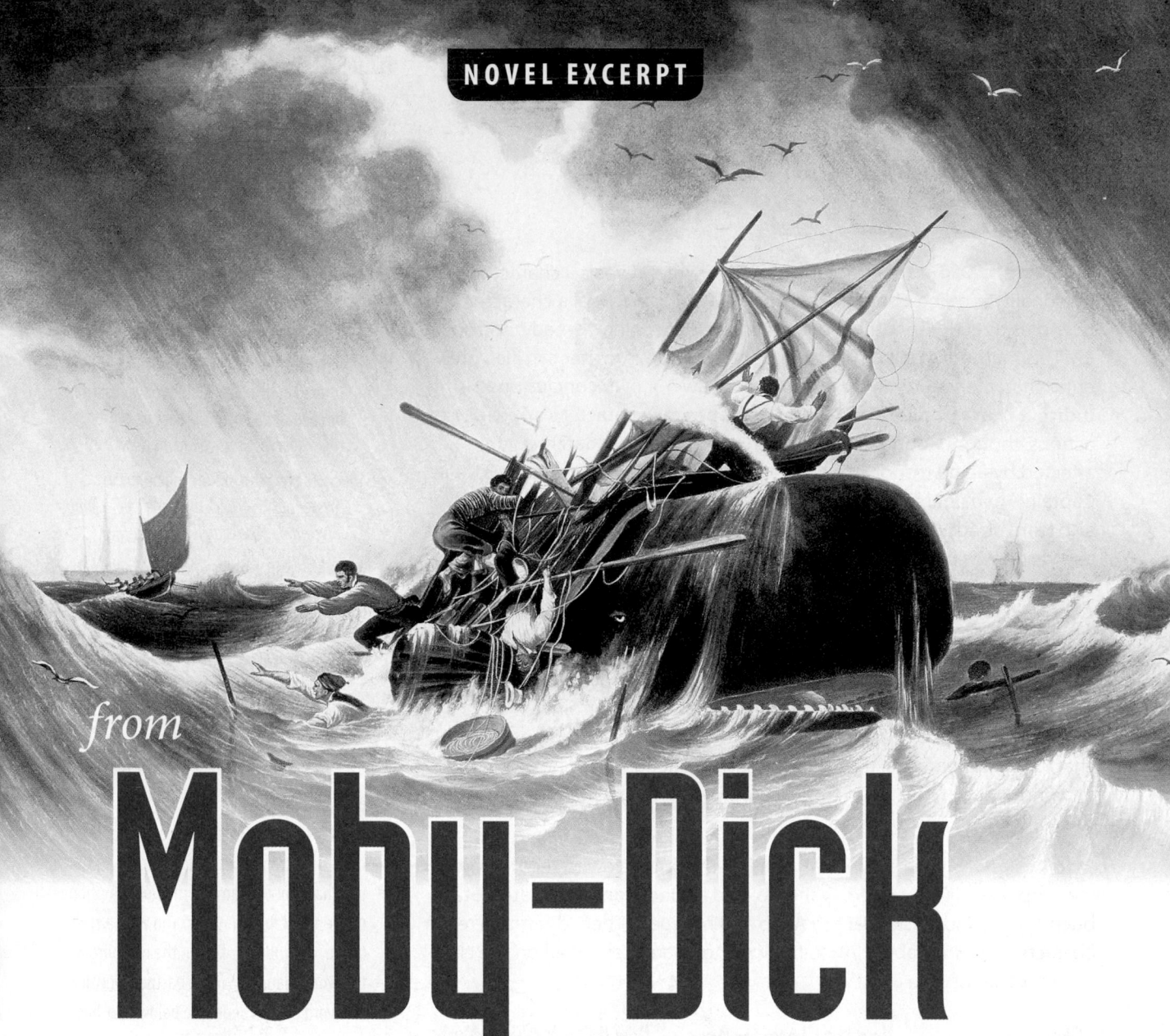

from

Moby-Dick

by **Herman Melville**

Read with a Purpose

Read to discover how the crew aboard the *Pequod* reacts to Captain Ahab's obsessive pursuit of Moby-Dick.

Build Background

Melville's epic novel, *Moby-Dick,* tells the story of one man's relentless pursuit of an elusive, seemingly invincible white whale. The man is the mysterious and obsessive Captain Ahab, commander of the whaling ship *Pequod.* Ahab is seeking revenge against Moby-Dick, the whale that years before took off his leg. His quest takes on a meaning that goes beyond simple vengeance. The *Pequod's* officers and crew are an assortment of men from all over the world, such as South Pacific Islanders and Massachusetts Indians. The harpooners are Queequeg, Tashtego, and Daggoo; the first, second, and third mates are Starbuck, Stubb, and Flask, respectively. The narrator of the novel, Ishmael, has joined the voyage as a common sailor. The book opens with one of the most famous sentences in literature: "Call me Ishmael."

The Sperm Whale in a Flurry from 'The Whale Fishery', published by Currier & Ives. Color lithograph.

The quarter-deck is a center of dramatic action in Moby-Dick. *Here Ahab calls the men to assemble on the deck and reveals his secret purpose—to track down and kill the great white whale. He binds the crew—even Starbuck, the reluctant first mate—to his relentless pursuit. The whaling voyage, which was to be an ordinary business venture, becomes instead the instrument of Ahab's vengeance.*

The Quarter-Deck

(Enter Ahab: Then all.)

It was not a great while after the affair of the pipe,[1] that one morning shortly after breakfast, Ahab, as was his wont, ascended the cabin gangway to the deck. There most sea captains usually walk at that hour, as country gentlemen, after the same meal, take a few turns in the garden.

Soon his steady, ivory stride was heard, as to and fro he paced his old rounds, upon planks so familiar to his tread, that they were all over dented, like geological stones, with the peculiar mark of his walk. Did you fixedly gaze, too, upon that ribbed and dented brow; there also, you would see still stranger footprints—the footprints of his one unsleeping, ever-pacing thought.

But on the occasion in question, those dents looked deeper, even as his nervous step that morning left a deeper mark. And, so full of his thought was Ahab, that at every uniform turn that he made, now at the mainmast and now at the binnacle,[2] you could almost see that thought turn in him as he turned, and pace in him as he paced; so completely possessing him, indeed, that it all but seemed the inward mold of every outer movement.

"D'ye mark him, Flask?" whispered Stubb; "the chick that's in him pecks the shell. 'Twill soon be out."

The hours wore on—Ahab now shut up within his cabin; anon, pacing the deck, with the same intense bigotry of purpose in his aspect.

It drew near the close of day. Suddenly he came to a halt by the bulwarks,[3] and inserting his bone leg into the auger hole there, and with one hand grasping a shroud, he ordered Starbuck to send everybody aft.

"Sir!" said the mate, astonished at an order seldom or never given on shipboard except in some extraordinary case.

"Send everybody aft," repeated Ahab. "Mastheads, there! Come down!"

When the entire ship's company were assembled, and with curious and not wholly unapprehensive faces were eyeing him, for he looked not unlike the weather horizon when a storm is coming up, Ahab, after rapidly glancing over the bulwarks, and then darting his eyes among the crew, started from his standpoint; and as though not a soul were nigh him resumed his heavy turns upon the deck. With bent head and half-slouched hat he continued to pace; unmindful of the wondering whispering among the men; till Stubb cautiously whispered to Flask, that Ahab must have summoned them there for the purpose of witnessing a pedestrian feat. But this did not last long. Vehemently pausing, he cried—

"What do ye do when ye see a whale, men?"

"Sing out for him!" was the impulsive rejoinder[4] from a score of clubbed[5] voices.

"Good!" cried Ahab, with a wild approval in his tones; observing the hearty animation into which his unexpected question had so magnetically thrown them.

"And what do ye next, men?"

"Lower away, and after him!"

"And what tune is it ye pull to, men?"

"A dead whale or a stove[6] boat!"

---

1. **affair of the pipe:** Ahab had thrown his pipe overboard one evening when he realized that he had no business with "this thing that is meant for sereneness."
2. **binnacle:** upright stand holding the ship's compass.

3. **bulwarks:** above-deck part of a ship's side.
4. **rejoinder:** answer.
5. **clubbed:** united.
6. **stove:** with a hole smashed in it.

Ⓐ **Literary Focus** **Characterization** What do you learn about Ahab from this description?

More and more strangely and fiercely glad and approving grew the countenance of the old man at every shout; while the mariners began to gaze curiously at each other, as if marveling how it was that they themselves became so excited at such seemingly purposeless questions. **Ⓑ**

But, they were all eagerness again, as Ahab, now half-revolving in his pivot hole, with one hand reaching high up a shroud, and tightly, almost convulsively grasping it, addressed them thus—

"All ye mastheaders have before now heard me give orders about a white whale. Look ye! d'ye see this Spanish ounce of gold?"—holding up a broad bright coin to the sun—"it is a sixteen-dollar piece, men. D'ye see it? Mr. Starbuck, hand me yon top-maul."[7]

While the mate was getting the hammer, Ahab, without speaking, was slowly rubbing the gold piece against the skirts of his jacket, as if to heighten its luster, and without using any words was meanwhile lowly humming to himself, producing a sound so strangely muffled and inarticulate that it seemed the mechanical humming of the wheels of his vitality in him.

Receiving the top-maul from Starbuck, he advanced toward the mainmast with the hammer uplifted in one hand, exhibiting the gold with the other, and with a high raised voice exclaiming: "Whosoever of ye raises me a white-headed whale with a wrinkled brow and a crooked jaw; whosoever of ye raises me that white-headed whale, with three holes punctured in his starboard fluke[8]—look ye, whosoever of ye raises me that same white whale, he shall have this gold ounce, my boys!"

"Huzza! huzza!" cried the seamen, as with swinging tarpaulins they hailed the act of nailing the gold to the mast.

"It's a white whale, I say," resumed Ahab, as he threw down the top-maul; "a white whale. Skin your eyes for him, men; look sharp for white water; if ye see but a bubble, sing out."

All this while Tashtego, Daggoo, and Queequeg had looked on with even more intense interest and surprise than the rest, and at the mention of the wrinkled brow and crooked jaw they had started as if each was separately touched by some specific recollection.

"Captain Ahab," said Tashtego, "that white whale must be the same that some call Moby-Dick."

"Moby-Dick?" shouted Ahab. "Do ye know the white whale then, Tash?"

"Does he fantail[9] a little curious, sir, before he goes down?" said the Gay-Header deliberately.

"And has he a curious spout, too," said Daggoo, "very bushy, even for a parmacety,[10] and mighty quick, Captain Ahab?"

"And he have one, two, tree—oh! good many iron in him hide, too, Captain," cried Queequeg disjointedly, "all twiske-tee be-twisk, like him—him—" faltering hard for a word, and screwing his hand round and round as though uncorking a bottle—"like him—him—"

"Corkscrew!" cried Ahab, "aye, Queequeg, the harpoons lie all twisted and wrenched in him; aye, Daggoo, his spout is a big one, like a whole shock of wheat, and white as a pile of our Nantucket wool after the great annual sheepshearing; aye, Tashtego, and he fantails like a split jib in a squall. Death and devils! men, it is Moby-Dick ye have seen—Moby-Dick—Moby-Dick!"

"Captain Ahab," said Starbuck, who, with Stubb and Flask, had thus far been eyeing his superior with increasing surprise, but at last seemed struck with a thought which somewhat explained all the wonder. "Captain Ahab, I have heard of Moby-Dick—but it was not Moby-Dick that took off thy leg?"

"Who told thee that?" cried Ahab; then pausing, "Aye, Starbuck; aye, my hearties all round; it was Moby-Dick that dismasted me; Moby-Dick that brought me to this dead stump I stand on now. Aye, Aye," he shouted, with a terrific, loud, animal sob, like

---

7. **top-maul:** heavy wooden hammer.
8. **starboard fluke:** right-hand side of the whale's tail.

9. **fantail:** spread the tail like a fan.
10. **parmacety** (pahr muh SEHT ee): slang for "spermaceti" (a sperm whale).

Ⓑ **Reading Focus** **Drawing Inferences** Based on the crew's reaction here, what inferences can you draw about these crewmen?

Vocabulary **luster** (LUHS tuhr) *n.:* brightness; shine.
inarticulate (ihn ahr TIHK yuh liht) *adj.:* not uttered in distinct syllables or words; mumbled.

Analyzing Visuals

Viewing and Interpreting
Compare the atmosphere in this painting to the atmosphere aboard the *Pequod* in this excerpt from *Moby-Dick*. If time allows, share your ideas with a small group or with the class as a whole.

The Spirit-Spout by George Klauba. Acrylic on panel, h 18" × w 14^1/$_2$"

that of a heart-stricken moose; "Aye, aye! it was that accursed white whale that razeed[11] me; made a poor pegging lubber[12] of me for ever and a day!" Then tossing both arms, with measureless imprecations[13] he shouted out: "Aye, aye! and I'll chase him round Good Hope and round the Horn, and round the Norway Maelstrom, and round perdition's flames before I give him up. And this is what ye have shipped for, men! to chase that white whale on both sides of land, and over all sides of earth, till he spouts black blood and rolls fin out. What say ye, men, will ye splice[14] hands on it, now? I think ye do look brave." **C**

"Aye, aye!" shouted the harpooners and seamen, running closer to the excited old man: "a sharp eye for the White Whale; a sharp lance for Moby-Dick!"

"God bless ye," he seemed to half sob and half shout. "God bless ye, men. Steward! Go draw the great measure of grog.[15] But what's this long face about, Mr. Starbuck; wilt thou not chase the White Whale? Art not game for Moby-Dick?"

---

11. **razeed** (ray ZEED): to razee is to make a wooden warship lower by removing the upper deck. Here, Ahab means that the whale reduced him to this low state.
12. **lubber:** big, slow, clumsy person.
13. **imprecations** (ihm pruh KAY shuhnz): curses.

14. **splice:** join.
15. **grog:** watered-down liquor drunk by sailors.

C Reading Focus **Drawing Inferences** What can you infer about Ahab's character from his words to the crew?

"I am game for his crooked jaw, and for the jaws of Death too, Captain Ahab, if it fairly comes in the way of the business we follow; but I came here to hunt whales, not my commander's vengeance. How many barrels will thy vengeance yield thee even if thou gettest it, Captain Ahab? It will not fetch thee much in our Nantucket market."

"Nantucket market! Hoot! But come closer, Starbuck; thou requirest a little lower layer. If money's to be the measurer, man, and the accountants have computed their great countinghouse the globe, by girdling it with guineas, one to every three parts of an inch; then, let me tell thee, that my vengeance will fetch a great premium *here*!"

"He smites his chest," whispered Stubb, "what's that for? Methinks it rings most vast, but hollow."

"Vengeance on a dumb brute!" cried Starbuck, "that simply smote thee from blindest instinct! Madness! To be enraged with a dumb thing, Captain Ahab, seems blasphemous." **D**

"Hark ye yet again—the little lower layer. All visible objects, man, are but as pasteboard masks. But in each event—in the living act, the undoubted deed—there, some unknown but still reasoning thing puts forth the moldings of its features from behind the unreasoning mask. If man will strike, strike through the mask! How can the prisoner reach outside except by thrusting through the wall? To me, the White Whale is that wall, shoved near to me. Sometimes I think there's naught beyond. But 'tis enough. He tasks me; he heaps me; I see in him outrageous strength, with an inscrutable malice sinewing it. That inscrutable thing is chiefly what I hate; and be the White Whale agent, or be the White Whale principal, I will wreak that hate upon him. Talk not to me of blasphemy, man; I'd strike the sun if it insulted me. For could the sun do that, then could I do the other; since there is ever a sort of fair play herein, jealousy presiding over all creations. But not my master, man, is even that fair play. Who's over me? Truth hath no confines. Take off thine eye! More intolerable than fiends' glarings is a doltish stare! So, so; thou reddenest and palest; my heat has melted thee to anger-glow. But look ye, Starbuck, what is said in heat, that thing unsays itself. There are men from whom warm words are small indignity. I meant not to incense thee. Let it go. Look! see yonder Turkish cheeks of spotted tawn—living, breathing pictures painted by the sun. The pagan leopards—the unrecking and unworshipping things, that live; and seek, and give no reasons for the torrid life they feel! The crew, man, the crew! Are they not one and all with Ahab, in this matter of the whale? See Stubb! he laughs! See yonder Chilean! he snorts to think of it. Stand up amid the general hurricane, thy one tossed sapling cannot, Starbuck! And what is it? Reckon it. 'Tis but to help strike a fin; no wondrous feat for Starbuck. What is it more? From this one poor hunt, then, the best lance out of all Nantucket, surely he will not hang back, when every foremast-hand has clutched a whetstone? Ah! constrainings seize thee; I see! the billow lifts thee! Speak, but speak!—Aye, aye! thy silence, then, *that* voices thee. *(Aside)* Something shot from my dilated nostrils, he has inhaled it in his lungs. Starbuck now is mine; cannot oppose me now, without rebellion."

"God keep me!—keep us all!" murmured Starbuck lowly. **E**

But in his joy at the enchanted, tacit[16] acquiescence of the mate, Ahab did not hear his foreboding invocation; nor yet the low laugh from the hold; nor yet the presaging vibrations of the winds in the cordage; nor yet the hollow flap of the sails against the masts, as for a moment their hearts sank in. For again Starbuck's downcast eyes lighted up with the stubbornness of life; the subterranean laugh died away; the winds blew on; the sails filled out; the ship heaved and rolled as before. Ah, ye admonitions and warnings! Why stay ye not when ye come? But rather are ye predictions than warnings, ye shadows! Yet not so much predictions from without, as verifications of the

---

16. **tacit:** implied but not expressed openly.

D **Literary Focus** Characterization This dialogue provides a strong characterization of Starbuck. What do Starbuck's words reveal about his personality?

E **Reading Focus** Drawing Inferences Based on the fact that Starbuck says this almost to himself and not to Ahab, what can you infer about how Starbuck's viewpoint has changed?

Vocabulary inscrutable (ihn SKROO tuh buhl) *adj:* mysterious. **wreak** (reek) *v.:* inflict.

foregoing things within. For with little external to constrain us, the innermost necessities in our being, these still drive us on.

"The measure! the measure!" cried Ahab.

Receiving the brimming pewter, and turning to the harpooneers, he ordered them to produce their weapons. Then ranging them before him near the capstan,[17] with their harpoons in their hands, while his three mates stood at his side with their lances, and the rest of the ship's company formed a circle round the group; he stood for an instant searchingly eyeing every man of his crew. But those wild eyes met his, as the bloodshot eyes of the prairie wolves meet the eye of their leader, ere he rushes on at their head in the trail of the bison; but, alas! only to fall into the hidden snare of the Indian.

"Drink and pass!" he cried, handing the heavy charged flagon to the nearest seaman. "The crew alone now drink. Round with it, round! Short drafts—long swallows, men; 'tis hot as Satan's hoof. So, so; it goes round excellently. It spiralizes in ye; forks out at the serpent-snapping eye. Well done; almost drained. That way it went, this way it comes. Hand it me—here's a hollow! Men, ye seem the years; so brimming life is gulped and gone. Steward, refill!

"Attend now, my braves. I have mustered ye all round this capstan; and ye, mates, flank me with your lances; and ye, harpooneers, stand there with your irons; and ye, stout mariners, ring me in, that I may in some sort revive a noble custom of my fisherman fathers before me. O men, you will yet see that— Ha! boy, come back? bad pennies come not sooner. Hand it me. Why, now, this pewter had run brimming again, wert not thou St. Vitus's imp[18]—away, thou ague! **F**

_____

17. **capstan:** similar to a winch; a large cylinder, usually on a ship's deck, around which cables are wound to lift heavy objects such as anchors and weights.
18. **St. Vitus's imp:** Saint Vitus is the patron saint of people ill with chorea, a nervous disorder characterized by irregular, jerking movements. An imp is a mischievous child or young demon. Ahab is complaining that the steward's clumsiness caused the pitcher of grog to be spilled.

"Advance, ye mates! Cross your lances full before me. Well done! Let me touch the axis." So saying, with extended arm, he grasped the three level, radiating lances at their crossed center; while so doing, suddenly and nervously twitched them; meanwhile, glancing intently from Starbuck to Stubb, from Stubb to Flask. It seemed as though, by some nameless, interior volition, he would fain have shocked into them the same fiery emotion accumulated within the Leyden jar[19] of his own magnetic life. The three mates quailed before his strong, sustained, and mystic aspect. Stubb and Flask looked sideways from him; the honest eye of Starbuck fell downright.

"In vain!" cried Ahab; "but, maybe, 'tis well. For did ye three but once take the full-forced shock, then mine own electric thing, _that_ had perhaps expired from out me. Perchance, too, it would have dropped ye dead. Perchance ye need it not. Down lances! And now, ye mates, I do appoint ye three cupbearers to my three pagan kinsmen there—yon three most honorable gentlemen and noblemen, my valiant harpooneers. Disdain the task? What, when the great Pope washes the feet of beggars, using his tiara for ewer?[20] Oh, my sweet cardinals! your own condescension, _that_ shall bend ye to it. I do not order ye; ye will it. Cut your seizings and draw the poles, ye harpooneers!"

Silently obeying the order, the three harpooneers now stood with the detached iron part of their harpoons, some three feet long, held, barbs up, before him.

"Stab me not with that keen steel! Cant[21] them; cant them over! know ye not the goblet end? Turn up the socket! So, so; now, ye cupbearers, advance. The irons! take them; hold them while I fill!" Forthwith, slowly going from one officer to the other, he brimmed the harpoon sockets with the fiery waters from the pewter.

_____

19. **Leyden jar:** device for storing electrical charges.
20. **tiara for ewer:** literally, "crown for a pitcher"; a reference to the practice in which the pope washes the feet of poor people on Holy Thursday in imitation of Jesus' washing the feet of his disciples.
21. **cant:** overturn or tilt.

F **Literary Focus** **Characterization** What does this moment of interruption to complain about the steward's clumsiness reveal about Ahab's personality?

Vocabulary **volition** (voh LIHSH uhn) _n._: will.

Like an Open-Doored Marble Tomb by George Klauba. Acrylic on panel, h 18" × w 14 ½"

"Now, three to three, ye stand. Commend the murderous chalices! Bestow them, ye who are now made parties to this indissoluble league. Ha! Starbuck! but the deed is done! Yon ratifying sun now waits to sit upon it. Drink, ye harpooneers! drink and swear, ye men that man the deathful whaleboat's bow—Death to Moby-Dick! God hunt us all, if we do not hunt Moby-Dick to his death!" The long, barbed steel goblets were lifted; and to cries and maledictions[22] against the White Whale, the spirits were simultaneously quaffed down with a hiss. Starbuck paled, and turned, and shivered.

22. **maledictions** (mal uh DIHK shuhnz): curses.

Once more, and finally, the replenished pewter went the rounds among the frantic crew; when, waving his free hand to them, they all dispersed; and Ahab retired within his cabin. **G**

G **Reading Focus** Drawing Inferences What can you infer about Starbuck from the way he responds to Ahab's speech? What can you infer about the rest of the crew from their actions?

SKILLS FOCUS **Literary Skills** Analyze characterization; analyze setting. **Reading Skills** Draw inferences about characters. **Vocabulary Skills** Identify antonyms. **Writing Skills** Develop characters using dialogue.

Respond and Think Critically

Reading Focus

Quick Check

1. What does Stubb observe about Ahab during the day, before the crew assembles for Ahab's speech?

2. What three details does Ahab use to identify Moby-Dick?

Read with a Purpose

3. How do different members of the crew respond to Ahab's obsession with Moby-Dick?

Reading Skills: Drawing Inferences About Characters

4. As you read, you recorded inferences about the crew's feelings toward Ahab. Add a column to your chart, and record what you can infer about Ahab from other characters' reactions to him.

Character	How the Character Reacts to Ahab and His Quest	How He Feels About Ahab	What You Can Infer About Ahab's Personality
Stubb	He whispers his opinions to others and does not challenge Ahab directly.	He is afraid of Ahab.	Ahab may have a tendency to be cruel.

✓ Vocabulary Check

Match each Vocabulary word with its antonym (word with opposite meaning):

5. luster
6. inarticulate
7. inscrutable
8. wreak
9. volition

a. eloquent
b. undo
c. obvious
d. indecision
e. dullness

Literary Focus

Literary Analysis

10. **Interpret** Explain Ahab's famous metaphor comparing visible objects to "pasteboard masks" (page 372). What do you think he means when he says "strike through the mask"?

11. **Evaluate** Do you think Captain Ahab's obsession is convincing? Explain.

Literary Skills: Characterization

12. **Draw Conclusions** Is Ahab passionately inspired or dangerously obsessed? Explain how his behavior or speech supports your answer.

Literary Skills Review: Setting

13. **Interpret** The **setting** is the time and place in which a story occurs. How does the setting of *Moby-Dick* contribute to its dramatic story?

Writing Focus

Think as a Reader/Writer

Use It in Your Writing Dialogue is one of the <u>principal</u> methods of characterization that Melville uses in this excerpt. Think of an interesting person you know whose personality is expressed in the way he or she speaks. Write a one-page dialogue that demonstrates how this person's speech helps to characterize him or her.

What Do You Think Now

We frequently think of inspiration as a creative force. Is this the case with Ahab? Explain your answer.

Writing Workshop

Short Story

Write with a Purpose

Write a short story that engages readers with a strong plot, complex characters, and a vivid setting. Your **purpose** for writing is to entertain your readers and to express yourself creatively. Your **audience** is classmates, your teacher, and others who can enjoy your story.

A Good Short Story

- creates interesting, complex characters
- takes place in a vivid setting
- initiates the action with a conflict that builds toward a climax and is resolved
- uses a clear, consistent point of view
- incorporates stylistic devices to enhance its style

See page 384 for complete rubric.

Think as a Reader/Writer
In this unit, you have studied some key techniques that writers use to create narratives. Now you'll use those same techniques to write a **short story.** Before you begin writing, read the following excerpt from Tim O'Brien's story "Speaking of Courage" on page 1196:

The war was over, and there was no place in particular to go. Paul Berlin followed the tar road in its seven-mile loop around the lake, then he started all over again, driving slowly, feeling safe inside his father's big Chevy, now and again looking out onto the lake to watch the boats and waterskiers and scenery. It was Sunday and it was summer, and things seemed pretty much the same. . . .

O'Brien introduces the main character, sets the scene, and hints at the conflict.

It was a good-sized lake. In high school he'd driven round and round and round with his friends and pretty girls, talking about urgent matters, worrying eagerly about the existence of God. . . . Then, there had not been a war. Still, it was the town's only lake, the only one in twenty-six miles, and at night the moon made a white swath across its waters, and on sunny days it was nice to look at, and that evening it would dazzle with the reflections of fireworks, and it was the center of things from the very start, always there to be driven around, still mesmerizing and quieting and a good audience for silence, a seven-mile flat circumference that could be traveled by slow car in twenty-five minutes. It was not such a good lake for swimming. After college, he'd caught an ear infection that had almost kept him out of the war. And the lake had drowned Max Arnold, keeping him out of the war entirely. . . . Before the war, they'd driven around the lake as friends, but now Max was dead and most of the others were living in Des Moines or Sioux City, or going to school somewhere, or holding down jobs. None of the girls was left. His father would not talk. His father had been in another war, so he knew the truth already, and he would not talk about it, and there was no one left to talk with.

He describes the main character and setting more fully.

He introduces the story's main conflict.

Reader/Writer Notebook

Use your **RWN** to complete the activities for this workshop.

Think About the Professional Model
With a partner, discuss the following questions about the model:

1. What do you think this story will be about? Why do you think so?
2. What details support the claim that everything is "pretty much the same"?

Prewriting

Explore Story Ideas

The eerie tales in Collection 5 are good examples of stories that start with an intriguing "What if?" premise. *What if a minister suddenly began wearing a dark veil* ("The Minister's Black Veil")? *What if a house could drive people to madness* ("The Fall of the House of Usher")? Using your imagination to explore different "What if?" scenarios is a good way to brainstorm story ideas. Since your purpose is to entertain readers, try to think of "What if?" questions whose answers might intrigue them. The **situation** you decide on is the starting point for developing the rest of your story.

Imagine Characters and Setting

Characters Once you have a story idea, imagine the **characters**—the people who will appear in the story. Short stories usually focus on one or two complex, interesting **main characters** and sometimes include a small number of **minor characters** as well. In your writing, use several **characterization** techniques to bring these individuals to life.

- Provide detailed **physical descriptions** of the character's **appearance** to reveal key character traits. How does the character look and move? What do his or her **actions** reveal? What distinctive **gestures** or **expressions** characterize him or her? Use **concrete sensory details** that describe the characters' behavior and actions to develop and reveal information about them.

- Show the **conflicts** the character faces. Is the character the cause of his or her own conflict? What personality traits come to light as the character faces the conflict? Does he or she grow because of the conflict?

- Use **dialogue** (the character's actual words) and **interior monologue** (a character's unspoken thoughts and feelings) to reveal personality and **perspective,** or **point of view.** How does the character speak and think? Is there any disconnect between what the character says to others, thinks to himself or herself, and does?

Setting Just as you have created interesting characters, imagine a vivid **setting,** or time and place, for your story. Locate each of the story's **scenes** and **incidents** in **specific places,** with unique sights, sounds, and smells that you describe with concrete **sensory details.** Limit your setting to one or two places to keep your short story focused.

Think About Purpose and Audience

As you plan your short story, keep your purpose and audience in mind. Your **purpose** in writing a short story is to entertain readers and to express yourself creatively. Your **audience** will be your teacher and classmates but also may include a wider audience of teens and young adult readers across the country. What effect do you want your story to have on them?

Idea Starters

- A real-life situation
- An interesting-looking person
- A news story
- A dream
- An inexplicable sound, smell, sight, or event

Your Turn _____

Get Started Using your own ideas or the suggestions on this page, brainstorm story ideas. In your **RWN,** write notes about the **characters** you will bring to life in your story and about the story's **setting.** Keep your **purpose** and **audience** in mind as your story begins to take shape.

Learn It Online
To see how one writer completed this assignment, see the model short story online.

go.hrw.com   L11-377   **Go**

Plot Your Story

To keep your readers interested in the situation, characters, and setting you've chosen, something has to happen. The **sequence of events** in a short story is called the **plot.** Most plots begin with an **exposition,** which introduces the characters, their setting, and their **conflict**—a problem or struggle of some kind. Next is the **rising action,** in which **complications** arise as the characters attempt to resolve their conflict. The conflict escalates until it reaches a breaking point, or **climax.** At the **denouement,** or **resolution,** the conflict is settled and the story ends. Here are some questions you can use to help you develop your plot:

- **Conflict:** What's the problem facing your main characters? Do they have a conflict with one another, or with some other external or internal force?

- **Rising Action:** What do the characters do as they struggle? How do their actions or decisions further complicate the problem? What complications are caused by outside forces?

- **Climax:** What happens to make the conflict reach a crisis, or breaking point? What does this crisis look like? feel like?

- **Denouement:** How is the crisis resolved? How have the characters changed by the end of the story? What is the significance of what has happened? What **theme,** or insight about life, do the events in the story reveal?

Decide when to vary the **pace** in your short story—the rate at which you relate events. You can build **suspense,** a feeling of uncertainty and curiosity about what will happen next in the story, by lingering over details that describe character or setting, or you can create **tension** by speeding up the narrative.

To map out your story's plot, create a plot plan like the one below.

Types of Conflict

External: Character struggles with outside forces, such as another character or something in his or her environment.

Internal: Character struggles with something inside himself or herself, such as insecurity or pride.

● Writing Tip

Don't be afraid to vary from your plot plan. Creative writing calls for being flexible at times. Revisit and revise your plot plan as often as needed.

Your Turn

Plot It Out To help you develop an engaging plot for your story, make a **plot plan** like the one on this page for your own story. As you plan, keep your **purpose** and **audience** in mind. What kinds of **conflict** would intrigue your readers, and what might surprise them?

Plot Plan

<u>Characters:</u> David and Nadine

<u>Setting:</u> kitchen at David's house

<u>Conflict:</u> A college letter has arrived; David hesitates to open it. His conflict is internal. He fights his nervousness and insecurities about his future.

<u>Rising action:</u> Nadine comes in, gets a drink of water, and reads the letter silently.

<u>Climax:</u> Nadine tells David that he is accepted to college in Boston.

<u>Denouement:</u> Nadine and David watch a movie together, knowing everything has changed.

Drafting

Organize and Draft Your Short Story

Although you'll present most plot points in **chronological order,** you may sometimes skip forward in time (**flash-forward**) or backward (**flashback**). Use the **Writer's Framework** to the right to be sure you have all the basics for your story.

Choose a Point of View

The **vantage point,** or **perspective,** from which a writer tells a story is called its **point of view.** For your story, choose from the following three most common points of view:

- **First person** The narrator, a character in the story, tells only what he or she knows and experiences. He or she uses first-person pronouns: *I, me, my, we, us.*
- **Third person limited** The narrator, who is not a character, tells the story, focusing on one character, describing only what that character knows and experiences. The narrator refers to all characters using third-person pronouns: *he, she,* and *they.*
- **Third person omniscient** An all-knowing narrator tells the story, using third-person pronouns. This narrator can tell what all characters are thinking and feeling, **shifting perspectives** from one character to another.

Consider Style

You can write more effectively and make your story more appealing to your readers by using **stylistic devices,** such as **imagery** (descriptive language that appeals to the senses), **figures of speech** (metaphor, simile, or personification), and **irony** (a contrast between appearances and reality).

Part of your style is also your use of sentence structure. To guide readers through shifts in time and place, your sentences should include **transitional expressions.**

Framework for a Short Story

Beginning
- Introduce the characters, setting, and conflict.

Middle
- Develop the characters.
- Introduce plot complications.
- Add stylistic devices—imagery, figures of speech, or irony.

End
- Bring the plot to a climax.
- Resolve the conflict.
- Reveal the final outcome.
- Make clear the significance of the events.

Grammar Link   Using Transitional Expressions

Transitional expressions create **coherence,** or a strong connection between ideas. In short stories they help the reader follow the progression of the plot. These words and phrases may be prepositions or adverbs. Most transitional phrases at the beginnings of sentences are separated from the main part of the sentence by a comma. Notice how Tim O'Brien uses transitional expressions to help his readers navigate the opening paragraphs of "Speaking of Courage."

> "**Then,** there had not been a war."
> "**Still,** it was the town's only lake. . . ."
> "**After college,** he'd caught an ear infection. . . ."
> "**Before the war,** they'd driven around the lake. . . ."

Reference Note   For more on transitional expressions, see the Writer's Handbook.

Your Turn

Write Your Draft Following the **plot plan** you created earlier and the **Writer's Framework** on this page, write a **draft** of your short story. Also, be sure to

- choose a **point of view** and stick to it
- use **stylistic devices** to enhance your writing
- create coherence by using **transitional expressions**

Peer Review

Working with a peer, review your draft. Answer each question in this chart to evaluate how each of your drafts could be improved. Then, use the tips and revision techniques to revise your draft. Revise as many times as necessary to make your short story effective.

Evaluating and Revising

Read the questions in the left-hand column of the chart and then use the tips in the middle column to help you make revisions to your short story. The right-hand column suggests techniques you can use to revise your draft.

Short Story: Guidelines for Content and Organization

Evaluation Question	Tip	Revision Technique
1. Does the story's beginning introduce the main characters and establish the setting? Does it initiate the conflict?	**Bracket** details about the main characters and setting. **Highlight** the event or situation that initiates the conflict.	**Add** details about the main characters and setting, including concrete, sensory details. **Add** a sentence that initiates the conflict.
2. Does the story have a clear point of view? Is the point of view developed consistently?	**Label** the point of view in the margin with *1* for first-person, *3L* for third-person limited, or *3O* for third-person omniscient. **Underline** phrases in your story that indicate the point of view.	**Delete** any information that the narrator would not reasonably know, especially for a first-person or third-person-limited narrator. **Reword** sentences as necessary to make the point of view consistent.
3. Is the plot developed with actions and decisions that complicate the problem? Does the conflict reach a climax?	**Star** each plot complication. **Double star** the story's climax.	**Add** actions or decisions that create complications. **Add** an event, action, decision, or realization that brings the conflict to a climax.
4. Does the story use dialogue, interior monologue, and concrete details to create complex characters?	**Draw a dotted line** under sentences that show a character's spoken words or unspoken thoughts and feelings. **Put parentheses** around any sensory details about characters.	**Add** dialogue and interior monologue to make characters more complex. **Elaborate** on characters with physical descriptions of appearance, behavior, and actions.
5. Does the story use stylistic devices, such as imagery, figures of speech, or irony?	**Circle** imagery, figurative language, and instances of irony.	**Replace** dull descriptions with figures of speech and sensory imagery. **Add irony** if it fits with your story's theme.
6. Does the story's end resolve the conflict and show the significance of the events?	**Bracket** the sentences that resolve the conflict. **Highlight** sentences that show the significance of the events.	**Add** sentences that resolve the conflict. **Elaborate** with a sentence or two that show the significance of the events.

Read this student's draft; note the comments on its structure and suggestions for how it could be made even stronger.

The Discovery

by Maile Cortese, Weddington High School

As David drove into the driveway, he became oddly calm. He turned down the radio so that he could hear his heart beating. Easing the door open, he stepped out of the car, walked down to the mailbox, and looked inside. "There it is." Hands shaking, he reached in for the letter.

David gently carried the envelope into the house as if it were made of glass. As he sat down at his kitchen table, he became numb. The envelope was addressed to him, but he didn't really feel like it was for him. He read the address line. "David Kalinger," he announced to no one in particular. "Yep, it's for me."

Fingers trembling, he slowly raised his hand to open it. He slid his thumb under the flap and tore the paper. The letter was sitting in the envelope so peacefully, waiting for someone to read its secret. Just as he was pulling the letter out of the envelope, Nadine strolled in through the side door. David sighed.

← Maile presents the **main character** and characterizes him with descriptions of his state of mind and his actions.

← She introduces **internal conflict.**

← She builds **suspense**—Nadine's arrival postpones the opening of the letter.

MINI-LESSON ▶ **How to Develop Plot with Dialogue**

Maile can develop the plot of the story even more effectively by intensifying the suspense she's already established. Dialogue is a good way to do that because conversation between the characters extends the moment and develops the characters and their relationship. It can also reveal information that is important to the plot. Maile decides to use dialogue to introduce the second character, create suspense, and reveal the nature of the letter.

Maile's Draft of Paragraph 3

Just as he was pulling the letter out of the envelope, Nadine came in through the side door. David sighed.

Maile's Revision of Paragraph 3

Just as he was pulling the letter out of the envelope, Nadine came in through the side door. David sighed.

ʌ"Nadine! What are you doing here?" he asked.

"I heard you were getting your acceptance letter today, so I just ran over here. Man, I'm so out of breath! Can I get a glass of water?" she panted as she reached into the cabinet.

"Sure, go ahead," David muttered, knowing she already had. As she sat down, he just stared at the envelope and held his breath.

Your Turn _____

Develop the Plot with Dialogue Read your draft, and then ask yourself these questions:

- What aspects of my characters' personalities and their relationships could I draw out through conversation?
- Where can I use dialogue instead of description to advance the plot?

Student Draft *continues*

Maile uses dialogue to continue → "So have you even looked at it yet?" Nadine asked.
the suspense.
David shook his head miserably. "Would you do it for me?" he pleaded.

Nadine gave him an inquisitive look but then quickly snatched the envelope, opened the letter, and started to read silently.

"What? What? Read it aloud! What are you doing?" he shouted in misery.

"Oh no, David. I was afraid of this," she said in a sorrowful voice, her face grim. He put his head in his hands, moaning softly.

The story reaches its climax when → "David, I'm not going to have you around here to keep me company any-
Nadine tells David the contents of more. You've been accepted! You're going to Boston!" she shouted triumphantly.
the letter.
David jumped to his feet, knocking over the chair, and tackled Nadine. "You'll be sorry!" he shouted, lunging for her.

They fell to the floor, breathless from laughing. The tackle finally ended in a huge bear hug.

MINI-LESSON ► **How to Conclude the Short Story**

Maile wanted to leave the reader with the resolution to the conflict of the story but also with some unanswered questions about the future of David and Nadine. She decided to add a denouement to the story that would hint at the unresolved future.

Maile's Draft of the Conclusion

David jumped to his feet, knocking over the chair, and tackled Nadine. "You'll be sorry!" he shouted, lunging for her.

They fell to the floor, breathless from laughing. The tackle finally ended in a huge bear hug.

Maile's Revision of the Conclusion

David jumped to his feet, knocking over the chair, and tackled Nadine. "You'll be sorry!" he shouted, lunging for her.

They fell to the floor, breathless from laughing. The tackle finally ended in a huge bear hug.

∧David set up the movie while Nadine made the popcorn, just like every other Friday night since they were young, but they both knew that nothing would ever be the same again.

Your Turn

Conclude Your Short Story

Ask a peer to read your final paragraphs and offer suggestions.

- Is the conflict resolved in a satisfying way?
- Have characters changed? If so, how? If not, does it matter to the story?
- Is the significance of what happened in the story clear?

Use your peer's suggestions to revise your conclusion.

Proofreading and Publishing

Proofreading

Before final publication of their stories, professional authors often examine page proofs to make sure that their stories are error-free. You also should look at the final draft of your story, or its "page proofs," to be certain that it does not contain distracting mistakes.

Since dialogue is frequently used in short stories, incorrect punctuation of dialogue is common in early drafts. **Proofread,** or **edit,** your short story to make sure you have punctuated the dialogue correctly.

Grammar Link Punctuating Dialogue

Since your short story will most likely include dialogue, you will need to make sure it is punctuated correctly. When used with quotation marks, **commas and periods** are placed within the closing quotation marks.

> "Oh, no, David. I was afraid of this," she said in a sorrowful voice, her face grim.

Question marks and exclamation points are placed inside the closing quotation marks if the quotation itself is a question or an exclamation. Otherwise, they are placed outside.

> "So have you even looked at it yet?" Nadine asked.

Reference Note For more on quotation marks, see the Language Handbook.

Publishing

A short story is more than a school assignment; it is a creative way to share your imagination with others. Try a few of these publishing ideas:

- Mail or e-mail your story to interested friends or relatives.
- Exchange a set of your class's short stories with stories from a junior high or high school in another country. Discuss what is gained and lost in the translation between cultures.
- Submit your story to your school's literary magazine or Web site.
- Submit your story to a short story contest. Ask your school librarian or media specialist to help you identify several contests.

Reflect on the Process
In your **RWN,** write a short response to each of the following questions:

1. If you wanted to tell the story again, this time from another point of view, what changes would you make, and why?
2. What element of your story—such as plot, characters, or style—was the most satisfying for you to write? the least satisfying? Explain.

Proofreading Tip

To help you catch mistakes or problems, exchange stories with a proofreading partner and check each other's work. Identify and correct errors in spelling, punctuation, usage, and sentence structure. Use the symbols for revising and proofreading found in the Writer's Handbook.

Your Turn _____
Proofread and Publish
Proofread your final draft. As you do, check dialogue to see that you have punctuated it correctly. Then, publish your completed work.

Scoring Rubric

Use one of the rubrics below to evaluate your short story from the Writing Workshop or your response to the on-demand prompt on the next page. Your teacher will tell you to use either the six- or the four-point rubric.

6-Point Scale

Score 6 *Demonstrates advanced success*
- focuses consistently on narrating a single incident or a unified sequence of incidents
- shows effective narrative sequence throughout, with smooth transitions
- offers a thoughtful, creative approach to the narration
- develops the story thoroughly, using precise and vivid descriptive and narrative details
- exhibits mature control of written language

Score 5 *Demonstrates proficient success*
- focuses on narrating a single incident or a unified sequence of incidents
- shows effective narrative sequence, with transitions
- offers a thoughtful approach to the narration
- develops the story competently, using descriptive and narrative details
- exhibits sufficient control of written language

Score 4 *Demonstrates competent success*
- focuses on narrating a single incident or a unified sequence of incidents, with minor distractions
- shows effective narrative sequence, with minor lapses
- offers a mostly thoughtful approach to the narration
- develops the story adequately, with some descriptive and narrative details
- exhibits general control of written language

Score 3 *Demonstrates limited success*
- includes some loosely related material that distracts from the writer's narrative focus
- shows some organization, with noticeable flaws in the narrative flow
- offers a routine, predictable approach to the narration
- develops the story with uneven use of descriptive and narrative detail
- exhibits limited control of written language

Score 2 *Demonstrates basic success*
- includes loosely related material that seriously distracts from the writer's narrative focus
- shows minimal organization, with major gaps in the narrative flow
- offers a narrative that merely skims the surface
- develops the story with inadequate descriptive and narrative detail
- exhibits significant problems with control of written language

Score 1 *Demonstrates emerging effort*
- shows little awareness of the topic and the narrative purpose
- lacks organization
- offers an unclear and confusing narrative
- develops the story with little or no detail
- exhibits major problems with control of written language

4-Point Scale

Score 4 *Demonstrates advanced success*
- focuses consistently on narrating a single incident or a unified sequence of incidents
- shows effective narrative sequence throughout, with smooth transitions
- offers a thoughtful, creative approach to the narration
- develops the story thoroughly, using precise and vivid descriptive and narrative details
- exhibits mature control of written language

Score 3 *Demonstrates competent success*
- focuses on narrating a single incident or a unified sequence of incidents, with minor distractions
- shows effective narrative sequence, with minor lapses
- offers a mostly thoughtful approach to the narration
- develops the story adequately, with some descriptive and narrative details
- exhibits general control of written language

Score 2 *Demonstrates limited success*
- includes some loosely related material that distracts from the writer's narrative focus
- shows some organization, with noticeable flaws in the narrative flow
- offers a routine, predictable approach to the narration
- develops the story with uneven use of descriptive and narrative detail
- exhibits limited control of written language

Score 1 *Demonstrates emerging effort*
- shows little awareness of the topic and the narrative purpose
- lacks organization
- offers an unclear and confusing narrative
- develops the story with little or no detail
- exhibits major problems with control of written language

Short Story

When responding to a prompt, use what you have learned from reading, writing your short story, and studying the rubric on page 384. Use the steps below to develop a response to the following prompt:

> ### Writing Prompt
> Write a short story in which characters react to an unexpected event in their own neighborhood. In your story, tell how the main character and others handle the unexpected event, and what happens as a result.

Study the Prompt

Begin by reading the prompt carefully. Circle or underline key words: *short story, characters, react, unexpected event, neighborhood, handle, result.*

Your **purpose** is to tell a story that entertains readers. The prompt tells you that you must quickly decide on the **setting** (a neighborhood) and the unexpected event. Your story will be about how the **characters** from the neighborhood react to the event and each other. The unexpected event creates the **conflict** that moves your story's **plot** forward. **Tip:** Spend about five minutes studying the prompt.

Plan Your Response

To quickly plan your response, brainstorm details, using a graphic organizer like the one below. Answer the questions to fill in the graphic:

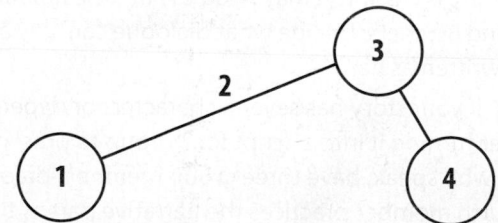

1. Exposition—What is the unexpected event? What are the sights, sounds, and smells of the neighborhood? What does the main character say, think, feel, and do as a result of the event? How does he or she interact with other characters? What conflict does the event create?

2. Rising Action—What complications arise as the characters try to resolve the conflict?

3. Climax—What is most exciting/suspenseful part of the story? Where does it happen? Who is involved?

4. Denouement—How is the conflict resolved? Do the neighborhood and characters change because of the unexpected event? If so, how?

Tip: Spend about ten minutes planning your response.

Respond to the Prompt

As you write your draft, try to maintain a consistent **point of view.** For instance, if you are telling the story from the first-person point of view of your main character, make sure that every sentence is from his or her perspective. A quick way to begin is to write a short **dialogue** between the characters that introduces them as well as establishes the setting and the conflict. **Tip:** Spend about twenty minutes writing your short story.

Improve Your Response

Revising Go back to the key aspects of the prompt. Does your story have a vivid setting and an interesting main character? Have you developed a plot that begins with an unexpected event and then tells what happens? Do sensory details and a consistent point of view help convey the story? If not, add these elements.

Proofreading Take a few minutes to edit your response to correct errors in grammar, spelling, punctuation, and capitalization. Make sure that your edits are neat and that the paper is legible.

Checking Your Final Copy Before you turn in your paper, read it one more time to catch any errors you may have missed. Take a few more minutes to correct the final copy of your story. **Tip:** Spend about five or ten minutes improving your draft.

Presenting a Story

Speak with a Purpose

Adapt your short story into an oral presentation. Practice telling your story, and then present it to your class.

Think as a Reader/Writer Like reading and writing, listening and speaking are related processes. Like a reader, a listener takes in and tries to understand someone's ideas. Like a writer, a speaker tries to convey ideas to others.

You have probably told stories to your family and friends in a relaxed atmosphere. Perhaps at dinner you related a funny incident that happened at school, or you told a friend a story about an adventure you had last summer. Now you can artfully share a story's meaning with a group of listeners by adapting it for an oral presentation.

Adapt Your Short Story

Consider Your Listeners

A reader has a chance to re-read a word, a passage, or an entire story. A listener, on the other hand, gets only one chance to understand your story. As you adapt your story for an oral presentation, keep these suggestions in mind.

- **Make Your Details Vivid** Readers have time to linger over language to form mental images of what a writer describes. Listeners do not. Look carefully at the sensory details you used in your short story to describe different sights, sounds, and smells. Read sensory passages aloud, and ask yourself if your language will create vivid images in listeners' minds.

- **Clarify Your Organization** You may need to strengthen the transitional words and phrases you used in your short story to help listeners follow the story events. On your own or with a classmate, review your narrative to make sure that one event clearly leads to the next and that important details have not been left out.

- **Limit Your Use of Dialogue** When reviewing the dialogue in your story, make sure the speaker's identity is clear. You may need to limit the amount of dialogue to avoid confusing listeners. Decide what dialogue can stay and what dialogue should be rewritten as narration.

- **Consider Reader's Theater** If your story has several characters or depends heavily on dialogue, consider turning it into a script for a group to present. If you have three characters who speak, have three group members practice the dialogue while a fourth member practices the narrative part of the story. Reader's theater does not require participants to memorize a story; instead, they can read from the script. The story should be well rehearsed, though, so that your readers bring the story to life with their voices.

Reader/Writer Notebook

Use your **RWN** to complete the activities for this workshop.

Deliver Your Short Story

Have a Point of View

When you present a short story orally, the **point of view,** or vantage point from which the story is told, will help determine what reading voice you use.

- In stories told from the **first-person point of view,** an "I" tells the story. If your story is written from this perspective, tell it as though you were the main character.
- Many stories are told from the **omniscient,** or all-knowing, **point of view.** The omniscient narrator can reveal the thoughts and feelings of all the characters. Use your own voice if your story is written from this point of view.

Polish Your Performance

After you have adapted your story for listeners and determined how the point of view will affect your delivery, use the tips in the checklist below to craft and practice your performance.

Tip for Polishing Your Performance	Done?
Know your text well. Read your story aloud several times so that you are very familiar with it. Find out how to pronounce difficult words.	
Use your voice to convey meaning. Portray different characters by changing the pitch of your voice, and vary your rate of speech to indicate changes in the story's action. Adapt your tone of voice to the story's mood.	
Use gestures and facial expressions to aid communication. Use your body, hands, and facial expressions to convey meaning and mood.	

Take Note

Make a set of notecards with key words or phrases to keep you on track and ensure that your narrative is coherent. Arrange your notecards in the order in which you want to tell the events.

During your presentation, do not keep your head down and your eyes locked on your notes. Look at your audience, and use eye contact to keep your listeners involved in the story. Glance at your notes only when truly necessary.

A Good Oral Presentation

- begins by engaging the audience in plot, characters, or setting
- organizes events so listeners can follow along easily
- uses sensory language to appeal to the audience
- uses effective verbal and nonverbal techniques

Speaking Tip

Practice telling your story alone until you know it very well. Experiment with varied facial expressions, gestures, and verbal techniques to suggest a range of moods and to portray different characters. Then, give your presentation to a friend or family member and ask for feedback on your story and delivery. Make adjustments as needed.

Learn It Online

Take your story a step further by adding images and sound. Check out Digital Storytelling online.

 go.hrw.com L11-387   Go

Literary Skills Review

Comparing Literature   **Directions:** Read the following poems. Then, read and respond to the questions that follow.

The Snow-Storm by **Ralph Waldo Emerson**

Announced by all the trumpets of the sky,
Arrives the snow, and, driving o'er the fields,
Seems nowhere to alight: the whited air
Hides hills and woods, the river, and the heaven,
5   And veils the farm-house at the garden's end.
The sled and traveller stopped, the courier's° feet
Delayed, all friends shut out, the housemates sit
Around the radiant fireplace, enclosed
In a tumultuous privacy of storm.

10   Come see the north wind's masonry.°
Out of an unseen quarry evermore
Furnished with tile, the fierce artificer°
Curves his white bastions° with projected roof
Round every windward stake, or tree, or door.
15   Speeding, the myriad°-handed, his wild work
So fanciful, so savage, nought° cares he
For number or proportion. Mockingly,
On coop or kennel he hangs Parian° wreaths;
A swan-like form invests the hidden thorn;
20   Fills up the farmer's lane from wall to wall,
Maugre° the farmer's sighs; and at the gate
A tapering turret° overtops the work.
And when his hours are numbered, and the world
Is all his own, retiring, as he were not,
25   Leaves, when the sun appears, astonished Art
To mimic in slow structures, stone by stone,
Built in an age, the mad wind's night-work,
The frolic architecture of the snow.

6. courier's: messenger's.

10. masonry: stonework. The poet suggests here that wind blows snow into shapes that look like stonework.
12. artificer (ahr TIHF uh suhr): craftsman.
13. bastions: fortifications.
15. myriad: countless.
16. nought: nothing.
18. Parian (PAIR ee uhn): made of fine white porcelain from the Greek city of Paros.

21. maugre (MAW guhr): in spite of.
22. turret: tower.

First Snow by **Mary Oliver**

The snow
began here
this morning and all day
continued, its white
5   rhetoric° everywhere
calling us back to *why, how,*
whence° such beauty and *what*
the meaning; such
an oracular° fever! flowing
10 past windows, an energy it seemed
would never ebb, never settle
less than lovely! and only now,
deep into night,
it has finally ended.
15 The silence
is immense,
and the heavens still hold
a million candles; nowhere
the familiar things:
20 stars, the moon,
the darkness we expect
and nightly turn from. Trees

glitter like castles
of ribbons, the broad fields
25 smolder° with light, a passing
creekbed lies
heaped with shining hills;
and though the questions
that have assailed us all day
30 remain—not a single
answer has been found—
walking out now
into the silence and the light
under the trees,
35 and through the fields,
feels like one.

---

25. **smolder:** to burn and smoke without flame.

---

5. **rhetoric** (REHT uhr ihk): persuasive use of words. By referring to the snow's rhetoric, Oliver suggests that the snow affects her like well-written persuasion.
7. **whence:** from where.
9. **oracular:** divinely inspired.

1. In line 5 of "The Snow-Storm," the poetic device is —
   A metaphor
   B simile
   C symbol
   D allusion

2. In the first stanza of Emerson's poem, what effect has the snowstorm had on the people?
   A They are happily playing in the snow.
   B They are working to clear the roads of snow.
   C They are unable to go anywhere because of the snow.
   D They are traveling to their destinations despite the snow.

3. In lines 10–14 of Emerson's poem, the poet refers to the north wind as —
   A a mighty beast
   B an unforgiving enemy
   C a long-lost friend
   D a builder of stone structures

4. In lines 10–17 of Emerson's poem, the wind's attitude can best be characterized as —
   A careful as a bricklayer's
   B lovingly playful
   C careless of consequences
   D angry at the snow for falling

5. In lines 17–18 of "The Snow-Storm," the poet uses which device to characterize the wind?
   A symbolism
   B alliteration
   C rhyme
   D personification

6. In lines 25–26 of Emerson's poem, which device of sound does the poet use?
   A symbol
   B alliteration
   C onomatopoeia
   D simile

7. In the first nine lines of "First Snow," which device does the poet use to characterize the snow?
   A onomatopoeia
   B personification
   C simile
   D metonymy

8. In Oliver's poem, what effect has the snow had on the night?
   A The night is now much brighter and quieter.
   B The night is more frightening than usual.
   C The night seems to last much longer.
   D The night is full of people walking around.

9. In line 18 of Oliver's poem, "a million candles" is which poetic device?

A personification

B assonance

C onomatopoeia

D metaphor

10. In lines 22–24 of Oliver's poem, trees are compared to what?

A "castles of ribbons"

B "broad fields"

C "creekbeds"

D "shining hills"

11. The meaning of lines 26–27 of "First Snow" is that —

A hills can be seen in the reflection from the creek water

B an avalanche has ruined the creek

C piles of gleaming snow have accumulated in the creekbed

D the hills are shining like diamonds

12. In Oliver's poem, what effect does the snow have on the speaker?

A The speaker feels angry because the storm is an inconvenience.

B The speaker marvels at the beauty of nature.

C The speaker realizes how destructive nature can be.

D The speaker takes no notice of the snow.

13. A theme common to both poems is —

A the beauty and majesty of nature

B the destructiveness of nature

C the unpredictability of nature

D humans' fear of nature

14. Which word best describes the tone of both poems?

A warmhearted

B irreverent

C humorous

D critical

Constructed Response

15. Briefly compare the use of images in "The Snow-Storm" and "First Snow." How does each poet use images to express an attitude toward the natural world? Be sure to support your response with evidence from the poems.

Vocabulary Skills Review

Analogies **Directions:** For each of the following items, choose the lettered pair of words that expresses the relationship most similar to the relationship between the pair of capitalized words.

1. BLITHE : CAREFREE ::

A biased : fair

B joyful : depressed

C anxious : worried

D lazy : powerful

2. STAGNANT : FLOWING ::

A rough : coarse

B difficult : puzzling

C vigorous : lively

D drowsy : alert

3. TUMULTUOUS : RIOT ::

A hilarious : grievance

B courageous : hero

C timid : clown

D cold : sun

4. AVARICE : GREED ::

A generosity : bitterness

B fear : courage

C confidence : self-respect

D honesty : deceitfulness

5. SOJOURN : BRIEF ::

A lemon : sour

B gravel : smooth

C water : dry

D metal : fragrant

6. PROSTRATE : UPRIGHT ::

A annual : yearly

B clear : hazy

C immense : large

D brilliant : shiny

7. WREAK : INFLICT ::

A preserve : spend

B ignore : notice

C trap : liberate

D honor : respect

8. INIQUITY : WICKEDNESS ::

A fragility : youthfulness

B reality : boldness

C purity : filth

D honesty : truthfulness

Academic Vocabulary

Directions: For each of the following analogy items, choose the pair of words that expresses the relationship most similar to the relationship between the pair of capitalized words.

9. IMPLICIT : STATED ::

A factor : criterion

B integral : unimportant

C transform : change

D principal : major

10. INTEGRAL : ESSENTIAL ::

A transform : paralyze

B principal : authority

C factor : unimportant

D implicit : inherent

Writing Skills Review

Editing a Short Story **Directions:** Read the following excerpt from a draft of a short story. Then, read and respond to the questions that follow.

(1) "My dad's going to ground me forever," Sean told his best friend, Anthony. (2) They stood there inspecting the damage to the side of Sean's dad's new extended-cab pickup truck. (3) The door on the passenger's side had a big dent in it where Sean had scraped a tree. (4) The two boys walked from the front to the back of the truck and leaned over several times to squint at the dent to see if it might disappear if they viewed it from a certain angle. (5) "Maybe you could tell your dad that it got bumped in the parking lot and you didn't see who did it," Anthony suggested.

---

1. To add characterization to the passage, which of the following could the writer add after sentence 3?

   A "I'm so stupid for denting Dad's truck," Sean thought.

   B The metallic paint was scratched for about four inches.

   C Anthony's mother called him on his cell phone at that moment.

   D Just then, Sean's father pulled up into the driveway.

2. The best way to add interest to the plot and slow down the pace of the story would be to —

   A contrast the different upbringings that Sean and Anthony had

   B flash back to the day Sean's dad bought the new truck

   C describe the neighborhood in which Sean lives

   D tell about the methods used to fix dents and scratches

3. Which adjective could replace the word *big* in sentence 3 to improve the precision of the writing?

   A large

   B plate-sized

   C small

   D full

4. To establish a humorous tone in the paragraph, the writer could —

   A describe the two boys' appearances in clear detail

   B add language that further depicts the apprehensive mood

   C write with a more lighthearted and relaxed vocabulary

   D include dialogue between Sean and his father

5. Which of the following sentences would add to the story's conflict?

   A "I'm glad you were with me when this happened, Anthony."

   B "I'm lucky that I didn't have a fatal crash, like so many teens do."

   C "That's the last time I'll back up without looking in the mirrors."

   D "That *would* be a nice way out, but I've never lied to my dad before."

FICTION
Moby-Dick

A literary masterpiece of the Romantic era, Herman Melville's novel is the epic tale of an obsession both dark and tragic. Captain Ahab, the strange captain of the whaling ship the *Pequod*, has one goal in life: to destroy the white whale that cost him his right leg. In his pursuit of the whale, Ahab risks everything—his crew, his ship, and ultimately even his sanity.

NONFICTION
Blue Highways: A Journey into America

Where is the true America—in a quiet corner by Walden Pond or on the asphalt of the country's back roads? Native American writer William Least Heat-Moon takes the traveling option and crosses the country in a van he calls Ghost Dancing. In the faces of people, in the beauty of the landscape, and in the small towns with names like Bear Wallow, Mud Lick, and Love Joy, Heat-Moon celebrates the human spirit and the American way of life—over the course of thirteen thousand miles.

NONFICTION
Arctic Dreams

With today's concerns about climate and the environment, nurturing our knowledge and appreciation of the Arctic is more important than ever. Barry Lopez records his experiences from fifteen extended trips to the Far North as he celebrates the animals, landscape, and people in places such as Alaska, the Canadian Arctic, and Greenland. Writing with vivid and stunning detail, Lopez transports readers to the natural treasures that are rarely visited but in danger of being lost.

POETRY
American Primitive

Emerson believed that in the presence of nature "a wild delight" would fill a person "in spite of real sorrows." Almost two hundred years later, poet Mary Oliver brings this philosophy to life in a book of poems that brings readers closer to nature. Whether exploring the danger of lightning, the joy of picking blackberries, or the wonder and sorrow of burying a stillborn kitten, these poems draw readers into the mysteries and beauty of the American wilderness that surrounds us.

FICTION
Middle Passage

A National Book Award winner, Charles Johnson's novel tells the story of Rutherford Calhoun, a newly freed slave trying to make his way in the New Orleans of 1830. Calhoun's harrowing adventure begins when he stows away on a ship without knowing it is a slave ship bound for Africa. Working as a cabin boy for the ship's captain, the protagonist works undercover to support a revolt brewing among the slaves on board.

FICTION
The Poe Shadow

Intrigued by the suspicious events surrounding the death of Edgar Allan Poe, Baltimore lawyer Quentin Clark investigates the author's final days. In the vein of Sherlock Holmes, this detailed mystery chronicles the events Clark's investigations set in motion. When Clark is charged with insanity and murder while attempting to preserve the memory of Poe, he is forced to defend himself. Novelist Matthew Pearl's well-researched historical elements offer new insights into Poe's fascinating life.

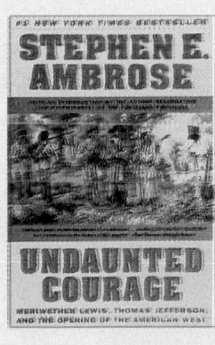

NONFICTION
Undaunted Courage

This biography of Meriwether Lewis documents the famous explorer's journey through the West with William Clark. It also explores the relationship between Lewis and President Thomas Jefferson, the man who charged Lewis with the mission of opening up the West. Author Stephen Ambrose's personal interest in the subject led him to take his research a step further. He spent several summers exploring the areas mentioned in Lewis and Clark's journals, gathering material to use for this account.

NONFICTION
Woman in the Nineteenth Century

Originally published in 1845, Margaret Fuller's classic feminist text examines issues related to women in nineteenth-century society—including prostitution, marriage, employment, and the right to vote. Inspired by her belief that women should be allowed to do the kind of work they wanted to, Fuller encouraged women to use education as a way to escape domestic life. Considered controversial for its time, this book sold out of its first printing in a week.

Learn It Online
For help choosing a book you'll like, check *NovelWise* online.

go.hrw.com L11-395   Go

A HOUSE DIVIDED:
The Civil War Era and Its Aftermath 1850–1890

COLLECTION 6
Up from Slavery

COLLECTION 7
The Ravages of War

COLLECTION 8
Whitman and Dickinson— American Masters

"'A house divided against itself cannot stand.' I believe this government cannot endure, permanently half slave and half free."

—Abraham Lincoln

What Do
You?
Think   How does conflict lead to change?

Learn It Online
Learn more about this historical period online.

go.hrw.com | L11-397 | Go

Battle of Pea Ridge Arkansas. United States Civil War batt e, March 3, 1862.
Nineteenth-century lithograph by Kurz and Allison.

A HOUSE DIVIDED:
The Civil War Era and Its Aftermath
1850–1890

This time line presents a snapshot of United States literary events, United States historical events, and world events from 1850 to 1890. During this period, widespread political and cultural changes took place in the United States and around the world.

Louisa May Alcott

UNITED STATES LITERARY EVENTS

1850

c. 1850 Sojourner Truth, abolitionist and women's rights advocate, dictates *Narrative of Sojourner Truth*

1852 Harriet Beecher Stowe publishes an influential novel about slavery, *Uncle Tom's Cabin; or Life Among the Lowly* ❯

1855 Frederick Douglass publishes *My Bondage and My Freedom*, a second version of his life story

1860

1862 Henry David Thoreau, author of *Walden, or Life in the Woods*, dies of tuberculosis at age 44

1865 William Cullen Bryant publishes his poem "Abraham Lincoln," mourning the president's death

1868–1869 Louisa May Alcott publishes a popular novel about growing up, *Little Women*

UNITED STATES HISTORICAL EVENTS

1850

early 1850s Susan B. Anthony and Elizabeth Cady Stanton lead U.S. women's rights movement

1852 More than twenty thousand Chinese immigrants settle in California

1857 Supreme Court's Dred Scott decision favors slaveholders

1859 John Brown, an abolitionist, leads a raid on the federal arsenal at Harpers Ferry, Virginia, and is hanged for treason

1860

April 1861 First shots of Civil War are fired at Fort Sumter, South Carolina

April 9, 1865 Confederate surrender at Appomattox Court House in Virginia ends Civil War ❯

1867 The United States purchases Alaska from Russia

1869 The first transcontinental railroad is completed

1869 The Cincinnati Red Stockings become the first professional team in baseball

The Granger Collection, New York.

WORLD EVENTS

1850

1853 Dutch painter Vincent van Gogh is born

1856 France's Gustave Flaubert publishes a classic realistic novel, *Madame Bovary*

1859 England's Charles Darwin explains his groundbreaking theory of evolution in *Origin of Species*

1860

1865 Lewis Carroll publishes *Alice's Adventures in Wonderland*

1869 Russian author Leo Tolstoy completes his panoramic novel *War and Peace*

The Granger Collection, New York.

SKILLS FOCUS **Literary Skills** Evaluate and analyze the philosophical, political, religious, ethical, and social influences of a historical period. **Reading Skills** Identify and understand chronological order; identify and understand graphic elements; use text organizers such as overviews, headings, and graphic features to locate and categorize information.

Your Turn

With a partner, review the time line and discuss the events that relate to change or conflict in society. Which events do you think had the most significant or lasting influence?

1870	1880	1890

1871 Stephen Crane, author of *The Red Badge of Courage*, is born in Newark, New Jersey

1876 Walt Whitman publishes a dual volume of poetry and prose on the occasion of the American centennial ❯

1878 Henry James publishes the novel *Daisy Miller*, a study of European and American manners

Walt Whitman

1884 Mark Twain publishes *Adventures of Huckleberry Finn* ❯

1886 Emily Dickinson dies

1889 Ambrose Bierce publishes "Chickamauga," considered one of the most graphic antiwar stories in American literature

The Granger Collection, New York

1870	1880	1890

1870 The Fifteenth Amendment to the U.S. Constitution, granting African American men the right to vote, goes into effect

1876 Alexander Graham Bell patents the first telephone

1877 The Compromise of 1877 removes federal troops from the South, ending Reconstruction

1881 Clara Barton organizes the American Red Cross ❯

1881 President James A. Garfield is assassinated in Washington, D.C.

1889 North Dakota, South Dakota, Montana, and Washington are admitted to the United States

1889 First Land Run in Oklahoma Territory

The Granger Collection, New York

1870	1880	1890

1873 French writer Jules Verne publishes *Around the World in Eighty Days*

1874 In Paris, Claude Monet organizes first exhibition of Impressionist paintings ❯

1879–1880 Russian novelist Fyodor Dostoyevsky publishes *The Brothers Karamazov*

White Waterlilies by Claude Monet

1883 The Indonesian volcano Krakatoa erupts, killing 36,000 people

1887 Sir Arthur Conan Doyle introduces the world to Sherlock Holmes in *A Study in Scarlet*

1889 Emmeline Pankhurst founds Women's Franchise League to work for British women's suffrage ❯

Emmeline Pankhurst

A HOUSE DIVIDED:

The Civil War Era and Its Aftermath
1850–1890

The Civil War, which lasted from 1861 to 1865, was a cataclysmic event that divided the nation. Four years of destruction and bloodshed left more than 600,000 soldiers dead and the South in ruins. Slavery was abolished, but African Americans still faced a struggle for freedom and equality. Reactions to the grim casualties of the war and to the rapid urban expansion of the postwar years led many writers and artists to abandon their Romantic ideals. A new literary movement, called realism, emerged.

KEY CONCEPTS

Slavery Leads to War

History of the Times Slavery was the major cause of the Civil War. After the election of Abraham Lincoln, who opposed slavery in the new territories, Southern states began seceding from the Union and joined to form the Confederate States of America.

Literature of the Times The suffering of enslaved African Americans found expression in slave narratives and spirituals. These accounts and songs vividly show the injustice of slavery and the determination to gain freedom.

Civil War Divides the Country

History of the Times Both North and South were motivated by ideology and economics. Northerners fought to end slavery and to preserve the Union. Southerners fought to uphold states' rights and to defend their way of life.

Literature of the Times Most literary works to come out of the war were of historical interest: diaries, letters, journals, and public documents. Apart from Whitman, few major writers witnessed the war firsthand.

The Country Rebuilds

History of the Times When the war ended, the South faced economic devastation. As Reconstruction began, the nation, which had lost its innocence through the experience of war, began to rebuild itself as a united country.

Literature of the Times The devastation of the Civil War caused disillusionment in many writers who turned away from Romanticism to realism. Realism focused on ordinary people instead of idealized heroes.

SKILLS FOCUS **Literary Skills** Evaluate and analyze the philosophical, political, religious, ethical, and social influences of a historical period. **Reading Skills** Read widely to increase knowledge of the student's culture, the culture of others, and the common elements across cultures; identify and understand elements of text structure (including headings and sections).

KEY CONCEPT

Slavery Leads to War

History of the Times

What had brought the United States to the point of civil war?[1] Today historians acknowledge a variety of causes, such as the economic, political, and social differences between the South and the North, but slavery lay at the heart of this conflict.

The agricultural South produced cash crops (sugar cane, tobacco, and cotton) for export to the North and to Europe. The South depended on the industrial North for financial, manufacturing, and commercial services. One of the major differences between the regions was that the South relied upon a labor force made up of nearly four million enslaved Africans. In addition, the North tended to regard the federal government as the primary authority over civil and economic life, whereas the South championed states' rights.

Increasing numbers of Northerners viewed slaveholding as a monstrous violation of the basic American principle of equality, but Southerners wanted to preserve the institution of slavery for economic and social reasons. The controversy over slavery worsened as new territories and states were admitted to the Union around 1850. Supporters of slavery saw an opportunity to create more slave states, while abolitionists[2] remained equally determined that slavery should not spread.

Literature of the Times

From the personal accounts of people held in slavery—such as Frederick Douglass and Harriet A. Jacobs—we learn firsthand about the horrors and injustices of slavery. Narratives of fugitive slaves were

---

1. **civil war:** war between groups of people in the same country.
2. **abolitionists:** opponents of slavery.

a popular form of literature, and at least sixty were published in the years before the war. None was more powerful than Douglass's autobiography, *My Bondage and My Freedom* (1855). In a plain style he gave eloquent expression to the human spirit that slavery could not crush.

Comprehension Check

What differences between the North and the South led to the outbreak of civil war in 1861?

Fast Facts

Historical Highlights

- The Civil War (1861–1865) results in the deaths of more than 600,000 soldiers.
- Slavery is formally abolished in 1865.
- Abraham Lincoln is assassinated in Ford's Theatre, Washington, D.C., on April 14, 1865.
- Great advances in technology include the telephone (1876), phonograph (1877), and electric light bulb (1879).

Literary Highlights

- Harriet Beecher Stowe's *Uncle Tom's Cabin* (1852) stirs abolitionists to protest the Fugitive Slave Act of 1850.
- Frederick Douglass publishes a version of his autobiography, *My Bondage and My Freedom* (1855), which helps fuel the antislavery cause.
- Walt Whitman publishes his first edition of *Leaves of Grass* in 1855.
- The literary movement realism takes shape.
- Emily Dickinson dies in 1886; her *Poems* is published in 1890.

 **Learn It Online**
Learn more about this historical period online.

| go.hrw.com | L11-401 | Go |

Civil War Divides the Country

History of the Times

The conflict between North and South reached a fever pitch and erupted into war after Confederate[1] guns fired on Fort Sumter, South Carolina, an important outpost of the federal government. As soldiers went off to battle, emotions ran high through a divided country.

Only slowly, after the outbreak of civil war in 1861, did most Americans realize the extent of the national tragedy. Those in both the North and the South who had believed that the war would end quickly, perhaps with a single decisive battle, had to face instead the mounting horrors of four long years of struggle.

Although the Northern and the Southern states disagreed on slavery and states' rights, the Civil War itself was universally regarded as a hellish, terrifying time of pain and sacrifice. The destruction and bloodshed of the war awakened Americans to a dark side of the national character. The number of soldier deaths was nearly as many as in all the other wars that this country has fought. In the end, the Union was preserved, but a fragile republic now had to find a future.

Literature of the Times

Although many works of historical interest—soldiers' letters and diaries, as well as journalistic writings—came out of the Civil War, works of literary significance were rare, prompting the question, Why did an event of such magnitude result in such a scanty literary output? Few major American writers experienced the Civil War firsthand.

---

1. **Confederate:** of the Confederate States of America, the nation formed by Southern states.

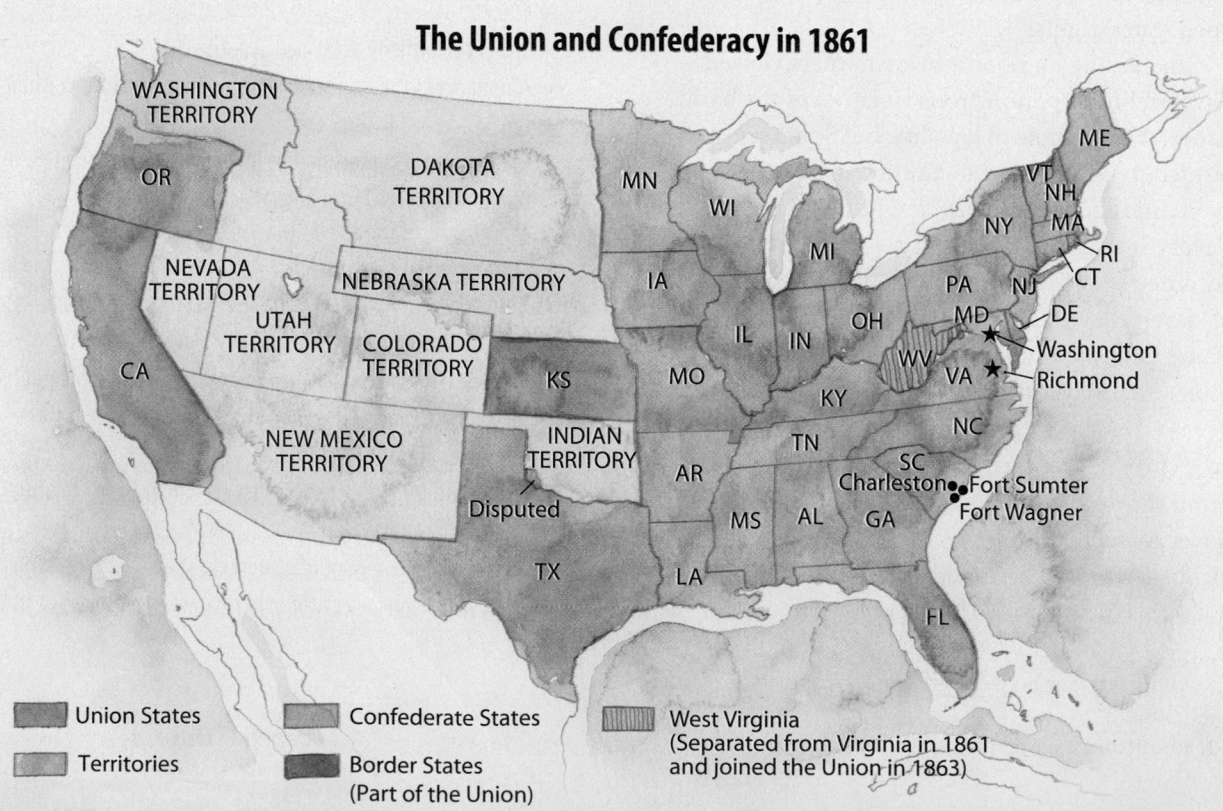

The Union and Confederacy in 1861

WASHINGTON TERRITORY

OR

DAKOTA TERRITORY

NEVADA TERRITORY

NEBRASKA TERRITORY

UTAH TERRITORY

COLORADO TERRITORY

CA

NEW MEXICO TERRITORY

INDIAN TERRITORY

Disputed

MN

WI

IA

MI

IL

IN

OH

MO

KS

KY

TN

AR

MS

AL

GA

TX

LA

ME

VT

NH

NY

MA

RI

CT

PA

NJ

MD

DE

★ Washington

WV

VA

★ Richmond

NC

SC

Charleston • Fort Sumter

Fort Wagner

FL

Union States

Territories

Confederate States

Border States (Part of the Union)

West Virginia (Separated from Virginia in 1861 and joined the Union in 1863)

In Concord, Massachusetts, Ralph Waldo Emerson had watched the Concord volunteers march off to war. When they returned a few months later from the First Battle of Bull Run in 1861, defeated and disillusioned, Emerson maintained his conviction that the war must be pursued. Henry David Thoreau, who had been a fervent abolitionist, died in 1862. Emily Dickinson remained in Amherst, Massachusetts, and the country's grief over the war seems not to have informed her poetry.

Herman Melville was fascinated by the war, but he never wrote a novel about it. He chose to treat the war in poetry that was often dark and foreboding. The poems are collected in *Battle-Pieces and Aspects of the War* (1866). These poems are based on newspaper accounts of battles as well as visits to battlefields. They record the heroism and futility of the fighting on both sides and demonstrate a respect for Southern as well as Northern troops. In some of Melville's poems, there is a sense of human nature being stripped bare, revealing humanity's basic evil.

Walt Whitman was one of the few American writers who did witness the Civil War firsthand. During the war Whitman served as a volunteer hospital visitor in Washington, D.C., comforting the wounded and writing to their loved ones. The condition of the wounded was appalling. Many of the injured had to remain on the battlefield for two or three days until the camp hospitals had room for them. Antiseptics were primitive, as were operating-room techniques. A major wound meant amputation or even death.

Whitman estimated that in three years as a camp hospital volunteer, he visited tens of thousands of wounded men. "I suffer'd, I was there," he had written earlier in *Song of Myself,* and now he was there in the real heart of America. In his poems he had presented a panoramic vision of America; now America passed through the hospital tents in the form of wounded men from every state in the Union and the Confederacy. Nevertheless, out of the horror that he viewed, Whitman was able to derive an optimistic vision of the American character, of "the actual soldier of 1862–1865 . . . with all his ways, his incredible dauntlessness, habits, practices, tastes, language, his fierce friendship, his appetite, rankness, his superb strength—and a hundred unnamed lights and shades."

Comprehension Check

Why did so few American writers respond to the war in their works?

Link to Today

Masters of Disguise

After the first shots of the Civil War were fired, young Frank Thompson answered the call to arms and joined up as a Union soldier. Pvt. Thompson of the 2nd Michigan Infantry fought in the siege of Yorktown and the blood-soaked Battle of Antietam. He was a good and loyal soldier, though all the while hiding his true identity from his comrades. Pvt. Thompson was, in reality, a woman named Sara Edmonds.

Today women are free to join the military and participate in combat, but not so during Edmonds's time. Women who wanted to go to war had no option but to masquerade as men. It is estimated that over four hundred women served in Civil War armies. Many enlisted for the same reasons as men: to escape from home, earn good pay, and experience a great adventure. By posing as men, however, female soldiers also gained freedoms denied to women at that time, such as full status as citizens, including the right to vote.

Soldier and Spy   In addition to soldiering, Sara Edmonds used her talent for disguise as a Union spy, infiltrating enemy lines for weeks at a time. Disguised first as a slave named Ned and later as "Bridget," an Irish peddler, Edmonds followed the Confederate army to gather information. In 1865, Edmonds published a bestselling memoir, *Nurse and Spy in the Union Army.*

Ask Yourself

How do you think Sara Edmonds would react to women's roles in the military today?

The Country Rebuilds

Photos showing early Confederate flags.

History of the Times

The South, devastated by war and then subjected by the federal government to shortsighted and sometimes vindictive policies of reconstruction, was slow to recover and take its place in the growing national prosperity.

In the North the situation was far different. Almost without pause the great industrial system that had produced the materials of war was turned to the production of civilian goods. In many respects the postwar decades simply continued trends already established before the war, such as advances in steel manufacturing, oil refining, electricity distribution, transportation, and communication.

As the economy expanded, immigration from abroad resumed, and once again, between 1870 and 1890, the nation's population doubled, with cities growing fastest of all.

Through the pain and tragedy of the Civil War, Americans had acquired new self-knowledge and strength. The nation would not again feel the supreme confidence in human potential that had been the faith of earlier generations, but it now had a firmer sense of human limitations.

> "If I were to speak of war, it would not be to show you the glories of conquering armies but the mischief and misery they strew in their tracks…. This is the side which history never shows."
>
> **—Clara Barton, Civil War nurse**

Link to Today

Civil War Slang

English is a slang-rich language, but most slang terms don't survive more than a generation or so. Here are some Civil War–era slang terms that people still use today.

fit to be tied—angry

greenbacks—money

I heard it through the grapevine—Telegraph wires, often used to transmit information during the war, were referred to as "grapevines." Soldiers would give this response when asked where they learned information.

hard knocks—tough break

been through the mill—had a hectic or bad day

snug as a bug—comfortable

scarce as hen's teeth—something rare

"Great Scott!"—an expression of astonishment or disbelief (referring to the nickname of the Union general Winfield Scott)

deadline—The Confederate prisoner of war camp at Andersonville, Georgia, had a small perimeter around the prison—the "dead line"—where, if anyone was caught, he would be immediately shot.

Ask Yourself

What slang words can you think of that come from events, people, or popular culture from the last few decades?

Literature of the Times

Modern readers think that one byproduct of a war is a literary account of it, largely in the form of novels and poems by people who participated in the war. During the Civil War era, however, the traditional literary forms were the letter and the journal, which were inadequate to express the horrifying details of the greatest cataclysm in the nation's history.

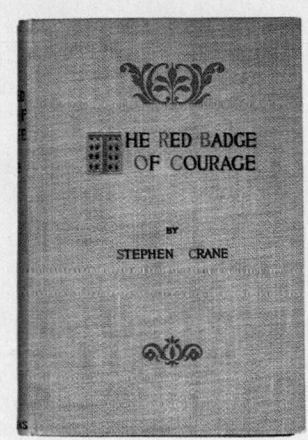

The literary form most appropriate for handling such strong material, would have been the realistic novel.[1] This type of novel rejects Romantic elements, such as larger-than-life heroes or overly dramatic situations, and instead focuses on detailed descriptions of real events and people. The realistic novel had not yet been fully developed in the United States. Thus, the great novel of the Civil War, *The Red Badge of Courage,* had to wait to be written by a man who was born six years after the war had ended: Stephen Crane. Driven by the desire to capture the sensations of an individual in battle conditions, an element of war not found in history books, Crane rightly chose the novel as the genre best suited to convey this remarkable story.

Comprehension Check

What literary form emerged in postwar America that was well suited to describe the horrors of the war?

---

1. **realistic novel:** a novel that presents a detailed depiction of ordinary characters and real-life situations.

Wrap Up

Talk About . . .

With a partner or in a small group, list and discuss the major changes that occurred in the United States as a result of the Civil War. How are the effects of the Civil War reflected in our society today?

Write About . . .

Walt Whitman wrote, "Future years will never know the seething hell . . . of the countless minor scenes and interiors . . . the real war will never get in the books." Do you agree with Whitman that books cannot convey the horror of war? Explain.

Academic Vocabulary for Unit 3

Talking and Writing About Literature
Academic Vocabulary is the language you'll use to write and talk about literature. Use these words to discuss the selections in this unit. These words will be underlined throughout the unit.

advocate (AD vuh kayt) *v.:* support; argue for. *Consider how slave narratives advocate for an end to slavery.*

criteria (kry TIHR ee uh) *n.:* standards on which an argument is based. *Examine whether an argument is based on valid criteria.*

fundamental (fuhn duh MEHN tuhl) *adj.:* essential; underlying. *What fundamental changes did the United States experience during and after the Civil War?*

principle (PRIHN suh puhl) *n.:* primary truth; rule of conduct. *In the Gettysburg Address, Lincoln reminds his audience of a principle to which the country is dedicated: equality.*

subsequent (SUHB sih kwuhnt) *adj.:* following; coming after. *Many subsequent poets have drawn from Whitman's and Dickinson's legacies.*

Your Turn

With a partner, summarize the main historical and literary events of the time period. Try to use the Academic Vocabulary words in your discussion.

Link to Today

Build Background

Kelly Ingram Park in Birmingham, Alabama, was the site of a civil rights demonstration in May 1963. Police used attack dogs against demonstrators, and firefighters blasted the demonstrators with pressure hoses. Today, the park serves as a memorial to the civil rights movement, with sculptures commemorating the historic events that took place there.

Author Note

Leonard Pitts, Jr. (1957–   ), a nationally syndicated newspaper columnist, was awarded the Pulitzer Prize for commentary in 2004. Born and raised in Southern California, Pitts has been writing professionally since the age of 18. His first column about the September 11 attacks so impressed readers that it generated more than 30,000 e-mails. Pitts lives in Bowie, Maryland, with his wife and five children.

Pulitzer Prize WINNER

Read with a Purpose Read this newspaper article to discover why the author believes that visiting this "battleground" of the civil rights movement is an important experience for his teenage sons today.

A Lesson Learned on the Road

by LEONARD PITTS, JR.

The Miami Herald

Sometimes, history is just a trick of the light. Sometimes, it's as if you have to incline your head to a certain angle, squint your eyes a certain way, before you can see the shadowy outlines of what used to be beneath the imposing actuality of what now is.

Which is as good an explanation as any of what I'm doing with my teen-age sons on a bright, chilly day in historic Kelly Ingram Park.

We've been on the road for six days out of this vague but persistent sense I had that they and I might benefit from some guy time, some undistracted hours in one another's company. Tonight we'll drive home, but I couldn't pass up the opportunity to bring them to one of my favorite places—arguably the most famous battlefield of the civil rights movement.

This city, which once—proudly—described itself as the most segregated in the South, has done an effective job of memorializing its role in the revolution that brought segregation down. Too effective, perhaps. While 16th St. Baptist Church, famous for the 1963 explosion that killed four little girls in Sunday school, still sits cater-corner[1] across the street, the rest of the area has changed dramatically.

If my memory and sense of direction are correct, the rooming house where Martin Luther King made his headquarters is a parking lot now. The storefronts against which people huddled for shelter from the water of high pressure hoses have been replaced by a civil rights museum. Meanwhile, the park itself, ground zero for the demonstrations, is filled with statues and inscriptions honoring the struggle that took place here.

---

1. **cater-corner:** diagonally.

Dr. Martin Luther King, Jr., March for Social and Economic Justice (top), January 18, 1999. Anti-segregation protesters seek shelter as firefighters use water hoses to break up a demonstration (above left), May 3, 1963. A young civil rights demonstrator is attacked by a police dog (left), May 3, 1963.

Elizabeth Eckford walking to Little Rock's Central High School on Sept. 4, 1957 (above). The white girl shouting at Eckford is Hazel Massery. Massery later regretted what she had done. In 1963, Massery apologized to Eckford. The two women (left) later became friends and have spoken publicly together about their experiences.

So it takes a little doing to get a sense of what it must have been like to be in this place then. To see the water cannon, hear the snarling dogs, feel the hammering of your own besieged heart. To put your life on the line as an agent of change. I am explaining these things to my sons and they are listening raptly. Which is gratifying, because when I was a teenager, I was pretty certain the past had nothing to do with me. I had little patience for my mother's Jim Crow tales,[2] less interest in my father's war stories. Then they died, taking with them all the things they knew and had seen, and it was a long time before I even realized all that I had lost. I thought history, while intermittently interesting, was a closed book, a finished story,

a period, end of paragraph, with no bearing on the urgencies of right now. By which I meant the 1970s and 1980s. Funny how fast "now" becomes "then."

So it is that I find myself struggling to help my sons understand what I did sooner than I did. That yesterday imposes upon today and shapes tomorrow. And that this means they have responsibilities here. Particularly because they are young African Americans, on whose behalf so much blood was shed, so many bones broken, so many lives lost.

We have come, in the words of "Lift Ev'ry Voice and Sing,"[3] to the "place for which our fathers sighed." Not the Promised Land, by any means. But still, a place where a young black person enjoys, at the very least, possibility.

---

2. **Jim Crow tales:** *Jim Crow* refers to the period of enforced segregation in the South from 1876 until the changes brought about by the civil rights movement of the mid-twentieth century.

3. **Lift Ev'ry Voice and Sing:** A moving spiritual, especially cherished by African Americans but with universal appeal.

Possibility elder generations could have scarcely dreamed. Possibility created for them at a bus stop in Montgomery, on a bridge in Selma, in a park in Birmingham.[4]

Possibility they are obliged to seize with both hands. And in doing so, recognize that history is not a closed book but an open one, not a finished story, but an unfolding one. Meaning that it's incumbent upon them to broaden what they have received and pass it to the generation that follows theirs.

My boys—you will forgive a father's pride— are bright, creative, talented young men. But they are young black men at a time when that description still closes doors, narrows eyes and hardens hearts. From where I sit, though, that's less an excuse for failure than a demand for excellence, courage, vision.

Sometimes, yes, history is a trick of the light. But sometimes, the future is, too.

Statue of Dr. Martin Luther King, Jr., Kelly Ingram Park, Birmingham, Alabama.

---

4. **bus stop in Montgomery . . . park in Birmingham:** Pitts refers to three important events in the civil rights movement—the 1955 arrest of Rosa Parks for refusing to give up her bus seat to a white man; the 1965 march across the Edmund Pettus Bridge in Selma, Alabama, when police attacked demonstrators with billy clubs and tear gas; and the civil rights demonstrations that occurred in Kelly Ingram Park during the 1960s.

Ask Yourself

1. **Read with a Purpose** Why does Leonard Pitts believe that it is important for his sons to visit the "battleground" of the civil rights movement?

2. Pitts admits that "when I was a teenager, I was pretty certain the past had nothing to do with me." What is your own attitude toward these historical events of half a century ago? Why is it important for us to study the past?

3. Looking back to his teenage years, Pitts says, "I thought history . . . was a closed book, a finished story, a period, end of paragraph, with no bearing on the urgencies of now." How and why has he changed his mind?

4. At the beginning and end of the essay, Pitts states that history is a "trick of the light." What do you think this statement means? Brainstorm ideas with a small group of your classmates.

Up from Slavery

LITERARY FOCUS
Slave Narratives

On to Liberty (1867) by Theodor Kaufmann. Detail.

CONTENTS

Link
to
Today

"My master had power and the law

on his side; I had a determined will.

There is might in each."

—Harriet A. Jacobs

Literary Focus

SKILLS FOCUS **Literary Skills** Evaluate and analyze the philosophical, political, religious, ethical, and social influences of a historical period.

Slave Narratives by **Leila Christenbury**

Characteristics of Slave Narratives

- Firsthand accounts written or recounted by slaves
- Tales of harrowing journeys from enslavement in the South to freedom in the North
- Detailed records of the mental as well as physical oppression of the narrator

> 'Tisn't he who has stood and looked on, that can tell you what slavery is—'tis who has endured.
>
> —John Little (1855)

These words by a fugitive slave appear in a **slave narrative**—a firsthand account written or orally recounted by a former slave. The majority of slave narratives were written during the Civil War and published by antislavery newspapers and journals. Slave narratives are <u>fundamentally</u> important both as historical documents that provide eyewitness accounts of the harsh realities of slavery and as autobiographies that give a voice to generations of enslaved people. They also constitute the beginning of a literary movement by African Americans in the United States.

The Origin of Slave Narratives

As the debate over slavery grew in the United States prior to the Civil War, antislavery activists, known as **abolitionists**, were determined to win the war of words by proving the evils of slavery. Abolitionists had been a part of American society since the founding of our nation. To fight against slavery they tried a variety of different tactics. They gave speeches to educate the public, and they pushed for public policies that, over time, made slavery illegal throughout the North. However, in their push for the total abolition of slavery in the United States, one of the abolitionists' most effective weapons was the testimony of those who best knew the bone-chilling facts about the inhumanity of slavery—former slaves themselves. Abolitionists began interviewing black runaways from the South while helping them escape to the North or to Canada on the Underground Railroad. These interviews were published in antislavery newspapers.

Frederick Douglass One of the best-known slave narratives, *Narrative of the Life of Frederick Douglass, an American Slave* (1845), gave its readers not only a remarkably accurate picture of slavery but also a compelling portrait of African American humanity. Douglass realized that a slave narrator had to be more than just an eyewitness to the brutality of slavery. The personal nature of an autobiography could also be a potent weapon against the racist myths that denigrated the humanity of black people.

Slave Narratives by Women Slave narratives by males typically stressed the author's heroic struggle for what Douglass called "my manhood." Formerly enslaved women, such as Sojourner Truth and Harriet A. Jacobs, spoke and wrote of their equally heroic efforts to preserve their self-respect as women in spite of slavery's attempts to turn them into its helpless, hopeless victims. In the following excerpt from a slave narrative, Mary Prince, a slave from the West Indies, recalls being sold at an auction:

> I then saw my sisters led forth, and sold to different owners; so that we had not the sad satisfaction of being partners in bondage. When the sale was over, my mother hugged and kissed us, and mourned over us, begging of us to keep up a good heart, and do our duty to our new masters. It was a sad parting; one went one way, one another, and our poor mammy went home with nothing.
>
> —Mary Prince (1831)

The Legacy of Slave Narratives

In the 1930s, the Works Progress Administration (WPA) Federal Writers' Project, an important Depression-era program that employed writers from around the country, conducted a series of interviews with some of the last surviving ex-slaves. The WPA compiled these valuable oral histories into a set of documents that were thought to be the last recorded slave narratives, though others have been uncovered since that time. Many of these narratives are striking because they provide eyewitness accounts of historical events, such as the following view of an event at the end of the Civil War.

> Marster and missus then went into the house got two large arm chairs put them on the porch facing the avenue and sat down side by side and remained there watching. In about an hour there was one of the blackest clouds coming up the avenue from the main road. It was the Yankee soldiers. . . . They called the slaves, saying, "You are free." Slaves were whooping and laughing and acting like they were crazy. . . .
>
> —Mary Anderson

The influence of slave narrative continues to be felt in more recent literature. Many scholars see the influence of the African American slave narrative in the autobiographies of modern African American writers, including Richard Wright's *Black Boy* (1945) and *The Autobiography of Malcolm X* (1965). In addition, the slave narrative has inspired important contemporary novels, including two Pulitzer Prize winners: William Styron's *The Confessions of Nat Turner* (1967) and Toni Morrison's *Beloved* (1987).

Portrait of Martha Rix, a former slave.

Ask Yourself

1. List three reasons that slave narratives are important.

2. What role did abolitionists play in the development and publication of slave narratives?

3. In your own words, describe the scene at the auction in the excerpt from Mary Prince's narrative.

4. What influence have slave narratives had on contemporary literature?

Learn It Online

Learn more about slave narratives online through *PowerNotes*.

go.hrw.com | L11-412 | **Go**

from **Narrative of the Life of Frederick Douglass**

SKILLS FOCUS **Literary Skills** Evaluate and analyze the philosophical, political, religious, ethical, and social influences of a historical period. **Reading Skills** Determine the writer's purpose or intent.

Analyzing Author's Purpose by **Kylene Beers**

Often an author is motivated to write because of personal circumstances. Through the text that the writer creates, these personal circumstances can become a focus of public interest and, in some cases, even a public cause. This is true of slave narratives in general and specifically of the highly regarded slave narrative by Frederick Douglass, *Narrative of the Life of Frederick Douglass, an American Slave.*

Authors rarely write for only one narrow purpose. They usually write to accomplish a set of related goals. Douglass's primary purpose for writing was to inform his readers about the inhumane conditions of slavery and to persuade readers to fight for change. However, he also had another purpose: to show oppressed slaves that it is possible to fight back against injustice.

To accomplish his primary purpose, Douglass used narration and description to tell of his experiences at the brutal hands of Mr. Covey. Note the descriptive details as Douglass relates an incident of becoming ill while carrying wheat to a fan in the fields owned by Mr. Covey:

> I was seized with a violent aching of the head, attended with extreme dizziness; I trembled in every limb.

As Douglass continues his story, he relates the sense of powerlessness and vulnerability that he felt:

> Finding what was coming, I nerved myself up, feeling it would never do to stop work. I stood as long as I could stagger to the hopper with grain. When I could stand no longer, I fell, and felt as if held down by an immense weight.

When Covey detects that work has stopped, he leaves his house to investigate and finds Douglass on the ground. Douglass uses descriptive details to help the reader see and experience Covey's cruelty:

> He then gave me a savage kick in the side, and told me to get up. I tried to do so, but fell back in the attempt. . . . While down in this situation, Mr. Covey took up the hickory slat with which Hughes had been striking off the half-bushel measure, and with it gave me a heavy blow upon the head, making a large wound, and the blood ran freely; and with this again told me to get up.

These vivid details create images that help Douglass achieve his purpose for writing: to make readers see the dehumanizing effects of slavery and to impel readers to take action against it.

Your Turn

Read the following passage from the narrative, and then discuss with a partner the techniques Douglass uses to accomplish his purpose.

> Mr. Covey seemed now to think he had me, and could do what he pleased; but at this moment—from whence came the spirit I don't know—I resolved to fight; and, suiting my action to the resolution, I seized Covey hard by the throat; and as I did so, I rose. He held on to me, and I to him. My resistance was so entirely unexpected, that Covey seemed taken all aback. He trembled like a leaf. This gave me assurance, and I held him uneasy, causing the blood to run where I touched him with the ends of my fingers.

Learn It Online

Practice analyzing an author's purpose with an interactive Reading Workshop online.

go.hrw.com   L11-413   **Go**

Preparing to Read

from Narrative of the Life of Frederick Douglass

What Do You Think

How does conflict lead to change?

🕐 QuickWrite

Think of a time when you experienced a turning point—a time when the way you viewed yourself underwent a sudden, dramatic change. In a paragraph, explain what caused this change. If you prefer, write about a turning point in the life of someone you know.

MEET THE WRITER

Frederick Douglass
(1817?–1895)

Frederick Douglass's experience and eloquence made him one of the most forceful opponents of slavery in American history.

A Hunger for Freedom

Douglass was born into slavery in Maryland and was separated from his mother soon after his birth. Since birth records were not kept for children born into slavery, Douglass was never sure of his exact age. Although Douglass received no formal education, he did teach himself to read with the help, at first, of members of the household he served. Later these same people became furious when they saw Douglass reading a book or newspaper; education, they decided, was incompatible with being enslaved.

When Douglass was about twenty-one, he escaped to Massachusetts, where he married and soon started to make public speeches in support of abolitionist <u>principles</u>. He later went to England, largely because of the danger he faced as a fugitive, especially after the publication of his autobiography *Narrative of the Life of Frederick Douglass, an American Slave.* In England he won support for the antislavery movement and became independent when British friends purchased his freedom.

Writing for a Cause

When he returned to the United States, in 1847, Douglass founded a newspaper, the *North Star.* (The name was chosen because escapees used this star as a guide north.) In his newspaper, Douglass championed the abolition of slavery. In 1855, he published a revised version of his life story, titled *My Bondage and My Freedom.* Douglass's narratives were widely read and very influential in the abolitionist cause.

After the Civil War, Douglass <u>advocated</u> for education as the surest way to rehabilitate his tragically scarred people. Today Douglass is revered for the courage with which he insistently proclaimed his profoundly humane values, and he is admired for the eloquence of his writing style.

Think About the Writer

Why do you think Douglass believed so strongly in education as a path to freedom and recovery?

Chester County Historical Society, West Chester, PA

Reader/Writer Notebook

Use your **RWN** to complete the activities for this selection.

Literary Focus

Diction A writer's or speaker's choice of words is **diction.** Writers and speakers select diction to suit their subject, purpose, and audience. Diction can be formal, informal, ornate, plain, and so on. Douglass provides us with a vivid account of an incident that occurred when he was a boy. He chooses ordinary, common words that are clear, effective, and precise.

Reading Focus

Analyzing Author's Purpose In many cases, writers combine several modes of expression—such as description, narration, exposition, and persuasion—in order to accomplish their **purpose.** Douglass's writing provides a good example. He does not rely solely on persuasion to prove that slavery is dehumanizing. As you read, look for details that show how Douglass *describes* his life as an enslaved person and *narrates* his experiences in order to persuade readers to take action against slavery.

Into Action As you read, record passages (noting where they appear) that are especially effective in helping Douglass advocate against slavery. In the left column of a chart like the one below, record each passage. In the right, explain why each passage is persuasive.

Passage	Why It's Persuasive
"...I broke down; my strength failed me; I was seized with a violent aching of the head, attended with extreme dizziness; I trembled in every limb. Finding what was coming, I nerved myself up, feeling it would never do to stop work." (p. 416)	It uses both description and narration to show the total powerlessness that characterized slaves' lives.

Vocabulary

epoch (EHP uhk) *n.:* noteworthy period of time. *The circumstances leading to Douglass's victory over Covey form an epoch in Douglass's history.*

comply (kuhm PLY) *v.:* obey; agree to a request or command. *Douglass refused to comply with Mr. Covey's command.*

subjected (suhb JEHKT ihd) *v.:* made to experience some action or treatment. *Douglass had been subjected to a brutal physical assault.*

interpose (ihn tuhr POHZ) *v.:* put forth in order to interfere. *Thomas was asked to interpose his authority in order to protect Douglass from Covey.*

gratification (grat uh fuh KAY shuhn) *n.:* satisfaction; delight. *Douglass's victory gave him increased self-confidence and a sense of gratification.*

Language Coach

Multiple-Meaning Words The word *subjected* is the past tense of the verb *subject,* which is also a very common noun and adjective. Look *subject* up in a dictionary to learn more about this word.

Writing Focus

Think as a Reader/Writer

Find It in Your Reading Douglass often uses a matter-of-fact **style** to describe dramatic events. In your *Reader/Writer Notebook,* record examples of Douglass's understated and matter-of-fact language. For each example, point out the dramatic event that Douglass is describing.

TechFocus As you read the selection, think about how Douglass might share his experiences if he were alive today.

 Learn It Online
Find out more about Frederick Douglass online at the Writers' Lives site.

go.hrw.com L11-415 **Go**

from

NARRATIVE OF THE LIFE OF
Frederick Douglass

by **Frederick Douglass**

Read with a Purpose

In this selection, Douglass describes "how a slave was made a man." As you read, note the events that lead to this important turning point in his life.

Build Background

In the following selection, Douglass provides a graphic account of a critical incident that occurred when he was sixteen years old. At the time, Douglass was "owned" by a man named Thomas, who had rented Douglass's services out for a year to a man named Covey. Earlier in his narrative, Douglass has explained to his readers "how a man was made a slave"; now he sets out to explain "how a slave was made a man."

THE BATTLE WITH MR. COVEY

I have already intimated that my condition was much worse, during the first six months of my stay at Mr. Covey's, than in the last six. The circumstances leading to the change in Mr. Covey's course toward me form an epoch in my humble history. You have seen how a man was made a slave; you shall see how a slave was made a man. On one of the hottest days of the month of August, 1833, Bill Smith, William Hughes, a slave named Eli, and myself, were engaged in fanning wheat.[1] Hughes was clearing the fanned wheat from before the fan, Eli was turning, Smith was feeding, and I was carrying wheat to the fan. The work was simple, requiring strength rather than intellect; yet, to one entirely unused to such work, it came very hard. **A**

About three o'clock of that day, I broke down; my strength failed me; I was seized with a violent aching of the head, attended with extreme dizziness; I trembled in every limb. Finding what was coming, I nerved myself up, feeling it would never do to stop work. I stood as long as I could stagger to the hopper with grain. When I could stand no longer, I fell, and felt as if held down by an immense weight. The fan of course stopped; everyone had his own work to do; and no one could do the work of the other, and have his own go on at the same time.

Mr. Covey was at the house, about one hundred yards from the treading yard where we were fanning. On hearing the fan stop, he left immediately, and came to the spot where we were. He hastily inquired what the matter was. Bill answered that I was sick, and there was no one to bring wheat to the fan. I had by this time crawled away under the side of the post-and-rail fence by which the yard was enclosed, hoping to find relief by getting out of the sun. He then asked where I was. He was told by one of the hands.

He came to the spot, and, after looking at me awhile, asked me what was the matter. I told him as well

---

1. **fanning wheat:** separating out usable grain by tossing in the air.

A **Reading Focus** **Analyzing Author's Purpose** What do you think is Douglass's purpose for writing about this episode? Use your own words.

Vocabulary **epoch** (EHP uhk) *n.:* noteworthy period of time.

Viewing and Interpreting How do the details in this picture (for example, the yoke on the wall, the ax lying on the floor, and the position of the two men) reflect the theme of Douglass's work?

The Life of Frederick Douglass (1939), Panel 10, by Jacob Lawrence. "The master of Douglass, seeing he was of a rebellious nature, sent him to a Mr. Covey, a man who had built up a reputation as a 'slave breaker.' A second attempt by Covey to flog Douglass was unsuccessful. This was one of the most important incidents in the life of Frederick Douglass: He was never again attacked by Covey. His philosophy: A slave easily flogged is flogged oftener; a slave who resists flogging is flogged less."

as I could, for I scarce had strength to speak. He then gave me a savage kick in the side, and told me to get up. I tried to do so, but fell back in the attempt. He gave me another kick, and again told me to rise. I again tried, and succeeded in gaining my feet; but, stooping to get the tub with which I was feeding the fan, I again staggered and fell. While down in this situation, Mr. Covey took up the hickory slat with which Hughes had been striking off the half-bushel measure, and with it gave me a heavy blow upon the head, making a large wound, and the blood ran freely; and with this again told me to get up. I made no effort to comply, having now made up my mind to let him do his worst. In a short time after

receiving this blow, my head grew better. Mr. Covey had now left me to my fate.

At this moment I resolved, for the first time, to go to my master, enter a complaint, and ask his protection. In order to [do] this, I must that afternoon walk seven miles; and this, under the circumstances, was truly a severe undertaking. I was exceedingly feeble; made so as much by the kicks and blows which I received, as by the severe fit of sickness to which I had been subjected. I, however, watched my chance, while Covey was looking in an opposite direction, and started for St. Michael's. I succeeded in getting a considerable distance on my way to the woods, when Covey discovered me, and called after me to come back, threatening what he would do if I did not come. I disregarded both his calls and his threats, and made my way to the woods as fast as my feeble state would allow; and thinking I might be overhauled by him if I kept the road, I walked through the woods, keeping far enough from the road to avoid detection, and near enough to prevent losing my way. **B**

I had not gone far before my little strength again failed me. I could go no farther. I fell down, and lay for a considerable time. The blood was yet oozing from the wound on my head. For a time I thought I should

---

B **Literary Focus** **Diction** In this paragraph, Douglass's writing style is matter-of-fact. How does Douglass's style help him achieve his purpose?

Vocabulary **comply** (kuhm PLY) *v.:* obey; agree to a request or command.
subjected (suhb JEHKT ihd) *v.:* made to experience some action or treatment.

bleed to death; and think now that I should have done so, but that the blood so matted my hair as to stop the wound. After lying there about three quarters of an hour, I nerved myself up again, and started on my way, through bogs and briers, barefooted and bareheaded, tearing my feet sometimes at nearly every step; and after a journey of about seven miles, occupying some five hours to perform it, I arrived at master's store. I then presented an appearance enough to affect any but a heart of iron. From the crown of my head to my feet, I was covered with blood. My hair was all clotted with dust and blood; my shirt was stiff with blood. My legs and feet were torn in sundry places with briers and thorns, and were also covered with blood. I suppose I looked like a man who had escaped a den of wild beasts, and barely escaped them. **C D**

In this state I appeared before my master, humbly entreating him to interpose his authority for my protection. I told him all the circumstances as well as I could, and it seemed, as I spoke, at times to affect him. He would then walk the floor, and seek to justify Covey by saying he expected I deserved it. He asked me what I wanted. I told him, to let me get a new home; that as sure as I lived with Mr. Covey again, I should live with but to die with him; that Covey would surely kill me; he was in a fair way for it. Master Thomas ridiculed the idea that there was any danger of Mr. Covey's killing me, and said that he knew Mr. Covey; that he was a good man, and that he could not think of taking me from him; that, should he do so, he would lose the whole year's wages; that I belonged to Mr. Covey for one year, and that I must go back to him, come what might; and that I must not trouble him with any more stories, or that he would himself *get hold of me.* After threatening me thus, he gave me a very large dose of salts, telling me that I might remain in St. Michael's that night (it being quite late), but that I must be off back to Mr. Covey's early in the morning; and that if I did not, he would *get hold of me,* which meant that he would whip me.

I remained all night, and, according to his orders, I started off to Covey's in the morning (Saturday morn-

ing), wearied in body and broken in spirit. I got no supper that night, or breakfast that morning. I reached Covey's about nine o'clock; and just as I was getting over the fence that divided Mrs. Kemp's fields from ours, out ran Covey with his cowskin, to give me another whipping. Before he could reach me, I succeeded in getting to the cornfield; and as the corn was very high, it afforded me the means of hiding. He seemed very angry, and searched for me a long time. My behavior was altogether unaccountable. He finally gave up the chase, thinking, I suppose, that I must come home for something to eat; he would give himself no further trouble in looking for me. I spent that day mostly in the woods, having the alternative before me—to go home and be whipped to death, or stay in the woods and be starved to death.

That night, I fell in with Sandy Jenkins, a slave with whom I was somewhat acquainted. Sandy had a free wife who lived about four miles from Mr. Covey's; and it being Saturday, he was on his way to see her. I told him my circumstances, and he very kindly invited me to go home with him. I went home with him, and talked this whole matter over, and got his advice as to what course it was best for me to pursue. I found Sandy an old advisor.[2] He told me, with great solemnity, I must go back to Covey; but that before I went, I must go with him into another part of the woods, where there was a certain *root,* which, if I would take some of it with me, carrying it *always on my right side,* would render it impossible for Mr. Covey, or any other white man, to whip me. He said he had carried it for years; and since he had done so, he had never received a blow, and never expected to while he carried it. I at first rejected the idea, that the simple carrying of a root in my pocket would have any such effect as he had said, and was not disposed to take it; but Sandy impressed the necessity with much earnestness, telling me it could do no harm, if it did no good. To please him, I at length took the root, and, according to his direction, carried it upon my right side. This was Sunday morning.

----

2. **an old advisor:** someone who can offer good advice.

C Reading Focus Analyzing Author's Purpose Why do you think Douglass describes his physical condition in so much detail?

D Literary Focus Diction Douglass compares himself to someone who has just "escaped a den of wild beasts." Why is this comparison ironic? How do the words "wild beasts" help Douglass achieve his purpose?

Vocabulary **interpose** (ihn tuhr POHZ) *v.*: put forth in order to interfere.

Root's working

I immediately started for home; and upon entering the yard gate, out came Mr. Covey on his way to meeting. He spoke to me very kindly, made me drive the pigs from a lot near by, and passed on towards the church. Now, this singular conduct of Mr. Covey really made me begin to think that there was something in the *root* which Sandy had given me; and had it been on any other day than Sunday, I could have attributed the conduct to no other cause than the influence of that root; and as it was, I was half inclined to think the *root* to be something more than I at first had taken it to be. All went well till Monday morning. On this morning, the virtue of the *root* was fully tested.

Long before daylight, I was called to go and rub, curry, and feed the horses. I obeyed, and was glad to obey. But while thus engaged, while in the act of throwing down some blades from the loft, Mr. Covey entered the stable with a long rope; and just as I was half out of the loft, he caught hold of my legs, and was about tying me. As soon as I found what he was up to, I gave a sudden spring, and as I did so, he holding to my legs, I was brought sprawling on the stable floor. Mr. Covey seemed now to think he had me, and could do what he pleased; but at this moment—from whence came the spirit I don't know—I resolved to fight; and, suiting my action to the resolution, I seized Covey hard by the throat; and as I did so, I rose. He held on to me, and I to him. My resistance was so entirely unexpected, that Covey seemed taken all aback. He trembled like a leaf. This gave me assurance, and I held him uneasy, causing the blood to run where I touched him with the ends of my fingers. Mr. Covey soon called out to Hughes for help. Hughes came, and, while Covey held me, attempted to tie my right hand. While he was in the act of doing so, I watched my chance, and gave him a heavy kick close under the ribs. This kick fairly sickened Hughes, so that he left me in the hands of Mr. Covey. **E**

This kick had the effect of not only weakening Hughes, but Covey also. When he saw Hughes bending over with pain, his courage quailed.[3] He asked me

3. **quailed:** faltered.

E Reading Focus Analyzing Author's Purpose Before saying that he had resolved to fight back, Douglass admits that "from whence came the spirit I don't know." How does this description of his state of mind add to the persuasiveness of his argument?

if I meant to persist in my resistance. I told him I did, come what might; that he had used me like a brute for six months, and that I was determined to be used so no longer. With that, he strove to drag me to a stick that was lying just out of the stable door. He meant to knock me down. But just as he was leaning over to get the stick, I seized him with both hands by his collar, and brought him by a sudden snatch to the ground. By this time, Bill came. Covey called upon him for assistance. Bill wanted to know what he could do. Covey said, "Take hold of him, take hold of him!" Bill said his master hired him out to work, and not to help to whip me; so he left Covey and myself to fight our own battle out. We were at it for nearly two hours. Covey at length let me go, puffing and blowing at a great rate, saying that if I had not resisted, he would not have whipped me half so much. The truth

The Life of Frederick Douglass (1939), Panel 12, by Jacob Lawrence. "It was in 1836 that Douglass conceived a plan of escape, also influencing several slaves around him. He told his co-conspirators what had been done, dared, and suffered by men to obtain the inestimable boon of liberty."

from Narrative of the Life of Frederick Douglass **419**

Douglass's Words Guide Archaeologists

More than 150 years after it was written, Frederick Douglass's autobiography is still revealing new facts about the lives of slaves. Archaeologists have used Douglass's writings, along with an eighteenth-century map, to explore the site of a slave village where Douglass spent two years of his childhood in the 1820s. Mark Leone, an archaeologist working on the excavation of the Wye House plantation in Maryland, says, "We have a priceless opportunity to assess the accuracy of Douglass's recollections."

According to Douglass, the slave village included a two-story brick building surrounded by huts on a "long green" that was "literally alive with slaves, of all ages, conditions, and sizes." Although the slave quarters disappeared more than a century ago, archaeologists have uncovered a brick foundation consistent with Douglass's description of the two-story house. Items such as spoons, knives, and bones from people's meals have also been discovered.

As archaeologist Lisa Kraus puts it, "The depth of history here is astonishing, and gives voice to the voiceless." Once again, Frederick Douglass has spoken for enslaved African Americans and ensured that their lives will be remembered.

Ask Yourself
How do the archaeological findings at Wye House support the historical accuracy of Douglass's writing?

---

was, that he had not whipped me at all. I considered him as getting entirely the worst end of the bargain; for he had drawn no blood from me, but I had from him. The whole six months afterward, that I spent with Mr. Covey, he never laid the weight of his finger upon me in anger. He would occasionally say, he didn't want to get hold of me again. "No," thought I, "you need not; for you will come off worse than you did before."

This battle with Mr. Covey was the turning point in my career as a slave. It rekindled the few expiring embers of freedom, and revived within me a sense of my own manhood. It recalled the departed self-confidence, and inspired me again with a determination to be free. The gratification afforded by the triumph was a full compensation for whatever else might follow, even death itself. He only can understand the deep satisfaction which I experienced, who has himself repelled by force the bloody arm of slavery. I felt as I never felt before. It was a glorious resurrection,[4] from the tomb of slavery, to the heaven of freedom. My long-crushed spirit rose, cowardice departed, bold defiance took its place; and I now resolved that, however long I might remain a slave in form, the day had passed forever when I could be a slave in fact. **F**

---

4. **resurrection:** coming back to life.

Vocabulary **gratification** (grat uh fuh KAY shuhn) *n.:* satisfaction; delight.

F **Literary Focus** Diction Douglass compares his new attitude to the religious experience of resurrection. How does the use of words with religious connotations help Douglass achieve his purpose?

Applying Your Skills

from **Narrative of the Life of Frederick Douglass**

Respond and Think Critically

Reading Focus

Quick Check

1. How does Thomas respond to Douglass's request for protection?

2. Explain how Sandy Jenkins helps Douglass.

Read with a Purpose

3. Douglass describes "how a slave was made a man." What events led to this turning point?

Reading Skills: Analyzing Author's Purpose

4. While reading, you recorded effective passages and explained why each is persuasive. Now, add a third column to your chart in which you analyze how diction adds power to each passage.

Passage	Why It's Persuasive	The Role of Diction
"...I broke down; my strength failed me; I was seized with a violent aching of the head, attended with extreme dizziness; I trembled in every limb. Finding what was coming, I nerved myself up, feeling it would never do to stop work." (p. 416)	It uses both description and narration to show the total powerlessness that characterized slaves' lives.	Words such as violent aching, dizziness, and trembled describe Douglass's acute illness. The phrase finding what was coming suggests that Douglass knew the severe consequences of taking a break.

Literary Focus

Literary Analysis

5. **Analyze** The root Douglass carried was thought to have supernatural powers. What made Douglass think the root was magical? What did he discover was more powerful than the root?

6. **Evaluate** Douglass writes, "He only can understand the deep satisfaction which I experienced, who has himself repelled by force the bloody arm of slavery." Do you agree with his statement? Can only someone who has been through a similar situation understand another person's experience? Explain.

Literary Skills: Diction

7. **Evaluate** Think about Douglass's purpose in writing this narrative. Consider Douglass's diction, including his objectivity and restraint in describing painful incidents. How does Douglass win over an audience that might be uneasy with the idea of a black man fighting a white man?

Literary Skills Review: Metaphor

8. **Interpret** A **metaphor** is a figure of speech that compares two unlike things without using comparison words such as *like* or *as*. Explain the metaphor implied in this line: "It [the battle with Covey] rekindled the few expiring embers of freedom." How is this metaphor related to the idea of rebirth?

Writing Focus

Think as a Reader/Writer

Use It in Your Writing Write a paragraph about someone facing a challenge. Use understated, matter-of-fact diction to describe the situation. Then, rewrite the paragraph using more dramatic language. Have a classmate read both versions. Discuss how the diction affects the tone and effect of each version.

 What Do **You Think Now** How can struggling against injustice affect the way a person views himself or herself? Explain.

Vocabulary Development

✓ Vocabulary Check

Match each Vocabulary word with its synonym.

1. epoch
2. comply
3. subjected
4. interpose
5. gratification

a. fulfillment
b. period
c. insert
d. obey
e. exposed

Vocabulary Skills: Context Clues

A word's **context**—the words and sentences that surround it—often gives clues to the word's meaning. The chart below shows how a close examination of context clues can reveal the meaning of the word *curry*.

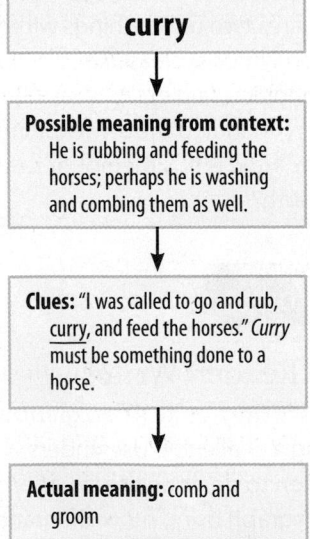

curry

↓

Possible meaning from context: He is rubbing and feeding the horses; perhaps he is washing and combing them as well.

↓

Clues: "I was called to go and rub, curry, and feed the horses." *Curry* must be something done to a horse.

↓

Actual meaning: comb and groom

The information around the word *curry* gives a number of clues about its meaning. As you read, context clues can help you make an informed guess about the meaning of an unfamiliar word. However, you should always use a dictionary to confirm your guess.

Your Turn

Look back at the selection, and see if there are any clues in the context that would help you figure out the meaning of each highlighted Vocabulary word. Record your findings in a chart like the one to the left.

Language Coach

Multiple-Meaning Words Many English words that are spelled the same have multiple meanings and sometimes different pronunciations. For example, the noun *subject* can mean "main idea" when it is pronounced "SUHB jehkt." The verb *subject,* which can mean "to bring under someone else's control," is pronounced "suhb JEHKT," with the emphasis on the second syllable. Look over the following list of words that have more than one meaning. Then, working with a partner, complete the chart using a dictionary. Practice pronouncing each word correctly with your partner.

Word	Part of speech and meaning	Part of speech and meaning	Same pronunciation?
produce	noun: farm or garden products	verb: to make something	no
address			
minute			
conflict			

Academic Vocabulary

Talk About
With a partner, discuss the <u>fundamental principles</u> that led Frederick Douglass to <u>advocate</u> against slavery.

Grammar Link

Verb Tense Consistency

Writers use **tense** to show at what point in time something happened. For example, in the excerpt you read from his narrative, Frederick Douglass used **past tense** to recount events that happened in the past. Unnecessarily changing verb tense in mid-sentence can create awkwardness and confusion. Unless you have a good reason for switching tenses, you should stick to one tense.

INCONSISTENT   Douglass received no formal education but teaches himself to read.

CONSISTENT   Douglass received no formal education but taught himself to read.

Your Turn

Check for consistency of verb tenses in the following sentences. If the tenses are consistent, write *correct*. If the tenses are not consistent, rewrite the sentence with the correct verb tense.

1. When Douglass was about twenty-one, he escapes to Massachusetts, where he changes his last name.

2. Because of the danger he faces as a fugitive slave, Douglass went to England.

3. When he returned to the United States, Douglass founded a newspaper.

Writing Application Choose a section of text—about ten sentences—from Douglass's work. Then, in your own words, re-write the text in the present tense, as if the action is happening right in front of your eyes. Be sure to use the present tense consistently. How are the two versions different?

CHOICES

As you respond to the Choices, use these **Academic Vocabulary** words as appropriate: advocate, criteria, fundamental, principle, subsequent.

REVIEW

Map the Narrative

Partner Activity Work with a partner to prepare a map of locations and a trail to show Douglass's route during the episode he recounts. For each location, add features—including buildings, tools, other objects, and people—to clarify which parts of the narrative happened there.

CONNECT

Explore Slave Narratives

Explore one of the many Web sites dedicated to preserving the written narratives and oral histories of former slaves, such as the Library of Congress's American Memory site. Choose an account you find particularly gripping. Then, present the narrative to your class in an oral report. Begin your report with a brief summary of the narrative. Be sure to use diction that fully expresses the horror of slavery.

EXTEND

Compare Communication

TechFocus Frederick Douglass shared his experiences as a slave by writing a book describing his life. Today, people have many different means of recording what happens in their lives, such as blogs, video diaries, documentaries, and digital stories. Choose a modern form of communication, and write a short essay comparing and contrasting it with a written narrative. Which form do you think would have a more powerful effect on an audience? What are the strengths and weaknesses of each form? Which would you choose to share your opinions on an issue you feel strongly about?

from Incidents in the Life of a Slave Girl

How does conflict lead to change?

QuickWrite

Think about a time when you or someone you know had to make a difficult decision that would affect others. What <u>criteria</u> were used to reach a decision? Write a few sentences reflecting on the decision and its effect on someone else.

Harriet A. Jacobs
(1813?–1897)

On the title page of her autobiography, Harriet Jacobs, a former slave, writes, "Northerners know nothing at all about Slavery. They think it is perpetual bondage only. They have no conception of the depth of *degradation* involved in that word, *Slavery. . . .*"

A Difficult Life

Harriet Jacobs was born into slavery in Edenton, North Carolina. Orphaned at the age of six, she was taken into the home of her mistress and trained as a house servant. She was taught how to read and write at a time when teaching these skills to enslaved people was illegal. When her mistress died, Jacobs was "willed" to her mistress's young niece and sent to live at the home of Dr. James Norcom.

Norcom subjected Jacobs to repeated harassment. Furious at her refusal of his advances, he sent her away to do hard labor as a plantation slave and then threatened to do the same to her two young children. Jacobs escaped and found shelter with the help of sympathetic relatives and friends, both black and white. In her grandmother's house in Edenton, she hid in a tiny crawl space above a storeroom for seven years—catching treasured glimpses of her children, whom Norcom had sold and who were living at the grandmother's house. In 1842, Jacobs escaped to New York City, where she was eventually reunited with her children. She spent the next ten years as a fugitive. In 1852, she finally gained her freedom.

Writing Her Story

Jacobs began writing the story of her life in 1853 and published it herself in 1861, using the pen name Linda Brent. *Incidents in the Life of a Slave Girl, Written by Herself* is an emotionally charged personal account and a fierce indictment of the slave system. After the publication of her book, Jacobs became active in the abolitionist movement, and she <u>advocated</u> tirelessly to relieve the poverty and suffering of other former slaves.

Think About the Writer   What does Harriet Jacobs's willingness to hide for seven years suggest about her situation as a slave?

Reader/Writer Notebook

Use your **RWN** to complete the activities for this selection.

Literary Focus

Style **Style** is the distinctive way a writer uses language. One aspect of Jacobs's style is her use of precise images that help readers imagine themselves in her shoes. Another element is her use of a highly informal **dialect** (local variations of spoken words). Notice the shift from standard language to dialect as the narrator tells her escape plan to her friend Sally:

> "Sally, they are going to carry my children to the plantation tomorrow. . . . Now, would you advise me to go back?"
> "No, chile, no," answered she. "When dey finds you is gone, dey won't want de plague ob de chillern."

Literary Perspectives Apply the literary perspective described on page 427 as you read this autobiographical narrative.

Reading Focus

Analyzing a Writer's Perspective Every writer has a unique viewpoint, or **perspective.** Harriet Jacobs's view of the world was <u>fundamentally</u> shaped by slavery. It established her identity and ruled her daily existence. Jacobs was more than a slave, though; she was also a woman, a mother, and a granddaughter.

Into Action As you read, use a graphic organizer like the one below to record language that shows Jacobs in each of her roles. Provide information about her roles as a slave, woman, mother, and granddaughter/niece.

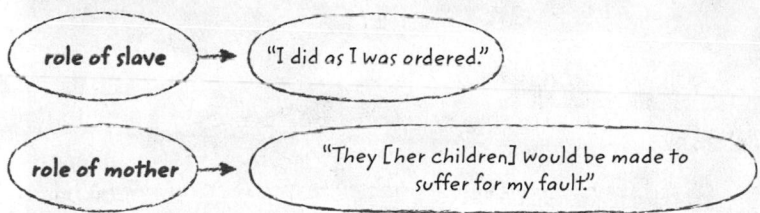

role of slave → "I did as I was ordered."

role of mother → "They [her children] would be made to suffer for my fault."

Writing Focus

Think as a Reader/Writer

Find It in Your Reading Jacobs varies her style by shifting between standard English and nonstandard English, in the form of **dialect.** As you read, notice how the use of dialect creates authenticity in characterization. In your *Reader/Writer Notebook,* note passages in which Jacobs shifts from the use of standard English to dialect.

Vocabulary

malice (MAL ihs) *n.:* ill will; desire to harm. *Jacobs fears that Mr. Flint will treat her with cruelty and malice.*

fervently (FUR vuhnt lee) *adv.:* with intense feeling. *With great passion, Jacobs prays fervently to God, begging for guidance and protection.*

provocation (prahv uh KAY shuhn) *n.:* something that stirs up action or feeling. *Many innocent slaves believe that they will be ill-treated by their masters without provocation.*

cunning (KUHN ihng) *adj.:* sly or crafty. *Cunning and resourceful, Jacobs creates a clever plan to escape Mr. Flint.*

compelled (kuhm PEHLD) *v.* used as *adj.:* driven; forced. *Fearing for her children, Jacobs feels compelled to escape.*

Language Coach

Word Parts *Mal—* is a Latin prefix meaning "bad." A similar prefix from Greek is *dys—.* What English words do you know that start with *mal—* or *dys—*?

Learn It Online
Get to know the Vocabulary words through Word Watch online.

go.hrw.com [L11-425] **Go**

from INCIDENTS IN THE LIFE OF A SLAVE GIRL

by **Harriet A. Jacobs**

Read with a Purpose

Read to discover the risks one woman is willing to take to escape a life of slavery.

Build Background

Harriet Jacobs's autobiography is an authentic historical narrative. She used language and dialect that were typical of her time but might be considered offensive by today's readers. Although *Incidents* *in the Life of a Slave Girl* is nonfiction, Jacobs used made-up names for the characters. The narrator, who says she is writing her autobiography, is called Linda Brent. Dr. James Norcom, the slaveholder who pursued Jacobs for years, is called Dr. or Mr. Flint. Mr. Sands is actually Samuel Sawyer, a white attorney who was an ally of Jacobs and the father of her children. Harriet Jacobs's grandmother was a free black woman who owned her own house.

THE FLIGHT

Mr. Flint was hard pushed for house servants, and rather than lose me he had restrained his malice. I did my work faithfully, though not, of course, with a willing mind. They were evidently afraid I should leave them. Mr. Flint wished that I should sleep in the great house instead of the servants' quarters. His wife agreed to the proposition, but said I mustn't bring my bed into the house, because it would scatter feathers on her carpet. I knew when I went there that they would never think of such a thing as furnishing a bed of any kind for me and my little one. I therefore carried my own bed, and now I was forbidden to use it. I did as I was ordered. But now that I was certain my children were to be put in their power, in order to give them a stronger hold on me, I resolved to leave them that night. I remembered the grief this step would bring upon my dear old grandmother; and nothing less than the freedom of my children would have induced me to disregard her advice. I went about my evening work with trembling steps. Mr. Flint twice called from his chamber door to inquire why the house was not locked up. I replied that I had not done my work. "You have had time enough to do it," said he. "Take care how you answer me!" **Ⓐ**

I shut all the windows, locked all the doors, and went up to the third story, to wait till midnight. How long those hours seemed, and how fervently I prayed that God would not forsake[1] me in this hour of utmost need! I was about to risk everything on the throw of a die; and if I failed, Oh what would become of me and my poor children? They would be made to suffer for my fault.

At half past twelve, I stole softly downstairs. I stopped on the second floor, thinking I heard a noise. I felt my way down into the parlor, and looked out of the window. The night was so intensely dark that I could see nothing. I raised the window very softly and jumped out. Large drops of rain were falling, and the darkness bewildered me. I dropped on my knees, and breathed a short prayer to God for guidance

---

1. **forsake:** abandon; give up.

and protection. I groped my way to the road, and rushed toward the town with almost lightning speed. I arrived at my grandmother's house, but dared not see her. She would say, "Linda,[2] you are killing me," and I knew that would unnerve me. I tapped softly at the window of a room occupied by a woman who had lived in the house several years. I knew she was a faithful friend, and could be trusted with my secret. I tapped several times before she heard me. At last she raised the window, and I whispered, "Sally, I have run away. Let me in, quick." She opened the door softly, and said in low tones, "For God's sake, don't. Your grandmother is trying to buy you and de chillern. Mr. Sands was here last week. He tole her he was going away on business, but he wanted her to go ahead about buying you and de chillern, and he

---

2. **Linda:** Jacobs's made-up name for herself.

Literary Perspectives

Analyzing Political Context Some critics believe that human history and institutions, even our ways of thinking, are determined by the ways in which our societies are organized. Two significant criteria shape political context: social class and gender. First, the class to which a person belongs determines his or her degree of economic, political, and social advantage. As a result, social classes invariably find themselves in conflict with each other. Membership in a social class also has a profound impact on one's beliefs, values, perceptions, and on ways of thinking and feeling. In Jacobs's account, consider the vast power difference between Linda Brent (Jacobs), a slave, and Dr. Flint, the slave owner. When considering gender, watch for Jacobs's difficulties that are specific to her status as a woman. (She is harassed by her slaveholder Dr. Flint; her status as mother also affects her escape and her subsequent actions.)

As you read, be sure to notice the questions in the text, which will guide you in using this perspective.

Ⓐ Reading Focus Analyzing a Writer's Perspective How does Jacobs's perspective as a mother influence her decision to run away?

Vocabulary malice (MAL ihs) *n.*: ill will; desire to harm.
fervently (FUR vuhnt lee) *adv.*: with intense feeling.

Viewing and Interpreting At the Lincoln Presidential Library in Springfield, Illinois, this display depicts slaves being sold. How does this scene add to Harriet Jacobs's insights into the institution of slavery?

would help her all he could. Don't run away, Linda. Your grandmother is all bowed down wid trouble now." **B**

I replied, "Sally, they are going to carry my children to the plantation tomorrow; and they will never sell them to anybody so long as they have me in their power. Now, would you advise me to go back?"

"No, chile, no," answered she. "When dey finds you is gone, dey won't want de plague ob de chillern; but where is you going to hide? Dey knows ebery inch ob dis house."

I told her I had a hiding place, and that was all it was best for her to know. I asked her to go into my

room as soon as it was light, and take all my clothes out of my trunk, and pack them in hers; for I knew Mr. Flint and the constable[3] would be there early to search my room. I feared the sight of my children would be too much for my full heart; but I could not go out into the uncertain future without one last look. I bent over the bed where lay my little Benny and baby Ellen. Poor little ones! Fatherless and motherless! Memories of their father came over me. He wanted to be kind to them; but they were not all to him, as they were to my womanly heart. I knelt and

---

B **Literary Focus** **Style** What effect does Sally's dialect have on the narrative? What does Sally's dialect indicate about the differences in education within the slave community?

---

3. **constable:** officer of the law, ranking just below sheriff.

prayed for the innocent little sleepers. I kissed them lightly, and turned away. **C**

As I was about to open the street door, Sally laid her hand on my shoulder, and said, "Linda, is you gwine all alone? Let me call your uncle."

"No, Sally," I replied, "I want no one to be brought into trouble on my account."

I went forth into the darkness and rain. I ran on till I came to the house of the friend who was to conceal me.

Early the next morning Mr. Flint was at my grandmother's inquiring for me. She told him she had not seen me, and supposed I was at the plantation. He watched her face narrowly, and said, "Don't you know anything about her running off?" She assured him that she did not. He went on to say, "Last night she ran off without the least provocation. We had treated her very kindly. My wife liked her. She will soon be found and brought back. Are her children with you?" When told that they were, he said, "I am very glad to hear that. If they are here, she cannot be far off. If I find out that any of my niggers have had anything to do with this damned business, I'll give 'em five hundred lashes." As he started to go to his father's, he turned round and added, persuasively, "Let her be brought back, and she shall have her children to live with her."

The tidings[4] made the old doctor rave and storm at a furious rate. It was a busy day for them. My grandmother's house was searched from top to bottom. As my trunk was empty, they concluded I had taken my clothes with me. Before ten o'clock every vessel northward bound was thoroughly examined, and the law against harboring[5] fugitives was read to all onboard. At night a watch was set over the town. Knowing how distressed my grandmother would be, I wanted to send her a message; but it could not be done. Everyone who went in or out of her house was closely watched. The doctor said he would take my children, unless she became responsible for them; which of course she willingly did. The next day was spent in searching. Before night, the following advertisement was posted at every corner, and in every public place for miles round:

$300 REWARD! Ran away from the subscriber,[6] an intelligent, bright mulatto[7] girl, named Linda, 21 years of age. Five feet four inches high. Dark eyes, and black hair inclined to curl; but it can be made straight. Has a decayed spot on a front tooth. She can read and write, and in all probability will try to get to the Free States. All persons are forbidden, under penalty of the law, to harbor or employ said slave. $150 will be given to whoever takes her in the state, and $300 if taken out of the state and delivered to me, or lodged in jail. **D**

Dr. Flint

Jacobs (Linda) passed a terrifying week in hiding. Then one night she heard her pursuers nearby. Afraid of capture, she rushed out of her friend's house and concealed herself in a thicket, where she was bitten by a poisonous reptile. Determined not to give up, Jacobs adopted the motto "Give me liberty, or give me death." With the aid of her friend Betty, she found shelter with the sympathetic wife of a local slaveholder. The woman urged Jacobs never to reveal who had helped her, and she hid the fugitive in a small upstairs storeroom.

MONTHS OF PERIL

I went to sleep that night with the feeling that I was for the present the most fortunate slave in town. Morning came and filled my little cell with light. I thanked the heavenly Father for this safe retreat. Opposite my window was a pile of feather beds. On the top of these I

---

4. tidings: news.
5. harboring: providing protection or shelter.

6. subscriber: literally, the person whose name is "written below"; that is, Dr. Flint.
7. mulatto: of mixed black and white ancestry.

C **Literary Perspectives** **Political Context** Why do you think Jacobs mentions the children's father in this scene? Compare the perspective of the children's father with that of Jacobs.

Vocabulary **provocation** (prahv uh KAY shuhn) *n.*: something that stirs up action or feeling.

D **Literary Focus** **Style** Why do you think that Jacobs includes Dr. Flint's advertisement of a reward? What does this element add to the narrative?

A white child with a slave nurse, 1858.

could lie perfectly concealed, and command a view of the street through which Dr. Flint passed to his office. Anxious as I was, I felt a gleam of satisfaction when I saw him. Thus far I had outwitted him, and I triumphed over it. Who can blame slaves for being cunning? They are constantly compelled to resort to it. It is the only weapon of the weak and oppressed against the strength of their tyrants. **E**

I was daily hoping to hear that my master had sold my children; for I knew who was on the watch to buy them. But Dr. Flint cared even more for revenge than he did for money. My brother William, and the good aunt who had served in his family twenty years, and my little Benny, and Ellen, who was a little over two years old, were thrust into jail, as a means of compelling my relatives to give some information about me. He swore my grandmother should never see one of them again till I was brought back. They kept these facts from me

for several days. When I heard that my little ones were in a loathsome jail, my first impulse was to go to them. I was encountering dangers for the sake of freeing them, and must I be the cause of their death? The thought was agonizing. My benefactress[8] tried to soothe me by telling me that my aunt would take good care of the children while they remained in jail. But it added to my pain to think that the good old aunt, who had always been so kind to her sister's orphan children, should be shut up in prison for no other crime than loving them. I suppose my friends feared a reckless movement on my part, knowing, as they did, that my life was bound up in my children. I received a note from my brother William. It was scarcely legible, and ran thus: "Wherever you are, dear sister, I beg of you not to come here. We are all much better off than you are. If you come, you will ruin us all. They would force you to tell where you had been, or they would kill you. Take the advice of your friends; if not for the sake of me and your children, at least for the sake of those you would ruin." **F**

Poor William! He also must suffer for being my brother. I took his advice and kept quiet. My aunt was taken out of jail at the end of a month, because Mrs. Flint could not spare her any longer. She was tired of being her own housekeeper. It was quite too fatiguing to order her dinner and eat it too. My children remained in jail, where brother William did all he could for their comfort. Betty went to see them sometimes, and brought me tidings. She was not permitted to enter the jail; but William would hold them up to the grated window while she chatted with them. When she repeated their prattle,[9] and told me how they wanted to see their ma, my tears would flow. Old Betty would exclaim, "Lors, chile! what's you crying 'bout? Dem young uns vil kill you dead. Don't be so chick'n-hearted! If you does, you vil nebber git thro' dis world."

---

8. **benefactress:** woman who gives aid.
9. **prattle:** chatter; babble.

E Literary Focus **Style** What images help you imagine this scene? Why do you think the narrator includes the words *weapon, weak, oppressed,* and *tyrants*?

Vocabulary **cunning** (KUHN ihng) *adj.:* sly or crafty. **compelled** (kuhm PEHLD) *v.* used as *adj.:* driven; forced.

F Reading Focus **Analyzing a Writer's Perspective** How do you think the narrator feels after reading William's letter? Do you think she has any regrets about running away? Why or why not?

Applying Your Skills

SKILLS FOCUS Literary Skills Analyze a writer's style; analyze conflict. **Reading Skills** Analyze a writer's perspective. **Vocabulary Skills** Identify antonyms. **Writing Skills** Use dialogue effectively.

from **Incidents in the Life of a Slave Girl**

Respond and Think Critically

Reading Focus

Quick Check

1. How does Dr. Flint try to use Jacobs's children as a means of manipulation?

2. What advice does Jacobs receive from her brother William?

Read with a Purpose

3. Consider the other characters in the text who help Jacobs. Why might these people put their own safety at risk to help her?

Reading Skills: Analyzing a Writer's Perspective

4. Review your notes about Jacobs's roles, and explain how Jacobs's use of language helps the reader understand the writer's perspective.

✔ Vocabulary Check

Match each Vocabulary word to its antonym (word with opposite meaning).

5. malice   **a.** persuaded
6. fervently   **b.** straightforward
7. provocation   **c.** goodwill
8. cunning   **d.** conciliation
9. compelled   **e.** unemotionally

Literary Focus

Literary Analysis

10. **Analysis** Cite details in the text that reveal Jacobs's character.

11. **Make Judgments** Re-read the text, and cite specific passages that mention Jacobs's religious influences. How do Jacobs's beliefs affect her viewpoint and decisions?

12. **Extend** What is Jacobs's purpose in writing and publishing her story? Judging from this excerpt, do you think she achieved her purpose? Explain.

13. **Literary Perspectives** How might Jacobs's situation have differed from that of a man in slavery?

Literary Skills: Style

14. **Analyze** Suspense is a fundamental element of Jacobs's style. What details in the narrative heighten suspense?

Literary Skills Review: Conflict

15. **Analyze** A character's **conflicts** can be **internal** (such as a struggle with conscience) or **external** (such as a struggle with another person or with society). How does Jacobs resolve one of her internal conflicts? How does her decision affect her external conflict?

Writing Focus

Think as a Reader/Writer

Use It in Your Writing Review your QuickWrite about a difficult decision that affected another person. Write a few sentences of dialogue that capture the way the other person reacted when he or she learned of the decision.

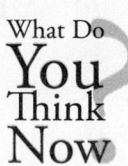 What Do **You Think Now** How might Harriet Jacobs's story inspire women of all backgrounds to fight for change in their lives?

Spirituals

Go Down, Moses

Swing Low, Sweet Chariot

Follow the Drinking Gourd

What Do You Think?

How does conflict lead to change?

QuickTalk

The spirituals sung by enslaved African Americans contributed significantly to American culture. Think about songs you listen to now. How might they reflect or define your culture? Discuss these questions in a small group.

INTRODUCTION

Spirituals

The moving and intensely emotional songs known as spirituals developed largely from the oral traditions of Africans held in slavery in the South before the Civil War. Spirituals, like other kinds of folk literature and music, were composed by anonymous artists and passed on orally. They often combine African melodies and rhythms with elements of white southern religious music. As the songs were passed from generation to generation by word of mouth, lines were changed and new stanzas were added, so sometimes numerous versions of a particular spiritual exist.

Expressions of Hope

Spirituals were concerned <u>fundamentally</u> with issues of freedom: spiritual freedom in the form of salvation and literal freedom from the shackles of slavery. Stories and figures from the Bible were especially prominent in the songs. Like the Biblical leader Moses, who delivered the ancient Israelites from slavery in Egypt, Harriet Tubman, herself an escaped slave, was famous for leading other enslaved people to freedom on the Underground Railroad. She was sometimes known as Moses. The song "Go Down, Moses" expressed the hope that a savior would again go "way down in Egypt land" and deliver runaways to freedom.

Some of the songs were code songs, or signal songs—that is, songs with details that provided runaways with directions, times, and meeting places for their escapes. For example, in "Follow the Drinking Gourd," the drinking gourd referred to was literally the shell of a vegetable related to the squash and melon that could be dried and hollowed out for holding water. Slaves, however, knew that the drinking gourd was also the Big Dipper, a group of stars. Two stars in the bowl of the Big Dipper pointed to the North Star, in the direction of freedom.

Think About the Spirituals

Can spirituals be considered a form of resistance against slavery? Explain.

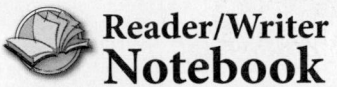

Reader/Writer Notebook

Use your **RWN** to complete the activities for these selections.

Literary Focus

Refrain A **refrain** is a word, phrase, line, or group of lines that is repeated for effect in a poem or song. In songs, refrains often express the most important idea or message in addition to achieving rhythmic or emotional effects. In the spirituals you are about to read, the refrains were often used as a call-and-response feature of group singing. **Call and response** was a pattern of exchange between a singer or storyteller and an audience in many African societies. Try reading the spirituals aloud in groups. Pick one person to read aloud "the call," and have the rest of the group respond with the refrain.

Reading Focus

Determining Purpose Spirituals served a variety of **purposes** for the enslaved people who sang them. Sung by a group working in the fields, spirituals were an expression of solidarity. They also served as a source of inspiration and hope that there would be an end to the people's suffering. In addition, some spirituals were code songs, providing listeners with instructions for escaping to freedom.

Into Action As you read the following spirituals, use a chart like the one below to take notes about the possible purposes of each song. As you look for details that help you determine purpose, pay particular attention to each song's refrain.

	Details That Help Me Determine Purpose	Possible Purposes
Go Down, Moses	Refrain: Let my people go.	To connect the slaves' condition to that of the Israelites in Egypt.
Swing Low, Sweet Chariot		
Follow the Drinking Gourd		

Language Coach

Related Words The spirituals you will read came from a people's desire to escape oppression—the cruel and crushing abuse of power. In "Go Down, Moses," the lyrics say that the people of Israel were "oppressed so hard they could not stand."

Along with *oppressed,* you have probably encountered the word *repressed.* *Oppressed* and *repressed* are very similar in meaning—they can both mean "to hold down by force"—yet *oppressed* has a more negative **connotation** (the feelings and associations that are attached to a word).

In a small group, discuss three other words that have the root *–press–* (perhaps *suppress, compress, depress*). Use reference sources such as dictionaries or usage guides to learn more about each word. Then, use each word in a sentence to show the differences in meaning.

Writing Focus

Think as a Reader/Writer

Find It in Your Reading As you read, identify repeated words and phrases that might have conveyed secret signals to the slaves. Record these words in your *Reader/Writer Notebook,* and make notes about what each one might have meant.

 Learn It Online
Follow spirituals into the twenty-first century with these Internet links.

go.hrw.com | L11-433 | **Go**

Go Down, Moses

Read with a Purpose

Read to learn how an enslaved people express their longing for liberation by invoking the situation of another enslaved people.

Build Background

Many Africans encountered Christianity for the first time when they were brought to America as slaves. Some enslaved Africans viewed the religion as hypocritical: Although it advocated brotherly love in principle, in practice slaveholders asserted ownership over and frequently mistreated fellow human beings. Still, many slaves were drawn to Biblical stories about oppressed people like themselves. Spirituals often allude to Biblical figures, places, and events, such as Moses and the Promised Land.

Go down, Moses,
Way down in Egypt land
Tell old Pharaoh°
To let my people go. **Ⓐ**

3. Pharaoh (FAIR oh): title of ancient Egyptian kings.

5   When Israel was in Egypt land
Let my people go
Oppressed so hard they could not stand
Let my people go.

Go down, Moses,
10   Way down in Egypt land
Tell old Pharaoh,
"Let my people go."

"Thus saith the Lord," bold Moses said,
"Let my people go;
15   If not I'll smite your firstborn dead°
Let my people go."

15. smite . . . dead: kill. When the Pharaoh refuses to let the Israelites go, the Lord inflicts a series of plagues on the Egyptians, finally killing the firstborn of every household.

Go down, Moses,
Way down in Egypt land,
Tell old Pharaoh,
20   "Let my people go!" **Ⓑ**

Ⓐ **Literary Focus** **Refrain** Enslaved people identified with the Israelites. How does the refrain in "Go Down, Moses" emphasize this identification?

Ⓑ **Reading Focus** **Determining Purpose** What do you think is the purpose of connecting the slaves' situation to that of the Israelites?

Analyzing Visuals

Poor Man's Cotton (1944)
by Hale Aspacio Woodruff

Viewing and Interpreting This image, like the songs it accompanies, reflects both suffering and strength. In what ways do this painting and the spirituals offer a glimpse into the feelings of people living under oppression?

Swing Low, Sweet Chariot

Watercolor by Alfred Heber Hutty (undated)
Morris Museum of Art, Augusta, Georgia.

Read with a Purpose Read to learn how an enslaved people use the image of a chariot to express their hope for freedom.

Swing low, sweet chariot,
Coming for to carry me home,°
Swing low, sweet chariot,
Coming for to carry me home.

5   I looked over Jordan° and what did I see
Coming for to carry me home,
A band of angels, coming after me,
Coming for to carry me home.

If you get there before I do,
10 Coming for to carry me home,
Tell all my friends I'm coming too,
Coming for to carry me home.

Swing low, sweet chariot,
Coming for to carry me home,
15 Swing low, sweet chariot,
Coming for to carry me home.   **A B**

2. The first two lines in this spiritual are a Biblical allusion to II Kings 2:1–12. When the prophet Elijah comes to the River Jordan, a chariot of fire and horses appear, and Elijah is taken up to heaven by a whirlwind.
5. Jordan: the Jordan River in the Middle East. In spirituals, *Jordan* was code for the Ohio River, which separated slave states from free states.

A Literary Focus Refrain What is the refrain of this song? How might this refrain have affected slaves who sang the song?

B Reading Focus Determining Purpose As a symbol of transport, what might the chariot signify? What might "home" signify? How do these symbols help convey the song's purpose?

Follow the Drinking Gourd

Cautious Advance Into the Light
by Janice Huse

Read with a Purpose Read to see how an enslaved people use a spiritual to encode directions for escape.

When the sun comes back and the first quail calls,
 Follow the drinking gourd,
For the old man° is a-waiting for to carry you to freedom
 If you follow the drinking gourd. **Ⓐ**

5 Follow the drinking gourd,
 Follow the drinking gourd,
For the old man is a-waiting for to carry you to freedom
 If you follow the drinking gourd.

The river bank will make a very good road,
10 The dead trees show you the way,
Left foot, peg foot traveling on
 Follow the drinking gourd.

Follow the drinking gourd,
 Follow the drinking gourd,
15 For the old man is a-waiting for to carry you to freedom
 If you follow the drinking gourd.

The river ends between two hills,
 Follow the drinking gourd.
There's another river on the other side,
20 Following the drinking gourd.

3. old man: refers to Peg Leg Joe, believed to be a carpenter who traveled from plantation to plantation teaching slaves this song.

Ⓐ Literary Focus Refrain The refrain's <u>fundamental</u> images—a drinking gourd and an old man—seem oddly benign. Why is this a suitable refrain for a code song?

Follow the drinking gourd,
     Follow the drinking gourd,
For the old man is a-waiting for to carry you to freedom
     If you follow the drinking gourd.

25   Where the little river meets the great big river,
     Follow the drinking gourd.
The old man is a-waiting for to carry you to freedom,
     If you follow the drinking gourd.

   Follow the drinking gourd,
30   Follow the drinking gourd,
For the old man is a-waiting for to carry you to freedom
     If you follow the drinking gourd. **Ⓑ**

Ⓑ **Reading Focus** **Determining Purpose** "Follow the Drinking Gourd" was used to teach slaves the escape route from Mississippi and Alabama. Which words in the spiritual do you think represent specific directions for escaped slaves to follow? Explain.

MUSIC LINK

Music of the Soul

The enormous popularity of African American music in the United States—spirituals, gospel music, blues, jazz, soul, rap—can be traced back to the years following the Civil War. In 1871, the Jubilee Singers from Fisk University, in Tennessee, made a series of tours in which they introduced the African American spiritual to general audiences in the United States. The result was a national recognition of the beauty of spirituals, which opened the mainstream American public to an ever-growing appreciation of different forms of African American music.

Ask Yourself

Review the spirituals. What specific elements of these songs might have made them so appealing to a wide audience? Why?

The Granger Collection, New York

Applying Your Skills

Spirituals

Respond and Think Critically

Reading Focus

Quick Check

1. In "Go Down, Moses," why does the Lord send Pharaoh a message? Who relays the message?

2. Summarize the speaker's desire in "Swing Low, Sweet Chariot."

3. How is a route of escape shared in "Follow the Drinking Gourd"?

Read with a Purpose

4. How do the spirituals use different images to express a longing for liberation?

Reading Skills: Determining Purpose

5. Review the possible purposes and details you listed in your chart. Then, in a new column comment on the overall purpose of each song.

	Details	Possible Purposes	Overall Purpose
Go Down, Moses	Refrain: Let my people go.	To connect the slaves' condition to that of the Israelites in Egypt.	To express the desire for someone who will lead people out of slavery.
Swing Low, Sweet Chariot			
Follow the Drinking Gourd			

Literary Focus

Literary Analysis

6. **Analyze** How could the call-and-response structure of spirituals have helped create a sense of solidarity among slaves working in the fields?

7. **Evaluate** Do you think reading and discussing slave narratives and spirituals can affect our understanding of slavery today? Why or why not?

8. **Make Judgments** Which spiritual evoked the deepest reaction from you? Why?

Literary Skills: Refrain

9. **Evaluate** Re-read the refrain of each song. Do the refrains convey to you mainly a sense of suffering and struggle, or of hope and relief? Explain.

Literary Skills Review: Symbolism

10. **Draw Conclusions** A **symbol** is a person, place, thing, or event that has meaning in itself and also stands for something more than itself. In "Swing Low, Sweet Chariot," what might the chariot and "home" symbolize in religious terms? How does examining the religious symbolism of these terms deepen your understanding of the song?

Writing Focus

Think as a Reader/Writer

Use It in Your Writing Write lyrics for a two-verse song that uses repeated words or phrases to convey a code or secret message to someone. You can use a simple tune such as "Row, Row, Row Your Boat." Choose your words carefully, and be prepared to explain the coded words.

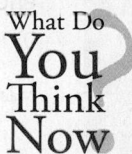

What Do You Think Now These spirituals reflect an intense desire for change. Do the songs suggest that slaves seek a violent or a peaceful means to secure their freedom? Explain.

Ain't I a Woman?

Sojourner Truth
(1797–1883)

Although Sojourner Truth never learned to read or write, her speeches <u>advocating</u> women's rights and denouncing slavery made her one of the most effective orators of her time.

A Call to Action

Sojourner Truth was born a slave in New York State. Her real name was Isabella Baumfree. As a child, she was sold to slaveholders who overworked and abused her. In 1827—shortly before New York passed laws abolishing slavery—Isabella escaped to freedom. While working in New York City, Isabella came under the influence of an evangelical preacher. She claimed that she received a call from God. In 1843 she changed her name to Sojourner ("traveler") Truth and began to travel throughout the United States, preaching religion, feminism, and abolition.

Truth's exceptional height, powerful voice, and flair for the dramatic made her a popular speaker. She sometimes shared the platform with Frederick Douglass. In 1850, she published her autobiography, *Narrative of Sojourner Truth: A Northern Slave,* which she had dictated to someone else.

Although Truth was frequently asked to speak at gatherings, she also appeared uninvited and would often interrupt to speak out on issues concerning women and slavery. Such was the case with her famous speech "Ain't I a Woman?" Before she spoke, others had argued that men were entitled to superior rights because of intellectual superiority and religious reasons.

Beloved Crusader

During the Civil War, Truth solicited and distributed supplies for African American regiments. She also helped fugitive slaves who had escaped to the North find work and housing. After the war, encouraged by suffragist Elizabeth Cady Stanton, Truth continued her work for women's rights. She petitioned Congress to give free tools and land in the West to former slaves to end their dependence on charity. By the time Truth died, nearly ninety years old, she had become a beloved national figure.

What Do You Think?

How does conflict lead to change?

QuickWrite

Think about something unfair that you would like to see changed. Why might someone disagree with you? Briefly state what you would like to see changed, and state one objection to that change that someone else might have.

Think About the Writer

Why do you think Sojourner Truth was attracted to the crusade for women's rights?

Reader/Writer Notebook

Use your **RWN** to complete the activities for this selection.

Literary Focus

Oratory The art of public speaking is called **oratory.** Orators, like poets, use the sounds of words as well as their meanings to communicate ideas. Orators employ **rhetoric**—the language of persuasion—to try to win over their audiences. In her speech, Sojourner Truth appeals to both **reason** and **emotion** as she argues for the <u>principles</u> she <u>advocates</u>—the equal rights of women and African Americans.

Reading Focus

Analyzing Rhetorical Devices Both speakers and writers use **rhetorical devices,** like the ones listed below, to make their words more effective.

- **rhetorical question:** a question that is asked for effect and that does not actually require an answer
- **repetition:** the recurrence of particular words, sounds, or ideas
- **allusion:** a reference to a person, place, or event from history or literature
- **counterargument:** an argument that anticipates and addresses the audience's or an opponent's objections and concerns
- **personal account:** example or account of an experience that supports the speaker's points

Into Action As you read Truth's speech, use a chart like the one below to record examples of the different rhetorical devices that she uses and note whether these devices appeal to logic or emotion.

Rhetorical Devices	Examples from Truth's Speech	Type of Appeal: Logical or Emotional?
counterargument	"That man over there says that women need to be helped into carriages. . . . Nobody ever helps me into carriages. . . . And ain't I a woman?"	logical and emotional

Writing Focus

Think as a Reader/Writer

Find It in Your Reading In her speech, Truth appeals to both logic and emotion to convince her audience. As you read, write down in your *Reader/Writer Notebook* some examples of each type of appeal.

Language Coach

Dialect Dialect is a way of speaking that is particular to a region or group of people. Sojourner Truth's speech "Ain't I a Woman?" contains dialect—phrases, contractions, and idioms that were particular to her historical context. In her speech, Truth uses dialect in addition to her use of standard English to express her ideas. When Truth gave her speech, her use of dialect reinforced her personal appeal as an authentic voice for the downtrodden, including phrases such as "out of kilter" for "not right" or "'twixt" for "between two things." With a partner, identify the standard English equivalents of the following examples of dialect from "Ain't I a Woman?": "ain't" and "all this here talking." Discuss how using the dialect versions of these terms helps Truth convey her message to her audience.

Learn It Online
Let this speech come alive. Listen to it online.

go.hrw.com   L11-441   **Go**

AIN'T I A WOMAN?

by **Sojourner Truth**

Read with a Purpose
Read to discover how Sojourner Truth counters the arguments of those who want to deny women equal rights.

Build Background
"Ain't I a Woman?" may be Sojourner Truth's best-known speech. It was delivered in May 1851 at a women's rights convention in Akron, Ohio. Since this speech was made without preparation, we have only records made by people who attended the convention. Several versions of the speech exist. The most commonly quoted version, which appears below, was written down by Frances Gage, president of the Woman's Rights Convention in Akron. It appeared in print in 1863, years after the speech had been given. It is in this text that the rhetorical question "Ain't I a Woman?" first appears.

Well, children, where there is so much racket there must be something out of kilter. I think that 'twixt the negroes of the South and the women at the North, all talking about rights, the white men will be in a fix pretty soon. But what's all this here talking about?

That man over there says that women need to be helped into carriages, and lifted over ditches, and to have the best place everywhere. Nobody ever helps me into carriages, or over mud-puddles, or gives me any best place! And ain't I a woman? Look at me! Look at my arm! I have plowed and planted, and gathered into barns, and no man could head me! And ain't I a woman? I could work as much and eat as much as a man—when I could get it—and bear the lash as well! And ain't I a woman? I have borne thirteen children, and seen them most all sold off to slavery,[1] and when I cried out with my mother's grief, none but Jesus heard me! And ain't I a woman? **Ⓐ**

Then they talk about this thing in the head; what's this they call it? [Intellect, someone whispers.] That's it, honey. What's that got to do with women's rights or negro's rights? If my cup won't hold but a pint, and yours hold a quart, wouldn't you be mean not to let me have my little half-measure full?

Then that little man in black there, he says women can't have as much rights as men, 'cause Christ wasn't a woman! Where did your Christ come from? Where did your Christ come from? From God and a woman! Man had nothing to do with Him. **Ⓑ**

If the first woman God ever made was strong enough to turn the world upside down all alone, these women together ought to be able to turn it back, and get it right side up again! And now they is asking to do it, the men better let them.

Obliged to you for hearing me, and now old Sojourner ain't got nothing more to say.

---

1. **thirteen children . . . slavery:** Truth actually bore five or six children to her husband, Thomas, to whom she was married around 1816. This allusion more accurately reflects her mother's experience.

Ⓐ Reading Focus Analyzing Rhetorical Devices How does Truth use the rhetorical device of counterargument to effectively address her opponents' claims?

Ⓑ Literary Focus Oratory Explain how Truth appeals to both logic and emotion to make her point. Which appeal do you think is more effective?

Applying Your Skills

SKILLS FOCUS **Literary Skills** Analyze characteristics of persuasion; analyze metaphor. **Reading Skills** Identify and understand appeals to reason; identify and understand appeals to emotion, including loaded words; identify and understand the use of counterclaims/counterarguments in a text. **Writing Skills** Address potential objections.

Ain't I a Woman?

Respond and Think Critically

Reading Focus

Quick Check

1. According to Truth, what is "out of kilter"?

2. How does Truth respond to the claim that women should always be given the best place?

Read with a Purpose

3. How does Truth counter the arguments of those who want to deny women their rights?

Reading Skills: Analyze Rhetorical Devices

4. While reading the speech, you recorded examples of the rhetorical devices that Truth uses to make her point. Now, look over your chart. Add a column, and analyze how the devices she uses help her achieve her purpose.

Rhetorical Devices	Examples from Truth's Speech	Type of Appeal: Logical or Emotional?	Rhetoric
counterargument	"That man over there says that women need to be helped into carriages...Nobody ever helps me into carriages... And ain't I a woman?"	logical and emotional	Her argument exposes the hypocrisy of the man's claim since she is a woman, yet never receives special treatment.

Literary Focus

Literary Analysis

5. **Interpret** How is the question "Ain't I a Woman?" used like a refrain repeated for effect? What point does she make with this question?

6. **Draw Conclusions** Why do you think Truth uses the words *children* and *honey* in addressing the audience? What effect do you think these words might have had on her listeners?

7. **Analyze** In what ways does Truth use humor to try to resolve conflict and bring about change?

8. **Evaluate** What do you think of Truth's speech? How do you think her audience might have responded to her message? Explain.

Literary Skills: Oratory

9. **Evaluate** In oratory, the sounds of words can add power to the speaker's argument. How does the rhetorical device of repetition create sound effects in Truth's speech? How does her use of sound add to her persuasive power?

Literary Skills Review: Metaphor

10. **Evaluate** A **metaphor** is a figure of speech that compares two unlike things without using a term of comparison such as *like* or *as*. How does Sojourner Truth use metaphor to refute the argument about intellect?

Writing Focus

Think as a Reader/Writer

Use It in Your Writing Review your QuickWrite about something that you wish to see changed. Write a paragraph using counterargument to address one objection from someone who may disagree.

 What Do **You Think Now** Do you think Truth's direct style and use of counterargument are effective, or do you think that she is too bold and confrontational? Explain.

For **CHOICES** see page 449. >

at the cemetery, walnut grove plantation, south carolina, 1989

What Do You Think

How does conflict lead to change?

QuickWrite

Think of a time when you or someone you know chose to deal with a difficult situation rather than avoid it. In a paragraph, reflect on this situation and on how addressing it led to a new awareness or understanding.

MEET THE WRITER

Lucille Clifton
(1936–)

Link to Today

Lucille Clifton was surrounded by stories from the beginning of her life. Although her parents had little education, they were avid readers who introduced their children to the poems of Paul Laurence Dunbar and Langston Hughes, prominent African American writers.

A Sense of Family

National Book Award WINNER

Clifton's father loved to tell stories of the family's history. These stories often revolved around his great-grandmother Caroline, who was kidnapped from Africa and enslaved in America in 1830. Caroline, who spent much of her life in slavery and became a respected midwife, loomed large in young Lucille's imagination, becoming a model of perseverance.

The <u>fundamentals</u> of Clifton's poems—slavery, family, her heritage, strong women, and the dignity of ordinary people—relate directly to the stories she heard as a child. In her poem "harriet," she addresses her grandmother, as well as the African American abolitionists Harriet Tubman and Sojourner Truth, asking them not to let her forget the lessons they taught her. *Generations,* her memoir, further explores these themes.

A Writer's Responsibility

Clifton has published twelve volumes of poetry. Her first poems were published by Langston Hughes in an anthology of African American poetry. Her first complete book of poems, *Good Times,* was selected by the *New York Times* as one of the ten best books of 1969. Clifton has twice been nominated for the Pulitzer Prize and won the National Book Award for *Blessing the Boats: New and Selected Poems 1988–2000* (2000).

Asked about her responsibility as an African American author, Clifton once replied:

> "I do feel a responsibility. . . . First, I'm going to write books that tend to celebrate life. . . . I also take seriously the responsibility of not lying. . . . It's a responsibility to the truth, and to my art as much as anything."

Think About the Writer In what ways is truth, even when painful, necessary for a full celebration of life?

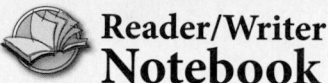 **Reader/Writer**
Notebook
Use your **RWN** to complete the activities for this selection.

Literary Focus

Repetition **Repetition** is the repeated use of the same sound, word, image, idea, or other element to enhance meaning and overall effect. In addition to building **rhythm** and creating musical effects, repetition can emphasize important ideas or create a certain **mood** or atmosphere. The repeated phrases in Clifton's poem give it an insistent tone that stresses her desire to make sure the slaves are remembered. The repetition of similar grammatical structures, or **parallelism,** creates a cadence that increases the solemn effect of her simple words.

Writing Focus

Think as a Reader/Writer

Find It in Your Reading In her poem, Clifton uses **repetition** to emphasize important ideas and to create a particular tone and mood. For example, the repetition of the line "nobody mentioned slaves" serves ironically to ensure that the slaves are mentioned. As you read, use a graphic organizer like the one below to record examples of repetition in your *Reader/ Writer Notebook*. List each example in the appropriate category to show what it contributes to the poem. Examples can be listed more than once.

TechFocus As you read Clifton's poem, think about how you would read the poem aloud in a podcast or video.

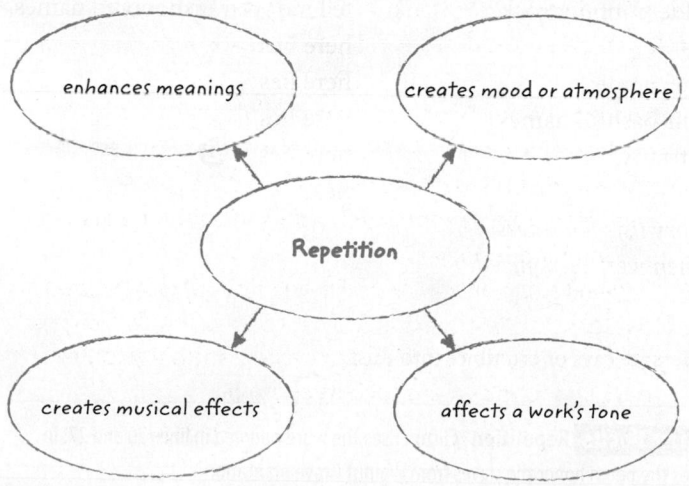

Language Coach

Fixed Expressions and Homonyms

A fixed expression is a group of words that often appear together. Fixed expressions tend to take on their own meaning so that the individual words within them lose their force. For example, a very old fixed expression you might come across on a tombstone is "Here lies . . .," followed by the name of the dead person. Clifton makes her readers think about these two words by repeating them, by not completing them, and finally by using a homonym (a word that has the same sound as another word, such as *hair* and *hare*.) What homonyms occur in the last two lines of the poem? How do they connect to bring meaning to the poem?

Learn It Online
Listen to the audio version of this poem online.

go.hrw.com   L11-445

Link to Today

This Link to Today shows how a contemporary writer confronts the injustices of slavery.

Read with a Purpose

As you read, ask yourself why the writer struggles to uncover the identities of forgotten slaves.

Build Background

The harsh realities of slavery are still part of our legacy as Americans today. Lucille Clifton wrote this moving poem after she took a tour of a former plantation in South Carolina. She talked with Bill Moyers, a television journalist, about that experience.

Clifton told Moyers that the plantation had a family burying ground. In the area leading up to the grounds, Clifton thought she saw the signs of old slave graves, but the guide didn't point them out. When Clifton challenged him about it and asked him to tell her more, she learned that the plantation had had an "inventory of ten slaves, but that they might have had more because women weren't counted." Clifton said, "Now, well, I had to find out about that! I mean, some things say, hey, like 'No!' Then when I learned that the women were not considered valuable enough to inventory, I definitely wanted to write about that."

at the cemetery, walnut grove plantation, south carolina, 1989

by **Lucille Clifton**

among the rocks
at walnut grove
your silence drumming
in my bones,
5 tell me your names.

nobody mentioned slaves
and yet the curious tools
shine with your fingerprints.
nobody mentioned slaves
10 but somebody did this work
who had no guide, no stone,
who moulders° under rock.

tell me your names,
tell me your bashful names
15 and i will testify.

*the inventory lists ten slaves
but only men were recognized.*

among the rocks
at walnut grove
20 some of these honored dead
were dark
some of these dark
were slaves
some of these slaves
25 were women
some of them did this
honored work. **Ⓐ**
tell me your names
foremothers, brothers,
30 tell me your dishonored names.
here lies
here lies
here lies
here lies **Ⓑ**
35 hear

---

12. **moulders:** decays or crumbles into dust.

Ⓐ **Literary Focus** Repetition Clifton uses the word *honored* in lines 20 and 27. In what way does the poem honor the slaves from Walnut Grove plantation?

Ⓑ **Literary Focus** Repetition Clifton repeats the phrase "here lies" in the last stanza. Explain at least two different meanings of this phrase.

The Funeral Procession (1947) by Ellis Wilson.
Aaron Douglas Collection, The Amistad Research Center at Tulane University, New Orleans, Louisiana.

Viewing and Interpreting What does the repetition of similar figures add to this image? How is this repetition similar to Clifton's use of repetition in the poem?

Applying Your Skills

at the cemetery, walnut grove
plantation, south carolina, 1989

Respond and Think Critically

Reading Focus

Quick Check

1. What happens at the Walnut Grove plantation cemetery that motivates Clifton to write the poem?

2. To whom is the speaker speaking throughout the poem?

3. List two adjectives that Clifton uses to describe the slaves' names. How do these adjectives reflect the poet's view of the slaves' fate?

Read with a Purpose

4. Why does the speaker struggle to uncover the identities of slaves whose lives have been forgotten?

Literary Focus

Literary Analysis

5. **Analyze** Clifton uses **apostrophe,** the addressing of a person or thing incapable of responding, throughout the poem. What effect does this use of apostrophe create?

6. **Interpret** During the interview, Bill Moyers asked Clifton what she wanted readers to do at the end of the poem. Clifton replied, "I want them to recognize that only half the truth was being told." How does the word *hear* in the last line call attention to her purpose?

7. **Draw Conclusions** Since slaves were considered property, why do you think women were not counted in the owner's inventory?

8. **Extend** Do you agree with Clifton that injustice in the world should be talked about? Do you think reading about the lives of enslaved people, such as Frederick Douglass and Harriet Jacobs, is important? Explain.

Literary Skills: Repetition

9. **Evaluate** Clifton repeats "here lies" four times at the end of the poem. What is the effect of this repetition?

10. **Analyze** Clifton calls some of the dead "honored" (line 20), and some of their work "honored" (line 27). Whose names are "dishonored" (line 30)? In what ways are they dishonored?

Literary Skills Review: Imagery

11. **Evaluate** The use of language to evoke a picture or a concrete sensation is called **imagery.** Identify examples of sight and sound imagery in the poem. How do these images contribute to the poem's mood?

Writing Focus

Think as a Reader/Writer

Use It in Your Writing As you read the poem, you recorded examples of repetition in your *Reader/Writer Notebook.* Think of someone or something you feel should not be forgotten. Then, write a poem that uses repetition to emphasize the need to remember.

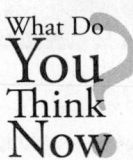 What Do You Think Now

What does this poem indicate about the need for conflict or confrontation to change the historical status of the deceased slaves?

SKILLS FOCUS **Literary Skills** Analyze characteristics of persuasion. **Writing Skills** Write comparison-contrast essays; write historical investigations. **Listening and Speaking Skills** Listen to comprehend or gain information; participate in group discussions; deliver informative presentations.

Ain't I a Woman? /
at the cemetery, walnut grove plantation, south carolina, 1989

CHOICES

As you respond to the Choices, use these **Academic Vocabulary** words as appropriate: <u>advocate</u>, <u>criteria</u>, <u>fundamental</u>, <u>principle</u>, <u>subsequent</u>.

REVIEW
Compare Types of Texts
Timed ⏱ Writing Both Sojourner Truth and Lucille Clifton use the power of words to <u>advocate</u> change. Review "Ain't I a Woman?" and "at the cemetery, walnut grove plantation, south carolina, 1989," and examine the rhetorical and poetic devices each speaker uses to make her points. As you re-read, consider the <u>fundamental</u> differences between poetry and public speaking. Then, write a brief essay in which you compare the two pieces and evaluate the effectiveness of poetry and oratory as means of exposing social injustice.

REVIEW
Discuss Poetry
Group Activity In her poem "harriet," Lucille Clifton addresses Sojourner Truth, saying, "if i be you / let me in my / sojourning / not forget / to ask my brothers / ain't i a woman too." In small groups, discuss how "at the cemetery, walnut grove plantation, south carolina, 1989" shows that Clifton has indeed remembered to ask Sojourner Truth's repeated question.

CONNECT
Research a Current Issue
Class Presentation Although we think of slavery as a part of the past, it still exists in many places in the world. Look up the Universal Declaration of Human Rights on the United Nations Web site, and read what it says about slavery. Then, research the practice of slavery in the world today. What forms does slavery take, and what is being done to stop it? Present your findings to the class, using charts and statistics to support your conclusions.

CONNECT
Conduct Historical Research
Look back at your response to the QuickWrite for "Ain't I a Woman?" Follow up on your response by researching some of the people who were involved in both the antislavery movement and the crusade for women's rights. Choose a few of these people, and write a report describing their activities and accomplishments.

EXTEND
Listen and Evaluate
Lucille Clifton regrets that the names and lives of deceased slaves have been forgotten. At the Library of Congress's American Memory Web site, listen to audio recordings of interviews with people who had been enslaved in the United States in the nineteenth century. Choose a few former slaves, and create a poster that includes their names and some of the information you learned from listening to their interviews. If possible, play parts of these audio recordings for your classmates.

Going Home (1992) by Willie Birch. Papier-mâché on mixed media.

EXTEND
Create an Audio Presentation
TechFocus Record yourself reading "at the cemetery, walnut grove plantation, south carolina, 1989" aloud in a podcast or a video recording such as those made for the Favorite Poem Project, which was created by Poet Laureate Robert Pinsky. Use your voice to convey the meaning you found in the poem. Also, consider the poem's use of repetition. How will you speak the repeated phrases? Share your podcast or video with your class.

The Ravages of War

LITERARY FOCUS
The Rise of Realism

Battle of Gettysburg: Picket's Charge by Peter F. Rothermel 16 ¾" × 32".

CONTENTS

"War is at best barbarism. . . .

Its glory is all moonshine. . . .

War is hell."

— **Union General William Tecumseh Sherman**

Literary Focus

SKILLS FOCUS Literary Skills Understand and analyze elements of literature from American Romanticism; understand and analyze elements of literature from the rise of realism.

The Rise of Realism by **Leila Christenbury**

> **Influences on American Realism**
>
> - Development of realism as a literary form in Europe, with a <u>fundamental</u> emphasis on ordinary characters in real-life situations
> - Disillusionment created by the brutality of the Civil War and the harshness of frontier life
> - Reactions to the social ills created by rapid industrialization and the growth of cities

Realism Takes Root

Before the Civil War, one of the most enduring subjects of prose fiction had been the exploits of larger-than-life heroes. Born of the chivalric romance, the **Romantic novel** presented readers with idealistic heroes engaged in exciting adventures.

The new literary movement known as **realism** represented a radical departure from the subjects and concerns of Romantic fiction. The great American fiction writers of the mid-nineteenth century—Edgar Allan Poe, Nathaniel Hawthorne, and Herman Melville—shared an aversion to simple realism. These writers <u>advocated</u> for the use of Romantic elements not simply to entertain readers but to reveal truths that would be hidden in a realistic story limited to what could actually happen. Partly because Romanticism had been the dominant literary form up until the Civil War, the poet Walt Whitman believed "the real war will never get in the books."

After the Civil War, however, a new generation of writers came of age. They were known as realists, writers who tried to represent faithfully the environment, the manners of daily life, and real events of ordinary lives.

Inside the Human Mind

Realism was not simply concerned with recording wallpaper patterns, hairstyles, or the subjects of conversations. It sought to explain why ordinary people behave the way they do. Realistic novelists often relied on the emerging sciences of human and animal behavior—biology, psychology, and sociology—as well as on their own insights and observations. Their subjects were drawn from the slums of the rapidly growing cities, from the factories that were quickly replacing farmlands, and from the lives of far-from-idealized characters—poor factory workers, corrupt politicians, and even prostitutes.

Foremost among the new generation of writers was Stephen Crane. Crane had profound psychological insight; his principal interest was the human character at moments of stress. He was the first of many modern American writers to juxtapose human illusions with the indifference of the universe. Of all the nineteenth-century realists, only Crane could describe a stabbing death (in his story "The Blue Hotel") in this coolly cynical manner: "[The blade] shot forward, and a human body, this citadel of virtue, wisdom, power, was pierced as easily as if it had been a melon."

It would take this sensibility to get the "real war" in the books at last.

Ask Yourself

1. How did the <u>criteria</u> of realist writers such as Stephen Crane differ from the standards of Romantic writers of the past?

2. Why was realism well suited to describe the horrors of war?

Learn It Online
Find more about Stephen Crane online at *NovelWise*.

go.hrw.com   L11-451   **Go**

Analyzing a Photograph

The Civil War was the first military conflict recorded by photographers, who could use the new medium for a realistic depiction of warfare.

Guidelines

Use the criteria of realism to analyze this photograph:

- Think about the arrangement of soldiers and battleground items. Does this scene look as if the photographer has posed his subjects?

- Examine the three soldiers looking toward the camera from the foreground. Do they illustrate the principles of a Romantic or a realist?

- Think about the photographer's purpose. Why might he have wanted to record this scene? What effect might he want the photograph to have on its viewers?

> **1.** What is the photographer trying to convey by emphasizing details of the soldiers' expressions and bandages?

> **2.** How does the emphasis on the figures in the foreground convey a realist's view of the war? Explain your response.

> **3.** How does the clutter in this scene contribute to a realistic impression of the war? Explain your answer.

Wounded Union soldiers after the Second Battle of Fredericksburg, May 3, 1863. Photograph by Mathew Brady.

Your Turn Analyze Realism in Photographs

Compare this image to the photographs on pages 483–485, which also depict wounded soldiers. Which photograph best illustrates the principles of realism? Be prepared to share your ideas with the class as a whole.

An Occurrence at Owl Creek Bridge

Analyzing Sequence of Events by Kylene Beers

Generally, writers present stories that follow a familiar structure—the expected move from beginning to middle to end. However, sometimes writers play with the standard sequence of events by using flashbacks. Ambrose Bierce's "An Occurrence at Owl Creek Bridge" departs from the expected sequence of events, with surprising results.

The story begins in the middle of the action as a military execution is about to take place. The condemned man, Peyton Farquhar, is a civilian Southern planter who is about to be hanged from a bridge, although Farquhar's offense is not revealed.

Bierce alters the sequence to explain why Farquhar faces execution by using a flashback in the story's second section. The **flashback** provides <u>fundamental</u> background information through a scene that occurred in the past—before the present scene on the bridge.

In the flashback, Farquhar discusses the destruction of the Owl Creek Bridge with a man who has hidden his real identity as a Federal scout. Read this excerpt from Part II of the story:

> The man says, "The commandant has issued an order . . . declaring that any civilian caught interfering with the railroad, its bridges, tunnels, or trains will be summarily hanged."

Farquhar then asks the man about guards and the condition of the bridge. Farquhar's inquiry seals his fate. By changing the sequence of events to give the reader critical information, Bierce explains why Farquhar faces execution at the Owl Creek Bridge.

Bierce alters the sequence of events again in Part III, when the story returns to the scene at the bridge. Focusing on Farquhar's imagination, Bierce shows how the mind can play tricks when a person is placed in a life-threatening situation. As he awaits death, his mind travels home, interrupting the natural sequence of events. Read the following passage from the story:

> How softly the turf had carpeted the untraveled avenue—he could no longer feel the roadway beneath his feet!
> Doubtless, despite his suffering, he had fallen asleep while walking, for now he sees another scene—perhaps he has merely recovered from a delirium. He stands at the gate of his own home.

Notice the clues Bierce uses to show that things aren't what they seem: "He could no longer feel the roadway beneath his feet"; "he had fallen asleep while walking, for now he sees another scene"; and "he stands at the gate of this own home."

By altering the sequence of events to include immediate action, flashback, and imagination, Ambrose Bierce makes his story more compelling.

Your Turn

Read this passage from Part III of the story. Then discuss the sequence of events with a partner.

> The baffled cannoneer had fired him a random farewell. He sprang to his feet, rushed up the sloping bank, and plunged into the forest.
> All that day he traveled, laying his course by the rounding sun. The forest seemed interminable; nowhere did he discover a break in it, not even a woodsman's road. He had not known that he lived in so wild a region. There was something uncanny in the revelation.

 Learn It Online
Find a graphic organizer online to help you analyze a sequence of events in fiction.

go.hrw.com   L11-453   **Go**

Preparing to Read

An Occurrence at Owl Creek Bridge

What Do You Think

How does conflict lead to change?

QuickWrite

Think about a serious conflict you or someone else has had. Did you or the person you know worry about it, imagine its resolution, or wish for escape? Write a paragraph about how serious and stressful situations affect one's thinking.

MEET THE WRITER

Ambrose Bierce
(1842–1914?)

Ambrose Bierce infused his writing with a dark vision of life that centers on warfare and the cruel joke it plays on humanity.

Humble Beginnings

Bierce was born in Ohio in 1842, the youngest child in the large family of an unsuccessful farmer. Bierce educated himself primarily by exploring his father's small library.

At age nineteen, Bierce joined the Ninth Indiana Volunteers and saw action at the bloody Civil War battles of Shiloh and Chickamauga. He was also part of General Sherman's march to the sea in 1864. Bierce was once severely wounded and was cited for bravery no fewer than fifteen times. After he left the army, Bierce went to San Francisco, where he began a successful career as a journalist.

"Bitter Bierce"

Bierce became editor of the San Francisco *News Letter* due to his growing reputation as a muckraking reporter, exposing public scandal and misconduct. When the financier Collis P. Huntington, head of the Southern Pacific Railroad, asked Bierce's price for silence on the railroad's tax fraud case, Bierce is said to have replied, "My price is about seventy-five million dollars, to be handed to the treasurer of the United States."

Bierce's disillusionment with deceit and greed continued to spur his pen, earning him the nickname "Bitter Bierce." He edited and contribute to humor magazines; he wrote a regular newspaper column, memoirs, and many short stories. Bierce's two volumes of stories represent his highest achievement. His fundamental theme is the impact of war on the individual.

In 1913, after asking his few friends to "forgive him in not perishing where he was," Bierce set off for Mexico to report on or join in its revolution. "Goodbye," he wrote. "If you hear of my being stood up against a Mexican stone wall and shot to rags please know that I think it a pretty good way to depart this life. It beats old age, disease, or falling down the cellar stairs." No subsequent word was ever heard from him.

Think About the Writer
If Bierce were alive today, what aspects of our society might make him feel disillusioned? Explain.

Ambrose Bierce by J.H.E. Partington (1843–1899). Oil on canvas (detail).

Reader/Writer Notebook

Use your **RWN** to complete the activities for this selection.

Literary Focus

Point of View A writer chooses a **point of view,** or vantage point, from which to tell a story. Bierce uses distinctly different points of view to accomplish his purpose. At the opening of the story, Bierce uses primarily an **objective point of view,** which records and reports the scenes without comment, much as a camera would. He then shifts to a **third-person-limited point of view,** focusing on the thoughts and feelings of the main character, Peyton Farquhar.

Literary Perspectives Apply the literary perspectives described on page 457 as you read this story.

Reading Focus

Analyzing Sequence of Events/Flashback Writers usually present events in a chronological sequence. Bierce's story begins with the impending execution of Peyton Farquhar. The action then shifts to a flashback in Part II. A **flashback** is a scene that interrupts the normal chronological sequence to depict something that happened earlier. Flashbacks provide important background information.

Into Action As you read, use a chart like the one below to follow the sequence of events in the story. For each part of the story, briefly summarize the action or events and provide an example of each point of view.

Part No.	Summary of Action	Point of View
Part I	Farquhar has been captured by Union soldiers and is about to be hanged.	objective; example: "The man's hands were behind his back...."

Vocabulary

ardently (AHR duhnt lee) *adv.:* in a way that is intensely passionate and eager. *Peyton Farquhar, a Southern planter, ardently supports the Southern cause.*

perilous (PEHR uh luhs) *adj.:* dangerous and risky. *He performs a perilous task in order to help the South.*

poignant (POYN yuhnt) *adj.:* deeply piercing, either emotionally or physically. *Farquhar experiences many stressful and poignant events.*

pivotal (PIHV uh tuhl) *adj.:* central; acting as a point around which other things turn. *Farquhar's escape is of pivotal importance.*

malign (muh LYN) *adj.:* harmful; evil. *His surroundings look threatening and seem to carry a malign meaning.*

Language Coach

Silent Letters English has many tricky words with spellings that aren't pronounced the way you would expect. Consider *bridge,* for instance. When you say *bridge,* you don't pronounce the *d.* In the word *poignant,* from the Vocabulary words above, the letter *g* is silent. What other word from the list above has a silent *g?*

Writing Focus

Think as a Reader/Writer

Find It in Your Reading In Part II of the story, Bierce uses **flashback** to provide information about why Farquhar, a Southern planter, is being hanged. As you read, notice how the author has created this scene to explain the situation. In your *Reader/Writer Notebook,* note the features of a narrative, such as **setting** and **dialogue,** that are used in the flashback.

Learn It Online
Prepare to plunge into this story with the video introduction online.

 go.hrw.com | L11-455 | Go

An Occurrence at Owl Creek Bridge

by **Ambrose Bierce**

Read with a Purpose

Read to discover how the author uses the story of one man, Peyton Farquhar, to make a general observation about the nature of war.

Build Background

Bierce's story is set in the Deep South during the Civil War (1861–1865). Peyton Farquhar, a Southern gentleman, is being hanged by Union soldiers for plotting to damage the Owl Creek Bridge, a bridge in Union-held territory. As Farquhar awaits execution, the perspective of the story changes, and readers accompany Farquhar on an incredible escape to his home and family. As you read this story, keep in mind that Southern (Confederate) soldiers wore gray uniforms, and Northern (Federal or Union) troops wore blue.

I

A man stood upon a railroad bridge in northern Alabama, looking down into the swift water twenty feet below. The man's hands were behind his back, the wrists bound with a cord. A rope closely encircled his neck. It was attached to a stout cross-timber above his head, and the slack fell to the level of his knees. Some loose boards laid upon the sleepers[1] supporting the metals of the railway supplied a footing for him and his executioners—two private soldiers of the Federal army, directed by a sergeant who in civil life may have been a deputy sheriff. At a short remove[2] upon the same temporary platform was an officer in the uniform of his rank, armed. He was a captain. A sentinel[3] at each end of the bridge stood with his rifle in the position known as "support," that is to say, vertical in front of the left shoulder, the hammer resting on the forearm thrown straight across the chest—a formal and unnatural position, enforcing an erect carriage of the body. It did not appear to be the duty of these two men to know what was occurring at the center of the bridge; they merely blockaded the two ends of the foot planking that traversed it. **(A)**

Beyond one of the sentinels nobody was in sight; the railroad ran straight away into a forest for a hundred yards, then, curving, was lost to view. Doubtless there was an outpost farther along. The other bank of the stream was open ground—a gentle acclivity[4] topped with a stockade of vertical tree trunks, loopholed for rifles, with a single embrasure through which protruded the muzzle of a brass cannon commanding the bridge. Midway of the slope between bridge and fort were the spectators—a single company of infantry in line, at "parade rest," the butts of the rifles on the ground, the barrels inclining slightly backward against the right shoulder, the hands crossed upon the stock. A lieutenant stood at the right of the line, the point of his sword upon the ground, his left hand resting upon

1. **sleepers:** railroad ties.
2. **remove:** distance.
3. **sentinel:** guard; sentry.
4. **acclivity:** uphill slope.

his right. Excepting the group of four at the center of the bridge, not a man moved. The company faced the bridge, staring stonily, motionless. The sentinels, facing the banks of the stream, might have been statues to adorn the bridge. The captain stood with folded arms, silent, observing the work of his subordinates, but making no sign. Death is a dignitary who when he comes announced is to be received with formal manifestations of respect, even by those most familiar with him. In the code of military etiquette, silence and fixity[5] are forms of deference.

The man who was engaged in being hanged was apparently about thirty-five years of age. He was a civilian, if one might judge from his habit, which was that of a planter. His features were good—a straight nose, firm mouth, broad forehead, from which his

5. **fixity:** steadiness; motionlessness.

(A) Literary Focus Point of View What point of view does the author use in this first paragraph—objective, omniscient, or third-person limited? What is the effect of this point of view?

Analyzing Visuals

Viewing and Interpreting
What does this photograph add to your grasp of the opening scene in "An Occurrence at Owl Creek Bridge"? Explain.

Film still from *An Occurrence at Owl Creek Bridge*, 1962.

long, dark hair was combed straight back, falling behind his ears to the collar of his well-fitting frock coat. He wore a moustache and pointed beard, but no whiskers; his eyes were large and dark gray, and had a kindly expression which one would hardly have expected in one whose neck was in the hemp. Evidently this was no vulgar assassin. The liberal military code makes provision for hanging many kinds of persons, and gentlemen are not excluded.   **B**

The preparations being complete, the two private soldiers stepped aside and each drew away the plank upon which he had been standing. The sergeant turned to the captain, saluted, and placed himself immediately behind that officer, who in turn moved apart one pace. These movements left the condemned man and the sergeant standing on the two ends of the same plank, which spanned three of the crossties of the bridge. The end upon which the civilian stood almost, but not quite, reached a fourth. This plank had been held in place by the weight of the captain; it was now held

by that of the sergeant. At a signal from the former, the latter would step aside, the plank would tilt and the condemned man go down between two ties. The arrangement commended itself to his judgment as simple and effective. His face had not been covered nor his eyes bandaged. He looked a moment at his "unsteadfast footing," then let his gaze wander to the swirling water of the stream racing madly beneath his feet. A piece of dancing driftwood caught his attention, and his eyes followed it down the current. How slowly it appeared to move! What a sluggish stream!   **C**

He closed his eyes in order to fix his last thoughts upon his wife and children. The water, touched to gold by the early sun, the brooding mists under the banks at some distance down the stream, the fort, the soldiers, the piece of drift—all had distracted him. And now he became conscious of a new disturbance. Striking through the thought of his dear ones was a sound which he could neither ignore nor understand, a sharp, distinct, metallic percussion like the stroke of

B **Reading Focus** **Analyzing Sequence of Events/Flashback**
Part I takes place in the story's present. How does starting the story in the middle of the action capture your attention?

C **Literary Focus** **Point of View** How does the point of view change here? How does this change in point of view affect your perception of the condemned man?

a blacksmith's hammer upon the anvil; it had the same ringing quality. He wondered what it was, and whether immeasurably distant or nearby—it seemed both. Its recurrence was regular, but as slow as the tolling of a death knell.[6] He awaited each stroke with impatience and—he knew not why—apprehension. The intervals of silence grew progressively longer; the delays became maddening. With their greater infrequency the sounds increased in strength and sharpness. They hurt his ear like the thrust of a knife; he feared he would shriek. What he heard was the ticking of his watch.

He unclosed his eyes and saw again the water below him. "If I could free my hands," he thought, "I might throw off the noose and spring into the stream. By diving I could evade the bullets and, swimming vigorously, reach the bank, take to the woods, and get away home. My home, thank God, is as yet outside their lines; my wife and little ones are still beyond the invader's farthest advance."

As these thoughts, which have here to be set down in words, were flashed into the doomed man's brain rather than evolved from it, the captain nodded to the sergeant. The sergeant stepped aside.

<h1 style="text-align:center">II</h1>

Peyton Farquhar was a well-to-do planter, of an old and highly respected Alabama family. Being a slave owner and, like other slave owners, a politician, he was naturally an original secessionist[7] and ardently devoted to the Southern cause. Circumstances of an imperious[8] nature, which it is unnecessary to relate here, had prevented him from taking service with the gallant army that had fought the disastrous campaigns ending with the fall of Corinth,[9] and he chafed[10] under the

---

6. **knell:** sound of a bell ringing slowly.
7. **secessionist:** one who favored the separation of Southern states from the Union.
8. **imperious:** urgent.
9. **Corinth:** Union forces under Gen. William S. Rosecrans (1819–1898) took Corinth, Mississippi, on October 4, 1862.
10. **chafed:** became impatient.

inglorious restraint, longing for the release of his energies, the larger life of the soldier, the opportunity for distinction. That opportunity, he felt, would come, as it comes to all in wartime. Meanwhile he did what he could. No service was too humble for him to perform in aid of the South, no adventure too perilous for him to undertake if consistent with the character of a civilian who was at heart a soldier, and who in good faith and without too much qualification assented to at least a part of the frankly villainous dictum[11] that all is fair in love and war. **(D)**

One evening while Farquhar and his wife were sitting on a rustic bench near the entrance to his grounds, a gray-clad soldier rode up to the gate and asked for a drink of water. Mrs. Farquhar was only too happy to serve him with her own white hands. While she was fetching the water, her husband approached the dusty horseman and inquired eagerly for news from the front.

"The Yanks are repairing the railroads," said the man, "and are getting ready for another advance. They have reached the Owl Creek bridge, put it in order, and built a stockade on the north bank. The commandant has issued an order, which is posted everywhere, declaring that any civilian caught interfering with the railroad, its bridges, tunnels, or trains will be summarily[12] hanged. I saw the order."

"How far is it to the Owl Creek Bridge?" Farquhar asked.

"About thirty miles."

"Is there no force on this side of the creek?"

"Only a picket post half a mile out, on the railroad, and a single sentinel at this end of the bridge."

"Suppose a man—a civilian and a student of hanging—should elude the picket post and perhaps get the better of the sentinel," said Farquhar, smiling, "what could he accomplish?"

The soldier reflected. "I was there a month ago," he replied. "I observed that the flood of last winter

---

11. **dictum:** statement; saying.
12. **summarily:** without delay.

(D) Literary Perspectives Analyzing Historical Context
How does the information in this paragraph help you understand the social and political influences affecting Farquhar?

Vocabulary   ardently (AHR duhnt lee) *adv.*: in a way that is intensely passionate and eager.
perilous (PEHR uh luhs) *adj.*: dangerous and risky.

had lodged a great quantity of driftwood against the wooden pier at this end of the bridge. It is now dry and would burn like tow."

The lady had now brought the water, which the soldier drank. He thanked her ceremoniously, bowed to her husband, and rode away. An hour later, after nightfall, he repassed the plantation, going northward in the direction from which he had come. He was a Federal scout. **Ⓔ**

III

As Peyton Farquhar fell straight downward through the bridge, he lost consciousness and was as one already dead. From this state he was awakened—ages later, it seemed to him—by the pain of a sharp pressure upon his throat, followed by a sense of suffocation. Keen, poignant agonies seemed to shoot from his neck downward through every fiber of his body and limbs. These pains appeared to flash along well-defined lines of ramification[13] and to beat with an inconceivably rapid periodicity. They seemed like streams of pulsating fire heating him to an intolerable temperature. As to his head, he was conscious of nothing but a feeling of fullness—of congestion. These sensations were unaccompanied by thought. The intellectual part of his nature was already effaced; he had power only to feel, and feeling was torment. He was conscious of motion. Encompassed in a luminous cloud, of which he was now merely the fiery heart, without material substance, he swung through unthinkable arcs of oscillation, like a vast pendulum. Then all at once, with terrible suddenness, the light about him shot upward with the noise of a loud plash; a frightful roaring was in his ears, and all was cold and dark. The power of thought was restored; he knew that the rope had broken and he had fallen into the stream. There was no additional strangulation; the noose about his neck was already suffocat-

---

13. **flash . . . ramification:** spread out rapidly along branches from one point.

ing him and kept the water from his lungs. To die of hanging at the bottom of a river!—the idea seemed to him ludicrous. He opened his eyes in the darkness and saw above him a gleam of light, but how distant, how inaccessible! He was still sinking, for the light became fainter and fainter until it was a mere glimmer. Then it began to grow and brighten, and he knew that he was rising toward the surface—knew it with reluctance, for he was now very comfortable. "To be hanged and drowned," he thought, "that is not so bad; but I do not wish to be shot. No; I will not be shot; that is not fair." **Ⓕ**

He was not conscious of an effort, but a sharp pain in his wrist apprised[14] him that he was trying to free his hands. He gave the struggle his attention, as an idler might observe the feat of a juggler, without interest in the outcome. What splendid effort!—what magnificent, what superhuman strength! Ah, that was a fine endeavor! Bravo! The cord fell away; his arms parted and floated upward, the hands dimly seen on each side in the growing light. He watched them with a new interest as first one and then the other pounced upon the noose at his neck. They tore it away and thrust it fiercely aside, its undulations resembling those of a water snake. "Put it back, put it back!" He thought he shouted these words to his hands, for the undoing of the noose had been succeeded by the direst pang that he had yet experienced. His neck ached horribly; his brain was on fire; his heart, which had been fluttering faintly, gave a great leap, trying to force itself out at his mouth. His whole body was racked and wrenched with an insupportable anguish! But his disobedient hands gave no heed to the command. They beat the water vigorously with quick, downward strokes, forcing him to the surface. He felt his head emerge; his eyes were blinded by the sunlight; his chest expanded convulsively, and with a supreme and crowning agony his lungs engulfed a great draft of air, which instantly he expelled in a shriek!

---

14. **apprised:** informed.

Ⓔ **Reading Focus** Analyzing Sequence of Events/Flashback At what point in the plot does the encounter between Farquhar and the "gray-clad soldier" occur? How does this flashback help you understand Farquhar's situation in Part I?

Ⓕ **Reading Focus** Analyzing Sequence of Events/Flashback Describe the sequence of events in this passage.

Vocabulary **poignant** (POYN yuhnt) *adj.:* deeply piercing, either emotionally or physically.

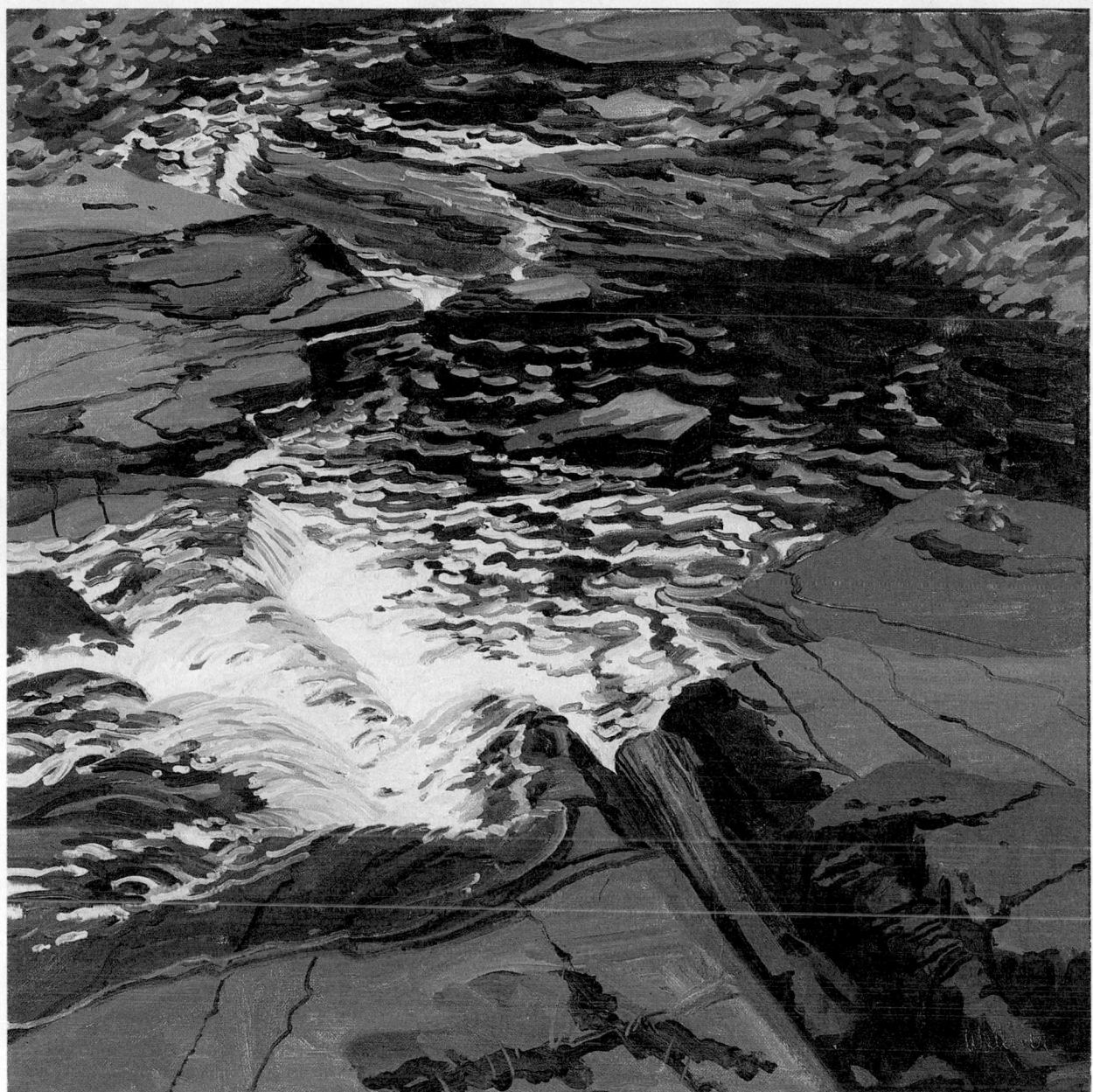

Study for River Falls (1990) by Neil Welliver. Oil on canvas, 24" × 24".

He was now in full possession of his physical senses. They were, indeed, preternaturally[15] keen and alert. Something in the awful disturbance of his organic system had so exalted and refined them that they made record of things never before perceived. He felt the ripples upon his face and heard their separate sounds as they struck. He looked at the forest on the bank of the stream, saw the individual trees, the leaves, and the veining of each leaf—saw the very insects upon them: the locusts, the brilliant-bodied flies, the gray spiders stretching their webs from twig to twig. He noted the prismatic colors in all the dewdrops upon a million blades of grass. The humming of the gnats that danced above the eddies of the stream, the beating of the dragonflies' wings, the strokes of the water spiders' legs, like oars which had

---

15. **preternaturally:** extraordinarily; abnormally.

lifted their boat—all these made audible music. A fish slid along beneath his eyes, and he heard the rush of its body parting the water.

He had come to the surface facing down the stream; in a moment the visible world seemed to wheel slowly round, himself the pivotal point, and he saw the bridge, the fort, the soldiers upon the bridge, the captain, the sergeant, the two privates, his executioners. They were in silhouette against the blue sky. They shouted and gesticulated, pointing at him. The captain had drawn his pistol, but did not fire; the others were unarmed. Their movements were grotesque and horrible, their forms gigantic.

Suddenly he heard a sharp report[16] and something struck the water smartly within a few inches of his head, spattering his face with spray. He heard a

---

16. **report:** explosive noise.

second report, and saw one of the sentinels with his rifle at his shoulder, a light cloud of blue smoke rising from the muzzle. The man in the water saw the eye of the man on the bridge gazing into his own through the sights of the rifle. He observed that it was a gray eye and remembered having read that gray eyes were keenest, and that all famous marksmen had them. Nevertheless, this one had missed.

A counterswirl had caught Farquhar and turned him half round; he was again looking into the forest on the bank opposite the fort. The sound of a clear, high voice in monotonous singsong now rang out behind him and came across the water with a distinctiveness that pierced and subdued all other sounds, even the beating of the ripples in his ears. Although no soldier, he had frequented camps enough to know the dread significance of that deliberate, drawling, aspirated chant; the lieutenant on shore was taking part in the

---

G **Literary Perspectives** Analyzing Credibility in Literature What elements of Farquhar's escape might be difficult to believe?

Vocabulary **pivotal** (PIHV uh tuhl) *adj.:* central; acting as a point around which other things turn.

H **Literary Focus** Point of View Farquhar notes the marksman's point of view. What does Farquhar's observation reveal about his own situation?

morning's work. How coldly and pitilessly—with what an even, calm intonation, presaging,[17] and enforcing tranquility in the men—with what accurately measured intervals fell those cruel words.

"Attention, company! . . . Shoulder arms! . . . Ready! . . . Aim! . . . Fire!"

Farquhar dived—dived as deeply as he could. The water roared in his ears like the voice of Niagara, yet he heard the dulled thunder of the volley and, rising again toward the surface, met shining bits of metal, singularly flattened, oscillating slowly downward. Some of them touched him on the face and hands, then fell away, continuing their descent. One lodged between his collar and neck; it was uncomfortably warm and he snatched it out.

As he rose to the surface, gasping for breath, he saw that he had been a long time underwater; he was perceptibly farther downstream—nearer to safety. The soldiers had almost finished reloading; the metal ramrods flashed all at once in the sunshine as they were drawn from the barrels, turned in the air, and thrust into their sockets. The two sentinels fired again, independently and ineffectually.

The hunted man saw all this over his shoulder; he was now swimming vigorously with the current. His brain was as energetic as his arms and legs; he thought with the rapidity of lightning.

"The officer," he reasoned, "will not make that martinet's[18] error a second time. It is as easy to dodge a volley as a single shot. He has probably already given the command to fire at will. God help me, I cannot dodge them all!"

An appalling plash within two yards of him was followed by a rushing sound, *diminuendo,*[19] which seemed to travel back through the air to the fort and died in an explosion which stirred the very river to its deeps! A rising sheet of water curved over him, fell down upon him, blinded him, strangled him! The cannon had taken a hand in the game. As he shook his head free from the commotion of the smitten water, he heard the deflected shot humming through the air ahead, and in an instant it was cracking and smashing the branches in the forest beyond.

"They will not do that again," he thought; the next time they will use a charge of grape.[20] I must keep my eye upon the gun; the smoke will apprise me—the report arrives too late; it lags behind the missile. That is a good gun."

Suddenly he felt himself whirled round and round—spinning like a top. The water, the banks, the forest, the now distant bridge, fort, and men—all were commingled and blurred. Objects were represented by their colors only; circular horizontal streaks of color—that was all he saw. He had been caught in a vortex and was being whirled on with a velocity of advance and gyration that made him giddy and sick. In a few moments he was flung upon the gravel at the foot of the left bank of the stream—the southern bank—and behind a projecting point which concealed him from his enemies. The sudden arrest of his motion, the abrasion of one of his hands on the gravel, restored him, and he wept with delight. He dug his fingers into the sand, threw it over himself in handfuls, and audibly blessed it. It looked like diamonds, rubies, emeralds; he could think of nothing beautiful which it did not resemble. The trees upon the bank were giant garden plants; he noted a definite order in their arrangement, inhaled the fragrance of their blooms. A strange, roseate light shone through the spaces among their trunks, and the wind made in their branches the music of aeolian harps.[21] He had no wish to perfect his escape—was content to remain in that enchanting spot until retaken.

A whiz and rattle of grapeshot among the branches high above his head roused him from his dream.

---

17. **presaging:** forewarning; predicting.
18. **martinet's:** A martinet believes in strict military discipline, with no exceptions.
19. *diminuendo* (duh mihn yoo EHN doh): decreasing in loudness.

20. **charge of grape:** cannon charge of small iron balls, called grapeshot.
21. **aeolian** (ee OH lee uhn) **harps:** stringed instruments that are played by the wind. Aeolus is the god of the wind in Greek mythology.

---

❶ Literary Focus Point of View What is strange about the thoughts going through Farquhar's mind? Why might Bierce have put such thoughts in his character's mind?

The baffled cannoneer had fired him a random farewell. He sprang to his feet, rushed up the sloping bank, and plunged into the forest.

All that day he traveled, laying his course by the rounding sun. The forest seemed interminable; nowhere did he discover a break in it, not even a woodsman's road. He had not known that he lived in so wild a region. There was something uncanny[22] in the revelation.

By nightfall he was fatigued, footsore, famishing. The thought of his wife and children urged him on. At last he found a road which led him in what he knew to be the right direction. It was as wide and straight as a city street, yet it seemed untraveled. No fields bordered it, no dwelling anywhere. Not so much as the barking of a dog suggested human habitation. The black bodies of the trees formed a straight wall on both sides, terminating on the horizon in a point, like a diagram in a lesson in perspective. Overhead, as he looked up through this rift in the wood, shone great golden stars looking unfamiliar and grouped in strange constellations. He was sure they were arranged in some order which had a secret and malign significance. The wood on either side was full of singular noises, among which—once, twice, and again—he distinctly heard whispers in an unknown tongue. **J**

His neck was in pain and lifting his hand to it he found it horribly swollen. He knew that it had a circle

> All is as he left it, and all bright and beautiful in the morning sunshine. He must have traveled the entire night.

of black where the rope had bruised it. His eyes felt congested; he could no longer close them. His tongue was swollen with thirst; he relieved its fever by thrusting it forward from between his teeth into the cold air. How softly the turf had carpeted the untraveled avenue—he could no longer feel the roadway beneath his feet!

Doubtless, despite his suffering, he had fallen asleep while walking, for now he sees another scene—perhaps he has merely recovered from a delirium. He stands at the gate of his own home. All is as he left it, and all bright and beautiful in the morning sunshine. He must have traveled the entire night. As he pushes open the gate and passes up the wide white walk, he sees a flutter of female garments; his wife, looking fresh and cool and sweet, steps down from the veranda to meet him. At the bottom of the steps she stands waiting, with a smile of ineffable[23] joy, an attitude of matchless grace and dignity. Ah, how beautiful she is! He springs forward with extended arms. As he is about to clasp her, he feels a stunning blow upon the back of the neck; a blinding white light blazes all about him with a sound like the shock of a cannon—then all is darkness and silence!

Peyton Farquhar was dead; his body, with a broken neck, swung gently from side to side beneath the timbers of the Owl Creek bridge. **K**

---

22. **uncanny:** eerie; weird.

23. **ineffable:** indescribable; unspeakable.

J **Literary Focus** Point of View How does the point of view add to the strangeness of the scene?

K **Literary Focus** Point of View Bierce returns to the objective point of view in his final sentence. What might be the reason for this sudden change at the end of the story? What comment on life and death might Bierce be making here?

Vocabulary **malign** (muh LYN) *adj.:* harmful; evil.

Respond and Think Critically

Reading Focus

Quick Check

1. How do Peyton Farquhar's political beliefs put him in jeopardy?

2. Summarize in one sentence what Farquhar imagines in Part III.

Read with a Purpose

3. What observation about the fundamental nature of war does Bierce make through the story of Peyton Farquhar?

Reading Skills: Analyzing Sequence of Events/Flashback

4. As you read, you examined the sequence of events and point of view. Review your chart. Add another column, and explain how the point of view Bierce uses in each part of the story is effective. Think about how point of view complements the event being described.

Part No.	Summary of Action	Point of View	Effectiveness
Part I	Farquhar has been captured by Union soldiers and is about to be hanged.	objective; example: "The man's hands were behind his back. . . ."	sets the scene and introduces us to the character; very visual

Literary Focus

Literary Analysis

5. **Analyze** Bierce does not tell the story in chronological order. How might the story's impact be different if the events were revealed in order?

6. **Interpret** Giving examples, explain how the events in Part III parallel what is really going on.

7. **Evaluate** Many readers find the story's conclusion powerful, but some argue that the ending is nothing more than a gimmick and cheats the reader. What do you think?

8. **Literary Perspectives** As you read, you considered two different approaches to making meaning, **analyzing historical context** and **analyzing credibility.** Explain how each perspective affected your interpretation of the story.

Literary Skills: Point of View

9. **Analyze** How does Bierce's use of point of view help you understand the mind of Peyton Farquhar? How does it contribute to the effectiveness of the surprise ending?

Literary Skills Review: Setting

10. **Interpret** The time and place in which a story takes place constitute its **setting.** How does setting influence the character of Peyton Farquhar, his situation, and the mood, or atmosphere, of the story? Consider aspects of the setting such as the historical period, the geographical location (the South), and the physical setting (the bridge, the river).

Writing Focus

Think as a Reader/Writer

Use It in Your Writing Review your QuickWrite about a serious conflict that led to a stressful situation. Using Bierce's flashback from Part II of the story as a model, write a flashback in your piece that provides background information about your conflict.

What Do You Think Now How does Farquhar's inner conflict while facing a life-and-death situation affect his mental state? Do you think this response is common in stressful situations? Explain.

An Occurrence at Owl Creek Bridge

Vocabulary Development

✓ Vocabulary Check

Match each Vocabulary word with its definition.

1. ardently   **a.** deeply moving
2. perilous   **b.** harmful
3. poignant   **c.** risky
4. pivotal   **d.** passionately
5. malign   **e.** central

Vocabulary Skills: Suffixes That Form Nouns

Suppose that you are going to a dressy event right after school. If you don't have time to change your clothes, you might just add to your school outfit to change your look. For instance, you might add a tie, scarf, hat, or piece of jewelry. Words can have the same flexibility. By adding a **suffix,** a word part that is attached to the end of a word, you can change the word's function. Some suffixes change an adjective or a verb into a noun. For instance, you can add the suffix *–ity* to the adjective *formal* to form the noun *formality.*

Note that some suffixes are simply added to the end of a word, as in *kind + –ness = kindness.* At other times, adding a suffix requires changing the spelling of the root. For instance, to form *tension,* the final letter *e* is dropped from *tense* before adding *–ion.*

Suffix	Word	Word + Suffix = Noun
–ance, –ence	emerge (verb)	emergence
–ancy, –ency	emerge (verb)	emergency
–ment	adjust (verb)	adjustment
–ness	kind (adjective)	kindness
–sion, –tion	tense (adjective)	tension
–ty	lax (adjective)	laxity

Your Turn

Write each word's part of speech. Then, turn each word into a noun by adding one of the suffixes from the chart on this page. Use a dictionary to see if the suffix you chose is correct, and write each word's definition.

Word/Part of Speech	Suffix	New Word (Noun)	Definition
swift (adj.)			
civil			
appear			
move			
exclude			

Language Coach

Silent Consonants Many English words have letters that aren't pronounced. In the Vocabulary word *malign,* for example, the *g* is silent. With a partner, identify the silent letter in each of these words from "An Occurrence at Owl Creek Bridge":

known, combed, judge, condemned, straight, slightly

Academic Vocabulary

Talk About

With a partner discuss the <u>fundamental</u> differences between Bierce's method of using flashbacks and a more traditional narrative without flashbacks.

Learn It Online
Find action-packed vocabulary lessons online.

go.hrw.com   L11-466   **Go**

Grammar Link

Adjective Clauses

You can improve the variety and flow of your sentences by using adjective clauses to show connections between ideas. An **adjective clause** is a subordinate clause that follows a noun or pronoun, specifying *what kind, which one,* or *how many.* Adjective clauses begin with a **relative pronoun,** such as *who, whom, whose, which,* or *that,* or with the **relative adverbs** *where* or *when.* You can use an adjective clause to combine two simple sentences into one complex sentence. Here are two simple sentences.

> Peyton Farquhar was unable to join the army. He wanted to help the cause of the South in some way.

Here the two simple sentences are joined by an adjective clause to form one complex sentence.

> Peyton Farquhar, who was unable to join the army, wanted to help the cause of the South in some way.

In the new sentence, the adjective clause modifies the proper noun *Peyton Farquhar.*

Your Turn

Combine each pair of sentences by using an adjective clause. Notice that when you use an adjective clause to combine sentences, you are eliminating repetition and simple syntax.

1. The Federal scout wears gray. Gray is the color that Confederate soldiers wear.
2. Peyton Farquhar is a well-to-do planter. He longs to be a soldier.
3. Peyton Farquhar stands upon the bridge. He had tried to sabotage the bridge.

Writing Application Choose a piece of your own writing, and find a pair of sentences that you can combine into one sentence by using an adjective clause. Rewrite the sentences.

CHOICES

As you respond to the Choices, use these **Academic Vocabulary** words as appropriate: <u>advocate</u>, <u>criteria</u>, <u>fundamental</u>, <u>principle</u>, <u>subsequent</u>.

REVIEW

Analyze Historical Context

Partner Activity With a partner, review the causes of the Civil War. (Refer to history textbooks and online references.) Discuss how the character of Peyton Farquhar clarifies <u>fundamental</u> divisions in the United States at that time. How do these divisions create an identity and mind-set for Farquhar? In what ways does Farquhar influence your understanding of the Civil War?

CONNECT

Research Critical Comments

The surprise ending of "An Occurrence at Owl Creek Bridge" has elicited much debate among literary critics. Look through an online literary database (your school or community librarian can refer you to one), and research responses critics have had to the story. Summarize your findings in two or three paragraphs.

EXTEND

Create a Storyboard

TechFocus As you read, you examined Bierce's use of flashbacks. Now, create a storyboard of "An Occurrence at Owl Creek Bridge." Be sure that your storyboard shows the difference between flashbacks and the present day of the narrative. Then, discuss how you would film these flashbacks if you were making a movie of the story. If time allows, share your ideas with the class as a whole.

A Mystery of Heroism

War Is Kind

What Do You Think

How does conflict lead to change?

QuickTalk

Are a soldier's impulsive actions during battle heroic or foolish? In a small group, discuss what makes someone a hero during a war.

Stephen Crane
(1871–1900)

Stephen Crane wrote gripping fictional and true accounts of life's dark side—of life on the streets and the horror of battle. A fundamental strength of his writing is his ability to depict the emotions aroused in situations of extreme stress.

Shocking Stories from the Streets

Stephen Crane was the youngest of fourteen children of a Methodist minister and his devout wife. Although frail as a child, Crane grew up—in upstate New York—yearning to become a baseball star. However, he decided to try to earn his living as a writer. At about age sixteen, Crane took a job at a news agency. Later, as a reporter in New York City, Crane was drawn to the city's underside. What he called his "artistic education" on the Bowery (Skid Row) left him hungry and often ill.

Crane's first significant fiction, *Maggie: A Girl of the Streets* (1893), was a somber, shocking novel based on his explorations of the city's slums and saloons. The novel revealed Crane as a pioneer of **naturalism,** a literary movement that dissected human instincts and behavior and examined the society that "conditioned" people to turn out as they did. The novel was impossibly grim for readers at the time and sold poorly.

War Chronicler and Adventurer

Crane's next novel, *The Red Badge of Courage* (1895), was a triumph. Crane filtered the events of the novel through the eyes of a young Civil War soldier named Henry Fleming. The novel made Crane a celebrity and a national expert on war.

Crane had a knack for interweaving his fiction with his real-life experiences. After being shipwrecked and enduring a thirty-hour struggle to survive on the open sea, he wrote the superb short story "The Open Boat." When he was a war correspondent, he covered the Greco-Turkish War in 1897 and the Spanish-American War a year later. These experiences took their toll on Crane's delicate health, but he continued to travel and write. He produced his second volume of poems, *War Is Kind,* in 1899. Crane died of tuberculosis at age twenty-eight.

Think About the Writer

Why do you think Crane might have been drawn to writing about the difficult aspects of life, such as poverty and war?

A Mystery of Heroism / War Is Kind

Reader/Writer Notebook

Use your **RWN** to complete the activities for these selections.

Literary Focus

Situational and Verbal Irony **Situational irony** occurs when there is a discrepancy between what is expected and what actually happens. For example, a soldier is wounded as he battles through war-torn terrain to rescue a fallen comrade, only to find out the comrade is safe. **Verbal irony** occurs when someone says one thing but means something else. Verbal irony can take the form of **understatement, exaggeration,** or **sarcasm.**

Reading Focus

Making Predictions In fiction, a **prediction** is an educated guess about subsequent events based on clues in the text and the reader's knowledge.

Into Action As you read "A Mystery of Heroism," use a chart like the one below, using clues and your own knowledge to make predictions.

My prediction about Collins	Collins will go for water and get killed.
Clues from the text	
Clues from my knowledge	When people dare me to do something, I often get angry and don't think things through.

Analyzing Tone Most often revealed by word choice, **tone** is a writer's attitude toward the subject of a work, the characters in it, or an audience.

Into Action As you read the "War Is Kind," write the words, phrases, or sentences that convey an ironic tone. Use a word web like the one below.

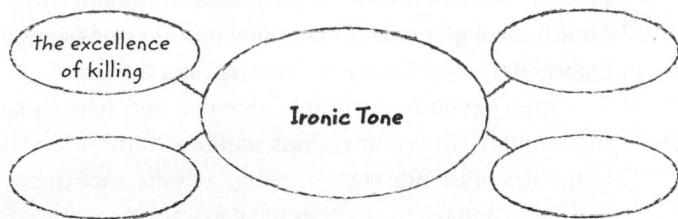

the excellence of killing

Ironic Tone

Writing Focus

Think as a Reader/Writer

Find It in Your Reading As you read "War Is Kind," record two examples of repetition in your *Reader/Writer Notebook,* and note their effect.

Vocabulary

onslaught (AHN slawt) *n.:* brutal, fierce attack. *The soldiers were attacked by an onslaught of bullets and cannon fire.*

obliterated (uh BLIHT uh rayt ihd) *v.:* completely destroyed. *Sections of the grassy meadow were obliterated during the battle.*

carnage (KAHR nihj) *n.:* extensive bloodshed. *The battle resulted in terrible carnage.*

eloquence (EHL uh kwuhns) *n.:* powerful expression. *One of the injured horses raised its head in eloquence before dying.*

ominous (AHM uh nuhs) *adj.:* threatening danger; menacing. *Collins spoke in an ominous tone to his comrades who jeered him.*

sullenly (SUHL uhn lee) *adv.:* in a resentfully silent manner; sulkily. *Collins felt pressure from his companions to go for water and moved sullenly away from them.*

provisional (pruh VIHZH uh nuhl) *adj.:* conditional; dependent on something else being done. *Collins earned the provisional respect of his comrades when he set out to bring back water.*

Language Coach

Connotations A word's connotations, or the feelings associated with it, can vary from mild to extreme. For example, *wreck* is a fairly mild synonym for *destroy,* while *obliterate* is an extreme one. Several words on the Vocabulary list above have extreme connotations.

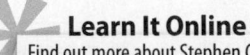

Learn It Online
Find out more about Stephen Crane at Writers' Lives.

go.hrw.com   L11-469   **Go**

A MYSTERY OF HEROISM

by Stephen Crane

Read with a Purpose
Read to discover how the author uses the story of one man's actions during battle to make a powerful statement about war.

Build Background
In war, the military chain of command makes it possible for an army to function. When reading stories about war, knowing the different military ranks can help you understand better not only the military action but also the relationships between soldiers. Here are ranks of soldiers mentioned in "A Mystery of Heroism," ranging from highest to lowest: colonel, lieutenant colonel, major, captain, lieutenant, sergeant, and private.

The dark uniforms of the men were so coated with dust from the incessant wrestling of the two armies that the regiment almost seemed a part of the clay bank which shielded them from the shells. On the top of the hill a battery[1] was arguing in tremendous roars with some other guns, and to the eye of the infantry, the artillerymen, the guns, the caissons,[2] the horses, were distinctly outlined upon the blue sky. When a piece was fired, a red streak as round as a log flashed low in the heavens, like a monstrous bolt of lightning. The men of the battery wore white duck trousers, which some-how emphasized their legs, and when they ran and crowded in little groups at the bidding of the shouting officers, it was more impressive than usual to the infantry.

Fred Collins of A Company was saying: "Thunder, I wisht I had a drink. Ain't there any water round here?" Then somebody yelled: "There goes th' bugler!" **A**

As the eyes of half of the regiment swept in one machinelike movement, there was an instant's picture of a horse in a great convulsive[3] leap of a death wound and a rider leaning back with a crooked arm and spread fingers before his face. On the ground was the crimson terror of an exploding shell, with fibers of flame that seemed like lances. A glittering bugle swung clear of the rider's back as fell headlong the horse and the man. In the air was an odor as from a conflagration.[4]

Sometimes they of the infantry looked down at a fair little meadow which spread at their feet. Its long, green grass was rippling gently in a breeze. Beyond it was the gray form of a house half torn to pieces by shells and by the busy axes of soldiers who had pursued firewood. The line of an old fence was now dimly marked by long weeds and by an occasional post. A shell had blown the well house to fragments. Little lines of gray smoke ribboning upward from some embers indicated the place where had stood the barn.

From beyond a curtain of green woods there came the sound of some stupendous scuffle as if two animals of the size of islands were fighting. At a distance there were occasional appearances of swift-moving men,

---

1. **battery:** set of heavy guns.
2. **caissons** (KAY sahnz): ammunition wagons.
3. **convulsive:** marked by a violent, involuntary spasm.
4. **conflagration** (kahn fluh GRAY shuhn): huge fire.

A **Literary Focus** **Situational Irony** What is the irony in this opening scene? Cite evidence to support your response.

Battle of Kelly's Field (1890) by Harry J. Kellogg.

Viewing and Interpreting What does this painting add to your understanding of the heroism required of soldiers facing battle? Explain your response.

horses, batteries, flags, and, with the crashing of infantry, volleys were heard, often, wild and frenzied cheers. In the midst of it all, Smith and Ferguson, two privates of A Company, were engaged in a heated discussion, which involved the greatest questions of the national existence. **B**

The battery on the hill presently engaged in a frightful duel. The white legs of the gunners scampered this way and that way and the officers redoubled their shouts. The guns, with their demeanors of stolidity[5] and courage, were typical of something infinitely self-possessed in this clamor of death that swirled around the hill.

One of a "swing" team was suddenly smitten quivering to the ground and his maddened brethren dragged his torn body in their struggle to escape from this turmoil and danger. A young soldier astride one of the leaders swore and fumed in his saddle and furiously jerked at the bridle. An officer screamed out an order so violently that his voice broke and ended the sentence in a falsetto[6] shriek.

The leading company of the infantry regiment was somewhat exposed and the colonel ordered it moved more fully under the shelter of the hill. There was the clank of steel against steel.

A lieutenant of the battery rode down and passed them, holding his right arm carefully in his left hand. And it was as if this arm was not at all a part of him, but belonged to another man. His sober and reflective charger[7] went slowly. The officer's face was grimy and

---

5. **stolidity** (stuh LIHD uh tee): absence of emotional reactions.

6. **falsetto:** artificially high voice.
7. **charger:** horse trained for battle.

B **Literary Focus** Situational Irony What is ironic about this passage? Explain.

perspiring and his uniform was tousled as if he had been in direct grapple with an enemy. He smiled grimly when the men stared at him. He turned his horse toward the meadow.

Collins of A Company said: "I wisht I had a drink. I bet there's water in that there ol' well yonder!"

"Yes; but how you goin' to git it?"

For the little meadow which intervened was now suffering a terrible onslaught of shells. Its green and beautiful calm had vanished utterly. Brown earth was being flung in monstrous handfuls. And there was a massacre of the young blades of grass. They were being torn, burned, obliterated. Some curious fortune of the battle had made this gentle little meadow the object of the red hate of the shells and each one as it exploded seemed like an imprecation[8] in the face of a maiden.

The wounded officer who was riding across this expanse said to himself: "Why, they couldn't shoot any harder if the whole army was massed here!"

A shell struck the gray ruins of the house and as, after the roar, the shattered wall fell in fragments, there was a noise which resembled the flapping of shutters during a wild gale of winter. Indeed the infantry paused in the shelter of the bank, appeared as men standing upon a shore contemplating a madness of the sea. The angel of calamity[9] had under its glance the battery upon the hill. Fewer white-legged men labored about the guns. A shell had smitten one of the pieces, and after the flare, the smoke, the dust, the wrath of this blow was gone, it was possible to see white legs stretched horizontally upon the ground. And at that interval to the rear, where it is the business of battery horses to stand with their noses to the fight awaiting the command to drag their guns out of the destruction or into it or wheresoever these incomprehensible humans demanded with whip and spur—in this line of passive and dumb spectators, whose fluttering hearts yet would not let them forget

Yorktown, Virginia, South end, May 1862. Battery No. 4 mounting 13-inch mortars.

the iron laws of man's control of them—in this rank of brute soldiers there had been relentless and hideous carnage. From the ruck[10] of bleeding and prostrate[11] horses, the men of the infantry could see one animal raising its stricken body with its forelegs and turning its nose with mystic and profound eloquence toward the sky.

Some comrades joked Collins about his thirst. "Well, if yeh want a drink so bad, why don't yeh go git it?"

"Well, I will in a minnet if yeh don't shut up."

A lieutenant of artillery floundered his horse straight down the hill with as great concern as if it were level ground. As he galloped past the colonel of the infantry, he threw up his hand in swift salute. "We've got to get out of that," he roared angrily. He was a black-bearded officer, and his eyes, which resembled beads, sparkled like those of an insane man. His jumping horse sped along the column of infantry.

---

8. **imprecation:** curse.
9. **calamity:** disaster; misfortune.

10. **ruck:** mass; crowd.
11. **prostrate:** lying flat on the ground.

C **Literary Focus** Situational Irony This story contains both elaborate description and straightforward plot and dialogue. What effect does Crane produce by using these contrasting elements?

D **Reading Focus** Making Predictions Judging from Collins's response to his comrades, what do you predict will happen next? Why?

Vocabulary **onslaught** (AHN slawt) *n.*: brutal, fierce attack.
obliterated (uh BLIHT uh rayt ihd) *v.*: completely destroyed.
carnage (KAHR nihj) *n.*: extensive bloodshed.
eloquence (EHL uh kwuhns) *n.*: powerful expression.

The fat major standing carelessly with his sword held horizontally behind him and with his legs far apart, looked after the receding horseman and laughed. "He wants to get back with orders pretty quick or there'll be no batt'ry left," he observed.

The wise young captain of the second company hazarded[12] to the lieutenant colonel that the enemy's infantry would probably soon attack the hill, and the lieutenant colonel snubbed him.

A private in one of the rear companies looked out over the meadow and then turned to a companion and said: "Look there, Jim." It was the wounded officer from the battery, who some time before had started to ride across the meadow, supporting his right arm carefully with his left hand. This man had encountered a shell apparently at a time when no one perceived him and he could now be seen lying face downward with a stirruped foot stretched across the body of his dead horse. A leg of the charger extended slantingly upward precisely as stiff as a stake. Around this motionless pair the shells still howled.

There was a quarrel in A Company. Collins was shaking his fist in the faces of some laughing comrades. "Dern yeh! I ain't afraid t' go. If yeh say much, I will go!"

"Of course, yeh will! Yeh'll run through that there medder, won't yeh?"

Collins said, in a terrible voice: "You see, now!" At this ominous threat his comrades broke into renewed jeers.

Collins gave them a dark scowl and went to find his captain. The latter was conversing with the colonel of the regiment.

"Captain," said Collins, saluting and standing at attention. In those days all trousers bagged at the knees. "Captain, I want t' git permission to go git some water from that there well over yonder!" **E**

_____
12. **hazarded:** risked saying.

The colonel and the captain swung about simultaneously and stared across the meadow. The captain laughed. "You must be pretty thirsty, Collins?"

"Yes, sir; I am."

"Well—ah," said the captain. After a moment he asked: "Can't you wait?"

"No, sir."

The colonel was watching Collins's face. "Look here, my lad," he said, in a pious[13] sort of a voice. "Look here, my lad." Collins was not a lad. "Don't you think that's taking pretty big risks for a little drink of water?"

"I dunno," said Collins, uncomfortably. Some of the resentment toward his companions, which perhaps had forced him into this affair, was beginning to fade. "I dunno wether 'tis."

The colonel and the captain contemplated him for a time.

"Well," said the captain finally.

"Well," said the colonel, "if you want to go, why go."

Collins saluted. "Much obliged t' yeh."

As he moved away, the colonel called after him. "Take some of the other boys' canteens with you an' hurry back now." **F**

"Yes, sir. I will."

The colonel and the captain looked at each other then, for it had suddenly occurred that they could not for the life of them tell whether Collins wanted to go or whether he did not.

They turned to regard Collins, and as they perceived him surrounded by gesticulating[14] comrades, the colonel said: "Well, by thunder! I guess he's going."

Collins appeared as a man dreaming. In the midst of the questions, the advice, the warnings, all the excited talk of his company mates, he maintained a curious silence.

_____
13. **pious:** seemingly virtuous.
14. **gesticulating** (jehs TIHK yuh layt ihng): gesturing, especially with the hands and arms.

_____

E Reading Focus **Making Predictions** Do you think the captain will grant permission to Collins? If so, will Collins go through with his plan? Cite clues in the text to support your prediction.

Vocabulary **ominous** (AHM uh nuhs) _adj.:_ threatening danger; menacing.

F Reading Focus **Making Predictions** Do you think that the captain's and the colonel's words and instructions will make it more or less likely that Collins will go through with his plan? Why?

They were very busy in preparing him for his ordeal. When they inspected him carefully, it was somewhat like the examination that grooms give a horse before a race; and they were amazed, staggered by the whole affair. Their astonishment found vent in strange repetitions.

"Are yeh sure a-goin'?" they demanded again and again.

"Certainly I am," cried Collins, at last furiously.

He strode sullenly away from them. He was swinging five or six canteens by their cords. It seemed that his cap would not remain firmly on his head, and often he reached and pulled it down over his brow.

There was a general movement in the compact column. The long animal-like thing moved slightly. Its four hundred eyes were turned upon the figure of Collins.

"Well, sir, if that ain't th' derndest thing. I never thought Fred Collins had the blood in him for that kind of business."

"What's he goin' to do, anyhow?"

"He's goin' to that well there after water."

"We ain't dyin' of thirst, are we? That's foolishness."

"Well, somebody put him up to it an' he's doin' it."

"Say, he must be a desperate cuss."

When Collins faced the meadow and walked away from the regiment, he was vaguely conscious that a chasm, the deep valley of all prides, was suddenly between him and his comrades. It was provisional, but the provision was that he return as a victor. He had blindly been led by quaint emotions and laid himself under an obligation to walk squarely up to the face of death.

But he was not sure that he wished to make a retraction[15] even if he could do so without shame.

> IT SEEMED TO HIM SUPERNATURALLY STRANGE THAT HE HAD ALLOWED HIS MIND TO MANEUVER HIS BODY INTO SUCH A SITUATION.

As a matter of truth he was sure of very little. He was mainly surprised.

It seemed to him supernaturally strange that he had allowed his mind to maneuver his body into such a situation. He understood that it might be called dramatically great.

However, he had no full appreciation of anything excepting that he was actually conscious of being dazed. He could feel his dulled mind groping after the form and color of this incident.

Too, he wondered why he did not feel some keen agony of fear cutting his sense like a knife. He wondered at this because human expression had said loudly for centuries that men should feel afraid of certain things and that all men who did not feel this fear were phenomena, heroes.

He was then a hero. He suffered that disappointment which we would all have if we discovered that we were ourselves capable of those deeds which we most admire in history and legend. This, then, was a hero. After all, heroes were not much.

No, it could not be true. He was not a hero. Heroes had no shames in their lives and, as for him, he remembered borrowing fifteen dollars from a friend and promising to pay it back the next day, and then avoiding that friend for ten months. When at home his mother had aroused him for the early labor of his life on the farm, it had often been his fashion to be irritable, childish, diabolical, and his mother had died since he had come to the war. **G**

He saw that in this matter of the well, the canteens, the shells, he was an intruder in the land of fine deeds. **H**

He was now about thirty paces from his comrades. The regiment had just turned its many faces toward him.

From the forest of terrific noises there suddenly emerged a little uneven line of men. They fired fiercely and rapidly at distant foliage on which appeared little

---

15. **retraction:** withdrawal.

Vocabulary **sullenly** (SUHL unh lee) *adv.*: in a resentfully silent manner; sulkily.
provisional (pruh VIHZH uh nuhl) *adj.*: conditional; dependent on something else being done.

G **Literary Focus** Situational Irony Why does the situation seem ironic to Collins when he discovers that he is a hero?

H **Reading Focus** Making Predictions Do you think Collins will succeed in getting the water from the well? What clues did you use to make your prediction?

puffs of white smoke. The spatter of skirmish firing was added to the thunder of the guns on the hill. The little line of men ran forward. A color sergeant fell flat with his flag as if he had slipped on ice. There was hoarse cheering from this distant field.

Collins suddenly felt that two demon fingers were pressed into his ears. He could see nothing but flying arrows, flaming red. He lurched from the shock of this explosion, but he made a mad rush for the house, which he viewed as a man submerged to the neck in a boiling surf might view the shore. In the air, little pieces of shell howled and the earthquake explosions drove him insane with the menace of their roar. As he ran, the canteens knocked together with a rhythmical tinkling.

As he neared the house, each detail of the scene became vivid to him. He was aware of some bricks of the vanished chimney lying on the sod. There was a door which hung by one hinge.

Rifle bullets called forth by the insistent skirmishers came from the far-off bank of foliage. They mingled with the shells and the pieces of shells until the air was torn in all directions by hootings, yells, howls. The sky was full of fiends who directed all their wild rage at his head.

When he came to the well, he flung himself face downward and peered into its darkness. There were furtive silver glintings some feet from the surface. He grabbed one of the canteens and, unfastening its cap, swung it down by the cord. The water flowed slowly in with an indolent[16] gurgle.

---

16. **indolent:** lazy.

And now as he lay with his face turned away, he was suddenly smitten with the terror. It came upon his heart like the grasp of claws. All the power faded from his muscles. For an instant he was no more than a dead man.

The canteen filled with a maddening slowness in the manner of all bottles. Presently he recovered his strength and addressed a screaming oath to it. He leaned over until it seemed as if he intended to try to push water into it with his hands. His eyes as he gazed down into the well shone like two pieces of metal and in their expression was a great appeal and a great curse. The stupid water derided[17] him.

There was the blaring thunder of a shell. Crimson light shone through the swift-boiling smoke and made a pink reflection on part of the wall of the well. Collins jerked out his arm and canteen with the same motion that a man would use in withdrawing his head from a furnace.

He scrambled erect and glared and hesitated. On the ground near him lay the old well bucket, with a length of rusty chain. He lowered it swiftly into the well. The bucket struck the water and then turning lazily over, sank. When, with hand reaching tremblingly over hand, he hauled it out, it knocked often against the walls of the well and spilled some of its contents.

In running with a filled bucket, a man can adopt but one kind of gait. So through this terrible field over which screamed practical angels of death Collins ran in the manner of a farmer chased out of a dairy by a bull. **❶**

His face went staring white with anticipation—anticipation of a blow that would whirl him around and down. He would fall as he had seen other men fall, the life knocked out of them so suddenly that

---

17. **derided:** mocked.

their knees were no more quick to touch the ground than their heads. He saw the long blue line of the regiment, but his comrades were standing looking at him from the edge of an impossible star. He was aware of some deep wheel ruts and hoof prints in the sod beneath his feet.

The artillery officer who had fallen in this meadow had been making groans in the teeth of the tempest of sound. These futile cries, wrenched from him by his agony, were heard only by shells, bullets. When wild-eyed Collins came running, this officer raised himself. His face contorted and blanched from pain, he was about to utter some great beseeching cry. But suddenly his face straightened and he called: "Say, young man, give me a drink of water, will you?"

Collins had no room amid his emotions for surprise. He was mad from the threats of destruction.

"I can't," he screamed, and in this reply was a full description of his quaking apprehension. His cap was gone and his hair was riotous. His clothes made it appear that he had been dragged over the ground by the heels. He ran on. **❷**

The officer's head sank down and one elbow crooked. His foot in its brass-bound stirrup still stretched over the body of his horse and the other leg was under the steed.

But Collins turned. He came dashing back. His face had now turned gray and in his eyes was all terror. "Here it is! Here it is!"

The officer was as a man gone in drink. His arm bended like a twig. His head drooped as if his neck was of willow. He was sinking to the ground, to lie face downward.

Collins grabbed him by the shoulder. "Here it is. Here's your drink. Turn over! Turn over, man, for God's sake!"

> COLLINS JERKED OUT HIS ARM AND CANTEEN WITH THE SAME MOTION THAT A MAN WOULD USE IN WITHDRAWING HIS HEAD FROM A FURNACE.

---

❶ Literary Focus Situational Irony How is the way Collins runs an example of situational irony?

❷ Reading Focus Making Predictions Will Collins keep running, or will he turn back to help the dying man? Explain the reasons behind your prediction.

Health Link: Surviving Trauma

Collins is surprised to find himself without fear at the thought of risking his life to get water. Psychologists now understand that during and sometimes after traumatic events like the battle described in this story, people experience what is known as dissociation. **Dissociation** involves a numbing of emotions and can lead to confusion, a disconnection from one's body, and a sense of surrealism about what is occurring. Although dissociation can help people survive terrible events like war, it can also make life very difficult later, when these emotions, detached in the mind from the experiences that caused them, can overwhelm traumatized people.

Ask Yourself

How does knowing about dissociation help you solve the "mystery" of heroism? How does it explain Collins's actions, the actions of the lieutenant on the field, and the ability of the guns to be "infinitely self-possessed" during such horrific battle?

Dulce Bellum Inexpertis (1979) by Randolph Harmes. Stained wood and thread, 11¾" × 9⅞" × 3½".

With Collins hauling at his shoulder, the officer twisted his body and fell with his face turned toward that region where lived the unspeakable noises of the swirling missiles. There was the faintest shadow of a smile on his lips as he looked at Collins. He gave a sigh, a little primitive breath like that from a child. **K**

Collins tried to hold the bucket steadily, but his shaking hands caused the water to splash all over the face of the dying man. Then he jerked it away and ran on.

The regiment gave him a welcoming roar. The grimed faces were wrinkled in laughter.

His captain waved the bucket away. "Give it to the men!"

The two genial,[18] skylarking[19] young lieutenants were the first to gain possession of it. They played over it in their fashion.

When one tried to drink, the other teasingly knocked his elbow. "Don't, Billie! You'll make me spill it," said the one. The other laughed.

Suddenly there was an oath, the thud of wood on the ground, and a swift murmur of astonishment from the ranks. The two lieutenants glared at each other. The bucket lay on the ground empty. **L**

18. **genial:** friendly; cheerful.
19. **skylarking:** frolicking; playful.

K Literary Focus **Situational Irony** What is ironic about the contrast between the facial expression of the dying man and the setting that is described in this passage? Why does he smile, and why is his smile childlike?

L Literary Focus **Situational Irony** Explain the story's final irony. What philosophic stance does it suggest?

WAR IS KIND

by **Stephen Crane**

Read with a Purpose
Read to discover the poet's true beliefs about war.

Build Background
Although Stephen Crane never fought in a battle, he interviewed Civil War veterans about their experiences. However, they offered him only dry facts and seemed unable to recall—or at least articulate—their thoughts and feelings about the war. Crane drew from his own imagination to fill in those thoughts and feelings and give them a larger meaning. In this poem, he quietly and intimately expresses his beliefs about the effects of war.

Do not weep, maiden, for war is kind.
Because your lover threw wild hands toward the sky
And the affrighted steed ran on alone,
Do not weep.
5   War is kind.

Hoarse, booming drums of the regiment,
Little souls who thirst for fight,
These men were born to drill and die.
The unexplained glory flies above them,
10   Great is the Battle-God, great, and his Kingdom—
A field where a thousand corpses lie.

Do not weep, babe, for war is kind.
Because your father tumbled in the yellow trenches,
Raged at his breast, gulped and died,
15   Do not weep.
War is kind.

A **Literary Focus** **Verbal Irony** Although the poet says in the first line that "war is kind," the poem's images are <u>fundamentally</u> opposed to the idea that war has a gentle, considerate side. Explain what the speaker is really saying about war.

Swift blazing flag of the regiment,
Eagle with crest of red and gold,
These men were born to drill and die.
20 Point for them the virtue of slaughter,
Make plain to them the excellence of killing
And a field where a thousand corpses lie. **Ⓑ**

Mother whose heart hung humble as a button
On the bright splendid shroud of your son,
25 Do not weep.
War is kind.

Ⓑ **Reading Focus** **Analyzing Tone** Identify the tone of this stanza. Which images help create the tone?

Analyzing Visuals

Viewing and Interpreting
Although this painting depicts soldiers departing for war, the mood of the scene has much in common with the mood of Crane's poem about death on the battlefield. With a partner, identify and discuss details in the painting that create its mournful mood.

Off to the Front (c. 1861). Artist unknown.
Oil on canvas, 27 1/4" × 30". Detail.
West Point Museum Art Collection, United States Military Academy, West Point, NY.

Applying Your Skills

A Mystery of Heroism / War Is Kind

Respond and Think Critically

Reading Focus

Read with a Purpose

1. What do you think of Crane's views on war?

Reading Skills: Making Predictions

A Mystery of Heroism

2. Review your prediction chart. Add a row to your chart, and tell what really happened. Were your predictions correct, or did the situational irony in the story surprise you?

My prediction about Collins	Collins will go for water and get killed.
Clues from the text	
Clues from my knowledge	When people dare me to do something, I often get angry and don't think things through.
What actually happened?	

Reading Skills: Analyzing Tone

War Is Kind

3. Revisit your word web, and note the words Crane uses to create an ironic tone. Which words or images were most effective?

Literary Focus

Literary Analysis

A Mystery of Heroism

4. Infer What do you think is Collins's motive for his daring act? In what sense might the "mystery" in the story's title refer to Collins's motivation?

5. Evaluate Crane depicts war as dehumanizing. What do you think of this view of war?

War Is Kind

6. Compare and Contrast How do the images of war presented in the second and fourth stanzas differ from the images of war presented in the rest of the poem?

7. Interpret What do you think is the "unexplained glory" (line 9)? Why is it "unexplained"?

Literary Skills: Irony

8. Analyze What situational irony occurs at the end of "A Mystery of Heroism"?

9. Interpret Explain why the poem's refrain below is an example of verbal irony.
> Do not weep.
> War is kind.

Literary Skills Review: Characterization

10. Evaluate Writers use details of character, as well as dialogue and descriptions of characters' thoughts and emotions, to achieve **characterization**. Analyze Collins's words and actions as well as his responses to other characters to decide whether Crane depicts him as a hero.

Writing Focus

Think as a Reader/Writer

Use It in Your Writing Write a short poem on a topic that is <u>fundamentally</u> important to you. Use repetition to support your poem's main idea.

 What Do You Think Now

Do you think that Crane's views on war are valid since he never fought in a war himself? Explain.

Vocabulary Development

✓ Vocabulary Check

Match each Vocabulary word with its definition.

1. onslaught
2. obliterated
3. carnage
4. eloquence
5. ominous
6. sullenly
7. provisional

a. expressiveness
b. resentfully
c. conditional
d. bloodshed
e. attack
f. destroyed
g. threatening

Vocabulary Skills: Prefixes and Suffixes

Just a few letters added to the beginning of a word (a **prefix**) or the end of a word (a **suffix**) can change a word's meaning and, often, its part of speech. When you find an unfamiliar word, look for prefixes and suffixes that provide clues to how the base form of the word changes. Keep in mind that –s, –ed, and –ing are inflectional suffixes (suffixes that indicate the tense or case of a word rather than change its meaning). Look at the examples in each of the following charts.

Prefix	Base Word	Prefix + Base Word
mis– (badly or wrongly; not)	treat	mistreat
di–, dis– (away; lack of)	infect	disinfect
over– (too much)	work	overwork
un– (not)	known	unknown

Suffix	Base Word	Base Word + Suffix
–ity (full of)	scarce	scarcity
–able, –ible (able to; likely to)	like	likable
–tion (action of; condition of)	condense	condensation
–ness (state or quality of being)	happy	happiness

Your Turn

For each of the following words, consult a dictionary to find the origins of the word, as well as the meanings of its prefix and suffix.

1. disappointment
2. incomprehensible
3. retraction
4. unspeakable
5. supernaturally

Language Coach

Connotations Connotations are the feelings associated with a word. Using a dictionary, create a scale like the one below for each of these "extreme" words: *onslaught, carnage.*

MILD   **EXTREME**

wrecked _ _ _ _ _ _ destroyed _ _ _ _ _ obliterated

Academic Vocabulary

Talk About

In a small group, develop a list of the fundamental traits of war, as depicted by Stephen Crane in "A Mystery of Heroism" and "War Is Kind." Discuss lines in the story or poem that illustrate each of the traits on your list.

 **Healing War's Wounds**

 How does conflict lead to change?

QuickWrite

Think about a crisis you or someone you know has experienced. How did you or the person you know cope with it? What changes occurred as a result of the crisis? Write a one-paragraph response in your *Reader/Writer Notebook.*

Informational Text Focus

Analyzing Author's Purpose An **author's purpose** is the author's reason for writing. The <u>fundamental</u> purpose of magazine articles is to inform readers about a particular subject. However, writers of informational texts can have other purposes as well, such as to entertain or persuade. One clue to an author's purpose is the language he or she uses to describe the subject of the article. In "Healing War's Wounds," Karen Breslau introduces Major Anthony Smith by describing him gleefully paddling a raft with his prosthetic arm. Breslau's depiction of Smith emphasizes that he has remained active and strong despite his injury.

Into Action As you read, use a chart like the one below to record the language Breslau uses to describe each soldier. Think about how Breslau's language conveys her purpose.

Soldier	Language Used to Describe the Soldier
Major Anthony Smith	"digging his paddle back into the water, growls with mock pirate glee" "endured more than 30 surgical procedures"

Writing Focus Preparing for **Constructed Response**

In your *Reader/Writer Notebook,* list the direct quotations the author uses to reflect the thoughts and feelings of the injured men. For example, she quotes Smith saying, "Hey, have any of y'all seen the crocodile that got my arm?" to show that Smith is able to joke about his injury. Ask yourself how the soldiers' own words add to your understanding of their struggles.

Reader/Writer Notebook

Use your **RWN** to complete the activities for this selection.

Vocabulary

prosthetic (prahs THEHT ihk) *adj.:* relating to an artificial replacement for a missing body part. *After losing his right arm to a grenade, the soldier was fitted with a prosthetic device.*

traumatic (traw MAT ihk) *adj.:* emotionally or physically severe. *A devastating wound can have lasting traumatic effects.*

holistic (hoh LIHS tihk) *adj.:* relating to the whole of something instead of its parts. *Holistic medicine treats the body and mind.*

orthopedic (awr thuh PEE dihk) *adj.:* medically related to the bones, joints, or muscles. *Orthopedic surgeons assess the damage caused by bone-shattering wounds.*

tourniqueted (TUR nuh keht ihd) *adj.:* fitted with a device to prevent blood loss from a major wound. *The surgeons began to operate on the patient's tourniqueted injured arm.*

Language Coach

Suffixes The suffix *–ic* usually signals an adjective. Some adjectives ending in *–ic,* such as *holistic,* have related nouns ending in *–ics,* signifying a field of study. Using a dictionary, find two more such nouns related to words above.

Learn It Online
Practice reading magazine articles like this one with the interactive Reading Workshop online.

go.hrw.com   L11-482   Go

Link to Today

This Link to Today shows how contemporary soldiers deal with the life-changing effects of military conflict.

Read with a Purpose

Read to discover how injured soldiers use extreme sports to regain their mental and physical health.

Build Background

The conflict in Iraq started in March 2003, when a coalition led by the United States entered the country and toppled the government of Saddam Hussein. In June 2004, an interim government was established. U.S. troops stationed in Iraq have been threatened by the insurgency, an ongoing and violent revolt against the interim government and the U.S. presence in Iraq. Because of medical advances, severely wounded soldiers often survive to face difficult and lengthy recoveries.

Anthony Smith braves the white water on Idaho's Salmon River.

Healing War's Wounds

by **Karen Breslau**

reprinted with permission from NEWSWEEK

SEPT. 11, 2006 ISSUE – "Hey, have any of y'all seen the crocodile that got my arm?" U.S. Army Maj. Anthony Smith hoists his prosthetic hook, tied to a paddle, as he floats down Idaho's Salmon River in a large blue raft, manned by a cackling crew of fellow amputees. Momentarily rattled, a group of rafters resting onshore stare as Smith's boat glides by, before someone on the beach points down the rapids and yells, "He went that-a-way." Smith, digging his paddle back into the water, growls with mock pirate glee. "You should see what happens when I'm in a restaurant and I say to the waitress 'Can you give me a hand?'" Ⓐ

Ⓐ **Informational Focus** Author's Purpose How does the author reveal her attitude toward the soldiers in the first paragraph of the article?

Vocabulary **prosthetic** (prahs THEHT ihk) *adj.:* relating to an artificial replacement for a missing body part.

Viewing and Interpreting
What emotions do you think the veteran in the paragliding harness was feeling at the moment the photograph was taken? What details of the scene help you identify his emotions?

U.S. Marine S/Sgt. Damion Jacobs paraglides over Sun Valley, Idaho.

He can laugh now. It's the surest sign yet of the progress he's made since April 24, 2004, when Smith, then a captain with an Arkansas National Guard unit stationed near Baghdad,[1] was struck by a rocket-propelled grenade. . . . As Smith staggered to his feet, insurgents[2] opened fire, shooting him four times. By the time medics[3] reached him minutes later, Smith had "flat-lined." Finding no pulse or respiration, they loaded him into a body bag and put his name on the list of those KIA, killed in action. Only as a soldier was preparing to zip shut the bag did she notice an air bubble in the blood oozing from Smith's neck wound. "They said, 'Hey, this guy's still alive,'" Smith says.

---

1. **Baghdad:** capital city of Iraq.
2. **insurgents:** loosely organized fighters who oppose the interim Iraqi government and the presence of the U.S. military in Iraq.
3. **medics:** trained military personnel who rescue wounded soldiers and administer life-saving first aid.

Two and a half years later, Smith recounts his own resurrection in vivid detail—not because he remembers (he was in a coma for six weeks), but because he has pieced the story together from conversations with his wife, Jackie, and the dozens of doctors who labored to save him. Smith has endured more than 30 surgical procedures to reconstruct his abdomen, the remains of his right arm, his burned face and the gaping wound in his hip, now painfully infected. He must be constantly monitored for signs of **traumatic** brain injury that may have resulted from the force of his skull's slamming against the inside of his helmet. **B**

Though Smith's tale of survival is extreme, it is no longer unheard of. . . . But it also presents a huge challenge for the military as this sizable population of wounded veterans returns to society, bearing complex disabilities that will require lifelong care.

B **Informational Focus** **Author's Purpose** Why do you think the author goes into detail about the extent of Smith's wounds? What purpose do these details serve?

Vocabulary **traumatic** (traw MAT ihk) *adj.:* emotionally or physically severe.

To address the problem, the military has adopted a holistic mind-body approach, deploying a fleet of experts ranging from orthopedic surgeons to therapists to work on the wounded. Doctors insist on group therapy to help cope with the guilt that often dogs survivors who have lost—or left—comrades on the battlefield. Of

special concern are the service members, like Smith, classified by the Pentagon as "severely injured"—having lost limbs or eyesight, or suffering burns, paralysis or debilitating brain injuries that will not emerge fully in some cases for years. "Technology has advanced to the point where we can salvage patients who would not have survived before," says Lt. Col. John McManus of the Army's Institute for Surgical Research in San Antonio, Texas. "The bigger test is psychological. Can we restore a life worth living?"

Vocabulary **holistic** (hoh LIHS tihk) *adj.*: relating to the whole of something instead of its parts.
orthopedic (awr thuh PEE dihk) *adj.*: medically related to the bones, joints, or muscles.

Analyzing Visuals

Viewing and Interpreting What mood is the photographer trying to capture in this picture? How does this mood relate to the goal of the Pentagon's experimental rehabilitation program?

U.S. Army Sp. Andrew Soule meets with disabled recreation advocate Erik Schultz on the bank of the Salmon River, Idaho.

The Pentagon has recently begun testing more experimental methods, rehabilitating wounded service members with extreme sports designed to build muscle—and self-confidence. . . . Patients who work out regularly, lifting weights and yanking pulleys from their wheelchairs, often with burned and mangled limbs, are rewarded with all-expenses-paid outdoor expeditions. It was just such an invitation that brought Smith, two other wounded service members and their wives to the Salmon River last month. . . . On the week's agenda: white-water rafting, paragliding, rock climbing and horseback riding. With the group is Erik Schultz, a backcountry sports enthusiast who was paralyzed in a skiing accident eight years ago. During his darkest depression, says Schultz, friends "literally dragged me" on a camping trip. After a week in the wilderness, "I was bursting with self-confidence. Things didn't seem that hard anymore." He hopes that his presence in a wheelchair, fly-fishing from a rocky beach and whooping his way down the river, will help "demystify" disabled life for the wounded service members. **C**

Free from their hospital routines, and the weight of their wounds, Smith and the others spend their days splashing like kids. U.S. Marine S/Sgt. Damion Jacobs, who lost his right leg below the knee to an IED[4] near Fallujah six months ago, removes his prosthetic and props

> After a week in the wilderness, "I was bursting with self-confidence. Things didn't seem that hard anymore."

it in the sand like a coffee table; he leans against it while watching the show. Jacobs plans to take his Marine Corps physical and return to active duty. Army Spc. Andrew Soule, an intense, dignified 25-year-old who has emerged as the star of BAMC's rehab program, says that before his injury, he wasn't "much of an athlete." A year ago Soule lost both legs and suffered a severe arm injury in a bomb blast in Afghanistan. Now he kayaks, hand-cycles and surfs. On the first day of the river trip, one of Soule's carbon-fiber prosthetics is fractured. He tosses the limb aside and, for the next five days, kayaks legless, dragging his body over rocky beaches, even climbing stairs, with his arms. "People have this tendency to overreact," says Soule, who left Texas A&M after 9/11 to join the Army. "They don't know how much you can do for yourself." **D**

Even Soule is amazed by how far he has come. As he lay tourniqueted on the ground last year next to the wreckage of his Humvee near the Pakistani border, waiting for a helicopter to rescue him, Soule's squad leader leaned over him and instructed the young soldier to repeat over and over, "I'm going to live. I'm going to live." It's a lesson he carried with him, down the Salmon River and beyond.

—Karen Breslau has served as a White House correspondent and is currently *Newsweek*'s San Francisco bureau chief © 2006 MSNBC.com

---

4. **IED:** improvised explosive device; the military term for a homemade bomb.

C **Informational Focus** Author's Purpose The author clearly admires the soldiers for participating in extreme adventure sports. What details in the paragraph show her admiration?

D **Informational Focus** Author's Purpose How did Andrew Soule respond when he broke one of his prosthetics on the first day of a river trip? What does his response tell you about the importance of the therapy profiled in the article?

Vocabulary **tourniqueted** (TUR nuh keht ihd) *adj.*: fitted with a device to prevent blood loss from a major wound.

SKILLS FOCUS Informational Skills
Analyze author's purpose. **Listening and Speaking Skills** Adapt to occasions when speaking: discussions. **Writing Skills** Write brief constructed responses, with specific support.

Respond and Think Critically

Informational Text Focus

Quick Check

1. Describe the military's "holistic mind-body approach" to treating injured soldiers.

2. How did spending a week in the wilderness boost Erik Schultz's self-confidence?

Read with a Purpose

3. How does participating in extreme sports benefit injured soldiers mentally and physically? Why is it important to treat both the physical and the psychological wounds of war?

Informational Skills: Author's Purpose

4. As you read, you recorded the language Breslau used to describe each soldier. Add a third column in which you explain why the author used the language she did. Write a sentence summing up the author's <u>fundamental</u> purpose.

Soldier	Language Used to Describe the Soldier	Author's Purpose
Major Anthony Smith	"digging his paddle back into the water, growls with mock pirate glee" "endured more than 30 surgical procedures"	to show that Smith is strong and active despite his injury

✓ Vocabulary Check

Which Vocabulary best completes each phrase?

5. holistic
6. tourniqueted
7. traumatic
8. prosthetic
9. orthopedic

a. a replacement, _____ limb
b. cutting-edge _____ surgery
c. a broad, _____ approach
d. a horrible, _____ experience
e. a badly wounded, _____ leg

Text Analysis

10. **Analyze** Breslau begins her article with a humorous anecdote, followed by a horrific description of Major Smith's near-fatal injuries. Why do you think she chose to begin the article this way?

11. **Interpret** Breslau refers to Major Smith's recovery as a "resurrection." Considering the facts surrounding his injury, how is this description appropriate?

12. **Evaluate** Re-read the article's closing sentence. What lesson do you think Soule carried with him? What lesson do you think Breslau wants readers to carry with them after reading her article?

Listening and Speaking

13. **Extend** While reading "Healing War's Wounds," you recorded information that the author includes to describe the soldiers in her article. With a small group of peers, discuss the information you recorded. As you talk, make a list of the soldiers' traits that your group admires.

Writing Focus Constructed Response

Briefly discuss how the author's use of quotations from injured soldiers contributes to your understanding of their struggle to recover in "Healing War's Wounds." Be sure to cite specific evidence from the article to support your response.

What Do You Think Now What have the experiences of the soldiers in this article taught you about coping with crisis or trauma? Use the text to support your response.

I Will Fight No More Forever

What Do You Think?

How does conflict lead to change?

QuickWrite

Think about a conflict between different groups of people within your community. Write a paragraph explaining the conflict and a possible resolution that would be fair to both groups.

MEET THE WRITER

Chief Joseph
(c. 1840–1904)

Born in what is now Oregon, Chief Joseph, or In-mut-too-yah-lat-lat, has become a symbol of the heroic spirit of the Nez Perce of the Pacific Northwest.

From Peace to Warfare

During the first half of the nineteenth century, the Nez Perce were friendly to European settlers. Many American Indians, including Joseph's father, converted to Christianity, and Joseph attended a mission school. After 1850, however, the influx of white settlers into the Pacific Northwest motivated U.S. officials to draw up treaties removing American Indians from their native lands and resettling them on small reservations. In 1871, Chief Joseph refused to sign a treaty that would send his people to a reservation. The United States responded with force, and the Nez Perce were drawn into battle.

Heroic Escape

In 1877, when the Nez Perce were ordered to move from their native Wallowa Valley in Oregon to the Lapwai Reservation in Idaho, Chief Joseph reluctantly agreed, hoping to avoid further bloodshed. Subsequently, he learned that three of his men had killed a group of white settlers. Fearing retaliation, he attempted to escape to Canada with his people. They retreated for more than a thousand miles, outmaneuvering and sometimes defeating U.S. troops. His people made it to within forty miles of the Canadian border before exhaustion and hunger forced them to stop.

Upon surrendering, the Nez Perce were taken to a reservation in Indian Territory (now part of Oklahoma), where many became sick and died. Chief Joseph pleaded with President Theodore Roosevelt to allow his people to return to their ancestral land. In 1885, the Nez Perce were moved to Colville Reservation in Washington State; they were never allowed to return to Wallowa Valley. On September 21, 1904, Chief Joseph died in Colville.

Think About the Writer

What does Chief Joseph's desire to avoid further bloodshed suggest about his values as a leader? Explain.

Hinmaton-Yalaktit ("Chief Joseph") (1840–1904) by Edward S. Curtis (1868–1952).

![Reader/Writer Notebook logo] **Reader/Writer Notebook**

Use your **RWN** to complete the activities for this selection.

SKILLS FOCUS **Literary Skills** Understand the characteristics of American Indian oratory, including repetition and tone. **Reading Skills** Identify emotional appeals in a text.

Literary Focus

American Indian Oratory For centuries, American Indians have relied fundamentally on spoken language for diplomacy, decision making, and preservation of their history and culture. In American Indian cultures, spoken language mystically links the natural and spiritual worlds and has the power to shape events. Thus, American Indians have often chosen their leaders in part for their eloquent **oratory.** Important speeches are even memorized exactly as spoken and passed on orally for generations.

Chief Joseph was a particularly eloquent speaker. "I Will Fight No More Forever" is well remembered today, more than one hundred years after the delivery of the speech. As you read, pay attention to the qualities that make it so powerful, especially **repetition** and **tone**.

Language Coach

Figurative Language Some words have a figurative or poetic meaning, as well as a literal meaning. *Heart*, for example, literally means an organ that pumps blood. Figuratively, it also refers to love, or a person's innermost feelings, or courage. Which sense of *heart* do you think Chief Joseph is using in the first lines of the selection on page 490? Explain your response.

Reading Focus

Recognizing Emotional Appeals Speakers and writers who want to move an audience to feel a certain way use emotional appeals. **Emotional appeals** consist of language and anecdotes that arouse strong feelings. In his speech, Chief Joseph uses emotional appeals to appease his captor, General Miles, and to arouse in him feelings of sympathy and sorrow.

Into Action As you read, use a chart like the one below to analyze the emotional appeals in Chief Joseph's speech. List examples of emotional appeals in the left-hand column. In the right-hand column, explain what gives each appeal its emotional power. Consider elements of American Indian oratory, such as repetition and tone.

Emotional Appeal	What Makes This an Effective Emotional Appeal?
"Looking Glass is dead. Toohoolhoolzote is dead. The old men are all dead."	The repetition of the word <u>dead</u> emphasizes the tragedy of the Nez Perce.

Writing Focus

Think as a Reader/Writer

Find It in Your Reading American Indian orators often used repetition to create rhythm, to reinforce a message, or to enhance an emotional effect. While you read the selection, watch for repetition. In your *Reader/Writer Notebook,* make a list of the sounds, words, images, and ideas that Chief Joseph repeats.

Learn It Online
Hear the power of this speech for yourself. Listen to the selection online.

go.hrw.com   LE11-489   **Go**

SPEECH

I WILL FIGHT NO MORE FOREVER

by **Chief Joseph**

Read with a Purpose

Read to discover why Chief Joseph declares that he will never fight again.

Build Background

In 1871, when Chief Joseph's father was dying, he urged his son, "You must stop your ears whenever you are asked to sign a treaty selling your home. . . . This country holds your father's body. Never sell the bones of your father and mother." Chief Joseph delivered the following speech when he surrendered to Gen. Nelson A. Miles of the U.S. Army on October 5, 1877. As you read, consider how his father's words might have affected Chief Joseph when he surrendered.

Tell General Howard[1] I know his heart. What he told me before, I have in my heart. I am tired of fighting. Our chiefs are killed. Looking Glass is dead. Toohoolhoolzote is dead. The old men are all dead. It is the young men who say yes and no. He who led on the young men is dead. It is cold and we have no blankets. The little children are freezing to death. My people, some of them, have run away to the hills and have no blankets, no food; no one knows where they are—perhaps freezing to death. I want to have time to look for my children and see how many I can find. Maybe I shall find them among the dead. Hear me, my chiefs, I am tired; my heart is sick and sad. From where the sun now stands I will fight no more forever. **Ⓐ Ⓑ**

1. **General Howard:** military commander who initially presented the Nez Perce with an ultimatum to give up their land and move to a reservation.

Ⓐ **Literary Focus** **American Indian Oratory** What words are repeated frequently throughout the speech? What effect does this repetition create?

Ⓑ **Reading Focus** **Recognizing Emotional Appeals** Near the end of his speech, Chief Joseph says, "I want to have time to look for my children and see how many I can find. Maybe I shall find them among the dead." What words and ideas give these lines their emotional power? How might they evoke the sympathy of General Miles?

Viewing and Interpreting How does the posture of the figures in the painting, as well as details of the landscape, convey the feelings Chief Joseph describes in his opening paragraph? Explain.

Chief Joseph Rides to Surrender by Howard Terpning (detail). Reproduced by permission of the Greenwich Workshop.

Applying Your Skills

SKILLS FOCUS **Literary Skills** Analyze the characteristics of American Indian oratory, including repetition and tone; analyze parallel structure. **Reading Skills** Analyze emotional appeals in a text. **Writing Skills** Enhance style for effective writing.

I Will Fight No More Forever

Respond and Think Critically

Reading Focus

Quick Check

1. Why do you think Chief Joseph mentions by name many of the people who have died?

2. What has happened to the leaders among Chief Joseph's people?

3. What does Chief Joseph mean when he says, "From where the sun now stands"?

Read with a Purpose

4. Why do you think Chief Joseph surrenders after he has fought so bravely? Which details from the selection shed light on his decision?

Reading Skills: Recognizing Emotional Appeals

5. As you read, you identified and analyzed the emotional appeals in Chief Joseph's speech. Now, review your chart. In a few sentences, explain which appeals had the strongest influence on you and why. Then, write a sentence or two that explain the combined effect of all the emotional appeals in the speech.

Emotional Appeal	What Makes This an Effective Emotional Appeal?
"Looking Glass is dead. Toohoolhoolzote is dead. The old men are all dead."	The repetition of the word dead emphasizes the tragedy of the Nez Perce.

Literary Focus

Literary Analysis

6. **Analyze** What does Chief Joseph mean when he says, "Tell General Howard I know his heart"? What is the purpose of establishing this connection with his audience?

7. **Infer** Judging by his speech, how would you describe Chief Joseph's relationship with his people? What phrases or sentences support your interpretation?

8. **Make Judgments** Does Chief Joseph's speech appeal to logic, emotion, or both? Explain your response.

Literary Skills: American Indian Oratory

9. **Interpret** What tone does Chief Joseph establish by using words such as *heart, tired, freezing,* and *dead*? Why do you think he chooses to establish this tone?

Literary Skills Review: Parallel Structure

10. **Analyze** The repetition of words or phrases that have similar grammatical structures is called **parallel structure.** What examples of parallelism can you find in this selection? Choose one example, and explain how it emphasizes one of the speaker's <u>fundamental</u> ideas.

Writing Focus

Think as a Reader/Writer

Use It in Your Writing Review the examples of repetition in your *Reader/Writer Notebook.* Then, write a paragraph in which you seek to end an argument with a friend or to encourage reconciliation between two fictional characters or two groups you've read about in the news. In your paragraph, use repetition to emphasize your tone or reinforce your message.

 What Do **You** **Think** **Now** How did years of conflict change Chief Joseph's view of conflict itself? How has this speech affected your own views regarding conflict?

Primary Sources on the Civil War

Soldiers' National Cemetery, Gettysburg National Military Park, Gettysburg, Pennsylvania.

Primary sources such as letters, diaries, historical documents, and speeches offer valuable insights into the personal experiences of individuals who lived during a particular time. Primary sources from the Civil War provide richly varied perspectives about this polarizing conflict to give us an intimate understanding of the sacrifices people made on both sides of the conflict. In this section, you will read letters, diary entries, and a speech by individuals whose lives were permanently altered by the war.

CONTENTS

What Do You Think

How does conflict lead to change?

 QuickWrite

At times of national crisis, we look to leaders for reassurance and advice. Write about a speech you've read or heard that addressed Americans at a time of crisis. How did the speaker's words affect you?

MEET THE WRITERS

Robert E. Lee
(1807–1870)

Robert E. Lee, the brilliant commander of all the Confederate armies, was loved by his troops and admired by his enemies. Lee was the son of the Revolutionary War cavalry leader Henry "Light Horse Harry" Lee, who gave the eulogy at the funeral of his friend George Washington.

Major Sullivan Ballou
(1829–1861)

Sullivan Ballou began his career as a lawyer and served as a clerk and speaker of the Rhode Island House of Representatives. Ballou joined the military at the outbreak of the Civil War in 1861. Shortly afterward, he was killed in the First Battle of Bull Run near Manassas, Virginia.

Mary Chesnut
(1823–1886)

During the Civil War, Mary Boykin Chesnut traveled with her husband, James Chesnut, on his military missions for the Confederacy. She wrote about her experiences in *A Diary from Dixie*. Her detailed observations and insights reflect her thorough understanding of Southern leadership and society.

Abraham Lincoln
(1809–1865)

Abraham Lincoln, nicknamed "Honest Abe" and "the Great Emancipator," served as president of the United States from 1861 to 1865. Lincoln is known for his eloquence in debate and clear expression of his ideals.

Think About the Writers

What experiences did all of these writers probably share? Can you think of anything about which they might have agreed?

Primary Sources on the Civil War

Reader/Writer Notebook

Use your **RWN** to complete the activities for these selections.

Informational Text Focus

Analyzing Primary Sources Letters, autobiographies, historical documents, and speeches are examples of **primary sources.** These are sources that provide original information, eyewitness testimony, or firsthand statements of ideas and opinion. As you read a primary source, look for unstated **beliefs** or **biases** that shape the text. For instance, The Gettysburg Address, a speech by President Abraham Lincoln, reveals a <u>fundamental</u> <u>principle</u>, the president's belief in the Union.

To understand an author's beliefs and biases, you also need to identify the intended **audience.** Two of these selections are letters. The intended audiences are family members, so the content is personal, candidly revealing the author's private feelings. The excerpt from *A Diary from Dixie* is a personal record of one woman's experiences and feelings. Like the letters, it adds the dimension of personal experience to history.

Into Action As you read, use a chart like the one below to make notes about each writer. List the writer's audience, and identify his or her beliefs and biases as they are revealed in the primary source. In the final column, tell how the writer's beliefs and audience affect the content.

Writer	Audience	Writer's Beliefs/ Biases	How Audience/ Beliefs Affect Content
Lee	his son	Southern; disagreed with secession	Lee can speak honestly about his feelings to his son.
Ballou			
Chesnut			
Lincoln			

Vocabulary

calamity (kuh LAM uh tee) *n.:* great misfortune; disaster. *The Civil War was a calamity for Southern cities like Atlanta.*

strife (stryf) *n.:* bitter struggle; conflict. *The inability to resolve the conflict peacefully led to strife and overwhelming loss.*

impelled (ihm PEHLD) *v.* used as *adj.:* urged; strongly driven. *A sense of honor made the men and women feel impelled to defend their ideals.*

exempt (ehg ZEHMPT) *adj.:* freed from a duty or other binding restriction. *Men who were unhealthy were exempt from military service.*

detract (dih TRAKT) *v.:* take away importance from. *Their defeat in battle did not detract from the courage of those who fought.*

Language Coach

Variations in Meaning The word *exempt* has several usages. In school, for example, students with high grades are sometimes *exempt* from exams. During the days of a military draft, individuals with certain medical conditions were *exempt* from serving in the military. When citizens file tax returns in the United States, they are *exempt* from taxes on some income donated to charitable organizations. You can even use the word to describe an attitude, such as someone you know at school acting as if he or she is *exempt* from school rules.

Writing Focus — Preparing for **Constructed Response**

In times of turmoil, writers often use words and phrases with highly charged emotional connotations. In her diary, for example, Mary Chesnut writes, "We are going to be wiped off the face of the earth." As you read these selections, note instances of emotional language in your *Reader/Writer Notebook.* What is the effect of this language?

 Learn It Online
Expand your understanding of the Vocabulary words with Word Watch.

| go.hrw.com | L11-495 | Go |

LETTER

Letter to His Son

by Robert E. Lee

January 23, 1861

I received Everett's[1] *Life of Washington* which you sent me, and enjoyed its perusal.[2] How his spirit would be grieved could he see the wreck of his mighty labors! I will not, however, permit myself to believe, until all ground of hope is gone, that the fruit of his noble deeds will be destroyed, and that his precious advice and virtuous example will so soon be forgotten by his countrymen. As far as I can judge by the papers, we are between a state of anarchy[3] and civil war. May God avert both of these evils from us! I fear that mankind will not for years be sufficiently Christianized to bear the absence of restraint and force. I see that four states[4] have declared themselves out of the Union; four more will apparently follow their example. Then, if the border states are brought into the gulf of revolution, one half of the country will be arrayed[5] against the other. I must try and be patient and await the end, for I can do nothing to hasten or retard it. **Ⓐ**

The South, in my opinion, has been aggrieved by the acts of the North, as you say. I feel the aggression and am willing to take every proper step for redress.[6] It is the principle I contend for, not individual or private benefit. As an American citizen, I take great pride in my country, her prosperity and institutions, and would defend any state if her rights were invaded. But I can anticipate no greater calamity for the country than a dissolution[7] of the Union. It would be an accumulation of all the evils we complain of, and I am willing to sacrifice everything but honor for its preservation. I hope, therefore, that all constitutional means will be exhausted before there is a resort to force. Secession is nothing but revolution. The framers of our Constitution

---

1. **Everett's:** Edward Everett (1794–1865) was an American statesman and orator who spoke at Gettysburg before Abraham Lincoln delivered his famous speech.
2. **perusal:** act of reading carefully.
3. **anarchy:** complete absence of government.
4. **four states:** South Carolina, Mississippi, Florida, and Alabama.
5. **arrayed:** set up; placed in order.
6. **redress:** correction for a wrong done.
7. **dissolution:** breaking up into parts.

Ⓐ **Informational Focus** **Analyzing Primary Sources** What are Lee's true feelings regarding secession? Which specific words or ideas in the paragraph reveal his feelings?

Vocabulary **calamity** (kuh LAM uh tee) *n.:* great misfortune; disaster.

never exhausted so much labor, wisdom, and forbearance in its formation, and surrounded it with so many guards and securities, if it was intended to be broken by every member of the Confederacy at will. It was intended for "perpetual union," so expressed in the preamble, and for the establishment of a government, not a compact,[8] which can only be dissolved by revolution or the consent of all the people in convention assembled. It is idle to talk of secession. Anarchy would have been established, and not a government, by Washington, Hamilton, Jefferson, Madison, and the other patriots of the Revolution. . . . Still, a Union that can only be maintained by swords and bayonets, and in which strife and civil war are to take the place of brotherly love and kindness, has no charm for me. I shall mourn for my country and for the welfare and progress of mankind. If the Union is dissolved, and the government disrupted, I shall return to my native state and share the miseries of my people; and, save in defense, will draw my sword on none. **B**

R E Lee

The Granger Collection, New York. *General Lee on his Famous Charger, 'Traveler,'* illustration from *Harper's Magazine* (1911) by Howard Pyle.

---

8. **compact:** agreement between two or more states.

B Informational Focus **Analyzing Primary Sources** In this letter, Lee's ethical principles seem to conflict with his political principles. Given that Lee was a loyal native of Virginia, what views in this letter would he probably not have shared during an interview with a Southern newspaper journalist?

Vocabulary strife (strÿf) *n.:* bitter struggle; conflict.

Read with a Purpose

Read this letter to understand the price a soldier is willing to pay for devotion to his country.

Build Background

In July 1861, Maj. Sullivan Ballou of Rhode Island wrote this letter to his wife, Sarah—a letter that reveals his devotion both to the Union cause and to his wife and family. A week later Ballou was killed near Manassas, Virginia, in the First Battle of Bull Run. Ironically, the letter was never mailed.

LETTER

Letter to Sarah Ballou

by **Major Sullivan Ballou**

July 14, 1861
Camp Clark, Washington

My very dear Sarah:

The indications are very strong that we shall move in a few days—perhaps tomorrow. Lest I should not be able to write again, I feel impelled to write a few lines that may fall under your eye when I shall be no more. . . .

I have no misgivings about, or lack of confidence in the cause in which I am engaged, and my courage does not halt or falter. I know how strongly American Civilization now leans on the triumph of the Government, and how great a debt we owe to those who went before us through the blood and sufferings of the Revolution. And I am willing—perfectly willing—to lay down all my joys in this life, to help maintain this Government, and to pay that debt. . . .

Ⓐ

Sarah, my love for you is deathless; it seems to bind me with mighty cables that nothing but Omnipotence[1] could break; and yet my love of Country comes over me like a strong wind and bears me unresistibly on with all these chains to the battlefield.

The memories of the blissful moments I have spent with you come creeping over me, and I feel most gratified to God and to you that I have enjoyed them so long. And hard it is for me to give them up and burn to ashes the hopes of future years, when, God willing, we might still have lived and loved together, and seen our sons grown up to honorable manhood around us. I have, I know, but few and small claims upon Divine Providence, but something whispers to me—perhaps it is the wafted prayer of my little Edgar, that I shall return to my loved ones unharmed. If I do not, my dear Sarah, never forget how much I love you, and when my last breath escapes me on the battlefield, it will whisper your name. Forgive my many faults, and the many pains I have caused you. How thoughtless and foolish I have oftentimes been! How gladly would I wash out with my tears every little spot upon your happiness. . . .

---

1. **Omnipotence:** one who has unlimited power (meaning God).

Ⓐ **Informational Focus** Analyzing Primary Sources In his letter, Ballou displays a <u>fundamental</u> awareness of the significance of his moment in history. How does Ballou relate his duties in the present moment to the past and the future?

Vocabulary **impelled** (ihm PEHLD) *v.* used as *adj:* urged; strongly driven.

But, O Sarah! If the dead can come back to this earth and flit unseen around those they loved, I shall always be near you; in the gladdest days and in the darkest nights . . . *always, always,* and if there be a soft breeze upon your cheek, it shall be my breath; as the cool air fans your throbbing temple, it shall be my spirit passing by. Sarah, do not mourn me dead; think I am gone and wait for thee, for we shall meet again. . . . **B**

Sullivan

A Union soldier with his wife.
The Granger Collection, New York.

B **Informational Focus** **Analyzing Primary Sources** In what ways does this letter offer a researcher more insight into the Civil War than an encyclopedia entry or a newspaper article would?

Read with a Purpose

Read to see how one Southern woman's diary portrays her personal experience of the Civil War.

Build Background

Mary Boykin Chesnut was the wife of James Chesnut, a former U.S. senator from South Carolina and an aide to Jefferson Davis, president of the Confederacy. During the course of the war, Mary Chesnut traveled from city to city in the South as the capital of the Confederacy changed. She kept up with the war news through her husband and their wide circle of knowledge-able and influential friends. Mary Chesnut was in Charleston, South Carolina, in April 1861, when the Civil War began with the attack on Fort Sumter. She was also present at the war's end. In Columbia, South Carolina, she received the increasingly discouraging news from the field.

from

A Diary from Dixie

by **Mary Chesnut**

The Granger Collection, New York.

September 1, 1864

The battle is raging at Atlanta, our fate hanging in the balance.

September 2, 1864

Atlanta is gone. Well that agony is over. Like David, when the child was dead, I will get up from my knees, will wash my face and comb my hair.[1] There is no hope, but we will try to have no fear. . . . **Ⓐ**

September 21, 1864

The president [of the Confederacy] has gone West. He has sent for Mr. Chesnut.

I went with Mrs. Rhett to hear Dr. Palmer [a minister]. I did not know before how utterly hopeless was our situation. This man is so eloquent; it was hard to listen and not give way. Despair was his word, and martyrdom. He offered us nothing more in this world than the martyr's crown. He is not for slavery, he says; he is for freedom, the freedom to govern our own country as we see fit. He is against foreign interference in our state matters. That is what Mr. Palmer went to war for, it appears. Every day shows that slavery is doomed the world over. For that he thanked God. He spoke of this time of our agony; and then came the cry: "Help us, Oh God! Vain is the help of man." So we came away shaken to the depths. . . . **Ⓑ**

The end has come, no doubt of the fact. . . . We are going to be wiped off the face of the earth. Now what is there to prevent Sherman taking General Lee in the rear. We have but two armies, and Sherman is between them now.

---

1. **Like David . . . comb my hair:** Chesnut alludes to 2 Samuel 12:20–23 in the Bible, where David weeps and prays for his sick child.

Ⓐ Informational Focus Analyzing Primary Sources What does Chesnut's Biblical allusion reveal about her personal beliefs?

Ⓑ Informational Focus Analyzing Primary Sources How does this passage reveal the differ-ent beliefs that existed among individuals within the Southern Confederacy?

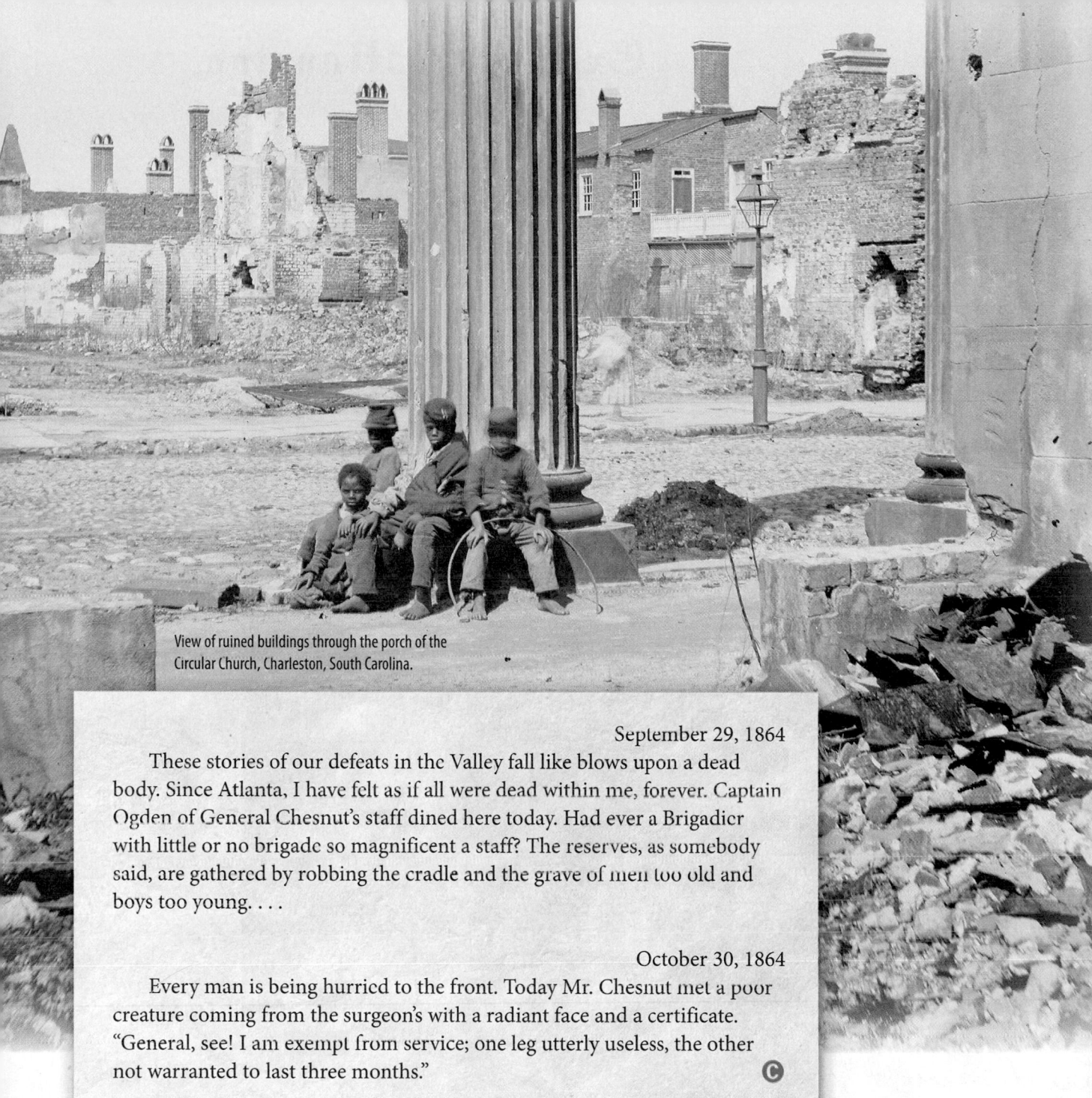

View of ruined buildings through the porch of the Circular Church, Charleston, South Carolina.

September 29, 1864

These stories of our defeats in the Valley fall like blows upon a dead body. Since Atlanta, I have felt as if all were dead within me, forever. Captain Ogden of General Chesnut's staff dined here today. Had ever a Brigadier with little or no brigade so magnificent a staff? The reserves, as somebody said, are gathered by robbing the cradle and the grave of men too old and boys too young. . . .

October 30, 1864

Every man is being hurried to the front. Today Mr. Chesnut met a poor creature coming from the surgeon's with a radiant face and a certificate. "General, see! I am exempt from service; one leg utterly useless, the other not warranted to last three months." **C**

C **Informational Focus** **Analyzing Primary Sources** What does this final entry suggest about the hope and morale among Southern men who are to be "hurried to the front" at this point in the war? How does the diary provide an outlet for Chesnut to speak bluntly?

Vocabulary **exempt** (ehg ZEHMPT) *adj.:* freed from a duty or other binding restriction.

Analyzing Visuals

Viewing and Interpreting What kind of voice do you associate with this image of Abraham Lincoln, and how does the image affect your reading of his famous Gettysburg Address? Explain.

The Gettysburg Address

Fourscore and seven[1] years ago our fathers brought forth on this continent a new nation, conceived[2] in Liberty, and dedicated to the proposition that all men are created equal.

Now we are engaged in a great civil war, testing whether that nation, or any nation so conceived and so dedicated, can long endure. We are met on a great battlefield of that war. We have come to dedicate a portion of that field as a final resting place for those who here gave their lives that that nation might live. It is altogether fitting and proper that we should do this. **A**

But, in a larger sense, we cannot dedicate—we cannot consecrate[3]—we cannot hallow[4]—this ground. The brave men, living and dead, who struggled here, have consecrated it far above our poor power to add or detract. The world will little note nor long remember what we say here, but it can never forget what they did here. It is for us the living, rather, to be dedicated here to the unfinished work which they who fought here have thus far so nobly advanced. It is rather for us to be here dedicated to the great task remaining before us—that from these honored dead we take increased devotion to that cause for which they gave the last full measure of devotion—that we here highly resolve that these dead shall not have died in vain—that this nation, under God, shall have a new birth of freedom—and that government of the people, by the people, for the people, shall not perish from the earth. **B**

Abraham Lincoln

1. **fourscore and seven:** eighty-seven. A score is a set of twenty.
2. **conceived:** developed; imagined.
3. **consecrate:** set apart as sacred or holy.
4. **hallow:** make holy.

A Informational Focus **Analyzing Primary Sources** What are Lincoln's beliefs about the importance of reuniting the country? Which words lead you to this conclusion?

B Informational Focus **Analyzing Primary Sources** What does Lincoln believe is at stake in the Civil War? How does this belief color his interpretation of what happened at the Battle of Gettysburg?

Vocabulary **detract** (dih TRAKT) *v.:* take away importance from.

Applying Your Skills

SKILLS FOCUS **Informational Skills** Analyze primary sources. **Vocabulary Skills** Identify and correctly use synonyms. **Listening and Speaking Skills** Use effective speaking strategies. **Writing Skills** Write a brief constructed response, with specific support.

Letter to His Son / Letter to Sarah Ballou / *from* A Diary from Dixie / The Gettysburg Address

Respond and Think Critically

Informational Text Focus

Quick Check

1. Why does Robert E. Lee admire George Washington? Explain.

2. Why is Major Ballou willing to lay down his life to help "maintain this Government"?

3. In her diary, why does Chesnut write that "the end has come"?

4. According to President Lincoln, how can the living ensure that the soldiers who sacrificed their lives at Gettysburg "shall not have died in vain"?

Read with a Purpose

5. What similar beliefs and concerns do the letters of Sullivan Ballou and Robert E. Lee reveal?

6. How do the writers of the Gettysburg Address and *A Diary from Dixie* express similar feelings about those who have died?

Informational Skills: Analyzing Primary Sources

7. Look over the chart you completed as you read. Then, write a brief commentary on the value each of these sources would have in a research report on the Civil War.

✔ Vocabulary Check

Match each Vocabulary word with its synonym.

8. calamity   **a.** excused

9. strife   **b.** forced

10. impelled   **c.** disaster

11. detract   **d.** diminish

12. exempt   **e.** conflict

Text Analysis

13. **Analyze** Why does Lee equate secession with revolution? Explain.

14. **Compare and Contrast** In Chesnut's diary, what belief does Dr. Palmer share with Northerners?

15. **Compare and Contrast** How is Lee's sense of duty to his country similar to Ballou's? What beliefs might have driven them to advocate for opposing sides in the war?

16. **Infer** Ballou tells his wife that he is bound to her by chains and cables, yet he is drawn to the battlefield by a strong wind symbolizing love for his country. What do these images reveal about his emotional state?

17. **Interpret** What do you think Lincoln means when he refers to "a new birth of freedom"? Explain your response.

Listening and Speaking

18. **Extend** In a group of four, read the two letters, the diary entry, and the speech aloud. Then, select a particularly effective paragraph from each one. Next, each group member will practice delivering one of the selected paragraphs—focusing on the rhythm and the emotional appeal of the words. Finally, share your performances with the class as a whole and discuss the various interpretations of these important voices from our past.

Writing Focus   Constructed Response

Briefly discuss the impact of emotional language in one of the primary sources you read. Be sure to support your response with specific evidence.

SKILLS FOCUS Informational **Skills** Compare and contrast primary sources. **Writing Skills** Write a compare-and-contrast essay; analyze nonfiction;

explore the significance of personal experiences, events, and conditions. **Listening and Speaking Skills** Offer insightful observations in discussions and conversations.

Primary Sources on the Civil War

Writing Focus

Writing a Comparison-Contrast Essay

Primary sources offer a mosaic of viewpoints, as well as a nuanced understanding of history. Using your reading chart, write a comparison-contrast essay about two of the primary sources on the Civil War. Use the following questions to help choose two sources and to guide your writing:

- Which source most increased your understanding of the Civil War on a national scale? Why?
- Which source most increased your understanding of how individual lives were affected by the Civil War? What did you learn?
- Which source(s) surprised you with information of which you were not already aware? What were the surprises?

Make a list of important similarities or differences (or both). Use an outline like the one below to help plan your essay.

Point-by-Point Comparison-Contrast

Point A:_____
    Source 1:_____
    Source 2:_____
Point B:_____
    Source 1:_____
    Source 2:_____
Point C:_____
    Source 1:_____
    Source 2:_____

An effective comparison-contrast essay

- clearly states major points at the outset
- follows a strong and consistent plan
- analyzes each point of comparison or contrast in detail
- uses smooth transitions

CHOICES

As you respond to the Choices, use the **Academic Vocabulary** words as appropriate: advocate, criteria, fundamental, principle, subsequent.

REVIEW
Research Primary Sources

Group Discussion With a small group, use the Internet to find additional letters, diaries, or other primary sources from the Civil War. Have each group member choose a single source and read it closely. Afterward, have a group discussion about these primary sources. What do they add to your understanding of the war? If time allows, share your thoughts with the rest of the class.

CONNECT
Analyze Bias

Timed ⌐Writing Select one of the four documents from Primary Sources on the Civil War. Write a detailed analysis of the writer's beliefs and how these beliefs affect the writer's attitude toward the Civil War.

EXTEND
Record Your Own Perceptions

Choose a current or recent national crisis that you have experienced in a fundamental way. Imagine that a high school student fifty years from now wants to know what this crisis was like for someone of the same age. Write a detailed personal account that captures the texture of your life during the crisis, as well as your thoughts and emotions.

What Do You Think Now

What changes did each side hope to achieve by fighting the Civil War? Do you think these changes could have been accomplished in a peaceful way? Explain.

Styles of Poetry

Sunset, Montclair (1892) by George Inness, Sr. (1825–1894).

"If you want me again, look for
me under your boot-soles."

— **Walt Whitman**

"This is my letter to the World
That never wrote to Me—"

SKILLS FOCUS Literary Skills Understand and analyze styles of poetry.

Styles of Poetry by Leila Christenbury

Influences on American Poetic Styles

- The emergence of free verse, with its open forms and rhythms
- America's expanding diversity and celebration of democracy
- The tight, meditative rhythms of hymns
- An emphasis on individuality and self-discovery

American Masters

In the middle of the nineteenth century, two fundamentally different writers planted the seeds of modern American poetry. One of those writers was Walt Whitman—a larger-than-life figure who struggled to get his poems published and who developed a broad, admiring audience during his lifetime. In contrast, the reclusive Emily Dickinson died unknown to the world of poetry, leaving a box full of unpublished poems.

The styles of these writers differ as much as their personalities. Whitman wrote in broad, flowing, conversational rhythms that came to characterize his innovative free-verse style. He compared his poetry to "liquid, billowy waves." Dickinson wrote in short, terse lines that use tight rhythms and slant rhymes. Whitman's writing often addresses the reader directly and places its message in the forefront. Dickinson's poems are usually more mysterious, and unraveling their meaning can sometimes be challenging.

Two Paths for American Poetry Whitman's career might be regarded as another classic American success story—the story of a pleasant young man who drifted into his thirties, working at one job after another, never finding himself until, at his own expense, he boldly published *Leaves of Grass* (1855). Although the book was mostly ignored at first—and considered too radical by many—Whitman continued to publish new, expanded editions. Over the course of his life, the poems gained more and more attention, eventually making Whitman famous around the world.

Dickinson, on the other hand, lived a mostly secluded life. Content to write in obscurity, she rarely left her house and made little effort to publish her poems. Dickinson's poetry was read by very few until after her death. Her fate is one of those ironies of history in which a writer dies unknown, only to receive widespread acclaim from subsequent generations.

Whitman and Dickinson blazed two separate but equally important trails in the journey toward modern American poetry. Whitman pioneered **free verse**—poetry without regular rhyme or meter. This style cleared a path for poets to explore a wide variety of forms and voices. His writing expanded the scope of what was considered poetic language and introduced new, natural rhythms. Aiming for the large, overall impression, he filled his pages with long lists as he strained to catalog everything in sight. His technique is based on **cadence**—the long, easy sweep of sound that echoes the Bible and the speeches of orators and preachers. Whitman used this style to celebrate universal brotherhood and the bright destiny of democracy. He had grand expectations and saw his poems as a way to pass his message along to future generations.

Dickinson had no such broad hopes for her poems. Each was written almost as a secret to herself—exploring private corners of her mind with a quiet but intense voice. Dickinson's crisp, focused style established another path that would be followed by generations of American poets. She wrote with the precision of a diamond cutter. Extremely careful in her choice of words, she wrought mystery from the minutiae of life, sometimes with startling effect. She would use one perfect word or phrase to fix a thought in the reader's mind. Her technique is economical, and her neat stanzas are controlled by the demands of **rhyme** and the meters she found in her hymn book.

Models for Future Poets

As the history of poetry shows, Whitman and Dickinson have served as models for later poets who have been drawn to the visions these two poets fulfilled and the techniques they mastered. Poetry as public speech written in the cadences of free verse remains a part of our literature; poetry as private observation, carefully crafted in rhyme and meter, still attracts young writers who tend to regard poems as experiences rather than statements.

Whitman's shadow has loomed so large over poetry that many writers have felt the need to address him directly in their work. One of Whitman's twentieth-century followers, Allen Ginsberg, does this in the opening of his poem "A Supermarket in California." Ginsberg was part of the "beat" generation, a group of American artists and writers whose work explored alternatives to conventional traditions and principles. His writing reflects the free-flowing cadences in Whitman's own work. Note the rhythms in Ginsberg's lines.

> What thoughts I have of you tonight, Walt Whitman, for I walked down the sidestreets under the trees with a headache self-conscious looking at the full moon.

Dickinson has also been cited by many major twentieth-century poets—such as William Carlos Williams—as a primary inspiration for their style. Although written nearly a century later, the poems of Sylvia Plath show Dickinson's influence. Plath was an innovative poet in her own right, but stanzas like this one from her poem "Sheep in Fog" clearly reflect techniques pioneered by Dickinson.

> The hills step off into whiteness.
> People or stars
> Regard me sadly, I disappoint them.

Whitman and Dickinson chose different paths but took parallel journeys. Together their work marks the beginning of modern American poetry.

Introduction to the London edition of Leaves of Grass, 1861. Autographed manuscript.

Ask Yourself

1. How are the lives and personalities of Whitman and Dickinson reflected in the kinds of poetry they wrote?

2. What are the main differences between the two poets' styles of writing?

3. Where can you find the influence of Whitman and Dickinson in popular poetry and writing today?

Learn It Online

Learn about these poets' styles the multimedia way—through *PowerNotes* online.

go.hrw.com L11-508 **Go**

Reading Focus

I Hear America Singing

SKILLS FOCUS **Reading Skills** Understand and analyze the use of text structure in poetry.

Analyzing Text Structures by **Kylene Beers**

The emergence of free verse <u>fundamentally</u> changed both the writing and reading of poetry. Poets were free to create new rhythms and forms, and readers were presented with ideas expressed in unusual ways. Without traditional rhyme and meter patterns to guide them, readers learned that thinking carefully about the structure of the text could help them build meaning. As a pioneer of free verse, Whitman created his own poetic technique through the use of structures such as parallelism, elliptical constructions, and inversion.

Parallel Structures The repetition of words or phrases that have similar grammatical structures is **parallelism.** Whitman uses parallel structure to unify his poems, build rhythm, and create other effects. His poem "I Hear America Singing" (page 513) is essentially one long declaration built with a collection of parallel phrases. As shown in the following lines, the parallelism gives the poem its form and creates its rhythms.

> The carpenter singing his as he measures his
>   plank or beam,
> The mason singing his as he makes ready for
>   work, or leaves off work . . .

The second line parallels the structure of the first almost exactly: the [worker] singing his as he [activity]. The second line also contains a smaller parallel structure at the end in "makes ready for work, or leaves off work."

Elliptical Constructions Whitman also makes use of some text structures that can create challenging lines. Sentences or parts of sentences with words intentionally left out are **elliptical constructions.** The meaning of the constructions can be inferred from nearby sentences or clauses with similar structures. Elliptical constructions are often combined with longer sentences to produce greater variety of style. Ellipsis also creates more concentrated writing that compresses ideas. Here is an example from "I Hear America Singing."

> Each singing what belongs to him or her and
>   to none else,
> The day what belongs to the day—

To understand the second line, compare the two lines. The lines are very similar, but the second line is missing the verb *singing*. From this you can infer that the speaker is saying, "The day *singing* what belongs to the day."

Inverted Word Order Whitman also uses **inversion,** the reversal of the normal word order in a sentence or phrase. Inversion can be used to create emphasis. Look at the opening line of the poem:

> I hear America singing, the varied carols I
>   hear . . .

The second half of the line differs from the normal word order: "I hear the varied carols." Inversion allows the line to begin and end with the words "I hear," creating a balanced effect.

Your Turn

Read the first five lines of "I Hear America Singing" and discuss with a partner how the grammatical structure of line 5 compares and contrasts with the grammatical structure of lines 3 and 4. Identify specific techniques or text structures at work in these lines.

Learn It Online
Practice analyzing text structures online with *PowerNotes*.

go.hrw.com   L11-509   **Go**

Walt Whitman
(1819–1892)

Walt Whitman was a fresh, radical voice embodying all the promise and contradictions of an emerging democratic nation.

Student of the World

Whitman was born on May 31, 1819, to parents of Dutch and English descent. They kept a farm in West Hills, Long Island, in what is today the town of Huntington. Whitman and his seven brothers and sisters grew up in circumstances that allowed them both the communal experience of country life and the urban experience of a new city, Brooklyn.

By the time Whitman was twenty, his feeling for the written word and his fascination with the boomtown atmosphere of Brooklyn led him to journalism. After ten years, he took a kind of working vacation—a difficult trip by train, horse-drawn coach, and riverboat to New Orleans. There he put his journalistic talent to work for the *Crescent* and his own talent for observation to work for himself. After a few months he returned to New York by way of the Great Lakes and a side trip to Niagara Falls. This journey had added to Whitman's limited sense of America the <u>fundamental</u> experience of a wilderness surrendering its vastness to civilization.

Back in Brooklyn, Whitman accepted an offer to serve as editor of the *Brooklyn Freeman*. For the next six or seven years he supplemented his income by working as a part-time carpenter and building contractor. All the while he was keeping notebooks and quietly putting together the sprawling collection of poems that would transform his life and change the course of American literature.

A Whitman Time Line

1819 Walt Whitman is born on Long Island, New York

1861 The Civil War begins

1820   **1850**   **1860**

1855 Whitman publishes first edition of *Leaves of Grass*

1862 Whitman travels to Virginia and begins caring for Civil War wounded; Abraham Lincoln issues Emancipation Proclamation

The Making of a Masterpiece

In 1855, Whitman published his collection at his own expense under the title *Leaves of Grass*. Too new and strange to win the attention of reviewers or readers with fixed ideas about poetry, the volume went all but unnoticed. To stir up interest, he sent samples to people whose endorsement he thought might be useful, including Ralph Waldo Emerson, who wrote to Whitman the most important letter of his life. Emerson praised Whitman's inventiveness and expressed his admiration for the unknown poet's writing. In the letter, he addressed Whitman with the famous line, "I greet you at the beginning of a great career."

Leaves of Grass is a masterpiece that Whitman was to expand and revise through many editions. Its process of growth did not end until the ninth, "deathbed," edition was published in 1891, thirty-six years after its first appearance. It is a spiritual autobiography that tells the story of an enchanted observer who says who he is at every opportunity and claims what he loves by naming it. "Camerado," he wrote, "this is no book / Who touches this touches a man."

Whitman's singular vision resulted in poetry that celebrated everything under the sun. Its sweep was easy, and its range was broad. He had invented a way of writing that perfectly accommodated his way of seeing. His form is loose enough to allow for long lists and catalogs abundant in detail; it is also flexible enough to include delicate moments of lyricism and stretches of blustery oratory. When Whitman died, in 1892, he had expanded American poetry to include the lyricism of simple speech and the grand design of the epic. By the end of his journey, which even takes him down into a kind of hell, the poet has also been transformed. The "I" has identified with every element in the universe and has been reborn as something divine. The poet has become the saving force that Whitman believed was the true role of the American poet.

Think About the Writer

How did Whitman's writing style and self-made approach to his career reflect what was happening in America at that time?

Key Elements of Whitman's Writing

- Free-verse form and flowing lines create rolling rhythms and cadences.
- Strong, direct, everyday language echoes the voices of common people.
- Focus on the diversity of the nation's people and places reflects America's emerging identity.
- Celebrations of self and nature support themes that explore the connectedness of all things.

1873 Whitman moves to Camden, New Jersey

1870   **1880**   **1890**   **1900**

1865 Civil War ends; Lincoln is assassinated; Whitman publishes *Drum-Taps,* including elegy for Lincoln, "When Lilacs Last in the Dooryard Bloom'd"

1882 Whitman's prose collection *Specimen Days* is published

1892 Whitman publishes *Leaves of Grass,* "Deathbed Edition"; Whitman dies of a stroke

Preparing to Read

SKILLS FOCUS **Literary Skills** Understand the use of catalogs in poetry. **Reading Skills** Analyze the use of text structure in poetry.

Reader/Writer Notebook

Use your **RWN** to complete the following activities for this selection.

Literary Focus

Catalog A **catalog** is a long list of related things, people, or events. Whitman frequently uses catalogs in his poetry. By selecting and naming workers and their "songs" in his poem "I Hear America Singing," Whitman celebrates the energetic spirit of the nation. A catalog also creates a kind of rhythm built on the **repetition** of sentence patterns.

Reading Focus

Analyzing Text Structures To create certain effects and convey meaning, Whitman uses text structures such as parallelism and elliptical construction in his poems. **Parallelism** is the repetition of words, phrases, clauses, or sentences that have the same grammatical structure. **Elliptical constructions** are phrases, clauses, or sentences with words left out. Their meaning can be inferred from nearby sentences with a similar structure.

Into Action Whitman uses parallel structure as he catalogs the different workers. As you read, identify each worker Whitman introduces. Use a chart like the one below to record the line number, the person's occupation, and the line from the text where the catalog appears.

Line #	Type of worker	Line
2	mechanic	"Those of mechanics, each one singing his as it should be blithe and strong,"

Vocabulary

blithe (blyth) *adj.*: happy and cheerful. *Whitman admires Americans' blithe nature.*

beam (beem) *n.*: large, long piece of timber for use in construction. *The speaker describes carpenters measuring beams.*

mason (MAY suhn) *n.*: worker who lays stone or brick. *The mason sings as he is about to begin his work.*

robust (roh BUHST) *adj.*: vigorous and healthy. *The robust young men enjoy singing as they socialize after work.*

melodious (muh LOH dee uhs) *adj.*: sweet sounding; musical. *Whitman uses melodious language and natural rhythms.*

Language Coach

Greek Root Words The word *melodious* comes from the Greek word *melōidia*, which means "song." How does knowing the root of *melodious* help you understand its meaning?

Writing Focus

Think as a Reader/Writer

Find It in Your Reading In your *Reader/Writer Notebook,* note some of the actions that Whitman catalogs throughout the poem.

TechFocus Whitman's poem creates a collage of scenes from American life during his era. As you read, think about how you might depict American society today in a multimedia presentation.

Learn It Online
Plunge into this poem with the video introduction online.

go.hrw.com | L11-512 | **Go**

I Hear America Singing

by **Walt Whitman**

Read with a Purpose
Read to discover how Whitman reveals the diversity and character of the American people.

Build Background
"I Hear America Singing" is one of Whitman's most famous poems, and it embodies the fundamental spirit of his powerful voice. The poem appears near the beginning of his collection *Leaves of Grass,* and it introduces one of Whitman's major themes—the tremendous variety and individuality in American life. In these lines, the poet celebrates the American enterprise, in all its varied forms.

I hear America singing, the varied carols I hear,
Those of mechanics, each one singing his as it should be blithe and strong,
The carpenter singing his as he measures his plank or beam,
The mason singing his as he makes ready for work, or leaves off work,
The boatman singing what belongs to him in his boat, the deckhand singing on the
5   steamboat deck,
The shoemaker singing as he sits on his bench, the hatter singing as he stands,
The wood-cutter's song, the plowboy's on his way in the morning, or at noon
      intermission or at sundown, **Ⓐ**
The delicious singing of the mother, or of the young wife at work, or of the girl sewing
      or washing,
Each singing what belongs to him or her and to none else,
10 The day what belongs to the day—at night the party of young fellows, robust, friendly,
Singing with open mouths their strong melodious songs. **Ⓑ**

Ⓐ **Literary Focus** **Catalog** What types of workers does Whitman name? What does this catalog celebrate?

Ⓑ **Reading Focus** **Analyzing Text Structures** How does "The day what belongs to the day" meet the criteria of an elliptical construction? What effect does the elliptical construction create?

Vocabulary **blithe** (blyth) *adj.:* happy and cheerful.
beam (beem) *n.:* large, long piece of timber for use in construction.
mason (MAY suhn) *n.:* worker who lays stone or brick.
robust (roh BUHST) *adj.:* vigorous and healthy.
melodious (muh LOH dee uhs) *adj.:* sweet sounding; musical.

Respond and Think Critically

Reading Focus

Quick Check

1. In the beginning of the poem, how does the speaker announce that he is about to present a list?

2. What are three occupations that Whitman mentions in this poem?

3. What does Whitman describe in the poem?

Read with a Purpose

4. What does the poem suggest about the diversity and character of Americans?

Reading Skills: Analyzing Text Structures

5. While reading, you used a chart to record information on each new worker that Whitman introduces. Now, review your chart. Write a sentence or two explaining the effect of Whitman's use of parallelism.

✔ Vocabulary Check

Choose the Vocabulary word that best completes each sentence.

blithe
beam
mason
robust
melodious

6. The foreman said the _____ needed to be trimmed to make it fit.

7. They were in love, and everyone could tell by the _____ look on their faces.

8. The sounds of the wind and ocean combined to create the _____ language of nature.

9. The builders needed a skilled _____ to complete the stonework.

10. The healthy boys appeared _____ and ready.

Literary Focus

Literary Analysis

11. Infer Why does the speaker say that each person's singing "should be blithe and strong"?

12. Interpret The nation's work songs are described as "varied carols" in the opening line. How does the phrase suggest both variety and harmony?

13. Infer What does this poem express about Whitman's belief in America's potential?

Literary Skills: Catalog

14. Interpret This whole poem can be viewed as a catalog. What is Whitman using the catalog to celebrate?

Literary Skills Review: Repetition

15. Evaluate A unifying property of repeated words, sounds, syllables, and other elements that appear in a work is called **repetition.** In "I Hear America Singing," what key word is repeated by the speaker? What is the effect of the repetition?

Writing Focus

Think as a Reader/Writer

Use It in Your Writing Think about a group of people, places, events, principles, or something else that you feel is worth celebrating. Write a poetic catalog that extends for several lines, in which you celebrate and define your subject.

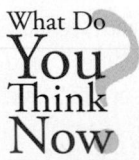

What Do **You Think Now** How do you think the struggles of common people can help transform a nation?

SKILLS FOCUS **Literary Skills** Analyze the use of catalogs in poetry; analyze repetition. **Reading Skills** Analyze the use of text structure in poetry. **Vocabulary Skills** Use context clues in words, sen- tences, and paragraphs to decode new vocabulary. **Writing Skills** Employ literary devices for effective writing; use writing as a tool for learning and research; deliver multimedia presentations. **Grammar Skills** Identify and correct sentence frag- ments; identify and correct run-on sentences.

Grammar Link

Avoiding Fragments and Run-ons

A **sentence fragment** is a group of words that is punc- tuated as if it were a complete sentence but that does not contain a subject and a verb or does not express a complete thought. **Phrases** do not contain both a verb and its subject; **subordinate clauses** do not express a complete thought. Both phrases and subordinate clauses become fragments when they stand alone.

> **PHRASE FRAGMENT** First published in 1855.
> **SENTENCE** First published in 1855, *Leaves of Grass* changed American poetry forever.

> **SUBORDINATE CLAUSE FRAGMENT** Because it was radically different.
> **SENTENCE** Because it was radically different, Whitman's poetry was largely ignored at first.

A **run-on sentence** is two or more sentences run together as if they were one. A *fused sentence* has no punctuation between independent clauses.

> "I Hear America Singing" describes Americans each person has his or her own job.

A *comma splice* has only a comma between clauses.

> These Americans are happy in their work, they sing to celebrate what they do.

Run-ons can be fixed by separating ideas into two sen- tences, by correctly joining the independent clauses, or by making one independent clause subordinate.

Your Turn

Writing Application Revise the following paragraph to correct sentence fragments and run-ons.

> The poem is about workers. Such as woodcutters and sewing girls. The speaker tells readers Ameri- cans are common people, their song is America's song. In poems like this one. Whitman showed readers a democratic country Whitman's America was alive with song.

CHOICES

As you respond to the Choices, use these **Academic Vocabulary** words as appropriate: advocate, criteria, fundamental, principle, subsequent.

REVIEW
Analyze Catalogs in a Poem
Group Discussion Review the types of people that Whitman catalogs in this poem. How many of these roles are prominent in society today? How have the roles of workers changed fundamentally since Whitman's time? Do you think the people in this poem provide an accurate reflection of everyday people today? In a small group, discuss your answers to these questions.

CONNECT
Live Another Life
Choose an occupation from the poem to research. Online or in the library, research that occupation in detail. Research what the job was like in Whitman's time or what it is like today. Then, write a short description of a typical day in that occupation during Whitman's time or now.

EXTEND
Take America's Picture
TechFocus Whitman's poem uses words to create a collage of American society in his time. Gather pictures, images, and sounds that reflect your view of American society today. Then, create a multimedia presentation that illustrates a broad view of Ameri- can society and culture. Show your presentation to your class, and discuss what similarities and differ- ences among Americans your presentation reveals.

from Song of Myself, Numbers 1, 6, 33

Reader/Writer Notebook

Use your **RWN** to complete the following activities for these selections.

Literary Focus

Free Verse Poetry written in **free verse** does not have a regular meter or rhyme scheme. Despite the lack of formal meter, free verse creates rhythm through **cadence,** the musical run of words that rises and falls in the lines. It also makes use of **alliteration** (repetition of similar consonant sounds), **assonance** (repetition of similar vowel sounds), **imagery** (language that appeals to the senses), and **parallel structure** (repetition of grammatically similar structures).

Literary Perspectives Apply the literary perspective described on page 518 as you read these poems.

Reading Focus

Paraphrasing Sometimes you may need to reword a line or a passage in a poem to simplify or clarify its meaning. When you encounter a puzzling line, **paraphrase** it, or restate it in your own words. Use a dictionary, if needed, to define any unfamiliar word and determine how the word is used in the poem. This strategy can help you understand the poem.

Into Action As you read the poems, locate any lines whose meaning is unclear. For each poem, make a chart like the one below. In the first column, record the lines and line numbers. In the second column, restate the text in your own words.

Lines from Song of Myself, no. 1	Paraphrase
Line 10: "Creeds and schools in abeyance"	Certain beliefs and schools or teachings are temporarily suspended.

Writing Focus

Think as a Reader/Writer

Find It in Your Reading Whitman uses the openness of **free verse** to create striking, individual lines of poetry. As you read, record in your *Reader/Writer Notebook* lines that you find memorable.

Vocabulary

harbor (HAHR buhr) *v.*: have and keep in the mind. *Whitman harbors an intense curiosity about the world around him.*

disposition (dihs puh ZIHSH uhn) *n.*: one's natural way of acting toward others or thinking about things. *In his poems, Whitman displays a hopeful disposition.*

transpire (tran SPYR) *v.*: develop or breathe out. *Whitman imagines that the grass transpires from the bodies of men.*

resuscitate (rih SUHS uh tayt) *v.*: return to life. *In his poem, Whitman imagines that the dead resuscitate.*

Language Coach

American and British Spelling Words ending in —*or,* like *harbor,* are spelled slightly differently in Great Britain and many other English-speaking nations, where the —*or* ending becomes —*our,* as in *harbour, colour,* and *favour.* If you read British novels or international Web sites, you may have noticed some spelling variations. These word pairs show the differences between American and British spellings: *theater/theatre, analyse/analyze, defence/defense, skillful/skilful.* Using a dictionary, identify the American spelling in each pair.

 Learn It Online
Find out more about Whitman's life—and explore his style further—with AuthorSpace online.

go.hrw.com | L11-516 | **Go**

POEM

from Song of Myself

1 I celebrate myself, and sing myself

by **Walt Whitman**

Read with a Purpose
Read to discover what Whitman celebrates about himself and others.

Build Background
Song of Myself is a work that is true to its title. In this long poem, Whitman tries to step into the experiences of other living things and share these experiences with the reader. This blend of imagination and empathy—the ability to share in another's thoughts and feelings—is at the heart of *Song of Myself.* The poem ends the first section of Whitman's collection *Leaves of Grass* and is divided into many parts, all of which could stand as individual poems themselves. In these different parts, Whitman juxtaposes a wide variety of scenes and emotions to provide glimpses of the broad American scene.

I celebrate myself, and sing myself,
And what I assume° you shall assume,
For every atom belonging to me as good belongs to you.   **A**

I loaf and invite my soul,
5 I lean and loaf at my ease observing a spear of summer grass.

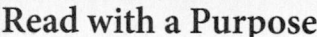
My tongue, every atom of my blood, form'd from this soil, this air,
Born here of parents born here from parents the same, and their
        parents the same,
I, now thirty-seven years old in perfect health begin,
Hoping to cease not till death.

10 Creeds and schools in abeyance,°
Retiring back a while sufficed at what they are, but never forgotten,
I harbor for good or bad, I permit to speak at every hazard,
Nature without check with original energy.   **B**

2. assume: Here, the word *assume* means "take on."

10. abeyance: temporary suspension; inactivity.

A **Literary Focus** **Free Verse** How does Whitman create rhythm and flow in these opening lines?

B **Reading Focus** **Paraphrasing** In your own words, restate this line. What does this line reveal about Whitman's view of nature?

Vocabulary harbor (HAHR buhr) *v.:* have and keep in the mind.

from Song of Myself

6 A child said *What is the grass?*

by **Walt Whitman**

> **Read with a Purpose** Read to discover connections among the images in Whitman's answer to a child's question.

A child said *What is the grass?* fetching it to me with full hands;
How could I answer the child? I do not know what it is any more than he.

I guess it must be the flag of my disposition, out of hopeful green stuff woven. **A**

Or I guess it is the handkerchief of the Lord,
5   A scented gift and remembrancer designedly dropt,
Bearing the owner's name someway in the corners, that we may see and remark,
    and say *Whose?*

Or I guess the grass is itself a child, the produced babe of the vegetation.

Or I guess it is a uniform hieroglyphic,°
And it means, Sprouting alike in broad zones and narrow zones,
10 Growing among black folks as among white,
Kanuck, Tuckahoe, Congressman, Cuff,° I give them the same,
    I receive them the same.

And now it seems to me the beautiful uncut hair of graves.

---

  8. hieroglyphic (hy uhr uh GLIHF ihk): picture symbol used in a writing system to represent sounds or words.
11. Kanuck (kuh NUHK), **Tuckahoe, . . . Cuff:** *Kanuck, Tuckahoe,* and *Cuff* are slang terms, now considered offensive, for a French Canadian, an inhabitant of the Virginia lowlands, and an African American, respectively.

A **Reading Focus** **Paraphrasing** In your own words, restate this line. What does this line reveal about the speaker?

Vocabulary **disposition** (dihs puh ZIHSH uhn) *n.:* one's natural way of acting toward others or thinking about things.

Literary Perspectives

Analyzing Biographical Information Biographical criticism looks for links between a writer's life and his or her published works. In Whitman's case, we see a deeply personal connection between his life and poems. As you read, remember that Whitman knew both rural and urban life and traveled widely—hence the diverse settings and people of his poems. Consider, too, how journalism would have trained him to observe events and how carpentry might have encouraged him to feel kinship with manual laborers.

As you read, notice the questions in the text, which will guide you in using this perspective.

Tenderly will I use you curling grass,
It may be you transpire from the breasts of young men,
15 It may be if I had known them I would have loved them,
It may be you are from old people, or from offspring taken soon out of their
      mothers' laps,
And here you are the mothers' laps.

The grass is very dark to be from the white heads of old mothers,
Darker than the colorless beards of old men,
20 Dark to come from under the faint red roofs of mouths. **B**

O I perceive after all so many uttering tongues,
And I perceive they do not come from the roofs of mouths for nothing.

I wish I could translate the hints about the dead young men and women,
And the hints about old men and mothers, and the offspring taken soon out of
      their laps.

25 What do you think has become of the young and old men?
And what do you think has become of the women and children?

They are alive and well somewhere,
The smallest sprout shows there is really no death,
And if ever there was it led forward life, and does not wait at the end to arrest it,
30 And ceas'd the moment life appear'd.

All goes onward and outward, nothing collapses,
And to die is different from what any one supposed, and luckier.

B **Literary Perspectives** **Biographical Information** How might Whitman's experience of rural life have influenced the imagery in lines 1–20? Explain.

Vocabulary **transpire** (tran SPYR) *v.*: develop or breathe out.

POEM

from Song of Myself

from **33** I understand the large hearts of heroes

by **Walt Whitman**

> **Read with a Purpose** Read to discover what the characters in the poem have in common.

I understand the large hearts of heroes,
The courage of present times and all times,
How the skipper saw the crowded and rudderless wreck of the
    steam-ship, and Death chasing it up and down the storm,
How he knuckled tight and gave not back an inch, and was faithful
    of days and faithful of nights,

And chalk'd in large letters on a board, *Be of good cheer,*
5   *we will not desert you;*
How he follow'd with them and tack'd with them three days and
    would not give it up,
How he saved the drifting company at last,
How the lank loose-gown'd women look'd when boated from the
    side of their prepared graves,
How the silent old-faced infants and the lifted sick, and the sharp-
    lipp'd unshaved men;
10 All this I swallow, it tastes good, I like it well, it becomes mine,
I am the man, I suffer'd, I was there. °

The disdain and calmness of martyrs,
The mother of old, condemn'd for a witch, burnt with dry wood,
    her children gazing on,
The hounded slave that flags in the race, leans by the fence,
    blowing, cover'd with sweat,
The twinges that sting like needles his legs and neck, the
15   murderous buckshot and the bullets,
All these I feel or am.

1–11. I understand . . . I was there: This stanza was inspired by an incident that occurred in 1853. According to reports in the New York *Weekly Tribune* of January 21, 1854, the ship *San Francisco* sailed from New York City on December 22, 1853, destined for South America. A violent storm hit the ship several hundred miles out of port, washing many passengers overboard. The captain of another ship helped rescue the survivors. A copy of the newspaper story was found among Whitman's papers after his death.

A **Reading Focus** **Paraphrasing** In your own words, tell what happens in the two scenes that Whitman describes. Why do you think he includes these tragic scenes in the poem?

Analyzing Visuals

Viewing and Interpreting According to Whitman's description of a slave's escape in this poem, what might the people in this painting face as they run for freedom?

I am the hounded slave, I wince at the bite of the dogs,
Hell and despair are upon me, crack and again crack the
    marksmen,
I clutch the rails of the fence, my gore dribs,° thinn'd with the ooze
    of my skin,
20 I fall on the weeds and stones,
The riders spur their unwilling horses, haul close,
Taunt my dizzy ears and beat me violently over the head with
    whip-stocks. **B**

19. dribs: dribbles.

B **Literary Focus** Free Verse How do the sound effects of this stanza (lines 17–22) reinforce the brutality of its subject matter?

Agonies are one of my changes of garments,
I do not ask the wounded person how he feels, I myself become the
　　wounded person,
25　My hurts turn livid upon me as I lean on a cane and observe.

I am the mash'd fireman with breast-bone broken,
Tumbling walls buried me in their debris,
Heat and smoke I inspired,° I heard the yelling shouts of my
　　comrades,
I heard the distant click of their picks and shovels,
30　They have clear'd the beams away, they tenderly lift me forth.

I lie in the night air in my red shirt, the pervading hush is for
　　my sake,
Painless after all I lie exhausted but not so unhappy,
White and beautiful are the faces around me, the heads are bared
　　of their fire-caps,
The kneeling crowd fades with the light of the torches.

35　Distant and dead resuscitate,
They show as the dial or move as the hands of me, I am the clock
　　myself.

I am an old artillerist, I tell of my fort's bombardment,
I am there again.

Again the long roll of the drummers,
40　Again the attacking cannon, mortars,
Again to my listening ears the cannon responsive.

I take part, I see and hear the whole,
The cries, curses, roar, the plaudits for well-aim'd shots,
The ambulanza° slowly passing trailing its red drip,
45　Workmen searching after damages, making indispensable repairs,
The fall of grenades through the rent roof, the fan-shaped
　　explosion,
The whizz of limbs, heads, stone, wood, iron, high in the air.

Again gurgles the mouth of my dying general, he furiously waves
　　with his hand,
He gasps through the clot *Mind not me—mind—the entrenchments.*

28. inspired: breathed in.

44. ambulanza (ahm boo
LAHNT suh): Italian for
"ambulance."

C **Literary Perspectives** **Biographical Information** How might Whitman's time
spent in the city, especially his work as a journalist, have <u>subsequently</u> influenced lines 26–30?

Vocabulary **resuscitate** (rih SUHS uh tayt) *v.:* return to life.

Applying Your Skills

SKILLS FOCUS Literary Skills Analyze the characteristics of free verse; analyze symbolic meaning. **Reading Skills** Use paraphrasing or retelling as a strategy for comprehension. **Writing Skills** Enhance style for effective writing.

from **Song of Myself, Numbers 1, 6, 33**

Respond and Think Critically

Reading Focus

Quick Check

1. In number 1 from *Song of Myself,* how does the speaker connect himself to America's heritage?

2. List some things to which Whitman compares the grass in number 6.

3. In number 33, why does the speaker consider the skipper a hero?

Read with a Purpose

4. How does Whitman relate himself to the experiences he presents in the three poems?

Reading Skills: Paraphrasing

5. Add a third column to your chart, and record the characteristics of free verse you find in each example.

Lines from Song of Myself, no. 1	Paraphrase	Characteristics of Free Verse
Line 10: "Creeds and schools in abeyance"	Certain beliefs and schools or teachings are temporarily suspended.	omitted words (elliptical construction)

Literary Focus

Literary Analysis

6. **Hypothesize** In number 1, why do you think Whitman repeats the word *loaf* (lines 4–5)? What effect does the repetition create?

7. **Interpret** In number 6, what idea is Whitman introducing when he describes the grass as "beautiful uncut hair of graves" (line 12)?

8. **Analyze** How does number 6 connect to and build upon the ideas presented in number 1?

9. **Infer** Based on your reading of number 33, how do you think Whitman defines heroism?

10. **Evaluate** In number 33, Whitman uses some disturbing images and tragic scenes to express the extremes of human experience. Do you think his imagery is effective? Explain.

11. **Evaluate** How do numbers 1 and 6 reflect the idea of humanity's connection to nature?

12. **Literary Perspectives** How does number 33 illustrate Whitman's admiration for everyday people?

Literary Skills: Free Verse

13. **Analyze** How do the characteristics of free verse you identified in the poems contribute to the effects and meaning? Explain your response.

Literary Skills Review: Symbolic Meaning

14. **Analyze** In poems, objects and images often have **symbolic meaning**—they represent larger ideas that go beyond their literal role in the poem. Explain the symbolic meaning of the grass in number 6.

Writing Focus

Think as a Reader/Writer

Use It in Your Writing Choose any topic that interests you, and write a short poem in free verse. Focus on creating lines that have a natural rhythm and flow when read aloud.

What Do **You Think Now** Whitman's poetry reveals his ability to step into the lives of others and empathize with people quite different from himself. Is this a common quality in people? Explain.

For more activities see page 529. >

Preparing to Read

from Song of Myself, Number 52

Reader/Writer Notebook

Use your **RWN** to complete the activities for this selection.

Literary Focus

Theme In literature, the **theme** is an insight about life that is expressed in the work. Because themes are rarely stated directly, a reader usually has to infer the theme from other elements in the work. To determine a poem's theme, first identify the work's general subject, such as "love." Then, consider what the images in the poem say about the subject. Number 52 is the final section of the poem *Song of Myself,* and in it Whitman restates some of the themes that run through the entire poem.

Literary Perspectives Apply the literary perspective described on page 518 as you read this poem.

Reading Focus

Comparing Themes Across Texts The final section of *Song of Myself* is not only the poet's farewell to the reader but also a **coda**—a summing up and restatement of the themes of the entire poem. As you read, recall the themes you previously encountered in Whitman's verse and think about how number 52 supports or contradicts those themes.

Into Action Some subjects in number 52 link to lines in *Song of Myself,* 1, 6, and 33. As you read, identify these subjects and record them on a chart. Note repeated subjects and the lines in number 52 where they appear. Then, write what the poem says about each subject.

Lines / Subject	What the Poem Says or Implies About the Subject (Theme)
Lines 1–4 / connection to nature	We are all part of the natural world.

Writing Focus

Think as a Reader/Writer

Find It in Your Reading To express his ideas and themes, Whitman includes concrete images in his poem. In your *Reader/Writer Notebook,* record some of the striking **images** Whitman uses to convey his ideas.

Vocabulary

loitering (LOY tuhr ihng) *n.:* the state of hanging about and wasting time. *The busy hawk seems to reproach Whitman for his idle loitering.*

bequeath (bih KWEETH) *v.:* give or leave by means of a will when one dies. *As a gesture of his connection to nature, Whitman bequeaths himself to the earth.*

Language Coach

Prefixes The word *bequeath* comes from the Old English prefix *be–* and the verb *cwethan,* "to say." *Be–,* combined with some verbs, is like adding *about* or *away* to the root verb. In one old sense, *bequeath* meant "to say (something) away formally." Today, the word *bequeath* is used mainly in wills (and, of course, in poems).

 Learn It Online

Let *PowerNotes* give you a different look at the instruction on this page.

go.hrw.com   L11-524

from Song of Myself

52 The spotted hawk swoops by

by **Walt Whitman**

Read with a Purpose
Read to discover how Whitman sees humanity's place in the natural world.

Build Background
In this final section, Whitman restates some of the themes that run throughout *Song of Myself*. Because the most insistently present element throughout *Song of Myself* is the mind and spirit of the speaker himself, this passage is highly personal. True to his confidence in himself, he also proclaims his importance—and his inescapability, even as he mocks his own egotism.

The spotted hawk swoops by and accuses me, he complains
    of my gab and my loitering. Ⓐ

I too am not a bit tamed, I too am untranslatable,
I sound my barbaric yawp° over the roofs of the world.

The last scud° of day holds back for me,
5 It flings my likeness after the rest and true as any on the shadow'd wilds,
It coaxes me to the vapor and the dusk.

---

3. yawp: a loud, harsh cry.
4. scud: windblown mist and low clouds.

Ⓐ **Literary Focus** **Theme** How does the image of the hawk relate to the main subjects of *Song of Myself*?

Vocabulary **loitering** (LOY tuhr ihng) *n.:* the state of hanging about and wasting time.

I depart as air, I shake my white locks at the runaway sun,
I effuse° my flesh in eddies,° and drift it in lacy jags.

I bequeath myself to the dirt to grow from the grass I love,   **B**
10   If you want me again look for me under your boot-soles.

You will hardly know who I am or what I mean,
But I shall be good health to you nevertheless,
And filter and fiber your blood.

Failing to fetch me at first keep encouraged,
15   Missing me one place search another,
I stop somewhere waiting for you.   **C**

_____

   8. effuse: spread out.   **eddies:** small whirlwinds.

_____

B **Reading Focus** **Comparing Themes Across Texts**   How does this line echo
subjects and themes from earlier sections of *Song of Myself*?

C **Literary Perspectives** **Biographical Information**   In the last two stanzas,
what is Whitman telling his readers? What is he offering to them?

Vocabulary **bequeath** (bih KWEETH) *v.:* give or leave by means of a will when
one dies.

Applying Your Skills

SKILLS FOCUS Literary Skills Analyze theme; analyze onomatopoeia. **Reading Skills** Compare themes across texts. **Writing Skills** Incorporate imagery in writing.

from **Song of Myself, Number 52**

Respond and Think Critically

Reading Focus

Quick Check

1. What qualities does the speaker share with the hawk?

2. Where does the speaker say the reader can find him? What does he mean by line 10?

Read with a Purpose

3. How does Whitman sees humanity's place in the natural world? How might his view differ in <u>principle</u> from other common beliefs?

Reading Skills: Comparing Themes Across Texts

4. Review the earlier sections from *Song of Myself*, and think about how the themes of those poems compare to the themes on your chart. Add a third column to the chart, and note which other *Song of Myself* poem or poems you have read that share the same theme.

Lines / Subject	What the Poem Says or Implies About the Subject (Theme)	Other Song of Myself Poems That Share This Theme
Lines 1–4 / connection to nature	We are all part of the natural world.	1, 6, 33

Literary Focus

Literary Analysis

5. **Interpret** What happens in lines 7–8? Explain the final bequest (line 9).

6. **Draw Conclusions** At what time of day do the events in the poem occur? Why is the setting appropriate for a poem that concludes Whitman's long sequence?

7. **Infer** How can Whitman be "good health" to the reader (line 12)?

8. **Analyze** The first line of *Song of Myself* is "I celebrate myself, and sing myself" (see page 517), and the last line is "I stop somewhere waiting for you." What do these last words reveal about Whitman's purpose for writing *Song of Myself*?

9. **Literary Perspectives** How does Whitman's description of himself in this poem compare with the information about him on pages 510–511?

Literary Skills: Theme

10. **Summarize** Re-read Whitman's verse. Then, summarize the themes stated in number 52, the coda, or end, to *Song of Myself*.

Literary Skills Review: Onomatopoeia

11. **Hypothesize** The use of a word whose sound imitates or suggests its meaning, such as *buzz*, is called **onomatopoeia**. Identify the onomatopoeia in the second stanza of number 52. Why do you think Whitman includes it in the poem?

Writing Focus

Think as a Reader/Writer

Use It in Your Writing Review the images that Whitman uses to establish the themes in number 52. Then, consider your own view of nature. Write a paragraph that uses imagery to help communicate your view. Make sure the words you choose strongly support the ideas you wish to convey about your subject.

 **What Do You Think Now**

How do you feel when you observe some particular aspect of nature? Do you find the powers of nature restorative? Explain.

from **Song of Myself, Numbers 1, 6, 33, 52**

Vocabulary Development

✓ Vocabulary Check

Match the Vocabulary words with their synonyms.

1. harbor
2. disposition
3. transpire
4. resuscitate
5. bequeath
6. loitering

a. develop
b. revive
c. endow
d. hold
e. wasting time
f. temperament

Vocabulary Skills: Multiple-Meaning Words

Many English words have multiple meanings and sometimes different pronunciations. For example, the noun *desert,* with stress on the first syllable, means "dry, barren, sandy region." The verb *desert,* with stress on the second syllable, means "abandon," as in this line from Whitman's *Song of Myself,* number 33:

> Be of good cheer, we will not **desert** you

Sometimes words carry multiple meanings even when the pronunciation and the part of speech don't change. To understand which meaning is intended, you must pay attention to the word's **context**—the surrounding words and sentences.

Using a Dictionary When you look up words like *desert,* you will find separate entries (or parts of an entry) for the word's uses as a verb and as a noun. Some dictionaries start with the word's oldest meaning and end with its most recent meaning. Other dictionaries start with the modern meanings and then list old, rare, or obsolete meanings.

Studying Origins Word origins often appear in brackets at the beginning of a dictionary entry. Some words have the same origin for all of their meanings. Other words, such as *desert* (noun) and *desert* (verb) have different origins—it is an accident of language history that the words ended up with the same spelling.

Your Turn

Use a dictionary to look up the origin and different meanings of the words listed below. Then, choose two of the words. Write sentences using each of them in two different contexts to show some of the word's different meanings.

1. air
2. mean
3. lobby
4. form

Language Coach

Prefixes It's difficult to see how a prefix adds to the meaning of a word when the root word is no longer being used (like *quethen* in *bequeath*). To get a better idea of how the prefix *be–* can affect a word's meaning, look at the words *bewail* and *bemoan*. What smaller verbs do you see within each of these words? In these words, *be–* means "thoroughly." How does knowing the meaning of the prefix help you understand these words? Use each word in a sentence.

Academic Vocabulary

Write About
In *Song of Myself*, upon what <u>principles</u> does Whitman seem to base his life? Do you think he considers his role in the universe as applicable to all people or unique to himself? Explain.

Grammar Link

Varying Sentence Beginnings

Sentences most often begin with subjects.

> **Whitman** revised *Leaves of Grass* nine times.

> The **poems** grew and evolved in each edition.

Varying sentence beginnings can help make writing more interesting to read. Sentences can begin with prepositional, participial, or infinitive phrases.

> **By revising,** Whitman kept the collection vital.

> **Included in every edition,** *Song of Myself* may be the most personal of Whitman's poems.

> **To express himself,** Whitman speaks directly to the reader.

Sentences can also begin with subordinate clauses.

> **When the speaker says, "I too am not a bit tamed,"** he may speak for Whitman himself.

Modifiers or conjunctive adverbs also begin sentences.

> **Usually,** the speaker of a poem is not the poet.

> **Nevertheless,** Whitman's voice is clear and powerful in *Song of Myself.*

Your Turn

Writing Application Revise the following paragraph to vary sentence beginnings. Begin at least one sentence with a phrase, at least one with a subordinate clause, and at least one with a modifier or conjunctive adverb.

> Whitman writes about dying in number 52 of *Song of Myself.* He does not see death as something sad. The speaker leaves the world "as air." He gives himself to the soil happily. He will still be with the world even after he is gone. He tells readers, "look for me under your boot-soles." He expresses joy if he expresses any feeling.

CHOICES

As you respond to the Choices, use these **Academic Vocabulary** words as appropriate: <u>advocate</u>, <u>criteria</u>, <u>fundamental</u>, <u>principle</u>, <u>subsequent</u>.

REVIEW

Compare and Contrast Inspiration

Timed └Writing In *Song of Myself,* Whitman finds inspiration in the natural world. Review the poem, and note how the speaker sees himself in nature. Are there any specific places or elements in nature with which you share a special connection or that you find inspiring? Where do you go to be inspired or to think about life? In an essay, discuss the <u>criteria</u> that a place or thing must meet in order to inspire you to think about life. Then, write about how your source of inspiration compares with Whitman's.

CONNECT

Search for Walt

At the end of *Song of Myself,* Whitman urges readers to seek him out. Although Whitman wants us to look for him in nature, you can also find him in the poems of others. Throughout the twentieth century, many poets—from Ezra Pound to Allen Ginsberg—address or refer to Whitman in their poems. In the library or online, search for a modern poem that includes a reference to Whitman. Write a paragraph discussing how the poem relates to Whitman and his themes.

EXTEND

Bring Images to Life

TechFocus From the swooping hawk in the beginning to the boot-soles near the end, Whitman's poem presents a flow of strong images. Think about how each image could be shown visually, and create a storyboard outlining how you would present the images as a short video. Using your storyboard as a guide, create a short video that depicts the flow of Whitman's images in the poem to present to your class.

Preparing to Read

A Sight in Camp in the Daybreak Gray and Dim

Reader/Writer
Notebook

Use your **RWN** to complete the activities for this selection.

Literary Focus

Symbol In literature a **symbol** is a person, place, thing, or event that has meaning in itself but also stands for something more than itself. A writer rarely makes a symbol obvious by directly stating what it means. Most symbols are more subtle; as the reader, you must make inferences to discover their broader meanings. In "A Sight in Camp in the Daybreak Gray and Dim," Whitman describes three different fallen soldiers who together form a powerful symbol of the devastating consequences of war.

Reading Focus

Visualizing the Text When you **visualize the text,** you see in your mind what it presents or describes. This also focuses your attention on key people, places, things, or events in the poem that may act as symbols. You can improve your ability to visualize the text by reading a few lines and then pausing to write a description of what you see in your mind. Another technique you might use to visualize the text is to make a quick drawing or sketch of what you picture as you read.

Into Action As you read, pause to describe in words or to make a quick sketch in your *Reader/Writer Notebook* of what you see in your mind. Make a list of which key elements in the poem act as symbols by standing for something more than themselves.

Writing Focus

Think as a Reader/Writer

Find It in Your Reading A symbol's ability to mean something greater than itself relies on how a writer portrays it. By focusing on just a few fundamental details, Whitman conveys the three soldiers' full humanity. As you read the poem, list in your *Reader/Writer Notebook* the details Whitman focuses on to describe each soldier. Do you notice any similarities or differences among these details?

Language Coach

Connotations A word's **connotations** are the feelings or ideas it inspires. A poet chooses each word carefully, searching for just the right connotations. Each pair of words below includes one word from "A Sight in Camp in the Daybreak Gray and Dim," followed by a synonym. (**Synonyms** are words with similar meanings, but they can have very different connotations.) With a partner, look up the words in each pair. Then, discuss the different connotations of each word.

   sleepless (line 2) / tired
   untended (line 4) / neglected
   gaunt (line 9) / thin
   comrade (line 10) / friend

 Learn It Online
Follow Whitman into the twenty-first century with these Internet links.

go.hrw.com | L11-530 | **Go**

A SIGHT IN CAMP
IN THE DAYBREAK GRAY
AND DIM

by **Walt Whitman**

Read with a Purpose
Read to discover how Whitman uses three individual soldiers to show the far-reaching costs of war.

Build Background
In December 1862, Whitman traveled to Virginia to care for his brother George, who had been wounded at the First Battle of Fredericksburg, a battle in which Union forces suffered devastating losses. Though George's injuries were minor, Whitman stayed on to assist the staffs of hospitals who were caring for the wounded. Whitman comforted and fed the injured and dying men, cleaned and bandaged their wounds, read to them, and wrote letters home to their families. By the end of the war, Whitman had probably inter-acted with thousands of soldiers.

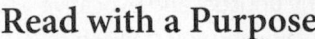

A sight in camp in the daybreak gray and dim,
As from my tent I emerge so early sleepless,
As slow I walk in the cool fresh air the path near by the hospital tent,
Three forms I see on stretchers lying, brought out there untended lying,
5   Over each the blanket spread, ample brownish woolen blanket,
Gray and heavy blanket, folding, covering all. **Ⓐ**

Curious I halt and silent stand,
Then with light fingers I from the face of the nearest the first just lift the blanket;
Who are you elderly man so gaunt° and grim, with well-gray'd hair, and flesh all sunken
     about the eyes?
10 Who are you my dear comrade°?

Then to the second I step—and who are you my child and darling?
Who are you sweet boy with cheeks yet blooming?
Then to the third—a face nor child nor old, very calm, as of beautiful yellow-white ivory;
Young man I think I know you—I think this face is the face of the Christ himself,
15 Dead and divine and brother of all, and here again he lies. **Ⓑ**

---

9. gaunt: thin and bony.
10. comrade: companion; fellow member of a group.

Ⓐ Reading Focus **Visualizing the Text** What do you visualize as you read lines 4–6 of the poem? What do you notice about how the "three forms" are described?

Ⓑ Literary Focus **Symbol** In what sense is the third dead soldier like Jesus Christ? Explain your response.

Applying Your Skills

A Sight in Camp in the Daybreak Gray and Dim

Respond and Think Critically

Reading Focus

Quick Check

1. At what time of day does the speaker come out of his tent? Why does he leave the tent?

2. What does the speaker's curiosity lead him to do?

3. Why does the speaker feel he knows the third face?

Read with a Purpose

4. According to the speaker, who is affected by war?

Reading Skills: Visualizing the Text

5. As you read the poem, you paused to describe or draw a sketch of the scenes depicted in it. Think about how pausing to visualize these scenes improved your comprehension of the poem. Write a sentence or two reflecting on the technique you chose and how it helped improve your understanding of the poem.

Literary Focus

Literary Analysis

6. **Compare and Contrast** The speaker includes the details that the air was "cool" and "fresh" (line 3). How do these details contrast with the images in subsequent lines?

7. **Analyze** What question does the speaker repeat in the poem? What is the effect of the repetition?

8. **Interpret** How would you explain what the speaker means in line 15? (Keep in mind that this is a civil war, in which "brother" kills "brother.")

9. **Infer** The point of the poem is never openly stated; that is, it remains implicit. How would you express the poet's message directly?

10. **Extend** Briographer Paul Zweig says that Whitman had a genius for the single line, "the verbal snapshot." Find two images in the poem that you think make particularly unusual and evocative verbal snapshots. Explain why you think so.

11. **Analyze** In *Leaves of Grass* the poet identifies with every part of the universe: body, soul, women, men, goodness, wickedness. Whom or what does he identify with in "A Sight in Camp in the Daybreak Gray and Dim"? Explain.

Literary Skills: Symbol

12. **Analyze** Review the list of symbols from the poem that you recorded in your *Reader/Writer Notebook* as you read. How does Whitman's use of symbolism enhance the meaning of this poem?

Literary Skills Review: Setting

13. **Interpret** The **setting** of a poem is the time and location in which the poem takes place. Describe the scene you see in the poem. Why does the poem take place at daybreak?

Writing Focus

Think as a Reader/Writer

Use It in Your Writing As you read the poem, you noted the select details on which Whitman focuses to convey the humanity of the three fallen soldiers. Write a paragraph describing a person you know. Focus on only a few carefully chosen details to convey a fuller portrait of his or her personality.

What Do You Think Now

How would you measure the costs of the Civil War against the positive changes it brought about?

from Specimen Days

Reader/Writer
Notebook
Use your **RWN** to complete the activities for this selection.

Informational Text Focus

Analyzing Rhetorical Devices A **rhetorical device** is a technique a writer uses to make an emotional appeal or evoke a response from a reader. Rhetorical devices can add clarity and force to writing, making it memorable. Two of the most obvious rhetorical devices Whitman uses are the **catalog,** an extensive list, to suggest inclusiveness and variety, and **repetition** of words and phrases to connect different people, places, or other elements to one another. Whitman also uses **parenthetical statements,** that is, statements set off by dashes or set in parentheses, to make his writing sound as if he is having a conversation with himself.

Into Action As you read, use a chart like the one below to list each catalog or parenthetical statement you encounter in the selection. In the second column of your chart, record the emotional response that each device evokes.

Rhetorical Device	Emotional Response
Parenthetical statement—"(and still, on recollection, find)"	It makes me respect Whitman because he has given much thought to the Civil War soldiers on both sides.
Catalog—"his incredible dauntlessness, habits, practices, tastes, language, his fierce friendship, his appetite, rankness, his superb strength and animality, lawless gait"	The words that describe the soldiers make me feel admiration for the soldiers' bravery and loyalty to their fellow soldiers.

Writing Focus   Preparing for **Constructed Response**

Whitman suggests that the truth of the war lay in the personal experience of soldiers—in what he calls "countless minor scenes." As you read the second paragraph of this journal excerpt, pay special attention to the fragment of narrative Whitman includes—his brief references to a single hospitalized soldier's suffering and to an incident involving seventeen soldiers killed in battle. How does the specific information in this passage contribute to Whitman's more general commentary on the war as a whole? Use your *Reader/Writer Notebook* to record your ideas.

Vocabulary

latent (LAY tuhnt) *adj.:* present but hidden or not active. *Whitman wanted to understand the latent individuality of each soldier.*

infernal (ihn FUR nuhl) *adj.:* as if coming from hell; detestable. *Whitman wrote about the infernal miseries of the Civil War.*

conveyed (kuhn VAYD) *v.:* communicated; made known. *Whitman thinks that the personal costs of the Civil War may never be conveyed to the public.*

interminable (ihn TUR muh nuh buhl) *adj.:* never stopping. *To soldiers in the war, the horrors seemed interminable.*

expenditure (ehk SPEHN duh chur) *n:* an amount spent. *Whitman notes the government's immense expenditure of money to support the Civil War.*

Language Coach

Related Words The prefix *in–* means "not," so the word *interminable* in the list above means "not terminable" or "not capable of ending." What do you think the related word *terminate* means? What about the word *terminal*? Use a dictionary to help you figure out the meanings of these related

Learn It Online
Practice the Vocabulary words with Word Watch online.

go.hrw.com   L11-533   GO

from

SPECIMEN DAYS

by **Walt Whitman**

Read with a Purpose
Read to learn of the grim realities of the Civil War from Whitman's firsthand account of his hospital experiences.

Build Background
Whitman first published *Specimen Days* in 1882, but he made his notes for the Civil War sections of the book at the time of the events themselves—while he was working as a government clerk and war correspondent in Washington, D.C. Whitman called his book *Specimen Days* because these journal entries offered "specimens" of his life. In the following excerpt, Whitman explores the human tragedy of the war—in the fields, among ordinary soldiers, and in the makeshift hospitals where Whitman worked—the part of the story of the war that was not told to the public.

THE REAL WAR WILL NEVER GET IN THE BOOKS

And so goodbye to the war. I know not how it may have been, or may be, to others—to me the main interest I found (and still, on recollection, find) in the rank and file of the armies, both sides, and in those specimens amid the hospitals, and even the dead on the field. To me the points illustrating the latent personal character and eligibilities of these States, in the two or three millions of American young and middle-aged men, North and South, embodied in those armies—and especially the one-third or one-fourth of their number, stricken by wounds or disease at some time in the course of the contest—were of more significance even than the political interests involved. (As so much of a race depends on how it faces death, and how it stands personal anguish and sickness. As, in the glints of emotions under emergencies, and the indirect traits and asides in Plutarch, we get far profounder clues to the antique world than all its more formal history.)

Future years will never know the seething hell and the black infernal background of countless minor scenes and interiors (not the official surface courteousness of the generals, not the few great battles), of the Secession war; and it is best they should not—the real war will never get in the books. In the mushy influences of current times, too, the fervid atmosphere and typical events of those years are in danger of being totally forgotten. I have at night watched by the side of a sick man in the hospital, one who could not live many hours. I have seen his eyes flash and burn as he raised himself and recurred to[1] the cruelties on his surrendered brother, and mutilations of the corpse afterward. (See, in the preceding pages, the incident at Upperville—the seventeen killed as in the description, were left there on the ground. After they dropped dead, no one touched them—all were made sure of, however. The carcasses were left for the citizens to bury or not, as they chose.)

---

1. **recurred to:** experienced again.

Vocabulary **latent** (LAY tuhnt) *adj.:* present but hidden or not active.
infernal (ihn FUR nuhl) *adj.:* as if coming from hell; detestable.

Robot Soldiers

The U.S. military now uses some robot soldiers in military missions. In 2005, the Pentagon predicted that robots will fight in actual combat within a decade. However, a robot soldier is not just a machine designed to kill; some robots actually perform complex military missions, just as a human soldier might. The U.S. military has used robots to dig for bombs and to search for enemies hiding in caves. One type of robot was created to fire from infantry front lines. The Pentagon hopes robot soldiers evolve to behave and reason as humans do, thus reducing the number of humans needed for combat.

Ask Yourself

How might Whitman's reactions have differed if robot soldiers had been used during the Civil War? Explain.

Such was the war. It was not a quadrille[2] in a ballroom. Its interior history will not only never be written—its practicality, minutiae of deeds and passions, will never be even suggested. The actual soldier of 1862–1865, North and South, with all his ways, his incredible dauntlessness, habits, practices, tastes, language, his fierce friendship, his appetite, rankness, his superb strength and animality, lawless gait, and a hundred unnamed lights and shades of camp, I say, will never be written—perhaps must not and should not be. **A B**

The preceding notes may furnish a few stray glimpses into that life, and into those lurid interiors, never to be fully conveyed to the future. The hospital part of the drama from 1861 to 1865, deserves indeed to be recorded. Of that many-threaded drama, with its sudden and strange surprises, its confounding of prophecies, its moments of despair, the dread of foreign interference, the interminable campaigns, the bloody battles, the mighty and cumbrous and green armies, the drafts and bounties—the immense money expenditure, like a heavy-pouring constant rain—with, over the whole land, the last three years of the struggle, an unending, universal mourning wail of women, parents, orphans—the marrow[3] of the tragedy concentrated in those Army Hospitals—(it seemed sometimes as if the whole interest of the land, North and South, was one vast central hospital, and all the rest of the affair but flanges)[4]—those forming the untold and unwritten history of the war— infinitely greater (like life's) than the few scraps and distortions that are ever told or written. Think how much, and of importance, will be—how much, civic and military, has already been—buried in the grave, in eternal darkness.

---

2. **quadrille** (kwuh DRIHL): a sophisticated French dance for four couples.

3. **marrow:** the most essential part.
4. **flanges** (FLAN jehz): protruding edges attached to another object to hold it in place.

A **Informational Focus** Rhetorical Devices Whitman provides a catalog of characteristics of "the actual soldier." What effect does this extensive list produce?

B **Informational Focus** Rhetorical Devices Why do you think Whitman repeats the phrase "never be written"? What purpose does the repetition serve?

Vocabulary **conveyed** (kuhn VAYD) *v.:* communicated; made known.
interminable (ihn TUR muh nuh buhl) *adj.:* never stopping.
expenditure (ehk SPEHN duh chur) *n.:* an amount spent.

SKILLS FOCUS Informational Skills
Analyze rhetorical devices. **Vocabulary
Skills** Identify synonyms. **Writing Skills**
Write brief constructed responses, with
specific support. **Listening and Speaking
Skills** Analyze the author's use of stylistic
devices.

from **Specimen Days**

Respond and Think Critically

Informational Text Focus

Quick Check

1. What happened to the bodies of fallen soldiers at Upperville? Why do you think Whitman mentions them?

2. Where does Whitman feel most of the war's real stories can be found?

Read with a Purpose

3. What have you learned from Whitman's firsthand account of the Civil War?

Informational Skills: Analyzing Rhetorical Devices

4. As you read, you listed examples of catalogs and parenthetical statements and noted the emotional responses the devices evoke. Now, write a few sentences reflecting on how these devices contribute to the selection as a whole.

Rhetorical Device	Emotional Response
Parenthetical statement—"(and still, on recollection, find)"	It makes me respect Whitman because he has given much thought to the Civil War soldiers on both sides.
Catalog—"his incredible dauntlessness, habits, practices, tastes, language ..."	The words that describe the soldiers make me feel admiration for the soldiers' bravery...

✔ Vocabulary Check

Match each Vocabulary word below with its synonym.

5. latent   a. horrible

6. infernal   b. expressed

7. conveyed   c. payment

8. interminable d. hidden

9. expenditure   e. unceasing

Text Analysis

10. **Interpret** Whitman says, "The real war will never get in the books." What do you think he means by this statement? Do you agree or disagree? Explain.

11. **Evaluate** What is the value of firsthand accounts such as *Specimen Days*? Explain.

12. **Evaluate** How does the excerpt from *Specimen Days* explore the idea that public accounts and private experiences sometimes tell very different stories? Explain.

13. **Analyze** What did you learn about the Civil War from Whitman's impressions and reflections?

Listening and Speaking

14. **Extend** With a partner, read the last paragraph of *Specimen Days* silently and note where parenthetical statements or catalogs appear. Then, read the same paragraph aloud. Note that you must briefly pause before reading any parenthetical statements aloud. How does this rhythm change when you read the catalogs aloud? Discuss how these different rhythms contribute to the way Whitman conveys his message.

Writing Focus Constructed Response

Briefly discuss how the specific information about a single hospitalized soldier's suffering and the incident involving seventeen soldiers killed in battle in the second paragraph of this excerpt contributes to the selection as a whole. Use specific evidence from the excerpt to support your response.

What Do **You Think Now** How do you think most people reconcile the violence of war with its outcome?

Preparing to Read

When I Heard the Learn'd Astronomer

Reader/Writer Notebook

Use your **RWN** to complete the activities for this selection.

Literary Focus

Parallelism The repetition of words, phrases, clauses, or sentences that have a similar grammatical structure is called **parallelism.** Whitman begins the poem "When I Heard the Learn'd Astronomer" with many dependent clauses arranged in a row—the first four lines all begin with the subordinating conjunction *When*. The poem is actually one long sentence containing many parallel dependent clauses. Whitman uses this grammatical structure to establish a pattern and to emphasize certain ideas. A writer's use of parallelism not only affects the **rhythm** of the poem but also adds to the **tone.** Important questions to ask include "How are the phrases different from each other?" and "What effect do these differences have on the rhythm, pacing, or tone of the poem?" Note the shift in rhythm that occurs in line 5 to reflect the negative effect of the astronomer's lecture on Whitman and the shift in tone that occurs in lines 6–8 to reflect Whitman's subsequent mystical experience of the stars.

Language Coach

Multiple-Meaning Words Words can have completely different meanings when used in different contexts. For instance, if you were talking about tennis and mentioned a court, you would be talking about the area where a game of tennis is played. If you were talking about a trial and mentioned a court, you would be referring to the place where a trial is held. The following poem contains words from the area of astronomy. Look up the words *proof, figure,* and *divide* in a dictionary. What do they mean in a scientific or mathematical context?

Writing Focus

Think as a Reader/Writer

Find It in Your Reading When you notice parallelism in a poem, you focus on what is similar about the words and phrases, but it is also useful to notice any differences between them. In your *Reader/Writer Notebook,* make a chart like the one below to identify each pair of parallel clauses in the poem and note the similarities and differences between them, including the poet's choice of words and the grammatical structures in each clause.

Parallel Dependent Clauses	Similarities	Differences
Line 1: "When I heard the learn'd astronomer" Line 3: "When I was shown the charts and diagrams, to add, divide, and measure them"	Both start with "When I" plus verb.	Verbs are different: <u>heard</u> in line 1 <u>was shown</u> in line 3

Learn It Online

Listen to the power of this poem for yourself with the audio recording online.

go.hrw.com L11-537 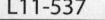 Go

When I Heard the Learn'd Astronomer

by **Walt Whitman**

Read with a Purpose
Read to learn about the poet's reaction to the astronomer's lecture and to the stars themselves.

Build Background
In the preface to *Leaves of Grass,* Whitman writes, "Exact science and its practical movements are no checks on the greatest poet but always his encouragement and support." Whitman seems to respect the role that science plays in the world, even insisting that poetry needs such support. Although elsewhere Whitman is both admiring of and receptive to science, in "When I Heard the Learn'd Astronomer," he seems to disdain the astronomer's scientific knowledge in favor of his own intuitive, even mystical response to the stars.

When I heard the learn'd astronomer,
When the proofs, the figures, were ranged in columns before me,
When I was shown the charts and diagrams, to add, divide, and measure them,
When I sitting heard the astronomer where he lectured with much applause in
      the lecture room, **Ⓐ Ⓑ**
5 How soon unaccountable I became tired and sick,
Till rising and gliding out I wander'd off by myself,
In the mystical moist night air, and from time to time,
Look'd up in perfect silence at the stars.

Ⓐ Literary Focus Parallelism How does the poet's use of parallelism affect the emotional impact of the first four lines?

Ⓑ Literary Focus Parallelism Where does Whitman use parallel structure within the parallel subordinate clauses? What effect does the additional parallelism have on the poem?

Preparing to Read

A Noiseless Patient Spider

Reader/Writer
Notebook

Use your **RWN** to complete the activities for this selection.

Literary Focus

Analogy An **analogy** is a comparison made between two things to show how they are alike. Writers often use analogies to reveal something about the things being compared in order to express a larger idea. In "A Noiseless Patient Spider," Whitman compares a spider spinning its web to his own soul reaching out for a connection with the universe. He begins by describing the spider's activities in detail. Then he describes himself in a similar way, inviting a comparison between the spider and his own soul.

Reading Focus

Visualizing Imagery In this poem, Whitman gives the reader an intricately detailed description of a spider's actions. This use of **imagery,** or language that evokes a picture or a concrete sensation, appeals to your senses as you read. The details help you visualize the imagery that the writer describes.

Into Action As you read "A Noiseless Patient Spider," notice that many of the images in the first stanza have parallels in the second. Use a chart like the one below to record the images from each line of the first stanza. Then, note any images in the second stanza that seem to correspond to the images you have listed from the first stanza.

Images from Stanza 1	Images from Stanza 2
Lines 1–2: "A noiseless patient spider" stands isolated on a promontory.	Lines 6–7: The poet's soul "stands"— detached, surrounded by space.

Writing Focus

Think as a Reader/Writer

Find It in Your Reading Whitman uses parallelism to draw an analogy between the spider and his own soul. In your *Reader/Writer Notebook*, list the actions that the spider performs. What do they suggest about how the speaker feels about his soul?

Learn It Online
Find interactive graphic organizers online to help you as you read.

go.hrw.com L11-539 **Go**

A Noiseless Patient Spider

by **Walt Whitman**

Read with a Purpose
Read to discover how a spider's actions can reflect human desires.

Build Background
Whitman's poetry expresses his <u>fundamental</u> connection not only to other people but also to nature. After observing a spider, Whitman finds a way to encompass both.

A noiseless patient spider,
I mark'd where on a little promontory° it stood isolated,
Mark'd how to explore the vacant vast surrounding,
It launch'd forth filament, filament, filament, out of itself,
5 Ever unreeling them, ever tirelessly speeding them. **Ⓐ**

And you O my soul where you stand,
Surrounded, detached, in measureless oceans of space,
Ceaselessly musing, venturing, throwing, seeking the spheres
        to connect them,
Till the bridge you will need be form'd, till the ductile° anchor hold,
10 Till the gossamer thread you fling catch somewhere, O my soul. **Ⓑ**

2. promontory: a high point of land or rock projecting into a body of water.

9. ductile: capable of being drawn out to an extreme thinness.

Ⓐ **Literary Focus** **Analogy** What important characteristic of the spider does the speaker emphasize? Why do you think the speaker emphasizes this characteristic?

Ⓑ **Reading Focus** **Visualizing Imagery** Paraphrase the images in these last two lines. How do they connect to the images in the previous stanza?

Applying Your Skills

When I Heard the Learn'd Astronomer /
A Noiseless Patient Spider

Respond and Think Critically

Reading Focus

Read with a Purpose

1. In "When I Heard . . .", how does the audience's reaction to the lecture differ from the speaker's reaction?

2. In "A Noiseless Patient Spider," what do the spider's actions reveal about humanity?

Reading Skills: Visualizing Imagery

3. As you read "A Noiseless Patient Spider," you noted images in the second stanza that corresponded to images in the first. Now, add a third column and explain the comparison.

Images from Stanza 1	Images from Stanza 2	Analogy
Lines 1–2: "A noiseless patient spider" stands isolated on a promontory.	Lines 6–7: The poet's soul "stands" — detached, surrounded by space.	Both the spider and the poet's soul are waiting, isolated.

Literary Focus

Literary Analysis

When I Heard the Learn'd Astronomer

4. **Analyze** How does line 5 serve as a transition in terms of the poem's meaning?

5. **Infer** What do you think the speaker is implying by contrasting the astronomer's lecture with the "perfect silence" outside the lecture hall?

A Noiseless Patient Spider

6. **Interpret** What is the speaker's attitude toward the spider? Which words reveal this attitude?

7. **Analyze** To what does the speaker hope to connect using the soul's "gossamer thread"?

Literary Skills: Parallelism/Analogy

When I Heard the Learn'd Astronomer

8. **Analyze** One way to identify the rhythmic effects of Whitman's parallelism is to read the lines aloud. Read the poem aloud, and describe its rhythmic effects.

A Noiseless Patient Spider

9. **Evaluate** If Whitman had stopped writing after the first stanza, how would the poem's meaning change?

Literary Skills Review: Apostrophe

10. **Analyze** The literary technique in which an absent person, object, or abstract idea is addressed as if it could hear or reply is called **apostrophe.** Where does Whitman use apostrophe in "A Noiseless Patient Spider?" What does Whitman's use of apostrophe add to the poem?

Writing Focus

Think as a Reader/Writer

Use It in Your Writing As you read Whitman's "When I Heard the Learn'd Astronomer," you noted the similarities and differences that occur between his parallel constructions. Write a short poem about someone who, like the astronomer, has an unusual job or vocation. Use parallel constructions in Whitman's style, and include your own catalog of the tools of the trade for that job, similar to the astronomer's charts and graphs Whitman mentions.

What Do You Think Now

How can conflict lead to a new perspective or a different way of seeing things?

Preparing to Read

Plenos poderes /
Fully Empowered

What Do You Think? How does conflict lead to change?

🕐 QuickTalk

Recall a time when you—or someone you know— was directly influenced by larger events in your community or somewhere else in the world. In a small group, discuss these events and their effects.

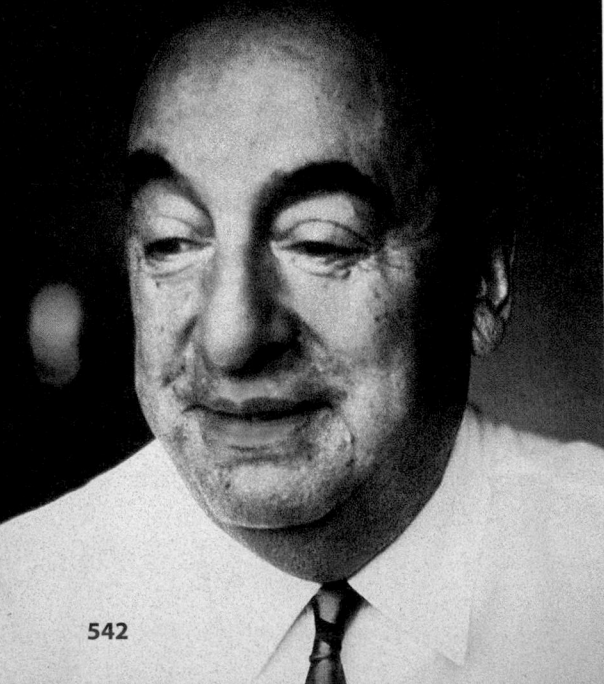

Pablo Neruda
(1904–1973)

Link to Today Readers celebrate Pablo Neruda for his humanism, his <u>advocacy</u> for peace and equality, and his love and respect for the natural world.

Poet with Promise

Nobel Prize WINNER

Born and educated in Chile, Pablo Neruda wrote that he went out "hunting poems" as a child. He received his first acclaim as a poet at the age of sixteen by winning first prize in a poetry competition. By the time he was twenty, the literary community already regarded him as a young poet with great promise. In addition to enjoying an enormously full and diverse life as a writer, Neruda served as a diplomat and a member of the Chilean senate for several years. When the Chilean government outlawed his political party and terminated his position in the senate, Neruda left his homeland to live in exile.

Many Homes, Many Poems

During his exile, Neruda lived in many countries around the world, including Burma (now known as Myanmar), Italy, Spain, France, Mexico, Russia, and China, before returning to Chile to resettle in Isla Negra in 1953. In 1971, he received the Nobel Prize in Literature. Known for his diverse range of poetic styles and voices, Neruda claims Walt Whitman as his "primary creditor." Pablo Neruda's poems are questions, riddles, political shouts, observations, homages, and introspective movements toward truth. Like Whitman, he influenced and inspired many of the great poets of the twentieth century.

Think About the Writer For Whitman and Neruda, how does their role as writers shape their relationship to the world around them?

 **Reader/Writer**
Notebook
Use your **RWN** to complete the activities for this selection.

Literary Focus

Metaphor A **metaphor** is a figure of speech that compares two unlike things without the use of comparison words such as *like* or *as*. In line 6, the metaphor "The black crop of the night" compares the darkness of night to a farmer's crop. Metaphors are <u>fundamental</u> to Neruda's poetic vision. Look for other metaphors as you read this poem and its English translation.

Reading Focus

Comparing and Contrasting Poems The poems of Whitman and Neruda share many of the same basic <u>principles</u>, even though the two writers emerged from different cultures, years apart. Their work often invites comparison. As you read Neruda's poem, look for images or phrases that remind you of lines from Whitman's *Song of Myself*.

Into Action As you read, use a chart like the one below to record phrases, images, and metaphors from Neruda's poem that remind you of lines from Whitman's poems. Copy each line, and note the Whitman poem in which you found each similar line. Then, in the third column, state how the lines from each poem are similar.

Lines from Neruda	Lines from Whitman	How the Lines Are Similar
"in a place where I can sing"	"I celebrate myself, and sing myself," number 1	They both declare that the poem is their song.

Writing Focus

Think as a Reader/Writer
Find It in Your Reading Neruda's **metaphors** are one of the elements in his poems that remind readers of Whitman. As you read, note in your *Reader/Writer Notebook* which metaphors recall the kinds of comparisons and images that Whitman uses in his poems.

Vocabulary

teeming (TEEM ihng) *v.* used as *adj.:* full of; alive with. *Neruda writes of streets teeming with energy.*

forge (fohrj) *v.:* heat and shape metal. *Neruda imagines forging keys as one step in the creative process.*

aspect (AS pehkt) *n.:* the way something looks; appearance. *Neruda examines death in all its aspects.*

waver (WAY vuhr) *v.:* move back and forth. *Asleep, the poet's soul wavers like a swimmer underwater.*

spasm (SPAZ uhm) *n.:* sudden, brief experience of intense energy or activity. *Neruda imagines his life as a creative spasm.*

Language Coach
Related Words One effective way to increase your vocabulary is to group related words in a cluster. *Teeming*, *waver*, and *spasm*, for example, are all words of energy and motion. Then, create a single mental picture for one cluster of words. For *teeming*, *waver*, and *spasm*, you could picture a street full of people in action, with fluttering motions as people wave, and sudden bursts of movement in the crowd.

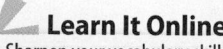 **Learn It Online**
Sharpen your vocabulary skills online with *WordSharp*.

| go.hrw.com | L11-543 | Go |

Link to Today

This Link to Today shows how the poetry of Walt Whitman inspired Pablo Neruda, a twentieth-century poet from South America.

Read with a Purpose
Read to hear the voice of Whitman in another language and time.

Build Background
Whitman and Neruda share a fundamental love of the earth and humanity. In different ways, both poets' lives also reflect a continuing devotion to civic life: Whitman as a journalist and hospital volunteer; Neruda as a professional diplomat. In the following poem, "Plenos poderes" ("Fully Empowered"), Neruda explores the source of his inspiration in a way that recalls Whitman's own explorations of self and writing. In fact, several lines in the poem can be read as allusions to Whitman's *Song of Myself.*

PLENOS PODERES

by **Pablo Neruda**

A puro sol escribo, a plena calle,
a pleno mar, en donde puedo canto,
sólo la noche errante me detiene
pero en su interrupción recojo espacio,
5   recojo sombra para mucho tiempo.

El trigo negro de la noche crece
mientras mis ojos miden la pradera
y así de sol a sol hago las llaves:
busco en la oscuridad las cerraduras
10   y voy abriendo al mar las puertas rotas
hasta llenar armarios con espuma.

Y no me canso de ir y de volver,
no me para la muerte con su piedra,
no me canso de ser y de no ser.

15   A veces me pregunto si de donde
si de padre o de madre o cordillera
heredé los deberes minerales,

los hilos de un océano encendido
y sé que sigo y sigo porque sigo
20   y canto porque canto y porque canto.

No tiene explicación lo que acontece
cuando cierro los ojos y circulo
como entre dos canales submarinos,
uno a morir me lleva en su ramaje
25   y el otro canta para que yo cante.

Así pues de no ser estoy compuesto
y como el mar asalta el arrecife
con cápsulas saladas de blancura
y retrata le piedra con la ola,
30   así lo que en la muerte me rodea
abre en mí la ventana de la vida
y en pleno paroxismo estoy durmiendo.
A plena luz camino por la sombra.

FULLY EMPOWERED

by **Pablo Neruda**   translated by Alastair Reid

I write in the clear sun, in the teeming street,
at full sea-tide, in a place where I can sing;
only the wayward night inhibits me,
but, interrupted by it, I recover space,
5   I gather shadows to last me a long time.

The black crop of the night is growing
while my eyes meanwhile take measure of
      the meadows.
So, from one sun to the next, I forge the keys.
In the darkness, I look for the locks
10   and keep on opening broken doors to the sea,
for it to fill the wardrobes° with its foam.   **Ⓐ**

And I do not weary of going and returning.
Death, in its stone aspect, does not halt me.
I am weary neither of being nor of
      non-being.   **Ⓑ**

15   Sometimes I puzzle over origins—
was it from my father, my mother, or
   the mountains
that I inherited debts to minerality,
the fine threads spreading from a sea on fire?
And I know that I keep on going for the
      going's sake,
20   and I sing because I sing and because I sing.

There is no way of explaining what does happen
when I close my eyes and waver
as between two lost channels under water.
One lifts me in its branches toward my dying,
25   and the other sings in order that I may sing.

And so I am made up of a non-being,
and, as the sea goes battering at a reef
in wave on wave of salty white-tops
and drags back stones in its retreating wash,
30   so what there is in death surrounding me
opens in me a window out to living,
and, in the spasm of being, I go on sleeping.
In the full light of day, I walk in the shade.

---

11. wardrobes: rooms, closets, or pieces of furniture
   for holding clothes.

Ⓐ **Literary Focus** **Metaphor** In this stanza, Neruda compares the foam of the sea to inspiration for his writing. What do you think the "keys" in line 8 unlock for the speaker? What do you think he means by "night" and "darkness"? Explain.

Ⓑ **Reading Focus** **Comparing and Contrasting Poems** Neruda suggests that death does not interfere with his work as a poet. Find an example of a similar theme in Whitman's writing.

Vocabulary **teeming** (TEEM ihng) *v.* used as *adj.:* full of; alive with.
forge (fohrj) *v.:* heat and shape metal.
aspect (AS pehkt) *n.:* the way something looks; appearance.
waver (WAY vuhr) *v.:* move back and forth.
spasm (SPAZ uhm) *n.:* sudden, brief experience of intense energy or activity.

Applying Your Skills

Plenos poderes / Fully Empowered

Respond and Think Critically

Reading Focus

Quick Check

1. What act does the speaker describe in the first stanza? What interrupts this act?

2. What entities does the speaker think may be responsible for his origins?

3. How does exploring death help the speaker better understand the living?

Read with a Purpose

4. Which characteristics of Whitman's poetic voice do you find in Neruda's poem? Explain.

Reading Skills: Comparing and Contrasting Poems

5. Review the chart you used to record lines in Neruda that remind you of lines from Whitman's poems. Then, briefly compare the two poets, focusing on imagery and metaphor. Cite examples from your chart.

✓ Vocabulary Check

Match each Vocabulary word with its definition.

6. waver
7. forge
8. teeming
9. spasm
10. aspect

a. brief, intense activity
b. move back and forth
c. heat and shape metal
d. appearance
e. alive with

Literary Focus

Literary Analysis

11. **Interpret** Explain Neruda's meaning in line 14.

12. **Infer** What might the speaker mean by his "debts to minerality" (line 17)?

13. **Draw Conclusions** Why does the speaker say in line 19 that he will "keep on going for the going's sake"? Support your answer with evidence from subsequent lines in the poem.

14. **Analyze** Analyze the themes in the poem, and explain why you think the poem is titled "Full Powers." What is the source of the speaker's creative power?

Literary Skills: Metaphor

15. **Compare and Contrast** Lines 21–25 compare the act of dreaming to drifting underwater. What do the "two lost channels" that the speaker "waver[s]" between represent?

Literary Skills Review: Repetition

16. **Analyze** The **repetition** of words, sounds, syllables, and other elements in a work acts as a unifying device. Note the use of repetition in line 20. How does the repetition in this line affect the meaning of the poem?

Writing Focus

Think as a Reader/Writer

Use It in Your Writing Look back at the **metaphors** you noted in your *Reader/Writer Notebook* as you read "Fully Empowered." Choose a favorite metaphor. Then, write a few lines explaining your criteria for choosing this metaphor and what it means to you.

 What Do You Think Now

Do you feel that Whitman and Neruda received inspiration from similar sources? Explain, referring to specific details in their work.

SKILLS FOCUS **Literary Skills** Understand and analyze the characteristics of a writer's style. **Reading Skills** Compare and contrast poems. **Writing Skills** Write an essay comparing and contrasting poems; identify and analyze literary elements; employ literary devices for effective writing.

Author Study: Walt Whitman

Writing Focus

Writing a Comparison-Contrast Essay

Walt Whitman's writing reflects the spirit of a growing, expanding United States, as the country recovered from the Civil War and progressed toward the twentieth century. Whitman's poetry echoes the natural rhythms of speech and the concerns of common people. At the same time, he contemplates subjects that have challenged and inspired many great minds over the centuries: war, nature, spirituality, and death.

Prewriting Choose two of Whitman's poems that have a striking similarity. Then, as you study them, look closely for significant differences. Your analysis should include differences in language, imagery, symbolism, and other aspects of Whitman's style.

Use a Venn diagram like the one below: In the middle, shaded area, record specific similarities between the two selections. In the two outer areas of the circles, record specific or unique aspects of the individual selections.

"I understand the large hearts of heroes"

"A Sight in Camp in the Daybreak Gray and Dim"

Consider the following suggestions to help focus your comparison , or choose a topic of your own:

- Focus on catalogs, repetition, and parallelism as features of Whitman's style.
- Analyze the traits of Whitman's free verse that give his poems their distinctive style.
- Focus on theme, symbols, or imagery.

Develop a Thesis Statement Using your notes and observations, develop a thesis that makes an assertion about what your poems have in common and how they contrast.

> *Sample Thesis:* Both poems address the challenge of devastating circumstances, but one employs a celebratory tone while the other has a muted, somber tone.

Drafting Begin with the strongest comparison linking the two poems; develop it in your first body paragraph. Then, depending on your analysis, your next body paragraph will develop an additional similarity or analyze a contrast. Each body paragraph will have two parts—one part for each poem. For example, if your essay compares the two poems listed in the Venn diagram on this page, the first part of each body paragraph will focus on "I understand the large hearts of heroes," while the second part will focus on "A Sight in Camp in the Daybreak Gray and Dim."

Text Evidence Use direct quotations from the selections to support each point you make. If you cannot find evidence in one of the selections, then rethink your analysis. Each paragraph should contain explanation and evidence from both selections.

Revising and Editing Re-read your draft to determine if you have fully supported your thesis with explanation and text evidence. Then, read to find grammar, usage, and mechanics errors. Prepare a final copy that is free of errors. Finally, share your essay with your class. Always seek a wider audience for a polished piece of writing.

What Do **You Think Now** Whitman's poems include a variety of people engaged in a broad range of struggles. What do you think is accomplished or achieved through these struggles?

* **Learn It Online**
Plan your essay with a graphic organizer.

go.hrw.com | L11-547 | Go

Emily Dickinson
(1830–1886)

How does conflict
lead to change?

QuickWrite Think of a time when
you lost something important to you. Write a
paragraph about how this loss changed your life
or changed how you think about life.

One portrait of Emily Dickinson that has persisted is that of an
eccentric recluse, shy and withdrawn, who went about dressed
in white and wrote poems in an upstairs bedroom in her father's
house. More recently, scholars and poets have come to see Dickinson in a new light, as a disciplined poet who chose isolation and
created a private life to fulfill her artistic goals.

Dickinson lived with her family in Amherst, Massachusetts.
Growing up, she took pleasure in her busy household and in the
seasonal games, parties, and outings of a village snowy cold in
winter and brilliantly green in summer. As she grew older, she did
not like being away from home, even for a short time. She attended
boarding school and spent one year at Mount Holyoke Female Seminary. She was an excellent student. Early on, she developed a habit
of questioning and challenging traditional ideas and authorities.

After her return from Mount Holyoke, Dickinson rarely left her
home. There were few important outward events in her life. Biog-
raphers have speculated that disappointment in love may explain
Dickinson's decision to withdraw from all social life except that
involving her immediate family.

The Recluse of Amherst

Emily Dickinson quietly and abruptly withdrew into a private life.
Her only activities were household tasks and writing poems that
she either kept to herself or sent as valentines, birthday greetings,
or notes to accompany gifts of a cherry pie or a batch of cookies.

In 1862, Dickinson sent a few poems to Thomas Wentworth Higginson. An editor of *The Atlantic Monthly*, Higginson encouraged the

A Dickinson Time Line

1830 Emily Dickinson is born
in Amherst, Massachusetts

1848 Dickinson spends
a year at Mount Holyoke
Female Seminary

1830　　**1840**　　**1850**

1855 Dickinson visits Philadelphia
and Washington, meeting a married
clergyman with whom, some think,
she falls in love

Amherst College Archives and Special Collections

E. Dickinson

work of younger poets. Higginson served as a kindly, distant "teacher" and "mentor." Eventually, Dickinson gave up hope of ever finding a wider audience than her few friends and relatives.

During her lifetime, Emily Dickinson published no more than a handful of her typically brief poems. She seemed to lack all concern for an audience, even going so far as to instruct her family to destroy any poems she might leave behind after her death. Still, she saw to it that bundles of handwritten poems were carefully wrapped and put away in places where, after her death, friendly, appreciative, and finally astonished eyes would find them. The poems were assembled and edited by different family members and friends; they were then published in installments so frequent that readers began to wonder when they would ever end.

Then, in 1955, a scholar named Thomas H. Johnson published a collection called *The Poems of Emily Dickinson*. Johnson, unlike Dickinson's earlier editors, attempted to remain faithful to Dickinson's original manuscripts.

A Legacy of Genius

When Emily Dickinson died at fifty-five, hardly anyone knew that the unusual, shy woman in their midst was a poet whose sharp, delicate voice would echo for generations to come. The self-imposed restrictions of Dickinson's life were more than matched by her ability to perceive the universal in the particular and the particular in the universal. These perceptions helped her create metaphors that embraced experiences far beyond the limited compass of Amherst village life. Some seventy years after her death, when the quarrels among her relatives who had inherited her manuscripts had died down and all her poems were finally published, she was recognized as one of the greatest poets America, and perhaps the world, had produced.

Think About the Writer

What one question would you ask Dickinson about her mysterious life?

Key Elements of Dickinson's Writing

- Strong images and metaphors enliven her work.
- Explorations of abstract concepts, such as truth and the soul, reveal profound insights.
- Personified concepts, like death and nature, add personality to the work.
- Unusual points of view provide a unique voice.
- Reflections on tiny details reveal great life in the smallest of things.
- Unconventional use of rhyme and punctuation creates subtle effects.

1861 Civil War begins

1864 Dickinson is treated for eye disease in Boston

1869 Dickinson no longer leaves her house in Amherst

Dickinson Homestead in Massachusetts.

1860

1870

1880

1890

1862 Dickinson begins correspondence with Thomas Wentworth Higginson

1870 Higginson is one of the few visitors to Amherst whom Dickinson meets in person

1886 Emily Dickinson dies

1890 Dickinson's *Poems* published by Higginson and Mabel Loomis Todd

Preparing to Read

SKILLS FOCUS Literary Skills Understand exact rhyme and slant rhyme. **Reading Skills** Analyze poem structure.

The Soul selects her own Society / This is my letter to the World

Reader/Writer
Notebook

Use your **RWN** to complete the activities for these selections.

Literary Focus

Slant Rhyme and Exact Rhyme **Rhyme** enhances a poem's musical quality and creates order by connecting words and ideas. **Exact rhyme** occurs when the accented syllables and all following syllables of two or more words share identical sounds (*mixture/fixture*). **Slant rhyme** is a close, but not exact, rhyming sound (*society/majority* or *nerve/love*).

Literary Perspectives Apply the literary perspective described on page 551 as you read these poems.

Reading Focus

Analyzing Poem Structure The structure of a poem, like the frame of a house, holds the poem together. Analyzing a poem's **rhyme scheme**— the pattern of rhymes—is a good way to begin examining its structure. As you read, notice how Dickinson uses both slant and exact rhymes.

Into Action For each poem, use a chart like the one below to record each pair of rhyming words you find, noting the stanza and lines in which they appear. In the third column, state whether the rhyme is exact or slant. After you finish reading, you will analyze the effects of the rhymes.

Stanza/Line	Rhyming Words	Slant or Exact Rhyme?
stanza 1, lines 1 and 3	Society/Majority	slant

Writing Focus

Think as a Reader/Writer

Find It in Your Reading The following poems show Dickinson's unusual and clever use of **rhyme.** Poets use rhyme as a way to create connections between the various parts of a poem. In your *Reader/Writer Notebook,* note the connections you find between the rhymed words.

Language Coach

Multiple-Meaning Words The word *soul* has many meanings. In the following poem, it refers to the deep, fundamental aspect of who a person is, a spiritual aspect that isn't influenced by appearance or age, for instance. Look up *soul* in a dictionary. Then, explain how the word is used in the following sentences:

He is a kind *soul*.
We went to the *soul* food restaurant.
She is the *soul* of the movement.
Their *souls* departed the earth.

Learn It Online
Explore Emily Dickinson's life further through the Writers' Lives site.

go.hrw.com L11-550 **Go**

POEM

The Soul selects her own Society

by **Emily Dickinson**

Read with a Purpose
Read to discover how the speaker's "soul" chooses her own company.

Build Background
In this poem, Dickinson explores the mysterious instinct that leads each one of us to prefer certain things and cherish certain people above all others. In Dickinson's view this instinct has less to do with the discriminations of the mind than with the yearnings of that spiritual part of us that some call the soul.

The Soul selects her own Society—
Then—shuts the Door—
To her divine Majority—
Present no more— **A**

5 Unmoved—she notes the Chariots—pausing—
At her low Gate—
Unmoved—an Emperor be kneeling
Upon her Mat—

I've known her—from an ample nation—
10 Choose One—
Then—close the Valves of her attention—
Like Stone— **B**

A **Literary Focus** Slant and Exact Rhyme Where do exact rhyme and slant rhyme occur in this stanza? What is the effect of mixing these two types of rhyme in the same stanza?

B **Literary Perspectives** Analyzing Style Why does Dickinson leave the poem "unfinished," using a dash to suggest a pause or break in the speaker's thoughts?

Literary Perspectives

Analyzing Style A writer's distinctive way of using language is his or her **style.** Emily Dickinson's style of writing is so distinct that some aspects of it are easily recognizable even by simply glancing at her poems. (For instance, consider the length of her poems and her use of punctuation and capitalization.) As you study her poems closely, however, pay attention to her word choice and use of rhyme and imagery. Before you begin reading, write down the elements of style that are mentioned in this paragraph and in the Key Elements listed on page 549. As you read, jot down notes and examples of Dickinson's use of each element of style.

As you read, be sure to notice the questions in the text, which will guide you in using this perspective.

This is my letter to the World

by **Emily Dickinson**

Memories (1885 or 1886) by William M. Chase. Oil on canvas, frame: 50 ¼" × 45 ⁵/₈". ©Munson-Williams-Proctor Institute Museum of Art, Utica, New York, 57.305.

Read with a Purpose
Read to discover the speaker's personal message to readers who don't know her.

Build Background
Emily Dickinson did not write her poetry for money or recognition. In "This is my letter to the World," Dickinson seems to be able to see into the future and know that her work would one day be held by "Hands" she could not see.

This is my letter to the World
That never wrote to Me—
The simple News that Nature told—
With tender Majesty

5   Her Message is committed
To Hands I cannot see—
for love of Her—Sweet—countrymen—
Judge tenderly—of Me   **A** **B**

A **Literary Perspectives** **Analyzing Style** What does the letter symbolize in line 1? Does the image of writing a letter have the same significance in line 2?

B **Reading Focus** **Analyzing Poem Structure** Dickinson splits the second stanza into two thoughts. Where does the split occur? What are the two thoughts the speaker presents? How is the second thought connected to the first?

Applying Your Skills

**The Soul selects her own Society /
This is my letter to the World**

Respond and Think Critically

Reading Focus

Quick Check

1. In "The Soul selects her own Society," how does the soul shut out those she does not choose?

2. In "This is my letter to the World," where does the speaker get her "News" (line 3)?

Read with a Purpose

3. What contradictory attitude toward the "World" is reflected in these two poems?

Reading Skills: Analyzing Poem Structure

4. Add a fourth column to your chart, and briefly note the effect of each pair of rhyming words on the reader. For instance, are they pleasing to the ear? Do they emphasize an idea?

Stanza/Line"	Rhyming Words	Slant or Exact Rhyme?	Rhyme's Effects
stanza 1, lines 1 and 3	Society/ Majority	slant	The rhyme emphasizes groups that the speaker distrusts.

Literary Focus

Literary Analysis

5. **Infer** In "The Soul selects her own Society," do you think the phrase "Valves of her attention" is derived from organic things (valves of the heart) or mechanical ones (valves of a faucet)? Why?

6. **Interpret** In "The Soul selects her own Society," what emotional effect does the word *stone* evoke? How is this effect further emphasized by the placement of *stone* in the poem?

7. **Extend** How might a sense of immortality be related to Dickinson's speaking of poetry as a "letter to the World"?

8. **Analyze** How do these poems reflect Dickinson's concerns with faith and immortality?

9. **Literary Perspectives** Review your notes about Dickinson's style, and use them to explain how Dickinson's use of language supports the messages of her poems and affects the reader.

Literary Skills: Slant Rhyme and Exact Rhyme

10. **Analyze** Write the rhyme scheme of each poem. Which lines rhyme exactly, and which use slant rhyme? Why do you think Dickinson includes slant rhyme in her poems? Explain.

Literary Skills Review: Symbol

11. **Interpret** In poetry, a **symbol** functions literally in the text while also representing a larger idea. Find two symbols in "The Soul selects her own Society," and explain what each represents.

Writing Focus

Think as a Reader/Writer

Use It in Your Writing Write a text message to the world, condensing what you want to say into a few concise lines, as Dickinson does in her "letter to the World." Use rhyme and slant rhyme at least once each in your text message. Then, write a short paragraph reflecting on the differences between your text message and Dickinson's poems on pages 551 and 552.

What Do **You Think Now** How might Dickinson's choices or conflicts about interacting with society have added tension to her poems?

The Soul selects her own Society /
This is my letter to the World

Grammar Link

Appositives

A noun or pronoun placed beside another noun or pronoun to identify or describe it is called an **appositive.**
An **appositive phrase** consists of an appositive and its modifiers.

> Emily Dickinson spent most of her life in one small village, *Amherst.*
> During her life, few knew about her poems, *some of the best written in America.*

An **essential** or **restrictive appositive** adds information that makes the sentence complete and clear. Because essential appositives are part of the sentence's basic meaning, they are not set off by commas.

> The poem seems to describe her isolation.
> The poem *"The Soul selects her own Society"* seems to describe her isolation.

A **nonessential** or **nonrestrictive appositive** is not essential to a sentence's meaning. These appositives are set off by commas because they interrupt sentences that would be clear and complete without them.

> Dickinson published few poems in her lifetime.
> Dickinson, *an accomplished poet,* published few poems in her lifetime.

Your Turn

Rewrite the following sentences, adding the italicized appositives. Use commas for nonessential appositives.

1. The great poet expresses contradictory emotions. *Emily Dickinson*

2. "The Soul selects her own Society" tells how the soul "shuts the Door." *one of her best-known poems*

3. This poem's speaker rejects society. *a recluse*

4. The book's editor restored Dickinson's original texts. *Thomas H. Johnson*

CHOICES

As you respond to the Choices, use these **Academic Vocabulary** words as appropriate: advocate, criteria, fundamental, principle, subsequent.

REVIEW

Write a Letter

Partner Work Many readers believe that "This is my letter to the World" is Emily Dickinson's appeal to the world from which she has withdrawn. What would this poem sound like as an actual letter? With a partner, rewrite the poem in the form of a letter, complete with salutation and valediction (closing). Compare your interpretation with those of your classmates.

CONNECT

State an Opinion

Timed └Writing In "The Soul selects her own Society," what advantages and disadvantages may there be in a selection as strict as this soul makes? What are the possible effects of allowing the soul's principles to determine one's friends? Explain your opinion in an essay, citing examples from the poem.

EXTEND

Produce a Play

Group Activity The themes of "The Soul selects her own Society" can apply to many social situations. Everyone can relate to feelings of acceptance and rejection. Think about ways for people to accept and associate with others who are different from them. Form a group, and write two or three short scenes for a play that touches on themes of social acceptance and rejection. Have the members of the group perform the play for the class.

Preparing to Read

Tell all the Truth but tell it slant

Reader/Writer Notebook

Use your **RWN** to complete the activities for this selection.

Literary Focus

Epigram An **epigram** is a short, clever poem or statement ending with a witty or ingenious twist in thought. The word *epigram* comes from a term meaning "inscription." In classical times, lines of great eloquence were frequently used as inscriptions on monuments or tombs. The ancient Greeks used the term to refer to any brief poem. The epigram became a popular literary form: In the hands of some Roman poets, the epigram even became a satirical weapon.

Epigrams often appear in fables, where they sum up the moral of the story. Many epigrams end in a satirical turn of thought. This "turn of thought" expresses something unexpected and gives a final twist to the meaning of the epigram. As you read "Tell all the Truth but tell it slant," determine the focus of the epigram and look for the "turn" or declaration at the end of the poem.

Language Coach

Definitions In "Tell all the Truth but tell it slant," Dickinson draws connections between truth and light. With a partner, skim the poem and underline words that are related to the concept of light. Then, look them up in a dictionary. (Keep in mind that even if you already know the words, it is helpful to read through their definitions to remind yourself of different aspects of meaning that the words can have.) Finally, discuss any connections you can make between the words you chose and the concept of truth.

Writing Focus

Think as a Reader/Writer

Find It in Your Reading Because epigrams are usually limited to a handful of lines, each word has <u>fundamental</u> importance. The poem's overall effect can be heavily influenced by a few key words. In your *Reader/Writer Notebook*, record words in the poem that have the most impact and note your reaction to these words. Use a graphic organizer like the one below to organize your thoughts.

key word <u>Circuit</u>	definition "indirect path"
my associations I think of the saying "beat around the bush."	my feelings seems both sneaky and clever

Learn It Online
Emily Dickinson's life is now very public. Find out more with these Internet links.

go.hrw.com   L11-555   **Go**

TELL ALL THE TRUTH BUT TELL IT SLANT

by **Emily Dickinson**

Drops of Rain (1903) by Clarence H. White (1871–1925). From *Camerawork*. National Gallery of Australia, Canberra.

Read with a Purpose Read to discover what it means to "Tell all the Truth but tell it slant."

Tell all the Truth but tell it slant—
Success in Circuit° lies
Too bright for our infirm Delight
The Truth's superb surprise
As Lightning to the Children eased
With explanation kind
The Truth must dazzle gradually
Or every man be blind— **A** **B**

2. **circuit:** indirect path.

A **Literary Focus** Epigram What is Dickinson making a plea for in this poem? Explain your response.

B **Literary Focus** Epigram What comparison is being made in lines 7–8? How do the lines give a final twist to the poem's meaning?

Preparing to Read

Success is counted sweetest

Reader/Writer
Notebook
Use your **RWN** to complete the activities for this selection.

Literary Focus

Rhythm In poetry, **rhythm** is the rise and fall of the voice, produced by the alternation of stressed and unstressed syllables. **Meter** is a regular pattern of stressed and unstressed syllables in a poem. For the most part, "Success is counted sweetest" uses the **iamb**—one unstressed syllable followed by one stressed syllable—as its basic metrical unit.

⌣ / ⌣ / ⌣ / ⌣
Success is counted sweetest

Additionally, writers create rhythm by using **rhyme,** types of **repetition,** variations in line length, and pauses.

Reading Focus

Annotating a Poem To **annotate a poem,** make notes about it as you read. For example, write down unfamiliar words and questions or comments about challenging lines. Read the footnotes to clarify meaning.

Into Action As you read, use a chart to record your annotations. In the first column, write lines from the poem that require close attention. In the second column, write comments, questions, or explanations about each. In the third column, note the techniques Dickinson uses to create rhythm.

Line(s)	Annotations	Techniques That Create Rhythm
"Success is counted sweetest / By those who ne'er succeed."	I wonder why Dickinson says this? I think successful people probably value their successes.	The poet uses "ne'er"— short for "never"— which does seem to fit the rhythm of the lines better.

Writing Focus

Think as a Reader/Writer
Find It in Your Reading In this poem, Dickinson uses rhyme and **alliteration** to create **rhythm.** In your *Reader/Writer Notebook,* record the rhyme scheme of each stanza and any examples of alliteration.

Language Coach

Multiple-Meaning Words The word *count* has a mathematical meaning, of course ("count from one to ten," for instance). It can also mean "to consider" or "to have value." Look at the following uses of *count*, and explain each meaning:

That doesn't *count.*
Count me in.

What might "Success is counted sweetest" mean?

Learn It Online
Listen to the rhythm of this poem through the audio recording online.

go.hrw.com   L11-557   **Go**

SUCCESS IS COUNTED SWEETEST

by **Emily Dickinson**

Read with a Purpose
Read to discover what Dickinson thinks about success.

Build Background
The poem "Success is counted sweetest" addresses some of the questions that readers might have for the poet today: How did she feel about her lack of success as a published poet during her life? Did she write for anyone other than herself and her family? In 1862, Dickinson sent this poem along with three others to Thomas Wentworth Higginson, a literary critic and editor for *The Atlantic Monthly*, seeking advice about her poems. It is one of several poems that show Dickinson's feelings about success and failure.

Success is counted sweetest
By those who ne'er succeed.
To comprehend a nectar°
Requires sorest° need. Ⓐ

5 Not one of all the purple Host°
Who took the Flag today
Can tell the definition
So clear of Victory

As he defeated—dying—
10 On whose forbidden ear
The distant strains of triumph
Burst agonized and clear! Ⓑ

3. nectar: name for the drink of the Greek and Roman gods; also, a term applied to any delicious beverage.
4. sorest: deepest; most extreme.
5. purple Host: royal army.

Ⓐ **Literary Focus** **Rhythm** What techniques does the poet use to create rhythm in this stanza? How does the rhyme scheme also help set the rhythm?

Ⓑ **Reading Focus** **Annotating a Poem** Use the information in the footnotes to rewrite stanza 1 as a single sentence in your own words. Now, rewrite your sentence, adding the ideas stated in stanza 3. How has Dickinson connected these two stanzas?

Applying Your Skills

Tell all the Truth but tell it slant /
Success is counted sweetest

Respond and Think Critically

Reading Focus

Quick Check

1. In "Tell all the Truth but tell it slant," what reasons does the speaker give for telling the truth "slant"?

2. In the beginning of "Success is counted sweetest," to what does the speaker compare the sweetness of success?

3. At the end of "Success is counted sweetest," who hears "the distant strains of triumph"?

Read with a Purpose

4. What does it mean to tell the truth slant? Is a truth told slant the same as a lie? Explain.

5. Do you agree with the view of success in "Success is counted sweetest"? Explain your criteria for defining success.

Reading Skills: Annotating a Poem

6. Review the annotations you wrote while reading "Success is counted sweetest," and use them to write a short explanation of the poem's message and how its rhythm affects its meaning.

Literary Focus

Literary Analysis

7. **Interpret** In "Tell the Truth but tell it slant," lines 5 and 6 provide an example to illustrate the poet's point about truth. Dickinson, who often compresses meaning, omits several words in these lines. How would you rephrase the lines to make a full sentence?

8. **Analyze** In "Success is counted sweetest," whose ear is mentioned in line 10? Why is the ear "forbidden"?

9. **Extend** In what way does the message of "Tell all the Truth but tell it slant" reflect the way Dickinson's poetry works?

10. **Extend** Explain how the image in the last stanza of "Success is counted sweetest" could refer to other situations in life.

Literary Skills: Epigram / Rhythm

11. **Evaluate** In epigrams, the "turn" often ends a poem in an unexpected way. In "Tell all the Truth but tell it slant," how is the last line surprising?

12. **Evaluate** How does the rhythm of "Success is counted sweetest" help you pay attention to what the poet is saying?

Literary Skills Review: Aphorism

13. **Extend** An **aphorism** is a brief, cleverly written statement that makes a wise observation about life. What aphorisms could you create from these poems?

Writing Focus

Think as a Reader/Writer

Use It in Your Writing Review the notes you took about Dickinson's word choice and rhyming techniques. Then, choose an abstract concept, such as truth, success, honor, or kindness. Write down your ideas for an epigram that focuses on this concept. List rhyming words you would include and alliteration you might use. Think about what "turn" you would include to deepen the epigram's meaning.

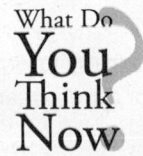
What Do You Think Now

How might speaking the truth cause conflict? In your opinion, what kinds of truths might need to be revealed "slant" (indirectly) or gradually?

Preparing to Read

Because I could not stop for Death

Reader/Writer
Notebook
Use your **RWN** to complete the activities for this selection.

Literary Focus

Irony In general, **irony** is a discrepancy between appearances and reality. The success of "Because I could not stop for Death" depends, fundamentally, on irony, on gradual comprehension, and on a lighthearted, witty **tone** that contrasts with the subject of the poem. As you read, pay careful attention to details that create an ironic twist.

Reading Focus

Summarizing a Text A **summary** presents the general idea of a passage or a complete work in brief form. To understand challenging literature, summarize the main events or ideas as you work through the text. In this poem Dickinson challenges the reader by using time in an unusual way.

Into Action Use a chart to summarize the events in each stanza and determine when the events occur. Then, note any irony in the stanza.

Stanza	Summary of the Stanza	When the Events Take Place	Irony
1	Death graciously stops the carriage to pick up the speaker, who seems in a hurry.	at the end of the speaker's life	Instead of being presented as a terrifying figure, Death is treated as a polite and gracious carriage driver.

Vocabulary

immortality (ihm awr TAL uh tee) *n.:* unending existence. *The speaker says that the carriage held Death and Immortality in addition to herself.*

civility (suh VIHL uh tee) *n.:* courteous or polite behavior. *According to the speaker, death behaves with great civility.*

surmised (suhr MYZD) *v.:* guessed or inferred with little supporting evidence. *The speaker surmised from the clues on her journey that she, like all humans, was traveling toward death.*

Language Coach

Frequently Misused Words Words that sound identical or almost the same can often confuse readers or writers. Consider the words *immortality* and *immorality*. *Immortality* means "unending existence." *Immorality* has quite a different meaning: "wicked, impure, or unprincipled character."

Writing Focus

Think as a Reader/Writer

Find It in Your Reading As you read, find examples of Dickinson's use of **irony**. In your *Reader/Writer Notebook,* note the examples of irony and infer what Dickinson was trying to achieve.

TechFocus Dickinson's poems are open to many interpretations. Consider how you might interpret this poem for others in an entry for a blog devoted to poetry.

Learn It Online
Step into this poem through the video introduction online.

 go.hrw.com | L11-560 | Go

Because I could not stop for Death

by Emily Dickinson

Read with a Purpose
Read to discover where the speaker is headed when she takes a carriage ride one day.

Build Background
Like many other metaphors in Dickinson's poetry, the one in this poem "tames" or "domesticates" the most awesome and <u>fundamental</u> of human experiences—death. The literal elements of the metaphor are simple: Dying is compared to an unexpected ride in a horse-drawn carriage. The poem presents readers with a broad range of possibilities and meanings.

Because I could not stop for Death—
He kindly stopped for me—
The Carriage held but just Ourselves—
And Immortality.

5   We slowly drove—He knew no haste
And I had put away
My labor and my leisure too,
For His Civility— **A**

A **Literary Focus** Irony What is ironic about the description of Death's personality? What is the emotional effect of this irony?

Vocabulary **immortality** (ihm awr TAL uh tee) *n.*: unending existence.
civility (suh VIHL uh tee) *n.*: courteous or polite behavior.

We passed the School, where Children strove
10   At Recess—in the Ring—
We passed the Fields of Gazing Grain—
We passed the Setting Sun—

Or rather—He passed Us—
The Dews drew quivering and chill—
15   For only Gossamer,° my Gown—
My Tippet—only Tulle°—

We paused before a House that seemed
A Swelling of the Ground—
The Roof was scarcely visible—
20   The Cornice°—in the Ground—   **B**

Since then—'tis Centuries—and yet
Feels shorter than the Day
I first surmised the Horses' Heads
Were toward Eternity—

15. gossamer: thin, soft material.
16. tippet . . . tulle: shawl made of fine netting.

20. cornice: molding at the top of a building.

B **Reading Focus** **Summarizing a Text** Both literally and symbolically, at what place has the speaker arrived in this stanza? What important truth about death does this poem share? Explain.

Vocabulary **surmised** (suhr MYZD) *v.*: guessed or inferred with little supporting evidence.

MUSIC LINK

American Geniuses

Brooklyn native Aaron Copland (1900–1990) is recognized as one of the greatest composers of the twentieth century. Sometimes called the "dean of American music," Copland infused his compositions with a distinctly American sound. In his song cycle *Twelve Poems of Emily Dickinson,* Copland used the poet's words as song lyrics. This poem, "Because I could not stop for Death," is included in Copland's cycle as a song titled "The Chariot" (the poem's title in earlier editions of Dickinson's poems).

Ask Yourself
What do Dickinson's poems have in common with song lyrics? What qualities in Dickinson's poems help them work well as songs? Why do you think a composer like Copland would be drawn to Dickinson for inspiration?

Preparing to Read

Much Madness is divinest Sense

Reader/Writer
Notebook

Use your **RWN** to complete the activities for this selection.

Literary Focus

Paradox A **paradox** is a statement that appears to be self-contradictory but actually reveals a kind of truth. In Shakespeare's *Romeo and Juliet*, for example, when Juliet says "Parting is such sweet sorrow," she uses a paradox: She is sad to be leaving Romeo, but kissing him goodbye is very sweet. The very title of this Dickinson poem, "Much Madness is divinest Sense," states an interesting paradox.

Reading Focus

Paraphrasing Dickinson's creative use of language and elements such as paradox can present challenges to the reader. If some of the lines in the poem puzzle you, pause to **paraphrase** them, or restate the lines in your own words. Look up any unfamiliar words in order to clarify meaning. Paraphrasing allows you to deepen your understanding of the poem.

Into Action As you read the poem, use a chart like the one below to record puzzling lines. In the second column, paraphrase the lines in your own words. In the third column, explain any paradox the lines contain.

Puzzling Lines	Paraphrase	Explanation of Paradox
"Much Madness is divinest Sense"	What seems insane is often inspired wisdom.	A person who appears mad may actually have more sense than someone who appears sane.

Writing Focus

Think as a Reader/Writer

Find It in Your Reading This poem is built on **paradoxes**. In your *Reader/Writer Notebook*, record each example you find of a paradox and note how the statement is self-contradictory.

TechFocus Readers may view the ideas in this poem in different ways. Consider what view or interpretation of this poem you might share with others in an entry for a blog devoted to poetry.

Vocabulary

discerning (dih SUR nihng) *v.*: used as *adj.*: sharp or shrewd in understanding. *The speaker says that a discerning eye will understand the paradox that "much madness is divinest sense."*

assent (uh SEHNT) *v.*: agree or express approval. *If you assent to the wishes of the majority, then you are sane.*

demur (dih MUR) *v.*: object or express disagreement. *If you demur and refuse to go along with the wishes of the majority, then you are mad.*

Language Coach

Frequently Misused Words You may find that **homophones,** words that have different meanings or spellings but are pronounced the same, are easy to misuse. For example, *assent* and *ascent* are pronounced the same. *Assent,* however, means "agree or express approval," whereas *ascent* can mean "movement upward," "rise in social standing," or "elevation."

Learn It Online
Get to know the Vocabulary words inside and out through Word Watch.

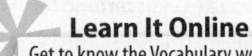

Much Madness is divinest Sense

by **Emily Dickinson**

Fall Begins (1976) by Alma Woodsey Thomas.

Read with a Purpose

Read to discover how this poem challenges our assumptions about madness and individuality.

Build Background

<u>Subsequent</u> to her death, Dickinson was often portrayed as an eccentric recluse. In fact, Dickinson lived as many other great poets (and quite a few "ordinary" people) have lived—deliberately choosing solitude for contemplation, reading, and writing. In "Much Madness is divinest Sense," the speaker presents a unique perspective on the topic of choosing your own path. This poem could be seen as Dickinson's response to those who might question her choice of solitude.

Much Madness is divinest Sense— **Ⓐ**
To a discerning Eye—
Much Sense—the starkest Madness—
'Tis the Majority
In this, as All, prevail—
Assent—and you are sane—
Demur—you're straightway dangerous—
And handled with a Chain— **Ⓑ**

Ⓐ Literary Focus Paradox How does the word *divinest* help create the contradiction in this line?

Ⓑ Reading Focus Paraphrasing Paraphrase the last three lines of the poem. How does Dickinson say that sanity is determined? Do you agree or disagree with her judgment? Explain your response.

Vocabulary discerning (dih SUR nihng) *v.:* used as *adj.:* sharp or shrewd in understanding.
assent (uh SEHNT) *v.:* agree or express approval.
demur (dih MUR) *v.:* object or express disagreement.

Applying Your Skills

Because I could not stop for Death /
Much Madness is divinest Sense

Respond and Think Critically

Reading Focus

Quick Check

1. In "Because I could not stop for Death," who is driving the carriage? Who (or what) else rides with the speaker?

2. Why is the speaker feeling a chill in the fourth stanza of "Because I could not stop for Death"?

3. According to the speaker in "Much Madness is divinest Sense," what are the main criteria for "madness" and "sense"?

Read with a Purpose

4. In "Because I could not stop for Death," where is the speaker headed? Were you surprised to discover the destination? Explain.

5. How does "Much Madness is divinest Sense" challenge our assumptions about madness?

Reading Skills: Summarizing a Text / Paraphrasing

6. Review your summaries and paraphrases for the two poems you read. Then, write a few sentences about Dickinson's use of irony and paradox to convey her message in each poem.

Literary Focus

Literary Analysis

7. **Interpret** What is significant about the sun passing the carriage in the fourth stanza of "Because I could not stop for Death"? How does the temperature now change?

8. **Analyze** Dickinson liked to use dashes—a mark of punctuation her early editors removed. How do dashes help emphasize certain ideas in "Much Madness is divinest Sense"?

9. **Interpret** How do these poems reflect Dickinson's ideas on immortality and her place in the world?

Literary Skills: Irony / Paradox

10. **Evaluate** In the second stanza of "Because I could not stop for Death," *civility* means "politeness; good manners." How does this kind of behavior on the part of both Death and the speaker extend the irony of the first stanza?

11. **Analyze** The paradoxes in "Much Madness is divinest Sense" are intended to reveal an unexpected truth about madness. What do you think that truth is?

Literary Skills Review: Personification

12. **Analyze** A figure of speech in which an object, idea, quality, or animal is given human qualities is **personification.** How is death personified in "Because I could not stop for Death"?

Writing Focus

Think as a Reader/Writer

Use It in Your Writing Irony and paradox are subtly different literary elements. **Irony** is based on appearances or expectations differing from reality. **Paradox** is based on a self-contradictory statement. Think of an aspect of life that everyone encounters that is either ironic or paradoxical. Then, explain the irony or paradox in a few sentences.

What Do **You Think Now** How are the ideas expressed in Dickinson's poems in conflict with conventional thinking? Explain.

**Because I could not stop for Death /
Much Madness is divinest Sense**

Vocabulary Development

✓ Vocabulary Check

Match each Vocabulary word with its synonym.

1. immortality		**a.** protest	
2. civility		**b.** observant	
3. surmised		**c.** comply	
4. discerning		**d.** endlessness	
5. assent		**e.** respect	
6. demur		**f.** assumed	

Vocabulary Skills: Affixes

Affixes are word parts that are added to the beginning or the end of a base word or root. A **prefix** is added to the beginning of a base word or root. A prefix such as *mis–, over–,* and *un–* always changes the meaning of the base word. A **suffix** is added to the end of a base word or root. **Inflectional suffixes,** like *–ed* and *–ing,* usually just change the tense, the person, or the number of a word (generally a verb). **Derivational suffixes,** like those listed in the chart below, change the meaning of a root or base word.

Suffix	Meanings	Example
–ity	state of; condition of	confidentiality
–ous	full of	pompous, tedious
–ness	quality or state of being	oddness, sickness

You can use derivational suffixes to help you decipher the meaning of unfamiliar words. By identifying the suffix and the root word, you can determine how the suffix changes the word's meaning. For example, in "Because I could not stop for Death," it might be difficult to determine the meaning of *civility* just by relying on the context clues in the poem. However, you can infer its meaning by identifying the root word, *civil,* and the suffix, *–ity,* as demonstrated in the following chart.

Root Word, Meaning	Suffix, Meaning	Full Word, Meaning
civil polite	*–ity* state of	*civility* polite behavior

Your Turn

Use the preceding chart as a model to create your own suffix-analysis chart for the following words from Dickinson's poems. Use a dictionary for help.

1. imprudent	**4.** dangerous
2. eternity	**5.** majority
3. starkest	

Language Coach

Frequently Misused Words Earlier you looked at the word pairs *immortality/immorality* and *assent/ascent.* Now, study the word pairs below. In your *Reader/Writer Notebook,* list the definitions of each pair's words. Then, circle the parts of the words that have different letters and note their spellings.

1. adverse/averse
2. eminent/imminent
3. formally/formerly
4. incite/insight

Academic Vocabulary

Talk About

In a small group, discuss the following question: In the decades <u>subsequent</u> to Dickinson's death, in what <u>fundamental</u> ways have the <u>criteria</u> for good poetry evolved? Explain.

Grammar Link

Adverb Clauses

A **clause** is a group of words that contains a verb and its subject. **Independent clauses** express complete thoughts and can stand alone as sentences. **Subordinate clauses** do not express complete thoughts and are not sentences.

> Emily Dickinson was considered eccentric. (independent)
> because she led a life of solitude (subordinate)

An **adverb clause** is a subordinate clause that acts as an adverb. Adverb clauses modify verbs, adjectives, or adverbs by telling *how, when, where, why, to what extent,* or *under what condition.*

> Dickinson wrote her poetry **while she lived a quiet life in Amherst, Massachusetts.**
> She might have become famous **if her work had been widely published during her life.**

Adverb clauses begin with **subordinating conjunctions,** such as *after, although, as, as if, because, before, if, in order that, once, since, though, unless, when,* and *where.* These words or groups of words show the relationship between the clause and the word it modifies.

Your Turn

Underline the adverb clauses in the sentences below. Identify the subordinating conjunctions and the words being modified.

1. As the poem begins, the speaker joins Death for a carriage ride.
2. Death is more casual than one might expect.
3. The speaker seems pleased even though she has died.

Writing Application Add adverb clauses to a piece of your own writing. First, underline all of the adverbs. Then, replace at least three adverbs with adverb clauses.

CHOICES

As you respond to the Choices, use these **Academic Vocabulary** words as appropriate: <u>advocate</u>, <u>criteria</u>, <u>fundamental</u>, <u>principle</u>, <u>subsequent</u>.

REVIEW

Analyze Imagery

Timed Writing In "Because I could not stop for Death," Emily Dickinson paints a vibrant picture of a carriage ride with Death. Review the poem, identifying its most powerful images and words. Use the following <u>criteria</u>: the pictures and emotions the images evoke for the reader; the connotations and associations of Dickinson's words. Explain your ideas in a short essay.

CONNECT

Research Critical Comments

Research Activity One of the most famous American poets, Emily Dickinson has invited praise as well as criticism. Using library or online resources, find two different critiques of "Because I could not stop for Death" or "Much Madness is divinest Sense." Discuss the following topics: How do the critiques differ? With which critique do you agree?

EXTEND

Post Your Point of View

TechFocus Both of these poems are open to varied interpretations, and they can generate lively discussion among readers. Write a blog entry that explains your interpretation of one of the poems. Either post the entry on a poetry blog and ask your classmates to respond online, or present your blog entry to the class and lead a class discussion about the poem.

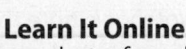

Learn It Online
Learn more about prefixes and suffixes online with *WordSharp.*

go.hrw.com | L11-567 | **Go**

I heard a Fly buzz—when I died /
My life closed twice before its close

Reader/Writer
Notebook
Use your **RWN** to complete the activities for these selections.

Literary Focus

Mood The **mood** of a literary work is the overall feeling or emotion that it arouses. A poem, for example, might make a reader feel sad or amused or frightened. Poems can create more than one feeling, but often they have one dominant mood. Mood is generally identified with one or two adjectives: *somber, hopeful.* Every element of an author's **style**—including rhythm, word choice, and sound effects—contributes to the mood. In the poem "I heard a Fly buzz—when I died," Dickinson's choice of the words *died* and *Stillness* in the first stanza helps establish the mood early on. As you read the following poems, look for other words and images that Dickinson uses to create the mood in each poem.

Into Action Use a graphic organizer like the one below to note words and images that work together to establish each poem's mood.

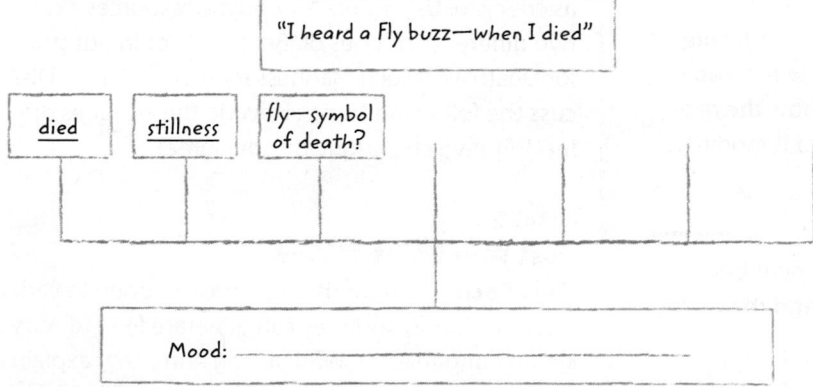

Language Coach

Word Definitions Before you read "I heard a Fly buzz—when I died," brainstorm possible adjectives that might describe the tone of a poem about death (perhaps *scary, peaceful,* or *tragic*). Use a thesaurus to help you list about ten words. Then, read the poem. Afterward, with a partner, discuss the adjectives you listed. Refer to a dictionary as needed to make sure you understand the full meaning of each adjective. Which ones actually describe the tone of Dickinson's poem? Which adjectives can you eliminate from your list? Select your top two adjectives from your lists, and share them with the class.

Writing Focus

Think as a Reader/Writer

Find It in Your Reading The feelings you experience as you read can guide you in determining the overall **mood** of a work of literature. In your *Reader/Writer Notebook,* note the different feelings evoked as you read each poem and record any words or images that contribute to the mood. Develop a reader's <u>criteria</u> for effective mood words.

Learn It Online
Examine Dickinson's style further through Author-Space online.

go.hrw.com ▕ L11-568 ▏ Go

I heard
a Fly buzz—
when I died

by **Emily Dickinson**

Morning Light (1995) by Alice Dalton Brown (b. 1939). Pastel on paper, 48.8 × 67.3 cm.

Read with a Purpose
Read to discover how a fly enables Dickinson to capture a chilling, mysterious moment just before death.

Build Background
"I heard a Fly buzz—when I died" is one of Dickinson's most brilliantly original works. The poem begins with such boldness and continues with such quick shifts of attention that we may not realize that we are hearing a voice from the dead.

> I heard a Fly buzz—when I died—
> The Stillness in the Room
> Was like the Stillness in the Air—
> Between the Heaves of Storm—
>
> 5   The Eyes around—had wrung them dry—
> And Breaths were gathering firm
> For that last Onset—when the King
> Be witnessed—in the Room— Ⓐ
>
> I willed my Keepsakes—Signed away
> 10 What portion of me be
> Assignable—and then it was
> There interposed a Fly—
>
> With Blue—uncertain stumbling Buzz—
> Between the light—and me—
> 15 And then the Windows failed—and then
> I could not see to see—

Ⓐ **Literary Focus** Mood What mood is conveyed in this stanza? Which words help to create the mood?

My life
closed twice
before its close

by **Emily Dickinson**

Evening (1859) by Jasper Francis Cropsey (1823–1900). Oil on canvas, 15 × 22.2 cm.

Read with a Purpose
Read to share Dickinson's experience of loss and the <u>subsequent</u> emotions that it stirs in her.

Build Background
The following poem deals with loss, which Dickinson experienced many times during her life. The line "My life closed twice before its close" could be referring to any number of people in her life: from the loss of two older male friends for whom she had great affection, Charles Wadsworth and Samuel Bowles, to the loss of her parents.

My life closed twice before its close—
It yet remains to see
If Immortality unveil
A third event to me

5 So huge, so hopeless to conceive
As these that twice befell.
Parting is all we know of heaven,
And all we need of hell.

A **Literary Focus** **Mood** What mood is evoked by the opening statement, "My life closed twice"? What do you think this statement might mean?

Applying Your Skills

SKILLS FOCUS Literary Skills Analyze mood; analyze irony; analyze paradox. **Writing Skills** Use word choice to create mood.

I heard a Fly buzz—when I died /
My life closed twice before its close

Respond and Think Critically

Reading Focus

Quick Check

1. According to stanzas 2 and 3 of "I heard a Fly buzz—when I died," how have the speaker and those around her prepared for her death?

2. At the end of "I heard a Fly buzz—when I died," where is the fly when the speaker notices it?

3. In "My life closed twice before its close," to what does the speaker compare *parting*?

Read with a Purpose

4. How are these two poems similar and different in their presentations of death?

Literary Focus

Literary Analysis

5. **Draw Conclusions** In the third stanza of "I heard a Fly buzz—when I died," what portion of the speaker is "assignable"? What portion, by implication, is not assignable?

6. **Interpret** What is the meaning of "the Windows failed" in line 15 of "I heard a Fly buzz—when I died"? Do you think Dickinson uses the word *windows* literally, or figuratively? Explain.

7. **Hypothesize** In "My life closed twice before its close" to what does "Immortality" in line 3 refer?

8. **Infer** In "My life closed twice before its close," the specific events that twice closed the speaker's life are not mentioned. What suggests that they were a kind of death?

9. **Extend** What private fears and disappointments might Dickinson's two poems address? How might they also relate to broader <u>fundamental</u> experiences of people everywhere?

10. **Evaluate** An extensive study of Dickinson's poetry shows that she swung between acceptance and denial of spiritual faith. How do these poems reflect her struggle?

Literary Skills: Mood

11. **Analyze** Review your graphic organizer in which you noted elements that help create mood. What is the overall mood of each poem? How does Dickinson's style set the mood of each poem?

Literary Skills Review: Irony and Paradox

12. **Analyze** In general, **irony** occurs when there is a discrepancy between what is expected and what actually happens. In "I heard a Fly buzz—when I died," whom are the dying person and those around her expecting to find in the room? What appears instead, and why is this situation ironic?

13. **Interpret** A **paradox** is a statement that appears self-contradictory but reveals a kind of truth. Explain the paradox in lines 7–8 of "My life closed twice before it closed."

Writing Focus

Think as a Reader/Writer

Use It in Your Writing Dickinson carefully crafted her words to create a specific mood in each of her poems. Choose a mood, and create a simple scene or setting that evokes that mood. Write a brief paragraph that establishes the mood through word choice. As you write, make sure that all of the elements in your paragraph contribute to the mood.

What Do
You Think Now In what ways do you think suffering and loss in someone's past might affect how that person views the future? Explain.

"I sing . . . because I am afraid"

Reader/Writer
Notebook
Use your **RWN** to complete the activities for this selection.

Informational Text Focus

Analyzing Primary Sources A **primary source** is firsthand, original information, such as a letter, autobiography, historical document, or interview. The following two letters written by Dickinson give the reader the kind of intimate, firsthand view that only primary sources can provide. Sometimes examining this kind of source can feel like traveling back in time and observing a subject yourself.

Primary sources are invaluable to researchers because they represent people's original thoughts, opinions, and perceptions. The letters of Emily Dickinson provide <u>fundamental</u> insight into the person behind the poetry.

Into Action As you read the letters, use a chart like the one below to keep track of information you learn about Dickinson. In the first column, record excerpts and details that provide information about her. In the second column, state what this information reveals about Dickinson's life and her personality and attitudes.

Excerpts / Details	What You Learn About Dickinson
"You asked how old I was?"	She never answers Higginson's question about her age. She seems to be avoiding the question.
"I made no verse, but one or two, until this winter, sir."	

Writing Focus   Preparing for **Constructed Response**

When you read the excerpts from Dickinson's letters, you will discover that Dickinson did not restrict her **figurative language** to her poetry, As you read the letter excerpts, note in your *Reader/Writer Notebook* any examples of metaphors, similes, and other figurative devices.

Language Coach

Identifying Definitions Before you read Emily Dickinson's letters, briefly skim over them. In your *Reader/Writer Notebook*, jot down any unfamiliar words. (Be sure to include *claimed* and *unconveyed:* Although these words may not seem unfamiliar, Dickinson uses them in a way you may not be used to seeing.) Next, look up each word in a dictionary. Re-read the sentence or sentences that surround the word, and select the definition that fits the best. Keep your notes handy as you read the letters through closely.

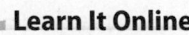
Learn It Online
Find out more about Dickinson's life through these Internet links.

go.hrw.com   L11-572   Go

"I sing . . . because I am afraid"

by **Emily Dickinson**

April 26, 1862

Mr. Higginson,—Your kindness claimed earlier gratitude, but I was ill, and write today from my pillow.

Thank you for the surgery; it was not so painful as I supposed. I bring you others, as you ask. . . .

You asked how old I was? I made no verse, but one or two, until this winter, sir.

I had a terror since September, I could tell to none; and so I sing, as the boy does of the burying ground, because I am afraid.

You inquire my books. For poets, I have Keats, and Mr. and Mrs. Browning. For prose, Mr. Ruskin, Sir Thomas Browne, and the Revelations.[1] I went to school, but in your manner of the phrase had no education. When a little girl, I had a friend who taught me Immortality; but venturing too near, himself, he never returned. Soon after my tutor died, and for several years my lexicon[2] was my only companion. Then I found one more, but he was not contented I be his scholar, so he left the land.

You ask of my companions. Hills, sir, and the sundown, and a dog large as myself, that my father bought me. They are better than beings because they know, but do not tell; and the noise in the pool at noon excels my piano.   (A)

---

1. **Revelations:** In the Bible, the book of Revelation is the last book of the New Testament.
2. **lexicon:** a dictionary, especially of Greek, Latin, or Hebrew.

(A) **Informational Focus** Primary Sources What biographical facts do you learn about Dickinson from this paragraph? What do her comments suggest about her personality and attitudes?

Thomas Wentworth Higginson (1823–1911). The Granger Collection, New York.

I have a brother and sister; my mother does not care for thought, and father, too busy with his briefs³ to notice what we do. He buys me many books, but begs me not to read them, because he fears they joggle the mind. They are religious, except me. . . .

But I fear my story fatigues you. I would like to learn. Could you tell me how to grow, or is it unconveyed, like melody or witchcraft?   **B**

You speak of Mr. Whitman. I never read his book, but was told that it was disgraceful. . .

July 1862

Could you believe me without? I had no portrait, now, but am small, like the wren; and my hair is bold, like the chestnut bur; and my eyes, like the sherry in the glass, that the guest leaves. Would this do just as well?   **C**

It often alarms father. He says death might occur, and he has molds [photographs] of all the rest, but has no mold of me. . . .

E. Dickinson

---

3. briefs: statements of the facts and the points of law of cases to be presented in court.

B **Informational Focus** **Primary Sources** Paraphrase Dickinson's question to Higginson. What does her question imply about the art of writing poetry?

C **Informational Focus** **Primary Sources** What does Dickinson mean when she says, "Could you believe me without?" Do you believe her? Explain your response.

Applying Your Skills

"I sing . . . because I am afraid"

SKILLS FOCUS Informational Skills
Analyze primary sources. **Writing Skills**
Write brief constructed responses, with
specific support. **Listening and Speaking
Skills** Offer insightful observations in discussions and conversations.

Respond and Think Critically

Informational Text Focus

Quick Check

1. What effect did the "terror" that Dickinson refers to in her letter have on her?

2. To whom or what in her life does Dickinson feel close?

3. How does Dickinson provide Higginson with a picture of herself?

Read with a Purpose

4. What do Emily Dickinson's letters tell you about her as a person that her poems do not?

Informational Skills: Analyzing Primary Sources

5. While reading the excerpts from Dickinson's letters, you analyzed details that gave you information about Emily Dickinson's life as well as insights into her personality and attitudes. Now that you have finished reading, review what you recorded in the chart. Referring to these letters, write a paragraph describing how Dickinson's life experiences and personality are reflected in her poems.

Excerpts / Details	What You Learn about Dickinson
"You asked how old I was?"	She never answers Higginson's question about her age. She seems to be avoiding the question.
"I made no verse, but one or two, until this winter, sir."	She did not start seriously writing poems until recently.

Text Analysis

6. **Analyze** Why do you think Dickinson refers to criticism about her poems as "surgery"? Do you think it is an appropriate metaphor? Explain.

7. **Infer** What can you infer about Dickinson's family life from the details in her letter? For example, how might she have felt about her parents' reluctance to advocate for her learning?

8. **Infer** Why might Dickinson not want people to have photographs of her? Why might she prefer to provide a "poetic" image of herself instead?

9. **Draw Conclusions** How does Dickinson evade Higginson's questions? What conclusions might you draw from her evasiveness?

10. **Make Judgments** In her first letter Dickinson refers to "the Revelations" as one of her books, yet claims she is not religious although other family members are. From what you know about her life and poetry, do you believe her? Explain.

11. **Compare and Contrast** How do Dickinson's letters reflect some of the same themes echoed in her poetry? Explain your response.

Listening and Speaking

12. **Extend** With a small group, discuss the insights into Dickinson these two excerpts from her letters provide. How do the letters add to your appreciation of her poetry? How might they contribute to a research paper on Dickinson's life?

Writing Focus Constructed Response

Briefly write about the effect of Dickinson's similes in the short excerpt from her letter of July 1862. Support your response with specific evidence from the letter.

What Do **You Think Now** How do you explain Dickinson's preference for the company of certain creatures and things over people? What insight into her nature does this information provide?

SKILLS FOCUS **Literary Skills** Understand metaphor.
Reading Skills Visualize imagery.

 Link to Today

Emily Dickinson

 What Do **You Think**

How does conflict lead to change?

 **QuickWrite**

Think of a time when you felt a <u>fundamental</u> connection to someone who lived before you, perhaps a relative or someone from history. In your *Reader/Writer Notebook,* write a few sentences exploring the connection.

Literary Focus

Metaphor A **metaphor** makes a comparison between two unlike things without specific words of comparison, such as *like, as,* or *than.* Some metaphors are stated directly: "Fame is a bee" (Emily Dickinson). Other metaphors are **implied**: "the bays where / day is anchored" (Lucha Corpi). In this implied metaphor, the poet suggests that the day is like a ship anchored in a harbor. Corpi uses both directly stated and implied metaphors.

Into Action As you read, use a chart like the one below to record Corpi's metaphors. Use the first column to record metaphors. In the second column, identify each metaphor as directly stated or implied.

Metaphor	Directly Stated or Implied?
"the bays where / day is anchored"	implied

Language Coach

Word Definitions Many English words come from Latin. The word *fundamental,* for example, comes from the same Latin word as *foundation,* which refers to the bottom of something. A <u>fundamental</u> truth is a basic truth. It is at the bottom, supporting other truths. If *fundamental* is a new word for you, picture it as the foundation of a house, holding the structure above it.

Writing Focus

Think as a Reader/Writer

Find It in Your Reading In this poem, Corpi uses **images** to appeal to the senses, helping readers imagine and respond to a scene. When Corpi speaks of "migrant / workers in search of / floating gardens," her image helps readers see the subject of the poem. As you read the poem, use your *Reader/Writer Notebook* to record images and note how each image makes you feel as a reader. What are your <u>criteria</u> for a successful image?

TechFocus As you read the poem, picture each stanza as one scene from a visual story in three parts. Film directors use this approach to create a storyboard before filming begins.

 **Reader/Writer Notebook**

Use your **RWN** to complete the activities for this selection.

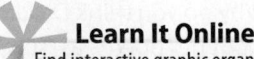 **Learn It Online**
Find interactive graphic organizers online to help you as you read.

go.hrw.com | L11-576 | Go

Link to Today

Read with a Purpose
Read to discover why the speaker feels a strong connection to Emily Dickinson.

Build Background
One of the most famous and talented of American poets, Emily Dickinson is the object of many tributes. Dickinson, a pioneer among women in the arts, is a special inspiration to other female poets, as is evident in the following poem by Lucha Corpi.

Author Note
Lucha Corpi (1945–   ) Born in a small town in Mexico, Lucha Corpi arrived in California at the age of nineteen. Currently, she lives and teaches in Oakland. The 1980 publication of *Palabras de Medioda / Noon Words* established her reputation as a poet. She has also had a successful career as a writer of fiction, including a series of mystery novels. Corpi claims justice as her inspiration: "I remember my grandmother saying, 'There is no justice in this world.' I think that's why I write—to bring justice into the world."

Emily Dickinson

by **Lucha Corpi**

Como tú, soy de ayer,
de las bahías en donde
se ancla el día a
esperar su propia hora.

5 Como yo, eres de hoy,
del andar de esa hora
en la que apenas palpita
lo que aún no ha nacido.

10 Somos cultivadoras de
indecibles, tejedoras
de singulares, campesinas
migratorias en busca de
chinampas aún sin
siembra y sin cosecha.

Like you, I belong to yesterday,
to the bays where
day is anchored to
wait for its hour.

5 Like me, you belong to today,
the progression of that hour
when what is unborn
begins to throb. **Ⓐ**

We are cultivators of
the unsayable, weavers
10 of singulars, migrant
workers in search of
floating gardens° as yet
unsown, as yet
unharvested. **Ⓑ**

---

13. **floating gardens:** small, artificial islands used in freshwater lakes to grow various crops. Organic matter in the lakes fertilizes these islands' rich soils.

Ⓐ Reading Focus Visualizing Imagery How does Corpi's image of the "unborn" beginning "to throb" relate to the idea of latent potential?

Ⓑ Literary Focus Metaphor To what three images does Corpi compare both herself and Emily Dickinson in lines 9–15? How are the comparisons valid?

Applying Your Skills

Emily Dickinson

Respond and Think Critically

Reading Focus

Quick Check

1. What suggests that the speaker is a poet?

2. Why do the first two stanzas seem to contradict each other?

3. To which categories of workers does the speaker compare herself and Dickinson?

Read with a Purpose

4. Why does the speaker feel such a strong connection with Emily Dickinson? What principles do they have in common? Given what you know of Dickinson's life, what kind of person do you think might feel a connection with Dickinson? Explain.

Literary Focus

Literary Analysis

5. **Analyze** What parallel structures does Corpi use in the first two stanzas of the poem? How do these parallel structures develop the speaker's relationship with Emily Dickinson?

6. **Evaluate** Given your reading of Dickinson's poems, do you think Corpi's metaphors and descriptions effectively capture Dickinson's qualities as a poet? Explain.

7. **Extend** Writers often compose tributes to their favorite writers of years past. Sometimes a tribute is meant to remind readers of a writer's importance in history. Other times, it is meant to show the relevance of a past writer's ideas and beliefs. Why do you think Corpi wrote this tribute to Emily Dickinson? What does she want to communicate through the tribute?

Literary Skills: Metaphor

8. **Analyze** In the final stanza, Corpi introduces farming metaphors. She mentions cultivators, migrant workers, gardens, and harvests. What effect does the farming metaphor have on you, and why do you think Corpi introduces migrant workers into the poem at this point? Explain your answer.

Literary Skills Review: Assonance

9. **Analyze** The repetition of similar vowel sounds followed by different consonant sounds, especially in words that are close together, is **assonance.** What examples of assonance can you find in "Emily Dickinson"? What effect does assonance have on the poem?

Writing Focus

Think as a Reader/Writer

Use It in Your Writing Corpi's images create three memorable scenes—one for each stanza of her poem. Think of someone with whom you feel a fundamental kinship. Using Corpi's poem as a model, write three short stanzas or sentences—starting with "Like you, I belong . . . ," "Like me, you belong . . . ," and "We are . . ." Use images to create a vivid scene for each stanza or sentence.

 What Do You Think Now

How does Corpi's poem echo the struggles that Dickinson faced during her life as a poet?

Wrap Up

SKILLS FOCUS Literary Skills Analyze a writer's style. **Reading Skills** Compare and contrast poems. **Writing Skills** Write comparison-contrast essays.

Author Study: Emily Dickinson

Writing Focus

Write a Comparison-Contrast Essay

Emily Dickinson compresses <u>fundamental</u> life experiences—such as death and success—and observations about abstract ideas—such as immortality and truth—into short, tightly woven poems expressing unique perspectives and <u>principles</u> to live by. As you read Dickinson's poems, you analyzed her use of rhyme, metaphor, and other literary techniques, including irony and paradox.

Prewriting Choose two of Dickinson's poems that have a striking similarity. Then, as you study the poems, look closely for the ways in which they differ.

Use a Venn diagram like the one below to record specific similarities between the two poems in the middle, shaded area and specific or unique aspects of the individual poems in the two outside circles.

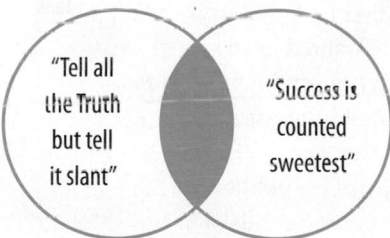

"Tell all the Truth but tell it slant"

"Success is counted sweetest"

Consider the following suggestions to help focus your comparison, or choose a topic of your own:

- Focus on an important poetic element in Dickinson's poetry, such as rhyme, slant rhyme, metaphor, irony, or paradox.
- Analyze a theme fundametal to Dickinson's view of the world.

Develop a Thesis Statement Using your notes and observations, develop a thesis that makes an assertion about what your poems have in common and how they contrast.

> *Sample Thesis:* The two poems use common, everyday experiences to discuss the inevitability of death, but each offers a unique perspective.

Drafting Begin with the strongest comparison linking the two poems; develop it in your first body paragraph. Then, depending on your analysis, your next body paragraph will develop an additional similarity or analyze a contrast. Each body paragraph will have two parts—one part for each poem. For example, if your essay compares the two poems listed in the Venn diagram on this page, the first part of each body paragraph will focus on "Tell all the Truth but tell it slant," while the second part will focus on "Success is counted sweetest."

Text Evidence Use direct quotations from the two poems to support each point you make. If you cannot find evidence in one of the poems, then rethink your analysis. Each paragraph should contain explanation and evidence from both poems.

Revising and Editing Re-read your draft to determine if you have fully supported your thesis with explanations and text evidence. Then, read for grammar, mechanics, and usage errors. Prepare a final copy that is free of errors. Share your essay with a group of peers or consider posting it on a classroom bulletin board.

What Do You Think Now

Based on what you've read of Emily Dickinson and her poetry, write a paragraph about how personal crises may have affected Emily Dickinson's outlook on life.

Writing Workshop

Historical Research Paper

Write with a Purpose

Write a historical research paper in which you present documented evidence that supports a thesis. Your **purpose** will be to investigate a historical event, draw conclusions, and then share your findings. Your **audience** may be your classmates and any reader who is interested in historical events.

A Good Historical Research Paper

- includes essential background information
- has a clear thesis statement
- considers differing perspectives
- synthesizes information from a variety of sources
- documents sources for information presented in the paper
- uses a formal, objective tone
- is well organized
- offers a thought-provoking conclusion

See page 592 for a complete rubric.

Reader/Writer Notebook

Use your **RWN** to complete the activities for this workshop.

Think as a Reader/Writer You have been reading historical accounts as well as literary responses that reflect history. Before you begin writing your own **historical research paper,** read this excerpt from Gordon S. Wood's *The Americanization of Benjamin Franklin.* In his biography, Wood examines how Franklin became widely known as a symbol of American values and beliefs.

Franklin is not an easy man to get to know. Although he wrote more pieces about more things than any of the other Founders, Franklin is never very revealing of himself. He always seems to be holding something back—he is reticent, detached, not wholly committed. We sense in Franklin the presence of calculated restraint—a restraint perhaps bred by his spectacular rise and the kind of hierarchical[1] and patronage-ridden[2] world he had to operate in. Certainly there were people in Philadelphia who never let him forget "his original obscurity," and that he had sprung from "the meanest Circumstances."[3] Despite his complaining that he was never able to order things in his life, we sense that he was always in control and was showing us only what he wanted us to see. Only at moments in the early 1770s and at the end of his life do we sense that the world was spinning out of his grasp.

Beyond the restrained and reserved character of his personal writings is the remarkable character of his public writings, especially his *Autobiography*—"this most famous of American texts," as one scholar calls it. Literary scholars have continually interpreted and reinterpreted the *Autobiography* but still cannot agree on what Franklin was trying to do in writing it. . . . His resembles a work of fiction in that we cannot be sure that the narrative voice is the same as the author's.

---

1. **hierarchical:** focused on rank, grade, etc.
2. **patronage-ridden:** filled with political deals and favors.
3. **the meanest Circumstances:** Franklin was one of 17 children born to a soap and candle maker.

Margin notes:
- Wood begins by stating his main idea.
- He supports his main idea with elaboration.
- He incorporates quotations from research to support ideas.
- Wood looks not only at other writers' research but also at Franklin's own writing.

Think About the Professional Model

With a partner, discuss the following questions about the model.

1. How does Wood show that he's using another person's ideas?
2. How does the elaboration in the first paragraph support the main idea?

Prewriting

Choose a Research Topic

You investigate a historical event so that you can draw your own conclusions about the event and its **significance,** or importance, to history. When you read a single record of a historical event—the attack on Pearl Harbor, the assassination of President John F. Kennedy, or the fall of the Berlin Wall—you are likely to be reading information that represents only one **perspective,** or **point of view,** on that event. To understand a historical event fully, you need to examine a wide variety of sources representing all relevant perspectives on the event.

As you consider a topic for your paper, look for a controversial event that interests you and for which you will be able to find a variety of sources. You should also make sure that the topic is narrow enough to be fully developed, yet not too narrow to support a full-length research paper. To choose an appropriate topic, answer the questions in the left column of the chart below. The sample answers are from the writer of the student model on page 588.

Questions	My Answers
What historical event am I interested in?	I'm interested in the Civil War.
How can I narrow this topic, if necessary?	I can focus on one important event: General Sherman's march from Atlanta to Savannah.
Can I find a variety of sources on this topic?	Yes—records and newspaper accounts written during the war, memoirs, and books written after the war are available.
Can I find sources representing all relevant perspectives on this topic?	Yes, there should be plenty of information representing various points of view, such as those of Northerners, Southerners, soldiers, and civilians.

If you're not sure what historical event you're interested in, thumb through a history book for intriguing topics or ask a history teacher to suggest interesting historical events for you to consider.

Think About Purpose and Audience

Once you have narrowed your topic, consider your **purpose** for writing this investigative paper: researching a historical event and sharing your findings with your **audience** (most likely your classmates and teacher). You should avoid, however, simply repeating facts. Instead, produce a paper that **synthesizes,** or combines, information gathered from various sources, analyzes it, and draws conclusions.

Idea Starters

- historical periods you have studied in school
- historical events depicted in novels, plays, or movies
- historical events involving your family, community, or state

Your Turn _____

Get Started Making notes in your **RWN,** use the questions in the chart on this page to find an appropriate topic for your historical research paper. Keep your **purpose** and **audience** in mind as you write.

 Learn It Online
For an example of a complete, double-spaced historical research paper, visit this interactive model.

go.hrw.com   L11-581   **Go**

Ask Research Questions

Clear **research questions** will help you focus your search for sources and will lead you to analyze the different perspectives on the historical event you're investigating. The writer of the student model came up with following research questions—

- *What are the facts of Sherman's march?*
- *What perspective is revealed by the written or spoken testimony of each group directly involved in or affected by the march?*
- *What were the perspectives of Northerners and Southerners not directly involved in or affected by the march?*

Find Answers to Research Questions

First, track down the answers to your research questions in a general reference work. You'll get an overview of your topic and gain valuable background information. In addition, articles in a general reference work usually mention other sources you can use in your research. For this step, consult a print or online encyclopedia or search the Internet for sites or pages that contain related keywords.

Once you have an overview of your topic, move on to specific sources that can help you answer your research questions. Be creative in developing a research strategy. Avoid restricting yourself to print or online sources. Your most valuable information might come from an interview with a historian, a visit to a museum, a letter (or e-mail) requesting additional information, or a visit to an actual historical site. Some sources may lead you to other sources.

- **Balance primary and secondary sources. Primary sources** are firsthand, original information, such as letters, autobiographies (like Ben Franklin's autobiography, used in the professional model), historical documents, and works of literature and art. **Secondary sources** include information derived from, or about, primary or other secondary sources. Examples include encyclopedias, documentaries, biographies, and history books.

- **Check the reliability and validity of sources.** A source is reliable and valid when its information is accurate and its ideas are presented objectively—without bias. Seek up-to-date information published by major universities or established, credible publishing companies.

- **Cover all relevant perspectives.** Look for sources that reveal the perspectives of a variety of historical authorities on your topic.

Record and Organize Information

Write complete and accurate information about all the sources you consult, even if you're not sure you will use them in your paper. On 3- x 5-inch index cards, create separate **source cards** for each source you use, or create an electronic file on your computer. Assign each source a number. Record full publishing information for each source and write short notes about the content and value of the source. Also note library call numbers or Web addresses (URLs). This information will help you later as you take notes and compile a *Works Cited* list.

Read and Take Notes Read each source carefully as you look for answers to your research questions. Use these guidelines for taking notes.

1. **Use 3- x 5-inch index cards, a notebook, or an electronic file to write down information you find.** Make your notes easy to sort and group by using a separate notecard or notebook page for each item of information. On the computer, key notes onto individual pages or make separate database or worksheet entries for each note.

2. **Write a label or heading.** In the upper left-hand corner of the card or file, identify the main idea of your note so that you do not have to re-read each note to remind yourself what it is about.

3. **Record each piece of information.**
   Quote directly: Use the writer's exact words, enclosed in quotation marks.
   Paraphrase: Rewrite a passage in your own words and style.
   Summarize: Present only the main points of a passage.

4. **Record the source number and page number(s).** In the upper right-hand corner of each note, write the number of your source card. Write page numbers at the bottom of your notes.

Here are one student's notecards for his paper on Sherman's march.

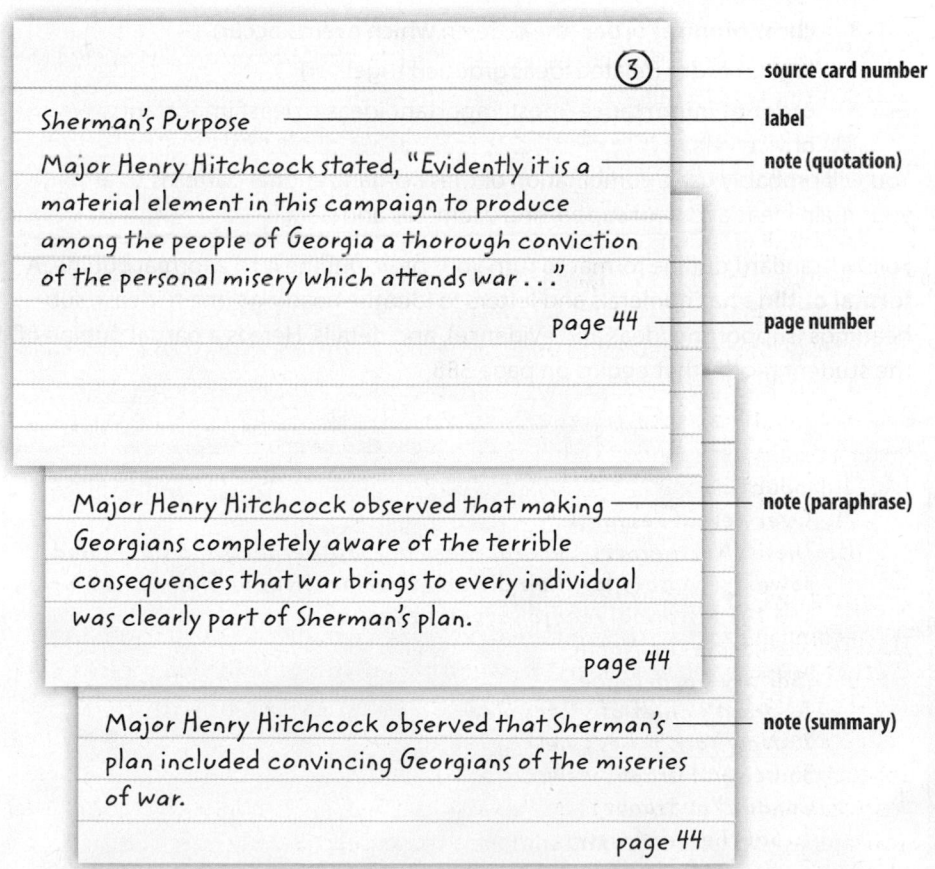

③ ——— source card number

Sherman's Purpose ——— label

Major Henry Hitchcock stated, "Evidently it is a ——— note (quotation)
material element in this campaign to produce
among the people of Georgia a thorough conviction
of the personal misery which attends war . . ."

page 44 ——— page number

Major Henry Hitchcock observed that making ——— note (paraphrase)
Georgians completely aware of the terrible
consequences that war brings to every individual
was clearly part of Sherman's plan.

page 44

Major Henry Hitchcock observed that Sherman's ——— note (summary)
plan included convincing Georgians of the miseries
of war.

page 44

● **Writing Tip**

Avoid **plagiarism**—a serious academic offense—by giving credit to authors whose words or ideas you use. You must credit all ideas you quote, paraphrase, or summarize.

Your Turn _____

Identify Sources and Take Notes Using the guidelines on these pages, ask and answer your research questions using reliable sources that offer a variety of perspectives. Then, record and organize your information.

Drafting

Write a Thesis Statement

How does all the information you have collected fit together? What larger point, or general conclusion, does the information support? Write a **thesis statement** that states your topic and your general conclusion about it. You can use this equation to create a **preliminary** thesis statement that will guide you in your writing, but you'll want to polish it for your final draft.

TOPIC: _____

+ CONCLUSION: _____

= THESIS: _____

Develop an Outline

Creating a basic **outline** or organizational plan helps you organize your ideas and ensure that they flow logically, with adequate support. Sort your notes into groups with similar headings or labels. Keep rearranging them until you find an order that makes sense. Most writers use one of these types of organization:

- **chronological order** (the order in which events occur)
- **logical order** (related ideas grouped together)
- **order of importance** (most important ideas to least important; or vice versa)

You will probably use a combination of these organizational patterns to arrange your main ideas and your supporting examples and details.

Follow standard outline format to turn your basic outline into a formal outline. A **formal outline** has numerals and letters to identify headings (main ideas), subheadings (supporting ideas and evidence), and details. Here is a partial outline of the student model that begins on page 588.

Framework for a Historical Research Paper

Introduction
- Grab the reader's interest.
- Give background information and an overview of your research.
- Include your thesis statement.

Body
- Develop each point from your outline in a separate paragraph.
- Support each main point with evidence—facts and details.
- Arrange your ideas logically.

Conclusion
- Restate your thesis.
- Summarize your main points.
- End with a closing thought.

I.   Introduction
  A. Overview of research
  B. Thesis: Northerners, General Sherman, Southerners, and slaves had powerful reasons for their different perspectives on Sherman's march, and the historical record supports them all.
II. The view from the North
  A. Military Importance
    1. Grant's chief of staff's view
    2. _New York Times's_ view
    3. General Grant's view
  B. Conduct of troops
    1. Southerners' view
    2. Public Resolution No. 4

Document Sources

Documenting a paper means identifying the sources of the information used in your paper. Give credit by **citing** all information from outside sources, except information that can be found in several sources or in standard reference books (for example, that Sherman was a Union army general during the Civil War).

Parenthetical Citations Sources of information enclosed in parentheses and placed within the body of your paper are called **parenthetical citations.** Parenthetical citations should be brief. In most citations, the author's last name and the page number are sufficient. The following chart shows the format that the Modern Language Association of America (MLA) suggests for the most common kinds of sources.

Guidelines for Parenthetical Citations	
Source with one author	Author's last name and the page number (if any) of the work cited: (Golay 36)
Source with more than one author	All authors' last names and the page number (if any): (Catton and Catton 103)
Source with no author	Title, or shortened version, and page number: (Brother 89)
An indirect source	Abbreviation *qtd. in* (quoted in) before the source and the page number: (qtd. in Miles 175)
Author's name given in the text	Page number only: (386)
Source with no pages (e.g., videos, interviews, Web sites)	Author only: (Inglehart)

⬤ Writing Tip

Always document sources of these types of information:

- direct quotations
- theories, ideas, and opinions other than your own
- data from surveys, research studies, and interviews conducted by others
- unusual, little-known, or questionable facts and statistics

Grammar Link Using Parenthetical Citations

A parenthetical citation in the text of your paper should provide just enough information to lead the reader to the full source entry in your *Works Cited* list. Always place the citation as close as possible to the material being documented. The following guidelines for parenthetical citations are from MLA:

- Always place the citation before the punctuation mark within a sentence that contains the information from the source.

  Sherman saw his march as a harsh but justified action against traitors to the United States who had "brought the war upon themselves" (Janda 16), an action calculated to bring a "quick end to a destructive war" (Hart 228).

- If a quotation ends a sentence, put the citation after the quotation mark, but before end punctuation.

  ...who was not capable of a long march" (qtd. in Nevin 44).

- Place the citation for a block quotation two spaces after the final punctuation mark.

  ... the last morsel of food has been taken from families. (qtd. in Clinton 1-11)

Reference Note

For more on formatting *Works Cited* lists, see the model on page 590.

● Writing Tip

Unlike a list of *Works Cited*, a *Bibliography* includes all the sources you consulted in researching your topic. Your teacher will indicated if you should develop a list of *Works Cited* or a *Bibliography*.

Your Turn _____

Draft Your Essay Following your outline and the Writer's Framework, write the first draft of your historical research paper. Remember to

- write a thesis statement that tells your topic and your general conclusion about it
- cite your sources, using correctly formatted parenthetical citations and a *Works Cited* list

Works Cited The *Works Cited* list contains all the sources, print and nonprint, that you credit in your paper. You do not credit sources that you consulted but did not cite in your paper. Use the following sample entries as a reference for preparing your *Works Cited* list. Notice that you include page numbers only for sources that are one part of a whole work, such as an article in a newspaper.

Guidelines for Recording Source Information

Print Encyclopedia Article Author's name, last name first (if provided); article title; encyclopedia name; edition number, followed by the abbreviation *ed.;* and year of publication.

Tebeau, Charlton W. "Sherman, William Tecumseh." The New Encyclopedia Britannica. 2007 ed.

Books Author's name, last name first; book title; place of publication; name of publishing company; and year of publication. For more than one author, additional author names are first name first.

One Author

Derry, Joseph T. Story of the Confederate States. Hinton, VA: Sprinkle, 1996.

Two Authors

Catton, William, and Bruce Catton. Two Roads to Sumter. New York: Book Sales, 2004.

Articles from Magazines, Newspapers, and Journals Author's name, last name first; article title; magazine, newspaper, or journal title; day, month and year of publication; edition; and beginning page number.

From a Weekly Magazine

Tolston, Jay. "The Man Who Would Shape the Future of War." U.S. News & World Report 2 July 2007: 78.

From a Daily Newspaper, with a Byline (a named writer)

Gross, Doug. "Georgia Uses Civil War Anniversary for Tourism." Augusta Chronicle 01 Apr 2007: G07.

From a Daily Newspaper, Without a Byline

"Civil War Sites Have Stories to Tell." Roanoke Times & World News 03 Jun 2007: 2.

Online Sources Author's name, last name first (if listed); title of document; title of site or database; date of electronic publication (if listed); name of sponsoring institution or organization; date information was accessed; and URL or name of online service.

"American Civil War." Encyclopedia Britannica. 2007. Encyclopedia Britannica Online. 18 Sept. 2009 <http://search.eb.com/eb/article-9006104>.

Film or Video Recording Title; director or artist's name, first name first; distributor; and year of release. For video recordings, include the original release date (if relevant) and the medium (for example, Videocassette, DVD).

The Civil War. Dir. Ken Burns. 1990. DVD. PBS Home Video, 2004.

Sound recording Title, artist, medium (if other than CD), manufacturer, and year of release.

Songs of the Civil War and Stephen Foster Favorites. Mormon Tabernacle Choir. Sony, 1991.

Interview Interviewee's name, last name first; interview type (personal, telephone, e-mail); and date of interview.

Gibson, Anne. E-mail interview. 14 Oct. 2009.

Evaluating and Revising

The following chart can help you determine whether you have clearly communicated the results of your historical research.

Historical Research Paper: Guidelines for Content and Organization

Evaluation Question	Tip	Revision Technique
1. **Does your introduction draw readers into the research, give an overview of the topic, and state the thesis?**	**Underline** the sentence that draws readers into the research; **bracket** the overview of research; **circle** the thesis statement.	**Add** a quotation or interesting detail to the first sentence. **Add** overview information, or **elaborate** on existing information. **Add** a sentence or two that states your thesis.
2. **Do several main ideas develop the thesis? Do facts and details support the main ideas?**	In the margin, **put a check mark** next to each main idea that develops the thesis. In the text, **put double check marks** next to at least one piece of supporting evidence for each idea.	**Add** main ideas to develop your thesis. **Delete** ideas that do not support the thesis. **Elaborate** on each idea with material from your research.
3. **Does the paper include summaries and paraphrases in addition to direct quotations?**	**Circle** all direct quotations. If direct quotations make up more than one third of the paper, revise.	**Replace** some direct quotations with paraphrases or summaries.
4. **Are sources cited when necessary? Are the citations in the correct MLA format?**	**Place stars** by direct quotations and by facts that are not common knowledge.	**Add** documentation for quoted, paraphrased, or summarized material. **Revise** incorrect citations.
5. **Are ideas presented in an order that makes sense?**	**Number** your main ideas. **Revise** if the order makes no sense or is unclear.	**Rearrange** the order of ideas for clarity. Try chronological or logical order.
6. **Does the conclusion restate the thesis and summarize the paper's main points? Does the essay end with a closing thought?**	**Bracket** the restatement of the thesis. **Highlight** the summary of main ideas. **Circle** the closing thought.	**Add** a sentence that returns the reader to the thesis of the paper. **Add** a summary of main ideas. **Add** a final idea, question, quotation, or anecdote to close the essay.

Peer Review

Working with a peer, use this chart to review your draft. If you need help answering the questions in the left-hand column, use the tips in the middle column. Then, revise your paper by making the changes suggested in the right-hand column. Be sure to take notes on your partner's suggestions.

Connor draws the reader in with interesting, suspenseful details and a direct quotation. →

He sets the scene with relevant background information. →

He provides an overview of perspectives uncovered by research. →

Connor's topic is clear, but what is his main idea about it? →

Read this student draft with comments on its structure and suggestions for how it could be made even stronger.

Student Draft

Sherman's March: A Civil War Controversy

by Connor Edmond of Riverbend High School

General William Tecumseh Sherman's army was ready. The sick and wounded and all excess baggage had been sent away. Captain Daniel Oakley of the 2nd Massachusetts wrote, "The army was reduced, one might say, to its fighting weight, no man being retained who was not capable of a long march" (qtd. in Nevin 44). General Sherman sent out last-minute dispatches before ordering the telegraph lines be cut, making it impossible for him and his army to communicate further with the Union. His last wire to General Grant reiterated the rationale for the march: "If the North can march an army right through the South, . . . it is proof positive that the North can prevail" (qtd. In Nevin 44). On November 12, 1864, Sherman set out with an army of 62,000 men on a 250-mile march from Atlanta to Savannah (Inglehart). His army destroyed a strip of land 60 miles wide and inflicted $100 million in damages (Holzer 172). While the annals of the American Civil War are filled with controversial actions, Sherman's march across Georgia remains one of the most debated. The U.S. government and many Northerners celebrated Sherman's action as a brilliant military success, but Sherman himself thought it a necessary, if harsh, part of war. Southerners whose homes were destroyed saw it as a lawless act of cruelty. Who was right?

MINI-LESSON ▶ **How to State Your Thesis**

In the draft above, Connor presents the topic of Sherman's march and gives background of the controversy surrounding it—but he doesn't provide his conclusion about it. He could strengthen his introduction by stating his thesis more clearly and explicitly to include both his topic and his conclusion about the topic.

Connor's Draft

. . . if harsh, part of war. Southerners whose homes were destroyed saw it as a lawless act of cruelty. Who was right?

Connor's Revision

. . . if harsh, part of war. Southerners whose homes were destroyed saw it as a lawless act of cruelty. Who was right? They all were. Northerners, General Sherman, and Southerners had powerful reasons for their different perspectives on Sherman's march, and the historical record supports them all.

Your Turn _____

Stating Your Thesis Read your draft, and then ask yourself:

- Does my thesis clearly state the topic of my paper?
- Does my thesis state the conclusion I have drawn from my research about the topic?

Southerners saw themselves not as traitors or rebels, but as citizens of a sovereign nation, the Confederate States of America. In their eyes, Sherman's march amounted to a foreign invasion. The manpower of the South had been drained, leaving women, children, and old men undefended at home. For enemy troops to come literally to their doors and take their property—including thousands of slaves who left their masters to follow Sherman's troops ("Sherman and the March")—was an outrage. Henrietta Lee voiced the feelings of many Southerners when she wrote to Union General David Hunter. "Your name will stand on history's pages as the Hunter of weak women, and innocent children: the Hunter to destroy defenseless villages and beautiful homes" (qtd. in Clinton 125).

To Southerners, the conduct of Sherman's troops seemed anything but gallant. The following statement by the Confederate Congress expresses the Southern view of Sherman's march:

> Houses are pillaged and burned, churches are defaced, towns are ransacked, clothing of women and infants is stripped from their persons, jewelry and mementoes of the dead are stolen . . . means of subsistence [survival] are wantonly [cruelly] wasted to produce beggary, . . . the last morsel of food has been taken from families. (qtd. in Clinton 111)

Doubtless fear and hatred of the advancing army gave rise to many rumors, and some accounts may have been exaggerated. However, credible testimony from Southern eyewitnesses concurs with the description above.

Connor states this paragraph's main idea: Southerners saw Sherman's march as an invasion.

He supports this main idea with paraphrased evidence.

He also supports his main idea with a direct quotation.

Connor omits words in this long quotation to shorten it, but adds words to help make it clearer.

He offers his own conclusion about evidence and ties this body paragraph to thesis statement.

MINI-LESSON ▶ **How to Integrate Quotations**

Sentence-length quotations should be integrated with either an introductory phrase followed by a comma or a full sentence followed by a colon. Connor revised the second paragraph of his draft, replacing the period with a colon.

Connor's Revision of Paragraph 2

Henrietta Lee voiced the feelings of many Southerners when she wrote to Union General David Hunter. "Your name will stand on history's pages as the Hunter of . . . .

If you are quoting just a few words from the source, make the quoted words part of your own sentence.

Example:
The phrase "gallantry and good conduct" might have been chosen to refute Southerners' claims of abuses (Sherman, <u>Memoirs</u> 590).

Your Turn _____

Integrating Quotations Ask a partner to go through your draft and mark any places where quotations are not smoothly integrated. Then, revise accordingly. For more information, see the Grammar Link on page 591.

Student Draft *continues*

Listing Works Cited

- Begin your *Works Cited* list on a separate page, after the essay.
- Center the words *Works Cited* above the list of sources.
- Begin each source entry on a separate line, aligned with the left margin; additional lines have a hanging indent of one-half inch.
- Double-space each entry. (Here they are single-spaced due to limited space.)
- List sources alphabetically by the authors' last names. If no author is listed, sort by title. Ignore *A, An,* and *The.*
- When two or more sources are written by the same author, list the author's name only in the first entry. For additional entries, use three hyphens (---) in place of the author's name, followed by a period.

Works Cited

Andrews, Eliza Frances. "The War-Time Journal of a Georgia Girl, 1864–1865: Electronic Edition." Documenting the American South. 2004. U of North Carolina at Chapel Hill. 14 May 2009 <http://docsouth.unc.edu/fpn/andrews/andrews.html>.

Brother Against Brother: Time-Life Books History of the Civil War. Fairfax, VA: Time-Life, 1995.

Clinton, Catherine. Tara Revisited: Women, War, and the Plantation Legend. New York: Abbeville, 1997.

Derry, Joseph T. Story of the Confederate States. Hinton, VA: Sprinkle, 1996.

Golay, Michael. A Ruined Land: The End of the Civil War. New York: Wiley, 2001.

Holzer, Harold. Witness to War: The Civil War: 1861–1865. New York: Berkley, 1996.

Inglehart, David. Fateful Lightning: A Narrative History of the Civil War. CD-ROM. Hebron, ME: Troubadour Interactive, 1998.

Janda, Lance. "Shutting the Gates of Mercy: The American Origins of Total War, 1860–1880." Journal of Military History 59.1 (1995): 7-26.

Miles, Jim. To the Sea: A History and Tour Guide of Sherman's March. Nashville: Cumberland, 2002.

Nevin, David, and the Editors of Time-Life Books. Sherman's March: Atlanta to the Sea. Alexandria: Time-Life, 1986.

"Sherman and the March to the Sea." Civil War Journal: The Commanders. Dir. Donna E. Lusitana. DVD. A&E Home Video, 2001.

Sherman, William Tecumseh. Memoirs of General W. T. Sherman. New York: Penguin, 2000.

---. "Special Field Orders Issued by Gen. Sherman, Nov. 9, 1864." GeorgiaInfo. 2004. Carl Vinson Institute of Government, U of Georgia. 14 May 2009 <http://www.cviog.uga.edu/Projects/gainfo/order2.htm>.

Proofreading and Publishing

Proofreading

So that your readers will fully appreciate your paper, **proofread,** or **edit,** it carefully. You don't want your readers to dismiss your work completely because they run into basic errors in grammar, spelling, and punctuation. Proofreading will help ensure that your paper follows the **conventions** of formal English and the documentation format required by your teacher.

One convention for quotations is that if you omit words from, or add words to, a quoted source, you must make it clear to readers that you've done so.

> ### Grammar Link Omitting or Adding Words in Quotations
>
> Whenever you provide a direct quotation from a source, be sure to integrate it smoothly and correctly into your text. Use three spaced periods (. . .), called **ellipsis points,** to mark omissions from the original quotation, and use **brackets** to mark additions. For example, look at the following block quotation from the student model.
>
> Houses are pillaged and burned, churches are defaced, towns are ransacked,
>
> clothing of women and infants is stripped from their persons, jewelry and
>
> mementoes of the dead are stolen . . . means of subsistence [survival] are
>
> wantonly [cruelly] wasted to produce beggary, . . . the last morsel of food has
>
> been taken from families." (qtd. in Clinton 111)

Publishing

Now that you've done the hard work researching and writing a historical research paper, don't let your accomplishment go unnoticed. Share your paper with a larger audience.

- Save your research paper as a writing sample to submit with a college or job application.
- Submit your paper to Web sites related to your topic.
- Ask your school librarian or media specialist to help you locate academic journals to which you might submit your paper.

Reflect on the Process
In your **RWN,** write a short response to the following questions.

1. How did your research experience affect your understanding of your topic? How did the experience affect your understanding of the study of history?
2. If you had to list four fundamental principles of research for a student younger than you, what would they be?

⬤ Proofreading Tip

You might be so familiar with your paper that you read over the errors. Ask one partner to proofread the essay and another partner to double-check the correctness of parenthetical citations and your *Works Cited* list. Pay particular attention to the placement and punctuation of parenthetical citations.

Your Turn _____

Proofread and Publish As you proofread, make sure that you have used ellipsis points and brackets correctly to show omissions and additions in quotations. Then, find and correct any other errors before publishing and reflecting on your writing experience.

Scoring Rubric

Use one of the rubrics below to evaluate expository essays: either your historical research paper from the Writing Workshop or your response to the on-demand prompt on the next page. Your teacher will tell you which rubric to use.

6-Point Scale

Score 6 *Demonstrates advanced success*
- focuses consistently on a clear thesis
- shows effective organization throughout, with smooth transitions
- offers thoughtful, creative ideas
- develops ideas thoroughly, using examples, details, and fully elaborated explanation
- exhibits mature control of written language

Score 5 *Demonstrates proficient success*
- focuses on a clear thesis
- shows effective organization, with transitions
- offers thoughtful ideas
- develops ideas competently, using examples, details, and well-elaborated explanation
- exhibits sufficient control of written language

Score 4 *Demonstrates competent success*
- focuses on a clear thesis, with minor distractions
- shows effective organization, with minor lapses
- offers mostly thoughtful ideas
- develops ideas adequately, with a mixture of general and specific elaboration
- exhibits general control of written language

Score 3 *Demonstrates limited success*
- includes some loosely related ideas that distract from the writer's expository focus
- shows some organization, with noticeable gaps in the logical flow of ideas
- offers routine, predictable ideas
- develops ideas with uneven elaboration
- exhibits limited control of written language

Score 2 *Demonstrates basic success*
- includes loosely related ideas that seriously distract from the writer's expository focus
- shows minimal organization, with major gaps in the logical flow of ideas
- offers ideas that merely skim the surface
- develops ideas with inadequate elaboration
- exhibits significant problems with control of written language

Score 1 *Demonstrates emerging effort*
- shows little awareness of the topic and purpose for writing
- lacks organization
- offers unclear and confusing ideas
- develops ideas in only a minimal way, if at all
- exhibits major problems with control of written language

4-Point Scale

Score 4 *Demonstrates advanced success*
- focuses consistently on a clear thesis
- shows effective organization throughout, with smooth transitions
- offers thoughtful, creative ideas
- develops ideas thoroughly, using examples, details, and fully elaborated explanation
- exhibits mature control of written language

Score 3 *Demonstrates competent success*
- focuses on a clear thesis, with minor distractions
- shows effective organization, with minor lapses
- offers mostly thoughtful ideas
- develops ideas adequately, with a mixture of general and specific elaboration
- exhibits general control of written language

Score 2 *Demonstrates limited success*
- includes some loosely related ideas that distract from the writer's expository focus
- shows some organization, with noticeable gaps in the logical flow of ideas
- offers routine, predictable ideas
- develops ideas with uneven elaboration
- exhibits limited control of written language

Score 1 *Demonstrates emerging effort*
- shows little awareness of the topic and purpose for writing
- lacks organization
- offers unclear and confusing ideas
- develops ideas in only a minimal way, if at all
- exhibits major problems with control of written language

Preparing for Timed Writing

Expository Essay

When responding to an expository prompt, use what you have learned from reading, writing your historical research paper, and studying the rubric on page 592. Use the steps below to develop a response to the following prompt.

> ## Writing Prompt
> You attend several classes in school every day. Decide which of these classes is your favorite. Then, explain why it is your favorite and what effect the class has on you or your life.

Study the Prompt

Begin by reading the prompt carefully. Circle or underline key words: *classes, favorite, why,* and *effect.* The key words in this prompt tell you that you will be writing an expository essay about your favorite class and its effect on your life. Remember that your **audience** is made up of adult readers who will probably associate *favorite* with positive effects. For this essay, choose a class that you know well and that has a positive effect on you. **Tip:** Spend about five minutes studying the prompt.

Plan Your Response

Brainstorm **reasons** why the class is your favorite. Be prepared to **elaborate** each reason with **evidence**—anecdotes of class activities or results of your participation in the class. The elaboration proves or illustrates *why* the class is your favorite. Then, brainstorm the **effects** the class has on your life. You will be answering *how?* questions, such as *how does this class affect me?* You may want to create a planning chart like this one.

Favorite Class: Biology

Why? (reasons)	How? (effect on me)
I like to study the environment.	I've joined a conservation club at school.
I like learning about staying healthy.	I have changed my diet.

Another approach to this prompt is to ask why a class is your favorite, list reasons, and look for a common **theme.** Instead of elaborating on *several* smaller effects the class has had on you, you elaborate on *one* large effect for the entire essay. One broad effect could be "I have decided on a career in biology." Both approaches are effective ways to respond to this kind of prompt. **Tip:** Spend about ten minutes planning your response.

Respond to the Prompt

Once you have decided on your reasons and the effect or effects on your life, you are ready to start writing. One way to begin quickly is to describe a scene that illustrates typical class activity. Then, state your **thesis,** which is an identification of the class and its biggest effect on you. Your body paragraphs will be the different reasons the class is your favorite. Don't forget to **elaborate** on each reason. Include anecdotes and examples, and address the effect or effects on your life. Your conclusion may be a look to the future, including the influence of this class. **Tip:** Spend about twenty minutes writing your draft.

Improve Your Response

Revising Review the key aspects of the prompt. Have you explained why the class is your favorite? Have you told what effect it has had on your life? Do details, examples, or anecdotes illustrate your ideas? If not, add these elements.

Proofreading Take a few minutes to edit your response so that you can correct errors in grammar, spelling, punctuation, and mechanics. Are your edits neat and your paper legible?

Checking Your Final Copy Before you turn in your response, read it one more time to catch any errors you may have missed. **Tip:** Save five or ten minutes to improve your paper.

Presenting Historical Research

Think as a Reader/Writer Professional historians routinely publish books and articles on the results of their research. They also introduce their research in oral presentations to their peers at conferences and meetings of historical organizations. To make these oral presentations interesting, historians use verbal and nonverbal techniques—techniques you will learn in order to turn your historical investigation into an oral presentation for your peers.

Adapt Your Report

Maintain Your Focus

Your **purpose** in giving an oral report of historical research is to present your findings in a clear, concise, and interesting way. Remember that your listeners have just one chance to hear and absorb your ideas, unlike readers who have the opportunity to re-read difficult passages in a written report. As you adapt your report for an oral presentation, think about which parts you may need to simplify for your audience. Use the tips below to help you.

- Begin with a thought-provoking quotation or an interesting incident to catch your listeners' attention right from the start.
- Consider providing additional background information, if needed. Then, state your **thesis** so that it clearly communicates conclusions about the topic.
- Use simpler vocabulary, and turn long, complicated sentences into shorter ones so that listeners can understand you.
- If you have to cut your paper because of time limitations, be sure to maintain a balance of **primary** and **secondary sources** that represent relevant **perspectives** on the topic and show you have analyzed several historical records. If you need to add information to your presentation, make sure you consider the **validity** and **reliability** of the new sources.
- Include a combination of rhetorical strategies: Use **exposition** to explain similarities and differences in the historical records and **persuasion** to convince readers of the validity of your conclusions. Look for places where you can effectively use **narration** and **description** to make audiences feel as if they are listening to an exciting story rather than a dull report on research results.
- Simplify your **conclusion.** Clearly restate your thesis and your main ideas. Leave your listeners with a thought-provoking quotation or idea.
- Cite sources only when necessary to identify the author of important quotations or the source of facts or ideas.

Present Your Report

The Natural Sound

Speakers who read a speech often sound stiff and dull. Extemporaneous speakers, on the other hand, usually have notecards or an outline to glance at as the need arises. They also rehearse their presentations until they feel confident that they know their material so well that they sound natural and spontaneous.

Prepare to deliver your presentation extemporaneously by writing on notecards your thesis, the main supporting ideas, and brief reminders of details you want to include. Arrange your notecards in the same pattern you used for your paper.

The Power of Visuals

Include visuals, such as charts, graphs, photographs, or props, at points in your presentation where they will enhance your words.

Do a Dress Rehearsal

Rehearse your oral report until you feel comfortable presenting it. You might want to videotape your presentation, practice in front of a mirror, or present your report to an audience of friends or family. Refer to the following table to improve your use of **verbal and nonverbal techniques.**

Verbal Techniques	Nonverbal Techniques
Tone: Maintain a formal tone to help your audience focus on the information.	**Eye contact:** Involve your audience by making eye contact with your listeners.
Volume: Speak loudly enough for everyone to hear you; emphasize important words by speaking slightly louder and with more force.	**Facial expression:** Allow your face to express your enthusiasm for the subject.
Pause: Pause for a moment after an important point to allow your audience to catch up with you.	**Gestures:** Use natural gestures as you speak; feel free to move around, but don't pace or fidget.
Rate: Speak slowly enough to allow your audience to follow you, but not so slowly that they become bored.	**Posture:** Use good posture to convey a sense of confidence.

A Good Oral Presentation

- examines a historical event from a variety of perspectives
- organizes ideas clearly so listeners can follow along easily
- clearly identifies the source of quoted material and important ideas
- uses visuals where appropriate
- uses effective verbal and nonverbal speaking techniques

Speaking Tip

Speak clearly using **formal English.** Also, be sure that your vocabulary is appropriate for your audience. For example, avoid terms that are likely to be unfamiliar to your audience. If your report requires the use of technical language, use the terms correctly and define them.

Literary Skills Review

Comparing Literature   The following two pieces of literature were written almost a hundred years apart. Both deal with the horrors of war.
Directions: Read the following novel excerpt and poem. Then, read each multiple-choice question that follows and write the letter of the best response.

> *Stephen Crane (1871–1900) was born after the Civil War, but his best-known work is* The Red Badge of Courage, *a short novel that supposedly takes place at the battle of Chancellorsville in Virginia. This classic work of fiction is told through the eyes of young Henry Fleming, a Union soldier.*
>
> *This excerpt from* The Red Badge of Courage *describes a column of soldiers headed into battle. The "youth" is Henry Fleming, Crane's protagonist in the novel.*

from
The Red Badge of Courage

by **Stephen Crane**

Presently the calm head of a forward-going column of infantry[1] appeared in the road. It came swiftly on. Avoiding the obstructions gave it the sinuous movement of a serpent. The men at the head butted mules with their musket stocks. They prodded teamsters[2] indifferent to all howls. The men forced their way through parts of the dense mass by strength. The blunt head of the column pushed. The raving teamsters swore many strange oaths.

---

1. **infantry:** foot soldiers.
2. **teamsters:** drivers of teams of horses used for hauling.

The commands to make way had the ring of a great importance in them. The men were going forward to the heart of the din. They were to confront the eager rush of the enemy. They felt the pride of their onward movement when the remainder of the army seemed trying to dribble down this road. They tumbled teams about with a fine feeling that it was no matter so long as their column got to the front in time. This importance made their faces grave and stern. And the backs of the officers were very rigid.

As the youth looked at them the black weight of his woe returned to him. He felt that he was regarding a procession of chosen beings. The separation was as great to him as if they had marched with weapons of flame and banners of sunlight. He could never be like them. He could have wept in his longings.

He searched about in his mind for an adequate malediction[3] for the indefinite cause, the thing upon which men turn the words of final blame. It—whatever it was— was responsible for him, he said. There lay the fault.

The haste of the column to reach the battle seemed to the forlorn young man to be something much finer than stout fighting. Heroes, he thought, could find excuses in that long seething lane. They could retire with perfect self-respect and make excuses to the stars.

He wondered what those men had eaten that they could be in such haste to force their way to grim chances of death. As he watched his envy grew until he thought that he wished to change lives with one of them. He would have liked to have used a tremendous force, he said, throw off himself and become a better. Swift pictures of himself, apart, yet in himself, came to him—a blue desperate figure leading lurid charges with one knee forward and a broken blade high—a blue, determined figure standing before a crimson and steel assault, getting calmly killed on a high place before the eyes of all. He thought of the magnificent pathos[4] of his dead body.

These thoughts uplifted him. He felt the quiver of war desire. In his ears, he heard the ring of victory. He knew the frenzy of a rapid successful charge. The music of the trampling feet, the sharp voices, the clanking arms of the column near him made him soar on the red wings of war. For a few moments he was sublime.[5]

---

3. **malediction:** curse.
4. **pathos:** the quality in something experienced or observed that arouses a sense of sorrow or pity.
5. **sublime:** noble; majestic.

> The poet Yusef Komunyakaa (1947–   ) won the Pulitzer Prize in 1994 for his poetry collection Neon Vernacular. Much of Komunyakaa's work, including "Camouflaging the Chimera," is based on his experiences in the Vietnam War, where he served as an information specialist.

Camouflaging the Chimera°

by Yusef Komunyakaa

We tied branches to our helmets.
We painted our faces & rifles
with mud from a riverbank,

blades of grass hung from the pockets
5   of our tiger suits.° We wove
ourselves into the terrain,
content to be a hummingbird's target.

We hugged bamboo & leaned
against a breeze off the river,
10 slow-dragging with ghosts

from Saigon to Bangkok,
with women left in doorways
reaching in from America.
We aimed at dark-hearted songbirds.

15 In our way station of shadows
rock apes° tried to blow our cover,

throwing stones at the sunset.
        Chameleons
crawled our spines, changing from day
to night: green to gold,
20 gold to black. But we waited
till the moon touched metal,

till something almost broke
inside us. VC° struggled
with the hillside, like black silk°

25 wrestling iron through grass.
We weren't there. The river ran
through our bones. Small animals took
        refuge
against our bodies; we held our breath,

ready to spring the L-shaped
30 ambush, as a world revolved
under each man's eyelid.

° **Chimera** (ky MIHR uh): a monster in Greek mythology. The word today also refers to a fanciful creation of the imagination.

5. **tiger suits:** camouflage uniforms with black and green stripes.

16. **rock apes:** apes or tailless monkeys known to throw rocks at humans, often scaring soldiers in Vietnam into thinking they were being attacked by the enemy.

---

23. **VC:** The Viet Cong were Communist forces that opposed the U.S. and South Vietnamese governments during the Vietnam War.

24. **black silk:** The Viet Cong wore black silk to camouflage themselves at night.

1. Which of the following statements is not true, based on the *The Red Badge of Courage* excerpt?

   A The soldiers are proud to go to battle.

   B The youth feels alienated from the soldiers leading the march.

   C The soldiers are delaying their charge into battle.

   D The youth imagines his own heroic death.

2. Which statement *best* represents the **situational irony** in the Crane excerpt?

   A Although the youth is fearless, he does not look forward to the battle.

   B The youth feels pride when looking at the enemy rather than when looking at his fellow soldiers.

   C The youth feels ecstatic when he fantasizes about his death.

   D Although he does not want to be a hero, the youth fights bravely.

3. Which of the animals mentioned in the Komunyakaa poem *best* **symbolizes** the soldiers?

   A Hummingbirds

   B Songbirds

   C Rock apes

   D Chameleons

4. The words that *best* describe the **tone** of Komunyakaa's poem are —

   A judgmental and condemning

   B adoring and extravagant

   C tense and apprehensive

   D bitter and sarcastic

5. Which statement accurately describes a contrast between the two selections?

   A Crane's piece is bitter, whereas Komunyakaa's poem is uplifting.

   B Crane's piece is written from one man's viewpoint, whereas Komunyakaa's poem uses the collective voice of a group of soldiers.

   C Crane's piece focuses on events the narrator remembers from the past, whereas Komunyakaa's poem takes place in the present.

   D Crane's piece emphasizes the loud sounds of the battle, whereas Komunyakaa's poem focuses on the smells of war.

6. Which of the following statements expresses a shared **theme** of these two selections?

   A Peace can be obtained only through bloodshed.

   B War requires ordinary people to perform extraordinary tasks.

   C Soldiers are incapable of true heroism.

   D Nature is ultimately ruined by war.

Constructed Response

7. Contrast the imagery in the prose passage and the poem. Use specific evidence to support your response.

Vocabulary Skills Review

SKILLS FOCUS **Vocabulary Skills** Identify and correctly use multiple-meaning words.

Multiple-Meaning Words **Directions:** Choose the sentence in which the meaning of the italicized word matches the meaning of the word as used by Walt Whitman.

1. "The carpenter singing his [carol] as he measures his plank or *beam*."
   A The *beam* of sunlight on the ocean made the waves sparkle.
   B This *beam* is a major support in the building's framework.
   C The station can *beam* its signal for miles.
   D The baby loved to *beam* at the silly adults.

2. "I shake my white *locks* at the runaway sun."
   A Whenever she leaves, she *locks* the door.
   B The boat passed through a series of *locks* before entering the canal.
   C The hardware store sells *locks* and keys.
   D The singer wore her hair in long, dark *locks*.

3. "When the proofs, the *figures*, were ranged in columns before me . . ."
   A In the distance, two small *figures* were visible.
   B He *figures* that the next gas station is close.
   C Traditionally, each of the Muses *figures* a different art.
   D She added up the *figures* on the board.

4. "The courage of *present* times and all times . . ."
   A It is my honor to *present* Walt Whitman.
   B It's better to live in the *present* than the past.
   C She wrapped the *present* with blue paper.
   D The officers were ordered to *present* their credentials.

5. "All this I swallow, it tastes good, I like it *well*, it becomes mine."
   A The tears began to *well* in his eyes.
   B A toddler fell into the *well* and was quickly rescued.
   C After a long recovery, John is feeling *well*.
   D That book is a *well* of information.

6. "The hounded slave that *flags* in the race, leans by the fence."
   A People hung *flags* in their windows after the tragedy.
   B His strength *flags* when he eats poorly.
   C The scholar put *flags* in the textbook he was studying.
   D The young woman beside the stalled car *flags* the police car down for help.

Academic Vocabulary

Select the synonym (word with a similar meaning) to the Academic Vocabulary word below.

7. *advocate*
   A advise
   B support
   C deny
   D claim

Writing Skills Review

SKILLS FOCUS Writing Skills Support ideas/theses with relevant evidence and details; rethink content and organization when revising.

Historical Research **Directions:** Read the following paragraph from a draft of a student's historical research paper. Then, answer the questions that follow.

Before the Battle of Gettysburg, Major General J.E.B. Stuart—with General Robert E. Lee's permission—attempted to take his cavalry unit completely around the Union army of the Potomac. Because the Union army was far more spread out than he had supposed, Stuart lost touch with Lee for ten days. General Lee was, therefore, unaware that the Union army had moved north of the Potomac River and thus believed he had positioned the Confederate army correctly. Lee was certain Stuart would have informed him if the Union army had changed its position. When Lee found out otherwise, he hastily moved his army into positions around Gettysburg. From there he was forced to fight before he was ready—just one of the reasons the Confederates lost the Battle of Gettysburg.

1. Which of the following research questions does the information in the paragraph *best* answer?

   A Who was the Confederate army's leader?

   B Why did the Confederate army lose the battle at Gettysburg?

   C Where did Major General Stuart fight during the Civil War?

   D How did the Civil War affect Southerners and Northerners?

2. To support the main idea, which sentence could the writer add?

   A Stuart was supposed to inform Lee of the Union army's location.

   B Stuart was one of the most flamboyant of Lee's subordinates.

   C The Battle of Gettysburg was an important battle of the war.

   D The battle site in Pennsylvania is now a national park.

3. To find more information, which primary source could the writer consult?

   A An encyclopedia article on the battle

   B A letter written by Major General Stuart

   C A journal article analyzing the battle

   D A biography of General Lee

4. If the writer wanted to include a visual in his paper, which would be best?

   A A time line showing the major battles of the Civil War

   B A table listing the number of soldiers in each unit of the Union army

   C A picture of the Confederate and Union soldiers' uniforms

   D A map illustrating the movements of Stuart's cavalry

5. To present this information in an oral presentation, the speaker should —

   A use only secondary sources because they will be more reliable

   B delete all references to sources

   C give only one perspective

   D weave parenthetical citation information into the speech

Read On

FICTION
The Living

Annie Dillard's historical novel describes the life of pioneers living in the Pacific Northwest in the late nineteenth century. Focusing on the challenges faced by those who settled in the Puget Sound area, Dillard underlines both the difficulty and the rewards of frontier life with a diverse cast of characters.

FICTION
Little Women

Outspoken, shy, simple, creative. The March sisters are as different as four young girls can be. However, when their father is sent to fight in the Civil War, they find themselves bound together through comedy, tragedy, and the challenges of growing up. This enduring story, whose events closely resemble those of author Louisa May Alcott's own life, offers an unforgettable portrait of coming-of-age during a turbulent time in history.

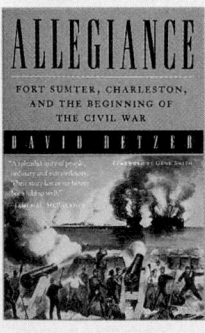

NONFICTION
Allegiance

This gripping account by David Detzer of the events leading up to the beginning of the Civil War focuses specifically on the drama surrounding Fort Sumter. Detzer's book is described as both well researched and engaging. His tale begins near the end of 1860 with the occupation of Fort Sumter and ends with the firing of the first shots and the opening of the war. Throughout, it describes the politics, uncertainty, and increasing tension that led to cannon fire on the fort.

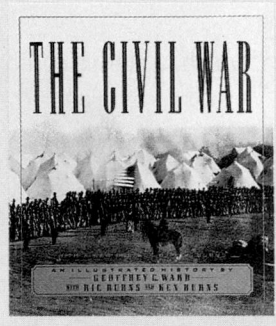

NONFICTION
The Civil War: An Illustrated History

For an inside look at the most dramatic war waged on U.S. soil, consider *The Civil War: An Illustrated History* by Geoffrey C. Ward and Ric and Ken Burns. This companion volume to the PBS series features essays; interviews; and an arresting series of photographs depicting generals, soldiers, and everyday citizens from the North and the South. The historical narrative and stunning images trace the war from the first shots at Fort Sumter through the bloody battlefields and finally to General Lee's surrender at Appomattox.

POETRY

José Martí: Selected Writings

Who's the most popular United States poet in Latin America? The answer is probably Walt Whitman. One of his greatest admirers was the Cuban poet José Martí, who introduced Whitman's work to Spanish-speaking audiences at the turn of the century. Whitman's influence on Martí's own verse is evident in *José Martí: Selected Writings,* translated by Esther Allen.

POETRY

Odes to Common Things

How do you feel about dictionaries, bread, socks, or chairs? The Chilean poet Pablo Neruda honors many of the objects we tend to forget in our daily lives. Crediting Walt Whitman as one of his main influences, Neruda writes poems that celebrate life with language both straightforward and metaphorical, lyrical and personal.

POETRY

Visiting Emily

Something about Emily Dickinson—her solitary life, her fierce, driven poems—has captured people's imaginations in a way few other writers have. *Visiting Emily* is a collection of poems gathered by editors Sheila Coghill and Thom Tommaro. The collection was inspired by the life and work of Emily Dickinson. Whether imitating Dickinson's trademark style or paying tribute to the woman herself, these poems keep a beautiful, mysterious legacy alive.

POETRY

negrospirituals. com

Nothing so intimately shares the hardships, hopes, and dreams of slaves as their songs known as spirituals. This Web site provides the history of spirituals, along with the singers and composers who made the songs come alive both before and after the Emancipation. Visitors to the site can search the lyrics to more than two hundred spirituals and even sample several audio files of songs performed by contemporary artists.

Learn It Online

Learn about more fiction and nonfiction works dealing with the Civil War on the *NovelWise* site online.

go.hrw.com   L11-603   Go

UNIT 4

The Age of Realism

1880–1914

COLLECTION 9
Regionalism and Local Color

COLLECTION 10
Realism and Naturalism

"What is character but the determination of incident? What is incident but the illustration of character?"

— **Henry James**

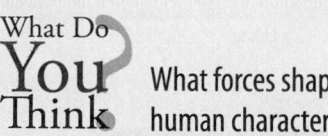

What Do You Think? What forces shape human character?

New York (1911) by George Bellows (1882–1925).
Collection of Mr. and Mrs. Paul Mellon. Image © Board of Trustees, National Gallery of Art, Washington.

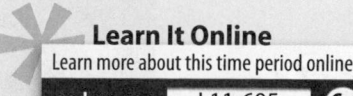

Learn It Online
Learn more about this time period online.
go.hrw.com L11-605 Go

The Age of Realism

1880–1914

This time line represents a snapshot of United States literary events, United States historical events, and world events from 1880 to 1914. During this period, the United States developed as an industrial nation, entered the world arena, and initiated reforms at home. In literature, realism emerged as the dominant style of writing.

UNITED STATES LITERARY EVENTS

1880

1881 Henry James publishes his novel *Portrait of a Lady* >

1884 Mark Twain publishes *Adventures of Huckleberry Finn*

1885 William Dean Howells publishes the realistic novel *The Rise of Silas Lapham*

1894 Kate Chopin publishes *Bayou Folk*

1890

1895 Stephen Crane publishes *The Red Badge of Courage*

1896 Paul Laurence Dunbar publishes *Lyrics of Lowly Life*

UNITED STATES HISTORICAL EVENTS

1880

1881 Clara Barton organizes the American Red Cross

1881 Booker T. Washington founds the Tuskegee Institute

1883 The Brooklyn Bridge opens

1885 Home Insurance Building, the first skyscraper, rises in Chicago

The Ferris Wheel at the Columbian Exposition in Chicago.

1890

1890 More than two hundred Sioux are killed by U.S. soldiers at Wounded Knee, South Dakota

< 1893 The World's Columbian Exposition showcases American technology and industry

1898 The Spanish-American War starts between the United States and Spain

WORLD EVENTS

1880

1881 Louis Pasteur develops a vaccine for rabies >

1885 Karl Benz produces the first gasoline-powered automobile

1890

1895 Wilhelm Roentgen discovers X-rays

1896 The first modern Olympic Games are held in Athens, Greece >

1899 Aspirin is patented

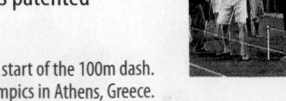

The start of the 100m dash. Olympics in Athens, Greece.

SKILLS FOCUS **Literary Skills** Evaluate and analyze the philosophical, political, religious, ethical, and social influences of a historical period. **Reading Skills** Identify and under- stand chronological order; identify and understand graphic elements; use text organizers such as overviews, headings, and graphic features to locate and categorize information.

Your Turn

With a partner, review the time line and select two events that may have shaped the way people viewed themselves and the world. Discuss how you think these events might have influenced human beliefs and behavior at the time they occurred. How might they have influenced beliefs and behavior since then?

1900 · 1910 · 1914

1900 Theodore Dreiser publishes the naturalistic novel *Sister Carrie*

1901 Frank Norris publishes the naturalistic novel *The Octopus: A Story of California*

1903 W.E.B. Du Bois publishes his influential essay collec- tion *The Souls of Black Folk*

1906 Upton Sinclair publishes ❯ *The Jungle,* drawing attention to unsafe, unsanitary conditions in the meat-packing industry

1910 Edwin Arlington Robinson publishes a collection of poems, *The Town Down the River*

1910 Jane Addams publishes *Twenty Years at Hull House* ❯

1913 Willa Cather publishes the novel *O Pioneers!*

Jane Addams with a young girl.

1900 · 1910 · 1914

1903 Wilbur and Orville Wright make the first airplane flight

1904 The United States takes over construction of the Panama Canal from the French

1907 Theodore Roosevelt sends the Great White Fleet on a voyage around the world

1913 Henry Ford announces conveyor-belt technology for mass-producing automobiles ❮

1914 The United States intervenes in the Mexican Revolution

Model T being assem- bled at Ford's plant.

1900 · 1910 · 1914

1900 Boxer Rebellion against foreign influence begins in China

1901 England's Queen Victoria dies

1905 Albert Einstein formulates his theory of relativity

1905 Japan wins the Russo- Japanese War

1910 Sigmund Freud publishes *The Origin and Development of Psychoanalysis*

❮ **1912** The ocean liner *Titanic* sinks while crossing the Atlantic

1913 Dr. Albert Schweitzer opens a hospital in French Equatorial Africa to battle disease

1914 World War I begins

The Age of Realism
1880–1914

After the Civil War, the United States was revitalized by a wave of immigration and westward expansion. Rapid industrial development brought the country wealth and new status as a world power but produced unsettling social problems. The Progressive Movement emerged in an attempt to improve American politics, business, and community life by embracing social and political reform. In literature, writers turned from Romanticism to realism, emphasizing ordinary characters and events and seeking to reflect life as it really was.

KEY CONCEPTS

New Settlers Go West

History of the Times A surge of westward expansion after the Civil War led to the confinement of Native Americans on reservations. Millions of immigrants arrived from Europe, filling the cities of the East and settling the West.

Literature of the Times Writers disillusioned by the Civil War turned from Romanticism to realism. Regional writers used local color to portray everyday life in particular settings.

The Perils of Prosperity

History of the Times Abundant resources and an endless supply of workers accelerated industrial development, which deepened social problems in cities. The United States began to exert influence in the Pacific and elsewhere.

Literature of the Times American realist writers sought to depict ordinary life and people accurately. Some writers reflected the insights of modern psychology when portraying human behavior.

Reforms Change Society

History of the Times A spirit of reform grew in reaction to the problems of industrialization. The Progressive Movement represented efforts to make government more responsive and businesses more ethical.

Literature of the Times Some writers influenced by Darwin and Freud began to view social problems as the result of biological forces that control human fate. This view is reflected in the literary movement called naturalism.

SKILLS FOCUS Literary Skills Evaluate and analyze the philosophical, political, religious, ethical, and social influences of a historical period. **Reading Skills** Read widely to increase knowledge of the student's culture, the culture of others, and the common elements across cultures; identify and understand elements of text structure (including headings and sections) information.

KEY CONCEPT

New Settlers Go West

History of the Times

Hundreds of thousands of Americans moved west after the Civil War, lured by an expanding rail system, available land, and the potential of farms, ranches, and mines. Far sooner than expected, the United States expanded to the Pacific and reached its continental limits. The census bureau declared the frontier closed in 1890. In a post-frontier United States, people would realize dreams of opportunity by building cities, forging industrial empires, and planting the American flag in distant outposts of the world.

The closing of the frontier had unfortunate consequences for Native Americans. In December 1890, army soldiers surrounded a band of Sioux near Wounded Knee Creek in South Dakota. Gunfire erupted, and more than two hundred Sioux men, women, and children were killed. The massacre at Wounded Knee was the last "battle" of the American Indian Wars and marked the end of an era for American Indians. Life and culture for most Native Americans existed within the confines of reservations thereafter.

Although the frontier had closed, the front doors of the United States remained open. Immigrants poured into the United States by the millions, adding momentum to western expansion and filling cities and factories in the East. The United States population leapt from 50 million people in 1880 to 76 million people by 1914.

Literature of the Times

American Romanticism, which was inadequate to express the horrors of the Civil War, wilted in the war's aftermath. A new generation of writers known as realists focused their attention on everyday life and ordinary human behavior.

American realism had its roots in regionalism, literature that emphasizes a specific geographic setting. Sarah Orne Jewett, Kate Chopin, Bret Harte, and others used techniques of local color writing to reflect the customs, speech, and character of people in different regions of the country.

Mark Twain is the best-known example of a regional writer whose realism far surpassed local bounds. His well-known novel *Adventures of Huckleberry Finn* (1885) combines a lyrical portrait of an American landscape with a biting picture of the inherent social injustices of pre–Civil War life.

Comprehension Check

Why might writers during this time have been attracted to realism rather than Romanticism?

Fast Facts

Historical Highlights

- The United States population booms from 1880 to 1914.
- A second industrial revolution occurs in the late nineteenth century.
- The Progressive Era begins in the 1890s and brings about needed reforms.

Literary Highlights

- Realism in America begins in the 1880s with local color writing by authors such as Sarah Orne Jewett.
- Naturalistic novels, such as Frank Norris's *The Octopus: A Story of California* (1901), offer grim portrayals of characters unable to control their fates.

Learn It Online

Learn more about the age of realism with the video "From Conflict to New Frontiers" online.

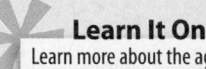 go.hrw.com   L11-609   **Go**

The Perils of Prosperity

History of the Times

In the aftermath of the Civil War, technological innovations unleashed an era of unparalleled industrial growth. Anchored by established coal, steel, and railroad industries, the American economy nurtured new technologies based on electricity, oil, and internal combustion. New inventions sprang up, from automobiles to airplanes, skyscrapers to motion pictures. Industry was fueled by a seemingly endless supply of raw materials and cheap labor.

New business strategies mirrored technological developments. Free of regulation, corporations merged into giant trusts,[1] or monopolies, to control wages, fix prices, wipe out competition, and concentrate power in the hands an elite few. These captains of industry were dominating economic and political figures and included Andrew Carnegie, J. P. Morgan, Jay Gould, and John D. Rockefeller. As industry

---

1. **trusts:** combinations of companies designed to control the production and price of goods and to eliminate competition.

advanced, the gap between rich and poor in the United States became a canyon. Carnegie earned more than twenty-three million dollars in 1900; a steel worker in one of his plants earned about five hundred dollars per year.

The United States was eager to translate its industrial might into a larger role on the world stage. It quickly snapped up Hawaii as a territory. After emerging from war with Spain as the victor, the United States added Cuba, Puerto Rico, Guam, and the Philippines to its territories. Theodore Roosevelt used American vigor and vision to complete the Panama Canal. Though the United States dominated the Western Hemisphere and was an important presence in the Pacific, it was completely unprepared to deal with war looming in Europe in 1914.

Literature of the Times

The American realism that emerged from regional writing aspired to make fiction true to life by describing ordinary characters, situations, and settings. Although they did not take direct

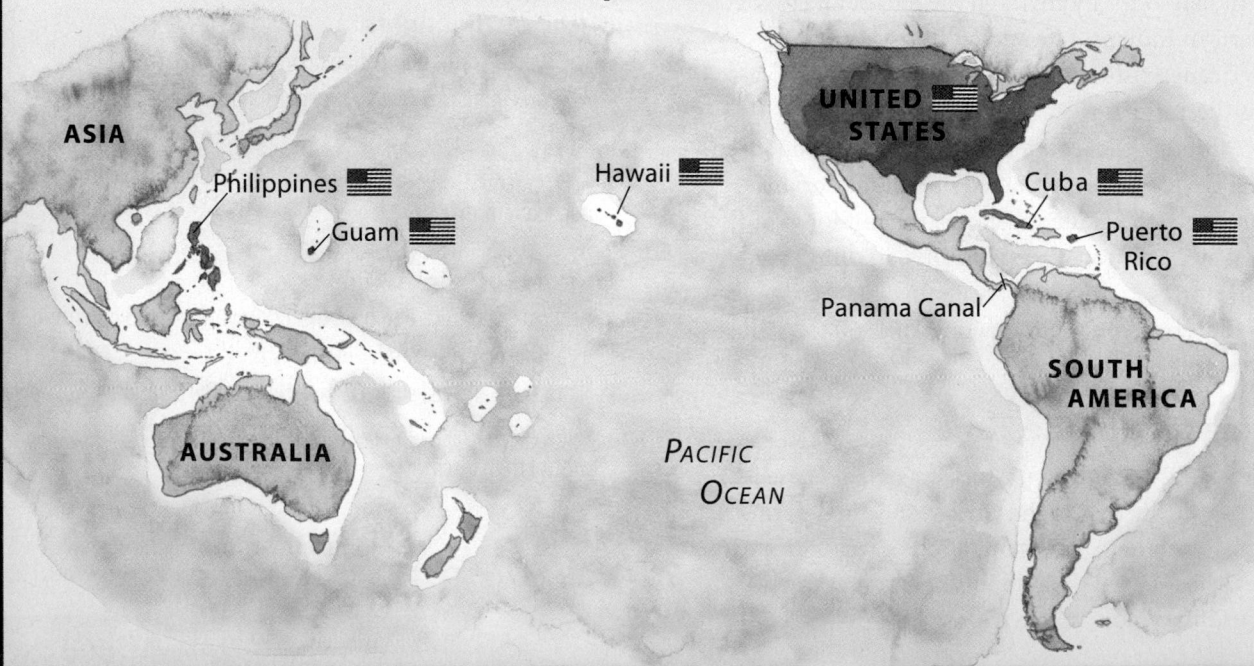

U.S. Expansion, 1898

inspiration from Europe, American writers were aware of an established European tradition of realism. William Dean Howells, editor of the influential magazine *The Atlantic Monthly,* became a tireless promoter of a distinctively American strain of realism. In his critical writings and novels, Howells modeled a "smiling realism" that portrayed an America where people may act foolishly, but their good qualities eventually win out.

Realistic novelists often relied on the emerging sciences of biology, psychology, and sociology, as well as their own observations and insights. Most realistic writers showed an interest in human motivation and psychology. For some writers, these interior issues were of enormous importance. The tradition of psychological realism found expression in the novels of Henry James, many of which reveal his interest in complex social and psychological situations. In a typical James novel, a straightforward American confronts the complexities of European society and either defeats or is defeated by them.

Like James, Stephen Crane (see Collection 7) had a deep interest in human psychology, especially when a character was under great stress. Crane's psychological dramas play out not in the gentle predicaments of William Dean Howells or the posh drawing rooms of Henry James but on a battlefield, in a tossing lifeboat, or in the gutter of a slum.

Comprehension Check

How did the economy of the United States help it become a global power during this era?

Money Talks

The end of the nineteenth century is often called the Gilded Age. Rich families of the era competed for power and position by displaying their wealth and extravagance.

Andrew Carnegie, however, believed that great wealth ought to be used for great good. He once wrote that "a man who dies rich dies disgraced." In 1901, he sold his steel empire and devoted the rest of his life to giving away his fortune. Carnegie is best known for building libraries across America, but he also promoted higher education, arts and culture, child welfare, scientific progress, and international peace. Though Carnegie died in 1919, many foundations funded by his wealth continue his philanthropic work today.

As in the industrial age, today's technologies have produced immense personal fortunes. Some beneficiaries of this boom have followed Carnegie's model. Software developer Bill Gates and his wife, Melinda, have created one of the world's largest charitable foundations. Investor Warren Buffett has dedicated most of his wealth to the Gates Foundation, linking the world's two largest personal fortunes for the promotion of education and health worldwide.

Ask Yourself

What similarities do you see in the way personal wealth is used today and the way it was used in the Gilded Age? Do you think Andrew Carnegie's beliefs about the responsible uses of wealth are common in today's culture? Why or why not?

Bill and Melinda Gates meeting with poor children in South Asia.

Reforms Change Society

History of the Times

The excesses of uncontrolled industrialism, the squalor of overcrowded cities, and deep social inequalities sparked a wide-ranging impulse for reform. This impulse was characteristic of the period known as the Progressive Era.

Remedies to social problems took many forms. In politics, President Theodore Roosevelt declared himself a trustbuster and campaigned against the powerful corporate structures that strangled commercial competition. His successors, Presidents Taft and Wilson, took similar actions by proposing laws and creating agencies to regulate banking, improve business competition, and protect the public interest. Robert La Follette and other activists won reforms at local, city, and state levels.

The labor movement was reborn as workers organized locally and across industries to protect wages, reduce working hours, and improve working conditions. Labor strikes sometimes had violent and even deadly outcomes. In 1894, workers at the Pullman railroad car factory went on strike when their wages were cut. Other unions honored the Pullman strike by freezing all rail traffic west of Chicago. More than two thousand United States soldiers were sent to break the strike. Violence and riots erupted; thirteen workers were killed.

In 1905, W.E.B. Du Bois joined with other African American leaders in creating the Niagara Movement,

an early step in the long quest to end segregation[2] and achieve civil rights. Elizabeth Cady Stanton and Susan B. Anthony continued the struggle for female suffrage and women's rights. Jane Addams was among the first people to take direct action to improve the lives of urban families by founding Hull House, which became a model for community settlement houses across the country. Naturalist John Muir led a conservation movement to protect landscapes and wildlife by creating national parks. From the slums to the wilderness, the Progressive Era sought lasting benefits for the American people.

---

2. **segregation:** isolation or separation of one racial group from others.

U.S. Cavalry escorting a train from Chicago during the Pullman strike (1894).

Link to Today

Investigative Reporting

Writers played an important role in the Progressive Era. Ida Tarbell, Lincoln Steffens, and other crusading journalists became known as muckrakers for their role in uncovering corruption and stirring up action. Most investigative journalism appeared in newspapers and popular magazines, but books played a decisive role, too. In 1906, Upton Sinclair's novel *The Jungle,* an exposé of the meatpacking industry, so shocked the nation that the Meat Inspection Act and the Pure Food and Drug Act became law within months of the book's publication.

Crime, corruption, abuse, and waste have not disappeared from American life, nor has the need for investigative reporters. Today's muckrakers, however, do not confine themselves to print. Some of the most effective critiques of present-day issues—from the fast-food industry to global warming—are done with a microphone and a video camera. Web sites have also become tools of social criticism, presenting text, images, and artifacts that assert a point of view.

Ask Yourself

In your view, what aspect of modern life most deserves a muckraking investigation?

John Muir (c. 1902).

Literature of the Times

For a number of writers in the Progressive Era, realism's effort to depict life accurately was insufficient. Writers known as naturalists followed the lead of the French novelist Émile Zola and relied on new scientific understandings to dissect human behavior. The work of Charles Darwin held that human beings are wholly subject to the natural laws of the universe. The insights of Sigmund Freud suggested that people are driven by subconscious motives they do not understand. If a mirror symbolizes realism's effort to reflect the human condition, then a microscope symbolizes naturalism's effort to expose the deep biological and environmental forces that determine human fate.

Frank Norris demonstrated that one can be both a naturalist and a muckraker in his best-known novel *The Octopus: A Story of California* (1901), which describes the strangling effects of the railroad on California farmers. Theodore Dreiser's *Sister Carrie* (1900) and Jack London's *The Call of the Wild* (1903) and *The Sea-Wolf* (1904) are models of naturalism.

The period from around the turn of the century until 1914 saw the continuation of many nineteenth-century trends. At the same time, however, writers tried out new styles and forms of expression in early experiments with modernism. Some writers, such as poet Edwin Arlington Robinson, with his memorable New England characters, worked to sustain earlier visions of America. Still, the currents of realism and naturalism sparked by the Civil War continued to dominate American literature.

Comprehension Check

How did writers of this age expose the need for reform?

Wrap Up

Talk About . . .

In a small group, discuss the relative merits of realism and Romanticism. What are the major qualities, strengths, and limitations of each movement? Which approach do you prefer, and why? Use each Academic Vocabulary word **listed below** in your discussion.

Write About . . .

Choose one writer who made a significant contribution during this era. Write a few paragraphs explaining how he or she reflected the political, economic, or social trends of the time.

Academic Vocabulary for Unit 4

Talking and Writing About Literature
To be a successful student, you should become familiar with Academic Vocabulary, the language you'll need to know in order to write and talk about literature. In this unit, you will encounter the Academic Vocabulary terms listed below. These words will be underlined throughout the unit.

capacity (kuh PAS uh tee) *n.:* ability. *Writers of the Progressive Era believed they had the capacity to bring about social reform.*

crucial (KROO shuhl) *adj.:* necessary. *Reforms were crucial to end exploitive working conditions.*

parameter (puh RAM uh tuhr) *n.:* limitation; boundary. *The suffragettes rejected the narrow parameters of women's social roles.*

relevant (REHL uh vuhnt) *adj.:* pertinent to the matter at hand. *Novelists of this time were more socially relevant than ever before.*

sustain (suh STAYN) *v.:* maintain or prolong. *Despite numerous setbacks, the workers were able to sustain their efforts.*

Your Turn

Copy the words from the Academic Vocabulary list into your *Reader/Writer Notebook.* Then, work with a partner to write a definition of each literary movement of this time period, making use of words from the list when possible.

Link to Today

In this Link to Today, a contemporary writer provides a humorous take on a winter pastime.

Read with a Purpose

Read to see how one author reflects on the frosty grandeur of the north.

Build Background

During Minnesota's bone-chilling winters, when temperatures plunge below zero and arctic blasts scour a frozen landscape, many people revel in wintertime pursuits. For instance, ice fishermen eagerly await "ice in," when frozen lakes become safe for walking. Fishermen cut holes in the thickening ice, lower their lines and baited hooks into frigid depths, and wait . . . and wait . . . and wait.

Author Note

Garrison Keillor (1942–) is an author, poet, performer, storyteller, and comedian. Born in Anoka, Minnesota, Keillor is best known as the creator of *A Prairie Home Companion,* an old-style radio variety show about the fictional town of Lake Wobegon. Keillor's skill in reflecting the rhythms and attitudes of small-town Minnesota recalls Mark Twain's evocations of his Missouri youth and makes Keillor the leading local colorist writing today.

A WALK ON THE ICE

by **Garrison Keillor**
Radio Essay, December 2005

Call me Hrothgar[1] the Savage, but when I look at men's fashions in magazines, the models all sullen and sensitive and obviously spending much too much time on their hair, wearing sweaters made from Persian cat fur woven with feathers of snowy owls, yours for $1,495, I feel a strong urge to put on a parka and insulated pants and walk out onto a frozen lake and cut a hole in the ice and fish.

I felt the urge rather strongly the other morning as I drove along the Mississippi River in Minneapolis, which was frozen over, while listening to a man talk on the radio about a book he'd written in which he explored his feelings about his father, whom he'd never felt close to. I said to him, "Oh, get over it." The ice is a good place for a man to go rather than waste time writing books about not knowing your father.

---

1. **Hrothgar:** Danish king in the medieval epic poem *Beowulf.*

Garrison Keillor speaking in Charlottesville, Virginia, on March 24, 2004.

The ice is a good place for a man to go rather than waste time writing books about not knowing your father.

In other parts of the country, you can climb to the top of a mountain and look around. Here, we walk out on the ice.

You could be living in south Minneapolis, in a neighborhood of comfortable homes with DSL and HBO and nearby shops selling latte and cranberry scones, but if you walk a few blocks to Lake Calhoun and stride out onto the ice, suddenly you are in Tolstoy's *War and Peace*,[2] waiting for Natasha and Prince Andrei to come lickety split through the birch forest in the sleigh. The moment you leave shore, you are gripped by a sense of grandeur.

This is all thanks to your mother, who warned you 11,000 times to stay off the ice lest you fall through, warnings that now serve to heighten the drama, which is further heightened by the fact that every year a few men, seeking a leadership role for themselves, drive their snowmobiles onto lakes before the ice is thick enough and drown, a Darwinian[3] moment indeed.

---

2. *War and Peace*: epic novel by Leo Tolstoy set in Russia in the early nineteenth century. Two main characters are Natasha Rostova and Prince Andrei Bolkonsky.
3. **Darwinian:** referring to Charles Darwin's theory of the survival of the fittest.

The water is cold and the laws of physics apply to us all. But a man must do what a man must do. It's in our circuitry. Little boys of sensitive, caring parents take the dolls that they've been given and rip the legs off and use them for pistols. It's just how they're wired.

A man needs grandeur in his life, more than calcium or vitamin E, so we can get loose of tedious regimentation and blather and escape from Gravity Week when Americans are reminded not to slip and fall, and we can march to a different drummer, one who leads us out onto the ice.

Think of grandeur as an alternative to therapy. Hercules[4] did. He had gone mad and done terrible things, as we all do from time to time, and he purified himself by performing heroic labors such as killing the nine-headed hydra and capturing Cerberus, the three-headed dog who guards the gates of Hades,[5] and in this way he regained his health, and so may we, if we are brave.

---

4. **Hercules:** a hero of Greek mythology.
5. **Hades:** the underworld, in Greek mythology.

In therapy, you complain about your dad not being available for you emotionally and you do it until you get tired of it and then you quit. It is whiny by nature. When you seek grandeur, you put your dad behind you and you get away from women and their endless questions (Why are you so quiet? What's wrong? What do you mean, "nothing's wrong"? What are you thinking? Why don't we ever talk? Are you listening to me? Do you think I'm too fat?) and you go off to do heroic deeds, such as write your autobiography, or drive to California, or build a cabin, or walk out on the ice.

I once led a group of winter visitors from California and North Carolina and Texas out onto White Bear Lake north of St. Paul. They had never done such a thing before. They stepped onto the ice gingerly, as if it might disintegrate under them, and walked out a hundred yards from shore, stopped, and looked around. It was a cold bright day and they trembled in the grandeur of the moment. They were speechless. They looked at me with tears in their eyes. Their noses were running. They wanted to tell me what a transforming experience this was for them, but it was indescribable, and anyway they knew I understood. We stayed as long as we needed to and then went back to the car. You don't have to go to Katmandu[6] to experience transcendence. It's right here in Minnesota.

---

6. **Katmandu:** capital of Nepal, a country that lies along the southern slopes of the Himalayan Mountains.

Ask Yourself

1. **Read with a Purpose** What about his fellow human beings amuses Keillor in this essay? Why does he praise ice fishing? Explain.

2. In the opening paragraph, how does exaggeration contribute to the essay's humor? What effect does Keillor create by contrasting the clothes of the male models with his "urge to put on a parka and insulated pants"?

3. In the fifth paragraph of the essay, the author uses humor to suggest something about the nature of men. What is he suggesting, and how does Keillor's use of humor affect your reaction to his idea?

4. This essay makes several references to grandeur. What do you think Keillor is saying about grandeur? Explain.

5. What do you imagine Keillor's visitors were thinking on the ice of White Bear Lake? How do you think you would react to such an experience? Explain your answer.

The Jolly Boatmen (1877–1878) by George Caleb Bingham (1811–1879).

CONTENTS

"Fiction is obliged to stick to possibilities. Truth isn't."

Regionalism by **Leila Christenbury**

Characteristics of Regionalism

- Desire to record, celebrate, and mythologize the vast diversity of the United States' different geographical regions
- Strict attention to recording accurately the speech, mannerisms, behavior, and beliefs of people in specific locales
- Local-color writing that "paints" the local scenes and tends toward the humorous or the sentimental

America's Diverse Regions

Regionalism in literature embraces not the universal but the particular, focusing on what specifically characterizes a geographical area and its people. Regional writers strive to capture the speech, dress, common beliefs, and social interactions of a given locale. Two of the most powerful American regional writers are Mark Twain and Bret Harte, both of whom captured for their readers local life, manners, and speech. In this collection you will read vivid examples of regionalism, set in locales such as the banks of the Mississippi River and the gold-mining camps of the West. As you read, look for details of time and place that capture the flavor of a particular region.

The growing interest in regionalism during the late 1800s resulted from changes occurring within the nation itself. As the United States rapidly expanded in the years after the Civil War and as greater numbers of immigrants entered the country, regionalist writers sought to record, celebrate, and mythologize the vast diversity of the American landscape and its people.

Regionalist writers attempt to re-create in careful detail both the <u>relevant</u> physical features of landscapes and towns and the often colorful characters who inhabit them. In *Life on the Mississippi,* for example, Mark Twain records the speech patterns and mannerisms of the steamboat pilot Mr. Bixby while conveying the beauty of the Mississippi River and the challenges involved in learning to pilot a steamboat. In regionalist writing, place is integral to the story itself, and the characters seem to belong to their particular locale.

Local Color The shift toward interest in particular regions led to the movement known as **local color.** Writers of local color use writing to "paint" local scenes. Many works in this style contain interesting, eccentric characters and whimsical humor. Local colorists often tend toward the romantic and sometimes the sentimental.

<u>Crucial</u> to local-color writing is the use of the **vernacular,** the language spoken by the people in a particular locality. Local colorists felt that the best way to capture a region's heart and soul was to let readers "hear" its authentic speech patterns. These writers often recorded regional dialect by presenting regional pronunciations rather than standard spellings. In Twain's "The Celebrated Jumping Frog of Calaveras County," for example, the Western miner Simon Wheeler uses phrases like "cal'klated to edercate" instead of "calculated to educate." The colorful characters and situations in local-color writing would be impossible to achieve without the use of the vernacular.

Ask Yourself

1. Why might nineteenth-century readers have been especially receptive to regionalist and local-color writing?
2. In your opinion, which qualities of regionalism might most appeal to today's readers?

Learn It Online
Go online to learn more about regionalism.

go.hrw.com   L11-619   **Go**

SKILLS FOCUS **Literary Skills** Understand and analyze regionalism.

Analyzing Regionalism in a Painting

Regionalism emphasizes the particular characteristics and positive attributes of a specific locale. Regionalist painters celebrate regions such as the Midwest in their works, often doing so in a way that is sympathetic and knowledgeable.

Guidelines

Use these guidelines to help you analyze how this painting reflects regionalism:

- What is the painting's title? What are the figures in the painting doing?
- Study the elements of this scene. How would you describe them?
- Does the painting express any humor? How?

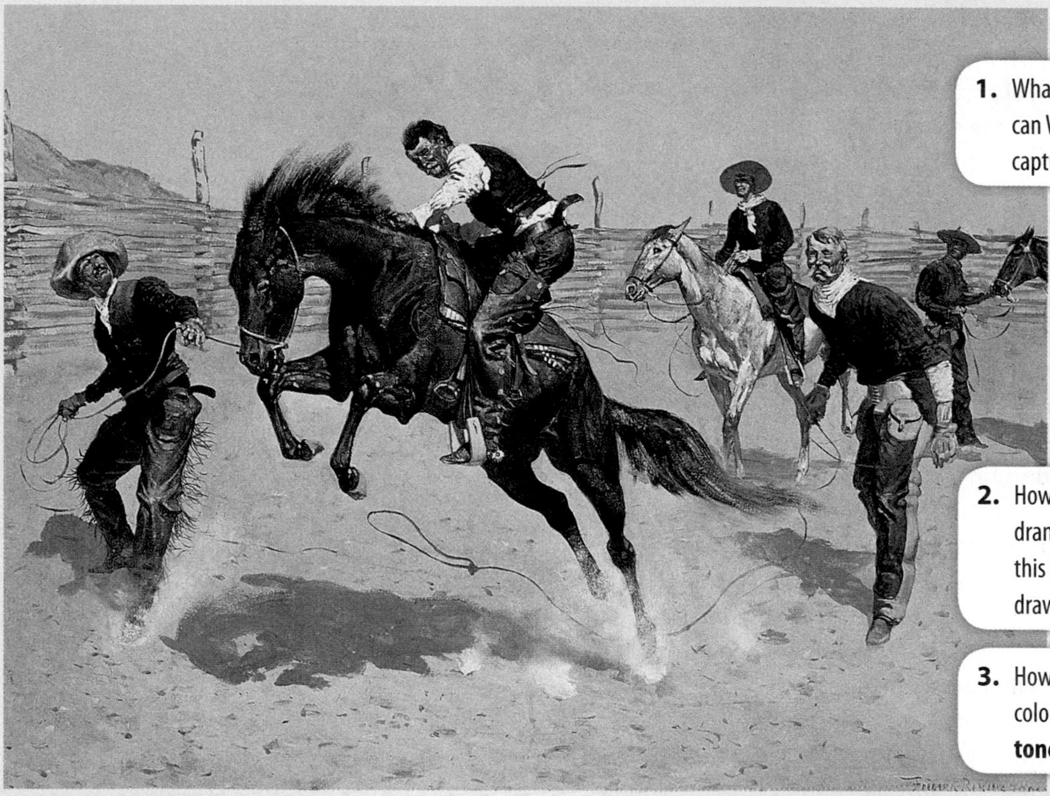

1. What aspects of the American West does this painting capture?

2. How does the artist add drama and excitement to this image? What elements draw your attention?

3. How would you describe the colors? What is the overall **tone** of the painting?

Turn Him Loose, Bill (c. 1893) by Frederic Remington (1861–1909).

Your Turn Analyze Regionalism in a Painting

Look at the painting on page 618. What characteristics of regionalism do you observe in the painting? How would you describe the figures and the locale? What is the tone of the painting?

SKILLS FOCUS Reading Skills Make predictions as a strategy for comprehension.

Predicting by **Kylene Beers**

When you watch a movie or read a book, do you ever guess what is going to happen next? At a movie do others become annoyed when you blurt out what you think may happen? Predicting is a natural response to anticipation and suspense.

To keep readers interested, filmmakers and fiction writers arrange the details of a story to create **suspense,** a feeling of uncertainty or curiosity about what will happen. A writer may also leave clues or build anticipation with **sensory details,** tempting you to guess a story's final outcome. You can predict story events by making educated guesses based on your prior knowledge and the information given in the text. In fact, you can make your very first predictions based on the title of a story.

> "The Outcasts of Poker Flat"

From the title above, you may predict that the story will feature characters who are forced out of a town and that the characters might be criminals.

The characters themselves—their thoughts, words, actions, and reactions—can provide clues that help you predict what will happen in the story. In the beginning of "The Outcasts of Poker Flat," the main character, Mr. Oakhurst, steps into Main Street in the town of Poker Flat. Notice that the writer, Bret Harte, focuses on how the other characters react to Oakhurst:

> Two or three men, conversing earnestly together, ceased as he approached and exchanged significant glances.

You might predict that something bad is going to happen to Oakhurst—as Oakhurst himself predicts.

In the following excerpt, Harte provides additional clues as he reveals Oakhurst's thoughts and actions when two characters, Tom and Piney, join the group of outcasts:

> Mr. Oakhurst seldom troubled himself with sentiment, still less with propriety; but he had a vague idea that the situation was not fortunate. . . . He then endeavored to dissuade Tom Simson from delaying further, but in vain. He even pointed out the fact that there was no provision, nor means of making a camp.

Oakhurst has a vague feeling that Tom should not stay—they have no way to feed or shelter additional company. Because Oakhurst's judgments have so far proven correct, you might predict that the situation will grow worse.

Your Turn

Because time and place can change the course of a story, descriptions of a story's **setting** may also help you make predictions. Read the following passage from "The Outcasts of Poker Flat," and then make predictions about what will happen in the story.

> He looked at the gloomy walls that rose a thousand feet sheer above the circling pines around him, at the sky ominously clouded, at the valley below, already deepening into shadow.

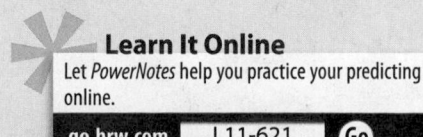

Learn It Online

Let *PowerNotes* help you practice your predicting online.

go.hrw.com   L11-621   **Go**

Preparing to Read

The Outcasts of Poker Flat

What Do You Think?

What forces shape human character?

⏱ QuickWrite

Think about a hardship that you or someone you know had to face. Write a paragraph describing the hardship and the way it changed the person who faced it.

Bret Harte
(1836–1902)

Bret Harte is remembered today for his stories and poems that capture the flavor of the American West. He is considered one of the classic writers of the genre now called Western pulp fiction.

Voice of the Wild West

Mark Twain once wrote, "Bret Harte was one of the pleasantest men I have ever known. He was also one of the unpleasantest men I have ever known." Francis Brett Hart (he later dropped the final *t* in Brett and added an *e* to Hart) arrived in California from Albany, New York, when he was about eighteen years old. He worked as a miner, a teacher, and a druggist's assistant before taking a job with the *Northern Californian* in 1859. He soon became a respected newspaper editor and a popular writer. During this time, he met writer Mark Twain, who admired the more experienced Harte and looked to him for advice.

Curiosity about the Western frontier had existed for a long time among Americans, and it grew during the gold rush of 1849. Although Harte's stories were written nearly twenty years later, the public was still hungry for tales about the colorful characters of the Wild West. Harte's ability to satisfy that hunger earned him nationwide fame as a realistic regionalist, a writer of "local color." From 1868 to 1871, Harte edited the *Overland Monthly*, a magazine published in San Francisco. Some of his best-known stories, including "The Luck of Roaring Camp" (1868) and "The Outcasts of Poker Flat" (1869), appeared during these years.

Gamblers, Gunfighters, and Gold

The basis for Harte's popularity was one of the very things that later made Mark Twain irate. Harte's Western characters were almost invariably noble, upstanding, and admirable. Beneath their rough exteriors, they were unfailingly dignified. Twain's Western characters, on the other hand, were, as Twain himself described, treacherous, filthy, and repulsive. Twain sometimes fumed over the romanticized, squeaky-clean vision of the West that Harte popularized.

Think About the Writer

Why do you think Harte may have "romanticized" his characters with nobler traits than the real people of the Wild West possessed?

Reader/Writer Notebook

Use your **RWN** to complete the activities for this selection.

Literary Focus

Characterization The process by which a writer reveals the personality of a character is called **characterization**. A writer can reveal a character in various ways:

- by directly stating what the character is like
- by describing the character's thoughts, words, and actions
- by showing how other characters react to him or her

As you read "The Outcasts of Poker Flat," notice the different ways in which Harte brings the characters in his story to life.

Reading Focus

Predicting When you make **predictions,** you use clues in the text, as well as your own experiences, to guess what might happen in a story. Understanding characters' personalities, motives (reasons for acting), and patterns of behavior can help you make accurate predictions.

Into Action As you read, use a chart like the one below to record relevant clues about characters in the story. Identify at least one example of characterization for each "outcast," noting where it appears. Use these clues to make predictions about what will happen to the characters.

Character	Clue	My Prediction
Mr. Oakhurst	"I reckon they're after somebody," he reflected; "likely, it's me." (p. 625)	The men who are after Mr. Oakhurst will try to harm him.

Writing Focus

Think as a Reader/Writer

Find It in Your Reading One way to learn about a character is by observing how other characters respond to him or her. As you read, pay close attention to how the characters in the story interact with one another. In your *Reader/Writer Notebook,* record notes about the interactions.

TechFocus As you read this story, think about how the events and characters might be portrayed in a modern news report.

Vocabulary

impropriety   (ihm pruh PRY uh tee) *n.:* improper conduct. *The citizens of Poker Flat decided to expel those who acted with impropriety.*

malevolence   (muh LEHV uh luhns) *n.:* the wish that evil may happen to others. *Mother Shipton speaks with malevolence when she becomes an outcast of Poker Flat.*

bellicose   (BEHL uh kohs) *adj.:* fond of fighting; warlike. *Although hostile at first, Uncle Billy feels less bellicose after drinking liquor.*

guileless   (GYL lihs) *adj.:* honest, sincere. *Tom proves too guileless to be a good gambler.*

amiability   (ay mee uh BIHL uh tee) *n.:* friendliness; pleasantness. *A feeling of amiability overcomes Mother Shipton when Tom and Piney arrive.*

jocular   (JAHK yuh luhr) *adj.:* joking; full of fun. *A jocular idea occurs to Uncle Billy, who almost cannot keep from laughing.*

extemporized   (ehk STEHM puh ryzd) *v.:* prepared offhand; made for the occasion. *Tom extemporized a covering for the roofless cabin by using pine boughs.*

Language Coach

Suffixes The suffix –*less* means "without" or "lacking." Take –*less* away from *guileless*. What do you think *guile* means? Check your guess in a dictionary. Does it mean what you expect it to mean?

Learn It Online
Listen to this story read aloud online.

go.hrw.com   L11-623   **Go**

The Outcasts of Poker Flat

by **Bret Harte**

Read with a Purpose

Read to discover the true nature of Harte's characters when they are forced to face hardship together.

Build Background

Harte's stories were popular because they seemed daringly realistic, but they always carried a neat, moralistic message for readers of the time. In a typical Harte story, good triumphs and evil is driven out. His Western characters are almost always honest, virtuous people. The gambler with a heart of gold, the gentle farmer driven to use a gun to fight evil, the rough dance-hall woman secretly motivated by compassion—these and other characters still inhabit Westerns written for movies and television. Bret Harte invented most of these character types.

As Mr. John Oakhurst, gambler, stepped into the main street of Poker Flat on the morning of the twenty-third of November, 1850, he was conscious of a change in its moral atmosphere since the preceding night. Two or three men, conversing earnestly together, ceased as he approached, and exchanged significant glances. There was a Sabbath lull in the air, which, in a settlement unused to Sabbath influences, looked ominous.

Mr. Oakhurst's calm, handsome face betrayed small concern in these indications. Whether he was conscious of any predisposing cause, was another question. "I reckon they're after somebody," he reflected; "likely it's me." He returned to his pocket the handkerchief with which he had been whipping away the red dust of Poker Flat from his neat boots, and quietly discharged his mind of any further conjecture. **Ⓐ**

In point of fact, Poker Flat was "after somebody." It had lately suffered the loss of several thousand dollars, two valuable horses, and a prominent citizen. It was experiencing a spasm of virtuous reaction, quite as lawless and ungovernable as any of the acts that had provoked it. A secret committee had determined to rid the town of all improper persons. This was done permanently in regard of two men who were then hanging from the boughs of a sycamore in the gulch, and temporarily in the banishment of certain other objectionable characters. I regret to say that some of these were ladies. It is but due to the sex, however, to state that their impropriety was professional, and it was only in such easily established standards of evil that Poker Flat ventured to sit in judgment.

Mr. Oakhurst was right in supposing that he was included in this category. A few of the committee had urged hanging him as a possible example, and a sure method of reimbursing themselves from his pockets of the sums he had won from them. "It's agin justice," said Jim Wheeler, "to let this yer young man from Roaring Camp—an entire stranger—carry away our money." But a crude sentiment of equity residing in the breasts of those who had been fortunate enough to win from Mr. Oakhurst overruled this narrower local prejudice.

Mr. Oakhurst received his sentence with philosophic calmness, none the less coolly that he was aware of the hesitation of his judges. He was too much of a gambler not to accept fate. With him life was at best an uncertain game, and he recognized the usual percentage in favor of the dealer.

A body of armed men accompanied the deported wickedness of Poker Flat to the outskirts of the settlement. Besides Mr. Oakhurst, who was known to be a coolly desperate man, and for whose intimidation the armed escort was intended, the expatriated party consisted of a young woman familiarly known as "The Duchess"; another who had won the title of "Mother Shipton";[1] and "Uncle Billy," a suspected sluice-robber[2] and confirmed drunkard. The cavalcade provoked no comments from the spectators, nor was any word uttered by the escort. Only, when the gulch which marked the uttermost limit of Poker Flat was reached, the leader spoke briefly and to the point. The exiles were forbidden to return at the peril of their lives.

As the escort disappeared, their pent-up feelings found vent in a few hysterical tears from the Duchess, some bad language from Mother Shipton, and a Parthian[3] volley of expletives from Uncle Billy. The philosophic Oakhurst alone remained silent. He listened calmly to Mother Shipton's desire to cut somebody's heart out, to the repeated statements of the Duchess that she would die in the road, and to the alarming oaths that seemed to be bumped out of Uncle Billy as he rode forward. With the easy good-humor characteristic of his class, he insisted upon exchanging his own riding-horse, "Five Spot," for the sorry mule which the Duchess rode. But even this act did not draw the party into any closer sympathy. The young woman readjusted her somewhat draggled plumes with a feeble, faded coquetry; Mother Shipton eyed

---

1. **"Mother Shipton":** an Englishwoman who was accused of witchcraft.
2. **sluice-robber:** Sluices were channels in which gold ore was washed. Robbing a sluice was a low form of stealing.
3. **Parthian:** In ancient times, the Parthians were said to have turned during their retreats and fired arrows at their enemy.

Ⓐ Literary Focus Characterization How does Harte create a clear picture of Oakhurst's character without saying directly what kind of man Oakhurst is?

Vocabulary impropriety (ihm pruh PRY uh tee) *n.:* improper conduct.

the possessor of "Five Spot" with malevolence, and Uncle Billy included the whole party in one sweeping anathema.[4]

The road to Sandy Bar—a camp that, not having as yet experienced the regenerating influences of Poker Flat, consequently seemed to offer some invitation to the emigrants—lay over a steep mountain range. It was distant a day's severe travel. In that advanced season, the party soon passed out of the moist, temperate regions of the foot-hills into the dry, cold, bracing air of the Sierras. The trail was narrow and difficult. At noon the Duchess, rolling out of her saddle upon the ground, declared her intention of going no farther, and the party halted.

The spot was singularly wild and impressive. A wooded amphitheatre, surrounded on three sides by precipitous cliffs of naked granite, sloped gently toward the crest of another precipice that overlooked the valley. It was, undoubtedly, the most suitable spot for a camp, had camping been advisable. But Mr. Oakhurst knew that scarcely half the journey to Sandy Bar was accomplished, and the party were not equipped or provisioned for delay. This fact he pointed out to his companions curtly, with a philosophic commentary on the folly of "throwing up their hand before the game was played out." But they were furnished with liquor, which in this emergency stood them in place of food, fuel, rest, and prescience.[5] In spite of his remonstrances, it was not long before they were more or less under its influence. Uncle Billy passed rapidly from a bellicose state into one of stupor, the Duchess became maudlin, and Mother Shipton snored. Mr. Oakhurst alone remained erect, leaning against a rock, calmly surveying them.

Mr. Oakhurst did not drink. It interfered with a profession which required coolness, impassiveness,

and presence of mind, and, in his own language, he "couldn't afford it." As he gazed at his recumbent fellow-exiles, the loneliness begotten of his pariah[6] trade, his habits of life, his very vices, for the first time seriously oppressed him. He bestirred himself in dusting his black clothes, washing his hands and face, and other acts characteristic of his studiously neat habits, and for a moment forgot his annoyance. The thought of deserting his weaker and more pitiable companions never perhaps occurred to him. Yet he could not help feeling the want of that excitement which, singularly enough, was most conducive to that calm equanimity for which he was notorious. He looked at the gloomy walls that rose a thousand feet sheer above the circling pines around him, at the sky ominously clouded, at the valley below, already deepening into shadow; and, doing so, suddenly he heard his own name called. **B**

A horseman slowly ascended the trail. In the fresh, open face of the new-comer Mr. Oakhurst recognized Tom Simson, otherwise known as "The Innocent," of Sandy Bar. He had met him some months before over a "little game" and had, with perfect equanimity, won the entire fortune—amounting to some forty dollars—of that guileless youth. After the game was finished, Mr. Oakhurst drew the youthful speculator behind the door and thus addressed him: "Tommy, you're a good little man, but you can't gamble worth a cent. Don't try it over again." He then handed him his money back, pushed him gently from the room, and so made a devoted slave of Tom Simson. **C**

There was a remembrance of this in his boyish and enthusiastic greeting of Mr. Oakhurst. He had started, he said, to go to Poker Flat to seek his fortune. "Alone?" No, not exactly alone; in fact (a giggle), he had run away with Piney Woods. Didn't Mr. Oakhurst remember Piney? She that used to wait on the table at the Temperance House? They had been engaged a long

---

4. **anathema** (uh NATH uh muh): a curse.
5. **prescience** (PREHSH ee uhns): knowledge of things before they happen; foresight.

---

6. **pariah** (puh RY uh): outcast; person belonging to a low or despised social class.

Vocabulary   **malevolence** (muh LEHV uh luhns) *n.*: the wish that evil may happen to others.
bellicose (BEHL uh kohs) *adj.*: fond of fighting; warlike.
guileless (GYL lihs) *adj.*: honest; sincere.

B Reading Focus **Predicting** What predictions can you make about the story's outcome based on the information that Mr. Oakhurst's vices "for the first time seriously oppressed him"?

C Reading Focus **Predicting** In light of the flashback about Oakhurst and Simson, what do you predict will happen between Oakhurst and Simson later in the story?

Photograph of the Hangman's Tree in California (c. 1945).

Viewing and Interpreting   Harte's writings made this real hangman's tree famous. What details does Harte include to depict the setting of this story convincingly?

time, but old Jake Woods had objected, and so they had run away, and were going to Poker Flat to be married, and here they were. And they were tired out, and how lucky it was they had found a place to camp and company. All this the Innocent delivered rapidly, while Piney, a stout, comely damsel of fifteen, emerged from behind the pine-tree, where she had been blushing unseen, and rode to the side of her lover.

Mr. Oakhurst seldom troubled himself with sentiment, still less with propriety; but he had a vague idea that the situation was not fortunate. He retained, however, his presence of mind sufficiently to kick Uncle Billy, who was about to say something, and Uncle Billy was sober enough to recognize in Mr. Oakhurst's kick a superior power that would not bear trifling. He then endeavored to dissuade Tom Simson from delaying further, but in vain. He even pointed out the fact that there was no provision, nor means of making a camp. But, unluckily, the Innocent met this objection by assuring the party that he was provided with an extra mule loaded with provisions, and by the discovery of a rude attempt at a log-house near the trail. "Piney can stay with Mrs. Oakhurst," said the Innocent, pointing to the Duchess, "and I can shift for myself."

Nothing but Mr. Oakhurst's admonishing foot saved Uncle Billy from bursting into a roar of laughter. As it was, he felt compelled to retire up the canyon until he could recover his gravity. There he confided the joke to the tall pine trees, with many slaps of his leg, contortions of his face, and the usual profanity. But when he returned to the party, he found them seated by a fire—for the air had grown strangely chill and the sky overcast—in apparently amicable conversation. Piney was actually talking in an impulsive, girlish fashion to the Duchess, who was listening with an interest and animation she had not shown for many days. **D**

The Innocent was holding forth, apparently with equal effect, to Mr. Oakhurst and Mother Shipton, who was actually relaxing into amiability. "Is this yer a d—d picnic?" said Uncle Billy, with inward scorn, as he surveyed the sylvan[7] group, the glancing firelight, and the tethered animals in the foreground. Suddenly an idea mingled with the alcoholic fumes that disturbed his brain. It was apparently of a jocular nature, for he felt impelled to slap his leg again and cram his fist into his mouth.

As the shadows crept slowly up the mountain, a slight breeze rocked the tops of the pine-trees, and moaned through their long and gloomy aisles. The ruined cabin, patched and covered with pine-boughs, was set apart for the ladies. As the lovers parted, they unaffectedly exchanged a kiss, so honest and sincere that it might have been heard above the swaying pines. The frail Duchess and the malevolent Mother Shipton were probably too stunned to remark upon this last evidence of simplicity, and so turned without a word to the hut. The fire was replenished, the men lay down before the door, and in a few minutes were asleep. **E**

Mr. Oakhurst was a light sleeper. Toward morning he awoke benumbed and cold. As he stirred the dying fire, the wind, which was now blowing strongly, brought to his cheek that which caused the blood to leave it,—snow!

He started to his feet with the intention of awakening the sleepers, for there was no time to lose. But, turning to where Uncle Billy had been lying, he found him gone. A suspicion leaped to his brain, and a curse to his lips. He ran to the spot where the mules had been tethered—they were no longer there. The tracks were already rapidly disappearing in the snow.

The momentary excitement brought Mr. Oakhurst back to the fire with his usual calm. He did not waken the sleepers. The Innocent slumbered peacefully, with a smile on his good-humored, freckled face; the virgin Piney slept beside her frailer sisters as sweetly as though attended by celestial guardians; and Mr.

---

7. **sylvan:** of the woods.

D **Literary Focus** Characterization Why is Billy laughing? Contrast Billy's actions with Oakhurst's actions. What do these actions reveal about each character?

E **Literary Focus** Characterization What does the description of the kiss and Mother Shipton's reaction to it suggest about the effect Tom and Piney have on Mother Shipton?

Vocabulary **amiability** (ay mee uh BIHL uh tee) *n.*: friendliness; pleasantness.
jocular (JAHK yuh luhr) *adj.*: joking; full of fun.

Image from the movie *The Outcasts of Poker Flat* (1952).

Oakhurst, drawing his blanket over his shoulders, stroked his mustaches and waited for the dawn. It came slowly in a whirling mist of snowflakes that dazzled and confused the eye. What could be seen of the landscape appeared magically changed. He looked over the valley, and summed up the present and future in two words, "Snowed in!"

A careful inventory of the provisions, which, fortunately for the party, had been stored within the hut, and so escaped the felonious fingers of Uncle Billy, disclosed the fact that with care and prudence, they might last ten days longer. "That is," said Mr. Oakhurst, *sotto voce*[8] to the Innocent, "if you're willing to board us. If you ain't—and perhaps you'd better not—you can wait till Uncle Billy gets back with provisions." For some occult reason, Mr. Oakhurst could not bring himself to disclose Uncle Billy's rascality, and so offered the hypothesis that he had wandered from the camp and had accidentally stampeded the animals. He dropped a warning to the Duchess and Mother Shipton, who of course knew the facts of their associate's defection. "They'll find out the truth about us *all* when they find out anything," he added, significantly, "and there's no good frightening them now." **F**

Tom Simson not only put all his worldly store at the disposal of Mr. Oakhurst, but seemed to enjoy the prospect of their enforced seclusion. "We'll have a good camp for a week, and then the snow'll melt, and we'll all go back together." The cheerful gaiety of the young man, and Mr. Oakhurst's calm infected the others. The Innocent, with the aid of pine boughs, extemporized a thatch for the roofless cabin, and the Duchess directed Piney in the rearrangement of the interior with a taste and tact that opened the blue eyes of that provincial maiden to their fullest extent. "I reckon now you're used to fine things at Poker Flat," said Piney. The Duchess turned away sharply to conceal something that reddened her cheeks through its professional tint, and Mother Shipton requested Piney not to "chatter." But when Mr. Oakhurst returned from a weary search for the trail, he heard the sound of happy laughter echoed from the rocks. He stopped in some alarm, and his thoughts first naturally reverted to the whiskey, which he had prudently cached.[9] "And yet it don't somehow sound like whiskey," said the gambler. It was not until he caught sight of the blazing fire through the still-blinding storm and the group around it that he settled to the conviction that it was "square fun."

8. *sotto voce* (SUHT oh VOH chee): in a low tone.

9. **cached** (kasht): hidden.

F **Literary Focus** Characterization Why do you suppose that Oakhurst discloses "Uncle Billy's rascality" only to the Duchess and Mother Shipton? What does this action reveal about Oakhurst's character?

Vocabulary **extemporized** (ehk STEHM puh ryzd): *v.:* prepared offhand; made for the occasion.

Whether Mr. Oakhurst had cached his cards with the whiskey as something debarred the free access of the community, I cannot say. It was certain that, in Mother Shipton's words, he "didn't say 'cards' once" during that evening. Haply the time was beguiled by an accordion, produced somewhat ostentatiously by Tom Simson from his pack. Notwithstanding some difficulties attending the manipulation of this instrument, Piney Woods managed to pluck several reluctant melodies from its keys, to an accompaniment by the Innocent on a pair of bone castanets. But the crowning festivity of the evening was reached in a rude camp-meeting hymn, which the lovers, joining hands, sang with great earnestness and vociferation. I fear that a certain defiant tone and Covenanters'[10] swing to its chorus, rather than any devotional quality, caused it speedily to infect the others, who at last joined in the refrain:

> *"I'm proud to live in the service of the Lord,*
> *And I'm bound to die in His army."*

The pines rocked, the storm eddied and whirled above the miserable group, and the flames of their altar leaped heavenward, as if in token of the vow. **Ⓖ**

At midnight the storm abated, the rolling clouds parted, and the stars glittered keenly above the sleeping camp. Mr. Oakhurst, whose professional habits had enabled him to live on the smallest possible amount of sleep, in dividing the watch with Tom Simson, somehow managed to take upon himself the greater part of that duty. He excused himself to the Innocent, by saying that he had "often been a week without sleep." "Doing what?" asked Tom. "Poker!" replied Oakhurst, sententiously; "when a man gets a streak of luck, he don't get tired. The luck gives in first. Luck," continued the gambler, reflectively, "is a mighty queer thing. All you know about it for certain is that it's bound to change. And it's finding out when it's going to change that makes you. We've had a streak of bad luck since we left Poker Flat,—you come along,

and slap you get into it, too. If you can hold your cards right along, you're all right. For," added the gambler, with cheerful irrelevance,

> *"I'm proud to live in the service of the Lord,*
> *And I'm bound to die in His army."*

The third day came, and the sun, looking through the white-curtained valley, saw the outcasts divide their slowly decreasing store of provisions for the morning meal. It was one of the peculiarities of that mountain climate that its rays diffused a kindly warmth over the wintry landscape, as if in regretful commiseration of the past. But it revealed drift on drift of snow piled high around the hut—a hopeless, uncharted, trackless sea of white lying below the rocky shores to which the castaways still clung. Through the marvelously clear air the smoke of the pastoral village of Poker Flat rose miles away. Mother Shipton saw it, and from a remote pinnacle of her rocky fastness, hurled in that direction a final malediction. It was her last vituperative attempt, and, perhaps for that reason, was invested with a certain degree of sublimity. It did her good, she privately informed the Duchess. "Just you go out there and cuss, and see." She then set herself to the task of amusing "the child," as she and the Duchess were pleased to call Piney. Piney was no chicken, but it was a soothing and original theory of the pair thus to account for the fact that she didn't swear and wasn't improper.

When night crept up again through the gorges, the reedy notes of the accordion rose and fell in fitful spasms and long-drawn gasps by the flickering camp-fire. But music failed to fill entirely the aching void left by insufficient food, and a new diversion was proposed by Piney—storytelling. Neither Mr. Oakhurst nor his female companions caring to relate their personal experiences, this plan would have failed, too, but for the Innocent. Some months before he had chanced upon a stray copy of Mr. Pope's[11] ingenious translation of the *Iliad*. He now proposed to narrate the principal incidents of that poem—having

---

10. **Covenanters':** Covenanters were Scottish Presbyterians who had made a covenant, or promise, to resist the rule of the Anglican Church.

11. **Mr. Pope's:** Alexander Pope (1688–1744), an English poet.

Ⓖ **Reading Focus** **Predicting** Based on the words of the hymn, the response of the wind and fire, and other clues in the paragraph, what prediction can you make about the outcome of the story?

thoroughly mastered the argument and fairly forgotten the words—in the current vernacular of Sandy Bar. And so, for the rest of that night, the Homeric demigods again walked the earth. Trojan bully and wily Greek wrestled in the winds, and the great pines in the canyon seemed to bow to the wrath of the son of Peleus.[12] Mr. Oakhurst listened with great satisfaction. Most especially was he interested in the fate of "Ash-heels," as the Innocent persisted in denominating the "swift-footed Achilles." **H**

So with small food and much of Homer and the accordion, a week passed over the heads of the outcasts. The sun again forsook them, and again from leaden skies the snowflakes were sifted over the land. Day by day closer around them drew the snowy circle, until at last they looked from their prison over drifted walls of dazzling white that towered twenty feet above their heads. It became more and more difficult to replenish their fires, even from the fallen trees beside them, now half hidden in the drifts. And yet no one complained. The lovers turned from the dreary prospect and looked into each other's eyes, and were happy. Mr. Oakhurst settled himself coolly to the losing game before him. The Duchess, more cheerful than she had been, assumed the care of Piney. Only Mother Shipton—once the strongest of the party—seemed to sicken and fade. At midnight on the tenth day, she called Oakhurst to her side. "I'm going," she said, in a voice of querulous weakness, "but don't say anything about it. Don't waken the kids. Take the bundle from under my head and open it." Mr. Oakhurst did so. It contained Mother Shipton's rations for the last week,

> The sun again forsook them, and again from leaden skies the snowflakes were sifted over the land.

untouched. "Give 'em to the child," she said, pointing to the sleeping Piney. "You've starved yourself," said the gambler. "That's what they call it," said the woman, querulously, as she lay down again, and, turning her face to the wall, passed quietly away. **I**

The accordion and the bones were put aside that day, and Homer was forgotten. When the body of Mother Shipton had been committed to the snow, Mr. Oakhurst took the Innocent aside, and showed him a pair of snowshoes, which he had fashioned from the old pack-saddle. "There's one chance in a hundred to save her yet," he said, pointing to Piney; "but it's there," he added, pointing toward Poker Flat. "If you can reach there in two days, she's safe." "And you?" asked Tom Simson. "I'll stay here," was the curt reply.

The lovers parted with a long embrace. "You are not going, too?" said the Duchess, as she saw Mr. Oakhurst apparently waiting to accompany him. "As far as the canyon," he replied. He turned suddenly and kissed the Duchess, leaving her pallid face aflame, and her trembling limbs rigid with amazement.

Night came, but not Mr. Oakhurst. It brought the storm again and the whirling snow. Then the Duchess, feeding the fire, found that someone had quietly piled beside the hut enough fuel to last a few days longer. The tears rose to her eyes, but she hid them from Piney.

The women slept but little. In the morning, looking into each other's faces, they read their fate. Neither spoke; but Piney, accepting the position of the stronger, drew near and placed her arm around the Duchess's waist. They kept this attitude for the rest of the day. That night the storm reached its greatest fury, and, rending asunder the protecting pines, invaded the very hut. **J**

---

12. **son of Peleus:** Achilles, whose wrath causes conflict in Homer's *Iliad*.

H **Reading Focus** **Predicting** Achilles, the Greek hero, was killed when an arrow pierced his vulnerable heel. Judging from this allusion, what new or revised predictions can you make about Oakhurst's fate?

I **Literary Focus** **Characterization** What effect have Piney and Tom Simson had on Mother Shipton's character? Explain.

J **Literary Focus** **Characterization** How has the relationship between the two young women changed? How have the women changed?

Toward morning they found themselves unable to feed the fire, which gradually died away. As the embers slowly blackened, the Duchess crept closer to Piney, and broke the silence of many hours: "Piney, can you pray?" "No, dear," said Piney, simply. The Duchess, without knowing exactly why, felt relieved, and, putting her head upon Piney's shoulder, spoke no more. And so reclining, the younger and purer pillowing the head of her soiled sister upon her virgin breast, they fell asleep.

The wind lulled as if it feared to waken them. Feathery drifts of snow, shaken from the long pine boughs, flew like white-winged birds and settled about them as they slept. The moon through the rifted clouds looked down upon what had been the camp. But all human stain, all trace of earthly travail, was hidden beneath the spotless mantle mercifully flung from above.

They slept all that day and the next, nor did they waken when voices and footsteps broke the silence of the camp. And when pitying fingers brushed the snow from their wan faces, you could scarcely have told from the equal peace that dwelt upon them, which was she that had sinned. Even the law of Poker Flat recognized this, and turned away, leaving them still locked in each other's arms. **(K)**

But at the head of the gulch, on one of the largest pine trees, they found the deuce of clubs[13] pinned to the bark with a bowie knife. It bore the following, written in pencil, in a firm hand:

> BENEATH THIS TREE
> LIES THE BODY OF
> JOHN OAKHURST,
> WHO STRUCK A STREAK OF BAD LUCK
> ON THE 23RD OF NOVEMBER, 1850,
> AND HANDED IN HIS CHECKS
> ON THE 7TH DECEMBER, 1850.

And pulseless and cold, with a Derringer[14] by his side and a bullet in his heart, though still calm as in life, beneath the snow lay he who was at once the strongest and yet the weakest of the outcasts of Poker Flat.

---

13. **deuce of clubs:** the two of clubs, the card with the lowest value in the deck.
14. **Derringer:** a short pistol with a large caliber, named after inventor Henry Derringer.

(K) Literary Focus Characterization Compare the descriptions of the faces of the two women. What point is the author making about the change in the Duchess's character?

Applying Your Skills

The Outcasts of Poker Flat

Respond and Think Critically

Reading Focus

Quick Check

1. Why are Oakhurst and the others forced to leave Poker Flat?

2. Why does Tom Simson act in the capacity of a "devoted slave" to Mr. Oakhurst?

3. What has happened to the characters by the story's end? Which two might still be alive?

Read with a Purpose

4. How does each outcast react to the difficulties of the situation? Faced with hardship, do the characters act nobly or treacherously? Explain.

Reading Skills: Predicting

5. Add a column to your chart, and for each prediction, indicate whether your prediction came true. Use your notes to answer this question: What changes in the characters surprised you?

Character	Clue	My Prediction	Yes/No
Mr. Oakhurst	"I reckon they're after somebody," he reflected; "likely it's me."	The men who are after Mr. Oakhurst will try to harm him.	yes

✓ Vocabulary Check

Match each Vocabulary word with its synonym.

6. impropriety   **a.** friendliness

7. malevolence   **b.** ill will

8. bellicose   **c.** improvised

9. guileless   **d.** hostile

10. amiability   **e.** sincere

11. jocular   **f.** joking

12. extemporized   **g.** indecency

Literary Focus

Literary Analysis

13. **Interpret** When Tom appears, Oakhurst has "a vague idea that the situation was not fortunate" (page 628). Why might Oakhurst be uneasy?

14. **Analyze** How does each of the outcasts—except Uncle Billy—change in the course of the story? What causes the changes?

15. **Interpret** In which ways is Oakhurst both the strongest and weakest of the outcasts?

Literary Skills: Characterization

16. **Analyze** Choose one character from the story, and analyze how Harte brings him or her to life. Which details reveal the most about the character? Cite at least three details from the text.

Literary Skills Review: Archetype

17. **Extend** An **archetype** is an imaginative pattern repeated through the ages. Harte is credited with inventing the Western **archetypal hero**— self-reliant, solitary, and fearless. The original Westerners were only human, yet why do most people prefer legend over reality?

Writing Focus

Think as a Reader/Writer

Use It in Your Writing Write a brief character sketch of a real or fictional person. Include at least one interaction with another character or person.

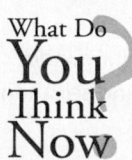

What Do **You Think Now** How does hardship help shape human character? How does it bring out the best in the story's outcasts?

SKILLS FOCUS Literary Skills Analyze characterization. **Writing Skills** Develop characters; establish and develop setting; write comparison-contrast essays.

Grammar Skills Use commas correctly to set off nonessential clauses and nonessential phrases.

Grammar Link

Using Commas with Nonessential Elements

A **nonessential element** is a word, phrase, or clause that adds to but is not necessary to the basic meaning of a sentence. Use commas to set off such elements.

> There was a Sabbath lull in the air, which, **in a settlement unused to Sabbath influences,** looked ominous.

An **appositive** is a noun or pronoun placed beside another noun or pronoun to identify or describe it. A **nonessential appositive** is set off with commas.

> As Mr. John Oakhurst, **gambler,** stepped into the main street of Poker Flat . . .

A **participial phrase** consists of a participle and all words related to the participle. A **nonessential participial** phrase is set off with commas.

> Two or three men, **conversing earnestly together,** ceased as he approached.

A **subordinate clause** is a group of words that contains a subject and a verb but does not express a complete thought. A **nonessential subordinate clause** is set off with commas.

> The Innocent was holding forth . . . to Mr. Oakhurst and Mother Shipton**, who was actually relaxing into amiability.**

Your Turn

Identify nonessential elements, and set them off with commas.

1. Harte born in New York moved to California.

2. Harte a newspaper editor began writing fiction.

3. Harte's stories which were popular in his time are not well known today.

Writing Application In a piece of your writing, add three nonessential elements to sentences and set them off with commas.

CHOICES

As you respond to the Choices, use these **Academic Vocabulary** words as appropriate: capacity, crucial, parameter, relevant, sustain.

REVIEW

Prepare an Investigative Report

TechFocus Imagine you are part of a news team sent to the scene of the incidents in "The Outcasts of Poker Flat." Prepare a news report that explains who the characters are and how and why they died. Provide characterization clues through relevant comments from local townspeople. Film your report, or perform it live for your class.

CONNECT

Compare Frontier Depictions

Choose a popular Western film or TV show, and write an essay comparing and contrasting it with "The Outcasts of Poker Flat." Does it perpetuate or sustain myths about the Old West? If so, which ones? Which depiction is more realistic? Some possible films for comparison are *Silverado, Shane,* and *High Noon.*

EXTEND

Write Your Own Western

Many of Harte's characters and plots were later used in other stories, films, and TV shows. Create your own Western character, and imagine his or her appearance, profession, mannerisms, and way of speaking. Write a short story or film script about a crucial challenge this character struggles to overcome. Remember to include a description of the setting of your Western.

Mark Twain

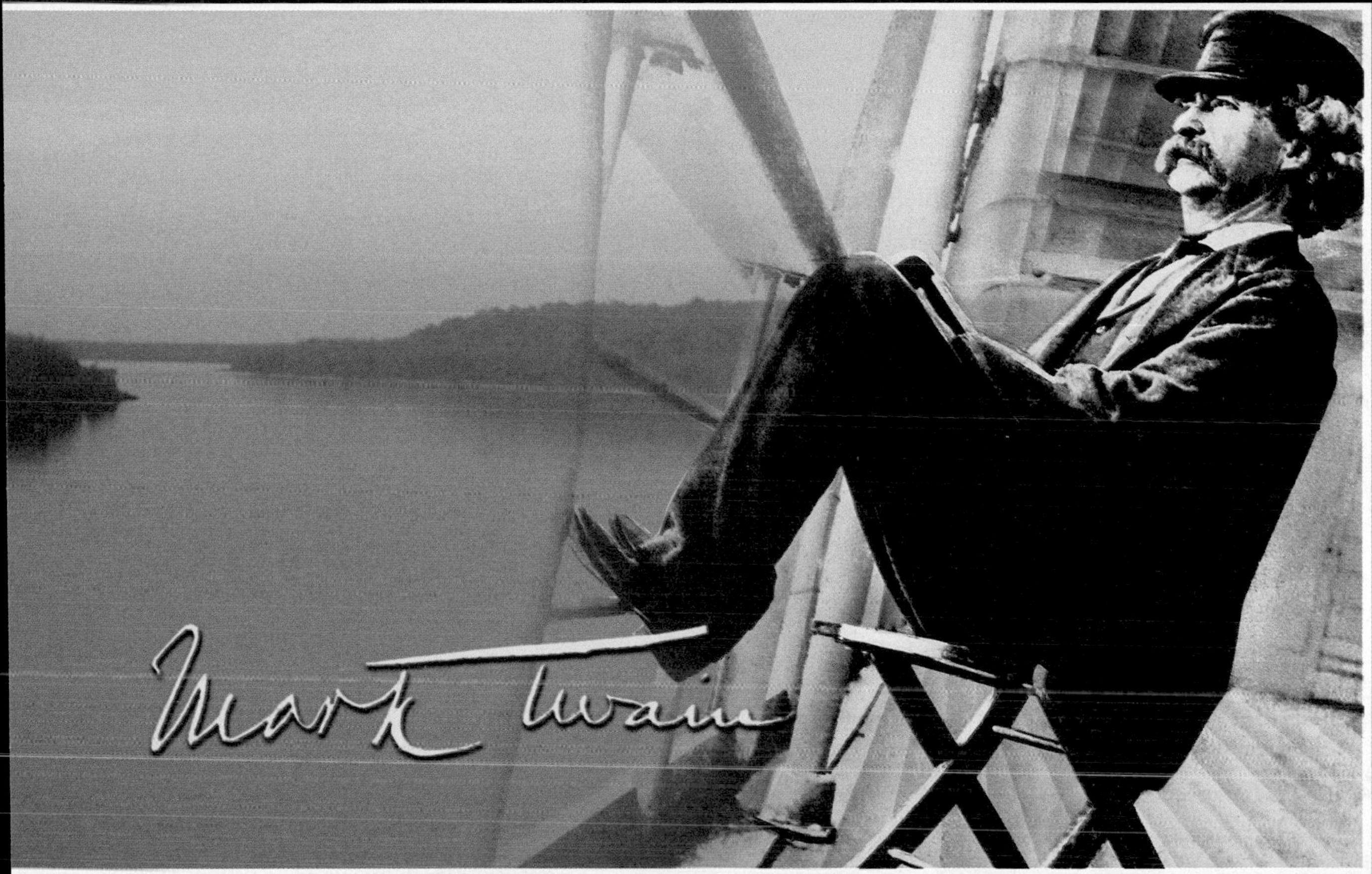

Mark Twain relaxes on a ship deck. March 15, 1901.
Twain's signature: The Granger Collection, New York.

What Do You Think?

What forces shape
human character?

 **QuickTalk**

How can laughter be a positive force? Think of times
when humor has brought about positive results.

CONTENTS

Mark Twain

(1835–1910)

Mark Twain is the most celebrated humorist in United States history. Twain's capacity for making us laugh has ensured his remarkable popularity, not just in his own time but in following generations.

"Mark Twain!"

Twain was born Samuel Langhorne Clemens in the backwoods of Missouri. His father, John Clemens, a bright, ambitious, but impractical Virginian, had married Jane Lampton, a witty, dynamic woman. When his store failed in 1839, Clemens moved his hopes and his family to Hannibal, Missouri—the Mississippi River town that Sam would later fashion into the setting of the most renowned boyhood in American literature, that of Tom Sawyer.

Sam's own carefree boyhood ended at twelve when his father died. To help support his mother and sister, he went to work setting type and editing copy for the newspaper started by his older brother Orion. At eighteen, Sam set out on his own. Over the next few years, he worked as a printer in various towns from Missouri to the East Coast. Smitten by a love for the magical steamboats that plied the Mississippi, he apprenticed himself to the great steamboat pilot Horace Bixby. It was the leadsman's cry of "Mark twain!"—announcing a water depth of two fathoms (twelve feet)—that provided Clemens with his celebrated pen name.

A Gold Mine of Humor

For a short time during the Civil War, Twain was a soldier with a company of Confederate irregulars, but he soon abandoned the military life for that of a gold prospector in Nevada. He found little gold there but discovered a rich mine of storytelling within himself. Twain's Missouri drawl and relaxed manner captivated audiences. In pretending not to recognize the coarseness or absurdity of his material, Twain maintained a deadpan attitude that added to his material's hilarity.

Twain soon turned his comic voice to prose, working as a journalist between 1862 and 1871. The 1865 publication of his version of an old tall tale, "The Celebrated Jumping Frog of Calaveras County," brought him widespread recognition as a humorist. Four years later, Twain's humorous dispatches from a Mediterranean tour were published as a satirical travelogue titled *The Innocents Abroad*. It sold well and launched Twain on a prosperous literary career.

An American Masterpiece

At thirty-five, with a rugged, worldly air about him, Twain was a dubious candidate for marriage, but he courted Olivia Langdon, the daughter of an affluent family from Elmira, New York, whom he married in 1870. In 1871, Twain moved to Hartford, Connecticut, where he built an enormous home, which thousands of tourists still visit today. The next year he published

A Twain Time Line

1853 Clemens sets out on his own and works as a printer in various towns and cities from Missouri to the East Coast

1861 Twain heads west to the Nevada Territory

1840   **1850**   **1860**

1835 Samuel Langhorne Clemens is born in Florida, Missouri

1856 Clemens apprentices himself to Mississippi River steamboat pilot Horace Bixby

1862 Twain begins working as a journalist

1865 "The Celebrated Jumping Frog of Calaveras County" is reprinted in newspapers across the country

Roughing It, drawing on his experiences as a tenderfoot in the West. Next he did a series for *The Atlantic Monthly* about his days as a riverboat pilot, which eventually became the book *Life on the Mississippi* (1883).

By the mid-1870s, Twain was also at work on *The Adventures of Tom Sawyer* (1876). In writing this celebration of boyhood, he made an imaginative return to the Hannibal of his childhood and succeeded in transforming it into a compelling myth.

A later novel, *Adventures of Huckleberry Finn* (1884), is a revelation of the illusions that existed in American life. Huck's journey on a raft with the escaped slave Jim dramatizes the grim realities of a slaveholding society. Twain caused a revolution in American literature through Huck's natural, slangy first-person narration. As Ernest Hemingway, speaking through a fictional character, later put it, "All modern American literature comes from one book by Mark Twain called *Huckleberry Finn.*" T. S. Eliot, a fellow Missourian, added that Twain's was "a new way of writing . . . a literary language based on American colloquial speech."

Loss and Legacy

Twain's later years were marked by financial and professional disappointment as well as personal tragedy. His fascination with business led him to invest, disastrously, in the Paige typesetting machine. The economic panic of 1893 bankrupted him. Then illness overtook the Clemens family. Susy, Twain's eldest daughter, died of meningitis in 1896; his wife died in 1904. In his final years the subject matter of Twain's work was his own disillusionment; the great comic writer appeared to be at war with the entire human race. Jean, his youngest daughter, died during an epileptic seizure in 1909. Four months later Twain was dead.

Think About the Writer — What do you think were the greatest influences on Twain's writing? Why?

Key Elements of Twain's Writing

- A **realistic approach** reflects the people and characteristics of different regions.

- **Vernacular speech,** the everyday language of people who live in a particular locality, brings characters and places to life.

- Colorful **figures of speech,** including **metaphor, simile,** and **hyperbole,** add humor and vitality.

1870 Twain marries Olivia Langdon

1872 Twain publishes *Roughing It,* a humorous view of frontier life in the 1860s

1883 Twain publishes *Life on the Mississippi*

1893 Twain goes bankrupt as a result of failed investments

1870   **1880**   **1890**   **1900**

1869 Twain publishes *The Innocents Abroad,* based on his European travels

1876 Twain publishes *The Adventures of Tom Sawyer*

1884 Twain publishes *Adventures of Huckleberry Finn*

1904 Twain's wife, Olivia, dies after a long illness

1910 Twain dies an embittered old man

Preparing to Read

SKILLS FOCUS Literary Skills Understand tall tales.
Reading Skills Understand vernacular.

Reader/Writer
Notebook

Use your **RWN** to complete the activities for this selection.

Literary Focus

Tall Tale "The Celebrated Jumping Frog of Calaveras County" is a classic example of the American **tall tale,** a humorous story characterized by outrageous exaggerations and events. Tall tales usually rely on <u>sustained</u> use of **hyperbole,** a figure of speech that uses exaggeration for effect. As you read, consider why Twain's tall tale continues to be popular.

Reading Focus

Understanding Vernacular Twain uses **vernacular**—the language commonly spoken by people in a particular place—to create vivid settings and characters. A vernacular usually includes these elements:

- **unique vocabulary** commonly used in a particular region, such as *a piece* to mean "a distance"
- **characteristic idioms,** or expressions that make no literal sense
- **dialect forms,** or local variations of spoken words, often containing differences in pronunciation, such as for *thish-yer* for "this here"

Into Action As you read, use a chart like the one below to record examples of the vernacular. In the second column, translate the word or phrase into standard English. Read aloud confusing words or phrases, and analyze their context to determine meaning. In the third column, explain how Twain's vernacular creates humor in the tall tale.

Vernacular	Standard English	How It Creates Humor in the Tall Tale
"lay for a chance to steal something" (p. 641)	to wait for an opportunity	It makes the bull pup seem comically tricky.

Writing Focus

Think as a Reader/Writer

Find It in Your Reading **Tall tales** often contain humorous comparisons. In Twain's tale, for example, Simon Wheeler describes a frog "whirling in the air like a doughnut." As you read, record in your *Reader/Writer Notebook* other examples of humorous comparisons.

Vocabulary

garrulous (GAR uh luhs) *adj.:* talking too much, especially about unimportant things. *Garrulous old Simon Wheeler tells the long tale of Jim Smiley and his frog.*

conjectured (kuhn JEHK chuhrd) *v.:* guessed. *The narrator's friend conjectured that Wheeler would relate the story of the celebrated jumping frog.*

infamous (IHN fuh muhs) *adj.:* having a bad reputation. *The infamous Jim Smiley would do anything to win a bet.*

dilapidated (duh LAP uh day tihd) *adj.:* partially ruined or decayed through neglect. *The speaker finds Wheeler dozing in an old, dilapidated tavern in an ancient mining camp.*

interminable (ihn TUR muh nuh buhl) *adj.:* endless; seeming to last forever. *As the afternoon wears on, Wheeler relates every detail in the interminable tale of Jim Smiley.*

Language Coach

Prefixes The Latin prefix *in*— sometimes means "in" or "into" (*inroad, inflame*). It can also mean "not" or "without" (*ingratitude, infinite*). Which meaning, if either, do you think it has in the word *interminable*? What about *infamous*? Explain.

Learn It Online

Visit AuthorSpace to learn more about Mark Twain's life and work.

go.hrw.com | L11-638 | **Go**

THE CELEBRATED JUMPING FROG OF CALAVERAS COUNTY

by **Mark Twain**

Read with a Purpose

Read to discover what happens when Jim Smiley bets his most celebrated jumping frog of Calaveras County against a stranger's frog.

Build Background

Mark Twain took a story he had heard while visiting a mining camp in California and turned it into a classic of American humor. In fact, this story is famous as an example of the American tall tale, an out-rageously exaggerated, humorous story that is obviously unbeliev-able. Twain first heard the tall tale about a frog contest during a chat around the stove in a mining camp's run-down tavern. After Twain's version of the story first appeared in a New York newspaper in 1865, the story became so popular that it was reprinted in newspapers across the country, helping make Twain a national celebrity. Twain's story demonstrates a <u>crucial</u> aspect of all humor: It's not only *what you say* but *how you say it* that makes people laugh.

In compliance with the request of a friend of mine, who wrote me from the East, I called on good-natured, garrulous old Simon Wheeler and inquired after my friend's friend, *Leonidas W.* Smiley, as requested to do, and I hereunto append the result. I have a lurking suspicion that *Leonidas W.* Smiley is a myth; that my friend never knew such a personage; and that he only conjectured that if I asked old Wheeler about him, it would remind him of his infamous *Jim* Smiley, and he would go to work and bore me nearly to death with some infernal reminiscence[1] of him as long and tedious it should be useless to me. If that was the design, it certainly succeeded.

I found Simon Wheeler dozing comfortably by the barroom stove of the old, dilapidated tavern in the ancient mining camp of Angel's, and I noticed that he was fat and baldheaded and had an expression of winning gentleness and simplicity upon his tranquil countenance.[2] He roused up and gave me good day. I told him a friend of mine had commissioned me to make some inquiries about a cherished companion of his boyhood named *Leonidas W.* Smiley—*Rev. Leonidas W.* Smiley—a young minister of the gospel, who he had heard was at one time a resident of Angel's Camp. I added that if Mr. Wheeler could tell me anything about this Rev. Leonidas W. Smiley, I would feel under many obligations to him.

Simon Wheeler backed me into a corner and blockaded me there with his chair and then sat me down and reeled off the monotonous narrative which follows this paragraph. He never smiled, he never frowned, he never changed his voice from the gentle-flowing key to which he tuned the initial sentence, he never betrayed the slightest suspicion of enthusiasm; but all through the interminable narrative there ran a vein of impressive earnestness and sincerity, which showed me plainly that so far from his imagining that there was anything ridiculous or funny about his story, he regarded it as a really important matter and admired its two heroes as men of transcendent genius in finesse.[3] To me, the spectacle of a man drifting serenely along through such a queer yarn without ever smiling was exquisitely absurd. As I said before, I asked him to tell me what he knew of Rev. Leonidas W. Smiley, and he replied as follows. I let him go on in his own way, and never interrupted him once:

---

1. **infernal reminiscence:** awful or unpleasant story of past experiences.

Vocabulary **garrulous** (GAR uh luhs) *adj.*: talking too much, especially about unimportant things.
conjectured (kuhn JEHK chuhrd) *v.*: guessed.
infamous (IHN fuh muhs) *adj.*: having a bad reputation.
dilapidated (duh LAP uh day tihd) *adj.*: partially ruined or decayed through neglect.
interminable (ihn TUR muh nuh buhl) *adj.*: endless; seeming to last forever.

---

2. **tranquil countenance:** calm face.
3. **transcendent genius in finesse** (fuh NEHS): exceptional skill and craftiness.

Analyzing Visuals

Viewing and Interpreting How does this image help illustrate the absurdity of Jim Smiley's passion for gambling?

There was a feller here once by the name of *Jim* Smiley, in the winter of '49—or maybe it was the spring of '50—I don't recollect exactly, somehow, though what makes me think it was one or the other is because I remember the big flume[4] wasn't finished when he first came to the camp; but anyway, he was the curiousest man about always betting on anything that turned up you ever see, if he could get anybody to bet on the other side; and if he couldn't, he'd change sides. Any way that suited the other man would suit him—any way just so's he got a bet, *he* was satisfied. But still he was lucky, uncommon lucky; he most always come out winner. He was always ready and laying for a chance; there couldn't be no solit'ry thing mentioned but that feller'd offer to bet on it and take any side you please, as I was just telling you. If there was a horse race, you'd find him flush,[5] or you'd find him busted at the end of it; if there was a dogfight, he'd bet on it; if there was a catfight, he'd bet on it; why if there was a chicken fight, he'd bet on it; why, if there was two birds setting on a fence, he would bet you which one would fly first; or if there was a camp meeting, he would be there reg'lar, to bet on Parson Walker, which he judged to be the best exhorter[6] about here, and so he was, too, and a good man. If he even seen a straddlebug start to go any-wheres, he would bet you how long it would take him to get wherever he was going to, and if you took him up, he would foller that straddlebug to Mexico but what he would find out where he was bound for and how long he was on the road. Lots of the boys here has seen that Smiley and can tell you about him. Why, it never made no difference to *him*—he would bet on *any*thing—the dangdest feller. Parson Walker's wife laid very sick once, for a good while, and it seemed as if they warn't going to save her; but one morning he come in, and Smiley asked how she was, and he said she was considerable better—thank the Lord for his inf'nit mercy—and coming on so smart that with the blessing of Prov'dence, she'd get well yet; and Smiley, before he thought, says, "Well, I'll risk twoandahalf that she don't, anyway." **(A)**

Thish-yer Smiley had a mare—the boys called her the fifteen-minute nag, but that was only in fun, you know, because, of course, she was faster than that—and he used to win money on that horse, for all she was so slow and always had the asthma, or the distemper, or the consumption, or something of that kind. They used to give her two or three hundred yards' start and then pass her underway; but always at the end of the race she'd get excited and desperate-like, and come cavort-ing[7] and straddling up, and scattering her legs around limber, sometimes in the air, and sometimes out to one side amongst the fences, and kicking up m-o-r-e dust, and raising m-o-r-e racket with her coughing and sneezing and blowing her nose—and always fetch up at the stand just about a neck ahead, as near as you could cipher it down.[8] **(B)**

And he had a little small bull pup, that to look at him you'd think he wa'n't worth a cent but to set around and look ornery and lay for a chance to steal something. But as soon as money was up on him, he was a different dog; his underjaw'd begin to stick out like the fo'castle[9] of a steamboat, and his teeth would uncover and shine savage like the furnaces. And a dog might tackle him, and bullyrag him, and bite him, and throw him over his shoulder two or three times, and Andrew Jackson—which was the name of the pup—Andrew Jackson would never let on but what *he* was satisfied and hadn't expected nothing else—and the bets being doubled and doubled on the other side all the time, till the money was all up; and then all of a sudden he would grab that other dog jest by the j'int of his hind leg and freeze to it—not chaw, you understand, but only jest grip and hang on till they throwed up the sponge,[10] if it was a year. Smiley always come out winner on that pup, till he harnessed a dog once that didn't have no hind legs, because they'd been sawed off by a circular saw, and when the thing had gone along far enough, and the money was all up, and

---

4. **flume:** human-made waterway.
5. **flush:** with a lot of money.
6. **exhorter:** preacher.

7. **cavorting:** running around playfully.
8. **cipher** (SY fuhr) **it down:** calculate it.
9. **fo'castle** (FOHK suhl): forecastle, the front part of a ship's upper deck.
10. **throwed up the sponge:** gave up.

(A) Reading Focus Understanding Vernacular How can you figure out the meaning of the words *solit'ry* and *reg'lar*? What other elements of dialect are evident in Wheeler's speech?

(B) Literary Focus Tall Tale How does Twain use humor to narrate the adventures of Smiley's horse? What elements in the description of the horse are exaggerations?

he come to make a snatch for his pet holt,[11] he saw in a minute how he'd been imposed on and how the other dog had him in the door, so to speak, and he 'peared surprised, and then he looked sorter discouraged-like, and didn't try no more to win the fight, and so he got shucked out bad. He give Smiley a look, as much as to say his heart was broke, and it was *his* fault, for putting up a dog that hadn't no hind legs for him to take holt of, which was his main dependence in a fight, and then he limped off a piece and laid down and died. It was a good pup, was that Andrew Jackson, and would have made a name for hisself if he'd lived, for the stuff was in him, and he had genius—I know it, because he hadn't no opportunities to speak of, and it don't stand to reason that a dog could make such a fight as he could under them circumstances, if he hadn't no talent. It always makes me feel sorry when I think of that last fight of his'n, and the way it turned out.

Well, thish-yer Smiley had rat tarriers, and chicken cocks, and tomcats, and all them kind of things, till you couldn't rest, and you couldn't fetch nothing for him to bet on but he'd match you. He ketched a frog one day, and took him home, and said he cal'klated to edercate him; and so he never done nothing for three months

---

11. **pet holt:** favorite grip.

Mike Nash and his daughter, Raychel, celebrate their winning frog at the Calaveras County Fair and Jumping Frog Jubilee in Angels Camp, California, May 21, 2006.

but set in his backyard and learn that frog to jump. And you bet you he *did* learn him, too. He'd give him a little punch behind, and the next minute you'd see that frog whirling in the air like a doughnut—see him turn one summerset, or maybe a couple, if he got a good start, and come down flat-footed and all right, like a cat. He got him up so in the matter of catching flies, and kept him in practice so constant, that he'd nail a fly every time as far as he could see him. Smiley said all a frog wanted was education, and he could do most anything—and I believe him. Why, I've seen him set Dan'l Webster down here on this floor—Dan'l Webster was the name of the frog—and sing out, "Flies, Dan'l, flies!" and quicker'n you could wink, he'd spring straight up, and snake a fly off'n the counter there, and flop down on the floor again as solid as a gob of mud, and fall to scratching the side of his head with his hind foot as indifferent as if he hadn't no idea he'd been doin' any more'n any frog might do. You never see a frog so modest and straightfor'ard as he was, for all he was so gifted. And when it come to fair-and-square jumping on a dead level, he could get over more ground at one straddle than any animal of his breed you ever see. Jumping on a dead level was his strong suit, you understand; and when it come to that, Smiley would ante up money on him as long as he had a red.[12] Smiley was monstrous proud of his frog, and well he might be, for fellers that had traveled and been everywheres all said he laid over any frog that ever *they* see.

Well, Smiley kept the beast in a little lattice box, and he used to fetch him downtown sometimes and lay for a bet. One day a feller—a stranger in the camp, he was—come across him with his box, and says:

"What might it be that you've got in the box?"

And Smiley says, sorter indifferent-like, "It might be a parrot, or it might be a canary, maybe, but it ain't—it's only just a frog."

---

12. **red:** penny (as in *red cent*).

C **Literary Focus** Tall Tale What elements of hyperbole, or exaggeration, does Twain include in his depiction of Smiley's pup Andrew Jackson? Which part of the description of the dogfight is outlandish? How do these elements contribute to the humor of the tale?

D **Reading Focus** Understanding Vernacular What does Wheeler mean when he says that Smiley "ketched a frog one day"? What other examples of dialect capture the flavor of Wheeler's speech? How do these examples contribute to the humor of Smiley's intent to "edercate" the frog?

And the feller took it, and looked at it careful, and turned it round this way and that, and says, "H'm—so 'tis. Well, what's *he* good for?"

"Well," Smiley says, easy and careless, "he's good enough for *one* thing, I should judge—he can outjump any frog in Calaveras County."

The feller took the box again, and took another long, particular look, and give it back to Smiley, and says, very deliberate, "Well, I don't see no p'ints[13] about that frog that's any better'n any other frog."

"Maybe you don't," Smiley says. "Maybe you understand frogs, and maybe you don't understand 'em; maybe you've had experience, and maybe you an't only a amature, as it were. Anyways, I've got *my* opinion, and I'll risk forty dollars that he can outjump any frog in Calaveras County."

And the feller studied a minute and then says, kinder sadlike, "Well, I'm only a stranger here, and I an't got no frog; but if I had a frog, I'd bet you."

And then Smiley says, "That's all right—that's all right—if you'll hold my box a minute, I'll go and get you a frog." And so the feller took the box, and put up his forty dollars along with Smiley's, and set down to wait.

So he set there a good while thinking and thinking to hisself, and then he got the frog out and prized[14] his mouth open and took a teaspoon and filled him full of quail shot[15]—filled him pretty near up to his chin—and set him on the floor. Smiley he went to the swamp and slopped around in the mud for a long time, and finally he ketched a frog, and fetched him in, and give him to this feller, and says:

"Now, if you're ready, set him alongside of Dan'l, with his forepaws just even with Dan'l, and I'll give the word." Then he says, "One—two—three—jump!" and him and the feller touched up the frogs from behind, and the new frog hopped off, but Dan'l give a heave, and hysted up his shoulders—so—like a Frenchman, but it wan't no use—he couldn't budge; he was planted as solid as an anvil,[16] and he couldn't no more stir than

if he was anchored out. Smiley was a good deal surprised, and he was disgusted too, but he didn't have no idea what the matter was, of course.

E

The feller took the money and started away; and when he was going out at the door, he sorter jerked his thumb over his shoulders—this way—at Dan'l, and says again, very deliberate, "Well, *I* don't see no p'ints about that frog that's any better'n any other frog."

Smiley he stood scratching his head and looking down at Dan'l a long time, and at last he says, "I do wonder what in the nation that frog throw'd off for—I wonder if there an't something the matter with him—he 'pears to look mighty baggy, somehow." And he ketched Dan'l by the nap of the neck and lifted him up and says, "Why, blame my cats, if he don't weigh five pound!" and turned him upside down, and he belched out a double handful of shot. And then he see how it was, and he was the maddest man—he set the frog down and took out after that feller, but he never ketched him. And—[Here Simon Wheeler heard his name called from the front yard and got up to see what was wanted.] And turning to me as he moved away, he said: "Just set where you are, stranger, and rest easy—I an't going to be gone a second."

F

But, by your leave, I did not think that a continuation of the history of the enterprising vagabond[17] *Jim Smiley* would be likely to afford me much information concerning the Rev. *Leonidas W.* Smiley, and so I started away.

At the door I met the sociable Wheeler returning, and he buttonholed[18] me and recommenced:

"Well, thish-yer Smiley had a yaller one-eyed cow that didn't have no tail, only jest a short stump like a bannanner, and—"

"Oh! hang Smiley and his afflicted cow!" I muttered, good-naturedly, and bidding the old gentleman good day, I departed.

---

13. **p'ints:** points, or physical qualities of an animal, used to judge breeding.
14. **prized:** pried.
15. **shot:** metal pellets used as ammunition for a shotgun.

16. **anvil:** iron or steel block on which metal objects are hammered into shape.
17. **vagabond:** someone who wanders from place to place without a home; drifter.
18. **buttonholed:** approached aggressively and delayed in conversation.

E **Literary Focus** Tall Tale What characteristics of the jumping frog competition indicate that this is a tall tale?

F **Reading Focus** Understanding Vernacular How does the use of the vernacular in this paragraph add to its comic effect?

Respond and Think Critically

Reading Focus

Quick Check

1. How does the first narrator in the story differ from the second narrator, Simon Wheeler?

2. Where does Twain use exaggeration to contribute to the story's humor?

3. Which frog wins the jumping contest? Why?

Read with a Purpose

4. How is Jim Smiley outwitted by the stranger in the camp? Is the ending unexpected? Explain.

Reading Skills: Understanding Vernacular

5. You have noted examples of the vernacular and translated them into standard English. You also noted how the vernacular added to the story's humor. Review your notes, and answer this question: Would the story be as effective if it were not written in the vernacular? Why or why not?

Vernacular	Standard English	How It Creates Humor...
"lay for a chance to steal something"	wait for an opportunity	It makes the bull pup seem comically tricky.

✓ Vocabulary Check

Match each Vocabulary word with its synonym.

6. dilapidated   a. endless

7. interminable   b. notorious

8. conjectured   c. run-down

9. garrulous   d. chattering

10. infamous   e. supposed

Literary Focus

Literary Analysis

11. **Analyze** "The Celebrated Jumping Frog of Calaveras County" is a story within a story. What is the basic plot of the frame story, the story at the beginning and the end?

12. **Interpret** Why does Twain choose to use a frog instead of another animal in his story?

13. **Infer** What can you infer about Wheeler and Smiley from Twain's use of the vernacular?

Literary Skills: Tall Tale

14. **Analyze** What message do you think Twain is trying to convey through this tall tale? Explain.

15. **Extend** Tall tales have long been popular entertainments. Explain why.

Literary Skills Review: Personification

16. **Evaluate** A figure of speech, **personification** gives an object or animal human feelings, thoughts, or attitudes. How does Wheeler's description of Smiley's frog as "modest" and "straightfor'ard" add humor to the tall tale?

Writing Focus

Think as a Reader/Writer

Use It in Your Writing The narrator leaves just as Wheeler is about to tell him about Smiley's *yaller one-eyed cow*. Write two paragraphs of Smiley's *yaller one-eyed cow* tale, and include humorous comparisons.

What Do **You Think Now** What do you think of Jim Smiley? What role does obsession play in shaping his character?

The Lowest Animal

Reader/Writer
Notebook
Use your **RWN** to complete the activities for this selection.

Literary Focus

Satire: The Weapon of Laughter Satire ridicules the shortcomings of people and institutions in an attempt to bring about change. One of the favorite techniques of the satirist is **exaggeration**—overstating something to make it look ridiculous. Another technique is **irony**—stating the opposite of what is really meant. As you read "The Lowest Animal," notice how Twain uses exaggeration and irony to satirize human nature.

Literary Perspectives Apply the literary perspective described on page 647 as you read the essay.

Reading Focus

Recognizing a Writer's Purpose In general, a writer's **purpose** can be to describe, to inform, to narrate, to entertain, to analyze, or to persuade. Satirists use humorous exaggeration because of its capacity to bring about real-world change, prompt people to reexamine their beliefs and values, or encourage the development of new attitudes and perspectives.

Into Action As you read "The Lowest Animal," use a chart like the one below to record examples of exaggeration and irony used to make a point. In the second column, comment on the point Twain makes.

Examples of Exaggeration and Irony	Twain's Point
"the Descent of Man from the Higher Animals" (p. 646)	It sounds like Twain believes animals are more advanced than humans.

Writing Focus

Think as a Reader/Writer

Find It in Your Reading Satirists frequently use **exaggeration** to point out social follies or absurdities. In "The Lowest Animal," for example, Twain writes that man "has made a graveyard of the globe," an obvious exaggeration. As you read "The Lowest Animal," record in your *Reader/Writer Notebook* other examples of exaggeration.

Vocabulary

dispositions (dihs puh ZIHSH uhns) *n.*: natural ways of acting or thinking. *Many types of animals have pleasant dispositions.*

verified (VEHR uh fyd) *v.*: proved something to be true. *Twain claims he verified his theories by conducting scientific experiments.*

caliber (KAL uh buhr) *n.*: quality or ability. *Humans show some differences in mental caliber.*

wantonly (WAHN tuhn lee) *adv.*: carelessly, often with ill will. *The earl wantonly hunted the buffalo and left many animals to die.*

transition (tran ZIHSH uhn) *n.*: passage from one condition, form, or stage to another. *Twain proposes that, in descending from the higher animals, humans have lost something in the transition.*

avaricious (av uh RIHSH uhs) *adj.*: greedy. *While humans can be avaricious, most animals will take only the things that they need.*

atrocious (uh TROH shuhs) *adj.*: very evil, savage, or brutal. *Many unjust laws have permitted atrocious acts to occur.*

Language Coach

Pronunciation Read each word on the list above aloud to become familiar with its sound. Notice which syllable is stressed in each word.

Learn It Online
Jump into Twain's perspective with an introductory video online.

go.hrw.com   L11-645   **Go**

The Lowest Animal

by **Mark Twain**

Read with a Purpose
Read to learn how Twain comes to the conclusion that human beings are inferior to other animals.

Build Background
In this essay, Twain satirizes human nature by describing a series of scientific experiments that he supposedly conducted at the London Zoological Gardens. He humorously addresses Charles Darwin's theory of evolution, which was developed in his books *On the Origin of Species* (1859) and *The Descent of Man* (1871). Twain takes one of Darwin's central ideas—that humans ascended from earlier ancestors, or the "lower animals"—and turns it upside down.

Man is the Reasoning Animal. Such is the claim.

I have been studying the traits and dispositions of the "lower animals" (so-called) and contrasting them with the traits and dispositions of man. I find the result humiliating to me. For it obliges me to renounce[1] my allegiance to the Darwinian theory of the Ascent of Man from the Lower Animals, since it now seems plain to me that that theory ought to be vacated in favor of a new and truer one, this new and truer one to be named the *De*scent of Man from the Higher Animals.

In proceeding toward this unpleasant conclusion, I have not guessed or speculated or conjectured, but have used what is commonly called the scientific method.[2] That is to say, I have subjected every postulate[3] that presented itself to the crucial test of actual experiment and have adopted it or rejected it according to the result. Thus, I verified and established each step of my course in its turn before advancing to the next. These experiments were made in the London Zoological Gardens and covered many months of painstaking and fatiguing work.

Before particularizing any of the experiments, I wish to state one or two things which seem to more properly belong in this place than further along. This in the interest of clearness. The massed experiments established to my satisfaction certain generalizations, to wit:

1. That the human race is of one distinct species. It exhibits slight variations—in color, stature, mental caliber, and so on—due to climate, environment, and so forth; but it is a species by itself and not to be confounded with any other.

---

1. **renounce:** give up; reject.

2. **scientific method:** research method in which a hypothesis is tested by careful, documented experiments.
3. **postulate** (PAHS chuh liht): assumption.

2. That the quadrupeds[4] are a distinct family, also. This family exhibits variations—in color, size, food preferences, and so on; but it is a family by itself.

3. That the other families—the birds, the fishes, the insects, the reptiles, etc.—are more or less distinct, also. They are in the procession. They are links in the chain which stretches down from the higher animals to man at the bottom.

Some of my experiments were quite curious. In the course of my reading, I had come across a case where, many years ago, some hunters on our Great Plains organized a buffalo hunt for the entertainment of an English earl—that, and to provide some fresh meat for his larder.[5] They had charming sport. They killed seventy-two of those great animals and ate part of one of them and left the seventy-one to rot. In order to determine the difference between an anaconda[6] and an earl—if any—I caused seven young calves to be turned into the anaconda's cage. The grateful reptile immediately crushed one of them and swallowed it, then lay back satisfied. It showed no further interest in the calves and no disposition to harm them. I tried this experiment with other anacondas, always with the same result. The fact stood proven that the difference between an earl and an anaconda is that the earl is cruel and the anaconda isn't; and that the earl wantonly destroys what he has no use for, but the anaconda doesn't. This seemed to suggest that the anaconda was not descended from the earl. It also seemed to suggest that the earl was descended from the anaconda, and had lost a good deal in the transition. **Ⓐ**

---

4. **quadrupeds:** four-footed animals.
5. **larder:** supply of food or place where food supplies are kept.
6. **anaconda:** long, heavy snake that crushes its prey.

Ⓐ **Literary Focus** Satire How can you tell that Twain is using satire to make his point? Do you think the satire is effective? Why or why not?

Vocabulary **wantonly** (WAHN tuhn lee) *adv.:* carelessly, often with ill will.
transition (tran ZIHSH uhn) *n.:* passage from one condition, form, or stage to another.

I was aware that many men who have accumulated more millions of money than they can ever use have shown a rabid hunger for more, and have not scrupled[7] to cheat the ignorant and the helpless out of their poor servings in order to partially appease[8] that appetite. I furnished a hundred different kinds of wild and tame animals the opportunity to accumulate vast stores of food, but none of them would do it. The squirrels and bees and certain birds made accumulations, but stopped when they had gathered a winter's supply and could not be persuaded to add to it either honestly or by chicane.[9] In order to bolster up a tottering reputation, the ant pretended to store up supplies, but I was not deceived. I know the ant.

---

7. **scrupled:** hesitated because of feelings of guilt.
8. **appease:** satisfy; pacify.
9. **chicane** (shih KAYN): clever deception; trickery.

Literary Perspectives

Analyzing Historical Context Writers create their works within the parameters of their historical context. This perspective will help you understand some of the major social issues during Twain's lifetime. Twain was born and raised in the slaveholding state of Missouri during the decades leading up to the Civil War. In fact, in his book *Adventures of Huckleberry Finn,* Twain addresses the horrible effects of slavery both on slaves and slave owners. Other issues regarding human rights were also gaining attention during Twain's lifetime; for example, women were beginning to organize for greater political rights. The plight of the poor was a growing concern because many hugely successful businessmen of the late 1800s, sometimes called robber barons, were profiting from the backbreaking labor of the lower classes. A rise in the prominence of scientific thought also occurred during this time. Scientific studies, such as those conducted by Charles Darwin, caused many to rethink traditional ideas about religion and to give greater credence to the influence of the environment on human behavior. How might Twain's essay reflect these changing attitudes toward slavery, work, women's rights, science, and religion?

As you read, be sure to notice the questions in the text, which will guide you in using this perspective.

These experiments convinced me that there is this difference between man and the higher animals: He is avaricious and miserly, they are not. **B**

In the course of my experiments, I convinced myself that among the animals man is the only one that harbors[10] insults and injuries, broods over them, waits till a chance offers, then takes revenge. The passion of revenge is unknown to the higher animals.

Roosters keep harems,[11] but it is by consent of their concubines;[12] therefore no wrong is done. Men keep harems, but it is by brute force, privileged by atrocious laws which the other sex was allowed no hand in making. In this matter man occupies a far lower place than the rooster. **C**

Cats are loose in their morals, but not consciously so. Man, in his descent from the cat, has brought the cat's looseness with him but has left the unconsciousness behind—the saving grace which excuses the cat. The cat is innocent, man is not.

Indecency, vulgarity, obscenity—these are strictly confined to man; he invented them. Among the higher animals there is no trace of them. They hide nothing; they are not ashamed. Man, with his soiled mind, covers himself. He will not even enter a drawing room with his breast and back naked, so alive are he and his mates to indecent suggestion. Man is the Animal that Laughs. But so does the monkey, as Mr. Darwin pointed out, and so does the Australian bird that is called the laughing jackass. No—Man is the Animal that Blushes. He is the only one that does it—or has occasion to.

At the head of this article we see how "three monks were burnt to death" a few days ago and a prior was "put to death with atrocious cruelty." Do we inquire into the details? No; or we should find out that the prior was subjected to unprintable mutilations. Man—when he is a North American Indian—gouges out his prisoner's eyes; when he is King John,[13] with a nephew to render untroublesome, he uses a red-hot iron; when he is a religious zealot[14] dealing with heretics[15] in the Middle Ages, he skins his captive alive and scatters salt on his back; in the first Richard's[16] time, he shuts up a multitude of Jewish families in a tower and sets fire to it; in Columbus's time he captures a family of Spanish Jews and—but *that* is not printable; in our day in England, a man is fined ten shillings for beating his mother nearly to death with a chair, and another man is fined forty shillings for having four pheasant eggs in his possession without being able to satisfactorily explain how he got them. Of all the animals, man is the only one that is cruel. He is the only one that inflicts pain for the pleasure of doing it. It is a trait that is not known to the higher animals. The cat plays with the frightened mouse; but she has this excuse, that she does not know that the mouse is suffering. The cat is moderate—unhumanly moderate: She only scares the mouse, she does not hurt it; she doesn't dig out its eyes, or tear off its skin, or drive splinters under its nails—man fashion; when she is done playing with it, she makes a sudden meal of it and puts it out of its trouble. Man is the Cruel Animal. He is alone in that distinction. **D**

---

10. **harbors:** clings to.
11. **harems:** groups of females who mate and live with one male.
12. **concubines:** secondary wives.

---

13. **King John:** king of England from 1199 to 1216, known for seizing the throne from his nephew Arthur.
14. **zealot** (ZEHL uht): overly enthusiastic person; fanatic.
15. **heretics** (HEHR uh tihks): people who hold beliefs opposed to those of the church.
16. **first Richard's:** refers to Richard I (1157–1199), also called Richard the Lion-Hearted, king of England from 1189 to 1199.

B **Reading Focus** **Recognizing Purpose** What is the outcome when Twain tries to persuade different wild and tame animals to hoard food? What purpose do the examples serve?

C **Literary Perspectives** **Analyzing Historical Context** What changing attitudes toward women's rights does Twain present in this paragraph?

D **Reading Focus** **Recognizing Purpose** Why does Twain include the examples about the various ways that men have demonstrated cruelty through the ages? Why do you think Twain relates information regarding the specific fines for crimes committed in England?

Vocabulary **avaricious** (av uh RIHSH uhs) *adj.:* greedy. **atrocious** (uh TROH shuhs) *adj.:* very evil, savage, or brutal.

These experiments convinced me that there is this difference between man and the higher animals: He is avaricious and miserly, they are not.

The higher animals engage in individual fights, but never in organized masses. Man is the only animal that deals in that atrocity of atrocities, war. He is the only one that gathers his brethren about him and goes forth in cold blood and with calm pulse to exterminate his kind. He is the only animal that for sordid wages will march out, as the Hessians[17] did in our Revolution, and as the boyish Prince Napoleon did in the Zulu war,[18] and help to slaughter strangers of his own species who have done him no harm and with whom he has no quarrel.

Man is the only animal that robs his helpless fellow of his country—takes possession of it and drives him out of it or destroys him. Man has done this in all the ages. There is not an acre of ground on the globe that is in possession of its rightful owner, or that has not been taken away from owner after owner, cycle after cycle, by force and bloodshed.

Man is the only Slave. And he is the only animal who enslaves. He has always been a slave in one form or another, and has always held other slaves in bondage under him in one way or another. In our day he is always some man's slave for wages and does that man's work; and this slave has other slaves under him for minor wages, and they do *his* work. The higher animals are the only ones who exclusively do their own work and provide their own living.

Man is the only Patriot. He sets himself apart in his own country, under his own flag, and sneers at the other nations, and keeps multitudinous uniformed assassins on hand at heavy expense to grab slices of other people's countries and keep *them* from grabbing slices of *his*. And in the intervals between campaigns, he washes the blood off his hands and works for "the universal brotherhood of man"—with his mouth.

Man is the Religious Animal. He is the only Religious Animal. He is the only animal that has the True Religion—several of them. He is the only animal that loves his neighbor as himself, and cuts his throat if his theology isn't straight. He has made a graveyard of the globe in trying his honest best to smooth his brother's path to happiness and heaven. He was at it in the time of the Caesars, he was at it in Mahomet's[19] time, he was at it in the time of the Inquisition, he was at it in France a couple of centuries, he was at it in England in Mary's day,[20] he has been at it ever since he first saw

E

---

17. **Hessians** (HEHSH uhnz): German soldiers who served for pay in the British army during the American Revolution.
18. **Prince Napoleon . . . Zulu war:** In search of adventure, Prince Napoleon, son of Napoleon III, joined the British campaign against Zululand (part of South Africa) in 1879.

---

19. **Mahomet's:** Muhammad (c. A.D. 570–632) was an Arab prophet and founder of Islam.
20. **in Mary's day:** during the reign of Queen Mary (1553–1558), who was given the nickname "Bloody Mary" when she ordered the deaths of many Protestants.

E **Literary Perspectives** Analyzing Historical Context
How might Twain's experiences of slavery while growing up in the South be relevant to this passage and his perspective on slavery?

the light, he is at it today in Crete—he will be at it somewhere else tomorrow. The higher animals have no religion. And we are told that they are going to be left out, in the hereafter. I wonder why. It seems questionable taste. **F**

Man is the Reasoning Animal. Such is the claim. I think it is open to dispute. Indeed, my experiments have proven to me that he is the Unreasoning Animal. Note his history, as sketched above. It seems plain to me that whatever he is, he is *not* a reasoning animal. His record is the fantastic record of a maniac. I consider that the strongest count against his intelligence is the fact that with that record back of him, he blandly sets himself up as the head animal of the lot; whereas by his own standards, he is the bottom one.

In truth, man is incurably foolish. Simple things which the other animals easily learn he is incapable of learning. Among my experiments was this. In an hour I taught a cat and a dog to be friends. I put them in a cage. In another hour I taught them to be friends with a rabbit. In the course of two days I was able to add a fox, a goose, a squirrel, and some doves. Finally a monkey. They lived together in peace, even affectionately.

Next, in another cage I confined an Irish Catholic from Tipperary, and as soon as he seemed tame, I added a Scottish Presbyterian from Aberdeen. Next a Turk from Constantinople, a Greek Christian from Crete, an Armenian, a Methodist from the wilds of Arkansas, a Buddhist from China, a Brahman from Benares. Finally, a Salvation Army colonel from Wapping. Then I stayed away two whole days. When I came back to note results, the cage of Higher Animals was all right, but in the other there was but a chaos of gory odds and

Analyzing Visuals

Viewing and Interpreting This humorous print depicts animals behaving like humans. What does the print imply about human behavior?

Print by the French illustrator J.J. Grandville.

ends of turbans and fezzes and plaids and bones and flesh—not a specimen left alive. These Reasoning Animals had disagreed on a theological detail and carried the matter to a higher court. **G**

F **Literary Focus** Satire What technique is Twain using when he contrasts humans with "the higher animals" that will be "left out, in the hereafter"?

G **Reading Focus** Recognizing Purpose Why do you think Twain ends his essay by describing this "experiment"?

Respond and Think Critically

Reading Focus

Quick Check

1. What theory does Twain set out to disprove?

2. What distinguishes a cat that harms a mouse from a human who does harm to others?

3. Describe Twain's last experiment with the two cages. What are the results of the experiment?

Read with a Purpose

4. How does Twain come to the conclusion that human beings are inferior to other animals? Support your answer with four examples.

Reading Skills: Recognizing a Writer's Purpose

5. Review your examples of irony and exaggeration, and consider what they reveal about Twain's religious, political, and social beliefs. Whom or what does Twain aim to improve? In one or two sentences, summarize the writer's overall purpose in this satirical essay.

Examples of Exaggeration and Irony	Twain's Point
"the Descent of Man from the Higher Animals"	It sounds like Twain believes animals are more advanced than humans.

Literary Focus

Literary Analysis

6. **Infer** Twain writes that "Man is the Animal that Blushes. He is the only one that does it—or has occasion to" (page 648). What does he mean?

7. **Analyze** What organizational pattern does Twain use to construct the essay?

8. **Evaluate** Evaluate Twain's philosophical beliefs, as revealed in this essay. How valid are his generalizations about people and their behavior?

9. **Analyze** What specific changes in human nature does Twain hope that this satire will encourage? How do Twain's ideas compare with yours?

10. **Literary Perspectives** What observations might have inspired Twain to write this essay? Why might he use humor to push the parameters of the conventional views of humankind?

Literary Skills: Satire

11. **Analyze** Satire often includes a writer's use of **verbal irony,** or stating one thing while meaning another. Which example of verbal irony did you think was the most effective? Why?

Literary Skills Review: Diction

12. **Evaluate** Twain's choice of words, his **diction,** includes loaded words, such as *slaughter, slave,* and *assassins,* to emphasize the immorality of human beings. How do these loaded words help sustain the power of Twain's satire?

Writing Focus

Think as a Reader/Writer

Use It in Your Writing Write a short satirical commentary on an aspect of society that is in need of improvement. Let your readers know that your ideas are satirical by taking your ideas to the extreme and by including exaggeration in your commentary.

What Do **You Think Now**

How can internal and external forces shape human behavior in negative ways?

Vocabulary Development

✓ Vocabulary Check

Match each Vocabulary word with its synonym.

1. atrocious	a. tendencies
2. avaricious	b. capability
3. caliber	c. carelessly
4. dispositions	d. confirmed
5. transition	e. horrible
6. verified	f. greedy
7. wantonly	g. change

Vocabulary Skills: Greek and Latin Roots in Math and Science

Many English words used in math and science have Greek or Latin **roots,** word parts that carry the core meaning of a word. This is due in part to the many scientific accomplishments of the Greeks and to the use of Latin as the common language of science for centuries. In "The Lowest Animal," Twain uses scientific and mathematical terms that have their origins in Greek and Latin roots—for example, *theory* and *quadrupeds*. In the following charts, you'll find these and other common words from math and science that have Greek and Latin roots.

Greek

Word	Root	Meaning	Meaning of Word
theory	–theor–	to look at, view	a principle explaining how something works
zoological	–log–, –logy	word, study	having to do with the study of animals
genesis	–gen–	to be born	beginning, origin

Latin

Word	Root	Meaning	Meaning of Word
verified	–ver–	true	proved true
scientific	–scien–	to know	systematic and exact
quadrupeds	–ped–	foot	animals with four feet
triangle	–ang–	corner, angle	figure with three angles and three sides

Your Turn

Complete the chart below with the root, the root meaning, and the word meaning for each term.

Word	Root	Root Meaning	Meaning of Word
epidermis			
habitat			
translucent			
symmetry			

Language Coach

Pronunciation The Vocabulary words from page 645 fall into two categories: Either the first or the second-to-last syllable is stressed. Categorize the words by how they are stressed, and note any patterns among the words in the second category.

Academic Vocabulary

Write About
How do the parameters of human nature limit our capacity for good?

Grammar Link

Using Dashes to Set off Parenthetical Elements

A **parenthetical element** is a word, expression, phrase, or sentence that interrupts the main thought of a sentence. Parenthetical elements are usually set off with commas or parentheses.

> Mark Twain was, of course, a great humorist.
> Some of his work (**"The Lowest Animal" is a good example**) is more bitter than funny.

When a parenthetical element represents an abrupt break in a sentence's thought, it is set off with dashes.

> This essay—**which I found shocking**—takes a dim view of humanity.

Dashes are sometimes used in place of *namely, in other words,* or *that is* to set off parenthetical explanations.

> "That the other families—**the birds, the fishes, the insects, the reptiles, etc.**—are more or less distinct, also."

Authors also use dashes to create pauses, often for ironic or satirical effect.

> "No—Man is the Animal that Blushes. He is the only one that does it—or has occasion to."

Your Turn

Add the italicized parenthetical elements to the following sentences, setting them off with dashes.

1. Mark Twain was the pen name of Samuel Langhorne Clemens. *a phrase shouted on steamboats*
2. Twain's fiction was deeply funny. *and realistic*
3. His novels changed American literature. *full of crude characters and language*
4. Later, the tone of Twain's work changed. *it became dark and disillusioned*

CHOICES

As you respond to the Choices, use these **Academic Vocabulary** words as appropriate: capacity, crucial, parameter, relevant, sustain.

REVIEW

Create Call-in Comments

TechFocus Imagine that Twain had had the capacity to broadcast this essay on a radio talk show. How would an audience have responded? Draft several comments listeners might have shared on the air, along with brief descriptions of each listener. If possible, record and share your comments.

CONNECT

Perform a Satirical Skit

Group Activity Work with a group to write a short satirical skit. Choose as your subject some aspect of society or humanity that needs improvement. Include an "experiment" in which you "prove" a point about society or humanity. All group members should play a role in the skit. If necessary, some students can play more than one role. Practice your skit, and then perform it for your class.

EXTEND

Present the Benefits of Science

In this essay Twain claims to use the scientific method to prove his points as he faults the human race for falling short of its ideals. Respond to Twain's essay by examining how some scientific discoveries have brought out the best in humans. Use library resources and Internet research to investigate three examples of how science has brought out positive qualities in human beings. Share your findings with your class in a speech or presentation.

Learn It Online
Find more about Twain through these Internet links.

go.hrw.com   L11-653   **Go**

Reader/Writer Notebook

Use your **RWN** to complete the activities for this selection.

Literary Focus

Extended Metaphor An **extended metaphor** extends a comparison over a number of lines or with several examples. Twain uses this technique to describe his apprenticeship piloting a Mississippi steamboat.

Literary Perspectives Apply the literary perspective described on page 657 as you read this memoir.

Reading Focus

Identifying Comic Devices Humor is hard to explain, but we do know that certain comic devices are frequently used in humorous writings:

- **Hyperbole:** outrageous exaggeration or overstatement
- **Comic comparisons:** similes and metaphors that link dissimilar things to create colorful images
- **Understatement:** saying less than what is really meant

Into Action As you read, record Twain's comic devices in a concept map.

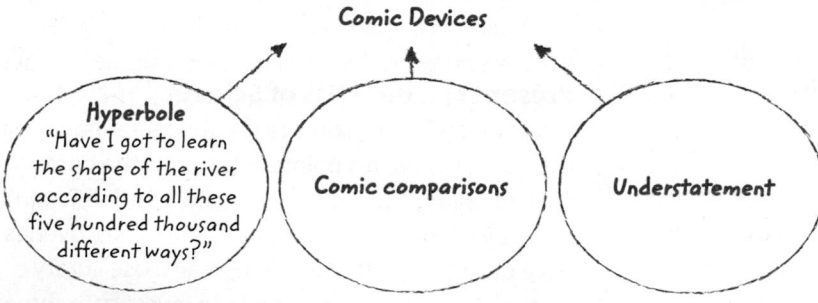

Comic Devices

Hyperbole
"Have I got to learn the shape of the river according to all these five hundred thousand different ways?"

Comic comparisons

Understatement

Writing Focus

Think as a Reader/Writer

Find It in Your Reading **Diction,** or word choice, conveys information about characters. For example, near the end of "Perplexing Lessons," Twain's use of technical language shows his navigational expertise. As you read, record examples of memorable diction in your *Reader/Writer Notebook.*

Vocabulary

inanimate (ihn AN uh miht) *adj.:* lifeless. *Twain compares his young brain to an inanimate mass of lumber.*

complacency (kuhm PLAY suhn see) *n.:* self-satisfaction. *As soon as the narrator feels a sense of complacency, Mr. Bixby challenges him with a tough question.*

serenely (suh REEN lee) *adv.:* calmly. *In spite of the darkness of the night, Mr. W——— serenely pilots the boat without speaking a word of alarm.*

benevolence (buh NEHV uh luhns) *n.:* kindness. *In an act of benevolence, the narrator plans to stay awake with Mr. W——— to provide him with useful information.*

eluding (ih LOOD ihng) *v.* used as *adj.:* remaining unexplained; baffling. *The river's shape, eluding understanding, mystified the apprentice.*

conspicuous (kuhn SPIHK yoo uhs) *adj.:* easily seen; clearly visible. *Though the log floating down the river was dark like the water, it was still conspicuous.*

somber (SAHM buhr) *adj.:* gloomy; dark. *The narrator once felt bewitched by the somber shadows that the forest cast over the river at sunset.*

Language Coach

Roots The root *–bene–* means "good" or "helpful." How does knowing this root help you understand the meaning of *benevolence*?

*** Learn It Online**
Learn more about two of Twain's novels on the *NovelWise* site online.

go.hrw.com   L11-654   Go

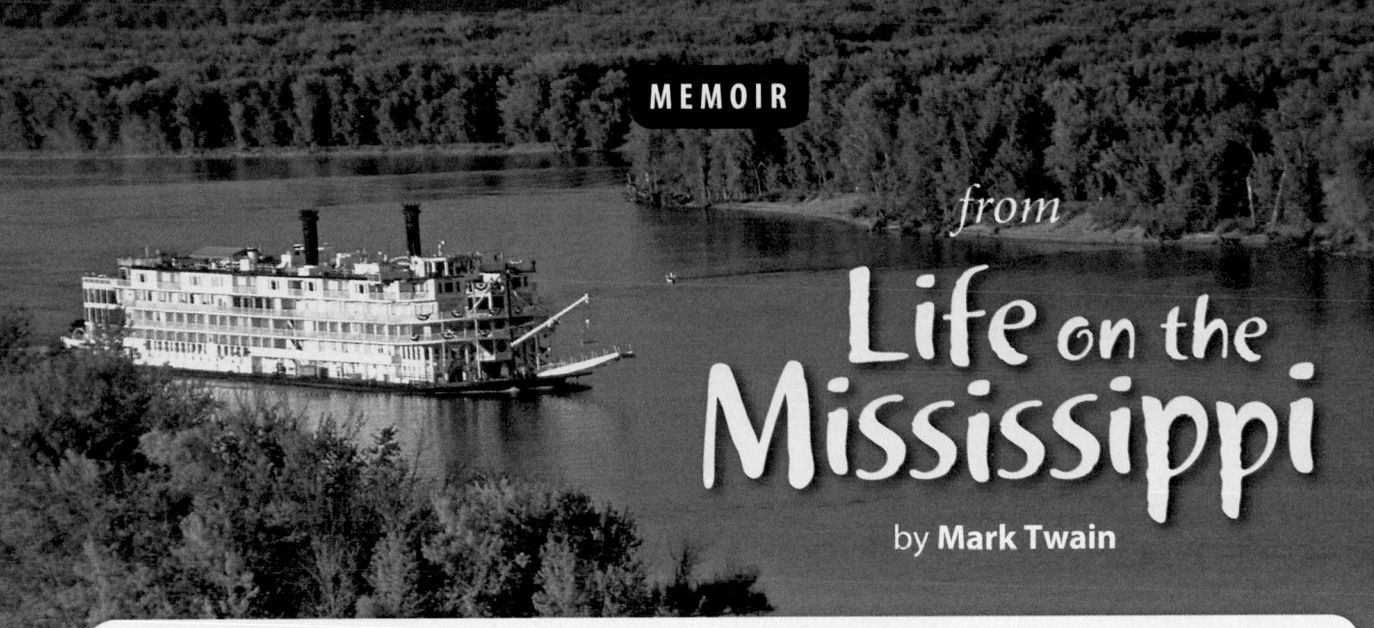

from Life on the Mississippi

by **Mark Twain**

Read with a Purpose

Read to enjoy Twain's humorous depiction of his struggles as an apprentice on a Mississippi River steamboat.

Build Background

As a youth, Twain was so fascinated by riverboats that he persuaded Horace Bixby, the locally famous pilot of the *Paul Jones,* to teach him how to navigate the river between New Orleans and St. Louis (a distance of about seven hundred miles) for five hundred dollars. Twain was not alone in his dream; many boys along the Mississippi, black and white, yearned to work on a steamboat. It didn't matter whether the job was clerk, engineer, mate, or pilot; life on the river meant adventure. "Once a day a cheap gaudy packet (boat) arrived upward from St. Louis," Twain wrote, "and another downward from Keokuk. Before these events, the day was glorious with expectancy; after them, the day was a dead and empty thing." Twain did succeed in becoming a steamboat pilot. These two chapters from *Life on the Mississippi* describe a time when he was still an apprentice, or "cub," pilot being trained by Horace Bixby.

Perplexing Lessons

At the end of what seemed a tedious while, I had managed to pack my head full of islands, towns, bars, "points," and bends;[1] and a curiously inanimate mass of lumber it was, too. However, inasmuch as I could shut my eyes and reel off a good long string of these names without leaving out more than ten miles of river in every fifty, I began to feel that I could take a boat down to New Orleans if I could make her skip those little gaps. But of course my complacency could hardly get start enough to lift my nose a trifle into the air, before Mr. Bixby would think of something to fetch it down again. One day he turned on me suddenly with this settler[2]—

"What is the shape of Walnut Bend?"

He might as well have asked me my grandmother's opinion of protoplasm.[3] I reflected respectfully, and then said I didn't know it had any particular shape. My gunpowdery chief went off with a bang, of course, and then went on loading and firing until he was out of adjectives.

I had learned long ago that he only carried just so many rounds of ammunition, and was sure to subside

---

1. **islands . . . bends:** geographic features used in river navigation. Each numbered point was a landmark on a curve or bend in the river.

2. **settler:** informal for "something (such as Bixby's question) that does a person in."
3. **protoplasm:** living matter basic to all plant and animal cells.

Vocabulary **inanimate** (ihn AN uh miht) *adj.:* lifeless.
complacency (kuhm PLAY suhn see) *n.:* self-satisfaction.

A **Reading Focus** **Identifying Comic Devices** How does the speaker create humor in this passage?

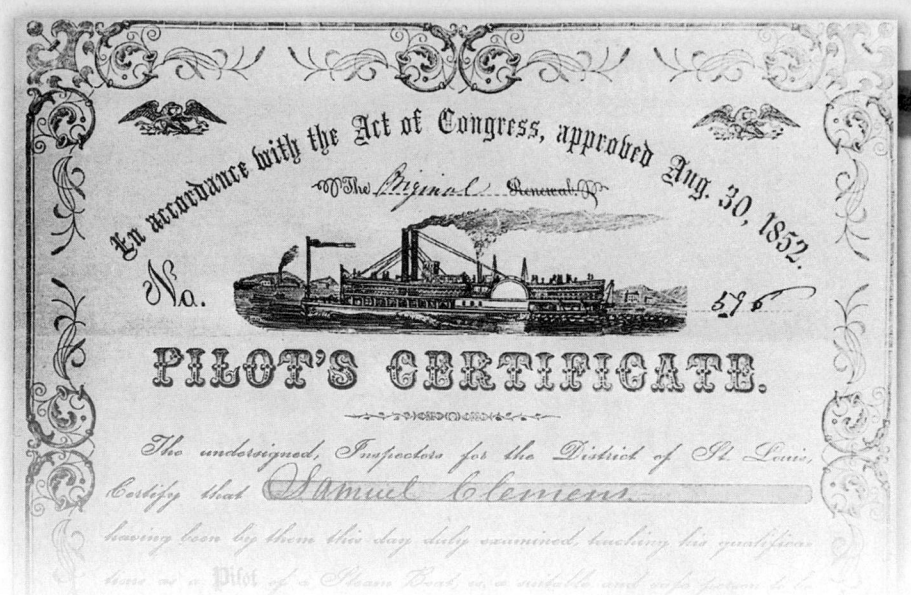

Analyzing Visuals

Viewing and Interpreting Samuel Clemens received his pilot's certificate in 1852. What does this excerpt reveal about the difficulties of learning to pilot a steamboat?

Pilot license of Samuel Clemens (Mark Twain).

into a very placable and even remorseful old smooth-bore[4] as soon as they were all gone. That word "old" is merely affectionate; he was not more than thirty-four. I waited. By and by he said— **B**

"My boy, you've got to know the *shape* of the river perfectly. It is all there is left to steer by on a very dark night. Everything else is blotted out and gone. But mind you, it hasn't the same shape in the night that it has in the day-time."

"How on earth am I ever going to learn it, then?"

"How do you follow a hall at home in the dark? Because you know the shape of it. You can't see it."

"Do you mean to say that I've got to know all the million trifling variations of shape in the banks of this interminable river as well as I know the shape of the front hall at home?"

"On my honor, you've got to know them *better* than any man ever did know the shapes of the halls in his own house."

"I wish I was dead!"

"Now I don't want to discourage you, but"—

"Well, pile it on me; I might as well have it now as another time."

"You see, this has got to be learned; there isn't any getting around it. A clear starlight night throws

such heavy shadows that if you didn't know the shape of a shore perfectly you would claw away from every bunch of timber, because you would take the black shadow of it for a solid cape;[5] and you see you would be getting scared to death every fifteen minutes by the watch.[6] You would be fifty yards from shore all the time when you ought to be within fifty feet of it. You can't see a snag[7] in one of those shadows, but you know exactly where it is, and the shape of the river tells you when you are coming to it. Then there's your pitch-dark night; the river is a very different shape on a pitch-dark night from what it is on a starlight night. All shores seem to be straight lines, then, and mighty dim ones, too; and you'd *run* them for straight lines only you know better. You boldly drive your boat right into what seems to be a solid, straight wall (you knowing very well that in reality there is a curve there), and that wall falls back and makes way for you. Then there's your gray mist. You take a night when there's one of these grisly, drizzly, gray mists, and then there

---

4. **smoothbore:** gun with no grooves inside its barrel.

5. **cape:** land projecting into water.
6. **by the watch:** The workday on a steamboat was divided into three four-hour periods, or watches, every twelve hours: two watches for work and one off-watch for rest.
7. **snag:** tree trunk dangerous to navigation because it is partly or completely underwater.

B **Literary Focus** Extended Metaphor In the previous two paragraphs, what two unlike things does Twain compare? How does Twain use this extended metaphor to create humor?

isn't *any* particular shape to a shore. A gray mist would tangle the head of the oldest man that ever lived. Well, then, different kinds of *moonlight* change the shape of the river in different ways. You see"—

"Oh, don't say any more, please! Have I got to learn the shape of the river according to all these five hundred thousand different ways? If I tried to carry all that cargo in my head it would make me stoop-shouldered." **C**

"*No!* you only learn *the* shape of the river, and you learn it with such absolute certainty that you can always steer by the shape that's *in your head,* and never mind the one that's before your eyes."

"Very well, I'll try it; but after I have learned it can I depend on it? Will it keep the same form and not go fooling around?"

Before Mr. Bixby could answer, Mr. W—— came in to take the watch, and he said—

"Bixby, you'll have to look out for President's Island and all that country clear away up above the Old Hen and Chickens. The banks are caving and the shape of the shores changing like everything. Why, you wouldn't know the point above 40.[8] You can go up inside the old sycamore snag,[9] now."

So that question was answered. Here were leagues[10] of shore changing shape. My spirits were down in the mud again. Two things seemed pretty apparent to me. One was, that in order to be a pilot a man had got to learn more than any one man ought to be allowed to know; and the other was, that he must learn it all over again in a different way every twenty-four hours. **D**

That night we had the watch until twelve. Now it was an ancient river custom for the two pilots to chat a bit when the watch changed. While the relieving pilot

---

8. **point above 40:** numbered navigational point on the river beyond the landmark numbered 40.
9. **inside . . . snag:** It may not be necessary, but still it can do no harm to explain that "inside" means between the snag and the shore. [Twain's note]
10. **leagues:** One league equals about 3 miles.

C **Reading Focus** **Identifying Comic Devices** What comic device does Twain use here?

D **Reading Focus** **Identifying Comic Devices** What comic technique does Twain use in this passage? What is the irony behind the humor here?

---

put on his gloves and lit his cigar, his partner, the retiring pilot, would say something like this—

"I judge the upper bar is making down a little at Hale's Point; had quarter twain with the lower lead and mark twain[11] with the other."

"Yes, I thought it was making down a little, last trip. Meet any boats?"

"Met one abreast the head of 21,[12] but she was away over hugging the bar, and I couldn't make her out entirely. I took her for the 'Sunny South'—hadn't any skylights forward of the chimneys."

And so on. And as the relieving pilot took the wheel his partner[13] would mention that we were in such-and-such a bend, and say we were abreast of such-and-such a man's wood-yard or plantation. This was courtesy; I supposed it was *necessity.* But Mr. W—— came on watch full twelve minutes late on this

---

11. **quarter . . . mark twain:** Two fathoms. Quarter twain is 2¼ fathoms, 13½ feet. Mark three is 3 fathoms. [Twain's note] These measures of water depth are calculated by using a lead weight attached to a rope. One fathom, or "mark one," equals 6 feet. Two fathoms, or "mark twain," equals 12 feet.
12. **abreast . . . 21:** beside landmark, or point, 21.
13. **partner:** "Partner" is technical for "the other pilot." [Twain's note]

Literary Perspectives

Analyzing Style This perspective builds on what you have learned about the techniques authors use to create recognizable styles. An author's style is a kind of literary fingerprint. Mark Twain, for example, uses sophisticated and precise diction when writing in his own voice, but the characters he creates speak in the vernacular of their regions. In *Life on the Mississippi,* Twain's style is humorous; he uses various comic devices, including exaggeration and understatement, to infuse humor into his writing, and he maintains a self-mocking tone to describe his youthful inexperience. When you analyze an author's style, consider sentence structure, vocabulary, figurative language, comic devices, use of dialogue, and recurring themes or topics.

As you read, notice the questions in the text, which will guide you in using this perspective.

particular night—a tremendous breach of etiquette; in fact, it is the unpardonable sin among pilots. So Mr. Bixby gave him no greeting whatever, but simply surrendered the wheel and marched out of the pilothouse without a word. I was appalled; it was a villainous night for blackness, we were in a particularly wide and blind part of the river, where there was no shape or substance to anything, and it seemed incredible that Mr. Bixby should have left that poor fellow to kill the boat trying to find out where he was. But I resolved that I would stand by him anyway. He should find that he was not wholly friendless. So I stood around, and waited to be asked where we were. But Mr. W—— plunged on serenely through the solid firmament of black cats that stood for an atmosphere, and never opened his mouth. Here is a proud devil, thought I; here is a limb of Satan that would rather send us all to destruction than put himself under obligations to me, because I am not yet one of the salt of the earth and privileged to snub captains and lord it over everything dead and alive in a steamboat. I presently climbed up on the bench; I did not think it was safe to go to sleep while this lunatic was on watch.

However, I must have gone to sleep in the course of time, because the next thing I was aware of was the fact that day was breaking, Mr. W—— gone, and Mr. Bixby at the wheel again. So it was four o'clock and all well—but me; I felt like a skinful of dry bones and all of them trying to ache at once.

Mr. Bixby asked me what I had stayed up there for. I confessed that it was to do Mr. W—— a benevolence—tell him where he was. It took five minutes for the entire preposterousness of the thing to filter into Mr. Bixby's system, and then I judge it filled him nearly up to the chin; because he paid me a

> I went to work now to learn the shape of the river; and of all the eluding and ungraspable objects that ever I tried to get mind or hands on.

compliment—and not much of a one either. He said—

"Well, taking you by-and-large, you do seem to be more different kinds of an ass than any creature I ever saw before. What did you suppose he wanted to know for?" **E**

I said I thought it might be a convenience to him.

"Convenience! D-nation! Didn't I tell you that a man's got to know the river in the night the same as he'd know his own front hall?"

"Well, I can follow the front hall in the dark if I know it *is* the front hall; but suppose you set me down in the middle of it in the dark and not tell me which hall it is; how am *I* to know?"

"Well you've *got* to, on the river!"

"All right. Then I'm glad I never said anything to Mr. W——"

"I should say so. Why, he'd have slammed you through the window and utterly ruined a hundred dollars' worth of window sash[14] and stuff."

I was glad this damage had been saved, for it would have made me unpopular with the owners. They always hated anybody who had the name of being careless, and injuring things. **F**

I went to work now to learn the shape of the river; and of all the eluding and ungraspable objects that ever I tried to get mind or hands on, that was the chief. I would fasten my eyes upon a sharp, wooded point that projected far into the river some miles ahead of me, and go to laboriously photographing its shape upon my brain; and just as I was beginning to succeed to my satisfaction, we would draw up toward it and the exasperating thing would begin to melt away and fold back into the bank! If there had been

---

14. **window sash:** frame that holds window glass.

Vocabulary **serenely** (suh REEN lee) *adv.:* calmly.
benevolence (buh NEHV uh luhns) *n.:* kindness.
eluding (ih LOOD ihng) *v.* used as *adj.:* remaining unexplained; baffling.

E **Reading Focus** **Identifying Comic Devices** How does Twain create a comic effect here through a reversal of the reader's expectations?

F **Reading Focus** **Identifying Comic Devices** What comic device does Twain use in this passage? How is this joke consistent with Bixby's character?

The Marvelous Mississippi River

The Mississippi River forms the backdrop of Twain's *Life on the Mississippi* and his masterpiece, *Adventures of Huckleberry Finn*. The longest river in North America and the third longest in the world, the Mississippi River provides a habitat, or native environment, for numerous plant, fish, and wildlife species that live in its waters and on its banks. However, some of these species have become threatened or endangered in recent years by habitat alterations, the result of natural events (such as the accumulation of sediment), or human activities (such as land development, dam construction, and pollution). Scientists monitor changes in local plant and wildlife so as to better understand and <u>sustain</u> their river habitats.

Ask Yourself
If Twain were alive today, how might he respond to the habitat alterations affecting native river plants, fish, and wildlife?

From the left, Erik Wilson, Jennifer Anderson, Lisa Hoffman, and Chad Pregracke remove trash from the Mississippi River.

---

a conspicuous dead tree standing upon the very point of the cape, I would find that tree inconspicuously merged into the general forest, and occupying the middle of a straight shore, when I got abreast of it! No prominent hill would stick to its shape long enough for me to make up my mind what its form really was, but it was as dissolving and changeful as if it had been a mountain of butter in the hottest corner of the tropics. Nothing ever had the same shape when I was coming downstream that it had borne when I went up. I mentioned these little difficulties to Mr. Bixby. He said—

"That's the very main virtue of the thing. If the shapes didn't change every three seconds they wouldn't be of any use. Take this place where we are now, for instance. As long as that hill over yonder is only one hill, I can boom right along the way I'm going; but the moment it splits at the top and forms a V, I know I've got to scratch to starboard[15] in a hurry,

or I'll bang this boat's brains out against a rock; and then the moment one of the prongs of the V swings behind the other, I've got to waltz to larboard[16] again, or I'll have a misunderstanding with a snag that would snatch the keelson[17] out of this steamboat as neatly as if it were a sliver in your hand. If that hill didn't change its shape on bad nights there would be an awful steamboat grave-yard around here inside of a year." **G**

It was plain that I had got to learn the shape of the river in all the different ways that could be thought of,—upside down, wrong end first, inside out, fore-and-aft, and "thortships"[18]—and then know what to do on gray nights when it hadn't any shape at all. So I set about it. In the course of time I began to

---

15. **scratch to starboard:** move quickly to the right side of the boat.

16. **larboard:** the left side of the boat.
17. **keelson:** wood or metal beams fastened along a boat's keel to strengthen it. The keel is the timber along the boat's bottom that supports the frame.
18. **fore-and-aft, and "thort-ships":** end to end and shore to shore.

Vocabulary **conspicuous** (kuhn SPIHK yoo uhs) *adj.*: easily seen; clearly visible.

G **Literary Perspectives** Analyzing Style Twain's use of figurative language is a distinctive element of his style. How does Twain use simile and metaphor to make Bixby's explanation clear?

get the best of this knotty lesson, and my self-compla-cency moved to the front once more. Mr. Bixby was all fixed, and ready to start it to the rear again. He opened on me after this fashion—

"How much water did we have in the middle crossing at Hole-in-the-Wall, trip before last?"

I considered this an outrage. I said—

"Every trip, down and up, the leadsmen[19] are singing through that tangled place for three quarters of an hour on a stretch. How do you reckon I can remember such a mess as that?"

"My boy, you've got to remember it. You've got to remember the exact spot and the exact marks the boat lay in when we had the shoalest[20] water, in everyone of the five hundred shoal places between St. Louis and New Orleans; and you mustn't get the shoal soundings and marks[21] of one trip mixed up with the shoal soundings and marks of another, either, for they're not often twice alike. You must keep them separate."

When I came to myself again, I said—

"When I get so that I can do that, I'll be able to raise the dead, and then I won't have to pilot a steam-boat to make a living. I want to retire from this busi-ness. I want a slush-bucket and a brush; I'm only fit for a roustabout.[22] I haven't got brains enough to be a pilot; and if I had I wouldn't have strength enough to carry them around, unless I went on crutches." **H**

"Now drop that! When I say I'll learn[23] a man the river, I mean it. And you can depend on it, I'll learn him or kill him."

Continued Perplexities

There was no use in arguing with a person like this. I promptly put such a strain on my memory that by and by even the shoal water and the countless cross-ing marks[24] began to stay with me. But the result was just the same. I never could more than get one knotty thing learned before another presented itself. Now I had often seen pilots gazing at the water and pretending to read it as if it were a book; but it was a book that told me nothing. A time came at last, how-ever, when Mr. Bixby seemed to think me far enough advanced to bear a lesson on water-reading. So he began— **I**

---

19. **leadsman:** workers who use a lead line to measure the water's depth.
20. **shoalest:** most shallow.
21. **soundings and marks:** measurements of water depth.

22. **roustabout:** deckhand; laborer in a boat.
23. **learn:** "Teach" is not in the river vocabulary. [Twain's note]
24. **crossing marks:** points on the river where a boat could cross safely.

H **Reading Focus** Identifying Comic Devices How does Twain use hyperbole to make clear how the young novice feels as he learns to navigate the river?

I **Literary Focus** Extended Metaphor How might reading the river be similar to reading a book?

"Do you see that long slanting line on the face of the water Now, that's a reef. Moreover, it's a bluff reef.[25] There is a solid sandbar under it that is nearly as straight up and down as the side of a house. There is plenty of water close up to it, but mighty little on top of it. If you were to hit it you would knock the boat's brains out. Do you see where the line fringes out at the upper end and begins to fade away?"

"Yes, sir."

"Well, that is a low place; that is the head of the reef. You can climb over there, and not hurt anything. Cross over, now, and follow along close under the reef—easy water there—not much current."

I followed the reef along till I approached the fringed end. Then Mr. Bixby said—

"Now get ready. Wait till I give the word. She won't want to mount the reef; a boat hates shoal water. Stand by—wait—WAIT—keep her well in hand. NOW cramp her down![26] Snatch her![27] Snatch her!"

He seized the other side of the wheel and helped to spin it around until it was hard down, and then we held it so. The boat resisted, and refused to answer for a while, and next she came surging to starboard, mounted the reef, and sent a long, angry ridge of water foaming away from her bows.[28]

"Now watch her; watch her like a cat, or she'll get away from you. When she fights strong and the tiller slips a little, in a jerky, greasy sort of way, let up on her a trifle; it is the way she tells you at night that the water is too shoal; but keep edging her up, little by little, toward the point. You are well up on the bar, now; there is a bar under every point, because the water that comes down around it forms an eddy and allows the sediment to sink. Do you see those fine lines on the face of the water that branch out like the ribs of a fan? Well, those are little reefs; you want to just miss the ends of them, but run them pretty close. Now look out—look out! Don't you crowd that slick, greasy-looking place; there ain't nine feet there; she won't stand it. She begins to smell it; look sharp, I tell you! Oh blazes, there you go! Stop the starboard wheel! Quick! Ship up to back! Set her back!"[29] **J**

The engine bells jingled and the engines answered promptly, shooting white columns of steam far aloft out of the 'scape pipes, but it was too late. The boat had "smelt"[30] the bar in good earnest; the foamy ridges that radiated from her bows suddenly disappeared,

25. **bluff reef:** hidden sandbar with a high, steep front. Its position is indicated by lines or ripples on the water.
26. **cramp her down:** turn the wheel sharply.
27. **Snatch her:** Act quickly.

28. **bows:** front part of a boat.
29. **Ship . . . back:** Put it in reverse.
30. **smelt:** dialect for "smelled." That is, the boat recognized water too shallow for safety.

J **Literary Perspectives** **Analyzing Style** Notice Bixby's vocabulary. How does Twain create a conversational or informal tone?

a great dead swell[31] came rolling forward and swept ahead of her, she careened far over to larboard, and went tearing away toward the other shore as if she were about scared to death. We were a good mile from where we ought to have been, when we finally got the upper hand of her again.

During the afternoon watch the next day, Mr. Bixby asked me if I knew how to run the next few miles. I said—

"Go inside the first snag above the point, outside the next one, start out from the lower end of Higgins's wood-yard, make a square crossing[32] and"—

"That's all right. I'll be back before you close up on the next point."

But he wasn't. He was still below when I rounded it and entered upon a piece of river which I had some misgivings about. I did not know that he was hiding behind a chimney to see how I would perform. I went gaily along, getting prouder and prouder, for he had never left the boat in my sole charge such a length of time before. I even got to 'setting' her and letting the wheel go, entirely, while I vaingloriously[33] turned my back and inspected the stern marks[34] and hummed a tune, a sort of easy indifference which I had prodigiously[35] admired in Bixby and other great pilots. Once I inspected rather long, and when I faced to the front again my heart flew into my mouth so suddenly that if I hadn't clapped my teeth together I should have lost it. One of those frightful bluff reefs was stretching its deadly length right across our bows! My head was gone in a moment; I did not know which end I stood on; I gasped and could not get my breath; I spun the wheel down with such rapidity that it wove itself together like a spider's web; the boat answered and turned square away from the reef, but

the reef followed her! I fled, and still it followed, still it kept—right across my bows! I never looked to see where I was going, I only fled. The awful crash was imminent—why didn't that villain come! If I committed the crime of ringing a bell, I might get thrown overboard. But better that than kill the boat. So in blind desperation I started such a rattling "shivaree"[36] down below as never had astounded an engineer in this world before, I fancy. Amidst the frenzy of the bells the engines began to back and fill in a furious way, and my reason forsook its throne—we were about to crash into the woods on the other side of the river. Just then Mr. Bixby stepped calmly into view on the hurricane deck.[37] My soul went out to him in gratitude. My distress vanished; I would have felt safe on the brink of Niagara, with Mr. Bixby on the hurricane deck. He blandly and sweetly took his tooth-pick out of his mouth between his fingers, as if it were a cigar—we were just in the act of climbing an overhanging big tree, and the passengers were scudding astern[38] like rats—and lifted up these commands to me ever so gently— Ⓚ

"Stop the starboard. Stop the larboard. Set her back on both."[39]

The boat hesitated, halted, pressed her nose among the boughs a critical instant, then reluctantly began to back away.

"Stop the larboard. Come ahead on it. Stop the starboard. Come ahead on it. Point her for the bar."

I sailed away as serenely as a summer's morning Mr. Bixby came in and said, with mock simplicity—

"When you have a hail,[40] my boy, you ought to tap the big bell three times before you land, so that the engineers can get ready."

I blushed under the sarcasm, and said I hadn't had any hail.

---

31. **great dead swell:** huge wave.
32. **make a square crossing:** go directly between crossing marks.
33. **vaingloriously** (vayn GLAWR ee uhs lee): with excessive pride or boastfulness.
34. **stern marks:** landmarks already passed and thus astern of, or behind, the boat.
35. **prodigiously** (pruh DIHJ uhs lee): greatly.

36. **"shivaree":** noisy celebration.
37. **hurricane deck:** topmost deck of a steamboat.
38. **scudding astern:** running to the back of the boat.
39. **Stop . . . both:** Halt the forward motion of the boat by stopping both the right and left paddle wheels, and put both wheels in reverse.
40. **hail:** call to land.

Ⓚ **Literary Perspectives** Analyzing Style How does Twain create suspense in this paragraph?

"Ah! Then it was for wood, I suppose. The officer of the watch will tell you when he wants to wood up."

I went on consuming and said I wasn't after wood.

"Indeed? Why, what could you want over here in the bend, then? Did you ever know of a boat following a bend up-stream at this stage of the river?"

"No sir,—and I wasn't trying to follow it. I was getting away from a bluff reef."

"No, it wasn't a bluff reef; there isn't one within three miles of where you were."

"But I saw it. It was as bluff as that one yonder."

"Just about. Run over it!"

"Do you give it as an order?"

"Yes. Run over it."

"If I don't, I wish I may die."

"All right; I am taking the responsibility." I was just as anxious to kill the boat, now, as I had been to save her before. I impressed my orders upon my memory, to be used at the inquest,[41] and made a straight break for the reef. As it disappeared under our bows I held my breath; but we slid over it like oil.

"Now don't you see the difference? It wasn't anything but a WIND reef. The wind does that."

"So I see. But it is exactly like a bluff reef. How am I ever going to tell them apart?"

"I can't tell you. It is an instinct. By and by you will just naturally KNOW one from the other, but you never will be able to explain why or how you know them apart."

It turned out to be true. The face of the water, in time, became a wonderful book—a book that was a dead language to the uneducated passenger, but which told its mind to me without reserve, delivering its most cherished secrets as clearly as if it uttered them with a voice. And it was not a book to be read once and thrown aside, for it had a new story to tell every day. Throughout the long twelve hundred miles there was never a page that was void of interest, never one that you could leave unread without loss, never one that you would want to skip, thinking you could find higher enjoyment in some other thing. There never was so wonderful a book written by man; never one whose interest was so absorbing, so unflagging, so sparkingly renewed with every re-perusal. The passenger who could not read it was charmed with a peculiar sort of faint dimple on its surface (on the rare occasions when he did not overlook it altogether); but to the pilot that was an ITALICIZED passage; indeed, it was more than that, it was a legend[42] of the largest capitals, with a string of shouting exclamation points at the end of it; for it meant that a wreck or a rock was buried there that could tear the life out of the strongest vessel that ever floated. It is the faintest and simplest expression the water ever makes, and the most hideous to a pilot's eye. In truth, the passenger who could not read this book saw nothing but all manner of pretty pictures in it painted by the sun and shaded by the clouds,

41. **inquest:** inquiry by a jury or panel investigating a crime.

42. **legend:** inscription.

L **Reading Focus** **Identifying Comic Devices** What creates the humor in this ironic situation?

whereas to the trained eye these were not pictures at all, but the grimmest and most dead-earnest of reading matter. Ⓜ

Now when I had mastered the language of this water and had come to know every trifling feature that bordered the great river as familiarly as I knew the letters of the alphabet, I had made a valuable acquisition. But I had lost something, too. I had lost something which could never be restored to me while I lived. All the grace, the beauty, the poetry had gone out of the majestic river! I still keep in mind a certain wonderful sunset which I witnessed when steamboating was new to me. A broad expanse of the river was turned to blood; in the middle distance the red hue brightened into gold, through which a solitary log came floating, black and conspicuous; in one place a long, slanting mark lay sparkling upon the water; in another the surface was broken by boiling, tumbling rings, that were as many-tinted as an opal; where the ruddy flush was faintest, was a smooth spot that was covered with graceful circles and radiating lines, ever so delicately traced; the shore on our left was densely wooded, and the somber shadow that fell from this forest was broken in one place by a long, ruffled trail that shone like silver; and high above the forest wall a clean-stemmed dead tree waved a single leafy bough that glowed like a flame in the unobstructed splendor that was flowing from the sun. There were graceful curves, reflected images, woody heights, soft distances; and over the whole scene, far and near, the dissolving lights drifted steadily, enriching it, every passing moment, with new marvels of coloring.

I stood like one bewitched. I drank it in, in a speechless rapture. The world was new to me, and I had never seen anything like this at home. But as I have said, a day came when I began to cease from noting the glories and the charms which the moon and the sun and the twilight wrought upon the river's face;

> ## The world was new to me, and I had never seen anything like this at home.

another day came when I ceased altogether to note them. Then, if that sunset scene had been repeated, I should have looked upon it without rapture, and should have commented upon it, inwardly, after this fashion: This sun means that we are going to have wind to-morrow; that floating log means that the river is rising, small thanks to it; that slanting mark on the water refers to a bluff reef which is going to kill somebody's steamboat one of these nights, if it keeps on stretching out like that; those tumbling 'boils' show a dissolving bar and a changing channel there; the lines and circles in the slick water over yonder are a warning that that troublesome place is shoaling up dangerously; that silver streak in the shadow of the forest is the "break" from a new snag,[43] and he has located himself in the very best place he could have found to fish for steamboats; that tall dead tree, with a single living branch, is not going to last long, and then how is a body ever going to get through this blind place at night without the friendly old landmark.

No, the romance and the beauty were all gone from the river. All the value any feature of it had for me now was the amount of usefulness it could furnish toward compassing the safe piloting of a steamboat. Since those days, I have pitied doctors from my heart. What does the lovely flush in a beauty's cheek mean to a doctor but a "break" that ripples above some deadly disease. Are not all her visible charms sown thick with what are to him the signs and symbols of hidden decay? Does he ever see her beauty at all, or doesn't he simply view her professionally, and comment upon her unwholesome condition all to himself? And doesn't he sometimes wonder whether he has gained most or lost most by learning his trade? Ⓝ

---

43. **"break" . . . snag:** ripple of line in the water indicating a newly fallen tree.

Ⓜ **Literary Focus** Extended Metaphor What two unlike things does Twain compare in this extended metaphor? When did Twain first introduce this metaphor, and why do you think he continues to use it at this particular part of the narrative?

Ⓝ **Literary Focus** Extended Metaphor Explain the extended metaphor in this paragraph. How does it communicate Twain's purpose?

Vocabulary **somber** (SAHM buhr) *adj.*: gloomy; dark.

Applying Your Skills

from **Life on the Mississippi**

SKILLS FOCUS **Literary Skills** Analyze extended metaphor; analyze diction; analyze style. **Reading Skills** Identify comic devices. **Writing Skills** Develop characters using dialogue.

Respond and Think Critically

Reading Focus

Quick Check

1. Why is learning the shape of the river such a great challenge?

2. How would you describe the relationship between Bixby and the young Twain? Support your answer with <u>relevant</u> details from the text.

3. How does Twain's view of the river change as he learns to be a steamboat pilot?

Read with a Purpose

4. How does Twain cope with the struggles and distress he often faces during his apprenticeship?

Reading Skills: Identifying Comic Devices

5. Review the concept map you completed as you read. Answer these questions: Which comic device does Twain use most frequently? Which devices or examples did you find funniest? What adjectives best describe Twain's humor?

Literary Focus

Literary Analysis

6. **Infer** Do you believe Bixby's assertion that Twain must learn the river better than he knows his own house, or is Bixby exaggerating? Explain.

7. **Make Judgments** Consider the episode in which Bixby lets Twain get into trouble before giving him quiet guidance. On the basis of your own experiences, do you think that Bixby is a good teacher? Give reasons for your answer.

8. **Interpret** What does Twain mean when he ruefully reports that "the romance and the beauty were all gone from the river"? Identify another instance of this type of experience in the memoir.

9. **Analyze** Twain must internalize the river's shape so he can navigate from memory with absolute certainty and avoid the variable impressions of his senses. How might this strategy be a metaphor for an approach to life in general?

10. **Literary Perspectives** What elements of Twain's style are characteristically his own? Explain.

Literary Skills: Extended Metaphor

11. **Evaluate** In "Continued Perplexities," Twain compares the river to a book that "had a new story to tell every day." List three comparisons Twain makes between reading a book and "reading" the river. Do you think this extended metaphor is an effective way of conveying the challenges of learning the river? Explain.

Literary Skills Review: Diction

12. **Compare and Contrast** A writer's choice of words is called **diction.** Contrast the diction used by Bixby, Twain the raw apprentice, and Twain the mature writer. Explain what purposes these differences serve.

Writing Focus

Think as a Reader/Writer

Use It in Your Writing Write a humorous conversation between two characters. Use the characters' **diction,** or word choice, to help you distinguish sufficiently between them. Allow part of the humor to arise from the characters' different ways of using language.

 What Do You Think Now

How does the process of learning the river help shape Twain's character? What qualities does it help Twain develop?

from Life on the Mississippi

Vocabulary Development

✓ Vocabulary Check

Choose the antonym of each Vocabulary word.

1. benevolence
2. complacency
3. eluding
4. inanimate
5. conspicuous
6. serenely
7. somber

a. understandable
b. alive
c. cheery
d. unnoticeable
e. anxiously
f. cruelty
g. self-doubt

Vocabulary Skills: Context Clues

A word's **context**—the words and sentences that surround it—often gives clues to the word's meaning. Look at some examples below from *Life on the Mississippi,* and notice how the context clues help illuminate the meaning of each boldface word.

"I went to work now to learn the shape of the river; and of all the **eluding** and ungraspable objects that ever I tried to get mind or hands on, that was the chief."
Context clues: *ungraspable, tried to get mind or hands on, went to work now to learn the shape*
My guess: difficult to understand
Dictionary meaning: remaining unexplained; baffling

"Now when I had mastered the language of this water and had come to know every trifling feature that bordered the great river as familiarly as I knew the letters of the alphabet, I had made a valuable **acquisition.** But I had lost something, too."
Context clues: *mastered; come to know; familiarly; valuable; lost something, too*
My guess: something gained
Dictionary meaning: something obtained or added

Your Turn

List context clues for each boldface word below, and infer its meaning. Then, use a dictionary to confirm whether your inference is correct.

1. ". . . he only carried just so many rounds of ammunition, and was sure to subside into a very **placable** and even remorseful old smoothbore as soon as they were all gone."

2. ". . . the foamy ridges that radiated from her bows suddenly disappeared, a great dead swell came rolling forward and swept ahead of her, she **careened** far over to larboard, and went tearing away toward the other shore."

3. "This was courtesy; I supposed it was *necessity.* But Mr. W——came on watch full twelve minutes late on this particular night,—a tremendous breach of **etiquette;** in fact, it is the unpardonable sin among pilots."

Language Coach

Roots Roots reveal a word's meaning. For example, knowing the root –*bene*– ("good") can help you understand the meaning other related words, such as *beneficial* ("helpful"). Consider the roots –*ludus*– and –*animus*–. Which Vocabulary words might be related to them?

Academic Vocabulary

Talk About
Bixby clearly made an impression on Twain. With a partner, talk about your favorite teachers. How did they <u>sustain</u> your attention and make lessons <u>relevant</u> for you?

SKILLS FOCUS **Literary Skills** Analyze a writer's style. **Vocabulary Skills** Use context clues in words, sentences, and paragraphs to decode new vocabulary. **Writing**

Skills Write comparison-contrast essays. **Listening and Speaking Skills** Participate in group discussions; demonstrate effective verbal techniques when speaking.

Author Study: Mark Twain

Writing Focus

Analyzing a Writer's Language

In "The Celebrated Jumping Frog of Calaveras County," "The Lowest Animal," and *Life on the Mississippi,* Mark Twain uses humor to convey his ideas. Devices such as irony, hyperbole, understatement, and comic metaphor help Twain accomplish his purpose—to entertain, persuade, or inform—in a memorable way.

Select your two favorite Twain selections. Then, identify Twain's purpose in each selection and note the ways humor helps him achieve his purpose in each. Write an essay analyzing how Twain uses two comic devices in each selection to inform, entertain, or persuade his audience. You should accomplish the following in your essay:

- Compare and contrast Twain's use of humor to achieve his purpose in at least two selections.
- Cite specific lines from the selections you are comparing, and use them to support your analysis.
- Discuss how Twain's use of each comic device helps him achieve his purpose.
- Begin with a paragraph that introduces your main points, and conclude with a paragraph that summarizes them.

Before you begin writing, use a chart like the one below to organize your ideas.

Comic Devices	Selection 1	Selection 2
hyperbole		
irony		
metaphor		
understatement		

CHOICES

As you respond to the Choices, use these **Academic Vocabulary** words as appropriate: capacity, crucial, parameter, relevant, sustain.

REVIEW

Perform an Oral Reading

Partner Activity With a partner, rehearse an oral reading of an excerpt from one of Twain's selections. To prepare, you might want to watch the video *Mark Twain Gives an Interview,* with the actor Hal Holbrook portraying Mark Twain. You may also want to use relevant props.

CONNECT

Discuss Twain's Humor

Group Discussion With classmates, discuss whether Twain's humor is like or unlike the humor of current humorists, citing specific examples. How do today's comics appeal to their audiences? Could Twain be a stand-up comic or a humorous writer these days?

EXTEND

Compare Two Views

Timed Writing The last three paragraphs of the excerpt from *Life on the Mississippi* examine two very different ways of looking at the river. Write an essay in which you compare and contrast two different views of something, such as the following examples:

- your feelings before and after taking a particular action
- how you see some aspect of your life now and how you saw it in the past
- a favorite place during the day and at night

What Do You Think Now

What forces do you think Twain felt were most important in shaping human character?

A Wagner Matinée

What Do You Think?

What forces shape human character?

QuickWrite

Most people can name at least one thing that's a source of great personal pleasure. Maybe it's an activity, such as fishing, or a place, like an art museum. In a paragraph, name something you enjoy and explain how it has influenced you. What might you or your life be like without it?

Willa Cather (1926) by Edward Steichen (1879–1973).

MEET THE WRITER

Willa Cather
(1873–1947)

Pulitzer Prize WINNER

Many of Willa Cather's works reflect the subject she knew best: the values of hardworking midwestern pioneer families. Cather believed these pioneers were the heart of the American dream.

Heart of the Prairie

The first of seven children, Willa Cather was born in rural Virginia. When she was nine, her family headed for the untried lands of the West and settled in Nebraska. Cather was stimulated by the hard life she saw around her, and she absorbed the stories of the immigrant families who were her neighbors.

As a first-year student at the University of Nebraska, Cather regularly contributed to a Lincoln newspaper. By the time she graduated in 1895, she had already won a reputation for brash, bright reviews. In 1903, while working as a journalist in Pittsburgh, she published her first book, a collection of verse titled *April Twilights*. This was followed in 1905 by a collection of short stories that includes "A Wagner Matinée."

Literary Success in New York

In 1906, Cather moved to New York and joined the staff of the dynamic muckraking magazine *McClure's*. For six years, she served as a writer and editor, immersed in the social and political currents of the time. In 1912, she resigned from the magazine to dedicate herself to writing fiction. In *O Pioneers!* (1913) and *My Ántonia* (1918), she chronicled the lives of immigrant families on the midwestern prairie.

Cather became increasingly uncomfortable with the modernist sensibility that swept through artistic and literary circles after World War I. Although she continued to produce finely crafted novels and stories—including the two masterpieces *The Professor's House* (1925) and *Death Comes for the Archbishop* (1927)—her creative vision remained rooted in the realities of the nineteenth century. She predicted that the new comforts of modern science would surely demand something of our spirit in return.

Think About the Writer

Why might Cather have believed that modern society would betray the pioneer ideal?

Reader/Writer Notebook

Use your **RWN** to complete the activities for this selection.

Literary Focus

Setting As in most of Willa Cather's works, **setting**—the <u>parameters</u> of time and location in which a story takes place—plays a central role in this story. Here, however, there are really two settings. The narrator contrasts rural Nebraska—where he, like Cather, spent his formative years—with Boston and its thriving cultural life. As you read, think about how the different settings help reveal the story's theme.

Reading Focus

Making Inferences A **theme** is the insight about human life that is revealed in a literary work. When you make **inferences** about a work's theme, you look beyond what is stated directly and think about ideas that are implied, or hinted at. As you read, be alert for details that seem to hint at a larger meaning. Pay close attention to the clues revealed in the descriptions of the story's two settings.

Into Action While you read, use a graphic organizer like the one below to record details that hint at a larger meaning. Then, explain what you can infer from each detail.

Detail

"They built a dugout in the red hillside, one of those cave dwellings whose inmates so often reverted to primitive conditions."

→

Inference

The words cave dwellings, inmates, and primitive suggest that Cather is commenting on the difficulty and lack of sophistication of life on the prairie.

Writing Focus

Think as a Reader/Writer

Find It in Your Reading Language that evokes a mental picture or concrete sensation of a person, a thing, a place, or an experience is called **imagery.** As you read "A Wagner Matinée," notice the striking images of the stark Nebraska **setting**—for example, "the cornfield that stretched to daybreak." In your *Reader/Writer Notebook,* record images of the Nebraska prairie that live on so vividly in the narrator's memory.

Vocabulary

legacy (LEHG uh see) *n.:* money or other property left to a person by the will of someone who has died. *Aunt Georgiana comes to Boston to receive a legacy left to her by a relative.*

grotesque (groh TEHSK) *adj.:* strange; absurd. *Years of hard work on the prairie have resulted in Aunt Georgiana's grotesque and pathetic figure.*

reverential (rehv uh REHN shuhl) *adj.:* deeply respectful. *The narrator has a reverential affection for his aunt, who brought much joy into his boyhood years.*

pious (PY uhs) *adj.:* devoted to one's religion. *Aunt Georgiana is a pious woman who finds consolation in her religious faith.*

inert (ihn URT) *adj.:* inactive; sluggish. *Upon entering the concert hall, Aunt Georgiana seemed less inert and began to notice her surroundings.*

trepidation (trehp uh DAY shuhn) *n.:* anxious uncertainty. *The narrator feels trepidation that his aunt will be embarrassed about her clothing.*

deluge (DEHL yooj) *n.:* rush; flood. *The narrator imagines that Aunt Georgiana is carried away by the deluge of music at the concert.*

Language Coach

Pronunciation French-derived words that end in *–que,* such as *unique* and *oblique,* end with a hard /k/ sound. Say the Vocabulary word above that follows this rule.

 Learn It Online
Learn more about Cather and her world with these Internet links.

go.hrw.com   L11-669   **Go**

A WAGNER MATINÉE

by **Willa Cather**

Read with a Purpose
Read to discover what the narrator comes to realize about his aunt's life when he takes her to a matinée at a concert hall.

Build Background
Many of Cather's works are set on the Nebraska frontier that she loved. She believed that midwestern farm life fostered important values, yet she was hardly a romantic who underestimated the hardships of that life or the harsh losses that many of her stoic characters had to endure. In addition to the frontier, the importance of the artistic life was a recurring subject in Cather's work. She had a great personal passion for music and was an accomplished musician. The story's title refers to the German composer Richard Wagner (1813–1883), a Romantic composer of the nineteenth century. A matinée is an afternoon performance of a play or concert.

I received one morning a letter, written in pale ink on glassy, blue-lined notepaper, and bearing the postmark of a little Nebraska village. This communication, worn and rubbed, looking as though it had been carried for some days in a coat pocket that was none too clean, was from my Uncle Howard and informed me that his wife had been left a small legacy by a bachelor relative who had recently died, and that it would be necessary for her to go to Boston to attend to the settling of the estate. He requested me to meet her at the station and render her whatever services might be necessary. On examining the date indicated as that of her arrival, I found it no later than tomorrow. He had characteristically delayed writing until, had I been away from home for a day, I must have missed the good woman altogether.

The name of Aunt Georgiana called up not alone her own figure, at once pathetic and grotesque, but opened before my feet a gulf of recollection so wide and deep, that, as the letter dropped from my hand, I felt suddenly a stranger to all the present conditions of my existence, wholly ill at ease and out of place amid the familiar surroundings of my study. I became, in short, the gangling farmer boy my aunt had known, scourged with chilblains[1] and bashfulness, my hands cracked and sore from the cornhusking. I felt the knuckles of my thumb tentatively, as though they were raw again. I sat again before her parlor organ, fumbling the scales with my stiff, red hands, while she, beside me, made canvas mittens for the huskers. **A**

The next morning, after preparing my landlady somewhat, I set out for the station. When the train arrived I had some difficulty in finding my aunt. She was the last of the passengers to alight, and it was not until I got her into the carriage that she seemed really to recognize me. She had come all the way in a day coach; her linen duster had become black with soot and her black bonnet gray with dust during the journey. When we arrived at my boardinghouse the landlady put her to bed at once and I did not see her again until the next morning.

---

1. **scourged with chilblains** (CHIHL blaynz): afflicted with an inflammation of the hands and feet, caused by exposure to cold.

A **Literary Focus** Setting Why does the narrator suddenly feel different about his surroundings?

Vocabulary **legacy** (LEHG uh see) *n.*: money or other property left to a person by the will of someone who has died.
grotesque (groh TEHSK) *adj.*: strange; absurd.

In the Loge (1878) by Mary Cassatt (1844–1926). Oil on canvas (32" × 26").
Photograph © 2009 Museum of Fine Arts, Boston.

Whatever shock Mrs. Springer experienced at my aunt's appearance, she considerately concealed. As for myself, I saw my aunt's misshapen figure with that feeling of awe and respect with which we behold explorers who have left their ears and fingers north of Franz Josef Land,[2] or their health somewhere along the upper Congo. My Aunt Georgiana had been a music teacher at the Boston Conservatory, somewhere back in the latter sixties. One summer, while visiting in the little village among the Green Mountains where her ancestors had dwelt for generations, she had kindled the callow[3] fancy of the most idle and shiftless of all the village lads, and had conceived for this Howard Carpenter one of those extravagant passions which a handsome country boy of twenty-one sometimes inspires in an angular, spectacled woman of thirty. When she returned to her duties in Boston, Howard followed her, and the upshot of this inexplicable infatuation was that she eloped with him, eluding the reproaches of her family and the criticisms of her friends by going with him to the Nebraska frontier. Carpenter, who, of course, had no money, had taken a homestead in Red Willow County, fifty miles from the railroad. There they had measured off their quarter section themselves by driving across the prairie in a wagon, to the wheel of which they had tied a red cotton handkerchief, and counting off its revolutions. They built a dugout in the red hillside, one of those cave dwellings whose inmates so often reverted to primitive conditions. Their water they got from the lagoons where the buffalo drank, and their slender stock of provisions was always at the mercy of bands of roving Indians. For thirty years my aunt had not been further than fifty miles from the homestead. **B**

But Mrs. Springer knew nothing of all this, and must have been considerably shocked at what was left of my kinswoman. Beneath the soiled linen duster

---

2. **Franz Josef Land:** group of islands in the Arctic Ocean.
3. **callow:** immature; inexperienced.

which, on her arrival, was the most conspicuous feature of her costume, she wore a black stuff[4] dress, whose ornamentation showed that she had surrendered herself unquestioningly into the hands of a country dressmaker. My poor aunt's figure, however, would have presented astonishing difficulties to any dressmaker. Originally stooped, her shoulders were now almost bent together over her sunken chest. She wore no stays,[5] and her gown, which trailed unevenly behind, rose in a sort of peak over her abdomen. She wore ill-fitting false teeth, and her skin was as yellow as a Mongolian's from constant exposure to a pitiless wind and to the alkaline water which hardens the most transparent cuticle into a sort of flexible leather. **C**

I owed to this woman most of the good that ever came my way in my boyhood, and had a reverential affection for her. During the years when I was riding herd for my uncle, my aunt, after cooking the three meals—the first of which was ready at six o'clock in the morning— and putting the six children to bed, would often stand until midnight at her ironing board, with me at the kitchen table beside her, hearing me recite Latin declensions and conjugations,[6] gently shaking me when my drowsy head sank down over a page of irregular verbs. It was to her, at her ironing or mending, that I read my first Shakespeare, and her old textbook on mythology was the first that ever came into my empty hands. She taught me my scales and exercises, too—on the little parlor organ, which her husband had bought her after fifteen years, during which she had not so much as seen any instrument, but an accordion that belonged to one of the Norwegian farmhands. She would sit beside me by the hour, darn-

---

4. **stuff:** cloth, usually woolen.
5. **stays:** corset, or figure-enhancing women's undergarment, stiffened as with whalebone.
6. **declensions and conjugations:** different forms of nouns, pronouns, adjectives, and verbs. Students often memorize these forms when studying Latin or other languages.

B **Literary Focus** Setting How does Cather depict the Nebraska frontier?

C **Literary Focus** Setting How had the narrator's aunt been physically transformed by her years spent in Nebraska?

Vocabulary reverential (rehv uh REHN shuhl) *adj.:* deeply respectful.

ing and counting while I struggled with the "Joyous Farmer," but she seldom talked to me about music, and I understood why. She was a pious woman; she had the consolations of religion and, to her at least, her martyrdom was not wholly sordid.[7] Once when I had been doggedly beating out some easy passages from an old score of *Euryanthe*[8] I had found among her music books, she came up to me and, putting her hands over my eyes, gently drew my head back upon her shoulder, saying tremulously,[9] "Don't love it so well, Clark, or it may be taken from you. Oh! Dear boy, pray that whatever your sacrifice may be, it be not that." **D**

When my aunt appeared on the morning after her arrival, she was still in a semisomnambulant[10] state. She seemed not to realize that she was in the city where she had spent her youth, the place longed for hungrily half a lifetime. She had been so wretchedly trainsick throughout the journey that she had no recollection of anything but her discomfort, and, to all intents and purposes, there were but a few hours of nightmare between the farm in Red Willow County and my study on Newbury Street. I had planned a little pleasure for her that afternoon, to repay her for some of the glorious moments she had given me when we used to milk together in the straw thatched cowshed and she, because I was more than usually tired, or because her husband had spoken sharply to me, would tell me of the splendid performance of the *Huguenots*[11] she had seen in Paris, in her youth. At two o'clock the Symphony Orchestra was to give a Wagner program, and I intended to take my aunt; though, as I conversed with her, I grew doubtful about her enjoyment of it. Indeed, for her own sake, I could only wish her taste for such things quite dead, and the long struggle mercifully ended at last. I suggested our visiting the

---

7. **sordid:** unethical; dishonest.
8. *Euryanthe*: Romantic opera by German composer Carl Maria von Weber.
9. **tremulously:** in a trembling or shaking manner.
10. **semisomnambulant:** confused and unperceiving, as if sleepwalking.

11. *Huguenots*: opera by Giacomo Meyerbeer about the violent struggle between Catholics and Protestants in sixteenth-century France.

D **Reading Focus** **Making Inferences** What do you think Aunt Georgiana means when she says, "Pray that whatever your sacrifice may be, it be not that"? What does this suggest about a possible theme?

Vocabulary **pious** (PY uhs) *adj.*: devoted to one's religion.

Conservatory and the Common before lunch, but she seemed altogether too timid to wish to venture out. She questioned me absently about various changes in the city, but she was chiefly concerned that she had forgotten to leave instructions about feeding half-skimmed milk to a certain weakling calf, "old Maggie's calf, you know, Clark," she explained, evidently having forgotten how long I had been away. She was further troubled because she had neglected to tell her daughter about the freshly opened kit of mackerel in the cellar, which would spoil if it were not used directly. **E** **F**

I asked her whether she had ever heard any of the Wagnerian operas, and found that she had not, though she was perfectly familiar with their respective situations, and had once possessed the piano score of *The Flying Dutchman.* I began to think it would have been best to get her back to Red Willow County without waking her, and regretted having suggested the concert. **G**

From the time we entered the concert hall, however, she was a trifle less passive and inert, and for the first time seemed to perceive her surroundings. I had felt some trepidation lest she might become aware of the absurdities of her attire, or might experience some painful embarrassment at stepping suddenly into the world to which she had been dead for a quarter of a century. But, again, I found how superficially I had judged her. She sat looking about her with eyes as impersonal, almost as stony, as those with which the granite Ramses[12] in a museum watches the froth and fret[13] that ebbs and flows about his pedestal—separated from it by the lonely stretch of centuries. I have seen this same aloofness in old miners who drift into the Brown Hotel at Denver, their pockets full of bullion,[14] their linen soiled, their haggard faces unshaven; standing in the thronged corridors as soli-

tary as though they were still in a frozen camp on the Yukon,[15] conscious that certain experiences have isolated them from their fellows by a gulf no haberdasher[16] could bridge.

We sat at the extreme left of the first balcony, facing the arc of our own and the balcony above us, veritable hanging gardens, brilliant as tulip beds. The matinée audience was made up chiefly of women. One lost the contour of faces and figures, indeed any effect of line whatever, and there was only the color of bodices past counting, the shimmer of fabrics soft and firm, silky and sheer; red, mauve, pink, blue, lilac, purple, ecru, rose, yellow, cream, and white, all the colors that an impressionist[17] finds in a sunlit landscape, with here and there the dead shadow of a frock coat. My Aunt Georgiana regarded them as though they had been so many daubs of tube paint on a palette.

When the musicians came out and took their places, she gave a little stir of anticipation and looked with quickening interest down over the rail at that invariable grouping, perhaps the first wholly familiar thing that had greeted her eye since she had left old Maggie and her weakling calf. I could feel how all those details sank into her soul, for I had not forgotten how they had sunk into mine when I came fresh from plowing forever and forever between green aisles of corn, where, as in a treadmill, one might walk from daybreak to dusk without perceiving a shadow of change. The clean profiles of the musicians, the gloss of their linen, the dull black of their coats, the beloved shapes of the instruments, the patches of yellow light thrown by the green shaded lamps on the smooth,

---

12. **Ramses:** one of the kings of ancient Egypt.
13. **froth and fret:** agitated waters moving around obstacles.
14. **bullion:** gold.

15. **Yukon:** territory in northwestern Canada.
16. **haberdasher:** one who sells men's clothing.
17. **impressionist:** Impressionism was a movement in French painting emphasizing the effects of light and color.

E **Reading Focus** Making Inferences To what is Clark referring when he speaks of Aunt Georgiana's struggle? Why does he hope the struggle has ended?

F **Literary Focus** Setting What do these worries about the farm reveal about Aunt Georgiana? What do they reveal about the time period?

G **Reading Focus** Making Inferences Explore the recurring motif of sleep. On page 670, Aunt Georgiana is put to bed. On page 673, she is described as "semisomnambulant." Here, Clark regrets waking her. What do you think the author wants to convey about Aunt Georgiana by using this recurring theme?

Vocabulary **inert** (ihn URT) *adj.:* inactive; sluggish.
trepidation (trehp uh DAY shuhn) *n.:* anxious uncertainty.

varnished bellies of the cellos and the bass viols in the rear, the restless, wind-tossed forest of fiddle necks and bows—I recalled how, in the first orchestra I had ever heard, those long bow strokes seemed to draw the heart out of me, as a conjurer's[18] stick reels out yards of paper ribbon from a hat.

The first number was the *Tannhäuser*[19] overture. When the horns drew out the first strain of the Pilgrim's chorus, my Aunt Georgiana clutched my coat sleeve. Then it was I first realized that for her this broke a silence of thirty years; the inconceivable silence of the plains. With the battle between the two motives, with the frenzy of the Venusberg theme and its ripping of strings, there came to me an overwhelming sense of the waste and wear we are so powerless to combat; and I saw again the tall, naked house on the prairie, black and grim as a wooden fortress; the black pond where I had learned to swim, its margin pitted with sundried cattle tracks; the rain-gullied clay banks about the naked house, the four dwarf ash seedlings where the dishcloths were always hung to dry before the kitchen door. The world there was the flat world of the ancients; to the east, a cornfield that stretched to daybreak; to the west, a corral that reached to sunset; between, the conquests of peace, dearer bought than those of war.

The overture closed, my aunt released my coat sleeve, but she said nothing. She sat staring at the orchestra through a dullness of thirty years, through the films made little by little by each of the three hundred and sixty-five days in every one of them. What, I wondered, did she get from it? She had been a good pianist in her day I knew, and her musical education had been broader than that of most music teachers of a quarter of a century ago. She had often told me of Mozart's[20] operas and Meyerbeer's, and I could remember hearing her sing, years ago, certain

---

18. **conjurer's:** magician's.
19. *Tannhäuser:* Wagner's opera about medieval German minstrels.
20. **Mozart's:** Wolfgang Amadeus Mozart (1756–1791), Austrian composer.

H **Literary Focus** Setting How does the Boston concert hall setting contrast with the Nebraska prairie in these three paragraphs?

MUSIC LINK

The Popularity of Opera

"A Wagner Matinée" contains references to some of the greatest operatic composers of all time: Wolfgang Amadeus Mozart, Giuseppe Verdi, and Richard Wagner. Opera is a form of musical theater that began in the seventeenth century and has remained popular ever since. Usually staged with extravagant sets and costumes, opera features highly skilled singers who are accompanied by an orchestra. Operatic composers often take their subjects from ancient myths and legends. Wagner's *Der Ring des Nibelungen* is a cycle of four music dramas based on Germanic and Norse myths and legends. In the last part of the *Ring* cycle, Hagen gives the hero, Siegfried, a potion that makes Siegfried forget his bride, Brünnhilde. Furious at Siegfried's betrayal, Brünnhilde conspires with Hagen to murder him. Shortly after Siegfried receives another potion, which restores his memory of Brünnhilde, Hagen stabs Siegfried in the back. As the *Ring* concludes, Brünnhilde sacrifices herself on Siegfried's funeral pyre.

Ask Yourself

Why do you think Cather chose to close the Wagner program with Siegfried's funeral march? How might Aunt Georgiana's emotional reaction have differed had the story been set during a time when musical recordings of opera were available?

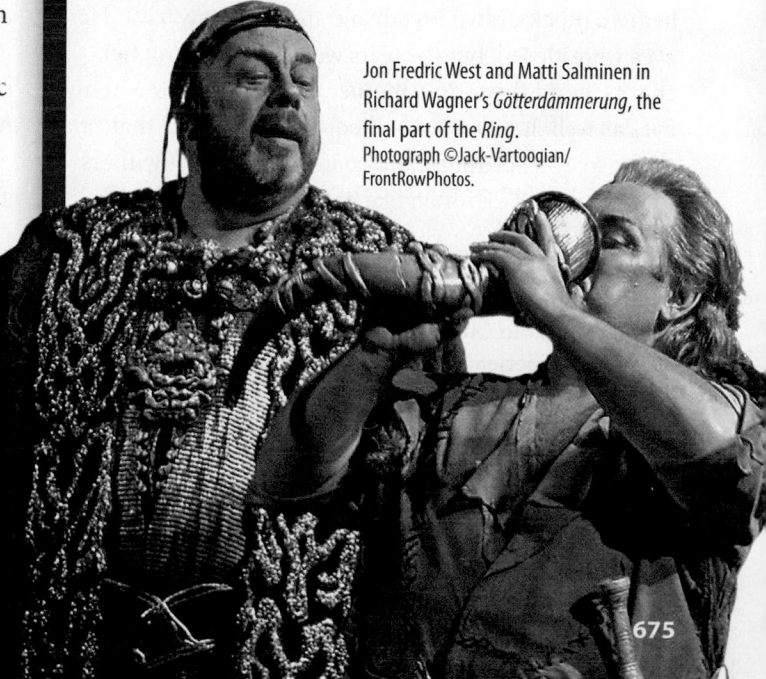

Jon Fredric West and Matti Salminen in Richard Wagner's *Götterdämmerung*, the final part of the *Ring*.
Photograph ©Jack-Vartoogian/FrontRowPhotos.

melodies of Verdi's.[21] When I had fallen ill with a fever in her house she used to sit by my cot in the evening—when the cool, night wind blew in through the faded mosquito netting tacked over the window and I lay watching a certain bright star that burned red above the cornfield—and sing "Home to our mountains, O, let us return!" in a way fit to break the heart of a Vermont boy near dead of homesickness already.

I watched her closely through the prelude to *Tristan and Isolde,* trying vainly to conjecture what that seething turmoil of strings and winds might mean to her, but she sat mutely staring at the violin bows that drove obliquely downward, like the pelting streaks of rain in a summer shower. Had this music any message for her? Had she enough left to at all comprehend this power which had kindled the world since she had left it? I was in a fever of curiosity, but Aunt Georgiana sat silent upon her peak in Darien.[22] She preserved this utter immobility throughout the number from *The Flying Dutchman,* though her fingers worked mechanically upon her black dress, as though, of themselves, they were recalling the piano score they had once played. Poor old hands! They had been stretched and twisted into mere tentacles to hold and lift and knead with; the palms unduly swollen, the fingers bent and knotted— on one of them a thin, worn band that had once been a wedding ring. As I pressed and gently quieted one of those groping hands, I remembered with quivering eyelids their services for me in other days.

Soon after the tenor began the "Prize Song,"[23] I heard a quick drawn breath and turned to my aunt. Her eyes were closed, but the tears were glistening on her cheeks, and I think, in a moment more, they were in my eyes as well. It never really died, then—the soul that can suffer so excruciatingly and so interminably; it withers to the outward eye only; like that strange moss which can lie on a dusty shelf half a century and yet, if placed in water, grows green again. She wept so throughout the development and elaboration of the melody. **❶**

During the intermission before the second half of the concert, I questioned my aunt and found that the "Prize Song" was not new to her. Some years before there had drifted to the farm in Red Willow County a young German, a tramp cowpuncher, who had sung the chorus at Bayreuth,[24] when he was a boy, along with the other peasant boys and girls. Of a Sunday morning he used to sit on his gingham-sheeted bed in the hands' bedroom which opened off the kitchen, cleaning the leather of his boots and saddle, singing the "Prize Song," while my aunt went about her work in the kitchen. She had hovered about him until she had prevailed upon him to join the country church, though his sole fitness for this step, in so far as I could gather, lay in his boyish face and his possession of this divine melody. Shortly afterward he had gone to town on the Fourth of July, been drunk for several days, lost his money at a faro[25] table, ridden a saddled Texan steer on a bet, and disappeared with a fractured collarbone. All this my aunt told me huskily, wanderingly, as though she were talking in the weak lapses of illness.

"Well, we have come to better things than the old *Trovatore*[26] at any rate, Aunt Georgie?" I queried, with a well-meant effort at jocularity.

Her lip quivered and she hastily put her handkerchief up to her mouth. From behind it she murmured, "And you have been hearing this ever since you left me, Clark?" Her question was the gentlest and saddest of reproaches.

The second half of the program consisted of four numbers from the *Ring,*[27] and closed with Siegfried's funeral march. My aunt wept quietly, but almost con-

---

21. **Verdi's:** Giuseppe Verdi (1813–1901), Italian composer.
22. **silent . . . Darien:** allusion to John Keats's "On First Looking into Chapman's Homer," a poem about Keats's awe at experiencing a great literary work.
23. **"Prize Song":** aria from the third act of Wagner's opera *Die Meistersinger von Nürnberg.*
24. **Bayreuth:** Bavarian city that hosts an annual festival of Wagnerian music.
25. **faro:** gambling game played with cards.
26. *Trovatore:* opera by the Italian composer Giuseppe Verdi.
27. *Ring:* Wagner's *Der Ring des Nibelungen,* a cycle of four music dramas based on traditional Germanic, Scandinavian, and Icelandic myths and legends.

---

❶ Reading Focus Making Inferences What sudden realization does the narrator have about his aunt? What details about his aunt's response to the music led him to this conclusion?

tinuously, as a shallow vessel overflows in a rainstorm. From time to time her dim eyes looked up at the lights which studded the ceiling, burning softly under their dull glass globes; doubtless they were stars in truth to her. I was still perplexed as to what measure of musical comprehension was left to her, she who had heard nothing but the singing of gospel hymns at Methodist services in the square frame schoolhouse on Section Thirteen for so many years. I was wholly unable to gauge how much of it had been dissolved in soapsuds, or worked into bread, or milked into the bottom of a pail.

The deluge of sound poured on and on; I never knew what she found in the shining current of it; I never knew how far it bore her, or past what happy islands. From the trembling of her face I could well believe that before the last numbers she had been carried out where the myriad graves are, into the gray, nameless burying grounds of the sea; or into some world of death vaster yet, where, from the beginning of the world, hope has lain down with hope and dream with dream and, renouncing,[28] slept.

The concert was over; the people filed out of the hall chattering and laughing, glad to relax and find the living level again, but my kinswoman made no effort to rise. The harpist slipped its green felt cover over his instrument; the flute players shook the water from their mouthpieces; the men of the orchestra went out one by one, leaving the stage to the chairs and music stands, empty as a winter cornfield.

I spoke to my aunt. She burst into tears and sobbed pleadingly. "I don't want to go, Clark, I don't want to go!"

I understood. For her, just outside the door of the concert hall, lay the black pond with the cattle-tracked bluffs; the tall, unpainted house, with weather-curled boards; naked as a tower, the crookbacked ash seedlings where the dishcloths hung to dry; the gaunt, molting turkeys picking up refuse about the kitchen door. **Ⓙ**

---

28. renouncing: giving up.

Vocabulary **deluge** (DEHL yooj) *n.*: rush; flood.

Ⓙ Literary Focus **Setting** Why does the narrator equate the world that lies beyond the concert hall with the bleak imagery of Aunt Georgiana's Nebraska home? What does this suggest about the loss in Aunt Georgiana's life?

Respond and Think Critically

Reading Focus

Quick Check

1. Why did the narrator's aunt move to Nebraska?

2. In what ways did Aunt Georgiana's life change as a result of her move to Nebraska?

3. Why does Clark feel that he owes his aunt a debt?

Read with a Purpose

4. What do you think Clark understands at the end of the story?

Reading Skills: Making Inferences

5. Review the graphic organizer that you completed while reading the story. Based on your inferences, what is the story's theme, and how do details about each setting develop the theme?

Detail	Inference
"They built a dugout in the red hillside, one of those cave dwellings whose inmates so often reverted to primitive conditions."	The words cave dwellings, inmates, and primitive suggest that Cather is commenting on the difficulty and lack of sophistication of life on the prairie.

Literary Focus

Literary Analysis

6. **Draw Conclusions** What does Aunt Georgiana's appearance upon her arrival in Boston tell you about her life in Nebraska?

7. **Infer** What emotions does Aunt Georgiana experience at the concert? Does she find that pleasure is worth the pain of longing? Explain.

8. **Analyze** Re-read the narrator's detailed description of the concert, paying close attention to the words used to describe the music. How is this central episode <u>crucial</u> to the story's theme?

9. **Evaluate** Aunt Georgiana says to the narrator, "Don't love it so well, Clark, or it may be taken from you." Do you agree with her, or do you have other ideas about how to cope with loss? Explain.

10. **Extend** If this story were written by a Romantic rather than a realist, how might Aunt Georgiana's visit to Boston have turned out? How might a Romantic writer have described the farm?

Literary Skills: Setting

11. **Interpret** The emotional effect of the music and the concert hall on Aunt Georgiana contrasts with the effect of the frontier. What responses do the details about each setting evoke?

Literary Skills Review: Narrator

12. **Analyze** Locate passages in which the first-person **narrator** is omniscient, or all knowing. How would you characterize the narrator? Why do you think Cather created a male narrator?

Writing Focus

Think as a Reader/Writer

Use It in Your Writing Write a descriptive paragraph in which you use striking imagery to describe a place that you have known well. Include sensory details and precise diction that evoke what it feels like to recall this memorable place.

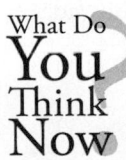

What Do You Think Now

How can the experience of a painful loss shape human character?

Vocabulary Development

✓ Vocabulary Check

Match each Vocabulary word with its synonym.

1. deluge
2. grotesque
3. inert
4. legacy
5. pious
6. reverential
7. trepidation

a. misshapen
b. religious
c. anxiety
d. flood
e. inheritance
f. respectful
g. inactive

Vocabulary Skills: Idioms

An **idiom** is an expression, particular to a certain lan- guage, that means something different from literal definitions of its parts. Study the examples of idioms in the following sentences. After each sentence is an explanation of the idiom's meaning.

Coach says he needs a day to <u>sleep on it</u> before making his final decision about the starting lineup.
When you sleep on it, you are not literally sleeping on any- thing—you are taking a day to think about something before making a decision.

Sarah was <u>feeling blue</u> because the dress she wanted to buy for the prom <u>costs an arm and a leg</u>.
When you feel blue, your skin does not literally turn blue—you are feeling a little sad. When something costs an arm and a leg, it does not literally require the removal of an arm and a leg—it is just very expensive.

Your Turn

Identify and explain the idioms in the sentences below. (Each item may have more than one idiom.)

1. "Boys, we are running late," my mother urged. "Step on it, or we'll miss the train!"

2. During the summer, we liked to hang out at the lake to swim, fish, and shoot the breeze.

3. The computer is broken—even the technician can't make heads or tails of the problem.

4. Jody didn't hit the books very hard, so she passed the test only by the skin of her teeth.

Language Coach

Pronunciation The letter *g* can be pronounced with a hard sound (*agree*) or a soft /j/ sound (*gen- der*). Often when followed by *e* or *i,* the *g* is soft. When followed by any other letter, or if at the end of a word, it is usually hard (*agog*). Say and write down the words from the Vocabulary list that con- tain a *g.* Is the *g* hard or soft? Do the words follow the pronunciation rules above?

Academic Vocabulary

Write About
Willa Cather was an accomplished musi- cian, and the powerful attraction to music is a theme that often recurs in her fiction. What are your thoughts on music? In what ways is it a <u>crucial</u> part of our humanity? Explain your views in a paragraph.

Learn It Online
Take your vocabulary knowledge further with Word Watch online.

go.hrw.com | L11-679 | Go

Realism and Naturalism

The Life Line (1884) by Winslow Homer.

CONTENTS

Link to Today

A man said to the universe:

"Sir, I exist!"

"However," replied the universe,

"The fact has not created in me

A sense of obligation."

—**Stephen Crane**

SKILLS FOCUS Literary Skills Evaluate genres and traditions in American literature; understand realism and naturalism.

Realism and Naturalism by **Leila Christenbury**

Characteristics of Realism and Naturalism

- Realism reacts against Romanticism's idealized heroes and sensational situations.
- Realism aims at an accurate and unsentimental depiction of social issues and problems.
- Naturalism seeks to present human behavior objectively, as a scientist would.
- Naturalism was influenced by Darwinism and the theories of psychology and sociology.

Humans Versus the Universe

In realist writing, characters face the kinds of problems and situations that readers might face in their own lives. Realists use sharp details and descriptions to provide an unflinching picture of a world that is sometimes unpleasant. Naturalist writers move beyond realism in their quest to dissect human behavior and show human beings as subject to natural forces beyond their control. Realism and naturalism are often stark, bold, and frank.

A Reaction Against Romanticism After the grim years of the Civil War, realists reacted against Romanticism, striving to show not larger-than-life heroes in extraordinary situations but everyday people in ordinary circumstances. The realists sought a "very minute fidelity" to the common course of events, especially emphasizing urban environments and characters from the lower classes. Realist fiction relies on careful description, regional dialect and everyday speech patterns, and a focus on the ethical struggles of daily life.

The Literature of Science Naturalism was inspired by the work of Charles Darwin, who broke new ground with his theory of natural selection, as well as by the emerging disciplines of psychology, the study of the human mind, and sociology, the study of human social behavior. For naturalists, human behavior is determined by forces beyond the individual's control. Naturalist characters are subject to natural laws of the universe and live like animals, by instinct, unable to control their own destinies. Naturalists seek truth in the universe—no matter how dark that truth seems—and tend to look at human life as a grim, losing battle.

Human Nature in the Wilderness Jack London was one of naturalism's leading voices, and his work brought the movement's stark perspective into popular culture. In his gripping wilderness tales, nature is a merciless force, indifferent to the humans who struggle for survival. Despite this bleak point of view, his characters demonstrate the vitality of the human spirit in the face of futility. The moments that London captures are dark but also honest and captivating. As a naturalist, London tries to show us humanity as it is in a cold universe—adrift but aware, like his character in the short story "To Build a Fire":

> Empty as the man's mind was of thought, he was keenly observant, and he noticed the changes in the creek, the curves and bends and timber jams, and always he sharply noted where he placed his feet.

Ask Yourself

1. What were some of the goals of realism?
2. In naturalist literature, what is the relationship between human beings and the natural world?

Learn It Online
Find more from Jack London on the *NovelWise* site online.

go.hrw.com   L11-681   **Go**

The Story of an Hour

What Do You Think?

What forces shape human character?

⚆ QuickWrite

Think of a time when you faced a problem you didn't know how to solve. Write a short paragraph describing how you felt and how the experience affected your behavior.

MEET THE WRITER

Kate Chopin
(1851–1904)

Although her work went unrecognized and was even scorned during her lifetime, Kate Chopin is now recognized as a writer of skill and perception, whose choice of theme was well ahead of its time.

The Emergence of a Rebel

Chopin was born Katherine O'Flaherty in St. Louis, Missouri, to an Irish immigrant father and a mother descended from French Creole aristocrats. Her prosperous parents encouraged her early interest in music and reading. She grew into a witty and popular young woman with a notably independent turn of mind. At nineteen, she married Oscar Chopin, a French Creole from New Orleans. The couple settled in Louisiana and reared a family of six children, but when she was thirty-one, her husband died suddenly from swamp fever. Chopin returned to St. Louis, where she began to write. She published one poem when she was thirty-eight, which was followed by a few short stories. In 1890, she published her first novel.

A Woman Ahead of Her Time

Chopin's short stories were praised for their accurate portrayal of the French Creole culture in the United States. Chopin's dominant theme, however, was much more controversial: the repression of women in Victorian America. This theme is presented most dramatically in her novel *The Awakening* (1899). The novel portrays a dissatisfied wife who breaks from the confines of her marriage and, in her quest for freedom, defies the Victorian ideals of motherhood and domesticity.

American critics condemned the novel as sordid and vulgar. It was removed from St. Louis libraries, some of Chopin's friends shunned her, and the local arts club denied her membership. Disheartened by this rejection, Chopin produced little more literature before her death in 1904. After her death, her work fell into obscurity and was not rediscovered until decades later. She is now seen as a literary pioneer who provided early insight into the modern American woman.

Think About the Writer

How do you think Chopin's writing career might have been different if her husband had lived?

 **Reader/Writer Notebook**

Use your **RWN** to complete the activities for this selection.

Literary Focus

Irony **Irony** occurs when there is a discrepancy between appearance and reality. **Situational irony** occurs when an event turns out to be different from what we expect. An ironic twist can send a narrative in an unexpected or surprising direction.

Kate Chopin's "The Story of an Hour" includes several ironic twists. As you read, note how Mrs. Mallard's emotional development and the story's conclusion unfold in unexpected ways.

Reading Focus

Analyzing Historical Context In the 1890s, when Chopin wrote this story, women in the United States could not vote, had few opportunities for education and employment, and could not live outside the param-eters of prescribed gender roles. Although women's rights activists were beginning to seek social justice, progress was slow. Chopin's story illumi-nates the position of women in Victorian society and marriage. Note how this historical context helps set up the story's ironic twists.

Into Action As you read, use the chart below to record attitudes toward marriage or women that the text reflects. In the second column, note how Mrs. Mallard's responses contrast with those attitudes and expectations.

Attitude toward women	Mrs. Mallard's response
Women are too fragile to be told bad news in a direct fashion.	Hearing the bad news actually strengthens her instead of weakening her.

Writing Focus

Think as a Reader/Writer

Find It in Your Reading In this story, Mrs. Mallard's reactions are not always what readers expect. As you read, record in your *Reader/Writer Notebook* the reactions that you find most surprising. Note the way in which you expect her to respond to each situation.

TechFocus A deeper knowledge of women's social status at the end of the nineteenth century can give you insight into Chopin's perspective in this story. As you read, consider how you might use online resources to help you better understand some of the issues presented in the text.

Vocabulary

abandonment (uh BAN duhn muhnt) *n.:* a yielding to natural impulses; freedom from self-control or restraint. *Mrs. Mallard imagines living a life of wild abandonment.*

tumultuously (too MUHL chu uhs lee) *adv.:* violently. *Mrs. Mallard wept tumultuously.*

vacant (VAY kuhnt) *adj.:* empty of thought. *When Mrs. Mallard first heard the news, her mind became vacant.*

illumination (ih loo muh NAY shuhn) *n.:* intellectual or spiritual enlightenment. *The news provides startling illumination.*

feverish (FEE vuhr ihsh) *adj.:* excited; rest-less. *Suddenly her thoughts grew feverish.*

Language Coach

Multiple-Meaning Words Words often have multiple meanings that are similar or closely related. In some cases a word has both a literal, or concrete, meaning and a figurative meaning. For example, the word *vacant* can be used to describe something that is literally empty, like a *vacant* room. In this story, however, *vacant* is used in a figurative way—describing someone who has an "empty" mind or seems to be thinking about nothing.

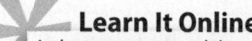 **Learn It Online**
Is there more to a word than just the definition? Find out with Word Watch online.

 go.hrw.com | L11-683 | **Go**

THE STORY OF AN HOUR

by **Kate Chopin**

Read with a Purpose
Read to discover how Mrs. Mallard reacts to news of her husband's untimely death.

Build Background
When Chopin wrote "The Story of an Hour," a woman was still looked upon as needing the protection and support of her husband. Many of Chopin's female characters, however, seek freedom from the conventional restraints of society, including marriage. Although women could own property and file for divorce when Chopin wrote this story, independent women were still frowned upon. The story explores many of the same issues that Chopin examined in her acclaimed novel, *The Awakening,* which caused a storm of controversy when it was first published.

Knowing that Mrs. Mallard was afflicted with a heart trouble, great care was taken to break to her as gently as possible the news of her husband's death.

It was her sister Josephine who told her, in broken sentences; veiled hints that revealed in half concealing. Her husband's friend Richards was there, too, near her. It was he who had been in the newspaper office when intelligence of the railroad disaster was received, with Brently Mallard's name leading the list of "killed." He had only taken the time to assure himself of its truth by a second telegram, and had hastened to forestall[1] any less careful, less tender friend in bearing the sad message. **Ⓐ**

She did not hear the story as many women have heard the same, with a paralyzed inability to accept

its significance. She wept at once, with sudden, wild abandonment, in her sister's arms. When the storm of grief had spent itself she went away to her room alone. She would have no one follow her.

There stood, facing the open window, a comfortable, roomy armchair. Into this she sank, pressed down by a physical exhaustion that haunted her body and seemed to reach into her soul.

She could see in the open square before her house the tops of trees that were all aquiver with the new spring life. The delicious breath of rain was in the air. In the street below a peddler was crying his wares. The notes of a distant song which some one was singing reached her faintly, and countless sparrows were twittering in the eaves.

There were patches of blue sky showing here and there through the clouds that had met and piled one above the other in the west facing her window.

---

1. **forestall:** to stop something from happening by acting ahead of time.

Ⓐ **Reading Focus** **Analyzing Historical Context** Why does Josephine, rather than Richards, tell Mrs. Mallard the news?

Vocabulary **abandonment** (uh BAN duhn muhnt) *n.*: a yielding to natural impulses; freedom from self-control or restraint.

Analyzing Visuals

Viewing and Interpreting Notice that there are no bars in the window, yet bars appear in the shadow on the floor. How do you interpret this image? In what ways is Mrs. Mallard's situation like that of the woman in this picture?

THERE WAS SOMETHING COMING TO HER AND SHE WAS WAITING FOR IT, FEARFULLY.

She sat with her head thrown back upon the cushion of the chair, quite motionless, except when a sob came up into her throat and shook her, as a child who has cried itself to sleep continues to sob in its dreams.

She was young, with a fair, calm face, whose lines bespoke repression[2] and even a certain strength. But now there was a dull stare in her eyes, whose gaze was fixed away off yonder on one of those patches of blue sky. It was not a glance of reflection, but rather indicated a suspension of intelligent thought.

There was something coming to her and she was waiting for it, fearfully. What was it? She did not know; it was too subtle and elusive[3] to name. But she felt it, creeping out of the sky, reaching toward her through the sounds, the scents, the color that filled the air.

Now her bosom rose and fell tumultuously. She was beginning to recognize this thing that was approaching to possess her, and she was striving to beat it back with her will—as powerless as her two white slender hands would have been.

---

2. **repression:** restraint.
3. **elusive:** difficult to understand.

When she abandoned herself a little whispered word escaped her slightly parted lips. She said it over and over under her breath: "free, free, free!" The vacant stare and the look of terror that had followed it went from her eyes. They stayed keen and bright. Her pulses beat fast, and the coursing blood warmed and relaxed every inch of her body. **Ⓑ**

She did not stop to ask if it were or were not a monstrous joy that held her. A clear and exalted perception enabled her to dismiss the suggestion as trivial.

She knew that she would weep again when she saw the kind, tender hands folded in death; the face that had never looked save with love upon her, fixed and gray and dead. But she saw beyond that bitter moment a long procession of years to come that would belong to her absolutely. And she opened and spread her arms out to them in welcome.

There would be no one to live for her during those coming years; she would live for herself. There would be no powerful will bending hers in that blind persistence with which men and women believe they have a right to impose a private will upon a fellow creature. A kind intention or a cruel intention made the act seem no less a crime as she looked upon it in

---

Vocabulary **tumultuously** (too MUHL chu uhs lee) *adv.*: violently.

vacant (VAY kuhnt) *adj.*: empty of thought.

Ⓑ **Literary Focus** **Irony** In what way does Mrs. Mallard's reaction in this paragraph differ from what you expect?

that brief moment of illumination. And yet she had loved him—sometimes. Often she had not. What did it matter! What could love, the unsolved mystery, count for in face of this possession of self-assertion which she suddenly recognized as the strongest impulse of her being!

"Free! Body and soul free!" she kept whispering.

Josephine was kneeling before the closed door with her lips to the keyhole, imploring for admission. "Louise, open the door! I beg; open the door—you will make yourself ill. What are you doing, Louise? For heaven's sake open the door."

"Go away. I am not making myself ill." No; she was drinking in a very elixir[4] of life through that open window.

Her fancy was running riot along those days ahead of her. Spring days, and summer days, and all sorts of days that would be her own. She breathed a quick prayer that life might be long. It was only yesterday she had thought with a shudder that life might be long.

_____
4. **elixir:** a legendary medicine that gives eternal life to those who drink it.

She arose at length and opened the door to her sister's importunities.[5] There was a feverish triumph in her eyes, and she carried herself unwittingly like a goddess of Victory. She clasped her sister's waist, and together they descended the stairs. Richards stood waiting for them at the bottom.

Some one was opening the front door with a latchkey. It was Brently Mallard who entered, a little travel-stained, composedly carrying his grip-sack and umbrella. He had been far from the scene of accident, and did not even know there had been one. He stood amazed at Josephine's piercing cry; at Richards' quick motion to screen him from the view of his wife.

But Richards was too late.

When the doctors came they said she had died of heart disease—of joy that kills.

_____
5. **importunities:** determined requests.

C **Reading Focus** **Analyzing Historical Context** This seems to be a clear sign that Mrs. Mallard was not happy in her marriage. Why do you think she felt she had to stay in her marriage?

D **Literary Focus** **Irony** What is ironic about Brently Mallard's appearance? How does his arrival affect his wife?

Vocabulary **illumination** (ih loo muh NAY shuhn) _n._: intellectual or spiritual enlightenment.
feverish (FEE vuhr ihsh) _adj._: excited; restless.

Respond and Think Critically

Reading Focus

Quick Check

1. Why does Josephine think news of Mr. Mallard's death must be broken to Mrs. Mallard gently?

2. What is Mrs. Mallard's first reaction to the news of her husband's death?

3. What does Mrs. Mallard's appearance convey as she emerges from her room?

Read with a Purpose

4. Summarize Mrs. Mallard's emotional shifts from the beginning to the end of the story.

Reading Skills: Analyzing Historical Context

5. While reading, you recorded how conventional attitudes about women contrasted with Mrs. Mallard's reactions to news of her husband's death. Review your chart, and write a brief paragraph explaining how these attitudes help set up the story's irony.

Attitude toward women	Mrs. Mallard's response
Women are too fragile to be told bad news in a direct fashion.	Hearing the bad news actually strengthens her instead of weakening her.

Literary Focus

Literary Analysis

6. **Make Judgments** Does Mrs. Mallard's reaction to the news of her husband's death seem typical for a grieving wife? Explain.

7. **Interpret** In what ways do the sights outside Mrs. Mallard's window reflect the feelings that are about to come over her?

8. **Infer** Why do you suppose Chopin does not describe Mrs. Mallard's thoughts and feelings at the end of the story?

9. **Analyze** What aspects of realism are apparent in "The Story of an Hour"?

10. **Draw Conclusions** Realist writers were skeptical of science because it reduced the complexities of life to concrete, measurable terms. How does the last line of the story reflect such skepticism?

11. **Extend** Many of Chopin's characters search for their identity by defying social customs. How do people today search for identity?

Literary Skills: Irony

12. **Analyze** What is ironic about Mrs. Mallard's death at the end of the story?

Literary Skills Review: Characterization

13. **Make Judgments** The process by which the writer reveals the personality of a character is called **characterization.** Describe ways in which Mrs. Mallard is and is not portrayed stereotypically in the story.

Writing Focus

Think as a Reader/Writer

Use It in Your Writing Review the moments in the story that you found most surprising. Write a short scene that seems to foreshadow a particular outcome, and then surprise the reader.

What Do **You Think Now** What point does Chopin make in this story? How do you think this point was received by readers in her day?

Vocabulary Development

✓ Vocabulary Check

Match each Vocabulary word with its synonym.

1. abandonment
2. tumultuously
3. vacant
4. illumination
5. feverish

a. wildly
b. emotionless
c. excited
d. recklessness
e. insight

Vocabulary Skills: Collocation

In English, certain words commonly occur together and appear in a particular order. These common word groupings are referred to as **collocations.**

For example, the Vocabulary word *abandonment* appears in this story as part of the collocation *wild abandonment*—a common word grouping that is frequently used to describe spontaneous, impulsive behavior. *Wild abandonment* is a collocation made up of an adjective and a noun, which is a common combination for collocations.

Collocations can be made up of a variety of word combinations. The following chart includes some examples of the many types of collocation combinations.

Parts of Speech	Collocation Example
adjective + noun	square meal
verb + noun	accept responsibility
adverb + adverb	quite easily
adverb + verb	strongly suggest
adverb + adjective + noun	totally unacceptable behavior

Your Turn

Review Chopin's "The Story of an Hour," and find four examples of collocation. Use a chart like the one on this page to record each example and identify the parts of speech that make up each collocation.

Language Coach

Multiple-Meaning Words Each of the Vocabulary words *vacant, illumination,* and *feverish* has both a concrete meaning and a figurative meaning. In this story, each word is used in a figurative way. Review how Chopin uses each of the words in the context of the story, and write three more sentences of your own using the words in the same figurative sense. Then, write sentences illustrating the words' concrete meanings.

Academic Vocabulary

Talk About
What social parameters limit Mrs. Mallard's options in life? Are these parameters still relevant today?

Learn It Online
Learn more about the Vocabulary words online.

go.hrw.com   L11-689   Go

Applying Your Skills

The Story of an Hour

Grammar Link

Active Voice and Passive Voice

The **voice** of a verb indicates whether the subject of the verb performs or receives the action. When a verb is in the **active voice,** its subject performs the action.

> Kate Chopin <u>wrote</u> "The Story of an Hour."
> Josephine <u>tells</u> Mrs. Mallard of her husband's death.

When a verb is in the **passive voice,** its subject receives the action. A passive construction includes the appropriate form of *be* plus the past participle of an action verb.

> "The Story of an Hour" <u>was written</u> by Kate Chopin.
> Mrs. Mallard <u>is told</u> of her husband's death by Josephine.

Use the passive voice sparingly. It is appropriate when the performer of the verb's action is unknown, when the performer of the action should not be revealed, or when the receiver of the action should be emphasized.

> Chopin's work <u>was scorned</u> during her lifetime.
> Her novels <u>were removed</u> from St. Louis libraries.

Your Turn

Rewrite the following sentences. Change the voice of the italicized verbs from passive to active or active to passive.

1. A friend *confirms* Mr. Mallard's death.

2. Josephine *is troubled* by Mrs. Mallard's reaction.

3. The thought of a life without her husband *thrills* Mrs. Mallard.

4. She *is killed* by Mr. Mallard's unexpected return.

Writing Application Pay careful attention to voice in a piece of your own writing. Circle all verbs in the passive voice. Underline any appropriate passive verbs. Rewrite sentences to change the remaining passive verbs to active voice.

CHOICES

As you respond to the Choices, use these **Academic Vocabulary** words as appropriate: <u>capacity</u>, <u>crucial</u>, <u>parameter</u>, <u>relevant</u>, <u>sustain</u>.

REVIEW

State Your View

There are many ways to view Mrs. Mallard's reaction to news of her husband's death. Some readers might view her response as an inspiring act of rebellion against the constraints of society. Others might simply find it to be a cold, unloving reaction. Review the story, and write a paragraph expressing your own view of Mrs. Mallard's reaction. Gather in a small group to discuss your view with your classmates.

CONNECT

Make a Presentation on Women's Lives

TechFocus Use the Internet to explore what life for women was like in the 1890s. You might find images of women's dress, information on their jobs, or writings about social customs by women of the time. Was Mrs. Mallard's situation typical for women of her time? How did women's experiences differ? Create a presentation of your findings and other relevant information to share with your class.

EXTEND

See Mrs. Mallard's Future

In "The Story of an Hour" Mrs. Mallard imagines a life of freedom without a husband, but in the end, her husband returns. Imagine, however, that her husband actually has died. What might happen in the next month or year of her life? Create a sequence of diary entries written by the recently widowed Mrs. Mallard, in which she describes her new life and how she feels now that she is on her own.

To Build a Fire

Analyzing Cause and Effect by **Kylene Beers**

One thing leads to another—that is the essence of **cause and effect.** In other words, for every action there is a reaction. Although causality is a basic premise of science, it also plays an important role in naturalist fiction. Naturalists show how human beings relate to an indifferent universe. By depicting stark cause-and-effect relationships, the naturalist reveals how nature adheres to its own strict rules, with no regard for human happiness.

Cause and effect is also an important element of storytelling. Advancing a story's action through cause and effect is one of the main ways in which writers build plot. Analyzing cause and effect can reveal themes in the text and help you understand how a plot is structured.

Naturalists use cause and effect to demonstrate how scientific principles govern the universe. In London's story "To Build a Fire," the fate of the protagonist is determined by the laws and parameters of nature. London shows cause-and-effect relationships on both a large and small scale, revealing the power of nature on many levels. The passage below from "To Build a Fire" takes place at the beginning of the man's fateful journey, yet it contains an idea that is vital to the story:

> As he turned to go on, he spat speculatively. There was a sharp, explosive crackle that startled him. He spat again. And again, in the air, before it could fall to the snow, the spittle crackled. He knew that at fifty below, spittle crackled on the snow, but this spittle had crackled in the air.

The spittle freezing shows the cause-and-effect relationship between temperature and liquid. The passage shows the harshness of the cold and reveals a cause-and-effect relationship central to the story.

The plot turns on several moments that capture key causes and effects. In these moments, the protagonist takes an action, and the effect alters the course of the story. In the following key moment, the man's actions have dire consequences:

> And then it happened. At a place where there were no signs, where the soft, unbroken snow seemed to advertise solidity beneath, the man broke through. It was not deep. He wet himself halfway to the knees before he floundered out to the firm crust.

This passage shows how the man's key actions have altered the course of the story. What happens afterward will be a result of his actions taken here.

Your Turn

Read the passage below from "To Build a Fire." What cause-and-effect relationship is revealed in this passage? In what ways does the man's situation reflect a naturalist premise for the story?

> He was sure to frost his cheeks; he knew that, and experienced a pang of regret that he had not devised a nose strap of the sort Bud wore in the cold snaps. Such a strap passed across the cheeks, as well, and saved them. But it didn't matter much, after all. What were frosted cheeks? A bit painful, that was all; they were never serious.

 **Learn It Online**

Try it as you read! Get your own interactive cause-and-effect chart online.

| go.hrw.com | L11-691 | Go |

Preparing to Read

To Build a Fire

What Do You Think?

What forces shape human character?

⏱ QuickWrite

Recall a time when you or someone you know ended up in a situation that was much more difficult or dangerous than expected. Write a short paragraph describing the experience and what lessons the experience taught.

MEET THE WRITER

Jack London
(1876–1916)

Jack London used his own youthful adventures on the sea and ice as inspiration for fifty volumes of fiction and essays. His stark, compelling stories have been thrilling readers since they were first published.

A Thirst for Adventure

John Griffith London was born into a poor family in San Francisco. When he was a boy, he delivered newspapers, worked on an ice wagon, set up pins in a bowling alley, and worked in a cannery. London read everything he could find in the public library, especially stories of real-life adventure. In his teens he plunged into danger. "I joined the oyster pirates in the bay; shipped as sailor on a schooner; took a turn at salmon fishing; shipped before the mast and sailed for the Japanese coast on a seal-hunting expedition."

London was still in his teens when he settled in Oakland. He began to write and sold a few pieces to local papers. After attending high school for one year, he passed the entrance exams for the University of California at Berkeley by cramming on his own. The combination of work, school, and writing proved too much, however, and he quit halfway through his freshman year. In 1897, he took off to prospect for gold in the Klondike—part of the Yukon Territory in northwestern Canada. London became sick and had to leave, but the experience convinced him that life is a struggle in which the strong survive and the weak do not.

"Wildly" Successful

London's first major success was a story collection, *The Son of the Wolf* (1900). Readers were thrilled by the shocking brutality of his stories, then hooked by the action and adventure. His most famous novel, *The Call of the Wild* (1903), introduced a sled dog named Buck, one of the most memorable animal characters in fiction. London became a millionaire from his writing. An alcoholic, he suffered from kidney disease and depression. He committed suicide in November 1916, at forty years old.

Think About the Writer

Judging from his own life and career, what kind of advice do you think London might give to a young writer?

Reader/Writer Notebook

Use your **RWN** to complete the activities for this selection.

Literary Focus

Naturalism The nineteenth-century literary movement known as **naturalism** was an extreme form of realism. It often depicted characters in a losing battle against an uncaring universe. Influenced by Charles Darwin (1809–1882) and his theories of natural selection and survival of the fittest, naturalist writers believed that human behavior is determined by heredity and environment. Relying on new theories in sociology and psychology, naturalists dissected human behavior with detachment and objectivity, like scientists dissecting laboratory specimens. Naturalists presented human beings as subject to natural forces beyond their control.

Literary Perspectives Apply the literary perspective described on page 695 as you read this story.

Reading Focus

Analyzing Cause and Effect Science tells us that for every action there is a reaction. In literature this is called **cause and effect.** In "To Build a Fire," the string of cause-and-effect relationships reflects the author's naturalist perspective. An action as small as a misstep or the lighting of a match can take on <u>crucial</u> importance in a plot.

Into Action As you read, use the chart below to record each significant action that the protagonist takes and note its effect. In the third column, note how the set of events reflects the principles of naturalism.

Action	Effect	How Events Reflect Naturalism
The man leaves the main Yukon trail.	He ends up alone in the wilderness.	Humans are vulnerable to the forces of nature.

Writing Focus

Think as a Reader/Writer

Find It in Your Reading **Juxtaposition** occurs when a writer puts two or more things side by side to emphasize the contrast between them. London juxtaposes reason and instinct—in the form of a man and a dog—to emphasize the weaknesses and limitations of reason in the face of nature's unforgiving power. As you read, makes notes in your *Reader/Writer Notebook* about each instance of juxtaposition.

Vocabulary

intangible (ihn TAN juh buhl) *adj.:* not capable of being touched or felt. *The danger that awaited the man was intangible, but real.*

protruding (proh TROOD ihng) *v.* used as *adj.:* thrusting forth; sticking out. *The protruding bundle held his food.*

apprehension (ap rih HEHN shuhn) *n.:* expectation of misfortune; fear. *As the man grew more desperate, the dog's apprehension grew.*

imperative (ihm PEHR uh tihv) *adj.:* not to be avoided; urgent. *In the Yukon, it is imperative that you prepare for the cold.*

extremities (ehk STREHM uh teez) *n.:* limbs of the body, especially the hands and feet. *The man's extremities were at the greatest risk of freezing.*

Language Coach

Parts of Speech A noun is a word that names a person, place, or thing (*Jack*, the *Yukon*, *snow*). An adjective is a word that changes a noun's meaning. Some adjectives can be only adjectives (*happy*, *homesick*), but others can also be nouns. In this story the word *imperative* is an adjective meaning "not to be avoided." As a noun, it can mean "necessity or duty." Nouns that come from adjectives often name abstract concepts. An imperative, for example, is not something concrete that you can touch, but an idea.

 **Learn It Online**
Jump into this story with the video introduction online.

go.hrw.com | L11-693 | Go

To Build a Fire

by **Jack London**

Read with a Purpose
Read to discover the danger of underestimating nature's power and of overestimating one's own.

Build Background
"To Build a Fire" must be the coldest story ever written. London draws on his own experience of prospecting for gold in the Yukon—a bleak region of northwestern Canada—to give authenticity to the story. This is ultimately far more than a classic "person versus nature" story. It is a grimly realistic tale about a man who is "quick and alert in the things of life, but . . . not in the significances"—an innocent who is not prepared for an unforgiving environment.

Day had broken cold and gray, exceedingly cold and gray, when the man turned aside from the main Yukon trail and climbed the high earth bank, where a dim and little-traveled trail led eastward through the fat spruce timberland. It was a steep bank, and he paused for breath at the top, excusing the act to himself by looking at his watch. It was nine o'clock. There was no sun or hint of sun, though there was not a cloud in the sky. It was a clear day, and yet there seemed an intangible pall[1] over the face of things, a subtle gloom that made the day dark, and that was due to the absence of sun. This fact did not worry the man. He was used to the lack of sun. It had been days since he had seen the sun, and he knew that a few more days must

pass before that cheerful orb, due south, would just peep above the skyline and dip immediately from view.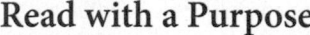

The man flung a look back along the way he had come. The Yukon lay a mile wide and hidden under three feet of ice. On top of this ice were as many feet of snow. It was all pure white, rolling in gentle undulations where the ice jams of the freeze-up had formed. North and south, as far as his eye could see, it was unbroken white, save for a dark hairline that curved and twisted from around the spruce-covered island to the south, and that curved and twisted away into the north, where it disappeared behind another spruce-covered island. This dark hairline was the trail—the main trail—that led south five hundred miles to the Chilkoot Pass, Dyea, and salt water; and that led north seventy miles to Dawson, and still on to the north a thousand miles to Nulato, and

_____
1. **pall:** overspreading atmosphere of gloom and depression.

Vocabulary **intangible** (ihn TAN juh buhl) _adj._: not capable of being touched or felt.

A **Literary Focus** Naturalism How does the protagonist's namelessness reflect London's naturalistic approach?

finally to St. Michael on the Bering Sea, a thousand miles and half a thousand more.

But all this—the mysterious, far-reaching hairline trail, the absence of sun from the sky, the tremendous cold, and the strangeness and weirdness of it all—made no impression on the man. It was not because he was long used to it. He was a newcomer in the land, a cheechako,[2] and this was his first winter. The trouble with him was that he was without imagination. He was quick and alert in the things of life, but only in the things, and not in the significances. Fifty degrees below zero meant eighty-odd degrees of frost. Such fact impressed him as being cold and uncomfortable, and that was all. It did not lead him to meditate upon his frailty as a creature of temperature, and upon man's frailty in general, able only to live within certain narrow limits of heat and cold, and from there on it did not lead him to the conjectural[3] field of immortality and man's place in the universe. Fifty degrees below zero stood for a bite of frost that hurt and that must be guarded against by the use of mittens, earflaps, warm moccasins, and thick socks. Fifty degrees below zero was to him just precisely fifty degrees below zero. That there should be anything more to it than that was a thought that never entered his head. **B**

As he turned to go on, he spat speculatively. There was a sharp, explosive crackle that startled him. He spat again. And again, in the air, before it could fall to the snow, the spittle crackled. He knew that at fifty below, spittle crackled on the snow, but this spittle had crackled in the air. Undoubtedly it was colder than fifty below—how much colder he did not know. But the temperature did not matter. He was bound for the old claim[4] on the left fork of Henderson Creek, where

---

2. **cheechako** (chee CHAYH koh): Chinook jargon for "newcomer" or "tenderfoot."
3. **conjectural:** based on guesswork or uncertain evidence.
4. **claim:** piece of land staked out by a miner.

B Reading Focus **Analyzing Cause and Effect** What consequences does the narrator imply might result from the man's lack of imagination and discernment?

Vocabulary **protruding** (proh TROOD ihng) *v.* used as *adj.:* thrusting forth; sticking out.

the boys were already. They had come over across the divide from the Indian Creek country, while he had come the roundabout way to take a look at the possibilities of getting out logs in the spring from the islands in the Yukon. He would be into camp by six o'clock; a bit after dark, it was true, but the boys would be there, a fire would be going, and a hot supper would be ready. As for lunch, he pressed his hand against the protruding bundle under his jacket. It was also under his shirt, wrapped up in a handkerchief and lying against the naked skin. It was the only way to keep the biscuits from freezing. He smiled agreeably to himself as he thought of those biscuits, each cut open and sopped in bacon grease, and each enclosing a generous slice of fried bacon.

He plunged in among the big spruce trees. The trail was faint. A foot of snow had fallen since the last sled had passed over, and he was glad he was without a sled, traveling light. In fact, he carried nothing but the lunch wrapped in the handkerchief. He was surprised, however, at the cold. It certainly was cold, he concluded, as he rubbed his numb nose and cheekbones with his mittened hand. He was a warm-whiskered man, but the hair on his face did not protect

Literary Perspectives

Analyzing Philosophical Context Jack London saw life as a savage struggle won by those best suited for survival by being in tune with nature. He regarded people as primitive beasts taking refuge behind a veneer of civilization. London believed that human nature is fierce and cruel and is tempered only by an equally spontaneous love. London was heavily influenced by the German philosopher Friedrich Nietzsche's idea of a "superman," who, by force of will, rises above the masses. London plotted his stories and built his characters with the principles of naturalism in mind. His short stories and novels dramatize his belief that "civilized" beings are either destroyed or re-created in savage environments.

As you read, be sure to notice the questions in the text, which will guide you in using this perspective.

the high cheekbones and the eager nose that thrust itself aggressively into the frosty air.

At the man's heels trotted a dog, a big native husky, the proper wolf dog, gray coated and without any visible or temperamental difference from its brother, the wild wolf. The animal was depressed by the tremendous cold. It knew that it was no time for traveling. Its instinct told it a truer tale than was told to the man by the man's judgment. In reality, it was not merely colder than fifty below zero; it was colder than sixty below, than seventy below. It was seventy-five below zero. Since the freezing point is thirty-two above zero, it meant that one hundred and seven degrees of frost obtained. The dog did not know anything about thermometers. Possibly in its brain there was no sharp consciousness of a condition of very cold such as was in the man's brain. But the brute had its instinct. It experienced a vague but menacing apprehension that subdued it and made it slink along at the man's heels, and that made it question eagerly every unwonted[5] movement of the man, as if expecting him to go into camp or to seek shelter somewhere and build a fire. The dog had learned fire, and it wanted fire, or else to burrow under the snow and cuddle its warmth away from the air.

The frozen moisture of its breathing had settled on its fur in a fine powder of frost, and especially were its jowls, muzzle, and eyelashes whitened by its crystaled breath. The man's red beard and moustache were likewise frosted, but more solidly, the deposit taking the form of ice and increasing with every warm, moist breath he exhaled. Also, the man was chewing tobacco, and the muzzle of ice held his lips so rigidly that he was unable to clear his chin when he expelled the juice. The result was that a crystal beard of the color and solidity of amber was increasing its length on his chin. If he fell down it would shatter itself, like glass, into brittle fragments. But he did not mind the appendage.[6] It was

____

5. **unwonted:** unusual.
6. **appendage:** something attached to another object.

the penalty all tobacco chewers paid in that country, and he had been out before in two cold snaps. They had not been so cold as this, he knew, but by the spirit thermometer[7] at Sixty Mile he knew they had been registered at fifty below and at fifty-five.

He held on through the level stretch of woods for several miles, crossed a wide flat, and dropped down a bank to the frozen bed of a small stream. This was Henderson Creek, and he knew he was ten miles from the forks. He looked at his watch. It was ten o' clock. He was making four miles an hour, and he calculated that he would arrive at the forks at half past twelve. He decided to celebrate that event by eating his lunch there.

The dog dropped in again at his heels, with a tail drooping discouragement, as the man swung along the creek bed. The furrow of the old sled trail was plainly visible, but a dozen inches of snow covered the marks of the last runners. In a month no man had come up or down that silent creek. The man held steadily on. He was not much given to thinking, and just then particularly, he had nothing to think about save that he would eat lunch at the forks and that at six o' clock he would be in camp with the boys. There was nobody to talk to; and, had there been, speech would have been impossible because of the ice muzzle on his mouth. So he continued monotonously to chew tobacco and to increase the length of his amber beard.

Once in a while the thought reiterated[8] itself that it was very cold and that he had never experienced such cold. As he walked along he rubbed his cheekbones and nose with the back of his mittened hand. He did this automatically, now and again changing hands. But rub as he would, the instant he stopped his cheekbones went numb, and the following instant the end of his nose went numb. He was sure to frost his cheeks;

____

7. **spirit thermometer:** alcohol thermometer. In places where the temperature often drops below the freezing point of mercury, alcohol is used in thermometers.
8. **reiterated:** repeated.

____

C Literary Focus **Naturalism** What does the verb *plunged* in the first sentence of this paragraph suggest about the man's personality? How would a naturalist view this trait?

Vocabulary **apprehension** (ap rih HEHN shuhn) *n.:* expectation of misfortune; fear.

D Reading Focus **Analyzing Cause and Effect** What causes the man to ignore the signs of extreme cold?

he knew that, and experienced a pang of regret that he had not devised a nose strap of the sort Bud wore in the cold snaps. Such a strap passed across the cheeks, as well, and saved them. But it didn't matter much, after all. What were frosted cheeks? A bit painful, that was all; they were never serious. **E**

Empty as the man's mind was of thought, he was keenly observant, and he noticed the changes in the creek, the curves and bends and timber jams, and always he sharply noted where he placed his feet. Once, coming around a bend, he shied abruptly, like a startled horse, curved away from the place where he had been walking, and retreated several paces back along the trail. The creek, he knew, was frozen clear to the bottom—no creek could contain water in that arctic winter—but he knew also that there were springs that bubbled out from the hillsides and ran along under the snow and on top of the ice of the creek. He knew that the coldest snaps never froze these springs, and he knew likewise their danger. They were traps. They hid pools of water under the snow that might be three inches deep, or three feet. Sometimes a skin of ice half an inch thick covered them, and in turn was covered by the snow. Sometimes there were alternate layers of water and ice skin, so that when one broke through he kept on breaking through for a while, sometimes wetting himself to the waist.

That was why he had shied in such panic. He had felt the give under his feet and heard the crackle of a snow-hidden ice skin. And to get his feet wet in such a temperature meant trouble and danger. At the very least it meant delay, for he would be forced to stop and build a fire, and under its protection to bare his feet while he dried his socks and moccasins. He stood and studied the creek bed and its banks, and decided that the flow of water came from the right. He reflected awhile, rubbing his nose and cheeks, then skirted to the left, stepping gingerly and testing the footing for each step. Once clear of the danger, he took a fresh chew of tobacco and swung along at his four-mile gait.

In the course of the next two hours he came upon several similar traps. Usually the snow above the hidden pools had a sunken, candied appearance that advertised the danger. Once again, however, he had a close call;

and once, suspecting danger, he compelled the dog to go on in front. The dog did not want to go. It hung back until the man shoved it forward, and then it went quickly across the white, unbroken surface. Suddenly it broke through, floundered to one side, and got away to firmer footing. It had wet its forefeet and legs, and almost immediately the water that clung to it turned to ice. It made quick efforts to lick the ice off its legs, then dropped down in the snow and began to bite out the ice that had formed between the toes. This was a matter of instinct. To permit the ice to remain would mean sore feet. It did not know this. It merely obeyed the mysterious prompting that arose from the deep crypts[9] of its being. But the man knew, having achieved a judgment on the subject, and he removed the mitten from his right hand and helped tear out the ice particles. He did not expose his fingers more than a minute, and was astonished at the swift numbness that smote[10] them. It certainly was cold. He pulled on the mitten hastily, and beat the hand savagely across his chest.

---

9. **crypts:** hidden recesses.
10. **smote:** powerfully struck.

E ▶ **Literary Perspectives** **Analyzing Philosophical Context**
Why do you think London often repeats that it is cold? How is this focus a reflection of his philosophical perspective?

At twelve o'clock the day was at its brightest. Yet the sun was too far south on its winter journey to clear the horizon. The bulge of the earth intervened between it and Henderson Creek, where the man walked under a clear sky at noon and cast no shadow. At half past twelve, to the minute, he arrived at the forks of the creek. He was pleased at the speed he had made. If he kept it up, he would certainly be with the boys by six. He unbuttoned his jacket and shirt and drew forth his lunch. The action consumed no more than a quarter of a minute, yet in that brief moment the numbness laid hold of the exposed fingers. He did not put the mitten on, but instead struck the fingers a dozen sharp smashes against his leg. Then he sat down on a snow-covered log to eat. The sting that followed upon the striking of his fingers against his leg ceased so quickly that he was startled. He had had no chance to take a bite of biscuit. He struck the fingers repeatedly and returned them to the mitten, baring the other hand for the purpose of eating. He tried to take a mouthful, but the ice muzzle prevented. He had forgotten to build a fire and thaw out. He chuckled at his foolishness, and as he chuckled he noted the numbness creeping into the exposed fingers. Also, he noted that the stinging which had first come to his toes when he sat down was already passing away. He wondered whether the toes were warm or numb. He moved them inside the moccasins and decided that they were numb. **F**

He pulled the mitten on hurriedly and stood up. He was a bit frightened. He stamped up and down until the stinging returned into the feet. It certainly was cold, was his thought. That man from Sulfur Creek had spoken the truth when telling how cold it sometimes got in the country. And he had laughed at him at the time! That showed one must not be too sure of things. There was no mistake about it, it *was* cold. He strode up and down, stamping his feet and threshing his arms, until reassured by the returning warmth. Then he got out matches and proceeded to make a fire. From the undergrowth, where high water of the previous spring had lodged a supply of seasoned twigs, he got his firewood. Working carefully from a small beginning, he soon had a roaring fire, over which he thawed the ice from his face and in the protection of which he ate his biscuits. For the moment the cold of space was outwitted. The dog took satisfaction in the fire, stretching out close enough for warmth and far enough away to escape being singed.

When the man had finished, he filled his pipe and took his comfortable time over a smoke. Then he pulled on his mittens, settled the earflaps of his cap firmly about his ears, and took the creek trail up the left fork. The dog was disappointed and yearned back toward the fire. This man did not know cold. Possibly all the generations of his ancestry had been ignorant of cold, of real cold, of cold one hundred and seven degrees below freezing point. But the dog knew; all its ancestry knew, and it had inherited the knowledge. And it knew that it was not good to walk abroad in such fearful cold. It was the time to lie snug in a hole in the snow and wait for a curtain of cloud to be drawn across the face of outer space whence this cold came. On the other hand, there was no keen intimacy between the dog and the man. The one was the toil slave of the other, and the only caresses it had ever received were the caresses of the whiplash and of harsh and menacing throat sounds that threatened the whiplash. So the dog made no effort to communicate its apprehension to the man. It was not concerned in the welfare of the man; it was for its own sake that it yearned back toward the fire. But the man whistled, and spoke to it with the sound of whiplashes, and the dog swung in at the man's heels and followed after.

The man took a chew of tobacco and proceeded to start a new amber beard. Also, his moist breath quickly powdered with white his moustache, eyebrows, and lashes. There did not seem to be so many springs on the left fork of the Henderson, and for half an hour the man saw no signs of any. And then it happened. At a place where there were no signs, where the soft, unbroken snow seemed to advertise solidity beneath, the man broke through. It was not deep. He wet himself halfway to the knees before he floundered out to the firm crust.

He was angry, and cursed his luck aloud. He had hoped to get into camp with the boys at six o'clock,

---

F **Reading Focus** **Analyzing Cause and Effect** Writers sometimes present effects first and name causes afterward. What are the effects of the man's forgetting to build a fire?

and this would delay him an hour, for he would have to build a fire and dry out his footgear. This was imperative at that low temperature—he knew that much; and he turned aside to the bank, which he climbed. On top, tangled in the underbrush about the trunks of several small spruce trees, was a high-water deposit of dry firewood—sticks and twigs, principally, but also larger portions of seasoned branches and fine, dry, last year's grasses. He threw down several large pieces on top of the snow. This served for a foundation and prevented the young flame from drowning itself in the snow it otherwise would melt. The flame he got by touching a match to a small shred of birch bark that he took from his pocket. This burned even more readily than paper. Placing it on the foundation, he fed the young flame with wisps of dry grass and with the tiniest dry twigs.

He worked slowly and carefully, keenly aware of his danger. Gradually, as the flame grew stronger, he increased the size of the twigs with which he fed it. He squatted in the snow, pulling the twigs out from their entanglement in the brush and feeding directly to the flame. He knew there must be no failure. When it is seventy-five below zero, a man must not fail in his first attempt to build a fire—that is, if his feet are wet. If his feet are dry, and he fails, he can run along the trail for a half a mile and restore his circulation. But the circulation of wet and freezing feet cannot be restored by running when it is seventy-five below. No matter how fast he runs, the wet feet will freeze the harder.

All this the man knew. The old-timer on Sulfur Creek had told him about it the previous fall, and now he was appreciating the advice. Already all sensation had gone out of his feet. To build the fire, he had been forced to remove his mittens, and the fingers had quickly gone numb. His pace of four miles an hour had kept his heart pumping blood to the surface of his body and to all the extremities. But the instant he

stopped, the action of the pump eased down. The cold of space smote the unprotected tip of the planet, and he, being on that unprotected tip, received the full force of the blow. The blood of his body recoiled before it. The blood was alive, like the dog, and like the dog it wanted to hide away and cover itself up from the fearful cold. So long as he walked four miles an hour, he pumped that blood, willy-nilly,[11] to the surface; but now it ebbed away and sank down into the recesses of his body. The extremities were the first to feel its absence. His wet feet froze the faster, and his exposed fingers numbed the faster, though they had not yet begun to freeze. Nose and cheeks were already freezing, while the skin of all his body chilled as it lost its blood. **G**

But he was safe. Toes and nose and cheeks would be only touched by the frost, for the fire was beginning to burn with strength. He was feeding it twigs the size of his finger. In another minute he would be able to feed it with branches the size of his wrist, and then he could remove his wet footgear, and, while it dried, he could keep his naked feet warm by the fire, rubbing them at first, of course, with snow. The fire was a success. He was safe. He remembered the advice of the old-timer on Sulfur Creek, and smiled. The old-timer had been very serious in laying down the law that no man must travel alone in the Klondike after fifty below. Well, here he was; he had had the accident; he was alone; and he had saved himself. Those old-timers were rather womanish, some of them, he thought. All a man had to do

---

11. **willy-nilly:** without choice.

G **Literary Focus** Naturalism Here London describes the process by which the human body shuts down in the cold. How does this description reflect the philosophy of naturalism?

Vocabulary **imperative** (ihm PEHR uh tihv) *adj.*: not to be avoided; urgent.
extremities (ehk STREHM uh teez) *n.*: limbs of the body, especially the hands and feet.

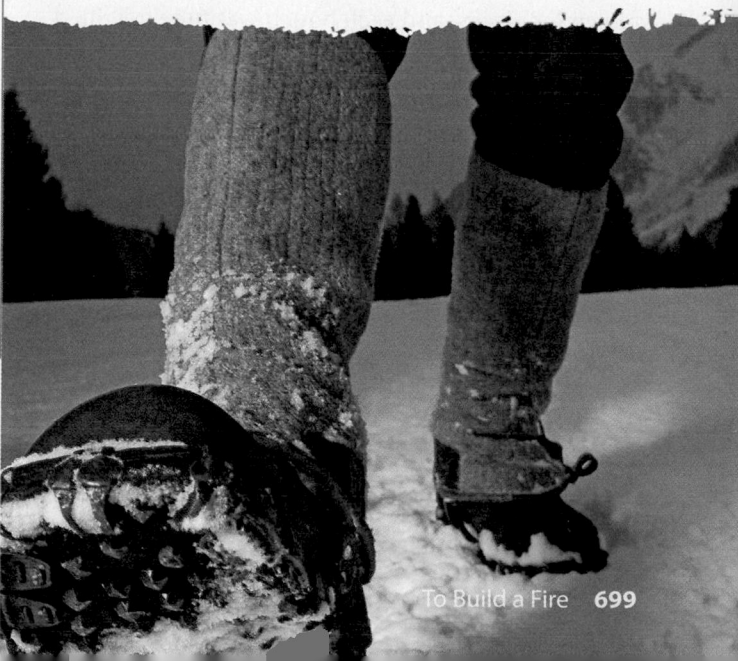

was to keep his head and he was all right. Any man who was a man could travel alone. But it was surprising, the rapidity with which his cheeks and nose were freezing. And he had not thought his fingers could go lifeless in so short a time. Lifeless they were, for he could scarcely make them move together to grip a twig, and they seemed remote from his body and from him. When he touched a twig, he had to look and see whether or not he had hold of it. The wires were pretty well down between him and his finger ends.

All of which counted for little. There was the fire, snapping and crackling and promising life with every dancing flame. He started to untie his moccasins. They were coated with ice; the thick German socks were like sheaths of iron halfway to the knees; and the moccasin strings were like rods of steel all twisted and knotted as by some conflagration.[12] For a moment he tugged with his numb fingers, then, realizing the folly of it, he drew his sheath knife.

But before he could cut the strings it happened. It was his own fault, or, rather, his mistake. He should not have built the fire under the spruce tree. He should have built it in the open. But it had been easier to pull the twigs from the bush and drop them directly on the fire. Now the tree under which he had done this carried a weight of snow on its boughs. No wind had blown for weeks, and each bough was fully freighted. Each time he had pulled a twig he had communicated a slight agitation to the tree—an imperceptible agitation, so far as he was concerned, but an agitation sufficient to bring about the disaster. High up in the tree one bough capsized its load of snow. This fell on the boughs beneath, capsizing them. This process continued, spreading out and involving the whole tree.

---

12. **conflagration:** large fire.

It grew like an avalanche, and it descended without warning upon the man and the fire, and the fire was blotted out! Where it had burned was a mantle of fresh and disordered snow. **(H)**

The man was shocked. It was as though he had just heard his own sentence of death. For a moment he sat and stared at the spot where the fire had been. Then he grew very calm. Perhaps the old-timer on Sulfur Creek was right. If he had only had a trail mate, he would have been in no danger now. The trail mate could have built the fire. Well, it was up to him to build the fire over again, and this second time there must be no failure. Even if he succeeded, he would most likely lose some toes. His feet must be badly frozen by now, and there would be some time before the second fire was ready.

> The man was shocked. It was as though he had just heard his own sentence of death.

Such were his thoughts, but he did not sit and think them. He was busy all the time they were passing through his mind. He made a new foundation for a fire, this time in the open, where no treacherous tree could blot it out. Next he gathered dry grasses and tiny twigs from the high-water flotsam.[13] He could not bring his fingers together to pull them out, but he was able to gather them by the handful. In this way he got many rotten twigs and bits of green moss that were undesirable, but it was the best he could do. He worked methodically, even collecting an armful of the larger branches to be used later when the fire gathered strength. And all the while the dog sat and watched him, a certain yearning wistfulness in its eyes, for it looked upon him as the fire provider, and the fire was slow in coming.

---

13. **high-water flotsam:** branches and debris washed ashore by a stream or river during the warm months, when the water is high.

(H) Reading Focus Analyzing Cause and Effect In this passage, London begins by saying "it happened." Then he describes a series of causes and effects that end in disaster—the extinguishing of the fire. Why does the man build his fire in the wrong place?

When all was ready, the man reached in his pocket for a second piece of birch bark. He knew the bark was there, and, though he could not feel it with his fingers, he could hear its crisp rustling as he fumbled for it. Try as he would, he could not clutch hold of it. And all the time, in his consciousness, was the knowledge that each instant his feet were freezing. This thought tended to put him in a panic, but he fought against it and kept calm. He pulled on his mittens with his teeth, and threshed his arms back and forth, beating his hands with all his might against his sides. He did this sitting down, and he stood up to do it; and all the while the dog sat in the snow, its wolf brush of a tail curled around warmly over its forefeet, its sharp wolf ears pricked forward intently as it watched the man. And the man, as he beat and threshed with his arms and hands, felt a great surge of envy as he regarded the creature that was warm and secure in its natural covering. **I**

After a time he was aware of the first faraway signals of sensation in his beaten fingers. The faint tingling grew stronger till it evolved into a stinging ache that was excruciating, but which the man hailed with satisfaction. He stripped the mitten from his right hand and fetched forth the birch bark. The exposed fingers were quickly going numb again. Next he brought out his bunch of sulfur matches. But the tremendous cold had already driven the life out of his fingers. In his effort to separate one match from the others, the whole bunch fell in the snow. He tried to pick it out of the snow, but failed. The dead fingers could neither touch nor clutch. He was very careful. He drove the thought of his freezing feet, and nose, and cheeks, out of his mind, devoting his whole soul to the matches. He watched, using the sense of vision in place of that of touch, and when he saw his fingers on each side of the bunch, he closed them—that is, he willed to close them, for the wires were down, and the fingers did not obey. He pulled the mitten on the right hand, and beat it fiercely against his knee. Then,

with both mittened hands, he scooped the bunch of matches, along with much snow, into his lap. Yet he was no better off. **J**

After some manipulation he managed to get the bunch between the heels of his mittened hands. In this fashion he carried it to his mouth. The ice crackled and snapped when by a violent effort he opened his mouth. He drew the lower jaw in, curled the upper lip out of the way, and scraped the bunch with his upper teeth in order to separate a match. He succeeded in getting one, which he dropped on his lap. He was no better off. He could not pick it up. Then he devised a way. He picked it up in his teeth and scratched it on his leg. Twenty times he scratched before he succeeded in lighting it. As it flamed he held it with his teeth to the birch bark. But the burning brimstone went up his nostrils and into his lungs, causing him to cough spasmodically.[14] The match fell into the snow and went out.

The old-timer on Sulfur Creek was right, he thought in the moment of controlled despair that ensued: After fifty below, a man should travel with a partner. He beat his hands, but failed in exciting any sensation. Suddenly he bared both hands, removing the mittens with his teeth. He caught the whole bunch between the heels of his hands. His arm muscles, not being frozen, enabled him to press the hand heels tightly against the matches. Then he scratched the bunch along his leg. It flared into flame, seventy sulfur matches at once! There was no wind to blow them out. He kept his head to one side to escape the strangling fumes, and held the blazing bunch to the birch bark. As he so held it, he became aware of sensation in his hand. His flesh was burning. He could smell it. Deep down below the surface he could feel it. The sensation developed into pain that grew acute. And still he endured it, holding the flame of matches clumsily to the bark that would not light

14. **spasmodically:** in a sudden, violent manner; fitfully.

I Literary Perspectives **Analyzing Philosophical Context** How does this passage reflect London's belief that those most in tune with nature are best suited to survive?

J Literary Focus **Naturalism** What does London imply by stating that the man devotes his whole *soul* to the task? Despite this reference to the man's soul, how does the passage as a whole reveal London's belief that impersonal forces will win out? How does the repetition of the phrase "he was no better off" reflect London's naturalistic approach?

readily because his own burning hands were in the way, absorbing most of the flame. **(K)**

At last, when he could endure no more, he jerked his hands apart. The blazing matches fell sizzling into the snow, but the birch bark was alight. He began laying dry grass and the tiniest twigs on the flame. He could not pick and choose, for he had to lift the fuel between the heels of his hands. Small pieces of rotten wood and green moss clung to the twigs, and he bit them off as well as he could with his teeth. He cherished the flame carefully and awkwardly. It meant life, and it must not perish. The withdrawal of blood from the surface of his body now made him begin to shiver, and he grew more awkward. A large piece of green moss fell squarely on the little fire. He tried to poke it out with his fingers, but his shivering frame made him poke too far, and he disrupted the nucleus of the little fire, the burning grasses and tiny twigs separating and scattering. He tried to poke them together again, but in spite of the tenseness of the effort, his shivering got away with him, and the twigs were hopelessly scattered. Each twig gushed a puff of smoke and went out. The fire provider had failed. As he looked apathetically[15] about him, his eyes chanced on the dog, sitting across the ruins of the fire from him, in the snow, making restless, hunching movements, slightly lifting one forefoot and then the other, shifting its weight back and forth on them with wistful eagerness. **(L)**

The sight of the dog put a wild idea into his head. He remembered the tale of the man, caught in a blizzard, who killed a steer and crawled inside the carcass, and so was saved. He would kill the dog and bury his hands in the warm body until the numbness went out of them. Then he could build another fire. He spoke to the dog, calling it to him; but in his voice was a strange note of fear that frightened the animal, who had never known the man to speak in such a way before. Something was the matter, and its suspicious nature sensed danger—it knew not what danger, but somewhere, somehow, in its brain arose an apprehension of the man. It flattened its ears down at the sound of the man's voice, and its restless, hunching movements and the liftings and shiftings of its forefeet became more pronounced; but it would not come to the man. He got on his hands and knees and crawled toward the dog. This unusual posture again excited suspicion, and the animal sidled mincingly[16] away. **(M)**

The man sat up in the snow for a moment and struggled for calmness. Then he pulled on his mittens, by means of his teeth, and got up on his feet. He glanced down at first in order to assure himself that he was really standing up, for the absence of sensation in his feet left him unrelated to the earth. His erect position in itself started to drive the webs of suspicion from the dog's mind; and when he spoke peremptorily,[17] with the sound of whiplashes in his voice, the dog rendered its customary allegiance and came to him. As it came within reaching distance, the man lost his control. His arms flashed out to the dog, and he experienced genuine surprise when he discovered that his hands could not clutch, that there was neither bend nor feeling in the fingers. He had forgotten for the moment that they were frozen and that they were freezing more and more. All this happened quickly, and before the animal could get away, he encircled its body with his arms. He sat down in the snow, and in this fashion held the dog, while it snarled and whined and struggled.

But it was all he could do, hold its body encircled in his arms and sit there. He realized that he could not kill the dog. There was no way to do it. With his helpless hands he could neither draw nor hold his sheath knife nor throttle the animal. He released it, and it plunged wildly away, its tail between its legs and still snarling. It halted forty feet away and surveyed him curiously, with ears sharply pricked forward. The man

---

15. **apathetically:** with little interest or concern; indifferently.

16. **sidled mincingly:** moved sideways with small steps.
17. **peremptorily:** in a commanding way.

(K) Reading Focus Analyzing Cause and Effect Why has the man reversed his opinion of the old-timer? What effect will this change produce?

(L) Literary Focus Naturalism How does the protagonist's failure to build a fire exemplify the philosophy of naturalism? How might the scene be handled by a Romantic writer?

(M) Literary Focus Naturalism What makes this brief scene even more bitterly naturalistic?

Analyzing Visuals

Viewing and Interpreting What does the image of this icy tree convey to you about the brutality of nature?

looked down at his hands in order to locate them, and found them hanging on the ends of his arms. It struck him as curious that one should have to use his eyes in order to find out where his hands were. He began threshing his arms back and forth, beating the mittened hands against his sides. He did this for five minutes, violently, and his heart pumped enough blood up to the surface to put a stop to his shivering. But no sensation was aroused in his hands. He had an impression that they hung like weights on the ends of his arms, but when he tried to run the impression down, he could not find it.

A certain fear of death, dull and oppressive, came to him. This fear quickly became poignant[18] as he realized that it was no longer a mere matter of freezing his fingers and toes, or of losing his hands and feet, but that it was a matter of life and death, with the chances against him. This threw him into a panic, and he turned and ran up the creek bed along the old, dim trail. The dog joined in behind and kept up with him. He ran blindly, without intention, in fear such as he

had never known in his life. Slowly, as he plowed and floundered through the snow, he began to see things again—the banks of the creek, the old timber jams, the leafless aspens, and the sky. The running made him feel better. He did not shiver. Maybe, if he ran on, his feet would thaw out; and, anyway, if he ran far enough, he would reach the camp and the boys. Without doubt he would lose some fingers and toes and some of his face; but the boys would take care of him, and save the rest of him when he got there. And, at the same time, there was another thought in his mind that said he would never get to the camp and the boys; that it was too many miles away, that the freezing had too great a start on him, and that he would soon be stiff and dead. This thought he kept in the background and refused to consider. Sometimes it pushed itself forward and demanded to be heard, but he thrust it back and strove to think of other things.

It struck him as curious that he could run at all on feet so frozen that he could not feel them when they struck the earth and took the weight of his body. He seemed to himself to skim along above the surface, and to have no connection with the earth. Somewhere

---

18. **poignant:** painfully affecting feelings; touching.

N **Reading Focus** **Analyzing Cause and Effect** What is happening in the man's mind here?

he had once seen a winged Mercury,[19] and he wondered if Mercury felt as he felt when skimming over the earth.

His theory of running until he reached camp and the boys had one flaw in it: He lacked the endurance. Several times he stumbled, and finally he tottered, crumpled up, and fell. When he tried to rise, he failed. He must sit and rest, he decided, and next time he would merely walk and keep on going. As he sat and regained his breath, he noted that he was feeling quite warm and comfortable. He was not shivering, and it even seemed that a warm glow had come to his chest and trunk. And yet, when he touched his nose or cheeks, there was no sensation. Running would not thaw them out. Nor would it thaw out his hands and feet. Then the thought came to him that the frozen portions of his body must be extending. He tried to keep this thought down, to forget it, to think of something else; he was aware of the panicky feeling that it caused, and he was afraid of the panic. But the thought asserted itself, and persisted, until it produced a vision of his body totally frozen. This was too much, and he made another wild run along the trail. Once he slowed down to a walk, but the thought of the freezing extending itself made him run again.

And all the time the dog ran with him, at his heels. When he fell down a second time, it curled its tail over its forefeet and sat in front of him, facing him, curiously eager and intent. The warmth and security of the animal angered him, and he cursed it till it flattened down its ears appeasingly. This time the shivering came more quickly upon the man. He was losing in this battle with the frost. It was creeping into his body from all sides. The thought of it drove him on, but he ran no more than a hundred feet when he staggered and pitched headlong. It was his last panic. When he had recovered his breath and control, he sat up and entertained in his mind the conception of meeting death with dignity. However, the conception did not come to him in such terms. His idea of it was that he had been making a fool of himself, running around like a chicken with its head cut off—such was the simile that occurred to him. Well, he was bound to freeze anyway, and he might as well take it decently. With this newfound peace of mind came the first glimmerings of drowsiness. A good idea, he thought, to sleep off to death. It was like taking an anesthetic.[20] Freezing was not so bad as people thought. There were lots worse ways to die. **O**

He pictured the boys finding his body next day. Suddenly he found himself with them, coming along the trail and looking for himself. And, still with them, he came around a turn in the trail and found himself lying in the snow. He did not belong with himself anymore, for even then he was out of himself, standing with the boys and looking at himself in the snow. It certainly was cold, was his thought. When he got back to the States, he could tell the folks what real cold was. He drifted on from this to a vision of the old-timer on Sulfur Creek. He could see him quite clearly, warm and comfortable, and smoking a pipe.

"You were right, old hoss; you were right," the man mumbled to the old-timer of Sulfur Creek. **P**

Then the man drowsed off into what seemed to him the most comfortable and satisfying sleep he had ever known. The dog sat facing him and waiting. The brief day drew to a close in a long, slow twilight. There were no signs of a fire to be made, and, besides, never in the dog's experience had it known a man to sit like that in the snow and make no fire. As the twilight drew on, its eager yearning for the fire mastered it, and with a great lifting and shifting of forefeet, it whined softly, then flattened its ears down in anticipation of being chidden[21] by the man. But the man remained silent. Later, the dog whined loudly. And still later it crept close to the man and caught the scent of death. This made the animal bristle and back away. A little longer it delayed, howling under the stars that leaped and danced and shone brightly in the cold sky. Then it turned and trotted up the trail in the direction of the camp it knew, where were the other food providers and fire providers.

---

19. **Mercury:** in Roman mythology, messenger of the gods, who is depicted wearing winged sandals and a winged hat.

20. **anesthetic:** medication that causes loss of the sensation of pain.
21. **chidden:** scolded.

O **Reading Focus** Analyzing Cause and Effect After the man accepts the inevitability of his death, how does his behavior change?

P **Literary Focus** Naturalism The man's recognition that the old-timer was right comes too late to save the man's life. What message do you think London is conveying in this story?

Applying Your Skills

SKILLS FOCUS Literary Skills Analyze naturalism; analyze characterization; analyze philosophical context. **Reading Skills** Analyze cause and effect.

To Build a Fire

Respond and Think Critically

Reading Focus

Quick Check

1. How does the man determine that it is colder than fifty below zero?

2. Why does the man fail to notice the water before he wets his feet?

3. At what point in the story does the dog become suspicious of the man?

Read with a Purpose

4. In what small yet critical ways does the man underestimate the danger of his trip? How do his body and mind fail him?

Reading Skills: Analyzing Cause and Effect

5. While reading, you recorded each significant action taken by the protagonist, its effect, and how the events reflect the principles of naturalism. Review your chart, and identify two actions that you think had the biggest impact on the protagonist's fate. Write a paragraph explaining why you think these actions were significant.

Action	Effect	How Events Reflect Naturalism
The man leaves the main Yukon trail.	He ends up alone in the wilderness.	Human beings are vulnerable to the forces of nature.

Literary Focus

Literary Analysis

6. **Analyze** How do the man and the dog differ in the ways that they approach the intense cold? What point is London making by means of this contrast?

7. **Interpret** Several times the man recalls advice given to him by the old-timer from Sulfur Creek. Why did the man not follow his advice?

8. **Make Judgments** London wrote another, more commercially acceptable ending for an earlier version of "To Build a Fire." In the first version the man survives, returns to camp, and learns an important lesson: Never travel alone. Do you think this ending improves the story or weakens it? Explain your opinion.

9. **Literary Perspectives** How does your knowledge of naturalism help you understand the perspective from which London wrote this story?

Literary Skills: Naturalism

10. **Extend** Re-read the description of naturalism (page 693). How does the story's **theme,** or insight about life, reflect key naturalist ideas?

Literary Skills Review: Characterization

11. **Make Judgments** London reveals the man's personality by showing the man's actions and relating his inner thoughts. Referring to these details, describe the man's character.

Writing Focus

Think as a Reader/Writer

Use It in Your Writing London's juxtaposition of reason with instinct ends with the death of the man and the survival of the dog. Think of two contrasting things, such as youth and old age, and write a short scene juxtaposing these ideas.

 What Do You Think Now

How do the events in the story cause the man to re-evaluate his ideas about the power of nature?

Vocabulary Development

✓ Vocabulary Check

Match the Vocabulary words with their antonyms.

1. intangible
2. protruding
3. apprehension
4. imperative
5. extremities

a. concave
b. tranquility
c. unnecessary
d. trunk
e. concrete

Vocabulary Skills: Word Origins

Where do words come from? You can determine the origins of a word by looking at its entry in a good dictionary or similar resource. A word's origin or its root usually has a meaning that is similar to that of the modern word. Examining a word's origins can help you gain a deeper understanding of its current meaning.

Using the Vocabulary word *intangible,* the example below demonstrates how you can make a word origin map to break down a word's meaning.

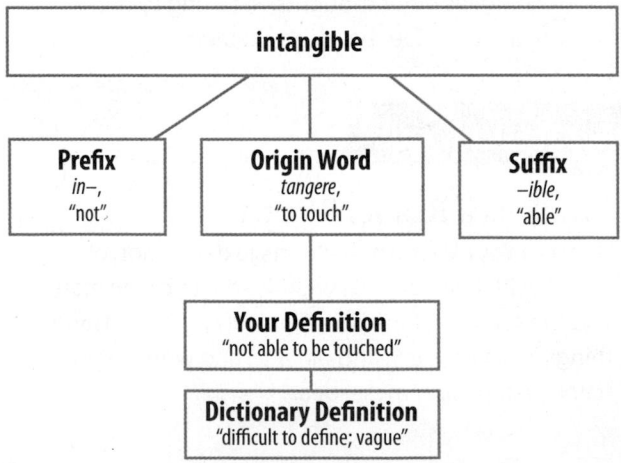

Your Turn

For each of the remaining Vocabulary words, fill out a word origin map like the one on this page. Use a dictionary for help. Some words will not have prefixes or suffixes. (Most dictionaries include prefixes, suffixes, and their meanings in the explanation of the word's origin. Sometimes, the word origin in the dictionary may send you to another word.)

Language Coach

Parts of Speech Both *intangible* and *imperative* can be used as either an adjective or a noun, depending on context. For each word, write two sentences—one that uses the word as an adjective and one that uses it as a noun. Exchange your sentences with those of a classmate, and check to make sure each example uses the word properly.

Academic Vocabulary

Write About
How does London <u>sustain</u> the suspense in "To Build a Fire"? As you read, were you surprised by your <u>capacity</u> to truly worry about the survival of this fictitious main character?

Learn It Online
Learn more about the Vocabulary words online.

go.hrw.com | L11-706 | Go

Grammar Link

Participial Phrases

A **participle** is a verb form used as an adjective. Present participles end in *–ing,* and past participles usually end in *–d* or *–ed*. Perfect participles are formed with *having* or *having been*.

> <u>Prospecting,</u> Jack London went to the Yukon.

> <u>Having seen</u> real danger, he wrote exciting and brutal stories of adventure.

A **participial phrase** consists of a participle and its modifiers and complements. The phrase is used as an adjective.

> "To Build a Fire" describes the final hours of a prospector <u>trapped in the bitter cold</u>.

> <u>Freezing to death</u>, he struggles to build a fire.

An **essential** participial phrase adds information that is necessary to a sentence's meaning and is not set off by commas.

> He pictured the boys <u>finding his body</u> the next day.

A **nonessential** participial phrase is not necessary to a sentence's basic meaning and is set off by commas.

> Suddenly he found himself with them, <u>coming along the trail</u> and <u>looking for himself</u>.

Your Turn

Underline the participial phrases in the following sentences. Set off nonessential phrases with commas.

1. The young Jack London inspired by the stories he read wanted to have real adventures.
2. Seeking gold he traveled to the Yukon in 1897.
3. He wrote vivid stories drawing on his experiences.

CHOICES

As you respond to the Choices, use these **Academic Vocabulary** words as appropriate: <u>capacity</u>, <u>crucial</u>, <u>parameter</u>, <u>relevant</u>, <u>sustain</u>.

REVIEW
Learn the Lesson
Group Discussion In this story, the man's lack of experience with conditions in the Yukon leads to his death. How could this be seen as a cautionary tale about the relationship of humans with nature? What is our <u>capacity</u> to survive in the wild? Gather in a group, and discuss these questions with your classmates.

CONNECT
Dig for Gold
This story draws from London's own experience as a young man in the Yukon. Find another article or story that depicts prospecting for gold in the Yukon or Alaska. Write an essay comparing the setting described in that piece with the setting depicted by London in "To Build a Fire."

EXTEND
Create a Dog's-Eye View
Timed └Writing The dog views the man as a provider, a possible threat, and a strange, foolish animal. Write a paragraph from the dog's point of view, recounting the man's final attempt to build and <u>sustain</u> a fire. Use details from the story to express the dog's point of view or perspective on the events.

Learn It Online
Journey further with Jack London through these Internet links.

go.hrw.com | L11-707 | Go

from **Left for Dead**

What Do You Think

What forces shape human character?

QuickWrite

Think of a time when you or someone you know rose to a challenge so daunting that no one believed success was possible. How did it change your outlook on life? Write a short paragraph explaining the experience.

Informational Text Focus

Identifying Details and Main Idea *Left for Dead* is a detailed, personal narrative of Beck Weathers's harrowing experience surviving a blizzard on Mount Everest. **Details** draw readers into the story and help build suspense, as well as support an implied **main idea.** To identify the main idea, ask yourself, "What did the narrator learn from his experience?"

Into Action In this excerpt, the narrative develops through a series of dangers that Weathers faced in his struggle for survival. As you read, record events in the left-hand column of a chart like the one below. In the middle column, list the details of the event, including the narrator's thoughts, feelings, and responses to the event. In the right-hand column, state the significance of the event.

Events	Details	Significance
Weathers awakens from a coma.	He is hypothermic and frostbitten, but he was "not ready to die," so he starts walking.	Although he is close to death, Weathers is determined to live.

Writing Focus Preparing for **Constructed Response**

The **point of view** determines what information the reader will know. For example, a first-person point of view allows the reader to know only what that one person knows. As you read, use your *Reader/Writer Notebook* to note any information or insights that could be provided only from this particular narrator's point of view.

Reader/Writer Notebook

Use your **RWN** to complete the activities for this selection.

Vocabulary

profoundly (pruh FOWND lee) *adv.*: deeply; completely. *Although Beck was profoundly hypothermic, he was determined to survive.*

encountered (ehn KOWN tuhrd) *v.*: met or confronted. *The climbers encountered many dangers while scaling Mount Everest.*

overwhelmed (oh vuhr HWEHLMD) *adj.*: overpowered. *Beck would not let himself become overwhelmed by fear during his struggle.*

expedition (ehks puh DIHSH uhn) *n.*: journey of exploration. *Luckily, Beck was saved by people on another climbing expedition.*

lurching (LURCH ihng) *adj.*: staggering. *Burleson was startled to see Beck Weathers lurching toward him.*

Language Coach

Word Origins The word *encountered* once meant "met in battle." Look at the definition above. Note how the word is used on page 710. How has its meaning changed? What part of the original sense remains?

from LEFT FOR DEAD

by **Beck Weathers**

On May 10, 1996, Dr. Seaborn ("Beck") Weathers was erroneously reported dead after lying exposed for eighteen hours in a massive blizzard high on the face of Mount Everest. A member of one of several expedition teams scaling Mount Everest at that time, Weathers never reached the summit. The high altitude affected his vision, leaving him wandering blindly and eventually unconscious. Eight climbers lost their lives during that blizzard, but Weathers determinedly clung to his life. The following excerpt tells about his struggle to return to camp after awakening from a deep coma the day after the storm.

I thought I was inured[1] to the idea of dying on the mountain. Such a death may even have seemed to me to have a romantic and noble quality. But even though I was prepared to die, I just wasn't ready. . . .

Both my hands were completely frozen. My face was destroyed by the cold. I was profoundly hypothermic.[2] I had not eaten in three days, or taken water for two days. I was lost and I was almost completely blind. Ⓐ

You cannot sweat that small stuff, I said to myself. You have to *focus* on that which must be done, and do that thing.

I began to move in that same repetitive, energy-conserving motion that my body knows so well. The ground was uneven, scattered with little ledges maybe five to eight inches deep that in the flat light of late afternoon were invisible to me.

---

1. **inured:** accustomed; used to.
2. **hypothermic:** of abnormally low body temperature.

Ⓐ **Informational Focus** Identifying Details and Main Idea How do the details in this short paragraph help you understand Weathers's chances of surviving his experience?

Vocabulary **profoundly** (pruh FOWND lee) *adv.:* deeply; completely.

Advance base camp for people climbing Mount Everest, on the mountain's north slope at about 21,000 feet; author Beck Weathers, soon after rescue.

Each time I encountered one of these hidden ledges, I would fall. At first, I instinctively put out my hands to break the fall, but I didn't want to compound the effects of the frostbite by further damaging my hands, so I held them close to my body and tried to turn on my back, or on my side, each time I slipped and fell. I hit the frozen ground pretty hard. . . . Then I'd get up and start again. . . .

I was overwhelmed by an enormous, encompassing sense of melancholy.[3] That I would not say goodbye to my family, that I would never again say "I love you" to my wife, that I would never again hold my children was just not acceptable.

"Keep moving," I said to myself again and again.

I began to hallucinate[4] again, getting awfully close to losing it. Things were really moving around.

Then I saw these two odd blue rocks in front of me, and I thought for one moment, Those might be

the tents! Just as quickly I said to myself, Don't! When you walk up to them and they are nothing but rocks, you're going to be discouraged and you might stop. *You cannot do that.* You are going to walk right up to them and you are going to walk right past them. It makes *no* difference.

I concentrated on these blue blurs, torn between believing they were camp and fearing they were not, until I got within a hundred feet of them—when suddenly a figure loomed up! It was Todd Burleson, the leader of yet another climbing expedition, who beheld a strange creature lurching toward him in the twilight.

Burleson later shared his first impression of me with a TV interviewer:

"I couldn't believe what I saw. This man had no face. It was completely black, solid black, like he had a crust over him. His jacket was unzipped down to his waist, full of snow. His right arm was bare and frozen over his head. We could not lower it. His skin looked like marble. White stone. No blood in it."

---

3. **melancholy:** sadness; gloom.
4. **hallucinate:** see what is not there; have delusions.

B **Informational Focus** Identifying Details and Main Idea What motivates Weathers to keep moving? What do you think is the most crucial point Weathers wants us to understand about human nature?

C **Informational Focus** Identifying Details and Main Idea What do these final, gruesome details say about Weathers's will to live? What do they suggest about the main idea behind this narrative?

Vocabulary **encountered** (ehn KOWN tuhrd) *v.*: met or confronted.
overwhelmed (oh vuhr HWEHLMD) *adj.*: overpowered.
expedition (ehks puh DIHSH uhn) *n.*: journey of exploration.
lurching (LURCH ihng) *adj.*: staggering.

Applying Your Skills

from **Left for Dead**

SKILLS FOCUS Informational Skills
Identify main ideas and supporting details.
Vocabulary Skills Identify and correctly
use synonyms. **Listening and Speaking
Skills** Listen actively; speak effectively.
Writing Skills Write brief constructed
responses, with specific support.

Respond and Think Critically

Informational Text Focus

Quick Check

1. What causes Weathers to fall repeatedly?

2. Why does Weathers purposely avoid breaking his fall with his hands?

3. Why does Weathers refuse to believe that the "two odd blue rocks" might be tents?

Read with a Purpose

4. How do Weathers's thoughts help him survive?

Informational Skills: Identifying Details and Main Idea

5. While reading, you recorded each event, the details of the event, and the significance of the event. Review your chart. What do you think Weathers wants his readers to learn from his experience? Write a few sentences explaining what you have learned.

Events	Details	Significance
Weathers awakens from a coma.	He is hypothermic and frostbitten, but he was "not ready to die," so he starts walking.	Although he is close to death, Weathers is determined to live.

✔ Vocabulary Check

Match each Vocabulary word with its synonym.

6. profoundly   a. overpowered

7. encountered   b. staggering

8. overwhelmed   c. deeply

9. expedition   d. confronted

10. lurching   e. exploration

Text Analysis

11. **Interpret** What do you think Weathers means when he says "you cannot sweat that small stuff" as he starts his journey back?

12. **Draw Conclusions** What role did Weathers have in his own survival? Explain.

13. **Compare and Contrast** How are the situations in "To Build a Fire" and the excerpt from *Left for Dead* similar? How are they different? How are the two men different psychologically? Explain your responses.

14. **Analyze** How does Weathers's mindset differ from that of London's protagonist? Explain.

15. **Make Judgments** Does Weather's story refute London's naturalistic message? Why or why not?

Listening and Speaking

16. **Draw Conclusions** As you read the excerpt from *Left for Dead*, you recorded details the author included about the effects of extreme cold on the human body. Discuss these effects with a small group of your classmates. What measures can climbers take to protect themselves from the extreme cold?

Writing Focus   Constructed Response

Write a short paragraph in which you discuss the value of first-person details in this excerpt from *Left for Dead*. Be sure to include specific evidence to support your response.

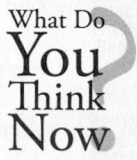

What Do **You Think Now** How do you think Weathers's experience has affected his perspective on life?

Richard Cory
Miniver Cheevy

Portrait of Edwin Arlington Robinson (1916)
by Lilla Cabot Perry. Detail.

What Do You Think?

What forces shape human character?

QuickWrite

Think about a time when someone's actions completely surprised you. Write a few sentences about your observations of the person's outward behavior and explain what took you by surprise.

MEET THE WRITER

Edwin Arlington Robinson
(1869–1935)

Robert Frost once noted that Robinson had "stayed content with the old way to be new." Although he wrote poetry in traditional forms, he did not churn out conventional verse.

A Rocky Beginning

Robinson was a Yankee from the rocky coast of Maine. Born at Head Tide in 1869, he lived for the next twenty-seven years in the town of Gardiner, except for two years when he attended Harvard. Gardiner became the Tilbury Town of his poems, the home of some of his most famous characters. Robinson's portrait poems are mostly about unfortunate, isolated lives. His two best-known figures appear in "Richard Cory" and "Miniver Cheevy," the poems that are included here.

A Bridge Between Centuries

When he was in his late twenties, Robinson moved to New York City, where he worked various jobs. After he spent a year in New York, Robinson's fortunes took a surprising turn for the better. Among the young poet's readers was the President of the United States, Theodore Roosevelt. When Roosevelt learned that the poet he admired was barely scraping by on a laborer's salary, he arranged to have the New York Custom House hire him as a clerk, a position Robinson held for almost five years. One year after Robinson resigned, he published *The Town Down the River* (1910) and dedicated the volume to Roosevelt. Another form of assistance came in an invitation from the famous MacDowell Colony—a center for composers, artists, and writers in Peterborough, New Hampshire. Robinson spent long working summers at the colony for the greater part of his life.

The strengths that distinguish Robinson are his wise and ironic views of human behavior. His bedrock realism informs even the most formal of his carefully wrought poems. His traditional forms link him to the nineteenth century, and his sense of irony links him to the modernists.

Think About the Writer

Why do you think Robinson chose to embrace irony and realism instead of Romanticism?

Richard Cory / Miniver Cheevy

Reader/Writer Notebook

Use your **RWN** to complete the activities for these selections.

Literary Focus

Language and Style: Connotations In Robinson's famous poem "Richard Cory," an unidentified speaker tells what happens to Cory, a prominent town citizen. Robinson never shows it outright, but he implies that the townspeople see Cory as the town's king. The poet achieves this effect by using words with connotations of royalty. Words get such **connotations,** or emotional overtones and associations, through shared usage.

Reading Focus

Reading Closely Poems often pack a broad range of <u>relevant</u> information and ideas into a few lines. Identifying subtle elements and deeper meanings requires **close reading**—a line-by-line examination of the poem's language and imagery. The language in these poems by Robinson contains **allusions**—historical and cultural references—and connotations that are best explored through close reading.

Into Action Create concept maps like the one below as you read each poem. Make one concept map for each stanza. In the center circle, jot down your interpretation of the stanza's meaning. In the outer circles, record the connotative words or phrases and allusions that convey that impression.

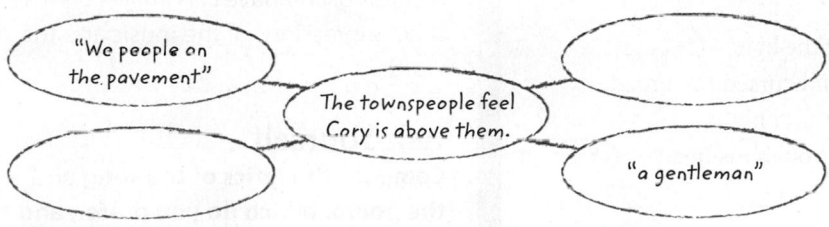

Vocabulary

imperially (ihm PIHR ee uhl lee) *adv.*: grandly; majestically. *Cory presented himself imperially.*

arrayed (uh RAYD) *adj.*: dressed. *Cory always appeared well arrayed in public.*

assailed (uh SAYLD) *v.*: set upon vigorously with hostile words. *Cheevy assailed the universe about his dull fate.*

renown (rih NOWN) *n.*: fame. *Cheevy sought a renown that he would never achieve.*

incessantly (ihn SEHS uhnt lee) *adv.*: continuous; without stop. *Cheevy thought about the past incessantly.*

Language Coach

Suffixes The suffix *–ly* is used to turn adjectives into adverbs. Adjectives modify, or change, nouns (*young* poet). Adverbs modify verbs (wrote *quickly*), adjectives (*quietly* desperate), or other adverbs (*very* carefully). When you learn a new adverb, you can usually add a new adjective to your vocabulary as well. For example, *imperially,* above, is formed by adding the suffix *–ly* to *imperial,* which can mean "grand or majestic." What adjective can you learn from the adverb *incessantly*? What would the adjective's definition be?

Writing Focus

Think as a Reader/Writer

Find It in Your Reading Because word associations often depend on a reader's personal experience, the impact and effect of connotations can vary. As you read, note in your *Reader/Writer Notebook* how Robinson compensates for this by using many different connotative words.

Learn It Online
Meet the other residents of Robinson's imagination through these Internet links.

go.hrw.com | L11-713 | **Go**

RICHARD CORY

by Edwin Arlington Robinson

Read with a Purpose
Read to discover how appearances can be deceiving.

Build Background
One of the persistent themes of early twentieth-century American poetry is that the conventions and behaviors common to small-town life are a facade that often obscures unpleasant realities. In this ironic poem, a small-town resident describes Richard Cory, a wealthy, refined man who is the envy of his less prosperous neighbors. Everything is not how it seems, however.

Whenever Richard Cory went downtown,
    We people on the pavement looked at him:
He was a gentleman from sole to crown,
    Clean favored, and imperially slim. **Ⓐ**

5   And he was always quietly arrayed,
    And he was always human when he talked;
But still he fluttered pulses when he said,
    "Good morning," and he glittered when he walked.

And he was rich—yes, richer than a king—
10   And admirably schooled in every grace:
In fine, we thought that he was everything
    To make us wish that we were in his place.

So on we worked, and waited for the light,
    And went without the meat, and cursed the bread;
15 And Richard Cory, one calm summer night,
    Went home and put a bullet through his head. **Ⓑ**

Ⓐ Literary Focus Language and Style: Connotations What does the poet imply by using the word *crown* instead of *head*? What other word in this stanza has a similar connotation?

Ⓑ Reading Focus Reading Closely How does the description of Cory's suicide contrast with the earlier descriptions of Cory in the poem? How is Cory's death ironic?

Vocabulary **imperially** (ihm PIHR ee uhl lee) *adv.:* grandly; majestically.
arrayed (uh RAYD) *adj.:* dressed.

MUSIC LINK

A Song Based on a Poem

The songwriter Paul Simon adapted Robinson's poem to compose lyrics for the song "Richard Cory." Locate a recording of the song, and distribute copies of the lyrics to the class. Play the recording, and have classmates discuss their impressions of the music and the words.

Ask Yourself
Compare the lyrics of the song and the poem. Which do you prefer, and why?

MINIVER CHEEVY

by **Edwin Arlington Robinson**

Read with a Purpose
Read to discover why Miniver Cheevy is drawn to splendid times in the distant past.

Build Background
The title "Miniver Cheevy" contains a clue to the poem's meaning. The word *miniver* refers to the white fur trim that can be seen on the costumes of royalty in medieval and Renaissance portraits. The subjects of such portraits are usually members of rich and powerful families, such as the Medici family. Other references in the poem also evoke heroic eras of the past.

Miniver Cheevy, child of scorn,   **A**
   Grew lean while he assailed the seasons;
He wept that he was ever born,
   And he had reasons.

5   Miniver loved the days of old
   When swords were bright and steeds were prancing:
The vision of a warrior bold
   Would set him dancing.

Miniver sighed for what was not,
10   And dreamed, and rested from his labors;
He dreamed of Thebes° and Camelot,°
   And Priam's° neighbors.

Miniver mourned the ripe renown
   That made so many a name so fragrant;
15   He mourned Romance, now on the town,°
   And Art, a vagrant.°

11. Thebes (theebz): a famous city in ancient Greece associated with many myths. **Camelot:** legendary site of King Arthur's court.
12. Priam's: In Homer's epic poem about the Trojan War, the *Iliad*, Priam is the king of Troy.
15. on the town: debased; corrupted.
16. vagrant: wanderer; beggar.

A **Literary Focus** **Language and Style: Connotations** Robinson calls Cheevy a "child of scorn." What emotional overtones does this phrase have?

Vocabulary **assailed** (uh SAYLD) *v.:* set upon vigorously with hostile words.
renown (rih NOWN) *n.:* fame.

Alfred, Son of Asher Wertheimer
(1901) by John Singer Sargent.

Miniver loved the Medici,°
    Albeit° he had never seen one;
He would have sinned incessantly
20   Could he have been one.

Miniver cursed the commonplace
    And eyed a khaki suit with loathing;
He missed the medieval grace
    Of iron clothing.°

25 Miniver scorned the gold he sought,
    But sore annoyed was he without it;
Miniver thought, and thought, and thought,
    And thought about it.   **B**

Miniver Cheevy, born too late,
30   Scratched his head and kept on thinking;
Miniver coughed, and called it fate,
    And kept on drinking.

17. Medici (MEHD uh chee): members of a wealthy Italian family during the Renaissance. They were famous for their power, their sponsorship of the arts, and their harsh rule over the city of Florence.
18. albeit: even though. The word combines and condenses "although it be."
24. iron clothing: armor worn by medieval knights.

B **Reading Focus** **Reading Closely** Why do you think Robinson repeats the word *thought* four times?

Vocabulary **incessantly** (ihn SEHS uhnt lee) *adv.:* continuously; without stop.

Applying Your Skills

Richard Cory / Miniver Cheevy

Respond and Think Critically

Reading Focus

Quick Check

1. According to the speaker in "Richard Cory," why do people envy Cory?

2. Name three historical or literary allusions in "Miniver Cheevy."

3. How does Cheevy cope with his lot in life?

Read with a Purpose

4. Why do you think Cory and Cheevy are so unhappy?

Reading Skills: Reading Closely

5. During your close reading of the poems, you recorded impressions of each stanza and connotative words or phrases that supported those impressions. Now, review your concept maps. What seems to be the main impression that each poem conveys? In a few sentences, explain what those impressions are and how a close reading of each poem reveals them.

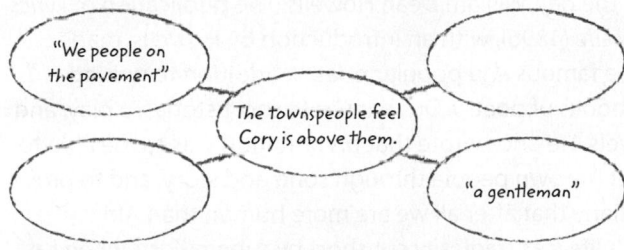

"We people on the pavement"

The townspeople feel Cory is above them.

"a gentleman"

✓ Vocabulary Check

Match each Vocabulary word with its synonym.

6. imperially   a. prestige

7. arrayed   b. attacked

8. assailed   c. magnificently

9. renown   d. ceaselessly

10. incessantly   e. attired

Literary Focus

Literary Analysis

11. **Infer** In "Richard Cory," what assumptions do people make about Cory because he is rich?

12. **Draw Conclusions** How might the hidden aspects of Cory's life account for his fate?

13. **Interpret** In "Miniver Cheevy," what do you think "child of scorn" means?

14. **Analyze** What does Cheevy think has happened to romance and art in his own time?

15. **Draw Conclusions** Do Cheevy's problems really stem from being "born too late"? Explain.

Literary Skills: Connotations

16. **Analyze** Find at least five words or phrases in "Richard Cory" with connotations of royalty. Replace each with a neutral one that has no strong connotations. How is the effect of the poem changed?

Literary Skills Review: Tone

17. **Analyze** The attitude a writer takes toward a subject or characters is called **tone.** How does the tone shift in the last stanza of each poem?

Writing Focus

Think as a Reader/Writer

Use It in Your Writing Write a poem that describes a unique character of your own creation. Choose words with connotations that support the poem's meaning.

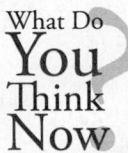

What Do You Think Now

Think about what these poems say about the relationship between appearance and character. What message do these poems have for readers today?

Preparing to Read

Douglass
We Wear the Mask

QuickWrite

Recall a time when you or someone you know felt pain or anxiety but chose to hide it. Write a few sentences about what was gained and lost by not revealing the pain or anxiety.

MEET THE WRITER

Paul Laurence Dunbar
(1872–1906)

During his brief life, Paul Laurence Dunbar became one of the first African American writers to attain national prominence and to support himself wholly by his writing.

An African American Pioneer

Dunbar, who was born in Dayton, Ohio, was the son of former slaves. Though poor and unschooled, his parents were ambitious for their son and predicted greatness for him. The only African American student in his high school class, Dunbar was the president of the literary society, editor of the school newspaper, and class poet.

After graduation, Dunbar took a job as an elevator operator and composed poems in his spare time. During a meeting in Dayton of the Western Association of Writers, a former teacher asked him to prepare an address of welcome. Dunbar delivered a poem. Impressed, the members of the association showed some of his poems to the famous writer James Whitcomb Riley, who responded with an encouraging letter of congratulations. Within a year Dunbar published his first volume of poetry, *Oak and Ivy* (1893).

Quick Ascent, Tragic Demise

A second collection, *Majors and Minors,* appeared the following year and received a laudatory review from the most influential critic of the day, William Dean Howells. The publication of *Lyrics of Lowly Life* (1896), with an introduction by Howells, made Dunbar a famous and popular poet. In addition to writing twelve books of poetry, Dunbar wrote short stories, a play, and five novels. He once wrote that his ambition was to "be able to interpret my own people through song and story, and to prove to the many that after all we are more human than African." Dunbar's life was tragically cut short by tuberculosis when he was only thirty-three.

Think About the Writer

What kinds of obstacles do you think Dunbar might have faced during his career as a writer?

Paul Laurence Dunbar as a young man, c. 1890.

Douglass

Reader/Writer Notebook

Use your **RWN** to complete the activities for this selection.

Literary Focus

Rhyme Scheme The pattern of rhymes in a poem is called a **rhyme scheme.** Rhyme scheme is commonly indicated by letters of the alphabet, with each rhyming sound represented by a different letter. For example, the rhyme scheme for the first four lines of "Douglass" is *abba:*

Ah, Douglass, we have fall'n on evil days,	*a*
Such days as thou, not even thou didst know,	*b*
When thee, the eyes of that harsh long ago	*b*
Saw, salient, at the cross of devious ways,	*a*

In addition to shaping a poem's musical qualities, a rhyme scheme can help <u>sustain</u> a tone, unify stanzas, and create structure within the poem.

"Douglass" is a **sonnet,** a fourteen-line poem that usually has two basic structures. The form Dunbar uses is the **Petrarchan,** or **Italian sonnet.** Its first eight lines, called the **octave,** ask a question or pose a problem. These lines usually have the rhyme scheme *abbaabba.* The last six lines, called the **sestet,** respond to the question or problem. These lines may have the rhyme scheme *cdecde* or some other pattern.

Into Action As you read "Douglass," determine the rhyme scheme in the octave and sestet. Then, comment on how the rhyme scheme influences the meaning of each line and the meaning of the entire poem.

Section	Rhyme Scheme	Effect on Meaning
Octave (lines 1–8)		
Sestet (lines 9–14)		

Writing Focus

Think as a Reader/Writer

Find It in Your Reading Petrarchan sonnets are made up of two parts—the octave and the sestet. Re-read the poem and think about how these two sections of the poem are different. What is the primary focus of the octave? What is the focus in the sestet? How does the two-part structure reinforce the meaning of "Douglass"? Jot down your responses in your *Reader/Writer Notebook.*

Vocabulary

salient (SAY lee uhnt) *adj.:* prominent; striking. *Dunbar's admiration of Douglass is one of the poem's salient features.*

tempest (TEHM pihst) *n.:* violent storm. *The speaker senses that he and his people are in the center of a tempest.*

dissension (dih SEHN shuhn) *n.:* hard feeling caused by a difference of opinion. *The speaker feels surrounded by dissension.*

Language Coach

Latin Roots The word *dissension* is rooted in the Latin word *sentire,* meaning "to feel." Many English words come from this root, such as *sense, sensitive,* and *consent.* With a partner, list at least five other words that come from this root. (Hint: Try applying the prefixes *in–* or *non–*, the suffixes *–ible, –tion,* and so on.)

Learn It Online
Hear this poem's rhyme scheme come to life online.

go.hrw.com   L11-719   **Go**

Douglass

by **Paul Laurence Dunbar**

The Life of Frederick Douglass, #30 (1939) by Jacob Lawrence.

Read with a Purpose
Read to discover why Dunbar laments the loss of Frederick Douglass.

Build Background
In 1893, Dunbar met Frederick Douglass, the famous African American lecturer, editor, and leader. Both men thought very highly of each other. In fact, Dunbar wrote several poems honoring the famous abolitionist. The poem "Douglass," published almost ten years after Douglass's death in 1895, contrasts Douglass's life with the time in which Dunbar was living. In it, the speaker laments the loss of Douglass and his leadership.

Ah, Douglass, we have fall'n on evil days,
    Such days as thou, not even thou didst know,
    When thee, the eyes of that harsh long ago
Saw, salient, at the cross of devious ways,
5 And all the country heard thee with amaze.
    Not ended then, the passionate ebb and flow,
    The awful tide that battled to and fro;
We ride amid a tempest of dispraise.   **Ⓐ**

Now, when the waves of swift dissension swarm,
10   And Honor, the strong pilot, lieth° stark,
Oh, for thy voice high-sounding o'er the storm,
    For thy strong arm to guide the shivering bark,°
The blast-defying power of thy form,
    To give us comfort through the lonely dark. **Ⓑ**

10. lieth: archaic form of *lies*.

12. bark: archaic for "ship."

Ⓐ Literary Focus **Rhyme Scheme** What is the rhyme scheme of the first eight lines? Why does the poet end line 5 with *amaze* instead of *amazement*?

Ⓑ Literary Focus **Rhyme Scheme** Notice how the rhyme scheme changes in the last six lines. How do the rhymes emphasize Dunbar's theme?

Vocabulary **salient** (SAY lee uhnt) *adj.:* prominent; striking.
tempest (TEHM pihst) *n.:* violent storm.
dissension (dih SEHN shuhn) *n.:* hard feeling caused by a difference of opinion.

Preparing to Read

We Wear the Mask

Reader/Writer Notebook

Use your **RWN** to complete the activities for this selection.

Literary Focus

Symbol In literature, a **symbol** is a person, place, thing, or event that represents an abstract idea or concept. Common examples include a rose as a symbol of love and darkness as a symbol of death.

In "We Wear the Mask," the mask is the central symbol, but much of the figurative language and imagery has symbolic meaning as well. As you read, note what the mask and other elements of the poem symbolize.

Reading Focus

Analyzing Author's Purpose An **author's purpose** can be to describe, to inform, to entertain, or to persuade. In some cases, the author's purpose is clear or even directly stated in the text. Sometimes, however, the purpose is less explicit and must be inferred from a close reading of the text. Dunbar often reveals his purpose by using symbolism and figurative language to express ideas.

Into Action Close examination of Dunbar's symbols and their meanings can help reveal his purpose for writing the poem. As you read, use a chart like the one below to record the poem's symbols and what they represent. In the last column, note what you think Dunbar's purpose was for choosing each element as a symbol.

Symbol	Meaning	Purpose
"torn and bleeding hearts"	African Americans' deep emotional pain and sadness	The violent, gruesome image reflects how severe the pain is.

Writing Focus

Think as a Reader/Writer

Find It in Your Reading In addition to their literal meanings within poems, symbols have the <u>capacity</u> to evoke emotional responses in the reader. As you read, use your *Reader/Writer Notebook* to record the feelings that the poem's symbols evoke in you.

Vocabulary

guile (gyl) *n.:* deceitfulness in dealing with others. *The speaker resents having to live a life of guile.*

myriad (MIHR ee uhd) *adj.:* innumerable; countless. *There are myriad reasons for his suffering.*

Language Coach

Pronunciation When the letter *g* is followed by *e* or *i*, it generally makes a soft *j* sound, as in *germ* or *engine*. As a rule, when the letter *u* comes between *g* and *e* or *i*, the *g* is hard and the *u* is silent—as in *guile*. However, this is one of those rules that has many exceptions. With a partner, pronounce each of the following words: *guilt, guess, guerrilla, tiger, fatigue, penguin, anguish, beguile*. To which words does the rule above apply? Which words are exceptions to the rule?

Learn It Online
Hear this poem in a whole new way online.

go.hrw.com   L11-721   **Go**

We Wear the Mask

by **Paul Laurence Dunbar**

Read with a Purpose

Read to discover one of the more subtle ways in which African Americans faced oppression.

Build Background

To Dunbar's great disappointment, the works that critics and the public most admired were his sentimental, supposedly authentic plantation lyrics written in African American dialect. However, Dunbar strove to write first and foremost as a poet of the English language, expressing universal values and feelings. In "We Wear the Mask," Dunbar explores the frustration and anguish that arose from the period's conflicting perceptions of African American identity. The poem deals with the incongruity between some African Americans' cheerful self-presentation and their inner state of anguish.

We wear the mask that grins and lies,
It hides our cheeks and shades our eyes,—
This debt we pay to human guile;
With torn and bleeding hearts we smile,
5   And mouth with myriad subtleties.

Why should the world be overwise,
In counting all our tears and sighs?
Nay, let them only see us, while
        We wear the mask.

10   We smile, but, O great Christ, our cries
To thee from tortured souls arise.   **Ⓐ**
We sing, but oh the clay is vile
Beneath our feet, and long the mile;
But let the world dream otherwise,
15   We wear the mask!   **Ⓑ**

Ⓐ **Reading Focus** **Analyzing Author's Purpose** Notice how the speaker contrasts the word *smile* with the "cries . . . from tortured souls." Why do you think the speaker makes this contrast?

Ⓑ **Literary Focus** **Symbol** What does the mask symbolize? Why do African Americans wear it?

Vocabulary **guile** (gyl) *n.*: deceitfulness in dealing with others.
myriad (MIHR ee uhd) *adj.*: innumerable; countless.

Analyzing Visuals

Viewing and Interpreting How might the words in Dunbar's poem apply to the people in this photograph? Even though they are not smiling, might they still be wearing "masks"?

Respond and Think Critically

Reading Focus

Quick Check

1. In "Douglass," for what does the speaker long?

2. What is the "mask" to which Dunbar refers in "We Wear the Mask"?

3. What social issues do both poems address?

Read with a Purpose

4. What do you think Frederick Douglass represents to Dunbar?

5. In "We Wear the Mask," what purpose does the mask serve for African Americans?

Reading Skills: Analyzing Author's Purpose

6. While reading "We Wear the Mask," you recorded symbols and their meanings, as well as why Dunbar chose each symbol. Based on the purposes that you listed for each of Dunbar's symbols, what can you infer about Dunbar's overall purpose for writing the poem?

Symbol	Meaning	Purpose
"torn and bleeding hearts"	African Americans' deep emotional pain and sadness	The violent, gruesome image reflects how severe the pain is.

✓ Vocabulary Check

Match each Vocabulary word with its antonym.

7. salient   **a.** calm

8. tempest   **b.** insignificant

9. dissension   **c.** honesty

10. guile   **d.** few

11. myriad   **e.** agreement

Literary Focus

Literary Analysis

12. Interpret How does the poet use metaphor to praise the strength of Frederick Douglass?

13. Draw Conclusions In "We Wear the Mask," what is the effect of the allusion to Christ?

14. Infer What is the theme of "We Wear the Mask"?

15. Extend Do you believe that hiding pain can make one stronger in the eyes of an oppressor?

Literary Skills: Rhyme Scheme / Symbol

16. Analyze In "Douglass," how does Dunbar use the rhyme scheme to reflect the changing temperament of the sea in lines 9–14?

17. Interpret In "We Wear the Mask," what is the symbol in lines 12–13? What does it represent?

Literary Skills Review: Refrain

18. Analyze A **refrain** is a line or group of lines repeated at intervals. What is the refrain in "We Wear the Mask"? How and why does it change in line 15?

Writing Focus

Think as a Reader/Writer

Use It in Your Writing Write a short poem about an object that has symbolic meaning for you. Use structural elements like rhyme scheme and stanza breaks to reinforce the emotional effect of the symbol.

 **What Do You Think Now** How do you think Dunbar's experiences as an African American in his time in history shaped his perspective?

Writing Workshop

Reflective Essay

Write with a Purpose

Write a reflective essay in which you explore an experience from your life and share its significance with readers. Your **purpose** is to express yourself. Your **audience** is your classmates, your teacher, and anyone else you think might be interested in your experience.

A Good Reflective Essay

- focuses on a single, meaningful experience
- includes narrative details that relate actions, thoughts, and feelings as well as depict dialogue and internal monologues
- conveys a complete image of the experience through descriptive details that appeal to the senses
- organizes events and details in an understandable order
- clearly expresses the significance of the experience

See page 732 for complete rubric.

Reader/Writer Notebook

Use your **RWN** to complete the activities for this workshop.

Think as a Reader/Writer

Many of the literary elements that you have analyzed are also important to reflective essays. Before you write your own **reflective essay,** read this excerpt from "Coming into the Country" (page 10), in which Gish Jen reflects on her experience as an immigrant to the United States.

In the Old World, there was one way of life, or 2, maybe 10. Here there are dozens, hundreds, all jammed in together, cheek by jowl, especially in the dizzying cities. Everywhere has a somewhere else just around the corner. We newish Americans leapfrog from world to world, reinventing ourselves en route. We perform our college selves, our waitress selves, our dot-com selves, our parent selves, our downtown selves, our Muslim, Greek, Hindi, South African selves. Even into the second or third generation, we speak different languages—more languages, often, than we know we know. We sport different names. I am Gish, Geesh, Jen, Lillian, Lil, Bilien, Ms. Jen, Miss Ren, Mrs. O'Connor. Or maybe we insist on one name. . . .

. . . It's a kind of high, switching spiels, eating Ethiopian, French, Thai, getting around. . . . Who could give up even the quotidian[1] luxury of choosing, that small swell of power: to walk or to drive? The soup or the salad? The green or the blue? We bubble with pleasure. It's me. I'm taking the plane. I'll take the sofa, the chair, the whole shebang—why not?

Why not, indeed? A most American question, a question that comes to dominate our most private self-talk. In therapy-speak, we Americans like to give ourselves permission. To do what? To take care of ourselves, to express ourselves, to listen to ourselves. We tune out the loudspeaker of duty, tune in to the whisper of desire. This is faint at first, but soon proves easily audible; indeed, irresistible. Why not go to town? Why not move away? Why not marry out? Why not? Why not? Why not?

> *Gish uses vivid details to capture readers' attention immediately.*

> *She uses first-person point of view (I, we).*

> *Gish uses sensory details to illustrate the countless choices suddenly available to her.*

> *She hints at the significance of experience—her first taste of overwhelming freedom of choice.*

1. **quotidian:** everyday; commonplace.

Think About the Professional Model

With a partner, discuss the following questions about the model.

1. Which details in the first paragraph do you find most interesting? Why?
2. How does repetition in the essay affect your understanding of the experience?

Prewriting

Think About Purpose and Audience

Your **purpose** in writing a reflective essay is to explore your experience and express its **significance,** or importance, to an audience. You'll not only discover and share the significance of the experience you describe, but you'll also go beyond the specifics to show how it compares and connects to the beliefs that you hold as important and the ideas that you have about life. Your **audience** will be your classmates and teacher, but might also include people who were involved in your experience. Also consider a wider audience of people you think your experience might entertain or inspire.

Choose an Experience

Think back on the experiences that have been important in your life. The experience you write about might be something as simple as feeding a pet or overhearing a conversation; however, it must be an experience that has taught you something about yourself or the world. For example, feeding a pet may have taught you responsibility and compassion for living things. To activate your memory, you might look at journals, scrapbooks, diaries, or photo albums. You might also try reading published reflective essays, memoirs, or autobiographies for ideas to inspire you. Keep your audience in mind when you are selecting an experience to explore. Which experiences will interest them? Be sure your experience is something you'll feel comfortable sharing with all your readers.

Reflect on Meaning

Once you've chosen an experience to explore, spend some time reflecting not only on what the experience meant to you at the time it occurred, but also on what it means to you now. As a springboard for reflection, answer the following questions:

- What did I feel during this experience? What did I feel when I thought about it shortly afterward? How do I feel about it now?
- What did I learn about others and myself from this experience?
- How did this experience influence what I believe about other people, human nature, or life in general? How have my beliefs changed or developed since then?

Sum It All Up

Now, write one or two sentences that sum up the significance of your experience. These sentences will appear at the end of your essay, but writing down your ideas now will remind you of the larger meaning you want to convey to readers. Every detail you include in your essay should help to communicate the meaning of your experience.

Idea Starters

- an unexpected friendship
- a frightening encounter
- a worthwhile task
- a visit to a new place
- an epiphany, or sudden insight

Your Turn _____

Get Started Making notes in your **RWN**, decide on the **experience** you will write about in your reflective essay. Then answer the **questions** on this page about the experience. Write a sentence that states the **significance** of the experience.

 Learn It Online
To see how one writer completed this assignment, see the model reflective essay online.

go.hrw.com | L11-725 | Go

⬤ Writing Tip

Here are some suggestions to help you recall as many details about your experience as you can.

- Close your eyes and visualize the experience.
- Discuss your experience with a friend or family member. Talking about it may help you remember more details. Someone who was present at the experience may recall details you have forgotten.
- Look through photos or souvenirs of the experience.

Gather and Arrange Details

Gather the **details** that will bring the experience to life and convince your readers that it is significant. First, list the individual **events** that made up the experience. Often, reflective essays use **chronological order**—the order in which events occurred—to relate the sequence of events that make up the experience. The writer of the student model that begins on page 729 created the following list of events that made up her experience.

> ### Events
> 1. drive out to farm from school
> 2. brush Mac
> 3. head down to dressage area
> 4. practice
> 5. walk Mac out of arena
> 6. feed Mac and clean up
> 7. drive back to town

Once you have a well-ordered list of events, brainstorm **narrative and descriptive details** that will help you create a more complete picture of each event. These details should describe the who, what, when, where, how, and why of the experience. The chart below gives explanations of the types of details to include along with examples from the student model.

Types of Details	Examples
Narrative Details	
Tell the **actions, thoughts,** and **feelings** of the people involved.	*I climb into the truck and shut the door. My mind is clear and spirit renewed.*
Include **dialogue** and **interior monologue,** your internal flow of thoughts.	*I am at the barn. I am home.*
Descriptive Details	
Use **sensory language** that appeals to the five senses (sight, hearing, smell, taste, and touch) to describe events, people, and places.	*The sweet smell of leather and warm scent of horse sweat from the saddle in my back seat overcome me.*
Incorporate **figurative language** (such as **similes** and **metaphors**) to create memorable images of your experience.	*The day's trials are blown out of the window. We are no longer two separate beings, but one.*

Within the chronological order of events, you can arrange details **spatially** or by **order of importance**. For example, you could describe an important person in your reflective essay from head to toe, or you could begin with his or her most prominent features, such as a sincere smile or huge, shovel-like hands.

Your Turn _____

Gather and Arrange Details To help you generate details for your essay, create a chart of narrative and descriptive details like the one on this page. Then, arrange the details in an order that makes sense. As you brainstorm and arrange details, keep your audience in mind. What do you need to tell readers so they can understand your experience and its significance?

Draft Your Reflective Essay

As you write your first draft, keep in mind the essentials of a good reflective essay listed on page 724. Review your prewriting notes and use the **Writer's Framework** to the right as a guide.

Consider Tone and Voice

Because reflective essays are personal in nature, your **tone**—the feeling you convey—should be informal. Your **voice**—the unique way you express yourself—should also come through. **Informal language,** such as contractions, slang, colloquialisms, and first-person pronouns *(I, me, my, we, us, ours),* are acceptable in this type of writing. In addition, you can make sentence-structure choices, such as adding **participial phrases,** to express tone and voice in your writing.

Framework for a Reflective Essay

Introduction
- Engage the reader's attention.
- Provide background information to establish a context for the experience.
- Hint at the significance of your experience.

Body
- Describe the people, places, and sequence of events.
- Include your thoughts and feelings.
- Make the order of the events clear.

Conclusion
- State the significance of the experience.
- Connect the experience to life in general.

● Writing Tip

A reflective essay is one of the few essays that should be written using first-person point of view (*I, me, my, we, us, ours*). Maintain a consistent first-person point of view throughout your essay.

Grammar Link Using Participial Phrases

Study the following sentences from "Coming into the Country." Note in particular how Gish Jen uses phrases at the ends of sentences to create a vibrant tone and to make her voice clear and personal.

> We newish Americans leapfrog from world to world, **reinventing ourselves en route.**

A **participle** is a verb form that is used as an adjective. A **participial phrase** consists of a participle and all words related to the participle. In the example sentence above, *reinventing* is the participle; *reinventing ourselves en route* is the participial phrase.

Participial phrases can also be used to add variety to the sentence beginnings in your essay. For instance, the example sentence above could be rewritten in the following way:

> **Reinventing ourselves en route,** we newish Americans leapfrog from world to world.

As you write your draft, use participial phrases to add life and variety to your sentences.

Reference Note For more on participles and participial phrases, see the Language Handbook.

Your Turn _____

Write Your Draft Using the narrative and descriptive details you have generated and the **Writer's Framework** on this page, write a draft of your reflective essay. Also consider how you can use participial phrases to express tone and voice in your writing. Always keep your purpose and audience in mind as you write.

Peer Review

Working with a partner, review your draft using the chart at the right.

- Point out detailed descriptions that are expressive and clear, as well as descriptions that need clarifying.
- In addition to constructive criticism, always give positive feedback about what the writer does well. Be especially careful not to critique the writer's experience.

Evaluating and Revising

Read the questions in the left-hand column of the chart and then use the tips in the middle column to help you make revisions to your reflective essay. The right-hand column suggests techniques you can use to revise your draft.

Reflective Essay: Guidelines for Content and Organization

Evaluation Question	Tip	Revision Technique
1. Does the introduction capture the reader's attention?	**Bracket** any attention-getting anecdote, question, or interesting statement.	**Replace** weak opening sentences with an anecdote, a question, or an interesting statement.
2. Does the introduction give a hint about the significance of the experience?	**Underline** the sentence or sentences in the introduction that hint at the significance of the experience.	**Add** a sentence or two that hint at the significance of the experience.
3. Is the sequence of events presented clearly and in an order that makes sense?	**Number** each event. If the sequence of events is not clear or logically organized, revise.	**Add** missing events, or **delete** events that do not relate to the experience. **Rearrange** events to make the order clear to the reader.
4. Do narrative and descriptive details describe the people, places, and events?	**Circle** the sentences that help readers imagine the events, people, and places.	**Add** details that clarify the experience, including details about what people do, say, or think, and **add** sensory details.
5. Is the tone appropriate to the experience? Does the writer's voice come through in the writing?	**Star** words or sentences that indicate tone. **Double star** words or sentences that show the reader's voice.	**Replace** words or sentences that do not fit the tone of the experience. **Reword** overly formal words, phrases, or sentences that do not convey a natural way of speaking.
6. Does the conclusion make the significance of the experience clear? Does it include a final statement that connects the experience to life in general?	**Underline** the sentence that relates to the meaning of the experience. **Double underline** the statement that relates to ideas about life in general.	**Add** a sentence that states the importance of the experience, or **revise** sentences so that they clearly convey the importance. **Add** a sentence that makes a generalization about life.

Read this student's draft with comments on its structure and suggestions for how it could be made even stronger.

Student Draft

Outside of a Horse

by Kim Moulton, Harrison High School

I climb into the truck and shut the door. The sweet smell of leather and warm scent of horse sweat from the saddle in my back seat overcome me. The motor kicks to life and windows roll down as if of their own accord, and we're off. The day's trials are blown out of the window, replaced with the cool October air and sounds of country music on the radio. Soon, the crowded blacktop morphs into a quiet gravel road. I am at the barn. I am home.

I grab the brush and begin brushing my horse, Mac. Any last remnants of the day's stress disappear once I swing my leg over his back and settle into the comfort of a well-broken-in saddle and company of an old friend. My mind is clear and spirit renewed. We head down to the dressage arena for a quick warm-up and prepare to work on perfecting our lateral work. I can feel Mac soften through his back and accept the bit, and we are no longer two separate beings, but one. We are a team, a force to be reckoned with.

← Kim's introduction grabs readers' attention with vivid details. Note sensory details that appeal to smell, hearing, touch, and sight.

← The last sentence of her first paragraph hints at the experience's significance.

← This paragraph describes the preparation for the day's ride.

MINI-LESSON ▶ **How to Set the Scene by Adding Details**

Abrupt shifts from one scene to another can be disorienting to readers. To help your readers move from one place to another, set the scene by adding details about the new setting. Kim added narrative and descriptive details to set the scene for her second paragraph, creating a transition and orienting the reader.

Kim's Draft of Paragraphs 1 and 2

. . . Soon, the crowded blacktop morphs into a quiet gravel road. I am at the barn. I am home.

I grab the brush and begin brushing my horse, Mac. Any last remnants of the day's stress disappear once I swing my leg over his back and settle into the comfort of a well-broken-in saddle and company of an old friend.

Kim's Revision of Paragraph 2

. . . Soon, the crowded blacktop morphs into a quiet gravel road. I am at the barn. I am home.

~~I grab the brush and begin brushing my horse, Mac.~~ Any last remnants of the day's stress disappear once I swing my leg over his back and settle into the comfort of a well-broken-in saddle and company of an old friend.

As I walk through the massive wooden doors, my horse's soft nicker greets me. The sound of my boots on the stained concrete aisle reverberates off the weathered cedar walls. My worries and stress fade away like the dirt on Mac's coat as I groom him.

Your Turn _____

Set the Scene Read your draft and then ask yourself, "What details can I add to help set the scene and provide transitions between scenes?" Add details as necessary.

Student Draft *continues*

Kim reflects on what riding has taught her.

She provides details to illustrate her point.

It is through riding that I became the student that I am today, and through school that I became the rider. Horseback riding teaches important qualities, such as patience, perseverance, and the yearning for perfection. Waiting for the right take-off spots in jumping, fighting to get that perfect balance of power and grace in dressage, and pushing the trust between horse and rider in cross-country translate easily into the skills needed to be successful in math, language arts, and science. I frequently call on the patience I have learned in riding lessons when helping struggling peers. If my grades in school ever fell below my parents' standard, my riding lessons would be gone. Therefore, I work hard both in and out of school to do well, making my parents' threat unnecessary. I want to get A's in all my classes; I want to keep improving. This attitude transfers into my riding as well. Even when I earn a 75 percent on a dressage test (a great score) or go clear in my jump course, I look for how I could improve. School and riding demand perfection, and I strive in both. They become a part of me, and I become a part of them.

Again, vivid sensory details help the reader to connect with Kim's experience and her reflections.

Kim sums up the significance of her experience—caring for and riding her horse make her a better person.

It was a good ride. We made considerable progress in our dressage, and I can see what areas need improvement. I pat Mac on the shoulder, telling him what a good boy he is, and walk him out of the arena. Once back at the barn, the refreshing mint smell of liniment fills both our nostrils. The steam rises from Mac's back as I remove my saddle and pad. After hosing him off, I return him to his stall. Mac's friendly whinny tells me that I am not preparing his hard-earned dinner fast enough, and I quickly deliver it to his bucket. I load my tack into the truck and begin my journey back to civilization. As Ronald Reagan once said, "There's nothing better for the inside of a man than the outside of a horse."

MINI-LESSON ▶ How to Add Interior Monologue

Kim can give her readers even greater insight into her thoughts and the meaning of her experience by including **interior monologue**—examples of her actual thoughts and feelings as the experience unfolded. She decided to add some thoughts to clarify her demand for perfection.

Kim's Revision to Paragraph 4

Even when I earn a 75 percent on a dressage test (a great score) or go clear in my jump course, I look for how I could improve. ∧*Thoughts such as, "Maybe if I had kept Mac rounder through that transition . . ." or "if I had cut that corner a little more . . ." always run through my head.* School and riding demand perfection, and I strive in both.

Your Turn _____

Add Interior Monologue Read your draft again to look for places where you could add what you were thinking or feeling at any given point. Of course, include only thoughts that will provide insight into your experience and that you feel comfortable sharing.

Proofreading and Publishing

Proofread

When people read your reflective essay, you want them to focus on your experience and its meaning, not on imperfections in grammar, punctuation, or spelling. **Proofread,** or **edit,** your paper individually, collaboratively, or both. Keep proofreading until your essay is error-free.

In reflective essays, you may express more than one action or describe somone or something using multiple details. When you do, make sure you use **parallel structure.**

Grammar Link Using Parallel Structure

Use **parallel structure** (the same grammatical form) to express ideas of equal weight. For instance, use parallel structure when you link coordinate ideas, when you compare and contrast ideas, and when you link ideas with correlative conjunctions (*both . . . and, either . . . or*). Kim uses parallel structures effectively throughout her essay. However, when she proofread her draft, she discovered a sentence that needed revision.

> I pat Mac on the shoulder, telling him what a good boy he is, and walk him out of the arena.

Notice how Kim revised the sentence to create parallel structure (*pat, tell, walk*).

Reference Note For more on parallel structure, see the Language Handbook.

Publish

Now that you've reflected on the significance of your experience, share what you have learned with others. Try one or more of the ideas below to share your reflective essay with a larger audience.

- If other people were involved in the experience, send them a copy of your reflection. Add photos, if you have them, to increase its visual appeal.
- Submit your essay to your high school's literary magazine or Web site.
- If your reflection centers around a certain place or activity, send it to related groups. For example, Kim, the writer of the student model, could have sent her essay to the riding association to which she belongs.

Reflect on the Process In your **RWN,** write a short response to each of the following questions.

1. How did you choose an experience for your essay? Do you think you made a good choice? Why or why not?
2. Did writing about the experience change your thoughts and feelings about it? Explain.
3. What would you do differently if you were to write another reflective essay?

Proofreading Tip

Proofread your paper more than once, each time looking for a specific type of error. For example, on your first read, check spelling; on your second read, check grammar, and so on. Clear your mind between proofreading passes by reading something else, such as a newspaper, magazine, or Web site.

Your Turn
Proofread and Publish

Proofread your draft. As you proofread, look for sentences that need revision to create parallel structures: for instance, items in a list, ideas linked with correlative conjunctions, and ideas being compared or contrasted. Then, publish a final copy of your reflection.

Scoring Rubric

Use one of the rubrics below to evaluate your reflective essay from the Writing Workshop or your response to the on-demand prompt on the next page. Your teacher will tell you to use either the six- or the four-point rubric.

6-Point Scale

Score 6 *Demonstrates advanced success*
- focuses consistently on narrating a single experience or a unified sequence of experiences
- shows effective narrative sequence throughout, with smooth transitions
- offers a thoughtful, creative approach to the reflection
- develops the reflection thoroughly, using vivid descriptive and narrative details
- exhibits mature control of written language

Score 5 *Demonstrates proficient success*
- focuses on narrating a single experience or a unified sequence of experiences
- shows effective narrative sequence, with transitions
- offers a thoughtful approach to the reflection
- develops the reflection competently, using descriptive and narrative details
- exhibits sufficient control of written language

Score 4 *Demonstrates competent success*
- focuses on narrating a single experience or a unified sequence of experiences, with minor distractions
- shows effective narrative sequence, with minor lapses
- offers a mostly thoughtful approach to the reflection
- develops the reflection adequately, with some descriptive and narrative details
- exhibits general control of written language

Score 3 *Demonstrates limited success*
- includes some loosely related material that distracts from the writer's narrative focus
- shows some organization, with noticeable flaws in the narrative flow
- offers a routine, predictable approach to the reflection
- develops the reflection with uneven use of descriptive and narrative detail
- exhibits limited control of written language

Score 2 *Demonstrates basic success*
- includes loosely related material that seriously distracts from the writer's narrative focus
- shows minimal organization, with major gaps in the narrative flow
- offers a reflection that merely skims the surface
- develops the reflection with inadequate descriptive and narrative detail
- exhibits significant problems with control of written language

Score 1 *Demonstrates emerging effort*
- shows little awareness of the topic and the narrative purpose
- lacks organization
- offers an unclear and confusing narrative
- develops the reflection with little or no detail
- exhibits major problems with control of written language

4-Point Scale

Score 4 *Demonstrates advanced success*
- focuses consistently on narrating a single experience or a unified sequence of experiences
- shows effective narrative sequence throughout, with smooth transitions
- offers a thoughtful, creative approach to the reflection
- develops the reflection thoroughly, using vivid descriptive and narrative details
- exhibits mature control of written language

Score 3 *Demonstrates competent success*
- focuses on narrating a single experience or a unified sequence of experiences, with minor distractions
- shows effective narrative sequence, with minor lapses
- offers a mostly thoughtful approach to the reflection
- develops the reflection adequately, with some descriptive and narrative details
- exhibits general control of written language

Score 2 *Demonstrates limited success*
- includes some loosely related material that distracts from the writer's narrative focus
- shows some organization, with noticeable flaws in the narrative flow
- offers a routine, predictable approach to the reflection
- develops the reflection with uneven use of descriptive and narrative detail
- exhibits limited control of written language

Score 1 *Demonstrates emerging effort*
- shows little awareness of the topic and the narrative purpose
- lacks organization
- offers an unclear and confusing narrative
- develops the reflection with little or no detail
- exhibits major problems with control of written language

Reflective Essay

When responding to a prompt requiring personal reflection, use what you have learned from reading, writing your reflective essay, and studying the rubric on page 732. Use the steps below to develop a response to the following prompt.

Writing Prompt

Write an essay reflecting on an experience that taught you something about yourself or about the world. In your essay, provide details to share with readers what happened and why the experience was significant to you.

Study the Prompt

Begin by reading the prompt carefully. Circle or underline key words: *reflecting, experience, taught you, yourself, the world, details,* and *significant.* Re-read the prompt to see if there is additional information that can help you.

Your **purpose** is to reflect on a specific experience that taught you something significant—important and meaningful to you. Use plenty of details, including thoughts and feelings, to help readers share the experience with you. **Tip:** Spend about five minutes studying the prompt.

Plan Your Response

Make a list of experiences that have taught you something. Before you pick one, determine if the lesson was significant and how it affected you. Then, choose the experience that you can write about most effectively in limited time. Next, brainstorm **narrative details** that tell *what happened,* in a chart like the one below.

	Details
Initial situation:	
First event or action:	
Second event or action:	
Third event or action:	
Significance of events / what you learned:	

Once you have outlined the experience and summed up its significance, brainstorm **descriptive details** that appeal to the senses. What did you see, hear, touch, smell, or taste at each stage of the experience? Choose details that help illuminate the significance of the experience. **Tip:** Spend about ten minutes planning your response.

Respond to the Prompt

Start writing, even if you are unsure about how to begin. The most important thing is to get your ideas on paper. Using the chart that you created, begin by setting the scene and describing the initial situation. Then write about the first thing that happened, using vivid narrative and descriptive details to describe people, places, and events. Be sure to include **dialogue** and your thoughts and feelings before, during, and after the experience. Continue in this way until you have fully described the experience. Finally, explain the significance of the experience by telling readers what you learned from it. **Tip:** Spend about twenty minutes writing your reflective essay.

Improve Your Response

Revising Go back to the key aspects of the prompt. Does your response relate and reflect on a specific experience that taught you something? Have you clearly stated the significance of the experience? Do narrative and descriptive details flesh out the experience? If not, add these elements.

Proofreading Take a few minutes to edit your response to correct errors in grammar, spelling, punctuation, and capitalization. Make sure that your edits are neat and the paper is legible.

Checking Your Final Copy Before you turn in your paper, read it one more time to catch any errors you may have missed. **Tip:** Save five or ten minutes to improve your paper.

Presenting a Reflective Essay

Speak with a Purpose

Adapt your reflective essay into an oral presentation, and deliver it to an audience.

Think as a Reader/Writer Writers and speakers try to convey ideas to an audience, while readers and listeners take in information and try to understand these ideas. Just as writers and readers take active roles in the creation and understanding of a story, speakers and listeners must take active steps in order for the message of an oral presentation to be successful. When you listen to a reflective essay, you want to connect the details of the essay to the speaker's larger message. A good listener asks the same questions a good reader would ask, such as, "What idea is the speaker trying to convey?" As an effective speaker, you need to concentrate on aspects of your presentation that bring your experience to life. For example, allowing your voice and body to express your emotions and making the people involved in your experience come alive for your listeners are two techniques that take your speech to the next level. Your tasks as a speaker are to engage your listeners and to make the presentation enjoyable.

Adapt Your Reflective Essay

Bring It to Life

While your essay relied on words alone, your presentation can use words as well as visuals, sounds, and actions to convey your experience and its significance. Your purpose, however, will be the same as that of your essay—to express and explore your thoughts and feelings about an experience. Use the following suggestions to adapt your essay for an effective presentation.

- **Don't just tell your experience—show it.** Instead of describing actions or appearances, for instance, act them out. Bring the people in your narrative to life by speaking their dialogue in a way that captures their unique personalities. Use visuals and sound effects, such as props, graphics, or music, to enhance your descriptions. For example, you may use an overhead projector to show images of the experience.

- **Strike a balance between showing the events and expressing their meaning.** Your audience will not understand why the experience is important to you unless you tell them. Narrate the events in chronological order, acting out details when you can, but also explain the events' significance. Help your listeners see the comparisons you are drawing between your experience and broader themes that show the insights you've gained about life.

- **Use clear, forceful, interesting language.** Incorporate concrete images that appeal to the five senses within your descriptions. Use figurative language, a metaphor or simile that draws a comparison between what you're describing—which may be new to your audience— and something familiar.

Reader/Writer Notebook

Use your **RWN** to complete the activities for this workshop.

Plan Your Delivery and Rehearse

Make a Note

To deliver your presentation effectively—without reading or memorizing—create notecards. Make cards that are brief and to the point. Each card will remind you of one part of your presentation, with brief cues for what you will say or do.

Delivering the Goods

How you say something is often just as important as what you say. When you give a presentation, let your voice and your body speak for you. Use the following chart to tailor your delivery techniques to your audience and purpose.

Delivery Techniques

Verbal Techniques	Nonverbal Techniques
Language: For the most part, use **standard American English** so that your presentation will be clear. However, you may use appropriate **informal expressions,** especially in dialogue.	**Eye contact:** Draw your audience into the story by making eye contact. This practice will give listeners the feeling that you are speaking directly to them.
Tone: Vary your tone of voice to fit the events you're narrating or to portray another person's voice. Use a light tone if events are funny and a sober tone if events are serious.	**Gestures:** When acting out events, make sure that your gestures are natural and give a sense of what's happening—without distracting the audience.
Volume: Vary the volume of your voice to fit the mood of the events, but make sure you always speak loudly enough to be heard.	**Facial expressions:** Let your feelings about the events show on your face. Use facial expressions to portray the moods of the people involved in your experience.

Act the Part

How will you remember what you're going to say? How will you present your visuals without fumbling, or play music without breaking the flow of your presentation? The only way to achieve command of the text and create skillful, artistic staging is to practice. Try one or more of the following rehearsal strategies.

- **Rehearse your presentation in front of a mirror.** Watch yourself to see if your gestures and facial expressions look natural.

- **Rehearse your presentation for family or friends.** Ask them for feedback—both compliments on what you've done well and suggestions on how to improve.

- **Videotape your rehearsals.** After you have rehearsed, view the video with a critical eye to determine how you can improve.

A Good Oral Presentation

- engages listeners' attention and interest at the beginning
- doesn't distract listeners with irrelevant details
- keeps listeners engaged by using transitions to connect narrative events with hints about the larger idea
- concludes with an idea that connects a personal reflection to a broader theme or message

⬤ **Speaking Tip**

Don't distract or overwhelm your audience with too many audiovisual elements. The focus of your presentation is the story of your experience. Evaluate when to use audiovisual elements to achieve the greatest effect.

 Learn It Online
Enhance your narrative with music and pictures—create your own digital story. Learn how online.

go.hrw.com L11-735 **Go**

Literary Skills Review

Comparing Literature **Directions:** Read the two poems. Then, read and respond to the questions that follow.

For a Dead Lady

by **Edwin Arlington Robinson**

No more with overflowing light
Shall fill the eyes that now are faded,
Nor shall another's fringe with night
Their woman-hidden world as they did.
5 No more shall quiver down the days
The flowing wonder of her ways,
Whereof no language may require
The shifting and the many-shaded.

The grace, divine, definitive,
10 Clings only as a faint forestalling;
The laugh that love could not forgive
Is hushed, and answers to no calling;
The forehead and the little ears
Have gone where Saturn keeps the years;
15 The breast where roses could not live
Has done with rising and with falling.

The beauty, shattered by the laws
That have creation in their keeping,
No longer trembles at applause,
20 Or over children that are sleeping;
And we who delve in beauty's lore
Know all that we have known before
Of what inexorable cause
Makes Time so vicious in his reaping.

Now and Then, America by **Pat Mora**

Who wants to rot
beneath dry, winter grass
in a numbered grave
in a numbered row
5 in a section labeled Eternal Peace
with neighbors plagued
by limp, plastic roses
springing from their toes?
Grant me a little life now and then, America.

10 Who wants to rot
as she marches through life
in a pinstriped suit
neck chained in a soft, silk bow
in step, in style, insane.
15 Let me in
to boardrooms wearing hot
colors, my hair long and free,
maybe speaking Spanish.
Risk my difference, my surprises.
20 Grant me a little life, America.

And when I die, plant *zempasúchitl*,°
flowers of the dead, and at my head
plant organ cactus, green fleshy
fingers sprouting, like in Oaxaca.°
25 Let desert creatures hide
in the orange blooms.
Let birds nest in the cactus stems.
Let me go knowing life flower and song
will continue right above my bones.

21. *zempasúchitl* (sem pah SOO chee tuhl): Mexican marigolds.
24. **Oaxaca** (wah HAH kah): state in southeastern Mexico.

1. In lines 21–24 of "For a Dead Lady," the speaker is saying that —

A those who study beauty will never know why time destroys it so viciously

B death is inevitable, but people who value beauty attempt to prevent it

C stories tell us everything we need to know about the beauty of the season of harvest

D death preserves beauty by keeping age from destroying it

2. What poetic device does Robinson use in line 24?

A Alliteration

B Personification

C Simile

D Onomatopoeia

3. What does Robinson mean by the lines, "The beauty, shattered by the laws / That have creation in their keeping" (lines 17-18)?

A Her loved ones will never see her face because it's covered in a casket.

B Someone harmed her, destroying her beauty.

C She was never a beautiful woman.

D Because of death, her beauty is gone.

4. In Mora's poem, what objection does the speaker make to traditional American burial practices?

A The tombs in a cemetery lie in indistinguishable rows and are decorated by plastic flowers.

B People don't take good care of the grass or tombstones in graveyards.

C Americans don't respect the natural cycle of life and death.

D The tombs do not show the names or display pictures of the deceased.

5. In Mora's poem, to what aspect of the typical American workplace does the speaker object?

A People's preference for speaking Spanish

B Stylish suits and soft, silk scarves

C Differences and surprises in the boardroom

D Pressure to dress and speak a certain way

6. In "Now and Then, America," the speaker is trying to express that she wants —

A more women to wear bright colors and speak Spanish

B the freedom to express her individuality and ethnic identity

C to be buried in a numbered grave, in a numbered row

D to be remembered as a smart and beautiful woman

7. How does the speaker of each poem seem to view life?

A Robinson's view is joyful, while Mora's view is skeptical.

B Robinson's view is disheartening, while Mora's view is angry.

C Robinson's view is accepting, while Mora's view is celebratory.

D Robinson's view is triumphant, while Mora's view is practical.

Constructed Response

8. Briefly compare the speakers' attitudes toward death in "For a Dead Lady" and "Now and Then, America." Be sure to support your response with evidence from the poems.

Vocabulary Skills Review

SKILLS FOCUS Vocabulary Skills
Understand denotation and connotation.

Denotation and Connotation   **Directions:** A word's **denotation** is its dictionary definition. **Connotation,** by contrast, refers to a word's emotional overtones—positive, negative, or neutral. Read each of the following short passages, and identify the connotation of the italicized word as positive, neutral, or negative.

1. My mother approached her childhood home in dismay; what she saw was an old, *dilapidated* building with broken windows and doors.

   A positive

   B neutral

   C negative

2. The students had different ideas regarding when the graduation ceremony would begin, so Annie made a phone call to the office and *verified* that commencement begins at noon.

   A positive

   B neutral

   C negative

3. Bob makes everyone laugh. He has the most *jocular* disposition of all my friends.

   A positive

   B neutral

   C negative

4. Winter holidays bring out the best in many people. These people perform acts of *benevolence* toward those who are less fortunate.

   A positive

   B neutral

   C negative

5. Eduardo didn't know anyone attending the party. When he walked in, he tried to put on a smile despite his *misgivings* about the situation.

   A positive

   B neutral

   C negative

6. Rosa's entrance into middle school this fall will mark her *transition* into her teenage years.

   A positive

   B neutral

   C negative

7. Time was running out, and Leah's *apprehension* grew by the second. She feared she wouldn't get the broken vase fixed before her mother came home.

   A positive

   B neutral

   C negative

8. After his seven-hour airplane trip, Gilberto rode along the coast, staring at the scenery. His mind was *vacant* of any stressful thoughts.

   A positive

   B neutral

   C negative

Academic Vocabulary

Directions: For each word, choose the correct antonym.

   9. *crucial*

      A symbolic

      B unimportant

      C essential

   10. *relevant*

      A pertinent

      B inapplicable

      C related

Writing Skills Review

Reflective Essay   **Directions:** Read the following paragraph from a draft of a student's reflective essay. Then, answer the questions below.

(1) My twin sister, Natasha, and I used to engage in unceasing hostilities. (2) We would fight over everything: clothes, bathroom space, chores, *everything*. (3) Then, the week after we turned fifteen, we got news that changed our lives. (4) Natasha had been feeling sick for a while, and medical tests determined that she had leukemia. (5) The type of leukemia she had held a strong chance of survival, but it would require chemotherapy and some sacrifice and determination from our family. (6) The thought of losing my sister made me reevaluate our relationship.

1. Which sentence could the writer add to communicate the lesson of the experience?

   A Leukemia is a terrible form of cancer.

   B Just because two people are twins doesn't make them close.

   C Natasha's leukemia made me realize how trivial our fights were.

   D Siblings should never fight.

2. To make a connection between the experience and life in general, which sentence could the writer add?

   A I learned that life is too precious to waste time fighting over trivial things.

   B I learned to love and appreciate my life.

   C I learned how the doctors planned to treat my sister's cancer.

   D I learned to value different people's points of view.

3. To include more narrative details, the writer could —

   A contrast her appearance with her sister's

   B describe the house where she and her sister live

   C use sensory language to describe the sisters' disagreements

   D describe her thoughts and feelings after hearing the bad news

4. To add a colloquial expression and maintain an informal voice, which sentence could the writer include in place of sentence 1?

   A My twin sister, Natasha, and I used to abominate each other.

   B My twin sister, Natasha, and I used to fight incessantly.

   C My twin sister, Natasha, and I never used to get along.

   D My twin sister, Natasha, and I used to quarrel ceaselessly.

5. The next paragraph of this essay would most likely —

   A go into detail about the sisters' fights

   B provide details about other family members

   C cite informative statistics about leukemia from a credible source

   D explain how the sisters' relationship changed as a result of Natasha's illness

6. If the writer were presenting the passage as a reflective presentation, she could best adapt the essay for her audience by —

   A using facial expressions to express her reaction to her sister's diagnosis of leukemia

   B providing only the details that show action and not meaning

   C speaking with a lighthearted tone

   D writing the complete essay on notecards

Read On

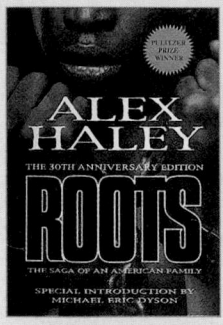

FICTION
Roots

When Alex Haley was a child, his grandmother told him tales of an ancestor known only as the African—a man torn from his Mandingo people and forced into slavery in America. When Haley grew up, he discovered that the African had a real name—Kunta Kinte—and that his story had the power to reach people everywhere. *Roots* is a fictionalized chronicle spanning the period between Kunta's birth in 1750 and the death of Haley's father, a college professor, in the twentieth century.

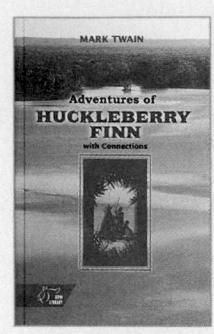

FICTION
Adventures of Huckleberry Finn

When Mark Twain takes a mischievous boy, a runaway slave, and a raft, and places them on the Mississippi River, the result is one of the greatest adventures in American literature. Mark Twain's masterpiece paints a satirical portrait of Southern life in the late nineteenth century with humor, colorful settings and characters, and wisdom. The novel has transcended time and place; it's no wonder that Ernest Hemingway wrote, "All modern American literature comes from one book by Mark Twain called *Huckleberry Finn*."

FICTION
My Ántonia

Willa Cather's classic novel puts a human face on the thousands of people who immigrated to the United States in the late nineteenth century. At the center of the story is Ántonia Shimerda, a young Bohemian immigrant whose family experiences the struggles and triumphs of building a new life in Nebraska. Ántonia's resilient spirit captures the heart and imagination of Jim Burden, the lonely neighbor boy who follows and narrates the story of Ántonia's eventful life.

AUTOBIOGRAPHY
Up From Slavery

Booker T. Washington's life story is an inspiring testament to the persistence of the human spirit and the transforming power of education. Born into slavery, Washington went on to found the esteemed Tuskegee Institute in Alabama, dedicated to the education of African Americans. *Up From Slavery* includes the story of Washington's career as a public speaker and advocate for civil rights.

FICTION

The Awakening

First published in 1899, Kate Chopin's *The Awakening* was a book ahead of its time about a woman ahead of her time. Its publication caused a scandal. In fact, the novel was so strongly condemned that it was out of print for decades after its initial publication. Chopin tells the story of Edna Pointellier and her difficult struggle to forge an identity on her own terms. Can Edna claim her life as her own in a society that wants women to stay in their place? Read this novel to find out if she succeeds.

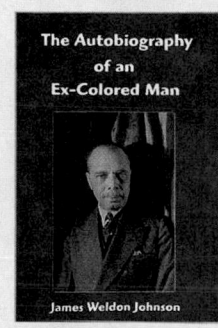

FICTION

The Autobiography of an Ex-Colored Man

James Weldon Johnson's novel describes the life of a boy with an African American mother and white father who is born in Georgia and later moves to Connecticut. At first unaware that he is not white, the boy learns of his mixed heritage while in school. He spends the rest of his life deciding which he identifies with more, his African American or his white ancestry. Johnson's novel provides an interesting social commentary and insight into race relations in the United States in the late nineteenth century.

FICTION

Ethan Frome

Winters in Starkville, Massachusetts, are harsh and lonely, and no one feels this loneliness more than Ethan Frome, who is stuck in his broken-down farmhouse with a sick and unpleasant wife. When his wife's attractive cousin, Mattie, comes to stay with the Fromes, Ethan feels a sense of hope and renewal that he hasn't felt in years, and he's overjoyed to learn that Mattie feels the same way. Edith Wharton's novel tells a classic story of ill-fated romance.

FICTION

The Portrait of a Lady

A masterpiece by Henry James, this novel follows a young American woman, Isabel Archer, on her journey to Europe after the death of her father. Wealthy but innocent, Isabel has her choice of potential suitors and the freedom, perhaps, to decide her own future. She discovers, however, that deception can hover just beneath the surface of Europe's civilized social behavior.

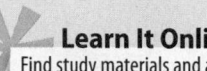

Learn It Online

Find study materials and a multimedia introduction to *Adventures of Huckleberry Finn* on *NovelWise*.

go.hrw.com | L11-741 | **Go**

The Moderns

1914–1939

"Men travel faster now, but I do not know if they go to better things."

— **Willa Cather**

What Do **You Think?**
How does progress challenge tradition and redefine society?

Evening Tones (1911–1917) by Oscar Bluemner.

 Learn It Online
What's this historical period all about? See the "Redefining the American Dream" video online.

go.hrw.com   L11-743   Go

The Moderns
1914–1939

This time line represents a snapshot of United States literary events, United States historical events, and world events from 1914 to 1939. The decades between the two world wars were marked by social upheaval and literary innovations that produced a movement known as Modernism.

UNITED STATES LITERARY EVENTS

1914

1915 T. S. Eliot publishes "The Love Song of J. Alfred Prufrock"

1915 Edgar Lee Masters reveals the shocking underside of small-town life in *Spoon River Anthology*

1916 Carl Sandburg publishes *Chicago Poems*

Edna St. Vincent Millay.

1920

1920 Sinclair Lewis publishes *Main Street,* a controversial novel examining mainstream American society

1922 T. S. Eliot publishes *The Waste Land*

< 1923 Edna St. Vincent Millay wins the Pulitzer Prize in poetry

1925 F. Scott Fitzgerald publishes his novel of the Jazz Age, *The Great Gatsby*

1925 First section of Ezra Pound's *Cantos* is published

UNITED STATES HISTORICAL EVENTS

1914

BUY A
United States Government Bond of the
SECOND
LIBERTY LOAN
of 1917
Help Your Country and Yourself

Lithograph (1917) urging Americans to buy war bonds.

1914 Panama Canal opens

< 1917 United States enters World War I

1918 President Woodrow Wilson presents his Fourteen Points, a plan for world peace

1920

1920 First commercial radio broadcast in the United States is aired

1920 Eighteenth Amendment (prohibiting the sale of alcohol) goes into effect (repealed in 1933)

1920 Nineteenth Amendment is ratified, granting U.S. women the right to vote **>**

1924 Nellie Tayloe Ross is elected in Wyoming as first female governor

MR. PRESIDENT WHAT WILL YOU DO FOR WOMAN SUFFRAGE

A picketer with the National Woman's Party, January 26, 1917.

WORLD EVENTS

1914

1914 World War I breaks out in Europe

1917 Russian Revolution ends czarist regime

1918 Spanish flu epidemic begins, claiming millions of lives worldwide

1919 Treaty of Versailles ends World War I **∨**

Treaty of Versailles by Sir William Orpen (1921) in *Bibby's Annual.*

1920

1920 League of Nations meets for the first time

1920 Mohandas Gandhi becomes leader of Indian Congress and leads campaign of civil disobedience

1922 Fascist government of Benito Mussolini comes to power in Italy

1922 Union of Soviet Socialist Republics is formed in Russia

744 Unit 5

SKILLS FOCUS Literary Skills Evaluate and analyze the philosophical, political, religious, ethical, and social influences of a historical period. Reading Skills Read widely to increase knowledge of the student's culture, the culture of others, and the common elements across cultures; identify and understand elements of text structure (including headings and sections).

Your Turn

Review the time line with a partner. Together, identify two historical or world events that you believe produced great changes in American society during this time period. In what ways do these developments continue to challenge or define our society today?

1926 — 1933 — 1939

1926 Langston Hughes publishes his first poetry collection, *The Weary Blues*

1929 Ernest Hemingway publishes his noted World War I novel, *A Farewell to Arms* ❯

1929 William Faulkner publishes *The Sound and the Fury*

1931 Eugene O'Neill's trilogy of plays, *Mourning Becomes Electra,* opens, shocking theatergoers with its stark portrayal of family rivalry

Movie poster for *A Farewell to Arms* (1932), staring Gary Cooper and Helen Hayes.

1936 Eudora Welty publishes her first short story, "Death of a Traveling Salesman"

1937 Zora Neale Hurston publishes *Their Eyes Were Watching God*

1939 John Steinbeck publishes *The Grapes of Wrath* and wins the Pulitzer Prize in literature ❯

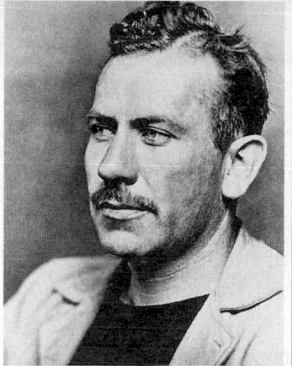

John Steinbeck.

1926 — 1933 — 1939

1927 Charles A. Lindbergh completes the first transatlantic solo flight by airplane

1927 *The Jazz Singer,* one of the first sound films with dialogue, opens

1929 U.S. stock market crashes, leading to the Great Depression

1933 Franklin D. Roosevelt becomes U.S. president; New Deal program to counter Great Depression begins

1935 Social Security Act is enacted

❮ **1937** Pioneering aviator Amelia Earhart disappears while flying around the world

1939 First commercial television broadcast in United States is aired

Famous aviator Amelia Earhart.

1926 — 1933 — 1939

1928 Sir Alexander Fleming discovers penicillin ⌄

1930 Jet engine is patented

1931 Electron microscope is invented

Alexander Fleming at microscope.

1933 Nazi leader Adolf Hitler comes to power in Germany

1936 Spanish Civil War begins

1937 Japan invades China

1939 Germany invades Poland; World War II begins in Europe ❯

German army photograph, World War II

The Moderns
1914–1939

World War I plunged the United States into an era of uncertainty and tremendous change on many levels—social, political, psychological, and spiritual. Each new decade brought upheaval, and each upheaval brought an adjustment in American attitudes, a shift away from the traditions and optimism of the past. These changes were reflected in a new period in American literature called modernism, a literary era characterized by experimentation and innovation.

KEY CONCEPTS

Upheaval and Challenges

History of the Times Drawn into World War I, the United States helped the Allies defeat the Central Powers. Over twenty million lives were lost before a truce was signed in November 1918. American idealism, however, had little influence in postwar Europe. Although America emerged as a victor, at home its values were beginning to be challenged.

Literature of the Times Poets took the first steps toward modernism by experimenting with form and technique. The poetic movements of symbolism and imagism developed as a result.

The Jazz Age

History of the Times The government's prohibition of alcohol could not quench the defiant spirit or booming economy of the Roaring Twenties. Women won the right to vote and took on more active social roles during the frenzy of postwar change. Popular mass culture flourished with the growth of the radio and the film industry.

Literature of the Times Novelists reflected both the spirit of the Jazz Age and the disillusionment of a "lost generation" living abroad. The Harlem Renaissance celebrated a flowering of African American art, music, and literature.

Fading Dreams

History of the Times The stock market crash in 1929 ushered in the Great Depression, flinging millions of Americans into unemployment and poverty. Anywhere from one fourth to one third of American workers were unemployed. The American dream—based on opportunity, progress, and free enterprise—seemed to have turned into a nightmare.

Literature of the Times Journalists, novelists, and poets depicted the personal and societal damage of the Great Depression. Writers' interest in Freudian psychology and psychoanalysis spurred a literary technique called stream of consciousness.

SKILLS FOCUS **Literary Skills** Evaluate and analyze the philosophical, political, religious, ethical, and social influences of a historical period. **Reading Skills** Read widely to increase knowledge of the student's culture, the culture of others, and the common elements across cultures; identify and understand elements of text structure (including headings and sections).

KEY CONCEPT

Upheaval and Challenges

History of the Times

In the summer of 1914, Europe erupted in a massive conflict, World War I, pitting the Allies (the British Empire, France and the Russian Empire) against the Central Powers (the German Empire, Austria-Hungary, the Ottoman Empire, and Bulgaria).

The United States remained neutral until 1917 when it joined the war on the side of the Allies. The addition of more than two million American soldiers tilted the war against the Central Powers, who surrendered in November 1918, but millions of soldiers and civilians had died in the war.

President Wilson had sent American soldiers overseas to "make the world safe for democracy," but that idealism did not survive the war. The United States recoiled into a period of disillusionment and isolationism, including falling farm prices, labor unrest, the "red menace" of radical politics, and resentment toward increased immigration.

However, postwar disillusionment was also liberating, transforming the habits and forms of tradition. Artists, musicians, and writers eagerly experimented with new styles, forms, and subject matter in a movement known as modernism.

Literature of the Times

World War I's devastation severely damaged the inherited assumptions of the American dream: belief in America as a land of opportunity, expectation of progress, and faith in individualism. In fact, the center of American literary life finally started to shift away from the Puritan tradition of New England, which had been the native region of America's most brilliant writers during the nineteenth century.

American poets began a dazzling period of experimentation, seeking new ways of seeing and thinking. Ezra Pound and T. S. Eliot used the technique of symbolism to fashion a new modernist poetry. Pound also spearheaded a related poetic movement, imagism, demanding precision in word choices and images. Poets like E. E. Cummings would sustain these styles for decades.

Some American poets rejected modernist trends. Robert Frost, the greatest of these poets, used plain New England speech and a mastery of verse forms to create an inimitable poetic voice.

Comprehension Check

How did the disillusionment of the postwar period influence the development of modernism?

Fast Facts

Historical Highlights

- World War I begins in 1914; the United States enters the conflict in 1917.
- The Nineteenth Amendment, ratified in 1920, gives women the right to vote.
- The New York stock market crash in 1929 starts the Great Depression.

Literary Highlights

- In the 1920s, a cultural movement known as the Harlem Renaissance showcases the unique contributions of African American writers such as Langston Hughes and Zora Neale Hurston.
- F. Scott Fitzgerald publishes *The Great Gatsby* in 1925, reflecting the glitter of the Jazz Age and the fading American dream.
- *The Sun Also Rises* brings Ernest Hemingway fame in 1926.

Learn It Online

Explore this historical period further online.

go.hrw.com L11-747 Go

The Jazz Age

Couple performing the Charleston.

History of the Times

In 1919, the Constitution was amended to prohibit the manufacture and sale of alcohol, which was singled out as a central social evil. Far from strengthening traditional values, Prohibition ushered in an age characterized by the bootlegger, the speak-easy, the short-skirted flapper, the rhythms of jazz, and the dangerous but lucrative profession of the gangster. Recording the Roaring Twenties and making the era a vivid chapter in our history, F. Scott Fitzgerald gave it its name: the Jazz Age.

The Jazz Age was powered by more than high spirits. Mass production had reduced the price of cars and other once-costly goods, putting them within the reach of the American middle class. Increasing access to electric power brought new products to market ranging from refrigerators to toasters. A sophisticated advertising industry arose to sell these products, making use of a new medium called "radio." The rapid cycle of production and consumption produced a booming economy.

Women won the right to vote in 1920, an event that coincided with their arrival in ever greater numbers in colleges and the workplace. Many young women began bobbing their hair and wearing shorter skirts in a daring modern fashion. They created the "flapper" look, a fashion statement equally effective in shocking parents and asserting independence, as they began to create a presence in artistic, intellectual, and social circles.

A vibrant popular culture also blossomed in the 1920s. Hollywood cranked out an average of eight hundred films a year, which were shown in elaborate movie palaces. About sixty million Americans— nearly half the population—went to the movies each week. Most Americans would continue to do so even after the Great Depression eclipsed the Jazz Age.

As energetic as the Roaring Twenties were in America, the pursuit of pleasure abroad was more attractive for some. F. Scott Fitzgerald was among the many American writers and artists who abandoned their own shores after the war for the expatriate[1] life in France. Living in Paris was not only cheap, but more exotic, filled with grace and luxury. This wave of expatriates was another signal that something had gone wrong with the American dream.

Literature of the Times

The writer linked most closely to the Jazz Age is F. Scott Fitzgerald, whose novels such as *The Great Gatsby* (1925) brought to life the flappers, tycoons, and other characters emblematic of the 1920s.

The most influential of all the post–World War I writers was Ernest Hemingway. Hemingway is perhaps most famous for his literary style, which affected the style of American prose fiction for several generations. Like the Puritans, who centuries earlier strove for a plain style, Hemingway reduced the flamboyance of literary language to the bare bones of the truth it must express. His novel *The Sun Also Rises* (1926) evokes the disillusionment of the "lost generation" of Americans living in postwar Europe.

---

1. **expatriate:** a person who leaves his or her homeland or birthplace to live in another country.

In the early 1920s, a group of black poets focused directly on the unique contributions of African American culture to America. Their poetry based its rhythms on spirituals and jazz, its lyrics on the blues, and its diction on the street talk of the ghettos.

Foremost among these poets were James Weldon Johnson, Langston Hughes, Claude McKay, and Countee Cullen. These poets brought literary distinction to the broad movement of painters, musicians, and writers known as the Harlem Renaissance. When African American poetry, hand in hand with the music echoing from New Orleans, Memphis, and Chicago, became part of the Jazz Age, it brought new appreciation of the role of black talent in American culture.

Comprehension Check

Who were the members of the "lost generation"? Why did they choose to leave the United States?

Link to Today

The American Hero

Ernest Hemingway introduced a new kind of hero to American literature, a tough man of action who upholds honor, courage, and endurance as a personal code. For Hemingway, heroism was not a matter of perfect character or public triumph. His heroes—soldiers, bullfighters, adventurers—were usually flawed and rarely victorious. Instead, they display "grace under pressure" by acting with skill, bravery, and decency when faced with overwhelming odds. The most important trait of this hero is thorough disillusionment. Hemingway's protagonists face their bleak fates alone, without the comfort of self-pity, illusion, or hope.

The "Hemingway hero" has had a lasting influence on American literature and films, living on in the standards and expectations we impose upon soldiers, officers of the law, cowboys, astronauts, and other heroic figures—real and imaginary—of our culture.

Ask Yourself

Identify some contemporary individuals whom you regard as heroes. What traits do they share with the Hemingway hero? How are they different?

Anthony Quinn in a film version of *The Old Man and the Sea* (1990).

Fading Dreams

History of the Times

With the stock market crash of 1929, the United States entered a dismal era known as the Great Depression. Stocks became worthless, banks and businesses were closed, and formerly secure citizens lost their jobs and savings. The Depression brought suffering to millions of Americans. At its worst, twelve million people were unemployed. Homelessness and begging were common. People waited in bread lines, hunted for food in garbage dumps, and slept in sewer pipes. Homeless families lived in tents and shacks in camps called Hoovervilles, named for President Herbert Hoover, who hesitated to slow the economic downslide.

Economic strain frayed the fabric of American society. When war veterans seeking benefits marched on Washington, D.C., in 1932, they were violently disbanded by federal troops. Racism and discrimination also increased in intensity. A long drought in the Great Plains added to the misery of thousands, forcing families from their barren farms and sending them west in hopes of finding work.

The Depression eroded America's sense of itself as a land of promise, progress, rugged individualism, and free enterprise. As faith in these values weakened, some Americans were attracted to socialism. This political system based on the beliefs of Karl Marx advocated

Dust Bowl farm (1938), Coldwater District, Texas. Photograph by Dorothea Lange.

a classless society and shared ownership of property. Though Americans became more aware of conflict between rich and poor, the class friction did not lead to revolution.

In 1933, President Franklin D. Roosevelt fought the effects of the Depression with various new ideas. Over the next several years, he attempted to rebuild the nation through a series of government-funded social programs known as the New Deal. Many New Deal programs eased the burdens of poverty and unemployment, and some, such as the Social Security Act, have had lasting effects on American life, but

Link to Today

Radio and Culture

By 1933, two thirds of American households owned at least one radio. Radio networks broadcast entertainment and news to every region, creating a national popular culture. An early proof of radio's growing influence on American life occurred on Halloween in 1938, when Orson Welles's radio play *Invasion from Mars* terrified thousands of Americans with fictional news bulletins of a Martian invasion. Hundreds of listeners assumed the imaginary events in the broadcast—based on H. G. Wells's novel *The War of the Worlds*—were real.

President Franklin D. Roosevelt was the first president to tap the immense potential of radio to communicate with Americans and unify the country. Beginning in 1933, he began broadcasting a series of "fireside chats" to inform and to reassure the American public during critical points of the Depression and, later, of World War II.

Though radio long ago surrendered most dramatic programming to television, it continues today as a news, talk, and music medium. Following the example of Roosevelt, presidents still make weekly radio addresses; radio talk-show hosts continue to influence millions of listeners.

Ask Yourself

In what ways do modern communications media unify American society? In your opinion, which medium today best fills the role that radio served in the 1930s?

legislation alone did not bring an end to the Depression. It would take another world war to return the United States to economic prosperity.

Literature of the Times

Sigmund Freud, the founder of psychoanalysis, had opened the workings of the unconscious mind to scrutiny. Interest grew in this new field of psychiatry in America, where it inspired writers to use a narrative technique called stream of consciousness. This technique abandoned chronology and attempted to imitate the moment-by-moment flow of a character's perceptions and memories. The Irish writer James Joyce used this technique to radically change the very concept of the novel in *Ulysses* (1922). Soon afterward, the American writers Katherine Anne Porter and William Faulkner also used it in their works. Faulkner, in particular, was a fearless experimenter with literary forms. In *The Sound and the Fury* (1929), Faulkner uses stream of consciousness to weave together several different viewpoints and several different moments in time.

The human cost of the Great Depression also engaged several modernist writers. One of the most significant results was John Steinbeck's novel *The Grapes of Wrath* (1939), which traces the sad odyssey of the Joad family from their bulldozed tenant farm in Oklahoma to the indignities of California labor camps. Steinbeck skillfully mingles the personal quests of the Joads with passionate exploration of the larger issue of social justice in America.

The writers of the modernist period imagined a new meaning for an American dream tarnished by world war and a devastating depression. Their bold experiments in form and subject matter produced some of the most enduring works in American literature.

Comprehension Check

What is the stream-of-consciousness narrative technique? How does it differ from other narrative techniques?

Wrap Up

Talk About...

In 1929, Gertrude Stein, a leading modernist writer, declared, "Everything is the same and everything is different." With a partner, discuss how this statement applies to the American dream of the early twentieth century and of today. Try to use the Academic Vocabulary words **listed below** in your discussion.

Write About...

A major war and economic disaster marked the first half of the twentieth century. What events will future historians focus on as defining the past ten years?

Academic Vocabulary for Unit 5

Talking and Writing About Literature

Academic Vocabulary is the language you use to write and talk about literature. Use these words to discuss the literature you read in this unit. These words will be underlined throughout the unit.

alternative (awl TUR nuh tihv) *n.*: a choice between two things. *Modernists sought fresh alternatives to art forms of the past.*

hierarchy (HY uh RAHR kee) *n.*: ranking persons or things higher or lower within categories. *When women won the vote in 1920, they redefined their place in the social hierarchy.*

ideology (y dee AHL uh jee) *n.*: a set of doctrines or opinions. *In the 1920s, established ideologies were open to question.*

inevitable (ihn EHV uh tuh buhl) *adj.*: unavoidable. *Some historians believe the Great Depression was an inevitable crisis.*

tradition (truh DIHSH uhn) *n.*: beliefs and customs handed down through generations. *T. S. Eliot and other poets steered away from literary tradition to invent a new kind of literature.*

Your Turn

 In your *Reader/Writer Notebook*, list factors that led to the growth of modernism. With other classmates, identify the three most significant factors. Write a sentence explaining each one. Use the Academic Vocabulary words in your sentences.

Link to Today

This Link to Today shows how you can transform literature during the act of reading.

Build Background

Toni Morrison encourages readers to experience the pulsing vitality of the modern era. Morrison says, "In listening and in reading, it is when I surrender to the language, enter it, that I see clearly." This attention to language is what connects her to American Nobelists of the modern era. Her essay will help you appreciate the passion for justice that informs Steinbeck's symbolism, the moral complexity beneath Hemingway's spare prose, and the radically innovative style that brings Faulkner's world to life.

Author Note

Toni Morrison (1931–), a novelist noted for her rich presentations of African American life, won the Nobel Prize in Literature in 1993. *Beloved,* which won the Pulitzer Prize in 1988, *Sula, The Bluest Eye,* and *Song of Solomon* are among her highly acclaimed novels. Educated at Howard and Cornell Universities, Morrison has taught at Howard, Yale, and Princeton. She is a dynamic participant in the African American literary tradition that has its roots in the Harlem Renaissance.

Nobel Prize WINNER

Read with a Purpose

Read to discover why reading is both a skill and an art.

The Reader as Artist
by Toni Morrison

from The Oprah Magazine

Mr. Head awakened to discover that the room was full of moonlight. He sat up and stared at the floor board—the color of silver—and then at the ticking[1] on his pillow, which might have been brocade, and after a second, he saw half of the moon five feet away in his shaving mirror, paused as if it were waiting for his permission to enter. It rolled forward and cast a dignifying light on everything. The straight chair against the wall looked stiff and attentive as if it were awaiting an order and Mr. Head's trousers, hanging to the back of it, had an almost noble air, like the garment some great man had just flung to his servant. . . .

The above opening to a short story by Flannery O'Connor is, to readers content with grasping information, straightforward enough. It introduces a character, Mr. Head, waking up at night and noticing moonlight. To readers who enjoy the practice of reading, the opening is much, much more.

Two approaches seem to me the difference between reading as a skill and reading as an art. The first is quite enough. From knowing what STOP means through understanding a scholarly essay or a legal brief,[2] the necessary skill varies greatly, can always be refined, and lets us negotiate life with some measure of control. Reading as art, not Art (once, depressingly called "critical" reading) is another matter. Like the avid devotion to other arts, it develops over time in any number of ways, takes all sorts of routes, and has many origins.

My own reading skills were enhanced in schools, but my pleasure in, my passion for the art of reading came long before. It came in childhood and it began with listening. Not only was I a radio child who grew up in the decades when radio was paramount, when being mesmerized[3] by the dramas and reenactments from a speaker box was commonplace, I was also surrounded by adults who told stories, reshaped and solicited them from each other as well as their children. The result was a heavy reliance on my own imagination to provide detail; the specific color of things, the feel of the weather, the space characters occupied, their physical features, their motives, why they behaved as they did, and especially the sound of their speech, where so much meaning lay. Listening required me to surrender to the narrator's world while remaining alert inside it.

---

1. **ticking:** striped fabric used to cover mattresses and pillows.

2. **brief:** a summary statement of facts, points of law, or legal arguments.

3. **mesmerized:** fascinated; hypnotized.

My own reading skills were enhanced in schools, but my pleasure in, my passion for the art of reading came long before. It came in childhood and it began with listening.

Chinese farmers listen to a storyteller at a storytelling temple fair, Chinese lantern festival. Shandong Province.

An African woman tells stories to her children. Mahwanke, Zimbabwe.

That Alice-in-Wonderland combination of willing acceptance coupled with intense inquiry is still the way I read literature: slowly, digging for the hidden, questioning or relishing the choices the author made, eager to envision what is there, noticing what is not. In listening and in reading, it is when I surrender to the language, enter it, that I see clearly. Yet only if I remain attentive to its choices can I understand deeply. Sometimes the experience is profound, harrowing, beautiful; other times enraging, contemptible, unrewarding. Whatever the consequence, the practice itself is riveting. I don't need to "like" the work; I want instead to "think" it.

In the opening sentences of Flannery O'Connor's story, she chose to direct her readers to Mr. Head's fantasy, his hopes. Lowly pillow ticking is like brocade, rich, elaborate. Moonlight turns a wooden floor to silver and "cast[s] a dignifying light" everywhere. His chair, "stiff and attentive," seems to await an order from him.

Even his trousers hanging on its back had "a noble air, like the garment some great man had just flung to his servant." So. Mr. Head has strong, perhaps unmanageable, dreams of majesty, of controlling servants to do his bidding, of rightful authority. Even the moon in his shaving mirror pauses "as if it were waiting for his permission to enter." We don't really have to wait (a few sentences on) to see his alarm clock sitting on an "overturned bucket," or to wonder why his shaving mirror is five feet away from his bed, to know a great deal about him—his pretension,[4] his insecurity, his pathetic yearnings—and anticipate his behavior as the story unfolds. In the accuracy of the 'ear' of the story, its shape, its supple economy and sheer knowingness, it seems to me virtually flawless and deliciously demanding. Which is to say, I can read it again and again, step into its world confident that my attentiveness will always yield wonder. …

---

4. **pretension:** a claim to importance, status, or worth.

Havasupai Indian Storyteller. Sedona, Arizona.

Toni Morrison talks with the Mocha Moms. Brooklyn, New York.

I can do this again: read it and be there once more, anytime I like. Sifting, adding, recapturing. Making the work work while it makes me do the same. Just like leaning into the radio; or sitting cross-legged at the feet of grandparents.

Skill is enough, but I prefer the art.

Analyzing Visuals

Viewing and Interpreting Reading is usually a passive pursuit, involving an individual and the printed word, yet the photographs on this page depict dynamic action, usually among several people. In a small group, discuss how these images relate to Morrison's message about reading. If time allows , share your group's perceptions with the class as a whole.

Ask Yourself

1. **Read with a Purpose** How does "reading as art" differ from "reading as skill," according to Toni Morrison?

2. How did listening to radio programs as a child help Morrison develop as a reader? Do you think contemporary radio, television, and film media offer the same benefit for readers today? Why or why not?

3. In your own words, explain what Morrison means when she says that she prefers to "think" a work of literature rather than to "like" it.

4. Re-read the quoted paragraph that begins the essay. In what ways have Morrison's insights changed your understanding of Mr. Head? How might you apply the information in this essay to your reading of poems and stories of the modern era?

Make It New!

LITERARY FOCUS
Symbolism and Imagism

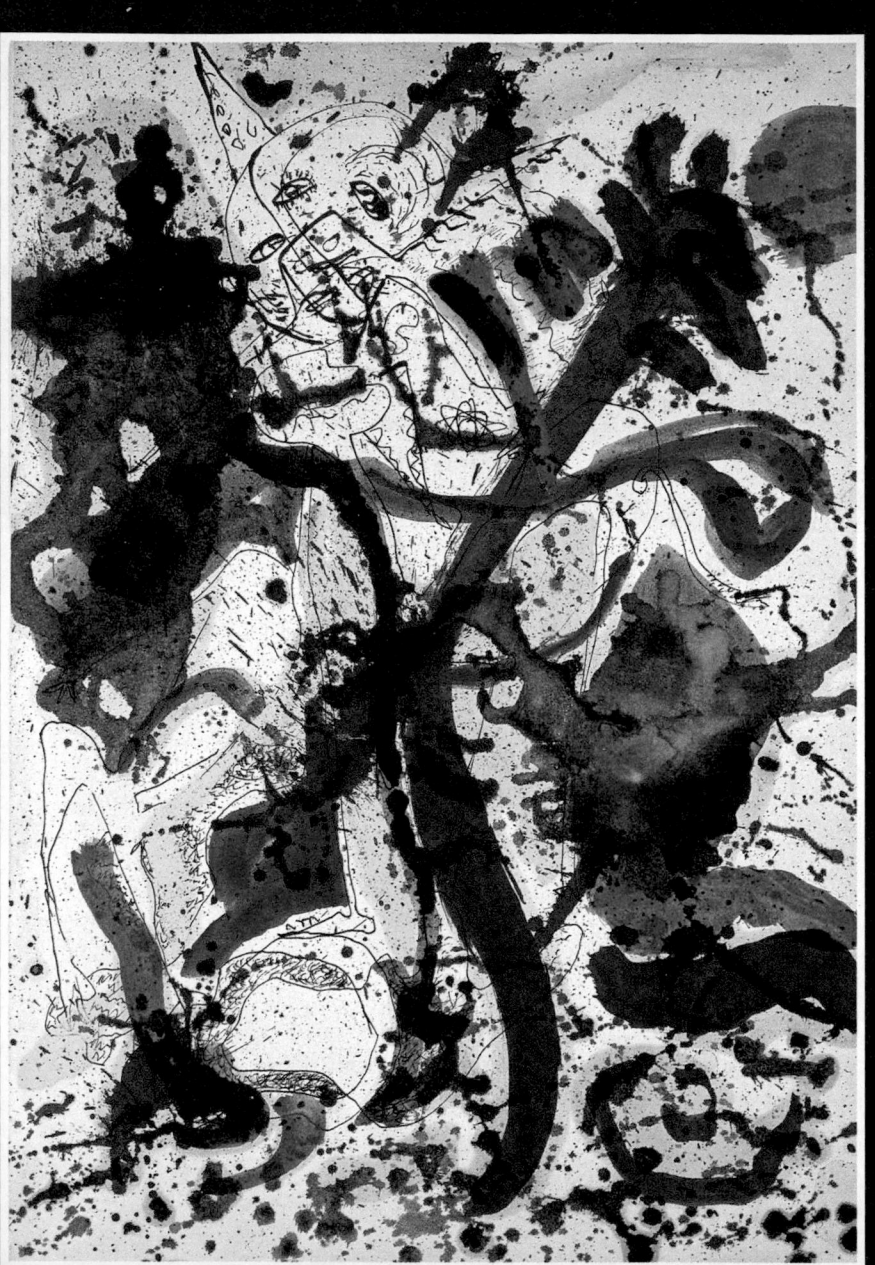

Untitled (ca. 1942–44) by Jackson Pollock.

CONTENTS

"Make it new!

Art is a joyous thing."

—**Ezra Pound**

Symbolism and Imagism by John Malcolm Brinnin

New Poetic Movements: Reactions to Tradition

- American symbolists rebel against the Romantics' focus on nature as a source of solace in the face of industrialization and mechanization.
- Imagism brings precision and concreteness to poetry in place of prettiness and decoration.
- Free verse overrides <u>traditional</u> poetic forms, which have set rhyme schemes and meters.

Sometime in the early twentieth century, Americans awoke to a sense that their own national culture had come of age. This was true in poetry and in painting, in music and in dance, even in the new architecture of the skyscraper. Ironically, American poets found their new inspiration in Paris rather than their homeland. Learning from the French symbolist poets, who dominated French literature from about 1875 to 1895, Americans were able to produce a new type of poetry through which the true American genius could speak.

Symbolism: The Search for a New Reality

Symbolism is a form of expression in which the world of appearances is violently rearranged by artists who seek to depict a different and more truthful version of reality. The symbolist poets did not merely describe objects; they tried to portray the emotional effects that objects can suggest. Do not be misled by the term *symbolism,* however: It has nothing to do with the religious, national, or psychological symbols with which we are all familiar. In fact, the symbolists were concerned with getting rid of such symbols, which they saw as having become dull and meaningless through overuse. The symbolists stressed instead the need for a trust in the nonrational. Imagination is more reliable than reason, the symbolists argued, and just as precise. With their emphasis on the mysterious and the intuitive, symbolists hoped to bring revelation—self-discovery—to readers through poems that lead the imagination to discover truths.

Symbolism was a new manifestation of the Romanticism that had swept through Europe and the United States in the nineteenth century. The Romantics had stressed the importance of feeling and the independence of the individual, and they had made a great stand against the mechanization of human life. In the natural world the Romantics found messages that spoke to the soul and gave it strength.

The symbolists, however, could find neither solace nor spiritual renewal in nature. By the start of the twentieth century, nature had been subjected to so much scientific classification and interpretation that it had been stripped of much of its mystery. Artists now faced the onslaught of the modern world, which suffered increased poverty, violence, and conflict in spite of advances in science and technology. The symbolist poets saw this new world as spiritually corrupt, and they faced it with a distaste amounting to outrage. They knew they could not transform or erase the modern world, though, so their revolt was spiritual. They tried to redefine what it meant to be human in a time when individualism was succumbing to the power of mass culture.

Imagism: "The *Exact* Word"

The two Americans who first came into close contact with symbolism and introduced the techniques of the movement to the United States were Ezra Pound (page 760) and T. S. Eliot (page 768). With the help of several British poets, a group of Americans led by Pound founded a school of thought perhaps better known and understood in the United States than symbolism itself. This school, **imagism,** flourished from 1912 to 1917.

Like the symbolists, imagists believed that poetry can be made purer by concentration on the precise, clear, unqualified image. Imagery alone, the imagists believed, could carry a poem's emotion and message. It could do this almost instantly, without all the elaborate metrics and stanza patterns that were part of poetry's traditional mode. The imagists took on the role of reformers. They would rid poetry of its prettiness, sentimentality, and artificiality, concentrating instead on the raw power of the image to communicate feeling and thought.

The imagists issued a "manifesto," or public declaration, proposing "to use the language of common speech," as well as "the *exact* word, not merely the decorative word." In the same spirit they called for a poetry "hard and clear, never blurred or indefinite." Some of the imagists' inspiration was drawn from Eastern art forms, particularly Japanese **haiku**, a verse form that often juxtaposes two distinct images and invites the reader to experience the emotion created by the juxtaposition.

Pound defined an image as "that which presents an intellectual and emotional complex in an instant of time." Here is a famous imagist poem that illustrates this concept:

> **In a Station of the Metro**
> The apparition of these faces in the crowd;
> Petals on a wet, black bough.
> —Ezra Pound

A New Poetic Order

Although poems with imagistic technique are commonplace today, at the time the imagists published their manifesto on poetry's nature and function, their theory created a great stir. It insisted that the range of poetic subject matter might include the kitchen sink as well as the rising of the moon, the trash can as well as the Chinese porcelain vase. The strongest opposition to the imagists was caused by their proposal "to create new rhythms—as the expression of new moods.... We do believe that the individuality of a poet may often be better expressed in free verse than in conventional forms." The first American practitioner of free verse was Walt Whitman, who, according to Pound, broke "the new wood." To tradition-minded poets, this **free verse**—poetry without regular rhyming and metrical patterns—was deplorable. It meant a loosening of poetic standards and an assault on the very craft of poetry. These poets did not yet realize that successful free verse was at least as difficult to create as verse written in traditional forms.

Although imagism was a short-lived movement, it gave rise to some of our greatest poets. Many in the forefront of imagism went beyond the movement's limitations and expanded its insights. Besides Pound, these poets included William Carlos Williams (page 778), Marianne Moore (page 784), and E. E. Cummings (page 806). Eventually, imagism came to stand for an entirely new order of poetry in the United States. Most Americans became familiar with the movement mainly as the school of free verse. But the imagist program was not only a call for a new method of organizing lines and stanzas but also an invitation to a new way of seeing and experiencing the world.

Ask Yourself

1. Why do you think the symbolists' focus on individualism was so appealing to American poets?

2. How did the imagists change poetry?

3. New generations often reject established ideas about poetry. Why do you think they do so?

Learn It Online
Meet symbolism and imagism through *PowerNotes*.
go.hrw.com   L11-758   **Go**

Analyzing Symbols in a Painting

Like stories and poems, the visual arts can employ images as **symbols** to express complex ideas and emotions.

Guidelines

Use these guidelines to explore the use of symbols in a painting.

- Think about the way the artist uses images. Does the painting contain one or more images that seem to have both a literal meaning and a larger, more complex meaning?

- Consider the larger meanings evoked by the images. What larger meanings does each image convey?

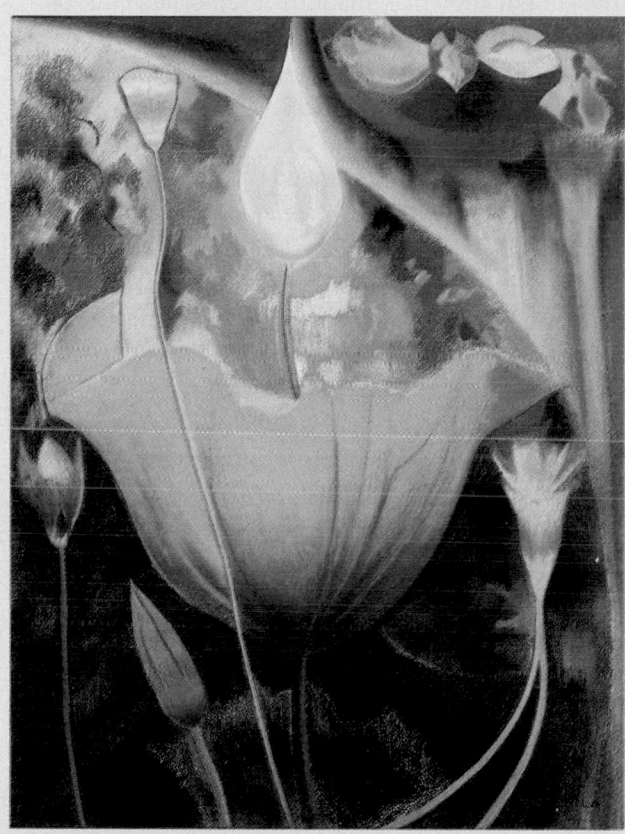

Abstraction (ca. 1913–1914) by Joseph Stella.

1. There seems to be a candle-wick and flame rising out of the main flower. What might this symbolize?

2. What larger meanings come to mind when you think of flowers? What else in this painting suggests these meanings?

3. What alternative title would you give this painting? Try to think of a title that captures both the literal and symbolic meanings of the images.

Your Turn   Analyze Symbolic Images

Identify a symbolic image in another artwork that you find in this unit. Write one or two paragraphs describing the image and explaining what you think it symbolizes.

Preparing to Read

The River-Merchant's Wife: A Letter

The Garden

⏱ **QuickWrite**

Have you ever been struck by the beauty or sadness of something you've seen? Write a short description of your memory, including as many vivid details as possible.

MEET THE WRITER

Ezra Pound
(1885–1972)

Ezra Pound is remembered by many as the man who was charged with treason during World War II and spent many years in a psychiatric hospital. However, the generations of poets who have come after Pound have kept alive a complex memory of a man whose career wavered between brilliance and episodic madness.

Make It New!

Pound was born in Idaho and grew up in Pennsylvania. In 1908, he settled in London and became a spokesperson for the new poetic movement known as imagism. A self-exiled critic of American life, he was also a torchbearer for any art that challenged the complacent middle class.

Pound—whose slogan was "Make it new!"—was a born teacher whose advice was sought by the most brilliant writers of the period. T. S. Eliot acknowledged Pound's influence by dedicating his great poem *The Waste Land* (1922) to him.

A Controversial Figure

After World War I, Pound's interest in economics and social theory led him to support Benito Mussolini, the Fascist dictator of Italy. When World War II broke out, Pound stayed in Italy and turned propagandist for Mussolini's policies. In his radio broadcasts from Italy—many of which were anti-Semitic—Pound denounced the United States and its allies.

In 1945, Pound was taken prisoner by the American army in Italy and was returned to the United States to be tried for treason. Psychiatrists judged him incompetent, and the poet was committed to a hospital for the criminally insane in 1946.

Twelve years later Pound was released through the intercession of writers, including Archibald MacLeish and Robert Frost, who argued that his literary contributions outweighed his lack of judgment. Pound returned to Italy. During Pound's last years, a reporter once asked him where he was living. "In hell," Pound answered. "Which hell?" the reporter asked. "Here," said Pound, pressing his heart. "Here."

Think About the Writer Do you think artists should be judged by a different standard from that used for other people? Should society be more forgiving of a genius? Explain.

The River-Merchant's Wife: A Letter / The Garden

SKILLS FOCUS Literary Skills Understand imagery. **Reading Skills** Use paraphrasing as a strategy for comprehension.

Reader/Writer Notebook

Use your **RWN** to complete the activities for these selections.

Literary Focus

Imagery Pound's poems are rich in **imagery**—language that evokes a picture or a concrete sensation of a person, a thing, a place, or an experience. "The River-Merchant's Wife: A Letter" is an adaptation of a poem by the great Chinese poet Li Po (701–762). Pound's poem is based on the images and feelings that he experienced when he read Li Po's poem in translation. In "The Garden," Pound's use of simple and concrete imagery helps the reader visualize a woman walking in a London park.

Reading Focus

Paraphrasing To make sure you understand a poem's meaning, **paraphrase** the lines as you read by restating them in your own words. Note unusual word order, and rewrite the phrases or lines in normal word order.

Into Action Paraphrase the lines of Pound's poems as you read. Use a two-column chart for each poem. In the first column, record lines from the poem; and in the second column, paraphrase them. Then, go back to the first column and underline any striking images in the poem.

Poem: "The River-Merchant's Wife: A Letter"

Lines	Paraphrase
(1–2) "While my <u>hair</u> was still <u>cut</u> straight across my forehead / <u>Played</u> I about the front gate, <u>pulling flowers</u>."	When I was still a child, I played in front of the house, picking flowers.

Writing Focus

Think as a Reader/Writer

Find It in Your Reading The words a poet chooses contribute to the poem's message and shape how we feel about the characters. For example, in "The Garden," Pound uses the image of a skein of loose silk. By comparing the woman to the skein of silk, he implies that she is emotionally fragile. As you read, record in your *Reader/Writer Notebook* any strong words that shape your image of each poem's main character.

TechFocus As you read these poems, consider how the poets might use digital sounds and images to convey their experiences.

Vocabulary

mingled (MIHNG guhld) *v.*: combined or blended in a mixture. *The wife hoped her remains would be mingled with her husband's remains after death.*

eddies (EHD eez) *n.*: small whirlpools. *The distant river contains swirling eddies.*

sorrowful (SAWR uh fuhl) *adj.*: full of sorrow or sadness. *The river-merchant's wife recalls the sorrowful noise of the monkeys.*

skein (skayn) *n.*: loosely coiled bundle of yarn or thread. *The poet compares a woman to a skein of silk.*

rabble (RAB uhl) *n.*: disorderly crowd. *The woman is surrounded by a rabble of poor children.*

Language Coach

Specific Nouns Some nouns are very precise. The words *skein* and *spool* can both describe thread. A skein names a coiled bundle of yarn or thread that is not wrapped around a hard core. A spool of thread is a coil of thread wrapped around a hard core, often made of wood or plastic.

Poets use specific nouns to create precise images. Think about similar words to understand the images a poet creates. Describe the difference between each pair of words.
1. *eddy* and *swirl*
2. *rabble* and *crowd*
3. *railing* and *fence*

Learn It Online
Hear these poems for yourself online.

go.hrw.com L11-761 **Go**

The River-Merchant's Wife: A Letter

by **Ezra Pound**

Read with a Purpose
Read to discover the longing one woman experiences in her life.

Build Background

In this letter-poem, Pound assumes the voice of a Chinese river-merchant's wife as she thinks about her growing love for her husband. This poem is a tribute to Li Po (701–762), a great Chinese poet. Pound had to cross generations, cultures, continents, and genders to write the poem; its intimate tone creates a bridge for the reader. If you have ever been moved to write a letter to someone you loved and missed, you will identify at once with the feelings of this eighth-century Chinese speaker.

While my hair was still cut straight across my forehead
Played I about the front gate, pulling flowers.
You came by on bamboo stilts, playing horse,
You walked about my seat, playing with blue plums.
5   And we went on living in the village of Chokan:
Two small people, without dislike or suspicion.   **A**

At fourteen I married My Lord you.
I never laughed, being bashful.
Lowering my head, I looked at the wall.
10   Called to, a thousand times, I never looked back.

At fifteen I stopped scowling,
I desired my dust to be mingled with yours
Forever and forever and forever.
Why should I climb the lookout?   **B**

A **Literary Focus** Imagery What emotions and character traits do the images in these lines suggest?

B **Reading Focus** Paraphrasing How would you paraphrase the last line in this stanza?

Vocabulary mingled (MIHNG guhld) v.: combined or blended in a mixture.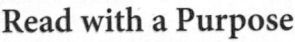

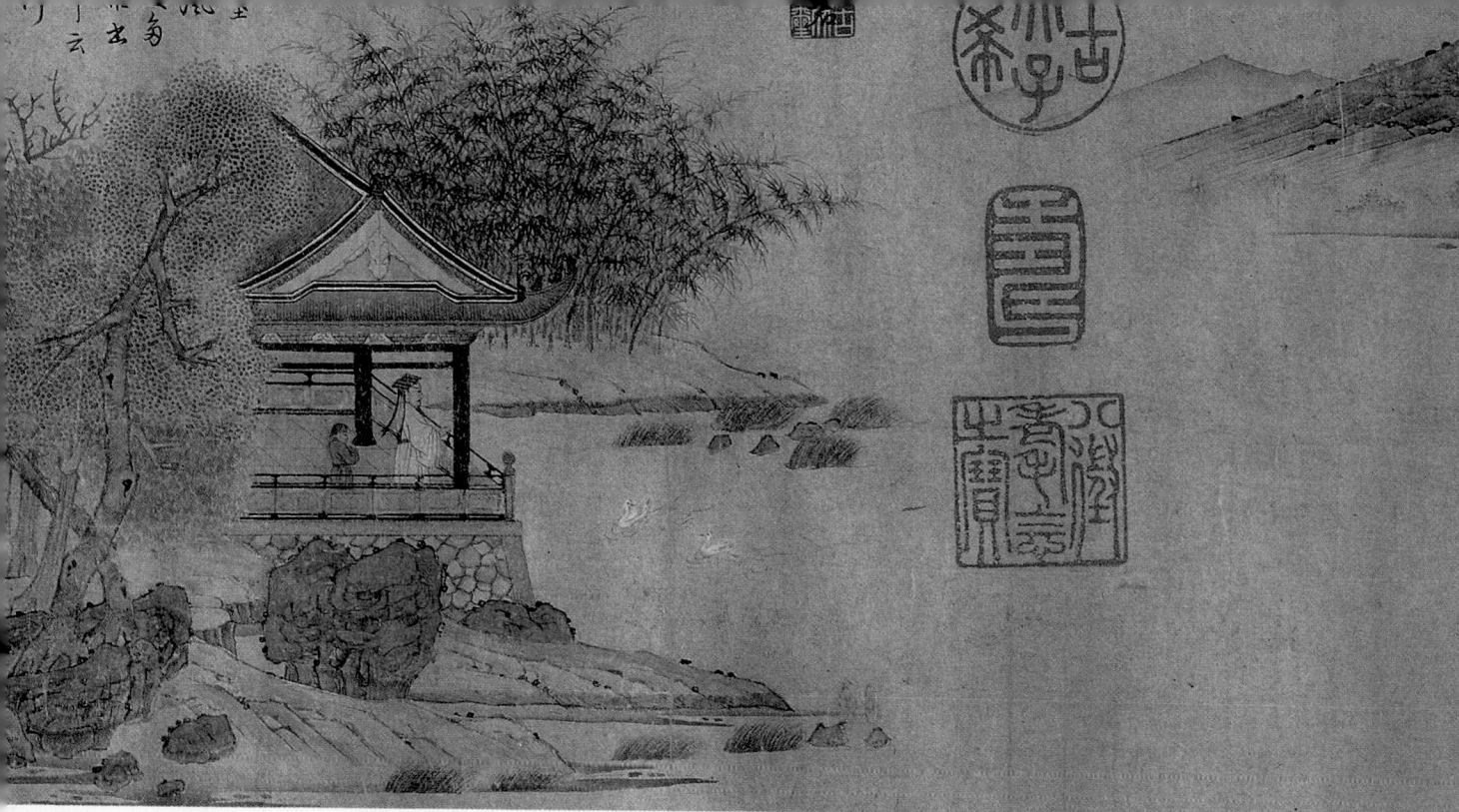

Wang Xizhi Watching Geese (detail)
(ca. 1295) by Qian Xuan.
Ex. coll.; C.C. Wang Family, Gift of the Dillon
Fund, 1973 (1973.120.6) © The Metropolitan
Museum of Art / Art Resource, NY.

15   At sixteen you departed
    You went into far Ku-to-yen, by the river of swirling eddies,
    And you have been gone five months.
    The monkeys make sorrowful noise overhead. **C**

    You dragged your feet when you went out.
20   By the gate now, the moss is grown, the different mosses,
    Too deep to clear them away!
    The leaves fall early this autumn, in wind.
    The paired butterflies are already yellow with August
    Over the grass in the West garden;
25   They hurt me. I grow older.
    If you are coming down through the narrows of the river Kiang,
    Please let me know beforehand.
    And I will come out to meet you
          As far as Cho-fu-Sa. **D**

                             —Li T'ai Po

C **Literary Focus** Imagery To what senses do the images "swirling eddies" and
"sorrowful noise" appeal? Why do you think Pound includes these descriptions?

D **Literary Focus** Imagery A series of images helps create a mood. What do these
images reveal about the speaker's feelings?

Vocabulary **eddies** (EHD eez) *n.*: small whirlpools.
sorrowful (SAWR uh fuhl) *adj.*: full of sorrow or sadness.

The Garden

by **Ezra Pound**

Read with a Purpose
Read to discover what the speaker assumes about a woman he observes in a park.

Build Background
"En robe de parade" is a quotation from the nineteenth-century French poet Albert Samain. It means "dressed for show" or, in military terms, "in full regalia." In this poem, the speaker observes a beautifully dressed woman walking in a London park called Kensington Gardens.

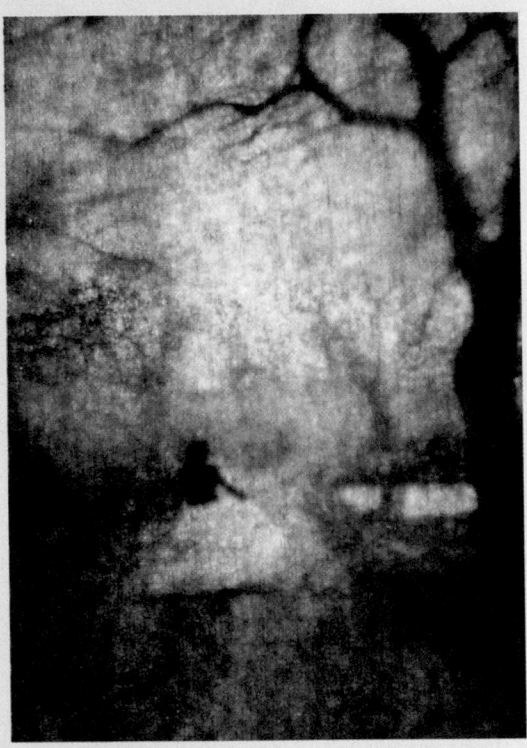

En robe de parade.
　　—Samain

Like a skein of loose silk blown against a wall
She walks by the railing of a path in Kensington Gardens,
And she is dying piecemeal
　　of a sort of emotional anemia. **Ⓐ**

5　And round about there is a rabble
Of the filthy, sturdy, unkillable infants of the very poor.
They shall inherit the earth.

In her is the end of breeding.
Her boredom is exquisite and excessive.
10　She would like someone to speak to her,
and is almost afraid that I
　　will commit that indiscretion. **Ⓑ**

Ⓐ Literary Focus Imagery To what does the poet compare the woman? Why do you think the poet uses the word *skein*?

Ⓑ Reading Focus Paraphrasing Paraphrase this stanza. What does it say about the woman?

Vocabulary skein (skayn) *n.:* loosely coiled bundle of yarn or thread.
rabble (RAB uhl) *n.:* disorderly crowd.

Applying Your Skills

SKILLS FOCUS Literary Skills Analyze imagery; analyze allusions. **Reading Skills** Use paraphrasing as a strategy for comprehension. **Writing Skills** Incorporate imagery in writing.

The River-Merchant's Wife: A Letter /
The Garden

Respond and Think Critically

Reading Focus

Quick Check

1. When did the river-merchant's wife fall in love with her husband?

2. How is the woman in "The Garden" different from others in her surroundings?

Read with a Purpose

3. How does the river-merchant's wife express her longing for her absent husband?

4. Why is the woman in "The Garden" unlikely to find happiness?

Reading Skills: Paraphrasing

5. Now that you have paraphrased the poems to better understand their meaning, review your chart. Note what associations each underlined image in the first column evokes. Write your response in the third column.

Poem: "The River-Merchant's Wife: A Letter"

Lines	Paraphrase	What the Image Evokes
(1–2) "While my hair was still <u>cut straight across my forehead</u> / Played I about the front gate, <u>pulling flowers.</u>"	When I was still a child, I played in front of the house, picking flowers.	innocence; a happy time; youth

Literary Focus

Literary Analysis

The River-Merchant's Wife: A Letter

6. **Infer** In the second stanza, what does the river-merchant's wife mean when she says, "I never laughed" and "I looked at the wall"?

7. **Infer** What is the significance of the mosses that are "too deep" to "clear them away" (line 21)?

The Garden

8. **Infer** Explain the phrase "emotional anemia" (line 4). How might this condition cause the woman to die "piecemeal"?

9. **Interpret** *Breeding* can mean "producing off-spring" or "upbringing." Explain the double meaning of the word in line 8.

Literary Skills: Imagery

10. **Infer** Why does the image of the paired butterflies in "The River-Merchant's Wife" affect the speaker?

Literary Skills Review: Allusion

11. **Extend** An **allusion** is a reference to someone or something known from history, religion, politics, or some other branch of culture. Line 7 of "The Garden," "They shall inherit the earth," alludes to the Bible (Matthew 5:5). There Jesus says, "Blessed are the meek, for they shall inherit the earth." What does the line mean in this context?

Writing Focus

Think as a Reader/Writer

Use It in Your Writing Review your QuickWrite description about something that moved you with its beauty or sadness. Revise your description by using new details and images. How does this change the meaning or emotional quality of your description?

What Do **You Think Now**

How is society being redefined in Pound's "The Garden"? Explain.

The River-Merchant's Wife: A Letter / The Garden

Vocabulary Development

 **Vocabulary Check**

Match each Vocabulary word with its definition.

1. mingled
2. eddies
3. sorrowful
4. skein
5. rabble

a. small whirlpools
b. coiled bundle of yarn
c. disorderly crowd
d. combined or blended
e. full of sadness

Vocabulary Skills: Suffixes

A **suffix** is a word part that is added to the end of a word or root (word base) to create a new word. The suffix –*ing*, added to a verb, can make that verb function as another part of speech. When the new word functions as an adjective, it is called a **participle**, as in "the **swimming** fish." When it functions as a noun, it is called a **gerund**, as in "I was was pulled over for **speeding**."

The suffix –*ing* can also change the form of a verb. Adding –*ing* to *live* changes the sentence *I live* to *I am living*. Here, *am living* is a **progressive** verb. The progressive verb form describes continuing action or a state of being.

Your Turn

Find each of the following words in Pound's poems. Tell whether they are used as participles, gerunds, or progressive verbs.

1. pulling
2. playing
3. scowling
4. swirling
5. breeding
6. dying

SKILLS FOCUS Vocabulary Skills
Understand suffixes. **Writing Skills** Write poetry; incorporate imagery in writing; develop descriptions with sensory details.

CHOICES

As you respond to the Choices, use these **Academic Vocabulary** words as appropriate: <u>alternative</u>, <u>hierarchy</u>, <u>ideology</u>, <u>inevitable</u>, <u>tradition</u>.

REVIEW

Create a Digital Story

TechFocus Ezra Pound used poetry to tell a story and convey emotions, but today's storytellers often use <u>alternative</u> artistic forms, such as film and digital media. Choose one of Pound's poems, and create a digital story version—a narrative enhanced with music and images—told from the speaker's point of view. Try to match the poem's mood and tone in your story. For more about digital stories, visit the Digital Storytelling mini-site at go.hrw.com.

CONNECT

Write the River-Merchant's Reply

Imagine that the river-merchant's wife is able to send her letter. Her husband receives it; then he composes a reply. What would he write? How would he write it? Write your version of his letter, in poem or prose form. Include imagery modeled after Pound's poetry.

EXTEND

Create Strong Imagery

Ezra Pound once expressed part of his poetic <u>ideology</u>: "It is better to present one Image in a lifetime than to produce voluminous works." Follow Pound's example, and describe something—an object, event, person—in prose, with plenty of detail and explanation. Then, select the strongest image from your description and use it to write a short poem. Choose words that will form an image in the reader's mind.

 **Learn It Online**
For more about digital stories visit the Digital Storytelling mini-site.

go.hrw.com   L11-766   **Go**

Reading Focus

SKILLS FOCUS **Reading Skills** Synthesize important ideas in a poem; identify historical context; analyze a writer's perspective.

The Love Song of J. Alfred Prufrock

Synthesizing Important Ideas in a Poem by **Kylene Beers**

One of your objects as a reader is to synthesize, or to bring together, elements of a work to form an impression of the whole. In reading a poem, you look at the literary tools that a writer uses to convey ideas, including figures of speech, imagery, form, and rhythm.

T. S. Eliot's poems reflect his ideas about the era in which he lived. He felt that life in the early twentieth century was unromantic and unheroic. He viewed people as spiritually empty and passive. In "The Love Song of J. Alfred Prufrock," these ideas emerge from the setting, the situation, the characters, and the speaker's thoughts and associations.

Identify the Historical Context

Although not every poem is explicitly tied to historical events or perspectives, knowing when and where a poem was written is helpful. T. S. Eliot published "The Love Song of J. Alfred Prufrock" during World War I. That's almost a century ago, before computers and the Internet. However, today's society has a good deal in common with Eliot's, as you can see in this passage from the poem:

> Let us go, through certain
>   half-deserted streets,
> The muttering retreats
> Of restless nights in one-night
>   cheap hotels
> And sawdust restaurants with
>   oyster-shells:

A city's half-deserted streets, cheap hotels, and mediocre restaurants can be seen in the twenty-first century.

See a Writer's Perspective

When you know the historical context of a poem, you can make connections between that context and the ideas the poem expresses. Knowing the context helps you see from the writer's perspective.

In Eliot's poem, instead of a "hero," a figure full of romance and grand successes, we meet an "antihero."

> Do I dare
> Disturb the universe?
> In a minute there is time
> For decisions and revisions…

The speaker is passive, disillusioned, and indecisive.

Connect to Today

Some ideas in a poem may apply only to their historical context, but some speak across time—such as the concept of an antihero. Scholar Joseph Campbell, in the PBS series *The Power of Myth,* observed that our times are hostile to heroism. According to Campbell, heroes are people of action, but the drudgery of modern life has turned many into observers rather than participants in life's adventures. As you read, think about which ideas in the poem are relevant today.

Your Turn

For each passage from "The Love Song of J. Alfred Prufrock," identify one thing you can learn about Eliot's time and one thing relevant to your own time.

1. For the yellow smoke that slides along the street
   Rubbing its back upon the window-panes;
   There will be time, there will be time
   To prepare a face to meet the faces that you meet;

2. (They will say: "How his hair is growing thin!")
   My morning coat, my collar mounting firmly to
     the chin,
   My necktie rich and modest, but asserted by a
     simple pin—

Learn It Online

Find the interactive *PowerNotes* presentation of this essay online.

go.hrw.com   L11-767   **Go**

Preparing to Read

The Love Song of J. Alfred Prufrock

What Do You Think

How does progress challenge <u>tradition</u> and redefine society?

QuickWrite

J. Alfred Prufrock is an insecure character, full of self-doubt, which hinders his ability to connect and communicate with others. What else can you think of that might hinder someone's ability to connect or communicate with others? Make a quick list.

T. S. Eliot
(1888–1965)

Nobel Prize WINNER

In 1948, Thomas Stearns Eliot was awarded the Nobel Prize in literature for his work as a pioneer of modern poetry. Eliot, once regarded as the most difficult and obscure poet of his era, ironically achieved celebrity and began drawing large audiences to his lectures and poetry readings.

Complex Poetry for a Complex World

T. S. Eliot was born in St. Louis, Missouri. Eliot's childhood awareness of his native city would show itself in his poetry, but only after he had moved far away from it. He graduated from Harvard University, did postgraduate work in Paris, and moved to London in 1914. There, he finally took up the business of literature. He became an active publisher, editor, and critic.

The most crucial influence on Eliot's early poems came from the late nineteenth-century French poets who, as a group, came to be known as the symbolists. These poets wanted to re-create states of mind and feeling, as opposed to reporting or confessing them. These beliefs became the basis of Eliot's poetic method. When people complained that the resulting poems were difficult to understand, Eliot replied that poetry had to be complex in order to express the complexities of modern life.

Words for a Wasteland

Eliot startled his contemporaries with "The Love Song of J. Alfred Prufrock" in 1915 and "Portrait of a Lady" in 1917. In 1922, with the encouragement of Ezra Pound, Eliot published *The Waste Land,* a long work considered the most significant poem of the early twentieth century. The poem describes a spiritually empty civilization that is paralyzed by indecision. The poem's intricate structure and dense network of allusions to world literature, Eastern religions, and anthropology intrigued critics. In 1925, Eliot published "The Hollow Men," a poem that brings the poet—and by extension, the world—to a point of despair beyond which lies either renewal or annihilation. His later poems explore religious themes and the search for faith.

Think About the Writer

Do you think Eliot's view of poetry is a common one? Why or why not?

![icon] **Reader/Writer**
Notebook

Use your **RWN** to complete the activities for this selection.

SKILLS FOCUS **Literary Skills** Understand dramatic monologue. **Reading Skills** Synthesize important ideas in a poem.

Literary Focus

Dramatic Monologue This poem is written as a **dramatic monologue**—a poem in which a character speaks directly to one or more listeners. The speaker is a man named Prufrock.

In a dramatic monologue, we must learn everything about the setting, the situation, the other characters, and the personality of the speaker through what the speaker tells us. Sometimes Prufrock's line of reasoning is interrupted by an unexpected thought. You will <u>inevitably</u> have to supply the missing connections in the speaker's stream of thoughts and associations.

Literary Perspectives Apply the literary perspective described on page 771 as you read this poem.

Reading Focus

Synthesizing Important Ideas in a Poem The speaker in a dramatic monologue often reveals his or her most private thoughts, inner longings, and deepest fears—all of which can reflect ideas about the period during which the poem is set.

Into Action As you read the poem, aim to get a general sense of Prufrock's thoughts, longings, and fears. Create a three-column chart. In column 2, summarize the speaker's thoughts and feelings in each stanza. After you've read the poem once, you will fill in a third column.

Stanza	Prufrock's Thoughts
1	He wants to take another person on a walk through the city in the evening. He does not want to talk about "the overwhelming question."

Vocabulary

tedious (TEE dee uhs) *adj.:* long and boring. *Prufrock thinks his private thoughts would probably seem tedious to others.*

digress (duh GREHS) *v.:* get off the main subject. *The rambling narrative style of the poem allows the speaker to digress easily from the topic.*

overwhelming (oh vuhr HWEHLM ihng) *adj.:* overpowering. *The idea of communicating intimately with another person is overwhelming and frightening to Prufrock.*

obtuse (uhb TOOS) *adj.:* slow to understand; stupid. *Prufrock feels that he is obtuse when it comes to relating to others.*

Language Coach

Antonyms Thinking about antonyms can help you recall the meanings of unfamiliar words. To remember that *tedious* means "long and boring," you can think about antonyms for the word, such as *exciting, interesting,* or *fascinating.* Can you think of at least one antonym for each word from the list above?

Writing Focus

Think as a Reader/Writer

Find It in Your Reading The speaking style of the poem's speaker is an important element of a **dramatic monologue**. What are the characteristics of Prufrock's speaking style? Does he use figures of speech, repetition, or other literary devices? In your *Reader/Writer Notebook*, note anything particular about his style.

Learn It Online
Find more about Eliot with these Internet links.

 L11-769

The Love Song of J. Alfred Prufrock

by **T. S. Eliot**

Read with a Purpose
Read to hear the thoughts of a man who is trapped by his own fears.

Build Background
T. S. Eliot begins this poem with an **epigraph**—a short quotation used to introduce a piece of writing. This quotation is from Dante's long narrative poem *The Divine Comedy* (1321). The speaker is Guido da Montefeltro, a man sent to Hell for dispensing evil advice. He speaks from a flame that quivers when he talks: "If I thought my answer were to one who ever could return to the world, this flame should shake no more; but since none ever did return alive from this depth, if what I hear be true, without fear of infamy I answer this" (*Inferno*, Canto 27, lines 61–66).

S'io credessi che mia risposta fosse
a persona che mai tornasse al mondo,
questa fiamma staria senza più scosse.
Ma per ciò che giammai di questo fondo
non tornò vivo alcun, s'i'odo il vero,
senza tema d'infamia ti rispondo.

Soho Twilight (c. 1924) by Christopher Richard Wynne Nevison.

Let us go then, you and I,
When the evening is spread out against the sky
Like a patient etherized° upon a table;
Let us go, through certain half-deserted streets, **Ⓐ**

5   The muttering retreats
Of restless nights in one-night cheap hotels
And sawdust restaurants with oyster-shells:
Streets that follow like a tedious argument
Of insidious intent

10   To lead you to an overwhelming question . . .
Oh, do not ask, "What is it?"
Let us go and make our visit. **Ⓑ**

In the room the women come and go
Talking of Michelangelo.°

3. etherized: made unconscious; under anesthesia.

14. Michelangelo: Michelangelo Buonarroti (1475–1564), a great artist of the Italian Renaissance.

Ⓐ **Literary Focus** **Dramatic Monologue** Dramatic monologues often have complex or multiple settings. What do you know about the setting so far?

Ⓑ **Literary Focus** **Dramatic Monologue** Whom do you think the speaker is addressing?

Vocabulary **tedious** (TEE dee uhs) *adj.*: long and boring.

15 The yellow fog that rubs its back upon the window-panes,
  The yellow smoke that rubs its muzzle on the window-panes,
  Licked its tongue into the corners of the evening,
  Lingered upon the pools that stand in drains,
  Let fall upon its back the soot that falls from chimneys,
20 Slipped by the terrace, made a sudden leap,
  And seeing that it was a soft October night,
  Curled once about the house, and fell asleep.

  And indeed there will be time
  For the yellow smoke that slides along the street
25 Rubbing its back upon the window-panes;
  There will be time, there will be time
  To prepare a face to meet the faces that you meet;
  There will be time to murder and create,
  And time for all the works and days of hands
30 That lift and drop a question on your plate;
  Time for you and time for me,
  And time yet for a hundred indecisions,
  And for a hundred visions and revisions,
  Before the taking of a toast and tea. **C**

35 In the room the women come and go
  Talking of Michelangelo.

  And indeed there will be time
  To wonder, "Do I dare?" and, "Do I dare?"
  Time to turn back and descend the stair,
40 With a bald spot in the middle of my hair—
  (They will say: "How his hair is growing thin!")
  My morning coat, my collar mounting firmly
    to the chin,
  My necktie rich and modest, but asserted by a simple pin—
  (They will say: "But how his arms and legs are thin!")
45 Do I dare
  Disturb the universe?
  In a minute there is time
  For decisions and revisions which a minute will reverse. **D**

C **Reading Focus** **Synthesizing Important Ideas in a Poem** What important idea do you sense from the repetition of "there will be time" and "time"? Think of the idea in terms of what you have read so far.

D **Literary Perspectives** **Analyzing Style** Notice that the speaker interrupts his train of thought to consider what others will say about him. What is the effect of these interruptions?

For I have known them all already, known them all—
50 Have known the evenings, mornings, afternoons,
I have measured out my life with coffee spoons;
I know the voices dying with a dying fall°
Beneath the music from a farther room.
     So how should I presume?

55 And I have known the eyes already, known them all—
The eyes that fix you in a formulated° phrase,
And when I am formulated, sprawling on a pin,
When I am pinned and wriggling on the wall,
Then how should I begin
60 To spit out all the butt-ends of my days and ways?
     And how should I presume?

And I have known the arms already, known them all—
Arms that are braceleted and white and bare
(But in the lamplight, downed with light brown hair!)
65 Is it perfume from a dress
That makes me so digress?
Arms that lie along a table, or wrap about a shawl.
     And should I then presume?
     And how should I begin?
          . . . . .
70 Shall I say, I have gone at dusk through narrow streets
And watched the smoke that rises from the pipes
Of lonely men in shirt-sleeves, leaning out of windows? . . .

I should have been a pair of ragged claws
Scuttling across the floors of silent seas.

          . . . . .
75 And the afternoon, the evening, sleeps so peacefully!
Smoothed by long fingers,
Asleep . . . tired . . . or it malingers,
Stretched on the floor, here beside you and me.
Should I, after tea and cakes and ices,
80 Have the strength to force the moment to its crisis?
But though I have wept and fasted, wept and prayed,

52. dying fall: in music, notes that fade away.

56. formulated: reduced to a formula and made insignificant.

Analyzing Visuals

Viewing and Interpreting
What is the mood suggested by this picture? Does this mood match the mood Eliot establishes in his poem?

New York by Night (c. 1922) by Christopher Richard Wynne Nevison.

E **Literary Focus** **Dramatic Monologue** A speaker in a dramatic monologue usually reveals inner longings and fears. What emotions does Prufrock's description of women's arms suggest?

Vocabulary **digress** (duh GREHS) *v.*: get off the main subject.

Though I have seen my head (grown slightly bald)
    brought in upon a platter,°
I am no prophet—and here's no great matter;
I have seen the moment of my greatness flicker,
And I have seen the eternal Footman hold my coat,
85   and snicker,
And in short, I was afraid. **F**

And would it have been worth it, after all,
After the cups, the marmalade, the tea,
Among the porcelain, among some talk of you and me,
90 Would it have been worth while,
To have bitten off the matter with a smile,
To have squeezed the universe into a ball
To roll it towards some overwhelming question,
To say: "I am Lazarus, come from the dead,
95 Come back to tell you all, I shall tell you all"—
If one, settling a pillow by her head,
    Should say: "That is not what I meant at all.
    That is not it, at all."

And would it have been worth it, after all,
100 Would it have been worth while,
After the sunsets and the dooryards and the sprinkled streets,
After the novels, after the teacups, after the skirts that trail
    along the floor—
And this, and so much more?—
It is impossible to say just what I mean!
But as if a magic lantern° threw the nerves in patterns on
105   a screen:
Would it have been worth while
If one, settling a pillow or throwing off a shawl,
And turning toward the window, should say:
    "That is not it at all,
110   That is not what I meant, at all." **G**
    . . . . .

No! I am not Prince Hamlet, nor was meant to be;
Am an attendant lord, one that will do

---

82. my head . . . a platter: biblical allusion to the execution of John the Baptist (Mark 6:17–28; Matthew 14:3–11). The dancing of Salome so pleased Herod Antipas, ruler of ancient Galilee, that he offered her any reward she desired. Goaded by her mother, who hated John, Salome asked for John's head. Herod ordered the prophet beheaded and his head delivered on a serving plate.

105. magic lantern: early type of projector that could magnify and project opaque photographs or book pages as well as transparent slides.

F **Reading Focus** **Synthesizing Important Ideas in a Poem** In this stanza, what larger idea is Prufrock conveying about life?

G **Literary Focus** **Dramatic Monologue** How would you characterize the woman who speaks in lines 109–110? What does she think of Prufrock?

Vocabulary **overwhelming** (oh vuhr HWEHLM ihng) *adj.:* overpowering.

At the Ball by Julius Leblanc Stewart (1855–1919).

To swell a progress,° start a scene or two,
Advise the prince; no doubt, an easy tool,
115 Deferential, glad to be of use,
Politic, cautious, and meticulous;
Full of high sentence,° but a bit obtuse;
At times, indeed, almost ridiculous—
Almost, at times, the Fool.

120 I grow old . . . I grow old . . .
I shall wear the bottoms of my trousers rolled.

Shall I part my hair behind? Do I dare to eat a peach?
I shall wear white flannel trousers, and walk upon the beach.
I have heard the mermaids singing, each to each.

125 I do not think that they will sing to me.

I have seen them riding seaward on the waves
Combing the white hair of the waves blown back
When the wind blows the water white and black.

We have lingered in the chambers of the sea
130 By sea-girls wreathed with seaweed red and brown
Till human voices wake us, and we drown. **Ⓗ**

113. swell a progress: fill out a scene in a play or pageant by serving as an extra.

117. high sentence: pompous talk.

Ⓗ **Literary Perspectives** **Analyzing Style** What expectation does the reader have after "Till human voices wake us"? What causes the irony in this line?

Vocabulary **obtuse** (uhb TOOS) *adj.:* slow to understand; stupid.

Applying Your Skills

The Love Song of J. Alfred Prufrock

Respond and Think Critically

Reading Focus

Quick Check

1. What does the famous simile in lines 2–3 reveal about the speaker's mind or will?

2. What are Prufrock's major concerns?

Read with a Purpose

3. What effect do Prufrock's fears have on his life? Which images convey this information? How?

Reading Skills: Synthesizing Important Ideas in a Poem

4. Re-read the poem. Now, record how Prufrock's thoughts reflect the following ideas about his time and ours: (1) People are passive observers, and (2) life is unromantic and unheroic.

Stanza	Prufrock's Thoughts	Connections to Prufrock's Time or Ours
1	He wants to take another person on a walk through the city in the evening. He does not want to talk about "the overwhelming question."	The city is half-deserted, restless, tedious, and run down. This description can apply to both times, depending on the mood of the observer.

Literary Focus

Literary Analysis

5. **Infer** What does line 51 imply about the way Prufrock has lived? What other measuring devices would suggest a different kind of life?

6. **Draw Conclusions** Lines 87–98 echo the complaint that a lack of communication between people is the cause of misunderstanding. What do you think Prufrock would like to tell people?

7. **Interpret** What references to women does Prufrock make? How do you think he feels about women and his attractiveness to them?

8. **Literary Perspectives** As you read, you considered aspects of Eliot's style that convey the mood, tone, and theme of the poem. Which technique do you think Eliot relies on most often in this poem to develop his style? Support your answer with examples.

Literary Skills: Dramatic Monologue

9. **Infer** Eliot's dramatic monologue allows us to see Prufrock's deep insecurities and self-consciousness, particularly in lines 37–44. What is Prufrock worried about in these lines?

Literary Skills Review: Extended Metaphor

10. **Analyze** An **extended metaphor** is a metaphor developed over a number of lines or with several examples. Lines 15–25 contain one of the most famous extended metaphors in modern poetry. What is being indirectly compared to what? What details extend the metaphor?

Writing Focus

Think as a Reader/Writer

Use It in Your Writing Write a few lines of a **dramatic monologue** spoken by someone giving advice to Prufrock on how to improve his life. Let your monologue reflect the free flow of the speaker's thought process by creating a particular speaking style for him or her.

What Do You Think Now How does Prufrock challenge tradition? Does he make any real progress?

The Love Song of J. Alfred Prufrock

Vocabulary Development

✔ Vocabulary Check

Use the Vocabulary words in your answers to the following questions.

1. What do you find more **tedious,** a long day stuck indoors or a three-hour car ride? Why?

2. Is an **obtuse** person more or less likely to believe anything you say? Explain.

3. If you **digress** while telling your best friend an interesting story, what might you be doing?

4. Why might an assignment feel **overwhelming?**

Vocabulary Skills: Suffixes Derived from Latin

A **suffix** is a word part that is added to the end of a base word or root. **Inflectional suffixes,** like –ed and –ing, usually just change the tense, the person, or the number of a word (generally a verb). **Derivational suffixes** actually change the meaning of a root or base word. Many derivational suffixes, such as –ous and –ion, have their origins in Latin.

When the suffix –ion, from the Latin ending –io, is added to a word, the suffix means "a state or condition," "the act of," or "the result of a state, act, or process." Quite simply, the suffix usually turns a verb into a noun. A demonstration, for example, is "the act of demonstrating."

The suffix –ous, from the Latin word ending –osus, means "full of" or "having the quality of." It is an adjective-forming suffix. It is exemplified in beauteous: "full of beauty."

Your Turn

Identify the suffix in each of the following words. Then, use the definition you know of each suffix and base word to write your own definition for the word. Check the accuracy of your definition in a dictionary.

1. indecision
2. cautious
3. revisions
4. question

Language Coach

Antonyms Some antonym pairs are obvious, such as *strong* and *weak*. Others require you to think about specific meanings. For example, *tedious* and *stimulating* are antonyms. *Tedious* means "long and boring," while *stimulating* can mean "causing interest or excitement." Match each word in the left column below with its antonym in the right column. Explain why the words in each pair are antonyms.

1. tedious   a. intelligent
2. digress   b. intriguing
3. overwhelming   c. insignificant
4. obtuse   d. focus

Academic Vocabulary

Talk About
With a partner, discuss the following questions: Are feelings of isolation an <u>inevitable</u> part of life? What <u>alternative</u> ways of viewing one's life can help relieve isolation?

SKILLS FOCUS Vocabulary Skills
Demonstrate word knowledge; use suffixes
to interpret words. **Writing Skills** Analyze
a poem; analyze unique aspects of the text.

Grammar Skills Identify the mood of verbs.
Listening and Speaking Skills Participate
in group discussions; make appropriate and
meaningful comments in discussions and

conversations; offer insightful observations in
discussions and conversations.

Grammar Link

Mood

Verbs may be in one of three **moods.** The **indicative mood** expresses facts, opinions, or questions.

> T. S. Eliot **was** a poet and an editor. [fact]
> I **believe** this is his best poem. [opinion]
> **Are** his poems hard to understand? [question]

The **imperative mood** expresses commands.

> **Read** this poem by T. S. Eliot for class. [command]
> **Tell** me how you interpret the poem. [request]

Verbs in the **subjunctive mood** express necessity, wishes, suggestions, or conditions contrary to fact. In the **present subjunctive,** the base form of the verb doesn't change, but you use *be* instead of *am, is,* or *are,* and drop the *–s* from third-person singular verbs.

> Eliot believed it essential that modern poems **be** as complex as modern life. [necessity]
> He recommends that she **leave** now. [suggestion]

The **past subjunctive** appears the same as the past tense, but in the case of the verb *to be,* you use *were.*

> I wish the poem **were** easier to understand. [wish]
> His poems would probably be less interesting if they **were** simpler. [condition contrary to fact]

Your Turn

Identify the mood of the italicized verbs in the following sentences as *indicative, imperative,* or *subjunctive.*

1. It is necessary that the student *read* carefully.

2. *Take* the time to read each footnote.

3. *Can* you *picture* the smoke Eliot describes?

Writing Application Practice mood with a piece of your own writing. Choose three sentences in the indicative mood, and rewrite each in the imperative or subjunctive mood.

CHOICES

As you respond to the Choices, use these **Academic Vocabulary** words as appropriate: alternative, hierarchy, ideology, inevitable, tradition.

REVIEW

Create Unusual Images

Eliot's poem is filled with unusual imagery, such as evening sprawled out like an unconscious patient, and yellow, catlike fog. Make a drawing, computer animation, or collage based on one of these images, and then create a written description of the image.

CONNECT

Discuss Prufrock

Class Discussion The poet Stephen Spender judges Prufrock harshly: "He is isolated, he cannot communicate. Although the fact that he is *conditioned* by the society in which he lives may account for his spiritual and sexual enervation, this does not excuse his moral cowardice." Discuss Spender's opinion. Do you agree with Spender? Explain.

EXTEND

Write About Prufrock

Timed Writing John Malcolm Brinnin wrote of Prufrock: "Focusing on one thing, he can't help thinking of something else. Everything actual has its counterpart in an image or a metaphor or a situation, by means of which Eliot can dramatize the dilemma of a man suffering a kind of emotional paralysis." Find evidence supporting Brinnin's analysis of Prufrock's psychology. Summarize your findings, and offer an alternative analysis in a short essay.

Learn It Online
For an interactive tutorial on suffixes, check out *WordSharp* online.

go.hrw.com   L11-777   **Go**

Preparing to Read

The Red Wheelbarrow
The Great Figure
This Is Just to Say

What Do You Think?

How does progress challenge tradition and redefine society?

🕐 QuickTalk

Why are people sometimes slow to recognize progress? With a group of classmates, think of occasions in history, literature, or your own life when people dismissed or overlooked something that eventually turned out to be revolutionary.

William Carlos Williams (1924) by Man Ray.

MEET THE WRITER

William Carlos Williams
(1883–1963)

The English Romantic poet William Wordsworth wrote that poetry should treat "incidents and situations from common life … in a selection of language really used by men." William Carlos Williams took this notion of poetic subject matter and language to heart and produced poetry that views ordinary people and objects in a fresh way.

The Bare Essentials

Williams was born in Rutherford, New Jersey, where he lived and practiced medicine as a pediatrician and obstetrician for most of his adult life. While studying medicine at the University of Pennsylvania, he came into contact with Ezra Pound. Pound's theories of imagism influenced Williams's early verse, which appeared in *Poems* (1909) and *The Tempers* (1913). During the next two decades, however, Williams went on to evolve his own alternative poetic style, which he called objectivism.

Williams defined the source of his poetry as "the local," by which he meant a strict focus on the reality of individual life and its surroundings. Williams looked for a return to the barest essentials in poetry. In this respect, he opposed such contemporaries as T. S. Eliot and Ezra Pound in their frequent use of allusions to art, history, religion, and foreign cultures.

No Ideas but in Things

Williams deliberately wrote in a spare, detached style about commonplace subjects, the very opposite of what many nineteenth-century American writers considered poetic material. Using as his slogan "No ideas but in things," Williams wrote of animals at the zoo, schoolgirls walking, or a piece of paper blowing down a street. As Marianne Moore, an admirer, noted, Williams's topics are traditionally "American"—crowds at the movies, mist rising from a duck pond, a ballgame. Williams's masterpiece is *Paterson*, a poem about life in an industrial city in New Jersey.

Think About the Writer What do you think Marianne Moore meant when she said that Williams's topics are "American"?

The Red Wheelbarrow / The Great Figure / This Is Just to Say

Reader/Writer Notebook

Use your **RWN** to complete the activities for these selections.

Literary Focus

Imagery The imagery in a poem helps us share on a sensory level the writer's own perceptions. **Imagery**—language that appeals to the senses—helps us see, hear, feel, taste, or smell what the poet wishes us to experience.

William Carlos Williams's "objectivist" approach emphasizes concrete objects and sensory experiences rather than abstract concepts or intellectual ideas. His poems, as a result, are rich in imagery. In these three short poems, Williams uses precise, simple language to describe his perception of seemingly ordinary things: a red wheelbarrow, a rumbling firetruck, and sweet, cold plums.

Literary Perspectives Apply the literary perspective described on page 782 as you read these poems.

Writing Focus

Think as a Reader/Writer

Find It in Your Reading As you read each poem, make a chart like the one below to record the vivid nouns, adjectives, and phrases that Williams uses to create imagery. In the left column, record words and phrases from the poem. In the right column, write the sense(s) you think he is appealing to with the words. What surprises you in each poem?

The Red Wheelbarrow

Imagery	Senses (sight, touch, taste, smell, sound)
"glazed with rain / water"	sight, touch

Vocabulary

glazed (glayzd) *v.* used as *adj.*: coated with a thin, shiny layer. *The glazed surface of the red wheelbarrow was transparent.*

unheeded (uhn HEE dihd) *v.* used as *adj.*: not noticed; disregarded. *The firetruck's number, unheeded by others, made an impression on Williams.*

icebox (YS bahks) *n.*: refrigerator. *The plums were stored in the icebox, where they would stay fresh.*

Language Coach

Related Words Some adjectives are formed from verbs. The adjective *glazed* is a form of the verb *glaze*, which means "to coat with a thin, shiny layer." You can use *glazed* as an adjective ("the glazed pot"), a past-tense verb ("He glazed the pot"), or a part of a verb phrase ("I have glazed the pot green.") The adjective *unheeded* is also a verb form. What do you think the verb *heed* means? Use *unheeded* in two sentences: first as an adjective and then as a part of a verb phrase, with *is*.

Learn It Online
Let these poems speak to you online.
go.hrw.com   L11-779   Go

The Red Wheelbarrow

by **William Carlos Williams**

Read with a Purpose
Read to discover the simple image on which "so much depends."

> so much depends
> upon
>
> a red wheel
> barrow
>
> 5 glazed with rain
> water **A**
>
> beside the white
> chickens. **B**

A **Literary Focus** Imagery In such a short poem, diction, or word choice, is especially important. Which words play a crucial role in creating the images in this poem?

B **Literary Focus** Imagery Why might the combined images of the wheelbarrow, the rainwater, and the chickens become something upon which "so much depends"?

Vocabulary **glazed** (glayzd) *v.* used as *adj.*: coated with a thin, shiny layer.

The Great Figure

by **William Carlos Williams**

Read with a Purpose
Read to find out what ordinary figure Williams describes as "great."

> Among the rain
> and lights
> I saw the figure 5
> in gold
> 5 on a red
> fire truck
> moving
> tense
> unheeded
> 10 to gong clangs
> siren howls
> and wheels rumbling
> through the dark city. **A**

A **Literary Focus** Imagery To what senses do the images in this poem appeal? What words does the poet use to appeal to those senses?

Vocabulary **unheeded** (uhn HEE dihd) *v.* used as *adj.*: not noticed; disregarded.

Analyzing Visuals

Viewing and Interpreting How does the imagery in this work of art compare to the imagery that Williams uses in "The Great Figure"?

This Is Just to Say

by **William Carlos Williams**

> **Read with a Purpose** Read to see how a simple apology can be poetic.

Literary Perspectives

Analyzing Credibility in Literature When you read a magazine article, a biography, or another work of nonfiction, you know it is important to consider the credibility of the author. How trustworthy and reliable is the information? Did the author do sufficient research? How often, however, do you consider the credibility of a poem's speaker? In order to understand a poem, evaluate the sincerity of the speaker's voice. How thoroughly should you trust what he or she says?

As your read, be sure to notice the questions in the text which will guide you in using this perspective.

I have eaten
the plums
that were in
the icebox

5   and which
you were probably
saving
for breakfast

Forgive me **Ⓐ**
10 they were delicious
so sweet
and so cold **Ⓑ**

Ⓐ **Literary Perspectives** **Analyzing Credibility in Literature** The speaker freely admits knowing that his audience was probably saving the plums for breakfast. How does this admission affect the sincerity of his request for forgiveness?

Ⓑ **Literary Focus** **Imagery** Which images in this poem appeal to the sense of taste, and which appeal to touch?

Vocabulary **icebox** (YS bahks) *n.*: refrigerator.

Applying Your Skills

SKILLS FOCUS **Literary Skills** Analyze imagery; analyze theme; analyze credibility. **Vocabulary Skills** Demonstrate knowledge of literal meanings of words and their usage. **Writing Skills** Incorporate imagery in writing.

The Red Wheelbarrow / The Great Figure /
This Is Just to Say

Respond and Think Critically

Reading Focus

Quick Check

1. Describe the setting of "The Red Wheelbarrow."

2. Which poem is more purely imagist, "The Red Wheelbarrow" or "The Great Figure"? Why?

3. Explain the meaning of the title "This Is Just to Say." How might the poem change if the words *I'm Sorry* followed the word *Say*?

Read with a Purpose

4. How do Williams's poems help readers see the poetic qualities in personal interactions with everyday objects?

✔ Vocabulary Check

Match each Vocabulary word with its definition.

5. glazed   a. unnoticed
6. icebox   b. glossed
7. unheeded   c. refrigerator

Literary Focus

Literary Analysis

The Red Wheelbarrow

8. **Infer** Think about what Williams has in mind when he says, "so much depends upon / a red wheel / barrow." What might he be saying about poetry or art? Do you agree with him?

9. **Analyze** The speaker opens with the dramatic assertion "so much depends / upon"—hinting that whatever follows will be extremely important. How does the rest of the poem overturn or meet the reader's expectations?

The Great Figure

10. **Compare and Contrast** The painter Charles Henry Demuth (1883–1935) was so struck by the imagery in "The Great Figure" that he painted *The Figure 5 in Gold* (page 781). What do you *see* in the painting? What do you *hear* in the poem?

11. **Evaluate** What one word is used metaphorically to describe the truck as if it were a person?

This Is Just to Say

12. **Hypothesize** Whom is the speaker addressing? What response do you think the speaker will receive, and why?

13. **Literary Perspectives** Do you think we are meant to believe that the speaker is truly sorry?

Literary Skills: Imagery

14. **Make Judgments** The imagists wanted poems to focus on common objects as they are, not to become metaphors or symbols. Which of these poems achieves this goal most successfully?

Literary Skills Review: Theme

15. **Evaluate** A poem's **theme** is the insight it offers into human life. Do these poems about simple, everyday objects reveal any insights about life?

Writing Focus

Think as a Reader/Writer

Use It in Your Writing Using these poems as models, write an imagist poem about something important to you. Use sensory images to convey the look, feel, sound, smell, and even taste of your subject.

 What Do You Think Now How does Williams's poetry challenge traditional notions about what serves as an appropriate topic for a poem?

Preparing to Read

MARIANNE MOORE
Poetry

ARCHIBALD MACLEISH
Ars Poetica

What Do You Think?

How does progress challenge <u>tradition</u> and redefine society?

🔘 QuickTalk

Both Moore and MacLeish attempt to define poetry from a modernist perspective. With a partner, discuss how you think a modernist might define poetry. How is this definition of poetry similar to <u>traditional</u> definitions? How is it different and new?

Marianne Moore
(1887–1972)

Pulitzer Prize WINNER

After graduating from Bryn Mawr College, outside Philadelphia, Marianne Moore worked as a teacher, a librarian, and an editor. All the while, she was writing and publishing her poems in the prestigious journals of the time.

By 1921, she was living in New York City and had just published her first collection of poetry, *Poems*. Among the literary celebrities in New York, she was easily identifiable by her antique capes and hats. In fact, the only thing modern about Moore was her poetry. She carefully pieced together her poems by combining her own writing with quotations and excerpts from social science and natural history journals. She once said, "If what I write is called poetry, it is because there is no other category in which to put it." Her poetry reflects some influence of the imagists, and it also makes use of the concrete in the <u>tradition</u> of William Carlos Williams. Some have said of Moore that no one was ever more indebted to other writers for material and, at the same time, more original.

Archibald MacLeish
(1892–1982)

Pulitzer Prize WINNER

Archibald MacLeish was born in Illinois and studied at Yale and Harvard Law School. During World War I he served as an ambulance driver in France and later as an artillery captain. After the war he worked as a lawyer, and in 1923 he moved his family to France, where he focused on writing. His poems from this period reflect the influence of the modernist writers he met in France, including Ezra Pound and T. S. Eliot.

MacLeish returned to the United States in 1928. In 1932, he published the epic poem *Conquistador*, about the Spanish conquest of Mexico. MacLeish won three Pulitzer Prizes, a National Book Award, and an Academy Award for Best Documentary.

Think About the Writers

What influences do the writing of Marianne Moore and Archibald MacLeish have in common?

Poetry /
Ars Poetica

Reader/Writer Notebook
Use your **RWN** to complete the activities for these selections.

Literary Focus

Imagery and Meaning The imagists believed that **imagery**—language that appeals to the senses—alone could carry a poem's meaning. Poets influenced by imagism, such as Marianne Moore and Archibald MacLeish, believed that imagery did more than set the mood and emotional tone of a poem. Their use of imagery was not merely to decorate, not merely to use many sensory images to describe something. Instead, they wanted to find the precise image to describe the poet's perception directly.

Reading Focus

Visualizing Imagery Imagist poets paid close attention to concrete details to convey their perceptions as accurately as possible and to make each poem not just a way to communicate a message to the reader, but its own unique experience.

Into Action For each poem make a chart like the one below. As you read, record in the first column some of the concrete images each poet uses. In the second column, note what each image evokes as you visualize it.

Image	Image evokes
"Poetry": "Hands that can grasp"	A hand reaching to touch

Writing Focus

Think as a Reader/Writer

Find It in Your Reading Moore and MacLeish use line and stanza breaks to draw readers' attention to important ideas. For example, MacLeish gives the words "But be" their own line to emphasize the concept that poems should re-create experiences rather than just describe them. As you read, record in your *Reader/Writer Notebook* examples of interesting line and stanza breaks. Make notes about how the breaks emphasize certain images or ideas.

Language Coach
Changing Suffixes Some nouns end with *–ence* or *–ance*. For many of these nouns, you can change the *–ce* to *–t* to create a related adjective. *Prominence* becomes *prominent*, an adjective that means "distinguished or widely known." Which adjective is related to *insolence*? What does that adjective mean?

Learn It Online
Get to know the Vocabulary words inside and out with Word Watch online.

go.hrw.com   L11-785   **Go**

Poetry

by **Marianne Moore**

Read with a Purpose
Read to discover why the poet says she dislikes poetry.

Build Background
Since the days of the Roman poet Horace (65–8 B.C.), poets have tried to explain what poetry is. Some poets have written poems about poetry, hoping to *show* rather than to tell what it is. Marianne Moore's "Poetry" and Archibald MacLeish's "Ars Poetica" (page 788) are in this <u>tradition</u> of poets writing about poetry.

I, too, dislike it: there are things that are important beyond all this fiddle.°
    Reading it, however, with a perfect contempt for it, one discovers in
    it after all, a place for the genuine.
       Hands that can grasp, eyes
5   that can dilate, hair that can rise
          if it must, these things are important not because a

high-sounding interpretation can be put upon them but because they are
    useful. When they become so derivative° as to become unintelligible,
    the same thing may be said for all of us, that we
10   do not admire what
       we cannot understand: the bat
          holding on upside down or in quest of something to

---

1. fiddle: slang for "nonsense."
8. derivative: based on the work of others; unoriginal.

A **Literary Focus** **Imagery and Meaning** Moore presents a series of concrete images while exploring the abstract question of what poetry should be. How do these images illustrate Moore's thinking about poetry?

Vocabulary **contempt** (kuhn TEHMPT) *n.:* the feeling that something is of no value; scorn.
unintelligible (uhn ihn TEHL uh juh buhl) *adj.:* unable to be understood.

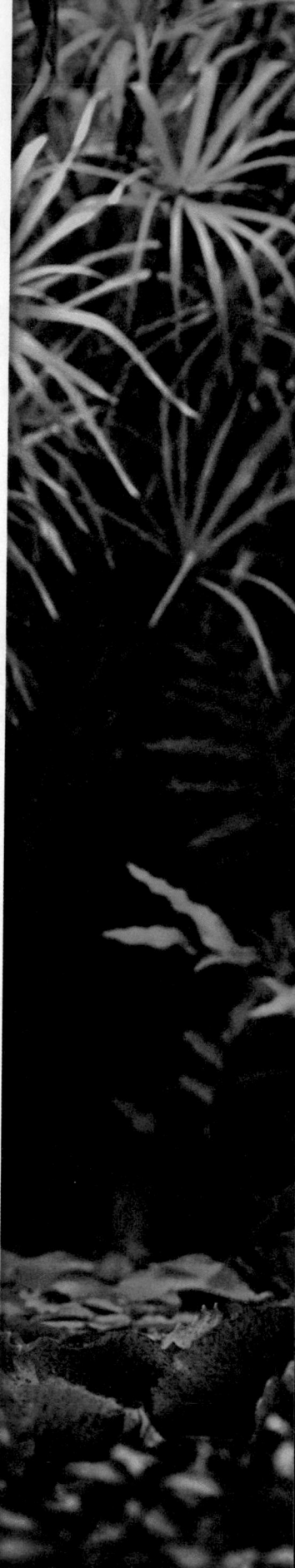

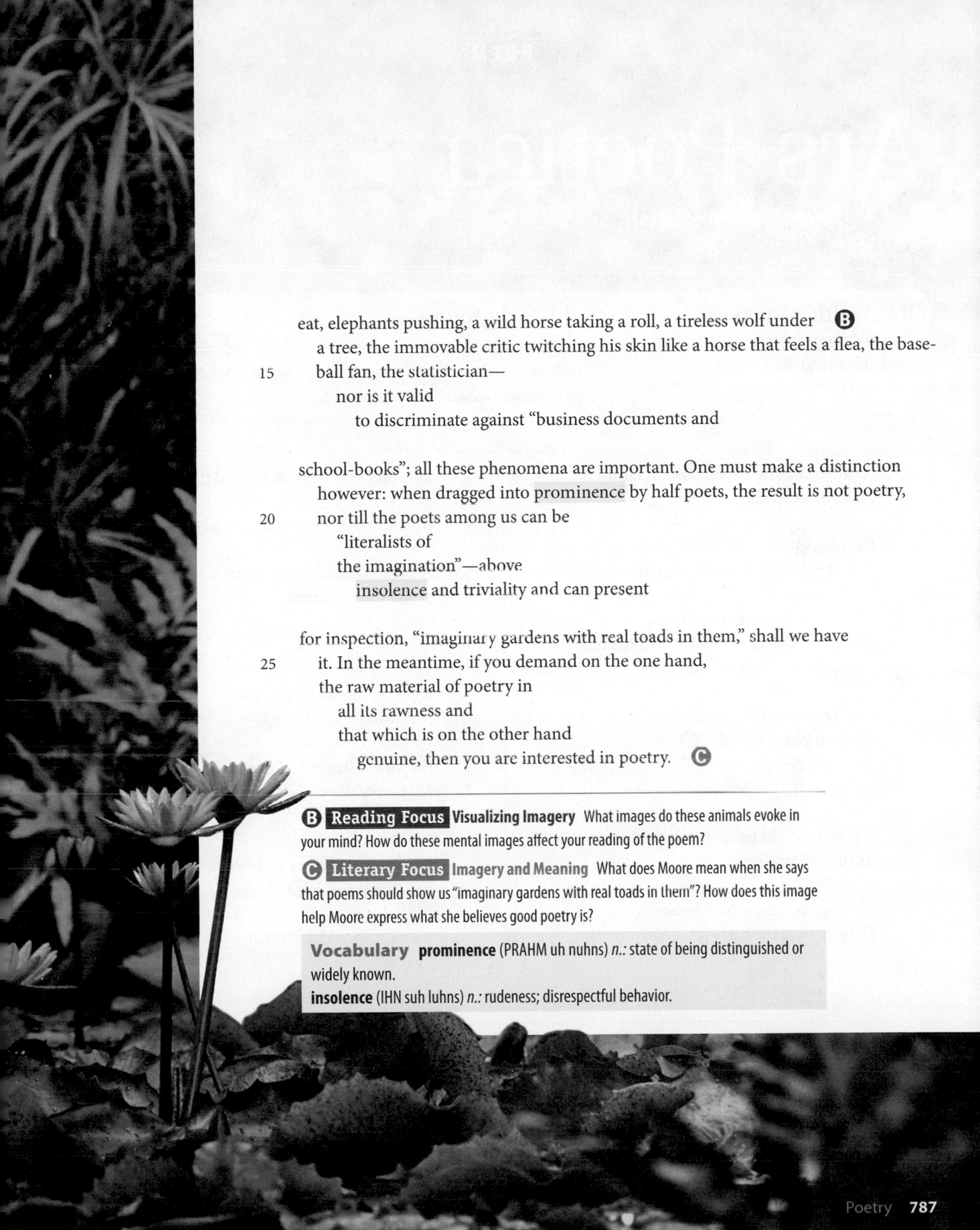

eat, elephants pushing, a wild horse taking a roll, a tireless wolf under **B**
a tree, the immovable critic twitching his skin like a horse that feels a flea, the base-
15 ball fan, the statistician—
nor is it valid
to discriminate against "business documents and

school-books"; all these phenomena are important. One must make a distinction
however: when dragged into prominence by half poets, the result is not poetry,
20 nor till the poets among us can be
"literalists of
the imagination"—above
insolence and triviality and can present

for inspection, "imaginary gardens with real toads in them," shall we have
25 it. In the meantime, if you demand on the one hand,
the raw material of poetry in
all its rawness and
that which is on the other hand
genuine, then you are interested in poetry. **C**

B **Reading Focus** **Visualizing Imagery** What images do these animals evoke in
your mind? How do these mental images affect your reading of the poem?

C **Literary Focus** **Imagery and Meaning** What does Moore mean when she says
that poems should show us "imaginary gardens with real toads in them"? How does this image
help Moore express what she believes good poetry is?

Vocabulary **prominence** (PRAHM uh nuhns) *n.*: state of being distinguished or
widely known.
insolence (IHN suh luhns) *n.*: rudeness; disrespectful behavior.

Ars Poetica

by **Archibald MacLeish**

Read with a Purpose
Read to discover one view of what a poem should and should not do.

Build Background
Ars poetica is Latin for "the art of poetry." MacLeish, like Ezra Pound and T. S. Eliot, believed that poetry should rely on concrete images to convey emotion, and that precise, genuine images do not need explanation to have meaning.

A poem should be palpable and mute
As a globed fruit,

Dumb
As old medallions to the thumb,

5 Silent as the sleeve-worn stone
Of casement ledges where the moss has
      grown—

A poem should be wordless
As the flight of birds.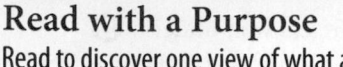

     •

A poem should be motionless in time
10 As the moon climbs,

Leaving, as the moon releases
Twig by twig the night-entangled trees,

Leaving, as the moon behind the winter
      leaves,
Memory by memory the mind—

15 A poem should be motionless in time
as the moon climbs.

     •

A poem should be equal to:
Not true.

For all the history of grief
20 An empty doorway and a maple leaf.

For love
The leaning grasses and two lights above
      the sea— **Ⓑ**

A poem should not mean
But be.

Ⓐ **Literary Focus** Imagery and Meaning What do the images in the first eight lines have in common? On the basis of these images, what does MacLeish think poetry should be?

Vocabulary **palpable** (PAL puh buhl) *adj.:* able to be touched or felt.

Ⓑ **Literary Focus** Imagery and Meaning How might these two images be "equal to," or stand for, love?

Applying Your Skills

Poetry /

Ars Poetica

Respond and Think Critically

Reading Focus

Quick Check

1. According to lines 4–8 of "Poetry," what kind of poetry does Moore like? According to lines 8–11, what kind of poetry does Moore dislike?

2. MacLeish's poem defines poetry by using a series of similes. List all the things MacLeish says poetry should be.

Read with a Purpose

3. How are Moore's and MacLeish's beliefs about poetry similar? How are they different?

Reading Skills: Visualizing Imagery

4. As you read, you recorded some of the images that you found in "Poetry" and "Ars Poetica," visualized them, and then recorded what they evoke. Add a third column to your chart. How does each image define what Moore or MacLeish believes poetry is? Refer to the poems themselves as needed. Then, summarize your findings in a paragraph.

Image	Image Evokes	Poetry Is
"Poetry": "Hands that can grasp"	A hand reaching to touch	a way to connect with what is real

✔ Vocabulary Check

Match each Vocabulary word with its antonym.

5. contempt   **a.** intangible

6. unintelligible   **b.** respect

7. palpable   **c.** admiration

8. prominence   **d.** clear

9. insolence   **e.** obscurity

Literary Focus

Literary Analysis

10. Analyze Whom do you think Moore is addressing in "Poetry"? What tone does she take with her audience?

11. Make Judgments In Moore's poem do you agree that "we / do not admire what / we cannot understand?" (lines 9–11)? Why?

12. Interpret How do the two images in line 20 of "Ars Poetica" suggest grief?

Literary Skills: Imagery and Meaning

13. Interpret Moore says that poets must be "literalists of the imagination." How is this related to her image of "imaginary gardens with real toads in them"?

Literary Skills Review: Simile

14. Analyze Some of MacLeish's **similes**, or comparisons that use *like* or *as*, are contradictory. For example, how can a poem be "wordless"? How does the poem explain these contradictions?

Writing Focus

Think as a Reader/Writer

Use It in Your Writing Review your notes about the line and stanza breaks in these poems. Then, choose a stanza or section from one of the poems and re-break the lines to change their emphasis or meaning. In a paragraph, describe how your version is different.

 What Do **You Think Now** How do these poems challenge your existing beliefs about poetry? What <u>alternative</u> ideas do they suggest about what poetry should be?

Preparing to Read

Chicago

What Do You Think?

How does progress challenge tradition and redefine society?

⏱ QuickTalk

In "Chicago," Sandburg challenges commonly held beliefs about Chicago by praising its pride and strength. With a group of classmates, discuss what people commonly believe about your hometown or another place of your choosing. How would you challenge these notions? What positive qualities would you bring to light?

MEET THE WRITER

Carl Sandburg
(1878–1967)

Carl Sandburg, a poetic spokesman for the toiling American worker, found his voice in the vernacular—slang, street talk, and common speech, with their clichés and plain expressions.

At the School of Hard Knocks

A descendant of Swedes who had settled in Galesburg, Illinois, Sandburg was not schooled so much in a classroom as in the proverbial school of hard knocks. Before he was twenty, he had traveled the Midwest from Illinois to Nebraska, supporting himself with odd jobs. The field and factory laborers that he met in his travels would one day people his own poetic landscape.

Sandburg volunteered, more from restlessness than from patriotism, to fight in the Spanish-American War that broke out in 1898. Eventually, he went to college in his hometown, and there he began to think of himself as a writer. This self-image became a reality when Sandburg was thirty-six. That year, the influential magazine *Poetry* published some of his poems, including "Chicago."

The Roughest of American Poets

Sandburg—who has been compared to Walt Whitman—used free verse and colloquial speech, which some critics disliked but which established him as a major literary figure. Sandburg's strong affirmation of American democratic ideology and of the inherent nobility of labor and the working person resulted in one of his best-known collections of poems, *The People, Yes* (1936).

While Sandburg seemed on the page to be the roughest of American poets, he was actually a gentle and thoughtful man. By the time he died in his ninetieth year, his craggy features and his boyish shock of hair had been familiar to Americans for more than fifty years. The author of two of the most popular poems of the century—"Chicago" (1914) and "Fog" (1916)—and of a six-volume biography of Abraham Lincoln (1926–1939) had become an American legend.

Think About the Writer

Given his subject matter, why might Sandburg have chosen to use free verse and colloquial speech rather than a more formal style?

 **Reader/Writer Notebook**

Use your **RWN** to complete the activities for this selection.

Literary Focus

Apostrophe Carl Sandburg's direct address to the city of Chicago is an example of **apostrophe.** Poets use apostrophe to address inanimate objects, abstract qualities, ideas, and dead or absent people. In this poem, the speaker addresses an entire city as though it were one person with many jobs—hog butcher, tool maker, railroad engineer, and freight handler.

Reading Focus

Analyzing Tone A writer's **tone** is the attitude he or she takes toward the subject of a work, the characters in it, or the audience. Tone is dependent on diction and style. Tone can usually be described in a single word: ironic, lighthearted, cynical, critical, and so on. Examine Sandburg's word choice to help you discover his tone.

Into Action Use webs like the one below to help you analyze the poet's tone. In the first web, list what "they" say about Chicago. Then, make another web and list what the speaker says to and about Chicago. Focus on words that stand out and reveal each side's attitude toward the city.

Writing Focus

Think as a Reader/Writer

Find It in Your Reading Sandburg constructs his poem like an argument: He presents the characteristics of Chicago that its critics point out and then counters them with an admiring portrait of the city's strengths. As you read, record in your *Reader/Writer Notebook* examples of this structure. What makes it interesting and effective?

TechFocus The poem "Chicago" provides a series of images that depict the difficult yet triumphant lives of its citizens. As you read, think about what images you would use to show others your own city or town.

Vocabulary

wanton (WAHN tuhn) *adj.*: without reason; unrestrained. *Poor people wear expressions of wanton hunger.*

coarse (kohrs) *adj.*: crude and unrefined. *The city may be coarse, but it is also alive and wonderful.*

toil (toyl) *n.*: hard work. *Amid the toil and struggle, the city sings.*

Language Coach

Homonyms Words that sound the same but have different spellings and meanings are called **homonyms.** The adjective *coarse* means "crude and unrefined." The word *course* can be a noun that means "class" or "path" as well as a verb that means "flow." Because both words sound the same, you need to pay attention to spelling, and context, to understand which word the author is using.

 **Learn It Online**
Listen to this poem read aloud online.

go.hrw.com | L11-791 | **Go**

CHICAGO

by **Carl Sandburg**

Read with a Purpose
Read to discover how a city can be celebrated for its brutal, industrial character.

Build Background
Throughout Chicago's development, its economy has depended on the city's importance as a hub of transportation. The city's location first helped it become an active port city and, later, the focus of the railroad system. As a result, industries that rely on shipping, such as manufacturing and meatpacking, flourished there.

Hog Butcher for the World,
Tool Maker, Stacker of Wheat,
Player with Railroads and the Nation's Freight Handler;
Stormy, husky, brawling,
5   City of the Big Shoulders:

They tell me you are wicked and I believe them, for I have seen your painted
        women under the gas lamps luring the farm boys.
And they tell me you are crooked and I answer: Yes, it is true I have seen the
        gunman kill and go free to kill again.   **A**
And they tell me you are brutal and my reply is: On the faces of women and
        children I have seen the marks of wanton hunger.
And having answered so I turn once more to those who sneer at this my city,
        and I give them back the sneer and say to them:
Come and show me another city with lifted head singing so proud to be alive
10   and coarse and strong and cunning.   **B**

A **Literary Focus** **Apostrophe** Sandburg does not just describe the city but addresses it directly. Why do you think he takes this approach? What does the use of direct address add to this poem?

B **Reading Focus** **Analyzing Tone** What is the speaker's attitude toward those who criticize Chicago? Support your answer with evidence from the text.

Vocabulary **wanton** (WAHN tuhn) *adj.:* without reason; unrestrained.
coarse (kohrs) *adj.:* crude and unrefined.

Flinging magnetic curses amid the toil of piling job on job, here is a tall bold
      slugger set vivid against the little soft cities;
Fierce as a dog with tongue lapping for action, cunning as a savage
      pitted against the wilderness,
          Bareheaded,
          Shoveling,
15   Wrecking,
          Planning,
          Building, breaking, rebuilding.
Under the smoke, dust all over his mouth, laughing with white teeth,
Under the terrible burden of destiny laughing as a young man laughs,
20 Laughing even as an ignorant fighter laughs who has never lost a battle,
Bragging and laughing that under his wrist is the pulse, and under his
      ribs the heart of the people,
          Laughing!
Laughing the stormy, husky, brawling laughter of Youth, half-naked,
      sweating, proud to be Hog Butcher, Tool Maker, Stacker of Wheat,
      Player with Railroads and Freight Handler to the Nation. **C**

C **Reading Focus** **Analyzing Tone** Why might the speaker compare Chicago to a youth rather than to an adult or an older person? How does this comparison reflect the speaker's attitude toward the city?

Vocabulary **toil** (toyl) *n.:* hard work.

Chicago

Respond and Think Critically

Reading Focus

Quick Check

1. An **epithet** is a descriptive word or phrase used to characterize a person or thing. To what aspects of Chicago do the epithets in the first three lines correspond?

2. How do people criticize the city of Chicago?

3. To what kind of person is Chicago compared?

Read with a Purpose

4. What does the speaker really think about Chicago? Support your answer with evidence from the text.

Reading Skills: Analyzing Tone

5. Review your webs listing what "they" say about Chicago and what the speaker says about Chicago. Then, write a paragraph about the poem's tone. Use words from your webs to support your ideas.

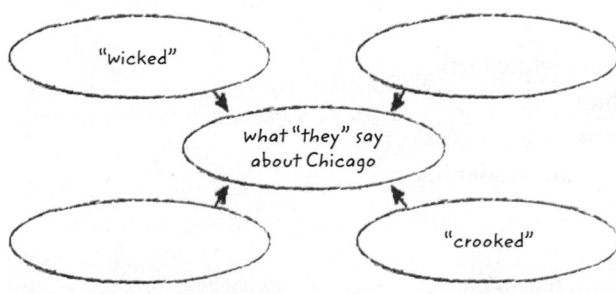

Literary Focus

Literary Analysis

6. **Interpret** Sandburg closes the poem with a series of epithets about Chicago. How do these epithets characterize the city, and why might Sandburg emphasize these images at this point?

7. **Analyze** Sandburg uses **personification,** a figure of speech in which something nonhuman is given human feelings or attitudes. What words and phrases give Chicago human qualities? How would you describe the city's personality?

8. **Extend** How have Chicago and other U.S. cities changed since this poem was written in 1914?

Literary Skills: Apostrophe

9. **Analyze** What images in the poem make Chicago the very embodiment of the rugged American individual? How does apostrophe help convey this sense of ruggedness and vitality?

Literary Skills Review: Theme

10. **Extend** The **American dream** consists of three central ideologies: a belief in the United States as a new Eden—a land of beauty, bounty, and promise; a feeling of optimism created by ever expanding opportunity; and confidence in the triumph of the individual. Sandburg praised ordinary people and celebrated a new kind of American hero. How does "Chicago" reveal a new take on this **theme**?

Writing Focus

Think as a Reader/Writer

Use It in Your Writing Review your notes on the structure of Sandburg's arguments. Write a poem about the place you discussed in the QuickTalk activity. Structure it as an argument: Present what "they" say, and then respond with what you know to be true.

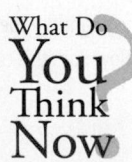

What Do You Think Now

In this poem, Chicago is depicted as a city of industry, work, and progress. How have these qualities affected the city in both positive and negative ways?

Vocabulary Development

✓ Vocabulary Check

Match each Vocabulary word with its antonym.

1. wanton   **a.** refined
2. coarse   **b.** rest
3. toil   **c.** restrained

Vocabulary Skills: Connotations

Words can have more than multiple meanings—they can also have connotations. **Connotations** are the feelings and associations attached to some words that go beyond a word's **denotation,** or its strict dictionary definition. Some words have strong **positive or negative connotations** that cause us to react either positively or negatively to their usage. For example, Sandburg uses the word *cunning* to describe Chicago; the connotation of *intelligence* is more positive than that of the related words *sneaky* or *devious*. Other words are fairly neutral—they provoke little or no emotional reaction.

Your Turn

For each of the following words from "Chicago," use context clues and your own personal experience to decide whether its connotation is positive, negative, or neutral: *stormy*, *brawling*, *proud*, *cunning*, and *pulse*.

Language Coach

Homonyms Words with the same sound but different spellings are **homonyms**. Pick the correct homonym in the following sentences.

1. He avoided (*course, coarse*) language in his writing.
2. Rhythmic beats (*course, coarse*) through the poem.

CHOICES

As you respond to the Choices, use these **Academic Vocabulary** words as appropriate: <u>alternative</u>, <u>hierarchy</u>, <u>ideology</u>, <u>inevitable</u>, <u>tradition</u>.

REVIEW
Research Historical Chicago

Class Presentation What was Chicago like at the beginning of the twentieth century? With a partner, use the library or the Internet to find out more about Chicago's history—how it became a city, what products it was known for, and how it changed during the Industrial Revolution. Create a presentation to share your findings with your classmates.

CONNECT
Create a Tourism Web Site

TechFocus How would you portray your own town to others? With a partner, create a tourism Web site that conveys the sights, sounds, and sense of your town or city. You can include slogans, pictures, quotations from citizens, audio clips, or even short videos. As an <u>alternative</u> to creating a Web site online, you can make a paper travel brochure.

EXTEND
Develop Social Awareness

Group Activity Hunger, violence, and homelessness are not problems that occur only in big cities like Chicago. In a small group, think about organizations you could contact to learn more about these issues in your community. What specific problems do people in your town face? What programs are offered in your town to help solve them? Use what you learn to prepare a short presentation for your class to share information about venues in your community through which students can volunteer to help solve these difficult problems.

Richard Bone
"Butch" Weldy
Mrs. George Reece

What Do You Think

How does progress challenge <u>tradition</u> and redefine society?

🕐 QuickTalk

Think about a news story in which something surprising was revealed or justice was denied someone. With a partner, discuss the story. What might prevent someone from speaking the truth or from making sure that justice is carried out?

Edgar Lee Masters
(1869–1950)

Edgar Lee Masters used his literary talent and personal memories to portray the hidden underside of small-town American life.

Small-Town Beginnings

Masters, like his contemporary Carl Sandburg, was a product of the Midwest, also known as the Corn Belt. Masters was born in Garnett, Kansas; when he was still a boy, his family moved to Illinois. As a young man with literary ambitions, Masters found small-town life oppressive. After studying law at his father's office in Lewistown, Illinois, Masters moved to Chicago, where he became the partner of a leading criminal lawyer. In his spare time, he wrote poems, plays, and essays, but, for a while, none of his work attracted much attention.

Spoon River

In 1914, a friend of Masters gave him a copy of *Select Epigrams from the Greek Anthology*, a collection of short Greek poems, many of them **epitaphs,** which in a few lines sum up an individual's life. These poems gave Masters the idea of writing their midwestern counterparts, uncovering the lives he had known in the small towns of southern Illinois. Instead of the <u>traditional</u> forms and meters he had used in his previous poetry, Masters chose to write his epitaphs in free verse.

Just as Sandburg had done, Masters found his voice in the free verse that characterized the second decade of the twentieth century. Though he published a great deal, Masters is primarily known today for just one book, *Spoon River Anthology* (1915), which became a landmark in American literature and made him famous. It is a collection of almost 250 epitaphs spoken by the ordinary inhabitants of a cemetery in the fictional town of Spoon River. In these autobiographical poems, Masters was able to reveal a whole life through a single incident.

Think About the Writer

Why do you think Masters gave voices to people who had died? What might they be able to say after death that they could not say during life?

Richard Bone / "Butch" Weldy / Mrs. George Reece

Reader/Writer Notebook

Use your **RWN** to complete the activities for these selections.

Literary Focus

Speaker The voice you hear when you read a poem is that of its **speaker,** who may or may not be the poet. The speakers in Masters' poems are the deceased inhabitants of the fictional town of Spoon River. As you read, note how Masters conveys the different personalities of each of his speakers through his or her unique voice.

Reading Focus

Using Oral Interpretation to Understand a Poem One of the most effective ways to understand a poem is to read it aloud. To help bring the speakers in Masters's poems to life, think about these questions:

- What is the tone of the poem? Is it sorrowful? Joyful? Matter-of-fact?
- Does the poem contain dialect, colloquial speech, or **idioms**—expressions particular to a language that mean something different from the literal definitions of each word? Is the language formal or informal?
- Which words should be stressed in each line? Where are the pauses in the poem—at the punctuation marks or at the line breaks?

Into Action Copy each of the three poems onto a sheet of paper. Read each poem aloud. As you read, underline the words that you naturally stress, along with any idioms or elements of dialect. Use a slash to mark places where you would pause in your reading, as in the example below.

> **"Richard Bone"**
> When I <u>first</u> came to Spoon River /
> I did not know whether what they told me
> Was <u>true</u> or <u>false</u>. /
> They would bring me the epitaph /

Writing Focus

Think as a Reader/Writer

Find It in Your Reading Masters creates different personalities in the Spoon River poems by giving each speaker a distinct style of speech. As you read each poem, record in your *Reader/Writer Notebook* the words or phrases that make each speaker's voice unique.

Vocabulary

chronicles (KRAHN uh kuhlz) *n.*: stories of past events; histories. *Richard Bone thinks of epitaphs as short chronicles of people's lives.*

influenced (IHN floo uhnsd) *v.*: persuaded. *Those who know the truth about a deceased person may be influenced by the living to hide it.*

soldering (SAHD uhr ihng) *v.* used as *adj.*: joining things tightly with melted metal. *Gasoline provided the fuel to heat the soldering irons.*

Language Coach

Word Origins The noun *chronicles* comes from the Greek *chronos,* meaning "time." How does the meaning of *chronos* relate to the meaning of the Vocabulary word *chronicles*? How does it relate to the meaning of these words: *synchronize, chronology, anachronism,* and *chronic*?

Learn It Online
Go online to hear an actor read these poems to you.

| go.hrw.com | L11-797 | |

Richard Bone by **Edgar Lee Masters**

Read with a Purpose
Read to discover what a stonecutter learned about his fellow townspeople and why he kept their secrets.

Build Background
In *Spoon River Anthology,* the deceased inhabitants of Spoon River are freed by death to talk without fear of consequences. Bit by bit, they fill in a picture of small-town life vastly different from the folksy, sentimental magazine-cover images of the time. Masters's speakers from beyond the grave bring buried truth into the daylight and, at the same time, a new kind of realism to poetry.

Richard Bone, like many other departed citizens of the town, is troubled by his conscience. Bone confesses his hypocrisy in quietly accepting false appearances. The name that Masters gives this speaker is a clue to his profession and to his nature. As a stonecutter in life, he engraved words that would identify skeletons; as a spokesperson for his own conscience, he speaks words that "cut to the bone."

When I first came to Spoon River
I did not know whether what they told me
Was true or false.
They would bring me the epitaph
5 And stand around the shop while I worked
And say "He was so kind," "He was wonderful,"
"She was the sweetest woman," "He was a consistent Christian."
And I chiseled for them whatever they wished,
All in ignorance of its truth.
10 But later, as I lived among the people here,
I knew how near to the life
Were the epitaphs that were ordered for them as they died.
But still I chiseled whatever they paid me to chisel
And made myself party to the false chronicles
15 Of the stones, **A**
Even as the historian does who writes
Without knowing the truth,
Or because he is influenced to hide it. **B**

A Literary Focus Speaker What do you learn about the speaker? Why do you think he feels compelled to tell the reader what he has done?

B Reading Focus Using Oral Interpretation Do you think that Richard Bone's voice contains any emotion here, or does he say this in a matter-of-fact tone? Explain.

Vocabulary   chronicles (KRAHN uh kuhlz) *n.:* stories of past events; histories.
influenced (IHN floo uhnsd) *v.:* persuaded.

"Butch" Weldy by Edgar Lee Masters

Read with a Purpose
Read for insight into a society where justice doesn't come from the courts.

Build Background
Many of the stories told in *Spoon River Anthology* are interlocking. The villain of the book is Deacon Thomas Rhodes, who "ran the church as well as the store and the bank." We hear about Rhodes from a number of his victims, including "Butch" Weldy. Butch also refers to Jack the Fiddler, a blind man who is buried in the Spoon River cemetery. Jack was killed when "Butch," who had been drinking, drove a carriage into a ditch.

After I got religion and steadied down
They gave me a job in the canning works,
And every morning I had to fill
The tank in the yard with gasoline,
5   That fed the blow-fires in the sheds
To heat the soldering irons.
And I mounted a rickety ladder to do it,
Carrying buckets full of the stuff.   **A**
One morning, as I stood there pouring,
10 The air grew still and seemed to heave,
And I shot up as the tank exploded,
And down I came with both legs broken
And my eyes burned crisp as a couple of eggs,
For someone left a blow-fire going,
15 And something sucked the flame in the tank.   **B**
The Circuit Judge said whoever did it
Was a fellow-servant of mine, and so
Old Rhodes' son didn't have to pay me.
And I sat on the witness stand as blind
20 As Jack the Fiddler, saying over and over,
"I didn't know him at all."

The White Dam (1939) by Raphael Gleitsmann.

Analyzing Visuals

Viewing and Interpreting Does the factory in this picture seem like a safe place to work? How closely does it resemble the picture you get from Weldy's description of the canning works?

A **Literary Focus** **Speaker** What do you learn about the speaker in these opening lines?

B **Reading Focus** **Using Oral Interpretation** How might "Butch" speak lines 10–15? What is his tone?

Vocabulary **soldering** (SAHD uhr ihng) *v.* used as *adj.*: joining things tightly with melted metal.

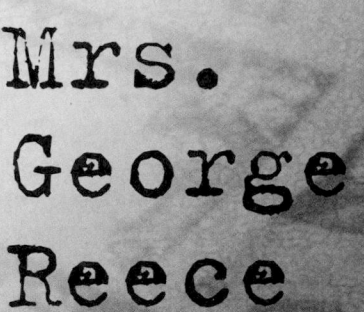

Mrs. George Reece

by **Edgar Lee Masters**

Read with a Purpose

Read to learn what gives Mrs. George Reece the strength to overcome tragedy in her life.

Build Background

This epitaph refers to a real-life bank failure in Lewistown, Illinois, in 1894, which Masters blamed on Henry Phelps (here renamed Thomas Rhodes) and Phelps's son. The bank collapse caused enormous hardships for the town's citizens, and Masters's father, a lawyer, helped prosecute the bank officials. None of the bank officials were sent to prison.

To this generation I would say:
Memorize some bit of verse of truth or beauty.
It may serve a turn in your life. **Ⓐ**
My husband had nothing to do
5   With the fall of the bank—he was only cashier.
The wreck was due to the president, Thomas Rhodes,
And his vain, unscrupulous son.
Yet my husband was sent to prison, **Ⓑ**
And I was left with the children,
10   To feed and clothe and school them.
And I did it, and sent them forth
Into the world all clean and strong,
And all through the wisdom of Pope, the poet:°
"Act well your part, there all the honor lies."

Motherhood by Bessie Porter Vonnoh. Bronze.

13. Pope, the poet: the English poet Alexander Pope (1688–1744), whose wise sayings are often quoted.

Ⓐ **Literary Focus** **Speaker** This speaker is referred to only as "Mrs. George Reece." What does her name say about her? Why did Masters choose her to be the poem's speaker?

Ⓑ **Reading Focus** **Using Oral Interpretation** How might Mrs. George Reece speak these lines? Is she angry, bitter, resigned, or something else?

Applying Your Skills

Richard Bone / "Butch" Weldy / Mrs. George Reece

Respond and Think Critically

Reading Focus

Read with a Purpose

1. Why do you think Richard Bone left so many things unsaid during his life?

2. What reason does the judge give for denying "Butch" compensation for the accident?

3. What idea or belief helps Mrs. George Reece overcome her husband's prison sentence?

Reading Skills: Using Oral Interpretation to Understand a Poem

4. With a partner, discuss how reading aloud and listening to the poems helps you understand each speaker's personality. Use your underlined copies of the poems as evidence.

✓ Vocabulary Check

Match each Vocabulary word with its definition.

5. soldering   **a.** records of events

6. chronicles   **b.** persuaded

7. influenced   **c.** joining together

Literary Focus

Literary Analysis

Richard Bone

8. **Interpret** What does Richard Bone come to realize about the people of Spoon River? What does he realize about himself?

9. **Compare and Contrast** How are epitaphs like historical chronicles?

"Butch" Weldy

10. **Analyze** What happened to Butch Weldy? Which details emphasize the danger of his job?

11. **Infer** What does "Butch" Weldy mean when he says, "I didn't know him at all"?

Mrs. George Reece

12. **Interpret** How does Pope's advice relate to the way Mrs. Reece responded to her tragedy?

13. **Extend** Could the situations and experiences in these poems be found in our society today?

Literary Skills: Speaker

14. **Make Judgments** The speaker of each poem is also the main character. Do you find qualities to admire in any of the speakers of these epitaphs?

Literary Skills Review: Situational Irony

15. **Evaluate** A discrepancy between what is expected to happen and what really does happen is called **situational irony.** What is ironic about the terrible things that happened to "Butch" Weldy after he "got religion" and settled down?

Writing Focus

Think as a Reader/Writer

Use It in Your Writing To write in a character's voice, a writer needs to understand that character—the character's age and situation, ideologies, regrets and hopes. Create a profile for a character; then, write the first few lines of a poem written from that person's perspective. Use Masters's epitaphs as a guide.

 What Do You Think Now

Did any of the speakers challenge the society of Spoon River in any way? What might they have done to bring about progress?

Domination of Black

Wallace Stevens
(1879–1955)

Wallace Stevens believed in the power of the imagination. He felt the poet's job was to provide ways of looking at the world that would stimulate the human imagination.

Pulitzer Prize WINNER

What Do You Think? How does progress challenge tradition and redefine society?

🕐 **QuickWrite**

In a dream, your mind makes associations between images, sensations, and ideas that may not occur to you during waking hours. Recall one of your recent dreams, and write a brief paragraph describing it. How might your dream redefine the way you view things in the waking world?

A Successful Lawyer

Wallace Stevens was born in Reading, Pennsylvania. He attended Harvard University and worked as a reporter for the New York *Herald Tribune.* Stevens graduated from law school in 1903. Shortly thereafter, he began to practice law in New York City, a career that he continued for over ten years. In 1916, he moved to Connecticut to work for the Hartford Accident and Indemnity Company, where he advanced in his career to become vice president of the company in 1934.

Between Imagination and Reality

Dedicated and successful in the world of business, Stevens had connections with the literary world as well. He was acquainted with the poets William Carlos Williams, Marianne Moore, and E. E. Cummings. He began to write his own poems, and although he was influenced by the imagists, Stevens was less interested in presenting a clear or realistic image than he was in the interaction of reality and imagination. Many of his poems attempt to make the reader aware of the physical world in new ways. He constantly points out the uncommon beauty of ordinary things, such as blackbirds ("Thirteen Ways of Looking at a Blackbird") and jars ("Anecdote of the Jar").

His first book, *Harmonium,* was published in 1923. The title, referring to a reed organ, reflects his interest in music, a pervasive theme in his work. Today *Harmonium* is considered one of the most important books of poetry of the twentieth century.

Stevens never abandoned his business career to become a full-time writer. Instead, he wrote poetry whenever he could find the time. After his *Collected Poems* was released in 1954, he received the Pulitzer Prize for Poetry. He is now considered a major American poet.

Think About the Writer What might Stevens's choice to continue his business career say about his view of poetry's place in society?

Reader/Writer
Notebook
Use your **RWN** to complete the activities for this selection.

Literary Focus

Mood The overall feeling or atmosphere present in a work of literature is referred to as **mood.** Writers evoke emotion through the words, images, rhythms, and sound effects they choose to include in their work. As you read "Domination of Black," pay close attention to the **connotations,** or emotional associations, of words. Also, look for how details of the setting, time of day and the season, contribute to the mood.

Reading Focus

Close Reading Stevens's poems often consist of images with associations like those made by the imaginative or dreaming mind. Closely examining the images, style, and mood in his poems can help you better understand them. In "Domination of Black," the time of the day and of the year is especially important, as are the repeated images of the falling leaves, the hemlocks, and the peacocks. These details help establish the mood of the poem.

Into Action As you read, note details that establish the **setting** (when and where) of the poem. Also, record images, colors, and other words that help establish the mood of the poem. Organize your thoughts in a chart like the one below.

Setting Details	Images	Mood Words
Stanza 1		
when: at night, in the fall where:	a fire in the night; fall colors of bushes and trees	night, fire
Stanza 2		

Vocabulary

striding (STRYD ihng) *v.:* walking with elongated steps. *The hemlocks looked as if they were striding across the ground.*

twilight (TWY lyt) *n.:* time between sunset and dark; faint light from the sun at this time of day. *The poet recalls the way the leaves looked in the evening twilight.*

boughs (bowz) *n.:* branches of a tree. *In autumn, leaves fall from the boughs.*

Language Coach

Precise Nouns Poets often use precise nouns to name specific times of day. Stevens describes a tree at twilight, the time between sunset and dark. Other words used to name this time are *dusk, nightfall,* and *sundown.* What images do you associate with each of these words? Explain the time of day named by each of these precise nouns: *dawn, nighttime, daybreak, evening, midday.*

Writing Focus

Think as a Reader/Writer

Find It in Your Reading The word *turning* is repeated several times in the poem; in fact, images in the poem seem to "turn" into other images. For example, the color of the firelight in the room flows into the image of autumn leaves, which flows into the image of the leaves blowing in the wind. In your *Reader/Writer Notebook,* keep track of how Stevens's images depend upon and transform each other.

Learn It Online
Explore the stories behind the Vocabulary words with Word Watch online.

DOMINATION OF BLACK

by **Wallace Stevens**

Read with a Purpose
Read to discover moods evoked by images in the poem.

Build Background
"Domination of Black" is a challenging poem that has been interpreted in various ways. The poem includes images of hemlock trees
and crying peacocks. The true hemlock is a tall tree with dark green
leaves, but the label "hemlock" is also applied to the poisonous plant
Conium maculatum—the source of the poison famously used by
the philosopher Socrates to carry out his own death sentence. The
mournful, wailing cry of the peacock sounds eerily human, almost
like a child in distress.

At night, by the fire
The colors of the bushes
And of the fallen leaves,
Repeating themselves,
5   Turned in the room,
Like the leaves themselves
Turning in the wind.
Yes: but the color of the heavy hemlocks
Came striding.
And I remembered the cry of the
10   peacocks.

The colors of their tails
Were like the leaves themselves
Turning in the wind,
In the twilight wind.
15   They swept over the room,
Just as they flew from the boughs of the
      hemlocks
Down to the ground.
I heard them cry—the peacocks.

Was it a cry against the twilight
20   Or against the leaves themselves
Turning in the wind,
Turning as the flames
Turned in the fire,
Turning as the tails of the peacocks
25   Turned in the loud fire,
Loud as the hemlocks
Full of the cry of the peacocks?
Or was it a cry against the hemlocks?

Out of the window,
30   I saw how the planets gathered
Like the leaves themselves
Turning in the wind.
I saw how the night came,
Came striding like the color of the heavy
      hemlocks
35   I felt afraid.
And I remembered the cry of the
      peacocks. **C**

A **Literary Focus** Mood What images in lines 1–18 suggest
death? How do these images shape the mood of the poem?

B **Literary Focus** Mood How does the repetition of the idea of
turning affect the mood of the second stanza (lines 11–28)?

C **Reading Focus** Close Reading What details and images in
the final stanza elaborate on the idea of turning—both real and metaphorical—in this poem?

Vocabulary **striding** (STRYD ihng) *v.:* walking with elongated
steps.
twilight (TWY lyt) *n.:* time between sunset and dark; faint light
from the sun at this time of day.
boughs (bowz) *n.:* branches of a tree.

Applying Your Skills

Domination of Black

Respond and Think Critically

Reading Focus

Quick Check

1. Where is the speaker of the poem?

2. How does the wind relate to the other images?

3. What does the speaker want to know about the peacocks?

Read with a Purpose

4. How do the repeated images in the poem change each time they are mentioned? What effect does this have on the mood?

Reading Skills: Close Reading

5. As you read, you noted the setting, images, colors, and other details that help establish the mood of the poem. Now, add a column to your chart. For each stanza, think of one or two words that describe the overall mood.

Setting	Images	Mood Words	Overall Mood
Stanza 1			
when: at night, in the fall where:	a fire in the night; fall colors of bushes and trees	night, fire	
Stanza 2			

✓ Vocabulary Check

Match each Vocabulary word with its synonym.

6. boughs   **a.** dusk

7. striding   **b.** walking

8. twilight   **c.** branches

Literary Focus

Literary Analysis

9. **Interpret** What does the title "Domination of Black" mean? How does it relate to the theme?

10. **Analyze** In line 35, the speaker suddenly says, "I felt afraid." What makes this line unique in the poem? Why did the poet include this line?

11. **Extend** Does the poet offer any answer to the question "Was it a cry against the twilight / Or against the leaves themselves… / Or was it a cry against the hemlocks?" Explain your response.

Literary Skills: Mood

12. **Analyze** The mood of the images and words echoes the emotional state of the speaker. How does this emotional state of the speaker change as the poem progresses? Support your answer.

Literary Skills Review: Imagery

13. **Evaluate** Stevens's poetry contains vibrant **imagery,** language that evokes a picture or concrete sensation of a person, thing, place, or experience. Choose images in the poem that appeal to the senses of sight and hearing. How effective are the images in conveying the poem's theme?

Writing Focus

Think as a Reader/Writer

Use It in Your Writing Choose two or three images from nature. Then, write a poem in which you slowly transform one image into another and back again.

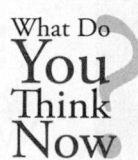
What Do You Think Now?

How does this poem challenge traditional notions of poetry?

Preparing to Read

what if a much of a which of a wind

somewhere i have never travelled, gladly beyond

What Do You Think

How does progress challenge tradition and redefine society?

QuickWrite

Have words alone ever seemed insufficient to express how you feel? Sometimes altering the appearance of words—capitalizing all the letters or italicizing a word—can enhance meaning. Write one or two sentences in which the meaning of a word or words is enhanced by its visual appearance.

The Granger Collection, New York.

E. E. Cummings
(1894–1962)

If there is such a thing as rugged individualism in poetry, E. E. Cummings is a prime example. All by himself, he challenged the conventions of English syntax and made typography and the division of words part of the shape and meaning of a poem.

A Unique Perspective

Edward Estlin Cummings was born in Cambridge, Massachusetts, the son of a Unitarian minister. He attended Harvard University at a time when French symbolism and free verse were major new influences on American poetry. Like other poets, Cummings found guidelines in the imagist manifesto that allowed him to experiment and to break old rules.

Trademark Typography

During World War I, Cummings volunteered for an ambulance corps privately financed by Americans and staffed by young men. Crossing to Bordeaux on a French troop ship threatened by German U-boats, Cummings had hardly begun his duties when a French censor, intercepting one of his typographically odd letters, imprisoned him on suspicion of espionage. Released within three months, Cummings drew on the experience to produce his first important book of prose, *The Enormous Room* (1922).

After World War I, Cummings returned to France. He was one of the American literary expatriates who found in Paris the freedom and inspiration the restrictive Puritan climate of their own country denied them. During this period, Cummings refined the eccentric shifts of syntax and typography that would become his trademark. In 1923, he published his first collection of verse, *Tulips and Chimneys,* which was followed by *&* (1925), *XLI Poems* (1925), and *is 5* (1926). His poetry is often marked by jubilant lyricism as he celebrates love, nature's beauty, and an almost Transcendentalist affirmation of the individual. He reserved his mischievous wit for the satire of the "unman," by which he meant the unthinking, unfeeling temperament of urban "humans."

Think About the Writer

How do Cummings's experiments with verse reflect Pound's famous slogan, "Make it new!"?

Reader/Writer Notebook

Use your **RWN** to complete the activities for these selections.

Literary Focus

Style A writer's **style** is the distinctive way he or she uses language. Sentence structure and length, word choice, imagery, syntax, and use of figurative language are all aspects of a writer's individual style. E. E. Cummings's unique style includes the unconventional use of capitalization, spacing, punctuation, and sentence structure. His punctuation is unorthodox, he uses parts of speech interchangeably, and his spacing is such that sometimes words bump into one another.

Reading Focus

Understanding Syntax The way words are arranged in a sentence is called **syntax.** In all languages, the syntax of sentences follows certain conventions or patterns so that readers can quickly make sense of what is said. Writers, particularly poets, sometimes experiment with syntax in order to find fresh ways to express experience. Cummings is known for his alternative syntax and usage. Finding basic sentence elements, such as the subject and verb(s), can help you make sense of his poems.

Into Action As you read the poems, find the beginning and end of each sentence. Then, locate the subject of the sentence and the verb or verbs associated with that subject. In the far right column, record other unusual aspects of his style. Use a chart like the one below for each poem.

Poem: "what if a much of a which of a wind"

Sentence	Subject	Verb	Other Aspects of Style
1	much	gives, bloodies, yanks	
2			no space after colon that follows fiend

Writing Focus

Think as a Reader/Writer

Find It in Your Reading Cummings is noted for playing with parts of speech, especially for using any word as a noun. As you read, note examples of this feature. When words that are normally verbs, adjectives, or adverbs are used as nouns, record them in your *Reader/Writer Notebook*. Think about how the meaning changes when the word is used as a noun.

Vocabulary

awry (uh RY) *adj.:* out of place; crooked. *The wind blows many things awry.*

flays (flayz) *v.:* whips; lashes. *The wind flays the landscape with rain and sleet.*

stifles (STY fuhlz) *v.:* smothers; extinguishes. *The wind stifles the forest.*

perceive (puhr SEEV) *v.:* observe; sense; understand. *The slightest gesture of the poet's beloved has more power over him than anything else he can perceive in the world.*

rendering (REHN duh rIhng) *v.* used as *adj.:* making; creating. *The poet's beloved takes breath after breath, rendering for him both death and eternal life.*

Language Coach

Connotations Poets choose words carefully for both their definitions and their **connotations,** the ideas associated with each word. The adjective *keen* means "sharp." The noun *keen* in line 9 means "a mournful cry," but it has a connotation of something sharp edged.

Sometimes you can figure out the connotations of a word by reading through its entire dictionary entry. That's because a word's multiple meanings tend to rub off on each other. Find *flay* in a dictionary, and read the entire entry. What connotations might have encouraged the poet to use *flays* rather than *whips* or *lashes* in line 9 of "what if a much of a which of a wind"?

Learn It Online
Find more about Cummings with these Internet links.

go.hrw.com | L11-807 | **Go**

what if a much of a which of a wind

by E. E. Cummings

Read with a Purpose

As you read this poem, think about what the speaker is saying about the tension between earthly destruction and the human spirit.

Build Background

In *New Poems,* Cummings wrote, "We are human beings;for whom birth is a supremely welcome mystery,the mystery of growing: the mystery which happens only and whenever we are faithful to ourselves. You and I wear the dangerous looseness of doom and find it becoming. Life, for eternal us,is now;and now is much too busy being a little more than everything to seem anything,catastrophic included. . . ." True humanity, in Cummings's view, is eternal and miraculous. In "what if a much of a which of a wind," Cummings explores this idea further. In spite of every kind of destruction, the speaker says, "the single secret will still be man."

what if a much of a which of a wind   **A**
gives the truth to summer's lie;
bloodies with dizzying leaves the sun
and yanks immortal stars awry?
5 Blow king to beggar and queen to seem
(blow friend to fiend:blow space to time)
—when skies are hanged and oceans drowned,
the single secret will still be man   **B**

A Literary Focus **Style** How would you describe the style of the poem's first line? What expectations does it set up for the poem as a whole?

B Reading Focus **Understanding Syntax** What happens to kings, queens, friends, space, sky, and oceans in lines 5–8? How would you restate the meaning of these lines in conventional syntax?

Vocabulary **awry** (uh RY) *adj.:* out of place; crooked.

what if a keen of a lean wind flays
10 screaming hills with sleet and snow:
strangles valleys by ropes of thing
and stifles forests in white ago?
Blow hope to terror;blow seeing to blind
(blow pity to envy and soul to mind)
15 —whose hearts are mountains,roots are trees,
it's they shall cry hello to the spring

what if a dawn of a doom of a dream
bites this universe in two,
peels forever out of his grave
20 and sprinkles nowhere with me and you?
Blow soon to never and never to twice
(blow life to isn't:blow death to was)
—all nothing's only our hugest home;
the most who die,the more we live **C**

C **Literary Focus** **Style** Cummings uses verbs, adjectives, and adverbs as nouns.
What examples can you find?

Vocabulary **flays** (flayz) *v.:* whips; lashes.
stifles (STY fuhlz) *v.:* smothers; extinguishes.

Analyzing Visuals

Viewing and Interpreting
In what ways do both the painting below and Cummings's poem break with traditional attitudes about creating images?

September Wind and Rain (1949) by Charles E. Burchfield (1893–1967).
Collection: Butler Institute of American Art, Youngstown, OH.

somewhere i have never travelled, gladly beyond by **E. E. Cummings**

Read with a Purpose
Read to discover the effect that the speaker's beloved has on him.

Build Background
Synesthesia is the practice of using an image that appeals to one sense but is expressed in terms of another, such as using a color to suggest a particular smell. In this love poem, for example, Cummings writes of the "color" of "texture" and says that the "voice" of his beloved's eyes is "deeper than all roses."

Der Kuss (The Kiss) (1907–1908) by Gustav Klimt. Oesterreichische Galerie, Vienna, Austria. Courtesy Erich Lessing / Art Resource, NY.

somewhere i have never travelled,gladly beyond
any experience,your eyes have their silence:
in your most frail gesture are things which enclose me,
or which i cannot touch because they are too near   **A**

5   your slightest look easily will unclose me
though i have closed myself as fingers,
you open always petal by petal myself as Spring opens
(touching skilfully,mysteriously)her first rose   **B**

or if your wish be to close me,i and
10   my life will shut very beautifully,suddenly,
as when the heart of this flower imagines
the snow carefully everywhere descending;

nothing which we are to perceive in this world equals
the power of your intense fragility:whose texture
15   compels me with the colour of its countries,
rendering death and forever with each breathing

(i do not know what it is about you that closes
and opens;only something in me understands
the voice of your eyes is deeper than all roses)
20   nobody,not even the rain,has such small hands

A **Literary Focus** Style What aspects of Cummings's style are apparent in this first stanza?

B **Reading Focus** Understanding Syntax Rewrite lines 6–8 in normal word order. How does this change the emotional effect of the lines?

Vocabulary **perceive** (puhr SEEV) *v.*: observe; sense; understand.
rendering (REHN duh rihng) *v.* used as *adj.*: making; creating.

SKILLS FOCUS **Literary Skills** Analyze the characteristics of a writer's style; analyze paradox. **Reading Skills** Understand syntax. **Vocabulary Skills** Identify synonyms. **Writing Skills** Enhance style for effective writing.

what if a much of a which of a wind /
somewhere i have never travelled,gladly beyond

Respond and Think Critically

Reading Focus

Read with a Purpose

1. What does the speaker of "what if a much…" say about the human spirit?

2. Describe the effect the speaker's beloved has on him in "somewhere i have never travelled.…"

Reading Skills: Understanding Syntax

3. You have dissected the sentences and noted aspects of style involving unusual grammar, punctuation, and syntax. Now, write two sentences summarizing the effect of this unique style.

✓ Vocabulary Check

Match each Vocabulary word with its synonym.

4. awry   **a.** smothers

5. flays   **b.** observe

6. stifles   **c.** whips

7. perceive   **d.** making

8. rendering   **e.** crooked

Literary Focus

Literary Analysis

what if a much of a which of a wind

9. Interpret What do you think Cummings means by the last two lines? Explain.

10. Analyze Explain the tone you hear in this poem—is it cynical, despairing, or triumphant?

11. Summarize Cummings opens each stanza with a question. What are the questions? What are the answers?

somewhere i have never travelled,gladly beyond

12. Analyze In the first three stanzas, what figures of speech show how the speaker feels about his love and how she affects him?

13. Interpret Explain what you think Cummings means by "death and forever" in stanza 4.

14. Interpret How can the rain be said to have small hands? What is the speaker suggesting about his love by using this beautiful and mysterious metaphor?

Literary Skills: Style

15. Make Judgments Find two or three examples of Cummings's distinctive use of punctuation and spacing in both poems. Then, comment on how each affects the meaning of the poem.

Literary Skills Review: Paradox

16. Analyze A **paradox** is a statement that appears contradictory but actually reveals a kind of truth. Find two paradoxes in these poems, and explain what they mean.

Writing Focus

Think as a Reader/Writer

Use It in Your Writing Write a poem using unconventional capitalization, punctuation, spacing, or sentence structure. Include one word that is normally a verb, adjective, or adverb, and use it as a noun.

What Do **You Think Now**

How does Cummings challenge and redefine traditional rules of grammar? Is his style effective? Explain.

Design / Nothing Gold Can Stay / Birches / Mending Wall / The Death of the Hired Man

What Do You Think

How does progress challenge tradition and redefine society?

QuickWrite

Think about a time when you observed something in nature that caused you to wonder about a larger idea. Write a few sentences describing the experience.

MEET THE WRITER

Robert Frost
(1874–1963)

Robert Frost sought to capture in his poetry the sound of common speech—what he called "the sound of sense." At the same time, however, he lifted common speech to the level of eloquence.

Beginnings in New England

Although Frost is most closely identified with New England, he was actually born in San Francisco, California. Frost was about ten years old before he first saw the New England landscapes and began to know the changing seasons he would later describe with the familiarity of a native son. The boy's move across the country was the result of his father's early death and his mother's decision to settle in the industrial town of Lawrence, Massachusetts. After high school, Frost entered Dartmouth College in New Hampshire. He decided after a few months that he was not yet ready for higher education, and he returned to Lawrence to work in the cotton mills and to write. His verse, however, found little favor with magazine editors.

Search for Identity

Married and with a growing family, Frost in his early twenties began to feel the need for a more formal education than his random, independent reading could provide. With financial assistance from his grandfather, Frost took his family to Cambridge, Massachusetts, where he entered Harvard. He stayed at Harvard for less than two years. He later wrote of his decision to leave: "Harvard had taken me away from the question of whether I could write or not."

By this time, Frost began to feel pressure to settle down in some profession. His wife Elinor appealed to his grandfather to buy them a farm in West Derry, New Hampshire. His grandfather, knowing that Frost's principal concern was poetry, asked, "Shall I give you a year? Will you settle down if I give you a year to try this out?" Frost replied, "Give me twenty." As it turned out, he spent ten long years on the "thirty acres, rather run down and poor, but with orchard, fields, pasture, woodland, and spring." He arranged his schedule to accommodate his poetry, milking his cows at midnight so that he could write poems in the late evening hours.

Frost eventually decided that the concentration necessary for writing poetry did not mix with the round-the-clock physical labor of working the land. Discouraged, he worked as a schoolteacher for a few years; then, in 1912, opting for a dramatic <u>alternative</u>, he took his family to England.

Inspiration in England

The move turned out to be a wise one. Inspired by meeting English and American poets, including Ezra Pound, Frost continued to write poetry, though he found his subjects in New England. In the three years he spent in England, he completed the two volumes that would make him famous—*A Boy's Will* (1913) and *North of Boston* (1914). These collections included several poems that would stand among Frost's best-known works: "The Tuft of Flowers," "Mending Wall," "The Death of the Hired Man," and "After Apple-Picking." These poems were marked by their realism and an impressive mastery of iambic rhythm, narrative dialogue, and dramatic monologue.

When Frost returned to New Hampshire in 1915, he was no longer an obscure scribbler intent on turning everyday New England life into poetry. Rather, he was an accomplished writer. In 1916, the publication of *Mountain Interval*—a collection that includes such favorites as "The Road Not Taken" and "Birches"—solidified his fame. For his subjects Frost often turned to the small farms of New England, the woods and mountains of that region, and its sturdy and self-reliant inhabitants. Frost once said that a poem should "begin in delight and end in wisdom." Readers of his work know that what begins as a description of a tuft of flowers often ends in a profound insight into life.

Poet of the People

Rewarded with many prizes (including four Pulitzer Prizes and a Congressional Medal), numerous honorary degrees, and the faithful attention of a wide readership, Frost spent the rest of his life as a lecturer and as a public performer who, as he put it, liked to "say" rather than to recite his poetry.

In his later years, Frost's public image was that of a lovable, fumbling old gent. Nevertheless, he was able to pierce the minds and hearts of those able to see beyond his playacting. In private, he was apt to put aside this guileless character and become a sometimes wicked commentator on the pretensions of rival poets. He could be just as cutting to gushing devotees, who

Portrait of Robert Lee Frost (1874–1963) by Clara E. Sipprell (c. 1955).

were unaware that he held in contempt the very flattery he demanded.

Frost was chosen to participate in the inauguration of President John F. Kennedy. On Inauguration Day in January 1961, he stood beside President Kennedy on the Capitol steps in Washington, D.C., and recited his poem "The Gift Outright." His art with words had brought him not only the friendship of a president, but also, by means of radio and television, the largest single audience in history for a poet until that time.

In a period when verbal experiment and exotic influences from abroad changed poetry, Frost remained devoted to <u>traditional</u> forms and stayed firmly rooted in American soil. He developed his talents with stubborn persistence, and he created a unique voice that remained unaffected by the clamor of modernism.

Think About the Writer

Why might Frost have developed a public persona that was different from his private self?

Preparing to Read

Reader/Writer Notebook

Use your **RWN** to complete the activities for this selection.

Literary Focus

Sonnet The lyric poem known as the **sonnet** consists of fourteen lines, usually written in iambic pentameter with a fixed rhyme scheme. In iambic pentameter, each line of poetry contains five iambs. An **iamb** is a metrical foot that has one unstressed syllable followed by a stressed syllable. There are two sonnet structures. In the **Petrarchan,** or Italian, sonnet, the **octave** (first eight lines) contains a question or problem. The rhyme scheme is *abba, abba*. The **sestet** (last six lines) proposes an answer or solution, with a rhyme scheme of *cde, cde*. In the **Shakespearean** alternative, three **quatrains** (four-line units), are followed by a concluding **couplet** (two rhyming lines). A common rhyme scheme is *abab, cdcd, efef, gg*.

Reading Focus

Analyzing Text Structure Frost's poem "Design" is an example of a Petrarchan sonnet with minor variations. Instead of posing the question or problem in the octave, Frost presents an observation about nature. He waits until lines 9–12 of the sestet to ask questions. In the final **couplet,** he gives his answer in the form of another question. Frost also uses a slight variation on the typical Petrarchan rhyme scheme of the sestet.

Into Action As you read, think about the relationship between the octave and the sestet. What images are found in the octave? Which questions about them does the speaker ask the sestet? Record the images in the chart below. Then, list the questions about them from the sestet.

Image from Octave	Question about it from Sestet (line no.)
dimpled spider, fat and white,	"What brought the kindred spider to that height," (line 11)

Writing Focus

Think as a Reader/Writer

Find It in Your Reading As you read, note the rhymes. Record the **rhyme scheme** in your *Reader/Writer Notebook*. How does the rhyme scheme of the sestet differ from that of a typical Petrarchan sonnet?

Vocabulary

rigid (RIHJ ihd) *adj.:* firm; stiff. *The moth's body was as rigid as a piece of paper.*

kindred (KIHN drihd) *adj.:* similar; related. *Frost observes kindred elements of nature: flower, spider, and moth.*

appall (uh PAWL) *v.:* horrify; fill with shock. *Nature can both delight and appall.*

Language Coach

Words Within Words The verb *appall* contains the word *pall*, which can mean "to become unpleasant." How are the meanings of *pall* and *appall* related? What noun can you find within the adjective *kindred*? How are the meanings of these words related?

 Learn It Online
Learn more about the Vocabulary words with Word Watch online.

go.hrw.com | L11-814 | Go

Design

by **Robert Frost**

Read with a Purpose
Read to discover what observation Frost makes about a spider, a moth, and a flowering plant.

Build Background
Frost was particularly proud of his sonnets, which are considered among the finest in the English language. He often expressed regret that more of them were not reprinted in the hundreds of anthologies in which his work appeared. In this sonnet, Frost uses the image of a spider and a moth on a heal-all to pose questions about nature. A heal-all is a flowering plant of the mint family, sometimes white in color. It is so named because the flowers, leaves, and stem are used in folk medicine to treat sore throats and other minor ailments.

I found a dimpled spider, fat and white,
On a white heal-all, holding up a moth
Like a white piece of rigid satin cloth—
Assorted characters of death and blight
5 Mixed ready to begin the morning right,
Like the ingredients of a witches' broth—
A snowdrop spider, a flower like a froth,°
And dead wings carried like a paper kite. **A**

What had that flower to do with being white,
10 The wayside blue and innocent heal-all?
What brought the kindred spider to that height,
Then steered the white moth thither° in the night?
What but design of darkness to appall?—
If design govern in a thing so small. **B**

7. froth: foam.

12. thither: archaic for "to there."

A **Literary Focus** Sonnet Is the meter regular or irregular? How do the meter and rhythm affect the tone?

B **Reading Focus** Analyzing Text Structure What questions does the speaker ask in the sestet? What is the answer in the final couplet?

Vocabulary **rigid** (RIHJ ihd) *adj.*: firm; stiff.
kindred (KIHN drihd) *adj.*: similar; related.
appall (uh PAWL) *v.*: horrify; fill with shock.

Reader/Writer Notebook

Use your **RWN** to complete the activities for this selection.

Literary Focus

Allusion Some poets make frequent use of allusions. An **allusion** is a reference, direct or indirect, to someone or something outside a literary work. A writer might refer to another work of literature or to events or persons in history, art, or contemporary life. When writers make allusions, they expect their readers to recognize the reference.

To understand "Nothing Gold Can Stay," you need to recognize two references Frost is making to other literary accounts.

- The first allusion is to the biblical story of Adam and Eve's expulsion from the Garden of Eden.
- The second allusion is to the Greek myth about the loss of the Golden Age, a time of innocent happiness that, like time in Eden, did not last.

Language Coach

Word Origins Knowing a word's origin can help you understand its meaning as well as the meanings of related words. The verb *subside* means "to sink to a low level or become less active." It comes from the Latin prefix *sub–*, which means "down" and a root that means "to settle."

- How do these word parts relate to the meaning of *subsides*?
- How does the same root affect the meaning of the word *reside*?
- How does the prefix *sub–* affect the meaning of the word *subterranean*?

Writing Focus

Think as a Reader/Writer

Find It in Your Reading As you read "Nothing Gold Can Stay," use a chart like the one below to record the poem's rhyme scheme in your *Reader/ Writer Notebook*. Also, note examples of repetition and alliteration in the poem.

Line	Repetition	Alliteration
1		"green is gold"

Learn It Online
Experience this poem read aloud online.

go.hrw.com   L11-816   **Go**

Nothing Gold Can Stay

by **Robert Frost**

Read with a Purpose
Read to discover how Frost uses nature to express an idea about perfection.

Build Background
Gold, whether it refers to the metal or the color, conjures up many images and meanings. Over the centuries, writers and artists have used gold as a symbol of perfection. In this poem, Frost observes that the color gold is also found in nature and that, like the perfection it symbolizes, it is temporary.

Nature's first green is gold,
Her hardest hue to hold.
Her early leaf's a flower;
But only so an hour.
Then leaf subsides° to leaf.
So Eden sank to grief,
So dawn goes down to day.
Nothing gold can stay. **A**

5. **subsides:** dies down or sinks.

A **Literary Focus** Allusion Adam and Eve are expelled from Eden for eating from the tree of knowledge. Do you think knowledge is better than the beauty and innocence of paradise? Might it be just as well that "nothing gold can stay"?

SKILLS FOCUS Literary Skills Analyze characteristics of sonnets; analyze allusions; analyze symbols. **Reading Skills** Analyze the use of text structure in poetry. **Vocabulary Skills** Use precise meaning.

Respond and Think Critically

Reading Focus

Read with a Purpose

Design

1. What has the speaker learned about nature through his observation of the flower, spider, and moth?

Nothing Gold Can Stay

2. How does the poem illustrate the transitory nature of perfect things?

Reading Skills: Analyzing Text Structure

3. Review the chart you created for "Design" to track images in the octave and questions the speaker asks about them in the sestet. Write a few sentences discussing what the speaker suggests the images have in common.

✔ Vocabulary Check

Match each Vocabulary word with its definition.

4. rigid
5. kindred
6. appall

a. similar
b. horrify
c. stiff

Literary Focus

Literary Analysis

Design

7. **Analyze** Look for ambiguity in Frost: His poems often suggest several meanings or contain contradictory details. In line 14, what reservation or doubt remains in his mind? How does this line affect the whole tone and meaning of the poem?

8. **Extend** The critic Laurence Perrine said that the poet "chillingly poses the problem of evil." If you agree, give reasons for your opinion. If you disagree, give an <u>alternative</u> theme for the poem.

Nothing Gold Can Stay

9. **Interpret** Think of what the first buds look like in spring, and then explain line 1.

10. **Infer** What natural process is described in line 5?

Literary Skills: Sonnet

11. **Analyze** In "Design," what key concepts do the rhyming words emphasize?

Literary Skills: Allusion

12. **Extend** In "Nothing Gold Can Stay," how does the poem's allusion to the expulsion from the Garden of Eden reflect the poem's theme?

Literary Skills Review: Symbol

13. **Hypothesize** In "Nothing Gold Can Stay," what different ideas might gold symbolize?

Writing Focus

Think as a Reader/Writer

Use It in Your Writing Write a Petrarchan sonnet in which you observe something in nature. Use rhyme scheme to express your ideas.

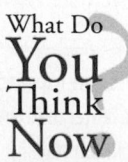

What Do **You Think Now** How do Frost's close observations of nature reveal larger truths about life?

Preparing to Read

Birches

Reader/Writer Notebook

Use your **RWN** to complete the activities for this selection.

Literary Focus

Blank Verse Many of Frost's poems, including "Birches," are written in **blank verse,** which is unrhymed iambic pentameter. This means that each line of the poem has five iambs. An **iamb** is one unaccented syllable followed by an accented syllable, such as in the word *across*.

Reading Focus

Reading Poetry Frost's blank verse sounds much like conversational English. As you read "Birches," you will hear the rise and fall of the speaker's voice. When you come to a period, make a full stop. When you see a comma, semicolon, or dash, pause slightly. If there is no mark of punctuation at the end of a line, read on to the next line without stopping.

Into Action As you read, notice that some of the lines are strict iambic pentameter   they adhere to the meter without any variation. Other lines are basically iambic, but there may be extra syllables or other variations in the meter. Use a chart to record which lines are loosely iambic. In the third column, explain how the line varies from strict iambic pentameter.

Line	Loose Iambic Pentameter	How the Line Varies
Line 5	"As ice storms do. Often you must have seen them"	It has one extra unaccented syllable at the end of the line.

Writing Focus

Think as a Reader/Writer

Find It in Your Reading Blank verse does not use end rhyme but relies instead on <u>alternative</u> sound effects. **Alliteration,** the repetition of the same or similar consonant sounds, is another sound device poets use. As you read, record examples of alliteration in your *Reader/Writer Notebook*.

TechFocus The poems "Design," "Nothing Gold Can Stay," and "Birches" all open with an image from nature. As you read, picture the images in your mind. How might a photograph of the same image look?

Vocabulary

enamel (ih NAM uhl) *n.*: a smooth, hard, shiny coating. *The ice covered the trees like enamel.*

shed (shehd) *v.*: cast off. *When the sun comes out, the trees shed their icy coating.*

subdued (suhb DOOD) *v.*: overcame by greater force; conquered. *The ice storm subdued the birch trees.*

poise (poyz) *n.*: balance. *Boys who climb trees must maintain their poise, or they might fall.*

Language Coach

Multiple-Meaning Words Some words, such as *shed* and *poise*, have multiple meanings. In this poem, *shed* is a verb meaning "to cast off," but it can also be a noun meaning "a structure built for shelter or storage." *Poise* can mean "physical balance," as in the poem, or it can mean "a dignified, self-confident manner."

 Learn It Online
Follow Frost across the Web with these links.

go.hrw.com   L11-819   **Go**

Birches

by **Robert Frost**

Read with a Purpose

Read to discover what the sight of birch trees covered in ice suggests to Frost about life.

Build Background

As spindly and awkward as a giraffe's legs, the birch trees of Robert Frost's New England have white bark ringed with black. Birches grow more quickly than do trees with harder wood, such as oak and maple. As a result, the birch trunks are remarkably pliable—a fact that gives this poem its realistic base. Children do, in fact, climb and swing on birch trees, which are commonly found in large groves in New England.

When I see birches bend to left and right
Across the lines of straighter darker trees,
I like to think some boy's been swinging them.
But swinging doesn't bend them down to stay
5   As ice storms do. Often you must have seen them   **A**
Loaded with ice a sunny winter morning
After a rain. They click upon themselves
As the breeze rises, and turn many-colored
As the stir cracks and crazes their enamel.
10   Soon the sun's warmth makes them shed crystal shells
Shattering and avalanching on the snow crust—
Such heaps of broken glass to sweep away
You'd think the inner dome of heaven had fallen.
They are dragged to the withered bracken° by the load,
15   And they seem not to break; though once they are bowed
So low for long, they never right themselves:
You may see their trunks arching in the woods
Years afterwards, trailing their leaves on the ground
Like girls on hands and knees that throw their hair
20   Before them over their heads to dry in the sun.
But I was going to say when Truth broke in
With all her matter of fact about the ice storm,
I should prefer to have some boy bend them
As he went out and in to fetch the cows—
25   Some boy too far from town to learn baseball,

14. bracken: large, coarse fern.

A **Literary Focus** **Blank Verse** What effect does the slight irregularity in meter have on the rhythm of the poem?

Vocabulary **enamel** (ih NAM uhl) *n.*: a smooth, hard, shiny coating.
shed (shehd) *v.*: cast off.

Whose only play was what he found himself,
Summer or winter, and could play alone.
One by one he subdued his father's trees
By riding them down over and over again **B**
30　Until he took the stiffness out of them,
And not one but hung limp, not one was left
For him to conquer. He learned all there was
To learn about not launching out too soon
And so not carrying the tree away
35　Clear to the ground. He always kept his poise
To the top branches, climbing carefully
With the same pains you use to fill a cup
Up to the brim, and even above the brim.
Then he flung outward, feet first, with a swish,
40　Kicking his way down through the air to the ground.
So was I once myself a swinger of birches.
And so I dream of going back to be.
It's when I'm weary of considerations,
And life is too much like a pathless wood
45　Where your face burns and tickles with the cobwebs
Broken across it, and one eye is weeping
From a twig's having lashed across it open.
I'd like to get away from earth awhile
And then come back to it and begin over.
50　May no fate willfully misunderstand me
And half grant what I wish and snatch me away
Not to return. Earth's the right place for love:
I don't know where it's likely to go better. **C**
I'd like to go by climbing a birch tree,
55　And climb black branches up a snow-white trunk
Toward heaven, till the tree could bear no more,
But dipped its top and set me down again.
That would be good both going and coming back.
One could do worse than be a swinger of birches. **D**

B **Literary Focus** **Blank Verse** How does line 29 differ from the usual meter of the poem? What effect does this change have on the rhythm of the poem?

C **Reading Focus** **Reading Poetry** Read lines 50–53 aloud, accenting the syllables in strict iambic pentameter. Then, read them more naturally, as if reading prose. What differences do you hear in your two readings?

D **Reading Focus** **Reading Poetry** How does the poet indicate that he wants to stress a particular word? How does he indicate places where you should pause or stop in your reading?

Vocabulary **subdued** (suhb DOOD) *v.*: overcame by greater force; conquered.
poise (poyz) *n.*: balance.

Respond and Think Critically

Reading Focus

Quick Check

1. How can the speaker tell that the birches he observes were not bent by a boy swinging on them?

2. Why does the speaker admire the young boy?

3. Why does the speaker wish to become a "swinger of birches" again?

Read with a Purpose

4. What do you think the playful activity of birch swinging symbolizes in the poem?

Reading Skills: Reading Poetry

5. As you read the poem, you recorded variations in the use of strict iambic pentameter. Now, look over your chart and write a sentence explaining why you think Frost chooses to include lines that deviate from strict iambic pentameter.

Line	Loose Iambic Pentameter	How the Line Varies
Line 5	"As ice storms do. Often you must have seen them"	It has one extra unaccented syllable at the end of the line.

Literary Focus

Literary Analysis

6. **Analyze** In lines 41–49, what does the speaker say he wishes he could do now when life is "like a pathless wood"?

7. **Interpret** How does the speaker correct himself in lines 50–53? In lines 54–57, what does he say he wants to do?

8. **Draw Conclusions** What do you think is the **moral,** or message, of Frost's poem? Explain.

9. **Evaluate** In a famous remark about the nature of poetry, Frost said that a poem "begins in delight and ends in wisdom." Do you think that this formula applies to "Birches"? Explain your view, including what you think Frost means by *delight* and *wisdom*.

Literary Skills: Blank Verse

10. **Compare and Contrast** Blank verse is close to the rhythm of natural, conversational English. What lines from "Birches" have the most casual, conversational tone? Why do you think so?

Literary Skills Review: Simile

11. **Analyze** A **simile** is a figure of speech that makes an explicit comparison between two unlike things, using a word such as *like, as, than,* or *resembles.* Two strong similes give this poem a richness that is both imaginative and the result of close observation. Find these similes in lines 18–20 and 44–47, and explain what is being compared. What does each simile help you see?

Writing Focus

Think as a Reader/Writer

Use It in Your Writing Write a short poem describing a scene in nature that reveals a universal truth about life. Write in blank verse, but you may vary the meter slightly to keep your poem from sounding singsong. Use the sound device of alliteration to achieve a musical effect.

 What Do You Think Now

How might the lessons of "not launching out too soon," not carrying the tree "clear to the ground," and "climbing carefully" apply to life in general?

SKILLS FOCUS **Literary Skills** Analyze blank verse; analyze similes. **Reading Skills** Read to understand poetry and elements of poetry. **Vocabulary Skills** Analyze

Germanic/Anglo-Saxon roots. **Writing Skills** Use descriptive language. **Listening and Speaking Skills** Offer insightful observations in discussions and conversations.

Vocabulary Development

✓ Vocabulary Check

Match each Vocabulary word with its definition.

1. enamel
2. shed
3. subdued
4. poise

a. overcome by force
b. cast off
c. balance
d. smooth, shiny coating

Vocabulary Skills: Germanic/Anglo-Saxon Roots

The imagery in "Birches" is vivid and appeals to the senses—notice lines like "crystal shells/Shattering and avalanching on the snow crust—" (lines 10–11) and "Then he flung outward, feet first, with a swish" (line 39). Much of this imagery depends on words that have Germanic origins. These words are often concrete, everyday words; for example, the word *birches*.

In contrast, words that have Latin origins are often more scientific or abstract; for example, *atmosphere* and *imagination*.

Your Turn

Which of the following words do you think have Germanic origins? Which do you think are from Latin? Take a guess. Then, look up the terms in a dictionary to discover if you are correct.

cracks   broken   subdued   black   conquered

Academic Vocabulary

Talk About

In "Birches," Frost seems to imagine an <u>alternative</u> world where we can all live a more carefree life. Do you find this notion appealing? Is it realistic in our <u>hierarchical</u> society? Why?

CHOICES

As you respond to the Choices, use these **Academic Vocabulary** words as appropriate: <u>alternative</u>, <u>hierarchy</u>, <u>ideology</u>, <u>inevitable</u>, <u>tradition</u>.

REVIEW
Use Scientific Perspective
Class Presentation Frost was interested in the natural world and used nature as a point of departure for self-expression and philosophical musing. To gain a deeper understanding of the natural phenomena that Frost refers to, research one of the following: gold (its atomic composition and chemical properties), the <u>hierarchy</u> of food chains, or ice storms. Share your findings with your classmates in an oral presentation.

CONNECT
Present Images from Nature
TechFocus Think of something in nature that has a powerful effect on you, and find a photograph of it or take your own. Then, write a paragraph describing the scene and explaining its importance. Present the photograph and your paragraph to your class.

EXTEND
Listen to Poems Set to Music
Randall Thompson, a well-known choral composer, set many of Frost's poems to music. His collection *Frostiana* includes the text of seven of Frost's poems, including "The Road Not Taken," "Stopping by Woods on a Snowy Evening," and "Choose Something Like a Star." Find a recording of these and, with a group, have a listening session. Afterward, discuss your reactions to hearing Frost's poems set to music.

Learn It Online
Explore word roots further online with *WordSharp*.

go.hrw.com   L11-823   **Go**

Reader/Writer Notebook

Use your **RWN** to complete the activities for this selection.

Literary Focus

Ambiguity "Mending Wall" is one of Frost's most controversial poems because of its **ambiguity**—that is, its quality of being open to two or more conflicting interpretations. The poem presents two views, and it is unclear which of the two <u>alternatives</u> the poem endorses. The neighbor expresses the <u>traditional</u> wisdom that walls are useful, while the speaker sees them as barriers that should be torn down. Many readers have wondered which attitude represents the view of the poet. There are also other ambiguities in the poem: For example, if the speaker dislikes walls, why does he begin the wall mending each spring?

> ### Language Coach
> **Connotations** A feeling or emotion that is evoked by a certain word is the word's **connotation,** which is different from the word's dictionary definition, or literal meaning. In this poem, *wall* has negative connotations to the speaker: isolation, separation, and aloofness.

Writing Focus

Think as a Reader/Writer

Find It in Your Reading As you read "Mending Wall," think about the two ways people have interpreted the meaning of the poem. What words, phrases, or lines lead you to believe that the poet agrees with the speaker? What details lead you to believe that the poet agrees with the neighbor? Use a chart like the one below to list the evidence for each interpretation in your *Reader/Writer Notebook*. Be sure to note where specific details appear in the poem.

Evidence that poet agrees with speaker	Evidence that poet agrees with neighbor
"Something there is that doesn't love a wall" (line1)	"He says again, 'Good fences make good neighbors.'" (line 45)

Learn It Online
Listen to "Mending Wall" online.

go.hrw.com   L11-824   **Go**

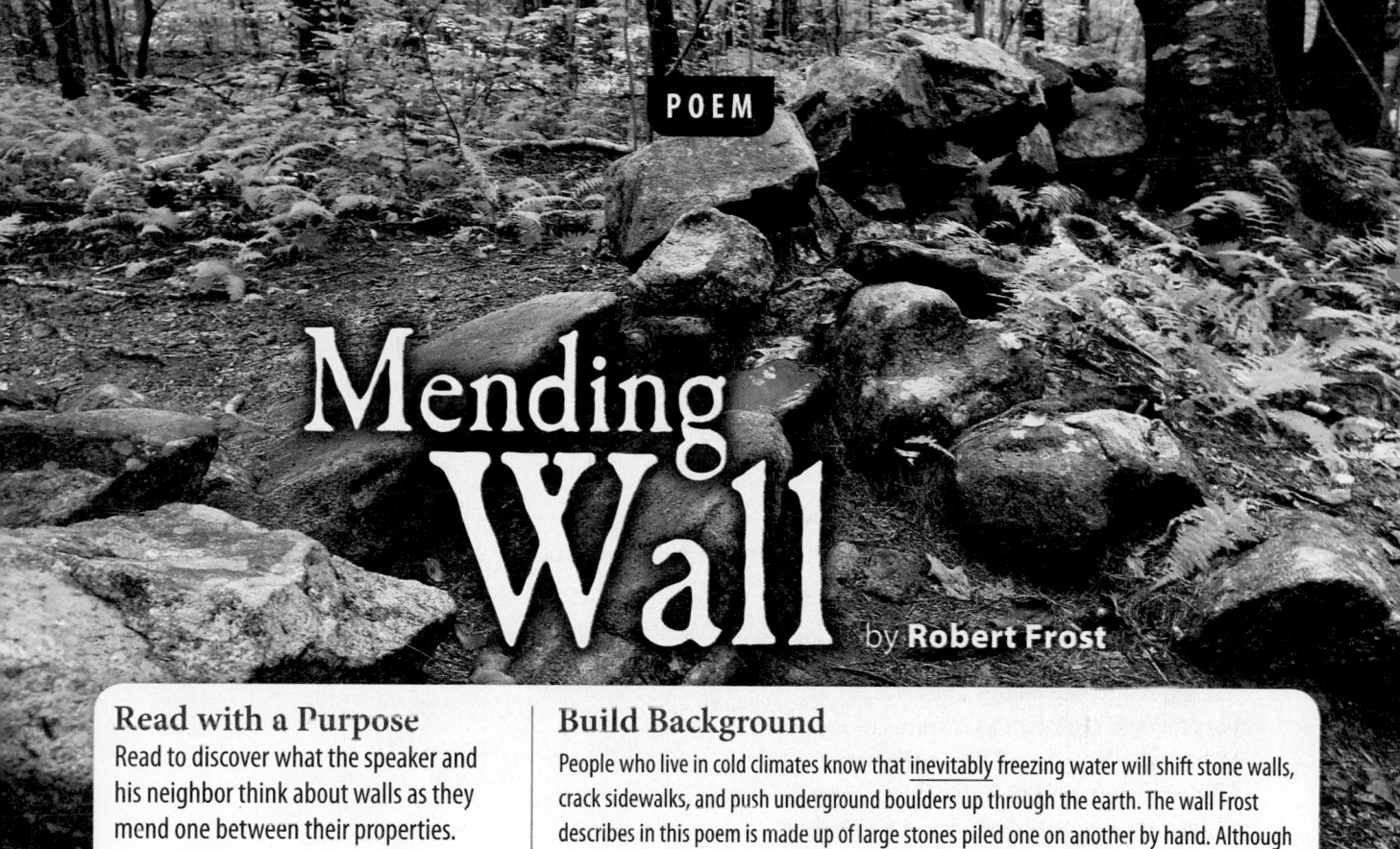

Mending Wall

by **Robert Frost**

Read with a Purpose

Read to discover what the speaker and his neighbor think about walls as they mend one between their properties.

Build Background

People who live in cold climates know that <u>inevitably</u> freezing water will shift stone walls, crack sidewalks, and push underground boulders up through the earth. The wall Frost describes in this poem is made up of large stones piled one on another by hand. Although low, such a wall can effectively mark the boundary between neighbors.

Something there is that doesn't love a wall,
That sends the frozen-ground-swell under it
And spills the upper boulders in the sun,
And makes gaps even two can pass abreast.
5 The work of hunters is another thing:
I have come after them and made repair
Where they have left not one stone on a stone,
But they would have the rabbit out of hiding,
To please the yelping dogs. The gaps I mean,
10 No one has seen them made or heard them made,
But at spring mending-time we find them there.
I let my neighbor know beyond the hill;
And on a day we meet to walk the line
And set the wall between us once again.
15 We keep the wall between us as we go.
To each the boulders that have fallen to each.
And some are loaves and some so nearly balls
We have to use a spell to make them balance:
"Stay where you are until our backs are turned!"
20 We wear our fingers rough with handling them.
Oh, just another kind of outdoor game,
One on a side. It comes to little more:

There where it is we do not need the wall:
He is all pine and I am apple orchard.
25 My apple trees will never get across
And eat the cones under his pines, I tell him.
He only says, "Good fences make good neighbors."
Spring is the mischief in me, and I wonder
If I could put a notion in his head:
30 "*Why* do they make good neighbors? Isn't it
Where there are cows? But here there are no cows.
Before I built a wall I'd ask to know
What I was walling in or walling out,
And to whom I was like to give offense.
35 Something there is that doesn't love a wall,
That wants it down." I could say "Elves" to him, **Ⓐ**
But it's not elves exactly, and I'd rather
He said it for himself. I see him there,
Bringing a stone grasped firmly by the top
40 In each hand, like an old-stone savage armed.
He moves in darkness as it seems to me,
Not of woods only and the shade of trees.
He will not go behind his father's saying,
And he likes having thought of it so well
45 He says again, "Good fences make good neighbors." **Ⓑ**

Ⓐ Literary Focus **Ambiguity** How does the speaker's behavior contradict the
opinion he voices about walls between neighbors?

Ⓑ Literary Focus **Ambiguity** How does the final line affect the reader's search for
the poem's overall meaning?

ART LINK

Dry-Stone Walling

Dry-stone walling is the practice of building stone walls without mortar. Correctly placed, the stones are held together by the forces of gravity and friction.
In other words, a stone's own weight holds it in place. Dry-stone walls can resist
weathering (breaking down) from freezing rain and snow much longer than
mortared walls can. Dry-stone walls are also easier to repair. They were used
extensively in Britain and Ireland, and, as a result, the practice took hold in colonial New England. Today, artists have revived this craft to create dry-stone sculpture. This method of sculpture uses the principles of dry-stone walling to create
aesthetically interesting functional walls as well as nonfunctional artworks.

Ask Yourself
**How does the absence of mortar in a dry-stone wall relate to the theme of
this poem?**

Applying Your Skills

Mending Wall

Respond and Think Critically

Reading Focus

Quick Check

1. What <u>inevitable</u> force is at work in lines 1–4 of the poem? Explain.

2. How would you interpret the neighbor's saying, "Good fences make good neighbors"?

3. Why does the speaker compare his neighbor to "an old-stone savage"?

Read with a Purpose

4. What do you think the speaker has learned from his yearly encounter with his neighbor as they rebuild the wall?

Literary Focus

Literary Analysis

5. **Infer** What makes the speaker say that "something" doesn't love a wall? Besides this "something," who else sometimes knocks down walls?

6. **Draw Conclusions** Describe what is happening in lines 13–16. According to the speaker, why is rebuilding the wall merely an "outdoor game" (lines 21–26)?

7. **Analyze** What questions does the speaker think should be settled before building a wall? Why does the speaker think that settling these questions is important?

8. **Hypothesize** Why does the speaker consider saying "Elves" (line 36) to his neighbor? What causes the speaker to change his mind?

9. **Interpret** What do you think the word *darkness* means in line 41? What could the simile in line 40 have to do with darkness?

10. **Extend** Frost creates two characters in this poem, and we come to know them by what they say, do, and think. What points of view in contemporary life do Frost's characters reflect?

11. **Evaluate** Do you believe that "Good fences make good neighbors"? Do you think that the generalization could apply in some situations but not all? Give your reasons.

Literary Skills: Ambiguity

12. **Compare and Contrast** The poem is ambiguous—it presents opposing views about the wall. Do you think Frost favors the view of the speaker or of the neighbor? Which details from the poem lead you to this interpretation?

Literary Skills Review: Symbols

13. **Interpret** A person, place, event, or thing that has meaning in itself but also stands for something more than itself is called a **symbol.** What do you think the wall in this poem symbolizes?

Writing Focus

Think as a Reader/Writer

Use It in Your Writing Write a short narrative, with dialogue, in which two characters take opposite sides of an issue. Using Frost's poem as a model, try to create ambiguity in your narrative. If time allows, consider writing your narrative in blank verse.

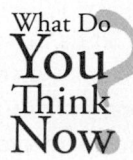 What Do You Think Now

What historical walls or boundaries have separated neighbors? Do you think they have been effective in accomplishing their purpose?

For **CHOICES** see page 836. >

Preparing to Read

SKILLS FOCUS Literary Skills Understand a narrative poem. **Reading Skills** Make inferences about characters.

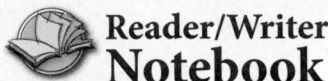

Reader/Writer Notebook

Use your **RWN** to complete the activities for this selection.

Literary Focus

Narrative Poetry A **narrative poem** is a poem that tells a story—a series of related events with a beginning, a middle, and an end. Most of "The Death of the Hired Man" consists of dialogue written in **blank verse**. The poem's main character, Silas (the hired man), does not speak for himself, yet his presence dominates the poem. We learn enough about Silas's background, habits, and <u>ideology</u> to feel that we know him. We also come to know the husband and wife whose dialogue tells the poem's story.

Literary Perspectives Apply the literary perspective described on page 829 as you read this poem.

Reading Focus

Making Inferences About Characters When you **infer,** you draw conclusions based on facts and evidence from the text and your own experience. As you read "The Death of the Hired Man," you can draw inferences about the characters based on what they say and do.

Into Action Read this narrative poem as if it were a short story. As you read, take notes about the plot and what you can infer from the conversation between Mary and Warren about Silas.

Line(s)	Mary's Actions/Inference	Warren's Actions/Inference
1–5	Mary hurries to tell Warren that Silas is back —Mary is anxious about Silas's return.	
6–7	Mary tells Warren, "Be kind."	

Writing Focus

Think as a Reader/Writer

Find It in Your Reading As you read the poem, record examples of realistic dialogue in your *Reader/Writer Notebook*. Comment on the methods Frost uses to make the **dialogue** sound authentic.

Vocabulary

beholden (bih HOHL duhn) *adj.:* indebted. *Silas does not feel beholden to Warren.*

grudge (gruhj) *v.:* withhold something from someone out of spite. *Warren's reaction is to grudge Silas a comfortable homecoming because Silas left without ditching the field.*

daft (daft) *adj.:* without sense; stupid. *Young Wilson may have seemed daft to Silas.*

Language Coach

Parts of Speech The verb *grudge* (line 49) means "to withhold something from someone out of spite." The noun *grudge* refers to "a sullen or unfriendly feeling." It is often used with the verb *hold* in the expression "hold a grudge." What do you think this expression means?

 Learn It Online

Get another glimpse of this poem through the *Power-Notes* introductory video online.

go.hrw.com | L11-828 | Go

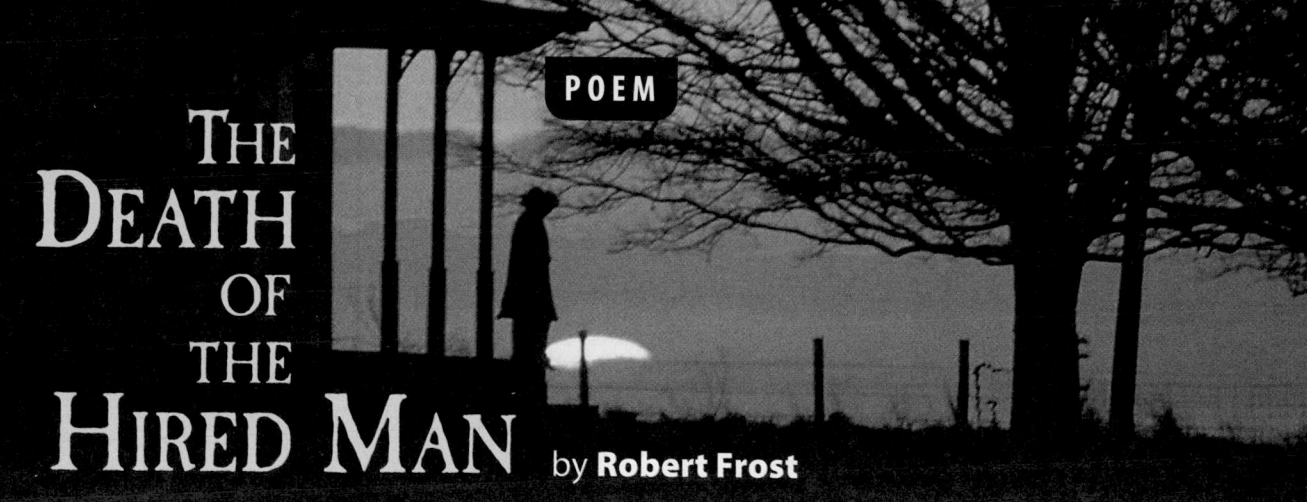

THE DEATH OF THE HIRED MAN
by **Robert Frost**

Read with a Purpose
Read to understand the conflict Warren and Mary, a couple in the poem, face when a hired man returns to their farm.

Build Background
A famous maxim comes from this poem: "Home is the place where, when you have to go there, / They have to take you in." The poem also offers another definition of home: "Something you somehow haven't to deserve." To some people, home is a definite place; to others, it is a state of mind, a sense of connection and belonging.

Mary sat musing on the lamp-flame at the table,
Waiting for Warren. When she heard his step,
She ran on tiptoe down the darkened passage
To meet him in the doorway with the news
5 And put him on his guard. "Silas is back."
She pushed him outward with her through the door
And shut it after her. "Be kind," she said. Ⓐ
She took the market things from Warren's arms
And set them on the porch, then drew him down
10 To sit beside her on the wooden steps.

"When was I ever anything but kind to him?
But I'll not have the fellow back," he said.
"I told him so last haying, didn't I?
If he left then, I said, that ended it.
15 What good is he? Who else will harbor° him
At his age for the little he can do?
What help he is there's no depending on.
Off he goes always when I need him most.
He thinks he ought to earn a little pay,
20 Enough at least to buy tobacco with,
So he won't have to beg and be beholden.
'All right,' I say, 'I can't afford to pay
Any fixed wages, though I wish I could.'

Ⓐ Reading Focus **Making Inferences About Characters** What can you infer about Warren from Mary's warning to him to "be kind"?

Vocabulary **beholden** (bih HOHL duhn) *adj.:* indebted.

15. harbor: provide safe shelter for.

Literary Perspectives

Analyzing Style Like many poets, Robert Frost has a recognizable style. Frost is known for his conversational diction as well as for his concrete images and characters drawn from rural New England. He has distinctive ways of using figurative language, imagery, diction, meter, and rhythm. For example, Frost uses blank verse almost exclusively, even though the trend among poets of his time was to explore free verse. As you read this poem, notice the clear, simple words Frost uses to describe the setting. Look for figurative language such as metaphors and similes, and pay attention to the colloquial, informal language in the dialogue, including the use of contractions such as *it's* and *I'd*.

As you read, be sure to notice the questions in the text, which will guide you in using this perspective.

'Someone else can.' 'Then someone else will have to.' **B**
25 I shouldn't mind his bettering himself
    If that was what it was. You can be certain,
    When he begins like that, there's someone at him
    Trying to coax him off with pocket money—
    In haying time, when any help is scarce.
30 In winter he comes back to us. I'm done."

    "Sh! not so loud: He'll hear you," Mary said.

    "I want him to: He'll have to soon or late." **C**

    "He's worn out. He's asleep beside the stove.
    When I came up from Rowe's I found him here,
35 Huddled against the barn door fast asleep,
    A miserable sight, and frightening, too—
    You needn't smile—I didn't recognize him—
    I wasn't looking for him—and he's changed.
    Wait till you see."

                    "Where did you say he'd been?"

40 "He didn't say. I dragged him to the house,
    And gave him tea and tried to make him smoke.
    I tried to make him talk about his travels.
    Nothing would do: He just kept nodding off."

    "What did he say? Did he say anything?"

    "But little."

45   "Anything? Mary, confess
    He said he'd come to ditch° the meadow for me."

    "Warren!"

            "But did he? I just want to know."

    "Of course he did. What would you have him say?
    Surely you wouldn't grudge the poor old man
50 Some humble way to save his self-respect.
    He added, if you really care to know,
    He meant to clear the upper pasture, too.
    That sounds like something you have heard before?
    Warren, I wish you could have heard the way
55 He jumbled everything. I stopped to look

46. ditch: dig drainage channels in.

B **Literary Focus** **Narrative Poetry** When did this conversation between Warren and Silas take place? What is the source of the conflict between them?

C **Reading Focus** **Making Inferences About Characters** What does this exchange (lines 31 and 32) reveal about Mary and Warren?

Vocabulary **grudge** (gruhj) *v.:* withhold something from someone out of spite.

Two or three times—he made me feel so queer°—
To see if he was talking in his sleep.
He ran on° Harold Wilson—you remember—
The boy you had in haying four years since.
60   He's finished school, and teaching in his college.
Silas declares you'll have to get him back.
He says they two will make a team for work:
Between them they will lay this farm as smooth!
The way he mixed that in with other things.
65   He thinks young Wilson a likely lad, though daft
On education—you know how they fought
All through July under the blazing sun,
Silas up on the cart to build the load,
Harold along beside to pitch it on."

70   "Yes, I took care to keep well out of earshot."

"Well, those days trouble Silas like a dream.
You wouldn't think they would. How some things linger!
Harold's young college-boy's assurance piqued° him.
After so many years he still keeps finding
75   Good arguments he sees he might have used.
I sympathize. I know just how it feels
To think of the right thing to say too late.
Harold's associated in his mind with Latin.
He asked me what I thought of Harold's saying
80   He studied Latin, like the violin,
Because he liked it—that an argument!
He said he couldn't make the boy believe
He could find water with a hazel prong°—
Which showed how much good school had ever done him.
85   He wanted to go over that. But most of all
He thinks if he could have another chance
To teach him how to build a load of hay—"

"I know, that's Silas' one accomplishment.
He bundles every forkful in its place,
90   And tags and numbers it for future reference,
So he can find and easily dislodge it
In the unloading. Silas does that well.
He takes it out in bunches like big birds' nests.
You never see him standing on the hay
95   He's trying to lift, straining to lift himself." **D**

"He thinks if he could teach him that, he'd be
Some good perhaps to someone in the world.
He hates to see a boy the fool of books.
Poor Silas, so concerned for other folk,
100   And nothing to look backward to with pride,

---

56. queer: uncomfortable; ill at ease.
58. ran on: kept talking about in a rambling way.

73. piqued: provoked.

83. hazel prong: forked branch used to find water underground.

D **Reading Focus** **Making Inferences About Characters** What do lines 88–95 suggest about Silas? What do they suggest about Warren?

Vocabulary **daft** (daft) *adj.:* without sense; stupid.

And nothing to look forward to with hope,
So now and never any different."

Part of a moon was falling down the west,
Dragging the whole sky with it to the hills.
105　Its light poured softly in her lap. She saw it
And spread her apron to it. She put out her hand
Among the harplike morning-glory strings,
Taut with the dew from garden bed to eaves,
As if she played unheard some tenderness
110　That wrought° on him beside her in the night. **E**
"Warren," she said, "he has come home to die:
You needn't be afraid he'll leave you this time."

"Home," he mocked gently.

　　　　　　　　　　"Yes, what else but home?
It all depends on what you mean by home.
115　Of course he's nothing to us, any more
Than was the hound that came a stranger to us
Out of the woods, worn out upon the trail."

"Home is the place where, when you have to go there,
They have to take you in."

　　　　　　　　　　"I should have called it
120　Something you somehow haven't to deserve." **F**

Warren leaned out and took a step or two,
Picked up a little stick, and brought it back
And broke it in his hand and tossed it by.
"Silas has better claim on us you think
125　Than on his brother? Thirteen little miles
As the road winds would bring him to his door.
Silas has walked that far no doubt today.
Why doesn't he go there? His brother's rich,
A somebody—director in the bank." **G**

"He never told us that."

　　　　　　　　　　"We know it, though."
130　"I think his brother ought to help, of course.
I'll see to that if there is need. He ought of right
To take him in, and might be willing to—
He may be better than appearances.
135　But have some pity on Silas. Do you think

110. **wrought:** worked.

E **Literary Perspectives** **Analyzing Style** What effect do the images in lines 103–110 have on the tone and mood of the poem?

F **Reading Focus** **Making Inferences About Characters** What do Warren's and Mary's different definitions of "home" suggest about their feelings toward Silas?

G **Literary Focus** **Narrative Poetry** What do you learn about Silas's family from Warren? What prevents Silas from seeking help from his family?

If he had any pride in claiming kin
Or anything he looked for from his brother,
He'd keep so still about him all this time?"

"I wonder what's between them."

                          "I can tell you.
140   Silas is what he is—we wouldn't mind him—
But just the kind that kinsfolk can't abide.
He never did a thing so very bad.
He don't know why he isn't quite as good
As anybody. Worthless though he is,
145   He won't be made ashamed to please his brother."

"*I* can't think Si ever hurt anyone."

"No, but he hurt my heart the way he lay
And rolled his old head on that sharp-edged chair-back.
He wouldn't let me put him on the lounge.
150   You must go in and see what you can do.
I made the bed up for him there tonight.
You'll be surprised at him—how much he's broken.
His working days are done; I'm sure of it."

"I'd not be in a hurry to say that."

155   "I haven't been. Go, look, see for yourself.
But, Warren, please remember how it is:
He's come to help you ditch the meadow.
He has a plan. You mustn't laugh at him.
He may not speak of it, and then he may.
160   I'll sit and see if that small sailing cloud
Will hit or miss the moon."

                       It hit the moon.
Then there were three there, making a dim row,
The moon, the little silver cloud, and she.

Warren returned—too soon, it seemed to her—
165   Slipped to her side, caught up her hand and waited.

"Warren?" she questioned.
                "Dead," was all he answered. **I**

H **Literary Focus** **Narrative Poetry** What does Mary do while Warren goes to check on Silas?

I **Literary Perspectives** **Analyzing Style** How does Warren's response to Mary's question reflect Frost's style?

Applying Your Skills

The Death of the Hired Man

Respond and Think Critically

Reading Focus

Quick Check

1. How does Warren feel about Silas?

2. Why does Silas return to Mary and Warren's farm?

3. Why does Silas say that he has come to ditch the meadow for Warren?

Read with a Purpose

4. How is the conflict in the poem resolved?

Reading Skills: Making Inferences About Characters

5. Review the chart you made as you read. In a short paragraph, explain how the couple's feelings toward Silas change throughout the poem.

Line(s)	Mary's Actions/Inference	Warren's Actions/Inference
1–5	Mary hurries to tell Warren that Silas is back —Mary is anxious about Silas's return.	
6–7	Mary tells Warren, "Be kind."	

Literary Focus

Literary Analysis

6. **Make Judgments** Some may say that Mary sees Silas's situation in an emotional sense, while Warren views it in a business sense. Do you agree?

7. **Hypothesize** Does the conclusion of this poem strike you as <u>inevitable</u>, or unavoidable? What would your feelings have been if Warren, instead of answering "Dead," had answered "Asleep"?

8. **Draw Conclusions** How would you state the poem's **theme,** or what it reveals about our lives?

9. **Evaluate** Find the two definitions of *home* offered in the poem. A critic has said that one definition is based on law and duty; and the other, on mercy. Identify each. Do you agree with the critic's observation?

10. **Literary Perspectives** Frost said that he aimed to give the speech of each character in his poetry a distinct sound. Based on your analysis of Frost's style in this poem, does he successfully differentiate Warren's and Mary's dialogue?

Literary Skills: Narrative Poetry

11. **Evaluate** A narrative is often told in **chronological order**—the order in which the events happened. Where does the telling of the events depart from chronological order? Explain.

Literary Skills Review: Setting

12. **Analyze** The **setting** is the time and location of a poem or story. Identify the details in lines 103–110 that create a vivid image of the setting. What does this setting tell you about Mary's character?

Writing Focus

Think as a Reader/Writer

Use It in Your Writing Think of the distinct way that two people in a conversation might speak to each other. Create a dialogue, as Frost has done, with a realistic sound, and have the two people state their personal <u>ideologies</u> about when to show mercy.

What Do **You Think Now** How is the <u>traditional</u> definition of *home* challenged and redefined in "The Death of the Hired Man"?

Vocabulary Development

✓ Vocabulary Check

Match each Vocabulary word with its definition.

1. grudge
2. daft
3. beholden

a. without sense
b. indebted
c. withhold from

Vocabulary Skills: Colloquial Language

An essential element of a writer's style is his or her diction. Recall that **diction** is a speaker or writer's choice of words and that word choice has a strong effect on the tone of a poem. Frost's diction is marked by his use of **colloquial speech**—the informal, everyday way in which people talk—and his conscious efforts to use conversational language. He has said of this effort:

> It has been a long time since I used any word not common in everyday speech. . . . I have sought only those words I have met up with as a boy in New Hampshire, working on farms during the summer vacations. I listened to the men with whom I worked, and found that I could make out their conversation as they talked together out of ear-shot, even when I had not plainly heard the words they spoke. When I started to carry their conversation over into poetry, I could hear their voices, and the sound posture differentiated between one and the other. It was the sense of sound I have been talking about. In some sort of way like this I have been able to write poetry, where characters talk, and, though not without infinite pains, to make it plain to the reader which character is saying the lines, without having to place his name before it, as is done in the drama.

Your Turn

Find the following examples of colloquial speech in Frost's "The Death of the Hired Man." List context clues that help you infer the meaning of each example.

1. haying
2. no depending on
3. bettering himself
4. ran on
5. fool of books

Language Coach

Parts of Speech Thinking about a word's part of speech can help you recognize its meaning in a sentence. Tell whether the word in italics is a verb, noun, or adverb. Then, explain its meaning.

1. Warren has been holding a *grudge* against Silas.
2. Mary is too open-hearted to *grudge* anyone anything.

Academic Vocabulary

Write About
Write a few sentences explaining how you feel about each of the three characters in the poem and their <u>ideologies</u> or actions.

SKILLS FOCUS Literary Skills Analyze the speaker of a poem. **Reading Skills** Read to research or information. **Writing Skills** Write to inform. **Grammar Skills** Combine related sentences correctly. **Listening and Speaking Skills** Participate in formal/informal discussions and conversations.

Mending Wall / The Death of the Hired Man

Grammar Link

Combining Sentences

Combining related sentences improves your writing style. Sentences that repeat much of the same information can be combined by inserting a key word or phrase from one sentence into the other. For example:

> Robert Frost began writing poetry as a young man.
> He wrote poems about New England life.
> Robert Frost began writing poetry **about New England life** as a young man.

Sentences that are equally important can be combined by **coordinating ideas**—forming sentences with compound subjects or predicates or forming compound sentences.

> Frost moved to England. His family moved, too.
> Frost **and** his family moved to England.

Sentences of unequal importance can be combined by **subordinating ideas,** or making the less important sentence into a subordinate clause.

> Frost returned to America in 1915. He was an accomplished poet.
> **When Frost returned to America in 1915,** he was an accomplished poet.

Your Turn

Combine the sentence pairs below in a variety of ways.

1. Frost was a prize-winning poet. He is still popular.

2. Most of his poetry is set in New England. It uses everyday language.

3. His poems are straightforward and realistic. He is considered a very conventional writer.

4. They are often unrhymed. They have strong rhythm.

CHOICES

As you respond to the Choices, use these **Academic Vocabulary** words as appropriate: <u>alternative</u>, <u>hierarchy</u>, <u>ideology</u>, <u>inevitable</u>, <u>tradition</u>.

REVIEW

Present a Dramatic Reading

Group Discussion Prepare a dramatic reading of "The Death of the Hired Man." With a small group, discuss how Mary and Warren speak in the poem. What tone of voice does each character use? Should Silas have his own voice? Do you have an <u>alternative</u> interpretation of a character? Practice with your group, and then present your reading to the class.

CONNECT

Classify Boundaries

Timed Writing Both "Mending Wall" and "The Death of the Hired Man" provide a look at the boundaries—physical, social, economic, and emotional—people put between themselves and others. Make a list classifying each boundary in each poem as physical, emotional, social, or economic. Then write a brief response in which you argue whether these boundaries are necessary.

EXTEND

Research Historical Walls

Hadrian's Wall, the Great Wall of China, and the Berlin Wall are famous examples of walls that divided people or nations. Research the history of one of these walls, including when and why it was built; who built it; and what happened to it. Write an essay detailing your findings. Be sure to address the question Frost poses: What were people "walling in or walling out"?

Preparing to Read

"I must have the pulse beat of rhythm . . ."

Reader/Writer Notebook

Use your **RWN** to complete the activities for this selection.

Informational Text Focus

Analyzing Primary Sources A **primary source** is original material—a firsthand account of information that has not been interpreted or edited by other writers. Primary sources include but are not limited to interviews, autobiographies, letters, speeches, oral histories, and eyewitness accounts. Since a primary source usually presents only one person's perspective on a topic, it may be biased. When you analyze a primary source, you can better understand a writer's perspective and works.

Into Action Keep the following questions in mind as you read and analyze the interview with Frost. As you read, use a graphic organizer like the one below to record your answers to the questions:

- Who is the intended audience? What assumptions does Frost make about the audience?
- How knowledgeable is Frost on the subject? How do you know?
- What does Frost think of free verse? What biases, if any, can you detect?
- How does Frost's interview give you a fuller understanding of poetry?

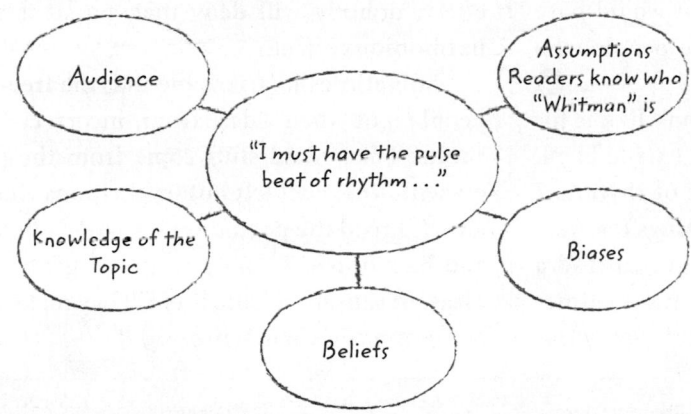

Writing Focus   Preparing for **Constructed Response**

This selection from an interview with Robert Frost contains elements of **persuasive writing** and speaking. What reasons does Frost give to convince his readers that blank verse is preferable to free verse? Record his reasons and examples in your *Reader/Writer Notebook*.

Vocabulary

accept (ak SEHPT) *v.*: include or give approval to. *It took a long time for Americans to accept Whitman as a great poet.*

influence (IHN floo uhns) *n.*: effect; ability to affect. *Frost and Whitman have both had an influence on American poetry.*

consciously (KAHN shuhs lee) *adv.*: intentionally; done with full awareness. *Frost consciously wrote blank verse rather than free verse.*

harmonious (hahr MOH nee uhs) *adj.*: going together in a pleasing, musical way. *Frost feels that the rhythm of blank verse is harmonious.*

distorted (dihs TAWRT ihd) *v.* used as *adj.*: twisted; not in normal form. *According to Frost, when his poems became distorted by the printer, they looked a little like free verse.*

Language Coach

Commonly Confused Words Note that *accept* means "to include or give approval." Be careful not to confuse this verb with the similar-sounding preposition *except,* which means "not including." Another pair of words that people sometimes confuse is *conscious* and *conscience.* What does each word mean?

 Learn It Online
Find interactive graphic organizers to use as you read online.

go.hrw.com   L11-837   Go

"I must have the pulse beat of rhythm..." by **Robert Frost**

from The New York Times

Read with a Purpose
Read to discover why Frost prefers <u>traditional</u> blank verse to modern free verse.

Build Background
In this excerpt from a 1923 interview with a *New York Times* reporter, Frost acknowledges American poetry's debt to Whitman, who wrote free verse—poetry that does not conform to a regular meter or a rhyme scheme—but also explains his own preference for blank verse, or unrhymed iambic pentameter. Frost sees modernist poets as achieving some striking, immediate effects but not creating anything of lasting beauty.

We're still a bit afraid. America, for instance, was afraid to accept Walt Whitman when he first sang the songs of democracy. His influence on American poetry began to be felt only after the French had hailed him as a great writer, a literary revolutionist. Our own poet had to be imported from France before we were sure of his strength.

Today almost every man who writes poetry confesses his debt to Whitman. Many have gone very much further than Whitman would have traveled with them. They are the people who believe in wide straddling. Ⓐ

I, myself, as I said before, don't like it for myself. I do not write free verse; I write blank verse. I must have the pulse beat of rhythm, I like to hear it beating under the things I write.

That doesn't mean I do not like to read a bit of free verse occasionally. I do. It sometimes succeeds in painting a picture that is very clear and startling. It's good as something created momentarily for its sudden startling effect; it hasn't the qualities, however, of something lastingly beautiful. Ⓑ

And sometimes my objection to it is that it's a pose. It's not honest. When a man sets out consciously to tear up forms and rhythms and measures, then he is not interested in giving you poetry. He just wants to perform; he wants to show you his tricks. He will get an effect; nobody will deny that, but it is not a harmonious effect.

Sometimes it strikes me that the free-verse people got their idea from incorrect proof sheets. I have had stuff come from the printers with lines half left out or positions changed about. I read the poems as they stood, distorted and half finished, and I confess I get a rather pleasant sensation from them. They make a sort of nightmarish half-sense. . . .

Ⓐ **Informational Focus** Analyzing Primary Sources
What is Frost explaining in the first two paragraphs? What details make him seem knowledgeable about the subject?

Ⓑ **Informational Focus** Analyzing Primary Sources
What kind of personal bias can you detect in this paragraph? Explain.

Vocabulary **accept** (ak SEHPT) *v.*: include or give approval to.
influence (IHN floo uhns) *n.*: effect; ability to affect.
consciously (KAHN shuhs lee) *adv.*: intentionally; done with full awareness.
harmonious (hahr MOH nee uhs) *adj.*: going together in a pleasing, musical way.
distorted (dihs TAWRT ihd) *v.* used as *adj.*: twisted; not in normal form.

Applying Your Skills

SKILLS FOCUS Informational Skills
Analyze primary sources. **Vocabulary Skills**
Identify and correctly use synonyms. **Writing
Skills** Write a brief constructed response,
with specific support. **Listening and
Speaking** Participate in group discussions.

"I must have the pulse beat of rhythm…"

Respond and Think Critically

Informational Text Focus

Quick Check

1. According to Frost, how did Americans come to accept the poetry of Whitman?

2. Why does Frost say he likes to write blank verse?

3. What is Frost's objection to free verse? Why does he feel this way?

Read with a Purpose

4. What about blank verse (or other metered verse) might make it "lastingly beautiful"?

Informational Skills: Analyzing Primary Sources

5. As you read "I must have the pulse beat of rhythm…," you analyzed the audience as well as the knowledge, beliefs, and biases of the speaker that are revealed in the interview. Now that you have finished reading, write a brief paragraph discussing how the interview affected you and how it contributes to your understanding of poetry.

✔ Vocabulary Check

Match each Vocabulary word with its synonym.

6. accept   a. intentionally

7. influence   b. twisted

8. consciously   c. musical

9. harmonious   d. include

10. distorted   e. effect

Text Analysis

11. **Draw Conclusions** What is Frost's attitude toward Walt Whitman? Cite details from the interview that support your opinion.

12. **Interpret** What do you think Frost means when he says, "Many have gone very much further than Whitman would have traveled with them"?

13. **Infer** What do you think Frost means when he says that free verse is "a pose"? Explain.

14. **Evaluate** What value does Frost sometimes see in free verse? Do you agree with Frost about this value? Explain.

Listening and Speaking

15. **Compare and Contrast** With a partner, choose one of Frost's poems from this collection and one of Whitman's poems from Collection 8. Read each poem aloud several times, trying to find the poet's rhythm with your voice. Discuss the differences between the two poems. If time allows, present your poems to the class and share your thoughts about how they contrast.

Writing Focus Constructed Response

Briefly discuss Frost's position on free verse and blank verse. Do you agree or disagree with his opinion? Use persuasive techniques to defend your own position. Be sure to cite specific evidence from the interview to develop your response.

What Do **You Think Now** Does Frost's writing in blank verse mean that his works cannot be progressive and challenge tradition? Explain your opinion.

Modernism

Gas (1940) by Edward Hopper.

"A writer's problem does
not change. He himself
changes, but his problem
remains the same."

— **Ernest Hemingway**

CONTENTS

Link
to
Today

SKILLS FOCUS **Literary Skills** Evaluate and analyze the philosophical, political, religious, ethical, and social issues of a historical period; understand modernism.

Modernism by **Leila Christenbury**

Characteristics of Modernism

- Sense of disillusionment and a loss of faith in the American dream
- Rejection of sentimentality and artificiality in favor of capturing reality
- Emphasis on bold experimentation in style and form, reflecting the fragmentation of society
- Interest in the individual and the inner workings of the human mind

Breakdown of Beliefs

The violence of World War I and the devastation of the Great Depression severely damaged the idealism of many Americans. Disillusioned, they began to distrust societal institutions and question the cultural, Puritan-based traditions that had guided American life for so many years. Modern life seemed vastly different from the lives of their parents and grandparents.

American fiction writers responded to this period of change by breaking with literary tradition. They created new approaches for telling stories that probed the complexities and uncertainties of the modern world.

Facing Reality Modernist writers believed in facing reality. The style and subject matter of Ernest Hemingway exemplify this trend. His spare style—strikingly different from the elaborate prose of the nineteenth century—boils down literature to the bare bones of the truth it must express.

Hemingway's novels and short stories deal frankly with the shattering realities of war. In novels such as *The Sun Also Rises,* his characters find themselves in an unpredictable, chaotic world. They are members of "the lost generation," a term coined by Gertrude Stein to describe disillusioned American expatriate writers living in Paris after the war. Confused, the characters respond to life's ambiguities by turning inward and clinging to their own sense of honor and decency.

The work of F. Scott Fitzgerald exposes the reality behind the crumbling American dream. More than any other writer, Fitzgerald captures the glittering life of what he called the Jazz Age—the booming decade between World War I and the Great Depression.

Fitzgerald's dazzling prose style is well suited to his subject matter. Novels such as *The Great Gatsby* showcase characters who are beautiful and glamorously wealthy, but unhappy. Fitzgerald believed that underneath its shiny surface, the nation was falling apart. Materialism and the pursuit of pleasure were rampant, and the gap between the elite and everyone else widened. Something had gone wrong with the American dream.

Modernist writer William Faulkner used a bold new style to describe an increasingly unfamiliar world. The innovative writer experimented to great effect with multiple points of view, disjointed images, and complex sentences—appropriate tools for examining a reality that felt increasingly complex. Many of his books, such as *The Sound and the Fury,* employ a **stream-of-consciousness** narrative technique. This approach reflects the interest in the workings of the unconscious mind, made popular both by Sigmund Freud and by the growing belief that individuals must look inside themselves to answer the questions raised by an endlessly changing world.

Ask Yourself

1. How did world events lead to disillusionment with traditional beliefs and values?
2. Explain how the work of one of the writers described above addresses the uncertainties of the modern world.

Learn It Online
Discover modernism through *PowerNotes* online.

go.hrw.com   L11-841   **Go**

Soldier's Home

Nobel Prize Acceptance Speech, 1954

What Do You Think?

How does progress challenge tradition and redefine society?

QuickTalk

Do people always make progress in life? Think about what might make a person want to stand still or go back in time, rather than move forward. Meet with a partner and discuss several examples.

Ernest Hemingway
(1899–1961)

Nobel Prize WINNER

Hemingway's life and work offer a bold definition of the modern hero. His vision centers on disillusionment with the conventions of an optimistic, patriotic society, and a belief that the essence of life is violence, from which there is no refuge.

A New Ideal of Heroism

For Hemingway, the hero must face life with a graceful stoicism. His ideal of rugged machismo, which may now seem superficial, powerfully affected generations of American readers. Hemingway launched a style of writing so forceful in its simplicity that it became a measure of excellence around the world.

Hemingway's life bore a notable resemblance to the lives of his fictional characters. Graduating from high school in 1917, just as the United States entered World War I, he yearned to enlist, but he was rejected by the army because of a boxing injury. He landed a job as a reporter and, a year later, reached the war as an ambulance driver for the Red Cross in Italy. He was soon wounded in the knee seriously. This wound was a central episode in Hemingway's real life and his creative one.

Author and Adventurer

In 1921, Hemingway set off for Paris. There, he worked at the craft of fiction and met other important writers. He gained widespread critical attention with the 1926 publication of *The Sun Also Rises,* which was based on his postwar experiences in Paris. Many readers of Hemingway's age embraced this book as a portrait of their own shattered lives.

Hemingway established himself as a worldwide adventurer, as though a heroic style was as important to his life as to his fiction. He went on to write several widely acclaimed books, including *A Farewell to Arms* (1929), *For Whom the Bell Tolls* (1940), and *The Old Man and the Sea* (1952), which won the Pulitzer Prize. In 1954, Hemingway won the Nobel Prize in literature. In his later years his health deteriorated and he suffered from depression. He committed suicide in 1961.

Think About the Writer

Why do you think Hemingway wanted so badly to take part in World War I?

Soldier's Home

Reader/Writer Notebook

Use your **RWN** to complete the activities for this selection.

Literary Focus

Protagonist: The Antihero In literature, the **protagonist** is the central character in the plot, the one who initiates the story's action. The **antihero** is a type of protagonist who appears in much modern literature. The antihero is an <u>alternative</u> to the <u>traditional</u> hero, who responds to challenges with courage and self-sacrifice. The modern antihero, like Krebs in "Soldier's Home," gives in to disillusionment, hopelessness, and inaction.

Reading Focus

Reading for Details Noting **details** helps readers understand the big picture, whether it is the main idea of a story or the personality of a character. In "Soldier's Home," Krebs's character slowly unfolds as Hemingway reveals more and more details about his feelings.

Into Action As you read, note details about what Krebs says, thinks, and does that illustrate how he is an antihero. Use a chart like the one below.

	Disillusionment	Hopelessness	Inaction
What Krebs says			
What Krebs thinks	Krebs wanted to talk about the war, but no one wanted to listen.		
What Krebs does			Krebs refuses to leave his house.

Writing Focus

Think as a Reader/Writer

Find It in Your Reading The **mood** of "Soldier's Home" fluctuates between hopeful and hopeless. In one moment, Krebs thinks that looking at girls is exciting, but he decides that it would be too much trouble to talk with a girl. In your *Reader/Writer Notebook,* list words and phrases that describe Krebs's positive and negative feelings.

TechFocus As you read, consider how modern technology might have changed the way Krebs was able to communicate with his family both during and after the war.

Vocabulary

hysteria (hihs TIHR ee uh) *n.:* uncontrolled excitement. *The soldiers were greeted with hysteria when they returned home from the war.*

atrocity (uh TRAHS uh tee) *n.* used as *adj.:* a horrible or brutal act. *After hearing so many atrocity stories, the people became desensitized.*

apocryphal (uh PAHK ruh fuhl) *adj.:* of questionable authority; false. *Krebs claimed that the events in many apocryphal war stories actually occurred.*

alliances (uh LY uhns ihz) *n.:* close associations entered into for mutual benefit. *Krebs, an outsider, found it difficult to enter a world that had so many existing feuds and alliances.*

intrigue (IHN treeg) *n.:* scheming; plotting. *He was uninterested in the complications and intrigue involved in the world of dating.*

Language Coach

Pronunciation Notice that the letter *y* has three different sounds in the words *hysteria, atrocity,* and *apocryphal.* Read these words aloud slowly. In which word or words does the letter *y* have the same vowel sound you hear in *free*? In which word does the letter *y* have the vowel sound you hear in *win*?

Learn It Online

Discover more about Hemingway on the Writers' Lives site online.

go.hrw.com | L11-843 | **Go**

SHORT STORY

SOLDIER'S HOME

by **Ernest Hemingway**

Read with a Purpose
Read to learn how a World War I veteran copes with life at home after the war.

Build Background
Soldiers who returned home from World War I were often described as shell-shocked—suffering from a mental and emotional condition of confusion, exhaustion, anxiety, and depression. In the past, the condition—now termed *post-traumatic stress disorder*—was not well understood, and friends and relatives often found themselves at a loss. They could not understand why some soldiers seemed unable to plunge back into civilian life.

Krebs went to the war from a Methodist college in Kansas. There is a picture which shows him among his fraternity brothers, all of them wearing exactly the same height and style collar. He enlisted in the Marines in 1917 and did not return to the United States until the second division returned from the Rhine[1] in the summer of 1919.

There is a picture which shows him on the Rhine with two German girls and another corporal. Krebs

and the corporal look too big for their uniforms. The German girls are not beautiful. The Rhine does not show in the picture. **Ⓐ**

By the time Krebs returned to his home town in Oklahoma the greeting of heroes was over. He came back much too late. The men from the town who had been drafted had all been welcomed elaborately on their return. There had been a great deal of hysteria. Now the reaction had set in. People seemed to think it was rather ridiculous for Krebs to be getting back so late, years after the war was over. **Ⓑ**

At first Krebs, who had been at Belleau Wood, Soissons, the Champagne, St. Mihiel and in the

---

1. **Rhine:** river that flows through Germany toward the North Sea.

Vocabulary hysteria (hihs TIHR ee uh) *n.:* uncontrolled excitement.

Ⓐ Reading Focus Reading for Details What do the details in this paragraph imply about Krebs's war experience?

Ⓑ Literary Focus Protagonist: The Antihero Why doesn't Krebs receive a hero's welcome upon his return home? How might this lack of fanfare have contributed to Krebs's sense of disillusionment?

Argonne[2] did not want to talk about the war at all. Later he felt the need to talk but no one wanted to hear about it. His town had heard too many atrocity stories to be thrilled by actualities. Krebs found that to be listened to at all he had to lie, and after he had done this twice he, too, had a reaction against the war and against talking about it. A distaste for everything that had happened to him in the war set in because of the lies he had told. All of the times that had been able to make him feel cool and clear inside himself when he thought of them; the times so long back when he had done the one thing, the only thing for a man to do, easily and naturally, when he might have done something else, now lost their cool, valuable quality and then were lost themselves. Ⓒ

His lies were quite unimportant lies and consisted in attributing to himself things other men had seen, done or heard of, and stating as facts certain apocryphal incidents familiar to all soldiers. Even his lies were not sensational at the pool room. His acquaintances, who had heard detailed accounts of German women found chained to machine guns in the Argonne forest and who could not comprehend, or were barred by their patriotism from interest in, any German machine gunners who were not chained, were not thrilled by his stories.

Krebs acquired the nausea in regard to experience that is the result of untruth or exaggeration, and when he occasionally met another man who had really been a soldier and they talked a few minutes in the dressing room at a dance he fell into the easy pose of the old soldier among other soldiers: that he had been badly, sickeningly frightened all the time. In this way he lost everything.

During this time, it was late summer, he was sleeping late in bed, getting up to walk down town to the library to get a book, eating lunch at home, reading on the front porch until he became bored and then walking down through the town to spend the hottest hours of the day in the cool dark of the pool room. He loved to play pool.

In the evening he practised on his clarinet, strolled down town, read and went to bed. He was still a hero to his two young sisters. His mother would have given him breakfast in bed if he had wanted it. She often came in when he was in bed and asked him to tell her about the war, but her attention always wandered. His father was non-committal. Ⓓ

Before Krebs went away to the war he had never been allowed to drive the family motor car. His father was in the real estate business and always wanted the car to be at his command when he required it to take clients out into the country to show them a piece of farm property. The car always stood outside the First National Bank building where his father had an office on the second floor. Now, after the war, it was still the same car.

Nothing was changed in the town except that the young girls had grown up. But they lived in such a complicated world of already defined alliances and shifting feuds that Krebs did not feel the energy or the courage to break into it. He liked to look at them, though. There were so many good-looking young girls. Most of them had their hair cut short. When he went away only little girls wore their hair like that or girls that were fast. They all wore sweaters and shirt waists with round Dutch collars. It was a pattern. He liked to look at them from the front porch as they walked on the other side of the street. He liked to watch them walking under the shade of the trees. He liked the round Dutch collars above their sweaters. He liked their silk stockings and flat shoes. He liked their bobbed hair and the way they walked.

When he was in town their appeal to him was not very strong. He did not like them when he saw them in the Greek's ice cream parlor. He did not want them themselves really. They were too complicated. There was something else. Vaguely he wanted a girl but he did not want to have to work to get her. He would

---

2. **Belleau** (beh LOH) **Wood . . . Argonne** (ARH gahn): sites of World War I battles that demonstrated the Allies' superior strength against the Germans.

Ⓒ **Literary Focus** **Protagonist: The Antihero** In Hemingway's work, lies often have a corrupting influence on the protagonist and can poison every aspect of an experience. How do lies cause—or at least contribute to—a change in Krebs's attitude toward his war experiences?

Ⓓ **Reading Focus** **Reading for Details** What do the details in this paragraph tell you about Krebs's relationships with his sisters and his parents?

Vocabulary **atrocity** (uh TRAHS uh tee) *n.* used as *adj.:* a horrible or brutal act.
apocryphal (uh PAHK ruh fuhl) *adj.:* of questionable authority; false.
alliances (uh LY uhns ihz) *n.:* close associations entered into for mutual benefit.

have liked to have a girl but he did not want to have to spend a long time getting her. He did not want to get into the intrigue and the politics. He did not want to have to do any courting. He did not want to tell any more lies. It wasn't worth it.

He did not want any consequences. He did not want any consequences ever again. He wanted to live along without consequences. Besides he did not really need a girl. The army had taught him that. It was all right to pose as though you had to have a girl. Nearly everybody did that. But it wasn't true. You did not need a girl. That was the funny thing. First a fellow boasted how girls mean nothing to him, that he never thought of them, that they could not touch him. Then a fellow boasted that he could not get along without girls, that he had to have them all the time, that he could not go to sleep without them.

That was all a lie. It was all a lie both ways. You did not need a girl unless you thought about them. He learned that in the army. Then sooner or later you always got one. When you were really ripe for a girl you always got one. You did not have to think about it. Sooner or later it would come. He had learned that in the army.

Now he would have liked a girl if she had come to him and not wanted to talk. But here at home it was all too complicated. He knew he could never get through it all again. It was not worth the trouble. That was the thing about French girls and German girls. There was not all this talking. You couldn't talk much and you did not need to talk. It was simple and you were friends. He thought about France and then he began to think about Germany. On the whole he had liked Germany better. He did not want to leave Germany.

> # You did not need a girl unless you thought about them.
>
> # He learned that in the army.

He did not want to come home. Still, he had come home. He sat on the front porch. **F**

He liked the girls that were walking along the other side of the street. He liked the look of them much better than the French girls or the German girls. But the world they were in was not the world he was in. He would like to have one of them. But it was not worth it. They were such a nice pattern. He liked the pattern. It was exciting. But he would not go through all the talking. He did not want one badly enough. He liked to look at them all, though. It was not worth it. Not now when things were getting good again.

He sat there on the porch reading a book on the war. It was a history and he was reading about all the engagements he had been in. It was the most interesting reading he had ever done. He wished there were more maps. He looked forward with a good feeling to reading all the really good histories when they would come out with good detail maps. Now he was really learning about the war. He had been a good soldier. That made a difference.

One morning after he had been home about a month his mother came into his bedroom and sat on the bed. She smoothed her apron.

"I had a talk with your father last night, Harold," she said, "and he is willing for you to take the car out in the evenings."

"Yeah?" said Krebs, who was not fully awake. "Take the car out? Yeah?"

"Yes. Your father has felt for some time that you should be able to take the car out in the evenings whenever you wished but we only talked it over last night."

"I'll bet you made him," Krebs said.

***

E **Literary Focus** Protagonist: The Antihero Why does Krebs want to live without any consequences? How does his attitude differ from that of the archetypal or traditional hero?

Vocabulary intrigue (IHN treeg) *n.*: scheming; plotting.

F **Literary Focus** Protagonist: The Antihero What internal conflicts does Krebs struggle with in this passage? How does he resolve these internal conflicts?

"No. It was your father's suggestion that we talk the matter over."

"Yeah. I'll bet you made him," Krebs sat up in bed.

"Will you come down to breakfast, Harold?" his mother said.

"As soon as I get my clothes on," Krebs said.

His mother went out of the room and he could hear her frying something downstairs while he washed, shaved and dressed to go down into the dining-room for breakfast. While he was eating breakfast his sister brought in the mail.

"Well, Hare," she said. "You old sleepy-head. What do you ever get up for?"

Krebs looked at her. He liked her. She was his best sister. **ⓖ**

"Have you got the paper?" he asked.

She handed him *The Kansas City Star* and he shucked off its brown wrapper and opened it to the sporting page. He folded *The Star* open and propped it against the water pitcher with his cereal dish to steady it, so he could read while he ate.

"Harold," his mother stood in the kitchen doorway, "Harold, please don't muss up the paper. Your father can't read his *Star* if it's been mussed."

"I won't muss it," Krebs said. **ⓗ**

His sister sat down at the table and watched him while he read.

"We're playing indoor over at school this afternoon," she said. "I'm going to pitch."

"Good," said Krebs. "How's the old wing?"[3]

"I can pitch better than lots of the boys. I tell them all you taught me. The other girls aren't much good."

"Yeah?" said Krebs.

"I tell them all you're my beau.[4] Aren't you my beau, Hare?"

"You bet."

"Couldn't your brother really be your beau just because he's your brother?"

"I don't know."

---

3. **wing:** arm.
4. **beau** (boh): boyfriend.

ⓖ Reading Focus **Reading for Details** Based on this brief interaction, why do you think this sister is Krebs's favorite?

ⓗ Reading Focus **Reading for Details** What does Mrs. Krebs's comment suggest about Harold's relationship with his father?

CULTURE LINK

The Roaring Twenties

Nothing symbolized the decade after World War I so well as the flapper—a liberated young woman who cropped her hair into a caplike shape, wore much simpler clothing than her Victorian-era counterpart, and boldly used rouge and lipstick. She kicked, shimmied, and swayed in a wild new dance called the Charleston.

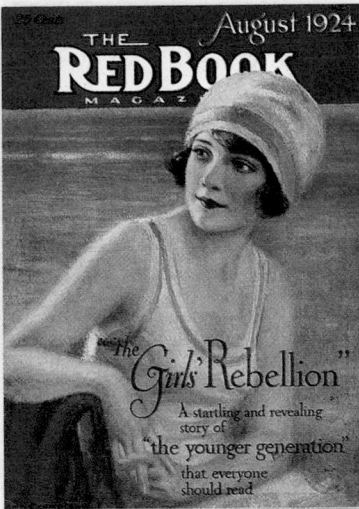

Cover of the *Redbook* magazine from August 1924.

Women and men alike, tired of the war and more aware of modernist thought, called for new social freedoms. Young people rebelled against the tight moral codes and the rigid hierarchies of their day. They scoffed at the prohibition on alcohol by inventing the private cocktail party. With the new availability of motorcars, people roared off to dances in places where no one knew them, where they could feel free of their inhibitions. Couples danced together closer than ever before, tangoing and fox-trotting cheek to cheek to the sound of the saxophone.

The twenties' emphasis on youth and openness is recognizably modern. At the time, many Americans were shocked and outraged by what they saw as the deterioration of culture and values. The 1920s were a rowdy, roisterous time—a decade that roared.

Ask Yourself

How do you think the cultural changes of the Roaring Twenties added to Harold Krebs's sense of isolation when he returned home from the war? Explain.

"Sure you know. Couldn't you be my beau, Hare, if I was old enough and if you wanted to?"

"Sure. You're my girl now."

"Am I really your girl?"

"Sure."

"Do you love me?"

"Uh, huh."

"Will you love me always?"

"Sure."

"Will you come over and watch me play indoor?"

"Maybe."

"Aw, Hare, you don't love me. If you loved me, you'd want to come over and watch me play indoor."

Krebs's mother came into the dining-room from the kitchen. She carried a plate with two fried eggs and some crisp bacon on it and a plate of buckwheat cakes.

"You run along, Helen," she said. "I want to talk to Harold."

She put the eggs and bacon down in front of him and brought in a jug of maple syrup for the buckwheat cakes. Then she sat down across the table from Krebs.

"I wish you'd put down the paper a minute, Harold," she said.

Krebs took down the paper and folded it.

"Have you decided what you are going to do yet, Harold?" his mother said, taking off her glasses.

"No," said Krebs.

"Don't you think it's about time?" His mother did not say this in a mean way. She seemed worried.

"I hadn't thought about it," Krebs said.

"God has some work for every one to do," his mother said. "There can be no idle hands in His Kingdom."

"I'm not in His Kingdom," Krebs said.

"We are all of us in His Kingdom."

Krebs felt embarrassed and resentful as always. ❶

"I've worried about you so much, Harold," his mother went on. "I know the temptations you must have been exposed to. I know how weak men are. I know what your own dear grandfather, my own father, told us about the Civil War and I have prayed for you. I pray for you all day long, Harold."

Krebs looked at the bacon fat hardening on his plate.

"Your father is worried, too," his mother went on. "He thinks you have lost your ambition, that you haven't got a definite aim in life. Charley Simmons, who is just your age, has a good job and is going to be married. The boys are all settling down; they're all determined to get somewhere; you can see that boys like Charley Simmons are on their way to being really a credit to the community." ❿

Krebs said nothing.

"Don't look that way, Harold," his mother said. "You know we love you and I want to tell you for your own good how matters stand. Your father does not want to hamper your freedom. He thinks you should be allowed to drive the car. If you want to take some of the nice girls out riding with you, we are only too pleased. We want you to enjoy yourself. But you are going to have to settle down to work, Harold. Your father doesn't care what you start in at. All work is honorable as he says. But you've got to make a start at something. He asked me to speak to you this morning and then you can stop in and see him at his office."

"Is that all?" Krebs said.

"Yes. Don't you love your mother, dear boy?"

"No," Krebs said.

His mother looked at him across the table. Her eyes were shiny. She started crying.

"I don't love anybody," Krebs said.

It wasn't any good. He couldn't tell her, he couldn't make her see it. It was silly to have said it. He had only hurt her. He went over and took hold of her arm. She was crying with her head in her hands.

"I didn't mean it," he said. "I was just angry at something. I didn't mean I didn't love you."

His mother went on crying. Krebs put his arm on her shoulder.

"Can't you believe me, mother?"

His mother shook her head.

"Please, please, mother. Please believe me."

"All right," his mother said chokily. She looked up at him. "I believe you, Harold."

Krebs kissed her hair. She put her face up to him.

"I'm your mother," she said. "I held you next to my heart when you were a tiny baby."

Krebs felt sick and vaguely nauseated.

---

❶ **Literary Focus** **Protagonist: The Antihero** What does this exchange reveal about Krebs's relationship with his mother?

❿ **Literary Focus** **Protagonist: The Antihero** Why is the mention of Charley Simmons important to the profile of Harold's character?

"I know, Mummy," he said. "I'll try and be a good boy for you."

"Would you kneel and pray with me, Harold?" his mother asked.

They knelt down beside the dining-room table and Krebs's mother prayed.

"Now, you pray, Harold," she said.

"I can't," Krebs said.

"Try, Harold."

"I can't."

"Do you want me to pray for you?"

"Yes."

So his mother prayed for him and then they stood up and Krebs kissed his mother and went out of the house. He had tried so to keep his life from being complicated. Still, none of it had touched him. He had felt sorry for his mother and she had made him lie. He would go to Kansas City and get a job and she would feel all right about it. There would be one more scene maybe before he got away. He would not go down to his father's office. He would miss that one. He wanted his life to go smoothly. It had just gotten going that way. Well, that was all over now, anyway. He would go over to the schoolyard and watch Helen play indoor baseball. **K**

K **Literary Focus** Protagonist: The Antihero How does the title of the story take on special meaning at the end of the first sentence in this paragraph?

Respond and Think Critically

Reading Focus

Quick Check

1. What can you tell about Krebs's goals and aspirations from the way he spends his time?

2. How do Krebs's interactions with his parents reflect his alienation from them?

3. Why does Krebs decide to leave home?

Read with a Purpose

4. Krebs faces both external and internal challenges. Which type of challenge is more difficult for Krebs? Why?

Reading Skills: Reading for Details

5. While reading the story, you created a chart that noted details about what Krebs says, thinks, and does that illustrate the ways in which he is an antihero. Review your chart. Then, using details from your chart, write a paragraph that explains why Krebs is an antihero.

Literary Focus

Literary Analysis

6. **Draw Conclusions** What does Krebs's statement "You did not need a girl unless you thought about them" (page 846) reveal about how he adapted to the hardships of war? How might such an adjustment affect his life at home?

7. **Interpret** Ernest Hemingway once remarked of his writing style, "I always try to write on the principle of the iceberg. There is seven-eighths of it underwater for every part that shows." What do you think Hemingway means? Use examples from "Soldier's Home" to interpret the "iceberg" principle. What parts of the story are underwater?

8. **Evaluate** Evaluate Krebs's approach to the postwar challenges he faced. In your opinion, which of his attitudes and actions are valid, partly valid, or completely invalid? Use a chart like the one below to organize your thoughts.

Valid	Partly Valid	Invalid

Literary Skills: Protagonist: The Antihero

9. **Interpret** Rather than conquering obstacles, the antihero may find obstacles overwhelming. Explain what the following statement reveals about Krebs's approach to obstacles: "Now he would have liked a girl if she had . . . not wanted to talk. But here at home it was all too complicated."

Literary Skills Review: Theme

10. **Infer** An insight about human life that is revealed in a literary work is a **theme.** It is a statement the writer wants to make about a specific subject. How would you state the theme of "Soldier's Home"? What does the story reveal to you about the way war can affect a young soldier?

Writing Focus

Think as a Reader/Writer

Use It in Your Writing Write two brief character sketches of yourself, people you know, or imaginary people. Describe the first character as you would a traditional hero. Describe the second character as you would an antihero.

What Do **You Think Now** Do you think Krebs yearns for an earlier time or looks forward to the future? Explain your answer.

Vocabulary Development

✔ Vocabulary Check

Match each Vocabulary word with its synonym.

1. intrigue
2. apocryphal
3. alliances
4. atrocity
5. hysteria

a. disputable
b. barbarism
c. frenzy
d. conspiracy
e. relationships

Vocabulary Skills: Greek and Latin Roots

Many English words are formed from Greek or Latin roots. Becoming familiar with these roots can help you improve your vocabulary.

A **root** is a word part that carries the core meaning of a word. In most cases, roots combine with prefixes or suffixes (or both) to form whole words. Groups of words with the same roots are called **word families.**

In "Soldier's Home," Hemingway uses words that have their origins in Greek and Latin roots. In the following chart, you'll find some examples:

Word	Root	Meaning of root	Meaning of word	Family words
apocryphal	–crypt– (Greek)	hidden place	of hidden or unknown authority	crypt, cryptogram, encrypt
elaborately	–labor– Latin	work	done with great care	labor, belabor, laborious
consisted	–sist– (Latin)	stand	made up of or composed of	resist, assistance
patriotic	–patr– (Greek/ Latin)	father	love of one's country	paternal, expatriate, patriot

Your Turn

For each root listed in the chart on the left, find at least one other word in the same word family. You may use a dictionary for help.

Language Coach

Pronunciation The letter *y* can have many different sounds. Here are three sounds the letter can have:

- In *atrocity*, it has the long /ee/ sound.
- In *hysteria*, it has the short /ih/ sound.
- In *apocryphal*, it has short /uh/ sound.

Read the following words aloud. Then, use a chart like the one below to classify how the letter *y* is pronounced in each word.

abundantly	emphysema	physician
anonymous	hypocrite	polygon
calamity	mysterious	pseudonym

/ee/	/ih/	/uh/

Academic Vocabulary

Talk About
Traditionally, how has our nation treated its returning warriors? Where do veterans stand in the hierarchy of our society?

✴ Learn It Online
Approach word roots a whole new way with *WordSharp* online.

go.hrw.com L11-851 Go

Grammar Link

Varying Sentence Beginnings

Much of Hemingway's writing consists of simple declarative sentences that are forceful in their simplicity. These sentences begin with a subject followed by a verb:

> <u>Krebs went</u> to the war from a Methodist college in Kansas.

In the hands of a weak writer, this pattern can become monotonous. **Varying sentence beginnings** improves the overall style of most writing.

> <u>Suffering from shellshock,</u> many soldiers were unable to adjust to civilian life. [participial phrase]

> <u>Disillusioned and isolated,</u> they found nothing they could relate to. [single-word modifiers]

> <u>Now</u> it seemed unimportant to talk about the war. [adverb]

> <u>Because his father needed the car for business,</u> Harold was not allowed to drive it. [adverb clause]

Your Turn

Writing Application Revise the following paragraph to vary sentence beginnings. Use modifying phrases, subordinate clauses, single-word modifiers, and sentence connectors such as conjunctive adverbs and coordinating conjunctions.

> Hemingway learned a lot about writing at the *Kansas City Star*. His powerful style comes supposedly from his training as a journalist. Readers noticed his sentences when he began writing fiction. They seemed very simple. They were much more complex, however.

CHOICES

As you respond to the Choices, use these **Academic Vocabulary** words as appropriate: <u>alternative</u>, <u>hierarchy</u>, <u>ideology</u>, <u>inevitable</u>, <u>tradition</u>.

REVIEW

Create War Blog Entries

TechFocus Imagine that Krebs had access to a digital camera and computer and was able to create a war blog. What do you think he would have wanted to communicate about his experiences? Create several blog entries from Krebs both during and after the war. Did his <u>ideology</u> change? Describe photographs he might have taken and posted on his blog.

CONNECT

Interview a Character

Today, it is not uncommon for people who have experienced unusual situations or challenges to tell their stories on television. With a partner, select one of the characters in the story to interview. Then, write a list of questions a news reporter or talk show host might ask the person.

EXTEND

Examine Contemporary Challenges

Class Presentation With a partner, use the school library or the Internet to research the challenges that soldiers returning from modern-day wars experience. Draw connections between these challenges and those that Krebs faced. When you have completed your research, present your findings to the class. Offer your peers the opportunity to ask questions, and provide sources where they can obtain additional information about this issue.

Learn It Online
Explore the trenches of World War I with these Internet links.

Preparing to Read

Nobel Prize Acceptance Speech, 1954

Reader/Writer
Notebook

Use your **RWN** to complete the activities for this selection.

Informational Text Focus

Determining a Speaker's Message The **speaker's message** is the main idea that he or she wants to communicate to the audience. In this speech, Hemingway expresses several ideas, including his thoughts about other writers, the writing life, and the true role of a writer. To determine Hemingway's message, consider why he includes each idea and how his various ideas relate to each other. What might Hemingway be trying to tell us?

Into Action As you read, use a chart like the one below to determine the speaker's message. First, identify key topics that Hemingway mentions in his speech. List those topics in the left column. For each topic, summarize what Hemingway says and explain why you think he includes it in his speech.

Topic	What Hemingway says	Why he includes it in his speech
other writers	Many great writers did not receive the Nobel Prize.	to show his humility, that he was no greater than those writers
his writing		

Writing Focus Preparing for **Constructed Response**

In his speech, Hemingway uses **negative constructions,** or phrases using *no, not,* and *nor.* For example, the first words of his speech are "Having no facility for speech making." As you read, record phrases with negative constructions in your *Reader/Writer Notebook*. Record notes about how these phrases affect the tone of the speech. Do they alter the speaker's message?

Vocabulary

discernible (dih SUR nuh buhl) *adj.:* able to be detected; perceptible. *A good writer's message might be discernible only after multiple close readings.*

stature (STACH uhr) *n.:* prominence; importance. *Does a writer's stature always reflect the quality of his writing?*

deteriorates (dih TIHR ee uh rayts) *v.:* becomes worse. *Hemingway says that a writer's work deteriorates as he or she gains fame.*

Language Coach

Word Origins The noun *stature* comes from the Latin word *stare,* meaning "to stand." You might think of someone's stature as being related to how high he or she stands within a community. The nouns *statute, status,* and *thermostat* come from the same root. Find these words in a dictionary. How does knowing the root help you better understand these words?

Learn It Online
Experience this speech for yourself online.

go.hrw.com   L11-853   **Go**

Nobel Prize Acceptance Speech, 1954
by **Ernest Hemingway**

Read with a Purpose
Read this speech to discover Hemingway's message about writing.

Having no facility for speech making and no command of oratory nor any domination of rhetoric, I wish to thank the administrators of the generosity of Alfred Nobel for this prize.

No writer who knows the great writers who did not receive the prize can accept it other than with humility. There is no need to list these writers. Everyone here may make his own list according to his knowledge and his conscience.

It would be impossible for me to ask the ambassador of my country to read a speech in which a writer said all of the things which are in his heart. Things may not be immediately discernible in what a man writes, and in this sometimes he is fortunate; but eventually they are quite clear and by these and the degree of alchemy[1] that he possesses he will endure or be forgotten.

Writing, at its best, is a lonely life. Organizations for writers palliate[2] the writer's loneliness, but I doubt if they improve his writing. He grows in public stature as he sheds his loneliness, and often his work deteriorates. For he does his work alone, and if he is a good enough writer he must face eternity, or the lack of it, each day. **(A)**

For a true writer each book should be a new beginning where he tries again for something that is beyond attainment. He should always try for something that has never been done or that others have tried and failed. Then sometimes, with great luck, he will succeed.

How simple the writing of literature would be if it were only necessary to write in another way what has been well written. It is because we have had such great writers in the past that a writer is driven far out past where he can go, out to where no one can help him.

I have spoken too long for a writer. A writer should write what he has to say and not speak it. Again I thank you.

---

1. **alchemy:** magical power to transform the ordinary into the extraordinary. Alchemy was a branch of medieval science, one aim of which was to change common metals such as lead into gold.
2. **palliate:** ease; lessen.

(A) Informational Focus Determining a Speaker's Message What philosophical belief does Hemingway reveal when he says that each day a writer "must face eternity, or the lack of it"?

Vocabulary **discernible** (dih SUR nuh buhl) *adj.*: able to be detected; perceptible.
stature (STACH uhr) *n.*: prominence; importance.
deteriorates (dih TIHR ee uh rayts) *v.*: becomes worse.

Applying Your Skills

Nobel Prize Acceptance Speech, 1954

SKILLS FOCUS Informational **Skills** Determine a speaker's message. **Vocabulary Skills** Demonstrate knowledge of literal meanings of words and their usage. **Listening and Speaking Skills** Organize and present oral interpretations: speeches. **Writing Skills** Write brief constructed responses, with specific support.

Respond and Think Critically

Informational Text Focus

Quick Check

1. Why does Hemingway think a writer should accept the Nobel Prize with humility?

2. How does Hemingway describe the life of a writer?

3. According to Hemingway, what do organizations for writers do? Why doesn't he believe that they improve writers' work?

Read with a Purpose

4. What does Hemingway's speech tell you about his life as a writer?

Informational Skills: Determining a Speaker's Message

5. Review the information in your chart. Draw lines to connect ideas that relate to each other, and record notes about the philosophical beliefs that these ideas share. Then, in a few sentences, explain what you think is Hemingway's overall message in his speech.

Topic	What Hemingway says	Why he includes it in his speech
other writers	Many great writers did not receive the Nobel Prize.	to show his humility, that he was no greater than those writers
his writing		

✔ Vocabulary Check

Match each Vocabulary word with its synonym.

6. discernible   **a.** worsens

7. stature   **b.** noticeable

8. deteriorates   **c.** prominence

Text Analysis

9. **Evaluate** Hemingway claims that he has "no facility for speech making." How would you evaluate Hemingway's speech-making ability? Support your answer with evidence from the text.

10. **Analyze** Hemingway states that it is because of the great writers of the past that a writer "is driven far out past where he can go." What does Hemingway mean? Does he see great writers as a hindrance, an inspiration, or something else?

11. **Hypothesize** What do you think Hemingway's opinion of a person who plagiarizes an essay for class would be?

Listening and Speaking

12. **Compare and Contrast** A speech can have many different purposes: to persuade, to inform, to motivate, or to accept acknowledgment. Compare Hemingway's acceptance speech to a speech that a candidate running for office might give. How do the purposes of these speeches differ? How does the content of each speech reflect its purpose?

Writing Focus   Constructed Response

Write a short speech accepting praise or thanks for an accomplishment or deed. Using the negative constructions in Hemingway's speech as a model, include phrases with *no*, *not*, or *nor*. Then, write a few sentences about how these phrases affect the tone and meaning of your speech. Support your response with specific evidence.

What Do You Think Now

Does Hemingway view the Nobel Prize as the pinnacle of his success? Explain why or why not.

Winter Dreams

What Do  You? Think

How does progress challenge <u>tradition</u> and redefine society?

⏱ QuickWrite

Write a paragraph about a time when you or someone you know achieved a goal that should have brought happiness, but instead brought dissatisfaction. Why do you think you or the person you know felt discontented?

MEET THE WRITER

F. Scott Fitzgerald
(1896–1940)

If ever there was a writer whose life and fiction were one, it was F. Scott Fitzgerald. Handsome, charming, and uncommonly gifted, he was not only part of the wonderful, reckless era of the 1920s—he helped to name it the Jazz Age. His works and his life exhibit the excesses of that legendary period.

Early Celebrity

Francis Scott Key Fitzgerald was born in 1896 in St. Paul, Minnesota. Spoiled in childhood, Fitzgerald was a failure at school and sports. He spent much of his time daydreaming and, while still in his teens, writing stories and plays. He continued to write at Princeton University, which he left for officers' training school when the United States entered World War I in 1917. He yearned for adventure but was never sent overseas. In camp, he worked on a novel that was twice turned down for publication.

Scribner's published a revised version of that novel, entitled *This Side of Paradise,* in 1920. The book was a sensation. In it, the old prewar world with its Victorian code of behavior has been dumped in favor of a gaudy spree of new freedoms. In Fitzgerald's novel, the Jazz Age had found its definition.

The Spiral Down

That same year, Fitzgerald married Zelda Sayre. At first, their marriage seemed to feed his literary ambitions. In 1925, Fitzgerald published what he called "something extraordinary"—*The Great Gatsby.* Its central triumph is its revelation of the rich in all their luxury and heedlessness, accompanied by an implicit condemnation of their way of life. In a remarkably concise work, Fitzgerald probed the ambiguities of the American dream.

Despite critical praise, *The Great Gatsby* was a financial disappointment. To support his and Zelda's expensive lifestyle, he turned out potboiling short stories and went to Hollywood to write movie scripts. In 1930, Zelda suffered a mental breakdown and never fully recovered. In 1934, Fitzgerald published *Tender Is the Night,* perhaps his finest novel. In its despair, the book is an epitaph for the Jazz Age and for the author himself.

Think About the Writer

How did Fitzgerald's novels reflect cultural, social, and economic factors of the times?

Reader/Writer Notebook

Use your **RWN** to complete the activities for this selection.

Literary Focus

Motivation The term **motivation** refers to the reasons that characters behave as they do. Motivation can come from internal sources (ambition, insecurity, shyness) or from external factors (poverty, an ambitious parent, the crash of the stock market). In sophisticated fiction, as in the complexity of life itself, motivation may come from many sources and is sometimes hard to pin down. Characters in many stories aren't even aware of their own motivations. In "Winter Dreams," when Dexter quits caddying, he says it is because he is too old, but the real reason has more to do with his reaction to an eleven-year-old girl.

Reading Focus

Making Inferences About Characters When you make an **inference**, you make an educated guess based on facts presented in the text and on your own life experience. As you read this story, think about these questions: Why does Dexter want to marry Judy? Why does Judy treat men so carelessly? Why does Dexter propose to Irene? Reflect on how details in the story and your own life experiences help you to understand the characters' motivations.

Into Action As you read, use concept maps like the one below to answer the questions listed above. Make one concept map for each question. List facts from the story and experiences from your own life that help you make inferences about the characters' motivations.

Writing Focus

Think as a Reader/Writer

Find It in Your Reading Fitzgerald uses uncommon adjectives to create vivid portraits of his characters. Think about how "monstrous conviction" and "precarious advantage" convey much more striking images than alternatives such as "big conviction" or "shaky advantage." As you read, note striking and unusual adjectives and record them in your *Reader/Writer Notebook*.

Vocabulary

malicious (muh LIHSH uhs) *adj.*: intentionally hurtful. *Did Judy hurt people because she was malicious, or because she was simply careless?*

reserve (rih ZURV) *n.*: self-restraint. *His conservative clothing conveyed a sense of reserve uncommon during the Jazz Age.*

petulance (PEHCH uh luhns) *n.*: irritability; impatience. *Judy's petulance worried Dexter, for he feared she was no longer happy with him.*

mirth (murth) *n.*: joyfulness. *Though Judy smiled, she conveyed no happiness or mirth.*

turbulence (TUR byuh luhns) *n.*: wild disorder. *Much of the turbulence in Dexter's life resulted from Judy's changing affections.*

ludicrous (LOO dih kruhs) *adj.*: laughable; absurd. *It was ludicrous to describe Judy as merely pretty; she was breathtaking.*

plaintive (PLAYN tihv) *adj.*: expressing sadness. *Judy's sadness showed in her plaintive eyes.*

Language Coach

Multiple Meanings The noun *reserve* can have several meanings. Fitzgerald uses it to mean "self-restraint." It can also mean "something kept back for later use," as in this sentence: *Our reserves will help us get through an emergency.* How can the word *reserve* be used as a verb?

 Learn It Online
Get the inside story behind the Vocabulary words with Word Watch online.

go.hrw.com   L11-857   **Go**

WINTER DREAMS

The Granger Collection, New York.

by F. Scott Fitzgerald

Read with a Purpose

Read to discover what happens when a man learns the truth about his dreams.

Build Background

This story is one of several that Fitzgerald wrote about the dreams and illusions that marked the Jazz Age. "Winter Dreams" was written in 1922, when Fitzgerald's stories were commanding top prices from *The Saturday Evening Post* and other popular magazines. The story opens around 1911, when fourteen-year-old Dexter is caddying for wealthy golfers, and it spans eighteen years of Dexter's life.

S ome of the caddies were poor as sin and lived in one-room houses with a neurasthenic[1] cow in the front yard, but Dexter Green's father owned the second best grocery store in Black Bear—the best one was "The Hub," patronized by the wealthy people from Sherry Island—and Dexter caddied only for pocket-money.

In the fall when the days became crisp and gray, and the long Minnesota winter shut down like the white lid of a box, Dexter's skis moved over the snow that hid the fairways[2] of the golf course. At these times the country gave him a feeling of profound melancholy—it offended him that the links should lie in enforced fallowness, haunted by ragged sparrows for the long season. It was dreary, too, that on the tees where the gay colors fluttered in summer there were now only the desolate sandboxes knee-deep in crusted ice. When he crossed the hills the wind blew cold as misery, and if the sun was out he

1. **neurasthenic** (nur uhs THEHN ihk): thin and weak, as though suffering from a nervous disorder.

2. **fairways:** mowed parts of a golf course. The fairway of most holes starts near the tee and ends near the green.

tramped with his eyes squinted up against the hard dimensionless glare.

In April the winter ceased abruptly. The snow ran down into Black Bear Lake scarcely tarrying[3] for the early golfers to brave the season with red and black balls. Without elation, without an interval of moist glory, the cold was gone.

Dexter knew that there was something dismal about this Northern spring, just as he knew there was something gorgeous about the fall. Fall made him clinch his hands and tremble and repeat idiotic sentences to himself, and make brisk abrupt gestures of command to imaginary audiences and armies. October filled him with hope which November raised to a sort of ecstatic triumph, and in this mood the fleeting brilliant impressions of the summer at Sherry Island were ready grist to his mill.[4] He became a golf champion and defeated Mr. T. A. Hedrick in a marvellous match played a hundred times over the fairways of his imagination, a match each detail of which he changed about untiringly—sometimes he won with almost laughable ease, sometimes he came up magnificently from behind. Again, stepping from a Pierce-Arrow automobile, like Mr. Mortimer Jones, he strolled frigidly into the lounge of the Sherry Island Golf Club—or perhaps, surrounded by an admiring crowd, he gave an exhibition of fancy diving from the spring-board of the club raft. . . . Among those who watched him in open-mouthed wonder was Mr. Mortimer Jones. **Ⓐ Ⓑ**

And one day it came to pass that Mr. Jones—himself and not his ghost—came up to Dexter with tears in his eyes and said that Dexter was the—best caddy in the club, and wouldn't he decide not to quit if Mr. Jones made it worth his while, because every other—caddy in the club lost one ball a hole for him—regularly—

"No, sir," said Dexter decisively, "I don't want to caddy any more." Then, after a pause: "I'm too old."

---

3. **tarrying:** waiting.
4. **grist to his mill:** something that can be used to advantage.

"You're not more than fourteen. Why the devil did you decide just this morning that you wanted to quit? You promised that next week you'd go over to the State tournament with me."

"I decided I was too old."

Dexter handed in his "A Class" badge, collected what money was due him from the caddy-master, and walked home to Black Bear Village.

"The best—caddy I ever saw," shouted Mr. Mortimer Jones over a drink that afternoon. "Never lost a ball! Willing! Intelligent! Quiet! Honest! Grateful!"

The little girl who had done this was eleven—beautifully ugly as little girls are apt to be who are destined after a few years to be inexpressibly lovely and bring no end of misery to a great number of men. The spark, however, was perceptible. There was a general ungodliness in the way her lips twisted down at the corners when she smiled, and in the—Heaven help us!—in the almost passionate quality of her eyes. Vitality is born early in such women. It was utterly in evidence now, shining through her thin frame in a sort of glow.

She had come eagerly out on to the course at nine o'clock with a white linen nurse and five small new golf clubs in a white canvas bag which the nurse was carrying. When Dexter first saw her she was standing by the caddy house, rather ill at ease and trying to conceal the fact by engaging her nurse in an obviously unnatural conversation graced by startling and irrelevant grimaces from herself.

"Well, it's certainly a nice day, Hilda," Dexter heard her say. She drew down the corners of her mouth, smiled, and glanced furtively around, her eyes in transit falling for an instant on Dexter.

Then to the nurse:

"Well, I guess there aren't very many people out here this morning, are there?"

The smile again—radiant, blatantly artificial—convincing. **Ⓒ**

Ⓐ **Reading Focus** Making Inferences About Characters
How do the seasons affect Dexter's moods? What do Dexter's moods suggest about his dreams?

Ⓑ **Literary Focus** Motivation What do Dexter's dreams suggest about his plans for the future?

Ⓒ **Reading Focus** Making Inferences About Characters
Fitzgerald uses contradictory words to describe Judy's smile. What does this suggest about the girl's character and the effect she has on others?

"I don't know what we're supposed to do now," said the nurse, looking nowhere in particular.

"Oh, that's all right. I'll fix it up."

Dexter stood perfectly still, his mouth slightly ajar. He knew that if he moved forward a step his stare would be in her line of vision—if he moved backward he would lose his full view of her face. For a moment he had not realized how young she was. Now he remembered having seen her several times the year before—in bloomers.[5]

Suddenly, involuntarily, he laughed, a short abrupt laugh—then, startled by himself, he turned and began to walk quickly away.

"Boy!"

Dexter stopped.

"Boy—"

Beyond question he was addressed. Not only that, but he was treated to that absurd smile, that preposterous smile—the memory of which at least a dozen men were to carry into middle age.

"Boy, do you know where the golf teacher is?"

"He's giving a lesson."

"Well, do you know where the caddy-master is?"

"He isn't here yet this morning."

"Oh." For a moment this baffled her. She stood alternately on her right and left foot.

"We'd like to get a caddy," said the nurse. "Mrs. Mortimer Jones sent us out to play golf, and we don't know how without we get a caddy."

Here she was stopped by an ominous glance from Miss Jones, followed immediately by the smile.

"There aren't any caddies here except me," said Dexter to the nurse, "and I got to stay here in charge until the caddy-master gets here."

"Oh."

Miss Jones and her retinue[6] now withdrew, and at a proper distance from Dexter became involved in a heated conversation, which was concluded by Miss Jones taking one of the clubs and hitting it on the ground with violence. For further emphasis she raised

it again and was about to bring it down smartly upon the nurse's bosom, when the nurse seized the club and twisted it from her hands.

"You damn little mean old *thing!*" cried Miss Jones wildly.

Another argument ensued. Realizing that the elements of the comedy were implied in the scene, Dexter several times began to laugh, but each time restrained the laugh before it reached audibility. He could not resist the monstrous conviction that the little girl was justified in beating the nurse.

The situation was resolved by the fortuitous[7] appearance of the caddy-master, who was appealed to immediately by the nurse.

"Miss Jones is to have a little caddy, and this one says he can't go."

"Mr. McKenna said I was to wait here till you came," said Dexter quickly.

"Well, he's here now." Miss Jones smiled cheerfully

---

5. **bloomers:** baggy pants gathered at the knee, formerly worn by females for athletic activities.

6. **retinue** (REHT'n oo): group of followers or servants attending a person of rank.

7. **fortuitous:** fortunate.

D **Reading Focus** Making Inferences About Characters

Why is Dexter so captivated by Judy?

at the caddy-master. Then she dropped her bag and set off at a haughty mince[8] toward the first tee.

"Well?" the caddy-master turned to Dexter. "What you standing there like a dummy for? Go pick up the young lady's clubs."

"I don't think I'll go out today," said Dexter.

"You don't—"

"I think I'll quit."

The enormity of his decision frightened him. He was a favorite caddy, and the thirty dollars a month he earned through the summer were not to be made elsewhere around the lake. But he had received a strong emotional shock, and his perturbation required a violent and immediate outlet. **E**

It is not so simple as that, either. As so frequently would be the case in the future, Dexter was unconsciously dictated to by his winter dreams.

II

Now, of course, the quality and the seasonability of these winter dreams varied, but the stuff of them remained. They persuaded Dexter several years later to pass up a business course at the State university—his father, prospering now, would have paid his way—for the precarious[9] advantage of attending an older and more famous university in the East, where he was bothered by his scanty funds. But do not get the impression, because his winter dreams happened to be concerned at first with musings on the rich, that there was anything merely snobbish in the boy. He wanted not association with glittering things and glittering people—he wanted the glittering things themselves. Often he reached out for the best without knowing why he wanted it—and sometimes he ran up against the mysterious denials and prohibitions in which life indulges. It is with one of those denials and not with his career as a whole that this story deals. **F**

He made money. It was rather amazing. After college he went to the city from which Black Bear Lake draws its wealthy patrons. When he was only twenty-three and had been there not quite two years, there were already people who liked to say: "Now *there's* a boy—" All about him rich men's sons were peddling bonds precariously, or investing patrimonies[10] precariously, or plodding through the two dozen volumes of the "George Washington Commercial Course," but Dexter borrowed a thousand dollars on his college degree and his confident mouth, and bought a partnership in a laundry.

It was a small laundry when he went into it but Dexter made a specialty of learning how the English washed fine woolen golf stockings without shrinking them, and within a year he was catering to the trade that wore knickerbockers.[11] Men were insisting that their Shetland hose and sweaters go to his laundry just as they had insisted on a caddy who could find golf balls. A little later he was doing their wives' lingerie as well—and running five branches in different parts of the city. Before he was twenty-seven he owned the largest string of laundries in his section of the country. It was then that he sold out and went to New York. But the part of his story that concerns us goes back to the days when he was making his first big success.

When he was twenty-three Mr. Hart—one of the gray-haired men who like to say "Now there's a boy"—gave him a guest card to the Sherry Island Golf Club for a weekend. So he signed his name one day on the register, and that afternoon played golf in a foursome with Mr. Hart and Mr. Sandwood and Mr. T. A. Hedrick. He did not consider it necessary to remark that he had once carried Mr. Hart's bag over this same links, and that he knew every trap and gully with his eyes shut—but he found himself glancing at the four caddies who trailed them, trying to catch a gleam or gesture that would remind him of himself, that would lessen the gap which lay between his present and his past.

---

8. **mince:** prim, affected walk.
9. **precarious:** uncertain.

10. **patrimonies:** inheritances.
11. **knickerbockers:** short, loose pants gathered at the knees, formerly worn by golfers.

E Literary Focus Motivation Why does Dexter quit his job?

F Literary Focus Motivation What does this paragraph suggest about Dexter's motivation for seeking "the glittering things"?

It was a curious day, slashed abruptly with fleeting, familiar impressions. One minute he had the sense of being a trespasser—in the next he was impressed by the tremendous superiority he felt toward Mr. T. A. Hedrick, who was a bore and not even a good golfer any more.

Then, because of a ball Mr. Hart lost near the fifteenth green, an enormous thing happened. While they were searching the stiff grasses of the rough there was a clear call of "Fore!"[12] from behind a hill in their rear. And as they all turned abruptly from their search a bright new ball sliced abruptly over the hill and caught Mr. T. A. Hedrick in the abdomen.

"By Gad!" cried Mr. T. A. Hedrick, "they ought to put some of these crazy women off the course. It's getting to be outrageous."

A head and a voice came up together over the hill: "Do you mind if we go through?"

"You hit me in the stomach!" declared Mr. Hedrick wildly.

"Did I?" The girl approached the group of men. "I'm sorry. I yelled 'Fore!'"

Her glance fell casually on each of the men—then scanned the fairway for her ball.

"Did I bounce into the rough?"

It was impossible to determine whether this question was ingenuous[13] or malicious. In a moment, however, she left no doubt, for as her partner came up over the hill she called cheerfully:

"Here I am! I'd have gone on the green except that I hit something." **G**

As she took her stance for a short mashie[14] shot, Dexter looked at her closely. She wore a blue gingham dress, rimmed at throat and shoulders with a white edging that accentuated her tan. The quality of exag-

---

12. **Fore:** warning cry that a golfer gives before hitting a ball down the fairway.
13. **ingenuous:** innocent; without guile.
14. **mashie:** number five iron (golf club).

geration, of thinness, which had made her passionate eyes and downturning mouth absurd at eleven, was gone now. She was arrestingly beautiful. The color in her cheeks was centered like the color in a picture—it was not a "high" color, but a sort of fluctuating and feverish warmth, so shaded that it seemed at any moment it would recede and disappear. This color and the mobility of her mouth gave a continual impression of flux, of intense life, of passionate vitality—balanced only partially by the sad luxury of her eyes.

She swung her mashie impatiently and without interest, pitching the ball into a sand-pit on the other side of the green. With a quick, insincere smile and a careless "Thank you!" she went on after it.

"That Judy Jones!" remarked Mr. Hedrick on the next tee, as they waited—some moments—for her to play on ahead. "All she needs is to be turned up and spanked for six months and then to be married off to an old-fashioned cavalry captain."

"My God, she's good-looking!" said Mr. Sandwood, who was just over thirty.

"Good-looking!" cried Mr. Hedrick contemptuously, "she always looks as if she wanted to be kissed! Turning those big cow-eyes on every calf in town!" **H**

It was doubtful if Mr. Hedrick intended a reference to the maternal instinct.

"She'd play pretty good golf if she'd try," said Mr. Sandwood.

"She has no form," said Mr. Hedrick solemnly.

"She has a nice figure," said Mr. Sandwood.

"Better thank the Lord she doesn't drive a swifter ball," said Mr. Hart, winking at Dexter.

Later in the afternoon the sun went down with a riotous swirl of gold and varying blues and scarlets, and left the dry, rustling night of Western summer. Dexter watched from the veranda of the Golf Club, watched the even overlap of the waters in the little wind, silver molasses under the harvest moon. Then the moon held a finger to her lips and the lake became a clear pool, pale and quiet. Dexter put on

---

G Reading Focus **Making Inferences About Characters**
What does the girl's behavior suggest about her character?

Vocabulary malicious (muh LIHSH uhs) *adj.:* intentionally hurtful.

H Reading Focus **Making Inferences About Characters**
What inferences can you draw about Mr. Hedrick's character from his comments about Judy?

his bathing suit and swam out to the farthest raft, where he stretched dripping on the wet canvas of the springboard.

There was a fish jumping and a star shining and the lights around the lake were gleaming. Over on a dark peninsula a piano was playing the songs of last summer and of summers before that—songs from "Chin-Chin" and "The Count of Luxemburg" and "The Chocolate Soldier"—and because the sound of a piano over a stretch of water had always seemed beautiful to Dexter he lay perfectly quiet and listened.

The tune the piano was playing at that moment had been gay and new five years before when Dexter was a sophomore at college. They had played it at a prom once when he could not afford the luxury of proms, and he had stood outside the gymnasium and listened. The sound of the tune precipitated in him a sort of ecstasy and it was with that ecstasy he viewed what happened to him now. It was a mood of intense appreciation, a sense that, for once, he was magnificently attuned to life and that everything about him was radiating a brightness and a glamour he might never know again.

A low, pale oblong[15] detached itself suddenly from the darkness of the Island, spitting forth the reverberate[16] sound of a racing motorboat. Two white streamers of cleft water rolled themselves out behind it and almost immediately the boat was beside him, drowning out the hot tinkle of the piano in the drone of its spray. Dexter raising himself on his arms was aware of a figure standing at the wheel, of two dark eyes regarding him over the lengthening space of water—then the boat had gone by and was sweeping in an immense and purposeless circle of spray round and round in the middle of the lake. With equal eccentricity one of the circles

> Everything about him was radiating a **brightness** and a **glamour** he might never know again.

flattened out and headed back toward the raft.

"Who's that?" she called, shutting off her motor. She was so near now that Dexter could see her bathing suit, which consisted apparently of pink rompers.[17]

The nose of the boat bumped the raft, and as the latter tilted rakishly, he was precipitated[18] toward her. With different degrees of interest they recognized each other.

"Aren't you one of those men we played through this afternoon?" she demanded.

He was.

"Well, do you know how to drive a motorboat? Because if you do I wish you'd drive this one so I can ride on the surfboard behind. My name is Judy Jones"—she favored him with an absurd smirk—rather, what tried to be a smirk, for, twist her mouth as she might, it was not grotesque, it was merely beautiful—"and I live in a house over there on the Island, and in that house there is a man waiting for me. When he drove up at the door I drove out of the dock because he says I'm his ideal." **①**

There was a fish jumping and a star shining and the lights around the lake were gleaming. Dexter sat beside Judy Jones and she explained how her boat was driven. Then she was in the water, swimming to the floating surfboard with a sinuous[19] crawl. Watching her was without effort to the eye, watching a branch waving or a seagull flying. Her arms, burned to butternut, moved sinuously among the dull platinum ripples, elbow appearing first, casting the forearm back with a cadence of falling water, then reaching out and down, stabbing a path ahead. **①**

They moved out into the lake; turning, Dexter saw that she was kneeling on the low rear of the now uptilted surfboard.

---

15. **oblong:** geometric figure longer than it is broad.
16. **reverberate:** reflected; echoed.

17. **rompers:** one-piece outfit with loose pants gathered at the knee.
18. **precipitated:** thrown headlong.
19. **sinuous:** curving back and forth; snakelike.

---

① Literary Focus Motivation Why does Judy leave the man waiting at her house?

① Reading Focus Making Inferences About Character What inferences can you draw about Judy's character based on the way she swims?

"Go faster," she called, "fast as it'll go."

Obediently he jammed the lever forward and the white spray mounted at the bow. When he looked around again the girl was standing up on the rushing board, her arms spread wide, her eyes lifted toward the moon.

"It's awful cold," she shouted. "What's your name?"

He told her.

"Well, why don't you come to dinner tomorrow night?"

His heart turned over like the flywheel[20] of the boat, and, for the second time, her casual whim gave a new direction to his life.

III

Next evening while he waited for her to come downstairs, Dexter peopled the soft deep summer room and the sunporch that opened from it with the men who had already loved Judy Jones. He knew the sort of men they were—the men who when he first went to college had entered from the great prep schools with graceful clothes and the deep tan of healthy summers. He had seen that, in one sense, he was better than these men. He was newer and stronger. Yet in acknowledging to himself that he wished his children to be like them he was admitting that he was but the rough, strong stuff from which they eternally sprang.

When the time had come for him to wear good clothes, he had known who were the best tailors in America, and the best tailors in America had made him the suit he wore this evening. He had acquired that particular reserve peculiar to his university, that set it off from other universities. He recognized the value to him of such a mannerism and he had adopted it; he knew that to be careless in dress and manner required more confidence than to be careful. But carelessness was for his children. His mother's name had been Krimslich. She was a Bohemian of the peasant class and she had talked broken English to the end of her days. Her son must keep to the set patterns.

---

20. **flywheel:** wheel that regulates the speed of a machine.

Vocabulary **reserve** (rih ZURV) *n.*: self-restraint.

The American Dream

Though readers today might equate Dexter's dream with the American dream, the term *American dream* did not appear in print until 1931, almost a decade after "Winter Dreams" was published. That year, historian James Truslow Adams coined the term. He wanted to use it as the title of his book *The Epic of America*, published in 1933, but his editor felt that "no red-blooded American would pay $3.50 for a dream." Adams argued back, "Red-blooded Americans have always been willing to gamble their last peso on a dream."

In 1931, the American dream was not a new concept. The vision of the United States as a promised land with unlimited resources and opportunities had existed since the time of the European settlers. However, it was not until Americans had to cope with the strain of the Great Depression—with its profound sense of lost opportunity—that the term came into widespread use.

Ask Yourself
What do you think Adams meant when he said that "Americans have always been willing to gamble their last peso on a dream"? Do you think this is true of Dexter? Why or why not?

A typical advertisement for a Nash automobile from an American magazine in 1934.
The Granger Collection, New York.

At a little after seven Judy Jones came downstairs. She wore a blue silk afternoon dress, and he was disappointed at first that she had not put on something more elaborate. This feeling was accentuated when, after a brief greeting, she went to the door of a butler's pantry and pushing it open called: "You can serve dinner, Martha." He had rather expected that a butler would announce dinner, that there would be a cocktail. Then he put these thoughts behind him as they sat down side by side on a lounge and looked at each other.

"Father and mother won't be here," she said thoughtfully.

He remembered the last time he had seen her father, and he was glad the parents were not to be here tonight—they might wonder who he was. He had been born in Keeble, a Minnesota village fifty miles farther north, and he always gave Keeble as his home instead of Black Bear Village. Country towns were well enough to come from if they weren't inconveniently in sight and used as footstools by fashionable lakes. **(K)**

They talked of his university, which she had visited frequently during the past two years, and of the nearby city which supplied Sherry Island with its patrons, and whither Dexter would return next day to his prospering laundries.

During dinner she slipped into a moody depression which gave Dexter a feeling of uneasiness. Whatever petulance she uttered in her throaty voice worried him. Whatever she smiled at—at him, at a chicken liver, at nothing—it disturbed him that her smile could have no root in mirth, or even in amusement. When the scarlet corners of her lips curved down, it was less a smile than an invitation to a kiss.

Then, after dinner, she led him out on the dark sun-porch and deliberately changed the atmosphere.

"Do you mind if I weep a little?" she said.

"I'm afraid I'm boring you," he responded quickly.

"You're not. I like you. But I've just had a terrible afternoon. There was a man I cared about, and this afternoon he told me out of a clear sky that he was poor as a church mouse. He'd never even hinted it before. Does this sound horribly mundane?"[21]

"Perhaps he was afraid to tell you."

"Suppose he was," she answered. "He didn't start right. You see, if I'd thought of him as poor—well, I've been mad about loads of poor men, and fully intended to marry them all. But in this case, I hadn't thought of him that way, and my interest in him wasn't strong enough to survive the shock. As if a girl calmly informed her fiancé that she was a widow. He might not object to widows, but—

"Let's start right," she interrupted herself suddenly. "Who are you, anyhow?" **(L)**

For a moment Dexter hesitated. Then:

"I'm nobody," he announced. "My career is largely a matter of futures."

"Are you poor?"

"No," he said frankly, "I'm probably making more money than any man my age in the Northwest. I know that's an obnoxious remark, but you advised me to start right."

There was a pause. Then she smiled and the corners of her mouth drooped and an almost imperceptible sway brought her closer to him, looking up into his eyes. A lump rose in Dexter's throat, and he waited breathless for the experiment, facing the unpredictable compound that would form mysteriously from the elements of their lips. Then he saw—she communicated her excitement to him, lavishly, deeply, with kisses that were not a promise but a fulfillment. They aroused in him not hunger demanding renewal but surfeit[22] that would demand more surfeit . . . kisses that were like charity, creating want by holding back nothing at all.

It did not take him many hours to decide that he had wanted Judy Jones ever since he was a proud, desirous little boy.

---

21. **mundane:** ordinary; everyday.
22. **surfeit:** discomfort resulting from excess or overindulgence.

(K) **Literary Focus** Motivation Why does Dexter lie about his hometown?

(L) **Literary Focus** Motivation Why does Judy ask Dexter who he is?

Vocabulary petulance (PEHCH uh luhns) *n.*: irritability; impatience.
mirth (murth) *n.*: joyfulness.

IV

It began like that—and continued, with varying shades of intensity, on such a note right up to the dénouement.[23] Dexter surrendered a part of himself to the most direct and unprincipled personality with which he had ever come in contact. Whatever Judy wanted, she went after with the full pressure of her charm. There was no divergence of method, no jockeying for position or premeditation of effects—there was a very little mental side to any of her affairs. She simply made men conscious to the highest degree of her physical loveliness. Dexter had no desire to change her. Her deficiencies were knit up with a passionate energy that transcended and justified them. **(M)**

When, as Judy's head lay against his shoulder that first night, she whispered, "I don't know what's the matter with me. Last night I thought I was in love with a man and tonight I think I'm in love with you—" —it seemed to him a beautiful and romantic thing to say. It was the exquisite excitability that for the moment he controlled and owned. But a week later he was compelled to view this same quality in a different light. She took him in her roadster to a picnic supper, and after supper she disappeared, likewise in her roadster, with another man. Dexter became enormously upset and was scarcely able to be decently civil to the other people present. When she assured him that she had not kissed the other man, he knew she was lying—yet he was glad that she had taken the trouble to lie to him. **(N)**

He was, as he found before the summer ended, one of a varying dozen who circulated about her. Each of them had at one time been favored above all others—about half of them still basked in the solace of occasional sentimental revivals. Whenever one showed signs of dropping out through long neglect, she granted him a brief honeyed hour, which encouraged him to tag along for a year or so longer. Judy made these forays[24] upon the helpless and defeated without malice, indeed half unconscious that there was anything mischievous in what she did.

When a new man came to town every one dropped out—dates were automatically cancelled.

The helpless part of trying to do anything about it was that she did it all herself. She was not a girl who could be "won" in the kinetic[25] sense—she was proof against[26] cleverness, she was proof against charm; if any of these assailed her too strongly she would immediately resolve the affair to a physical basis, and under the magic of her physical splendor the strong as well as the brilliant played her game and not their own. She was entertained only by the gratification of her desires and by the direct exercise of her own charm. Perhaps from so much youthful love, so many youthful lovers, she had come, in self-defense, to nourish herself wholly from within.

Succeeding Dexter's first exhilaration came restlessness and dissatisfaction. The helpless ecstasy of losing himself in her was opiate rather than tonic.[27] It was fortunate for his work during the winter that those moments of ecstasy came infrequently. Early in their acquaintance it had seemed for a while that there was a deep and spontaneous mutual attraction—that first August, for example—three days of long evenings on her dusky veranda, of strange wan kisses through the late afternoon, in shadowy alcoves or behind the protecting trellises of the garden arbors, of mornings when she was fresh as a dream and almost shy at meeting him in the clarity of the rising day. There was all the ecstasy of an engagement about it, sharpened by his realization that there was no engagement. It was during those three days that, for the first time, he had asked her to marry him. She said "maybe some day," she said "kiss me," she said "I'd like to marry you," she said "I love you"—she said—nothing.

---

23. **dénouement** (day noo MAHN): final outcome.

24. **forays:** raids.
25. **kinetic:** coming about through action or energy.
26. **proof against:** able to withstand.
27. **opiate . . . tonic:** calming rather than stimulating.

(M) Literary Focus Motivation Fitzgerald says that Judy goes directly after whatever she wants. What exactly does she want?

(N) Reading Focus Making Inferences About Characters There are elements of Judy's character that Dexter does not like, yet he doesn't want to change her. How do you explain this contradiction?

The three days were interrupted by the arrival of a New York man who visited at her house for half September. To Dexter's agony, rumor engaged them. The man was the son of the president of a great trust company. But at the end of a month it was reported that Judy was yawning. At a dance one night she sat all evening in a motorboat with a local beau, while the New Yorker searched the club for her frantically. She told the local beau that she was bored with her visitor, and two days later he left. She was seen with him at the station, and it was reported that he looked very mournful indeed.

On this note the summer ended. Dexter was twenty-four, and he found himself increasingly in a position to do as he wished. He joined two clubs in the city and lived at one of them. Though he was by no means an integral part of the stag-lines[28] at these clubs, he managed to be on hand at dances where Judy Jones was likely to appear. He could have gone out socially as much as he liked—he was an eligible young man, now, and popular with downtown fathers. His confessed devotion to Judy Jones had rather solidified his position. But he had no social aspirations and rather despised the dancing men who were always on tap for the Thursday or Saturday parties and who filled in at dinners with the younger married set. Already he was playing with the idea of going East to New York. He wanted to take Judy Jones with him. No disillusion as to the world in which she had grown up could cure his illusion as to her desirability. **O**

Remember that—for only in the light of it can what he did for her be understood.

> She had treated him with **interest,** with **encouragement,** with **malice,** with **indifference,** with **contempt.**

Eighteen months after he first met Judy Jones he became engaged to another girl. Her name was Irene Scheerer, and her father was one of the men who had always believed in Dexter. Irene was light-haired and sweet and honorable, and a little stout, and she had two suitors whom she pleasantly relinquished when Dexter formally asked her to marry him. **P**

Summer, fall, winter, spring, another summer, another fall—so much he had given of his active life to the incorrigible[29] lips of Judy Jones. She had treated him with interest, with encouragement, with malice, with indifference, with contempt. She had inflicted on him the innumerable little slights and indignities possible in such a case—as if in revenge for having ever cared for him at all. She had beckoned him and yawned at him and beckoned him again and he had responded often with bitterness and narrowed eyes. She had brought him ecstatic happiness and intolerable agony of spirit. She had caused him untold inconvenience and not a little trouble. She had insulted him, and she had ridden over him, and she had played his interest in her against his interest in his work—for fun. She had done everything to him except to criticize him—this she had not done—it seemed to him only because it might have sullied[30] the utter indifference she manifested and sincerely felt toward him.

When autumn had come and gone again it occurred to him that he could not have Judy Jones. He had to beat this into his mind but he convinced himself at last. He lay awake at night for a while and argued it over. He told himself the trouble and the pain she had caused him, he enumerated her glaring defi-

---

28. **stag-lines:** lines of unaccompanied men at a dance, waiting for available dance partners.

29. **incorrigible:** incapable of correction or reform.
30. **sullied:** tainted; soiled.

O Reading Focus | Making Inferences About Characters
Have Dexter's dreams changed? Explain why or why not.

P Literary Focus | Motivation Why does Dexter become engaged to Irene?

ciencies as a wife. Then he said to himself that he loved her, and after a while he fell asleep. For a week, lest he imagined her husky voice over the telephone or her eyes opposite him at lunch, he worked hard and late, and at night he went to his office and plotted out his years.

At the end of a week he went to a dance and cut in on her once. For almost the first time since they had met he did not ask her to sit out with him or tell her that she was lovely. It hurt him that she did not miss these things—that was all. He was not jealous when he saw that there was a new man tonight. He had been hardened against jealousy long before.

He stayed late at the dance. He sat for an hour with Irene Scheerer and talked about books and about music. He knew very little about either. But he was beginning

to be master of his own time now, and he had a rather priggish[31] notion that he—the young and already fabulously successful Dexter Green—should know more about such things. **Q**

That was in October, when he was twenty-five. In January, Dexter and Irene became engaged. It was to be announced in June, and they were to be married three months later.

The Minnesota winter prolonged itself interminably, and it was almost May when the winds came soft and the snow ran down into Black Bear Lake at last. For the first time in over a year Dexter was enjoying a certain tranquility of spirit. Judy Jones had been in Florida, and afterward in Hot Springs, and somewhere she had been engaged, and somewhere she had broken it off. At first, when Dexter had definitely given her up, it had made him sad that people still linked them together and asked for news of her, but when he began to be placed at dinner next to Irene Scheerer people didn't ask him about her any more—they told him about her. He ceased to be an authority on her.

May at last. Dexter walked the streets at night when the darkness was damp as rain, wondering that so soon, with so little done, so much of ecstasy had gone from him. May one year back had been marked by Judy's poignant, unforgivable, yet forgiven turbulence—it had been one of those rare times when he fancied she had grown to care for him. That old penny's worth of happiness he had spent for this bushel of content. He knew that Irene would be no more than a curtain spread behind him, a hand moving among gleaming teacups, a voice calling to children . . . fire and loveliness were gone, the magic of nights and the wonder of the varying hours and seasons . . . slender lips, downturning, dropping to his lips and bearing him up into a heaven of eyes. . . . The thing was deep in him. He was too strong and alive for it to die lightly. **R**

In the middle of May when the weather balanced for a few days on the thin bridge that led to deep sum-

---

31. **priggish:** annoyingly precise and proper.

Q **Literary Focus** Motivation Why does Dexter decide at this time of his life that he should know more about books and music?

R **Reading Focus** Making Inferences About Characters What do Dexter's thoughts suggest about his feelings toward Irene? Toward Judy? About marriage?

Vocabulary **turbulence** (TUR byuh luhns) n.: wild disorder.

mer he turned in one night at Irene's house. Their engagement was to be announced in a week now—no one would be surprised at it. And tonight they would sit together on the lounge at the University Club and look on for an hour at the dancers. It gave him a sense of solidity to go with her—she was so sturdily popular, so intensely "great."

He mounted the steps of the brownstone house and stepped inside.

"Irene," he called.

Mrs. Scheerer came out of the living room to meet him.

"Dexter," she said, "Irene's gone upstairs with a splitting headache. She wanted to go with you but I made her go to bed."

"Nothing serious, I—"

"Oh, no. She's going to play golf with you in the morning. You can spare her for just one night, can't you, Dexter?"

Her smile was kind. She and Dexter liked each other. In the living room he talked for a moment before he said good-night.

Returning to the University Club, where he had rooms, he stood in the doorway for a moment and watched the dancers. He leaned against the doorpost, nodded at a man or two—yawned.

"Hello, darling."

The familiar voice at his elbow startled him. Judy Jones had left a man and crossed the room to him— Judy Jones, a slender enameled doll in cloth of gold: gold in a band at her head, gold in two slipper points at her dress's hem. The fragile glow of her face seemed to blossom as she smiled at him. A breeze of warmth and light blew through the room. His hands in the pockets of his dinner jacket tightened spasmodically. He was filled with a sudden excitement.

"When did you get back?" he asked casually.

"Come here and I'll tell you about it."

She turned and he followed her. She had been away—he could have wept at the wonder of her return. She had passed through enchanted streets, doing things that were like provocative music. All mysterious happenings, all fresh and quickening hopes, had gone away with her, come back with her now.

She turned in the doorway.

"Have you a car here? If you haven't, I have."

"I have a coupé."

In then, with a rustle of golden cloth. He slammed the door. Into so many cars she had stepped—like this—like that—her back against the leather, so—her elbow resting on the door—waiting. She would have been soiled long since had there been anything to soil her—except herself—but this was her own self outpouring.

With an effort he forced himself to start the car and back into the street. This was nothing, he must remember. She had done this before, and he had put her behind him, as he would have crossed a bad account from his books. **S**

He drove slowly downtown and, affecting abstraction, traversed the deserted streets of the business section, peopled here and there where a movie was giving out its crowd or where consumptive[32] or pugilistic[33] youth lounged in front of pool halls. The clink of glasses and the slap of hands on the bars issued from saloons, cloisters of glazed glass and dirty yellow light.

She was watching him closely and the silence was embarrassing, yet in this crisis he could find no casual word with which to profane[34] the hour. At a convenient turning he began to zigzag back toward the University Club.

"Have you missed me?" she asked suddenly.

"Everybody missed you."

He wondered if she knew of Irene Scheerer. She had been back only a day—her absence had been almost contemporaneous with his engagement. **T**

"What a remark!" Judy laughed sadly—without sadness. She looked at him searchingly. He became absorbed in the dashboard.

---

32. **consumptive:** destructive; wasteful.
33. **pugilistic:** eager to fight.
34. **profane:** curse.

S **Literary Focus** **Motivation** Why does Dexter agree to go for a ride with Judy if, as he says, he has "put her behind him"?

T **Reading Focus** **Making Inferences About Characters** Why does Dexter wonder whether Judy knows about Irene?

"You're handsomer than you used to be," she said thoughtfully. "Dexter, you have the most rememberable eyes."

He could have laughed at this, but he did not laugh. It was the sort of thing that was said to sophomores. Yet it stabbed at him.

"I'm awfully tired of everything, darling." She called every one darling, endowing the endearment with careless, individual comraderie. "I wish you'd marry me."

The directness of this confused him. He should have told her now that he was going to marry another girl, but he could not tell her. He could as easily have sworn that he had never loved her.

"I think we'd get along," she continued, on the same note, "unless probably you've forgotten me and fallen in love with another girl."

Her confidence was obviously enormous. She had said, in effect, that she found such a thing impossible to believe, that if it were true he had merely committed a childish indiscretion—and probably to show off. She would forgive him, because it was not a matter of any moment but rather something to be brushed aside lightly.

"Of course you could never love anybody but me," she continued. "I like the way you love me. Oh, Dexter, have you forgotten last year?"

"No, I haven't forgotten."

"Neither have I!"

Was she sincerely moved—or was she carried along by the wave of her own acting?

"I wish we could be like that again," she said, and he forced himself to answer:

"I don't think we can."

"I suppose not. . . . I hear you're giving Irene Scheerer a violent rush." Ⓤ

There was not the faintest emphasis on the name, yet Dexter was suddenly ashamed.

"Oh, take me home," cried Judy suddenly; "I don't want to go back to that idiotic dance—with those children."

Then, as he turned up the street that led to the residence district, Judy began to cry quietly to herself. He had never seen her cry before.

The dark street lightened, the dwellings of the rich loomed up around them, he stopped his coupé in front of the great white bulk of the Mortimer Joneses house, somnolent,[35] gorgeous, drenched with the splendor of the damp moonlight. Its solidity startled him. The strong walls, the steel of the girders, the breadth and beam and pomp of it were there only to bring out the contrast with the young beauty beside him. It was sturdy to accentuate her slightness—as if to show what a breeze could be generated by a butterfly's wing.

He sat perfectly quiet, his nerves in wild clamor, afraid that if he moved he would find her irresistibly in his arms. Two tears had rolled down her wet face and trembled on her upper lip.

"I'm more beautiful than anybody else," she said brokenly, "why can't I be happy?" Her moist eyes tore at his stability—her mouth turned slowly downward with an exquisite sadness: "I'd like to marry you if you'll have me, Dexter. I suppose you think I'm not worth having, but I'll be so beautiful for you, Dexter."

A million phrases of anger, pride, passion, hatred, tenderness fought on his lips. Then a perfect wave of emotion washed over him, carrying off with it a sediment of wisdom, of convention,[36] of doubt, of honor. This was his girl who was speaking, his own, his beautiful, his pride.

"Won't you come in?" He heard her draw in her breath sharply.

Waiting.

"All right," his voice was trembling, "I'll come in." Ⓥ

V

It was strange that neither when it was over nor a long time afterward did he regret that night. Looking at it from the perspective of ten years, the fact that Judy's flare for him endured just one month seemed of little importance. Nor did it matter that by his yielding he subjected himself to a deeper agony in the end and gave serious hurt to Irene Scheerer and to Irene's

---

35. **somnolent:** sleepy.
36. **convention:** accepted practices of social behavior.

Ⓤ **Literary Focus** Motivation Why does Judy take a renewed interest in Dexter?

Ⓥ **Literary Focus** Motivation Why does Dexter accept Judy's invitation?

parents, who had befriended him. There was nothing sufficiently pictorial about Irene's grief to stamp itself on his mind.

Dexter was at bottom hard-minded. The attitude of the city on his action was of no importance to him, not because he was going to leave the city, but because any outside attitude on the situation seemed superficial. He was completely indifferent to popular opinion. Nor, when he had seen that it was no use, that he did not possess in himself the power to move fundamentally or to hold Judy Jones, did he bear any malice toward her. He loved her, and he would love her until the day he was too old for loving—but he could not have her. So he tasted the deep pain that is reserved only for the strong, just as he had tasted for a little while the deep happiness.

Even the ultimate falsity of the grounds upon which Judy terminated the engagement, that she did not want to "take him away" from Irene—Judy, who had wanted nothing else—did not revolt him. He was beyond any revulsion or any amusement. **Ⓦ**

He went East in February with the intention of selling out his laundries and settling in New York—but the war came to America in March and changed his

---

Ⓦ Reading Focus Making Inferences About Characters
Biographer Matthew J. Bruccoli writes, "Fitzgerald developed a new American figure: the determined girl-woman. Not the cartoon flapper, but the warm, courageous, attractive, and chastely independent young woman competing at life and love for the highest stakes—her future." Does Judy fit this description? Explain.

plans. He returned to the West, handed over the management of the business to his partner, and went into the first officers' training camp in late April. He was one of those young thousands who greeted the war with a certain amount of relief, welcoming the liberation from webs of tangled emotion.

VI

This story is not his biography, remember, although things creep into it which have nothing to do with those dreams he had when he was young. We are almost done with them and with him now. There is only one more incident to be related here, and it happens seven years farther on.

It took place in New York, where he had done well—so well that there were no barriers too high for him. He was thirty-two years old, and, except for one flying trip immediately after the war, he had not been West in seven years. A man named Devlin from Detroit came into his office to see him in a business way, and then and there this incident occurred, and closed out, so to speak, this particular side of his life.

"So you're from the Middle West," said the man Devlin with careless curiosity. "That's funny—I thought men like you were probably born and raised on Wall Street. You know—wife of one of my best friends in Detroit came from your city. I was an usher at the wedding."

Dexter waited with no apprehension of what was coming.

"Judy Simms," said Devlin with no particular interest; "Judy Jones she was once."

"Yes, I knew her." A dull impatience spread over him. He had heard, of course, that she was married—perhaps deliberately he had heard no more.

"Awfully nice girl," brooded Devlin meaninglessly, "I'm sort of sorry for her."

"Why?" Something in Dexter was alert, receptive, at once.

"Oh, Lud Simms has gone to pieces in a way. I don't mean he ill-uses her, but he drinks and runs around—"

"Doesn't she run around?"

"No. Stays at home with her kids."

"Oh."

"She's a little too old for him," said Devlin.

"Too old!" cried Dexter. "Why, man, she's only twenty-seven."

He was possessed with a wild notion of rushing out into the streets and taking a train to Detroit. He rose to his feet spasmodically. **(X)**

"I guess you're busy," Devlin apologized quickly. "I didn't realize—"

"No, I'm not busy," said Dexter, steadying his voice. "I'm not busy at all. Not busy at all. Did you say she was—twenty-seven? No, I said she was twenty-seven."

"Yes, you did," agreed Devlin dryly.

"Go on, then. Go on."

"What do you mean?"

"About Judy Jones."

Devlin looked at him helplessly.

"Well, that's—I told you all there is to it. He treats her like the devil. Oh, they're not going to get divorced or anything. When he's particularly outrageous she forgives him. In fact, I'm inclined to think she loves him. She was a pretty girl when she first came to Detroit."

A pretty girl! The phrase struck Dexter as ludicrous.

"Isn't she—a pretty girl, anymore?"

"Oh, she's all right."

"Look here," said Dexter, sitting down suddenly, "I don't understand. You say she was a 'pretty girl' and now you say she's 'all right.' I don't understand what you mean—Judy Jones wasn't a pretty girl, at all. She was a great beauty. Why, I knew her, I knew her. She was—"

Devlin laughed pleasantly.

"I'm not trying to start a row," he said. "I think Judy's a nice girl and I like her. I can't understand how a man like Lud Simms could fall madly in love with her, but he did." Then he added: "Most of the women like her."

Dexter looked closely at Devlin, thinking wildly that there must be a reason for this, some insensitivity in the man or some private malice.

Vocabulary   **ludicrous** (LOO dih kruhs) *adj.*: laughable; absurd.

(X) Literary Focus Motivation   Why does Dexter want to take a train to Detroit?

"Lots of women fade just like that," Devlin snapped his fingers. "You must have seen it happen. Perhaps I've forgotten how pretty she was at her wedding. I've seen her so much since then, you see. She has nice eyes."

A sort of dullness settled down upon Dexter. For the first time in his life he felt like getting very drunk. He knew that he was laughing loudly at something Devlin had said, but he did not know what it was or why it was funny. When, in a few minutes, Devlin went, he lay down on his lounge and looked out the window at the New York skyline into which the sun was sinking in dull lovely shades of pink and gold.

He had thought that having nothing else to lose he was invulnerable at last—but he knew that he had just lost something more, as surely as if he had married Judy Jones and seen her fade away before his eyes.

The dream was gone. Something had been taken from him. In a sort of panic he pushed the palms of his hands into his eyes and tried to bring up a picture of the waters lapping on Sherry Island and the moonlit veranda, and gingham on the golf links and the dry sun and the gold color of her neck's soft down. And her mouth damp to his kisses and her eyes plaintive with melancholy and her freshness like new fine linen in the morning. Why, these things were no longer in the world! They had existed and they existed no longer.

For the first time in years the tears were streaming down his face. But they were for himself now. He did not care about mouth and eyes and moving hands. He wanted to care, and he could not care. For he had gone away and he could never go back anymore. The gates were closed, the sun was gone down, and there was no beauty but the gray beauty of steel that withstands all time. Even the grief he could have borne was left behind in the country of illusion, of youth, of the richness of life, where his winter dreams had flourished.

"Long ago," he said, "long ago, there was something in me, but now that thing is gone. Now that thing is gone, that thing is gone. I cannot cry. I cannot care. That thing will come back no more." **Z**

Y **Reading Focus** **Making Inferences About Characters** How has Judy changed? What brought about these changes in Judy? Are they believable?

Z **Reading Focus** **Making Inferences About Character** How has Dexter changed? What brought about these changes in Dexter? What effect will they have on his future?

Vocabulary **plaintive** (PLAYN tihv) *adj.*: expressing sadness.

Applying Your Skills

Winter Dreams

SKILLS FOCUS Literary Skills Analyze character motivation; analyze climax. **Reading Skills** Make inferences about characters. **Vocabulary Skills** Identify synonyms. **Writing Skills** Develop characters.

Respond and Think Critically

Reading Focus

Quick Check

1. Why does Dexter react the way he does when he first meets Judy?

2. How do Judy and Dexter become reacquainted as adults? How do their attitudes about dating and their relationship compare?

Read with a Purpose

3. At the end of the story, what loss does Dexter lament? Use evidence to support your answer.

Reading Skills: Making Inferences About Characters

4. As you read, you recorded information that would help you make inferences about the characters' motivations. Add a fourth oval to each map. In each new oval, make an inference based on the information in the preceding ovals.

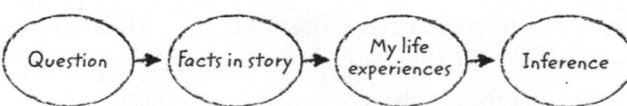

Question → Facts in story → My life experiences → Inference

✓ Vocabulary Check

Match each Vocabulary word with its synonym.

5. ludicrous   a. spiteful
6. mirth   b. melancholy
7. plaintive   c. restraint
8. petulance   d. glee
9. turbulence   e. preposterous
10. reserve   f. peevishness
11. malicious   g. chaos

Literary Focus

Literary Analysis

12. **Draw Conclusions** In *Richard III,* Shakespeare refers to "the winter of our discontent." How do Dexter's "winter dreams" reflect discontent?

13. **Interpret** A recurring theme in Fitzgerald's work is the pursuit of the American dream. Define what Fitzgerald sees as the American dream.

14. **Extend** Are this story's themes universal, or specific to the Jazz Age? Draw comparisons with other narratives you have read in your response.

Literary Skills: Motivation

15. **Analyze** A character's motivation can provide reasons for his or her behavior. Dexter is motivated by dreams of success. With a partner, discuss how Dexter pursues these dreams. Is the outcome <u>inevitable</u>? Why or why not?

Literary Skills Review: Climax

16. **Interpret** A story's **climax** is the point in the plot that creates the greatest intensity or interest. Which event marks the climax of this story? Why?

Writing Focus

Think as a Reader/Writer

Use It in Your Writing Review the adjectives you recorded in your *Reader/Writer Notebook.* Use similarly vivid adjectives in a brief character profile of someone you know.

What Do **You Think Now** Does "Winter Dreams" applaud or lament the changes in society that developed during the Jazz Age? Explain.

Making Inferences by Kylene Beers

In your daily life, you make inferences all the time. If you leave a movie theater and see that the streets and cars are wet, you infer that it has rained. **Inferences** are educated guesses based on facts and on your own knowledge and experience.

You make inferences when you read, too. When you draw an inference about a character or event, you are making an educated guess based on what you read and what you already know. Making inferences requires paying careful attention to details. It also involves thinking about what is hinted at, or implied.

In William Faulkner's "A Rose for Emily," we can learn about Miss Emily, the eccentric main character, by making inferences based on descriptions in the text. For example, in the first paragraph the author introduces us to Miss Emily by describing her funeral.

> When Miss Emily Grierson died, our whole town went to her funeral: the men through a sort of respectful attention for a fallen monument, the women mostly out of curiosity to see the inside of her house . . . .

From this description, we can infer that Miss Emily must have been important, since the whole town attends her funeral. Sometimes, however, we can make inferences based on the details that are not included. Because there is no mention of feelings of love or loss, we can infer that Miss Emily must have led a lonely life.

Faulkner then gives us more information about Miss Emily by describing her house.

> It was a big, squarish frame house that had once been white, decorated with cupolas and spires and scrolled balconies in the heavily lightsome style of the seventies, set on what had once been our most select street.

Notice the details that Faulkner uses to describe the house, which is an integral part of the story's setting. The paint on Miss Emily's house has faded, the style is no longer in fashion, and even the street is no longer as respected as it once was. By examining these details and reading between the lines, you can infer that Miss Emily, like her house, has lost status and prominence as the years have passed.

As you read "A Rose for Emily," look beneath the surface of the text to make inferences not only about Miss Emily, but also about Faulkner's opinions on the social conventions of the South.

Your Turn

Read the following passage about Miss Emily's response to a series of letters about a tax bill. Meet with a partner and discuss what you can infer about Miss Emily's opinion of herself and her community from the details in the text and from your own knowledge.

> On the first of the year they mailed her a tax notice. February came, and there was no reply. They wrote her a formal letter, asking her to call at the sheriff's office at her convenience. A week later the mayor wrote her himself, offering to call or to send his car for her and received in reply a note on paper of an archaic shape in a thin, flowing calligraphy in faded ink, to the effect that she no longer went out at all.

Learn It Online

For tips on making inferences in longer works, visit *NovelWise* online.

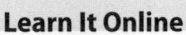 L11-875

A Rose for Emily

Nobel Prize Acceptance Speech, 1950

What Do You Think

How does progress challenge <u>tradition</u> and redefine society?

QuickTalk

In a small group, brainstorm specific examples of individuals or groups who choose not to accept forward movement in society. Discuss why they are uninterested in progress and how this position affects their lives.

William Faulkner
(1897–1962)

Nobel Prize WINNER

Few literary places are as famous as the imagined world of William Faulkner, Yoknapatawpha County, Mississippi, the scene of his most celebrated stories. This imaginary place is similar to Oxford, Mississippi, where Faulkner lived for most of his life.

A Life Without Focus

Faulkner was a mediocre student who quit high school in the tenth grade. Rejected by the U.S. Army at the outbreak of World War I, he enlisted in the Royal Air Force of Canada, only to see the war end before he was commissioned. When Faulkner returned home to Oxford, Mississippi, he took some courses at the university and did poorly in English. With neither profession nor skill and a marked distaste for regular employment, he seemed to his neighbors a moody and puzzling young man.

Finding a Theme

In 1924, Faulkner left Oxford for New Orleans, where he met the writer Sherwood Anderson. Impressed and encouraged by Anderson, Faulkner tried his hand at fiction. In five months, he completed a first novel, *Soldier's Pay*.

Faulkner found his great theme: the American South as a microcosm for the universal themes of time, the passions of the human heart, and the destruction of the wilderness. Faulkner saw the South as a nation unto itself, with a strong sense of its noble past, despite the humiliating defeat in the Civil War and the enforced acceptance of the North's values. Faulkner started to explore these themes in *Sartoris* and *The Sound and the Fury*, both published in 1929. *The Sound and the Fury* was a literary milestone because of Faulkner's bold manipulation of point of view and its stream-of-consciousness narrative technique.

In the decade that followed, Faulkner produced a succession of dazzling books. He portrayed the South accurately, perceptively, and with a poignant ambivalence—on the one hand, affectionate; on the other, critical. In 1950 Faulkner received the Nobel Prize in Literature.

Think About the Writer Why might Faulkner have found the American South such a rich and intriguing setting?

A Rose for Emily

Reader/Writer Notebook

Use your **RWN** to complete the activities for this selection.

Literary Focus

Setting The time and location in which a story takes place is its **setting.** Setting also includes the customs and social conditions of a time—including, in this case, racial stereotyping. If parts of this story give off an offensive odor, it arises from the racial slurs used by some of the characters. Although we find this language offensive, we must remember that Faulkner used it to portray realistically the <u>ideology</u> of a racially segregated town of the rural South in the early twentieth century.

Literary Perspectives Apply the literary perspective described on page 879 as you read this story.

Reading Focus

Making Inferences About Characters When you make an **inference** about literary characters, you use the facts in the text plus the knowledge you have gained through your own experiences to make assumptions about them. As you read the story, think about Miss Emily's bizarre behavior. Try to determine whether her behavior is merely madness or an extension of qualities admired in her community.

Into Action As you read, record examples of Miss Emily's strange behavior. Note details from the story and information from your life experience that may help you understand her actions.

Miss Emily's behavior	Details from the story	Prior knowledge
She never leaves her house.	The town is changing; the next generation is introducing modern ideas.	The elderly are often seen as relics of the past and treated without respect.

Writing Focus

Think as a Reader/Writer

Find It in Your Reading Faulkner's descriptions of objects help to convey a **mood** of gloom and decay. For example, he describes Miss Emily's house as a "fallen monument" and her letter as written in "faded ink." Note other descriptions of objects that convey the story's gloomy mood, and record them in your *Reader/Writer Notebook*.

Vocabulary

archaic (ahr KAY ihk) *adj.:* old-fashioned. *The archaic paper reflected an era long gone.*

vindicated (VIHN dih kayt ihd) *v.* used as *adj.:* proved correct. *The townspeople felt vindicated when Miss Emily did not marry.*

pauper (PAW puhr) *n.:* extremely poor person. *She had no inheritance, so the proud woman was actually a pauper.*

circumvent (sur kuhm VEHNT) *v.:* avoid by cleverness or deceit. *The townspeople wanted to circumvent Miss Emily's cousins.*

virulent (VIHR yoo luhnt) *adj.:* full of hate; venomous. *Her father's protectiveness had been so virulent that it stifled Miss Emily.*

tranquil (TRANG kwuhl) *adj.:* calm; quiet. *Year after year, she sat at the window looking perfectly tranquil.*

perverse (puhr VURS) *adj.:* odd; contrary. *What perverse secret did the townspeople uncover at the end of the story?*

acrid (AK rihd) *adj.:* bitter; irritating. *Undisturbed for years, the room had an acrid smell.*

Language Coach
Forming Nouns from Adjectives

Adding a suffix can change many adjectives to nouns. Attach the suffix *–ity* to the adjective *tranquil* to form the noun *tranquility,* which means "a state of being calm or quiet." What noun can you form from the adjective *perverse*?

Learn It Online
Get a glimpse of Miss Emily's world through the introductory video online.

go.hrw.com | L11-877 | **Go**

A ROSE FOR EMILY

by **William Faulkner**

Read with a Purpose
Read to discover the secret that the townspeople uncover after a reclusive old woman dies.

Build Background
Faulkner, a master of the Southern Gothic tale, knew firsthand the American South and its powerful <u>traditions</u>—small-town social castes and changing social values, the politeness that marks routine interactions and the struggle to find joy in life.

The facts of this story tell a lurid tale, as sensational as any you might see headlined in scandal magazines. What primarily turns this account of outrageous human behavior into literature, though, is the relationship between the event and its setting. As the story of one eccentric woman unfolds, we learn some important truths about the rest of her community: its loyalty to family and the past, its pride, its faithfulness to old values, its fierce independence, and its scorn for outsiders and change.

I

When Miss Emily Grierson died, our whole town went to her funeral: the men through a sort of respectful affection for a fallen monument, the women mostly out of curiosity to see the inside of her house, which no one save an old manservant—a combined gardener and cook—had seen in at least ten years. **Ⓐ**

It was a big, squarish frame house that had once been white, decorated with cupolas[1] and spires and scrolled balconies in the heavily lightsome style of the seventies,[2] set on what had once been our most select street. But garages and cotton gins had encroached and obliterated even the august names of that neigh-

borhood; only Miss Emily's house was left, lifting its stubborn and coquettish decay above the cotton wagons and the gasoline pumps—an eyesore among eyesores. And now Miss Emily had gone to join the representatives of those august names where they lay in the cedar-bemused cemetery among the ranked and anonymous graves of Union and Confederate soldiers who fell at the battle of Jefferson. **Ⓑ**

Alive, Miss Emily had been a tradition, a duty, and a care; a sort of hereditary obligation upon the town, dating from that day in 1894 when Colonel Sartoris, the mayor—he who fathered the edict that no Negro woman should appear on the streets without an apron—remitted her taxes, the dispensation dating from the death of her father on into perpetuity.[3] Not that Miss Emily would have accepted charity. Colonel

---

1. **cupolas** (KYOO puh luhz): small, dome-shaped structures built on a roof.
2. **the seventies:** the 1870s.

3. **perpetuity** (pur puh TOO uh tee): eternity.

Ⓐ **Reading Focus** **Making Inferences** We meet Miss Emily through others' responses to her death. What can you infer about her from learning why the men and women attended her funeral?

Ⓑ **Literary Focus** **Setting** How does this description of setting reveal the changing economic and social conditions in Miss Emily's town?

Sartoris invented an involved tale to the effect that Miss Emily's father had loaned money to the town, which the town, as a matter of business, preferred this way of repaying. Only a man of Colonel Sartoris' generation and thought could have invented it, and only a woman could have believed it.

When the next generation, with its more modern ideas, became mayors and aldermen, this arrangement created some little dissatisfaction. On the first of the year they mailed her a tax notice. February came, and there was no reply. They wrote her a formal letter, asking her to call at the sheriff's office at her convenience. A week later the mayor wrote her himself, offering to call or to send his car for her and received in reply a note on paper of an archaic shape in a thin, flowing calligraphy in faded ink, to the effect that she no longer went out at all. The tax notice was also enclosed, without comment.

They called a special meeting of the Board of Aldermen. A deputation waited upon her, knocked at the door through which no visitor had passed since she ceased giving china-painting lessons eight or ten years earlier. They were admitted by the old Negro into a dim hall from which a stairway mounted into still more shadow. It smelled of dust and disuse—a close, dank smell. The Negro led them into the parlor. It was furnished in heavy, leather-covered furniture. When the Negro opened the blinds of one window they could see that the leather was cracked; and when they sat down, a faint dust rose sluggishly about their thighs spinning with slow motes in the single sun-ray. On a tarnished gilt easel before the fireplace stood a crayon portrait of Miss Emily's father. **C**

They rose when she entered—a small, fat woman in black, with a thin gold chain descending to her waist and vanishing into her belt, leaning on an ebony cane with a tarnished gold head. Her skeleton was small and spare; perhaps that was why what would have been merely plumpness in another was obesity in her. She looked bloated, like a body long submerged in motionless water, and of that pallid hue. Her eyes, lost in the fatty ridges of her face, looked like two small pieces of coal pressed into

a lump of dough as they moved from one face to another while the visitors stated their errand.

She did not ask them to sit. She just stood in the door and listened quietly until the spokesman came to a stumbling halt. Then they could hear the invisible watch ticking at the end of the gold chain.

Her voice was dry and cold. "I have no taxes in Jefferson. Colonel Sartoris explained it to me. Perhaps one of you can gain access to the city records and satisfy yourselves."

"But we have. We are the city authorities, Miss Emily. Didn't you get a notice from the sheriff, signed by him?"

"I received a paper, yes," Miss Emily said. "Perhaps he considers himself the sheriff . . . I have no taxes in Jefferson."

"But there is nothing on the books to show that, you see. We must go by the—"

"See Colonel Sartoris. I have no taxes in Jefferson."

"But, Miss Emily—"

Literary Perspectives

Analyzing Credibility in Literature The strange tale of Emily's life is told through a narrator speaking as a plural "we" rather than as a singular "I." The narrative voice is collective; it represents the people of Jefferson, Mississippi, who seem to have spent decades watching and talking about Emily and her family. Emily is the focus of this story, but she does not get to tell her own story. We see her (and her actions) through the eyes of a town that clearly has strong opinions about her. As you read, look for details that reveal the townspeople's attitudes toward Emily and her father, and toward their status as the faded elite of the community. Do their beliefs and personal views influence their portrayal of Emily? What does their portrayal say about the culture of the South at the time?

As you read, note the questions in the text, which will guide you in using this perspective.

C **Literary Focus** Setting What mood, or emotional atmosphere, does this setting convey to you?

Vocabulary archaic (ahr KAY ihk) adj.: old-fashioned.

"See Colonel Sartoris." (Colonel Sartoris had been dead almost ten years.) "I have no taxes in Jefferson. Tobe!" The Negro appeared. "Show these gentlemen out." **ⓓ**

II

So she vanquished them, horse and foot, just as she had vanquished their fathers thirty years before about the smell. That was two years after her father's death and a short time after her sweetheart—the one we believed would marry her—had deserted her. After her father's death she went out very little; after her sweetheart went away, people hardly saw her at all. A few of the ladies had the temerity[4] to call, but were not received, and the only sign of life about the place was the Negro man—a young man then—going in and out with a market basket.

"Just as if a man—any man—could keep a kitchen properly," the ladies said; so they were not surprised when the smell developed. It was another link between the gross, teeming world and the high and mighty Griersons.

A neighbor, a woman, complained to the mayor, Judge Stevens, eighty years old.

"But what will you have me do about it, madam?" he said.

"Why, send her word to stop it," the woman said. "Isn't there a law?"

"I'm sure that won't be necessary," Judge Stevens said. "It's probably just a snake or a rat that nigger of hers killed in the yard. I'll speak to him about it."

The next day he received two more complaints, one from a man who came in diffident deprecation.[5] "We really must do something about it, Judge. I'd be the last one in the world to bother Miss Emily, but we've got to do something." That night the Board of Aldermen met—three graybeards and one younger man, a member of the rising generation.

"It's simple enough," he said. "Send her word to have her place cleaned up. Give her a certain time to do it in, and if she don't . . ."

"Dammit, sir," Judge Stevens said, "will you accuse a lady to her face of smelling bad?"

So the next night, after midnight, four men crossed Miss Emily's lawn and slunk about the house like burglars, sniffing along the base of the brickwork and at the cellar openings while one of them performed a regular sowing motion with his hand out of a sack slung from his shoulder. They broke open the cellar door and sprinkled lime there, and in all the outbuildings. As they recrossed the lawn, a window that had been dark was lighted and Miss Emily sat in it, the light behind her, and her upright torso motionless as that of an idol. They crept quietly across the lawn and into the shadow of the locusts that lined the street. After a week or two the smell went away.

That was when people had begun to feel really sorry for her. People in our town, remembering how old lady Wyatt, her great-aunt, had gone completely crazy at last, believed that the Griersons held themselves a little too high for what they really were. None of the young men were quite good enough for Miss Emily and such. We had long thought of them as a tableau,[6] Miss Emily a slender figure in white in the background, her father a spraddled silhouette in the foreground, his back to her and clutching a horsewhip, the two of them framed by the back-flung front door. So when she got to be thirty and was still single, we were not pleased exactly, but vindicated; even with insanity in the family she wouldn't have turned down all of her chances if they had really materialized. **ⓔ**

When her father died, it got about that the house was all that was left to her; and in a way, people were glad. At last they could pity Miss Emily. Being left

---

4. **temerity** (tuh MEHR uh tee): foolish boldness; rashness.
5. **diffident deprecation:** timid disapproval.

6. **tableau** (TAB loh): striking dramatic scene, usually motionless.

ⓓ Reading Focus **Making Inferences** What does this detail about Colonel Sartoris suggest about Emily?

ⓔ Literary Perspectives **Analyzing Credibility** What does this paragraph reveal about the townspeople's view of Emily and her family? Do these opinions seem to be based in fact?

Vocabulary **vindicated** (VIHN dih kayt ihd) *v.* used as *adj.*: proved correct.

alone, and a pauper, she had become humanized. Now she too would know the old thrill and the old despair of a penny more or less. **(F)**

The day after his death all the ladies prepared to call at the house and offer condolence and aid, as is our custom. Miss Emily met them at the door, dressed as usual and with no trace of grief on her face. She told them that her father was not dead. She did that for three days, with the ministers calling on her, and the doctors, trying to persuade her to let them dispose of the body. Just as they were about to resort to law and force, she broke down, and they buried her father quickly.

We did not say she was crazy then. We believed she had to do that. We remembered all the young men her father had driven away, and we knew that with nothing left, she would have to cling to that which had robbed her, as people will.

III

She was sick for a long time. When we saw her again, her hair was cut short, making her look like a girl, with a vague resemblance to those angels in colored church windows—sort of tragic and serene.

The town had just let the contracts for paving the sidewalks, and in the summer after her father's death they began the work. The construction company came with niggers and mules and machinery, and a foreman named Homer Barron, a Yankee—a big, dark, ready man, with a big voice and eyes lighter than his face. The little boys would follow in groups to hear him cuss the niggers, and the niggers singing in time to the rise and fall of picks. Pretty soon he knew everybody in town. Whenever you heard a lot of laughing anywhere about the square, Homer Barron would be in the center of the group. Presently we began to see him and Miss Emily on

> After her father's death she went out very little; after her sweetheart went away, people hardly saw her at all.

Sunday afternoons driving in the yellow-wheeled buggy and the matched team of bays from the livery stable.

At first we were glad that Miss Emily would have an interest, because the ladies all said, "Of course a Grierson would not think seriously of a Northerner, a day laborer." But there were still others, older people, who said that even grief could not cause a real lady to forget noblesse oblige[7]—without calling it noblesse oblige. They just said, "Poor Emily. Her kinsfolk should come to her." She had some kin in Alabama; but years ago her father had fallen out with them over the estate of old lady Wyatt, the crazy woman, and there was no communication between the two families. They had not even been represented at the funeral.

And as soon as the old people said, "Poor Emily," the whispering began. "Do you suppose it's really so?" they said to one another. "Of course it is. What else could . . ." This behind their hands; rustling of craned[8] silk and satin behind jalousies[9] closed upon the sun of Sunday afternoon as the thin, swift, clop-clop-clop of the matched team passed: "Poor Emily." **(G)**

She carried her head high enough—even when we believed that she was fallen. It was as if she demanded more than ever the recognition of her dignity as the last Grierson; as if it had wanted that touch of earthiness to reaffirm her imperviousness. Like when she bought the rat poison, the arsenic. That was over a year after they had begun to say

---

7. **noblesse oblige** (noh BLEHS oh BLEEZH): French for "nobility obliges." It refers to the supposed obligation of the upper classes to act nobly or kindly toward the lower classes.
8. **craned:** stretched.
9. **jalousies** (JAL uh seez): windows, shades, or doors made of overlapping, adjustable slats.

(F) Reading Focus **Making Inferences** Why does Emily's situation after her father's death make the townspeople glad?

(G) Literary Focus **Analyzing Credibility** Do you think the narrator really feels sympathy for Emily? Explain.

Vocabulary **pauper** (PAW puhr) *n.*: extremely poor person.

"Poor Emily," and while the two female cousins were visiting her.

"I want some poison," she said to the druggist. She was over thirty then, still a slight woman, though thinner than usual, with cold, haughty black eyes in a face the flesh of which was strained across the temples and about the eye-sockets as you imagine a lighthouse-keeper's face ought to look. "I want some poison," she said.

"Yes, Miss Emily. What kind? For rats and such? I'd recom—"

"I want the best you have. I don't care what kind."

The druggist named several. "They'll kill anything up to an elephant. But what you want is—"

"Arsenic," Miss Emily said. "Is that a good one?"

"Is . . . arsenic? Yes, ma'am. But what you want—"

"I want arsenic."

The druggist looked down at her. She looked back at him, erect, her face like a strained flag. "Why, of course," the druggist said. "If that's what you want. But the law requires you to tell what you are going to use it for."

Miss Emily just stared at him, her head tilted back in order to look him eye for eye, until he looked away and went and got the arsenic and wrapped it up. The Negro delivery boy brought her the package; the druggist didn't come back. When she opened the package at home there was written on the box, under the skull and bones: "For rats." **H**

IV

So the next day we all said, "She will kill herself"; and we said it would be the best thing. When she had first begun to be seen with Homer Barron, we had said, "She will marry him." Then we said, "She will persuade him yet," because Homer himself had remarked—he liked men, and it was known that he drank with the younger men in the Elks' Club—that he was not a marrying man. Later we said, "Poor Emily," behind the jalousies as they passed on Sunday afternoon in the glittering buggy, Miss Emily with her head high and Homer Barron with his hat cocked and a cigar in his teeth, reins and whip in a yellow glove. **I**

Then some of the ladies began to say that it was a disgrace to the town and a bad example to the young people. The men did not want to interfere, but at last the ladies forced the Baptist minister—Miss Emily's people were Episcopal—to call upon her. He would never divulge what happened during that interview, but he refused to go back again. The next Sunday they again drove about the streets, and the following day the minister's wife wrote to Miss Emily's relations in Alabama.

So she had blood-kin under her roof again and we sat back to watch developments. At first nothing happened. Then we were sure that they were to be married. We learned that Miss Emily had been to the jeweler's and ordered a man's toilet set[10] in silver, with the letters H. B. on each piece. Two days later we learned that she had bought a complete outfit of men's clothing, including a nightshirt, and we said, "They are married." We were really glad. We were glad because the two female cousins were even more Grierson than Miss Emily had ever been.

So we were not surprised when Homer Barron—the streets had been finished some time since—was gone. We were a little disappointed that there was not a public blowing-off, but we believed that he had gone on to prepare for Miss Emily's coming, or to give her a chance to get rid of the cousins. (By that time it was a cabal,[11] and we were all Miss Emily's allies to help circumvent the cousins.) Sure enough, after another week they departed. And, as we had expected all along, within three days Homer Barron was back in town. A neighbor saw the Negro man admit him at the kitchen door at dusk one evening. **J**

---

10. **toilet set:** set of grooming aids, such as a hand mirror, hairbrush, and comb.
11. **cabal** (kuh BAL): small group involved in a secret intrigue.

H **Literary Perspectives** Analyzing Credibility Is it believable that the pharmacist would give Miss Emily the poison despite her refusal to state her purpose for buying it? Why?

I **Literary Focus** Setting How do the townspeople's responses to Emily's purchase show their attitudes toward her?

J **Literary Perspectives** Analyzing Credibility
The townspeople speculate that Homer Barron's disappearance relates to his imminent marriage to Miss Emily—despite the fact that he has been described as not the marrying type. How might the townspeople's values have led them to this conclusion?

Vocabulary **circumvent** (sur kuhm VEHNT) v.: avoid by cleverness or deceit.

And that was the last we saw of Homer Barron. And of Miss Emily for some time. The Negro man went in and out with the market basket, but the front door remained closed. Now and then we would see her at a window for a moment, as the men did that night when they sprinkled the lime, but for almost six months she did not appear on the streets. Then we knew that this was to be expected too; as if that quality of her father which had thwarted her woman's life so many times had been too virulent and too furious to die.

When we next saw Miss Emily, she had grown fat and her hair was turning gray. During the next few years it grew grayer and grayer until it attained an even pepper-and-salt iron-gray, when it ceased turning. Up to the day of her death at seventy-four it was still that vigorous iron-gray, like the hair of an active man.

From that time on her front door remained closed, save for a period of six or seven years, when she was about forty, during which she gave lessons in china-painting. She fitted up a studio in one of the down-stairs rooms, where the daughters and granddaughters of Colonel Sartoris' contemporaries were sent to her with the same regularity and in the same spirit that they were sent to church on Sundays with a twenty-five-cent piece for the collection plate. Meanwhile her taxes had been remitted. **K**

Then the newer generation became the backbone and the spirit of the town, and the painting pupils grew up and fell away and did not send their children to her with boxes of color and tedious brushes and pictures cut from the ladies' magazines. The front door closed upon the last one and remained closed for good. When the town got free postal delivery, Miss Emily alone refused to let them fasten the metal numbers above her door and attach a mailbox to it. She would not listen to them. **L**

Daily, monthly, yearly we watched the Negro grow grayer and more stooped, going in and out with the market basket. Each December we sent her a tax notice, which would be returned by the post office a week later,

K Reading Focus Making Inferences How is sending pupils to Miss Emily like donating money to church?

L Reading Focus Making Inferences Why does Miss Emily refuse a mailbox?

Vocabulary virulent (VIHR yoo luhnt) adj.: full of hate; venomous.

Analyzing Visuals

Viewing and Interpreting Notice the lack of color in the background and the woman's dress. What do these details tell you about the mood of the painting and the mood of the story?

My Mother (1921) (detail) by George Wesley Bellows.
Photography © The Art Institute of Chicago.

unclaimed. Now and then we would see her in one of the downstairs windows—she had evidently shut up the top floor of the house—like the carven torso of an idol in a niche, looking or not looking at us, we could never tell which. Thus she passed from generation to generation—dear, inescapable, impervious, tranquil, and perverse.

And so she died. Fell ill in the house filled with dust and shadows, with only a doddering Negro man to wait on her. We did not even know she was sick; we had long since given up trying to get any information from the Negro. He talked to no one, probably not even to her, for his voice had grown harsh and rusty, as if from disuse.

She died in one of the downstairs rooms, in a heavy walnut bed with a curtain, her gray head propped on a pillow yellow and moldy with age and lack of sunlight.

V

The Negro met the first of the ladies at the front door and let them in, with their hushed, sibilant[12] voices and their quick, curious glances, and then he disappeared. He walked right through the house and out the back and was not seen again.

The two female cousins came at once. They held the funeral on the second day, with the town coming to look at Miss Emily beneath a mass of bought flowers, with the crayon face of her father musing profoundly above the bier[13] and the ladies sibilant and macabre;[14] and the very old men—some in their brushed Confederate uniforms—on the porch and the lawn, talking of Miss Emily as if she had been a contemporary of theirs, believing that they had danced with her and courted her perhaps, confusing time with its mathematical progression, as the old do, to whom all the past is not a diminishing road but, instead, a huge meadow which no winter ever quite touches, divided from them now by the narrow bottle-neck of the most recent decade of years.

---

12. **sibilant:** hissing.
13. **bier** (bihr): coffin and its supporting platform.
14. **macabre** (muh KAH bruh): focused on the gruesome; horrible.

Already we knew that there was one room in that region above stairs which no one had seen in forty years, and which would have to be forced. They waited until Miss Emily was decently in the ground before they opened it.

The violence of breaking down the door seemed to fill this room with pervading dust. A thin, acrid pall as of the tomb seemed to lie everywhere upon this room decked and furnished as for a bridal: upon the valance curtains of faded rose color, upon the rose-shaded lights, upon the dressing table, upon the delicate array of crystal and the man's toilet things backed with tarnished silver, silver so tarnished that the monogram was obscured. Among them lay a collar and tie, as if they had just been removed, which, lifted, left upon the surface a pale crescent in the dust. Upon a chair hung the suit, carefully folded; beneath it the two mute shoes and the discarded socks. **(M)**

The man himself lay in the bed.

For a long while we just stood there, looking down at the profound and fleshless grin. The body had apparently once lain in the attitude of an embrace, but now the long sleep that outlasts love, that conquers even the grimace of love, had cuckolded[15] him. What was left of him, rotted beneath what was left of the nightshirt, had become inextricable from the bed in which he lay; and upon him and upon the pillow beside him lay that even coating of the patient and biding dust.

Then we noticed that in the second pillow was the indentation of a head. One of us lifted something from it, and leaning forward, that faint and invisible dust dry and acrid in the nostrils, we saw a long strand of iron-gray hair. **(N)**

---

15. **cuckolded:** betrayed; usually used to describe a husband whose wife has been unfaithful.

Vocabulary **tranquil** (TRANG kwuhl) *adj.*: calm; quiet.
perverse (puhr VURS) *adj.*: odd; contrary.
acrid (AK rihd) *adj.*: bitter; irritating.

(M) **Literary Focus** Setting What mood does this description of the room create?

(N) **Reading Focus** Making Inferences What does the strand of hair imply? What do you think motivated Miss Emily to act as she did?

Applying Your Skills

A Rose for Emily

Respond and Think Critically

Reading Focus

Quick Check

1. How would you describe the town in which Miss Emily lives and dies?

2. Why does the minister's wife send for Miss Emily's relations?

3. How does Miss Emily spend the last decades of her life?

Read with a Purpose

4. Why do the townspeople fail to discover Miss Emily's secret before her death?

Reading Skills: Making Inferences About Characters

5. Review the information in your chart. Add a fourth column and make inferences based on your understanding of Miss Emily's character.

Miss Emily's behavior	Details from the story	Prior knowledge	Inference about Miss Emily
She never leaves her house.	The town is changing; the next generation is introducing modern ideas.	The elderly are seen as relics of the past and treated without respect.	Miss Emily is afraid the townspeople will challenge her aristocratic view of herself.

Literary Focus

Literary Analysis

6. **Draw Conclusions** Colonel Sartoris's white lie to Miss Emily about her taxes is an attempt to spare her pride. How does the town's shift in attitude about taxes reflect wider social and economic changes in the South?

7. **Analyze** What significance do you see in the long strand of iron-gray hair on the pillow in the upstairs bedroom? What do you think happened there? Why?

8. **Literary Perspectives** What passages in this story most strongly reveal the narrator's views on Emily and her family? What do those passages tell you about the town and the town's values and beliefs? In the end, do all of their judgments about Emily seem fair?

Literary Skills: Setting

9. **Analyze** Historical details in this story reveal a great deal about its setting. What do you learn about the times from the white townspeople's attitudes toward the African Americans who live in Jefferson? Have such attitudes changed today? Explain your response.

Literary Skills Review: Symbolism

10. **Interpret** A **symbol** is a person, place, thing, or event that has a meaning of its own, but also stands for something else. Consider what roses usually symbolize. Then, defend the title of the story, or propose an <u>alternative</u> title.

Writing Focus

Think as a Reader/Writer

Use It in Your Writing Imagine another part of Miss Emily's house, such as a kitchen, closet, or basement. Describe the area, using details in Faulkner's story as a model. Make sure your description includes details that help convey the story's gloomy mood.

 What Do You Think Now

Why does Miss Emily resist change and try to live in the past?

A Rose for Emily

Vocabulary Development

✓ Vocabulary Check

Match each Vocabulary word with its synonym.

1. tranquil
2. circumvent
3. pauper
4. perverse
5. vindicated
6. acrid
7. virulent
8. archaic

a. caustic
b. serene
c. outdated
d. hateful
e. justified
f. beggar
g. evade
h. contrary

Vocabulary Skills: Latin Affixes

Prefixes and suffixes are examples of **affixes,** word parts that are attached to the beginning or end of a base word or root to help make a new word. Knowing some frequently used affixes from Latin can help you quickly unlock the meanings of some difficult words.

Prefixes are added to the beginning of a base word and always change its meaning. The following chart shows some examples of Latin prefixes.

Latin Prefixes	Meanings	Examples
co–, col–, com–	with; together	coauthor, collide, compute
circum–	around	circumvent, circumnavigate
di–, dis–	away; lack of	dilute, disconnect
re–	again; back	research, redo

Suffixes are added to the end of a base word or root. **Inflectional suffixes,** like –ed and –ing, usually just change the tense, the person, or the number of a word (generally a verb). **Derivational suffixes,** like the ones listed in the chart that follows, change the meaning of a root or base word.

Latin Suffixes	Meanings	Examples
–ance, –ence	state or quality of being	assistance, deference
–ity	state of; condition of	possibility, eternity
–ous	full of	ingenuous, vaporous
–tion	action of, condition of	inspiration, participation

Your Turn

Use the charts on this page to help you answer the following questions.

1. What is the smallest number of people needed to *coauthor* a book?
2. Where might a ship go if it were to *circumnavigate* the world?
3. How might someone show *deference* to an elder?
4. What might you add to lemon juice to *dilute* it?
5. Would someone who is *ingenuous* tell a lie?

Language Coach

Forming Nouns from Adjectives Many adjectives have related nouns. Describe how each of the following nouns is related to a Vocabulary word and explain its meaning.

1. tranquility   2. virulence   3. archaism

Academic Vocabulary

Talk About

How <u>inevitable</u> is it that today's conventional <u>ideology</u> will be handed down as <u>tradition</u>?

Grammar Link

Troublesome Modifiers

A **modifier** makes the meaning of another word more specific. The two kinds of modifiers are **adjectives** and **adverbs.** Adjectives modify nouns, and adverbs modify verbs, adjectives, and other adverbs. Some **troublesome modifiers** frequently cause confusion. For example, *bad* is an adjective, while *badly* is an adverb.

> When Faulkner was young, his prospects were **bad.**
> He wanted **badly** to succeed as a writer.

Well can be either an adverb or an adjective, but *good* is an adjective and does not modify verbs.

> Faulkner's work was not always **well** received.
> No matter how **good** his novels were, they were too bold and different for some readers.

Slow also can be an adjective or an adverb. *Slowly* is an adverb and is the better form for most adverb uses.

> Fame was **slow** to come to Faulkner.
> His reputation built **slowly,** over many years.

Your Turn

Choose the correct modifiers from the pairs in parentheses in the following sentences.

1. "A Rose for Emily" is a (*real, really*) unusual story.
2. Emily is an old woman who is used to being treated (*good, well*) by the whole town.
3. People complain about a (*bad, badly*) smell coming from Emily's house.
4. Faulkner's description of a small Southern town is very (*good, well*).

Writing Application Use the words in each pair in sentences that illustrate their function as adjectives or adverbs.

    bad, badly   *good, well*   *real, really*   *slow, slowly*

CHOICES

As you respond to the Choices, use these **Academic Vocabulary** words as appropriate: <u>alternative</u>, <u>hierarchy</u>, <u>ideology</u>, <u>inevitable</u>, <u>tradition</u>.

REVIEW

Analyze Faulkner's Mood

Timed ⌐Writing As you read "A Rose for Emily," you recorded passages of description related to the mood of the tale. Write a short essay analyzing how Faulkner uses descriptive details to convey this story's Gothic mood. Be sure to cite specific evidence from the story to support your analysis.

CONNECT

Investigate Miss Emily

Today, a sensational story like this one would <u>inevitably</u> make the cable news. Create your own investigative report like one a news show might air. It could involve interviews with townspeople, sketches of the house and what was found there, and background information on Emily and her family. You might also consider what information modern forensic technology might provide for your report. If you have access to a camera, film your investigative report. If not, present it live to your class.

EXTEND

Be a Good Neighbor

Group Discussion How should people treat neighbors who are reclusive or eccentric? Should they try to include them in social activities or leave them alone? With a group, debate this question. Focus on Emily's case and on specific examples from literature, film, or the news.

Learn It Online
Take a trip to Faulkner's world with these Internet links.

go.hrw.com   L11-887   **Go**

Reader/Writer
Notebook
Use your **RWN** to complete the activities for this selection.

Informational Text Focus

Analyzing an Author's Beliefs An **author's beliefs** are the ideas that he or she wants to communicate to the audience. To analyze an author's beliefs about a particular topic, identify what he or she says directly. Then, identify the patterns or similarities in these statements, and think about what larger philosophical ideas they reveal. As you read the following speech, analyze Faulkner's beliefs about the ultimate purpose of writers and writing.

Into Action As you read, use a web like the one below to record Faulkner's statements about writers and literature.

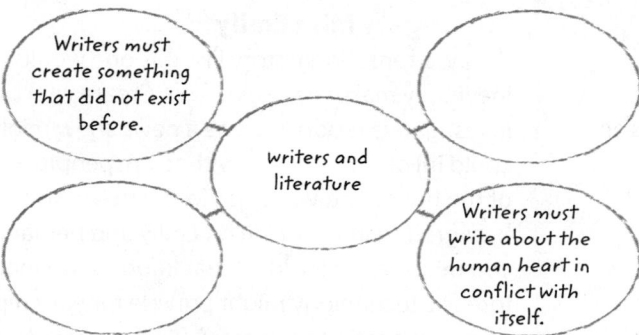

Writers must create something that did not exist before.

writers and literature

Writers must write about the human heart in conflict with itself.

Writing Focus Preparing for **Constructed Response**

In his speech, Faulkner often draws attention to his main ideas through **repetition** and **parallel structure.** For example, in the last paragraph, Faulkner repeats the idea that human beings will not merely endure but will <u>inevitably</u> prevail. He uses parallel structure when he speaks of the writer: "He writes not of love but of lust. . . . He writes not of the heart but of the glands." As you read, record in your *Reader/Writer Notebook* examples of repetition and parallel structure that Faulkner uses to convey some of his most important ideas.

Vocabulary

commensurate (kuh MEHN shuhr iht) *adj.:* equal to; proportional. *Faulkner found a use for his acclaim commensurate with its purpose and meaning.*

pinnacle (PIHN uh kuhl) *n.:* highest point; apex. *His acceptance of the Nobel Prize was a pinnacle from which to tell the world about his beliefs.*

ephemeral (ih FEHM uhr uhl) *adj.:* short-lived; fleeting. *Unless a story is about universal truths, it will prove to be shallow and ephemeral.*

Language Coach
Formal Versus Informal Language
Some words sound more formal than others. In this speech, Faulkner uses the word *commensurate* when he might have used the phrase *equal to.* They have almost the same meaning, but *commensurate*—which means "equal in measure or length"—has a specificity that makes it rarer. People may only use it when they feel the situation calls for the most precise language, as in a formal speech. Do the other Vocabulary words feel formal or informal? What words might Faulkner have used instead?

Learn It Online
Hear an actor bring this speech to life online.

go.hrw.com   L11-888   Go

Nobel Prize Acceptance Speech, 1950

by **William Faulkner**

Read with a Purpose
Read to learn what Faulkner asks young writers to do—and why.

Build Background
Faulkner expresses anxieties widely felt in the wake of World War II. In 1945, the United States detonated the first nuclear bombs over Hiroshima and Nagasaki. The devastation stunned the world. By 1949, the Soviet Union became the second nuclear power, triggering fears of global nuclear war.

I feel that this award was not made to me as a man, but to my work—a life's work in the agony and sweat of the human spirit, not for glory and least of all for profit, but to create out of the materials of the human spirit something which did not exist before. So this award is only mine in trust. It will not be difficult to find a dedication for the money part of it commensurate with the purpose and significance of its origin. But I would like to do the same with the acclaim too, by using this moment as a pinnacle from which I might be listened to by the young men and women already dedicated to the same anguish and travail, among whom is already that one who will someday stand here where I am standing.

Our tragedy today is a general and universal physical fear so long sustained by now that we can even bear it. There are no longer problems of the spirit. There is only the question: Whenw will I be blown up? Because of this, the young man or woman writing today has forgotten the problems of the human heart in conflict with itself which alone can make good writing because only that is worth writing about, worth the agony and the sweat.

He must learn them again. He must teach himself that the basest of all things is to be afraid; and, teaching himself that, forget it forever, leaving no room in his workshop for anything but the old verities and truths of the heart, the old universal truths lacking which any story is ephemeral and doomed— love and honor and pity and pride and compassion and sacrifice. Until he does so, he labors under a curse. He writes not of love but of lust, of defeats in which

Vocabulary **commensurate** (kuh MEHN shuhr iht) *adj.:* equal to; proportional.
pinnacle (PIHN uh kuhl) *n.:* highest point; apex.
ephemeral (ih FEHM uhr uhl) *adj.:* short-lived; fleeting.

nobody loses anything of value, of victories without hope and, worst of all, without pity or compassion. His griefs grieve on no universal bones, leaving no scars. He writes not of the heart but of the glands. **A**

Until he relearns these things, he will write as though he stood among and watched the end of man. I decline to accept the end of man. It is easy enough to say that man is immortal simply because he will endure: that when the last dingdong of doom has clanged and faded from the last worthless rock hanging tideless in the last red and dying evening, that even then there will still be one more sound: that of his puny inexhaustible voice, still talking. I refuse to accept this. I believe that man will not merely endure: he will prevail. He is immortal, not because he alone among creatures has an inexhaustible voice, but because he has a soul, a spirit capable of compassion and sacrifice and endurance. The poet's, the writer's, duty is to write about these things. It is his privilege to help man endure by lifting his heart, by reminding him of the courage and honor and hope and pride and compassion and pity and sacrifice which have been the glory of his past. The poet's voice need not merely be the record of man, it can be one of the props, the pillars to help him endure and prevail. **B**

Willbac Faulkner

The Granger Collection, New York.

William Faulkner (right) accepts the 1949 Nobel Prize in Literature from King Gustaf VI of Sweden.

A Informational Focus Analyzing an Author's Beliefs What does Faulkner mean when he says that fear leads writers to write "not of the heart but of the glands"? How does this distinction help you to understand Faulkner's beliefs about the purpose of writing?

B Informational Focus Analyzing an Author's Beliefs What is the ultimate purpose of a poet or writer according to Faulkner?

Applying Your Skills

SKILLS FOCUS **Informational Skills** Analyze an author's beliefs. **Vocabulary Skills** Demonstrate knowledge of literal meanings of words and their usage. **Writing Skills** Write brief constructed responses with specific support. **Listening and Speaking Skills** Evaluate persuasive presentations.

Nobel Prize Acceptance Speech, 1950

Respond and Think Critically

Informational Text Focus

Quick Check

1. How does Faulkner's speech reflect the anxieties felt in the wake of World War II?

2. Why does Faulkner urge writers to write of universal truths rather than the end of humankind?

Read with a Purpose

3. How does Faulkner think writers can help human beings to endure and prevail?

Informational Skills: Analyzing an Author's Beliefs

4. As you read, you used a web to record statements about writers and literature. Review the information in your web, and think about how the statements relate to one another. Draw lines to connect statements that convey similar ideas or reveal a pattern. Then, in a paragraph, sum up Faulkner's beliefs about writers and writing.

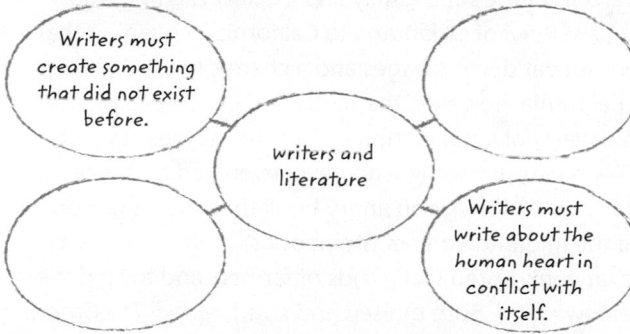

Writers must create something that did not exist before.

writers and literature

Writers must write about the human heart in conflict with itself.

✓ Vocabulary Check

Match each Vocabulary word to its synonym.

5. commensurate   a. apex

6. pinnacle   b. temporary

7. ephemeral   c. equivalent

Text Analysis

8. **Analyze** Faulkner states that any story that does not deal with ultimate truths is "doomed." Why do you think Faulkner believes this? Do you agree?

9. **Evaluate** Why do you think Faulkner's speech is so highly regarded?

10. **Extend** Faulkner says, "I believe that man will not merely endure: he will prevail." Is this message still relevant today? Explain.

11. **Compare and Contrast** In this speech, Faulkner urges writers to tackle "the old universal truths… love and honor and pity and pride and compassion and sacrifice." Do you think Faulkner follows his own advice in "A Rose for Emily"?

Listening and Speaking

12. **Analyze** Discourse that uses emotional appeals and reason to convince a reader to think or act in a certain way is called **persuasion. Persuasive devices** include loaded words and figurative language that arouse the emotions of the audience as well as appeals to logic such as evidence, facts, and statistics. With a partner, identify emotional and logical appeals in Faulkner's speech.

Writing Focus   Constructed Response

What do you think makes writing lasting and powerful? Compose one or two paragraphs explaining your vision of great writing. Use repetition and parallel structure to emphasize your most important points.

What Do You Think Now

How can literature help the human race endure and progress during difficult times?

Preparing to Read

from *The Grapes of Wrath*, Chapter 17

What Do You Think How does progress challenge tradition and redefine society?

QuickTalk

Think about the ways in which technology affects workers' lives. With a partner, talk about examples of the positive and negative effects of technological progress on working people.

John Steinbeck
(1902–1968)

Nobel Prize WINNER

When John Steinbeck received the Nobel Prize in literature in 1962, the Academy cited his "great feeling for nature" and his sympathy for "the oppressed, the misfits, the distressed." He is chiefly remembered today for his stories about common people, their dignity, and their dreams.

Working at Odd Jobs

Steinbeck was born in California's Salinas Valley. After graduating from high school, he spent some time at Stanford University without taking a degree. He worked as a mason's assistant, fruit picker, apprentice painter, laboratory assistant, caretaker, surveyor, and journalist. These jobs gave him enduring empathy for the downtrodden, which was to color much of his work.

Writing in the Field

Steinbeck wrote seventeen novels, in addition to stories, plays, and screenplays. His first major success came in 1937 with *Of Mice and Men,* a short, bestselling novel that Steinbeck himself adapted for the Broadway theater. Steinbeck followed this success by living and working with some Oklahoma farmers—known as Okies—over the next two years. The result was his strongest and most enduring novel, *The Grapes of Wrath* (1939). This novel tells of the Joad family and their forced migration from the Dust Bowl of Oklahoma to California, the region that promised work at decent wages and a chance to buy land. Once in California, however, the Joads find only the exploitation and poverty of labor camps. Gradually, they learn what *Okies* really means—people who never even had a chance.

    The Grapes of Wrath is an angry book that speaks out on behalf of the migrant workers. Steinbeck sharply criticizes a system that bankrupted thousands of farmers and turned them from their own land. Both praised and condemned, *The Grapes of Wrath* became the most widely read novel of the 1930s. It won a Pulitzer Prize in 1940. Steinbeck continued to write through the 1960s, but his work from the 1930s defines him.

Think About the Writer How might Steinbeck's experiences working with the Okies have inspired him to write *The Grapes of Wrath*? Explain.

Reader/Writer Notebook

Use your **RWN** to complete the activities for this selection.

Literary Focus

Tone A writer's attitude toward his or her subject, characters, or audience is called **tone.** Tone depends on **diction** and **style.** Tone can usually be described in a single word, for example, *ironic, solemn, affectionate, humorous.* In *The Grapes of Wrath,* Steinbeck writes reverently of migrant workers, but his reverence cannot mask his anger at the injustice of their situation. Steinbeck's word choice reveals his attitudes.

Literary Perspectives Apply the literary perspective described on page 895 as you read this novel excerpt.

Reading Focus

Analyzing Repetition The **repetition** of words, sounds, syllables, phrases, or text structures can create rhythm, reinforce messages, and establish a tone. Repetition can also offer clues to a writer's attitude and purpose. To analyze repetition, look at the elements the writer chooses to repeat. Where do they appear in the text? How do they sound?

Into Action As you read, note examples of repetition in a chart like the one below.

Line with repetition	Repeated words or phrases within line
"In the daylight they scuttled like bugs...they clustered like bugs near to shelter and to water." (p. 895)	like bugs

Writing Focus

Think as a Reader/Writer

Find It in Your Reading If you are used to thinking of adjectives as descriptive words, the writing adage "Describe with verbs!" may seem paradoxical. However, when used precisely, verbs can serve as an <u>alternative</u> to adjectives, as when Steinbeck speaks of the migrant people who *scuttled, clustered,* and *huddled.* As you read, use your *Reader/Writer Notebook* to keep track of the verbs Steinbeck uses to present people in motion.

Vocabulary

migrant (MY gruhnt) *adj.*: migrating. *The migrant workers moved often to take advantage of seasonal work.*

perplexed (puhr PLEHKST) *v.* used as *adj.*: confused, puzzled. *Families, perplexed at the failure of their farms, scrambled to find new means of surviving.*

transcend (tran SEHND) *v.*: surpass; go above. *The effects of the Dust Bowl transcend the cares of a handful of families; it was a major human tragedy.*

ostracism (AHS truh sihz uhm) *n.*: banishment; act of being shut out or excluded. *Because the group members depend on each other for survival, ostracism is the worst punishment an individual can receive.*

endanger (ehn DAYN juhr) *v.*: put in danger; jeopardize. *People were careful not to endanger the pregnant and the sick.*

lusted (LUHS tihd) *v.*: strongly desired. *The uprooted families lusted for new homes and farms.*

Language Coach

Prefixes The prefix *en*– can mean "make; put in." The word *endanger* means to "put in danger." How does this prefix help you understand the origin of the word *encourage?*

Learn It Online
Use the reading tips and strategies on the *NovelWise* mini-site to help you with this novel excerpt.

go.hrw.com   L11-893   **Go**

from

The Grapes of Wrath

C H A P T E R   17

by **John Steinbeck**

Wraparound jacket of the first edition (1939).
The Granger Collection, New York.

Read with a Purpose

Read to learn how people who leave everything they have ever known create a new, makeshift community.

Build Background

In the 1930s, a severe drought wiped out thousands of acres of farmland in the heartland of the United States. A series of dust storms swept away the topsoil, making it impossible for farmers to till the land and support their families. The afflicted region became known as the Dust Bowl. With no relief in sight, many people headed west in the hope of finding work to feed their families. Leaving with whatever they could carry, these people traveled the cross-country highways from Oklahoma, Arkansas, Kansas, Missouri, Texas, and other states. Their iconic struggle influenced artists as diverse as the songwriters Woody Guthrie and Bob Dylan, photographers Dorothea Lange and Walker Evans, and writers James Agee, Nathanael West, and John Steinbeck. Throughout *The Grapes of Wrath,* Steinbeck interrupts the narrative with passages like this one, which describes the greater social movements taking place and presents the backdrop for the Joad family's tale of aspiration and heartbreak.

There grew up government in the worlds, with leaders, with elders. A man who was wise found that his wisdom was needed in every camp; a man who was a fool could not change his folly with his world. And a kind of insurance developed in these nights. A man with food fed a hungry man, and thus insured himself against hunger. And when a baby died a pile of silver coins grew at the door flap, for a baby must be well buried, since it has had nothing else of life. An old man may be left in a potter's field,[2] but not a baby.

A certain physical pattern is needed for the building of a world—water, a river bank, a stream, a spring, or even a faucet unguarded. And there is

---

2. **potter's field:** an area set aside to bury people who were poor or unknown.

needed enough flat land to pitch the tents, a little brush or wood to build the fires. If there is a garbage dump not too far off, all the better; for there can be found equipment—stove tops, a curved fender to shelter the fire, and cans to cook in and to eat from.

And the worlds were built in the evening. The people, moving in from the highways, made them with their tents and their hearts and their brains. **E**

In the morning the tents came down, the canvas was folded, the tent poles tied along the running board, the beds put in place on the cars, the pots in their places. And as the families moved westward, the technique of building up a home in the evening and tearing it down with the morning light became fixed; so that the folded tent was packed in one place, the cooking pots counted in their box. And as the cars

E **Literary Focus** **Tone** How would you describe Steinbeck's attitude toward the migrant people in the first three paragraphs on this page?

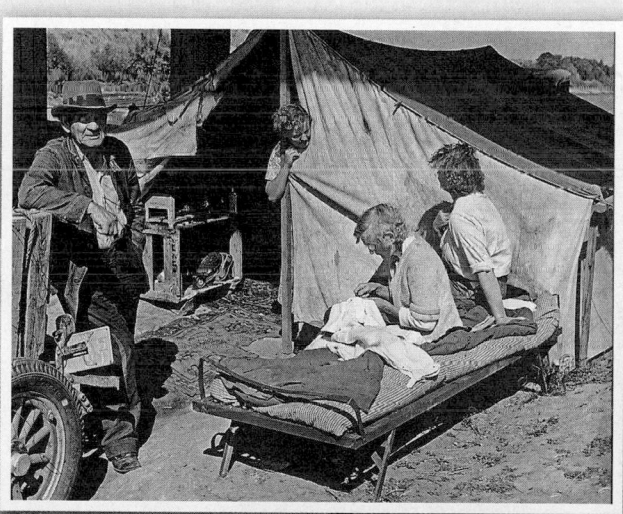

Analyzing Visuals

Viewing and Interpreting Examine the black-and-white photographs—on pages 896–899—of migrants during the Great Depression. What do the details in these images add to the picture of migrants created by Steinbeck in the adjacent excerpt from *The Grapes of Wrath*? Explain your response.

moved westward, each member of the family grew into his proper place, grew into his duties; so that each member, old and young, had his place in the car; so that in the weary, hot evenings, when the cars pulled into the camping places, each member had his duty and went to it without instruction: children to gather wood, to carry water; men to pitch the tents and bring down the beds; women to cook the supper and to watch while the family fed. And this was done without command. The families, which had been units of which the boundaries were a house at night, a farm by day, changed their boundaries. In the long hot light, they were silent in the cars moving slowly westward; but at night they integrated with any group they found. **F**

Thus they changed their social life—changed as in the whole universe only man can change. They were not farm men any more, but migrant men. And the thought, the planning, the long staring silence that had gone out to the fields, went now to the roads, to the distance, to the West. That man whose mind had been bound with acres lived with narrow concrete miles. And his thought and his worry were not any more with rainfall, with wind and dust, with the thrust of the crops. Eyes watched the tires, ears listened to the clattering motors, and minds struggled with oil, with gasoline, with the thinning rubber between air and road. Then a broken gear was tragedy. Then water in the evening was the yearning, and food over the fire. Then health to go on was the need and strength to go on, and spirit to go on. The wills thrust westward ahead of them, and fears that had once apprehended drought or flood now lingered with anything that might stop the westward crawling. **G**

The camps became fixed—each a short day's journey from the last.

And on the road the panic overcame some of the families, so that they drove night and day, stopped

---

F **Reading Focus** **Analyzing Repetition** Steinbeck begins this paragraph with a string of tasks. What effects do repetitive word choices and structures create in this passage?

G **Literary Perspectives** **Analyzing Political Context** The migrants' concerns have shifted from nature to machines. What might Steinbeck be saying about the connection between technology and tragedy? How is technology related to social advantage?

to sleep in the cars, and drove on to the West, flying from the road, flying from movement. And these lusted so greatly to be settled that they set their faces into the West and drove toward it, forcing the clashing engines over the roads.

But most of the families changed and grew quickly into the new life. And when the sun went down——

Time to look out for a place to stop.

And—there's some tents ahead.

The car pulled off the road and stopped, and because others were there first, certain courtesies were necessary. And the man, the leader of the family, leaned from the car.

Can we pull up here an' sleep?

Why, sure, be proud to have you. What State you from?

Come all the way from Arkansas.

They's Arkansas people down that fourth tent.

That so?

And the great question, How's the water?

Well, she don't taste so good, but they's plenty.

Well, thank ya.

No thanks to me.

But the courtesies had to be. The car lumbered over the ground to the end tent, and stopped. Then down from the car the weary people climbed, and stretched stiff bodies. Then the new tent sprang up; the children went for water and the older boys cut brush or wood. The fires started and supper was put on to boil or to fry. Early comers moved over, and States were exchanged, and friends and sometimes relatives discovered.

Oklahoma, huh? What county?

Cherokee.

Why, I got folks from there. Know the Allens? They's Allens all over Cherokee. Know the Willises?

Why sure. **H**

And a new unit was formed. The dusk came, but before the dark was down the new family was of the camp. A word had been passed with every family. They were known people—good people.

H **Literary Perspectives** **Analyzing Political Context** How might the migrants' courtesies in the midst of hardship reflect a social message?

Vocabulary **lusted** (LUHS tihd) *v.:* strongly desired.

Applying Your Skills

from The Grapes of Wrath, Chapter 17

Respond and Think Critically

Reading Focus

Quick Check

1. Why do the migrant families become expert at setting up camp?

2. How do the migrant families provide a sense of security and order within the camps?

Read with a Purpose

3. How do people find their places within the hierarchy of the shifting migrant groups?

Reading Skills: Analyzing Repetition

4. While reading this novel excerpt, you noted examples of repetition. Now, add a column to your chart. In it, note how each example of repetition affects Steinbeck's tone.

Line with repetition	Repeated words or phrases within line	Effect on tone
"In the daylight they scuttled like bugs... they clustered like bugs near to shelter and to water." (p. 895)	like bugs	Shows how desperate they are living in subhuman conditions

Literary Focus

Literary Analysis

5. **Analyze** In this chapter, Steinbeck breaks with traditional narrative form to present the circumstances that surround his main characters without including them. What is the effect of this technique? In the absence of a protagonist, what or whom do you care about most?

6. **Draw Conclusions** At the end of this excerpt, why do you think Steinbeck presents dialogue without identifying the speakers?

7. **Analyze** Steinbeck shows the evolution of the migrants' social order, from instincts to rights to rules to laws. What might he be saying about societies in general?

8. **Literary Perspectives** Migrant workers of the 1930s met with scorn, prejudice, and outright hostility. What social classes receive similar treatment today? Who profits from their situation? Is it possible for a society to exist free from exploitation? Explain.

Literary Skills: Tone

9. **Compare and Contrast** A writer's **tone** is his or her attitude toward a story's characters, subject, or audience. Who is Steinbeck's intended audience? What is his attitude toward them? Compare and contrast his tone toward his subject with his tone toward his audience.

Literary Skills Review: Dialect

10. **Evaluate** Locate passages in which the characters use **dialect,** a way of speaking that is characteristic of a specific group of people. What does their use of dialect convey about the speakers?

Writing Focus

Think as a Reader/Writer

Use It in Your Writing Think about a road trip—real or imaginary—that you have taken or would like to

 **What Do You Think Now** How do the migrant people overcome hardships and persevere in the face of threats to their way of life?

SKILLS FOCUS Literary Skills Analyze tone; analyze dialect. **Reading Skills** Analyze repetition. **Vocabulary Skills**

Understand connotation. **Writing Skills** Employ precise language for effective writing; employ literary devices for effective writing.

Vocabulary Development

✔ Vocabulary Check

Match each Vocabulary word with its synonym.

1. ostracism
2. migrant
3. transcend
4. perplexed
5. endanger
6. lusted

a. traveling
b. threaten
c. confused
d. surpass
e. desired
f. rejection

Vocabulary Skills: Connotations

Connotation helps writers establish tone by conveying emotions associated with a word's meaning. A connotation, whether positive or negative, is subjective. The word *wealth* may have a positive connotation ("prosperity") or a negative one ("excess"), depending on the bias of the person using the word.

Your Turn

Each group of words below denotes, or means, roughly the same thing, but each word has a slightly different connotation. For each group, write a few sentences describing the differences between the words, explaining how some are more negative, positive, or neutral.

1. ostracism, exile, exclusion
2. migrant, wandering, vagrant
3. perplexed, baffled, unsure

Language Coach

Prefix Explain the meaning of each word. Use a dictionary to check your answers.

1. encode 3. ennoble 5. enshrine

CHOICES

As you respond to the Choices, use these **Academic Vocabulary** words as appropriate: <u>alternative</u>, <u>hierarchy</u>, <u>ideology</u>, <u>inevitable</u>, <u>tradition</u>.

REVIEW
Record the Codes

Create a written document to record all the rights, rules, laws, and punishments the migrant people create to maintain order and peace in this excerpt from *The Grapes of Wrath*. Why do you think the migrants left these laws unwritten? Explain your response.

CONNECT
Describe Modern Migrants

If this story were set today, what group of people would it depict? Where would they travel? What difficulties would they encounter? Why would they be on the road? To what position in the social or economic <u>hierarchy</u> would they aspire? Write a few paragraphs of fiction about migrants today. Express your attitude toward your characters and their situation in the tone of your narrative.

EXTEND
Create a "Photo" Collection

TechFocus Visit the Library of Congress's American Memory collection online to view photographs of the migrants of the 1930s and 1940s. Use these pictures to visualize the people and places in *The Grapes of Wrath*. What do you think the characters would have photographed if they had cameras? Create a "photo" collection for the text by sketching the people and events in the novel excerpt as if the characters had taken photographs of them. Label the pictures as the characters might have.

Learn It Online
Learn more about Steinbeck through these Internet links.

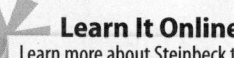 go.hrw.com L11-901   Go

Preparing to Read

A Worn Path

What Do You Think How does progress challenge <u>tradition</u> and redefine society?

QuickTalk

Sometimes an ordinary journey can turn out to be difficult. With a partner, discuss a journey that you or someone you know undertook. Discuss the purpose and outcome of the journey and any hardships encountered. Did the journey lead to greater self-knowledge or understanding? Explain.

Eudora Welty
(1909–2001)

Pulitzer Prize WINNER

Eudora Welty's life and writing are strongly connected to her Mississippi home. Her short stories and novels provide fascinating accounts of the people and places of the American South.

Home in Mississippi

Eudora Welty was born in the quintessentially Southern city of Jackson, Mississippi, where she lived almost her whole life. As the daughter of an insurance man and a schoolteacher, she enjoyed a <u>traditional</u> Southern girlhood. She recalled pleading with her brothers to teach her golf, sharing with them an enthusiasm for baseball, and bicycling to the library while wearing *two* petticoats to forestall the librarian's sarcastic remark, "I can practically see through you."

Welty attended Mississippi State College for Women, graduated from the University of Wisconsin, and did graduate work at Columbia University, anticipating a career in advertising. However, the Depression sent her home to Jackson with a belief that she would succeed as a writer of fiction.

Blessed with a Visual Mind

Welty's first collections of stories, *A Curtain of Green* and *The Wide Net,* appeared in the 1940s. These were followed by *The Golden Apples* (1949), one of her best-known volumes of short stories. Then came a novella, *The Ponder Heart* (1954), which was made into a Broadway play. *Losing Battles,* her comic novel about a family reunion in the rural South, was published in 1970. Two years later she produced the Pulitzer Prize–winning *The Optimist's Daughter,* a gripping novel about family conflicts.

Welty is recognized for painstaking accuracy in colloquial, or everyday, speech. She was fascinated by words and by snatches of overheard dialogue. Welty was blessed with a visual mind, and she said that this gift makes for "the best shorthand a writer can have." She once wrote, "To watch everything about me I regarded grimly and possessively as a need." That need became an enviable artistic vision.

Think About the Writer How can a quiet life also be an active life?

Reader/Writer Notebook

Use your **RWN** to complete the activities for this selection.

Literary Focus

Theme A story's main insight into human life is its **theme.** Theme is almost never directly stated. Instead, the writer hopes that readers will enter into the experiences of the characters and share the discoveries they make as they face **conflict.** When you think about the theme of a story, think about what happens to the main **character.** Does the character discover or learn something? Does the character accomplish something important? As you read "A Worn Path," think about how following the woman on her path might help you understand your own path in life.

Reading Focus

Identifying Details To discover the theme of a story, pay attention to the **details,** the smaller, intricate parts that form the story's whole. A detail might take the form of a character description, a bit of **dialogue,** an interesting object, or a **figure of speech**. These words and phrases can hint at the deeper significance of the story's events.

Into Action Use a chart to record details from the story. Focus on details about characters and the journey. As you identify details, ask yourself what each detail reveals about Phoenix Jackson and her journey.

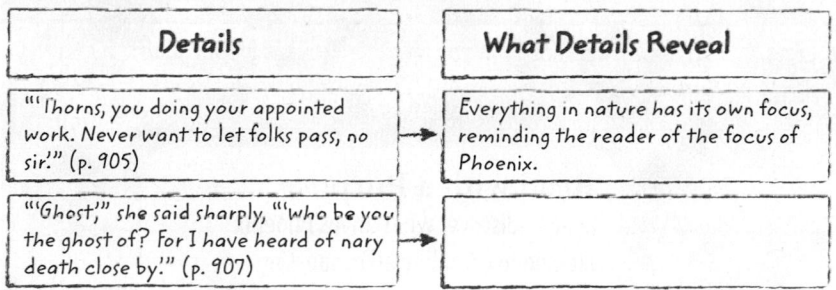

Details	What Details Reveal
"'Thorns, you doing your appointed work. Never want to let folks pass, no sir!'" (p. 905)	Everything in nature has its own focus, reminding the reader of the focus of Phoenix.
"'Ghost,'" she said sharply, "'who be you the ghost of? For I have heard of nary death close by.'" (p. 907)	

Vocabulary

persistent (puhr SIHS tuhnt) *adj.:* continuing. *As she walked, the old woman tapped her cane, making a steady, persistent noise.*

illumined (ih LOO muhnd) *v.:* lit up. *Hope illumined her face like a lamp.*

intent (ihn TEHNT) *adj.:* purposeful. *The old woman's fingers were intent on keeping her dress from tearing on the thorny bush.*

appointed (uh POYN I uhd) *v.* used as *adj.:* assigned. *The thorny bush's appointed work was to keep people from passing by.*

solemn (SAHL uhm) *adj.:* serious. *The old woman's face remained solemn when the nurse asked her about her grandson.*

Language Coach

Word Origins The verb *illumined* comes from the Latin word meaning "light." *Illumination* and *luster* are related to the same root. So is the noun *luminary,* which means "a notable or famous person." How do you think the meaning of *luminary* connects to its Latin origin?

Writing Focus

Think as a Reader/Writer

Find It in Your Reading In "A Worn Path," Welty vividly re-creates Phoenix's journey by using sensory **details** based on the senses of sight, smell, sound, taste, and touch. For example, Phoenix's tapping cane makes a "grave and persistent noise in the still air, that seemed meditative like the chirping of a solitary little bird." As you read, use your *Reader/Writer Notebook* to record other examples of details that appeal to the senses.

Learn It Online
Listen to the story read aloud online.

go.hrw.com   L11-903   **Go**

A WORN PATH

by **Eudora Welty**

Read with a Purpose

Read to discover what drives Phoenix Jackson to complete an exhausting journey.

Build Background

"A Worn Path" takes place during the Great Depression of the 1930s, a time when one fourth to one third of America's workers were unemployed. As a result, many people were forced to rely on charity for food, medicine, and even shelter. As you read this story, look for clues to the hard life of America's poor during this time period.

It was December—a bright frozen day in the early morning. Far out in the country there was an old Negro woman with her head tied in a red rag, coming along a path through the pinewoods. Her name was Phoenix Jackson. She was very old and small and she walked slowly in the dark pine shadows, moving a little from side to side in her steps, with the balanced heaviness and lightness of a pendulum in a grandfather clock. She carried a thin, small cane made from an umbrella, and with this she kept tapping the frozen earth in front of her. This made a grave and persistent noise in the still air, that seemed meditative like the chirping of a solitary little bird.

She wore a dark striped dress reaching down to her shoe tops, and an equally long apron of bleached sugar sacks, with a full pocket: all neat and tidy, but every time she took a step she might have fallen over her shoelaces, which dragged from her unlaced shoes. She looked straight ahead. Her eyes were blue with age. Her skin had a pattern all its own of numberless branching wrinkles and as though a whole little tree stood in the middle of her forehead, but a golden color ran underneath, and the two knobs of her cheeks were illumined by a yellow burning under the dark. Under the red rag her hair came down on her neck in the frailest of ringlets, still black, and with an odor like copper. **A**

Now and then there was a quivering in the thicket. Old Phoenix said, "Out of my way, all you foxes, owls, beetles, jack rabbits, coons, and wild animals! . . . Keep out from under these feet, little bobwhites. . . . Keep the big wild hogs out of my path. Don't let none of those come running in my direction. I got a long way." Under her small black-freckled hand her cane, limber as a buggy whip, would switch at the brush as if to rouse up any hiding things.

On she went. The woods were deep and still. The sun made the pine needles almost too bright to look at, up where the wind rocked. The cones dropped as light as feathers. Down in the hollow was the mourning dove—it was not too late for him.

The path ran up a hill. "Seem like there is chains about my feet, time I get this far," she said, in the voice of argument old people keep to use with themselves. "Something always take a hold of me on this hill—pleads I should stay."

After she got to the top she turned and gave a full, severe look behind her where she had come. "Up through pines," she said at length. "Now down through oaks." **B**

Her eyes opened their widest, and she started down gently. But before she got to the bottom of the hill a bush caught her dress.

Her fingers were busy and intent, but her skirts were full and long, so that before she could pull them free in one place they were caught in another. It was not possible to allow the dress to tear. "I in the thorny bush," she said. "Thorns, you doing your appointed work. Never want to let folks pass, no sir. Old eyes thought you was a pretty little green bush."

Finally, trembling all over, she stood free, and after a moment dared to stoop for her cane.

"Sun so high!" she cried, leaning back and looking, while the thick tears went over her eyes. "The time getting all gone here." At the foot of this hill was a place where a log was laid across the creek.

"Now comes the trial," said Phoenix.

Putting her right foot out, she mounted the log and shut her eyes. Lifting her skirt, leveling her cane fiercely before her, like a festival figure in some parade, she began to march across. Then she opened her eyes and she was safe on the other side.

"I wasn't as old as I thought," she said. **C**

But she sat down to rest. She spread her skirts on the bank around her and folded her hands over her knees. Up above her was a tree in a pearly cloud of mistletoe. She did not dare to close her eyes, and when a little boy brought her a plate with a slice of marble

---

A Reading Focus **Identifying Details** What does the description of Phoenix's face reveal about her? How is Phoenix herself like a worn path?

B Reading Focus **Identifying Details** What details show that Phoenix has traveled this path before?

C Literary Focus **Theme** What do you learn about Phoenix from the way she responds to the thorny bush and the log bridge?

Vocabulary **persistent** (puhr SIHS tuhnt) *adj.*: continuing.
illumined (ih LOO muhnd) *v.*: lit up.
intent (ihn TEHNT) *adj.*: purposeful.
appointed (uh POYNT uhd) *v.* used as *adj.*: assigned.

Analyzing Visuals

Viewing and Interpreting
The path in this photograph is uphill and mostly in shadow. How does this image relate to Phoenix Jackson's path in the story?

cake on it she spoke to him. "That would be acceptable," she said. But when she went to take it there was just her own hand in the air. **D**

So she left that tree, and had to go through a barbed-wire fence. There she had to creep and crawl, spreading her knees and stretching her fingers like a baby trying to climb the steps. But she talked loudly to herself: She could not let her dress be torn now, so late in the day, and she could not pay for having her arm or her leg sawed off if she got caught fast where she was.

At last she was safe through the fence and risen up out in the clearing. Big dead trees, like black men with one arm, were standing in the purple stalks of the withered cotton field. There sat a buzzard.[1]

"Who you watching?"

In the furrow[2] she made her way along.

"Glad this not the season for bulls," she said, looking sideways, "and the good Lord made his snakes to curl up and sleep in the winter. A pleasure I don't see no two-headed snake coming around that tree, where it come once. It took a while to get by him, back in the summer."

She passed through the old cotton and went into a field of dead corn. It whispered and shook and was taller than her head. "Through the maze now," she said, for there was no path. **E**

Then there was something tall, black, and skinny there, moving before her.

---

1. **buzzard:** a large scavenger bird that eats the remains of dead animals. Buzzards are often symbolic of death.

2. **furrow:** groove in the land made by a plow.

D **Literary Focus** **Theme** What does Phoenix imagine when she sits down to rest? What does this vision reveal about her motivation for making the journey?

E **Reading Focus** **Identifying Details** The images of the black trees, the buzzard, the old cotton, and the field of dead corn vividly illustrate the winter landscape. What greater significance might these images have?

At first she took it for a man. It could have been a man dancing in the field. But she stood still and listened, and it did not make a sound. It was as silent as a ghost.

"Ghost," she said sharply, "who be you the ghost of? For I have heard of nary death close by."

But there was no answer—only the ragged dancing in the wind.

She shut her eyes, reached out her hand, and touched a sleeve. She found a coat and inside that an emptiness, cold as ice.

"You scarecrow," she said. Her face lighted. "I ought to be shut up for good," she said with laughter. "My senses is gone. I too old. I the oldest people I ever know. Dance, old scarecrow," she said, "while I dancing with you." **F**

She kicked her foot over the furrow, and with mouth drawn down, shook her head once or twice in a little strutting way. Some husks blew down and whirled in streamers about her skirts.

Then she went on, parting her way from side to side with the cane, through the whispering field. At last she came to the end, to a wagon track where the silver grass blew between the red ruts. The quail were walking around like pullets[3], seeming all dainty and unseen.

"Walk pretty," she said. "This the easy place. This the easy going."

She followed the track, swaying through the quiet bare fields, through the little strings of trees silver in their dead leaves, past cabins silver from weather, with the doors and windows boarded shut, all like old women under a spell sitting there. "I walking in their sleep," she said, nodding her head vigorously.

In a ravine she went where a spring was silently flowing through a hollow log. Old Phoenix bent and drank. "Sweet gum makes the water sweet," she said, and drank more. "Nobody know who made this well, for it was here when I was born."

The track crossed a swampy part where the moss hung as white as lace from every limb. "Sleep on, alligators, and blow your bubbles." Then the track went into the road. **G**

---

3. **pullets:** young hens.

Deep, deep the road went down between the high green-colored banks. Overhead the live oaks met, and it was as dark as a cave.

A black dog with a lolling tongue came up out of the weeds by the ditch. She was meditating, and not ready, and when he came at her she only hit him a little with her cane. Over she went in the ditch, like a little puff of milkweed.

Down there, her senses drifted away. A dream visited her, and she reached her hand up, but nothing reached down and gave her a pull. So she lay there and presently went to talking. "Old woman," she said to herself, "that black dog come up out of the weeds to stall you off, and now there he sitting on his fine tail, smiling at you."

A white man finally came along and found her—a hunter, a young man, with his dog on a chain. "Well, Granny!" he laughed. "What are you doing there?"

"Lying on my back like a June bug waiting to be turned over, mister," she said, reaching up her hand.

He lifted her up, gave her a swing in the air, and set her down. "Anything broken, Granny?"

"No sir, them old dead weeds is springy enough," said Phoenix, when she had got her breath. "I thank you for your trouble."

"Where do you live, Granny?" he asked, while the two dogs were growling at each other.

"Away back yonder, sir, behind the ridge. You can't even see it from here."

"On your way home?"

"No sir, I going to town."

"Why, that's too far! That's as far as I walk when I come out myself, and I get something for my trouble." He patted the stuffed bag he carried, and there hung down a little closed claw. It was one of the bobwhites, with its beak hooked bitterly to show it was dead. "Now you go on home, Granny!"

"I bound to go to town, mister," said Phoenix. "The time come around."

He gave another laugh, filling the whole landscape. "I know you old colored people! Wouldn't miss going to town to see Santa Claus!"

F Reading Focus **Identifying Details** Why is Phoenix afraid of the scarecrow at first? Why does she dance with it?

G Reading Focus **Identifying Details** Describe Phoenix's response to the natural world. What insight does this response provide into her character?

But something held old Phoenix very still. The deep lines in her face went into a fierce and different radiation.[4] Without warning, she had seen with her own eyes a flashing nickel fall out of the man's pocket onto the ground.

"How old are you, Granny?" he was saying.

"There is no telling, mister," she said, "no telling."

Then she gave a little cry and clapped her hands and said, "Git on away from here, dog! Look! Look at that dog!" She laughed as if in admiration. "He ain't scared of nobody. He a big black dog." She whispered, "Sic him!"

"Watch me get rid of that cur," said the man. "Sic him, Pete! Sic him!"

Phoenix heard the dogs fighting, and heard the man running and throwing sticks. She even heard a gunshot. But she was slowly bending forward by that time, further and further forward, the lids stretched down over her eyes, as if she were doing this in her sleep. Her chin was lowered almost to her knees. The yellow palm of her hand came out from the fold of her apron. Her fingers slid down and along the ground under the piece of money with the grace and care they would have in lifting an egg from under a setting hen. Then she slowly straightened up, she stood erect, and the nickel was in her apron pocket. A bird flew by. Her lips moved. "God watching me the whole time. I come to stealing."

The man came back, and his own dog panted about them. "Well, I scared him off that time," he said, and then he laughed and lifted his gun and pointed it at Phoenix.

She stood straight and faced him.

"Doesn't the gun scare you?" he said, still pointing it.

"No, sir, I seen plenty go off closer by, in my day, and for less than what I done," she said holding utterly still.

He smiled, and shouldered the gun. "Well, Granny," he said, "you must be a hundred years old, and scared of nothing. I'd give you a dime if I had any money with me. But you take my advice and stay home, and nothing will happen to you."

"I bound to go on my way, mister," said Phoenix. She inclined her head in the red rag. Then they went in different directions, but she could hear the gun shooting again and again over the hill. **H**

She walked on. The shadows hung from the oak trees to the road like curtains. Then she smelled woodsmoke, and smelled the river, and she saw a steeple and the cabins on their steep steps. Dozens of little black children whirled around her. There ahead was Natchez shining. Bells were ringing. She walked on.

In the paved city it was Christmas time. There were red and green electric lights strung and criss-crossed everywhere, and all turned on in the daytime. Old Phoenix would have been lost if she had not distrusted her eyesight and depended on her feet to know where to take her. **I**

She paused quietly on the sidewalk where people were passing by. A lady came along in the crowd, carrying an armful of red-, green-, and silver-wrapped presents; she gave off perfume like the red roses in hot summer, and Phoenix stopped her.

"Please, missy, will you lace up my shoe?" She held up her foot.

"What do you want, Grandma?"

"See my shoe," said Phoenix. "Do all right for out in the country, but wouldn't look right to go in a big building."

"Stand still then, Grandma," said the lady. She put her packages down on the sidewalk beside her and laced and tied both shoes tightly.

"Can't lace 'em with a cane," said Phoenix. "Thank you, missy. I doesn't mind asking a nice lady to tie up my shoe, when I gets out on the street."

Moving slowly and from side to side, she went into the big building, and into a tower of steps, where she walked up and around and around until her feet knew to stop.

She entered a door, and there she saw nailed up on the wall the document that had been stamped with the gold seal and framed in the gold frame, which matched the dream that was hung up in her head.

---

4. **radiation:** pattern.

H Literary Focus **Theme** What might Phoenix's determination to continue her journey imply thematically?

I Literary Focus **Theme** How does Phoenix's reliance on her feet emphasize the title and theme?

Analyzing Visuals

Viewing and Interpreting
What might this photograph of a Southern city in the 1930s reveal about Phoenix Jackson's destination in "A Worn Path"? Explain your response.

"Here I be," she said. There was a fixed and ceremonial stiffness over her body.

"A charity case, I suppose," said an attendant who sat at the desk before her.

But Phoenix only looked above her head. There was sweat on her face, the wrinkles in her skin shone like a bright net.

"Speak up, Grandma," the woman said. "What's your name? We must have your history, you know. Have you been here before? What seems to be the trouble with you?"

Old Phoenix only gave a twitch to her face as if a fly were bothering her.

"Are you deaf?" cried the attendant.

But then the nurse came in.

"Oh, that's just old Aunt Phoenix," she said. "She doesn't come for herself—she has a little grandson. She makes these trips just as regular as clockwork. She lives away back off the Old Natchez Trace." She bent down. "Well, Aunt Phoenix, why don't you just take a seat? We won't keep you standing after your long trip." She pointed.

The old woman sat down, bolt upright in the chair.

"Now, how is the boy?" asked the nurse.

Old Phoenix did not speak.

"I said, how is the boy?"

But Phoenix only waited and stared straight ahead, her face very solemn and withdrawn into rigidity.

J **Reading Focus** **Identifying Details** Why might the stiffness of Phoenix's body be "ceremonial"?

K **Literary Focus** **Theme** Why has Welty withheld the reason for Phoenix's journey until this point? Explain your response.

Vocabulary **solemn** (SAHL uhm) *adj.*: serious.

"Is his throat any better?" asked the nurse. "Aunt Phoenix, don't you hear me? Is your grandson's throat any better since the last time you came for the medicine?"

With her hands on her knees, the old woman waited, silent, erect and motionless, just as if she were in armor.

"You mustn't take up our time this way, Aunt Phoenix," the nurse said. "Tell us quickly about your grandson, and get it over. He isn't dead, is he?"

At last there came a flicker and then a flame of comprehension across her face, and she spoke.

"My grandson. It was my memory had left me. There I sat and forgot why I made my long trip."

"Forgot?" The nurse frowned. "After you came so far?"

Then Phoenix was like an old woman begging a dignified forgiveness for waking up frightened in the night. "I never did go to school, I was too old at the Surrender," she said in a soft voice. "I'm an old woman without an education. It was my memory fail me. My little grandson, he is just the same, and I forgot it in the coming." **L**

"Throat never heals, does it?" said the nurse, speaking in a loud, sure voice to old Phoenix. By now she had a card with something written on it, a little list. "Yes. Swallowed lye.[5] When was it?—January—two-three years ago—"

Phoenix spoke unasked now. "No, missy, he not dead, he just the same. Every little while his throat begin to close up again, and he not able to swallow. He not get his breath. He not able to help himself. So the time come around, and I go on another trip for the soothing medicine."

"All right. The doctor said as long as you came to get it, you could have it," said the nurse. "But it's an obstinate case."

"My little grandson, he sit up there in the house all wrapped up, waiting by himself," Phoenix went on. "We is the only two left in the world. He suffer and it don't seem to put him back at all. He got a sweet look. He going to last. He wear a little patch quilt and peep out holding his mouth open like a little bird. I remembers so plain now. I not going to forget him again, no, the whole enduring time. I could tell him from all the others in creation."

"All right." The nurse was trying to hush her now. She brought her a bottle of medicine. "Charity," she said, making a check mark in a book.

Old Phoenix held the bottle close to her eyes, and then carefully put it into her pocket.

"I thank you," she said.

"It's Christmas time, Grandma," said the attendant. "Could I give you a few pennies out of my purse?"

"Five pennies is a nickel," said Phoenix stiffly.

"Here's a nickel," said the attendant.

Phoenix rose carefully and held out her hand. She received the nickel and then fished the other nickel out of her pocket and laid it beside the new one. She stared at her palm closely, with her head on one side.

Then she gave a tap with her cane on the floor.

"This is what come to me to do," she said. "I going to the store and buy my child a little windmill they sells, made out of paper. He going to find it hard to believe there such a thing in the world. I'll march myself back where he waiting, holding it straight up in this hand." **M**

She lifted her free hand, gave a little nod, turned around, and walked out of the doctor's office. Then her slow step began on the stairs, going down. **N**

---

5. **lye:** a highly caustic alkali compound used in making soaps and cleaning. Lye is corrosive enough to burn through aluminum; it can badly damage skin, eyes, and other body tissues.

L **Reading Focus** **Identifying Details** What explanation does Phoenix give for her forgetfulness? Do you accept her excuse? Why or why not?

M **Literary Focus** **Theme** What greater significance does Phoenix's gift for her grandson have?

N **Literary Focus** **Theme** What does the metaphor of a "worn path" suggest about life? Explain.

Applying Your Skills

SKILLS FOCUS **Literary Skills** Analyze theme; analyze archetypes. **Reading Skills** Identify details. **Vocabulary Skills** Demonstrate knowledge of literal meanings of words and their usage. **Writing Skills** Develop descriptions with sensory details.

A Worn Path

Respond and Think Critically

Reading Focus

Quick Check

1. Phoenix encounters several omens of death, like the buzzard and the scarecrow. What do her responses to these omens tell you about her?

2. List the obstacles that Phoenix overcomes during her journey. What might they represent?

3. How is Phoenix treated by the people she encounters on her journey? Explain.

Read with a Purpose

4. What is the result of Phoenix's perilous journey? What does the journey reveal about her?

Reading Skills: Identifying Details

5. Review the chart of details that you kept while reading "A Worn Path." Then, explain how the details relate to the story's theme.

✔ Vocabulary Check

Fill in each blank with the appropriate Vocabulary word from the following list: **appointed, illumined, intent, persistent, solemn.**

At the agency's **6.** _____ hour, hundreds of citizens, driven by **7.** _____ hunger, lined up for food. The hall was dark and poorly **8.** _____, but the people, **9.** _____ on getting something to eat, barely noticed. The atmosphere was quiet and **10.** _____.

Literary Focus

Literary Analysis

11. **Interpret** A phoenix is a mythical bird that sets itself on fire and is reborn from the ashes. Why is *Phoenix* a fitting name for the main character?

12. **Extend** Is Phoenix Jackson a heroine in the traditional sense of the word? Explain, giving examples of other heroines in literature or film.

13. **Evaluate** Many readers leave "A Worn Path" wondering whether or not Phoenix's grandson is actually alive. Do you think he is alive? Explain.

Literary Skills: Theme

14. **Analyze** Welty once wrote that the "worn path" is a metaphor for "the habit of love." Explain what Welty means by "the habit of love," and why this habit might be compared to a worn path. How does this metaphor suggest the story's theme?

Literary Skills Review: Archetype

15. **Extend** An **archetype** is an imaginative pattern that is repeated through the ages. Many writers have used the archetype of a journey to make larger observations about life. What parallels exist between Phoenix's journey and life itself?

Writing Focus

Think as a Reader/Writer

Use It in Your Writing In one or two paragraphs, describe a physical or symbolic journey. You may base the description upon a real or imaginary journey. Make your journey come alive for the reader by using descriptive language that appeals to the senses.

What Do You Think Now How does Phoenix define herself through her journey? In what ways does her journey challenge traditional social hierarchies?

The Jilting of Granny Weatherall

Katherine Anne Porter
(1890–1980)

What Do You Think? How does progress challenge tradition and redefine society?

QuickTalk

With a partner, discuss how views on gender roles have changed in your lifetime. Have they changed much? What has been the nature of the changes?

Pulitzer Prize WINNER

Katherine Anne Porter is regarded as one of the greatest American short story writers of the twentieth century. Her fiction centers on internal realization, rather than on external action.

Early Struggles

Porter was born in a Texas log cabin. She was raised, mostly by her grandmother, as part of a sprawling family on close terms with hardship and deprivation. Her schooling was fragmentary.

The first of Porter's four marriages took place when she was sixteen. She was consistently impatient with lasting marital relationships, yet she disliked being alone. She struggled during early years to define herself as an individual, as a Southern woman, and as the writer that she was slowly becoming.

After her Texas youth, Porter traveled widely, living at various times in New York City's Greenwich Village, New England, Washington, Mexico, Paris, and Berlin. She supported herself as a newspaper reporter and a translator.

A Self-Taught Success

As a creative writer, Porter was largely self-taught. She worked slowly and painstakingly, and she did not begin publishing until she was over thirty. Her first book of stories, *Flowering Judas* (1930), grew out of her experiences in Mexico after World War I. Much of Porter's work presents southern women caught up in a web of custom and obligation. Her main themes focus on the burden of past evil and the strain with which that evil holds us captive in the present.

After the publication of her finest story collection, *Pale Horse, Pale Rider* (1939), Porter's growing audience eagerly awaited a promised novel. In 1941, Porter began writing *Ship of Fools,* which took twenty years to complete. The novel is about the seeds of World War II—a bitter portrait of the Nazi state and the human race's capacity for cruelty. When it finally appeared in 1962, it enjoyed a wide popular success and received the National Book Award and the Pulitzer Prize.

Think About the Writer How might Porter's struggle to define herself have influenced her writing?

Reader/Writer Notebook

Use your **RWN** to complete the activities for this selection.

Literary Focus

Stream of Consciousness The modernist style of writing that conveys the inner—and sometimes chaotic—workings of a character's mind is called **stream of consciousness.** In this story, stream of consciousness gives readers the impression that they are listening to Granny Weatherall's thoughts and memories as they flow through her mind. Sometimes contradictory, sometimes ambiguous or unclear, the ideas and thoughts shift back and forth from past to present. Writers often use this narrative style when a character is under great pressure or stress.

Literary Perspectives Apply the literary perspective described on page 915 as you read this story.

Reading Focus

Close Reading A stream-of-consciousness story requires **close reading,** or sifting carefully through clues to discover the work's deeper meaning. Pay attention to verb tenses, since they can help you distinguish past from present. Look for quotation marks; Granny Weatherall thinks many things that she does not say. Finally, be patient. Sometimes, the only way to understand what you have just read is to keep reading and re-reading.

Into Action As you read, use a chart like the one below to track the sequence of Granny Weatherall's mental and emotional associations. Look closely at the words and phrases that trigger certain memories.

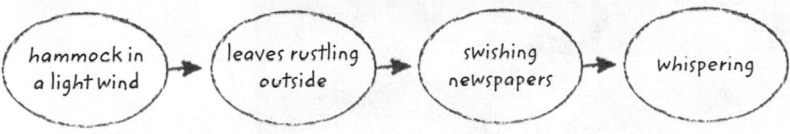

Writing Focus

Think as a Reader/Writer

Find It in Your Reading To show the reader what Granny sees in her mind's eye, Porter uses many **figures of speech**—words or phrases that describe one thing in terms of something else and that are not meant to be taken literally. Figures of speech accurately represent the sometimes illogical associations. At the beginning of the story, for example, Granny sees Doctor Harry float "like a balloon around the foot of the bed." As you read, use your *Reader/Writer Notebook* to record other figures of speech.

Language Coach

Verb Forms When you learn a new verb, learn all of its forms. Regular verbs use the endings *–s, –ed,* and *–ing.* The base form of *rummaging* is *rummage.* Its related forms are *rummages* and *rummaged.* How do the endings change the meaning of the verb? What are the other forms of the verbs *disputed* and *dwindled*?

 Learn It Online
Use Word Watch to take your vocabulary knowledge to the next level.

go.hrw.com   L11-913   **Go**

The Jilting of Granny Weatherall

by **Katherine Anne Porter**

Lamps and Tulips by Susan Ryder. Oil on canvas.

Read with a Purpose
Read to learn how Granny Weatherall confronts her past.

Build Background
Today, instead of saying that someone has been jilted, we might say that he or she has been dumped. Still, the word *dumped* doesn't mean as much to us as *jilted* would have meant to someone of Granny Weatherall's era. Katherine Anne Porter—and some of her characters—came of age before women in the United States had the right to vote. In those years, a broken engagement was much more serious than it is today. In a society that considered marriage the highest possible achievement for a woman, being abandoned by a fiancé was a calamity. Without a husband, a woman might not have the means to support herself. Along with the emotional pain and shame one would expect, being jilted carried enormous negative social and financial implications.

She flicked her wrist neatly out of Doctor Harry's pudgy careful fingers and pulled the sheet up to her chin. The brat ought to be in knee breeches. Doctoring around the country with spectacles on his nose! "Get along now, take your schoolbooks and go. There's nothing wrong with me."

Doctor Harry spread a warm paw like a cushion on her forehead where the forked green vein danced and made her eyelids twitch. "Now, now, be a good girl, and we'll have you up in no time."

"That's no way to speak to a woman nearly eighty years old just because she's down. I'd have you respect your elders, young man."

"Well, Missy, excuse me." Doctor Harry patted her cheek. "But I've got to warn you, haven't I? You're a marvel, but you must be careful or you're going to be good and sorry."

"Don't tell me what I'm going to be. I'm on my feet now, morally speaking. It's Cornelia. I had to go to bed to get rid of her."

Her bones felt loose, and floated around in her skin, and Doctor Harry floated like a balloon around the foot of the bed. He floated and pulled down his waistcoat and swung his glasses on a cord. "Well, stay where you are, it certainly can't hurt you." **(A)**

"Get along and doctor your sick," said Granny Weatherall. "Leave a well woman alone. I'll call for you when I want you. . . . Where were you forty years ago when I pulled through milk leg[1] and double pneumonia? You weren't even born. Don't let Cornelia lead you on," she shouted, because Doctor Harry appeared to

float up to the ceiling and out. "I pay my own bills, and I don't throw my money away on nonsense!" **(B)**

She meant to wave goodbye, but it was too much trouble. Her eyes closed of themselves, it was like a dark curtain drawn around the bed. The pillow rose and floated under her, pleasant as a hammock in a light wind. She listened to the leaves rustling outside the window. No, somebody was swishing newspapers: No, Cornelia and Doctor Harry were whispering together. She leaped broad awake, thinking they whispered in her ear.

"She was never like this, *never* like this!" "Well, what can we expect?" "Yes, eighty years old. . . ."

Well, and what if she was? She still had ears. It was like Cornelia to whisper around doors. She always kept things secret in such a public way. She was always being tactful and kind. Cornelia was dutiful; that was the trouble with her. Dutiful and good: "So good and dutiful," said Granny, "that I'd like to spank her." She saw herself spanking Cornelia and making a fine job of it. **(C)**

"What'd you say, Mother?"

Granny felt her face tying up in hard knots.

"Can't a body think, I'd like to know?"

---

1. **milk leg:** painful swelling of the leg, usually as a result of an infection during childbirth.

(A) Reading Focus Close Reading What is happening to Granny at this point? How do you know?

(B) Literary Perspectives Analyzing Political Context In what manner does Doctor Harry address Granny? What does Granny's response suggest about her attitude toward male authority figures?

(C) Literary Perspectives Analyzing Political Context Based on Granny's description, how does Cornelia fulfill the stereotypical role of a good woman? How does Granny rebel against this attitude toward womanhood?

Vocabulary **tactful** (TAKT fuhl) *adj.:* skilled in saying and doing the right thing.

Literary Perspectives

Analyzing Political Context The study of gender in literature is the study of how concepts of masculinity and femininity influence an author's work. Use the political context perspective to think about the importance of gender relationships in this story. In American society, men have historically had greater political rights and more economic opportunities than women. Women have often felt that their social and economic needs or wants are secondary to men's. In addition, many women have been raised to feel that they must strongly compete against each other for men's affections. How might Granny Weatherall's actions have been influenced by these and other social structures that give priority to male interests? How might her view of life have been determined by the political and social ideologies of her day? In what ways does she rebel against these traditional ideas?

As you read, be sure to notice the questions in the text, which will guide you in using this perspective.

"I thought you might want something."

"I do. I want a lot of things. First off, go away and don't whisper."

She lay and drowsed, hoping in her sleep that the children would keep out and let her rest a minute. It had been a long day. Not that she was tired. It was always pleasant to snatch a minute now and then. There was always so much to be done, let me see: tomorrow.

Tomorrow was far away and there was nothing to trouble about. Things were finished somehow when the time came; thank God there was always a little margin over for peace: Then a person could spread out the plan of life and tuck in the edges orderly. It was good to have everything clean and folded away, with the hairbrushes and tonic bottles sitting straight on the white embroidered linen: the day started without fuss and the pantry shelves laid out with rows of jelly glasses and brown jugs and white stone-china jars with blue whirligigs and words painted on them: coffee, tea, sugar, ginger, cinnamon, allspice: and the bronze clock with the lion on top nicely dusted off. The dust that lion could collect in twenty-four hours! The box in the attic with all those letters tied up, well, she'd have to go through that tomorrow. All those letters—George's letters and John's letters and her letters to them both—lying around for the children to find afterward made her uneasy. Yes, that would be tomorrow's business. No use to let them know how silly she had been once. **D**

While she was rummaging around she found death in her mind and it felt clammy and unfamiliar. She had spent so much time preparing for death there was no need for bringing it up again. Let it take care of itself now. When she was sixty she had felt very old, finished, and went around making farewell trips to see her children and grandchildren, with a secret in her mind: This is the very last of your mother, children! Then she made her will and came down with a long fever. That was all just a notion like a lot of other things, but it was lucky too, for she had once for all got over the idea of dying for a long time. Now she

couldn't be worried. She hoped she had better sense now. Her father had lived to be one hundred and two years old and had drunk a noggin[2] of strong hot toddy[3] on his last birthday. He told the reporters it was his daily habit, and he owed his long life to that. He had made quite a scandal and was very pleased about it. She believed she'd just plague Cornelia a little.

"Cornelia! Cornelia!" No footsteps, but a sudden hand on her cheek. "Bless you, where have you been?"

"Here, Mother."

"Well, Cornelia, I want a noggin of hot toddy."

"Are you cold, darling?"

"I'm chilly, Cornelia. Lying in bed stops the circulation. I must have told you that a thousand times."

Well, she could just hear Cornelia telling her husband that Mother was getting a little childish and they'd have to humor her. The thing that most annoyed her was that Cornelia thought she was deaf, dumb, and blind. Little hasty glances and tiny gestures tossed around her and over her head saying, "Don't cross her, let her have her way, she's eighty years old," and she sitting there as if she lived in a thin glass cage. Sometimes Granny almost made up her mind to pack up and move back to her own house where nobody could remind her every minute that she was old. Wait, wait, Cornelia, till your own children whisper behind your back!

In her day she had kept a better house and had got more work done. She wasn't too old yet for Lydia to be driving eighty miles for advice when one of the children jumped the track, and Jimmy still dropped in and talked things over: "Now, Mammy, you've a good business head, I want to know what you think of this? . . ." Old. Cornelia couldn't change the furniture around without asking. Little things, little things! They had been so sweet when they were little. Granny wished the old days were back again with the children young and everything to be done over. It had been a

---

2. **noggin:** mug.
3. **hot toddy:** drink made of liquor mixed with hot water, sugar, and spices.

D **Literary Focus** Stream of Consciousness Ironically, in the midst of her disordered mental state, Granny is concerned with cleaning and tidying. What does Granny's concern with cleanliness and orderliness indicate about her?

Vocabulary **rummaging** (RUHM ihj ihng) *v.:* searching thoroughly by moving things about.
clammy (KLAM ee) *adj.:* cold and damp.

Morning Post by Fairlie Harmar. Oil on canvas.

hard pull, but not too much for her. When she thought of all the food she had cooked, and all the clothes she had cut and sewed, and all the gardens she had made—well, the children showed it. There they were, made out of her, and they couldn't get away from that. Sometimes she wanted to see John again and point to them and say, Well, I didn't do so badly, did I? But that would have to wait. That was for tomorrow. She used to think of him as a man, but now all the children were older than their father, and he would be a child beside her if she saw him now. It seemed strange and there was something wrong in the idea. Why, he couldn't possibly recognize her. She had fenced in a hundred acres once, digging the postholes herself and clamping the wires with just a Negro boy to help. That changed a woman. John would be looking for a young woman with the peaked Spanish comb in her hair and the painted fan. Digging postholes changed a woman. Riding country roads in the winter when women had their babies was another thing: sitting up nights with sick horses and sick Negroes and sick children and hardly ever losing one. John, I hardly ever lost one of them! John would see that in a minute, that would be something he could understand, she wouldn't have to explain anything! **E**

It made her feel like rolling up her sleeves and putting the whole place to rights again. No matter if Cornelia was determined to be everywhere at once, there were a great many things left undone on this place. She would start tomorrow and do them. It was good to be strong enough for everything, even if all you made melted and changed and slipped under your hands, so that by the time you finished you almost forgot what you were working for. What was it I set

---

E **Literary Perspectives** **Analyzing Political Context** Why would Granny's husband John "be a child beside her if she saw him now"? In light of political views of women during Porter's time, how might "digging postholes change a woman"?

Reflections (1893) by William Merritt Chase.
Collection of Margaret and Raymond Horowitz.

Analyzing Visuals

Viewing and Interpreting The woman's face is visible only in a reflection. What do you think this means? Why is the woman staring in the mirror? How does this remind you of Granny's situation?

out to do? she asked herself intently, but she could not remember. A fog rose over the valley, she saw it marching across the creek swallowing the trees and moving up the hill like an army of ghosts. Soon it would be at the near edge of the orchard, and then it was time to go in and light the lamps. Come in, children, don't stay out in the night air. **F**

Lighting the lamps had been beautiful. The children huddled up to her and breathed like little calves waiting at the bars in the twilight. Their eyes followed the match and watched the flame rise and settle in a blue curve, then they moved away from her. The lamp was lit, they didn't have to be scared and hang on to mother any more. Never, never, never more. God, for all my life I thank Thee. Without Thee, my God, I could never have done it. Hail, Mary, full of grace.[4] **G**

I want you to pick all the fruit this year and see that nothing is wasted. There's always someone who can use it. Don't let good things rot for want of using. You waste life when you waste good food. Don't let things get lost. It's bitter to lose things. Now, don't let me get to thinking, not when I am tired and taking a little nap before supper. . . .

The pillow rose about her shoulders and pressed against her heart and the memory was being squeezed out of it: Oh, push down the pillow, somebody: It would smother her if she tried to hold it. Such a fresh breeze blowing and such a green day with no threats in it. But he had not come, just the same. What does a woman do when she has put on the white veil and set out the white cake for a man and he doesn't come? She tried to remember. No, I swear he never harmed me but in that. He never harmed me but in that . . . and

---

4. **Hail . . . grace:** the beginning of a traditional prayer in the Roman Catholic Church. A later line of the prayer refers to Mary's child as "the fruit of your womb," an association that may trigger Granny's next association about wasting fruit.

what if he did? There was the day, the day, but a whirl of dark smoke rose and covered it, crept up and over into the bright field where everything was planted so carefully in orderly rows. That was hell, she knew hell when she saw it. For sixty years she had prayed against remembering him and against losing her soul in the deep pit of hell, and now the two things were mingled in one and the thought of him was a smoky cloud from hell that moved and crept in her head when she had just got rid of Doctor Harry and was trying to rest a minute. Wounded vanity, Ellen, said a sharp voice in the top of her mind. Don't let your wounded vanity get the upper hand of you. Plenty of girls get jilted. You were jilted, weren't you? Then stand up to it. Her eyelids wavered and let in streamers of blue-gray light like tissue paper over her eyes. She must get up and pull the shades down or she'd never sleep. She was in bed again and the shades were not down. How could that happen? Better turn over, hide from the light, sleeping in the light gave you nightmares. "Mother, how do you feel now?" and a stinging wetness on her forehead. But I don't like having my face washed in cold water! **H**

Hapsy? George? Lydia? Jimmy? No, Cornelia, and her features were swollen and full of little puddles. "They're coming, darling, they'll all be here soon." Go wash your face, child, you look funny.

Instead of obeying, Cornelia knelt down and put her head on the pillow. She seemed to be talking but there was no sound. "Well, are you tongue-tied? Whose birthday is it? Are you going to give a party?"

Cornelia's mouth moved urgently in strange shapes. "Don't do that, you bother me, daughter."

"Oh, no, Mother. Oh, no . . ."

Nonsense. It was strange about children. They disputed your every word. "No what, Cornelia?"

"Here's Doctor Harry."

"I won't see that boy again. He just left five minutes ago."

"That was this morning, Mother. It's night now. Here's the nurse."

F

G

H

"This is Doctor Harry, Mrs. Weatherall. I never saw you look so young and happy!"

"Ah, I'll never be young again—but I'd be happy if they'd let me lie in peace and get rested."

She thought she spoke up loudly, but no one answered. A warm weight on her forehead, a warm bracelet on her wrist, and a breeze went on whispering, trying to tell her something. A shuffle of leaves in the everlasting hand of God, He blew on them and they danced and rattled. "Mother, don't mind, we're going to give you a little hypodermic."[5] "Look here, daughter, how do ants get in this bed? I saw sugar ants yesterday." Did you send for Hapsy too? **Ⓘ**

It was Hapsy she really wanted. She had to go a long way back through a great many rooms to find Hapsy standing with a baby on her arm. She seemed to herself to be Hapsy also, and the baby on Hapsy's arm was Hapsy and himself and herself, all at once, and there was no surprise in the meeting. Then Hapsy melted from within and turned flimsy as gray gauze and the baby was a gauzy shadow, and Hapsy came up close and said, "I thought you'd never come," and looked at her very searchingly and said, "You haven't changed a bit!" They leaned forward to kiss, when Cornelia began whispering from a long way off, "Oh, is there anything you want to tell me? Is there anything I can do for you?" **Ⓙ**

Yes, she had changed her mind after sixty years and she would like to see George. I want you to find George. Find him and be sure to tell him I forgot him. I want him to know I had my husband just the same and my children and my house like any other woman. A good house too and a good husband that I loved and fine children out of him. Better than I hoped for even. Tell him I was given back everything he took away and more. Oh, no, oh, God, no, there was something else besides the house and the man and the children. Oh, surely they were not all? What was it? Something not given back. . . . Her breath crowded down under her

---

5. **hypodermic:** injection of medicine.

ribs and grew into a monstrous frightening shape with cutting edges; it bored up into her head, and the agony was unbelievable: Yes, John, get the Doctor now, no more talk, my time has come. **Ⓚ**

When this one was born it should be the last. The last. It should have been born first, for it was the one she had truly wanted. Everything came in good time. Nothing left out, left over. She was strong, in three days she would be as well as ever. Better. A woman needed milk in her to have her full health. **Ⓛ**

"Mother, do you hear me?"

"I've been telling you—"

"Mother, Father Connolly's here."

"I went to Holy Communion only last week. Tell him I'm not so sinful as all that."

"Father just wants to speak to you."

He could speak as much as he pleased. It was like him to drop in and inquire about her soul as if it were a teething baby, and then stay on for a cup of tea and a round of cards and gossip. He always had a funny story of some sort, usually about an Irishman who made his little mistakes and confessed them, and the point lay in some absurd thing he would blurt out in the confessional showing his struggles between native piety and original sin.[6] Granny felt easy about her soul. Cornelia, where are your manners? Give Father Connolly a chair. She had her secret comfortable understanding with a few favorite saints who cleared a straight road to God for her. All as surely signed and sealed as the papers for the new Forty Acres. Forever . . . heirs and assigns forever. Since the day the wedding cake was not cut, but thrown out and wasted. The whole bottom dropped out of the world, and there she was blind and sweating with nothing under her feet and the walls falling away. His hand had caught her under the breast, she had not fallen, there was the freshly polished floor with the green rug on it, just as

---

6. **original sin:** in Christian theology, the sin of disobedience committed by Adam and Eve, the first man and first woman, which is passed on to all persons.

Ⓘ Literary Focus Stream of Consciousness How do Granny's sensory perceptions trigger emotional associations?

Ⓙ Reading Focus Close Reading What do the "great many rooms" represent? Who is Hapsy?

Ⓚ Literary Perspectives Analyzing Political Context What criteria define conventional social views of womanhood, according to Granny? How does she feel about these criteria?

Ⓛ Reading Focus Close Reading Why might Granny associate death with childbirth?

before. He had cursed like a sailor's parrot and said, "I'll kill him for you." Don't lay a hand on him, for my sake leave something to God. "Now, Ellen, you must believe what I tell you...."

So there was nothing, nothing to worry about any more, except sometimes in the night one of the children screamed in a nightmare, and they both hustled out shaking and hunting for the matches and calling, "There, wait a minute, here we are!" John, get the doctor now, Hapsy's time has come. But there was Hapsy standing by the bed in a white cap. "Cornelia, tell Hapsy to take off her cap. I can't see her plain."

Her eyes opened very wide and the room stood out like a picture she had seen somewhere. Dark colors with the shadows rising toward the ceiling in long angles. The tall black dresser gleamed with nothing on it but John's picture, enlarged from a little one, with John's eyes very black when they should have been blue. You never saw him, so how do you know how he looked? But the man insisted the copy was perfect, it was very rich and handsome. For a picture, yes, but it's not my husband. The table by the bed had a linen cover and a candle and a crucifix. The light was blue from Cornelia's silk lampshades. No sort of light at all, just frippery. You had to live forty years with kerosene lamps to appreciate honest electricity. She felt very strong and she saw Doctor Harry with a rosy nimbus around him.

"You look like a saint, Doctor Harry, and I vow that's as near as you'll ever come to it."

"She's saying something."

"I heard you, Cornelia. What's all this carrying-on?"

"Father Connolly's saying—"

> What if he did run away and leave me to face the priest by myself? I found another a whole world better.

Cornelia's voice staggered and bumped like a cart in a bad road. It rounded corners and turned back again and arrived nowhere. Granny stepped up in the cart very lightly and reached for the reins, but a man sat beside her and she knew him by his hands, driving the cart. She did not look in his face, for she knew without seeing, but looked instead down the road where the trees leaned over and bowed to each other and a thousand birds were singing a Mass. She felt like singing too, but she put her hand in the bosom of her dress and pulled out a rosary, and Father Connolly murmured Latin in a very solemn voice and tickled her feet.[7] My God, will you stop that nonsense? I'm a married woman. What if he did run away and leave me to face the priest by myself? I found another a whole world better. I wouldn't have exchanged my husband for anybody except St. Michael[8] himself, and you may tell him that for me with a thank you in the bargain. (M)

Light flashed on her closed eyelids, and a deep roaring shook her. Cornelia, is that lightning? I hear thunder. There's going to be a storm. Close all the windows. Call the children in.... "Mother, here we are, all of us." "Is that you, Hapsy?" "Oh, no, I'm Lydia. We drove as fast as we could." Their faces drifted above her, drifted away. The rosary fell out of her hands and Lydia put it back. Jimmy tried to help, their hands fumbled together, and Granny closed two fingers

---

7. **murmured . . . feet:** The priest is performing the sacramental last rites of the Roman Catholic Church, which include anointing the dying person's feet with oil.
8. **St. Michael:** the most powerful of the four archangels in Jewish and Christian doctrine. In Christian art, he is usually depicted as a handsome knight in white armor.

(M) **Literary Focus** Stream of Consciousness Who is the man sitting beside her in the cart? How would you explain the associations in this passage?

around Jimmy's thumb. Beads wouldn't do, it must be something alive. She was so amazed her thoughts ran round and round. So, my dear Lord, this is my death and I wasn't even thinking about it. My children have come to see me die. But I can't, it's not time. Oh, I always hated surprises. I wanted to give Cornelia the amethyst[9] set—Cornelia, you're to have the amethyst set, but Hapsy's to wear it when she wants, and, Doctor Harry, do shut up. Nobody sent for you. Oh, my dear Lord, do wait a minute. I meant to do something about the Forty Acres, Jimmy doesn't need it and Lydia will later on, with that worthless husband of hers. I meant to finish the altar cloth and send six bottles of wine to Sister Borgia for her dyspepsia.[10] I want to send six bottles of wine to Sister Borgia, Father Connolly, now don't let me forget.

Cornelia's voice made short turns and tilted over and crashed. "Oh, Mother, oh, Mother, oh, Mother . . ."

---

9. **amethyst:** purple or violet quartz gemstone, used in jewelry.
10. **dyspepsia:** indigestion.

"I'm not going, Cornelia. I'm taken by surprise. I can't go."

You'll see Hapsy again. What about her? "I thought you'd never come." Granny made a long journey outward, looking for Hapsy. What if I don't find her? What then? Her heart sank down and down, there was no bottom to death, she couldn't come to the end of it. The blue light from Cornelia's lampshade drew into a tiny point in the center of her brain, it flickered and winked like an eye, quietly it fluttered and dwindled. Granny lay curled down within herself, amazed and watchful, staring at the point of light that was herself; her body was now only a deeper mass of shadow in an endless darkness and this darkness would curl around the light and swallow it up. God, give a sign!

For the second time there was no sign. Again no bridegroom and the priest in the house. She could not remember any other sorrow because this grief wiped them all away. Oh, no, there's nothing more cruel than this—I'll never forgive it. She stretched herself with a deep breath and blew out the light.

Vocabulary **dwindled** (DWIHN duhld) *v.:* diminished.

N **Reading Focus** **Close Reading** What sign does Granny want?

O **Reading Focus** **Close Reading** How do you interpret the final sentence? What does the light stand for?

SKILLS FOCUS **Literary Skills** Analyze stream of consciousness; analyze ambiguity; analyze political context. **Reading Skills** Close reading. **Writing Skills** Enhance style for effective writing.

Respond and Think Critically

Reading Focus

Quick Check

1. Why is Granny revisiting her old memories?

2. How does Granny feel about each of her children? How do you know?

3. Whom does Granny most wish to see? Where does that person appear in the story?

Read with a Purpose

4. How is Granny haunted by her past? Does she ever make peace with her past?

Reading Skills: Close Reading

5. As you read, you used flowcharts to keep track of what triggers Granny Weatherall's memories. Now circle the ideas, figures of speech, and images that appear more than once. Write a few sentences about how and why these recurring elements might drive Granny's thoughts.

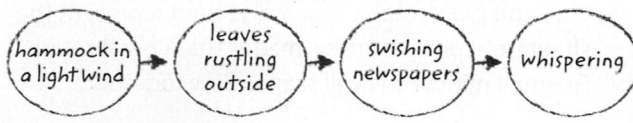

Literary Focus

Literary Analysis

6. **Hypothesize** Why do you think that the character Weatherall is identified as "Granny" and not by her first name, Ellen, in the story's title?

7. **Analyze** What does Granny mean when she thinks, "That was hell, she knew hell when she saw it" (p. 919)? How does she feel about heaven?

8. **Evaluate** When Granny recalls George, she thinks, "Find him and be sure to tell him I forgot him" (p. 920). What is ironic about this statement? How did George really affect Granny's life?

9. **Infer** The end of the story suggests that Granny is jilted once again. Who jilts her this time?

10. **Extend** Granny's last thoughts revolve around a rejection that occurred six decades ago. Do you find this believable? Why or why not?

11. **Literary Perspectives** Does Granny successfully resist <u>traditional</u> definitions of female social roles? Why or why not?

Literary Skills: Stream of Consciousness

12. **Draw Conclusions** Granny's stream of consciousness becomes especially chaotic, revealing thoughts she cannot control or fears that she does not want to face. List examples from the story, and explain why her thoughts are chaotic.

Literary Skills Review: Ambiguity

13. **Extend** Deliberately suggesting two or more different meanings is a writing technique called **ambiguity.** Granny feels that she was "given back everything" that was taken away by the jilting. Yet then she says that it was "not given back." Discuss why she might be of two minds about the jilting.

Writing Focus

Think as a Reader/Writer

Use It in Your Writing In one or two paragraphs, write a stream-of-consciousness narrative for a character who is experiencing trauma, or stress of some kind. Incorporate figures of speech that help readers understand what your character is experiencing in his or her mind.

What Do **You Think Now** How has Granny challenged <u>traditional</u> attitudes about gender? How is she still defined by those attitudes? Explain.

Applying Your Skills

The Jilting of Granny Weatherall

SKILLS FOCUS **Vocabulary Skills** Use context clues in words, sentences, and paragraphs to decode new vocabulary. **Writing Skills** Analyze a short story; write media scripts; employ literary devices for effective writing.

Vocabulary Development

✓ Vocabulary Check

Match each Vocabulary word to its antonym.

1. clammy
2. jilted
3. tactful
4. disputed
5. rummaging
6. vanity
7. dwindled

a. accepted
b. examining
c. arid
d. agreed
e. rude
f. humility
g. increased

Vocabulary Skills: Context Clues

Context is the sentence or passage in which a word is located. Often, context contains clues to the word's meaning. In the example below, notice how context clues help reveal the meaning of the underlined word.

Don't let your wounded vanity get the upper hand... You were jilted, weren't you? Then stand up to it.

Context clues: wounded, jilted, stand up to it
My guess at meaning: Vanity is something that could be hurt by a rejection, like pride or self-respect.
Dictionary definition: "excessive pride"

Your Turn

Use context clues to determine the meaning of the underlined word.

The light was blue from Cornelia's silk lampshades... She felt very strong and she saw Doctor Harry with a rosy nimbus around him. "You look like a saint..."

Language Coach

Verbs Forms Choose the correct verb.

1. She (*rummaging, rummaged*) through the house.
2. As the last light of day (*dwindle, dwindles*), the birds (*warble, warbles*) quietly.

CHOICES

As you respond to the Choices, use these **Academic Vocabulary** words as appropriate: alternative, hierarchy, ideology, inevitable, tradition.

REVIEW

Analyze Gender Roles

Timed Writing Write a brief essay about what womanhood means to Ellen Weatherall. How has her social and political context influenced her thoughts, feelings, and choices? How has she rebelled against or succumbed to certain ideas about gender? How does her impending death affect the way she feels about her choices? Use examples from the story to support your claims.

CONNECT

Visualize the Story

TechFocus Imagine that you are directing a film version of "The Jilting of Granny Weatherall." Create a storyboard showing the flow of images that would occur within the film. Take advantage of the fact that film can show events that are unrestricted in time and place. Make your storyboard represent the stream-of-consciousness images that flow through Granny's mind. How will scenes flow together?

EXTEND

Record Your Thoughts

Write an episode from your life, using stream-of-consciousness narration. Before writing your story, you may want to reflect on your thought processes and record some notes about how your mind works. Which ideas and emotions lead to others? Why? Write from a first-person point of view. After you write your episode, think about the process of writing in stream of consciousness. Does it require more or less discipline than writing in a more traditional style? Why?

Preparing to Read

Link to Today

The Fight Against Alzheimer's

What Do You Think

How does progress challenge <u>tradition</u> and redefine society?

⏱ **QuickTalk**

Recall a time when you tried to remember something but your memory failed you. In a small group, share the experience and how you felt at the time.

Informational Text Focus

Organizing Information As you read expository—or informative—articles, look for ways to organize and retain what you have learned. Helpful strategies include listing or charting the writer's main points, summarizing key ideas, and examining an article to see how the writer has organized information. The best strategy is the one that works for you.

Into Action As you read, notice how the writer organizes events to tell a real-life story and how he includes facts to inform you about his subject. Use a chart like the one below to note what happens in the story the writer presents, as well as the facts the writer includes with the events.

Events	Facts
eight students get together (p. 926)	ages 56–81, five with early Alzheimer's (p. 926)

Writing Focus   Preparing for **Constructed Response**

Direct quotations can give an article interest and credibility. They can also show the human side of a news story—not just what is happening, but how people feel about it. Nonfiction writers must choose which words in a quotation to incorporate and how to work them into the text. As you read, use your *Reader/Writer Notebook* to record one or two of the article's direct quotations. Underline the information provided in the quotation and note how it personalizes the story.

Reader/Writer Notebook

Use your **RWN** to complete the activities for this selection.

Vocabulary

progressive (pruh GREHS ihv) *adj.:* becoming more severe over time. *The progressive disease would soon result in memory loss.*

eclectic (ehk LEHK tihk) *adj.:* made up of a variety of elements. *Her eclectic hobbies include chess, painting, and puzzles.*

camaraderie (kah muh RAH duhr ee) *n.:* lighthearted rapport among friends. *There was camaraderie among the classmates.*

gravitate (GRAV uh tayt) *v.:* move together. *The patients gravitate toward each other.*

tailored (TAY luhrd) *v.:* made to specific requirements. *The woman tailored her week around club meetings.*

stigma (STIHG muh) *n.:* a mark of disgrace or shame. *The stigma of having a disease was not going to keep him from making friends.*

Language Coach

Roots *Gravitate* comes from the Latin root *gravis,* meaning "heavy." Use this root to help you understand other English words. *Gravity,* for example, is the force that makes us "heavy" on the earth.

Learn It Online
Organize your thoughts with the interactive graphic organizers online.

go.hrw.com   L11-925   **Go**

Read with a Purpose

Read to learn how one program helps people with Alzheimer's disease fight memory loss.

Build Background

Everyone forgets things now and then, but some people forget more often than others. For people with Alzheimer's, forgetting becomes the rule rather than the exception. Alzheimer's is a progressive disease in which a person's memory gradually fails. Eventually, the patient will not even recognize family members. There is no cure for Alzheimer's, but medical researchers are constantly looking for ways to slow the progression of the disease and keep individuals' memories as intact as possible. Some researchers have discovered that stimulating the brain helps people keep memories alive. This discovery makes it possible for people in the early stages of Alzheimer's to stay alert and in touch with their memories.

The Fight Against Alzheimer's

by BILL GLAUBER from MILWAUKEE JOURNAL SENTINEL

MILWAUKEE, Wis. Somewhere between memory and loss there is this: a class of eight students who range in age from 56 to 81. Five are in the early stage of Alzheimer's disease. Three suffer ailments that threaten their cognitive[1] health.

They exercise their minds with Sudoku puzzles and worksheets where they complete a phrase. ("Live and let live. Honesty is the best policy.") They work the senses. (Hear that? It's a horn. Smell that? It's a garlic clove.)

Most of all, they talk, relate, laugh, and for a few hours are free to be who they are, the way they are. **Ⓐ**

"There is no reason to fear coming here. There is nothing scary about it," says Robert (Gus) Shanower, 56, in a low whisper of a voice, struggling with the effects of vascular dementia[2] triggered by small strokes.

The Early Bird Club is a place of hope amid heartbreak, a potentially groundbreaking program tried in only a handful of communities nationwide.

Twice a week, four hours at a clip, there is a fight for memory at the Harwood Place Retirement Community in Wauwatosa, Wisconsin. Alzheimer's can't yet be cured—it's a progressive brain disorder that affects 4.5 million Americans. **Ⓑ**

But maybe, just maybe, through a program like this, the early stages of the disease can somehow be slowed, memory retained.

That's the hope, the goal. They're not selling a miracle here. They're

---

1. **cognitive:** having to do with cognition, or the mental process of knowing.

2. **vascular dementia:** a deterioration of mental faculties resulting from a lack of proper blood supply in the brain.

Ⓐ Informational Focus Organizing Information What activities stimulate memory?

Ⓑ Informational Focus Organizing Information Which part of this short paragraph relates events in a story, and which part provides information about the writer's subject?

Vocabulary progressive (pruh GREHS ihv) *adj.*: becoming more severe over time.

Shirley Cicerello, left, and another participant in the Early Bird Club paint scenes that come to them while listening to music.

selling education, a social gathering, memory enhancement for those who suffer from mild memory loss.

"What we're trying to do is stimulate their minds, get them thinking of stuff, stuff they had long forgotten," says Jennifer Nowak, a warm, engaging 36-year-old who heads the class.

Nowak is a director of community services for Lutheran Living Services. But here, in a room off a main dining area, she's a teacher, friend and cheerleader for an eclectic group bound by a determination to not surrender to a disease.

When the class began in early January, three people attended. Slowly but surely, the message got out. A recent class included eight students huddled around a couple of tables. Four days later, 10 people showed up.

There is camaraderie. Newcomers are welcome. People who had similar professions gravitate to one another.

There is even some gentle joking. The students are given a checklist of potential warning signs for Alzheimer's, including one about losing car keys in unusual places such as the trash can or the freezer.

"Who drives?" one man asks. Laughter fills the room.

The key is stimulation to keep the brain working, the limbs moving: talk, work, even a gentle stroll after lunch.

Vocabulary **eclectic** (ehk LEHK tihk) *adj.:* made up of a variety of elements.
camaraderie (kah muh RAH duhr ee) *n.:* lighthearted rapport among friends.
gravitate (GRAV uh tayt) *v.:* move together.

There are similar programs in Oklahoma, Minnesota and California. The model comes from Napa, California, created by Kristin Einberger, supervisor of an older adult program. She named it "Mind Boosters" and tailored the program for "people who are fully aware they have issues with their memories," those who would feel out of place in groups designed for those in the mid to late stages of the disease. **C**

"We called it an early memory loss group," Einberger says. "The Big A [Alzheimer's] is still a stigma."

She doesn't have hard data, but Einberger claims the program makes a difference to the students.

"Alzheimer's is progressive," she says. "It's my belief we can make a difference and maybe we can keep them at this [early] stage longer than if they were sitting home on the couch completely isolated."

Spend a few days with the class and a few things stand out.

There's homework, the students filling out worksheets, stretching their minds with math and history, rustling papers in three-ring binders.

Pictures also play a large part. They're designed to stir questions, jar memories as the class creates a group story, applying names to characters. A photo of a Tupperware party from the 1950s triggers reminders of the way things used to be, when ranch homes and plastic containers were all the rage.

"This is crazy," one woman says in the midst of a story the class creates, a story that revolves around a chicken salad lunch and neighbors carpooling to the party.

But by the end, the woman has bought into the subject. And when someone says the party ends with martinis, the woman deadpans, "I never had a martini

A woman plays checkers with her grandchild. Games such as chess and checkers can maintain and improve mental fitness.

at a Tupperware party. I missed out." Again, laughter fills the room.

There's a lot of love in the room, too. Love based on a shared struggle.

"You have to have a sense of humor," Nowak says. "You have to appreciate these people as individuals."

By trial and error, the class learns what works, what doesn't, the puzzles, the homework, the sounds, the smells. **D**

With that whispery voice, Shanower says, "This gives a person something to do."

And it gives the students something more. Hope in a struggle for memory.

C **Informational Focus** Organizing Information This paragraph introduces other programs for coping with memory loss. How does it add to the story of the Early Bird Club, and what kind of information does it provide?

D **Informational Focus** Organizing Information Summarize the methods and goals of the program described in this article.

Vocabulary **tailored** (TAY luhrd) v.: made to specific requirements.

stigma (STIHG muh) n.: a mark of disgrace or shame.

SKILLS FOCUS Informational Skills Organize and record new information in systematic ways, such as notes, charts, and graphic organizers. **Vocabulary Skills** Demonstrate knowledge of literal meanings of words and their usage. **Listening and Speaking Skills** Adapt to purpose when speaking. **Writing Skills** Write brief constructed responses, with specific support.

Respond and Think Critically

Informational Text Focus

Quick Check

1. Describe the Early Bird Club's approach to helping people with memory impairments.

2. How does brain stimulation benefit people with Alzheimer's disease?

Read with a Purpose

3. For Alzheimer's patients, memory loss is inevitable. How do people try to fight it?

Informational Skills: Organizing Information

4. As you read, you used a chart to show the relationship between events and facts in this article. By presenting these particular events and facts, the writer suggests an idea about Alzheimer's and programs that cope with memory loss. Look over your chart carefully. Then, write a single sentence stating the article's main idea.

Events	Facts
eight students get together (p. 926)	ages 56—81, five with early Alzheimer's (p. 926)

✓ Vocabulary Check

Match each Vocabulary word with its definition.

5. gravitate   a. specifically designed

6. progressive   b. having varied tastes

7. stigma   c. move toward

8. eclectic   d. increasing in severity

9. tailored   e. negative reputation

10. camaraderie   f. friendly feeling

Text Analysis

11. **Interpret** Why is "the Big A" considered a stigma?

12. **Evaluate** One of the activities involves creating a story that revolves around chicken salad and carpooling. Which is more important: the story itself or the act of creating the story? Explain.

13. **Make Judgments** Describe three benefits of the Early Bird Club. If you were a person in the early stages of Alzheimer's disease, which benefit would be the most important to you? Explain.

Listening and Speaking

14. **Extend** While reading "The Fight Against Alzheimer's," you listed some of the activities that programs use to help people retain their memories. Now, imagine that you are leading such a program. Create an activity designed to challenge participants' minds. Lead a group of your classmates through the activity. How would your activity stimulate participants' memories?

Writing Focus   Constructed Response

Talk to two or three classmates, friends, or relatives about their significant memories and why these memories are important to them. Record these talks or write down comments that strike you as particularly interesting. Then, write a response about the importance of memory. Include several direct quotations.

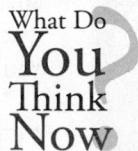

What Do You Think Now

What have the experiences of the participants in this program taught you about coping with a progressive disease?

The Secret Life of Walter Mitty

What Do You Think

How does progress challenge tradition and redefine society?

QuickWrite

How can humor challenge tradition by testing our beliefs and assumptions? Write a few sentences about how humor provides a fresh perspective on social structures we may take for granted.

James Thurber
(1894–1961)

A supremely gifted cartoonist and a writer of essays, sketches, and stories, James Thurber is considered one of the greatest American humorists of the twentieth century.

A Humorous Self-Portrait

Thurber once mocked the typical puffed-up biographies of literary figures by presenting this self-portrait:

> James Thurber was born in Columbus Ohio, where so many awful things happened to him, on December 8, 1894. . . . He began to write when he was ten years old . . . and to draw when he was fourteen. . . . Quick to arouse, he is very hard to quiet and people often just go away. . . . He never listens when anybody else is talking, preferring to keep his mind a blank until they get through, so he can talk. . . . He is Sagittarius with the moon in Aries and gets along fine with persons born between the 20th and 24th of August.

Thurber did grow up in Columbus, where he attended Ohio State University. He worked as a reporter in Columbus and Chicago for a number of years. He moved east, went to work for *The New Yorker* magazine in 1927, and remained on its staff for the rest of his life. In addition to writing many collections of essays, stories, and children's books, he collaborated on a successful Broadway play.

"You Can't Explain Thurber"

Thurber's humor often turned on the chaos of contemporary American life. His works often focused on the "little man," who cannot quite assert himself. Thurber defined humor as "a kind of emotional chaos told about calmly and quietly in retrospect."

The writer Mark Van Doren, a friend of Thurber's, said of him: "He was an extraordinary man . . . with so many quick changes: gentle and fierce, fascinating and boring, sophisticated and boorish, kind and cruel, broad-minded and parochial. You can't explain Thurber."

Think About the Writer

How might the chaos of contemporary life provide a rich source for humor?

 **Reader/Writer Notebook**

Use your **RWN** to complete the activities for this selection.

Literary Focus

Parody A work that ridicules another work by imitating or exaggerating some aspect of its style or content is called a **parody.** You have probably encountered parodies of shows, songs, and films in humor magazines, TV sitcoms, commercials, and movies. In "The Secret Life of Walter Mitty," the title character lapses into daydreams that parody different types of stories or films. As you read, try to determine the kinds of stories or films that each daydream parodies.

Reading Focus

Analyzing Cause and Effect In this famous story, James Thurber uses the basic plot structure of **cause and effect** in a highly original way. He creates a pattern of free association in which trivial details from Mitty's everyday life trigger grand adventures in Mitty's imagination. Thus, a mundane and trivial cause has a momentous imaginary effect, giving Mitty at least a temporary triumph over reality.

Into Action As you read the story, note the unheroic detail that triggers each heroic daydream. Note also Mitty's character in each daydream, the subject each daydream parodies, and what snaps Mitty out of each fantasy.

Cause of day-dream	Mitty's character in daydream	Subject of parody	Cause of daydream's end
Driving with his wife into town	Naval commander	War/adventure story	Mrs. Mitty says, "Not so fast!"

Writing Focus

Think as a Reader/Writer

Find It in Your Reading Writers of parody often use **hyperbole,** or dramatic exaggeration. Elements that are excessive, outrageous, or ridiculous increase a parody's humor. In one of Mitty's daydreams, for example, a character exclaims, "The Old Man ain't afraid of Hell!"—the sort of over-the-top statement common in wartime melodrama. As you read this story, use your *Reader/Writer Notebook* to record other examples of exaggerated, outrageous, or ridiculous elements.

Vocabulary

rakishly (RAY kihsh lee) *adv.:* in a casual, stylish manner. *The commander's cap was pulled rakishly over one eye.*

distraught (dihs TRAWT) *adj.:* highly troubled. *Dr. Renshaw looked distraught after a difficult operation.*

haggard (HAG uhrd) *adj.:* wasted or worn in appearance. *Dr. Renshaw's haggard appearance was a result of long hours spent in the operating room.*

insolent (IIN suh luhnt) *adj.:* boldly disrespectful. *Irritated with Mitty's lack of attention, the parking-lot attendant parked Mitty's car with insolent skill.*

bickering (BIHK uhr ihng) *v.* used as *adj.:* quarreling over something unimportant; squabbling. *Raising his hand, Mitty calmly silenced the bickering attorneys.*

pandemonium (pan duh MOH nee uhm) *n.:* wild confusion. *When Mitty claimed that he could have killed the victim, pandemonium broke loose in the courtroom.*

inscrutable (ihn SKROO tuh buhl) *adj.:* mysterious. *With a fleeting smile on his lips, the inscrutable Walter Mitty proudly faced the firing squad.*

Language Coach

Words Ending in *–ing* The word *bickering* is an adjective in the example sentence above; but in this sentence, it is a noun: *Stop that bickering!* Use each of these words first as a adjective and then as a noun: *daydreaming, awakening, driving, nagging.*

 Learn It Online

Find a graphic organizer, activities, and links for this story online.

go.hrw.com | L11-931 | **Go**

THE SECRET LIFE OF WALTER MITTY

by **James Thurber**

Read with a Purpose
Read to learn what kind of person Mitty becomes in each of his daydreams.

Build Background
This story became instantly popular when it was published in *The New Yorker* in 1939. Since then, the name "Walter Mitty" has become synonymous with a person who is prone to romantic daydreaming. In fact, the term is defined in *Webster's Third New International Dictionary* as "a commonplace unadventurous person who seeks escape from reality through daydreaming and typically imagines himself leading a glamorous life and becoming famous." Although Mitty is based on the age-old stereotype of a belittled husband, Thurber's character is also an original—no one else dreams his dreams in quite the same way as Mitty dreams them.

"We're going through!" The commander's voice was like thin ice breaking. He wore his full-dress uniform, with the heavily braided white cap pulled down rakishly over one cold gray eye. "We can't make it, sir. It's spoiling for[1] a hurricane, if you ask me." "I'm not asking you, Lieutenant Berg," said the commander. "Throw on the power lights! Rev her up to 8,500! We're going through!" The pounding of the cylinders increased: ta-pocketa-pocketa-pocketa-pocketa-pocketa. The commander stared at the ice forming on the pilot window. He walked over and twisted a row of complicated dials. "Switch on No. 8 auxiliary!" he shouted. "Switch on No. 8 auxiliary!" repeated Lieutenant Berg. "Full strength in No. 3 turret!" shouted the commander. "Full strength in No. 3 turret!" The crew, bending to their various tasks in the huge, hurtling eight-engined navy hydroplane, looked at each other and grinned. "The Old Man'll get us through," they said to one another. "The Old Man ain't afraid of Hell!" . . . Ⓐ

"Not so fast! You're driving too fast!" said Mrs. Mitty. "What are you driving so fast for?"

"Hmm?" said Walter Mitty. He looked at his wife, in the seat beside him, with shocked astonishment. She seemed grossly unfamiliar, like a strange woman who had yelled at him in a crowd. "You were up to fifty-five," she said. "You know I don't like to go more than forty. You were up to fifty-five." Walter Mitty drove on toward Waterbury in silence, the roaring of the SN202 through the worst storm in twenty years of navy flying fading in the remote, intimate airways of his mind. "You're tensed up again," said Mrs. Mitty. "It's one of your days. I wish you'd let Dr. Renshaw look you over." Ⓑ

Walter Mitty stopped the car in front of the building where his wife went to have her hair done. "Remember to get those overshoes while I'm having my hair done," she said. "I don't need overshoes," said Mitty. She put her mirror back into her bag. "We've been all through that," she said, getting out of the car. "You're not a young man any longer." He raced the engine a little. "Why don't you wear your gloves? Have you lost your gloves?" Walter Mitty reached in a pocket and brought out the gloves. He put them on, but after she had turned and gone into the building and he had driven on to a red light, he took them off again. "Pick it up, brother!" snapped a cop as the light changed, and Mitty hastily pulled on his gloves and lurched ahead. He drove around the streets aimlessly for a time, and then he drove past the hospital on his way to the parking lot. Ⓒ

. . . "It's the millionaire banker, Wellington McMillan," said the pretty nurse. "Yes?" said Walter Mitty, removing his gloves slowly. "Who has the case?" "Dr. Renshaw and Dr. Benbow, but there are two specialists here, Dr. Remington from New York and Mr. Pritchard-Mitford from London. He flew over." A door opened down a long, cool corridor and Dr. Renshaw came out. He looked distraught and haggard. "Hello, Mitty," he said. "We're having the devil's own time with McMillan, the millionaire banker and close personal friend of Roosevelt. Obstreosis of the ductal tract. Tertiary. Wish you'd take a look at him." "Glad to," said Mitty.

In the operating room there were whispered introductions: "Dr. Remington, Dr. Mitty. Mr. Pritchard-Mitford, Dr. Mitty." "I've read your book on streptothricosis," said Pritchard-Mitford, shaking hands. "A brilliant performance, sir." "Thank you," said Walter Mitty. "Didn't know you were in the States, Mitty," grumbled Remington. "Coals to Newcastle,[2] bringing Mitford and me up here for a tertiary." "You are very kind," said Mitty. A huge, complicated

---

1. **it's spoiling for:** slang for "conditions are right for."

2. **coals to Newcastle:** unnecessary effort. Newcastle, England, was a major coal-producing city.

Ⓐ **Literary Focus** Parody What details in this opening paragraph reveal that it is parody?

Ⓑ **Reading Focus** Analyzing Cause and Effect Why does Mitty's wife seem "grossly unfamiliar" to him at this moment? What does this suggest both about the reason he daydreams and about the effect of his daydreaming on their relationship?

Ⓒ **Reading Focus** Analyzing Cause and Effect What may have caused Mitty to race the engine a little?

Vocabulary rakishly (RAY kihsh lee) adv.: in a casual, stylish manner.
distraught (dihs TRAWT) adj.: highly troubled.
haggard (HAG uhrd) adj.: wasted or worn in appearance.

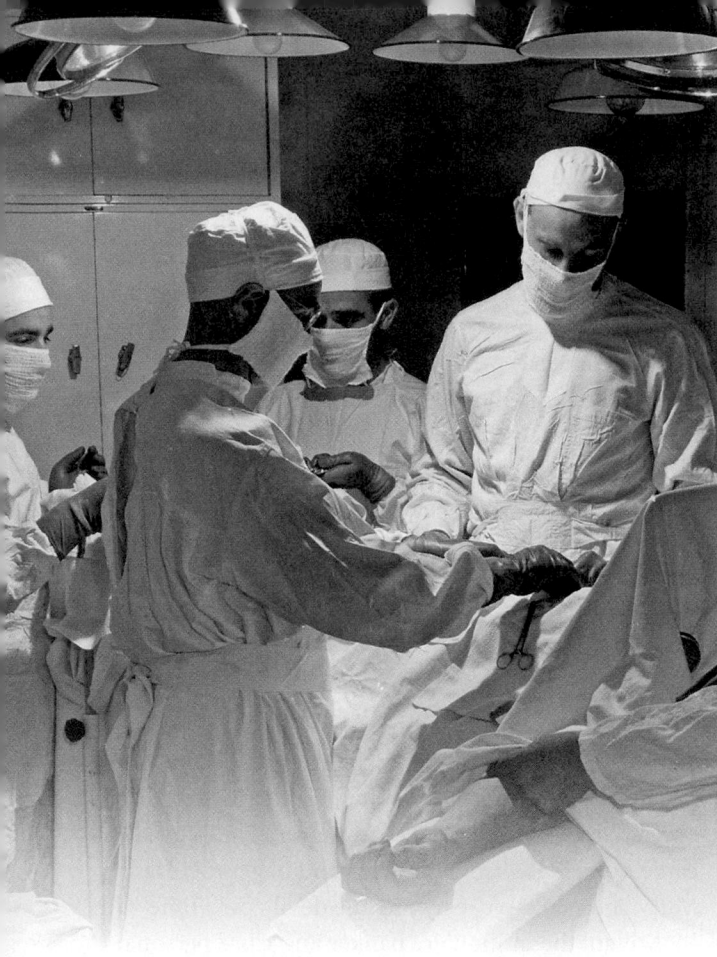

uncertain faces of the two great specialists. "If you wish," he said. They slipped a white gown on him; he adjusted a mask and drew on thin gloves; nurses handed him shining . . .

"Back it up, Mac! Look out for that Buick!" Walter Mitty jammed on the brakes. "Wrong lane, Mac," said the parking-lot attendant, looking at Mitty closely. "Gee. Yeh," muttered Mitty. He began cautiously to back out of the lane marked "Exit Only." "Leave her sit there," said the attendant. "I'll put her away." Mitty got out of the car. "Hey, better leave the key." "Oh," said Mitty, handing the man the ignition key. The attendant vaulted into the car, backed it up with insolent skill, and put it where it belonged.

They're so damn cocky, thought Walter Mitty, walking along Main Street; they think they know everything. Once he had tried to take his chains[3] off, outside New Milford, and he had got them wound around the axles. A man had had to come out in a wrecking car and unwind them, a young, grinning garageman. Since then Mrs. Mitty always made him drive to a garage to have the chains taken off. The next time, he thought, I'll wear my right arm in a sling; they won't grin at me then. I'll have my right arm in a sling, and they'll see I couldn't possibly take the chains off myself. He kicked at the slush on the sidewalk. "Overshoes," he said to himself, and he began looking for a shoe store.

When he came out into the street again, with the overshoes in a box under his arm, Walter Mitty began to wonder what the other thing was his wife had told him to get. She had told him, twice, before they set out from their house for Waterbury. In a way he hated these weekly trips to town—he was always getting something wrong. Kleenex, he thought, Squibb's,[4] razor blades? No. Toothpaste, toothbrush, bicarbonate, carborundum, initiative and referendum? He gave it

---

machine, connected to the operating table, with many tubes and wires, began at this moment to go pocketa-pocketa-pocketa. "The new anesthetizer is giving way!" shouted an intern. "There is no one in the East who knows how to fix it!" "Quiet, man!" said Mitty, in a low, cool voice. He sprang to the machine, which was now going pocketa-pocketa-queep-pocketa-queep. He began fingering delicately a row of glistening dials. "Give me a fountain pen!" he snapped. Someone handed him a fountain pen. He pulled a faulty piston out of the machine and inserted the pen in its place. "That will hold for ten minutes," he said. "Get on with the operation." A nurse hurried over and whispered to Renshaw, and Mitty saw the man turn pale. "Coreopsis has set in," said Renshaw nervously. "If you would take over, Mitty?" Mitty looked at him and at the craven figure of Benbow, who drank, and at the grave,

---

3. **chains:** chains attached to automobile tires to increase traction in snow and ice.
4. **Squibb's:** Squibb (now part of Bristol-Myers Squibb) was a U.S. pharmaceutical company that manufactured a variety of prescription drugs and health care products. It is not clear which product Mitty is thinking about.

D **Literary Focus** **Parody** What medical stereotype does Thurber parody here? How do the misused or made-up words, the medical jargon, and the incident with the fountain pen contribute to the parody?

Vocabulary **insolent** (IHN suh luhnt) *adj.:* boldly disrespectful.

up. But she would remember it. "Where's the what's-its-name?" she would ask. "Don't tell me you forgot the what's-its-name." A newsboy went by shouting something about the Waterbury trial.

. . . "Perhaps this will refresh your memory." The district attorney suddenly thrust a heavy automatic at the quiet figure on the witness stand. "Have you ever seen this before?" Walter Mitty took the gun and examined it expertly. "This is my Webley-Vickers 50.80," he said calmly. An excited buzz ran around the courtroom. The judge rapped for order. "You are a crack shot with any sort of firearms, I believe?" said the district attorney, insinuatingly. "Objection!" shouted Mitty's attorney. "We have shown that the defendant could not have fired the shot. We have shown that he wore his right arm in a sling on the night of the fourteenth of July." Walter Mitty raised his hand briefly and the bickering attorneys were stilled. "With any known make of gun," he said evenly, "I could have killed Gregory Fitzhurst at three hundred feet *with my left hand.*" Pandemonium broke loose in the courtroom. A woman's scream rose above the bedlam and suddenly a lovely, dark-haired girl was in Walter Mitty's arms. The district attorney struck at her savagely. Without rising from his chair, Mitty let the man have it on the point of the chin. "You miserable cur!"[5] . . .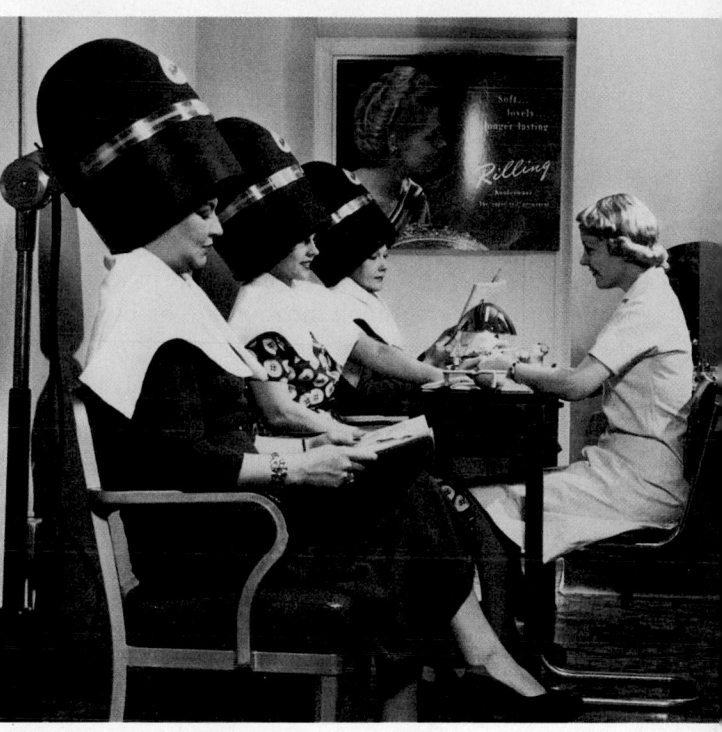

"Puppy biscuit," said Walter Mitty. He stopped walking and the buildings of Waterbury rose up out of the misty courtroom and surrounded him again. A woman who was passing laughed. "He said 'Puppy biscuit,'" she said to her companion. "That man said 'Puppy biscuit' to himself." Walter Mitty hurried on. He went into an A & P, not the first one he came to but a smaller one farther up the street. "I want some biscuit for small, young dogs," he said to the clerk. "Any special brand, sir?" The greatest pistol shot in the world thought a moment. "It says 'Puppies Bark for It' on the box," said Walter Mitty. **F**

His wife would be through at the hairdresser's in fifteen minutes, Mitty saw in looking at his watch, unless they had trouble drying it; sometimes they had trouble drying it. She didn't like to get to the hotel first; she would want him to be there waiting for her as usual. He found a big leather chair in the lobby, facing a window, and he put the overshoes and the puppy biscuit on the floor beside it. He picked up an old copy of *Liberty* and sank down into the chair. "Can Germany Conquer the World Through the Air?" Walter Mitty looked at the pictures of bombing planes and of ruined streets.

. . . "The cannonading has got the wind up in young Raleigh, sir," said the sergeant. Captain Mitty looked up at him through tousled hair. "Get him to bed," he said wearily. "With the others. I'll fly alone." "But you can't, sir," said the sergeant anxiously.

---

5. **cur:** cowardly or contemptible person; also, a mongrel dog.

E **Literary Focus** **Parody** What stereotype does Thurber parody by describing the female in Mitty's arms as "a lovely, dark-haired girl"?

F **Reading Focus** **Analyzing Cause and Effect** What association does Mitty make with the word *cur* in his daydream? How does this differ from previous interruptions to Mitty's daydreams?

Vocabulary **bickering** (BIHK uhr ihng) *v.* used as *adj.:* quarreling over something unimportant; squabbling.
pandemonium (pan duh MOH nee uhm) *n.:* wild confusion.

"It takes two men to handle that bomber and the Archies[6] are pounding hell out of the air. Von Richtman's circus[7] is between here and Saulier." "Somebody's got to get to that ammunition dump," said Mitty. "I'm going over. Spot of brandy?" He poured a drink for the sergeant and one for himself. War thundered and whined around the dugout and battered at the door. There was a rending of wood and splinters flew through the room. "A bit of a near thing," said Captain Mitty carelessly. "The box barrage is closing in," said the sergeant. "We only live once, Sergeant," said Mitty, with his faint, fleeting smile. "Or do we?" He poured another brandy and tossed it off. "I never see a man could hold his brandy like you, sir," said the sergeant. "Begging your pardon, sir." Captain Mitty stood up and strapped on his huge Webley-Vickers automatic. "It's forty kilometers through hell, sir," said the sergeant. Mitty finished one last brandy. "After all," he said softly, "what isn't?" The pounding of the cannon increased; there was the rat-tat-tatting of machine guns, and from somewhere came the menacing pocketa-pocketa-pocketa of the new flame-throwers. Walter Mitty walked to the door of the dugout humming "Auprès de Ma Blonde."[8] He turned and waved to the sergeant. "Cheerio!" he said. . . .

Something struck his shoulder. "I've been looking all over this hotel for you," said Mrs. Mitty. "Why do you have to hide in this old chair? How did you expect me to find you?" "Things close in," said Walter Mitty vaguely. "What?" Mrs. Mitty said. "Did you get the what's-its-name? The puppy biscuit? What's in that box?" "Overshoes," said Mitty. "Couldn't you have put them on in the store?" "I was thinking," said

Walter Mitty. "Does it ever occur to you that I am sometimes thinking?" She looked at him. "I'm going to take your temperature when I get you home," she said. **H**

They went out through the revolving doors that made a faintly derisive whistling sound when you pushed them. It was two blocks to the parking lot. At the drugstore on the corner she said, "Wait here for me. I forgot something. I won't be a minute." She was more than a minute. Walter Mitty lighted a cigarette. It began to rain, rain with sleet in it. He stood up against the wall of the drugstore, smoking. . . . He put his shoulders back and his heels together. "To hell with the handkerchief," said Walter Mitty scornfully. He took one last drag on his cigarette and snapped it away. Then, with that faint, fleeting smile playing about his lips, he faced the firing squad; erect and motionless, proud and disdainful, Walter Mitty the Undefeated, inscrutable to the last. **I**

---

6. **Archies:** German antiaircraft guns or gunners in World War I.
7. **circus:** squadron of planes.
8. **"Auprès de Ma Blonde"** (oh PRAY duh mah blohnd): French song. The title means "Near My Blonde."

G **Literary Focus** Parody What is the target of this parody? Why do you think that Mitty is imagining himself in this kind of story?

H **Reading Focus** Analyzing Cause and Effect What does this conversation reveal about the relationship between Mitty and his wife? How do the two of them cause each other's behavior?

I **Reading Focus** Analyzing Cause and Effect What prompts Mitty to imagine that he is facing a firing squad? How does he face it? What does this suggest about how he feels about his life?

Vocabulary **inscrutable** (ihn SKROO tuh buhl) *adj.:* mysterious.

Applying Your Skills

SKILLS FOCUS Literary Skills Analyze parody; analyze irony. Reading Skills Analyze cause and effect. Vocabulary

Skills Understand denotation and connotation. Writing Skills Employ elements of an author's style effectively.

The Secret Life of Walter Mitty

Respond and Think Critically

Reading Focus

Quick Check

1. How does Mitty feel about his real-life errands?

2. How do people in real life react to Mitty?

3. How do his fantasies contrast with his real life?

Read with a Purpose

4. What sort of person is Mitty in each of his daydreams? What does Mitty's tendency to daydream reveal about his character?

Reading Skills: Analyzing Cause and Effect

5. Use your cause-and-effect chart to answer the following questions: What is the overriding cause of Mitty's tendency to daydream? Why do Mitty's daydreams parody popular movie and story styles? Do Mitty's problems with the world cause his daydreams, or do his daydreams cause his real-life interactions to be inept? Explain.

✓ Vocabulary Check

Connotations are the feelings attached to words. Use a chart like the one below to compare the connotations of each pair of words. Mark a > if the word on the left seems more intense than the one on the right. Mark a < if the word on the left seems weaker.

6. rakishly	<	flamboyantly
7. distraught		upset
8. haggard		tired
9. insolent		audacious
10. bickering		debating
11. pandemonium		noise
12. inscrutable		puzzling

Literary Focus

Literary Analysis

13. **Interpret** What is the meaning of the last line of the story? How might Mitty be "undefeated"?

14. **Extend** In a tribute to Thurber, writer E . B. White recalled Thurber's belief that humor "may do some good." Explore some of the effects of humor in this story. What good can come out of reading this story? What insight into human nature does the story reveal?

Literary Skills: Parody

15. **Make Judgments** Mitty's daydreams parody, or make fun of, genre movies and novels with stereotyped characters and dialogue. Why does Thurber make fun of movies and stories about war heroes, doctor heroes, and courtroom dramas? Explain.

Literary Skills Review: Irony

16. **Analyze** Recall that **irony** involves a discrepancy between what we expect to happen—or what we think is appropriate—and what does happen. What is the central irony of Mitty's life? What might this irony be saying about modern life?

Writing Focus

Think as a Reader/Writer

Use It in Your Writing Write a one or two-paragraph parody of a popular style of movie or TV show. Incorporate elements of hyperbole into your parody.

What Do You Think Now How does Mitty respond to modern life? Do you think Mitty would be inclined to embrace tradition, or would he be excited by progress? Explain.

The Life You Save May Be Your Own

What Do You Think?

How does progress challenge tradition and redefine society?

QuickTalk

In the struggle to adapt to rapid progress, people sometimes abandon worthy values or ideals. With a partner, talk about some ideals no longer valued in modern society. Are they lost forever, or might they be recovered? Explain.

Flannery O'Connor
(1925–1964)

Although Flannery O'Connor limited herself to a rural, Southern literary terrain, her works are so striking and original that they have earned a permanent place in American literature.

"Sickness Is a Place"

Flannery O'Connor was born in Savannah, Georgia, and spent almost all of her short life in nearby Milledgeville, where her family had lived since the Civil War. She graduated from the Georgia State College for Women and then went to the Writers' Workshop at the University of Iowa. She wrote steadily from 1948 until her early death sixteen years later.

For many years, she suffered from lupus, a painful disease of the immune system that had also killed her father. The illness kept her more confined and immobile as the years went on. "I have never been anywhere but sick," O'Connor wrote. "In a sense sickness is a place, more instructive than a long trip to Europe, and it's always a place where there's no company, where nobody can follow. Sickness before death is a very appropriate thing, and I think those who don't have it miss one of God's mercies."

A Unique Vision

From the first, O'Connor was recognized as a satirist of astonishing originality and energy, whose targets were smugness, optimism, and self-righteousness. The essential element of her life and work is that she remained a Roman Catholic without the slightest wavering of faith. A thunder-and-lightning Christian ideology fills every story and novel she wrote. Her attraction to the grotesque and the violent puts off some readers who fail to appreciate that the violent motifs in her short stories and novels grow from her passionate Christian vision of secular society.

What O'Connor wants to tell us is that, in our rationality, we have lost the one essential—a spiritual center for our lives. O'Connor seems to be saying that we have become so accustomed to the lack of God in our lives that a writer must use violent means to make a point.

Think About the Writer

Why might a devout Christian like Flannery O'Connor be drawn to characters without a spiritual center, like hypocrites and swindlers?

 **Reader/Writer**
Notebook
Use your **RWN** to complete the activities for this selection.

Literary Focus

Foreshadowing The use of hints and clues to suggest what will happen later in a plot is called **foreshadowing.** Writers use foreshadowing to build **suspense,** the feeling of uncertainty and curiosity about what will happen next in the story. As you read "The Life You Save May Be Your Own," pay close attention to clues that keep you on the edge of your seat.

Reading Focus

Making Predictions A **prediction** is a particular kind of inference. When you make predictions, you use the hints and clues of foreshadowing to make guesses about what will happen further along in a story. Hints and clues can take the form of **dialogue**, actions, images, figurative language, or descriptions of **character** and **setting**.

Into Action Use a chart like the one below to record your predictions about what will happen in the story. In the first column, record evidence from the story. In the second column, make your predictions about what will happen.

Clues from Story	My Predictions
"'Lady,'" he said..., "'I'd give a fortune to live where I could see me a sun do that every evening.'" (p. 941)	Mr. Shiftlet may be flattering Mrs. Crater because he will try to get something from her later on.

Writing Focus

Think as a Reader/Writer
Find It in Your Reading Flannery O'Connor uses striking **imagery,** language that evokes a picture or a concrete sensation of a person, a place, a thing, or an experience. Her imagery often enhances **atmosphere**, reveals character, foreshadows events, or hints at deeper meanings. For example, early in the story (page 941), Mr. Shiftlet raises his arms in such a way that "his figure formed a crooked cross." This description presents a clear image of Shiftlet, but it also foreshadows his deceptiveness and alludes to O'Connor's frequent theme of Christian redemption. Use your *Reader/ Writer Notebook* to record examples of other unusual or memorable images from the story.

 Learn It Online
Get to know the Vocabulary words inside and out with Word Watch online.

go.hrw.com   L11-939   **Go**

The Life You Save May Be Your Own

by **Flannery O'Connor**

Read with a Purpose
Read to discover how the title of the story relates to its theme.

Build Background

Flannery O'Connor is one of the most famous writers of Southern Gothic, an influential style that involves outlandish, grotesque, or otherwise distorted happenings in the American South. The style takes its name from the fiction of 1790s England, which drew on themes of medievalism and sensationalism. In Gothic writing, events and characters often have a deep, brooding horror and a sometimes supernatural sense of mystery; in Southern Gothic writing, however, these qualities may turn out to be darkly ironic. Other Southern Gothic writers include William Faulkner, Tennessee Williams, and Truman Capote.

Like all of O'Connor's writing, this story takes place in the rural South, a region struggling with the transition from agriculture to modern industrial life. The characters speak in dialect. Mr. Shiftlet probably lost his arm in World War II, in which the United States fought from 1941 to 1945.

The old woman and her daughter were sitting on their porch when Mr. Shiftlet came up their road for the first time. The old woman slid to the edge of her chair and leaned forward, shading her eyes from the piercing sunset with her hand. The daughter could not see far in front of her and continued to play with her fingers. Although the old woman lived in this desolate spot with only her daughter and she had never seen Mr. Shiftlet before, she could tell, even from a distance, that he was a tramp and no one to be afraid of. His left coat sleeve was folded up to show there was only half an arm in it and his gaunt figure listed[1] slightly to the side as if the breeze were pushing him. He had on a black town suit and a brown felt hat that was turned up in the front and down in the back and he carried a tin toolbox by a handle. He came on, at an amble,[2] up her road, his face turned toward the sun which appeared to be balancing itself on the peak of a small mountain. (A)

The old woman didn't change her position until he was almost into her yard; then she rose with one hand fisted on her hip. The daughter, a large girl in a short blue organdy dress, saw him all at once and jumped up and began to stamp and point and make excited speechless sounds.

Mr. Shiftlet stopped just inside the yard and set his box on the ground and tipped his hat at her as if she were not in the least afflicted;[3] then he turned toward the old woman and swung the hat all the way off. He had long black slick hair that hung flat from a part in the

---

1. **listed:** tilted.

2. **amble:** leisurely pace.
3. **afflicted:** developmentally disabled.

Vocabulary   **desolate** (DEHS uh liht) *adj.:* deserted.
gaunt (gawnt) *adj.:* very thin and bony.

(A) **Literary Focus** Foreshadowing What might Mr. Shiftlet's name suggest about his role in the story that follows?

Analyzing Visuals

Viewing and Interpreting In this painting, dark clouds ominously foreshadow a coming storm. How does O'Connor foreshadow dark events in her story?

middle to beyond the tips of his ears on either side. His face descended in forehead for more than half its length and ended suddenly with his features just balanced over a jutting steel-trap jaw. He seemed to be a young man but he had a look of composed dissatisfaction as if he understood life thoroughly.

"Good evening," the old woman said. She was about the size of a cedar fence post and she had a man's gray hat pulled down low over her head.

The tramp stood looking at her and didn't answer. He turned his back and faced the sunset. He swung both his whole and his short arm up slowly so that they indicated an expanse of sky and his figure formed a crooked cross. The old woman watched him with her arms folded across her chest as if she were the owner of the sun, and the daughter watched, her head thrust forward and her fat helpless hands hanging at the wrists. She had long pink-gold hair and eyes as blue as a peacock's neck. **B**

He held the pose for almost fifty seconds and then he picked up his box and came on to the porch and dropped down on the bottom step. "Lady," he said in a firm nasal voice, "I'd give a fortune to live where I could see me a sun do that every evening." **C**

"Does it every evening," the old woman said and sat back down. The daughter sat down too and watched him with a cautious sly look as if he were a bird that had

B **Literary Focus** Foreshadowing What might the image of the crooked cross suggest? What does this image foreshadow about what will happen in the story?

C **Reading Focus** Making Predictions Do you think that Mr. Shiftlet will get his wish? Explain.

come up very close. He leaned to one side, rooting in his pants pocket, and in a second he brought out a package of chewing gum and offered her a piece. She took it and unpeeled it and began to chew without taking her eyes off him. He offered the old woman a piece but she only raised her upper lip to indicate she had no teeth.

Mr. Shiftlet's pale sharp glance had already passed over everything in the yard—the pump near the corner of the house and the big fig tree that three or four chickens were preparing to roost in—and had moved to a shed where he saw the square rusted back of an automobile. "You ladies drive?" he asked.

"That car ain't run in fifteen year," the old woman said. "The day my husband died, it quit running."

"Nothing is like it used to be, lady," he said. "The world is almost rotten."

"That's right," the old woman said. "You from around here?"

"Name Tom T. Shiftlet," he murmured, looking at the tires.

"I'm pleased to meet you," the old woman said. "Name Lucynell Crater and daughter Lucynell Crater. What you doing around here, Mr. Shiftlet?"

He judged the car to be about a 1928 or '29 Ford. "Lady," he said, and turned and gave her his full attention, "lemme tell you something. There's one of these doctors in Atlanta that's taken a knife and cut the human heart—the human heart," he repeated, leaning forward, "out of a man's chest and held it in his hand," and he held his hand out, palm up, as if it were slightly weighted with the human heart, "and studied it like it was a day-old chicken, and lady," he said, allowing a long significant pause in which his head slid forward and his clay-colored eyes brightened, "he don't know no more about it than you or me."

"That's right," the old woman said.

"Why, if he was to take that knife and cut into every corner of it, he still wouldn't know no more than you or me. What you want to bet?"

"Nothing," the old woman said wisely. "Where you come from, Mr. Shiftlet?"

He didn't answer. He reached into his pocket and brought out a sack of tobacco and a package of cigarette papers and rolled himself a cigarette, expertly with one hand, and attached it in a hanging position to his upper lip. Then he took a box of wooden matches from his pocket and struck one on his shoe. He held the burning match as if he were studying the mystery of flame while it traveled dangerously toward his skin. The daughter began to make loud noises and to point to his hand and shake her finger at him, but when the flame was just before touching him, he leaned down with his hand cupped over it as if he were going to set fire to his nose and lit the cigarette.

He flipped away the dead match and blew a stream of gray into the evening. A sly look came over his face. "Lady," he said, "nowadays, people'll do anything

---

D **Reading Focus** **Making Predictions** Why does Mr. Shiftlet make this speech to Mrs. Crater? What can you predict about his future actions on the basis of his speech?

anyways. I can tell you my name is Tom T. Shiftlet, and I come from Tarwater, Tennessee, but you never have seen me before: How you know I ain't lying? How you know my name ain't Aaron Sparks, lady, and I come from Singleberry, Georgia, or how you know it's not George Speeds and I come from Lucy, Alabama, or how you know I ain't Thompson Bright from Toolafalls, Mississippi?"

"I don't know nothing about you," the old woman muttered, irked.[4]

"Lady," he said, "people don't care how they lie. Maybe the best I can tell you is, I'm a man; but listen lady," he said and paused and made his tone more ominous still, "what is a man?"

The old woman began to gum a seed. "What you carry in that tin box, Mr. Shiftlet?" she asked.

"Tools," he said, put back. "I'm a carpenter."

"Well, if you come out here to work, I'll be able to feed you and give you a place to sleep but I can't pay. I'll tell you that before you begin," she said.

There was no answer at once and no particular expression on his face. He leaned back against the two-by-four that helped support the porch roof. "Lady," he said slowly, "there's some men that some things mean more to them than money." The old woman rocked without comment and the daughter watched the trigger that moved up and down in his neck. He told the old woman then that all most people were interested in was money, but he asked what a man was made for. He asked her if a man was made for money, or what. He asked her what she thought she was made for but she didn't answer, she only sat rocking and wondered if a one-armed man could put a new roof on her garden house. He asked a lot of questions that she didn't answer. He told her that he was twenty-eight years old and had lived a varied life. He had been a gospel singer, a foreman on the railroad, an assistant in an undertaking parlor, and he come over the radio for three months with Uncle Roy and his Red Creek Wranglers. He said he had fought and

bled in the Arm Service of his country and visited every foreign land and that everywhere he had seen people that didn't care if they did a thing one way or another. He said he hadn't been raised thataway.

A fat yellow moon appeared in the branches of the fig tree as if it were going to roost there with the chickens. He said that a man had to escape to the country to see the world whole and that he wished he lived in a desolate place like this where he could see the sun go down every evening like God made it to do.

"Are you married or are you single?" the old woman asked. **E**

There was a long silence. "Lady," he asked finally, "where would you find you an innocent woman today? I wouldn't have any of this trash I could just pick up."

The daughter was leaning very far down, hanging her head almost between her knees watching him through a triangular door she had made in her over turned hair; and she suddenly fell in a heap on the floor and began to whimper. Mr. Shiftlet straightened her out and helped her get back in the chair.

"Is she your baby girl?" he asked.

"My only," the old woman said, "and she's the sweetest girl in the world. I would give her up for nothing on earth. She's smart too. She can sweep the floor, cook, wash, feed the chickens, and hoe. I wouldn't give her up for a casket of jewels." **F**

"No," he said kindly, "don't ever let any man take her away from you."

"Any man come after her," the old woman said, "'ll have to stay around the place."

Mr. Shiftlet's eye in the darkness was focused on a part of the automobile bumper that glittered in the distance. "Lady," he said, jerking his short arm up as if he could point with it to her house and yard and pump, "there ain't a broken thing on this plantation that I couldn't fix for you, one-arm jackleg[5] or not. I'm a man,"

---

4. **irked:** annoyed; irritated.

---

5. **jackleg:** amateur; someone not correctly trained. O'Connor is probably playing with the other meaning of *jackleg,* "a dishonest person."

E **Reading Focus** **Making Predictions** Why might Mrs. Crater question Mr. Shiftlet about his marital status?

F **Reading Focus** **Making Predictions** Why is Mrs. Crater trying to convince Mr. Shiftlet that her "afflicted" daughter is "smart"? What prediction can you make about her future actions?

he said with a sullen dignity, "even if I ain't a whole one. I got," he said, tapping his knuckles on the floor to emphasize the immensity of what he was going to say, "a moral intelligence!" and his face pierced out of the darkness into a shaft of doorlight and he stared at her as if he were astonished himself at this impossible truth. **(G)**

The old woman was not impressed with the phrase. "I told you you could hang around and work for food," she said, "if you don't mind sleeping in that car yonder."

"Why listen, lady," he said with a grin of delight, "the monks of old slept in their coffins!"

"They wasn't as advanced as we are," the old woman said.

The next morning he began on the roof of the garden house while Lucynell, the daughter, sat on a rock and watched him work. He had not been around a week before the change he had made in the place was apparent. He had patched the front and back steps, built a new hog pen, restored a fence, and taught Lucynell, who was completely deaf and had never said a word in her life, to say the word "bird." The big rosy-faced girl followed him everywhere, saying "Burrttddt ddbirrrttdt," and clapping her hands. The old woman watched from a distance, secretly pleased. She was ravenous for a son-in-law. **(H)**

Mr. Shiftlet slept on the hard narrow back seat of the car with his feet out the side window. He had his razor and a can of water on a crate that served him as a bedside table and he put up a piece of mirror against the back glass and kept his coat neatly on a hanger that he hung over one of the windows.

In the evenings he sat on the steps and talked while the old woman and Lucynell rocked violently in their chairs on either side of him. The old woman's three mountains were black against the dark blue sky and were visited off and on by various planets and by the moon after it had left the chickens. Mr. Shiftlet pointed out that the reason he had improved this plantation was because he had taken a personal interest in it. He said he was even going to make the automobile run.

He had raised the hood and studied the mechanism and he said he could tell that the car had been built in the days when cars were really built. You take now, he said, one man puts in one bolt and another man puts in another bolt and another man puts in another bolt so that it's a man for a bolt. That's why you have to pay so much for a car: you're paying all those men. Now if you didn't have to pay but one man, you could get you a cheaper car and one that had had a personal interest taken in it, and it would be a better car. The old woman agreed with him that this was so.

Mr. Shiftlet said that the trouble with the world was that nobody cared, or stopped and took any trouble. He said he never would have been able to teach Lucynell to say a word if he hadn't cared and stopped long enough.

"Teach her to say something else," the old woman said.

"What you want her to say next?" Mr. Shiftlet asked.

The old woman's smile was broad and toothless and suggestive. "Teach her to say 'sugarpie,'" she said.

Mr. Shiftlet already knew what was on her mind.

The next day he began to tinker with the automobile and that evening he told her that if she would buy a fan belt, he would be able to make the car run.

The old woman said she would give him the money. "You see that girl yonder?" she asked, pointing to Lucynell who was sitting on the floor a foot away, watching him, her eyes blue even in the dark. "If it was ever a man wanted to take her away, I would say, 'No man on earth is going to take that sweet girl of mine away from me!' but if he was to say, 'Lady, I don't want to take her away, I want her right here,' I would say, 'Mister, I don't blame you none. I wouldn't pass up a chance to live in a permanent place and get the sweetest girl in the world myself. You ain't no fool,' I would say."

"How old is she?" Mr. Shiftlet asked casually.

"Fifteen, sixteen," the old woman said. The girl was nearly thirty but because of her innocence it was impossible to guess.

(G) Literary Focus Foreshadowing What do Mr. Shiftlet's glance at the car and his comments about his "moral intelligence" suggest about what will happen next?

(H) Reading Focus Making Predictions Do you think Mrs. Crater will get her wish? Explain.

"It would be a good idea to paint it too," Mr. Shiftlet remarked. "You don't want it to rust out." ❶

"We'll see about that later," the old woman said.

The next day he walked into town and returned with the parts he needed and a can of gasoline. Late in the afternoon, terrible noises issued from the shed and the old woman rushed out of the house, thinking Lucynell was somewhere having a fit. Lucynell was sitting on a chicken crate, stamping her feet and screaming, "Burrddttt! bddurrddtttt!" but her fuss was drowned out by the car. With a volley of blasts it emerged from the shed, moving in a fierce and stately way. Mr. Shiftlet was in the driver's seat, sitting very erect. He had an expression of serious modesty on his face as if he had just raised the dead.

That night, rocking on the porch, the old woman began her business, at once. "You want you an innocent woman, don't you?" she asked sympathetically. "You don't want none of this trash."

"No'm, I don't," Mr. Shiftlet said.

"One that can't talk," she continued, "can't sass you back or use foul language. That's the kind for you to have. Right there," and she pointed to Lucynell sitting cross-legged in her chair, holding both feet in her hands.

"That's right," he admitted. "She wouldn't give me any trouble."

"Saturday," the old woman said, "you and her and me can drive into town and get married."

Mr. Shiftlet eased his position on the steps.

"I can't get married right now," he said. "Everything you want to do takes money and I ain't got any."

"What you need with money?" she asked.

"It takes money," he said. "Some people'll do anything anyhow these days, but the way I think, I wouldn't marry no woman that I couldn't take on a trip like she was somebody. I mean take her to a hotel and treat her. I wouldn't marry the Duchesser Windsor,[6] he said firmly, "unless I could take her to a hotel and giver something good to eat.

"I was raised thataway and there ain't a thing I can do about it. My old mother taught me how to do."

"Lucynell don't even know what a hotel is," the old woman muttered. "Listen here, Mr. Shiftlet," she said, sliding forward in her chair, "you'd be getting a permanent house and a deep well and the most innocent girl in the world. You don't need no money. Lemme tell you something: there ain't any place in the world for a poor disabled friendless drifting man."

The ugly words settled in Mr. Shiftlet's head like a group of buzzards in the top of a tree. He didn't answer at once. He rolled himself a cigarette and lit it and then he said in an even voice, "Lady, a man is divided into two parts, body and spirit."

The old woman clamped her gums together.

---

6. **Duchesser Windsor:** the duchess of Windsor, the American woman whom King Edward VIII of England gave up his throne to marry. The duchess of Windsor was one of the most elegant women of her time.

---

❶ **Reading Focus** Making Predictions Mr. Shiftlet abruptly changes the subject. What can you predict about his true motivations and his future behavior?

"A body and a spirit," he repeated. "The body, lady, is like a house: it don't go anywhere; but the spirit, lady, is like an automobile: always on the move, always . . ."

"Listen, Mr. Shiftlet," she said, "my well never goes dry and my house is always warm in the winter and there's no mortgage on a thing about this place. You can go to the courthouse and see for yourself. And yonder under that shed is a fine automobile." She laid the bait carefully. "You can have it painted by Saturday. I'll pay for the paint."

In the darkness, Mr. Shiftlet's smile stretched like a weary snake waking up by a fire. After a second he recalled himself and said, "I'm only saying a man's spirit means more to him than anything else. I would have to take my wife off for the weekend without no regards at all for cost. I got to follow where my spirit says to go." **J**

"I'll give you fifteen dollars for a weekend trip," the old woman said in a crabbed voice. "That's the best I can do."

"That wouldn't hardly pay for more than the gas and the hotel," he said. "It wouldn't feed her."

"Seventeen-fifty," the old woman said. "That's all I got so it isn't any use you trying to milk me. You can take a lunch."

Mr. Shiftlet was deeply hurt by the word "milk." He didn't doubt that she had more money sewed up in her mattress but he had already told her he was not interested in her money. "I'll make that do," he said and rose and walked off without treating[7] with her further.

On Saturday the three of them drove into town in the car that the paint had barely dried on and Mr. Shiftlet and Lucynell were married in the Ordinary's office[8] while the old woman witnessed. As they came out of the courthouse, Mr. Shiftlet began twisting his neck in his collar. He looked morose and bitter as if he had been insulted while someone held him. "That didn't satisfy me none," he said. "That was just some-

---

7. **treating:** dealing; negotiating.
8. **Ordinary's office:** judge's office.

thing a woman in an office did, nothing but paper-work and blood tests. What do they know about my blood? If they was to take my heart and cut it out," he said, "they wouldn't know a thing about me. It didn't satisfy me at all."

"It satisfied the law," the old woman said sharply.

"The law," Mr. Shiftlet said and spit. "It's the law that don't satisfy me."

He had painted the car dark green with a yellow band around it just under the windows. The three of them climbed in the front seat and the old woman said, "Don't Lucynell look pretty? Looks like a baby doll." Lucynell was dressed up in a white dress that her mother had uprooted from a trunk and there was a Panama hat on her head with a bunch of red wooden cherries on the brim. Every now and then her placid expression was changed by a sly isolated little thought like a shoot of green in the desert. "You got a prize!" the old woman said.

Mr. Shiftlet didn't even look at her. **K**

They drove back to the house to let the old woman off and pick up the lunch. When they were ready to leave, she stood staring in the window of the car, with her fingers clenched around the glass. Tears began to seep sideways out of her eyes and run along the dirty creases in her face. "I ain't ever been parted with her for two days before," she said.

Mr. Shiftlet started the motor.

"And I wouldn't let no man have her but you because I seen you would do right. Good-bye, Sugarbaby," she said, clutching at the sleeve of the white dress. Lucynell looked straight at her and didn't seem to see her there at all. Mr. Shiftlet eased the car forward so that she had to move her hands.

The early afternoon was clear and open and surrounded by pale blue sky. Although the car would go only thirty miles an hour, Mr. Shiftlet imagined a terrific climb and dip and swerve that went entirely to his head so that he forgot his morning bitterness. He had always wanted an automobile but he had never been able to afford one before. He drove very fast because he wanted to make Mobile by nightfall.

J Literary Focus **Foreshadowing** What is suggested by the comparison of Mr. Shiftlet's smile to a "weary snake waking up by a fire"? What might Mr. Shiftlet be planning?

K Reading Focus **Making Predictions** What does this detail lead you to predict about the honeymoon?

Vocabulary **morose** (muh ROHS) *adj.*: gloomy.

"Hitchhiker," Mr. Shiftlet explained. "I can't wait. I got to make Tuscaloosa."

The boy bent over again and very carefully touched his finger to a strand of the golden hair and Mr. Shiftlet left. **L**

He was more depressed than ever as he drove on by himself. The late afternoon had grown hot and sultry and the country had flattened out. Deep in the sky a storm was preparing very slowly and without thunder as if it meant to drain every drop of air from the earth before it broke. There were times when Mr. Shiftlet preferred not to be alone. He felt too that a man with a car had a responsibility to others and he kept his eye out for a hitchhiker. Occasionally he saw a sign that warned: "Drive carefully. The life you save may be your own."

The narrow road dropped off on either side into dry fields and here and there a shack or a filling station stood in a clearing. The sun began to set directly in front of the automobile. It was a reddening ball that through his windshield was slightly flat on the bottom and top. He saw a boy in overalls and a gray hat standing on the edge of the road and he slowed the car down and stopped in front of him. The boy didn't have his hand raised to thumb the ride, he was only standing there, but he had a small cardboard suitcase and his hat was set on his head in a way to indicate that he had left somewhere for good. "Son," Mr. Shiftlet said, "I see you want a ride."

The boy didn't say he did or he didn't but he opened the door of the car and got in, and Mr. Shiftlet started driving again. The child held the suitcase on his lap and folded his arms on top of it. He turned his head and looked out the window away from Mr. Shiftlet. Mr. Shiftlet felt oppressed. "Son," he said after a minute, "I got the best old mother in the world so I reckon you only got the second best."

Occasionally he stopped his thoughts long enough to look at Lucynell in the seat beside him. She had eaten the lunch as soon as they were out of the yard and now she was pulling the cherries off the hat one by one and throwing them out the window. He became depressed in spite of the car. He had driven about a hundred miles when he decided that she must be hungry again and at the next small town they came to, he stopped in front of an aluminum-painted eating place called The Hot Spot and took her in and ordered her a plate of ham and grits. The ride had made her sleepy and as soon as she got up on the stool, she rested her head on the counter and shut her eyes. There was no one in The Hot Spot but Mr. Shiftlet and the boy behind the counter, a pale youth with a greasy rag hung over his shoulder. Before he could dish up the food, she was snoring gently.

"Give it to her when she wakes up," Mr. Shiftlet said. "I'll pay for it now."

The boy bent over her and stared at the long pink-gold hair and the half-shut sleeping eyes. Then he looked up and stared at Mr. Shiftlet. "She looks like an angel of Gawd," he murmured.

L **Reading Focus** **Making Predictions** What do you think will happen when Lucynell wakes up?

The boy gave him a quick dark glance and then turned his face back out the window.

"It's nothing so sweet," Mr. Shiftlet continued, "as a boy's mother. She taught him his first prayers at her knee, she give him love when no other would, she told him what was right and what wasn't, and she seen that he done the right thing. Son," he said, "I never rued[9] a day in my life like the one I rued when I left that old mother of mine."

The boy shifted in his seat but he didn't look at Mr. Shiftlet. He unfolded his arms and put one hand on the door handle.

"My mother was a angel of Gawd," Mr. Shiftlet said in a very strained voice. "He took her from heaven and giver to me and I left her." His eyes were instantly clouded over with a mist of tears. The car was barely moving.

The boy turned angrily in the seat. "You go to the devil!" he cried. "My old woman is a fleabag and yours is a stinking polecat!" and with that he flung the door open and jumped out with his suitcase into the ditch.

Mr. Shiftlet was so shocked that for about a hundred feet he drove along slowly with the door still open. A cloud, the exact color of the boy's hat and shaped like a turnip, had descended over the sun, and another, worse looking, crouched behind the car. Mr. Shiftlet felt that the rottenness of the world was about to engulf him. He raised his arm and let it fall again to his breast. "Oh Lord!" he prayed. "Break forth and wash the slime from this earth!"

The turnip continued slowly to descend. After a few minutes there was a guffawing peal of thunder from behind and fantastic raindrops, like tin-can tops, crashed over the rear of Mr. Shiftlet's car. Very quickly he stepped on the gas and with his stump sticking out the window he raced the galloping shower into Mobile.

---

9. **rued** (rood): regretted.

SKILLS FOCUS Literary Skills Analyze foreshadowing; analyze irony. **Reading Skills** Make predictions as a strategy for comprehension. **Vocabulary Skills** Understand synonyms. **Writing Skills** Develop descriptions with sensory details.

The Life You Save May Be Your Own

Respond and Think Critically

Reading Focus

Quick Check

1. Explain how Mr. Shiftlet exploits the Craters. How does Mrs. Crater want to exploit him?

2. What does Mr. Shiflet take from Mrs. Crater?

Read with a Purpose

3. Where does the title of this story come from? How does it relate to the story's theme?

Reading Skills: Making Predictions

4. While reading, you kept a chart of your predictions for the story. Add a third column to the chart and record whether your predictions were correct. Then, write a paragraph explaining how O'Connor uses foreshadowing to increase the story's suspense.

Clues from Story	My Predictions	Yes or No?
"'Lady,'" he said..., "'I'd give a fortune to live where I could see me a sun do that every evening.'" (p. 941)	Mr. Shiftlet may be flattering Mrs. Crater because he will try to get something from her later on.	Yes

✓ Vocabulary Check

Match each Vocabulary word with its definition.

5. morose   a. deserted
6. gaunt   b. swallow up
7. desolate   c. thin
8. ominous   d. laughing
9. guffawing   e. gloomy
10. engulf   f. threatening

Literary Focus

Literary Analysis

11. **Evaluate** O'Connor's aunt preferred an alternative ending in which Shiftlet returns for Lucynell. What do you think of the story's original ending?

12. **Analyze** Does the story depict a conflict between innocence and evil, or a world in which everyone is morally questionable? Explain.

13. **Make Judgments** How do the characters distort the archetype of the diligent, self-reliant hero?

Literary Skills: Foreshadowing

14. **Interpret** How do the images of Mr. Shiftlet's figure forming "a crooked cross" and his smile "stretched like a weary snake" serve as **foreshadowing** clues?

Literary Skills Review: Irony

15. **Analyze** What evidence from the story suggests that Shiftlet feels he is morally superior to most other people? What **irony,** or discrepancy between appearances and reality, do you sense in Mr. Shiftlet's view of his own morality?

Writing Focus

Think as a Reader/Writer

Use It in Your Writing Write a description of a place, incorporating foreshadowing in your description to suggest that an ominous event will occur there. Use vivid imagery to create an atmosphere of foreboding.

What Do You Think Now Mr. Shiftlet talks a great deal about life and what his needs are. How do his actions contrast with his statements? What does he really want in life?

The Harlem Renaissance

LITERARY FOCUS
The Harlem Renaissance

Ices I (1960) by Jacob Lawrence.

CONTENTS

"I, too, sing America."

— **Langston Hughes**

The Harlem Renaissance by **Leila Christenbury**

Influences on American Culture

- African American talent in music, writing, and art was introduced to mainstream America.
- Autobiographies provided firsthand accounts of the black experience.
- Dialects of African American vernacular speech enriched the English language.
- African Americans were recognized and celebrated for their contributions to American culture.

The Harlem Renaissance

The place is Harlem, a densely populated section of New York City in which African Americans live and work. The time line is short, extending from the end of World War I through the mid-1930s. The event is nothing less than a renaissance, an explosion of creativity in poetry, prose, drama, music, and art.

Harlem Comes to Life After World War I, an exodus to the North known as the Great Migration brought thousands of African Americans together in New York City. Musicians, writers, painters, and students congregated to form a mecca of cultural affirmation and inspiration.

Geographically, the center of that movement was Harlem, the section of the borough of Manhattan that stands north of 110th Street. Its spiritual center, however, was not a place on the map but a place in the consciousness of a people whose gifts had long been ignored, patronized as "quaint," or otherwise relegated to the margins of American culture. A new appreciation grew of the role of black talent in American culture when, hand in hand with the music echoing from New Orleans, Memphis, and Chicago, black poetry became part of the Jazz Age.

Langston Hughes wrote, "It was the period when the Negro was in vogue." Marcus Garvey's "Back to Africa" movement was in full swing. Blues and jazz were becoming popular. An all-black Broadway show called *Shuffle Along* opened in 1921, introducing audiences to performers Josephine Baker, Paul Robeson, and Florence Mills. The art world was changed by the modernist European artists Pablo Picasso and Georges Braque, whose work was influenced by African art. Mainstream America was developing a new respect for African art and culture.

In the words of educator and critic Alain Locke, this cultural revolution helped the African American become accepted as "a collaborator and participant in American civilization." Writers like Jean Toomer and Zora Neale Hurston wrote about the African American experience, while artists like Aaron Douglas and William H. Johnson painted it. Photographer James Van Der Zee recorded it with his camera. Trumpet player Louis Armstrong and pianist Fletcher Henderson set it to music, while vocalists Bessie Smith and Ma Rainey sang it.

Harlem newspapers and journals, such as *The Crisis* and *Opportunity,* published the work of African American writers and sponsored literary contests to support intellectually gifted youth. These contests encouraged creative writing and rewarded young writers' efforts with cash prizes and introductions to the most esteemed writers of the time.

African American writers strengthened the influence of black talent in America, focusing on different aspects of black life worldwide. They addressed inequalities of race, class, religion, and gender. Some writers attacked racism; others addressed social issues within black communities. The flourishing of African American writing helped affirm that black dialects were a vital part of American English.

The African American Voice Many writers, including Claude McKay and Countee Cullen, continued to write in standard English. While their works had a new tone, the forms and language they used were traditional. Other writers drew on African American oral tradition—dialect,

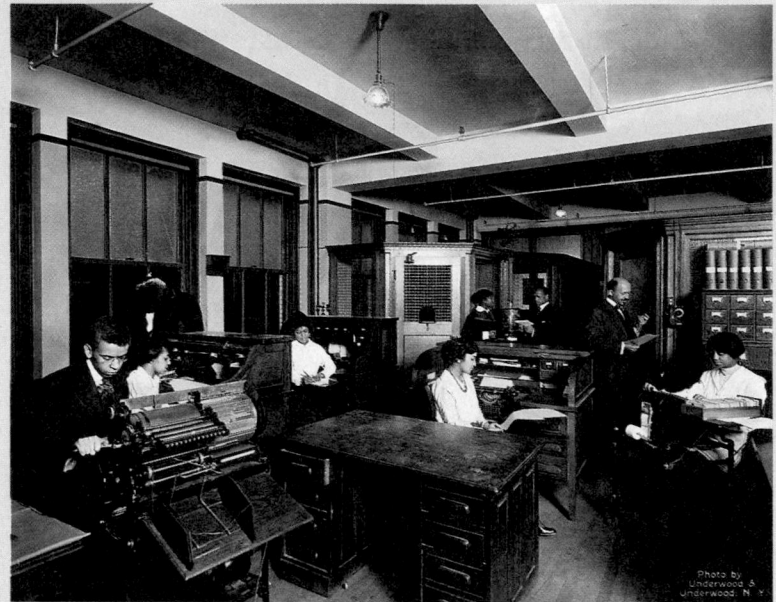

Civil rights activist W.E.B. Du Bois in the office of the NAACP'S magazine *The Crisis* (top right).

His first, *The Big Sea,* contains a famous section on the Harlem Renaissance called "When the Negro Was in Vogue." Zora Neale Hurston wrote a celebrated—and controversial—autobiography, *Dust Tracks on a Road* (1949). Along with poetry, fiction, and drama, autobiographical writing taught the country about African American experiences of racism, family life, politics, and social inequality.

Decline of the Harlem Renaissance By the early 1930s, the Great Depression had depleted the funds that had provided financial support to African American writers, institutions, and publications. This made it difficult for established artists to continue nurturing new talent. Nevertheless, American culture was forever changed. The foundation was laid for writers such as Richard Wright, Ralph Ellison, James Baldwin, Gwendolyn Brooks, Alice Walker, Toni Morrison, Maya Angelou, Terry McMillan, Rita Dove, and many other African American artists. They could now make their feelings and experiences part of the American artistic expression: "I, too, sing America."

the blues, folk tales, spirituals, and work songs. Two pioneers in adapting oral traditions in their work were writers Langston Hughes and Zora Neale Hurston. Hughes was sensitive to the rhythms of African American music, and he was successful in capturing the inflections of African American speech. During the 1920s, Hughes, who invented blues and jazz poetry, read his poems to the accompaniment of jazz bands. Hurston drew on Southern black speech patterns to create a literary language filled with wit and metaphor.

African American Autobiography As American readers grew more familiar with the black experience, autobiography became the preferred genre for some African American writers. The tradition of the African American autobiography began with the genre of slave narratives, which reached a peak in the years before the Civil War. Narratives by Olaudah Equiano, Harriet Jacobs, and Frederick Douglass had helped bring about the emancipation of slaves. A masterpiece of auto-biography, *Up from Slavery* (1901), had been written by Booker T. Washington.

In the years after the Harlem Renaissance, the genre of autobiography became more and more popular. Langston Hughes wrote two autobiographies.

Ask Yourself

1. How did the Harlem Renaissance help African Americans become more accepted in American society?

2. What are some themes and characteristics of the Harlem Renaissance?

Learn It Online

Learn more about the Harlem Renaissance with *PowerNotes* online.

go.hrw.com | L11-952 | Go

Reading Focus

from **Dust Tracks on a Road**

SKILLS FOCUS Reading Skills Identify historical context.

Identifying Historical Context by **Kylene Beers**

Not too long ago, an apple was something you ate, surfing required a board, a web was home to a spider, and a virus infected a human body. Now, though, when people say they have an Apple, spent the afternoon surfing, are still amazed at the Web, or have a virus, there can be some confusion! Words mean different things at different times. Additionally, views on human rights and particular practices change over time. As you read, especially as you read a text written in another time, understanding the **historical context** will help you reach valid conclusions about the text.

When you read a novel or an autobiography, how do you know when it takes place? In literature, the time period is a very important part of the setting. Think about current events and ideas that shape your world, such as political and <u>ideological</u> issues, environmental concerns, or new technology. All of these have an impact on your life. If you were to write your own autobiography, current events would probably make their way into your writing.

Frequently, dialogue serves to indicate the time period in which a work of literature takes place. Archaic language and antiquated grammar tell a reader that a piece was written a long time ago. Often literature will contain slang terms that capture the flavor of a particular time and place.

Read the following excerpt from Zora Neale Hurston's *Dust Tracks on a Road*. Which details give you clues about the time period?

> I used to take a seat on top of the gatepost and watch the world go by. One way to Orlando ran past my house, so the carriages and cars would pass before me. The movement made me glad to see it. Often the white travelers would hail me, but more often I hailed them, and asked, "Don't you want me to go a piece of the way with you?"

The reference to carriages and cars tells you that this selection takes place at a time when one could see both carriages and cars on a road. The road appears to be a country road, not a highway, which runs past the narrator's house. These details suggest a time around the early part of the twentieth century. The narrator's request to go "a piece of the way," meaning "a short distance," is rural Southern dialect, which establishes the setting for the narrative.

Read the following excerpt from the same text, and pay special attention to the last sentence.

> I'd ride up the road for perhaps a half-mile, then walk back. I did not do this with the permission of my parents, nor with their foreknowledge. When they found out about it later, I usually got a whipping. My grandmother worried about my forward ways a great deal. She had known slavery and to her my brazenness was unthinkable.

This passage gives you a clue to the period Hurston is writing about. Her grandmother who "had known slavery" is still alive. This detail sets the narrative several decades after emancipation.

Your Turn

Read the rest of the selection from *Dust Tracks on a Road*. Why is the historical period important to Hurston's writing? How did the social, political, and racial issues of the time affect Hurston's childhood?

Learn It Online
FInd more tips and strategies for reading historical works online at the *NovelWise* mini-site.

go.hrw.com L11-953 **Go**

Preparing to Read

from Dust Tracks on a Road

What Do You Think?

How does progress challenge tradition and redefine society?

🕐 QuickTalk

How important do you think the ability to read is in modern life? What inspires children to read? Discuss these questions briefly with a classmate.

Zora Neale Hurston
(c. 1891–1960)

By means of her own determination and talent, Hurston escaped poverty to find glamour and fame in New York City. "I have been in Sorrow's kitchen and licked out all the pots," Hurston wrote. "Then I have stood on the peaky mountain wrapped in rainbows, with a harp and sword in my hands." Sadly, her life ended back in Sorrow's kitchen.

She Jumped at the Sun

Hurston's family moved to Eatonville when Hurston was very young. Her father was a preacher, carpenter, and eventually mayor; her mother was a schoolteacher who urged her talented daughter to "jump at the sun."

In 1904 her mother died, and Zora, passed between relatives and friends, had to support herself. She eventually enrolled at Howard University in Washington, D.C., where she published her first story in 1921.

Sorrow's Kitchen Again

In 1925, Hurston set out for New York City to attend Barnard College. Hurston was soon immersed in the Harlem Renaissance. At Barnard, anthropologist Franz Boas encouraged her to travel through the South gathering folk tales from African American oral traditions. Eventually, she published two collections of folklore, *Mules and Men* (1935) and *Tell My Horse* (1938).

Hurston's most famous novel, *Their Eyes Were Watching God,* the story of an African Amercian woman's search for emotional and spiritual fulfillment, was published in 1937. Throughout the last twenty years of her life, Hurston continued to produce fiction and nonfiction, including her autobiography, *Dust Tracks on a Road.* In time, however, she began to have difficulty finding a market for her work, some of which was criticized in the African American community for celebrating the life of black people rather than confronting the white community for its discrimination. She died in a Florida welfare home in 1960. Today, Hurston is recognized as one of the most original of the Harlem Renaissance writers, and much of her work is again in print.

Think About the Writer

What does Hurston's dedication to education as a young adult lead you to believe about her earlier experiences in school?

Reader/Writer Notebook

Use your **RWN** to complete the activities for this selection.

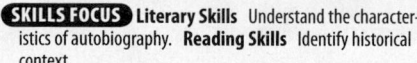

Literary Focus

Autobiography An **autobiography** is an account of the writer's own life. In that <u>tradition</u>, Hurston's autobiography is an American classic—passionate, lively, sometimes brutally honest. In the selection from her autobiography that follows, Hurston narrates, with her customary wit and enthusiasm, an important experience from her childhood.

Literary Perspectives Apply the literary perspective described on page 957 as you read this autobiographical excerpt.

Reading Focus

Identifying Historical Context This autobiography was published in 1942, and the events described in it took place many years before that, near the beginning of the last century. The world that Hurston lived in was very different from our own. Through the descriptions of her experiences and surroundings, however, we can learn what it was like to be a young black student in the South about a hundred years ago. We also learn about the social and <u>ideological</u> issues that defined her era.

Into Action As you read, look for details that reveal the historical context of the work. Gather them in a chart like the one below. Then, note what the details reveal about the period.

	Details from the text	What they tell me about the historical period
Through the descriptions, I learned ...	The teacher dismisses one class and calls another to the front of the room.	Children of different grade levels shared a classroom.
Through the dialogue, I learned ...		

Writing Focus

Think as a Reader/Writer

Find It in Your Reading Hurston's distinctive voice comes through loud and clear in her autobiography. As you read, use your *Reader/Writer Notebook* to list some of the expressions and **idioms** that give this story particular appeal.

Vocabulary

hail (hayl) *v.*: greet. *When she was a child, Hurston liked to hail strangers as they passed by her house.*

brazenness (BRAY zuhn nehs) *n.*: boldness. *Hurston's grandmother worried that Zora's brazenness would cause trouble.*

caper (KAY puhr) *n.*: foolish prank. *Mr. Calhoun wanted to put on a good show for the visitors from Minnesota; he didn't want any capers in the classroom that day.*

realm (rehlm) *n.*: kingdom. *Hurston's realm was Eatonville, Florida, until she left there after her mother's death.*

avarice (AV uhr ihs) *n.*: greed. *Hurston loved the new pennies, not because of avarice, but because of their beauty.*

profoundly (proh FOWND lee) *adv.*: deeply. *The story of Hercules profoundly affected Zora because Hercules followed Duty rather than Pleasure.*

Language Coach

Idioms Expressions particular to a certain language that mean something different from the literal definitions of their parts are **idioms**. Hurston uses the idioms "go a piece of the way," "carried the point," and "kicked the bucket." What do the expressions mean?

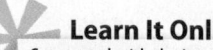
Learn It Online
Get started with the introductory video online.

go.hrw.com | L11-955 | Go

from

Dust Tracks on a Road

by **Zora Neale Hurston**

Read with a Purpose
Read to learn about the events that helped make Hurston a lifelong lover of stories and tales.

Build Background
The story takes place in a small African American community in central Florida in the early years of the twentieth century. At one point in the story, Hurston goes to the Park House Hotel in Maitland, which is now a suburb of Orlando. Russell C. Calhoun ran the school Zora attended and founded several all-black schools in segregated central Florida in 1889. As for the myths and legends and books Hurston loved—see how many you can recognize. Some might have been a part of your own imaginative world when you were her age.

I used to take a seat on top of the gatepost and watch the world go by. One way to Orlando ran past my house, so the carriages and cars would pass before me. The movement made me glad to see it. Often the white travelers would hail me, but more often I hailed them, and asked, "Don't you want me to go a piece of the way with you?"

They always did. I know now that I must have caused a great deal of amusement among them, but my self-assurance must have carried the point, for I was always invited to come along. I'd ride up the road for perhaps a half-mile, then walk back. I did not do this with the permission of my parents, nor with their foreknowledge. When they found out about it later, I usually got a whipping. My grandmother worried about my forward ways a great deal. She had known slavery and to her my brazenness was unthinkable.

"Git down offa dat gatepost! You li'l sow, you! Git down! Setting up dere looking dem white folks right in de face! They's gowine to lynch you, yet. And don't stand in dat doorway gazing out at 'em neither. Youse too brazen to live long." **Ⓐ**

Nevertheless, I kept right on gazing at them, and "going a piece of the way" whenever I could make it. The village seemed dull to me most of the time. If the village was singing a chorus, I must have missed the tune. **Ⓑ**

Perhaps a year before the old man[1] died, I came to know two other white people for myself. They were women.

It came about this way. The whites who came down from the North were often brought by their friends to visit the village school. A Negro school was something strange to them, and while they were always sympathetic and kind, curiosity must have been present, also. They came and went, came and went. Always, the room was hurriedly put in order, and we were threatened with a prompt and bloody death if we cut one caper while the visitors were present. We always sang a spiritual, led by Mr. Calhoun himself. Mrs. Calhoun always stood in the back, with a palmetto switch[2] in her hand as a squelcher. We were all little angels for the duration, because we'd better be. She would cut her eyes[3] and give us a glare that meant trouble, then turn her face toward the visitors and beam as much as to say it was a great privilege and pleasure to teach lovely children like us. They couldn't see that palmetto hickory in her hand behind all those benches, but we knew where our angelic behavior was coming from.

Usually, the visitors gave warning a day ahead and we would be cautioned to put on shoes, comb

---

1. **old man:** a white farmer who knew Hurston's family, took her fishing, and gave her advice.

2. **palmetto switch:** a whip made from the stem of a large, fanlike leaf of the palmetto, a type of palm tree. Teachers sometimes used these switches to discipline students.

3. **cut her eyes:** slang for "look scornfully."

Black Girl with Wings by Laura James. Acrylic on canvas.

our heads, and see to ears and fingernails. There was a close inspection of every one of us before we marched in that morning. Knotty heads, dirty ears, and finger-nails got hauled out of line, strapped, and sent home to lick the calf[4] over again. **C**

This particular afternoon, the two young ladies just popped in. Mr. Calhoun was flustered, but he put on the best show he could. He dismissed the class that he was teaching up at the front of the room, then called the fifth grade in reading. That was my class.

So we took our readers and went up front. We stood up in the usual line, and opened to the lesson. It was the story of Pluto and Persephone.[5] It was new

───────

4. **lick the calf:** slang for "wash up."
5. **Pluto and Persephone:** In classical mythology, Pluto, or Hades, is the god who rules the underworld; Perse-phone, also known as Proserpina, is his wife, queen of the underworld. In this version of the origin of the sea-sons, Hurston uses the names of Roman and Greek gods interchangeably.

and hard to the class in general, and Mr. Calhoun was very uncomfortable as the readers stumbled along, spelling out words with their lips, and in mumbling undertones before they exposed them experimentally to the teacher's ears.

Then it came to me. I was fifth or sixth down the line. The story was not new to me, because I had read my reader through from lid to lid, the first week that Papa had bought it for me.

That is how it was that my eyes were not in the book, working out the paragraph which I knew would be mine by counting the children ahead of me. I was observing our visitors, who held a book between them, following the lesson. They had shiny hair, mostly brownish. One had a looping gold chain around her neck. The other one was dressed all over in black and white with a pretty finger ring on her left hand. But the thing that held my eyes were their fingers. They were long and thin, and very white, except up near the tips. There they were baby pink. I had never seen such hands. It was a fascinating discovery for me. I wondered how they felt. I would have given those hands more attention, but the child before me was almost through. My turn next, so I got on my mark, bringing my eyes back to the book and made sure of my place. Some of the stories I had reread several times, and this Greco-Roman myth was one of my favorites. I was exalted by it, and that is the way I read my paragraph. **D**

"Yes, Jupiter[6] had seen her (Persephone). He had seen the maiden picking flowers in the field. He had seen the chariot of the dark monarch pause by the maiden's side. He had seen him when he seized Persephone. He had seen the black horses leap down Mount Aetna's[7] fiery throat. Persephone was now in Pluto's dark realm and he had made her his wife."

───────

6. **Jupiter:** in Roman mythology, king of the gods.
7. **Mount Aetna's:** Mount Aetna (also spelled *Etna*) is a volcanic mountain in eastern Sicily.

───────

C Reading Focus Historical Context What does this passage tell you about the way white society viewed the all-black schools in the South at the time?

D Literary Perspectives Analyzing Style How does Hurston's use of sentence variety make her writing effective?

Vocabulary realm (rehlm) *n.:* kingdom.

The two women looked at each other and then back to me. Mr. Calhoun broke out with a proud smile beneath his bristly moustache, and instead of the next child taking up where I had ended, he nodded to me to go on. So I read the story to the end, where flying Mercury, the messenger of the Gods, brought Persephone back to the sunlit earth and restored her to the arms of Dame Ceres, her mother, that the world might have springtime and summer flowers, autumn and harvest. But because she had bitten the pomegranate while in Pluto's kingdom, she must return to him for three months of each year, and be his queen. Then the world had winter, until she returned to earth.

The class was dismissed and the visitors smiled us away and went into a low-voiced conversation with Mr. Calhoun for a few minutes. They glanced my way once or twice and I began to worry. Not only was I barefooted, but my feet and legs were dusty. My hair was more uncombed than usual, and my nails were not shiny clean. Oh, I'm going to catch it now. Those ladies saw me, too. Mr. Calhoun is promising to 'tend to me. So I thought. **E**

Then Mr. Calhoun called me. I went up thinking how awful it was to get a whipping before company. Furthermore, I heard a snicker run over the room. Hennie Clark and Stell Brazzle did it out loud, so I would be sure to hear them. The smart aleck was going to get it. I slipped one hand behind me and switched my dress tail at them, indicating scorn.

"Come here, Zora Neale," Mr. Calhoun cooed as I reached the desk. He put his hand on my shoulder and gave me little pats. The ladies smiled and held out those flower-looking fingers toward me. I seized the opportunity for a good look.

"Shake hands with the ladies, Zora Neale," Mr. Calhoun prompted and they took my hand one after the other and smiled. They asked me if I loved school, and I lied that I did. There was *some* truth in it, because I liked geography and reading, and I liked to play at recess time. Whoever it was invented writing and arithmetic got no thanks from me. Neither did I like the arrangement where the teacher could sit up there with a palmetto stem and lick me whenever he saw fit. I hated things I couldn't do anything about. But I knew better than to bring that up right there, so I said yes, I *loved* school. **F**

"I can tell you do," Brown Taffeta gleamed. She patted my head, and was lucky enough not to get sandspurs in her hand. Children who roll and tumble in the grass in Florida are apt to get sandspurs in their hair. They shook hands with me again and I went back to my seat.

When school let out at three o'clock, Mr. Calhoun told me to wait. When everybody had gone, he told me I was to go to the Park House, that was the hotel in Maitland, the next afternoon to call upon Mrs. Johnstone and Miss Hurd. I must tell Mama to see that I was clean and brushed from head to feet, and I must wear shoes and stockings. The ladies liked me, he said, and I must be on my best behavior.

The next day I was let out of school an hour early, and went home to be stood up in a tub of suds and be scrubbed and have my ears dug into. My sandy hair sported a red ribbon to match my red and white checked gingham dress, starched until it could stand alone. Mama saw to it that my shoes were on the right feet, since I was careless about left and right. Last thing, I was given a handkerchief to carry, warned again about my behavior, and sent off, with my big brother John to go as far as the hotel gate with me. **G**

First thing, the ladies gave me strange things, like stuffed dates and preserved ginger, and encouraged me to eat all that I wanted. Then they showed me their Japanese dolls and just talked. I was then handed a copy of *Scribner's Magazine*, and asked to read a place that was pointed out to me. After a paragraph or two, I was told with smiles, that that would do.

I was led out on the grounds and they took my picture under a palm tree. They handed me what was to me then a heavy cylinder done up in fancy paper, tied with a ribbon, and they told me goodbye, asking me not to open it until I got home.

E **Literary Focus** Autobiography What important autobiographical details has the writer supplied so far?

F **Literary Focus** Autobiography Hurston confesses that there were things she liked about school and things she didn't. Why did she like the things she named? Why did she dislike other parts of school?

G **Reading Focus** Historical Context Why was Hurston's mother so careful about her daughter's appearance when Zora Neale was invited to visit the white women at their hotel?

My brother was waiting for me down by the lake, and we hurried home, eager to see what was in the thing. It was too heavy to be candy or anything like that. John insisted on toting it for me.

My mother made John give it back to me and let me open it. Perhaps, I shall never experience such joy again. The nearest thing to that moment was the telegram accepting my first book. One hundred goldy-new pennies rolled out of the cylinder. Their gleam lit up the world. It was not avarice that moved me. It was the beauty of the thing. I stood on the mountain. Mama let me play with my pennies for a while, then put them away for me to keep.

That was only the beginning. The next day I received an Episcopal hymnbook bound in white leather with a golden cross stamped into the front cover, a copy of *The Swiss Family Robinson,* and a book of fairy tales.

I set about to commit the song words to memory. There was no music written there, just the words. But there was to my consciousness music in between them just the same. "When I survey the Wondrous Cross" seemed the most beautiful to me, so I committed that to memory first of all. Some of them seemed dull and without life, and I pretended they were not there. If white people liked trashy singing like that, there must be something funny about them that I had not noticed

---

Vocabulary **avarice** (AV uhr ihs) *n.:* greed.

The Rape of Persephone by Hades
(English School, 19th century).

before. I stuck to the pretty ones where the words
marched to a throb I could feel. **(H)**

A month or so after the two young ladies returned
to Minnesota, they sent me a huge box packed with
clothes and books. The red coat with a wide circular
collar and the red tam pleased me more than any of the
other things. My chums pretended not to like anything
that I had, but even then I knew that they were jealous. Old Smarty had gotten by them again. The clothes
were not new, but they were very good. I shone like the
morning sun.

But the books gave me more pleasure than the
clothes. I had never been too keen on dressing up. It

called for hard scrubbings with Octagon soap suds getting in my eyes, and none too gentle fingers scrubbing
my neck and gouging in my ears.

In that box were *Gulliver's Travels, Grimm's Fairy
Tales, Dick Whittington, Greek and Roman Myths,* and
best of all, *Norse Tales.* Why did the Norse tales strike
so deeply into my soul? I do not know, but they did.
I seemed to remember seeing Thor swing his mighty
short-handled hammer as he sped across the sky in
rumbling thunder, lightning flashing from the tread of
his steeds and the wheels of his chariot. The great and
good Odin, who went down to the well of knowledge
to drink, and was told that the price of a drink from

(H) **Literary Focus** Analyzing Style How does Hurston's diction
and choice of detail make this paragraph more lively and interesting?

from Dust Tracks on a Road   **961**

that fountain was an eye. Odin drank deeply, then plucked out one eye without a murmur and handed it to the grizzly keeper, and walked away. That held majesty for me.

Of the Greeks, Hercules moved me most. I followed him eagerly on his tasks. The story of the choice of Hercules as a boy when he met Pleasure and Duty, and put his hand in that of Duty and followed her steep way to the blue hills of fame and glory, which she pointed out at the end, moved me profoundly. I resolved to be like him. The tricks and turns of the other gods and goddesses left me cold. There were other thin books about this and that sweet and gentle little girl who gave up her heart to Christ and good works. Almost always they died from it, preaching as they passed. I was utterly indifferent to their deaths. In the first place I could not conceive of death, and in the next place they never had any funerals that amounted to a hill of beans, so I didn't care how soon they rolled up their big, soulful, blue eyes and kicked the bucket. They had no meat on their bones. **Ⓘ**

But I also met Hans Andersen[8] and Robert Louis Stevenson.[9] They seemed to know what I wanted to hear and said it in a way that tingled me. Just a little below these friends was Rudyard Kipling[10] in his Jungle Books. I loved his talking snakes as much as I did the hero.

I came to start reading the Bible through my mother. She gave me a licking one afternoon for repeating something I had overheard a neighbor telling her. She locked me in her room after the whipping, and the Bible was the only thing in there for me to read. I happened to open to the place where David was doing some mighty smiting, and I got interested. David went here and he went there, and no matter where he went, he smote 'em hip and thigh. Then he sung songs to his harp awhile, and went out and smote some more. Not one time did David stop and preach about sins and things. All David wanted to know from God was who to kill and when. He took care of the other details himself. Never a quiet moment. I liked him a lot. So I read a great deal more in the Bible, hunting for some more active people like David. Except for the beautiful language of Luke and Paul, the New Testament still plays a poor second to the Old Testament for me. The Jews had a God who laid about Him[11] when they needed Him. I could see no use waiting till Judgment Day to see a man who was just crying for a good killing, to be told to go and roast.[12] My idea was to give him a good killing first, and then if he got roasted later on, so much the better. **Ⓙ**

> I was utterly indifferent to their deaths. In the first place I could not conceive of death, and in the next place they never had any funerals that amounted to a hill of beans.

---

8. **Hans Andersen:** Hans Christian Andersen (1805–1875), Danish writer known primarily for his fairy tales.
9. **Robert Louis Stevenson:** (1850–1894), Scottish writer of adventure stories such as *Kidnapped* and *Treasure Island*.
10. **Rudyard Kipling . . . Books:** Kipling (1865–1936) was an English writer born in India. His *Jungle Book* and *Second Jungle Book* contain stories of the adventures of Mowgli, a boy raised by animals in the jungles of India.
11. **laid about Him:** slang for "struck blows in every direction."
12. **roast:** slang for "burn in Hell."

Ⓘ Literary Focus Autobiography What does Hurston reveal about her values and character here?

Vocabulary profoundly (proh FOWND lee) *adv.*: deeply.

Ⓙ Literary Focus Analyzing Style How do stylistic features, such as sentence length, diction, and the use of slang, make the final paragraph more effective?

SKILLS FOCUS **Literary Skills** Identify characteristics of autobiograpy; analyze setting; analyze style. **Reading Skills** Identify historical context. **Writing Skills** Employ elements of an author's style effectively.

from **Dust Tracks on a Road**

Respond and Think Critically

Reading Focus

Quick Check

1. Why is Hurston's grandmother afraid of her granddaughter's boldness?

2. Who visits Hurston's school?

3. What do the visitors send from Minnesota?

4. What are the narrator's favorite books?

Read with a Purpose

5. What details show that Hurston, even as a child, responded to language and to storytelling?

Reading Skills: Identifying Historical Context

6. Review the list of details about the historical context that you gathered as you read. Then, summarize your findings in two or three paragraphs, focusing on the details that shed the most light on the historical realities and important social issues that Hurston reveals.

Literary Focus

Literary Analysis

7. **Analyze** Which of Hurston's comments give you particular insight into her personality? For example, what do you learn from her responses to the story of David in the Bible?

8. **Infer** What details indicate that even as a young girl Zora wanted to get away from the constraints of her small town and see the wider world?

9. **Infer** Why do you think the two visitors came to Zora's school?

10. **Analyze** Hurston's unmistakable voice comes through clearly in this autobiography. What is her tone? Does she reveal any bitterness? Explain.

11. **Make Judgments** Some other writers of the Harlem Renaissance criticized Hurston for not emphasizing the oppression of African Americans by the white establishment. Is their criticism just? Instead of political and social issues, what does she focus on in her autobiography?

12 **Literary Perspectives** How does Hurston's writing style allow her to express a child's perspective without sounding childish?

Literary Skills: Autobiography

13. **Compare and Contrast** What do you learn from an autobiography that you probably would not learn from a biography? On the other hand, what can a biography tell you that an autobiography cannot?

Literary Skills Review: Setting

14. **Extend** The **setting** of a piece of literature Is the time and place in which the story occurs. How would the excerpt from *Dust Tracks on a Road* have been different if it had taken place fifty years earlier? Fifty years later?

Writing Focus

Think as a Reader/Writer

Use It in Your Writing Write about something that happened to you in your own early education. Make sure your story contains two or three idioms.

What Do
You
Think
Now

How important is the ability to read today? Can progress be made if children cannot read? Explain.

Vocabulary Development

✓ Vocabulary Check

Match each Vocabulary word with its definition.

1. hail
2. brazenness
3. caper
4. realm
5. avarice
6. profoundly

a. daring
b. deeply
c. acknowledge
d. desire for money
e. wild act
f. dominion

Vocabulary Skills: Diction—Using Slang

Slang is idiomatic, informal language that is not considered standard English usage. Slang usually develops from the attempt to find fresh and new ways of saying something. Often slang originates in particular groups within a larger culture. When you talk with your friends, you probably use slang. Groups like skateboarders have coined many slang words: Do you know what *gnarly*, *vert*, and *yoinker* mean? Often slang expressions move into mainstream English or just go out of style. Meanwhile, new slang expressions are coined every day.

Sometimes a slang word becomes so common that it passes into mainstream English. *Jazz*, *groovy*, *disco*, and *chocoholic* are a few examples.

If you do research on the Internet, you can find all sorts of slang. Conversations on blogs and discussion boards have created a new category of slang that is unique to the virtual world. The abbreviation *LOL* for *laugh out loud* is an example.

Your Turn

Look up some words that you and your friends use that you think might be slang. What standard English expression means the same thing? What is the slang term's origin?

Language Coach

Idioms Idioms are combinations of words that don't necessarily make literal sense. You've probably heard someone say, "She's a really smart cookie." You know that the speaker doesn't mean she is soft and chewy or that she is made of chocolate chips and raisins.

On the left are three idioms from Hurston's story. Match each idiom with the correct meaning from the list on the right.

1. *cut her eyes*
2. *lick the calf*
3. *laid about him*

a. "wash up"
b. "struck blows in every direction"
c. "look scornfully"

Academic Vocabulary

Write About
Hurston was particularly drawn to exciting stories about strong heroes such as Thor and David. How do you think these stories helped her transcend conventional ideological beliefs about the limitations of women and African Americans?

Learn It Online
Spend more time exploring the Vocabulary words by visiting Word Watch.

go.hrw.com   L11-964   **Go**

Grammar Link

Avoiding Misplaced and Dangling Modifiers

A **modifier** is a word, a phrase, or a clause that makes the meaning of another word more specific. **Adjectives** and **adverbs** are modifiers. A **misplaced modifier** is a modifier that refers to the wrong word in a sentence, usually because it is too far from the correct word.

Single-word modifiers, such as *only, always, often, almost, even,* and *nearly* should be placed directly in front of or after the words or phrases they describe.

MISPLACED Zora Neale <u>only</u> rode part of the way with the travelers.

CLEAR Zora Neale rode only part of the way with the travelers.

A **dangling modifier** doesn't logically modify *any* word in a sentence. The most common example is called a **dangling participle.** An introductory **participial phrase** (a word group beginning with an *ing* or an *–ed* verb form) should modify the noun or the pronoun that comes directly after it.

DANGLING <u>Sitting on the gatepost</u>, the carriages and cars passed Zora Neale's house. [It was Zora Neale who was sitting on the gatepost, not the carriages and cars.]

CLEAR Sitting on the gatepost, Zora Neale watched the carriages and cars pass by her house.

Your Turn

Identify the misplaced or dangling modifier in each of these sentences. Then, correct each sentence.

1. Afraid, Mr. Calhoun called Zora Neale up to his desk.

2. Resolving to be like Hercules, the other Greek gods were ignored by Zora Neale.

CHOICES

As you respond to the Choices, use these **Academic Vocabulary** words as appropriate: <u>alternative</u>, <u>hierarchy</u>, <u>ideology</u>, <u>inevitable</u>, <u>tradition</u>.

REVIEW

Summarize to Explore Hurston's Style

Timed ⌐Writing In the last paragraph of this excerpt from *Dust Tracks on a Road,* Hurston re-tells the story of David in a lively and engaging style. Reread this paragraph and pay careful attention to her style of writing. Then, choose a story that you know well. It might be a short story that you have recently read. <u>Alternatively</u>, it might be a movie that you have seen several times. In a brief paragraph, re-tell this story, using elements of Hurston's style to bring humor and excitement to your version.

CONNECT

Interpret the Story in a Performance

Group Activity With a group, prepare this excerpt from *Dust Tracks on a Road* for performance. Assign scriptwriters, a director, actors, costume designers, and set designers. You might also need a narrator to tell parts of the story. Consider using music to enhance the mood of the story.

EXTEND

Learn More About Eatonville

Presentation With a partner, do research on the town of Eatonville, Florida, as it is today. Be sure to find out about the attempts to preserve Eatonville, the annual Zora Neale Hurston Festival of Arts and Humanities, and the museum honoring Hurston. Work with your partner to present your findings to your classmates.

Learn It Online
Explore Zora Neale Hurston's life and work at Author-Space online.

go.hrw.com   L11-965   **Go**

Preparing to Read

A Black Man Talks of Reaping

What Do You Think?

How does progress challenge tradition and redefine society?

QuickWrite

Can you think of times in history when progress has failed to reach some of the people on the lowest rung of the economic ladder? Write a paragraph in which you describe such a time.

Arna Bontemps (detail) (1953) by Betsy Graves Reyneau.

Arna Bontemps
(1902–1973)

At one point in his life, Arna Bontemps was asked to destroy his books to prove he was not a radical. He refused to do so.

A Body of Work

Bontemps was born in Louisiana and grew up in the Watts district of Los Angeles. After graduating from Pacific Union College in California in 1923, he moved to New York to teach in Harlem. He arrived at the height of the Harlem Renaissance. By the mid-twenties, his poetry had appeared in the prestigious African American magazines *Opportunity* and *The Crisis*.

Affected by the Scottsboro Case

In 1931, Bontemps moved to Huntsville, Alabama, to teach at a junior college. Shortly thereafter, in nearby Scottsboro, an all-white jury convicted nine African American teenagers of rape and sentenced them to death. Later, one of the "victims" admitted to lying. The case was brought to the U.S. Supreme Court. Because the so-called Scottsboro boys had been under-represented, the court ordered a new trial. This time the boys were represented by the legal arm of the Communist Party. Eventually they were all freed. (The case inspired Harper Lee to write *To Kill a Mockingbird*.)

With racial tensions and fear at a high pitch, the college asked Bontemps to prove he was not a political radical by burning certain books by African American writers that he kept in his private library. Instead of destroying his books—by such writers as James Weldon Johnson and W.E.B. Du Bois—he resigned and moved his family back to California.

Bontemps went on to write children's books, as well as biographies of George Washington Carver, Frederick Douglass, and Booker T. Washington. Critics think his finest work is *Black Thunder* (1936), the true story of a failed slave rebellion. Bontemps produced only one book of poetry, *Personals* (1963), but, together with Langston Hughes, he published valuable anthologies of African American poetry and folklore.

Think About the Writer What does Bontemps's refusal to destroy his books reveal about his values—and his courage?

Reader/Writer Notebook

Use your **RWN** to complete the activities for this selection.

Literary Focus

Extended Metaphor A **metaphor** directly compares two unlike things, without using a word of comparison such as *like* or *as*: "Life is a journey"; "the car licks up the miles." An **extended metaphor** is developed—or extended—over several lines or even an entire work. In the following poem, notice how Bontemps uses planting and harvesting a field as an extended metaphor for the hardships that many rural African Americans experienced in the early part of the twentieth century.

Reading Focus

Understanding Line Breaks To understand a poem's unique **rhythm**, pay close attention to where its lines begin and end and to the punctuation throughout each line. When you come to a period in a poem, whether at the end of a line or in the middle of a line, make a full stop. When you come to a comma, semicolon, or dash, pause slightly. If there is no punctuation at the end of a line, read right on to the next line without pausing.

Into Action As you read, use a chart like the one below to identify where each line of the poem breaks. In the first column, write each line. In the second column, note whether the line ends with a period, a semicolon, or has no punctuation.

Line	Punctuation at line break?
Line 1: "I have sown beside all waters in my day."	Period

Writing Focus

Think as a Reader/Writer

Find It in Your Reading Bontemps uses a formal **meter** and **rhyme scheme** in "A Black Man Talks of Reaping." In your *Reader/Writer Notebook* record the rhyming words used in the poem, and identify the rhyme scheme.

Vocabulary

sown (sohn) *v*.: scattered seed; planted. *The speaker says he has sown seeds for many years.*

stark (stahrk) *adj*.: bleak; bare. *The farmer planted so that he would have food during a stark year.*

reaping (REEP ihng) *v*. used as *n*.: gathering or harvesting a crop. *The speaker says that for all his reaping he has received little reward.*

glean (gleen) *v*.: gather produce left behind after reaping. *The speaker's children glean in fields they have not planted.*

Language Coach

Usage Note Historically, "to glean" was to pick up whatever fruit or grain was left in a field after a harvest. In ancient times, gleaning was considered a right of poor people, though the practice was sometimes challenged by landowners. Today, the U.S. Department of Agriculture recognizes the efforts of charitable organizations to glean fields to provide food for poor people. The more common modern meaning, though, is to gather something—such as information—from various sources. Create sentences using both definitions of *glean*.

Learn It Online
Listen to this poem online.

go.hrw.com	L11-967	Go

A Black Man Talks of Reaping

by **Arna Bontemps**

Read with a Purpose

This poem alludes to a Biblical passage from Paul's letter to the Galatians (6:7): "Whatsoever a man soweth, that shall he also reap." Read to discover what the poem says about this idea.

Build Background

Sharecropping is a system of agricultural production in which a landowner allows a farmer to use the land in exchange for a share of the crops produced. After the Civil War, share-cropping often kept African American farmers in constant debt to white landowners. In this poem, the speaker laments the fact that he and his family work hard to plant a crop yet can keep only a small portion of it.

I have sown beside all waters in my day.
I planted deep, within my heart the fear
that wind or fowl would take the grain away.
I planted safe against this stark, lean year. **A**

5 I scattered seed enough to plant the land
in rows from Canada to Mexico
but for my reaping only what the hand
can hold at once is all that I can show.

Yet what I sowed and what the orchard yields
10 my brother's sons are gathering stalk and root;
small wonder then my children glean in fields
they have not sown, and feed on bitter fruit. **B**

A **Reading Focus** **Line Breaks** Where would you pause in reading this stanza?

B **Literary Focus** **Extended Metaphor** What words suggest that this poem is about something more than literally planting seeds and harvesting a crop?

Vocabulary **sown** (sohn) v.: scattered seed; planted.
stark (stahrk) adj.: bleak; bare.
reaping (REEP ihng) v. used as n.: gathering or harvesting a crop.
glean (gleen) v.: gather produce left behind after reaping.

Analyzing Visuals

Viewing and Interpreting Think about how this image relates to the ideas in the poem. How does the tree in the man's hand reflect the situation the speaker describes?

Men Exist for the Sake of One Another, Teach Them Then or Bear with Them. (Great Ideas of Western Man series) (1958) by Jacob Lawrence.

Applying Your Skills

A Black Man Talks of Reaping

Respond and Think Critically

Reading Focus

Quick Check

1. What has the speaker done "in his day"?

2. What has the speaker gained from all his work?

3. Who has gathered the fruits of what the speaker planted?

4. What do the speaker's children do?

Read with a Purpose

5. Explain the poem's allusion to the biblical saying "whatsoever a man soweth, that shall he also reap." What does the poem say about this idea?

Reading Skills: Understanding Line Breaks

6. Using the chart you created as you read, prepare the poem to be read aloud. Before you read, add a third column, indicating where you will make full stops, where you will pause briefly, and where you will read right on to the next line without stopping. This will provide a road map to help you read the poem aloud accurately.

Line	Punctuation at line break?	When reading aloud
1: "I have sown beside all waters in my day."	Period	Make a full stop

✓ Vocabulary Check

Explain your answers to these questions.

7. Does **sown** mean "planted" or "harvested"?

8. If something is **stark**, is it pleasant or bleak?

9. If farmers are **reaping** a crop, are they planting it or harvesting it?

Literary Focus

Literary Analysis

10. **Infer** Who are his "brother's sons" in line 10?

11. **Interpret** How would you interpret the last two lines of the poem? What are the "fields" his children glean in? What is the "bitter fruit"?

12. **Analyze** What is the tone of the poem? Can you read the poem as a kind of protest or warning?

Literary Skills: Extended Metaphor

13. **Analyze** Throughout the poem, images of planting and harvesting a field are used as an extended metaphor for personal struggles. What double meanings does the speaker give to sowing, planting, reaping, and fruit?

Literary Skills Review: Allusion

14. **Evaluate** The first line of the poem is an **allusion** to the Biblical verse Isaiah 32:20: "Blessed are ye that sow beside all waters, that send forth thither the ox and the ass." Why do you think Bontemps alludes to this verse? Does the speaker feel blessed? Why or why not?

Writing Focus

Think as a Reader/Writer

Use It in Your Writing Bontemps writes in a traditional poetic form, using meter and a regular rhyming pattern. Check the rhyming words and rhyme scheme you recorded in your notebook. Write a poem, at least one stanza long, using the same rhyme scheme.

 What Do You Think Now

What comment does the poem make on how the black man has profited from all his work?

Tableau

Incident

Countee Cullen
(1903–1946)

Strongly influenced by the poetry of the English Romantics (his favorite poet was John Keats), Countee Cullen thought of himself primarily as a lyric poet in the Romantic tradition, not as a black poet writing about social and racial themes. Nevertheless, Cullen found himself inevitably drawn to such themes.

A Bright Future

Cullen, who some feel is the central literary figure of the Harlem Renaissance, was always secretive about his early life. Probably abandoned by his birth mother, who contacted him only after he became famous, he grew up in New York City as the adopted son of Reverend and Mrs. Frederick Cullen. He was a brilliant student and was already writing accomplished poems in traditional forms while still in high school. He graduated Phi Beta Kappa from New York University in 1925. While in college, Cullen won the coveted Witter Bynner Poetry Prize. He published *Color,* his first volume of poetry, that same year.

Passion and Craftsmanship

After earning a master's degree from Harvard, where he wrote his thesis on Edna St. Vincent Millay, Cullen worked as an assistant editor of the African American magazine *Opportunity*. His poems were published in such influential periodicals as *Harper's, Poetry,* and *The Crisis.* In 1927, he published *Copper Sun,* a collection of poems, and *Caroling Dusk,* an anthology of poetry by African Americans. In the introduction to *Caroling Dusk,* Cullen called on black poets not to abandon traditional forms and to avoid the restrictions of solely racial themes.

At the peak of his career, Cullen married the daughter of the famous black writer W.E.B. Du Bois. He published two other collections of poems, *The Ballad of the Brown Girl* and *The Black Christ.* Cullen's poems were perfectly crafted and passionate, very much like the work of Millay, whose poetry readings in New York City he attended. Like many poets, Cullen was unable to make a living as a writer during the Great Depression of the 1930s, and he began teaching in Harlem public schools.

What Do  **You Think** How does progress challenge tradition and redefine society?

QuickTalk

With a partner, spend a few minutes discussing this question: How does entrenched racism affect children?

Countee Porter Cullen (detail) (c. 1925) by Winold Reiss.

Think About the Writer Why might Cullen have not wanted to define himself primarily as a black poet writing about social and racial themes?

Tableau / Incident

Reader/Writer Notebook

Use your **RWN** to complete the activities for these selections.

Literary Focus

Metaphor and Simile A **metaphor** is an imaginative comparison between two dissimilar things. Some metaphors are stated directly, using a linking verb: *That boy is a blaze of lightning*. Often metaphors are indirect: *That boy blazed across the room*. **Similes** also compare two dissimilar things, but similes use specific words of comparison, such as *like* or *as*: *That boy is like a blaze of lightning*. Both metaphors and similes are able to communicate powerful feelings.

Reading Focus

Comparing and Contrasting Poems When you **compare and contrast** two poems, you focus on specific elements of each to discover how they are similar to, or differ from, one another. These elements may include each poem's **theme**, **speaker**, **rhyme scheme**, **tone**, metaphors, similes, and so on.

Into Action In the first column of a chart like the one below, record specific literary elements as you read each poem. In the second column, include an example of each element from "Tableau." Then, do the same in column three for "Incident." If you cannot find an example, leave the space blank.

Elements	Tableau	Incident
simile	"lightning brilliant as a sword"	

Writing Focus

Think as a Reader/Writer

Find It in Your Reading Read Cullen's poetry aloud to hear its distinctive sound effects. What examples of rhyme and alliteration do you hear? (**Alliteration** is the repetition of consonant sounds in words that are close together.) In your *Reader/Writer Notebook* list examples of Cullen's sound effects.

Language Coach

Connotations Every word has a dictionary definition. Many words also have strong connotations—that is, they suggest certain feelings or ideas. The words a poet chooses for a poem's title are especially important. One way to think about connotations in a title is to consider what other words a writer might have chosen. The noun *incident* means "event; happening." It has several very different connotations: some suggest that the event is unfortunate and very serious; others suggest that the event is minor. Why might Cullen have chosen this word for his title? What connotations might have encouraged him to choose the title "Tableau" instead of "Scene"? Use a dictionary or thesaurus to find out more about *tableau*.

Learn It Online
Learn more about Cullen with these Internet links.

go.hrw.com   L11-971   Go

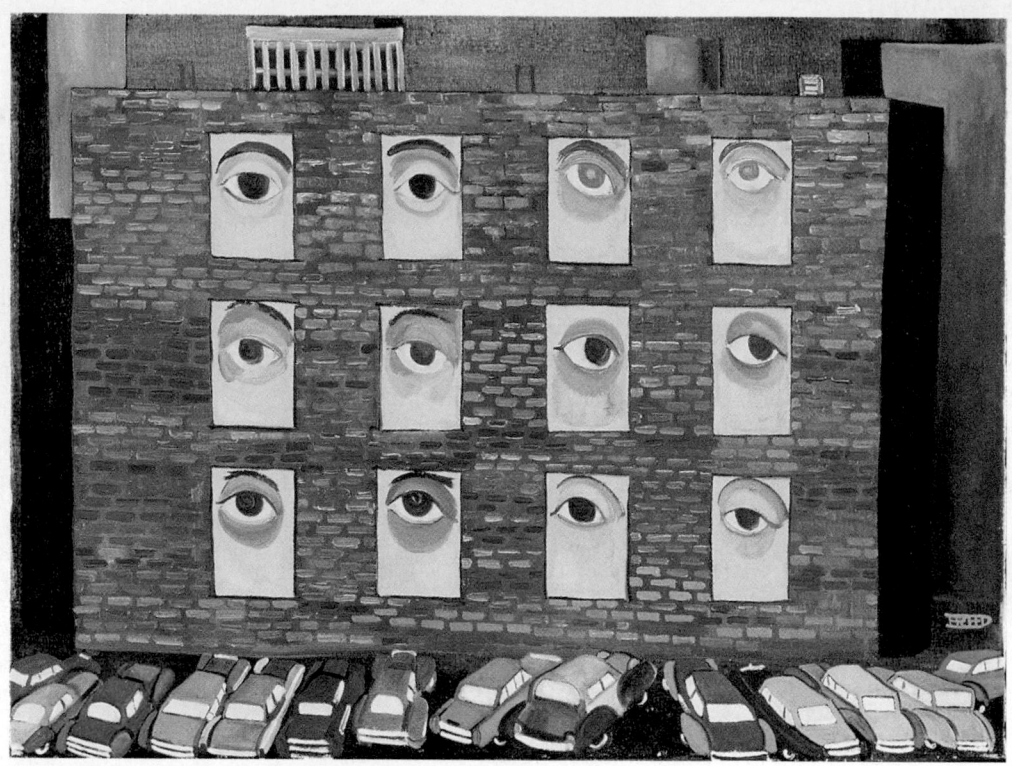

Eyes of the City (1972) by Frank Freed.

Tableau by **Countee Cullen**
(For Donald Duff)

Read with a Purpose
Read to find out how the speaker feels about the tableau he describes.

Build Background
A *tableau* is "a scene or an action stopped cold," like a frame stopped in a reel of film. The word *sable* in line 4 means "dark or black." A sable is an animal (also called a marten) prized for its beautiful dark fur.

Locked arm in arm they cross the way,
   The black boy and the white,
The golden splendor of the day,
   The sable pride of night. **Ⓐ**

5 From lowered blinds the dark folk stare,
   And here the fair folk talk,
Indignant that these two should dare
   In unison to walk.

Oblivious to look and word
10   They pass, and see no wonder
That lightning brilliant as a sword
   Should blaze the path of thunder. **Ⓑ**

Ⓐ **Literary Focus** **Metaphor and Simile** What metaphors describe the boys?

Ⓑ **Literary Focus** **Metaphor and Simile** What literary devices describe the boys here?

Incident by **Countee Cullen**

Read with a Purpose
As you read, consider why Cullen chose to write about racism from the perspective of a child.

Build Background
This poem links personal and political meanings. An incident that occurs one summer in Baltimore is a turning point for the speaker, who experiences the lasting effects of racial name-calling. Despite the fact that the children are similar in size and age, the incident underscores their social inequality. The poem is a powerful protest against racism.

Once, riding in old Baltimore,
    Heart-filled, head-filled with glee,
I saw a Baltimorean
    Keep looking straight at me.

5   Now I was eight and very small,
    And he was no whit bigger,
And so I smiled, but he poked out
    His tongue, and called me "Nigger."

I saw the whole of Baltimore
10   From May until December;
Of all the things that happened there
    That's all that I remember. **Ⓐ**

Ⓐ Reading Focus **Comparing and Contrasting Poems** How is this poem like Cullen's poem "Tableau"? How is it different?

Applying Your Skills

Tableau / Incident

Respond and Think Critically

Reading Focus

Quick Check

1. What exactly are the two boys in the tableau doing?

2. How do the adults in "Tableau" feel about what they see from their windows?

3. Who are the two people in "Incident," and what occurs between them?

Read with a Purpose

4. How does the speaker in each poem feel about the people he is describing? Cite evidence from the poems to support your answer.

Reading Skills: Comparing and Contrasting Poems

5. Review the chart you made comparing and contrasting certain elements in these poems. Choose one element that appears to be different in both poems. Write a paragraph in which you discuss the different effect this element creates in each poem.

Literary Focus

Literary Analysis

6. **Evaluate** What must a reader know about the social context of "Tableau" to understand why such a commonplace thing as a friendship between two boys could evoke such an indignant response? Are you surprised that in this case both "fair folk" and "dark folk" disapprove?

7. **Make Judgments** What do you think leads the "Baltimorean" in "Incident" to act as he does? Are his actions more or less disturbing because he is a child? Explain your responses.

8. **Extend** Do you think that the content and messages of "Tableau" and "Incident" are relevant only to the time in which Cullen wrote them? Could these events still happen today? Explain.

9. **Interpret** How might these poems be thought of as companion poems that illustrate pictures of race relations?

Literary Skills: Metaphor and Simile

10. **Analyze** "Tableau" contains two sets of metaphors. What comparisons are made in the first stanza? What comparisons are made in the third? What **simile** appears in line 11?

Literary Skills Review: Theme

11. **Interpret** Remember that **theme** is the insight about human life that is revealed in a literary work. What is the theme of "Tableau"? What is the theme of "Incident"?

Writing Focus

Think as a Reader/Writer

Use It in Your Writing Check your *Reader/Writer Notebook* to review the sound effects Cullen uses in "Incident." Then, write a brief poem of your own, perhaps also called "Incident," about something that happened to you. Try to use rhymes and alliteration, as Cullen does; you might also want to imitate his meter. Open with "Once, in . . ."

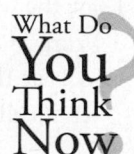

What Do You Think Now

Do you think progress in race relations has challenged the attitudes revealed by some of the characters in these poems? Discuss your responses.

Langston Hughes

Langston Hughes

(1902–1967)

Langston Hughes once described his work as an attempt to "explain and illuminate the Negro condition in America." He succeeded in doing both with vigor and compassion.

> I had been . . . a writer who wrote mostly because, when I felt bad, writing kept me from feeling worse; it put my inner emotions into exterior form, and gave me an outlet for words that never came in conversation.

A True Poet Discovered

One evening in 1925, the poet Vachel Lindsay was eating dinner in the Wardman Park Hotel in Washington, D.C. The busboy, a twenty-three-year-old African American, left three poems near Lindsay's plate. Lindsay was so impressed by the poems that he presented them in his reading that night, telling the audience that he had discovered a true poet—a young black man who was working as a busboy in the hotel restaurant. Over the next few days, articles about the "busboy poet" appeared in newspapers up and down the East Coast.

The busboy, Langston Hughes, was no beginning writer. In fact, when Hughes shyly approached Lindsay, his first book of poetry, *The Weary Blues*, was about to be published by a prestigious New York company. Individual poems had already appeared in numerous publications.

Lindsay warned the young poet about literary "lionizers" who might exploit him for their own purposes: "Hide and write and study and think. I know what factions do. Beware of them." Hughes responded: "If anything is important, it is my poetry, not me. I do not want folks to know me, but if they know and like some of my poems I am glad. Perhaps the mission of an artist is to interpret beauty to the people—the beauty within themselves. That is what I want to do, if I consciously want to do anything with poetry."

Early Experiences

Before this encounter, Hughes had attended Columbia University and worked his way to Africa and back as a crew member on an ocean freighter. Ambitious and energetic, Hughes had learned early on to rely on himself. He spoke German and Spanish; he had lived in Mexico, France, and Italy. In the years that followed his "overnight" celebrity, he earned his degree at Lincoln University and wrote fifteen volumes of poetry, six novels, three books of short stories, eleven plays, and a variety of nonfiction works.

Born in Joplin, Missouri, Hughes spent most of his childhood in Lawrence, Kansas, with his grandmother.

A Hughes Time Line

1902 Born in Joplin, Missouri

Circa 1916–1917 Begins writing poetry (eighth grade)

1921 Publishes "The Negro Speaks of Rivers" in *The Crisis*, a monthly magazine published by the National Association for the Advancement of Colored People (NAACP)

Circa 1917–1921 Publishes his work in a high school literary magazine, *Central High Monthly Magazine*

1910   **1920**   **1930**

1925 Wins a poetry prize sponsored by the magazine *Opportunity: Journal of Negro Life;* poet Vachel Lindsay discovers Hughes and calls him a "true poet"

1926 Publishes his first book of poetry, *The Weary Blues;* wins first prize in the Witter Bynner Undergraduate Poetry Contest at Lincoln University

Langston Hughes as a young man.
The Granger Collection, New York.

After she died, he moved to Illinois, and then to Ohio, to live with his mother and stepfather.

Hughes began writing poems in the eighth grade, and he began publishing his work as a high school student in his high school literary magazine. He read voraciously and admired the work of Edgar Lee Masters, Vachel Lindsay, Amy Lowell, Carl Sandburg, and Walt Whitman. At the age of nineteen, Hughes published his poem "The Negro Speaks of Rivers" in *The Crisis* magazine, a national publication. In this poem, Hughes developed his own poetic voice.

Influences and Inspiration

The most important influences on Hughes's poetry were Walt Whitman and Carl Sandburg. Both poets broke from traditional poetic forms, using free verse to express the common humanity of all people regardless of age, gender, race, and class. Encouraged by the examples of Whitman and Sandburg, Hughes celebrated the experiences of African Americans. He infused his poetry with the musical quality of black speech, and he incorporated jazz rhythms and the repetitive structure of the blues.

Hughes's work also addressed historical events such as the Great Depression. Many poems explored Harlem, the place Hughes called the "great dark city." In 1931, Hughes collaborated with writer Zora Neale Hurston to write a play called *Mule Bone,* based on a folk tale Hurston collected in the South. Hughes and Hurston wanted to create "a comedy of Negro life" and a rebirth of African American theater, but *Mule Bone* was never staged in their lifetimes. It was performed in 1991, sixty years after it was written. Hughes was also responsible for the founding of several black theater companies.

Think About the Writer

Hughes told Lindsay he did not want people to know him, but "if they know and like some of my poems I am glad." What does this reveal about Hughes?

Key Elements of Hughes's Writing

- **Hughes often wrote in free verse** and adopted the characteristics of everyday black speech, but he sometimes used conventional poetic forms.

- **Jazz rhythms** and the metrical forms of the blues in Hughes's poetry reflect the music of the Harlem Renaissance.

- **Themes** centered on the experiences of African Americans.

1930 Publishes first novel, *Not Without Laughter*

1934 Publishes a collection of short stories called *The Ways of White Folks*

1940 Publishes an autobiography, *The Big Sea*

1950 Publishes *Simple Speaks His Mind,* a collection of sketches about Jesse B. Semple, a streetwise Harlem everyman

1930　　　　**1940**　　　　**1950**　　　　**1960**

1929 Receives degree from Lincoln University, an African American institution in Pennsylvania

1937 Becomes a newspaper correspondent during the Spanish Civil War

1967 *The Panther and the Lash,* a collection of poems published posthumously, addresses the anger felt by the black community in the 1960s

 **Reader/Writer**
Notebook
Use your **RWN** to complete the activities for this selection.

Literary Focus

Rhythm In poetry, **rhythm** is the rise and fall of the speaker's voice, produced by alternating stressed and unstressed syllables. Hughes uses several kinds of rhythms: the "syncopated tune" of a piano, the rhythm of everyday speech, the soulful rhythm of the blues, and even the formal rhythm of traditional poetry.

Reading Focus

Understanding the Writer's Context Think of a time you read a poem before learning about the author. After you learned about the author's life and work, did your knowledge enhance your understanding of the poem? Understanding the **writer's context** can provide helpful clues. For example, knowing that Hughes began writing "The Weary Blues" in a small Harlem cabaret—a kind of nightclub—while listening to an African American piano player helps you understand its style. In his writing, Hughes incorporates elements of his life—Southern black speech, lyrics of the first blues he ever heard, and <u>traditional</u> poetic forms learned in school.

Into Action As you read, use a chart like the one below to list examples from the poem that might provide insight into the writer's context. In the second column, provide a possible meaning for your example.

Examples	Possible Meaning
"poor piano," "rickety stool"	The singer is poor and his future uncertain.

Writing Focus

Think as a Reader/Writer

Find It in Your Reading Blues music influenced Hughes's writing style. As you read, notice how Hughes captures the rhythms of speech and music in words. In your *Reader/Writer Notebook,* write down examples that illustrate Hughes's style.

Vocabulary

syncopated (SIHNG kuh pay tihd) *adj.:* in music, having accented beats where they would normally be unaccented. *The song had a syncopated rhythm.*

croon (kroon) *n.:* song sung in a low voice. *The blues singer performed a soulful croon.*

pallor (PAL uhr) *n.:* unnatural lack of color. *The singer's pallor was due to exhaustion.*

melody (MEHL uh dee) *n.:* the arrangement of musical tones that forms a tune. *He played the melody on the piano.*

melancholy (MEHL uhn kahl ee) *adj.:* sad or suggestive of sadness. *We discussed the poem's melancholy tone.*

Language Coach

Prefixes Sometimes people use the expression "in sync" to suggest that two things are happening at the same time, or simultaneously. This expression comes from the word *synchronize.* The prefix *syn–* is Greek in origin and means "together with." Which word on the Vocabulary list is related to *synchronize?*

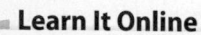 **Learn It Online**
Take this poem further with these project ideas.

go.hrw.com   L11-978   Go

THE WEARY BLUES

by **Langston Hughes**

Read with a Purpose

As you read, think about the relationship between blues music and the experiences of African Americans in the United States at the time this poem was written.

Build Background

Lenox Avenue is a main street in Harlem, where street musicians often played blues and jazz during the Harlem Renaissance. Blues music has African origins, particularly in work songs and the field call-and-response hollers of slaves. Ragtime and blues became especially popular after World War I, when singers like Mamie Smith, Ma Rainey, and Bessie Smith began performing and producing records.

Droning a drowsy syncopated tune,
Rocking back and forth to a mellow croon,
    I heard a Negro play.
Down on Lenox Avenue the other night
5 By the pale dull pallor of an old gas light
    He did a lazy sway . . .
    He did a lazy sway . . .
To the tune o' those Weary Blues. **A**
With his ebony hands on each ivory key **B**
10 He made that poor piano moan with melody.
    O Blues!
Swaying to and fro on his rickety stool
He played that sad raggy tune like a musical fool.
    Sweet Blues!
15 Coming from a black man's soul.
    O Blues!

Book cover of *The Weary Blues* (1926), the collection in which this poem first appeared.

A **Literary Focus** **Rhythm** What is the pattern of the rhyming lines in the first eight lines of the poem? How do the line lengths vary? What effect does this have on the rhythm?

B **Reading Focus** **Understanding the Writer's Context** Think about the social and economic prospects for African Americans at the time that Hughes wrote this poem. How does Hughes indirectly allude to poverty and inequality in this poem?

Vocabulary **syncopated** (SIHNG kuh pay tihd) *adj.:* in music, having accented beats where they would normally be unaccented.
croon (kroon) *n.:* a song sung in a low voice.
pallor (PAL uhr) *n.:* unnatural lack of color.
melody (MEHL uh dee) *n.:* the arrangement of musical tones that forms a tune.

In a deep song voice with a melancholy tone
I heard that Negro sing, that old piano moan—
    "Ain't got nobody in all this world,
20   Ain't got nobody but ma salf.
    I's gwine to quit ma frownin'
    And put ma troubles on the shelf."   C
Thump, thump, thump, went his foot on the floor.
He played a few chords then he sang some more—
25   "I got the Weary Blues
    And I can't be satisfied.
    Got the Weary Blues
    And can't be satisfied—
    I ain't happy no mo'
30   And I wish that I had died."
And far into the night he crooned that tune.
The stars went out and so did the moon.
The singer stopped playing and went to bed
While the Weary Blues echoed through his head.
35   He slept like a rock or a man that's dead.

C **Literary Focus** **Rhythm**   How does the rhythm change when Hughes quotes the
blues singer of his poem?

Vocabulary   **melancholy** (MEHL uhn kahl ee) *adj.:* sad or suggestive of sadness.

The Blues

When asked about the origins of the blues, a veteran New Orleans fiddler once said: "The blues? Ain't no first blues! The blues always been." The
first form of blues, country blues, developed in several parts of the United
States, most notably the Mississippi Delta, around 1900. Country blues
tunes were typically sung by men—usually sharecroppers. The subject was
often the relationship between men and women. As the contemporary
blues singer B. B. King once said, the blues is about a man losing his woman.

From the start, blues music was improvisational—it changed with
every singer and performance. Parts of lyrics were inevitably borrowed
from other songs or based on folk songs or figures of speech. Lines might
be repeated two or three times, with different accents and emphases, then
answered or completed by a rhyming line.

Ask Yourself
**How does Hughes's poem re-create the sounds and feelings he expe-
rienced while listening to the blues in a Harlem cabaret?**

The Weary Blues

Respond and Think Critically

Reading Focus

Quick Check

1. How does Hughes describe the tune being played?

2. Describe the singer's actions as he plays the piano and sings.

3. What did the singer do after he finished playing for the evening?

Read with a Purpose

4. Why do you think Hughes chose to describe this scene in such detail?

Reading Skills: Understanding the Writer's Context

5. While reading the poem, you listed examples that might provide insight into the writer's context. Now that you have finished reading, review your list. Then, add a column to your chart and explain what insight each example offers into the writer's context.

Examples	Possible Meaning	Insight Offered
"poor piano," "rickety stool"	means the singer is poor and his future uncertain	Hughes seems to understand and identify with the singer's experiences.

Literary Focus

Literary Analysis

6. **Interpret** What scene do you see as you read this poem?

7. **Compare and Contrast** How does the message of the blues singer's first verse contrast with that of the second verse?

8. **Interpret** What similes in the poem's last line describe how the singer sleeps? What do you think the last five words suggest?

9. **Evaluate** Think about how the blues singer, the listener, and you feel as you hear the blues song. How would you describe the overall mood of the poem? What words help create this mood?

Literary Skills: Rhythm

10. **Interpret** Describe how the poem's structure suggests the rhythms of blues music.

Literary Skills Review: Alliteration and Onomatopoeia

11. **Analyze** Hughes uses alliteration and onomatopoeia to create his music. **Alliteration** is the repetition of similar consonant sounds in words that are close together. **Onomatopoeia** is the use of words that actually sound like what they name (*swish*, *slap*, and *pop* are examples). Find examples of alliteration and onomatopoeia in the poem. (Hint: Try reading the poem aloud.)

Writing Focus

Think as a Reader/Writer

Use It in Your Writing Re-read the examples of Hughes's style that you collected as you first read this poem. Then, think of a poem or song whose style you like very much. Compare the stylistic elements of that poem or song to those in the "The Weary Blues."

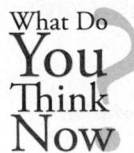 What Do **You Think Now** How do you think the listener feels about the singer? How do you feel about the singer?

For **CHOICES** see page 994.

The Weary Blues

Vocabulary Development

Vocabulary Check

Match each Vocabulary word with the word or phrase closest in meaning.

1. syncopated   **a.** extreme paleness
2. croon   **b.** sequence of notes; a tune
3. pallor   **c.** having a beat with unusual accents
4. melody   **d.** sorrowful
5. melancholy   **e.** "bluesy" song

Vocabulary Skills: Connotations

Words have the power to convey intense emotion and inspire strong feelings in readers. A one-word insult can communicate hate and loathing, while a term of endearment can make a person feel warm and loved. A dictionary can provide a word's standard meaning, or **denotation,** but it cannot communicate everything that the word implies. When you describe a word's meaning in terms of emotion or feeling, you are describing the word's **connotation.**

Example: *croon*
Denotation—a song sung in a low voice
Connotation—implies a sense of warmth, gentleness, and sometimes sadness

Your Turn

Using a table similar to the one below, write the Vocabulary words and their meanings. Include each word's denotation and connotation.

Vocabulary Word	Denotation	Connotation

Language Coach

Prefixes Understanding the meaning of prefixes can help you figure out the meanings of unfamiliar words. The prefix *syn–* tells you that the meaning of the word will have something to do with "together." For example, a *synonym* is a word that shares a meaning with another word. When the prefix *syn–* is used before a word or root beginning with the letters *b, m,* or *p, syn–* becomes *sym–.*

Use a dictionary to look up the meanings of the following words. How does the prefix *syn–* contribute to the meaning of each word?

symbiosis
synagogue
synthesis

List other words that begin with *syn–.*

Academic Vocabulary

Talk About
What does "The Weary Blues" suggest about the connections between the traditions of music and poetry? Do music and poetry inevitably share some common elements? What might those elements be? Discuss these questions with a partner or in a small group.

 **Learn It Online**
Explore connotations the interactive way—through *WordSharp* online.

go.hrw.com   L11-982   Go

Preparing to Read

The Negro Speaks of Rivers

 **Reader/Writer**
Notebook

Use your **RWN** to complete the activities for this selection.

Literary Focus

Repetition Poets create rhythm and musical effects by using **repetition**—a unifying property of repeated words, sounds, syllables, and other elements that appear in a work. A repeated word or line in a poem or song is called a **refrain.** Repetition emphasizes important ideas and builds feelings and expectations in the reader.

Reading Focus

Visualizing the Text Writers use words to help readers **visualize the text,** or form mental images. These images appeal to our senses of sight, hearing, smell, taste, and touch. They can stir our imaginations and move our emotions. In this poem, Hughes uses the recurring image of a river.

Into Action As you read, use a chart like the one below to list words or phrases from the poem that evoke a mental image. In the second column, briefly describe the image created in your mind's eye.

Words or Phrases	Description of Image
"rivers ancient as the world"	old, clean waters undisturbed by people

TechFocus As you read, think about the images and sounds that this poem suggests to you. How might you share your impressions on a Web site?

Writing Focus

Think as a Reader/Writer

Find It in Your Reading In his autobiography, Hughes writes: "Now it was just sunset and we crossed the Mississippi … and I began to think what that river … had meant to Negroes in the past. … Then I began to think of other rivers in our past—the Congo, and the Niger, and the Nile in Africa." Hughes uses rivers as a **symbol** for experiences of black people around the world. In your *Reader/Writer Notebook*, make a list of words and phrases that illustrate Hughes's use of symbolism.

Language Coach

Multiple-Meaning Words Many words have more than one meaning. For example, the verb *raise* can have these meanings:

"to lift up high"
"to build"
"to collect (money) for a purpose"
"to bring up"

Which meanings are used in the following sentences?

1. I raised a house along the Congo River.
2. The committee raised enough money for a tour to the pyramids.
3. He raised his hands above his head as he looked at the sun setting on the river.

Can you find other words in the poem that have multiple meanings?

 **Learn It Online**
Learn more about Hughes online.

go.hrw.com   L11-983   **Go**

THE NEGRO SPEAKS OF RIVERS

by **Langston Hughes**

When They Speak of Rivers (1998)
by Phoebe Beasley.
© Phoebe Beasley.

Read with a Purpose
Read to discover how the poet uses ancient rivers as a symbol for wisdom and experience.

Build Background

In literature, water is often a symbol of the life force, and deep waters frequently symbolize wisdom. Hughes has used both meanings in this poem to convey the eternal wisdom of his ancestors. In many African <u>traditions</u>, ancestors are honored and revered. In this poem, Hughes celebrates the ancient knowledge of his ancestors that lives on in him; he pays homage to his heritage and his people.

I've known rivers:
I've known rivers ancient as the world and older than the flow
    of human blood in human veins. **Ⓐ**

My soul has grown   deep like rivers.

I bathed in the Euphrates when dawns were young.
5   I built my hut near the Congo and it lulled me to sleep.
I looked upon the Nile and raised the pyramids above it.
I heard the singing of the Mississippi when Abe Lincoln went
    down to New Orleans, and I've seen its muddy bosom turn
    all golden in the sunset. **Ⓑ**

I've known rivers:
Ancient, dusky rivers.

10   My soul has grown   deep like rivers.

Ⓐ **Literary Focus** **Repetition** Notice the phrases that Hughes repeats in this poem, such as "I've known rivers" and "My soul has grown deep like rivers." What is the effect of this repetition?

Ⓑ **Reading Focus** **Visualizing the Text** Imagine what the Mississippi River must look like when it turns golden in the sunset. What emotions does this image evoke for you as you read the poem?

Applying Your Skills

SKILLS FOCUS Literary Skills Analyze repetition; analyze tone. **Reading Skills** Visualize the text. **Writing Skills** Employ literary devices for effective writing.

The Negro Speaks of Rivers

Respond and Think Critically

Reading Focus

Quick Check

1. What specific rivers does the speaker name?

2. How old are the rivers the speaker mentions?

3. What comparison occurs more than once in the poem?

Read with a Purpose

4. What words and phrases in the poem serve to develop the ancient rivers as a symbol of human wisdom and experience?

Reading Skills: Visualizing the Text

5. While reading the poem, you listed words and phrases that help the reader visualize the text. Now that you have finished reading, review your list. Then, add a column to your chart and describe the emotion each image evokes.

Words or Phrases	Description of Image	Emotional Response
"rivers ancient as the world"	old, clean waters undisturbed by people	nostalgic longing

Literary Focus

Literary Analysis

6. **Interpret** This speaker speaks for a multitude of people. Who or what does the poet imagine is the "I" in this poem?

7. **Analyze** What special connections might African Americans have with each of these rivers?

8. **Infer** What might the change in the river's color suggest?

Literary Skills: Repetition

9. **Make Judgments** What instances of repetition occur in the poem? What line acts as a refrain? What emotional effect does repetition create in this poem?

Literary Skills Review: Tone

10. **Draw Conclusions** After you read Hughes's poem aloud, think about the tone you hear. Remember that **tone** is the writer's attitude toward his or her work or audience. Which word best describes that tone: *sad*? *bitter*? *thoughtful*? *joyful*? Give details from the poem to support your response.

Writing Focus

Think as a Reader/Writer

Use It in Your Writing Symbols add a depth of meaning to a written work because they draw upon the reader's knowledge and experience. In this poem, Hughes uses the Mississippi River and rivers in Africa and Asia as symbols of the triumphs and tribulations of black people around the world. Select a symbol that has meaning for you, and write a poem that builds upon your symbol just as Hughes built a poem upon rivers. You might choose to write about an object or place that is especially important to you.

What Do You Think Now

According to the speaker, what have the rivers witnessed?

*For **CHOICES** see page 994.* >

Reader/Writer
Notebook

Use your **RWN** to complete the activities for this selection.

Literary Focus

Mood In literature, **mood** refers to the overall emotion created by a work. A poem might make a reader feel sad or amused or thoughtful. While some poems evoke more than one emotional response, often a poem is characterized by one dominant mood. As you read, look for words and images that create a particular mood.

Literary Perspectives Apply the literary perspective described on page 987 as you read this poem.

Reading Focus

Identifying Historical Themes Writers often use historical events as the foundation for their work. The Harlem Renaissance writers responded to the oppression and feelings of powerlessness that pervaded their lives. Hughes wrote several poems using the title "Harlem." The poem that you will read is set during the Great Depression of the 1930s, a time when even a one-cent increase in the price of bread could be disastrous.

Into Action As you read, use a chart like the one below to find details that identify the historical theme. Paraphrase them in the second column.

Details	Paraphrase
"the edge of hell"	a tough place to live

Writing Focus

Think as a Reader/Writer

Find It in Your Reading Hughes's poem is written in **free verse,** or poetry that does not follow a specific meter or rhyme scheme. As you read, take note of details that help you identify this poem as free verse. Use your *Reader/Writer Notebook* to record your thoughts.

Language Coach

Finding the Root The English language has been heavily influenced by other languages—including some languages no longer spoken today. Many English words can be traced back to Latin, ancient Greek, and Old English. The root, or base part of a word, can be used to form many different words. For example, the word *memory* comes from the Latin word *memor,* meaning "mindful." What word repeated several times in "Harlem" also comes from the root *memor*?

Learn It Online
Find more from Hughes with these Internet links.

go.hrw.com   L11-986   **Go**

HARLEM

by **Langston Hughes**

Read with a Purpose
Read to understand the perspective of an African American in Harlem facing a prejudiced world.

Build Background
In the early twentieth century, many African Americans lived in poverty. Racism prevented many black people from getting jobs and renting apartments. In this poem, Hughes explores the African American struggle to lead dignified lives despite racial oppression.

Here on the edge of hell
Stands Harlem—
Remembering the old lies,
The old kicks in the back,
5 The old "Be patient"
They told us before.   **A**

Sure, we remember.   **B**
Now when the man at the corner store
Says sugar's gone up another two cents,
10 And bread one,
And there's a new tax on cigarettes—
We remember the job we never had,
Never could get,
And can't have now
15 Because we're colored.   **C**

So we stand here
On the edge of hell
In Harlem
And look out on the world
20 And wonder
What we're gonna do
In the face of what
We remember.

Literary Perspectives

Analyzing Political Context Analyze the political context of the poem by considering the social and cultural characteristics of the United States during this time period. Hundreds of thousands of African Americans had left the South during the Great Migration. They hoped to find jobs, housing, and educational opportunities that had been denied to them in the rural South. Harlem became the cultural capital for black people and was called the Mecca of the New Negro. However, the reality was different from the dream. Racist attitudes in northern states kept many African Americans in an endless cycle of poverty. Many white-owned businesses refused to hire black people, while white landlords often refused to rent to black tenants. The politics of race created an oppressive environment for African Americans, breeding resentment and bitterness. How do these emotions come through in Hughes's poem? How has the speaker been affected by political and social circumstances?

As you read, be sure to notice the question in the text, which will guide you in using this perspective.

A **Reading Focus** **Identifying Historical Themes** How does racism affect the lives of African Americans in Harlem?

B **Literary Focus** **Mood** What does the phrase "we remember" reveal about the mood of the poem?

C **Literary Perspectives** **Analyzing Political Context** How does Hughes's poem comment on the politics of race?

SKILLS FOCUS Literary Skills Analyze mood; analyze tone. **Reading Skills** Identify historical themes. **Writing Skills** Employ elements of an author's style effectively.

Respond and Think Critically

Reading Focus

Quick Check

1. Name the specific hardships and injustices that the people of Harlem remember, according to the speaker.

2. What did the man at the corner store say?

3. Why are the people mentioned in the poem unable to get jobs?

Read with a Purpose

4. How would you describe the speaker's perspective on racism? What words from the poem best convey this perspective?

Reading Skills: Identifying Historical Themes

5. While reading the poem, you listed details that helped identify the poem's historical theme. Now that you have finished reading, review your list. Then, add a column to your chart and explain what each detail reveals about the historical period.

Details	Paraphrase	Information revealed about time period
"the edge of hell"	a tough place to live	African Americans in Harlem lived very difficult lives, especially during the Depression.

Literary Focus

Literary Analysis

6. **Analyze** What does Hughes create by repeating the word *remember*?

7. **Draw Conclusions** Why does the speaker mention seemingly minor price increases in the second stanza?

8. **Evaluate** The word *old* appears three times in the first stanza. Is this repetition effective? Explain.

9. **Literary Perspectives** Analyze the poem's final stanza. Is it an expression of powerlessness, of opposition, or of something else? Be sure you can defend your analysis with evidence from the text.

Literary Skills: Mood

10. **Analyze** What mood does the speaker create with his description of the poem's setting: "Here on the edge of hell / Stands Harlem—(lines 1–2)"?

Literary Skills Review: Tone

11. **Infer** Describe the tone of the poem. Remember that the **tone** is the attitude a writer takes toward the subject of a work, the characters in it, or the audience.

Writing Focus

Think as a Reader/Writer

Use It in Your Writing The use of free verse helps Hughes imitate spoken language. Using "Harlem" as a model, write your own poem in free verse.

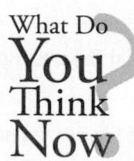 What Do **You Think Now** The Depression was especially hard on the people of Harlem. Do you think Hughes's words had the power to bring changes to his community? Explain.

For **CHOICES** see page 994. ❯

Preparing to Read

Heyday in Harlem *from* The Big Sea

Reader/Writer
Notebook

Use your **RWN** to complete the activities for this selection.

Informational Text Focus

Analyzing an Author's Argument An **argument** is a form of persuasion that appeals to reason in order to convince readers to think or act in a certain way. Primary source documents such as newspapers, diaries, letters, memoirs, and autobiographies can help you understand an author's thinking about an event or time period. In this excerpt from his memoir *The Big Sea,* Hughes describes the years when African American culture in Harlem became fashionable among the white elite of New York.

Into Action As you read, use a chart like the one below to record Hughes's arguments and the reasons he gives for his beliefs.

Hughes's Argument	Reasons for Belief
Harlem was a stylish place for white people.	White celebrities flocked to clubs and parties.

Writing Focus   Preparing for **Constructed Response**

Like all good writers, Hughes does not just state his opinion; he supports his assertions and ideas with textual evidence. As you read this memoir, use your *Reader/Writer Notebook* to keep track of the details from the text that support Hughes's argument. Keep in mind that evidence can take many forms, including personal anecdotes, or stories, dates, and other historical facts.

Vocabulary

monied (MUHN eed) *adj.:* wealthy. *At the time, Harlem was a popular destination for monied whites.*

patronage (PAY truh nihj) *n.:* business provided by customers. *Segregated establishments did not want the patronage of African Americans.*

distinguished (dihs TIHNG gwihsht) *adj.:* renowned or socially important. *Many distinguished guests attended house-rent parties in Harlem.*

vogue (vohg) *n.:* fashion. *It was in vogue for wealthy whites to attend cultural events in Harlem.*

impromptu (ihm PRAHMP too) *adj.:* on the spur of the moment; without preparation. *Impromptu singing and dancing were common types of entertainment.*

Language Coach

Words from French Several words related to this selection come from French, including *memoir, impromptu,* and *vogue.* The suffix *–age,* meaning "related to" or "belonging to," also comes from French. This suffix is sometimes attached to words for people, such as *orphanage* and *personage.* Which word from the Vocabulary list is like these words?

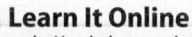

Learn It Online
Explore the Vocabulary words with Word Watch.

go.hrw.com   L11-989   Go

Read with a Purpose

While reading the selection, pay special attention to Hughes's use of satire, a type of writing that ridicules the shortcomings of people or institutions in an attempt to bring about a change, to critique the social atmosphere of the Harlem Renaissance.

Build Background

Langston Hughes published his first autobiography, *The Big Sea,* in 1940, about ten years after the Harlem Renaissance had faded. In "Heyday in Harlem," taken from "When the Negro Was in Vogue" in *The Big Sea,* Hughes describes the lively social scene at the height of the movement. During the Roaring Twenties, upper-class social climbers often hosted and attended parties in order to meet famous musicians, artists, and writers. With so many African Americans producing great works of art and literature, the white social elite <u>inevitably</u> became fascinated with black life and culture.

HEYDAY IN HARLEM

from The Big Sea by Langston Hughes

White people began to come to Harlem in droves. For several years they packed the expensive Cotton Club on Lenox Avenue. But I was never there, because the Cotton Club was a Jim Crow club[1] for gangsters and monied whites. They were not cordial to Negro patronage, unless you were a celebrity like Bojangles.[2] So Harlem Negroes did not like the Cotton Club and never appreciated its Jim Crow policy in the very heart of their dark community. . . .

It was a period when, at almost every Harlem upper-crust dance or party, one would be introduced to various distinguished white celebrities there as guests. It was a period when almost any Harlem Negro of any social importance at all would be likely to say casually: "As I was remarking the other day to Heywood—," meaning Heywood Broun.[3] Or: "As I said to George—," referring to George Gershwin.[4] It was a period when local and visiting royalty were not at all uncommon in Harlem. And when the parties of A'Lelia Walker, the Negro heiress, were filled with guests whose names would turn any Nordic[5] social climber green with envy. . . . It was a period when every season there was at least one hit play on Broadway acted by a Negro cast. And when books by Negro authors were being published with much greater frequency and much more publicity than ever before or since in history. It was a period when white writers wrote about Negroes more successfully (commercially speak-

---

1. **Jim Crow club:** segregated nightclub.
2. **Bojangles:** Bill "Bojangles" Robinson (1879–1949), star of black musical comedies and vaudeville.
3. **Heywood Broun** (1888–1939): American journalist of the 1920s and 1930s.
4. **George Gershwin** (1898–1937): well-known American composer of both popular and classical music who was influenced by jazz and blues.
5. **Nordic:** of Northern European origins.

Vocabulary **monied** (MUHN eed) *adj.:* wealthy.
patronage (PAY truh nihj) *n.:* business provided by customers.
distinguished (dihs TIHNG gwihsht) *adj.:* renowned or socially important.

ing) than Negroes did about themselves. It was the period (God help us!) when Ethel Barrymore[6] appeared in blackface[7] in *Scarlet Sister Mary*! It was the period when the Negro was in vogue. . . .

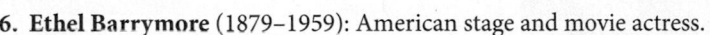

Then it was that house-rent parties began to flourish—and not always to raise the rent either. But, as often as not, to have a get-together of one's own, where you could do the black-bottom[8] with no stranger behind you trying to do it, too. Nontheatrical, nonintellectual Harlem was an unwilling victim of its own vogue. It didn't like to be stared at by white folks. But perhaps the downtowners never knew this—for the cabaret owners, the entertainers, and the speakeasy[9] proprietors treated them fine—as long as they paid.

The Saturday night rent parties that I attended were often more amusing than any night club, in small apartments where God knows who lived—because the guests seldom did—but where the piano would often be augmented by a guitar, or an odd cornet,[10] or somebody with a pair of drums walking in off the street. And where awful bootleg whiskey and good fried fish or steaming chitterling[11] were sold at very low prices. And the dancing and singing and impromptu entertaining went on until dawn came in at the windows. **B**

6. **Ethel Barrymore** (1879–1959): American stage and movie actress.
7. **blackface:** theatrical makeup used to darken actors' skin to mimic the appearance of blacks.
8. **black-bottom:** popular dance of the late 1920s.
9. **speakeasy:** club where alcoholic drinks were sold illegally during Prohibition.
10. **cornet:** brass instrument resembling the trumpet.
11. **chitterling:** food made from the small intestines of pigs that have been deep-fried in hot oil.

A Informational Focus **Analyzing an Author's Argument** What is Hughes's attitude toward the period when "the Negro was in vogue" among wealthy white Americans? What phrases reveal his feelings?

B Informational Focus **Analyzing an Author's Argument** How does Hughes feel about the people—both black and white—whom he describes here?

Vocabulary **vogue** (vohg) *n.:* fashion.
impromptu (ihm PRAHMP too) *adj.:* on the spur of the moment; without preparation.

These parties, often termed whist[12] parties or dances, were usually announced by brightly colored cards stuck in the grille of apartment house elevators. Some of the cards were highly entertaining in themselves:

> *Some wear pajamas, some wear pants, what does it matter just so you can dance, at*
>
> ## *A Social Whist Party*
>
> GIVEN BY
>
> **MR. & MRS. BROWN**
>
> AT
>
> **258 W. 115TH STREET, APT. 9**
> **SATURDAY EVE., SEPT. 14, 1929**
>
> *The music is sweet and everything good to eat!*

Almost every Saturday night when I was in Harlem I went to a house-rent party. I wrote lots of poems about house-rent parties, and ate thereat many a fried fish and pig's foot—with liquid refreshments on the side. I met ladies' maids and truck drivers, laundry workers and shoeshine boys, seamstresses and porters. I can still hear their laughter in my ears, hear the soft slow music, and feel the floor shaking as the dancers danced. **C**

Jitterbugging in Harlem in the 1930s.

---

12. **whist:** a card game popular during the nineteenth and early twentieth centuries.

C **Informational Focus** Analyzing an Author's Argument   Why do you think Hughes wrote about house-rent parties?

Applying Your Skills

SKILLS FOCUS Informational Skills
Analyze an author's arguments. **Vocabulary Skills** Demonstrate knowledge of literal meanings of words and their usage. **Listening and Speaking Skills** Identify emotional appeals when listening.

Writing Skills Write brief constructed responses, with specific support.

Heyday in Harlem *from* The Big Sea

Respond and Think Critically

Informational Text Focus

Quick Check

1. What was a "Harlem upper-crust dance" like?

2. What were house-rent parties?

Read with a Purpose

3. How does Hughes use satire to critique the social atmosphere of the Harlem Renaissance?

Informational Skills: Analyzing an Author's Argument

4. While reading the memoir, you took notes to help you understand Hughes's thinking about Harlem in the 1920s and 1930s. Now, add a third column to your chart and record your own response to Hughes's arguments.

Hughes's Argument	Reasons for Belief	Response to Arguments
It was just a passing fad for white people to visit Harlem.	White celebrities flocked to clubs and parties.	

✓ Vocabulary Check

Choose the Vocabulary word that best completes each sentence: **monied, patronage, distinguished, vogue, impromptu.**

5. Many _____ visitors, such as George Gershwin, came to Harlem in the 1920s and 1930s.

6. The Cotton Club was mostly for _____ whites.

7. House-rent parties could be very _____ events.

8. Ironically, some jazz clubs did not welcome the _____ of African Americans.

9. Hughes argues that Harlem became a victim of its own _____.

Text Analysis

10. **Summarize** In a few sentences, describe the main idea of this selection.

11. **Interpret** What word or phrase best describes the selection's tone?

12. **Analyze** What does Hughes mean when he says, "Nontheatrical, nonintellectual Harlem was an unwilling victim of its own vogue"?

13. **Make Judgments** What characterizes this selection as a memoir rather than as an autobiography?

14. **Analyze** How does Hughes's use of repetition enhance his narrative? Why do you think he chose to use this literary technique as much as he did? Is there anything about his subject that makes repetition particularly appropriate?

Listening and Speaking

15. **Evaluate** Hughes uses satire to draw attention to the irony of African Americans being discriminated against in their own neighborhoods, even at a time when black culture was in style. Read this excerpt aloud with a group and explain how the irony affected your emotional reaction while listening.

Writing Focus Constructed Response

Discuss the evidence that you collected in your *Reader/Writer Notebook*. How does Hughes choose his evidence? What makes his choices effective? Be sure to cite details from the text to support your argument.

What Do You Think Now

What, if anything, do you think Hughes accomplishes by writing about the past?

SKILLS FOCUS **Literary Skills** Evaluate and analyze the philosophical, political, religious, ethical, and social influences of a historical period; understand the Harlem Renaissance. **Writing Skills** Perform literary analysis. **Listening and Speaking Skills** Deliver informative presentations; deliver oral responses to literature.

The Weary Blues / The Negro Speaks of Rivers / Harlem / Heyday in Harlem

CHOICES

As you respond to the Choices, use these **Academic Vocabulary** words as appropriate: alternative, hierarchy, ideology, inevitable, tradition.

REVIEW
Research the Poets Who Inspired Hughes

Timed └Writing Hughes was inspired by the poets Walt Whitman and Carl Sandburg because they broke free from traditional poetic forms and used free verse to celebrate the spirit of humanity. Choose one of these two poets and learn more about his life and work. Write an essay in which you discuss the poet's attitude toward the world and poetry.

Investigate the Harlem Renaissance

Class Presentation Find out more about some of the writers and artists of the Harlem Renaissance. You may want to read more of Hughes's poetry or research some of the musicians mentioned in his memoir *The Big Sea*. Alternatively, you could investigate the works of other writers of that time, such as Claude McKay or Jessie Fauset. You might investigate one of the great Harlem Renaissance artists, such as Aaron Douglas or William H. Johnson. Write a brief research report on a topic related to the Harlem Renaissance. Share your findings with the rest of the class.

CONNECT
Speak from the Soul

Oral Reading Paying careful attention to punctuation and line breaks, prepare an oral reading of "The Weary Blues" and "Harlem" that expresses each poem's unique **rhythm** and **mood.** Make a recording of your reading and share it with your classmates. You might also want to add music or visual effects to your recorded reading.

Create a Poem Web Site

TechFocus Think about the images that these poems created in your mind as you read. Choose one poem, and create a Web site for that poem. Your Web site should include images that the poem suggests to you, as well as sounds and text. Try to convey the effect the poem had on you as a reader through your Web site.

EXTEND
Make Music

Paired Activity Jazz evolved from African American folk music. Its roots lie in African musical and dance rhythms, European harmonies, American gospel sounds, and the work songs that flourished among plantation workers. These last two forms, along with "sorrow songs," influenced the rise of the blues, which in turn contributed to jazz. Visit your school or local library to learn more about jazz and blues music. Working with a partner, prepare an oral presentation for the class and play brief samples of the various types of music that you researched.

Capture the Image

The Harlem Renaissance was a cultural phenomenon involving literature, art, and theater. Now that you have studied a selection of literature from this period, create a visual image of one of the literary selections you have read. Your image can be a photograph, a painting, a collage, or any other visual representation.

SKILLS FOCUS **Reading Skills** Read in order to research self-selected and assigned topics. **Writing Skills** Support ideas/thesis with relevant evidence and details; elaborate with explanations; compare literary works; compare themes or literary elements.

Author Study: Langston Hughes

Writing Focus

Analyzing a Writer's Language

Langston Hughes incorporated the sounds of spoken language and blues-inspired rhythm and repetition into his prose and poetry, creating a music all his own.

Write an essay in which you analyze Hughes's use of language by comparing and contrasting the selections in this Author Study. Look closely at "The Weary Blues," "The Negro Speaks of Rivers," "Harlem," and "Heyday in Harlem" to identify the ways in which these selections are similar *and* different or unique.

Identify Similarities and Differences Look closely at the notes in your *Reader/Writer Notebook* to determine how the selections are alike and how they differ. Re-read the selections if necessary. Then, ask yourself the following questions:

- Do the four selections use a similar tone? How do the writer's word choices indicate his tone or attitude about the subjects in each selection?

- Does the writer use the same or different contexts for all the selections? Are the contexts historical? Are they contemporary to Hughes?

- Does the writer use similar images in the selections? To what senses do his images appeal?

- What is the effect of allusions and references to specific places in the four selections?

Use these and your own ideas to identify points of comparison or contrast in the four selections by Hughes. For each point you choose to focus on, find examples from the texts to support your comparison-contrast. Use carefully chosen quotations from the texts that support your claims.

Organize Your Essay In a comparison-contrast essay, it is generally best to begin with a discussion of similarities and then discuss differences. Use the following framework for a **point-by-point** organization for your essay on Hughes.

- **Introduction:** Identify the historical context for the writer and his works. Include titles of selections and the writer's name. Provide a **thesis statement** that makes an assertion about the similarities and differences of the selections.

- **Body paragraph 1:** Establish a basis of **similarity** among the four works: for instance, the rhythm, repetition, and cadences of natural speech. Use examples from each selection to support your claims.

- **Body paragraphs 2, 3, and 4** (the number will vary depending on the similarities and differences you identify): Establish *another* basis of **similarity** or *introduce* a **difference** that you can discuss using examples from each of Hughes's selections. Be sure to identify at least one difference and use that as your last body paragraph.

- **Conclusion:** Restate your thesis, focusing on similarities and differences in the writer's works.

Before you begin writing, review the criteria for a good comparison-contrast essay.

An Effective Comparison-Contrast Essay

- clearly states the basis of the comparison and contrast in a thesis
- organizes ideas using the point-by-point method
- uses and cites textual evidence to support each point of comparison and contrast
- contains few or no errors in spelling, punctuation, and usage

What Do You Think Now In what ways has the writing of Langston Hughes inspired change and challenged <u>traditional</u> ways of thinking?

Learn It Online
See a sample comparison-contrast essay online.
go.hrw.com | L11-995 | Go

Link to Today

from **Coming Up Harlem**

What Do You Think

How does progress challenge <u>tradition</u> and redefine society?

QuickWrite

Think of a cultural event that has had an impact on you—it might be in the field of art, literature, film, theater, music, or dance. Write a journal entry describing this cultural event, and explain why it is important to you.

Informational Text Focus

Analyzing Diction Diction, or word choice, is a strong component of style. Diction can be formal, informal, colloquial, ornate, plain, abstract, and so on. A writer's diction depends on the intended audience, purpose for writing, and subject. Analyzing diction helps you identify a writer's attitude toward his or her subject. As you read, think about why the author may have chosen particular words instead of others.

Into Action As you read, use a chart like the one below to list words that are central to the writer's description of the revival in Harlem. Then, list one or more synonyms that the writer could have used.

Word Choice	Alternative Words
"boutique" (p. 997)	shop, store

Writing Focus Preparing for **Constructed Response**

The author includes several **anecdotes**—brief stories about individual Harlem residents. What do anecdotes add to the text that generalizations, summaries, or descriptions do not? What effect do the anecdotes in this article have on you as a reader? Record your ideas in your *Reader/Writer Notebook*.

Vocabulary

revival (rih VY vuhl) *n.:* renewal; a restoration to use, popularity, or life. *Harlem is enjoying a revival of its history and art.*

resurgence (rih SUR juhns) *n.:* a return; a comeback. *A resurgence of interest in the town houses drove up prices.*

renovated (REHN uh vayt ihd) *adj.:* repaired, updated; restored. *The renovated buildings are beautiful again.*

homage (HAHM ihj) *n.:* respect; reverence. *By celebrating its culture, the community pays homage to its past.*

Language Coach

Synonyms Words that have the same meaning as other words are synonyms. Which Vocabulary word is a synonym for the underlined word in the sentence "The <u>modernized</u> town house attracted a buyer"?

Reader/Writer Notebook

Use your **RWN** to complete the activities for this selection.

Learn It Online

Find more graphic organizers online to help you as you read.

go.hrw.com L11-996   **Go**

File   Edit   View   Favorites   Tools   Help

Back   Forward   Stop   Refresh   Home   Search   Favorites   History   Mail   Print

Address _____ ▽ → Go

Link to Today

This Link to Today shows how the New York community of Harlem is experiencing a second renaissance.

Read with a Purpose

Read to learn how renovations in Harlem honor the community's cultural roots.

Build Background

Since the Great Depression, Harlem has suffered from urban decay, becoming a dangerous center of crime and drugs. Many people there live in poverty, and many buildings are in disrepair. In the past few years, however, Harlem has begun to recover as a fresh wave of creative energy has suffused the neighborhood. People are calling this new artistic movement a "second renaissance." Recent renovations have restored many of Harlem's historic buildings and brownstone houses, helping to bring the neighborhood back to life.

Photograph: Houses under reconstruction. One side of this Harlem apartment building has been renovated.

from Coming Up HARLEM

by Peter Hellman   *from* Smithsonianmag.com

A revival of the fabled New York community inspires pride.

At 6:30 one recent morning, Paulette Gay was already working at The Scarf Lady, her four-year-old boutique on Lenox Avenue, a faded Harlem thoroughfare showing vivid signs of renewal. Because the sidewalk is normally deserted at that hour, Gay was surprised to see someone peering in the store window—a giant of a man with a shaved head and piercing eyes. He looked familiar. Gay stuck her head out the door and said, "Aren't you—?" **A**

He was. Kareem Abdul-Jabbar, the basketball great, who was born in the neighborhood and had long been a celebrated resident of Los Angeles, was back in Harlem. Gay asked him what he was doing

A **Informational Focus** Diction   Which word in this paragraph focuses the reader's attention on the revival of Harlem?

Vocabulary   **revival** (rih VY vuhl) *n.*: renewal; a restoration to use, popularity, or life.

out so early. "He explained that, being a very private person, he prefers to stroll around before anyone else is out," she says. (At over 7-foot-1 and with a famous visage, he undoubtedly has trouble going unnoticed.) Abdul-Jabbar bought a town house in Harlem this past winter, according to Kareem Productions.

He joins a wave of black artists, activists, scholars and home-seekers lately drawn to one of the world's signature African-American communities. The poet Maya Angelou and the singer Roberta Flack have bought houses in Harlem. Harvard professor Henry Louis Gates, Jr., who is among the nation's best-known intellectuals, is on the hunt for a Harlem town house.

Harlem, a community in northern Manhattan that hit bottom in the 1980s when poverty, neglected housing, and drug-related crime took their toll, is enjoying a lively second renaissance. Some Harlemites dismiss the resurgence as little more than a real estate boom, because the neighborhood's magnificent 19th-century town houses are being snapped up at a rapid rate. You'll also hear that the cultural scene doesn't compare with Harlem's first flowering, in the 1920s, which was animated by extraordinary creativity in politics, the arts, and especially the written word. But if it's true there are no stand-ins today for fiery W.E.B. Du Bois, gentle Langston Hughes, or patrician Duke Ellington, the second renaissance is still taking shape.

Highbrow, mainstream, pop, hiphop, avant-garde— Harlem's cultural and artistic revival is evident on nearly every block. At the partially renovated Apollo Theater, the curtain went up in July on *Harlem Song*, a Broadway-style musical directed by George C. Wolfe, producer of the Joseph Papp Public Theater/New York Shakespeare Festival. On St. Nicholas

Vocabulary **resurgence** (ri SUR jens) *n.:* a return; a comeback
renovated (REN uh vey tihd) *adj.:* repaired; updated; restored..

Analyzing Visuals

Connecting to the Text
Do you believe that graffiti, such as can be seen in this photograph, is an art form? Explain.

Hip-hop artist The Mighty Mike C of the Fearless 4 (left) takes photos with a tourist at the Graffiti Hall of Fame in Harlem.

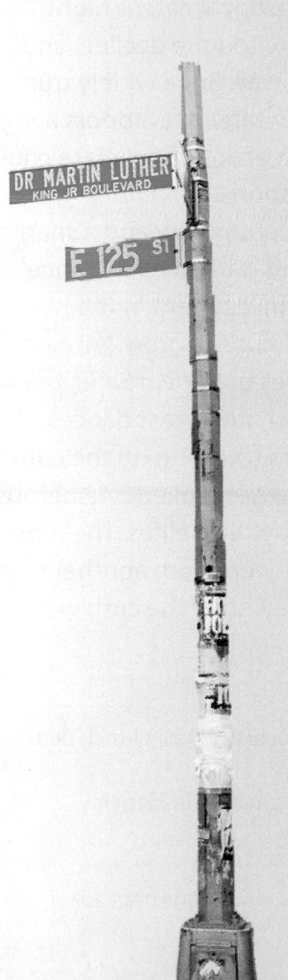

Avenue, the three-year-old Classical Theater of Harlem recently staged *King Lear* in its garden court, with Paul Butler playing the title role as an African tribal chief in purple and cinnamon robes. In a 1909 firehouse on Hancock Place, George Faison, choreographer of *The Wiz*, a Broadway hit in the 1970s, is creating a performing arts complex with two theaters, three rehearsal studios, and a library. **B**

Half a dozen new eateries have taken hold, from the upscale and raffish Jimmy's Uptown, at 2207 Seventh Avenue, to the sedate Sugar Hill Bistro, situated in a 19th-century town house on West 145th Street. Sugar Hill is a nickname for a part of northwest Harlem in which wealthy blacks began to settle in the 1920s, who in the parlance had lots of "sugar," or cash. On Mother's Day, the bistro's ground-floor lounge was filled with people as a singer belted out the words to "This Little Light of Mine." The microphone was passed from table to table so diners could deliver the refrain: "Let it shine, let it shine, let it shine." The easygoing warmth evident here, Harlemites will tell you, is a community trait. Indeed, it's as easy to strike up a conversation with a stranger in Harlem as it is difficult in midtown. **C**

The new Harlem pays homage to the old, as Dr. Dineo Khabele, an owner of Sugar Hill Bistro, suggested. The bistro is owned by three young black couples, all recently settled in the neighborhood, who never intended to become restaurateurs. . . . Jumpstarted by a $300,000 loan from the Empowerment Zone, they bought a then-vacant town house and redid it top to bottom. The bistro has a first-floor bar leading to a rear garden, a second-floor dining room, and a third-floor gallery and cultural space. "It reminds me of what I've heard about A'Lelia Walker's upper-floor room where people could gather," says Khabele, referring to the premier hostess of the first Harlem renaissance, a wealthy patroness of the arts who called her salon the Dark Tower, after a poem by Countee Cullen.[1]

Harlem is defined by a set of geographic coordinates, to be sure, but also by a feeling, or sensibility. For that reason, the Morris-Jumel Mansion on Edgecombe Avenue at West 160th Street may be said to be part of Harlem, though it's technically just north of the 155th Street administrative boundary. The stately home, which dates from 1765 and which George Washington used as his headquarters for a month during the Revolutionary

---

1. **Countee Cullen:** African American poet and schoolteacher; prominent literary figure of the Harlem Renaissance.

B Informational Focus Diction Based on the diction in this paragraph, how would you characterize the writer's attitude toward today's Harlem?

C Informational Focus Diction Which words help to characterize the mood in Harlem today? Explain.

Vocabulary **homage** (HAHM ij) *n.:* respect; reverence.

Link
to
Today

War, incorporates perhaps the first octagonal room in the Colonies. Shady gardens surround the house, which, improbably, sits on a kind of schist proscenium[2] overlooking the towers of an enormous public housing project on the site of the old Polo Grounds, where the New York Giants played baseball. The Morris-Jumel Historic District, as the neighborhood is called, feels like Harlem, with its dignified homes, including 16 Jumel Terrace, which once belonged to the incomparable singer, actor, and fighter for social justice, Paul Robeson.

D

The nightclubs of the first Harlem renaissance are gone. Last June, a plaque was belatedly dedicated to mark the Seventh Avenue site of the Savoy Ballroom, once the "Home of Happy Feet" and the Lindy Hop.[3] It's now a housing project. Nothing marks the site of the original Cotton Club a block away. A club by that name today on West 125th Street caters largely to tourists, with offerings like a Sunday gospel brunch.

The Apollo Theater, which introduced or helped launch the careers of artists such as Ella Fitzgerald, Sarah Vaughn, and James Brown, deteriorated over the years, despite the popularity of its Wednesday amateur night shows. A ballyhooed[4] 1992 renovation barely stemmed the decline, and a more extensive, $53 million renovation is under way. But a widely trumpeted plan to incorporate the shuttered Victoria Theater a few doors away was postponed in September due to fears that the economic climate could result in lower-than-budgeted revenues and donations.

The postponement was a blow to some in the community and a snag in its otherwise dazzling comeback. But the second Harlem renaissance is far bigger than any one reconstruction project. Investment in the place remains strong, and its undeniable mystique continues to grow. You can sense that energy at the sold-out performances of *Harlem Song,* the Apollo's first long-running show, in which a supercharged cast dances and sings its way through twenty musical numbers touching on the community's history. On the night I attended, the audience looked prosperous and included members of the city's financial and political elites. The most familiar songs, like 1933's "Drop Me Off in Harlem," were from another heyday, but the natty throng and the limousines jockeying at the curb were very much of this one.

---

2. **schist proscenium:** stage-like outcropping formed of schist, a type of rock that splits easily into slabs or flakes.
3. **Lindy Hop:** lively form of swing dance for couples, originating in Harlem.
4. **ballyhooed:** announced with great fanfare or publicity.

D **Informational Focus** Diction How does the writer's word choice help to create a vivid mental image of a part of Harlem? Explain.

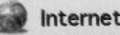

Applying Your Skills

SKILLS FOCUS Informational Skills
Identify and understand patterns of
organization; identify comparison-
contrast organization. **Vocabulary**

Skills Demonstrate word knowledge.
Listening and Speaking Skills Interview
subject. **Writing Skills** Write brief constructed responses, with specific support.

from **Coming Up Harlem**

Respond and Think Critically

Informational Text Focus

Quick Check

1. What kinds of cultural elements characterized the first Harlem Renaissance?

2. What recent changes does the article describe?

3. List examples that help show how Harlem is changing.

Read with a Purpose

4. How can people create change in a difficult situation?

Informational Skills: Analyzing Diction

5. In "Coming Up Harlem" the writer uses purpose-ful word choices. Refer to the table you created while you were reading the article. Add a column in which you explain how the diction affects meaning and helps establish the tone of the article.

Word Choice	Synonyms	How the diction affects meaning and tone
"boutique" (p. 997)	shop, store	A "boutique" is an upscale shop; the word choice shows that a market for high-end goods is developing in Harlem.
"giant" (p. 997)	big, tall	

✔ Vocabulary Check

Match each Vocabulary word with its definition.

6. revival
7. resurgence
8. renovated
9. homage

a. honor
b. coming to life again
c. continuing again
d. refurbished

Text Analysis

10. **Compare and Contrast** In what ways are Harlem's two cultural rebirths similar? In what ways are they different? Explain.

11. **Infer** The author calls Harlem "one of the world's signature African-American communities" and states that it has an "undeniable mystique." What can you infer about Harlem from these statements?

12. **Analyze** What is meant by the statement, "The new Harlem pays homage to the old"? Explain.

13. **Extend** What is the significance of the restoration currently taking place in Harlem? How can restoration projects inspire creativity?

Listening and Speaking

14. **Extend** Think of something new and exciting in your school, neighborhood, or community. In a small group, discuss the developments. Share **anecdotes** that illuminate what makes the developments exciting.

Writing Focus   Constructed Response

Briefly discuss how anecdotes help to develop the main idea of "Coming Up Harlem." Imagine removing the anecdotes from the article. What, besides information, would be lost? How else could you deliver that information to the reader? Be sure to support your response with specific evidence from the article.

What Do
You
Think
Now

How has the recent "cultural revival" influenced the community of Harlem? Use the text to support your response.

Writing Workshop

Literary Analysis

Write with a Purpose

Write a literary analysis of a novel. Your **purpose** is to inform others of your insights about the novel. The **audience** for this literary analysis will be your teacher, students, and others who are interested in reading this novel or others by the same author.

A Good Literary Analysis

- focuses on a clear and reasonable conclusion about the work based on literary elements the author uses
- supports conclusions with evidence and elaboration
- demonstrates a clear and detailed analysis of the text
- shows effective organization throughout

See page 1010 for complete rubric.

Think as a Reader/Writer
Analyzing literary works you read adds depth to your understanding of them. By writing a **literary analysis** of a novel, you can help others discover the deeper layers of meaning you have found and add to their appreciation of the novel. Before you begin your own analysis, read the following excerpt from Toni Morrison's "The Reader as Artist" (page 752).

> In the opening sentences of Flannery O'Connor's story, she chose to direct her readers to Mr. Head's fantasy, his hopes. Lowly pillow ticking[1] is like brocade, rich, elaborate. Moonlight turns a wooden floor to silver and "cast[s] a dignifying light" everywhere. His chair, "stiff and attentive," seems to await an order from him. Even his trousers hanging on its back had "a noble air, like the garment some great man had just flung to his servant." So. Mr. Head has strong, perhaps unmanageable, dreams of majesty, of controlling servants to do his bidding, of rightful authority. Even the moon in his shaving mirror pauses "as if it were waiting for his permission to enter." We don't really have to wait (a few sentences on) to see his alarm clock sitting on an "overturned bucket," or to wonder why his shaving mirror is five feet away from his bed, to know a great deal about him—his pretension,[2] his insecurity, his pathetic yearnings—and anticipate his behavior as the story unfolds. In the accuracy of the 'ear' of the story, its shape, its supple economy and sheer knowingness, it seems to me virtually flawless and deliciously demanding. Which is to say, I can read it again and again, step into its world confident that my attentiveness will always yield wonder. . . .
>
> I can do this again: read it and be there once more, anytime I like. Sifting, adding, recapturing. Making the work work while it makes me do the same.
>
> ---
>
> 1. **ticking:** striped fabric used to cover mattresses and pillows.
> 2. **pretension:** a claim to importance, status, or worth.

← Morrison **quotes** directly from the text as **evidence.**

← She **elaborates** upon the **evidence** she presents.

← She draws a **conclusion** about the literary work.

Reader/Writer Notebook

Use your **RWN** to complete the activities for this workshop.

Think About the Professional Model
With a partner, discuss the following questions about the professional model.

1. How do the quotations from O'Connor's story help Morrison make her points?
2. What does Morrison do after she makes a point about the writing?

Prewriting

Choose a Novel

Begin by choosing an appropriate novel—one that you like or that prompts a strong reaction in you. The novel should be complex enough for you to create a thoughtful analysis.

Read and Analyze the Novel

Read the novel first for enjoyment and general understanding, taking notes in your *Reader/Writer Notebook* on passages you might wish to revisit in your analysis. Then, re-read (or skim) the novel, taking additional notes. To develop a **comprehensive understanding** of the author's ideas, refresh your memory of literary elements and stylistic devices from the chart below. Answer the analysis questions to give you an overview of the novel and organize your thoughts.

Literary Elements	Analysis Questions
Character—an individual in the story	How do the important characters in the novel think, talk, and act? Do their actions or attitudes change over the course of the novel?
Setting—the time and location of the story	Where and when does the novel take place? What mood does the setting suggest? How does the setting affect the plot?
Plot—the series of related events in the story	What is the central conflict, or problem, of the story? How does the outcome of the story relate to the theme or meaning?
Point of View—the perspective or vantage point from which the story is told	Is the story told by a first-person or a third-person narrator? How much does the narrator know? What does the narrator think about the characters and events in the story?
Theme—the idea or insight the novel reveals about life	What truths does the novel express about human nature, experiences, problems, or relationships? What details reflect this theme?
Symbol—something that has meaning in itself and also stands for something else	Do any objects or elements show up repeatedly? Does any person, place, or thing represent an abstract idea, such as hope, faith, greed, freedom, or cruelty?
Stylistic Devices	
Imagery—language that appeals to the senses	What feelings do descriptions of people, places, and actions suggest? What effects are created through the use of imagery?
Diction—the author's choice of words	Is the author's word choice straightforward, or is the language connotative (having meaning beyond a simple definition)? How does the word choice affect the tone and mood of the story?
Figurative Language—imaginative comparisons not meant to be taken literally	Does the author use similes, metaphors, personification, or symbols? If so, what effects do these comparisons create?

Idea Starters

- novels by authors in this book whose works you have enjoyed
- novels recommended by friends, teachers, librarians, or family members
- novels on which movies or TV miniseries have been based (be careful; many stray considerably from the original source)
- novels reviewed in magazines, in newspapers, or on the Web

Your Turn

Get Started Take notes in your **RWN** as you read and analyze the novel you have chosen. Use the chart on this page to decide which **literary elements** and **stylistic devices** stand out in the novel you have selected.

Learn It Online
To see how one writer completed this assignment, see the model literary analysis online.

go.hrw.com   L11-1003   **Go**

Think About Audience and Purpose

When you write a literary analysis, you need to consider your **purpose** for writing—to inform others of your insights about the novel. You should also consider your **audience,** which will include your teacher and classmates. Always provide **context** and use specific examples so that a reader who has not read the novel will be able to understand and appreciate your analysis.

Write a Thesis Statement

To plan your essay, focus on one or two literary elements over the entire course of the novel. Look at your notes to decide which element seems most important or interesting. Identify a few major points that make that element so strong—for example, the most surprising plot events or the characters whose lives demonstrate the theme. Then, write a sentence or two that presents your insights about the novel—a conclusion based on the major points about your chosen element. This sentence, your working **thesis statement,** will serve as a guide as you plan and write your analysis. If necessary, you can revise this statement later.

Gather Evidence

To convice readers that your thesis is valid, you must find evidence to prove it. Your most important support will be **literary evidence**—detailed references to the text of the novel. Literary evidence includes **quotations, paraphrases,** and **summaries** of specific details and passages in the text. Be sure whenever you quote from the novel that you have copied the quotation exactly as it appears in the novel.

Although most of your evidence will come from the **primary source** (the novel itself), you might also find evidence in **secondary sources,** reference materials such as encyclopedias, periodicals, author biographies, or literary criticism. Such sources can bolster your major points and provide background information that your readers may need to understand the context of the novel. When you use material from secondary sources, however, always document your sources to avoid **plagiarism**—using other authors' words or ideas without giving them proper credit. For more on documenting sources, see page 585.

Elaborate Explain how each piece of evidence supports your thesis and develops your main points. To do this, **elaborate** on the importance of each idea and its connection to your thesis. As part of your elaboration, explain how the author uses ambiguities, nuances, and complexities, and how those devices relate to your thesis.

- **ambiguities:** language or situations that can be interpreted in more than one way or have more than one meaning
- **nuances:** fine shades of meaning, especially any changes in the way the author expresses a recurring idea
- **complexities:** details in the novel that at first seem contradictory or confusing, requiring some thought to understand thoroughly

Peer Review

Share your thesis statement with another student. Ask your partner if he or she can tell what your paper will be about from reading just your thesis statement. If not, discuss together your insights about the novel, and create a clearer, more precise statement.

Your Turn _____

Write a Thesis and Gather Evidence When you have completed an analysis of the novel and its theme and literary elements, draft a working thesis statement to use for your essay. Begin reviewing your notes to find evidence to support your thesis.

Drafting

Organizing Ideas

How you arrange your ideas will depend on your thesis statement. What is the best organizational structure to help you prove the thesis? If you are examining how an element such as character changes over time, you may want to use **chronological order.** If you are examining the role of literary elements in developing theme, you may use **order of importance,** finishing your essay with your most important point. You may wish to use a combination of both orders—ranking each element by importance, then discussing the elements chronologically, as they appear in the novel. Whatever order you choose, think about whether readers will find it logical and coherent.

Using a Writer's Framework

Most essays are divided into three sections: the introduction, the body, and the conclusion. Review the **Writer's Framework** to the right to see what elements to include in each section.

When you write a literary analysis, you may use supporting evidence in the form of fragments of direct quotations from the original text. As you write your draft, be sure to punctuate these fragments correctly.

Framework for a Literary Analysis

Introduction
- Identify the novel's author and title.
- Present background information that provides a context for your analysis.
- Include a clear thesis statement.

Body
- Organize major points in a logical order.
- Include literary evidence from the novel or secondary sources.
- Elaborate on how evidence supports major points.

Conclusion
- Restate your thesis and summarize your major points.
- End with a memorable statement—an idea your readers can ponder.

Grammar Link Punctuating Fragments in Quotations

When you quote fragments in your analysis, blend them smoothly with your own syntax to add powerful and specific evidence.

Toni Morrison uses fragments as evidence in her analysis of Flannery O'Connor's story.

> His chair, "stiff and attentive," seems to await an order from him.

The fragment above is **not** capitalized, but it is enclosed in quotation marks. Morrison made the style choice to put O'Connor's words after the noun they modify, *chair,* and to enclose them in commas.

In the next example, Morrison's sentence does not require additional punctuation; however, notice that the fragment's original punctuation contains a comma, which is retained.

> Even his trousers hanging on its back had "a noble air, like the garment some great man had just flung to his servant."

Reference Note For more on punctuating quotations, see the Language Handbook.

Your Turn

Write Your Draft Using your **prewriting notes** and the **Writer's Framework,** write your first draft. Ask yourself:

- Which elements stood out in my reading? What role do they play?
- What insight can I develop and support with literary evidence?
- How can I smoothly add quotations to my essay?

Peer Review

Before you revise, trade papers with a peer and ask for input about where you need to integrate literary evidence more smoothly into your paper. Answer each question in the chart to the right to determine where and how your draft could be improved.

Evaluating and Revising

Your analysis is not complete until you've revised it carefully. Use the guidelines below to look critically at content and organization. With a partner, work from the left to the right, answering questions about your draft and making suggested revisions.

Literary Analysis: Guidelines for Content and Organization

Evaluation Question	Tip	Revision Technique
1. Does the introduction include the author's name, the novel's title, and background information?	**Underline** the name of the author and the title of the novel. **Double underline** background information that provides context.	**Add** the name of the author or the title of the novel. **Add** details about the author's life and other work or the novel's setting, if important.
2. Does the introduction present a clear thesis that identifies the main point of the analysis?	**Bracket** the thesis statement.	**Add** a conclusion about the novel or a clearer statement of the literary element or elements to be analyzed.
3. Does each body paragraph develop a major point that supports the thesis?	**Label** the major point of each body paragraph in the margin next to the paragraph.	**Replace** sentences or paragraphs that don't support the thesis. **Elaborate** on the thesis as needed.
4. Does evidence from the novel support each major point?	**Draw a jagged line** under each piece of evidence. **Draw an arrow** from the evidence to the point it supports.	**Add** quotations, paraphrases, and summaries. **Elaborate** on how evidence supports each point.
5. Are the major points organized effectively?	**Number** the sequence of ideas for chronological order. For order of importance, **underline** the most important point.	**Reorder** a chronological presentation in correct time order. For order of importance, **reorder** so the most important point is discussed last.
6. Does the conclusion sum up the main points of the essay and bring it to a close?	**Underline** the sentence or sentences that restate the focus of the essay.	**Add** a sentence or two that restate the thesis. **Elaborate** with a memorable closing statement.

Read this student draft and notice the comments on its strengths and suggestions on how it could be improved.

Dysfunctional Communication

by Paige Horne, Coastal High School

After the terrorist attacks of September 11, 2001, Americans experienced feelings of vengeance, distress, and fear. Never before had America been attacked on its own soil. Never before had so much uncertainty about the future existed in America. The incomprehensibly violent actions of the terrorists left Americans shattered and vulnerable. In the novel *Extremely Loud and Incredibly Close,* Jonathan Safron Foer vividly captures America's crippling distress.

Foer uses victims of the tragedy and their response to it in the novel. When the planes hit the World Trade Center, Thomas Schell, whom we meet only in flashbacks, is trapped inside the building. Schell leaves his wife and son, Oskar, five telephone messages during the crisis. Initially, Thomas's intention is to assure his family that he is safe: "I'm OK. They are telling us to stay where we are and wait for the firemen. I'll give you another call when I have a better idea or know what is going on"(25). By repeating what the emergency services personnel tells him, Schell tries to convince himself and his family that everything is going to be fine. Foer uses Thomas and his messages of false hope to illustrate an all too common and ineffective form of communication.

← The introductory paragraph sets the **context** for the novel and provides the **title** and **author.**

← Paige **summarizes** the plot to develop her first **major point.**

← She **quotes directly** from the novel as **evidence.**

MINI-LESSON ▶ How to Write a Thesis Statement

The first step in developing a thesis statement is to review your notes about the novel and decide which literary elements you want to emphasize. The second step is to decide on how the elements relate to the novel's theme. Your thesis statement should give readers a preview of your analysis by telling them the theme and elements the essay will discuss.

Paige's introduction is dramatic and effective, but she fails to provide a thesis statement that will guide her readers through the analysis. Paige decides to focus on symbols of communication and link those to the theme of failed communication in a time of suffering.

Paige's Revision of Paragraph 1

In the novel, *Extremely Loud and Incredibly Close,* Jonathan Safron Foer vividly captures America's distress after the terrorist attacks. *Despite the fact that today's technology presents a myriad of ways to communicate, Foer asserts that communication fails in times of personal suffering.*

● Writing Tip

The student model uses parenthetical citations to show the page numbers in the novel where quotations appear. For information on parenthetical citations, see page 585.

Your Turn _____

Write a Thesis Re-read the draft of your essay. As you wrote, did you develop any ideas that were not included in your thesis statement? If so, revise your thesis.

Student Draft *continues*

This paragraph develops the idea that Oskar fails to communicate. →

When Oskar returns home from school, his father's five messages await. Oskar "listened to them and listened to them again, and before [he] had time to figure out what to do, or what to think or feel the phone started ringing. . . . [He] saw that it was his father"(15). Oskar understands that his father is trapped inside the burning building; however, when Thomas calls for a sixth time, Oskar does not answer. He refuses to deal with the reality of his father's desperate cries.

This paragraph further develops the **theme** with Oskar and his grandmother. →

Oskar and his paternal grandmother are both deeply affected by the death of Oskar's father. They communicate via walkie-talkie rather than face to face. Oskar is unable to articulate his feelings directly to anyone and resorts to using an indirect, electronic method of communication to share his feelings. Using Oskar and his grandmother, Foer asserts that people who face adversity often communicate behind barriers.

This paragraph develops the grandparents as additional **examples**. →

The relationship between Oskar's grandparents was complex. A few months into their marriage, they started marking off areas in their apartment—areas in which the other could not enter. They referred to them as a "Nothing Place." His grandmother explains, "There came a point when our apartment was more Nothing than Something" (111). Throughout the marriage they live independently in one apartment, completely isolated from one another. The "Nothing Place" is a model of solitary confinement where communication does not exist. Oskar's grandparents are symbols of the complete failure of communication.

The conclusion **restates the theme,** giving the reader a new thought to contemplate. →

Foer's unique novel, *Extremely Loud and Incredibly Close,* reveals the theme of failed communication through its major characters. Every character suffers from a tragic experience. Although each individual reacts differently, all are united by their dysfunctional methods of communication. Foer suggests that even in a modern world immersed in technology, human communication fails.

MINI-LESSON ▶ How to Link Each Idea to the Thesis

Each of Paige's body paragraphs develops a unique symbol of failed communication. Paragraph 3 summarizes Oskar's response to his father's messages, and uses textual evidence, but fails to link the summary and quotation to the thesis statement. She realizes this and adds the following statement to link Oskar's example to the theme of failed communication.

Paige's Revision of Paragraph 3

. . . when Thomas calls for a sixth time, Oskar does not answer. He refuses to deal with the reality of his father's desperate cries.∧*Foer uses Oskar as a tragic example of individuals who refuse to communicate and as a consequence suffer the loss forever.*

Your Turn _____

Link Supporting Points to the Thesis Re-read your draft to determine if you have made the link between the thesis statement and the supporting points clear. If not, add a statement that specifically links the two.

Proofreading and Publishing

Proofreading

All writers make mistakes. A good writer catches and corrects mistakes before the work is published. Carefully check your draft—individually and collaboratively with a peer—for grammar, usage, spelling, and punctuation errors before you submit the final copy. Since your analysis discusses literature, you should check it to make sure you have correctly used the **literary present tense.**

Grammar Link Using Literary Present Tense

When you discuss literature, you should use **literary present tense** to discuss events in the work. Because the events in a novel you have analyzed are constantly unfolding for new readers, the present tense is the standard. While proofreading, Paige found two errors in tense. She corrected the past-tense verbs by changing them to the present tense.

The relationship between Oskar's grandparents ~~was~~ *is* complex. . . .

They ~~referred~~ *refer* to them as a "Nothing Place."

Publishing

Your literary analysis presents your unique perspective on the novel you have examined. Share your literary analysis with a wider audience.

- Collaborate with other students on a booklet of related analyses. Collect analyses about the same author's works. Bind your booklet, and add it to a class or library display of student work.
- Create a bulletin board for your class. Arrange your literary analysis next to a photo of the novel's author.
- Find a Web site about the author of the novel you analyzed. Send an e-mail message to ask the creators of the site if they will publish your analysis.

Reflect on the Process
Now that your literary analysis is complete, take time to reflect on your writing. Writing responses to the following questions will help you identify and build on what you learned in this workshop. Use your **RWN** to reflect on the writing process.

1. How did you choose the focus of your analysis? What other elements of the novel or major points might you have analyzed instead?
2. How has writing the analysis deepened your understanding of the novel?
3. What important revisions did you make to the draft? How did they improve it?
4. What will you do differently when you write another literary analysis?

● Proofreading Tip

Proofread your analysis four times, using one pass each for grammar, usage, spelling, and punctuation. Between reads, try to read something else—a magazine, a newspaper, or a Web site—to clear your mind. If you have questions about whether you have correctly used literary present tense, ask a classmate for help.

Your Turn
Proofread and Publish
Proofread your revised analysis to correct any errors in grammar, usage, or mechanics. Be sure to use literary present tense where appropriate. Make a final copy of your analysis and publish it.

Scoring Rubric

Use one of the rubrics below to evaluate your literary analysis from the Writing Workshop or your response to the on-demand prompt on the next page. Your teacher will tell you to use either the six- or the four-point rubric.

6-Point Scale

Score 6 *Demonstrates advanced success*
- focuses consistently on a clear thesis
- shows effective organization throughout, with smooth transitions
- offers thoughtful, creative analysis of the literary work
- develops ideas thoroughly, using fully elaborated textual support
- exhibits mature control of written language

Score 5 *Demonstrates proficient success*
- focuses on a clear thesis
- shows effective organization, with transitions
- offers thoughtful analysis of the literary work
- develops ideas competently, using well-elaborated textual support
- exhibits sufficient control of written language

Score 4 *Demonstrates competent success*
- focuses on a clear thesis, with minor distractions
- shows effective organization, with minor lapses
- offers mostly thoughtful analysis of the literary work
- develops ideas adequately, with a mixture of general and specific elaboration
- exhibits general control of written language

Score 3 *Demonstrates limited success*
- includes some loosely related ideas that distract from the writer's focus
- shows some organization, with noticeable gaps in the logical flow of ideas
- offers routine, predictable ideas about the literary work
- develops ideas with little textual support and uneven elaboration
- exhibits limited control of written language

Score 2 *Demonstrates basic success*
- includes loosely related ideas that seriously distract from the writer's focus
- shows minimal organization, with major gaps in the logical flow of ideas
- offers ideas that show only a surface understanding of the literary work
- develops ideas with inadequate textual support and elaboration
- exhibits significant problems with control of written language

Score 1 *Demonstrates emerging effort*
- shows little awareness of the topic and purpose for writing
- lacks organization
- offers unclear ideas that show a confused understanding of the literary work
- develops ideas with minimal textual support and elaboration, if any
- exhibits major problems with control of written language

4-Point Scale

Score 4 *Demonstrates advanced success*
- focuses consistently on a clear thesis
- shows effective organization throughout, with smooth transitions
- offers thoughtful, creative analysis of the literary work
- develops ideas thoroughly, using fully elaborated textual support
- exhibits mature control of written language

Score 3 *Demonstrates competent success*
- focuses on a clear thesis, with minor distractions
- shows effective organization, with minor lapses
- offers mostly thoughtful analysis of the literary work
- develops ideas adequately, with a mixture of general and specific elaboration
- exhibits general control of written language

Score 2 *Demonstrates limited success*
- includes some loosely related ideas that distract from the writer's focus
- shows some organization, with noticeable gaps in the logical flow of ideas
- offers routine, predictable ideas about the literary work
- develops ideas with little textual support and uneven elaboration
- exhibits limited control of written language

Score 1 *Demonstrates emerging effort*
- shows little awareness of the topic and purpose for writing
- lacks organization
- offers unclear ideas that show a confused understanding of the literary work.
- develops ideas with minimal textual support and elaboration, if any
- exhibits major problems with control of written language

Preparing for Timed Writing

Literary Analysis

When responding to a literary analysis prompt, use what you have learned from reading, writing your literary analysis of a novel, and studying the rubric on page 1010. Use the steps below to develop a response to the following prompt.

Writing Prompt

The plot of every novel occurs in at least one major setting: the time and location in which the story takes place. Think about a novel that you have read in which the setting is an important factor in the story's conflict. Write an essay explaining the importance of the setting on the plot in a novel of your choice.

Study the Prompt

Re-read the prompt, underlining its key words: *plot, novel, setting, time, location, important factor,* and *conflict.* Your task is to choose a novel in which the setting significantly influences the conflict. Remember that setting is not just a location, but may also be a time period marked by events such as the American Revolution. **Tip:** Spend about five minutes studying the prompt.

Plan Your Response

When you search your memory for a novel, ask yourself *why* and *how* the setting is significant to each novel you remember well. Quickly answer these questions:

1. What is the novel's time and location?
2. Does the setting cause or contribute to the conflict?
3. Does the setting help or hinder the resolution of the conflict?
4. Does the setting help define the characters?
5. Does a change in the setting affect the characters or plot?

If you answered *yes* to one or more of questions 2-6 for your novel, you can elaborate on your answers to develop your essay. Review your answers to help you write a **thesis statement** that clearly states the role of setting in the novel. **Tip:** Spend about ten minutes planning your response.

Respond to the Prompt

Using your thesis statement and your notes, begin writing your draft. Follow these guidelines:

- The **introduction** should specifically describe the setting of the novel. The thesis statement will assert the role of the setting. Include the title and author of the work as well.

- The **body** of the essay should address the major points of your analysis in a logical order. Consider using **chronological order:** highlight major events in the novel as they occur, relate them to the setting, and comment on each one. Or you may wish to use **order of importance:** choose two or three points to make about the setting, and develop each in a separate paragraph.

- In the **conclusion,** restate your thesis. You may want to leave the reader with an image of the setting at a key point in the novel.

Tip: Spend about twenty minutes writing your draft.

Improve Your Response

Revising Save enough time to read your essay before turning it in. Determine if you have specifically described the setting at the beginning of the essay. If not, add details. Have you maintained a consistent organizational strategy? If not, clarify the sequence of events or your major points. Have you explained each point with examples and explanation? If not, revise.

Proofreading Proofread your essay to correct errors in grammar, spelling, punctuation, and capitalization. Make sure all your edits are neat, and erase any stray marks.

Checking your final copy Before you turn in your final copy, read it again to catch any errors you may have missed. **Tip:** Save five or ten minutes to improve your paper.

Presenting a Literary Analysis

Speak with a Purpose

Adapt your written literary analysis into an oral response to literature, and deliver it to your class.

Think as a Reader/Writer Writing an essay isn't the only way for you to share your analysis of a novel. You can also tell a group of listeners your ideas in an **oral response to literature.** However, you'll need to adjust your written ideas and techniques when you present them to a listening audience.

Remember that you crafted your written literary analysis for an audience of classmates and teachers. As you prepare your oral response to literature for the same audience, think of their needs as listeners rather than readers.

Adapt Your Analysis

Reorganize the Content

You will need to reorganize your material to prepare your listeners for the ideas you plan to present. Focus your speech on the most important points about the literary elements or devices you analyzed in your essay. Use the tips below to help you:

- **Keep It Short** If you have a time limit, plan your presentation with the time limit in mind. Even without a time limit, focus on a limited number of points and pieces of evidence to hold your listeners' interest.

- **Adapt Your Thesis Statement** Shorten or simplify your written thesis statement to make it easier for listeners to understand. Summarize your main points up front to prepare listeners for the ideas you will present.

- **Focus Your Content** Select the most important points from your written analysis. Remember that main points can include descriptions and explanations of literary elements such as **universal themes,** point of view, symbolism, **imagery,** and the author's choice of **language,** and other **unique aspects** of the text.

- **Include Evidence** Support your thesis and each major point you discuss with accurate and detailed references to the text or to other works. Identify the title and author of any secondary source you quote.

- **Elaborate** Show how your evidence relates to the assertion your thesis makes about the work. If appropriate, explain any significant **ambiguities, nuances,** or **complexities** in the work to help you develop your major points or your elaboration.

- **Use Rhetorical Techniques** To make your presentation easier for listeners to follow and remember, use **rhetorical questions** and **parallel structure**. A presentation on *The Great Gatsby* might begin with a rhetorical question such as, "Which is more important, love or money?" A presentation on characters might use the same grammatical form to make a comparison—for example, "While *Gatsby has loved* only Daisy, *Daisy has loved* Tom and his money as well as Gatsby."

Reader/Writer Notebook

Use your **RWN** to complete the activities for this workshop.

Direct Your Listener

Like your written literary analysis, your presentation will follow **chronological order** or **order of importance.**

- Plan to give listeners clues that indicate the order you will use, such as *first, then,* and *finally* for chronological order, or *for one thing, further,* and *most important* for order of importance. Be especially careful to use these clues as transitions between the major points of your presentation.

- Make brief notes on notecards, and number the cards in the correct order in which you will present the information.

- If presentation software such as PowerPoint is available, consider making presentation slides to help you organize your analysis and give your listeners visual support as they follow along. Convert your thesis into a single slide listing the major points of your presentation in block letters, clearly visible from the back of the presentation area. Make another slide for each of your major points. You can even make a slide for each of the major quotations you plan to use as you speak.

- Plan a closing statement that will effectively conclude your presentation. If time allows, plan to ask your listeners if they have any questions.

Deliver Your Literary Analysis

To give a successful presentation, you must master the material you will present and fine-tune the details of your speech. To do this, try these rehearsal strategies:

Strategy 1: Record	Strategy 2: Reflect	Strategy 3: Rehearse
• Make a video or audio recording of your presentation. • Play it back, noting two specific ways you might improve it. • Practice and record again as needed.	• Practice your presentation in front of a mirror. • First, concentrate on nonverbal elements, such as facial expressions and gestures. • Next, work on verbal elements, such as volume and enunciation.	• Present your literary analysis to a group of friends or family, and ask for feedback. • Give your presentation to another group of listeners. • Repeat this process until you feel confident.

Once you are comfortable and confident with both your material and the performance details of your delivery, present your literary analysis to your classmates. Afterwards, make notes on what went well and what could have been improved. Use these notes to help improve the quality of future presentations.

A Good Literary Analysis

- simplifies the thesis statement so that listeners can follow easily
- focuses on a limited number of main points
- summarizes main points early in the presentation
- supports the thesis and each main point with evidence from the text or from an outside source
- demonstrates that the speaker has mastered the material
- shows that the speech has been practiced

 Speaking Tip

When reading an excerpt aloud, read each line carefully, paying close attention to phrasing and writer's words come alive with your voice.

Learn It Online

Pictures or music can make your presentation more compelling. Visit MediaScope to learn more.

go.hrw.com   L11-1013   **Go**

Literary Skills Review

Comparing Literature   **Directions:** Read the following poems. Then, read and respond to the questions that follow.

The two poems that follow are concerned with the state of America in the twentieth century. The first was written in the 1920s by Claude McKay, who was born in 1890 in Jamaica and later became one of the leading writers of the Harlem Renaissance. The other poem was written more than fifty years later by the activist poet Allen Ginsberg, who was born in 1926 and who for many years made his home on the teeming Lower East Side of New York City.

America

by **Claude McKay**

Although she feeds me bread of bitterness°,
And sinks into my throat her tiger's tooth,
Stealing my breath of life, I will confess
I love this cultured hell that tests my youth!
5   Her vigor flows like tides into my blood,
Giving me strength erect against her hate.
Her bigness sweeps my being like a flood.
Yet as a rebel fronts° a king in state,
I stand within her walls with not a shred
10   Of terror, malice, not a word of jeer.
Darkly I gaze into the days ahead,
And see her might and granite wonders there,
Beneath the touch of Time's unerring hand,
Like priceless treasures sinking in the sand.

---

1. **bread of bitterness:** allusion to Psalm 80:5: "Thou feedest them with the bread of tears; and givest them tears to drink in great measure."
8. **fronts:** confronts.

Homework

by **Allen Ginsberg**

Homage Kenneth Koch

If I were doing my Laundry I'd wash my dirty Iran
I'd throw in my United States, and pour on the Ivory Soap, scrub
    up Africa, put all the birds and elephants back in
    the jungle,
I'd wash the Amazon river and clean the oily Carib & Gulf of
    Mexico,
Rub that smog off the North Pole, wipe up all the pipelines in
    Alaska,
Rub a dub dub for Rocky Flats and Los Alamos, Flush that
5   sparkly Cesium out of Love Canal
Rinse down the Acid Rain over the Parthenon & Sphinx,
    Drain the Sludge out of the Mediterranean basin &
    make it azure again,
Put some blueing back into the sky over the Rhine, bleach the
    little Clouds so snow return white as snow,
Cleanse the Hudson Thames & Neckar, Drain the Suds out
    of Lake Erie
Then I'd throw big Asia in one giant Load & wash out the
    blood & Agent Orange,
Dump the whole mess of Russia and China in the wringer,
    squeeze out the tattletail Gray of U.S. Central American
10   police state,
& put the planet in the drier & let it sit 20 minutes or an Aeon
    till it came out clean.

April 26, 1980

Literary Skills Review CONTINUED

1. In the first four lines of McKay's poem, what does he confess about his feelings for America?

   A He dislikes her.

   B He loves her.

   C He does not understand her.

   D He wishes to leave her.

2. In the first four lines, how does McKay **personify** America?

   A As a tiger

   B As a mother

   C As a nurse

   D As a nightmare

3. Consider McKay's background and the time he wrote this poem. How would you explain what he means by "her hate" in line 6?

   A He refers to America's size.

   B He refers to racism.

   C He refers to prejudice against poets.

   D He refers to hatred of the poor.

4. Which words *best* describe the **tone** of lines 11–14 of "America"?

   A Defiant and sad

   B Terrified and mocking

   C Admiring and triumphant

   D Bitter and angry

5. The central **conflict** in "America" takes place between —

   A the speaker's contradictory feelings

   B the king and the rebel

   C the tiger and the poet

   D America and her tragic fate

6. In lines 8–10 of "America," the speaker does not revolt against America because —

   A time will destroy America

   B he loves the country

   C he moves to Europe

   D he feels powerless

7. In "America," what does the speaker see as the future of the country?

   A America will be overcome by violence.

   B America will lead the world.

   C America's glory will not endure.

   D America will no longer exist.

8. In the laundry **metaphor** that runs throughout "Homework," what does the speaker want cleaned up?

   A Urban decay and rural poverty

   B Pornographic books and films

   C Scandals in Washington, D.C.

   D Political and environmental problems

9. In Ginsberg's poem, how long does the speaker say he'll wait for the wash to come "out clean"?

A Until the end of time

B A minute or two

C Twenty minutes or an aeon

D Half an hour

10. Which word *best* describes Ginsberg's **tone**?

A Tragic

B Threatening

C Playful

D Bitter

11. With which statement would the speaker of "Homework" most likely agree?

A The world's problems are easy to solve.

B The speaker has a responsibility to help the world.

C The world's problems are unsolvable.

D The world is a great place to live.

12. Which statement is true of *both* "America" and "Homework"?

A The speakers of both poems describe their love of their home.

B Both poets refer to America as a female.

C Both poets have a negative outlook for the future.

D Both poets use metaphors to describe their feelings.

13. With which of the following statements about the United States do you think McKay and Ginsberg would agree?

A America and the world are not perfect and need reform.

B We should not let the natural world become polluted.

C Individuals are powerless in society today.

D This is the best of all possible worlds.

14. What do McKay and Ginsberg have in common with other twentieth-century American writers, such as Hemingway and Fitzgerald?

A They prefer lyrical, romantic language.

B They have a critical attitude toward modern life.

C They all have amusing tones.

D They think that American society is perfect.

Constructed Response

15. Contrast the imagery of water in these two poems. Support your response with specific evidence from the poems.

Vocabulary Skills Review

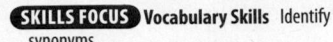
Synonyms **Directions:** Use context clues and your prior knowledge to help you identify synonyms for the italicized Vocabulary words.

1. The lieutenant knew that the order to withdraw troops came from an *apocryphal* source.

   A reliable

   B fictional

   C outlying

   D confidential

2. Everyone in the waiting room looked very *solemn*.

   A rigid

   B tired

   C agitated

   D serious

3. Jorge's neighbors *hailed* him as they passed by on their bikes.

   A avoided

   B destroyed

   C greeted

   D saw

4. Some writers use *archaic* language to establish an old-fashioned tone.

   A antiquated

   B current

   C immature

   D stylized

5. The *bedlam* created by the war made communication difficult.

   A battle

   B comfort

   C order

   D turmoil

6. As the demanding customers left, the waiter's *perturbation* was obvious.

   A satisfaction

   B confusion

   C frustration

   D circumstance

7. Josie's parents were *distraught* when she did not return home last night.

   A giddy

   B troubled

   C lethargic

   D disgusted

8. The *pauper* had a hard time feeding her family.

   A criminal

   B professor

   C beggar

   D glutton

Academic Vocabulary

Directions: For each word, choose the correct synonym.

9. *inevitable*

   A unstable

   B expelling

   C occurring

   D unavoidable

10. *hierarchy*

    A pretense

    B order

    C authority

    D excessive

Writing Skills Review

Edit a Literary Analysis **Directions:** Read the following paragraph from a literary analysis. Then, answer the questions that follow.

(1) In the novel *Passing,* the two main characters are masked. (2) The novel proved Nella Larsen one of the most influential writers of the Harlem Renaissance. (3) Although the characters in *Passing,* Clare and Irene, come from African American families, both are able to "pass" as white women. (4) Early in the novel, Irene describes Clare's face as an "ivory mask" that she uses to break away "from all that was familiar and friendly to take [her] chance in another environment" (24). (5) Irene also passes, and at the end of the novel "her face ha[s] become a mask" that she uses to hide her emotions (99). (6) While masking themselves allows Clare and Irene entrance into other social spheres, they soon learn the greater consequences of not being true to themselves.

1. Which sentence could replace sentence 1 to express a clearer perspective?

    A *Passing* uses the metaphor of a mask to show how characters hide their true identities.

    B *Passing* contrasts Clare and Irene's lifestyles and families.

    C *Passing* explains how and why light-skinned African Americans entered white society.

    D *Passing,* a Harlem Renaissance novel, explores issues of race.

2. Which sentence would best explain the quotations in sentence 4?

    A Passing distances Clare from family, friends, and heritage.

    B Irene passes because she enjoys fooling others.

    C By passing, Clare experiences white society.

    D Clare doesn't miss the friends and family she leaves behind.

3. To further support his viewpoint, the student could—

    A summarize his major points

    B include more detailed and accurate references to the text

    C write another paragraph, focusing on the consequences of passing

    D ignore ambiguities and complexities within the text

4. Which sentence should be moved to another paragraph to improve coherence?

    A 2

    B 4

    C 5

    D 6

5. To present this analysis orally, the student should—

    A make the thesis statement longer and more complex

    B read the entire analysis aloud from note cards

    C rehearse one time only

    D focus on the strongest main points and evidence

Read On

FICTION
A Farewell to Arms

Read the opening page of this novel and you won't want to put it down. Ernest Hemingway was wounded on the Italian front during World War I. A decade later, he published this riveting narrative of a soldier's life on the front and the romance that engulfs him in a hospital for the wounded. Hemingway's prose here is spare and imagistic, and the story upholds the meaningfulness of individual lives in the face of war's drudgery and horror.

FICTION
The Great Gatsby

Jay Gatsby is rich and handsome and throws fantastic parties—so why does he stand outside his opulent Long Island mansion, gazing longingly at a light across the water? The narrator, Nick Carraway, tries to unlock the puzzle in *The Great Gatsby,* F. Scott Fitzgerald's novel of American dreams and disappointments during the Jazz Age. Meet Daisy Buchanan, torn between her wealthy husband and the lure of doomed romance. Take an exhilarating ride through the Roaring Twenties. No other novel has more eloquently recorded the contradictions of that turbulent era.

FICTION
Everything That Rises Must Converge

In the title story to this masterful collection, Flannery O'Connor exposes a foolish woman and her resentful son to an encounter that shatters not only their relationship but the way they see their world. It can be difficult to like O'Connor's people, but they are always interesting, and the revelations her narratives have in store for characters and readers alike will keep you turning pages to the very end.

FICTION
The Collected Stories of Eudora Welty

This collection includes forty-one stories—all of Welty's published short fiction—with a preface by the author. Welty's ear for dialogue, her gift for humor, and her ability to create characters we care about are everywhere in evidence here. Treat yourself to "Why I Live at the P.O.," published early in Welty's career, in which a quirky postmistress relates the hilarious misadventures of family life gone awry. *The Collected Stories* was honored with the National Book Award.

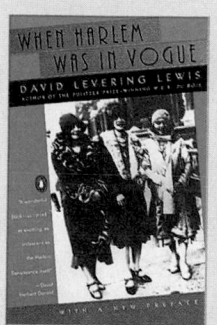

NONFICTION
When Harlem Was in Vogue

From about 1919 to 1932, New York City experienced a blossoming of African American culture known as the Harlem Renaissance (see pages 951–952). Langston Hughes, Zora Neale Hurston, and James Weldon Johnson are just three of the many creative talents featured in *When Harlem Was in Vogue,* David Levering Lewis's highly readable social history. Harlem has had many lives. Take a trip back to one of its most inspiring eras.

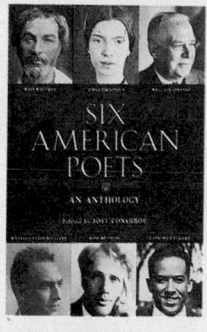

POETRY
Six American Poets

Editor Joe Conarroe has collected 247 poems from some of the most important voices in modern American poetry: Walt Whitman, Emily Dickinson, William Carlos Williams, Wallace Stevens, Robert Frost, and Langston Hughes. The poetry collected here is breathtaking in its range—from Whitman's expansive, euphoric free verse to Williams's little jewels, from Dickinson's terse insights to Hughes's melodious heartbreak. Introductory essays and author biographies provide valuable context for some of the best American poetry of any period.

NONFICTION
Let Us Now Praise Famous Men

James Agee's writing combines with Walker Evans's photographs to depict the lives of three sharecropping families living in the South in the 1930s. Originally intended for an article in *Fortune* magazine, the research performed by Agee and Evans led to the creation of a powerful full-length book instead. The combination of lyrical but unflinching prose with starkly evocative photographs is magical; it will transport you to an important time and place in the American story.

DRAMA
Our Town

Our Town first opened in 1938 and was an immediate hit. It won a Pulitzer Prize for Thornton Wilder and went on to become one of the most frequently produced plays by an American author. Set in small-town New England at the beginning of the twentieth century, the play features a Stage Manager who speaks directly to the audience and a cast of characters who reflect on love, happiness, and sorrow in America's rural past.

Learn It Online
Explore other novels at *NovelWise.*

go.hrw.com | L11-1021 | **Go**

The Contemporary Period

1939 to Present

"Everything is connected
in the end."

— **Don DeLillo, from *Underworld***

What Do
You?
Think

What human needs
and desires do we
have in common?

Christo and Jeanne-Claude. *Running Fence. Sonoma and Marin Counties, California (1972–1976).*
Photo: Jeanne-Claude. ©Christo 1976.

Learn It Online
Learn more about this historical period by watching a
short video introduction online.

go.hrw.com | L11-1023 | Go

The Contemporary Period

1939 to Present

This time line represents a snapshot of United States literary and historical events and world events from 1939 to the present. During this period of widespread political and cultural change, the United States emerged victorious from World War II, the Cold War ended, and American society began to emphasize cultural and ethnic inclusion.

UNITED STATES LITERARY EVENTS

1940

1940 Richard Wright publishes his brutal novel *Native Son*

1945 Tennessee Williams's play *The Glass Menagerie* opens on Broadway

1948 William Faulkner publishes *Intruder in the Dust*

1949 Arthur Miller's tragedy *Death of a Salesman* opens

The Granger Collection, New York.

1950

1951 J. D. Salinger publishes his novel *The Catcher in the Rye*

1952 Ralph Ellison publishes his novel *Invisible Man*

1959 Lorraine Hansberry's play *A Raisin in the Sun* opens

‹ 1960 Harper Lee publishes her novel *To Kill a Mockingbird*

1962 John Steinbeck wins the Nobel Prize in literature

1965 *The Autobiography of Malcolm X* is published

1966 Truman Capote publishes his "nonfiction novel" *In Cold Blood*

UNITED STATES HISTORICAL EVENTS

1940

1941 Japan's attack on Pearl Harbor, Hawaii, draws the U.S. into World War II

1944 Franklin Delano Roosevelt is elected to a historic fourth term as president of the United States

1948 President Truman issues an executive order that integrates the U.S. armed forces

1950

1954 U.S. Supreme Court rules that segregation in public schools is unconstitutional

1957 Dalip Singh Saund becomes the first U.S. citizen of Indian Sikh descent to serve in the U.S. House of Representatives

1963 President Kennedy is assassinated

1969 Two U.S. astronauts become the first human beings to walk on the moon **›**

WORLD EVENTS

1940

1944 Allies begin final drive against German forces on D-day, June 6

1945 U.S. explodes atomic bombs over Hiroshima (August 6) and Nagasaki (August 9)

1945 United Nations is established **∨**

The flag of the United Nations.

1950

1953 Korean War ends with division of the country into North Korea and South Korea

1957 Soviet Union launches first artificial satellite, *Sputnik I*, beginning a "space race" with the United States

1961 U.S. invasion of Bay of Pigs, in Cuba, fails

1965 U.S. involvement in the Vietnam War escalates **∨**

Vietnam Veterans Memorial in Washington, D.C.

Your Turn

In a small group, review the time line and discuss an event or a work of literature that relates to our common needs and desires as human beings. Discuss how these needs and desires span all cultures.

1970   1990   2010

1970 Maya Angelou publishes her autobiography *I Know Why the Caged Bird Sings*

1975 E. L. Doctorow publishes *Ragtime,* a novel mixing fictional and real characters

1976 Alex Haley publishes *Roots,* a fictional history of his family beginning with its African origins

1982 Alice Walker publishes her novel *The Color Purple*

1990 Tim O'Brien publishes his novel about the Vietnam War, *The Things They Carried*

1991 Sandra Cisneros publishes the story collection *Woman Hollering Creek*

1993 Toni Morrison wins the Nobel Prize in Literature

2000 Jhumpa Lahiri wins the Pulitzer Prize for her short story collection *Interpreter of Maladies*

2005 American playwright Arthur Miller dies

2007 American novelist Kurt Vonnegut dies

1970   1990   2010

1974 Watergate scandal forces Richard M. Nixon to resign as president of the United States ▼

1986 U.S. space shuttle *Challenger* explodes soon after liftoff

1987 Ronald Reagan signs a treaty with the Soviet Union reducing medium-range nuclear weapons

1995 Bomb explosion kills 168 at the Murrah Federal Building, in Oklahoma City, Oklahoma

2001 Terrorist attacks at the World Trade Center in New York, at the Pentagon in Washington, D.C., and on a plane over Pennsylvania kill thousands ▶

2005 Hurricane Katrina, one of the worst natural disasters in U.S. history, ravages New Orleans

U.S. flag is draped over the Pentagon in Washington, D.C., after terrorist attacks of 9/11.

1970   1990   2010

1973 Peace treaty provides for a cease-fire in Vietnam and withdrawal of U.S. forces

1979 Iranian militants seize the U.S. embassy in Tehran and take 52 Americans captive, beginning a 444-day hostage crisis

1989 Pro-democracy demonstrations are crushed in Tiananmen Square, in Beijing, China

1991 Soviet Union is dissolved

2003 U.S.-led coalition invades Iraq ▶

2004 A tsunami leaves 250,000 people missing or dead in southeast Asia

2007 Pratibha Patil is elected the first female President of India

A U.S. soldier on patrol in Iraq.

The Contemporary Period
1939 to Present

Since the Great Depression ended and World War II erupted in 1939, the world has changed dramatically. Wartime atrocities from the Holocaust to ethnic cleansing in contemporary Darfur, and the growing influence of technology in our lives, have changed perceptions of humanity and morality. The literature produced during the contemporary period often explores human nature and the psychological effects of traumatic war experiences and cultural conflicts.

KEY CONCEPTS

War Changes the World

History of the Times Germany's invasion of Poland in 1939 escalated into a worldwide conflict. The German army continued to invade European countries, sending millions to their deaths in concentration camps. The United States was pulled into World War II in 1941 when Japan attacked Pearl Harbor. The war ended in 1945 after the surrender of Germany and the bombing of Japan.

Literature of the Times Elie Wiesel's memoir *Night* and John Hersey's nonfiction chronicle *Hiroshima* describe the horrors that civilians endured during the war. Many others write about similar experiences coping with a chaotic world.

Cold War and Social Conflict

History of the Times Both the United States and the Soviet Union emerged from World War II as political superpowers. Although no direct military conflict ensued, the two nations spent the next four decades in an arms race that nearly resulted in full-scale war. The Cold War ended with the collapse of the Soviet Union in 1991.

Literature of the Times During these tumultuous times, many writers challenged political and social conventions. The madness of the war-torn world was viewed as an inescapable condition of modern life.

Our Global World

History of the Times Technological advances in the second half of the twentieth century encouraged trade and communication between nations that had previously had little contact with one another. A single global market emerged. Business chains providing both goods and services have spread across the globe.

Literature of the Times Postmodern literature explores multiple meanings and multiple worlds. Characteristics of postmodern literature include nontraditional forms, cultural diversity, and a blending of fiction and nonfiction.

SKILLS FOCUS **Literary Skills** Evaluate and analyze the philosophical, political, religious, ethical, and social influences of a historical period. **Reading Skills** Read widely to increase knowledge of the student's culture, the culture of others, and the common elements across cultures.

UNIT 6 INTRODUCTION

KEY CONCEPT

War Changes the World

History of the Times

The second great war of the twentieth century officially began in 1939, when Britain and France declared war on Germany after Hitler's armies invaded Poland. On December 7, 1941, Japanese warplanes attacked the U.S. naval base at Pearl Harbor, in Hawaii. The raid killed approximately 2,400 Americans and destroyed or damaged 21 ships and 323 aircraft. Until then, the United States had remained technically neutral in World War II, which many had considered a foreign problem. This attitude of indifference melted in the outrage over Japan's attack. Americans threw their energy into the war effort. Factories stopped making cars and began making tanks. With so many men off fighting, women, for the first time, entered the workforce in droves. Caught up in the fears and suspicions of war, thousands of Japanese Americans were interned in camps until the long and painful war ended in 1945.

Literature of the Times

As the war ended and the United States emerged from the Depression, writers began to attempt to make sense of the horror and absurdity of the war. Veterans wrote about their experiences; among these works we find Norman Mailer's *The Naked and the Dead*, Joseph Heller's *Catch-22*, and Kurt Vonnegut's *Slaughterhouse-Five*. Different voices spoke up as well. An angry African American (*Native Son*), an emotionally fragile girl (*The Glass Menagerie*), and a tragically lost salesman (*Death of a Salesman*) were among the representative protagonists who appeared during the 1940s, a time when the certainties of the past were suddenly called into question.

(opposite) The 2005 Presidential Scholars gather for a group photo in the East Room of the White House in Washington, Monday, June 27, 2005.

Comprehension Check

How were social developments in the United States and abroad reflected in literature written in the 1940s?

Fast Facts

Historical Highlights

- The United States enters World War II, 1941–1945
- First atomic bombs used against Japan, 1945
- Cuban Missile Crisis ends when Soviet Union withdraws nuclear-armed rockets from Cuba and America does likewise in Turkey, 1962
- Soviet Union collapses, 1991
- Terrorists crash airplanes into U.S. Pentagon and World Trade Center, 2001
- United States invades Iraq, 2003

Literary Highlights

- John Hersey's narrative *Hiroshima,* about the dropping of an atomic bomb on a civilian population, becomes a national event (1946).
- Ralph Ellison's novel *Invisible Man,* dramatizing the evils of racial segregation, gives impetus to nationwide civil rights movement (1952).
- With her publication of *The Joy Luck Club,* Amy Tan becomes one of the first prominent Asian American novelists (1989).
- Tim O'Brien's novel *The Things They Carried* chronicles the Vietnam War (1990).

Learn It Online
Go online to learn more about the history and literature of this period.

go.hrw.com   L11-1027   **Go**

Cold War and Social Conflict

History of the Times

The United States emerged from World War II an economic and political powerhouse, but U.S. dominance did not go unchallenged for long. Soon after the war ended, the Soviet Union seized control of most of Eastern Europe and installed one-party Communist governments behind what Winston Churchill called an "iron curtain." The Cold War had begun.

The United States had developed nuclear weapons in 1945. When the Soviet Union caught up in the 1950s and 1960s, the ideological conflict between the two nations hardened into a long and expensive arms race. Smaller countries, such as South Korea and Vietnam, became bloody battle-grounds on which the great powers played out their rivalries. Fear of unthinkable destruction kept both superpowers from using "the bomb," but the ever-present threat made anxiety a constant feature of modern life.

The long-simmering Cold War reached a climax in 1962, when the Soviet Union tried to ship missiles to its ally Cuba. President Kennedy sent warships to the island, heading off the Soviet vessels. The threat was withdrawn, averting a possible global catastrophe.

In the late 1980s, the Soviet Union began to unravel. In 1991, it buckled, brought down by internal failures and the cost of the arms race. A new Russian republic emerged, and with it the end of the Cold War.

Literature of the Times

The rapidly expanding empire of the Soviet Union and the United States' response to it influenced writers such as Arthur Miller to explore the culture of fear that was developing in America. Miller wrote *The Crucible* as a response to the "Red hunt," which took place in America in the 1950s. Miller found parallels between the "Red hunt"

(below) A German crowd celebrates the fall of the Berlin Wall in 1989. Throughout the Cold War, the Berlin Wall separated East and West Berlin, with the Soviet Union controlling the eastern half. Its fall signaled the decline of the Soviet Union and the beginning of a new era in Europe.

and the witch hunts that took place in Salem, Massachusetts, in 1692.

Writers such as John Hersey (*Hiroshima*) and Truman Capote (*In Cold Blood*) developed a new genre, called literary journalism, which incorporates many devices previously associated strictly with fiction, such as narration, suspense, and characterization, to explore the significance of real-life acts of violence.

Other writers responded to the madness of the war-torn world with hard-edged laughter at life's tragic ironies. The term *gallows humor*—ironic humor arising from an acknowledgment of the absurd or grotesque—was often used to describe the work of writers such as Joseph Heller and Philip Roth.

Robert Lowell, Sylvia Plath, and Anne Sexton opted to turn toward the interior, writing often brutally frank poems about their personal lives. They became known as "confessional poets."

During the 1960s, social upheaval surrounding the Vietnam War sparked a widespread re-examination of social values, with a new emphasis on the rights of the individual. Issues involving racism and civil rights dominated the thinking of writers such as James Baldwin and Malcolm X, whose autobiography, published in 1965, became a rallying point for disaffected African Americans.

Comprehension Check

How did writers respond to the "culture of fear" in post–World War II America?

Video Games

During and after World War II, it was common for young children (especially boys) to "play soldier," imitating adults who had seen combat by pretending to shoot, stab, bomb, or otherwise destroy the "bad guys." As memory of the war faded, attitudes toward killing and violence changed as well. Many parents began to promote activities of a more peaceable nature.

In the 1980s, a new phenomenon appeared among America's youth: the video game. Though no physical violence is involved, many games today include "virtual" violence by portraying horrific acts of criminality, killing, and bloodshed. The explicit style of such games, which realistically depict dismemberment and sadistic cruelty, has become a matter of serious concern for many parents, caregivers, and educators.

Ask Yourself

What do you think has contributed to the rise in violence among America's youth? How might our society influence their actions?

Our Global World

History of the Times

Affordable air travel, reliable communications, and closer economic ties between nations have led to a global culture.

Thanks to advances in transportation and the development of the Internet and other telecommunications, trade among nations has increased exponentially, forming a single, global marketplace. Benefits to consumers include low prices and a dazzling variety of goods. The dangers include the loss of jobs and even whole industries, as manufacturers move their operations to cheaper labor sources abroad. Global commerce has also sometimes led to imports of unregulated, unsafe foods and other products.

The era of the computer chip has also threatened Ralph Waldo Emerson's ideal of the rugged individual. Many Americans feel that they have become anonymous consumers, known only by a computer password or credit card number. They worry, too, that their privacy is unprotected and that their thoughts and even their dreams are being shaped by mass advertising, mass journalism, and mass entertainment.

Literature of the Times

Who should write literature? Which authors are essential for students to read? As the end of the twentieth century approached, proponents of multiculturalism challenged views of what writers should write and what students should read. As a result, American literature after the Cold War era became unprecedentedly diverse, more accurately reflecting a country that values democracy and inclusion as its defining political philosophies.

Literature written by women and people of color is now widely read and recognized. Toni Morrison, a female African American writer, won the Nobel Prize in Literature in 1993, the first woman of color to do so. Her novel *Beloved* was named the most influential work of American

literature of the past 25 years in a *New York Times* poll in 2006. African American Pulitzer Prize winner Alice Walker, Asian American writer Amy Tan, and Hispanic writer Richard Rodriguez have become established authors whose works are widely taught in American schools. Reconceiving the American dream on their own terms, the authors produce works that often deal with the creation of self and the desire for autonomy.

Writers from previous decades who may have been overlooked on the basis of race, gender, or both have also seen a resurgence of interest in their works. Richard Wright, James Baldwin, and Malcom X's autobiographical works are now widely taught as powerful works heralding social change.

American literature continues to undergo change as writers experiment with nontraditional forms, such as memoirs, graphic novels, and postmodern writings that blend fiction and nonfiction. In our global world, many writers are also exploring the Internet as an alternative way to reach a new audience of readers. Writers and readers alike are embracing the new literacies required to live sucessfully in the twenty-first century.

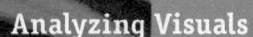

Analyzing Visuals

Viewing and Interpreting
How would you expect the people depicted in the collage at left to describe their lives? What kinds of stories, characters, and themes would they be interested in reading about? Explain.

Wrap Up

Talk About...
With a partner, re-read the sections describing the Cold War. Which nations were involved in that struggle? How did this struggle affect American literature? Try to use each Academic Vocabulary word **listed below** at least once in your discussion.

Write About...
Global communications have led to new opportunities and new problems. Write about how recent technological changes have affected your life. What changes have had a positive or negative impact?

Academic Vocabulary for Unit 6

Talking and Writing About Literature
Academic Vocabulary is the language you use to write and talk about literature. Use these words to discuss the literature you read in this unit. These words will be underlined throughout the unit.

component (kuhm POH nuhnt) *n.:* one of the parts that make up a whole. *One component of postmodernism is the use of nontraditional forms.*

diverse (duh VURS) *adj.:* varied. *America is a very diverse nation.*

intrinsic (ihn TRIHN sihk) *adj.:* essential; inherent. *Characterization is an intrinsic part of good fiction.*

potential (puh TEHN shuhl) *adj.:* expressing possibility. *A potential problem in the genre of nonfiction writing is truth or accuracy of the events depicted.*

transmit (trans MIHT) *v.:* pass along; communicate. *American modernist writers transmitted many of their new styles and forms to postmodern writers.*

Your Turn
With a partner, create a summary of the main historical events and kinds of literature produced during the contemporary period. Try to use the Academic Vocabulary words in your analysis.

Read with a Purpose

Read to learn how one family remembers relatives and preserves memories with mementoes handed down through the generations.

Build Background

China, or chinaware, is any of various ornamental and useful ceramic dishes, usually made of porcelain and valued as family heirlooms. Some china patterns have brilliant colors and designs, while others are very simple in appearance.

In this essay, Goodman refers to Hurricane Katrina, which devastated New Orleans and surrounding areas in August 2005.

Author Note

Pulitzer Prize WINNER

Ellen Goodman is a newspaper columnist for the *Boston Globe*. Her columns and books earned her a Pulitzer Prize for Distinguished Commentary with the *Boston Globe* in 1980, as well as numerous other awards from professional, civic, and human-rights organizations.

Thanksgiving Memories

BY ELLEN GOODMAN

BOSTON — We are taking my grandmother's china out for a spin. The plates, cups and saucers, wrapped carefully like ancient artifacts, will make their annual pilgrimage one doorway and one generation down the street from my aunt's house to my own.

On Thanksgiving, four generations will eat off the dishes of a fifth, although this year the people finally outnumber the place settings and the youngest quartet will be safely relegated to plastic plates and sippy cups. I am not a china kind of hostess, but I was awarded temporary custody of these dishes when I inherited Thanksgiving. To have the holiday without my grandmother's china would seem more disrespectful to her memory than the blasphemy we already commit when we put her plates in our dishwasher.

It is remarkable how we attach memory and meaning to mere stuff. And which stuff? Why is it that my grandmother's dishes remain from the rich inventory of her life?

Last August, Hurricane Katrina drove people from their homes with barely enough time to cull a backpack of goods from a lifetime of possessions. From my safe, dry perch I wondered exactly how I would fill such a grab bag. With photographs? Letters? What else? But at some point we all have to decide how to triage our memories. Or have others decide for us.

Since last Thanksgiving, my mother's life has been downsized to a single room. Over time, as she went from house to apartment to assisted living, we had repeatedly strip-searched her rooms for what mattered most to take along. But when the flood waters of old age and ill health rose dangerously in her own life, she was rescued to a room now decorated with photographs, a 90th-birthday book and a single bureau.

The home that this homemaker created with as much care and flair as a set designer has gone into its own diaspora.[1] A buffet was sent to one granddaughter, wing chairs to a nephew. Two of the dining chairs that I sat on as a child will be pulled up to my own table this holiday. But things that we had neither space nor taste for went to a hospice and a consignment shop. It's only stuff, we said to each other. The stuff of stories and lives.

Have you ever seen photo albums in an antique store or flea market and wondered how they ended up in this orphanage? Didn't anybody want them, know them anymore? Can we, on the other hand, get laden down with too much history?

In the shadow of all this, my husband and I have been rummaging through our storage room, triaging what stays and what goes. There is a box of letters from my father to a war buddy. Will I be the last generation that hears his voice in the typewritten words? There are the soup pots, also my grandmother's legacy, known only to me. There is the eccentric jeweled pin that so reminds me—but only me—of my great-aunt Polly.

How much should we save for our kids? How much should we saddle them with?

In some ways every generation balances the pleasure of traditions, legacies, roots, with the equally American appeal of a fresh start. I wonder how much stuff, and stories, our children can carry with them to their own table and still have room for the new. How much, on the other hand, do restless people long for their connection to the past?

Only a handful at our table—six of the 26 —actually knew my grandmother. The others know the condensed version: the lobster-lover, the cleaning fanatic. As for my father, who married my mother one Thanksgiving long ago, his wit and generosity of spirit have been inevitably condensed to a box of letters, a litany of family stories, a collection of photographs and a campaign poster from his political adventures.

We pare down and salvage, attach stories to a teacup and forget sometimes the complexity of an individual. Our own histories will someday have to squeeze into a portfolio as small and portable as a DVD.

Still, every Thanksgiving, when the china seems to unite a family as fond and diverse as the mix-and-match silverware, I tip my hat to tradition. I make room for the extra table we bought for the newest members of our tribe, the ones on booster seats and in high chairs. As I count out their plastic plates and sippy cups, I am allowed to believe that the small people who cut their teeth on family traditions this year will one day cut their turkey on bone china.

White, of course, with a slim gold rim.

---

1. **diaspora:** group migration; dispersion.

Ask Yourself

1. Read with a Purpose What are some advantages and disadvantages of saving items from the past?

2. What does the author mean when she says she "inherited Thanksgiving"?

3. Why does the author attach personal meaning to certain mementoes?

The Wages of War

LITERARY FOCUS
War Literature

CONTENTS

Link to Today

"I hate war as only a soldier who has lived it can, only as one who has seen its brutality, its futility, its stupidity."

—Gen. Dwight D. Eisenhower

From *A Pacific Sketchbook* (1943–44) by George M. Harding
(Captain in the Marine Corps Reserves).

War Literature by Leila Christenbury

Characteristics of War Literature

- Provides firsthand accounts or portrays experiences of war
- Gives insight into the physical as well as psychological consequences of war
- Often explores themes of humanity, faith, and morality

War Literature

Unavoidable or not, wars are terrible events in the lives of the soldiers who fight them and the civilians who are often caught up in the conflict. The authors in this collection face the ultimate challenge for a writer: to put into words experiences that defy description. The terror and destruction of World War II, including the suffering and pain of soldiers and civilians, are described in this literature in detail. In poetry, memoir, journalistic reports, and even a graphic novel, the writers in this collection explore the nature of war from diverse points of view. What can you conclude about war from these writers and their subjects?

To Convey the Incomprehensible Inevitably, warfare, with its unspeakable cruelties and absurdities, is diminished by any attempt to capture it verbally. Yet, each of the selections here takes us deep into the abyss of World War II, communicating an indelible sense of that conflict and its effects.

Only twenty-one years after World War I ended, the world was plunged into another horror. World War II began in 1939 when Germany invaded Poland, beginning a quest to conquer all of Europe. On December 7, 1941, Japanese forces bombed Pearl Harbor in the Hawaiian Islands. The next day the United States declared war on Japan. Germany and Italy then declared war on the United States, and by December 11, the United States was at war in Europe as well.

The war in Europe ended with the fall of Berlin and the surrender of Germany on May 8, 1945. The Japanese emperor surrendered four months later, but only after the Japanese cities of Hiroshima and Nagasaki were destroyed by atomic bombs.

In just five lines, Randall Jarrell's poem "The Death of the Ball Turret Gunner" powerfully conveys the vulnerability of soldiers in combat. Jarrell, who trained U.S. pilots in World War II, makes a soldier the poem's speaker. Despite its brevity, or perhaps because of it, the poem viscerally and unforgettably communicates one man's experience of the intrinsic horrors of war.

Authors in this collection also write about inequality and discrimination within the army itself. Army units were segregated during World War II, and African American soldiers were often treated unfairly and were not recognized for their service. Journalist Brenda Payton wonders about the justice of a military system that permitted African American airmen to risk (and lose) their lives in battle but did not permit them to share an officers' club with whites. "Honor at Last" tells their story.

Elie Wiesel's *Night,* a first-person account of the Nazi death camps, presents an almost unbearable look at the daily horrors suffered by Jews as part of what Hitler called "the Final Solution"—total extermination of the entire European Jewish population. The Nazis also targeted Romanies, people with disabilities, Slavic peoples (such as Russians and Poles), homosexuals, and political or religious dissidents and sent them to forced-labor and death camps.

This memoir, told from the point of view of a fifteen-year-old prisoner of concentration camps, takes readers on a nightmare journey through the Holocaust. Readers experience the trauma and despair of concentration camp life, from deportation to the final death march. Wiesel wrote *Night* as a testimony to the suffering and misery that he and millions of others endured at the hands of the Nazis.

Art Spiegelman's *Maus* chronicles many of these same atrocities, but through a form that came into being long after World War II: the graphic novel. In creating his classic series of historically accurate tales, Spiegelman also raises cartooning, long considered merely pop culture, to the status of serious art. Using various animals to represent different groups of people, he tells the story of his father's survival of the Holocaust. The characteristics of the animals are symbolic of human attributes; cats who hunt and kill mice represent Nazis who hunt and kill Jews, who are helpless in the face of the Holocaust. A cat's tendency to play with a mouse before killing it mirrors the Nazi practice of torturing Jews with starvation and hard labor. Converting humans into cats and mice innovatively portrays this devastating event, while never sacrificing its truth.

Victims' Voices The authors John Hersey and Mitsuye Yamada remind us of war's terrible randomness—that once the shooting starts, no one is safe. The dangers of war are not limited to soldiers and officers; civilians often become victims of war caught in the crossfire between fighting nations. It is estimated that approximately 55 percent of the deaths in World War II were civilian casualties. It is estimated that Russia alone lost about 18 million people in the war. When the U.S. military entered Germany after its surrender, they found the concentration camps the Nazis had abandoned in which millions of Jews and other persecuted groups had perished.

Hersey's landmark book *Hiroshima,* excerpted here as "A Noiseless Flash," recounts the effects of a unique military action: the dropping of an atomic bomb on a civilian population in Hiroshima, Japan. The lives of six survivors, presented in moment-to-moment snapshots of their daily lives, enables the reader not just to know these innocent victims but, more importantly, to care personally about them. Through their eyes, Americans could experience this catastrophe as if it were happening to them and to their friends and neighbors. It is possible for readers to imagine being victims of such an attack themselves, as the victims of the Hiroshima bombing were merely going about their daily lives when their world collapsed. Through Hersey's vivid narrative and his

gift for characterization, the unimaginable becomes horrifyingly real.

Yamada's poem "Desert Run" brings the war home, re-creating its emotional ravages through the imagery of a bleak American landscape. After the Japanese sneak attack at Pearl Harbor, thousands of Japanese Americans were herded by the U.S. government into "detention" camps to prevent Japanese spy activity during the war. Yamada and her family were among them. Memories of the injustice, confinement, and persecution that resulted continue to inform the themes of Yamada's poems.

In this collection, writers who served in the military during the war and writers who witnessed it from a civilian's perspective delve into the horrors of World War II. Here authors explore the devastating consequences of the war in Europe and Japan, as well as the psychological impact of surviving and recovering from such destruction.

Ask Yourself

1. What is so difficult about writing war literature?

2. What are some of the common characteristics that works of war literature share?

3. How do the authors in this collection convey the war experience to readers who have never witnessed it?

Learn It Online
Go online to learn more about this historical period.

go.hrw.com   L11-1036   **Go**

The Death of the Ball Turret Gunner

Visualizing by **Kylene Beers**

People say a picture is worth a thousand words. Authors use words to paint a picture in a reader's mind. The artist and the author both want to put a thought or idea into your mind. One gives you the image and lets you create the words; the other gives you the words so that you can create the image. As you read, pause occasionally and ask yourself, "If I turned what I'm reading into a movie, what would I see?" This will help you visualize, or see, the text, thus giving yourself one more way to understand it.

Visualizing also helps us connect the story with our own experiences. If a detail seems funny, scary, or beautiful, it might remind us of something that especially amused, frightened, or impressed us in the past. However, the images we visualize are even better than what we recall, because they are enhanced by our imagination. We see them, as Shakespeare said, in our "mind's eye."

Good readers try to visualize as they read, forming mental pictures of what the writer is describing. In some cases, this means imagining a place that is important to the story. In other cases, it means using details from the text to form a mental picture of a character. Good writers provide easy-to-imagine clues. What, for example, might this character look like?

> He had a roundish head, and his tiny ears stood out like the handles on a jug. Above them, stiff gray hair splayed in all directions. His large, pink-rimmed blue eyes watered constantly, and his full, rubbery lips pursed and unpursed. If not for a large mole on it, his chin would disappear completely into the folds of his leathery neck.

An important element in visualizing a text is an attention to diction, or word choice. In "The Death of the Ball Turret Gunner," Jarrell uses the word *hunched* to describe the gunner. What image does this word create? How might that image have been different if Jarrell had decided to use the phrase *curled up* instead? These are the kinds of questions you should ask as you read and visualize the text.

In this collection, you will be asked to imagine scenes of destruction ("A Noiseless Flash"), scenes of cruelty (from *Night*), and a harsh landscape ("Desert Run"). You will also meet fully drawn characters from all walks of life. While you read, note places where the descriptions appeal strongly to sight, sound, or the other senses. Think about the images the text conjures up, and be prepared to discuss these images afterward.

Your Turn

Writers use figurative language to help readers visualize what they are expressing in words. Read this line and allow the imagery to create a picture in your mind.

> *My skin turned pink brown in the bright desert light.*

Write a paragraph that describes the scene you visualize after reading this line. What picture is created in your mind after reading this line?

Think about the literary works featured in this collection. In one selection, you will read text accompanied by graphics. Why do you think this writer might find it important for readers to see the face of war? How do you think visuals can enhance our understanding of a text?

Learn It Online
Find an interactive *PowerNotes* presentation for this essay online.

go.hrw.com | L11-1037 | **Go**

The Death of the Ball Turret Gunner

QuickWrite

Images of war, in prose, in poetry, and through the media, have a lasting impact on many who view them. Write about images of war that are the most vivid and lasting for you.

Randall Jarrell
(1914–1965)

Randall Jarrell was considered one of America's leading poets and perhaps its best literary critic during the mid-1900s.

Wartime Poet

Born in Nashville, Tennessee, Jarrell was brought up in California. His childhood experiences included close observation of the gaudy remnants of the old Hollywood, a personal acquaintance with the MGM lion, and an appreciation of the difference between fantasy and fact. This divide between showbiz illusion and real life became a theme in much of his poetry.

After graduating from Vanderbilt University in 1938, Jarrell taught literature and writing at various colleges and universities in the United States. His first book of poems, *Blood for a Stranger,* appeared in 1942. That year, he joined the Army Air Corps, serving as a celestial navigation trainer of pilots assigned to fly B-29 bombers, a common type of warplane used during World War II. From these experiences came two notable poetry collections, *Little Friend, Little Friend* (1945) and *Losses* (1948). Many critics rank these books among the best American contributions to World War II literature.

A Mysterious Death

Though sensitive as a poet, Jarrell could also be a harsh critic of his fellow writers. In *A Sad Heart at the Supermarket,* a 1962 collection of articles and essays, he flays bad literature with a devastatingly caustic wit. In poetry, however, his wit shows itself only in his good humor ("I feel like the first men who read Wordsworth. / It's so simple I can't understand it") and in a toleration of the absurd aspects of American life. From 1956 to 1958, he was named poetry consultant to the Library of Congress. His poetry collection *The Woman at the Washington Zoo* won the National Book Award in 1961.

Jarrell died when struck by a car while walking along a North Carolina highway in 1965. His tragic death raised a question: Was it actually a suicide? There was no question, however, of the loss to Jarrell's fellow poets and to American letters.

Think About the Writer What might Jarrell think about present-day conflicts in America? Do you think his writing would be optimistic or pessimistic?

Reader/Writer Notebook

Use your **RWN** to complete the activities for this selection.

Literary Focus

Implied Metaphor Some **metaphors** are stated directly. Carson McCullers, for example, uses a metaphor as the title of her book *The Heart Is a Lonely Hunter*. Other metaphors are implied, or hinted at, and we must figure out these **implied metaphors** from the language the writer uses. An implied metaphor is a comparison between two unlike things that is suggested but not stated directly.

Literary Perspectives Apply the literary perspective described on page 1040 as you read this poem.

Language Coach

Word Origins In World War II, *flak* (sometimes spelled *flack*) referred to German antiaircraft guns or the exploding shells these guns fired. It comes from combining the beginnings of the three parts of *Fliegerabwehrkanonen*, a German word meaning "flyer defense canons." *Flak* has also come to mean "loud, insistent criticism". Why might this meaning have arisen? Which use of *flak* do you expect to find in the poem?

Reading Focus

Visualizing To understand the deeper meaning of a written work, you can visualize it, or picture it in your mind. Writers use **imagery** to evoke a picture or concrete sensation. In Yusef Komunyaaka's poem "Camouflaging the Chimera," the poet creates an impression of war through descriptive details and sensory images. How does Komunyaaka help you visualize the experience of war in these stanzas?

> We tied branches to our helmets.
> We painted our faces & rifles
> with mud from a riverbank,
>
> blades of grass hung from the pockets
> 5 of our tiger suits. We wove
> ourselves into the terrain,
> content to be a hummingbird's target.

Into Action As you read Jarrell's experience of war, use a chart like the one below to record memorable imagery from the poem. Describe the picture the words <u>transmit</u> to you.

What it says	*What you picture*
"I fell into the State"	*tumbling backward*

Writing Focus

Think as a Reader/Writer

Find It in Your Reading As you read Jarrell's poem, think about how he uses the words *sleep* and *wake*. In your *Reader/Writer Notebook*, explain how he uses these words with opposite meanings and to what effect.

Learn It Online
Check out the *PowerNotes* introduction to this poem online.

go.hrw.com   L11-1039

Read with a Purpose
Read to understand one poet's point of view about World War II.

Build Background
A ball turret was a transparent plastic sphere set into the belly of a B-17 or B-24 bomber plane during World War II. Inside were two machine guns, operated by a soldier who had to sit curled in a fetal position between the guns. Ball turret gunners had to have a small build so that they could fit in the tiny compartment with the machine guns. They could rotate the ball turret 360 degrees horizontally and 90 degrees vertically to track targets. The temperature in the compartment could become frigid at high altitudes, especially during the winter.

Aerial Gunner (1942) by Peter Hurd.

The Death of the Ball Turret Gunner

by **Randall Jarrell**

From my mother's sleep I fell into the State,
And I hunched in its belly till my wet fur froze.   **Ⓐ**
Six miles from earth, loosed from its dream of life,
I woke to black flak° and the nightmare fighters.
When I died they washed me out of the turret with a hose.   **Ⓑ Ⓒ**

---

4. **black flak:** antiaircraft fire.

Ⓐ Literary Focus **Implied Metaphor** To what is the ball turret compared?

Ⓑ Reading Focus **Visualizing the Text** What is the effect of the image in the last line of the poem?

Ⓒ Literary Perspectives **Analyzing Historical Context** What larger message might the poem be sending about warfare?

Literary Perspectives

Analyzing Historical Context Historical context refers to how the social, economic, cultural, intellectual, religious, and political circumstances of a time period influence a work of literature. In this poem, the context is World War II. The wartime draft required young men to leave their families, fight the enemy, save lives, and perhaps die for their country. Many soldiers believed that this was the noblest work any citizen could do. As you read, consider the historical context in which the poem was written. For example, the speaker in this poem says he "fell into the State." Do you think he considers himself a patriotic hero for his military service? How is his youth reflected in the image of him in the "belly" of the bomber? Does his struggle against the "nightmare fighters" make sense to him?

As you read, use the question in the text to guide you in using this perspective.

Respond and Think Critically

Reading Focus

Quick Check

1. What is a ball turret?
2. What is flak?
3. Why does the gunner experience freezing?
4. In what position is a "hunched" body?

Read with a Purpose

5. How would you define Jarrell's attitude toward war?

Reading Skills: Visualizing the Text

6. What image do you see after reading the line, "And I hunched in its belly till my wet fur froze (line 2)"?
7. What might the inside of the turret look like as it is washed out with a hose?
8. As you read, you described the mental pictures evoked by strong imagery. Now, complete the chart below. For each line from the poem, tell what picture you form in your mind and what feelings it evokes.

What it says	What you picture	Feelings evoked
"I fell into the State"	tumbling backward	helplessness, fright, confusion

Literary Focus

Literary Analysis

9. **Interpret** What is this poem really about? What statement about war does the poet make in only five lines?

10. **Make Judgments** Why do you think this poem is identified as the most famous poem to come out of World War II? What about it makes it especially memorable?

11. **Literary Perspectives** What does this poem reveal about <u>potential</u> attitudes toward "the State" in postwar America? Explain.

Literary Skills: Implied Metaphor

12. **Interpret** Explain the **implied metaphor** in the poem. To what is the ball turret gunner compared? What specific words develop this metaphor?

Literary Skills Review: Mood

13. **Analyze** The overall emotion created by a work of literature is the **mood**. All the elements of literature, including sound effects, rhythm, and word choice, contribute to a work's mood. Explain how Jarrell uses these literary elements to create mood in his poem. How would you describe the mood of the poem?

Writing Focus

Think as a Reader/Writer

Use It in Your Writing Using your QuickWrite about images of war, and using forms of the words *sleep* and *wake*, write a five-line poem that captures your feelings about war. Share your poem with the class.

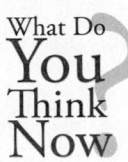

What Do You Think Now? How do you think Randall Jarrell felt about the role of soldiers in the war?

Honor at Last

What Do You Think

What human needs and desires do we have in common?

QuickWrite

Think of someone who should be publicly recognized for having done something special. Write a paragraph explaining why the person should be honored. Remember to support your ideas with specific, concrete evidence.

Informational Text Focus

Analyzing an Author's Arguments An **argument** is a form of persuasion that appeals to reason to convince an audience to think or act in a certain way. To strengthen their arguments, authors often cite facts, show statistics, and display <u>intrinsic</u> evidence. In this selection, Brenda Payton says that the honors conferred on the airmen were long overdue. In your analysis, pay close attention to the historical facts, anecdotes, and other evidence she uses to support her argument.

Into Action As you read, use a chart like the one below to record the author's arguments and supporting evidence. As you record the facts, think about why an author uses this supporting evidence to persuade a reader.

Argument	Supporting Evidence
Tuskegee Airmen paved the way for the integration of the armed forces.	They risked arrest by protesting segregation at Freeman Field in 1945.

Writing Focus Preparing for **Constructed Response**

As you read, note how the actions of the Tuskegee Airmen surprised their critics and changed history forever.

Vocabulary

rotunda (roh TUHN duh) *n.:* a building shaped inside and outside like a cylinder, usually covered with a dome. *The families met in the Capitol's large rotunda.*

fascism (FASH ihz uhm) *n.:* an authoritarian and nationalistic right-wing system of government and social organization. The term was first used of the totalitarian right-wing nationalist regime of Benito Mussolini in Italy (1922–1943). *Soldiers from the United States fought fascism during World War II.*

palpable (PAL puh buhl) *adj.:* able to be touched or felt. *The pride that people felt for the Tuskegee Airmen was palpable.*

Language Coach

Word Derivation When used as an adjective, *spirited* means "enlivened" or "excited". Both the noun and the adjective form derive from the word *spirit,* referring to unseen, possibly supernatural forces.

Reader/Writer Notebook
Use your **RWN** to complete the activities for this selection.

Learn It Online
Practice reading newspaper articles like this one with the interactive Reading Workshop online.

| go.hrw.com | L11-1042 | Go |

Link to Today

This Link to Today reflects on the "long overdue" awarding of military heroes' medals, half a century after they were earned, and what their recognition means to the soldiers they honor and their families.

Read with a Purpose

Read to discover how the United States finally recognized the Tuskegee Airmen's valiant service in World War II.

Build Background

Before 1940, African Americans were not allowed to fly U.S. military planes. Under pressure from civil rights organizations and black journalists, the army inaugurated the so-called Tuskegee Experiment, which was a pursuit squadron made up of African American pilots, navigators, instructors, maintenance and support crews, and other military personnel. Performing heroically in battle, these men became one of the war's most highly respected combat units.

HONOR AT LAST

by BRENDA PAYTON *from* THE (HAYWARD) DAILY REVIEW

APRIL 3, 2007 ISSUE – I forgot to look at the medal. I took a bunch of pictures of my dad holding his replica of the Congressional Gold Medal awarded to the Tuskegee Airmen last week.

"Turn this way," I said. "Hold it at this angle." But I forgot to look at it.

The Rotunda of the United States Capitol was packed. In fact, in order to seat the 300 Tuskegee Airmen and their wives, U.S. Rep. Charles Rangel, co-sponsor of the bill establishing the medal, had to ask people to move to an overflow room. Family members had come from all over the country to see what most had never expected: the government's recognition of the achievements of the Tuskegee Airmen. Sixty years later.

At the beginning of World War II, the armed forces were still segregated and the U.S. Army Air Corps (later renamed the U.S. Air Force) did not train Negro pilots. In response to a lawsuit, it agreed to an experiment training pilots and crews at Tuskegee University, an experiment it expected to fail. Ⓐ

But the Tuskegee Airmen, as the men came to be known, defied the odds. They amassed a remarkable record defending the bombers they escorted on missions in Europe. They challenged racial segregation and paved the way for the integration of the armed forces which today is our nation's most successfully integrated institution. They fought fascism abroad and racism at home.

My dad, James B. Williams, was a first lieutenant and an engineering officer with the 477th Bombardment Group, 619th squadron. His story highlights the fight against racism at home. While stationed at Freeman Field in Indiana

---

Ⓐ **Informational Focus** Analyzing the Author's Arguments What technique does the writer use to present her argument?

Vocabulary **rotunda** (roh TUHN duh) *n.:* building shaped inside and outside like a cylinder, usually covered with a dome.
fascism (FASH ihz uhm) *n.:* an authoritarian and nationalistic right-wing system of government and social organization.

in 1945, the men were told to sign an order establishing a whites-only officers' club. He and 100 other Tuskegee Airmen refused to sign. He told his superior officer if he couldn't enjoy the privileges of being an officer, then he shouldn't be one.

The group was spirited off the base. A camera hidden in a brown paper bag captured a picture of the group that ran on the front pages of Negro newspapers across the country. They were arrested for disobeying a direct order by a superior officer, an offense punishable by death in time of war. The charges were later dropped but a letter of reprimand, stating they were a discredit to their country and their race, stayed in their individual files until 1995.

After the 1945 incident, members of the group met with top officials about the need to integrate the armed forces. Some historians have said the protest at Freeman Field was the beginning of the end of segregation in the armed services; in 1948 President Harry Truman signed executive order 9981, integrating the forces.

In the Capitol Rotunda, the air seemed to contain more oxygen than usual. The exhilaration was palpable, like static electricity. We waited for what seemed like hours. I worried about how the men, in their 80s and 90s, were holding up.

Then they entered. The crowd rose and the men walked to their seats to continuous applause. Some were in wheelchairs, some used walkers. Overall they were surprisingly sound. Their hair, silver, thinned. If their steps had slowed, their backs were still straight.

They were the picture of dignity. Their wives were stylish, their white hair catching the light coming in through the Rotunda's high windows.

I wished a section had been reserved for young African Americans. I wished they could feel the pride in that room. It was immense. **B**

Speaker after speaker thanked the men for their service. Sen. Carl Levin, co-sponsor with Rangel. U.S. Rep. Carolyn Kilpatrick. House Speaker Nancy Pelosi. President Bush. "An honor long overdue" was a repeated phrase. Former Secretary of State Colin Powell asked a profound question.

"Why did you serve a nation that would not serve you? When the conflict was over you returned to the same conditions. You still believed in a vision of what the declaration and constitution set forth of what America could be. Thank you for what you did for African Americans. Thank you for what you've done for America," he said. **C**

The 300 at the ceremony accepted for the hundreds who have already passed on. Each year at the Tuskegee Airmen convention, the list of Lonely Eagles, the deceased, is longer and longer. Five died since January. One died the week before the award ceremony, long overdue.

I asked my dad how it felt.

"I think it was pretty rewarding," he said. "I think we deserved it. I was happy to see they went to the extent of doing it." He said he never imagined the group would get that kind of recognition. We couldn't stop telling him how proud we are. He was beaming.

I'm not sure if the glow he's radiating is permanent. The congratulations keep coming in. While visiting the Aerospace Museum in Washington, D.C., people noticed his Tuskegee Airmen cap and came up to shake his hand. On the flight home, the airline bumped him and my mother up to first class. I think he may have had his Tuskegee Airmen cap permanently attached to his head.

That procession of elderly African American men, parading into the Rotunda of the United States Capitol to finally get their due. I'll never forget that sight.

B Informational Focus **Analyzing the Author's Arguments** How does the author's word choice enhance the article?

C Informational Focus **Analyzing the Author's Arguments** Who is the author's target audience for this article?

Vocabulary **palpable** (PAL puh buhl) *adj.*: able to be touched or felt.

INFORMATIONAL TEXT FOCUS
Applying Your Skills

SKILLS FOCUS Informational Skills
Analyze the author's arguments. **Vocabulary Skills** Demonstrate knowledge of literal meanings of words and their usage. **Writing Skills** Write brief constructed responses, with specific support. **Listening and Speaking Skills** Participate in group discussions.

Honor at Last

Respond and Think Critically

Informational Text Focus

Quick Check

1. Is the honors ceremony a major Washington, D.C., event? What details support your answer?

2. What establishment at Freeman Field, Indiana, did the Tuskegee Airmen refuse to support? Why?

3. What momentous change in the American military did the airmen bring about, starting with the Freeman Field incident?

Read with a Purpose

4. How might things be different if the airmen had not stood up for their rights? What characteristics of the men were <u>intrinsic</u> to their success in doing so?

Informational Skills: Analyzing the Author's Arguments

5. As you read, you recorded the author's arguments and supporting evidence. Add a third column in which you explain why this supporting evidence bolsters her argument.

Argument	Supporting Evidence	Why It Strengthens the Argument
Tuskegee Airmen paved the way for the integration of the armed forces.	They risked arrest by protesting segregation at Freeman Field in 1945.	Evidence shows they took a risky stand for what was right.

✓ Vocabulary Check

Match each Vocabulary word with its definition.

6. rotunda   **a.** able to be touched or felt

7. fascism   **b.** dictatorial system of government

8. palpable   **c.** large, round hall or room

Text Analysis

9. **Analyze** Payton says that one of the honorees died the week before the award ceremony. Why does she choose this moment to repeat the phrase "long overdue"? What extra force does it have in this context?

10. **Interpret** When Payton says that the Tuskegee Airmen "defied the odds," what does she mean?

11. **Evaluate** What does the article's closing sentence tell you about Payton's feelings? What special reason does she have to relish this moment?

Listening and Speaking

12. **Analyze** While reading "Honor at Last," you recorded evidence that the author includes. With a group, discuss the information you recorded. List the facts that your group found most convincing, and explain why.

Writing Focus   Constructed Response

How did the Tuskegee Airmen pave the way for future generations of African Americans in the United States Armed Forces? Use at least two specific examples from "Honor at Last" in your response.

What Do You Think Now   Do you think an honor that is delayed holds the same meaning as one that is not?

Preparing to Read

from Night

What Do You Think?

What human needs and desires do we have in common?

QuickWrite

Imagine surviving a near-death experience, such as a terrible illness. Would you wish to share your experience with others? Write a paragraph or two expressing your opinion.

MEET THE WRITER

Elie Wiesel
(1928–   )

Nobel Prize WINNER

In March of 1944, when Elie Wiesel (EHL-ee vee-ZEHL) was fifteen, his life changed forever. At the time, Wiesel was living in the little town where he was born—Sighet, a remote village in the Carpathian Mountains of Hungary. In 1944, the German army invaded Hungary. Soon, Wiesel, his family, and some fifteen thousand other Jews from his region were rounded up and deported to concentration camps in Nazi-occupied Poland.

The Camps

Wiesel experienced unremitting horror in several concentration camps. He saw his mother and youngest sister sent to die in a gas chamber. He witnessed his father's terrible death, and he saw many fellow prisoners tortured and murdered by the Nazis.

After the liberation of Buchenwald in 1945, Wiesel could not bring himself to write about the Holocaust, for fear "that words might betray it." He also remembered a promise he had made to himself: "If, by some miracle, I survive, I will devote my life to testifying on behalf of all those whose shadows will be bound to mine forever."

Testifying for Humanity

The result of this promise was *Night,* Wiesel's harrowing memoir of his experiences under the Nazi terror, published in 1956. That year he came to the United States as a reporter to cover the United Nations. Seven years later he became an American citizen, and today he is a professor at Boston University.

For more than four decades as a novelist, dramatist, journalist, religious scholar, and international activist, Wiesel has been a powerful advocate for human dignity. Seeking to maintain global awareness of Nazi atrocities and to prevent similar crimes against humanity, he has spoken out against human rights abuses in places such as Cambodia, South Africa, and the former Soviet Union. Such work won him a Nobel Peace Prize in 1986.

Think About the Writer

Why do you think Wiesel was concerned "that words might betray" the Holocaust? What does that mean? Why might it be difficult to write about such an event?

Reader/Writer Notebook

Use your **RWN** to complete the activities for this selection.

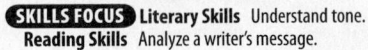

SKILLS FOCUS **Literary Skills** Understand tone.
Reading Skills Analyze a writer's message.

Literary Focus

Tone The attitude a writer takes toward the subject of a literary work, the characters in it, or its audience is called **tone**. Word choice, sentence construction, and selection of details all contribute to tone. The overall tone of a work can usually be described in a single word: for example, *serious, lighthearted,* or *critical.* In some cases, a work may reveal more than one tone, since an author's tone can develop and shift throughout a work. As you read, be attentive to the details in the text that reveal Wiesel's tone.

Reading Focus

Analyzing a Writer's Message Besides <u>transmitting</u> facts, a writer evaluates and interprets them—in other words, finds greater meaning in those facts. What he or she chooses to include or exclude, and how the details are presented, convey the writer's message. *Night* is a memoir, a firsthand account of a personal experience. However, Wiesel does not directly state a message. Instead, he allows his experiences to speak for themselves so readers may draw their own conclusions.

Into Action In addition to sharing his own experiences, Wiesel includes descriptions of several other concentration camp prisoners, including his own father. As you read, use a graphic organizer to keep track of key <u>components</u> of each prisoner's personality.

Other Prisoners	Description of Personality
Mrs. Schächter	shattered by deportation of husband; lost her mind; cries out at night about fire no one else can see; warns others of coming doom

Vocabulary

irrevocably (ih REHV uh kuh blee) *adv.:* permanently, irreversibly. *After the Holocaust, Wiesel's life was irrevocably changed.*

abyss (uh BIHS) *n.:* a deep, immeasurable space, gulf, or cavity. *The darkness made the abyss seem even more ominous.*

convoy (KAHN voy) *n.:* a group of vehicles accompanied by an escort. *The convoy left the train station.*

sage (sayj) *n.:* a profoundly wise person. *The people in the village asked the sage to help them resolve their conflicts.*

poignant (POYN yuhnt) *adj.:* moving or emotionally touching. *Night is a poignant account of the Holocaust.*

Language Coach

Prefixes A prefix is a word part that is attached to the beginning of a root to make a new word. *Irrevocably* refers to something that cannot be changed. *Revoke* means "take something away." What do you think the prefix *ir-* means? Note that *ir-* is a form of the prefix *in-*.

Writing Focus

Think as a Reader/Writer

Find It in Your Reading If a subject is very serious or important, allowing the events to speak for themselves is often effective. **Understatement** is one of the techniques Wiesel uses to convey the terrors of life in concentration camps. Use your *Reader/Writer Notebook* to keep track of passages in which Wiesel uses understatement.

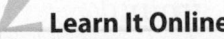
Learn It Online
Go online to access an interactive Reading Workshop on Analyzing a Writer's Message.

go.hrw.com L11-1047   **Go**

Study C (detail)(1995) by Samuel Bak.

from NIGHT

by **Elie Wiesel**
translated by **Marion Wiesel**

Read with a Purpose

As you read, discover how constant misery and suffering affected the prisoners in the concentration camp.

Build Background

During the Holocaust, Nazis deported millions of Jews to death camps or forced labor camps. Once there, those who appeared weak or sick were sent to gas chambers to be killed. Families were torn apart; those who were not victims of the gas chambers often died from disease or starvation. Near the end of the war, the Nazis forced the prisoners out of the camps on death marches in an effort to get rid of any evidence of concentration camps.

The following selection contains three excerpts from Wiesel's memoir.

The train stopped in Kaschau, a small town on the Czechoslovakian border. We realized then that we were not staying in Hungary. Our eyes opened. Too late.

The door of the car slid aside. A German officer stepped in accompanied by a Hungarian lieutenant, acting as his interpreter.

"From this moment on, you are under the authority of the German Army. Anyone who still owns gold, silver, or watches must hand them over now. Anyone who will be found to have kept any of these will be shot on the spot. Secondly, anyone who is ill should report to the hospital car. That's all."

The Hungarian lieutenant went around with a basket and retrieved the last possessions from those who chose not to go on tasting the bitterness of fear.

"There are eighty of you in the car," the German officer added. "If anyone goes missing, you will all be shot, like dogs."

The two disappeared. The doors clanked shut. We had fallen into the trap, up to our necks. The doors were nailed, the way back irrevocably cut off. The world had become a hermetically sealed[1] cattle car.

There was a woman among us, a certain Mrs. Schächter.[2] She was in her fifties and her ten-year-old son was with her, crouched in a corner. Her husband and two older sons had been deported with the first transport, by mistake. The separation had totally shattered her.

I knew her well. A quiet, tense woman with piercing eyes, she had been a frequent guest in our house. Her husband was a pious man who spent most of his days and nights in the house of study. It was she who supported the family.

Mrs. Schächter had lost her mind. On the first day of the journey, she had already begun to moan. She kept asking why she had been separated from her family. Later, her sobs and screams became hysterical.

---

1. **hermetically sealed:** airtight.
2. **Schächter** (SHAHK tuhr).

On the third night, as we were sleeping, some of us sitting, huddled against each other, some of us standing, a piercing cry broke the silence:

"Fire! I see a fire! I see a fire!"

There was a moment of panic. Who had screamed? It was Mrs. Schächter. Standing in the middle of the car, in the faint light filtering through the windows, she looked like a withered tree in a field of wheat. She was howling, pointing through the window:

"Look! Look at this fire! This terrible fire! Have mercy on me!"

Some pressed against the bars to see. There was nothing. Only the darkness of night.

It took us a long time to recover from this harsh awakening. We were still trembling, and with every screech of the wheels, we felt the abyss opening beneath us. Unable to still our anguish, we tried to reassure each other:

"She is mad, poor woman . . ."

Someone had placed a damp rag on her forehead. But she nevertheless continued to scream:

"Fire! I see a fire!"

Her little boy was crying, clinging to her skirt, trying to hold her hand:

"It's nothing, Mother! There's nothing there . . . Please sit down . . ." He pained me even more than did his mother's cries.

Some of the women tried to calm her:

"You'll see, you'll find your husband and sons again . . . In a few days . . ."

She continued to scream and sob fitfully.

"Jews, listen to me," she cried. "I see a fire! I see flames, huge flames!"

It was as though she were possessed by some evil spirit.

We tried to reason with her, more to calm ourselves, to catch our breath, than to soothe her:

"She is hallucinating because she is thirsty, poor woman . . . That's why she speaks of flames devouring her . . ."

But it was all in vain. Our terror could no longer be contained. Our nerves had reached a breaking point.

Our very skin was aching. It was as though madness had infected all of us. We gave up. A few young men forced her to sit down, then bound and gagged her.

Silence fell again. The small boy sat next to his mother, crying. I started to breathe normally again as I listened to the rhythmic pounding of the wheels on the tracks as the train raced through the night. We could begin to doze again, to rest, to dream . . .

And so an hour or two passed. Another scream jolted us. The woman had broken free of her bonds and was shouting louder than before:

"Look at the fire! Look at the flames! Flames everywhere . . ."

Once again, the young men bound and gagged her. When they actually struck her, people shouted their approval:

"Keep her quiet! Make that madwoman shut up. She's not the only one here . . ."

She received several blows to the head, blows that could have been lethal. Her son was clinging desperately to her, not uttering a word. He was no longer crying.

The night seemed endless. By daybreak, Mrs. Schächter had settled down. Crouching in her corner, her blank gaze fixed on some faraway place, she no longer saw us.

She remained like that all day, mute, absent, alone in the midst of us. Toward evening she began to shout again:

"The fire, over there!"

She was pointing somewhere in the distance, always the same place. No one felt like beating her anymore. The heat, the thirst, the stench, the lack of air, were suffocating us. Yet all that was nothing compared to her screams, which tore us apart. A few more days and all of us would have started to scream. **C**

But we were pulling into a station. Someone near a window read to us:

"Auschwitz.[3]"

Nobody had ever heard that name.

---

3. **Auschwitz:** half of the Auschwitz-Birkenau Nazi German concentration and death camp, a forced-labor and extermination center run by the German Nazis during World War II (1939–1945).

The train did not move again. The afternoon went by slowly. Then the doors of the wagon slid open. Two men were given permission to fetch water.

When they came back, they told us that they had learned, in exchange for a gold watch, that this was the final destination. We were to leave the train here. There was a labor camp on the site. The conditions were good. Families would not be separated. Only the young would work in the factories. The old and the sick would find work in the fields.

Confidence soared. Suddenly we felt free of the previous nights' terror. We gave thanks to God.

Mrs. Schächter remained huddled in her corner, mute, untouched by the optimism around her. Her little one was stroking her hand.

Dusk began to fill the wagon. We ate what was left of our food. At ten o' clock in the evening, we were all trying to find a position for a quick nap and soon we were dozing. Suddenly:

"Look at the fire! Look at the flames! Over there!"

With a start, we awoke and rushed to the window yet again. We had believed her, if only for an instant. But there was nothing outside but darkness. We returned to our places, shame in our souls but fear gnawing at us nevertheless. As she went on howling, she was struck again. Only with great difficulty did we succeed in quieting her down.

The man in charge of our wagon called out to a German officer strolling down the platform, asking him to have the sick woman moved to a hospital car.

"Patience," the German replied, "patience. She'll be taken there soon."

Around eleven o' clock, the train began to move again. We pressed against the windows. The convoy was rolling slowly. A quarter of an hour later, it began to slow down even more. Through the windows, we saw barbed wire; we understood that this was the camp.

We had forgotten Mrs. Schächter's existence. Suddenly there was a terrible scream:

"Jews, look! Look at the fire! Look at the flames!"

And as the train stopped, this time we saw flames rising from a tall chimney into a black sky.

Mrs. Schächter had fallen silent on her own. Mute again, indifferent, absent, she had returned to her corner.

C **Reading Focus** **Analyzing a Writer's Message** How do the other people on the train react to Mrs. Schächter?

Vocabulary convoy (KAHN voy) *n.:* a group of vehicles accompanied by an escort.

We stared at the flames in the darkness. A wretched stench floated in the air. Abruptly, our doors opened. Strange-looking creatures, dressed in striped jackets and black pants, jumped into the wagon. Holding flashlights and sticks, they began to strike at us left and right, shouting:

"Everybody out! Leave everything inside. Hurry up!"

We jumped out. I glanced at Mrs. Schächter. Her little boy was still holding her hand.

In front of us, those flames. In the air, the smell of burning flesh. It must have been around midnight. We had arrived. In Birkenau.[4]

The following section of Night *takes place in Buna (BOO nuh), another camp in Poland, where Wiesel and his father were sent from Auschwitz. It documents the horrifying process of selection, in which the Nazis separated those prisoners judged fit to perform slave labor from those who were to be killed immediately. It was after such a selection that Wiesel's mother and sister were murdered in the Auschwitz gas chamber.*

Our *Blockälteste*[5] had not been outside a concentration camp since 1933. He had already been through all the slaughterhouses, all the factories of death. Around nine o'clock, he came to stand in our midst:

"Achtung!"[6]

There was instant silence.

"Listen carefully to what I am about to tell you." For the first time, his voice quivered. "In a few moments, selection will take place. You will have to undress completely. Then you will go, one by one, before the SS[7] doctors. I hope you will all pass. But you must try to increase your chances. Before you go into the next room, try to move your limbs, give yourself some color. Don't walk slowly, run! Run as if you had the devil at your heels! Don't look at the SS. Run, straight in front of you!"

An example of a Star of David patch that Jews were forced to wear in Nazi-controlled Europe during the war.

He paused and then added:

"And most important, don't be afraid!"

That was a piece of advice we would have loved to be able to follow.

I undressed, leaving my clothes on my cot. Tonight, there was no danger that they would be stolen.

Tibi and Yossi, who had changed Kommandos at the same time I did, came to urge me:

"Let's stay together. It will make us stronger."

Yossi was mumbling something. He probably was praying. I had never suspected that Yossi was religious. In fact, I had always believed the opposite. Tibi was silent and very pale. All the block inmates stood naked between the rows of bunks. This must be how one stands for the Last Judgment. **(D)**

"They are coming!"

Three SS officers surrounded the notorious Dr. Mengele,[8] the very same who had received us in Birkenau. The *Blockälteste* attempted a smile. He asked us:

"Ready?"

---

4. **Birkenau** (BEER kuh now): half of the Auschwitz-Birkenau Nazi German concentration and death camp.
5. *Blockälteste* (BLAHK ahl test uh): German for "head of the block, or barrack."
6. *Achtung!* (AHKH tung): German for "attention!"
7. **SS**: abbreviation for Schutzstaffel (SHOOTS shteh fehl), German for "protection squad," the elite Nazi guards who oversaw the operation of the concentration camps.

8. **Dr. Mengele:** Joseph Mengele (1911–1979) was a Nazi doctor and SS officer infamous for torturing camp prisoners, often children, sometimes in pseudoscientific experiments.

(D) **Reading Focus** Analyzing a Writer's Message What is Wiesel's message about faith and its importance?

Yes, we were ready. So were the SS doctors. Dr. Mengele was holding a list: our numbers. He nodded to the *Blockälteste*: we can begin! As if this were a game.

The first to go were the "notables" of the block, the *Stubenälteste*, the Kapos,[9] the foremen, all of whom were in perfect physical condition, of course! Then came the ordinary prisoners' turns. Dr. Mengele looked them over from head to toe. From time to time, he noted a number. I had but one thought: not to have my number taken down and not to show my left arm.

---

9. *Stubenälteste,* **the Kapos:** prisoners appointed by the Nazis to oversee other prisoners, in exchange for better treatment.

In front of me, there were only Tibi and Yossi. They passed. I had time to notice that Mengele had not written down their numbers. Someone pushed me. It was my turn. I ran without looking back. My head was spinning: you are too skinny . . . you are too weak . . . you are too skinny, you are good for the ovens . . . The race seemed endless; I felt as though I had been running for years . . . You are too skinny, you are too weak . . . At last I arrived. Exhausted. When I had caught my breath, I asked Yossi and Tibi:

"Did they write me down?"

"No," said Yossi. Smiling, he added, "Anyway, they couldn't have. You were running too fast . . ."

I began to laugh. I was happy. I felt like kissing him. At that moment, the others did not matter! They had not written me down. **E**

Those whose numbers had been noted were standing apart, abandoned by the whole world. Some were silently weeping.

A few days passed. We were no longer thinking about the selection. We went to work as usual and loaded the heavy stones onto the freight cars. The rations had grown smaller; that was the only change.

We had risen at dawn, as we did every day. We had received our black coffee, our ration of bread. We were about to head to the work yard as always. The *Blockälteste* came running:

"Let's have a moment of quiet. I have here a list of numbers. I shall read them to you. All those called will not go to work this morning; they will stay in camp."

Softly, he read some ten numbers. We understood. These were the numbers from the selection. Dr. Mengele had not forgotten.

The *Blockälteste* turned to go to his room. The ten prisoners surrounded him, clinging to his clothes:

"Save us! You promised . . . We want to go to the depot, we are strong enough to work. We are good workers. We can . . . we want . . ."

He tried to calm them, to reassure them about their fate, to explain to them that staying in the camp did not mean much, had no tragic significance: "After all, I stay here every day . . ."

E **Literary Focus** Tone What is Wiesel's tone right after he passes the selection? Is he actually happy?

The argument was more than flimsy. He realized it and, without another word, locked himself in his room.

The bell had just rung.

"Form ranks!"

Now, it no longer mattered that the work was hard. All that mattered was to be far from the block, far from the crucible of death, from the center of hell. **F**

I saw my father running in my direction. Suddenly, I was afraid.

"What is happening?"

He was out of breath, hardly able to open his mouth.

"Me too, me too . . . They told me too to stay in the camp."

They had recorded his number without his noticing.

"What are we going to do?" I said anxiously.

But it was he who tried to reassure me:

"It's not certain yet. There's still a chance. Today, they will do another selection . . . a decisive one . . ."

I said nothing.

He felt time was running out. He was speaking rapidly, he wanted to tell me so many things. His speech became confused, his voice was choked. He knew that I had to leave in a few moments. He was going to remain alone, so alone . . . **G**

"Here, take this knife," he said. "I won't need it anymore. You may find it useful. Also take this spoon. Don't sell it. Quickly! Go ahead, take what I'm giving you!"

My inheritance . . .

"Don't talk like that, Father." I was on the verge of breaking into sobs. "I don't want you to say such things. Keep the spoon and knife. You will need them as much as I. We'll see each other tonight, after work."

He looked at me with his tired eyes, veiled by despair. He insisted:

"I am asking you . . . Take it, do as I ask you, my son. Time is running out. Do as your father asks you . . ."

Our Kapo shouted the order to march.

The Kommando headed toward the camp gate. Left, right! I was biting my lips. My father had remained near the block, leaning against the wall.

Then he began to run, to try to catch up with us. Perhaps he had forgotten to tell me something . . . But we were marching too fast . . . Left, right!

We were at the gate. We were being counted. Around us, the din of military music. Then we were outside.

All day I plodded around like a sleepwalker. Tibi and Yossi would call out to me, from time to time, trying to reassure me. As did the Kapo who had given me easier tasks that day. I felt sick at heart. How kindly they treated me. Like an orphan. I thought: Even now, my father is helping me.

I myself didn't know whether I wanted the day to go by quickly or not. I was afraid of finding myself alone that evening. How good it would be to die right here!

At last, we began the return journey. How I longed for an order to run! The military march. The gate. The camp. I ran toward Block 36.

Were there still miracles on this earth? He was alive. He had passed the second selection. He had still proved his usefulness . . . I gave him back his knife and spoon.

Akiba Drumer has left us, a victim of the selection. Lately, he had been wandering among us, his eyes glazed, telling everyone how weak he was: "I can't go on . . . It's over . . ." We tried to raise his spirits, but he wouldn't listen to anything we said. He just kept repeating that it was all over for him, that he could no longer fight, he had no more strength, no more faith. His eyes would suddenly go blank, leaving two gaping wounds, two wells of terror.

He was not alone in having lost his faith during those days of selection. I knew a rabbi, from a small town in Poland. He was old and bent, his lips constantly trembling. He was always praying, in the block, at work, in the ranks. He recited entire pages from the Talmud, arguing with himself, asking and answering himself endless questions. One day, he said to me:

"It's over. God is no longer with us."

And as though he regretted having uttered such words so coldly, so dryly, he added in his broken voice,

---

F **Reading Focus** **Analyzing a Writer's Message** What does this paragraph suggest about the power of evil?

G **Literary Focus** **Tone** What is the emotional effect of this paragraph?

"I know. No one has the right to say things like that. I know that very well. Man is too insignificant, too limited, to even try to comprehend God's mysterious ways. But what can someone like myself do? I'm neither a sage nor a just man. I am not a saint. I'm a simple creature of flesh and bone. I suffer hell in my soul and my flesh. I also have eyes and I see what is being done here. Where is God's mercy? Where's God? How can I believe, how can anyone believe in this God of Mercy?"

Poor Akiba Drumer, if only he could have kept his faith in God, if only he could have considered this suffering a divine test, he would not have been swept away by the selection. But as soon as he felt the first chinks in his faith, he lost all incentive to fight and opened the door to death.

When the selection came, he was doomed from the start, offering his neck to the executioner, as it were. All he asked of us was:

"In three days, I'll be gone . . . Say Kaddish[10] for me."

We promised: in three days, when we would see the smoke rising from the chimney, we would think of him. We would gather ten men and hold a special service. All his friends would say Kaddish.

Then he left, in the direction of the hospital. His step was almost steady and he never looked back. An ambulance was waiting to take him to Birkenau.

There followed terrible days. We received more blows than food. The work was crushing. And three days after he left, we forgot to say Kaddish.

The next section of Night *occurs toward the end of Wiesel's eleven months in the concentration camps. It opens during a brutal march toward a new camp, Gleiwitz (GLY vihtz). The Nazi guards have forced the prisoners to run for miles in the snow without adequate rest or clothing. As a result, hundreds will die before they reach the dangerously overcrowded barracks.*

The door of the shed opened. An old man appeared. His mustache was covered with ice, his lips were blue. It was Rabbi Eliahou,[11] who had headed a small congregation in Poland. A very kind man, beloved by everyone in the camp, even by the Kapos and the *Blockälteste.* Despite the ordeals and deprivations, his face continued to radiate his innocence. He was the only rabbi whom nobody ever failed to address as "Rabbi" in Buna. He looked like one of those prophets of old, always in the midst of his people when they needed to be consoled. And, strangely, his words never provoked anyone. They did bring peace. **(H)**

As he entered the shed, his eyes, brighter than ever, seemed to be searching for someone.

"Perhaps someone here has seen my son?"

He had lost his son in the commotion. He had searched for him among the dying, to no avail. Then he had dug through the snow to find his body. In vain.

For three years, they had stayed close to one another. Side by side, they had endured the suffering, the blows; they had waited for their ration of bread and they had prayed. Three years, from camp to camp, from selection to selection. And now—when the end seemed near—fate had separated them.

When he came near me, Rabbi Eliahou whispered, "It happened on the road. We lost sight of one another during the journey. I fell behind a little, at the rear of the column. I didn't have the strength to run anymore. And my son didn't notice. That's all I know. Where has he disappeared? Where can I find him? Perhaps you've seen him somewhere?"

"No, Rabbi Eliahou, I haven't seen him."

And so he left, as he had come: a shadow swept away by the wind.

He had already gone through the door when I remembered that I had noticed his son running beside me. I had forgotten and so had not mentioned it to Rabbi Eliahou!

But then I remembered something else: his son *had* seen him losing ground, sliding back to the rear of the column. He had seen him. And he had continued to run in front, letting the distance between them become greater.

---

10. **Kaddish:** Jewish prayer in praise of God, one form of which is recited to mourn a death.

11. **Eliahou** (el ee AH hoo).

Vocabulary **sage** (sayj) *n.:* a profoundly wise person.

(H) **Literary Focus** Tone How does Wiesel convey his attitude toward Rabbi Eliahou?

SONS ABANDONED
THE REMAINS OF THEIR FATHERS
WITHOUT A TEAR.

A terrible thought crossed my mind: What if he had wanted to be rid of his father? He had felt his father growing weaker and, believing that the end was near, had thought by this separation to free himself of a burden that could diminish his own chance for survival.

It was good that I *had* forgotten all that. And I was glad that Rabbi Eliahou continued to search for his beloved son.

And in spite of myself, a prayer formed inside me, a prayer to this God in whom I no longer believed. **I**

"Oh God, Master of the Universe, give me the strength never to do what Rabbi Eliahou's son has done."

There was shouting outside, in the courtyard. Night had fallen and the SS were ordering us to form ranks.

We started to march once more. The dead remained in the yard, under the snow without even a marker, like fallen guards. No one recited Kaddish over them. Sons abandoned the remains of their fathers without a tear.

On the road, it snowed and snowed, it snowed endlessly. We were marching more slowly. Even the guards seemed tired. My wounded foot no longer hurt, probably frozen. I felt I had lost that foot. It had become detached from me like a wheel fallen off a car. Never mind. I had to accept the fact: I would have to live with only one leg. The important thing was not to dwell on it. Especially now. Leave those thoughts for later.

Our column had lost all appearance of discipline. Everyone walked as he wished, as he could. No more gunshots. Our guards surely *were* tired.

But death hardly needed their help. The cold was conscientiously doing its work. At every step, somebody fell down and ceased to suffer. **J**

From time to time, SS officers on motorcycles drove the length of the column to shake off the growing apathy:

"Hold on! We're almost there!"

"Courage! Just a few more hours!"

"We're arriving in Gleiwitz!"

These words of encouragement, even coming as they did from the mouths of our assassins, were of great help. Nobody wanted to give up now, just before the end, so close to our destination. Our eyes searched the horizon for the barbed wire of Gleiwitz. Our only wish was to arrive there quickly.

By now it was night. It had stopped snowing. We marched a few more hours before we arrived. We saw the camp only when we stood right in front of its gate. **K**

The Kapos quickly settled us into the barrack. There was shoving and jostling as if this were the ultimate haven, the gateway to life. People trod over numbed bodies, trampled wounded faces. There were no cries, only a few moans. My father and I were thrown to the ground by this rolling tide. From beneath me came a desperate cry:

"You're crushing me . . . have mercy!"

The voice was familiar.

"You're crushing me . . . mercy, have mercy!"

The same faint voice, the same cry I had heard somewhere before. This voice had spoken to me one day. When? Years ago? No, it must have been in the camp.

"Mercy!"

Knowing that I was crushing him, preventing him from breathing, I wanted to get up and disengage myself to allow him to breathe. But I myself was crushed under the weight of other bodies. I had

---

I **Reading Focus** **Analyzing a Writer's Message** How does Wiesel's belief in God change throughout the memoir?

J **Literary Focus** **Tone** How does the climate affect the prisoners during the death march?

K **Literary Focus** **Tone** How does Wiesel's tone change between his arrival at Auschwitz and the end of the death march?

difficulty breathing. I dug my nails into unknown faces. I was biting my way through, searching for air. No one cried out.

Suddenly I remembered. Juliek![12] The boy from Warsaw who played the violin in the Buna orchestra . . .

"Juliek, is that you?"

"Eliezer[13] . . . The twenty-five whiplashes . . . Yes . . . I remember."

He fell silent. A long moment went by.

"Juliek! Can you hear me, Juliek?"

"Yes . . ." he said feebly. "What do you want?"

He was not dead.

"Are you all right, Juliek?" I asked, less to know his answer than to hear him speak, to know he was alive.

"All right, Eliezer . . . All right . . . Not too much air . . . Tired. My feet are swollen. It's good to rest, but my violin . . ."

I thought he'd lost his mind. His violin? Here?

"What about your violin?"

He was gasping:

"I . . . I'm afraid . . . They'll break . . . my violin . . . I . . . I brought it with me."

I could not answer him. Someone had lain down on top of me, smothering me. I couldn't breathe through my mouth or my nose. Sweat was running down my forehead and my back. This was it; the end of the road. A silent death, suffocation. No way to scream, to call for help.

I tried to rid myself of my invisible assassin. My whole desire to live became concentrated in my nails. I scratched, I fought for a breath of air. I tore at decaying flesh that did not respond. I could not free myself of that mass weighing down my chest. Who knows? Was I struggling with a dead man?

I shall never know. All I can say is that I prevailed. I succeeded in digging a hole in that wall of dead and dying people, a small hole through which I could drink a little air.

"Father are you there?" I asked as soon as I was able to utter a word.

I knew that he could not be far from me.

"Yes!" a voice replied from far away, as if from another world. "I am trying to sleep."

He was trying to sleep. Could one fall asleep here? Wasn't it dangerous to lower one's guard, even for a moment, when death could strike at any time?

Those were my thoughts when I heard the sound of a violin. A violin in a dark barrack where the dead were piled on top of the living? Who was this madman who played the violin here, at the edge of his own grave? Or was it a hallucination?

It had to be Juliek.

He was playing a fragment of a Beethoven concerto. Never before had I heard such a beautiful sound. In such silence.

How had he succeeded in disengaging himself? To slip out from under my body without my feeling it?

The darkness enveloped us. All I could hear was the violin, and it was as if Juliek's soul had become his bow. He was playing his life. His whole being was gliding over the strings. His unfulfilled hopes. His charred past, his extinguished future. He played that which he would never play again.

I shall never forget Juliek. How could I forget this concert given before an audience of the dead and dying? Even today, when I hear that particular piece by Beethoven, my eyes close and out of the darkness emerges the pale and melancholy face of my Polish comrade bidding farewell to an audience of dying men.

I don't know how long he played. I was overcome by sleep. When I awoke at daybreak, I saw Juliek facing me, hunched over, dead. Next to him lay his violin, trampled, an eerily poignant little corpse. **L**

---

12. **Juliek** (YOU lee ek).
13. **Eliezer** (ah lee AH zhur).

Vocabulary **poignant** (POYN yuhnt) *adj.*: moving or emotionally touching.

L **Reading Focus** Analyzing a Writer's Message Wiesel wrote this memoir as a testimony to the horrors he witnessed, as well as to advocate for the protection of human rights. Do you think he achieved these goals with *Night*?

Applying Your Skills

from **Night**

Respond and Think Critically

Reading Focus

Quick Check

1. To what does the German officer compare the Jews when he threatens to shoot them?

2. Why does Wiesel's father give him a spoon and knife?

3. What does Juliek do just before he dies?

Read with a Purpose

4. How does the constant misery in the camp affect the prisoners?

Reading Skills: Analyzing a Writer's Message

5. Review the chart you made about the other concentration camp prisoners Wiesel describes. Add a third column to your chart. Speculate on how the description of each of them specifically contributes to Wiesel's overall message.

Other Prisoners	Description	How does this person contribute to Wiesel's message?
Mrs. Schächter	shattered by deportation of husband; lost her mind; cries out at night about fire no one else can see; warns others of coming doom.	No one believes her about the fires, but it turns out she is right. It is too easy to believe that terrible events are not really happening when they actually are.

Literary Focus

Literary Analysis

6. Analyze Why do you think it was so important for the prisoners not to lose faith?

7. Summarize Describe the train ride from Hungary to Auschwitz.

8. Evaluate Why does Wiesel make a point of telling the reader how quickly the prisoners forgot about those who died?

9. Make Judgments When Wiesel accepted the Nobel Peace Prize, he said that "indifference" is the "greatest source of evil and danger in the world." He also said that if humanity ever forgets the Holocaust, then "we are guilty, we are accomplices." Do you agree with this political point of view? Explain your position.

Literary Skills: Tone

10. Analyze How would you describe the tone of the scene in which Wiesel's father gives him his inheritance?

11. Interpret Explain ways in which Wiesel's tone could be described as philosophical. Use evidence from the text to support your answer.

Literary Skills Review: Mood

12. Analyze In literature, **mood** refers to the feelings aroused by words and images. What is the mood of the scene in the cattle cars? What details help create the mood?

Writing Focus

Think as a Reader/Writer

Use It in Your Writing Write about an event or situation that you think would elicit a strong emotion from a reader. Use **understatement** to emphasize the most poignant parts of the event or situation. Use Wiesel's memoir as a model to help you avoid telling the reader what he or she should be feeling.

 What Do You Think Now

What dark side of human nature does Wiesel's memoir reveal?

from **Night**

Vocabulary Development

Vocabulary Check

Match each Vocabulary word with its synonym.

1. irrevocably   **a.** scholar
2. abyss   **b.** permanently
3. convoy   **c.** moving
4. sage   **d.** procession
5. poignant   **e.** void

Vocabulary Skills: Precise Meanings

Wiesel's memoir was written in French in 1958 and later translated into English. Go back to the selection and locate each Vocabulary word. Fill out a chart like the one below. Has the translator chosen her words carefully? If a more descriptive synonym were substituted, would the emotional impact of the sentence change?

irrevocably	sage
abyss	poignant
convoy	

Word
abyss

Synonyms
chasm, hole

Does the sentence have the same impact when you use these synonyms?

1. With every screech of the wheels, we felt a **chasm** open under us. (yes)
2. With every screech of the wheels, we felt a **hole** open under us. (no, it loses emotion)

Your Turn

Using the table below, write down the Vocabulary words and their basic synonyms. Then, think of a more descriptive synonym that has a similar impact.

Vocabulary Word	Basic Synonym	Descriptive Synonym
poignant	moving	heartrending

Language Coach

Prefixes A prefix is a word part that is attached to the beginning of a root to make a new word. In the sentences below, find the root of the italicized words. Then, identify the prefix from the following table. Explain how the prefix affects the meaning of the word.

ex–: out, out of   *in–*: not or in, within
ir–: not   *re–*: again, back

1. The people on the train tried to *reassure* one another that things would get better.
2. One passenger *exchanged* gold for information from a guard.
3. It would be *irresponsible* to leave his shoes where they could be stolen.
4. Many *inmates* of the camp starved to death.

Academic Vocabulary

Write About

Write about the <u>components</u> of Wiesel's memoir that surprised you the most. What made them surprising to you?

Grammar Link

Varying Sentence Structure

Writing that uses the same kinds of sentences again and again can become predictable and often monotonous. For example:

> The guards appeared. They asked for identification. We showed them our papers. They ordered us to wait. We stood in the rain. It was getting dark. There was nothing to eat.

Too many long, involved sentences can have a similar effect, blunting the sentence's impact:

> The ride was long and difficult, with many hardships for the prisoners to endure, and being nailed inside the cattle cars meant that there was no chance of escape and little fresh air to breathe.

Using a combination of long and short sentences can be very effective in creating a sense of drama:

> As it prepared to destroy London during World War II, the mighty German air force had about 2,600 fighters armed and ready for battle. The English had one fourth as many. During what came to be known as the Battle of Britain, the Germans dropped thousands of bombs and, for weeks, fought the English spitfires nearly every day. The outcome shocked the world. Though heavily outmanned and outgunned, English pilots cut the German air force to ribbons and wrecked Hitler's plan for an invasion. The tide of the war had turned.

Your Turn

Writing Application Think of a highly dramatic event, such as a closely contested hockey game or a verbal confrontation between two bitter rivals. Write down some ideas for what might happen. Then, write a paragraph about the incident. Vary the length and structure of the sentences, and see how gripping and suspenseful your description can be.

CHOICES

As you respond to the Choices, use these **Academic Vocabulary** words as appropriate: component, diverse, intrinsic, potential, transmit.

REVIEW

Define Human Behavior

Group Discussion How can people treat each other with cruelty? What influences us to behave with compassion or cruelty toward others? Do you believe human beings are intrinsically good or evil? Discuss these questions with your classmates in a small group.

CONNECT

Research Who Wiesel Is Today

Partner Work Wiesel was liberated from Buchenwald, another concentration camp, in 1945. In addition to writing *Night*, Wiesel has had many other important accomplishments. With a partner, research Wiesel's life after 1945 to the present. Create a multimedia presentation about Wiesel's life since leaving the camps to share with your class.

EXTEND

Learn About Other Persecuted Groups

TechFocus Using a variety of online sources, research one of the other groups the Nazis targeted to be sent to concentration camps. Why did the Nazis target this group? How many of them died? Locate testimony provided by a survivor of such a group about his or her experience.

Learn It Online
Find more information on *Night* by visiting these Internet links.

go.hrw.com | L11-1059 | **Go**

Preparing to Read

Reader/Writer Notebook

Use your **RWN** to complete the activities for this selection.

Literary Focus

Tone The term **tone** can apply to more than a person's manner of speaking or writing. It can refer to pictures as well. *Maus* is a **graphic novel,** a genre that combines narrative with drawings in comic-strip format. The tone of a graphic novel depends on both the pictures and the words that are used to tell the story. As you read the excerpt from *Maus*, pay attention to its tone. How do you think Spiegelman feels about his subject?

Reading Focus

Responding to Graphics The drawings and format used in graphic novels add an extra dimension to telling a story. As you read this excerpt from *Maus*, think about the author's purpose in using the format of a graphic novel to tell his story. While reading the excerpt, notice ways in which the pictures transmit facts and evoke feelings.

Into Action Focus on how Vladek is revealed through his actions, appearance, thoughts, and dialogue. Use a cluster diagram like the one below to record details that relate to Vladek.

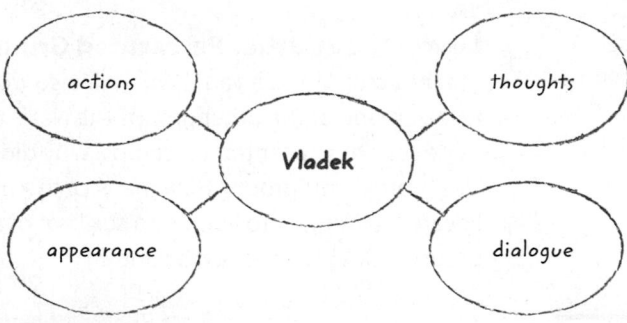

Writing Focus

Think as a Reader/Writer

Find It in Your Writing Nearly all the writing in a graphic novel is in the form of dialogue. In your *Reader/Writer Notebook,* note the dialogue spoken by the narrator and the way it creates a clear characterization.

Vocabulary

deport (dee POHRT) *v.:* send or carry off; transport, especially forcibly. *The Nazis were preparing to deport the Jews to camps.*

ghetto (GEHT oh) *n.:* a densely populated section of a city inhabited predominantly by members of an ethnic or other minority group, often as a result of social or economic restrictions. *The Nazis took away the Jews' rights and forced them to live in terrible conditions in the ghetto.*

bunker (BUHNG kuhr) *n.:* a storehouse or chamber made of earth or concrete, built mostly or entirely below ground. *Vladek and his wife hide in the bunker after the Nazis begin to expel the Jews from the ghetto.*

Language Coach

Word Origins The word *bunker,* dating from 1750 to 1760, probably comes from the Scottish word *bonkar,* meaning "a sturdy box or chest that was used both for storage and as a seat." It came to denote any enclosed storage space. What word for a type of bed can be found inside the word *bunker*?

Learn It Online
There's more to words than just definitions. Get the whole story online.

go.hrw.com | L11-1060 | Go

FROM MAUS

by **Art Spiegelman**

Read with a Purpose

Read to discover how a writer's attitude about a subject can be conveyed through visuals and dialogue in a graphic novel.

Build Background

Art Spiegelman is a political cartoonist and satirist, best known for his politically charged memoir *Maus,* a graphic novel. In it he recounts his father's struggles to survive the Holocaust, and he explores his troubled relationship with his father. He uses animals to represent the <u>diverse</u> ethnic groups that were most affected by the war, portraying Europe's Jews as mice, the Nazis as cats (Katzies), Americans as dogs, and Poles as pigs. *Maus* was released in two volumes: *Maus I: A Survivor's Tale* (also known as *Maus I: My Father Bleeds History*) and *Maus II: And Here My Troubles Began*. His final installment earned him a Pulitzer Prize in 1992.

This excerpt takes place in 1943 in Srodula, a town in southern Poland. The story is told by Spiegelman's father, Vladek.

C **Reading Focus** **Responding to Graphics** How is the character Lolek depicted visually and through dialogue?

D **Literary Focus** **Tone** How does Spiegelman place emphasis on certain lines of dialogue?

from *Maus* **1063**

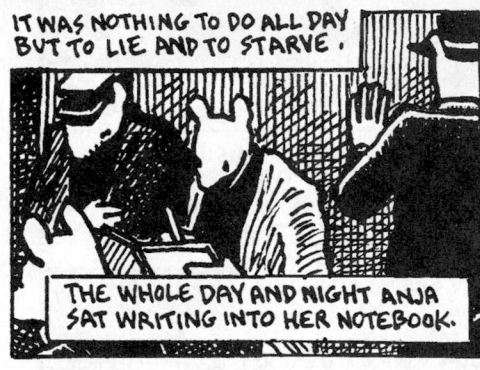

E **Literary Focus** Tone What tone is implied by the line "No, it's only wood. But chewing it feels a little like eating food"?

F **Reading Focus** Responding to Graphics Why might the artist start out with a large panel at the top of the page and end with three small panels at the bottom?

SKILLS FOCUS **Literary Skills** Analyze tone; analyze character motivation. **Reading Skills** Respond to graphics. **Writing Skills** Develop characters using dialogue.

Respond and Think Critically

Reading Focus

Quick Check

1. Why are the Katzies taking the mice (Jews) into custody?

2. Why was Lolek so confident he was safe?

3. What dangers did the mice face in the bunker?

Read with a Purpose

4. Why does Spiegelman use visuals as well as words to express political commentary? What are some of the advantages of this approach?

Reading Skills: Responding to Graphics

5. Review the cluster diagram that you used to collect information about Vladek. Now, write a brief description of the <u>diverse</u> techniques that Spiegelman uses to reveal Vladek's character. Focus especially on how Spiegelman uses graphic elements to reveal this character.

✔ Vocabulary Check

Complete each sentence with the appropriate Vocabulary word: **deport, ghetto, bunker.**

6. The conditions in the _____ were terrible.

7. The men were afraid that the army wanted to _____ their families.

8. The _____ was built to protect the people from bombs.

Literary Focus

Literary Analysis

9. **Interpret** What is meant by the line, "No, Darling! To die, it's easy. . . . But you have to struggle for life!" on page 1063?

10. **Compare and Contrast** In what ways are the excerpts from Wiesel's memoir *Night* (page 1048) and Spiegelman's graphic novel similar or different? Use a Venn diagram to organize your thoughts.

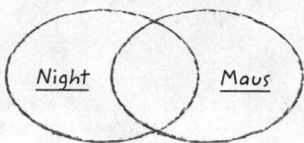

11. **Evaluate** Why do you think Spiegelman chose not to use color in his graphic novel?

Literary Skills: Tone

12. **Interpret** In speaking we use voice inflections to show our tone. How does Spiegelman show a character's voice inflections in his graphic novel?

Literary Skills Review: Motivation

13. **Extend** **Motivation** refers to the reasons for a character's behavior. What do you think Vladek's motivation for telling this story might be?

Writing Focus

Think as a Reader/Writer

Use it in your Writing Write a continuation of this story by creating three original panels of visuals and dialogue. Remember to include dialogue, which is an <u>intrinsic</u> part of a graphic novel. Also be sure that the visuals you include vividly illustrate the characters' situation.

 **What Do You Think Now** Can a graphic novel be as powerful and effective as a prose novel? Review the selection, noting examples from the text to support your opinion.

A Noiseless Flash
from Hiroshima

What human needs and
desires do we have in
common?

QuickWrite

If you were witness to a catastrophic event, such as
a war, how might it affect you? Write a paragraph or
two expressing your thoughts and feelings.

John Hersey
(1914–1993)

Pulitzer
Prize
WINNER

The great scientist Albert Einstein ordered a
thousand copies of it. *The New Yorker* magazine
devoted an entire issue to it. The Book-of-the-
Month Club gave it to members free, saying
that no book "could be of more importance at this moment to
the human race." The book is *Hiroshima,* and the author is John
Hersey.

World Traveler and Writer

John Hersey was born in China and lived there until age ten. He
graduated from Yale University and studied at Cambridge University in England. He reported for *Time* and *Life* magazines from
the South Pacific and the Mediterranean during World War II.

Not satisfied with simply reporting facts, he became a novelist as well. His best-selling *A Bell for Adano* won a Pulitzer Prize
in 1945. The book analyzes the American military government's
struggles to establish democracy in the formerly fascist Italy.

The Nonfiction Novel

With the 1946 publication of *Hiroshima,* Hersey launched a new
literary form: the nonfiction novel which combines narrative
and journalistic techniques. He took an almost incomprehensible act, the dropping of an atomic bomb on a civilian population, and showed how it affected the lives of six survivors.
Through their eyes, readers could experience this catastrophe
as if it were happening to their own friends and neighbors.

Hiroshima became a national event. The American Broadcasting Company (ABC) had the book read aloud on its radio
stations. Hersey became famous as a writer who could make
history understandable. While teaching at his alma mater, Yale
University, he continued to write fiction that dramatized social
issues and grappled with modern atrocities.

Hiroshima remains Hersey's crowning achievement, both
as a record of inhumanity and as a testimony of conscience on
behalf of the writer, his nation, and all peoples of the world.

Think
About the
Writer

If John Hersey were writing about
social and political issues today, what
events might he choose to cover?

Reader/Writer
Notebook

Use your **RWN** to complete the activities for this selection.

Literary Focus

Subjective and Objective Reporting In **subjective reporting,** a writer openly expresses personal emotions and attitudes toward the events and characters in his or her writing. In **objective reporting,** a writer keeps his or her emotions at a distance and focuses on observable, verifiable facts. Objective reporting is <u>intrinsically</u> factual, so, often, the only way we can understand the writer's feelings about the subject is to analyze closely the details the writer has chosen to include or to leave out. With this in mind, why might some consider Hersey's book a political document?

Literary Perspectives Apply the literary perspective described on page 1069 as you read this reportage.

Reading Focus

Reading Closely for Details Hersey describes the effects of the atomic bombing of Hiroshima by focusing on six witnesses' stories, each with his or her own section in the text. As you read, note the many precise details about each person Hersey uses to lend his account authenticity. Why does Hersey particularly concentrate on these six witnesses?

Into Action Use a graphic organizer like the one below. Choose three of the six witnesses, and take brief notes on key details that Hersey provides about each of them, such as their jobs, their specific locations, and so on.

Character	Description/Characteristics
Dr. Fujii	doctor; prosperous; wife and children staying in Osaka
Mrs. Nakamura	

Writing Focus

Think as a Reader/Writer

Find It in Your Reading Hersey's narrative uses a cinematic approach much like that employed by a movie or documentary filmmaker. Without offering any authorial commentary or explanation, it simply focuses on six survivors of the atomic blast. The descriptions are like filmed close-ups: sharply detailed views of people going about their daily lives, then reacting to the bomb. As you read, use your *Reader/Writer Notebook* to record ideas about how this technique lends a sense of reality and authenticity to each scene. Why would Hersey take such care in his portrayals?

Language Coach

Noun-Forming Suffixes A suffix is a word part that attaches to the end of a word or root. The suffix *—ence* turns a verb—an action word—into a noun, which names a person, place, or thing. What verb is the root of *abstinence*?

A NOISELESS FLASH

from Hiroshima

by **John Hersey**

Read with a Purpose
Read to discover how six civilians survived the Hiroshima atomic bombing.

Build Background

War erupted between the United States and Japan on December 7, 1941, when Japanese bombers broke the stillness of a Sunday morning and blasted the U.S. naval base at Pearl Harbor in Hawaii. By August 1945, the war in Europe had ended, but the United States and its allies had not yet defeated Japan. To bring the long war to a close, the United States used its newest and most lethal weapon. The atomic bombs struck twice—first the Japanese city of Hiroshima and then, three days later, the city of Nagasaki. It was the world's first—and to date, its last—use of atomic weapons in war. Between 70,000 and 80,000 people were killed in Hiroshima. In Nagasaki, 35,000 to 40,000 people perished.

View of the mushroom cloud forming over Hiroshima from an Air Force plane soon after the atomic bomb was dropped.

At exactly fifteen minutes past eight in the morning, on August 6, 1945, Japanese time, at the moment when the atomic bomb flashed above Hiroshima, Miss Toshiko Sasaki, a clerk in the personnel department of the East Asia Tin Works, had just sat down at her place in the plant office and was turning her head to speak to the girl at the next desk. At that same moment, Dr. Masakazu Fujii was settling down cross-legged to read the Osaka *Asahi*[1] on the porch of his private hospital, overhanging one of the seven deltaic rivers which divide Hiroshima; Mrs. Hatsuyo Nakamura, a tailor's widow, stood by the window of her kitchen, watching a neighbor tearing down his house because it lay in the path of an air-raid-defense fire lane; Father Wilhelm Kleinsorge, a German priest of the Society of Jesus,[2] reclined in his underwear on a cot on the top floor of his order's three-story mission house, reading a Jesuit magazine, *Stimmen der Zeit*;[3] Dr. Terufumi Sasaki, a young member of the surgical staff of the city's large, modern Red Cross Hospital, walked along one of the hospital corridors with a blood specimen for a Wassermann test[4] in his hand; and the Reverend Mr. Kiyoshi Tanimoto, pastor of the Hiroshima Methodist Church, paused at the door of a rich man's house in Koi, the city's western suburb, and prepared to unload a handcart full of things he had evacuated from town in fear of the massive B-29 raid which everyone expected Hiroshima to suffer. A hundred thousand people were killed by the atomic bomb, and these six were among the survivors. They still wonder why they lived when so many others died. Each of them counts many small items of chance or volition—a step taken in time, a decision to go indoors, catching one streetcar instead of the next—that spared him. And now each knows that in the act of survival he lived a dozen lives and saw more death than he ever thought he would see. At the time, none of them knew anything. **(A)**

The Reverend Mr. Tanimoto got up at five o'clock that morning. He was alone in the parsonage, because for some time his wife had been commuting with their year-old baby to spend nights with a friend in Ushida, a suburb to the north. Of all the important cities of Japan, only two, Kyoto[5] and Hiroshima, had not been visited in strength by *B-san,* or Mr. B, as the Japanese, with a mixture of respect and unhappy familiarity, called the B-29; and Mr. Tanimoto, like all his neighbors and friends, was almost sick with anxiety. He had heard uncomfortably detailed accounts of mass raids on Kure, Iwakuni, Tokuyama, and other nearby towns; he was sure Hiroshima's turn would come soon. He had slept badly the night before, because there had been several air-raid warnings. Hiroshima had been getting such warnings almost every night for weeks, for at that time the B-29s were using Lake Biwa, northeast of Hiroshima, as a rendezvous point,

---

1. *Asahi:* Japanese for "morning sun." The Osaka *Asahi* is the city newspaper.
2. **Society of Jesus:** Roman Catholic religious order of priests and brothers, also known as the Jesuit (JEHZH oo iht) order.
3. *Stimmen der Zeit* (SHTIHM uhn dehr tsyt): German for "Voices of the Times."
4. **Wassermann test:** test used to diagnose syphilis.

---

5. **Kyoto** (kee OH toh): city some two hundred miles east of Hiroshima.

Literary Perspectives

Analyzing Historical Context Some works of literature are timeless. *Hiroshima,* however, is deeply rooted in historical events. It was published one year after the bombing of Hiroshima. American life was just beginning to return to normal. Throughout the war years, Americans were not encouraged to think of the Japanese as objects of sympathy. They were objects of deep hatred. Hersey's account of the bombing, however, struck a chord with the U.S. public. War-weary Americans still wanted to know what happened to Hiroshima. Hersey's account is a window into that period. As you read, think about how the historical context affected Hersey's style of writing, his tone, and his choice of detail. Think about what made this account so relevant in 1946 and what makes it relevant today.

As you read, be sure to notice the questions in the text, which will guide you in using this perspective.

(A) Literary Focus Subjective and Objective Reporting Why does Hersey write the first paragraph as if it were a newspaper article?

Vocabulary **rendezvous** (RAHN day voo) *n.* used as *adj.:* designated for a meeting.

and no matter what city the Americans planned to hit, the Super-fortresses streamed in over the coast near Hiroshima. The frequency of the warnings and the continued abstinence of Mr. B with respect to Hiroshima had made its citizens jittery; a rumor was going around that the Americans were saving something special for the city.

Mr. Tanimoto is a small man, quick to talk, laugh, and cry. He wears his black hair parted in the middle and rather long; the prominence of the frontal bones just above his eyebrows and the smallness of his moustache, mouth, and chin give him a strange, old-young look, boyish and yet wise, weak and yet fiery. He moves nervously and fast, but with a restraint which suggests that he is a cautious, thoughtful man. He showed, indeed, just those qualities in the uneasy days before the bomb fell. Besides having his wife spend the nights in Ushida, Mr. Tanimoto had been carrying all the portable things from his church, in the close-packed residential district called Nagaragawa, to a house that belonged to a rayon manufacturer in Koi, two miles from the center of town. The rayon man, a Mr. Matsui, had opened his then unoccupied estate to a large number of his friends and acquaintances, so that they might evacuate whatever they wished to a safe distance from the probable target area. Mr. Tanimoto had had no difficulty in moving chairs, hymnals, Bibles, altar gear, and church records by pushcart himself, but the organ console and an upright piano required some aid. A friend of his named Matsuo had, the day before, helped him get the piano out to Koi; in return, he had promised this day to assist Mr. Matsuo in hauling out a daughter's belongings. That is why he had risen so early. **Ⓑ**

Mr. Tanimoto cooked his own breakfast. He felt awfully tired. The effort of moving the piano the day before, a sleepless night, weeks of worry and unbalanced diet, the cares of his parish—all combined to make him feel hardly adequate to the new day's work. There was another thing, too: Mr. Tanimoto had studied theology at Emory College, in Atlanta, Georgia; he had graduated in 1940; he spoke excellent English;

he dressed in American clothes; he had corresponded with many American friends right up to the time the war began; and among a people obsessed with a fear of being spied upon—perhaps almost obsessed himself—he found himself growing increasingly uneasy. The police had questioned him several times, and just a few days before, he had heard that an influential acquaintance, a Mr. Tanaka, a retired officer of the Tokyo Kisen Kaisha steamship line, an anti-Christian, a man famous in Hiroshima for his showy philanthropies and notorious for his personal tyrannies, had been telling people that Tanimoto should not be trusted. In compensation, to show himself publicly a good Japanese, Mr. Tanimoto had taken on the chairmanship of his local *tonarigumi*, or Neighborhood Association, and to his other duties and concerns this position had added the business of organizing air-raid defense for about twenty families.

Before six o'clock that morning, Mr. Tanimoto started for Mr. Matsuo's house. There he found that their burden was to be a *tansu*, a large Japanese cabinet, full of clothing and household goods. The two men set out. The morning was perfectly clear and so warm that the day promised to be uncomfortable. A few minutes after they started, the air-raid siren went off—a minute-long blast that warned of approaching planes but indicated to the people of Hiroshima only a slight degree of danger, since it sounded every morning at this time, when an American weather plane came over. The two men pulled and pushed the handcart through the city streets. Hiroshima was a fan-shaped city, lying mostly on the six islands formed by the seven estuarial[6] rivers that branch out from the Ota River; its main commercial and residential districts, covering about four square miles in the center of the city, contained three-quarters of its population, which had been reduced by several evacuation programs from a wartime peak of 380,000 to about 245,000. Factories and other residential districts, or suburbs, lay compactly around the edges of

---

6. **estuarial** (ehs choo EHR ee uhl): on the estuary, or mouth, of a river, where freshwater meets saltwater.

Ⓑ Reading Focus **Reading Closely for Details** How does Mr. Tanimoto's appearance reflect his personality?

Vocabulary **abstinence** (AB stuh nuhns) *n.:* the act of refraining from a behavior.
notorious (noh TOHR ee uhs) *adj.:* widely and unfavorably known.

The *Enola Gay*, the plane that dropped the atomic bomb on Hiroshima, returning to base.

the city. To the south were the docks, an airport, and the island-studded Inland Sea. A rim of mountains runs around the other three sides of the delta. Mr. Tanimoto and Mr. Matsuo took their way through the shopping center, already full of people, and across two of the rivers to the sloping streets of Koi, and up them to the outskirts and foothills. As they started up a valley away from the tight-ranked houses, the all-clear sounded. (The Japanese radar operators, detecting only three planes, supposed that they comprised a reconnaissance.)[7] Pushing the handcart up to the rayon man's house was tiring, and the men, after they had maneuvered their load into the driveway and to the front steps, paused to rest awhile. They stood with a wing of the house between them and the city. Like most homes in this part of Japan, the house consisted of a wooden frame and wooden walls supporting a heavy tile roof. Its front hall, packed with rolls of bedding and clothing, looked like a cool cave full of fat cushions. Opposite the house, to the right of the front door, there was a large,

finicky rock garden. There was no sound of planes. The morning was still; the place was cool and pleasant. **C**

Then a tremendous flash of light cut across the sky. Mr. Tanimoto has a distinct recollection that it traveled from east to west, from the city toward the hills. It seemed a sheet of sun. Both he and Mr. Matsuo reacted in terror—and both had time to react (for they were 3,500 yards, or two miles, from the center of the explosion). Mr. Matsuo dashed up the front steps into the house and dived among the bedrolls and buried himself there. Mr. Tanimoto took four or five steps and threw himself between two big rocks in the garden. He bellied up very hard against one of them. As his face was against the stone, he did not see what happened. He felt a sudden pressure, and then splinters and pieces of board and fragments of tile fell on him. He heard no roar. (Almost no one in Hiroshima recalls hearing any noise of the bomb. But a fisherman in his sampan[8] on the Inland Sea near Tsuzu, the man with whom Mr. Tanimoto's mother-in-law and sister-in-law were living, saw the flash and heard a tremendous explosion;

---

7. **reconnaissance**: exploratory mission.

8. **sampan**: small, flat-bottomed boat.

C **Reading Focus** **Reading Closely for Details** What is the author's purpose for describing the geography of Hiroshima and the surrounding towns?

he was nearly twenty miles from Hiroshima, but the thunder was greater than when the B-29s hit Iwakuni, only five miles away.)

When he dared, Mr. Tanimoto raised his head and saw that the rayon man's house had collapsed. He thought a bomb had fallen directly on it. Such clouds of dust had risen that there was a sort of twilight around. In panic, not thinking for the moment of Mr. Matsuo under the ruins, he dashed out into the street. He noticed as he ran that the concrete wall of the estate had fallen over—toward the house rather than away from it. In the street, the first thing he saw was a squad of soldiers who had been burrowing into the hillside opposite, making one of the thousands of dugouts in which the Japanese apparently intended to resist invasion, hill by hill, life for life; the soldiers were coming out of the hole, where they should have been safe, and blood was running from their heads, chests, and backs. They were silent and dazed.

Under what seemed to be a local dust cloud, the day grew darker and darker. **D**

At nearly midnight, the night before the bomb was dropped, an announcer on the city's radio station said that about two hundred B-29s were approaching southern Honshu[9] and advised the population of Hiroshima to evacuate to their designated "safe areas." Mrs. Hatsuyo Nakamura, the tailor's widow, who lived in the section called Noboricho and who had long had a habit of doing as she was told, got her three children—a ten-year-old boy, Toshio, an eight-year-old girl, Yaeko, and a five-year-old girl, Myeko—out of bed and dressed them and walked with them to the military area known as the East Parade Ground, on the northeast edge of the city. There she unrolled some mats and the children lay down on them. They slept until about two, when they were awakened by the roar of the planes going over Hiroshima.

As soon as the planes had passed, Mrs. Nakamura started back with her children. They reached home a little after two-thirty and she immediately turned on the radio, which, to her distress, was just then broadcasting a fresh warning. When she looked at the children and saw how tired they were, and when she thought of the number of trips they had made in past weeks, all to no purpose, to the East Parade Ground, she decided that in spite of the instructions on the radio, she simply could not face starting out all over again. She put the children in their bedrolls on the floor, lay down herself at three o'clock, and fell asleep at once, so soundly that when the planes passed over later, she did not waken to their sound.

The siren jarred her awake at about seven. She arose, dressed quickly, and hurried to the house of Mr. Nakamoto, the head of her Neighborhood Association, and asked him what she should do. He said that she should remain at home unless an urgent warning—a series of intermittent blasts of the siren—was sounded. She returned home, lit the stove in the kitchen, set some rice to cook, and sat down to read that morning's Hiroshima *Chugoku*.[10] To her relief, the all-clear sounded at eight o'clock. She heard the children stirring, so she went and gave each of them a handful of peanuts and told them to stay on their bedrolls, because they were tired from the night's walk. She had hoped that they would go back to sleep, but the man in the house directly to the south began to make a terrible hullabaloo of hammering, wedging, ripping, and splitting. The prefectural government,[11] convinced, as everyone in Hiroshima was, that the city would be attacked soon, had begun to press with threats and warnings for the completion of wide fire lanes, which, it was hoped, might act in conjunction with the rivers to localize any fires started by an incendiary[12] raid; and the neighbor was reluctantly sacrificing his home to the city's safety. Just the day before, the prefecture had ordered all able-bodied girls from the secondary schools to spend a few days helping

---

9. **Honshu:** largest island of Japan. Hiroshima is in southern Honshu.

10. *Chugoku:* newspaper named for the region where Hiroshima is located.
11. **prefectural government:** regional administration of each Japanese district, called a prefecture.
12. **incendiary:** designed to cause fires.

D Literary Focus **Subjective and Objective Reporting** Does Hersey successfully avoid bias in his writing?

to clear these lanes, and they started work soon after the all-clear sounded. **E**

Mrs. Nakamura went back to the kitchen, looked at the rice, and began watching the man next door. At first, she was annoyed with him for making so much noise, but then she was moved almost to tears by pity. Her emotion was specifically directed toward her neighbor, tearing down his home, board by board, at a time when there was so much unavoidable destruction, but undoubtedly she also felt a generalized, community pity, to say nothing of self-pity. She had not had an easy time. Her husband, Isawa, had gone into the Army just after Myeko was born, and she had heard nothing from or of him for a long time, until, on March 5, 1942, she received a seven-word telegram: "Isawa died an honorable death at Singapore." She learned later that he had died on February 15th, the day Singapore fell, and that he had been a corporal. Isawa had been a not particularly prosperous tailor, and his only capital was a Sankoku sewing machine. After his death, when his allotments stopped coming, Mrs. Nakamura got out the machine and began to take in piecework[13] herself, and since then had supported the children, but poorly, by sewing. **F**

---

13. **piecework:** work paid at a fixed rate for each piece completed.

E Reading Focus **Reading Closely for Details** Why do you think Hersey includes such specific details in this paragraph?

F Literary Perspectives **Analyzing Historical Context** Do you think readers in 1946 would have felt sympathy for Mrs. Nakamura? Why or why not? Is Hersey presenting her sympathetically?

Hiroshima, Japan, 1945

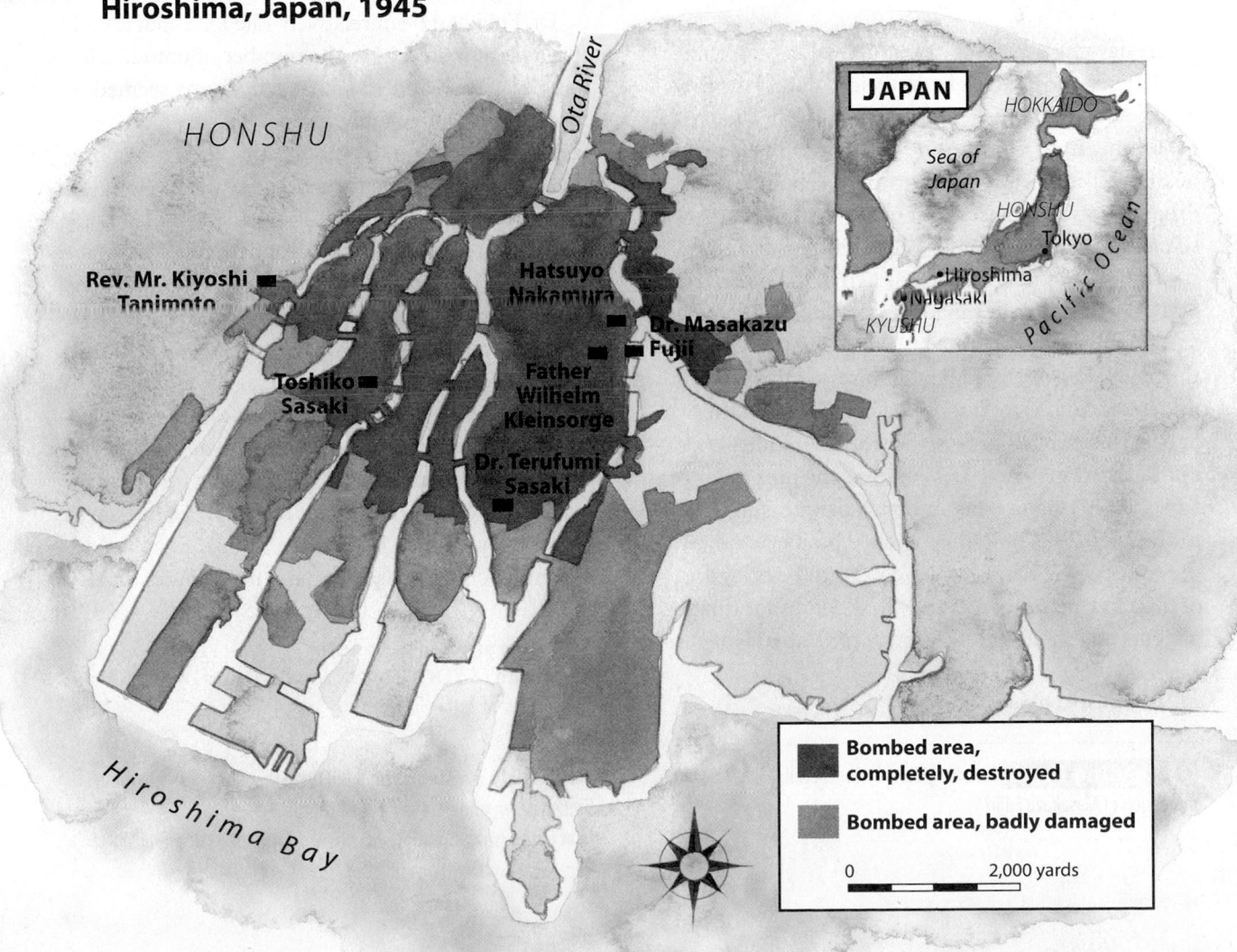

HONSHU

Ota River

Rev. Mr. Kiyoshi Tanimoto

Hatsuyo Nakamura

Dr. Masakazu Fujii

Toshiko Sasaki

Father Wilhelm Kleinsorge

Dr. Terufumi Sasaki

Hiroshima Bay

JAPAN

HOKKAIDO

Sea of Japan

HONSHU

Tokyo

Hiroshima

Nagasaki

KYUSHU

Pacific Ocean

Bombed area, completely, destroyed

Bombed area, badly damaged

0   2,000 yards

As Mrs. Nakamura stood watching her neighbor, everything flashed whiter than any white she had ever seen. She did not notice what happened to the man next door; the reflex of a mother set her in motion toward her children. She had taken a single step (the house was 1,350 yards, or three-quarters of a mile, from the center of the explosion) when something picked her up and she seemed to fly into the next room over the raised sleeping platform, pursued by parts of her house.

Timbers fell around her as she landed, and a shower of tiles pummeled her; everything became dark, for she was buried. The debris did not cover her deeply. She rose up and freed herself. She heard a child cry, "Mother, help me!," and saw her youngest—Myeko, the five-year-old—buried up to her breast and unable to move. As Mrs. Nakamura started frantically to claw her way toward the baby, she could see or hear nothing of her other children.

In the days right before the bombing, Dr. Masakazu Fujii, being prosperous, hedonistic,[14] and at the time not too busy, had been allowing himself the luxury of sleeping until nine or nine-thirty, but fortunately he had to get up early the morning the bomb was dropped to see a house guest off on a train. He rose at six, and half an hour later walked with his friend to the station, not far away, across two of the rivers. He was back home by seven, just as the siren sounded its sustained warning. He ate breakfast and then, because the morning was already hot, undressed down to his underwear and went out on the porch to read the paper. This porch—in fact, the whole building—was curiously constructed. Dr. Fujii was the proprietor of a peculiarly Japanese institution: a private, single-doctor hospital. This building, perched beside and over the water of the Kyo River, and next to the bridge of the same name, contained thirty rooms for thirty patients and their kinfolk—for, according to Japanese

_____
14. **hedonistic:** pleasure loving.

G **Reading Focus** **Reading Closely for Details** What is your impression of Masakazu Fujii?

custom, when a person falls sick and goes to a hospital, one or more members of his family go and live there with him, to cook for him, bathe, massage, and read to him, and to offer incessant familial sympathy, without which a Japanese patient would be miserable indeed. Dr. Fujii had no beds—only straw mats—for his patients. He did, however, have all sorts of modern equipment: an X-ray machine, diathermy[15] apparatus, and a fine tiled laboratory. The structure rested two-thirds on the land, one-third on piles over the tidal waters of the Kyo. This overhang, the part of the building where Dr. Fujii lived, was queer-looking, but it was cool in summer and from the porch, which faced away from the center of the city, the prospect of the river, with pleasure boats drifting up and down it, was always refreshing. Dr. Fujii had occasionally had anxious moments when the Ota and its mouth branches rose to flood, but the piling was apparently firm enough and the house had always held. **G**

Dr. Fujii had been relatively idle for about a month because in July, as the number of untouched cities in Japan dwindled and as Hiroshima seemed more and more inevitably a target, he began turning patients away, on the ground that in case of a fire raid he would not be able to evacuate them. Now he had only two patients left—a woman from Yano, injured in the shoulder, and a young man of twenty-five recovering from burns he had suffered when the steel factory near Hiroshima in which he worked had been hit. Dr. Fujii had six nurses to tend his patients. His wife and children were safe; his wife and one son were living outside Osaka, and another son and two daughters were in the country on Kyushu.[16] A niece was living with him, and a maid and a manservant. He had little to do and did not mind, for he had saved some money. At fifty, he was healthy, convivial, and calm, and he was pleased to pass the evenings drink-

_____
15. **diathermy:** heat treatment.
16. **Kyushu** (KYOO SHOO): southernmost of the principal islands of Japan.

Vocabulary **debris** (duh BREE) *n.:* the remains of anything broken down or destroyed; ruins; rubble.
sustained (suh STAYND) *v.* used as *adj.:* ongoing, continuous.
convivial (kuhn VIHV ee uhl) *adj.:* jovial, sociable.

ing whiskey with friends, always sensibly and for the sake of conversation. Before the war, he had affected brands imported from Scotland and America; now he was perfectly satisfied with the best Japanese brand, Suntory.

Dr. Fujii sat down cross-legged in his underwear on the spotless matting of the porch, put on his glasses, and started reading the Osaka *Asahi*. He liked to read the Osaka news because his wife was there. He saw the flash. To him—faced away from the center and looking at his paper—it seemed a brilliant yellow. Startled, he began to rise to his feet. In that moment (he was 1,550 yards from the center), the hospital leaned behind his rising and, with a terrible ripping noise, toppled into the river. The doctor, still in the act of getting to his feet, was thrown forward and around and over; he was buffeted and gripped; he lost track of everything, because things were so speeded up; he felt the water.

Dr. Fujii hardly had time to think that he was dying before he realized that he was alive, squeezed tightly by two long timbers in a V across his chest, like a morsel suspended between two huge chopsticks— held upright, so that he could not move, with his head miraculously above water and his torso and legs in it. The remains of his hospital were all around him in a mad assortment of splintered lumber and materials for the relief of pain. His left shoulder hurt terribly. His glasses were gone. **(H)**

Father Wilhelm Kleinsorge, of the Society of Jesus, was, on the morning of the explosion, in rather frail condition. The Japanese wartime diet had not sustained him, and he felt the strain of being a foreigner in an increasingly xenophobic[17] Japan; even a German, since the defeat of the Fatherland,[18] was

---

17. **xenophobic** (zehn uh FOH bihk): fearing or disliking foreigners.
18. **defeat of the Fatherland:** Germany surrendered to the Allies on May 7, 1945, approximately three months before the bombing of Hiroshima.

(H) **Literary Focus** Subjective and Objective Reporting Why might Hersey want to avoid being too subjective?

Godzilla and the Atomic Bomb

"The theme of the film, from the beginning, was the terror of the bomb. Mankind had created the bomb, and now nature was going to take revenge on mankind."

—*Tomoyuki Tanaka*, Godzilla *producer*

The original *Godzilla* movie was released in Tokyo on November 3, 1954, nine years after atomic bombs were dropped on Hiroshima and Nagasaki. The producer of the original *Godzilla* movie, Tomoyuki Tanaka, witnessed the destruction caused by the atomic bomb. In his movie, Godzilla is a prehistoric monster who has been awakened and has undergone mutations as a result of atomic tests in the ocean. Godzilla levels Tokyo before a scientist successfully kills him with an oxygen destroyer.

Ask Yourself
How can a subjective, fictional story sometimes shed light on objective reality?

Poster for the Japanese movie *Gojira (Godzilla)*, 1954.

unpopular. Father Kleinsorge had, at thirty-eight, the look of a boy growing too fast—thin in the face, with a prominent Adam's apple, a hollow chest, dangling hands, big feet. He walked clumsily, leaning forward a little. He was tired all the time. To make matters worse, he had suffered for two days, along with Father Cieslik, a fellow-priest, from a rather painful and urgent diarrhea, which they blamed on the beans and black ration bread they were obliged to eat. Two other priests then living in the mission compound, which was in the Noboricho section—Father Superior LaSalle and Father Schiffer—had happily escaped this affliction.

Father Kleinsorge woke up about six the morning the bomb was dropped, and half an hour later—he was a bit tardy because of his sickness—he began to read Mass in the mission chapel, a small Japanese-style wooden building which was without pews, since its worshipers knelt on the usual Japanese matted floor, facing an altar graced with splendid silks, brass, silver, and heavy embroideries. This morning, a Monday, the only worshipers were Mr. Takemoto, a theological student living in the mission house; Mr. Fukai, the secretary of the diocese;[19] Mrs. Murata, the mission's devoutly Christian housekeeper; and his fellow-priests. After Mass, while Father Kleinsorge was reading the Prayers of Thanksgiving, the siren sounded. He stopped the service and the missionaries retired across the compound to the bigger building. There, in his room on the ground floor, to the right of the front door, Father Kleinsorge changed into a military uniform which he had acquired when he was teaching at the Rokko Middle School in Kobe and which he wore during air-raid alerts.   **I**

After an alarm, Father Kleinsorge always went out and scanned the sky, and in this instance, when he stepped outside, he was glad to see only the single weather plane that flew over Hiroshima each day about this time. Satisfied that nothing would happen, he went in and breakfasted with the other Fathers on substitute coffee and ration bread, which, under

the circumstances, was especially repugnant to him. The Fathers sat and talked awhile, until, at eight, they heard the all-clear. They went then to various parts of the building. Father Schiffer retired to his room to do some writing. Father Cieslik sat in his room in a straight chair with a pillow over his stomach to ease his pain, and read. Father Superior LaSalle stood at the window of his room, thinking. Father Kleinsorge went up to a room on the third floor, took off all his clothes except his underwear, and stretched out on his right side on a cot and began reading his *Stimmen der Zeit*.

After the terrible flash—which, Father Kleinsorge later realized, reminded him of something he had read as a boy about a large meteor colliding with the earth—he had time (since he was 1,400 yards from the center) for one thought: A bomb has fallen directly on us. Then, for a few seconds or minutes, he went out of his mind.   **J**

Father Kleinsorge never knew how he got out of the house. The next things he was conscious of were that he was wandering around in the mission's vegetable garden in his underwear, bleeding slightly from small cuts along his left flank; that all the buildings round about had fallen down except the Jesuits' mission house, which had long before been braced and double-braced by a priest named Gropper, who was terrified of earthquakes; that the day had turned dark; and that Murata-*san*, the housekeeper, was nearby, crying over and over, "*Shu Jesusu, awaremi tamai!* Our Lord Jesus, have pity on us!"

On the train on the way into Hiroshima from the country, where he lived with his mother, Dr. Terufumi Sasaki, the Red Cross Hospital surgeon, thought over an unpleasant nightmare he had had the night before. His mother's home was in Mukai-hara, thirty miles from the city, and it took him two hours by train and tram to reach the hospital. He had slept uneasily all night and had wakened an hour earlier than usual, and, feeling sluggish and slightly feverish, had debated whether to go to the hospital at all; his sense of duty finally forced him to go, and he had started out on an earlier train than he took most mornings.

---

19. **diocese**: church district administered by a bishop.

I Reading Focus **Reading Closely for Details** Why is it important for the reader to know the times at which the survivors woke up and arrived at work?

J Literary Perspectives **Analyzing Historical Context** How do you think Hersey's readers would have reacted to this paragraph in 1946? How does Hersey's tone reflect his awareness of his 1946 audience?

The dream had particularly frightened him because it was so closely associated, on the surface at least, with a disturbing actuality. He was only twenty-five years old and had just completed his training at the Eastern Medical University, in Tsingtao, China. He was something of an idealist and was much distressed by the inadequacy of medical facilities in the country town where his mother lived. Quite on his own, and without a permit, he had begun visiting a few sick people out there in the evenings, after his eight hours at the hospital and four hours' commuting. He had recently learned that the penalty for practicing without a permit was severe; a fellow-doctor whom he had asked about it had given him a serious scolding. Nevertheless, he had continued to practice. In his dream, he had been at the bedside of a country patient when the police and the doctor he had consulted burst into the room, seized him, dragged him outside, and beat him up cruelly. On the train, he just about decided to give up the work in Mukai-hara, since he felt it would be impossible to get a permit, because the authorities would hold that it would conflict with his duties at the Red Cross Hospital.

At the terminus, he caught a streetcar at once. (He later calculated that if he had taken his customary train that morning, and if he had had to wait a few minutes for the streetcar, as often happened, he would have been close to the center at the time of the explosion and would surely have perished.) He arrived at the hospital at seven-forty and reported to the chief surgeon. A few minutes later, he went to a room on the first floor and drew blood from the arm of a man in order to perform a Wassermann test. The laboratory containing the incubators[20] for the test was on the third floor. With the blood specimen in his left hand, walking in a kind of distraction he had felt all morning, probably because of the dream and his restless night, he started along the main corridor on

20. **incubators:** equipment providing a favorable environment for the growth of cell cultures.

his way toward the stairs. He was one step beyond an open window when the light of the bomb was reflected, like a gigantic photographic flash, in the corridor. He ducked down on one knee and said to himself, as only a Japanese would, "Sasaki, *gambare!* Be brave!" Just then (the building was 1,650 yards from the center), the blast ripped through the hospital. The glasses he was wearing flew off his face; the bottle of blood crashed against one wall; his Japanese slippers zipped out from under his feet—but otherwise, thanks to where he stood, he was untouched. **Ⓚ**

HE HAD TIME... FOR ONE THOUGHT: A BOMB HAS FALLEN DIRECTLY ON US.

Dr. Sasaki shouted the name of the chief surgeon and rushed around to the man's office and found him terribly cut by glass. The hospital was in horrible confusion: Heavy partitions and ceilings had fallen on patients, beds had overturned, windows had blown in and cut people, blood was spattered on the walls and floors, instruments were everywhere, many of the patients were running about screaming, many more lay dead. (A colleague working in the laboratory to which Dr. Sasaki had been walking was dead; Dr. Sasaki's patient, whom he had just left and who a few moments before had been dreadfully afraid of syphilis, was also dead.) Dr. Sasaki found himself the only doctor in the hospital who was unhurt.

Dr. Sasaki, who believed that the enemy had hit only the building he was in, got bandages and began to bind

Vocabulary **idealist** (y DEE uh lihst) *n.*: a person who cherishes high principles or goals.

Ⓚ **Literary Focus** Subjective and Objective Reporting Is the fragment "said to himself, as only a Japanese would" objective or subjective?

(below and center) Hiroshima soon after the atomic-bomb blast.

Analyzing Visuals

Viewing and Interpreting How do these photographs help you visualize the effect of the atomic bombings on Hiroshima and Nagasaki?

the wounds of those inside the hospital; while outside, all over Hiroshima, maimed and dying citizens turned their unsteady steps toward the Red Cross Hospital to begin an invasion that was to make Dr. Sasaki forget his private nightmare for a long, long time.

Miss Toshiko Sasaki, the East Asia Tin Works clerk, who is not related to Dr. Sasaki, got up at three o'clock in the morning on the day the bomb fell. There was extra housework to do. Her eleven-month-old brother, Akio, had come down the day before with a serious stomach upset; her mother had taken him to the Tamura Pediatric Hospital and was staying there with him. Miss Sasaki, who was about twenty, had to cook breakfast for her father, a brother, a sister, and herself, and—since the hospital, because of the war, was unable to provide food—to prepare a whole day's

meals for her mother and the baby, in time for her father, who worked in a factory making rubber earplugs for artillery crews, to take the food by on his way to the plant. When she had finished and had cleaned and put away the cooking things, it was nearly seven. The family lived in Koi, and she had a forty-five-minute trip to the tin works, in the section of town called Kannon-machi. She was in charge of the personnel records in the factory. She left Koi at seven, and as soon as she reached the plant, she went with some of the other girls from the personnel department to the factory auditorium. A prominent local Navy man, a former employee, had committed suicide the day before by throwing himself under a train—a death considered honorable enough to warrant a memorial service, which was to be held at the tin works at ten o' clock that morning. In the large hall, Miss Sasaki and

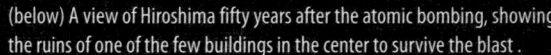

(below) A view of Hiroshima fifty years after the atomic bombing, showing the ruins of one of the few buildings in the center to survive the blast .

the others made suitable preparations for the meeting. This work took about twenty minutes.

Miss Sasaki went back to her office and sat down at her desk. She was quite far from the windows, which were off to her left, and behind her were a couple of tall bookcases containing all the books of the factory library, which the personnel department had organized. She settled herself at her desk, put some things in a drawer, and shifted papers. She thought that before she began to make entries in her lists of new employees, discharges, and departures for the Army, she would chat for a moment with the girl at her right. Just as she turned her head away from the windows, the room was filled with a blinding light. She was paralyzed by fear, fixed still in her chair for a long moment (the plant was 1,600 yards from the center).

Everything fell, and Miss Sasaki lost consciousness. The ceiling dropped suddenly and the wooden floor above collapsed in splinters and the people up there came down and the roof above them gave way; but principally and first of all, the bookcases right behind her swooped forward and the contents threw her down, with her left leg horribly twisted and breaking underneath her. There, in the tin factory, in the first moment of the atomic age, a human being was crushed by books. **L** **M**

L **Reading Focus** **Reading Closely for Details** Why does Hersey emphasize the fact that Miss Sasaki was "crushed by books"?

M **Literary Focus** **Subjective and Objective Reporting** Does the author remain completely objective?

A Noiseless Flash *from* Hiroshima

Respond and Think Critically

Reading Focus

Quick Check

1. What do the six survivors do for a living?

2. Why did many residents of Hiroshima have family who lived in other cities?

3. What was daily life in Hiroshima like in the months leading up to the bombing?

4. What responsibility does Dr. Sasaki face after the bomb falls?

Read with a Purpose

5. How did these six people manage to survive an attack that killed thousands?

Reading Skills: Reading Closely for Details

6. As you read "A Noiseless Flash," you recorded details Hersey includes about three of the witnesses. Add a third <u>component</u> to your chart titled "Words to Describe Bombing." Briefly record some of the words each witness used to describe his or her direct experience of the bombing. Think about how each person's choice of words contributes to the story as a whole.

Character	Description/ Characteristics	Words to Describe Bombing
Dr. Fujii	doctor; prosperous; wife and children staying in Osaka	"Toppled into the river"; "buffeted and gripped"

Literary Focus

Literary Analysis

7. **Summarize** What did Mrs. Nakamura do the night and the morning before the bomb fell?

8. **Interpret** Explain the significance of the term *B-san.*

9. **Infer** Why does the author tell how far each survivor was from the center of the explosion?

10. **Literary Perspectives** What made this account relevant to readers in 1946? What answers might readers have been searching for? Is our purpose for reading it today different? Explain.

Literary Skills: Subjective and Objective Reporting

11. **Evaluate** Is this selection more subjective or objective? Why do you think so? Make a list of specific words that support your opinion of the text as subjective or objective.

Literary Skills Review: Characterization

12. **Analyze** How does the author describe, or **characterize,** the six survivors? What details does he include that make them realistic for the reader?

Writing Focus

Think as a Reader/Writer

Use It in Your Writing Imitating the cinematic technique that Hersey uses in his writing, write a brief character sketch of a person as if you are following your character with a camera. Hersey uses cinematic details to highlight important characteristics of each survivor. Use your "camera" the same way to convey essential information to your reader about the person you describe.

What Do **You Think Now**

How does Hersey convey the shock and horror of the bombing? Are words sometimes insufficient to <u>transmit</u> an enormity such as the Hiroshima bombing? Explain.

Vocabulary Development

✓ Vocabulary Check

Answer the following questions. Be sure you can justify your responses.

1. Would the middle of the street be a good place for a **rendezvous**?

2. If a dinner guest told you of her **abstinence** from dairy products, would you serve her a glass of milk?

3. If a gangster is **notorious,** are the police probably on the lookout for him?

4. Would a park full of **debris** be a good place for children to play?

5. Does a **sustained** alarm continue to ring for a long time?

6. Would you invite a **convivial** person to a party?

7. Does an **idealist** have many skeptical ideas?

Language Coach

Noun-Forming Suffixes A suffix is a word part that attaches to the end of a word or root. Each of the following suffixes forms a noun: –cy, –ence, –ety, and –ist. Find nouns containing these suffixes in the sentences below. Then, write down as many words related to those nouns as you can think of.

EXAMPLE: "Mr. Tanimoto, like all his neighbors and friends, was almost sick with *anxiety*."

Related words: *anxious, anguish, anger*

1. "The frequency of the warnings and the continued abstinence of Mr. B with respect to Hiroshima had made its citizens jittery . . . "

2. "He was something of an idealist and was much distressed by the inadequacy of medical facilities in the country town where his mother lived."

SKILLS FOCUS Literary Skills Analyze subjective and objective reporting; analyze characterization; analyze historical context. Reading Skills Read closely for details. Vocabulary Skills Demonstrate word knowledge. Writing Skills Use descriptive language; describe a person; explore the significance of personal experiences, events, and conditions; use writing as a tool for learning and research.

CHOICES

As you respond to the Choices, use these **Academic Vocabulary** words as appropriate: component, diverse, intrinsic, potential, transmit.

REVIEW
Discuss an Event
Timed ⌐**Writing** Write a brief passage about an event of national or historical importance within the last five years that has had an effect on your life. Explain in detail the integral components of the event and the impact it has had on you and others.

CONNECT
Research War Reports
Use the library or Internet to locate various pieces of reportage on a recent war, such as the Vietnam War or the war in Iraq. As you read, note instances in which the writers of these pieces seem to have been influenced by Hersey's nonfiction narrative style in *Hiroshima*.

EXTEND
Explore Historical Context
Partner Activity With a partner, research how America's decision to drop the atomic bomb on Hiroshima and Nagasaki came to pass. Who made the decision? What factors contributed to it? What were some of the reactions to the bombings? Write a brief report about your findings and present it to your class.

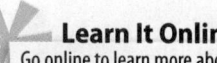
Learn It Online
Go online to learn more about the decision to use the atomic bomb on Hiroshima and Nagasaki.

 go.hrw.com L11-1081 Go

Desert Run

What human needs and desires do we have in common?

QuickTalk

Imagine being unjustly removed from the society in which you were born and raised. What would it feel like to be on the outside looking in? Do you think you would want to return to your old surroundings once you were released? Why or why not? Discuss your thoughts with a group, sharing experiences and anecdotes from your own life or the lives of others.

Mitsuye Yamada
(1923–   )

In her writing, Mitsuye Yamada focuses on issues of race and gender discrimination, which she experienced firsthand as a Japanese American woman growing up during World War II. Yamada's identity is divided between two worlds. Her work as a writer and an English professor reflects the internal and external conflicts she experiences "straddling" two cultures.

Between Two Worlds

Yamada was born in Japan on July 5, 1923. Three years later, her family moved to Seattle, Washington, where her father worked for the U.S. Immigration Service and served as president of a Japanese poetry society. He instilled in his daughter a love of literature and a deep respect for Japanese culture.

Breaking from Tradition

After the Japanese attacked Pearl Harbor, in 1941, President Roosevelt signed a law calling for the detention of all persons of Japanese ancestry in internment camps. In 1942, Yamada and her family were sent to a "relocation" camp in Idaho. Two thirds of detainees were U.S. citizens by birth, yet some of the them were held for years and were never charged with a crime.

Yamada and her brother were allowed to leave the camp after pledging allegiance to America and renouncing loyalty to the emperor of Japan. However, Yamada's parents refused to forsake their cultural heritage and remained in the camp. Yamada never forgot the humiliation that her family and her people suffered under this racist policy. Her first publication, *Camp Notes and Other Poems,* recounts the events of that time, and subsequent books of poetry, such as *Desert Run: Poems and Stories,* also deal with themes of captivity and mistreatment. Poetry, she says, is "a continuous process of making connections as I live my life. It holds my life together."

In 1981, Yamada and poet Nellie Wong created a biographical documentary called *Mitsuye and Nellie: Two Asian-American Woman Poets,* in which they break the tradition of silence and candidly tell about their families' hardships.

Think About the Writer

Why is it important to respect and honor one's cultural heritage? Why is it difficult when others do not respect cultural differences?

Reader/Writer Notebook

Use your **RWN** to complete the activities for this selection.

Literary Focus

Figures of Speech A **figure of speech** is a word or phrase that describes one thing in terms of something else and is not meant to be taken literally. Figurative language takes <u>diverse</u> forms. **Personification** gives objects or animals human qualities. **Hyperbole** uses exaggeration or overstatement for effect. A **symbol** is a figure of speech in which a person, place, thing, or event stands for something else. For example, a skull and crossbones is a public symbol of death. Remember that **similes** and **metaphors** are also common types of figurative language.

Reading Focus

Using Context Clues If you come across a word you don't understand, it helps to look at its context, or the words and sentences surrounding it, for clues to its meaning. There are several different types of context clues. Three common types are

- **definition, or restatement**—Look for an actual definition or rephrasing of the word in more familiar terms.
- **synonyms**—Look for clues that the unfamiliar word is similar in meaning to a familiar word or phrase.
- **contrasting words**—Sometimes an unfamiliar word is contrasted with a familiar word or concept.

Into Action Use a chart like the one below to record words from the poem that are difficult or unfamiliar. For each word, note the clues to its meaning that you find in the surrounding lines.

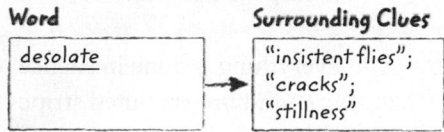

Word	Surrounding Clues
desolate	"insistent flies"; "cracks"; "stillness"

Language Coach

Common Word Pairs Some words are frequently paired. The adjective *peripheral* means "at the edge of something." You will often find it in the phrase *peripheral vision*, which refers to the edges of a person's field of sight. *Marrow* can mean "the center or essence of something," but is more commonly near the word *bone*. Bone marrow is the soft tissue that fills the cavities of bones. What does the word pair *discreet distance* mean?

Writing Focus

Think as a Reader/Writer

Find It in Your Reading Yamada uses animal **imagery** to convey meaning in her poem. As you read the poem, note in your *Reader/Writer Notebook* the animals she mentions and record your thoughts about what the imagery implies.

Learn It Online
Go online to listen to this poem.

go.hrw.com | L11-1083 | **Go**

DESERT RUN
by **Mitsuye Yamada**

The obelisk below marks the site of the Manzanar War Relocation Center, which held nearly 10,000 Japanese Americans during World War II.

I

I return to the desert
where criminals
were abandoned to wander
away to their deaths
5   where scorpions
spiders
snakes
lizards
and rats
10   live in outcast harmony Ⓐ
where the sculptor's wreck
was reclaimed
by the gentle drifting sands.

We approach the dunes while
15   the insistent flies bother our ears
the sound of crunching gravel under
our shoes cracks the desolate stillness
and opens our way.

Everything is done in silence here:
20   the wind fingers fluted stripes
over mounds and mounds of sand
the swinging grasses sweep
patterns on the slopes
the sidewinder passes out of sight. Ⓑ
25   I was too young to hear silence before.

Ⓐ **Literary Focus** **Figures of Speech** How do the criminals and the various desert creatures act as metaphors for the speaker's situation?

Ⓑ **Reading Focus** **Using Context Clues** What do you think a "sidewinder" is? On what context clues did you base your guess?

A soldier (right) escorts Japanese Americans to a relocation center in 1942.

II

I spent 547 sulking days here
in my own dreams
there was not much to marvel at
I thought
30   only miles of sagebrush and
lifeless sand.

I watched the most beautiful
sunsets in the world and saw nothing
forty years ago
35   I wrote my will here
my fingers moved slowly in the
hot sand the texture of whole wheat flour
three words: I died here
the winds filed them away.

40   I am back to claim my body
my carcass lies
between the spiny branches
of two creosote bushes
it looks strangely like a small calf
45   left to graze and die
half of its bones are gone
after all these years   **C**

but no matter
I am satisfied
50   I take a dry stick
and give myself
a ritual burial.

III

Like the bull snakes brought
into this desert by the soldiers
55   we were transported here
to drive away rattlers
in your nightmares
we were part of some one's plan
to spirit away spies
60   in your peripheral vision.

My skin turned pink brown
in the bright desert light
I slithered in the matching sand
doing what you put me here to do
65   we were predators at your service
I put your mind at ease.

I am that odd creature
the female bull snake
I flick my tongue in your face
70   an image trapped in your mirror.
You will use me or
you will honor me in a shrine
to keep me pure.   **D**

C **Literary Focus** Figures of Speech   What two things does the speaker compare in lines 40–47? What is the effect of the simile?

D **Reading Focus** Using Context Clues   How do the words "keep me pure" help you understand what a "shrine" is?

IV

At night the outerstellar darkness
75 above is only an arm's length away
I am pressed by the silence around me
the stars are bold as big as quarters **E**
against the velvet blue sky
their beams search for the marrow
80 of my bones
I shiver as I stumble my way to
the outhouse.

In the morning we find
kangaroo rats
85 have built mounds of messy homes
out of dry sticks and leavings
behind our wagon
They have accepted our alien presence.
The night creatures keep a discreet
90 distance.

V

The desert is the lungs of the world.
This land of sudden lizards and nappy ants
is only useful when not used
We must leave before we feel we can
95 change it.
When we leave the dirt roads
my body is thankful for the
paved ride the rest of the way
home.
100 Rows of yucca trees with spiked crowns
wave stiffly at us
Some watch us arms akimbo.

I cannot stay in the desert
where you will have me nor
105 will I be brought back in a cage
to grace your need for exotica. **F**
I write these words at night
for I am still a night creature
but I will not keep a discreet distance
110 If you must fit me to your needs
I will die
and so will you.

E Literary Focus Figures of Speech Which figure of speech is used in this line—metaphor, simile, or hyperbole? How can you tell?

F Reading Focus Using Context Clues What do you think the word "exotica" means based on its context?

SKILLS FOCUS **Literary Skills** Analyze figures of speech; analyze tone. **Reading Skills** Use context clues to determine the meaning of words. **Writing Skills** Incorporate imagery in writing.

Respond and Think Critically

Reading Focus

Quick Check

1. How would you describe the landscape in the poem?

2. What happened to the speaker in this landscape?

3. To what animal does the speaker compare herself in part III?

4. What happens to the speaker in part V?

Read with a Purpose

5. In what way does the desert landscape add to the speaker's emotions?

Reading Skills: Using Context Clues

6. In line 20, the word *fluted* is used to describe an aspect of the desert. From the context, do you think this refers to something seen rather than heard? Support your answer with references to specific parts of the poem.

7. Look back at the flow chart you completed as you read the poem. Add a third item to your chart titled "Meaning." Then, write down what you think the word means in the context of the poem.

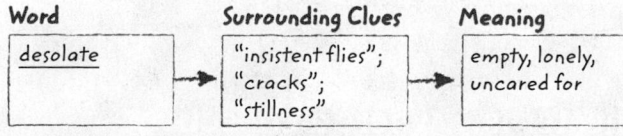

Word	Surrounding Clues	Meaning
desolate	"insistent flies"; "cracks"; "stillness"	empty, lonely, uncared for

Literary Focus

Literary Analysis

8. **Interpret** Why do you think the author uses words like *abandoned* and *outcast* in the first stanza?

9. **Analyze** What is the significance of the 547 days mentioned in part II?

10. **Extend** What can be difficult about visiting a place from one's past?

Literary Skills: Figures of Speech

11. **Analyze** List the similes you find in this poem.

12. **Interpret** Explain the figure of speech in this line: "The desert is the lungs of the world" (line 91).

13. **Draw Conclusions** Explain why these lines are an example of personification: "Rows of yucca trees with spiked crowns / wave stiffly at us / Some watch us arms akimbo" (lines 100–103).

Literary Skills Review: Tone

14. **Evaluate** Remember that **tone** is the attitude a writer takes toward the subject of a work. How does Yamada choose specific words to convey how she feels about her subject? How would you describe the tone of the poem?

Writing Focus

Think as a Reader/Writer

Use It in Your Writing Use the notes you compiled about animal imagery to write your own descriptive paragraph or poem about an animal that is special to you in some way. As in "Desert Run," let the aspects of the landscape and nature help you tap into the emotions associated with this animal.

What Do **You Think Now** How did the speaker's experience change her views of her fellow citizens? Are her feelings justified, in your opinion?

Contemporary Drama

Actors Audra McDonald, Sean Combs, and Phylicia Rashad take a curtain call after a 2004 production of *A Raisin in the Sun*.

CONTENTS

"To me the theater is…where a collective
mass of people, through the genius of
some author, is able to project its terrors
and its hopes and to symbolize them."

— **Arthur Miller**

American Drama by Robert Anderson

Characteristics of Twentieth-Century American Drama

- Focuses frequently on social issues and on the lives of ordinary people
- Provides in-depth exploration of the inner lives of characters
- Shifts gradually from more realistic to more experimental productions by the end of the century

Contemporary Drama

Drama is probably the most difficult form of writing; it certainly seems to take the longest to learn. According to a saying, young poets are eighteen, young novelists are twenty-four, and young playwrights are thirty.

George S. Kaufman, a noted American writer of comedies during the 1920s and 1930s, said that writing plays was not an art but a trick. Art or trick, it is difficult, possibly because a play is not finished as soon as it is written. There remains the painful and pleasurable process of bringing the play's potential to life on stage, with the help of a director, actors, set designer, costume designer, lighting technician, stagehands, musicians—and a responsive audience. Producing a play is a team effort, and much can go wrong.

When a play is not successful, it is usually because the writer has failed to conceive the story in dramatic terms. Playwrights must place their characters in a situation involving **conflict** and then make the audience understand that it is not just any conflict. The character or characters must have something vital at stake. The major character who faces conflict is the **protagonist**, who drives the action forward. The protagonist's **external conflict** is usually with his or her opponent, the **antagonist.** Also warring with the protagonist are intrinsic doubts and fears, his or her **internal conflict.** Authors bring these elements to life by way of **exposition;** they "expose" the background of the situation with details.

American Drama

Eugene O'Neill (1888–1953) is generally considered the first important figure in American drama. Decades after the 1920 production of his first full-length play, *Beyond the Horizon,* he is still regarded as the most important playwright the United States has produced. American drama before O'Neill consisted mostly of shows and entertainments. These wildly theatrical spectacles often featured such delights as chariot races and burning cities, staged by means of special effects that dazzled audiences. Melodramas and farces were also written for famous actors, much as television shows today are created to display the personalities and talents of popular performers. In fact, O'Neill's own father, James O'Neill, spent the better part of his life touring in a spectacular melodrama based on Alexander Dumas's *The Count of Monte Cristo.*

There was great theatrical activity in the United States in the nineteenth century, a time when there were no movies, radio, or television. Every town of any size had its theater or "opera house" in which touring companies performed. Given the hunger for entertainment, one may wonder how no significant American drama was staged in the century that produced, among others, Melville, Emerson, Whitman, Dickinson, and Twain.

One explanation is that theater has usually followed the other arts, rather than leading the way toward new directions. Robert Sherwood, one of a group of notable American playwrights between 1920 and 1940, once said, "Drama travels in the caboose of literature." Theater seems to take up new attitudes, subject matter, and forms only after they have been transmitted by the other arts. For the most part, theater tends to dramatize accepted attitudes and values.

The reason is that theater is a social art, one we attend as part of a large group; we seem to respond to something new much more slowly as a group than we do as individuals. When you laugh or cry in the theater, your response is noticed. You are, in a sense, giving your approval, and this approval may be subject to criticism or condemnation by those sitting around you who are not laughing or crying. Furthermore, you may not be shocked to *read* about your secret thoughts, dreams, and desires, but if you see them shown on stage as you sit among a large audience, you may refuse to respond, refuse to acknowledge them. You may even rise up and stalk out of the theater.

Thus, the novel and, to some extent, the poetry of the nineteenth and early twentieth centuries were more daring than the theater in giving us a record of experience, in showing us life as it *is* lived rather than as it *should* be lived.

The Influence of Europe

European drama, which was to influence modern American drama profoundly, matured near the end of the nineteenth century with the achievements of three playwrights: the Norwegian Henrik Ibsen, the Swede August Strindberg, and the Russian Anton Chekhov.

Ibsen tackled subjects such as guilt, sexuality, and mental illness—subjects that had never before been so realistically and disturbingly portrayed on stage. Strindberg brought to his characterizations an unprecedented level of psychological complexity. Along with Ibsen and Strindberg, Chekhov shifted the subject matter of drama from wildly theatrical displays of external action to internal action and emotions, as well as the concerns of everyday life. Chekhov once remarked, "People don't go to the North Pole and fall off icebergs. They go to the office and quarrel with their wives and eat cabbage soup."

Ibsen, Strindberg, and Chekhov bequeathed to their American counterparts plays about life as it is actually lived. They presented characters and situations realistically, in what has been called the "slice of life" dramatic technique.

Redirecting Realism

Realistic drama rejected previous romanticized approaches. Instead, playwrights favored settings, characters, actions, and emotions drawn directly from ordinary life and sought to mirror that life as accurately as possible. Early in the twentieth century, realism became the dominant mode of American drama. As with all theatrical revolutions, the movement toward realism began apart from the commercial theater. However, very soon after the new drama succeeded in little theaters off Broadway (about 1916), the commercial theater adopted realism, too.

In 1916 and 1917, two small theater groups in New York—the Provincetown Players and the Washington Square Players—began to produce new American plays. They provided a congenial home for new American playwrights, notably Eugene O'Neill, whose first one-act plays about the sea were produced by the Provincetown Players in Greenwich Village in 1916. (New movements in the theater have often begun with one-act plays. In addition to O'Neill, Tennessee Williams, Clifford Odets, and Edward Albee all started with short plays.) These theater groups seemed to have no program. They were not sure what they were for, but they were sure what they were against: the established commercial theater. They would produce any play, in any style, that commercial theater would not touch.

O'Neill gravitated to such theaters. Well aware of Sigmund Freud and his new theories about the complex self, O'Neill tried especially hard to reveal more than realism—or Naturalism—could normally reveal. "The old naturalism," he wrote, "no longer applies. We have taken too many snapshots of each other in every graceless position; we have endured too much from the banality of surfaces."

In *The Great God Brown* (1926), O'Neill experimented with using masks to differentiate between two sides of a personality. In *Days Without End* (1934), he had two actors play one character to achieve the same end.

Post–World War II Playwrights

The post-World War II years brought two important figures to prominence in American drama: Arthur Miller (1915–2005) and Tennessee Williams (1911–1983). Although other playwrights, such as William Inge

Elizabeth Franz and Brian Dennehy in the 50th Anniversary Broadway production of Arthur Miller's *Death of a Salesman* (1999).

(1913–1973), have contributed striking and effective plays, Miller and Williams remain the dominant figures in the second half of the century. Miller and Williams represent the two principal movements in modern American drama: realism, and realism combined with an attempt at something more imaginative. American playwrights have continued to try to break away from pure realism or to blend it with more poetic expression, as in Miller's *Death of a Salesman* (1949), Williams's *The Glass Menagerie* (1944), and Thornton Wilder's *Our Town* (1938) and *The Skin of Our Teeth* (1942).

Delving into personal matters and complexity of character, Tennessee Williams became the playwright of our souls. In play after play, he probed the psychological intricacies of his characters, especially of his female characters: Amanda and Laura in *The Glass Menagerie* (1944), Blanche in *A Streetcar Named Desire* (1947), and Alma in *Summer and Smoke* (1948).

The components of Williams's plays are generally realistic, even when the scenes involve colorful and intense characters. However, Williams often added less realistic, more imaginative touches to his plays, such as "music in the wings" or symbolic props, like Laura's unicorn in *The Glass Menagerie* or the looming statue of Eternity in *Summer and Smoke.* He conceived his plays in visually arresting, colorful, theatrical environments— an effort in which he was aided by the imaginative

designer Jo Mielziner, who designed the sets for many of his plays.

Current Trends in American Drama

Realism in drama was conceived as a revolt against crude theatricalism. Currently, there is a revolt against realism itself in American drama. Naturally, the movement is toward theatricalism again, with its emphasis on stage effects and imaginative settings. The revolt does not confine itself to a particular manner of staging; instead, it extends to the texture of language and plot in the scripts themselves.

The moral and religious certainties that once bound people together exert little or no force on many modern audiences. Some people believe that survival itself depends on a willingness to accept life as formless or meaningless.

Some American playwrights found this new outlook on life impossible to express in the orderly "beginning, middle, end" format of realism. They borrowed from Europe a theater of fragmentation, impressions, and stream of consciousness that was called expressionist. **Expressionist drama** is aimed at the revelation of characters' inner consciousness without reference to a logical sequence of surface actions. Many writers who used expressionist techniques in drama came to be called playwrights of the Theater of the Absurd. Samuel Beckett (1906–1989) and Eugene Ionesco (1912–1994) are among the founders of the Theater of the Absurd. The drama critic Martin Esslin has written this about the Absurdists:

"The action of a play of the Theater of the Absurd is not intended to tell a story but to communicate a pattern of poetic images. To give but one example: Things happen in [Samuel Beckett's] *Waiting for Godot* (1952), but these things do not constitute a plot or a story; they are an image of Beckett's intuition that *nothing really ever happens* in man's existence."

The trouble with a static play that mirrors a static life is that the play itself is static. It is an image, a picture, and a picture can absorb our interest for only so long because it lacks the progression and development, the <u>intrinsic</u> drama of a story. We can observe a situation without development for only a short period of time. Perhaps this is why so many of the Absurdist plays *are* only one act, such as Beckett's *Krapp's Last Tape* (1958) and Ionesco's *The Bald Soprano* (1950).

The most significant Absurdist in the United States has been Edward Albee (1928–   ). Albee is not a pure Absurdist since, like all innovative playwrights, he experiments with <u>diverse</u> forms. From 1959 to 1970, Albee produced a play every year. These works ranged from his startling one-act debut, *The Zoo Story* (1959), through the Absurdist play *The American Dream* (1961), to the savage and electrifying domestic drama *Who's Afraid of Virginia Woolf?* (1962), which made Albee world famous.

Experimental drama has increased the options that are open to playwrights. There are practically no conventions in the theater anymore; there is simply a stage and an audience. Playwrights are free to load the stage with scenery, lights, and special effects, but they are equally free—as the playwright was in the age of Shakespeare—to have an actor gesture toward one side of an utterly bare stage and say, "This is the Forest of Arden."

Producing a Play

The English plays of the late Middle Ages were called miracle plays because they often dealt with stories of miracles from the Bible or the lives of saints. Any modern-day American play might also be called a miracle play because it is a miracle that it was written and even more of a miracle that it was produced. In the United States today, drama is dependent on money. Only a few institutional theaters are able to present plays with little or no regard for profit. Most of the plays that are produced (and that therefore stand a chance of becoming part of our dramatic literature) are put on with the goal of making money.

Playbills for *Death of a Salesman* and *The Glass Menagerie*.
PLAYBILL®. All rights reserved. Used by permission.

To produce any writer's new play on Broadway today costs a minimum of half a million dollars. The **producers** (people who advance the money) willing to take such a risk are rare, although such risks *are* taken every season. Even though it operates in a very costly manner, the professional Broadway theater, to its credit, has been the launching pad for most of the distinguished plays in American dramatic literature. Recently, regional theaters throughout the country have been presenting new plays by both new and established playwrights. The Broadway producers often visit, look, and take whatever they want for production. For the most part, only a successful Broadway production gives a playwright enough income to plunge in and take the years necessary to write the next play. For that reason, Broadway remains the goal of most playwrights.

There are many stops on the way to New York, some of which will become full stops. Over ten thousand plays are copyrighted every year; this number probably represents only half of the plays actually written. Perhaps several hundred new plays are produced on stage *somewhere* around the country; maybe ten of those appear on Broadway.

Producers could not hope to cope with reading thousands and thousands of plays, so playwrights must generally find an agent who will handle their work. The agent is the producer's first line of defense.

Knowing their various tastes, the agent submits a play to likely producers who may take three months to a year to read it. They may admire the play but still be unwilling to produce it. One playwright used to say, "If they take you to lunch, they're not going to invest in your play." A good lunch is a consolation prize, and many playwrights have eaten very well off plays that were never produced.

However, if the producer should decide to finance the play, he or she then sits down with the playwright to go over changes suggested for the script or ideas for directors and actors. Authors maintain control over their scripts, and the playwright is very much involved in the selection of the director and the actors. Of course, since the theater is a collaborative medium, the playwright tries to get along with the producer. Nevertheless, if the playwright and producer discover during these preliminary talks that they have incompatible ideas, they can shake hands and part.

The director becomes the playwright's surrogate at rehearsals. In a sense, the director takes the play away from the playwright, and, finally, the actors take it away from both of them.

Rehearsals are both pleasurable and tense. Many components must mesh as the actors move forward to the climactic moment of opening night. Note that all the elements of drama itself are also present at play rehearsals: striving for a goal, having something at stake, and dealing with external and internal conflicts.

The Show Must Go On!

The play opens in a smaller city for a tryout run or in New York for previews. Sometimes all goes well, and the production needs only some refining and sharpening. More often, the play needs work, like rewriting. Edward Albee commented on his sense of worth and value as a writer: "[T]he final evaluation of a play has nothing to do with immediate audience or critical response. The playwright, along with any writer, composer, painter in this society, has got to have a terribly private view of his own value, of his own work. He's got to listen to his own voice primarily."

Sometimes the play needs new sets, new costumes, sometimes a new director or a new star. Chaos reigns until opening night when all the cast will suddenly come down with laryngitis, intestinal upsets, sinus trouble, or splitting headaches. Somehow, the curtain rises, and the show goes on.

The day after the opening, there may or not be a line of eager theatergoers at the box office. If there is, the playwright has created what may later be called an American classic, which will be performed around the world and will find its way into the anthologies you study in school. If there isn't a line, the playwright will quickly look around for a way to make a living while writing the next play—if he or she has the courage. The second instance is the more usual. The theater has been called the "fabulous invalid," always teetering on the edge of extinction. If so, playwrights themselves might be called the walking wounded—working, barely surviving, but finally enduring to try once again.

Ask Yourself

1. Explain the relationship between the protagonist and the antagonist in drama. How does this relationship mirror relationships in our everyday lives?

2. Compare and contrast "realistic drama" and "expressionist drama." Use a Venn diagram to record similarities and differences between the two types of theater. Then, explain which type of drama you would prefer to watch and why.

Learn It Online

Learn about drama through *PowerNotes* online.

go.hrw.com   L11-1093   **Go**

What Do You Think? What human needs and desires do we have in common?

🕐 **QuickWrite**

Have you, or has someone you know, ever been falsely accused of something? In a paragraph or two, explain the situation and how it was resolved.

Arthur Miller
(1915–2005)

The social injustices that this writer witnessed firsthand inspired him to write some of America's most famous dramas.

Early Success

Arthur Miller, considered by many to be the preeminent American playwright of the second half of the twentieth century, was born in New York City. His father's business was destroyed by the Great Depression, and the family suffered financial hardship.

In high school, Miller preferred sports to literature. But while attending the University of Michigan, he wrote *No Villain,* an award-winning play, switched his major from journalism to English, and became a playwright.

Red Hunts / Witch Hunts

Broadway produced Miller's first successful play, *All My Sons,* the New York Drama Critics' winner for 1947. The play's message about the need for moral responsibility would be repeated in Miller's future works. Two years later, Miller joined top-ranking American playwrights when the production of *Death of a Salesman,* his masterpiece, won him the Pulitzer Prize and the New York Drama Critics' Circle Award, among others.

In the 1950s, Senator Joseph McCarthy accused many prominent people, especially in the arts and show business, of being Communists in his infamous "Red hunts." Miller's friend and the director of his plays, Elia Kazan, denounced eight colleagues to McCarthy in 1952. *The Crucible* was produced the following year, calling to the public's mind what fear and lack of social responsibility can do as a "witch hunt" transpires. In 1954 Miller was denied a passport to attend the play's Belgian premiere. In 1956, McCarthy called upon Miller himself to "name names," but he refused to inform on his neighbors and friends.

Miller continued to write until his death, but he never surpassed the successes of *Death of a Salesman* and *The Crucible,* his most widely produced plays.

Think About the Writer Miller's sense of morality caused him to write about issues like the "Red hunt." If Miller were writing today, what issues might he write about?

Why I Wrote *The Crucible:*
An artist's answer to politics

by **Arthur Miller**

As I watched *The Crucible* taking shape as a movie over much of the past year, the sheer depth of time that it represents for me kept returning to mind. As those powerful actors blossomed on the screen, and the children and the horses, and the crowds and the wagons, I thought again about how I came to cook all this up nearly fifty years ago, in an America almost nobody I know seems to remember clearly. . . .

I remember those years—they formed *The Crucible's* skeleton—but I have lost the dead weight of the fear I had then. Fear doesn't travel well; just as it can warp judgment, its absence can diminish memory's truth. What terrifies one generation is likely to bring only a puzzled smile to the next. . . .

[Senator] McCarthy's power to stir fears of creeping Communism was not entirely based on illusion, of course. . . . From being our wartime ally, the Soviet Union rapidly became an expanding empire. In 1949, Mao Zedong took power in China. Western Europe also seemed ready to become Red, especially Italy, where the Communist Party was the largest outside Russia, and was growing. . . . McCarthy—brash and ill-mannered but to many authentic and true—boiled it all down to what anyone could understand: We had "lost China" and would soon lose Europe as well, because the State Department—staffed, of course, under Democratic presidents—was full of treasonous

pro-Soviet intellectuals. It was as simple as that. . . .

The Crucible was an act of desperation. . . . By 1950 when I began to think of writing about the hunt for Reds in America, I was motivated in some great part by the paralysis that had set in among many liberals who, despite their discomfort with the inquisitors' violations of civil rights, were fearful, and with good reason, of being identified as covert Communists if they should protest too strongly. . . .

I visited Salem for the first time on a dismal spring day in 1952. . . . In the gloomy courthouse there I read the transcripts of the witchcraft trials of 1692, as taken down in a primitive shorthand by ministers who were spelling each other. But there was one entry in Upham[1] in which the thousands of pieces I had come across were jogged into place. It was from a report written by the Reverend Samuel Parris, who was one of the chief instigators of the witch-hunt. "During the examination of Elizabeth Proctor, Abigail Williams, and Ann Putnam"—the two were "afflicted" teen-age accusers, and Abigail was Parris's niece—"both made offer to strike at said Proctor; but when Abigail's hand came near, it opened, whereas it was made up, into a fist before, and came down exceeding lightly as it drew near to said Proctor, and at length, with open and

---

1. **Charles W. Upham:** a mayor of Salem who published a two-volume study of the trials in 1867.

extended fingers, touched Proctor's hood very lightly. Immediately Abigail cried out her fingers, her fingers, her fingers burned. . . ."

In this remarkably observed gesture of a troubled young girl, I believed, a play became possible. Elizabeth Proctor had been the orphaned Abigail's mistress, and they had lived together in the same small house until Elizabeth fired the girl. By this time, I was sure, John Proctor had bedded Abigail, who had to be dismissed most likely to appease Elizabeth. There was bad blood between the two women now. That Abigail started, in effect, to condemn Elizabeth to death with her touch, then stopped her hand, then went through with it, was quite suddenly the human center of all this turmoil.

All this I understood. I had not approached the witchcraft out of nowhere or from purely social and political considerations. My own marriage of twelve years was teetering and I knew more than I wished to know about where the blame lay. That John Proctor the sinner might overturn his paralyzing personal guilt and become the most forthright voice against the madness around him was a reassurance to me, and, I suppose, an inspiration: It demonstrated that a clear moral outcry could still spring even from an ambiguously unblemished soul. Moving crabwise across the profusion of evidence, I sensed that I had at last found something of myself in it, and a play began to accumulate around this man.

—from *The New Yorker*; October 21 and 28, 1996

Hollywood writers arrive at court: Samuel Ortiz, Ring Lardner, Jr., Albert Maltz, Alvah Bessie, Lester Cole, Herbert Bieberman, and Edward Dmytryk face trial. 1950.

U.S. House of Representatives Committee on Un-American Activities investigates alleged Communist activities in the movie industry. 1947.

Drawing Conclusions by **Kylene Beers**

Although presents may come wrapped up neatly in a package, ideas in a text are rarely presented that way. Instead, authors reveal some messages directly but leave others unstated for readers to figure out on their own. To figure out a text, you make **inferences**—that is, you combine your own knowledge of the world with a careful reading of the text. When an inference leads you to a definite, final understanding of some part of the text, you are drawing (or reaching) **conclusions**.

The Crucible is set in Salem, Massachusetts, during the cold, dreary winter of 1691 and 1692. To write the play, Miller drew on historical accounts of the events that led to the Salem witch trials. When the daughter and the niece of Reverend Samuel Parris began having seizures, developed lesions on their skin, and seemed to be choked by invisible hands, a doctor diagnosed the girls as victims of malicious witchcraft.

Urged to name those responsible for bewitching them, the girls accused two unpopular women from the village, and Tituba, a slave from Barbados. During the subsequent trial the girls writhed and moaned and behaved as if they were being choked. The witch hunt had begun.

As you read Arthur Miller's interpretation of this historical event, think about his reasons for presenting characters in certain ways. Remember that *The Crucible* is a play, so most of the action is <u>transmitted</u> through dialogue and through interactions between characters. Pay attention to what characters say, how they say it, and how they react to the words and actions of other characters. You should also think about the possible motivations behind each character's actions.

It is not enough, however, just to have a set of opinions about the play. Drawing valid conclusions means being able to cite evidence to back up and support your ideas. Therefore, collecting evidence serves two purposes: Gathering it helps you draw valid conclusions, and citing it later will allow you to support and defend those conclusions. Use a chart to help you record the major characters' actions and dialogue.

Character	Character's Actions	Conclusion
Abigail Williams	Act One: First she denies accusations of witchcraft; later, admits to being forced to dance with the Devil.	She changes her story to become the accuser instead of the accused.

What do you think the author is implying in the following lines from Act Two?

> Why do you never wonder if Parris be innocent, or Abigail? Is the accuser always holy now? Were they born this morning as clean as God's fingers? I'll tell you what's walking Salem—vengeance is walking Salem. We are what we always were in Salem, but now the little crazy children are jangling the keys of the kingdom, and common vengeance writes the law!

Between June and September of 1692, nineteen people were hanged. One man, Giles Corey, who had refused to plead either innocent or guilty, was crushed to death under a pile of stones. In *The Crucible,* his last words are "More weight."

Your Turn

As the story of *The Crucible* unfolds, think about the truths we learn about the people of Salem village. How do you think the death of Giles Corey relates to events that took place during Arthur Miller's own lifetime? What conclusions can you draw about the author's motivations for including this character?

Learn It Online
Find graphic organizers online to help you as you read.

go.hrw.com   L11-1097   **Go**

Reader/Writer Notebook

Use your **RWN** to complete the activities for this selection.

Literary Focus

Motivation The reason for a character's behavior is **motivation.** Just like real people, fictional characters often have complex motivations, and their actions can result from several motivating factors. In *The Crucible,* Miller shows <u>diverse</u> and conflicting motivations at work in his characters.

Literary Perspectives Apply the literary perspective described on page 1100 as you read this play.

Reading Focus

Drawing Conclusions About Characters To understand a complex dramatic work like *The Crucible,* you need to interpret it. You should **draw conclusions,** or form opinions, about who the characters really are, why they behave the way they do, and what the larger meaning of their situation might be. As you read *The Crucible,* notice what the dialogue and actions <u>transmit</u> about the characters' values, emotions, motivations, and personal histories.

Into Action As you read each act, use a chart like the one below to record lines of dialogue that reveal key information about a character. After you finish reading, you can refer to your chart to draw conclusions about the characters.

Character	Dialogue (Act)
Parris	"I do not preach for children, Rebecca. It is not the children who are unmindful of their obligations toward this ministry." (Act One)

Writing Focus

Think as a Reader/Writer

Find It in Your Reading Miller uses stage directions to supplement the dialogue of his characters. The facial expressions, actions, and gestures of the actors convey information to the audience. In your *Reader/Writer Notebook,* record stage directions that help you understand the dialogue.

Vocabulary

theocracy (thee AHK ruh see) *n.:* a government ruled by religious authority. *Salem was ruled by a rigid Puritan theocracy.*

dissembling (dih SEHM blihng) *v.* used as *n.:* the hiding of one's feelings or motives. *Parris did not suspect Tituba of lying or dissembling.*

partisan (PAHR tih zuhn) *n.:* a strong supporter in a cause. *Some became partisans for the girls, but others opposed their actions.*

avidly (AV ihd lee) *adv.:* eagerly. *Abigail avidly pursues John Proctor, whom she loves.*

blasphemy (BLAS fuh mee) *n.:* words or actions that disrespect something sacred. *Hale thinks the village is guilty of blasphemy.*

deposition (DEHP uh ZIHSH uhn) *n.:* testimony given under oath at a trial. *John Proctor was forced to give a deposition.*

beguile (bih GYL) *v.:* mislead; deceive. *Rebecca will not allow the men to beguile her.*

adamant (AD uh muhnt) *adj.:* not giving in; immovable. *John Proctor was adamant and refused to give in to pressure.*

Language Coach

Parts of Speech The ending of a word may reveal that word's part of speech. The suffix *–tion* is usually at the end of nouns; the suffix *–ly* is often at the end of adverbs. Which Vocabulary words contain suffixes?

Learn It Online
Plunge into this play with the online video introduction.

go.hrw.com   L11-1098   Go

The Crucible

by **Arthur Miller**

Read with a Purpose

Read this play to discover how dialogue and actions reveal a character's values, emotions, motivations, and personal history.

Build Background

The Crucible is based on the witch trials that took place in 1692, in Salem, Massachusetts. Elizabeth Parris, daughter of Reverend Samuel Parris, and Abigail Williams, his niece, began acting strangely. Since no medical cause for their behavior could be found, doctors concluded that the girls were bewitched. Soon other girls began exhibiting the same behavior, crying out the names of women they knew and sparking the witch hunt. Over the next eight months, twenty-seven people were convicted, nineteen were hanged, one was crushed to death, and more than one hundred were imprisoned.

The Crucible *was first presented by Kermit Bloomgarden at the Martin Beck Theatre, New York City, January 22, 1953, with the following cast.*

Cast of Characters *(in order of appearance)*

Reverend Parris, *Fred Stewart*
Betty Parris, *Janet Alexander*
Tituba, *Jacqueline Andre*
Abigail Williams, *Madeleine Sherwood*
Susanna Walcott, *Barbara Stanton*
Mrs. Ann Putnam, *Jane Hoffman*
Thomas Putnam, *Raymond Bramley*
Mercy Lewis, *Dorothy Joliffe*
Mary Warren, *Jennie Egan*
John Proctor, *Arthur Kennedy*
Rebecca Nurse, *Jean Adair*
Giles Corey, *Joseph Sweeney*
Reverend John Hale, *E. G. Marshall*
Elizabeth Proctor, *Beatrice Straight*
Francis Nurse, *Graham Velsey*
Ezekiel Cheever, *Don McHenry*
Marshal Herrick, *George Mitchell*

Judge Hathorne, *Philip Coolidge*
Deputy Governor Danforth, *Walter Hampden*
Sarah Good, *Adele Fortin*
Hopkins, *Donald Marye*

Staged by Jed Harris
Settings by Boris Aronson
Costumes made and designed by Edith Lutyens

The play is set in Salem, Massachusetts, in 1692.

Act One (An Overture)
Home of Rev. Samuel Parris.

Act Two
John Proctor's house, eight days later.

Act Three
Salem meeting house, serving as the General Court.

Act Four
A cell in Salem jail, fall 1692.

Act One (An Overture)

A small upper bedroom in the home of REVEREND
SAMUEL PARRIS, *Salem, Massachusetts, in the spring
of the year 1692.*

*There is a narrow window at the left. Through its
leaded panes the morning sunlight streams. A candle
still burns near the bed, which is at the right. A chest,
a chair, and a small table are the other furnishings. At
the back a door opens on the landing of the stairway
to the ground floor. The room gives off an air of clean
spareness. The roof rafters are exposed, and the wood
colors are raw and unmellowed.*

As the curtain rises, REVEREND PARRIS *is
discovered kneeling beside the bed, evidently in prayer.
His daughter,* BETTY PARRIS, *aged ten, is lying on the
bed, inert.*

At the time of these events Parris was in his
middle forties. In history he cut a villainous path, and
there is very little good to be said for him. He believed
he was being persecuted wherever he went, despite his
best efforts to win people and God to his side. In meeting, he felt insulted if someone rose to shut the door
without first asking his permission. He was a widower
with no interest in children, or talent with them. He
regarded them as young adults, and until this strange
crisis he, like the rest of Salem, never conceived that
the children were anything but thankful for being permitted to walk straight, eyes slightly lowered, arms at
the sides, and mouths shut until bidden to speak. **Ⓐ**

His house stood in the "town"—but we today
would hardly call it a village. The meeting house was
nearby, and from this point outward—toward the
bay or inland—there were a few small-windowed,
dark houses snuggling against the raw Massachusetts
winter. Salem had been established hardly forty years
before. To the European world the whole province
was a barbaric frontier inhabited by a sect of fanat-
ics who, nevertheless, were shipping out products of
slowly increasing quantity and value.

No one can really know what their lives were like.
They had no novelists—and would not have permitted
anyone to read a novel if one were handy. Their creed
forbade anything resembling a theater or "vain enjoyment." They did not celebrate Christmas, and a holiday from work meant only that they must concentrate
even more upon prayer.

Which is not to say that nothing broke into this
strict and somber way of life. When a new farmhouse
was built, friends assembled to "raise the roof," and
there would be special foods cooked and probably
some potent cider passed around. There was a good
supply of ne'er-do-wells in Salem, who dallied at the
shovelboard in Bridget Bishop's tavern. Probably more
than the creed, hard work kept the morals of the place
from spoiling, for the people were forced to fight the
land like heroes for every grain of corn, and no man
had very much time for fooling around.

That there were some jokers, however, is indicated
by the practice of appointing a two-man patrol whose
duty was to "walk forth in the time of God's worship
to take notice of such as either lye about the meeting
house, without attending to the word and ordinances,
or that lye at home or in the fields without giving
good account thereof, and to take the names of such
persons, and to present them to the magistrates,
whereby they may be accordingly proceeded against."
This predilection for minding other people's business
was time-honored among the people of Salem, and
it undoubtedly created many of the suspicions which
were to feed the coming madness. It was also, in my
opinion, one of the things that a John Proctor would
rebel against, for the time of the armed camp had

Ⓐ **Reading Focus** **Drawing Conclusions About Characters**
What can you infer about Parris from the statement, "he felt insulted if
someone rose to shut the door without first asking his permission"?

almost passed, and since the country was reasonably—although not wholly—safe, the old disciplines were beginning to rankle. But, as in all such matters, the issue was not clearcut, for danger was still a possibility, and in unity still lay the best promise of safety.

The edge of the wilderness was close by. The American continent stretched endlessly west, and it was full of mystery for them. It stood, dark and threatening, over their shoulders night and day, for out of it Indian tribes marauded from time to time, and Reverend Parris had parishioners who had lost relatives to these heathen.

The parochial snobbery of these people was partly responsible for their failure to convert the Indians. Probably they also preferred to take land from heathens rather than from fellow Christians. At any rate, very few Indians were converted, and the Salem folk believed that the virgin forest was the Devil's last preserve, his home base and the citadel of his final stand. To the best of their knowledge the American forest was the last place on earth that was not paying homage to God.

For these reasons, among others, they carried about an air of innate resistance, even of persecution. Their fathers had, of course, been persecuted in England. So now they and their church found it necessary to deny any other sect its freedom, lest their New Jerusalem[1] be defiled and corrupted by wrong ways and deceitful ideas.

They believed, in short, that they held in their steady hands the candle that would light the world. We have inherited this belief, and it has helped and hurt us. It helped them with the discipline it gave them. They were a dedicated folk, by and large, and they had to be to survive the life they had chosen or been born into in this country. **Ⓑ**

The proof of their belief's value to them may be taken from the opposite character of the first Jamestown settlement, farther south, in Virginia. The Englishmen who landed there were motivated mainly by a hunt for profit. They had thought to pick off the wealth of the new country and then return rich to England. They were a band of individualists, and a much more ingratiating group than the Massachusetts men. But Virginia destroyed them. Massachusetts tried to kill off the Puritans, but they combined; they set up a communal society which, in the beginning, was little more than an armed camp with an autocratic and very devoted leadership. It was, however, an autocracy by consent, for they were united from top to bottom by a commonly held ideology whose perpetuation was the reason and justification for all their sufferings. So their self-denial, their purposefulness, their suspicion of all vain pursuits, their hard-handed justice were altogether perfect instruments for the conquest of this space so antagonistic to man.

But the people of Salem in 1692 were not quite the dedicated folk that arrived on the *Mayflower*. A vast differentiation had taken place, and in their own time a revolution had unseated the royal government and substituted a junta which was at this moment in power. The times, to their eyes, must have been out of joint, and to the common folk must have seemed as insoluble and complicated as do ours today. It is not hard to see how easily many could have been led to believe that the time of confusion had been brought upon them by deep and darkling forces. No hint of such speculation appears on the court record, but social disorder in any age breeds such mystical suspicions, and when, as in Salem, wonders are brought forth from below the social surface, it is too much to expect people to hold back very long from laying on the victims with all the force of their frustrations.

The Salem tragedy, which is about to begin in these pages, developed from a paradox. It is a paradox in whose grip we still live, and there is no prospect yet that we will discover its resolution. Simply, it was this: for good purposes, even high purposes, the people of Salem developed a theocracy, a combine of state and religious power whose function was to keep the community together, and to prevent any kind of disunity that might open it to destruction by material or ideological enemies. It was forged for a necessary purpose

---

1. **New Jerusalem:** in the New Testament (Revelation 21), the holy city of Heaven.

Ⓑ **Literary Perspectives** Analyzing Credibility What do you think Miller is saying about the beliefs of the characters in his play and of some of his contemporaries?

Vocabulary **theocracy** (thee AHK ruh see) *n.:* a government ruled by religious authority.

and accomplished that purpose. But all organization is and must be grounded on the idea of exclusion and prohibition, just as two objects cannot occupy the same space. Evidently the time came in New England when the repressions of order were heavier than seemed warranted by the dangers against which the order was organized. The witch-hunt was a perverse manifestation of the panic which set in among all classes when the balance began to turn toward greater individual freedom.

When one rises above the individual villainy displayed, one can only pity them all, just as we shall be pitied someday. It is still impossible for man to organize his social life without repressions, and the balance has yet to be struck between order and freedom.

The witch-hunt was not, however, a mere repression. It was also, and as importantly, a long overdue opportunity for everyone so inclined to express publicly his guilt and sins, under the cover of accusations against the victims. It suddenly became possible—and patriotic and holy—for a man to say that Martha Corey had come into his bedroom at night, and that, while his wife was sleeping at his side, Martha laid herself down on his chest and "nearly suffocated him." Of course it was her spirit only, but his satisfaction at confessing himself was no lighter than if it had been Martha herself. One could not ordinarily speak such things in public.

Long-held hatreds of neighbors could now be openly expressed, and vengeance taken, despite the Bible's charitable injunctions. Land-lust, which had been expressed by constant bickering over boundaries and deeds, could now be elevated to the arena of morality; one could cry witch against one's neighbor and feel perfectly justified in the bargain. Old scores could be settled on a plane of heavenly combat between Lucifer and the Lord; suspicions and the envy of the miserable toward the happy could and did burst out in the general revenge. **C**

REVEREND PARRIS *is praying now, and, though we cannot hear his words, a sense of his confusion hangs about him. He mumbles, then seems about to weep; then he weeps, then prays again; but his daughter does not stir on the bed.*

The door opens, and his Negro slave enters. TITUBA *is in her forties.* PARRIS *brought her with him from Barbados, where he spent some years as a merchant before entering the ministry. She enters as one does who can no longer bear to be barred from the sight of her beloved, but she is also very frightened because her slave sense has warned her that, as always, trouble in this house eventually lands on her back.*

Tituba, *already taking a step backward:* My Betty be hearty soon?
Parris: Out of here!
Tituba, *backing to the door:* My Betty not goin' die . . .
Parris, *scrambling to his feet in a fury:* Out of my sight! *She is gone.* Out of my— *He is overcome with sobs. He clamps his teeth against them and closes the door and leans against it, exhausted.* Oh, my God! God help me! *Quaking with fear, mumbling to himself through his sobs, he goes to the bed and gently takes* BETTY's *hand.* Betty. Child. Dear child. Will you wake, will you open up your eyes! Betty, little one . . .

He is bending to kneel again when his niece, ABIGAIL WILLIAMS, *seventeen, enters—a strikingly beautiful girl, an orphan, with an endless capacity for dissembling. Now she is all worry and apprehension and propriety.*

Abigail: Uncle? *He looks to her.* Susanna Walcott's here from Doctor Griggs.
Parris: Oh? Let her come, let her come.
Abigail, *leaning out the door to call to* SUSANNA, *who is down the hall a few steps:* Come in, Susanna.

SUSANNA WALCOTT, *a little younger than* ABIGAIL, *a nervous, hurried girl, enters.*

Parris, *eagerly:* What does the doctor say, child?
Susanna, *craning around* PARRIS *to get a look at* BETTY: He bid me come and tell you, reverend sir, that he cannot discover no medicine for it in his books.
Parris: Then he must search on.
Susanna: Aye, sir, he have been searchin' his books since he left you, sir. But he bid me tell you, that you might look to unnatural things for the cause of it.
Parris, *his eyes going wide:* No—no. There be no unnatural cause here. Tell him I have sent for

C Literary Perspectives **Analyzing Credibility** How could this desire for vengeance cloud the credibility of the witchcraft claims that people made?

Vocabulary **dissembling** (dih SEHM blihng) *v.* used as *n.:* the hiding of one's feelings or motives.

Reverend Hale of Beverly, and Mr. Hale will surely confirm that. Let him look to medicine and put out all thought of unnatural causes here. There be none.  **D**

Susanna: Aye, sir. He bid me tell you. *She turns to go.*

Abigail: Speak nothin' of it in the village, Susanna.

Parris: Go directly home and speak nothing of unnatural causes.

Susanna: Aye, sir. I pray for her. *She goes out.*

Abigail: Uncle, the rumor of witchcraft is all about; I think you'd best go down and deny it yourself. The parlor's packed with people, sir. I'll sit with her.

Parris, *pressed, turns on her:* And what shall I say to them? That my daughter and my niece I discovered dancing like heathen in the forest?

Abigail: Uncle, we did dance; let you tell them I confessed it—and I'll be whipped if I must be. But they're speakin' of witchcraft. Betty's not witched.

Parris: Abigail, I cannot go before the congregation when I know you have not opened with me. What did you do with her in the forest?

Abigail: We did dance, uncle, and when you leaped out of the bush so suddenly, Betty was frightened and then she fainted. And there's the whole of it.

Parris: Child. Sit you down.

Abigail, *quavering, as she sits:* I would never hurt Betty. I love her dearly.

Parris: Now look you, child, your punishment will come in its time. But if you trafficked with spirits in

---

D **Literary Focus** Motivation Why is Parris adamant that there is "no unnatural cause here"?

Analyzing Visuals

Viewing and Interpreting How do facial expressions and body language in this movie still contribute to the mood the playwright establishes in Act One? Explain your response.

Bruce Davison as Reverend Parris, Winona Ryder (right) as Abigail Williams in film version of *The Crucible*. 1996.

the forest I must know it now, for surely my enemies will, and they will ruin me with it. **E**

Abigail: But we never conjured spirits.

Parris: Then why can she not move herself since midnight? This child is desperate! ABIGAIL *lowers her eyes.* It must come out—my enemies will bring it out. Let me know what you done there. Abigail, do you understand that I have many enemies?

Abigail: I have heard of it, uncle.

Parris: There is a faction that is sworn to drive me from my pulpit. Do you understand that?

Abigail: I think so, sir.

Parris: Now then, in the midst of such disruption, my own household is discovered to be the very center of some obscene practice. Abominations are done in the forest—

Abigail: It were sport, uncle!

Parris, *pointing at* BETTY: You call this sport? *She lowers her eyes. He pleads:* Abigail, if you know something that may help the doctor, for God's sake tell it to me. *She is silent.* I saw Tituba waving her arms over the fire when I came on you. Why was she doing that? And I heard a screeching and gibberish coming from her mouth. She were swaying like a dumb beast over that fire!

Abigail: She always sings her Barbados songs, and we dance.

Parris: I cannot blink what I saw, Abigail, for my enemies will not blink it. I saw a dress lying on the grass.

Abigail, *innocently:* A dress?

Parris—*it is very hard to say:* Aye, a dress. And I thought I saw—someone naked running through the trees!

Abigail, *in terror:* No one was naked! You mistake yourself, uncle!

Parris, *with anger:* I saw it! *He moves from her. Then, resolved:* Now tell me true, Abigail. And I pray you feel the weight of truth upon you, for now my ministry's at stake, my ministry and perhaps your cousin's life. Whatever abomination you have done, give me all of it now, for I dare not be taken unaware when I go before them down there.

Abigail: There is nothin' more. I swear it, uncle.

Parris, *studies her, then nods, half convinced:* Abigail, I have fought here three long years to bend these stiff-necked people to me, and now, just now when some good respect is rising for me in the parish, you compromise my very character. I have given you a home, child, I have put clothes upon your back—now give me upright answer. Your name in the town—it is entirely white, is it not?

Abigail, *with an edge of resentment:* Why, I am sure it is, sir. There be no blush about my name.

Parris, *to the point:* Abigail, is there any other cause than you have told me, for your being discharged from Goody[2] Proctor's service? I have heard it said, and I tell you as I heard it, that she comes so rarely to the church this year for she will not sit so close to something soiled. What signified that remark?

Abigail: She hates me, uncle, she must, for I would not be her slave. It's a bitter woman, a lying, cold, sniveling woman, and I will not work for such a woman!

Parris: She may be. And yet it has troubled me that you are now seven month out of their house, and in all this time no other family has ever called for your service. **F**

Abigail: They want slaves, not such as I. Let them send to Barbados for that. I will not black my face for any of them! *With ill-concealed resentment at him:* Do you begrudge my bed, uncle?

Parris: No—no.

Abigail, *in a temper:* My name is good in the village! I will not have it said my name is soiled! Goody Proctor is a gossiping liar!

Enter MRS. ANN PUTNAM. *She is a twisted soul of forty-five, a death-ridden woman, haunted by dreams.*

Parris, *as soon as the door begins to open:* No—no, I cannot have anyone. *He sees her, and a certain deference springs into him, although his worry remains.* Why, Goody Putnam, come in.

Mrs. Putnam, *full of breath, shiny-eyed:* It is a marvel. It is surely a stroke of hell upon you.

Parris: No, Goody Putnam, it is—

---

2. **Goody:** formerly a title (short for *goodwife*) for a woman, especially a housewife or older woman.

E **Literary Focus** Motivation If Parris claims Betty is not sick from "unnatural causes," why would he accuse her and Abigail of "trafficking with spirits"? Explain.

F **Reading Focus** Drawing Conclusions About Characters What might Parris be accusing Abigail of? Why is it so troubling that she has been out of work for seven months?

Mrs. Putnam, *glancing at* BETTY: How high did she fly, how high?

Parris: No, no, she never flew—

Mrs. Putnam, *very pleased with it:* Why, it's sure she did. Mr. Collins saw her goin' over Ingersoll's barn, and come down light as bird, he says!

Parris: Now, look you, Goody Putnam, she never— *Enter* THOMAS PUTNAM, *a well-to-do, hard-handed landowner, near fifty.* Oh, good morning, Mr. Putnam.

Putnam: It is a providence the thing is out now! It is a providence. *He goes directly to the bed.*

Parris: What's out, sir, what's—?

MRS. PUTNAM *goes to the bed.*

Putnam, *looking down at* BETTY: Why, *her* eyes is closed! Look you, Ann.

Mrs. Putnam: Why, that's strange. *To* PARRIS: Ours is open.

Parris, *shocked:* Your Ruth is sick?

Mrs. Putnam, *with vicious certainty:* I'd not call it sick; the Devil's touch is heavier than sick. It's death, y'know, it's death drivin' into them, forked and hoofed.

Parris: Oh, pray not! Why, how does Ruth ail?

Mrs. Putnam: She ails as she must—she never waked this morning, but her eyes open and she walks, and hears naught, sees naught, and cannot eat. Her soul is taken, surely.

PARRIS *is struck.*

Putnam, *as though for further details:* They say you've sent for Reverend Hale of Beverly?

Parris, *with dwindling conviction now:* A precaution only. He has much experience in all demonic arts, and I—

Mrs. Putnam: He has indeed; and found a witch in Beverly last year, and let you remember that.

Parris: Now, Goody Ann, they only thought that were a witch, and I am certain there be no element of witchcraft here.

Putnam No witchcraft! Now look you, Mr. Parris—

Parris: Thomas, Thomas, I pray you, leap not to witchcraft. I know that you—you least of all, Thomas, would ever wish so disastrous a charge laid upon me. We cannot leap to witchcraft. They will howl me out of Salem for such corruption in my house.

A word about Thomas Putnam. He was a man with many grievances, at least one of which appears justified. Some time before, his wife's brother-in-law, James Bayley, had been turned down as minister of Salem. Bayley had all the qualifications, and a two-thirds vote into the bargain, but a faction stopped his acceptance, for reasons that are not clear.

Thomas Putnam was the eldest son of the richest man in the village. He had fought the Indians at Narragansett, and was deeply interested in parish affairs. He undoubtedly felt it poor payment that the village should so blatantly disregard his candidate for one of its more important offices, especially since he regarded himself as the intellectual superior of most of the people around him.

His vindictive nature was demonstrated long before the witchcraft began. A former Salem minister, George Burroughs, had had to borrow money to pay for his wife's funeral, and, since the parish was remiss in his salary, he was soon bankrupt. Thomas and his brother John had Burroughs jailed for debts the man did not owe. The incident is important only in that Burroughs succeeded in becoming minister where Bayley, Thomas Putnam's brother-in-law, had been rejected; the motif of resentment is clear here. Thomas Putnam felt that his own name and the honor of his family had been smirched by the village, and he meant to right matters however he could. **G**

> My name is good in the village! I will not have it said my name is soiled! Goody Proctor is a gossiping liar!

G **Literary Focus** **Motivation** How might Putnam's family history prejudice the way Putnam sees Parris, or any other minister?

Another reason to believe him a deeply embittered man was his attempt to break his father's will, which left a disproportionate amount to a stepbrother. As with every other public cause in which he tried to force his way, he failed in this.

So it is not surprising to find that so many accusations against people are in the handwriting of Thomas Putnam, or that his name is so often found as a witness corroborating the supernatural testimony, or that his daughter led the crying-out at the most opportune junctures of the trials, especially when—But we'll speak of that when we come to it.

Putnam—*at the moment he is intent upon getting* PARRIS, *for whom he has only contempt, to move toward the abyss:* Mr. Parris, I have taken your part in all contention here, and I would continue; but I cannot if you hold back in this. There are hurtful, vengeful spirits layin' hands on these children.

Parris: But, Thomas, you cannot—

Putnam: Ann! Tell Mr. Parris what you have done.

Mrs. Putnam: Reverend Parris, I have laid seven babies unbaptized in the earth. Believe me, sir, you never saw more hearty babies born. And yet, each would wither in my arms the very night of their birth. I have spoke nothin', but my heart has clamored intimations. And now, this year, my Ruth, my only—I see her turning strange. A secret child she has become this year, and shrivels like a sucking mouth were pullin' on her life too. And so I thought to send her to your Tituba— (H)

Parris: To Tituba! What may Tituba—?

Mrs. Putnam: Tituba knows how to speak to the dead, Mr. Parris.

Parris: Goody Ann, it is a formidable sin to conjure up the dead!

Mrs. Putnam: I take it on my soul, but who else may surely tell us what person murdered my babies?

Parris, *horrified:* Woman!

Mrs. Putnam: They were murdered, Mr. Parris! And mark this proof! Mark it! Last night my Ruth were ever so close to their little spirits; I know it, sir. For how else is she struck dumb now except some power of darkness would stop her mouth? It is a marvelous sign, Mr. Parris!

Putnam: Don't you understand it, sir? There is a murdering witch among us, bound to keep herself in the dark. PARRIS *turns to* BETTY, *a frantic terror rising in him.* Let your enemies make of it what they will, you cannot blink it more.

Parris, *to* ABIGAIL: Then you were conjuring spirits last night.

Abigail, *whispering:* Not I, sir—Tituba and Ruth.

Parris, *turns now, with new fear, and goes to* BETTY, *looks down at her, and then, gazing off:* Oh, Abigail, what proper payment for my charity! Now I am undone.

Putnam: You are not undone! Let you take hold here. Wait for no one to charge you—declare it yourself. You have discovered witchcraft— (I)

Parris: In my house? In my house, Thomas? They will topple me with this! They will make of it a—

Enter MERCY LEWIS, *the* PUTNAMS' *servant, a fat, sly, merciless girl of eighteen.*

Mercy: Your pardons. I only thought to see how Betty is.

Putnam: Why aren't you home? Who's with Ruth?

Mercy: Her grandma come. She's improved a little, I think—she give a powerful sneeze before.

Mrs. Putnam: Ah, there's a sign of life!

Mercy: I'd fear no more, Goody Putnam. It were a grand sneeze; another like it will shake her wits together, I'm sure. *She goes to the bed to look.*

Parris: Will you leave me now, Thomas? I would pray a while alone.

Abigail: Uncle, you've prayed since midnight. Why do you not go down and—

Parris: No—no. *To* PUTNAM: I have no answer for that crowd. I'll wait till Mr. Hale arrives. *To get* MRS. PUTNAM *to leave:* If you will, Goody Ann . . .

Putnam: Now look you, sir. Let you strike out against the Devil, and the village will bless you for it! Come down, speak to them—pray with them. They're thirsting for your word, Mister! Surely you'll pray with them.

Parris, *swayed:* I'll lead them in a psalm, but let you say nothing of witchcraft yet. I will not discuss it. The

---

(H) **Reading Focus** Drawing Conclusions About Characters
What kind of mother might Mrs. Putnam be to her only child Ruth?

(I) **Literary Focus** Motivation Should Parris take this advice? Why or why not?

1106 Unit 6 • Collection 15

cause is yet unknown. I have had enough contention since I came; I want no more.

Mrs. Putnam: Mercy, you go home to Ruth, d'y'hear?

Mercy: Aye, mum.

MRS. PUTNAM *goes out.*

Parris, *to* ABIGAIL: If she starts for the window, cry for me at once.

Abigail: I will, uncle.

Parris, *to* PUTNAM: There is a terrible power in her arms today. *He goes out with* PUTNAM.

Abigail, *with hushed trepidation:* How is Ruth sick?

Mercy: It's weirdish, I know not—she seems to walk like a dead one since last night.

Abigail, *turns at once and goes to* BETTY, *and now, with fear in her voice:* Betty? BETTY *doesn't move. She shakes her.* Now stop this! Betty! Sit up now!

BETTY *doesn't stir.* MERCY *comes over.*

Mercy: Have you tried beatin' her? I gave Ruth a good one and it waked her for a minute. Here, let me have her.

Abigail, *holding* MERCY *back:* No, he'll be comin' up. Listen, now; if they be questioning us, tell them we danced—I told him as much already.

Mercy: Aye. And what more?

Abigail: He knows Tituba conjured Ruth's sisters to come out of the grave.

Mercy: And what more?

Abigail: He saw you naked.

Mercy, *clapping her hands together with a frightened laugh:* Oh, Jesus!

Enter MARY WARREN, *breathless. She is seventeen, a subservient, naïve, lonely girl.*

Mary Warren: What'll we do? The village is out! I just come from the farm; the whole country's talkin' witchcraft! They'll be callin' us witches, Abby!

Mercy, *pointing and looking at* MARY WARREN: She means to tell, I know it.

Mary Warren: Abigail, we've got to tell. Witchery's a hangin' error, a hangin' like they done in Boston two year ago! We must tell the truth, Abigail! You'll only be whipped for dancin', and the other things!

Abigail: Oh, *we'll* be whipped!

Mary Warren: I never done none of it, Abigail. I only looked!

Mercy, *moving menacingly toward* MARY: Oh, you're a great one for lookin', aren't you, Mary Warren? What a grand peeping courage you have!

BETTY, *on the bed, whimpers.* ABIGAIL *turns to her at once.*

Abigail: Betty? *She goes to* BETTY. Now, Betty, dear, wake up now. It's Abigail. *She sits* BETTY *up and furiously shakes her.* I'll beat you, Betty! BETTY *whimpers.* My, you seem improving. I talked to your papa and I told him everything. So there's nothing to—

Betty, *darts off the bed, frightened of* ABIGAIL, *and flattens herself against the wall:* I want my mama!

Abigail, *with alarm, as she cautiously approaches* BETTY: What ails you, Betty? Your mama's dead and buried.

Betty: I'll fly to Mama. Let me fly! *She raises her arms as though to fly, and streaks for the window, gets one leg out.*

Abigail, *pulling her away from the window:* I told him everything; he knows now, he knows everything we—

Betty: You drank blood, Abby! You didn't tell him that!

Abigail: Betty, you never say that again! You will never—

Betty: You did, you did! You drank a charm to kill John Proctor's wife! You drank a charm to kill Goody Proctor!

Abigail, *smashes her across the face:* Shut it! Now shut it!

Betty, *collapsing on the bed:* Mama, Mama! *She dissolves into sobs.*

Abigail: Now look you. All of you. We danced. And Tituba conjured Ruth Putnam's dead sisters. And that is all. And mark this. Let either of you breathe a word, or the edge of a word, about the other things, and I will come to you in the black of some terrible night and I will bring a pointy reckoning that will shudder you. And you know I can do it; I saw Indians smash my dear parents' heads on the pillow next to mine, and I have seen some reddish work done at night, and I can make you wish you had never seen the sun go

---

J Reading Focus Drawing Conclusions About Characters
How does Betty know that Abigail didn't tell Parris about the blood?

down! *She goes to* BETTY *and roughly sits her up.* Now, you—sit up and stop this! **(K)**

But BETTY *collapses in her hands and lies inert on the bed.*

Mary Warren, *with hysterical fright:* What's got her? ABIGAIL *stares in fright at* BETTY. Abigail, she's going to die! It's a sin to conjure, and we—

Abigail, *starting for* MARY: I say shut it, Mary Warren!

Enter JOHN PROCTOR. *On seeing him,* MARY WARREN *leaps in fright.*

Proctor was a farmer in his middle thirties. He need not have been a partisan of any faction in the town, but there is evidence to suggest that he had a sharp and biting way with hypocrites. He was the kind of man—powerful of body, even-tempered, and not easily led—who cannot refuse support to partisans without drawing their deepest resentment. In Proctor's presence a fool felt his foolishness instantly—and a Proctor is always marked for calumny therefore.

But as we shall see, the steady manner he displays does not spring from an untroubled soul. He is a sinner, a sinner not only against the moral fashion of the time, but against his own vision of decent conduct. These people had no ritual for the washing away of sins. It is another trait we inherited from them, and it has helped to discipline us as well as to breed hypocrisy among us. Proctor, respected and even feared in Salem, has come to regard himself as a kind of fraud. But no hint of this has yet appeared on the surface, and as he enters from the crowded parlor below it is a man in his prime we see, with a quiet confidence and an unexpressed, hidden force. Mary Warren, his servant, can barely speak for embarrassment and fear.

Mary Warren: Oh! I'm just going home, Mr. Proctor.

Proctor: Be you foolish, Mary Warren? Be you deaf? I forbid you leave the house, did I not? Why shall I pay you? I am looking for you more often than my cows!

Mary Warren: I only come to see the great doings in the world.

Proctor: I'll show you a great doin' on your arse one of these days. Now get you home; my wife is waitin' with your work! *Trying to retain a shred of dignity, she goes slowly out.*

Mercy Lewis, *both afraid of him and strangely titillated:* I'd best be off. I have my Ruth to watch. Good morning, Mr. Proctor.

MERCY *sidles out. Since* PROCTOR's *entrance,* ABIGAIL *has stood as though on tiptoe, absorbing his presence, wide-eyed. He glances at her,* then goes to BETTY *on the bed.*

Abigail: Gah! I'd almost forgot how strong you are, John Proctor!

Proctor, *looking at* ABIGAIL *now, the faintest suggestion of a knowing smile on his face:* What's this mischief here?

Abigail, *with a nervous laugh:* Oh, she's only gone silly somehow.

Proctor: The road past my house is a pilgrimage to Salem all morning. The town's mumbling witchcraft.

Abigail: Oh, posh! *Winningly she comes a little closer, with a confidential, wicked air.* We were dancin' in the woods last night, and my uncle leaped in on us. She took fright, is all.

Proctor, *his smile widening:* Ah, you're wicked yet, aren't y'! *A trill of expectant laughter escapes her, and she dares come closer, feverishly looking into his eyes.* You'll be clapped in the stocks before you're twenty.

He takes a step to go, and she springs into his path.

Abigail: Give me a word, John. A soft word. *Her concentrated desire destroys his smile.*

Proctor: No, no, Abby. That's done with. **(L)**

Abigail, *tauntingly:* You come five mile to see a silly girl fly? I know you better.

Proctor, *setting her firmly out of his path:* I come to see what mischief your uncle's brewin' now. *With final emphasis:* Put it out of mind, Abby.

(K) **Literary Focus** Motivation Is this an admission that Abigail is a witch, or is she just trying to scare them? Why?

Vocabulary **partisan** (PAHR tih zuhn) *n.:* a strong supporter in a cause.

(L) **Literary Focus** Motivation What is "done with"? Why is Abigail comfortable teasing Proctor this way? Explain.

"We never touched, Abby." Abigail Williams, played by Winona Ryder, with John Proctor, played by Daniel Day-Lewis (right).

Abigail, *grasping his hand before he can release her:* John—I am waitin' for you every night.

Proctor: Abigail, I never give you hope to wait for me.

Abigail, *now beginning to anger—she can't believe it:* I have something better than hope, I think!

Proctor: Abigail, you'll put it out of mind. I'll not be comin' for you more.

Abigail: You're surely sportin' with me.

Proctor: You know me better.

Abigail: I know how you clutched my back behind your house and sweated like a stallion when ever I come near! Or did I dream that? It's she put me out, you cannot pretend it were you. I saw your face when she put me out, and you loved me then and you do now!

Proctor: Abby, that's a wild thing to say—

Abigail: A wild thing may say wild things. But not so wild, I think. I have seen you since she put me out; I have seen you nights.

Proctor: I have hardly stepped off my farm this sevenmonth.

Abigail: I have a sense for heat, John, and yours has drawn me to my window, and I have seen you looking up, burning in your loneliness. Do you tell me you've never looked up at my window?

Proctor: I may have looked up.

Abigail, *now softening:* And you must. You are no wintry man. I know you, John. I know you. *She is weeping.* I cannot sleep for dreamin'; I cannot dream but I wake and walk about the house as though I'd find you comin' through some door. *She clutches him desperately.*

Proctor, *gently pressing her from him, with great sympathy but firmly:* Child—

Abigail, *with a flash of anger:* How do you call me child!

Proctor: Abby, I may think of you softly from time to time. But I will cut off my hand before I'll ever reach for you again. Wipe it out of mind. We never touched, Abby.

Abigail: Aye, but we did.

M **Reading Focus** Drawing Conclusions About Characters

Why does Abigail characterize herself as a "wild thing"?

Proctor: Aye, but we did not.

Abigail, *with a bitter anger:* Oh, I marvel how such a strong man may let such a sickly wife be—

Proctor, *angered—at himself as well:* You'll speak nothin' of Elizabeth!

Abigail: She is blackening my name in the village! She is telling lies about me! She is a cold, sniveling woman, and you bend to her! Let her turn you like a—

Proctor, *shaking her:* Do you look for whippin'?

A psalm is heard being sung below.

Abigail, *in tears:* I look for John Proctor that took me from my sleep and put knowledge in my heart! I never knew what pretense Salem was, I never knew the lying lessons I was taught by all these Christian women and their covenanted men! And now you bid me tear the light out of my eyes? I will not, I cannot! You loved me, John Proctor, and whatever sin it is, you love me yet! *He turns abruptly to go out. She rushes to him.* John, pity me, pity me!

The words "going up to Jesus" are heard in the psalm, and BETTY *claps her ears suddenly and whines loudly.*

Abigail: Betty? *She hurries to* BETTY, *who is now sitting up and screaming.* PROCTOR *goes to* BETTY *as* ABIGAIL *is trying to pull her hands down, calling "Betty!"*

Proctor, *growing unnerved:* What's she doing? Girl, what ails you? Stop that wailing!

The singing has stopped in the midst of this, and now PARRIS *rushes in.*

Parris: What happened? What are you doing to her? Betty! *He rushes to the bed, crying, "Betty, Betty!"* MRS. PUTNAM *enters, feverish with curiosity, and with her* THOMAS PUTNAM *and* MERCY LEWIS. PARRIS, *at the bed, keeps lightly slapping* BETTY'S *face, while she moans and tries to get up.*

Abigail: She heard you singin' and suddenly she's up and screamin'.

Mrs. Putnam: The psalm! The psalm! She cannot bear to hear the Lord's name!

Parris: No, God forbid. Mercy, run to the doctor! Tell him what's happened here! MERCY LEWIS *rushes out.* Ⓝ

Mrs. Putnam: Mark it for a sign, mark it!

REBECCA NURSE, *seventy-two, enters. She is white-haired, leaning upon her walking-stick.*

Putnam, *pointing at the whimpering* BETTY: That is a notorious sign of witchcraft afoot, Goody Nurse, a prodigious sign!

Mrs. Putnam: My mother told me that! When they cannot bear to hear the name of—

Parris, *trembling:* Rebecca, Rebecca, go to her, we're lost. She suddenly cannot bear to hear the Lord's—

GILES COREY, *eighty-three, enters. He is knotted with muscle, canny, inquisitive, and still powerful.*

Rebecca: There is hard sickness here, Giles Corey, so please to keep the quiet.

Giles: I've not said a word. No one here can testify I've said a word. Is she going to fly again? I hear she flies.

Putnam: Man, be quiet now!

Everything is quiet. REBECCA *walks across the room to the bed. Gentleness exudes from her.* BETTY *is quietly whimpering, eyes shut.* REBECCA *simply stands over the child, who gradually quiets.*

And while they are so absorbed, we may put a word in for Rebecca. Rebecca was the wife of Francis Nurse, who, from all accounts, was one of those men for whom both sides of the argument had to have respect. He was called upon to arbitrate disputes as though he were an unofficial judge, and Rebecca also enjoyed the high opinion most people had for him. By the time of the delusion, they had three hundred acres, and their children were settled in separate homesteads within the same estate. However, Francis had originally rented the land, and one theory has it that, as he gradually paid for it and raised his social status, there were those who resented his rise.

Another suggestion to explain the systematic campaign against Rebecca, and inferentially against Francis, is the land war he fought with his neighbors, one of whom was a Putnam. This squabble grew to the proportions of a battle in the woods between partisans of both sides, and it is said to have lasted for two days. As for Rebecca herself, the general

---

Ⓝ **Literary Focus** **Motivation** Why would Parris instruct Mercy to get the doctor at this time?

opinion of her character was so high that to explain how anyone dared cry her out for a witch—and more, how adults could bring themselves to lay hands on her—we must look to the fields and boundaries of that time.

As we have seen, Thomas Putnam's man for the Salem ministry was Bayley. The Nurse clan had been in the faction that prevented Bayley's taking office. In addition, certain families allied to the Nurses by blood or friendship, and whose farms were contiguous with the Nurse farm or close to it, combined to break away from the Salem town authority and set up Topsfield, a new and independent entity whose existence was resented by old Salemites.

That the guiding hand behind the outcry was Putnam's is indicated by the fact that, as soon as it began, this Topsfield-Nurse faction absented themselves from church in protest and disbelief. It was Edward and Jonathan Putnam who signed the first complaint against Rebecca; and Thomas Putnam's little daughter was the one who fell into a fit at the hearing and pointed to Rebecca as her attacker. To top it all, Mrs. Putnam—who is now staring at the bewitched child on the bed—soon accused Rebecca's spirit of "tempting her to iniquity," a charge that had more truth in it than Mrs. Putnam could know.

Mrs. Putnam, *astonished:* What have you done?

REBECCA, *in thought, now leaves the bedside and sits.*

Parris, *wondrous and relieved:* What do you make of it, Rebecca?

Putnam, *eagerly:* Goody Nurse, will you go to my Ruth and see if you can wake her?

Rebecca, *sitting:* I think she'll wake in time. Pray calm yourselves. I have eleven children, and I am twenty-six times a grandma, and I have seen them all through their silly seasons, and when it come on them they will run the Devil bowlegged keeping up with their mischief. I think she'll wake when she tires of it. A child's spirit is like a child, you can never catch it by running after it; you must stand still, and, for love, it will soon itself come back.

Proctor: Aye, that's the truth of it, Rebecca.

Mrs. Putnam: This is no silly season, Rebecca. My Ruth is bewildered, Rebecca; she cannot eat.

Rebecca: Perhaps she is not hungered yet. *To* PARRIS:

I hope you are not decided to go in search of loose spirits, Mr. Parris. I've heard promise of that outside.

Parris: A wide opinion's running in the parish that the Devil may be among us, and I would satisfy them that they are wrong.

Proctor: Then let you come out and call them wrong. Did you consult the wardens before you called this minister to look for devils?

Parris: He is not coming to look for devils!

Proctor: Then what's he coming for?

Putnam: There be children dyin' in the village, Mister!

Proctor: I seen none dyin'. This society will not be a bag to swing around your head, Mr. Putnam. *To* PARRIS: Did you call a meeting before you—?

Putnam: I am sick of meetings; cannot the man turn his head without he have a meeting?

Proctor: He may turn his head, but not to Hell!

Rebecca: Pray, John, be calm. *Pause. He defers to her.* Mr. Parris, I think you'd best send Reverend Hale back as soon as he come. This will set us all to arguin' again in the society, and we thought to have peace this year. I think we ought rely on the doctor now, and good prayer.

Mrs. Putnam: Rebecca, the doctor's baffled!

Rebecca: If so he is, then let us go to God for the cause of it. There is prodigious danger in the seeking of loose spirits. I fear it, I fear it. Let us rather blame ourselves and—

Putnam: How may we blame ourselves? I am one of nine sons; the Putnam seed have peopled this province. And yet I have but one child left of eight—and now she shrivels!

Rebecca: I cannot fathom that.

Mrs. Putnam, *with a growing edge of sarcasm:* But I must! You think it God's work you should never lose a child, nor grandchild either, and I bury all but one? There are wheels within wheels in this village, and fires within fires!

Putnam, *to* PARRIS: When Reverend Hale comes, you will proceed to look for signs of witchcraft here.

Proctor, *to* PUTNAM: You cannot command Mr. Parris. We vote by name in this society, not by acreage.

Putnam: I never heard you worried so on this society, Mr. Proctor. I do not think I saw you at Sabbath meeting since snow flew.

Proctor: I have trouble enough without I come five mile to hear him preach only hellfire and bloody damnation. Take it to heart, Mr. Parris. There are many others who stay away from church these days because you hardly ever mention God anymore.

Parris, *now aroused:* Why, that's a drastic charge!

Rebecca: It's somewhat true; there are many that quail to bring their children—

Parris: I do not preach for children, Rebecca. It is not the children who are unmindful of their obligations toward this ministry.

Rebecca: Are there really those unmindful?

Parris: I should say the better half of Salem village—

Putnam: And more than that!

Parris: Where is my wood? My contract provides I be supplied with all my firewood. I am waiting since November for a stick, and even in November I had to show my frostbitten hands like some London beggar!

Giles: You are allowed six pound a year to buy your wood, Mr. Parris.

Parris: I regard that six pound as part of my salary. I am paid little enough without I spend six pound on firewood.

Proctor: Sixty, plus six for firewood—

Parris: The salary is sixty-six pound, Mr. Proctor! I am not some preaching farmer with a book under my arm; I am a graduate of Harvard College.

Giles: Aye, and well instructed in arithmetic!

Parris: Mr. Corey, you will look far for a man of my kind at sixty pound a year! I am not used to this poverty; I left a thrifty business in the Barbados to serve the Lord. I do not fathom it, why am I persecuted here? I cannot offer one proposition but there be a howling riot of argument. I have often wondered if the Devil be in it somewhere; I cannot understand you people otherwise.

Proctor: Mr. Parris, you are the first minister ever did demand the deed to this house—

Parris: Man! Don't a minister deserve a house to live in?

Proctor: To live in, yes. But to ask ownership is like

> ## A minister is the Lord's man in the parish; a minister is not to be so lightly crossed and contradicted.

you shall own the meeting house itself; the last meeting I were at you spoke so long on deeds and mortgages I thought it were an auction.

Parris: I want a mark of confidence, is all! I am your third preacher in seven years. I do not wish to be put out like the cat whenever some majority feels the whim. You people seem not to comprehend that a minister is the Lord's man in the parish; a minister is not to be so lightly crossed and contradicted—

Putnam: Aye!

Parris: There is either obedience or the church will burn like Hell is burning!

Proctor: Can you speak one minute without we land in Hell again? I am sick of Hell!

Parris: It is not for you to say what is good for you to hear!

Proctor: I may speak my heart, I think!

Parris, *in a fury:* What, are we Quakers?[3] We are not Quakers here yet, Mr. Proctor. And you may tell that to your followers!

Proctor: My followers!

Parris—*now he's out with it:* There is a party in this church. I am not blind; there is a faction and a party.

Proctor: Against you?

Putnam: Against him and all authority!

Proctor: Why, then I must find it and join it.

There is shock among the others.

Rebecca: He does not mean that.

Putnam: He confessed it now!

Proctor: I mean it solemnly, Rebecca; I like not the smell of this "authority."

Rebecca: No, you cannot break charity with your minister. You are another kind, John. Clasp his hand, make your peace.

---

3. **Quakers:** Most Quakers believe that no rite or formally trained priest is needed to commune with God; instead, divine truth can be found in one's "inner light."

Ⓞ Literary Focus **Motivation** Why does Parris make such an abrupt change in the subject here? What does this action reveal?

Proctor: I have a crop to sow and lumber to drag home. *He goes angrily to the door and turns to* COREY *with a smile.* What say you, Giles, let's find the party. He says there's a party.

Giles: I've changed my opinion of this man, John. Mr. Parris, I beg your pardon. I never thought you had so much iron in you.

Parris, *surprised:* Why, thank you, Giles! *(P)*

Giles: It suggests to the mind what the trouble be ~~over all Town~~ among us all these years. *To all:* Think on it. Wherefore is everybody suing everybody else? Think on it now, it's a deep thing, and dark as a pit. I have been six time in court this year—

Proctor, *familiarly, with warmth, although he knows he is approaching the edge of* GILES' *tolerance with this:* Is it the Devil's fault that a man cannot say you good morning without you clap him for defamation? You're old, Giles, and you're not hearin' so well as you did.

Giles—*he cannot be crossed:* John Proctor, I have only last month collected four pound damages for you publicly sayin' I burned the roof off your house, and I—

Proctor, *laughing:* I never said no such thing, but I've paid you for it, so I hope I can call you deaf without charge. Now come along, Giles, and help me drag my lumber home. *(Q)*

Putnam: A moment, Mr. Proctor. What lumber is that you're draggin', if I may ask you?

Proctor: My lumber. From out my forest by the riverside.

Putnam: Why, we are surely gone wild this year. What anarchy is this? That tract is in my bounds, it's in my bounds, Mr. Proctor.

Proctor: In your bounds! *Indicating* REBECCA: I bought that tract from Goody Nurse's husband five months ago.

Putnam: He had no right to sell it. It stands clear in my grandfather's will that all the land between the river and—

Proctor: Your grandfather had a habit of willing land that never belonged to him, if I may say it plain.

Giles: That's God's truth; he nearly willed away my north pasture but he knew I'd break his fingers before he'd set his name to it. Let's get your lumber home, John. I feel a sudden will to work coming on.

Putnam: You load one oak of mine and you'll fight to drag it home!

Giles: Aye, and we'll win too, Putnam—this fool and I. Come on! *He turns to* PROCTOR *and starts out.*

Putnam: I'll have my men on you, Corey! I'll clap a writ on you!

Enter REVEREND JOHN HALE *of Beverly.* ~~Question 5.~~

Mr. Hale is nearing forty, a tight-skinned, eager-eyed intellectual. This is a beloved errand for him; on being called here to ascertain witchcraft he felt the pride of the specialist whose unique knowledge has at last been publicly called for. Like almost all men of learning, he spent a good deal of his time pondering the invisible world, especially since he had himself encountered a witch in his parish not long before. That woman, however, turned into a mere pest under his searching scrutiny, and the child she had allegedly been afflicting recovered her normal behavior after Hale had given her his kindness and a few days of rest in his own house. However, that experience never raised a doubt in his mind as to the reality of the underworld or the existence of Lucifer's many-faced lieutenants. And his belief is not to his discredit. Better minds than Hale's were—and still are—convinced that there is a society of spirits beyond our ken. One cannot help noting that one of his lines has never yet raised a laugh in any audience that has seen this play; it is his assurance that "We cannot look to superstition in this. The Devil is precise." Evidently we are not quite certain even now whether diabolism is holy and not to be scoffed at. And it is no accident that we should be so bemused.

Like Reverend Hale and the others on this stage, we conceive the Devil as a necessary part of a respectable view of cosmology. Ours is a divided empire in which certain ideas and emotions and actions are of God, and their opposites are of Lucifer. It is as impossible for most men to conceive of a morality without sin as of an earth without "sky." Since 1692 a great but superficial change has wiped out God's beard and the Devil's horns, but the world is still gripped between

---

(P) Reading Focus Drawing Conclusions About Characters
What has changed Giles's opinion of Parris?

(Q) Reading Focus Drawing Conclusions About Characters
Why do you think Giles and Proctor can fight amicably, but Proctor and Putnam cannot?

two diametrically opposed absolutes. The concept of unity, in which positive and negative are attributes of the same force, in which good and evil are relative, ever-changing, and always joined to the same phenomenon—such a concept is still reserved to the physical sciences and to the few who have grasped the history of ideas. When it is recalled that until the Christian era the underworld was never regarded as a hostile area, that all gods were useful and essentially friendly to man despite occasional lapses; when we see the steady and methodical inculcation into humanity of the idea of man's worthlessness—until redeemed—the necessity of the Devil may become evident as a weapon, a weapon designed and used time and time again in every age to whip men into a surrender to a particular church or church-state.

Our difficulty in believing the—for want of a better word—political inspiration of the Devil is due in great part to the fact that he is called up and damned not only by our social antagonists but by our own side, whatever it may be. The Catholic Church, through its Inquisition,[4] is famous for cultivating Lucifer as the arch-fiend, but the Church's enemies relied no less upon the Old Boy to keep the human mind enthralled. Luther[5] was himself accused of alliance with Hell, and he in turn accused his enemies. To complicate matters further, he believed that he had had contact with the Devil, and had argued theology with him. I am not surprised at this, for at my own university a professor of history—a Lutheran, by the way—used to assemble his graduate students, draw the shades, and commune in the classroom with Erasmus.[6] He was never, to my knowledge, officially scoffed at for this, the reason being that the university officials, like most of us, are the children of a history which still sucks at the Devil's teats. At this writing, only England has held back before the temptations of contemporary diabolism. In the countries of the Communist ideology, all resistance of any import is linked to the totally malign capitalist succubi,[7] and in America any man who is not reactionary in his views is open to the charge of alliance with the Red hell. Political opposition, thereby, is given an inhumane overlay which then justifies the abrogation of all normally applied customs of civilized intercourse. A political policy is equated with moral right, and opposition to it with diabolical malevolence. Once such an equation is effectively made, society becomes a congerie of plots and counterplots, and the main role of government changes from that of the arbiter to that of the scourge of God.

The results of this process are no different now from what they ever were, except sometimes in the degree of cruelty inflicted, and not always even in that department. Normally the actions and deeds of a man were all that society felt comfortable in judging. The secret intent of an action was left to the ministers, priests, and rabbis to deal with. When diabolism rises, however, actions are the least important manifests of the true nature of a man. The Devil, as Reverend Hale said, is a wily one, and, until an hour before he fell, even God thought him beautiful in Heaven.

The analogy, however, seems to falter when one considers that, while there were no witches then, there are Communists and capitalists now, and in each camp there is certain proof that spies of each side are at work undermining the other. But this is a snobbish objection and not at all warranted by the facts. I have no doubt that people *were* communing with, and even worshiping, the Devil in Salem, and if the whole truth could be known in this case, as it is in others, we should discover a regular and conventionalized propitiation of the dark spirit. One certain evidence of this is the confession of Tituba, the slave of Reverend Parris, and another is the behavior of the children who were known to have indulged in sorceries with her. Ⓡ

---

4. **Inquisition:** techniques of suppression and punishment used in the thirteenth century by the Roman Catholic Church against people thought to hold heretical beliefs.
5. **Luther:** Martin Luther (1483–1546), a German theologian and leader of the Protestant Reformation.
6. **Erasmus** (ih RAZ muhs) (c. 1466–1536): Dutch scholar and humanist, who came into conflict with Luther over predestination. (Erasmus believed in free will.)

---

7. **succubi** (SUHK yoo by): plural of *succubus,* the term for a female evil spirit or demon thought in medieval times to have sexual intercourse with sleeping men.

Ⓡ **Literary Perspectives** **Analyzing Credibility** How does Miller's assertion that "there were no witches then" affect your view of the children in the play? Why does Miller tell us this outright?

There are accounts of similar *klatches* in Europe, where the daughters of the towns would assemble at night and, sometimes with fetishes, sometimes with a selected young man, give themselves to love, with some bastardly results. The Church, sharp-eyed as it must be when gods long dead are brought to life, condemned these orgies as witchcraft and interpreted them rightly, as a resurgence of the Dionysiac[8] forces it had crushed long before. Sex, sin, and the Devil were early linked, and so they continued to be in Salem, and are today. From all accounts there are no more puritanical mores in the world than those enforced by the Communists in Russia, where women's fashions, for instance, are as prudent and all-covering as any American Baptist would desire. The divorce laws lay a tremendous responsibility on the father for the care of his children. Even the laxity of divorce regulations in the early years of the revolution was undoubtedly a revulsion from the nineteenth-century Victorian immobility of marriage and the consequent hypocrisy that developed from it. If for no other reasons, a state so powerful, so jealous of the uniformity of its citizens, cannot long tolerate the atomization of the family. And yet, in American eyes at least, there remains the conviction that the Russian attitude toward women is lascivious. It is the Devil working again, just as he is working within the Slav who is shocked at the very idea of a woman's disrobing herself in a burlesque show. Our opposites are always robed in sexual sin, and it is from this unconscious conviction that demonology gains both its attractive sensuality and its capacity to infuriate and frighten.

Coming into Salem now, Reverend Hale conceives of himself much as a young doctor on his first call. His painfully acquired armory of symptoms, catchwords, and diagnostic procedures is now to be put to use at last. The road from Beverly is unusually busy this morning, and he has passed a hundred rumors that make him smile at the ignorance of the yeomanry in this most precise science. He feels himself allied with the best minds of Europe—kings, philosophers, scientists, and ecclesiasts of all churches. His goal is light, goodness and its preservation, and he knows the exaltation of the blessed whose intelligence, sharpened by minute examinations of enormous tracts, is finally called upon to face what may be a bloody fight with the Fiend himself. Ⓢ

---

8. **Dionysiac** (dy uh NIHS ee ak): like Dionysus (dy uh NIH suhs), the ancient Greek god of wine and revelry; wild, ecstatic, sensuous, frenzied.

Ⓢ **Literary Perspectives** Analyzing Credibility How does the juxtaposition of Miller's beliefs about the McCarthy hearings with the introduction of Reverend Hale influence your view of the minister?

SCIENCE LINK

Ergot Poisoning and the Salem Witch Trials

Wheat infected with ergot.

Could the strange behavior exhibited by several members of Salem village in 1692 have been caused by a fungus that affects rye, wheat, and other cereal grasses? The fungus, called ergot, grows in warm, damp environments—the kind of environment found in parts of Salem village, where swampy meadows thrive. According to behavioral psychologist Linnda Caporael, the effects of ergot poisoning match the symptoms reported during the Salem witch trials. These symptoms include such things as violent muscle spasms, vomiting, delusions, hallucinations, and crawling sensations on the skin.

Ask Yourself
It is common for people to use scientific theories to explain bizzare events of the past. Why do you think they do so?

He appears loaded down with half a dozen heavy books.

Hale: Pray you, someone take these!

Parris, *delighted:* Mr. Hale! Oh! it's good to see you again! *Taking some books:* My, they're heavy! **T**

Hale, *setting down his books:* They must be; they are weighted with authority.

Parris, *a little scared:* Well, you do come prepared!

Hale: We shall need hard study if it comes to tracking down the Old Boy. *Noticing* REBECCA: You cannot be Rebecca Nurse?

Rebecca: I am, sir. Do you know me?

Hale: It's strange how I knew you, but I suppose you look as such a good soul should. We have all heard of your great charities in Beverly.

Parris: Do you know this gentleman? Mr. Thomas Putnam. And his good wife Ann.

Hale: Putnam! I had not expected such distinguished company, sir.

Putnam, *pleased:* It does not seem to help us today, Mr. Hale. We look to you to come to our house and save our child.

Hale: Your child ails too?

Mrs. Putnam: Her soul, her soul seems flown away. She sleeps and yet she walks. . . .

Putnam: She cannot eat.

Hale: Cannot eat! *Thinks on it. Then, to* PROCTOR *and* GILES COREY: Do you men have afflicted children?

Parris: No, no, these are farmers. John Proctor— **U**

Giles Corey: He don't believe in witches.

Proctor, *to* HALE: I never spoke on witches one way or the other. Will you come, Giles?

Giles: No—no, John, I think not. I have some few queer questions of my own to ask this fellow.

Proctor: I've heard you to be a sensible man, Mr. Hale. I hope you'll leave some of it in Salem.

PROCTOR *goes.* HALE *stands embarrassed for an instant.*

Parris, *quickly:* Will you look at my daughter, sir? *Leads* HALE *to the bed.* She has tried to leap out the window; we discovered her this morning on the highroad, waving her arms as though she'd fly.

Hale, *narrowing his eyes:* Tries to fly.

Putnam: She cannot bear to hear the Lord's name,

Mr. Hale; that's a sure sign of witchcraft afloat.

Hale, *holding up his hands:* No, no. Now let me instruct you. We cannot look to superstition in this. The Devil is precise; the marks of his presence are definite as stone, and I must tell you all that I shall not proceed unless you are prepared to believe me if I should find no bruise of Hell upon her.

Parris: It is agreed, sir—it is agreed—we will abide by your judgment.

Hale: Good then. *He goes to the bed, looks down at* BETTY. *To* PARRIS: Now, sir, what were your first warning of this strangeness?

Parris: Why, sir—I discovered her—*indicating* ABIGAIL—and my niece and ten or twelve of the other girls, dancing in the forest last night.

Hale, *surprised:* You permit dancing?

Parris: No, no, it were secret—

Mrs. Putnam, *unable to wait:* Mr. Parris's slave has knowledge of conjurin', sir.

Parris, *to* MRS. PUTNAM: We cannot be sure of that, Goody Ann—

Mrs. Putnam, *frightened, very softly:* I know it, sir. I sent my child—she should learn from Tituba who murdered her sisters.

Rebecca, *horrified:* Goody Ann! You sent a child to conjure up the dead?

Mrs. Putnam: Let God blame me, not you, not you, Rebecca! I'll not have you judging me any more! *To* HALE: Is it a natural work to lose seven children before they live a day?

Parris: Sssh!

REBECCA, *with great pain, turns her face away. There is a pause.*

Hale: Seven dead in childbirth.

Mrs. Putnam, *softly:* Aye. *Her voice breaks; she looks up at him. Silence.* HALE *is impressed.* PARRIS *looks to him. He goes to his books, opens one, turns pages, then reads. All wait, avidly.*

Parris, *hushed:* What book is that?

Mrs. Putnam: What's there, sir?

Hale, *with a tasty love of intellectual pursuit:* Here is all the invisible world, caught, defined, and calculated. In these books the Devil stands stripped of all

T **Reading Focus** **Drawing Conclusions About Characters**
Why might Parris refer to Reverend Hale as "Mr. Hale"?

U **Literary Focus** **Motivation** Why does Parris tell Hale that Proctor and Corey are farmers?

1116 Unit 6 • Collection 15

his brute disguises. Here are all your familiar spirits—your incubi[9] and succubi; your witches that go by land, by air, and by sea; your wizards of the night and of the day. Have no fear now—we shall find him out if he has come among us, and I mean to crush him utterly if he has shown his face! *He starts for the bed.*

Rebecca: Will it hurt the child, sir?

Hale: I cannot tell. If she is truly in the Devil's grip we may have to rip and tear to get her free.

Rebecca: I think I'll go, then. I am too old for this. *She rises.*

Parris, *striving for conviction:* Why, Rebecca, we may open up the boil of all our troubles today!

Rebecca: Let us hope for that. I go to God for you, sir.

Parris, *with trepidation— and resentment:* I hope you do not mean we go to Satan here! *Slight pause.*

Rebecca: I wish I knew. *She goes out; they feel resentful of her note of moral superiority.*

Putnam, *abruptly:* Come, Mr. Hale, let's get on. Sit you here.

Giles: Mr. Hale, I have always wanted to ask a learned man—what signifies the readin' of strange books?

Hale: What books?

Giles: I cannot tell; she hides them.

Hale: Who does this?

Giles: Martha, my wife. I have waked at night many a time and found her in a corner, readin' of a book. Now what do you make of that?

Hale: Why, that's not necessarily—

Giles: It discomfits me! Last night—mark this—I tried and tried and could not say my prayers. And then she close her book and walks out of the house, and suddenly—mark this—I could pray again!

Old Giles must be spoken for, if only because his fate was to be so remarkable and so different from that of all the others. He was in his early eighties at this time,

> # What victory would the Devil have to win a soul already bad? It is the best the Devil wants.

and was the most comical hero in the history. No man has ever been blamed for so much. If a cow was missed, the first thought was to look for her around Corey's house; a fire blazing up at night brought suspicion of arson to his door. He didn't give a hoot for public opinion, and only in his last years—after he had married Martha—did he bother much with the church. That she stopped his prayer is very probable, but he forgot to say that he'd only recently learned any prayers and it didn't take much to make him stumble over them. He was a crank and a nuisance, but withal a deeply innocent and brave man. In court, once, he was asked if it were true that he had been frightened by the strange behavior of a hog and had then said he knew it to be the Devil in an animal's shape. "What frighted you?" he was asked. He forgot everything but the word "frighted," and instantly replied, "I do not know that I ever spoke that word in my life."

Hale: Ah! The stoppage of prayer—that is strange. I'll speak further on that with you.

Giles: I'm not sayin' she's touched the Devil, now, but I'd admire to know what books she reads and why she hides them. She'll not answer me, y' see.

Hale: Aye, we'll discuss it. *To all:* Now mark me, if the Devil is in her you will witness some frightful wonders in this room, so please to keep your wits about you. Mr. Putnam, stand close in case she flies. Now, Betty, dear, will you sit up? PUTNAM *comes in closer, ready-handed.* HALE *sits* BETTY *up, but she hangs limp in his hands.* Hmmm. *He observes her carefully. The others watch breathlessly.* Can you hear me? I am John Hale, minister of Beverly. I have come to help you, dear. Do you remember my two little girls in Beverly? *She does not stir in his hands.*

Parris, *in fright:* How can it be the Devil? Why would he choose my house to strike? We have all manner of licentious people in the village!

Hale: What victory would the Devil have to win a soul already bad? It is the best the Devil wants, and who is better than the minister?

---

9. **incubi** (IHN kyuh by): plural of *incubus,* the term for an evil male spirit or demon thought in medieval times to have sexual intercourse with sleeping women.

Giles: That's deep, Mr. Parris, deep, deep!

Parris, *with resolution now:* Betty! Answer Mr. Hale! Betty!

Hale: Does someone afflict you, child? It need not be a woman, mind you, or a man. Perhaps some bird invisible to others comes to you—perhaps a pig, a mouse, or any beast at all. Is there some figure bids you fly? *The child remains limp in his hands. In silence he lays her back on the pillow. Now, holding out his hands toward her, he intones:* In nomine Domini Sabaoth sui filiique ite ad infernos.[10] *She does not stir. He turns to* ABIGAIL, *his eyes narrowing.* Abigail, what sort of dancing were you doing with her in the forest?

Abigail: Why—common dancing is all.

Parris: I think I ought to say that I—I saw a kettle in the grass where they were dancing.

Abigail: That were only soup.

Hale: What sort of soup were in this kettle, Abigail?

Abigail: Why, it were beans—and lentils, I think, and—

Hale: Mr. Parris, you did not notice, did you, any living thing in the kettle? A mouse, perhaps, a spider, a frog—? **Ⓥ**

Parris, *fearfully:* I—do believe there were some movement—in the soup.

Abigail: That jumped in, we never put it in!

Hale, *quickly:* What jumped in?

Abigail: Why, a very little frog jumped—

Parris: A frog, Abby!

Hale, *grasping* ABIGAIL: Abigail, it may be your cousin is dying. Did you call the Devil last night?

Abigail: I never called him! Tituba, Tituba . . . **Ⓦ**

Parris, *blanched:* She called the Devil?

---

10. **In nomine Domini Sabaoth sui filiique ite ad infernos:** Latin for "In the name of the Lord of Hosts and his son, get thee to hell."

Abigail, what sort of dancing were you doing with her in the forest?

Hale: I should like to speak with Tituba.

Parris: Goody Ann, will you bring her up? MRS. PUTNAM *exits.*

Hale: How did she call him?

Abigail: I know not—she spoke Barbados.

Hale: Did you feel any strangeness when she called him? A sudden cold wind, perhaps? A trembling below the ground?

Abigail: I didn't see no Devil! *Shaking* BETTY: Betty, wake up. Betty! Betty!

Hale: You cannot evade me, Abigail. Did your cousin drink any of the brew in that kettle?

Abigail: She never drank it!

Hale: Did you drink it?

Abigail: No, sir!

Hale: Did Tituba ask you to drink it?

Abigail: She tried, but I refused.

Hale: Why are you concealing? Have you sold yourself to Lucifer?

Abigail: I never sold myself! I'm a good girl! I'm a proper girl!

MRS. PUTNAM *enters with* TITUBA, *and instantly* ABIGAIL *points at* TITUBA.

Abigail: She made me do it! She made Betty do it!

Tituba, *shocked and angry:* Abby!

Abigail: She makes me drink blood!

Parris: Blood!!

Mrs. Putnam: My baby's blood?

Tituba: No, no, chicken blood. I give she chicken blood!

Hale: Woman, have you enlisted these children for the Devil?

Tituba: No, no, sir, I don't truck with no Devil!

Hale: Why can she not wake? Are you silencing this child?

Tituba: I love me Betty!

Hale: You have sent your spirit out upon this child, have you not? Are you gathering souls for the Devil?

Ⓥ Reading Focus **Drawing Conclusions About Characters** How does Hale "lead" Parris to give particular answers? Explain.

Ⓦ Literary Focus **Motivation** Why does Abigail immediately call out "Tituba"?

Abigail: She sends her spirit on me in church; she makes me laugh at prayer!

Parris: She have often laughed at prayer!

Abigail: She comes to me every night to go and drink blood!

Tituba: You beg *me* to conjure! She beg *me* make charm—

Abigail: Don't lie! *To* HALE: She comes to me while I sleep; she's always making me dream corruptions!

Tituba: Why you say that, Abby?

Abigail: Sometimes I wake and find myself standing in the open doorway and not a stitch on my body! I always hear her laughing in my sleep. I hear her singing her Barbados songs and tempting me with—

Tituba: Mister Reverend, I never—

Hale, *resolved now:* Tituba, I want you to wake this child.

Tituba: I have no power on this child, sir.

Hale: You most certainly do, and you will free her from it now! When did you compact with the Devil? Ⓧ

Tituba: I don't compact with no Devil!

Parris: You will confess yourself or I will take you out and whip you to your death, Tituba!

Putnam: This woman must be hanged! She must be taken and hanged!

Tituba, *terrified, falls to her knees:* No, no, don't hang Tituba! I tell him I don't desire to work for him, sir.

Parris: The Devil?

Hale: Then you saw him! TITUBA *weeps.* Now Tituba, I know that when we bind ourselves to Hell it is very hard to break with it. We are going to help you tear yourself free—

Tituba, *frightened by the coming process:* Mister Reverend, I do believe somebody else be witchin' these children.

Hale: Who?

Tituba: I don't know, sir, but the Devil got him numerous witches.

Hale: Does he! *It is a clue.* Tituba, look into my eyes. Come, look into me. *She raises her eyes to his fearfully.* You would be a good Christian woman, would you not, Tituba?

Tituba: Aye, sir, a good Christian woman.

Hale: And you love these little children?

Tituba: Oh, yes, sir, I don't desire to hurt little children.

Hale: And you love God, Tituba?

Tituba: I love God with all my bein'.

Hale: Now, in God's holy name—

Tituba: Bless Him. Bless Him. *She is rocking on her knees, sobbing in terror.*

Hale: And to His glory—

Tituba: Eternal glory. Bless Him—bless God . . .

Hale: Open yourself, Tituba—open yourself and let God's holy light shine on you.

Tituba: Oh, bless the Lord.

Hale: When the Devil comes to you does he ever come—with another person? *She stares up into his face.* Perhaps another person in the village? Someone you know.

Parris: Who came with him?

Putnam: Sarah Good? Did you ever see Sarah Good with him? Or Osburn?

Parris: Was it man or woman came with him?

Tituba: Man or woman. Was—was woman.

Parris: What woman? A woman, you said. What woman?

Tituba: It was black dark, and I—

Parris: You could see him, why could you not see her?

Tituba: Well, they was always talking; they was always runnin' round and carryin' on—

Parris: You mean out of Salem? Salem witches?

Tituba: I believe so, yes, sir.

Now HALE *takes her hand. She is surprised.*

Hale: Tituba. You must have no fear to tell us who they are, do you understand? We will protect you. The Devil can never overcome a minister. You know that, do you not?

Tituba—*she kisses* HALE's *hand:* Aye, sir, oh, I do.

Hale: You have confessed yourself to witchcraft, and that speaks a wish to come to Heaven's side. And we will bless you, Tituba.

Tituba, *deeply relieved:* Oh, God bless you, Mr. Hale!

Hale, *with rising exaltation:* You are God's instrument put in our hands to discover the Devil's agents among us. You are selected, Tituba, you are chosen to help us cleanse our village. So speak utterly, Tituba, turn your

---

Ⓧ **Literary Focus** Motivation What causes Hale to believe Abigail's testimony?

back on him and face God—face God, Tituba, and God will protect you.

Tituba, *joining with him:* Oh, God, protect Tituba!

Hale, *kindly:* Who came to you with the Devil? Two? Three? Four? How many?

TITUBA *pants and begins rocking back and forth again, staring ahead.*

Tituba: There was four. There was four.

Parris, *pressing in on her:* Who? Who? Their names, their names!

Tituba, *suddenly bursting out:* Oh, how many times he bid me kill you, Mr. Parris!

Parris: Kill me!

Tituba, *in a fury:* He say Mr. Parris must be kill! Mr. Parris no goodly man, Mr. Parris mean man and no gentle man, and he bid me rise out of my bed and cut your throat! *They gasp.* But I tell him "No! I don't hate that man. I don't want kill that man." But he say, "You work for me, Tituba, and I make you free! I give you pretty dress to wear, and put you way high up in the air, and you gone fly back to Barbados!" And I say, "You lie, Devil, you lie!" And then he come one stormy night to me, and he say, "Look! I have *white* people belong to me." And I look—and there was Goody Good. **Y**

Parris: Sarah Good!

Tituba, *rocking and weeping:* Aye, sir, and Goody Osburn.

Mrs. Putnam: I knew it! Goody Osburn were midwife to me three times. I begged you, Thomas, did I not? I begged him not to call Osburn because I feared her. My babies always shriveled in her hands!

Hale: Take courage, you must give us all their names. How can you bear to see this child suffering? Look at her, Tituba. *He is indicating* BETTY *on the bed.* Look at her God-given innocence; her soul is so tender; we must protect her, Tituba; the Devil is out and preying on her like a beast upon the flesh of the pure lamb. God will bless you for your help.

ABIGAIL *rises, staring as though inspired, and cries out.*

Abigail: I want to open myself! *They turn to her, startled. She is enraptured, as though in a pearly light.* I want the light of God, I want the sweet love of Jesus! I danced for the Devil; I saw him; I wrote in his book; I go back to Jesus; I kiss His hand. I saw Sarah Good with the Devil! I saw Goody Osburn with the Devil! I saw Bridget Bishop with the Devil! **Z**

As she is speaking, BETTY *is rising from the bed, a fever in her eyes, and picks up the chant.*

Betty, *staring too:* I saw George Jacobs with the Devil! I saw Goody Howe with the Devil!

Parris: She speaks! *He rushes to embrace* BETTY. She speaks!

Hale: Glory to God! It is broken, they are free!

Betty, *calling out hysterically and with great relief:* I saw Martha Bellows with the Devil!

Abigail: I saw Goody Sibber with the Devil! *It is rising to a great glee.*

Putnam: The marshal, I'll call the marshal!

PARRIS *is shouting a prayer of thanksgiving.*

Betty: I saw Alice Barrow with the Devil!

The curtain begins to fall.

Hale, *as* PUTNAM *goes out:* Let the marshal bring irons!

Abigail: I saw Goody Hawkins with the Devil!

Betty: I saw Goody Bibber with the Devil!

Abigail: I saw Goody Booth with the Devil!

On their ecstatic cries

The curtain falls

Y **Literary Focus** Motivation Why might Tituba make this accusation?

Z **Literary Focus** Motivation Why does Abigail change her story so abruptly and completely?

Applying Your Skills

The Crucible, Act One

Respond and Think Critically

Reading Focus

Quick Check

1. When Abigail is alone with Proctor, what claim does she make?

2. Why are both Mrs. Putnam and Abigail interested in Tituba's "conjuring"?

3. What symptoms do Betty and Ruth display?

Read with a Purpose

4. Make a time line that places in rough chronological order events such as the murder of Abigail's parents, the dispute over the election of the minister, the battle over Francis Nurse's land, and the death of Mrs. Putnam's babies.

Reading Skills: Drawing Conclusions About Characters

5. Add a third column to the chart you created as you read the first act of the play. Label the column "Interpretation," and write about the characters' values, emotions, and motives.

Character	Dialogue (Act)	Interpretation
Parris	"I do not preach for children, Rebecca. It is not the children who are unmindful of their obligations toward this ministry." (Act One)	

Literary Focus

Literary Analysis

6. **Summarize** What is Hale's view of his mission in Salem? What does he mean when he says that the devil is "precise"?

7. **Compare and Contrast** What comparisons can you make between Abigail's relationship with the other girls and her relationship with Proctor?

8. **Literary Perspectives** Among the characters from Act One, which do you think is the most credible? The least credible? Explain.

Literary Skills: Motivation

9. **Hypothesize** What concerns might Reverend Parris have about Betty's affliction?

10. **Infer** What do you think is Abigail's motivation to "open" herself and begin naming names?

Literary Skills Review: Figures of Speech

11. **Analyze** A **figure of speech** describes one thing in terms of something else and is not meant to be taken literally. How does Miller's figurative language, "dark houses snuggling against the raw Massachusetts winter," lend to the mood of *The Crucible*?

Writing Focus

Think as a Reader/Writer

Use It in Your Writing Write a dramatic scene with at least three characters. Using Miller's play as a model, include stage directions to supplement your dialogue and <u>transmit</u> more information about the characters.

What Do You Think Now

When someone is accused of a crime today, do people still have a tendency to side with the accuser? Explain your answer.

For **CHOICES** see page 1167. ❯

The Crucible
Act Two

Read with a Purpose Read Act Two of *The Crucible* to learn what motivates the members of the Proctor household.

Act Two

The common room of PROCTOR'*s house, eight days later.*

At the right is a door opening on the fields outside. A fireplace is at the left, and behind it a stairway leading upstairs. It is the low, dark, and rather long living room of the time. As the curtain rises, the room is empty. From above, ELIZABETH *is heard softly singing to the children. Presently the door opens and* JOHN PROCTOR *enters, carrying his gun. He glances about the room as he comes toward the fireplace, then halts for an instant as he hears her singing. He continues on to the fireplace, leans the gun against the wall as he swings a pot out of the fire and smells it. Then he lifts out the ladle and tastes. He is* not quite pleased. *He reaches to a cupboard, takes a pinch of salt, and drops it into the pot. As he is tasting again, her footsteps are heard on the stair. He swings the pot into the fireplace and goes to a basin and washes his hands and face.* ELIZABETH *enters.*

Elizabeth: What keeps you so late? It's almost dark.
Proctor: I were planting far out to the forest edge.
Elizabeth: Oh, you're done then.

Proctor: Aye, the farm is seeded. The boys asleep?
Elizabeth: They will be soon. *And she goes to the fireplace, proceeds to ladle up stew in a dish.*
Proctor: Pray now for a fair summer.
Elizabeth: Aye.
Proctor: Are you well today?
Elizabeth: I am. *She brings the plate to the table, and, indicating the food:* It is a rabbit.
Proctor, *going to the table:* Oh, is it! In Jonathan's trap?
Elizabeth: No, she walked into the house this afternoon; I found her sittin' in the corner like she come to visit.
Proctor: Oh, that's a good sign walkin' in.
Elizabeth: Pray God. It hurt my heart to strip her, poor rabbit. *She sits and watches him taste it.*
Proctor: It's well seasoned.   **Ⓐ**
Elizabeth, *blushing with pleasure:* I took great care. She's tender?
Proctor: Aye. *He eats. She watches him.* I think we'll see green fields soon. It's warm as blood beneath the clods.
Elizabeth: That's well.

PROCTOR *eats, then looks up.*

Proctor: If the crop is good I'll buy George Jacobs' heifer. How would that please you?

Ⓐ Literary Focus Motivation Why does Proctor compliment the dish when he has just added seasoning to the stew? Explain.

Elizabeth: Aye, it would.

Proctor, *with a grin:* I mean to please you, Elizabeth.

Elizabeth—*it is hard to say:* I know it, John.

He gets up, goes to her, kisses her. She receives it. With a certain disappointment, he returns to the table. **B**

Proctor, *as gently as he can:* Cider?

Elizabeth, *with a sense of reprimanding herself for having forgot:* Aye! *She gets up and goes and pours a glass for him. He now arches his back.*

Proctor: This farm's a continent when you go foot by foot droppin' seeds in it.

metifor and HYPERbols [handwritten]

Elizabeth, *coming with the cider:* It must be.

Proctor, *he drinks a long draught, then, putting the glass down:* You ought to bring some flowers in the house.

Elizabeth: Oh! I forgot! I will tomorrow.

Proctor: It's winter in here yet. On Sunday let you come with me, and we'll walk the farm together; I never see such a load of flowers on the earth. *With good feeling he goes and looks up at the sky through the open doorway.* Lilacs have a purple smell. Lilac is the smell of nightfall, I think. Massachusetts is a beauty in the spring! *Justaposition with righter Death. Sens new Birth* [handwritten] **C**

Elizabeth: Aye, it is.

There is a pause. She is watching him from the table as he stands there absorbing the night. It is as though she would speak but cannot. Instead, now, she takes up his plate and glass and fork and goes with them to the basin. Her back is turned to him. He turns to her and watches her. A sense of their separation rises.

acting [handwritten vertical]

Proctor: I think you're sad again. Are you?

Elizabeth—*she doesn't want friction, and yet she must:* You come so late I thought you'd gone to Salem this afternoon. *Iry TO Say he DID not visit aBBY* [handwritten]

Proctor: Why? I have no business in Salem.

Elizabeth: You did speak of going, earlier this week.

Proctor—*he knows what she means:* I thought better of it since.

Elizabeth: Mary Warren's there today.

Proctor: Why'd you let her? You heard me forbid her to go to Salem any more!

Elizabeth: I couldn't stop her.

Proctor, *holding back a full condemnation of her:* It is a fault, it is a fault, Elizabeth—you're the mistress here, not Mary Warren.

Elizabeth: She frightened all my strength away.

Proctor: How may that mouse frighten you, Elizabeth? You—

Elizabeth: It is a mouse no more. I forbid her go, and she raises up her chin like the daughter of a prince and says to me, "I must go to Salem, Goody Proctor; I am an official of the court!"

Proctor: Court! What court?

Elizabeth: Aye, it is a proper court they have now. *Hails importor The Perry People* [handwritten] They've sent four judges out of Boston, she says, weighty magistrates of the General Court, and at the head sits the Deputy Governor of the Province.

Proctor, *astonished:* Why, she's mad.

Elizabeth: I would to God she were. There be fourteen people in the jail now, she says. **PROCTOR** *simply looks at her, unable to grasp it.* And they'll be tried, and the court have power to hang them too, she says.

Proctor, *scoffing, but without conviction:* Ah, they'd never hang—

Elizabeth: The Deputy Governor promise hangin' if they'll not confess, John. The town's gone wild, I think. She speak of Abigail, and I thought she were a saint, to hear her. Abigail brings the other girls into the court, and where she walks the crowd will part like the sea for Israel. And folks are brought before them, and if they scream and howl and fall to the floor—the person's clapped in the jail for bewitchin' them.

Proctor, *wide-eyed:* Oh, it is a black mischief. **D**

The town's gone wild, I think.

B **Reading Focus** Drawing Conclusions About Characters
Why is Proctor disappointed?

C **Reading Focus** Drawing Conclusions About Characters
Why is it significant that Proctor would choose Sunday for the walk?

D **Reading Focus** Drawing Conclusions About Characters
What is Proctor's attitude toward the people who claim to have been bewitched?

Elizabeth: I think you must go to Salem, John. *He turns to her.* I think so. You must tell them it is a fraud.

Proctor, *thinking beyond this:* Aye, it is, it is surely.

Elizabeth: Let you go to Ezekiel Cheever—he knows you well. And tell him what she said to you last week in her uncle's house. She said it had naught to do with witchcraft, did she not?

Proctor, *in thought:* Aye, she did, she did. *Now a pause.*

Elizabeth, *quietly, fearing to anger him by prodding:* God forbid you keep that from the court, John. I think they must be told.

Proctor, *quietly, struggling with his thought:* Aye, they must, they must. It is a wonder they do believe her.

Elizabeth: I would go to Salem now, John—let you go tonight.

Proctor: I'll think on it.

Elizabeth, *with her courage now:* You cannot keep it, John.

Proctor, *angering:* I know I cannot keep it. I say I will think on it!

Elizabeth, *hurt, and very coldly:* Good, then, let you think on it. *She stands and starts to walk out of the room.*

Proctor: I am only wondering how I may prove what she told me, Elizabeth. If the girl's a saint now, I think it is not easy to prove she's fraud, and the town gone so silly. She told it to me in a room alone—I have no proof for it.

Elizabeth: You were alone with her?

Proctor, *stubbornly:* For a moment alone, aye.

Elizabeth: Why, then, it is not as you told me.

Proctor, *his anger rising:* For a moment, I say. The others come in soon after.

Elizabeth, *quietly—she has suddenly lost all faith in him:* Do as you wish, then. *She starts to turn.*

Proctor: Woman. *She turns to him.* I'll not have your suspicion any more.

Elizabeth, *a little loftily:* I have no—

Proctor: I'll not have it!

Elizabeth: Then let you not earn it.

Proctor, *with a violent undertone:* You doubt me yet?

Elizabeth, *with a smile, to keep her dignity:* John, if it were not Abigail that you must go to hurt, would you falter now? I think not.

Proctor: Now look you—

Elizabeth: I see what I see, John.

Proctor, *with solemn warning:* You will not judge me more, Elizabeth. I have good reason to think before I charge fraud on Abigail, and I will think on it. Let you look to your own improvement before you go to judge your husband any more. I have forgot Abigail, and—

Elizabeth: And I.

Proctor: Spare me! You forget nothin' and forgive nothin'. Learn charity, woman. I have gone tiptoe in this house all seven month since she is gone. I have not moved from there to there without I think to please you, and still an everlasting funeral marches round your heart. I cannot speak but I am doubted, every moment judged for lies, as though I come into a court when I come into this house!

Elizabeth: John, you are not open with me. You saw her with a crowd, you said. Now you—

Proctor: I'll plead my honesty no more, Elizabeth.

Elizabeth—*now she would justify herself:* John, I am only—

Proctor: No more! I should have roared you down when first you told me your suspicion. But I wilted, and, like a Christian, I confessed. Confessed! Some dream I had must have mistaken you for God that day. But you're not, you're not, and let you remember it! Let you look sometimes for the goodness in me, and judge me not.

Elizabeth: I do not judge you. The magistrate sits in your heart that judges you. I never thought you but a good man, John—*with a smile*—only somewhat bewildered.

Proctor, *laughing bitterly:* Oh, Elizabeth, your justice would freeze beer! *He turns suddenly toward a sound outside. He starts for the door as* MARY WARREN *enters. As soon as he sees her, he goes directly to her and grabs her by her cloak, furious.* How do you go to Salem when I forbid it? Do you mock me? *Shaking her:* I'll whip you if you dare leave this house again! **Ⓔ** *Strangely, she doesn't resist him but hangs limply by his grip.*

Mary Warren: I am sick, I am sick, Mr. Proctor. Pray, pray, hurt me not. *Her strangeness throws him off, and her evident pallor and weakness. He frees her.* My insides are all shuddery; I am in the proceedings all day, sir.

Proctor, *with draining anger—his curiosity is draining*

Ⓔ Literary Focus Motivation What do you believe is the source of Proctor's fury?

it: And what of these proceedings here? When will you proceed to keep this house, as you are paid nine pound a year to do—and my wife not wholly well?

As though to compensate, MARY WARREN *goes to* ELIZABETH *with a small rag doll.* voдve

Mary Warren: I made a gift for you today, Goody Proctor. I had to sit long hours in a chair, and passed the time with sewing.

Elizabeth, *perplexed, looking at the doll:* Why, thank you, it's a fair poppet.[1]

Mary Warren, *with a trembling, decayed voice:* We must all love each other now, Goody Proctor.

Elizabeth, *amazed at her strangeness:* Aye, indeed, we must.

_____

1. **poppet:** doll; puppet.

Mary Warren, *glancing at the room:* I'll get up early in the morning and clean the house. I must sleep now. *She turns and starts off.*

Proctor: Mary. *She halts.* Is it true? There be fourteen women arrested?

Mary Warren: No, sir. There be thirty-nine now— *She suddenly breaks off and sobs and sits down, exhausted.*

Elizabeth: Why, she's weepin'! What ails you, child?

Mary Warren: Goody Osburn—will hang! *There is a shocked pause, while she sobs.* **Ⓕ**

Proctor: Hang! *He calls into her face.* Hang, y'say?

Mary Warren, *through her weeping:* Aye.

Proctor: The Deputy Governor will permit it?

_____

Ⓕ Literary Focus Motivation What is Mary's attitude toward the accused women at this point?

Analyzing Visuals

The girls of Salem "scream and howl and fall to the floor. . . ."

Viewing and Interpreting How do the facial expressions and body language of the girls in the photograph help <u>transmit</u> the impression that they are bewitched? Explain your response.

Mary Warren: He sentenced her. He must. *To ameliorate it:* But not Sarah Good. For Sarah Good confessed, y'see.

Proctor: Confessed! To what?

Mary Warren: That she—*in horror at the memory*—she sometimes made a compact with Lucifer, and wrote her name in his black book—with her blood—and bound herself to torment Christians till God's thrown down—and we all must worship Hell forevermore. **G**

Pause.

Proctor: But—surely you know what a jabberer she is. Did you tell them that?

Mary Warren: Mr. Proctor, in open court she near to choked us all to death.

Proctor: How, choked you?

Mary Warren: She sent her spirit out.

Elizabeth: Oh, Mary, Mary, surely you—

Mary Warren, *with an indignant edge:* She tried to kill me many times, Goody Proctor!

Elizabeth: Why, I never heard you mention that before.

Mary Warren: I never knew it before. I never knew anything before. When she come into the court I say to myself, I must not accuse this woman, for she sleep in ditches, and so very old and poor. But then—then she sit there, denying and denying, and I feel a misty coldness climbin' up my back, and the skin on my skull begin to creep, and I feel a clamp around my neck and I cannot breathe air; and then—*entranced*—I hear a voice, a screamin' voice, and it were my voice—and all at once I remember everything she done to me!

Proctor: Why? What did she do to you?

Mary Warren, *like one awakened to a marvelous secret insight:* So many time, Mr. Proctor, she come to this very door, beggin' bread and a cup of cider—and mark this: whenever I turned her away empty, she *mumbled.*

Elizabeth: Mumbled! She may mumble if she's hungry.

Mary Warren: But *what* does she mumble? You must remember, Goody Proctor. Last month—a Monday, I think—she walked away, and I thought my guts would burst for two days after. Do you remember it?

Elizabeth: Why—I do, I think, but—

Mary Warren: And so I told that to Judge Hathorne, and he asks her so. "Goody Osburn," says he, "what curse do you mumble that this girl must fall sick after turning you away?" And then she replies—*mimicking an old crone*—"Why, your excellence, no curse at all. I only say my commandments; I hope I may say my commandments," says she!

Elizabeth: And that's an upright answer.

Mary Warren: Aye, but then Judge Hathorne say, "Recite for us your commandments!"—*leaning avidly toward them*—and of all the ten she could not say a single one. She never knew no commandments, and they had her in a flat lie!

Proctor: And so condemned her?

Mary Warren, *now a little strained, seeing his stubborn doubt:* Why, they must when she condemned herself.

Proctor: But the proof, the proof! **H**

Mary Warren, *with greater impatience with him:* I told you the proof. It's hard proof, hard as rock, the judges said.

Proctor—*he pauses an instant, then:* You will not go to court again, Mary Warren.

Mary Warren: I must tell you, sir, I will be gone every day now. I am amazed you do not see what weighty work we do.

Proctor: What work you do! It's strange work for a Christian girl to hang old women!

Mary Warren: But, Mr. Proctor, they will not hang them if they confess. Sarah Good will only sit in jail some time—*recalling*—and here's a wonder for you; think on this. Goody Good is pregnant!

Elizabeth: Pregnant! Are they mad? The woman's near to sixty!

Mary Warren: They had Doctor Griggs examine her, and she's full to the brim. And smokin' a pipe all these years, and no husband either! But she's safe, thank God, for they'll not hurt the innocent child. But be that not a marvel? You must see it, sir, it's God's work we do. So I'll be gone every day for some time. I'm—I am an official of the court, they say, and I— *She has been edging toward offstage.*

G **Literary Perspectives** Analyzing Credibility Why would those who confess to witchcraft be pardoned while those who profess to love God be hanged? Explain your response.

H **Reading Focus** Drawing Conclusions About Characters Why isn't Proctor convinced by Mary's statements?

Vocabulary **avidly** (AV ihd lee) *adv.:* eagerly.

Proctor: I'll official you! *He strides to the mantel, takes down the whip hanging there.*

Mary Warren, *terrified, but coming erect, striving for her authority:* I'll not stand whipping any more!

Elizabeth, *hurriedly, as* PROCTOR *approaches:* Mary, promise now you'll stay at home—

Mary Warren, *backing from him, but keeping her erect posture, striving, striving for her way:* The Devil's loose in Salem, Mr. Proctor; we must discover where he's hiding!

Proctor: I'll whip the Devil out of you! *With whip raised he reaches out for her, and she streaks away and yells.*

Mary Warren, *pointing at* ELIZABETH: I saved her life today!

Silence. His whip comes down.

Elizabeth, *softly:* I am accused?

Mary Warren, *quaking:* Somewhat mentioned. But I said I never see no sign you ever sent your spirit out to hurt no one, and seeing I do live so closely with you, they dismissed it.

Elizabeth: Who accused me?   ❶

Mary Warren: I am bound by law, I cannot tell it. *To* PROCTOR: I only hope you'll not be so sarcastical no more. Four judges and the King's deputy sat to dinner with us but an hour ago. I—I would have you speak civilly to me, from this out.

Proctor, *in horror, muttering in disgust at her:* Go to bed.

Mary Warren, *with a stamp of her foot:* I'll not be ordered to bed no more, Mr. Proctor! I am eighteen and a woman, however single!

Proctor: Do you wish to sit up? Then sit up.

Mary Warren: I wish to go to bed!

Proctor, *in anger:* Good night, then!

Mary Warren: Good night. *Dissatisfied, uncertain of herself, she goes out. Wide-eyed, both* PROCTOR *and* ELIZABETH *stand staring.*

Elizabeth, *quietly:* Oh, the noose, the noose is up!

Proctor: There'll be no noose.

Elizabeth: She wants me dead. I knew all week it would come to this!

Proctor, *without conviction:* They dismissed it. You heard her say—

Elizabeth: And what of tomorrow? She will cry me out until they take me!

Proctor: Sit you down.

Elizabeth: She wants me dead, John, you know it!

Proctor: I say sit down! *She sits, trembling. He speaks quietly, trying to keep his wits.* Now we must be wise, Elizabeth.

Elizabeth, *with sarcasm, and a sense of being lost:* Oh, indeed, indeed!

Proctor: Fear nothing. I'll find Ezekiel Cheever. I'll tell him she said it were all sport.

Elizabeth: John, with so many in the jail, more than Cheever's help is needed now, I think. Would you favor me with this? Go to Abigail.

Proctor, *his soul hardening as he senses . . . :* What have I to say to Abigail?

Elizabeth, *delicately:* John—grant me this. You have a faulty understanding of young girls. There is a promise made in any bed—

Proctor, *striving against his anger:* What promise!

Elizabeth: Spoke or silent, a promise is surely made. And she may dote on it now—I am sure she does—and thinks to kill me, then to take my place.

PROCTOR's *anger is rising; he cannot speak.*

Elizabeth: It is her dearest hope, John, I know it. There be a thousand names; why does she call mine? There be a certain danger in calling such a name—I am no Goody Good that sleeps in ditches, nor Osburn, drunk and half-witted. She'd dare not call out such a farmer's wife but there be monstrous profit in it. She thinks to take my place, John.

Proctor: She cannot think it! *He knows it is true.*

Elizabeth, *"reasonably":* John, have you ever shown her somewhat of contempt? She cannot pass you in the church but you will blush—

Proctor: I may blush for my sin.

Elizabeth: I think she sees another meaning in that blush.

Proctor: And what see you? What see you, Elizabeth?

Elizabeth, *"conceding":* I think you be somewhat ashamed, for I am there, and she so close.

Proctor: When will you know me, woman? Were I stone I would have cracked for shame this seven month!

---

❶ **Literary Focus** Motivation Who would have the strongest motivation to accuse Elizabeth of witchcraft? Why?

Elizabeth: Then go and tell her she's a whore. Whatever promise she may sense—break it, John, break it.

Proctor, *between his teeth:* Good, then. I'll go. *He starts for his rifle.*

Elizabeth, *trembling, fearfully:* Oh, how unwillingly!

Proctor, *turning on her, rifle in hand:* I will curse her hotter than the oldest cinder in hell. But pray, begrudge me not my anger!

Elizabeth: Your anger! I only ask you—

Proctor: Woman, am I so base? Do you truly think me base?

Elizabeth: I never called you base.

Proctor: Then how do you charge me with such a promise? The promise that a stallion gives a mare I gave that girl!

Elizabeth: Then why do you anger with me when I bid you break it?

Proctor: Because it speaks deceit, and I am honest! But I'll plead no more! I see now your spirit twists around the single error of my life, and I will never tear it free!

Elizabeth, *crying out:* You'll tear it free—when you come to know that I will be your only wife, or no wife at all! She has an arrow in you yet, John Proctor, and you know it well!

Quite suddenly, as though from the air, a figure appears in the doorway. They start slightly. It is MR. HALE. *He is different now—drawn a little, and there is a quality of deference, even of guilt, about his manner now.*

Hale: Good evening.

Proctor, *still in his shock:* Why, Mr. Hale! Good evening to you, sir. Come in, come in.

Hale, *to* ELIZABETH: I hope I do not startle you.

Elizabeth: No, no, it's only that I heard no horse—

Hale: You are Goodwife Proctor.

Proctor: Aye; Elizabeth.

Hale, *nods, then:* I hope you're not off to bed yet.

Proctor, *setting down his gun:* No, no. HALE *comes further into the room. And* PROCTOR, *to explain his nervousness:* We are not used to visitors after dark, but you're welcome here. Will you sit you down, sir?

Hale: I will. *He sits.* Let you sit, Goodwife Proctor.

She does, never letting him out of her sight. There is a pause as HALE *looks about the room.*

Proctor, *to break the silence:* Will you drink cider, Mr. Hale?

Hale: No, it rebels my stomach; I have some further traveling yet tonight. Sit you down, sir. PROCTOR *sits.* I will not keep you long, but I have some business with you.

Proctor: Business of the court?

Hale: No—no, I come of my own, without the court's authority. Hear me. *He wets his lips.* I know not if you are aware, but your wife's name is—mentioned in the court.

Proctor: We know it, sir. Our Mary Warren told us. We are entirely amazed.

Hale: I am a stranger here, as you know. And in my ignorance I find it hard to draw a clear opinion of them that come accused before the court. And so this afternoon, and now tonight, I go from house to house—I come now from Rebecca Nurse's house and—

Elizabeth, *shocked:* Rebecca's charged!

Hale: God forbid such a one be charged. She is, however—mentioned somewhat.

Elizabeth, *with an attempt at a laugh:* You will never believe, I hope, that Rebecca trafficked with the Devil.

Hale: Woman, it is possible.

Proctor, *taken aback:* Surely you cannot think so.

Hale: This is a strange time, Mister. No man may longer doubt the powers of the dark are gathered in monstrous attack upon this village. There is too much evidence now to deny it. You will agree, sir?

Proctor, *evading:* I—I have no knowledge in that line. But it's hard to think so pious a woman be secretly a Devil's bitch after seventy year of such good prayer. **(K)**

Hale: Aye. But the Devil is a wily one, you cannot deny it. However, she is far from accused, and I know she will not be. *Pause.* I thought, sir, to put some questions as to the Christian character of this house, if you'll permit me.

Proctor, *coldly, resentful:* Why, we—have no fear of questions, sir.

(J) **Reading Focus** **Drawing Conclusions About Characters**
Is protecting her own reputation the only reason Elizabeth wants Proctor to "break his promise"?

(K) **Literary Focus** **Motivation** Why won't Proctor reveal what he knows about Abigail and the other girls?

Hale: Good, then. *He makes himself more comfortable.* In the book of record that Mr. Parris keeps, I note that you are rarely in the church on Sabbath Day.

Proctor: No, sir, you are mistaken.

Hale: Twenty-six time in seventeen month, sir. I must call that rare. Will you tell me why you are so absent?

Proctor: Mr. Hale, I never knew I must account too that man for I come to church or stay at home. My wife were sick this winter.

Hale: So I am told. But you, Mister, why could you not come alone?

Proctor: I surely did come when I could, and when I could not I prayed in this house.

Hale: Mr. Proctor, your house is not a church; your theology must tell you that.

Proctor: It does, sir, it does; and it tells me that a minister may pray to God without he have golden candlesticks upon the altar.

Hale: What golden candlesticks?

Proctor: Since we built the church there were pewter candlesticks upon the altar; Francis Nurse made them, y'know, and a sweeter hand never touched the metal. But Parris came, and for twenty week he preach nothin' but golden candlesticks until he had them. I labor the earth from dawn of day to blink of night, and I tell you true, when I look to heaven and see my money glaring at his elbows—it hurt my prayer, sir, it hurt my prayer. I think, sometimes, the man dreams cathedrals, not clapboard meetin' houses.

Hale, *thinks, then:* And yet, Mister, a Christian on Sabbath Day must be in church. *Pause.* Tell me—you have three children?

Proctor: Aye. Boys.

Hale: How comes it that only two are baptized?

Proctor, *starts to speak, then stops, then, as though unable to restrain this:* I like it not that Mr. Parris should lay his hand upon my baby. I see no light of God in that man. I'll not conceal it.

Hale: I must say it, Mr. Proctor; that is not for you to decide. The man's ordained, therefore the light of God is in him.

Proctor, *flushed with resentment but trying to smile:*

No man may longer doubt the powers of the dark are gathered in monstrous attack upon this village.

What's your suspicion, Mr. Hale?

Hale: No, no, I have no—

Proctor: I nailed the roof upon the church, I hung the door—

Hale: Oh, did you! That's a good sign, then.

Proctor: It may be I have been too quick to bring the man to book, but you cannot think we ever desired the destruction of religion. I think that's in your mind, is it not?

Hale, *not altogether giving way:* I—have—there is a softness in your record, sir, a softness.

Elizabeth: I think, maybe, we have been too hard with Mr. Parris. I think so. But sure we never loved the Devil here.

Hale, *nods, deliberating this. Then, with the voice of one administering a secret test:* Do you know your Commandments, Elizabeth?

Elizabeth, *without hesitation, even eagerly:* I surely do. There be no mark of blame upon my life, Mr. Hale. I am a covenanted Christian woman.

Hale: And you, Mister?

Proctor, *a trifle unsteadily:* I—am sure I do, sir.

Hale, *glances at her open face, then at* JOHN, *then:* Let you repeat them, if you will.

Proctor: The Commandments.

Hale: Aye.

Proctor, *looking off, beginning to sweat:* Thou shalt not kill.

Hale: Aye.

Proctor, *counting on his fingers:* Thou shalt not steal. Thou shalt not covet thy neighbor's goods, nor make unto thee any graven image. Thou shalt not take the name of the Lord in vain; thou shalt have no other gods before me. *With some hesitation:* Thou shalt remember the Sabbath Day and keep it holy. *Pause. Then:* Thou shalt honor thy father and mother. Thou shalt not bear false witness. *He is stuck. He counts back on his fingers, knowing one is missing.* Thou shalt not make unto thee any graven image.

Hale: You have said that twice, sir.

Proctor, *lost:* Aye. *He is flailing for it.*

Elizabeth, *delicately:* Adultery, John.

Proctor, *as though a secret arrow had pained his heart:* Aye. *Trying to grin it away—to* HALE: You see, sir, between the two of us we do know them all. HALE *only looks at* PROCTOR, *deep in his attempt to define this man.* PROCTOR *grows more uneasy.* I think it be a small fault.

Hale: Theology, sir, is a fortress; no crack in a fortress may be accounted small. *He rises; he seems worried now. He paces a little, in deep thought.* **L**

Proctor: There be no love for Satan in this house, Mister.

Hale: I pray it, I pray it dearly. *He looks to both of them, an attempt at a smile on his face, but his misgivings are clear.* Well, then—I'll bid you good night.

Elizabeth, *unable to restrain herself:* Mr. Hale. *He turns.* I do think you are suspecting me somewhat? Are you not?

Hale, *obviously disturbed—and evasive:* Goody Proctor, I do not judge you. My duty is to add what I may to the godly wisdom of the court. I pray you both good health and good fortune. *To* JOHN: Good night, sir. *He starts out.*

Elizabeth, *with a note of desperation:* I think you must tell him, John.

Hale: What's that?

Elizabeth, *restraining a call:* Will you tell him?

Slight pause. HALE *looks questioningly at* JOHN.

Proctor, *with difficulty:* I—I have no witness and cannot prove it, except my word be taken. But I know the children's sickness had naught to do with witchcraft.

Hale, *stopped, struck:* Naught to do—?

Proctor: Mr. Parris discovered them sportin' in the woods. They were startled and took sick.

Pause.

Hale: Who told you this?

Proctor, *hesitates, then:* Abigail Williams.

Hale: Abigail!

Proctor: Aye.

Hale, *his eyes wide:* Abigail Williams told you it had naught to do with witchcraft!

Proctor: She told me the day you came, sir.

Hale, *suspiciously:* Why—why did you keep this?

Proctor: I never knew until tonight that the world is gone daft with this nonsense.

Hale: Nonsense! Mister, I have myself examined Tituba, Sarah Good, and numerous others that have confessed to dealing with the Devil. They have *confessed* it.

Proctor: And why not, if they must hang for denyin' it? There are them that will swear to anything before they'll hang; have you never thought of that?

Hale: I have. I—I have indeed. *It is his own suspicion, but he resists it. He glances at* ELIZABETH, *then at* JOHN. And you—would you testify to this in court?

Proctor: I—had not reckoned with goin' into court. But if I must I will.

Hale: Do you falter here?

Proctor: I falter nothing, but I may wonder if my story will be credited in such a court. I do wonder on it, when such a steady-minded minister as you will suspicion such a woman that never lied, and cannot, and the world knows she cannot! I may falter somewhat, Mister; I am no fool. **M**

Hale, *quietly—it has impressed him:* Proctor, let you open with me now, for I have a rumor that troubles me. It's said you hold no belief that there may even be witches in the world. Is that true, sir?

Proctor—*he knows this is critical, and is striving against his disgust with* HALE *and with himself for even answering:* I know not what I have said, I may have said it. I have wondered if there be witches in the world—although I cannot believe they come among us now.

Hale: Then you do not believe—

Proctor: I have no knowledge of it; the Bible speaks of witches, and I will not deny them.

Hale: And you, woman?

Elizabeth: I—I cannot believe it.

Hale, *shocked:* You cannot!

Proctor: Elizabeth, you bewilder him!

Elizabeth, *to* HALE: I cannot think the Devil may own a woman's soul, Mr. Hale, when she keeps an upright way, as I have. I am a good woman, I know it; and if you believe I may do only good work in the world, and yet be secretly bound to Satan, then I must tell you, sir, I do not believe it.

L **Reading Focus** **Drawing Conclusions About Characters** Why does Hale attach so much significance to Proctor's forgetting a commandment?

M **Literary Perspectives** **Analyzing Credibility** Why do you think Miller has Proctor express his doubts that he would be "credited in such a court"? Explain your response.

Hale: But, woman, you do believe there are witches in—

Elizabeth: If you think that I am one, then I say there are none.

Hale: You surely do not fly against the Gospel, the Gospel—

Proctor: She believe in the Gospel, every word!

Elizabeth: Question Abigail Williams about the Gospel, not myself!

HALE *stares at her.*

Proctor: She do not mean to doubt the Gospel, sir, you cannot think it. This be a Christian house, sir, a Christian house.

Hale: God keep you both; let the third child be quickly baptized, and go you without fail each Sunday in to Sabbath prayer; and keep a solemn, quiet way among you. I think—

GILES COREY *appears in doorway.*

Giles: John!

Proctor: Giles! What's the matter?

Giles: They take my wife.

FRANCIS NURSE *enters.*

Giles: And his Rebecca!

Proctor, *to* FRANCIS: Rebecca's in the *jail!*

Francis: Aye, Cheever come and take her in his wagon. We've only now come from the jail, and they'll not even let us in to see them.

Elizabeth: They've surely gone wild now, Mr. Hale!

Francis, *going to* HALE: Reverend Hale! Can you not speak to the Deputy Governor? I'm sure he mistakes these people—

Hale: Pray calm yourself, Mr. Nurse.

Francis: My wife is the very brick and mortar of the church, Mr. Hale—*indicating* GILES—and Martha Corey, there cannot be a woman closer yet to God than Martha.

Hale: How is Rebecca charged, Mr. Nurse?

Francis, *with a mocking, half-hearted laugh:* For murder, she's charged! *Mockingly quoting the warrant:* "For the marvelous and supernatural murder of Goody Putnam's babies." What am I to do, Mr. Hale?

Hale, *turns from* FRANCIS, *deeply troubled, then:*

Believe me, Mr. Nurse, if Rebecca Nurse be tainted, then nothing's left to stop the whole green world from burning. Let you rest upon the justice of the court; the court will send her home, I know it.

Francis: You cannot mean she will be tried in court!

Hale, *pleading:* Nurse, though our hearts break, we cannot flinch; these are new times, sir. There is a misty plot afoot so subtle we should be criminal to cling to old respects and ancient friendships. I have seen too many frightful proofs in court—the Devil is alive in Salem, and we dare not quail to follow wherever the accusing finger points!

Proctor, *angered:* How may such a woman murder children?

Hale, *in great pain:* Man, remember, until an hour before the Devil fell, God thought him beautiful in Heaven.

Giles: I never said my wife were a witch, Mr. Hale; I only said she were reading books!

Hale: Mr. Corey, exactly what complaint were made on your wife?

Giles: That bloody mongrel Walcott charge her. Y'see, he buy a pig of my wife four or five year ago, and the pig died soon after. So he come dancin' in for his money back. So my Martha, she says to him, "Walcott, if you haven't the wit to feed a pig properly, you'll not live to own many," she says. Now he goes to court and claims that from that day to this he cannot keep a pig alive for more than four weeks because my Martha bewitch them with her books!

Enter EZEKIEL CHEEVER. *A shocked silence.*

Cheever: Good evening to you, Proctor.

Proctor: Why, Mr. Cheever. Good evening.

Cheever: Good evening, all. Good evening, Mr. Hale.

Proctor: I hope you come not on business of the court.

Cheever: I do, Proctor, aye. I am clerk of the court now, y'know.

Enter MARSHAL HERRICK, *a man in his early thirties, who is somewhat shamefaced at the moment.*

Giles: It's a pity, Ezekiel, that an honest tailor might have gone to Heaven must burn in Hell. You'll burn for this, do you know it?

N | **Literary Focus** Motivation Why does Elizabeth risk raising Hale's suspicion by denying the existence of witches?

O | **Literary Perspectives** Analyzing Credibility How does this statement contradict Hale's earlier assertion to Francis about Rebecca?

Cheever: You know yourself I must do as I'm told. You surely know that, Giles. And I'd as lief[2] you'd not be sending me to Hell. I like not the sound of it, I tell you; I like not the sound of it. *He fears* PROCTOR, *but starts to reach inside his coat.* Now believe me, Proctor, how heavy be the law, all its tonnage I do carry on my back tonight. *He takes out a warrant.* I have a warrant for your wife.

Proctor, *to* HALE: You said she were not charged!

Hale: I know nothin' of it. *To* CHEEVER: When were she charged?

Cheever: I am given sixteen warrant tonight, sir, and she is one.

Proctor: Who charged her?

Cheever: Why, Abigail Williams charge her.

Proctor: On what proof, what proof?

Cheever, *looking about the room:* Mr. Proctor, I have little time. The court bid me search your house, but I like not to search a house. So will you hand me any poppets that your wife may keep here?

Proctor: Poppets?

Elizabeth: I never kept no poppets, not since I were a girl.

Cheever, *embarrassed, glancing toward the mantel where sits* MARY WARREN's *poppet:* I spy a poppet, Goody Proctor.

Elizabeth: Oh! *Going for it:* Why, this is Mary's.

Cheever, *shyly:* Would you please to give it to me?

Elizabeth, *handing it to him, asks* HALE: Has the court discovered a text in poppets now?

Cheever, *carefully holding the poppet:* Do you keep any others in this house?

Proctor: No, not this one either till tonight. What signifies a poppet?

Cheever: Why, a poppet—*he gingerly turns the poppet over*—a poppet may signify— Now, woman, will you please to come with me? **P**

---

2. **lief** (leef): gladly.

Proctor: She will not! *To* ELIZABETH: Fetch Mary here.

Cheever, *ineptly reaching toward* ELIZABETH: No, no, I am forbid to leave her from my sight.

Proctor, *pushing his arm away:* You'll leave her out of sight and out of mind, Mister. Fetch Mary, Elizabeth.

ELIZABETH *goes upstairs.*

Hale: What signifies a poppet, Mr. Cheever?

Cheever, *turning the poppet over in his hands:* Why, they say it may signify that she— *He has lifted the poppet's skirt, and his eyes widen in astonished fear.* Why, this, this—

Proctor, *reaching for the poppet:* What's there?

Cheever: Why—*he draws out a long needle from the poppet*—it is a needle! Herrick, Herrick, it is a needle!

HERRICK *comes toward him.*

Proctor, *angrily, bewildered:* And what signifies a needle!

Cheever, *his hands shaking:* Why, this go hard with her, Proctor, this—I had my doubts, Proctor, I had my doubts, but here's calamity. *To* HALE, *showing the needle:* You see it, sir, it is a needle!

Hale: Why? What meanin' has it? **Q**

Cheever, *wide-eyed, trembling:* The girl, the Williams girl, Abigail Williams, sir. She sat to dinner in Reverend Parris's house tonight, and without word nor warnin' she falls to the floor. Like a struck beast, he says, and screamed a scream that a bull would weep to hear. And he goes to save her, and, stuck two inches in the flesh of her belly, he draw a needle out. And demandin' of her how she come to be so stabbed, she—*to* PROCTOR *now*—testify it were your wife's familiar spirit pushed it in.

Proctor: Why, she done it herself! *To* HALE: I hope you're not takin' this for proof, Mister!

HALE, *struck by the proof, is silent.*

P **Reading Focus** Drawing Conclusions About Characters
Why doesn't Cheever answer this critical question of Proctor's?

Q **Literary Perspectives** Analyzing Credibility If a poppet is so significant, why doesn't Hale know the meaning behind it?

1132 Unit 6 • Collection 15

Cheever: 'Tis hard proof! *To* HALE: I find her a poppet Goody Proctor keeps. I have found it, sir. And in the belly of the poppet a needle's stuck. I tell you true, Proctor, I never warranted to see such proof of Hell, and I bid you obstruct me not, for I—

Enter ELIZABETH *with* MARY WARREN. PROCTOR, *seeing* MARY WARREN, *draws her by the arm to* HALE.

Proctor: Here now! Mary, how did this poppet come into my house?

Mary Warren, *frightened for herself, her voice very small:* What poppet's that, sir?

Proctor, *impatiently, pointing at the doll in* CHEEVER's *hand:* This poppet, this poppet.

Mary Warren, *evasively, looking at it:* Why, I—I think it is mine.

Proctor: It is your poppet, is it not?

Mary Warren, *not understanding the direction of this:* It—is, sir.

Proctor: And how did it come into this house?

Mary Warren, *glancing about at the avid faces:* Why—I made it in the court, sir, and—give it to Goody Proctor tonight.

Proctor, *to* HALE: Now, sir—do you have it?

Hale: Mary Warren, a needle have been found inside this poppet.

Mary Warren, *bewildered:* Why, I meant no harm by it, sir. _ADmitens To needen_

Proctor, *quickly:* You stuck that needle in yourself?

Mary Warren: I—I believe I did, sir, I—

Proctor, *to* HALE: What say you now?

Hale, *watching* MARY WARREN *closely:* Child, you are certain this be your natural memory? May it be, perhaps, that someone conjures you even now to say this? **R**

Mary Warren: Conjures me? Why, no, sir, I am entirely myself, I think. Let you ask Susanna Walcott—she saw me sewin' it in court. *Or better still:* Ask Abby, Abby sat beside me when I made it. _ABbys Needs_

Proctor, *to* HALE, *of* CHEEVER: Bid him begone. Your mind is surely settled now. Bid him out, Mr. Hale.

Elizabeth: What signifies a needle?

Hale: Mary—you charge a cold and <u>cruel murder on</u> Abigail.

Mary Warren: <u>Murder! I charge no—</u>

Hale: Abigail were stabbed tonight; a needle were found stuck into her belly— **S**

Elizabeth: And she charges me?

Hale: Aye.

Elizabeth, *her breath knocked out:* <u>Why—! The girl is murder! She must be ripped out of the world!</u> _ABBg should Be south._

Cheever, *pointing at* ELIZABETH: You've heard that, sir! Ripped out of the world! Herrick, you heard it!

Proctor, *suddenly snatching the warrant out of* CHEEVER's *hands:* Out with you.

Cheever: Proctor, you dare not touch the warrant.

Proctor, *ripping the warrant:* Out with you!

Cheever: You've ripped the Deputy Governor's warrant, man!

Proctor: Damn the Deputy Governor! Out of my house!

Hale: Now, Proctor, Proctor!

Proctor: Get y'gone with them! You are a broken minister.

Hale: Proctor, if she is innocent, the court— _ABBy Parr'es Postmams_

Proctor: If *she* is innocent! Why do you never wonder if Parris be innocent, or Abigail? Is the accuser always holy now? Were they born this morning as clean as God's fingers? I'll tell you what's walking Salem—vengeance is walking Salem. We are what we always were in Salem, but now the little crazy children are jangling the keys of the kingdom, and common vengeance writes the law! This warrant's vengeance! I'll not give my wife to vengeance!

Elizabeth: I'll go, John—

Proctor: You will not go!

Herrick: I have nine men outside. You cannot keep her. The law binds me, John, I cannot budge.

Proctor, *to* HALE, *ready to break him:* Will you see her taken?

Hale: Proctor, the court is just—

Proctor: Pontius Pilate![3] God will not let you wash your hands of this! _god Convection._

Elizabeth: John—I think I must go with them.

---

3. **Pontius Pilate** (PUHN chuhs PY luht) (first century A.D.): Roman official who reluctantly condemned Jesus to death. Pilate is said to have declared, "I am innocent of the blood of this just man" (Matthew 27:24).

R Literary Focus **Motivation** Why does Hale suggest that Mary does not remember events correctly?

S Reading Focus **Drawing Conclusions About Characters** Why do Hale and the others continue to believe Abigail?

He cannot bear to look at her. Mary, there is bread enough for the morning; you will bake, in the afternoon. Help Mr. Proctor as you were his daughter—you owe me that, and much more. *She is fighting her weeping. To* PROCTOR: When the children wake, speak nothing of witchcraft—it will frighten them. *She cannot go on.*

Proctor: I will bring you home. I will bring you soon.

Elizabeth: Oh, John, bring me soon!

Proctor: I will fall like an ocean on that court! Fear nothing, Elizabeth.

Elizabeth, *with great fear:* I will fear nothing. *She looks about the room, as though to fix it in her mind.* Tell the children I have gone to visit someone sick.

She walks out the door, HERRICK *and* CHEEVER *behind her. For a moment,* PROCTOR *watches from the doorway. The clank of chain is heard.*

Proctor: Herrick! Herrick, don't chain her! *He rushes out the door. From outside:* Damn you, man, you will not chain her! Off with them! I'll not have it! I will not have her chained!

There are other men's voices against his. HALE, *in a fever of guilt and uncertainty, turns from the door to avoid the sight;* MARY WARREN *bursts into tears and sits weeping.* GILES COREY *calls to* HALE. 🅣

Giles: And yet silent, minister? It is fraud, you know it is fraud! What keeps you, man?

PROCTOR *is half braced, half pushed into the room by two deputies and* HERRICK.

Proctor: I'll pay you, Herrick, I will surely pay you!

Herrick, *panting:* In God's name, John, I cannot help myself. I must chain them all. Now let you keep inside this house till I am gone! *He goes out with his deputies.*

PROCTOR *stands there, gulping air. Horses and a wagon creaking are heard.*

Hale, *in great uncertainty:* Mr. Proctor—

Proctor: Out of my sight!

Hale: Charity, Proctor, charity. What I have heard in her favor, I will not fear to testify in court. God help

me, I cannot judge her guilty or innocent—I know not. Only this consider: the world goes mad, and it profit nothing you should lay the cause to the vengeance of a little girl.

Proctor: You are a coward! Though you be ordained in God's own tears, you are a coward now!

Hale: Proctor, I cannot think God be provoked so grandly by such a petty cause. The jails are packed—our greatest judges sit in Salem now—and hangin's promised. Man, we must look to cause proportionate. Were there murder done, perhaps, and never brought to light? Abomination? Some secret blasphemy that stinks to Heaven? Think on cause, man, and let you help me to discover it. For there's your way, believe it, there is your only way, when such confusion strikes upon the world. *He goes to* GILES *and* FRANCIS. Let you counsel among yourselves; think on your village and what may have drawn from heaven such thundering wrath upon you all. I shall pray God open up our eyes.

HALE *goes out.*

Francis, *struck by* HALE's *mood:* I never heard no murder done in Salem.

Proctor—*he has been reached by* HALE's *words:* Leave me, Francis, leave me.

Giles, *shaken:* John—tell me, are we lost?

Proctor: Go home now, Giles. We'll speak on it tomorrow.

Giles: Let you think on it. We'll come early, eh?

Proctor: Aye. Go now, Giles.

Giles: Good night, then.

GILES COREY *and* FRANCIS NURSE *go out. After a moment:*

Mary Warren, *in a fearful squeak of a voice:* Mr. Proctor, very likely they'll let her come home once they're given proper evidence.

Proctor: You're coming to the court with me, Mary. You will tell it in the court.

Mary Warren: I cannot charge murder on Abigail.

Proctor, *moving menacingly toward her:* You will tell the court how that poppet come here and who stuck the needle in.

🅣 **Literary Focus** Motivation How could Proctor clear up the misconceptions voiced by Hale? Why doesn't he? Explain your response.

Vocabulary **blasphemy** (BLAS fuh mee) *n.:* words or actions that disrespect something sacred.

Mary Warren: She'll kill me for sayin' that! PROCTOR *continues toward her.* Abigail'll charge lechery on you, Mr. Proctor!

Proctor, *halting:* She's told you!

Mary Warren: I have known it, sir. She'll ruin you with it, I know she will.

Proctor, *hesitating, and with deep hatred of himself:* Good. Then her saintliness is done with. MARY *backs from him.* We will slide together into our pit; you will tell the court what you know.

Mary Warren, *in terror:* I cannot, they'll turn on me—

PROCTOR *strides and catches her, and she is repeating, "I cannot, I cannot!"*

Proctor: My wife will never die for me! I will bring your guts into your mouth but that goodness will not die for me!

Mary Warren, *struggling to escape him:* I cannot do it, I cannot!

Proctor, *grasping her by the throat as though he would strangle her:* Make your peace with it! Now Hell and Heaven grapple on our backs, and all our old pretense is ripped away—make your peace! *He throws her to the floor, where she sobs, "I cannot, I cannot . . ." And now, half to himself, staring, and turning to the open door:* Peace. It is a providence, and no great change; we are only what we always were, but naked now. *He walks as though toward a great horror, facing the open sky.* Aye, naked! And the wind, God's icy wind, will blow!

And she is over and over again sobbing, "I cannot, I cannot, I cannot," as

The curtain falls

ⓤ **Reading Focus** Drawing Conclusions About Characters

What change in Proctor's character is revealed by his insistence that Mary tell the court the whole truth?

Applying Your Skills

SKILLS FOCUS **Literary Skills** Analyze character motivation; analyze figures of speech. **Reading Skills** Draw inferences about characters.

The Crucible, Act Two

Respond and Think Critically

Reading Focus

Quick Check

1. At the beginning of the act, why does Elizabeth want John to go to Salem?

2. What gift does Mary Warren give to Elizabeth?

3. According to Elizabeth, what is Abigail's true objective in court?

4. Why is Rebecca Nurse in jail?

5. To what does John Proctor want Mary to testify?

Read with a Purpose

6. Describe the most significant <u>components</u> of the relationship between John and Elizabeth Proctor. Explain the metaphor of the "everlasting funeral" that John sees in Elizabeth's heart.

Reading Skills: Drawing Conclusions About Characters

7. Why does Hale become suspicious of the Proctors? What is the irony in Hale's urging Proctor to show "charity"?

8. Use your chart from Acts One and Two to write a summary stating your opinion of the following characters: Reverend Parris, Mary Warren, John Proctor, Giles Corey, and one other character of your choice. Include a final statement in which you draw conclusions about the characters and explain reasons for their behavior.

Literary Focus

Literary Analysis

9. **Make Judgments** What do you think are the real reasons Mary gives Elizabeth the gift?

10. **Analyze** Describe Proctor's internal conflict. How could it relate to a broader conflict in the play between public and private selves?

11. **Literary Perspectives** Are Mary's accusations against Sarah Good credible? Does Mary herself believe them? Explain.

Literary Skills: Motivation

12. **Draw Conclusions** Regarding Mary's visions and accusations, what clues does Miller give for her motivation?

Literary Skills Review: Figures of Speech

13. **Interpret** A word or phrase that describes one thing in terms of something else is a **figure of speech.** Identify the figure of speech from the following line in Act Two. Then, interpret its meaning: Lilac is the smell of nightfall, I think. Massachusetts is a beauty in the spring! (page 1123)

Writing Focus

Think as a Reader/Writer

Use It in Your Writing Several stage directions in *The Crucible* describe characters' thoughts, revealing unspoken conflicts. At one point, for example, Elizabeth Proctor *"is watching [John] from the table. . . . It is as though she would speak but cannot"* (page 1123). Briefly discuss what this stage direction adds to your understanding of the Proctors' relationship.

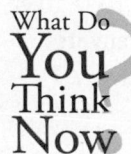 **What Do You Think Now** At this point in the play, who would you say is the protagonist, or central character? What does this character not have in common with the others.

For **CHOICES** see page 1167.

The Crucible

Act Three

> **Read with a Purpose** Read to understand the characters' motivation for falsely accusing members of their own community of witchcraft.

Act Three

[handwritten notes: suspicious, newz + Thomas, hwan, change room]

The vestry room of the Salem meeting house, now serving as the anteroom of the General Court. *[handwritten: clove rooms]*

As the curtain rises, the room is empty, but for sunlight pouring through two high windows in the back wall. The room is solemn, even forbidding. Heavy beams jut out, boards of random widths make up the walls. At the right are two doors leading into the meeting house proper, where the court is being held. At the left another door leads outside.

There is a plain bench at the left, and another at the right. In the center a rather long meeting table, with stools and a considerable armchair snugged up to it.

Through the partitioning wall at the right we hear a prosecutor's voice, JUDGE HATHORNE's, asking a question; then a woman's voice, MARTHA COREY's, replying.

Hathorne's Voice: Now, Martha Corey, there is abundant evidence in our hands to show that you have given yourself to the reading of fortunes. Do you deny it?

Martha Corey's Voice: I am innocent to a witch. I know not what a witch is.

Hathorne's Voice: How do you know, then, that you are not a witch?

Martha Corey's Voice: If I were, I would know it.

Hathorne's Voice: Why do you hurt these children? *[handwritten: ?]*

[handwritten: Rebeca news ABBY???]

Martha Corey's Voice: I do not hurt them. I scorn it!

Giles' Voice, *roaring:* I have evidence for the court!

Voices of townspeople rise in excitement.

Danforth's Voice: You will keep your seat!

Giles' Voice: Thomas Putnam is reaching out for land!

Danforth's Voice: Remove that man, Marshal!

Giles' Voice: You're hearing lies, lies!

A roaring goes up from the people.

Hathorne's Voice: Arrest him, Excellency!

Giles' Voice: I have evidence. Why will you not hear my evidence?

The door opens and GILES is half carried into the vestry room by HERRICK. FRANCIS NURSE enters, trailing anxiously behind GILES.

Giles: Hands off, damn you, let me go!

Herrick: Giles, Giles!

Giles: Out of my way, Herrick! I bring evidence—

Herrick: You cannot go in there, Giles; it's a court!

Enter HALE from the court.

Hale: Pray be calm a moment.

Giles: You, Mr. Hale, go in there and demand I speak.

Hale: A moment, sir, a moment.

Giles: They'll be hangin' my wife!

JUDGE HATHORNE enters. He is in his sixties, a bitter, remorseless Salem judge.

Hathorne: How do you dare come roarin' into this court! Are you gone daft, Corey?

Giles: You're not a Boston judge yet, Hathorne. You'll not call me daft!

Enter DEPUTY GOVERNOR DANFORTH and, behind him, EZEKIEL CHEEVER and PARRIS. On his appearance, silence falls. DANFORTH is a grave man in his sixties, of some humor and sophistication that do not, however, interfere with an exact loyalty to his position and his cause. He comes down to GILES, who awaits his wrath.

Danforth, *looking directly at GILES:* Who is this man?

Parris: Giles Corey, sir, and a more contentious—

Giles, *to PARRIS:* I am asked the question, and I am old enough to answer it! *To DANFORTH, who impresses him and to whom he smiles through his strain:* My name is Corey, sir, Giles Corey. I have six hundred acres, and timber in addition. It is my wife you be condemning now. *He indicates the courtroom.*

Danforth: And how do you imagine to help her cause with such contemptuous riot? Now be gone. Your old age alone keeps you out of jail for this.

Giles, *beginning to plead:* They be tellin' lies about my wife, sir, I—

Danforth: Do you take it upon yourself to determine what this court shall believe and what it shall set aside? **(A)**

Giles: Your Excellency, we mean no disrespect for—

Danforth: Disrespect indeed! It is disruption, Mister. This is the highest court of the supreme government of this province, do you know it?

Giles, *beginning to weep:* Your Excellency, I only said she were readin' books, sir, and they come and take her out of my house for—

We burn a hot fire here; it melts down all concealment.

Danforth, *mystified:* Books! What books?

Giles, *through helpless sobs:* It is my third wife, sir; I never had no wife that be so taken with books, and I thought to find the cause of it, d'y'see, but it were no witch I blamed her for. *He is openly weeping.* I have broke charity with the woman, I have broke charity with her. *He covers his face, ashamed.* DANFORTH *is respectfully silent.*

Hale: Excellency, he claims hard evidence for his wife's defense. I think that in all justice you must—

Danforth: Then let him submit his evidence in proper affidavit.[1] You are certainly aware of our procedure here, Mr. Hale. *To* HERRICK: Clear this room. **(B)**

Herrick: Come now, Giles. *He gently pushes COREY out.*

Francis: We are desperate, sir; we come here three days now and cannot be heard.

Danforth: Who is this man?

Francis: Francis Nurse, Your Excellency.

Hale: His wife's Rebecca that were condemned this morning.

Danforth: Indeed! I am amazed to find you in such uproar. I have only good report of your character, Mr. Nurse.

Hathorne: I think they must both be arrested in contempt, sir.

Danforth, *to* FRANCIS: Let you write your plea, and in due time I will—

Francis: Excellency, we have proof for your eyes; God forbid you shut them to it. The girls, sir, the girls are frauds.

Danforth: What's that?

Francis: We have proof of it, sir. They are all deceiving you.

DANFORTH *is shocked, but studying* FRANCIS.

---

1. **affidavit:** written statement made under oath before a legal authority.

(A) Literary Focus Motivation What preconceptions might prevent Danforth from hearing evidence that would acquit the accused?

(B) Reading Focus Drawing Conclusions About Characters Why has Hale lost the authority he possessed at the beginning of the play? Explain your response.

Hathorne: This is contempt, sir, contempt!

Danforth: Peace, Judge Hathorne. Do you know who I am, Mr. Nurse?

Francis: I surely do, sir, and I think you must be a wise judge to be what you are.

Danforth: And do you know that near to four hundred are in the jails from Marblehead to Lynn, and upon my signature?

Francis: I—

Danforth: And seventy-two condemned to hang by that signature?

Francis: Excellency, I never thought to say it to such a weighty judge, but you are deceived.

Enter GILES COREY *from left. All turn to see as he beckons in* MARY WARREN *with* PROCTOR. MARY *is keeping her eyes to the ground;* PROCTOR *has her elbow as though she were near collapse.*

Parris, *on seeing her, in shock:* Mary Warren! *He goes directly to bend close to her face.* What are you about here?

Proctor, *pressing* PARRIS *away from her with a gentle but firm motion of protectiveness:* She would speak with the Deputy Governor.

Danforth, *shocked by this, turns to* HERRICK: Did you not tell me Mary Warren were sick in bed?

Herrick: She were, Your Honor. When I go to fetch her to the court last week, she said she were sick.

Giles: She has been strivin' with her soul all week, Your Honor; she comes now to tell the truth of this to you.

Danforth: Who is this?

Proctor: John Proctor, sir. Elizabeth Proctor is my wife.

Parris: Beware this man, Your Excellency, this man is mischief.

Hale, *excitedly:* I think you must hear the girl, sir, she—

Danforth, *who has become very interested in* MARY WARREN *and only raises a hand toward* HALE: Peace. What would you tell us, Mary Warren?

PROCTOR *looks at her, but she cannot speak.*

Proctor: She never saw no spirits, sir.

Danforth, *with great alarm and surprise, to* MARY: Never saw no spirits!

Giles, *eagerly:* Never.

Proctor, *reaching into his jacket:* She has signed a deposition, sir—

Danforth, *instantly:* No, no, I accept no depositions. *He is rapidly calculating this; he turns from her to* PROCTOR. Tell me, Mr. Proctor, have you given out this story in the village?

Proctor: We have not.

Parris: They've come to overthrow the court, sir! This man is—

Danforth: I pray you, Mr. Parris. Do you know, Mr. Proctor, that the entire contention of the state in these trials is that the voice of Heaven is speaking through the children?

Proctor: I know that, sir.

Danforth, *thinks, staring at* PROCTOR, *then turns to* MARY WARREN: And you, Mary Warren, how came you to cry out people for sending their spirits against you?

Mary Warren: It were pretense, sir.

Danforth: I cannot hear you.

Proctor: It were pretense, she says.

Danforth: Ah? And the other girls? Susanna Walcott, and—the others? They are also pretending?

Mary Warren: Aye, sir.

Danforth, *wide-eyed:* Indeed. Pause. *He is baffled by this. He turns to study* PROCTOR's *face.*

Parris, *in a sweat:* Excellency, you surely cannot think to let so vile a lie be spread in open court!

Danforth: Indeed not, but it strike hard upon me that she will dare come here with such a tale. Now, Mr. Proctor, before I decide whether I shall hear you or not, it is my duty to tell you this. We burn a hot fire here; it melts down all concealment.

Proctor: I know that, sir.

C **Reading Focus** **Drawing Conclusions About Characters**
How does Danforth's position in society validate his belief that the accused in Salem are witches?

D **Literary Focus** **Motivation** Why would Danforth instruct Giles and Francis to write an affidavit with their proof but not accept Mary Warren's written testimony?

Vocabulary **deposition** (DEHP uh ZIHSH uhn) *n.:* testimony given under oath at a trial.

Danforth: Let me continue. I understand well, a husband's tenderness may drive him to extravagance in defense of a wife. Are you certain in your conscience, Mister, that your evidence is the truth? *examin youcozens*

Proctor: It is. And you will surely know it.

Danforth: And you thought to declare this revelation in the open court before the public?

Proctor: I thought I would, aye—with your permission.

Danforth, *his eyes narrowing:* Now, sir, what is your purpose in so doing?

Proctor: Why, I—I would free my wife, sir.

Danforth: There lurks nowhere in your heart, nor hidden in your spirit, any desire to undermine this court?

Proctor, *with the faintest faltering:* Why, no, sir. *under min ABBY*

Cheever, *clears his throat, awakening:* I— Your Excellency.

Danforth: Mr. Cheever.

Cheever: I think it be my duty, sir—*Kindly, to* PROCTOR: You'll not deny it, John. *To* DANFORTH: When we come to take his wife, he damned the court and ripped your warrant.

Parris: Now you have it!

Danforth: He did that, Mr. Hale?

Hale, *takes a breath:* Aye, he did.

Proctor: It were a temper, sir. I knew not what I did.

Danforth, *studying him:* Mr. Proctor.

Proctor: Aye, sir.

Danforth, *straight into his eyes:* Have you ever seen the Devil?

Proctor: No, sir.

Danforth: You are in all respects a Gospel Christian? *pow not silus to church*

Proctor: I am, sir.

Parris: Such a Christian that will not come to church but once in a month!

Danforth, *restrained—he is curious:* Not come to church?

Proctor: I—I have no love for Mr. Parris. It is no secret. But God I surely love. *truu*

Cheever: He plow on Sunday, sir.

Danforth: Plow on Sunday!

Cheever, *apologetically:* I think it be evidence, John. I am an official of the court, I cannot keep it. **E**

Proctor: I—I have once or twice plowed on Sunday. I have three children, sir, and until last year my land give little.

Giles: You'll find other Christians that do plow on Sunday if the truth be known.

Hale: Your Honor, I cannot think you may judge the man on such evidence. *on Procteg sio.*

Danforth: I judge nothing. *Pause. He keeps watching* PROCTOR, *who tries to meet his gaze.* I tell you straight, Mister—I have seen marvels in this court. I have seen people choked before my eyes by spirits; I have seen them stuck by pins and slashed by daggers. I have until this moment not the slightest reason to suspect that the children may be deceiving me. Do you understand my meaning?

Proctor: Excellency, does it not strike upon you that so many of these women have lived so long with such upright reputation, and—

Parris: Do you read the Gospel, Mr. Proctor?

Proctor: I read the Gospel.

Parris: I think not, or you should surely know that Cain were an upright man, and yet he did kill Abel.[2]

Proctor: Aye, God tells us that. *To* DANFORTH: But who tells us Rebecca Nurse murdered seven babies by sending out her spirit on them? It is the children only, and this one will swear she lied to you.

DANFORTH *considers, then beckons* HATHORNE *to him.* HATHORNE *leans in, and he speaks in his ear.* HATHORNE *nods.*

Hathorne: Aye, she's the one.

Danforth: Mr. Proctor, this morning, your wife send me a claim in which she states that she is pregnant now.

Proctor: My wife pregnant!

Danforth: There be no sign of it—we have examined her body.

Proctor: But if she say she is pregnant, then she must be! That woman will never lie, Mr. Danforth.

Danforth: She will not?

Proctor: Never, sir, never.

Danforth: We have thought it too convenient to be credited. However, if I should tell you now that I will let her be kept another month; and if she begin to show

---

2. **Cain . . . Abel:** According to the Book of Genesis, Cain, the oldest son of Adam and Eve, killed his brother Abel.

E **Literary Focus** **Motivation** Why does Cheever reveal incriminating evidence against Proctor?

her natural signs, you shall have her living yet another year until she is delivered—what say you to that? *JOHN PROCTOR is struck silent.* Come now. You say your only purpose is to save your wife. Good, then, she is saved at least this year, and a year is long. What say you, sir? It is done now. *In conflict,* PROCTOR *glances at* FRANCIS *and* GILES. Will you drop this charge?

Proctor: I—I think I cannot.

Danforth, *now an almost imperceptible hardness in his voice:* Then your purpose is somewhat larger.

Parris: He's come to overthrow this court, Your Honor!

Proctor: These are my friends. Their wives are also accused—

Danforth, *with a sudden briskness of manner:* I judge you not, sir. I am ready to hear your evidence.

Proctor: I come not to hurt the court; I only—

Danforth, *cutting him off:* Marshal, go into the court and bid Judge Stoughton and Judge Sewall declare recess for one hour. And let them go to the tavern, if they will. All witnesses and prisoners are to be kept in the building.

Herrick: Aye, sir. *Very deferentially:* If I may say it, sir, I know this man all my life. It is a good man, sir.

Danforth—*it is the reflection on himself he resents:* I am sure of it, Marshal. HERRICK *nods, then goes out.* Now, what deposition do you have for us, Mr. Proctor? And I beg you be clear, open as the sky, and honest.

Proctor, *as he takes out several papers:* I am no lawyer, so I'll—

Danforth: The pure in heart need no lawyers. Proceed as you will.

Proctor, *handing* DANFORTH *a paper:* Will you read this first, sir? It's a sort of testament. The people signing it declare their good opinion of Rebecca, and my wife, and Martha Corey. DANFORTH *looks down at the paper.*

Parris, *to enlist* DANFORTH'S *sarcasm:* Their good opinion! *But* DANFORTH *goes on reading, and* PROCTOR *is heartened.*

F

Proctor: These are all landholding farmers, members of the church. *Delicately, trying to point out a paragraph:* If you'll notice, sir—they've known the women many years and never saw no sign they had dealings with the Devil.

PARRIS *nervously moves over and reads over* DANFORTH'S *shoulder.*

Danforth, *glancing down a long list:* How many names are here?

Francis: Ninety-one, Your Excellency.

Parris, *sweating:* These people should be summoned. DANFORTH *looks up at him questioningly.* For questioning.

Francis, *trembling with anger:* Mr. Danforth, I gave them all my word no harm would come to them for signing this.

Parris: This is a clear attack upon the court!

Hale, *to* PARRIS, *trying to contain himself:* Is every defense an attack upon the court? Can no one—?

Parris: All innocent and Christian people are happy for the courts in Salem! These people are gloomy for it. *To* DANFORTH *directly:* And I think you will want to know, from each and every one of them, what discontents them with you!

Hathorne: I think they ought to be examined, sir.

Danforth: It is not necessarily an attack, I think. Yet—

Francis: These are all covenanted Christians, sir.

Danforth: Then I am sure they may have nothing to fear. *Hands* CHEEVER *the paper.* Mr. Cheever, have warrants drawn for all of these—arrest for examination. *To* PROCTOR: Now, Mister, what other information do you have for us? FRANCIS *is still standing, horrified.* You may sit, Mr. Nurse.

G

Francis: I have brought trouble on these people; I have—

> ## All innocent and Christian people are happy for the courts in Salem! These people are gloomy for it.

F Literary Focus **Motivation** Why might the court refrain from hanging a pregnant woman?

G Literary Perspectives **Analyzing Credibility** How does Miller make Danforth's actions believable?

The Crucible, Act Three **1141**

Danforth: No, old man, you have not hurt these people if they are of good conscience. But you must understand, sir, that a person is either with this court or he must be counted against it, there be no road between. This is a sharp time, now, a precise time—we live no longer in the dusky afternoon when evil mixed itself with good and befuddled the world. Now, by God's grace, the shining sun is up, and them that fear not light will surely praise it. I hope you will be one of those. MARY WARREN *suddenly sobs.* She's not hearty, I see.

Proctor: No, she's not, sir. *To* MARY, *bending to her, holding her hand, quietly:* Now remember what the angel Raphael said to the boy Tobias.[3] Remember it.

Mary Warren, *hardly audible:* Aye.

Proctor: "Do that which is good, and no harm shall come to thee."

Mary Warren: Aye.

Danforth: Come, man, we wait you.

MARSHAL HERRICK *returns, and takes his post at the door.*

Giles: John, my deposition, give him mine.

Proctor: Aye. *He hands* DANFORTH *another paper.* This is Mr. Corey's deposition.

Danforth: Oh? *He looks down at it. Now* HATHORNE *comes behind him and reads with him.*

Hathorne, *suspiciously:* What lawyer drew this, Corey?

Giles: You know I never hired a lawyer in my life, Hathorne.

Danforth, *finishing the reading:* It is very well phrased. My compliments. Mr. Parris, if Mr. Putnam is in the court, will you bring him in? HATHORNE *takes the deposition, and walks to the window with it.* PARRIS *goes into the court.* You have no legal training, Mr. Corey?

Giles, *very pleased:* I have the best, sir—I am thirty-three time in court in my life. And always plaintiff, too.

Danforth: Oh, then you're much put-upon.

Giles: I am never put-upon; I know my rights, sir, and I will have them. You know, your father tried a case of mine—might be thirty-five year ago, I think.

Danforth: Indeed.

Giles: He never spoke to you of it?

---

3. **Raphael . . . Tobias:** In the Old Testament Apocrypha, the archangel Raphael guides Tobias, an exiled Jew.

Danforth: No, I cannot recall it.

Giles: That's strange, he give me nine pound damages. He were a fair judge, your father. Y'see, I had a white mare that time, and this fellow come to borrow the mare— *Enter* PARRIS *with* THOMAS PUTNAM. *When he sees* PUTNAM, GILES' *ease goes; he is hard.* Aye, there he is.

Danforth: Mr. Putnam, I have here an accusation by Mr. Corey against you. He states that you coldly prompted your daughter to cry witchery upon George Jacobs that is now in jail.

Putnam: It is a lie.

Danforth, *turning to* GILES: Mr. Putnam states your charge is a lie. What say you to that?

Giles, *furious, his fists clenched:* A fart on Thomas Putnam, that is what I say to that!

Danforth: What proof do you submit for your charge, sir?

Giles: My proof is there! *Pointing to the paper.* If Jacobs hangs for a witch he forfeit up his property— that's law! And there is none but Putnam with the coin to buy so great a piece. This man is killing his neighbors for their land! **Ⓗ**

Danforth: But proof, sir, proof.

Giles, *pointing at his deposition:* The proof is there! I have it from an honest man who heard Putnam say it! The day his daughter cried out on Jacobs, he said she'd given him a fair gift of land.

Hathorne: And the name of this man?

Giles, *taken aback:* What name?

Hathorne: The man that give you this information.

Giles, *hesitates, then:* Why, I—I cannot give you his name.

Hathorne: And why not?

Giles, *hesitates, then bursts out:* You know well why not! He'll lay in jail if I give his name!

Hathorne: This is contempt of the court, Mr. Danforth!

Danforth, *to avoid that:* You will surely tell us the name.

Giles: I will not give you no name. I mentioned my wife's name once and I'll burn in hell long enough for that. I stand mute.

Danforth: In that case, I have no choice but to arrest

Ⓗ Reading Focus Drawing Conclusions About Characters
What have we learned about Putnam that makes it likely Giles's claim is truthful?

you for contempt of this court, do you know that?

Giles: This is a hearing; you cannot clap me for contempt of a hearing.

Danforth: Oh, it is a proper lawyer! Do you wish me to declare the court in full session here? Or will you give me good reply?

Giles, *faltering:* I cannot give you no name, sir, I cannot.

Danforth: You are a foolish old man. Mr. Cheever, begin the record. The court is now in session. I ask you, Mr. Corey—

Proctor, *breaking in:* Your Honor—he has the story in confidence, sir, and he—

Parris: The Devil lives on such confidences! *To DANFORTH:* Without confidences there could be no conspiracy, Your Honor!

Hathorne: I think it must be broken, sir.

Danforth, *to GILES:* Old man, if your informant tells the truth let him come here openly like a decent man. But if he hide in anonymity I must know why. Now sir, the government and central church demand of you the name of him who reported Mr. Thomas Putnam a common murderer.

Hale: Excellency—

Danforth: Mr. Hale.

Hale: We cannot blink it more. There is a prodigious fear of this court in the country—

Danforth: Then there is a prodigious guilt in the country. Are *you* afraid to be questioned here?

Hale: I may only fear the Lord, sir, but there is fear in the country nevertheless.

Danforth, *angered now:* Reproach me not with the fear in the country; there is fear in the country because there is a moving plot to topple Christ in the country!

Hale: But it does not follow that everyone accused is part of it.

Danforth: No uncorrupted man may fear this court, Mr. Hale! None! *To GILES:* You are under arrest in contempt of this court. Now sit you down and take counsel with yourself, or you will be set in the jail until you decide to answer all questions. **ⓘ**

GILES COREY *makes a rush for* PUTNAM. PROCTOR *lunges and holds him.*

Proctor: No, Giles!

Giles, *over* PROCTOR's *shoulder at* PUTNAM: I'll cut your throat, Putnam, I'll kill you yet!

Proctor, *forcing him into a chair:* Peace, Giles, peace. *Releasing him.* We'll prove ourselves. Now we will. *He starts to turn to* DANFORTH.

Giles: Say nothin' more, John. *Pointing at* DANFORTH: He's only playin' you! He means to hang us all!

MARY WARREN *bursts into sobs.*

Danforth: This is a court of law, Mister. I'll have no effrontery here!

Proctor: Forgive him, sir, for his old age. Peace, Giles, we'll prove it all now. *He lifts up* MARY's *chin.* You cannot weep, Mary. Remember the angel, what he say to the boy. Hold to it, now; there is your rock. MARY *quiets. He takes out a paper, and turns to* DANFORTH. This is Mary Warren's deposition. I—I would ask you remember, sir, while you read it, that until two week ago she were no different than the other children are today. *He is speaking reasonably, restraining all his fears, his anger, his anxiety.* You saw her scream, she howled, she swore familiar spirits choked her; she even testified that Satan, in the form of women now in jail, tried to win her soul away, and then when she refused—

Danforth: We know all this.

Proctor: Aye, sir. She swears now that she never saw Satan; not any spirit, vague or clear, that Satan may have sent to hurt her. And she declares her friends are lying now.

PROCTOR *starts to hand* DANFORTH *the deposition, and* HALE *comes up to* DANFORTH *in a trembling state.*

Hale: Excellency, a moment. I think this goes to the heart of the matter.

Danforth, *with deep misgivings:* It surely does.

Hale: I cannot say he is an honest man; I know him little. But in all justice, sir, a claim so weighty cannot be argued by a farmer. In God's name, sir, stop here; send him home and let him come again with a lawyer— **ⓙ**

Danforth, *patiently:* Now look you, Mr. Hale—

Hale: Excellency, I have signed seventy-two death warrants; I am a minister of the Lord, and I dare not take a life without there be a proof so immaculate no slightest qualm of conscience may doubt it.

ⓘ Literary Perspectives Analyzing Credibility Does Giles's refusal to name his informant help or hurt his credibility?

ⓙ Literary Focus Motivation Why does Hale want Proctor to have a lawyer before Mary's deposition is argued?

Danforth: Mr. Hale, you surely do not doubt my justice.

Hale: I have this morning signed away the soul of Rebecca Nurse, Your Honor. I'll not conceal it, my hand shakes yet as with a wound! I pray you, sir, *this* argument let lawyers present to you.

Danforth: Mr. Hale, believe me; for a man of such terrible learning you are most bewildered—I hope you will forgive me. I have been thirty-two year at the bar, sir, and I should be confounded were I called upon to defend these people. Let you consider, now— *To* PROCTOR *and the others:* And I bid you all do likewise. In an ordinary crime, how does one defend the accused? One calls up witnesses to prove his innocence. But witchcraft is *ipso facto,*[4] on its face and by its nature, an invisible crime, is it not? Therefore, who may possibly be witness to it? The witch and the victim. None other. Now we cannot hope the witch will accuse herself; granted? Therefore, we must rely upon her victims—and they do testify, the children certainly do testify. As for the witches, none will deny that we are most eager for all their confessions. Therefore, what is left for a lawyer to bring out? I think I have made my point. Have I not?

Hale: But this child claims the girls are not truthful, and if they are not—

Danforth: That is precisely what I am about to consider, sir. What more may you ask of me? Unless you doubt my probity?[5]

Hale, *defeated:* I surely do not, sir. Let you consider it, then.

Danforth: And let you put your heart to rest. Her deposition, Mr. Proctor.

PROCTOR *hands it to him.* HATHORNE *rises, goes beside* DANFORTH, *and starts reading.* PARRIS *comes to his other side.* DANFORTH *looks at* JOHN PROCTOR, *then proceeds to read.* HALE *gets up, finds position near the judge, reads too.* PROCTOR *glances at* GILES.

---

4. *ipso facto:* by that very fact.
5. **probity:** integrity.

FRANCIS *prays silently, hands pressed together.* CHEEVER *waits placidly, the sublime official, dutiful.* MARY WARREN *sobs once.* JOHN PROCTOR *touches her head reassuringly. Presently* DANFORTH *lifts his eyes, stands up, takes out a kerchief and blows his nose. The others stand aside as he moves in thought toward the window.*

Parris, *hardly able to contain his anger and fear:* I should like to question—

Danforth—*his first real outburst, in which his contempt for* PARRIS *is clear:* Mr. Parris, I bid you be silent! *He stands in silence, looking out the window. Now, having established that he will set the gait:* Mr. Cheever, will you go into the court and bring the children here? CHEEVER *gets up and goes out upstage.* DANFORTH *now turns to* MARY. Mary Warren, how came you to this turnabout? Has Mr. Proctor threatened you for this deposition?

Mary Warren: No, sir.

Danforth: Has he ever threatened you?

Mary Warren, *weaker:* No, sir.

Danforth, *sensing a weakening:* Has he threatened you?

Mary Warren: No, sir.

Danforth: Then you tell me that you sat in my court, callously lying, when you knew that people would hang by your evidence? *She does not answer.* Answer me!

Mary Warren, *almost inaudibly:* I did, sir.

Danforth: How were you instructed in your life? Do you not know that God damns all liars? *She cannot speak.* Or is it now that you lie?

Mary Warren: No, sir—I am with God now.

Danforth: You are with God now.

Mary Warren: Aye, sir.

Danforth, *containing himself:* I will tell you this—you are either lying now, or you were lying in the court, and in either case you have committed perjury and you will go to jail for it. You cannot lightly say you lied, Mary. Do you know that?

Mary Warren: I cannot lie no more. I am with God, I am with God.

K **Reading Focus** **Drawing Conclusions About Characters**
Why should it be easier now for Mary to tell the truth?

> I pray you, sir, *this* argument let lawyers present to you.

Analyzing Visuals

Viewing and Interpreting
Identify the elements in this image that transmit the play's increasing tension in Act Three. Discuss your ideas with a small group of your peers.

"Do you witch her?"

But she breaks into sobs at the thought of it, and the right door opens, and enter SUSANNA WALCOTT, MERCY LEWIS, BETTY PARRIS, *and finally* ABIGAIL. CHEEVER *comes to* DANFORTH.

Cheever: Ruth Putnam's not in the court, sir, nor the other children.

Danforth: These will be sufficient. Sit you down, children. *Silently they sit.* Your friend, Mary Warren, has given us a deposition. In which she swears that she never saw familiar spirits, apparitions, nor any manifest of the Devil. She claims as well that none of you have seen these things either. *Slight pause.* Now, children, this is a court of law. The law, based upon the Bible, and the Bible, writ by Almighty God, forbid the practice of witchcraft, and describe death as the penalty thereof. But likewise, children, the law and Bible damn all bearers of false witness. *Slight pause.* Now then. It does not escape me that this deposition may be devised to blind us; it may well be that Mary Warren has been conquered by Satan, who sends her here to distract our sacred purpose. If so, her neck will break

for it. But if she speak true, I bid you now drop your guile and confess your pretense, for a quick confession will go easier with you. *Pause.* Abigail Williams, rise. ABIGAIL *slowly rises.* Is there any truth in this?

Abigail: No, sir.

Danforth, *thinks, glances at* MARY, *then back to* ABIGAIL: Children, a very augur bit[6] will now be turned into your souls until your honesty is proved. Will either of you change your positions now, or do you force me to hard questioning?

Abigail: I have naught to change, sir. She lies.

Danforth, *to* MARY: You would still go on with this?

Mary Warren, *faintly:* Aye, sir. **Ⓛ**

Danforth, *turning to* ABIGAIL: A poppet were discovered in Mr. Proctor's house, stabbed by a needle. Mary Warren claims that you sat beside her in the court when she made it, and that you saw her make it and witnessed how she herself stuck her needle into it for safe-keeping. What say you to that?

6. **augur bit:** drilling tool with pointed end and spiral grooves. (The conventional spelling is *auger*.)

Ⓛ Reading Focus **Drawing Conclusions About Characters**
Why doesn't Mary speak with conviction?

Abigail, *with a slight note of indignation:* It is a lie, sir.

Danforth, *after a slight pause:* While you worked for Mr. Proctor, did you see poppets in that house?

Abigail: Goody Proctor always kept poppets.

Proctor: Your Honor, my wife never kept no poppets. Mary Warren confesses it was her poppet.

Cheever: Your Excellency.

Danforth: Mr. Cheever.

Cheever: When I spoke with Goody Proctor in that house, she said she never kept no poppets. But she said she did keep poppets when she were a girl.

Proctor: She has not been a girl these fifteen years, Your Honor.

Hathorne: But a poppet will keep fifteen years, will it not?

Proctor: It will keep if it is kept, but Mary Warren swears she never saw no poppets in my house, nor anyone else.

Parris: Why could there not have been poppets hid where no one ever saw them?

Proctor, *furious:* There might also be a dragon with five legs in my house, but no one has ever seen it.

Parris: We are here, Your Honor, precisely to discover what no one has ever seen.

Proctor: Mr. Danforth, what profit this girl to turn herself about? What may Mary Warren gain but hard questioning and worse?

Danforth: You are charging Abigail Williams with a marvelous cool plot to murder, do you understand that?

Proctor: I do, sir. I believe she means to murder.

Danforth, *pointing at* ABIGAIL, *incredulously:* This child would murder your wife?

Proctor: It is not a child. Now hear me, sir. In the sight of the congregation she were twice this year put out of this meetin' house for laughter during prayer.

Danforth, *shocked, turning to* ABIGAIL: What's this? Laughter during—!

Parris: Excellency, she were under Tituba's power at that time, but she is solemn now.

Giles: Aye, now she is solemn and goes to hang people!

Danforth: Quiet, man.

Hathorne: Surely it have no bearing on the question, sir. He charges contemplation of murder.

Danforth: Aye. *He studies* ABIGAIL *for a moment, then:* Continue, Mr. Proctor.

Proctor: Mary. Now tell the Governor how you danced in the woods.

Parris, *instantly:* Excellency, since I come to Salem this man is blackening my name. He—

Danforth: In a moment, sir. *To* MARY WARREN, *sternly, and surprised:* What is this dancing?

Mary Warren: I— *She glances at* ABIGAIL, *who is staring down at her remorselessly. Then, appealing to* PROCTOR: Mr. Proctor—

Proctor, *taking it right up:* Abigail leads the girls to the woods, Your Honor, and they have danced there naked—

Parris: Your Honor, this—

Proctor, *at once:* Mr. Parris discovered them himself in the dead of night! There's the "child" she is!

Danforth—*it is growing into a nightmare, and he turns, astonished, to* PARRIS: Mr. Parris—

Parris: I can only say, sir, that I never found any of them naked, and this man is—

Danforth: But you discovered them dancing in the woods? *Eyes on* PARRIS, *he points at* ABIGAIL. Abigail?

Hale: Excellency, when I first arrived from Beverly, Mr. Parris told me that.

Danforth: Do you deny it, Mr. Parris?

Parris: I do not, sir, but I never saw any of them naked.

Danforth: But she have *danced?*

Parris, *unwillingly:* Aye, sir.

DANFORTH, *as though with new eyes, looks at* ABIGAIL.

Hathorne: Excellency, will you permit me? *He points at* MARY WARREN.

Danforth, *with great worry:* Pray, proceed.

Hathorne: You say you never saw no spirits, Mary,

> # You are charging Abigail Williams with a marvelous cool plot to murder, do you understand that?

Ⓜ **Literary Focus** Motivation Why does Parris lie about what he witnessed?

were never threatened or afflicted by any manifest of the Devil or the Devil's agents.

Mary Warren, *very faintly:* No, sir.

Hathorne, *with a gleam of victory:* And yet, when people accused of witchery confronted you in court, you would faint, saying their spirits came out of their bodies and choked you—

Mary Warren: That were pretense, sir.

Danforth: I cannot hear you.

Mary Warren: Pretense, sir.

Parris: But you did turn cold, did you not? I myself picked you up many times, and your skin were icy. Mr. Danforth, you—

Danforth: I saw that many times.

Proctor: She only pretended to faint, Your Excellency. They're all marvelous pretenders.

Hathorne: Then can she pretend to faint now?

Proctor: Now?

Parris: Why not? Now there are no spirits attacking her, for none in this room is accused of witchcraft. So let her turn herself cold now, let her pretend she is attacked now, let her faint. *He turns to* MARY WARREN. Faint!

Mary Warren: Faint?

Parris: Aye, faint. Prove to us how you pretended in the court so many times.

Mary Warren, *looking to* PROCTOR: I—cannot faint now, sir.

Proctor, *alarmed, quietly:* Can you not pretend it?

Mary Warren: I— *She looks about as though searching for the passion to faint.* I—have no *sense* of it now, I—

Danforth: Why? What is lacking now?

Mary Warren: I—cannot tell, sir, I—

Danforth: Might it be that here we have no afflicting spirit loose, but in the court there were some?

Mary Warren: I never saw no spirits.

Parris: Then see no spirits now, and prove to us that you can faint by your own will, as you claim.

Mary Warren, *stares, searching for the emotion of it, and then shakes her head:* I—cannot do it.

Parris: Then you will confess, will you not? It were attacking spirits made you faint!

Mary Warren: No, sir, I—

Parris: Your Excellency, this is a trick to blind the court!

Mary Warren: It's not a trick! *She stands.* I—I used to faint because I—I thought I saw spirits.

Danforth: *Thought* you saw them!

Mary Warren: But I did not, Your Honor.

Hathorne: How could you think you saw them unless you saw them?

Mary Warren: I—I cannot tell how, but I did. I—I heard the other girls screaming, and you, Your Honor, you seemed to believe them, and I— It were only sport in the beginning, sir, but then the whole world cried spirits, spirits, and I—I promise you, Mr. Danforth, I only thought I saw them but I did not.

DANFORTH *peers at her.*

Parris, *smiling, but nervous because* DANFORTH *seems to be struck by* MARY WARREN's *story:* Surely Your Excellency is not taken by this simple lie.

Danforth, *turning worriedly to* ABIGAIL: Abigail. I bid you now search your heart and tell me this—and beware of it, child, to God every soul is precious and His vengeance is terrible on them that take life without cause. Is it possible, child, that the spirits you have seen are illusion only, some deception that may cross your mind when—

Abigail: Why, this—this—is a base question, sir.

Danforth: Child, I would have you consider it—

Abigail: I have been hurt, Mr. Danforth; I have seen my blood runnin' out! I have been near to murdered every day because I done my duty pointing out the Devil's people—and this is my reward? To be mistrusted, denied, questioned like a—

Danforth, *weakening:* Child, I do not mistrust you—

Abigail, *in an open threat:* Let *you* beware, Mr. Danforth. Think you to be so mighty that the power of Hell may not turn *your* wits? Beware of it! There is— *Suddenly, from an accusatory attitude, her face turns, looking into the air above—it is truly frightened.*

Danforth, *apprehensively:* What is it, child?

Abigail, *looking about in the air, clasping her arms about her as though cold:* I—I know not. A wind, a cold wind, has come. *Her eyes fall on* MARY WARREN.

Mary Warren, *terrified, pleading:* Abby!

Mercy Lewis, *shivering:* Your Honor, I freeze!

Proctor: They're pretending!

N **Literary Focus** **Motivation** What made Mary and the other girls able to faint before, but not on command? Explain your response.

O **Literary Perspectives** **Analyzing Credibility** Why does the court question Mary's credibility?

Hathorne, *touching* ABIGAIL's *hand:* She is cold, Your Honor, touch her!

Mercy Lewis, *through chattering teeth:* Mary, do you send this shadow on me?

Mary Warren: Lord, save me!

Susanna Walcott: I freeze, I freeze!

Abigail, *shivering visibly:* It is a wind, a wind!

Mary Warren: Abby, don't do that!

Danforth, *himself engaged and entered by* ABIGAIL: Mary Warren, do you witch her? I say to you, do you send your spirit out?

With a hysterical cry MARY WARREN *starts to run.* PROCTOR *catches her.*

Mary Warren, *almost collapsing:* Let me go, Mr. Proctor, I cannot, I cannot—

Abigail, *crying to Heaven:* Oh, Heavenly Father, take away this shadow!

Without warning or hesitation, PROCTOR *leaps at* ABIGAIL *and, grabbing her by the hair, pulls her to her feet. She screams in pain.* DANFORTH, *astonished, cries,* "What are you about?" *and* HATHORNE *and* PARRIS *call,* "Take your hands off her!" *and out of it all comes* PROCTOR's *roaring voice.* The Truth comes out

Proctor: How do you call Heaven! Whore! Whore!

HERRICK *breaks* PROCTOR *from her.*

Herrick: John!

Danforth: Man! Man, what do you—

Proctor, *breathless and in agony:* It is a whore!

Danforth, *dumfounded:* You charge—?

Abigail: Mr. Danforth, he is lying!

Proctor: Mark her! Now she'll suck a scream to stab me with, but—

Danforth: You will prove this! This will not pass!

Proctor, *trembling, his life collapsing about him:* I have known her, sir. I have known her.

Danforth: You—you are a lecher?

Francis, *horrified:* John, you cannot say such a—

Proctor: Oh, Francis, I wish you had some evil in you that you might know me! *To* DANFORTH: A man will not cast away his good name. You surely know that.

Danforth, *dumfounded:* In—in what time? In what place?

Proctor, *his voice about to break, and his shame great:* In the proper place—where my beasts are bedded. On the last night of my joy, some eight months past. She used to serve me in my house, sir. *He has to clamp his jaw to keep from weeping.* A man may think God sleeps, but God sees everything, I know it now. I beg you, sir, I beg you—see her what she is. My wife, my dear good wife, took this girl soon after, sir, and put her out on the highroad. And being what she is, a lump of vanity, sir— *He is being overcome.* Excellency, forgive me, forgive me. *Angrily against himself, he turns away from the Governor for a moment. Then, as though to cry out is his only means of speech left:* She thinks to dance with me on my wife's grave! And well she might, for I thought of her softly. God help me, I lusted, and there *is* a promise in such sweat. But it is a whore's vengeance, and you must see it; I set myself entirely in your hands. I know you must see it now.

Danforth, *blanched, in horror, turning to* ABIGAIL: You deny every scrap and tittle of this? ⓟ

Abigail: If I must answer that, I will leave and I will not come back again!

DANFORTH *seems unsteady.*

Proctor: I have made a bell of my honor! I have rung the doom of my good name—you will believe me, Mr. Danforth! My wife is innocent, except she knew a whore when she saw one!

Abigail, *stepping up to* DANFORTH: What look do you give me? DANFORTH *cannot speak.* I'll not have such looks! *She turns and starts for the door.*

Danforth: You will remain where you are! HERRICK *steps into her path. She comes up short, fire in her eyes.* Mr. Parris, go into the court and bring Goodwife Proctor out.

Parris, *objecting:* Your Honor, this is all a—

Danforth, *sharply to* PARRIS: Bring her out! And tell her not one word of what's been spoken here. And let you knock before you enter. PARRIS *goes out.* Now we shall touch the bottom of this swamp. *To* PROCTOR: Your wife, you say, is an honest woman.

Proctor: In her life, sir, she have never lied. There are them that cannot sing, and them that cannot weep—

ⓟ **Literary Focus** **Motivation** Why would Danforth ask Abigail to deny Proctor's allegations?

my wife cannot lie. I have paid much to learn it, sir.

Danforth: And when she put this girl out of your house, she put her out for a harlot?

Proctor: Aye, sir.

Danforth: And knew her for a harlot?

Proctor: Aye, sir, she knew her for a harlot.

Danforth: Good then. *To* ABIGAIL: And if she tell me, child, it were for harlotry, may God spread His mercy on you! *There is a knock. He calls to the door.* Hold! *To* ABIGAIL: Turn your back. Turn your back. *To* PROCTOR: Do likewise. *Both turn their backs—* ABIGAIL *with indignant slowness.* Now let neither of you turn to face Goody Proctor. No one in this room is to speak one word, or raise a gesture aye or nay. *He turns toward the door, calls:* Enter! *The door opens.* ELIZABETH *enters with* PARRIS. PARRIS *leaves her. She stands alone, her eyes looking for* PROCTOR. Mr. Cheever, report this testimony in all exactness. Are you ready?

Cheever: Ready, sir.

Danforth: Come here, woman. ELIZABETH *comes to him, glancing at* PROCTOR'*s back.* Look at me only, not at your husband. In my eyes only.

Elizabeth, *faintly:* Good, sir.

Danforth: We are given to understand that at one time you dismissed your servant, Abigail Williams.

Elizabeth: That is true, sir.

Danforth: For what cause did you dismiss her? *Slight pause. Then* ELIZABETH *tries to glance at* PROCTOR. You will look in my eyes only and not at your husband. The answer is in your memory and you need no help to give it to me. Why did you dismiss Abigail Williams?

Elizabeth, *not knowing what to say, sensing a situation, wetting her lips to stall for time:* She—dissatisfied me. *Pause.* And my husband.

Danforth: In what way dissatisfied you?

Elizabeth: She were— *She glances at* PROCTOR *for a cue.*

Danforth: Woman, look at me! ELIZABETH *does.* Were she slovenly? Lazy? What disturbance did she cause?

Elizabeth: Your Honor, I—in that time I were sick. And I—My husband is a good and righteous man. He is never drunk as some are, nor wastin' his time at the shovelboard, but always at his work. But in my sickness—you see, sir. I were a long time sick after my last baby, and I thought I saw my husband somewhat turning from me. And this girl— *She turns to* ABIGAIL.

Danforth: Look at me.

Elizabeth: Aye, sir. Abigail Williams— *She breaks off.*

Danforth: What of Abigail Williams?

Elizabeth: I came to think he fancied her. And so one night I lost my wits, I think, and put her out on the highroad.

Danforth: Your husband—did he indeed turn from you?

Elizabeth, *in agony:* My husband—is a goodly man, sir.

Danforth: Then he did not turn from you.

Elizabeth, *starting to glance at* PROCTOR: He—

Danforth, *reaches out and holds her face, then.* Look at me! To your own knowledge, has John Proctor ever committed the crime of lechery? *In a crisis of indecision she cannot speak.* Answer my question! Is your husband a lecher!

Elizabeth, *faintly:* No, sir.   **Q**

Danforth: Remove her, Marshal.

Proctor: Elizabeth, tell the truth!

Danforth: She has spoken. Remove her!

Proctor, *crying out:* Elizabeth, I have confessed it!

Elizabeth: Oh, God! *The door closes behind her.*

Proctor: She only thought to save my name!

Hale: Excellency, it is a natural lie to tell; I beg you, stop now before another is condemned! I may shut my conscience to it no more—private vengeance is working through this testimony! From the beginning this man has struck me true. By my oath to Heaven,

---

Q **Literary Focus** **Motivation** What motivates Elizabeth to lie?

I believe him now, and I pray you call back his wife before we—

Danforth: She spoke nothing of lechery, and this man has lied!

Hale: I believe him! *Pointing at* ABIGAIL: This girl has always struck me false! She has—

ABIGAIL, *with a weird, wild, chilling cry, screams up to the ceiling.*

Abigail: You will not! Begone! Begone, I say!

Danforth: What is it, child? *But* ABIGAIL, *pointing with fear, is now raising up her frightened eyes, her awed face, toward the ceiling—the girls are doing the same—and now* HATHORNE, HALE, PUTNAM, CHEEVER, HERRICK, *and* DANFORTH *do the same.* What's there? *He lowers his eyes from the ceiling, and now he is frightened; there is real tension in his voice.* Child! *She is transfixed—with all the girls, she is whimpering open-mouthed, agape at the ceiling.* Girls! Why do you—?

Mercy Lewis, *pointing:* It's on the beam! Behind the rafter!

Danforth, *looking up:* Where!

Abigail: Why—? *She gulps.* Why do you come, yellow bird?

Proctor: Where's a bird? I see no bird!

Abigail, *to the ceiling:* My face? My face?

Proctor: Mr. Hale—

Danforth: Be quiet!

Proctor, *to* HALE: Do you see a bird?

Danforth: Be quiet!!

Abigail, *to the ceiling, in a genuine conversation with the "bird," as though trying to talk it out of attacking her:* But God made my face; you cannot want to tear my face. Envy is a deadly sin, Mary.

Mary Warren, *on her feet with a spring, and horrified, pleading:* Abby!

Abigail, *unperturbed, continuing to the "bird":* Oh, Mary, this is a black art to change your shape. No, I can-

not, I cannot stop my mouth; it's God's work I do.

Mary Warren: Abby, I'm *here!*

Proctor, *frantically:* They're pretending, Mr. Danforth!

Abigail—*now she takes a backward step, as though in fear the bird will swoop down momentarily:* Oh, please, Mary! Don't come down.

Susanna Walcott: Her claws, she's stretching her claws!

Proctor: Lies, lies.

Abigail, *backing further, eyes still fixed above:* Mary, please don't hurt me!

Mary Warren, *to* DANFORTH: I'm not hurting her!

Danforth, *to* MARY WARREN: Why does she see this vision?

Mary Warren: She sees nothin'!

Abigail, *now staring full front as though hypnotized, and mimicking the exact tone of* MARY WARREN's *cry:* She sees nothin'!

Mary Warren, *pleading:* Abby, you mustn't!

Abigail and All the Girls, *all transfixed:* Abby, you mustn't!

Mary Warren, *to all the girls:* I'm here, I'm here!

Girls: I'm here, I'm here!

Danforth, *horrified:* Mary Warren! Draw back your spirit out of them!

Mary Warren: Mr. Danforth!

Girls, *cutting her off:* Mr. Danforth!

Danforth: Have you compacted with the Devil? Have you?

Mary Warren: Never, never!

Girls: Never, never!

Danforth, *growing hysterical:* Why can they only repeat you?

Proctor: Give me a whip—I'll stop it!

Mary Warren: They're sporting. They—!

Girls: They're sporting!

Mary Warren, *turning on them all hysterically and stamping her feet:* Abby, stop it!

Girls, *stamping their feet:* Abby, stop it!

Mary Warren: Stop it!

> **From the beginning this man has struck me true. By my oath to Heaven, I believe him now, and I pray you call back his wife.**

Ⓡ

Ⓡ **Reading Focus** **Drawing Conclusions About Characters**
Why does Danforth believe the other girls instead of Mary?

Girls: Stop it!

Mary Warren, *screaming it out at the top of her lungs, and raising her fists:* Stop it!!

Girls, *raising their fists:* Stop it!!

MARY WARREN, *utterly confounded, and becoming overwhelmed by* ABIGAIL's—*and the girls'—utter conviction, starts to whimper, hands half raised, powerless, and all the girls begin whimpering exactly as she does.*

Danforth: A little while ago you were afflicted. Now it seems you afflict others; where did you find this power?

Mary Warren, *staring at* ABIGAIL: I—have no power.

Girls: I have no power.

Proctor: They're gulling you, Mister!

Danforth: Why did you turn about this past two weeks? You have seen the Devil, have you not?

Hale, *indicating* ABIGAIL *and the girls:* You cannot believe them!

Mary Warren: I—

Proctor, *sensing her weakening:* Mary, God damns all liars!

Danforth, *pounding it into her:* You have seen the Devil, you have made compact with Lucifer, have you not?

Proctor: God damns liars, Mary!

MARY *utters something unintelligible, staring at* ABIGAIL, *who keeps watching the "bird" above.*

Danforth: I cannot hear you. What do you say? MARY *utters again unintelligibly.* You will confess yourself or you will hang! *He turns her roughly to face him.* Do you know who I am? I say you will hang if you do not open with me!

Proctor: Mary, remember the angel Raphael—do that which is good and—

Abigail, *pointing upward:* The wings! Her wings are spreading! Mary, please, don't, don't—!

Hale: I see nothing, Your Honor!

Danforth: Do you confess this power! *He is an inch from her face.* Speak!

Abigail: She's going to come down! She's walking the beam!

Danforth: Will you speak!

Mary Warren, *staring in horror:* I cannot!

Girls: I cannot!

Parris: Cast the Devil out! Look him in the face! Trample him! We'll save you, Mary, only stand fast against him and—

Abigail, *looking up:* Look out! She's coming down!

She and all the girls run to one wall, shielding their eyes. And now, as though cornered, they let out a gigantic scream, and MARY, *as though infected, opens her mouth and screams with them. Gradually* ABIGAIL *and the girls leave off, until only* MARY *is left there, staring up at the "bird," screaming madly. All watch her, horrified by this evident fit.* PROCTOR *strides to her.*

Proctor: Mary, tell the Governor what they—*He has hardly got a word out, when, seeing him coming for her, she rushes out of his reach, screaming in horror.*

Mary Warren: Don't touch me—don't touch me! *At which the girls halt at the door.*

Proctor, *astonished:* Mary!

Mary Warren, *pointing at* PROCTOR: You're the Devil's man! Ⓢ

He is stopped in his tracks.

Parris: Praise God!

Girls: Praise God!

Proctor, *numbed:* Mary, how—?

Mary Warren: I'll not hang with you! I love God, I love God.

Danforth, *to* MARY: He bid you do the Devil's work?

Mary Warren, *hysterically, indicating* PROCTOR: He come at me by night and every day to sign, to sign, to—

Danforth: Sign what?

Parris: The Devil's book? He come with a book?

Mary Warren, *hysterically, pointing at* PROCTOR, *fearful of him:* My name, he want my name. "I'll murder you," he says, "if my wife hangs! We must go and overthrow the court," he says!

DANFORTH's *head jerks toward* PROCTOR, *shock and horror in his face.*

Proctor, *turning, appealing to* HALE: Mr. Hale!

Mary Warren, *her sobs beginning:* He wake me every night, his eyes were like coals and his fingers claw my

Ⓢ **Literary Focus** **Motivation** Why does Mary suddenly recant, and rejoin the girls?

neck, and I sign, I sign . . .

Hale: Excellency, this child's gone wild!

Proctor, *as* DANFORTH's *wide eyes pour on him:* Mary, Mary!

Mary Warren, *screaming at him:* No, I love God; I go your way no more. I love God, I bless God. *Sobbing, she rushes to* ABIGAIL. Abby, Abby, I'll never hurt you more! *They all watch, as* ABIGAIL, *out of her infinite charity, reaches out and draws the sobbing* MARY *to her, and then looks up to* DANFORTH.

Danforth, *to* PROCTOR: What are you? PROCTOR *is beyond speech in his anger.* You are combined with anti-Christ,[7] are you not? I have seen your power; you will not deny it! What say you, Mister?

Hale: Excellency—

Danforth: I will have nothing from you, Mr. Hale! *To* PROCTOR: Will you confess yourself befouled with Hell, or do you keep that black allegiance yet? What say you?

---

7. **anti-Christ:** in the New Testament Christ's great enemy, expected to spread evil before Christ conquers him and the world ends (1 John 2:18).

Proctor, *his mind wild, breathless:* I say—I say—God is dead!

Parris: Hear it, hear it!

Proctor, *laughs insanely, then:* A fire, a fire is burning! I hear the boot of Lucifer, I see his filthy face! And it is my face, and yours, Danforth! For them that quail to bring men out of ignorance, as I have quailed, and as you quail now when you know in all your black hearts that this be fraud—God damns our kind especially, and we will burn, we will burn together!

Danforth: Marshal! Take him and Corey with him to the jail!

Hale, *starting across to the door:* I denounce these proceedings!

Proctor: You are pulling Heaven down and raising up a whore!

Hale: I denounce these proceedings, I quit this court! *He slams the door to the outside behind him.*

Danforth, *calling to him in a fury:* Mr. Hale! Mr. Hale!

The curtain falls

T **Literary Focus** **Motivation** Why would Proctor make this statement, knowing it will cause trouble for him?

Applying Your Skills

SKILLS FOCUS **Literary Skills** Analyze character motivation; analyze mood. **Reading Skills** Draw inferences about characters.

The Crucible, Act Three

Respond and Think Critically

Reading Focus

Quick Check

1. As the act begins, why does Giles Corey interrupt Judge Hathorne?
2. How does Mary respond when Danforth asks her to explain her behavior?
3. What does Danforth do with the list of people supporting Rebecca and Martha?
4. What test does Danforth devise to determine why Abigail was put out of the Proctor house?
5. What is Abigail's "vision"?

Read with a Purpose

6. What does Hale mean when he asks if every defense is an attack upon the court? By the end of this act, would you say that Hale is a dynamic character, who has changed, or a static character, who has not changed? Use details from the play to support your response.

Reading Skills: Drawing Conclusions About Characters

7. Explain why Giles Corey feels that he cannot present his one piece of evidence requested by the judge.
8. At this point in the play, what conclusions have you drawn about Abigail? Support your response with evidence from your chart.

Literary Focus

Literary Analysis

9. **Analyze** What does Danforth's reaction to Giles's outburst at the beginning of the act suggest about his character?
10. **Interpret** Why does the court debate whether Proctor plows on Sunday? What is the significance of this debate?
11. **Literary Perspectives** Elizabeth Proctor is known to be intrinsically honest. Explain whether her lie to Danforth undermines her credibility.

Literary Skills: Motivation

12. **Make Judgments** When John reveals his true relationship to Abigail, what do you think he also reveals about his character and his motivation?

Literary Skills Review: Mood

13. **Analyze** The overall emotion transmitted by a work of literature is its **mood**. Dramatic works often include comic relief—the inclusion of a comic episode or element to relieve emotional tension by shifting temporarily to a lighter mood. Do you think Giles Corey's earthy dialogue provides comic relief in *The Crucible*? Explain.

Writing Focus

Think as a Reader/Writer

Use It in Your Writing Write a brief dialogue between two characters in which one attempts to make the other, who is innocent, appear guilty of wrongdoing. Include stage directions to show the innocent character's reactions and to reveal the secret intent of the accuser.

What Do You Think Now? Elizabeth Proctor lies to Danforth. Does her lie make her seem more like other characters in the play? Why or why not?

For **CHOICES** see page 1167.

The Crucible

Act Four

Drinking together normal 9 pont Drink.

Read with a Purpose Read the last act of *The Crucible* to understand what motivates a character to risk his life in the name of truth.

Act Four

A cell in Salem jail, that fall.

nite = Deqth.

At the back is a high barred window; near it, a great, heavy door. Along the walls are two benches.

People denie

The place is in darkness but for the moonlight seeping through the bars. It appears empty. Presently footsteps are heard coming down a corridor beyond the wall, keys rattle, and the door swings open. MARSHAL HERRICK *enters with a lantern.*

He is nearly drunk, and heavy-footed. He goes to a bench and nudges a bundle of rags lying on it.

Herrick: Sarah, wake up! Sarah Good! *He then crosses to the other bench.*

Sarah Good, *rising in her rags:* Oh, Majesty! Comin', comin'! Tituba, he's here, His Majesty's come!

Herrick: Go to the north cell; this place is wanted now. *He hangs his lantern on the wall.* TITUBA *sits up.*

Tituba: That don't look to me like His Majesty; look to me like the marshal.

Herrick, *taking out a flask:* Get along with you now, clear this place. *He drinks, and* SARAH GOOD *comes and peers up into his face.*

Sarah Good: Oh, is it you, Marshal! I thought sure you be the Devil comin' for us. Could I have a sip of cider for me goin'-away?

Herrick, *handing her the flask:* And where are you off to, Sarah?

Tituba, *as* SARAH *drinks:* We goin' to Barbados, soon the Devil gits here with the feathers and the wings.

Herrick: Oh? A happy voyage to you.

Sarah Good: A pair of bluebirds wingin' southerly, the two of us! Oh, it be a grand transformation, Marshal! *She raises the flask to drink again.*

Herrick, *taking the flask from her lips:* You'd best give me that or you'll never rise off the ground. Come along now.

Tituba: I'll speak to him for you, if you desires to come along, Marshal.

Herrick: I'd not refuse it, Tituba; it's the proper morning to fly into Hell.

Tituba: Oh, it be no Hell in Barbados. Devil, him be pleasureman in Barbados, him be singin' and dancin' in Barbados. It's you folks—you riles him up 'round here; it be too cold 'round here for that Old Boy. He freeze his soul in Massachusetts, but in Barbados he just as sweet and—*A bellowing cow is heard, and* TITUBA *leaps up and calls to the window:* Aye, sir! That's him, Sarah! Ⓐ

Sarah Good: I'm here, Majesty! *They hurriedly pick up*

Ⓐ **Literary Focus** **Motivation** Why do Sarah and Tituba pretend to be waiting for the devil to come?

Viewing and Interpreting Study the faces of Proctor and Elizabeth. They seem to be staring into the distance, far beyond the town official before them. Where might they be looking? What idea from the play do the actors convey here? Explain your response.

their rags as HOPKINS, *a guard, enters.*

Hopkins: The Deputy Governor's arrived.

Herrick, *grabbing* TITUBA: Come along, come along.

Tituba, *resisting him:* No, he comin' for me. I goin' home!

Herrick, *pulling her to the door:* That's not Satan, just a poor old cow with a hatful of milk. Come along now, out with you!

Tituba, *calling to the window:* Take me home, Devil! Take me home!

Sarah Good, *following the shouting* TITUBA *out:* Tell him I'm goin', Tituba! Now you tell him Sarah Good is goin' too!

In the corridor outside TITUBA *calls on—"Take me home, Devil; Devil take me home!" and* HOPKINS' *voice orders her to move on.* HERRICK *returns and begins to push old rags and straw into a corner. Hearing footsteps, he turns, and enter* DANFORTH *and* JUDGE HATHORNE. *They are in greatcoats and wear hats against the bitter cold. They are followed in by* CHEEVER, *who carries a dispatch case and a flat wooden box containing his writing materials.*

Herrick: Good morning, Excellency.

Danforth: Where is Mr. Parris?

Herrick: I'll fetch him. *He starts for the door.*

Danforth: Marshal. HERRICK *stops.* When did Reverend Hale arrive?

Herrick: It were toward midnight, I think.

Danforth, *suspiciously:* What is he about here?

Herrick: He goes among them that will hang, sir. And he prays with them. He sits with Goody Nurse now. And Mr. Parris with him.

Danforth: Indeed. That man have no authority to enter here, Marshal. Why have you let him in?

Herrick: Why, Mr. Parris command me, sir. I cannot deny him. **B**

Danforth: Are you drunk, Marshal?

Herrick: No, sir; it is a bitter night, and I have no fire here.

Danforth, *containing his anger:* Fetch Mr. Parris.

Herrick: Aye, sir.

Danforth: There is a prodigious stench in this place.

Herrick: I have only now cleared the people out for you.

Danforth: Beware hard drink, Marshal.

Herrick: Aye, sir. *He waits an instant for further orders. But* DANFORTH, *in dissatisfaction, turns his back on him, and* HERRICK *goes out. There is a pause.* DANFORTH *stands in thought.*

Hathorne: Let you question Hale, Excellency; I should not be surprised he have been preaching in Andover lately.

Danforth: We'll come to that; speak nothing of Andover. Parris prays with him. That's strange. *He blows on his hands, moves toward the window, and looks out.*

Hathorne: Excellency, I wonder if it be wise to let Mr. Parris so continuously with the prisoners. DANFORTH *turns to him, interested.* I think, sometimes, the man has a mad look these days.

Danforth: Mad?

Hathorne: I met him yesterday coming out of his house, and I bid him good morning—and he wept and went his way. I think it is not well the village sees him so unsteady.

Danforth: Perhaps he have some sorrow.

Cheever, *stamping his feet against the cold:* I think it be the cows, sir.

Danforth: Cows?

Cheever: There be so many cows wanderin' the highroads, now their masters are in the jails, and much disagreement who they will belong to now. I know Mr. Parris be arguin' with farmers all yesterday—there is great contention, sir, about the cows. Contention make him weep, sir; it were always a man that weep for contention. *He turns, as do* HATHORNE *and* DANFORTH, *hearing someone coming up the corridor.* DANFORTH *raises his head as* PARRIS *enters. He is gaunt, frightened, and sweating in his greatcoat.*

Parris, *to* DANFORTH, *instantly:* Oh, good morning, sir, thank you for coming, I beg your pardon wakin' you so early. Good morning, Judge Hathorne.

Danforth: Reverend Hale have no right to enter this—

Parris: Excellency, a moment. *He hurries back and shuts the door.*

Hathorne: Do you leave him alone with the prisoners?

Danforth: What's his business here?

Parris, *prayerfully holding up his hands:* Excellency, hear me. It is a providence. Reverend Hale has returned to bring Rebecca Nurse to God.

Danforth, *surprised:* He bids her confess?

Parris, *sitting:* Hear me. Rebecca have not given me a word this three month since she came. Now she sits with him, and her sister and Martha Corey and two or three others, and he pleads with them, confess their crimes and save their lives. **C**

Danforth: Why—this is indeed a providence. And they soften, they soften?

Parris: Not yet, not yet. But I thought to summon you, sir, that we might think on whether it be not wise, to—*He dares not say it.* I had thought to put a question, sir, and I hope you will not—

Danforth: Mr. Parris, be plain, what troubles you?

Parris: There is news, sir, that the court—the court must reckon with. My niece, sir, my niece—I believe she has vanished.

B **Literary Focus** Motivation Why would Parris continue to work with Hale when they are now on opposite sides of the court proceedings?

C **Literary Focus** Motivation Why would Hale ask the prisoners to confess to a crime he knows they did not commit?

Danforth: Vanished!

Parris: I had thought to advise you of it earlier in the week, but—

Danforth: Why? How long is she gone?

Parris: This be the third night. You see, sir, she told me she would stay a night with Mercy Lewis. And next day, when she does not return, I send to Mr. Lewis to inquire. Mercy told him she would sleep in *my* house for a night.

Danforth: They are both gone?!

Parris, *in fear of him:* They are, sir.

Danforth, *alarmed:* I will send a party for them. Where may they be?

Parris: Excellency, I think they be aboard a ship. DAN-FORTH *stands agape.* My daughter tells me how she heard them speaking of ships last week, and tonight I discover my—my strong-box is broke into. *He presses his fingers against his eyes to keep back tears.*

Hathorne, *astonished:* She have robbed you?

Parris: Thirty-one pound is gone. I am penniless. *He covers his face and sobs.*

Danforth: Mr. Parris, you are a brainless man! *He walks in thought, deeply worried.*

Parris: Excellency, it profit nothing you should blame me. I cannot think they would run off except they fear to keep in Salem any more. *He is pleading.* Mark it, sir, Abigail had close knowledge of the town, and since the news of Andover has broken here—

Danforth: Andover is remedied. The court returns there on Friday, and will resume examinations.

Parris: I am sure of it, sir. But the rumor here speaks rebellion in Andover, and it—

Danforth: There is no rebellion in Andover!

Parris: I tell you what is said here, sir. Andover has thrown out the court, they say, and will have no part of witchcraft. There be a faction here, feeding on that news, and I tell you true, sir, I fear there will be riot here.

Hathorne: Riot! Why at every execution I have seen naught but high satisfaction in the town.

Parris: Judge Hathorne—it were another sort that hanged till now. Rebecca Nurse is no Bridget that lived three year with Bishop before she married him. John Proctor is not Isaac Ward that drank his family to ruin. *To* DANFORTH: I would to God it were not so, Excellency, but these people have great weight yet in the town. Let Rebecca stand upon the gibbet[1] and send up some righteous prayer, and I fear she'll wake a vengeance on you.

D

Hathorne: Excellency, she is condemned a witch. The court have—

Danforth, *in deep concern, raising a hand to* HATHORNE: Pray you. *To* PARRIS: How do you propose, then?

Parris: Excellency, I would postpone these hangin's for a time.

Danforth: There will be no postponement.

There is news, sir, that the court—the court must reckon with. My niece, sir, my niece —I believe she has vanished.

Parris: Now Mr. Hale's returned, there is hope, I think—for if he bring even one of these to God, that confession surely damns the others in the public eye, and none may doubt more that they are all linked to Hell. This way, unconfessed and claiming innocence, doubts are multiplied, many honest people will weep for them, and our good purpose is lost in their tears.

Danforth, *after thinking a moment, then going to* CHEEVER: Give me the list.

CHEEVER *opens the dispatch case, searches.*

Parris: It cannot be forgot, sir, that when I summoned the congregation for John Proctor's excommunication there were hardly thirty people come to hear it. That speak a discontent, I think, and—

Danforth, *studying the list:* There will be no postponement.

---

1. **gibbet** (JIHB iht): gallows, or structure from which a person is executed by hanging.

D Reading Focus **Drawing Conclusions About Characters**
What is Parris saying about the character of Nurse and Proctor, compared to those who have already been hanged? Explain your response.

Parris: Excellency—

Danforth: Now, sir—which of these in your opinion may be brought to God? I will myself strive with him till dawn. *He hands the list to* PARRIS, *who merely glances at it.*

Parris: There is not sufficient time till dawn.

Danforth: I shall do my utmost. Which of them do you have hope for?

Parris, *not even glancing at the list now, and in a quavering voice, quietly:* Excellency—a dagger— *He chokes up.*

Danforth: What do you say?

Parris: Tonight, when I open my door to leave my house—a dagger clattered to the ground. *Silence.* DAN-FORTH *absorbs this. Now* PARRIS *cries out:* You cannot hang this sort. There is danger for me. I dare not step outside at night!

REVEREND HALE *enters. They look at him for an instant in silence. He is steeped in sorrow, exhausted, and more direct than he ever was.*

Danforth: Accept my congratulations, Reverend Hale; we are gladdened to see you returned to your good work.

Hale, *coming to* DANFORTH *now:* You must pardon them. They will not budge.

HERRICK *enters, waits.*

Danforth, *conciliatory:* You misunderstand, sir; I cannot pardon these when twelve are already hanged for the same crime. It is not just.

Parris, *with failing heart:* Rebecca will not confess?

Hale: The sun will rise in a few minutes. Excellency, I must have more time.

Danforth: Now hear me, and beguile yourselves no more. I will not receive a single plea for pardon or postponement. Them that will not confess will hang. Twelve are already executed; the names of these seven are given out, and the village expects to see them die this morning. Postponement now speaks a floundering on my part; reprieve or pardon must cast doubt upon the guilt of them that died till now. While I speak God's law, I will not crack its voice with whimpering. If retaliation is your fear, know this—I should hang ten thousand that dared to rise against the law, and an ocean of salt tears could not melt the resolution of the statutes. Now draw yourselves up like men and help me, as you are bound by Heaven to do. Have you spoken with them all, Mr. Hale?

Hale: All but Proctor. He is in the dungeon.

Danforth, *to* HERRICK: What's Proctor's way now?

Herrick: He sits like some great bird; you'd not know he lived except he will take food from time to time.

Danforth, *after thinking a moment:* His wife—his wife must be well on with child now.

Herrick: She is, sir.

Danforth: What think you, Mr. Parris? You have closer knowledge of this man; might her presence soften him?

Parris: It is possible, sir. He have not laid eyes on her these three months. I should summon her.

Danforth, *to* HERRICK: Is he yet adamant? Has he struck at you again?

Herrick: He cannot, sir, he is chained to the wall now.

Danforth, *after thinking on it:* Fetch Goody Proctor to me. Then let you bring him up.

Herrick: Aye, sir. HERRICK *goes. There is silence.*

Hale: Excellency, if you postpone a week and publish to the town that you are striving for their confessions, that speak mercy on your part, not faltering.

Danforth: Mr. Hale, as God have not empowered me like Joshua to stop this sun from rising,[2] so I cannot

> **You misunderstand, sir; I cannot pardon these when twelve are already hanged for the same crime. It is not just.**

---

2. **Joshua . . . rising:** In the Bible, Joshua, the successor of Moses, commands the sun and moon to stand still while his people take vengeance on their enemies.

E **Literary Focus** **Motivation** How does Danforth justify hanging more innocent people?

Vocabulary **beguile** (bih GYL) *v.:* mislead; deceive.
adamant (AD uh muhnt) *adj.:* not giving in; immovable.

withhold from them the perfection of their punishment.

Hale, *harder now:* If you think God wills you to raise rebellion, Mr. Danforth, you are mistaken!

Danforth, *instantly:* You have heard rebellion spoken in the town?

Hale: Excellency, there are orphans wandering from house to house; abandoned cattle bellow on the high-roads, the stink of rotting crops hangs everywhere, and no man knows when the harlots' cry will end his life—and you wonder yet if rebellion's spoke? Better you should marvel how they do not burn your province! **F**

Danforth: Mr. Hale, have you preached in Andover this month?

Hale: Thank God they have no need of me in Andover.

Danforth: You baffle me, sir. Why have you returned here?

Hale: Why, it is all simple. I come to do the Devil's work. I come to counsel Christians they should belie themselves. *His sarcasm collapses.* There is blood on my head! Can you not see the blood on my head!!

Parris: Hush! *For he has heard footsteps. They all face the door.* HERRICK *enters with* ELIZABETH. *Her wrists are linked by heavy chain, which* HERRICK *now removes. Her clothes are dirty; her face is pale and gaunt.* HERRICK *goes out.*

Danforth, *very politely:* Goody Proctor. *She is silent.* I hope you are hearty?

Elizabeth, *as a warning reminder:* I am yet six month before my time.

Danforth: Pray be at your ease, we come not for your life. We—*uncertain how to plead, for he is not accustomed to it.* Mr. Hale, will you speak with the woman?

Hale: Goody Proctor, your husband is marked to hang this morning.

Pause.

Elizabeth, *quietly:* I have heard it.

Hale: You know, do you not, that I have no connection with the court? *She seems to doubt it.* I come of my own, Goody Proctor. I would save your husband's life, for if he is taken I count myself his murderer. Do you understand me?

Elizabeth: What do you want of me?

Hale: Goody Proctor, I have gone this three month

like our Lord into the wilderness. I have sought a Christian way, for damnation's doubled on a minister who counsels men to lie.

Hathorne: It is no lie, you cannot speak of lies.

Hale: It is a lie! They are innocent!

Danforth: I'll hear no more of that!

Hale, *continuing to* ELIZABETH: Let you not mistake your duty as I mistook my own. I came into this village like a bridegroom to his beloved, bearing gifts of high religion; the very crowns of holy law I brought, and what I touched with my bright confidence, it died; and where I turned the eye of my great faith, blood flowed up. Beware, Goody Proctor—cleave to no faith when faith brings blood. It is mistaken law that leads you to sacrifice. Life, woman, life is God's most precious gift; no principle, however glorious, may justify the taking of it. I beg you, woman, prevail upon your husband to confess. Let him give his lie. Quail not before God's judgment in this, for it may well be God damns a liar less than he that throws his life away for pride. Will you plead with him? I cannot think he will listen to another.

Elizabeth, *quietly:* I think that be the Devil's argument. **G**

Hale, *with a climactic desperation:* Woman, before the laws of God we are as swine! We cannot read His will!

Elizabeth: I cannot dispute with you, sir; I lack learning for it.

Danforth, *going to her:* Goody Proctor, you are not summoned here for disputation. Be there no wifely tenderness within you? He will die with the sunrise. Your husband. Do you understand it? *She only looks at him.* What say you? Will you contend with him? *She is silent.* Are you stone? I tell you true, woman, had I no other proof of your unnatural life, your dry eyes now would be sufficient evidence that you delivered up your soul to Hell! A very ape would weep at such calamity! Have the Devil dried up any tear of pity in you? *She is silent.* Take her out. It profit nothing she should speak to him!

Elizabeth, *quietly:* Let me speak with him, Excellency.

Parris, *with hope:* You'll strive with him? *She hesitates.*

Danforth: Will you plead for his confession or will you not?

F Literary Perspectives **Analyzing Credibility** How does the warning of rebellion in Salem undermine Danforth's authority?

G Reading Focus **Drawing Conclusions About Characters** For what reasons does Elizabeth reject Hale's argument?

Elizabeth: I promise nothing. Let me speak with him.

A sound—the sibilance of dragging feet on stone. They turn. A pause. HERRICK *enters with* JOHN PROCTOR. *His wrists are chained. He is another man, bearded, filthy, his eyes misty as though webs had overgrown them. He halts inside the doorway, his eye caught by the sight of* ELIZABETH. *The emotion flowing between them prevents anyone from speaking for an instant. Now* HALE, *visibly affected, goes to* DANFORTH *and speaks quietly.*

Hale: Pray, leave them, Excellency.
Danforth, *pressing* HALE *impatiently aside:* Mr. Proctor, you have been notified, have you not? PROCTOR *is silent, staring at* ELIZABETH. I see light in the sky, Mister; let you counsel with your wife, and may God help you turn your back on Hell. PROCTOR *is silent, staring at* ELIZABETH.
Hale, *quietly:* Excellency, let—

DANFORTH *brushes past* HALE *and walks out.* HALE *follows.* CHEEVER *stands and follows,* HATHORNE *behind.* HERRICK *goes.* PARRIS, *from a safe distance, offers:*

Parris: If you desire a cup of cider, Mr. Proctor, I am sure I—PROCTOR *turns an icy stare at him, and he breaks off.* PARRIS *raises his palms toward* PROCTOR. God lead you now. PARRIS *goes out.*

Alone, PROCTOR *walks to her, halts. It is as though they stood in a spinning world. It is beyond sorrow, above it. He reaches out his hand as though toward an embodiment not quite real, and as he touches her, a strange soft sound, half laughter, half amazement, comes from his throat. He pats her hand. She covers his hand with hers. And then, weak, he sits. Then she sits, facing him.*

Proctor: The child?
Elizabeth: It grows.
Proctor: There is no word of the boys?
Elizabeth: They're well. Rebecca's Samuel keeps them.
Proctor: You have not seen them?
Elizabeth: I have not. *She catches a weakening in herself and downs it.*
Proctor: You are a—marvel, Elizabeth.
Elizabeth: You—have been tortured?
Proctor: Aye. *Pause. She will not let herself be drowned in the sea that threatens her.* They come for my life now.
Elizabeth: I know it.

Pause.

Proctor: None—have yet confessed?
Elizabeth: There be many confessed.
Proctor: Who are they?
Elizabeth: There be a hundred or more, they say. Goody Ballard is one; Isaiah Goodkind is one. There be many.
Proctor: Rebecca?
Elizabeth: Not Rebecca. She is one foot in Heaven now; naught may hurt her more.
Proctor: And Giles?
Elizabeth: You have not heard of it?
Proctor: I hear nothin', where I am kept.
Elizabeth: Giles is dead.

He looks at her incredulously.

Proctor: When were he hanged?
Elizabeth, *quietly, factually:* He were not hanged. He would not answer aye or nay to his indictment; for if he denied the charge they'd hang him surely, and auction out his property. So he stand mute, and died Christian under the law. And so his sons will have his farm. It is the law, for he could not be condemned a wizard without he answer the indictment, aye or nay. **H**
Proctor: Then how does he die?
Elizabeth, *gently:* They press him, John.
Proctor: Press?
Elizabeth: Great stones they lay upon his chest until he plead aye or nay. *With a tender smile for the old man:* They say he give them but two words. "More weight," he says. And died.
Proctor, *numbed—a thread to weave into his agony:* "More weight."
Elizabeth: Aye. It were a fearsome man, Giles Corey.

Pause.

Proctor, *with great force of will, but not quite looking at her:* I have been thinking I would confess to them, Elizabeth. *She shows nothing.* What say you? If I give them that?
Elizabeth: I cannot judge you, John.

H **Reading Focus** **Drawing Conclusions About Characters**
What does Giles's refusal to answer the indictment reveal about his values?

1160 Unit 6 • Collection 15

Pause.

Proctor, *simply—a pure question:* What would you have me do?

Elizabeth: As you will, I would have it. *Slight pause.* I want you living, John. That's sure.

Proctor—*he pauses, then with a flailing of hope:* Giles' wife? Have she confessed?

Elizabeth: She will not.

Pause.

Proctor: It is a pretense, Elizabeth.

Elizabeth: What is?

Proctor: I cannot mount the gibbet like a saint. It is a fraud. I am not that man. *She is silent.* My honesty is broke, Elizabeth; I am no good man. Nothing's spoiled by giving them this lie that were not rotten long before.

Elizabeth: And yet you've not confessed till now. That speak goodness in you.

Proctor: Spite only keeps me silent. It is hard to give a lie to dogs. *Pause, for the first time he turns directly to her.* I would have your forgiveness, Elizabeth.

Elizabeth: It is not for me to give, John, I am—

Proctor: I'd have you see some honesty in it. Let them that never lied die now to keep their souls. It is pretense for me, a vanity that will not blind God nor keep my children out of the wind. *Pause.* What say you?

Elizabeth, *upon a heaving sob that always threatens:* John, it come to naught that I should forgive you, if you'll not forgive yourself. *Now he turns away a little, in great agony.* It is not my soul, John, it is yours. *He stands, as though in physical pain, slowly rising to his feet with a great immortal longing to find his answer. It is difficult to say, and she is on the verge of tears.* Only be sure of this, for I know it now: Whatever you will do, it is a good man does it. *He turns his doubting, searching gaze upon her.* I have read my heart this three month, John. *Pause.* I have sins of my own to count. It needs a cold wife to prompt lechery.

Proctor, *in great pain:* Enough, enough—

Elizabeth, *now pouring out her heart:* Better you should know me!

Proctor: I will not hear it! I know you!

Elizabeth: You take my sins upon you, John—

Proctor, *in agony:* No, I take my own, my own!

Elizabeth: John, I counted myself so plain, so poorly made, no honest love could come to me! Suspicion kissed you when I did; I never knew how I should say my love. It were a cold house I kept! *In fright, she swerves, as* HATHORNE *enters.*

Hathorne: What say you, Proctor? The sun is soon up.

PROCTOR, *his chest heaving, stares, turns to* ELIZABETH. *She comes to him as though to plead, her voice quaking.*

Elizabeth: Do what you will. But let none be your judge. There be no higher judge under Heaven than Proctor is! Forgive me, forgive me, John—I never knew such goodness in the world! *She covers her face, weeping.*

PROCTOR *turns from her to* HATHORNE; *he is off the earth, his voice hollow.*

Proctor: I want my life.

Hathorne, *electrified, surprised:* You'll confess yourself?

Proctor: I will have my life.

Hathorne, *with a mystical tone:* God be praised! It is a providence! *He rushes out the door, and his voice is heard calling down the corridor:* He will confess! Proctor will confess!

Proctor, *with a cry, as he strides to the door:* Why do you cry it? *In great pain he turns back to her.* It is evil, is it not? It is evil.

Elizabeth, *in terror, weeping:* I cannot judge you, John, I cannot!

Proctor: Then who will judge me? *Suddenly clasping his hands:* God in Heaven, what is John Proctor, what is John Proctor? *He moves as an animal, and a fury is riding in him, a tantalized search.* I think it is honest, I think so; I am no saint. *As though she had denied this he calls angrily at her:* Let Rebecca go like a saint; for me it is fraud!

Voices are heard in the hall, speaking together in suppressed excitement.

Elizabeth: I am not your judge, I cannot be. *As though giving him release:* Do as you will, do as you will!

---

❶ Literary Focus **Motivation** Proctor told the truth in court. Why does he now say "My honesty is broke"?

Proctor: Would you give them such a lie? Say it. Would you ever give them this? *She cannot answer.* You would not; if tongs of fire were singeing you you would not! It is evil. Good, then—it is evil, and I do it!

HATHORNE *enters with* DANFORTH, *and, with them,* CHEEVER, PARRIS, *and* HALE. *It is a businesslike, rapid entrance, as though the ice had been broken.*

Danforth, *with great relief and gratitude:* Praise to God, man, praise to God; you shall be blessed in Heaven for this. CHEEVER *has hurried to the bench with pen, ink, and paper.* PROCTOR *watches him.* Now then, let us have it. Are you ready, Mr. Cheever?

Proctor, *with a cold, cold horror at their efficiency:* Why must it be written?

Danforth: Why, for the good instruction of the village, Mister; this we shall post upon the church door! *To* PARRIS, *urgently:* Where is the marshal?

Parris, *runs to the door and calls down the corridor:* Marshal! Hurry!

Danforth: Now, then, Mister, will you speak slowly, and directly to the point, for Mr. Cheever's sake. *He is on record now, and is really dictating to* CHEEVER, *who writes.* Mr. Proctor, have you seen the Devil in your life? PROCTOR's *jaws lock.* Come, man, there is light in the sky; the town waits at the scaffold; I would give out this news. Did you see the Devil?

Proctor: I did.

Parris: Praise God!

Danforth: And when he come to you, what were his demand? PROCTOR *is silent.* DANFORTH *helps.* Did he bid you to do his work upon the earth?

Proctor: He did.

Danforth: And you bound yourself to his service? DANFORTH *turns, as* REBECCA NURSE *enters, with* HERRICK *helping to support her. She is barely able to walk.* Come in, come in, woman!

Rebecca, *brightening as she sees* PROCTOR: Ah, John! You are well, then, eh?

PROCTOR *turns his face to the wall.*

Danforth: Courage, man, courage—let her witness your good example that she may come to God herself. Now hear it, Goody Nurse! Say on, Mr. Proctor. Did you bind yourself to the Devil's service?

Rebecca, *astonished:* Why, John!

Proctor, *through his teeth, his face turned from* REBECCA: I did.

Danforth: Now, woman, you surely see it profit nothin' to keep this conspiracy any further. Will you confess yourself with him?

Rebecca: Oh, John—God send his mercy on you!

Danforth: I say, will you confess yourself, Goody Nurse?

Rebecca: Why, it is a lie, it is a lie; how may I damn myself? I cannot, I cannot.

Danforth: Mr. Proctor. When the Devil came to you did you see Rebecca Nurse in his company? PROCTOR *is silent.* Come, man, take courage—did you ever see her with the Devil?

Proctor, *almost inaudibly:* No.

DANFORTH, *now sensing trouble, glances at* JOHN *and goes to the table, and picks up a sheet—the list of condemned.*

Danforth: Did you ever see her sister, Mary Easty, with the Devil?

Proctor: No, I did not.

Danforth, *his eyes narrow on* PROCTOR: Did you ever see Martha Corey with the Devil?

Proctor: I did not.

Danforth, *realizing, slowly putting the sheet down:* Did you ever see anyone with the Devil?

Proctor: I did not.

Danforth: Proctor, you mistake me. I am not empowered to trade your life for a lie. You have most certainly seen some person with the Devil. PROCTOR *is silent.* Mr. Proctor, a score of people have already testified they saw this woman with the Devil.

Proctor: Then it is proved. Why must I say it?

Danforth: Why "must" you say it! Why, you should rejoice to say it if your soul is truly purged of any love for Hell!

Proctor: They think to go like saints. I like not to spoil their names.

Danforth, *inquiring, incredulous:* Mr. Proctor, do you think they go like saints?

Proctor, *evading:* This woman never thought she done the Devil's work. **J**

Danforth: Look you, sir. I think you mistake your duty here. It matters nothing what she thought—she

---

J Literary Focus **Motivation** If Proctor has decided to confess, why does he evade the questioning now? Explain your response.

is convicted of the unnatural murder of children, and you for sending your spirit out upon Mary Warren. Your soul alone is the issue here, Mister, and you will prove its whiteness or you cannot live in a Christian country. Will you tell me now what persons conspired with you in the Devil's company? PROCTOR *is silent.* To your knowledge was Rebecca Nurse ever—

Proctor: I speak my own sins; I cannot judge another. *Crying out, with hatred:* I have no tongue for it. **Ⓚ**

Hale, *quickly to* DANFORTH: Excellency, it is enough he confess himself. Let him sign it, let him sign it.

Parris, *feverishly:* It is a great service, sir. It is a weighty name; it will strike the village that Proctor confess. I beg you, let him sign it. The sun is up, Excellency!

Danforth, *considers; then with dissatisfaction:* Come, then, sign your testimony. *To* CHEEVER: Give it to him. CHEEVER *goes to* PROCTOR, *the confession and a pen in hand.* PROCTOR *does not look at it.* Come, man, sign it.

Proctor, *after glancing at the confession:* You have all witnessed it—it is enough.

Danforth: You will not sign it?

Proctor: You have all witnessed it; what more is needed?

Danforth: Do you sport with me? You will sign your name or it is no confession, Mister! *His breast heaving with agonized breathing,* PROCTOR *now lays the paper down and signs his name.*

Parris: Praise be to the Lord!

PROCTOR *has just finished signing when* DANFORTH *reaches for the paper. But* PROCTOR *snatches it up, and now a wild terror is rising in him, and a boundless anger.*

Danforth, *perplexed, but politely extending his hand:* If you please, sir.

Proctor: No.

Danforth, *as though* PROCTOR *did not understand:* Mr. Proctor, I must have—

Proctor: No, no. I have signed it. You have seen me. It is done! You have no need for this.

Parris: Proctor, the village must have proof that—

Proctor: Damn the village! I confess to God, and God has seen my name on this! It is enough!

Danforth: No, sir, it is—

Proctor: You came to save my soul, did you not? Here! I have confessed myself; it is enough!

Danforth: You have not con—

Proctor: I have confessed myself! Is there no good penitence but it be public? God does not need my name nailed upon the church! God sees my name; God knows how black my sins are! It is enough! **Ⓛ**

Danforth: Mr. Proctor—

Proctor: You will not use me! I am no Sarah Good or Tituba, I am John Proctor! You will not use me! It is no part of salvation that you should use me!

Danforth: I do not wish to—

Proctor: I have three children—how may I teach them to walk like men in the world, and I sold my friends?

Danforth: You have not sold your friends—

Proctor: Beguile me not! I blacken all of them when this is nailed to the church the very day they hang for silence!

Danforth: Mr. Proctor, I must have good and legal proof that you—

Proctor: You are the high court, your word is good enough! Tell them I confessed myself; say Proctor broke his knees and wept like a woman; say what you will, but my name cannot—

Danforth, *with suspicion:* It is the same, is it not? If I report it or you sign to it?

Proctor—*he knows it is insane:* No, it is not the same! What others say and what I sign to is not the same!

Danforth: Why? Do you mean to deny this confession when you are free?

Proctor: I mean to deny nothing!

Danforth: Then explain to me, Mr. Proctor, why you will not let—

> # Now, woman, you surely see it profit nothin' to keep this conspiracy any further. Will you confess yourself with him?

Ⓚ Literary Perspectives Analyzing Credibility How is the statement "I cannot judge another" a condemnation of the court itself?

Ⓛ Reading Focus Drawing Conclusions About Characters What sin does Danforth believe Proctor is talking about? What sin does Proctor feel most guilty about?

Proctor, *with a cry of his whole soul:* Because it is my name! Because I cannot have another in my life! Because I lie and sign myself to lies! Because I am not worth the dust on the feet of them that hang! How may I live without my name? I have given you my soul; leave me my name!

Danforth, *pointing at the confession in* PROCTOR's *hand:* Is that document a lie? If it is a lie I will not accept it! What say you? I will not deal in lies, Mister! PROCTOR *is motionless.* You will give me your honest confession in my hand, or I cannot keep you from the rope. PROCTOR *does not reply.* Which way do you go, Mister?

His breast heaving, his eyes staring, PROCTOR *tears the paper and crumples it, and he is weeping in fury, but erect.*

Danforth: Marshal!

Parris, *hysterically, as though the tearing paper were his life:* Proctor, Proctor! **Ⓜ**

Hale: Man, you will hang! You cannot!

Proctor, *his eyes full of tears:* I can. And there's your first marvel, that I can. You have made your magic now, for now I do think I see some shred of goodness in John Proctor. Not enough to weave a banner with, but white enough to keep it from such dogs. **Ⓝ**

ELIZABETH, *in a burst of terror, rushes to him and weeps against his hand.* Give them no tear! Tears pleasure them! Show honor now, show a stony heart and sink them with it! *He has lifted her, and kisses her now with great passion.*

Rebecca: Let you fear nothing! Another judgment waits us all!

Danforth: Hang them high over the town! Who weeps for these, weeps for corruption! *He sweeps out past them.* HERRICK *starts to lead* REBECCA, *who*

almost collapses, but PROCTOR *catches her, and she glances up at him apologetically.*

Rebecca: I've had no breakfast.

Herrick: Come, man.

HERRICK *escorts them out,* HATHORNE *and* CHEEVER *behind them.* ELIZABETH *stands staring at the empty doorway.*

Parris, *in deadly fear, to* ELIZABETH: Go to him, Goody Proctor! There is yet time!

From outside a drumroll strikes the air. PARRIS *is startled.* ELIZABETH *jerks about toward the window.*

Parris: Go to him! *He rushes out the door, as though to hold back his fate.* Proctor! Proctor!

Again, a short burst of drums.

Hale: Woman, plead with him! *He starts to rush out the door, and then goes back to her.* Woman! It is pride, it is vanity. *She avoids his eyes, and moves to the window. He drops to his knees.* Be his helper! What profit him to bleed? Shall the dust praise him? Shall the worms declare his truth? Go to him, take his shame away!

Elizabeth, *supporting herself against collapse, grips the bars of the window, and with a cry:* He have his goodness now. God forbid I take it from him!

The final drumroll crashes, then heightens violently. HALE *weeps in frantic prayer, and the new sun is pouring in upon her face, and the drums rattle like bones in the morning air.*

The curtain falls

Ⓜ Reading Focus **Drawing Conclusions About Characters**
Why is it so important to Parris that Proctor, who has only bad feelings for him, be spared from hanging?

Ⓝ Reading Focus **Drawing Conclusions About Characters**
What goodness has Proctor found within himself?

Applying Your Skills

SKILLS FOCUS **Literary Skills** Analyze character motivation; understand and analyze elements of American drama; analyze credibility. **Reading Skills** Draw conclusions about characters. **Writing Skills** Analyze unique aspects of the text.

The Crucible, Act Four

Respond and Think Critically

Reading Focus

Quick Check

1. Why has Reverend Hale returned to Salem?

2. What news about Abigail does Parris give to Danforth?

3. What two things does Elizabeth say she is unable to do for John?

4. Why does Danforth want a written confession from Proctor?

5. What does Parris fear about the response of the people in Andover?

Read with a Purpose

6. Why does Proctor ultimately choose his own "goodness" instead of confessing to an act he didn't commit?

Reading Skills: Drawing Conclusions About Characters

7. Review your chart. What, in your opinion, is the difference between the way Proctor and Hale resolve the conflicts between their public and private lives? Whose solution is better? Could similar conflicts be found in people today? Support your answers with examples from the text and from life.

Literary Focus

Literary Analysis

8. **Summarize** Describe the events that precede the sudden disappearance of Abigail and Mercy.

9. **Make Judgments** Why does Hale counsel Elizabeth to persuade John Proctor to lie? Do you think he is right to do so? Explain your response.

10. **Interpret** How do you interpret Arthur Miller's statement that John and Elizabeth inhabit a world "beyond sorrow, above it"?

11. **Literary Perspectives** Has Hale become more credible over the course of the play? Explain.

Literary Skills: Motivation

12. **Infer** What motivation does Proctor have for confessing?

Literary Skills Review: American Drama

13. **Evaluate** In drama, **realism** attempts to depict life as it is lived, without idealizing or romanticizing it. Robert Anderson credits Arthur Miller with transforming realism in American drama, writing plays that demonstrate "realism combined with…something more imaginative" (page 1091). Is *The Crucible* pure realism, or is it transformed by something more imaginative? Cite evidence from Act Four to support your response.

Writing Focus

Think as a Reader/Writer

Use It in Your Writing Stage directions may include physical descriptions of a scene or the characters that provide us with insight into the play itself. *The Crucible*'s final stage direction is, "*the new sun is pouring in upon [Elizabeth's] face, and the drums rattle like bones in the morning air.*" What theme does this stage direction transmit? Explain your response.

What Do **You Think Now**

What needs and desires do Elizabeth and John Proctor share? How are they different?

Vocabulary Development

✓ Vocabulary Check

Match each Vocabulary word with its definition.

1. adamant
2. deposition
3. beguile
4. dissembling
5. blasphemy
6. theocracy
7. avidly
8. partisan

a. religious rule
b. eagerly
c. immovable
d. biased supporter
e. hiding one's motives
f. testimony under oath
g. cursing or profanity
h. mislead

Vocabulary Skills: Connotations

A **denotation** is the dictionary definition of a word. In context, however, many words assume additional meanings, or **connotations**. A **connotation** is the emotional overtones attached to a word or phrase. Read the following sentence:

> There is a prodigious *stench* in this place.

What connotation is associated with the word *stench*?

Your Turn

Read the definitions of *crucible* below and use them to explain the title of the play. What connotations are associated with the word *crucible*? Why do you think Miller chose this title?

crucible (KROO sih buhl) *n.*: lamp, pot, jug, earthen pot

1. a container made of a substance that can resist great heat, for melting, fusing, or catching ores, metals, etc.
2. the hollow at the bottom of an ore furnace, where the molten metal collects
3. a severe test or trial

Language Coach

Parts of Speech Word endings often indicate the word's part of speech. The suffix *–tion* usually comes at the end of a noun, such as *suggestion*. The suffixes *–ous* and *–ate* often come at the end of adjectives, such as *monstrous* and *passionate*. The suffix *–ate* can also end verbs, such as *invalidate*.

Identify the part of speech of each word below. Then use a dictionary to check your answer and find the definition.

1. immaculate
2. perdition
3. pontificate
4. facetious
5. immolate
6. arduous
7. imputation
8. intricate

Academic Vocabulary

Write About
In *The Crucible*, many underline{components} contribute to the situation spiraling so rapidly out of control. Write about an experience in which you lost control of a situation. What could you have done to prevent it?

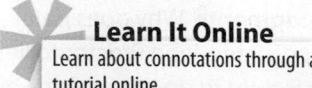

Learn It Online
Learn about connotations through a *WordSharp* tutorial online.

go.hrw.com L11-1166   **Go**

Grammar Link

Choosing Vivid Nouns and Verbs

Most sentences contain at least one noun and one verb. Choosing **vivid nouns** and **vivid verbs** will make your writing more engaging and informative for your reader.

In the right-hand column of the chart below is a sentence that communicates a message, but would do so more effectively with the addition of vivid nouns or verbs.

The middle column shows the same sentence with vivid nouns replacing the less lively ones. Vivid nouns help your reader understand specifically who or what you are describing and provide additional information to your reader.

The third column shows the sentence with a vivid verb added as well. Vivid verbs help your reader feel the action.

Sentence without vivid nouns or verbs	With vivid nouns	With vivid verbs
She did not tell the truth about her feelings for John.	She did not tell the truth about her **passion** for John.	She **lied** about her passions for John.
She fooled the audience with a story about scary things.	She fooled the audience with a story about **demons** and **witchcraft.**	She **beguiled** the audience with a story about demons and witchcraft.

Your Turn

Rewrite each of the following sentences by replacing the underlined words with vivid nouns or verbs. Remember to be specific so that your reader knows exactly what you mean.

1. She <u>went</u> to the judge <u>to discuss</u> her <u>situation</u>.
2. The girls <u>left</u> and <u>took</u> the man's *things*.

CHOICES

As you respond to the Choices, use these **Academic Vocabulary** words as appropriate: <u>component</u>, <u>diverse</u>, <u>intrinsic</u>, <u>potential</u>, <u>transmit</u>.

REVIEW

Analyze a Character

Timed Writing Write an analysis of one of the characters in *The Crucible*. Focus on the conflicts that character faces, the motivation behind the character's actions, discoveries the character makes, and changes the character undergoes. Provide evidence from the text to support your analysis.

CONNECT

Discuss Groups in Conflict

Group Discussion In *The Crucible*, some characters are accused of being evil or allied with the Devil. Enemies, whether they be nations at war or rival political factions, often demonize each other in this way. By the end of the play, however, it is clear the true conflicts in Salem are not that simple. Why do people in conflict sometimes treat each other as incarnations of evil? What does doing so achieve?

EXTEND

Discuss Conscience and Society

Paired Activity Miller said he wrote *The Crucible* with the conviction that "there were moments when an individual conscience was all that could keep the world from falling apart." With a partner, discuss your response to this statement. Do you think the play demonstrates a triumph or a failure of individual conscience? Create a list of <u>diverse</u> real-life examples to support your point.

Learn It Online
Explore Miller's inspirations for *The Crucible* through these Internet links.

go.hrw.com L11-1167 **Go**

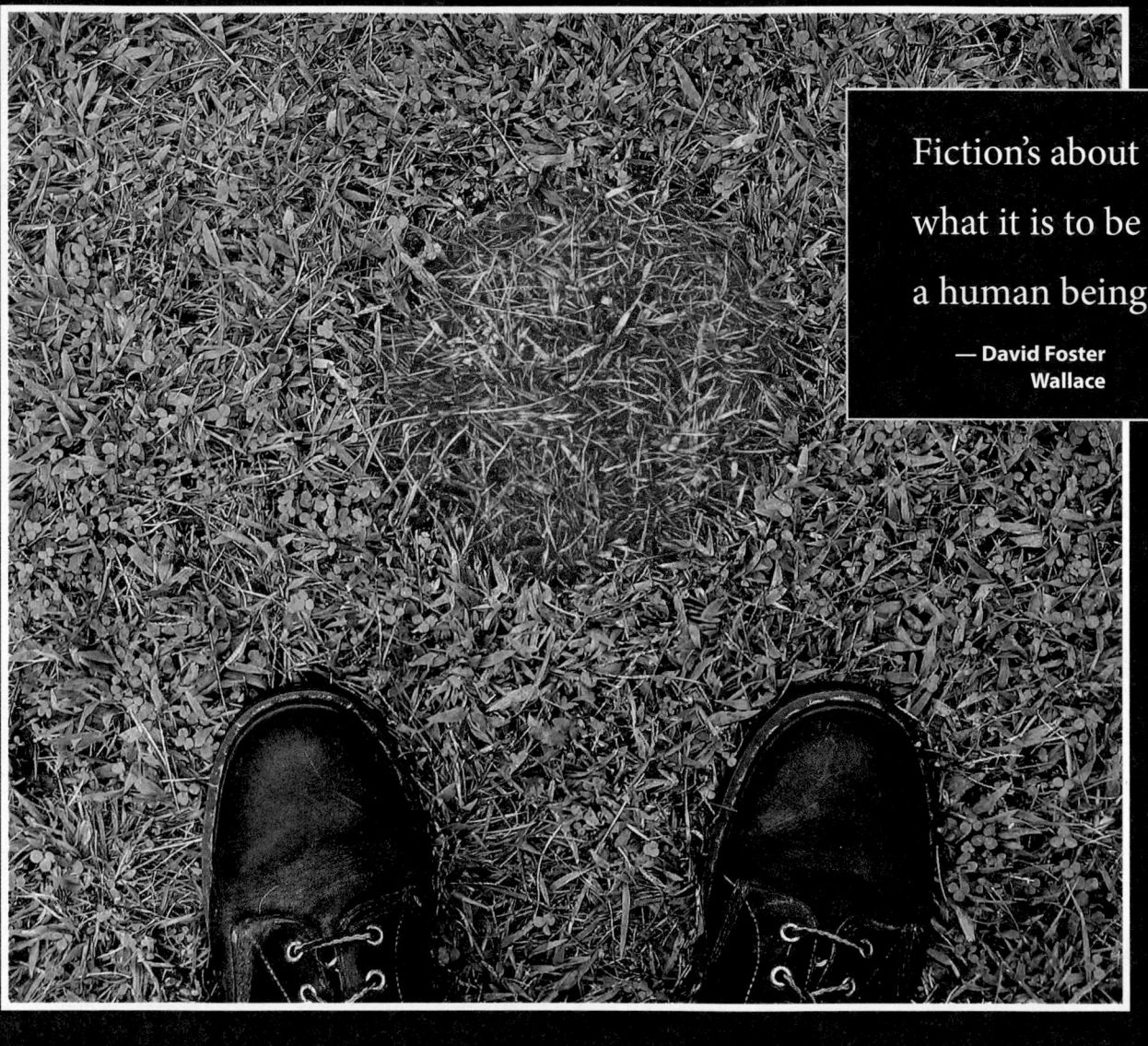

> Fiction's about
> what it is to be
> a human being.
>
> — **David Foster
> Wallace**

CONTENTS

Characterization by **Leila Christenbury**

Functions of Characterization

- Defines a character's personality
- Reveals hopes and fears of the characters
- Makes characters lively and realistic
- Helps advance the plot and communicate the theme

For many readers, the best thing about stories is the chance to meet interesting characters. How a writer reveals a character's personality is called **characterization,** and it is carried out in various ways:

- by telling us what the character is like
- by describing how the character looks and dresses
- by letting us hear the character speak
- by revealing the character's private thoughts and feelings
- by revealing the character's effect on other people
- by showing the character in action

The success of the short stories in this collection depends on you, the reader, believing that these imaginary people are real. Look for various components of character development. What does the writer tell you about the character? How does the character act? What does the character say and think? What is directly stated about this character, and what is implied? Finally, look for the one thing that all good literature contains: dynamic characters who, in the course of the narrative, show change. What kinds of changes, small or large, do these characters undergo?

Static Versus Dynamic Characters

Bernard Malamud's short story "The Magic Barrel" (page 1174) presents us with two intriguing men, a marriage broker and a religious scholar who is seeking a wife. As the story works its way through their relationship, we find that one of them remains basically unchanged from beginning to end. He is considered a **static,** or unchanging, **character.** In contrast, events force the other man to undergo a major shift in his thinking, and he emerges as quite a different character at the end of the story. He is a **dynamic,** or changing, **character.** What this man learns about himself is a significant element of the tale.

In his short story "Son" (page 1188), John Updike presents an array of related characters: grandfathers, fathers, and sons. The generational differences between them are pronounced—but so are their similarities. By tracing their personalities and noticing ways in which they succeed, fail, change, and remain static as parents and children, we understand important things about our own families and ourselves. Ultimately, some characters will grow more than others, just as in real life. As you read, ask yourself how each character changes and why.

Round Versus Flat Characters

When a character is revealed in great detail and when we see deeply into his or her personality, it is as if we are being shown a three-dimensional version of that person. Characters like these are called **round** because we, seeing several perspectives, gain a clear impression of their internal and external conflicts.

An example of a round character is Paul Berlin, the Vietnam veteran who appears in Tim O'Brien's "Speaking of Courage" (page 1197). While Berlin drives robotically around and around a lake, we follow his thoughts as he replays horrors of the war, evaluates his own conduct as a soldier, and holds imaginary conversations with his father. Through his ruminations and his actions we learn a lot about Paul's personality and life. By the end of the story, we feel that he is a real person in a complicated and difficult situation.

At the opposite extreme, some characters have so little depth that they appear to be nothing but cardboard cutouts. Not surprisingly, these are called **flat characters.**

Anne Tyler's "Teenage Wasteland" (page 1216) presents one such character, a tutor named Cal. Called upon to help prevent a troubled young man from failing in school, Cal responds with an <u>intrinsic</u>, lazy carelessness that never varies—or helps. This is not a flaw in Tyler's short story but an accurate portrayal of a certain stereotypical character.

Identifying with Characters

The quality of characterization depends directly on the extent to which we identify with these people, or imaginatively and sympathetically compare ourselves to them. Strange as it may seem, feeling empathy for fictional characters can happen even if our life experiences are quite different from theirs. A case in point is Raymond Carver's subtle snapshot of a young married couple in "Everything Stuck to Him" (page 1208).

In Carver's short story, the characters don't even have names; they're just "the boy" and "the girl." What happens between them could not be more ordinary, yet Carver's precise rendering of their clothing, actions, and words makes them seem real to the reader. He succinctly shows us exactly how a disagreement arises between the married couple, what the issues are, and what's *really* at stake. We know who these caring, conflicted,

inarticulate characters are, and we identify with them in some way because, in our hearts, they are us.

Julia Alvarez provides a similar model through the young narrator of her short story "Daughter of Invention" (page 1227). Alvarez's story involves familial **conflicts,** with generational differences intensified further by a clash of cultures. Her characterization of the funny and irresistibly good-natured "Cukita," as her mother calls her, is so well executed that we're rooting for her at every turn.

We understand what motivates Waverly Jong, the feisty seven-year-old protagonist of Amy Tan's "Rules of the Game" (page 1241). Saddled with bossy older brothers and a nagging mom, she discovers in herself a special talent that sets her free. Who among us could fail to identify with this spunky child—and rejoice in her liberation?

As you read these selections, look for static, dynamic, round, and flat characters. Which of them do you identify with most, and which do you identify with least? What details help you define their characters?

Ask Yourself

In a brief paragraph, explain which short story described in the essay you are most interested in reading. Why does this story interest you? Use information from the essay to help support your answer.

Learn It Online

Explore characterization the multimedia way—through *PowerNotes* online.

go.hrw.com L11-1170 **Go**

Analyzing a Movie Still

Movies, like printed stories, use <u>diverse</u> techniques for establishing the personalities of their characters.

Guidelines

To explore **characterization** in this still from the movie *Smoke Signals*,

- think about how the director has organized the scene—study the characters' surroundings and the locations of the characters within their surroundings.

- observe the characters' clothes, posture, and facial expressions. What do you notice about these characters?

- look for similarities and differences: How are the two characters alike? How do they differ?

1. What do you infer from the characters' positions in the frame and their postures?

2. How does facial expression lend to **characterization**?

3. The characters' hair and clothes are similar in some ways but **characterize** them differently. How?

Movie still from *Smoke Signals*, screenplay by Sherman Alexie, based on stories by Sherman Alexie. Adam Beach as Victor Joseph (left), Evan Adams as Thomas Builds-the-Fire (right).

Your Turn Analyze Characterization in a Movie Still

Use an Internet site to locate a still from one of your favorite movies. With a partner, discuss which <u>components</u> of the movie still reveal the characters' personalities.

The Magic Barrel

Bernard Malamud
(1914–1986)

National Book Award WINNER

What Do You Think

What human needs and desires do we have in common?

QuickWrite

Think about a life-changing decision you or someone you know might have to make, such as changing schools. What questions should be asked before deciding? List these questions. Then, write a paragraph or two describing how to reach a good decision.

Although Bernard Malamud crafted tales that draw on the experiences of Jewish people, Malamud preferred not to be pigeonholed. He wrote *about* Jews, but he wrote *for* all people.

"Somebody Has to Cry"

Malamud's characters usually live at a level of bare physical subsistence. Though we feel compassion for them, they do not display the least self-pity. Even if their lives are sad, Malamud's characters are triumphant because they survive heroically against the odds we all face.

Malamud's own upbringing was bleak. He was the older of two sons of a Russian immigrant. His mother died when he was fourteen. He grew up in Brooklyn in a household without pictures on the walls, books, or music. In particular, it was the suffering of European Jews during World War II that convinced Malamud he had something to say as a writer. "Somebody has to cry," he said, "even if it's a writer, twenty years later."

Although Malamud's stories are often about the struggle for survival in a difficult world, they are always informed by love, and, indeed, his characters are largely redeemed by love.

A World Where Good and Evil Matter

Many writers in the last half of the twentieth century broke with earlier traditions in storytelling and experimented with forms and style. Their characters are adrift in a world that seems devoid of meaning. Malamud was different. In his carefully plotted stories, a reader might hear echoes of the nineteenth-century storyteller and moralist Nathaniel Hawthorne, whose characters live in a world where good and evil are forces with which to contend.

In addition to several volumes of short stories, Malamud produced seven novels. His short story collection *The Magic Barrel* received a National Book Award for fiction in 1959.

Think About the Writer Why do you think Malamud chose to write about the Jewish experience? Do all great authors write from their own experiences?

Reader/Writer
Notebook

Use your **RWN** to complete the activities for this selection.

Literary Focus

Static and Dynamic Characters In literature, some characters remain the same throughout the story, ending with the same <u>intrinsic</u> ideas, attitudes, and feelings they had at the start. They are called **static characters.** In contrast, some characters change in important ways as the story progresses. They are called **dynamic characters.** As you read "The Magic Barrel," take note of which characters are static and which are dynamic.

Reading Focus

Drawing Conclusions About Characters While we are reading, it is important to figure out why characters say and do certain things in order to understand their personalities and motivations. In doing so, we are **drawing conclusions** about the characters. As you read this selection, pause after each page and draw conclusions about the characters; continue reading to see if your conclusions are correct.

Into Action As you read, use a chart like the one below to note details that lead you to a conclusion about the characters. In the left column, note each detail you find; in the right column, draw your conclusion. The first one has been done for you.

Detail	Conclusion
Salzman's portfolio had been worn thin with use.	He has been a matchmaker for many years.

Writing Focus

Think as a Reader/Writer

Find It in Your Reading Writers use a variety of grammatical structures to add descriptive details about their characters. Malamud frequently employs the participial phrase, a verb form used as an adjective with its accompanying modifiers, to do so. The present participle ends in *–ing,* and the past participle ends in *–ed.* Notice the participial phrase in italics in this sentence: "Around the corner, Salzman, *leaning against a wall*, chanted prayers for the dead." As you read, record in your *Reader/Writer Notebook* some of Malamud's most effective uses of participles to describe his characters.

Vocabulary

meager (MEE guhr) *adj.:* poor, scanty, inadequate. *Leo's room was meager, except for an abundance of books.*

rabbinical (ruh BIHN uh kuhl) *adj.:* relating to rabbis, or spiritual leaders in the Jewish religion. *Leo attended Yeshiva University for his rabbinical studies.*

matchmaker (MACH may kuhr) *n.:* a person who arranges marriages by introducing possible mates. *As a matchmaker, Salzman offered Leo several candidates for mates.*

dowry (DOW ree) *n.:* the money or property that a wife brings to her husband at marriage. *Salzman could not understand Leo's disinterest in the woman's dowry.*

clientele (kly uhn TEHL) *n.:* the clients or customers of a business. *Despite being a client himself, Leo did not approve of the rest of Salzman's clientele.*

trepidation (trehp uh DAY shuhn) *n.:* tremulous fear, alarm, or agitation. *Salzman appeared filled with trepidation at Leo's passion for his daughter.*

Language Coach

Suffixes The suffix *–ical* can mean "relating to" and can be used to change nouns into related adjectives. The noun *rabbi* adds an *n* in addition to the suffix to form the adjective *rabbinical.* Identify a noun related to each of these adjectives: *tyrannical, fanatical, hypocritical, theological.*

Learn It Online
Practice your vocabulary knowledge with Word Watch.

go.hrw.com | L11-1173 | Go

⇥ THE MAGIC BARREL ⇤

by **Bernard Malamud**

Read with a Purpose
As you read, ask yourself what Leo Finkle discovers about himself, love, and personal redemption.

Build Background
The practice of matchmaking in the Jewish community has a long history, going back to the Torah itself. "The Magic Barrel" was first published in 1954, when many Orthodox Jews still relied on professional matchmakers. It was considered an honorable profession, as matching two people who are perfectly suited to each other is no simple task. It was typical for marriage brokers to match people based on age, profession, intellect, income, and family status. In more recent times, the typical matchmaker began to earn a negative reputation as a conniving, deceitful person who lacked integrity.

Not long ago there lived in uptown New York, in a small, almost meager room, though crowded with books, Leo Finkle, a rabbinical student in the Yeshivah University.[1] Finkle, after six years of study, was to be ordained in June and had been advised by an acquaintance that he might find it easier to win himself a congregation if he were married. Since he had no present prospects of marriage, after two tormented days of turning it over in his mind, he called in Pinye Salzman, a marriage broker whose two-line advertisement he had read in the *Forward*.[2]

The matchmaker appeared one night out of the dark fourth-floor hallway of the graystone rooming house where Finkle lived, grasping a black, strapped portfolio that had been worn thin with use. Salzman, who had been long in the business, was of slight but dignified build, wearing an old hat, and an overcoat too short and tight for him. He smelled frankly of fish, which he loved to eat, and although he was missing a few teeth, his presence was not displeasing, because of an amiable manner curiously contrasted with mournful eyes. His voice, his lips, his wisp of beard, his bony fingers were animated, but give him a moment of repose and his mild blue eyes revealed a depth of sadness, a characteristic that put Leo a little at ease although the situation, for him, was inherently tense. **(A)**

He at once informed Salzman why he had asked him to come, explaining that his home was in Cleveland, and that but for his parents, who had married comparatively late in life, he was alone in the world. He had for six years devoted himself almost entirely to his studies, as a result of which, understandably, he had found himself without time for a social life and the company of young women. Therefore he thought

---

1. **Yeshivah University:** school in New York City that is a general college and a seminary for the training of Orthodox Jewish rabbis.
2. *Forward:* the *Jewish Daily Forward*, a Yiddish newspaper in New York City.

Vocabulary **meager** (MEE guhr) *adj.:* poor, scanty, inadequate.
rabbinical (ruh BIHN uh kuhl) *adj.:* relating to rabbis, or spiritual leaders in the Jewish religion.
matchmaker (MACH may kuhr) *n.:* a person who arranges marriages by introducing possible mates.

(A) Reading Focus **Drawing Conclusions About Characters**
What is your impression of Salzman after reading this description?

it the better part of trial and error—of embarrassing fumbling—to call in an experienced person to advise him on these matters. He remarked in passing that the function of the marriage broker was ancient and honorable, highly approved in the Jewish community, because it made practical the necessary without hindering joy. Moreover, his own parents had been brought together by a matchmaker. They had made, if not a financially profitable marriage—since neither had possessed any worldly goods to speak of—at least a successful one in the sense of their everlasting devotion to each other. Salzman listened in embarrassed surprise, sensing a sort of apology. Later, however, he experienced a glow of pride in his work, an emotion that had left him years ago, and he heartily approved of Finkle. **B**

The two went to their business. Leo had led Salzman to the only clear place in the room, a table near a window that overlooked the lamp-lit city. He seated himself at the matchmaker's side but facing him, attempting by an act of will to suppress the unpleasant tickle in his throat. Salzman eagerly unstrapped his portfolio and removed a loose rubber band from a thin packet of much-handled cards. As he flipped through them, a gesture and sound that physically hurt Leo, the student pretended not to see and gazed steadfastly out the window. Although it was still February, winter was on its last legs, signs of which he had for the first time in years begun to notice. He now observed the round white moon, moving high in the sky through a cloud menagerie,[3] and watched with half-open mouth as it penetrated a huge hen, and dropped out of her like an egg laying itself. Salzman, though pretending through eyeglasses he had just slipped on, to be engaged in scanning the writing on the cards, stole occasional

---

3. **menagerie:** collection of animals.

B **Reading Focus** **Drawing Conclusions About Characters**
Why does Leo Finkle feel the need to explain his background?

glances at the young man's distinguished face, noting with pleasure the long, severe scholar's nose, brown eyes heavy with learning, sensitive yet ascetic[4] lips, and a certain, almost hollow quality of the dark cheeks. He gazed around at shelves upon shelves of books and let out a soft, contented sigh. **C**

When Leo's eyes fell upon the cards, he counted six spread out in Salzman's hand.

"So few?" he asked in disappointment.

"You wouldn't believe me how much cards I got in my office," Salzman replied. "The drawers are already filled to the top, so I keep them now in a barrel, but is every girl good for a new rabbi?"

Leo blushed at this, regretting all he had revealed of himself in a curriculum vitae[5] he had sent to Salzman. He had thought it best to acquaint him with his strict standards and specifications, but in having done so, felt he had told the marriage broker more than was absolutely necessary.

He hesitantly inquired, "Do you keep photographs of your clients on file?"

"First comes family, amount of dowry, also what kind promises," Salzman replied, unbuttoning his tight coat and settling himself in the chair. "After comes pictures, rabbi."

"Call me Mr. Finkle. I'm not yet a rabbi."

Salzman said he would, but instead called him doctor, which he changed to rabbi when Leo was not listening too attentively. **D**

Salzman adjusted his horn-rimmed spectacles, gently cleared his throat and read in an eager voice the contents of the top card:

"Sophie P. Twenty four year. Widow one year. No children. Educated high school and two years college. Father promises eight thousand dollars. Has wonderful wholesale business. Also real estate. On the mother's side comes teachers, also one actor. Well known on Second Avenue."

Leo gazed up in surprise. "Did you say a widow?"

"A widow don't mean spoiled, rabbi. She lived with her husband maybe four months. He was a sick boy she made a mistake to marry him."

"Marrying a widow has never entered my mind."

"This is because you have no experience. A widow, especially if she is young and healthy like this girl, is a wonderful person to marry. She will be thankful to you the rest of her life. Believe me, if I was looking now for a bride, I would marry a widow."

Leo reflected, then shook his head.

Salzman hunched his shoulders in an almost imperceptible gesture of disappointment. He placed the card down on the wooden table and began to read another:

"Lily H. High school teacher. Regular. Not a substitute. Has savings and new Dodge car. Lived in Paris one year. Father is successful dentist thirty-five years. Interested in professional man. Well Americanized family. Wonderful opportunity.

"I knew her personally," said Salzman. "I wish you could see this girl. She is a doll. Also very intelligent. All day you could talk to her about books and theater and what not. She also knows current events."

"I don't believe you mentioned her age?"

"Her age?" Salzman said, raising his brows. "Her age is thirty-two years."

Leo said after a while, "I'm afraid that seems a little too old."

Salzman let out a laugh. "So how old are you, rabbi?"

"Twenty-seven."

"So what is the difference, tell me, between twenty-seven and thirty-two? My own wife is seven years older than me. So what did I suffer?—Nothing. If a Rothschild's daughter[6] wants to marry you, would you say on account her age, no?" **E**

---

4. **ascetic:** severe.
5. **curriculum vitae:** Latin for "course of life"; a résumé.

---

6. **Rothschild's daughter:** The Rothschilds are a wealthy banking family.

C **Reading Focus** Drawing Conclusions About Characters
How does the description of Finkle's apartment help characterize him?

D **Literary Focus** Static and Dynamic Characters Does Salzman appear to be a more static or more dynamic character so far? Explain your answer.

E **Reading Focus** Drawing Conclusions About Characters
What does this statement reveal about Salzman's view of marriage?

Vocabulary **dowry** (DOW ree) *n.:* the money or property that a wife brings to her husband at marriage.

Lucy (1936) by Lasar Segall (1891 Vilna–1957 Sao Paulo), Oil on canvas, 58.5 × 40 cm. Collection of the Musée National d'Art Moderne, Centre Georges Pompidou, Paris, France.

"Yes," Leo said dryly.

Salzman shook off the no in the yes. "Five years don't mean a thing. I give you my word that when you will live with her for one week you will forget her age. What does it mean five years—that she lived more and knows more than somebody who is younger? On this girl, God bless her, years are not wasted. Each one that it comes makes better the bargain!"

"What subject does she teach in high school?"

"Languages. If you heard the way she speaks French, you will think it is music. I am in the business twenty-five years, and I recommend her with my whole heart. Believe me, I know what I'm talking, rabbi."

"What's on the next card?" Leo said abruptly. Salzman reluctantly turned up the third card:

"Ruth K. Nineteen years. Honor student. Father offers thirteen thousand cash to the right bridegroom. He is a medical doctor. Stomach specialist with marvelous practice. Brother-in-law owns own garment business. Particular people."

Salzman looked as if he had read his trump card.

"Did you say nineteen?" Leo asked with interest.

"On the dot."

"Is she attractive?" He blushed. "Pretty?"

Salzman kissed his finger tips. "A little doll. On this I give you my word. Let me call the father tonight and you will see what means pretty!"

But Leo was troubled. "You're sure she's that young?"

"This I am positive. The father will show you the birth certificate."

''Are you positive there isn't something wrong with her?" Leo insisted.

"Who says there is wrong?"

"I don't understand why an American girl her age should go to a marriage broker."

A smile spread over Salzman's face.

"So for the same reason you went, she comes."

Leo flushed. "I am pressed for time."

Salzman, realizing he had been tactless, quickly explained. "The father came, not her. He wants she should have the best, so he looks around himself. When we will locate the right boy he will introduce him and encourage. This makes a better marriage than if a young girl without experience takes for herself. I don't have to tell you this."

"But don't you think this young girl believes in love?" Leo spoke uneasily.

Salzman was about to guffaw but caught himself and said soberly, "Love comes with the right person, not before."

Leo parted dry lips but did not speak. Noticing that Salzman had snatched a glance at the next card, he cleverly asked, "How is her health?"

"Perfect," Salzman said, breathing with difficulty. "Of course, she is a little lame on her right foot from an auto accident that it happened to her when she was twelve years, but nobody notices on account she is so brilliant and also beautiful."

F **Literary Focus** Static and Dynamic Characters How has Salzman's character changed or stayed the same?

G **Reading Focus** Drawing Conclusions About Characters Why does Leo turn red?

Leo got up heavily and went to the window. He felt curiously bitter and upbraided[7] himself for having called in the marriage broker. Finally, he shook his head.

"Why not?" Salzman persisted, the pitch of his voice rising.

"Because I detest stomach specialists."

"So what do you care what is his business? After you marry her do you need him? Who says he must come every Friday night in your house?"

Ashamed of the way the talk was going, Leo dismissed Salzman, who went home with heavy, melancholy eyes.

Though he had felt only relief at the marriage broker's departure, Leo was in low spirits the next day. He explained it as arising from Salzman's failure to produce a suitable bride for him. He did not care for his type of clientele. But when Leo found himself hesitating whether to seek out another matchmaker, one more polished than Pinye, he wondered if it could be—his protestations to the contrary, and although he honored his father and mother—that he did not, in essence, care for the matchmaking institution? This thought he quickly put out of mind yet found himself still upset. All day he ran around in the woods—missed an important appointment, forgot to give out his laundry, walked out of a Broadway cafeteria without paying and had to run back with the ticket in his hand; had even not recognized his landlady in the street when she passed with a friend and courteously called out, "A good evening to you, Doctor Finkle." By nightfall, however, he had regained sufficient calm to sink his nose into a book and there found peace from his thoughts. **H**

Almost at once there came a knock on the door. Before Leo could say enter, Salzman, commercial cupid, was standing in the room. His face was gray and meager, his expression hungry, and he looked as if he would expire[8] on his feet. Yet the marriage broker managed, by some trick of the muscles, to display a broad smile. **I**

---

7. **upbraided:** criticized.
8. **expire:** die.

"So good evening. I am invited?"

Leo nodded, disturbed to see him again, yet unwilling to ask the man to leave.

Beaming still, Salzman laid his portfolio on the table. "Rabbi, I got for you tonight good news."

"I've asked you not to call me rabbi. I'm still a student."

"Your worries are finished. I have for you a first-class bride."

"Leave me in peace concerning this subject." Leo pretended lack of interest.

"The world will dance at your wedding."

"Please, Mr. Salzman, no more."

"But first must come back my strength," Salzman said weakly. He fumbled with the portfolio straps and took out of the leather case an oily paper bag, from which he extracted a hard, seeded roll and a small, smoked whitefish. With a quick motion of his hand he stripped the fish out of its skin and began ravenously to chew. "All day in a rush," he muttered.

Leo watched him eat.

"A sliced tomato you have maybe?" Salzman hesitantly inquired.

"No."

The marriage broker shut his eyes and ate. When he had finished he carefully cleaned up the crumbs and rolled up the remains of the fish, in the paper bag. His spectacled eyes roamed the room until he discovered, amid some piles of books, a one-burner gas stove. Lifting his hat he humbly asked, "A glass tea you got, rabbi?"

Conscience-striken, Leo rose and brewed the tea. He served it with a chunk of lemon and two cubes of lump sugar, delighting Salzman. **J**

After he had drunk his tea, Salzman's strength and good spirits were restored.

"So tell me, rabbi," he said amiably, "you considered some more the three clients I mentioned yesterday?"

"There was no need to consider."

"Why not?"

"None of them suits me."

H **Literary Focus** Static and Dynamic Characters   How does Leo respond to the matchmaking process? Why does it affect him this way?

I **Reading Focus** Drawing Conclusions About Characters
What does Salzman's smile suggest about his character?

J **Literary Focus** Static and Dynamic Characters   Why does Leo resist Salzman?

Vocabulary   **clientele** (kly uhn TEHL) *n*.: the clients or customers of a business.

"What then suits you?"

Leo let it pass because he could give only a confused answer.

Without waiting for a reply, Salzman asked, "You remember this girl I talked to you—the high school teacher?"

"Age thirty-two?"

But, surprisingly, Salzman's face lit in a smile. "Age twenty-nine."

Leo shot him a look. "Reduced from thirty-two?"

"A mistake." Salzman avowed. "I talked today with the dentist. He took me to his safety deposit box and showed me the birth certificate. She was twenty-nine years last August. They made her a party in the mountains where she went for her vacation. When her father spoke to me the first time I forgot to write the age and I told you thirty-two, but now I remember this was a different client, a widow."

"The same one you told me about? I thought she was twenty-four?"

"A different. Am I responsible that the world is filled with widows?"

"No, but I'm not interested in them, nor for that matter, in school teachers."

Salzman pulled his clasped hands to his breast. Looking at the ceiling he devoutly exclaimed, "Yiddishe kinder,[9] what can I say to somebody that he is not interested in high school teachers? So what then you are interested?"

Leo flushed but controlled himself.

"In what else will you be interested," Salzman went on, "if you not interested in this fine girl that she speaks four languages and has personally in the bank ten thousand dollars? Also her father guarantees further twelve thousand. Also she has a new car, wonderful clothes, talks on all subjects, and she will give you a first-class home and children. How near do we come in our life to paradise?"

"If she's so wonderful, why wasn't she married ten years ago?"

"Why?" said Salzman with a heavy laugh. "—Why? Because she is *partikiler*. This is why. She wants the *best*."

---

9. **Yiddishe kinder:** Yiddish for "Jewish children."

Leo was silent, amused at how he had entangled himself. But Salzman had aroused his interest in Lily H., and he began seriously to consider calling on her. When the marriage broker observed how intently Leo's mind was at work on the facts he had supplied, he felt certain they would soon come to an agreement.

Late Saturday afternoon, conscious of Salzman, Leo Finkle walked with Lily Hirschorn along Riverside Drive. He walked briskly and erectly, wearing with distinction the black fedora he had that morning taken with trepidation out of the dusty hat box on his closet shelf, and the heavy black Saturday coat he had thoroughly whisked clean. Leo also owned a walking stick, a present from a distant relative, but quickly put temptation aside and did not use it. Lily, petite and not unpretty, had on something signifying the approach of spring. She was au courant,[10] animatedly, with all sorts of subjects, and he weighed her words and found her surprisingly sound—score another for Salzman, whom he uneasily sensed to be somewhere around, hiding perhaps high in a tree along the street, flashing the lady signals with a pocket mirror; or perhaps a cloven-hoofed Pan,[11] piping nuptial[12] ditties as he danced his invisible way before them, strewing wild buds on the walk and purple grapes in their path, symbolizing fruit of a union, though there was of course still none.

Lily startled Leo by remarking, "I was thinking of Mr. Salzman, a curious figure, wouldn't you say?" **K**

Not certain what to answer, he nodded.

She bravely went on, blushing, "I for one am grateful for his introducing us. Aren't you?"

He courteously replied, "I am."

"I mean," she said with a little laugh—and it was all in good taste, or at least gave the effect of being not in bad—"do you mind that we came together so?"

---

10. **au courant:** French for "in the current," meaning up-to-date on news or events.

11. **Pan:** Greek god of the woodlands, often shown with the feet and horns of a goat. Pan was a merry god who played the pipes and was always in love with one nymph or another.

12. **nuptial:** having to do with weddings or marriage.

Vocabulary **trepidation** (trehp uh DAY shuhn) *n.*: tremulous fear, alarm, or agitation.

K **Reading Focus** **Drawing Conclusions About Characters**
Why does Lily's statement startle Leo?

He was not displeased with her honesty, recognizing that she meant to set the relationship aright, and understanding that it took a certain amount of experience in life, and courage, to want to do it quite that way. One had to have some sort of past to make that kind of beginning.

He said that he did not mind. Salzman's function was traditional and honorable—valuable for what it might achieve, which, he pointed out, was frequently nothing.

Lily agreed with a sigh. They walked on for a while and she said after a long silence, again with a nervous laugh, "Would you mind if I asked you something a little bit personal? Frankly, I find the subject fascinating." Although Leo shrugged, she went on half embarrassedly, "How was it that you came to your calling? I mean was it a sudden passionate inspiration?" Leo, after a time, slowly replied, "I was always interested in the Law."[13]

"You saw revealed in it the presence of the Highest?"

He nodded and changed the subject. "I understand that you spent a little time in Paris, Miss Hirschorn?" **L**

"Oh, did Mr. Salzman tell you, Rabbi Finkle?"

Leo winced but she went on, "It was ages ago and almost forgotten. I remember I had to return for my sister's wedding."

---

13. **the Law:** the first five books of the Hebrew Bible, also called the Torah. These books along with all the commentary written on them make up the Jewish Law.

And Lily would not be put off. "When," she asked in a trembly voice, "did you become enamored of God?"

He stared at her. Then it came to him that she was talking not about Leo Finkle, but of a total stranger, some mystical figure, perhaps even passionate prophet that Salzman had dreamed up for her—no relation to the living or dead. Leo trembled with rage and weakness. The trickster had obviously sold her a bill of goods, just as he had him, who'd expected to become acquainted with a young lady of twenty-nine, only to behold, the moment he laid eyes upon her strained and anxious face, a woman past thirty-five and aging rapidly. Only his self-control had kept him this long in her presence.

"I am not," he said gravely, "a talented religious person," and in seeking words to go on, found himself possessed by shame and fear. "I think," he said in a strained manner, "that I came to God not because I loved Him, but because I did not."

This confession he spoke harshly because its unexpectedness shook him. **M**

Lily wilted. Leo saw a profusion of loaves of bread go flying like ducks high over his head, not unlike the winged loaves by which he had counted himself to sleep last night. Mercifully, then, it snowed, which he would not put past Salzman's machinations.[14]

---

14. **machinations:** plots; schemes.

L **Reading Focus** **Drawing Conclusions About Characters**
Why does Leo change the subject?

M **Literary Focus** **Static and Dynamic Characters** How does this revelation show a change in Finkle's character?

Ketubah, a Jewish marriage contract, from Shiraz, Iran, 1925, depicting roses, birds and the traditional heraldic lions.

He was infuriated with the marriage broker and swore he would throw him out of the room the minute he reappeared. But Salzman did not come that night, and when Leo's anger had subsided, an unaccountable despair grew in its place. At first he thought this was caused by his disappointment in Lily, but before long it became evident that he had involved himself with Salzman without a true knowledge of his own intent. He gradually realized—with an emptiness that seized him with six hands—that he had called in the broker to find him a bride because he was incapable of doing it himself. This terrifying insight he had derived as a result of his meeting and conversation with Lily Hirschorn. Her probing questions had somehow irritated him into revealing—to himself more than her—the true nature of his relationship to God, and from that it had come upon him, with shocking force, that apart from his parents, he had never loved anyone. Or perhaps it went the other way, that he did not love God so well as he might, because he had not loved man. It seemed to Leo that his whole life stood starkly revealed and he saw himself for the first time as he truly was—unloved and loveless. This bitter but somehow not fully unexpected revelation brought him to a point of panic, controlled only by extraordinary effort. He covered his face with his hands and cried. **Ⓝ**

The week that followed was the worst of his life. He did not eat and lost weight. His beard darkened and grew ragged. He stopped attending seminars and almost never opened a book. He seriously considered leaving the Yeshivah, although he was deeply troubled at the thought of the loss of all his years of study—saw them like pages torn from a book, strewn over the city—and at the devastating effect of this decision upon his parents. But he had lived without knowledge of himself, and never in the Five Books and all the Commentaries—mea culpa[15]—had the truth been revealed to him. He did not know where to turn, and in all this desolating loneliness there was no *to whom,* although he often thought of Lily but not once could bring himself to go downstairs and make the call. He became touchy and irritable, especially with his land-

---

15. **mea culpa:** Latin for "by my fault."

lady, who asked him all manner of personal questions; on the other hand, sensing his own disagreeableness, he waylaid her on the stairs and apologized abjectly, until mortified, she ran from him. Out of this, however, he drew the consolation that he was a Jew and that a Jew suffered. But gradually, as the long and terrible week drew to a close, he regained his composure and some idea of purpose in life: to go on as planned. Although he was imperfect, the ideal was not. As for his quest of a bride, the thought of continuing afflicted him with anxiety and heartburn, yet perhaps with this new knowledge of himself he would be more successful than in the past. Perhaps love would now come to him and a bride to that love. And for this sanctified seeking who needed a Salzman?

The marriage broker, a skeleton with haunted eyes, returned that very night. He looked, withal, the picture of frustrated expectancy—as if he had steadfastly waited the week at Miss Lily Hirschorn's side for a telephone call that never came. **Ⓞ**

Casually coughing, Salzman came immediately to the point: "So how did you like her?"

Leo's anger rose and he could not refrain from chiding the matchmaker: "Why did you lie to me, Salzman?"

Salzman's pale face went dead white, the world had snowed on him.

"Did you not state that she was twenty-nine?" Leo insisted.

"I give you my word—"

"She was thirty-five, if a day. *At least* thirty-five."

"Of this don't be too sure. Her father told me—"

"Never mind. The worst of it was that you lied to her."

"How did I lie to her, tell me?"

"You told her things about me that weren't true. You made me out to be more, consequently less than I am. She had in mind a totally different person, a sort of semi-mystical Wonder Rabbi."

"All I said, you was a religious man."

"I can imagine."

Salzman sighed. "This is my weakness that I have," he confessed. "My wife says to me I shouldn't be a salesman, but when I have two fine people that they would be wonderful to be married, I am so happy

---

Ⓝ Literary Focus Static and Dynamic Characters What causes Leo to cry?

Ⓞ Reading Focus Drawing Conclusions About Characters What do Leo's objections to Lily suggest about his character?

that I talk too much." He smiled wanly.[16] "This is why Salzman is a poor man."

Leo's anger left him. "Well, Salzman, I'm afraid that's all."

The marriage broker fastened hungry eyes on him. "You don't want any more a bride?"

"I do," said Leo, "but I have decided to seek her in a different way. I am no longer interested in an arranged marriage. To be frank, I now admit the necessity of premarital love. That is, I want to be in love with the one I marry."

"Love?" said Salzman, astounded. After a moment he remarked, "For us, our love is our life, not for the ladies. In the ghetto they—"

"I know, I know," said Leo. "I've thought of it often. Love, I have said to myself, should be a by-product of living and worship rather than its own end. Yet for myself I find it necessary to establish the level of my need and fulfill it."

Salzman shrugged but answered, "Listen, rabbi, if you want love, this I can find for you also. I have such beautiful clients that you will love them the minute your eyes will see them." **P**

Leo smiled unhappily. "I'm afraid you don't understand."

But Salzman hastily unstrapped his portfolio and withdrew a manila packet from it.

"Pictures," he said, quickly laying the envelope on the table.

Leo called after him to take the pictures away, but as if on the wings of the wind, Salzman had disappeared.

March came. Leo had returned to his regular routine. Although he felt not quite himself yet—lacked energy—he was making plans for a more active social life. Of course it would cost something, but he was an expert in cutting corners; and when there were no corners left he would make circles rounder. All the while Salzman's pictures had lain on the table, gathering dust. Occasionally as Leo sat studying, or enjoying a cup of tea, his eyes fell on the manila envelope, but he never opened it.

The days went by and no social life to speak of developed with a member of the opposite sex—it was

difficult, given the circumstances of his situation. One morning Leo toiled up the stairs to his room and stared out the window at the city. Although the day was bright his view of it was dark. For some time he watched the people in the street below hurrying along and then turned with a heavy heart to his little room. On the table was the packet. With a sudden relentless gesture he tore it open. For a half-hour he stood by the table in a state of excitement, examining the photographs of the ladies Salzman had included. Finally, with a deep sigh he put them down. There were six, of varying degrees of attractiveness, but look at them long enough and they all became Lily Hirschorn: all past their prime, all starved behind bright smiles, not a true personality in the lot. Life, despite their frantic yoohooings, had passed them by; they were pictures in a briefcase that stank of fish. After a while, however, as Leo attempted to return the photographs into the envelope, he found in it another, a snapshot of the type taken by a machine for a quarter. He gazed at it a moment and let out a cry.

Her face deeply moved him. Why, he could at first not say. It gave him the impression of youth—spring flowers, yet age—a sense of having been used to the bone, wasted; this came from the eyes, which were hauntingly familiar, yet absolutely strange. He had a vivid impression that he had met her before, but try as he might he could not place her although he could almost recall her name, as if he had read it in her own handwriting. No, this couldn't be; he would have remembered her. It was not, he affirmed, that she had an extraordinary beauty—no, though her face was attractive enough; it was that *something* about her moved him. Feature for feature, even some of the ladies of the photographs could do better; but she leaped forth to his heart—had *lived*, or wanted to— more than just wanted, perhaps regretted how she had lived—had somehow deeply suffered: It could be seen in the depths of those reluctant eyes, and from the way the light enclosed and shone from her, and within her, opening realms of possibility: This was her own. Her he desired. His head ached and eyes narrowed with the intensity of his gazing, then as if an obscure fog had

---

16. **wanly:** feebly.

P Literary Focus **Static and Dynamic Characters** What does this statement reveal about Salzman? Explain your response.

blown up in the mind, he experienced fear of her and was aware that he had received an impression, somehow, of evil. He shuddered, saying softly, it is thus with us all. Leo brewed some tea in a small pot and sat sipping it without sugar, to calm himself. But before he had finished drinking, again with excitement he examined the face and found it good: good for Leo Finkle. Only such a one could understand him and help him seek whatever he was seeking. She might, perhaps, love him. How she had happened to be among the discards in Salzman's barrel he could never guess, but he knew he must urgently go find her. **Q**

Leo rushed downstairs, grabbed up the Bronx[17] telephone book, and searched for Salzman's home address. He was not listed, nor was his office. Neither was he in the Manhattan book. But Leo remembered having written down the address on a slip of paper after he had read Salzman's advertisement in the "personals" column of the *Forward*. He ran up to his room and tore through his papers, without luck. It was exasperating. Just when he needed the matchmaker he was nowhere to be found. Fortunately Leo remembered to look in his wallet. There on a card he found his name written and a Bronx address. No phone number was listed, the reason—Leo now recalled—he had originally communicated with Salzman by letter. He got on his coat, put a hat on over his skullcap and hurried to the subway station. All the way to the far end of the Bronx he sat on the edge of his seat. He was more than once tempted to take out the picture and see if the girl's face was as he remembered it, but he refrained, allowing the snapshot to remain in his inside coat pocket, content to have her so close. When the train pulled into the station he was waiting at the door and bolted out. He quickly located the street Salzman had advertised.

The building he sought was less than a block from the subway, but it was not an office building, nor even a loft, nor a store in which one could rent office space. It was a very old tenement house. Leo found Salzman's name in pencil on a soiled tag under the bell and climbed three dark flights to his apartment. When he

17. **the Bronx:** one of the five boroughs of New York City.

knocked, the door was opened by a thin, asthmatic, gray-haired woman, in felt slippers.

"Yes?" she said, expecting nothing. She listened without listening. He could have sworn he had seen her, too, before but knew it was an illusion.

"Salzman—does he live here? Pinye Salzman," he said, "the matchmaker?"

She stared at him a long minute. "Of course."

He felt embarrassed. "Is he in?" **R**

"No." Her mouth, though left open, offered nothing more.

"The matter is urgent. Can you tell me where his office is?"

"In the air." She pointed upward.

"You mean he has no office?" Leo asked.

"In his socks."

He peered into the apartment. It was sunless and dingy, one large room divided by a half-open curtain, beyond which he could see a sagging metal bed. The near side of the room was crowded with rickety chairs, old bureaus, a three-legged table, racks of cooking utensils, and all the apparatus of a kitchen. But there was no sign of Salzman or his magic barrel, probably also a figment of the imagination. An odor of frying fish made Leo weak to the knees.

"Where is he?" he insisted. "I've got to see your husband."

At length she answered, "So who knows where he is? Every time he thinks a new thought he runs to a different place. Go home, he will find you."

"Tell him Leo Finkle."

She gave no sign she had heard.

He walked downstairs, depressed.

But Salzman, breathless, stood waiting at his door.

Leo was astounded and overjoyed. "How did you get here before me?"

"I rushed."

"Come inside."

They entered. Leo fixed tea, and a sardine sandwich for Salzman. As they were drinking he reached behind him for the packet of pictures and handed them to the marriage broker.

Salzman put down his glass and said expectantly, "You found somebody you like?"

Q **Literary Focus** Static and Dynamic Characters What do we learn about Leo's view of love in this paragraph?

R **Reading Focus** Drawing Conclusions About Characters Why does Leo still feel embarrassed?

"Not among these."

The marriage broker turned away.

"Here is the one I want." Leo held forth the snapshot.

Salzman slipped on his glasses and took the picture into his trembling hand. He turned ghastly and let out a groan.

"What's the matter?" cried Leo.

"Excuse me. Was an accident this picture. She isn't for you."

Salzman frantically shoved the manila packet into his portfolio. He thrust the snapshot into his pocket and fled down the stairs.

Leo, after momentary paralysis, gave chase and cornered the marriage broker in the vestibule. The landlady made hysterical outcries but neither of them listened.

"Give me back the picture, Salzman."

"No." The pain in his eyes was terrible.

"Tell me who she is then."

"This I can't tell you. Excuse me."

He made to depart, but Leo, forgetting himself, seized the matchmaker by his tight coat and shook him frenziedly.

"Please," sighed Salzman. "Please."

Leo ashamedly let him go. "Tell me who she is," he begged. "It's very important for me to know."

"She is not for you. She is a wild one—wild, without shame. This is not a bride for a rabbi."

"What do you mean wild?"

"Like an animal. Like a dog. For her to be poor was a sin. This is why to me she is dead now."

"In God's name, what do you mean?"

"Her I can't introduce to you," Salzman cried.

"Why are you so excited?"

"Why, he asks," Salzman said, bursting into tears. "This is my baby, my Stella, she should burn in hell."

Leo hurried up to bed and hid under the covers. Under the covers he thought his life through. Although he soon fell asleep he could not sleep her out of his mind. He woke, beating his breast. Though he prayed to be rid of her, his prayers went unanswered. Through days of torment he endlessly struggled not to love her; fearing success, he escaped it. He then concluded to convert her to goodness, himself to God. The idea alternately nauseated and exalted him. **S**

He perhaps did not know that he had come to a final decision until he encountered Salzman in a Broadway cafeteria. He was sitting alone at a rear table, sucking the bony remains of a fish. The marriage broker appeared haggard, and transparent to the point of vanishing.

Salzman looked up at first without recognizing him. Leo had grown a pointed beard and his eyes were weighted with wisdom.

"Salzman," he said, "love has at last come to my heart."

"Who can love from a picture?" mocked the marriage broker.

"It is not impossible."

"If you can love her, then you can love anybody. Let me show you some new clients that they just sent me their photographs. One is a little doll."

"Just her I want," Leo murmured.

"Don't be a fool, doctor. Don't bother with her."

"Put me in touch with her, Salzman," Leo said humbly. "Perhaps I can be of service."

Salzman had stopped eating and Leo understood with emotion that it was now arranged.

Leaving the cafeteria, he was, however, afflicted by a tormenting suspicion that Salzman had planned it all to happen this way.

Leo was informed by letter that she would meet him on a certain corner, and she was there one spring night, waiting under a street lamp. He appeared, carrying a small bouquet of violets and rosebuds. Stella stood by the lamppost, smoking. She wore white with red shoes, which fitted his expectations, although in a troubled moment he had imagined the dress red, and only the shoes white. She waited uneasily and shyly. From afar he saw that her eyes—clearly her father's—were filled with desperate innocence. He pictured, in her, his own redemption. Violins and lit candles revolved in the sky. Leo ran forward with flowers outthrust. **T**

Around the corner, Salzman, leaning against a wall, chanted prayers for the dead.

S Reading Focus **Drawing Conclusions About Characters**
Why does this thought nauseate but also exalt Leo?

T Reading Focus **Drawing Conclusions About Characters**
What is your impression of Stella? What did Leo expect her to be like?

Applying Your Skills

SKILLS FOCUS **Literary Skills** Analyze static and dynamic characters; analyze characterization. **Reading Skills** Draw inferences about characters **Vocabulary Skills** Demonstrate knowledge of literal meanings of words and their usage.

The Magic Barrel

Respond and Think Critically

Reading Focus

Quick Check

1. What is the "magic barrel"? Do readers ever see it? What does the title add to the story?

2. Why does Leo Finkle fall in love with the woman in the photograph?

3. By the end of the story, have Leo and Salzman both gotten what they want? Explain.

Read with a Purpose

4. What does Leo discover about himself and about love?

Reading Skills: Drawing Conclusions About Characters

5. Add a third column labeled "After Reading" to your chart. Think about how your conclusions have changed or stayed the same now that you have finished the story. Add your final conclusions to the chart.

Detail	Conclusion	After Reading
Salzman's portfolio had been worn thin with use.	He has been a matchmaker for many years.	He doesn't seem to be very successful.

✔ Vocabulary Check

Match each Vocabulary word with its definition.

6. rabbinical
7. meager
8. dowry
9. trepidation
10. clientele
11. matchmaker

a. alarm
b. customers
c. scanty
d. relating to rabbis
e. arranger of marriages
f. money or goods brought by wife to marriage

Literary Focus

Literary Analysis

12. **Analyze** How would you explain the **paradox**—or seeming contradiction—in Leo's confession to Lily as to why he came to God?

13. **Draw Conclusions** Why do you think Salzman is chanting prayers for the dead at the story's end?

14. **Make Judgments** Do you think Salzman arranged the match between Leo and Stella after all? Explain your answer.

Literary Skills: Static and Dynamic Characters

15. **Make Judgments** How does Leo change throughout the story? Does Salzman change, or is he a static character?

Literary Skills Review: Dialogue

16. **Analyze** How does Malamud use dialogue to enhance characterization in "The Magic Barrel"? Cite evidence to support your response.

Writing Focus

Think as a Reader/Writer

Use It in Your Writing Write a paragraph in which you describe the traits of someone you know well. Use at least three participial phrases in your description. Try to put some at the beginnings and some at the ends of sentences. Use Malamud's participial phrases as models for your own.

What Do **You Think Now** Do Leo and Salzman want the same things out of life? Are their wants and needs shared by many people around the world?

Preparing to Read

Son

What Do You Think?

What human needs and desires do we have in common?

QuickTalk

Pick an issue that commonly arises within families, such as use of the family car. List feelings and attitudes intrinsic to the issue for both parents and children. Be prepared to discuss these responses with a small group.

John Updike
(1932–   )

Pulitzer Prize WINNER

Gifted with what seems like total recall of American middle-class life, Updike also displays a skill with language that can evoke responses to the most ordinary and familiar events, endowing them with importance.

Capturing Small-Town America

John Updike grew up in the small town of Shillington, Pennsylvania. After graduating *summa cum laude* from Harvard University in 1954, Updike studied drawing in England for a year and, on his return to the United States, went to work for *The New Yorker* magazine, in which many of his short stories have appeared. After two years, he made the courageous decision to support his young family entirely by writing. He left New York for Massachusetts and has since produced a long list of impressive novels, stories, poems, memoirs, and critical essays.

Among his most famous and probably most enduring works is the "Rabbit" series—*Rabbit, Run* (1960); *Rabbit Redux* (1971); *Rabbit Is Rich* (1981), which earned the Pulitzer Prize for fiction, the American National Book Award, and the National Book Critics Circle Award; and *Rabbit at Rest* (1990), which won another Pulitzer Prize. These novels chronicle the life of Harry "Rabbit" Angstrom, a former high school star athlete who feels trapped by small-town life. In these novels, Updike portrays forty years of American social behavior.

Closeness and Conflict

Updike's fiction often deals with the complexity and uncertainty of human relationships and how people struggle to connect with or to escape from each other. A number of his stories deal with adolescence and the relationship between parents and children. The story that follows is about several generations of fathers and sons. In some ways, it echoes Updike's own family background. Updike's father was a teacher. Updike's son David, who may have provided the inspiration for this story, is, like his father, a writer.

Think About the Writer

What does Updike's decision to make his living solely through his writing say about him? Do you think it was a hard decision for him to make?

Reader/Writer Notebook

Use your **RWN** to complete the activities for this selection.

Literary Focus

Theme In literary works, **theme** is the insight about human life that is revealed through characters and events. Theme should not be confused with **subject**. A subject is a topic, such as "relationships between fathers and sons." The theme is a statement the writer transmits about that subject. Theme is rarely stated directly; the reader must infer the meaning of a story from its characters' experiences. As you read "Son," see if you can identify one or more major themes having to do with relationships between fathers and sons.

Reading Focus

Analyzing Sequence of Events The order in which things happen is called **sequence of events**. Events in stories usually occur in clear, chronological order. Authors may, however, vary the sequence, so events do not take place in chronological order. Instead, the story may jump backward or forward in time. Clues such as specific dates or historical events may help you establish the sequence of events in a story so you can follow them more easily.

Into Action As you read, notice how events are arranged in Updike's story. "Son" has eight separate scenes. In each scene of the story, look for any clues that tell you when that scene takes place. Use a chart like the one below to record the clues you find.

Scene	Clues to Sequence of Events
One	"…this tiring year of 1973"

Writing Focus

Think as a Reader/Writer

Find It in Your Reading Writers use sentence structure like punctuation to emphasize points that they want their readers to notice. John Updike uses short, repetitive sentences to make observations about the characters in "Son." Simple sentence structure and repetition of the subject *he* appear throughout the story in sentences such as "He prefers to be elsewhere" and "He wishes for perfection." As you read, notice the effect of these simple sentences in comparison to other sentences. Copy some of the most effective ones in your *Reader/Writer Notebook*.

Language Coach

Word Origins The word *mincingly* has its roots in the Latin word *minutus*, meaning "small." A dancer's exaggeratedly tiny steps might be called *mincing*. How does this Latin root affect the meanings of the words *miniature* and *minutia*?

Learn It Online
Listen to this story online.

go.hrw.com   L11-1187   Go

Son

by John Updike

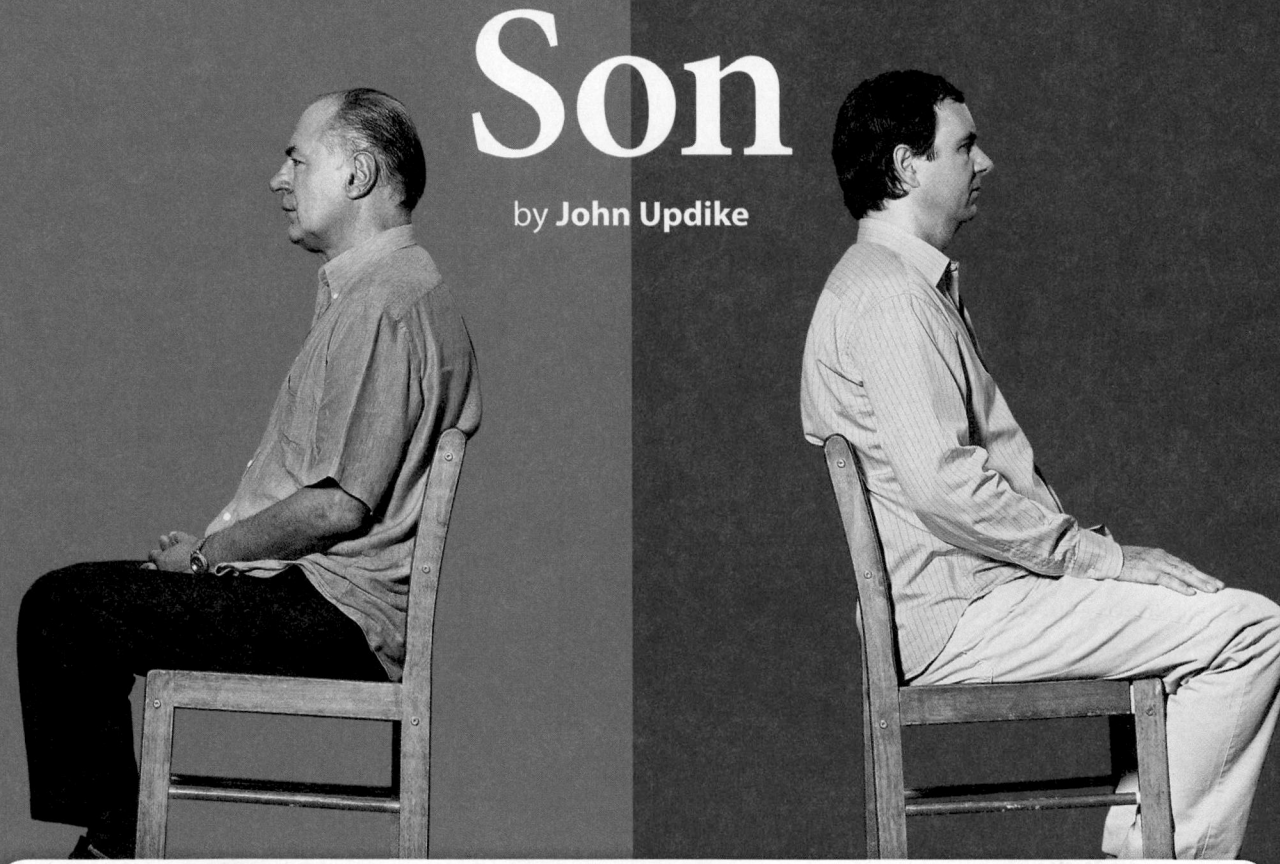

Read with a Purpose

Read to piece together the history of a group of fathers and sons, and to discover what they have in common.

Build Background

This story is presented in a series of eight vignettes, or short scenes. The story is told out of chronological order, and the setting of the vignettes abruptly shifts back and forth. (Watch for places where dates and places are mentioned.) In these scenes, Updike tells the story of four men, both fathers and sons. As you read, determine who the narrator is and how he relates to the other characters.

He is often upstairs, when he has to be home. He prefers to be elsewhere. He is almost sixteen, though beardless still, a man's mind indignantly captive in the frame of a child. I love touching him, but don't often dare. The other day, he had the flu, and a fever, and I gave him a back rub, marvelling at the symmetrical knit of muscle, the organic tension. He is high-strung. Yet his sleep is so solid he sweats like a stone in the wall of a well. He wishes for perfection. He would like to destroy us, for we are, variously, too fat, too jocular,[1] too sloppy, too affectionate, too grotesque and heedless in our ways. His mother smokes too much. His younger brother chews with his mouth open. His older sister leaves unbuttoned the top button of her blouses. His younger sister tussles with the dogs, getting them overexcited, avoiding doing her homework. Everyone in the house talks nonsense. He would be a better father than his father. But time has tricked him, has made him a son. After a quarrel, if he cannot go outside and kick a ball, he retreats to a corner of the house and reclines on the beanbag chair in an attitude of strange— infantile or leonine—torpor.[2] We exhaust him, without meaning to. He takes an interest in the newspaper now, the front page as well as the sports, in this tiring year of 1973. **(A)**

He is upstairs, writing a musical comedy. It is a Sunday in 1949. He has volunteered to prepare a high-school assembly program; people will sing. Songs of the time go through his head, as he scribbles new words. *Up in de mornin', down at de school, work like a debil for my grades.* Below him, irksome voices grind on, like machines working their way through tunnels. His parents each want something from the other. "Marion, you don't understand that man like I do; he has a heart of gold." His father's charade is very complex: the

---

1. **jocular:** jolly; joking.
2. **torpor:** sluggishness; dullness.

world, which he fears, is used as a flail[3] on his wife. But from his cringing attitude he would seem to an outsider the one being flailed. With burning red face, the woman accepts the role of aggressor as penance for the fact, the incessant shameful fact, that *he* has to wrestle with the world while she hides here, in solitude, at home. This is normal, but does not seem to them to be so. Only by convolution[4] have they arrived at the dominant/submissive relationship society has assigned them. For the man is maternally kind and with a smile hugs to himself his jewel, his certainty of being victimized; it is the mother whose tongue is sharp, who sometimes strikes. "Well, he gets you out of the house, and I guess that's gold to you." His answer is "Duty calls," pronounced mincingly. "The social contract is a balance of compromises." This will infuriate her, the son knows; as his heart thickens, the downstairs overflows with her hot voice. *"Don't wear that smile at me! And take your hands off your hips; you look like a sissy!"* Their son tries not to listen. When he does, visual details of the downstairs flood his mind: the two antagonists, circling with their coffee cups; the shabby mismatched furniture; the hopeful books; the docile framed photographs of the dead, docile and still like cowed students. This matrix[5] of pain that bore him— he feels he is floating above it, sprawled on the bed as on a cloud, stealing songs as they come into his head *(Across the hallway from the guidance room / Lives a French instructor called Mrs. Blum),* contemplating the view from the upstairs window (last summer's burdock[6] stalks like the beginnings of an alphabet, an apple tree holding three rotten apples as if pondering

---

3. **flail:** kind of whip.
4. **convolution:** process that is extremely involved and complicated.
5. **matrix:** point of origin or development; here, some event or situation from which his pain originates.
6. **burdock:** plant with large leaves and prickly, purple flower heads.

(A) **Literary Focus** **Theme** In the first scene, Updike writes of a young man who longs for his family to be perfect. How does this desire affect his relationship with his family?

Vocabulary **symmetrical** (sih MEHT ruh kuhl) *adj.:* well-proportioned; balanced.
leonine (LEE uh nyn) *adj.:* resembling or suggestive of a lion.
charade (shuh RAYD) *n.:* act, blatant pretense.
mincingly (MIHN sihng lee) *adv.:* in a manner affectedly dainty, nice, or elegant.

why they failed to fall), yearning for Monday, for the ride to school with his father, for the bell that calls him to homeroom, for the excitements of class, for Broadway, for fame, for the cloud that will carry him away, out of this, out. **B C**

He returns from his paper-delivery route and finds a few Christmas presents for him on the kitchen table. I must guess at the year. 1913? Without opening them, he knocks them to the floor, puts his head on the table, and falls asleep. He must have been consciously dramatizing his plight: His father was sick, money was scarce, he had to work, to win food for the family when he was still a child. In his dismissal of Christmas, he touched a nerve: his love of anarchy, his distrust of the social contract. He treasured this moment of revolt; else why remember it, hoard a memory so bitter, and confide it to his son many Christmases later? He had a teaching instinct, though he claimed that life miscast him as a schoolteacher. I suffered in his classes, feeling the confusion as a persecution of him, but now wonder if his rebellious heart did not court confusion, not as Communists do, to intrude their own order, but, more radical still, as an end pleasurable in itself, as truth's very body. Yet his handwriting (an old pink permission slip recently fluttered from a book where it had been marking a page for twenty years) was always considerately legible, and he was sitting up doing arithmetic the morning of the day he died. **D**

And letters survive from that yet prior son, written in brown ink, in a tidy tame hand, home to his mother from the Missouri seminary where he was preparing for his vocation. The dates are 1887, 1888, 1889. Nothing much happened: He missed New Jersey, and was teased at a church social for escorting a widow. He wanted to do the right thing, but the little sheets of faded penscript exhale a dispirited calm, as if his heart already knew he would not make a successful minister, or live to be old. His son, my father, when old, drove hundreds of miles out of his way to visit the Missouri town from which those letters had been sent. Strangely, the town had not changed; it looked just as he had imagined, from his father's descriptions: tall wooden houses, rain-soaked, stacked on a bluff. The town was a sepia postcard mailed homesick home and preserved in an attic. My father cursed: His father's old sorrow bore him down into depression, into hatred of life. My mother claims his decline in health began at that moment.

He is wonderful to watch, playing soccer. Smaller than the others, my son leaps, heads, dribbles, feints, passes. When a big boy knocks him down, he tumbles on the mud, in his green-and-black school uniform, in an ecstasy of falling. I am envious. Never for me the jaunty pride of the school uniform, the solemn ritual of the coach's pep talk, the camaraderie of shook hands and slapped backsides, the shadow-striped hush of late afternoon and last quarter, the solemn vaulted universe of official combat, with its cheering mothers and referees exotic as zebras and the bespectacled time keeper alert with his claxon.[7] When the boy scores a goal, he runs into the arms of his teammates with upraised arms and his face alight as if blinded by triumph. They lift him from the earth in a union of muddy hugs. What spirit! What valor! What skill! His father, watching from the sidelines, inwardly registers only one complaint: He feels the boy, with his talent, should be more aggressive. **E**

---

7. **claxon:** more correctly, Klaxon, the trademark for a type of electric horn used in sporting events to mark ends of time periods.

B Reading Focus Analyzing Sequence of Events The second section takes place in 1949. How has changing the sequence of events shifted the point of view?

C Literary Focus Theme The second scene of the story ends with the son's desire for "the cloud that will carry him away, out of this, out." How do these words relate to the theme of this scene?

D Reading Focus Analyzing Sequence of Events What does the shift in verb tense tell you about the sequence of events? Who is the "he" referred to in this section? Who is narrating it?

E Literary Focus Theme How would you describe the father-son relationship in this scene?

Vocabulary sepia (SEE pee uh) *adj.:* reddish brown in color.
camaraderie (kah muh RAH duh ree) *n.:* comradeship; good-fellowship.

Interior with Jim by Harry Sefarbi (20th century).

They drove across the Commonwealth of Pennsylvania to hear their son read in Pittsburgh. But when their presence was announced to the audience, they did not stand; the applause groped for them and died. My mother said afterwards she was afraid she might fall into the next row if she tried to stand in the dark. Next morning was sunny, and the three of us searched for the house where once they had lived. They had been happy there; I imagined, indeed, that I had been conceived there, just before the slope of the Depression steepened and fear gripped my family. We found the

---

8. **Turgenev:** Ivan Turgenev (1818–1883), Russian writer, author of a novel called *Fathers and Sons*.

library where she used to read Turgenev,[8] and the little park where the bums slept close as paving stones in the summer night; but their street kept eluding us, though we circled in the car. On foot, my mother found the tree. She claimed she recognized it, the sooty linden tree she would gaze into from their apartment windows. The branches, though thicker, had held their pattern. But the house itself, and the entire block, was gone. Stray bricks and rods of iron in the grass suggested that the demolition had been recent. We stood on the empty spot and laughed. They knew it was right, because the railroad tracks were the right distance away. In confirmation, a long freight train pulled itself east around the curve, its great weight gliding as if on a river current; then a silver passenger train came gliding as effortlessly in the other direction. The curve of the tracks tipped the cars slightly toward us. The Golden Triangle,[9] gray and hazed, was off to our left, beyond a forest of bridges. We stood on the grassy rubble that morning, where something once had been, beside the tree still there, and were intensely happy. Why? We knew. **F** **G**

"'No,' Dad said to me, 'the Christian ministry isn't a job you choose, it's a vocation for which you got to receive a call.' I could tell he wanted me to ask him. We never talked much, but we understood each other, we were both scared devils, not like you and the kid. I asked him, Had he ever received the call? He said No. He said No, he never had. Received the call. That was a terrible thing, for him to admit. And I was the one he told. As far as I knew he never admitted it to anybody, but he admitted it to me. He felt like hell about it, I could tell. That was all we ever said about it. That was enough." **H**

He has made his younger brother cry, and justice must be done. A father enforces justice. I corner the rat in our bedroom; he is holding a cardboard mailing tube like a sword. The challenge flares white-hot; I roll my weight toward him like a rock down a mountain, and knock the weapon from his hand. He smiles. Smiles! Because my facial expression is silly? Because he is glad that he can still be overpowered, and hence is still protected? Why? I do not hit him. We stand a second, father and son, and then as nimbly as on the soccer field he steps around me and out the door. He slams the door. He shouts obscenities in the hall, slams all the doors he can find on the way to his room. Our moment of smilingly shared silence was the moment

9. **Golden Triangle:** triangular piece of land formed by the junction of the Allegheny and Monongahela rivers.

of compression; now the explosion. The whole house rocks with it. Downstairs, his siblings and mother come to me and offer advice and psychological analysis. I was too aggressive. He is spoiled. What they can never know, my grief alone to treasure, was that lucid many-sided second of his smiling and my relenting, before the world's wrathful pantomime of power resumed.

As we huddle whispering about him, my son takes his revenge. In his room, he plays his guitar. He has greatly improved this winter; his hands getting bigger is the least of it. He has found in the guitar an escape. He plays the Romanza[10] wherein repeated notes, with a sliding like the heart's valves, let themselves fall along the scale:

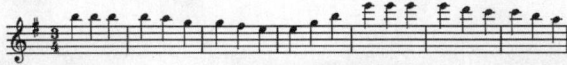

The notes fall, so gently he bombs us, drops feathery notes down upon us, our visitor, our prisoner. **I**

10. **Romanza:** very romantic piece of music.

F **Reading Focus** **Analyzing Sequence of Events** In this scene of the story, what are some of the words Updike uses to indicate the passage of time?

G **Literary Focus** **Theme** What do you think the main idea is in section six?

H **Literary Focus** **Theme** Who is the narrator in this section? What is the obstacle the father and son face in their struggle to communicate with each other?

I **Literary Focus** **Theme** Who wins the battle in this incident? How do you know? Is the power struggle in this section related to similar events in any of the previous sections?

SKILLS FOCUS Literary Skills Analyze theme; analyze a writer's style. Reading Skills Analyze the sequence of events in a text. Vocabulary Skills Demonstrate knowledge of literal meanings of words and their usage. Writing Skills Use varied sentence structure.

Respond and Think Critically

Reading Focus

Read with a Purpose

1. How would you describe generational conflicts of fathers and sons in this story? Do these conflicts change over time or remain the same?

Reading Skills: Analyzing Sequence of Events

2. As you read, you listed clues to the sequence of events in this story. Now, use your chart to determine how the various characters in this story are related. Add a third column and write down who appears in each scene. Then, answer these questions: How does the narrator relate to these other characters? Why did Updike tell his story in this particular order?

Scene	Clues to Sequence of Events	Main Characters in Scene
One	"...This tiring year of 1973"	Narrator and his son

✓ Vocabulary Quick Check

Answer the following questions with a sentence that shows your knowledge of the Vocabulary word.

3. When might a book have a **sepia** tint to it?

4. What features would a **leonine** face have?

5. Why might people laugh if you walked **mincingly** during a serious ceremony?

6. What groups might have a strong **camaraderie**?

7. What is an example of a **symmetrical** shape?

8. Should you believe in a **charade**?

Literary Focus

Literary Analysis

9. **Interpret** At the end of scene five, why does the narrator say that he wishes his son were "more aggressive"? What does this say about the family?

10. **Analyze** How would you describe the narrator's tone, or attitude, in telling this story? How does the narrator feel about the people in his family?

11. **Interpret** What is the significance of the father's calling his son "our visitor, our prisoner" at the story's end?

Literary Skills: Theme

12. **Analyze** What components of family interactions are common to all eight scenes? What theme can you construct from these features?

Literary Skills Review: Style

13. **Analyze** How would you describe Updike's writing style, especially his sentence structure and word choice? In what ways do his stylistic choices enhance the meaning of this story?

Writing Focus

Think as a Reader/Writer

Use It in Your Writing As you read "Son," you recorded examples of Updike's use of short, repetitive sentences. Now, write a paragraph describing a person you know well. Using Updike's style as a model, include repetitive, short sentences to emphasize character traits.

 What did the conflicts between fathers and sons teach you about relationships? Do you think generational conflicts today are any different?

Preparing to Read

Speaking of Courage

What Do You Think?

What human needs and desires do we have in common?

QuickWrite

Imagine yourself or someone you know fighting in a war far from home. In a letter to family or friends, what kinds of experiences might surface? Which ones might you *not* write about?

MEET·THE·WRITER

Tim O'Brien
(1946–   )

National Book Award WINNER

As a writer, Tim O'Brien's main concerns have been with the "big issues": courage, and how to get it; justice, and how to achieve it; how to do the right thing in an evil situation. Such concerns inform his novels, stories, and memoirs.

War Stories

O'Brien was born in Austin, Minnesota, and graduated from Macalester College. Drafted in 1968, he served with the U.S. Army in Vietnam and was awarded the Purple Heart. After he returned from the war, he did graduate work in English at Harvard, then became a reporter for the *Washington Post*.

O'Brien's Vietnam experiences became a major source for his writing. In 1973 he published *If I Die in a Combat Zone, Box Me Up and Ship Me Home,* a collection of anecdotes and observations based on his military experiences. The book was widely praised for its authenticity, particularly by his fellow veterans.

O'Brien's first novel, *Northern Lights,* appeared the following year. It dealt with a war veteran returning to civilian life. *Going After Cacciato,* a second novel, followed in 1978. It depicted a soldier's fantasy of quitting the East Asian battlefield and walking all the way to Paris. *Going After Cacciato* won the prestigious National Book Award in 1979. His purpose in writing it, O'Brien explained, was "to have readers care about what's right and wrong and about the difficulty of doing right, the difficulty of saying no to a war."

The Living and the Dead

In 1990, O'Brien published *The Things They Carried,* a fictional memoir made up of interconnected stories. The title story deals with the physical objects a soldier carries into battle, such as weapons and letters from home, as well as intangible things such as fears and memories. O'Brien has said, "I believe in stories, in their incredible power to keep people alive, to keep the living alive, and the dead."

Think About the Writer

Why do you think O'Brien wants his readers to "care about what's right and wrong"? What does this tell you about him?

Reader/Writer Notebook

Use your **RWN** to complete the activities for this selection.

SKILLS FOCUS Literary Skills Understand conflict.
Reading Skills Analyze historical context, especially political and social influences of the time.

Literary Focus

Conflict A **conflict** is a struggle between opposing forces or characters. An **external conflict** can involve two people or can pit a person against a natural or artificial force. An **internal conflict** involves opposing forces within a person's mind. "Speaking of Courage" focuses mainly on an internal conflict in the mind of Paul Berlin. As you read, notice how the writer transmits this character's conflict.

Literary Perspectives Apply the literary perspective described on page 1197 as you read this story.

Reading Focus

Identifying Historical Context The setting of a story includes not only its time and place but also its **historical context**—the social and political environment of a particular time and place. Atmosphere, characterization, and the central conflicts of a story often flow directly from historical context, as they do in this selection.

Into Action As you read, take notes on contrasts between the attitudes and values of Paul Berlin's small-town Iowa home and the terrible realities of his recent combat experience in Vietnam. Use a Venn diagram to compare and contrast them. Label one side "Iowa" and the other side "Vietnam." Insert any similarities in the space where the circles overlap.

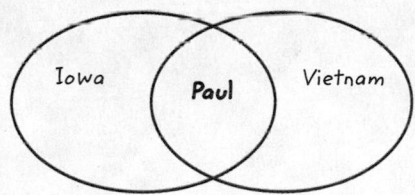

Iowa Paul Vietnam

Writing Focus

Think as a Reader/Writer

Find It in Your Reading Writers often use a story's setting symbolically. The lake's circular shoreline, for example, reflects the repetitive thoughts that run through Paul Berlin's mind as he drives around and around, unable to change course. What might be the symbolism of the Fourth of July fireworks over the lake in the story? Record these and other potential symbols in the setting in your *Reader/Writer Notebook*.

Vocabulary

affluent (AF loo uhnt) *n.*: prosperous; rich. *The affluent enjoyed a view of the lake, while those with less money did not.*

tepid (TEHP ihd) *adj.*: moderately warm; lukewarm. *The lake was tepid rather than cool in the summer.*

mesmerizing (MEHS muh ryz ihng) *adj.*: fascinating, hypnotizing. *Paul's experiences in the war were mesmerizing to him.*

drone (drohn) *n.*: dull, monotonous sound. *The boat's motor made a steady drone.*

recede (rih SEED) *v.*: become more distant and indistinct. *The more alienated he felt, the more the town seemed to recede from him.*

valor (VAL uhr) *n.*: courage, bravery. *Paul won seven medals, but none were for valor in combat.*

profundity (pruh FUHN duh tee) *n.*: deep significance, intellectual depth. *People around Paul failed to understand the profundity of his experience in Vietnam.*

tactile (TAK tuhl) *adj.*: perceptible to the touch; tangible. *The medal's cold, smooth metal was tactile under his fingers.*

Language Coach

Root Words The Latin verb *cedere* means "to go." *Cedere* forms the root of many English words such as *proceed*, meaning "go forth," and *intercede*, meaning "go between." Which word above comes from this same root?

  Learn It Online
Explore the historical context of this story with these Internet links.

go.hrw.com L11-1195   **Go**

Speaking of Courage

by **Tim O'Brien**

Quitsa, Martha's Vineyard (1995) by John Laub.

Read with a Purpose
Read to find out why Paul Berlin feels so alienated from his family and his town after the war.

Build Background
After the Vietnam War, many soldiers returned to a civilian life that seemed empty and pointless. They often felt disconnected from their families and neighbors who had not experienced the war firsthand. Since the war in Vietnam was widely protested, people did not care to hear about the soldiers' horrid experiences or stories of bravery in combat. In his story, O'Brien mentions the Silver Star, which is the fourth-highest military decoration that can be granted to a member of the United States Army for gallantry in action.

The war was over, and there was no place in particular to go. Paul Berlin followed the tar road in its seven-mile loop around the lake, then he started all over again, driving slowly, feeling safe inside his father's big Chevy, now and again looking out onto the lake to watch the boats and waterskiers and scenery. It was Sunday and it was summer, and things seemed pretty much the same. The lake was the same. The houses were the same, all low-slung and split level and modern, porches and picture windows facing the water. The lots were spacious. On the lake-side of the road, the houses were handsome and set deep in, well-kept and painted, with docks jutting out into the lake, and boats moored and covered with canvas, and gardens, and sometimes even gardeners, and stone patios with barbecue spits and grills, and wooden shingles saying who lived where. On the other side of the road, to his left, the houses were also handsome, though less expensive and on a smaller scale and with no docks or boats or wooden shingles. The road was a sort of boundary between the affluent and the almost affluent, and to live on the lake-side of the road was one of the few natural privileges in a town of the prairie—the difference between watching the sun set over cornfields or over the lake. **(A)**

It was a good-sized lake. In high school he'd driven round and round and round with his friends and pretty girls, talking about urgent matters, worrying eagerly about the existence of God and theories of causation,[1] or wondering whether Sally Hankins, who lived on the lake-side of the road, would want to pull into the shelter of Sunset Park. Then, there had not been a war. But there had always been the lake. It had been dug out by the southernmost advance of the Wisconsin glacier. Fed by neither springs nor streams, it was a tepid, algaed lake that depended on fickle prairie rains for replenishment. Still, it was the town's only lake, the only one in twenty-six miles, and at night the moon made a white swath across its waters, and on sunny days it was nice to look at, and that evening it would dazzle with the reflections of fireworks, and it was the center of things from the very start, always there to be driven around, still mesmerizing and quieting and a good audience for silence, a seven-mile flat circumference that could be traveled by slow car in twenty-five minutes. It was not such a good lake for swimming. After college, he'd caught an ear infection that had almost kept him out of the war. And the lake had drowned Max Arnold, keeping him out of the war entirely. Max had been one who liked to talk about the existence of God. "No, I'm not saying *that*," he would say carefully against the drone of the engine. "I'm saying it is possible as an idea, even necessary as an idea, a final cause in the whole structure of causation." Now he knew, perhaps. Before the war, they'd driven around the lake as friends, but now Max was dead and most of the others were living in Des Moines or Sioux City, or going to school somewhere, or holding down jobs. None of the girls was left. Sally Hankins was mar-

---

1. **theories of causation:** philosophical theories holding that events are connected through cause-and-effect relationships.

(A) Literary Perspectives Analyzing Credibility Why is it significant that this scene is described by someone who has just witnessed war?

Vocabulary affluent (AF loo uhnt) *n.*: prosperous; rich.
tepid (TEHP ihd) *adj.*: moderately warm; lukewarm.
mesmerizing (MEHS muh ryz ihng) *adj.*: fascinating, hypnotizing.
drone (drohn) *n.*: dull, monotonous sound.

Literary Perspectives

Analyzing Credibility in Literature The short story "Speaking of Courage" follows a young soldier named Paul Berlin who has recently returned home from battle duty in Vietnam. The credibility of the narrator depends on his ability to balance his experience of the external world with his internal thoughts and emotions. It also depends on whether he seems credible, or real, as a character. To what extent do Paul's thoughts and feelings color his perception of the people and places he encounters? Why is this the case? Is his point of view less credible or more credible as a result? Does it make him more credible or less credible as a character? What can we learn from Paul's perspective?

As you read, be sure to notice the questions in the text, which will guide you in using this perspective.

ried. His father would not talk. His father had been in another war, so he knew the truth already, and he would not talk about it, and there was no one left to talk with. **B**

He turned on the radio. The car's big engine fired machinery that blew cold air all over him. Clockwise, like an electron spinning forever around its nucleus, the big Chevy circled the lake, and he had little to do but sit in the air-conditioning, both hands on the wheel, letting the car carry him in orbit. It was a lazy Sunday. The town was small. Out on the lake, a man's motorboat had stalled, and the fellow was bent over the silver motor with a wrench and a frown, and beyond him there were waterskiers and smooth July waters and two mud hens. **C**

The road curved west. The sun was low in front of him, and he figured it was close to five o'clock. Twenty after, he guessed. The war had taught him to figure time. Even without the sun, waking from sleep, he could usually place it within fifteen minutes either way. He wished his father were there beside him, so he could say, "Well, looks about five-twenty," and his father would look at his watch and say, "Hey! How'd you do that?" "One of those things you learn in the war," he would say. "I know exactly what you mean," his father would then say, and the ice would be broken, and then they would be able to talk about it as they circled the lake.

He drove past Slater Park and across the causeway and past Sunset Park. The radio announcer sounded tired. He said it was five-thirty. The temperature in Des Moines was eighty-one degrees, and "All you on the road, drive carefully now, you hear, on this fine Fourth of July." Along the road, kicking stones in front of them, two young boys were hiking with knap-sacks and toy rifles and canteens. He honked going by, but neither boy looked up. Already he'd passed them six times, forty-two miles, nearly three hours.

He watched the boys recede in his rearview mirror. They turned purply colored, like clotted blood, before finally disappearing. **D**

"How many medals did you win?" his father might have asked.

"Seven," he would have said, "though none of them were for valor."

"That's all right," his father would have answered, knowing full well that many brave men did not win medals for their bravery, and that others won medals for doing nothing. "What are the med-als you won?"

And he would have listed them, as a kind of starting place for talking about the war: the Combat Infantryman's Badge, the Air Medal, the Bronze Star (without a V-device for valor), the Army Commendation Medal, the Vietnam Campaign Medal, the Good Conduct Medal, and the Purple Heart, though it wasn't much of a wound, and there was no scar, and it didn't hurt and never had. While none of them was for valor, the decorations still looked good on the uniform in his closet, and if any-one were to ask, he would have explained what each signified, and eventually he would have talked about the medals he did not win, and why he did not win them, and how afraid he had been. **E**

"Well," his father might have said, "that's an impressive list of medals, all right."

"But none were for valor."

"I understand."

And that would have been the time for telling his father that he'd almost won the Silver Star, or maybe even the Medal of Honor.

"I almost won the Silver Star," he would have said.

"How's that?"

"Oh, it's just a war story."

"What's wrong with war stories?" his father would have said.

B Reading Focus **Identifying Historical Context** What does the author mean by the sentence "His father had been in another war, so he knew the truth already"?

C Literary Perspectives **Analyzing Credibility** Why might the town feel especially small to the main character? What might this reveal about his state of mind?

D Reading Focus **Identifying Historical Context** How does the Fourth of July lend to this story's historical context? Explain.

E Literary Perspectives **Analyzing Credibility** Why does O'Brien list all the medals that Paul Berlin won?

Vocabulary recede (rih SEED) *v.*: become more distant and indistinct.
valor (VAL uhr) *n.*: courage; bravery.

"Nothing, except I guess nobody wants to hear them." **F**

"Tell me," his father would have said.

And then, circling the lake, he would have started the story by saying what a crazy hot day it had been when Frenchie Tucker crawled like a snake into the clay tunnel and got shot in the neck, going on with the story in great detail, telling how it smelled and what the sounds had been, everything, then going on to say how he'd almost won the Silver Star for valor.

"Well," his father would have said, "that's not a very pretty story."

"I wasn't very brave."

"You have seven medals."

"True, true," he would have said, "but I might have had eight," but even so, seven medals was pretty good, hinting at courage with their bright colors and heavy metals. "But I wasn't brave," he would have admitted.

"You weren't a coward, either," his father would have said.

"I might have been a hero."

"But you weren't a coward," his father would have insisted.

"No," Paul Berlin would have said, holding the wheel slightly right of center to produce the constant clockwise motion, "no, I wasn't a coward, and I wasn't brave, but I had the chance." He would have explained, if anyone were there to listen, that his most precious medal, except for the one he did not win, was the Combat Infantryman's Badge. While not strictly speaking a genuine medal—more an insignia of soldierdom—the CIB meant that he had seen the war as a real soldier, on the ground. It meant he'd had the opportunity to be brave, it meant that. It meant, too, that he'd . . . seen Frenchie Tucker crawl into the tunnel so that just his feet were left showing, and heard the sound when he got shot in the neck. With its crossed rifles and silver and blue colors, the CIB was really not such a bad decoration, not as good as the Silver Star or Medal of Honor, but still evidence that he'd once been there with the chance to be very brave. "I wasn't brave," he would have said, "but I might have been."

The road descended into the outskirts of town, turning northwest past the junior college and tennis courts, then past the city park where tables were spread with sheets of colored plastic as picnickers listened to the high school band, then past the municipal[2] docks where a fat woman stood in pedal-pushers and white socks, fishing for bullheads.[3] There were no other fish in the lake, excepting some perch and a few worthless carp. It was a bad lake for swimming and fishing both.

He was in no great hurry. There was no place in particular to go. The day was very hot, but inside the Chevy the air was cold and oily and secure, and he liked the sound of the big engine and the radio and the air-conditioning. Through the windows, as though seen through one-way glass, the town shined like a stop-motion photograph, or a memory. The town could not talk, and it would not listen, and it was really a very small town anyway. "How'd you like to hear about the time I almost won the Silver Star for valor?" he might have said. The Chevy seemed to know its way around the lake. **G**

It was late afternoon. Along an unused railway spur, four men were erecting steel launchers for the evening fireworks. They were dressed alike in khaki trousers, work shirts, visored caps and black boots. They were sweating. Two of them were unloading crates of explosives from a city truck, stacking the crates near the steel launchers. They were talking. One of them was laughing. "How'd you like to hear about it?" he might have murmured, but the men did not look up. Later they would blow color into the sky. The lake would be like a mirror, and the picnickers would sigh. The colors would open wide. "Well, it was this crazy hot day," he would have said to anyone who asked, "and Frenchie Tucker took off his helmet and pack and crawled into the tunnel with a forty-five and a knife, and the whole platoon stood in a circle around the mouth of the tunnel to watch him go down. 'Don't

---

2. **municipal:** of or pertaining to a town or city or its local government.
3. **bullheads:** type of freshwater catfish with hornlike growths near its mouth.

F **Literary Perspectives** Analyzing Credibility Does this imaginary conversation between Paul and his father seem believable? Based on what you have read, can you imagine it taking place like this?

G **Literary Focus** Conflict How is Paul Berlin in conflict with his surroundings?

get blowed away," said Stink Harris, but Frenchie was already inside and he didn't hear. You could see his feet wiggling, and you could smell the dirt and clay, and then, when he got shot through the neck, you could smell the gunpowder and you could see Frenchie's feet jerk, and that was the day I could have won the Silver Star for valor."

The Chevy rolled smoothly across the old railroad spur. To his right, there was only the open lake. To his left, the lawns were scorched dry like October corn. Hopelessly, round and round, a rotating sprinkler scattered water into Doctor Mason's vegetable garden. In August it would get worse. The lake would turn green, thick with bacteria and decay, and the golf course would dry up, and dragonflies would crack open for lack of good water. The summer seemed permanent.

The big Chevy curled past the A&W[4] and Centennial Beach, and he started his seventh revolution around the lake.

He followed the road past the handsome low-slung houses. Back to Slater Park, across the causeway, around to Sunset Park, as though riding on tracks.

Out on the lake, the man with the stalled motorboat was still fiddling with the engine.

The two boys were still trudging on their hike. They did not look up when he honked.

The pair of mud hens floated like wooden decoys.

---

4. **A&W:** chain of drive-in fast-food restaurants.

Analyzing Visuals

Viewing and Interpreting Compare this lithograph with the painting shown on page 1196. How do such widely contrasting images relate to the protagonist's conflict in "Speaking of Courage"?

The waterskiers looked tan and happy, and the spray behind them looked clean.

It was all distant and pretty. ⓗ

Facing the sun again, he figured it was nearly six o'clock. Not much later the tired announcer in Des Moines confirmed it, his voice seeming to rock itself into a Sunday afternoon snooze.

Too bad, he thought. If Max were there, he would say something meaningful about the announcer's fatigue, and relate it to the sun low and red now over the lake, and the war, and courage. Too bad that all the girls had gone away. And his father, who already knew the difficulties of being brave, and who preferred silence.

Circling the lake, with time to talk, he would have told the truth. He would not have faked it. Starting with the admission that he had not been truly brave, he would have next said he hadn't been a coward, either. "I almost won the Silver Star for valor," he would have said, and, even so, he'd learned many important things in the war. Like telling time without a watch. He had learned to step lightly. He knew, just by the sound, the difference between friendly and enemy mortars,[5] and with time to talk and with an audience, he could explain the difference in great detail. He could tell people that the enemy fired 82-millimeter mortar rounds, while we fired 81's, and that this was a real advantage to the enemy since they could steal our rounds and shoot them from their own weapons. He knew many lies. Simple, unprofound things. He knew it is a lie that only stupid men are brave. He knew that a man can die of fright, literally, because it had happened just that way to Billy Boy Watkins after his foot had been blown off. Billy Boy had been scared to death. Dead of a heart attack caused by fright, according to Doc Peret, who would know. He knew, too, that it is a lie, the old saying that you never hear the shot that gets you, because Frenchie Tucker was shot in the neck, and after they dragged him out of the tunnel he lay there and told everyone his great discovery; he'd heard it coming the whole way, he said excitedly; and then he raised his thumb and bled through his mouth, grinning at the great discovery. So the old saying was surely a lie, or else Frenchie Tucker was lying himself, which under the circumstances was hard to believe. He knew a lot of things. They were not new or profound, but they were true. He knew that he might have won a Silver Star, like Frenchie, if he'd been able to finish what Frenchie started in the foul tunnel. He knew many war stories, a thousand details, smells and the confusion of the senses, but nobody was there to listen, and nobody knew a damn about the war because nobody believed it was really a war at all. It was not a war for war stories, or talk of valor, and nobody asked questions about the details, such as how afraid you can be, or what the particular sounds were, or whether it hurts to be shot, or what you think about and hear and see on ambush, or whether you can really tell in a firefight which way to shoot, which you can't, or how you become brave enough to win the Silver Star, or how it smells of sulfur against your cheek after firing eighteen fast rounds, or how you crawl on hands and knees without knowing direction, and how, after crawling into the red-mouthed tunnel, you close your eyes like a mole and follow the tunnel walls and smell Frenchie's fresh blood and know a bullet cannot miss in there, and how there is nowhere to go but forward or backward, eyes closed, and how you can't go forward, and lose all sense, and are dragged out by the heels, losing the Silver Star. All the details, without profundity, simple and age old, but nobody wants to hear war stories because they are age old and not new and not profound, and because everyone knows already that it hadn't been a war like other wars. If Max or his father were ever to ask, or anybody, he would say, "Well, first off, it was a war the same as any war," which would not sound profound at all, but which would be the truth. Then he would explain what he meant in great detail, explaining that, right or wrong or win or lose, at root it had been a real war, regardless of corruption in high places or politics or sociology or the existence of God. His father knew it already, though. Which was why he didn't ask. And

---

5. **mortars:** cannons used to fire explosive shells.

ⓗ **Literary Perspectives** Analyzing Credibility Why do things seem distant to Paul? Are they distant, or is Paul pulling away?

Vocabulary **profundity** (pruh FUHN duh tee) *n.*: deep significance; intellectual depth.

Max could not ask. It was a small town, but it wasn't the town's fault, either.

He passed the sprawling ranch-style homes. He lit a cigarette. He had learned to smoke in the war. He opened the window a crack but kept the air-conditioner going full, and again he circled the lake. His thoughts were the same. Out on the lake, the man was frantically yanking the cord to his stalled outboard motor. Along the causeway, the two boys marched on. The pair of mud hens sought sludge at the bottom of the lake, heads under water and tails bobbing.

Six-thirty, he thought. The lake had divided into two halves. One half still glistened. The other was caught in shadow. Soon it would be dark. The crew of workers would shoot the sky full of color, for the war was over, and the town would celebrate independence. He passed Sunset Park once again, and more houses, and the junior college and tennis courts, and the picnickers and the high school band, and the municipal docks where the fat woman patiently waited for fish.

Already, though it wasn't quite dusk, the A&W was awash in neon lights.

He maneuvered his father's Chevy into one of the parking slots, let the engine idle, and waited. The place was doing a good holiday business. Mostly kids in their fathers' cars, a few farmers in for the day, a few faces he thought he remembered, but no names. He sat still. With the sound of the engine and air-conditioning and radio, he could not hear the kids laughing, or the cars coming and going and burning rubber. But it didn't matter, it seemed proper, and he sat patiently and watched while mosquitoes and June bugs swarmed off the lake to attack the orange-colored lighting. A slim, hipless, deft young blonde delivered trays of food, passing him by as if the big Chevy were invisible, but he waited. The tired announcer in Des Moines gave the time, seven o'clock. He could trace the fall of dusk in the orange lights which grew brighter and sharper. It was a bad war for medals. But the Silver Star would have been nice. Nice to have been brave. The tactile, certain substance of the Silver Star, and

how he could have rubbed his fingers over it, remembering the tunnel and the smell of clay in his nose, going forward and not backward in simple bravery. He waited patiently. The mosquitoes were electrocuting themselves against a Pest-Rid machine. The slim young carhop ignored him, chatting with four boys in a Firebird, her legs in nylons even in mid-summer. **J**

He honked once, a little embarrassed, but she did not turn. The four boys were laughing. He could not hear them, or the joke, but he could see their bright eyes and the way their heads moved. She patted the cheek of the driver.

He honked again, twice. He could not hear the sound. The girl did not hear, either.

He honked again, this time leaning on the horn. His ears buzzed. The air-conditioning shot cold air into his lap. The girl turned slowly, as though hearing something very distant, not at all sure. She said something to the boys, and they laughed, then she moved reluctantly toward him. EAT MAMA BURGERS said the orange and brown button on her chest. "How'd you like to hear about the war," he whispered, feeling vengeful. "The time I almost won the Silver Star."

She stood at the window, straight up so he could not see her face, only the button that said, EAT MAMA BURGERS. "Papa Burger, root beer, and french fries," he said, but the girl did not move or answer. She rapped on the window.

"Papa Burger, root beer, and french fries," he said, rolling it down.

She leaned down. She shook her head dumbly. Her eyes were as lovely and fuzzy as cotton candy.

"Papa Burger, root beer, and french fries," he said slowly, pronouncing the words separately and distinctly for her.

She stared at him with her strange eyes. "You blind?" she chirped suddenly. She gestured toward an intercom attached to a steel post. "You blind or something?"

"Papa Burger, root beer, and french fries."

"Push the button," she said, "and place your order."

I **Literary Focus** Conflict Why does the idea of "not being truly brave" but "not being a coward either" keep running through the main character's mind?

J **Literary Perspectives** Analyzing Credibility Paul feels invisible. What does this reveal about him?

Vocabulary **tactile** (TAK tuhl) *adj.*: perceptible to the touch; tangible.

Then, first punching the button for him, she returned to her friends in the Firebird. **K**

"Order," commanded a tinny voice.

"Papa Burger, root beer, and french fries."

"Roger-dodger," the voice said. "Repeat: one Papa, one beer, one fries. Stand by. That's it?"

"Roger," said Paul Berlin.

"Out," said the voice, and the intercom squeaked and went dead.

"Out," said Paul Berlin.

When the slim carhop brought him his tray, he ate quickly, without looking up, then punched the intercom button.

"Order," said the tinny voice.

"I'm done."

"That's it?"

"Yes, all done."

"Roger-dodger, over n' out," said the voice.

"Out."

On his ninth revolution around the lake he passed the hiking boys for the last time. The man with the stalled motorboat was paddling toward shore. The mud hens were gone. The fat woman was reeling in her line. The sun had left a smudge of watercolor on the horizon, and the bandshell[6] was empty, and Doctor Mason's sprinkler went round and round.

On his tenth revolution, he switched off the air-conditioning, cranked open a window, and rested his elbow comfortably on the sill, driving with one hand. He could trace the contours of the tunnel. He could talk about the scrambling sense of being lost, though he could not describe it even in his thoughts. He could talk about the terror, but he could not describe it or even feel it anymore. He could talk about emerging to see sunlight, but he could not feel the warmth, or see the faces of the men who looked away, or talk about his shame. There was no one to talk to, and nothing to say.

On his eleventh revolution, the sky went crazy with color.

He pulled into Sunset Park and stopped in the shadow of a picnic shelter. After a time, he got out and walked down to the beach and stood with his arms folded and watched the fireworks. For a small town, it was a pretty good show.

---

6. **bandshell:** open-air stage with a rear sounding board shaped like the shell of a scallop.

K **Reading Focus** **Identifying Historical Context** Why is the intercom an important detail in this setting?

Respond and Think Critically

Reading Focus

Quick Check

1. Why is it symbolic that the story takes place on July 4?

2. What does Paul wish his father would do?

3. List the things Paul has learned from the war.

Read with a Purpose

4. According to Paul, why don't people want to hear about the war?

Reading Skills: Identifying Historical Context

5. Review the Venn diagram you created to compare and contrast the attitudes and values Paul encounters in Iowa and in Vietnam. What similarities did you list in the overlapping section of the circles? Write a paragraph discussing how the two environments contribute to the conflict at the heart of O'Brien's story.

✓ Vocabulary Check

Match each Vocabulary word with its definition.

6. recede	a. bravery	
7. profundity	b. tangible	
8. mesmerizing	c. become distant	
9. tepid	d. deep significance	
10. tactile	e. dull sound	
11. drone	f. hypnotic	
12. valor	g. lukewarm	

Literary Focus

Literary Analysis

13. **Analyze** Why is it so difficult for Paul and his father to talk about their war experiences?

14. **Interpret** What things does Paul do repeatedly in this story? What do these repetitions reveal about his state of mind?

15. **Draw Conclusions** Do you think Paul would feel significantly different if he had won the Silver Star for valor? Explain.

16. **Analyze** What is ironic about the scene in which Paul uses the intercom at the A&W drive-in (pages 1202–1203)? Explain your response.

17. **Literary Perspectives** Throughout the story, Paul insists that he wasn't very brave in the war. Do you think he is being fair to himself? Do we have any reasons to doubt him? Why or why not?

Literary Skills: Conflict

18. **Analyze** What is Paul's internal conflict? Is it resolved by the end of the story?

19. **Analyze** What external conflicts do we see in the events Paul remembers from Vietnam?

Literary Skills Review: Theme

20. **Interpret** What insight into life, or **theme,** does O'Brien develop in this story?

Writing Focus

Think as a Reader/Writer

Use It in Your Writing As you read, you noted O'Brien's use of symbolic settings. Review the entries in your *Reader/Writer Notebook* to find a setting that you could revise to make it more symbolic. Add symbolic details that provide clues, or you may write your own original description of a symbolic setting.

What Do **You Think Now** What do you think Paul needs to help him get out of the rut that he's in? Do you think he will find a way to live with his past?

SKILLS FOCUS **Literary Skills** Analyze conflict; analyze theme. **Reading Skills** Analyze historical context, especially political and social influences of the time. **Vocabulary Skills** Demonstrate word knowledge. **Writing Skills** Write comparison-contrast essays. **Grammar Skills** Combine related sentences correctly. **Listening and Speaking Skills** Offer insightful observations in discussions and conversations.

Grammar Link

Combining Sentences

Short, choppy sentences can be combined to create longer, fluid sentences. You can combine sentences by taking a key word (or another form of the word) from one sentence and inserting it into another.

ORIGINAL	Jack London describes the man's attempt to build a fire. The description is vivid.
COMBINED	Jack London **vividly** describes the man's attempt to build a fire. [The adjective *vivid* becomes the adverb *vividly*.]

Sentences can be combined by joining ideas that are equally important. By using coordinating conjunctions (*and, but, or, yet*) or correlative conjunctions (*both . . . and, either . . . or, neither . . . nor, not only . . . but also*), you can turn coordinate ideas into compound sentences.

ORIGINAL	Robert Frost did not receive the Nobel Prize. Carl Sandburg never received it.
COMBINED	**Neither Robert Frost nor Carl Sandburg** received the Nobel Prize.

You can also form a compound sentence by linking independent clauses with a semicolon and a conjunctive adverb or with just a semicolon.

ORIGINAL	We planned to go swimming. The weather did not cooperate.
COMBINED	We planned to go swimming; **however,** the weather did not cooperate.

Your Turn

Combine the sentences in the ways described above.

1. Paul drove in circles around the lake. He felt lonely and aimless.

2. Paul honked at the boys every time he passed them. They never looked up.

CHOICES

As you respond to the Choices, use these **Academic Vocabulary** words as appropriate: component, diverse, intrinsic, potential, and transmit.

REVIEW

Compare and Contrast

Write a two-paragraph comparison-contrast essay. In the first paragraph, discuss the differences between the two worlds in the story: the typical small-town life of Paul's home and the horrors of war-torn Vietnam. Then, in a second paragraph discuss the conflicts that Paul faces in both places. What did he fight against in Vietman? What does he struggle with now that he has returned home?

CONNECT

Research Historical Context

TechFocus With a partner, identify two or three people who were alive during the war in Vietnam and old enough to remember or participate in the conflict. Using a video camera, record an interview with each person about the conflict in Vietnam. In what ways did people talk about the war? What was kept silent?

EXTEND

Discuss the Concept of Courage

Group Activity What is courage? In a small group, define what courage means to you. Create a list of diverse examples of people who have acted courageously in dangerous situations, but whose bravery may have been overlooked or gone unrewarded. What makes these people courageous? How could they be rewarded for their valor?

Learn It Online
Go online to find graphic organizers to help you gather and arrange your ideas and research.

go.hrw.com	L11-1205	Go

Preparing to Read

Everything Stuck to Him

What Do You Think

What human needs and desires do we have in common?

QuickWrite

Think about someone you know or have read about. List four or five things that this person or character does habitually or routinely—things characteristic of him or her. Then, write a few paragraphs describing a typical day in his or her life, including these characteristics.

Raymond Carver
(1938–1988)

Raymond Carver uses stripped-down language to explore the overlooked lives of working-class people. "They're my people. I know them. I could never write down to them."

People on the Edge

"We didn't have any youth," Raymond Carver recalled about the rough days he spent growing up in a working class family in Yakima, Washington, where his father worked in a lumber mill and his mother as a waitress and a clerk. Married soon after high school and twice a father by age twenty, Carver supported his family by pumping gas, sweeping floors, and picking tulips.

Given this background, it is no surprise that in his stories—as critic Thomas R. Edwards has noted—"people worry about whether their old cars will start, [and] unemployment or personal bankruptcy are present dangers." However, Carver's characters, typically mechanics or waitresses, often survive their struggles, and there is a sense of hope in many of his stories.

Among the Masters

In the late 1950s, Carver moved his family to California, where he entered college and studied writing. He continued on to the University of Iowa's highly regarded Writers' Workshop. In the late 1960s, he began publishing stories and poems, some dealing with favorite topics such as hunting and fishing. Carver experienced a breakthrough in 1976 with the widely acclaimed collection *Will You Please Be Quiet, Please?* In 1977, he won a prestigious Guggenheim fellowship. "I never figured I'd make a living writing short stories....I'm pleased and happy with the way things turned out. But I was surprised."

In 1981, Carver published another story collection, *What We Talk About When We Talk About Love,* and in 1983 his collection *Cathedral* enjoyed enormous critical and popular success. By then, critics were comparing him to Stephen Crane, Ernest Hemingway, and other literary masters. "His eye is so clear," wrote *The Washington Post* book reviewer Jonathan Yardley, "it almost breaks your heart.

Think About the Writer If Carver were writing today, what jobs might his characters have? What problems might they talk about?

© Marion Ettlinger.

Reader/Writer Notebook

Use your **RWN** to complete the activities for this selection.

Literary Focus

Style The way a writer uses language is called **style.** Style is a combination of many things: sentence structure, word choice, use of figures of speech, and so forth. Most writers develop individual styles—plain, technical, flowery, effusive—that reflect their own sense of rightness and truth. One of the most striking <u>components</u> of Raymond Carver's writing is his style. Carver's prose has a chiseled quality, as if he has chipped away at every unnecessary word. His style includes some oddities, however. He uses no quotation marks around dialogue, and he often doesn't give his characters names. As you read the selection, think of words that describe Carver's unique style and record examples that illustrate his style.

Reading Focus

Learning Through Questioning Great fiction enables us to discover surprising depths of feeling in ordinary events we often take for granted. In Carver's story, planning a hunting trip, soothing a baby, or simply making breakfast provides clues to the inner lives of a troubled young married couple. By asking questions about what goes on beneath these ordinary events, you will learn what the young couple's story really is.

Into Action Use a chart like the one below to list ordinary events in the story. Next, ask a question to help you discover what that event conceals about the characters and their situation.

Event	Question
The boy wants to go hunting.	Why does he want to go hunting?

Writing Focus

Think as a Reader/Writer

Find It in Your Reading Carver's **dialogue** contains many **colloquial expressions,** or informal words and phrases of conversational language, such as "crazy in love" and "are you getting the picture?" These lend credibility to the characters and to the action. As you read, use your *Reader/Writer Notebook* to make a list of colloquial expressions and be prepared to discuss what they mean.

Vocabulary

coincide (koh ihn SYD) *v.:* occupy the same time or place; agree. *They argued because they could not make their different viewpoints coincide.*

striking (STRY kihng) *adj.:* Impressive; attractive; dramatic. *He liked his sister-in-law's striking good looks.*

fitfully (FIHT fuhl lee) *adv.:* irregularly; in fits and starts. *The mother worried because her baby cried fitfully.*

Language Coach

Multiple Meanings The word *striking* has multiple meanings: It can mean "Impressive or attractive," as noted above. It is also a form of the verb *strike,* meaning "to hit." Can you guess how the first meaning grew out of the second?

The words *snap*, *gear*, and *nail*, all from the selection you are about to read, also have multiple meanings. Jot down the meaning that you know. As you read, notice whether the meanings in the selection are the same as those you wrote down.

Learn It Online
Get to know the Vocabulary words inside and out with Word Watch online.

go.hrw.com L11-1207 **Go**

Everything Stuck to Him

by **Raymond Carver**

Read with a Purpose

Read to discover how, years later, a small sequence of events can take on great significance.

Build Background

In "Everything Stuck to Him," Carver uses a device in which one story is enclosed within another. He begins with a frame story in which a father and daughter meet in Italy. She asks to hear about her childhood. In the inner story, the father recalls the early years of the marriage. The frame story and the inner story provide insight into the relationship of the characters and the meaning of the story's title.

She's in Milan[1] for Christmas and wants to know what it was like when she was a kid.

Tell me, she says. Tell me what it was like when I was a kid. She sips Strega,[2] waits, eyes him closely.

She is a cool, slim, attractive girl, a survivor from top to bottom.

That was a long time ago. That was twenty years ago, he says.

You can remember, she says. Go on.

What do you want to hear? he says. What else can I tell you? I could tell you about something that happened when you were a baby. It involves you, he says. But only in a minor way.

Tell me, she says. But first fix us another so you won't have to stop in the middle.

He comes back from the kitchen with drinks, settles into his chair, begins.

They were kids themselves, but they were crazy in love, this eighteen-year-old boy and this seventeen-year-old girl when they married. Not all that long afterwards they had a daughter.

The baby came along in late November during a cold spell that just happened to coincide with the peak of the waterfowl season. The boy loved to hunt, you see. That's part of it.

The boy and girl, husband and wife, father and mother, they lived in a little apartment under a dentist's office. Each night they cleaned the dentist's place

upstairs in exchange for rent and utilities. In summer they were expected to maintain the lawn and the flowers. In winter the boy shoveled snow and spread rock salt on the walks. Are you still with me? Are you getting the picture?

I am, she says.

That's good, he says. So one day the dentist finds out they were using his letterhead for their personal correspondence. But that's another story.

He gets up from his chair and looks out the window. He sees the tile rooftops and the snow that is falling steadily on them.

Tell the story, she says.

The two kids were very much in love. On top of this they had great ambitions. They were always talk-

---

1. **Milan**: city in northwestern Italy.
2. **Strega**: sweet Italian liqueur.

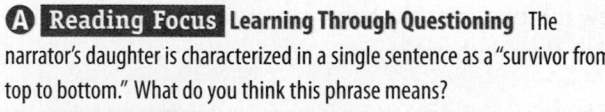

Ⓐ **Reading Focus** **Learning Through Questioning** The narrator's daughter is characterized in a single sentence as a "survivor from top to bottom." What do you think this phrase means?

Ⓑ **Literary Focus** **Style** Why does Carver use the frame story technique, a story enclosed in another story, for this narrative?

Ⓒ **Reading Focus** **Learning Through Questioning** How would you characterize "the boy" and "the girl" of the inner story? Why?

Ⓓ **Literary Focus** **Style** What is Carver implying by using the words *girl* and *boy* to refer to the married couple?

Vocabulary **coincide** (koh ihn SYD) *v.*: occupy the same time or place; agree.

ing about the things they were going to do and the places they were going to go.

Now the boy and girl slept in the bedroom, and the baby slept in the living room. Let's say the baby was about three months old and had only just begun to sleep through the night.

On this one Saturday night after finishing his work upstairs, the boy stayed in the dentist's office and called an old hunting friend of his father's.

Carl, he said when the man picked up the receiver, believe it or not, I'm a father.

Congratulations, Carl said. How is the wife?

She's fine, Carl. Everybody's fine.

That's good, Carl said, I'm glad to hear it. But if you called about going hunting, I'll tell you something. The geese are flying to beat the band. I don't think I've ever seen so many. Got five today. Going back in the morning, so come along if you want to.

I want to, the boy said. **E**

The boy hung up the telephone and went downstairs to tell the girl. She watched while he laid out his things. Hunting coat, shell bag, boots, socks, hunting cap, long underwear, pump gun.

What time will you be back? the girl said.

Probably around noon, the boy said. But maybe as late as six o'clock. Would that be too late?

It's fine, she said. The baby and I will get along fine. You go and have some fun. When you get back, we'll dress the baby up and go visit Sally.

The boy said, Sounds like a good idea.

Sally was the girl's sister. She was striking. I don't know if you've seen pictures of her. The boy was a little in love with Sally, just as he was a little in love with Betsy, who was another sister the girl had. The boy used to say to the girl, If we weren't married, I could go for Sally.

What about Betsy? the girl used to say. I hate to admit it, but I truly feel she's better looking than Sally and me. What about Betsy?

Betsy too, the boy used to say.

After dinner he turned up the furnace and helped her bathe the baby. He marveled again at the infant who had half his features and half the girl's. He powdered the tiny body. He powdered between fingers and toes.

He emptied the bath into the sink and went upstairs to check the air. It was overcast and cold. The grass, what there was of it, looked like canvas, stiff and gray under the street light.

Snow lay in piles beside the walk. A car went by. He heard sand under the tires. He let himself imagine what it might be like tomorrow, geese beating the air over his head, shotgun plunging against his shoulder.

Then he locked the door and went downstairs.

In bed they tried to read. But both of them fell asleep, she first, letting the magazine sink to the quilt.

It was the baby's cries that woke him up.

The light was on out there, and the girl was standing next to the crib rocking the baby in her arms. She put the baby down, turned out the light, and came back to the bed.

He heard the baby cry. This time the girl stayed where she was. The baby cried fitfully and stopped. The boy listened, then dozed. But the baby's cries woke him again. The living room light was burning. He sat up and turned on the lamp.

I don't know what's wrong, the girl said, walking back and forth with the baby. I've changed her and fed her, but she keeps on crying. I'm so tired I'm afraid I might drop her.

You come back to bed, the boy said. I'll hold her for a while.

He got up and took the baby, and the girl went to lie down again.

Just rock her for a few minutes, the girl said from the bedroom. Maybe she'll go back to sleep.

The boy sat on the sofa and held the baby. He jiggled it in his lap until he got its eyes to close, his own eyes closing right along. He rose carefully and put the baby back in the crib.

It was a quarter to four, which gave him forty-five minutes. He crawled into bed and dropped off. But a few minutes later the baby was crying again, and this time they both got up.

E **Reading Focus** **Learning Through Questioning** Why does the boy call his father's old hunting friend?

The boy did a terrible thing. He swore.

For God's sake, what's the matter with you? the girl said to the boy. Maybe she's sick or something. Maybe we shouldn't have given her the bath.

The boy picked up the baby. The baby kicked its feet and smiled.

Look, the boy said, I really don't think there's anything wrong with her.

How do you know that? the girl said. Here, let me have her. I know I ought to give her something, but I don't know what it's supposed to be.

The girl put the baby down again. The boy and the girl looked at the baby, and the baby began to cry.

The girl took the baby. Baby, baby, the girl said with tears in her eyes.

Probably it's something on her stomach, the boy said.

The girl didn't answer. She went on rocking the baby, paying no attention to the boy.

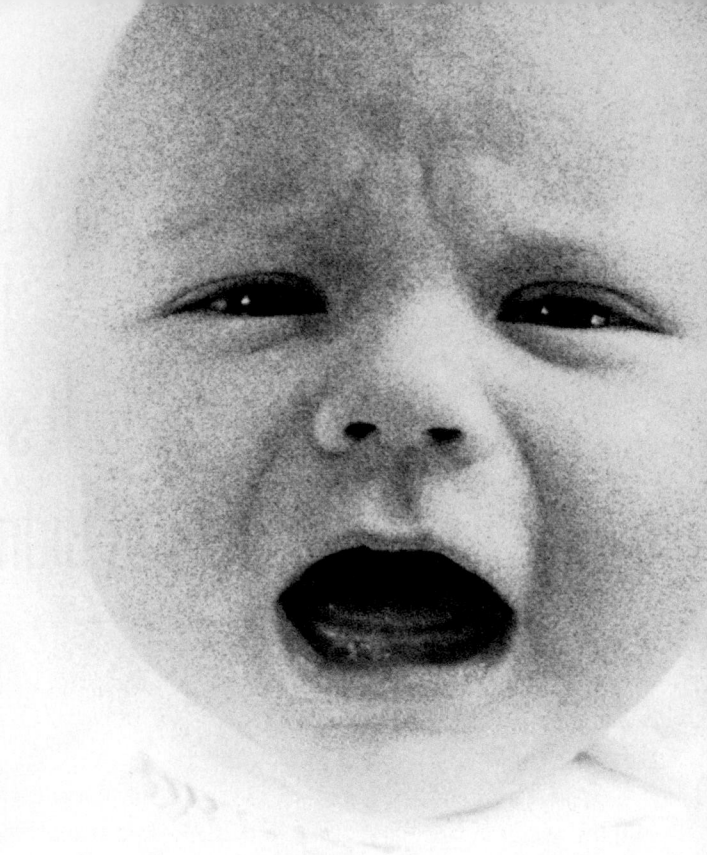

The boy waited. He went to the kitchen and put on water for coffee. He drew his woolen underwear on over his shorts and T-shirt, buttoned up, then got into his clothes.

What are you doing? the girl said.

Going hunting, the boy said.

I don't think you should, she said. I don't want to be left alone with her like this.

Carl's planning on me going, the boy said. We've planned it.

I don't care about what you and Carl planned, she said. And I don't care about Carl, either. I don't even know Carl.

You've met Carl before. You know him, the boy said. What do you mean you don't know him?

That's not the point and you know it, the girl said.

What is the point? the boy said. The point is we planned it.

The girl said, I'm your wife. This is your baby. She's sick or something. Look at her. Why else is she crying?

I know you're my wife, the boy said.

The girl began to cry. She put the baby back in the crib. But the baby started up again. The girl dried her eyes on the sleeve of her nightgown and picked the baby up.

The boy laced up his boots. He put on his shirt, his sweater, his coat. The kettle whistled on the stove in the kitchen.

You're going to have to choose, the girl said. Carl or us. I mean it.

What do you mean? the boy said.

You heard what I said, the girl said. If you want a family, you're going to have to choose.

They stared at each other. Then the boy took up his hunting gear and went outside. He started the car. He went around to the car windows and, making a job of it, scraped away the ice.

He turned off the motor and sat awhile. And then he got out and went back inside.

The living-room light was on. The girl was asleep on the bed. The baby was asleep beside her.

The boy took off his boots. Then he took off everything else. In his socks and his long underwear, he sat on the sofa and read the Sunday paper.

The girl and the baby slept on. After a while, the boy went to the kitchen and started frying bacon.

The girl came out in her robe and put her arms around the boy.

Hey, the boy said.

I'm sorry, the girl said.

It's all right, the boy said.

Hey, the boy said.
I'm sorry, the girl said.
It's all right, the boy said.
I didn't mean to snap like that.
It was my fault, he said.

I didn't mean to snap like that.

It was my fault, he said.

You sit down, the girl said. How does a waffle sound with bacon?

Sounds great, the boy said. **(F)**

She took the bacon out of the pan and made waffle batter. He sat at the table and watched her move around the kitchen.

She put a plate in front of him with bacon, a waffle. He spread butter and poured syrup. But when he started to cut, he turned the plate into his lap.

I don't believe it, he said, jumping up from the table.

If you could see yourself, the girl said.

The boy looked down at himself, at everything stuck to his underwear.

I was starved, he said, shaking his head.

You were starved, she said, laughing.

He peeled off the woolen underwear and threw it at the bathroom door. Then he opened his arms and the girl moved into them.

We won't fight anymore, she said.

The boy said, We won't.

He gets up from his chair and refills their glasses.

That's it, he says. End of story. I admit it's not much of a story.

I was interested, she says.

He shrugs and carries his drink over to the window. It's dark now but still snowing.

Things change, he says. I don't know how they do. But they do without your realizing it or wanting them to.

Yes, that's true, only—But she does not finish what she started.

She drops the subject. In the window's reflection he sees her study her nails. Then she raises her head. Speaking brightly, she asks if he is going to show her the city, after all.

He says, Put your boots on and let's go.

But he stays by the window, remembering. They had laughed. They had leaned on each other and laughed until the tears had come, while everything else—the cold, and where he'd go in it—was outside, for a while anyway. **(G)**

(F) Literary Focus **Style** Why does the author use such short sentences during the couple's reconciliation?

(G) Reading Focus **Learning Through Questioning** What does this final memory suggest about the boy and the girl?

SKILLS FOCUS **Literary Skills** Analyze a writer's style; analyze characterization.
Reading Skills Learn through questioning.
Vocabulary Skills Identify antonyms.

Writing Skills Develop characters using dialogue.

Everything Stuck to Him

Respond and Think Critically

Reading Focus

Quick Check

1. What is the setting, and who are the characters in the frame story?

2. In the inner story, what is the setting, and who are the characters? Which characters appear in both stories?

Read with a Purpose

3. After telling the inner story, the man says "things change." What do you think has changed since the inner story took place?

Reading Skills: Learning Through Questioning

4. As you read "Everything Stuck to Him," you listed questions about ordinary scenes to explore what they transmit about the inner lives of the story's characters. Add a third column to your chart in which you record what you think each scene reveals about the young couple.

Event	Question	Answer
The boy wants to go hunting.	Why does he want to go hunting?	He feels stifled by his marriage.

✔ Vocabulary Check

Match each Vocabulary word with its antonym.

5. coincide   **a.** unattractive

6. striking   **b.** regularly

7. fitfully   **c.** disagree

Literary Focus

Literary Analysis

8. **Interpret** The title refers to an incident in the inner story. Why is this incident important?

9. **Draw Conclusions** What emotions do you think the boy experienced as he "sat awhile" in the car?

10. **Infer** Near the end of the frame story (page 1212), the daughter replies, "Yes, that's true, only—" She does not finish. What do you think she intended to say, and why did she stop?

Literary Skills: Style

11. **Hypothesize** One aspect of Carver's style in this story is the omission of names for the main characters. Why does he use *boy* and *girl* instead of *man* and *woman* or *father* and *mother*?

Literary Skills Review: Characterization

12. **Extend** Writers reveal character through **characterization**. How does the character of the daughter help you understand her parents and their relationship?

Writing Focus

Think as a Reader/Writer

Use It in Your Writing Write an original dialogue using some of the colloquial expressions you found in the story. With a partner, read the dialogue to the class.

What Do **You Think Now** How have the family dynamics changed in this story? How has the daughter been affected?

Preparing to Read

Teenage Wasteland

What Do You Think

What human needs and desires do we have in common?

🕐 QuickWrite

Write briefly about relationships between teenagers and adults. Do you believe it is possible for adults to understand teenagers, or do teenagers have certain needs that adults cannot understand?

Anne Tyler
(1941–)

Pulitzer Prize WINNER

As a child, Anne Tyler lived with her family in various Quaker communities in the United States and thinks her attraction to writing came from her sense of being set apart from others. She frequently writes about people's struggle to connect to one another. "My fondest hope . . . is that readers will feel . . . that for awhile they have actually stepped inside another person's life and come to feel related to that person."

Exploring the Family

Anne Tyler was born in Minneapolis and grew up in North Carolina. She was an imaginative child and started to write stories by the time she was seven years old. Tyler graduated from Duke University and did postgraduate work in Russian studies at Columbia University. She has lived most of her adult life in Baltimore, the setting for many of her novels.

Tyler's favorite theme is the quiet drama of family life and "how people endure together." In the family, she says, with all its conflicts, lies a "perfect breeding ground for plot." Tyler has said about her method of writing: "I do write long, long character notes—family background, history, details of appearance— much more than will ever appear in the novel. I think this is what lifts a book from that early calculated, artificial stage."

Imagining Other Lives

Tyler has also commented that many novels lack "quiet, gentle, basically good people." A reviewer echoed her words in saying, "Her fiction is a quiet, gentle reminder of the goodness to be found in most ordinary lives. In a noisy, violent world, this is surely not to be sniffed at—and neither is her extremely fine writing."

Tyler's most popular novel to date is *The Accidental Tourist* (1985), about a travel writer whose family is horribly torn apart when his son is murdered in a fast-food restaurant. The book was made into an Oscar-winning movie in 1988. In 1989, Tyler won the Pulitzer Prize for *Breathing Lessons,* the story of a married couple who yearn to repair their son's broken marriage.

Think About the Writer

Anne Tyler makes extensive notes about her characters before writing. Why might she take more notes than she will include in the final work?

Reader/Writer Notebook

Use your **RWN** to complete the activities for this selection.

Literary Focus

Characterization The way a writer <u>transmits</u> the personality of characters is called **characterization.** Writers use two basic methods: direct characterization and indirect characterization. When writers use **direct characterization,** they reveal things directly. When they use **indirect characterization,** they force readers to put clues together to infer what a character is like. In her story "Teenage Wasteland," Anne Tyler sees deeply into her characters and paints a richly detailed series of portraits of them. As you read, be alert for the details that make characters come alive on the page.

Reading Focus

Making Predictions One good way to understand what you read is to pause from time to time to make predictions about it. A **prediction** is an educated guess about what will happen next, based on clues that suggest or foreshadow what is to come. As you resume reading, you can check to see if your predictions turn out to be accurate.

Into Action Analyze events in the story to make predictions about what could <u>potentially</u> happen next. Use a chart like the one below to record events and your predictions about their outcomes.

Event	Prediction
Donny meets Cal.	Donny will dislike Cal.

Writing Focus

Think as a Reader/Writer

Find It in Your Reading Anne Tyler uses the dash throughout the story "Teenage Wasteland." The dash is an effective punctuation mark that signals a break in thought or speech or a continuation or clarification of a thought. Tyler uses a dash frequently to build her description of a character: "He used to have very blond hair—almost white" or "he wore it longer—past his collar even." As you read, copy some of Tyler's uses of the dash in your *Reader/Writer Notebook* as models for your own writing.

Vocabulary

morass (muh RAS) *n.:* any confusing or troublesome situation; entanglement. *Donny's difficult situation became a morass for which his parents saw no easy solution.*

amiably (AY mee uh blee) *adv.:* in a friendly, agreeable way. *Cal behaved amiably at first, but became increasingly controlling.*

perturbed (puhr TURBD) *v.* used as *adj.:* uneasy; anxious; ill at ease. *The restrictions placed on him at school and at home made Donny perturbed.*

shambled (SHAM buhld) *v.:* proceeded awkwardly; shuffled. *Donny shambled reluctantly to his new school.*

evasive (ih VAY sihv) *adj.:* tending or seeking to evade. *Daisy became suspicious because Donny was evasive about telling the truth.*

forlorn (fawr LAWRN) *adj.:* lonely and sad; forsaken. *Her inability to understand her son's situation made Daisy forlorn.*

Language Coach

Word Origins The word *forlorn* comes from the Middle English prefix *for–* and the word *lorn*, which means "abandoned." Old English words that begin with *for–* tend to have negative associations. To forget, for example, is to lose the memory of something.

 Learn It Online
Find interactive graphic organizers online.

go.hrw.com   L11-1215

TEENAGE WASTELAND

by **Anne Tyler**

Marc (April) (2003) by Elizabeth Peyton.

Read with a Purpose
Read to discover whether a troubled teenager's parents can reconnect with him.

Build Background
In this story about a troubled American family, Tyler explores the world of Matt and Daisy Coble, who are enduring the alienated behavior of their teenage son. But Tyler's story also examines another conflict: the conflict between how parents and teenagers may see the same situation from strikingly different points of view.

He used to have very blond hair—almost white—cut shorter than other children's so that on his crown a little cowlick always stood up to catch the light. But this was when he was small. As he grew older, his hair grew darker, and he wore it longer—past his collar even. It hung in lank, taffy-colored ropes around his face, which was still an endearing face, fine-featured, the eyes an unusual aqua blue. But his cheeks, of course, were no longer round, and a sharp new Adam's apple jogged in his throat when he talked. **A**

In October, they called from the private school he attended to request a conference with his parents. Daisy went alone; her husband was at work. Clutching her purse, she sat on the principal's couch and learned that Donny was noisy, lazy, and disruptive, always fooling around with his friends, and he wouldn't respond in class.

In the past, before her children were born, Daisy had been a fourth-grade teacher. It shamed her now to sit before this principal as a parent, a delinquent

A **Literary Focus** **Characterization** What do you learn about this character from Tyler's description of him in the first paragraph?

parent, a parent who struck Mr. Lanham, no doubt, as unseeing or uncaring. "It isn't that we're not concerned," she said. "Both of us are. And we've done what we could, whatever we could think of. We don't let him watch TV on school nights. We don't let him talk on the phone till he's finished his homework. But he tells us he doesn't *have* any homework or he did it all in study hall. How are we to know what to believe?"

From early October through November, at Mr. Lanham's suggestion, Daisy checked Donny's assignments every day. She sat next to him as he worked, trying to be encouraging, sagging inwardly as she saw the poor quality of everything he did—the sloppy mistakes in math, the illogical leaps in his English themes, the history questions left blank if they required any research.

Daisy was often late starting supper, and she couldn't give as much attention to Donny's younger sister. "You'll never guess what happened at . . ." Amanda would begin, and Daisy would have to tell her, "Not now, honey."

By the time her husband Matt came home, she'd be snappish. She would recite the day's hardships—the fuzzy instructions in English, the botched history map, the morass of unsolvable algebra equations. Matt would look surprised and confused, and Daisy would gradually wind down. There was no way, really, to convey how exhausting all this was. **B**

In December, the school called again. This time, they wanted Matt to come as well. She and Matt had to sit on Mr. Lanham's couch like two bad children and listen to the news: Donny had improved only slightly, raising a D in history to a C, and a C in algebra to a B-minus. What was worse, he had developed new problems. He had cut classes on at least three occasions. Smoked in the furnace room. Helped Sonny Barnett break into a freshman's locker. And last week, during athletics, he and three friends had been seen off the school grounds; when they returned, the coach had smelled beer on their breath.

Daisy and Matt sat silent, shocked. Matt rubbed his forehead with his fingertips. Imagine, Daisy thought, how they must look to Mr. Lanham: an overweight housewife in a cotton dress and a too-tall, too-thin insurance agent in a baggy, frayed suit. Failures, both of them—the kind of people who are always hurrying to catch up, missing the point of things that everyone else grasps at once. She wished she'd worn nylons instead of knee socks. **C**

It was arranged that Donny would visit a psychologist for testing. Mr. Lanham knew just the person. He would set this boy straight, he said.

When they stood to leave, Daisy held her stomach in and gave Mr. Lanham a firm, responsible handshake.

Donny said the psychologist was a jackass and the tests were really dumb; but he kept all three of his appointments, and when it was time for the follow-up conference with the psychologist and both parents, Donny combed his hair and seemed unusually sober and subdued. The psychologist said Donny had no serious emotional problems. He was merely going through a difficult period in his life. He required some academic help and a better sense of self-worth. For this reason, he was suggesting a man named Calvin Beadle, a tutor with considerable psychological training.

In the car going home, Donny said he'd be damned if he'd let them drag him to some stupid dork tutor. His father told him to watch his language in front of his mother.

That night, Daisy lay awake pondering the term "self-worth." She had always been free with her praise. She had always told Donny he had talent, was smart, was good with his hands. She had made a big to-do over every little gift he gave her. In fact, maybe she had gone too far, although, Lord knows, she had meant every word. Was that his trouble?

She remembered when Amanda was born. Donny had acted lost and bewildered. Daisy had been alert to that, of course, but still, a new baby keeps you so

---

B Literary Focus **Characterization** What details does Tyler use to describe Daisy?

C Literary Focus **Characterization** Daisy often imagines how she and her husband appear to the principal. What does that tell you about Daisy?

Vocabulary **morass** (muh RAS) *n.*: any confusing or troublesome situation; entanglement.

busy. Had she really done all she could have? She longed—she ached—for a time machine. Given one more chance, she'd do it perfectly—hug him more, praise him more, or perhaps praise him less. Oh, who can say . . .

The tutor told Donny to call him Cal. All his kids did he said. Daisy thought for a second that he meant his own children, then realized her mistake. He seemed too young, anyhow, to be a family man. He wore a heavy brown handlebar mustache. His hair was as long and stringy as Donny's, and his jeans as faded. Wire-rimmed spectacles slid down his nose. He lounged in a canvas director's chair with his fingers laced across his chest, and he casually, amiably questioned Donny, who sat upright and glaring in an armchair.

"So they're getting on your back at school," said Cal. "Making a big deal about anything you do wrong."

"Right," said Donny.

"Any idea why that would be?"

"Oh, well, you know, stuff like homework and all," Donny said.

"You don't do your homework?"

"Oh, well, I might do it sometimes but not just exactly like they want it." Donny sat forward and said, "It's like a prison there, you know? You've got to go to every class, you can never step off the school grounds."

"You cut classes sometimes?"

"Sometimes," Donny said, with a glance at his parents.

Cal didn't seem perturbed. "Well," he said, "I'll tell you what. Let's you and me try working together three nights a week. Think you could handle that? We'll see if we can show that school of yours a thing or two. Give it a month; then if you don't like it, we'll stop. If *I* don't like it, we'll stop. I mean, sometimes people just don't get along, right? What do you say to that?"

"Okay," Donny said. He seemed pleased. **D** **E**

"Make it seven o'clock till eight, Monday, Wednesday, and Friday," Cal told Matt and Daisy. They nodded. Cal shambled to his feet, gave them a little salute, and showed them to the door.

This was where he lived as well as worked, evidently. The interview had taken place in the dining room, which had been transformed into a kind of office. Passing the living room, Daisy winced at the rock music she had been hearing, without registering it, ever since she had entered the house. She looked in and saw a boy about Donny's age lying on a sofa with a book. Another boy and a girl were playing Ping-Pong in front of the fireplace. "You have several here together?" Daisy asked Cal.

"Oh, sometimes they stay on after their sessions, just to rap. They're a pretty sociable group, all in all. Plenty of goof-offs like young Donny here."

He cuffed Donny's shoulder playfully. Donny flushed and grinned.

Climbing into the car, Daisy asked Donny, "Well? What did you think?"

But Donny had returned to his old evasive self. He jerked his chin toward the garage. "Look," he said. "He's got a basketball net."

Now on Mondays, Wednesdays, and Fridays, they had supper early—the instant Matt came home. Sometimes, they had to leave before they were really finished. Amanda would still be eating her dessert. "Bye, honey. Sorry," Daisy would tell her.

Cal's first bill sent a flutter of panic through Daisy's chest, but it was worth it, of course. Just look at Donny's face when they picked him up: alight and full of interest. The principal telephoned Daisy to tell her how Donny had improved. "Of course, it hasn't shown up in his grades yet, but several of the teachers have noticed how his attitude's changed. Yes sir, I think we're onto something here."

At home, Donny didn't act much different. He still seemed to have a low opinion of his parents. But Daisy supposed that was unavoidable—part of being fifteen. He said his parents were too "controlling"—a

---

D **Literary Focus** **Characterization** What do you learn about Cal from his appearance and the way he speaks to Donny?

E **Reading Focus** **Making Predictions** What effect do you think Cal will have on Donny, if any?

Vocabulary **amiably** (AY mee uh blee) *adv.:* in a friendly, agreeable way.
perturbed (puhr TURBD) *v.* used as *adj.:* uneasy; anxious; ill at ease.
shambled (SHAM buhld) *v.:* proceeded awkwardly; shuffled.
evasive (ih VAY sihv) *adj.:* tending or seeking to evade.

word that made Daisy give him a sudden look. He said they acted like wardens. On weekends, they enforced a curfew. And any time he went to a party, they always telephoned first to see if adults would be supervising. "For God's sake!" he said. "Don't you trust me?" **F**

"It isn't a matter of trust, honey . . ." But there was no explaining to him.

His tutor called one afternoon. "I get the sense," he said, "that this kid's feeling . . . underestimated, you know? Like you folks expect the worst of him. I'm thinking we ought to give him more rope."

"But see, he's still so suggestible," Daisy said. "When his friends suggest some mischief—smoking or drinking or such—why, he just finds it very hard not to go along with them."

"Mrs. Coble," the tutor said, "I think this kid is hurting. You know? Here's a serious, sensitive kid, telling you he'd like to take on some grown-up challenges, and you're giving him the message that he can't be trusted. Don't you understand how that hurts?"

"Oh," said Daisy.

"It undermines his self-esteem—don't you realize that?"

"Well, I guess you're right," said Daisy. She saw Donny suddenly from a whole new angle: his pathetically poor posture, that slouch so forlorn that his shoulders seemed about to meet his chin . . . oh, wasn't it awful being young? She'd had a miserable adolescence herself and had always sworn no child of hers would ever be that unhappy.

They let Donny stay out later, they didn't call ahead to see if the parties were supervised, and they were careful not to grill him about his evening. The tutor had set down so many rules! They were not allowed any questions at all about any aspect of school, nor were they to speak with his teachers. If a teacher had some complaint, she should phone Cal. Only one

teacher disobeyed—the history teacher, Miss Evans. She called one morning in February. "I'm a little concerned about Donny, Mrs. Coble."

"Oh, I'm sorry, Miss Evans, but Donny's tutor handles these things now . . ."

"I always deal directly with the parents. You are the parent," Miss Evans said, speaking very slowly and distinctly. "Now, here is the problem. Back when you were helping Donny with his homework, his grades rose from a D to a C, but now they've slipped back, and they're closer to an F."

"They are?"

"I think you should start overseeing his homework again."

"But Donny's tutor says . . ."

"It's nice that Donny has a tutor, but you should still be in charge of his homework. With you, he learned it. Then he passed his tests. With the tutor, well, it seems the tutor is more of a crutch. 'Donny,' I say, 'a quiz is coming up on Friday. Hadn't you better be listening instead of talking?' 'That's okay, Miss Evans,' he says. 'I have a tutor now.' Like a talisman!¹ I really think you ought to take over, Mrs. Coble." **G**

"I see," said Daisy. "Well, I'll think about that. Thank you for calling."

Hanging up, she felt a rush of anger at Donny. A talisman! For a talisman, she'd given up all luxuries, all that time with her daughter, her evenings at home!

She dialed Cal's number. He sounded muzzy. "I'm sorry if I woke you," she told him, "but Donny's history teacher just called. She says he isn't doing well."

"She should have dealt with me."

"She wants me to start supervising his homework again. His grades are slipping."

"Yes," said the tutor, "but you and I both know there's more to it than mere grades, don't we? I care

---

1. **talisman:** charm thought to have magical powers.

> "YOU CUT CLASSES SOMETIMES?"
>
> "SOMETIMES," DONNY SAID, WITH A GLANCE AT HIS PARENTS.

F **Literary Focus** **Characterization** Why does Donny have problems with authority figures in his life? Why does he respond well to Cal, but not to other adults?

G **Reading Focus** **Making Predictions** How do you think Donny will respond to his mother's supervision of his homework?

Vocabulary **forlorn** (fawr LAWRN) *adj.*: lonely and sad; forsaken.

about the *whole* child—his happiness, his self-esteem. The grades will come. Just give them time."

When she hung up, it was Miss Evans she was angry at. What a narrow woman!

It was Cal this, Cal that, Cal says this, Cal and I did that. Cal lent Donny an album by the Who. He took Donny and two other pupils to a rock concert. In March, when Donny began to talk endlessly on the phone with a girl named Miriam, Cal even let Miriam come to one of the tutoring sessions. Daisy was touched that Cal would grow so involved in Donny's life, but she was also a little hurt, because she had offered to have Miriam to dinner and Donny had refused. Now he asked her to drive them to Cal's house without a qualm.[2] **H**

This Miriam was an unappealing girl with blurry lipstick and masses of rough red hair. She wore a short, bulky jacket that would not have been out of place on a motorcycle. During the trip to Cal's she was silent, but coming back, she was more talkative. "What a neat guy, and what a house! All those kids hanging out, like a club. And the stereo playing rock . . . gosh, he's not like a grown-up at all! Married and divorced and everything, but you'd think he was our own age."

"Mr. Beadle was married?" Daisy asked.

"Yeah, to this really controlling lady. She didn't understand him a bit."

"No, I guess not," Daisy said. **I**

Spring came, and the students who hung around at Cal's drifted out to the basketball net above the garage. Sometimes, when Daisy and Matt arrived to pick up Donny, they'd find him there with the others—spiky and excited, jittering on his toes beneath the backboard. It was staying light much longer now, and the neighboring fence cast narrow bars across the bright grass. Loud music would be spilling from Cal's windows. Once it was the Who, which Daisy recognized from the time that Donny had borrowed

the album. "*Teenage Wasteland*,"[3] she said aloud, identifying the song, and Matt gave a short, dry laugh. "It certainly is," he said. He'd misunderstood; he thought she was commenting on the scene spread before them. In fact, she might have been. The players looked like hoodlums, even her son. Why, one of Cal's students had recently been knifed in a tavern. One had been shipped off to boarding school in midterm; two had been withdrawn by their parents. On the other hand, Donny had mentioned someone who'd been studying with Cal for five years. "Five years!" said Daisy. "Doesn't anyone ever stop needing him?"

Donny looked at her. Lately, whatever she said about Cal was read as criticism. "You're just feeling competitive," he said. "And controlling."

She bit her lip and said no more.

In April, the principal called to tell her that Donny had been expelled. There had been a locker check, and in Donny's locker they found five cans of beer and half a pack of cigarettes. With Donny's previous record, this offense meant expulsion. **J**

Daisy gripped the receiver tightly and said, "Well, where is he now?"

"We've sent him home," said Mr. Lanham. "He's packed up all his belongings, and he's coming home on foot."

Daisy wondered what she would say to him. She felt him looming closer and closer, bringing this brand-new situation that no one had prepared her to handle. What other place would take him? Could they enter him in a public school? What were the rules? She stood at the living room window, waiting for him to show up. Gradually, she realized that he was taking too long. She checked the clock. She stared up the street again. **K**

---

3. **"*Teenage Wasteland*"**: words repeated in the song "Baba O'Riley" from a 1971 album by the British rock group The Who. The song is often referred to as "Teenage Wasteland."

---

2. **qualm:** uneasy feeling; doubt.

H **Literary Focus** Characterization Donny's attitude with Cal and at school is different from his attitude at home with his parents. What does that reveal about Donny's character and the conflicts that he faces?

I **Literary Focus** Characterization What does Miriam's description of Cal reveal about him?

J **Reading Focus** Making Predictions How do you think Donny, his parents, and Cal will react to Donny's expulsion from school? How might Donny's situation be resolved?

K **Literary Focus** Characterization Daisy repeatedly appeals to "the rules." What does her reliance on the rules tell you about her personality?

When an hour had passed, she phoned the school. Mr. Lanham's secretary answered and told her in a grave, sympathetic voice that yes, Donny Coble had most definitely gone home. Daisy called her husband. He was out of the office. She went back to the window and thought a while, and then she called Donny's tutor.

"Donny's been expelled from school," she said, "and now I don't know where he's gone. I wonder if you've heard from him?"

There was a long silence. "Donny's with me, Mrs. Coble," he finally said.

"With you? How'd he get there?"

"He hailed a cab, and I paid the driver."

"Could I speak to him, please?"

There was another silence. "Maybe it'd be better if we had a conference," Cal said.

"I don't *want* a conference. I've been standing at the window picturing him dead or kidnapped or something, and now you tell me you want a—"

"Donny is very, very upset. Understandably so," said Cal. "Believe me, Mrs. Coble, this is not what it seems. Have you asked Donny's side of the story?"

"Well, of course not, how could I? He went running off to you instead."

"Because he didn't feel he'd be listened to."

"But I haven't even—"

"Why don't you come out and talk? The three of us," said Cal, "will try to get this thing in perspective."

"Well, all right," Daisy said. But she wasn't as reluctant as she sounded. Already she felt soothed by the calm way Cal was taking this.

Cal answered the doorbell at once. He said, "Hi, there," and led her into the dining room. Donny sat slumped in a chair, chewing the knuckle of one thumb. "Hello, Donny," Daisy said. He flicked his eyes in her direction.

"Sit here, Mrs. Coble," said Cal, placing her opposite Donny. He himself remained standing, restlessly pacing. "So," he said.

Daisy stole a look at Donny. His lips were swollen, as if he'd been crying.

"You know," Cal told Daisy, "I kind of expected something like this. That's a very punitive[4] school you've got him in—you realize that. And any half-

Woman with a Newspaper by Richard Diebenkorn (1922–1993).
© Estate of Richard Diebenkorn.

decent lawyer will tell you they've violated his civil rights. Locker checks! Where's their search warrant?"

"But if the rule is—" Daisy said.

"Well, anyhow, let him tell you his side."

She looked at Donny. He said, "It wasn't my fault. I promise."

"They said your locker was full of beer."

"It was a put-up job! See, there's this guy that doesn't like me. He put all these beers in my locker and started a rumor going, so Mr. Lanham ordered a locker check."

"What was the boy's name?" Daisy asked.

"Huh?"

"Mrs. Coble, take my word, the situation is not so unusual," Cal said. "You can't imagine how vindictive[5] kids can be sometimes."

4. **punitive:** focused on punishment.

5. **vindictive:** looking for revenge.

"What was the boy's *name*," said Daisy, "so that I can ask Mr. Lanham if that's who suggested he run a locker check."

"You don't believe me," Donny said.

"And how'd this boy get your combination in the first place?"

"Frankly," said Cal, "I wouldn't be surprised to learn the school was in on it. Any kid that marches to a different drummer,[6] why, they'd just love an excuse to get rid of him. The school is where I lay the blame."

"Doesn't *Donny* ever get blamed?"

"Now, Mrs. Coble, you heard what he—"

"Forget it," Donny told Cal. "You can see she doesn't trust me."

Daisy drew in a breath to say that of course she trusted him—a reflex. But she knew that bold-faced, wide-eyed look of Donny's. He had worn that look when he was small, denying some petty misdeed with the evidence plain as day all around him. Still, it was hard for her to accuse him outright. She temporized[7] and said, "The only thing I'm sure of is that they've kicked you out of school, and now I don't know what we're going to do."

"We'll fight it," said Cal.

"We can't. Even you must see we can't."

"I could apply to Brantly," Donny said.

Cal stopped his pacing to beam down at him. "Brantly! Yes. They're really onto where a kid is coming from, at Brantly. Why, *I* could get you into Brantly. I work with a lot of their students."

Daisy had never heard of Brantly, but already she didn't like it. And she didn't like Cal's smile, which struck her now as feverish and avid[8]—a smile of hunger.

On the fifteenth of April, they entered Donny in a public school, and they stopped his tutoring sessions.

Donny fought both decisions bitterly. Cal, surprisingly enough, did not object. He admitted he'd made no headway with Donny and said it was because Donny was emotionally disturbed. **(L)**

Donny went to his new school every morning, plodding off alone with his head down. He did his assignments, and he earned average grades, but he gathered no friends, joined no clubs. There was something exhausted and defeated about him.

The first week in June, during final exams, Donny vanished. He simply didn't come home one afternoon, and no one at school remembered seeing him. The police were reassuring, and for the first few days, they worked hard. They combed Donny's sad, messy room for clues; they visited Miriam and Cal. But then they started talking about the number of kids who ran away every year. Hundreds, just in this city. "He'll show up, if he wants to," they said. "If he doesn't, he won't."

Evidently, Donny didn't want to.

It's been three months now and still no word. Matt and Daisy still look for him in every crowd of awkward, heartbreaking teenage boys. Every time the phone rings, they imagine it might be Donny. Both parents have aged. Donny's sister seems to be staying away from home as much as possible.

At night, Daisy lies awake and goes over Donny's life. She is trying to figure out what went wrong, where they made their first mistake. Often, she finds herself blaming Cal, although she knows he didn't begin it. Then at other times she excuses him, for without him, Donny might have left earlier. Who really knows? In the end, she can only sigh and search for a cooler spot on the pillow. As she falls asleep, she occasionally glimpses something in the corner of her vision. It's something fleet[9] and round, a ball—a basketball. It flies up, it sinks through the hoop, descends, lands in a yard littered with last year's leaves and striped with bars of sunlight as white as bones, bleached and parched and cleanly picked. **(M)**

---

6. **different drummer:** reference to a passage from Henry David Thoreau's *Walden*: "If a man does not keep pace with his companions, perhaps it is because he hears a different drummer. Let him step to the music which he hears, however measured or far away."

7. **temporized:** evaded making a decision in order to buy time.

8. **avid:** greedy; having an intense desire for something.

9. **fleet:** swift; fast.

(L) Literary Focus Characterization What does the description of Cal's smile reveal about him? Why do Donny's parents take him out of therapy?

(M) Reading Focus Making Predictions What do you think will happen to Donny and his family in the future? Do you think his parents understand him better than they did earlier?

SKILLS FOCUS Literary Skills Analyze characterization; analyze static and dynamic characters. **Reading Skills** Make predictions as a strategy for comprehension. **Vocabulary Skills** Demonstrate knowledge of literal meanings of words and their usage. **Writing Skills** Employ elements of an author's style effectively.

Respond and Think Critically

Reading Focus

Quick Check

1. Describe the problem that exists in the Coble family at the start of the story.

2. Why is Donny expelled from school?

3. What effect does Donny's running away have on the rest of the family?

Read with a Purpose

4. How do the value systems of Donny and his parents differ? What conflicts result?

Reading Skills: Making Predictions

5. As you read, you recorded predictions about what would happen in the story. Add another column to your chart and record what actually happens. Were your predictions correct?

Event	Prediction	What Actually Happens
Donny meets Cal.	Donny will dislike Cal.	Donny likes Cal.

✓ Vocabulary Quick Check

Be sure you can justify your response to each question about the Vocabulary words below.

6. How does someone act who is **evasive**?

7. How quickly would you move if you **shambled** to your next class?

8. Your room is a **morass**. How can you change it?

9. How would you describe a **forlorn** expression?

10. What kind of person would talk **amiably** with you?

11. How might you respond if a friend is **perturbed**?

Literary Focus

Literary Analysis

12. **Make Judgments** Why do you think Donny leaves home?

13. **Interpret** At the end of the story, Daisy visualizes a basketball going through a hoop. What might this image symbolize for her?

Literary Skills: Characterization

14. **Analyze** What do Cal's interactions with Donny and the other teenagers suggest about his character? Does he truly care about them?

Literary Skills Review: Static and Dynamic Characters

15. **Compare and Contrast** In literature, **static** characters are characters that remain the same throughout the story, while **dynamic** characters go through important changes. Which main characters in this story are static, and which are dynamic? How do the dynamic characters change?

Writing Focus

Think as a Reader/Writer

Use It in Your Writing Choose a descriptive paragraph from your *Reader/Writer Notebook* to revise. Use a dash effectively in at least three sentences to indicate either a shift in thought or a continuation or clarification of thought. Share your paragraph with a classmate.

What Do **You Think Now** What needs does Donny have? What does Donny's family desire for him? How do these needs and desires clash?

Daughter of Invention

What human needs and desires do we have in common?

⏱ **QuickWrite**

Write a few lines about a misunderstanding between two family members or two friends.

Julia Alvarez
(1950–   )

"All my childhood I had dressed like an American, eaten American foods, and befriended American children. I had gone to an American school and spent most of the day speaking and reading English. . . . All my childhood I had longed for this moment of arrival. And here I was, an American girl, coming home at last."

With these words, Julia (pronounced HOO lee uh) Alvarez describes stepping back into America.

Politics Becomes Prose

Although born in New York City, Alvarez spent her early childhood in the Dominican Republic. In 1960, just before her father was to be arrested for his involvement in a secret plot to overthrow the dictator Rafael Trujillo Molina, Alvarez and her family were tipped off by an American agent and escaped to the United States.

Paradoxically, her homecoming was filled with the difficulties of adjusting to a brand-new life. Learning contemporary American English was only one part of the adjustment. Alvarez also had to learn to compromise in order to resolve conflicts between American customs and her parents' more traditional views. This theme is at the heart of her fiction—particularly her short stories and her best-known work, the novel *How the Garcia Girls Lost Their Accents* (1991).

This novel, a series of fifteen interlocking stories, tells how the Garcia family, with its four daughters, struggles to overcome a variety of cultural and generational conflicts. Comparisons with Alvarez's own family make it clear that the novel is highly autobiographical. Alvarez's 1994 novel, *In the Time of the Butterflies,* is a fictionalized account of the lives and deaths of three sisters, Patria, Minerva, and Maria Teresa Mirabal, the wives of political prisoners in the Dominican Republic. In 1960, shortly after visiting their husbands in jail, the real-life women were murdered by thugs connected to the Trujillo regime. Alvarez's 1997 novel *¡Yo!* is populated with some of the *Garcia Girls* characters. Alvarez has clearly forged, out of memory and imagination, a novelist's sensibility.

Think About the Writer How has Alvarez reconciled her American upbringing and her Dominican background? How does she explore this theme in her writing?

 **Reader/Writer**
Notebook
Use your **RWN** to complete the activities for this selection.

Literary Focus

Conflict One important <u>component</u> of literature is **conflict;** without conflict, there would not be much of a story. "Daughter of Invention" derives its strength and much of its fun from the clash between the traditional values of Latin American parents and the liberal values of their New York–raised daughter. Each major character experiences both **external conflicts** (clashes with other people, a government, or society in general) and **internal conflicts** (problems that exist within his or her own mind).

Reading Focus

Making Inferences About Characters As a skilled reader, you will want to go beneath the surface of a story and understand why characters think and act as they do. In other words, you will make **inferences,** or educated guesses, about the <u>potential</u> behavior of the characters, based both on clues provided in the story and on your own experience with people.

Into Action Pick one character from the story, and using a web like the one below, record actions, likes, dislikes, and other characteristics that reveal this character's unique personality, including his or her responses to internal and external conflict.

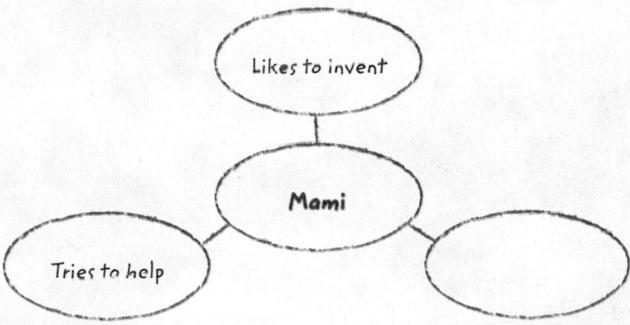

Vocabulary

disembodied (dihs ehm BAHD eed) *adj.:* freed from the body. *Her father's glasses watched the household like a disembodied guard.*

labyrinth (LAB uh rihnth) *n.:* maze; bewildering complex. *The narrator explored the labyrinth of her feelings through her writing.*

communal (kah MYOO nuhl) *adj.:* used or shared by everyone in a group. *Writing the speech became a communal experience.*

eulogy (YOO luh jee) *n.:* speech expressing high praise or commendation. *She had to write a eulogy praising the nuns.*

noncommittal (nahn kuh MIHT uhl) *adj.:* not committing oneself to a particular view or course of action. *Instead of being noncommittal, the narrator's first speech had a strong point of view .*

florid (FLAWR ihd) *adj.:* flowery; excessively ornate; showy. *His children had trouble understanding their father's florid diction.*

Language Coach

Antonyms You can remember some words' meanings by thinking about their opposites, or antonyms. One antonym for *florid* is *concise*. If florid writing is painfully excessive, concise writing is pleasingly brief. Another antonym for florid is *colorless*. Colorless writing is just as painful to read as florid writing, but for the opposite reason.

Writing Focus

Think as a Reader/Writer
Find It in Your Reading As you read, notice how Alvarez uses **humor** to guide our response to each of the characters. Use your *Reader/Writer Notebook* to record lines or events from the story that you find humorous. What makes something <u>intrinsically</u> funny? Is it the situation? the language? the characterization? Think about what makes each example you record humorous.

 Learn It Online
Learn more about Alvarez's life at the Writers' Lives site online.

go.hrw.com | L11-1225 | **Go**

Daughter of Invention

by **Julia Alvarez**

Read with a Purpose
Read to explore the differences between the cultural values of the narrator and those of her Dominican parents.

Build Background
From 1930 to 1961, the Dominican Republic was ruled by the dictator Rafael Trujillo, who murdered thousands of Haitian and Dominican civilians. Under his rule, freedom and basic rights were nearly nonexistent, and people lived in constant fear. One of the contemptuous nicknames given to him was "Chapita," which means "bottle cap." This was a reference to his interest in collecting bottle caps when he was a child. He was assassinated in May 1961, and the Dominican Republic has since moved toward a representative democracy.

Perfume (2001) (detail) by Graciela Genoves.

She wanted to invent something, my mother. There was a period after we arrived in this country, until five or so years later, when my mother was inventing. They were never pressing, global needs she was addressing with her pencil and pad. She would have said that was for men to do, rockets and engines that ran on gasoline and turned the wheels of the world. She was just fussing with little house things, don't mind her. Ⓐ

She always invented at night, after settling her house down. On his side of the bed my father would be conked out for an hour already, his Spanish newspaper draped over his chest, his glasses, propped up on his bedside table, looking out eerily at the darkened room like a disembodied guard. But in her lighted corner, like some devoted scholar burning the midnight oil, my mother was inventing, sheets pulled to her lap, pillows propped up behind her, her reading glasses riding the bridge of her nose like a schoolmarm's. On her lap lay one of those innumerable pads of paper my father always brought home from his office, compliments of some pharmaceutical company, advertising tranquilizers or antibiotics or skin cream; in her other hand, my mother held a pencil that looked like a pen with a little cylinder of lead inside. She would work on a sketch of something familiar, but drawn at such close range so she could attach a special nozzle or handier handle, the thing looked peculiar. Once, I mistook the spiral of a corkscrew for a nautilus shell, but it could just as well have been a galaxy forming. Ⓑ

It was the only time all day we'd catch her sitting down, for she herself was living proof of the *perpetuum mobile*[1] machine so many inventors had sought over the ages. My sisters and I would seek her out now when she seemed to have a moment to talk to us: We were having trouble at school or we wanted her to persuade my father to give us permission to go into the city or to a shopping mall or a movie—in broad daylight! My mother would wave us out of her room. "The problem with you girls . . ." I can tell you right now what the problem always boiled down to: We wanted to become Americans and my father—and my mother, at first—would have none of it. Ⓒ

"You girls are going to drive me crazy!" She always threatened if we kept nagging. "When I end up in Bellevue,[2] you'll be safely sorry!"

She spoke in English when she argued with us, even though, in a matter of months, her daughters were the fluent ones. Her English was much better than my father's, but it was still a mishmash of mixed-up idioms and sayings that showed she was "green behind the ears," as she called it.

If my sisters and I tried to get her to talk in Spanish, she'd snap, "When in Rome, do unto the Romans . . ."

I had become the spokesman for my sisters, and I would stand my ground in that bedroom. "We're not going to that school anymore, Mami!"

"You have to." Her eyes would widen with worry. "In this country, it is against the law not to go to school. You want us to get thrown out?"

"You want us to get killed? Those kids were throwing stones today!"

"Sticks and stones don't break bones . . ." she chanted. I could tell, though, by the look on her face, it was as if one of those stones the kids had aimed at us had hit her. But she always pretended we were at fault. "What did you do to provoke them? It takes two to tangle, you know." Ⓓ

"Thanks, thanks a lot, Mom!" I'd storm out of that room and into mine. I never called her *Mom* except when I wanted her to feel how much she had failed us in this country. She was a good enough Mami, fussing

---

1. *perpetuum mobile*: Latin for "perpetual motion."

2. **Bellevue:** large New York City hospital known for its psychiatric department.

Ⓐ **Reading Focus** Making Inferences About Characters
What inferences can you make about the mother from this paragraph?

Ⓑ **Reading Focus** Making Inferences About Characters
How would you characterize the narrator's attitude toward her mother in the two opening paragraphs? Explain your response.

Ⓒ **Literary Focus** Conflict What causes conflict to arise between the daughters and their parents?

Ⓓ **Literary Focus** Conflict How does the mother react to her daughters' conflict? Why do you think she reacts this way?

Vocabulary disembodied (dihs ehm BAHD eed) *adj.:* freed from the body.

Technology Link: Female American Inventors

Hedy Lamarr, a movie star from Hollywood's golden age, was also an inventor.

The narrator's mother in "Daughter of Invention" is one in a long list of female inventors in America. Since 1793, U.S. patents have been granted for inventions created by women, ranging from the brown paper bag, the modern coffeepot, and the disposable diaper to the first computer program, cancer treatments, and construction methods for dams and reservoirs. Even glamorous female film stars got the itch to create inventions. Hedy Lamarr, a mid-twentieth-century movie star, helped the U.S. and its allies defeat Germany. With composer George Antheil, she invented a secret communication system that manipulated radio frequencies so top-secret messages could not be intercepted by enemy forces. Thousands have escaped death by wearing bulletproof vests made with Kevlar. They owe their lives to Stephanie Kwolek, who invented the synthetic fiber with five times the strength of steel, patenting it in 1966. A research scientist, Kwolek obtained 28 patents over her 40-year career and was inducted into the National Inventors Hall of Fame in 1995.

Ask Yourself

Why do you think the mother in Alvarez's story doesn't try to patent her inventions? What does it mean to be an "American" inventor? Use evidence from the story to support your answer.

and scolding and giving advice, but a terrible girl-friend parent, a real failure of a Mom.

Back she'd go to her pencil and pad, scribbling and tsking and tearing off paper, finally giving up, and taking up her *New York Times*. Some nights, though, she'd get a good idea, and she'd rush into my room, a flushed look on her face, her tablet of paper in her hand, a cursory knock on the door she'd just thrown open: "Do I have something to show you, Cukita!"

This was my time to myself, after I'd finished my homework, while my sisters were still downstairs watching TV in the basement. Hunched over my small desk, the overhead light turned off, my lamp shining poignantly on my paper, the rest of the room in warm,

soft, uncreated darkness, I wrote my secret poems in my new language.

"You're going to ruin your eyes!" My mother would storm into my room, turning on the overly bright overhead light, scaring off whatever shy passion I had just begun coaxing out of a labyrinth of feelings with the blue thread of my writing.

"Oh Mami!" I'd cry out, my eyes blinking up at her. "I'm writing." **E**

"Ay, Cukita." That was her communal pet name for whoever was in her favor. "Cukita, when I make a million, I'll buy you your very own typewriter." (I'd been nagging my mother for one just like the one father had bought her to do his order forms at home.) "Gravy on

---

Vocabulary **labyrinth** (LAB uh rihnth) *n.:* maze; bewildering complex.
communal (kah MYOO nuhl) *adj.:* used or shared by everyone in a group.

E **Reading Focus** Making Inferences About Characters
How would you describe the narrator?

the turkey" was what she called it when someone was buttering her up. She'd butter and pour. "I'll hire you your very own typist."

Down she'd plop on my bed and hold out her pad to me. "Take a guess, Cukita?" I'd study her rough sketch a moment: soap sprayed from the nozzle head of a shower when you turned the knob a certain way? Coffee with creamer already mixed in? Time-released water capsules for your plants when you were away? A key chain with a timer that would go off when your parking meter was about to expire? (The ticking would help you find your keys easily if you mislaid them.) The famous one, famous only in hindsight, was the stick person dragging a square by a rope—a suitcase with wheels? "Oh, of course," we'd humor her. "What every household needs: a shower like a car wash, keys ticking like a bomb, luggage on a leash!" By now, as you can see, it'd become something of a family joke, our Thomas Edison Mami, our Benjamin Franklin Mom.

Her face would fall. "Come on now! Use your head." One more wrong guess, and she'd tell me, pressing with her pencil point the different highlights of this incredible new wonder. "Remember that time we took the car to Bear Mountain, and we re-ah-lized that we had forgotten to pack an opener with our pick-a-nick?" (We kept correcting her, but she insisted this is how it should be said.) "When we were ready to eat we didn't have any way to open the refreshments cans?" (This before flip top lids, which she claimed had crossed her mind.) "You know what this is now?" A shake of my head. "Is a car bumper, but see this part is a removable can opener. So simple and yet so necessary, no?" **F**

"Yeah, Mami. You should patent it." I'd shrug. She'd tear off the scratch paper and fold it, carefully, corner to corner, as if she were going to save it. But then, she'd toss it in the wastebasket on her way out of the room and give a little laugh like a disclaimer.[3] "It's half of one or two dozen of another . . ."

I suppose none of her daughters was very encouraging. We resented her spending time on those dumb inventions. Here, we were trying to fit in America

among Americans; we needed help figuring out who we were, why these Irish kids whose grandparents were micks two generations ago, why they were calling us spics. Why had we come to the country in the first place? Important, crucial, final things, you see, and here was our own mother, who didn't have a second to help us puzzle any of this out, inventing gadgets to make life easier for American moms. Why, it seemed as if she were arming our own enemy against us! **G**

One time, she did have a moment of triumph. Every night, she liked to read *The New York Times* in bed before turning off her light, to see what the Americans were up to. One night, she let out a yelp to wake up my father beside her, bolt upright, reaching for his glasses which, in his haste, he knocked across the room. "Que pasa? Que pasa?"[4] What is wrong? There was terror in his voice, fear she'd seen in his eyes in the Dominican Republic before we left. We were being watched there; he was being followed; he and mother had often exchanged those looks. They could not talk, of course, though they must have whispered to each other in fear at night in the dark bed. Now in America, he was safe, a success even; his Centro Medico in Brooklyn was thronged with the sick and the homesick. But in dreams, he went back to those awful days and long nights, and my mother's screams confirmed his secret fear: We had not gotten away after all; they had come for us at last.

"Ay, Papi, I'm sorry. Go back to sleep, Cukito. It's nothing, nothing really." My mother held up the *Times* for him to squint at the small print, back page headline, one hand tapping all over the top of the bedside table for his glasses, the other rubbing his eyes to wakefulness.

"Remember, remember how I showed you that suitcase with little wheels so we would not have to carry those heavy bags when we traveled? Someone stole my idea and made a million!" She shook the paper in his face. She shook the paper in all our faces that night. "See! See! This man was no bobo![5]

---

3. **disclaimer:** refusal to accept responsibility; denial.

4. **Que pasa?:** Spanish for "What's going on?"
5. **bobo:** Spanish for "fool."

F Reading Focus **Making Inferences About Characters** Why does the narrator's mother throw her ideas for inventions into the wastebasket?

G Literary Focus **Conflict** Why do the daughters resent Mami's inventions?

He didn't put all his pokers on a back burner. I kept telling you, one of these days my ship would pass me by in the night!" She wagged her finger at my sisters and my father and me, laughing all the while, one of those eerie laughs crazy people in movies laugh. We had congregated in her room to hear the good news she'd been yelling down the stairs, and now we eyed her and each other. I suppose we were all thinking the same thing: Wouldn't it be weird and sad if Mami did end up in Bellevue as she'd always threatened she might?

"*Ya, ya!* Enough!" She waved us out of her room at last. "There is no use trying to drink spilt milk, that's for sure."

It was the suitcase rollers that stopped my mother's hand; she had weather vaned a minor brainstorm. She would have to start taking herself seriously. That blocked the free play of her ingenuity. Besides, she had also begun working at my father's office, and at night, she was too tired and busy filling in columns with how much money they had made that day to be fooling with gadgets! **(H)**

She did take up her pencil and pad one last time to help me out. In ninth grade, I was chosen by my English teacher, Sister Mary Joseph, to deliver the teacher's day address at the school assembly. Back in the Dominican Republic, I was a terrible student. No one could ever get me to sit down to a book. But in New York, I needed to settle somewhere, and the natives were unfriendly, the country inhospitable, so I took root in the language. By high school, the nuns were reading my stories and compositions out loud to my classmates as examples of imagination at work.

This time my imagination jammed. At first I didn't want and then I couldn't seem to write that speech. I suppose I should have thought of it as a "great honor," as my father called it. But I was mortified. I still had a pronounced lilt to my accent, and I did not like to speak in public, subjecting myself to my classmates' ridicule. Recently, they had begun to

warm toward my sisters and me, and it took no great figuring to see that to deliver a eulogy for a convent full of crazy, old overweight nuns was no way to endear myself to the members of my class. **(I)**

But I didn't know how to get out of it. Week after week, I'd sit down, hoping to polish off some quick, noncommittal little speech. I couldn't get anything down.

The weekend before our Monday morning assembly I went into a panic. My mother would just have to call in and say I was in the hospital, in a coma. I was in the Dominican Republic. Yeah, that was it! Recently, my father had been talking about going back home to live.

My mother tried to calm me down. "Just remember how Mister Lincoln couldn't think of anything to say at the Gettysburg, but then, Bang! 'Four score and once upon a time ago,'" she began reciting. Her version of history was half invention and half truths and whatever else she needed to prove a point. "Something is going to come if you just relax. You'll see, like the Americans say, 'Necessity is the daughter of invention.' I'll help you."

All weekend, she kept coming into my room with help. "Please, Mami, just leave me alone, please," I pleaded with her. But I'd get rid of the goose only to have to contend with the gander. My father kept poking his head in the door just to see if I had "fulfilled my obligations," a phrase he'd used when we were a little younger, and he'd check to see whether we had gone to the bathroom before a car trip. Several times that weekend around the supper table, he'd recite his valedictorian speech from when he graduated from high school. He'd give me pointers on delivery, on the great orators and their tricks. (Humbleness and praise and falling silent with great emotion were his favorites.)

My mother sat across the table, the only one who seemed to be listening to him. My sisters and I were forgetting a lot of our Spanish, and my father's formal, florid diction was even harder to under-

---

(H) **Literary Focus** **Conflict** What is the mother's external conflict?

(I) **Literary Focus** **Conflict** What are the main causes of the narrator's internal conflict?

Vocabulary **eulogy** (YOO luh jee) *n.*: speech expressing high praise or commendation.
noncommittal (nahn kuh MIHT uhl) *adj.*: not committing oneself to a particular view or course of action.
florid (FLAWR ihd) *adj.*: flowery; excessively ornate; showy.

stand. But my mother smiled softly to herself, and turned the Lazy Susan at the center of the table around and around as if it were the prime mover,[6] the first gear of attention. **ⓙ**

That Sunday evening, I was reading some poetry to get myself inspired: Whitman in an old book with an engraved cover my father had picked up in a thrift shop next to his office a few weeks back. "I celebrate myself and sing myself . . ." "He most honors my style who learns under it to destroy the teacher." The poet's words shocked and thrilled me. I had gotten used to the nuns, a literature of appropriate sentiments, poems with a message, expurgated texts. But here was a flesh and blood man, belching and laughing and sweating in poems. "Who touches this book touches a man."

That night, at last, I started to write, recklessly, three, five pages, looking up once only to see my father passing by the hall on tiptoe. When I was done, I read over my words, and my eyes filled. I finally sounded like myself in English!

As soon as I had finished that first draft, I called my mother to my room. She listened attentively, as she had to my father's speech, and in the end, her eyes were glistening too. Her face was soft and warm and proud. "That is a beautiful, beautiful speech, Cukita. I want for your father to hear it before he goes to sleep. Then I will type it for you, all right?" **ⓚ**

Down the hall we went, the two of us, faces flushed with accomplishment. Into the master bedroom where my father was propped up on his pillows, still awake, reading the Dominican papers,

> "You'll see, like the Americans say, **'Necessity is the daughter of invention.'** I'll help you."

already days old. He had become interested in his country's fate again. The dictatorship had been toppled. The interim government was going to hold the first free elections in thirty years. There was still some question in his mind whether or not we might want to move back. History was in the making, freedom and hope were in the air again! But my mother had gotten used to the life here. She did not want to go back to the old country where she was only a wife and a mother (and a failed one at that, since she had never had the required son). She did not come straight out and disagree with my father's plans. Instead, she fussed with him about reading the papers in bed, soiling those sheets with those poorly printed, foreign tabloids. "*The Times* is not that bad!" she'd claim if my father tried to humor her by saying they shared the same dirty habit.

The minute my father saw my mother and me, filing in, he put his paper down, and his face brightened as if at long last his wife had delivered a son, and that was the news we were bringing him. His teeth were already grinning from the glass of water next to his bedside lamp, so he lisped when he said, "Eh-speech, eh-speech!"

"It is so beautiful, Papi," my mother previewed him, turning the sound off on his TV. She sat down at the foot of the bed. I stood before both of them, blocking their view of the soldiers in helicopters landing amid silenced gun reports and explosions. A few weeks ago it had been the shores of the Dominican Republic. Now it was the jungles of Southeast Asia they were saving. My mother gave me the nod to begin reading.

I didn't need much encouragement. I put my nose to the fire, as my mother would have said, and read from start to finish without looking up. When I was

---

6. **prime mover:** in philosophy, the self-moved being that is the source of all motion; in machinery, the source of power, such as a windmill or an engine.

ⓙ Reading Focus Making Inferences About Characters
How would you characterize the relationship of the family members in this scene?

ⓚ Literary Focus Conflict How does the narrator solve her problem of being unable to write a speech?

done, I was a little embarrassed at my pride in my own words. I pretended to quibble with a phrase or two I was sure I'd be talked out of changing. I looked questioningly to my mother. Her face was radiant. She turned to share her pride with my father.

But the expression on his face shocked us both. His toothless mouth had collapsed into a dark zero. His eyes glared at me, then shifted to my mother, accusingly. In barely audible Spanish, as if secret microphones or informers were all about, he whispered, "You will permit her to read *that*?"

My mother's eyebrows shot up, her mouth fell open. In the old country, any whisper of a challenge to authority could bring the secret police in their black V.W.'s. But this was America. People could say what they thought. "What is wrong with her speech?" my mother questioned him.

"What ees wrrrong with her eh-speech?" My father wagged his head at her. His anger was always more frightening in his broken English. As if he had mutilated the language in his fury—and now there was nothing to stand between us and his raw, dumb anger. "What is wrong? I will tell you what is wrong. It shows no gratitude. It is boastful. 'I celebrate myself'? 'The best student learns to destroy the teacher'?" He mocked my plagiarized words. "That is insubordinate. It is improper. It is disrespecting of her teachers—" In his anger he had forgotten his fear of lurking spies: Each wrong he voiced was a decibel higher than the last outrage. Finally, he was yelling at me, "As your father, I forbid you to say that eh-speech!" **L**

My mother leapt to her feet, a sign always that she was about to make a speech or deliver an ultimatum. She was a small woman, and she spoke all her pronouncements standing up, either for more protection or as a carry-over from her girlhood in convent schools where one asked for, and literally took, the floor in order to speak. She stood by my side, shoulder to shoulder; we looked down at my father. "That is no tone of voice, Eduardo—" she began.

By now, my father was truly furious. I suppose it was bad enough I was rebelling, but here was my mother joining forces with me. Soon he would be surrounded by a house full of independent American

women. He too leapt from his bed, throwing off his covers. The Spanish newspapers flew across the room. He snatched my speech out of my hands, held it before my panicked eyes, a vengeful, mad look in his own, and then once, twice, three, four, countless times, he tore my prize into shreds.

"Are you crazy?" My mother lunged at him. "Have you gone mad? That is her speech for tomorrow you have torn up!"

"Have *you* gone mad?" He shook her away. "You were going to let her read that . . . that insult to her teachers?"

"Insult to her teachers!" My mother's face had crumpled up like a piece of paper. On it was written a love note to my father. Ever since they had come to this country, their life together was a constant war. "This is America, Papi, America!" she reminded him now. "You are not in a savage country anymore!"

I was on my knees, weeping wildly, collecting all the little pieces of my speech, hoping that I could put it back together before the assembly tomorrow morning. But not even a sibyl[7] could have made sense of all those scattered pieces of paper. All hope was lost. "He broke it, he broke it," I moaned as I picked up a handful of pieces.

Probably, if I had thought a moment about it, I would not have done what I did next. I would have realized my father had lost brothers and comrades to the dictator Trujillo.[8] For the rest of his life, he would be haunted by blood in the streets and late night disappearances. Even after he had been in the States for years, he jumped if a black Volkswagen passed him on the street. He feared anyone in uniform: the meter maid giving out parking tickets, a museum guard approaching to tell him not to touch his favorite Goya at the Metropolitan.[9] **M**

---

7. **sibyl:** in ancient Greece and Rome, a woman who foretold the future.

8. **Trujillo:** Rafael Leonidas Trujillo Molina, general who took over as president of the Dominican Republic and ruled oppressively from 1930 to 1938 and from 1942 until 1961, when he was assassinated.

9. **Goya . . . Metropolitan:** painting by the Spanish artist Francisco José de Goya y Lucientes at the Metropolitan Museum of Art in New York City.

L **Reading Focus** Making Inferences About Characters
What might cause the father to react this way?

M **Literary Focus** Conflict How do conflicts experienced in his past influence the father's actions?

Portrait of a Girl (Retrato de Nina) (1942) by Jesus Guerrer Galvan.

I took a handful of the scraps I had gathered, stood up, and hurled them in his face. "Chapita!" I said in a low, ugly whisper. "You're just another Chapita!"

It took my father only a moment to register the hated nickname of our dictator, and he was after me. Down the halls we raced, but I was quicker than he and made it to my room just in time to lock the door as my father threw his weight against it. He called down curses on my head, ordered me on his authority as my father to open that door this very instant! He throttled that doorknob, but all to no avail. My mother's love of gadgets saved my hide that night. She had hired a locksmith to install good locks on all the bedroom doors after our house had been broken into while we were away the previous summer. In case burglars broke in again, and we were in the house, they'd have a second round of locks to contend with before they got to us.

"Eduardo," she tried to calm him down. "Don't you ruin my new locks."

He finally did calm down, his anger spent. I heard their footsteps retreating down the hall. I heard their door close, the clicking of their lock. Then, muffled voices, my mother's peaking in anger, in persuasion, my father's deep murmurs of explanation and of self-defense. At last, the house fell silent, before I heard, far off, the gun blasts and explosions, the serious, self-important voices of newscasters reporting their TV war.

A little while later, there was a quiet knock at my door, followed by a tentative attempt at the doorknob. "Cukita?" my mother whispered. "Open up, Cukita."

"Go away," I wailed, but we both knew I was glad she was there, and I needed only a moment's protest to save face before opening that door.

What we ended up doing that night was putting together a speech at the last moment. Two brief pages of stale compliments and the polite commonplaces on teachers, wrought by necessity without much invention by mother for daughter late into the night in the basement on the pad of paper and with the same pencil she had once used for her own inventions, for I was too upset to compose the speech myself. After it was drafted, she typed it up while I stood by, correcting her misnomers and mis-sayings. **Ⓝ**

She was so very proud of herself when I came home the next day with the success story of the assembly. The nuns had been flattered, the audience had stood up and given "our devoted teachers a standing ovation," what my mother had suggested they do at the end of my speech.

She clapped her hands together as I re-created the moment for her. "I stole that from your father's speech, remember? Remember how he put that in at the end?" She quoted him in Spanish, then translated for me into English.

That night, I watched him from the upstairs hall window where I'd retreated the minute I heard his

> He called down curses on my head, ordered me on his authority as my father to open that door this very instant! He throttled that doorknob, but all to no avail.

car pull up in front of our house. Slowly, my father came up the driveway, a grim expression on his face as he grappled with a large, heavy cardboard box. At the front door, he set the package down carefully and patted all his pockets for his house keys—precisely why my mother had invented her ticking key chain. I heard the snapping open of the locks downstairs. Heard as he struggled to maneuver the box through the narrow doorway. Then, he called my name several times. But I would not answer him.

"My daughter, your father, he love you very much," he explained from the bottom of the stairs. "He just want to protect you." Finally, my mother came up and pleaded with me to go down and reconcile with him. "Your father did not mean to harm. You must pardon him. Always it is better to let bygones be forgotten, no?"

I guess she was right. Downstairs, I found him setting up a brand new electric typewriter on the kitchen table. It was even better than the one I'd been begging to get like my mother's. My father had outdone himself with all the extra features: a plastic carrying case with my initials, in decals, below the handle, a brace to lift the paper upright while I typed, an erase cartridge, an automatic margin tab, a plastic hood like a toaster cover to keep the dust away. Not even my mother, I think, could have invented such a machine! **Ⓞ**

But her inventing days were over just as mine were starting up with my schoolwide success. That's why I've always thought of that speech my mother wrote for me as her last invention rather than the suitcase rollers everyone else in the family remembers. It was as if she had passed on to me her pencil and pad and said, "Okay, Cukita, here's the buck. You give it a shot."

Ⓝ Literary Focus Conflict What kinds of changes does the mother help make to her daughter's speech?

Ⓞ Literary Focus Conflict How is the typewriter a symbolic way for the father to resolve the conflict with his daughter?

Applying Your Skills

Daughter of Invention

Respond and Think Critically

Reading Focus

Quick Check

1. Which of the mother's ideas for an invention is a huge success for somebody else?

2. Why did the daughters resent the time their mother spent on inventions?

3. What is the mother's reaction to her daughter's speech?

4. How does the daughter insult her father after he destroys her speech?

5. How do the father and daughter become reconciled?

Read with a Purpose

6. What does the father's violent rejection of the speech tell us about him? Why is the mother's reaction to the speech different from his?

Reading Skills: Making Inferences About Characters

7. As you read, you recorded actions and other characteristics that transmit the personality of one of the characters from the story. Now, add the inferences that you have made about the character below each characteristic in your chart.

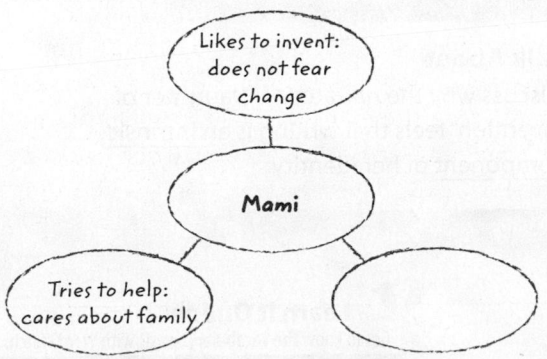

Literary Focus

Literary Analysis

8. **Infer** What is the actual cause of the father's anger? How does he resolve this conflict?

9. **Hypothesize** How does her mother's creativity affect the narrator? How does the narrator's creativity affect her mother?

Literary Skills: Conflict

10. **Draw Conclusions** How does the culture and language barrier between the narrator and her parents cause conflict?

Literary Skills Review: Figures of Speech

11. **Interpret** A **figure of speech** is a word or phrase that describes one thing in terms of something else and that is not meant to be taken literally. The narrator says that her mother had "weather vaned a minor brainstorm" (page 1230). How is the narrator using the image of a weather vane to explain her mother's ideas?

Writing Focus

Think as a Reader/Writer

Use It in Your Writing Think about someone in your life who makes you laugh. Then, recall details of a humorous story involving that person. Next, write a short passage about that incident, using humor to create an impression of that person.

 What Do **You Think Now**

Why does the father's love for his daughter cause him to destroy her speech?

SKILLS FOCUS Vocabulary Skills
Use suffixes to interpret and create words; demonstrate knowledge of literal meanings of words and their usage.

Vocabulary Development

✓ Vocabulary Check

Complete each sentence with the appropriate Vocabulary word: **disembodied, labyrinth, communal, eulogy, noncommittal, florid.**

1. All our neighbors shared the _____ garden.
2. A ghost is a _____ person.
3. The poet's elaborate, _____ style was tiring.
4. The mayor gave a _____ at the funeral.
5. The forest was a _____ of twisted branches.
6. "I might," was my _____ reply.

Vocabulary Skills: Suffixes

Some suffixes added to words indicate smallness or affection. For example, in English, the **diminutive suffix** –ette added to *kitchen* forms *kitchenette,* a small kitchen. The suffix –ling added to *duck* results in *duckling.* In Spanish, words ending in –o and –a are changed to words ending in –ito and –ita to form the diminutive. Here is a list of examples:

Word Ending in –o or –a	Meaning	Word Ending in –ito or –ita	Meaning
señora	married woman	señorita	little girl or unmarried woman
perro	dog	perrito	puppy

Re-read "Daughter of Invention" to find other examples of words ending in –o or –a, and add them to the chart. What other Spanish words do you know that fit this pattern?

Your Turn

The numbered words below are from French, Italian, and Portuguese. The lettered words have endings that denote littleness or smallness. Match the words from the same language.

1. cigare   **a.** cafezinho
2. lingue   **b.** cigarette
3. café   **c.** linguine

Language Coach

Antonyms Thinking of words' antonyms, or opposites, can help you expand your vocabulary. In some cases, the possibilities for antonyms seems limited: *good/bad; black/white.* Other cases are not so straightforward. A negative word such as *florid,* for example, has both positive antonyms (like *concise*) and negative antonyms (like *colorless*). For each item below, choose the word that is not an antonym and explain your choice.

1. noncommittal
   a. revealing   **b.** definite   **c.** careful
2. communal
   a. shared   **b.** individual   **c.** private

Academic Vocabulary

Talk About
Discuss why the narrator of "Daughter of Invention" feels that writing is an <u>intrinsic component</u> of her identity.

Learn It Online
Get to know the Vocabulary words with Word Watch.

go.hrw.com L11-1236 **Go**

Analyzing a Writer's Message by **Kylene Beers**

Sometimes I think it would be nice if the author added an epilogue to what he or she had written that started like this, "In case you missed it, my message for this story is . . ." Other times, I like the "aha" moments that I have when I discover a writer's message myself. The reality is that skilled readers know both experiences. They appreciate that authors have something they are trying to say, even if their meaning is unclear. At the same time, readers enjoy analyzing and interpreting literary works according to their own worldviews. As you read, stop occasionally and ask yourself why the author might have written a particular statement or passage. Then, ask yourself what that statement means to you.

Dig Beneath the Surface

The first time we read something, all we usually notice is the surface story: what happens to whom. If we want to know more—to understand the characters better or to find out why things happen—we need to read the selection a second time, and maybe even a third. Re-reading a text helps us formulate questions in our mind, so we're looking for the right answers.

We know, for example, that "Rules of the Game" is about a young Chinese American girl who becomes a chess champion. The plot revolves around her development as a chess player and her relationship with her family. What message is the author trying to send by relating these events? What is Tan's reason for telling this story in this particular way?

While some details in the selection might seem irrelevant to the story as a whole, if we notice those details and ask ourselves why the author chose to include them, we can begin to understand the author's message. Why, for example, would the author begin the selection with an anecdote about Waverly's mother teaching her to "bite back her tongue"? We learn later that Waverly applies this lesson to chess, when she learns the importance of keeping secrets about playing the game from her opponent.

The reader might also wonder why the author includes the scene in which Waverly's mother reads from a chess instruction book. This might seem especially pointless since she cannot read English well. We know, however, that this scene has been included for a reason. Waverly's mother is sending her children an important message about being an immigrant. In complaining about "American rules," she is conveying her anger at the unfair way in which immigrants are treated.

The game of chess is also used to convey messages to the reader. We might ask why Waverly begins to excel at chess only when she is taught by a complete stranger instead of by her brothers, who are both very competitive players. We begin to see how chess is something she can excel at without their interference. Her impatience with her mother also teaches us about the family dynamics in her home, sending messages about respect and pride in a Chinese American family. As you read the story, see if that theme is part of a larger message about children and their families.

Your Turn

Analyzing a writer's message requires active reading and questioning. As you read "Rules of the Game," practice strategies for analyzing a writer's message. Stop periodically as you read and ask yourself why the author may have included a particular scene or statement from the narrator or other characters. Then ask yourself what this particular scene or statement means to you and to the story as a whole. Be prepared to discuss what you think Tan's message or theme is in "Rules of the Game."

Learn It Online
Learn more with *PowerNotes* online.

go.hrw.com   L11-1237   Go

Rules of the Game

What Do You Think?

What human needs and desires do we have in common?

⏱ QuickWrite

Tan makes good use of local color, including vivid details that convey the setting of "Rules of the Game." If you were writing about a particular neighborhood in your town or city, what details would describe it best?

MEET THE WRITER

Amy Tan
(1952–   )

Amy Tan had not planned to become a fiction writer. In fact, for years she worked as a freelance writer for high-technology companies, a career in which flights of imagination are not permitted. To ease the pressures of her job, she decided to take jazz piano lessons—and she began writing fiction. The result was the emergence of a dazzling new storyteller.

Uprooted Childhood

Tan's parents had fled Communist China and come to the United States shortly before she was born in Oakland, California. Her mother, a nurse, was originally from Shanghai; her father, an engineer and Baptist minister, came from Beijing.

After Tan's father and younger brother both died of brain tumors when she was just fifteen, her mother took her away from their "diseased" house to Switzerland, where she finished high school. Her mother expected her talented daughter to become a neurosurgeon, as well as a pianist in her spare time. Instead, after returning to the United States, Tan enrolled at San Jose University and majored in English.

Mother as Muse

Amy Tan's mother had a gift for narrative, and though the two were sometimes at odds, Tan's mother came to be an inspiration for many of Tan's writings. Tan's first story, "Rules of the Game," was included in *The Joy Luck Club*, published in 1989. In this highly popular collection, which later became a movie, four Chinese American women tell stories about their Chinese-born mothers, who all belong to a mah-jongg club in San Francisco. Other novels involving familial relationships are *The Kitchen God's Wife* (1991) and *The Hundred Secret Senses* (1995).

Tan's mother died in 1999, and the final days of her life helped shape Tan's fourth bestseller, *The Bonesetter's Daughter* (2001). Tan says that her mother will continue to serve as her muse. "She is a voice . . . She'll insist that she has a role in the next book. She's not done with me yet."

Think About the Writer

In "Rules of the Game," Tan portrays a complex set of feelings that exist between mother and daughter. How might these feelings reflect Tan's own experiences?

Reader/Writer
Notebook
Use your **RWN** to complete the activities for this selection.

Literary Focus

Motivation A character's **motivation** refers to the underlying reasons for his or her behavior. A writer can reveal motivation directly by telling us what makes a character tick. More often, a writer uses indirect methods, revealing a character's motivations through his or her speech and actions. The reader must sift through details to make inferences about the character's motives. In this story, notice how Waverly's interest in chess changes her family dynamics. What are the true motivations behind the final showdown between Waverly and her mother?

Literary Perspectives Apply the literary perspective described on page 1241 as you read this story.

Reading Focus

Analyzing a Writer's Message In good literature, things don't just happen without a reason. Often, literary events help writers <u>transmit</u> an idea, theme, or message to readers. Here, Waverly is in conflict with her mother and in competition with her brothers. As the story explores this conflict and the characters' motivations, it delivers a message about all children, their parents, and their siblings.

Into Action Use a graphic organizer like the one below. In the first column, list events that trigger a change in the relationships between Waverly and other characters as she becomes increasingly successful at chess. In the second column briefly describe what change occurs.

Event	What Happens Next
Vincent wins a chess set and teaches Waverly to play.	Vincent quits playing, and Waverly becomes a chess champion.

Writing Focus

Think as a Reader/Writer
Find It in Your Reading As you read, notice ways in which the game of chess, with its two warring sides, is used in the story as a **metaphor** for other conflicts among characters and between cultures. Use your *Reader/Writer Notebook* to record some examples.

Vocabulary

ancestral (an SEHS truhl) *adj.:* inherited. *China is the family's ancestral home.*

intricate (IHN truh kiht) *adj.:* complex; complicated. *She loved the intricate moves the game of chess requires.*

obscured (uhb SKYURD) *v.:* concealed; hidden. *She deliberately obscured her knowledge of the game's secrets from her opponents.*

retort (rih TAWRT) *n.:* a quick, sharp answer. *Waverly's retort to Luu Po's humorous remark was to place the box holding chess pieces on the bench.*

touted (TOWT ihd) *v.:* highly praised. *The media touted her as a future chess master.*

prodigy (PRAHD uh jee) *n.:* extremely gifted person. *Her skill at playing the game so well at a young age made her a chess prodigy.*

concessions (kuhn SEHSH uhnz) *n.:* acts of giving in. *Would she have to make concessions to her mother to keep the peace?*

Language Coach

Frequently Misused Words The word *prodigy* is sometimes confused with the word *genius*. Both words refer to people with extraordinary abilities, but a *genius* is someone of great intellect or understanding, such as Newton or Einstein. A *prodigy* is usually young and has a talent for mastering difficult things, such as math or music.

 **Learn It Online**
Meet this story through the video introduction online.

go.hrw.com   L11-1239

RULES OF THE GAME

from
The Joy Luck Club

by **Amy Tan**

Dragon's Gate, Chinatown, San Francisco (1986) by Alek Rapoport.

Read with a Purpose

As you read, think about the relationship between the narrator's family and her growing success at chess.

Build Background

Chess is an ancient game. It was played many centuries ago in India, Persia, and China. Some believe that the game originated in India. By the year 1000, the game had spread throughout Europe. Europeans gave the chess pieces the names they have today. The modern game of chess dates from around 1450, when the rules for basic moves were modified and adopted widely.

I was six when my mother taught me the art of invisible strength. It was a strategy for winning arguments, respect from others, and eventually, though neither of us knew it at the time, chess games. "Bite back your tongue," scolded my mother when I cried loudly, yanking her hand toward the store that sold bags of salted plums. At home, she said, "Wise guy, he not go against wind. In Chinese we say, Come from South, blow with wind—poom!—North will follow. Strongest wind cannot be seen."

The next week I bit back my tongue as we entered the store with the forbidden candies. When my mother finished her shopping, she quietly plucked a small bag of plums from the rack and put it on the counter with the rest of the items.

My mother imparted her daily truths so she could help my older brothers and me rise above our circumstances. We lived in San Francisco's Chinatown. Like most of the other Chinese children who played in the back alleys of restaurants and curio shops, I didn't think we were poor. My bowl was always full, three five-course meals every day, beginning with a soup full of mysterious things I didn't want to know the names of. **A** **B**

We lived on Waverly Place, in a warm, clean, two-bedroom flat that sat above a small Chinese bakery specializing in steamed pastries and dim sum. In the early morning, when the alley was still quiet, I could smell fragrant red beans as they were cooked down to a pasty sweetness. By daybreak, our flat was heavy with the odor of fried sesame balls and sweet curried chicken crescents. From my bed, I would listen as my father got ready for work, then locked the door behind him, one-two-three clicks. **C**

At the end of our two-block alley was a small sandlot playground with swings and slides well-shined down the middle with use. The play area was bordered by wood-slat benches where old-country people sat cracking roasted watermelon seeds with their golden teeth and scattering the husks to an impatient gathering of gurgling pigeons. The best playground, however, was the dark alley itself. It was crammed with daily mysteries and adventures. My brothers and I would peer into the medicinal herb shop, watching old Li dole out onto a still sheet of white paper the right amount of insect shells, saffron-colored seeds, and pungent leaves for his ailing customers. It was said that he once cured a woman dying of an ancestral curse that had eluded the best of American doctors. Next to the pharmacy was a printer who specialized in gold-embossed wedding invitations and festive red banners.

Farther down the street was Ping Yuen Fish Market. The front window displayed a tank crowded with doomed fish and turtles struggling to gain footing on the slimy green-tiled sides. A handwritten sign informed tourists, "Within this store, is all for food, not for pet." Inside, the butchers with their blood-stained white smocks deftly gutted the fish while customers cried out their orders and shouted, "Give me your freshest," to which the butchers always protested, "All are freshest." On less crowded market days, we would inspect the crates of live frogs and crabs which we were warned not to poke, boxes of dried cuttlefish, and row upon row of iced prawns, squid,

A **Reading Focus** **Analyzing a Writer's Message** The narrator says that she did not know her family was poor. What does this tell you about her and the way she was raised?

B **Literary Focus** **Motivation** Why does the narrator's mother want to teach her children "the art of invisible strength"?

C **Literary Perspectives** **Analyzing Biographical Information** How does the smell of food cooking relate to Tan's background and to Waverly's family?

Vocabulary **ancestral** (an SEHS truhl) *adj.:* inherited.

and slippery fish. The sanddabs made me shiver each time; their eyes lay on one flattened side and reminded me of my mother's story of a careless girl who ran into a crowded street and was crushed by a cab. "Was smash flat," reported my mother.

At the corner of the alley was Hong Sing's, a four-table café with a recessed stairwell in front that led to a door marked "Tradesmen." My brothers and I believed the bad people emerged from this door at night. Tourists never went to Hong Sing's, since the menu was printed only in Chinese. A Caucasian man with a big camera once posed me and my playmates in front of the restaurant. He had us move to the side of the picture window so the photo would capture the roasted duck with its head dangling from a juice-covered rope. After he took the picture, I told him he should go into Hong Sing's and eat dinner. When he smiled and asked me what they served, I shouted, "Guts and duck's feet and octopus gizzards!" Then I ran off with my friends, shrieking with laughter as we scampered across the alley and hid in the entryway grotto of the China Gem Company, my heart pounding with hope that he would chase us.

My mother named me after the street that we lived on: Waverly Place Jong, my official name for important American documents. But my family called me Meimei, "Little Sister." I was the youngest, the only daughter. Each morning before school, my mother would twist and yank on my thick black hair until she had formed two tightly wound pigtails. One day, as she struggled to weave a hard-toothed comb through my disobedient hair, I had a sly thought.   **D**

I asked her, "Ma, what is Chinese torture?" My mother shook her head. A bobby pin was wedged between her lips. She wetted her palm and smoothed the hair above my ear, then pushed the pin in so that it nicked sharply against my scalp.

"Who say this word?" she asked without a trace of knowing how wicked I was being. I shrugged my shoulders and said, "Some boy in my class said Chinese people do Chinese torture."

"Chinese people do many things," she said simply. "Chinese people do business, do medicine, do painting.

Not lazy like American people. We do torture. Best torture."   **E**

My older brother Vincent was the one who actually got the chess set. We had gone to the annual Christmas party held at the First Chinese Baptist Church at the end of the alley. The missionary ladies had put together a Santa bag of gifts donated by members of another church. None of the gifts had names on them. There were separate sacks for boys and girls of different ages.

One of the Chinese parishioners had donned a Santa Claus costume and a stiff paper beard with cotton balls glued to it. I think the only children who thought he was the real thing were too young to know that Santa Claus was not Chinese. When my turn came up, the Santa man asked me how old I was. I thought it was a trick question; I was seven according to the American formula and eight by the Chinese calendar. I said I was born on March 17, 1951. That seemed to satisfy him. He then solemnly asked if I had been a very, very good girl this year and did I believe in Jesus Christ and obey my parents. I knew the only answer to that. I nodded back with equal solemnity.

Having watched the other children opening their gifts, I already knew that the big gifts were not necessarily the nicest ones. One girl my age got a large coloring book of biblical characters, while a less greedy girl who selected a smaller box received a glass vial of lavender toilet water.[1] The sound of the box was also important. A ten-year-old boy had chosen a box that jangled when he shook it. It was a tin globe of the world with a slit for inserting money. He must have thought it was full of dimes and nickels, because when he saw that it had just ten pennies, his face fell with such undisguised disappointment that his mother slapped the side of his head and led him out of the church hall, apologizing to the crowd for her son who had such bad manners he couldn't appreciate such a fine gift.

As I peered into the sack, I quickly fingered the remaining presents, testing their weight, imagining what

---

1. **toilet water:** perfumed after-bath skin freshener.

they contained. I chose a heavy, compact one that was wrapped in shiny silver foil and a red satin ribbon. It was a twelve-pack of Life Savers and I spent the rest of the party arranging and rearranging the candy tubes in the order of my favorites. My brother Winston chose wisely as well. His present turned out to be a box of intricate plastic parts; the instructions on the box proclaimed that when they were properly assembled he would have an authentic miniature replica of a World War II submarine.

Vincent got the chess set, which would have been a very decent present to get at a church Christmas party, except it was obviously used and, as we discovered later, it was missing a black pawn and a white knight. My mother graciously thanked the unknown benefactor, saying, "Too good. Cost too much." At which point, an old lady with fine white, wispy hair nodded toward our family and said with a whistling whisper, "Merry, merry Christmas."

When we got home, my mother told Vincent to throw the chess set away. "She not want it. We not want it," she said, tossing her head stiffly to the side with a tight, proud smile. My brothers had deaf ears. They were already lining up the chess pieces and reading from the dog-eared instruction book. **F**

I watched Vincent and Winston play during Christmas week. The chessboard seemed to hold elaborate secrets waiting to be untangled. The chessmen were more powerful than Old Li's magic herbs that cured ancestral curses. And my brothers wore such serious faces that I was sure something was at stake that was greater than avoiding the tradesmen's door to Hong Sing's.

"Let me! Let me!" I begged between games when one brother or the other would sit back with a deep sigh of relief and victory, the other annoyed, unable to let go of the outcome. Vincent at first refused to let me play, but when I offered my Life Savers as replacements for the buttons that filled in for the missing pieces, he relented. He chose the flavors: wild cherry for the black pawn and peppermint for the white knight. Winner could eat both. **G**

As our mother sprinkled flour and rolled out small doughy circles for the steamed dumplings that would be our dinner that night, Vincent explained the rules, pointing to each piece. "You have sixteen pieces and so do I. One king and queen, two bishops, two knights, two castles, and eight pawns. The pawns can only move forward one step, except on the first move. Then they can move two. But they can only take men by moving crossways like this, except in the beginning, when you can move ahead and take another pawn."

"Why?" I asked as I moved my pawn. "Why can't they move more steps?"

"Because they're pawns," he said.

"But why do they go crossways to take other men? Why aren't there any women and children?"

"Why is the sky blue? Why must you always ask stupid questions?" asked Vincent. "This is a game. These are the rules. I didn't make them up. See. Here. In the book." He jabbed a page with a pawn in his hand. "Pawn. P-A-W-N. Pawn. Read it yourself."

My mother patted the flour off her hands. "Let me see book," she said quietly. She scanned the pages quickly, not reading the foreign English symbols, seeming to search deliberately for nothing in particular.

"This American rules," she concluded at last. "Every time people come out from foreign country, must know rules. You not know, judge say, Too bad, go back. They not telling you why so you can use their way go forward. They say, Don't know why, you find out yourself. But they knowing all the time. Better you take it, find out why yourself." She tossed her head back with a satisfied smile. **H**

I found out about all the whys later. I read the rules and looked up all the big words in a dictionary. I borrowed books from the Chinatown library. I studied each chess piece, trying to absorb the power each contained.

I learned about opening moves and why it's important to control the center early on; the shortest distance between two points is straight down the middle. I learned about the middle game and why tactics between

---

F **Reading Focus** Analyzing a Writer's Message Why does Waverly's mother want to throw away the used chess set?

G **Literary Focus** Motivation Why does Vincent refuse to let Waverly play chess at first?

H **Literary Perspectives** Analyzing Biographical Information As a Chinese immigrant, how does the mother interpret the "rules"?

Vocabulary intricate (IHN truh kiht) *adj.*: complex; complicated.

two adversaries are like clashing ideas; the one who plays better has the clearest plans for both attacking and getting out of traps. I learned why it is essential in the endgame to have foresight, a mathematical understanding of all possible moves, and patience; all weaknesses and advantages become evident to a strong adversary and are obscured to a tiring opponent. I discovered that for the whole game one must gather invisible strengths and see the endgame before the game begins. **Ⓘ**

I also found out why I should never reveal "why" to others. A little knowledge withheld is a great advantage one should store for future use. That is the power of chess. It is a game of secrets in which one must show and never tell. **Ⓙ**

I loved the secrets I found within the sixty-four black and white squares. I carefully drew a hand-made chessboard and pinned it to the wall next to my bed, where at night I would stare for hours at imaginary battles. Soon I no longer lost any games or Life Savers, but I lost my adversaries. Winston and Vincent decided they were more interested in roaming the streets after school in their Hopalong Cassidy[2] cowboy hats.

On a cold spring afternoon, while walking home from school, I detoured through the play-ground at the end of our alley. I saw a group of old men, two seated across a folding table playing a game of chess, others smoking pipes, eating peanuts, and watching. I ran home and grabbed Vincent's chess set, which was bound in a cardboard box with rubber bands. I also carefully selected two prized rolls of Life Savers. I came back to the park and approached a man who was observing the game.

"Want to play?" I asked him. His face widened with surprise and he grinned as he looked at the box under my arm.

---

2. **Hopalong Cassidy:** cowboy hero of movies and television from the 1930s through the early 1950s.

"Little sister, been a long time since I play with dolls," he said, smiling benevolently. I quickly put the box down next to him on the bench and displayed my retort.

Lau Po, as he allowed me to call him, turned out to be a much better player than my brothers. I lost many games and many Life Savers. But over the weeks, with each diminishing roll of candies, I added new secrets. Lau Po gave me the names. The Double Attack from the East and West Shores. Throwing Stones on the Drowning Man. The Sudden Meeting of the Clan. The Surprise from the Sleeping Guard. The Humble Servant Who Kills the King. Sand in the Eyes of Advancing Forces. A Double Killing Without Blood.

There were also the fine points of chess etiquette. Keep captured men in neat rows, as well-tended prisoners. Never announce "Check" with vanity, lest someone with an unseen sword slit your throat. Never hurl pieces into the sandbox after you have lost a game, because then you must find them again, by yourself, after apologizing to all around you. By the end of the summer, Lau Po had taught me all he knew, and I had become a better chess player. **Ⓚ**

A small weekend crowd of Chinese people and tourists would gather as I played and defeated my opponents one by one. My mother would join the crowds during these outdoor exhibition games. She sat proudly on the bench, telling my admirers with proper Chinese humility, "Is luck."

A man who watched me play in the park suggested that my mother allow me to play in local chess tournaments. My mother smiled graciously, an answer that meant nothing. I desperately wanted to go, but I bit back my tongue. I knew she would not let me play among strangers. So as we walked home I said in a small voice that I didn't want to play in the local tournament. They would have American rules. If I lost, I would bring shame on my family.

"Is shame you fall down nobody push you," said my mother.

Ⓘ **Literary Focus** Motivation Waverly makes an independent effort to learn as much as she can about chess. What motivates her to do this?

Ⓙ **Reading Focus** Analyzing a Writer's Message Waverly discovers that chess is a game of secrets in which "a little knowledge withheld is a great advantage." Does this lesson apply to her life in general?

Ⓚ **Literary Focus** Motivation Why does Lau Po teach Waverly all his chess strategies and secrets?

Vocabulary **obscured** (uhb SKYURD) *v.*: concealed; hidden. **retort** (ri TAWRT) *n.*: a quick, sharp answer.

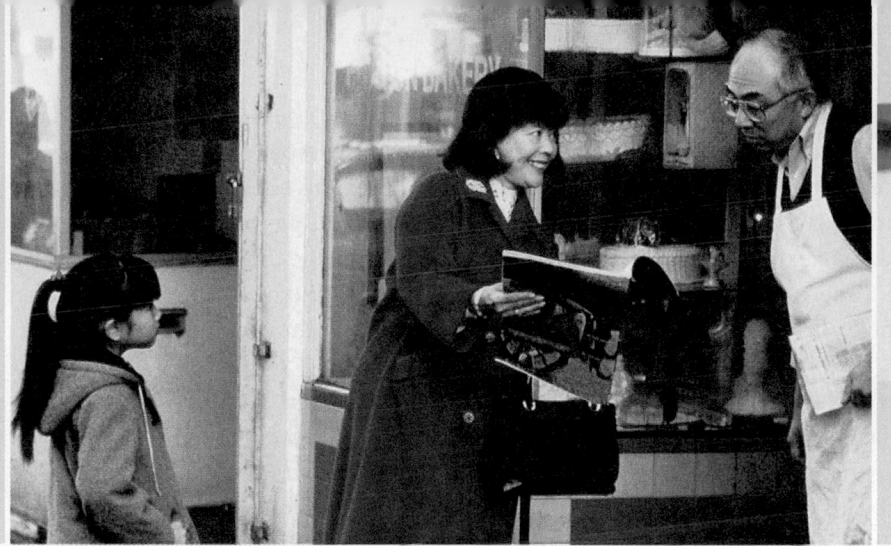

Analyzing Visuals

Viewing and Interpreting Placing the woman in the scarlet coat at the center of the image makes her its focal point. How is Waverly's mother at the center of her daughter's story?

A still image from the movie
The Joy Luck Club (1993).

During my first tournament, my mother sat with me in the front row as I waited for my turn. I frequently bounced my legs to unstick them from the cold metal seat of the folding chair. When my name was called, I leapt up. My mother unwrapped something in her lap. It was her *chang*, a small tablet of red jade which held the sun's fire. "Is luck," she whispered, and tucked it into my dress pocket. I turned to my opponent, a fifteen-year-old boy from Oakland. He looked at me, wrinkling his nose.

As I began to play, the boy disappeared, the color ran out of the room, and I saw only my white pieces and his black ones waiting on the other side. A light wind began blowing past my ears. It whispered secrets only I could hear.

"Blow from the South," it murmured. "The wind leaves no trail." I saw a clear path, the traps to avoid. The crowd rustled. "Shhh! Shhh!" said the corners of the room. The wind blew stronger. "Throw sand from the East to distract him." The knight came forward ready for the sacrifice. The wind hissed, louder and louder. "Blow, blow, blow. He cannot see. He is blind now. Make him lean away from the wind so he is easier to knock down."

"Check," I said, as the wind roared with laughter. The wind died down to little puffs, my own breath.

My mother placed my first trophy next to a new plastic chess set that the neighborhood Tao society had given to me. As she wiped each piece with a soft cloth, she said, "Next time win more, lose less."

"Ma, it's not how many pieces you lose," I said. "Sometimes you need to lose pieces to get ahead."

"Better to lose less, see if you really need."

At the next tournament, I won again, but it was my mother who wore the triumphant grin.

"Lost eight piece this time. Last time was eleven. What I tell you? Better off lose less!" I was annoyed, but I couldn't say anything. **L**

I attended more tournaments, each one farther away from home. I won all games, in all divisions. The Chinese bakery downstairs from our flat displayed my growing collection of trophies in its window, amidst the dust-covered cakes that were never picked up. The day after I won an important regional tournament, the window encased a fresh sheet cake with whipped-cream frosting and red script saying, "Congratulations, Waverly Jong, Chinatown Chess Champion." Soon after that, a flower shop, headstone engraver, and funeral parlor offered to sponsor me in national tournaments. That's when my mother decided I no longer had to do the dishes. Winston and Vincent had to do my chores. **M**

"Why does she get to play and we do all the work," complained Vincent.

"Is new American rules," said my mother. "Meimei play, squeeze all her brains out for win chess. You play, worth squeeze towel."

L Reading Focus **Analyzing a Writer's Message** Why is Waverly annoyed by her mother? Why does Waverly feel she cannot respond to her mother?

M Literary Focus **Motivation** What motivates Waverly's mother to give Waverly's chores to her brothers?

By my ninth birthday, I was a national chess champion. I was still some 429 points away from grand-master status,[3] but I was touted as the Great American Hope, a child prodigy and a girl to boot. They ran a photo of me in *Life* magazine next to a quote in which Bobby Fischer[4] said, "There will never be a woman grand master." "Your move, Bobby," said the caption.

The day they took the magazine picture I wore neatly plaited braids clipped with plastic barrettes trimmed with rhinestones. I was playing in a large high school auditorium that echoed with phlegmy coughs and the squeaky rubber knobs of chair legs sliding across freshly waxed wooden floors. Seated across from me was an American man, about the same age as Lau Po, maybe fifty. I remember that his sweaty brow seemed to weep at my every move. He wore a dark, malodorous suit. One of his pockets was stuffed with a great white kerchief on which he wiped his palm before sweeping his hand over the chosen chess piece with great flourish.

In my crisp pink-and-white dress with scratchy lace at the neck, one of two my mother had sewn for these special occasions, I would clasp my hands under my chin, the delicate points of my elbows poised lightly on the table in the manner my mother had shown me for posing for the press. I would swing my patent leather shoes back and forth like an impatient child riding on a school bus. Then I would pause, suck in my lips, twirl my chosen piece in midair as if undecided, and then firmly plant it in its new threatening place, with a triumphant smile thrown back at my opponent for good measure.

I no longer played in the alley of Waverly Place. I never visited the playground where the pigeons and old men gathered. I went to school, then directly home to learn new chess secrets, cleverly concealed advantages, more escape routes.

But I found it difficult to concentrate at home. My mother had a habit of standing over me while I plotted out my games. I think she thought of herself as my protective ally. Her lips would be sealed tight, and after each move I made, a soft "Hmmmmph" would escape from her nose.

"Ma, I can't practice when you stand there like that," I said one day. She retreated to the kitchen and made loud noises with the pots and pans. When the crashing stopped, I could see out of the corner of my eye that she was standing in the doorway. "Hmmmph!" Only this one came out of her tight throat.

My parents made many concessions to allow me to practice. One time I complained that the bedroom I shared was so noisy that I couldn't think. Thereafter, my brothers slept in a bed in the living room facing the street. I said I couldn't finish my rice; my head didn't work right when my stomach was too full. I left the table with half-finished bowls and nobody complained. But there was one duty I couldn't avoid. I had to accompany my mother on Saturday market days when I had no tournament to play. My mother would proudly walk with me, visiting many shops, buying very little. "This my daughter Wave-ly Jong," she said to whoever looked her way. **Ⓝ**

One day, after we left a shop I said under my breath, "I wish you wouldn't do that, telling everybody I'm your daughter." My mother stopped walking. Crowds of people with heavy bags pushed past us on the sidewalk, bumping into first one shoulder, then another.

"Aiii-ya. So shame be with mother?" She grasped my hand even tighter as she glared at me.

I looked down. "It's not that, it's just so obvious. It's just so embarrassing."

"Embarrass you be my daughter?" Her voice was cracking with anger.

"That's not what I meant. That's not what I said."

"What you say?"

I knew it was a mistake to say anything more, but I heard my voice speaking. "Why do you have to use

---

3. **grand-master status:** top rank in international chess competition.
4. **Bobby Fischer** (1943–2008): American chess master, the youngest player in the world to attain the rank of grand master, in 1958.

Vocabulary **touted** (TOWT ihd) *v.:* highly praised.
prodigy (PRAHD uh jee) *n.:* extremely gifted person.
concessions (kuhn SEHSH uhnz) *n.:* acts of giving in.

Ⓝ Literary Focus Motivation What motivates Waverly's mother to take Waverly to the market?

me to show off? If you want to show off, then why don't you learn to play chess?" **O**

My mother's eyes turned into dangerous black slits. She had no words for me, just sharp silence.

I felt the wind rushing around my hot ears. I jerked my hand out of my mother's tight grasp and spun around, knocking into an old woman. Her bag of groceries spilled to the ground.

"Aii-ya! Stupid girl!" my mother and the woman cried. Oranges and tin cans careened down the sidewalk. As my mother stooped to help the old woman pick up the escaping food, I took off.

I raced down the street, dashing between people, not looking back as my mother screamed shrilly, "Meimei! Meimei!" I fled down an alley, past dark, curtained shops and merchants washing the grime off their windows. I sped into the sunlight, into a large street crowded with tourists examining trinkets and souvenirs. I ducked into another dark alley, down another street, up another alley. I ran until it hurt and I realized I had nowhere to go, that I was not running from anything. The alleys contained no escape routes.

My breath came out like angry smoke. It was cold. I sat down on an upturned plastic pail next to a stack of empty boxes, cupping my chin with my hands, thinking hard. I imagined my mother, first walking briskly down one street or another looking for me, then giving up and returning home to await my arrival. After two hours, I stood up on creaking legs and slowly walked home. **P**

The alley was quiet and I could see the yellow lights shining from our flat like two tiger's eyes in the night. I climbed the sixteen steps to the door, advancing quietly up each so as not to make any warning

> "Ma, I can't practice when you stand there like that," I said one day. She retreated to the kitchen and made loud noises with the pots and pans.

sounds. I turned the knob; the door was locked. I heard a chair moving, quick steps, the locks turning—click! click! click!—and then the door opened.

"About time you got home," said Vincent. "Boy, are you in trouble."

He slid back to the dinner table. On a platter were the remains of a large fish, its fleshy head still connected to bones swimming upstream in vain escape. Standing there waiting for my punishment, I heard my mother speak in a dry voice.

"We not concerning this girl. This girl not have concerning for us."

Nobody looked at me. Bone chopsticks clinked against the inside of bowls being emptied into hungry mouths. **Q**

I walked into my room, closed the door, and lay down on my bed. The room was dark, the ceiling filled with shadows from the dinnertime lights of neighboring flats.

In my head, I saw a chessboard with sixty-four black and white squares. Opposite me was my opponent, two angry black slits. She wore a triumphant smile. "Strongest wind cannot be seen," she said.

Her black men advanced across the plane, slowly marching to each successive level as a single unit. My white pieces screamed as they scurried and fell off the board one by one. As her men drew closer to my edge, I felt myself growing light. I rose up into the air and flew out the window. Higher and higher, above the alley, over the tops of tiled roofs, where I was gathered up by the wind and pushed up toward the night sky until everything below me disappeared and I was alone.

I closed my eyes and pondered my next move. **R**

O **Reading Focus** Analyzing a Writer's Message What does Waverly mean when she tells her mother, "If you want to show off, then why don't you learn to play chess?"

P **Literary Focus** Motivation Why does Waverly run away from her mother after their disagreement? Why does she wait to return home?

Q **Reading Focus** Analyzing a Writer's Message Why does Waverly's mother and the rest of her family refuse to acknowledge Waverly's presence?

R **Reading Focus** Analyzing a Writer's Message What kind of game are Waverly and her mother really playing? How effective an opponent does Waverly's mother turn out to be?

Applying Your Skills

Rules of the Game

Respond and Think Critically

Reading Focus

Quick Check

1. Describe where Waverly lives.

2. How do the Jongs acquire their first chess set?

3. How does Waverly persuade her brothers to let her play chess?

4. What are some ways in which Waverly's mother shows her pride in Waverly's accomplishments?

Read with a Purpose

5. How does playing chess provide Waverly with a chance to establish a separate identity from that of her family? Does this make her stronger or not?

Reading Skills: Analyzing a Writer's Message

6. How do Waverly's relationships in the family change as she becomes a chess champion? Review the chart you created to record these changes. Add a third row in which you record how the relationship changed as a result of this event.

Event	What Happens Next	How Does It Change Their Relationship?
Vincent wins a chess set and teaches Waverly to play.	Vincent quits playing, and Waverly becomes a chess champion.	Vincent resents it when Waverly becomes the family favorite.

Literary Focus

Literary Analysis

7. **Interpret** What kinds of rules does Waverly's mother want her children to learn and why?

8. **Infer** What is Mrs. Jong's motivation for showing off her daughter? Why does Waverly resent her mother's actions?

9. **Analyze** What might the story be suggesting about the potential effects of success of one family member on the family as a whole?

10. **Analyze** What do you think Waverly's fantasy at the end of the story means? What do you predict as her "next move"?

11. **Interpret** What multiple meanings might the word *rules* in the story's title have?

12. **Literary Perspectives** How might this story be different if Waverly's parents were not immigrants?

Literary Skills: Motivation

13. **Hypothesize** What is the motivation behind Waverly's actions in the story?

Literary Skills Review: Conflict

14. **Analyze** Why does Waverly rely on logic and strategy to resolve her **conflicts,** or battles with herself and other forces? Does it always work?

Writing Focus

Think as a Reader/Writer

Use It in Your Writing Write a brief story in which you use the metaphor of a game to portray a conflict between two characters. The game you use as a metaphor may be chess or any other game with which you are familiar.

 What Do You Think Now

How can learning to play a game such as chess help us discover what we have in common with others?

1248 Unit 6 • Collection 16

Vocabulary Development

SKILLS FOCUS Literary Skills Analyze character motivation; analyze conflict. Reading Skills Analyze a writer's message.

Vocabulary Skills Identify synonyms. Writing Skills Employ literary devices for effective writing.

✓ Vocabulary Check

Match each Vocabulary word with its definition.

1. ancestral
2. intricate
3. obscured
4. retort
5. concessions
6. touted
7. prodigy

a. incisive or witty answer
b. acts of giving in
c. complex or complicated
d. concealed or hidden
e. extremely gifted person
f. highly praised
g. inherited

Vocabulary Skills: Synonyms

A **synonym** is a word that has the same, or almost the same, meaning as another word. The verb *play* has several synonyms, which depend for their meanings on the context in which they appear. One synonym for *play* is *compete*—as in playing in a game to win ("A man who watched me play in the park suggested that my mother allow me to play in local chess tournaments"). You can also play with no other purpose than to enjoy yourself and frolic away your day. Another synonym for *play* is *deceive*. Hopefully, you would not deceive someone in order to win a game. The graphic organizer below shows three synonyms for the verb *play*. Each one clearly demonstrates a specific meaning of the word.

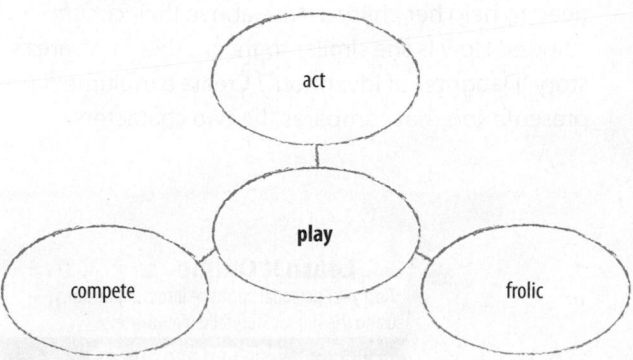

Your Turn

On a separate sheet of paper, draw a similar graphic organizer for each of the following words. Then, think about how each word is subtly different.

battle   defeat   victory   game

Language Coach

Frequently Misused Words Some words get misused because they have similar definitions, like *prodigy* ("an extremely talented person") and *genius* ("an extremely intelligent person"). Other words, like *ingenious* and *ingenuous*, get misused because they sound similar. In the left column below are several Vocabulary words from the selection. Each one is frequently confused with a similar word from the right column. Write a sentence using each word to the left correctly. Look up the words to the right in the dictionary as needed.

1. prodigy   genius
2. intricate   intimate
3. retort   reply
4. successive   successful

Academic Vocabulary

Talk About

In what way is life <u>potentially</u> like a game? Does life have <u>intrinsic</u> rules, or do we all make up our own rules? Discuss these questions in a small group.

Applying Your Skills

SKILLS FOCUS Writing Skills Write narratives; perform literary analysis. **Grammar Skills** Use transitional expressions.

Rules of the Game

Grammar Link

Using Transitional Expressions

Transitional expressions are words or phrases that provide a smooth flow from one idea to the next. They make your writing more coherent and logical. Transitional expressions often show **chronological** or **spatial** relationships. They may also show connections based on **comparison and contrast, cause and effect,** or **exemplification-restatement**. In the following passages from "Rules of the Game," notice the transitional words that connect the sentences:

> I knew she would not let me play among strangers. **So** as we walked home I said in a small voice that I didn't want to play in the local tournament. [*So* indicates a cause-and-effect relationship.]

> One time I complained that the bedroom I shared was so noisy that I couldn't think. **Thereafter,** my brothers slept in a bed in the living room facing the street. [*Thereafter* indicates a chronological relationship.]

In the first example the transitional word *so* explains why Waverly says what she does to her mother—her motivation. In the second example the word *thereafter* tells the order in which these two events occurred.

Your Turn

Writing Application In the following passages, add transitional expressions to strengthen the connection between ideas.

1. In Amy Tan's story "Rules of the Game," Waverly's brother Vincent gets a chess set at a Christmas party. Their mother tells him to throw it away.

2. Waverly learns to play chess better than her brothers. They lose interest in playing with her.

3. Waverly becomes a chess champion. Her mother is proud of her. Waverly is uncomfortable with her mother's pride.

CHOICES

As you respond to the Choices, use these **Academic Vocabulary** words as appropriate: component, diverse, intrinsic, potential, transmit.

REVIEW

Respond to a Review

Timed └Writing In a review of *The Joy Luck Club,* critic Susan Dooley wrote the following comment:

> These women from China find trying to talk to their daughters like trying to plug a foreign appliance into an American outlet. The current won't work. Impulses collide and nothing flows through the wires except anger and exasperation.

Using specific examples from the story, explain how this comment applies to "Rules of the Game."

CONNECT

Write a Narrative About Competing

It has been said that competition is a great teacher. We learn from being involved in competitive sports and other activities. Write a narrative essay about a time when you were involved in some kind of competition and learned from the experience.

EXTEND

Compare and Contrast Characters

Group Activity In a group, discuss Tan's characterization of the mother in her story. Think about the mother's role in her family and why she feels an intrinsic need to help her children "rise above their circumstances." How is she similar to the mother in Alvarez's story "Daughter of Invention"? Create a multimedia presentation that compares the two characters.

Learn It Online
Turn your personal narrative into a digital story—using the Digital Storytelling mini-site.

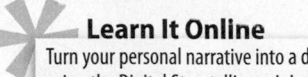
go.hrw.com   L11-1250   Go

Themes Across Genres

Denied Adolescence (2006) by Gaetano Belverde.

A theme that recurs in literature is the desire of human beings to find meaning in their experiences—to understand their relationship to others and to the natural world. As you read a short story about lost childhood, an essay that explores the natural world, and a cartoon about the ultimate meaning of life, examine how this theme is treated across different genres.

CONTENTS

The Sky Blue Ball

What Do You Think

What human needs and desires do we have in common?

⏱ QuickWrite

Have you ever had a pet, a toy, or something else that meant everything to you? Write a brief paragraph about it and its significance to you, and be prepared to discuss your feelings with a partner.

Joyce Carol Oates
(1938–   )

National Book Award WINNER

Author of numerous books, including stories, poems, essays, and novels, Joyce Carol Oates continues to capture the psychology of the human soul in her writing.

Working-Class Writer

Joyce Carol Oates, today a Princeton professor, waged a "daily scramble for existence" while growing up on a farm in Erie County, New York. It is this area of upstate New York that often serves as the locale for her work. A storyteller from childhood, Joyce was given a typewriter at age fourteen and trained herself to write, producing "novel after novel" through high school and college.

Oates's hardworking habits have led to a prolific portfolio of writings. Her first collection of stories, *By the North Gate*, was published in 1963. She is a recipient of the National Book Award, the PEN/Malamud Award for Excellence in Short Fiction, and the 2005 Prix Femina, among numerous other honors. Along the way, she has earned a preeminent place among the greats of contemporary American literature. She has even found time to produce suspense novels under the pseudonyms of Rosamund Smith and Lauren Kelly.

Chronicler of the American Experience

Oates has said, "I am a chronicler of the American experience." Many critics have pointed out the pervasiveness of violence in her fiction. Her work often deals with bad things happening to ordinary people. A number of her stories are about teenage girls. Through her writing, she tries to hammer out what she has called "the human soul caught in the stampede of time."

Oates has experimented with <u>diverse</u> genres and styles. While most of her work is in the realistic tradition, in the 1980s she turned to Gothic fiction conventions in her novel *Bellefleur*. By the 1990s, she had begun a series of family chronicles.

Think About the Writer

Why do you think Joyce Carol Oates writes about "bad things that happen to ordinary people"?

Reader/Writer
Notebook
Use your **RWN** to complete the activities for this selection.

Literary Focus

Symbol A **symbol** is a person, a place, a thing, or an event that has <u>intrinsic</u> meaning and also stands for something much more than itself. Often symbols stand for abstract ideas or qualities. The dove, for instance, is used as a symbol of peace. A skull symbolizes death. A red rose symbolizes love. A flag symbolizes an entire country. These are all public symbols; everyone agrees on what they mean. Writers may also create an imaginary world with its own symbols. As you read "The Sky Blue Ball," see if you can tell what the ball of the title represents to the narrator.

Reading Focus

Interpreting Details The narrator in "The Sky Blue Ball" recalls an episode from her adolescence that has a special meaning for her. As she waits at the wall, she reflects, "there I stood, fourteen years old, a long-limbed weed of a girl, no longer a child yet panting and bleeding from the knees, the palms of my hands, too, chafed and scraped and dirty; there I stood alone in front of a moldering brick wall waiting for—what?" Pay attention to the **details** of setting, like the wall, that reflect the narrator's state of mind. While reading, ask yourself how each detail helps you understand what the episode means to her.

Into Action As you read, use a chart like the one below to record images and details that stand out to you. Explain what those details tell you about the narrator or her situation, and think about what they might symbolize in the story.

Detail from text	What it says about the narrator or her situation
The wall is the color of "dried blood" (p. 1254).	This image is unsettling and suggests that the narrator is in a bad place.

Vocabulary

spherical (SFEHR uh kuhl) *adj.:* having the form of a sphere; globular. *The spherical ball flew over the high, flat wall.*

resilient (rih ZIHL yuhnt) *adj.:* able to return to original form after being bent, compressed, or stretched. *The toy was miraculously resilient after so many years.*

volition (voh LIHSH uhn) *n.:* conscious choice; will; determination. *Her refusal to stop searching was an act of volition.*

intransigent (ihn TRAN suh juhnt) *adj.:* uncompromising. *She was intransigent in her desire to see who was on the other side of the wall.*

insurmountable (ihn suhr MOWNT uh buhl) *adj.:* not capable of being overcome. *She knew that for a child the wall would have been an insurmountable obstacle.*

Language Coach

Shades of Meaning The meaning of an adjective can change when it is used to describe different nouns. A *resilient* ball has the ability to be restored to its original shape after hard use. A resilient human is able to "bounce back" emotionally after a major trauma. What would a resilient track shoe be like? What about a resilient smile?

Writing Focus

Think as a Reader/Writer

Find It in Your Reading Oates makes good use of natural objects—plants and animals—as inspiration for her thoughts. As you read, use your *Reader/Writer Notebook* to take note of the things she chooses to emphasize, and see what conclusions she makes regarding their meaning.

Learn It Online
Find out more about these Vocabulary words with Word Watch online.

| go.hrw.com | L11-1253 | Go |

The Sky Blue Ball

by **Joyce Carol Oates**

Read with a Purpose

Read to discover how an unexpected game of catch causes a young girl to examine her place in the world.

Build Background

Like the narrator of *The Sky Blue Ball,* Joyce Carol Oates grew up on a farm. Her family did not have much money, and she was educated in a one-room schoolhouse. The narrator feels self-conscious about her family's financial status and the fact that they still live in a rural town, while her other relatives have moved to the wealthier town of Strykersville. She feels inferior to and alienated from the children with whom she goes to school, and she is delighted at the opportunity to have a friendship that is independent of class lines.

In a long-ago time when I didn't know *Yes I was happy, I was myself and I was happy.* In a long-ago time when I wasn't a child any longer yet wasn't entirely not-a-child. In a long-ago time when I seemed often to be alone, and imagined myself lonely. *Yet this is your truest self: alone, lonely.*

One day I found myself walking beside a high brick wall the color of dried blood, the aged bricks loose and moldering, and over the wall came flying a spherical object so brightly blue I thought it was a bird!—until it dropped a few yards in front of me, bouncing at a crooked angle off the broken sidewalk, and I saw that it was a rubber ball. A child had thrown a rubber ball over the wall, and I was expected to throw it back. **Ⓐ**

Hurriedly I let my things fall into the weeds, ran to snatch up the ball, which looked new, smelled new, spongy and resilient in my hand like a rubber ball I'd played with years before as a little girl; a ball I'd loved and had long ago misplaced; a ball I'd loved and had

Ⓐ Literary Focus Symbol What might the brick wall symbolize? Which details provide clues?

Vocabulary **spherical** (SFEHR uh kuhl) *adj.*: having the form of a sphere; globular.
resilient (rih ZIHL yuhnt) *adj.*: able to return to original form after being bent, compressed, or stretched.

forgotten. "Here it comes!" I called, and tossed the ball back over the wall; I would have walked on except, a few seconds later, there came the ball again, flying back.

A game, I thought. *You can't quit a game.*

So I ran after the ball as it rolled in the road, in the gravelly dirt, and again snatched it up, squeezing it with pleasure, how spongy how resilient a rubber ball, and again I tossed it over the wall; feeling happiness in swinging my arm as I hadn't done for years since I'd lost interest in such childish games. And this time I waited expectantly, and again it came!—the most beautiful sky blue rubber ball rising high, high into the air above my head and pausing for a heartbeat before it began to fall, to sink, like an object possessed of its own willful volition; so there was plenty of time for me to position myself beneath it and catch it firmly with both hands.

"Got it!"

I was fourteen years old and did not live in this neighborhood, nor anywhere in the town of Strykersville, New York (population 5,600). I lived on a small farm eleven miles to the north and I was brought to Strykersville by school bus, and consequently I was often alone; for this year, ninth grade, was my first at the school and I hadn't made many friends. And though I had relatives in Strykersville these were not relatives close to my family; they were not relatives eager to acknowledge me; for we who still lived in the country, hadn't yet made the inevitable move into town, were perceived inferior to those who lived in town. And, in fact, my family was poorer than our relatives who lived in Strykersville.

At our school teachers referred to the nine farm children bussed there as "North Country children." We were allowed to understand that "North Country children" differed significantly from Strykersville children. **(B)**

I was not thinking of such things now, I was smiling thinking it must be a particularly playful child on the other side of the wall, a little girl like me; like the little girl I'd been; though the wall was ugly and forbidding with rusted signs EMPIRE MACHINE PARTS and PRIVATE PROPERTY NO TRESPASSING. On the other side of the Chautauqua & Buffalo railroad yard was a street of small wood-frame houses; it must have been in one of these that the little girl, my invisible playmate, lived. She must be much younger than I was; for fourteen-year-old girls didn't play such heedless games with strangers, we grew up swiftly if our families were not well-to-do.

I threw the ball back over the wall, calling, "Hi! Hi, there!" But there was no reply. I waited; I was standing in broken concrete, amid a scrubby patch of weeds. Insects buzzed and droned around me as if in curiosity, yellow butterflies no larger than my smallest fingernail fluttered and caught in my hair, tickling me. The sun was bright as a nova in a pebbled-white soiled sky that was like a thin chamois cloth about to be lifted away and I thought, *This is the surprise I've been waiting for.* For somehow I had acquired the belief that a surprise, a nice surprise, was waiting for me. I had only to merit it, and it would happen. (And if I did not merit it, it would not happen.) Such a surprise could not come from God but only from strangers, by chance.

Another time the sky blue ball sailed over the wall, after a longer interval of perhaps thirty seconds; and at an unexpected angle, as if it had been thrown away from me, from my voice, purposefully. Yet there it came, as if it could not not come: my invisible playmate was obliged to continue the game. I had no hope of catching it but ran blindly into the road (which was partly asphalt and partly gravel and not much traveled except by trucks) and there came a dump truck headed at me, I heard the ugly shriek of brakes and a deafening angry horn and I'd fallen onto my knees, I'd cut my knees that were bare, probably I'd torn my skirt, scrambling quickly to my feet, my cheeks smarting with shame, for wasn't I too grown a girl for such behavior? "Get the hell out of the road!" a man's voice was furious in rectitude, the voice of so many adult men of my acquaintance, you did not question such voices, you did not doubt them, you ran quickly to get out of their way, already I'd snatched up the ball, panting like a dog, trying to hide the ball in my skirt as I turned, shrinking and ducking so the truck driver couldn't see my face, for what if he was someone who

---

(B) **Reading Focus** **Interpreting Details** Based on details in the text so far, what are the implied differences between Strykerville and North Country children?

Vocabulary **volition** (voh LIHSH uhn) *n.:* conscious choice; will; determination.

knew my father, what if he recognized me, knew my name. But already the truck was thundering past, already I'd been forgotten. **C**

Back then I ran to the wall, though both my knees throbbed with pain, and I was shaking as if shivering, the air had grown cold, a shaft of cloud had pierced the sun. I threw the ball back over the wall again, underhand, so that it rose high, high—so that my invisible playmate would have plenty of time to run and catch it. And it disappeared behind the wall and I waited, I was breathing hard and did not investigate my bleeding knees, my torn skirt. More clouds pierced the sun and shadows moved swift and certain across the earth like predator fish. After a while I called out hesitantly, "Hi? Hello?" It was like a ringing telephone you answer but no one is there. You wait, you inquire again, shyly, "Hello?" A vein throbbed in my forehead, a tinge of pain glimmered behind my eyes, that warning of pain, of punishment, following excitement. The child had drifted away, I supposed; she'd lost interest in our game, it if was a game. And suddenly it seemed silly and contemptible to me, and sad: there I stood, fourteen years old, a long-limbed weed of a girl, no longer a child yet panting and bleeding from the knees, the palms of my hands, too, chafed and scraped and dirty; there I stood alone in front of a moldering brick wall waiting for—what?

It was my school notebook, my several textbooks I'd let fall into the grass and I would afterward discover that my math textbook was muddy, many pages damp and torn; my spiral notebook in which I kept careful notes of the intransigent rules of English grammar and sample sentences diagrammed was soaked in a virulent-smelling chemical and my teacher's laudatory comments in red and my grades of A (for all my grades at Strykersville Junior High were A, of that I was obsessively proud) had become illegible as if they were grades of C, D, F. I should have taken up my books and walked hurriedly away and put the sky

blue ball out of my mind entirely but I was not so free, through my life I've been made to realize that I am not free, as others appear to be free, at all. For the "nice" surprise carries with it the "bad" surprise and the two are intricately entwined and they cannot be separated, nor even defined as separate. So though my head pounded I felt obliged to look for a way over the wall. Though my knees were scraped and bleeding I located a filthy oil drum and shoved it against the wall and climbed shakily up on it, dirtying my hands and arms, my legs, my clothes, even more. And I hauled myself over the wall, and jumped down, a drop of about ten feet, the breath knocked out of me as I landed, the shock of impact reverberating through me, along my spine, as if I'd been struck a sledge-hammer blow to the soles of my feet. At once I saw that there could be no little girl here, the factory yard was surely deserted, about the size of a baseball diamond totally walled in and overgrown with weeds pushing through cracked asphalt, thistles, stunted trees, and clouds of tiny yellow butterflies clustered here in such profusion I was made to see that they were not beautiful creatures, but mere insects, horrible. And rushing at me as if my very breath sucked them at me, sticking against my sweaty face, and in my snarled hair. **D**

Yet stubbornly I searched for the ball. I would not leave without the ball. I seemed to know that the ball must be there, somewhere on the other side of the wall, though the wall would have been insurmountable for a little girl. And at last, after long minutes of searching, in a heat of indignation I discovered the ball in a patch of chicory. It was no longer sky blue but faded and cracked; its dun-colored rubber showed through the venous-cracked surface, like my own ball, years ago. Yet I snatched it up in triumph, and squeezed it, and smelled it—it smelled of nothing: of the earth: of the sweating palm of my own hand. **E**

C **Literary Focus** **Symbol** What does the game of catch represent for the narrator?

D **Reading Focus** **Interpreting Details** Which details in this paragraph reveal the strong emotions that the narrator experiences when she makes this surprising discovery?

E **Literary Focus** **Symbol** How has the ball changed? What did it represent at the beginning? What does it represent now?

Vocabulary **intransigent** (ihn TRAN suh juhnt) *adj.:* uncompromising.
insurmountable (ihn suhr MOWNT uh buhl) *adj.:* not capable of being overcome.

The Sky Blue Ball

Respond and Think Critically

Reading Focus

Quick Check

1. In "The Sky Blue Ball," how old is the narrator?

2. What is the setting of this story? Describe it in a few sentences.

3. How does the girl feel about finding the ball? Of what does it remind her?

Read with a Purpose

4. Why does a ball landing near the narrator cause her to examine her life so deeply?

Reading Skills: Interpreting Details

5. As you read, you recorded details from the text and interpreted their meaning. Now that you have finished reading, review your chart. Write a brief paragraph on how Oates carefully chooses details to give symbolic meaning to the story.

✓ Vocabulary Check

Complete each sentence with a Vocabulary word: **spherical, resilient, volition, intransigent, insurmountable.**

6. His position on the need for quality was ____ .

7. Many balloons are_____ when inflated.

8. Against my _____, I had to wash the car.

9. Despite heartbreak, his spirit remained ____ .

10. The icy hill was _____ .

Literary Focus

Literary Analysis

11. **Interpret** What is the significance of the fact that the narrator is not in her own neighborhood?

12. **Make Judgments** The person who tosses the ball over the wall is not identified. Why not? Does this make the story more effective or less?

13. **Interpret** What does the narrator mean when she says that she is "not so free" (page 1256)?

14. **Hypothesize** Why is the narrator determined to retrieve the ball? Why does she feel triumphant when she finds it?

Literary Skills: Symbol

15. **Draw Conclusions** Why did the author choose a rubber ball as a meaningful symbol?

Literary Skills Review: Imagery

16. **Compare and Contrast** The use of vivid language that appeals to a reader's senses (touch, smell, sound, sight, and taste) is **imagery.** How does Oates use imagery to bring the setting and her narrator's experiences to life? Find two passages that are especially effective and describe what her imagery adds.

Writing Focus

Think as a Reader/Writer

Use It in Your Writing Write a paragraph about an object that reminds you of childhood, your own childhood or just the concept of childhood. What does the item symbolize or represent? What mental images or emotions do you associate with this object?

 What Do **You Think Now** What is the best thing about playing games? What needs or desires does playing games fulfill?

SKILLS FOCUS Literary Skills Understand the use of catalog. **Reading Skills** Identify and understand patterns of organization.

 **Reader/Writer**
Notebook
Use your **RWN** to complete the activities for this selection.

Literary Focus

Catalog A **catalog** is a list of related things, people, or events. Writers use catalogs to emphasize comprehensiveness and variety. You can find effective uses of catalog as a literary device in age-old religious writings, in epics, and in the poetry of Walt Whitman. Notice how Brian Doyle uses catalog to express the diversity and richness of the natural world.

Reading Focus

Analyzing Patterns of Organization How a writer organizes information is important to the overall effect of a piece of literature. Doyle starts by describing something very tiny, then something very large, and then things of various sizes. Why? How does this organization serve his argument about human beings? Notice this pattern and others, such as his use of catalog, and think about how they are used to convey meaning.

Into Action Use a chart like the one below to catalog the objects that Doyle discusses in his essay.

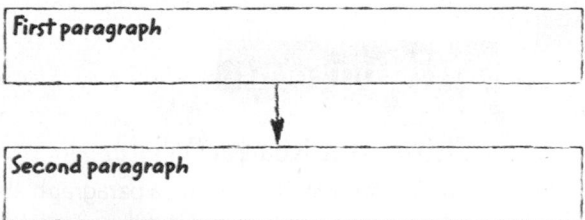

First paragraph

Second paragraph

Writing Focus

Think as a Reader/Writer

Find It in Your Reading Doyle's essay provides detailed information about the natural world. He makes comparisons to objects familiar to most readers so that the new information is clear. For example, Doyle compares the size of the hummingbird's heart to a "pencil eraser." As you read, copy some of Doyle's most effective comparisons in your *Reader/Writer Notebook* and think about what makes them so compelling.

Vocabulary

elephantine (ehl uh FAN tyn) *adj.*: huge; ponderous; clumsy. *In comparison to the tiny hummingbird, humans are elephantine.*

infinitesimal (ihn fih nuh TEHS uh muhl) *adj.*: extremely small; minute. *Compared to the blue whale's heart, the hummingbird's is infinitesimal.*

mitochondria (my tuh KAHN dree uh) *n.*: the part of a cell that produces energy for the cell. *Due to their intense need for oxygen, hummingbirds' hearts have more mitochondria.*

aneurysms (AN yuh rihz uhmz) *n. pl.*: damage or defects in arteries or veins that can cause death. *The hummingbird has more aneurysms than any other creature.*

Language Coach

Using Context Clues to a word's meaning are often found in its context—the words that surround it. In the essay, Doyle observes a hummingbird, a very small creature. He uses *elephantine* to describe a human ear in relationship to a tiny hummingbird. Even without the definition above, you can guess that *elephantine* means "huge." The words *frigid*, *torpor*, and *sludging* all occur in the selection's second paragraph. Read the paragraph; then, with a partner, try to guess the meaning of each word.

 Learn It Online
Find interactive graphic organizers online.

go.hrw.com | L11-1258 | **Go**

Read with a Purpose

Read to learn about the heart, how small or big it can be, and what it embodies in a metaphorical sense.

Build Background

The natural world has captivated and mystified people since the dawn of human history. We are often fascinated with the extremes in nature: tiny, complex organisms that function at a high level of efficiency, as well as enormous animals that make us feel insignificant in comparison. From hummingbirds to blue whales, the animal kingdom shows us how vast and powerful nature can be.

In the following essay, Brian Doyle talks about the natural properties of the heart. He begins with the hummingbird and its absurdly small heart. Slowly, however, he expands his discussion to the properties of the heart that cannot be measured or weighed.

Author Note

Brian Doyle's essays have appeared in *The American Scholar, The Atlantic Monthly, Harper's,* and other prestigious periodicals. He teaches at the University of Portland, writes book reviews, and is a columnist for an Australian newspaper. He is the author of several books of essays, including *The Wet Engine,* a lengthy meditation on the heart.

"Joyas Voladoras"

by **Brian Doyle**

Consider the hummingbird for a long moment. A hummingbird's heart beats ten times a second. A hummingbird's heart is the size of a pencil eraser. A hummingbird's heart is a lot of the hummingbird. *Joyas voladoras,* flying jewels, the first white explorers in the Americas called them, and the white men had never seen such creatures, for hummingbirds came into the world only in the Americas, nowhere else in the universe, more than three hundred species of them whirring and zooming and nectaring in hummer time zones nine times removed from ours, their hearts hammering faster than we could clearly hear if we pressed our elephantine ears to their infinitesimal chests. **Ⓐ**

Each one visits a thousand flowers a day. They can dive at sixty miles an hour. They can fly backward. They can fly more than five hundred miles without pausing to rest. But when they rest they come close to death: on frigid nights, or when they are starving, they retreat into torpor, their metabolic rate slowing to a fifteenth of their normal sleep rate, their hearts

Ⓐ **Literary Focus** Catalog Where does Doyle use the catalog device? What is its effect?

Vocabulary **elephantine** (ehl uh FAN teen) *adj.:* huge; ponderous; clumsy.
infinitesimal (ihn fih nuh TEHS uh muhl) *adj.:* extremely small; minute.

Hummingbirds (1994) by Pat Culler. Oil on panel.

sludging nearly to a halt, barely beating, and if they are not soon warmed, if they do not soon find that which is sweet, their hearts grow cold, and they cease to be. Consider for a moment those hummingbirds who did not open their eyes again today, this very day, in the Americas: bearded helmetcrests and booted racket-tails, violet-tailed sylphs and violet-capped woodnymphs, crimson topazes and purple-crowned fairies, red-tailed comets and amethyst woodstars, rainbow-bearded thornbills and glittering-bellied emeralds, velvet-purple coronets and golden-bellied star-frontlets, fiery-tailed awlbills and Andean hillstars, spatuletails and pufflegs, each the most amazing thing you have never seen, each thunderous wild heart the size of an infant's fingernail, each mad heart silent, a brilliant music stilled. **B**

Hummingbirds, like all flying birds but more so, have incredible enormous immense ferocious metabolisms. To drive those metabolisms they have racecar hearts that eat oxygen at an eye-popping rate. Their hearts are built of thinner, leaner fibers than ours. Their arteries are stiffer and more taut. They have more mitochondria

Vocabulary **mitochondria** (my tuh KAHN dree uh) *n.:* the part of a cell that produces energy for the cell.

B Reading Focus **Analyzing Patterns of Organization** Why does Doyle list the names of so many varieties of hummingbirds?

in their heart muscles—anything to gulp more oxygen. Their hearts are stripped to the skin for the war against gravity and inertia, the mad search for food, the insane idea of flight. The price of their ambition is a life closer to death; they suffer more heart attacks and aneurysms and ruptures than any other living creature. It's expensive to fly. You burn out. You fry the machine. You melt the engine. Every creature on earth has approximately two billion heartbeats to spend in a lifetime. You can spend them slowly, like a tortoise, and live to be two hundred years old, or you can spend them fast, like a hummingbird, and live to be two years old.

The biggest heart in the world is inside the blue whale. It weighs more than seven tons. It's as big as a room. It *is* a room, with four chambers. A child could walk around in it, head high, bending only to step through the valves. The valves are as big as the swinging doors in a saloon. This house of a heart drives a creature a hundred feet long. When this creature is born it is twenty feet long and weighs four tons. It is waaaaay bigger than your car. It drinks a hundred gallons of milk from its mama every day and gains two hundred pounds a day, and when it is seven or eight years old it endures an unimaginable puberty and then it essentially disappears from human ken, for next to nothing is known of the mating habits, travel patterns, diet, social life, language, social structure, diseases, spirituality, wars, stories, despairs, and arts of the blue whale. There are perhaps ten thousand blue whales in the world, living in every ocean on earth, and of the largest mammal who ever lived we know nearly nothing. But we know this: the animals with the largest hearts in the world generally travel in pairs, and their penetrating moaning cries, their piercing yearning tongue, can be heard underwater for miles and miles. **C** **D**

Every creature on earth has approximately **two billion** heartbeats to spend in a lifetime.

Mammals and birds have hearts with four chambers. Reptiles and turtles have hearts with three chambers. Fish have hearts with two chambers. Insects and mollusks have hearts with one chamber. Worms have hearts with one chamber, although they may have as many as eleven single-chambered hearts. Unicellular bacteria have no hearts at all; but even they have fluid eternally in motion, washing from one side of the cell to the other, swirling and whirling. No living being is without interior liquid motion. We all churn inside.

So much held in a heart in a lifetime. So much held in a heart in a day, an hour, a moment. We are utterly open with no one, in the end—not mother and father, not wife or husband, not lover, not child, not friend. We open windows to each but we live alone in the house of the heart. Perhaps we must. Perhaps we could not bear to be so naked for fear of a constantly harrowed heart. When young we think there will come

---

C **Literary Focus** Catalog What kinds of facts does Doyle catalog about the hummingbird and the blue whale? Why?

D **Reading Focus** Analyzing Patterns of Organization Why does the author emphasize the extremes in nature, from hummingbirds to blue whales?

Vocabulary **aneurysms** (AN yuh rihz uhmz) *n. pl.*: damage or defects in arteries or veins that can cause death.

Alexander: *Open Up Your Heart* (1998) by Burhan Dogancay.

one person who will savor and sustain us always; when we are older we know this is the dream of a child, that all hearts finally are bruised and scarred, scored and torn, repaired by time and will, patched by force of character, yet fragile and rickety forevermore, no matter how ferocious the defense and how many bricks you bring to the wall. You can brick up your heart as stout and tight and hard and cold and impregnable as you possibly can and down it comes in an instant, felled by a woman's second glance, a child's apple breath, the shatter of glass in the road, the words "I have something to tell you," a cat with a broken spine dragging itself into the forest to die, the brush of your mother's papery ancient hand in the thicket of your hair, the memory of your father's voice early in the morning echoing from the kitchen where he is making pancakes for his children. **E**

E **Literary Focus** **Catalog** Why does the author focus on the hearts of the animals that he describes?

Applying Your Skills

SKILLS FOCUS **Literary Skills** Analyze the use of catalog; analyze imagery. **Reading Skills** Identify and understand patterns of organization. **Vocabulary**

Skills Demonstrate word knowledge. **Writing Skills** Employ elements of an author's style effectively.

"Joyas Voladoras"

Respond and Think Critically

Reading Focus

Quick Check

1. About how long does a hummingbird live?

2. How large is a blue whale's heart?

3. How does a human heart rate compare with that of a hummingbird?

Read with a Purpose

4. What do you think Doyle means by the line, "we live alone in the house of the heart" (page 1261)?

Reading Skills: Analyzing Patterns of Organization

5. As you read, you recorded the catalog of facts and objects in each paragraph. Now that you have finished reading, expand your chart to explain how those cataloged facts and objects affected your reading of the essay.

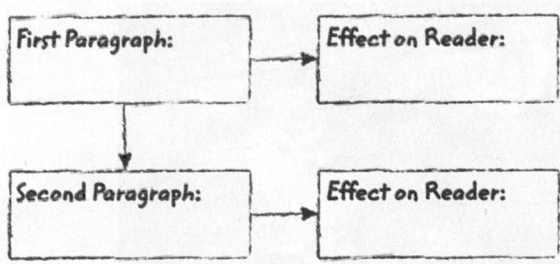

Literary Focus

Literary Analysis

10. **Evaluate** How does Doyle express his love of and passion for nature?

11. **Evaluate** Why does Doyle begin his essay with a detailed and scientific comparison of the very different hearts of a hummingbird and a whale?

12. **Interpret** What is Doyle suggesting by saying that all animals "churn inside" (page 1261)?

Literary Skills: Catalog

13. **Hypothesize** Why does the author catalog facts in ornate, elaborate language?

14. **Analyze** How does the author's use of catalog create rhythm? What does this rhythm add?

Literary Skills Review: Imagery

15. **Analyze** How does Doyle's use of **imagery,** or language the appeals to the senses, enhance the effectiveness of this essay? Cite examples.

Writing Focus

Think as a Reader/Writer

Use It in Your Writing Think about a topic pertaining to the natural world that you know well or one that you would like to research. Write two or three informative paragraphs about this topic. As you write, use at least two comparisons similar to those employed by Doyle to make the information clearer to your reader.

Vocabulary Check

Write a sentence using each of the Vocabulary words:

6. elephantine

7. infinitesimal

8. mitochondria

9. aneurysms

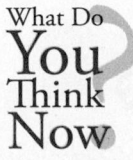

What Do You Think Now Are elements of nature, such as plants and animals, ordinary? Do we tend to take them for granted?

CALVIN AND HOBBES

by Bill Watterson

Themes Across Genres

Writing Focus

1. Write a Comparison-Contrast Essay
Comparing and contrasting authors' themes across genres presents challenges but can also offer real insights into literature. In this case, comparing and contrasting a visual representation (such as a cartoon) and written selections of different genres that address similar themes provides a unique opportunity to focus on how authors and artists use images in words and art.

Identify Similarities and Differences

To compare and contrast across genres, you must first determine a basis of similarity. In other words, there needs to be something significant that connects the works. The short story "The Sky Blue Ball," the essay "Joyas Voladoras," and the *Calvin and Hobbes* cartoon all explore the vulnerability of the heart and comment on the emotions that make us human. After re-reading the selections, ask yourself the following questions to determine similarities and differences.

- What aspects of the human heart does each work address?
- Do the authors employ similar or different imagery and figurative language?
- Do the characteristics of the genres themselves create differences among the works?
- Do the authors express similar or different themes?

First, you should focus on commonalities. Then, you should focus on identifying significant differences. (Do not use the fact that the three represent different genres as a significant difference.)

Organize and Draft Your Essay

A point-by-point organizational method is effective for comparing and contrasting three selections. In each body paragraph, address a point of similarity or difference and, using textual evidence, refer to each of the three selections. Use the following outline to plan your comparison-contrast essay.

I. Paragraph One/ Introduction
Provide selection titles, authors, and genres; identify the basis for comparison.

II. Paragraph Two
Develop the basis of similarity (in this case, theme).

III. Paragraph Three
Discuss another similarity or the first difference.

IV. Additional Paragraphs
(The number of paragraphs will vary depending on the points you want to discuss.) Discuss another similarity or difference. The final body paragraph should be a significant difference among the three selections.

V. Final Paragraph / Conclusion
Restate the major similarities and differences; include any overarching conclusions.

2. Timed ⌐Writing The cartoon, the essay by Doyle, and the short story by Oates explore the very human state of yearning for answers to life's most basic questions: Who am I? Am I happy? Am I loved? In an essay, explain how the questions explored in these three selections relate to your own life. Provide specific examples of your own search for answers to these or other basic questions.

Contemporary Nonfiction

LITERARY FOCUS
Autobiographical Writing

CONTENTS

"I would hurl words
into this darkness and
wait for an echo. If
an echo sounded, no
matter how faintly,
I would send other
words to tell . . . to
create a sense of the
hunger for life that
gnaws in us all, to
keep alive in our
hearts a sense of the
inexpressibly human."

— **Richard Wright**

New Orleans (2001) by Gwen Knight. Serigraph, edition of 100 (22 × 20 inches).

SKILLS FOCUS Literary Skills Understand and analyze the characteristics of autobiography.

Autobiographical Writing by Leila Christenbury

Characteristics of Autobiographical Writing

- Personal writing exhibiting reflection and introspection
- Interpretive account of events on the part of the author, usually with the understanding that readers will judge or evaluate the interpretation
- Explanation of the writer's sources of inspiration or reasons for writing

Reflection and Introspection

An **autobiography** is an account of a writer's own life (from the prefix *auto–*, meaning "self," and the word *biography*, meaning "story of a life"). When a published writer tells the story of his or her own life, we expect to learn how that person became a writer and on which experiences the writer drew to produce his or her work. In autobiographies we also look for subjective details—we want to know how the writer felt about his or her family, friends, and experiences. It is these authentic, firsthand details that distinguish autobiography from biography.

Autobiography is a connected narrative that shows reflection and introspection on the part of the author. It is not so much a recounting of events as an interpretation of them. The purpose of the autobiographical writer is to make public the private events in the writer's life. The fact that others are reading—and judging—is often at the heart of autobiography.

The Importance of Memory

In her autobiography, *One Writer's Beginnings*, Eudora Welty states, "Writing fiction has developed in me . . . a sense of where to look for the threads, how to follow, how to connect, find in the thick of the tangle what clear line persists. The strands are all there: To the memory nothing is ever really lost."

One of the oldest bits of advice to an aspiring writer is "write what you know." Taking that advice, just about every good writer discovers that personal experience is what gives vitality and authenticity to literature. It is no surprise then that autobiographies of writers often include detailed memories of childhood experiences that paved the way for the adult to become a writer. For example, writer Alice Walker draws upon childhood memories as inspiration for her poems, essays, and novels. Similarly, Sandra Cisneros draws ideas for her work from her family and her culture.

Sometimes, childhood experiences are recollections of extreme hardships or painful struggles with identity. In his autobiography, *Black Boy*, Richard Wright unflinchingly describes life after his father abandons the family. James Baldwin discusses the tension between defining himself as a writer and as an African American in his "Autobiographical Notes." In *The Woman Warrior*, Maxine Hong Kingston explores the subject of assimilation by using a young Chinese American girl as her narrator.

As you read this collection, think about how the writers shape their stories. Can you tell how they want to be remembered or viewed by their readers?

Ask Yourself

1. Describe the thought process involved in autobiographical writing.
2. What impact can childhood experiences have on an individual's decision or need to write?

Learn It Online
Explore autobiographical writing with *PowerNotes*.
go.hrw.com L11-1267 GO

from Black Boy

Richard Wright
(1908–1960)

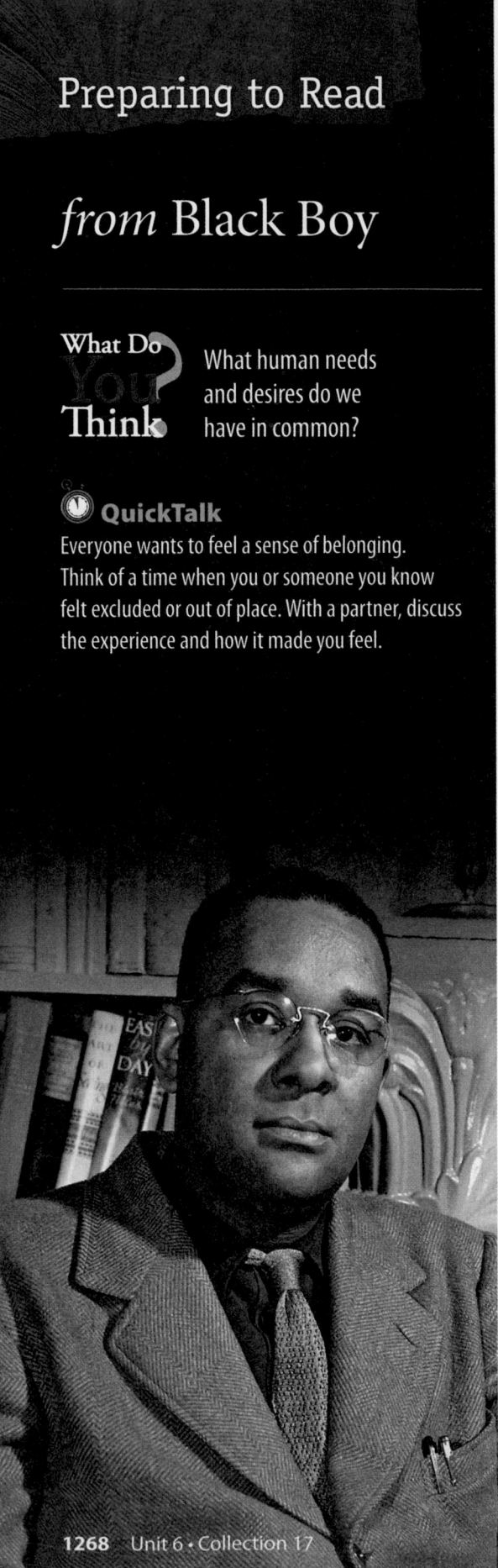

What Do You Think? What human needs and desires do we have in common?

QuickTalk

Everyone wants to feel a sense of belonging. Think of a time when you or someone you know felt excluded or out of place. With a partner, discuss the experience and how it made you feel.

Richard Wright is typically described as the first African American writer to expose American racism to a large white audience. This cool academic assessment fails to emphasize the angry, relentless drive of his most famous novel, *Native Son* (1940), or of his autobiography, *Black Boy* (1945). Wright is hard to label, yet it is clear that African American writers who followed him have had to emerge from his shadow.

Saved by Books

Wright's life began in poverty. His father, a Mississippi share-cropper, abandoned his family when Wright was five; when the boy was twelve, his mother could no longer support the family. Raised by various relatives, he learned the bitter lessons of survival in the ghetto. He remembered living with "the sustained expectation of violence." By borrowing a white man's library card, he was finally able to gain access to books. Wright once said: "It had been only through books—at best, no more than vicarious cultural transfusions—that I had managed to keep myself alive. . . ."

Before he was twenty, Wright fled the South forever, moving to Chicago and then to New York. He joined the WPA Federal Writers Project, a Depression-era government organization that provided a livelihood for unemployed writers. He explored Marxism and eventually joined the Communist party at a time when many people thought it offered hope for a better society. Disillusioned with its politics, Wright left the party in 1944.

Critical Success and Later Life

Wright achieved his first real recognition with his novel *Native Son*. His autobiography, *Black Boy,* secured Wright's fame and became a bestseller. He struggled to understand the historical and cultural place of African Americans in modern life, visiting Africa and recording his observations, but he felt as much an alien in Africa as anywhere else. He died in Paris, where he spent the last fourteen years of his life in self-imposed exile.

Think About the Writer In what ways do you think Wright's early experiences of poverty and abandonment influenced his writing?

Reader/Writer Notebook

Use your **RWN** to complete the activities for this selection.

Literary Focus

Dialogue We often associate **dialogue,** the directly quoted words of people speaking to one another, with drama and fiction. Dialogue is also an important <u>component</u> of contemporary nonfiction, particularly in **autobiography** and journalism. In Wright's autobiography, most of the scenes are dramatized by means of dialogue, giving it the feel of a novel, even though he is writing about actual events from his own life.

TechFocus As you read the excerpt, think about how you might present it in a podcast. How will you use Wright's dialogue to bring this autobiography to life?

Reading Focus

Interpreting Details Writers use specific details to add color and depth to their work. When you **interpret details** from a text, you gain insight into a writer's intended meaning. As you read, notice the details Wright uses to describe his father's character.

Into Action Use a chart like the one below to record the details in Wright's first description of his father (page 1271) and his final description (page 1279). Details may include his father's physical traits, actions, and effect on his son.

Father in Memphis	Father 25 years later
night porter	sharecropper
imposing, forbidding	smiling toothlessly, white hair, body bent, eyes glazed

Writing Focus

Think as a Reader/Writer

Find It in Your Reading When writers describe an incident, they often list the series of events leading up to that incident in **chronological order** to show how and why the incident took place. Take note of how Wright reveals the events that lead to his placement in an orphanage. Use your *Reader/Writer Notebook* to record the sequence in which Wright presents these events.

Vocabulary

enthralled (ehn THRAWLD) *v.:* fascinated. *The machines enthralled the young Wright.*

clamor (KLAM uhr) *n.:* loud noise; loud demand or complaint. *His hunger created a clamor in his empty stomach.*

dispirited (dihs PIHR uh tihd) *adj.:* discouraged. *After long days away from her family, Wright's mother returned home dispirited.*

frenzy (FREHN zee) *n.:* frantic behavior; wildness. *Wright worked himself into a frenzy as he fought off the bullies who attacked him.*

ardently (AHR duhnt lee) *adv.:* intensely; eagerly. *His mother found some peace in her ardently held religious beliefs.*

futile (FYOO tuhl) *adj.:* useless; pointless. *Reasoning with his father was futile.*

eluded (ih LOOD ihd) *v.:* escaped detection or notice. *The meaning of his interactions with his father eluded him.*

withering (WIHTH uhr ihng) *v.* used as *adj.:* drying up; weakening. *Wright noticed his father's withering body.*

Language Coach

Final Vowel Sounds When the pattern *i*-consonant-*e* occurs at the end of a multi-syllable word, like *futile*, it can be difficult to determine the correct pronunciation of the letter *i*. Here are some examples:

hostile: Final *i* sound is /uh/ or /y/.
massive: Final *i* sound is /ih/.
routine: Final *i* sound is /ee/.

 Learn It Online
Learn more about Wright with these Internet links.

go.hrw.com [L11-1269] **Go**

from
Black
BOY

by **Richard Wright**

Jim (1930) by William H. Johnson.

Read with a Purpose
Read to learn about how the hunger Wright endured as a child affected his view of the world.

Build Background
Black Boy, widely considered to be Wright's masterpiece, appeared in 1945. It tells the story of Wright's early life in the South. The second part of Wright's autobiography, written in the 1940s, is called *American Hunger* and covers the story of Wright's life after he left the South and traveled to Chicago in 1927.

Wright wrestled with various hungers all his life, from the physical hunger he experienced as a poverty-stricken child to the hunger to express himself as a writer and to forge his own identity as an African American. This excerpt from *Black Boy* reveals how he came to terms with his father's abandonment and his family's ensuing poverty.

One day my mother told me that we were going to Memphis on a boat, the *Kate Adams*, and my eagerness thereafter made the days seem endless. Each night I went to bed hoping that the next morning would be the day of departure.

"How big is the boat?" I asked my mother.

"As big as a mountain," she said.

"Has it got a whistle?"

"Yes."

"Does the whistle blow?"

"Yes."

"When?"

"When the captain wants it to blow."

"Why do they call it the *Kate Adams*?"

"Because that's the boat's name."

"What color is the boat?"

"White."

"How long will we be on the boat?"

"All day and all night."

"Will we sleep on the boat?"

"Yes, when we get sleepy, we'll sleep. Now, hush." **A**

For days I had dreamed about a huge white boat floating on a vast body of water, but when my mother took me down to the levee on the day of leaving, I saw a tiny, dirty boat that was not at all like the boat I had imagined. I was disappointed and when time came to go on board I cried and my mother thought that I did not want to go with her to Memphis, and I could not tell her what the trouble was. Solace came when I wandered about the boat and gazed at Negroes throwing dice, drinking whiskey, playing cards, lolling on boxes, eating, talking, and singing. My father took me down into the engine room and the throbbing machines enthralled me for hours.

In Memphis we lived in a one-story brick tenement. The stone buildings and the concrete pavements looked bleak and hostile to me. The absence of green, growing things made the city seem dead. Living space for the four of us—my mother, my brother, my father, and me—was a kitchen and a bedroom. In the front and rear were paved areas in which my brother and I could play, but for days I was afraid to go into the strange city streets alone.

It was in this tenement that the personality of my father first came fully into the orbit of my concern. He worked as a night porter in a Beale Street drugstore and he became important and forbidding to me only when I learned that I could not make noise when he was asleep in the daytime. He was the lawgiver in our family and I never laughed in his presence. I used to lurk timidly in the kitchen doorway and watch his huge body sitting slumped at the table. I stared at him with awe as he gulped his beer from a tin bucket, as he ate long and heavily, sighed, belched, closed his eyes to nod on a stuffed belly. He was quite fat and his bloated stomach always lapped over his belt. He was always a stranger to me, always somehow alien and remote. . . . **B**

Hunger stole upon me so slowly that at first I was not aware of what hunger really meant. Hunger had always been more or less at my elbow when I played, but now I began to wake up at night to find hunger standing at my bedside, staring at me gauntly. The hunger I had known before this had been no grim, hostile stranger; it had been a normal hunger that had made me beg constantly for bread, and when I ate a crust or two I was satisfied. But this new hunger baffled me, scared me, made me angry and insistent. Whenever I begged for food now my mother would pour me a cup of tea which would still the clamor in my stomach for a moment or two; but a little later I would feel hunger nudging my ribs, twisting my empty guts until they ached. I would grow dizzy and my vision would dim. I became less active in my play, and for the first time in my life I had to pause and think of what was happening to me.

"Mama, I'm hungry," I complained one afternoon.

"Jump up and catch a kungry," she said, trying to make me laugh and forget.

"What's a *kungry*?"

"It's what little boys eat when they get hungry," she said.

A Literary Focus **Dialogue** Based on this dialogue, how would you describe the young Wright? How would you describe his mother?

B Reading Focus **Interpreting Details** Which details support the idea that Wright's father was a "stranger"?

Vocabulary **enthralled** (ehn THRAWLD) *v.*: fascinated.
clamor (KLAM uhr) *n.*: loud noise; loud demand or complaint.

Analyzing Visuals

Viewing and Interpreting
The young boy sits pressed closely between the women in the painting. How could his position reflect Wright's situation as a child?

A Mother's Strength (2001) by Colin Bootman.

"What does it taste like?"

"I don't know."

"Then why do you tell me to catch one?"

"Because you said that you were hungry," she said, smiling.

I sensed that she was teasing me and it made me angry.

"But I'm hungry. I want to eat."

"You'll have to wait."

"But I want to eat now."

"But there's nothing to eat," she told me.

"Why?"

"Just because there's none," she explained.

"But I want to eat," I said, beginning to cry.

"You'll just have to wait," she said again.

"But why?"

"For God to send some food."

"When is He going to send it?"

"I don't know."

"But I'm hungry!" **C**

She was ironing and she paused and looked at me with tears in her eyes.

"Where's your father?" she asked me.

I stared in bewilderment. Yes, it was true that my father had not come home to sleep for many days now and I could make as much noise as I wanted. Though I had not known why he was absent, I had been glad that he was not there to shout his restrictions at me. But it had never occurred to me that his absence would mean that there would be no food.

"I don't know," I said.

"Who brings food into the house?" my mother asked me.

"Papa," I said. "He always brought food."

"Well, your father isn't here now," she said.

"Where is he?"

"I don't know," she said.

"But I'm hungry," I whimpered, stomping my feet.

"You'll have to wait until I get a job and buy food," she said.

As the days slid past, the image of my father became associated with my pangs of hunger, and whenever I felt hunger I thought of him with a deep biological bitterness. **D**

C Literary Focus **Dialogue** What does this exchange reveal about Wright's mother?

D Reading Focus **Interpreting Details** How does Wright's view of his father change? Why?

My mother finally went to work as a cook and left me and my brother alone in the flat each day with a loaf of bread and a pot of tea. When she returned at evening she would be tired and dispirited and would cry a lot. Sometimes, when she was in despair, she would call us to her and talk to us for hours, telling us that we now had no father, that our lives would be different from those of other children, that we must learn as soon as possible to take care of ourselves, to dress ourselves, to prepare our own food; that we must take upon ourselves the responsibility of the flat while she worked. Half frightened, we would promise solemnly. We did not understand what had happened between our father and our mother and the most that these long talks did to us was to make us feel a vague dread. Whenever we asked why father had left, she would tell us that we were too young to know. **E**

One evening my mother told me that thereafter I would have to do the shopping for food. She took me to the corner store to show me the way. I was proud; I felt like a grownup. The next afternoon I looped the basket over my arm and went down the pavement toward the store. When I reached the corner, a gang of boys grabbed me, knocked me down, snatched the basket, took the money, and sent me running home in panic. That evening I told my mother what had happened, but she made no comment; she sat down at once, wrote another note, gave me more money, and sent me out to the grocery again. I crept down the steps and saw the same gang of boys playing down the street. I ran back into the house.

"What's the matter?" my mother asked.

"It's those same boys," I said. "They'll beat me."

"You've got to get over that," she said. "Now, go on."

"I'm scared," I said.

"Go on and don't pay any attention to them," she said.

I went out of the door and walked briskly down the sidewalk, praying that the gang would not molest me. But when I came abreast of them someone shouted.

"There he is!"

They came toward me and I broke into a wild run toward home. They overtook me and flung me to the pavement. I yelled, pleaded, kicked, but they wrenched the money out of my hand. They yanked me to my feet, gave me a few slaps, and sent me home sobbing. My mother met me at the door.

"They b-beat m-me," I gasped. "They t-t-took the m-money."

I started up the steps, seeking the shelter of the house.

"Don't you come in here," my mother warned me.

I froze in my tracks and stared at her.

"But they're coming after me," I said.

"You just stay right where you are," she said in a deadly tone. "I'm going to teach you this night to stand up and fight for yourself." **F**

She went into the house and I waited, terrified, wondering what she was about. Presently she returned with more money and another note; she also had a long heavy stick.

"Take this money, this note, and this stick," she said. "Go to the store and buy those groceries. If those boys bother you, then fight."

I was baffled. My mother was telling me to fight, a thing that she had never done before.

"But I'm scared," I said.

"Don't you come into this house until you've gotten those groceries," she said.

"They'll beat me; they'll beat me," I said.

"Then stay in the streets; don't come back here!"

I ran up the steps and tried to force my way past her into the house. A stinging slap came on my jaw. I stood on the sidewalk, crying.

"Please, let me wait until tomorrow," I begged.

"No," she said. "Go now! If you come back into this house without those groceries, I'll whip you!" **G**

She slammed the door and I heard the key turn in the lock. I shook with fright. I was alone upon the dark, hostile streets and gangs were after me. I had the choice of being beaten at home or away from home. I clutched the stick, crying, trying to reason. If I were beaten at home, there was absolutely nothing that I could do about it; but if I were beaten in the streets,

---

E **Reading Focus** **Interpreting Details** What details hint at how Wright's life changed after his father left?

Vocabulary **dispirited** (dihs PIHR uh tihd) *adj.:* discouraged.

F **Literary Focus** **Dialogue** From the dialogue, what do you learn about the mother's character and motivation?

G **Reading Focus** **Interpreting Details** How would you interpret the mother's actions?

I had a chance to fight and defend myself. I walked slowly down the sidewalk, coming closer to the gang of boys, holding the stick tightly. I was so full of fear that I could scarcely breathe. I was almost upon them now.

"There he is again!" the cry went up.

They surrounded me quickly and began to grab for my hand.

"I'll kill you!" I threatened.

They closed in. In blind fear I let the stick fly, feeling it crack against a boy's skull. I swung again, lamming another skull, then another. Realizing that they would retaliate if I let up for but a second, I fought to lay them low, to knock them cold, to kill them so that they could not strike back at me. I flayed with tears in my eyes, teeth clenched, stark fear making me throw every ounce of my strength behind each blow. I hit again and again, dropping the money and the grocery list. The boys scattered, yelling, nursing their heads, staring at me in utter disbelief. They had never seen such frenzy. I stood panting, egging them on, taunting them to come on and fight. When they refused, I ran after them and they tore out for their homes, screaming. The parents of the boys rushed into the streets and threatened me, and for the first time in my life I shouted at grownups, telling them that I would give them the same if they bothered me. I finally found my grocery list and the money and went to the store. On my way back I kept my stick poised for instant use, but there was not a single boy in sight. That night I won the right to the streets of Memphis. . . . **H**

After my father's desertion, my mother's ardently religious disposition dominated the household and I was often taken to Sunday school where I met God's representative in the guise of a tall, black preacher. One Sunday my mother invited the tall, black preacher to a dinner of fried chicken. I was happy, not because the preacher was coming but because of the chicken. One or two neighbors also were invited. But no sooner had the preacher arrived than I began to resent him, for I learned at once that he, like my father, was used to having his own way. The hour for dinner came and I was wedged at the table between talking and laughing adults. In the center of the table was a huge platter of golden-brown fried chicken. I compared the bowl of soup that sat before me with the crispy chicken and decided in favor of the chicken. The others began to eat their soup, but I could not touch mine.

"Eat your soup," my mother said.

"I don't want any," I said.

"You won't get anything else until you've eaten your soup," she said.

The preacher had finished his soup and had asked that the platter of chicken be passed to him. It galled me. He smiled, cocked his head this way and that, picking out choice pieces. I forced a spoonful of soup down my throat and looked to see if my speed matched that of the preacher. It did not. There were already bare chicken bones on his plate, and he was reaching for more. I tried eating my soup faster, but it was no use; the other people were now serving themselves chicken and the platter was more than half empty. I gave up and sat staring in despair at the vanishing pieces of fried chicken.

"Eat your soup or you won't get anything," my mother warned.

I looked at her appealingly and could not answer. As piece after piece of chicken was eaten, I was unable to eat my soup at all. I grew hot with anger. The preacher was laughing and joking and the grownups were hanging on his words. My growing hate of the preacher finally became more important than God or religion and I could no longer contain myself. I leaped up from the table, knowing that I should be ashamed of what I was doing, but unable to stop, and screamed, running blindly from the room

"That preacher's going to eat *all* the chicken!" I bawled. **I**

The preacher tossed back his head and roared with laughter, but my mother was angry and told me that I was to have no dinner because of my bad manners. **J**

H **Reading Focus** Interpreting Details Why is this an important episode in Wright's life?

Vocabulary frenzy (FREHN zee) *n.*: frantic behavior; wildness.
ardently (AHR duhnt lee) *adv.*: intensely; eagerly.

I **Reading Focus** Interpreting Details What details reveal Wright's frustration?

J **Literary Focus** Dialogue What is the effect of the dialogue in this scene? Why can Wright not answer his mother?

Fighting Hunger

Today, about 37% of Americans live in poverty. An estimated 12.9 million of them are under the age of 18. An organization called America's Second Harvest works in all 50 states to provide food for hungry people. This group distributes more than two billion pounds of food annually to people in need. As many as nine million children in this country benefit from charitable organizations such as America's Second Harvest and local food banks, devoted to feeding the hungry.

Ask Yourself
What can you do to help fight hunger?

Volunteers lending a hand at a food bank in Sacramento.

When I awakened one morning my mother told me that we were going to see a judge who would make my father support me and my brother. An hour later all three of us were sitting in a huge crowded room. I was overwhelmed by the many faces and the voices which I could not understand. High above me was a white face which my mother told me was the face of the judge. Across the huge room sat my father, smiling confidently, looking at us. My mother warned me not to be fooled by my father's friendly manner; she told me that the judge might ask me questions, and if he did I must tell him the truth. I agreed, yet I hoped that the judge would not ask me anything.

For some reason the entire thing struck me as being useless; I felt that if my father were going to feed me, then he would have done so regardless of what a judge said to him. And I did not want my father to feed me; I was hungry, but my thoughts of food did not now center about him. I waited, growing restless, hungry. My mother gave me a dry sandwich and I munched and stared, longing to go home. Finally I heard my mother's name called; she rose and began weeping so copiously that she could not talk for a few moments; at last she managed to say that her husband had deserted her and two children, that her children were hungry, that they stayed hungry, that she worked, that she was trying to raise them alone. Then my father was called; he came forward jauntily, smiling. He tried to kiss my mother, but she turned away from him. I only heard one sentence of what he said. **(K)**

"I'm doing all I can, Your Honor," he mumbled, grinning.

It had been painful to sit and watch my mother crying and my father laughing and I was glad when we were outside in the sunny streets. Back at home my mother wept again and talked complainingly about the unfairness of the judge who had accepted my father's word. After the court scene, I tried to forget my father; I did not hate him; I simply did not want to think of him. Often when we were hungry my mother would beg me to go to my father's job and ask him for a dollar, a dime, a nickel . . . But I would never consent to go. I did not want to see him.

(K) Reading Focus Interpreting Details What do the details in this passage reveal about Wright's attitude toward his father?

My mother fell ill and the problem of food became an acute, daily agony. Hunger was with us always. Sometimes the neighbors would feed us or a dollar bill would come in the mail from my grandmother. It was winter and I would buy a dime's worth of coal each morning from the corner coalyard and lug it home in paper bags. For a time I remained out of school to wait upon my mother, then Granny came to visit us and I returned to school.

At night there were long, halting discussions about our going to live with Granny, but nothing came of it. Perhaps there was not enough money for railroad fare. Angered by having been hauled into court, my father now spurned us completely. I heard long, angrily whispered conversations between my mother and grandmother to the effect that "that woman ought to be killed for breaking up a home." What irked me was the ceaseless talk and no action. If someone had suggested that my father be killed, I would perhaps have become interested; if someone had suggested that his name never be mentioned, I would no doubt have agreed; if someone had suggested that we move to another city, I would have been glad. But there was only endless talk that led nowhere and I began to keep away from home as much as possible, preferring the simplicity of the streets to the worried, futile talk at home.

Finally we could no longer pay the rent for our dingy flat; the few dollars that Granny had left us before she went home were gone. Half sick and in despair, my mother made the rounds of the charitable institutions, seeking help. She found an orphan home that agreed to assume the guidance of me and my brother provided my mother worked and made small payments. My mother hated to be separated from us, but she had no choice.

The orphan home was a two-story frame building set amid trees in a wide, green field. My mother ushered me and my brother one morning into the building and into the presence of a tall, gaunt, mulatto woman who called herself Miss Simon. At once she took a fancy to me and I was frightened speechless; I was afraid of her the moment I saw her and my fear lasted during my entire stay in the home.

The house was crowded with children and there was always a storm of noise. The daily routine was blurred to me and I never quite grasped it. The most abiding feeling I had each day was hunger and fear. The meals were skimpy and there were only two of them. Just before we went to bed each night we were given a slice of bread smeared with molasses. The children were silent, hostile, vindictive, continuously complaining of hunger. There was an overall atmosphere of nervousness and intrigue, of children telling tales upon others, of children being deprived of food to punish them.

The home did not have the money to check the growth of the wide stretches of grass by having it mown, so it had to be pulled by hand. Each morning after we had eaten a breakfast that seemed like no breakfast at all, an older child would lead a herd of us to the vast lawn and we would get to our knees and wrench the grass loose from the dirt with our fingers. At intervals Miss Simon would make a tour of inspection, examining the pile of pulled grass beside each child, scolding or praising according to the size of the pile. Many mornings I was too weak from hunger to pull the grass; I would grow dizzy and my mind would become blank and I would find myself, after an interval of unconsciousness, upon my hands and knees, my head whirling, my eyes staring in bleak astonishment at the green grass, wondering where I was, feeling that I was emerging from a dream . . . **Ⓛ**

During the first days my mother came each night to visit me and my brother, then her visits stopped. I began to wonder if she, too, like my father, had disappeared into the unknown. I was rapidly learning to distrust everything and everybody. When my mother did come, I asked her why had she remained away so long and she told me that Miss Simon had forbidden her to visit us, that Miss Simon had said that she was spoiling us with too much attention. I begged my mother to take me away; she wept and told me to wait, that soon she would take us to Arkansas. She left and my heart sank.

Miss Simon tried to win my confidence; she asked me if I would like to be adopted by her if my mother consented and I said no. She would take me into her apartment and talk to me, but her words had no effect.

Vocabulary futile (FYOO tuhl) *adj.*: useless; pointless.

Ⓛ Reading Focus Interpreting Details Which details reveal the most about the poverty of the orphanage?

Dread and mistrust had already become a daily part of my being and my memory grew sharp, my senses more impressionable; I began to be aware of myself as a distinct personality striving against others. I held myself in, afraid to act or speak until I was sure of my surroundings, feeling most of the time that I was suspended over a void. My imagination soared; I dreamed of running away. Each morning I vowed that I would leave the next morning, but the next morning always found me afraid. **Ⓜ**

One day Miss Simon told me that thereafter I was to help her in the office. I ate lunch with her and, strangely, when I sat facing her at the table, my hunger vanished. The woman killed something in me. Next she called me to her desk where she sat addressing envelopes.

"Step up close to the desk," she said. "Don't be afraid."

I went and stood at her elbow. There was a wart on her chin and I stared at it.

"Now, take a blotter from over there and blot each envelope after I'm through writing on it," she instructed me, pointing to a blotter that stood about a foot from my hand.

I stared and did not move or answer.

"Take the blotter," she said.

I wanted to reach for the blotter and succeeded only in twitching my arm.

"Here," she said sharply, reaching for the blotter and shoving it into my fingers.

She wrote in ink on an envelope and pushed it toward me. Holding the blotter in my hand, I stared at the envelope and could not move.

"Blot it," she said.

I could not lift my hand. I knew what she had said; I knew what she wanted me to do; and I had heard her correctly. I wanted to look at her and say something, tell her why I could not move; but my eyes were fixed upon the floor. I could not summon enough courage while she sat there looking at me to reach over the yawning space of twelve inches and blot the wet ink on the envelope.

"Blot it!" she spoke sharply.

Gamin (c.1929) by Augusta Savage.

Still I could not move or answer.

"Look at me!"

I could not lift my eyes. She reached her hand to my face and I twisted away.

"What's wrong with you?" she demanded. **Ⓝ**

I began to cry and she drove me from the room. I decided that as soon as night came I would run away. The dinner bell rang and I did not go to the table, but hid in a corner of the hallway. When I heard the dishes rattling at the table, I opened the door and ran down the walk to the street. Dusk was falling. Doubt made me stop. Ought I go back? No; hunger was back there, and fear. I went on, coming to concrete sidewalks. People passed me. Where was I going? I did not know.

Ⓜ Reading Focus **Interpreting Details** What do the details in this paragraph tell you about Wright's development? Which details reveal the most about him?

Ⓝ Literary Focus **Dialogue** Why do you think Wright chose to describe these events through dialogue? Explain.

The farther I walked the more frantic I became. In a confused and vague way I knew that I was doing more running *away* from than running *toward* something. I stopped. The streets seemed dangerous. The buildings were massive and dark. The moon shone and the trees loomed frighteningly. No, I could not go on. I would go back. But I had walked so far and had turned too many corners and had not kept track of the direction. Which way led back to the orphan home? I did not know. I was lost.

I stood in the middle of the sidewalk and cried. A "white" policeman came to me and I wondered if he was going to beat me. He asked me what was the matter and I told him that I was trying to find my mother. His "white" face created a new fear in me. I was remembering the tale of the "white" man who had beaten the "black" boy. A crowd gathered and I was urged to tell where I lived. Curiously, I was too full of fear to cry now. I wanted to tell the "white" face that I had run off from an orphan home and that Miss Simon ran it, but I was afraid. Finally I was taken to the police station where I was fed. I felt better. I sat in a big chair where I was surrounded by "white" policemen, but they seemed to ignore me. Through the window I could see that night had completely fallen and that lights now gleamed in the streets. I grew sleepy and dozed. My shoulder was shaken gently and I opened my eyes and looked into a "white" face of another policeman who was sitting beside me. He asked me questions in a quiet, confidential tone, and quite before I knew it he was not "white" any more. I told him that I had run away from an orphan home and that Miss Simon ran it. **O**

It was but a matter of minutes before I was walking alongside a policeman, heading toward the home. The policeman led me to the front gate and I saw Miss Simon waiting for me on the steps. She identified me and I was left in her charge. I begged her not to beat me, but she yanked me upstairs into an empty room and lashed me thoroughly. Sobbing, I slunk off to bed, resolved to run away again. But I was watched closely after that.

My mother was informed upon her next visit that I had tried to run away and she was terribly upset.

"Why did you do it?" she asked.

"I don't want to stay here," I told her.

"But you must," she said. "How can I work if I'm to worry about you? You must remember that you have no father. I'm doing all I can."

"I don't want to stay here," I repeated.

"Then, if I take you to your father . . ."

"I don't want to stay with him either," I said.

"But I want you to ask him for enough money for us to go to my sister's in Arkansas," she said.

Again I was faced with choices I did not like, but I finally agreed. After all, my hate for my father was not so great and urgent as my hate for the orphan home. My mother held to her idea and one night a week or so later I found myself standing in a room in a frame house. My father and a strange woman were sitting before a bright fire that blazed in a grate. My mother and I were standing about six feet away, as though we were afraid to approach them any closer. **P**

"It's not for me," my mother was saying. "It's for your children that I'm asking you for money."

"I ain't got nothing," my father said, laughing.

"Come here, boy," the strange woman called to me. I looked at her and did not move.

"Give him a nickel," the woman said. "He's cute."

"Come here, Richard," my father said, stretching out his hand.

I backed away, shaking my head, keeping my eyes on the fire.

"He is a cute child," the strange woman said.

"You ought to be ashamed," my mother said to the strange woman. "You're starving my children."

"Now, don't you-all fight," my father said, laughing. **Q**

"I'll take that poker and hit you!" I blurted at my father.

He looked at my mother and laughed louder.

"You told him to say that," he said.

"Don't say such things, Richard," my mother said.

"You ought to be dead," I said to the strange woman.

O **Reading Focus** **Interpreting Details** What is the significance of the word *white* in this paragraph? Why is it in quotation marks?

P **Reading Focus** **Interpreting Details** What do the details of the setting suggest about the father's honesty?

Q **Literary Focus** **Dialogue** How does Wright use dialogue to reveal the personalities of the father, the girlfriend, and the mother?

The woman laughed and threw her arms about my father's neck. I grew ashamed and wanted to leave.

"How can you starve your children?" my mother asked.

"Let Richard stay with me," my father said.

"Do you want to stay with your father, Richard?" my mother asked.

"No," I said.

"You'll get plenty to eat," he said.

"I'm hungry now," I told him. "But I won't stay with you."

"Aw, give the boy a nickel," the woman said.

My father ran his hand into his pocket and pulled out a nickel.

"Here, Richard," he said.

"Don't take it," my mother said.

"Don't teach him to be a fool," my father said. "Here, Richard, take it."

I looked at my mother, at the strange woman, at my father, then into the fire. I wanted to take the nickel, but I did not want to take it from my father.

"You ought to be ashamed," my mother said, weeping. "Giving your son a nickel when he's hungry. If there's a God, He'll pay you back."

"That's all I got," my father said, laughing again and returning the nickel to his pocket. **ⓡ**

We left. I had the feeling that I had had to do with something unclean. Many times in the years after that the image of my father and the strange woman, their faces lit by the dancing flames, would surge up in my imagination so vivid and strong that I felt I could reach out and touch it; I would stare at it, feeling that it possessed some vital meaning which always eluded me.

A quarter of a century was to elapse between the time when I saw my father sitting with the strange woman and the time when I was to see him again, standing alone upon the red clay of a Mississippi plantation, a sharecropper,[1] clad in ragged overalls,

holding a muddy hoe in his gnarled, veined hands—a quarter of a century during which my mind and consciousness had become so greatly and violently altered that when I tried to talk to him I realized that, though ties of blood made us kin, though I could see a shadow of my face in his face, though there was an echo of my voice in his voice, we were forever strangers, speaking a different language, living on vastly distant planes of reality. That day a quarter of a century later when I visited him on the plantation—he was standing against the sky, smiling toothlessly, his hair whitened, his body bent, his eyes glazed with dim recollection, his fearsome aspect of twenty-five years ago gone forever from him— I was overwhelmed to realize that he could never understand me or the scalding experiences that had swept me beyond his life and into an area of living that he could never know. I stood before him, poised, my mind aching as it embraced the simple nakedness of his life, feeling how completely his soul was imprisoned by the slow flow of the seasons, by wind and rain and sun, how fastened were his memories to a crude and raw past, how chained were his actions and emotions to the direct, animalistic impulses of his withering body . . . **ⓢ**

From the white landowners above him there had not been handed to him a chance to learn the meaning of loyalty, of sentiment, of tradition. Joy was as unknown to him as was despair. As a creature of the earth, he endured, hearty, whole, seemingly indestructible, with no regrets and no hope. He asked easy, drawling questions about me, his other son, his wife, and he laughed, amused, when I informed him of their destinies. I forgave him and pitied him as my eyes looked past him to the unpainted wooden shack. From far beyond the horizons that bound this bleak plantation there had come to me through my living the knowledge that my father was a black peasant who had gone to the city seeking life, but who had failed in the city; a black peasant whose life had been hopelessly snarled in the city, and who had at last fled the city—that same city which had lifted me in its burning arms and borne me toward alien and undreamed-of shores of knowing. **ⓣ**

---

1. **sharecropper**: farmer who works a piece of land for its owner and gets a small portion of the crop in return.

ⓡ Literary Focus Dialogue Why does Wright just silently refuse the offer of money? What does this say about him?

ⓢ Reading Focus Interpreting Details How has Wright's father changed? How has Wright himself changed?

ⓣ Reading Focus Interpreting Details In the last two paragraphs, which details reveal how Wright and his father have changed?

Vocabulary eluded (ih LOOD ihd) v.: escaped detection or notice.

withering (WIHTH uhr ihng) v. used as adj.: drying up; weakening.

Respond and Think Critically

Reading Focus

Quick Check

1. What was life like for Wright and his family when they arrived in Memphis?

2. What happened when the young Wright went to buy groceries?

3. How did Wright feel about his father during most of his childhood?

Read with a Purpose

4. To what degree did hunger determine Wright's actions? Does it push him to do things?

Reading Skills: Interpreting Details

5. While reading, you listed details from Wright's first and last description of his father. Review your list; then, add a row to your chart in which you interpret the details you recorded to show how Wright's father changed over time.

Father in Memphis	Father 25 years later	Interpretation
night porter	sharecropper	has become poor

Literary Focus

Literary Analysis

6. **Interpret** When Wright's mother sent him back to face the boys who robbed him, what lesson was she trying to teach him?

7. **Draw Conclusions** Wright describes his feelings about the policeman who found him: "...before I knew it he was not 'white' any more." What do his initial fear of the policeman and this comment reveal about Wright's beliefs about white people?

8. **Infer** What caused Wright's parents to separate? What are some of the clues in the text upon which we can base our inferences about this?

9. **Interpret** Why does Wright refuse to blot the envelopes for Miss Simon? Where else in the text does he refuse to do something?

Literary Skills: Dialogue

10. **Interpret** Wright uses dialogue to dramatize scenes of great emotional conflict. Find and read two of these scenes and then describe how well they reveal Wright's emotions.

Literary Skills Review: Characterization

11. **Infer** The way an author reveals a character's personality to the reader is **characterization.** Why couldn't Wright eat his soup while the preacher was eating the chicken? What does this incident reveal about the boy's character?

Writing Focus

Think as a Reader/Writer

Use It in Your Writing Sequencing events in chronological order can help readers understand how an event came to be. Think of an experience that has meaning for you, and then write a few paragraphs describing that experience. Make sure you describe the sequence of events in chronological order. Then ask yourself how else you could have sequenced the events. What would be the advantages and disadvantages to these alternative methods of sequencing?

What Do
**You
Think
Now** Which of Wright's needs and desires were not met during his childhood?

Vocabulary Development

SKILLS FOCUS Literary Skills Analyze dialogue in nonfiction; analyze characterization. Reading Skills Interpret/analyze details.

Vocabulary Skills Identify and correctly use synonyms. Writing Skills Narrate a sequence of events. Listening and Speaking Skills Deliver informative presentations.

✔ Vocabulary Check

Match the Vocabulary words with their definitions.

1. enthralled 3. clamor 5. dispirited 7. frenzy
2. withering 4. eluded 6. ardently 8. futile

a. escaped notice d. loud noise g. fascinated
b. wildness e. discouraged h. pointless
c. drying up f. eagerly

Vocabulary Skills: Synonym Maps

Synonyms are words that have similar meanings, but not all synonyms are interchangeable. Create a chart like the one below. Use a dictionary or a thesaurus to find a synonym for each Vocabulary word. Then, go back to the text and replace each Vocabulary word with the synonym you have found. For each word, evaluate whether the synonym works as well as the original word in the context of the sentence.

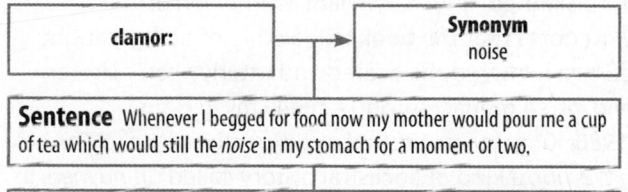

| clamor: | → | **Synonym** noise |

Sentence Whenever I begged for food now my mother would pour me a cup of tea which would still the *noise* in my stomach for a moment or two.

Evaluation *Noise* could also work, but *clamor* suggests an intolerable noise level and is more powerful.

Your Turn

Using a chart like the one above, evaluate the synonyms that you find for each Vocabulary word.

Language Coach

Final Vowel Sounds Group these words into four categories by the final *i* sound: /uh/, /ih/, /ee/, or /y/.

magazine discipline peregrine
determine subjective predestine
futile asinine tactile

CHOICES

As you respond to the Choices, use these **Academic Vocabulary** words as appropriate: component, diverse, intrinsic, potential, transmit.

REVIEW

Create a Podcast

TechFocus With a partner, create a podcast of a section of this autobiography. As you read, use Wright's dialogue and your own voices to bring the episode to life. Consider how you might use vocal cues and sound effects to help convey Wright's themes.

CONNECT

Research Economic Issues

Partner Work With a partner, research what five cents could have bought in 1917 so that you can determine what Wright was refusing when he did not take his father's nickel. Create a time line to chart the change in what that sum could buy over the years. Next, find out what it would have cost three people (one adult and two children) to travel by bus from Memphis, Tennessee, to Little Rock, Arkansas. Calculate the price of the tickets in 1917, and then guess how much money Wright's mother requested from his father.

EXTEND

Learn About Orphanages

In the late nineteenth and early twentieth centuries, it was not uncommon for poverty-stricken parents to seek potential homes for their children outside the family as a matter of survival. Research the orphanage as an institution in the United States in the 1910s and 1920s. Consider the administration, the living conditions, the population of children, and the rate of adoption in U.S. orphanages. Share your findings with the class.

The Girl Who Wouldn't Talk

 **What Do You Think** What human needs and desires do we have in common?

QuickWrite

Wanting to be understood may be a universal desire. Think of a time when you or someone you know chose to stay silent rather than risk being misunderstood. Write a brief paragraph about this experience.

MEET THE WRITER

Maxine Hong Kingston
(1940–   )

Maxine Hong Kingston burst onto the literary scene in 1976 with an extraordinary and innovative book—*The Woman Warrior: Memoirs of a Girlhood Among Ghosts.* When the book won the National Book Critics Circle Award for general nonfiction, Kingston gained national attention.

Student and Teacher

Kingston was born in California of Chinese immigrant parents and grew up in the Chinatown of Stockton, California. She was named for an American woman in the gambling house where her father worked for a time. She earned a B.A. from the University of California at Berkeley in 1962 and married the actor Earll Kingston. After their son was born, the Kingstons lived in Hawaii, where Maxine taught English at the high school and college levels, before returning to California.

A Fusion of Styles

In *The Woman Warrior,* Kingston uses components of autobiography, myth, poetic meditation, and fiction to convey her memories and feelings about growing up in a strange world (the United States) populated by what she and her family thought of as white-skinned "ghosts." William McPherson of *The Washington Post* notes that the book tells a story of being "caught between two highly sophisticated and utterly alien cultures, both vivid, often menacing, and equally mysterious."

In 1980, Kingston published a companion piece to *The Woman Warrior,* a kind of ancestral history called *China Men.* In 1988, Kingston published an extravagant novel called *Tripmaster Monkey: His Fake Book,* blending Chinese history and myth and vivid storytelling.

Despite critical acclaim, Kingston has remained relatively private. She seldom gives interviews, and her memoirs do not answer all of the questions raised by her writing. In the selection that follows, even a careful reader will not be able to decide what is truth, what is fiction, and what is simply left unsaid. This ambiguity gives Kingston's work much of its haunting quality.

Think About the Writer Why do you think writers like Kingston choose to write about painful episodes from their childhoods?

![Reader/Writer Notebook logo]

Reader/Writer Notebook

Use your **RWN** to complete the activities for this selection.

Literary Focus

Characterization Like fiction writers, nonfiction writers use all the devices of **characterization** to bring the people in their texts to life. Notice how Kingston reveals the <u>diverse</u> personalities of her narrator and the other characters by describing how they look, how they dress, how they act, and when they speak or do not speak. She shows us how her characters affect others and what other people think of them.

Reading Focus

Making Inferences About Characters As you read literary works, you make inferences about the characters and events. **Inferences** are educated guesses based on details in the text and on your own experiences. Making inferences about characters is a process. When you read about complex characters, your inferences may change as you gather more information about the characters. Keep in mind that you should always be able to support your inferences with details and quotations from the text.

Into Action As you read, use a Venn diagram like the one below. Record specific information from the story to describe the speech, actions, and appearance of the narrator and the silent girl. List any characteristics the girls share in the overlapping circles in the middle of the diagram.

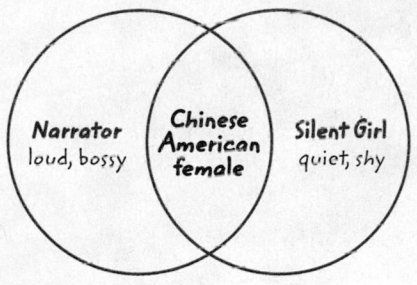

Vocabulary

loitered (LOY tuhrd) *v.:* lingered aimlessly. *Children often loitered after school to play.*

nape (nayp) *n.:* back of the neck. *When I sat behind her, I could see the nape of her neck.*

habitually (huh BIHCH u uh lee) *adv.:* usually; by habit. *It bothered me that she was habitually silent.*

sarcastic (sahr KAS tihk) *adj.:* scornful; mocking. *The teacher's frustration showed in her sarcastic tone when she spoke to the boy.*

temples (TEHM puhlz) *n.:* sides of the forehead, just above and in front of the ears. *I pulled the hair at her temples until she cried.*

Language Coach

Multiple Meanings Many words have multiple meanings. The same word will have completely different definitions depending on the context in which it is used. For example, the word *temple* means the sides of the forehead just above the ears. A completely different meaning of the word *temple* is a building used for worship, such as a synagogue or church.

Writing Focus

Think as a Reader/Writer

Find It in Your Reading Repetitive sentence beginnings can be used as an effective rhetorical device to emphasize an author's ideas. Kingston frequently begins sentences with "I" and follows the pronoun with strong verbs such as *hated, shook,* and *stared.* Copy some of these **repetitions** into your *Reader/Writer Notebook* and consider why Kingston chose to use this syntactical pattern.

Learn It Online
Explore the vocabulary words further online.

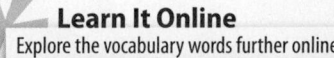
go.hrw.com L11-1283 **Go**

THE GIRL WHO WOULDN'T TALK

from THE WOMAN WARRIOR

by **Maxine Hong Kingston**

Read with a Purpose
Read to discover how silence can speak more loudly than words.

Build Background
The Chinese American family in this excerpt from *The Woman Warrior* lives in Stockton, California. Just before the episode starts, the narrator describes Chinese voices, which she says are louder than American voices. Describing her own voice, the narrator says, "You could hear splinters in my voice, bones rubbing jagged against one another. I was loud, though. I was glad I didn't whisper." The "ghosts" that the narrator mentions are white Americans, who seem strange to this Chinese family.

Normal Chinese women's voices are strong and bossy. We American-Chinese girls had to whisper to make ourselves American feminine. Apparently we whispered even more softly than the Americans. Once a year the teachers referred my sister and me to speech therapy, but our voices would straighten out, unpredictably normal, for the therapists. Some of us gave up, shook our heads, and said nothing, not one word. Some of us could not even shake our heads. At times shaking my head no is more self-assertion than I can manage. Most of us eventually found some voice, however faltering. We invented an American-feminine speaking personality, except for that one girl who could not speak up even in Chinese school. **Ⓐ**

She was a year older than I and was in my class for twelve years. During all those years she read aloud but would not talk. Her older sister was usually beside her; their parents kept the older daughter back to protect the younger one. They were six and seven years old when they began school. Although I had flunked kindergarten, I was the same age as most other students in our class; my parents had probably lied about my age, so I had had a head start and came out even. My younger sister was in the class below me; we were normal ages and normally separated. The parents of the quiet girl, on the other hand, protected both daughters. When it sprinkled, they kept them home from school. The girls did not work for a living the way we did. But in other ways we were the same.

We were similar in sports. We held the bat on our shoulders until we walked to first base. (You got a strike only when you actually struck at the ball.) Sometimes the pitcher wouldn't bother to throw to us. "Automatic walk," the other children would call, sending us on our way. By fourth or fifth grade, though, some of us would try to hit the ball. "Easy out," the other kids would say. I hit the ball a couple of times. Baseball was nice in that there was a definite spot to run to after hitting the ball. Basketball confused me because when I caught the ball I didn't know whom to throw it to. "Me. Me," the kids would be yelling. "Over here." Suddenly it would occur to me I hadn't

memorized which ghosts were on my team and which were on the other. When the kids said, "Automatic walk," the girl who was quieter than I kneeled with one end of the bat in each hand and placed it carefully on the plate. Then she dusted her hands as she walked to first base, where she rubbed her hands softly, fingers spread. She always got tagged out before second base. She would whisper-read but not talk. Her whisper was as soft as if she had no muscles. She seemed to be breathing from a distance. I heard no anger or tension.

I joined in at lunchtime when the other students, the Chinese too, talked about whether or not she was mute, although obviously she was not if she could read aloud. People told how *they* had tried *their* best to be friendly. *They* said hello, but if she refused to answer, well, they didn't see why they had to say hello anymore. She had no friends of her own but followed her sister everywhere, although people and she herself probably thought I was her friend. I also followed her sister about, who was fairly normal. She was almost two years older and read more than anyone else.

I hated the younger sister, the quiet one. I hated her when she was the last chosen for her team and I, the last chosen for my team. I hated her for her China doll hair cut. I hated her at music time for the wheezes that came out of her plastic flute. **Ⓑ**

Once afternoon in the sixth grade (that year I was arrogant with talk, not knowing there were going to be high school dances and college seminars to set me back), I and my little sister and the quiet girl and her big sister stayed late after school for some reason. The cement was cooling, and the tetherball poles made shadows across the gravel. The hooks at the rope ends were clinking against the poles. We shouldn't have been so late; there was laundry work to do and Chinese school to get to by 5:00. The last time we had stayed late, my mother had phoned the police and told them we had been kidnapped by bandits. The radio stations broadcast our descriptions. I had to get home before she did that again. But sometimes if you loitered long enough in the schoolyard, the other children would have gone home and you could play

---

Ⓐ Reading Focus Making Inferences About Characters
What pressure is placed on the Chinese American girls, and how do they handle it?

Ⓑ Literary Focus Characterization What do the narrator's social interactions reveal about her?

Vocabulary loitered (LOY tuhrd) *v.*: lingered aimlessly.

with the equipment before the office took it away. We were chasing one another through the playground and in and out of the basement, where the playroom and lavatory were. During air raid drills (it was during the Korean War, which you knew about because every day the front page of the newspaper printed a map of Korea with the top part red and going up and down like a window shade), we curled up in this basement. Now everyone was gone. The playroom was army green and had nothing in it but a long trough with drinking spigots in rows. Pipes across the ceiling led to the drinking fountains and to the toilets in the next room. When someone flushed you could hear the water and other matter, which the children named, running inside the big pipe above the drinking spigots. There was one playroom for girls next to the girls' lavatory and one playroom for boys next to the boys' lavatory. The stalls were open and the toilets had no lids, by which we knew that ghosts have no sense of shame or privacy.

Inside the playroom the lightbulbs in cages had already been turned off. Daylight came in x-patterns through the caging at the windows. I looked out and, seeing no one in the schoolyard, ran outside to climb the fire escape upside down, hanging on to the metal stairs with fingers and toes.

I did a flip off the fire escape and ran across the schoolyard. The day was a great eye, and it was not paying much attention to me now. I could disappear with the sun; I could turn quickly sideways and slip into a different world. It seemed I could run faster at this time, and by evening I would be able to fly. As the afternoon wore on we could run into the forbidden places—the boys' big yard, the boys' playroom. We could go into the boys' lavatory and look at the urinals. The only time during school hours I had crossed the boys' yard was when a flatbed truck with a giant thing covered with canvas and tied down with ropes had parked across the street. The children had told one another that it was a gorilla in captivity; we couldn't decide whether the sign said "Trail of the Gorilla" or "Trial of the Gorilla." The thing was as big as a house. The teachers couldn't stop us from

hysterically rushing to the fence and clinging to the wire mesh. Now I ran across the boys' yard clear to the Cyclone fence and thought about the hair that I had seen sticking out of the canvas. It was going to be summer soon, so you could feel that freedom coming on too.

I ran back into the girls' yard, and there was the quiet sister all by herself. I ran past her, and she followed me into the girls' lavatory. My footsteps rang hard against cement and tile because of the taps I had nailed into my shoes. Her footsteps were soft, padding after me. There was no one in the lavatory but the two of us. I ran all around the rows of twenty-five open stalls to make sure of that. No sisters. I think we must have been playing hide-and-go-seek. She was not good at hiding by herself and usually followed her sister; they'd hide in the same place. They must have gotten separated. In this growing twilight, a child could hide and never be found.

I stopped abruptly in front of the sinks, and she came running toward me before she could stop herself, so that she almost collided with me. I walked closer. She backed away, puzzlement, then alarm in her eyes.

"You're going to talk," I said, my voice steady and normal, as it is when talking to the familiar, the weak, and the small. "I am going to make you talk, you sissy-girl." She stopped backing away and stood fixed. **C**

I looked into her face so I could hate it close up. She wore black bangs, and her cheeks were pink and white. She was baby-soft. I thought that I could put my thumb on her nose and push it bonelessly in, indent her face. I could poke dimples into her cheeks. I could work her face around like dough. She stood still, and I did not want to look at her face anymore; I hated fragility. I walked around her, looked her up and down the way the Mexican and Negro girls did when they fought, so tough. I hated her weak neck, the way it did not support her head but let it droop; her head would fall backward. I stared at the curve of her nape. I wished I was able to see what my own neck looked like from the back and sides. I hoped it did not look like hers; I wanted a stout neck. I grew my hair long to hide

---

Vocabulary **nape** (nayp) *n.*: back of the neck.

C **Reading Focus** **Making Inferences About Characters**
What do you infer about the narrator from her statement that she had a steady voice when talking to "the familiar, the weak, and the small"?

it in case it was a flower-stem neck. I walked around to the front of her to hate her face some more. **Ⓓ Ⓔ**

I reached up and took the fatty part of her cheek, not dough, but meat, between my thumb and finger. This close, and I saw no pores. "Talk," I said. "Are you going to talk?" Her skin was fleshy, like squid out of which the glassy blades of bones had been pulled. I wanted tough skin, hard brown skin. I had callused my hands; I had scratched dirt to blacken the nails, which I cut straight across to make stubby fingers. I gave her face a squeeze. "Talk." When I let go, the pink rushed back into my white thumbprint on her skin. I walked around to her side. "Talk!" I shouted into the side of her head. Her straight hair hung, the same all these years, no ringlets or braids or permanents. I squeezed her other cheek. "Are you? Huh? Are you going to talk?" She tried to shake her head, but I had hold of her face. She had no muscles to jerk away. Her skin seemed to stretch. I let go in horror. What if it came away in my hand? "No, huh?" I said, rubbing the touch of her off my fingers. "Say 'No,' then," I said. I gave her another pinch and a twist. "Say 'No.'" She shook her head, her straight hair turning with her head, not swinging side to side like the pretty girls'. She was so neat. Her neatness bothered me. I hated the way she folded the wax paper from her lunch; she did not wad her brown paper bag and her school papers. I hated her clothes—the blue pastel cardigan, the white blouse with the collar that lay flat over the cardigan, the homemade flat, cotton skirt she wore when everybody else was wearing flared skirts. I hated pastels; I would wear black always. I squeezed again, harder, even though her cheek had a weak rubbery feeling I did not like. I squeezed one cheek, then the other, back and forth until the tears ran out of her eyes as if I had pulled them out. "Stop crying," I said, but although she habitually followed me around, she did not obey. Her eyes dripped; her nose dripped. **Ⓕ** She wiped her eyes with her papery fingers. The skin

on her hands and arms seemed powdery-dry, like tracing paper, onion paper. I hated her fingers. I could snap them like breadsticks. I pushed her hands down. "Say 'Hi,'" I said. "'Hi.' Like that. Say your name. Go ahead. Say it. Or are you stupid? You're so stupid, you don't know your own name, is that it? When I say, 'What's your name?' you just blurt it out, O.K.? What's your name?" Last year the whole class had laughed at a boy who couldn't fill out a form because he didn't know his father's name. The teacher sighed, exasperated and was very sarcastic, "Don't you notice things? What does your mother call him?" she said. The class laughed at how dumb he was not to notice things. "She calls him father of me," he said. Even we laughed although we knew that his mother did not call his father by name, and a son does not know his father's name. We laughed and were relieved that our parents had had the foresight to tell us some names we could give the teachers. "If you're not stupid," I said to the quiet girl, "what's your name?" She shook her head, and some hair caught in the tears; wet black hair stuck to the side of the pink and white face. I reached up (she was taller than I) and took a strand of hair. I pulled it. "Well, then, let's honk your hair," I said. "Honk. Honk." Then I pulled the other side—"ho-o-n-nk"—a long pull; "ho-o-n-n-nk" -a longer pull. I could see her little white ears, like white cutworms curled underneath the hair. "Talk!" I yelled into each cutworm.

I looked right at her. "I know you talk," I said. "I've heard you." Her eyebrows flew up. Something in those black eyes was startled, and I pursued it. "I was walking past your house when you didn't know I was there. I heard you yell in English and in Chinese. You weren't just talking. You were shouting. I heard you shout. You were saying, 'Where are you?' Say that again. Go ahead, just the way you did at home." I yanked harder on the hair, but steadily, not jerking. I did not want to pull it out. "Go ahead. Say, 'Where are you?'

Ⓓ Reading Focus Making Inferences About Characters How does the narrator hope she appears in contrast to the silent girl?

Ⓔ Literary Focus Characterization Which details in the story so far have revealed the most about the silent girl? What does the way she responds to the narrator's bullying tell you about her?

Ⓕ Reading Focus Making Inferences About Characters What can we infer about the narrator based on what she hates about the silent girl's appearance?

Vocabulary **habitually** (huh BIHCH u uh lee) *adv.*: usually; by habit.
sarcastic (sahr KAS tihk) *adj.*: scornful; mocking.

Say it loud enough for your sister to come. Call her. Make her come help you. Call her name. I'll stop if she comes. So call. Go ahead." **G**

She shook her head, her mouth curved down, crying. I could see her tiny white teeth, baby teeth. I wanted to grow big strong yellow teeth. "You do have a tongue," I said. "So use it." I pulled the hair at her temples, pulled the tears out of her eyes. "Say, 'Ow'" I said. "Just 'Ow.' Say, 'Let go.' Go ahead. Say it. I'll honk you again if you don't say, 'Let me alone.' Say, 'Leave me alone,' and I'll let you go. I will. I'll let go if you say it. You can stop this anytime you want to, you know. All you have to do is tell me to stop. Just say, 'Stop.' You're just asking for it, aren't you? You're just asking for another honk. Well then, I'll have to give you another honk. Say, 'Stop.'" But she didn't. I had to pull again and again.

Sounds did come out of her mouth, sobs, chokes, noises that were almost words. Snot ran out of her nose. She tried to wipe it on her hands, but there was too much of it. She used her sleeve. "You're disgusting," I told her. "Look at you, snot streaming down your nose, and you won't say a word to stop it. You're such a nothing." I moved behind her and pulled the hair growing out of her weak neck. I let go. I stood silent for a long time. Then I screamed, "Talk!" I would scare the words out of her. If she had had little bound feet, the toes twisted under the balls, I would have jumped up and landed on them—crunch!—stomped on them with my iron shoes. She cried hard, sobbing aloud. "Cry, 'Mama,'" I said. "Come on. Cry, 'Mama.' Say, 'Stop it.'" **H**

I put my finger on her pointed chin. "I don't like you. I don't like the weak little toots you make on your flute. Wheeze. Wheeze. I don't like the way you don't swing at the ball. I don't like the way you're the last one chosen. I don't like the way you can't make a fist for tetherball. Why don't you make a fist? Come on. Get tough. Come on. Throw fists." I pushed at her long hands; they swung limply at her sides. Her fingers were so long, I thought maybe they had an extra joint. They couldn't possibly make fists like other people's. "Make a fist," I said. "Come on. Just fold those fingers up; fingers on the inside, thumbs on the outside. Say something. Honk me back. You're so tall, and you let me pick on you. **I**

"Would you like a hanky? I can't get you one with embroidery on it or crocheting along the edges, but I'll get you some toilet paper if you tell me to. Go ahead. Ask me. I'll get it for you if you ask." She did not stop crying. "Why don't you scream, 'Help'?" I suggested. "Say, 'Help.' Go ahead." She cried on. "O.K. O.K. Don't talk. Just scream, and I'll let you go. Won't that feel good? Go ahead. Like this." I screamed not too loudly. My voice hit the tile and rang it as if I had thrown a rock at it. The stalls opened wider and the toilets wider and darker. Shadows leaned at angles I had not seen before. It was very late. Maybe a janitor had locked me in with this girl for the night. Her black eyes blinked and stared, blinked and stared. I felt dizzy from hunger. We had been in this lavatory together forever. My mother would call the police again if I didn't bring my sister home soon. "I'll let you go if you say just one word," I said. "You can even say 'a' or 'the,' and I'll let you go. Come on. Please." She didn't shake her head anymore, only cried steadily, so much water coming out of her. I could see the two duct holes where the tears welled out. Quarts of tears but no words. I grabbed her by the shoulder. I could feel bones. The light was coming in queerly through the frosted glass with the chicken wire embedded in it. Her crying was like an animal's—a seal's—and it echoed around the basement. "Do you want to stay here all night?" I asked. "Your mother is wondering what happened to her baby. You wouldn't want to have her mad at you. You'd better say something." I shook her shoulder. I

"I'LL LET YOU GO IF YOU SAY **JUST ONE WORD,"** I SAID.

pulled her hair again. I squeezed her face. "Come on! Talk! Talk! Talk!" She didn't seem to feel it anymore when I pulled her hair. "There's nobody here but you and me. This isn't a classroom or a playground or a crowd. I'm just one person. You can talk in front of one person. Don't make me pull harder and harder until you talk." But her hair seemed to stretch; she did not say a word. "I'm going to pull harder. Don't make me pull anymore, or your hair will come out and you're going to be bald. Do you want to be bald? You don't want to be bald, do you?" **J**

Far away, coming from the edge of town, I heard whistles blow. The cannery was changing shifts, letting out the afternoon people, and still we were here at school. It was a sad sound—work done. The air was lonelier after the sound died.

"Why won't you talk?" I started to cry. What if I couldn't stop, and everyone would want to know what happened? "Now look what you've done," I scolded. "You're going to pay for this. I want to know why. And you're going to tell me why. You don't see

I'm trying to help you out, do you? Do you want to be like this, dumb (do you know what dumb **K** means?), your whole life? Don't you ever want to be a cheerleader? Or a pompom girl? What are you going to do for a living? Yeah, you're going to have to work because you can't be a housewife. Somebody has to marry you before you can be a housewife. And you, you are a plant. Do you know that? That's all you are if you don't talk. If you don't talk, you can't have a personality. You'll have no personality and no hair. You've got to let people know you have a personality and a brain. You think somebody is going to take care of you all your stupid life? You think you'll always have your big sister? You think somebody's going to marry you, is that it? Well, you're not the type that gets dates, let alone gets married. Nobody's going to notice you. And you have to talk for interviews, speak right up in front of the boss. Don't you know that? You're so dumb. Why do I waste my time on you?" Sniffling and snorting, I couldn't stop crying and talking at the same time. I kept wiping my

---

J **Reading Focus** Making Inferences About Characters The narrator is hungry and afraid of staying so late in the building. Why does she continue to torment the silent girl?

K **Literary Focus** Characterization Why does the narrator start to cry? Why does she insist that she is trying to help the silent girl?

nose on my arm, my sweater lost somewhere (probably not worn because my mother said to wear a sweater). It seemed as if I had spent my life in that basement, doing the worst thing I had yet done to another person. "I'm doing this for your own good," I said. "Don't you dare tell anyone I've been bad to you. Talk. Please talk."

I was getting dizzy from the air I was gulping. Her sobs and my sobs were bouncing wildly off the tile, sometimes together, sometimes alternating. "I don't understand why you won't say just one word," I cried, clenching my teeth. My knees were shaking, and I hung on to her hair to stand up. Another time I'd stayed too late, I had had to walk around two Negro kids who were bonking each other's head on the concrete. I went back later to see if the concrete had cracks in it. "Look. I'll give you something if you talk. I'll give you my pencil box. I'll buy you some candy. O.K.? What do you want? Tell me. Just say it, and I'll give it to you. Just say, 'yes,' or, 'O.K.,' or, 'Baby Ruth.'" But she didn't want anything.

I had stopped pinching her cheek because I did not like the feel of her skin. I would go crazy if it came away in my hands. "I skinned her," I would have to confess.

Suddenly I heard footsteps hurrying through the basement, and her sister ran into the lavatory calling her name. "Oh, there you are," I said. "We've been waiting for you. I was only trying to teach her to talk. She wouldn't cooperate, though." Her sister went into one of the stalls and got handfuls of toilet paper and wiped her off. Then we found my sister, and we walked home together. "Your family really ought to force her to speak," I advised all the way home. "You mustn't pamper her." **L**

The world is sometimes just, and I spent the next eighteen months sick in bed with a mysterious illness. There was no pain and no symptoms, though the middle line in my left palm broke in two. Instead of starting junior high school, I lived like the Victorian recluses[1] I

1. **Victorian recluses:** characters in Victorian novels who, because of some illness or incapacity, lived shut away from the world.

read about. I had a rented hospital bed in the living room, where I watched soap operas on TV, and my family cranked me up and down. I saw no one but my family, who took good care of me. I could have no visitors, no other relatives, no villagers. My bed was against the west window, and I watched the seasons change the peach tree. I had a bell to ring for help. I used a bedpan. It was the best year and a half of my life. Nothing happened.

But one day my mother, the doctor, said, "You're ready to get up today. It's time to get up and go to school." I walked about outside to get my legs working, leaning on a staff I cut from the peach tree. The sky and trees, the sun were immense—no longer framed by a window, no longer grayed with a fly screen. I sat down on the sidewalk in amazement—the night, the stars. But at school I had to figure out again how to talk. I met again the poor girl I had tormented. She had not changed. She wore the same clothes, hair cut, and manner as when we were in elementary school, no make-up on the pink and white face, while the other Asian girls were starting to tape their eyelids. She continued to be able to read aloud. But there was hardly any reading aloud anymore, less and less as we got into high school. **M**

I was wrong about nobody taking care of her. Her sister became a clerk-typist and stayed unmarried. They lived with their mother and father. She did not have to leave the house except to go to the movies. She was supported. She was protected by her family, as they would normally have done in China if they could have afforded it, not sent off to school with strangers, ghosts, boys. **N**

L **Literary Focus** Characterization Why does the narrator's manner change when the silent girl's sister enters the room?

M **Reading Focus** Making Inferences About Characters Why is it significant that the narrator "had to figure out again how to talk"?

N **Reading Focus** Making Inferences About Characters According to the narrator, how has this confrontation affected her own life story?

Applying Your Skills

SKILLS FOCUS **Literary Skills** Analyze characterization; analyze imagery. **Reading Skills** Make inferences about characters. **Vocabulary Skills** Demonstrate knowledge of word meanings and their usage. **Writing Skills** Employ elements of an author's style effectively.

The Girl Who Wouldn't Talk

Respond and Think Critically

Reading Focus

Quick Check

1. What reasons does the narrator give for hating the silent girl?

2. How does the narrator try to make the silent girl talk? How does the girl respond?

3. What happens to the narrator to make her say that "the world is sometimes just"?

Read with a Purpose

4. Why does the girl's silence bother the narrator?

Reading Skills: Making Inferences About Characters

5. Review the Venn diagram you created to gather information about the narrator and the silent girl as you read the story. Now, write a paragraph about what the narrator and the silent girl have in common. What can you infer about the narrator from the traits she shares with the silent girl?

✔ Vocabulary Check

Match each Vocabulary word with its definition.

6. loitered
7. nape
8. habitually
9. sarcastic
10. temples

a. mocking
b. sides of the forehead
c. lingered
d. usually
e. back of the neck

Literary Focus

Literary Analysis

11. **Hypothesize** The silent girl is obviously able to speak. Why do you think she does not speak?

12. **Draw Conclusions** What conclusion can you draw from the fact that the narrator says that her time in bed "was the best year and a half of my life"? What discoveries about herself or about the silent girl might she have made during that time?

13. **Extend** Was this story uncomfortable to read? Why or why not?

Literary Skills: Characterization

14. **Analyze** How does the ongoing verbal assault in this story help to characterize the narrator and the silent girl? Which details about their interaction reveal the most about these two characters?

Literary Skills Review: Imagery

15. **Evaluate** The use of language to evoke a picture of a person, a place, or a thing is called **imagery.** Find the images that the narrator uses to describe the silent girl's physical appearance, such as her clothing and her skin. Why does the narrator dislike the girl's appearance so much?

Writing Focus

Think as a Reader/Writer

Use It in Your Writing Review your *Reader/Writer Notebook* to find a draft that you will revise to include repetitive sentence structure and strong verbs. Looking to Kingston's writing as a model, use repetitive sentence structure and strong verbs in your draft to emphasize the ideas and emotions that you want your reader to recognize.

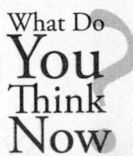 What Do You Think Now

What needs and desires might best be conveyed through silence? Is silence itself a universal need? Explain.

from In Search of Our Mothers' Gardens

What Do You Think?

What human needs and desires do we have in common?

QuickWrite

Write a brief paragraph explaining why you or someone you know might enjoy exploring creative interests such as writing, painting, or playing an instrument.

MEET THE WRITER

Alice Walker
(1944–   )

Pulitzer Prize WINNER

In her poetry, essays, and novels, Alice Walker has celebrated the endurance, the strength, and the creativity of African American women like her mother—unsung women who carried immense familial and social burdens even as they struggled against low status and a complete lack of recognition.

Inspiration in Bloom

Walker was born in Eatonton, Georgia, and grew up on a succession of farms in the area. Her father was a sharecropper, and her mother labored side by side with him in the fields, cared for their eight children, and still never failed, wherever they were living, to cultivate a large and beautiful flower garden. Her mother's hard work and determination to enrich her own life have served as an inspiration to Walker throughout her career.

Influences and Success

A childhood accident that blinded Walker in one eye made her feel disfigured and outcast for a time. Seeking solace, she turned to writing poetry and reading. Walker later attended Spelman College in Atlanta for two and a half years, before transferring to Sarah Lawrence College, near New York City. There she studied with the noted poet Muriel Rukeyser and graduated in 1965.

During her college years, Walker was active in the civil rights movement in Georgia and Mississippi, and she traveled in Africa. Many of the poems in her first published collection, *Once: Poems* (1968), were inspired by these activities. After graduating from college, Walker began a career of teaching and writing. She was among the first to teach university courses on the work of African American women writers, and she has since brought an understanding of their work to a wider audience.

In addition to poetry, short stories, and essays, Walker has written a number of well-received novels, including the Pulitzer Prize-winning *The Color Purple* (1982).

Think About the Writer

How have Walker's life experiences influenced her writing? Why do you think she has been described as a "woman at peace with herself and with the universe"?

Reader/Writer Notebook

Use your **RWN** to complete the activities for this selection.

Literary Focus

Personal Essay There are two types of essays: formal essays and informal essays, sometimes called personal essays. A **personal essay** is a short prose work of nonfiction that explores a topic in a personal way. Some of the best personal essays show how the individual experience of the writer connects with larger, more universal concerns. Such essays typically tap deeply into the emotional life of the writer.

Literary Perspectives Apply the literary perspective described on page 1295 as you read this essay.

Reading Focus

Identifying the Main Idea: Outlining Personal essays are often discursive, even rambling —that is, they are not as tightly organized as more formal essays. For that reason, it may be harder to recognize the main idea in a personal essay, but a careful reader can use outlining to help discover it.

Into Action Walker's essay includes several different topics, including her mother's life history and the creativity of African American women. Together, all of these topics connect with each other to contribute to the essay's main idea. As you read the essay, use a chart like the one below to group paragraphs together according to the topics to which they refer.

Paragraphs	Subject
1-4	Walker's mother: early marriage and motherhood; field worker; her creativity at home
4-7	

Writing Focus

Think as a Reader/Writer

Find It in Your Reading Personal essays, as well as other types of writing, can be brought to life by using **anecdotes,** or brief stories that are amusing or interesting. Watch for Walker's use of anecdotes. Use your *Reader/Writer Notebook* to describe how and when Walker uses anecdotes as integral <u>components</u> of her essay.

Vocabulary

vibrant (VY bruhnt) *adj.*: full of energy. *Walker pays tribute to the vibrant creative spirit that often goes unrecognized.*

medium (MEE dee uhm) *n.*: material for an artist. *Her artistic medium was her garden.*

profusely (pruh FYOOS lee) *adv.*: in great quantities. *The flowers bloomed profusely.*

conception (kuhn SEHP shuhn) *n.*: mental formation of ideas. *The flower gardens represent her conception of beauty.*

ingenious (ihn JEEN yuhs) *adj.*: clever. *African American women have found ingenious ways to express individual creativity.*

Language Coach

Word Histories Complete the chart below by using a dictionary to research the origin, or **etymology,** of the Vocabulary words. The etymology usually appears in brackets following the word's pronunciation. (In some cases, like *vibrant* below, you may find the etymology in the entry for a closely related word—in this case, *vibrate*.)

	Language of Origin	Original Word	Related Word
ingenious	Latin	*ingenium,* inborn talent; skill	genius
vibrant			
medium			
conception			
profusely			

 Learn It Online

Learn more about Walker with these Internet links.

go.hrw.com   L11-1293   **Go**

from OUR MOTHERS' GARDENS
IN SEARCH OF

by **Alice Walker**

Amadeus V (2004) by Johnathan Green. Oil on masonite, 11″ × 14″.
From the collection of Janice and Michael Danzig.

Read with a Purpose
Read to learn about examples of creativity that occur in "wild and unlikely places."

Build Background
The selection that follows is the second part of an essay about the creative spirit of African American women. In the first part of Walker's essay, she describes the harsh lives of black women in the South and wonders how they kept their creativity alive in an inhospitable climate. She suggests that in looking for the source of black women's creativity, she found the answer to be very close to home.

In the late 1920s my mother ran away from home to marry my father. Marriage, if not running away, was expected of seventeen-year-old girls. By the time she was twenty, she had two children and was pregnant with a third. Five children later, I was born. And this is how I came to know my mother: She seemed a large, soft, loving-eyed woman who was rarely impatient in our home. Her quick, violent temper was on view only a few times a year, when she battled with the white landlord who had the misfortune to suggest to her that her children did not need to go to school.

She made all the clothes we wore, even my brothers' overalls. She made all the towels and sheets we used. She spent the summers canning vegetables and fruits. She spent the winter evenings making quilts enough to cover all our beds.

During the "working" day, she labored beside—not behind—my father in the fields. Her day began before sunup, and did not end until late at night. There was never a moment for her to sit down, undisturbed, to unravel her own private thoughts; never a time free from interruption—by work or the noisy inquiries of her many children. And yet, it is to my mother—and all our mothers who were not famous—that I went in search of the secret of what has fed that muzzled and often mutilated, but vibrant, creative spirit that the black woman has inherited, and that pops out in wild and unlikely places to this day. **Ⓐ Ⓑ**

But when, you will ask, did my overworked mother have time to know or care about feeding the creative spirit?

The answer is so simple that many of us have spent years discovering it. We have constantly looked high, when we should have looked high—and low.

For example: In the Smithsonian Institution in Washington, D.C., there hangs a quilt unlike any other in the world. In fanciful, inspired, and yet simple and identifiable figures, it portrays the story of the Crucifixion. It is considered rare, beyond price. Though it follows no known pattern of quilt-making, and though it is made of bits and pieces of worthless rags, it is obviously the work of a person of powerful imagination and deep spiritual feeling. Below this quilt I saw a note that says it was made by "an anonymous Black woman in Alabama, a hundred years ago." **Ⓒ**

If we could locate this "anonymous" black woman from Alabama, she would turn out to be one of our grandmothers—an artist who left her mark in the only materials she could afford, and in the only medium her position in society allowed her to use.

Ⓐ Literary Perspectives Analyzing Political Context Describe Walker's mother's life and her attitude toward her family.

Ⓑ Literary Focus Personal Essay What does the author reveal here about the purpose of her essay?

Ⓒ Reading Focus Identifying the Main Idea What main idea in the previous paragraphs does this example support?

Vocabulary vibrant (VY bruhnt) *adj.*: full of energy.
medium (MEE dee uhm) *n.*: material for an artist.

Literary Perspectives

Analyzing Political Context Writers live and work in the real world. As a result, their writing often reflects the social and political issues of the period in which it is written. A writer's gender, or sex, can be a factor in how he or she views these issues. In most cultures throughout history, women have occupied a secondary position in society; therefore, many artistically inclined women have been forced to create with whatever materials were handy. The struggle to establish an artistic presence—even if the audience is only family—has urged many women to do creative work and transmit their creative talents and impulses to the next generation of women.

As you read, be sure to notice the questions in the text, which will guide you in using this perspective.

As Virginia Woolf[1] wrote further, in *A Room of One's Own:*

Yet genius of a sort must have existed among women as it must have existed among the working class. [Change this to "slaves" and "the wives and daughters of sharecroppers."] Now and again an Emily Brontë[2] or a Robert Burns[3] [change this to "a Zora Hurston or a Richard Wright"] blazes out and proves its presence. But certainly it never got itself on to paper. When, however, one reads of a witch being ducked, of a woman possessed by devils [or "Sainthood"[4]], of a wise woman selling herbs [our root workers], or even a very remarkable man who had a mother, then I think we are on the track of a lost novelist, a suppressed poet, of some mute and inglorious Jane Austen...[5] Indeed, I would venture to guess that Anon, who wrote so many poems without signing them, was often a woman. . . . **D**

And so our mothers and grandmothers have, more often than not anonymously, handed on the creative spark, the seed of the flower they themselves never hoped to see: or like a sealed letter they could not plainly read. **E**

And so it is, certainly, with my own mother. Unlike "Ma" Rainey's[6] songs, which retained their creator's

> AND SO OUR MOTHERS AND GRANDMOTHERS HAVE . . . HANDED ON THE CREATIVE SPARK.

name even while blasting forth from Bessie Smith's[7] mouth, no song or poem will bear my mother's name. Yet so many of the stories that I write, that we all write, are my mother's stories. Only recently did I fully realize this: that through years of listening to my mother's stories of her life, I have absorbed not only the stories themselves, but something of the manner in which she spoke, something of the urgency that involves the knowledge that her stories—like her life—must be recorded. It is probably for this reason that so much of what I have written is about characters whose counterparts in real life are so much older than I am. **F**

But the telling of these stories, which came from my mother's lips as naturally as breathing, was not the only way my mother showed herself as an artist. For stories, too, were subject to being distracted, to dying without conclusion. Dinners must be started, and cotton must be gathered before the big rains. The artist that was and is my mother showed itself to me only after many years. This is what I finally noticed:

Like Mem, a character in *The Third Life of Grange Copeland,*[8] my mother adorned with flowers whatever shabby house we were forced to live in. And not just your typical straggly country stand of zinnias, either.

---

1. **Virginia Woolf:** English novelist and critic. In *A Room of One's Own* (1929), Woolf says that, in order to write, a woman must have a room of her own (privacy) and the means to support herself (money).
2. **Emily Brontë:** English novelist and poet, best known for her novel *Wuthering Heights* (1847).
3. **Robert Burns:** eighteenth-century Scottish poet.
4. **"Sainthood":** In the early part of this essay, Walker talks about certain black women in the South called Saints. Intensely spiritual, these women were driven to madness because they could find no release for their creativity.
5. **Jane Austen**: English novelist, best known for *Pride and Prejudice* (1813).
6. **"Ma" Rainey:** nickname of Gertrude Malissa Nix Pridgett Rainey. She was the first great African American professional blues vocalist and is considered to be the mother of the blues.

7. **Bessie Smith:** One of the greatest of blues singers, Smith achieved professional status with the help of Ma Rainey and became known in her lifetime as the "Empress of the Blues."
8. *The Third Life of Grange Copeland:* Alice Walker's first novel, published in 1970.

D **Literary Perspectives** Analyzing Political Context
Why do you think Walker includes Virginia Woolf's thoughts in her essay?

E **Literary Focus** Personal Essay What does the "sealed letter" in this sentence suggest about the lives of the mothers and grandmothers?

F **Literary Focus** Personal Essay How do the mother's "stories of her life" inspire her daughter's creativity?

She planted ambitious gardens—and still does—with over fifty different varieties of plants that bloom profusely from early March until late November. Before she left home for the fields, she watered her flowers, chopped up the grass, and laid out new beds. When she returned from the fields she might divide clumps of bulbs, dig a cold pit,[9] uproot and replant roses, or prune branches from her taller bushes or trees—until night came and it was too dark to see.

Whatever she planted grew as if by magic, and her fame as a grower of flowers spread over three counties. Because of her creativity with her flowers, even my memories of poverty are seen through a screen of blooms—sunflowers, petunias, roses, dahlias, forsythia, spirea, delphiniums, verbena . . . and on and on.

And I remember people coming to my mother's yard to be given cuttings from her flowers; I hear again the praise showered on her because whatever rocky soil she landed on, she turned into a garden. A garden so brilliant with colors, so original in its design, so magnificent with life and creativity, that to this day people drive by our house in Georgia—perfect strangers and imperfect strangers—and ask to stand or walk among my mother's art.

I notice that it is only when my mother is working in her flowers that she is radiant, almost to the point of being invisible —except as Creator: hand and eye. She is involved in work her soul must have. Ordering the universe in the image of her personal conception of Beauty.

Her face, as she prepares the Art that is her gift, is a legacy of respect she leaves to me, for all that illuminates and cherishes life. She has handed down respect for the possibilities—and the will to grasp them.

9. **cold pit:** shallow pit, usually covered with glass, that is used for rooting plants or sheltering young plants from temperature variations in the spring.

For her, so hindered and intruded upon in so many ways, being an artist has still been a daily part of her life. This ability to hold on, even in very simple ways, is work black women have done for a very long time.

This poem is not enough, but it is something, for the woman who literally covered the holes in our walls with sunflowers:

> They were women then
> My mama's generation
> Husky of voice—Stout of
> Step
> With fists as well as
> Hands
> How they battered down
> Doors
> And ironed
> Starched white
> Shirts
> How they led
> Armies
> Headragged Generals
> Across mined
> Fields
> Booby-trapped
> Kitchens
> To discover books
> Desks
> A place for us
> How they knew what we
> Must know
> Without knowing a page
> Of it
> Themselves.

Guided by my heritage of a love of beauty and a respect for strength—in search of my mother's garden, I found my own.

G **Reading Focus** **Identifying the Main Idea** What previously stated idea does this information support?

H **Literary Perspectives** **Analyzing Political Context** What does this passage reveal about Walker's mother?

I **Literary Focus** **Personal Essay** How does the inclusion of Walker's original poem contribute to the essay as a whole?

J **Literary Perspectives** **Analyzing Political Context** According to Walker's poem, what were the women of her mother's generation trying to accomplish?

Vocabulary **profusely** (pruh FYOOS lee) *adv.:* in great quantities.
conception (kuhn SEHP shuhn) *n.:* mental formation of ideas.

And perhaps in Africa over two hundred years ago, there was just such a mother; perhaps she painted vivid and daring decorations in oranges and yellows and greens on the walls of her hut; perhaps she sang—in a voice like Roberta Flack's[10]—*sweetly* over the compounds of her village; perhaps she wove the most stunning mats or told the most ingenious stories of all the village storytellers. Perhaps she was herself a poet—though only her daughter's name is signed to the poems that we know.

Perhaps Phillis Wheatley's[11] mother was also an artist.

Perhaps in more than Phillis Wheatley's biological life is her mother's signature made clear. **Ⓚ**

---

10. **Roberta Flack:** popular African American singer-songwriter.

11. **Phillis Wheatley** (c. 1753–1784): American poet, born in Africa and brought to America in slavery. Wheatley is often referred to as the first African American poet.

Vocabulary **ingenious** (ihn JEEN yuhs) *adj.:* clever.

Ⓚ **Reading Focus** **Identifying the Main Idea** What connection does Walker suggest she has with Wheatley?

Applying Your Skills

SKILLS FOCUS **Literary Skills** Analyze a personal, or informal, essay; analyze paradox; analyze political context. **Reading Skills** Identify the main idea by outlining.

Vocabulary Skills Use context clues to determine the meanings of words. **Writing Skills** Employ elements of an author's style effectively.

from **In Search of Our Mothers' Gardens**

Respond and Think Critically

Reading Focus

Quick Check

1. Describe the kind of life Walker's mother led while Walker was growing up.

2. What secret does Walker wish to discover by examining her mother's life and the lives of women like her?

3. How does Walker's mother express creativity?

Read with a Purpose

4. What legacy has Walker's mother left her? Why is it important to her?

Reading Skills: Identifying the Main Idea: Outlining

5. Review the outline of topics that you created as you read the essay. What do they all have in common? With a partner, discuss your outlines and determine the essay's main idea: What is Walker saying about women and creativity?

✔ Vocabulary Check

Complete each sentence with the appropriate Vocabulary word.

medium
vibrant
conception
ingenious
profusely

6. Oils are the artist's favorite _____.

7. The inventor came up with a(n) _____ solution to the problem.

8. Weeds sprouted _____ in the untended garden.

9. Pictures in _____ colors covered the walls.

10. She expressed her _____ of beauty in her garden.

Literary Focus

Literary Analysis

11. **Interpret** What metaphor does Walker use to describe how African American women handed down their "creative spark" over the generations?

12. **Hypothesize** What do you think Walker means when she says she found her own "garden" in her process of searching for her mother's?

13. **Literary Perspectives** What might Walker have learned from her mother the storyteller? from her mother the gardener? from her mother the woman?

Literary Skills: Personal Essay

14. **Analyze** In this essay, Walker relates her experience to a universal issue. What is that issue, and how does Walker connect herself to it?

Literary Skills Review: Paradox

15. **Make Judgments** In the last five lines of her poem, Walker presents a **paradox,** an apparent contradiction. State the paradox in your own words. What knowledge is Walker discussing?

Writing Focus

Think as a Reader/Writer

Use It in Your Writing Anecdotes can add insight to a personal essay. Add an anecdote to a personal essay in your *Reader/Writer Notebook*. Be sure the anecdote illustrates a point you are making in the essay.

 **What Do You Think Now** Why is expressing creativity a uniquely human characteristic? What do we gain from it?

Preparing to Read

Autobiographical Notes

What Do You Think What human needs and desires do we have in common?

QuickWrite

Many people belong to groups such clubs or teams. These groups can offer a sense of identity and belonging. Write about a group you belong to and explain what you gain from your membership.

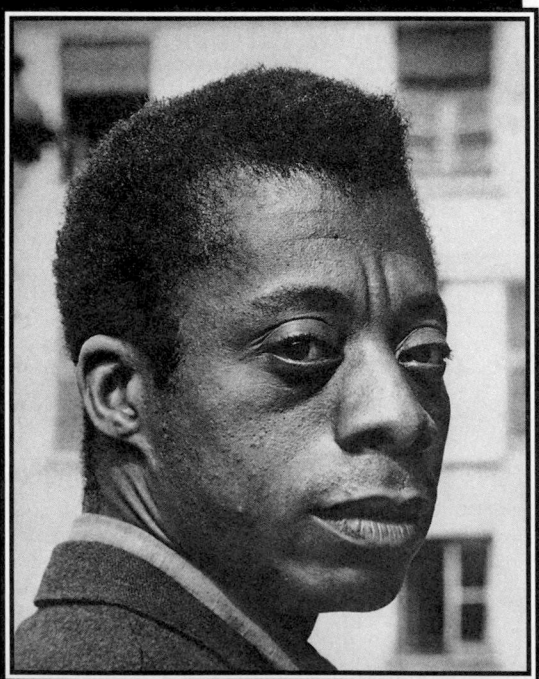

James Baldwin
(1924–1987)

James Baldwin felt compelled to write at length about being an African American because, he wrote, "it was the gate I had to unlock before I could hope to write about anything else." His essays flow from his conviction that a writer's duty is "to examine attitudes, to go beneath the surface, to tap the source."

Early Critical Success

One of the most controversial and stirring writers of the twentieth century, James Baldwin was born and raised in New York City's Harlem, where his stepfather was the minister of a small evangelical church. As a young man, Baldwin read voraciously and served as a junior minister for a few years at the Fireside Pentecostal Assembly. At the age of 24, he used funds from a fellowship to move to Europe. While living in Paris, he completed his first—and some say best—novel, *Go Tell It on the Mountain* (1953). *Notes of a Native Son,* a collection of autobiographical essays published in 1955, established Baldwin as an American writer of the first rank. The critic Irving Howe said Baldwin was among "the two or three greatest essayists this country has ever produced."

Advocate Against Injustice

Although he lived much of his life in France, Baldwin never relinquished his U.S. citizenship. While abroad, he wrote in a variety of forms, including novels, plays, essays, poetry, and book reviews.

In the 1950s, the decade that witnessed the early growth of the American civil rights movement, Baldwin's audacious, searing scrutiny of racial injustice played a major role in forcing leaders, black and white, to come to terms with one of the nation's most anguishing problems—the treatment of African Americans. In 1963 he published *The Fire Next Time,* a groundbreaking book on race relations that had wide influence. Until his death, he remained a prominent, humane advocate of racial justice in American life.

Think About the Writer Baldwin wrote about American life but lived in Europe. What unique perspective do you think this gave him on race?

Reader/Writer Notebook

Use your **RWN** to complete the activities for this selection.

Literary Focus

Tone Because Baldwin is writing his autobiography, his main subjects are himself and his life experience. The **tone** of Baldwin's essay reflects his <u>intrinsic</u> attitude toward himself and the world in which he lives. Baldwin conveys that attitude through the words he chooses and through the style or manner in which he arranges those words. Tone can often be summed up with one or two adjectives, such as *ironic*, *humorous*, or *light-hearted*. A detailed analysis of a writer's subject and **style** can help readers examine the way in which a particular tone is achieved.

Reading Focus

Evaluating an Author's Argument An **argument** is a form of persuasion that appeals to reason, rather than emotion, to persuade an audience to think or act in a certain way. In this essay, Baldwin assesses his life and tells us what conclusions he has drawn about a number of important subjects, such as the racial divide in American society and the dilemma of the African American writer. Baldwin presents his argument by stating assertions about these subjects. He then strengthens each assertion with evidence and reasons that support his argument.

Into Action As you read, use a chart like the one below. In the first column, record some of Baldwin's major assertions. Then, in the second column, list the reasons he gives for making each assertion.

Assertions	Reasons
"... the things which hurt him and the things which helped him cannot be divorced from each other." (p. 1303)	"... [the writer] could be helped in a certain way only because he was hurt in a certain way ..." (p. 1303)

Writing Focus

Think as a Reader/Writer

Find It in Your Reading Baldwin makes use of parenthetical asides throughout the essay: "...[I]t's my melancholy conviction that I've scarcely ever had enough to eat (this is because it's *impossible* to eat enough if you're worried about your next meal). . . ." Because these parenthetical comments are often addressed to the reader, they create a casual, conversational tone. As you read, note how Baldwin uses parenthetical statements, and record two or three examples in your *Reader/Writer Notebook*.

Vocabulary

bleak (bleek) *adj.:* cheerless. *Baldwin describes his childhood as bleak.*

censored (SEHN suhrd) *v.:* cut or changed to remove material deemed objectionable. *The editor censored Baldwin's story.*

conundrum (kuh NUHN druhm) *n.:* riddle. *Writers explore life's difficult conundrums.*

coherent (koh HIHR uhnt) *adj.:* clear, logical, consistent. *An honest examination of the past makes the present coherent.*

crucial (KROO shuhl) *adj.:* critical; decisive. *Baldwin made a crucial discovery about himself when he was a young man.*

interloper (IHN tuhr LOHP uhr) *n.:* intruder; meddler. *He felt that he was an interloper when he tried to adopt European heritage.*

appropriate (uh PROH pree ayt) *v.:* take over. *Baldwin felt that he had to appropriate European history in order to make it his.*

pulverized (PUHL vuh ryzd) *v.:* crushed; destroyed. *Baldwin's hopes and ambitions were not pulverized by a difficult childhood.*

Language Coach

Vowel Combinations The spelling of the Vocabulary word *bleak* illustrates the *ea* vowel combination. The pronunciation is exactly the same as the long *e* sound of the double *e* in words such as *cheek* and *sweet*. With a partner, make a list of words that are spelled with the *ea* vowel combination, but pronounced with a long *e* sound.

Learn It Online
Listen to the tone of this essay come alive in the audio recording online.

go.hrw.com   L11-1301

Autobiographical Notes

by **James Baldwin**

Read with a Purpose

Read to learn about the conflicts and challenges that Baldwin faces as an African American writer.

Build Background

"Autobiographical Notes" offers a compelling portrait of Baldwin's development as a writer and thinker. For much of the selection, he reflects on what he sees as the difficult position of the African American writer. He believes that writers who happen to be African American must not only achieve some kind of clarity regarding the "Negro problem" in America, but must also establish a clear position on Western culture in general, a culture in which they are considered "interlopers," or intruders.

I was born in Harlem thirty-one years ago. I began plotting novels at about the time I learned to read. The story of my childhood is the usual bleak fantasy, and we can dismiss it with the restrained observation that I certainly would not consider living it again. In those days my mother was given to the exasperating[1] and mysterious habit of having babies. As they were born, I took them over with one hand and held a book with the other. The children probably suffered, though they have since been kind enough to deny it, and in this way I read *Uncle Tom's Cabin* and *A Tale of Two Cities* over and over and over again; in this way, in fact, I read just about everything I could get my hands on—except the Bible, probably because it was the only book I was encouraged to read. I must also confess that I wrote—a great deal—and my first professional triumph, in any case, the first effort of mine to be seen in print, occurred at the age of twelve or thereabouts, when a short story I had written about the Spanish revolution won some sort of a prize in an extremely short-lived church newspaper. I remember the story was censored by the lady editor, though I don't remember why, and I was outraged. **Ⓐ**

Also wrote plays, and songs, for one of which I received a letter of congratulations from Mayor La Guardia,[2] and poetry, about which the less said, the better. My mother was delighted by all these goings-on, but my father wasn't; he wanted me to be a preacher. When I was fourteen I became a preacher, and when I was seventeen I stopped. Very shortly thereafter I left home. For God knows how long I struggled

---

1. **exasperating:** irritating; very annoying.

2. **Mayor La Guardia:** Fiorello La Guardia, mayor of New York City from 1934 to 1945.

Vocabulary   bleak (bleek) *adj.*: cheerless.
censored (SEHN suhrd) *v.*: cut or changed to remove material deemed objectionable.

Ⓐ Literary Focus   Tone What is Baldwin's tone in this paragraph? Which phrases create that tone?

with the world of commerce and industry—I guess they would say they struggled with *me*—and when I was about twenty-one I had enough done of a novel to get a Saxton Fellowship. When I was twenty-two the fellowship was over, the novel turned out to be unsalable, and I started waiting on tables in a Village[3] restaurant and writing book reviews—mostly, as it turned out, about the Negro problem, concerning which the color of my skin made me automatically an expert. Did another book, in company with photographer Theodore Pelatowski, about the store-front churches in Harlem. This book met exactly the same fate as my first—fellowship, but no sale. (It was a Rosenwald Fellowship.) By the time I was twenty-four I had decided to stop reviewing books about the Negro problem—which, by this time, was only slightly less horrible in print than it was in life—and I packed my bags and went to France, where I finished, God knows how, *Go Tell It on the Mountain*.

Baldwin in his New York City apartment in 1963.

Any writer, I suppose, feels that the world into which he was born is nothing less than a conspiracy against the cultivation of his talent—which attitude certainly has a great deal to support it. On the other hand, it is only because the world looks on his talent with such a frightening indifference that the artist is compelled to make his talent important. So that any writer, looking back over even so short a span of time as I am here forced to assess, finds that the things which hurt him and the things which helped him cannot be divorced from each other; he could be helped in a certain way only because he was hurt in a certain way; and his help is simply to be enabled to move from one conundrum to the next—one is tempted to say that he moves from one disaster to the next. When one begins looking for influences one finds them by the score. I haven't thought much about my own, not enough anyway; I hazard that the King James Bible, the rhetoric of the store-front church, something ironic and violent and perpetually understated in Negro speech—and something of Dickens' love for bravura[4]—have something to do with me today; but I wouldn't stake my life on it. Likewise, innumerable people have helped me in many ways; but finally, I suppose, the most difficult (and most rewarding) thing in my life has been the fact that I was born a Negro and was forced, therefore, to effect some kind of truce with this reality. (Truce, by the way, is the best one can hope for.) **B C**

---

3. **Village:** Greenwich Village, a section of Manhattan noted as a center for writers and other artists.

4. **bravura:** showy, brilliant style.

Vocabulary **conundrum** (kuh NUHN druhm) *n.*: riddle.

B **Reading Focus** **Evaluating an Author's Argument** How does Baldwin support his opinion?

C **Reading Focus** **Evaluating an Author's Argument** What does Baldwin mean by "truce"?

One of the difficulties about being a Negro writer (and this is not special pleading, since I don't mean to suggest that he has it worse than anybody else) is that the Negro problem is written about so widely. The bookshelves groan under the weight of information, and everyone therefore considers himself informed. And this information, furthermore, operates usually (generally, popularly) to reinforce traditional attitudes. Of traditional attitudes there are only two—For or Against—and I, personally, find it difficult to say which attitude has caused me the most pain. I am speaking as a writer; from a social point of view I am perfectly aware that the change from ill-will to good-will, however motivated, however imperfect, however expressed, is better than no change at all. **D**

But it is part of the business of the writer—as I see it—to examine attitudes, to go beneath the surface, to tap the source. From this point of view the Negro problem is nearly inaccessible. It is not only written about so widely; it is written about so badly. It is quite possible to say that the price a Negro pays for becoming articulate is to find himself, at length, with nothing to be articulate about. ("You taught me language," says Caliban to Prospero,[5] "and my profit on't is I know how to curse.") Consider: the tremendous social activity that this problem generates imposes on whites and Negroes alike the necessity of looking forward, of working to bring about a better day. This is fine, it keeps the waters troubled; it is all, indeed, that has made possible the Negro's progress. Nevertheless, social affairs are not generally speaking the writer's prime concern, whether they ought to be or not; it is absolutely necessary that he establish between himself and these affairs a distance

which will allow, at least, for clarity, so that before he can look forward in any meaningful sense, he must first be allowed to take a long look back. In the context of the Negro problem neither whites nor blacks, for excellent reasons of their own, have the faintest desire to look back; but I think that the past is all that makes the present coherent, and further, that the past will remain horrible for exactly as long as we refuse to assess it honestly. **E**

I know, in any case, that the most crucial time in my own development came when I was forced to recognize that I was a kind of bastard of the West; when I followed the line of my past I did not find myself in Europe but in Africa. And this meant that in some subtle way, in a really profound way, I brought to Shakespeare, Bach, Rembrandt, to the stones of Paris, to the cathedral at Chartres, and to the Empire State Building, a special attitude. These were not really my creations, they did not contain my history; I might search in them in vain forever for any reflection of myself. I was an interloper; this was not my heritage. At the same time I had no other heritage which I could possibly hope to use—I had certainly been unfitted for the jungle or the tribe. I would have to appropriate these white centuries, I would have to make them mine—I would have to accept my special attitude, my special place in this scheme—otherwise I would have no place in *any* scheme. What was the most difficult was the fact that I was forced to admit something I had always hidden from myself, which the American Negro has had to hide from himself as the price of his public progress; that I hated and feared white people. This did not mean that I loved black people; on the contrary, I despised them, possibly because they failed to produce Rembrandt. In effect, I hated and feared the world. And this meant, not only that I thus gave the world an altogether murderous power over me, but also that in such a self-destroying limbo[6] I could never hope to write.

---

5. **Caliban to Prospero:** In Act I, Scene 2 of *The Tempest* by William Shakespeare, Caliban, a rough creature, is a slave, whom Prospero, his master, tries to civilize.

D **Reading Focus** **Evaluating an Author's Argument** Why is Baldwin conflicted about literature that deals with the "Negro problem"?

E **Literary Focus** **Tone** How would you describe Baldwin's tone in this paragraph? What specific details reveal the most about his tone?

Vocabulary **coherent** (koh HIHR uhnt) *adj.:* clear, logical, consistent.
crucial (KROO shuhl) *adj.:* critical; decisive.
interloper (IHN tuhr LOHP uhr) *n.:* intruder; meddler.
appropriate (uh PROH pree ayt) *v.:* take over.

One writes out of one thing only—one's own experience. Everything depends on how relentlessly one forces from this experience the last drop, sweet or bitter, it can possibly give. This is the only real concern of the artist, to recreate out of the disorder of life that order which is art. The difficulty then, for me, of being a Negro writer was the fact that I was, in effect, prohibited from examining my own experience too closely by the tremendous demands and the very real dangers of my social situation. **F**

I don't think the dilemma outlined above is uncommon. I do think, since writers work in the disastrously explicit medium of language, that it goes a little way toward explaining why, out of the enormous resources of Negro speech and life, and despite the example of Negro music, prose written by Negroes has been generally speaking so pallid[7] and so harsh. I have not written about being a Negro at such length because I expect that to be my only subject, but only because it was the gate I had to unlock before I could hope to write about anything else. I don't think that the Negro problem in America can be even discussed coherently without bearing in mind its context; its context being the history, traditions, customs, the moral assumptions and preoccupations of the country; in short, the general social fabric. Appearances to the contrary, no one in America escapes its effects and everyone in America bears some responsibility for it. I believe this the more firmly because it is the overwhelming tendency to speak of this problem as though it were a thing apart. But in the work of Faulkner, in the general attitude and certain specific passages in Robert Penn Warren, and, most significantly, in the advent of Ralph Ellison, one sees the beginnings—at least—of a more genuinely penetrating search. Mr. Ellison, by the way, is the first Negro novelist I have ever read to utilize in language,

and brilliantly, some of the ambiguity and irony of Negro life.

About my interests: I don't know if I have any, unless the morbid desire to own a sixteen-millimeter camera and make experimental movies can be so classified. Otherwise, I love to eat and drink—it's my melancholy conviction that I've scarcely ever had enough to eat (this is because it's *impossible* to eat enough if you're worried about the next meal)—and I love to argue with people who do not disagree with me too profoundly, and I love to laugh. I do *not* like bohemia,[8] or bohemians, I do not like people whose principal aim is pleasure, and I do not like people who are *earnest* about anything. I don't like people who like me because I'm a Negro; neither do I like people who find in the same accident grounds for contempt. I love America more than any other country in the world, and, exactly for this reason, I insist on the right to criticize her perpetually. I think all theories are suspect, that the finest principles may have to be modified, or may even be pulverized by the demands of life, and that one must find, therefore, one's own moral center and move through the world hoping that this center will guide one aright. I consider that I have many responsibilities, but none greater than this: to last, as Hemingway says, and get my work done. **G**

I want to be an honest man and a good writer. **H**

---

8. **bohemia:** any nonconformist, unconventional community, often made up of writers and other artists.

---

6. **limbo:** borderland state of uncertainty and oblivion.
7. **pallid:** dull; lacking in vitality.

F **Reading Focus** Evaluating an Author's Argument
What argument is Baldwin making about the writing process?

Vocabulary **pulverized** (PUHL vuh ryzd) *v.*: crushed; destroyed.

G **Literary Focus** Tone How does Baldwin's tone in this paragraph differ from the tone of the preceding paragraphs?

H **Reading Focus** Evaluating an Author's Argument
How might this essay be an attempt to reconcile these two goals?

Applying Your Skills

SKILLS FOCUS Literary Skills Analyze tone; analyze persuasive devices. Reading Skills Evaluate an author's arguments. Vocabulary Skills Demonstrate knowl- edge of literal meanings of words and their usage. Writing Skills Employ elements of an author's style effectively.

Autobiographical Notes

Respond and Think Critically

Reading Focus

Quick Check

1. What was Baldwin's childhood like?

2. What does Baldwin see as the business of a writer?

3. According to the essay, what was the most cru- cial time in Baldwin's development? What did he learn about himself during that time?

4. What does Baldwin say is his greatest responsi- bility?

Read with a Purpose

5. What are the conflicts, internal and external, that Baldwin faces as an African American writer?

Reading Skills: Evaluating an Author's Argument

6. While reading, you listed two critical parts of Baldwin's argument: his assertions and his rea- sons for making each assertion. Now, examine what Baldwin's **diction,** or his choice of specific language, adds to his argument. How does his diction reveal his tone? How does his tone make his argument more persuasive? Cite specific examples that you have included in your chart.

✓Vocabulary Check

Match each Vocabulary word with its definition.

7. censored   10. conundrum   13. crucial
8. pulverized   11. interloper   14. appropriate
9. bleak   12. coherent

a. take over   d. smashed   f. miserable
b. intruder   e. puzzle   g. important
c. well thought out   h. removed or changed

Literary Focus

Literary Analysis

15. **Interpret** According to Baldwin, how does a writer make use of his or her experience? Do you think Baldwin practices what he preaches in this essay? Support your response with details from the text.

16. **Draw Conclusions** What do you think were Baldwin's goals in writing these autobiographical notes? Do you think he achieved his goals?

Literary Skills: Tone

17. **Analyze** What tone does Baldwin take toward his subject matter? What specific words and details help you identify his tone?

Literary Skills Review: Persuasion

18. **Draw Conclusions** Using appeals to reason and emotions to convince a reader of some- thing is called **persuasion.** Has Baldwin per- suaded you to accept his view of the role of the writer, especially the African American writer, in Western society? Why or why not?

Writing Focus

Think as a Reader/Writer

Use It in Your Writing Revise one of the personal essays in your *Reader/Writer Notebook* by adding two or three parenthetical expressions to provide explan- atory information. Re-read your essay. How do the parenthetical comments affect your essay's tone?

What Do You Think Now

During the time in his life that Baldwin focuses on in this excerpt, what were his needs and desires? How successful was he in meeting those needs and desires?

SKILLS FOCUS Reading Skills Identify and understand a writer's background.

Understanding a Writer's Background

by **Kylene Beers**

For years I enjoyed a poem titled "Forgive My Guilt" by Robert P. Tristram Coffin without knowing anything about the poet. Then, I read about him and discovered he was an American writer who served in World War I. When I re-read the poem knowing that, I saw a whole new way of reading that poem. I still loved the poem, but knowing about the poet gave me new insight into his writing. If you take the time to get to know the backgrounds of poets and authors of the texts you read, you too might discover some <u>potential</u> meanings that you didn't know were there.

Some of the best writers have an uncanny ability to discover the essential that is hidden in the everyday, the universal that is hidden in the local. In her autobiographical essay "Straw into Gold: The Metamorphosis of the Everyday," Sandra Cisneros tells about the raw material she has transformed into literature— raw material gleaned from everyday life. She describes family experiences and other influences that shaped her as a writer. Her entire life, she suggests, is an illustration of how everyday experiences can be imaginatively transformed into art.

In her essay, Cisneros reveals her insecurity and self-doubt, which she overcomes on her path to success. Read the following passage:

> I've managed to do a lot of things in my life I didn't think I was capable of and which many others didn't think I was capable of either. Especially because I am a woman, a Latina, an only daughter in a family of six men…. In our culture men and women don't leave their father's house except by way of marriage. . . . I broke a terrible taboo.

Cisneros discusses not only the self-doubt often experienced by young people, but also a self-doubt that stems from culture and gender. Understanding the cultural idiosyncrasies with which a writer is raised helps the reader understand whether an obstacle is a mountain or a molehill. For Cisneros, leaving her parents' home as an unmarried woman was a true breakthrough, one that gave her the strength to move on to even more challenging endeavors.

Your Turn

Read the following passage from Cisneros's essay, and then discuss with a partner how the writer's background influences your interpretation. How would your interpretation change if she had a different cultural background?

> I've done all kinds of things I didn't think I could do since then. I've gone to a prestigious university, studied with famous writers, and taken an MFA degree. I've taught poetry in schools in Illinois and Texas. I've gotten an NEA grant and run away with it as far as my courage would take me. . . . I've lived on an island. I've been to Venice twice. I've lived in Yugoslavia. . . . I've lived in a village in the pre-Alps and witnessed the daily parade of promenaders.

Learn It Online
For more information on Cisneros, go online.

go.hrw.com | L11-1307 | **Go**

Straw into Gold

What Do You Think What human needs and desires do we have in common?

QuickWrite

Think about your own cultural background or the backgrounds of some of your friends. Then, write about how a person's cultural heritage can influence his or her personality, goals, needs, or dreams.

MEET THE WRITER

Sandra Cisneros
(1954–   )

Sandra Cisneros has said that she experienced a major turning point at the University of Iowa when she realized that her history was different from that of her classmates. They "had been bred as fine hothouse flowers. I was a yellow weed among the city's cracks."

A Lonely Childhood

Cisneros remembers her Chicago childhood as solitary, even though, she says, her parents would be hard pressed to remember it that way. The nine members of her Mexican American family lived in cramped apartments where the only room with any privacy was the bathroom. As the only female child in a family with six sons, Cisneros often felt as solitary as an only child. To Cisneros, solitude proved important. If she had had a sister or a best friend, Cisneros thinks, she would not have buried herself in books.

Finding Her Voice

Cisneros received a bachelor's degree from Loyola University, in Chicago, and then earned a master's at The Writers' Workshop at the University of Iowa. There she began writing in earnest. Finding her own voice did not come easily or quickly for Cisneros; she did not realize for a long time that her best writer's voice was the voice of the home she grew up in, a voice that was a combination of her mother's South Side Chicago "tough" street English and her father's gentle, lulling Spanish. The result is a style that suggests a unique synthesis of the disparate languages of her childhood. Cisneros writes in an English often heavily informed by Spanish diction and grammatical structure.

Cisneros's first novel, *The House on Mango Street* (1983), won the American Book Award of the Before Columbus Foundation. In 1991, she published *Woman Hollering Creek and Other Stories*. In 1995, she was awarded a prestigious long-term fellowship by the John D. and Catherine T. MacArthur Foundation.

Think About the Writer How did Cisneros's solitude as a child contribute to her writing career?

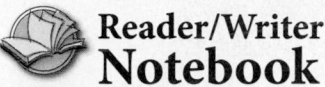

Reader/Writer Notebook

Use your **RWN** to complete the activities for this selection.

SKILLS FOCUS **Literary Skills** Understand allusions. **Reading Skills** Identify and understand a writer's background.

Literary Focus

Allusion An **allusion** is a reference to someone or something that is known from history, literature, religion, politics, sports, science, or some other cultural field. Writers expect readers to understand their allusions—a confidence based on the assumption of a shared culture. The title of Cisneros's essay is an allusion: Do you recognize the old folk tale she is referencing? As you read, think about what she is suggesting through this allusion.

Literary Perspectives Apply the literary perspective described on page 1311 as you read this essay.

Reading Focus

Understanding a Writer's Background Since personal experience is often an important resource for writers, understanding a writer's cultural background can be a key to understanding and appreciating his or her writing. A writer's cultural background is made up of such <u>components</u> as the place and time in which the writer grew up as well as the racial, ethnic, religious, and political traditions and values of the writer's family and community. Although writers usually move beyond their beginnings and make value choices of their own, they are rarely untouched by their culture of origin.

Into Action As you read, jot down the elements of Cisneros's background that she says have influenced her writing, and note how she responds to each element.

Cultural background	Cisneros's response to it
Women are expected to marry and then leave home.	Cisneros leaves home early, before marriage.

Writing Focus

Think as a Reader/Writer

Find It In Your Reading An **idiom** is an expression meaning something different from the literal definitions of its parts. Two examples of common idioms are "falling in love" and "I lost my head." As you read, watch for Cisneros's use of idioms. Use your *Reader/Writer Notebook* to make a list of idioms Cisneros uses in her essay.

Vocabulary

subsisting (suhb SIHST ihng) *v.* used as *adj.*: staying alive. *Subsisting on beans and bread, Cisneros tried to make her grant money last longer.*

intuitively (ihn TOO uh tihv lee) *adv.*: without conscious reasoning. *Creative writing came intuitively for Cisneros.*

ventured (VEHN chuhrd) *v.*: dared or risked going. *Cisneros ventured out into the wide world by herself.*

taboo (tuh BOO) *n.*: social restriction. *By leaving home before her brothers, Cisneros broke a cultural taboo.*

nomadic (noh MAD ihk) *adj.*: wandering. *Her unsettled childhood was very nomadic.*

nostalgia (nahs TAL juh) *n.*: longing. *She turned her nostalgia for home into a theme.*

flourished (FLUR ihshd) *v.*: thrived; prospered. *Cisneros's mother planted a garden that flourished under her care.*

prestigious (prehs TIHJ uhs) *adj.*: impressive; having distinction. *Cisneros has received several prestigious honors in her career.*

Language Coach

Antonyms A word that has the opposite, or nearly the opposite, meaning of another word is an **antonym.** For example, *permissible* and *acceptable* are antonyms for the Vocabulary word *taboo.*

 Learn It Online
Go online to read more about Sandra Cisneros and her essay.

go.hrw.com   L11-1309   **Go**

Straw into Gold

The Metamorphosis of the Everyday

by **Sandra Cisneros**

Mexican Heart (2006) by Hilary Simon.

Read with a Purpose
Read to discover how Cisneros's family has influenced her writing.

Build Background
In this personal essay, Cisneros alludes to the fairy tale "Rumpelstiltskin," in which a woman is given the impossible task of spinning straw into gold. Like the character in this fairy tale, Cisneros succeeds in her impossible task and finds a new meaning of her own in the old tale. Although fairy tales convey universal messages, they can also take on new and diverse meanings as our culture and society change.

When I was living in an artists' colony in the south of France, some fellow Latin-Americans who taught at the university in Aix-en-Provence invited me to share a home-cooked meal with them. I had been living abroad almost a year then on an NEA[1] grant, subsisting mainly on French bread and lentils so that my money could last longer. So when the invitation to dinner arrived, I accepted without hesitation. Especially since they had promised Mexican food.

What I didn't realize when they made this invitation was that I was supposed to be involved in preparing the meal. I guess they assumed I knew how to cook Mexican food because I am Mexican. They wanted specifically tortillas, though I'd never made a tortilla in my life.

It's true I had witnessed my mother rolling the little armies of dough into perfect circles, but my mother's family is from Guanajuato; they are *provincianos,* country folk. They only know how to make flour tortillas. My father's family, on the other hand, is *chilango*[2] from Mexico City. We ate corn tortillas but we didn't make them. Someone was sent to the corner tortilleria to buy some. I'd never seen anybody make corn tortillas. Ever. **Ⓐ**

Somehow my Latino hosts had gotten a hold of a packet of corn flour, and this is what they tossed my way with orders to produce tortillas. *Así como sea.* Any ol' way, they said and went back to their cooking.

Why did I feel like the woman in the fairy tale who was locked in a room and ordered to spin straw into gold? I had the same sick feeling when I was required to write my critical essay for the MFA[3] exam—the only piece of noncreative writing necessary in order to get my graduate degree. How was I to start? There were rules involved here, unlike writing a poem or story, which I did intuitively. There was a step by step process needed and I had better know it. I felt as if making tortillas—or writing a critical paper, for that matter—were tasks so impossible I wanted to break down into tears.

Somehow though, I managed to make tortillas—crooked and burnt, but edible nonetheless. My hosts were absolutely ignorant when it came to Mexican food; they thought my tortillas were delicious. (I'm glad my mama wasn't there.) Thinking back and look-

---

1. **NEA:** National Endowment for the Arts, a federal agency that grants money to selected organizations and individuals so they may engage in creative pursuits.
2. *chilango:* variation of "Shilango," name used by people of coastal Veracruz for those who live inland, especially the poor people of Mexico.
3. **MFA:** Master of Fine Arts.

Ⓐ Reading Focus Understanding a Writer's Background
What does this paragraph reveal about Cisneros's background?

Vocabulary subsisting (suhb SIHST ihng) *v.* used as *adj.:* staying alive.
intuitively (ihn TOO uh tihv lee) *adv.:* without conscious reasoning.

Literary Perspectives

Analyzing Political Context The social group to which writers—or other individuals—belong can influence their attitudes toward themselves, toward society, and toward their work. Historically, women and minority groups have found it difficult to achieve success in the dominant society. Some obstacles have been imposed by society itself through laws and restrictions, while other obstacles have been imposed by culture or custom. For example, Cisneros breaks a cultural taboo by leaving home before marriage. The struggle to end discrimination against women, African Americans, and other minority groups has brought major changes to American society. In literature—both fiction and nonfiction—we find records of this struggle. Thinking about a writer's relationship to the dominant society and about the role that societal and cultural expectations have played in his or her life can offer valid and useful insights into a writer's work.

As you read, be sure to notice the questions in the text, which will guide you in using this perspective.

ing at an old photograph documenting the three of us consuming those lopsided circles I am amazed. Just as I am amazed I could finish my MFA exam.

I've managed to do a lot of things in my life I didn't think I was capable of and which many others didn't think I was capable of either. Especially because I am a woman, a Latina, an only daughter in a family of six men. My father would've liked to have seen me married long ago. In our culture men and women don't leave their father's house except by way of marriage. I crossed my father's threshold with nothing carrying me but my own two feet. A woman whom no one came for and no one chased away. **B**

To make matters worse, I left before any of my six brothers had ventured away from home. I broke a terrible taboo. Somehow, looking back at photos of myself as a child, I wonder if I was aware of having begun already my own quiet war. **C**

I like to think that somehow my family, my Mexicanness, my poverty, all had something to do with shaping me into a writer. I like to think my parents were preparing me all along for my life as an artist even though they didn't know it. From my father I inherited a love of wandering. He was born in Mexico City but as a young man he traveled into the U.S. vagabonding. He eventually was drafted and thus became a citizen. Some of the stories he has told about his first months in the U.S. with little or no English surface in my stories in *The House on Mango Street* as well as others I have in mind to write in the future. From him I inherited a sappy heart. (He still cries when he watches Mexican soaps—especially if they deal with children who have forsaken their parents.)

My mother was born like me—in Chicago but of Mexican descent. It would be her tough streetwise

voice that would haunt all my stories and poems. An amazing woman who loves to draw and read books and can sing an opera. A smart cookie.

When I was a little girl we traveled to Mexico City so much I thought my grandparents' house on La Fortuna, number 12, was home. It was the only constant in our nomadic ramblings from one Chicago flat to another. The house on Destiny Street, number 12, in the colonia Tepeyac would be perhaps the only home I knew, and that nostalgia for a home would be a theme that would obsess me.

My brothers also figured greatly in my art. Especially the older two; I grew up in their shadows. Henry, the second oldest and my favorite, appears often in poems I have written and in stories which at times only borrow his nickname, Kiki. He played a major role in my childhood. We were bunk-bed mates. We were co-conspirators. We were pals. Until my oldest brother came back from studying in Mexico and left me odd woman out for always. **D**

What would my teachers say if they knew I was a writer now? Who would've guessed it? I wasn't a very bright student. I didn't much like school because we moved so much and I was always new and funny looking. In my fifth-grade report card I have nothing but an avalanche of C's and D's, but I don't remember being that stupid. I was good at art and I read plenty of library books and Kiki laughed at all my jokes. At home I was fine, but at school I never opened my mouth except when the teacher called on me.

When I think of how I see myself it would have to be at age eleven. I know I'm thirty-two on the outside, but inside I'm eleven. I'm the girl in the picture with skinny arms and a crumpled skirt and crooked hair. I didn't like school because all they saw was the out-

---

B **Literary Focus** Allusion What allusions to Mexican culture does Cisneros make when she describes herself as "a woman whom no one came for and no one chased away"?

C **Literary Perspectives** Analyzing Political Context Cisneros says that she broke a cultural taboo by leaving her parents' home unmarried. How do you think breaking free of social taboos might empower a person?

D **Reading Focus** Understanding a Writer's Background How does Cisneros think her parents "prepared" her for life as an artist?

Vocabulary **ventured** (VEHN chuhrd) *v.:* dared or risked going.
taboo (tuh BOO) *n.:* social restriction.
nomadic (noh MAD ihk) *adj.:* wandering.
nostalgia (nahs TAL juh) *n.:* longing.

Analyzing Visuals

Viewing and Interpreting Cisneros titles her essay "Straw into Gold." What details in this picture could a writer spin into the "gold" of a good story?

side me. School was lots of rules and sitting with your hands folded and being very afraid all the time. I liked looking out the window and thinking. I liked staring at the girl across the way writing her name over and over again in red ink. I wondered why the boy with the dirty collar in front of me didn't have a mama who took better care of him.

I think my mama and papa did the best they could to keep us warm and clean and never hungry. We had birthday and graduation parties and things like that, but there was another hunger that had to be fed. There was a hunger I didn't even have a name for. Was this when I began writing? **E F**

In 1966 we moved into a house, a real one, our first real home. This meant we didn't have to change schools and be the new kids on the block every couple of years. We could make friends and not be afraid we'd have to say goodbye to them and start all

E **Literary Perspectives** **Analyzing Political Context** Why might it be significant that Cisneros did not "have a name" for the hunger she felt?

F **Reading Focus** **Understanding a Writer's Background** Writers use unexpected connections as metaphors. What connections between her background and her present life does Cisneros discover here?

over. My brothers and the flock of boys they brought home would become important characters eventually for my stories—Louie and his cousins, Meme Ortiz and his dog with two names, one in English and one in Spanish.

My mother flourished in her own home. She took books out of the library and taught herself to garden—to grow flowers so envied we had to put a lock on the gate to keep out the midnight flower thieves. My mother has never quit gardening. **G**

This was the period in my life, that slippery age when you are both child and woman and neither, I was to record in *The House on Mango Street*. I was still shy. I was a girl who couldn't come out of her shell.

How was I to know I would be recording and documenting the women who sat their sadness on an elbow and stared out a window? It would be the city streets of Chicago I would later record, as seen through a child's eyes.

I've done all kinds of things I didn't think I could do since then. I've gone to a prestigious university, studied with famous writers, and taken an MFA degree. I've taught poetry in schools in Illinois and Texas. I've gotten an NEA grant and run away with it as far as my courage would take me. I've seen the bleached and bitter mountains of the Peloponnesus.[4] I've lived on an island. I've been to Venice twice. I've lived in Yugoslavia. I've been to the famous Nice[5] flower market behind the opera house. I've lived in a village in the pre-Alps and witnessed the daily parade of promenaders.

I've moved since Europe to the strange and wonderful country of Texas, land of polaroid-blue skies and big bugs. I met a mayor with my last name. I met famous Chicana and Chicano artists and writers and *políticos*.

Texas is another chapter in my life. It brought with it the Dobie-Paisano Fellowship, a six-month residency on a 265-acre ranch. But most important, Texas brought Mexico back to me.

I couldn't think of anything else I'd rather be than a writer.

In the days when I would sit at my favorite people-watching spot, the snakey Woolworth's counter across the street from the Alamo (the Woolworth's which has since been torn down to make way for progress), I couldn't think of anything else I'd rather be than a writer. I've traveled and lectured from Cape Cod to San Francisco, to Spain, Yugoslavia, Greece, Mexico, France, Italy, and now today to Texas. Along the way there has been straw for the taking. With a little imagination, it can be spun into gold. **H I**

---

4. **Peloponnesus:** the large peninsula on the mainland of Greece.
5. **Nice** (nees): port city in southern France.

G **Literary Perspectives** Analyzing Political Context
What are the effects of moving into the family's "first real home"?

Vocabulary **flourished** (FLUR ihshd) *v.:* thrived; prospered.
prestigious (prehs TIHJ uhs) *adj.:* impressive; having distinction.

H **Reading Focus** Understanding a Writer's Background
How has Texas brought Cisneros's Mexican background back to her?

I **Literary Focus** Allusion Cisneros ties the end of the essay to its beginning by alluding again to the fairy tale. What tools has she used to achieve her metamorphosis?

Applying Your Skills

Straw into Gold

Respond and Think Critically

Reading Focus

Quick Check

1. What similarities does Cisneros see between making tortillas and writing a critical essay?

2. Describe Cisneros's experiences at elementary school. How do they connect with her later role as a writer?

3. Why does Cisneros think that wanting a home is a theme with which she is obsessed?

Read with a Purpose

4. How did Cisneros's family and childhood influence her development as a writer?

Reading Skills: Understanding a Writer's Background

5. While reading the essay, you took notes about the background elements that have influenced Cisneros's writing and her response to them. Now that you have finished reading, review your notes. Add a column to your chart. Explain how each background element has influenced her writing.

Cultural background	Cisneros's response to it	How does it influence her writing?
Women are expected to marry and then leave home.	Cisneros leaves home early, before marriage.	It frees her to become a writer; she writes about her mother.

Literary Focus

Literary Analysis

6. **Interpret** How would you interpret the essay's subtitle, "The Metamorphosis of the Everyday," as it relates to events in Cisneros's life and to her writing?

7. **Infer** What can you tell about Cisneros from the list of things she has done in her life?

8. **Literary Perspectives** Cisneros says she has done many things that she didn't believe she was capable of doing. How do you think the cultural and social environment in which Cisneros grew up affected her view of her own capability? What social factors might have caused Cisneros to change her opinion of herself?

Literary Skills: Allusion

9. **Interpret** The title of the essay includes an allusion to the folk tale of Rumpelstiltskin. In the essay itself, how does Cisneros use that magical story as a metaphor for her writing? How does the title point to the essay's main idea?

Literary Skills Review: Style

10. **Analyze** A writer's **style** is the distinctive way in which he or she uses language. Identify some fresh images and figures of speech in the essay that reveal Cisneros to be an accomplished writer. How would you describe her style? (Is it formal? conversational? poetic?)

Writing Focus

Think as a Reader/Writer

Use It in Your Writing Writers can use idioms to make their writing more expressive. Review the entries in your *Reader/Writer Notebook* to find one that would be enhanced by adding idioms. Add at least two idioms to this entry and evaluate their effect on your writing.

What needs and desires does Cisneros express in her essay? Are these needs and desires common or unique?

Applying Your Skills

Straw into Gold

Vocabulary Development

✓ Vocabulary Check

Use a Vocabulary word to answer each question below. Use each word only once.

subsisting
intuitively
ventured
taboo
nomadic
nostalgia
flourished
prestigious

1. Which word would you use to describe what last year's bumper crop did?

2. Which word describes how a dog is living if it eats only what it finds on the street?

3. Which word might a DJ use to describe her audience's longing for oldies?

4. Which word could you use to describe the most influential law firm in the country?

5. Which word can be used to describe the lifestyle of wandering sheepherders?

6. Which word refers to forbidden behavior?

7. Which word describes the actions of a person who has left a safe or well-known area?

8. Which word is the opposite of *consciously*?

Vocabulary Skills: Word Origins

The English language has absorbed words from different languages, including Greek, Latin, and German. As technology makes the world a smaller place, English continues to absorb foreign words. The Vocabulary word *taboo* may have its origins in several South Pacific languages. Tongan, a Polynesian language, has a word *ta-bu* that means "sacred." The Hawaiian word *kapu* means "sacred, holy, or consecrated," and the Maori word *tapu* means "prohibited." The first known use of *taboo* was by Captain James Cook, who explored the South Pacific between 1768 and 1779.

A dictionary will tell you the source of most modern English words. Sometimes you might need to check more than one entry to find a word's origin.

intuitively: from the Latin *intuitus,* past participle of *intueri* meaning "to look at" [origin found under *intuition*]

ventured: a shortened form of *aventure,* which is a form of *adventure* from the Old French *auenture* meaning "about to happen" [origin found under *adventure*]

Your Turn

Use a dictionary to find the word origins for the rest of the Vocabulary words: *subsisting, nomadic, nostalgia, flourished,* and *prestigious.*

Language Coach

Antonyms A word that has the opposite, or nearly the opposite, meaning of another word is an antonym. For example, an antonym for the Vocabulary word *nomadic,* which means "wandering," is *sedentary,* meaning "not migratory; not physically active." Match each Vocabulary word listed in the left-hand column with its antonym in the right-hand column.

1. subsisting   **a.** settled

2. nomadic   **b.** disreputable

3. flourished   **c.** perishing

4. prestigious   **d.** declined

Academic Vocabulary

Talk About
Cisneros lists several <u>components</u> of her development as a writer. In a small group, discuss the <u>components</u> of your life that have shaped your interests and personality.

SKILLS FOCUS Vocabulary Skills
Research word origins, including Greek,
Latin, and Anglo-Saxon words. **Writing
Skills** Explore the significance of personal
experiences, events, and conditions. **Grammar Skills** Identify and use parallel grammatical structures. **Listening and Speaking
Skills** Deliver informative presentations.

Grammar Link

Parallel Structure

Parallel structure is the repetition of words, phrases, clauses, or sentences that have the same grammatical form. Parallel structure can emphasize ideas that are equal in weight. The key to parallel structure is balance. You must pair a noun with a noun, a verb with a verb, a prepositional phrase with a prepositional phrase, a clause with the same kind of clause.

> Thinking back and looking at an old photograph documenting the three of us consuming those lopsided circles I am amazed.

> We were bunk-bed mates. We were co-conspirators. We were pals.

Your Turn

Rewrite each of the following sentences so that they are parallel in structure.

1. Cisneros's mother loves to draw, to read, and singing.

2. For Cisneros, home was where she could be herself and in school she was quiet.

3. Her mother's family ate flour tortillas and the family of her father was eating corn tortillas.

4. Cisneros has traveled, gives lectures, and written in many countries.

5. She has gone to a good university. In a school she taught poetry. There is an island where she once lived.

Writing Application Write a brief personal narrative that is modeled on "Straw into Gold." To add emphasis and rhythm to your prose, use at least three examples of parallel sentence structure. As shown in the examples above, your repetitions can join elements within a sentence, or they can connect independent sentences.

CHOICES

As you respond to the Choices, use these **Academic Vocabulary** words as appropriate: component, diverse, intrinsic, potential, transmit.

REVIEW

Connect to Other Fairy Tales

Timed ┗ Writing With a small group, brainstorm a list of fairy tales other than "Rumpelstiltskin." Briefly summarize the plot of each fairy tale. Then, working on your own, write a brief essay making a connection between one of the fairy tales on your list and some aspect of your own life.

CONNECT

Create a Cultural Mural

Survey your parents or other adult family members or friends to find out which components of their cultural backgrounds give them the most pride. What skills and traditions did they learn as children and continue to practice as adults? Which do they most want their children to continue? Which do they feel are being lost? Compile your results with the results of classmates, and create a mural that represents the cultural values and backgrounds of your community.

EXTEND

Research Mexican Culture

Oral Presentation Like Cisneros, the Mexican American labor leader Cesar Chavez attended many schools as a child. In 1962, he began to organize the group that later became the United Farm Workers, a union to help protect migrant farm workers. Research other Mexicans or Mexican Americans who have made significant contributions to society. Share your findings with the class in an oral presentation.

Learn It Online
Find graphic organizers online to help you organize information and formulate a response.

go.hrw.com | L11-1317 | Go

Contemporary Poetry

Above the Clouds I (1962/1963) by Georgia O'Keeffe.
Oil on canvas. 36 ⅛" × 48 ¼".

"Poetry is life distilled."

— **Gwendolyn Brooks**

CONTENTS

Poetry and Personal Experience
by **Leila Christenbury**

Characteristics of Personal Poetry

- Explores subjects of which the poet has personal experience
- Communicates ideas in a literal and figurative sense
- Enhances readers' understanding of universal themes and ideas

Getting Personal

Poetry is often personal. Even when poems are about big topics—war, nature, death, love, loss—they are almost always presented through the poet's individual lens. Part of what makes a poem appealing is the reader's sense of sharing an experience with the poet. This sense is called **empathy,** experiencing the feelings of another person. Much of poetry's power lies in its ability to make us see the world in a new way and to remind us of how much we have in common.

How can we learn to empathize with a poet and to experience the emotions and ideas offered in a poem? It takes a little work, but the effort is rewarding. Follow these steps:

1. **Think about the title** for a moment. Titles often provide important clues to a poem's meaning.

2. With the title in mind, **read the entire poem through.** Doing so will give you an overview of its major ideas and images. As you read, be sure to listen to the sounds of the poem. Poetry is sound and meaning.

3. **Re-read the poem, restating the lines in language you understand.** It is easy to get confused by line breaks, inverted sentences, unfamiliar words, and figures of speech. You will not fully understand a poem if you do not understand the literal meaning of each line. For example, here are the opening lines of Dickinson's "Tell all the Truth but tell it slant":

> Tell all the Truth but tell it slant—
> Success in Circuit lies

You might restate these lines this way: "Tell important truths indirectly. You will communicate them better if you are roundabout."

4. **Connect the poem's ideas.** Most poems have an argument, or proposition, of some kind. Dickinson's poem, for example, contains a simile likening us to children whose fear of lightning is eased though gentle explanation. This simile supports the argument of the poem—that the direct truth can overwhelm.

5. **Connect the poem's ideas to yourself.** Once you've finished, sit back and reflect a moment on what the poem means to you. Can you relate to the ideas? Does the poem make your own experience seem richer or more complex?

Ask Yourself

1. What is the significance of the relationship between reader and poet?

2. Why do you think many poems seem to need to be "translated," or restated by readers?

Learn It Online
Learn more about poetry through *PowerNotes*.

go.hrw.com   L11-1319   **Go**

Preparing to Read

The Unknown Citizen

What Do You Think?

What human needs and desires do we have in common?

QuickTalk

Auden often wrote about public subjects in a personal way that defied ideology. What public subjects do you think concern people personally today? Discuss this question with a partner.

W. H. Auden
(1907–1973)

Pulitzer Prize WINNER

Wystan Hugh Auden is widely considered one of the greatest poets of the twentieth century. His work covers subjects from politics to the search for love. Auden's essays and reviews made him one of the most influential social critics of his day. Since his death, Auden's influence has not waned, and his poems continue to have relevance. After the attacks of September 11, 2001, for example, quotations from his poem "Musée des Beaux Arts," about human indifference to suffering, appeared in news articles as well as on the subway walls of New York City.

Complex Political Views

After leaving Oxford in 1928, Auden lived in Weimar, Germany. There, while right- and left-wing parties were struggling for dominance, Auden was exposed to the political and economic unrest that would be a subject of his poetry for years to come. Returning to Britain in 1929, he became the leader of a left-wing literary group. Many of these writers idealistically headed to Spain in 1937 to support the Spanish Republican Army's fight against the fascist rebels; Auden intended to drive an ambulance. When he realized, however, that the Republicans were supported by Stalin's Soviet Union, Auden's political views became increasingly complex. By the end of the 1930s, Auden abandoned his role as a left-wing political poet.

From England to America and Back Again

In 1939, on the eve of World War II, Auden moved to the United States, prompted by an invitation to teach at the University of Michigan. His English colleagues felt he was deserting his country at a critical time, just as World War II was about to break out. Though Auden became a naturalized U.S. citizen in 1946, he spent the final years of his life back in Oxford. His poetry, meanwhile, moved from political topics to emotional and religious exploration. *The Age of Anxiety* (1947), which opens in a wartime bar in New York City, became one of the defining works of the postwar literary era and won him a Pulitzer Prize.

Think About the Writer

If Auden were alive today, what political and social issues might he address in his poetry and essays?

Reader/Writer Notebook

Use your **RWN** to complete the activities for this selection.

Literary Focus

Irony The literary technique called **irony** sets up a discrepancy or incongruity between appearances and reality. An example of **verbal irony** happens when someone says something but means the opposite. **Situational irony** occurs when it turns out to be the opposite of what we expect or what we think would be appropriate. A more specialized kind of irony— **dramatic irony**—is when a reader or audience knows something that a character in a story does not know.

There is also a literary mode called irony: In literature written in the ironic mode there is no hero, people have lost individual freedom, and their quests or searches for something of value are failures. Irony has been the dominant literary mode of the past century.

Auden is known for his ironic style, which often—unexpectedly— combines clever wordplay and versification with serious religious and political ideas. This poem is firmly in the ironic mode; instead of a noble hero we find a nameless bureaucrat who is praised for his conformity.

Literary Perspectives Apply the literary perspective described on page 1323 as you read this poem.

Language Coach

Suffixes In the word *eugenist,* the suffix *–ist* means "an expert." A eugenist is an expert in the science of genes and heredity. The suffix *–ist* can also mean "a person who does or makes something," "a person who plays a musical instrument," or "a person who believes in a cause or philosophy."

Use the suffix *–ist* to identify each of these people: an expert in psychology, someone who plays the violin, and someone who believes in ideals.

Reading Focus

Analyzing Tone **Tone** is the attitude that a writer takes toward the subject of a work, the characters in it, or the audience. When people speak, you can tell from the tone of their voices how they feel. In poetry, tone is transmitted through sound, word choice, and imagery. Verbal irony, for example, produces an ironic tone.

Into Action As you read, use a chart like the one below to note key details in the poem and the tone each detail conveys. Be sure to consider the sounds of the poem —how do the rhymes and rhythms create tone?

Details	Tone
"he was a saint" (line 4)	mocking

Writing Focus

Think as a Reader/Writer

Find It in Your Reading This poem presents a list of the unknown citizen's specific characteristics. As you read, use your *Reader/Writer Notebook* to list the details describing the unknown citizen that you think are most informative or most revealing.

Learn It Online
Listen to this poem online.

go.hrw.com L11-1321 **Go**

THE UNKNOWN CITIZEN

by **W. H. Auden**

(To JS/07/M/378
This Marble Monument
Is Erected by the State)

Read with a Purpose
Read to find out what the State feels is necessary for human happiness.

Build Background
The poem's title alludes to the grand monuments erected by nations all over the world to honor soldiers who died for their country. In the tombs usually lie the remains of an unidentified fallen soldier. In the United States, the Tomb of the Unknowns is in Washington, D.C. Inscribed on the tomb are these words:

> HERE RESTS
> IN HONORED GLORY
> AN AMERICAN SOLDIER
> KNOWN BUT TO GOD

He was found by the Bureau of Statistics to be
One against whom there was no official complaint,
And all the reports on his conduct agree
That, in the modern sense of an old-fashioned word,
    he was a saint,
5 For in everything he did he served the Greater Community. **Ⓐ**
He worked in a factory and never got fired,
Except for the War till the day he retired
He worked in a factory and never got fired,
But satisfied his employers, Fudge Motors Inc. **Ⓑ**

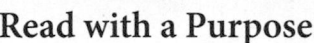

Ⓐ Literary Focus Irony According to the State, what is the modern sense of the word *saint*? Do you think Auden agrees with this definition of *saint*?

Ⓑ Reading Focus Analyzing Tone What tone does the writer reveal when he names the factory Fudge Motors?

Yet he wasn't a scab° or odd in his views,

10 For his Union reports that he paid his dues,
(Our report on his Union shows it was sound)
And our Social Psychology workers found
That he was popular with his mates and liked a drink.
The Press are convinced that he bought a paper every day

15 And that his reactions to advertisements were normal in every way.
Policies taken out in his name prove that he was fully insured,
And his Health-card shows he was once in hospital but left it cured.
Both Producers Research and High-Grade Living declare
He was fully sensible to the advantages of the Installment Plan

20 And had everything necessary to the Modern Man,
A gramophone, a radio, a car, and a frigidaire.° **C**
Our researchers into Public Opinion are content
That he held the proper opinions for the time of year;
When there was peace, he was for peace; when there was war, he went. **D**

25 He was married and added five children to the population,
Which our Eugenist° says was the right number
        for a parent of his generation,
And our teachers report that he never interfered
        with their education.
Was he free? Was he happy? The question is
        absurd:
Had anything been wrong, we should certainly
        have heard.

---

9. **scab** (skab): a worker who refuses to join a labor union or a labor strike and takes the job of a striking worker.

21. **gramophone** (GRAM uh fohn) and **frigidaire** (frihj uh DAIR): old-fashioned words for a record player and refrigerator.

26. **Eugenist** (YOO juhn ihst): person who studies hereditary improvement through selective breeding.

C Literary Perspectives **Philosophical Context** What does Auden want you to think of this philosophy of human happiness? How does it relate to capitalism's equation of happiness with material gain?

D Literary Perspectives **Philosophical Context** What happens to a society in which individuals do not think for themselves?

Literary Perspectives

Analyzing Philosophical Context Nearly all enduring literature deals with the "big questions" of life—the philosophical questions that all of us think about from time to time. *What does it mean to be a human being? What does it mean to live a good life? What is the role of an individual in society?* These questions concern ethics. **Ethics** is the branch of philosophy that focuses on issues of right and wrong, or justice and injustice. The question of what it means to be an ethical person is at the heart of this poem. In "The Unknown Citizen," we see what Auden thinks of a society where people are reduced to numbers and statistics and live under the total control of the State.

As you read, be sure to notice the questions in the text, which will guide you in using this perspective.

Respond and Think Critically

Reading Focus

Quick Check

1. Why has the State erected this monument to the unknown citizen?

2. When asked if the man was free and happy, what does the State reply?

Read with a Purpose

3. The State says that this citizen "had everything necessary to the Modern Man." What are the things that the State believes necessary?

Reading Skills: Analyzing Tone

4. While reading, you used a chart to note details that convey the writer's tone—his attitude toward the citizen and toward the State. Review your notes now and write a sentence summing up Auden's tone in this poem. How does he really feel about this citizen and the State that has erected a monument to him?

Literary Focus

Literary Analysis

5. **Infer** Auden satirizes the citizen's society in this poem. What, by implication, does Auden think an ideal society should be like?

6. **Analyze** Auden chose as the title of his poem the name of monuments that honor people who have died for their countries. How does this title make Auden's poem even more ironic?

7. **Analyze** What details in the poem mock the tendency to reduce individuals to statistics?

8. **Extend** Do people like Auden's unknown citizen exist today? Explain.

9. **Literary Perspectives** Is this materialistic philosophy about what constitutes happiness and freedom still common today?

Literary Skills: Irony

10. **Evaluate** Use the chart below to note details that tell you the poem is in the ironic mode:

Features of Ironic Mode	Details from Poem
A. Loss of heroic protagonist B. Loss of individual freedom C. Failure to find something of value in life	

Literary Skills Review: Characterization

11. **Make Judgments** The process by which a writer reveals the personality of a character is **characterization.** Auden presents a character by describing how he behaves, what he values, and how the State evaluates him. What kind of person is this unknown citizen? On what details do you base your evaluation?

Writing Focus

Think as a Reader/Writer

Use It in Your Writing As you read, you noted the specific ironic ways in which Auden characterizes the citizen. How do you think our society would define the "perfect" citizen? Can you think of any traits that our society particularly admires? What kind of behavior does it discourage? How similar is our society to the one described in Auden's poem?

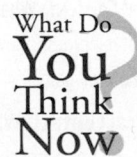 **What Do You Think Now** What do you think Auden might say about materialism, bureaucracy, and social control today?

CHOICES

As you respond to the Choices, use these **Academic Vocabulary** words as appropriate: component, diverse, intrinsic, potential, transmit.

REVIEW

Perform a Choral Reading

Prepare "The Unknown Citizen" for a choral reading. In a choral reading, some lines are spoken by a group of readers and others are spoken by individuals. In assigning the lines, be aware of the rhymes and of where the sentences begin and end, as well as the tone that you want to convey. You might use a musical accompaniment or create masks for your readers. Present your performance to the class.

Define a Saint

According to the statistics on the citizen in Auden's poem, he is a "saint." Think about how you would define a saintly person, and write your own poem about him or her. Try to include the characteristics that have been overlooked in Auden's State.

CONNECT

Compare Attitudes Toward Authority

Group Discussion Locate and read a copy of "Game," a short story by Donald Barthelme, and compare it to Auden's poem. In a small group, discuss how authority is represented in each text and what attitude toward authority each author seems to hold. Then, talk about the concept of authority as it relates to your everyday life, the lives of your friends, and the condition of your town, state, or country. How does your attitude toward authority compare to the attitudes held by Auden and Barthelme?

Form a Consensus

Group Discussion In a small group, discuss what it means to be a happy and productive member of today's society. Create a list of deeds and characteristics that you believe are intrinsic to an ideal citizen today. Present your conclusions to the class.

EXTEND

Analyze Auden's Irony

Timed Writing Auden's poem "The Unknown Citizen" catalogs the diverse virtues of a man, as viewed by the eyes of his society. The poem's ironic tone, however, reveals how Auden really feels. In an expository essay, explain how the use of irony in the poem reveals Auden's theme. Use examples from the poem to support your claims.

Describe the Imperfect Citizen

Write a brief description of what might happen to the unknown citizen if the State later found out he had, in fact, committed a crime. Write this description in the form of a newspaper article in a State-run newspaper. Describe your idea of what the State might consider a crime, based on details in the poem. Try to duplicate Auden's dry, ironic tone in your fake newpaper article.

The Fish
One Art

 What human needs and desires do we have in common?

🕐 **QuickWrite**

Think about the symbols in your life. What objects, animals, or places represent powerful emotions, beliefs, or ideas? Choose a symbol, write about what it represents, and explain why it is important to you.

Elizabeth Bishop
(1911–1979)

Pulitzer Prize WINNER

For many of the important poets of her time, Elizabeth Bishop has been a "poet's poet"—an acknowledged master of the highest art and most meticulous craft. She has also been an unacknowledged inspiration for many other poets who are still trying to solve the mystery of her deceptive simplicity.

A Dark Childhood

Bishop spent her early years in a Nova Scotia village—a childhood marked by the death of her father when she was only eight months old and darkened by the long mental illness of her mother. These circumstances in effect made her an orphan whose upbringing was entrusted to relatives. After she turned five, she never saw her mother again.

At the time of her mother's death in a psychiatric hospital, Bishop was a student at Vassar College. After graduation she embarked on a career devoted to poetry and, by means of a private income, travel. In her travels she discovered two places that detained her for years—Key West, Florida, and Rio de Janeiro, Brazil. *Questions of Travel* (1965), the title she gave to one of her books, might serve as an index to the story of a life told in poems that are always "letters from abroad." In these poems, places provide temporary settings for an endless inquiry into the nature of perception and reality.

Poems Reveal Her Character

In the final years of her life, Bishop lived in Boston and taught at Harvard. A shy woman with a taste for the exotic as well as a love of the everyday, Bishop conducted herself with a scrupulous conventionality, much at odds with the audacity and profundity of her imagination. Her poems most truly reveal her character: a combination of the conservatism and moral uprightness that was often associated with the North and the casual sensuousness and cheerfully untidy sprawl that some people associated with the everyday outdoor life of the South. For Elizabeth Bishop, geography was less a matter of maps and place names than of states of mind and areas of feeling.

Think About the Writer Bishop was not a "confessional" poet. What power can there be in works that are more suggestive than explicit?

The Fish

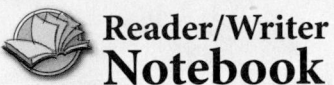
Reader/Writer
Notebook
Use your **RWN** to complete the activities for this selection.

Literary Focus

Symbol A **symbol** is a person, a place, a thing, or an event that has meaning in itself and also stands for something much more than itself. Often symbols stand for abstract ideas or qualities. The dove, for instance, is used as a symbol of peace. A skull symbolizes death. A red rose symbolizes love. A flag symbolizes an entire country. These are all public symbols; their meaning is conventional. Writers may also create private symbols. As you read this poem, think about what this old fish might symbolize to the speaker.

Reading Focus

Analyzing Details Bishop crafts her poems with meticulous attention to details. This poem, like most poetry, is compressed and therefore works by power of suggestion. This compression magnifies the importance of every detail. To understand this poem, you must note the details and understand the <u>potential</u> significance of each one. Ask yourself, "Why did the poet choose this detail and not another?"

Into Action As you read, record key details that Bishop uses in describing the fish. Use a chart like the one below.

	Details describing the fish
Skin	"like ancient wall-paper" (line 11)
Eyes	
Face and jaw	

Vocabulary

venerable (VEHN uhr uh buhl) *adj.:* old and respected. *The fish's age and ability to survive make him venerable for the poet.*

bilge (bihlj) *n.:* dirty water that gathers in the bottom of a boat. *She found the fish beautiful as it lay there in the oily bilge.*

thwarts (thwawrts) *n. pl.:* seats on a boat. *We sat on the thwarts of the canoe as we dropped our fishing lines into the water.*

gunnels (GUHN uhlz) *n. pl.:* gunwales; the upper edges of the sides of a boat. *Bishop dropped the fish over the gunnels and into the water.*

Language Coach

Related Words When you learn a new word, you can also learn related words that share the same root of the word. For example, the adjective *venerable* means "old and respected." What do you think the related verb *venerate* means? What does the related noun *veneration* mean? You can check your answers in a dictionary.

Writing Focus

Think as a Reader/Writer

Find It in Your Reading Bishop uses **similes** throughout this poem—especially to describe the fish. In your *Reader/Writer Notebook,* write down some of these similes. After you finish reading the poem, re-read the similes you selected to see whether they help explain the speaker's action in the poem's last line.

 Learn It Online
Explore the Vocabulary words with Word Watch.

go.hrw.com   L11-1327   **Go**

The Fish
by **Elizabeth Bishop**

Read with a Purpose
Read to find out how the speaker feels about this fish.

Build Background
Bishop grew up in Nova Scotia and later lived for many years in Key West in Florida, on North Haven Island in Maine, and near Boston Harbor. Most likely during some of these years, she fished from a rowboat. This poem uses many words connected with rowboats: *bilge* is the dirty water that gathers in the bottom of the boat; a *bailer* is a bucket used to bail water out of the boat; *thwarts* are the seats on the boat; and *gunnels* (gunwales) are the upper edges of the sides of the boat. The *wire leader* hanging from the fish's mouth would have been used to attach the hook to the fish line. As in all her poems, Bishop here writes in detail of something she knows very well.

I caught a tremendous fish
and held him beside the boat
half out of water, with my hook
fast in a corner of his mouth.
5   He didn't fight.
He hadn't fought at all.
He hung a grunting weight,
battered and venerable
and homely. Here and there
10   his brown skin hung in strips
like ancient wall-paper,
and its pattern of darker brown
was like wall-paper:
shapes like full-blown roses
15   stained and lost through age. **A**
He was speckled with barnacles,
fine rosettes of lime,
and infested
with tiny white sea-lice,
20   and underneath two or three
rags of green weed hung down.
While his gills were breathing in
the terrible oxygen

   —the frightening gills
25   fresh and crisp with blood,
that can cut so badly—
I thought of the coarse white flesh
packed in like feathers,
the big bones and the little bones,
30   the dramatic reds and blacks
of his shiny entrails,
and the pink swim-bladder
like a big peony. **B**
I looked into his eyes
35   which were far larger than mine
but shallower, and yellowed,
the irises backed and packed
with tarnished tinfoil
seen through the lenses
40   of old scratched isinglass.
They shifted a little, but not
to return my stare. **C**
—It was more like the tipping
of an object toward the light.
45   I admired his sullen face,
the mechanism of his jaw,

A **Literary Focus** Symbol On the basis of the characteristics of the fish the poet includes in the opening lines, what might the fish symbolize?

Vocabulary **venerable** (VEHN uhr uh buhl) *adj.*: old and respected.

B **Reading Focus** Analyzing Details What details help you visualize the fish? Do these details create an attractive or unattractive image?

C **Reading Focus** Analyzing Details What details describe the fish's eyes? To what does the speaker compare the eyes?

Trout Leap (1993) by Paul Riley.

and then I saw
that from his lower lip
—if you could call it a lip—
50 grim, wet, and weapon-like,
hung five old pieces of fish-line,
or four and a wire leader
with the swivel still attached,
with all their five big hooks
55 grown firmly in his mouth.
A green line, frayed at the end
where he broke it, two heavier lines,
and a fine black thread
still crimped from the strain and snap
60 when it broke and he got away.
Like medals with their ribbons
frayed and wavering,

a five-haired beard of wisdom
trailing from his aching jaw. **D**
65 I stared and stared
and victory filled up
the little rented boat,
from the pool of bilge
where oil had spread a rainbow
70 around the rusted engine
to the bailer rusted orange,
the sun cracked thwarts,
the oarlocks on their strings,
the gunnels—until everything
75 was rainbow, rainbow, rainbow! **E**
And I let the fish go.

Vocabulary **bilge** (bihlj) *n.:* dirty water that gathers in the bottom of a boat.
thwarts (thwawrts) *n. pl.:* seats on a boat.
gunnels (GUHN uhlz) *n. pl.:* gunwales; the upper edges of the sides of a boat.

D **Reading Focus** Analyzing Details To what does the speaker compare the five lines and hooks that have grown into the fish's mouth? How do these comparisons shape the way you view the fish?

E **Literary Focus** Symbol What could a rainbow symbolize? Why would Bishop compare this fish to a rainbow?

Preparing to Read

One Art

Reader/Writer Notebook

Use your **RWN** for completing the activities for this selection.

Literary Focus

Villanelle A **villanelle** (vihl uh NEHL) is an intricately patterned, nineteen-line lyric poem. A traditional villanelle follows this structure:

- The poem consists of five three-line stanzas and a final four-line stanza.
- The first line is repeated as the end of the second and fourth stanzas.
- The third line is repeated as the last line of the third and fifth stanzas.
- These two repeated, or **refrain**, lines also make up the two final lines.
- The **rhyme scheme** is *aba* except in the last stanza, where it is *abaa*.

This complex form of poetry presents many challenges: the poet must maintain a steady **rhythm**, find enough rhyming words for the *a* or *b* endings of all nineteen lines, and construct the poem in such a way that the emotional intensity reaches a crescendo in the final stanza. Most importantly, the poet wants to create the impression that the poem is not labored at all, but is a spontaneous expression of emotion.

Writing Focus

Think as a Reader/Writer

Find It in Your Reading Irony plays a large part in this poem, as it does in a great many modern works of literature. Irony is saying one thing and meaning the opposite. If you have had a terrible day and you tell a friend that your day was "terrific," you are being ironic. (You will probably say it with a depressed tone of voice to <u>transmit</u> the irony.) As you read, make a chart like the one below in your *Reader/Writer Notebook* to keep track of lines and phrases that suggest an ironic tone. Underline any words that seem especially ironic.

Details that suggest an ironic tone (line #)	How is this ironic?
"<u>practice</u> losing farther" (line 7)	Why would anyone want to "practice" losing anything?

Language Coach

Related Words Poets often use forms of the same word to create echoes of both meaning and sound. How are the words *loss, lost,* and *losing* related? Tell the part of speech of each word and give its definition. Name the basic form of the verb from which they are formed. Then, choose another simple verb and see how many related words you can find.

Learn It Online

Follow Elizabeth Bishop across the Internet with these links.

go.hrw.com   L11-1330   **Go**

Coney Island III (1990) (detail) by Max Ferguson.

One Art

by **Elizabeth Bishop**

Read with a Purpose
What personal experiences and difficulties does Bishop express in this poem?

The art of losing isn't hard to master;
so many things seem filled with the intent
to be lost that their loss is no disaster.

Lose something every day. Accept the fluster
5   of lost door keys, the hour badly spent.
The art of losing isn't hard to master.

Then practice losing farther, losing faster:
places, and names, and where it was you meant
to travel. None of these will bring disaster.

10   I lost my mother's watch. And look! my last, or
next to-last, of three loved houses went.
The art of losing isn't hard to master.

I lost two cities, lovely ones. And, vaster,
some realms I owned, two rivers, a continent.
15   I miss them, but it wasn't a disaster.

—Even losing you (the joking voice, a gesture
I love) I shan't have lied. It's evident
the art of losing's not too-hard to master
though it may look like (*Write* it!) like disaster.

 Literary Focus Villanelle How does the poem conform to the structure of the villanelle? Where does it vary from the traditional form?

Respond and Think Critically

Reading Focus

Quick Check

1. What is the setting of "The Fish"?

2. What is the "art" Bishop is talking about in "One Art"?

Read with a Purpose

The Fish

3. How do the speaker's feelings toward the fish change thoughout the poem?

One Art

4. Do you think "art" helps the speaker deal with the emotional pain in her life? Explain.

Reading Skills: Analyzing Details

5. Refer to the chart you made while you read "The Fish," citing the details that describe the fish. Why do you think the author chose the details that she did?

Literary Focus

Literary Analysis

The Fish

6. **Interpret** Why is the oxygen "terrible" in line 23?

7. **Interpret** Why does the speaker call the fish hooks "medals" in line 61?

8. **Interpret** In lines 65–67, as the speaker stared at the fish, "victory filled up" the boat. Whose victory is it? Who or what is the enemy?

9. **Draw Conclusions** Why does the speaker in "The Fish" let the fish go?

One Art

10. **Infer** What do you think is the worst loss for the speaker?

11. **Interpret** Why do you think the speaker orders "*Write* it!" in the last line of "One Art"? Does the speaker mean what she says, or is she putting up a good front? Explain.

Literary Skills: Symbol/Villanelle

12. **Analyze** In "The Fish" what clues suggest that the fish might have a symbolic meaning? What could the rainbow at the end symbolize?

13. **Compare and Contrast** Can you guess why the poet chose to change the traditional form of the villanelle? Does this change affect the meaning of the poem?

Literary Skills Review: Imagery

14. **Evaluate** "The Fish" includes imagery, or language used to evoke a picture or concrete sensation, that helps us share the speaker's experience of this fishing trip. What images help you picture the fish and the boat?

Writing Focus

Think as a Reader/Writer

Use It in Your Writing As you read, you noted in your *Reader/Writer Notebook* examples of similes ("The Fish") and details that reveal an ironic tone ("One Art"). Review your notes and write a villanelle using similes and irony. You might write about an animal or about an "art" that we all eventually learn.

What Do You Think Now When is it appropriate to hang on to something you want? When might you need to let it go? How would you know?

Vocabulary Development

✓ Vocabulary Check

Match the Vocabulary words with their definitions.

1. venerable   **a.** a boat's seats
2. bilge   **b.** sides of a boat
3. thwarts   **c.** worthy of respect
4. gunnels   **d.** water at the bottom of a boat

Vocabulary Skills: Technical Vocabulary

Technical vocabulary in a work of literature can lend credibility and authority to the piece, but it can also make the writing difficult to understand. In "The Fish," Bishop uses many terms that are unique to the areas of fishing and sailing. Readers with experience in these activities will understand this vocabulary right away, but many readers will have to look the words up in a dictionary. Sometimes you can guess a word's meaning by its **context,** or the surrounding words and sentences. Knowing technical vocabulary can give you a better understanding of the work, as well as provide you with more vivid images.

Language Coach

Related Words When words are related, they share the same root. For example, the verb *admire* is related to the noun *admiration*, the adjective *admirable*, and the adverb *admirably*. Complete this chart by finding the related words indicated in the second column.

Word	Related Words
tremendous (adjective) (line 1, "The Fish")	adverb:
wavering (verb) (line 62, "The Fish")	adverb:
master (verb) (line 1, "One Art")	adjective:
disaster (noun) (line 9, "One Art")	adjective:
evident (adjective) (line 17, "One Art")	noun: adverb:

CHOICES

As you respond to the Choices, use these **Academic Vocabulary** words as appropriate: component, diverse, intrinsic, potential, transmit.

REVIEW
Make a Group Collage

A collage is an art form in which diverse objects such as newspaper, cloth, pressed flowers, and stones are pasted together to form a picture or abstract illustration of some sort. Since "The Fish" is very visual, try making a collage to illustrate it. You will first have to isolate the images you want to illustrate; then go on a hunt to locate them. You could assign different tasks to the group: some could go through newspapers and magazines for images, others could collect natural objects like flowers, and others could decide how they will illustrate the fish itself. Collages can also contain words: What words from the poem would you feature in your collage?

CONNECT
Relate an Experience

Timed ⌐Writing People often think that their routine activities will continue on without interruption. Suddenly, however, something happens that changes everything. Write an autobiographical narrative about a time when your routine changed because of something unexpected. (It does not have to be something bad.) Explain what happened and how the change affected you.

EXTEND
Tell the Fish's Story

Write a short poem telling the poem's story from the fish's point of view. You might begin with the line "I was caught" and end with the line "I was let go." How does the fish feel about being caught? How does he feel about being freed?

The Bells

🕐 QuickTalk

How do you feel about poems that express frank feelings about matters that could be considered private and personal? What effect can such poems have on their readers? Discuss with a partner your thoughts about these topics.

MEET THE WRITER

Anne Sexton
(1928–1974)

Pulitzer Prize WINNER

From the beginning of her literary career, Anne Sexton was recognized as a spirit in turmoil. Sexton's poetry was an eruption of her emotional life into art. The titles of her most gripping volumes indicate a preoccupation with her own anxiety and depression: *To Bedlam and Part Way Back* (1960), *Live or Die* (1966), *The Death Notebooks* (1974), and *The Awful Rowing Toward God* (1975).

A Late Start

Anne Sexton did not start writing poetry until she was 28. She was born in Newton, Massachusetts, and attended the public schools in nearby Wellesley. In 1947, she enrolled in the Garland School, a finishing school for women, and in 1948, she married. She worked for a time as a fashion model and gave birth to two daughters. Then, in 1956, she began to write poetry. Sexton attracted the notice of the respected poet Robert Lowell in his graduate writing seminar at Boston University. She also developed strong friendships with other important poets, including Sylvia Plath. In 1966, only ten years after she began writing poetry, Sexton won the Pulitzer Prize for *Live or Die*.

A Shock to the Senses

Sexton admitted that her poetry was intended to be a shock to the senses. In her collection called *All My Pretty Ones* (1962), she said, quoting Franz Kafka, that a "book should serve as the axe for the frozen sea within us." Her books opened up a wider vision of the lives of contemporary women. Many of her poems portray women in times of crisis.

Sexton formed a rock-music group called Anne Sexton and Her Kind, in which she read her poetry while her six-piece band played. Sexton's mentor, Robert Lowell, said that no one ever fell asleep at Sexton's poetry readings. "I see her," Lowell remarked, "as having the large, transparent, breakable, and increasingly ragged wings of a dragonfly—her poor, shy, driven life, the blind terror behind her bravado, her deadly increasing pace . . . her bravery while she lasted."

Think About the Writer

Sexton thought that a "book should serve as the axe for the frozen sea within us." What do you think this means?

Reader/Writer Notebook

Use your **RWN** to complete the activities for this selection.

Literary Focus

Imagery The use of language to evoke a picture or a concrete sensation of a person, a thing, a place, or an experience is called **imagery.** Although most images are visual, images may also appeal to the senses of taste, smell, hearing, and touch. In poetry, imagery is used to help us participate in an experience and to evoke emotional responses. Imagery is so important in poetry that we can even make distinctions among poets based purely on the <u>diverse</u> images they use.

Reading Focus

Paraphrasing Rewriting or rephrasing a text using your own words is called **paraphrasing.** Paraphrasing helps you clarify a text so you can be sure you understood what you read. When you paraphrase, you must restate all figures of speech in your own words, to be sure you know what they mean. If you are paraphrasing a poem, you must supply words that the poet might have omitted. You must also rewrite sentences that do not use standard subject-verb-object order. A paraphrase is usually about the same length as the original text, though it can also be much longer. A paraphrase, of course, can never be a substitute for the original text.

Into Action As you read, paraphrase the poem. The first four lines are done as an example. Use a graphic organizer like the one below:

Original Lines	Paraphrase
"Today the circus poster is scabbing off the concrete wall and the children have forgotten if they knew at all."	The circus poster on the concrete wall is starting to peel off like a scab peeling off a sore. The children have forgotten about the circus, if they knew it at all.

Writing Focus

Think as a Reader/Writer

Find It in Your Reading Sexton uses imagery to help you participate in this experience from her childhood. As you read, use your *Reader/Writer Notebook* to write down some of the images that you find especially effective.

Language Coach

Verb Forms When you come across an unfamiliar verb, first define its basic meaning. A dictionary lists the basic form of each verb, without endings like *–s, –ed,* or *–ing.* To define the verb *trembled,* you can look up the basic form—*tremble*—in a dictionary. Then, think about how a verb ending affects the meaning. *Tremble* means "to shake or shiver slightly." What do the verbs *trembled* and *trembling* mean? Try using each verb form in a sentence.

Learn It Online
Take your exploration of this poem further with the project ideas online.

go.hrw.com   L11-1335   **Go**

POEM

The Bells
by **Anne Sexton**

Read with a Purpose
Read to discover why this experience is a special memory for the speaker.

Build Background
Though less common today than in years past, traveling circuses still visit many towns and cities in America. Posters advertise the coming of the circus, which often features three performance areas, called "rings," under the "big top" tent. In the rings, several kinds of entertainment—acrobatics, animal acts, clowning, and so on—occur simultaneously.

Today the circus poster
is scabbing off the concrete wall
and the children have forgotten **Ⓐ**
if they knew at all.
5 Father, do you remember?
Only the sound remains,
the distant thump of the good elephants,
the voice of the ancient lions
and how the bells
10 trembled for the flying man.
I, laughing,
lifted to your high shoulder
or small at the rough legs of strangers, **Ⓑ**
was not afraid.
15 You held my hand

and were instant to explain
the three rings of danger.
Oh see the naughty clown
and the wild parade
20 while love love
love grew rings around me.
This was the sound where it began;
our breath pounding up to see
the flying man breast out
25 across the boarded sky **Ⓒ**
and climb the air.
I remember the color of music
and how forever
all the trembling bells of you
30 were mine.

Ⓐ **Literary Focus** Imagery What tone do these images create?

Ⓑ **Literary Focus** Imagery What do the images in the first thirteen lines help you see and hear?

Ⓒ **Reading Focus** Paraphrasing In your own words, describe what you think the "boarded sky" is.

Applying Your Skills

The Bells

Respond and Think Critically

Reading Focus

Quick Check

1. What prompted the speaker to remember the circus of her childhood?

2. To whom is the poem addressed?

3. Which details in the poem tell you how the speaker felt about her time at the circus?

Read with a Purpose

4. What is the most important part of the speaker's experience at the circus?

Reading Skills: Paraphrasing

5. While reading, you paraphrased the poem. Now, review your chart and think about why paraphrasing is a valuable skill.

> **Original Lines**
> "Today the circus poster
> is scabbing off the concrete wall
> and the children have forgotten
> if they knew at all."

> **Paraphrase**
> The circus poster on the concrete wall is starting to peel off like a scab peeling off a sore. The children have forgotten about the circus, even if they went to it.

Literary Focus

Literary Analysis

6. **Infer** What lines suggest how the speaker feels about her father? Do you find any hint that she felt the lack of her father's love in her life? Explain.

7. **Interpret** Why does the speaker describe the circus rings as "three rings of danger" (line 17)? How would you interpret the other "rings" she mentions in the poem?

8. **Interpret** What does sound add to this poem? Re-read it aloud and pay careful attention to what rhythm and sound effects add to the meaning of the poem.

Literary Skills: Imagery

9. **Evaluate** "The Bells" contains several examples of imagery. Which images help you experience this day at the circus?

10. **Analyze** Describing a perception of one sense in terms of another sense is called **synesthesia** (sihn ehs THEE zhuh). What senses does the poet mix in line 27?

Literary Skills Review: Style

11. **Make Judgments** The unique way in which a writer uses language is his or her **style**. Style can be plain, ornate, suggestive, or colloquial (meaning "like everyday speech"). How would you characterize Sexton's style?

Writing Focus

Think as a Reader/Writer

Use It in Your Writing As you read, you noted images that helped you share Sexton's experience. Write a poem of your own in which you use images to share an incident from your childhood. You might open with the phrase "I remember."

What Do **You Think Now** How would Sexton's account of the circus she attended with her father differ if she had told it in a memoir?

Mirror
Mushrooms

What human needs and desires do we have in common?

QuickWrite

Many poets give voices to inanimate objects or nonhuman organisms. The voices they give to these things reveal little about the things themselves, but they reveal a great deal about the poets. What reflections might the voice of a mirror convey? What might mushrooms have to say?

MEET THE WRITER

Sylvia Plath
(1932–1963)

Pulitzer Prize WINNER

Until her death, Sylvia Plath was, to most appearances, a model of achievement. Her success, however, could neither fully mask nor calm a fearsome inner turmoil.

Ambition to Be a Writer

Born in Boston, Plath spent her early years in the nearby seaside town of Winthrop. Her father, a professor of biology, was from Germany. Her mother, a teacher of office skills, was of Austrian descent. From the Freudian point of view typical of the times, Plath believed that her emotional suffering was caused by her father's death when she was only eight years old.

Plath published her first poem in a Boston newspaper around the time of her father's death. Her early success was short-lived, however—45 rejection slips later, she finally landed a story in *Seventeen* magazine when she was eighteen. Plath was awarded a scholarship to Smith College, and she won a much-coveted fiction prize from *Mademoiselle* magazine in her junior year. After Smith, she went to Cambridge University in England on a Fulbright fellowship. There she met the noted English poet Ted Hughes, whom she married in 1956. In 1960, Plath's first book of poetry, *The Colossus,* was published, and their daughter, Frieda, was born. Their son, Nicholas, was born in 1962. The marriage was stormy from the start.

Struggles with Illness

Throughout her life, Plath struggled with depression—years before effective drug therapy was available. As a teenager, she had been overcome by depression and attempted suicide, an experience that became the basis for her autobiographical novel, *The Bell Jar* (1963). Her *Ariel* poems, published shortly after her death, deal bitterly and frankly with the death of her father and with her own illness. In the winter of 1963, separated from her husband and caring for two young children in an unheated London flat, she attempted suicide again. This time she succeeded.

What is the appeal of works that expose the writer's personal life?

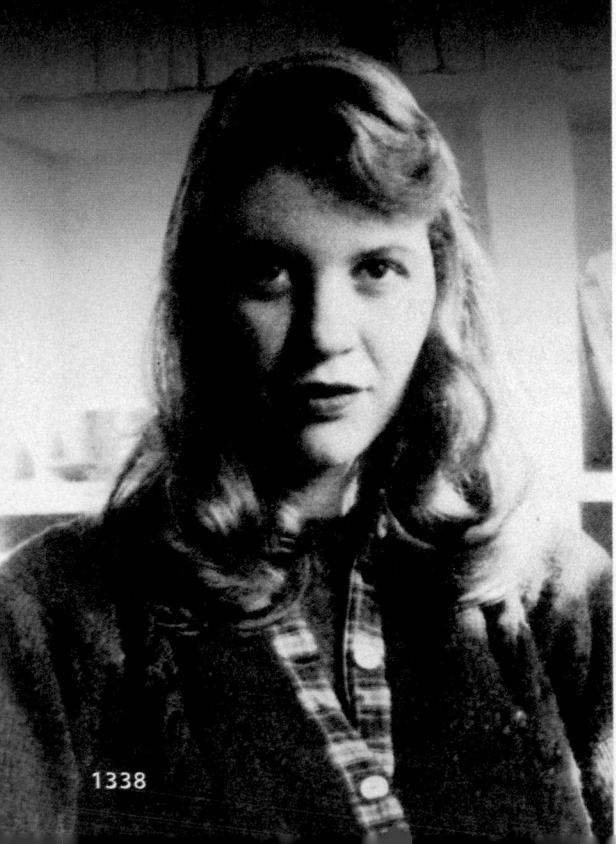

Mirror

Reader/Writer Notebook

Use your **RWN** to complete the activities for this selection.

Literary Focus

Personification The figure of speech in which an object or animal is given human features, thoughts, or attitudes is called **personification.** Like other figures of speech, such as metaphors and similes, personification helps readers see things in <u>potentially</u> new and unique ways. Using these stylistic devices adds to the rhetorical and aesthetic impact of your story—that is, they help you write more effectively and make your story more appealing to readers. In this poem, Plath personifies the mirror, giving it a voice as well as the ability to see and think.

Reading Focus

Drawing Conclusions About Meaning Poetry can be subtle or cryptic in its meaning. Sometimes asking a series of questions can help you to **draw conclusions** about the meaning of a poem. As you read a poem, ask yourself the following questions:

- What does the writer want me to *see*? What **images** are presented and emphasized?
- What **figures of speech** are used in the poem?
- What does the writer want me to *feel*? What **mood** is created by the images and figures of speech?
- What does the writer want me to *understand*? What is the main **theme** or message of the poem?

Into Action Use a web like the one below to list what you think the writer wants you to see and feel in the poem.

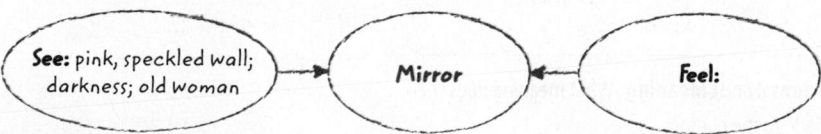

See: pink, speckled wall; darkness; old woman → **Mirror** ← **Feel:**

Writing Focus

Think as a Reader/Writer

Find It in Your Reading Writers can use **personification** to enhance the tone and description of their writing. Notice how Plath uses personification to bring the mirror to life. Use your *Reader/Writer Notebook* to record examples of Plath's use of personification.

Vocabulary

preconceptions (pree kuhn SEHP shuhnz) *n. pl.*: opinions formed beforehand. *I had no preconceptions about Sylvia Plath before I sat down last night to read her poetry.*

agitation (aj uh TAY shuhn) *n.*: violent motion or disturbance. *The agitation of the young woman's hands reveals her anxiety.*

Language Coach

Connotations Connotations are feelings that are associated with a word. They can be positive or negative. The word *preconception* refers to "ideas formed beforehand." This word often has negative connotations because it implies that someone formed an opinion before having firsthand experience of something. Tell which word in each pair below has stronger negative connotations, and explain each of your choices in a brief sentence:

1. cruel, unkind
2. liars, phonies
3. terrible, awful

 Learn It Online
Learn more about Plath at the Writers' Lives site online.

go.hrw.com | L11-1339 | **Go**

Mirror
by **Sylvia Plath**

Read with a Purpose
Read to discover clues to the identity of the poem's speaker.

Build Background
When we hear lyric poetry, we hear a voice speaking to us. Often the speaker of the poem is identifiable as the poet. At other times, the voice talking to us in the poem is identifiable as someone or something else. In this lyric poem, Plath imagines what an object with no voice at all would sound like if it could speak.

I am silver and exact. I have no preconceptions.
Whatever I see I swallow immediately
Just as it is, unmisted by love or dislike.
I am not cruel, only truthful—
5   The eye of a little god, four-cornered.   **A**
Most of the time I meditate on the opposite wall.
It is pink, with speckles. I have looked at it so long
I think it is a part of my heart. But it flickers.
Faces and darkness separate us over and over.
10   Now I am a lake. A woman bends over me,   **B**
Searching my reaches for what she really is.
Then she turns to those liars, the candles or the moon.
I see her back, and reflect it faithfully.
She rewards me with tears and an agitation of hands.
15   I am important to her. She comes and goes.
Each morning it is her face that replaces the darkness.
In me she has drowned a young girl, and in me an old woman   **C**
Rises toward her day after day, like a terrible fish.

A **Reading Focus** **Drawing Conclusions About Meaning** What meaning does the phrase "The eye of a little god, four-cornered" add to the poem?

B **Literary Focus** **Personification** How does the personality of a mirror differ from that of a lake in this poem?

C **Reading Focus** **Drawing Conclusions About Meaning** Explain what the poet means when she says, "In me she has drowned a young girl."

Vocabulary **preconceptions** (pree kuhn SEHP shuhnz) *n. pl.:* opinions formed beforehand.
agitation (aj uh TAY shuhn) *n.:* violent motion or disturbance.

Mushrooms

Reader/Writer
Notebook

Use your **RWN** to complete the activities for this selection.

Literary Focus

Tone The attitude a writer or speaker takes toward the subject of a work, toward the characters in the work, or toward the audience is **tone**. Tone, which results from the complex interplay of diction and style, can often be described in one word (playful, sarcastic, critical, bitter, affectionate, sinister, and so on). If you have not caught the tone of a work, you have not fully understood it.

Into Action As you read "Mushrooms," listen for the tone conveyed by the poem's speakers. In a chart like the one below, record lines from the poem that strike you as having a particular tone.

Line from poem	Tone
"Nobody sees us" (line 7)	mysterious

Language Coach

Idioms An **idiom** is an expression unique to a language that cannot be understood literally. In the last line of "Mushrooms," the phrase "our foot's in the door" is idiomatic. When you "get your foot in the door," you take a small opportunity that has the potential to turn into something bigger and better. Your foot wedges open the door just a little; later, the door may open wider and you may be able to get your whole body through it. What is the meaning of these other English idioms that use the word *foot*?

1. Put your foot in your mouth
2. Put your best foot forward
3. Start off on the wrong foot

Writing Focus

Think as a Reader/Writer

Find It in Your Reading **Personification** is a figure of speech in which an object or an animal is given human characteristics or other components of being human. In your *Reader/Writer Notebook* note the differences in how Plath uses personification in "Mushrooms" and how she uses it in "Mirror."

Learn It Online
Looking for a project idea? Check out these ideas online.
go.hrw.com | L11-1341 | Go

MUSHROOMS

by **Sylvia Plath**

> **Read with a Purpose** Read to discover clues to the identity of the personified speaker.

Overnight, very
Whitely, discreetly,
Very quiet ⒜

Our toes, our noses
5   Take hold on the loam,
Acquire the air.

Nobody sees us,
Stops us, betrays us;
The small grains make room.

10   Soft fists insist on
Heaving the needles,
The leafy bedding,

Even the paving.
Our hammers, our rams,
15   Earless and eyeless,

Perfectly voiceless,
Widen the crannies,
Shoulder through holes. We

Diet on water,
20   On crumbs of shadow,
Bland-mannered, asking

Little or nothing.
So many of us!
So many of us!

25   We are shelves, we are
Tables, we are meek,
We are edible,

Nudgers and shovers
In spite of ourselves.
30   Our kind multiplies:

We shall by morning
Inherit the earth.
Our foot's in the door. ⒝

Ⓐ **Literary Focus** **Tone** What tone does the first stanza establish?

Ⓑ **Literary Focus** **Tone** What words in the last four stanzas particularly influence the tone?

Applying Your Skills

SKILLS FOCUS **Literary Skills** Analyze personification; analyze tone; analyze imagery. **Reading Skills** Draw inferences such as conclusions, generalizations, and pre-

dictions, and support them using the text. **Vocabulary Skills** Demonstrate word knowledge.

Mirror / Mushrooms

Respond and Think Critically

Reading Focus

Quick Check

1. In "Mirror," why does the woman cry and wring her hands when she looks at her reflection?

2. What are some of the things to which the poet compares the mushrooms in "Mushrooms"?

Read with a Purpose

3. What clues does Plath provide to make clear that the speaker of "Mirror" is a mirror? What clues make clear that the speakers of "Mushrooms" are mushrooms?

Reading Skills: Drawing Conclusions About Meaning

4. As you read, what conclusions can you draw about the real subject of "Mirror"? Is it really about a mirror? Explain.

✔ Vocabulary Check

5. Do you have **preconceptions** about some type of food? What are they?

6. If you saw signs of **agitation** in the face of a friend, what might explain it?

Literary Focus

Literary Analysis

7. Interpret The last line of "Mirror" contains the striking image of "a terrible fish." How would you interpret this image? What emotional overtones does the image of a terrible fish have for you?

8. Draw Conclusions In "Mushrooms," for what or whom might the mushrooms be a metaphor? Explain.

9. Make Judgments "Blessed are the meek, for they shall inherit the earth" is from Matthew 5:5 in the Bible. Why might the speakers in "Mushrooms" allude to this saying (line 32)?

Literary Skills: Personification/ Tone

10. Analyze What kind of person does the mirror personify? What kind of people do the mushrooms personify? How does Plath make you feel about the mirror and the mushrooms?

11. Compare and Contrast What tones do you hear in these poems by Plath? Are they similar? Explain.

Literary Skills Review: Imagery

12. Evaluate The use of language to evoke sensory impressions—of sight, smell, sound, taste, and touch—is called **imagery.** A writer's choice of imagery can create an emotional response. What images in these two poems are most vivid to you? What emotional response did you have to the images?

Writing Focus

Think as a Reader/Writer

Use It in Your Writing Plath uses personification to help us imagine what a mirror and mushrooms might say if they could speak. Write a poem in which you allow some ordinary object, plant, or animal to speak. What personality would your speaker have? What might your speaker say about the human condition?

What Do You Think Now

How does Plath view the need to establish an identity as both a benefit and as a detriment? Is this the case for most people?

The Bean Eaters

In Honor of David Anderson Brooks, My Father

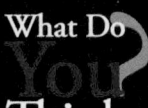

What Do You Think What human needs and desires do we have in common?

 QuickTalk

How can poetry be read as a form of protest about social and political issues? Discuss this question with a partner.

Gwendolyn Brooks
(1917–2000)

Pulitzer Prize WINNER

Born in Kansas, Gwendolyn Brooks grew up in Chicago, the city whose African American community she celebrated as Bronzeville in her poetry. Brooks was honored not only for her literary achievement but also for her efforts on behalf of young African American writers, to whom she gave practical advice and tireless encouragement. For many of these young writers, Brooks opened doors to self-realization and professional careers.

Common Speech as Poetry

Gwendolyn Brooks established her credentials early. In her first two volumes of poetry—*A Street in Bronzeville* (1945) and *Annie Allen* (1949), for which she was awarded the Pulitzer Prize—she used conventional poetic forms to present portraits of African American city dwellers. Later, Brooks turned to more open forms and more extensive use of common speech. This transition was sparked by the insistence of young African American poets that their poetry use the rhythms and vernacular of urban African American speech and culture. In her work, Brooks also reflected the expansion of African American consciousness during the 1950s and 1960s, when the civil rights movement renewed pride among the followers of Martin Luther King, Jr.

A Generous Talent

Brooks's best known work of fiction, *Maud Martha* (1953), is the story of a young African American woman forging her identity in the face of self-doubt and racism. One critic wrote, "It is a powerful, beautiful dagger of a book, as generous as it can possibly be. It teaches more, more quickly, more lastingly, than a thousand pages of protest." In her later years, Brooks became the first African American woman to serve as Poet Laureate Consultant in Poetry to the Library of Congress. Known for her generosity, Brooks often sponsored literary awards and gave prizes out of her own funds. Though she received many honors, she never let praise cloud her vision.

Think About the Writer Brooks's life spans most of the twentieth century. What events during that time might influence an African American writer?

The Bean Eaters /
In Honor of David Anderson Brooks, My Father

Reader/Writer
Notebook
Use your **RWN** to complete the activities for these selections.

Literary Focus

The Uses of Rhyme **Rhyme** is the repetition of vowel sounds in accented syllables and succeeding syllables. In years past, a poet's use of rhyme was a matter of following rules and conventions and staying within traditional verse forms. Contemporary poets use rhyme more freely, often to convey the **mood** of a poem. It can suggest a sense of control and order, calm balance, or even grim finality. A poem, like a song, may have its own beat that conveys specific emotions. Rhyme also helps create a poem's **rhythm,** its music, which in turn contributes to the poem's mood.

Writing Focus

Think as a Reader/Writer
Find It in Your Reading As you read Brooks's poems, listen for her use of rhyme. Remember that while some words have **exact rhyme,** in which the accented syllable and all succeedng syllables rhyme, other words, like *forever* and *fever*, are **approximate rhymes**—they contain sounds that are similar but not identical. In your *Reader/Writer Notebook*, use a chart like the one below to list the rhyming words in each poem.

	Exact Rhyme	Approximate Rhyme
"The Bean Eaters"	"pair" (line 1) and "affair" (line 2)	
"In Honor of David Anderson Brooks, My Father"		"forever" (line 6) and "fever" (line 8)

Learn It Online
Learn more about Gwendolyn Brooks at the Writers' Lives site.

go.hrw.com L11-1345 Go

The Bean Eaters

by **Gwendolyn Brooks**

Old Love (1995) by Francks Deceus.

Read with a Purpose
Read to learn about a couple's humble life together.

Build Background
The editors of *African American Writers* say this poem treats a
common theme of Brooks's, "the notion of the tiny, cramped physical and emotional space of the poor, which can be redeemed by the
power of memory or the imagination to provide 'a streak or two
streaks of sun.'"

They eat beans mostly, this old yellow pair.
Dinner is a casual affair.
Plain chipware on a plain and creaking wood,
Tin flatware.   **A**

5   Two who are Mostly Good.
Two who have lived their day,
But keep on putting on their clothes
and putting things away.

And remembering . . .
10   Remembering, with twinklings and twinges,
As they lean over the beans in their rented back room that
        is full of beads and receipts and dolls and cloths, tobacco
        crumbs, vases and fringes.   **B**

A **Literary Focus** Rhyme What rhymes does Brooks use in this first stanza?

B **Literary Focus** Rhyme What internal rhymes are contained in the last two
lines of the poem?

In Honor of David Anderson Brooks, My Father

by **Gwendolyn Brooks**

July 30, 1883–November 21, 1959

Read with a Purpose
Read this poem to discover how Brooks
mourns her father's death.

A dryness is upon the house
My father loved and tended.
Beyond his firm and sculpted door
His light and lease have ended. **Ⓐ**

5   He walks the valleys, now—replies
To sun and wind forever.
No more the cramping chamber's chill,
No more the hindering fever.

Now out upon the wide clean air
10   My father's soul revives,
All innocent of self-interest
And the fear that strikes and strives.

He who was Goodness, Gentleness,
And Dignity is free,
15   Translates to public Love
Old private Charity. **Ⓑ**

Ⓐ Literary Focus Rhyme By the fourth line, a
definite rhyme scheme is apparent. What is it?

Ⓑ Literary Focus Rhyme How does the rhyme of
"free" and "charity" create a sense of closure?

Applying Your Skills

SKILLS FOCUS Literary Skills Analyze the uses of rhyme; analyze tone. **Writing Skills** Employ elements of an author's style effectively.

The Bean Eaters /
In Honor of David Anderson Brooks, My Father

Respond and Think Critically

Reading Focus

Quick Check

1. What details in "The Bean Eaters" tell you that this couple does not have much money?

2. In "In Honor of David Anderson Brooks, My Father," where does the speaker imagine her father is now?

Read with a Purpose

3. What feelings for the old couple and for her father does the poet convey in "The Bean Eaters" and "In Honor of David Anderson Brooks, My Father"?

Literary Focus

Literary Analysis

4. **Interpret** What does the speaker mean in "The Bean Eaters" when she says that the old couple are "Mostly Good"? Why is this phrase capitalized?

5. **Analyze** In "The Bean Eaters," what is the difference between "twinklings" and "twinges" in line 10? How would you restate each of these sensations in your own words?

6. **Interpret** In the first line of "In Honor of David Anderson Brooks, My Father," what might the speaker mean when she says "a dryness is upon the house"?

7. **Interpret** What is the "cramping chamber's chill" that Brooks mentions in line 7 of "In Honor of David Anderson Brooks, My Father"?

8. **Summarize** How would you paraphrase, or restate in your own words, lines 13–16 of "In Honor of David Anderson Brooks, My Father"?

9. **Intrepret** "The Bean Eaters" is about a couple's humble life, while "In Honor of David Anderson Brooks, My Father" is about the death of Brooks's father. What themes do the two poems have in common?

Literary Skills: The Uses of Rhyme

10. **Compare and Contrast** Compare Brooks's use of rhyme to create different rhythms in the two poems. What effect does rhythm have on each poem's mood and message? Why might Brooks have chosen to use a strong, obvious rhythm in one poem and not the other?

Literary Skills Review: Tone

11. **Make Judgments** The attitude a writer takes toward the subject or characters of a work, or toward the audience, is **tone.** What tone (or tones) does Brooks convey toward the characters in these poems?

Writing Focus

Think as a Reader/Writer

Use It in Your Writing Using Brooks's poems as models, write your own poem using rhyming sounds at the ends of lines. You might write about a person who has died or about people you know who have struggled but remained dignified and proud. Think about how the use of rhyme affects the tone and message of your poem.

 What Do You Think Now

What social influences do you think helped shape the characters and the settings of each poem? Do these influences still exist today?

Man Listening to Disc

Summarizing a Text by **Kylene Beers**

Summarizing a Text

One critical difference between skilled readers and less skilled readers is the ability to summarize a text. It's just not realistic to think that as you read you will remember literally everything you have read. Instead, as you read, you are constantly summarizing—condensing and putting into your own words—what you have read. When you can't do that, it's a good sign that you need to re-read and rethink what you've been reading.

Benefits of Summarizing

Summarizing is like using a mental filing system. When you summarize, you collect and group main ideas into categories, just as you might gather individual papers into files. When you summarize, you mentally group those files in "folders." This process helps you store information accurately.

Physical files help you quickly find what you need. Rather than rummaging randomly through a pile of documents, you can find a tab with a key word and instantly pull out the desired files. It's the same with summarizing. By keeping mental "tabs" on what you're reading, you can keep information straight in your head and retrieve it quickly afterward. By failing to summarize, you run the risk of losing track of an argument, getting confused, or forgetting important details.

Strategies for Summarizing Poems

Like paragraphs, stanzas in poetry are often organized around a single idea or image. If a stanza does not contain a topic sentence, look for **key words** that point to a central idea. When you finish the stanza, you can use these key words to help you summarize the stanza. Sometimes, you can identify key words by noting words that are repeated. Other times, sound effects, figurative language, and other forms of emphasis will provide clues.

Readers use various strategies for summarizing. Here are a few:

- **Highlighting** Use a highlighter to mark main ideas or important details that you want to return to later. (However, do not highlight in books you don't own.)
- **Annotation** Annotate the text as you read. Some readers write down comments or notes on what they are reading as they move through the poem.
- **Sequencing** Identify a series of related ideas by giving them a numerical or alphabetical order. If writing or highlighting isn't possible, mentally note each item as you read and remember the total number of items. You can also order them according to time (*first, then, next, finally*), space (*on the left, to the right, ahead, around*), importance, or some other principle.
- **Visualizing** Form a mental image that shows items and their relationship. You might picture the most important idea as a large circle, for example, and lesser ideas might branch out from it. Other possibilities include visualizing or sketching a time line, an arrangement of boxes, or a formal outline. In the poem you are about to read, the speaker is walking through Manhattan. Visualizing and perhaps sketching the speaker's literal journey downtown may help you understand the figurative journey the speaker makes.

Your Turn

Select one of the strategies listed above and use it to summarize this Reading Focus essay, a favorite poem, or another text of your choice. If this strategy works for you, continue to use it as you read the selections in this unit. If not, choose another strategy and try again.

Learn It Online
Learn how to summarize longer works at *NovelWise*.

go.hrw.com | L11-1349 | **Go**

Man Listening to Disc

What human needs and desires do we have in common?

QuickTalk

Why do you think music is vital to our lives? How important is music to you and to your friends? Discuss the importance of music with a partner.

MEET THE WRITER

Billy Collins
(1941–)

When Billy Collins was named poet laureate of the United States in 2001, he said, "It came completely out of the blue, like a soft wrecking ball from outer space." This contradictory image of a soft wrecking ball is characteristic of Collins's poetry—surprising, playful, almost casual, but with a hint of danger.

A Reader-Friendly Academic

Born in New York City, Billy Collins has been a professor of English at the City University of New York for more than thirty years—as he modestly puts it, a "lifter of chalk in the Bronx." During his career he has won many poetry awards and wide popularity—some have called him the most popular poet in America—largely because his poems are not written strictly for an audience of academics. Collins tries to be reader friendly:

> I have one reader in mind, someone who is in the room with me, and who I'm talking to, and I want to make sure I don't talk too fast, or too glibly. Usually I try to create a hospitable tone at the beginning of a poem. Stepping from the title to the first lines is like stepping into a canoe. A lot of things can go wrong.

An American Original

Billy Collins's collections include *The Apple That Astonished Paris* (1988); *Questions About Angels* (1991); *The Art of Drowning* (1995); and *Sailing Alone Around the Room* (2001). He runs poetry workshops during the summer and has recorded many of his poems. Collins's poems may at first seem deceptively straightforward, but they usually convey a subtle message. As his fellow poet Edward Hirsch says: "Billy Collins is an American original, a metaphysical poet with a funny bone and a sly questioning intelligence. . . . His poems—witty, playful, and beautifully turned—bump up against the deepest human mysteries."

Think About the Writer

In 2003 Collins edited a collection of poems for high school students called *Poetry 180: A Turning Back to Poetry*. If you were to advise Collins on the kinds of poetry he should include in such a collection, what would you say?

Reader/Writer Notebook

Use your **RWN** to complete the activities for this selection.

Literary Focus

Style The distinctive way a writer uses language is called **style.** Style can be ornate, plain, informal, elegant, personal, complex, and so on. People are sometimes criticized for having "more style than substance." In literature and the arts, however, style and substance are deeply intertwined. In fact, the best writers make style an <u>intrinsic</u> part of the substance of their works. The Puritan plain style reflects an entire community's faith in simplicity. Whitman's free-verse style embodies his boldness and innovation. Hemingway's muscular prose conveys his belief in the value of graceful strength in both literature and life. As you read, consider how you would characterize Collins's style.

Reading Focus

Summarizing a Text As you read a poem, it is important to stop and think about the poem's main ideas, images, or message. In doing so, you are **summarizing** the poem. After you complete each stanza of this poem, pause and summarize who the characters are and what they have done or experienced at that point. Consider, too, how the poet's style helps convey key elements of the poem.

Into Action Keeping a timeline can help you gather information you need to summarize the poem. Copy the time line below. As you read, note, in order, the main character's actions and what he sees and hears.

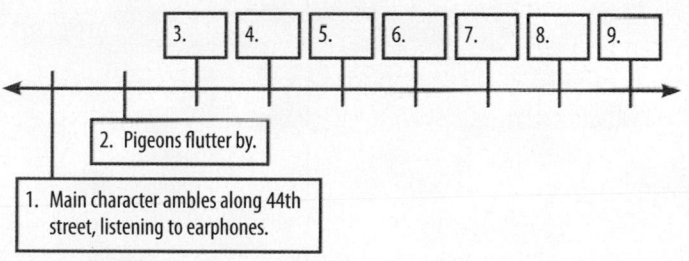

Writing Focus

Think as a Reader/Writer

Find It in Your Reading This poem refers to specific musicians the speaker hears as he ambles along the city streets listening to a disc. In your *Reader/Writer Notebook*, write down the names of the musicians he is listening to and the instruments he hears.

Vocabulary

ambling (AM blihng) *v.* used as *n.:* walking at an easy, slow pace. *The speaker likes ambling along the city street while listening to jazz.*

profusion (pruh FYOO zhuhn) *n.:* great abundance. *On the sidewalk, there was a profusion of bread crumbs for the pigeons.*

suffused (suh FYOOZD) *v.* used as *adj.:* overspread (as with a color, liquid, or dye). *The speaker feels suffused with the music from the saxophone.*

aggregation (ag ruh GAY shuhn) *n.:* collection of separate things into one group or whole. *The speaker imagines himself and the musicians he hears on the headset as an aggregation of people.*

Language Coach

Frequently Confused Words Words that have similar spellings are easy to confuse. The word *suffused* in this poem could be confused with the word *sufficed*. *Suffice* means "to be enough." Which word, *suffused* or *sufficed*, best completes each of these sentences?

1. A piece of toast _____ for his breakfast.
2. A golden light _____ the room.

Now explain the different meanings of these easily confused word pairs:

1. *profusion* and *confusion*
2. *aggregation* and *aggravation*

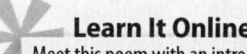

Learn It Online
Meet this poem with an introductory video online.

go.hrw.com   L11-1351   **Go**

Man Listening to Disc

by **Billy Collins**

Read with a Purpose Read to discover how this speaker feels as he listens to music while he walks downtown.

This is not bad—
ambling along 44th Street
with Sonny Rollins for company,
his music flowing through the soft calipers°
5   of these earphones,

as if he were right beside me
on this clear day in March,
the pavement sparkling with sunlight,
pigeons fluttering off the curb,
10 nodding over a profusion of bread crumbs.

In fact, I would say
my delight at being suffused
with phrases from his saxophone—
some like honey, some like vinegar—
15 is surpassed only by my gratitude

to Tommy Potter for taking the time
to join us on this breezy afternoon
with his most unwieldy bass
and to the esteemed Arthur Taylor
20 who is somehow managing to navigate

4. calipers: instruments used to measure the diameter or thickness of some small object.

Vocabulary **ambling** (AM blihng) *v.* used as *n.*: walking at an easy, slow pace.
profusion (pruh FYOO zhuhn) *n.*: great abundance.
suffused (suh FYOOZD) *v.* used as *adj.*: overspread (as with a color, liquid, or dye).

this crowd with his cumbersome drums.
And I bow deeply to Thelonious Monk
for figuring out a way
to motorize—or whatever—his huge piano
25   so he could be with us today. **Ⓐ**

The music is loud yet so confidential
I cannot help feeling even more
like the center of the universe
than usual as I walk along to a rapid
30   little version of "The Way You Look Tonight,"

and all I can say to my fellow pedestrians,
to the woman in the white sweater,
the man in the tan raincoat and the heavy glasses,
who mistake themselves for the center of the universe—
35   all I can say is watch your step

because the five of us, instruments and all,
are about to angle over
to the south side of the street
and then, in our own tightly knit way,
40   turn the corner at Sixth Avenue. **Ⓑ**

And if any of you are curious
about where this aggregation,
this whole battery-powered crew,
is headed, let us just say
45   that the real center of the universe,

the only true point of view,
is full of the hope that he,
the hub of the cosmos
with his hair blown sideways,
50   will eventually make it all the way downtown.

Analyzing Visuals

Viewing and Interpreting The artist uses letters to represent music. Collins refers to "phrases from" a saxophone. How is music like writing or speech?

Blue Note (2005) by Gil Mayers.

Ⓐ **Literary Focus** **Style** What details in the poem so far make it sound like someone having an informal conversation with the reader?

Ⓑ **Reading Focus** **Summarizing** What has happened in the poem up to this point?

Vocabulary **aggregation** (ag ruh GAY shuhn) *n.:* collection of separate things into one group or whole.

Respond and Think Critically

Reading Focus

Quick Check

1. Where and when is the poem set? How do you know?

2. What does the speaker imagine is happening in lines 1–25?

3. What does the speaker want to say to the other pedestrians?

Read with a Purpose

4. How does the music make the speaker feel? Cite specific lines that show his response to it.

Reading Skills: Summarizing a Text

5. While you were reading, you made a time line of the speaker's actions in the poem. Refer to your notes now and summarize what happens in the poem. What kind of journey does this poem depict?

Literary Focus

Literary Analysis

6. **Analyze** What does the simile in lines 13–14 tell us about the music to which the main character is listening?

7. **Interpret** What makes the music "loud yet so confidential" (line 26)?

8. **Interpret** In the last stanza, who is the "hub of the cosmos"?

9. **Interpret** Think about the speaker and how the music makes him feel on his journey downtown. What do you think the main point of the poem is?

10. **Extend** Have you ever listened to music with a headset and felt the way Collins's speaker feels? Explain.

Literary Skills: Style

11. **Evaluate** Using more than one descriptive word (such as *humorous*), how would you describe Collins's style in this poem? How does his style compare with the style of other poets, such as Gwendolyn Brooks?

12. **Analyze** Notice how Collins uses run-on lines so that one stanza often flows right into the next stanza. How does this style reflect the speaker's experiences in the poem?

Literary Skills Review: Imagery

13. **Analyze** Language that appeals to the senses is called **imagery.** Images are usually visual, but they can also appeal to the senses of sound, smell, taste, and touch. What images help you share the experience of the speaker in this poem?

Writing Focus

Think as a Reader/Writer

Use It in Your Writing In your *Reader/Writer Notebook* you noted the names of musicians and instruments the speaker listens to in the poem. Make a brief list of your favorite musical artists. Then, using Collins's poem as a model, write a poem about what it would be like to take a leisurely walk while listening to this music. What does the music sound like? What might you see along the way? How would the music make you feel?

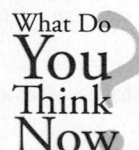 What Do You Think Now

Do you think the speaker's feelings as he listens to music are universal? What do you think our lives would be like without music?

Vocabulary Development

✓ Vocabulary Check

Answer these questions about the Vocabulary words.

1. What is the difference between **ambling** and striding or marching?

2. If you have a **profusion** of homework, how much homework do you have?

3. If a room is **suffused** with light, how does it look?

4. If you say there is an **aggregation** of people on the sidewalk, do you mean there is no one there or do you mean a crowd is present?

Vocabulary Skills: Recognizing Roots

The English language comes from the ancient family of languages called Indo-European languages. These languages include most of the languages spoken today in Europe and southwestern Asia and India. The principal Indo-European languages and language groups include Albanian, Anatolian, Armenian, Baltic, Celtic, Germanic, Greek, Indo-Iranian, Italic, and Slavic. (English comes from the Germanic language group.) Languages today from Ireland to India are descendants of one language that was spoken thousands of years ago.

Some Indo-European roots are listed in the left-hand column below. Use the root words to help you define the words listed in the right-hand column.

Roots	Words
–aud–, –audi–: "hear"	audio, audition
–dict–: "say or assert"	diction, dictator
–mater–, –matr–: "mother"	maternity
–pater–, –patr–: "father"	patriot, paternity
–phono–: "sound"	telephone, cacophony
-vid–, –vis–: "see"	video, visualize

CHOICES

As you respond to the Choices, use these **Academic Vocabulary** words as appropriate: component, diverse, intrinsic, potential, and transmit.

REVIEW
Map the Speaker's Journey

Make your own map of the journey taken by the speaker in the poem. On your map, draw and label the diverse things he sees and the streets he passes. (You might use a map of New York City to locate the streets Collins mentions and landmarks on the route.) You could illustrate your map with images from the poem.

CONNECT
Share an Experience

Timed ⏱ Writing In a brief essay, describe an experience that made you feel like "the hub of the universe," just as the music did for the speaker in the poem. Tell where you were and what happened to make you feel, for a second, that the world revolved around you. Be sure to write about an experience you are willing to share.

EXTEND
Research the Role of Poet Laureate

Class Presentation Billy Collins, like Rita Dove, served as Poet Laureate of the United States. Research the role of Poet Laureate. Who decides who will be Poet Laureate? How long does the position last? What are the Poet Laureate's responsibilities? Create an informative presentation about the Poet Laureate to share with your class.

The Latin Deli: An Ars Poetica

Judith Ortiz Cofer

(1952–   )

What human needs and desires do we have in common?

QuickTalk

If you were to move to a place where you had to learn a new language, what would you miss about your first language? Discuss this question with a partner.

"My family is one of the main topics of my poetry," says Judith Ortiz Cofer, "the ones left behind on the island of Puerto Rico, and the ones who came to the United States. In tracing their lives, I discover more about mine." This impulse toward self-definition and self-discovery emerges in Cofer's stories, essays, and poems.

Bridging Two Cultures

Cofer was born in Puerto Rico. "We lived in Puerto Rico until my brother was born in 1954," Cofer has written. "Soon after, because of economic pressures, my father joined the United States Navy." Cofer's family then moved to Paterson, New Jersey, when her father was assigned a job in the Brooklyn Navy Yard. Subsequently, Cofer's childhood was divided between a mainland American urban environment and Puerto Rico. She lived mostly in Paterson, but moved to Puerto Rico temporarily when her father was at sea.

"Things We All Must Leave Behind"

Cofer earned a master's degree in English and has taught at the University of Miami and the University of Georgia. Her first publication, *Latin Women Pray,* appeared in 1980. Since then, she has published several volumes of poetry and a book of personal essays. Her semiautobiographical first novel, *The Line of the Sun* (1989), is about a family that moves from Puerto Rico to Paterson and is caught between two cultures. Some consider Cofer's *The Latin Deli,* a collection of poetry and prose, to be her most powerful work. An engaging blend of poetry and lyrical prose, it is a mosaic of responses to cultural differences. As Cofer has said, "The place of birth itself becomes a metaphor for the things we all must leave behind. My poetry is a study of this process of change, assimilation, and transformation."

Think About the Writer

Cofer says that it was a challenge not only to learn English, but to master it and reach her ultimate goal—to write poetry in it. What particular problems do you think people face when they write poetry in a second language?

Reader/Writer Notebook

Use your **RWN** to complete the activities for this selection.

Literary Focus

Concrete and Abstract Language **Concrete language** names a person, place, or thing that can be perceived by one or more of the senses (sight, sound, smell, taste, touch). **Abstract language** names an idea or concept, something that cannot be seen, heard, smelled, tasted, or touched. Examples of concrete language are *grass, stone, mud, chili, Harlem*. Examples of abstract language are *peace, justice, honor, deceit*. Cofer's poem is a striking example of the effective use of concrete language.

Literary Perspectives Apply the literary perspective described on page 1358 as you read this poem.

Reading Focus

Identifying Key Words In this poem certain **key words** tell us what the poem is about and help transmit what the writer wants to communicate. Key words may describe specific people or situations in the poem and help you understand how they reflect the poem's theme.

Into Action As you read, use a chart like the one below to record key words. Identify words from the poem that belong in the same category because they share a specific characteristic. For example, several Spanish words appear in the poem. Gather these words together under "Key Words" in the first column. Underline any words that are examples of concrete language. Identify the category they share in the second column.

Key Word(s)	Category
dólares, El Norte, Suspiros, Merengues, jamón y queso	Spanish words

Vocabulary

disillusions (dihs ih LOO zhuhnz) *n. pl.:* states of freedom from illusion. *Although the customers speak of their disillusions, the mood in the store is always sympathetic.*

conjuring (KAHN juhr ihng) *v.* used as *adj.:* causing to happen as if by magic. *Cofer is like a magician conjuring beautiful poetry out of ordinary conversations.*

Language Coach

Prefixes A **prefix** attaches to the beginning of a word and changes the word's meaning. The prefix *dis–* means "without" or "away." The noun *illusions* means "false impressions." You can add the prefix *dis–* to form the word *disillusion*, which means "the state of being without illusions." Use the meaning of the prefix *dis–* to unlock the meaning of these words: *discomfort, disrepair, disrespectful.*

Writing Focus

Think as a Reader/Writer

Find It in Your Reading Cofer describes the woman running the deli as someone who "spends her days selling canned memories." In your *Reader/Writer Notebook,* record the "memories" that are made tangible again by the list of products for sale in the deli.

Learn It Online
Plunge into this poem the multimedia way—through *PowerNotes* online.

 go.hrw.com L11-1357

The Latin Deli: An Ars Poetica

by **Judith Ortiz Cofer**

Read with a Purpose
Read to learn about the poetry that the speaker finds in an ordinary delicatessen that caters to people of Spanish descent.

Build Background
Ars poetica is a Latin term meaning "the art of poetry." On pages 786 and 788 you will find other poems that talk about the art of poetry and that define what poetry should be. Cofer sees poetry as operating in a very different place—not in a literary magazine or classroom but in a city delicatessen, or "deli."

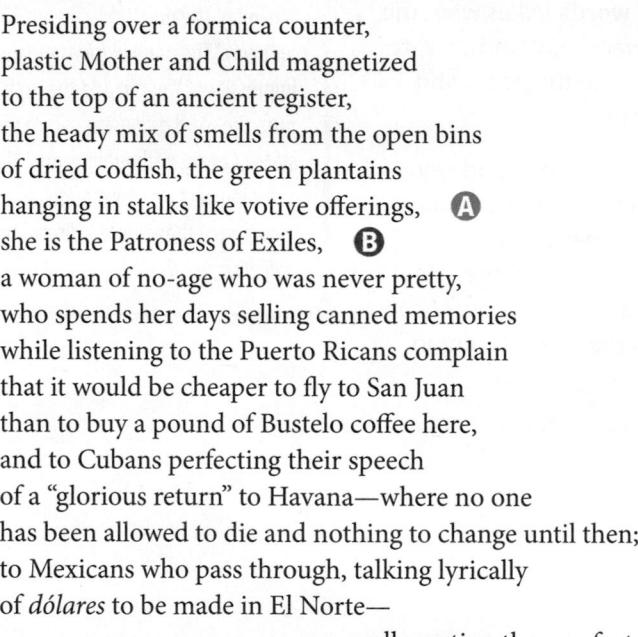

Presiding over a formica counter,
plastic Mother and Child magnetized
to the top of an ancient register,
the heady mix of smells from the open bins
5 of dried codfish, the green plantains
hanging in stalks like votive offerings,   **A**
she is the Patroness of Exiles,   **B**
a woman of no-age who was never pretty,
who spends her days selling canned memories
10 while listening to the Puerto Ricans complain
that it would be cheaper to fly to San Juan
than to buy a pound of Bustelo coffee here,
and to Cubans perfecting their speech
of a "glorious return" to Havana—where no one
15 has been allowed to die and nothing to change until then;
to Mexicans who pass through, talking lyrically
of *dólares* to be made in El Norte—

                                        all wanting the comfort

---

Ⓐ Literary Focus Concrete and Abstract Language
What examples of concrete language can you find in lines 4–6?

Ⓑ Reading Focus Identifying Key Words The first object mentioned in the deli is a plastic statue of Mary and the Christ child on the cash register. How do these key words "Mother and Child" provide clues to the theme of the poem?

Literary Perspectives

Analyzing Biographical Information
Biographical information—where and when a writer was born, where the writer grew up, the writer's education, ethnicity, and gender—can sometimes give you insight into the writer's work. During Cofer's childhood, she shuttled between Paterson, N.J., and Puerto Rico. As you read the poem, think about what parallels you see between Cofer, the woman who runs the deli, and the deli's customers. How does Cofer's experience growing up in two different locations help you understand and analyze the poem?

As you read, be sure to notice the questions in the text, which will guide you in using this perspective.

of spoken Spanish, to gaze upon the family portrait
20 of her plain wide face, her ample bosom
resting on her plump arms, her look of maternal interest
as they speak to her and each other
of their dreams and their disillusions—
how she smiles understanding,
25 when they walk down the narrow aisles of her store
reading the labels of packages aloud, as if
they were the names of lost lovers: *Suspiros,*
Merengues, the stale candy of everyone's childhood.
                                    She spends her days
30 slicing *jamón y queso* and wrapping it in wax paper
tied with string: plain ham and cheese
that would cost less at the A&P, but it would not satisfy
the hunger of the fragile old man lost in the folds
of his winter coat, who brings her lists of items
35 that he reads to her like poetry, or the others,
whose needs she must divine, conjuring up products
from places that now exist only in their hearts—
closed ports she must trade with. **C**

C **Literary Perspectives** Analyzing Biographical Information Why does Cofer
include Spanish words in the poem?

Vocabulary **disillusions** (dihs ih LOO zhuhnz) *n. pl.:* states of freedom from illusion.
conjuring (KAHN juhr ihng) *v.* used as *adj.:* causing to happen as if by magic.

Applying Your Skills

The Latin Deli: An Ars Poetica

Respond and Think Critically

Reading Focus

Quick Check

1. How does the poet describe the woman who runs the deli?

2. Describe in your own words the feelings and motivations of the different Spanish-speaking customers who come to the deli.

Read with a Purpose

3. Why does Cofer believe the Spanish words spoken by the deli customers are a kind of beautiful poetry?

Reading Skills: Identifying Key Words

4. While you were reading, you noted key words in a chart and the category to which they belong. Choose one of your lists of key words. How do they contribute to the poem's theme?

Literary Focus

Literary Analysis

5. **Interpret** What does it mean that the woman is the "Patroness of Exiles" (line 7)?

6. **Interpret** How would you explain what the poet means by "canned memories" in line 9?

7. **Analyze** Why do the customers read "the labels of packages aloud" in the deli (line 26)?

8. **Interpret** In line 37 the speaker mentions "places that now exist only in their hearts." What does she mean?

9. **Literary Perspectives** What details from Cofer's personal history might be reflected in this poem?

Literary Skills: Concrete and Abstract Language

10. **Analyze** What examples of concrete language help make this poem very specific? How do they help convey the customers' emotions?

Literary Skills Review: Style

11. **Make Judgments** The distinctive way in which a writer uses language is called **style.** Which word or words would you use to describe Cofer's style? Cite examples from the poem to support your response.

Writing Focus

Think as a Reader/Writer

Use It in Your Writing Refer to the notes you took in your *Reader/Writer Notebook* about the list of items that are sold in the Latin deli. Now, make a list of items in a store that represent you, your history, and your interests. Write a short poem in which you describe a store that sells these items and explain how the items represent you.

What Do **You Think Now** Have your responses to the question about the importance of language changed? Explain.

Vocabulary Development

Vocabulary Check

Answer these questions about the Vocabulary words.

1. What are the differences between **illusions** and **disillusions**?

2. Other than magicians, who else might be involved in **conjuring** things?

Vocabulary Skills: Foreign Words Used in English

Many Spanish words have entered the English lexicon because the United States has a large Spanish-speaking population. Think of a few Spanish words commonly used in English, such as *patio, adobe,* and *canyon.* What do these words mean in each language?

Language Coach

Prefixes Knowing a prefix can help you understand the meaning of words. The prefix *dis–* can mean "without" or "away." Define each pair of words below, explaining how the prefix changes the meaning. Use a dictionary to check your answers.

1. organized, disorganized
2. loyal, disloyal
3. infect, disinfect
4. reputable, disreputable

Academic Vocabulary

Talk About

In what forms are important cultural traditions <u>transmitted</u> to help people remain connected to their heritage? In a small group, think of some examples.

CHOICES

As you respond to the Choices, use these **Academic Vocabulary** words as appropriate: <u>component</u>, <u>diverse</u>, <u>intrinsic</u>, <u>potential</u>, and <u>transmit</u>.

REVIEW
Make a Collage of Details

Presentation Review the specific images Cofer includes in this poem. Then, make a collage that unites a number of the concrete images from the poem. Remember that a collage is a collection of images taken from all sorts of places. Its <u>components</u> can include newsprint, stones, flowers, cloth, photographs, and drawings of your own. Present your collage in class and explain the images you chose to include.

CONNECT
Describe a Place

Timed Writing Write an essay describing a place you know very well. It could be a store or a room in your house or a room in school. It could also be a place in a yard or on the subway. Use as many concrete details as you can. Include an explanation of why the place is significant to you.

EXTEND
Compare Ars Poetica Poems

Archibald MacLeish also wrote a poem with "Ars Poetica" in its title (page 788). Making specific reference to each poem, write a paragraph comparing how MacLeish describes the "art of poetry" with how Cofer describes it. Do they define poetry the same way or differently? Make sure you include evidence from each poem to support your response.

Preparing to Read

Testimonial

What Do You Think?

What human needs and desires do we have in common?

QuickWrite

As you have grown older, what is one important way you have changed? Write a paragraph discussing this change.

Rita Dove
(1952–   )

Pulitzer Prize WINNER

About her Pulitzer Prize–winning sequence of poems called *Thomas and Beulah,* loosely based on the lives of her great-grandparents, Rita Dove says: "I know that when I was writing the poems that went into *Thomas and Beulah* . . . I realized that what I was trying to tell, let's say, was not a narrative as we know narratives but actually the moments that matter most in our lives. I began to think, how do we remember our lives? How do we think of our lives or shape our lives in our own consciousnesses, and I realized that we don't actually think of our lives in very cohesive strands but we remember as beads on a necklace, moments that matter to us, come to us in flashes, and the connections are submerged."

The Joys and Trials of Family Life

Dove, born and raised in Akron, Ohio, attended the Writers' Workshop at the University of Iowa, where she earned a master's degree. She eventually became professor of English at the University of Virginia, Charlottesville. From 1993 to 1995, she was Poet Laureate of the United States.

Dove's life as a mother has also had a major influence on her later poetry. Dove says that after her daughter, Aviva, was born, she felt she was living "the story of many women who all have three full-time jobs: You teach, you do parenting, and you try to write, too. I just was tired all the time. I remember the days when I came back home and fell asleep over dessert."

Historical Themes

Besides writing on personal subjects, Dove weaves historical themes, including race relations, into her verse. As she told *The Washington Post,* "Obviously, as a black woman, I am concerned with race. But certainly not every poem of mine mentions the fact of being black. They are poems about humanity, and sometimes humanity happens to be black. I cannot run from, I *won't* run from, any kind of truth."

Think About the Writer

The central concern of much of Dove's poetry is how memory shapes who we are. What do you think shapes "who we are"?

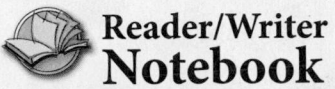

Reader/Writer Notebook

Use your **RWN** to complete the activities for this selection.

Literary Focus

Sound Effects Some **sound effects** in poetry are obvious and hard to miss. Others don't call much attention to themselves. Skillful poets use a wide range of sound effects to create rich and surprising verbal music.

- **Rhyme,** for example, especially end rhyme, is the sound effect most listeners or readers notice first.
- **Onomatopoeia**—the use of language to imitate sounds, such as the words *hiss, slap,* and *buzz*—is also easy to spot.
- **Alliteration**—the repetition of consonant sounds—can require more attention.
- **Assonance**—the repetition of vowel sounds—can be even more subtle, yet it can produce memorable music.

Read the poem aloud to hear its <u>diverse</u> sound effects, and note how they make you feel.

Writing Focus

Think as a Reader/Writer

Find It in Your Reading As you read the poem, notice the metaphors Dove uses to describe herself "when the earth was new." In your *Reader/Writer Notebook*, use a chart like the one below to record these metaphors. In the second column, note your thoughts about the meaning and significance of each metaphor

Metaphor	Meaning/Significance
"filigree and flame"	delicate; intricate; vibrant (but potentially destructive)

Language Coach

Related Words Related words come from the same basic form of a word. This basic form is called the root. The noun *testimonial* means "a tribute." A testimonial is a kind of witness to something done well. It is related to these words:

> *Testify* (verb) means "to make a factual statement about something witnessed."
>
> *Testimony* (noun) means "evidence that a witness gives in court."
>
> What do the meanings of these related words have in common?

What are the roots of the following words? Explain the meanings of these related words.

1. *ignite* and *ignition*
2. *blessings* and *blessed*
3. *promise* and *promising*

Learn It Online
Find out more about Rita Dove at the Writers' Lives site.

go.hrw.com   L11-1363   **Go**

TESTIMONIAL by **Rita Dove**

Read with a Purpose
What "testimonial" is Rita Dove giving in this poem?

Build Background
In a tribute to Gwendolyn Brooks, Dove said, "There is a tradition in the black church: we call it Testifying. It is the brave and humbling act of standing up among one's family, friends, and neighbors to bare one's soul, and to bear witness by acknowledging those who have sustained and nurtured the testifier along the way." Rita Dove read this poem, called "Testimonial," at a commencement ceremony at Howard University, where she was being honored.

Back when the earth was new
and heaven just a whisper,
back when the names of things
hadn't had time to stick;

5   back when the smallest breezes
melted summer into autumn,
when all the poplars quivered
sweetly in rank and file . . . **A**

the world called, and I answered.
10 Each glance ignited to a gaze.
I caught my breath and called that life,
swooned between spoonfuls of lemon sorbet.

I was pirouette and flourish,
I was filigree and flame.
15 How could I count my blessings
when I didn't know their names? **B**

Back when everything was still to come,
luck leaked out everywhere.
I gave my promise to the world,
20 and the world followed me here.

Booly Booly Girl (2004) by Marsha Hatcher.

A **Literary Focus** **Sound Effects** Where in the first two stanzas does Dove use alliteration by repeating the sound of *s* or *th*? What effect does this produce?

B **Literary Focus** **Sound Effects** Where does Dove use rhyme in stanza 4?

Applying Your Skills

SKILLS FOCUS **Literary Skills** Analyze sound effects in poetry; analyze concrete and abstract language. **Writing Skills** Employ literary devices for effective writing.

Testimonial

Respond and Think Critically

Reading Focus

Quick Check

1. What is Dove describing in the first two stanzas?

2. What does the word "here" refer to in line 20?

Read with a Purpose

3. What testimonial is Rita Dove giving in this poem? Why do you think she does so?

Literary Focus

Literary Analysis

4. **Infer** What is Dove describing in lines 1–9?

5. **Hypothesize** What could be the "call" that the world makes in line 9? What promise do you think Dove gives the world, according to line 19?

6. **Interpret** Could Dove be talking about falling in love in the third stanza? Explain.

7. **Evaluate** How would you describe the tone of lines 13–16? Use details from the poem to support your response.

8. **Analyze** Dove uses alliteration in lines 13–14 to describe her younger self as "flourish," "filigree and flame." On the basis of these sound effects, what kind of person do you think she was?

9. **Analyze** What has changed for the speaker over the course of the poem? What would you say is the main theme of the poem?

Literary Skills: Sound Effects

10. **Analyze** Dove uses sound effects to create rich and pleasing verbal music. Find lines in which the poet uses alliteration and rhyme. How do the sound effects Dove uses in the last stanza of the poem differ from those she uses in the first stanza? How does her use of sound effects support the poem's theme?

Literary Skills Review: Concrete and Abstract Language

11. **Analyze** Language that uses specific words and details to describe something, such as *poplars*, is **concrete language**. Language that deals with generalities and ideas, such as *love*, is **abstract language**. Look at the poem again. What examples of concrete and abstract language can you find? Would you say that "Testimonial" is, as a whole, an abstract poem or a concrete poem? Explain.

Writing Focus

Think as a Reader/Writer

Use It in Your Writing Refer to your *Reader/Writer Notebook*, in which you have recorded the unusual metaphors Dove uses in her poem. What makes them effective? Imagine you were writing a similar poem "testifying" about an important moment in your life. What metaphors would you use to describe yourself? Be as creative as you can.

 What Do You Think Now

Do you think most people looking back at an earlier time in their lives would respond similarly to the way Dove did, no matter where they live or what their culture? Explain.

What For

What human needs and desires do we have in common?

QuickTalk

How important do you think stories are to children? What can stories do for a child? With a partner, talk about the questions. Consider children everywhere, not just those in your own family or neighborhood.

MEET THE WRITER

Garrett Hongo
(1951–   )

Garrett Hongo's poetry grows out of his experiences as a fourth-generation Japanese American. He believes it is his privilege and responsibility to tell his family's story.

From Volcano to Los Angeles

Hongo was born in Volcano, Hawaii, a small town below the summit of the Kilauea volcano. When he was six, his family moved to the Los Angeles area. He graduated from Pomona College in California and earned a master of fine arts degree from the University of California at Irvine in 1980. He has taught creative writing at several universities.

Hongo's first poetry collection was *Yellow Light* (1982), which includes homages to Japanese American history and to the laborers who helped build this country, people like his father and grandfather. His second collection, *The River of Heaven* (1988), captured the attention of critics and was a finalist for the Pulitzer Prize. Subjects of the poems in that book include the volcanoes of Hawaii, the gritty city streets of Los Angeles, and the death of his father. His memories of growing up are found in *Volcano: A Memoir of Hawaii* (1995).

Poems Equal to His Father's Heart

Garrett Hongo says he writes for his father, Albert Kazuyoshi Hongo. "I want to be his witness," Hongo says of his father, "to testify to his great and noble life, in struggle against anger, in struggle against his own loneliness and isolation for being a Hawaiian Japanese who immigrated to Los Angeles without much family or community. He was a great example to me of a man who refused to hate, or, being different himself, to be afraid of difference, who accepted the friendship of all the strange and underprivileged ostracized by the rest of 'normal' society—Vietnamese, Mexicans, Southern blacks, reservation Indians relocated to the city—and I want my poems to be equal to his heart."

Think About the Writer Do you think poetry can change people's hearts and affect the way they deal with other people in the world? Explain your response.

Reader/Writer Notebook

Use your **RWN** to complete the activities for this selection.

Literary Focus

Refrain A **refrain** is a word, phrase, line, or group of lines that is repeated; refrains are especially common in poetry. In ballads, refrains have long been used to build suspense—and also to help the singer remember the song. In modern poetry, refrains are used to emphasize certain ideas and to create emotional effects. In many poems, refrains contribute to the structure of the poem.

Reading Focus

Analyzing Poem Structure Poetic **structure** involves various <u>components</u>, such as meter, rhyme, repetition, and syntax. Some poems are built on very rigid structures. A **villanelle,** as you learned on page 1330, is a nineteen-line poem consisting of five three-line stanzas, a final four-line stanza, a strict rhyme scheme, and complex rules governing the repetition of certain lines. A **haiku,** originally a Japanese form of poetry, is written in three lines with five, seven, and five syllables, respectively.

Hongo's poem has a looser structure, but a logic controls his poem nevertheless. He has built his poem on stanzas introduced by a refrain, each stanza giving a different view of the child the speaker once was.

Into Action As you read, use a chart like the one below to identify the topic of each stanza of the poem. Write down the refrain that opens each stanza.

	Topic	Refrain
Stanza 1	poet's childhood love of spells and stories	Line 1: "At six I lived for spells"
Stanza 2		

Writing Focus

Think as a Reader/Writer

Find It in Your Reading **Imagery** is the use of language that appeals to a reader's sense (sight, touch, taste, sound, or smell) to evoke a vivid picture or sensation. In your *Reader/Writer Notebook,* make a list of some of the images in Hongo's poem that you find especially evocative.

Language Coach

Silent Letters Many English words contain letters that are not sounded when they are spoken aloud. For example, the word *hymn* in line 3 is pronounced /hihm/. The *n* is silent. These words from the poem are not pronounced the way they are spelled. How is each of these words pronounced? Use a dictionary if you are not sure.

> trough
> pneumatic

Here are some other English words with silent letters. How is each of these words pronounced?

1. rare
2. sea
3. lei
4. night
5. condemn

Learn It Online
Find graphic organizers online to help you as you read.

go.hrw.com L11-1367 **Go**

WHAT FOR

by **Garrett Hongo**

Read with a Purpose In this poem, the speaker looks back on his childhood. Read to find out how he feels about his experiences—and what his father endured.

Analyzing Visuals

Viewing and Interpreting
What do the details in this image suggest about the poem's setting?

Tongan Tradition (Father and Son)
by Timothy J. Terry.

At six I lived for spells:
how a few Hawaiian words could call
up the rain, could hymn like the sea
in the long swirl of chambers
5 curling in the nautilus of a shell,
how Amida's° ballads of the Buddhaland
in the drone of the priest's liturgy
could conjure money from the poor
and give them nothing but mantras,°
10 the strange syllables that healed desire.

---

6. **Amida's:** *Amida* is Japanese for "Amitōbha," Sanskrit for "infinite light." Amida is the great savior worshiped by members of the Pure Land sect, one of the most popular Buddhist sects in eastern Asia.

9. **mantras:** hymns or other portions of a sacred text, chanted or intoned as incantations or prayers.

I lived for stories about the war
my grandfather told over *hana* cards,°
slapping them down on the mats
with a sharp Japanese *kiai*.°

15 I lived for songs my grandmother sang
stirring curry into a thick stew,
weaving a calligraphy of Kannon's° love
into grass mats and straw sandals.

I lived for the red volcano dirt
20 staining my toes, the salt residue
of surf and sea wind in my hair,
the arc of a flat stone skipping
in the hollow trough of a wave. **Ⓐ**

I lived a child's world, waited
25 for my father to drag himself home,
dusted with blasts of sand, powdered rock,
and the strange ash of raw cement,
his deafness made worse by the clang
of pneumatic drills, sore in his bones
30 from the buckings of a jackhammer.
He'd hand me a scarred lunchpail,
let me unlace the hightop G.I. boots,
call him the new name I'd invented
that day in school, write it for him
35 on his newspaper. He'd rub my face
with hands that felt like gravel roads,
tell me to move, go play, and then he'd
walk to the laundry sink to scrub,
rinse the dirt of his long day
40 from a face brown and grained as koa° wood. **Ⓑ**

---

12. *hana* cards: cards used in a Japanese game in which players attempt to match
pairs of flower patterns. *Hana* is Japanese for "flower."
14. *kiai*: a Japanese onomatopoeic word for the sound made by slapping down
hana cards.
17. Kannon's: In Japanese Buddhism, Kannon is the bodhisattva ("Buddha to be")
of infinite compassion and mercy.
40. koa: Hawaiian mimosa tree valued for its wood and bark.

Ⓐ Reading Focus Analyzing Poem Structure What structural elements does Hongo use
to join the three stanzas at the top of this page?

Ⓑ Reading Focus Analyzing Poem Structure How is this stanza different from the three
that come before it? Why do you think Hongo varies the stanzas in this way?

I wanted to take away the pain
in his legs, the swelling in his joints,
give him back his hearing,
clear and rare as crystal chimes,
45   the fins of glass that wrinkled
and sparked the air with their sound.

I wanted to heal the sores that work
and war had sent to him,
let him play catch in the backyard
50   with me, tossing a tennis ball
past papaya trees without the shoulders
of pain shrugging back his arms.

I wanted to become a doctor of pure magic,
to string a necklace of sweet words
55   fragrant as pine needles and plumeria,°
fragrant as the bread my mother baked,
place it like a lei of cowrie shells
and *pikake*° flowers around my father's neck,
and chant him a blessing, a sutra.° **C D**

---

55. plumeria: a kind of fragrant, flowering, tropical
    American trees.
58. *pikake*: Hawaiian for "Arabian jasmine."
59. sutra: one of the sacred scriptures of Buddhism.

C Reading Focus **Analyzing Poem Structure** Compare the three
stanzas on this page with the three at the top of the previous page. How are they
different? How are they similar?

D Literary Focus **Refrain** How do the refrains enhance the emotional
effect of each stanza in the poem?

Applying Your Skills

SKILLS FOCUS **Literary Skills** Analyze refrain; analyze tone. **Reading Skills** Analyze poem structure. **Writing Skills** Write poetry.

What For

Respond and Think Critically

Reading Focus

Quick Check

1. Describe the setting introduced in the first four stanzas of the poem.

2. In the poem, what is the speaker's relationship with his father like?

Read with a Purpose

3. How does the speaker feel about his childhood and about his father's life?

Reading Skills: Analyzing Poem Structure

4. While reading the poem, you identified the topic of each stanza and the refrain that opens each stanza. Review your notes. How does the structure of the poem help you understand the title "What For"?

Literary Focus

Literary Analysis

5. **Compare and Contrast** How do the images describing the speaker's father contrast with the images that the speaker remembers in the first four stanzas?

6. **Interpret** What do you think the speaker means when he says, "I wanted to become a doctor of pure magic" (line 53)?

7. **Interpret** What does the speaker want to do for his father in the last stanza? Do you think that in writing this poem he has accomplished it?

8. **Extend** One of the central teachings of Buddhism is that "life is suffering"—that sickness, pain, and loss are an unavoidable part of living. Does this poem reflect that belief? Explain.

Literary Skills: Refrain

9. **Interpret** What mood do you think the refrains lend to the poem? Explain.

Literary Skills Review: Tone

10. **Analyze** The writer's attitude toward his or her subject or audience is **tone**. Describe the speaker's tone toward his childhood and toward his family. How does the speaker's tone change? What tone do you hear in the first four stanzas? What tone do you hear in the fifth stanza? What tone do you hear in the final three stanzas?

Writing Focus

Think as a Reader/Writer

Use It in Your Writing As you read the poem, you noted in your *Reader/Writer Notebook* images that were especially evocative. Now, write a poem of your own in which you use images to evoke the world you knew as a child. Use the refrains "I lived for" and "I wanted." You may choose to write about your own childhood or about the childhood of someone you know. Think about how imagery helps your reader understand your speaker's experiences.

 What Do **You Think Now** Hongo refers to the stories he heard as a child from his grandparents. Do you think the experiences of the older generation are still important to children today? Explain.

The Beep Beep Poem

Nikki Giovanni
(1943–)

What Do You Think? What human needs and desires do we have in common?

QuickTalk

Discuss a time when you or someone you know used the written word to make a statement about an important issue. Why might people choose to respond to political or social events through writing?

Nikki Giovanni has, at last count, been awarded 21 honorary doctorates; written more than two dozen books; and had her *Nikki Giovanni Poetry Collection,* a spoken-word CD, rank as a finalist for a 2003 Grammy Award. Also, in 2003, she published *The Collected Poetry of Nikki Giovanni, 1968–1998.* She was the first recipient of the Rosa Parks Women of Courage Award.

"Princess of Black Poetry"

Giovanni, whose given name is Yolande Cornelia, was born in Knoxville, Tennessee, and grew up in Cincinnati, Ohio. She graduated from Fisk University in Nashville and did graduate work at the University of Pennsylvania and Columbia University School of Fine Arts. Giovanni is affectionately called the Princess of Black Poetry because of the large, enthusiastic crowds she attracts whenever she gives public readings of her work. Behind all Giovanni's poetry, according to one critic, are the "creation of racial pride and the communication of individual love." Giovanni says of her writing, "I write out of my own experiences—which also happen to be the experiences of my people."

From the Ivory Tower to Pop Culture

Nikki Giovanni is currently a University Distinguished Professor at Virginia Tech, where she has taught writing and literature since 1987. Not flattered when her students write poems that sound like hers, she says, "I already sound like me. I want my students to hear their own voices." Though she dwells in academia, Giovanni is also a lover of pop culture. She is a fan of *Star Trek* and a proponent of hip-hop, though she also argues "it's important to involve young people in spirituals."

Think About the Writer Giovanni became a poet during the sixties, a decade of great political and social turbulence. How might this social context have influenced her poetry?

Reader/Writer Notebook

Use your **RWN** to complete the activities for this selection.

Literary Focus

Parallelism Used to create rhythm and emphasis in poetry, **parallelism** is the repetition of words, phrases, clauses, or sentences that have identical or similar grammatical structures. Parallelism in sentence construction improves writing style and readability. As you read, think about why Giovanni uses it and what effect it has on the poem.

Reading Focus

Analyzing Author's Message It is often easy to determine what a poem is about. A poem may be about a poet's father or about a specific experience or event. That is the subject of a poem. The **message** of a poem, however, can be more difficult to determine and to understand fully. The places to look for clues are in the parts of the poem that are emphasized. Ideas at the beginning of stanzas or ideas in short lines in the middle of stanzas are usually important. Repetition and parallelism, too, often emphasize significant ideas.

Into Action As you read, write down details that help you analyze the author's message. Use a chart like the one below to note the <u>diverse</u> details that help convey the message.

Details
Repetition: "but there's almost nothing / that hasn't been said / and said and said" (lines 2–4)
Parallelism: "i wrote a poem," "i composed a ditty," "i love to drive my car" (lines 21, 26, 33)

Language Coach

Synonyms Synonyms are words that have the same or nearly the same meaning. The speaker in this poem finds solace in a warm bath. Synonyms for *solace* include *comfort*, *consolation*, and *relief*. Identify at least one synonym for each of these words from this poem: *tyrants, constant, baffled, sensitivity, ascend*. Use a thesaurus if necessary.

Writing Focus

Think as a Reader/Writer

Find It in Your Reading Giovanni repeats grammatical structures in the poem to achieve specific effects. As you read, note these repetitions in your *Reader/Writer Notebook*. Consider how the repetitions and shifts lead the reader to the poem's conclusion.

Learn It Online
Listen to the parallelism in this poem online.

go.hrw.com   L11-1373   **Go**

THE BEEP BEEP POEM

by Nikki Giovanni

Read with a Purpose
Read to learn how the poet draws a parallel between driving and writing poetry.

Build Background
Kent State University in Ohio was the scene of a tragic confrontation between troops in the National Guard and students protesting the movement of U.S. soldiers into Cambodia during the Vietnam War. On May 4, 1970, four students were killed and nine wounded when National Guard troops opened fire during a noontime demonstration.

I should write a poem
but there's almost nothing
that hasn't been said
and said and said
5   beautifully, ugly, blandly
excitingly
      stay in school
      make love not war
      death to all tyrants
10   where have all the flowers gone
and don't they understand at kent state
the troopers will shoot . . . again **A**

i could write a poem
because i love walking
15   in the rain
and the solace of my naked
body in a tub of warm water
cleanliness may not be next
to godliness but it sure feels
20   good

i wrote a poem
for my father but it was so constant
i burned it up
he hates change
25   and i'm baffled by sameness

i composed a ditty
about encore american and worldwide news
but the editorial board
said no one would understand it
30   as if people have to be tricked
into sensitivity
though of course they do **B**

i love to drive my car
hours on end
35   along back country roads
i love to stop for cider and apples and acorn
      squash
three for a dollar
i love my CB when the truckers talk
and the hum of the diesel in my ear
40   i love the aloneness of the road
when I ascend descending curves
the power within my toe delights me
and i fling my spirit down the highway
i love the way i feel
45   when i pass the moon and i holler to the stars
i'm coming through

Beep Beep **C**

A **Reading Focus** **Analyzing Author's Message** What is Giovanni's message in this stanza, when she mentions Kent State?

B **Reading Focus** **Analyzing Author's Message** What is Giovanni saying about the American public here?

C **Literary Focus** **Parallelism** What does the repetition of "i love" add to the final stanza?

Applying Your Skills

The Beep Beep Poem

Respond and Think Critically

Reading Focus

Quick Check

1. In the opening stanza, what discourages the speaker from writing a poem?

2. What does the speaker mean when she says that she is "baffled by sameness"?

Read with a Purpose

3. How does Giovanni draw a parallel between driving and writing poetry?

Reading Skills: Analyzing Author's Message

4. While reading, you listed several components of the poem that help you analyze the author's message. Now that you have finished reading, review your notes. How do details in the poem, such as repetitions and the use of parallelism, help you analyze Giovanni's message? What is the message of the poem?

Literary Focus

Literary Analysis

5. **Interpret** Why has the poet indented four lines in the first stanza? What do these lines have in common? How do they relate to the theme?

6. **Make Judgments** What values are important to the author? Support your response with details from the text.

7. **Infer** Why do you think the poet shifts from talking about writing poems to describing long drives? What does this shift reveal about the poet as an individual?

8. **Interpret** What is the meaning of the last two words of the poem, "Beep Beep"?

9. **Extend** People often say that Americans are "in love with their cars." Is it true? Explain.

Literary Skills: Parallelism

10. **Analyze** "The Beep Beep Poem" has several instances of parallelism. How does the use of parallelism help create rhythm in the poem?

Literary Skills Review: Style

11. **Evaluate** Many writers have a unique, distinctive **style.** Style can be plain, descriptive, ornate, and so on. After reading "The Beep Beep Poem," identify aspects of Giovanni's style. How would you describe her style?

Writing Focus

Think as a Reader/Writer

Use It in Your Writing As you read, you collected information on Giovanni's use of repetition. Now, write a short poem in which three or more lines (or stanzas) begin with a short repeated phrase.

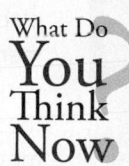 What Do You Think Now

How might social and political incidents have influenced Giovanni's writing and her outlook on life?

Providence

What human needs and desires do we have in common?

QuickWrite

Think about a vivid memory from your childhood. What makes the memory stand out to you? What details do you remember best? Write a paragraph describing your memory and its importance to you.

Natasha Trethewey
(1966–   )

Pulitzer Prize WINNER

Through her poetry, Natasha Trethewey tells the story of the working poor in the American South. Collective memory is a common theme of her work; many of her poems focus on "things that aren't memorialized, and how we remember and what it is that we forget." Trethewey reclaims the stories of the forgotten by presenting their reflections upon the scenes of daily life.

A Difficult Beginning

Natasha Trethewey was born to an African American mother and white father in Gulfport, Mississippi. At the time, interracial marriage was still illegal in Mississippi, and as a girl Trethewey often noticed people staring whenever her family went out together. As she grew up, her father—a poet himself—encouraged her to express herself through poetry. She later earned degrees in poetry from Hollins University and the University of Massachusetts.

Reclaiming Lost History

The difficult memories of growing up as an outsider and the sudden death of her mother led to Trethewey's desire to speak for the forgotten. Trethewey's first poetry collection, *Domestic Work*, came out in 2000. In it, she uses images of the lives of domestic workers as a window into their private thoughts, hopes, and dreams. Her next collection, *Native Guard*, began in part from an observation: In her hometown of Gulfport, a plaque commemorated Confederate soldiers, but nothing commemorated African American Union soldiers. *Native Guard* is in part her monument to these men. Interwoven with poems of the forgotten soldiers are poems commemorating Trethewey's mother. In 2007, *Native Guard* was awarded the Pulitzer Prize for poetry.

Think About the Writer

History is a common subject in Trethewey's poetry. Why do you think that Trethewey has chosen to confront history through poetry rather than some other way?

Reader/Writer Notebook

Use your **RWN** to complete the activities for this selection.

Literary Focus

Enjambment Enjambment is the running on of meaning from the end of one line of verse into the next without a punctuated pause. Poets often use enjambment to add rhythmic <u>diversity</u>. Enjambment is contrasted with an end-stopped line (a line that is a grammatical unit followed by punctuation). Enjambed lines allow the poet to create a pause in the middle of a sentence. As you read "Providence," think about how enjambments affect your reading speed and your understanding of the lines.

Reading Focus

Analyzing Characteristics of Free Verse Although **free verse** lacks regular rhyme and meter, it still contains many of the same poetic devices that traditional poetry does. The lack of a formal structure—an alternating rhyme scheme or a set number of stanzas—allows the poet to have complete freedom to mold the lines to communicate images and ideas.

Into Action As you read, analyze Trethewey's use of poetic devices. Look for examples of repetition, imagery, and enjambment. Then, describe the effect that each has on your reading of the poem. Collect the information in a chart like the one below.

	Example (line #)	Significance or effect
Repetition	Repetition of all sound in lines 9–10: rec<u>all</u>, <u>all</u>, sm<u>all</u>	
Imagery		
Enjambment		

Language Coach

Words in Context Words can have specific meanings in specific settings, or contexts. The word *footage* can mean the total length of something in feet. In the context of a TV news report, however, it refers to scenes recorded on film or video. Film is recorded on thin strips. Their length is measured in feet; the total length is the footage. Explain the meanings of these words in the context of film and news: *shot, tape, live, angle, pan, zoom.*

Writing Focus

Think as a Reader/Writer

Find It in Your Reading In your *Reader/Writer Notebook,* take note of Trethewey's use of contrast in "Providence." Note in particular the tension she creates between land and water and between the time before the full impact of the storm and after. Record the details of these and any other contrasts in your *Reader/Writer Notebook,* and think about what they add to the poem.

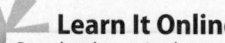

Learn It Online
But what does enjambment sound like? Find out with the audio recording online.

| go.hrw.com | L11-1377 | Go |

PROVIDENCE

by **Natasha Trethewey**

Build Background

Hurricane Camille made landfall along the coast of Mississippi on August 17, 1969, having traveled from the waters west of the Cayman Islands over western Cuba and across the Gulf of Mexico. It was powerful enough to destroy all the instruments set up to record the speed of its winds. Weather researchers estimate that wind speeds reached 200 miles per hour. One of the deadliest hurricanes in American history, Camille killed 256 people as it whipped from Mississippi into Tennessee and Kentucky and then across the Virginias. It caused nearly $1.5 billion in damages—a huge loss at the time, though it is dwarfed by the estimated $75 billion loss in New Orleans and along the Mississippi coast caused by Hurricane Katrina in 2005.

What's left is footage: the hours before
      Camille, 1969—hurricane
          parties, palm trees leaning
in the wind,
5   fronds blown back,

a woman's hair. Then after:
      the vacant lots,
      boats washed ashore, a swamp

where graves had been. I recall   **A**

10   how we huddled all night in our small house,
      moving between rooms,
         emptying pots filled with rain.

The next day, our house—
      on its cinderblocks—seemed to float

15   in the flooded yard: no foundation

beneath us, nothing I could see
      tying us   to the land.
      In the water, our reflection
         trembled,
20   disappeared
   when I bent to touch it. **B**

A **Literary Focus** **Enjambment** How does enjambment add to the description of destruction in lines 6–9?

B **Reading Focus** **Free Verse** What poetic elements or devices give structure and form to lines 13–21? How do these elements and sound effects reinforce the poet's message?

SKILLS FOCUS **Literary Skills** Analyze enjambment; analyze setting. **Reading Skills** Analyze characteristics of free verse. **Writing Skills** Write poetry; describe a place.

Respond and Think Critically

Reading Focus

Quick Check

1. What is the meaning of the title of this poem, "Providence"?

2. How does the speaker protect the inside of her house during the hurricane?

Read with a Purpose

3. How does the speaker feel about Camille? Angry? Sad? Resigned? Explain.

Reading Skills: Analyzing Characteristics of Free Verse

4. As you read, you collected examples of repetition, imagery, and enjambment in the poem. Make sure that you have at least three examples of each device. Now, comment on the effect that each has on the meaning of the poem. Summarize your comments in a brief paragraph about the structure of this poem.

	Example (line #)	Significance or effect
Repetition	Repetition of all sound in lines 9–10: recall, all, small	Reinforces the speaker's memories, the length of the night, and how helpless the house was.
Imagery		

Literary Focus

Literary Analysis

5. **Infer** In line 7, why are the lots "vacant"? What is the speaker describing?

6. **Evaluate** Is the structure of this poem appropriate for its subject matter? How does the poem's form reinforce its meaning?

7. **Analyze** How is the image in lines 5–6 ironic? What does this image reveal about the development of the speaker's tone?

8. **Interpret** In line 17, Trethewey uses a long space in the middle of the line. Why does she do so? What does it suggest?

9. **Interpret** What does the image of the speaker's reflection trembling and disappearing suggest? Why does the poet choose to end with this image?

Literary Skills: Enjambment

10. **Analyze** How does enjambment affect the rhythm of the poem? How would this poem be different if the poet had chosen to end each line with a punctuated pause?

Literary Skills Review: Setting

11. **Analyze** The time and place of a text are its **setting.** What is the setting of "Providence," and what role does it play in the poem? Why is this poem's setting significant?

Writing Focus

Think as a Reader/Writer

Use It in Your Writing Review your notes about the use of contrasts in "Providence." Then, write a short poem or prose paragraph in which you use contrast to describe a scene that once looked one way but was later profoundly altered by a powerful force. Include details that emphasize the change.

What Do You Think Now

Compare "Providence" to the Build Background section to its left. Can facts and statistics fully capture experience? What human need does poetry address?

Trying to Name What Doesn't Change

What Do You Think?

What human needs and desires do we have in common?

QuickWrite

Think about the role that change plays in your life. Maybe your personality, clothes, or favorite activities are constantly changing, or maybe you don't encounter much change from day to day. Consider the question, "Do human beings need change?" Then, write a paragraph in response.

MEET THE WRITER

Naomi Shihab Nye
(1952–   )

Naomi Shihab Nye doesn't believe that poetry is a solitary art. Instead, she sees it as a form of dialogue. In an interview with journalist Bill Moyers, she says poetry is "conversation with the world, conversation with those words on the page allowing them to speak back to you—conversation with yourself."

Diverse Roots

Naomi Shihab Nye was born in St. Louis, Missouri. She has a diverse background: Her mother was American and her father was Palestinian. When she was a teenager, her family moved to Jerusalem, where she attended high school for one year. When the family returned to the United States, they settled in San Antonio, Texas, where she has lived for many years.

As an Arab American woman, Nye often draws upon her cultural heritage. When she was a child, her father told her many stories of his life in Palestine, stories she incorporates into her work. In addition, Nye is a leading voice of the American Southwest. She writes, "My poems and stories often begin with the voices of our neighbors, mostly Mexican American, always inventive and surprising."

One of Nye's books, *19 Varieties of Gazelle: Poems of the Middle East,* was a finalist for the National Book Award.

The "Job" of Poetry

According to Nye, poetry has an unusual power to humanize people. Nye writes poems and stories that highlight our shared humanity and emphasize the value of peace. She firmly believes that "it will be peace, not violence, that fixes things."

Nye has seen the power of poetry at work in the classrooms she visits. She says that after she read two third-grade girls a few poems by writers in Iraq, the girls said, "We never thought about there being children in Iraq before." Nye thought, "Well, those poems did their job, because now [the girls] will think about everything a little bit differently. "

Think About the Writer

What do you think Naomi Shihab Nye thinks the "job" of poetry is?

Reader/Writer Notebook

Use your **RWN** to complete the activities for this selection.

Literary Focus

Theme A **theme** is an insight or truth about human life that is <u>transmitted</u> through a piece of imaginative literature, such as a poem, a story, or a play. Themes are rarely stated directly; the goal of most literature is not to deliver a sermon or a moral lesson. Instead, the writer expects you, the reader, to participate in the story, poem, or play and experience the theme on your own. If you are reading a story or play, you may experience this revelation about life as the characters do. If you are reading a poem, you may think about key images and metaphors that seem to point to a truth about life.

Theme is not the same as subject, which can be expressed in a word or two. Theme is the revelation you discover about the subject. To express a theme, you have to use at least one sentence.

Language Coach

Adjective Endings The suffix *—y* can be added to many nouns to form descriptive adjectives. In this poem, the noun *spider* uses the *—y* ending to create an adjective: *spidery*. Use the *—y* ending to make adjectives out of these nouns from the poem:

weed	star
wood	cat
soup	bush
rose	brain

Which words have to change their spelling when the *—y* ending is added? Use a dictionary to confirm your responses.

Reading Focus

Interpreting Details To discover a theme, you must pay close attention to **details**. In the poem "Trying to Name What Doesn't Change," several points of view are given about the subject of change. Each point of view is based on observed details.

Into Action As you read, write down details used to name things that change and things that don't change. Use a graphic organizer like the one below to record details for each opinion.

Subject	How does it change or not change?
Train tracks	They stay the same because they do not grow or develop. (1st stanza)

Writing Focus

Think as a Reader/Writer

Find It in Your Reading As you read the poem, look for specific images that help you see, hear, or taste what changes or doesn't change. Record these images in your *Reader/Writer Notebook*.

Learn It Online
To learn more about theme in longer works, visit *NovelWise* online.

go.hrw.com   L11-1381

TRYING TO NAME WHAT DOESN'T CHANGE

by **Naomi Shihab Nye**

> ### Read with a Purpose
> Read to learn people's differing thoughts about the nature of change.

Roselva says the only thing that doesn't change
is train tracks. She's sure of it.
The train changes, or the weeds that grow up spidery
by the side, but not the tracks.
5　I've watched one for three years, she says,
and it doesn't curve, doesn't break, doesn't grow.

Peter isn't sure. He saw an abandoned track
near Sabinas, Mexico, and says a track without a train
is a changed track. The metal wasn't shiny anymore,
10　The wood was split and some of the ties were gone.

Every Tuesday on Morales Street
butchers crack the necks of a hundred hens.
The widow in the tilted house
spices her soup with cinnamon.
15　Ask her what doesn't change. **Ⓐ**

Stars explode.
The rose curls up as if there is fire in the petals.
The cat who knew me is buried under the bush. **Ⓑ**

The train whistle still wails its ancient sound
20　but when it goes away, shrinking back
from the walls of the brain,
it takes something different with it every time.

Ⓐ Reading Focus Interpreting Details How do the details in
this stanza alter the tone of the poem?

Ⓑ Literary Focus Theme What do the images in lines 16–18
contribute to the poem's ideas about change?

Applying Your Skills

Trying to Name What Doesn't Change

SKILLS FOCUS **Literary Skills** Analyze theme; analyze free verse. **Reading Skills** Interpret details. **Writing Skills** Respond to poetry.

Respond and Think Critically

Reading Focus

Quick Check

1. What is the difference between Roselva's and Peter's ideas about change? With whom does the speaker seem to agree?

2. In what way is a "track without a train" a "changed track" (lines 8–9)?

Read with a Purpose

3. What different perspectives on the nature of change are presented in the poem? Explain.

Reading Skills: Interpreting Details

4. While reading the poem, you recorded details that relate to the theme of the poem. You should have collected at least one detail for each stanza. Complete your chart by adding a third column and commenting on what each detail says about life. Then, write a brief summary of the information in your chart.

Subject	How does it change or not change?	What it says about life
Train tracks	They stay the same because they do not grow or develop (1st stanza).	This lack of change or growth is not necessarily positive.

Literary Focus

Literary Analysis

5. Make Judgments Do you think Roselva would change her opinion about train tracks after hearing Peter's ideas? Why or why not?

6. Interpret Why does Nye have the widow live in a "tilted house" (line 13)? What does this detail add to the poem?

7. Interpret Why did Nye include the detail about where the cat is buried? How does this image contribute to the theme?

8. Summarize In your own words, summarize the final stanza of the poem.

9. Analyze Think about all of the things in this poem that do change. What are some common characteristics of the changes they undergo? How do these common elements affect the mood of the poem?

Literary Skills: Theme

10. Analyze In one or two brief sentences, state the theme of this poem in your own words. Then, write a brief paragraph in which you agree or disagree with Nye's idea or ideas.

Literary Skills Review: Free Verse

11. Evaluate Poetry that is written without a strict rhyme scheme and meter is called **free verse.** Free-verse poets use the **rhythms of conversation,** occasional **rhymes, alliteration, images,** and **metaphors.** Which of these poetic elements do you find in Nye's poem?

Writing Focus

Think as a Reader/Writer

Use It in Your Writing Write a response to Nye's poem, using specific details like the ones you noted in your *Reader/Writer Notebook*. Think about how these details relate to the theme of the poem.

What Do **You Think Now** Do you think most people yearn for something in the world that is constant, that does not change? Explain.

Preparing to Read

Prayer *from* Three Paumanok Pieces

What Do You Think?

What human needs and desires do we have in common?

🕐 QuickTalk

Talk with a partner about a place you have spent time or where you have lived. Describe your memories of that place and how it has sshaped who you are.

MEET THE WRITER

Norbert Krapf
(1943–   )

Much of Norbert Krapf's work explores his past by investigating places where he and his ancestors have lived. Krapf has said, "My passion for origins has been inseparable from my compulsion to write poems. I find it impossible to live, fully, in the present without understanding where I have lived in the past."

Child of the Midwest

Norbert Krapf was born and raised in Jasper, Indiana. He stayed in Indiana to pursue a bachelor's degree and graduate degrees in English and American literature. He eventually received a Ph.D. from the University of Notre Dame. It was not until he left Indiana to begin teaching at Long Island University that he began to write poetry.

Nature and art are frequently featured in Krapf's poetry, particularly nature in southern Indiana and northern European art. Krapf has frequently collaborated with artists from Germany and Indiana, and his poem "Back Home" was selected to be featured as a part of a stained-glass panel for Indianapolis's airport.

The Importance of Place

Leaving Indiana uprooted Krapf and led him to explore his origins. He began to study German language and history, and, in particular, the region of Franconia. He has since been selected twice to serve as the Senior Fulbright Professor of American Poetry at the universities of Freiburg and Erlangen-Nuremberg.

Krapf taught at Long Island University for thirty-four years, eventually becoming the director of the C. W. Post Poetry Center. In that time, the New York metropolitan region also became an inspiration for much of his work. In 2000, he released *Bittersweet Along the Expressway: Poems of Long Island*. The poem "Prayer" was written for an anthology commemorating the terrorist attacks of September 11, 2001.

Think About the Writer Norbert Krapf did not start writing poetry until he left his home in Indiana. What purpose do you think poetry served in his adopted home?

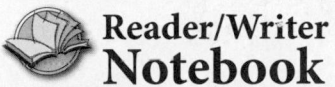

Reader/Writer Notebook

Use your **RWN** to complete the activities for this selection.

Literary Focus

Apostrophe In a work of literature, **apostrophe** is the direct address of a thing, place, abstract idea, or dead or absent person. The object of the speaker's address is often spoken to in a way that suggests it might actually respond with words or with actions. In this poem, the speaker addresses a famous poet, Walt Whitman. When poets use apostrophe, you can be sure that the object of their address has been very carefully chosen. As you read "Prayer," think about the message that the poet might be sending by addressing a poem on this subject to Whitman, who died in 1892.

Reading Focus

Understanding Allusions In "Prayer," Krapf speaks to Whitman and makes a number of **allusions,** or historical and literary references, to Whitman's poetry and distinctive style of writing, and to some of the major events in Whitman's life. Whitman did not fight in the Civil War (1861–1865), but he experienced it firsthand when he helped his wounded brother at Fredericksburg and when he worked as a nurse in Washington, D.C. He also lived much of his life in New York City, especially Brooklyn.

Into Action Some of the allusions in the poem are very specific. Unless you are very familiar with Whitman's poetry, you will miss a few. Use this chart to gather details that seem to relate to Whitman's life and art.

Allusions to . . .	Example
Whitman's poems	
Whitman's war experience	
Whitman's time in New York City	

Language Coach

Connotations A word's **connotations** are the feelings or emotions that it evokes in the reader, beyond its dictionary definition. In this poem, Krapf uses poems with strong connotations to evoke emotions in the reader. Write down connotations of each of these words from the poem:

1. sanctuary
2. ghostly
3. underbelly
4. caper
5. implore
6. resolve

Writing Focus

Think as a Reader/Writer

Find It in Your Reading Krapf's poem about the destruction of the World Trade Center contains a catalog of representative groups that were affected by that tragedy. As you read, collect details on these groups and record them in your *Reader/Writer Notebook*.

Learn It Online
Listen to this poem online.

go.hrw.com   L11-1385   Go

PRAYER by **Norbert Krapf**

from Three Paumanok Pieces

Read with a Purpose
Read to hear the speaker talk to a fellow poet, Walt Whitman, about the aftermath of September 11, 2001.

Build Background

The poet Walt Whitman (1819–1892) is one of our nation's strongest literary voices. To read about his life and to read some of his poetry, see pages 510–541. Whitman's poetry is written in a bold free verse. His long, flowing lines celebrate the vitality and variety of American life and praise the natural beauty of its land. During his life, the United States was torn apart by the Civil War. Whitman's poems about the war do not flinch at its awful devastation, but they hold out a promise that the war's terrible wounds will heal in time.

Come back, Walt Whitman, we need you now in the hour of our grief.
Come back, Camerado,° wind your way back to Ground Zero° where you belong. **A**
Wrap your arm around the shoulder of a fireman who lost his best friend,
tell the policemen how brave were their fellows at the moment of collapse,
5   rub your fingers between the ears of the dog that has sniffed hour after hour
for the smell of human flesh,
stand at attention when workers find in the rubble the body of a brother,
amble over to the Armory and say a word to long lines of those with
pictures of loved ones pinned to their chests,
10   tell the husband how beautiful and good his missing wife is,
tell the wife how courageous her husband was to help his colleagues,
promise the sister you will hunt with her for her lost brother just as you hunted
for your own brother George at Fredericksburg, **B**
hold steady the mother and father who lost their son weeks before he was to marry,
hug the student from Queens who, after her class in the suburbs, rode your word-ferry across
15   time and space, sobbed to her teacher how they had found the body of her firefighter,
comfort the family of the Brooklyn student who came to this country from Syria for asylum and
    will now return home only in spirit,

---

2. **Camerado:** comrade or friend. This invented word was used by Whitman in his poem "Starting from Paumanok."
   Ground Zero: The site in New York City where the towers of the World Trade Center once stood. The terrorist attacks on September 11, 2001, caused the towers to collapse, killing approximately 2,750 people.

A **Literary Focus** Apostrophe Why does the poet say that Walt Whitman belongs at Ground Zero?

B **Reading Focus** Understanding Allusions How might Walt Whitman's experiences at Fredericksburg have been like the experiences of some of the people at Ground Zero?

guide to sanctuary the refugees who, clothed in ash and ghostly powder, hobbled across
    Brooklyn Bridge toward your old haunts,
you who know so well the underbelly of this city and the pulse of her people.

Come back to smoking Manahatta,° Father Walt, where you walked the streets
20   with immigrants from many lands and rode the omnibus and listened to Italian opera
and American folk songs and applauded the singer and ferried back to Brooklyn,
convince us the lilac will blossom° again and release its fragrance into the air,
help us believe the mockingbird will trill and caper and the hermit thrush sing
and children will smile, shout and play in these streets and parks again.

25   Come back, implore the wounded moon to pour her mysterious ministrations on us,
petition the splendid silent sun to come out and shine long while wounds heal,
teach us a language that rises into prayer as we lift one another, **C**
help us not to fear our grief as we remember the thousands lost,
look over us as we read the poem-prayers that inform our resolve
30   to become larger than before, open-hearted, strong, wise, patient,
keep waiting for us in the grass that grows beneath our boot-soles. **D**

---

19. Manahatta: The Lenni Lenape people's name for what is now Manhattan Island.
22. lilac will blossom: an allusion to Whitman's "When Lilacs Last in the Dooryard Bloom'd."

C **Literary Focus** **Apostrophe** How does the figure of Whitman change at the end of the poem?

D **Reading Focus** **Understanding Allusions** This line alludes to a poem from Whitman's *Leaves of Grass*.
See page 526, lines 9 and 10. Why might Krapf have included this allusion?

Applying Your Skills

SKILLS FOCUS Literary Skills Analyze apostrophe; analyze theme. **Reading Skills** Analyze allusions. **Writing Skills** Write poetry.

Prayer *from* **Three Paumanok Pieces**

Respond and Think Critically

Reading Focus

Quick Check

1. What details in this poem reveal the setting?

2. For what is the speaker praying?

Read with a Purpose

3. Why might it comfort the poem's speaker to view the events of September 11, 2001, against the backdrop of Whitman's life and art?

Reading Skills: Understanding Allusions

4. While you were reading, you recorded examples of allusions from the poem. Now that you have finished reading, add another column to your chart explaining how each allusion affects the poem.

Allusions to . . .	Example (line #)	Effect
Whitman's poetry	The long lines reflect Whitman's style (all lines).	This allows the poet to speak with Whitman's voice.
Whitman's war experiences	"body of a brother" (line 7)	
Whitman's time in New York City		

Literary Focus

Literary Analysis

5. **Analyze** How does the repetition of the phrase, "Come back, Walt Whitman," affect the tone of the poem? How does this repetition connect to the idea of prayer evoked by the title?

6. **Interpret** How do you interpret the image of "your word-ferry" in line 15? What does it mean in the context of the poem?

7. **Interpret** In the last two stanzas, there is a great deal of nature imagery: the lilac, the hermit thrush, the mockingbird, the moon, the sun, and the grass. In what way is this imagery significant? What role does nature play in the poem?

8. **Extend** Many of the poems you have read deal with things that happened before you were born. How is it different to read a poem about an event that happened during your life?

Literary Skills: Apostrophe

9. **Infer** What kind of person is Krapf's Walt Whitman? In a short paragraph, describe what Whitman is like. Then, comment on why he is an appropriate figure to turn to for comfort in this time of need.

Literary Skills Review: Theme

10. **Interpret** What is the **theme,** or message about life, of "Prayer"? Which specific details help you identify the theme?

Writing Focus

Think as a Reader/Writer

Use It in Your Writing Think about an event or experience that affected you greatly. Write a poem that describes how you and three or four people from your circle of friends and family were changed by the event.

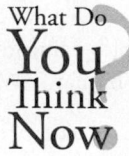

What Do You Think Now

What do you think motivated Krapf to write about these events?

Themes Across Cultures

Metamorphosis, a moment of powerful transformation, is a theme found in literature throughout the world. Transformation can take place inwardly or outwardly and can range from a shift in appearance or behavior to a dramatic change in a character's point of view. Such changes often occur in reaction to external forces or triggers—a piece of tragic news or the revelation of a painful hidden truth. As you read, examine how five writers approach this theme across different genres and from different cultural perspectives.

CONTENTS

Preparing to Read

Elsewhere
(For Stephen Spender)

What Do You Think?

What human needs and desires do we have in common?

QuickWrite

How would you define freedom? What are its most important components? Write a brief paragraph in which you explain your definition.

Derek Walcott
(1930–   )

Nobel Prize WINNER

When he was eighteen, Derek Walcott borrowed two hundred dollars to print his first book of poems, then stood on the street corners of Saint Lucia, in the West Indies, to sell it. Decades later, having forged a unique style blending English and Caribbean elements, he won the 1992 Nobel Prize in literature. It has been a remarkable journey for a remarkable man.

A Wealth of Sources

Walcott was born and raised in the former British colony of Saint Lucia. His parents were educators, but the island was his greatest teacher. The land and the sea provided him with endless imagery. He absorbed the music, art, and languages of the mix of African, French, and English cultures around him. Walcott went to the University of the West Indies, in Jamaica, and then moved to Trinidad, where he still lives. A frequent visitor to the United States, he teaches writing at Boston University.

Walcott's poems, gathered in collections such as *Sea Grapes* (1976) and *Midsummer* (1984), convey passionate intensity in language that is both intimate and formal, lyrical and political. Classical mythology, historical allusions, and complex extended metaphors move naturally through his lines, which resonate with the vocal rhythms, diction, and dialects of the speech of the islands. One of his most remarkable books, *Omeros* (1990), uses Homer's *Iliad* and *Odyssey* as the basis for a West Indian story, fusing themes of wandering and exile, culture and history, identity and justice.

A Multifaceted Talent

Honored as a poet, Walcott has also built a career as a dramatist and founded the Trinidad Theatre Workshop. He is a gifted painter as well. His book-length poem *Tiepolo's Hound* (2000) is illustrated with dozens of his vibrant watercolors.

"Elsewhere" makes a powerful appeal. It insists that oppression and censorship affect us all, no matter where they take place.

Think About the Writer

Walcott grew up in a former British colony. How do you think this affected his ideas about freedom?

Reader/Writer Notebook

Use your **RWN** to complete the activities for this selection.

Literary Focus

Repetition The repeated use of the same sound, image, or idea to enhance a poem's meaning and overall effect is called **repetition**. In a poem, repetition is more than a sound effect. Poets also use repetition to convey meaning, emphasize ideas, clarify images, build rhythms, create moods, and evoke emotional responses. When you read a poem aloud, listen for repetition. What is the writer trying to achieve by repeating certain components of the poem such as sounds, words, images, and ideas?

Reading Focus

Analyzing Themes Across Cultures Walcott often writes of political crimes and social injustice. The themes of the right to freedom, the fight for justice, and the need to safeguard human rights are not unique to the West Indies where Walcott was born and raised. They are shared by societies and cultures around the world. As you read, note how Walcott draws on these themes to evoke recognizable, familiar emotions.

Into Action Using a chart like the one below, record at least three specific details from the poem, and describe the emotions that each detail evokes.

Detail from poem	Emotions
"Somewhere there was a small harvest / of bodies in the truck." (lines 10–11)	Horror, compassion

Writing Focus

Think as a Reader/Writer

Find It in Your Reading Walcott uses similes in this poem to intensify the statements. A **simile** is a comparison that includes the words *like* or *as*. While reading, notice where the similes occur and what comparisons are being made, and record them in your *Reader/Writer Notebook*.

Vocabulary

shawled (shawld) *adj.*: wearing or covered with a shawl. *The beach was deserted, except for a shawled woman.*

harvest (HAHR vihst) *n.*: a gathering in of crops or objects. *The bodies made a gruesome harvest.*

camouflage (KAM uh flahzh) *n.*: a disguise or false appearance adopted in order to conceal. *The landscape looked beautiful, but it was camouflage that concealed terrible events.*

summary (SUHM uh ree) *adj.*: carried out quickly and without proper formalities. *A summary hit to the skull could be fatal.*

Language Coach

Multiple-Meaning Words When you read a word with more than one meaning, first identify how the word is used. Is it used as a noun, verb, adjective, or adverb? The answer will help you decide which meaning the writer is using. The word *summary* has more than one meaning. As an adjective, *summary* can mean "carried out quickly." As a noun, *summary* means "a brief statement that gives the main points." How does the meaning of the noun *harvest* differ from the meaning of the verb *harvest*?

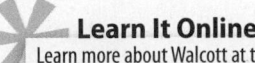 **Learn It Online**
Learn more about Walcott at the Writers' Lives site online.

go.hrw.com   L11-1391   Go

ELSEWHERE

by **Derek Walcott**

(For Stephen Spender)

Read with a Purpose
Read to learn about the global impact of social and political oppression.

Build Background
Derek Walcott's *The Arkansas Testament* (1987) is divided into two sections: "Here" and "Elsewhere." In the first section the poems focus on Saint Lucia—its landscape, language, and culture. In the second section (in which the poem "Elsewhere" appears), Wolcott expands his scope as he moves beyond his concern about Caribbean colonialism to the effects of political and cultural oppression worldwide.

"Elsewhere" is dedicated to Sir Stephen Spender (1909–1995), a British writer noted for his poems of social protest and his eloquent sympathy for victims of war and oppression, especially during the Spanish Civil War and World War II. For Walcott, Spender was a model of how to combine poetry and activism.

Somewhere a white horse gallops with its mane
plunging round a field whose sticks
are ringed with barbed wire, and men
break stones or bind straw into ricks.°

5   Somewhere women tire of the shawled sea's
weeping, for the fishermen's dories°
still go out. It is blue as peace.
Somewhere they're tired of torture stories.

That somewhere there was an arrest.
10 Somewhere there was a small harvest
of bodies in the truck. Soldiers rest
somewhere by a road, or smoke in a forest.

Somewhere there is the conference rage
at an outrage. Somewhere a page
15 is torn out, and somehow the foliage
no longer looks like leaves but camouflage.

4. ricks: stacks of hay.

6. dories: rowboats.

Vocabulary   shawled (shawld) *adj.*: wearing or covered with a shawl.
harvest (HAHR vihst) *n.*: a gathering in of crops or objects.
camouflage (KAM uh flahzh) *n.*: a disguise or false appearance in order to conceal.

Somewhere there is a comrade,  **Ⓐ**
a writer lying with his eyes wide open
on a mattress ticking,° who will not read
20   this, or write. How to make a pen?

And here we are free for a while, but
elsewhere, in one-third, or one-seventh
of this planet, a summary rifle butt
breaks a skull into the idea of a heaven **Ⓑ**

25   where nothing is free, where blue air
is paper-frail, and whatever we write
will be stamped twice, a blue letter, **Ⓒ**
its throat slit by the paper knife° of the state.

Through these black bars
30   hollowed faces stare. Fingers
grip the cross bars of these stanzas
and it is here, because somewhere else

their stares fog into oblivion
thinly, like the faceless numbers
35   that bewilder you in your telephone
diary. Like last year's massacres.

The world is blameless. The darker crime
is to make a career of conscience,
to feel through our own nerves the silent scream
40   of winter branches, wonders read as signs.

19. ticking: strong fabric, usually striped, used for mattress covers.

28. paper knife: a knife with a blade of metal, wood, ivory, plastic, or other material, used to cut open letters and the pages of books.

Ⓐ **Literary Focus** Repetition Why does Walcott repeat the word *somewhere* in the first five stanzas? What effect does this have on the poem?

Ⓑ **Reading Focus** Analyzing Themes Across Cultures In line 21, Walcott uses the first-person plural *we*. To whom does *we* refer? Why does Walcott include it at this point in the poem?

Ⓒ **Literary Focus** Repetition What is the significance of the color blue, and why is it repeated throughout the poem?

Vocabulary summary (SUHM uh ee) *adj.:* carried out quickly and without proper formalities.

Analyzing Visuals

Viewing and Interpreting Why is it significant that this woman's mouth is bound? How does this image remind you of themes in Walcott's poem?

Political Prisoner (1976) by Rupert Garcia.

Respond and Think Critically

Reading Focus

Quick Check

1. Walcott presents a series of images of oppression. Identify at least three of these images.

2. The poem changes dramatically at line 21. What image of violence occurs in this stanza?

3. What are the "cross bars" in the eighth and ninth stanzas?

4. What is the shocking simile in lines 34–36?

Read with a Purpose

5. What is Walcott saying about social and political injustice and the suffering it causes?

Reading Skills: Analyzing Themes Across Cultures

6. In your chart, you described the emotions that the details in Walcott's poem evoke. Add a third column in which you note what social change Walcott advocates in response to those emotions.

Detail from poem	Emotion	Social change
"Somewhere there was a small harvest/ of bodies in the truck."	Horror, compassion	Stop massacring people.

Literary Focus

Literary Analysis

7. **Infer** Who are the "hollowed faces" who "stare" through the "black bars"? What response does Walcott suggest "we" have to them?

8. **Analyze** In line 20, Walcott asks, "...How to make a pen?" What does he mean by this? Who needs the pen and for what purpose?

9. **Interpret** Why is Walcott's poem called "Elsewhere"? Explain.

10. **Hypothesize** In the final stanza, what does it mean that "the darker crime/ is to make a career of conscience"? How should a sympathetic person respond to the world's suffering?

Literary Skills: Repetition

11. **Analyze** What words does Walcott keep repeating? What emotional effect does this repetition have?

Literary Skills Review: Literary Criticism

12. **Draw Conclusions** In his book on Derek Walcott, literary critic John Thieme says that "Elsewhere" is "less concerned with attacking political injustice than exposing the inadequacy of armchair liberalism." Why might Thieme come to this conclusion? Do you agree? Explain why or why not, using specific references to the poem to support your response.

Writing Focus

Think as a Reader/Writer

Use It in Your Writing Write a poem in which you describe how one person acts compassionately to ease the suffering of another. Include three similes in your poem to describe this compassion in action.

 What Do **You Think Now** How can shared needs and desires bring people together and encourage them to care about one another?

SKILLS FOCUS **Literary Skills** Analyze repetition; analyze text using approaches to literary criticism. **Reading Skills** Analyze themes across cultures. **Vocabulary Skills**

Understand figurative language; demonstrate knowledge of literal meanings of words and their usage. **Writing Skills** Identify and analyze literary elements.

Vocabulary Development

✓ Vocabulary Check

Match each Vocabulary word with its definition.

1. harvest
2. shawled
3. summary
4. camouflage

a. disguise
b. with covered shoulders
c. reaping or gathering
d. determined rapidly

Vocabulary Skills: Figurative Language

Many poets enhance similes, metaphors, and imagery with multiple-meaning words that guide readers toward a poem's larger meaning. For example, the word *camouflage* is reminiscent of the military because soldiers often wear camouflage to disguise themselves. The simile in line 16 of "Elsewhere" implicitly evokes ideas of war and the military. Fully understanding *camouflage*'s connotations helps readers explore the simile in more depth.

Your Turn

Find the words *shawled, harvest,* and *summary* in the poem. Then, explain how the multiple meanings or connotations of each word contribute to the similes or metaphors in which they appear.

Language Coach

Multiple-Meaning Words Many words have more than one meaning. Identifying a word's part of speech can help you decide which meaning is used in a sentence. Read each definition for the following word and explain which meaning is used in each sentence.

summary *n.*: a brief statement that gives main points; *adj.*: carried out rapidly

1. She made a summary review of her notes.
2. After reading the poem, she wrote a brief summary to help her recall the key events.

CHOICES

As you respond to the Choices, use these **Academic Vocabulary** words as appropriate: component, diverse, intrinsic, potential, transmit.

REVIEW
Analyze Figurative Language

Timed └ Writing Review "Elsewhere" and identify five examples of figurative language from the poem. Then, write an essay in which you analyze the role that each example of figurative language plays in the poem. What does the use of figurative language add to the poem that literal language cannot?

CONNECT
Discuss Ideas of Freedom

Partner Work One topic that Walcott addresses in "Elsewhere" is the concept of freedom. With a partner, discuss how freedom is explored and represented in the poem. Then, compare the representations of freedom in "Elsewhere" with your own thoughts about freedom. What does freedom mean to you? How do your ideas of freedom compare to Walcott's?

EXTEND
Address a Social Issue

In "Elsewhere," Walcott transmits his thoughts about social issues. Follow Walcott's model by writing a poem about a social issue that affects you strongly, such as an event in your community or an issue with global implications. If necessary, research your topic to strengthen your background knowledge before writing.

Preparing to Read

Medusa

What Do You Think

What human needs and desires do we have in common?

QuickTalk

With a partner, discuss whether people or characters that we label as monsters—be they from famous works of literature or real life—have familiar human needs and desires. Might these monsters have something in common with us? What can we learn about ourselves from them?

Agha Shahid Ali
(1949–2001)

The poems of Agha Shahid Ali embrace multiple heritages and cross literary traditions. They sound simultaneously ancient and modern, Eastern and Western.

A Multilingual Background

Agha Shahid Ali was born in New Delhi, India, and educated at an Irish Catholic school in the Kashmir region. Ali grew up in a culturally diverse home where his family recited poetry in Persian, Urdu, Hindi, and English. He called Urdu, a language of Pakistan and India, his "mother tongue," but said English was his first language: "When I wrote my first poems, at the age of ten, they were in English. I did not 'choose' to write them in English; it just happened that way."

Kashmir to America

After graduating from the University of Kashmir and earning a master's degree in English literature from Delhi University, Ali began lecturing and published his first poetry collection. He then earned a Ph.D. at Pennsylvania State University and studied and taught at colleges in Arizona, Utah, and Massachusetts.

A prolific writer, Ali published eight more collections of verse over the next quarter century, some bearing whimsical titles such as *A Nostalgist's Map of America* and *A Walk Through the Yellow Pages*. His poems often blend history, myth, popular culture, and personal memory into dreamlike scenes. His poems bridge cultures and centuries, and like all nostalgists, he finds the past very much alive in the present.

One of his last poetry collections, *Rooms Are Never Finished* (2001), was a National Book Award finalist. A reviewer wrote that if the collection "is the work of a hyphenated American, it's of a new kind: an exile more than an immigrant, for whom English is not particularly British or American but the international language, and whose imagination is supple and cultivated enough to draw on different cultures simultaneously." As Ali noted, "The point is you are a universe....There is the Muslim in me, there is the Hindi in me, there is the Western in me."

Think About the Writer

How might Ali's diverse upbringing have influenced his views about identity?

 **Reader/Writer**
Notebook
Use your **RWN** to complete the activities for this selection.

Literary Focus

Archetypes **Archetypes** are repeated patterns that help us tell ourselves the stories of our own lives. In our reading, we have all encountered archetypal characters (like the superhero), archetypal plots (like the perilous journey or the Cinderella story), archetypal places (like the monster's cave), and archetypal images (like snakes).

Many archetypes appear in myths. Metamorphosis—a change in shape or form—is also an archetype. You might recall Greek myths in which people metamorphose into animals, flowers, rivers, and constellations. Today special effects in film can morph anybody into anything. As long as caterpillars continue to transform into butterflies and tadpoles into frogs, we will probably continue to find metamorphosis a powerful archetype in storytelling.

Reading Focus

Analyzing Themes Across Cultures Greek myths continue to be a source of inspiration to writers because they deal with themes and concepts that people from a variety of cultures can potentially relate to and understand, such as loneliness, longing, joy, and affection. In this poem, the writer finds a new meaning in the myth of Medusa.

Into Action Use a chart like the one below to record details from the poem and explain what cross-cultural themes they address.

Detail from poem	Cross-cultural themes
"I too was human, I who now live here / at the end of the world / with two aging sisters, spinsters"	alienation, isolation, loneliness

Writing Focus

Think as a Reader/Writer

Find It in Your Reading Much of "Medusa" is an **interior monologue,** or an extended passage expressing a character's thoughts. As you read, ask yourself what Medusa's words tell us about her personality. Record a few examples from her internal monologue in your *Reader/Writer Notebook.*

Learn It Online
Learn more about Ali and his work with these Internet links.

go.hrw.com   L11-1397   Go

MEDUSA

by Agha Shahid Ali

Read with a Purpose
Gain a new perspective on a famous mythological monster by reading her story in her own words.

Build Background
According to Greek myth, Medusa was a monster who turned anyone who looked at her snake-covered head to stone. Perseus defeated her while she slept. By not looking directly at Medusa, but only at her reflection in his metal shield, he was able to cut off her head.

"I must be beautiful.
Or why would men be speechless
at my sight? I have populated the countryside
with animals of stone
5   and put nations painlessly to sleep.

I too was human, I who now live here
at the end of the world
with two aging sisters, spinsters
massaging poisons into our scalps
10   and sunning our ruffled snakes,

and dreading the night, when
under the warm stars
we recall men we have loved,
their gestures now forever refusing us. **Ⓐ**

15   Then why let anything remain
when whatever we loved
turned instantly to stone?
I am waiting for the Mediterranean
to see me: It will petrify.
20   And as caravans from Africa begin to cross it,
I will freeze their cargo of slaves. **Ⓑ**

Soon, soon, the sky will have eyes:
I will fossilize its dome into cracked blue,
I who am about to come
25   into God's full view
from the wrong side of the mirror
into which He gazes."

And so she dreams
till the sun-crimsoned shield
30   blinds her into nightmare:
her locks, falling from their roots,
crawl into rocks to die.
Perseus holds the sword above her neck.
Restless in her sleep, she,
35   for the last time, brushes back
the hissing curls from her forehead. **Ⓒ**

Ⓐ Literary Focus Archetypes Which archetype does Medusa represent? How does she challenge this definition of herself?

Ⓑ Reading Focus Analyzing Themes Across Cultures How does the poem treat the themes of social rejection, longing, and revenge?

Ⓒ Literary Focus Archetypes Does Perseus fit the archetype of the hero in this poem? Why or why not?

SKILLS FOCUS **Literary Skills** Analyze archetypes; analyze irony. **Reading Skills** Analyze themes across cultures. **Writing Skills** Employ elements of an author's style effectively.

Respond and Think Critically

Reading Focus

Quick Check

1. Why does Medusa think she is beautiful?

2. What do Medusa and her sisters do at night?

3. What scheme does Medusa have for the Mediterranean Sea and for caravans crossing it?

4. In the final stanza, what is about to happen?

Read with a Purpose

5. How does having Medusa tell her own story affect your view of her and her battle with Perseus?

Reading Skills: Analyzing Themes Across Cultures

6. As you read, you kept a chart to record cross-cultural themes in "Medusa." Review the themes you identified. Choose one of the themes and write a brief paragraph about how it affects your view of Medusa for better or worse.

Detail from poem	Cross-cultural themes
"I too was human, I who now live here / at the end of the world / with two aging sisters, spinsters"	alienation, isolation, loneliness

Literary Focus

Literary Analysis

7. **Analyze** Living things dread Medusa, but what does Medusa dread? Why?

8. **Interpret** What motive for revenge is suggested by lines 15–17? Explain your answer.

9. **Infer** Medusa is both a victim of metamorphosis and one of its greatest agents. How does Medusa feel about her own metamorphosis? How does she hope to use metamorphosis in order to obtain revenge?

Literary Skills: Archetypes

10. **Extend** Many people see Medusa as an archetypal villain or monster. Based on what you learned from the poem, do you agree with this classification of Medusa or not? Support your response with evidence from the text.

Literary Skills Review: Irony

11. **Analyze** Irony is a discrepancy between appearances and reality. **Situational irony** takes place when there is a discrepancy between what is expected to happen and what really does happen. In lines 24–27, Medusa imagines that God is gazing into a mirror. In light of what happens to Medusa next, why are these lines ironic?

Writing Focus

Think as a Reader/Writer

Use It in Your Writing Invent a character who, like Medusa, is a human with supernatural powers who has been rejected by society. Write a short passage about him or her, using the technique of **interior monologue** to reveal the character's thoughts, feelings, and attitudes.

What Do You Think Now

What needs and desires do most people have in common with Medusa?

Preparing to Read

When Mr. Pirzada Came to Dine

What Do  **You Think**

What human needs and desires do we have in common?

🕐 **QuickTalk**

Have you or any of your classmates ever had to move from one neighborhood to another? From one part of the country to another? From one country to another? In a small group, discuss what making a transition to an unfamiliar place is like.

Jhumpa Lahiri
(1967–)

Pulitzer Prize WINNER

Most young writers can only dream of the success that Jhumpa Lahiri has found. Propelled by a stint at the Provincetown Fine Arts Work Center in Provincetown, Massachusetts, her career took off. "It was something of a miracle. In seven months I got an agent, sold a book, and had a story published in *The New Yorker*. I've been extremely lucky." Behind that luck lies a great deal of searching, uncertainty, and writing, writing, writing.

Indian or American?

Born in London to parents who had emigrated from Calcutta, India, Lahiri grew up in Rhode Island. Her experience as an Indian American has been essential in forging her identity as a writer. "One of the things I was always aware of growing up was conflicting expectations. I was expected to be Indian by Indians and American by Americans."

Lahiri graduated from Barnard College, in New York City, with a degree in English literature and has since earned a doctorate in Renaissance studies. However, scholarship has never replaced writing as her life's ambition.

Interpreting Maladies

Lahiri's first collection of stories, *Interpreter of Maladies,* won the Pulitzer Prize in fiction in 2000, a rare honor for a first book. The title, she explains, grew out of an encounter with a man who worked as a translator for a doctor whose patients did not speak English. The man's occupation intrigued her, and she came to see his role as a metaphor for her own life as a writer. "I think it best expresses the predicament at the heart of the book: the dilemma, the difficulty, and often the impossibility of communicating emotional pain to others, as well as expressing it to ourselves. In some senses I view my position as a writer, insofar as I attempt to articulate these emotions, as an interpreter as well." "When Mr. Pirzada Came to Dine" depicts characters dealing with the "maladies," the difficulties and limits of commitment, compassion, and communication.

Think About the Writer How might Lahiri's Indian American identity be connected to the way in which she sees her role as a writer?

 **Reader/Writer**
Notebook
Use your **RWN** to complete the activities for this selection.

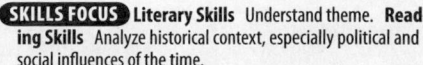

Literary Focus

Theme A **theme** is an insight about human life that is revealed in a literary work. Themes are rarely stated directly. Most often, a reader has to infer the theme of a work after considerable thought.

To uncover the theme of a story, it is better to ask, "What does this story reveal to me?" than to ask, "What does this story teach?" Most fiction writers do not want to moralize; rather, they want readers to recognize truths about human existence. The ability to identify a complex and subtle theme is an indication of a reader's deeper understanding of a story.

Literary Perspectives Apply the literary perspective described on page 1403 as you read this story.

Reading Focus

Analyzing Historical Context Major political or economic shifts, social mores or customs, and prevailing religious beliefs are all components authors use to portray people, places, and conflicts in their historical contexts. Consider how "When Mr. Pirzada Came to Dine" may have been shaped by the historical context in which it is set.

Into Action As you read, create a Venn diagram like the one below. Label the left circle "East Pakistan" and the right circle "United States." List details from the story that provide clues to the historical context in East Pakistan in the left circle and to the historical context in the U.S. in the right circle. Include details they have in common where the two circles overlap.

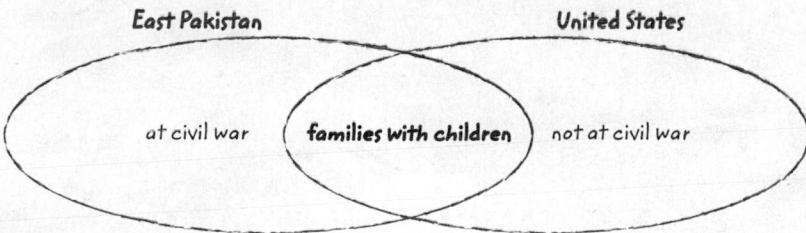

East Pakistan

United States

at civil war · **families with children** · not at civil war

Writing Focus

Think as a Reader/Writer

Find It in Your Reading Lahiri employs a cinematic **style** to tell this story, providing movie-like close-ups of characters and activities. In your *Reader/Writer Notebook*, keep track of details that give a strong visual sense of the characters and what they do.

Vocabulary

ascertaining (as uhr TAYN ihng) *v.*: finding out with certainty. *Mr. Pirzada was ascertaining his family's safety when he visited.*

autonomy (aw TAHN uh mee) *n.*: independence; self-government. *India gained autonomy from Great Britain in 1947.*

austere (aw STIHR) *adj.*: very plain. *Worried for Mr. Pirzada, the family ate an austere diet.*

impeccably (ihm PEHK uh blee) *adj.*: perfectly; without error or defect. *He was impeccably dressed in a suit and silk tie.*

imperceptible (ihm puhr SEHP tuh buhl) *adj.*: so slight as not to be noticed. *His bow was nearly imperceptible.*

rotund (roh TUHND) *adj.*: round; plump. *He loved to eat, so he had a rotund figure.*

deplored (dih PLAWRD) *v.*: condemned as wrong; disapproved of. *Lilia's father deplored the brutal treatment of the refugees.*

reiteration (ree iht uh RAY shuhn) *n.*: repetition. *Each cruel act committed in the war seemed a reiteration of the last.*

Language Coach

Word Origins Words often take on new meanings over time. The word *austere* comes from a Greek word that means "harsh" or "bitter." In English, the word gradually changed its meaning. First it meant "severe self-discipline." By the nineteenth century, it also came to mean "very plain."

 Learn It Online
Explore the Vocabulary words with Word Watch online.

| go.hrw.com | L11-1401 | Go |

WHEN MR. PIRZADA CAME TO DINE

by **Jhumpa Lahiri**

Read with a Purpose

Read to find out what it means to develop compassion for other people.

Build Background

After ruling India for nearly two hundred years, in 1947 the British agreed to a transfer of power. Because the Muslim minority demanded a separate state, the British partitioned the Indian subcontinent into predominantly Hindu India and predominantly Muslim Pakistan. Pakistan itself was divided into two geographically, ethnically, and linguistically separate parts, East and West Pakistan.

By the autumn of 1971, when this story takes place, East Pakistan, led by Sheikh Mujib Rahman, was demanding independence. The government of West Pakistan, directed by Yahyah Kahn, reacted with brutal force, driving ten million refugees into India. As a result, India intervened, quickly forcing the Pakistani army to surrender. In mid-December 1971, Bangladesh, the former East Pakistan, was established as an independent state.

Dacca, East Pakistan (1962).

I N THE AUTUMN of 1971 a man used to come to our house, bearing confections[1] in his pocket and hopes of ascertaining the life or death of his family. His name was Mr. Pirzada, and he came from Dacca, now the capital of Bangladesh, but then a part of Pakistan. That year Pakistan was engaged in civil war. The eastern frontier, where Dacca was located, was fighting for autonomy from the ruling regime in the west. In March, Dacca had been invaded, torched, and shelled by the Pakistani army. Teachers were dragged onto streets and shot, women dragged into barracks and raped. By the end of the summer, three hundred thousand people were said to have died. In Dacca Mr. Pirzada had a three-story home, a lecture-ship in botany at the university, a wife of twenty years, and seven daughters between the ages of six and six-teen whose names all began with the letter *A*. "Their mother's idea," he explained one day, producing from his wallet a black-and-white picture of seven girls at a picnic, their braids tied with ribbons, sitting cross-legged in a row, eating chicken curry off of banana leaves. "How am I to distinguish? Ayesha, Amira, Amina, Aziza, you see the difficulty." **Ⓐ**

Each week Mr. Pirzada wrote letters to his wife, and sent comic books to each of his seven daughters, but the postal system, along with most everything else in Dacca, had collapsed, and he had not heard word of them in over six months. Mr. Pirzada, meanwhile, was in America for the year, for he had been awarded a grant from the government of Pakistan to study the foliage[2] of New England. In spring and summer he had gathered data in Vermont and Maine, and in autumn he moved to a university north of Boston,

where we lived, to write a short book about his dis-coveries. The grant was a great honor, but when con-verted into dollars it was not generous. As a result, Mr. Pirzada lived in a room in a graduate dormitory, and did not own a proper stove or a television set of his own. And so he came to our house to eat dinner and watch the evening news.

At first I knew nothing of the reason for his visits. I was ten years old, and was not surprised that my parents, who were from India, and had a number of Indian acquaintances at the university, should ask Mr. Pirzada to share our meals. It was a small campus, with narrow brick walkways and white pillared buildings, located on the fringes of what seemed to be an even smaller town. The supermarket did not carry mustard oil, doctors did not make house calls, neighbors never dropped by without an invitation, and of these things, every so often, my parents complained. In search of compatriots,[3] they used to trail their fingers, at the

_____
3. **compatriots:** people from the same country.

Literary Perspectives

Analyzing Political Context Analyze the political context of the story by considering the political upheaval in India and Pakistan during the time this story takes place. Pakistan was divided into East Pakistan and West Pakistan, the two sides separated by Indian territory. West Pakistan dominated the divided country politically and economically, even though East Pakistan was more populous. East Pakistan was underrepresented in the government and mili-tary and faced overwhelming oppression and poverty. The ensuing civil war between East and West Pakistan resulted in the decima-tion of the country and drove many people from their homes and into India. The large number of refugees overwhelmed refugee camps, which led to deaths from cholera and malnutrition. How does this political context affect the characters in Lahiri's story?

As you read, be sure to notice the questions in the text, which will guide you in using this perspective.

_____
1. **confections:** candies and other sweet things.
2. **foliage:** leaves, as on a plant or tree.

Ⓐ Literary Focus Theme What does the inclusion of personal and political information in the first paragraph suggest about the story's theme?

Vocabulary **ascertaining** (as uhr TAYN ihng) *v.:* finding out with certainty.
autonomy (aw TAHN uh mee) *n.:* independence; self-government.

Partition of India, 1947

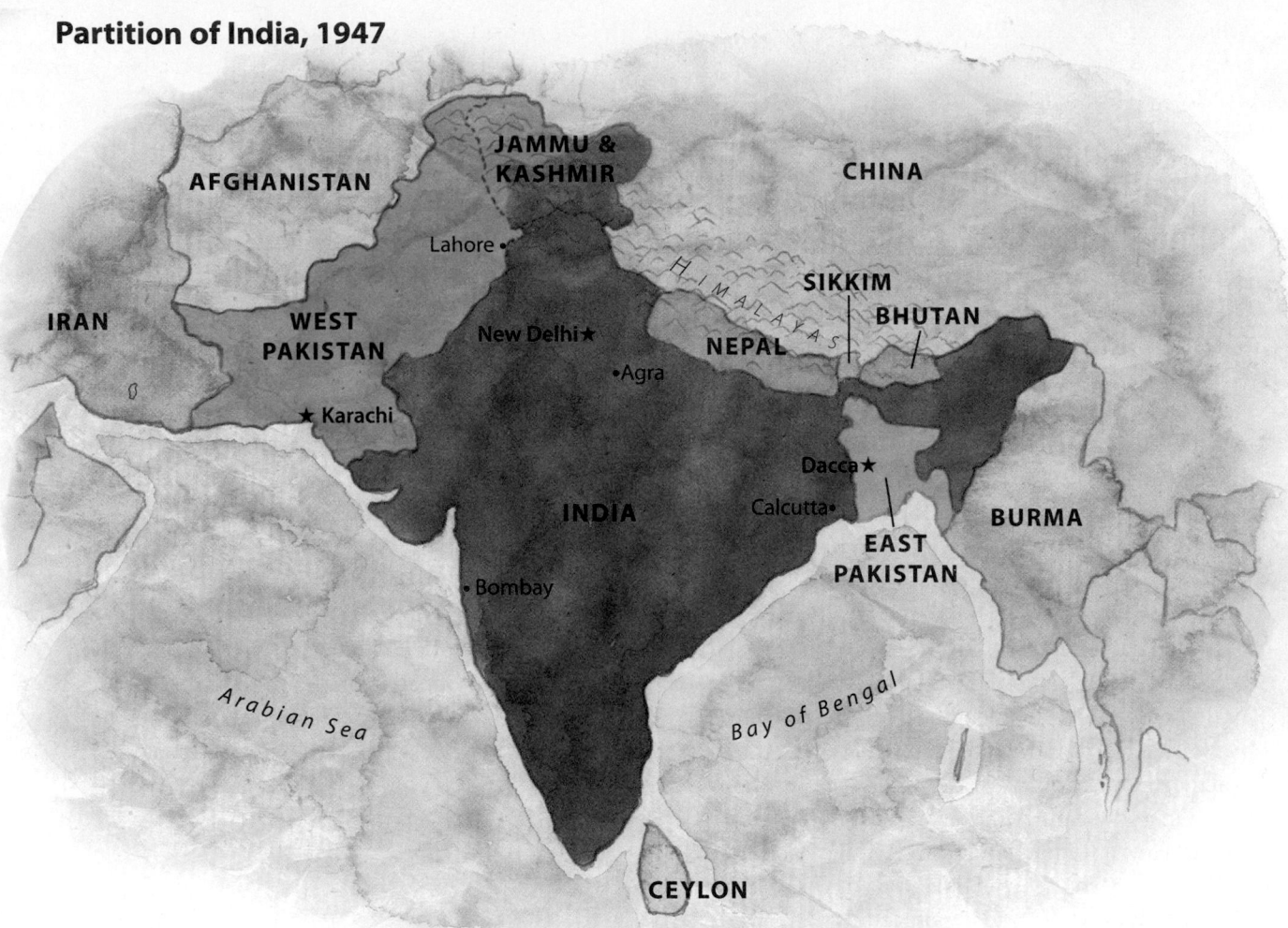

start of each new semester, through the columns of the university directory, circling surnames familiar to their part of the world. It was in this manner that they discovered Mr. Pirzada, and phoned him, and invited him to our home. **B**

I have no memory of his first visit, or of his second or his third, but by the end of September I had grown so accustomed to Mr. Pirzada's presence in our living room that one evening, as I was dropping ice cubes into the water pitcher, I asked my mother to hand me a fourth glass from a cupboard still out of my reach. She was busy at the stove, presiding over a skillet of fried spinach with radishes, and could not hear me because of the drone of the exhaust fan and the fierce scrapes of her spatula. I turned to my father, who was leaning against the refrigerator, eating spiced cashews from a cupped fist.

"What is it, Lilia?"

"A glass for the Indian man."

"Mr. Pirzada won't be coming today. More importantly, Mr. Pirzada is no longer considered Indian," my father announced, brushing salt from the cashews out of his trim black beard. "Not since Partition.[4] Our country was divided. 1947."

When I said I thought that was the date of India's independence from Britain, my father said, "That too. One moment we were free and then we were sliced up," he explained, drawing an X with his finger on the

4. **Partition:** division of the British-ruled Indian subcontinent in 1947, creating the independent dominions of India and Pakistan. Pakistan was further divided into two parts—West Pakistan and East Pakistan.

B **Literary Focus** **Theme** Why do Lilia's parents invite Mr. Pirzada to their home?

countertop, "like a pie. Hindus here, Muslims there. Dacca no longer belongs to us." He told me that during Partition Hindus and Muslims had set fire to each other's homes. For many, the idea of eating in the other's company was still unthinkable. **C**

It made no sense to me. Mr. Pirzada and my parents spoke the same language, laughed at the same jokes, looked more or less the same. They ate pickled mangoes with their meals, ate rice every night for supper with their hands. Like my parents, Mr. Pirzada took off his shoes before entering a room, chewed fennel seeds after meals as a digestive, drank no alcohol, for dessert dipped austere biscuits into successive cups of tea. Nevertheless my father insisted that I understand the difference, and he led me to a map of the world taped to the wall over his desk. He seemed concerned that Mr. Pirzada might take offense if I accidentally referred to him as an Indian, though I could not really imagine Mr. Pirzada being offended by much of anything. "Mr. Pirzada is Bengali, but he is a Muslim," my father informed me. "Therefore he lives in East Pakistan, not India." His finger trailed across the Atlantic, through Europe, the Mediterranean, the Middle East, and finally to the sprawling orange diamond that my mother once told me resembled a woman wearing a sari with her left arm extended. Various cities had been circled with lines drawn between them to indicate my parents' travels, and the place of their birth, Calcutta, was signified by a small silver star. I had been there only once and had no memory of the trip. "As you see, Lilia, it is a different country, a different color," my father said. Pakistan was yellow, not orange. I noticed that there were two distinct parts to it, one much larger than the other, separated by an expanse of Indian territory; it was as if California and Connecticut constituted a nation apart from the U.S. **D** **E**

My father rapped his knuckles on top of my head. "You are, of course, aware of the current situation? Aware of East Pakistan's fight for sovereignty?"[5]

I nodded, unaware of the situation.

We returned to the kitchen, where my mother was draining a pot of boiled rice into a colander. My father opened up the can on the counter and eyed me sharply over the frames of his glasses as he ate some more cashews. "What exactly do they teach you at school? Do you study history? geography?"

"Lilia has plenty to learn at school," my mother said. "We live here now, she was born here." She seemed genuinely proud of the fact, as if it were a reflection of my character. In her estimation, I knew, I was assured a safe life, an easy life, a fine education, every opportunity. I would never have to eat rationed food, or obey curfews, or watch riots from my rooftop, or hide neighbors in water tanks to prevent them from being shot, as she and my father had. "Imagine having to place her in a decent school. Imagine her having to read during power failures by the light of kerosene lamps. Imagine the pressures, the tutors, the constant exams." She ran a hand through her hair, bobbed to a suitable length for her part-time job as a bank teller. "How can you possibly expect her to know about Partition? Put those nuts away."

"But what does she learn about the world?" My father rattled the cashew can in his hand. "What is she learning?" **F**

We learned American history, of course, and American geography. That year, and every year, it seemed, we began by studying the Revolutionary War. We were taken in school buses on field trips to visit Plymouth Rock, and to walk the Freedom Trail, and

5. **sovereignty** (SAHV ruhn tee): independent political authority.

C **Reading Focus** **Analyzing Historical Context** Why does Lilia's father no longer consider Mr. Pirzada to be Indian? Does this change her father's attitude toward him?

D **Reading Focus** **Analyzing Historical Context** Why does Lilia's father insist that she look at the map?

E **Literary Perspectives** **Analyzing Political Context** What does the description of the map reveal about the power structure in East and West Pakistan?

F **Literary Perspectives** **Analyzing Political Context** What difference of opinion do Lilia's parents have about her education?

Vocabulary **austere** (aw STIHR) *adj.:* very plain.

to climb to the top of the Bunker Hill Monument. We made dioramas out of colored construction paper depicting George Washington crossing the choppy waters of the Delaware River, and we made puppets of King George wearing white tights and a black bow in his hair. During tests we were given blank maps of the thirteen colonies, and asked to fill in names, dates, capitals. I could do it with my eyes closed.

The next evening Mr. Pirzada arrived, as usual, at six o'clock. Though they were no longer strangers, upon first greeting each other, he and my father maintained the habit of shaking hands.

"Come in, sir. Lilia, Mr. Pirzada's coat, please."

He stepped into the foyer, impeccably suited and scarved, with a silk tie knotted at his collar. Each evening he appeared in ensembles[6] of plums, olives, and chocolate browns. He was a compact man, and though his feet were perpetually splayed,[7] and his belly slightly wide, he nevertheless maintained an efficient posture, as if balancing in either hand two suitcases of equal weight. His ears were insulated by tufts of graying hair that seemed to block out the unpleasant traffic of life. He had thickly lashed eyes shaded with a trace of camphor,[8] a generous moustache that turned up playfully at the ends, and a mole shaped like a flattened raisin in the very center of his left cheek. On his head he wore a black fez made from the wool of Persian lambs, secured by bobby pins,

> THE NEXT EVENING MR. PIRZADA ARRIVED, AS USUAL, AT SIX O'CLOCK.

without which I was never to see him. Though my father always offered to fetch him in our car, Mr. Pirzada preferred to walk from his dormitory to our neighborhood, a distance of about twenty minutes on foot, studying trees and shrubs on his way, and when he entered our house, his knuckles were pink with the effects of crisp autumn air.

"Another refugee, I am afraid, on Indian territory."

"They are estimating nine million at the last count," my father said.

Mr. Pirzada handed me his coat, for it was my job to hang it on the rack at the bottom of the stairs. It was made of finely checkered gray-and-blue wool, with a striped lining and horn buttons, and carried in its weave the faint smell of limes. There were no recognizable tags inside, only a hand-stitched label with the phrase "Z. Sayeed, Suitors" embroidered on it in cursive with glossy black thread. On certain days a birch or maple leaf was tucked into a pocket. He unlaced his shoes and lined them against the baseboard; a golden paste clung to the toes and heels, the result of walking through our damp, unraked lawn. Relieved of his trappings, he grazed my throat with his short, restless fingers, the way a person feels for solidity behind a wall before driving in a nail. Then he followed my father to the living room, where the television was tuned to the local news. As soon as they were seated, my mother appeared from the kitchen with a plate of mincemeat kebabs with coriander chutney. Mr. Pirzada popped one into his mouth.

"One can only hope," he said, reaching for another, "that Dacca's refugees are as heartily fed. Which reminds me." He reached into his suit pocket and gave me a small plastic egg filled with cinnamon hearts.

---

6. **ensembles:** outfits; costumes.
7. **splayed:** spread out; turned outward.
8. **camphor:** fragrant substance made from the camphor tree. Camphor is often used for medicinal purposes.

Vocabulary   impeccably (ihm PEHK uh blee) *adj.*: perfectly; without error or defect.

"For the lady of the house," he said with an almost imperceptible splay-footed bow.

"Really, Mr. Pirzada," my mother protested. "Night after night. You spoil her."

"I only spoil children who are incapable of spoiling."

It was an awkward moment for me, one which I awaited in part with dread, in part with delight. I was charmed by the presence of Mr. Pirzada's rotund elegance, and flattered by the faint theatricality of his attentions, yet unsettled by the superb ease of his gestures, which made me feel, for an instant, like a stranger in my own home. It had become our ritual, and for several weeks, before we grew more comfortable with one another, it was the only time he spoke to me directly. I had no response, offered no comment, betrayed no visible reaction to the steady stream of honey-filled lozenges, the raspberry truffles, the slender rolls of sour pastilles. I could not even thank him, for once, when I did, for an especially spectacular peppermint lollipop wrapped in a spray of purple cellophane, he had demanded, "What is this thank-you? The lady at the bank thanks me, the cashier at the shop thanks me, the librarian thanks me when I return an overdue book, the overseas operator thanks me as she tries to connect me to Dacca and fails. If I am buried in this country, I will be thanked, no doubt, at my funeral."

It was inappropriate, in my opinion, to consume the candy Mr. Pirzada gave me in a casual manner. I coveted each evening's treasure as I would a jewel, or a coin from a buried kingdom, and I would place it in a small keepsake box made of carved sandalwood beside my bed, in which, long ago in India, my father's mother used to store the ground areca nuts she ate after her morning bath. It was my only memento of a grandmother I had never known, and until Mr. Pirzada came to our lives, I could find nothing to put inside it. Every so often before brushing my teeth and laying out my clothes for school the next day, I opened the lid of the box and ate one of his treats.

That night, like every night, we did not eat at the dining table, because it did not provide an unobstructed view of the television set. Instead we huddled around the coffee table, without conversing, our plates perched on the edges of our knees. From the kitchen my mother brought forth the succession of dishes: lentils with fried onions, green beans with coconut, fish cooked with raisins in a yogurt sauce. I followed with the water glasses, and the plate of lemon wedges, and the chili peppers, purchased on monthly trips to Chinatown and stored by the pound in the freezer, which they liked to snap open and crush into their food.

Before eating, Mr. Pirzada always did a curious thing. He took out a plain silver watch without a band, which he kept in his breast pocket, held it briefly to one of his tufted ears, and wound it with three swift flicks of his thumb and forefinger. Unlike the watch on his wrist, the pocket watch, he had explained to me, was set to the local time in Dacca, eleven hours ahead. For the duration of the meal the watch rested on his folded paper napkin on the coffee table. He never seemed to consult it.

Now that I had learned Mr. Pirzada was not an Indian, I began to study him with extra care, to try to figure out what made him different. I decided that the pocket watch was one of those things. When I saw it that night, as he wound it and arranged it on the coffee table, an uneasiness possessed me; life, I realized, was being lived in Dacca first. I imagined Mr. Pirzada's daughters rising from sleep, tying ribbons in their hair, anticipating breakfast, preparing for school. Our meals, our actions, were only a shadow of what had already happened there, a lagging ghost of where Mr. Pirzada really belonged. **G**

At six-thirty, which was when the national news began, my father raised the volume and adjusted the antennae. Usually I occupied myself with a book, but that night my father insisted that I pay attention. On the screen I saw tanks rolling through dusty streets, and fallen buildings, and forests of unfamiliar trees into which East Pakistani refugees had fled, seeking safety over the Indian border. I saw boats with fan-shaped sails floating on wide coffee-colored rivers, a barricaded university, newspaper offices burned to the ground. I turned to look at Mr. Pirzada; the images

---

Vocabulary **imperceptible** (ihm puhr SEHP tuh buhl) *adj.*: so slight as not to be noticed.
rotund (roh TUHND) *adj.*: round; plump.

G **Literary Focus** **Theme** What does Lilia realize about Mr. Pirzada's dinners with her family?

flashed in miniature across his eyes. As he watched, he had an immovable expression on his face, composed but alert, as if someone were giving him directions to an unknown destination.

During the commercial my mother went to the kitchen to get more rice, and my father and Mr. Pirzada deplored the policies of a general named Yahyah Khan.[9] They discussed intrigues I did not know, a catastrophe I could not comprehend. "See, children your age, what they do to survive," my father said as he served me another piece of fish. But I could no longer eat. I could only steal glances at Mr. Pirzada, sitting beside me in his olive-green jacket, calmly creating a well in his rice to make room for a second helping of lentils. He was not my notion of a man burdened by such grave concerns. I wondered if the reason he was always so smartly dressed was in preparation to endure with dignity whatever news assailed him, perhaps even to attend a funeral at a moment's notice. I wondered, too, what would happen if suddenly his seven daughters were to appear on television, smiling and waving and blowing kisses to Mr. Pirzada from a balcony. I imagined how relieved he would be. But this never happened.

That night when I placed the plastic egg filled with cinnamon hearts in the box beside my bed, I did not feel the ceremonious satisfaction I normally did. I tried not to think about Mr. Pirzada, in his lime-scented overcoat, connected to the unruly, sweltering world we had viewed a few hours ago in our bright, carpeted living room. And yet for several moments that was all I could think about. My stomach tightened as I worried whether his wife and seven daughters were now members of the drifting, clamoring[10] crowd that had flashed at intervals on the screen. In an effort to banish the image, I looked around my room, at the yellow canopied bed with matching flounced curtains, at framed class pictures mounted on white-and-violet papered walls, at the penciled inscriptions by the closet door where my father recorded my height on each of my birthdays. But the more I tried to distract myself, the more I began to convince myself that Mr. Pirzada's family was in all likelihood dead. Eventually I took a square of white chocolate out of the box, and unwrapped it, and then I did something I had never done before. I put the chocolate in my mouth, letting it soften until the last possible moment, and then as I chewed it slowly, I prayed that Mr. Pirzada's family was safe and sound. I had never prayed for anything before, had never been taught or told to, but I decided, given the circumstances, that it was something I should do. That night when I went to the bathroom, I only pretended to brush my teeth, for I feared that I would somehow rinse the prayer out as well. I wet the brush and rearranged the tube of paste to prevent my parents from asking any questions, and fell asleep with sugar on my tongue.

No one at school talked about the war followed so faithfully in my living room. We continued to study the American Revolution, and learned about the injustices of taxation without representation, and memorized passages from the Declaration of Independence. During recess the boys would divide in two groups, chasing each other wildly around the swings and seesaws, Redcoats against the colonies. In the classroom our teacher, Mrs. Kenyon, pointed frequently to a map that emerged like a movie screen from the top of the chalkboard, charting the route of the *Mayflower*, or showing us the location of the Liberty Bell. Each week two members of the class gave a report on a particular aspect of the Revolution, and so one day I was sent to the school library with my friend Dora to learn about the surrender at Yorktown. Mrs. Kenyon handed us a slip of paper with the names of three books to look up in the card catalog. We found them right away, and sat down at a low round table to read and take notes. But I could not concentrate. I returned to the blond-wood shelves, to a section I had noticed labeled "Asia." I saw books about China, India, Indonesia, Korea. Eventually I found a book titled *Pakistan: A Land and Its People*. I sat on a footstool and opened the book. The laminated[11] jacket crackled in my grip. I began

---

9. **Yahyah Khan** (1917–1980): president of Pakistan from 1969 to 1971. Khan used brutal force to try to upset East Pakistan's bid for independence.
10. **clamoring:** noisy; demanding.

Vocabulary **deplored** (dih PLAWRD) *v.:* condemned as wrong; disapproved of.

turning the pages, filled with photos of rivers and rice fields and men in military uniforms. There was a chapter about Dacca, and I began to read about its rainfall, and its jute production. I was studying a population chart when Dora appeared in the aisle.

"What are you doing back here? Mrs. Kenyon's in the library. She came to check up on us."

I slammed the book shut, too loudly. Mrs. Kenyon emerged, the aroma of her perfume filling up the tiny aisle, and lifted the book by the tip of its spine as if it were a hair clinging to my sweater. She glanced at the cover, then at me.

"Is this book a part of your report, Lilia?"

"No, Mrs. Kenyon."

---

11. **laminated:** covered with a thin sheet of plastic.

"Then I see no reason to consult it," she said, replacing it in the slim gap on the shelf. "Do you?" **H**

As weeks passed, it grew more and more rare to see any footage from Dacca on the news. The report came after the first set of commercials, sometimes the second. The press had been censored, removed, restricted, rerouted. Some days, many days, only a death toll was announced, prefaced by a reiteration of the general situation. More poets were executed, more villages set ablaze. In spite of it all, night after night, my parents and Mr. Pirzada enjoyed long, leisurely meals. After the television was shut off, and the dishes washed and dried, they joked, and told stories, and dipped biscuits in their tea. When they tired of discussing political matters, they discussed, instead,

---

Vocabulary **reiteration** (ree iht uh RAY shuhn) *n.:* repetition.

H **Reading Focus** **Analyzing Historical Context** What does the scene with Mrs. Kenyon reveal about Lilia's American education?

the progress of Mr. Pirzada's book about the deciduous trees of New England, and my father's nomination for tenure, and the peculiar eating habits of my mother's American coworkers at the bank. Eventually I was sent upstairs to do my homework, but through the carpet I heard them as they drank more tea, and listened to cassettes of Kishore Kumar,[12] and played Scrabble on the coffee table, laughing and arguing long into the night about the spellings of English words. I wanted to join them, wanted, above all, to console Mr. Pirzada somehow. But apart from eating a piece of candy for the sake of his family and praying for their safety, there was nothing I could do. They played Scrabble until the eleven o'clock news, and then, sometime around midnight, Mr. Pirzada walked back to his dormitory. For this reason I never saw him leave, but each night as I drifted off to sleep, I would hear them, anticipating the birth of a nation on the other side of the world. ⓘ

One day in October Mr. Pirzada asked upon arrival, "What are these large orange vegetables on people's doorsteps? A type of squash?"

"Pumpkins," my mother replied. "Lilia, remind me to pick one up at the supermarket."

"And the purpose? It indicates what?"

"You make a jack-o'-lantern," I said, grinning ferociously. "Like this. To scare people away."

"I see," Mr. Pirzada said, grinning back. "Very useful."

The next day my mother bought a ten-pound pumpkin, fat and round, and placed it on the dining table. Before supper, while my father and Mr. Pirzada were watching the local news, she told me to decorate it with markers, but I wanted to carve it properly like others I had noticed in the neighborhood.

"Yes, let's carve it," Mr. Pirzada agreed, and rose from the sofa. "Hang the news tonight." Asking no questions, he walked into the kitchen, opened a drawer, and returned, bearing a long serrated knife. He glanced at me for approval. "Shall I?"

I nodded. For the first time we all gathered around the dining table, my mother, my father, Mr. Pirzada, and I. While the television aired unattended, we covered the tabletop with newspapers. Mr. Pirzada draped his jacket over the chair behind him, removed a pair of opal cuff links, and rolled up the starched sleeves of his shirt.

"First go around the top, like this," I instructed, demonstrating with my index finger.

He made an initial incision and drew the knife around. When he had come full circle, he lifted the cap by the stem; it loosened effortlessly, and Mr. Pirzada leaned over the pumpkin for a moment to inspect and inhale its contents. My mother gave him a long metal spoon with which he gutted the interior until the last bits of string and seeds were gone. My father, meanwhile, separated the seeds from the pulp and set them out to dry on a cookie sheet, so that we could roast them later on. I drew two triangles against the ridged surface for the eyes, which Mr. Pirzada dutifully carved, and crescents for eyebrows, and another triangle for the nose. The mouth was all that remained, and the teeth posed a challenge. I hesitated.

"Smile or frown?" I asked.

"You choose," Mr. Pirzada said.

As a compromise I drew a kind of grimace, straight across, neither mournful nor friendly. Mr. Pirzada began carving, without the least bit of intimidation,[13] as if he had been carving jack-o'-lanterns his whole life. He had nearly finished when the national news began. The reporter mentioned Dacca, and we all turned to listen: An Indian official announced that unless the world helped to relieve the burden of East Pakistani refugees, India would have to go to war against Pakistan. The reporter's face dripped with sweat as he relayed the information. He did not wear a tie or a jacket, dressed instead as if he himself were about to take part in the battle. He shielded his scorched face as he hollered things to the cameraman. The knife slipped from Mr. Pirzada's hand and made a gash dipping toward the base of the pumpkin.

---

12. **Kishore Kumar:** popular Indian singer.

13. **intimidation:** fear; timidity.

ⓘ **Literary Perspectives** Analyzing Political Context Why do Mr. Pirzada and Lilia's parents have long meals and play Scrabble "in spite of" the news about life in Pakistan in this paragraph?

"Please forgive me." He raised a hand to one side of his face, as if someone had slapped him there. "I am—it is terrible. I will buy another. We will try again."

"Not at all, not at all," my father said. He took the knife from Mr. Pirzada, and carved around the gash, evening it out, dispensing altogether with the teeth I had drawn. What resulted was a disproportionately large hole the size of a lemon, so that our jack-o'-lantern wore an expression of placid astonishment, the eyebrows no longer fierce, floating in frozen surprise above a vacant, geometric gaze.

For Halloween I was a witch. Dora, my trick-or-treating partner, was a witch too. We wore black capes fashioned from dyed pillowcases and conical hats with wide cardboard brims. We shaded our faces green with a broken eye shadow that belonged to Dora's mother, and my mother gave us two burlap sacks that had once contained basmati rice, for collecting candy. That year our parents decided that we were old enough to roam the neighborhood unattended. Our plan was to walk from my house to Dora's, from where I was to call to say I had arrived safely, and then Dora's mother would drive me home. My father equipped us with flashlights, and I had to wear my watch and synchronize it with his. We were to return no later than nine o'clock.

When Mr. Pirzada arrived that evening, he presented me with a box of chocolate-covered mints.

"In here," I told him, and opened up the burlap sack. "Trick or treat!"

"I understand that you don't really need my contribution this evening," he said, depositing the box. He

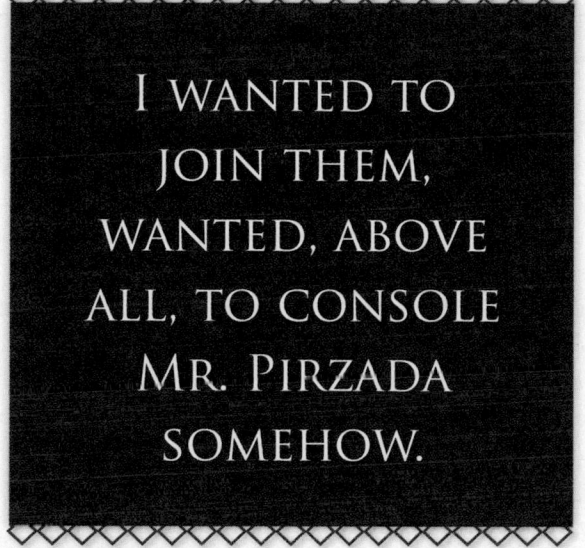

I WANTED TO JOIN THEM, WANTED, ABOVE ALL, TO CONSOLE MR. PIRZADA SOMEHOW.

gazed at my green face, and the hat secured by a string under my chin. Gingerly he lifted the hem of the cape, under which I was wearing a sweater and a zipped fleece jacket. "Will you be warm enough?"

I nodded, causing the hat to tip to one side.

He set it right. "Perhaps it is best to stand still." The bottom of our staircase was lined with baskets of miniature candy, and when Mr. Pirzada removed his shoes, he did not place them there as he normally did, but inside the closet instead. He began to unbutton his coat, and I waited to take it from him, but Dora called me from the bathroom to say that she needed my help drawing a mole on her chin. When we were finally ready, my mother took a picture of us in front of the fireplace, and then I opened the front door to leave. Mr. Pirzada and my father, who had not gone into the living room yet, hovered in the foyer. Outside it was already dark. The air smelled of wet leaves, and our carved jack-o'-lantern flickered impressively against the shrubbery by the door. In the distance came the sounds of scampering feet, and the howls of the older boys who wore no costume at all other than a rubber mask, and the rustling apparel of the youngest children, some so young that they were carried from door to door in the arms of their parents.

"Don't go into any of the houses you don't know," my father warned.

Mr. Pirzada knit his brows together. "Is there any danger?" **J**

"No, no," my mother assured him. "All the children will be out. It's a tradition."

"Perhaps I should accompany them?" Mr. Pirzada suggested. He looked suddenly tired and small, stand-

---

J [Literary Perspectives] **Analyzing Political Context** What is currently happening in Dacca that makes Mr. Pirzada worry about the girls on Halloween?

ing there in his splayed, stockinged feet, and his eyes contained a panic I had never seen before. In spite of the cold I began to sweat inside my pillowcase.

"Really, Mr. Pirzada," my mother said, "Lilia will be perfectly safe with her friend."

"But if it rains? If they lose their way?"

"Don't worry," I said. It was the first time I had uttered those words to Mr. Pirzada, two simple words I had tried but failed to tell him for weeks, had said only in my prayers. It shamed me now that I had said them for my own sake.

He placed one of his stocky fingers on my cheek, then pressed it to the back of his own hand, leaving a faint green smear. "If the lady insists," he conceded, and offered a small bow.

We left, stumbling slightly in our black pointy thrift-store shoes, and when we turned at the end of the driveway to wave good-bye, Mr. Pirzada was standing in the frame of the doorway, a short figure between my parents, waving back.

"Why did that man want to come with us?" Dora asked.

"His daughters are missing." As soon as I said it, I wished I had not. I felt that my saying it made it true, that Mr. Pirzada's daughters really were missing, and that he would never see them again.

"You mean they were kidnapped?" Dora continued. "From a park or something?"

"I didn't mean they were missing. I meant, he misses them. They live in a different country, and he hasn't seen them in a while, that's all." **K**

We went from house to house, walking along pathways and pressing doorbells. Some people had switched off all their lights for effect, or strung rubber bats in their windows. At the McIntyres' a coffin was placed in front of the door, and Mr. McIntyre rose from it in silence, his face covered with chalk, and deposited a fistful of candy corns into our sacks. Several people told me that they had never seen an Indian witch before. Others performed the transaction without comment. As we paved our way with the parallel beams of our flashlights, we saw eggs cracked in the middle of the road, and cars covered with shaving cream, and toilet paper garlanding the branches of trees. By the time we reached Dora's house, our hands were chapped from carrying our bulging burlap bags, and our feet were sore and swollen. Her mother gave us bandages for our blisters and served us warm cider and caramel popcorn. She reminded me to call my parents to tell them I had arrived safely, and when I did, I could hear the television in the background. My mother did not seem particularly relieved to hear from me. When I replaced the phone on the receiver, it occurred to me that the television wasn't on at Dora's house at all. Her father was lying on the couch, reading a magazine, with a glass of wine on the coffee table, and there was saxophone music playing on the stereo. **L**

After Dora and I had sorted through our plunder,[14] and counted and sampled and traded until we were satisfied, her mother drove me back to my house. I thanked her for the ride, and she waited in the driveway until I made it to the door. In the glare of her headlights I saw that our pumpkin had been shattered, its thick shell strewn in chunks across the grass. I felt the sting of tears in my eyes, and a sudden pain in my throat, as if it had been stuffed with the sharp tiny pebbles that crunched with each step under my aching feet. I opened the door, expecting the three of them to be standing in the foyer, waiting to receive me, and to grieve for our ruined pumpkin, but there was no one. In the living room Mr. Pirzada, my father, and mother were sitting side by side on the sofa. The television was turned off, and Mr. Pirzada had his head in his hands.

What they heard that evening, and for many evenings after that, was that India and Pakistan were drawing closer and closer to war. Troops from both sides lined the border, and Dacca was insisting on nothing short of independence. The war was to be waged on East Pakistani soil. The United States was siding with West Pakistan, the Soviet Union with India and what was soon to be Bangladesh. War was declared officially on December 4, and twelve days later, the Pakistani army, weakened by having to fight three thousand miles from their source of supplies,

---

14. **plunder:** loot.

K **Literary Perspectives** Analyzing Political Context Why does Lilia correct what she said to Dora about Mr. Pirzada and his family?

L **Reading Focus** Analyzing Historical Context Lilia notes that the television is not on at Dora's house. What does her observation imply about Dora's family?

surrendered in Dacca. All of these facts I know only now, for they are available to me in any history book, in any library. But then it remained, for the most part, a remote mystery with haphazard clues. What I remember during those twelve days of the war was that my father no longer asked me to watch the news with them, and that Mr. Pirzada stopped bringing me candy, and that my mother refused to serve anything other than boiled eggs with rice for dinner. I remember some nights helping my mother spread a sheet and blankets on the couch so that Mr. Pirzada could sleep there, and high-pitched voices hollering in the middle of the night when my parents called our relatives in Calcutta to learn more details about the situation. Most of all I remember the three of them operating during that time as if they were a single person, sharing a single meal, a single body, a single silence, and a single fear. Ⓜ

In January, Mr. Pirzada flew back to his three-story home in Dacca, to discover what was left of it. We did not see much of him in those final weeks of the year; he was busy finishing his manuscript, and we went to Philadelphia to spend Christmas with friends of my

Ⓜ **Literary Focus** Theme   What does Lilia observe about the interaction of her parents and Mr. Pirzada after war is declared?

parents. Just as I have no memory of his first visit, I have no memory of his last. My father drove him to the airport one afternoon while I was at school. For a long time we did not hear from him. Our evenings went on as usual, with dinners in front of the news. The only difference was that Mr. Pirzada and his extra watch were not there to accompany us. According to reports Dacca was repairing itself slowly, with a newly formed parliamentary government. The new leader, Sheikh Mujib Rahman,[15] recently released from prison, asked countries for building materials to replace more than one million houses that had been destroyed in the war. Countless refugees returned from India, greeted, we learned, by unemployment and the threat of famine. Every now and then I studied the map above my father's desk and pictured Mr. Pirzada on that small patch of yellow, perspiring heavily, I imagined, in one of his suits, searching for his family. Of course, the map was outdated by then.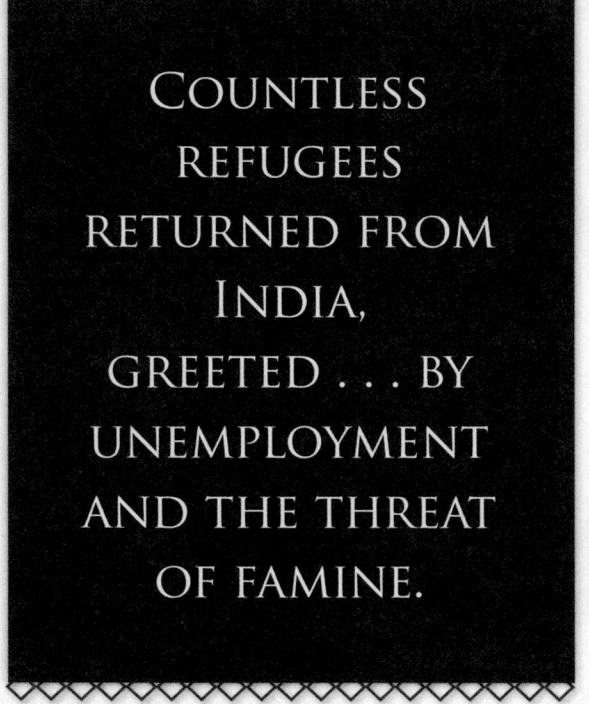

Finally, several months later, we received a card from Mr. Pirzada commemorating the Muslim New Year, along with a short letter. He was reunited, he wrote, with his wife and children. All were well, having survived the events of the past year at an estate belonging to his wife's grandparents in the mountains of Shillong. His seven daughters were a bit taller, he wrote, but otherwise they were the same, and he still could not keep their names in order. At the end of the letter he thanked us for our hospitality, adding that although he now understood the meaning of the words "thank you," they still were not adequate to express his gratitude. To celebrate the good news, my mother prepared a special dinner that evening, and when we sat down to eat at the coffee table, we toasted our water glasses, but I did not feel like celebrating. Though I had not seen him for months, it was only then that I felt Mr. Pirzada's absence. It was only then, raising my water glass in his name, that I knew what it meant to miss someone who was so many miles and hours away, just as he had missed his wife and daughters for so many months. He had no reason to return to us, and my parents predicted, correctly, that we would never see him again. Since January, each night before bed, I had continued to eat, for the sake of Mr. Pirzada's family, a piece of candy I had saved from Halloween. That night there was no need to. Eventually, I threw them away. **O** **P**

> ## COUNTLESS REFUGEES RETURNED FROM INDIA, GREETED . . . BY UNEMPLOYMENT AND THE THREAT OF FAMINE.

---

15. **Sheikh Mujib Rahman** (1920–1975): Bengali leader who demanded independence for East Pakistan. He became the first prime minister of Bangladesh in 1972 and its president in 1975.

N **Reading Focus** **Analyzing Historical Context** How would the map have changed after the war? Why is it "outdated"?

O **Literary Focus** **Theme** Throughout this story, the whereabouts and safety of Mr. Pirzada's family were always in question. Were Mr. Pirzada's worries justified? Why or why not?

P **Literary Focus** **Theme** Why does Lilia "not feel like celebrating"? What does Mr. Pirzada's absence suddenly mean to her?

Applying Your Skills

SKILLS FOCUS Literary Skills Analyze theme; analyze characterization. **Reading Skills** Analyze historical context, especially political and social influences of the time.

When Mr. Pirzada Came to Dine

Respond and Think Critically

Reading Focus

Quick Check

1. Describe the members of Mr. Pirzada's family in East Pakistan/Bangladesh.

2. Why are the adults so interested in television reports about East and West Pakistan?

3. How does Mr. Pirzada try to help the family celebrate Halloween?

4. What becomes of Mr. Pirzada and his family?

Read with a Purpose

5. How does Lilia learn compassion for others?

Reading Skills: Analyzing Historical Context

6. As you read, you recorded details that reflected the differences, as well as the similarities, between the historical contexts of East Pakistan and the United States in the story. Write a few sentences in which you discuss the similiarities between the two that you listed in the overlapping portion of the Venn diagram.

Literary Focus

Literary Analysis

7. **Infer** Why does Lilia's family invite Mr. Pirzada to dinner despite the fact that he is not Indian?

8. **Interpret** Why does Mr. Pirzada set his silver watch to Dacca time rather than U.S. time?

9. **Infer** Why is it so difficult for Lilia to console Mr. Pirzada openly? Why does she feel ashamed when she tells him, "Don't worry"?

10. **Literary Perspectives** What is the significance of Lilia studying the American Revolution in school during the story?

Literary Skills: Theme

11. **Analyze** What, in your own words, is the **theme**, or insight about human life, that the story brings to light?

Literary Skills Review: Characterization

12. **Interpret** Mr. Pirzada brings gifts of candy to Lilia throughout most of the story. What does this reveal about his **character**? What does Lilia's response to the gifts reveal about her personality as the story goes on? Use evidence from the text to support your response.

Writing Focus

Think as a Reader/Writer

Use It in Your Writing If you were a writer with a cinematic style, how might you describe your classroom? Look around for possible movie-like close-ups of people and activities, and record these in sharp detail. Then write a paragraph about this setting, but refrain from making any judgments about it. See how much you can communicate purely through strong visual impression.

What Do **You Think Now**

Why is the urge to be understood by others such a common human desire?

When Mr. Pirzada Came to Dine

Vocabulary Development

✓ Vocabulary Check

Complete each sentence with a Vocabulary word:

ascertaining
autonomy
austere
impeccably
imperceptible
rotund
deplored
reiteration

1. The hippo had a(n) _____ belly.

2. She drew the tree _____; every leaf was in place.

3. I am _____ the tragic fate of the victim.

4. Something you cannot see or hear is _____.

5. Freedom is another term for political _____.

6. The lack of color made the room look _____.

7. Each twin was a perfect _____ of the other.

8. Both sides in the war _____ each other.

Vocabulary Skills: Using Print and Online Reference Sources

Most words have multiple senses in which they can be used. The Vocabulary word *rotund*, for instance, means "round"; however, it can be used to describe both shapes (a rotund, or plump, person) and sounds (a rotund, or full-toned, speech). Can you see how these meanings, though similar, are subtly different? The best way to see all the different senses in which a word may be used is to look it up in the dictionary.

Your Turn _____

Look up each of the following Vocabulary words in a dictionary, either a printed copy or an online version. Write one sentence for each of the word's different meanings. Be sure your sentences are written to differentiate each meaning of a word from the other meanings of that word clearly.

1. austere   3 deplore
2. autonomy   4. imperceptible

Language Coach

Word Origins Learning the origin of a word can help you understand its meaning and its history. Match each Vocabulary word with its origin. Use a dictionary to check your answers.

1. ascertaining   5. impeccably
2. austere   6. imperceptible
3. autonomy   7. reiteration
4. deplored   8. rotund

a. Latin word meaning "round; like a wheel."

b. French words meaning "to" and "certain."

c. Latin words meaning "not" and "to sin."

d. Greek word meaning "harsh; bitter."

e. Latin words meaning "not" and "grasp; take."

f. Greek words meaning "self" and "law."

g. Latin words meaning "repeat" and "again."

h. Latin words meaning "entirely" and "weep."

Academic Vocabulary

Talk About

"When Mr. Pirzada Came to Dine" suggests that people with <u>diverse</u> backgrounds and characteristics can learn to feel compassion for each other. Discuss how people can overcome their differences to do this.

Grammar Link

Varying Sentence Structure

Writing that uses the same kinds of sentences again and again can become predictable and often monotonous. Varying the length and structure of sentences can make your writing more vibrant and interesting. Including too many short, choppy sentences will produce writing that sounds childish and stilted. Including too many long, involved sentences can have the opposite effect, blunting the sentences' impact. Using a mix of simple, compound, complex, and compound-complex sentences in your writing, as in the passage below, can be effective in creating variety and interest and in directing your reader's attention to important points. Notice how the final, short sentence ("But I could no longer eat") makes a stronger impression because the sentences before it vary in length.

> During the commercial my mother went to the kitchen to get more rice, and my father and Mr. Pirzada deplored the policies of a general named Yahyah Khan. They discussed intrigues I did not know, a catastrophe I could not comprehend. "See, children your age, what they do to survive," my father said as he served me another piece of fish. But I could no longer eat.

Your Turn

Writing Application The paragraph below is boring and repetitive because all of its sentences sound the same. Rewrite it, using a variety of sentence structures to make it more powerful. Add or subtract information from the paragraph as necessary.

> Lilia's family lived in New England. Mr. Pirzada lived in their town. They invited him for dinner. He brought Lilia presents. They ate Indian food. They watched TV. The news told about East Pakistan. East Pakistan was very violent. East Pakistan was experiencing a revolution. Mr. Pirzada's family lived there. He worried about them.

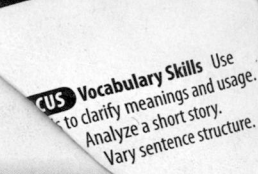

Vocabulary Skills Use ... to clarify meanings and usage. Analyze a short story. Vary sentence structure.

CHOICES

As you respond to the Choices, use these **Academic** words as appropriate: component, diverse, intrinsic, potency, transmit.

REVIEW

Report the War

Imagine that you were a newspaper reporter in East Pakistan during the 1971 revolution. What events might you have witnessed as members of religious and ethnic groups were driven out of their homes, forced to walk hundreds of miles, and cruelly mistreated? Make some notes based on what you read in Lahiri's story. Supplement your notes with research conducted in the library or online. Then, write your own account as if you are reporting directly from the scene.

CONNECT

Explore Symbolism

Timed └**Writing** Write a brief essay describing the jack-o'-lantern from the time when Mr. Pirzada carves it until Lilia returns from trick-or-treating to find it smashed. How does the jack-o'-lantern come to symbolize the characters' diverse emotional states?

EXTEND

Plan a "Welcome to America" Dinner

Plan a dinner for a family who have recently moved in next door from another part of the world. Plan out a menu and discussion points. What should you serve? What should you tell the family about your country? What questions might you ask?

Learn It Online
Learn more about Lahiri and the background behind this story with these Internet links.

go.hrw.com | L11-1417 | Go

What human needs
and desires do we
have in common?

⏱ **QuickWrite**

Think about a time when you or someone you
know discovered that something you thought to
be true was actually false. How did you react to
the discovery? Write about that discovery and
your reaction to it.

Edwidge Danticat
(1969–   )

In Haiti a storyteller asks "*Krik?*" meaning "Are you ready for a
story?" The circle of listeners answers "*Krak!*" meaning "Yes, we're
ready to listen!" In this way, stories begin, take shape, and play
their role in community life. In her own way, Edwidge Danticat,
a Haitian American novelist and short-story writer, keeps that
tradition alive.

Culture Shock

Edwidge Danticat (EHD wehj dahn tih KAH) came to the United
States from Haiti when she was twelve, joining her parents,
who had emigrated years earlier. She remembers the shock:
"It was all so different. I didn't speak the language. . . . I sought
solace in books, read a lot, and kept journals written in fragmented Creole, French, and English."

Danticat went to high school in Brooklyn, New York, earned
a degree in French at Barnard College, and received a master of
fine arts in writing at Brown University. Her first novel, *Breath,
Eyes, Memory* (1994), is the gripping story of a Haitian immigrant girl deeply bonded to the generations of women who
have come before, yet who defines herself as American by the
time she reaches adulthood.

Speaking for Us All

Breath, Eyes, Memory was followed by *Krik? Krak!* (1995), a collection of short stories nominated for the National Book Award.
Poverty, dreams, love, migration, social and emotional barriers,
the delights and disappointments of family life—Danticat's stories reflect firsthand experience, yet her themes are universal.

Danticat's second novel, *The Farming of Bones* (1998), takes
a courageous step back into Haitian history. Set in 1937, this
chronicle of struggle and triumph centers on the massacre of
Haitians by the Dominican Republic dictator Rafael Trujillo. The
grim title refers to the backbreaking work done by Caribbean
sugar-cane workers. In 2007, Danticat published *Brother, I'm
Dying*, a family memoir.

Think About the Writer   How might moving from one culture to another
have inspired Danticat's desire to write? How is
writing a way to negotiate such a change?

Reader/Writer
Notebook

Use your **RWN** to complete the activities for this selection.

Literary Focus

Irony A discrepancy between appearance and reality is called **irony.**
Verbal irony occurs when someone says one thing but (perhaps unwittingly) means something else. **Situational irony** takes place when there is a discrepancy between what is expected to happen, or what would be appropriate to happen, and what actually happens. **Dramatic irony** occurs when the character in a play or story thinks something to be true, but the reader knows better. Keep an eye out for these types of irony as you read "The Book of the Dead."

Reading Focus

Close Reading for Details In some stories, seemingly minor details of plot, setting, and characterization can nevertheless communicate important meanings. Good readers are careful to notice such details, or even to re-read passages that might contain important details.

Into Action As you read, look for significant details that convey a larger meaning or reveal important information about the story's characters, plot, or theme. Record these details in a chart like the one below.

Details from text (p. #)	Meaning
"I do this because it is one more thing I have longed to have in common with my parents." (p. 1421)	The narrator wants a deep connection to her heritage.

Writing Focus

Think as a Reader/Writer
Find It in Your Reading As you read, notice how the author provides readers with vivid, specific details about the characters' physical appearances. Record these details in your *Reader/Writer Notebook,* and consider what each vivid physical description might imply about that character's personality. How might a character's physical appearance be <u>intrinsically</u> connected to his or her inner traits?

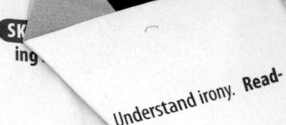
Understand irony. Read-

Language Coach
Remembering Word Meanings
Different strategies will help you remember different words.
1. Some words sound like what they mean. The word *staccato* has an abrupt, harsh sound. What sounds do you hear in *cicadas?*
2. Forming a strong image can help you remember a word. To remember that *chartreuse* is a yellowish green, imagine a school bus painted chartreuse instead of yellow.
3. Write a catchy slogan. What store might use the slogan "Get your *gaudy* goods here"?

Learn It Online
Listen to this story online.

go.hrw.com   L11-1419   **Go**

THE BOOK OF THE DEAD

by **Edwidge Danticat**

Village Scene (20th Century) by Yves Phonard.

Read with a Purpose
Read to discover what the narrator finds out about her father.

Build Background
Haiti, a country in the West Indies, occupies the western portion of the island of Hispaniola, which lies between Cuba and Puerto Rico in the Caribbean Sea. Beautiful, <u>diverse</u>, tropical, mountainous, but very poor, Haiti has a long history of political instability. In the period most relevant to "The Book of the Dead," Haiti was ruled by the oppressive Duvalier regime when the narrator's father was a young man.

My father is gone. I am slouched in a cast-aluminum chair across from two men, one the manager of the hotel where we're staying and the other a policeman. They are waiting for me to explain what has become of him, my father.

The manager—"Mr. Flavio Salinas," the plaque on his office door reads—has the most striking pair of chartreuse eyes I have ever seen on a man with an island-Spanish lilt to his voice.

The officer is a baby-faced, short white Floridian with a pot belly.

"Where are you and your daddy from, Ms. Bienaimé?" he asks.

I answer "Haiti," even though I was born and raised in East Flatbush, Brooklyn, and have never visited my parents' birthplace. I do this because it is one more thing I have longed to have in common with my parents.

The officer plows forward. "You down here in Lakeland from Haiti?"

"We live in New York. We were on our way to Tampa."

I find Manager Salinas's office gaudy. The walls are covered with orange-and-green wallpaper, briefly interrupted by a giant gold-leaf-bordered print of a Victorian cottage that somehow resembles the building we're in. Patting his light-green tie, he whispers reassuringly, "Officer Bo and I will do the best we can to help you find your father."

We start out with a brief description: "Sixty-four, five feet eight inches, two hundred and twenty pounds, moon-faced, with thinning salt-and-pepper hair. Velvet-brown eyes—"

"Velvet-brown?" says Officer Bo.

"Deep brown—same color as his complexion."

My father has had partial frontal dentures for ten years, since he fell off his and my mother's bed when his prison nightmares began. I mention that,

too. Just the dentures, not ___ up the claw-shaped marks th___ down along his cheek to the corn___ I also bring only visible reminder of the year he___ left ear Dimanche, the Port-au-Prince prison in___ uth—the after the Lord's Day. ___rt

"Does your daddy have any kind of mental ill___ amed senility?" asks Officer Bo.

"No."

"Do you have any pictures of your daddy?"

I feel like less of a daughter because I'm not carrying a photograph in my wallet. I had hoped to take some pictures of him on our trip. At one of the rest stops I bought a disposable camera and pointed it at my father. No, no, he had protested, covering his face with both hands like a little boy protecting his cheeks from a slap. He did not want any more pictures taken of him for the rest of his life. He was feeling too ugly.

"That's too bad," says Officer Bo. "Does he speak English, your daddy? He can ask for directions, et cetera?"

"Yes."

"Is there anything that might make your father run away from you—particularly here in Lakeland?" Manager Salinas interjects. "Did you two have a fight?"

I had never tried to tell my father's story in words before now, but my first sculpture of him was the reason for our trip: a two-foot-high mahogany figure of my father, naked, crouching on the floor, his back arched like the curve of a crescent moon, his downcast eyes fixed on his short stubby fingers and the wide palms of his hands. It was hardly revolutionary, minimalist at best, but it was my favorite of all my attempted representations of him. It was the way I had imagined him in prison. **Ⓑ**

The last time I had seen my father? The previous night, before falling asleep. When we pulled into the pebbled

---

Ⓐ **Literary Focus** Irony *Dimanche* is a French word for "Sunday," which is often called "the Lord's Day." Why is this name ironic?

Ⓑ **Reading Focus** **Close Reading** This paragraph stands in place of a straight answer to Manager Salinas's question. What can you infer about the narrator's unspoken answer?

Vocabulary **chartreuse** (shahr TROOZ) *adj.*: a light, yellowish green.
gaudy (GAW dee) *adj.*: too bright and flashy to be in good taste; cheap and showy.

...alm and banana trees, it ...driveway, d... ...e restaurants in the area were ...was almo... ...g to do but shower and go to bed. ...closed. T... ...se here," my father said when ...it had the same orange-and-green ..."It ... ...linas's office, and the plush green carpet ...he sa... ...walls. "Look, Annie," he said, "it is like ...wall... ...er our feet." He was always searching for a ma... ...gr... of paradise, my father.

...He picked the bed closest to the bathroom, ...emoved the top of his gray jogging suit, and unpacked ...is toiletries. Soon after, I heard him humming, as he always did, in the shower.

After he got into bed, I took a bath, pulled my hair back in a ponytail, and checked on the sculpture—just felt it a little bit through the bubble padding and carton wrapping to make sure it wasn't broken. Then I slipped under the covers, closed my eyes, and tried to sleep.

I pictured the client to whom I was delivering the sculpture: Gabrielle Fonteneau, a young woman about my age, an actress on a nationally syndicated television series. My friend Jonas, the principal at the East Flatbush elementary school where I teach drawing to fifth-graders, had shown her a picture of my *Father* sculpture, and, the way Jonas told it, Gabrielle Fonteneau had fallen in love with it and wished to offer it as a gift to her father on his birthday.

Since this was my first big sale, I wanted to make sure that the piece got there safely. Besides, I needed a weekend away, and both my mother and I figured that my father, who watched a lot of television, both in his barbershop and at home, would enjoy meeting Gabrielle, too. But when I woke up the next morning, my father was gone.

I showered, put on my driving jeans and a T-shirt, and waited. I watched a half hour of midmorning local news, smoked three mentholated cigarettes even though we were in a nonsmoking room, and waited some more. By noon, four hours had gone by. And it was only then that I noticed that the car was still there but the sculpture was gone.

I decided to start looking for my father: in the east garden, the west garden, the dining room, the exercise room, and in the few guest rooms cracked open while the maid changed the sheets; in the little convenience store at the Amoco gas station nearby; even in the Salvation Army thrift shop that from a distance seemed to blend into the interstate. All that waiting and looking actually took six hours, and I felt guilty for having held back so long before going to the front desk to ask, "Have you seen my father?"

I feel Officer Bo's fingers gently stroking my wrist. Up close he smells like fried eggs and gasoline, like breakfast at the Amoco. "I'll put the word out with the other boys," he says. "Salinas here will be in his office. Why don't you go back to your room in case he shows up there?"

I return to the room and lie in the unmade bed, jumping up when I hear the click from the electronic key in the door. It's only the housekeeper. I turn down the late-afternoon cleaning and call my mother at the beauty salon where she perms, presses, and braids hair, next door to my father's barbershop. But she isn't there. So I call my parents' house and leave the hotel number on their machine. "Please call me as soon as you can, Manman. It's about Papi."

Once, when I was twelve, I overheard my mother telling a young woman who was about to get married how she and my father had first met on the sidewalk in front of Fort Dimanche the evening that my father was released from jail. (At a dance, my father had fought with a soldier out of uniform who had him arrested and thrown in prison for a year.) That night, my mother was returning home from a sewing class when he stumbled out of the prison gates and collapsed into her arms, his face still bleeding from his last beating. They married and left for New York a year later. "We were like two seeds planted in a rock," my mother had told the young woman, "but somehow when our daughter, Annie, came, we took root." **D**

My mother soon calls me back, her voice staccato with worry.

C **Literary Focus** Irony Why does the description of the hotel room seem ironic given the narrator's circumstances?

D **Reading Focus** Close Reading What is the purpose of this anecdote about Annie's parents?

Vocabulary staccato (stuh KAH toh) *adj.*: made up of short bursts of sound.

"Where is Papi?"

"I lost him."

"How you lost him?"

"He got up before I did and disappeared."

"How long he been gone?"

"Eight hours," I say, almost not believing myself that it's been that long.

My mother is clicking her tongue and humming. I can see her sitting at the kitchen table, her eyes closed, her fingers sliding up and down her flesh-colored stockinged legs.

"You call police?"

"Yes."

"What they say?"

"To wait, that he'll come back."

My mother is thumping her fingers against the phone's mouthpiece, which is giving me a slight ache in my right ear.

"Tell me where you are," she says. "Two more hours and he's not there, call me, I come."

I dial Gabrielle Fonteneau's cellular-phone number. When she answers, her voice sounds just as it does on television, but more silken and seductive without the sitcom laugh track.

"To think," my father once said while watching her show, "Haitian-born actresses on American television."

"And one of them wants to buy my stuff," I'd added.

When she speaks, Gabrielle Fonteneau sounds as if she's in a place with cicadas, waterfalls, palm trees, and citronella candles to keep the mosquitoes away. I realize that I, too, am in such a place, but I can't appreciate it.

"So nice of you to come all this way to deliver the sculpture," she says. "Jonas tell you why I like it so much? My papa was a journalist in Port-au-Prince. In 1975, he wrote a story criticizing the dictatorship, and he was arrested and put in jail."

"Fort Dimanche?"

"No, another one," she says. "Caserne. Papa kept track of days there by scraping lines with his fingernails on the walls of his cell. One of the guards didn't like this, so he pulled out all his fingernails with pliers."

The Book of the Dead

The title of Danticat's story refers to an ancient Egyptian collection of magical spells and formulas. The earliest examples we have of this book date from around 1600 B.C., but parts of the text may have been composed as early as 2400 B.C. A copy was often placed in the burial chamber of wealthy Egyptians, since only the rich could afford to pay someone to copy the long text onto papyrus. The ancient Egyptians believed the afterlife was filled with danger, and many of the spells in the book are intended to protect and guide the dead during their journey to the underworld. Colorful illustrations depicting the afterlife adorn many existing copies. The full collection includes approximately 200 chapters, though no copy has been found containing every single chapter.

Ask Yourself

Why might Danticat have called this story "The Book of the Dead"? Are there objects in the story that serve a similar purpose for the characters as the historical *Book of the Dead* served for the ancient Egyptians?

I think of the photo spread I saw in the *Haitian Times* of Gabrielle Fonteneau and her parents in their living room in Tampa. Her father was described as a lawyer, his daughter's manager; her mother a court stenographer. There was no hint in that photograph of what had once happened to the father. Perhaps people don't see anything in my father's face, either, in spite of his scars. **E**

"We celebrate his birthday on the day he was released from prison," she says. "It's the hands I love so much in your sculpture. They're so strong."

I am drifting away from Gabrielle Fonteneau when I hear her say, "So when will you get here? You have instructions from Jonas, right? Maybe we can make you lunch. My mother makes great *lanbi*."[1]

"I'll be there at twelve tomorrow," I say. "My father is with me. We are making a little weekend vacation of this." **F**

My father loves museums. When he isn't working in his barbershop, he's often at the Brooklyn Museum. The ancient Egyptian rooms are his favorites.

"The Egyptians, they was like us," he likes to say. The Egyptians worshiped their gods in many forms and were often ruled by foreigners. The pharaohs were like the dictators he had fled. But what he admires most about the Egyptians is the way they mourned.

"Yes, they grieve," he'll say. He marvels at the mummification that went on for weeks, resulting in bodies that survived thousands of years.

My whole adult life, I have struggled to find the proper manner of sculpting my father, a man who learned about art by standing with me most of the Saturday mornings of my childhood, mesmerized by the golden masks, the shawabtis,[2] and Osiris, ruler of the underworld.

---

1. *lanbi:* Creole for "conch," a type of shellfish.
2. **shawabtis:** figures that are buried with ancient Egyptian mummies. *Shawabtis* contain passages from the *Book of the Dead* and are meant to represent a mummy's servants in the afterlife.

When my father finally appears in the hotel-room doorway, I am awed by him. Smiling, he looks like a much younger man, further bronzed after a long day at the beach.

"Annie, let your father talk to you." He walks over to my bed, bends down to unlace his sneakers. "*On ti koze,* a little chat."

"Where were you? Where is the sculpture, Papi?" I feel my eyes twitching, a nervous reaction I inherited from my mother.

"That's why we need to chat," he says. "I have objections with your statue."

He pulls off his sneakers and rubs his feet with both hands.

"I don't want you to sell that statue," he says. Then he picks up the phone and calls my mother.

"I know she called you," he says to her in Creole. "Her head is so hot. She panics so easily. I was just out walking, thinking."

I hear my mother lovingly scolding him and telling him not to leave me again. When he hangs up the phone, he picks up his sneakers and puts them back on.

"Where is the sculpture?" My eyes are twitching so hard now that I can barely see.

"Let us go," he says. "I will take you to it."

As my father maneuvers the car out of the parking lot, I tell myself he might be ill, mentally ill, even though I have never detected anything wrong beyond his prison nightmares. I am trying to piece it together, this sudden yet familiar picture of a parent's vulnerability. When I was ten years old and my father had the chicken pox, I overheard him say to a friend on the phone, "The doctor tells me that at my age chicken pox can kill a man." This was the first time I realized that my father could die. I looked up the word *kill* in every dictionary and encyclopedia at school, trying to comprehend what it meant, that my father could be eradicated from my life.

My father stops the car on the side of the highway near a man-made lake, one of those artificial creations

---

E **Literary Focus** **Irony** How does the narrator's suggestion here make her father's feelings about being photographed seem ironic?

F **Literary Focus** **Irony** Sometimes a fine line divides ironic statements and lies. How would you categorize Annie's statement to Gabrielle Fonteneau?

Vocabulary **vulnerability** (vuhl nuhr uh BIHL uh tee) *n.:* openness to attack or injury.
eradicated (ih RAD uh kayt ihd) *v.:* gotten rid of; destroyed completely.

Analyzing Visuals

Viewing and Interpreting How would you describe the mood of this Haitian painting? How does it differ from the description of the sculpture of her father that the story's narrator provides?

Agoue and His Wife (1945) by Hector Hyppolite.

of the modern tropical city, with curved stone benches surrounding stagnant water. There is little light to see by except a half-moon. He heads toward one of the benches, and I sit down next to him, letting my hands dangle between my legs.

"Is this where the sculpture is?" I ask.

"In the water," he says.　　**G**

"OK," I say. "But please know this about yourself. You are an especially harsh critic."

My father tries to smother a smile.

"Why?" I ask.

He scratches his chin. Anger is a wasted emotion, I've always thought. My parents got angry at unfair politics in New York or Port-au-Prince, but they never got angry at my grades—at all the B's I got in everything but art classes—or at my not eating vegetables or occasionally vomiting my daily spoonful of cod-liver oil. Ordinary anger, I thought, was a weakness. But now I am angry. I want to hit my father, beat the craziness out of his head.

"Annie," he says. "When I first saw your statue, I wanted to be buried with it, to take it with me into the other world."

"Like the ancient Egyptians," I say.

He smiles, grateful, I think, that I still recall his passions.

"Annie," he asks, "do you remember when I read to you from the Book of the Dead?"

"Are you dying?" I say to my father. "Because I can only forgive you for this if you are. You can't take this back."

He is silent for a moment too long.

I think I hear crickets, though I cannot imagine where they might be. There is the highway, the cars racing by, the half-moon, the lake dug up from the depths of the ground, the allée[3] of royal palms beyond. And there is me and my father.

_____

3. **allée:** walkway between two rows of evenly planted trees.

"You remember the judgment of the dead," my father says, "when the heart of a person is put on a scale. If it is heavy, then this person cannot enter the other world."

It is a testament to my upbringing that I am not yelling at him.

"I don't deserve a statue," he says, even while looking like one: the Madonna of Humility, for example, contemplating her losses in the dust.

"Annie, your father was the hunter," he says. "He was not the prey."

"What are you saying?" I ask.

"We have a proverb," he says. "'One day for the hunter, one day for the prey.' Your father was the hunter. He was not the prey." Each word is hard won as it leaves my father's mouth, balanced like those hearts on the Egyptian scale.　　**H**

"Annie, when I saw your mother the first time, I was not just out of prison. I was a guard in the prison. One of the prisoners I was questioning had scratched me with a piece of tin. I went out to the street in a rage, blood all over my face. I was about to go back and do something bad, very bad. But instead comes your mother. I smash into her, and she asks me what I am doing there. I told her I was just let go from prison and she held my face and cried in my hair."

"And the nightmares, what are they?"

"Of what I, your father, did to others."

"Does Manman know?"

"I told her, Annie, before we married."　　**I**

I am the one who drives back to the hotel. In the car, he says, "Annie, I am still your father, still your mother's husband. I would not do these things now."

When we get back to the hotel room, I leave a message for Officer Bo, and another for Manager Salinas, telling them that I have found my father. He has slipped into the bathroom, and now he runs the shower at full force. When it seems that he is never coming out, I call my mother at home in Brooklyn.

G **Literary Focus** **Irony** The discrepancy between the father's feelings of reverence for the sculpture and his disposing of it is an example of situational irony. How does this sudden twist contribute to the suspense of the plot?

H **Reading Focus** **Close Reading** What might Annie's father mean by calling himself "the hunter...not the prey"? Why do you think he makes this statement about himself in the third person?

I **Literary Focus** **Irony** In what way is this new information about the father ironic?

"How do you love him?" I whisper into the phone.

My mother is tapping her fingers against the mouthpiece.

"I don't know, Annie," she whispers back, as though there is a chance that she might also be overheard by him. "I feel only that you and me, we saved him. When I met him, it made him stop hurting the people. This is how I see it. He was a seed thrown into a rock, and you and me, Annie, we helped push a flower out of the rock."

When I get up the next morning, my father is already dressed. He is sitting on the edge of his bed with his back to me, his head bowed, his face buried in his hands. If I were sculpting him, I would make him a praying mantis, crouching motionless, seeming to pray while waiting to strike. **J**

With his back still turned, my father says, "Will you call those people and tell them you have it no more, the statue?"

"We were invited to lunch there. I believe we should go."

He raises his shoulders and shrugs. It is up to me.

The drive to Gabrielle Fonteneau's house seems longer than the twenty-four hours it took to drive from New York: the ocean, the palms along the road, the highway so imposingly neat. My father fills in the silence in the car by saying, "So now you know, Annie, why your mother and me, we have never returned home."

The Fonteneaus' house is made of bricks of white coral, on a cul-de-sac[4] with a row of banyans[5] separating the two sides of the street.

> ## YOU AND ME, ANNIE, WE HELPED PUSH A FLOWER OUT OF THE ROCK.

Silently, we get out of the car and follow a concrete path to the front door. Before we can knock, an older woman walks out. Like Gabrielle, she has stunning midnight-black eyes and skin the color of sorrel,[6] with spiraling curls brushing the sides of her face. When Gabrielle's father joins her, I realize where Gabrielle Fonteneau gets her height. He is more than six feet tall.

Mr. Fonteneau extends his hands, first to my father and then to me. They're large, twice the size of my father's. The fingernails have grown back, thick, densely dark, as though the past had nestled itself there in black ink. **K**

We move slowly through the living room, which has a cathedral ceiling and walls covered with Haitian paintings—Obin, Hyppolite, Tiga, Duval-Carrié. Out on the back terrace, which towers over a nursery of orchids and red dracaenas, a table is set for lunch.

Mr. Fonteneau asks my father where his family is from in Haiti, and my father lies. In the past, I thought he always said a different province because he had lived in all those places, but I realize now that he says this to keep anyone from tracing him, even though twenty-six years and eighty more pounds shield him from the threat of immediate recognition.

When Gabrielle Fonteneau makes her entrance, in an off-the-shoulder ruby dress, my father and I stand up.

"Gabrielle," she says, when she shakes hands with my father, who blurts out spontaneously, "You are one of the flowers of Haiti."

Gabrielle Fonteneau tilts her head coyly.

"We eat now," Mrs. Fonteneau announces, leading me and my father to a bathroom to wash up before the meal. Standing before a pink seashell-shaped sink, my father and I dip our hands under the faucet flow.

---

4. **cul-de-sac:** dead-end street; blind alley.
5. **banyans:** tropical fig trees.

6. **sorrel:** small, leafy plants of the buckwheat family, typically reddish brown in color.

J **Reading Focus** **Close Reading** Why does the narrator compare her father to a praying mantis? What does it reveal about her?

K **Reading Focus** **Close Reading** What does this detail about Mr. Fonteneau's nails say about his character?

"Annie," my father says, "we always thought, your mother and me, that children could raise their parents higher. Look at what this girl has done for her parents."

During the meal of conch, plantains, and mushroom rice, Mr. Fonteneau tries to draw my father into conversation. He asks when my father was last in Haiti.

"Twenty-six years," my father replies.

"No going back for you?" asks Mrs. Fonteneau.

"I have not had the opportunity," my father says.

"We go back every year to a beautiful place overlooking the ocean in the mountains in Jacmel," says Mrs. Fonteneau.

"Have you ever been to Jacmel?" Gabrielle Fonteneau asks me.

I shake my head no.

"We are fortunate," Mrs. Fonteneau says, "that we have another place to go where we can say our rain is sweeter, our dust is lighter, our beach is prettier."

"So now we are tasting rain and weighing dust," Mr. Fonteneau says, and laughs.

"There is nothing like drinking the sweet juice from a green coconut you fetched yourself from your own tree, or sinking your hand in sand from the beach in your own country," Mrs. Fonteneau says.

"When did you ever climb a coconut tree?" Mr. Fonteneau says, teasing his wife.

I am imagining what my father's nightmares might be. Maybe he dreams of dipping his hands in the sand on a beach in his own country and finds that what he comes up with is a fist full of blood. **L**

After lunch, my father asks if he can have a closer look at the Fonteneaus' backyard garden. While he's taking the tour, I confess to Gabrielle Fonteneau that I don't have the sculpture.

"My father threw it away," I say.

Gabrielle Fonteneau frowns.

"I don't know," she says. "Was there even a sculpture at all? I trust Jonas, but maybe you fooled him, too. Is this some scam, to get into our home?"

"There was a sculpture," I say. "Jonas will tell you that. My father just didn't like it, so he threw it away."

She raises her perfectly arched eyebrows, perhaps out of concern for my father's sanity or my own.

"I'm really disappointed," she says. "I wanted it for a reason. My father goes home when he looks at a piece of art. He goes home deep inside himself. For a long time, he used to hide his fingers from people. It's like he was making a fist all the time. I wanted to give him this thing so that he knows we understand what happened to him." **M**

"I am truly sorry," I say.

Over her shoulders, I see her parents guiding my father through rows of lemongrass. I want to promise her that I will make her another sculpture, one especially modeled on her father. But I don't know when I will be able to work on anything again. I have lost my subject, the father I loved as well as pitied.

In the garden, I watch my father snap a white orchid from its stem and hold it out toward Mrs. Fonteneau, who accepts it with a nod of thanks.

"I don't understand," Gabrielle Fonteneau says. "You did all this for nothing."

I wave to my father to signal that we should perhaps leave now, and he comes toward me, the Fonteneaus trailing slowly behind him.

With each step he rubs the scars on the side of his face.

Perhaps the last person my father harmed had dreamed this moment into my father's future—his daughter seeing those marks, like chunks of warm plaster still clinging to a cast, and questioning him about them, giving him a chance to either lie or tell the truth. After all, we have the proverb, as my father would say: "Those who give the blows may try to forget, but those who carry the scars must remember." **N**

L **Reading Focus** Close Reading Why might the narrator's father pick up "a fist full of blood" from a beach in Haiti?

M **Reading Focus** Close Reading What detail in the sculpture made it seem to Gabrielle to be an appropriate gift for her father?

N **Literary Focus** Irony What is ironic about this proverb as it relates to the narrator's father?

Applying Your Skills

SKILLS FOCUS **Literary Skills** Analyze irony; analyze symbols. **Reading Skills** Close reading. **Vocabulary Skills** Demonstrate knowledge of literal meanings of words and their usage. **Writing Skills** Use descriptive language.

The Book of the Dead

Respond and Think Critically

Reading Focus

Quick Check

1. What has Annie created to honor her father?

2. Why is Annie taking a trip with her father? Where do they go?

3. What misunderstanding did the narrator have about her father and the prison?

Read with a Purpose

4. What discovery does Annie make? How does her perception of her father change as a result?

Reading Skills: Close Reading for Details

5. Review the chart you made listing details from the text. Add a third column in which you note what the details reveal about the characters.

Details from text	Meaning	What they reveal
"I do this because it is one more thing I have longed to have in common with my parents." (p. 1421)	The narrator wants a deep connection to her heritage.	Her family and background are important to her.

✔ Vocabulary Check

Match each Vocabulary word with its definition.

6. chartreuse   **a.** cricketlike insects

7. gaudy   **b.** destroyed

8. staccato   **c.** cheap and showy

9. cicadas   **d.** openness to attack

10. vulnerability   **e.** yellowish green

11. eradicated   **f.** abrupt

Literary Focus

Literary Analysis

12. **Extend** What particular historical events shape this story? Describe the events and their effect.

13. **Infer** What can you conclude about Annie's father from what he does with the statue?

14. **Interpret** What does Annie lose in this story? Which of her several losses affects her the most?

Literary Skills: Irony

15. **Make Judgments** The main irony in this story relates to Annie's father. What is ironic about his life? Is he the opposite of what he said he was, or is the situation more complex than that? Explain.

Literary Skills Review: Symbol

16. **Compare and Contrast** A **symbol** has meaning in itself but also stands for something else. At the beginning of the story, what does the statue symbolize for Annie? for her father? What does it symbolize for them at the end?

Writing Focus

Think as a Reader/Writer

Use It in Your Writing Write a vivid physical description of a real or imaginary person. In your description, rather than stating your character's personality traits directly, hint at his or her characteristics through specific, colorful physical details.

What Do You Think Now

Is it important for people to face the truth about themselves and others? How might facing the truth be both beneficial and detrimental?

Preparing to Read

 **What Do You Think?** What human needs and desires do we have in common?

⏱ **QuickWrite**

Think about how you have changed over the years. Do you have mixed feelings about some of the changes that have taken place in your life? Explain.

Literary Focus

Diction A writer's choice of words is called **diction.** Diction can be formal, colloquial, full of slang, poetic, flowery, plain, abstract, concrete, and so on. Diction depends on the writer's purpose, subject, and audience. Some words, for example, are suited to formal discussions, but sound out of place in casual conversation. Diction can have a powerful effect on the tone of a piece of writing.

Reading Focus

Analyzing Tone The attitude a writer takes toward the subject of a work, its characters, or the audience is known as **tone.** The primary components of tone are a writer's diction and choice of details. Tone can be playful, ironic, objective, sarcastic, reverent, critical, or angry.

Into Action Describe the tone of this excerpt from *Days of Obligation* as you read. In a chart like the one below, record some details from the text and choose a word or two that characterize Rodriguez's tone as he relates those details.

Details from text	Tone
"The best metaphor of America remains the dreadful metaphor—the Melting Pot."	ironic, sarcastic

Writing Focus

Think as a Reader/Writer

Find It in Your Reading The use of memory and **flashback** in an essay can trigger emotions such as regret, nostalgia, or longing. In your *Reader/Writer Notebook*, record examples of flashback that you find in this excerpt, and jot down your thoughts about the emotions they evoke.

 **Reader/Writer Notebook**

Use your **RWN** to complete the activities for this selection.

Vocabulary

elision (ih LIHZH uhn) *n.:* omission of a vowel, consonant, or syllable in pronunciation. *The girl's elision suggested that English was not her native language.*

naïveté (nah eev uh TAY) *n.:* state or quality of being inexperienced or unsophisticated. *She demonstrated naïveté about American customs.*

chrome (krohm) *n.:* a lustrous, hard, metallic element used in alloy steels. *Her voice grew hard as chrome as she discussed city life.*

assimilated (uh SIHM uh layt ihd) *v.* used as *adj.:* conformed or adjusted to the customs and attitudes of a group or nation. *After a few years in her new country, the Chinese immigrant became assimilated.*

Language Coach

Suffixes The suffix *–ion* can be added to a verb to form a noun. The verb *discuss* means "to talk about." When the suffix *–ion* is added, the word becomes *discussion.* Sometimes, word forms change when adding *–ion.* The verb *elide* means "to omit in pronunciation." Which Vocabulary word is related to *elide*? How does this verb change when adding *–ion*?

✳ **Learn It Online**
Practice your vocabulary with Word Watch online.

go.hrw.com | L11-1430 | Go

from

Days of Obligation:
An Argument with My Mexican Father

by **Richard Rodriguez**

Read with a Purpose
Read to discover the complex feelings an immigrant has about adapting to American culture.

Build Background
Although America is a nation of immigrants, in which <u>diverse</u> cultures blend together to form a unique, vibrant culture, immigrants are still sometimes ashamed of their inexperience with English and American culture. An accent or superficial cultural differences can make them feel isolated from others. These feelings often encourage children to assimilate into their new culture so that they can have a feeling of belonging.

The best metaphor of America remains the dreadful metaphor—the Melting Pot. Fall into the Melting Pot, ease into the Melting Pot, or jump into the Melting Pot—it makes no difference—you will find yourself a stranger to your parents, a stranger to your own memory of yourself. **A**

A Chinese girl walks to the front of the classroom, unfolds several ruled pages, and begins to read her essay to a trio of judges (I am one of her judges).

The voice of the essay is the voice of an immigrant. Stammer and elision approximate naïveté (the judges squirm in their chairs). The narrator remembers her night-long journey to the United States aboard a Pan Am jet. The moon. Stars. Then a memory within a memory: in the darkened cabin of the plane, sitting next to her sleeping father, the little girl remembers bright China.

Many years pass.

The narrator's voice hardens into an American voice; her diction takes on rock and chrome. There is an ashtray on the table. The narrator is sitting at a sidewalk café in San Francisco. She is sixteen years old. She is with friends. The narrator notices a Chinese girl passing on the sidewalk. The narrator remembers bright China. The passing girl's face turns toward hers. The narrator recognizes herself in the passing girl—herself less assimilated. Their connective glance lasts only seconds. The narrator is embarrassed by her double—she remembers the cabin of the plane, her sleeping father, the moon, stars. The stranger disappears. **B**

End of essay.

The room is silent as the Chinese student raises her eyes from the text.

One judge breaks the silence. Do you think your story is a sad story?

No, she replies. It is a true story.

What is the difference?

(Slowly, then.)

When you hear a sad story you cry, she says. When you hear a true story, you cry even more. **C**

A **Literary Focus** Diction What is the difference between falling, easing, or jumping into the Melting Pot?

B **Literary Focus** Diction What is the effect of using the words *rock* and *chrome* to describe the narrator's voice?

C **Reading Focus** Analyzing Tone How does the girl's final statement affect the overall tone of the work?

Vocabulary **elision** (ih LIHZH uhn) *n.:* omission of a vowel, consonant, or syllable in pronunciation.
naïveté (nah eev uh TAY) *n.:* state or quality of being inexperienced or unsophisticated.
chrome (krohm) *n.:* a lustrous, hard, metallic element used in alloy steels.
assimilated (uh SIHM uh layt ihd) *v.* used as *adj.:* conformed or adjusted to the customs and attitudes of a group or nation.

from Days of Obligation...

SKILLS FOCUS Literary Skills Analyze diction; analyze a writer's style. **Reading Skills** Identify/analyze tone. **Vocabulary Skills** Demonstrate word knowledge **Writing Skills** Employ elements of an author's style effectively.

Respond and Think Critically

Reading Focus

Quick Check

1. According to Rodriguez what metaphor best describes America?

2. With what memory does the young girl begin her essay?

3. Why does the passing stranger catch the narrator's attention?

Read with a Purpose

4. How does the Chinese girl feel about her assimilation?

Reading Skills: Analyzing Tone

5. While reading the essay, you recorded the tone of several quotations from the text. Now that you have finished reading, complete a third column of the chart by explaining what the tone of each quotation reveals about Rodriguez's attitude toward assimilation.

Details from text	Tone	Author's attitude
"The best metaphor of America remains the dreadful metaphor—the Melting Pot."	ironic, sarcastic	Rodriguez feels that assimilation may have negative consequences.

✔ Vocabulary Check

Match each Vocabulary word with its definition.

6. elision   **a.** metallic element

7. naïveté   **b.** omission

8. chrome   **c.** adjusted to

9. assimilated   **d.** inexperience

Literary Focus

Literary Analysis

10. **Extend** What conflicts are intrinsic to the relationship between immigrant children and their parents?

11. **Hypothesize** Why does the "voice of an immigrant" make the judges squirm?

12. **Analyze** Why is the narrator embarrassed by the girl who reminds her of "herself less assimilated"?

Literary Skills: Diction

13. **Compare and Contrast** What might the author be implying when he describes China as "bright"? What does Rodriguez's **diction**, or choice of words, imply about America?

Literary Skills Review: Style

14. **Evaluate** The distinctive way in which a writer uses language is called **style.** How would you describe Rodriguez's writing style in this excerpt? How do his diction and sentence structure contribute to his style?

Writing Focus

Think as a Reader/Writer

Use It in Your Writing Review the examples of flashback that you recorded as you read. Now, write about a transformation you have experienced, using a flashback to illustrate how that change took place. Include concrete details to make your flashback vivid.

What Do **You Think Now**

How is the Chinese student affected by her need to belong? Do you think she would do things differently if she had the chance?

Bend It Like Beckham

"BEND IT LIKE BECKHAM" © 2003 Twentieth Century Fox. All Rights Reserved.

Themes Across Cultures

Writing Focus

1. Write a Comparison-Contrast Essay

One could argue that the pieces by Walcott, Ali, Lahiri, Danticat, and Rodriguez all concern the theme of place—that is, each work explores the question of how a place can shape our view of ourselves and others. However, they may be connected in other ways as well. Select one such connection and use it as a starting point for writing a comparison-contrast essay.

Prewriting

Gather Ideas Begin by comparing and contrasting the selections using a chart like this one.

	Narrator	Setting	Tone	Theme
Selection #1				
Selection #2				
Selection #3				
Selection #4				
Selection #5				

Choose three of the five selections that have a strong basis of similarity but also contain unique differences.

Develop a Thesis Statement Using your notes, develop a thesis statement that makes an assertion about both the similarities and differences between the selections you chose. Always begin with a basis of similarity before focusing on the differences.

Drafting

Use the point-by-point method of organization to present information in your essay. Begin by stating your thesis. In your first body paragraph, develop your thesis by explaining a major similarity between the three selections. Your next body paragraphs should explain additional similarities and differences that support your thesis. Discuss all three selections in each paragraph.

Text Evidence Use direct quotations from each selection to support each point. Punctuate the quotations correctly and blend them into your own writing.

Before you begin writing, review the elements of a point-by-point comparison-contrast.

- **Introductory paragraph**—Identifies authors and titles of selections; presents thesis
- **Body paragraph 1**—Develops the basis of similarity (for example, theme)
- **Body paragraphs 2–4**—Discuss other similarities or the most important difference
- **Last body paragraph**—Discusses and explains remaining differences
- **Concluding paragraph**—Restates similarities and differences in a new context

Revising and Editing

Review the criteria for a good comparison-contrast essay before you begin revising.

- States the basis of the comparison in a thesis
- Uses point-by-point method to organize ideas
- Uses and cites textual evidence to support each point of comparison and contrast

2. Timed Writing

The movie poster (p. 1434), Rodriguez's essay, and Danticat's short story all explore what it means to live in one culture and maintain the memories and traditions of another. In an essay, explain what these documents suggest about how straddling two cultures shapes one's life. Provide specific examples from each document in your response.

What Do You Think Now? How do the authors in this collection address human rights and emotions? Through what topics do they choose to explore these themes?

Writing Workshop

Nonfiction Analysis

Write with a Purpose

Write an essay that analyzes literary nonfiction. Your **purpose** is to explain the nonfiction work to your **audience**—your classmates, teacher, and anyone else interested in your subject—so that they better appreciate and understand the selection.

Think as a Reader/Writer

Many of the contemporary works you have read in this unit are classified as nonfiction because they are based on fact. Nonfiction, when in the hands of skilled writers, has literary qualities as lively and compelling as those in fiction. By writing a **nonfiction analysis,** you can learn how the writer uses language to convey significant ideas both effectively and artistically. Now it is your turn to analyze and explain a nonfiction text to others. To familiarize yourself with literary nonfiction, start by reading this passage from Alice Walker's essay "In Search of Our Mothers' Gardens" (page 1295):

> This is how I came to know my mother: She seemed a large, soft, loving-eyed woman who was rarely impatient. . . . Her quick, violent temper was on view only a few times a year, when she battled with the white landlord who had the misfortune to suggest that her children did not need to go to school. . . .
>
> During the "working" day, [my mother] labored beside— not behind—my father in the fields. Her day began before sunup, and did not end until late at night. There was never a moment for her to sit down, undisturbed, to unravel her own private thoughts; never a time free from interruption—by work or the noisy inquiries of her many children. And yet, it is to my mother—and all our mothers who were not famous—that I went in search of the secret of what has fed that muzzled and often mutilated, but vibrant, creative spirit that the black woman has inherited, and that pops out in wild and unlikely places to this day. But when, you will ask, did my overworked mother have time to know or care about feeding the creative spirit? The answer is so simple that many of us have spent years discovering it. We have constantly looked high, when we should have looked high—and low.

← Walker's essay focuses on the **topic** of her mother.

← Walker's **attitude** toward her subject shows through her **choice of words and details.**

← She reveals an **insight** about life.

A Good Nonfiction Analysis

- focuses on a reasonable conclusion about the nonfiction work based on its literary elements
- supports conclusions with precise and relevant textual evidence
- elaborates on examples, clearly linking them to the thesis
- shows effective organization throughout

See page 1444 for complete rubric.

Think About the Professional Model

With a partner, discuss the following questions about the model:

1. What verbs and adjectives does Walker use to describe her mother?
2. What different aspects of her mother's personality do Walker's details show?

Reader/Writer Notebook

Use your **RWN** to complete the activities for this workshop.

Prewriting

Choose a Topic

You may already know of an interesting work of literary nonfiction, such as an essay, a memoir, or a letter, that you would like to analyze. If not, scan this book's table of contents, or look at anthologies of nonfiction for ideas. You may also ask your teachers or school librarian to recommend writers or selections in current magazines or newspapers or on the Internet. Select a nonfiction text complex enough to analyze in a well-planned, thoughtful essay.

Think About Audience and Purpose

The **purpose** of your analysis is to explain how the nonfiction writer achieves his or her specific **rhetorical** and **aesthetic goals**. In other words, you will explain what makes the writing effective and artistically appealing. Your **audience** will be your teacher, classmates, and others who are interested in the writer or topic.

Analyze the Work

During your first reading of the nonfiction selection, identify the **writer's purpose,** and develop a general understanding of the work's ideas. During your second reading, use the questions in the chart below to analyze which literary elements the writer uses and what effect they have on the work. The sample answers are based on the professional model on page 1436.

Analysis Questions	Sample Answers
What **theme,** or insight about human life, is revealed in the work?	African American women have always found ways to sustain their creative spirits.
What is the work's **tone**—the writer's attitude toward the subject and audience?	The writer's tone is respectful and determined without being overly sentimental.
What emotional state, or **mood,** does the work evoke?	The work evokes pride and respect for all African American women, especially for the writer's mother.

Style, a writer's distinctive use of language, is another important literary element. To analyze the **stylistic devices** a writer uses, look for the devices listed below, and try to determine what effect each has on the work you're analyzing.

- **Irony**—a contrast, or discrepancy, between expectation and reality
- **Diction**—choice of words; can be formal, informal, plain, ornate, and so on
- **Imagery**—language that appeals to the senses; can evoke emotions
- **Sound effects**—effects such as the **repetition** of vowel or consonant sounds **(assonance, alliteration),** sound patterns **(rhythm),** or words and phrases

Other stylistic devices include **allusion, figurative language,** and **parallelism.** See the Handbook of Literary and Historical Terms for more.

Idea Starters

- essays by writers you enjoy
- essays on topics that interest you
- contemporary and historical essayists
- published memoirs of people you admire

Your Turn

Analyze the Selection Making notes in your **RWN,** evaluate the writer's use of **literary elements,** including **theme** and **stylistic devices.** As you make notes, think about your **purpose** and **audience.**

Learn It Online
To see how one writer completed this assignment, see the model nonfiction analysis online.

 go.hrw.com L11-1437   **Go**

State and Support Your Thesis

A nonfiction selection expresses the writer's ideas about a topic or experience. As you analyze the selection's literary elements, determine which ones contribute most to making the writer's perspective clear and memorable. Your **thesis statement** then identifies these elements and expresses your main idea about them. A thesis for an analysis of "In Search of Our Mothers' Gardens" might read:

> Alice Walker uses diction and imagery to convey effectively her theme that African American women have always found ways to sustain their creative spirits.

Next, support your thesis statement with precise and relevant **textual evidence—direct quotations, paraphrases,** and **summaries** of the text. Provide at least two examples for each element that you select. An analysis of the diction used in "In Search of Our Mothers' Gardens" might include a statement like this, which quotes the text and explains why the quoted words are important:

> Strong verbs, such as "battled" and "labored," reflect the strength of the writer's mother. African American women fought and worked hard not only physically but also mentally and spiritually to keep their creativity alive.

Organize Your Ideas

Make sure the organization of your essay is clear and logical by using one of these two common organizational patterns for analysis:

- **Chronological order** traces the writer's development of ideas and shows how the literary elements support them throughout the piece.
- **Order of importance** arranges the discussion of the author's ideas and the use of literary elements to support those ideas from most important to least important or vice versa.

Create an Outline

An **outline** is a way of organizing your thoughts and ideas into logical patterns. With an outline, you can see relationships among your ideas so that you can present them clearly as you draft. Your outline might begin like the one below:

> I. Introduction
>   A. Attention-getting statement, quotation, or anecdote
>   B. Introduce writer and nonfiction work to be analyzed
>   C. List of main points to be covered in essay
>   D. Thesis statement
> II. First body paragraph with first main point
>   A. Transitional sentence
>   B. Topic sentence explaining the first main point
>   C. Support
>   1. First example of textual evidence
>   a. Elaboration

Your Turn

Prepare to Draft Write a working **thesis statement,** and review your **RWN** for **textual evidence** to support your thesis. In preparation for drafting your analysis, create an **outline** that lists the major points you plan to address. Share your outline with a peer. Think about the feedback you receive, and revise your outline as needed.

Drafting

Follow Your Outline

Use your outline to draft your essay. As you write, keep in mind the characteristics of a good nonfiction analysis (page 1436).

Use Textual Evidence

When writing a nonfiction analysis, you must use **evidence** from the text to explain your reasoning. You can present evidence from the text in three ways:

- **Quotations** are brief excerpts from the text copied into your essay exactly as they appear in the work. Quotations are enclosed in quotation marks.
- **Paraphrases** rephrase a portion of the text in your own words. Phrases such as *according to* or *the writer says* indicate that the thoughts belong to the writer of the work.
- **Summaries** are highly condensed restatements of a text's main points. Use summaries to give an overview of the whole work or large sections you cannot discuss at greater length.

After presenting textual evidence in support of a main point, **elaborate,** or explain *how* the example supports the point and thesis. When you use textual evidence, be sure to follow standard punctuation guidelines as indicated below.

Grammar Link Using Textual Evidence

Proper punctuation indicates to the reader that the writer is using textual evidence. Follow these rules to use quotations, paraphrases, and summaries:

- Quotation marks enclose the exact words from the text. Periods and commas also belong within the quotation marks.

> "It is considered rare, beyond price."

- When introducing a quotation as an example, use an introductory phrase followed by a comma and the quotation. In this case, the first word of the quotation should be capitalized.

> **For example,** "It is considered rare, beyond price."

- Direct quotations can be long and difficult to weave into your text. Use paraphrases or summaries to state your point and your example more concisely.

> **Walker says** that the quilt hanging in the Smithsonian is **rare and priceless.**

- A quotation and paraphrase can sometimes be combined. In the following example, the first word of the quotation should be lowercase, because it is integrated with the rest of the sentence:

> For example, Walker says that the Smithsonian quilt "is considered rare, beyond price."

Reference Note For more on punctuating quotations, see the Language Handbook.

Writing Tip

Use a computer's cut-and-paste tools to experiment with the organization of your analysis, moving whole paragraphs or large text blocks around to see where they will be most effective.

Your Turn

Draft your Analysis Following your outline, write a draft of your essay. Answer the following questions before you write:

- What **textual evidence** will you use to support your thesis?
- What information will you **quote? paraphrase? summarize?** How will you decide?

Peer Review

Work with a peer reviewer to evaluate your essay. Answer each question in the chart to the right to determine where and how your draft could be improved. Make sure you take notes about the revisions that you and your partner discuss. Give your partner feedback on his or her comments. Which suggestions did you use? Which ones did you not use? Why not? These comments will help your partner become a more effective peer reviewer.

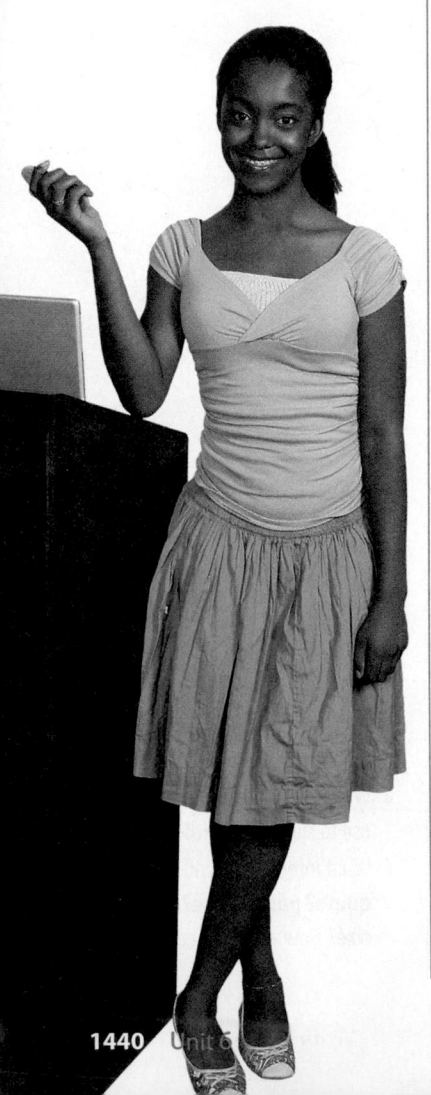

Evaluating and Revising

Read the questions in the left-hand column of the chart, and then use the tips in the middle column to help you make revisions to your essay. The right-hand column suggests techniques you can use to revise your draft.

Nonfiction Analysis: Guidelines for Evaluating and Revising

Evaluation Question	Tip	Revision Technique
1. **Does the analysis identify the literary elements used in the nonfiction selection?**	**Circle** the literary elements identified in the introduction. **Draw arrows** from each element in the introduction to the body paragraph or paragraphs that discuss it.	**Add** references to literary elements to your introduction and body paragraphs if needed.
2. **Does the thesis statement express a main idea about the use of literary elements?**	**Bracket** your thesis statement.	**Reword** your thesis if the relationship between the thesis and literary elements is not clear.
3. **Is the thesis supported with textual evidence?**	**Highlight in yellow** each example of textual evidence. **Label with a Q, P, or S** the direct quotations, paraphrases, and summaries.	**Add** direct quotations, paraphrases, or summaries if you do not have at least two pieces of textual evidence to support each literary element discussed.
4. **Is the textual evidence well elaborated?**	**Highlight in blue** each explanation that links a direct quotation, paraphrase, or summary to your thesis. Each yellow highlight should be followed by a blue highlight.	**Add** a sentence or two of elaboration to each piece of evidence that is not clearly linked to the thesis.
5. **Is your essay organized clearly?**	**Number** your paragraphs in the margin. Compare with your outline. Do the paragraphs follow the order laid out in your outline?	**Rearrange** sentences or paragraphs that deviate from the planned structure.

Read this student draft and notice the comments on its strengths and suggestions on how it could be improved.

Transformed by Language
by Jake Reynolds, Anderson High School

Born of Mexican and Apache heritage, Jimmy Baca, writing in "Coming into Language," reveals his experience of facing prejudice and rejection. Baca finds a positive outlet for his struggles through language. He reveals the process of transformation through the use of simile and metaphor.

Baca is a symbol for human beings whose good intentions have been over-looked by an ignorant society. Growing up in "the poverty and squalor of barrio life," he lived in an orphanage during his adolescence, following the death of his parents. His lack of parental nurturing and failure to receive a strong education results in an "inarticulateness"—an inability to express himself except in rage and self-destructive acts. Baca experiences the wrath of a society that judges on first impression alone. Society convicts Baca of crimes without providing evidence and acts on "suspicion" alone, leaving him feeling "like a target" and feeling "the hang-rope tighten around [his] neck." Baca's figurative comparison of his miser-able position to a "target" or to choking to death at his own hanging reveals society's tendency to single out and persecute unwanted human beings, chok-ing such victims of their individuality, their voice, their rights as individuals.

← Jake's **introduction** identifies the nonfiction text's **author** and **title;** then he states his **thesis.**

← The organizational structure is **chronological,** beginning with Baca's childhood.

← Jake **quotes** Baca's **similes** and **metaphors,** then **elaborates** on them.

MINI-LESSON ▶ How to Provide Background Information

Jake chose a writer who may not be familiar to the readers of his analysis. Because nonfiction often reveals so much about its writer, Jake decided to pro-vide more background information about Baca and this selection to help readers appreciate and understand his analysis.

Jake's Revision of Paragraph 1

Born of Mexican and Apache heritage, *poet* Jimmy *Santiago* Baca, ~~writing in~~ *published in 1992 his memoir* Working in the Dark: Reflections of a Poet in the Barrio, *from which the essay* "Coming into Language," *is taken. This essay* reveals his experiences of facing prejudice and rejection. *Ultimately,* Baca finds a posi-tive outlet for his struggles through language. *While incarcerated in the 1970s, he taught himself to read and write at 21. In the essay, h*~~He~~ reveals the process of transformation through the use of metaphor. *Baca has become one of America's foremost poets, holding the Wallace Stevens Endowed Chair at Yale University and winning numerous awards for his poetry.*

Your Turn _____
Provide Background Information

Re-read your draft's introduction to determine if you have included enough background information about the writer and context of the nonfiction work you are analyzing. If you haven't, add more information to help your reader understand and appreciate the selection and your analysis.

The essay continues to follow **chronological order.** →

Jake introduces and **elaborates** on the metaphor of magic. →

Baca recalls a clarifying moment: "I shot my arms through the bars, grabbed one of the attendant's university textbooks, and tucked it in my overalls. It was the only way I had of protesting." In prison, Baca finds a positive outlet for his frustration as he turns to reading and writing "to avenge the betrayals [and] purge the bitterness of injustice." He says that language was the "magic that could liberate and transport" him to places far from the prison. The metaphor of magic is used to capture the process of transformation that occurs, allowing him both to disappear, escaping the injustice around him, and to re-create himself in another form. Magic! The transformation of language allows him to reappear as someone else and become a part of the society that had once rejected him. Baca's positive resolution through language gives hope to other victims of prejudice and discrimination. The metaphor of magic captures that sense of transformation and metamorphosis.

The conclusion **restates** Jake's **thesis,** touching on the relationship between Baca's use of metaphor and his message. →

Jimmy Santiago Baca finds the power of language and a new way of life while in prison. In his essay "Coming into Language," Baca uses figurative language to reveal how both discrimination and exclusion defined his early life. Then, language itself transformed him, giving him new life.

MINI-LESSON ▸ **How to Transition Between Ideas**

A transition in writing—whether it is a word, a phrase, or even a sentence—reaches *across* or *over* ideas, connecting one idea to another. When you use transitions, you not only connect ideas but you also show explicitly *how* they are connected. Jake realized that his transition between paragraphs two and three was weak. He revised to make the transition between ideas clearer by using repetition of ideas, connecting "voice" and "'inarticulateness.'"

Jakes Draft of Paragraphs 2 and 3

. . . society's tendency to single out and persecute unwanted human beings, choking such victims of their individuality, their voice, their rights as individuals.

Baca recalls a clarifying moment: "I shot my arms through the bars, grabbed one of the attendant's university textbooks, and tucked it in my overalls.

Jake's Revision of Paragraph 3

. . . society's tendency to single out and persecute unwanted human beings, choking such victims of their individuality, their voice, their rights as individuals. *Baca fully realizes this loss of voice, this "inarticulateness" while in prison. It is there that he first realizes he has no means to communicate. He is bereft of a way to reveal his true intentions to the world.*

∧Baca recalls a clarifying moment: "I shot my arms through the bars, grabbed one of the attendant's university textbooks, and tucked it in my overalls.

Your Turn _____

Transition Between Ideas

Re-read your draft, focusing on the main ideas that you have presented. Are the main ideas connected to each other? If not, add words, phrases, or sentences to provide better transition between paragraphs.

Proofreading and Publishing

Proofreading

Before turning in the final draft of your analysis, make sure you **proofread,** or **edit,** your work for errors in grammar, usage, and mechanics. Trade papers with a partner for one last peer review. Reading your papers aloud to each other can help you identify mistakes, such as **subject-verb agreement** errors.

Grammar Link **Achieving Subject-Verb Agreement**

Agreement of subject and verb can be particularly challenging when you are writing long, complex sentences, especially those with compound subjects. Compound subjects joined by *and* generally take a plural verb because two items form the subject. As he was proofreading, Jake found one sentence in paragraph two that he had to correct. He had a compound subject and needed to make his verb plural.

> His lack of parental nurturing and failure to receive a strong education results in an "inar-
>
> ticulateness"—an inability to express himself except in rage and self-destructive acts. [the
>
> subjects are *lack* and *failure;* the plural verb is *result*]

Reference Note For more on subject-verb agreement, see the Language Handbook.

Publishing

Now that the work of analyzing and writing is done, it is time to publish the results of your effort. Here are some ways to share your analysis:

- Turn your essay into a multimedia presentation. Find audio or video clips and other appropriate images to enhance your presentation.

- Contact your school or public library for a listing of literary clubs that invite speakers. Volunteer to read the nonfiction work you have analyzed (or excerpts, if the work is longer) and your analysis of it at a club meeting.

- Contact your community library. Volunteer to provide a program that includes your analysis, biographical information on your author, and a reading of the original nonfiction work you have analyzed.

- Search the Internet for a Web site dedicated to the writer whose work you have analyzed. Submit your essay for publication. If there is no dedicated Web site, consider creating one.

Reflect on the Process
Use your **RWN** to reflect on the writing process. Write a short response to each of the following questions:

1. What techniques were most helpful to you as you analyzed the nonfiction work about which you decided to write?

2. How did using an outline help you draft your essay? Explain.

3. How did the peer review process help you revise and edit your essay? How could you improve the feedback process in future peer situations?

● **Proofreading Tip**

Review the instances in which you refer to the nonfiction work's title. Refer to the Language Handbook to make sure you've followed the rules for capitalizing and punctuating titles.

Your Turn _____
Proofread and Publish

Proofread your essay for errors. As you proofread, check for subject-verb agreement errors, especially in sentences with compound subjects. Then, publish your essay to share your insights with your intended audience.

Scoring Rubric

Use one of the rubrics below to evaluate your nonfiction analysis from the Writing Workshop or your response to the expository on-demand prompt on the next page. Your teacher will tell you to use either the six- or the four-point rubric.

6-Point Scale

Score 6 *Demonstrates advanced success*
- focuses consistently on a clear thesis
- shows effective organization throughout, with smooth transitions
- offers thoughtful, creative ideas
- develops ideas thoroughly, using examples, details, and fully elaborated explanation
- exhibits mature control of written language

Score 5 *Demonstrates proficient success*
- focuses on a clear thesis
- shows effective organization, with transitions
- offers thoughtful ideas
- develops ideas competently, using examples, details, and well-elaborated explanation
- exhibits sufficient control of written language

Score 4 *Demonstrates competent success*
- focuses on a clear thesis, with minor distractions
- shows effective organization, with minor lapses
- offers mostly thoughtful ideas
- develops ideas adequately, with a mixture of general and specific elaboration
- exhibits general control of written language

Score 3 *Demonstrates limited success*
- includes some loosely related ideas that distract from the writer's expository focus
- shows some organization, with noticeable gaps in the logical flow of ideas
- offers routine, predictable ideas
- develops ideas with uneven elaboration
- exhibits limited control of written language

Score 2 *Demonstrates basic success*
- includes loosely related ideas that seriously distract from the writer's expository focus
- shows minimal organization, with major gaps in the logical flow of ideas
- offers ideas that merely skim the surface
- develops ideas with inadequate elaboration
- exhibits significant problems with control of written language

Score 1 *Demonstrates emerging effort*
- shows little awareness of the topic and purpose for writing
- lacks organization
- offers unclear and confusing ideas
- develops ideas in only a minimal way, if at all
- exhibits major problems with control of written language

4-Point Scale

Score 4 *Demonstrates advanced success*
- focuses consistently on a clear thesis
- shows effective organization throughout, with smooth transitions
- offers thoughtful, creative ideas
- develops ideas thoroughly, using examples, details, and fully elaborated explanation
- exhibits mature control of written language

Score 3 *Demonstrates competent success*
- focuses on a clear thesis, with minor distractions
- shows effective organization, with minor lapses
- offers mostly thoughtful ideas
- develops ideas adequately, with a mixture of general and specific elaboration
- exhibits general control of written language

Score 2 *Demonstrates limited success*
- includes some loosely related ideas that distract from the writer's expository focus
- shows some organization, with noticeable gaps in the logical flow of ideas
- offers routine, predictable ideas
- develops ideas with uneven elaboration
- exhibits limited control of written language

Score 1 *Demonstrates emerging effort*
- shows little awareness of the topic and purpose for writing
- lacks organization
- offers unclear and confusing ideas
- develops ideas in only a minimal way, if at all
- exhibits major problems with control of written language

Expository Essay: Cause and Effect

When responding to an expository prompt, use what you have learned from reading, writing your nonfiction analysis, and studying the rubric on page 1444. Use the steps below to develop a response to the following prompt:

Writing Prompt

Age requirements for obtaining a driver's license in the United States vary from state to state. Consider the driving age in your state, and write an expository essay that explains the events that would likely occur if your state's driving age were raised or lowered.

Study the Prompt

Begin by reading the prompt carefully. Circle or underline key words: *driving age, in your state, raised or lowered.* Re-read the prompt to see if there is any additional information that can help you.

Your **purpose** is to explain what you think the possible **effects** would be if the driving age in your state were raised or lowered. Begin by deciding whether to write about the age being raised or lowered. Then, think about the events you think this change would **cause. Tip:** Spend about five minutes studying the prompt.

Plan Your Response

Create an organizer that lists the following information:

Current driving age: _____		
Choose one: Raise to _____; Lower to _____		
Cause	**Effects**	
Change in the driving age	1.	
	2.	
	3.	

- Write down **facts, examples,** and other **details** that will support your explanation of the relationship between cause and effect.
- Write a one-sentence **thesis statement** that explains the cause-effect relationship.

Tip: Spend about ten minutes planning your response.

Respond to the Prompt

Using your thesis statement and your notes, draft your response. Follow these guidelines:

- The **introduction** should identify the change in the driving age that you have chosen (cause) and suggest that there will be specific results (effects) of the change. One creative way to begin is with a hypothetical newspaper headline stating the change. A brief dialogue could follow, with two people discussing the change and its effects. Include your thesis statement.

- The **body** of the essay should address each effect in a **logical order.** You may want to organize the effects in the following order: second most significant, least significant, and most significant. Each effect should be supported with facts and specific examples.

- In the **conclusion,** make sure to restate your thesis and summarize the cause-effect relationship. End with a memorable statement.

Tip: Spend about twenty minutes writing your draft.

Improve Your Response

Revising Go back to the key aspects of the prompt. Does your response explain what you think would happen if the driving age in your state were raised or lowered? Is your essay logically and effectively organized?

Proofreading Take a few minutes to proofread to correct errors in grammar, spelling, punctuation, and capitalization. Make sure your edits are neat and your paper is legible.

Checking Your Final Copy Before you turn in your paper, read it one more time to catch any errors you may have missed and to make any finishing touches.

Tip: Save five or ten minutes to improve your paper.

Analyzing Media

Think as a Reader/Writer You can often choose what you read. Today, however, you are bombarded by information, images, and sounds beyond your control. Television, advertisements, the Internet, and other media of the digital age have made it increasingly important to understand how media messages work. This workshop will show you how to apply analytical skills to the media that surround you and how to combine media into a presentation of your own.

Analyzing Media

It is not possible to imagine a day without e-mail, the Internet, television, radio, books, or newspapers. Clearly, receiving and decoding media messages are part of daily life. These messages reach their intended audiences through two categories of **media sources.**

- **Print media sources** include books, newspapers, magazines, pamphlets, advertising fliers, billboards, and posters.
- **Electronic media sources** include radio, television, videos, the Internet, blogs, and podcasts.

In the twenty-first century, of course, many digital media combine several kinds of information, not to mention multiple modes of delivery. A typical home computer, for example, can give you access to political news on the Web sites of reputable newspapers; to carefully crafted political information on the Web sites of national political parties and candidates; to political blogs by individuals of every political persuasion; and to Web sites posting film clips that include both professional and amateur political advertisements.

Media for the Twenty-first Century

To function successfully in today's world, you must be able to read and analyze three kinds of media:

- **Informational media** Advances in computer technology have brought with them an information explosion. Thanks to the Internet, you can access search engines, online databases, newspaper Web sites, blogs, and hundreds of thousands of other Web-based resources when you need information. Much of what is available on the Web, however, is not reliable.
- **Commercial advertisements** Every day, you are exposed to a flood of commercial images. Learning how advertisements work can help you to make informed choices.
- **Political advertisements** Our political process is shaped, in large part, by the advertising media. Understanding this kind of advertising can help you to participate effectively in the political process.

Reader/Writer Notebook

Use your **RWN** to complete the activities for this workshop.

SKILLS FOCUS **Reading Skills** Analyze editorials, advertisements, documentaries, and other texts for bias and use of common persuasive techniques; evaluate the credibility of information sources and their appropriateness for varied needs. **Writing Skills** Compare print media and electronic media. **Listening and Speaking Skills** Understand and identify logical fallacies and propaganda techniques.

Media Literacy

Critical readers and viewers use media literacy concepts to analyze, interpret, and evaluate media messages. The left column of the following chart will help you understand basic media literacy concepts. The suggestions in the right column will help you analyze the media messages you receive.

Media Literacy Concepts

Concept	Application
1. People—alone or in groups—write, edit, select, illustrate, or compose every media message.	When you look at a Web page, try to find who is behind the information on the page—the name of the individual or group. Always be on the alert for bias in the media you encounter.
2. Like a story or poem, a media message reflects a particular point of view—sometimes a combined point of view.	When you see an eyewitness account on televised news, remember that it reflects at least three points of view: the witness speaking in the video clip, the technician who edited the original video footage, and the television station airing it.
3. Your interpretation of a media message is based on your knowledge.	Discover as much as you can about the media that shape your world. As you learn more about how media work, you will be a more effective citizen of the digital age.
4. Every media message has a purpose—to inform, persuade, or entertain, but always to persuade.	As you observe media messages, always look for a persuasive purpose and the persuasive methods that support the purpose.
5. Media producers shape messages according to the characteristics of the medium in use.	Notice specific characteristics of the medium that media producers use to emphasize a message.

A Good Media Analysis

- identifies the medium and its message
- considers the creator of the message and his or her purpose
- discerns how the form or style of the medium affects its message
- recognizes the strategies used in creating or expressing the message
- infers what may have been left out of the message and why
- evaluates the effectiveness of the message

Learn It Online
Analyze web pages and more at MediaScope.

go.hrw.com   L11-1447   **Go**

Recognizing Propaganda

Media producers use the techniques of propaganda to achieve their purposes and to shape their messages for their intended audiences. To be an effective media consumer, you must be able to analyze and evaluate the use of these methods. The following chart describes some of the most common propaganda strategies in use today.

Media Strategies

Strategy	Examples
Ad Hominem Attack Also known as name-calling, this approach is common in political advertising, in which one candidate or group tries to persuade voters by smearing the reputation of another candidate or group.	In a common variation on the political attack ad, a disapproving voice repeats the name of a candidate and, with each repetition, names something negative the candidate supposedly has done or cast a vote for. Attack ads present heavily edited evidence, almost always out of context.
Card Stacking Advertisers stack the cards when they emphasize the appealing aspects of their product—or their candidate—and leave out any negative traits.	An ad favoring a particular political candidate generally selects only favorable information; an attack ad selects only what makes the candidate look bad.
Celebrity Endorsement This method uses the testimony of someone well known to support a product, a cause, or a candidate.	Commercial advertising has long featured rock stars, movie stars, and athletes. Increasingly, however, political advertising includes testimonials by famous people.
Escape Advertisers exploit the universal human desire to get away from everyday routines or pressures.	Television commercials for beverages and other products frequently picture white-water rafting or other outdoor adventures. Political ads sometimes take advantage of this impulse by picturing a candidate in the great outdoors, even on horseback.
Facts and Figures Propaganda exploits our tendency to see data as proof, selecting facts and figures to make the favored candidate—or product—look appealing.	Attack ads tend to cite negative evidence from a candidate's voting record.
Glittering Generalities Abstract words with a positive emotional appeal give propaganda persuasive power.	Ads in favor of a particular candidate use phrases such as "truth, justice, and the American way." Attack ads use words and phrases that have the reverse effect.
Lifestyle This method associates a product—or a political candidate—with an appealing way of living.	Favorable political ads try to show a candidate living the kind of life that target voters would approve. Attack ads associate candidates with values that voters would oppose.

Presentation Tip

Ensure a successful multimedia presentation by learning as much as you can about how today's media work. Before you choose a topic, examine as many political advertisements as possible, looking for the propaganda methods presented on the adjacent chart. If time allows, use the Internet to research other persuasive methods used by advertisers in the digital age.

Nonconformity Advertisers exploit American culture's emphasis on indviduality by suggesting that purchasing a particular product demonstrates noncomformity.	Favorable political ads frequently picture a presidential candidate as someone willing to make difficult, even "unpopular" choices.
Peer Approval By contrast with the appeal to nonconformity, this method exploits the need for approval by implying that a particular product—or political—position will ensure approval by others.	Clothing ads geared for adolescent audiences freqently depict models in a group of people who smile and show their approval. Political ads that picture a candidate in the midst of an approving crowd are using the same appeal.
Plain Folks / Snob Appeal The Plain Folks method appeals to the ordinary citizen in you, while the Snob Appeal approach exploits the desire to be part of a select group.	Since politicians are in the business of being elected, a favorable political ad pictures the politician as one of the people. By contrast, attack ads frequently imply that a candidate is a snob, "out of touch" with the people.

Learn It Online
Learn more about political advertisements
at MediaScope.

go.hrw.com   L11-1449   **Go**

Preparing a Multimedia Analysis

Now that you have studied strategies common to the propaganda of advertising, you will analyze a political advertisement or a group of related political advertisements and shape your analysis into a multimedia presentation, using words, images, and sound. In choosing a suitable subject for this presentation, consider your own interests, as well as the political advertising that is prominent when you are ready to begin. During an election season, for example, you might want to analyze one or more advertisements for a particular candidate or party. If you have an interest in political history, consider focusing on political advertising during an important historical campaign. You could also focus on advertising for a local political issue.

Select Words, Images, and Sound You will use words to present the major ideas in your analysis, images to illustrate your ideas, and sound to enhance what your words and images convey. Use the following chart to help you assemble the components of your presentation.

Media	Content	Format
Text	• the major points of your presentation • important facts, figures, or quotations	• Use PowerPoint or a similar approach to present major points in large lettering, attractively formatted. • An LCD projector will display the text of your presentation on a large screen. • A document camera will enlarge facts, figures, and quotations and display them on a large screen.
Images	• color reproductions of still images from the advertisement(s) your presentation analyzes • video clips from the advertisement(s) your presentation analyzes	• You can use PowerPoint to project still images and even video clips. • You can also use an LCD projector, a video projector, or a document camera to project images.
Sound	• video clips with sound—for advertisements that have a soundtrack • your own voice to conduct the presentation	• The methods listed above can be used to project sound. • Use speakers appropriate for the size of the room and your audience. • Practice projecting your voice; use a microphone and speakers, if appropriate.

Presentation Tip

Before planning your multimedia presentation, check with your campus library or media center to see what kind of presentation equipment is available to you. Many schools also make training and support available to students. In addition, you can take advantage of interactive training software that is available for presentation software and for equipment such as LCD projectors.

Research Your Topic Remember the purpose of your presentation—to analyze the persuasive methods at work in a political advertisement. You may choose to analyze a print or televised ad. If time allows, you might wish to analyze a group of related ads. Once you have chosen an advertisement, analyze it thoroughly, looking for the media strategies presented on pages 1448–1449. After you identify your ad's primary methods of persuasion, do some more research on these methods so that you can explain them effectively when you make your presentation.

Consider Your Audience As you prepare your presentation, think about the characteristics and needs of your audience. The following questions will help you analyze your audience:

- What will my audience know about my chosen subject?
- What will my audience want to know?
- What methods can I use to capture and hold my audience's attention?
- What media would work best in presenting my topic?
- What combination of media will my audience find most interesting?

Maximize Your Impact The most appropriate text, image, or sound effect might be ineffective and even distracting if it is not designed properly. Pay close attention to the quality of the material you choose. Think carefully about how to incorporate it into your presentation. Use the following design principles to create the maximum impact on your audience.

- **Text** Limit the amount of text that you expect your audience to read. For each screen or slide, display information in list form, if possible. Present three to five listed items per slide—or one impressive quotation. Choose a plain, non-serif font in a size that your audience will be able to read from the back of the presentation area. If you begin with a list of major points, consider repeating the slide with this list, as needed, for emphasis.

- **Images** Since your purpose is to analyze the persuasive techniques at work in print or televised advertising, high-quality slides or video clips are essential. Be sure images are large enough and clear enough to be seen by everyone in the presentation area. Consider a four-step process for any image or video you analyze: (1) Introduce the image or clip. (2) Show your audience the image or clip without commenting. (3) Show and briefly discuss a slide listing the points you want to make about the image or clip. (4) Show the image or clip again, and point out the features you want your audience to notice. Use a wand-shaped pointer about the length of a yardstick to pinpoint details in any advertisement you share with your audience.

- **Sound** If you present televised advertising, be sure that your equipment is loud enough for your presentation area. Use speakers, if necessary. Practice projecting your voice to the back of the presentation area. If possible, use a microphone and speakers.

A Good Multimedia Presentation

- effectively combines text with images and sound
- presents a clear thesis and evidence that supports it
- organizes information and ideas in a logical way
- considers the needs of the audience

● **Presentation Tip**
Consider the **purpose** and **audience** when selecting a topic. When you know why and for whom you are presenting, you should be better able to focus your thoughts and establish a direction for your presentation. In this workshop, your purpose is to inform, and your audience will be your teachers and classmates.

✳ **Learn It Online**
Plan your multimedia presentation online with MediaScope.

 L11-1451

Develop a Thesis Statement

The thesis statement for your presentation will identify the most important persuasive strategies at work in the advertisement or group of advertisements you have chosen to analyze. For the sake of your audience, consider presenting your thesis statement as a list of bulleted points—on a single slide or screen, using large, non-serif letters, clearly visible from the back of the presentation area.

Organize Your Presentation

To help ensure that the audience finds your presentation easy to follow, plan its organization carefully. Follow the steps in the chart below to effectively combine the spoken content and the multimedia support you've chosen.

Organizing a Multimedia Presentation

1. Compose your thesis statement and create a single slide or screen presenting the major points of your thesis as a bulleted list.

2. Create a single slide or screen for each of the major points listed on your thesis slide or screen. Each of these screens will introduce a major part of your presentation.

3. Plan the visual backup for each major point in your presentation. What image or video clip will you show your audience? How will you point out the persuasive strategy you want to highlight at this point in your presentation?

4. Plan the textual support for each major point in your presentation. Set up one or more slides or screens to display the information and ideas you want your audience to remember.

5. If it would be useful to remind your audience of any major point or points, make duplicate slides or screens of these to insert in your presentation, as appropriate.

6. Plan your conclusion. Consider repeating your thesis slide. If time allows, consider showing your audience a new advertisement that uses the techniques your presentation analyzed. Ask members of the audience to identify these techniques.

7. Plan how you will integrate the components of your analysis—words, images, and sound—into a seamless presentation. Make an outline, chart, or storyboard to consult as you rehearse.

● Presentation Tip

As you develop your presentation, place yourself in the position of your audience.

- What will convey your ideas with impact so you capture their interest and attention?
- Where might they become confused?
- How will visuals support, rather than detract from, your key points?

Practice Your Presentation Throughout the process of planning and developing your presentation, you've probably given serious consideration to the effect it will have on your intended audience. Now is the time to determine whether all of the elements work together as planned. Gather a group of friends or family members, and rehearse your presentation. Deliver it exactly as you would for the intended audience of your final presentation. If you need use of the school's audiovisual equipment, arrange a rehearsal before or after school.

As you rehearse, express interest in and enthusiasm about your topic. After all, your delivery holds the whole presentation together. Speak confidently, enunciate clearly, and avoid vocalized pauses, such as *um* or *ah*. Use nonverbal behavior—eye contact, facial expressions, and gestures—to your advantage. Be familiar with your presentation equipment, and don't turn your back on the audience when using it. After your rehearsal, use the questions in the chart below to ask your audience for feedback.

Audience Feedback

Which section of the spoken part of the presentation was most memorable? Why did it succeed?

Which of the multimedia elements of the presentation were most effective? Why did you think so?

How well did the presentation combine spoken words with text, images, and sounds? Explain.

What parts of the multimedia presentation, if any, did you find confusing? Why?

How did the delivery itself affect the presentation? Explain.

What did you learn about propaganda techniques in advertising? Where in the presentation would you like more information?

Revise Your Presentation Adjust the content and delivery of your presentation according to your rehearsal audience's responses. Do further research, if indicated, to strengthen the content of your analysis. If necessary, revise slides or screens for greater clarity or adjust the way you present still images or video clips. Then, practice delivering your presentation for a second time to make sure all the problems have been eliminated. Check and double-check your presentation equipment. The effectiveness of an excellent presentation depends on your efficient management of your equipment. Because a multimedia presentation coordinates so many different parts, anticipate possible trouble and be prepared for emergencies.

● Viewing Tip

As a viewer of media, don't ignore or discount your gut reaction to an image, but use your head, too. Think about why you reacted to the image as you did. Ask yourself these questions:

- What made me react that way?
- Is my reaction the one the image maker wanted me to have? Why might he or she have tried to evoke a particular reaction?
- How does my reaction to the image affect my understanding of the issue or story the image accompanies?

Literary Skills Review

Compare and Contrast Literature from Two Different Literary Periods

Directions: Read the following poems. Then, read each multiple-choice question that follows and choose the letter of the best response.

Each of the following poems was written by an American woman during a time of war. "September, 1918" was written by Amy Lowell when the final, horrific battles of World War I were claiming tens of thousands of lives in France. Julia Alvarez's poem "How I Learned to Sweep" recalls how television brought the violent images of Vietnam's jungle warfare into American living rooms during the 1960s and 1970s.

September, 1918 by **Amy Lowell**

This afternoon was the color of water falling through sunlight;
The trees glittered with the tumbling of leaves;
The sidewalks shone like alleys of dropped maple leaves;
And the houses ran along them laughing out of square, open windows.
5 Under a tree in the park,
Two little boys, lying flat on their faces,
Were carefully gathering red berries
To put in a pasteboard box.
Some day there will be no war.
10 Then I shall take out this afternoon
And turn it in my fingers,
And remark the sweet taste of it upon my palate,
And note the crisp variety of its flights of leaves.
Today I can only gather it
15 And put it into my lunch-box,
For I have time for nothing
But the endeavor to balance myself
Upon a broken world.

How I Learned to Sweep by **Julia Alvarez**

My mother never taught me sweeping. . . .
One afternoon she found me watching
TV. She eyed the dusty floor
boldly, and put a broom before
5   me, and said she'd like to be able
to eat her dinner off that table,
and nodded at my feet, then left.
I knew right off what she expected
and went at it. I stepped and swept;
10 the TV blared the news; I kept
my mind on what I had to do,
until in minutes, I was through.
Her floor was as immaculate
as a just-washed dinner plate.
15 I waited for her to return
and turned to watch the President,
live from the White House, talk of war:
in the Far East our soldiers were
landing in their helicopters
20 into jungles their propellers

swept like weeds seen underwater
while perplexing shots were fired
from those beautiful green gardens
into which these dragonflies
25 filled with little men descended.
I got up and swept again
as they fell out of the sky.
I swept all the harder when
I watched a dozen of them die . . .
30 as if their dust fell through the screen
upon the floor I had just cleaned.
She came back and turned the dial;
The screen went dark. *That's beautiful,*
she said, and ran her clean hand through
35 my hair, and on, over the windowsill, coffee table, rocker, desk,
and held it up—I held my breath—
That's beautiful, she said, impressed,
she hadn't found a speck of death.

Literary Skills Review CONTINUED

1. What **mood** is created by the images in the first eight lines of "September, 1918"?

   A deep longing

   B looming dread

   C carefree innocence

   D quiet sadness

2. How would you describe the speaker's **attitude** in lines 9–18 of "September, 1918"?

   A losing hope

   B troubled but hopeful

   C disillusioned and angry

   D frightened of the future

3. In the implied comparison in lines 10–13 of "September, 1918," the afternoon is compared to a—

   A glass globe

   B leaf from a tree

   C child's ball

   D piece of fruit

4. The speaker puts the afternoon into her lunchbox because he or she—

   A has become tired of it

   B has become distracted by it

   C has become excited by it

   D has become saddened by it

5. The **irony** at the center of Lowell's poem is the contrast between—

   A the beautiful fall day and the reality of war

   B the boys' innocence and the speaker's despair

   C the present and the past

   D the boys at home and the boys at war

6. In addition to the dust on the floor, what else is the speaker of "How I Learned to Sweep" trying to sweep away?

   A her mother's presence

   B her dislike of housework

   C her fear of dying

   D the deaths of the soldiers

7. What is the **tone** of the last two lines of Alvarez's poem?

   A angry

   B ironic

   C hopeful

   D disappointed

8. What does the mother **symbolize** in Alvarez's poem?

   A the obsession with keeping a clean house

   B the need for disciplining young children

   C the desire to avoid thinking about the dead soldiers

   D the hope of respectfully honoring the dead soldiers

9. By the end of Alvarez's poem, the dust on the floor has become identified with—

A the garden on television

B the dragonflies

C the dead soldiers

D weeds underwater

10. Both poems make a statement about war by—

A directly stating their opposition to war

B showing how war hurts innocent people

C contrasting war with ordinary life

D graphically describing the horrors of war

11. An important difference between the two poems is that—

A Lowell uses rhythm, but Alvarez does not

B Lowell uses imagery, but Alvarez does not

C Alvarez uses end rhymes, but Lowell does not

D Alvarez uses onomatopoeia, but Lowell does not

Constructed Response

12. Briefly discuss the contrast in "September, 1918" and "How I Learned to Sweep" between the images in the poem and the narrator's awareness of war. Be sure to support your response with evidence from the poems.

Vocabulary Skills Review

Analogies   **Directions:** For each of the following items, choose the lettered pair of words that expresses a relationship that is most similar to the relationship between the pair of capitalized words.

1. *INTERLOPER* : INTRUDES ::
   A plumber : toilet
   B burglar : steals
   C leader : follows
   D drives : rides

2. *MALICIOUS* : BENEVOLENT ::
   A beautiful : gorgeous
   B strong : courageous
   C gentle : aggressive
   D violent : demanding

3. *PALPABLE* : TOUCH ::
   A painted : see
   B audible : hear
   C upset : feel
   D hungry : taste

4. *MORTIFIED* : EMBARRASSED ::
   A drizzled : flurried
   B forgetful : regretful
   C faithful : disloyal
   D arrogant : proud

5. *MALODOROUS* : SKUNK ::
   A robin : bird
   B deceitful : cheater
   C fair : tyrant
   D teacher : faculty

6. *ABOMINABLE* : DISGUSTING ::
   A ferocious : tame
   B accident : blame
   C mistaken : correct
   D horrifying : scary

7. *EULOGY* : SPEECH ::
   A envelope : letter
   B comedy : play
   C death : burial
   D writer : typist

8. *AUSTERE* : LUXURIOUS ::
   A harsh : severe
   B secure : safe
   C restful : vacation
   D elegant : plain

Academic Vocabulary

Directions: Complete each of the following word analogies.

9. *COMPONENT* : WHOLE ::
   A chapter : novel
   B song : music
   C thoughtless : considerate
   D inevitable : unavoidable

10. *DIVERSE* : VARIED ::
   A transmit : convey
   B happy : ecstatic
   C intrinsic : value
   D similar : different

Writing Skills Review

Edit an Analysis of Nonfiction **Directions:** Read the following paragraph from a draft of a student's analysis of nonfiction. Then, answer the questions below it.

(1) In her memoir "The Girl Who Wouldn't Talk," Maxine Hong Kingston retells a disturbing memory about a childhood acquaintance in order to reveal unpleasant but important truths about herself. (2) Kingston, a Chinese American, writes about her experiences growing up in California. (3) At first glance, her memoir is a description of her interactions with a Chinese girl whom Kingston "hated" for her shyness, inability to play sports, and refusal to talk. (4) Throughout the memoir, however, Kingston uses literary techniques to suggest that she hates the girl who won't talk only because Kingston sees the girl's own qualities in herself.

(5) The narrator's dialogue, which sounds typical of a sixth grader, contrasts with her more "adult" narration. (6) This contrast suggests that Kingston, as an adult narrator, is commenting on—and condemning—her own childish behavior.

---

1. Which sentence states the essay's thesis?

A 1

B 3

C 5

D 6

2. Which of the following additions to the introductory paragraph would *best* support the author's thesis?

A an accurate description of the story's major events

B a sentence identifying specific literary techniques that Kingston uses in her memoir

C a personal anecdote about the author's experiences with childhood friends

D a brief biography of Kingston, including details about her childhood

3. Which sentence would provide the *best* introduction to the second paragraph?

A Kingston uses many literary techniques, such as vivid narration, in her memoir.

B Although Kingston uses a childlike voice in parts of her memoir, she is really an adult.

C Kingston's use of realistic dialogue is more impressive than her use of narration.

D Kingston combines thoughtful narration with powerful, realistic dialogue.

4. Which type of sentence could the writer add after sentence 5 to strengthen the essay's argument?

A a sentence that identifies the author's favorite line from the memoir

B a sentence that quotes the most realistic line of dialogue from the memoir

C a sentence that explains how Kingston uses language to communicate with the reader

D a sentence that uses examples to illustrate the contrast between the dialogue and narration

5. Which sentence is *least* relevant to the author's thesis?

A 2

B 4

C 5

D 6

Read On

FICTION

The Things They Carried

A Bible used as a pillow, a pebble kept under the tongue, a can of peaches—these objects may puzzle us, but they mean the world to the young soldiers depicted in Tim O'Brien's brilliant narrative of the Vietnam War. This work of interconnected short stories straddles the line between reality and imagination, relating the stories of soldiers both on and off the battlefield.

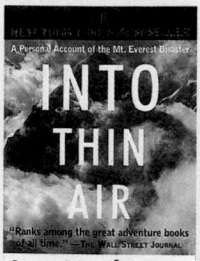

NONFICTION

Into Thin Air

A journalist who had, for the most part, put mountain climbing behind him, Jon Krakauer braved Mount Everest, the climber's dream and nightmare. Krakauer's 1996 climb turned into a catastrophe, with eight participants killed and several others stranded on the mountain by a terrible storm. This nonfiction narrative tells the story in riveting detail.

FICTION

Beloved

Toni Morrison (p. 752) writes of the debilitating effects of the oppression of African Americans on victim and perpetrator alike; she also explores the other side of the coin: the richness of the African American community and its traditions. Morrison's novel tells the story of a mother's desperate attempt to save her children from slavery.

POETRY

Unsettling America

More people are writing poetry than ever before, and happily, the audience for poetry is also growing. This volume, edited by Maria M. Gillan and Jennifer Gillan, contains thematically grouped poems by American poets of many cultures. These poems illustrate the richness of experience that defines Americans.

NONFICTION
Long Walk to Freedom

In 1990, Nelson Mandela was released from a South African prison twenty-seven years after being sentenced for his leadership role in the struggle against apartheid, a system of oppressive racial segregation. What happened next fulfilled the wildest dreams of millions of South Africans and human rights advocates: Apartheid laws were dismantled, and Mandela was elected president of a multiracial South African government. He was later honored with the Nobel Peace Prize. Mandela's autobiography details the struggles and setbacks that make the outcome of his lifelong journey so extraordinary.

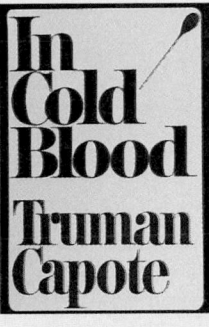

NONFICTION
In Cold Blood

In 1959, a Kansas farming family of four were murdered in their home. In 1966, Truman Capote's masterful account of the aftermath, replete with interviews of the captured murderers, was selling out of bookstores across the country. This nonfiction novel—which seemed to spawn a new genre—attracted readers with its psychological portraits and precise prose. The seemingly fictional account of actual events made a celebrity of its author and a mint for Hollywood studios when the film industry brought the book to the big screen in 1967.

WEB SITE
www.poets.org

Search this extensive database by poet or poem for more information on your favorite examples of free verse, sonnet, or villanelle, and present and past masters of rhyme, meter, and stanza. Weekly features and highlights include new poems, information on new poets, and essays. You can even listen to audio clips of poets reading their own work.

POETRY
The Voice at 3:00 A.M.

Serbian American poet Charles Simic is one of the most prolific writers of the twentieth century, and one of the most celebrated. A Pulitzer Prize winner, he is also the fifteenth Poet Laureate of the United States. Readers interested in exploring Simic's work have more than sixty titles to choose from, including prose selections, translations, and eighteen books of poetry. *The Voice at 3:00 A.M.* is an inviting introduction to several of his more recent poems.

Learn It Online
Explore other titles online at *NovelWise*.

go.hrw.com L11-1461 **Go**

Resource Center

Handbook of Literary and Historical Terms

For more information about a topic or to see related entries, turn to the page(s) indicated with each entry. Also, at the end of some entries in this handbook you will find cross-references to other entries that provide closely related information. For instance, at the end of *Alliteration* is a cross-reference to *Assonance*.

ABSTRACT LANGUAGE **A term used to describe language that deals with generalities and intangible concepts.** Words such as *happiness, despair, hope, beauty,* and *evil* are examples of the abstract. Abstract language is useful in dealing with philosophical ideas.

See page 1537.
See also *Concrete Language.*

ALLEGORY **A story or poem in which characters, settings, and events stand for other people or events or for abstract ideas or qualities.** An allegory can be read on one level for its literal meaning and on a second level for its symbolic, or allegorical, meaning. The most famous allegory in the English language is *The Pilgrim's Progress* (1678) by the English Puritan writer John Bunyan, in which Christian, on his journey to the Celestial City, meets such personages as Mr. Worldly Wiseman, Hopeful, and Giant Despair and travels to such places as the Slough of Despond, the Valley of Humiliation, and Doubting Castle. Puritans were trained to see their own lives as allegories of biblical experiences. Nathaniel Hawthorne and Edgar Allan Poe's fictions are often called allegorical.

See page 334.

ALLITERATION **The repetition of the same or similar consonant sounds in words that are close together.** Alliteration is used to create musical effects and to establish mood. In the following line from "The Tide Rises, the Tide Falls" (page 226) by Henry Wadsworth Longfellow, the repetition of the *s* sound is an example of alliteration:

> But the sea, the sea in darkness calls

See pages 359, 516.
See also *Assonance, Onomatopoeia, Rhyme.*

ALLUSION **A reference to someone or something that is known from history, literature, religion, politics, sports, science, or some other branch of culture.** T. S. Eliot drew on his knowledge of the Bible when he alluded to the raising of Lazarus from the dead in "The Love Song of J. Alfred Prufrock" (page 770). The title of Sandra Cisneros's essay "Straw into Gold" (page 1310) is an allusion to the folk tale about Rumpelstiltskin.

You won't understand the cartoon below unless you recognize the fairy tale it alludes to.

See pages 63, 320, 816, 1309.

"They're offering a deal–you can pay court costs and damages, they drop charges of breaking and entering."

Drawing by Maslin ©1988 The New Yorker Magazine.

AMBIGUITY **A technique by which a writer deliberately suggests two or more different, and sometimes conflicting, meanings in a work.** Langston Hughes's poem "Harlem" (page 987) has an ambiguous ending. The tone of William Carlos Williams's poem "This Is Just to Say" (page 782) is charmingly ambiguous.

See pages 824, 923.

AMERICAN DREAM **A uniquely American vision of the country consisting of three central ideas.** The American dream consists of a belief in America as a new Eden—a land of beauty, bounty, and unlimited promise; a feeling of optimism, created by ever expanding opportunity; and a confidence in triumph of the individual. Aspects of the American dream are reflected in the literature of all periods in American history.

See pages 746, 794, 864.

ANALOGY **A comparison made between two things to show how they are alike.** In *The Crisis, No. 1* (page 132), Thomas Paine draws an analogy between a thief breaking into a house and the king of England interfering in the affairs of the American Colonies.

See pages 131, 539.

ANAPEST **A metrical foot that has two unstressed syllables followed by one stressed syllable.** The word coexist (˘ ˘ ´) is an example of an anapest.

See also *Dactyl, Foot, Iamb, Iambic Pentameter, Meter, Spondee, Trochee.*

ANECDOTE **A very brief story, told to illustrate a point or serve as an example of something.** In Thomas Paine's *The Crisis, No. 1* (page 132), the tale of the Tory tavern keeper and his child is an anecdote.

See page 996.

ANTAGONIST **The opponent who struggles against or blocks the hero, or protagonist, in a story.** In *The Narrative of the Life of Frederick Douglass* (page 416), Mr. Covey is Douglass's antagonist. Mrs. Mitty is Mr. Mitty's antagonist in Thurber's story "The Secret Life of Walter Mitty" (page 932).

See also *Protagonist.*

ANTHROPOMORPHISM **Attributing human characteristics to an animal or inanimate object.** Writers often anthropomorphize animals or objects in order to achieve humorous or satirical effects.

See also *Personification.*

APHORISM **A brief, cleverly worded statement that makes a wise observation about life.** Benjamin Franklin's *Poor Richard's Almanack* (page 171) is a book of aphorisms. Ralph Waldo Emerson's style is **aphoristic**—he incorporates many pithy sayings into his essays (which is why he is so quotable).

See pages 165, 559.
See also *Proverb.*

ARCHETYPE **A very old imaginative pattern that appears in literature across cultures and is repeated through the ages.** An archetype can be a character, a plot, an image, a theme, or a setting. The plot in which a man sells his soul to the devil, as in "The Devil and Tom Walker" (page 290), is a recurring pattern in folk tales and other literature from around the world. The tragic hero is an example of an archetypal character that appears again and again in literature. The pattern of the journey, or quest, is a plot that recurs repeatedly in American literature.

See pages 19, 633, 911.

ARGUMENT **A form of persuasion that appeals to reason, rather than emotion, to convince an audience to think or act in a certain way.** The Declaration of Independence (page 141) is a famous example of a closely reasoned argument.

See page 280.
See also *Persuasion.*

ASSONANCE **The repetition of similar vowel sounds followed by different consonant sounds, especially in words close together.** Notice the repeated sounds of *i* in these lines from "The Tide Rises, the Tide Falls" (page 226) by Henry Wadsworth Longfellow. Read the lines aloud to hear the verbal music created by assonance.

> The tide rises, the tide falls,
> The twilight darkens, the curlew calls

See pages 516, 1363.
See also *Alliteration, Onomatopoeia, Rhyme.*

ATMOSPHERE **The mood or feeling created in a piece of writing.** A story's atmosphere might be peaceful, festive, menacing, melancholy, and so on. Elie Wiesel's *Night* (page 1048), for example, creates an atmosphere of terror and sadness.

See also *Mood, Setting.*

AUTOBIOGRAPHY **An account of the writer's own life.** Benjamin Franklin's *The Autobiography* (page 166) is one of the most famous autobiographies in American literature. An excerpt from Richard Wright's autobiography, *Black Boy*, is on page 1270.

See pages 165, 955, 1269.

BALLAD **A song or poem that tells a story.** The typical ballad tells a tragic story in the form of a monologue or dialogue. Ballads usually have a simple, steady rhythm, a simple rhyme pattern, and a refrain, all of which make them easy to memorize. Ballads composed by unknown singers and passed on orally from one generation to the next are called **folk ballads.** **Literary ballads** are written to imitate the sounds and subjects of folk ballads. A strong tradition of folk ballads and literary ballads exists in the United States. Country-and-western music, for example, frequently features songs written to imitate the older ballads. Here is the start of a favorite ballad, telling the story of Betsy and Ike:

> Oh don't you remember sweet Betsy from Pike,
> Who crossed the big mountains with her lover Ike,
> With two yoke of oxen, a big yellow dog,
> A tall Shanghai rooster, and one spotted hog?
> *Chorus*
> Singing dang fol dee dido,
> Singing dang fol dee day.

BIOGRAPHY **An account of someone's life written by another person.** One of the most famous biographies in American literature is Carl Sandburg's multivolume account of the life of Abraham Lincoln. A more recent, bestselling biography is David McCullough's *John Adams,* about one of our nation's founders and presidents.

BLANK VERSE **Poetry written in unrhymed iambic pentameter.** Blank verse has a long history in English literature. It was used notably by such poets as Shakespeare and Milton in the sixteenth and seventeenth centuries and by Robert Frost in the twentieth.

See pages 819, 828.
See also *Iambic Pentameter.*

CADENCE **The natural, rhythmic rise and fall of a language as it is normally spoken.** Cadence is different from **meter,** in which stressed and unstressed syllables of a poetic line are carefully counted to conform to a regular pattern. Walt Whitman was a master of imitating the cadence of spoken American English in his free verse.

See pages 507, 516.
See also *Free Verse, Meter, Rhythm.*

CAESURA **A pause or break within a line of poetry.** Some pauses are indicated by punctuation; others are suggested by phrasing or meaning. In the lines below, the caesuras are marked by double vertical lines. These pauses are indicated by punctuation.

> Announced by all the trumpets of the sky,
> Arrives the snow, || and, || driving o'er the fields,
> Seems nowhere to alight: || the whited air
> Hides hills and woods . . .
>
> —Ralph Waldo Emerson, from "The Snow-Storm"

CATALOG **A list of things, people, or events.** Cataloging was a favorite device of Walt Whitman, who included long, descriptive lists throughout *Leaves of Grass.*

See page 512.

CHARACTER **An individual in a story or play.** A character always has human traits, even if the character is an animal, as in Aesop's fables, or a god, as in the Greek and Roman myths. The process by which the writer reveals the personality of a character is called **characterization.** A writer can reveal a character in the following ways:

- by telling us directly what the character is like: sneaky, generous, mean to pets, and so on
- by describing how the character looks and dresses
- by letting us hear the character speak
- by revealing the character's private thoughts and feelings
- by revealing the character's effect on other people— showing how other characters feel or behave toward the character
- by showing the character in action

The first method of revealing a character is called **direct characterization.** When a writer uses this method, we do not have to figure out what a character's personality is like—the writer tells us directly. The other five methods of revealing a character are known as **indirect characterization.** When a writer uses these methods, we have to exercise our own judgment, putting clues together to infer what a character is like—just as we do in real life when we are getting to know someone.

Characters are often classified as static or dynamic. A **static character** is one who does not change much in the course of a story. A **dynamic character,** on the other hand, changes in some important way as a result of the story's action. Characters can also be classified as flat or round. **Flat characters** have few personality traits. They can be summed up by a single phrase: the loyal sidekick, the buffoon, the nosy neighbor. In contrast, **round characters** have more dimension to their personalities—they are complex, just as real people are.

> See pages 857, 1169, 1283.
> See also *Motivation, Stereotype.*

CLICHÉ A word or phrase, often a figure of speech, that has become lifeless because of overuse. Some examples of clichés are "green with envy," "quiet as a mouse," and "pretty as a picture."

CLIMAX That point in a plot that creates the greatest intensity, suspense, or interest. The climax is usually the point at which the conflict in the story is resolved.

> See page 874.

COMEDY In general, a story that ends with a happy resolution of the conflicts faced by the main character or characters. In many comedies the conflict is provided when a young couple who wish to marry are blocked by adults. In many comedies the main character has moved into a world of greater freedom at the end. In literature the word *comedy* is not synonymous with *humor.* Some comedies are humorous; some are not.

> See also *Tragedy.*

CONCEIT An elaborate metaphor or other figure of speech that compares two things that are startlingly different. Often a conceit is also a very lengthy comparison. The conceit was a popular figure of speech in seventeenth-century English metaphysical poetry. In American literature the poems of Emily Dickinson (page 548) are known for their conceits. In more recent literary history, T. S. Eliot (page 768) also used conceits.

> See also *Figure of Speech, Metaphor.*

CONCRETE LANGUAGE A term for language that uses specific words and details to describe a particular subject. Concrete language deals with the specifics of a subject. Words that engage the senses of hearing, touch, sight, smell, and taste are important examples of concrete language. A *fuzzy puppy with a round belly* is an example of concrete language.

> See page 1365.
> See also *Abstract Language.*

CONFESSIONAL SCHOOL A group of poets who wrote in the 1950s. Confessional poets include Robert Lowell, Sylvia Plath, Anne Sexton, and John Berryman. The confessional poets wrote frank and sometimes brutal poems about their personal lives.

> See page 1029.

CONFLICT The struggle between opposing forces or characters in a story. A conflict can be internal, involving opposing forces within a person's mind. In James Thurber's "The Secret Life of Walter Mitty" (page 932), for example, the title character has a comical internal conflict between his desire for heroism and his cowardice in the face of a formidable spouse. **External** conflicts can exist between two people, between a person and a force of nature or a machine, or between a person and a whole society. In one segment of Julia Alvarez's "Daughter of Invention" (page 1226), the narrator is in conflict with both her father and mother. Many stories have both internal and external conflicts.

> See pages 903, 1195, 1225.
> See also *Setting.*

CONNOTATION The associations and emotional overtones that have become attached to a word or phrase, in addition to its strict dictionary definition. The words *determined, firm, rigid, stubborn,* and *pigheaded* have similar dictionary definitions, or **denotations,** but widely varying connotations, or overtones of meaning. *Determined* and *firm* both suggest an admirable kind of resoluteness; *rigid* suggests an inability to bend and a kind of mindless refusal to change. *Stubborn* and *pigheaded,* on the other hand, have even more negative connotations. *Stubborn* has associations with a mule, and *pigheaded* with the pig, which, wrongly or not, is an animal often associated with mindless willfulness. Here are some other words that are more or less synonymous but which have vastly different connotations: *fastidious* and *fussy; daydreamer* and *escapist; scent, odor, smell,* and *stink.* Words with strong connotations are often called **loaded** words or **suggestive** words.

See page 713.

CONSONANCE **The repetition of the same or similar final consonant sounds on accented syllables or in important words.** The words *ticktock* and *singsong* contain examples of consonance. Some modern poets use consonance in place of rhyme.

COUPLET **Two consecutive rhyming lines of poetry.** If the two rhyming lines express a complete thought, they are called a **closed couplet.** The following lines are from a poem built on a series of closed couplets:

> If ever wife was happy in a man,
> Compare with me, ye women, if you can.
>
> —Anne Bradstreet, from "To My Dear and Loving Husband"

DACTYL **A metrical foot of three syllables in which the first syllable is stressed and the next two are unstressed.** The word *tendency* ('˘˘) is a dactyl.

See also *Anapest, Foot, Iamb, Iambic Pentameter, Meter, Spondee, Trochee.*

DARK ROMANTICS **A group of nineteenth-century writers who explored the dark side of human nature.** The Dark Romantics include Nathaniel Hawthorne, Herman Melville, and Edgar Allan Poe. In contrast to the optimistic nature of the Transcendentalist writers, the Dark Romantics explored the potentially evil side of humanity. Often their writings explored the psychological effects of guilt, sin, and madness.

See page 209.

DEISM **An eighteenth-century philosophy based on rationalism.** Deists believed that God created the world and its natural laws, but takes no other part in it. In contrast to the Puritans, deists believed in humanity's innate goodness and perfectibility. Many of the founders of the United States were deists.

See page 8.

DENOUEMENT **The conclusion (or resolution) of a story.** In French the word means "unraveling." At this point in a story, all the mysteries are unraveled, the conflicts are resolved, and all the questions raised by the plot are answered. Much modern fiction ends without a denouement, leaving the reader with a sense of incompleteness—just as life itself often offers only incomplete or ambiguous resolutions to problems.

See also *Plot, Resolution.*

DESCRIPTION **One of the four major forms of discourse, in which language is used to create a mood or emotion.** Description does this by using words that appeal to our senses: sight, hearing, touch, smell, and taste. Walt Whitman gives a vivid description of a Civil War battlefield in *Specimen Days* (page 534). N. Scott Momaday gives a wonderful description of a unique landmark in the opening paragraph of the selection from *The Way to Rainy Mountain* (page 32). The other three major forms of discourse are **exposition, narration,** and **persuasion.**

DIALECT **A way of speaking that is characteristic of a certain social group or of the inhabitants of a certain geographical area.** Dialects may differ from one another in vocabulary, pronunciation, and grammar. The dialect that has become dominant in America is known as Standard English. This is the dialect used most often on national radio news and television news broadcasts. Many writers try to capture dialects to give their stories local color, humor, or an air of authenticity. Some writers who are known for their skilled use of dialect are Mark Twain, Eudora Welty, William Faulkner, and Langston Hughes.

See pages 638, 900.
See also *Vernacular.*

DIALOGUE **The directly quoted words of people speaking to one another.** Writers use dialogue to advance the plot and develop characters.

See pages 939, 1269.
See also *Dialect, Diction, Tone.*

DICTION **A speaker's or writer's choice of words.** Diction can be formal, informal, colloquial, full of slang, poetic, ornate, plain, abstract, concrete, and so on. Diction depends on the writer's subject, purpose, and audience. Some words, for example, are suited to informal conversations but are inappropriate in a formal speech. Diction has a powerful effect on the **tone** of a piece of writing.

See also *Tone.*

DRAMATIC MONOLOGUE **A poem in which a character speaks to one or more listeners whose responses are not known.** The reactions of the listener must be inferred by the reader. From the speaker's words the reader learns about the setting, the situation, the identity of the other characters, and the personality of the speaker. The outstanding dramatic monologue in American literature is T. S. Eliot's "The Love Song of J. Alfred Prufrock" (page 770).

See page 769.

ELEGY **A poem of mourning, usually about someone who has died.** Most elegies are written to mark a particular person's death, but some extend their subject to reflect on life, death, and the fleeting nature of beauty. William Cullen Bryant's poem "Thanatopsis" (page 220) is an elegy. The excerpt from N. Scott Momaday's *The Way to Rainy Mountain* (page 32) is partly elegiac in that it mourns the death of a particular person and, by extension, the passing of an entire way of life.

ENJAMBMENT **The running on of sense from the end of one line of verse into the next, without a punctuated pause.** Poets often use enjambment to add rhythmic diversity. Enjambment is contrasted with an end-stopped line (a line that is a grammatical unit and ends with punctuation). Enjambed lines allow the poet to create a pause in the middle of a sentence. This mental and physical "breath" creates an unexpected moment for the reader.

EPIC **A long narrative poem, written in heightened language, which recounts the deeds of a heroic character who embodies the values of a particular society.** Epics in English include *Beowulf* (c. 700) and John Milton's *Paradise Lost* (1667). Some critics of Walt Whitman's *Leaves of Grass* see his collection as an American epic in which the hero is the questing poet.

EPITHET **A descriptive word or phrase that is frequently used to characterize a person or a thing.** The epithet "the father of our country" is often used to characterize George Washington. New York City's popular epithet, "the Big Apple," is frequently used by advertisers. Epics such as Homer's *Odyssey* and *Iliad* frequently use **stock epithets** over and over again to describe certain characters or places: "patient Penelope," "wily Odysseus," and "earthshaker" for Poseidon.

ESSAY **A short piece of nonfiction prose in which the writer discusses some aspect of a subject.** The word *essay* come from French *essai,* meaning "to try," a derivation that suggests that the essay form is not an exhaustive treatment of a subject. Essays are sometimes classified as **formal** or **informal** (or personal). The essay form was especially popular in the twentieth century, particularly among American writers. Some famous American essayists of the past include Thomas Paine (page 130), Ralph Waldo Emerson (page 238), and Henry David Thoreau (page 252). More recent essayists include E. B. White, Alice Walker (page 1292), James Baldwin (page 1300), Annie Dillard (page 210), and Joan Didion.

See page 1293.

EXPOSITION **One of the four major forms of discourse, in which something is explained or set forth.** Exposition is most commonly used in nonfiction. The word *exposition* also refers to that part of a plot in which the reader is given important background information on the characters, their setting, and their problems. Such exposition is usually provided at the opening of a story or play. See the opening paragraph of Nathaniel Hawthorne's "The Minister's Black Veil" (page 304) for an example. The other three major forms of discourse are **description, narration,** and **persuasion.**

See also *Plot.*

FABLE **A very short story told in prose or poetry that teaches a practical lesson about how to succeed in life.** In many fables the characters are animals that behave like people. The most ancient fabulist is the Greek Aesop; the most famous American fabulist is James Thurber (page 930), who wrote *Fables for Our Time* and *Further Fables for Our Time.*

FARCE **A type of comedy in which ridiculous and often stereotyped characters are involved in silly far-fetched situations.** The humor in a farce is often physical and slapstick, with characters being hit in the face with pies or running into closed doors. American cinema has produced many farces, including those starring Laurel and Hardy, Abbott and Costello, and the Marx Brothers.

FIGURE OF SPEECH **A word or phrase that describes one thing in terms of something else and that is not meant to be taken literally.** Figures of speech almost always involve a comparison of two things that are basically very dissimilar. Hundreds of figures of speech have been identified by scholars; the most common ones are **simile, metaphor, personification,** and **symbol.** Figures of speech more generally called **figurative language,** are basic to everyday speech. Statements like "She is a tower of strength" and "He is a pain in the neck" are figures of speech.

See pages 244, 1083.
See also *Conceit, Metaphor, Personification, Simile, Symbol.*

FIRESIDE POETS **A group of nineteenth-century poets from Boston including Henry Wadsworth Longfellow, John Greenleaf Whittier, Oliver Wendell Holmes, and James Russell Lowell.** Their poems were often read by the fireside as family entertainment and memorized and recited by students in classrooms. They were also known as the Schoolroom Poets.

See page 216.

FLASHBACK **A scene that interrupts the normal chronological sequence of events in a story to depict something that happened at an earlier time.** Although the word was coined to describe a technique used by moviemakers, the technique itself is at least as old as ancient Greek literature. Much of Homer's epic poem the *Odyssey* is a flashback. Willa Cather uses frequent flashbacks to reveal the past of Georgiana in "A Wagner Matinée" (page 670).

See page 453.

FOIL **A character who acts as a contrast to another character.** In Maxine Hong Kingston's "The Girl Who Wouldn't Talk" (page 1284), the quiet girl who takes refuge in her Chinese family is a foil for the narrator who is aggressively trying to fit into American society.

FOOT **A metrical unit of poetry.** A foot always contains at least one stressed syllable and, usually, one or more unstressed syllables. An **iamb** is a common foot in English poetry: It consists of an unstressed syllable followed by a stressed syllable (˘ ′).

See also *Anapest, Blank Verse, Dactyl, Iamb, Iambic Pentameter, Meter, Spondee, Trochee.*

FORESHADOWING **The use of hints and clues to suggest what will happen later in a plot.** A writer might use foreshadowing to create suspense or to prefigure later events. In "To Build a Fire" (page 694), for example, Jack London places hints throughout the text that foreshadow the story's conclusion.

FRAME STORY **A literary device in which a story is enclosed in another story, a tale within a tale.** The best-known example of a frame story is the Persian collection *The Thousand and One Nights* (also known as *Arabian Nights*). Raymond Carver uses the frame device in "Everything Stuck to Him" (page 1208). His story begins and ends with a frame in which an unnamed man tells a woman a story. The story that the man tells is the main body of Carver's tale.

FREE ENTERPRISE **The practice of allowing private businesses to operate competitively for profit with little government regulation.** Free enterprise was threatened by Marxist beliefs. Several novelists of the 1920s and 1930s satirized the free-enterprise system and the gross materialism of American business of the time. Sinclair Lewis's *Babbitt* (1922) is a major example.

FREE VERSE **Poetry that does not conform to regular meter or rhyme scheme.** Poets who write in free verse try to reproduce the natural rhythms of spoken language. Free verse uses the traditional poetic elements of **imagery, figures of speech, repetition, internal rhyme, alliteration, assonance,** and **onomatopoeia.** The first American practitioner of free verse was Walt Whitman (page 510). Some of Whitman's heirs are William Carlos Williams (page 778), Carl Sandburg (page 790), and Allen Ginsberg (page 1015).

See pages 507, 758.
See also *Cadence, Meter, Rhythm.*

HAIKU **A short, unrhymed poem developed in Japan in the fifteenth century.** A haiku consists of three unrhymed lines and a total of seventeen syllables. The first and third lines of a traditional haiku have five syllables each, and the middle line has seven syllables. Haiku often convey feelings through a descriptive snapshot of a natural object or scene. Imagists like Ezra Pound were influenced by the haiku form.

See page 758.

HARLEM RENAISSANCE **A cultural movement of the early 1920s led by African American artists, writers, musicians, and performers located in Harlem.** After World War I, vast numbers of African Americans migrated north and settled in the New York City neighborhood called Harlem. Important contributors to the Harlem Renaissance were the writers Langston Hughes and Countee Cullen, the artists Jacob Lawrence and Aaron Douglas, and the performers Paul Robeson and Josephine Baker.

See pages 746, 749, 951–952.

HYPERBOLE **A figure of speech that uses an incredible exaggeration, or overstatement, for effect.** In "The Celebrated Jumping Frog of Calaveras County" (page 639), Mark Twain uses hyperbole for comic effect. In his poetry, Walt Whitman often uses overstatement to create a larger-than-life persona, or speaker, as in the line below.

> I sound my barbaric yawp over the roofs of the world.
>
> —Walt Whitman, *Song of Myself*, 54

See page 1083.
See also *Understatement*.

IAMB **A metrical foot in poetry that has an unstressed syllable followed by a stressed syllable, as in the word *protect*.** The iamb (ˇ ′) is a common foot in poetry written in English.

See pages 225, 228.
See also *Anapest, Blank Verse, Dactyl, Foot, Iambic Pentameter, Meter, Spondee, Trochee.*

IAMBIC PENTAMETER **A line of poetry that contains five iambic feet.** The iambic pentameter line is most common in English and American poetry. Shakespeare and John Milton, among others, used iambic pentameter in their major works. So did such American poets as William Cullen Bryant, Ralph Waldo Emerson, Robert Frost, and Wallace Stevens. Here, for example, is the opening line of a poem by Emerson:

> In Máy, whĕn séa-wĭnds pierced oŭr sólitŭdes
>
> —Ralph Waldo Emerson, from "The Rhodora"

See page 228.
See also *Blank Verse, Foot, Iamb, Meter, Scanning.*

IDIOM **An expression particular to a certain language that means something different from the literal definitions of its parts.** "Falling in love" is an American idiom, as is "I lost my head."

See also *Figure of Speech.*

IMAGERY **The use of language to evoke a picture or a concrete sensation of a person, a thing, a place, or an experience.** Although most images appeal to the sense of sight, they may appeal to the sense of taste, smell, hearing, and touch as well.

See pages 105, 131, 356, 448.

IMAGISM **A twentieth-century movement in European and American poetry that advocated the creation of hard, clear images, concisely expressed in everyday speech.** The leading Imagist poets in America were Ezra Pound, Amy Lowell, H. D. [Hilda Doolittle], and William Carlos Williams.

See pages 757, 758.

IMPRESSIONISM **A nineteenth-century movement in literature and art that advocated recording one's personal impressions of the world, rather than attempting a strict representation of reality.** Some famous American impressionists in art are Mary Cassatt, Maurice Prendergast, and William Merritt Chase. In fiction, Stephen Crane pioneered a kind of literary impressionism in which he portrayed not objective reality but one character's impressions of reality. Crane's impressionistic technique is best seen in his novel *The Red Badge of Courage.*

INCONGRUITY **The deliberate joining of opposites or of elements that are not appropriate to each other.** T. S. Eliot's famous opening simile in "The Love Song of J. Alfred Prufrock" (page 770) joins two incongruous elements: a sunset and a patient knocked out by ether on an operating table. Incongruity can also be used for humor: We laugh at the sight of an elephant dressed in a pink tutu because the two elements are incongruous. Writers also use incongruity for dramatic effect by creating a tension between how characters act and the situation they find themselves in. An example would be a someone acting normal in a very absurd situation.

INTERIOR MONOLOGUE **A narrative technique that records a character's internal flow of thoughts, memories, and associations.** Parts of James Joyce's *Ulysses* and William Faulkner's *The Sound and the Fury* are written as interior monologues.

See also *Stream of Consciousness.*

INTERNAL RHYME **Rhyme that occurs within a line of poetry or within consecutive lines.** The first line of the following couplet includes an internal rhyme.

> And so, all the night-**tide,** I lie down by the **side**
> Of my darling—my darling—my life and my bride. . . .
>
> —Edgar Allan Poe, from "Annabel Lee"

See also *Rhyme.*

INVERSION **The reversal of the normal word order in a sentence or phrase.** An English sentence is normally built on subject-verb-complement, in that order. An inverted sentence reverses one or more of those elements. In poetry written many years ago, writers often inverted word order as a matter of course, in order to have words conform to the meter, or to create rhymes. The poetry of Anne Bradstreet contains many inversions, as in the first line of the poem on the burning of her house:

> In silent night when rest I took

In prose, inversion is often used for emphasis, as when Patrick Henry, in his fiery speech to the Virginia Convention (page 122), thundered "Suffer not yourselves to be betrayed with a kiss" (instead of "Do not suffer [allow] yourselves," and so on).

See pages 95, 219, 509.

IRONY **In general, a discrepancy between appearances and reality.** There are three main types of irony:

1. **Verbal irony** occurs when someone says one thing but really means something else. The first line of Stephen Crane's poem "War Is Kind" is an example of verbal irony: "Do not weep, maiden, for war is kind." The speaker really believes that war is not kind and warrants weeping.
2. **Situational irony** takes place when there is a discrepancy between what is expected to happen, or what would be appropriate to happen, and what really does happen. A famous use of situational irony is in Stephen Crane's "A Mystery of Heroism" (page 470), in which a soldier risks his life to get water that is then spilled.
3. **Dramatic irony** is so called because it is often used on stage. In this kind of irony a character in the play or story thinks one thing is true, but the audience or reader knows better. In Edwin

Arlington Robinson's "Miniver Cheevy" (page 715), Miniver thinks he is too refined for his time, but to the reader he seems foolish and somewhat pathetic.

See pages 469, 560, 571, 645, 1419.

LYRIC POEM **A poem that does not tell a story but expresses the personal feelings or thoughts of a speaker.** The many lyric poems in this textbook include "Thanatopsis" by William Cullen Bryant (page 220) and the optimistic "what if a much of a which of a wind" by E. E. Cummings (page 808).

MAGIC REALISM **A genre developed in Latin America that juxtaposes the everyday with the marvelous or magical.** Myths, folk tales, religious beliefs, and tall tales are the raw material for many magic realist writers. Gabriel García Márquez's work, particularly his novel *One Hundred Years of Solitude* (1967), established him as a master of the genre. Other prominent Latin American magic realists include Jorge Luis Borges, Julio Cortázar, and Isabel Allende. Among American writers, Donald Barthelme and Thomas Pynchon have been influenced by magic realism.

MARXISM **The political and economic philosophy developed by Karl Marx and his followers in the mid-nineteenth century.** In contrast to capitalists, Marxists believe greater economic unity can be reached by a classless society.

MEMOIR **A type of autobiography that often focuses on a specific time period or historical event.** Elie Wiesel's *Night* (page 1048) is a memoir about the author's harrowing experience in a concentration camp.

See also *Autobiography.*

METAPHOR **A figure of speech that makes a comparison between two unlike things without the use of such specific words of comparison as *like, as, than,* or *resembles.*** There are several kinds of metaphor:

1. A **directly stated metaphor** states the comparison explicitly: "Fame is a bee" (Emily Dickinson).
2. An **implied metaphor** does not state explicitly the two terms of the comparison: "I like to see it lap the Miles" (Emily Dickinson) contains an implied metaphor in which the verb *lap* implies a comparison between "it," which is a train, and

some animal that "laps" up water.

3. An **extended metaphor** is a metaphor that is extended or developed over a number of lines or with several examples. Dickinson's poem beginning "Fame is a bee" is an extended metaphor: The comparison of fame to a bee is extended for four lines.

> Fame is a bee.
> It has a song—
> It has a sting—
> Ah, too, it has a wing.

4. A **dead metaphor** is a metaphor that has been used so often that the comparison is no longer vivid: "The head of the house," "the seat of government," and a "knotty problem" are all dead metaphors.

5. A **mixed metaphor** is a metaphor that fails to make a logical comparison because its mixed terms are visually or imaginatively incompatible. If you say, "The president is a lame duck who is running out of gas," you've lost control of your metaphor and have produced a statement that is ridiculous (ducks do not run out of gas).

See pages 233, 244, 253, 421, 543, 576, 971, 1039.
See also *Conceit, Figure of Speech, Simile.*

METER   A pattern of stressed and unstressed syllables in poetry. The meter of a poem is commonly indicated by using the symbol (´) for stressed syllables and the symbol (˘) for unstressed syllables. This is called **scanning** the poem.

Meter is described as **iambic, trochaic, dactylic,** or **anapestic.** These scanned lines from "Richard Cory" (page 714) are iambic: They are built on iambs—unstressed syllables followed by stressed syllables.

> Ănd hé wăs álwăys quíetlý arráyed
> Ănd hé wăs álwăys húmăn whĕn hĕ tálked

See also *Anapest, Cadence, Dactyl, Foot, Free Verse, Iamb, Iambic Pentameter, Rhythm, Scanning, Spondee, Trochee.*
See page 225.

METONYMY   A figure of speech in which a person, place, or thing is referred to by something closely associated with it. Referring to a king or queen as "the crown" is an example of metonymy, as is calling a car "wheels."

See also *Synecdoche.*

MODERNISM   A term for the bold new experimental styles and forms that swept the arts during the first third of the twentieth century. Modernism called for changes in subject matter, in fictional styles, in poetic forms, and in attitudes. T. S. Eliot and Ezra Pound are associated with the modernist movement in poetry. Their aim was to rid poetry of its nineteenth-century prettiness and sentimentality.

See page 746.
See also *Imagism, Symbolism.*

MOOD   The overall emotion created by a work of literature. Mood can usually be described with one or two adjectives, such as *bittersweet, playful,* or *scary.* All the elements of literature, including sound effects, rhythm, and word choice, contribute to a work's mood. The mood of William Faulkner's "A Rose for Emily" (page 878) is dark and murky, just like the house described in the story.

See pages 289, 803, 986.
See also *Atmosphere, Setting.*

MOTIVATION   The reasons for a character's behavior. In order for us to understand why characters act the way they do, their motivation has to be believable, at least in terms of the story. At times a writer directly reveals motivation; in subtler fiction we must use details from the story to infer motivation.

See pages 857, 1098, 1239.
See also *Character.*

MYTH   An anonymous traditional story that is basically religious in nature and that usually serves to explain a belief, ritual, or mysterious natural phenomenon. Most myths have grown out of religious rituals, and almost all of them involve the exploits of gods and humans. Works of magic realism often draw on myths or mythlike tales.

See pages 15–16.

NARRATIVE **The form of discourse that tells about a series of events.** Narration is used in all kinds of literature: fiction, nonfiction, and poetry. Usually a narrative is told in **chronological order**—in the order in which events occurred. The other three major forms of discourse are **description, exposition,** and **persuasion.**

NARRATIVE POEM **A poem that tells a story—a series of related events with a beginning, a middle, and an end.** A narrative poem also features characters and, frequently, dialogue. Henry Wadsworth Longfellow is famous for his long narrative poems based on figures from myth and from European and American history. *The Song of Hiawatha* and *Evangeline* are major examples of his narrative poems.

See page 828.

NARRATOR **In fiction, the one who tells the story.** Narrators differ in their degree of participation in the story: (1) **Omniscient narrators** are all-knowing and outside the action; they can take us into the minds and hearts of all the characters and behind all the events unfolding in the story; (2) **first-person narrators** are either witnesses to or participants in the story; (3) **third-person-limited narrators** are omniscient narrators too, but they zoom in on one character and allow us to experience the story through this one character's perceptions.

See also *Point of View.*

NATURALISM **A nineteenth-century literary movement that was an extension of realism and that claimed to portray life exactly as if it were being examined through a scientist's microscope.** The naturalists relied heavily on the new fields of psychology and sociology. They tended to dissect human behavior with complete objectivity, the way a scientist would dissect a specimen in the laboratory. The naturalists were also influenced by Darwinian theories of the survival of the fittest. Naturalists believed that human behavior is determined by heredity and environment; they felt that people have no recourse to supernatural forces and that human beings, like animals, are subject to laws of nature beyond their control. The outstanding naturalists among American writers are Theodore Dreiser, Jack London, and Frank Norris. Some people consider John Steinbeck's *The Grapes of Wrath* a naturalistic novel, in which characters are the pawns of economic conditions.

See pages 681, 693.
See also *Realism.*

OCTAVE **An eight-line poem, or the first eight lines of a Petrarchan, or Italian, sonnet.** In a Petrarchan sonnet the octave states the subject of the sonnet or poses a problem or question.

See also *Sestet, Sonnet.*

ODE **A lyric poem, usually long, on a serious subject and written in dignified language.** In ancient Greece and Rome, odes were written to be read in public at ceremonial occasions. In modern literature, odes tend to be more private, informal, and reflective.

ONOMATOPOEIA **The use of a word whose sound imitates or suggests its meaning.** The word *buzz* is onomatopoeic; it imitates the sound it names.

See page 1363.

OXYMORON **A figure of speech that combines opposite or contradictory terms in a brief phrase.** *Sweet sorrow, deafening silence,* and *living death* are common oxymorons. (Some jokesters claim that phrases such as *jumbo shrimp, congressional leadership,* and *limited nuclear war* are also oxymorons.)

PARABLE **A relatively short story that teaches a moral, or lesson, about how to lead a good life.** The most famous parables are those told by Jesus in the Bible.

See pages 263, 304.

PARADOX **A statement that appears self-contradictory but reveals a kind of truth.** Many writers like to use paradox because it allows them to express the complexity of life by showing how opposing ideas can be both contradictory and true. Emily Dickinson often used paradoxes, as in "I taste a liquor never brewed" and "Much Madness is divinest Sense" (page 564).

See pages 268, 571, 811.

PARALLEL STRUCTURE **The repetition of words or phrases that have similar grammatical structures (also called *parallelism*).** Lincoln, in his Gettysburg Address (page 503), uses several memorable parallel structures, as when he refers to "government of the people, by the people, for the people."

See pages 139, 277, 492, 512.

PARODY **A work that makes fun of another work by imitating some aspect of the writer's style.** Parodies often achieve their effects by humorously exaggerating certain features in the original work.

See page 931.

PASTORAL **A type of poem that depicts country life in idyllic, idealized terms.** The term *pastoral* comes from the Latin word for "shepherd" (which survives today in our word *pastor*). Originally, in the Latin verse of ancient Rome, pastorals were about the loves of shepherds and nymphs and the simple idealized pleasures of country life. (Any work of literature that treats rural life as it really is would not be pastoral.) Today the term has a looser meaning, referring to any poem that portrays an idyllic rural setting or expresses nostalgia for an age or place of lost innocence. England has a long pastoral tradition; America has almost no pastoral tradition at all. The term *pastoral* is often used, misleadingly, to refer to poets who write about rural life. Robert Frost, for example, has been called a pastoral poet. No poet's work could be further from the idealized pastoral tradition. Frost is a deeply ironic, even dark poet.

PERSONIFICATION **A figure of speech in which an object or animal is given human feelings, thoughts, or attitudes.** Personification is a type of metaphor in which two dissimilar things are compared. In "Mirror" (page 1340), Sylvia Plath personifies a mirror by giving it human thoughts and characteristics.

See pages 27, 227, 244, 565.
See also *Anthropomorphism,
Figure of Speech.*

PERSUASION **One of the four forms of discourse, which uses reason and emotional appeals to convince a reader to think or act in a certain way.** Persuasive techniques are used in the Declaration of Independence (page 141), in Patrick Henry's "Give me liberty, or give me death" speech (page 122), and in Thomas Paine's *The Crisis, No. 1* (page 132). Persuasion is almost exclusively used in nonfiction, particularly in essays and speeches. The other three major forms of discourse are **description, exposition,** and **narration.**

See pages 121, 158.
See also *Argument.*

PLAIN STYLE **A way of writing that stresses simplicity and clarity of expression.** The plain style was favored by most Puritan writers, who avoided unnecessary ornamentation in all aspects of their lives, including church ritual and even the style of church structures. Simple sentences, everyday words from common speech, and clear and direct statements characterize the plain style. This style can be seen in Anne Bradstreet's works. One of the chief exponents of the plain style in recent American literature was Ernest Hemingway.

See pages 53, 103.
See also *Style.*

PLOT **The series of related events in a story or play, sometimes called the story line.** Most short story plots contain the following elements: **exposition,** which tells us who the characters are and introduces their conflict; **complications,** which arise as the characters take steps to resolve their conflicts; the **climax,** that exciting or suspenseful moment when the outcome of the conflict is imminent; and a **resolution** or **denouement,** when the story's problems are all resolved and the story ends.

The plots of dramas and novels are more complex because of their length. A schematic representation of a typical dramatic plot is shown below. It is based on a pyramid developed by the nineteenth-century German critic Gustav Freitag. The **rising action** refers to all the actions that take place before the **turning point** (sometimes called the **crisis**). The turning point is the point at which the hero experiences a decisive reversal of fortune: In a comedy, things begin to work out well at that turning point; in a tragedy they get worse and worse. (In Shakespeare's plays the turning point takes place in the third act. In *Romeo and Juliet,* for example, after he kills Tybalt in the third act, Romeo's fate is sealed and he experiences one disaster after another.) All the action after the turning point is called **falling action** because it leads to the final resolution (happy or unhappy) of the conflict. The major **climax** in most plays and novels takes place just before the ending; in Shakespeare's plays the final climax takes place in the fifth, or last, act. (In *Romeo and Juliet* the major climax takes place in the last act when the two young people kill themselves.)

Dramatic Plot

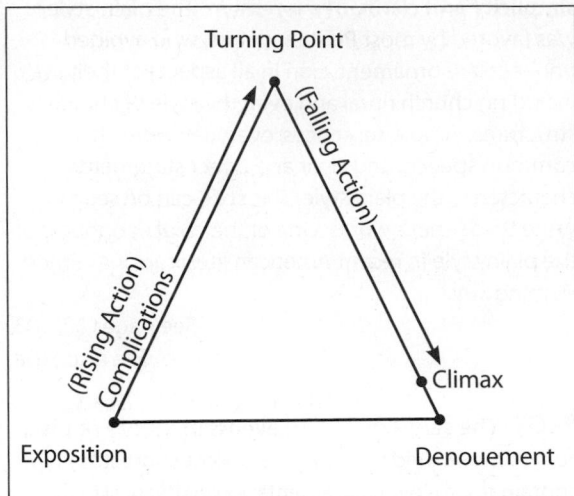

See pages 289, 300.
See also *Climax, Denouement, Exposition, Resolution.*

POINT OF VIEW **The vantage point from which the writer tells a story.** In broad terms, there are four main points of view: **first person, third person limited, omniscient,** and **objective.**

1. In the **first-person point of view,** one of the characters in the story tells the story, using first-person pronouns such as *I* and *we.* With this point of view, we can know only what the narrator knows. Mark Twain's novel *Adventures of Huckleberry Finn* is told from the first-person point of view, by the novel's main character, a boy named Huck Finn. One of the great pleasures of that novel, in fact, is that its point of view allows us to hear Huck's very distinct voice and dialect. It also allows us to see the complex adult world through the eyes of a young boy who is often victimized by that world.

2. In the **third-person-limited point of view,** an unknown narrator (usually thought of as the author) tells the story, but this narrator zooms in to focus on the thoughts and feelings of only one character. (This point of view gets its name because the narrator refers to all the characters as he, she, and they; this narrator does not refer to himself or herself with the first-person pronoun *I.*) Like the first-person point of view, however, this point of view also limits us to the perceptions of one character, but in this case the narrator can tell us many things that the character is unaware of. For example, Eudora Welty tells "A Worn Path" (page 904) from the third-person-limited point of view, which zooms in on her protagonist, an old woman

named Phoenix Jackson. At one point, Welty's narrator tells us that Phoenix was "like an old woman begging a dignified forgiveness."

3. In the **omniscient point of view,** an omniscient, or all-knowing, narrator tells the story, also using the third-person pronouns. However, this narrator, instead of focusing on one character only, often tells us everything about many characters: their motives, weaknesses, hopes, childhoods, and sometimes even their futures. This narrator can also comment directly on the characters' actions. Nathaniel Hawthorne's "The Minister's Black Veil" (page 304) is told from the omniscient point of view.

4. In the **objective point of view,** a narrator who is totally impersonal and objective tells the story, with no comment on any characters or events. The objective point of view is like the point of view of a movie camera; it is totally impersonal, and what we know is only what the camera might see. This narrator never gives any direct revelation of the characters' thoughts or motives. Ernest Hemingway uses this objective point of view, which is why his stories often seem so puzzling to readers. "What happened?" we ask. The *reader* must infer what happens in Hemingway's stories, just as in real life we have to infer the motives, thoughts, and feelings of people we meet.

See page 455.

POSTMODERNISM **A term for the dominant trend in the arts since 1945 characterized by experiments with nontraditional forms and the acceptance of multiple meanings.** The lines between real and imaginary worlds are often blurred in postmodern texts, as is the boundary between fiction and nonfiction. Other characteristics of postmodern texts are cultural diversity and an often playful self-consciousness, which is an acknowledgment that literature is not a mirror that accurately reflects the world, but a created world unto itself. Some well-known postmodern writers are Donald Barthelme, Toni Morrison, and Philip Roth.

See pages 1026, 1030.

PROTAGONIST **The central character in a story, the one who initiates or drives the action.** The protagonist might or might not be the story's hero; some protagonists are actually the villains in the story.

See page 843.
See also *Antagonist.*

PROVERB **A short, pithy statement that expresses a common truth or experience.** Many of Benjamin Franklin's sayings, such as "Fish and visitors smell in three days," have become proverbs in American culture.

See also *Aphorism.*

PSYCHOANALYSIS **A method of examining the unconscious mind, developed primarily by the Austrian physician Sigmund Freud (1865–1939).** Psychoanalysis is based on the assumption that many mental and emotional disorders are the result of the conscious mind repressing factors that persist in the unconscious and can cause conflicts. Modern writers often use the techniques of psychoanalysis. In "The Secret Life of Walter Mitty" (page 932), James Thurber uses the psychoanalytic technique of free association to give us a picture of a man with (comically) repressed desires.

See page 751.

PUN **A play on words based on the multiple meanings of a single word or on words that sound alike but mean different things.** An example of the first type of pun is a singer explaining her claim that she was locked out of an audition because she couldn't find the right key. The second kind of pun can be found in the opening lines of Shakespeare's *Julius Caesar,* where a man who repairs shoes claims to be a mender of men's souls (soles). Puns are often used for humor, but some puns are a serious element in poetry.

QUATRAIN **A poem consisting of four lines, or four lines of a poem that can be considered as a unit.** The typical ballad stanza, for example, is a quatrain.

RATIONALISM **The belief that human beings can arrive at truth by using reason, rather than by relying on the authority of the past, on religious faith, or on intuition.** The Declaration of Independence (page 141) is a document based on rationalist principles.

See pages 8, 117.

REALISM **A style of writing, developed in the nineteenth century, that attempts to depict life accurately, as it really is, without idealizing or romanticizing it.** Instead of writing about the long ago or far away, the realists concentrated on contemporary life and on middle- and lower-class lives in particular. Among the outstanding realistic novelists in America are Stephen Crane, Willa Cather, and John Steinbeck. European playwrights who wrote realistic dramas, including Henrik Ibsen, August Strindberg, and Anton Chekhov, discarded artificial plots in favor of themes centering on contemporary society. They also rejected extravagant language in favor of simple, everyday diction.

See pages 451, 681.

See also *Naturalism, Romanticism.*

REFRAIN **A word, phrase, line, or group of lines that is repeated, for effect, several times in a poem.** Refrains are often used in ballads and other narrative poems. "Nevermore" is a refrain in Poe's "The Raven" (page 360).

See page 433.

REGIONALISM **Literature that emphasizes a specific geographic setting and that reproduces the speech, behavior, and attitudes of the people who live in that region.** Among the great regional writers of the twentieth century are Sinclair Lewis (Midwest); John Steinbeck (California); and William Faulkner, Flannery O'Connor, and Eudora Welty (South).

See page 619.

REPETITION **A unifying property of repeated words, sounds, syllables, and other elements that appear in a work.** Repetition occurs in most poetry and in some prose. Repetition is used to create rhythm, to reinforce a message, and to enhance a mood or emotional affect. **Rhyme, refrain, assonance, dissonance,** and other literary devices are all based on the repetition of certain sounds.

See pages 445, 546, 983, 1391.

See also *Assonance, Consonance, Refrain, Rhyme.*

RESOLUTION **The conclusion of a story, when all or most of the conflicts have been settled.** The resolution is also often called the *denouement.*

See also *Denouement, Plot.*

RHETORICAL QUESTION **A question that is asked for effect and that does not actually require an answer.** In his speech to the Virginia Convention (page 122), Patrick Henry asks several rhetorical questions. Such questions presume the audience agrees with the speaker on the answers.

RHYME **The repetition of vowel sounds in accented syllables and all succeeding syllables.** *Listen* and *glisten* rhyme, as do *chime* and *sublime.* When words within the same line of poetry have repeated sounds, we have an example of **internal rhyme. End rhyme**

refers to rhyming words at the end of lines.

The pattern of rhymes in a poem is called a **rhyme scheme.** Rhyme scheme is commonly indicated with letters of the alphabet, each rhyming sound represented by a different letter of the alphabet. For example, the rhyme scheme of the following lines is abab.

> Tell me not, in mournful numbers,   *a*
> Life is but an empty dream!—   *b*
> For the soul is dead that slumbers,   *a*
> And things are not what they seem.   *b*
>
> —Henry Wadsworth
> Longfellow, "A Psalm of Life"

Approximate rhymes (also called **off rhymes, half rhymes, imperfect rhymes,** or **slant rhymes**) are words that have some correspondence in sound but not an exact one. Examples of approximate rhymes are often found in Emily Dickinson's poems. *Flash* and *flesh* are approximate rhymes, as are *stream* and *storm,* and *early* and *barley.* Approximate rhyme has the effect of catching the reader off guard: Where you expect a perfect rhyme, you get only an approximation. The emotional effect is something like that of the sound of a sharp or flat note in music.

See also *Internal Rhyme, Rhythm, Slant Rhyme.*

RHYTHM   The alternation of stressed and unstressed syllables in language. Rhythm occurs naturally in all forms of spoken and written English. The most obvious kind of rhythm is produced by **meter,** the regular pattern of stressed and unstressed syllables found in some poetry. Writers can also create less structured rhythms by using rhyme, repetition, pauses, and variations in line length and by balancing long and short words or phrases.

See pages 557, 978.
See also *Cadence, Free Verse, Meter, Rhyme.*

ROMANCE   In general, a story in which an idealized hero or heroine undertakes a quest and is successful. In a romance, beauty, innocence, and goodness usually prevail over evil. Romances are traditionally set in the distant past and use a great deal of fantasy. The laws of nature are often suspended in a romance, so that the hero often has supernatural powers, as we see in the adventures of King Arthur and his knights. Stories set in the American West are in the romance mode, except that the supernatural elements are eliminated (though the sheriff-hero usually has a nearly magical skill with

his gun). Today we also use the word *romance* to refer to a kind of popular escapist love story, which often takes place in an exotic setting. A popular contemporary romance in the traditional sense is the bestselling trilogy by J.R.R. Tolkien, *The Lord of the Rings.*

ROMANTICISM   **A revolt against rationalism that affected literature and the other arts, beginning in the late eighteenth century and remaining strong throughout most of the nineteenth century.** Romanticism is marked by these characteristics: (1) a conviction that intuition, imagination, and emotion are superior to reason; (2) a conviction that poetry is superior to science; (3) a belief that contemplation of the natural world is a means of discovering the truth that lies behind mere reality; (4) a distrust of industry and city life and an idealization of rural life and of the wilderness; (5) an interest in the more "natural" past and in the super natural. Romanticism affected so many creative people that it was bound to take many different forms; the result is that it is difficult to define the word in a way that includes everyone who might be called a Romantic. In the nineteenth century, for example, Romantics were outspoken in their love of nature and contempt for technology. In the twentieth century, however, as nature was taken over by real-estate developers and highways, some writers took a romantic view of machines, buildings, and other products of technology.

See pages 202–209, 215–216.
See also *Realism.*

ROMANTIC NOVEL   **A novel with a happy ending that presents readers with characters engaged in adventures filled with courageous acts, daring chases, and exciting escapes.** James Fenimore Cooper is known for novels such as *The Last of the Mohicans* (1826) and *The Deerslayer* (1841), which are filled with romantic adventures.

See page 216.

SATIRE   **A type of writing that ridicules the shortcomings of people or institutions in an attempt to bring about a change.** Satire can cover a wide range of tones, from gentle spoofing to savage mockery. In "The Secret Life of Walter Mitty" (page 932), James Thurber pokes fun at the domesticated American male's tendency to escape into heroic fantasies. Satire is always intensely moral in its purpose. Mark Twain, in his essay "The Lowest Animal" (page 646), satirizes the moral infirmity of the entire human race by ironically comparing the behavior of humans with that of the animals and finding the latter to be morally superior.

See pages 73, 645.

SCANNING **The analysis of a poem to determine its meter.** When you scan a poem, you describe the pattern of stressed and unstressed syllables in each line. Stresses, or accents, are indicated by the symbol (´) and unstressed syllables by the symbol (˘).

> To hím who ĭn thĕ lóve ŏf Natŭre hólds
> Commúnĭon wĭth hĕr vísĭblĕ fórms, shĕ spéaks
> Ă várĭoŭs lánguăge: fŏr hĭs gáyĕr hoúrs
> Shĕ hás ă voíce ŏf gládnĕss, ănd ă smíle.
>
> —William Cullen Bryant, from "Thanatopsis"

See also *Anapest, Blank Verse, Dactyl, Foot, Iamb, Iambic Pentameter, Meter, Spondee, Trochee.*

SESTET **Six lines of poetry, especially the last six lines of a Petrarchan, or Italian, sonnet.** In the Petrarchan sonnet the sestet offers a comment on the subject or problem presented in the first eight lines, or the octave, of the poem.

See pages 228, 719, 814.
See also *Octave, Sonnet.*

SETTING **The time and location in which a story takes place.** Setting can have several functions in fiction:

1. Setting is often used to create **conflict.** In the purest and often simplest form of a story, a character is in conflict with some element of a setting. The narrator in Jack London's "To Build a Fire" (page 694), for example, is in conflict with extreme cold (the cold wins).
2. Often the setting helps to create **atmosphere** or **mood.** Edgar Allan Poe's setting of a dungeon in "The Pit and the Pendulum" (page 345) creates a mood of horror.
3. Setting can also create and delineate **character.** In William Faulkner's "A Rose for Emily" (page 878), Miss Emily Grierson's old-fashioned house with its musty rooms reflects her refusal to live in the present.

See pages 31, 669, 877.

SHORT STORY **A brief work of prose fiction.** A short story has a simpler plot than a novel and is not long enough to be published as a volume of its own. Short stories usually focus on a few characters and one major event. Edgar Allan Poe has often been called one of the originators and masters of the modern short story. Some of the great American short story writers include Nathaniel Hawthorne, Flannery O'Connor, Eudora Welty, and Raymond Carver.

SIMILE **A figure of speech that makes an explicit comparison between two unlike things, using a word such as like, as, than, or resembles.**

> Helen, thy beauty is to me
> Like those Nicéan barks of yore
>
> —Edgar Allan Poe, from "To Helen"

See also *Figure of Speech, Metaphor.*

SLANT RHYME **A rhyming sound that is not exact.** *Follow/fellow* and *mystery/mastery* are examples of slant or approximate rhyme. Emily Dickinson frequently uses the subtleties of slant rhyme.

See page 550.
See also *Rhyme.*

SOLILOQUY **A long speech made by a character in a play while no other characters are on stage.** A soliloquy is different from a monologue in that the speaker appears to be thinking aloud, not addressing a listener.

SONNET **A fourteen-line poem, usually written in iambic pentameter, that has one of two basic structures.** The **Petrarchan sonnet,** also called the **Italian sonnet,** is named after the fourteenth-century Italian poet Petrarch. Its first eight lines, called the **octave,** ask a question or pose a problem. These lines have a rhyme scheme of *abba, abba.* The last six lines, called the **sestet,** respond to the question or problem. These lines have a rhyme scheme of *cde, cde.*

The form used to such perfection by William Shakespeare is known as the **English, Elizabethan,** or **Shakespearean sonnet.** It has three four-line units, or **quatrains,** and it concludes with a **couplet.** The most common rhyme scheme for the Shakespearean sonnet is *abab, cdcd, efef, gg.*

Longfellow wrote many sonnets, such as "The Cross of Snow" (page 229), as did Edna St. Vincent Millay, Robert Frost, and E. E. Cummings.

See pages 719, 814.
See also *Octave, Sestet.*

SOUND EFFECTS **The use of sounds to create specific literary effects.** Writers use devices such as **rhythm, rhyme, meter, alliteration, onomatopoeia, assonance, consonance,** and **repetition** to make the sounds of a work convey and enhance its meaning.

SPEAKER **The voice that addresses the reader in a poem.** The speaker may be the poet or a persona, a character whose voice and concerns do not necessarily reflect those of the poet. The speaker of T. S. Eliot's "The Love Song of J. Alfred Prufrock" (page 770) is one of the most famous personas in literature. The speaker in Sylvia Plath's poem "Mirror" (page 1340) is the personified mirror itself.

See page 797.

SPEECH **A formal address delivered to an audience, or the printed version of the same address.** Speeches are most commonly delivered by politicians, political activists, and other types of public figures. Patrick Henry's "Speech to the Virginia Convention" (page 122) is an example of a political speech given to sway an audience's opinion on an important issue.

SPONDEE **A metrical foot consisting of two syllables, both of which are stressed.** The words *true-blue* and *nineteen* are made of spondees. When Walt Whitman writes "Beat! beat! drums," he uses spondees. Spondaic feet are rarely used extensively because of their *thump-thump* sound. However, poets sometimes use spondees to provide a brief change from an iambic or trochaic beat or to provide emphasis.

See also *Anapest, Dactyl, Foot, Iamb, Iambic Pentameter, Meter, Trochee.*

STANZA **A group of consecutive lines that forms a structural unit in a poem.** Stanzas come in varying numbers of lines, though four is the most common. On the page, stanzas are separated by spaces. Stanza patterns are determined by the number of lines, the kind of feet in each line, and metrical and rhyme schemes, if any.

STEREOTYPE **A fixed idea or conception of a character or a group of people that does not allow for any individuality and is often based on religious, social, or racial prejudices.** Some common stereotypes are the unsophisticated farmer, the socially inept honor student, the dumb athlete, and the lazy teenager. Stereotypes, also called **stock characters,** are often deliberately used in comedies and in melodramas, where they receive instant recognition from the audience and make fully fleshed characterization unnecessary. In Thurber's "The Secret Life of Walter Mitty" (page 932), Walter and Mrs. Mitty are stock characters—the henpecked husband and the domineering wife.

See page 300.
See also *Character.*

STREAM OF CONSCIOUSNESS **A style of writing that portrays the inner (and often chaotic) workings of a character's mind.** The stream-of-consciousness technique usually consists of a recording of the random flow of ideas, memories, associations, images, and emotions, as they arise spontaneously in a character's mind. This flow of the contents of a character's mind is called an **interior monologue.** William Faulkner, in his novel *The Sound and the Fury,* uses a stream-of-consciousness technique. Two other great writers that successfully use a stream-of-consciousness technique are the Irish writer James Joyce and the English writer Virginia Woolf.

See pages 841, 913.

STYLE **The distinctive way in which a writer uses language.** Style can be plain, ornate, metaphorical, spare, descriptive, and so on. Style is determined by such factors as sentence length and complexity, syntax, use of figurative language and imagery, and diction.

See also *Plain Style, Stream of Consciousness, Tone.*

SUBJECTIVE AND OBJECTIVE WRITING **Subjectivity, in terms of writing, suggests that the writer's primary purpose is to express personal experiences, feelings, and ideas.** Objectivity suggests that the writer's purpose is to report facts, avoiding personal judgments and feelings. Subjective writing is typified by autobiographies and memoirs. Objective writing is used mostly in news reporting and other types of journalism. This is not to say that all writing must be one or the other. In fact, most writing will have elements of subjective and objective writing.

SURREALISM **A movement in art and literature that started in Europe during the 1920s.** Surrealists wanted to replace conventional realism with the full expression of the unconscious mind, which they considered to be more real than the "real" world of appearances. Surrealists, influenced by the psychoanalytic theories of Sigmund Freud, tried not to censor the images that came from their dreams or to impose logical connections on these images. This resulted in surprising combinations of "inner" and "outer" reality—a "suprareality." Surrealism affected writers as diverse as T. S. Eliot and Donald Barthelme. Two famous surrealist artists are the Spaniard Salvador Dali (1904–1989) and the Belgian René Magritte (1898–1967).

SUSPENSE **A feeling of uncertainty and curiosity about what will happen next in a story.** A key element in fiction and drama, suspense is one of the hooks a writer uses to keep the audience interested.

See page 939.

SYMBOL **A person, a place, a thing, or an event that has meaning in itself and that also stands for something more than itself.** We can distinguish between **public** and **personal symbols.** The dove, for example, is a public symbol of peace—that is, it is widely accepted the world over as such a symbol. The bald eagle is a public symbol that stands for the United States; a picture of a skull and crossbones is a public symbol of death; two snakes coiled around a staff is a widely accepted symbol of the medical profession.

Most symbols used in literature are personal symbols; even though a symbol may be widely used, a writer will usually adapt it in some imaginative, personal way so that it can suggest not just one, but a myriad of meanings. One of the most commonly used symbols in literature, for example, is the journey, which can stand for a search for truth, for redemption from evil, or for discovery of the self and freedom.

The writers known as the Dark Romantics—Poe, Hawthorne, and Melville—used symbolism heavily in their works. One of American literature's most famous symbols is Melville's white whale, Moby-Dick, used to symbolize the inexpressible nature of evil.

See pages 303, 344, 530.
See also *Figure of Speech.*

SYMBOLISM **A literary movement that originated in late-nineteenth-century France, in which writers rearranged the world of appearances in order to reveal a more truthful version of reality.** The symbolists believed that direct statements of feeling were inadequate. Instead, they called for new and striking imaginative images to evoke complexities of meaning and mood. The French symbolists were influenced by the poetry and critical writings of the American writer Edgar Allan Poe. The poetry of Ezra Pound, T. S. Eliot, and Wallace Stevens is in the symbolist tradition.

See pages 757–759.

SYNECDOCHE **A figure of speech in which a part represents the whole.** The capital city of a nation, for example, is often spoken of as though it were the government: *Washington and Moscow are both claiming popular support for their positions.* In "The Love Song of J. Alfred Prufrock" (page 770), T. S. Eliot writes "And I have known the arms already. . . ." *Arms* stands for all the women he has known.

See also *Metonymy.*

SYNESTHESIA **The juxtaposition of one sensory image with another image that appeals to an unrelated sense.** In synesthesia an image of sound might be conveyed in terms of an image of taste as in "sweet laughter," or an image that appeals to the sense of touch might be combined with an image that appeals to the sense of sight, as in the example from Emily Dickinson: "golden touch."

TALL TALE **An outrageously exaggerated, humorous story that is obviously unbelievable.** Tall tales are part of folk literature of many countries, including the United States. Perhaps the most famous tall tale in American literature is Mark Twain's "The Celebrated Jumping Frog of Calaveras County" (page 639).

THEME **The insight about human life that is revealed in literary work.** Themes are rarely stated directly in literature. Most often, a reader has to infer the theme of a work after considerable thought. Theme is different from **subject.** A story's subject might be stated as "growing up," "love," "heroism," or "fear." The theme is the statement the writer wants to make about that subject: "For most young people, growing up is a process that involves the pain of achieving self-knowledge." Theme must be summarized in at least one complete sentence; most themes are complex enough to require several sentences, or even an essay.

See pages 219, 903, 1401.

TONE **The attitude a writer takes toward the subject of a work, the characters in it, or the audience.** In speaking we use voice inflections and even body language to show how we feel about what we are saying. Writers manipulate language in an attempt to achieve the same effect. For example, John Hersey takes an objective tone in telling about the nuclear explosion in *Hiroshima* (see "A Noiseless Flash," page 1068). In contrast, the tone in Patrick Henry's speech to the Virginia Convention (page 122) is subjective, even impassioned. Tone is dependent on **diction** and **style,** and we cannot say we have understood any work of literature until we have sensed the writer's tone. Tone can usually be described in a single word: objective, solemn, playful, ironic, sarcastic, critical, reverent, irreverent, philosophical, cynical, and so on.

See pages 893, 1301, 1341.
See also *Diction, Style.*

TRAGEDY **In general, a story in which a heroic character either dies or comes to some other unhappy end.** In most tragedies the main character is in an enviable, even exalted, position when the story begins (in classical tragedies and in Shakespeare's plays, the tragic hero is of noble origin, often a king or queen, prince or princess). The character's downfall generally occurs because of some combination of fate, an error in judgment, or a personality failure known as a **tragic flaw** (Creon's stubbornness in *Antigone* or Hamlet's indecision, for example). The tragic character has usually gained wisdom at the end of the story, in spite of suffering defeat or even death. Our feeling on reading or viewing a tragedy is usually exaltation—despite the unhappy ending—because we have witnessed the best that human beings are capable of.

See also *Comedy.*

TRANSCENDENTALISM **A nineteenth-century movement in the Romantic tradition, which held that every individual can reach ultimate truths through spiritual intuition, which transcends reason and**

sensory experience. The Transcendental movement was centered in Concord, Massachusetts, home of its leading exponents, Ralph Waldo Emerson and Henry David Thoreau. The basic tenets of the Transcendentalists were (1) a belief that God is present in every aspect of nature, including every human being; (2) the conviction that everyone is capable of apprehending God through the use of intuition; (3) the belief that all of nature is symbolic of the spirit. A corollary of these beliefs was an optimistic view of the world as good and evil as nonexistent.

See page 206.

TROCHEE **A metrical foot made up of an accented syllable followed by an unaccented syllable, as in the word *taxi*.** A trochee, the opposite of an iamb, is sometimes used to vary iambic rhythm.

See also *Anapest, Dactyl, Foot, Iamb, Iambic Pentameter, Meter, Spondee.*

UNDERSTATEMENT **A statement that says less than what is meant.** Understatement, paradoxically, can make us recognize the truth of something by saying that just the opposite is true. If you are sitting down to enjoy a ten-course meal and say, "Ah! A little snack before bedtime," you are using an understatement to emphasize the tremendous amount of food you are about to eat. Understatement is often used to make an ironic point; it can also be used for humor.

See page 638.
See also *Hyperbole.*

VERNACULAR **The language spoken by the people who live in a particular locality.** Regionalist writers try to capture the vernacular of their area.

See pages 619, 638.
See also *Dialect.*

VILLANELLE **A nineteen-line poem consisting of five tercets (three-line stanzas) with the rhyme scheme *aba* and with a final quatrain (four-line stanza) of *abaa*.** Two well-known villanelles in the English language are Dylan Thomas's "Do Not Go Gentle into That Good Night" and Elizabeth Bishop's "One Art" (page 1331).

The World of Work

You will use reading and writing skills almost every day of your life. For example, a police officer must write coherent reports. A parent must understand school policies. A car buyer must understand the contract. A dissatisfied employee must document unfair treatment in an effective memo. In your life and in the world of work, you will use reading and writing skills to learn new information, to communicate effectively, and to get the results you want.

Reading

Reading is an important decision-making tool that helps you analyze information, weigh arguments, and make informed choices. Much of the real-life reading you will do will come from **informative documents** and **persuasive documents**.

Informative Documents

Informative documents focus on providing facts and information, and they can be good places to check when you want to verify or clarify information from other sources. For example, suppose a co-worker sends you an e-mail complaining about a new vacation policy. Before responding, you can read the memo that explains the policy to see if your co-worker has understood the information correctly. Informative documents include **consumer documents** and **workplace documents**.

CONSUMER DOCUMENTS As a consumer, you will face thousands of buying decisions. Maybe you've heard the warning: "Let the buyer beware!" That warning means that buyers are responsible for reading and understanding information about products and services. This information can be found in consumer documents, which spell out details about products and the legal rights and responsibilities of the buyer and the companies that produce and sell the product. Consumer documents you're likely to see include

warranties, contracts, product information, and **instruction manuals.**

■ **Warranties** describe what happens if the product breaks down or doesn't work properly. Warranties such as the one below note how long the product is covered for repair or replacement, which repairs the warranty does and does not cover, and how to receive repair service.

> The MovieBuff DVD player is guaranteed to be free of defects in material or workmanship under normal use for a period of one (1) year from the date of purchase. Equipment covered by the warranty will be repaired by MovieBuff merchants WITHOUT CHARGE, except for insurance, transportation, and handling charges. A copy of this warranty card and proof of purchase must be enclosed when returning equipment for warranty service. The warranty does not apply in the following cases:
>
> • if loss or damage to the equipment is due to abuse
>
> • if the equipment is defective due to leaking batteries or liquid damage
>
> • if the equipment has been serviced by unauthorized repair technicians

■ **Contracts** give details about an agreement that the buyer enters into with a company. For example, a buyer might sign a membership contract at a local gym. The contract defines the terms of the agreement, the length of the membership, the benefits of membership, and the responsibilities of the buyer and the gym. Both parties must sign a contract to show that they understand and agree to its terms.

BodyFitness Membership Contract

A one-year membership, effective the date of this signed contract, to BodyFitness Gym includes the following services:

1. Unlimited access to the equipment, classes, and locker room facilities

2. Three sessions with a personal trainer to develop a fitness plan

3. Assistance by staff in operating equipment

Member agrees to the following terms:

1. The monthly membership fee will be paid by the tenth of each month for a full year. A charge of 5 percent will be added to late payments.

2. Members who discontinue membership will be required to pay all past-due charges and the remaining months of the membership.

3. After one year, membership may be renewed on a month-to-month basis.

BodyFitness representative   Member signature and date

■ **Product information** describes the basic features and materials of a product. Product information on a laptop computer box would give the processor speed, hard-drive space, monitor size, and other specifications of the computer.

■ **Instruction manuals** tell the owner how to set up, operate, and troubleshoot problems with the product. Instruction manuals also include safety precautions, diagrams, and descriptions of the product's features.

WORKPLACE DOCUMENTS When you work, you want to know what's expected of you, when changes are made in procedures, and when important meetings are being held. This information comes in workplace documents, such as **memos** and **procedure manuals.** Knowing how to read these documents can make you an informed and effective worker.

■ **Memos** are the standard form of communication in many businesses. They provide direct, concise, and clearly organized messages to announce or summarize meetings, request action, or provide important information. To read a memo effectively, first check the subject line at the top to learn the topic of the memo. As you read, notice headings or bullets that indicate the main ideas, and pay attention to the purpose of the memo: Is it summarizing information, requesting action, or providing facts, such as dates and prices? You will know whether and how to respond by understanding the purpose of the memo.

■ **Procedure manuals** detail the steps to follow for conducting business, operating machinery, reporting problems, or requesting vacation time—anything a company wants done in a certain way. Procedure manuals are often used to train new employees and to clarify procedures for existing employees so the company runs in a smooth and predictable way. As you read a procedure manual, pay attention to the step-by-step instructions so you know exactly how to carry out the procedures.

Persuasive Documents

Some persuasive documents may sound informative. For example, a policy statement by a city commission on changing the curfew is persuasive. Its purpose is to persuade citizens to support the changes, even though it may rely heavily on facts to make its argument. Learning to recognize and analyze the features and rhetorical devices used in a persuasive public document can help you learn about what is happening in your community and watch out for your own interests. Common persuasive public documents include **policy statements, political platforms, speeches,** and **debates.**

■ A **policy statement** outlines a group's position on an issue and sometimes provides the rationale for its position. For example, the school board might issue a policy statement explaining why it supports or rejects allowing soft-drink machines in schools. The policy statement gives the major points for the school board's position and may make a logical appeal or use rhetorical devices, such as an analogy, to support its position. A policy statement may also include a call to action. Many groups issue policy statements to endorse upholding or changing specific laws. The audience for a policy statement is the public who must vote on the issue or the lawmakers who are creating legislation concerning it.

■ A **political platform** describes the direction a political candidate or party wants to take if elected. It details specific positions and goals on a variety of issues and describes the principles that guide these positions, often through ethical appeals. The positions and goals are known as the **planks** of the platform. Some platforms also address opposing viewpoints, although the audience for a platform is usually friendly to the candidate.

A platform is intended to arouse support and to persuade undecided voters. Here is an excerpt concerning recycling from a mayoral candidate's platform.

Greenville is a community that has long deserved its name—it is a place of tree-lined streets, clear lakes, and green meadows. It is time to preserve this beauty for our children and grandchildren by instituting a recycling program. Our landfills are near capacity, and statistics show that we are collecting 28 percent more garbage than we did just five years ago. A recycling program may be expensive to implement, but I believe Greenville's citizens are willing to make small sacrifices for long-term gains. If elected, I would push the city council to begin a recycling program and explore ways to fund this program.

■ A persuasive **speech** may establish a fact, strengthen or change a person's belief, or move a person to action. A persuasive speaker may use a variety of logical, emotional, and ethical appeals to make arguments, address listener concerns, and rebut counterclaims. Logical appeals, based on facts and solid reasoning, give a speaker the strongest credibility. However, emotional and ethical appeals, which may target a listener's sympathy or sense of duty, may be even more persuasive to a listener who is not carefully analyzing the message. (For more on **persuasive speeches,** see page 192.)

■ A **debate** involves two teams who systematically discuss a controversial topic to determine which

side has the stronger argument. The issue is called the **proposition,** and the case includes the reasons and evidence a side uses for its position. After both sides present their **cases,** they may **refute** each other's arguments, attacking or trying to disprove the opposing side's points.

CRITIQUING PERSUASIVE DOCUMENTS

Learning to critique the validity and truthfulness of the various arguments and appeals that are used in persuasive documents can help you avoid being easily misled. Here are some questions to guide you.

■ To whom does the document appeal—a friendly or a hostile audience? Are that audience's concerns and counterclaims addressed in a convincing and appropriate way?

■ What kinds of appeals does the document make? Does it appeal primarily to logic and reason, to emotions such as sympathy and anger, or to ethics and authority? How powerful are the appeals that are used?

■ Can you distinguish between facts and opinions? Can factual claims be confirmed through other sources, including informative public documents? Can any statements of opinion be analyzed for meaning?

■ Is the writer or speaker credible and knowledgeable? Are respectable and credible sources of information being used?

Your Turn Choose a persuasive public document, and critique it. Analyze the document's features, rhetorical devices, and appeals, and identify the call to action, if any. Consult at least one informative public document, such as a city ordinance or the minutes from a city council meeting, to verify information presented in the persuasive document.

Writing

In the adult world, to win your dream job you'll have to write a letter and a résumé. To help your company improve quality, you'll have to write a memo outlining your plan. Effective writing makes things happen in the world of work, from getting hired to sharing ideas.

Job Applications and Résumés

Your ticket to the world of work usually comes in the form of a job application or résumé. A **job application** is a form that asks for specific information. To complete a job application completely and accurately, read the instructions carefully. Type or write neatly in blue or black ink. Include all information requested. If a question does not apply to you, write *N/A* or *not applicable* in the blank. Proofread your completed form, and neatly correct errors. Avoid cross-outs. Finally, submit the form to the correct person.

A **résumé** summarizes your background and experience in an easy-to-read format. It should be written with your potential employer in mind. That means you should use the appropriate tone, level, and type of language for the employer and highlight skills that would appeal to him or her. An advertising company, for example, might enjoy a creative approach. A lawyer's office, however, would probably appreciate a serious tone with formal language. Here are some more tips to help you create an effective résumé.

■ Give complete information about work experience, including job title, dates of employment, company, and location.

■ Do not use *I;* instead, use short, parallel phrases that describe duties and activities.

■ Proofread carefully. Mistakes on a résumé make the writer seem careless.

Workplace Documents

Writing effectively on the job includes knowing how to write concise, easy-to-understand memos. Standard memo format includes the date, the recipient, the sender, and the subject at the top of the document. In a professional and courteous tone, the memo should answer *who, what, when, where, why,* and *how* for the reader. The following memo gets right to the point, communicating clearly and directly.

Date: October 8, 2009

To: Isabel Gutierrez

From: David Fossi

Subject: Internship Program

The Human Resources Department met yesterday to plan an internship program for high school students. These recommendations were made:

1. Internships will last nine weeks to fit the school calendar.

2. No more than one intern at a time may be assigned to a department.

3. Interns will be selected based on an application letter, teacher recommendations, and grade-point average. Each department will be responsible for interviewing and selecting candidates.

Please let me know by November 20th if your department is interested in participating in this program. I will also need a brief description of the kinds of duties an intern would participate in during the internship.

Word-Processing Features

Creating clear content for documents is essential, but presenting that content in a predictable, easy-to-read way is just as important. Give your ideas greater impact and add to the readability of your documents by using word-processing features. Use the following suggestions to format documents correctly and to integrate databases, graphics, or spreadsheets.

FORMATTING DOCUMENTS Presenting workplace information effectively involves formatting documents by setting the **margins, fonts,** and **spacing** to enhance impact and readability.

■ **Margins** are the blank space that surrounds the text on a page. Most word-processing programs automatically set margins, but you can adjust these default margins as needed.

■ **A font** is a complete set of characters (including letters, numbers, and punctuation marks) in a particular size and design. Choose a font that suits your purpose and is businesslike and easy to read. To maintain a professional appearance, avoid mixing several fonts in one document. For more on **fonts,** see page 1496.

■ **Line spacing** is the white space between lines of

text. Most word processors allow you to choose single- or double-space measurements. Most letters and memos are single-spaced to conserve space, but longer reports are often double-spaced to allow room for handwritten edits and comments.

INTEGRATING DATABASES, GRAPHICS, AND SPREADSHEETS Suppose you are writing a memo summarizing sales figures for each sales person in a company. To make this information clear, you might include a bar graph or a spread sheet that lists the figures. Integrate databases, graphics, or spreadsheets into documents when they will support your ideas or help readers grasp information. These features should be placed close to the related text and be clearly explained. For help in integrating databases, graphics,

and spreadsheets into documents, consult the Help feature of your word-processing program or ask your teacher to help you.

A MODEL RÉSUMÉ Word-processing features can help you create a winning résumé. Follow these guidelines to format a résumé effectively.

- ■ Make sure the résumé is not cluttered. Use wide margins for the top, bottom, and sides, and use double-spacing between sections to make the résumé easy to scan for information.

- ■ Use a font size of at least ten points. Consider using a different font, boldface, and a larger point size for your name and headings. Be sure all fonts are easy to read.

    This example uses a typical résumé format.

MALIK MILLER

489 Oceanside Drive

San Pedro, CA 90731

(310) 555-0162

E-mail: mmiller@sbahs.k12.ca.us

Education: Junior: Susan B. Anthony High School

Grade-point average: 3.0 (B)

Major studies: Writing and computer graphics courses

Work Experience:

Summer 2003   **Public Relations Volunteer**

Habitat for Humanity, San Pedro

- Helped write and design layout for newsletter
- Input data for mailing list

Summer 2002   **Office Assistant**

Saunders Realty, Rancho Palos Verdes

- Proofread letters and documents
- Answered phones and greeted customers

Skills: Typing: 50 words per minute

Computers: Word processing, publication layout, graphics

Activities: Copyeditor, yearbook; member of Future Business Leaders of America

References: Dr. Shavonne Newman, Principal   Scott Saunders, Owner

Susan B. Anthony High School   Saunders Realty

(310) 555-0029   (310) 555-0196

Your Turn Create a résumé for your dream job. Include experiences and skills you have that would appeal to your potential employer. Then, present this information in a clear, concise, and eye-catching way.

Writer's Handbook

The Writing Process

You have a writing assignment due tomorrow. Your plan was to dash something off quickly and turn it in, so why are you stuck? What is keeping your ideas from flowing effortlessly onto the page? Realizing that writing is a process involving many steps can help you get unstuck. The chart below explains the stages of the writing process.

Stages of the Writing Process	
Prewriting	• Choose and narrow a topic, and choose a form. • Identify your purpose and audience. • Gather information about the topic. • Begin to organize the information. • Draft a sentence that expresses your main point and your perspective on the topic.
Drafting	• Draft an introduction that gets your readers' attention. • Provide background information. • Follow a plan or an organizational pattern that makes sense. • State your main points, and elaborate on them. • Wrap things up with a conclusion.
Evaluating and Revising	• Evaluate your draft. • Revise the draft's content, organization, and style.
Proofreading and Publishing	• Proofread for spelling, punctuation, and grammar mistakes. • Share your finished writing with readers. • Reflect on your writing experience.

This process is **recursive,** which means that as you research, write, and revise you can always go back and repeat steps in the process. Suppose you are drafting a report and discover that you need additional facts to elaborate on a point. Simply go back to the prewriting task of gathering information. Then, pick up where you left off, insert the new information, and continue the process.

As you progress through each stage in the writing process, make sure you do the following.

- **Keep your ideas coherent and focused.** Present a tightly reasoned argument that will help you achieve your specific purpose. Every idea should focus on the point you make in your thesis statement.
- **Share your own perspective.** Give readers a piece of your mind by clearly communicating your viewpoint on the topic. Leave no doubt about who is the speaker in your writing, whether that person is you as a writer or a character you create to narrate a fictional piece.
- **Keep your audience in mind.** Use your understanding of your specific audience's backgrounds and interests to make your writing speak directly to them. If you have the option, choose a form that will be familiar or appealing to your readers—for example, a song, poem, memoir, editorial, screenplay, pamphlet, or letter.
- **Plan to publish.** Develop every piece as if it might be submitted for publication. When you proofread, work with a classmate who can help you find errors and inconsistencies. Use the following questions to guide you. The numbers in parentheses indicate the sections in which instruction on each topic begins in the Language Handbook.

Questions For Proofreading

1. Is every sentence complete, not a fragment or run-on? (9d, e)

2. Are punctuation marks used correctly? (12a–r, 13a–n)

3. Do sentences and proper nouns and adjectives begin with a capital letter? (11a, c)

4. Does each verb agree in number with its subject? (2a) Are verb forms and tenses used correctly? (3a–c)

5. Are subject and object forms of personal pronouns used correctly? (4a–d) Does every pronoun agree with a clear antecedent in number and gender?

To mark corrections, use the following symbols

Symbols For Revising And Proofreading

Symbol	Example	Meaning of Symbol
≡	Spence college	Capitalize a lowercase letter.
/	our Best friend	Lowercase a capital letter.
∧	the on fourth of July	Insert a missing word, letter, or punctuation mark.
∧	the capital of Iowa Ohio	Replace a word.
ℓ	hoped for to go	Delete a word, letter, or punctuation mark.

RESOURCE CENTER Writer's Handbook

Paragraphs

The Parts of a Paragraph

Paragraphs come in all sorts of shapes and sizes. They can be as short as one sentence or as long as many pages; they can seamlessly connect several items or develop a single idea.

In works of nonfiction, including essays that you write for school, paragraphs usually develop one main idea. These main-idea paragraphs are often made up of a **topic sentence, supporting sentences,** and a **clincher sentence,** as explained in the chart below.

Parts of Paragraphs	
Topic Sentence	• states the main idea, or central focus, of the paragraph • is often the first or second sentence of a paragraph • can be placed at or near the end of a paragraph to create surprise or to summarize ideas
Supporting Sentences	• support or prove the main idea in the topic sentence • use the following kinds of details: *sensory details*—images of sight, sound, taste, smell, and texture *facts*—statements that can be proved true *examples*—specific instances or illustrations of a general idea; examples must be relevant to the main idea and precise rather than general *anecdotes*—brief biographical or autobiographical stories used to illustrate a main idea *analogies*—comparisons between ideas familiar to readers and unfamiliar concepts being explained
Clincher Sentence	• is a final sentence that emphasizes or summarizes the main idea • can help readers grasp the main idea of a longer paragraph

Tip Not all paragraphs have or need topic sentences. In fiction, paragraphs rarely include topic sentences. Paragraphs in nonfiction works that relate a sequence of events or steps frequently do not contain topic sentences. In much of the writing you do for school, however, you'll find topic sentences useful. They provide a focus for readers, and they keep you from straying off the topic as you develop the rest of your paragraph.

Tip Many paragraphs—even those that develop a main idea—do not use a clincher sentence. Use clinchers sparingly in your writing to avoid boring readers by restating an obvious main idea.

PUTTING THE PARTS TOGETHER Look carefully at the parts of the following paragraph. Notice that the topic sentence at the beginning expresses the main idea.

> In the past forty years, however, anthropologists have done some very thorough digging into the life of the North American Indians and have discovered a bewildering variety of cultures and societies beyond anything the schoolbooks have taught. There were Indian societies that dwelt in permanent settlements, and others that wandered; some were wholly democratic, and others had very rigid class systems based on property. Some were ruled by gods carried around on litters; some had judicial systems; to some the only known punishment was torture. Some lived in caves, others in tepees of bison skins, others in cabins. There were tribes ruled by warriors or by women, by sacred elders or by councils. . . .There were tribes who worshiped the bison or a matriarch or the maize they lived by. There were tribes that had never heard of war, and there were tribes debauched by centuries of fighting. In short, there was a great diversity of Indian nations, speaking over five hundred languages.
>
> Alistair Cooke, *Alistair Cooke's America*

Topic Sentence

Supporting Sentences

Clincher Sentence

Qualities of Paragraphs

You wouldn't build a house without thinking about how the boards, bricks, and shingles fit together. Paragraphs need to be just as carefully constructed. A well-written paragraph has **unity** and **coherence.**

UNITY Unity simply means that a paragraph "hangs together." In other words, all the supporting sentences work together to develop a focused main idea. A paragraph should have unity whether the main idea is directly stated or merely suggested. Unity is achieved when all sentences relate to a stated or implied main idea or when all sentences relate to a sequence of events. In paragraphs that relate a series of actions or events, you can achieve unity by providing all the steps in the sequence, with no digressions.

COHERENCE In a coherent paragraph, the relationship between ideas is clear—the paragraph flows smoothly. You can go a long way toward making paragraphs coherent by paying attention to two things:

- the structure, or **order,** you use to arrange your ideas
- the **connections** you make between ideas

Tip At times, you may need to use multiple orders. In explaining an effect, for example, you may trace it **chronologically** from its cause. If one effect has four simultaneous causes, you would place these causes in **logical order or order of importance.** To avoid confusing your readers, use multiple orders in a sustained way and only when necessary.

Types of Order

Order	When To Use	How It Works
Chronological	• to tell a story • to explain a process • to show cause and effect	shows how things change over time
Spatial	• to describe	provides details according to their location—near to far, top to bottom, left to right, and so on
Order of Importance	• to inform • to persuade	arranges ideas and details from most important to least or vice versa, depending on which order the writer considers most effective
Logical	• to explain or classify —often by defining, dividing a subject into parts, or comparing and contrasting	groups ideas together in a way that shows the relationships between them

In addition to presenting details in an order that makes sense, a paragraph that has coherence also shows how these details are connected. You can show connections by using **direct references** (or repetition of ideas), **transitional expressions,** and **parallelism.**

Connecting Ideas

Connecting Strategy	How To Use It
Direct References, or Repetition of Ideas	• Refer to a noun or pronoun used earlier in the paragraph. • Repeat a word used earlier. • Use a word or phrase that means the same thing as one used earlier.
Transitional Expressions	• Compare ideas (*also, and, another, just as, like, likewise, moreover, similarly, too*). • Contrast ideas (*although, but, however, in spite of, instead, nevertheless, on the other hand, still, yet*). • Show cause and effect (*as a result, because, consequently, since, so that, therefore*). • Show time (*after, at last, at once, before, eventually, finally, first, later, meanwhile, next, soon, then, thereafter, when, while*). • Show place (*above, across, around, before, beyond, down, here, in, inside, into, next, over, there, to, under*). • Show importance (*first, last, mainly, more important, then, to begin with*).
Parallelism	• Use the same grammatical forms or structures to balance related ideas in a sentence. • Sparingly, use the same sentence structures to show connections between related ideas in a paragraph or composition.

Tip Direct references and transitional expressions can also build coherence in longer compositions, leading readers from one sentence, paragraph, or idea to another. Try not to overuse these connecting strategies in your writing, though, as doing so can result in writing that sounds artificial and stilted.

YOUR TURN Choose a broad topic that interests you, and then use the instruction in this section to develop two paragraphs on the topic, following these steps:

• Think of two ways to organize ideas about the topic—for example, you could organize ideas about school in chronological order to narrate the events in a typical school day or in spatial order to describe the campus.
• Plan a topic sentence, a variety of supporting details (see page 1490), and a clincher sentence for each of the two paragraphs you will write.
• Draft your paragraphs, following the organizational patterns you have chosen. Eliminate any ideas that detract from your focus, and connect ideas using direct references, transitional expressions, and parallelism.

The Writer's Language

After your ideas are on paper, complete and organized, revise your writing for **style**—the way you communicate those ideas. Consider your **voice** and **tone, word choice, sentence variety,** and your use of **rhetorical devices** to develop a style that will fit your audience and purpose and the type of writing you have chosen.

A SOUND ALL ITS OWN Revise to give your writing a natural **voice** and an appropriate **tone.**

VOICE A writer's voice reveals his or her personality. A writer's voice should sound distinctive and natural, never stilted or forced. Read your own writing aloud to decide whether it sounds like you. Make sure your natural voice comes through loud and clear.

TONE Tone reveals the writer's attitude toward a given topic and audience. As with voice, tone can be revealed through word choice and sentence structure. Select a tone that fits your **purpose.** For example, if your main purpose is to entertain, you won't use a serious tone because that could interfere with your goal. Also, consider how formal or informal your tone should be, based on your audience. Are you addressing your friends, classmates, and family members? In that case, your tone will probably be informal. If you are addressing your teacher or a group of strangers, it is best to use a formal tone.

Notice the differences in the following sentences.

FORMAL TONE   Going for a difficult run at dawn prepares me for the challenges of the day.

INFORMAL TONE   Nothing gets me ready to slay the day's dragons like a tough run at dawn.

PRECISELY MY POINT To make your writing fresh and vivid, revise your word choice. Replace vague language with **precise verbs, nouns,** and **adjectives.** Instead of dull verbs, like *talk,* use more precise verbs, such as *mumble* or *chatter.* Isn't "Second Avenue, choked with honking taxis and stalled delivery trucks" more vivid than "a noisy, crowded street"? Create a clear, striking picture of your subject.

Many words have special **connotations**—that is, they create a particular emotional effect. For example, the word *cowardly* has a negative connotation. The word *frightened* expresses the same idea in a more positive way. Notice connotations as you revise.

VARIETY IS THE SPICE OF LIFE Aim for a variety of sentence lengths in your writing—a short, simple sentence here, and a longer, more complex one there. Review each piece to give it a mix of simple, compound, and complex sentences and to vary the beginnings of your sentences. For example, if most of your sentences start with a subject, occasionally move a phrase from later in the sentence to the beginning.

A RHETORICAL POINT To make your writing more effective, use the **rhetorical devices** of parallelism, repetition, and analogy.

PARALLELISM Use the same grammatical forms to connect related ideas within a sentence. Also, consider linking two ideas that appear in different sentences by using the same sentence structure. Use this latter technique sparingly to create an "echo" in readers' minds that will help them see the connections between important points.

REPETITION Repeating words or phrases can cement important ideas in readers' minds and make your writing more coherent. Significant words, when repeated, can also create an emotional response, as in Martin Luther King, Jr.'s famous "I Have a Dream" speech.

ANALOGY An analogy is an extended comparison between two things. You can use an analogy to explain something unfamiliar to readers by using terms they will understand, or you can enhance your tone through an analogy, such as this one: "The island emerged from the ocean in the same way that movie monsters suddenly appear from the darkness."

A DESCRIPTIVE MODEL As you read the following passage, notice its voice and tone, word choice, sentence variety, and rhetorical devices.

> ### A Writer's Model
>
> The day I went to Alcatraz was as bleak as the island prison's past. It was cold and windy, and the waters of the bay were gunmetal gray. Along with the other tourists, my family and I crowded onto the ferry to the island, and the boat set out. Alcatraz loomed out of the waters of the bay, its peak crowned with concrete prison buildings and an old lighthouse. Gray, gray, everything looked gray. Later I would notice that wildflowers grew all over the island. At that moment, though, there was no color to be seen.

Analogy
Precise language

Voice and tone

Repetition

Tone

YOUR TURN Revise the following paragraph to improve its style.

I went to the Muir Woods last Saturday with my friend. We saw a big cross section of a redwood tree that showed that the tree was very old. We walked in the forest all day. The trees were tall. There were lots of other people walking in the forest. Afterward we went to the gift shop. I bought a bracelet made of redwood. It reminds me of the forest.

Designing Your Writing

A poorly designed document won't communicate even strong information effectively. In a well-designed document, the design supports the content, making it easy for readers to navigate through ideas and using visuals to share information that is difficult to communicate in words. You can create effective design and visuals by hand, or you can use advanced publishing software and graphics programs to design pages and to integrate databases, graphics, and spreadsheets into your documents.

Page Design

USER-FRIENDLY As a reader, you know that some document designs make text look inviting and others make you want to stop reading. As a writer, design your documents to be as appealing and easy to read as possible. Use these design elements to improve readability:

COLUMNS AND BLOCKS **Columns** arrange text in separate sections printed side by side. A **block** is a rectangle of text shorter than a page separated from other text by white space. The text in advertisements is usually set in blocks so that it may be read quickly. Text in reference books and newspapers usually appears in columns.

BULLETS A **bullet** (·) is a symbol used to separate information into lists like the one on page 1493. Bullets attract attention and help readers remember the information included in the lists.

HEADINGS AND SUBHEADINGS A **heading** at the beginning of a section of text, such as a chapter, gives a general idea of what that section will be about. A **subheading** indicates a new idea within the section. Several subheadings often appear under one heading. Headings and subheadings are usually set in larger type or in a different style than the rest of the text.

PULL-QUOTES Many magazine articles catch your attention with pull-quotes. A **pull-quote** is a significant sentence from the text that is printed in a large font and set in a box.

WHITE SPACE **White space** is any area on a page where there is little or no text, visuals, or graphics. Usually, white space is limited to the margins and the spaces between words, lines, columns, and blocks. Advertisements usually have more white space than do books or articles.

CAPTIONS **Captions** are lines of text that explain the meaning or importance of photographs or illustrations and connect them to the main text. Captions may appear in italics or in smaller type than the main text.

CONTRAST **Contrast** refers to the balance of light and dark areas on a page. Dark areas are those that contain blocks of text or graphics. Light areas have little type. A page with high contrast, or roughly balanced light and dark areas, is easier to read than a page with low contrast, such as one that is filled with text and images.

EMPHASIS **Emphasis** is how a page designer indicates which information on a page is important. For example, the front page of a newspaper uses photographs and large headlines to place emphasis on a particular story. Because readers' eyes are drawn naturally to color, large print, and graphics, these elements are often used to create emphasis.

Type

JUST MY TYPE The kind of type you choose affects the readability of your documents. You can use type to provide emphasis and interest by varying the case and the font of your letters.

CASE You can vary case in your documents in the following ways.

- **Uppercase letters** Words in all uppercase, or capital, letters attract readers' attention and may be used in headings or titles. Text in all capital letters can be difficult to read. Therefore, use it sparingly.

- **Initial letter** An initial letter is a large first letter used to draw readers into an essay. You can draw your initial letter by hand, or you can enlarge a letter using a word-processing program.

- **Small caps** Small caps are uppercase letters reduced in size. They appear in abbreviations of time, such as 9:00 A.M. and A.D. 1500. Small caps may be combined with capitals for an artistic effect.

FONT A **font** is one complete set of characters (such as letters, numbers, and punctuation marks) of a given size and design. All fonts belong to one of the three categories shown in the chart on the next page.

Categories of Fonts

Category	Explanation	Uses
decorative, or **script**	elaborately designed characters that convey a distinct mood or feeling	Decorative fonts are difficult to read and should be used sparingly for an artistic effect.
serif	characters with small strokes (serifs) attached at each end	Because the strokes on serif characters help guide the reader's eyes from letter to letter, serif type is often used for large bodies of text.
sans serif	characters formed of straight lines, with no serifs (*sans serif means "without strokes"*)	Sans serif fonts are easy to read and are used for headings, subheadings, callouts, and captions.

■ **Font size** The size of the type in a document is called the font size or point size. Many newspapers use type measured at 12 points, with larger type for headings and smaller type for captions.

■ **Font style** Most text is set in *roman* (not slanted) style. *Italic,* or slanted, style has special uses, as for captions or book titles. Underscored or bold-face type can be used for emphasis.

Visuals

GET VISUAL Some ideas can be communicated more effectively visually than as part of the text. For instance, a line graph showing how your club's membership has grown over the last four years would be more effective than simply writing about the information. If available, use technology, such as computer software and graphics programs, to create visuals and to integrate databases, graphics, and spreadsheets into documents. Whether you create them with software or by hand, the following types of visuals can help you effectively share ideas.

GRAPHS A **bar graph** can compare quantities at a glance or indicate the parts of a whole. A **line graph** such as the example below can compare trends or show how two or more variables interact. Both kinds of graphs can show trends or changes over time.

Tip You can copy databases or spreadsheets and paste them into word-processed documents. For example, imagine that you are writing a letter to your school administration asking for more money for the prom. Your letter will be more effective if you include in the letter a spreadsheet showing the budget and estimated expenses for the prom.

EXAMPLE

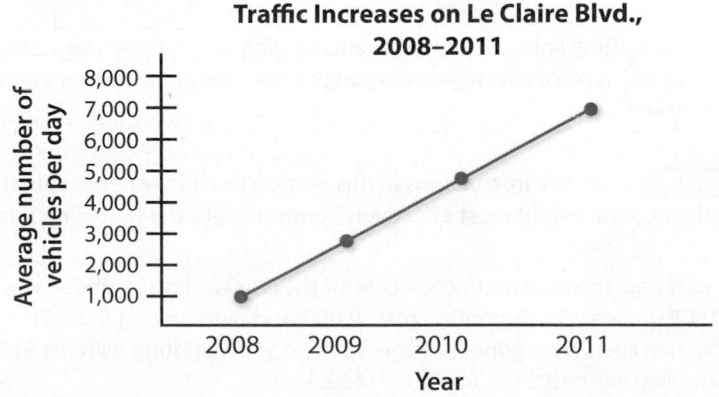

TABLES By using rows and columns, tables provide detailed information that is arranged in an accessible, organized way. A **spreadsheet** is a special kind of table created on a computer. The cells of a spreadsheet are associated with mathematical equations. Spreadsheets are especially useful for budgets or schedules in which the numbers are variables in an equation. In the spreadsheet below, the last row totals the figures in each column.

EXAMPLE

Club Account Balances by Month				
Month	**September**	**October**	**November**	**December**
deposit (dues)	150.00	150.00	165.00	165.00
deposit (other)	75.00	38.00	17.75	119.00
total	225.00	188.00	182.75	284.00

PICTURES You may scan a drawing or photograph into your document on the computer or paste it in manually. Place a picture as close as possible to the reference in the text, and use a caption.

CHARTS Charts show relationships among ideas or data. Two types of charts you are likely to use are flowcharts and pie charts. A **flowchart** uses geometric shapes linked by arrows to show the sequence of events in a process. A **pie chart** is a circle that is divided into wedges. Each wedge represents a certain percentage of the total, and a legend tells what concept each wedge color represents.

EXAMPLE

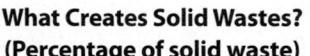

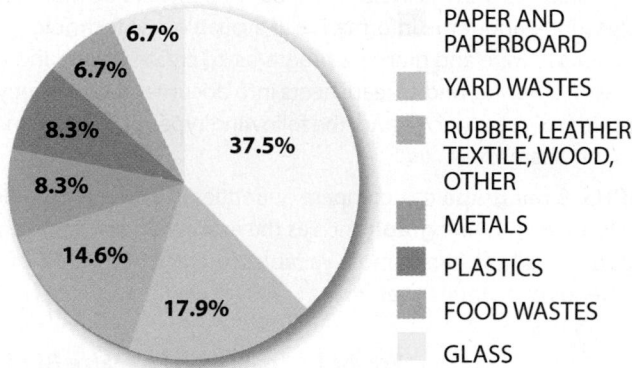

TIME LINES Time lines identify the events dealing with a particular subject that have taken place over a given period of time. (See page 2 for an example of a time line.)

YOUR TURN Use the instructions in this section to choose and create the visual you think would most effectively communicate the following information.

Last year, the total production cost for the Eureka High yearbook was $2,000. Paper cost $400, printing cost $1,000, and binding cost $600. This year, production costs have gone up. Paper will cost $500, printing will cost $1,250, and binding will cost $725, for a total of $2,475.

Language Handbook

1. The Parts Of Speech

Part Of Speech	Definition	Examples
NOUN	Names person, place, thing, or idea	poet, Sylvia Plath, city, Chicago, awards, Nobel Prize, *Of Mice and Men*, books, crew, Harlem Renaissance, realism
PRONOUN	Takes place of one or more nouns or pronouns	
Personal	Refers to one(s) speaking (first person), spoken to (second person), or spoken about (third person)	I, me, my, mine, we, us, our, ours you, your, yours he, him, his, she, her, hers, it, its they, them, their, theirs
Reflexive	Refers to subject; directs action of verb back to subject	myself, ourselves, yourself, yourselves, himself, herself, itself, themselves
Intensive	Refers to and emphasizes noun or another pronoun	(same as examples for Reflexive)
Demonstrative	Refers to specific one(s) of a group	this, that, these, those
Interrogative	Introduces question	what, which, who, whom, whose
Relative	Introduces subordinate clause	that, which, who, whom, whose
Indefinite	Refers to one(s) not specifically named	all, anyone, both, each, either, everybody, many, none, nothing, someone
ADJECTIVE	Modifies noun or pronoun; tells *what kind, which one,* or *how many/how much*	**a large black** box, **an able-bodied** worker, **that** one, **the five Iroquois** nations, **enough** time, **less** money
VERB	Shows action or state of being	
Action	Expresses physical or mental activity	write, receive, run, think, imagine, know
Linking	Connects subject with word identifying or describing it	appear, be, seem, become, feel, look, smell, sound, taste
Helping (Auxiliary)	Helps another verb express time, voice, or mood	be, have, may, can, shall, will, would
ADVERB	Modifies verb, adjective, or adverb; tells *how, when, where,* or *to what extent*	speaks **clearly, quite** interesting, **rather** calmly, arrived **there late**
PREPOSITION	Relates noun or pronoun to another word	about, at, by, for, of, in, on, through, according to, in front of, out of
CONJUNCTION	Joins words or word groups	
Coordinating	Joins words or word groups used in the same way	and, but, for, nor, or, so, yet

Correlative	Paired conjunctions that join parallel words or word groups	both . . . and, not only . . . but (also), either . . . or, neither . . . nor
Subordinating	Begins subordinate clause; connects it to independent clause	although, as if, because, since, so that, unless, when, where, while
INTERJECTION	Expresses emotion	hey, oh, ouch, wow, well, hooray

Your Turn Using Specific Adjectives

In the following paragraph, replace the underlined adjectives with adjectives that are more specific.

[1] When Clark learned that Aunt Georgiana was coming to Boston, he felt <u>funny</u>. [2] She once had taught music in Boston, but then she had eloped with the <u>poor</u> and <u>boring</u> Howard Carpenter. [3] Clark was <u>happy</u>, though, for the <u>good</u> care she had given him as a boy; indeed, he had a <u>great</u> affection for her. [4] Now, he wanted to treat her to a <u>nice</u> performance by the symphony orchestra, in Boston's <u>pretty</u> concert hall. [5] As the <u>fine</u> orchestra played, Clark watched the look on his aunt's <u>tired</u>, <u>old-looking</u> face change from aloofness to <u>real</u> sadness.

2. Agreement

AGREEMENT OF SUBJECT AND VERB

2a. A verb should agree in number with its subject. Singular subjects take singular verbs. Plural subjects take plural verbs.

SINGULAR   The **character lives** on a farm.

PLURAL   **Both** of these stories **are** funny.

2b. The number of the subject is not changed by a phrase or clause following the subject.

SINGULAR   **Langston Hughes**, who wrote poems, **was** part of the Harlem Renaissance.

PLURAL   **The students** in Ms. Rey's class **are** eager to use the new software.

2c. Indefinite pronouns may be singular, plural, or either.

(1) The following indefinite pronouns are singular: *anybody, anyone, anything, each, either, one, everybody, everyone, everything, neither, nobody, no one, nothing, somebody, someone, something.*

Neither of the books **contains** that story.

(2) The following indefinite pronouns are plural: *both, few, many, several.*

Both of the poems **were written** by Claude McKay.

(3) The indefinite pronouns *all, any, most, none,* and *some* are singular when they refer to singular words and plural when they refer to plural words.

SINGULAR   **Some** of her artwork **is** beautiful. [*Some* refers to *artwork.*]

PLURAL   **Some** of her paintings **are** beautiful. [*Some* refers to *paintings.*]

2d. A *compound subject* may be singular or plural.

(1) Subjects joined by *and* usually take a plural verb.

Hemingway, Steinbeck, and Morrison are Nobel Prize winners.

A compound subject that names only one person or thing takes a singular verb.

Roderick Usher's **sister and** sole **companion is** Madeline.

(2) Singular subjects joined by *or* or *nor* take a singular verb.

Amy or Eric plans to report on icebergs.

Neither the **rain nor** the **wind has stopped.**

(3) When a singular subject and a plural subject are joined by *or* or *nor*, the verb agrees with the subject nearer the verb.

Neither the **performers nor** the **director was** eager to rehearse the scene again.

2e. The verb agrees with its subject even when the verb precedes the subject, such as in sentences beginning with *here, there,* or *where.*

Here **is** [*or* here**'s**] a **copy** of the letter.

Here **are** [*not* here's] two **copies** of the letter.

2f. A *collective noun* (such as *class, herd,* or *jury*) is singular in form but names a group of persons or things. A collective noun takes a singular verb when the noun refers to the group as a unit and takes a plural verb when the noun refers to the parts or members of the group.

SINGULAR   The **cast** of *A Raisin in the Sun* **makes** its debut on Friday night. [The cast as a whole will debut.]

PLURAL   After the play, the **cast are joining** their families for a celebration. [Members of the cast are joining their families.]

2g. An expression of an amount (a length of time, a statistic, or a fraction, for example) is singular when the amount is thought of as a whole or when it refers to a singular word. An amount is plural when it is thought of as many parts or when it refers to a plural word.

SINGULAR   **Twenty years was** a long time for Rip Van Winkle to sleep. [one unit]

PLURAL   **Fifty percent** of the students **have** already **read** *Walden.* [The percentage refers to *students.*]

2h. The title of a creative work (such as a book, song, film, or painting) or the name of an organization, a country, or a city (even if the name is plural in form) takes a singular verb.

"Birches" was written by Robert Frost.

The **United States calls** its flag "Old Glory."

2i. A verb agrees with its subject, not with its predicate nominative.

SINGULAR   One **symptom** of flu **is** sore muscles.

PLURAL   Sore **muscles are** one symptom of flu.

AGREEMENT OF PRONOUN AND ANTECEDENT

A pronoun usually refers to a noun or another pronoun, called its *antecedent.*

2j. A pronoun agrees with its antecedent in number and gender. Singular pronouns refer to singular antecedents. Plural pronouns refer to plural antecedents. A few singular pronouns indicate gender (neuter, feminine, masculine).

Marianne Moore published **her** first book of poems in 1921. [singular, feminine]

Payton Farquhar thinks **he** has escaped. [singular, masculine]

Benjamin Franklin wrote, "**Three** may keep a secret if two of **them** are dead." [plural]

2k. Indefinite pronouns may be singular, plural, or either.

(1)   Singular pronouns are used to refer to the indefinite pronouns *anybody, anyone, anything, each, other, everybody, everyone, everything, neither, nobody, no one, nothing, one, somebody, someone,* and *something.* The gender of any of these pronouns is often determined by a word in a phrase following the pronoun.

Each of the **girls** has memorized **her** part.

One of the **boys** gave **his** interpretation of "Nothing Gold Can Stay."

If the antecedent may be either masculine or feminine, use masculine and feminine pronouns to refer to it.

Anyone who is qualified for the job may submit **his** or **her** application.

NOTE: Whenever possible, revise the sentence to avoid this awkward construction.

Those who **are** qualified for the job may submit **an** application.

(2)   Plural pronouns are used to refer to the indefinite pronouns *both, few, many,* and *several.*

Both of the finalists in the piano competition played **their** best.

(3)   Singular or plural pronouns may be used to refer to the indefinite pronouns *all, any, most, none,* and *some.* These indefinite pronouns are singular when they refer to singular words and are plural when they refer to plural words.

SINGULAR   **All** of our **planning** achieved **its** purpose.

PLURAL   **All** of your **suggestions** had **their** good points.

2l. A plural pronoun is used to refer to two or more singular antecedents joined by *and.*

Leah and Mario read **their** sonnets to the class.

2m. A singular pronoun is used to refer to two or more singular antecedents joined by *or* or *nor*.

Neither **Cindy nor Carla** thinks **she** is ready.

2n. When a singular and a plural antecedent are joined by *or* or *nor*, the pronoun agrees with the nearer antecedent.

Either **Jerry or** the **twins** will bring **their** stereo.

2o. A collective noun (such as *audience, family,* or *team*) takes a singular pronoun when the noun refers to the group as a unit and takes a plural pronoun when the noun refers to the parts or members of the group.

| SINGULAR | The **debate club** elected **its** new officers. |
| PLURAL | The **debate club** will practice **their** speeches this week. |

2p. The title of a creative work (such as a book, song, film, or painting) or the name of an organization, a country, or a city (even if it is plural in form) takes a singular pronoun.

After Mr. Kim read "**Mushrooms**," we discussed **it**.

Anderson Outfitters advertises **itself** well.

Your Turn **Revising Sentences**

Sentences with antecedents joined by *or* or *nor* can sometimes be misleading. Revise the following sentences to keep the meaning clear.

1. Either the boys or Mom will miss her favorite TV show this afternoon.
2. Neither she nor I, however, would miss my chance to meet the family's favorite author.
3. We or you should save you a place in line to have our books signed.
4. If you see Mike or Helen, tell her that we bought an extra copy of the book.
5. None of us have ever heard her or another writer read his or her works before.

3. Using Verbs

REGULAR AND IRREGULAR VERBS

Every verb has four basic forms called the **principal parts:** the *base form*, the *present participle*, the *past*, and the *past participle*. A verb is classified as *regular* or *irregular* depending on the way it forms the past and past participle.

3a. A *regular verb* forms its past and past participle by adding *–d* or *–ed* to the base form. An *irregular verb* forms the past and the past participle in some other way.

Common Regular And Irregular Verbs			
BASE FORM	PRESENT PARTICIPLE	PAST	PAST PARTICIPLE
Regular			
ask	(is) asking	asked	(have) asked
attack	(is) attacking	attacked	(have) attacked
drown	(is) drowning	drowned	(have) drowned
plan	(is) planning	planned	(have) planned
try	(is) trying	tried	(have) tried
use	(is) using	used	(have) used

Irregular			
be	(is) being	was, were	(have) been
begin	(is) beginning	began	(have) begun
catch	(is) catching	caught	(have) caught
drive	(is) driving	drove	(have) driven
go	(is) going	went	(have) gone
lead	(is) leading	led	(have) led
shake	(is) shaking	shook	(have) shaken
swim	(is) swimming	swam	(have) swum
throw	(is) throwing	threw	(have) thrown

TENSES AND THEIR USES

3b. The *tense* of a verb indicates the time of the action or the state of being expressed by the verb.

Tense/ Formation	Meaning	Examples
PRESENT (base form)	Expresses action or state of being that is occurring now	We **understand** now.
	Shows customary or habitual action or state of being	For breakfast I **eat** cereal and **drink** orange juice.
	Conveys a general truth	The earth **revolves** once around the sun each year.
	Makes a historical event seem current (the **historical present**)	Several of the *Mayflower* passengers **die** before the ship **reaches** Plymouth.
	Summarizes the plot or topic of a literary work (the **literary present**)	*Moby-Dick* **tells** the story of a vengeful sea captain who **pursues** a white whale.
	Expresses future time	The workshop **begins** tomorrow.
PAST (past form)	Shows action or state of being that occurred in the past but did not continue into the present	Pepe **grabbed** his rifle and **crawled** into the brush.
FUTURE (*will* or *shall* + base form)	Shows action or state of being that will occur	Elisa **will play** the part of Beneatha Younger in tonight's performance. I **will** [or **shall**] **serve** as her understudy.
PRESENT PERFECT (*have* or *has* + past participle)	Shows action or state of being that occurred at some indefinite time in the past	**Have** you **read** any stories by Sandra Cisneros?
	Shows action or state of being that began in the past and continues into the present	My sister **has been** a Girl Scout for at least two years.
PAST PERFECT (*had* + past participle)	Shows action or state of being that was completed in the past before another action or state of being occurred	Miss Emily returned the tax notice that she **had received.**
FUTURE PERFECT (*will have* or *shall have* + past participle)	Shows action or state of being that will be completed in the future before some other future occurrence	By the time Rip Van Winkle returns to his village, the Revolutionary War **will have occurred.**

3c. Avoid unnecessary shifts in tense.

INCONSISTENT   Shiftlet marries Lucynell and then abandoned her.

CONSISTENT   Shiftlet **marries** Lucynell and then **abandons** her.

CONSISTENT   Shiftlet **married** Lucynell and then **abandoned** her.

When describing events that occur at different times, use verbs in different tenses to show the order of events.

> She now **works** for *The New York Times*, but she **worked** for *The Wall Street Journal* last year.

ACTIVE VOICE AND PASSIVE VOICE

3d. *Voice* is the form a verb takes to indicate whether the subject of the verb performs or receives action.

A verb is in the *active voice* when its subject performs action.

> Julia Alvarez **wrote** "Daughter of Invention."

A verb is in the *passive voice* when its subject receives action. A passive voice verb is always a verb phrase that includes a form of *be* and the past participle of an action verb.

> "Daughter of Invention" **was written** by Julia Alvarez.

3e. Use the passive voice sparingly.

In general, the passive voice is less direct and less forceful than the active voice. In some cases, the passive voice may sound awkward.

AWKWARD PASSIVE   A memorable speech was delivered by William Faulkner when the Nobel Prize was accepted by him in 1950.

ACTIVE   William Faulkner delivered a memorable speech when he accepted the Nobel Prize in 1950.

Your Turn **Using Active and Passive Voice**

Although the active voice is generally preferred in writing, the passive voice sometimes makes better sense. All of the following sentences use the passive voice. Decide which sentences would be more effective in the active voice, and then rewrite those sentences accordingly.

1. Has a book ever been read by you to raise money?
2. Many charities have been helped in this way.
3. More than five hundred book readings were registered during this year's Readathon.
4. Approximately ten dollars was raised by each reading for a community charity.
5. A homeless shelter was given half of the total; the rest went to an after-school tutoring program.

---

4. Using Pronouns

CASE

Case is the form that a noun or a pronoun takes to indicate its use in a sentence. In English, there are three cases: *nominative, objective,* and *possessive.*

A noun's form is the same for both the nominative case and the objective case. A noun changes form only in the possessive case. Most personal pronouns, however, have one form for each case. The form a pronoun takes depends on its function in a sentence.

THE NOMINATIVE CASE

4a. A subject of a verb is in the nominative case.

> **They** were happy that **he** was home from the war at last. [*They* is the subject of *were,* and *he* is the subject of *was.*]

THE OBJECTIVE CASE

4b. A predicate nominative is in the nominative case.

> The one who jilts Granny Weatherall is **he**. [*He* follows *is* and identifies the subject *one.*]

4c. An object of a verb is in the objective case.

> Since my stepbrother and stepsister don't have cars, I usually give **them** a ride to school. [*Them* is the direct object of the verb *give.*]

> The Jazz Age collage earned Don and **her** blue ribbons. [*Don and her* is a compound indirect object of the verb *earned.*]

4d. An object of a preposition is in the objective case

> Did you send copies of *Blue Highways* to **him**? [*Him* is an object of the preposition *to.*]

THE POSSESSIVE CASE

4e. A noun or a pronoun preceding a gerund is in the possessive case

> Warren did not appreciate **Silas's** [*or* **his**] leaving during haying time. [*Silas's* or *his* modifies *leaving*, a gerund used as the direct object of the verb *appreciate*.]

SPECIAL PRONOUN PROBLEMS

4b. An appositive is in the same case as the noun or pronoun to which it refers.

> The Ushers, **Madeline and he,** live in a gloomy mansion. [The appositive, *Madeline and he*, refers to the subject, *Ushers*, which is in the nominative case.]

4c. The pronoun *who* (*whoever*) is in the nominative case. The pronoun *whom* (*whomever*) is in the objective case.

> **Who** wrote *Dangling Man*? [*Who* is the subject of *wrote*.]
>
> With **whom** did Moss Hart write the play? [*Whom* is the object of *with*.]

4d. A pronoun ending in *–self* or *–selves* should not be used in place of a personal pronoun.

> You were a great help to Lupe and **me** [*not* myself].

4e. A pronoun following *than* or *as* in an elliptical construction is in the same case as it would be if the construction were completed.

An *elliptical construction* is a clause from which words have been omitted. Notice how the meaning of each of the following sentences depends on the pronoun form in the elliptical construction.

NOMINATIVE CASE	I have known Ana longer **than she.** [I have known Ana longer than she has known Ana.]
OBJECTIVE CASE	I have known Ana longer **than her.** [I have known Ana longer than I have known her.]

CLEAR PRONOUN REFERENCE

4f. A pronoun should refer clearly to its antecedent. Avoid an ambiguous, a general, a weak, or an indefinite reference by (1) rephrasing the sentence, (2) replacing the pronoun with a noun, or (3) giving the pronoun a clear antecedent.

AMBIGUOUS	Jody talked to Billy as he was working. [*He* refers to either *Jody* or *Billy*.]
CLEAR	As Billy was working, Jody talked to him.
GENERAL	Dark clouds descended on the house. This seemed to bewilder Roderick. [*This* has no specific antecedent.]
CLEAR	The dark clouds that descended on the house seemed to bewilder Roderick.
WEAK	He was superstitious. One of these was that black cats bring bad luck. [The antecedent of *these* is not expressed.]
CLEAR	He was superstitious. One of his superstitions was that black cats bring bad luck.
INDEFINITE	In this book, it explains the origins of words. [*It* is not necessary.]
CLEAR	This book explains the origins of words.

Personal Pronouns		
Singular		
	NOMINATIVE	**OBJECTIVE**	**POSSESSIVE**
FIRST PERSON	I	me	my, mine
SECOND PERSON	you	you	your, yours
THIRD PERSON	he, she, it	him, her, it	his, her, hers, its
Plural		
	NOMINATIVE	**OBJECTIVE**	**POSSESSIVE**
FIRST PERSON	we	us	our, ours
SECOND PERSON	you	you	your, yours
THIRD PERSON	they	them	their, theirs

Your Turn Revising Pronoun References

A pronoun should refer clearly to its antecedent. In the following sentences, however, some pronouns have more than one possible antecedent, no antecedent, or a vague antecedent. Rewrite each sentence to correct faulty pronoun references.

1. Well, I have to write another essay of literary analysis. This always is a problem for me.
2. In the assignment, it says that we should compare two primary source documents from the Civil War.
3. Scott suggested that I include the letter from Major Sullivan Ballou. I will think about him.
4. I know I want to write about Mary Chesnut. That is a certainty!
5. Both writers were rather idealistic, but the horrors of war shattered it for Chesnut.

5. Using Modifiers

WHAT IS A MODIFIER?

A *modifier* is a word or group of words that limits the meaning of another word or group of words. The two kinds of modifiers are *adjectives* and *adverbs*.

COMPARISON OF MODIFIERS

5a. *Comparison* refers to the change in the form of an adjective or an adverb to show increasing or decreasing degrees in the quality the modifier expresses.

The three degrees of comparison are *positive*, *comparative*, and *superlative*.

(1) Most one-syllable modifiers form the comparative and superlative degrees by adding –er (*less*) and –est (*least*).
(2) Some two-syllable modifiers form the comparative and superlative degrees by adding –er and –est; others form the comparative and superlative degrees by using *more* and *most*. All two-syllable modifiers form decreasing comparisons by using *less* and *least*.
(3) Modifiers of more than two syllables form the comparative and superlative degrees by using *more (less)* and *most (least)*.

Positive	Comparative	Superlative
neat	neater	neatest
simple	simpler	simplest
calmly	more calmly	most calmly
optimistic	less optimistic	least optimistic

(4) Some modifiers form the comparative and superlative degrees in other ways.

Positive	Comparative	Superlative
bad	worse	worst
far	farther (further)	farthest (furthest)
good (well)	better	best
little	less	least
many (much)	more	most

5b. Use the comparative degree when comparing two things. Use the superlative degree when comparing more than two.

COMPARATIVE Both puppies are cute, but the **more active** one seems **healthier.**

SUPERLATIVE Of the four plays, I think *Death of a Salesman* was the **most moving.**

5c. Avoid using a double comparison or a double negative. A *double comparison* is the use of two comparative forms (usually –er and *more*) or two superlative forms (usually –est and *most*) to modify the same word. A *double negative* is the use of two negative words when one is enough.

Samuel Clemens is **better** [*not* more better] known as Mark Twain.

She did**n't** say **anything** [*not* nothing].

5d. Include the word *other* or *else* when comparing one member of a group with the rest of the group.

Esteban is taller than anyone **else** on the team.

5e. Avoid comparing items that cannot logically be compared.

> ILLOGICAL   Hemingway's style is perhaps more imitated than any other American writer. [A style is compared to a writer.]
>
> LOGICAL   Hemingway's style is perhaps more imitated than **that of** any other American writer. [Two styles are compared.]

PLACEMENT OF MODIFIERS

5f. Avoid using a *misplaced modifier*—a word, phrase, or clause that sounds awkward because it modifies the wrong word or group of words.

To correct a misplaced modifier, place the word, phrase, or clause as close as possible to the word or words you intend it to modify.

> MISPLACED   Thoreau listened to the song of a robin looking at the pond. [Was the robin or Thoreau looking at the pond?]
>
> CLEAR   **Looking at the pond**, Thoreau listened to the song of a distant robin.

5g. Avoid using a *dangling modifier*—a modifying word, phrase, or clause that does not sensibly modify any word or words in a sentence.

You may correct a dangling modifier by
- adding a word or words that the dangling word, phrase, or clause can refer to sensibly
- adding a word or words to the dangling word, phrase, or clause
- rewording the sentence

> DANGLING   Alone, the mountain is virtually impossible to climb. [Who or what is alone?]
>
> CLEAR   **For a person alone**, the mountain is virtually impossible to climb.
>
> CLEAR   The mountain is virtually impossible **for a person** to climb **alone**.
>
> DANGLING   After winning the Pulitzer Prize, the novel *Maud Martha* was written. [Who won the Pulitzer Prize?]
>
> CLEAR   After winning the Pulitzer Prize, **Gwendolyn Brooks wrote** the novel *Maud Martha*.
>
> CLEAR   After **Gwendolyn Brooks won** the Pulitzer Prize, **she wrote** the novel *Maud Martha*.

Your Turn   Revising Comparisons

The comparisons in the following sentences are not logical. Rewrite each sentence so that the comparison is as clear and logical as possible.

1. In *Moby-Dick*, Melville presents symbols whose interpretations are more varied than traditional works.
2. Captain Ahab is more complex than any literary character I know.
3. In my opinion, Melville's imagery is the most mysterious of any writer from that era.
4. I believe that the levels of meaning in *Moby-Dick* are more complex than Hawthorne's *The Scarlet Letter*.
5. Don't you think that this novel's importance is even greater than Melville's own *Billy Budd*?

---

6. Phrases

6a. A *phrase* is a group of related words that is used as a single part of speech and that does not contain both a verb and its subject.

> **At two o'clock** [adverb phrase], the event **of the year** [adjective phrase], the company picnic, **will commence** [verb phrase].

PREPOSITIONAL PHRASES

6b. A *prepositional phrase* begins with a preposition and ends with an *object of the preposition*, a word or word group that functions as a noun.

> **On the pillow** lay a strand **of gray hair**. [*Pillow* is the object of the preposition *on*. *Hair* is the object of the preposition *of*.]

(1) An *adjective phrase* is a prepositional phrase that modifies a noun or a pronoun. The adjective phrase usually follows the word it modifies. That word may be the object of another preposition.

> Cassie made fry bread, using a recipe **like that of her ancestors**. [*Like that* modifies the noun *recipe*. *Of her ancestors* modifies the pronoun *that*, which is the object of the preposition *like*.]

(2) An *adverb phrase* is a prepositional phrase that modifies a verb, an adjective, or an adverb. An adverb phrase tells *how, when, where, why,* or *to what extent* (*how long* or *how far*).

> **During the Civil War**, Louisa May Alcott worked **as a nurse**. [Each phrase modifies the verb *worked*. *During the Civil War* tells *when* and *as a nurse* tells *how*.]

VERBALS AND VERBAL PHRASES

6c. A *verbal* is a form of a verb used as a noun, an adjective, or an adverb. A *verbal phrase* consists of a verbal and any of its modifiers or complements.

Verbal/ Verbal Phrase	Function/ Formation	Examples
PARTICIPLE/ PARTICIPIAL PHRASE	Used as an adjective Present participle: ends in –*ing* Past participle: usually ends in –*d* or –*ed*, but may be irregularly formed	The explorer could hear something **moving.** [modifies the pronoun *something*] **Obsessed with revenge,** Captain Ahab pursued the white whale. [modifies the noun *Captain Ahab*] Samuel Clemens, **better known as Mark Twain,** was born in Florida, Missouri, in 1835. [modifies the noun *Samuel Clemens* (irregular)]
GERUND/ GERUND PHRASE	Used as a noun Always ends in –*ing*	**Exercising** is a good health habit. [subject] Dexter enjoyed **working at the golf club.** [direct object] Walter Mitty dreamed of **being a pilot.** [object of the preposition] One way to build your vocabulary is **reading good literature.** [predicate nominative]
INFINITIVE/ INFINITIVE PHRASE	Used as a noun, an adjective, or an adverb Usually begins with the word *to*	My main goal for the marathon is **to finish.** [noun functioning as a predicate nominative] My plan **to finish the novel last night** didn't quite work out. [adjective modifying *plan*] However, I will be happy **to give you my opinion of this famous novel.** [adverb modifying *happy*]

The Infinitive Clause

6d. Unlike other verbals, an infinitive may have a subject. If so, it is called an *infinitive clause.*

> Our teacher asked **us to read "Thanatopsis."** [*Us* is the subject of the infinitive *to read*. The entire infinitive clause is the direct object of *asked.*]

> Did anyone see **Darlene leave the room**? [*Darlene* is the subject of the infinitive *(to) leave*. The entire infinitive clause is the direct object of *did see.*]

APPOSITIVES AND APPOSITIVE PHRASES

6e. An *appositive* is a noun or a pronoun placed beside (usually after) another noun or pronoun to identify or explain it. An *appositive phrase* consists of an appositive and its modifiers.

An appositive or appositive phrase usually follows the word it identifies or explains.

> We went to the Navajo Gallery to see R. C. Gorman's artwork *Freeform Lady.* [The appositive *Freeform Lady* identifies the noun *artwork.*]

> The gallery, **an undiscovered treasure,** is one of my favorite places. [The appositive phrase *an undiscovered treasure* refers to *gallery.*]

> Can you believe that I **myself** plan to become an artist? [The appositive *myself* refers to *I.*]

For emphasis, however, an appositive or appositive phrase may come at the beginning of a sentence.

> **A young painter,** Jaune Quick-to-See Smith shows a deep awareness of her French, Shoshone, and Cree heritage.

Appositives are sometimes introduced by a colon or by the expressions *or, namely, such as, for example, i.e.,* or *e.g.*

> The shelter is accepting donations of the following items: canned **food, blankets,** and winter **coats.**

> Beneficial insects, **such as ladybugs** and **praying mantises,** can help control the population of harmful insects in a garden.

Your Turn   Using Phrases

In the following sentences, fill in each blank to complete each adjective phrase or adverb phrase.

1. Rocket ships and aliens appear with ___ in novels that explore a future of ___.
2. As I read such stories, I often imagine myself doing battle with ___ or just sailing through ___.
3. Darker works, like ___ , present a future in which people live sad lives of ___.
4. When I reach the end of ___ , I appreciate today's world all the more, despite ___.
5. Come see me about ___—my bookshelves are filled with ___!

7. Clauses

7a. A *clause* is a group of words that contains a verb and its subject and that is used as part of a sentence. There are two kinds of clauses: the *independent clause* and the *subordinate clause*.

THE INDEPENDENT CLAUSE

7b. An *independent* (or *main*) *clause* expresses a complete thought and can stand by itself as a sentence.

SUBJECT	VERB
Emily Dickinson	**wrote** hundreds of poems.

THE SUBORDINATE CLAUSE

7c. A *subordinate* (or *dependent*) *clause* does not express a complete thought and cannot stand by itself as a sentence.

	SUBJECT	VERB
that	**we**	**read**

The thought expressed by a subordinate clause becomes complete when the clause is combined with an independent clause.

The last book **that we read** was *Blue Highways*.

THE ADJECTIVE CLAUSE

7d. An *adjective clause* is a subordinate clause that modifies a noun or a pronoun.

An adjective clause follows the word or words it modifies and usually begins with a relative pronoun. The relative pronoun (1) relates the adjective clause to the word or words the clause modifies and (2) performs a function within the adjective clause.

Li recommends every poem **that Denise Levertov has written**. [The relative pronoun *that* relates the adjective clause to the noun *poem* and serves as the direct object of the verb *has written*.]

An adjective clause may begin with a relative adverb such as *when* or *where*.

From 1914 to 1931, Isak Denisen lived in Kenya, **where she operated a coffee plantation**.

Sometimes the relative pronoun or relative adverb is not expressed.

The book [**that**] I am reading is her biography.

THE NOUN CLAUSE

7e. A *noun clause* is a subordinate clause that may be used as a subject, a predicate nominative, a direct object, an indirect object, or an object of a preposition.

Words commonly used to introduce noun clauses include *how, that, what, whether, who(m),* and *why*.

A catchy slogan is **what we will need for this campaign**. [predicate nominative]

Students say **that I am a good teacher**. [direct object]

The director will give **whomever does best in this audition** the lead role. [indirect object]

The word that introduces the noun clause may or may not have a function within the clause.

Do any of you know **who wrote *Spoon River Anthology***? [The word *who* introduces the noun clause and serves as the subject of the verb *wrote*.]

She told Walter **that he was driving too fast and should slow down**. [The word *that* introduces the noun clause but does not have any function within it.]

THE ADVERB CLAUSE

7f. An *adverb clause* is a subordinate clause that modifies a verb, an adjective, or an adverb.

An adverb clause, which may come before or after the word or words it modifies, tells *how, when, where, why, to what extent,* or *under what condition.* An adverb clause is introduced by a **subordinating conjunction,** which relates the adverb clause to the word or words that it modifies.

> William Cullen Bryant wrote the first version of "Thanatopsis" **when he was a teenager.** [The adverb clause modifies the verb *wrote,* telling *when* Bryant wrote the first version.]

Zoë can explain naturalism to you better **than I.** [The adverb clause modifies the adjective *better,* telling *to what extent* Zoë can better explain naturalism.]

The Elliptical Clause

7g. Part of a clause may be left out when the meaning can be understood from the context of the sentence. Such a clause is called an *elliptical clause.*

> Roger knew the rule better **than Elgin** [**did**].
> **While** [**he was**] **living at Walden Pond,** Thoreau wrote his first book.

Your Turn Combining Sentences

Combine each of the following pairs of sentences by making one of the independent clauses into a subordinate clause.

1. Mrs. Sommers receives fifteen dollars. She does not have a plan for it at first.
2. She finally decides. She will use the money to buy clothes for her children.
3. She shops for the children. She sees and then buys a pair of silk stockings for herself.
4. The money once seemed so abundant. It begins to disappear in a spending spree.
5. The day ends. Mrs. Sommers has indulged her long-denied desires.

---

8. Sentence Structure

SENTENCE OR FRAGMENT?

8a. A *sentence* is a group of words that has a subject and a verb and expresses a complete thought.

> Benjamin Franklin lived in London and in Paris.

Only a sentence should begin with a capital letter and end with either a period, a question mark, or an exclamation point. A group of words that either does not contain a subject and a verb or does not express a complete thought is called a *sentence fragment.*

> FRAGMENT   Collapses during a storm.
> SENTENCE   The House of Usher collapses during a storm.

SUBJECT AND PREDICATE

8b. A sentence consists of two parts: a subject and a predicate. A *subject* tells *whom* or *what* the sentence is about. A *predicate* tells something about the subject.

In the following examples, the words labeled *subject* make up the **complete subject,** and the words labeled *predicate* make up the **complete predicate.**

SUBJECT	PREDICATE
Walt Whitman	wrote *Leaves of Grass.*

PREDICATE	SUBJECT	PREDICATE
Why did	Phoenix	walk to town?

The Simple Subject

8c. A *simple subject* is the main word or group of words that tells *whom* or *what* the sentence is about.

> **Harold Krebs,** the protagonist of the story, returns home from the war. [The complete subject is *Harold Krebs, the protagonist of the story.*]

The Simple Predicate

8d. A *simple predicate* is a verb or verb phrase that tells something about the subject.

> **Did** Judy **marry** Dexter? [The complete predicate is *did marry Dexter.*]

The Compound Subject and the Compound Verb

8e. A *compound subject* consists of two or more subjects that are joined by a conjunction—usually *and* or *or*—and that have the same verb.

Reuben and **I** are discussing "A Wagner Matinée."

8f. A *compound verb* consists of two or more verbs that are joined by a conjunction—usually *and, but,* or *or*—and that have the same subject.

I **recognized** the song but **had forgotten** its title.

How to Find the Subject of a Sentence

8g. To find the subject of a sentence, ask *Who?* or *What?* before the verb.

(1) The subject of a sentence is never within a prepositional phrase.

On the quarter-deck stood **Captain Ahab.** [Who stood? Captain Ahab stood. *Quarter deck* is the object of the preposition *on.*]

(2) The subject of a sentence expressing a command or a request is always understood to be *you*, but *you* may not appear in the sentence.

COMMAND   Identify two of the most striking characteristics of E. E. Cummings's poetry. [Who is being told to identify? *You* is understood.]

The subject of a command or a request is *you*, even when a sentence contains a **noun of direct address**—a word naming the one or ones spoken to.

REQUEST   Jordan, [**you**] please read aloud Jimmy Santiago Baca's "Fall."

(3) The subject of a sentence expressing a question usually follows the verb or a part of the verb phrase. Turning the question into a statement will often help you find the subject.

QUESTION   Was Pearl Buck awarded the Nobel Prize in literature in 1938? [Who was awarded?]

STATEMENT   **Pearl Buck** was awarded the Nobel Prize in literature in 1938.

QUESTION   Where is the dog's leash? [Where is what?]

STATEMENT   The dog's **leash** is where.

(4) The word *there* or *here* is never the subject of a sentence.

Here are your **gloves.** [What are here? Gloves are.]

COMPLEMENTS

8h. A *complement* is a word or group of words that completes the meaning of a verb. There are four main kinds of complements: *direct object, indirect object, objective complement,* and *subject complement.*

Type of Complement	Description	Examples
DIRECT OBJECT	Noun, pronoun, or word group that functions as a noun and tells *who* or *what* receives the action of a transitive verb	Kerry called **me** at noon. [called whom? *me*] Captain Ahab sacrifices his **ship** and almost **all** of his crew. [sacrifices what? *ship* and *all*—compound direct object]
INDIRECT OBJECT	Noun, pronoun, or word group that comes between a transitive verb and a direct object and tells *to whom, to what, for whom,* or *for what* the action of the verb is done	Emily Dickinson sent **Thomas Wentworth Higginson** four poems. [sent to whom? Thomas Wentworth Higginson] Ms. Cruz showed **José** and **me** photos of her visit to Walden Pond. [showed to whom? José and me—compound indirect object]
OBJECTIVE COMPLEMENT	Noun, pronoun, adjective, or word group that helps complete the meaning of a transitive verb by identifying or modifying the direct object	Everyone considered her **dependable**. [The adjective *dependable* modifies the direct object *her*.] Many literary historians call Poe **the master of the macabre**. [The word group *the master of the macabre* modifies the direct object *Poe*.]

Type of Complement	Description	Examples
SUBJECT COMPLEMENT	Word or word group that completes the meaning of the verb and identifies or modifies the subject	
Predicate Nominative	A word or group of words that follows a linking verb and refers to the same person or thing as the subject of the verb	Of the applicants, Carlos is the most competent **one**. [The pronoun *one* refers to the subject *Carlos*.] The main characters are **Aunt Georgiana** and **Clark**. [The nouns *Aunt Georgiana* and *Clark* refer to the subject *characters*.]
Predicate Adjective	An adjective that follows a linking verb and modifies the subject	Eben Flood felt very **lonely**. [The adjective *lonely* modifies the subject *Eben Flood*.] Shiftlet is **sly** and **scheming**. [The adjectives *sly* and *scheming* modify the subject *Shiftlet*.]

SENTENCES CLASSIFIED ACCORDING TO STRUCTURE

8i. According to structure, sentences are classified as *simple, compound, complex,* or *compound-complex.*

(1) A *simple sentence* has one independent clause and no subordinate clauses.

Thornton Wilder's *Our Town* is my favorite play.

(2) A *compound sentence* has two or more independent clauses but no subordinate clauses.

Jack London was a prolific writer; he wrote nearly fifty books in less than twenty years. [two independent clauses joined by a semicolon]

(3) A *complex sentence* has one independent clause and at least one subordinate clause.

Before we read the novel [subordinate clause], let's discuss the author [independent clause].

(4) A *compound-complex sentence* contains two or more independent clauses and at least one subordinate clause.

The two eyewitnesses described [independent clause] what they saw [subordinate clause], but their reports differed [independent clause].

SENTENCES CLASSIFIED ACCORDING TO PURPOSE

8j. Sentences may be classified according to purpose.

(1) A *declarative sentence* makes a statement. It is followed by a period.

Kirsten asked what the problem was**.**

(2) An *interrogative sentence* asks a question. It is followed by a question mark.

Have you ever read *Blue Highways***?**

(3) An *imperative sentence* makes a request or gives a command. It usually is followed by a period.

Please give me the dates for the class meetings**.**

(4) An *exclamatory sentence* expresses strong feeling. It is followed by an exclamation point.

What a noble leader he was**!**

Your Turn Combining Sentences

You can combine sentences by using compound subjects or compound verbs. For the following sentence pairs, decide if you need a compound subject or a compound verb. Then, combine the sentences.

1. The people stared with disbelief. They wondered about their minister's sanity.
2. Loud whispers disturbed the worshipful calmness within the meeting-house. The shuffling of feet disturbed the calmness, as well.
3. Mr. Hooper entered his pulpit. He preached a sermon about secret, unconfessed sin.
4. Afterward, Mr. Hooper's greetings were met by stares and an awkward silence. His blessings were met by stares and silence, too.

9. Sentence Style

WAYS TO ACHIEVE CLARITY

Coordinating Ideas

9a. To *coordinate* two or more ideas, or to give them equal emphasis, link them with a connecting word, an appropriate mark of punctuation, or both.

> Edgar Allan Poe wrote "The Raven"**;** Edgar Lee Masters wrote *Spoon River Anthology.*

Subordinating Ideas

9b. To *subordinate* an idea, or to show that one idea is related to but less important than another, use an adverb clause or an adjective clause.

An *adverb clause* begins with a subordinating conjunction, which shows how the adverb clause relates to the main clause. Usually, the relationship is *time, cause or reason, purpose or result,* or *condition.*

> **Whenever I think of Boston,** I think of Glen. [time]
>
> Janet got a major role in *Our Town* **because she is one of the best actors in our school.** [cause]
>
> Let's finish now **so that we won't have to come back tomorrow.** [purpose or result]

An *adjective clause* usually begins with *who, whom, whose, which, that,* or *where.*

> Tamisha is the one **whose essay won first prize.**

Using Parallel Structure

9c. Use the same grammatical form (*parallel structure*) to express ideas of equal weight.

(1) Use parallel structure when you link coordinate ideas.

> The company guaranteed **that salaries would be increased** and **that working days would be shortened.** [noun clause linked to noun clause]

(2) Use parallel structure when you compare or contrast ideas.

> **Thinking** logically is as important as **calculating** accurately. [gerund compared with gerund]

(3) Use parallel structure when you link ideas with correlative conjunctions (such as *both . . . and, either . . . or, neither . . . nor,* and *not only . . . but also*).

> With *Ship of Fools,* Katherine Anne Porter proved her talents not only **as a short-story writer** but also **as a novelist.** [The correlative conjunctions come directly before the parallel terms.]

OBSTACLES TO CLARITY

Sentence Fragments

9d. Avoid using a *sentence fragment*—a word or word group that either does not contain a subject and a verb or does not express a complete thought.

Attach the fragment to the sentence that comes before or after it, or add words to or delete words from the fragment to make it a complete sentence.

FRAGMENT	Nina Otero was one of the first Mexican American women. To hold a major public post in New Mexico.
SENTENCE	Nina Otero was one of the first Mexican American women **to hold a major public post in New Mexico.**

Run-on Sentences

9e. Avoid using a *run-on sentence*—two or more complete thoughts that run together as if they were one complete thought.

There are two kinds of run-on sentences.

- A *fused sentence* has no punctuation at all between the complete thoughts.
- A *comma splice* has just a comma between the complete thoughts.

FUSED SENTENCE	Emerson praised Whitman's poetry most other poets sharply criticized its break with tradition.
COMMA SPLICE	Emerson praised Whitman's poetry, most other poets sharply criticized its break with tradition.

You may correct a run-on sentence in one of the following ways. Depending on the relationship you want to show, one method will often prove to be more effective than another.

Method of Correction	Example
Make two sentences.	Emerson praised Whitman's poetry. **M**ost other poets sharply criticized its break with tradition.
Use a comma and a coordinating conjunction.	Emerson praised Whitman's poetry, **but** most other poets sharply criticized its break with tradition.
Change one of the independent clauses to a subordinate clause.	Emerson praised Whitman's poetry, **although most other poets sharply criticized its break with tradition.**
Use a semicolon.	Emerson praised Whitman's poetry; most other poets sharply criticized its break with tradition.
Use a semicolon and a conjunctive adverb followed by a comma.	Emerson praised Whitman's poetry; **however,** most other poets sharply criticized its break with tradition.

Unnecessary Shifts in Sentences

9f. *Avoid making unnecessary shifts in subject, in verb tense, and in voice.*

AWKWARD	Athletes should be at the parking lot by 7:00 so that you can leave by 7:15. [shift in subject]
BETTER	**Athletes** should be at the parking lot by 7:00 so that **they** can leave by 7:15.
AWKWARD	She walked into the room and says, "The lights of the car outside are on." [shift in verb tense]
BETTER	She **walked** into the room and **said,** "The lights of the car outside are on."
AWKWARD	Russell Means portrayed Chingachgook in *The Last of the Mohicans,* and an outstanding performance was delivered. [shift in voice]
BETTER	Russell Means **portrayed** Chingachgook in *The Last of the Mohicans,* and he **delivered** an outstanding performance.

REVISING FOR VARIETY

9g. **Use a variety of sentence beginnings.**

The following examples show how a writer can revise sentences to avoid beginning with the subject every time.

Method of Revision	Example
Begin with the subject (basic structure).	*Billy Budd* was published in 1924 and helped revive an interest in Melville's other works.
Begin with a participial phrase.	**Published in 1924,** *Billy Budd* helped revive an interest in Melville's other works.
Begin with a prepositional phrase.	**In 1924,** *Billy Budd* was published and helped revive interest in Melville's other works.
Begin with an adverb clause.	**When** *Billy Budd* **was published in 1924,** it helped revive interest in Melville's other works.

Varying Sentence Structure

9h. **Use a mix of simple, compound, complex, and compound-complex sentences in your writing.**

San Francisco is famous for its scenic views. [simple] Because the city sprawls over forty-two hills, driving through San Francisco is like riding a roller coaster. [complex] Atop one of San Francisco's hills is Chinatown; atop another is Coit Tower. [compound] The most popular place to visit is the San Francisco Bay area, where the Golden Gate Bridge and Fisherman's Wharf attract a steady stream of tourists. [complex]

Revising to Reduce Wordiness

9i. **Avoid using unnecessary words in your writing.**

The following guidelines suggest some ways to revise wordy sentences.

(1) Take out a whole group of unnecessary words.

WORDY	After climbing down to the edge of the river, we boarded a small houseboat that was floating on the surface of the water.
BETTER	After climbing down to the edge of the river, we boarded a small houseboat.

(2) Replace pretentious words and expressions with straightforward ones.

WORDY The young woman, who was at some indeterminate point in her teenage years, sported through her hair a streak of pink dye that could be considered extremely garish.

BETTER The **teenager** sported a streak of **shocking**-pink dye in her hair.

(3) Reduce a clause to a phrase.

WORDY Emily Dickinson fell in love with Charles Wadsworth, who was a Presbyterian minister.

BETTER Emily Dickinson fell in love with Charles Wadsworth, **a Presbyterian minister.**

(4) Reduce a phrase or a clause to one word.

WORDY One of the writers from the South was William Faulkner.

BETTER One of the **Southern** writers was William Faulkner.

Your Turn Revising Sentences

Revise the following sentences so that ideas of the same weight have the same grammatical form. (Note: Some sentences require more than one revision.)

1. Henry presented this choice to the assembled legislators: They could be either free people or slavery would be their lot.
2. Listening to painful truths is hard, he said, but to sacrifice freedom for a less-troubled life is neither wise nor does it seem right.
3. He urged his listeners to understand all of the truth, to understand the worst of it, and they should prepare a response.
4. Pointing to the increase in Britain's military presence, and after a note about Britain's failure to respond to colonial petitions, Henry called for patriots to act now rather than waiting any longer.
5. Henry asked, "Why stand we here idle?" and his conclusion was the challenge to "give me liberty, or I would rather die!"

10. Sentence Combining

COMBINING SENTENCES FOR VARIETY

Combining by Inserting Words and Phrases

10a. Combine related sentences by taking a key word (or using another form of the word) from one sentence and inserting it into another.

ORIGINAL Jack London describes the man's attempt to build a fire. The description is vivid.

COMBINED Jack London **vividly** describes the man's attempt to build a fire. [The adjective *vivid* becomes the adverb *vividly*.]

10b. Combine related sentences by taking (or creating) a phrase from one sentence and inserting it into another.

ORIGINAL Our class is reading "Everyday Use." **Alice Walker wrote the story.**

COMBINED Our class is reading "Everyday Use" **by Alice Walker.** [prepositional phrase]

Combining by Coordinating Ideas

10c. Combine related sentences whose ideas are equally important by using an appropriate coordinating conjunction (*and, but, or, nor, for, yet*) or correlative conjunction (*both . . . and, either . . . or, neither . . . nor, not only . . . but also*).

ORIGINAL **Robert Frost** did not receive the Nobel Prize. **Carl Sandburg** never received it, either.

COMBINED **Neither Robert Frost nor Carl Sandburg** received the Nobel Prize.

You also can form a compound sentence by linking independent clauses with a semicolon and a conjunctive adverb or with just a semicolon.

We planned a picnic; **however,** the weather did not cooperate.

Southwestern cities are among the fastest-growing in the nation; water supply is therefore a crucial issue for these desert boom towns.

Combining by Subordinating Ideas

10d. Combine related sentences whose ideas are not equally important by placing the less important idea in a subordinate clause.

ORIGINAL   The National Air and Space Museum is in Washington, D.C. It contains exhibits on the history of aeronautics.

COMBINED   The National Air and Space Museum, **which contains exhibits on the history of aeronautics,** is in Washington, D.C. [adjective clause]

ORIGINAL   Shiftlet married Lucynell. He wanted her mother's car.

COMBINED   Shiftlet married Lucynell **because he wanted her mother's car.** [adverb clause]

ORIGINAL   Judy Jones was married. Devlin told Dexter this.

COMBINED   Devlin told Dexter **that Judy Jones was married.** [noun clause]

Your Turn Combining Sentences

Choose a sentence-combining technique to connect each of the following pairs of related sentences in a logical way.

1. Emily Dickinson's father was a well-known lawyer. Emily Dickinson's father frequently had prominent visitors.
2. Dickinson's childhood seemed active and normal in every way. There was little sign of the recluse poet to come.
3. As a young adult, she felt drained by public activities. She began to keep to herself, at home, more and more.
4. Emily Dickinson wrote hundreds of poems. Only seven of them were published during her lifetime.
5. After Emily's death, Lavinia Dickinson found Emily's collection of poems and helped prepare them for publication. Emily Dickinson's genius might have remained a secret forever.

11. CAPITALIZATION

11a. Capitalize the first word in every sentence.

The author Leslie Marmon Silko was born in Albuquerque, New Mexico.

Stop!

(1) Capitalize the first word of a sentence following a colon.

The police commissioner issued a surprising statement: In light of new evidence, the Brooks burglary case will be reopened.

(2) Capitalize the first word of a direct quotation that is a complete sentence.

Chief Joseph declared, "From where the sun now stands I will fight no more forever."

(3) Traditionally, the first word of a line of poetry is capitalized.

I placed a jar in Tennessee,
And round it was, upon a hill.
            —Wallace Stevens, from "Anecdote of the Jar"

11b. Capitalize the first word in the salutation and the closing of a letter.

Dear Maria,   Dear Sir or Madam: Sincerely,

11c. Capitalize proper nouns and proper adjectives.

A *common noun* is a general name for a person, place, thing, or idea. A *proper noun* is the specific name of a particular person, place, thing, or idea. A *proper adjective* is formed from a proper noun. Common nouns are capitalized only if they begin a sentence (or, in most cases, a line of poetry) or a direct quotation or if they are part of a title.

Common Nouns	Proper Nouns	Proper Adjectives
poet	Homer	Homeric epithet
country	Japan	Japanese diplomat

In most proper nouns made up of two or more words, do *not* capitalize articles (*a, an, the*), short prepositions (those with fewer than five letters, such as *at, of, for, to, with*), the mark of the infinitive (*to*), and coordinating conjunctions (*and, but, for, nor, or, so, yet*).

Army of the Potomac   "Writing to Persuade"

(1) Capitalize the names of most persons and animals.

GIVEN NAMES	Julia	Richard
SURNAMES	Alvarez	Wright
ANIMALS	Moby-Dick	White Fang

(2) Capitalize geographical names.

Type of Name	Examples
Countries	Mozambique, Costa Rica
Continents	North America, Asia
Islands	Catalina Island, Isle of Pines
Mountains	Blue Ridge Mountains, Dinali
Other Land Forms	Cape Cod, Isthmus of Panama, Mojave Desert, Horse Cave
Bodies of Water	Great Lakes, Strait of Hormuz, Amazon River, Lake Huron
Parks	Mississippi Headwaters State Forest, Gates of the Arctic National Park
Roads, Streets, and Highways	Morningside Drive, Thirty-first Street, Michigan Avenue, Interstate 55, Route 30, Pennsylvania Turnpike
Towns, Cities	Boston, Rio de Janeiro, South Bend, St. Petersburg
Counties, Townships, Provinces	Mercer County, Lawrence Township Manitoba, Shanghai
States and Territories	Wisconsin, Nuevo León, Yukon Territory, The Virgin Islands
Regions	New England, the West Coast the Sunbelt, the Southwest

(3) Capitalize the names of organizations, teams, business firms, institutions, buildings and other structures, and government bodies.

Type of Name	Examples
Organizations	National Science Foundation, Future Farmers of America
Teams	Detroit Pistons, Texas Rangers
Business Firms	General Electric, Marvel Entertainment, Inc.
Institutions	Mayo Clinic, Library of Congress
Buildings and Other Structures	Meadowlawn Junior High School the Golden Gate Bridge, the Pyramid of Khufu
Government Bodies	Atomic Energy Commission, United States Marine Corps

(4) Capitalize the names of historical events and periods, special events, holidays and other calendar items, and time zones.

Type of Name	Examples
Historical Events and Periods	Boston Tea Party, Roaring Twenties, Battle of Saratoga, French Revolution, Middle Ages
Special Events	Olympics, Ohio State Fair, Sunshine Festival, U.S.-Africa Business Summit
Holidays and Calendar Items	Wednesday, September, Fourth of July, Hispanic Heritage Month
Time Zones	Mountain Standard Time (MST), Eastern Daylight Time (EDT)

(5) Capitalize the brand names of business products.

Borden milk   Colonial bread   Zenith television

Notice in the examples that the noun that follows a brand name is not capitalized.

(6) Capitalize the names of nationalities, races, and peoples.

Chinese   Jewish   Hopi   Caucasian

(7) Capitalize the names of ships, trains, aircraft, spacecraft, monuments, awards, and planets, and any other particular places, things, or events.

Type of Name	Examples
Ships	*Cunard Princess*, **U.S.S.** *Forrestal*
Trains	*Orient Express, North Coast Limited*
Aircraft	*Spirit of St. Louis, Air Force One*
Spacecraft	*Atlantis, Apollo 11*
Monuments	Lincoln Memorial, Statue of Liberty, Arc de Triomphe
Awards	Academy Award, Pulitzer Prize
Planets, Stars, Heavenly Bodies	Jupiter, Orion, Ursa Minor, the Milky Way
Other Particular Things, Places, and Events	Silk Route, Treaty Oak, Underground Railroad, the Muses, Hurricane Andrew, Marshall Plan

11d. Do not capitalize the names of school subjects, except for names of languages and course names followed by a number.

Spanish   chemistry   Chemistry II

11e. Capitalize titles.

(1) Capitalize a title belonging to a particular person when it comes before the person's name. Also capitalize initials and abbreviations such as *Jr., M.D.,* and *Ph.D.* after a name.

General Davis   Ms. Diaz   President Kennedy

Kelly **T.** Jones, **M.D.**   Enrique Sánchez, **Ph.D.**

In general, do not capitalize a title used alone or following a name. Some titles, however, are by tradition capitalized. If you are unsure of whether or not to capitalize a title, check in a dictionary.

Who is the governor of Kansas?

A title is usually capitalized when it is used alone in direct address.

Have you reached your decision, **Governor**?

(2) Capitalize words showing family relationships except when preceded by a possessive.

Aunt Amy   my aunt   Mother   Bill's mother

(3) Capitalize the names of religions and their followers, holy days and celebrations, holy writings, and specific deities and venerated beings.

Type of Name	Examples
Religions and Followers	Islam, Baha'i, Judaism, Muslim, Christian, Hindu
Holy Days and Celebrations	Epiphany, Rosh Hashanah, Ramadan
Holy Writings	Bible, Upanishads
Specific Deities	God, Thor, Vishnu

(4) Capitalize the first and last words and all important words in titles of books, periodicals, poems, stories, essays, speeches, plays, historical documents, movies, radio and television programs, works of art, musical compositions, and cartoons.

Unimportant words in a title include articles (*a, an, the*), short prepositions (those with fewer than five letters, such as *of, to, in, for, from, with*), and coordinating conjunctions (*and, but, for, nor, or, so, yet*)—unless they are the first word in the official title.

Type of Name	Examples
Books	*The Call of the Wild* / *Into Thin Air*
Periodicals	*Car and Driver* / *Atlantic Monthly*
Poems	"Once by the Pacific"
Stories	"The Fall of the House of Usher"
Essays and Speeches	"The Lost Worlds of Ancient America," / "I Have a Dream"
Plays	*A Raisin in the Sun*
Historical Documents	Declaration of Independence, Ninety-Five Theses
Movies	*Raiders of the Lost Ark*
Radio and TV Programs	*Car Talk, CSI: Crime Scene Investigation*
Works of Art	*Double Dutch on the Golden Gate Bridge*
Musical Compositions	"Lift Every Voice and Sing" / *Nixon in China*
Cartoons	*Where I'm Coming From*

Your Turn Using Correct Capitalization

Correct the errors in capitalization in the following paragraph.

[1] Following his Father's death in 1847, Samuel Clemens became an Apprentice Printer in the Town of Hannibal. [2] Within a few Years, He was writing for the Newspaper that his Brother, Orion, owned. [3] At the age of Eighteen, Clemens moved on to Printing work in several Eastern Cities, but he came Home a few Years later. [4] Then, in 1857, while taking a Trip down the Mississippi River to New Orleans, Clemens got to know Bixby, a Steamboat Pilot. [5] Clemens decided that He, too, would become a Pilot—a Decision that eventually gave him the Pseudonym "Mark Twain."

12. PUNCTUATION

END MARKS

12a. A statement (declarative sentence) is followed by a period.

> Felipe asked whether Edgar Allan Poe was primarily a poet, an essayist, or a short-story writer.

12b. A question (interrogative sentence) is followed by a question mark.

> Have you read any of Edgar Allan Poe's poetry?

12c. A request or command (imperative sentence) is followed by either a period or an exclamation point.

> Answer the phone, please.
>
> Turn that music down now!

12d. An exclamation (exclamatory sentence) is followed by an exclamation point.

> What an imagination Edgar Allan Poe had!

An exclamation point also may be used after an interjection that precedes a sentence that ends in an exclamation point.

> Hey! Wait for me!

12e. An abbreviation usually is followed by a period.

Some common abbreviations, including many for units of measurement, are written without periods.

AM/FM, FBI, IOU, PBS, PC, ROTC, SOS, cc, db, ft, lb, kw, ml, psi, rpm [Use a period with the abbreviation *in.* (*inch*) to avoid confusion with the word *in.*]

Type of Abbreviation	Examples
Personal Names	N. Scott Momaday E. A. Robinson
Organizations and Companies	Assn. Ltd. Co. Corp. Inc. Org.
Titles Used with Names	Dr. Jr. Mrs. Ph.D.
Times of Day	A.M. (*or* a.m.) P.M. (*or* p.m.)
Years	B.C. [written after the date] A.D. [written before the date]
Addresses	Ave. Blvd. St. P.O. Box
States	Ark. Fla. R.I. N. Mex.

COMMAS

12f. Use commas to separate items in a series.

> The main characters are Huck, Tom, and Jim.

If all the items in a series are linked by *and, or,* or *nor,* do not use commas to separate them.

> Saul Bellow **and** Isaac Bashevis Singer **and** Toni Morrison won Nobel Prizes.

12g. Use a comma to separate two or more adjectives preceding a noun.

> Lincoln was a noble, compassionate, wise leader.

12h. Use a comma before *and, but, or, nor, for, so,* and *yet* when they join independent clauses.

> I read an excerpt from Amy Tan's *The Joy Luck Club,* and now I want to read the entire book.

You may omit the comma before *and, but, or,* or *nor* if the clauses are very short and there is no chance of misunderstanding.

12i. Use commas to set off nonessential clauses and nonessential participial phrases.

A *nonessential* clause or phrase is one that can be left out without changing the meaning of the sentence.

NONESSENTIAL CLAUSE	Eudora Welty, **who was born in Mississippi,** uses her home state in many of her stories.
NONESSENTIAL PHRASE	Lee, **noticing my confusion,** rephrased her question.

An *essential* clause or phrase is one that can't be left out without changing the meaning of the sentence. Essential clauses and phrases are *not* set off by commas.

ESSENTIAL CLAUSE	Material **that is quoted verbatim** should be placed in quotation marks.
ESSENTIAL PHRASE	The only word **spoken by the raven** is *nevermore.*

12j. Use a comma after certain introductory elements.

(1) Use a comma after a one-word adverb such as *first, next, yes,* or *no* and after any mild exclamation such as *well* or *why* at the beginning of a sentence.

> **Yes,** Hemingway is my favorite author.

(2) Use a comma after an introductory participial phrase or introductory adverb clause.

Standing on the quarter-deck, Captain Ahab spoke to his crew. [participial phrase]

After he had driven around the lake, he decided to go to the restaurant. [adverb clause]

(3) Use a comma after two or more introductory prepositional phrases.

At the end of the story, Walter Mitty imagines that he is facing a firing squad.

12k. Use commas to set off elements that interrupt a sentence.

(1) Appositives and appositive phrases usually are set off by commas.

My favorite book by Claude McKay, *Banjo,* was first published in 1929.

Sometimes an appositive is so closely related to the word or words it refers to that it should not be set off by commas.

The poet **Maya Angelou** read one of her poems on Inauguration Day.

(2) Terms of direct address are set off by commas.

Your essay, **Theo,** was well organized.

(3) Parenthetical expressions are set off by commas.

Parenthetical expressions are remarks that add incidental information or that relate ideas to each other.

Simón Bolívar liberated much of South America from Spanish rule; he went on, **moreover,** to become the most powerful person on the continent.

12l. Use a comma in certain conventional situations.

(1) Use a comma to separate items in dates and addresses.

On Tuesday, October 23, 2007, my niece Leslie Ann was born.

Please address all further inquiries to 92 Keystone Crossings, Indianapolis, IN 46240. [Notice that a comma is not used between a state abbreviation and a ZIP Code.]

(2) Use a comma after the salutation of a friendly letter and after the closing of any letter.

Dear Rosa,　　Sincerely yours,

(3) Use a comma to set off an abbreviation such as *Jr., Sr., RN, M.D., Ltd.,* or *Inc.*

Is Juan Fuentes, Jr., your cousin?

My father has worked for Global Networks, Inc., for five years, now.

SEMICOLONS

12m. Use a semicolon between independent clauses that are closely related in thought and are not joined by *and, but, for, nor, or, so,* or *yet.*

"Tart words make no friends; a spoonful of honey will catch more flies than a gallon of vinegar."
　—Benjamin Franklin, *Poor Richard's Almanack*

12n. Use a semicolon between independent clauses joined by a conjunctive adverb or a transitional expression.

A *conjunctive adverb* (such as *consequently, however,* or *therefore*) or a *transitional expression* (such as *for example, as a result,* or *in other words*) indicates the relationship of the independent clauses that it joins.

Dexter knew that Judy was selfish and insensitive; **however**, he continued to adore her. [Notice that a comma is placed after the conjunctive adverb.]

12o. Use a semicolon before a coordinating conjunction to join independent clauses that contain commas.

During the nineteenth century—the era of such distinguished poets as Longfellow, Whittier, and Holmes—most poetry was written in traditional metrical patterns; but one poet, Walt Whitman, rejected the conventional verse forms.

12p. Use a semicolon between items in a series if the items themselves contain commas.

The summer reading list includes *Behind the Trail of Broken Treaties,* by Vine Deloria, Jr.; *House Made of Dawn,* by N. Scott Momaday; and *Blue Highways: A Journey into America,* by William Least Heat-Moon.

COLONS

12q. Use a colon to mean "note what follows."

(1) Use a colon before a list of items, especially after expressions such as *follows* and *the following*.

The magazine article profiles the following famous American authors of the nineteenth century: Edgar Allan Poe, Nathaniel Hawthorne, and Herman Melville.

(2) Use a colon before a quotation that lacks a speaker tag such as *he said* or *she remarked*.

Dad's orders were clear: "Everybody up and at 'em."

(3) Use a colon before a long, formal statement or quotation.

Patrick Henry concluded his fiery speech with these words: "I know not what course others may take; but as for me, give me liberty, or give me death!"

12r. Use a colon in certain conventional situations.

5:20 P.M. [between the hour and the minute]

Deuteronomy 5:6–21 [between chapter and verse in references to passages from the Bible]

Dear Sir: [after the salutation of a business letter]

"Cold Kills: Hypothermia" [between a title and a subtitle]

Your Turn Using Semicolons Correctly

The following sentences use semicolons to connect shorter sentences. Decide whether each sentence is better expressed as a single sentence or as two or more sentences. Rewrite the sentences that you think would be clearer if separated.

1. The Reverend Parris, a self-righteous man, prayed by the bedside of his daughter Betty, a possible victim of witchcraft; he also had sent word to the Reverend Hale, known for his understanding of witchcraft, asking for his help.
2. Earlier, Parris had discovered Betty and some of her friends dancing in the forest; his slave, Tituba, had been with them.
3. He questioned Abigail Williams, his niece, about the dancing, the cause of Betty's condition, and the girls' interest in the occult; Abigail denied the charge of witchcraft; furthermore, she said that Parris was only worried about losing his job.
4. Thomas and Ann Putnam arrived with news about Ruth, their daughter; they reported Ruth's claim that she saw Betty flying over a barn.
5. It was the first charge of witchcraft; unfortunately, it would not be the last; and by the end of the story, innocent people would be executed as witches.

---

13. Punctuation

ITALICS

Italics are printed characters that slant to the right, *like this.* To indicate italics in handwritten or typewritten work, use underlining.

| PRINTED | Who wrote *Black Boy*? |
| HANDWRITTEN | Who wrote <u>Black Boy</u>? |

13a. Use italics (underlining) for titles of books, plays, long poems, periodicals, newspapers, works of art, films, television series, long musical compositions, recordings, comic strips, court cases, trains, ships, aircraft, and spacecraft.

Type of Title	Examples
Books	*The Scarlet Letter, Fifth Chinese Daughter*
Plays	*The Crucible, West Side Story*
Long Poems	*I Am Joaquin,* the *Epic of Gilgamesh*
Periodicals	*Reader's Digest, Newsweek*
Newspapers	*The Wall Street Journal,* the *Austin American-Statesman*
Works of Art	*The Kiss, The Starry Night*
Films	*Forrest Gump, The Bridge on the River Kwai*
TV Series	*Heroes, Wheel of Fortune*

Type of Title	Examples
Long Musical Compositions	*Liverpool Oratorio, Hiawatha's Wedding Feast*
Recordings	*Achtung Baby, Sketches of Spain*
Comic Strips	*Garfield, Over the Hedge*
Court Cases	*Plessy v. Ferguson, Bailey v. Alabama*
Trains, Ships	*Empire Builder, Queen Mary*
Aircraft, Spacecraft	*Solar Challenger, Apollo 11*

13b. Use italics (underlining) for words, letters, numerals, and symbols referred to as such and for foreign words that have not been adopted into English.

> Should the use of *their* for *there* be considered a spelling error or a usage error?

> The teacher couldn't tell whether I had written a script *S*, the number *5*, or an *&*.

> All U.S. coins are now stamped with the inscription *e pluribus unum*.

QUOTATION MARKS

13c. Use quotation marks to enclose a *direct quotation*—a person's exact words.

> Chief Joseph said, "The earth is the mother of all people, and all people should have equal rights upon it."

Notice that a direct quotation begins with a capital letter. However, if the quotation is only part of a sentence, it does not begin with a capital letter.

> "I'm leaving now," said Gwen, "**B**ecause I must be home by 10:00." [Each part of the divided quotation is enclosed in quotation marks.]

(1) When the second part of a divided quotation is a new sentence, it begins with a capital letter.

> "Teddy Roosevelt was the first U.S. President to express concern about the depletion of the nation's natural resources," explained Mr. Fuentes. "**H**e established a conservation program that expanded the national park system."

(2) When used with quotation marks, other marks of punctuation are placed according to the following rules.

Rule	Examples
Commas and **periods** always are placed inside the closing quotation marks.	"On the other hand," he said, "your decision may be correct."
Semicolons and **colons** always are placed outside the closing quotation marks.	My neighbor said, "Sure, I'll buy a subscription"; it was lucky that I asked her on payday. Edna St. Vincent Millay uses the following devices "Spring": alliteration, slant rhyme, and personification.
Quotation marks and **exclamation points** are placed inside the closing quotation marks if the quotation itself is a question or an exclamation. Otherwise, they are placed outside.	"What a tortured soul the Reverend Dimmesdale is!" said Mr. Klein. Was it you who wrote the poem "Upon Turning Seventeen"?

(3) When quoting a passage that consists of more than one paragraph, put quotation marks at the beginning of each paragraph but at the end of only the last paragraph.

> "As he neared the house, each detail of the scene became vivid to him. He was aware of some bricks of the vanished chimney lying on the sod. There was a door which hung by one hinge.

> "Rifle bullets called forth by the insistent skirmishers came from the far-off bank of foliage. They mingled with the shells and the pieces of shells until the air was torn in all directions by hootings, yells, howls. The sky was full of fiends who directed all their wild rage at his head."

> —Stephen Crane, "A Mystery of Heroism"

(4) Use single quotation marks to enclose a quotation within a quotation.

> The teacher said, "Jorge, please explain what Emerson meant when he said, 'To be great is to be misunderstood.'"

(5) When writing *dialogue* (conversation), begin a new paragraph every time the speaker changes, and enclose the speaker's words in quotation marks.

"How far is it to the Owl Creek bridge?" Farquhar asked.

"About thirty miles."

"Is there no force on this side the creek?"

"Only a picket post half a mile out, on the railroad, and a single sentinel at this end of the bridge."

—Ambrose Bierce, "An Occurrence at Owl Creek Bridge"

13d. Use quotation marks to enclose titles of short works, such as short stories, poems, essays, articles, songs, episodes of television series, and chapters and other parts of books.

Type of Title	Examples
Short Stories	"The Magic Barrel" "The Tell-Tale Heart"
Poems	"The Latin Deli" "Thanatopsis"
Essays	"On the Mall" "The Creative Process"
Articles	"Old Poetry and Modern Music"
Songs	"On Top of Old Smoky"
TV Episodes	"The Flight of the Condor"
Chapters and Parts of Books	"The World Was New" "The Colonies' Struggle for Freedom"

ELLIPSIS POINTS

13e. Use three spaced periods called *ellipsis points* (. . .) to mark omissions from quoted material and pauses in a written passage.

ORIGINAL   The second half of the program consisted of four numbers from the *Ring* and closed with Siegfried's funeral march. My aunt wept quietly, but almost continuously, as a shallow vessel overflows in a rainstorm. From time to time her dim eyes looked up at the lights which studded the ceiling, burning softly under their dull glass globes; doubtless they were stars in truth to her. I was still perplexed as to what measure of musical comprehension was left to her, she who had heard nothing but the singing of gospel hymns at Methodist services in the square frame schoolhouse on Section Thirteen for so many years.
—Willa Cather, "A Wagner Matinée"

(1) If the quoted material that comes before the ellipsis points is not a complete sentence, use three ellipsis points with a space before the first point.

The narrator notes, "The second half of the program . . . closed with Siegfried's funeral march."

(2) If the quoted material that comes before or after the ellipsis points is a complete sentence, use an end mark before the ellipsis points.

The narrator observes, "My aunt wept quietly. . . ."

(3) If one or more sentences are omitted, place ellipsis points after the end mark that precedes the omitted material.

Recalling the experience, the narrator says, "My aunt wept quietly, but almost continuously, as a shallow vessel overflows in a rainstorm. . . . I was still perplexed as to what measure of musical comprehension was left to her, she who had heard nothing but the singing of gospel hymns at Methodist services in the square frame schoolhouse on Section Thirteen for so many years."

APOSTROPHES

13f. Use an apostrophe in forming the possessive of nouns and indefinite pronouns.

Rule	Examples
To form the possessive of a **singular noun,** add an apostrophe and an *s*.	the minister's veil Ross's opinion
To form the possessive of a **plural noun ending in *s*,** add only the apostrophe. If the **plural noun does not end in *s*,** add an apostrophe and an *s*.	the authors' styles the Ushers' house men's fashions children's toys
To form the possessive of an **indefinite pronoun,** add an apostrophe and an *s*.	each one's time everybody's opinion

Rule	Examples
Form the possessive of only the last word in a compound word, in the name of an organization or business firm, or in a word group showing joint possession.	father-in-law's gloves Roz and Denise's idea Taylor, Sanders, and Weissman's law office
Form the possessive of each noun in a word group showing individual possession of similar items. When a possessive pronoun is part of a word group showing joint possession, each noun in the word group is also possessive.	Baldwin's and Ellison's writings Jane's and Kathryn's coats Walter Mitty's and **her** relationship
When used as possessives, words that indicate time or amounts of money require apostrophes.	a week's vacation five dollars' worth

13g. Use an apostrophe to show where letters, words, or numbers have been omitted in a contraction.

they had . . . **they'd**   Kerry is . . . **Kerry's**
let us . . . **let's**   of the clock . . . **o'clock**
where is . . . **where's**   1997 . . . **'97**

The word *not* can be shortened to *–n't* and added to a verb, usually without changing the spelling of the verb.

is not—**isn't**   has not—**hasn't**   will not—**won't**

13h. Use an apostrophe and an *s* to form the plurals of all lowercase letters, some uppercase letters, numerals, and some words referred to as words.

There are two *r's* and two *s's* in *embarrassed*.

Tom abandoned Lucynell soon after their *I do's*.

You may add only an *s* to form the plurals of such items—except lowercase letters—if the plural forms will not cause misreading.

Compact discs (**CDs**) were introduced in the **1980s**.

HYPHENS

13i. Use a hyphen to divide a word at the end of a line.

When dividing a word at the end of a line, remember the following rules:

(1) Do not divide a one-syllable word.

Peyton Farquhar was captured, and he was finally **hanged** [*not* hang-ed] from the bridge.

(2) Divide a word only between syllables.

Ernest Hemingway's *A Farewell to Arms* was **pub-lished** [*not* publ-ished] in 1929.

(3) Divide an already hyphenated word at the hyphen.

Stephen Crane died at the age of **twenty-eight**. [*not* twen-ty-eight]

(4) Do not divide a word so that one letter stands alone.

One fine autumn day, Rip Van Winkle fell fast **asleep** [*not* a-sleep] in the mountains.

13j. Use a hyphen with compound numbers from twenty-one to ninety-nine and with fractions used as modifiers.

six hundred **twenty-five**
a **two-thirds** majority [*but* **two thirds** of the class]

DASHES

13k. Use dashes to set off abrupt breaks in thoughts.

The poor condition of this road—it really needs to be paved—makes this route unpopular.

13l. Use dashes to set off an appositive or a parenthetical expression that contains commas.

Many nineteenth-century poets—Whitman and Dickinson, for example—led remarkable lives.

PARENTHESES

13m. Use parentheses to enclose informative or explanatory material of minor importance.

Harriet Tubman (c. 1820–1913) is remembered for her work in the Underground Railroad.

Thoreau lived at Walden Pond for two years. (See the map on page 350.)

BRACKETS

13n. Use brackets to enclose an explanation within quoted or parenthetical material.

Hilda Doolittle (commonly known as H. D. [1886-1961]) is remembered for her Imagist poetry.

Your Turn   Eliminating Parentheses

Sometimes parentheses distract rather than help, especially in formal writing. In each of the following sentences, decide whether the parentheses are distracting. If they are, rewrite the sentence, eliminating the parenthetical comment.

1. The letter from Major Sullivan Ballou (written in 1861), with its passionate last words to his wife (whom he loved dearly), never fails to move me.
2. "The Fall of the House of Usher" (and how I love Poe's stories!) is a dark but fascinating tale about the connection between twins.
3. I like the poems of Walt Whitman (1819–1892) because he treats all of humanity as his family.
4. "Daughter of Invention," by Julia Alvarez (a more modern work), shows that parents (even when they differ in their opinions) can work together for the good of their child.
5. Amy Tan's "Rules of the Game" (which relates a mother and daughter's interaction to games of chess) reminds us that some family relationships are difficult.

14. SPELLING

UNDERSTANDING WORD STRUCTURE

Many English words are made up of roots and affixes (prefixes and suffixes).

Roots

14a. The *root* of a word is the part that carries the word's core meaning.

Roots	Meanings	Examples
–bio–	life	biology, symbiotic
–duc–, –duct–	lead	educate, conductor
–mit–, –miss–	send	remit, emissary
–port–	carry, bear	transport, portable, airport
–spec–	watch, look	spectator, spectacle, speculate

Prefixes

14b. A *prefix* is one or more letters or syllables added to the beginning of a word or word part to create a new word.

Prefixes	Meanings	Examples
a–	lacking, without	amorphous, apolitical
dia–	through, across, apart	diagonal, diameter, diagnose, dialogue
inter–	between, among	international, intercede, interface, interfere
mis–	badly, wrongly	mistake, misfire, misspell, misdeed

Suffixes

14c. A *suffix* is one or more letters or syllables added to the end of a word or word part to create a new word.

Suffixes	Meanings	Examples
–ation, –ition	action, result	repetition, starvation
–er	doer, native of	baker, westerner
–ible	able, likely, fit	edible, possible, divisible
–or	doer, office, action	director, juror, error

SPELLING RULES
ie and *ei*

14d. Write *ie* when the sound is long e, except after *c*.

believe   field   ceiling   receive

EXCEPTIONS

either   leisure   seize   protein

14e. Write *ei* when the sound is not long e.

eight   neighbor   weigh   foreign

EXCEPTIONS

ancient   view   friend   efficient

–cede, *–ceed*, and *–sede*

14f. The only English word ending in *–sede* is *supersede*. The only words ending in *–ceed* are *exceed*, *proceed*, and *succeed*. Most other words with this sound end in *–cede*.

concede   intercede   precede   precede   secede

Adding Prefixes

14g. When adding a prefix, do not change the spelling of the root.

mis + spell = **mis**spell

inter + national = **inter**national

Adding Suffixes

14h. When adding the suffix *–ness* or *–ly*, do not change the spelling of the original word.

plain + ness = plain**ness**   casual + ly = casual**ly**

EXCEPTIONS

For most words ending in *y*, change the *y* to *i* before adding *–ness* or *–ly*.

empty + ness = empt**iness**   busy + ly = bus**ily**

14i. Drop the final silent *e* before a suffix beginning with a vowel.

care + ing = car**ing**   dose + age = dos**age**

EXCEPTIONS

Keep the final silent *e*
- in a word ending in *ce* or *ge* before a suffix beginning with *a* or *o*: peac**eable**, courag**eous**
- in *dye* and in *singe*, before *–ing*: dy**eing**, sing**eing**
- in *mile* before *–age*: mil**eage**

14j. Keep the final silent *e* before a suffix beginning with a consonant.

hope + ful= hop**eful**   love + ly = lov**ely**

EXCEPTIONS

awe + ful = aw**ful**   whole + ly = whol**ly**
nine + th = nin**th**   argue + ment = argu**ment**

14k. For words ending in *y* preceded by a consonant, change the *y* to *i* before any suffix that does not begin with *i*.

thirsty + est = thirst**iest**   plenty + ful = plent**iful**

14l. For words ending in *y* preceded by a vowel, keep the *y* when adding a suffix.

joy + ful = jo**yful**   obey + ing = obe**ying**

EXCEPTIONS

day—da**ily**   lay—la**id**
pay—pa**id**   say—sa**id**

14m. Double the final consonant before a suffix that begins with a vowel if the word both

(1) has only one syllable or has the accent on the last syllable
    and
(2) ends in a single consonant preceded by a single vowel.

thin + est = thi**nnest**   occur + ed = occu**rred**

EXCEPTIONS

- For words ending in *w* or *x*, do not double the final consonant.
    new + er = new**er**   relax + ing = relax**ing**
- For words ending in *c*, add *k* before the suffix instead of doubling the *c*.
    picnic + k + ed = picnic**ked**

Forming the Plurals of Nouns

14n. Remembering the following rules will help you spell the plural forms of nouns.

(1) For most nouns, add *–s*.

players   islands   Jeffersons

(2) For nouns ending in *s*, *x*, *z*, *ch*, or *sh*, add *–es*.

classes   matches   taxes   Chávezes

(3) For nouns ending in *y* preceded by a vowel, add *–s*.

monkeys   alloys   McKays

(4) For nouns ending in *y* preceded by a consonant, change the *y* to *i* and add *–es*.

flies   countries   trophies

EXCEPTIONS

For proper nouns, add *–s*: Kennedys

(5) For some nouns ending in *f* or *fe*, add *–s*. For others, change the *f* or *fe* to *v* and add *–es*. For proper nouns, add *–s*.

gulfs   roofs   leav**es**   kniv**es**
wol**ves**   Tallchiefs   Wolfes

(6) For nouns ending in *o* preceded by a vowel, add *–s*.

studio**s**   stereo**s**   Ignacio**s**

(7) For nouns ending in *o* preceded by a consonant, add *–es*.

tomato**es**   hero**es**   veto**es**

For some nouns ending in *o* preceded by a consonant, either *–s* or *–es* may be added.

zero**s** *or* zero**es**   mosquito**s** *or* mosquito**es**

(8) The plurals of a few nouns are formed in irregular ways.

t**ee**th   women   m**i**ce   g**ee**se

(9) For a few nouns, the singular and the plural forms are the same.

Sheep   trout   aircraft   Japanese   Sioux

(10) For most compound nouns, form the plural of only the last word of the compound.

bookshel**ves**   baby sitter**s**   ten-year-old**s**

(11) For compound nouns in which one of the words is modified by the other word or words, form the plural of the noun modified.

sister**s**-in-law   runner**s**-up   mountain goat**s**

(12) For some nouns borrowed from other languages, the plural is formed as in the original languages.

alga—alg**ae**   hypothesis—hypothes**es**
ellipsis—ellips**es**   phenomenon—phenomen**a**

(13) To form the plurals of figures, most uppercase letters, signs, and words used as words, add an *–s* or both an apostrophe and an *–s*.

1990—1990**s** *or* 1990**'s**   *C*—*C***s** *or* *C***'s**
and— *and***s** *or* *and***'s**   &—&**s** *or* &**'s**

To prevent confusion, add both an apostrophe and an *–s* to form the plural of all lowercase letters, certain uppercase letters, and some words used as words.

The word *Mississippi* contains four *s*'s and four *i*'s. [Without an apostrophe, the plural of *i* could be confused with *is*.]

Because I mistakenly thought that Flannery O'Connor was a man, I used *his*'s instead of *her*'s in my essay. [Without an apostrophe, the plural of *his* would look like *hiss*, and the plural of *her* would look like *hers*.]

Your Turn Using Prefixes and Suffixes

Rewrite the following wordy sentences. Replace each underlined group or groups of words with a word (or a shorter phrase) that uses a prefix or a suffix from rules 14b and 14c.

1. Who might go on trial for the <u>act of destroying</u> of "the melancholy House of Usher"?
2. Could a jury convict Coyote, the trickster <u>who lacks morals</u>, of a crime?
3. I think that the people who enslaved Olaudah Equiano were guilty of some crime <u>that went across nations</u>!
4. Fred Collins might present evidence to clear him of cowardice, but I'm not sure that his evidence would be <u>able to be permitted</u>.
5. Unless I have <u>judged the situation wrongly</u>, the "trials" in *The Crucible* reveal <u>an action of devotedness</u> to fear.

---

15. GLOSSARY OF USAGE

The **Glossary of Usage** is an alphabetical list of words and expressions with definitions, explanations, and examples. Some examples in this list are labeled *standard*, *nonstandard*, *formal*, or *informal*. **Standard** and **formal** identify usage that is appropriate in serious writing and speaking (such as compositions and speeches). *Informal* indicates standard English commonly used in conversation and in everyday writing (such as personal letters). **Nonstandard** identifies usage that does not follow the guidelines of standard English usage.

accept, except   *Accept* is a verb meaning "to receive." *Except* may be either a verb meaning "to leave out" or a preposition meaning "excluding."

I will **accept** another yearbook assignment. [verb]

Should the military services **except** women from combat duty? [verb]

I have read all of Willa Cather's novels **except** *My Ántonia*. [preposition]

affect, effect *Affect* is a verb meaning "to influence." *Effect* may be either a verb meaning "to bring about or accomplish" or a noun meaning "the result [of an action]."

How did the House of Usher **affect** the narrator?

Renewed interest in *Moby-Dick* during the 1920s **effected** a change in Melville's reputation.

What **effect** did the war have on Paul Berlin?

All ready, already *All ready* means "prepared." *Already* means "previously."

Are you **all ready** to give your report?

We have **already** read that story.

all together, altogether *All together* means "everyone or everything in the same place." *Altogether* means "entirely."

My family will be **all together** for the holidays.

The president is **altogether** opposed to the bill.

allusion, illusion An *allusion* is an indirect reference to something. An *illusion* is a mistaken idea or a misleading appearance.

In her stories, Flannery O'Connor makes numerous **allusions** to the Bible.

Illusions of success haunt Willy Loman.

Makeup can be used to create an **illusion.**

almost, most Avoid using *most* for *almost* in all writing other than dialogue.

Almost [*not* Most] everyone was surprised by the ending of "An Occurrence at Owl Creek Bridge."

a lot Avoid this expression in formal situations by using *many* or *much.*

amount, number Use *amount* to refer to a singular word. Use *number* to refer to a plural word.

The library has a large **amount** of material about the Harlem Renaissance. [*Amount* refers to *material.*]

The library has a large **number** of books about the Harlem Renaissance. [*Number* refers to *books.*]

and, but In general, avoid beginning a sentence with *and* or *but* in formal writing.

and etc. *Etc.* stands for the Latin words *et cetera,* meaning "and others" or "and so forth." Always avoid using *and* before *etc.* In general, avoid using *etc.* in formal situations. Use an unabbreviated English expression instead.

We are studying twentieth-century American novelists: Ernest Hemingway, Margaret Walker, Jean Toomer, **and others** [*or* etc., but not *and etc.*].

and/or Avoid using this confusing construction. Decide which alternative, *and* or *or,* expresses what you mean, and use it alone.

any more, anymore The expression *any more* specifies a quantity. *Anymore* means "now; nowadays."

Do you know **any more** Caddo folk tales?

Kam doesn't work at the record store **anymore.**

any one, anyone The expression *any one* specifies one member of a group. *Anyone* is a pronoun meaning "one person, no matter which."

Any one of you can play the part.

Anyone can try out for the part.

at Avoid using *at* after a construction beginning with *where.*

Where was Chief Joseph [*not* Where was Chief Joseph at] when he gave his surrender speech?

a while, awhile *A while* means "a period of time." *Awhile* means "for a short time."

Let's sit here for **a while** and listen to the band.

Let's wait here **awhile.**

bad, badly *Bad* is an adjective. *Badly* is an adverb. In standard English, *bad* should follow a sense verb, such as *feel, look, sound, taste,* or *smell,* or other linking verb.

NONSTANDARD If the meat smells badly, don't eat it.

STANDARD If the meat smells **bad,** don't eat it.

because In formal situations, do not use the construction *reason . . . because.* Instead, use *reason . . . that.*

The **reason** for the eclipse is **that** [*not* because] the moon has come between the Earth and the sun.

being as, being that Avoid using either of these expressions in place of *since* or *because.*

Because [*not* Being as *or* Being that] Ms. Ribas is a gemologist, she may know what these stones are.

beside, besides *Beside* is a preposition meaning "by the side of" or "next to." *Besides* may be either a preposition meaning "in addition to" or "other than" or an adverb meaning "moreover."

Rip Van Winkle laid his rifle **beside** him on the ground. [preposition]

No one **besides** Lurleen has read all of *Leaves of Grass.* [preposition]

I'm not in the mood to go shopping; **besides,** I have an English test tomorrow. [adverb]

between, among Use *between* to refer to only two items or to more than two when comparing each item individually to each of the others.

The money from the sale of the property was evenly divided **between** Sasha and Antonio.

Don't you know the difference **between** a simile, a metaphor, and an analogy? [Each figure of speech is compared individually to each of the others.]

Use *among* to refer to more than two items when you are not considering each item in relation to each other item individually.

The money from the sale of the property was evenly divided **among** the four relatives.

bring, take   *Bring* means "to come carrying something." *Take* means "to go carrying something."

I'll **bring** my Wynton Marsalis CD when I come.

Rip Van Winkle **took** his gun and his dog to hunt.

cannot (can't) help but   Avoid using *but* followed by an infinitive after the expression *cannot (can't)* help. Instead, use a gerund after the expression.

| NONSTANDARD | I can't help but [to] tap my foot whenever I hear mariachi music. |
| STANDARD | I can't help **tapping** my foot whenever I hear mariachi music. |

compare, contrast   Used with *to, compare* means "to look for similarities." Used with *with, compare* means "to look for similarities and differences." *Contrast* is always used to point out differences.

Write a simile **comparing** a manufactured product **to** something in nature.

How do the haiku of Taniguchi Buson **compare with** those of Matsuo Bashō?

The teacher **contrasted** the writing styles of Walt Whitman and Emily Dickinson.

double subject   Do not use an unnecessary pronoun after the subject of a sentence.

Judy Jones [*not* Judy Jones she] fascinates Dexter Green.

due to   Avoid using *due to* for "because of" or "owing to."

The game was delayed **because of** [*not* due to] rain.

each and every   The expression *each and every* is redundant. Instead, use either *each* or *every* alone.

Every [*not* Each and every] resident of Jefferson attended Miss Emily Grierson's funeral.

either, neither   *Either* usually means "one or the other of two." *Neither* usually means "not one or the other of two." Avoid using *either* or *neither* when referring to more than two.

Consider writing about the Jazz Age, the Harlem Renaissance, or the Great Depression; **any one** [*not* either] of those topics would be interesting.

emigrate, immigrate   *Emigate* means "to leave a country or a region to settle elsewhere." *Immigrate* means "to come into a country or a region to settle there."

Claude McKay **emigrated** from Jamaica in 1912.

Claude McKay **immigrated** to the U.S. in 1912.

every day, everyday   *Every day* means "each day." *Everyday* means "daily" or "usual."

Parson Hooper wore the black veil **every day.**

Walking the dog is one of my **everyday** chores.

every one, everyone   *Every one* specifies every person or thing of those named. *Everyone* means "every person; everybody."

Every one of these poems was written by Kim.

Has **everyone** read "The Bells"?

farther, further   Use *farther* to express physical distance. Use *further* to express abstract relationships of degree or quantity.

We swam **farther** than we usually do.

After discussing "The Road Not Taken" **further,** we agreed with Karl's interpretation of the poem.

fewer, less   Use *fewer* to modify a plural noun and *less* to modify a singular noun.

We should use **fewer** paper towels. [plural]

We should use **less** paper. [singular]

good, well   Do not use the adjective *good* to modify a verb. Instead, use the adverb *well*, meaning "capably" or "satisfactorily." As an adjective, *well* means "in good health" or "satisfactory in appearance or condition."

The school orchestra played **well.** [adverb]

He says that he feels quite **well.** [adjective]

It's midnight, and all is **well.** [adjective]

had ought, hadn't ought   Do not use *had* or *hadn't* with *ought.*

His scores **ought** [*not* had ought] to be back by now.

half   Avoid using an indefinite article (*a* or *an*) both before and after *half.*

We've waited for **half an hour** [*or* **a half hour**].

if, whether   Avoid using *if* for *whether* in indirect questions and in expressions of doubt.

Dickinson wanted to know **whether** [*not* if] her poems were "alive."

imply, infer   *Imply* means "to suggest indirectly." *Infer* means "to interpret" or "to draw a conclusion."

> The speaker of "Thanatopsis" **implies** that nature can allay one's fear of death.

> I **infer** from the poem that nature can cure many ills.

in, into   *In* generally shows location. *Into* generally shows direction.

> Randall Jarrell was born **in** Nashville, Tennessee.

> When Rip walked **into** the village, everybody stared.

irregardless, regardless   *Irregardless* is nonstandard. Use *regardless* instead.

> **Regardless** [*not* Irregardless] of our pleas, Dad said that we had to go to bed.

its, it's   *Its* is the possessive form of *it*. *It's* is the contraction of *it is* or *it has*.

> The crew prepares for **its** fight with Moby-Dick.

> **It's** [It is] Captain Ahab's obsession.

> **It's** [It has] been many years since Ahab lost his leg.

kind of, sort of   In formal situations, avoid using these terms for the adverb *somewhat* or *rather*.

> INFORMAL   Roderick became kind of agitated.

> FORMAL   Roderick became rather **agitated.**

kind(s), sort(s), type(s)   With the singular form of each of these nouns, use *this* or *that*. With the plural form, use *these* or *those*.

> **This kind** of gas is safe, but **those kinds** aren't.

learn, teach   *Learn* means "to gain knowledge." *Teach* means "to provide with knowledge."

> The more you **teach** someone else, the more you **learn** yourself.

lie, lay   The verb *lie* means "to rest" or "to stay, to recline, or to remain in a certain state or position." Its principal parts are *lie, lying, lay,* and *lain*. *Lie* never takes an object. The verb *lay* means "to put [something] in a place." Its principal parts are *lay, laying, laid,* and *laid*. *Lay* usually takes an object.

> Their land **lay** in the shadow of Rainy Mountain. [no object]

> Eduardo **laid** the strips of grilled meat on the tortilla. [*Strips* is the object of *laid*.]

like, as   In formal situations, do not use *like* for the conjunction *as* to introduce a subordinate clause.

> INFORMAL   He sings like Caruso once did.

> FORMAL   He sings **as** Caruso once did.

like, as if   In formal situations, avoid using the preposition *like* for the conjunction *as if* or *as though* to introduce a subordinate clause.

> INFORMAL   The singers sounded like they had not rehearsed.

> FORMAL   The singers sounded **as if** [*or* **as though**] they had not rehearsed.

of   *Of* is a preposition. Do not use *of* in place of *have* after verbs such as *could, should, would, might, must,* and *ought* [*to*]. Also, do not use *had of* for *had*.

> You ought to **have** [*not* of] studied harder.

> If he **had** [*not* had of] remembered the name of the author of "Mending Wall," he **would have** [*not* would of] made a perfect score.

Avoid using *of* after other prepositions such as *inside, off,* and *outside*.

> Chian-Chu dived **off** [*not* off of] the side of the pool into the water.

on to, onto   In the expression *on to, on* is an adverb and *to* is a preposition. *Onto* is a preposition.

> Dexter held **on to** his winter dreams.

> The cat leapt gracefully **onto** the windowsill.

or, nor   Use *or* with *either;* use *nor* with *neither*.

> On Tuesdays the school cafeteria offers a choice of **either** a taco salad **or** a pizza.

> I wonder why **neither** Ralph Ellison **nor** Robert Frost received the Nobel Prize in literature.

rise, raise   The verb *rise* means "to go up" or "to get up." Its principal parts are *rise, rising, rose,* and *risen*. *Rise* never takes an object. The verb *raise* means "to cause [something] to rise" or "to lift up." Its principal parts are *raise, raising, raised,* and *raised*. *Raise* usually takes an object.

> The queen **rose** from her throne. [no object]

> The movers **raised** the boxes onto their shoulders. [*Boxes* is the object of *raised*.]

sit, set   The verb *sit* means "to rest in an upright, seated position." Its principal parts are *sit, sitting, sat,* and *sat*. *Sit* seldom takes an object. The verb *set* means "to put [something] in a place." Its principal parts are *set, setting, set,* and *set*. *Set* usually takes an object.

> The raven **sat** on the bust of Pallas. [no object]

> Eben **set** the jug down. [*Jug* is the object of *set*.]

some, somewhat   In formal situations, use *somewhat* instead of *some* to mean "to some extent."

> My grades have improved **somewhat** [*not* some].

than, then *Than* is a conjunction used in comparisons. *Then* is an adverb meaning "at that time" or "next."

> Tyrone is more studious **than** I am.

> First, mix the wet ingredients; **then,** add the flour and other dry ingredients.

their, there, they're *Their* is a possessive form of *they*. As an adverb, *there* means "at that place." *There* can also be used to begin a sentence. *They're* is the contraction of *they are*.

> The performers are studying **their** lines.

> I will be **there** after rehearsal. [adverb]

> **There** will be four acts in the play. [expletive]

> **They're** performing a play by Lorraine Hansberry.

theirs, there's *Theirs* is a possessive form of the pronoun *they*. *There's* is the contraction of *there is* or *there has*.

> These posters are ours; **theirs** are the ones on the opposite wall.

> **There's** [There is] a biography of W.E.B. DuBois in the library.

> **There's** [There has] been a change in plans.

them Do not use *them* as an adjective. Use *those*.

> **Those** [*not* Them] lines illustrate Poe's use of internal rhyme.

this here, that there Avoid using *here* or *there* after *this* or *that*.

> **This** [*not* This here] magazine has an article about Andrea Lee.

try and, try to Use *try to*, not *try and*.

> I will **try to** [*not* try and] finish my report on John Updike.

type, type of Avoid using the noun *type* as an adjective. Add *of* after *type*.

> I prefer this **type of** [*not* type] shirt.

ways Use *way*, not *ways*, when referring to distance.

> My home in Wichita is a long **way** [*not* ways] from Tokyo, where my pen pal lives.

when, where Avoid using *when* or *where* to begin a definition.

> NONSTANDARD A predicament is when you are in an embarrassing situation.

> STANDARD A predicament is **an embarrassing situation.**

where Avoid using *where* for *that*.

> I read **that** [*not* where] the Smithsonian Institution has preserved many of William H. Johnson's paintings.

who, which, that *Who* refers to persons only. *Which* refers to things only. *That* may refer to either persons or things.

> Wasn't Beethoven the composer **who** [*or* **that**] wrote music even after he lost his hearing?

> First editions of Poe's first book, **which** is titled *Tamerlane and Other Poems*, are worth thousands of dollars.

> Is this the only essay **that** James Baldwin wrote?

> I've never met or even seen the person **that** [*or* **who**] delivers our newspaper each morning.

who's, whose *Who's* is the contraction of *who is* or *who has*. *Whose* is the possessive form of *who*.

> **Who's** [Who is] going to portray the Navajo detective in the play?

> **Who's** [Who has] been using my computer?

> **Whose** artwork is this?

your, you're *Your* is a possessive form of *you*. *You're* is the contraction of *you are*.

> Is this **your** book?

> I hope **you're** [you are] able to come to graduation.

Your Turn Using Formal Usage

The following sentences contain examples of informal or nonstandard usage. Rewrite each sentence to establish formal, standard usage.

1. The reason I like to write is because writing makes me feel like I'm sharing my thoughts and dreams with a good friend.

2. Most every time I begin or work on a piece of writing, the activity energizes me, irregardless of my mood.

3. Inspiration is when the mind and emotions are stimulated—and I can't help but pull out a notebook and make some notes when I'm inspired by a writing idea.

4. For example, in this here notebook I've recorded ideas and drafts for stories, essays, articles, and etc.

5. I would of liked to meet a famous short-story writer from the past, but I sort of think that I'm honoring a lot of them by being a writer myself.

Glossary

The glossary that follows is an alphabetical list of words found in the selections in this book. Use this glossary just as you would use a dictionary – to find out the meaning of unfamiliar words. (Some technical, foreign, and more obscure words in this book are not listed here but instead are defined for you in the footnotes that accompany many of the selections.)

Mary words in the English language have more than one meaning. This glossary gives the meanings that apply to the words as they are used in the selections in this book. Words closely related in form and meaning are usually listed together in one entry (for instance, *cower* and *cowered*), and the definition is given for the first form.

The following abbreviations are used:

adj.	adjective
adv.	adverb
n.	noun
v.	verb

Each word's pronunciation is given in parentheses. For more information about the words in this glossary or for information about words not listed here, consult a dictionary.

A

abandonment (uh BAN duhn muhnt) *n.* a yielding to natural impulses; freedom from self-control or restraint.

abject (AB jehkt) *adj.* hopeless.

abstinence (AB stuh nuhns) *n.* the act of refraining from a behavior.

abyss (uh BIHS) *n.* a deep, immeasurable space, gulf, or cavity.

accept (ak SEHPT) *v.* include or give approval to.

acrid (AK rihd) *adj.* bitter; irritating.

adamant (AD uh mant) *adj.* not giving in; immovable.

admonishing (ad MAHN ihsh ihng) *v.* used as *adj.* gently warning.

adorn (uh DAWRN) *v.* enhance, as with ornaments.

adversary (AD vuhr sehr ee) *n.* opponent.

afflictions (uh FLIHK shuhnz) *n.* pains; hardships.

affluent (AF lu uhnt) *adj.* prosperous; rich.

aggregation (ag ruh GAY shuhn) *n.* collection of separate things into one mass or whole.

agitation (aj uh TAY shuhn) *n.* violent motion or disturbance.

alacrity (uh LAK ruh tee) *n.* promptness in responding; eagerness.

alliances (uh LY uhns ihz) *n. pl.* close associations entered into for mutual benefit.

ambling (AM blihng) *v.* walking at an easy, slow pace.

amiability (ay mee uh BIHL uh tee) *n.* friendliness; pleasantness.

amiably (AY mee uh blee) *adv.* in a friendly, agreeable way.

anarchy (AN uhr kee) *n.* disorder and confusion; lawlessness.

ancestral (an SEHS truhl) *adj.* inherited.

aneurysms (AN yuh rihz uhmz) *n. pl.* damage or defects in arteries or veins that can cause death.

antipathy (an TIHP uh thee) *n.* strong dislike.

apocryphal (uh PAHK ruh fuhl) *adj.* of questionable authority; false.

appall (uh PAWL) *v.* horrify; fill with shock.

application (ap luh KAY shuhn) *n.* act of using; putting to use.

appointed (uh POYNT uhd) *v.* used as *adj.* assigned.

apprehension (ap rih HEHN shuhn) *n.* expectation of misfortune; fear.

appropriate (uh PROH pree ayt) *v.* take over.

arbitrary (AHR buh trehr ee) *adj.* based on personal preference or whim.

archaic (ahr KAY ihk) *adj.* old-fashioned.

ardently (AHR duhnt lee) *adv.* in a way that is intensely passionate and eager.

arduous (AHR ju uhs) *adj.* difficult.

arouse (uh ROWZ) *v.* stir to action.

arrayed (uh RAYD) *adj.* dressed.

ascertaining (as uhr TAYN ihng) *v.* finding out with certainty.

aspect (AS pehkt) *n.* the way something looks; appearance.

assailed (uh SAYLD) *v.* set upon vigorously with hostile words.

assent (uh SEHNT) *n.* agreement.

assent (uh SEHNT) *v.* agree or express approval.

assimilated (uh SIHM uh layt ihd) *adj.* conformed or adjusted to the customs and attitudes of a group, nation, etc.

atrocious (uh TROH shuhs) *adj.* very evil, savage, or brutal.

atrocity (uh TRAHS uh tee) *n.* a horrible or brutal act.

austere (aw STIHR) *adj.* very plain.

autonomy (aw TAHN uh mee) *n.* independence; self-government.

avarice (AV uhr ihs) *n.* greed; desire for wealth.

avaricious (av uh RIHSH uhs) *adj.* greedy.

aversion (uh VUR zhuhn, -shuhn) *n.* strong or fixed dislike.

avert (uh VURT) *v.* turn away; prevent.

avidly (AV ihd lee) *adv.* eagerly.

awry (uh RY) *adj.* out of place; crooked.

B

beam (beem) *n.* large, long piece of timber for use in construction.

beguile (bih GYL) *v.* mislead; deceive.

beholden (bih HOHL duhn) *adj.* indebted.

bellicose (BEHL uh kohs) *adj.* fond of fighting; warlike.

belligerents (buh LIHJ uhr uhnts) *n.* nations, states, or their citizens at war.

benevolence (buh NEHV uh luhns) *n.* kindness.

berate (bih RAYT) *v.* scold harshly.

beseeched (bih SEECHT) *v.* begged.

bickering (BIHK uhr ihng) *v.* used as *adj.* quarreling over something unimportant; squabbling.

bilge (bihlj) *n.* dirty water that gathers in the bottom of a boat.

blasphemy (BLAS fuh mee) *n.* words or actions that disrespect something sacred.

bleak (bleek) *adj.* cheerless.

blight (blyt) *n.* anything that takes away hope or causes ruin.

blithe (blyth) *adj.* happy; cheerful; carefree.

boughs (bowz) *n. pl.* branches of a tree.

brazenness (BRAY zuhn ness) *n.* boldness.

breached (breechd) *v.* broke through.

bunker (BUHNG kuhr) *n.* a storehouse or chamber made of earth or concrete, built mostly or entirely below ground.

C

calamity (kuh LAM uh tee) *n.* great misfortune; disaster.

caliber (KAL uh buhr) *n.* quality or ability.

camaraderie (kah muh RAH duh ree) *n.* comradeship; good-fellowship; lighthearted rapport among friends.

camouflage (KAM uh flahzh) *n.* a disguise or false appearance adopted in order to conceal.

caper (KAY puhr) *n.* foolish prank.

carnage (KAHR nihj) *n.* extensive bloodshed.

censored (SEHN suhrd) *v.* cut or changed to remove material deemed objectionable.

charade (shuh RAYD) *n.* act; blatant pretense.

chartreuse (shahr TROOZ) *adj.* a light, yellowish green.

chastisement (chas TYZ muhnt) *n.* punishment.

chrome (krohm) *n.* a lustrous, hard, metallic element used in alloy steels.

chronicles (KRAHN uh kuhlz) *n.* stories of past events; histories.

cicadas (sih KAY duhz) *n. pl.* cricketlike insects that make loud, shrill sounds.

circumvent (sur kuhm VEHNT) *v.* avoid by cleverness or deceit.

civility (suh VIHL uh tee) *n.* courteous or polite behavior.

clammy (KLAM ee) *adj.* cold and damp.

clamor (KLAM uhr) *n.* loud noise; loud demand or complaint.

clientele (kly uhn TEHL) *n.* the clients or customers of a business.

clod (klod) *n.* lump of dirt or soil.

coarse (kohrs) *adj.* crude and unrefined.

coherent (koh HIHR uhnt) *adj.* clear, logical, consistent.

coincide (koh ihn SYD) *v.* occupy the same time or place; to agree.

commensurate (kuh MEHN shuhr iht) *adj.* equal to; proportional.

communal (kah MYOO nuhl) *adj.* used or shared by everyone in a group.

compelled (kuhm PEHLD) *adj.* driven; forced.

complacency (kuhm PLAY suhn see) *n.* self-satisfaction.

comply (kuhm PLY) *v.* obey; agree to a request or command.

conceded (kuhn SEE dihd) *v.* admitted; acknowledged.

conception (kuhn SEHP shuhn) *n.* mental formation of ideas.

concessions (kuhn SEHSH uhnz) *n.* acts of giving in.

conferred (kuhn FURD) *v.* talked things over; consulted.

conjectured (kuhn JEHK chuhrd) *v.* guessed.

conjuring (KAHN juhr ihng) *v.* causing to be or to happen by magic or as if by magic.

consciously (KAHN shuhs lee) *adv.* intentionally; done with full awareness.

conspicuous (kuhn SPIHK yu uhs) *adj.* easily seen; clearly visible.

consultation (kahn suhl TAY shuhn) *n.* a meeting to seek information or exchange ideas.

consume (kuhn SOOM) *v.* burn away; destroy.

contempt (kuhn TEHMPT) *n.* the feeling that something is of no value; scorn.

conundrum (kuh NUHN druhm) *n.* riddle.
conveyed (kuhn VAYD) *v.* communicated; made known.
conviction (kuhn VIHK shuhn) *n.* firm belief.
convivial (kuhn VIHV ee uhl) *adj.* jovial, sociable.
convoy (KAHN voy) *n.* a group of vehicles accompanied by an escort.
copious (KOH pee uhs) *adj.* more than enough; plentiful.
covenant (KUHV uh nuhnt) *n.* binding agreement; compact.
croon (kroon) *n.* song sung in a low voice.
crucial (KROO shuhl) *adj.* critical; decisive.
crypt (krihpt) *n.* underground burial chamber.
cunning (KUHN ihng) *adj.* sly or crafty.

D

daft (daft) *adj.* without sense; stupid.
debris (duh BREE) *n.* the remains of anything broken down or destroyed; ruins; rubble.
deluge (DEHL yooj) *n.* rush; flood.
demur (dih MUR) *v.* object or express disagreement.
deplored (dih PLAWRD) *v.* condemned as wrong; disapproved of.
deport (dih POHRT) *v.* send or carry off; transport, especially forcibly.
deposition (DEHP uh ZIHSH uhn) *n.* testimony given under oath at a trial.
derision (dih RIHZH uhn) *n.* ridicule or contempt.
desolate (DEHS uh liht) *adj.* deserted.
despotism (DEHS puh tihz uhm) *n.* rule by a tyrant or king with unlimited power.
deteriorates (dih TIHR ee uh rayts) *v.* becomes worse.
determined (dih TUR muhnd) *v.* decided; concluded.
detract (dih TRAKT) *v.* take away importance from.
digress (duh GREHS) *v.* get off the main subject.
dilapidated (duh LAP uh day tihd) *adj.* partially ruined or decayed through neglect.
discernible (duh ZUR nuh buhl, -SUR-) *adj.* able to be detected; perceptible.
discerning (dih SUR nihng) *v.* used as *adj.* sharp or shrewd in understanding.
discourse (DIHS kawrs) *n.* a written or spoken conversation.
disdained (dihs DAYND) *v.* refused; disapproved; scorned.
disembodied (dihs ehm BAHD eed) *adj.* freed from the body.
disillusions (dihs ih LOO zhuhns) *n. pl.* states of freedom from illusion.
dispirited (dihs PIHR uh tihd) *adj.* discouraged.

disposition (dihs puh ZIHSH uhn) *n.* one's natural way of acting toward others or thinking about things.
disputed (dihs PYOOT ihd) *v.* disagreed with.
dissembling (dih SEHM blihng) *n.* hiding one's feelings or motives.
dissension (dih SEHN shuhn) *n.* hard feeling caused by a difference of opinion.
distinguished (dihs TIHNG gwihsht) *adj.* renowned or socially important.
distorted (dihs TAWRT ihd) *v.* used as *adj.* twisted; not in normal form.
distraught (dihs TRAWT) *adj.* highly troubled.
dominion (duh MIHN yuhn) *n.* rule; the right to govern.
dowry (DOW ree) *n.* the money or property that a wife brings to her husband at marriage.
drone (drohn) *n.* dull, monotonous sound.
dwindled (DWIHN duhld) *v.* diminished.

E

earnest (UR nihst) *adj.* strong and firm in purpose; serious.
eclectic (ehk LEHK tihk) *adj.* made up of a variety of elements.
eddies (EHD eez) *n.* small whirlpools.
egotism (EE guh tihz uhm) *n.* thinking excessively of oneself.
elephantine (ehl uh FAN tyn) *adj.* huge; ponderous; clumsy.
elision (i LIZH uhn) *n.* omission of a vowel, consonant, or syllable in pronunciation.
eloquence (EHL uh kwuhns) *n.* expressive or graceful manner of speech; powerful expression.
eluded (ih LOOD ihd) *v.* escaped detection or notice.
eluding (ih LOOD ihng) *adj.* remaining unexplained; baffling.
emaciated (ih MAY shee ay tihd) *adj.* unusually thin.
enamel (ih NAM uhl) *n.* a smooth, hard, shiny coating.
encountered (ehn KOWN tuhrd) *v.* met or confronted.
endanger (ehn DAYN juhr) *v.* put in danger, jeopardize.
endures (ehn DURZ) *v.* keeps on; continues.
engulf (ehn GUHLF) *v.* swallow up.
enmities (EHN muh teez) *n. pl.* hatreds.
enthralled (ehn THRAWLD) *v.* fascinated.
entreated (ehn TREET ihd) *v.* asked sincerely; begged.
ephemeral (ih FEHM uhr uhl) *adj.* short-lived; fleeting.
epoch (EHP uhk) *n.* noteworthy period of time.
eradicate (ih RAD uh kayt) *v.* eliminate; get rid of or destroy completely. —**eradicated** *v.* used as *adj.*
ethereal (ih THIHR ee uhl) *adj.* not of the earth; spiritual.

eulogy (YOO luh jee) *n.* speech expressing high praise or commendation.

evading (ih VAY dihng) *v.* getting away from by trickery; avoiding.

evasive (ih VAY sihv) *adj.* tending or seeking to evade.

exempt (ehg ZEHMPT) *adj.* freed from a duty or other binding restriction.

expedient (ehk SPEE dee uhnt) *n.* convenience; means to an end.

expedition (ehks puh DIHSH uhn) *n.* journey of exploration.

expenditure (ehk SPEHN duh chuhr) *n.* an amount spent.

extemporized (ehk STEHM puh ryzd) *v.* prepared offhand; made for the occasion.

extremities (ehk STREHM uh teez) *n.* the limbs of the body, especially hands and feet.

F

facilitate (fuh SIHL uh tayt) *v.* make easier.

fascism (FASH ihz uhm) *n.* an authoritarian and nationalistic right-wing system of government and social organization. The term was first used of the totalitarian right-wing nationalist regime of Benito Mussolini in Italy (1922–43).

fervently (FUR vuhnt lee) *adv.* with intense feeling.

feverish (FEE vuhr ihsh) *adj.* excited; restless.

fitfully (FIHT fuhl lee) *adv.* irregularly; in fits and starts.

flays (flayz) *v.* whips; lashes.

florid (FLAWR ihd) *adj.* flowery; excessively ornate; showy.

flourished (FLUR ihshd) *v.* thrived; prospered.

foment (foh MEHNT) *v.* stimulate; provoke.

forge (fohrj) *v.* to heat and shape metal.

forlorn (fawr LAWRN) *adj.* lonely and sad; forsaken; deserted; miserable; hopeless.

frenzy (FREHN zee) *n.* frantic behavior; wildness.

frugality (froo GAL uh tee) *n.* thrift.

futile (FYOO tuhl) *adj.* useless; pointless.

G

garrulous (GAR uh luhs) *adj.* talking too much, especially about unimportant things.

gaudy (GAW dee) *adj.* too bright and flashy to be in good taste; cheap and showy.

gaunt (gawnt) *adj.* very thin and bony.

ghetto (GEHT oh) *n.* a densely populated section of a city inhabited predominantly by members of an ethnic or other minority group, often as a result of social or economic restrictions.

glazed (glayzd) *adj.* coated with a thin, shiny layer.

glean (gleen) *v.* gather produce left behind after reaping a harvest.

glory (GLOHR ee) *n.* great beauty; splendor.

gratification (grat uh fuh KAY shuhn) *n.* satisfaction; delight.

gravitate (GRAV uh tayt) *v.* move together.

grotesque (groh TEHSK) *adj.* strange; absurd.

grudge (gruhj) *v.* withhold something from someone out of spite.

guffawing (guh FAW ihng) *v.* used as *adj.* loudly and coarsely laughing.

guileless (GYL lihs) *adj.* honest; sincere.

gunnels (GUHN uhl) *n. pl.* gunwales, the upper edges of the sides of a boat.

H

habitually (huh BIHCH oo uh lee) *adv.* usually; by habit.

haggard (HAG uhrd) *adj.* looking wasted or worn from pain, hunger, worry, or fatigue.

hail (hayl) *v.* greet.

halo (HAY loh) *n.* circular band of light.

harbor (HAHR buhr) *v.* have and keep in the mind.

harmonious (hahr MOH nee uhs) *adj.* going together in a pleasing, musical way.

harvest (HAHR vihst) *n.* a gathering in of crops or objects.

haughty (HAW tee) *adj.* arrogant.

holistic (hoh LIHS tihk) *adj.* relating to the whole of something instead of its parts.

homage (HOM ihj) *n.* respect; reverence.

hysteria (hihs TIHR ee uh) *n.* uncontrolled excitement.

I

icebox (YS bahks) *n.* refrigerator.

idealist (y DEE uh lihst) *n.* a person who cherishes high principles or goals.

illumination (ih loo muh NAY shuhn) *n.* intellectual or spiritual enlightenment.

illumined (ih LOO muhnd) *v.* lit up.

immortality (ihm awr TAL uh tee) *n.* unending existence.

impeccably (ihm PEHK uh blee) *adv.* perfectly; without error or defect.

impelled (ihm PEHLD) *v.* used as *adj.* urged; strongly driven.

imperative (ihm PEHR uh tihv) *adj.* not to be avoided; urgent.

imperceptible (ihm puhr SEHP tuh buhl) *adj.* so slight as not to be noticed.

imperially (ihm PIHR ee uhl lee) *adv.* grandly; majestically.

impious (ihm PY uhs) *adj.* irreverent.

impromptu (ihm PRAHMP too) *adj.* on the spur of the moment; without preparation.

impropriety (ihm pruh PRY uh tee) *n.* improper conduct.

impunity (ihm PYOO nuh tee) *n.* immunity from harm or punishment.

inanimate (ihn AN uh miht) *adj.* lifeless.

incensed (ihn SEHNST) *adj.* infuriated; angry.

incessantly (ihn SEHS uhnt lee) *adv.* without stopping; constantly; continuously.

inconceivable (ihn kuhn SEE vuh buhl) *adj.* unimaginable; beyond understanding.

inert (ihn URT) *adj.* inactive; sluggish.

infamous (IHN fuh muhs) *adj.* having a bad reputation.

infernal (ihn FUR nuhl) *adj.* as if coming from hell; detestable.

infinitesimal (ihn fih nuh TEHS uh muhl) *adj.* extremely small; minute.

infirm (ihn FURM) *adj.* physically weak.

influence (IHN floo uhns) *n.* effect; ability to affect.

influenced (IHN floo uhnsd) *v.* persuaded.

ingenious (ihn JEEN yuhs) *adj.* clever.

inhabited (ihn HAB uh tihd) *adj.* lived in.

inherent (ihn HIHR uhnt) *adj.* inborn; built-in.

iniquity (ih NIHK wuh tee) *n.* wickedness.

inordinate (ihn AWR duh niht) *adj.* excessive.

inscrutable (ihn SKROO tuh buhl) *adj.* mysterious.

insidious (ihn SIHD ee uhs) *adj.* sly; sneaky.

insolence (IHN suh luhns) *n.* rudeness; disrespectful behavior.

insolent (IHN suh luhnt) *adj.* boldly disrespectful.

insurmountable (ihn suhr MOWNT tuh buhl) *adj.* not capable of being overcome.

insurrection (ihn suh REHK shuhn) *n.* rebellion; revolt.

intangible (ihn TAN juh buhl) *adj.* not capable of being touched or felt.

integrate (IHN tuh grayt) *v.* form into a whole.

integrity (ihn TEHG ruh tee) *n.* sound moral principles; honesty.

intent (ihn TEHNT) *adj.* purposeful.

interloper (IHN tuhr lohp uhr) *n.* intruder; meddler.

interminable (ihn TUR muh nuh buhl) *adj.* never stopping; endless; seeming to last forever.

interpose (ihn tuhr POHZ) *v.* put forth in order to interfere.

intransigent (ihn TRAN suh juhnt) *adj.* uncompromising.

intricate (IHN truh kiht) *adj.* complex; complicated.

intrigue (IHN treeg) *n.* scheming; plotting.

intuitively (ihn TOO uh tihv lee) *adv.* without conscious reasoning.

inviolate (ihn VY uh liht) *adj.* uncorrupted.

irrevocably (ih REHV uh kuh blee) *adv.* permanently, irreversibly.

J

jilted (JIHLT ihd) *v.* rejected as a lover.

jocular (JAHK yuh luhr) *adj.* joking, full of fun.

K

kindred (KIHN drihd) *adj.* similar; related.

L

labyrinth (LAB uh rinth) *n.* maze; bewildering complex.

lamentable (luh MEHN tuh buhl) *adj.* regrettable; distressing.

lamented (luh MEHN tihd) *v.* cried out in sorrow.

latent (LAY tuhnt) *adj.* present but hidden or not active.

legacy (LEHG uh see) *n.* money or other property left to a person by the will of someone who has died.

leonine (LEE uh nyn) *n.* resembling or suggestive of a lion.

lethargy (LEHTH uhr jee) *n.* abnormal drowsiness.

loathsome (LOHTH suhm) *adj.* arousing hatred.

loitered (LOY tuhrd) *v.* lingered aimlessly.

loitering (LOY tuhr ihng) *n.* the state of hanging about and wasting time.

lucid (LOO sihd) *adj.* clearheaded; not confused.

ludicrous (LOO duh kruhs) *adj.* laughable; absurd.

lurching (LURCH ing) *v.* staggering.

lusted (LUH stehd) *v.* strongly desired.

luster (LUHS tuhr) *n.* brightness; shine.

lustrous (LUHS truhs) *adj.* shining; glossy.

luxuriant (luhg ZHUR ee uhnt) *adj.* rich; abundant.

M

malevolence (muh LEHV uh luhns) *n.* the wish that evil may happen to others.

malice (MAL ihs) *n.* ill will; desire to harm.

malicious (muh LIHSH uhs) *adj.* intentionally hurtful.

malign (muh LYN) *adj.* harmful; evil.

manifest (MAN uh fehst) *adj.* apparent; clear.

martyrdom (MAHR tuhr duhm) *n.* painful death of a martyr.

mason (MAY suhn) *n.* worker who lays stone or brick.

matchmaker (MACH may kuhr) *n.* a person who arranges marriages by introducing possible mates.

meager (MEE guhr) *adj.* poor, scanty, inadequate.

medium (MEE dee uhm) *n.* material for an artist.

melancholy (MEHL uhn kahl ee) *adj.* sad or suggestive of sadness; sorrowful.

melodious (muh LOH dee uhs) *adj.* sweet sounding; musical.

melody (MEHL uh dee) *n.* the arrangement of musical tones that forms a tune.

mesmerizing (MEHS muh ryz ihng) *adj.* fascinating, hypnotizing.

migrant (MY gruhnt) *adj.* migrating.

mincingly (MIHN sihng lee) *adv.* in a manner affectedly dainty, nice, or elegant.

mingled (MIHNG guhld) *v.* combined or blended in a mixture.

mirth (murth) *n.* happiness; joyfulness.

mitigation (miht uh GAY shuhn) *n.* moderation; softening.

mitochondria (my tuh KAHN dree uh) *n. pl.* the part of a cell that produces energy for the cell.

monied (MUHN eed) *adj.* wealthy.

morass (muh RAS) *n.* any confusing or troublesome situation; entanglement.

morbid (MAWR bihd) *adj.* diseased; unhealthy.

morose (muh ROHS) *adj.* gloomy.

N

naïveté (nah eev TAY) *n.* state or quality of being inexperienced or unsophisticated.

nape (nayp) *n.* back of the neck.

nomadic (noh MAD ihk) *adj.* wandering.

nominal (NAHM uh nuhl) *adj.* existing in name only; not real.

noncommittal (nahn kuh MIHT uhl) *adj.* not committing oneself to a particular view or course of action.

nostalgia (nahs TAL juh) *n.* longing.

notorious (noh TAWR ee uhs) *adj.* widely and unfavorably known.

O

obliterate (uh BLIHT uh rayt) *v.* erase or destroy completely. —**obliterated** *v.* used as *adj.*

obscured (uhb SKYURD) *v.* concealed; hidden.

obscurity (uhb SKYUR uh tee) *n.* darkness; the condition of being unknown.

obstinate (AHB stuh niht) *adj.* stubborn.

obtuse (uhb TOOS) *adj.* slow to understand; stupid.

ominous (AHM uh nuhs) *adj.* of bad omen; threatening danger; menacing.

onslaught (AHN slawt) *n.* brutal, fierce attack.

opaque (oh PAYK) *adj.* not transparent; not admitting light.

opprobrium (uh PROH bree uhm) *n.* shameful conduct.

orthopedic (awr thuh PEE dihk) *adj.* medically related to the bones, joints, or muscles.

ostentatious (ahs tehn TAY shuhs) *adj.* deliberately attracting notice.

ostracism (AHS truh sihz uhm) *n.* banishment; act of being shut out or excluded.

overwhelmed (oh vuhr HWHEHLMD) *adj.* overpowered.

overwhelming (oh vuhr HWEHLM ihng) *adj.* overpowering.

P

pallor (PAL uhr) *n.* unnatural lack of color.

palpable (PAL puh buhl) *adj.* able to be touched or felt; obvious; perceivable.

pandemonium (pan duh MOH nee uhm) *n.* wild confusion.

partisan (PAHR tih zuhn) *n.* a strong supporter in a cause.

patronage (PAY truh nihj) *n.* business provided by customers.

pauper (PAW puhr) *n.* extremely poor person.

pensively (PEHN sihv lee) *adv.* thoughtfully or seriously.

perceive (puhr SEEV) *v.* observe; sense; understand.

perfidy (PUR fuh dee) *n.* betrayal of trust.

perilous (PEHR uh luhs) *adj.* dangerous and risky.

perplexed (puhr PLEHKST) *adj.* confused, puzzled.

persistent (puhr SIHS tuhnt) *adj.* continuing.

personas (puhr SOH nuhz) *n.* public personalities.

perturbed (puhr TURBD) *v.* used as *adj.* uneasy; anxious; ill at ease.

pervaded (puhr VAY dihd) *v.* spread throughout.

perverse (puhr VURS) *adj.* odd; contrary.

perverted (puhr VUR tihd) *v.* misdirected; corrupted.

petulance (PEHCH uh luhns) *n.* irritability; impatience.

pinnacle (PIHN uh kuhl) *n.* highest point; apex.

pious (PY uhs) *adj.* devoted to one's religion.

piteous (PIHT ee uhs) *adj.* deserving pity or compassion.

pivotal (PIHV uh tuhl) *adj.* central; acting as a point around which other things turn.

plaintive (PLAYN tihv) *adj.* expressing sadness.

plausibility (plaw zuh BIHL uh tee) *n.* believability.

plod (plahd) *v.* walk slowly or with difficulty.

plunder (PLUHN duhr) *n.* goods seized, especially during wartime.

poignant (POYN yuhnt) *adj.* deeply piercing, either emotionally or physically; very moving emotionally.

poise (poyz) *n.* balance.

posterity (pahs TEHR uh tee) *n.* generations to come.

precarious (prih KAIR ee uhs) *adj.* uncertain; insecure; risky.

preconceptions (prih kuhn SEHP shuhnz) *n. pl.* opinions formed beforehand.

predominating (prih DAHM uh nay tihng) *adj.* having great influence or power.

preeminently (pree EHM uh nuhnt lee) *adv.* above all else.

prerogative (prih RAHG uh tihv) *n.* exclusive right or privilege.

prestigious (prehs TIHJ uhs) *adj.* impressive; having distinction.

pretense (PREE tehns) *n.* false claim.

prevalent (PREHV uh lehnt) *adj.* widely existing; frequent.

procured (pruh KYURD) *v.* brought about; caused.

prodigy (PRAHD uh jee) *n.* extremely gifted person.

profane (pruh FAYN) *adj.* not religious; contemptuous; disrespectful.

profoundly (pruh FOWND lee) *adv.* deeply; completely.

profundity (pruh FUHN duh tee) *n.* profound quality; having deep significance.

profusely (pruh FYOOS lee) *adv.* in great quantities.

profusion (pruh FYOO zhuhn) *n.* great abundance.

progressive (pruh GREHS ihv) *adj.* becoming more severe over time.

prominence (PRAHM uh nuhns) *n.* state of being distinguished or widely known.

prosthetic (prahs THEHT ihk) *adj.* relating to an artificial replacement for a missing body part.

prostrate (PRAHS trayt) *adj.* lying flat.

protruding (proh TROOD ihng) *v.* thrusting forth; sticking out.

provisional (pruh VIHZH uh nuhl) *adj.* conditional; dependent on something else being done.

provocation (prahv uh KAY shuhn) *n.* something that stirs up action or feeling.

prudence (PROO duhns) *n.* carefulness.

pseudonymous (soo DAHN uh muhs) *adj.* bearing a false name.

pulverized (PUHL vuh ryzd) *v.* crushed; destroyed.

R

rabbinical (ruh BIHN uh kuhl) *adj.* relating to rabbis, or spiritual leaders in the Jewish religion.

rabble (RAB uhl) *n.* disorderly crowd.

rakishly (RAY kihs lee) *adv.* in a casual, stylish manner.

ravage (RAV ihj) *n.* violent destruction.

ravines (ruh VEENZ) *n.* long, narrow valleys with steep sides.

realm (rehlm) *n.* kingdom.

reaping (REEP ihng) *v.* used as *n.* gathering or harvesting a crop.

recede (rih SEED) *v.* become more distant and indistinct.

rectitude (REHK tuh tood) *n.* correctness.

redress (rih DREHS) *n.* correction for a wrong done.

reiteration (ree iht uh RAY shuhn) *n.* repetition.

relinquished (rih LIHNG kwihshd) *v.* given up.

remnants (REHM nuhnts) *n.* remains.

remuneration (rih myoo nuh RAY shuhn) *n.* payment.

render (REHN duhr) *v.* cause to become; make; create.

rendezvous (RAHN duh voo) *n.* used as *adj.* designated for a meeting.

renovated (REHN uh vayt ihd) *adj.* repaired; updated; restored.

renown (rih NOWN) *n.* fame.

repentance (rih PEHN tuhns) *n.* sorrow for doing wrong; regret.

reserve (rih ZURV) *n.* self-restraint.

resilient (rih ZIHL yuhnt) *adj.* able to return to original form after being bent, compressed, or stretched.

resolute (REHZ uh loot) *adj.* determined; unwavering.

resurgence (rih SUR juhns) *n.* a return; a comeback.

resuscitate (rih SUHS uh tayt) *v.* return to life.

reticent (REHT uh suhnt) *adj.* hesitant to speak; quiet.

retort (rih TAWRT) *n.* a severe, incisive, or witty reply.

reverential (rehv uh REHN shuhl) *adj.* deeply respectful.

revival (rih VY vuhl) *n.* renewal; a restoration to use, popularity, or life.

revive (rih VYV) *v.* return to life.

rhetorical (rih TAWR uh kuhl) *adj.* intended especially for display; artificial.

rigid (RIHJ ihd) *adj.* firm; stiff.

robust (roh BUHST) *adj.* vigorous and healthy.

rotund (roh TUHND) *adj.* round; plump.

rotunda (roh TUHN duh) *n.* a building shaped inside and outside like a cylinder, usually covered with a dome.

rummaging (RUHM ihj ihng) *v.* searching thoroughly by moving things about.

S

sage (sayj) *n.* a profoundly wise person.

salient (SAY lee uhnt) *adj.* prominent; striking.

sarcastic (sahr KAS tihk) *adj.* scornful; mocking.

segregation (sehg ruh GAY shuhn) *n.* separation of one racial group from another or from the rest of society.

sepia (SEE pee uh) *adj.* reddish brown in color.

serenely (suh REEN lee) *adv.* calmly.

shambled (SHAM buhld) *v.* proceeded awkwardly; shuffled.

shawled (shawld) *adj.* wearing or covered with a shawl.

shed (shehd) *v.* cast off.

skein (skayn) *n.* loosely coiled bundle of yarn or thread.

sojourn (SOH jurn) *n.* short stay.

solace (SAHL ihs) *v.* comfort.

soldering (SAHD uhr ihng) *v.* used as *adj.* joining things tightly with melted metal.

solemn (SAHL uhm) *adj.* serious.

somber (SAHM buhr) *adj.* gloomy; dark.

sorrowful (SAWR uh fuhl) *adj.* full of sorrow or sadness.

sovereign (SAHV ruhn) *n.* person, group, or nation having supreme control.

sown (sohn) *v.* scattered seed; planted.

spasm (SPAZ uhm) *n.* a sudden brief experience of intense energy or activity.

spherical (SFEHR uh kuhl) *adj.* having the form of a sphere; globular.

spurned (spurnd) *v.* rejected.

staccato (stuh KAH toh) *adj.* made up of short bursts of sound.

stagnant (STAG nuhnt) *adj.* not flowing or moving.

stark (stahrk) *adj.* bleak; bare.

stature (STACH uhr) *n.* prominence; importance.

stifles (STY fuhlz) *v.* smothers; extinguishes.

stigma (STIHG muh) *n.* a mark of disgrace or shame.

striding (STRYD ihng) *v.* walking with elongated steps.

strife (stryf) *n.* bitter struggle; conflict.

striking (STRY kihng) *adj.* impressive; attractive; dramatic.

subdued (suhb DOOD) *v.* overcome by greater force; conquered.

subjected (suhb JEHKT ihd) *v.* made to experience some action or treatment.

subsequent (SUHB suh kwuhnt) *adj.* following.

subsisting (suhb SIHST ihng) *v.* staying alive.

suffused (suh FYOOZ) *v.* overspread (as with a color, liquid, or dye).

sullenly (SUHL uhn lee) *adv.* in a resentfully silent manner; sulkily.

summary (SUHM uhr ee) *adj.* carried out quickly and without proper formalities.

sundry (SUHN dree) *adj.* various; several.

superficial (soo puhr FIHSH uhl) *adj.* on the surface; shallow.

superfluous (soo PUR floo uhs) *adj.* more than is needed or wanted; useless.

supplication (suhp luh KAY shuhn) *n.* plea; prayer.

surmised (suhr MYZD) *v.* guessed or inferred with little supporting evidence.

sustained (suh STAYND) *v.* used as *adj.* ongoing, continuous.

symmetrical (si MEHT ruh kuhl) *adj.* well-proportioned; balanced.

syncopated (SIHNG kuh pay tihd) *adj.* melody in which accents are placed on normally unaccented beats.

T

taboo (tuh BOO) *n.* social restriction.

tactful (TAKT fuhl) *adj.* skilled in saying and doing the right thing.

tactile (TAK tuhl) *adj.* perceptible to the touch; tangible.

tailored (TAY luhrd) *v.* made to specific requirements.

tedious (TEE dee uhs) *adj.* long and boring; tiring; dreary.

teeming (TEE mihng) *adj.* full of; alive with.

tempest (TEHM pihst) *n.* violent storm.

temples (TEH IM puhlz) *n.* sides of the forehead, just above and in front of the ears.

tenuous (TEHN yoo uhs) *adj.* slight; insubstantial; not firm.

tenure (TEHN yuhr) *n.* length of time that an office is held.

tepid (TEHP ihd) *adj.* moderately warm; lukewarm.

theocracy (thee AHK ruh see) *n.* a government ruled by religious authority.

thwarts (thwawrts) *n.* seats on a boat.

toil (toyl) *n.* hard work.

tourniqueted (TUR nuh keht ihd) *adj.* fitted with a device to prevent blood loss from a major wound.

touted (TOWT ihd) *v.* highly praised.

tranquil (TRANG kwuhl) *adj.* calm; quiet.

transcend (tran SEHND) *v.* surpass, go above.

transcendent (tran SEHN duhnt) *adj.* excelling; surpassing.

transition (tran ZIHSH uhn) *n.* passage from one condition, form, or stage to another.

transparent (trans PAIR uhnt) *adj.* able to be seen through.

transpire (tran SPYR) *v.* develop or breathe out.

traumatic (traw MAT ihk) *adj.* emotionally or physically severe.

trepidation (trehp uh DAY shuhn) *n.* anxious uncertainty; tremulous fear, alarm, or agitation.

tumultuous (too MUHL choo uhs) *adj.* very noisy, disorderly, or violent; greatly agitated or disturbed. —**tumultuously** *adv.*

turbulence (TUR byuh luhns) *n.* wild disorder.

twilight (TWY lyt) *n.* time between sunset and dark; faint light from the sun at this time of day.

tyranny (TIHR uh nee) *n.* cruel use of power.

U

unfurl (uhn FURL) *v.* spread out or unfold.

unheeded (uhn HEE dihd) *adj.* not noticed; disregarded.

unintelligible (uhn ihn TEHL uh juh buhl) *adj.* unable to be understood.

V

vacant (VAY kuhnt) *adj.* empty of thought.

valor (VAL uhr) *n.* courage, bravery.

vanity (VAN uh tee) *n.* something valueless; excessive pride.

venerable (VEHN uhr uh buhl) *adj.* old and respected or deserving respect.

ventured (VEHN chuhrd) *v.* dared or risked going.

venturous (VEHN chuhr uhs) *adj.* bold; daring; adventurous.

verified (VEHR uh fyd) *v.* proved something to be true.

vibrant (VY bruhnt) *adj.* full of energy.

vigilant (VIHJ uh luhnt) *n.* those who are watchful.

vindicated (VIHN duh kayt ihd) *v.* used as *adj.* proved correct.

virulent (VIHR yuh luhnt) *adj.* full of hate; venomous.

vogue (vohg) *n.* fashion.

volition (voh LIHSH uhn) *n.* conscious choice; will; determination.

vulnerability (vuhl nuhr uh BIHL uh tee) *n.* being open to attack or injury.

W

wanton (WAHN tuhn) *adj.* without reason; unrestrained; careless, often with ill will. —**wantonly** *adv.*

waver (WAY vuhr) *v.* to move back and forth.

withering (WIHTH uhr ihng) *v.* used as *adj.* drying up; weakening.

wreak (reek) *v.* inflict.

Spanish Glossary

A

a medida *loc. adj.* hecho según requerimientos específicos.

abandono *sust.* acto de ceder a los impulsos naturales; libertad del autocontrol o las limitaciones.

abatido *adj.* abandonado; triste; sin esperanzas.

abismo *sust.* espacio, golfo o cavidad inmensa y profunda.

aborrecible *adj.* que despierta odio.

abrumado *adj.* aturdido.

abrumador *adj.* que aturde.

abstinencia *sust.* acto de evitar un comportamiento.

abyecto *adj.* sin esperanzas.

acatar *v.* obedecer; aceptar una orden o un pedido.

acertijo *sust.* adivinanza.

acomodado *adj.* próspero; rico.

acongojado *adj.* lleno de pena o tristeza.

acorde *adj.* igual; proporcional.

adinerado *adj.* rico.

admitir *v.* incluir o aprobar algo.

adversario *sust.* oponente.

afabilidad *sust.* actitud amigable; amabilidad.

afablemente *adv.* de manera agradable y amistosa.

afán *v.* trabajo duro.

aflicción *sust.* dolor; malestar.

agitación *sust.* movimiento o alboroto violento.

agobio *sust.* cansancio; pesadez.

agredir *v.* atacar a alguien enérgicamente con palabras duras.

agrio *adj.* amargo; irritante.

albañil *sust.* persona que trabaja en la construcción con ladrillos o piedra.

albergar *v.* guardar una idea en la mente.

alianza *sust.* asociación que se crea para el beneficio mutuo.

alicaído *adj.* desanimado.

altivo *adj.* arrogante.

alumbrar *v.* iluminar.

aluvión *sust.* torrente, inundación.

amblar *v.* caminar a un ritmo lento y tranquilo.

ameno *adj.* jovial, sociable.

amonestar *v.* reprender con severidad.

análogo *adj.* similar; relacionado.

anarquía *sust.* desorden y confusión; ausencia de leyes.

ancestral *adj.* heredado.

aneurisma *sust.* inflamación permanente de las arterias o las venas.

animadversión *sust.* enemistad.

animosidad *sust.* gran antipatía.

añoranza *sust.* nostalgia.

apacible *adj.* tranquilo; sereno.

apartar *v.* alejar.

aplicación *sust.* acción de usar o poner en uso.

apócrifo *adj.* de autoridad cuestionable; falso.

aprensión *sust.* expectativa de que ocurra una desgracia; temor.

apropiar *v.* quedarse con algo.

arbitrario *adj.* basado en una preferencia personal o un capricho.

arbitrio *sust.* medio o recurso para lograr un objetivo.

arcaico *adj.* antiguo.

ardientemente *adv.* con intensidad; con entusiasmo.

arduo *adj.* difícil.

armonioso *adj.* que se combina de forma agradable y musical.

arrastrarse *v.* avanzar con torpeza.

arriesgar *v.* poner en peligro.

asentimiento *sust.* aprobación.

asentir *v.* aceptar o expresar aprobación.

asiduamente *adv.* habitualmente.

asimilado *adj.* que se ajusta a las costumbres y actitudes de un grupo, una nación, etcétera.

asolar *v.* destruir completamente.

aspecto *sust.* manera en que luce algo; apariencia.

atraer *v.* acercar.

atrocidad *sust.* acción horrible o brutal.

atroz *adj.* muy malo, salvaje o brutal.

audaz *adj.* valiente; atrevido; aventurero.

austero *adj.* muy sencillo.

autocomplacencia *sust.* autosatisfacción.

autonomía *sust.* independencia; autogobierno.

avaricia *sust.* codicia; afán de riqueza.

avaro *adj.* codicioso.

aventurado *adj.* peligroso y arriesgado.

aventurar *v.* animarse o arriesgarse a ir.

aversión *sust.* rechazo profundo y constante.

ávidamente *adv.* con entusiasmo.

avieso *adj.* retorcido; contrario.

B

banda a banda *loc. adj.* dispuesto de un lado a otro de un bote.

belicoso *adj.* que le agrada pelear.

beligerante *sust.* nación, estado o ciudadanos que están en guerra.

benevolencia *sust.* amabilidad.

blasfemia *sust.* palabras o acciones que faltan el respeto a algo sagrado.

boga *sust.* moda.

borda *sust.* bordes superiores de los costados de un barco.

bravura *sust.* coraje; valentía.

búnker *sust.* depósito o cámara hecha de tierra o cemento, construida en su mayoría o totalmente bajo tierra.

C

calamidad *sust.* desdicha; desgracia; gran desgracia; desastre.

calibre *sust.* cualidad o capacidad.

camaradería *sust.* relación alegre entre amigos; fraternidad.

camuflaje *sust.* disfraz o apariencia falsa adoptada para disimular.

canción melódica *sust.* canción cantada en voz baja.

cándido *adj.* sincero; honesto.

candor *sust.* estado o cualidad de ser inexperto o ingenuo.

caravana *sust.* grupo de vehículos acompañado por una escolta.

carcajear *v.* reír en voz alta y de manera ordinaria.

carnicería *sust.* gran matanza.

casamentero *sust.* persona que concierta matrimonios presentando a las posibles parejas.

causar *v.* hacer; crear.

cautela *sust.* reserva.

cautivante *adj.* fascinante; que hipnotiza.

cavilosamente *adv.* pensativamente.

censurar *v.* cortar o cambiar para eliminar material que se considera inaceptable.

chal *adj.* paño de seda o lana que se usa sobre los hombros.

chartreuse *adj.* verde claro amarillento.

chillón *adj.* demasiado brillante y llamativo para ser de buen gusto; vulgar y extravagante.

cigarra *sust.* insecto parecido al grillo que emite un sonido fuerte y agudo.

clamor *sust.* ruido fuerte; reclamo o queja fuerte.

clientela *sust.* los clientes de una empresa.

codiciar *v.* desear ardientemente algo.

coherente *adj.* claro, lógico, consistente.

colmado *adj.* lleno de algo.

compeler *v.* obligar; forzar.

comunitario *adj.* que se usa o se comparte entre todos los miembros de un grupo.

conceder *v.* admitir; reconocer.

concentración *sust.* reunión.

concepción *sust.* formación mental de las ideas.

concesión *sust.* acto de ceder.

concordar *v.* ocupar el mismo espacio o existir al mismo tiempo; estar de acuerdo.

conferir *v.* hablar sobre un tema; consultar.

conjeturar *v.* adivinar.

conjurar *v.* hacer que algo ocurra por medio de la magia o como si fuera por obra de magia.

conmovedor *adj.* emotivo o emocionante.

consejo *sust.* reunión para obtener información o intercambiar ideas.

consolar *v.* reconfortar.

conspicuo *adj.* claramente visible; fácil de ver.

consternado *adj.* muy preocupado.

consternar *v.* horrorizar; llenar de sorpresa.

consumir *v.* extinguir; destruir.

contrición *sust.* pesar o dolor por un mal causado; arrepentimiento.

convenio *sust.* pacto; acuerdo.

convicción *sust.* creencia firme.

copioso *adj.* más que suficiente; abundante.

cosecha *sust.* recolección de cultivos o cosas.

cosechar *v.* recoger un cultivo.

crepúsculo *sust.* período entre la puesta del sol y la noche; en este momento del día, el sol brilla con una luz tenue.

cripta *sust.* tumba subterránea.

cromo *sust.* elemento metálico duro y brilloso que se usa en las aleaciones de acero.

crónica *sust.* relato de sucesos pasados; historia.

crucial *adj.* crítico; decisivo.

cuestionar *v.* expresar desacuerdo.

D

deambular *v.* caminar sin dirección, perdiendo el tiempo.

declaración *sust.* testimonio que se da bajo juramento en un juicio.

deliberadamente *adv.* intencionalmente; hecho con total consciencia.

demacrado *adj.* que luce cansado por dolor, hambre, preocupación o fatiga.

demacrado *adj.* que se ve cansado y consumido.

deplorable *adj.* lamentable; angustiante.

deplorar *v.* condenar algo por ser incorrecto;

reprobar.

deportar *v.* enviar o llevar; transportar, especialmente por la fuerza.

derramar *v.* desechar.

desamparado *adj.* solo y triste; abandonado.

desatendido *adj.* desoído; ignorado.

descarnado *adj.* muy delgado y huesudo.

descaro *sust.* atrevimiento.

descollar *v.* exceder en tamaño; sobresalir.

desconcertante *v.* sin explicación; sorprendente.

desdén *sust.* sentimiento de que algo no tiene valor; desprecio.

desdeñar *v.* rechazar; desaprobar; despreciar.

desenfadado *adj.* desenvuelto, informal.

desgarrador *adj.* profundamente doloroso, ya sea a nivel emocional o físico.

designar *v.* nombrar.

desilusión *sust.* estado de la ausencia de ilusión.

desistir *v.* renunciar.

desolado *adj.* desierto; inhóspito; pelado.

desollar *v.* azotar; fustigar.

desplegar *v.* desdoblar o extender, como una bandera.

despotismo *sust.* gobierno en manos de un tirano o un rey con poder ilimitado.

desvencijado *adj.* descuidado o arruinado por falta de cuidado.

deteriorar *v.* empeorar.

determinar *v.* decidir; concluir; establecer con certeza.

detractar *v.* quitar importancia a algo.

devastación *sust.* destrucción violenta.

devoto *adj.* muy dedicado a la propia religión.

diálogo *sust.* conversación escrita u oral.

diplomático *adj.* que tiene capacidad para decir y hacer lo correcto.

disensión *sust.* discusión provocada por una diferencia de opiniones.

disimular *v.* ocultar sentimientos o motivos.

dispendio *sust.* cantidad gastada.

disputa *sust.* lucha; conflicto.

distinguido *adj.* de renombre o socialmente importante.

distorsionar *v.* torcer; dar una forma anormal.

divagar *v.* desviarse del tema principal.

diverso *adj.* variado, muchos.

dominio *sust.* control; poder de gobernar; reino.

dote *sust.* dinero o propiedades que una esposa aporta a su esposo al casarse.

dúctil *adj.* que puede volver a su forma original después de ser doblado, comprimido o estirado.

E

ecléctico *adj.* compuesto de una variedad de elementos.

efímero *adj.* fugaz; breve.

egotismo *sust.* pensamiento excesivo sobre uno mismo.

ejercicio *sust.* duración de un cargo o puesto.

elisión *sust.* "omisión de una vocal, una consonante o una sílaba en la pronunciación.

elocuencia *sust.* manera expresiva y elegante de hablar; gran capacidad de expresión..

eludir *v.* evitar ser detectado o descubierto.

elusivo *adj.* que tiende a evadir.

embestida *sust.* ataque brutal e intenso.

embrollo *sust.* situación confusa y problemática; enredo.

encrespar *v.* enfurecer; enfadar.

encubrir *v.* ocultar; esconder.

endeble *adj.* físicamente débil.

endeudado *adj.* que está en deuda.

engalanado *adj.* adornado.

engañar *v.* confundir; hacer creer lo que no es.

época *sust.* período de tiempo notable.

erradicar *v.* eliminar; deshacerse de algo; destruirlo por completo.

escandaloso *adj.* muy famoso por motivos negativos.

escarmiento *sust.* castigo.

escarnio *sust.* burla, desprecio.

esclarecimiento *sust.* ilustración intelectual o espiritual.

escombro *sust.* resto de algo roto o destruido; ruinas.

esmalte *sust.* revestimiento suave, duro y brillante.

esmirriado *adj.* muy delgado.

espasmo *sust.* experiencia breve y repentina de actividad o energía intensa.

espigar *v.* recoger la producción que quedó después de cosechar un cultivo.

esplendor *sust.* grandeza.

esporádicamente *adv.* de manera irregular; de vez en cuando.

estabilidad *sust.* equilibrio.

estadía *sust.* permanencia temporal en un lugar.

estancado *adj.* que no fluye o no se mueve.

estigma *sust.* marca de verguenza.

etéreo *adj.* que no pertenece a la tierra; espiritual.

evadir *v.* evitar algo con astucia; esquivar.

evasivo *adj.* que no se compromete con una visión o un accionar en particular.

exento *adj.* libre de un deber u otra restricción.

exiguo *adj.* pobre, escaso, inadecuado.

exorbitante *adj.* excesivo.

expedición *sust.* viaje de exploración.

expresar *v.* comunicar; expresar.

extremidades *sust.* los miembros del cuerpo, especialmente las manos y los pies.

exuberante *adj.* rico; abundante.

F

farsa *sust.* engaño; simulación descarada.

fascinar *v.* encantar.

fascismo *sust.* sistema de gobierno y organización social autoritario y nacionalista de derecha. El término se usó por primera vez para caracterizar el régimen totalitario nacionalista de derecha de Benito Mussolini en Italia (1922–1943).

febril *adj.* excitado, inquieto.

fechoría *sust.* broma tonta.

fervientemente *adv.* de manera apasionada e intensa.

florecer *v.* crecer; prosperar.

florido *adj.* que tiene demasiados adornos; llamativo.

fomentar *v.* estimular; promover.

forjar *v.* calentar y dar forma a los metales.

frenesí *sust.* comportamiento frenético; desenfreno.

frugalidad *sust.* ahorro.

funesto *adj.* de mal agüero; amenazador; triste.

G

gárrulo *adj.* que habla mucho, especialmente de cosas sin importancia.

glaseado *adj.* cubierto con una capa delgada y brillante.

globular *adj.* que tiene forma de esfera; esférico.

gloria *sust.* gran belleza; esplendor.

gratificación *sust.* satisfacción; placer.

gratuito *adj.* sin razón, desmedido.

grotesco *adj.* ridículo; absurdo.

gueto *sust.* sección densamente poblada de una ciudad, habitada principalmente por miembros de un grupo étnico u otro grupo minoritario, por lo general como resultado de restricciones sociales o económicas.

H

habitar *v.* vivir en un lugar.

halo *sust.* círculo de luz.

histeria *sust.* emoción descontrolada.

holgazanear *v.* permanecer en un lugar sin una ocupación.

holístico *adj.* relacionado con la totalidad de algo y no con sus partes por separado.

homenaje *sust.* respetar; venerar.

hoscamente *adv.* de manera silenciosa y resentida; de mala gana.

hurgar *v.* buscar meticulosamente moviendo cosas.

I

idealista *sust.* persona que tiene principios o metas elevadas.

impecablemente *adv.* perfectamente; sin errores ni defectos.

impedir *v.* evitar.

impeler *v.* impulsar; dar empuje para que algo ocurra.

imperceptible *adj.* tan leve que no se nota.

imperioso *adj.* que no debe evitarse; urgente.

implorar *v.* rogar.

impregnar *v.* esparcir (un color, un líquido o una tintura).

improvisado *adj.* repentino; sin preparación.

improvisar *v.* preparado en el momento; hecho para la ocasión.

impunidad *sust.* impunidad ante un daño o castigo.

inamovible *adj.* que no cede; inflexible.

inanimado *adj.* sin vida.

inarticulado *adj.* que no se expresa en sílabas o palabras claras; confuso.

inaudito *adj.* que nunca antes ocurrió.

incesantemente *adv.* sin detenerse; constantemente.

incitación *sust.* algo que provoca una acción o un sentimiento.

inclinarse *v.* saludar.

inconcebible *adj.* que no se puede imaginar; que va más allá de la comprensión.

incorporar *v.* combinar o mezclar.

incorpóreo *adj.* similar a un espíritu; liberado del cuerpo.

incorrección *sust.* conducta inadecuada.

indigente *sust.* persona extremadamente pobre.

inducir *v.* hacer que algo suceda; impulsar.

inerte *adj.* inactivo; inmóvil.

inescrutable *adj.* misterioso.

infame *adj.* que tiene mala reputación.

inferir *v.* adivinar o concluir a partir de pocas pruebas.

infernal *adj.* perteneciente o relativo al infierno; desagradable.

infinitesimal *adj.* indefinidamente o sumamente pequeño; mínimo.

infligir *v.* causar algo negativo.

influencia *sust.* efecto; capacidad de afectar.

infortunio *sust.* algo que provoca desesperanza o ruina.

infranqueable *adj.* que no se puede superar.

infringir *v.* romper.

ingenioso *adj.* inteligente.

inherente *adj.* innato; que es parte de la naturaleza de algo.

ininteligible *adj.* incomprensible.

iniquidad *sust.* maldad.

inmaculado *adj.* puro.

inmortalidad *sust.* existencia que no tiene fin.

inquietud *sust.* inseguridad que produce ansiedad.

insensato *adj.* sin sentido; estúpido.

insidioso *adj.* malicioso; traicionero.

insolencia *sust.* grosería; comportamiento irrespetuoso.

insolente *adj.* descaradamente irrespetuoso.

insurrección *sust.* levantamiento; rebelión.

intangible *adj.* que no se puede tocar ni sentir.

integrar *v.* formar un todo.

integridad *sust.* principios morales firmes; honestidad.

interminable *adj.* que no se detiene nunca; continuo; que parece durar para siempre.

interponer *v.* poner algo con el objeto de interferir.

intransigente *adj.* inflexible.

intriga *sust.* conspiración, maquinación.

intrincado *adj.* complejo; complicado.

intruso *sust.* que se ha introducido sin derecho.

intuitivamente *adv.* sin razonamiento consciente.

irreverente *adj.* que no expresa el respeto debido.

irrevocablemente *adv.* permanentemente, irreversiblemente.

irritabilidad *sust.* mal genio; falta de paciencia.

itinerante *adj.* que migra.

J

jocoso *adj.* gracioso; chistoso.

júbilo *sust.* alegría.

L

laberinto *sust.* complejo desconcertante.

ladino *sust.* astuto o hábil.

lastimero *adj.* digno de compasión; que expresa tristeza.

latente *adj.* existente pero escondido o inactivo.

legado *sust.* dinero u otra propiedad que se da a una persona mediante el testamento de alguien que falleció.

leonino *adj.* relacionado con un león o parecido a él.

letargo *sust.* somnolencia anormal.

licenciosamente *adv.* sin cuidado y, en general, con mala intención.

lividez *sust.* falta de color antinatural.

loa *sust.* discurso que expresa elogios y admiración.

lobreguez *sust.* oscuridad.

lúcido *adj.* claro en el razonamiento; que no está confundido.

lustre *sust.* brillo; resplandor.

lustroso *adj.* brillante; luminoso.

M

madeja *sust.* atado de hilo enrollado sin apretar.

malevolencia *sust.* deseo de que les sucedan cosas malas a otras personas.

malicia *sust.* mala intención; deseo de dañar.

malicioso *adj.* intencionalmente hiriente.

manifiesto *adj.* obvio; evidente.

marchitar *v.* secar; debilitar.

martirio *sust.* muerte dolorosa de un mártir.

mastodóntico *adj.* enorme, pesado o torpe.

medio *sust.* material para un artista.

melancólico *adj.* triste o que sugiere tristeza.

melodía *sust.* disposición de notas musicales que forman una canción.

melodioso *adj.* de sonido agradable; musical.

menguar *v.* disminuir.

menospreciar *v.* rechazar.

mitigación *sust.* factor que modera o suaviza.

mitocondria *sust.* organismos microscópicos que ayudan a las células a convertir los alimentos en energía que el cuerpo puede usar.

mórbido *adj.* enfermo; malsano.

muchedumbre *sust.* multitud alborotada.

N

nevera *sust.* refrigerador.

nómade *adj.* que deambula.

nominal *adj.* que existe en nombre pero no en la realidad.

nuca *sust.* parte de atrás del cuello.

nuclear *adj.* central; que actúa como el centro alrededor del cual giran otras cosas.

O

objetar *v.* oponerse o expresar desacuerdo.

obliterar *v.* borrar o eliminar.

obtuso *adj.* lento para comprender; estúpido.

ominoso *adj.* de mal agüero; amenazador.

opaco *adj.* que no es transparente; que no deja pasar la luz.

oprobio *sust.* conducta vergonzosa.

ornar *v.* mejorar algo con adornos.

ortopédico *adj.* relacionado con el área de la medicina que se ocupa de los huesos, las articulaciones o los músculos.

oscilar *v.* moverse de un lado a otro.

ostensible *adj.* que puede detectarse; perceptible.

ostentoso *adj.* que atrae mucho la atención.

ostracismo *sust.* destierro; acto de ser expulsado o excluido.

P

palpable *adj.* obvio; que se puede percibir.
palpable *adj.* que se puede tocar o sentir.
pandemónium *sust.* gran confusión.
partidario *sust.* firme seguidor de una causa.
patrocinio *sust.* empresa sostenida por los clientes.
pegajoso *adj.* frío y húmedo.
percibir *v.* observar; notar; comprender.
perdurar *v.* mantenerse o prolongarse.
perfidia *sust.* traición.
pernicioso *adj.* dañino; malvado.
perplejo *adj.* confundido, desorientado.
persistente *adj.* continuo.
persistir *v.* continuar; durar.
personaje *sust.* personalidad pública.
perspicaz *adj.* inteligente y de comprensión aguda.
persuadir *v.* influir.
pertinaz *adj.* terco.
perturbado *adj.* inquieto; ansioso.
pervertir *v.* dar malos consejos o ejemplos; corromper.
pináculo *sust.* cumbre; cima.
plañir *v.* llorar y sollozar de tristeza.
plantar *v.* rechazar a alguien como amante.
posteridad *sust.* las generaciones que vendrán.
postrado *adj.* tendido.
precario *adj.* inseguro; inestable; riesgoso.
preconcepto *sust.* opinión formada de antemano.
predominante *adj.* que existe ampliamente; corriente.
preponderante *adj.* que tiene una gran influencia o poder.
prerrogativa *sust.* privilegio o derecho exclusivo.
presteza *sust.* rapidez y entusiasmo para responder.
prestigioso *adj.* admirable; que tiene distinción.
pretensión *sust.* reclamación falsa.
primordialmente *adv.* ante todo lo demás.
privar *v.* ocultar algo a alguien por maldad.
procurar *v.* conseguir; causar.
prodigio *sust.* persona muy talentosa.
prodigioso *adj.* admirable; atractivo; espectacular.
profano *adj.* que no es religioso; despectivo, irrespetuoso.
profundidad *sust.* algo muy significativo.
profusamente *adv.* en grandes cantidades.
profusión *sust.* gran abundancia.
progresivo *adj.* que se agrava con el tiempo.
proliferación *sust.* expansión de pensamientos e ideas.

prominencia *sust.* gran distinción o reconocimiento.
prominente *adj.* saliente; destacado.
promocionar *v.* elogiar mucho.
propagar *v.* expandir o extender por todo el lugar.
protésico *adj.* relacionado al reemplazo artificial de una parte del cuerpo que falta.
provisional *adj.* condicional; que depende de otra cosa.
prudencia *sust.* cuidado.
pseudónimo *sust.* nombre falso.
pulverizar *v.* aplastar; destruir.

Q

quebrada *sust.* valle angosto entre montañas.

R

rabínico *adj.* relativo a los rabinos, o líderes espirituales de la religión judía.
rectitud *sust.* corrección.
reiteración *sust.* repetición.
reivindicar *v.* probar que algo es correcto.
remilgadamente *adv.* de manera muy refinada o elegante.
remuneración *sust.* pago.
renacimiento *sus.* renovación; resurgimiento.
reñir *v.* pelear por algo que no es importante; discutir.
renombre *sust.* fama.
renovado *adj.* restaurar; modernizar.
réplica *sust.* respuesta severa, aguda o ingeniosa.
reprender *v.* advertir con delicadeza.
resarcimiento *sust.* reparar un mal ocasionado.
restaurar *v.* arreglar; renovar.
resucitar *v.* volver a la vida.
resuelto *adj.* decidido; firme.
resultar *v.* llegar a ser.
resurgimiento *sust.* volver a aparecer; surgir de nuevo.
reticente *adj.* que duda en hablar; reservado.
retirar *v.* hacerse más distante y menos definido.
retórico *adj.* que se usa solamente para crear un efecto o por razones de estilo; artificial.
reverencial *adj.* muy respetuoso.
revivir *v.* volver a la vida.
rígido *adj.* firme; duro.
risueño *adj.* feliz y alegre; despreocupado.
robusto *adj.* fuerte y saludable.
rollizo *adj.* redondo; regordete.
rotonda *sust.* edificio con forma de cilindro tanto dentro como fuera, normalmente cubierto con una cúpula.

S

sabio *sust.* persona con mucha sabiduría.

saqueo *sust.* acción de apoderarse violentamente de los objetos que se hallan en un lugar, especialmente en tiempos de guerra.

sarcástico *adj.* desdeñoso; burlón.

segregación *sust.* separación de un grupo racial de otro o del resto de la sociedad.

sembrar *v.* esparcir semillas; plantar.

señorialmente *adv.* grandiosamente; majestuosamente.

sentina *sust.* agua sucia que se acumula en la parte inferior de un barco.

sepia *adj.* de color marrón rojizo, como las fotografías viejas.

serenamente *adv.* calmadamente.

sien *sust.* costados de la frente, sobre los oídos y delante de ellos.

simétrico *adj.* proporcionado; equilibrado.

simplificar *v.* hacer más fácil.

sincopado *adj.* melodía en la que los acentos están en notas que normalmente no están acentuadas.

soberano *sust.* persona, grupo o nación que tiene control supremo.

sofocar *v.* ahogar; extinguir.

soldar *v.* unir cosas fuertemente con metal derretido.

solemne *adj.* serio.

sombrío *adj.* tenebroso; oscuro.

somero *adj.* llevado a cabo rápidamente y sin las formalidades adecuadas.

someter *v.* imponer a alguien una acción o un tratamiento; dominar con una fuerza superior; conquistar.

staccato *adj.* formado por irrupciones cortas de sonido.

subsistente *adj.* que se mantiene vivo.

sucesivo *adj.* siguiente.

sumamente *adv.* profundamente; completamente.

sumir *v.* envolver.

superficial *adj.* sin profundidad.

superfluo *adj.* que está de más; innecesario.

súplica *sust.* ruego; plegaria.

suplicar *v.* pedir sinceramente; rogar.

suscitar *v.* despertar una respuesta de alguien o algo.

T

tabú *sust.* restricción social.

taciturno *adj.* triste y silencioso.

talla *sust.* importancia; valor.

tambalear *v.* moverse hacia adelante y hacia atrás.

tangible *adj.* perceptible al tacto; táctil.

tedioso *adj.* cansador; aburrido.

temperamento *sust.* el modo personal de actuar ante otras personas o de hablar acerca de algo.

tempestad *sust.* tormenta violenta.

templado *adj.* moderadamente caliente.

tenaz *adj.* perseverante; firme en su propósito.

tenue *adj.* leve; de poca sustancia; débil.

teocracia *sust.* gobierno dirigido por una autoridad religiosa.

terrón *sust.* terrón de tierra.

tiniebla *sust.* estado de ignorancia o falta de conocimiento.

tiranía *sust.* uso cruel del poder.

topar *v.* encontrar o enfrentar.

torbellino *sust.* pequeño remolino.

torcido *adj.* encorvado.

torniquete *sust.* instrumento para evitar la pérdida de sangre cuando se amputa una extremidad del cuerpo.

tosco *adj.* ordinario y grosero.

totalidad *sust.* recolección de cosas separadas para formar una masa o un conjunto.

transición *sust.* paso de una condición, forma o estado a otro.

transparente *adj.* cualidad de los objetos a través de los que se puede ver.

trascendente *adj.* sobresaliente; incomparable.

trascender *v.* superar, sobrepasar.

traumático *adj.* emocional o físicamente grave.

trepidación *sust.* temblor por miedo, alarma o inquietud.

trivialidad *sust.* algo sin valor.

tumultuosamente *adv.* violentamente.

tumultuoso *adj.* muy ruidoso, desordenado o agitado.

turbulencia *sust.* gran desorden.

U

urbanidad *sust.* conducta respetuosa o amable.

V

vacío *adj.* sin pensamiento.

vanidad *sust.* orgullo excesivo.

vano *adj.* inútil; sin sentido.

vástago *sust.* rama de un árbol.

vehementemente *adv.* con mucha fuerza o intensidad.

venerable *adj.* viejo y respetado.

verificar *v.* probar que algo es verdadero.

verosimilitud *sust.* credibilidad.

vestigio *sust.* resto.

vibrante *adj.* lleno de energía.

viga *sust.* pedazo de madera largo y grueso listo para usar en una construcción.

vigilante *sust.* alguien que está siempre alerta.

virulento *adj.* lleno de odio; nocivo.

volición *sust.* elección consciente; voluntad; determinación.

vulnerabilidad *sust.* condición de estar expuesto a un ataque o una lesión.

Z

zancada *sust.* paso largo.

zumbido *sust.* sonido sordo y monótono.

Academic Vocabulary Glossary

The Academic Vocabulary Glossary in this section is an alphabetical list of the Academic Vocabulary words found in this textbook. Use this glossary just as you would use a dictionary—to find out the meanings of words used in your literature class to talk about and write about literary and informational texts and to talk about and write about concepts and topics in your other academic classes.

For each word, the glossary includes the pronunciation, part of speech, and meaning. A Spanish version of the glossary immediately follows the English version. For more information about the words in the Academic Vocabulary Glossary, please consult a dictionary.

ENGLISH

A

advocate (AD vuh kayt) *v.* support; argue for.
alternative (awl TUR nuh tihv) *n.* a choice between two things.
aspect (AS pehkt) *n.* a side of something; part.

C

capacity (kuh PAS uh tee) *n.* ability.
cite (syt) *v.* quote as an authority; give as an example.
component (kuhm POH nuhnt) *n.* one of the parts that make up a whole.
contemporary (kuhn TEHM puh rehr ee) *adj.* living or happening at the same time.
criteria (kry TIHR ee uh) *n.* standards on which an argument is based.
crucial (KROO shuhl) *adj.* necessary.

D

diverse (duh VURS) *adj.* varied.

F

factor (FAK tuhr) *n.* one element in a situation.
fundamental (fuhn duh MEHN tuhl) *adj.* essential; underlying.

H

hierarchy (HY uh rahr kee) *n.* ranking persons or things higher or lower within categories.

I

ideology (y dee AHL uh jee) *n.* a set of doctrines or opinions.
implicit (ihm PLIHS iht) *adj.* implied; suggested yet not plainly expressed.
inevitable (ihn EHV uh tuh buhl) *adj.* unavoidable.
integral (IHN tuh gruhl) *adj.* necessary for completeness; essential.
interpret (ihn TUR priht) *v.* explain the meaning of.
intrinsic (ihn TRIHN sihk) *adj.* essential; inherent.

P

parameter (puh RAM uh tuhr) *n.* limitation; boundary.
perspective (puhr SPEHK tihv) *n.* point of view.
potential (puh TEHN shuhl) *adj.* expressing possibility.
principal (PRIHN suh puhl) *adj.* most important; main.
principle (PRIHN suh puhl) *n.* primary truth; rule of conduct.

R

relevant (REHL uh vuhnt) *adj.* pertinent to the matter at hand.

S

subsequent (SUHB sih kwuhnt) *adj.* following; coming after.
sustain (suh STAYN) *v.* maintain or prolong.

T

tradition (truh DIHSH uhn) *n.* beliefs and customs handed down through generations.
transform (trans FAWRM) *v.* change in form or condition.
transmit (trans MIHT) *v.* pass along; communicate.

SPANISH

A

abogar *v.* defender; hablar a favor de alguien.
alternativa *sust.* opción entre dos cosas.
aspecto *sust.* parte o faceta de algo.

C

citar *v.* hacer mención de alguien o algo; dar como ejemplo.

Academic Vocabulary Glossary

componente *sust.* una de las partes que forman un todo.

contemporáneo *adj.* que existe o sucede en el mismo tiempo que otra cosa o persona.

criterio *sust.* estándar sobre el que se basa un argumento.

crucial *adj.* necesario.

D

diverso *adj.* variado.

F

factor *sust.* uno de los elementos de una situación.

facultad *sust.* capacidad.

fundamental *adj.* esencial; vital.

I

ideología *sust.* conjunto de doctrinas u opiniones.

implícito *adj.* insinuado; sugerido pero no expresado de manera clara o directa.

indefectible *adj.* inevitable.

indispensable *adj.* necesario para completar algo; esencial.

interpretar *v.* explicar el significado de algo.

intrìnseco *adj.* esencial; inherente.

J

jerarquía *sust.* clasificación de personas o cosas en categorías más altas o más bajas.

M

margen *sust.* límite.

P

perdurar *v.* mantenerse o prolongarse.

perspectiva *sust.* punto de vista.

pertinente *adj.* relevante para el tema en cuestión.

potencial *adj.* que expresa posibilidad.

primordial *adj.* de mucha importancia; principal.

principio *sust.* verdad primaria; norma de conducta.

S

sucesivo *adj.* siguiente; a continuación de otro.

T

tradición *sust.* creencias y costumbres transmitidas de generación en generación.

transformar *v.* cambiar la forma o la condición de algo.

transmitir *v.* pasar; comunicar.

ACKNOWLEDGMENTS

For permission to reprint copyrighted material, grateful acknowledgment is made to the following sources:

"Plenos Poderes" from *Plenos Poderes* by Pablo Neruda. Copyright © 1962 by Pablo Neruda and Fundación Pablo Neruda; copyright renewed © 2007 by Herederos Pablo Neruda. Reproduced by permission of **Agencia Literaria Carmen Balcells, S.A.**

"Coyote Finishes His Work" from *Giving Birth to Thunder, Sleeping with His Daughter* by Barry Holstun Lopez. Copyright © 1977 by Barry Holstun Lopez. All rights reserved. Reproduced by permission of **Andrews McMeel Publishing.**

"The Latin Deli: An Ars Poetica" by Judith Ortiz Cofer from *The Americas Review,* vol. 19, no. 1. Copyright © 1991 by Judith Ortiz Cofer. Published by **Arte Público Press–University of Houston, 1991.** Reproduced by permission of the publisher.

"Emily Dickinson" (English and Spanish version) from *Palabras de Mediodía/Noon Words* by Lucha Corpi, translated by Catherine Rodríguez-Nieto. Copyright © 1980 by Lucha Corpi and Catherine Rodríguez-Nieto. Reproduced by permission of **Arte Público Press - University of Houston, Houston, TX.**

"Now and Then, America" from *Borders* by Pat Mora. Copyright © 1986 by Pat Mora. Published by Arte Público Press–University of Houston, 1986. Reproduced by permission of **Arte Público Press - University of Houston, Houston, TX.**

"Sonnet XXX" (retitled "Love is not all") of *Fatal Interview* from *Collected Poems* by Edna St. Vincent Millay. Copyright © 1931, 1958 by Edna St. Vincent Millay and Norma Millay Ellis. Published by HarperCollins. All rights reserved. Reproduced by permission of **Elizabeth Barnett, Literary Executor.**

"Autobiographical Notes" and excerpts from *Notes of a Native Son* by James Baldwin. Copyright © 1955 and renewed © 1983 by James Baldwin. Reproduced by permission of **Beacon Press, Boston.**

"How I Learned to Sweep" from *Homecoming* by Julia Alvarez. Copyright © 1984, 1996 by Julia Alvarez. Published by Plume, an imprint of Dutton Signet, a division of Penguin Group (USA). Originally published by Grove Press. All rights reserved. Reproduced by permission of **Susan Bergholz Literary Services, New York, NY, and Lamy, NM.**

"Daughter of Invention" from *How the García Girls Lost Their Accents* by Julia Alvarez. Copyright © 1991 by Julia Alvarez. Published by Plume, an imprint of Dutton Signet, a division of Penguin Group (USA). Originally published in hardcover by Algonquin Books of Chapel Hill. All rights reserved. Reproduced by permission of **Susan Bergholz Literary Services, New York, NY, and Lamy, NM.**

"Straw into Gold" by Sandra Cisneros. Copyright © 1987 by Sandra Cisneros. First published in *The Texas Observer,* September 1987. All rights reserved. Reproduced by permission of **Susan Bergholz Literary Services, New York, NY, and Lamy, NM.**

"Visions and Interpretations" from *Rose* by Li-Young Lee. Copyright © 1986 by Li-Young Lee. Reproduced by permission of **BOA Editions, Ltd.**

"at the cemetery, walnut grove plantation, south carolina, 1989" from *Quilting: Poems 1987–1990* by Lucille Clifton. Copyright © 1991 by Lucille Clifton. Reproduced by permission of **BOA Editions, Ltd.**

"The Bean Eaters" from *Blacks* by Gwendolyn Brooks. Copyright © 1991 by Gwendolyn Brooks. Published by Third World Press, Chicago, 1991. Reproduced by permission of **Brooks Permissions.**

"In Honor of David Anderson Brooks, My Father" from *Blacks* by Gwendolyn Brooks. Copyright © 1991 by Gwendolyn Brooks. Published by Third World Press, Chicago, 1991. Reproduced by permission of **Brooks Permissions.**

From "Lucille Clifton" from *The Language of Life: A Festival of Poets* by Bill Moyers. Copyright © 1995 by Public Affairs Television, Inc. and David Grubin Productions, Inc. Reproduced by permission of **Doubleday, a division of Random House, Inc., www.randomhouse.com.**

"Joyas Voladoras" by Brian Doyle from *The American Scholar,* Autumn 2004. Copyright © 2004 by **Brian Doyle.** Reproduced by permission of the author.

"The Fall of the House of Usher (graphic adaptation)" from *Graphic Classics: Edgar Allan Poe,* edited by Tom Pomplun, adapted by Matt Howarth. Copyright © 2004 by **Eureka Productions.** Reproduced by permission of the publisher.

"Trying to Name What Doesn't Change" from *Words Under the Words: Selected Poems* by Naomi Shihab Nye. Copyright © 1995 by Naomi Shihab Nye. Reproduced by permission of **Far Corner Books, Portland, OR.**

"The Fish" from *The Complete Poems 1927–1979* by Elizabeth Bishop. Copyright © 1979, 1983 by Alice Helen Methfessel. Reproduced by permission of **Farrar, Straus and Giroux, LLC.**

"One Art" from *The Complete Poems 1927–1979* by Elizabeth Bishop. Copyright © 1979, 1983 by Alice Helen Methfessel. Reproduced by permission of **Farrar, Straus and Giroux, LLC.**

"The Death of the Ball Turret Gunner" from *The Complete Poems* by Randall Jarrell. Copyright © 1969 and renewed © 1997 by Mary von S. Jarrell. Reproduced by permission of **Farrar, Straus and Giroux, LLC.**

"The Magic Barrel" from *The Magic Barrel* by Bernard Malamud. Copyright © 1950, 1958 and renewed © 1977, 1986 by Bernard Malamud. Reproduced by permission of **Farrar, Straus and Giroux, LLC** and electronic format by permission of **Russell & Volkening, Inc.** as agents for the author.

"Coming Up Harlem" by **Peter Hellman** from *Smithsonian Magazine* Web site, November 2002, accessed February 11, 2008 at http://www.smithsonianmag.com/travel/harlem.html. Copyright © 2002 by Peter Hellman. Reproduced by permission of the author.

From "When the Negro Was in Vogue" (retitled "Heyday in Harlem") from *The Big Sea* by Langston Hughes. Copyright © 1940 by Langston Hughes; copyright renewed © 1968 by Arna Bontemps and George Houston Bass. Reproduced by permission of **Hill and Wang, a division of Farrar, Straus and Giroux, LLC** and electronic format by **Harold Ober Associates Incorporated.**

Slightly adapted from *Night* by Elie Wiesel, translated by Marion Wiesel. Copyright © 1972, 1985 by Elie Wiesel; translation copyright © 2006 by Marion Wiesel. Reproduced by permission of **Hill and Wang, a division of Farrar, Straus and Giroux LLC** and electronic format by permission of **Georges Borchardt, Inc.**

"When Mr. Pirzada Came to Dine" from *Interpreter of Maladies* by Jhumpa Lahiri. Copyright © 1999 by Jhumpa Lahiri. All rights reserved. Reproduced by permission of **Houghton Mifflin Company,** www.hmco.com.

"Ars Poetica" from *Collected Poems 1917–1982* by Archibald MacLeish. Copyright © 1985 by The Estate of Archibald MacLeish. All rights reserved. Reproduced by permission of **Houghton Mifflin Company.**

"The Bells" from *To Bedlam and Part Way Back* by Anne Sexton. Copyright © 1960 by Anne Sexton; copyright renewed © 1988 by Linda G. Sexton. All rights reserved. Reproduced by permission of **Houghton Mifflin Company** and electronic format by permission of **SLL/Sterling Lord Literistic, Inc.**

"Young" from *All My Pretty Ones* by Anne Sexton. Copyright © 1962 by Anne Sexton; copyright renewed © 1990 by Linda G. Sexton. All rights reserved. Reproduced by permission of **Houghton Mifflin Company** and electronic format by permission of **SLL/Sterling Lord Literistic, Inc.**

"Providence" from *Native Guard: Poems* by Natasha Trethewey. Copyright © 2006 by Natasha Trethewey. All rights reserved. Reproduced by permission of **Houghton Mifflin Company.**

"Why I Wrote *The Crucible*" by Arthur Miller from *The New Yorker,* October 21 and 28, 1996. Copyright © 1996 by Arthur Miller. Reproduced by permission of **International Creative Management, Inc.**

From "On James Baldwin" by Toni Morrison from *The New York Times Book Review,* December 20, 1987. Copyright © 1987 by Toni Morrison. Reproduced by permission of **International Creative Management, Inc.**

From "The Reader as Artist" by Toni Morrison from *The Oprah Magazine,* July 2006. Copyright © 2006 by Toni Morrison. Reproduced by permission of **International Creative Management, Inc.**

"A Walk on the Ice" by Garrison Keillor from *Salon* web site, accessed on May 9, 2007 at http://dir.salon.com/story/opinion/feature/2005/12/07/garrison_keillor/index.html. Published in *The Old Scout/Salon Magazine,* December 7, 2007. Copyright © 2005 by **Garrison Keillor.** Reproduced by permission of the author, c/o Prairie Home Productions, LLC.

From "Letter from Birmingham City Jail" by Martin Luther King, Jr. Copyright © 1963 by Martin Luther King, Jr.; copyright renewed © 1991 by Coretta Scott King. Reproduced by permission of **The Estate of Martin Luther King, Jr., c/o Writers House, LLC, as agent for the proprietor, New York, NY.**

"The Book of the Dead" from *The Dew Breaker* by Edwidge Danticat. Copyright © 2004 by Edwidge Danticat. Originally published in *The New Yorker,* June 1999. Reproduced by permission of **Alfred A. Knopf, a division of Random House, Inc.,** www.randomhouse.com and audio format by permission of **Aragi, Inc.**

"A Noiseless Flash" from *Hiroshima* by John Hersey. Copyright 1946 and renewed © 1974 by John Hersey. Reproduced by permission of **Alfred A. Knopf, a division of Random House, Inc.** and online format by permission of **The Estate of John Hersey.**

"The Weary Blues" from *The Collected Poems of Langston Hughes,* edited by Arnold Rampersad with David Roessel, Associate Editor. Copyright © 1994 by The Estate of Langston Hughes. Reproduced by permission of **Alfred A. Knopf, a division of Random House, Inc.** and electronic format by permission of **Harold Ober Associates Incorporated.**

"Harlem [1]" from *The Selected Poems of Langston Hughes.* Copyright 1926 by Alfred A. Knopf, Inc.; copyright renewed 1954 by Langston Hughes. Copyright © 1994 by The Estate of Langston Hughes. Reproduced by permission of **Alfred A. Knopf, a division of Random House, Inc.** and electronic format by **Harold Ober Associates Incorporated.**

"The Girl Who Wouldn't Talk" from *The Woman Warrior* by Maxine Hong Kingston. Copyright © 1975, 1976 by Maxine Hong Kingston. Reproduced by permission of **Alfred A. Knopf, a division of Random House, Inc.,** www.randomhouse.com.

"Mushrooms" from *The Colossus and Other Poems* by Sylvia Plath. Copyright © 1962 by Sylvia Plath. Reproduced by permission **Alfred A. Knopf, a division of Random House, Inc.** and electronic format by permission of **Edwards Fuglewicz.**

"Domination of Black" from *The Collected Poems of Wallace Stevens.* Copyright 1954 by Wallace Stevens; copyright renewed © 1982 by Holly Stevens. Reproduced by permission of **Alfred A. Knopf, a division of Random House, Inc.,** www.randomhouse.com.

"Son" from *The Early Stories, 1953–1975* by John Updike. Copyright © 2003 by John Updike. Reproduced by permission of **Alfred A. Knopf, a division of Random House, Inc.,** www.randomhouse.com.

PICTURE CREDITS

The illustrations and photographs on the Contents pages are picked up from pages in the textbook.
Credits for those can be found either on the textbook page on which they appear or in the listing below.

Picture Library/The Bridgeman Art Library; **202** (t), The Beinecke Rare Book and Manuscript Library, Yale University Library; (c), Courtesy Norfolk Southern Corporation; (b), ©Ann Ronan Picture Library/HIP/The Image Works; **203** (b), ©Image Select/ Art Resource, NY; **204,** Prints & Photographs Division, Library of Congress, [cph 3b52137]; **206** (l), Prints & Photographs Division, Library of Congress, [rbpe 01501500]; (r), *Girls' Evening School*, (c. 1840) by Unidentified artist, American. Graphite pencil and watercolor on paper. Catalogue Raisonne: Karolik cat.1235, fig.313 (folk artists). Sheet: 34.3 X 45.9cm (13 1/2 X 18 1/16in.). Museum of Fine Arts, Boston. Gift of Maxim Karolik for the M. and M. Karolik Collection of American Watercolors and Drawings, 1800–1875. 53.2431; **207,** ©Jack Naylor Collection/ Picture Research Consultants and Archives; **208,** ©AP Photo/ Greg Gibson; **211** (l), ©Bettmann/CORBIS; (r), ©Tom & Pat Leeson/Photo Researchers, Inc.; **213,** ©Steve Kazlowski/Danita Delimont; **214,** ©Worcester Art Museum, Massachusetts, USA/ The Bridgeman Art Library; **215,** ©Mary Evans Picture Library/ The Image Works; **216,** ©Frank Connor, 20th Century Fox/ Morgan Creek/The Kobal Collection; **217,** *View of the Round-Top in the Catskill Mountains* (1827) by Thomas Cole (1801–1848, American). Oil on panel, 47.31 x 64.45 cm (18 5/8 x 25 3/8 in.). Museum of Fine Arts, Boston. Gift of Martha C. Karolik for M. and M. Karolik Collection of American Paintings, 1815–1865. 47.1200; **218,** *William Cullen Bryant* (1833) by James Frothingham (1786–1864, American). Oil on canvas, 53.66 x 44.13 cm (21 1/8 x 17 3/8 in.). Museum of Fine Arts, Boston. Gift of Maxim Karolik for the M. and M. Karolik Collection of American Paintings, 1815–1865. 62.271; **220–221** (bkgd), ©Gary John Norman/Digital Vision/Getty Images; **221** (inset), ©Collection of the New York Historical Society, USA/The Bridgeman Art Library; **222** (t), ©Gary John Norman/Digital Vision/Getty Images; (b), ©Brooklyn Museum of Art, New York, USA, Bequest of Charles A. Schieren/The Bridgeman Art Library; **224,** ©Hulton Archives/Getty Images; **226,** ©Kristi J. Black/ CORBIS; **229,** ©Jim Mires/Alamy; **231,** By permission of the Houghton Library, Harvard University, Cambridge, Massachusetts; **232,** ©Bettmann/CORBIS; **234,** ©Scott Camazine/Photo Researchers, Inc.; **238,** *Ralph Waldo Emerson* (c.1867) by William Henry Furness, Jr., Oil on canvas, 45 3/4 x 36 3/16 in. Courtesy of the Pennsylvania Academy of the Fine Arts, Philadelphia. Gift of Horace Howard Furness, 1899.8; **240** (bkgd), ©Amy Neunsinger/Riser/Getty Images; (c), ©Smithsonian American Art Museum, Washington, DC/Art Resource, NY; **241, 242** (all), ©Amy Neunsinger/Riser/Getty Images; **246–247,** ©Metropolitan Museum of Art, New York, USA/The Bridgeman Art Library; **250,** ©Art Resource, NY; **254** (t, b), ©Mike Grandmaison/CORBIS; **256** (l, r), ©Sean Justice/CORBIS; (c), ©The Pierpont Morgan Library/Art Resource, NY; **256–257** (bkgd), ©Visions of America, LLC/Alamy; **259** (l), ©Jan Bengtsson/Etsa/ CORBIS; (r), ©Gary Bell/zefa/CORBIS; **260** (l), ©Gunter Marx Photography/CORBIS; (r), ©Sam Diephuis/CORBIS; **262,** ©Tim Laman/National Geographic Image Collection; **267,** ©Robert Visser/Greenpeace; **269,** ©altrendo images/Getty Images; **270,** ©Rudi Von Briel/PhotoEdit, Inc.; **271,** ©Jim West/Alamy; **273,** ©altrendo images/Getty Images; **276** (l), ©Vithalbhai Collection/ DPA/The Image Works; (r), ©Flip Schulke/CORBIS; **279,** ©Bettmann/CORBIS; **282,** ©Charles Moore/Blackstar; **285,** ©Eric Slomanson/ZUMA Press; **286,** ©Nora Good/Masterfile; **290,** ©Pete Leonard/zefa/CORBIS; **293** (bkgd), ©Matt Henry Gunther/ Stone/Getty Images; (inset), ©Comstock Images/Alamy; **294– 295,** ©Jeremy Woodhouse/CORBIS; **298,** ©Jeremy Woodhouse/

Photodisc/Getty Images; **304** (t), ©Mediscan/CORBIS; (b), ©Marcos Appelt/Arcangel Images; **309,** Houghton Mifflin Company; **311,** ©G.E. Kidder Smith/CORBIS; **316,** ©Photodisc/ PunchStock; **318,** Private Collection ©The Bridgeman Art Library; **319** (cl), ©Universal Pictures/Photofest; (cr), ©A.I.P./The Kobal Collection; (bc), ©Warner Brothers/Photofest; **321,** Courtesy Everett Collection; **327,** ©Mary Evans Picture Library/ The Image Works; **331,** Courtesy Everett Collection; **345** (bkgd), (c), ©Mary Evans Picture Library/The Image Works; **347,** ©Scala/ Art Resource, NY; **351,** © Bernard Annebicque/CORBIS; **354,** ©Erich Lessing/Art Resource, NY; **360** (bkgd), ©Arthur Morris/ CORBIS; (inset), ©Polka Dot Images/JUPITERimages; **362,** ©The Marsden Archive/Alamy; **366,** ©CORBIS; **368,** ©Peabody Essex Museum, Salem, Massachusetts, USA/The Bridgeman Art Library; **371, 374,** ©George Klauba/Ann Nathan Gallery; **380,** HRW Photo; **394** (tl), Cover image from *Moby-Dick* by Herman Melville. Copyright ©1967 by Bantam Books, a division of Random House, Inc. Reproduced by permission of the publisher; (tr), Cover image from *Blue Highways* by William Least Heat-Moon. Copyright ©1982, 1999 by William Least Heat-Moon. Reproduced by permission of Little, Brown and Company, a subsidiary of Hachette Book Group USA; (bl), Cover image from *Arctic Dreams* by Barry Lopez. Copyright ©1986 by Barry Holstun Lopez. Reproduced by permission of Vintage Books, a division of Random House, Inc.; (br), Cover image from *American Primitive* by Mary Oliver. Copyright ©1983 by Mary Oliver. Reproduced by permission of Little, Brown and Company, a subsidiary of Hachette Book Group USA; **395** (tl), Cover image from *Middle Passage* by Charles Johnson. Copyright ©1990 by Charles Johnson. Reproduced by permission of Scribner, an imprint of Simon & Schuster Adult Publishing Group; (tr), Cover image from *The Poe Shadow* by Matthew Pearl. Copyright ©2006, 2007 by Matthew Pearl. Reproduced by permission of Random House, Inc.; (bl), Cover image from *Undaunted Courage* by Stephen E. Ambrose. Copyright ©1996 by Ambrose-Tubbs, Inc. Reproduced by permission of Simon & Schuster, Inc.; (br), Cover image from *Woman in the Nineteenth Century* by Margaret Fuller. Copyright ©1999 by Dover Publications, Inc. Reproduced by permission of the publisher; **396–397,** Prints & Photographs Division, Library of Congress, [pga 01888]; **398** (tl), ©Swim Ink 2, LLC/CORBIS; (tr), ©Bettmann/CORBIS; **399** (tl), ©CORBIS; (bl), ©Scala /Art Resource, NY; (br), ©The Art Archive/Culver Pictures; **400,** Prints & Photographs Division, Library of Congress, [ppmsca 08230]; **402, 404** (all), ©Tria Giovan/CORBIS; **405,** *Red Badge of Courage*, Stephen Crane, Special Collections Research Center, Syracuse University Library; **407** (t), ©Kathy McLaughlin/ The Image Works; (c), ©Bettmann/CORBIS; (b), ©AP Photo/Bill Hudson; **408** (all), ©Arkansas Democrat-Gazette, 2007; **409,** ©Jeff Greenberg/The Image Works; **410,** Private Collection, Photo ©Christie's Images/The Bridgeman Art Library; **412,** ©CORBIS; **417,** Photo: The Jacob and Gwendolyn Lawrence Foundation/Art Resource, NY. © 2009 The Jacob and Gwendolyn Lawrence Foundation, Seattle/Artists Rights Society (ARS), New York. From the Collection of the Hampton University; **419,** Photo: The Jacob and Gwendolyn Lawrence Foundation/Art Resource, NY. © 2009 The Jacob and Gwendolyn Lawrence Foundation, Seattle/Artists Rights Society (ARS), New York; **420,** ©AP Photo/Kathleen Lange; **424,** Gilbert Studios, Washington, D.C. c.1894; **426,** ©Bettmann/CORBIS; **428,** ©Brooks Kraft/ CORBIS; **430,** ©Missouri Historical Society; **432** (t), "Go Down Moses, Moses; Let My People Go.", Item #: Music #708, Historic American Sheet Music. Rare Book, Manuscript, and Special

Collections Library, Duke University; (b), "Negro Spiritual Song, Swing Low, Sweet Chariot", Item #: Music #570,no.10, Historic American Sheet Music. Rare Book, Manuscript, and Special Collections Library, Duke University; **434–435** (bkgd), ©Bettmann/CORBIS; **435,** ©The Newark Museum/Art Resource, NY; **436–437,** (bkgd) ©Bettmann/CORBIS; **437,** ©Janice Huse; **438** (t), ©Bettmann/CORBIS; **440,** ©Schomberg Center/Art Resource, NY; **444,** Photo Courtesy of St. Mary's College of Maryland; **449,** Courtesy of the Arthur Roger Gallery; **450,** ©State Museum of Pennsylvania, Pennsylvania Historical and Museum Commission; **452,** Prints & Photographs Division, Library of Congress; **454,** ©Huntington Library/SuperStock; **456** (bkgd), ©Look Photography/Beateworks/CORBIS; (inset), ©DAJ/Getty Images; **458,** ©Films Du Centaure/The Kobal Collection; **461,** Courtesy Alexandre Gallery, New York; **462,** ©Frank Krahmer/Masterfile; **464,** ©Look Photography/Beateworks/CORBIS; **468,** © Kean Collection/Hulton Archive/Getty Images; **471,** ©Harry J. Kellogg/Minnesota Historical Society; **472,** Prints & Photographs Division, Library of Congress, [LC-DIG-cwpb-01001]; **475,** Cooper-Hewitt, National Design Museum, Smithsonian Institution, Gift of Charles Savage Homer, Jr., 1912-12-100; **477,** ©National Vietnam Veterans Art Museum; **483, 484, 485,** ©Brent Stirton/Getty Images News/Getty Images; **488,** ©National Portrait Gallery, Smithsonian Institution, Washington, DC/Art Resource, NY; **490–491,** ©2007 Howard Terpning, Courtesy of The Greenwich Workshop, Inc.; **493,** ©Lester Lefkowitz/CORBIS; **497** (b), Private Collection ©The Bridgeman Art Library; **498–499** (bkgd), Prints & Photographs Division, Library of Congress; **500–501,** Prints & Photographs Division, Library of Congress, [cwpb 03049]; **502** (inset), Private Collection ©The Bridgeman Art Library; **503,** National Archives; **506,** ©Private Collection, David Findlay Jr. Fine Art, NYC, USA/The Bridgeman Art Library; **508,** ©The Pierpont Morgan Library/Art Resource, NY; **510,** ©The Art Archive/National Archives Washington, DC; **511,** ©Bernard Hoffman/Time & Life Pictures/Getty Images; **517,** ©Robin Allen/Index Stock Imagery, Inc.; **519,** ©Terra Foundation for American Art, Chicago/Art Resource, NY; **525,** ©John Foxx/Stockbyte/Getty Images; **526,** ©Tay Rees/The Image Bank/Getty Images; **531,** Fair Street Pictures; **534,** ©Bettmann/CORBIS; **535,** ©Jonathan Montgomery/epa/CORBIS; **538,** ©Corbis Premium Collection/Alamy; **540,** ©Robert Llewellyn/Workbook Stock/JUPITER images; **542,** ©Ozkok/SIPA Press; **544–545,** ©Comstock/PunchStock; **549** (b), ©James Marshall/CORBIS; **551,** ©INSADCO Photography/Alamy; **556,** Clarence H. White, United States of America 1871–1925 Mexico City, Mexico, *Drops of Rain* 1903, photogravure off an original negative, 19.4 X 15.4 cm; **558,** Prints & Photographs Division, Library of Congress, [pga 01849]; **561,** ©Brown Brothers; **562,** ©ArenaPal/Topham/The Image Works; **564,** ©Smithsonian American Art Museum, Washington, DC/Art Resource, NY; **569,** ©Private Collection, Courtesy Fischbach Gallery, New York/The Bridgeman Art Library; **570,** Private Collection, Photo ©Bonhams, London, UK/The Bridgeman Art Library; **573,** Prints & Photographs Division, Library of Congress, [LC-USZ62-73367]; **587,** Eric Camden/Harcourt; **602** (tl), Cover image from *The Living* by Annie Dillard. Copyright ©1992 by Annie Dillard. Reproduced by permission of HarperCollins Publishers Inc.; (tr), Cover image from *Little Women* by Louisa May Alcott. Copyright ©1989 by Viking Penguin, a division of Penguin Group (USA) Inc. Reproduced by permission of the publisher; (bl), Cover image from *Allegiance* by David Detzer. Copyright ©2001 by David Detzer. Reproduced by permission of Harcourt, Inc.; (br), Cover

image from *The Civil War: An Illustrated History* by Geoffrey C. Ward with Ric Burns and Ken Burns. Copyright ©1990 by American Documentaries, Inc. Reproduced by permission of Alfred A. Knopf, a division of Random House Inc.; **603** (tl), Cover image from *José Martí: Selected Writing*, translation and selection by Esther Allen. Translation and selection copyright ©2002 by Esther Allen. Reproduced by permission of Penguin Group (USA) Inc.; (tr), Cover image from *Odes to Common Things* by Pablo Neruda. Copyright ©1994 by Pablo Neruda; translation copyright ©1994 by Ken Krabbenhoft. Reproduced by permission of Bulfinch Press, a subsidiary of Hachette Book Group USA; (bl), Cover image from *Visiting Emily*, edited by Sheila Coghill and Thom Tammaro. Copyright ©2000 by the University of Iowa Press. Reproduced by permission of the publisher; (br), © Image Source/CORBIS, **606** (t, c), ©Bettmann/CORBIS; (bl), ©Ann Ronan Picture Library/HIP/The Image Works; (br), ©Topham/The Image Works; **607** (tl), *The Jungle*, Upton Sinclair, Special Collections Research Center, Syracuse University Library; (tr, c), ©Bettmann/CORBIS; (b), ©Hulton-Deutsch Collection/CORBIS; **608,** ©CORBIS; **611,** ©Gates Foundation/CORBIS; **612,** ©North Wind/North Wind Picture Archives; **613,** Prints & Photographs Division, Library of Congress, [cph 3b00011]; **615,** ©AP Photo/The Daily Progress, Rachel Zahumensky; **616,** © 2009 Jeff Schultz/AlaskaStock Images; **618,** ©Terra Foundation for American Art, Chicago/Art Resource, NY; **620,** ©Anschutz Collection, Colorado, USA/Peter Newark Western Americana/The Bridgeman Art Library; **622,** PictureHistory; **624,** ©Christophe Boisvieux/CORBIS; **627,** ©Nina Leen/Time & Life Pictures/Getty Images; **629,** ©20th Century Fox/The Kobal Collection; **632** (l), ©Goodshoot/CORBIS; (r) ©Christophe Boisvieux/CORBIS; (inset card), ©Cut and Deal/PunchStock; (inset knife), ©MedioImages/CORBIS; **635** (bkgd), ©Philip Gould/CORBIS; (r), ©Bettmann/CORBIS; **636,** From the collection of the Mark Twain House; **637,** Prints & Photographs Division, Library of Congress, [cph 3g04294]; **639,** (r) ©AP Photo/Ron Harris; **640,** ©Jeff White/Frogtown; **642,** ©AP Photo/Ron Harris; **646,** Prints & Photographs Division, Library of Congress, [cph 3c12728]; **650,** ©The New York Public Library/Art Resource, NY; **655,** ©Julie Habel/CORBIS; **656,** ©Bettmann/CORBIS; **659,** ©Layne Kennedy/Time & Life Pictures/Getty Images; **660–661,** ©Joseph Sohm/Visions of America/CORBIS; **663,** Steamboat pilot in the wheelhouse, c.1870 ©Private Collection, Peter Newark American Picture/The Bridgeman Art Library; **668,** Digital image ©The Museum of Modern Art/Licensed by SCALA/Art Resource, NY. With permission, Joanna T. Steichen; **671,** *In the Loge* (1878) by Mary Cassatt (1844–1926, American). Oil on canvas, 81.28 x 66.04 cm (32 x 26 in). Museum of Fine Arts, Boston. The Hayden Collection-Charles Henry Hayden Fund, 10.35; **673,** ©Private Collection, James Goodman Gallery, New York, USA/The Bridgeman Art Library; **677,** ©Michael Rougier/Time & Life Pictures/Getty Images; **680,** The George W. Elkins Collection, 1924. ©The Philadelphia Museum of Art/Art Resource, NY; **682,** ©Missouri Historical Society; **685,** ©Michael Pole/CORBIS; **686** (l), ©Annette Fournet/CORBIS; **686–687,** ©Gildo Nicolo Spadoni/Images.com; **692,** ©The New York Public Library/Art Resource, NY; **694,** ©Mark Cassino/SuperStock; **697,** © 2009 Jeff Schultz/AlaskaStock Images; **699,** ©Mark Seelen/zefa/CORBIS; **703,** ©Edwin Remsberg/Alamy; **709,** ©Michael C. Klesius/National Geographic/Getty Images; **710** (l), ©AP Photo/Dave Watson; (r), ©REUTERS/Gopal Chitrakar; **712,** Courtesy of Colby College Special Collections, Waterville, Maine; **715,** ©Image Source/CORBIS; **716,** ©Tate Gallery,

London, Great Britain/Art Resource, NY; **718,** ©Ohio Historical Society; **720,** Photo: The Jacob and Gwendolyn Lawrence Foundation, Seattle/Art Resource, NY. © 2009 The Jacob and Gwendolyn Lawrence Foundation, Seattle/Artists Rights Society (ARS), New York; **722,** ©Ohio Historical Society; **728,** Victoria Smith/HRW; **740** (tl), Cover image from *Roots* by Alex Haley. Copyright ©1974 by Alex Haley; copyright renewed ©2004 by Myran Haley, Cynthia Haley, Lydia Haley, and William Haley. Reproduced by permission of Vanguard Press, a member of Perseus Books Group; (tr), Cover image from *The Adventures of Huckleberry Finn* by Mark Twain. Reproduced by permission of Holt, Rinehart and Winston; **(bl),** Cover image from *My Ántonia* by Willa Cather. Copyright © 2003 by Barnes & Noble Books. Cover design by Dutton & Sherman; cover art "Spring" by Camille Pissarro. Reproduced by permission of **Barnes & Noble Books;** (br), Cover image from *Up From Slavery* by Booker T. Washington. Copyright ©2000 by Signet Classic. Reproduced by permission of Penguin Group (USA) Inc.; **741** (tl), Cover image from *The Awakening* by Kate Chopin. Copyright ©1993 by Dover Publications, Inc. Reproduced by permission of the publisher; **(tr),** Cover image from *The Autobiography of an Ex-Colored Man* by James Weldon Johnson. Copyright © 2007 by **Filiquarian Publishing, LLC.** Reproduced by permission of the publisher; (bl), Cover image of *Ethan Frome* by Edith Wharton. Copyright ©2005 by Holt, Rinehart and Winston. Cover Illustration, *Mountain Winter*, Woodcut (15" X 10") copyright ©1979 by Sabra Field. Reproduced by permission of Holt, Rinehart and Winston; (br), Cover image from *The Portrait of a Lady* by Henry James. Reproduced by permission of Penguin Books Ltd. (UK); **742–743,** ©Smithsonian American Art Museum, Washington, DC/Art Resource, NY; **744** (t), ©Bettmann/CORBIS; (cl), Prints & Photographs Division, Library of Congress, [cph 3g08038]; (cr), Prints & Photographs Division, Library of Congress, [cph 3a00941]; (b), ©Mary Evans Picture Library; **745** (tl), Courtesy Everett Collection; (tr, c, br), ©AP Photo; (bl), ©Bettmann/CORBIS, **746,** ©Bettmann/CORBIS; **748,** ©Hulton-Deutsch Collection/CORBIS; **749,** ©Fuisz Productions/Courtesy Everett Collection; **750,** Farm Security Administration - Office of War Information Photograph Collection, Prints & Photographs Division, Library of Congress, [fsa 8b32396]; **752,** ©Deborah Feingold/CORBIS; **754** (l), ©Wu Hong/epa/CORBIS; (r), ©Gideon Mendel/CORBIS; **755** (l), ©Catherine Karnow/CORBIS; (r), ©AP Photo/Gino Domenico; **756,** Scottish National Gallery of Modern Art, Edinburgh, UK, © DACS/The Bridgeman Art Library. © 2009 The Pollock-Krasner Foundation/Artists Rights Society (ARS), NY; **759,** ©Collection of The Newark Museum, Gift of Mrs. Rhoda Weintraub Ziff, 1983. 93.264. The Newark Museum/Art Resource, NY; **760,** ©E.O. Hoppé/CORBIS; **764,** ©Rebecca Floyd/Images.com; **768,** ©Bettmann/CORBIS; **770,** Private Collection, ©The Fine Art Society, London, UK/The Bridgeman Art Library; **772,** Private Collection, ©Agnew's, London, UK/The Bridgeman Art Library; **774,** Private Collection, ©Whitford & Hughes, London, UK/The Bridgeman Art Library; **778,** National Portrait Gallery, Smithsonian Institution, Washington, DC/Art Resource, NY. © 2009 Man Ray Trust/Artists Rights Society (ARS), New York/ADAGP, Paris; **784** (t), ©Hulton Archive/Getty Images; (b), ©Keystone/Hulton Archive/Getty Images; **786–787,** ©Remi Benali/CORBIS; **788,** ©Carson Ganci/Design Pics/CORBIS; **790,** ©The New York Public Library/Art Resource, NY; **793,** Collection of the Illinois State Museum/Photo by Gary Andrashko; **796,** ©Bettmann/CORBIS; **798,** ©Robert Shafer/Brand X Pictures/Getty Images; **799,** *The White Dam*, 1939 by Raphael Gleitsmann

(1910-1995, American). Oil on masonite board, 97.8 x 112.7 cm. © The Cleveland Museum of Art, Leonard C. Hanna, Jr. Fund, 1996.325; **800** (bkgd), ©Jennifer Kennard/CORBIS; (inset), ©The Sullivan Collection/The Bridgeman Art Library; **802,** ©Bettmann/CORBIS; **804,** ©Kelly Redinger/DesignPics/PunchStock; **809,** *September Wind and Rain* (1949) by Charles Ephraim Burchfield (1893–1967), Watercolor on paper mounted on board, 22" x 48" (55.88 x 121.92 cm), Museum purchase, 953-W-102. Reproduced with permission from the Charles E. Burchfield Foundation. Courtesy D.C. Moore Gallery ©Butler Institute of American Art, Youngstown, Ohio; **810,** Detail. Oesterreichische Galerie, Vienna, Austria. Courtesy Erich Lessing/Art Resource, NY; **812,** ©Bettmann/CORBIS; **813,** ©National Portrait Gallery, Smithsonian Institution, Washington, DC/Art Resource, NY; **815,** ©WestEnd61/PunchStock; **817,** ©WizData/Images.com; **820–821** (all), ©Pat O'Hara/CORBIS; **825,** ©AP Photo/Jim Cole; **826,** ©Jerry and Marcy Monkman/Images.com; **829,** ©Patrick Bennett/CORBIS; **830,** ©Frank Lane Picture Agency/CORBIS; **831,** ©Hanson Ng/Design Pics/PunchStock; **832–833,** ©Cynthia Diane Pringle/CORBIS; **833** (t), ©Image Source/Images.com; **840,** Mrs. Simon Guggenheim Fund. (577.1943). The Museum of Modern Art, New York, NY, U.S.A. Digital Image ©The Museum of Modern Art/Licensed by SCALA/Art Resource, NY; **842,** ©Hulton Archive/Getty Images; **844** (l), Ernest Hemingway Collections, Manuscript Division, Department of Rare Books and Special Collections/Princeton University Library; (r), HRW Photo; **847,** HRW Photo; **849, 856,** ©Bettmann/CORBIS; **860,** The interrupted play, illustration from 'La Gazette du Bon Ton', 1925 by Pierre Mourque. Private Collection ©The Bridgeman Art Library; **868,** ©The New York Public Library/Art Resource, NY; **871,** ©Bibliotheque des Arts Decoratifs, Paris, France, Archives Charmet/The Bridgeman Art Library; **873,** ©The New York Public Library/Art Resource, NY; **876,** ©Bettmann/CORBIS; **878** (l), ©Images.com/CORBIS; (r), ©Photos.com/JUPITERimages; **881,** ©Images.com/CORBIS; **883,** George Wesley Bellows, American, 1882–1925. *My Mother*, March 1921, detail. Oil on canvas, 83 X 49in. (210.8 X 124.5cm), Frank Russell Waksworth Memorial, 1923.975. Reproduction, The Art Institute of Chicago; **890** (b), ©AP Photo/Files; **892,** ©Hulton-Deutsch Collection/CORBIS; **894** (bkgd), ©Photodisc/PunchStock; **896** (Inset), ©Bettmann/CORBIS; **896–897** (bkgd), ©Thinkstock/PunchStock; **897** (inset left), ©Horace Bristol/CORBIS; (inset right), ©Bettmann/CORBIS; **898** (inset), Farm Security Administration - Office of War Information Photograph Collection, Prints & Photographs Division, Library of Congress, [fsa 8b29855]; **898–899** (bkgd), ©Digital Vision/PunchStock; **899** (inset), Farm Security Administration - Office of War Information Photograph Collection, Prints & Photographs Division, Library of Congress, [fsa 8b29790]; **902,** ©Philip Gould/CORBIS; **904** (bkgd), Farm Security Administration - Office of War Information Photograph Collection, Prints & Photographs Division, Library of Congress, [LC-USF33-030590-M3]; (inset), Prints & Photographs Division, Library of Congress, [LC-USZ62-125143]; **906,** ©John Elk/Bruce Coleman, Inc.; **909,** PictureHistory; **912,** ©Bernard Gotfryd/Hulton Archive/Getty Images; **914,** Private Collection, ©Manya Igel Fine Arts, London, UK/The Bridgeman Art Library; **917,** Private Collection ©Bonhams, London, UK/The Bridgeman Art Library; **918,** Private Collection, photo courtesy of Adelson Galleries, New York; **922,** ©Kamil Vojnar/Photonica/Getty Images; **927,** ©McClatchy-Tribune Information Services. All Rights Reserved. Reprinted with permission; **928,** ©Index Stock/PhototakeUSA.com; **930,** ©AP Photo; **932,** ©H. Armstrong

INDEX OF SKILLS

The Index of Skills is divided into the following categories:

The boldface page numbers indicate an extensive treatment of the topic.

LITERARY SKILLS

Abstract language, **1357,** 1358, 1360, 1365, **1464**

African American tradition, the, **951–952**

Allegory, **334, 1464**

Alliteration, 131, **359,** 516, 981, **1363,** 1383, **1464**

Allusion, 60, **63,** 66, 67, 70, 237, 320, 717, 765, **816,** 817, 969, **1315, 1464**

Ambiguity, **824,** 826, 827, 923, **1464**

American dream, 794, **1465**

Analogy, **539,** 540, 541, **1465, 1495**

Analysis, literary. *See* Literary analysis.

Analyzing style, **123,** 125, 127, 133, 136, **141,** 143, 148, 149, **551,** 552

Analyzing Visuals
movie still, **1171**
Native American art, **17**
paintings, **217, 620, 759,** 1175
photograph, **452**
regionalism in a painting, **620**
symbols in a painting, **759**

Anapest, **1465**

Anecdote, **1465**

Antagonist, **1089, 1465**

Anthropomorphism, **1465**

Antihero, **843,** 844, 845, 846, 848, 849, 850

Aphorism, **165,** 172, 173, 559, **1465**

Apostrophe, **448,** 541, **791,** 792, 794, **1385,** 1386, 1387, 1388

Appeal, rhetorical, 441

Archetypal hero, 633

Archetype, **19,** 20, 23, 25, 26, 27, 633, 911, **1397,** 1398, 1399, **1465**

Argument, questions used in, **280,** 281, 283, **1465**

Assonance, **516,** 578, 1363, **1465**

Atmosphere, **320,** 324, 327, 328, 330, 333, 334, **336,** 343, **1465**

Audience, **45,** 47, 48, 49, 70, 343

Author's purpose, **156,** 157, 161, 173, 283

Autobiography, **165,** 168, 170, 173, **955,** 957, 959, 962, 963, **1267,** 1269, **1466**

Ballad, **1465**

Biographical information, **518,** 519, 522, 526, **1245,** 1246, 1252, **1358,** 1359

Biography, **1465**

Blank verse, **819,** 820, 821, 822, 828, **1466**

Cadence, 507, 516, **1465**

Caesura, **1465**

Call and response, **433**

Captivity narratives, **43, 62**

Catalog, **512,** 513, 514, **1258,** 1259, 1261, 1263, **1466**

Character, **1466–1467**
dynamic/static, 1125, **1169, 1173,** 1176, 1177, 1178, 1180, 1181, 1182, 1183, 1184, 1185, 1227, **1467**
motivation, **857,** 859, 861, 863, 865, 866, 867, 868, 869, 870, 872, 874, **1098,** 1108, 1110, 1112, 1116, 1118, 1119, 1120, 1121, 1122, 1124, 1125, 1127, 1128, 1131, 1133, 1134, 1136, 1138, 1139,1140, 1141, 1142, 1143, 1146, 1147, 1148, 1149, 1150, 1151, 1152, 1153, 1154, 1156, 1158, 1159, 1161, 1162, 1165, 1166, 1243, 1244, 1245, 1246, 1247, 1248
round/flat, **1173,** 1467
and theme, 903

Characterization, 90, **367,** 369, 372, 373, 375, **1169–1170, 1466–1467**
in autobiography, **1283**
direct/indirect, **367, 1215, 1466–1467**
in memoir, **1283,** 1285, 1287, 1288, 1289, 1290, 1291, 1292
in poetry, 1328
in reportage, 1080

in short story, 480, **623,** 625, 628, 629, 631, 632, 633, 688, 705, 1213, 1217, 1218, 1219, 1220, 1222, 1223, 1224, 1227, 1415

Chronological order, **834**

Civil War, **400, 402–403**

Cliché, **1467**

Climax, 874, **1467**

Cold War, **1026, 1028–1029**

Comedy, **1467**

Comparing and contrasting texts, 149, 173, 181, 194–195, 388–391, 596–599, 736–737, 1014–1017, 1454–1457

Conceit, **101,** 102, 103, 431, **1467**

Concrete language, **1357,** 1360, 1365, **1467**

Confessional school, **1467**

Conflict, 903, **1093, 1195,** 1202, 1204, **1225,** 1227, 1229, 1230,1231, 1232, 1235, 1236, 1238, 1239, **1467**

Connotation, in literature, **713, 771,** 824, **1467**

Consonance, **1468**

Constructed Response, 195, 391, 599, 737, 1017, 1457

Couplet, **228,** 814, **1468**

Credibility, **457,** 462, 465, **782,** 783, **879,** 880, 881, 882, **1100,** 1101, 1102, 1114, 1115, 1130, 1131, 1132, 1134, 1143, 1147, 1163, 1167, **1197,** 1198, 1199, 1201, 1202

Dactyl, **1468**

Dark Romantics, **1468**

Deism, 117, **1468**

Denouement, **1468**

Description, **1468**

Dialect, 900, **1468**

Dialogue, 939, **1269,** 1271, 1272, 1273, 1274,1277, 1278, 1279, 1280, **1468**

Diction, 289, **415,** 417, 418, 420, 421, 651, 665, 893, **1430,** 1432, 1433, **1468**

Direct characterization, **367, 1466**

WRITING SKILLS

INDEX OF AUTHORS AND TITLES

Page numbers in italic type refer to the pages on which author biographies appear.